PAGE 56 **ON THE ROAD**

[...]ON GUIDE

[...]tings

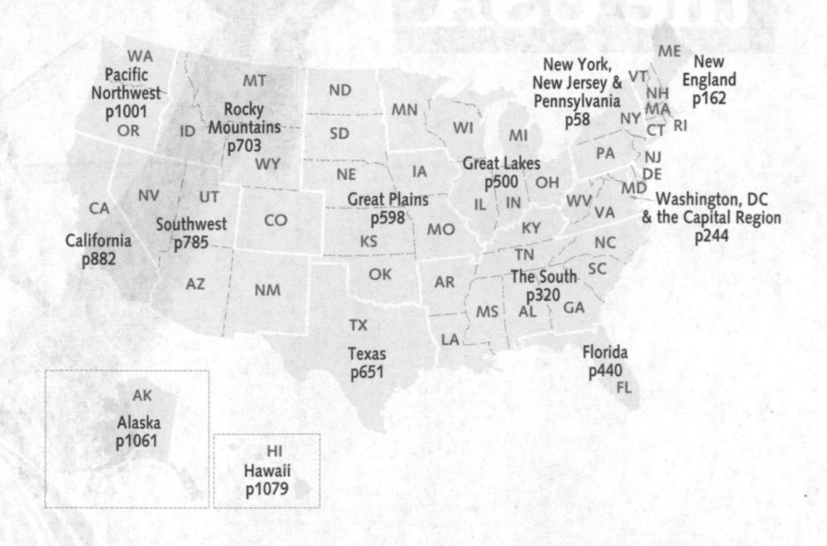

PAGE 1153 **SURVIVAL GUIDE**

VITAL PRACTICAL INFORMATION TO HELP YOU HAVE A SMOOTH TRIP

Directory A–Z 1154
Transportation 1168
Index 1187
Map Legend 1204

THIS EDITION WRITTEN AND RESEARCHED BY

Regis St Louis

Amy C Balfour, Michael Benanav, Andrew Bender, Glenda Bendure, Sara Benson, Alison Bing, Jeff Campbell, Nate Cavalieri, Sarah Chandler, Jim DuFresne, Lisa Dunford, Ned Friary, Bridget Gleeson, Michael Grosberg, Beth Kohn, Mariella Krause, Emily Matchar, Bradley Mayhew, Carolyn McCarthy, Kevin Raub, Brendan Sainsbury, Andrea Schulte-Peevers, Ryan Ver Berkmoes, John A Vlahides, Karla Zimmerman

welcome to the USA

Bright Lights, Big Cities

America is the birthplace of LA, Las Vegas, Chicago, Miami, Boston and New York City – each a brimming metropolis whose name alone conjures a million different notions of culture, cuisine and entertainment. Look more closely, and the American quilt unfurls in all its surprising variety: the eclectic music scene of Austin, the easygoing charms of antebellum Savannah, the ecoconsciousness of free-spirited Portland, the magnificent waterfront of San Francisco, and the captivating old quarters of New Orleans, still rising up from its waterlogged ashes.

On the Road Again

This is a country of road trips and great open skies, where four million miles of highways lead past red-rock deserts, below towering mountain peaks, and across fertile wheat fields that roll off toward the horizon. The sun-bleached hillsides of the Great Plains, the lush rain forests of the Pacific Northwest and the scenic country lanes of New England are a few fine starting points for the great American road trip.

Food-Loving Nation

Cuisine is another way of illuminating the American experience. On one evening in the US, thick barbecue ribs and smoked

Enormous and staggeringly diverse, America harbors an astounding collection of natural and cultural wonders, from teeming city streets to mountains, plains and forests covering vast swaths of the continent.

(left) Statue of Liberty (p63), New York City.
(below) Burger and fries.

brisket come piping hot at a Texas roadhouse; over 1500 miles away, talented chefs blend organic, fresh-off-the-farm produce with Asian accents at award-winning West Coast restaurants. A smattering of locals get their fix of bagels and lox at a century-old deli in Manhattan's Upper West Side, while several states away, plump pancakes and fried eggs disappear in a hurry under the clatter of cutlery at a 1950s-style diner. Steaming plates of fresh lobster served off a Maine pier, oysters and champagne in a fashion-forward wine bar in California, beer and pizza at a Midwestern pub – these are just a few ways to dine à la Americana.

Cultural Behemoth

The world's third-largest nation has made tremendous contributions to the arts. Georgia O'Keeffe's wild landscapes, Robert Rauschenberg's surreal collages, Alexander Calder's elegant mobiles and Jackson Pollock's drip paintings have entered the vernacular of modern 20th-century art. Cities like Chicago and New York have become veritable drawing boards for the great architects of the modern era. Musically speaking, America has few peers on the world stage. From the soulful blues born in the Mississippi Delta to the bluegrass of Appalachia and Detroit's Motown sound, plus jazz, funk, hip-hop, country, and rock and roll – America has invented sounds that are integral to modern music.

❯USA

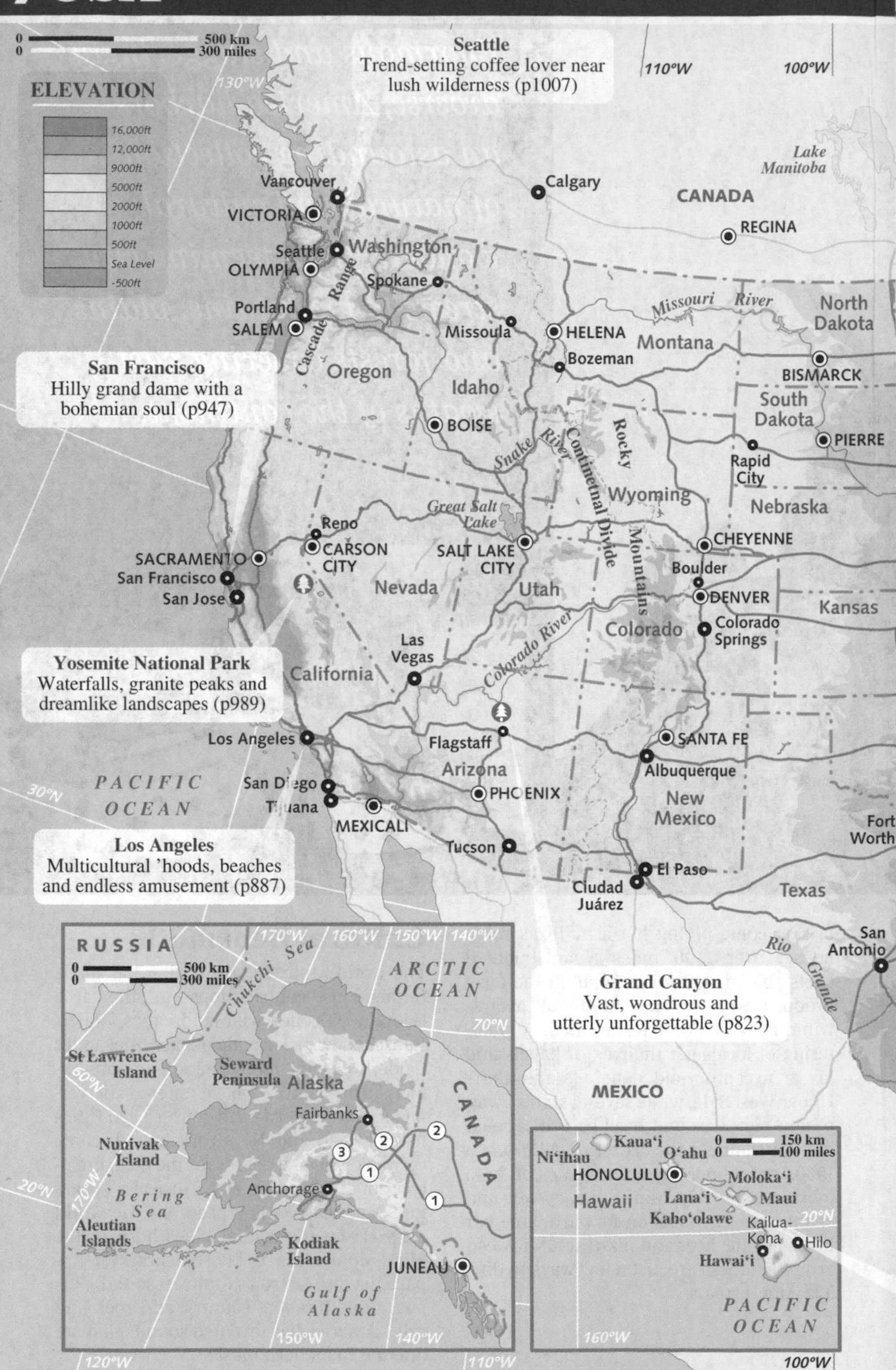

Seattle
Trend-setting coffee lover near lush wilderness (p1007)
San Francisco
Hilly grand dame with a bohemian soul (p947)
Yosemite National Park
Waterfalls, granite peaks and dreamlike landscapes (p989)
Los Angeles
Multicultural 'hoods, beaches and endless amusement (p887)
Grand Canyon
Vast, wondrous and utterly unforgettable (p823)
0 500 km
0 300 miles
ELEVATION
16,000ft
12,000ft
9000ft
5000ft
2000ft
1000ft
500ft
Sea Level
-500ft
130°W
110°W
100°W
120°W
30°N
Lake Manitoba
CANADA
Calgary
REGINA
Vancouver
VICTORIA
Seattle
Washington
OLYMPIA
Spokane
Cascade Range
Portland
SALEM
Missoula
HELENA
Missouri River
Montana
North Dakota
Bozeman
BISMARCK
South Dakota
PIERRE
Oregon
Idaho
BOISE
Snake River
Continental Divide
Rocky Mountains
Rapid City
Wyoming
Nebraska
Great Salt Lake
Reno
CARSON CITY
SACRAMENTO
San Francisco
San Jose
SALT LAKE CITY
CHEYENNE
Boulder
DENVER
Kansas
Nevada
Utah
Colorado
Colorado Springs
Colorado River
Las Vegas
California
Flagstaff
SANTA FE
Albuquerque
Los Angeles
Arizona
PACIFIC OCEAN
San Diego
Tijuana
MEXICALI
PHOENIX
New Mexico
Fort Worth
Tucson
El Paso
Ciudad Juárez
Texas
San Antonio
Rio Grande
MEXICO
RUSSIA
0 500 km
0 300 miles
Chukchi Sea
ARCTIC OCEAN
170°W
160°W
150°W
140°W
70°N
60°N
20°N
St Lawrence Island
Seward Peninsula
Alaska
CANADA
Fairbanks
Nunivak Island
Anchorage
Bering Sea
Aleutian Islands
Kodiak Island
JUNEAU
Gulf of Alaska
Kaua'i
Ni'ihau
O'ahu
0 150 km
0 100 miles
HONOLULU
Moloka'i
Hawaii
Lana'i
Maui
Kaho'olawe
Kailua-Kona
Hilo
Hawai'i
PACIFIC OCEAN

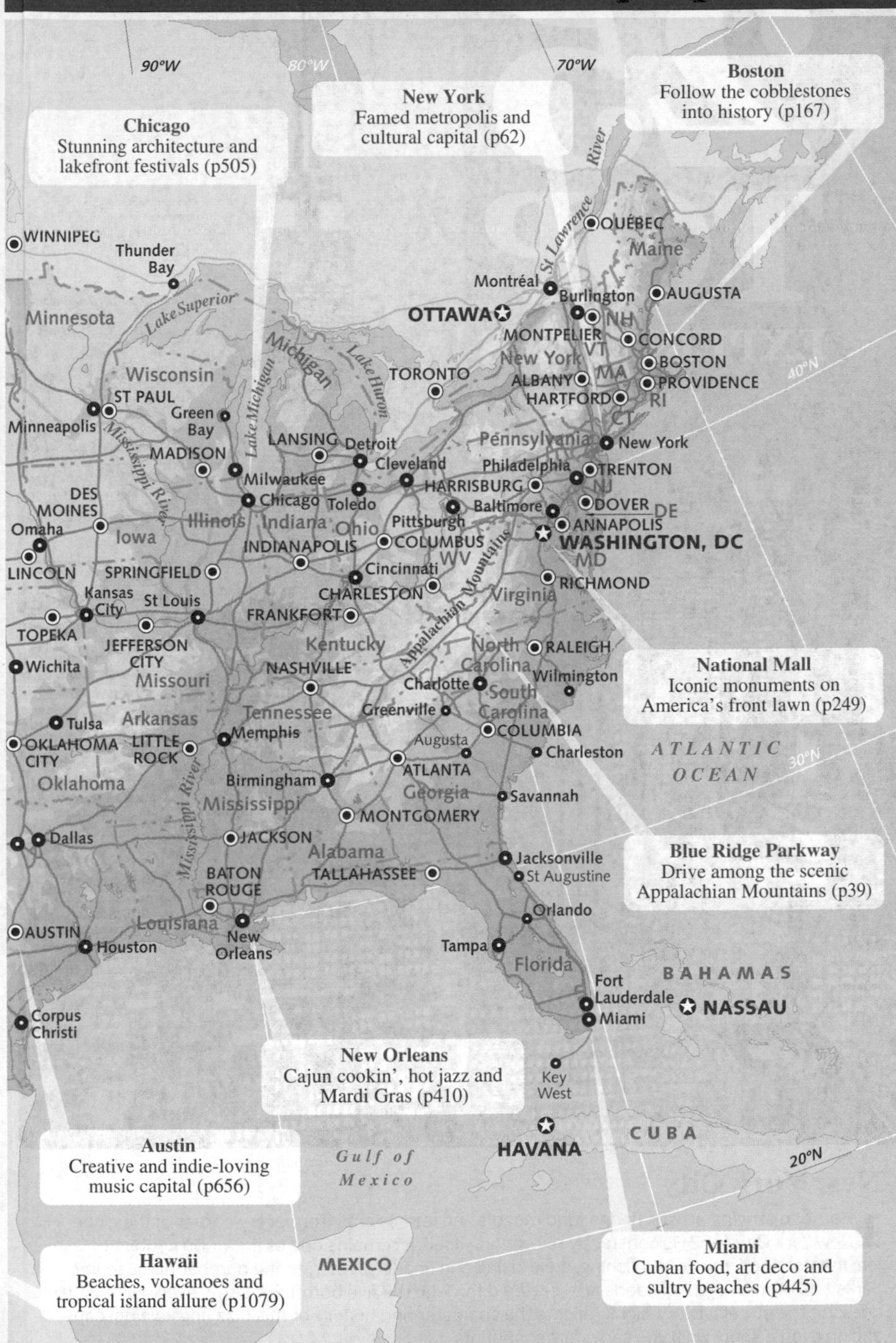

Chicago
Stunning architecture and lakefront festivals (p505)
New York
Famed metropolis and cultural capital (p62)
Boston
Follow the cobblestones into history (p167)
National Mall
Iconic monuments on America's front lawn (p249)
Blue Ridge Parkway
Drive among the scenic Appalachian Mountains (p39)
New Orleans
Cajun cookin', hot jazz and Mardi Gras (p410)
Austin
Creative and indie-loving music capital (p656)
Hawaii
Beaches, volcanoes and tropical island allure (p1079)
Miami
Cuban food, art deco and sultry beaches (p445)
90°W
80°W
70°W
40°N
30°N
20°N
WINNIPEG
Thunder Bay
Lake Superior
Minnesota
Wisconsin
Lake Michigan
Michigan
Lake Huron
St Lawrence River
QUÉBEC
Maine
Montréal
OTTAWA
Burlington
AUGUSTA
NH
MONTPELIER
VT
CONCORD
New York
MA
BOSTON
TORONTO
ALBANY
PROVIDENCE
HARTFORD
RI
CT
ST PAUL
Minneapolis
Green Bay
Mississippi River
LANSING
Detroit
Pennsylvania
New York
MADISON
Milwaukee
Cleveland
Philadelphia
TRENTON
NJ
DES MOINES
Chicago
Toledo
HARRISBURG
Baltimore
DOVER
DE
Omaha
Illinois
Indiana
Ohio
Pittsburgh
ANNAPOLIS
Iowa
INDIANAPOLIS
COLUMBUS
WASHINGTON, DC
WV
MD
LINCOLN
SPRINGFIELD
Cincinnati
Appalachian Mountains
RICHMOND
Kansas City
St Louis
CHARLESTON
Virginia
TOPEKA
FRANKFORT
Kentucky
North Carolina
RALEIGH
JEFFERSON CITY
Wichita
Missouri
NASHVILLE
Wilmington
Charlotte
South Carolina
Tennessee
Greenville
Tulsa
Arkansas
Memphis
COLUMBIA
OKLAHOMA CITY
LITTLE ROCK
Augusta
Charleston
ATLANTIC OCEAN
ATLANTA
Oklahoma
Birmingham
Georgia
Savannah
Mississippi
MONTGOMERY
Dallas
JACKSON
Alabama
Jacksonville
St Augustine
BATON ROUGE
TALLAHASSEE
Orlando
AUSTIN
Louisiana
New Orleans
Houston
Tampa
Florida
BAHAMAS
Fort Lauderdale
NASSAU
Miami
Corpus Christi
Key West
HAVANA
CUBA
Gulf of Mexico
MEXICO

25 TOP EXPERIENCES

RICHARD I'ANSON/LONELY PLANET IMAGES ©

New York City

1 Home to striving artists, hedge fund moguls and immigrants from every corner of the globe, New York City (p62) is constantly reinventing itself. It remains one of the world centers of fashion, theater, food, music, publishing, advertising and finance. A staggering number of museums, parks and ethnic neighborhoods are scattered through the five boroughs. Do as every New Yorker does: hit the streets. Every block reflects the character and history of this dizzying kaleidoscope, and on even a short walk you can cross continents.

RICHARD I'ANSON/LONELY PLANET IMAGES ©

Grand Canyon

2 You've seen it on film, heard about it from all and sundry who've made the trip. Is it worth the hype? The answer is a resounding yes. The Grand Canyon (p823) is vast and nearly incomprehensible in age – it took 6 million years for the canyon to form and some rocks exposed along its walls are 2 billion years old. Peer over the edge and you'll confront the great power and mystery of this earth we live on. Once you see it, no other natural phenemenon quite compares.

JOHN ELK III/LONELY PLANET IMAGES ©

Route 66

3 This ribbon of concrete was the USA's original road trip, connecting Chicago with Los Angeles in 1926. You'll find neon signs, motor courts, pie-filled diners and drive-in theaters along the way. The route was bypassed by I-40 in 1984, but many original sites remain, and tracing Route 66 (p35) today is a journey through small-town America. Whether you do the whole length or just a stretch, you'll come face to face with classic, nostalgic Americana. National Route 66 Museum (p647), Elk City

New Orleans

4 New Orleanians live to eat. The French, Spanish, Sicilians, Filipinos, Haitians, former Yugoslavians, Irish and Germans have all contributed to the gastro-amalgamation, making New Orleans (p410) one of the most food-centric cities in the USA. Sure, there's unique history, gorgeous architecture and amazing music, but, in the end, a visit here turns out to be all about the food. Get out of the French Quarter and eat with the locals in Riverbend, Uptown, Faubourg Maringy and the Bywater for a true taste of N'awlins. Soft-shell crab with new potatoes and almonds

Yellowstone National Park

5 Stunning natural beauty, amazing geology and some of the best wildlife watching in North America: these are just a few reasons why Yellowstone (p744) has such star power among the world's national parks. Divided into five distinct regions, this place is huge – almost 3500 sq miles – and you could spend many days exploring the park's wonders. Highlights include massive geysers, waterfalls, fossil forests, rugged mountains, scenic overlooks and gurgling mud pools – with some 1100 miles of hiking trails providing the best way to take it all in. Morning Glory Pool, Upper Geyser Basin (p745)

PETER PTSCHELINZEW/LONELY PLANET IMAGES ©

New England in Fall

6 It's a major event, one approaching epic proportions in New England (p162): watching the leaves change color. You can do it just about anywhere – all you need is one brilliant tree. But if you're most people, you'll want lots of trees. From the Litchfield Hills in Connecticut and the Berkshires in Massachusetts to Stowe in northern Vermont, entire hillsides blaze in brilliant crimsons, oranges and yellows. Covered bridges and white-steeple churches with abundant maple trees put Vermont and New Hampshire in the forefront of leaf-peeping heaven. New Hampshire (p222)

JOHN ELK III/LONELY PLANET IMAGES ©

San Francisco & Wine Country

7 Amid the clatter of old-fashioned trams and thick fog that sweeps in by night, San Francisco's (p947) diverse hill and valley neighborhoods invite long days of wandering, with great indie shops, world-class restaurants and bohemian nightlife. Round a corner to waterfront views, and you'll be hooked. If you can tear yourself away, the lush vineyards (p975) of Napa, Sonoma and the Russian River Valley lie just north. Touring vineyards, drinking great wine and lingering over farm-to-table meals – it's all part of the wine-country experience. Golden Gate Bridge (p960), San Francisco

Chicago

8 The Windy City (p505) will blow you away with its cloud-scraping architecture, lakefront beaches and world-class museums. But its true mojo is its blend of high culture and earthy pleasures. Is there another city that dresses its Picasso sculpture in local sports team gear? Where residents queue for hot dogs in equal measure to North America's top restaurant? Winters are brutal, but come summer, Chicago fetes the warm days with food and music festivals. John Hancock Center (p513)

Walt Disney World

9 Want to set the bar high? Call yourself 'the happiest place on earth.' Walt Disney World (p493) does, and then pulls out all the stops to deliver the exhilarating sensation that you are the most important character in the show. Despite all the frantic rides, entertainment and nostalgia, the magic is watching your own child swell with belief after they have made Goofy laugh, been curtsied to by Cinderella, guarded the galaxy with Buzz Lightyear, and battled Darth Maul like your very own Jedi knight. Walt Disney World, Orlando

The Deep South

10 Steeped in history and complex regional pride, the Deep South (p320) is America at its weirdest and most fascinating, from the moss-draped South Carolina swamps to the cinder block juke joints of the steamy Mississippi Delta to the isolated French-speaking enclaves of the Louisiana bayou. Famous for its slow pace, the Deep South is all about enjoying life's small pleasures: sucking down fresh Gulf oysters at an Alabama seafood shack, strolling Savannah's antebellum alleys, sipping sweet tea on the porch with new friends. Oak Alley Plantation (p427), Vacherie

Las Vegas

11 Sin City (p790) is a neon-fueled ride through the nerve center of American strike-it-rich fantasies. See billionaires' names gleam from the marquees of luxury hotels. Hear a raucous soundscape of slot machines, clinking martini glasses, and the hypnotic beats of DJs spinning till dawn. Sip cocktails under palm trees and play blackjack by the pool. Visit Paris, the Wild West and a tropical island, all in one night. It's all here and it's open 24 hours, all for the price of a poker chip (and a little luck).

Pacific Coast Highway

12 Stunning coastal highways (p38) wind their way down the US West Coast from Canada all the way to the Mexican border and offer dramatic scenery that's hard to match anywhere in the world. Clifftop views over crashing waves, sunlit rolling hills, fragrant eucalyptus forests and lush redwoods. There are wild and remote beaches, idyllic towns and fishing villages, and primeval rain forest. Amid the remote natural beauty you can mix things up with big-city adventures, dipping into Seattle, Portland, San Francisco and Los Angeles. Coastal poppies, Big Sur (p941)

Miami

13 How does one city get so lucky? Most content themselves with one or two attributes, but Miami (p445) seems to have it all. Beyond the stunning beaches and Art Deco Historic District, there's culture at every turn. In cigar-filled dancehalls, Havana expats dance to *son* and boleros, in exclusive nightclubs stiletto-heeled, fiery-eyed Brazilian models shake to Latin hip-hop, and in the park old men clack dominos. To top it off, street vendors and restaurants dish out flavors from the Caribbean, Cuba, Argentina and Spain. Ocean Drive (p447), Miami Beach

National Mall

14 Nearly 2 miles long and lined with iconic monuments and hallowed marble buildings, the National Mall (p249) is the epicenter of Washington, DC's political and cultural life. In the summer, massive music and food festivals are staged here, while year-round visitors wander the halls of America's finest museums lining the green. For exploring American history, there's no better place to ruminate, whether tracing your hand along the Vietnam War Memorial or ascending the steps of Lincoln Memorial, where Martin Luther King Jr gave his famous 'I Have a Dream' speech.

CAROL POLICH/LONELY PLANET IMAGES ©

Yosemite National Park

15 Yosemite's iconic glacier-carved valley never fails to get the heart racing, even when it's loved bumper-to-bumper in summer. In springtime, get drenched by the spray of its thundering snowmelt waterfalls and twirl singing to the *Sound of Music* in high-country meadows awash with wildflowers. Yosemite's scenery (p989) is intoxicating, with dizzying rock walls and formations, and ancient giant sequoia trees. If you look for it, you'll find solitude and space in the 1100 sq miles of development-free wilderness. Yosemite Falls (p991)

DAVID TOMLINSON/LONELY PLANET IMAGES ©

Rocky Mountains

16 The Rockies (p703) are home to the highest peaks in the lower 48. Craggy peaks, raging rivers, age-old canyons and national parks set the scene. Go skiing and snowboarding down pristine, powdery slopes in the winter, hike and mountain bike amid springtime wildflowers or feel the rush of white water on sundrenched summer afternoons. You can also recharge at microbreweries, farm-to-table restaurants and refreshing hot springs. Bison, Grand Teton National Park (p750)

Blue Ridge Parkway

17 In the southern Appalachian Mountains of Virginia and North Carolina, you can take in sublime sunsets, watch for wildlife and lose all sense of the present-day while staring off at the vast wilderness surrounding this 469-mile roadway (p39). Dozens of great hikes take you deeper into nature, from easy trails along lakes and streams to challenging scrambles up to eagles' nest heights. Camp or spend the night at forest lodges, and don't miss the great bluegrass and mountain music scene of nearby towns.

Austin & San Antonio

18 One of Texas' brightest stars, eco-friendly Austin (p656) is a great dining, drinking and shopping city, with a creative, bohemian vibe courtesy of its university and renegade subculture. Austin is one of America's music capitals with a dizzying variety of sounds playing out on stages nightly. Two major music fests showcase the best of the best. Southwest of Austin, San Antonio (p666) beguiles visitors with its pretty Riverwalk, lively festivals (including the 10-day San Antonio fest) and rich history (from serene Spanish missions to the battle-scarred Alamo). Riverside dining, San Antonio

Boston & Cape Cod

19 Start by tracing the footsteps of early Tea Partiers like Paul Revere and Sam Adams on Boston's (p167) famed Freedom Trail. After following the road through American revolutionary history, go romp around the campus of Harvard University and do a little rebel-rousing yourself at one of the city's famed clubs. Then cool off by hitting the beaches of the Cape Cod National Seashore (p190), hopping on a whale-watching cruise and getting lost in the wild dunes of Provincetown. Freedom Trail (p174), Boston

EMILY RIDDELL/LONELY PLANET IMAGES ©

Seattle

21 A cutting-edge Pacific Rim city with an uncanny habit of turning locally hatched ideas into global brands, Seattle (p1007) has earned its place in the pantheon of 'great' US metropolises, with a world-renowned music scene, a mercurial coffee culture, and a penchant for internet-driven innovation. But, while Seattle's trendsetters rush to unearth the next big thing, city traditionalists guard its soul with distinct urban neighborhoods, a homegrown food culture, and what is arguably the nation's finest public market, Pike Place. Space Needle (p1011)

MARK NEWMAN/LONELY PLANET IMAGES ©

Native American Sites

20 The Southwest is Native American country (p1120) with a fantastic array of sites covering both the distant past and the present. In Colorado and Arizona, you can visit the ancient clifftop homes of Puebloan peoples who lived among this dramatic and rocky landscape before mysteriously abandoning it. For living cultures, pay a visit to the Navajo Nation. Amid spectacular scenery, you can hire a guide and trek to the bottom of the sacred Canyon de Chelly, overnight on the reservation land and purchase handicrafts directly from the artisans. Puebloan cliff houses, Cortez

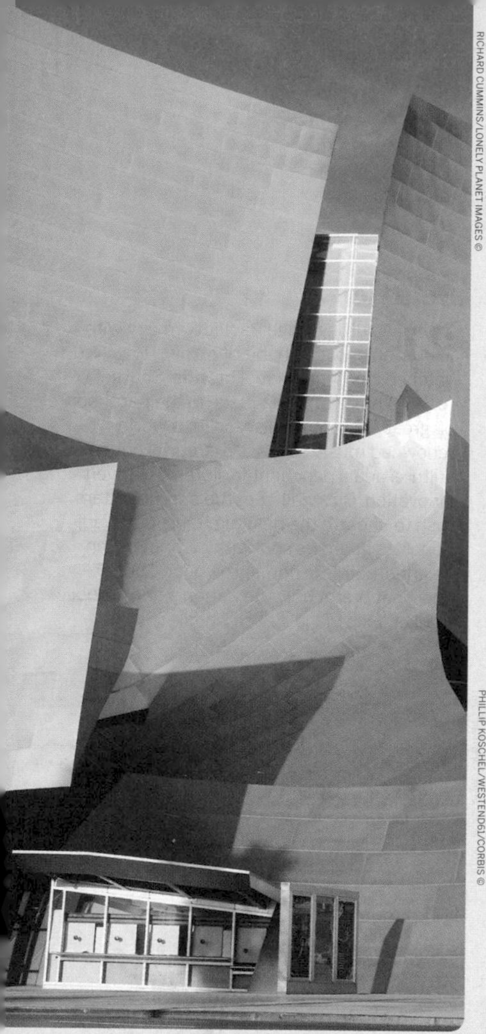

RICHARD CUMMINS/LONELY PLANET IMAGES ©

Los Angeles

22 Although it's the entertainment capital of the world, Los Angeles (p887) is more than two-dimensional silver-screen star. This is the city of odd-loving Venice Beach, art galleries and dining in Santa Monica, indie-loving neighborhoods like Los Feliz and Silverlake, surf-loving beaches like Malibu, and rugged and wild Griffith Park. And this is just the beginning. Dig deeper and you'll find an assortment of museums displaying every kind of ephemera, a cultural renaissance happening downtown and vibrant multi-ethnic 'hoods where great food lies just around the corner. Walt Disney Concert Hall (p890)

Texas Barbecue

23 Texas barbecue (p652) is an obsession. Who makes the best is the subject of countless newspaper and magazine articles. But with the endless varieties of sauces and rubs, it's probably best just to grab a plate and find out for yourself. Don't bother looking for the latest and greatest; the real treasures are the joints that look like they've been around for decades. And if you're wondering how to eat it without making a mess, don't. Just grab some napkins and dig in.

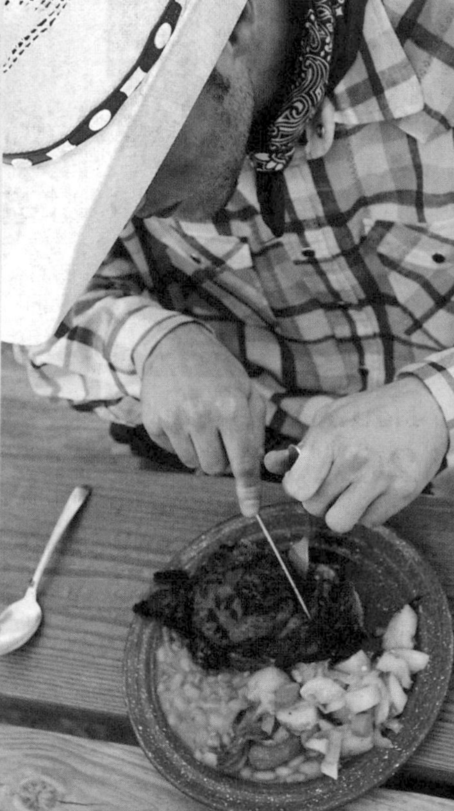

PHILLIP KOSCHEL/WESTEND61/CORBIS ©

RICK GERHARTER/LONELY PLANET IMAGES ©

Middle Americana

24 Endless open roads, stunning parks like the Badlands and great food in Kansas City are just some of the myriad allures of the Great Plains (p598). Surprises abound, some much more surprising than you'd expect: Nebraska's Carhenge, South Dakota's Corn Palace (just down the road from the huckster mecca of Wall Drug) and Kansas' fantabulous space museum plus its wild art in Lucas are but a few. Start down iconic old roads like US50 and you'll find so many diversions that the journey is the point of the trip. Corn Palace (p625), Mitchell

SABRINA DALBESIO/LONELY PLANET IMAGES ©

Hawaii

25 Hawaii (p1079) is a magical place. Where else can you find tropical rain forest, smoking volcanoes, thundering waterfalls and beautiful beaches all in such a condensed area? There's great hiking and kayaking by ancient seacliffs, surfing (for pros and learners alike) and that intangible island allure that makes you take things slow and relish the great food and vistas. Hawaii also has a culture all of its own, with a laid-back Polynesian vibe. It's all rather addictive, so plan to stick around longer than you originally intend. Hanauma Bay (p1086)

need to know

Currency

» US dollar ($)

Language

» English

When to Go

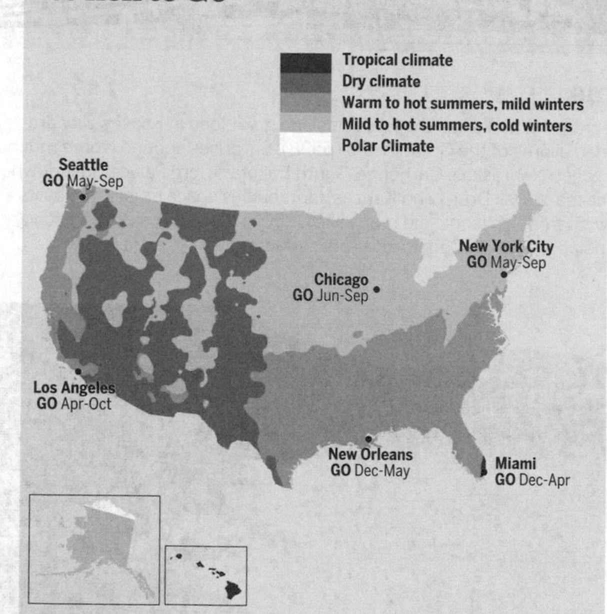

High Season (Jun–Aug)

» Warm days across the country, with generally high temperatures

» Busiest season, with big crowds and higher prices

» In ski resort areas, January to March is high season

» Shoulder Season (Oct & Apr–May)

» Milder temps, fewer crowds

» Spring flowers (April); fiery autumn colors (October) in many parts

Low Season (Nov–Mar)

» Wintery days, with snowfall in the north, and heavier rains in some regions

» Lowest prices for accommodation (aside from ski resorts and warmer getaway destinations)

Your Daily Budget

Budget: less than

$100

» Dorm beds: $20-30; campgrounds: $15-30; budget motels: $60

» Free activities (beach days, free concerts, free museums)

» Travel off-season; avoid resort areas

Midrange:

$150-$250

» Double room in midrange hotel: $100-200

» Decent-restaurant dinner: $50-80 for two

» Car hire: from $30 per day

Top end: more than

$250

» Lodging in a resort: from $250

» Dining in top restaurants: $60-100 per person

» Big nights out (plays, concerts, nightclubs): $60-200

Money

» ATMs widely available. Credit cards accepted at most hotels, restaurants and shops.

Visas

» Visitors from Canada, the UK, Australia, New Zealand, Japan and many EU countries don't need visas for under 90-day stays. Other nations might (see http://travel.state.gov).

Cell Phones

» Only foreign phones that operate on tri- or quad-band frequencies will work in the USA. Or purchase inexpensive cell phones with a pay-as-you-go plan here.

Driving

» Drive on the right; steering wheel is on the left side of the car.

Websites

» **Lonely Planet** (www.lonelyplanet.com/usa) Destination information, hotel bookings, travel forum, photos.

» **Away.com** (www.away.com) Boundless ideas for outdoor and urban adventure travel across the 50 states.

» **Festivals.com** (www.festivals.com) Find America's best celebrations; live-music, food, drink and dance.

» **New York Times Travel** (http://travel.nytimes.com) Travel news, practical advice and engaging features.

» **Roadside America** (www.roadsideamerica.com) For all things weird and wacky.

Exchange Rates

Australia	A$1	US$1.03
Canada	C$1	US$0.98
Europe	€1	US$1.37
Japan	¥100	US$1.29
New Zealand	NZ$1	US$0.78
UK	UK£1	US$1.60

For current exchange rates see www.xe.com

Important Numbers

To call any regular number, dial the area code, followed by the seven-digit number.

Emergency	☎911
USA Country Code	☎1
Directory Assistance	☎411
International directory assistance	☎00
International access code from the USA	☎011

Arriving

» **JFK, New York** (p112)
Airtrain to Jamaica Station, then LIRR to Penn Station: $12-14
Taxi to Manhattan: $45, plus toll and tip

» **Los Angeles International (LAX)** (p910)
LAX Flyaway Bus to Union Station: $7
Door-to-door Prime Time & Supershuttle: $16-28
Taxi to downtown: $47

» **Miami International** (p459)
Airport Flyer Express Bus to Lincoln Rd & Washington Ave, South Beach: $2.35
Taxi to Miami Beach: $32

Time Zones in the USA

There are four time zones in the continental US:

EST Eastern (which is GMT – 5 hours): NYC, New England and Atlanta
CST Central (GMT – 6 hours): Chicago, New Orleans and Houston
MST Mountain (GMT – 7 hours): Denver, Santa Fe, Phoenix
PST Pacific (GMT – 8 hours): Seattle, San Francisco, Las Vegas

Most of Alaska is one hour behind Pacific time (GMT – 9), while Hawaii is two hours behind Pacific time.

So if it's 9pm in New York, it's 8pm in Chicago, 7pm in Denver, 6pm in Los Angeles, 4pm in Anchorage and 3pm in Honolulu.

Daylight Savings Time pushes the clocks ahead an hour and runs from the second Sunday in March to the first Sunday in November. A few places (like Hawaii and Arizona) don't observe daylight savings time.

what's new

For this new edition of USA, our authors have hunted down the fresh, the transformed, the hot and the happening. These are some of our favorites. For up-to-the-minute recommendations, see lonelyplanet.com/usa.

Food Truck City

1 No longer the domain of hot dogs and soggy pretzels, food trucks are taking America by storm. You'll find incredibly diverse gourmet fare – dumplings, free-range herb-roasted chicken, lobster rolls, thin-crust pizzas, banh mi, BBQ, Colombian arepas, creme brulee and much much more. Find the best variety of trucks in NYC, LA, San Francisco, Austin and Portland. You can track down the action on twitter.

The High Line

2 NYC's much loved new greenway, the Highline (p73), has opened stage two, meaning you can now walk for almost a mile peacefully above the traffic following the former railroad tracks.

Art-loving Boston

3 Boston's Museum of Fine Arts (p171) opened a spectacular new multimillion-dollar Art of the Americas wing with over 50 galleries of American art, covering everything from pre-Columbian to contemporary American works.

Bike-Friendly Nation

4 Cities across the country have added adding hundreds of miles of bike lanes. Boston and DC even have bike-sharing programs, making it easy to go for a pedal.

Napa is Now

5 Downtown Napa (p975) is popping, with enticing new restaurants and the now fully functioning Oxbow Market, with artisinal bakers, cheesemongers, and yet more sustainable restaurants.

A Moveable Feast

6 Denver's latest trend is its underground dining, held in random locations like plane hangars, fields and warehouses with top chefs and theme menus (see www.hushdenver.com).

Wizards and Such

7 In Florida, Universal Orlando (p489) opened the Wizarding World of Harry Potter in 2010, to great acclaim. It's currently the hottest theme park experience of the moment.

Hello, Dalí

8 Also in Florida, the spectacular Salvador Dalí Museum (p485) opened the doors of its theatrical new home, complete with geodesic atrium, in the waterfront town of St Petersburg.

Destination Dining

9 At Chicago's Next (p526), chef Grant Achatz chooses a place and time period, say Paris 1906, and serves a multi-course meal of that era. Every three months he changes everything.

Greening NYC

10 NYC is all about parks and green living these days, with new waterfront parks in Brooklyn (near the Brooklyn Bridge) and all along Manhattan's West Side.

if you like...

Beaches

Coastlines on two oceans and the Gulf of Mexico (not to mention those tropical Hawaiian islands) make for some tough choices for beach-lovers, from the rugged and wild shores of Maine to the surf-loving beauties of Southern California.

Point Reyes National Seashore The water is cold but the scenery is magical along this 110-mile stretch of untamed coastline in Northern California (p973).

South Beach Famous the world over, South Beach is less about wave frolicking than taking in the passing people parade crossing Miami's favorite playground (p447).

Cape Cod National Seashore Massive sand dunes, picturesque lighthouses and cool forests invite endless exploring on the Massachusetts cape (p190).

Montauk Past Fire Island and the Hamptons, at the eastern tip of Long Island lies windswept Montauk, with pretty shoreline, beach camping and an 18th-century (still functioning) lighthouse (p115).

Santa Monica This LA beauty captivates with its two-pack of beach fun and urban allure. Hit the shore, then go celeb-spotting at edgy art galleries and high-end bistros (p897).

Theme Parks

America's theme parks come in many varieties – from old-fashioned cotton candy and rollercoaster fun to multiday immersions in pure Peter-Pan-style make-believe. Some parks are impressive enough to plan a whole itinerary around.

Disney With one on either coast, Disney makes things easy when you're ready to delve into this enchanting fairy-tale world. (p493) and (p913).

Dollyworld A paean to the much-loved country singer Dolly Parton, with Appalachian-themed rides and attractions in the hills of Tennessee (p370).

Legoland Everyone's favorite building block gets its due in this creative hands-on park for the younger set outside of San Diego (p927).

Cedar Park The Valhalla of roller coasters is this massive theme park near Sandusky, Ohio. Masochists line up for the Top Thrill Dragster, one of the world's highest and fastest roller coasters (p547).

Universal Studios Florida You'll need a few days to exhaust this massive complex, with action-filled theme parks and a water park, with something for all ages (p489).

Wine

The American wine industry has grown in leaps and bounds in recent years, becoming the world's fourth-largest producer along the way. Visiting wineries isn't just about tasting first-rate drops, but drinking in the pretty countryside and sampling the enticing farmstands and delectable bistros that often sprout alongside vineyards.

Napa Home to over 230 vineyards, Napa is synonymous with world-class winemaking. You'll find superb varietals, gourmet bites and beautiful scenery in which to enjoy them (p975).

Willamette Valley Outside of Portland, Oregon, this fertile region produces some of the tastiest pinot noirs on the planet (p1046).

Finger Lakes Wine Trail Upstate New York is a prime growing wine region (particularly for ice wine). After a few quaffs, you can walk it off at the lovely state parks in the area (p118).

Virginia Wine Country This up-and-coming wine district makes for some great vineyard rambles among countryside packed with history – you can even sample the wines grown on Thomas Jefferson's old estate (p307).

» National Museum of Natural History (p253), Washington, DC

Great Food

The classic American dining experience: making a mess at a Maine lobster shack, plowing through BBQ in Texas Hill Country, feasting at world-famous restaurants in New York and California and finding farm-to-table locavore-loving spots all across the country. It's all this and much more.

New York City Whether you crave steak frites, linguini con vongole, sushi, chicken tikka masala or gourmet hot dogs, globe-trotting Gotham has you covered (p97).

Chicago No 'Second City' when it comes to dining, Chicago earns rave reviews for its fantastic culinary scene, with great Greek, Thai and molecular gastronomy, famously deep-dish pizzas and much more (p523).

San Francisco A bewildering array of temptations await food-minded diners: real-deal taquerias and trattorias, world-class Vietnamese, magnificent farmers markets and critically acclaimed chefs firing up the best of California cuisine (p964).

Hill Country Texas smokes them all – at least when it comes to barbecue meats. Carnivores shouldn't miss the legendary capital of mouth-watering brisket (p664).

Hiking

The stage is set: soaring mountains, mist-covered rainforests, red-rock canyons and craggy clifftops overlooking wild, wind-swept seas. These are just a few places where you can hike the great American wilderness.

Appalachian Trail Even if you chose not to walk all 2178 miles of this mother-of-all hiking trails, the AT is well worth a visit – 14 different states provide access (p44).

Marin County Across the Golden Gate Bridge from SF, in one day you can hike amid towering redwoods at Muir Woods then head to the nearby headlands for an unforgettably scenic walk overlooking the Pacific (p972).

North Cascades Glaciers, jagged peaks and alpine lakes are all part of the scenery at this wild and remote wilderness with some superb hiking (p1029).

Acadia National Park Maine's coastal beauty reaches high art on the hiking trails coursing through and over this dramatic park with its sea cliffs, forests, boulder-strewn peaks and rich wildlife (p239).

Museums & Galleries

Visiting the local museum can mean gazing at world-class collections (if you happen to be standing in New York's Upper East Side) or contemplating brilliant folk art (if you find yourself in Lucas, Kansas), while art galleries serve up a mix of the classic, the avant-garde and the downright indescribable (not to mention free wine at openings).

New York City Spend a few weeks ploughing through the city's museums and galleries and you'll barely scratch the surface. Come again a few weeks later and you'll see entirely new collections – that's the beauty (and despair!) of the NYC art scene (p63).

Washington, DC The capital has treasured halls dedicated to outer space, history and art (western, eastern, African, Native American) – plus woolly mammoths; and they're all free (p249).

Art Basel Art lovers descend upon Miami each year to take in edgy exhibitions, music and copious amounts of alcohol at this massive revelry-loving art fair (p455).

If you like... outdoor music
Red Rocks Park has a 9000-seat amphitheater dramatically set between 400ft-high red sandstone rocks. The acoustics are phenomenal, which is why many artists record live albums here (p711).

Off-beat America

When you tire of traipsing through museums and ticking off well-known sights (perhaps because some guidebook suggested you shouldn't miss it), unbuckle your safety belt and throw yourself into the strange world of American kitsch and nonesuch. Really, you won't want to miss it.

Foamhenge A magnificent homage to Styrofoam, this is Stonehenge redux, done to scale and appropriately tranquil around sunset – there's even a resident wizard (also made of Stryofoam) watching over the mystifying proceedings (p312).

Emma Crawford Coffin Races Paint your coffin, add wheels and join the races at this spirited free-for-all held just before Halloween in Colorado Springs (p717).

NashTrash Tours Nashville's tall-haired 'Jugg Sisters' take visitors on a deliciously tacky journey through Nashville's spicier side (p363).

Spam Museum What's not to love about Spam? The tinned meat has fed armies, inspired poets and even been adopted into the culinary family in some parts (ahem, Hawaii). Pay your respects at the tiny altar of Spam (p593).

Architecture

Whether you're a devotee of Frank Lloyd Wright or simply enjoy gazing at beautifully designed buildings, the US has some aesthetic head-turners. With the rapidly changing nature of American cities, you can come back again next year, and see a completely different architectural landscape.

Chicago If you think New York is tall, try Chicago, birthplace of the skyscraper and home of the nation's tallest building. To see works by all the 20th-century greats, sign up for a tour given by the Chicago Architectural Foundation (p505).

Fallingwater A few hours from Pittsburgh, this 1939 Frank Lloyd Wright masterpiece seamlessly blends into the forested landscape and the waterfall over which the house is built (p161).

New York City Despite the relentless buzz on the ground, there's as much happening overhead as there is on the streets. Much photographed classics include the art-deco Chrysler Building, the spiraling Guggenheim and the majestic Brooklyn Bridge (p63).

Miami Miami's art-deco district is a Technicolor dream come to life – and the largest collection of Deco buildings found anywhere in the world (p445).

Wildlife

Home to soaring eagles, masticating buffaloes and bellowing sea lions – not to mention coyotes, alligators and grizzlies – America has a treasure chest of wildlife. Among the hits: whale-watching off the coasts, moose sightings up north and great birdwatching all over (even Manhattan's Central Park).

Alligators The road signs will alert you: Florida is gator country; head to the Everglades for the chance to see these prehistoric creatures in their swampy homeland (p463).

Grizzlies The mighty Grizzly lives out west and generally eats whatever he wants. Your best chance to see them in the wild is in Montana's Glacier National Park (p761).

Whales Pack your binoculars and head out to Washington state's San Juan Islands for a glimpse of breaching whales on their annual migration (p1027).

Elk In the pristine wilderness of Yellowstone, the noble elk is just one of many animal species you might see – along with bison, wolves, eagles and gulp, brown bears (p744).

If you like... mountain climbing

Sign up for a challenging five-day guided climb to the summit of 14,411ft Mt Rainier (p1031).

If you like... kayaking

Head to Alaska's Tracy Arm, a steep-sided fjord lined with icebergs that's an enchanting destination for an extended paddle (p1069).

Native American Culture

The continent's first peoples have a connection to the land and its animals, which stretches back many generations. To learn more about Native American culture, and to see historic sites and flourishing tribes, plan a trip through the southwest.

Washington, DC Appropriately, the capital holds the nation's finest museum dedicated to Native peoples. Multimedia exhibits provide an excellent introduction to the different customs, practices and spiritual beliefs of tribes from every corner of the Americas (p248)

Mesa Verde Carved into the mountains of Southern Colorado, this fascinating site was mysteriously abandoned by Ancestral Puebloan peoples (p740)

Pine Ridge Indian Reservation Visit the tragic site where Lakota men, women and children were massacred by US Cavalry in 1890, then visit nearby Wall, to learn more about the Lakota (p627)

Navajo Nation In Arizona, you can travel on Navajo land, visit spectacular scenery, stay in a sandstone guesthouse beautifully integrated into the environment and purchase crafts directly from the artisans (p829)

Historical Sights

The East Coast is where you'll find the original 13 colonies. To delve into the past, head south and west, where Spanish explorers and indigenous peoples, left their mark.

Philadelphia The nation's first capital is where the idea of America as an independent nation first coalesced. Excellent museums and multimedia exhibits, not to mention 300-year-old buildings help tell the story (p134).

Boston The ghosts of the past live on in the cobblestone streets and house museums of historic Boston. Visit Paul Revere's former home, walk the graveyard where 18th-century patriots lie buried and hear the creak of the decks aboard the 1797 USS Constitution (p167).

Williamsburg Be transported back to the 1700s in the preserved town of Williamsburg, the largest living history museum on the planet (p299).

Washington, DC Visit the theater where John Wilkes Booth shot America's favorite president, the steps of Lincoln Memorial where Martin Luther King Jr gave his famous 'I have a dream' speech and the Watergate Hotel, which destroyed Nixon's presidency (p248).

Beer & Microbreweries

In case you haven't heard, Americans don't drink much Budweiser anymore. Microbreweries have exploded in popularity, and you'll never be far from a finely crafted pint. Colorado, Washington and Oregon are particularly famed for their breweries.

Magic Hat Brewery Vermont, which has more microbreweries per capita than any other state in America, deserves special mention – and Magic Hat makes for a refreshing and entertaining beer outing (p220).

Mountain Sun Pub & Brewery Boulder's favorite microbrewery serves an array of excellent drafts, plus good food and regular music jams (p721).

Fullsteam In Durham, NC, Fullsteam is the first 'Southern brewery' of its kind, with sweet potato beer, kudzu beer and other unusual but surprisingly successful drops (p333).

Portland Valhalla for beer lovers, Portland has over 30 microbreweries within city limits including the famous McMenamin brothers and the Bridgeport, one of America's first brewpubs (p1042).

LOU JONES/LONELY PLANET IMAGES ©

» Buskers, Santa Monica Pier (p897)

Geologic Wonders

The American landscape is littered with awe-inspiring sights, particularly out west. With red rock deserts, petrified forests, blasting geysers and one massive hole in the ground, you might feel like you've stepped onto another planet.

Grand Canyon Needing little introduction, the Grand Canyon is mesmerizing. It's a mile deep and 10 miles across and was carved over 6 million years. Take your time when you go (p823).

Yellowstone Massive geysers, rainbow-colored thermal pools and the supervolcano it all sits on – this 3472-sq-mile national park certainly puts on a dazzling show (p744).

Hawai'i Volcanoes National Park Home to two active volcanoes, this park is the place to go for a look at lava deserts, smoldering craters and, with luck, the sight of molten lava rolling into the ocean (p1091).

Carlsbad Caverns Take a two-mile walk along a subterranean passage to arrive in the great room – a veritable underground cathedral concealed in this massive cave system (p881).

Live Music

Americans may not agree on a national soundtrack, but they do know where to catch a good live band – whether they're after Memphis blues, Appalachian bluegrass, New Orleans jazz, fist-pumping rock, country crooning, brassy funk, bouncing hip-hop, sultry salsa and much much more.

Austin Home to more than 200 venues and the country's biggest music fest, Austin proudly wears the music crown – with a stunning variety of talent playing on stages nightly (p661).

New Orleans The Big Easy has a soundtrack as intoxicating as the city itself – room-filling big-band jazz that slips easily into funk, plus blues, zydeco, Cajun and indie rock (p424).

Nashville Lots of country stars got their start singing on the bright stages of Nashville. But this river city is more than a one-trick pony with bluegrass, blues, folk and plenty of rough-and-tumble honky-tonk (p366).

Los Angeles LA is a magnet for aspiring stars and that means some seriously talented street performers. Of course, don't miss the legendary Sunset Strip clubs for A list artists (p907).

Sports

No matter when you visit, there will be something happening in the arena of sport – whether it's baseball, basketball, football, hockey or soccer. While big pro games are fun to attend, don't overlook minor leagues or college sporting events, which can be an equally good time.

Fenway Park Seeing the Red Sox play at venerated Fenway Park – the nation's oldest baseball park – is reason enough to come to Boston (p182).

New York Although most folks think New Yorkers go more for opera and champagne than ballparks and hotdogs, this city is mad for sport – with pro teams in hockey, soccer, basketball (two), football (two) and baseball (two) (p109).

Chicago The Windy City has a soft spot for its (five) pro sports teams – even if they're woefully bad like the Cubs, who have the worst record of any team, any sport. Don't miss the chance to see them play their hearts out at historic Wrigley Field (p529).

month by month

Top Events

1. **Mardi Gras,** February or March
2. **South by Southwest,** March
3. **National Cherry Blossom Festival,** March
4. **Chicago Blues Festival,** June
5. **Independence Day,** July

January

The New Year starts off with a shiver, as snowfall blankets large swaths of the country. Ski resorts kick into high gear, while sun-lovers seek refuge in warmer climes (especially Florida).

Mummers Parade

Philadelphia's biggest event is this brilliant parade (p144), where local clubs spend months creating costumes and mobile scenery in order to win top honors on New Year's Day. String bands and clowns add to the general good cheer at this long-running fest.

Chinese New Year

In late January or early February, you'll find colorful celebrations and feasting anywhere there's a Chinatown. NYC throws a festive parade, though San Francisco's is the best, with floats, firecrackers, bands and plenty of merriment.

Sundance Film Festival Film

The legendary Sundance Film Festival (www.sundance.org; p845) brings Hollywood stars, indie directors and avid filmgoers to Park City, UT, for a 10-day indie extravaganza in late January. Plan well in advance, as passes sell out fast.

February

Aside from mountain getaways, many Americans dread February with its long dark nights and frozen days. For foreign visitors, this can be the cheapest time to travel, with ultra-discount rates for flights and hotels.

Mardi Gras

Held in late February or early March, on the day before Ash Wednesday, Mardi Gras (Fat Tuesday) is the finale of Carnival. New Orleans' celebrations (p418) are legendary as colorful parades, masquerade balls, feasting and plenty of hedonism rule the day.

March

The first blossoms of spring arrive (at least in the south – the north still shivers in the chill). In the mountains, it's still high season for skiing. Meanwhile, drunken spring breakers descend on Florida.

St Patricks Day

On the 17th, the patron saint of Ireland is honored with brass bands and ever-flowing pints of Guinness; huge parades occur in New York, Boston and Chicago (which goes all-out by dyeing the Chicago River green).

National Cherry Blossom Festival

The brilliant blooms of Japanese cherry blossoms around DC's Tidal Basin are celebrated with concerts, parades, taiko drumming, kite-flying and 90 other events during the five-week fest (p261). More than one million go each year, so don't forget to book ahead.

South by Southwest

Each year Austin, Texas, becomes ground zero for one of the biggest music fests (p657) in North America. Over 2000 performers play at nearly 100 venues. SXSW is also a major film festival and interactive fest – a platform for ground-breaking ideas.

April

The weather is warming up, but April can still be unpredictable with chilly weather mixed with a few, teasingly warm days up north. Down south, it's a fine time to travel.

Jazz Fest

On the last weekend in April, New Orleans hosts the country's best jazz jam (p418), with top-notch acts (local resident Harry Connick Jr often headlines) and plenty of good cheer. In addition to world-class jazz, there's also great food and crafts.

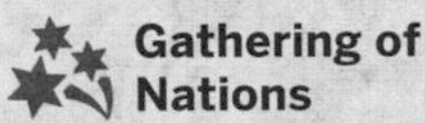

Gathering of Nations

For an immersion in indigenous culture, head to Albuquerque for the Gathering of Nations (www.gatheringofnations.com; p860), the largest Native American pow-wow in the world. You'll find traditional dance, music, food, crafts and the crowning of Miss Indian World.

May

May is true spring and one of the loveliest times to travel, with blooming wildflowers and generally mild sunny weather. Summer crowds and high prices have yet to arrive.

Cinco de Mayo

Celebrate Mexico's victory over the French with salsa music and pitchers of margaritas across the country. Denver throws one of the best Cinco de Mayos (p711), with music on three stages and dozens of food and craft stalls.

June

Summer is here. Americans spend more time at outdoor cafes and restaurants, and head to the shore or to national parks. School is out; vacationers fill the highways and resorts bringing higher prices.

Red Earth Native American Cultural Festival

In early June, Oklahoma City becomes the epicenter of Native American culture, when indigenous artists, performers and craftmakers from all over North America light up the city. With over 100 tribes attending, it's an incredibly diverse affair. See p645.

Gay Pride

In some cities, gay pride celebrations last a week, but in San Francisco, it's a month-long party, where the last weekend in June sees giant parades (p961). You'll find other great pride events at major cities across the country.

Chicago Blues Festival

It's the globe's biggest free blues fest (www.chicagobluesfestival.us; p521), with three days of the music that made Chicago famous. More than 640,000 people unfurl blankets by the multiple stages that take over Grant Park in early June.

Mermaid Parade

In Brooklyn, Coney Island celebrates summer's steamy arrival with a kitsch-loving parade (p93). Skimpily attired but brilliantly imaginative mermaids and horn-blowing mermen march through Coney Island. Afterwards, everyone (at least those not afraid of NY Harbor Water) takes a dip in the ocean.

CMA Music Festival

Legions of Country music fans from every corner of the globe come to Nashville for the chance to hear a few of the nation's top singers (www.cmaworld.com; p363). More than 400 artists perform at stages on Riverfront Park and LP Field.

Telluride Bluegrass Festival

The banjo gets its due at this festive, boot-stomping music jam (www.planetbluegrass.com; p738) in Colorado mountain country. You'll find nonstop performances, excellent regional food stalls and great locally crafted microbrews. It's good all-comers entertainment and many folks even camp.

July

With summer in full swing, Americans break out the backyard barbecues or head for the beach. The prices are high and the crowds can be fierce, but it's one of the liveliest times to visit.

Independence Day

The nation celebrates its birthday with a bang as nearly every town and city stages a massive fireworks show. Quick to the draw, Chicago goes off on the 3rd. Washington, DC; New York, Philadelphia and Boston are all great spots.

Oregon Brewers Festival

The beer-loving city of Portland pulls out the stops and pours a heady array of handcrafted perfection (www.oregonbrewfest.com; p1039). Featuring 80 different beers from around the country, there are plenty of choices; and it's nicely set along the banks of the Willamette River.

Pageant of the Masters

This eight-week arts fest (www.LagunaFestivalofArts.org; p915) brings a touch of the surreal to Laguna Beach, CA. On stage, meticulously costumed actors create living pictures – imitations of famous works of art – which is accompanied by narration and an orchestra.

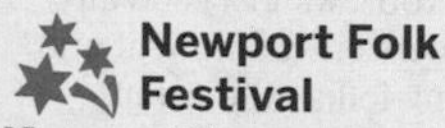

Newport Folk Festival

Newport, RI, a summer haunt of the well-heeled, hosts a world-class music fest (www.newportfolkfest.com; p205) in late July. Top folk artists from every corner of America and beyond take to the stage at this fun, all-welcoming event.

August

Expect blasting heat in August, with temperatures and

(above) Thanksgiving Day Parade, New York City.
(below) Mardi Gras, New Orleans.

humidity less bearable the further south you go. You'll find people-packed beaches, high prices and empty cities on weekends, when residents escape to the nearest waterfront.

Lollapalooza

Once upon a time, this mondo rock fest (www.lollapalooza.com; p521) traveled city to city; now its permanent home is in Chicago. It's a raucous event, with 130 bands – including many A-listers – spilling off eight stages in Grant Park the first Friday-to-Sunday in August.

Iowa State Fair

If you've never been to a state fair, now's your chance (www.iowastatefair.org; p617). You'll find country crooning, wondrous carvings (in butter), livestock shows, sprawling food stalls and a down-home good time in America's heartland. Runs over 10 days in mid August.

September

With the end of summer, cooler days arrive, making for pleasant outings nationwide. The kids are back in school, and concert halls, gallery spaces and performing arts venues kick off a new season.

Burning Man Festival

Over one week, some 50,000 revelers, artists and assorted free spirits descend on Nevada's Black Rock Desert to create a temporary metropolis of art installations, theme camps and environmental curiosities. It culminates in the burning of a giant stick figure (www.burningman.com; p805).

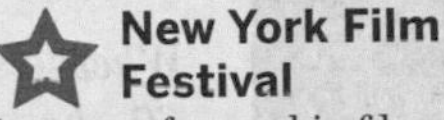

New York Film Festival

Just one of many big film fests (www.filmlinc.com; p93) in NYC (Tribeca Film Fest in late April is another), this one features world premiers from across the globe, plus Q&As with indie- and prominent directors alike. Lincoln Center plays host.

October

Temperatures are falling, as autumn brings fiery colors to northern climes. It's high season where the leaves are most brilliant (New England); elsewhere expect lower prices and fewer crowds.

Halloween

It's not just for kids; adults celebrate Halloween at masquerade parties. In NYC, you can don a costume and join the Halloween parade up Sixth Avenue. West Hollywood in Los Angeles is the places to see California's most outrageous outfits.

Fantasy Fest

Key West's answer to Mardi Gras brings more than 100,000 revelers to the subtropical enclave on the week leading up to Halloween. Expect parades, colorful floats, costume parties, the selecting of a conch king and queen and plenty of alcohol-fueled merriment. (www.fantasyfest.net; p472).

November

No matter where you go, this is generally low season, with cold winds discouraging visitors and lower prices (although airfares skyrocket around Thanksgiving). There's much happening culturally in the city.

Thanksgiving

On the fourth Thursday of November, Americans gather with family and friends over day-long feasts – roast turkey, sweet potatoes, cranberry sauce, wine, pumpkin pie and loads of other dishes. New York City hosts a huge parade, and there's pro football on TV.

December

Winter arrives as ski season kicks off in the Rockies (out east conditions aren't usually ideal until January). Aside from winter sports, December means heading inside and curling up by the fire.

Art Basel

This massive arts fest (www.artbaselmiamibeach.com; p455) is four days of cutting-edge art, film, architecture and design. More than 250 major galleries from across the globe come to the event, with works by some 2000 artists; plus much hobnobbing with a glitterati crowd in Miami Beach.

New Year's Eve

Americans are of two minds when it comes to ringing in the New Year. Some join festive crowds to celebrate; others plot a getaway to escape the mayhem. Whichever you choose, plan well in advance. Expect high prices (especially in NYC).

itineraries

Whether you've got six days or 60, these itineraries provide a starting point for the trip of a lifetime. Want more inspiration? Head online to lonelyplanet.com/thorntree to chat with other travelers.

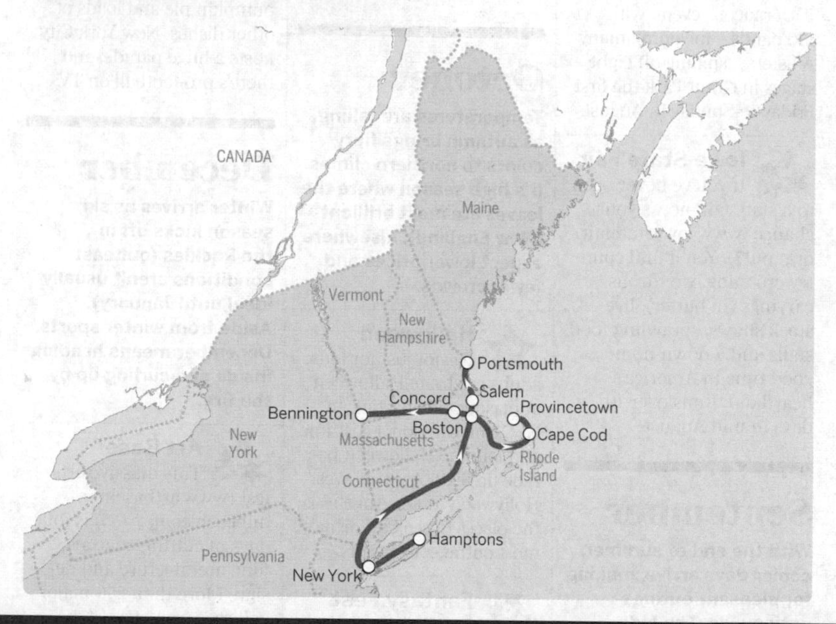

Two to Three Weeks
East Coasting

The great dynamo of art, fashion and culture, **New York City** is America at her most urbane. Spend four days exploring the metropolis, visiting memorable people-watching hoods such as the West and East Villages, the Lower East Side, Soho, Nolita and the Upper West Side, with a museum hop down the Upper East Side. Have a ramble in Central Park, stroll the High Line and take a detour to Brooklyn. After big-city culture, catch your breath at the pretty beaches and enticing charms of the **Hamptons** on Long Island. Back in NYC, catch the train to **Boston**, for two days visiting historic sights, dining in the North End and pub-hopping in Cambridge. Strike out for **Cape Cod**, with its idyllic dunes, forests and pretty shores. Leave time for **Provincetown**, the Cape's liveliest settlement. Back in Boston, hire a car and take a three-day jaunt taking in New England's back roads, covered bridges, picturesque towns and beautiful scenery, staying at heritage B&Bs en route. Highlights include **Salem** and **Concord** in Massachusetts; **Bennington**, Vermont; and **Portsmouth**, New Hampshire. If time allows, head all the way up to **Maine** for lobster feasts amid beautifully rugged coastline.

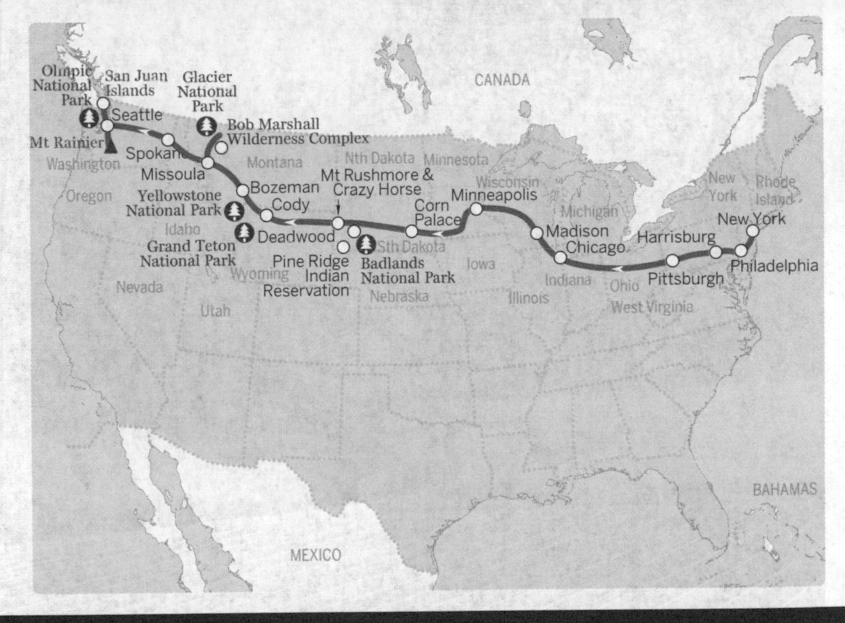

Three Weeks
Northern Expedition

For a different take on the transcontinental journey, plan a route through the north. From **New York City**, head west toward **Harrisburg** via **Philadelphia**, but stop first to explore the idyllic backroads of Pennsylvania Dutch Country. Next is **Pittsburg**, a surprising town of picturesque bridges and green spaces, cutting-edge museums and lively neighborhoods. Enter Ohio by interstate, but quickly step back in time on a drive through old-fashioned Amish Country. Big-hearted **Chicago** – aka Second City, the Windy City – is the Midwest's greatest city. Stroll or bike the lakefront, marvel at famous artwork and grand architecture, and take a culinary journey amid Chicago's celebrated restaurant scene. Head north to **Madison**, a youthful green-loving university town.

Detour north to the land of 10,000 lakes (aka Minnesota) for a stop in friendly, arty **Minneapolis**, followed by a visit to its quieter historic twin, **St Paul**, across the river.

Return to I-90 and activate cruise control, admiring the corn (and the **Corn Palace**) and the flat, flat South Dakota plains. Hit the brakes for the **Badlands National Park** and plunge into the Wild West. In the Black Hills, contemplate the nation's complex history at the massive monuments of **Mt Rushmore** and **Crazy Horse**. Watch mythic gunfights in **Deadwood** and learn about Native American culture at **Pine Ridge Indian Reservation**.

Halfway across Wyoming, cruise into **Cody** to catch a summer rodeo. Then take in the wonders of **Yellowstone National Park**, home to geysers, alpine lakes and waterfalls, with magnificent wildlife watching. Next, hike past jewel-like lakes and soaring peaks in **Grand Teton National Park**. Through rural Montana, the outdoorsy towns of **Bozeman** and **Missoula** make fun stops. Hit the boutique- and cafe scene, enjoy a fabulous meal, then head off again into the alpine beauty of **Glacier National Park** followed by a trek through the **Bob Marshall Wilderness Complex**.

After a few days out in the wild, surprising **Spokane** is a great place to recharge, with a pleasant riverfront and historic district sprinkled with enticing eating and drinking spots. For more cosmopolitan flavor, keep heading west to **Seattle**, a forward-thinking, eco-minded city with cafe culture, abundant nightlife and speedy island escapes on Puget Sound. If you still have time, the region has some great places to explore, including **Mt Rainier**, **Olympic National Park**, and the **San Juan Islands**.

» (above) Vineyard, Napa Valley (p975)
» (left) General store in a small Texan town

STEPHEN SAKS/LONELY PLANET IMAGES ©

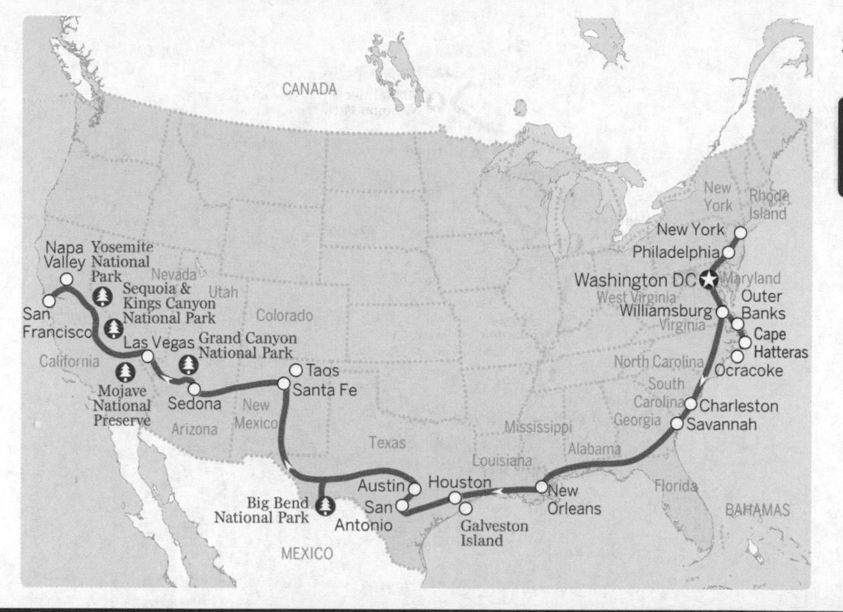

One Month
Coast to Coast

The Great American road trip: It's been mythologized hundreds of ways. Now live the dream, driving the length and breadth of the USA. Start in **New York City** (but hire a car in cheaper New Jersey) and hit the road. First stop: **Philadelphia**, a historic city with a burgeoning food, art and music scene. Continue on to **Washington, DC**. The nation's capital has a dizzying array of sights, plus great dining (crab feasts, global fare) and revelry, after the museums close. Continue south through Virginia, taking a detour to visit the fantastic historic settlement of colonial **Williamsburg**. Stick to the coast as you drive south, visiting **Cape Hatteras** with its pristine dunes, marshes and woodlands. Catch the ferry to remote **Ocracoke Island** where the wild ponies run. Further down, take in the antebellum allure of **Charleston** and **Savannah**, two of the south's most captivating destinations. Next it's on to jazz-loving **New Orleans**, with a soundtrack of smokin' hot funk brass bands, and succulent Cajun and Creole food.

The big open skies of Texas are next. Hit the beach at **Galveston Island** outside **Houston**. Follow the Mission Trail and stroll the tree-lined riverwalk in thriving **San Antonio**, then revel in the great music and drinking scene in **Austin**. Afterwards, eat your way through barbecue-loving Hill Country, then walk it off in jaw-dropping **Big Bend National Park**. Head north to New Mexico, following the Turquoise Trail up to artsy **Santa Fe** and far-out **Taos**. Roll west to red-rock **Sedona**, one of Arizona's loveliest and – to Native American tribes – most sacred places. The awe-inspiring **Grand Canyon** is next. Stay in the area to maximize time near this great wonder. Try your luck amid the bright lights of (luck be a lady tonight?) **Las Vegas**, then skirt the vast desert wilderness of **Mojave National Preserve** on your ride into California. From there, it's onto the lush towering forests of majestic **Sequoia & Kings Canyon National Parks** in the Sierra Nevada, followed by hiking and wildlife watching in **Yosemite**, California's most revered national park. The last stop is in hilly **San Francisco**, an enchanting city spread between ocean and bay with beautiful vistas, world-class dining and bohemian-loving nightlife. If there's time, tack on a grand finale drinking in the vineyards and gourmet produce of **Napa Valley**.

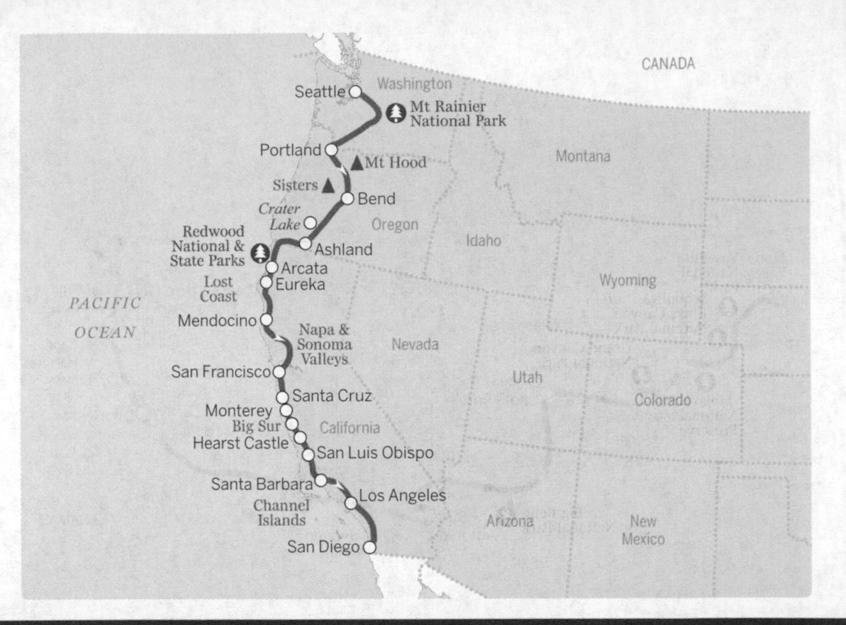

Three Weeks

The Left Coast

Geographically and politically, the West Coast couldn't be further from Washington, DC. This is a trip for those who lean left, and who like their nature ancient and wild, and their horizons and beaches wide-open.

Start in **Seattle**, taking in sprawling food markets, microbreweries and waterfront scenery. Heading south, visit **Mt Rainier National Park**, with superb hiking and relaxing inns nestled beneath the snow-covered peak. Continue on to the cutting-edge city of **Portland**, known for its sprawling parks, environmentally minded residents and progressive urbanism – plus food carts, coffeehouse culture and great nightlife to boot. After your culture fix, jump into nature's bounty by driving east along the Columbia River Gorge. Then turn south and make for **Mt Hood** for winter skiing and summer hiking. Further adventures await in the **Sisters**, a trio of 10,000ft peaks, and the striking blue waters of **Crater Lake**. Catch a Shakespearian play in sunny **Ashland**, then trade the mountains for the foggy coast. Enter California via Hwy 199 and take a stroll through the magnificent old-growth forests in **Redwood National & State Parks**.

Hug the coast as it meanders south through funky **Arcata** and seaside **Eureka**, lose yourself on the **Lost Coast**, then catch Hwy 1 through quaint **Mendocino** whose scenic headlands and rugged shoreline make for a requisite wander.

Make your way inland to the **Napa & Sonoma Valleys** for a wash-up and wine tasting amid rolling vineyards. Then continue south to the romantically hilly, ever free-spirited **San Francisco**.

Return to scenic Hwy 1 through surf-loving **Santa Cruz**, stately bayfront **Monterey** and beatnik-flavored **Big Sur**, where you can get scruffy again. In no time you'll reach the surreal **Hearst Castle** and laid-back, collegiate **San Luis Obispo**.

Roll into Mediterranean-esque **Santa Barbara**, then hop aboard a ferry in Ventura to the wildlife-rich **Channel Islands**. The pull from **Los Angeles** is strong. Go ahead, indulge your fantasies of **Hollywood** then cruise through LA's palm-lined neighborhoods – from Santa Monica to Los Feliz, Beverly Hills to Long Beach. After wracking up a few sins in the city of Angels, move on down to picture-perfect **San Diego**, visiting the historic Mission, the world-famous zoo, and of course those enticing beaches.

Road Trips & Scenic Drives

Best Experiences

Seeing dazzling coastal scenery on the Pacific Coast Highway.

Discovering charming, rarely visited destinations on Route 66.

Watching dramatic sunsets over the Appalachian Mountains on the Blue Ridge Parkway.

Listening to Memphis blues at a jumping music joint off the Great River Road.

Best Time

April to October

Key Starting Points

Chicago or Los Angeles – Route 66

Seattle or San Diego – Pacific Coast Highway

Waynesboro, VA or Cherokee, NC – Blue Ridge Parkway

Itasca State Park, MN or Venice, LA – Great River Road

Major Sights

Grand Canyon – Route 66

Point Reyes National Seashore – Pacific Coast Highway

Peaks of Otter – Blue Ridge Parkway

Shawnee National Park – Great River Road

Fill up the gas tank and buckle up. Everyone knows road-tripping is the ultimate way to see America. You can drive up, down, across, around or straight through every state on the continental US. Revel in yesteryear along Route 66, marvel at spectacular sunsets on the Pacific Coast Highway, or carve your own path through the Appalachian Mountains or along the mighty Mississippi. The great American experience is about so many things – bluegrass and beaches, Cajun food and farmers markets, rolling vineyards and redwood forests, and big cities and small towns in which to retreat after days well spent beneath those wide open skies. And there's no better way to get a taste for America in all its complexity and contradiction that setting off on the classic four-wheeled journey.

For more road-tripping ideas, turn to the Itineraries chapter (p30).

Route 66

For a classic American road trip, nothing beats good ol' Route 66. Nicknamed the nation's 'Mother Road' by novelist John Steinbeck, this string of small-town main streets and country byways first connected big-shouldered Chicago with the waving palm trees of Los Angeles in 1926.

Why Go?

Whether you seek to explore retro Americana or simply want to experience big horizons and captivating scenery far from the maddening crowd, Route 66 will take you there. The winding journey passes some of the USA's greatest outdoor attractions – not just the Grand Canyon, but also the Mississippi River, Arizona's Painted Desert and Petrified Forest National Park, and, at road's end, the Pacific beaches of sun-kissed Southern California.

Other highlights along the way: old-fashioned museums stocked with strange and wondrous objects from the past, Norman Rockwell-ish soda fountains, classic mom-and-pop diners, working gas stations that seem to have fallen right out of an old James Dean film clip and ghost towns (or soon-to-be ghost towns) hunkering on the edge of the desert.

Culturally speaking, Route 66 can be an eye-opener. Discard your preconceptions of small-town American life and unearth the joys of what bicoastal types dismissively term 'flyover' states. Mingle with farmers in Illinois and country-and-western stars in Missouri. Hear the legends of cowboys and Indians in Oklahoma. Visit Native American tribal nations and contemporary pueblos across the Southwest, all the while discovering the traditions of the USA's indigenous peoples. Then follow the trails of miners and desperados deep into the Old West.

When to Go

The best time to travel Route 66 is May to September, when the weather is warm and you can take advantage open-air activities. Take caution if you travel in the height of summer (July and August) as the heat can be unbearable – particularly in desert areas. Avoid traveling in the winter (December to March), when snow can lead to perilous driving conditions or outright road closures.

The Route

The journey starts in Chicago, just west of Michigan Ave and runs for some 2400 miles across eight states before terminating in Los Angeles near the Santa Monica pier. The road remains a never-ending work in progress as old sections get resurrected or disappear owing to the rerouting of other major roads.

For a run-down of some of the highlights and attractions along the way, see the following state sections, listed from east to west:

Illinois (p534)
Missouri (p610)
Kansas (p640)
Oklahoma (p647)
Texas (p694)
Arizona (p831)

History of the Mother Road

Route 66 didn't really hit its stride until the Great Depression, when migrant farm-

BEFORE YOU HIT THE ROAD

A few things to remember to ensure your road trip is as happy-go-lucky as possible:

» Join an automobile club (p1173) that provides members with 24-hour emergency roadside assistance and discounts on lodging and attractions; some international clubs have reciprocal agreements with US automobile associations, so check first and bring your member card from home.

» Check the spare tire, tool kit (eg jack, jumper cables, ice scraper, tire pressure gauge) and emergency equipment (eg flashers) in your car; if you're renting a vehicle and these essential safety items are not provided, consider buying them.

» Bring good maps (p1159), especially if you're touring off-road or away from highways; don't rely on a GPS unit – they can malfunction, and in remote areas such as deep canyons or thick forests they may not even work.

» Always carry your driver's license (p1173) and proof of insurance (p1173).

» If you're an international traveler, review the USA's road rules (p1176) and common road hazards (p1176).

» Fill up the tank often, because gas stations can be few and far between on the USA's scenic byways.

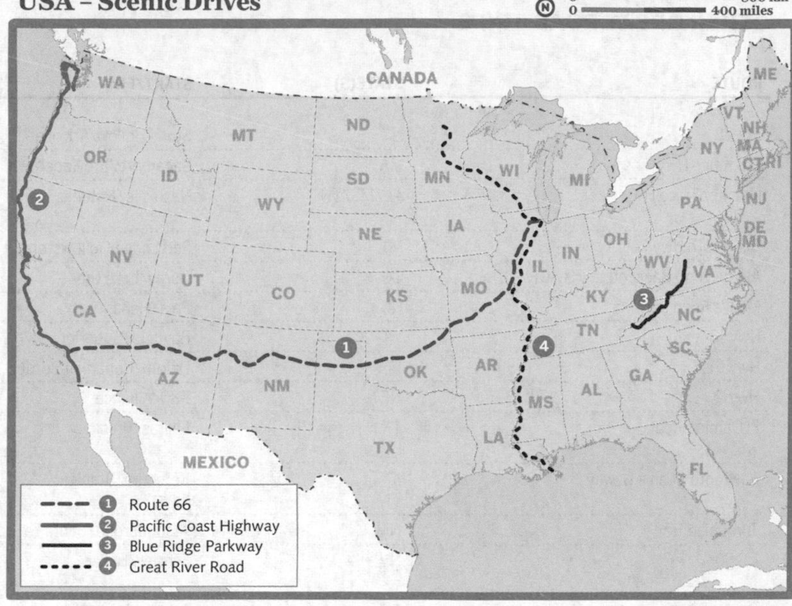

ers followed it as they fled the Dust Bowl across the Great Plains. Later, during the post-WWII baby boom, newfound prosperity encouraged many Americans to hit the road and 'get their kicks' on Route 66.

Almost as soon as it came of age, however, Route 66 began to lose steam. The shiny blacktop of an ambitious new interstate system started systematically paving over Route 66, bypassing its mom-and-pop diners, drugstore soda fountains and once-stylish motor courts. Railway towns were forgotten and way stations for travelers became dusty. Even entire towns began to disappear.

By the time Route 66 was officially decommissioned in 1984, preservation associations of Mother Road fans had sprung up. Today you can still get your kicks on Route 66, following gravel frontage roads and blue-line highways across the belly of America. It's like a time warp – connecting places where the 1950s seem to have stopped just yesterday.

Getting Lost

You need to be an amateur sleuth to follow Route 66 these days. Historical realignments of the route, dead-ends in farm fields and tumbleweed-filled desert patches, and rough, rutted driving conditions are par for the course. Remember that getting lost every now and then is inevitable. But never mind, since what the road offers is so valuable: a leap back through time to see what America once was, and still sometimes is. Nostalgia never tasted so sweet.

Resources

Before you hit the road, arm yourself with useful maps and key insider tips to help you make the most of your trip.

Historic Route 66 (www.historic66.com) Excellent website, with turn-by-turn directions for each state.

Here It Is: Route 66 Maps with directions (traveling both east-to-west and west-to-east) that you'll definitely want to take along for the ride.

Route 66: EZ66 Guide for Travelers by Jerry McClanahan, earns high marks for its glossy easy-to-follow maps.

Route 66: The Mother Road by Michael Wallis, is a fascinating look at the history and lore of the great road with old photographs bringing it all to life.

OTHER GREAT ROAD TRIPS

ROUTE	STATE(S)	START/END
Rte 28	NY	Stony Hollow/Arkville
Old Kings Hwy	MA	Sagamore/Provincetown
Natchez Trace Hwy	AL/MS/TN	Nashville/Natchez
Beartooth Hwy	MT	Red Lodge/Yellowstone
Alpine Loop Backcountry Byway	CO	Ouray/Lake City
Maui's Road to Hana	HI	Paia/Hana
Hwy 13	WI	Bayfield/Superior
Hwy 61	IA	Duluth/Canadian Border
Hwy 2	NE	I-80/Alliance
El Camino Real	TX	Lajitas/Presidio
Sawtooth Scenic Byway	ID	Ketchum/Stanley
Turquoise Trail	NM	Albuquerque/Santa Fe
US 50	NV	Fernley/Baker
Historic Columbia River Hwy	OR	Portland/Portland
Monument Valley	UT	Monument Valley
VT 100	VT	Stamford/Newport
Kancamagus Hwy	VT	Conway/Lincoln

Pacific Coast Highway

The classic west coast journey through California, Oregon and Washington takes in cosmopolitan cities, surf towns and charming coastal enclaves ripe for exploration. For many travelers, the real appeal of the Pacific Coast Highway is the magnificent scenery – wild and remote beaches, clifftop views overlooking crashing waves, rolling hills and lush forests (redwoods, eucalyptus trees) – that sometimes lies just beyond a city's outskirts.

Why Go?

The Pacific Coast Highway is an epic adventure for water babies, surfers, kayakers, scuba divers and every other kind of outdoor enthusiast, including landlubbers. Or if you're a more laid-back road-tripper, who just dreams of cruising alongside the ocean in a cherry-red convertible, drifting from sunrise to sunset, the insanely scenic PCH can deliver that, too.

The PCH is a road trip for lovers, nomadic ramblers, bohemians, beatniks and curiosity seekers keen to search out every nook and cranny of forgotten beachside hamlets and pastoral farm towns along the way.

The Route

Technically 'the PCH' is one of several coastal highways, including Hwy 101, stretching nearly 2000 miles from Tijuana, Mexico to British Columbia, Canada. The route connects the dots between some of the West Coast's most striking cities, starting from surf-style San Diego, through hedonistic Los Angeles and offbeat San Francisco in California, then moving north to equally alternative-minded and arty Seattle, Washington.

When the urban streets start to make you feel claustrophobic, just head out back on the open road and hit the coast again, heading north or south. The direction doesn't

SIGHTS & ACTIVITIES	BEST TIME	MORE INFO
Catskills mountains, lakes, rivers, hiking, leaf-peeping, tubing	May-Sep	p119
historic districts, period homes, coastal scenery	Apr-Oct	p189
'Old South' history, archaeological sites, scenic waterways, biking, camping, hiking,	Mar-Nov	p368
wildflowers, mountains, alpine scenery, camping	Jun-Sep	p757
Mountains, views, valleys, abandoned mines	Jun-Sep	p736
jungle waterfalls, beaches, hiking, swimming, surfing	year-round	p1095
lakeside beaches, forests, farmlands, nature walks	May-Sep	p581
state parks, waterfalls, quaint towns, hiking	May-Sep	p595
grass-covered sand-dunes, open vistas	May-Sep	p637
vast desert & mountain landscapes, hot springs, hiking, horseback riding	Feb-Apr & Oct-Nov	p696
jagged mountains, verdant forests, backpacking, hiking, wildlife watching	May-Sep	p767
mining towns, quirky museums & folk art, cycling, hiking	Mar-May & Sep-Nov	p859
'Loneliest Road in America', epic wilderness, biking, hiking, spelunking	May-Sep	p807
scenery, waterfalls, wildflowers, cycling, hiking	Apr-Sep	p1049
iconic buttes, movie-set locations; 4WD tours, horseback riding	year-round	p830
rolling pastures, green mountains, hiking, skiing	Jun-Sep	p218
craggy mountains, streams & waterfalls, camping, hiking, swimming	May-Sep	p225

really matter – the views and hidden places you find along the way make for rewarding exploring.

You could bypass metro areas and just stick to the places in between, like the almost too-perfect beaches of California's Orange County ('the OC') and Santa Barbara (the 'American Riviera'); wacky Santa Cruz, a university town and surfers' paradise; redwood forests along the Big Sur coast and north of Mendocino; the sand dunes, seaside resorts and fishing villages of coastal Oregon; and finally, the wild lands of Washington's Olympic Peninsula, with its primeval rain forest, and bucolic San Juan Islands, served by coastal ferries.

When to Go

There's no very bad time of year to drive the PCH, although northern climes will be rainier and snowier during winter. Peak travel season is June through August, which isn't always the best time to see the road – as many stretches of the coast are socked in by fog during early summer (locals call it 'June Gloom'). The shoulder seasons before Memorial Day (ie April and May) and after Labor Day (ie September and October) can be ideal, with sunny days, crisply cool nights and fewer crowds.

Blue Ridge Parkway

Snaking for some 469 miles through the southern Appalachian Mountains, the Blue Ridge Parkway is the land of great hiking and wildlife watching, old-fashioned music and captivating mountainous scenery – all of which make for a memorable and easily accessible road trip.

Construction on the parkway began in 1935 under President Franklin D Roosevelt and it was one of the great New Deal projects that helped put people back to work. It was a huge effort that took over 52 years to complete, with the final section laid in 1987.

ROADSIDE ODDITIES: ROUTE 66

Kitschy, time-warped and just plain weird roadside attractions? Route 66 has got 'em in spades. Here are a few beloved Mother Road landmarks to make your own scavenger hunt:

» Gemini Giant (p534) in Illinois

» Pacific's Black Madonna Shrine and Red Oak II outside Carthage in Missouri

» Blue Whale (p647) in Oklahoma

» Devil's Rope Museum (p694), Cadillac Ranch and Bug Ranch (p659) in Texas

» Seligman's Snow Cap Drive-In and Holbrook's WigWam Motel and Meteor Crater in Arizona (p831)

» Roy's Motel & Cafe in Amboy, in the middle of California's Mojave Desert

Why Go?

Watch the sunset over this wilderness of forest and mountain, tranquil streams and blissful silence – and you might feel like you've gone back a few centuries. Although it skirts dozens of towns and a few metropolitan areas, the Blue Ridge Parkway feels far removed from modern-day America. Here, rustic log cabins with rocking chairs on the front porch still dot the rolling hillsides, while signs for folk-art shops and live bluegrass music joints entice travelers onto side roads. History seems to permeate the air of these rolling backwoods – once home to Cherokee tribal people and later early colonial homesteads and Civil War battlefields.

There are great places to sleep and eat. Early-20th-century mountain and lakeside resorts still welcome families like old friends, while log-cabin diners dish up heaping piles of buckwheat pancakes with blackberry preserves and a side of country ham.

When you need to work off all that good Southern cooking, over 100 hiking trails can be accessed along the Blue Ridge Parkway, from gentle nature walks and easily summited peaks to rough-and-ready tramps along the legendary Appalachian Trail (p44). Or clamber on a horse and ride off into the refreshingly shady forests. Then go canoeing, kayaking or inner tubing along rushing rivers, or dangle a fishing line over the side of a rowboat on petite lakes. And who says you even have to drive? The parkway makes an epic trip for long-distance cyclists, too.

The Route

This rolling, scenic byway still connects Virginia's Shenandoah National Park with Great Smoky Mountains National Park, straddling the North Carolina–Tennessee border. Towns include Boone and Asheville in North Carolina; and Galax and Roanoke in Virginia, with Charlottesville, VA, also within a short drive of the park. Cities within range of the parkway are Washington, DC (140 miles) and Richmond, VA (95 miles).

When to Go

Keep in mind that the weather can vary greatly, depending on your elevation. While mountain peaks are snowed in during winter, the valleys can still be invitingly warm. Most visitor services along the parkway are only open from April through October. May is best for wildflowers, although most people come for leaf-peeping during fall. Spring and fall are good times for birdwatching, with nearly 160 species having been spotted in the skies over the parkway. Expect big crowds if you go during the summer or early autumn.

Resources

Blue Ridge Parkway (www.blueridgeparkway.org) Maps, activities and places to stay along the way. Can also download here the free *Blue Ridge Parkway Travel Planner.*

Hiking the Blue Ridge Parkway, by Randy Johnson, has in-depth trail descriptions, topographic trail maps and other essential info for hikes both short and long (including overnight treks).

Recreation.gov (www.recreation.gov) Can reserve some campsites through this site.

Great River Road

Established in the late 1930s, the Great River Road is an epic journey from the Mississippi's headwaters in the northern lakes of

Minnesota, floating downstream all the way to the river's mouth on the Gulf of Mexico near New Orleans. For a look at America across cultural divides – north-south, urban-rural, Baptist-bohemian – this is the road trip to make.

Why Go?

You'll be awed by the sweeping scenery as you meander alongside North America's second-longest river, from the rolling plains of Iowa down to the sunbaked cotton fields of the Mississippi Delta. Limestone cliffs, dense forests, flower-filled meadows and steamy swamps are all part of the backdrop – along with smokestacks, riverboat casinos and urban sprawl: this is the good, the bad and the ugly of life on the Mississippi. The portrait though isn't complete without mentioning the great music, lip-smacking food and down-home welcome at towns well off the beaten path on this waterfront itinerary.

Small towns provide a glimpse into American culture: there's Hibbing, MN, where folk rocker Bob Dylan grew up; Brainerd, MN, as seen in the Coen Brothers' film *Fargo;* Spring Green, WI, where architect Frank Lloyd Wright cut his teeth; pastoral Hannibal, MO, boyhood home of Mark Twain; and Metropolis, IL, where you'll find Superman's quick-change phone booth.

The southern section of this route traces American musical history, from rock and roll in St Louis to Memphis blues and New Orleans jazz. And you won't go hungry either, with retro Midwestern diners, Southern barbecue joints and smokehouses, and Cajun taverns and dance halls in Louisiana.

The Route

The Great River Road is not really one road at all, but a collection of roads that follow the 2300-mile-long Mississippi River, and takes travelers through 10 different states. Major urban areas that provide easy access to the road include New Orleans, Memphis, St Louis and Minneapolis.

When to Go

The best time to travel is from May to October, when the weather is warmest. Avoid going in the winter (or else stick to the deep south) when you'll have to contest with snowstorms.

Resources

Mississippi River Travel (www.experience mississippiriver.com) 'Ten states, one river' is the slogan for this official site, which is a great resource for history, outdoor recreation, live music and more.

USA Outdoors

Best Wildlife Watching

Bears in **Glacier National Park, MT**
Elk, bison and gray wolves in **Yellowstone National Park, WY**
Alligators, manatees and sea turtles in the **Florida Everglades**
Whales and dolphins on **Monterey Bay, CA**

Top Aquatic Activities

White-water rafting on the **New River, WV**
Surfing perfect waves in **Oahu, HI**
Diving and snorkeling off the **Florida Keys**
Kayaking pristine **Penobscot Bay, ME**

Best Multiday Adventures

Hiking the **Appalachian Trail**
Mountain-biking **Kokopelli's Trail, UT**
Climbing 13,770ft Grand Teton in **Grand Teton National Park, WY**
Canoeing, portaging and camping in the vast **Boundary Waters, MN**

Best Winter Activities

Downhill skiing in **Vail, CO**
Snowboarding in **Stowe, VT**
Cross-country skiing off **Lake Placid, NY**

Towering redwoods, alpine lakes, rolling hills, chiseled peaks, lunarlike deserts and a dramatic coastline of unrivaled beauty: the USA has no shortage of spectacular settings for a bit of outdoor adventure – and so far, we've described just one state (California). In the other 49 lie an astounding collection of natural wonders, from red-rock canyons and lush rainforests to snow-covered mountains and vast stretches of wilderness devoid of people but full of endless possibility.

No matter your weakness – hiking, biking, kayaking, rafting, surfing, horseback riding, rock climbing – you'll find world-class places to commune with the great outdoors. And if you're thinking of trying something new, the USA is a great place to take a course or hone your craft.

For outdoor activities, the USA has excellent infrastructure and a wealth of resources for planning an adventure – whether that entails trekking some (or all!) of the Appalachian Trail, mountain biking in Moab or carving up the legendary powder ski runs in the Rockies; for something more obscure you can kayak Washington's San Juan Islands, ski the maple woods of Vermont or canoe and camp in Minnesota's Boundary Waters. This really is just the beginning, with few limits save your own imagination.

For an overview of the nation's top national parks, see p769.

Hiking & Trekking

Fitness-focused Americans take great pride in their formidable network of trails – literally tens of thousands of miles – and there's no better way to experience the countryside up close and at your own pace.

The wilderness is amazingly accessible, making for easy exploration. National parks are ideal for short and long hikes, and if you're hankering for nights in the wilderness beneath star-filled skies, plan on securing a backcountry permit in advance, especially in places like the Grand Canyon – spaces are limited, particularly during summer.

Beyond the parks, you'll find troves of trails in every state. There's no limit to the places you can explore, from the sun-blasted hoodoos and red spires in Arizona's Chiricahua Mountains to the dripping trees and mossy nooks in Washington's Hoh River Rainforest (p1022); from the dogwood-choked Wild Azalea Trail in Louisiana to the tropical paradise of Kaua'i's Na Pali Coast (p1097). Almost anywhere you go, there's great hiking and backpacking within easy striking distance. All you need is a sturdy pair of shoes (sneakers or hiking boots) and a water bottle.

Hiking Resources

» **Survive Outdoors** (www.surviveoutdoors.com) Dispenses safety and first-aid tips, plus helpful photos of dangerous critters.

» **Wilderness Survival** by Gregory Davenport, is easily the best book on surviving nearly every contingency.

» **American Hiking Society** (www.americanhiking.org) Links to local hiking clubs and 'volunteer vacations' building trails.

» **Backpacker** (www.backpacker.com) Premier national magazine for backpackers, from novices to experts.

» **Rails-to-Trails Conservancy** (www.railstotrails.org) Converts abandoned railroad corridors into hiking and biking trails; publishes free trail reviews at www.traillink.com.

Cycling

Cycling's popularity grows by the day in the USA, with cities (including New York) adding more cycle lanes and becoming more bike-friendly and an increasing number of greenways dotting the countryside. You'll find die-hards in every town, and outfitters offering guided trips for all levels and durations. For the best advice on rides and rentals, stop by a local bike shop or do an internet search of the area you plan to visit.

Many states offer social multiday rides, such as Ride the Rockies in Colorado. For a modest fee, you can join the peloton on a scenic, well-supported route; your gear is ferried ahead to that night's camping spot. Other standout rides include Arizona's Mt

HONE YOUR SKILLS (OR LEARN SOME NEW ONES)

Whether you're eager to catch a wave or dangle from a cliff, learn some new outdoor tricks in these high-thrill programs.

» **Club Ed Surf Camp** (www.club-ed.com) Learn to ride the waves from Manresa Beach to Santa Cruz, CA, with field trips to the surfing museum and surfboard companies included.

» **Craftsbury Outdoor Center** (www.craftsbury.com) Come here for sculling, cross-country skiing and running amid the forests and hills of Vermont.

» **Joshua Tree Rock Climbing School** (www.joshuatreerockclimbing.com) Local guides lead beginners to experts on 7000 different climbs in Joshua Tree National Park, CA.

» **Nantahala Outdoor Center** (www.noc.com) Learn to paddle like a pro at this North Carolina-based school, which offers world-class instruction in canoeing and kayaking in the Great Smoky Mountains.

» **Otterbar Lodge Kayak School** (www.otterbar.com) Top-notch whitewater kayaking instruction is complemented by saunas, hot tubs, salmon dinners and a woodsy lodge tucked away on California's north coast.

» **Steep and Deep Ski Camp** (www.jacksonhole.com/info/ski.ac.steepski.asp) Finesse skiing extreme terrain (and snagging first tracks) then wind down over dinner parties. You can also ski with Olympian Tommy Moe.

TOP TRAILS IN THE USA

Ask 10 people for their top trail recommendations and it's possible that no two answers will be alike. The country is so varied and distances so enormous, there's little consensus. That said, you can't go wrong with the following all-star sampler.

» **Appalachian Trail** (www.appalachiantrail.org) Completed in 1937, the country's longest footpath is more than 2100 miles long, crosses six national parks, traverses eight national forests and hits 14 states from Georgia to Maine.

» **Pacific Crest Trail** (PCT; www.pcta.org) Follows the spines of the Cascades and Sierra Nevada, traipsing 2650 miles from Canada to Mexico, passing through six of North America's seven ecozones.

» **John Muir Trail in Yosemite** (p992) 222 miles of scenic bliss, from Yosemite Valley up to Mt Whitney.

» **Enchanted Valley, Olympic National Park, WA** (p1022) Magnificent mountain views, roaming wildlife and lush rainforests – all on a 13-mile out-and-back trail.

» **Great Northern Traverse, Glacier National Park, MT** (p761) A 58-mile haul that cuts through the heart of grizzly country and crosses the Continental Divide.

» **Kalalau Trail, Na Pali Coast, Kaua'i, HI** (p1097) Wild Hawaii at its finest – 11 miles of lush waterfalls, hidden beaches, verdant valleys and crashing surf.

» **Mount Katahdin, Baxter State Park, ME** (p243) A 9.5-mile hike over the 5268ft summit, with panoramic views of the park's 46 peaks.

» **South Kaibab/North Kaibab Trail, Grand Canyon, AZ** (p825) A multiday cross-canyon tramp down to the Colorado River and back up to the rim.

» **South Rim, Big Bend National Park, TX** (p694) A 13-mile loop through the ruddy, 7000ft Chisos Mountains, with views into Mexico.

» **Tahoe Rim Trail, Lake Tahoe, CA** (p998) This 165-mile all-purpose trail circumnavigates the lake from high above, affording glistening Sierra views.

Lemmon, a thigh-zinging 28-mile climb from the Sonoran Desert floor to the 9157ft summit and Tennessee's Cherohala Skyway, 51 glorious miles of undulating road and Great Smoky Mountain views.

Top Cycling Towns

» **San Francisco, CA** A pedal over the Golden Gate Bridge lands you in the stunningly beautiful, and stunningly hilly, Marin Headlands.

» **Madison, WI** More than 120 miles of bike paths, taking in the city's pretty lakes, parks and university campus.

» **Boulder, CO** Outdoors-loving town with loads of great biking paths, including the 16-mile Boulder Creek Trail.

» **Austin, TX** Indie-rock-loving town with nearly 200 miles of trails and great year-round weather.

» **Burlington, VT** Bike haven in the Northeast, with great rides, the best-known along Lake Champlain.

» **Portland, OR** A trove of great cycling (on- and off-road) in the Pacific Northwest.

Surfing

Hawaii

Blessed is the state that started it all, where the best swells generally arrive between November and March.

Waikiki (South Shore of Oahu) Hawaii's ancient kings rode waves on wooden boards well before 19th-century missionaries deemed the sport a godless activity. With warm water and gentle rolling waves, Waikiki is perfect for novices, offering long and sudsy rides.

Pipeline & Sunset Beach (North Shore of Oahu) Home to the classic tubing wave, which form as deep-water swells break over reefs into shallows, these are expert-only spots but well worth an ogle.

West Coast/California

Huntington Beach, CA, (aka Surf City, USA) The quintessential surf capital, with perpetual sun and a 'perfect' break, particularly during winter when the winds are calm.

Black's Beach, San Diego, CA This 2-mile sandy strip at the base of 300ft cliffs in La Jolla is known as one of the most powerful beach breaks in SoCal, thanks to an underwater canyon just offshore.

Huntington Beach, CA Surfer central is a great place to take in the scene - and some lessons.

Oceanside Beach, Oceanside, CA One of SoCal's prettiest beaches boasts one of the world's most consistent surf breaks come summer. It's a family-friendly spot.

Rincon, Santa Barbara, CA Arguably one of the planet's top surfing spots; nearly every major surf champion on the globe has taken Rincon for a ride.

Steamer Lane & Pleasure Point, Santa Cruz, CA There are 11 world-class breaks, including the point breaks over rock bottoms at these two sweet spots.

Swami's, Encinitas, CA Located below Seacliff Roadside Park, this popular surfing beach has multiple breaks guaranteeing you some fantastic waves.

East Coast

The Atlantic seaboard states harbor some terrific and unexpected surfing spots – especially if you're after more moderate swells. You'll find the warmest waters off Florida's Gulf Coast, where jetties, piers, and sandbars offer up many fine surfing opportunities.

Cocoa Beach, Melbourne Beach, FL Small crowds and mellow waves make it a paradise for beginners and longboarders. Just south is the Inlet, known for consistent surf and crowds to match.

Reef Rd, Palm Beach, FL This stellar spot features exposed beach and reef breaks with consistent surf, especially at low tide; winter is best.

Cape Hatteras Lighthouse, NC This very popular area has several quality spots and infinitely rideable breaks that gracefully handle swells of all sizes and winds from any direction.

Long Island, Montauk, NY More than a dozen surfing areas dot the length of Long Island from Montack's oft-packed Ditch Plains to Nassau County's Long Beach, with its 3-mile stretch of curling waves.

Casino Pier, Seaside Heights, NJ Both sides of the pier offer arguably the longest tube rides in NJ - just be prepared to compete with the crowds and entitled locals.

Point Judith, Narragansett, RI Rhode Island has premier surfing, with 40 miles of coastline and more than 30 surf spots, including this rocky point break offering long rollers as well as hollow barrels. Not for beginners.

MAD FOR MOUNTAIN BIKING

Mountain-biking enthusiasts will find trail nirvana in Boulder, CO; Moab, UT; Bend, OR; Ketchum, ID; and Marin, CA, where Gary Fisher and Co bunny-hopped the sport forward by careening down the rocky flanks of Mt Tamalpais on home-rigged bikes. Other great destinations include the following:

» **Kokopelli's Trail, UT** One of the premier mountain-biking trails in the Southwest stretches 140 miles on mountainous terrain between Loma, CO, and Moab, UT. Other nearby options include the 206-mile, hut-to-hut ride between Telluride, CO, and Moab, UT, and the shorter but very challenging 38-mile ride from Aspen to Crested Butte – an equally stunning ride.

» **Maah Daah Hey Trail, ND** A 96-mile jaunt over rolling buttes along the Little Missouri River.

» **Sun Top Loop, WA** A 22-mile ride with challenging climbs and superb views of Mt Rainier and surrounding peaks on the western slopes of Washington's Cascade Mountains.

» **Downieville Downhill, Downieville, CA** Not for the faint of heart, this piney trail, located near its namesake Sierra foothill town in Tahoe's National Forest, skirts river-hugging cliffs, passes through old-growth forest and drops 4200ft in under 14 miles.

» **Finger Lakes Trail, Letchworth State Park, NY** A little-known treasure, 35 miles south of Rochester in upstate New York, featuring more than 20 miles of singletrack along the rim of the 'Grand Canyon of the East'.

» **McKenzie River Trail, Wilamette National Forest, OR** (www.mckenzierivertrail.com) Twenty-two miles of blissful single-track winding through deep forests and volcanic formations. The town of McKenzie is located about 50 miles east of Eugene (p1047).

» **Porcupine Rim, Moab, UT** (p848) A 30-mile loop from town, this venerable high-desert romp features stunning views and hairy downhills.

Coast Guard Beach, Eastham, MA Part of the Cape Cod National Seashore, this family-friendly beach is known for its consistent shortboard/longboard swell all summer long.

White-Water Rafting

East of the Mississippi, West Virginia has an arsenal of legendary white water. First, there's the New River Gorge National River (p318), which, despite its name, is one of the oldest rivers in the world. Slicing from North Carolina into West Virginia, it cuts a deep gorge, known as the Grand Canyon of the East, producing frothy rapids in its wake. Then there's the Gauley, arguably among the world's finest white water. Revered for its ultrasteep and turbulent chutes, this venerable Appalachian river is a watery roller-coaster, dropping more than 668ft and churning up 100-plus rapids in a mere 28 miles. Six more rivers, all in the same neighborhood, offer training grounds for less-experienced river rats.

Out west there's no shortage of scenic and spectacular rafting, from Utah's Cataract Canyon, a thrilling romp through the red rocks of Canyonlands National Park, to the Rio Grande in Texas, a lazy run through limestone canyons. The North Fork of the Owyhee – which snakes from the high plateau of southwest Oregon to the rangelands of Idaho – is rightfully popular and features towering hoodoos. In California, both the Tuolumne and American Rivers surge with moderate-to-extreme rapids while in Idaho, the Middle Fork of the Salmon River has it all: abundant wildlife, thrilling rapids, a rich homesteader history, waterfalls and hot springs. If you're organized enough to plan a few years in advance, book a spot on the Colorado River, the quintessential river trip. And if you're not after white-knuckle rapids, fret not – many rivers have sections suitable for peaceful float trips or inner-tube drifts you can traverse with a cold beer in hand.

Kayaking & Canoeing

For exploring flatwater (no rapids or surf), opt for a kayak or canoe. While kayaks are seaworthy, they are not always suited for carrying bulky gear. For big lakes and the seacoast (including the San Juan Islands), use a sea kayak. For month-long wilderness trips – including the 12,000 miles of watery routes in Minnesota's Boundary Waters or Alabama's Bartram Canoe Trail, with 300,000 acres of marshy delta bayous, lakes and rivers – use a canoe.

You can kayak or canoe almost anywhere in the USA. Rentals and instruction are yours for the asking, from Wisconsin's Apostle Islands National Seashore and Utah's celebrated Green River (p848) to Hawaii's Na Pali Coast (p1097). Hire kayaks in Maine's Penobscot Bay to poke around the briny waters and spruce-fringed islets, or join a full-moon paddle in Sausalito's Richardson Bay, CA.

Skiing & Other Winter Sports

You can hit the slopes in 40 states, making for tremendous variety in terrain and ski-town vibe. Colorado has some of the best skiing in the nation, though California, Vermont and Utah are all top-notch destinations for the alpine experience. The ski season typically runs from mid-December to April, though some resorts have longer seasons. In summer, many resorts are great places to go mountain biking and hiking courtesy of chair lifts. Ski packages (including airfare, hotel and lift tickets) are easy to find through resorts, travel agencies and online travel booking sites; these packages can be a good deal if your main goal is to ski.

Wherever you ski, it won't come cheap. Find the best deals by going midweek, purchasing multiday tickets, heading to lesser-known 'sibling' resorts (like Alpine Meadows near Lake Tahoe) or checking out mountains that cater to locals including Vermont's Mad River Glen (p218), Santa Fe Ski Area (p866) and Colorado's Wolf Grade.

Top Ski & Snowboard Resorts

Vermont's first-rate Stowe (p218) draws seasoned souls – freeze your tail off on the lifts, but thaw out nicely après ski in timbered bars with local brews. Find more snow, altitude and attitude out west at Vail, CO (p729), Squaw Valley, CA (p999) and high-glitz Aspen, CO (p731). For an unfussy scene and steep vertical chutes, try Alta, UT (p844), Telluride, CO (p738), Jackson, WY (p751) and Taos, NM (p872). In Alaska, slopes slice through spectacular terrain outside Juneau, Anchorage and Fairbanks. Mt Aurora Ski-Land has the most northerly chairlift in North America and, from spring to summer, the shimmering green-blue aurora borealis.

Rock Climbing

Scads of climbers flock to Joshua Tree National Park, an otherworldly shrine in southern California's sun-scorched desert. There, amid craggy monoliths and the country's oldest trees, they pay pilgrimage on more than 8000 routes, tackling sheer vertical, sharp edges and bountiful cracks with aplomb. Or not. Fortunately, a top-notch climbing school offers classes for all levels (see p43).

In Zion National Park, UT, multiday canyoneering classes teach the fine art of going *down:* rappelling off sheer sandstone cliffs into glorious, red-rock canyons filled with trees. Some of the sportier pitches are made in dry suits, down the flanks of roaring waterfalls into ice-cold pools.

Other great climbing spots:

Wyoming's Grand Teton National Park (p750) A great spot for climbers of all levels: beginners can take basic climbing courses; the more experienced can join two-day expeditions up to the top of Grand Teton itself: a 13,770ft peak with majestic views.

City of Rocks National Reserve, ID More than 500 routes up wind-scoured granite and pinnacles 60 stories tall.

Yosemite National Park, CA (p989) A hallowed shrine for rock climbers, offers superb climbing courses for first timers as well as for those craving a night in a hammock 1000ft above terra firma.

Bishop, CA (p997) South of the park and favored by many top climbers, this sleepy town in the Eastern Sierra is gateway to excellent climbing in the nearby Owens River Gorge and Buttermilk Hills.

Red Rock Canyon, NV (p802) Ten miles west of Las Vegas is some of the world's finest sandstone climbing.

Enchanted Rock State Natural Area, TX Located 70 miles west of Austin, this national park with its huge pink granite dome, has hundreds of routes and stellar views of the Texas Hill Country.

Rocky Mountain National Park, CO Offers alpine climbing near Boulder.

Flatirons, CO Also near Boulder, has fine multi-pitch ascents.

Shawangunk Ridge, NY (p117) Located within a two-hour drive north of New York City, this ridge stretches some 50 miles, and the 'Gunks' are where many East Coast climbers tied their first billets.

Climbing & Canyoneering Resources

American Canyoneering Association (www.canyoneering.net) An online canyons database and links to courses, local climbing groups and more.

Climbing (www.climbing.com) Cutting-edge rock-climbing news and information since 1970.

SuperTopo (www.supertopo.com) One-stop shop for rock-climbing guidebooks, free topo maps and route descriptions.

Scuba Diving & Snorkeling

The most exotic underwater destination in the USA is Hawaii. There, in shimmering aquamarine waters that stay warm year-round, you'll besmn treated to a psychedelic display of surreal colors and shapes. Swim alongside sea turtles, octopuses and fiesta-colored parrot-fish – not to mention lava tubes and black coral. Back on shore, cap off the reverie with a Kona brew and *poke* made from just-caught ahi tuna.

The best diving is off the coast or between the islands, so liveaboards are the way to go for scuba buffs. From the green turtles and WWII wrecks off the shores of Oahu to the undersea lava sculptures near little Lana'i, the Aloha State offers endless underwater bliss – but plan ahead, as the dive sites change with the seasons.

On the continental USA, Florida has the lion's share of great diving, with more than 1000 miles of coastline subdivided into 20 unique undersea areas. There are hundreds of sites and countless dive shops offering equipment and guided excursions. South of West Palm Beach, you'll find clear waters and fantastic year-round diving with ample reefs. In the Panhandle, or northern part of the state, you can scuba in the calm and balmy waters of the Gulf of Mexico; off Pensacola and Destin, there are fabulous wreck dives; and you can dive with manatees near Crystal River.

The Florida Keys, a curving string of 31 islets, are the crown jewel; expect a brilliant mix of marine habitats, North America's only living coral garden and the occasional shipwreck. Key Largo is home to the John Pennekamp Coral Reef State Park with over 200 miles of underwater bliss.

There's terrific diving and snorkeling (and much warmer water) beyond the mangrove swamps of the Florida Keys, FL, boasting the world's third-largest coral system. Look for manatees off Islamorada (p467) or take an expedition to Dry Tortugas (p471), where the expansive reef swarms with barracuda, sea turtles and a couple of hundred sunken ships.

Other Underwater Destinations

Hanauma Bay Nature Preserve, Oahu, HI (p1086) Despite the crowds, this is still one of the world's great spots for snorkeling, with more than 450 resident species of reef fish.

Point Lobos State Reserve, CA (p941) Some of best shore-diving in California, with shallow reefs, caves, pinnacles, sea stars, torpedo rays, sea lions, seals and otters. The **Monterey Bay Dive Company** (www.montereyscubadiving.com) is a handy resource for sites and guides.

The Channel Islands, CA (p937) Lying between Santa Barbara and Los Angeles, harbor spiny lobsters, angel sharks and numerous dive sites best accessed by liveaboard charter.

Jade Cove (about 10 miles south of Lucia on Hwy 1) This aptly named spot has the world's only underwater concentration of jade, making for an unforgettable dive.

Cape Hatteras National Seashore, NC Along the northern coast of North Carolina, divers can explore historical wrecks from the Civil War (and encounter tiger sand sharks); there are also numerous options for dive charters within the Outer Banks and the Cape Lookout areas.

Lake Ouachita, AR The largest lake in Arkansas is ringed by forested mountains and known for its pristine waters and some 30 distinct dive spots. Camp along the lakeshore and, quite literally, dive in. It's also the site of a 16-mile water-based trail, the first of its kind in the country.

Great Lakes, MI The USA's most unexpected dive spot? Michigan's Lakes Superior and Huron, with thousands of shipwrecks lying strewn on the sandy bottoms – just don't expect to see any angelfish!

Horseback Riding

Cowboy wannabes will be happy to learn that horseback riding of every style, from Western to bareback, is available across the USA. Out west, you'll find truly memorable experiences – everything from week-long expeditions through the canyons of southern Utah and cattle wrangling in Wyoming, to pony rides along the Oregon coast. Finding horses is easy; rental stables and riding schools are located around and in many of the national parks. Experienced equestrians can explore alone or in the company of guides familiar with local flora, fauna and history. Half- and full-day group trail rides, which usually include lunch in a wildflower-speckled meadow, are popular and plentiful.

California is terrific for riding, with fog-swept trails leading along the cliffs of Point Reyes National Seashore, longer excursions through the high-altitude lakes of the Ansel Adams Wilderness, and multiday pack trips in Yosemite and Kings Canyon. Utah's Capitol Reef (p852) and Canyonlands (p850) also provide spectacular four-hoofed outings, as do the mountains, arroyos and plains of Colorado, Arizona, New Mexico, Montana and Texas.

Dude ranches come in all varieties, from down-duvet luxurious to barn-duty authentic on working cattle ranches. They're found in most of the western states, and even some eastern ones (such as Tennessee and North Carolina). Real-life cowboys are included.

Travel with Children

Best Regions for Kids in the USA

New York, New Jersey & Pennsylvania

New York City has museums, carriage rides and row-boating in Central Park, cruises on the Hudson and theme restaurants in Times Square. Head to the NJ shore for boardwalk fun, and to Pennsylvania for Amish Country horse-and-buggy rides.

California

See stars in Hollywood and get behind the movie magic at Universal Studios, hit the beaches then head south to Disneyland and the San Diego Zoo. In Northern California, see redwoods and the Golden Gate Bridge.

Washington, DC, & the Capital Region

Washington has unrivalled allure for families, with museums, a panda-loving zoo, and open spaces on the Mall. Virginia's Williamsburg is a slice of 18th-century America with costumed interpreters and fanciful activities.

Florida

Orlando's Walt Disney World is well worth planning a vacation around. Afterwards, hit the state's beautiful beaches.

From coast to coast, you'll find superb attractions for all ages in the USA: bucket-and-spade fun at the beach, amusement parks, zoos, eye-popping aquariums and natural history exhibits, hands-on science museums, camping adventures, battlefields, hikes in wilderness reserves, leisurely bike rides through serene countryside (easy-going and challenging alike), and plenty of other activities likely to wow the young ones. The great outdoors is a good place to start: most national and state parks gear at least some exhibits, trails and programs (junior ranger activities and the like) towards families with kids.

Traveling with children can bring a whole new dimension to the American experience. You may make deeper connections, as locals (especially those with their own children) brighten and coo and embrace your family like long-lost cousins. From the city to the country, most facilities are ready to accommodate a child's needs.

The USA for Kids

Dining with Children

Child- and family-friendly activities are listed throughout this guide in the On the Road chapters, and major cities have a section devoted specifically to kids.

The US restaurant industry seems built on family-style service: children are not just accepted almost everywhere, but usually are encouraged by special children's menus with smaller portions and lower prices. In some restaurants children under a certain age even eat for free. Restaurants usually provide high chairs and booster seats. Some restaurants may also offer children crayons and puzzles, and occasionally live performances by cartoon-like characters.

Restaurants without children's menus don't necessarily discourage kids, though higher-end restaurants might; however, even at the nicer places, if you show up early enough (right at dinner time opening hours), you can usually eat without too much stress – and you'll likely be joined by other foodie couples with kids. You can ask if the kitchen will make a smaller order of a dish (also ask how much it will cost), or if they will split a normal-size main dish between two plates for the kids. Chinese, Mexican and Italian restaurants seem to be the best bet for finicky young eaters.

Farmers markets are growing in popularity in the USA, and every sizeable town has at least one a week. This is a good place to assemble a first-rate picnic, sample the local specialties and support independent growers in the process. After getting your stash, head to the park or waterfront, which is probably nearby.

Accommodations

Motels and hotels typically have rooms with two beds, which are ideal for families. Some also have roll-away beds or cribs that can be brought into the room for an extra charge – but keep in mind these are usually Pack 'n Plays, which not all children sleep well in. Some hotels offer 'kids stay free' programs for children up to 12 or sometimes 18 years old. Be wary of B&Bs, as many of these don't allow children; ask when reserving.

Babysitting

Resort hotels may have on-call babysitting services; otherwise, ask the front-desk staff or concierge to help you make arrangements. Always ask if babysitters are licensed and bonded, what they charge per hour per child, whether there's a minimum fee, and if they charge extra for transportation or meals. Most tourist bureaus list local resources for childcare and recreation facilities, medical services and so on.

To find family-oriented sights and activities, accommodations, restaurants and entertainment throughout this book, just look for the child-friendly icon (👪).

Necessities, Driving & Flying

Many public toilets have a baby-changing table (sometimes in men's toilets too), and gender-neutral 'family' facilities appear in airports.

Medical services and facilities in America are of a high standard, and items such as baby food, formula and disposable diapers are widely available – including organic options – in supermarkets across the country.

Every car-rental agency should be able to provide an appropriate child seat, since these are required in every state, but you need to request it when booking and expect to pay around $10 more per day.

Domestic airlines don't charge for children under two. Those two and up must have a seat, and discounts are unlikely. Rarely, some resorts (eg Disneyland) offer a 'kids fly free' promotion. Amtrak and other train operators run similar deals (with kids up to age 15 riding free) on various routes.

Discounts for Children

Child concessions often apply for tours, admission fees, and transport, with some discounts as high as 50% off the adult rate. However, the definition of 'child' can vary from under 12 to under 16 years. Some popular sights also have discount rates for families, which will save a few dollars compared to buying individual tickets. Most sights also give free admission to children under two years.

Planning

Weather and crowds are all-important considerations when planning a US family getaway. The peak travel season across the country is from June to August, when schools are out and the weather is warmest. Expect high prices and abundant crowds – meaning long lines at amusement and water parks, fully booked resort areas and heavy traffic on the roads; you'll need to reserve well in advance for popular destinations. The same holds true for winter resorts (in the Rockies, Tahoe, Catskills) during its high season of January to March.

Children's Highlights

Outdoor Adventure

» Kayaking, canoeing or taking guided walks in the Florida Everglades

» Watching powerful geysers, spying wildlife and taking magnificent hikes in Yellowstone National Park

» Gazing across one of earth's great wonders at Grand Canyon National Park

» Exploring the wild and pristine wilderness of Olympic National Park, one of the world's only temperate rain forests

» Going white-water rafting in the New River Gorge National Park, West Virginia

Theme Parks & Zoos

» Bronx Wildlife Conservation Park, NY – One of the nation's biggest and best zoos is just a subway ride from Manhattan

» Walt Disney World, Florida – With four action-packed parks spread across 20,000 acres, this is the place your children will long remember

» Disneyland, California – Kids four and up appreciate the original park, while teenagers go nuts next door at California Adventure

» SeaWorld – Killer-whale and dolphin shows, rides and loads of other amusements at these aquatic parks in Florida and California

» San Diego Zoo – A fantastic place to see creatures great and small, this pioneering zoo has more than 4000 animals (880 species)

Traveling in Time

» Donning 18th-century garb and mingling with costumed interpreters in the history-rich settings of Plimoth, Williamsburg, Yorktown and Jamestown

» Plugging your ears as soldiers in 19th-century garb fire muskets and cannons at Fort Mackinac, Michigan

» Go on a walking tour of Boston's Freedom Trail with Ben Franklin (or at least his 21st century lookalike)

» Strolling in the footsteps of one of America's greatest presidents at the Lincoln Home in Springfield, Illinois

» Rattling along in a horse-drawn carriage through the historic streets of St Augustine, Florida

Rainy-Day Activities

» National Air & Space Museum, Washington, DC – rockets, spacecraft, old-fashioned biplanes and ride simulators will inspire any budding aviator

» American Museum of Natural History, New York City – kids of all ages will enjoy a massive planetarium, immense dinosaur skeletons and 30 million other artifacts

» City Museum, St Louis – a packed funhouse of unusual exhibits, plus a Ferris wheel on the roof

» Port Discovery Museum, Baltimore – three stories of adventure and (cleverly disguised) learning, including an Egyptian tomb, farmers market, train, art studio and physics stations

» Pacific Science Center, Seattle – Fascinating, hands-on exhibits, plus an IMAX theater, planetarium and laser shows

Eating

» Getting messy eating scrumptious Maryland blue crabs at open-air restaurants along the Chesapeake Bay

» Turn the clock back a few generations at the 1950s retro Ellens Stardust Diner in NYC

» Dive face-first (no plates or cutlery provided) into Texas' best barbecue at City Market in Luling

» Tasting the world's best deep-dish pizza (and scrawling your name on the wall) at Gino's East in Chicago

» Assembling a gourmet picnic from the weekend farmers market at San Francisco's ferry building

Helpful Resources for Families

For all-around information and advice, check out Lonely Planet's *Travel with Children*. For outdoor advice, read *Kids in the Wild: A Family Guide to Outdoor Recreation* by Cindy Ross and Todd Gladfelter, and Alice Cary's *Parents' Guide to Hiking & Camping*.

Family Travel Files (www.thefamilytravelfiles.com) Ready-made vacation ideas, destination profiles and travel tips.

Go City Kids (www.gocitykids.com) Excellent coverage of kid-centric activities and entertainment in more than 50 US cities.

Kids.gov (www.kids.gov) Eclectic, enormous national resource; download songs and activities, or even link to the CIA Kids' Page.

regions at a glance

Deciding where to go can be daunting in the massive USA. The East Coast has big-city allure, picturesque towns (especially New England), historic attractions, bountiful feasts (Maine lobsters, Maryland crabs) and outdoor beauty (beaches, islands, mountains).

The West Coast has memorable urban exploring (San Francisco, LA, Seattle), stunning scenery (dramatic coastline, redwoods, high Sierra) and feasting aplenty (wineries, award-winning restaurants).

In between, there's much: soulful music and belly-pleasing fare in the south; big skies and Native American culture in the Rockies, Southwest and Great Plains; live music and barbecue in Texas; and off-the-beaten path adventures in the Great Lakes.

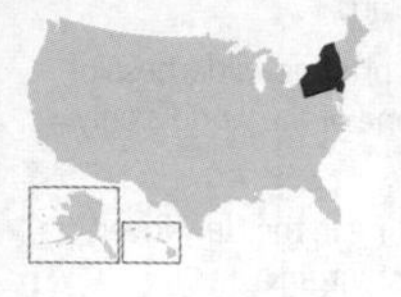

New York, New Jersey & Pennsylvania

Arts ✓✓✓
History ✓✓✓
Outdoors ✓✓✓

Arts

Home to the MET, MOMA and Broadway – and that's just NYC. Buffalo, Philadelphia, Pittsburgh also have a share of world-renowned cultural institutions.

History

From preserved Gilded Age mansions in the Hudson Valley, Independence National Historic Park in Philadelphia and sites dedicated to formative moments in the nation's founding, the region gives an interactive education.

Outdoors

The outdoors lurks beyond the city's gaze, with hiking in the Adirondack wilderness and Catskills, rafting down the Delaware River and Atlantic Ocean and frolics along the Jersey Shore or Hamptons.

p58

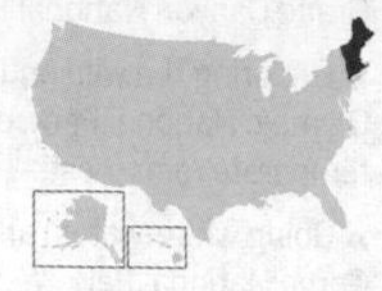

New England

Seafood ✓✓✓
History ✓✓✓
Beaches ✓✓✓

Seafood

New England is justifiably famous for its fresh seafood. The coast is peppered with seaside eateries where you can feast on fresh oysters, lobster and fish as you watch the dayboats haul in their catch.

History

From the Pilgrims landing in Plymouth and the witch hysteria in Salem to Paul Revere's revolutionary ride, New England has shaped American history.

Beaches

Cape Cod, Martha's Vineyard and Block Island – New England is a summer mecca for sand and sea worshippers. The region's scores of beaches run the gamut from kid-friendly tidal flats to gnarly open-ocean surf.

p162

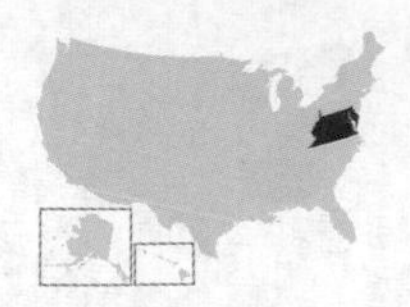

DC & the Capital Region

Arts ✓✓✓
History ✓✓✓
Food ✓✓✓

Arts
Washington has a superb collection of museums and galleries. You'll also find down-home mountain music on Virginia's Crooked Red, famous theaters and edgy art in Baltimore.

History
For historical lore, Jamestown, Williamsburg and Yorktown offer windows into Colonial America, while Civil War battlefields litter the Virginia countryside. There are fascinating presidential estates like Mount Vernon and Monticello.

Food
Feasts await: Maryland blue crabs, oysters and seafood platters; international restaurants in DC and farm-to-table dining rooms in Baltimore, Charlottesville, Staunton and Rehoboth.

p244

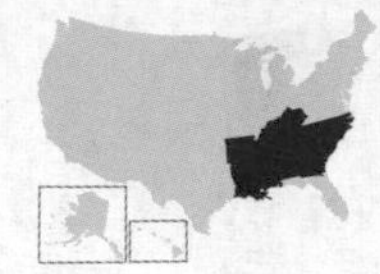

The South

Food ✓✓✓
Music ✓✓✓
Charm ✓✓✓

Food
From Georgia BBQ to Mississippi soul food to the Cajun-Creole smorgasbord in Louisiana, the South is a diverse, artery clogging, magnificent, place to eat.

Music
Nowhere on earth has a soundtrack as influential as the South. Head to music meccas for the authentic experience: country in Nashville, blues in Memphis and big-band jazz in New Orleans.

Charm
Picture-book towns like Charleston and Savannah among others have captivated visitors with their historic tree-lined streets, antebellum architecture and down-home welcome.

p320

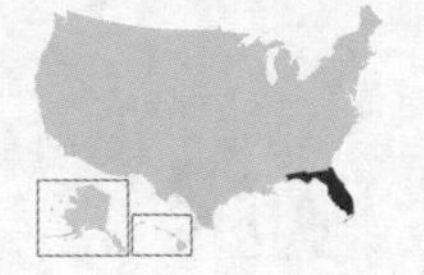

Florida

Fun ✓✓✓
Wildlife ✓✓✓
Beaches ✓✓✓

Fun
Florida has a complicated soul: it's the home of Miami's art deco district and Little Havana, plus historical attractions in St Augustine, theme parks in Orlando and museums and island heritage in Key West.

Wildlife
Immerse yourself in aquatic life on a snorkeling or diving trip. For bigger beasts, head off on a whale-watching cruise, or spy alligators – along with egrets, eagles, manatees and other wildlife – on an Everglades trip.

Beaches
You'll find an array of sandy shores from steamy South Beach to upscale Palm Beach, island allure on Sanibel and Captiva and panhandle rowdiness in Pensacola.

p440

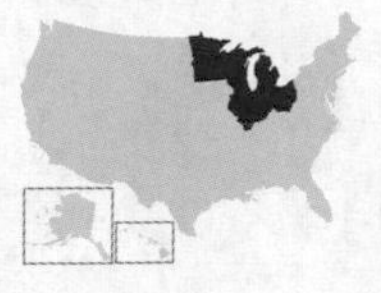

Great Lakes

Food ✓✓✓
Music ✓✓✓
Attractions ✓✓

Food
From Beard-award-winning restaurants in Chicago and Minneapolis to fresh-from-the-dairy milkshakes, the Midwest's farms, orchards and breweries satisfy the palate.

Music
Home to the Rock and Roll Hall of Fame, blowout fests like Lollapalooza and thrashing clubs in all the cities, the Midwest rocks, baby.

Attractions
A big ball of twine, a mustard museum, a cow-doo throwing contest: the quirks rise from the Midwest's backyards and back roads, wherever there are folks with a passion, imagination and maybe a little too much time on their hands.

p500

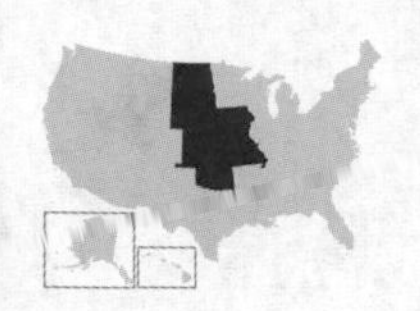

Great Plains

Road Trips ✓✓✓
Geology ✓✓
Nightlife ✓✓

Road Trips

Beneath big open skies, a two-lane highway passes sunlit fields, rolling river valleys and dramatic peaks on its journey to the horizon – all par for the course (along with oddball museums and cozy cafes) on the great American road trip.

Geology

The Badlands are b-a-a-a-d in every good sense. These geologic wonders are matched by the wildlife-filled beauty of the Black Hills and Theodore Roosevelt National Park.

Nightlife

Out in the wilds, streets roll up at sunset but in St Louis and Kansas City, that's when the fun begins. Legendary jazz, blues and rock are played in clubs and bars big and small.

p598

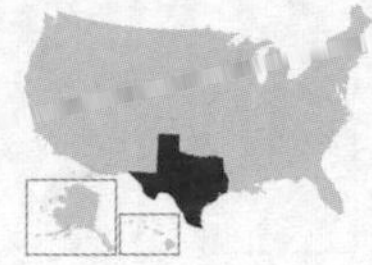

Texas

Barbecue ✓✓✓
Live Music ✓✓✓
Outdoors ✓✓

Barbecue

Meat lovers, you've died and gone to heaven (vegetarians, you're somewhere else). Some of the best barbecue on earth is served up in Lockhart near Austin, although you can dig in to brisket, ribs and sausage all across the state.

Live Music

Austin has proclaimed itself (and no one's arguing) the 'Live Music Capital of the World,' and you can two-step to live bands on worn wooden floors at honky-tonks and dance halls all around the state.

Outdoors

Canyons, mountains and hot springs set the scene for memorable outings in Texas. Go rafting on the Big Bend River or get your beach fix along the pretty Southern Gulf Coast.

p651

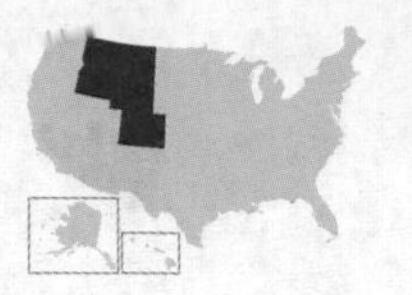

Rocky Mountains

Outdoors ✓✓✓
Culture ✓✓✓
Landscapes ✓✓✓

Outdoors

Skiing, hiking and boating make the Rockies a playground for adrenaline junkies. Hundreds of races and group rides, and an incredible infrastructure of parks, trails and cabins.

Culture

Once a land of Stetsons and prairie dresses, today's Rocky folk are more often spotted in lycra, mountain bike nearby, sipping a microbrew or latte at a cafe. Hard playing and slow living still rule.

Landscapes

The snow-covered Rocky Mountains are pure majesty. With chiseled peaks, clear rivers and red-rock contours, the Rockies contain some of the world's most famous parks and bucketloads of clean mountain air.

p703

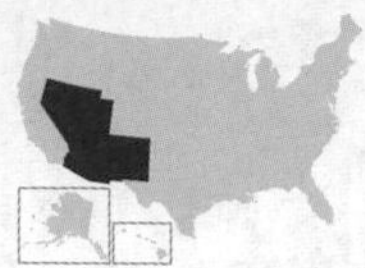

Southwest

Scenery ✓✓✓
Outdoors ✓✓✓
Cultures ✓✓✓

Scenery

Home to spectacular national parks, the Southwest is famous for the jaw-dropping Grand Canyon, the dramatic red buttes of Monument Valley and the vast Carlsbad Caverns – just a few of many regional wonders.

Outdoors

Ski powdery slopes at Park City, splash and frolic in Slide Rock State Park, skitter down dunes at White Sands and hike to your heart's content at Brice, Zion and countless other spots.

Cultures

This is Native American country, and visiting the Hopi and Navajo Nations provide a fine introduction to America's first peoples. For a journey back in time, explore clifftop dwellings abandoned by ancient Puebloan peoples.

p785

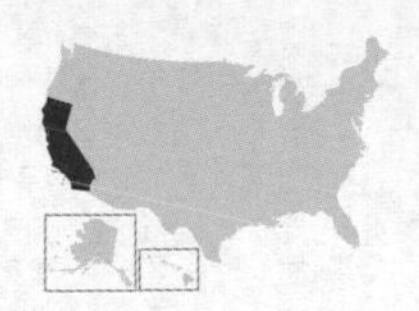

California

Beaches ✓✓✓
Outdoors ✓✓✓
Eating ✓✓✓

Beaches

With more than 1100 miles of coast, California rules the sands: rugged, pristine beaches in the north and people-packed beauties in the south, with great surfing, sea kayaking or simply beach-walking all along the coast.

Outdoors

Snow-covered mountains, glittering sea and old-growth forests set the stage for skiing, hiking, biking, wave frolicking, wildlife-watching and more.

Eating

Fertile fields, talented chefs and an insatiable appetite for the new make California a major culinary destination. Browse food markets, sample the produce at lush vineyards and eat well in California's many celebrated dining rooms.

p882

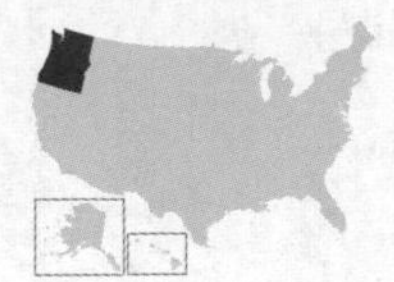

Pacific Northwest

Food & Wine ✓✓
Skiing ✓✓
Parks ✓✓✓

Food & Wine

'Up-and-coming' is the word in Portland and Seattle where chefs blend fish caught in local waters with vegetables harvested in the Eden-like valleys surrounding the Columbia River. Then there's Washington wine.

Skiing

From year-round ski areas, to rustic cross-country, to the snowboarding heaven that is Mt Baker; the region with the highest snowfalls in North America delivers unparalleled winter-sports.

Parks

The northwest has four national parks, including three Teddy Roosevelt-era classics – Olympic, Mount Rainier, and Crater Lake – each bequeathed with historic lodges; plus a wilder addition – the North Cascades.

p1001

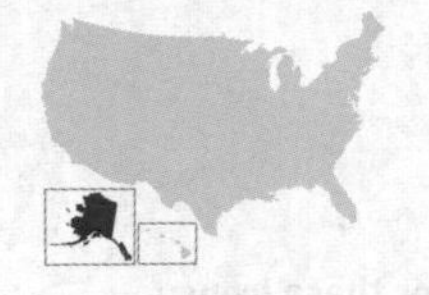

Alaska

Wildlife ✓✓✓
Glaciers ✓✓✓
Food & Drink ✓

Wildlife

Alaska offers some of the best wildlife viewing opportunities in the country. Seeing the sight of breaching whales and foraging bears Southeast Alaska is unforgettable, while Denali National Park is home to caribou, dall sheep, moose and yet more bears.

Glaciers

If you want to explore glaciers in the USA, Alaska is the place to go. Glacier Bay National Park is the crown jewel for the cruise ships and a favourite for kayakers looking for an icy wilderness.

Food & Drink

Alaska's restaurant scene is not Manhattan, but the seafood is magnificent and you may make a friend or two – Alaskans are always up for a drink.

p1061

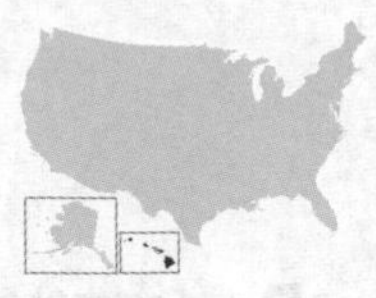

Hawaii

Beaches ✓✓✓
Adventure ✓✓✓
Scenery ✓✓✓

Beaches

There's great sunning and people watching on Waikiki (among dozens of other spots); stunning black-sand beaches on the Hamakua Coast, and world-class surfing all over Hawaii.

Adventure

You can trek through rain forest, kayak the Na Pali coast, descend on mule ride into the Kalaupapa Peninsula, and go eye-to-eye with aquatic life in marvelous Hanauma Bay.

Scenery

Hawaii has its head-turners, and we're not just talking people: volcanoes, ancient rainforests, picturesque waterfalls, clifftop vistas and jungle-lined valleys – not to mention the sparkling seas surrounding the islands.

p1079

Look out for these icons:

TOP CHOICE Our author's recommendation

A green or sustainable option

FREE No payment required

NEW YORK, NEW JERSEY & PENNSYLVANIA.... 58
NEW YORK CITY.........62
NEW YORK STATE.........113
Long Island.........114
NEW JERSEY.........127
Jersey Shore.........130
PENNSYLVANIA.........134
Philadelphia.........134
Pittsburgh.........155

NEW ENGLAND.....162
MASSACHUSETTS.........167
Boston.........167
Cape Cod.........185
Martha's Vineyard.........195
RHODE ISLAND.........201
Providence.........201
Newport.........203
CONNECTICUT.........207
Hartford.........210
VERMONT.........212
Burlington.........219
NEW HAMPSHIRE.........222
Portsmouth.........223
Manchester.........224
MAINE.........230
Portland.........233
Acadia National Park.........239
Bar Harbor.........240

WASHINGTON, DC & THE CAPITAL REGION.........244
WASHINGTON, DC.........248
MARYLAND.........270
Baltimore.........271
Annapolis.........281
DELAWARE.........287
VIRGINIA.........291
Fredericksburg.........295
Richmond.........296
WEST VIRGINIA.........315

THE SOUTH.......320
NORTH CAROLINA.........324
Charlotte.........333
SOUTH CAROLINA.........339
Charleston.........340
Columbia.........350
TENNESSEE.........350
Memphis.........351
Nashville.........359
KENTUCKY.........370
Louisville.........371
GEORGIA.........378
Atlanta.........379
Savannah.........391
ALABAMA.........397
Birmingham.........397
MISSISSIPPI.........402
Mississippi Delta.........403
Jackson.........407
LOUISIANA.........409
New Orleans.........410
ARKANSAS.........433
Little Rock.........434

FLORIDA.........440
SOUTH FLORIDA.........445
Miami.........445
Fort Lauderdale.........459
The Everglades.........463
ATLANTIC COAST.........474
Daytona Beach.........476
Jacksonville.........480
WEST COAST.........481
Tampa.........481
St Petersburg.........484
CENTRAL FLORIDA.........489
Orlando.........489
Walt Disney World Resort.493
FLORIDA PANHANDLE.........495

GREAT LAKES.....500
ILLINOIS.........505
Chicago.........505
INDIANA.........535
Indianapolis.........536
OHIO.........542
Cleveland.........542
Amish Country.........548
Columbus.........549
Cincinnati.........551
MICHIGAN.........555
Detroit.........555
WISCONSIN.........572
Milwaukee.........572
MINNESOTA.........582

See the Index for a full list of destinations covered in this book.

On the Road

Minneapolis............582
St Paul................590

GREAT PLAINS.... 598

MISSOURI...............602
St Louis...............603
Kansas City............612
IOWA...................616
Des Moines.............617
NORTH DAKOTA...........620
SOUTH DAKOTA...........624
NEBRASKA...............634
Omaha..................634
KANSAS.................639
Wichita................639
OKLAHOMA...............644
Oklahoma City..........644

TEXAS 651

SOUTH-CENTRAL TEXAS..653
Austin.................656
San Antonio............666
Houston................672
SOUTHERN GULF COAST 680
DALLAS-FORT WORTH..682
WEST TEXAS.............694
Big Bend National Park..694
Guadalupe Mountains National Park..........702

ROCKY MOUNTAINS...... 703

COLORADO...............709
Denver.................709
WYOMING................741
Cheyenne...............742
Yellowstone National Park..........744
Grand Teton National Park..........750
MONTANA................754
Bozeman................754
Missoula...............758
Glacier National Park...761
IDAHO..................763
Boise..................763

SOUTHWEST.......785

NEVADA.................790
Las Vegas..............790
ARIZONA................808
Phoenix................809
Flagstaff..............818
Grand Canyon National Park..........823
Tucson.................832
UTAH...................837
Salt Lake City.........838
NEW MEXICO.............857
Albuquerque............858
Santa Fe...............863
Taos...................871

CALIFORNIA...... 882

LOS ANGELES............887
SOUTHERN CALIFORNIA COAST..............911
Disneyland & Anaheim...911
San Diego..............916
PALM SPRINGS & THE DESERTS..............927
Palm Springs...........928
Joshua Tree National Park............930
Death Valley National Park...................933
Big Sur................940
SAN FRANCISCO & THE BAY AREA...........947
San Francisco..........947
NORTHERN CALIFORNIA..975
Wine Country...........975
Sacramento.............984
SIERRA NEVADA..........989
Yosemite National Park..989
Sequoia & Kings Canyon National Parks.........994
Lake Tahoe.............998

PACIFIC NORTHWEST......1001

WASHINGTON.............1007
Seattle................1007
OREGON.................1034
Portland...............1034

ALASKA..........1061

SOUTHEAST ALASKA.. 1064
ANCHORAGE..............1074

HAWAII...........1079

O'AHU..................1082
HAWAI'I THE BIG ISLAND.................1087
MAUI...................1091
KAUA'I.................1095

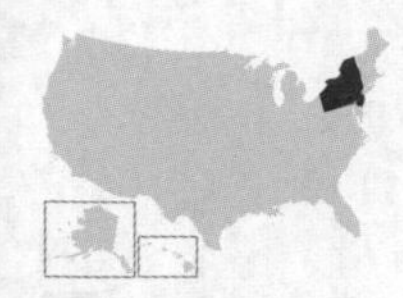

New York, New Jersey & Pennsylvania

Includes »

New York City 62
New York State 113
Long Island 114
Hudson Valley 116
Catskills 118
Capital Region 121
New Jersey 127
Jersey Shore 130
Pennsylvania 134
Philadelphia 134
Pennsylvania Dutch Country 151
Pittsburgh 154

Best Places to Eat

» Blue Hill (p100)
» Morimoto (p145)
» The Breslin (p100)
» Anchor Bar (p125)
» Primanti Bros (p159)

Best Places to Stay

» Bowery Hotel (p94)
» Mohonk Mountain House (p117)
» Saugerties Lighthouse (p118)
» Morris House Hotel (p144)
» Caribbean Motel (p133)

Why Go?

Where else could you visit an Amish family's farm, camp on a mountaintop, read the Declaration of Independence and view New York, New York from the 86th floor of an art-deco landmark - all in a few days? Even though it's the most densely populated part of the US, it's full of places where jaded city dwellers escape to seek simple lives, where artists retreat for inspiration, and pretty houses line main streets in small towns set amid stunning scenery.

Urban adventures in NYC, historic and lively Philadelphia and river-rich Pittsburgh are a must. Miles and miles of glorious beaches are within reach, from glamorous Long Island to the Jersey Shore – the latter ranges from stately to kitschy. The mountain wilderness of the Adirondacks reaches skyward just a day's drive north of New York City, a journey that perfectly encapsulates this region's heady character.

When to Go

New York City

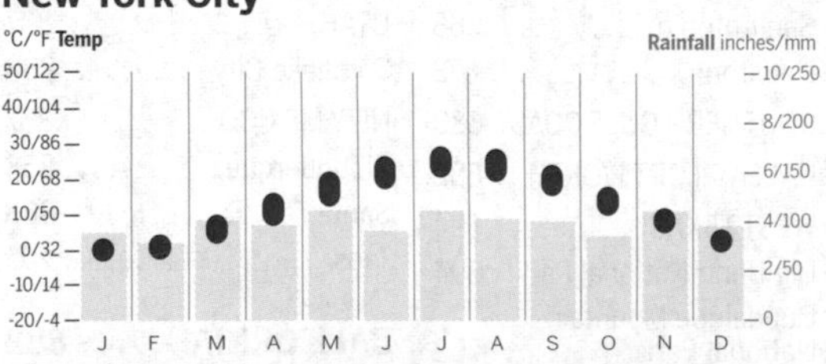

Oct–Nov Autumn in NYC brings cool temps, festivals, the marathon and gearing up for holiday season.

Feb Winter sports buffs head to the mountains of the Adirondacks, Catskills and Poconos.

31 May–5 Sep Memorial Day through Labor Day is for beaches from Montauk to Cape May.

Transportation

The big cities all have airports, but New York's John F Kennedy is the region's major international gateway. Alternatives include Newark Liberty International Airport and La Guardia, in Queens, with mostly domestic flights. Philadelphia and Pittsburgh also have small international airports.

Greyhound buses serve main cities and towns, while Peter Pan Bus Lines and Adirondack Trailways are two regional bus lines. Amtrak provides rail services linking New York with much of New Jersey, as well as Philadelphia and Pittsburgh. Most popular day trips, at least from New York City, are easily accessible by one of the three commuter-rail lines. If you're driving, the main north–south highway is the I-95.

NATIONAL & STATE PARKS

Parklands and recreation areas are in big supply here, as is wildlife, which is at first surprising to many who associate these states only with large urban areas. Black bears, bobcats and even elk can be found in forested parts of the states; more common are various species of deer. Falcons, eagles, hawks and migrating species of birds stop over in the region, some even within only a few miles of New York City.

In New York alone, you'll find hundreds of state parks, ranging from waterfalls around Ithaca to wilderness in the Adirondacks. In New Jersey, float down the Delaware River, grab some sun at the Cape May beach and hike the forested Kittatinny Valley in the north. Pennsylvania includes a huge array of thick forests, rolling parklands and a significant portion of the Appalachian National Scenic Trail, a 2175-mile footpath that snakes its way from Maine to Georgia.

Top Five Scenic Drives

» **Catskills, New York – Rte 23A to 214 to 28**: This takes you past forested hills, rushing rivers and spectacular falls.

» **North Central, Pennsylvania – Rte 6**: A drive through this rugged stretch of mountains and woodlands includes gushing creeks, wildlife and state forests.

» **Lake Cayuga, New York – Rte 80**: Head north from Ithaca above the lake past dozens of wineries.

» **Delaware Water Gap, New Jersey – Old Mine Rd**: One of the oldest roads in the US past beautiful vistas of the Delaware River and rural countryside.

» **Brandywine Valley, Pennsylvania – Rte 100, 52 and 163**: Only 25 miles through rolling horse country and lovely farmland.

THE HIGH LINE

Originally built in the 1930s to lift freight trains off Manhattan's streets, the High Line is now a brilliantly designed elevated park that embraces the natural and industrial, from the Meatpacking District to Chelsea.

Fast Facts

» Hub cities: New York City (population 8,175,000), Philadelphia (population 1,526,000)

» New York to Philadelphia: 97 miles

» New York to Niagara Falls: 408 miles

» Time zone: Eastern Standard

» Number of politicians resigned or jailed after scandal: enough to fill the legislature

Did You Know?

From November to April harbor seals, as well as other seal species, migrate to the waters of the Jersey Shore, Long Island Sound and NYC, from Staten Island to beaches in the Bronx.

Resources

» New York State Tourism (www.iloveny.com) Info, maps, travel advice available by phone.

» New Jersey Travel & Tourism (www.visitnj.org) Statewide tips on sights, accommodations and festivals.

» Pennsylvania Travel and Tourism (www.visitpa.com) Maps, videos and suggested itineraries.

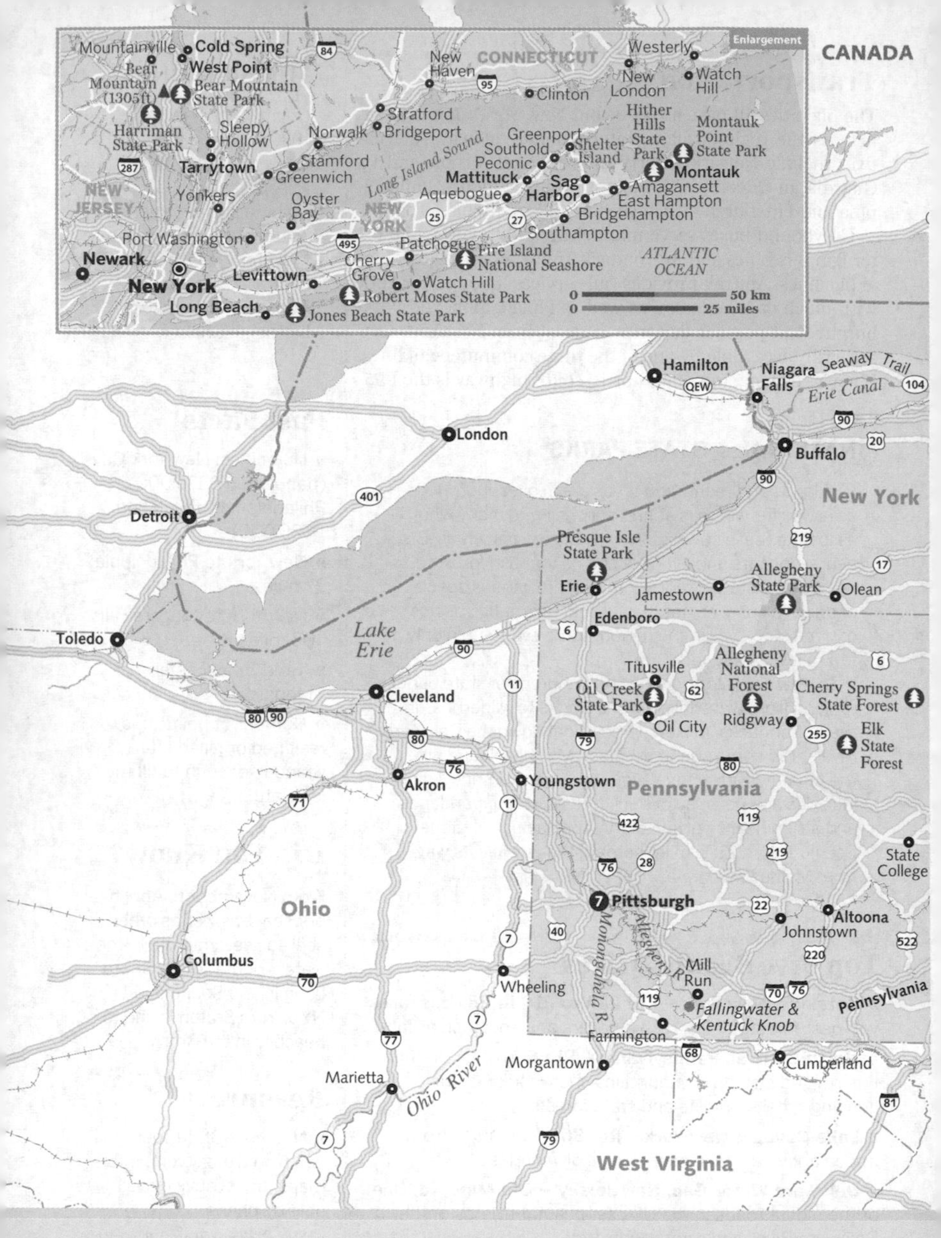

New York, New Jersey & Pennsylvania Highlights

1. Traveling round the world without ever leaving the kaleidoscope of neighborhoods and cultures that is **New York City** (p62)

2. Enjoying the kitsch and calm of the **Jersey Shore** (p130)

3. Absorbing the story of the birth of the nation in Philadelphia's **Independence National Historic Park** (p135)

4. Walking the densely forested paths of the unspoiled **Catskills** (p118)

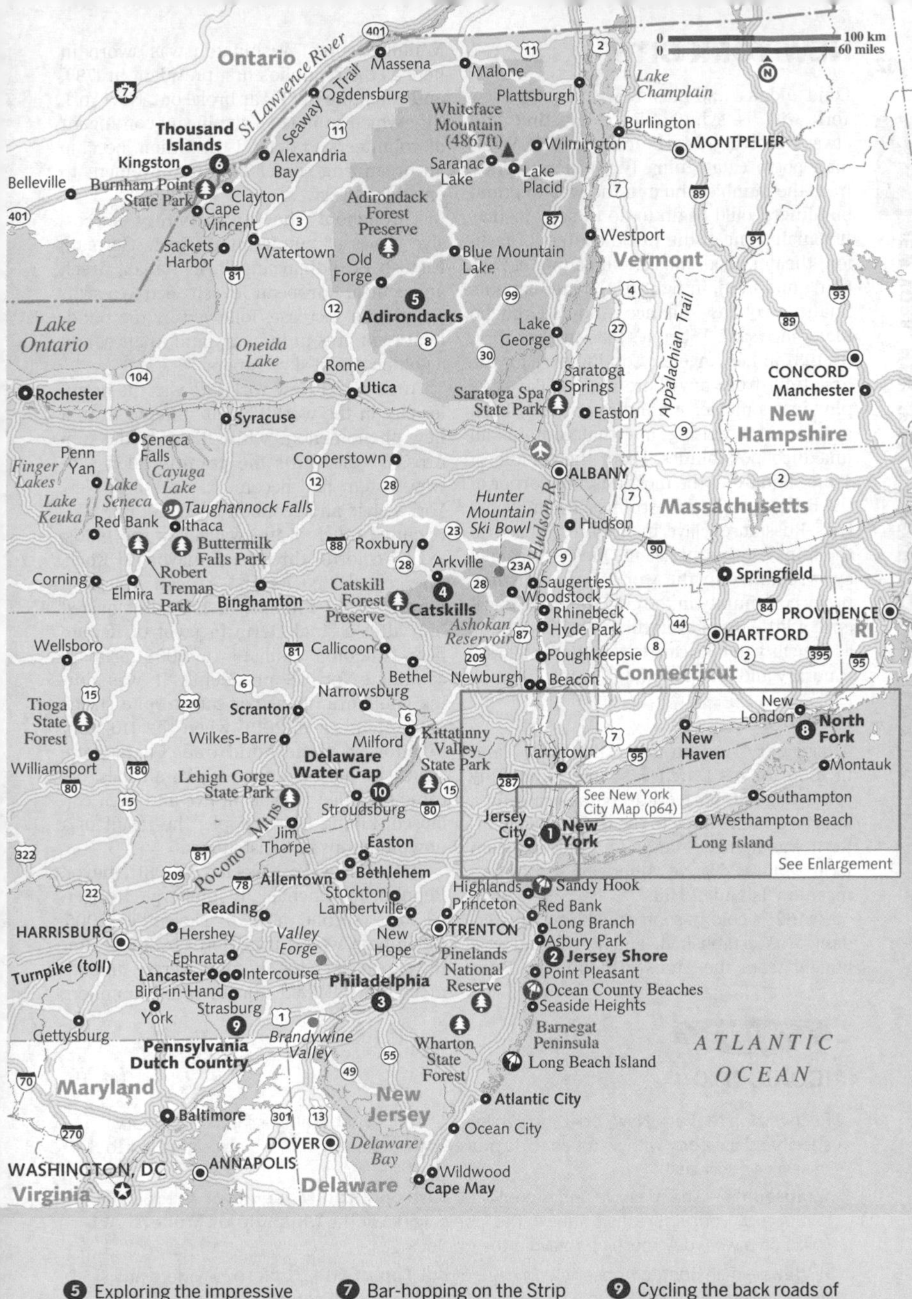

5 Exploring the impressive wilderness beauty of the **Adirondacks** (p122)

6 Camping along the shores of the St Lawrence River in the **Thousand Islands** (p123)

7 Bar-hopping on the Strip in **Pittsburgh** (p154)

8 Wine tasting on Long Island's **North Fork** (p116)

9 Cycling the back roads of **Pennsylvania Dutch Country** (p151)

10 0 Floating past bucolic scenery in the **Delaware Water Gap** (p129)

NEW YORK CITY

Loud and fast and pulsing with energy, New York City is symphonic, exhausting and always evolving. Maybe only a Walt Whitman poem cataloguing typical city scenes, from the humblest hole-in-the-wall to grand buildings, could begin to do the city justice. It remains one of the world centers of fashion, theater, food, music, publishing, advertising and even, in light of the late-naughts financial collapse, finance. And as Groucho Marx once said, 'When it's 9:30 in New York, it's 1937 in Los Angeles.' Coming here for the first time from anywhere else is like stepping into a movie, one you've probably been unknowingly writing, one that contains all imagined possibilities. From the middle of Times Square to the most obscure corner of the Bronx, you'll find extremes. From Brooklyn's Russian enclave in Brighton Beach to the mini South America in Queens, virtually every country in the world has a bustling proxy community in the city. You can experience a little bit of everything on a visit here, as long as you take care to travel with a loose itinerary and an open mind.

History

After Henry Hudson first claimed this land in 1609 for his Dutch East India Company sponsors, he reported it to be 'as beautiful a land as one can hope to tread upon.' Soon after it was named 'Manhattan,' derived from local Munsee Native American words and meaning 'Island of Hills.'

By 1625 a colony, soon called New Amsterdam, was established, and the island was bought from the Munsee Indians by Peter Minuit. George Washington was sworn in here as the republic's first president in 1789, and when the Civil War broke out, New York City, which supplied a significant contingent of volunteers to defend the Union, became an organizing center for the movement to emancipate slaves.

Throughout the 19th century successive waves of immigrants – Irish, German, English, Scandinavian, Slavic, Italian, Greek and central European Jewish – led to a swift population increase, followed by the building of empires in industry and finance, and a golden age of skyscrapers.

After WWII New York City was the premier city in the world, but it suffered from a new phenomenon: 'white flight' to the suburbs. By the 1970s the graffiti-ridden subway system had become a symbol of New York's civic and economic decline. But NYC regained much of its swagger in the 1980s, led by colorful three-term mayor Ed Koch. The city elected its first African American mayor, David Dinkins, in 1989, but ousted him after a single term in favor of Republican Rudolph Giuliani (a 2008 primary candidate for US president). It was during Giuliani's reign that catastrophe struck on September 11, 2001, when the 110-story twin towers of the World Trade Center were struck by hijacked commercial airlines, became engulfed in balls of fire and then collapsed, killing 3000 people, the result of a now-infamous terrorist attack.

In 2001 New York elected its 108th mayor, Republican Michael Bloomberg. Reelected for a second term in November 2005, Bloomberg won a third term in 2009 after the passage of a highly controversial amendment that allowed him to run. Bloomberg

DON'T MISS

ICONIC NYC

Recognizing that any New York City highlights list is inevitably abbreviated, necessary shorthand for a city with so much to do and see, the following offers a few sights not to miss on a short visit:

» **Museums** – The massive and exceptional **Metropolitan Museum of Art** (p83) can occupy your entire visit. Take in the iconic works at the **Museum of Modern Art** (p75) on a weekday morning to avoid the gridlock.

» **Views** – The open-air observation deck of the **Top of the Rock** (p79) offers an unparalleled perspective. On a nighttime stroll, stop midway across the **Brooklyn Bridge** (p63) for one of the more romantic sights the city has to offer.

» **Green Space** – Whatever the season, a walk through **Central Park** (p82) is the quintessential New York experience. To get a sense of how much of the city lives, head out to Brooklyn's **Prospect Park** (p88) for a weekend picnic.

NEW YORK, NEW JERSEY & PENNSYLVANIA IN...

One Week

Start off with a gentle introduction in **Philadelphia**, birthplace of American independence. After a day of touring the historic sites and a night of sampling the hoppin' nightlife, head into New Jersey for a bucolic night in **Cape May**. Sample another beachtown like **Wildwood** or **Atlantic City** further north along the **Jersey Shore**, landing in **New York City** the following day. Spend the rest of your visit here, blending touristy must-dos – such as the **Top of the Rock** and **Central Park** – with vibrant nightlife and eclectic dining adventures, perhaps in the city's bustling **East Village**.

Two Weeks

Begin with several days in **New York City**, then a night somewhere in the **Hudson Valley**, before reaching the **Catskills**. After touring this bucolic region, head further north to **Saratoga Springs** and **Lake George**. The outdoor-minded will want to explore the forested **Adirondack Mountains** before looping back south and west with a night in college-town **Ithaca**. From here you can head to **Buffalo** and **Niagara Falls** or south to the **Poconos** of northern Pennsylvania. The southern portion of the state has loads of historic sites as well as **Lancaster County** where you can stay on a working Amish farm. From here it's a short jaunt to **Philadelphia**, which deserves at least a couple of nights. Follow it up with a stay at a quaint B&B in **Cape May**, a day of boardwalk amusements in **Wildwood** and casino fun in **Atlantic City**.

is known as an independent political pragmatist, and his administration has earned both raves and criticism for its dual pursuit of environmental and development goals (the citywide nonsmoking law has proved popular, while congestion pricing to combat gridlock failed to get approval).

Sights

LOWER MANHATTAN

TOP CHOICE Brooklyn Bridge BRIDGE

(Map p66) Marianne Moore's description of the world's first suspension bridge – which inspired poets from Walt Whitman to Jack Kerouac even before its completion – as a 'climatic ornament, a double rainbow' is perhaps most evocative. Walking across the grand Brooklyn Bridge is a rite of passage for New Yorkers and visitors alike – with this in mind, walk no more than two abreast or else you're in danger of colliding with runners and speeding cyclists. With an unprecedented span of 1596ft, it remains a compelling symbol of US achievement and a superbly graceful structure, despite the fact that its construction was plagued by budget overruns and the death of 20 workers. Among the casualties was designer John Roebling, who was knocked off a pier in 1869 while scouting a site for the western bridge tower and later died of tetanus poisoning. The bridge and the smooth pedestrian/cyclist path, beginning just east of City Hall, affords wonderful views of Lower Manhattan and Brooklyn. Observation points under the two stone support towers have illustrations showing panoramas of the waterfront at various points in New York's history. On the Brooklyn side, the ever-expanding **Brooklyn Bridge Park** and restaurants of **Dumbo** are excellent end points for your stroll.

Statue of Liberty MONUMENT

(Map p64; ☎212-363-3200; www.nps.gov/stli; New York Harbor, Liberty Island; ⊙9:30am-5pm) In a city full of American icons, the Statue of Liberty is perhaps the most famous. Conceived as early as 1865 by French intellectual Edouard Laboulaye as a monument to the republican principals shared by France and the USA, it's still generally recognized as a symbol for at least the ideals of opportunity and freedom to many. French sculptor Frédéric-Auguste Bartholdi traveled to New York in 1871 to select the site, then spent more than 10 years in Paris designing and making the 151ft-tall figure *Liberty Enlightening the World*. It was then shipped to New York, erected on a small island in the harbor and unveiled in 1886. Structurally, it consists of an iron skeleton (designed by Gustave Eiffel) with a copper skin attached to it by stiff but flexible metal bars.

New York City

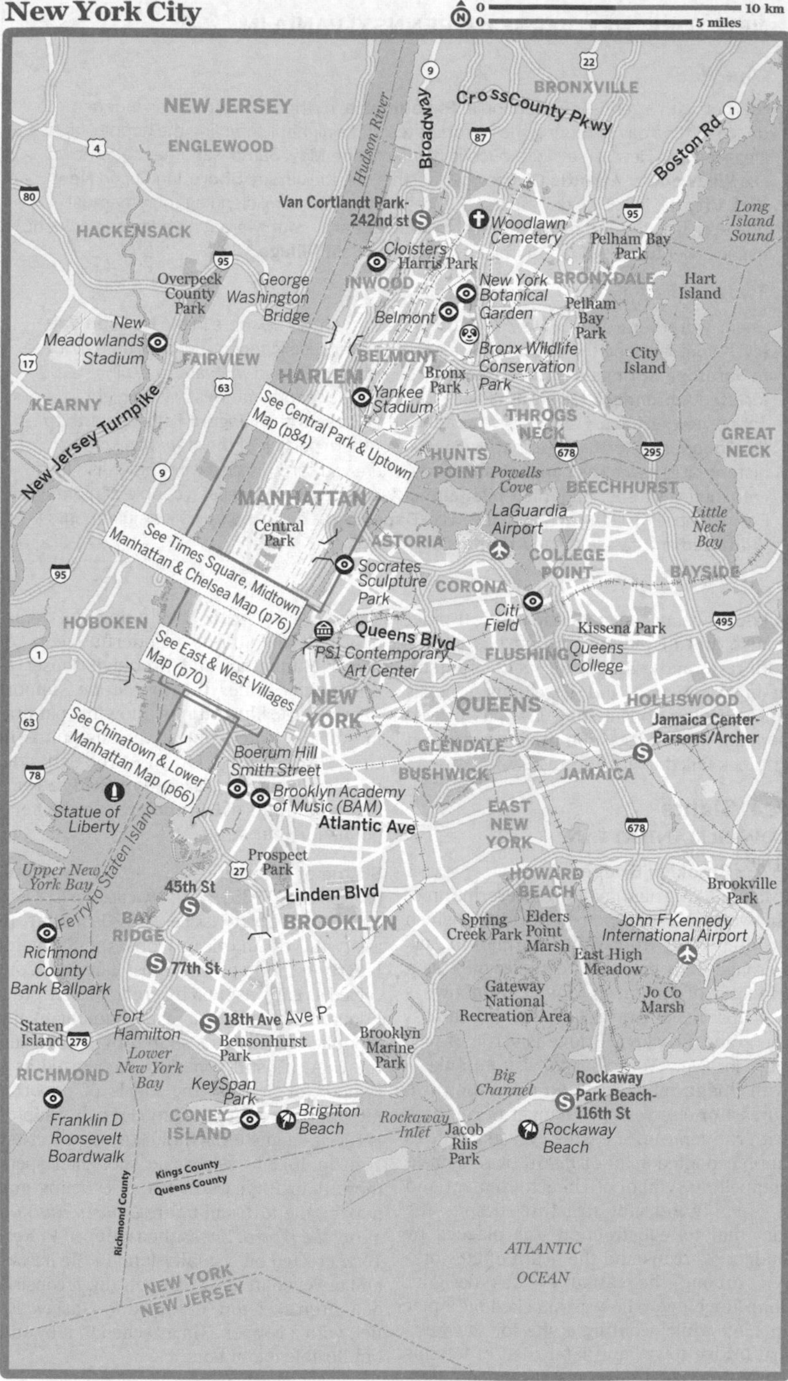

0 10 km
0 5 miles
NEW JERSEY
ENGLEWOOD
HACKENSACK
Overpeck County Park
George Washington Bridge
New Meadowlands Stadium
FAIRVIEW
KEARNY
New Jersey Turnpike
HOBOKEN
Hudson River
Broadway
Cross County Pkwy
BRONXVILLE
Boston Rd
Van Cortlandt Park-242nd st
Woodlawn Cemetery
Pelham Bay Park
Long Island Sound
Cloisters
Harris Park
INWOOD
New York Botanical Garden
BRONXDALE
Hart Island
Belmont
BELMONT
Pelham Bay Park
City Island
Bronx Wildlife Conservation Park
Bronx Park
HARLEM
Yankee Stadium
THROGS NECK
GREAT NECK
See Central Park & Uptown Map (p84)
HUNTS POINT
Powells Cove
BEECHHURST
MANHATTAN
LaGuardia Airport
Little Neck Bay
Central Park
ASTORIA
COLLEGE POINT
See Times Square, Midtown Manhattan & Chelsea Map (p76)
Socrates Sculpture Park
CORONA
BAYSIDE
Citi Field
Queens Blvd
Kissena Park
PS1 Contemporary Art Center
FLUSHING
Queens College
See East & West Villages Map (p70)
NEW YORK
QUEENS
HOLLISWOOD
Jamaica Center-Parsons/Archer
GLENDALE
See Chinatown & Lower Manhattan Map (p66)
Boerum Hill Smith Street
BUSHWICK
JAMAICA
Brooklyn Academy of Music (BAM)
Statue of Liberty
Atlantic Ave
EAST NEW YORK
Ferry to Staten Island
Prospect Park
Upper New York Bay
45th St
Linden Blvd
HOWARD BEACH
Brookville Park
BAY RIDGE
BROOKLYN
Spring Creek Park
Elders Point Marsh
John F Kennedy International Airport
Richmond County Bank Ballpark
77th St
East High Meadow
Gateway National Recreation Area
Jo Co Marsh
Staten Island
Fort Hamilton
18th Ave
Ave P
Bensonhurst Park
Brooklyn Marine Park
Lower New York Bay
RICHMOND
KeySpan Park
Big Channel
Rockaway Park Beach-116th St
CONEY ISLAND
Brighton Beach
Rockaway Inlet
Jacob Riis Park
Rockaway Beach
Franklin D Roosevelt Boardwalk
Kings County
Queens County
Richmond County
ATLANTIC OCEAN
NEW YORK
NEW JERSEY

The crown is again open to the public – numbers are limited, however, so reservations are required, as far in advance as possible. For those without crown reservations, a visit to Statue of Liberty National Monument means you can wander the grounds and enjoy the view from the 16-story observation deck; a specially designed glass ceiling lets you look up into the statue's striking interior. The trip to its island, via ferry, is usually visited in conjunction with nearby Ellis Island. **Ferries** (Map p66; ☎201-604-2800, 877-523-9849; www.statuecruises.com; adult/child $13/5; ⏲every 30min 9am-5pm, extended summer hr) leave from Battery Park. South Ferry and Bowling Green are the closest subway stations. Ferry tickets (additional $3 for crown admission) include admission to both sights and reservations can be made in advance.

Ellis Island MUSEUM

The way-station from 1892 to 1954 for more than 12 million immigrants who were hoping to make new lives in the United States, Ellis Island conjures up the humble and sometimes miserable beginnings of the experience of coming to America – as well as the fulfillment of dreams. More than three thousand died in the island's hospital and more than two percent were denied admission. Ferries to the Statue of Liberty make a second stop at the **immigration station** on Ellis Island (Map p64). The handsome main building has been restored as the **Immigration Museum** (☎212-363-3200; www.ellisisland.org; New York Harbor; audio guide $8; ⏲9:30am-5pm), with fascinating exhibits and a film about immigrant experiences, the processing of immigrants and how the influx changed the USA.

National September 11 Memorial & Museum MEMORIAL

After a decade of cost overruns, delays and politicking the redevelopment of the World Trade Center site destroyed by the attacks of September 11, 2001 is finally coming to fruition. Half of the area's 16 acres is dedicated to honoring victims and preserving history, while the remaining space will be occupied by office towers, a transport hub and performing arts center. The Memorial opened to the public on September 12, 2011. Its focus is two large pools with cascading waterfalls set in the footprints of the north and south towers. Bronze parapets surrounding the pools are inscribed with the names of those killed in the attacks. Hundreds of swamp whitewood trees will provide shade to the site. Visitor passes (free) can be reserved through the memorial's website (www.national911memorial.org; the museum is scheduled to open in September 2012). Construction of the $3.2 billion One World Trade Center, formerly known as the Freedom Tower and the signature building of the site, has reached the 65th floor as of the summer of 2011 (the scheduled opening is for 2014); at 1776ft its antenna tower will make it the tallest building in the US. The Santigago Calatrava-designed WTC Transit Hub will open in 2014. You can check progress on the site or reserve passes by stopping by the **9/11 Memorial Preview Site** (Map p66; ☎212-267-2047; www.911memorial.org; 20 Vesey St; ⏲10am-7pm, to 6pm Sun), which has exhibits and information on the rebuilding or go to www.wtcprogress.com.

Nearby is the **Tribute WTC Visitor Center** (Map p66; ☎866-737-1184; www.tributewtc.org; 120 Liberty St; admission $10; ⏲10am-6pm Mon, Wed-Sat, noon-6pm Tue, to 5pm Sun), which provides exhibits, first-person testimony and **walking tours** of the site ($15 per person and includes museum admission, several from 11am to 3pm Sunday to Friday, and to 4pm Saturday); though the status of this center is unclear once the memorial and museum are open.

Some of the best views of the construction site are from the atrium in One World Financial Center, an office building across the West Side Hwy.

FREE **Governor's Island National Monument** PARK

(Map p64; ☎212-825-3045; www.nps.gov/gois) Most New Yorkers have gazed out on this mysterious path of green in the harbor, less than half a mile from the southern tip of Manhattan, without a clue as to its purpose. Although it was once reserved only for the army or coast guard personnel who were based here, these days the general public can visit. The 22-acre Governor's Island National Monument is accessible by riding the **ferry** (☎212-514-8285; www.nps.gov/gois; ⏲10am-3pm Wed-Fri, 10am-5pm Sat & Sun, summer only) leaving from the **Battery Marine Terminal** (Map p66; cnr South & Whitehall Sts) next to the Staten Island Ferry Whitehall Terminal in very lower Manhattan. Guided **walking tours** (⏲10am-1pm Wed & Thu), an hour and a half long, are run by the park service; tickets are available first-come, first-served an hour in advance at

Chinatown & Lower Manhattan

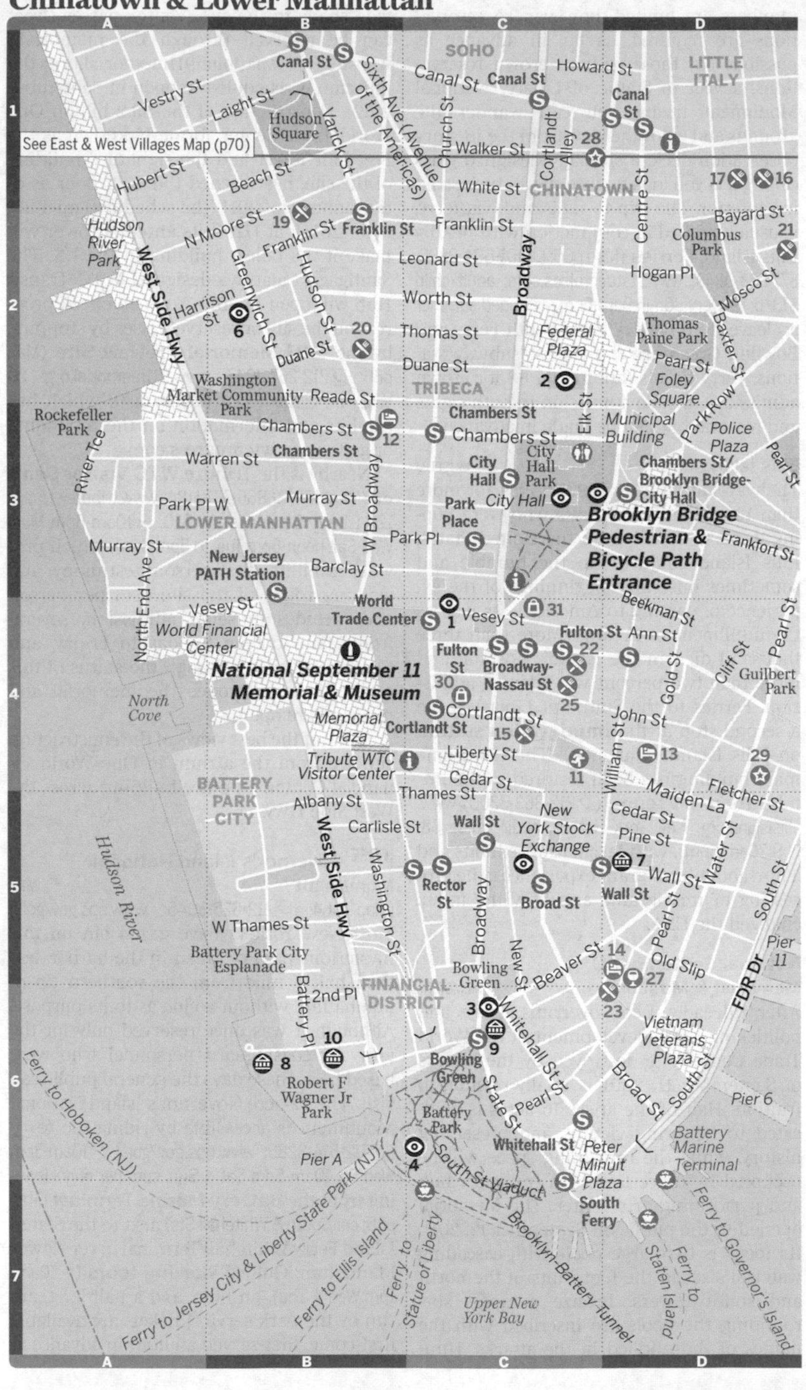

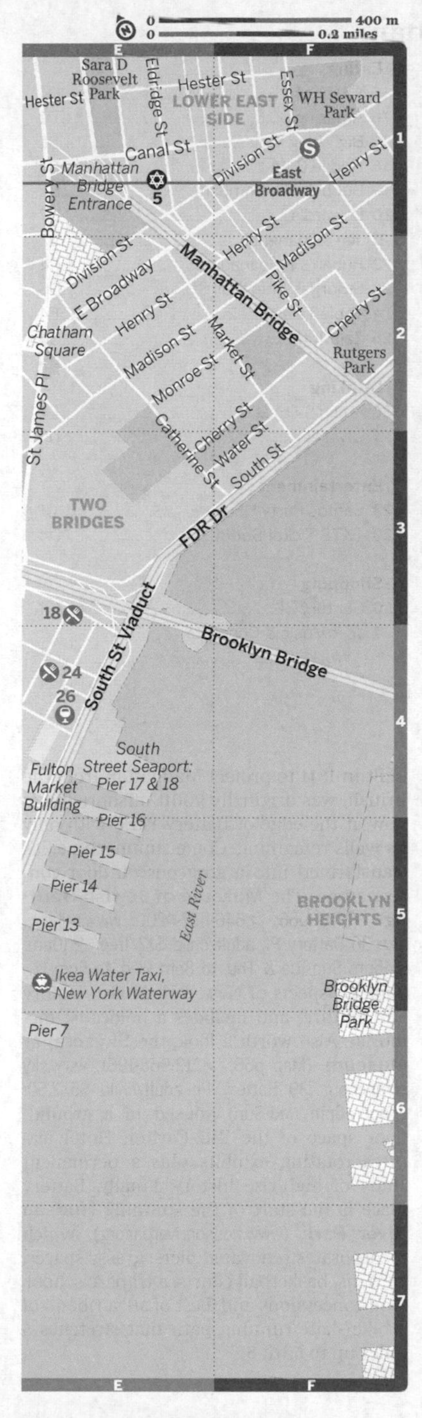

the Battery Marine Terminal. Highlights include two 19th-century fortifications – Fort Jay and the three-tiered, sandstone Castle Williams – plus open lawns, massive shade trees and unsurpassed city views.

South Street Seaport NEIGHBORHOOD
Known more for the large commercial mall jutting out over the East River on Pier 17, this 11-block enclave of cobblestoned streets and restored historic buildings has been revitalized into an area worthy of a walk. The Fulton Fish Market is long gone but a combination of residents and tourists mix in a handful of bars and restaurants housed in restored mid-19th-century buildings. When in the area it's worth considering hopping on the **Ikea water taxi** (Map p66; ⏲every 40min 2-6:40pm Mon-Fri, 11am-7:40pm Sat & Sun) operated by the Swedish furniture store from Pier 11 (six blocks south of South Street Seaport) to its store in Red Hook, Brooklyn. Besides offering the chance to get out on the water and take in breathtaking views of the city, it's free for customers (free for all Saturday and Sunday, otherwise $5).

Bowling Green Park & Around PARK
(Map p66; cnr State & Whitehall Sts) At Bowling Green Park, British residents relaxed with quiet games in the late 17th century. The large **bronze bull** here is a tourist photo stop. The **National Museum of the American Indian** (Map p66; ☎212-514-3700; www.nmai.si.edu; 1 Bowling Green; admission free; ⏲10am-5pm, to 8pm Thu), housed in the gorgeous and historic Alexander Hamilton US Customs House, has quite an extensive collection of Native American arts, crafts and exhibits, plus a library and a great gift shop. Just up Broadway from here is the **African Burial Ground** (Map p66; ☎212-637-2019; www.nps.gov/afbg; Ted Weiss Federal Bldg, 1st fl, 290 Broadway, btwn Duane & Reade Sts; admission free; ⏲10am-4pm Tue-Sat), where the skeletal remains of more than 400 free and enslaved African men and women were discovered during preliminary construction of a downtown office building in 1991.

WALL STREET & THE FINANCIAL DISTRICT

Of course once-venerable banks including Lehman Brothers and Bear Stearns have shuttered and thousands of jobs were lost in the worldwide economic crash of late 2007/early 2008, however the neighborhood and financial industry have rebounded. Still, these days, in the mind of Main St, **Wall**

Chinatown & Lower Manhattan

Top Sights

Brooklyn Bridge Pedestrian & Bicycle Path Entrance ... C3
National September 11 Memorial & Museum ... B4

Sights

1 9/11 Memorial Preview Site ... C4
2 African Burial Ground ... C2
3 Bowling Green Park ... C6
Bronze Bull ... (see 3)
4 Castle Clinton ... C6
5 Eldridge Street Synagogue ... E1
6 Harrison Street Townhouses ... B2
7 Museum of American Finance ... D5
8 Museum of Jewish Heritage ... B6
9 National Museum of the American Indian ... C6
10 Skyscraper Museum ... B6

Activities, Courses & Tours

11 Federal Reserve ... C4

Sleeping

12 Cosmopolitan Hotel ... B3
13 Gild Hall Wall Street ... D4
14 Wall Street Inn ... D5

Eating

15 Alfanoose ... C4
16 Amazing 66 ... D1
17 Big Wong King ... D1
18 Bridge Café ... E3
19 Bubby's Pie Company ... B2
20 Edward's ... B2
21 Joe's Shanghai ... D2
22 Ruben's Empanadas ... C4
23 Smorgas Chef Wall St ... D6
24 Table Tales ... E4
25 Zaitstaff ... C4

Drinking

26 Fresh Salt ... E4
27 Ulysses ... D5

Entertainment

28 Santos Party House ... C1
29 TKTS Ticket Booth ... D4

Shopping

30 Century 21 ... C4
31 J&R Music & Computer World ... C4

Street is synonymous with shortsighted greed and decadent irresponsibility. Both an actual street and the metaphorical home of US commerce, its etymological origin is the wooden barrier built by Dutch settlers in 1653 to protect Nieuw Amsterdam from Native Americans and the British. A comprehensive overview, warts and all, of the US economy is explained in fascinating up-to-date exhibits at the **Museum of American Finance** (Map p66; ☎212-908-4110; www.moaf.org; 48 Wall St; adult/child $8/free; ⏰10am-4pm Tue-Sat) housed in the venerable former home of the Bank of New York. To get an up-close and personal view of what makes the world go round, sign up for an hour-plus tour of the **Federal Reserve** (Map p66; ☎212-825-6990; www.nps.gov/feha; 26 Wall St; admission free; ⏰9am-5pm).

Battery Park & Around NEIGHBORHOOD

The southwestern tip of Manhattan Island has been extended with landfill over the years to form Battery Park, so named for the gun batteries that used to be housed at the bulkheads. **Castle Clinton**, a fortification built in 1811 to protect Manhattan from the British, was originally 900ft offshore but is now at the edge of Battery Park, with only its walls remaining. Come summertime, it's transformed into a gorgeous outdoor concert arena. The **Museum of Jewish Heritage** (Map p66; ☎646-437-4200; www.mjhnyc.org; 36 Battery Pl; adult/child $12/free; ⏰10am-5:45pm Sun-Tue & Thu, to 8pm Wed, to 5pm Fri) depicts aspects of New York Jewish history and culture, and includes a holocaust memorial. Also worth a look, the **Skyscraper Museum** (Map p66; ☎212-968-1961; www.skyscraper.org; 39 Battery Pl; adult/child $5/2.50; ⏰noon-6pm Wed-Sun) housed in a ground-floor space of the Ritz-Carlton Hotel features rotating exhibits plus a permanent study of high-rise history. Finally, Battery Place is the start of the stunning **Hudson River Park** (www.hudsonriverpar.org), which incorporates renovated piers, grassy spaces, gardens, basketball courts, a trapeze school, food concessions and, best of all, a ribbon of a bike/skate/running path that stretches 5 miles up to 59th St.

TRIBECA & SOHO

The 'TRIangle BElow CAnal St,' bordered roughly by Broadway to the east and Chambers St to the south, is the more downtown of these two sister 'hoods. It has old warehouses, very expensive loft apartments and chichi restaurants. On the historic side, the **Harrison Street town houses** (Map p66; Harrison St) west of Greenwich St, were built between 1804 and 1828 and are New York's largest remaining collection of Federal architecture.

SoHo has nothing to do with its London counterpart, but instead, like Tribeca, takes its name from its geographical placement: SOuth of HOuston St. SoHo is filled with block upon block of cast-iron industrial buildings that date to the period just after the Civil War, when this was the city's leading commercial district. It had a Bohemian/artsy heyday that had ended by the 1980s, and now this super-gentrified area is a major shopping destination, home to chain stores and boutiques alike and to hordes of consumers, especially on weekends.

SoHo's hip cup overfloweth to the northern side of Houston St and east side of Lafayette St, where two small areas, **NoHo** ('north of Houston') and **NoLita** ('north of Little Italy'), respectively, are known for excellent shopping – lots of small, independent and stylish clothing boutiques for women – and dining. Add them to SoHo and Tribeca for a great experience of strolling, window-shopping and cafe-hopping, and you'll have quite a lovely afternoon.

CHINATOWN & LITTLE ITALY

More than 150,000 Chinese-speaking residents live in cramped tenements and crowded apartments in Chinatown, the largest Chinese community that exists outside of Asia (though there are two other major Chinatowns in the city – Sunset Park in Brooklyn and Flushing, in Queens). In the 1990s, the neighborhood also attracted a growing number of Vietnamese immigrants, who set up their own shops and opened inexpensive restaurants here; depending on what street you're on, you'll often notice more of a Vietnamese than Chinese presence.

The best reason to visit Chinatown is to experience a feast for the senses – it's the only spot in the city where you can simultaneously see whole roasted pigs hanging in butcher-shop windows, get whiffs of fresh fish and hear the twangs of Cantonese and Vietnamese rise over the calls of knock-off-Prada-bag hawkers on Canal St.

Museum of Chinese in America MUSEUM

(Map p70; ☎212-619-4785; www.mocanyc.org; 215 Centre St; adult/child $7/free; ⏰11am-5pm Mon, to 9pm Thu, 10am-5pm Fri-Sun) Strikingly designed and cutting edge interactive exhibits trace the history and cultural impact of Chinese communities in the US. Lectures, film series and walking tours as well.

Little Italy NEIGHBORHOOD

Once known as a truly authentic pocket of Italian people, culture and eateries, Little Italy is a barely-there remnant that's constantly shrinking (Chinatown keeps encroaching). Still, loyal Italian Americans, mostly from the suburbs, flock here to gather around red-and-white-checked tablecloths at one of a handful of longtime red-sauce restaurants. Join them for a stroll along **Mulberry Street**, and take a peek at the **Old St Patrick's Cathedral** (Map p70; 263 Mulberry St), which became the city's first Roman Catholic cathedral in 1809 and remained so until 1878, when its more famous uptown successor was completed. The former **Ravenite Social Club** (Map p70; 247 Mulberry St), now a fancy shoe shop, is a reminder of the not-so-long-ago days when mobsters ran the neighborhood. Originally known as the Alto Knights Social Club, where big hitters like Lucky Luciano spent time, the Ravenite was a favorite hangout of John Gotti (and the FBI) before his arrest and life sentencing in 1992.

LOWER EAST SIDE

First came the Jews, then the Latinos, and now, of course, the hipsters. Today the place, once the densest neighborhood in the world, is focused on being cool – by cramming into low-lit lounges, live-music clubs and trendy bistros. Luxury high-rise condominiums and boutique hotels coexist with public housing projects (read Richard Price's novel *Lush Life* for entertaining insight into this class conflict). Nevertheless, 40% of residents are still immigrants and two-thirds speak a language other than English at home.

Eldridge Street Synagogue RELIGIOUS

(Map p66; ☎212-219-0302; www.eldridgestreet.org; 12 Eldridge St, btwn Canal & Division Sts) Built in 1887 with Moorish and Romanesque ornamental work, this synagogue attracted as many as 1000 worshippers on the High Holidays at the turn of the 20th century. But membership dwindled in the 1920s with restricted immigration laws, and by the 1950s the temple closed altogether. A 20-year restoration project was finally completed in 2007 and now the synagogue holds Friday-evening and Saturday-morning worship services, hosts weddings and offers **tours** (adult/child $10/6; ⏲10am-5pm Sun-Thu, on the half-hour) of the building. Perhaps the most breathtaking aspect of the interior is the new massive circular **stained-glass window** above the ark (space where torahs are kept). The synagogue helps organize the early-June **Egg Cream and Egg Roll Festival**, a celebration of Jewish and Chinese cultural and gastronomic traditions.

Lower East Side Tenement Museum TOUR
(Map p70; ☎212-982-8420; www.tenement.org; 90 Orchard St, at Broome St; tours $17; ⏲visitor center 10am-5:30pm, tours 10:15am-5pm) To keep the humble past in perspective, this museum puts the neighborhood's heartbreaking heritage on full display in several reconstructed tenements. Plans call for a reconstruction of a butcher shop and saloon on the ground floor. Visits are available only as part of variously themed scheduled tours, which typically operate every 40 or 50 minutes.

EAST VILLAGE

Bordered roughly by 14th St, Lafayette St, E Houston St and the East River, the East Village has gentrified in the last decade or so, much to the horror of longtime tenants and punk-kid squatters, who have been around for decades. These days real-estate developers have the upper hand – although the 'hood has not yet shaken its image as an edgy, radical, be-yourself kind of place.

Tompkins Square Park PARK
This park between Seventh and Tenth Sts and Aves A and B is an unofficial border between the East Village (to the west) and Alphabet City (to the east). It was once an Eastern European immigrant area; you'll

East & West Villages

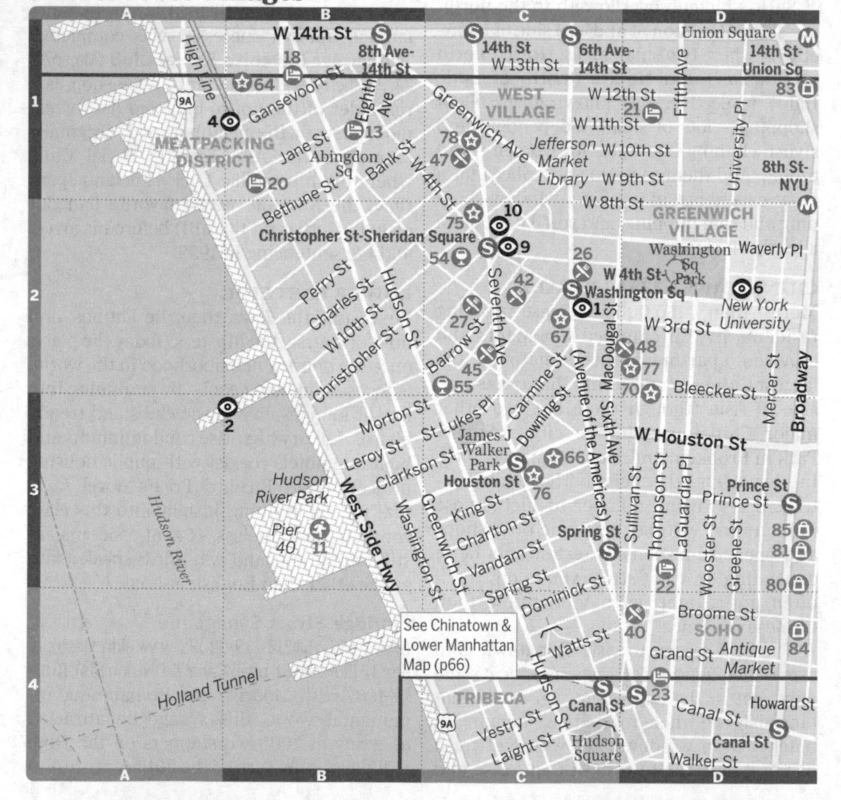

still see old Ukrainians and Poles in the park, but they'll be alongside punks, students, panhandlers and a slew of dog-walking yuppies.

New Museum of Contemporary Art MUSEUM

(Map p70; ☎212-219-1222; www.newmuseum.org; 235 Bowery, at Prince St; adult/child $12/free; ⏰11am-6pm Wed, Fri, Sat & Sun, to 9pm Thu) Housed in an architecturally ambitious building on a formerly gritty Bowery strip, this is the city's sole museum dedicated to contemporary art. There's the added treat of a city viewing platform, which provides a unique perspective on the constantly changing neighborhood landscape.

Russian & Turkish Baths SPA

(Map p70; ☎212-505-0665; www.russianturkishbaths.com; 268 E 10th St; admission $30; ⏰noon-10pm Mon, Tue, Thu & Fri, from 9am Sat, 8am-1pm Sun) The historic bathhouse is a great place to work out your stress in one of the four hot rooms; traditional massages are also offered. It's authentic and somewhat grungy, and you're as likely to share a sauna with a downtown couple on a date, a well-known actor looking for a time-out or an actual Russian.

Astor Place & Around NEIGHBORHOOD

(Map p70) At the west end of St Mark's Pl, Astor Place was once an elite neighborhood and some of its impressive original Greek Revival residences remain. These days a large Starbucks anchors one corner and a K-Mart another, while a tall glass condominium dominates the skyline across the street. The landmark rotating sculpture – 'the Cube' – remains, as do the young skateboarders who congregate here.

Cooper Union HISTORIC BUILDING

(Map p70; www.cooper.edu; 51 Astor Pl) The large brownstone Cooper Union is a public college founded by glue millionaire Peter Cooper in 1859. Abraham Lincoln gave his 'Right

East & West Villages

Top Sights

Lower East Side Tenement Museum....F3
New Museum of Contemporary Art......E3

Sights

1 Cage....C2
2 Christopher Street Pier....B3
3 Cooper Union....E2
4 High Line Southern Terminus....B1
5 Museum of Chinese in America....E4
6 New York University....D2
7 Old St Patrick's Cathedral....E3
8 Ravenite Social Club....E3
9 Sheridan Square....C2
10 Stonewall Inn....C2

Activities, Courses & Tours

11 Downtown Boathouse....B3
12 Russian & Turkish Baths....F1

Sleeping

13 Abingdon Guest House....B1
14 Bowery Hotel....E2
15 East Village Bed & Coffee....G2
16 Gem Hotel....E3
17 Hotel Azure....E4
18 Hotel Gansevoort....B1
19 Hotel on Rivington....F3
20 Jane Hotel....B1
21 Larchmont Hotel....D1
22 Sixty Thompson....D3
23 Soho Grand Hotel....D4
24 SoLita SoHo....E4

Eating

25 Bánh Mì Saigon Bakery....E4
26 Blue Hill....C2
27 Buvette....C2
28 Counter....F2
29 Donut Plant....F4
30 Economy Candy....F3
31 Egg Custard King....F4
32 Fat Radish....F4
33 Focolare....E4
34 Fonda Nolita....E3
35 Il Bagatto....F2
36 Katz's Delicatessen....F3
37 Kuma Inn....F3
38 La Esquina Taqueria....E4
39 Momofuku Noodle Bar....F1
40 Mooncake Foods....D4
41 Peasant....E3
42 Perilla....C2
43 Ruby's....E3
44 Russ & Daughters....F3
45 Snack Taverna....C2
46 Souvlaki GR....F3
Spitzer's Corner....(see 19)
47 Taïm....C1
48 Thelewala....D2
49 Torrisi Italian Specialties....E3
50 Vanessa's Dumpling House....F4
51 Veselka....E1
52 Xi'an Famous Foods....F1

Drinking

53 Decibel....E1
54 Fat Cat....C2
55 Henrietta Hudson....C2
56 KGB Bar....E2
57 Mayahuel....E2
58 McSorley's Old Ale House....E2
59 Mulberry Project....E4
60 Schiller's Liquor Bar....F3
61 Welcome to the Johnsons....F3

Entertainment

62 Anthology Film Archives....E2
63 Beauty & Essex....F3
64 Cielo....B1
65 Delancey Lounge....G3
66 Film Forum....C3
67 IFC Center....C2
68 Joe's Pub....E2
69 Landmark Sunshine Cinema....F3
70 Le Poisson Rouge....D2
71 Mercury Lounge....F3
72 New York Theater Workshop....E2
73 Ontological Theater....E1
74 PS 122....F1
Public Theater....(see 68)
75 Smalls....C2
76 SOBs....C3
77 Sullivan Room....D2
Village Lantern....(see 77)
78 Village Vanguard....C1
79 Webster Hall....E1

Shopping

80 Bloomingdale's SoHo....D3
81 Eastern Mountain Sports....D3
82 McNally Jackson Books....E3
83 Strand Bookstore....D1
84 Topshop....D4
85 Uniqlo....D3

Makes Might' speech condemning slavery before his election to the White House in the college's Great Hall.

WEST (GREENWICH) VILLAGE

Once a symbol for all things artistic, outlandish and Bohemian, this storied and popular neighborhood – the birthplace of the gay-rights movement as well as former home of Beat poets and important artists – feels worlds away from busy Broadway, and in fact almost European. Known by most visitors as 'Greenwich Village,' although that term is not used by locals, it has narrow streets lined with well-groomed and high-priced real estate, as well as cafes and restaurants, making it an ideal place to wander.

Washington Square Park & Around PARK

(Map p70) This park began as a 'potter's field' – a burial ground for the penniless – and its status as a cemetery protected it from development. It is now a completely renovated and incredibly well-used park, especially on the weekend. Children use the playground, NYU students catch some rays and friends meet 'under the arch,' the renovated landmark on the park's northern edge, designed in 1889 by society architect Stanford White. Dominating a huge swath of property in the middle of the Village, New York University, one of the largest in the country, defines the area around the park and beyond architecturally and demographically. The undersized basketball court, the **Cage** (cnr Sixth Ave & W 3rd St), considered one of the more competitive playgrounds in the city, draws onlookers and top ballers – the more people-watching, the more showboating.

Christopher Street Pier (Pier 45) PLAZA

(Map p66; Christopher St, at the Hudson River; closes 1am) Developers of the Hudson River Park Project paid special attention to this prime waterfront spot, adding a lawn and flower bed, wooden deck, tented shade shelters, benches and a grand stone fountain at its entrance.

Sheridan Square & Around NEIGHBORHOOD

The western edge of the Village is home to Sheridan Square, a small, triangular park where life-size white statues by George Segal honor the gay community and gay pride movement that began in the nearby renovated **Stonewall Inn** sitting just across the street from the square. A block further east, an appropriately bent street is officially named Gay St. Although gay social scenes have in many ways moved further uptown to Chelsea, **Christopher Street** is still the center of gay life in the Village.

MEATPACKING DISTRICT

Nestled between the far West Village and the southern border of Chelsea is the gentrified and now inappropriately named Meatpacking District. The neighborhood was once home to 250 slaughterhouses – today only eight butchers remain – and was best known for its groups of tranny hookers, racy S&M sex clubs and, of course, its sides of beef. These days the hugely popular High Line park has only intensified an every increasing proliferation of trendy wine bars, eateries, nightclubs, high-end designer clothing stores, chic hotels and high-rent condos.

TOP CHOICE **High Line** PARK

(Map p66; www.thehighline.org; 7am-10pm) With the completion of the High Line, a 30ft-high abandoned stretch of elevated railroad track transformed into a long ribbon of parkland (from Gansevoort St to W 34th St; entrances are at Gansevoort, 14th, 16th, 18th, 20th and 30th Sts; elevator access at all but 18th St), there's finally some greenery amid the asphalt jungle. Only three stories above the streetscape, this thoughtfully and carefully designed mix of contemporary, industrial and natural elements is nevertheless a refuge and escape from the ordinary. A glass-front **amphitheater** with bleacher-like seating sits just above 10th Ave – bring some food and join local workers on their lunch break. Rising on concrete stilts over the High Line, the **Standard** is one of the celebrated destinations of the moment, with two choice drinking spots and a grill (plus hotel rooms where high-paying guests sometimes expose themselves in front of their floor-to-ceiling windows in a towel – or less). The second phase, a half-mile stretch from 20th to 30th Sts, the northern end not far from Penn Station, opened in the summer of 2011. The **Whitney Museum of American Art** (long located on the Upper East Side), has broken ground on construction of its new meatpacking district home on Gansevoort St scheduled for a 2015 opening.

CHELSEA

This 'hood is popular for two main attractions: one, the parade of gorgeous gay men (known affectionately as 'Chelsea boys') who roam Eighth Ave, darting from gyms to trendy happy hours; and two, it's one of the

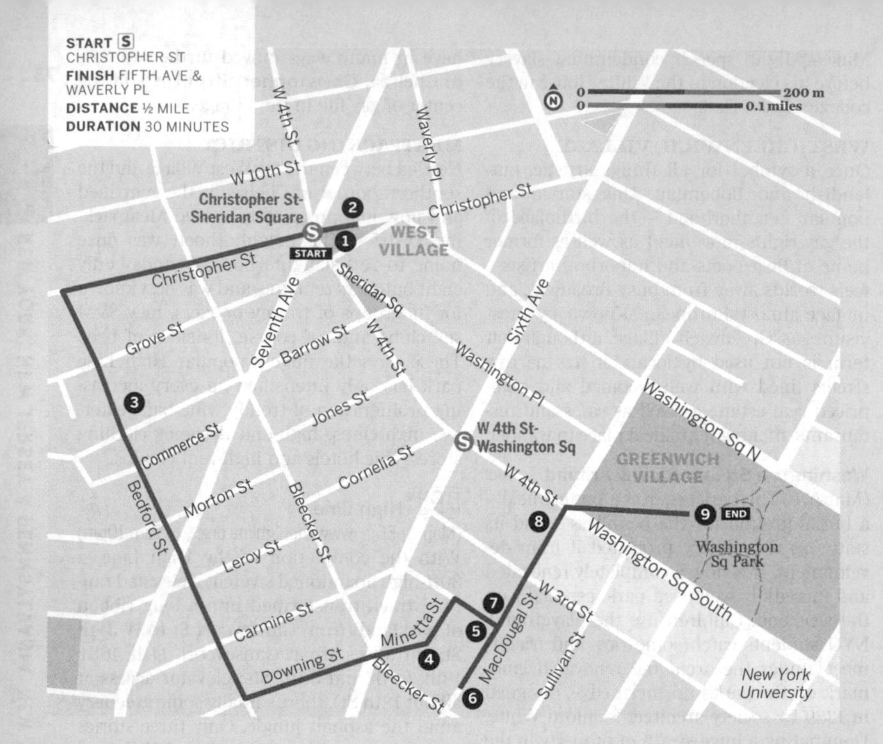

Waking Tour
Village Radicals

Manhattan's most unruly maze of streets can be found in Greenwich Village, historically a hotbed for upstarts, radicals, Bohemians, poets, folk singers, feminists and freedom-seeking gays and lesbians. To begin, disembark the subway at Christopher St and stop at tiny ❶ **Christopher Park**, where two white, life-size statues of same-sex couples (Gay Liberation, 1992) stand guard. On its north side is the legendary ❷ **Stonewall Inn**, where a clutch of fed-up drag queens rioted for their civil rights in 1969, signaling the start of the gay revolution. Cross Seventh Ave South and continue west along Christopher St, still known as the pulse of gay life here. Turn left onto quaint Bedford St; stop and peer into ❸ **Chumley's**, the site of a prohibition-dodging socialist-run speakeasy. Continue along Bedford St for several blocks, make a left on Downing St and cross Sixth Ave. Continue east on the crooked Minetta St, home to the unremarkable Panchito's Mexican Restaurant which recently painted over the faded sign for the ❹ **Fat Black Pussycat** – called The Commons in 1962, when a young Bob Dylan wrote and first performed 'Blowin' in the Wind' here. Turn right on Minetta Lane and right on MacDougal St to find the historic ❺ **Minetta Tavern**, which opened as a speakeasy in 1922, its walls now lined with photos of celebs who have visited. Also on this block is the former site of the ❻ **Folklore Center**, where Izzy Young established a hangout for folk artists including Dylan, who found his first audience at the music venue ❼ **Cafe Wha?**. Double back along MacDougal to the current Research Fellows & Scholars Office of the NYU School of Law, the former site of the ❽ **Liberal Club**, a meeting place for free thinkers, including Jack London and Upton Sinclair, founded in 1913. Beyond here is the southwest entrance to ❾ **Washington Square Park**, which has a long history as a magnet for radicals. Wrap up the tour by leaving the park at the iconic arch and head up Fifth Ave.

hubs of the city's art-gallery scene – it's currently home to nearly 200 modern-art exhibition spaces, most of which are clustered west of Tenth Ave. Find specific galleries at www.westchelseaarts.com.

Rubin Museum of Art MUSEUM
(Map p76; ☎212-620-5000; www.rmanyc.org; 150 W 17th St at Seventh Ave; adult/child $10/free; ⏰11am-5pm Mon & Thu, to 7pm Wed, to 10pm Fri, to 6pm Sat & Sun) Dedicated to art of the Himalayas and surrounding regions, this museum's impressive collections include embroidered textiles from China, metal sculptures from Tibet, intricate Bhutanese paintings, as well as ritual objects and dance masks from various Tibetan regions, spanning from the 2nd to the 19th centuries.

Chelsea Piers HEALTH & FITNESS
(Map p76; ☎212-336-6666; www.chelseapiers.com; W 23rd St, at Hudson River) A waterfront sports center that caters to the athlete in everyone. It's got a four-level driving range, indoor ice rink, jazzy bowling alley, Hoop City for basketball, a sailing school for kids, batting cages, a huge gym, indoor rock-climbing walls – the works.

FLATIRON DISTRICT

At the intersection of Broadway, Fifth Ave and 23rd St, the famous (and absolutely gorgeous) 1902 **Flatiron Building** has a distinctive triangular shape to match its site. It was New York's first iron-frame high-rise, and the world's tallest building until 1909. Its surrounding district is a fashionable area of boutiques, loft apartments and a growing high-tech corridor, the city's answer to Silicon Valley between here and neighboring Chelsea. Peaceful **Madison Square Park** bordered by 23rd and 26th Sts, and Fifth and Madison Aves, has an active dog run, rotating outdoor sculptures, shaded park benches and a popular burger joint. Several blocks to the east is the **Museum of Sex** (Map p76; ☎212-689-6337; www.museumofsex.com; 233 Fifth Ave, at W 27th St; admission $18; ⏰10am-8pm Sun-Thu, to 9m Fri & Sat), a somewhat intellectualized homage to intercourse. Only 18 and over admitted.

UNION SQUARE

A true town square, albeit one with a grassy interior, Union Square is a hive of activity with all manner of New Yorkers rubbing elbows, sharing hacky sacks and eyeing each other. A major renovation has brought a showpiece playground and public toilets to the northern end while the steps of the southern end are the place for antiwar and other liberal-leaning demonstrators.

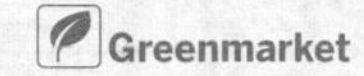

Greenmarket Farmers Market FOOD MARKET
(Map p76; ☎212-788-7476; www.grownyc.org; 17th St, btwn Broadway & Park Ave S; ⏰8am-6pm Mon, Wed, Fri & Sat) On most days, Union Square's north end hosts the most popular of the nearly 50 greenmarkets throughout the five boroughs, where even celebrity chefs come for just-picked rarities including fiddlehead ferns, heirloom tomatoes and fresh curry leaves.

GRAMERCY PARK

This area, loosely comprising the 20s east of Madison Ave, is named after one of New York's loveliest parks; it's for residents only, though, and you need a key to get in! If you're strolling by, peer through the gates and get a good look at what you're missing.

Theodore Roosevelt's Birthplace HISTORIC SITE
(Map p76; ☎212-668-2251; www.nps.gov/thrb; 28 E 20th St, btwn Park Ave & Broadway; admission $3; ⏰9am-5pm Tue-Sat) A National Historic Site; however, this building is simply a re-creation – the actual house where the 26th president was born was demolished in his lifetime.

MIDTOWN

The classic NYC fantasy – shiny skyscrapers, teeming mobs of worker bees, Fifth Ave store windows, taxi traffic – and some of the city's most popular attractions can be found here. Long ago when print ruled and newspaper and magazines were the cultural currency of the day, Midtown was actually also the literary district – the prime movers and shakers used to meet at the Algonquin Hotel. Major media companies such as the *New York Times* are still based here.

Museum of Modern Art MUSEUM
(MoMA; Map p76; ☎212-708-9400; www.moma.org; 11 W 53rd St, btwn Fifth & Sixth Aves; adult/child $20/free, free 4-8pm Fri; ⏰10:30am-5:30pm, to 8pm Fri, closed Tue) A veritable art universe of more than 100,000 pieces, the 75-year old Museum of Modern Art houses one of the more significant collections of works in the world. A controversial renovation project designed by the architect Yoshio Taniguchi doubled the museum's capacity to 630,000 sq ft on six floors. Most of the big hitters – Matisse,

Times Square, Midtown Manhattan & Chelsea

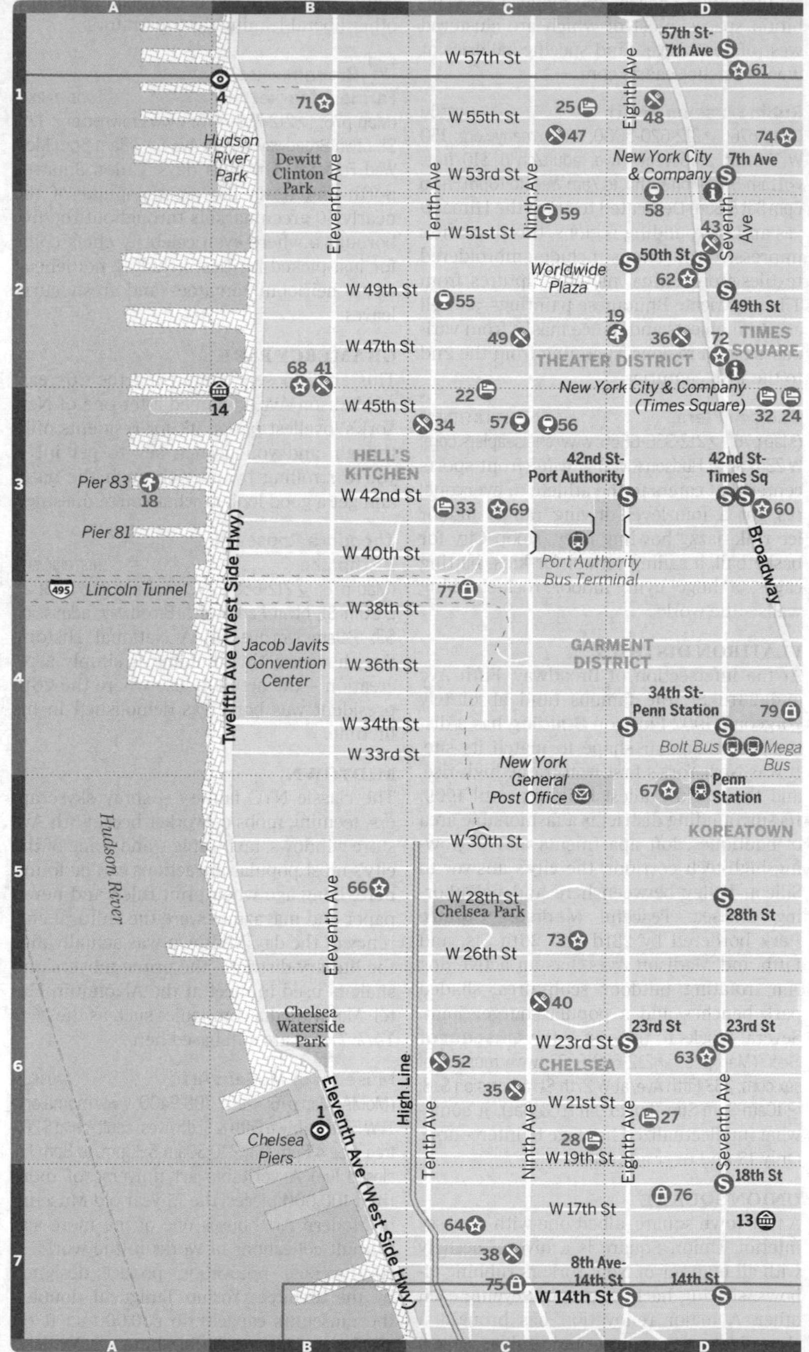

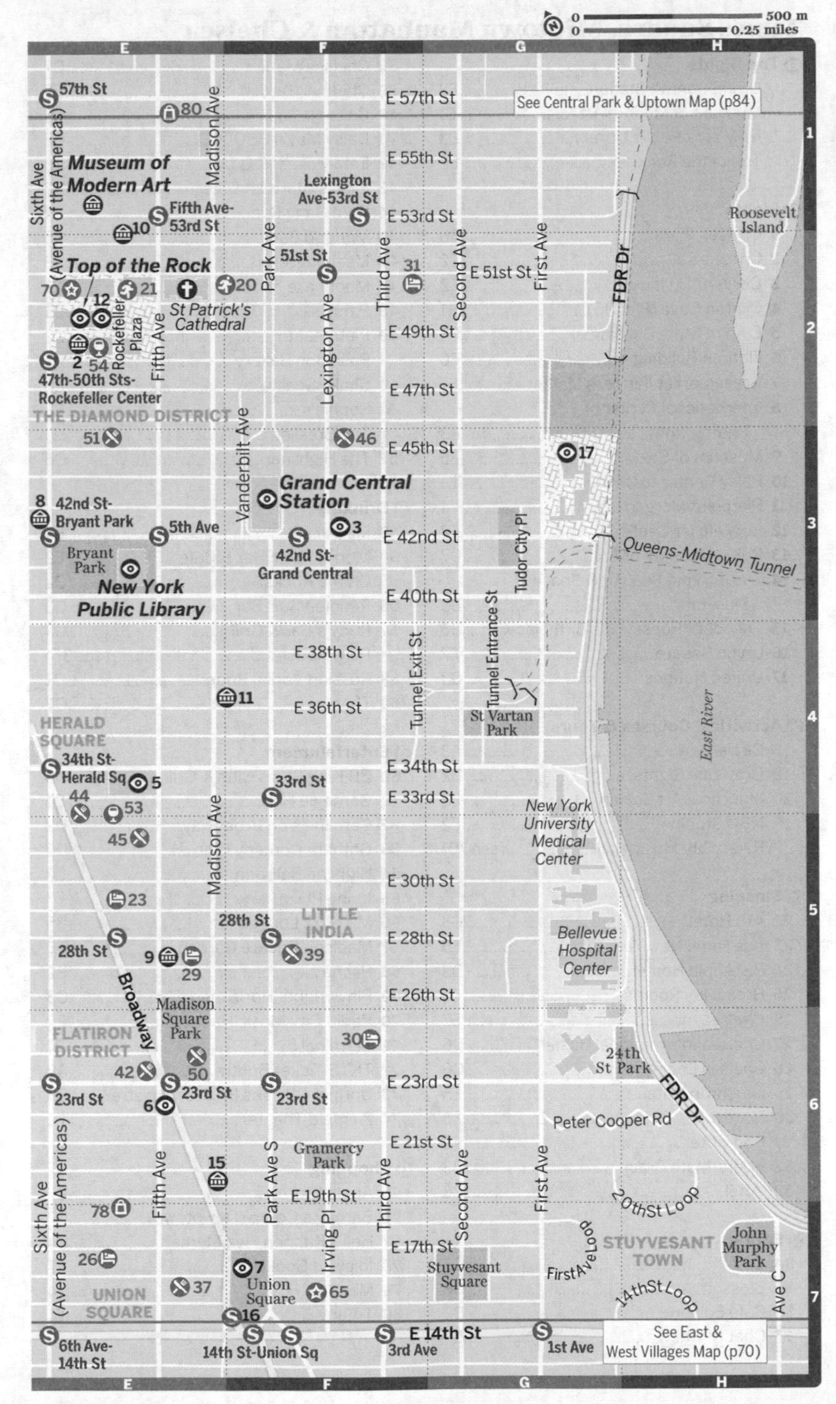
0 500 m
0 0.25 miles
See Central Park & Uptown Map (p84)
57th St
E 57th St
Museum of Modern Art
Fifth Ave-53rd St
Lexington Ave-53rd St
E 55th St
E 53rd St
Roosevelt Island
Top of the Rock
51st St
E 51st St
St Patrick's Cathedral
Rockefeller Plaza
47th-50th Sts-Rockefeller Center
E 49th St
E 47th St
THE DIAMOND DISTRICT
E 45th St
Grand Central Station
42nd St-Bryant Park
5th Ave
42nd St-Grand Central
E 42nd St
Bryant Park
New York Public Library
Queens-Midtown Tunnel
E 40th St
E 38th St
E 36th St
St Vartan Park
Tunnel Exit St
Tunnel Entrance St
Tudor City Pl
East River
HERALD SQUARE
34th St-Herald Sq
33rd St
E 34th St
E 33rd St
New York University Medical Center
E 30th St
28th St
LITTLE INDIA
E 28th St
Bellevue Hospital Center
Broadway
Madison Square Park
E 26th St
FLATIRON DISTRICT
24th St Park
23rd St
E 23rd St
FDR Dr
Peter Cooper Rd
Gramercy Park
E 21st St
E 19th St
20th St Loop
E 17th St
Stuyvesant Square
First Ave Loop
STUYVESANT TOWN
John Murphy Park
Union Square
UNION SQUARE
14th St Loop
Ave C
6th Ave-14th St
14th St-Union Sq
E 14th St
3rd Ave
1st Ave
See East & West Villages Map (p70)
Sixth Ave (Avenue of the Americas)
Fifth Ave
Madison Ave
Vanderbilt Ave
Park Ave
Park Ave S
Irving Pl
Lexington Ave
Third Ave
Second Ave
First Ave
E F G H
1 2 3 4 5 6 7
80 10 70 12 21 20 31 2 54 51 46 8 3 17 11 5 44 53 45 23 9 29 39 30 42 50 6 15 78 26 7 37 65 16

Times Square, Midtown Manhattan & Chelsea

Top Sights

Grand Central Station ... F3
Museum of Modern Art ... E1
New York Public Library ... E3
Top of the Rock ... E2

Sights

1 Chelsea Piers ... B6
2 Christie's ... E2
3 Chrysler Building ... F3
4 Clinton Cove (Pier 96) ... B1
5 Empire State Building ... E4
6 Flatiron Building ... E6
7 Greenmarket Farmers Market ... F7
8 International Center of Photography ... E3
9 Museum of Sex ... E5
10 Paley Center for Media ... E1
11 Pierpoint Morgan Library ... F4
12 Rockefeller Center ... E2
13 Rubin Museum of Art ... D7
14 The Intrepid Sea, Air & Space Museum ... B3
15 Theodore Roosevelt's Birthplace ... E6
16 Union Square ... F7
17 United Nations ... G3

Activities, Courses & Tours

18 Circle Line ... A3
19 Gray Line Sightseeing ... D2
20 Municipal Art Society ... F2
21 NBC Studios ... E2
Radio City Music Hall ... (see 70)

Sleeping

22 414 Hotel ... C3
23 Ace Hotel New York City ... E5
24 Big Apple Hostel ... D3
25 Broadway Rooms ... C1
26 Chelsea Inn ... E7
27 Chelsea International Hostel ... D6
28 Chelsea Lodge ... C6
29 Gershwin Hotel ... E5
30 Marcel ... F6
31 Pod Hotel ... F2
32 Room-Mate Grace ... D3
33 Yotel ... C3

Eating

34 44 & X ... C3
35 Blossom ... C6
36 Café Edison ... D2
37 Chat N' Chew ... E7
38 Chelsea Market ... C7
39 Chennai Garden ... F5
40 Co. ... C6
41 Daisy May's BBQ ... B2
42 Eataly ... E6
43 Ellen's Stardust Diner ... D2
44 Kum Gang San ... E4
45 Mandoo Bar ... E5
46 Mechango Tei ... F3
47 Mooncake Foods ... C1
48 Patsy's ... D1
49 Pietrasanta ... C2
Poseidon Bakery ... (see 57)
50 Shake Shack ... E6
51 Sophie's ... E3
The Breslin ... (see 23)
52 The Highliner ... C6

Drinking

53 Mé Bar ... E4
54 Morrell Wine Bar & Café ... E2
55 On the Rocks ... C2
56 Réunion Surf Bar ... C3
57 Rudy's Bar & Grill ... C3
Rum House ... (see 36)
58 Russian Vodka Room ... D1
59 Therapy ... C2

Entertainment

60 BB King Blues Club & Grill ... D3
61 Carnegie Hall ... D1
62 Caroline's on Broadway ... D2
63 Gotham Comedy Club ... D6
64 Highline Ballroom ... C7
65 Irving Plaza ... F7
66 M2 Ultra Lounge ... B5
67 Madison Square Garden ... D5
68 Pacha ... B2
69 Playwrights Horizons ... C3
70 Radio City Music Hall ... E2
71 Terminal 5 ... B1
72 TKTS Ticket Booth ... D2
73 Upright Citizens Brigade Theatre ... C5
74 Ziegfeld Theater ... D1

Shopping

75 Apple Store ... C7
76 Barney's Co-op (Downtown) ... D7
77 Hell's Kitchen Flea Market ... C4
78 Idlewild Books ... E7
79 Macy's ... D4
80 Tiffany & Co ... E1

Picasso, Cézanne, Rothko, Pollock and many others – are housed in the central five-story atrium. Be prepared for long entrance lines and crowds.

Times Square & Theater District NEIGHBORHOOD

(Map p76) There are few images more universally iconic than the glittering orb dropping from Times Square on New Year's Eve – the first one descended 100 years ago. Smack in the middle of Midtown Manhattan, this area around the intersection of Broadway and Seventh Ave, with its gaudy billboards and glittery marquees, has become so intertwined with New York City in the minds of non-New Yorkers that regardless of how Disneyfied it has become, it's still considered quintessential New York. Once again 'the Crossroads of the World' and unrecognizable from its '70s-era seediness of strip clubs, hookers and pickpockets, the square draws 35 million visitors annually. Massive chains like American Eagle and themed stores like Hershey's pull in folks and multiplex theaters draw crowds with large screens and stadium seating. In an effort to make the area more pedestrian-friendly and diminish the perpetual gridlock, Broadway from 47th to 42nd St was turned into a vehicle-free zone.

The Times Square area is at least equally famous as New York's official **Theater District**, with dozens of Broadway and off-Broadway theaters located in an area that stretches from 41st to 54th Sts, between Sixth and Ninth Aves. The Times Square branch of **New York City & Company** (☎212-763-1560; www.timessquarenyc.org; 1560 Broadway, btwn 46th & 47th Sts; ⏲9am-7pm Mon-Fri, 8am-8pm Sun) sits smack in the middle of this famous crossroads, inside the beautifully restored landmark Embassy Theater. Broadway, the road, once ran all the way to the state capitol in Albany.

Rockefeller Center HISTORIC BUILDING, TOUR

(Map p76) It was built during the height of the Great Depression in the 1930s, and construction of the 22-acre Rockefeller Center, including the landmark art-deco skyscraper gave jobs to 70,000 workers over nine years and was the first project to combine retail, entertainment and office space in what is often referred to as a 'city within a city.' The 360-degree views from the tri-level observation deck of the **Top of the Rock** (☎212-698-2000; www.topoftherocknyc.com; main entrance 50th St, btwn Fifth & Sixth Aves; adult/child $22/15; ⏲8am-midnight) are absolutely stunning and should not be missed; on a clear day you can see quite a distance across the river into New Jersey. The 67th and 69th floors have outdoor terraces. In winter the ground floor outdoor space is abuzz with ice-skaters and Christmas-tree gawkers. Within the complex is the 1932, 6000-seat **Radio City Music Hall** (☎212-247-4777; www.radiocity.com; 1260 Sixth Ave; tours adult/child $22.50/16; ⏲tours 11am-3pm Mon-Sun). To get an inside look at this former movie palace and protected landmark that's been gorgeously restored in all its art-deco grandeur join one of the frequent guided tours that leave the lobby every half-hour. Fans of the NBC TV show *30 Rock* will recognize the 70-story GE Building as the network headquarters. Tours of the **NBC studios**, (☎212-664-3700; www.nbcstudiotour.com; 30 Rockefeller Plaza; adult/child $20/17; ⏲8:30am-5:30pm Mon-Sat, to 6:30pm Fri & Sat, 9:15am-4:30pm Sun) leave from the lobby of the GE Building every 15 minutes; note that children under six are not admitted. *The Today Show* broadcasts live 7am to 11am daily from a glass-enclosed street-level studio near the fountain.

FREE **New York Public Library** LIBRARY, MUSEUM

(Map p76; ☎212-340-0833; www.nypl.org; Fifth Ave, at 42nd St; ⏲10am-6pm Tue-Sat) Flanked by two huge marble lions nicknamed 'Patience' and 'Fortitude' by former mayor Fiorello LaGuardia, the stairway leading up to the New York Public Library is a grand entrance. The massive, superb beaux-arts building stands as testament to the value of learning and culture in the city, as well as to the wealth of the philanthropists who made its founding possible. A magnificent 3rd-floor reading room has a painted ceiling and bountiful natural light – rows of long wooden tables are occupied by students, writers and the general public working away at laptops. This, the main branch of the entire city library system, has galleries of manuscripts on display, as well as fascinating temporary exhibits. Immediately behind the library is beautifully maintained **Bryant Park**, a grassy expanse furnished with tables and chairs, and even a lending library, chessboards and Ping Pong tables in warm weather (free wi-fi too), as well as an ice-skating rink in winter.

Empire State Building HISTORIC BUILDING
(Map p76; ☎212-736-3100; www.esbnyc.org; 350 Fifth Ave, at E 34th St; adult/child $20/15; ⌚8am-2am) Catapulted to Hollywood stardom both as the planned meeting spot for Cary Grant and Deborah Kerr in *An Affair to Remember*, and the vertical perch that helped to topple King Kong, the classic Empire State Building is one of New York's most famous members of the skyline. It's a limestone classic built in just 410 days, or seven million man-hours, during the depths of the Depression at a cost of $41 million. On the site of the original Waldorf-Astoria Hotel, the 102-story, 1472ft (to the top of the antenna) Empire State Building opened in 1931 after 10 million bricks were laid, 6400 windows installed and 328,000 sq ft of marble laid. Today you can ride the elevator to observatories on the 86th and 102nd floors (for the latter it's an additional $17), but be prepared for crowds; try to come very early or very late (and purchase your tickets ahead of time, online or pony up for more expensive 'express passes') for an optimal experience.

Grand Central Station HISTORIC BUILDING
(Map p76; www.grandcentralterminal.com; 42nd St, at Fifth Ave) Built in 1913 as a prestigious terminal by New York Central and Hudson River Railroad, Grand Central Station is no longer a romantic place to begin a cross-country journey, as it's now the terminus for Metro North commuter trains to the northern suburbs and Connecticut. But even if you're not boarding a train to the 'burbs, it's worth exploring the grand, vaulted main concourse and gazing up at the restored ceiling, decorated with a star map that is actually a 'God's-eye' image of the night sky. There's a high-end food market and the lower level houses a truly excellent array of eateries, while the balcony has a cozy '20s-era salon kind of bar called the **Campbell Apartment**.

Fifth Avenue & Around NEIGHBORHOOD
Immortalized in both film and song, Fifth Ave first developed its high-class reputation in the early 20th century, when it was considered desirable for its 'country' air and open spaces. The series of mansions called **Millionaire's Row** extended right up to 130th St, though most of the heirs to the millionaire mansions on Fifth Ave above 59th St sold them for demolition or converted them to the cultural institutions that now make up Museum Mile.

The avenue's Midtown stretch still boasts upmarket shops and hotels, including Trump Tower (725 Fifth Ave, at 56th St) and the Plaza (cnr Fifth Ave and Central Park South). While a number of the more exclusive boutiques have migrated to Madison Ave – leaving outposts of Gap and H&M in their wake – several superstars still reign over Fifth Ave above 50th St, including the famous Tiffany & Co.

Pierpont Morgan Library MUSEUM
(Map p76; ☎212-685-0008; www.morganlibrary.org; 29 E 36th St at Madison Ave; adult/child $15/10; ⌚10:30am-5pm Tue-Thu, to 9pm Fri, 10am-6pm Sat & Sun) The beautifully renovated library is part of the 45-room mansion once owned by steel magnate JP Morgan. His collection features a phenomenal array of manuscripts, tapestries and books, a study filled with Italian Renaissance artwork, a marble rotunda and the three-tiered East Room main library.

United Nations Headquarters TOUR
(Map p76; ☎212-963-8687; www.un.org/tours; First Ave, btwn 42nd & 48th Sts; tours adult/child $16/9; ⌚tours 9:45am-4:45pm) The UN is technically on a section of international territory overlooking the East River. Take a guided 45-minute tour of the facility and you'll get to see the General Assembly, where the annual fall convocation of member nations takes place, the Security Council Chamber (depending on schedules) and also the Economic & Social Council Chamber. There is a park to the south of the complex which is home to several sculptures with a peace theme. English-language tours of the UN complex depart frequently; limited tours in several other languages are also available.

Paley Center for Media MUSEUM
(Map p76; ☎212-621-6800; www.paleycenter.org; 25 W 52nd St; adult/child $10/5, theater $6; ⌚noon-6pm Fri-Wed, to 8pm Thu) TV fanatics who spent their childhood glued to the tube and proudly claim instant recall of all of Fonzi's *Happy Days* exploits can hold their heads high. This is the 'museum' for them. Search through a catalogue of more than 100,000 US TV and radio programs and advertisements and a click of the mouse will play your selection on one of the library's computer screens. A comfy theater shows some great specials on broadcasting history, and there are frequent events and screenings.

Intrepid Sea, Air & Space Museum MUSEUM
(Map p76; ☎212-245-0072; www.intrepidmuseum.org; Pier 86, Twelfth Ave at 46th St; adult/child $24/12; ⊙10am-5pm, to 6pm Sat & Sun) The USS Intrepid, a hulking aircraft carrier that survived both a WWII bomb and kamikaze attacks has been transformed into a military museum with high-tech exhibits and fighter planes and helicopters for view on the outdoor flight deck. The pier area contains the guided-missile submarine *Growler,* a decommissioned Concorde and in 2012 the *Enterprise* space shuttle.

International Center of Photography MUSEUM
(Map p76; ☎212-857-0000; www.icp.org; 1133 Sixth Ave, at 43rd St; adult/child $12/free; ⊙10am-6pm Tue-Sun, to 8pm Fri) The city's most important showcase for major photographers, especially photojournalists. Its past exhibitions have included work by Henri Cartier-Bresson, Matthew Brady and Robert Capa.

Herald Square & Around NEIGHBORHOOD
This crowded convergence of Broadway, Sixth Ave and 34th St is best known as the home of **Macy's** department store, where you can still ride some of the remaining original wooden elevators to floors ranging from home furnishings to lingerie. But the busy square gets its name from a long-defunct newspaper, the *Herald,* and the small, leafy park here bustles during business hours. (The indoor mall south of Macy's on Sixth Ave houses the standard array of suburban chain stores.) In order to cut down on some of the area gridlock, Broadway, from 33rd to 35th St has been closed to traffic and turned into a pedestrian plaza.

West of Herald Sq, the **Garment District** has most of New York's fashion design offices, and while not much clothing is actually made here anymore, for anyone into pawing through dreamy selections of fabrics, buttons, sequins, lace and zippers it is the place to shop.

From 31st St to 36th St, between Broadway and Fifth Ave, **Koreatown** is an interesting and lively neighborhood with an expanding number of good restaurants and authentic karaoke spots.

Hell's Kitchen (Clinton) NEIGHBORHOOD
For years, the far west side of Midtown was a working-class district of tenements and food warehouses known as Hell's Kitchen – supposedly its name was muttered by a cop in reaction to a riot in the neighborhood in 1881. A 1990s economic boom seriously altered the character and developers reverted to using the cleaned-up name Clinton, a moniker originating from the 1950s; locals are split on usage. New restaurants exploded along Ninth and Tenth Aves between about 37th and 55th Sts, and now it's a great place to grab a pre- or post-theater meal. Antique-lovers should visit the **Hell's Kitchen Flea Market** (Map p76; ☎212-243-5343; www.hellskitchenfleamarket.com; W 39th St, btwn Ninth & Tenth Aves; ⊙7am-5pm Sat & Sun), boasting 170 vendors of vintage clothing, antique jewelry, period furniture and many more treasures.

Museum of Arts and Design MUSEUM
(Map p84; ☎212-299-7777; www.madmuseum.org; 2 Columbus Circle; adult/child $15/free; ⊙11am-6pm Tue-Sun, to 9pm Thu) On the southern side of the circle, exhibiting a diverse international collection of modern, folk, craft and fine art pieces. The plush and trippy design of the 9th floor **restaurant** complements fantastic views of Central Park.

Chrysler Building HISTORIC BUILDING
(Map p76; 405 Lexington Ave) Just east of Grand Central Station, the Chrysler Building, an art-deco masterpiece that's adorned with motorcar motifs, was completed in 1930 to be the headquarters for Walter P Chrysler and his automobile empire. Luckily, because visitors can't go up in the building (it's full of offices), it's most magnificent when viewed from a distance.

SOLD!

Even if your idea of a significant art purchase is a Van Gogh postcard, the adrenalin-pumping thrill of an art auction combines the best of museum-going and high-end shopping. Both **Christie's** (☎212-636-2000; www.christies.com; 20 Rockefeller Plaza) and **Sotheby's** (☎212-606-7000; www.sothebys.com; 1334 York Ave, at 72nd St), two of the city's and world's most prominent auction houses are open to the public. Whether it's a collection of Warhol canvases or old European masterworks, the prices remain generally stratospheric – keep your hands down or else your casual twitch will be taken for a bid and you could be on the hook for tens of millions of dollars.

UPPER WEST SIDE

Shorthand for liberal, progressive and intellectual New York – think Woody Allen movies (although he lives on the Upper East Side) and Seinfeld – this neighborhood comprising the west side of Manhattan from Central Park to the Hudson River, and from Columbus Circle to 110th St, is no longer as colorful as it once was. Upper Broadway has been taken over by banks, pharmacies and national retail chain stores and many of the mom-and-pop shops and bookstores are long gone. You'll still find massive, ornate apartments and a diverse mix of stable, upwardly mobile folks (with many actors and classical musicians sprinkled throughout), and some lovely green spaces – **Riverside Park** stretches for 4 miles between W 72nd St and W 158th St along the Hudson River, and is a great place for strolling, running, cycling or simply gazing at the sun as it sets over the Hudson River.

Central Park PARK

(Map p84; ☎212-310-6600; www.centralparknyc.org; btwn 57th & 110th Sts & Fifth Ave & Central Park; 👪) It's hard to imagine what the city would be like without this refuge from the claustrophobia, from the teeming sidewalks and clogged roadways. This enormous wonderland of a park, sitting right in the middle of Manhattan, provides both metaphorical and spiritual oxygen to its residents. The park's 843 acres were set aside in 1856 on the marshy northern fringe of the city. The landscaping (the first in a US public park), by Frederick Law Olmsted and Calvert Vaux, was innovative in its naturalistic style, with forested groves, meandering paths and informal ponds. Highlights include **Sheep Meadow** (mid-park from 66th to 69th Sts), where tens of thousands of people lounge and play on warm weather weekends; **Strawberry Fields** at 72nd St, dedicated to John Lennon, who lived at (and was murdered in front of) the **Dakota apartment building** across the street; the sparkling **Jacqueline Kennedy Onassis Reservoir**, encircled by joggers daily; **Central Park Zoo** (☎212-439-6500; www.wcs.org; 64th St, at Fifth Ave; adult/child $10/5; ⊙10am-5pm Mon-Fri, to 5:30pm Sat & Sun); the formal, tree-lined promenade called the **Mall**, which culminates at the elegant **Bethesda Fountain**; and the **Ramble**, a rest stop for nearly 250 migratory species of birdlife – early morning is best for sightings. A favorite tourist activity is to rent a **horse-drawn carriage** (Map p84; 30min tour $35 plus generous tip) at 59th St (Central Park South) or hop in a **pedicab** (30min tours $30); the latter congregate at Central Park West and 72nd St. For more information while you're strolling, visit the **Dairy Building visitor centre** (Map p84; ☎212-794-6564; Central Park, at 65th St; ⊙10am-5pm Tue-Sat) in the southern section of the park.

Lincoln Center ARTS CENTER

(Map p84; ☎212-875-5456; www.lincolncenter.org; cnr Columbus Ave & Broadway) Only a few unfinished elements remain to complete the billion-dollar-plus redevelopment of the world's largest performing arts center. The dramatically redesigned Alice Tully Hall anchors one end of the property and other stunning venues surround a massive fountain; public spaces, including the roof lawn of the North Plaza (an upscale restaurant is underneath), have been upgraded. The lavishly designed **Metropolitan Opera House** (MET), the largest opera house in the world, seats 3900 people. Fascinating one-hour **tours** (☎212-875-5350; adult/child $15/8) of the complex leave from the lobby of Avery Fisher Hall from 10:30am to 4:30pm daily; these vary from architectural to backstage tours. Free wi-fi is available on the property as well as at the **David Rubenstein Atrium** (Broadway, btwn 62nd & 63rd Sts), a modern public space featuring a lounge area, cafe, information desk and a ticket center offering day-of discounts to Lincoln Center performances.

TOP CHOICE **American Museum of Natural History** MUSEUM

(Map p84; ☎212-769-5100; www.amnh.org; Central Park West, at 79th St; suggested admission adult/child $16/9, extra for space shows, IMAX shows & special exhibits; ⊙10am-5:45pm; 👪) Founded in 1869, this museum includes more than 30 million artifacts, interactive exhibits and loads of taxidermy. It's most famous for its three large dinosaur halls, an enormous (fake) blue whale that hangs from the ceiling above the Hall of Ocean Life and the elaborate **Rose Center for Earth & Space**. Just gazing at its facade – a massive glass box that contains a silver globe, home to space-show theaters and the planetarium – is mesmerizing, especially at night, when all of its otherworldly features are aglow.

New York Historical Society MUSEUM

(Map p84; ☎212-873-3400; www.nyhistory.org; 170 Central Park W, at 77th St; adult/child $10/6;

⏲10am-6pm Tue-Sun) This museum, founded in 1804 and widely credited with being the city's oldest, received a full-scale makeover in 2011. The quirky and wide-ranging permanent collection, including original watercolors from John James Audubon's *Birds of America* will be housed in a spruced-up contemporary exhibition space; there's a new auditorium, library and restaurant as well.

MORNINGSIDE HEIGHTS

The Upper West Side's northern neighbor, comprises the area of Broadway and west up to about 125th St. Dominating the neighborhood is **Columbia University**, the highly rated Ivy League college, which features a spacious, grassy central quadrangle.

Cathedral of St John the Divine CHURCH

(Map p84; ☎212-316-7540; 1047 Amsterdam Ave, at 112th St; ⏲7am-6pm, to 7pm Sun) A decades-long restoration of this Episcopal cathedral, the largest place of worship in the USA, is a truly stunning accomplishment. High Mass, held at 11am Sunday, often with sermons by well-known intellectuals.

UPPER EAST SIDE

The Upper East Side (UES) is home to New York's greatest concentration of cultural centers, including the grand dame that is the Metropolitan Museum of Art (see below), and many refer to Fifth Ave above 57th St as Museum Mile. The real estate, at least along Fifth, Madison and Park Aves, is some of the most expensive in the world. Home to ladies who lunch as well as frat boys who drink, the neighborhood becomes decidedly less chichi the further east you go.

Metropolitan Museum of Art MUSEUM

(Map p84; ☎212-535-7710; www.metmuseum.org; 1000 Fifth Ave, at 82nd St; suggested donation $25, children free; ⏲9:30am-5:30pm Tue-Thu & Sun, to 9pm Fri & Sat) With more than five million visitors a year, the Met is New York's most popular single-site tourist attraction, with one of the richest coffers in the arts world. The Met is a self-contained cultural city-state, with two million individual objects in its collection and an annual budget of over $120 million; its 19th-century European paintings and sculpture galleries have been greatly expanded and refurbished.

Highlight rooms here include Egyptian Art, American Paintings and Sculpture, Arms and Armor, Modern Art, Greek and Roman Art, European Paintings and the gorgeous rooftop, which offers bar service and spectacular views throughout the summer. Note that the suggested donation (which is, truly, a *suggestion*) includes same-day admission to the Cloisters.

TOP CHOICE **Frick Collection** MUSEUM

(Map p84; ☎212-288-0700; www.frick.org; 1 E 70th St; admission $18; ⏲10am-6pm Tue-Sat, 11am-5pm Sun) This spectacular art collection sits in a mansion built by Henry Clay Frick in 1914; it's a shame that the 2nd floor of the residence isn't open for viewing. The 12 richly furnished rooms on the ground floor display paintings by Titian, Vermeer, El Greco, Goya and other masters. Perhaps the best asset here is that it's rarely crowded, providing a welcome break from the swarms of gawkers at larger museums, especially on weekends.

Solomon R Guggenheim Museum MUSEUM

(Map p84; ☎212-423-3500; www.guggenheim.org; 1071 Fifth Ave; adult/child $18/free; ⏲10am-5:45pm Sat-Wed, to 7:45pm Fri) The inspired work of Frank Lloyd Wright, and its sweeping spiral of a staircase is a superb sculpture, holding 20th-century paintings by Picasso, Pollock, Chagall and Kandinsky.

Neue Galerie MUSEUM

(Map p84; ☎212-628-6200; www.neuegalerie.org; 1048 Fifth Ave, at 86th St; adult $15, children under 12 not admitted; ⏲11am-6pm Thu-Mon) Housed in a stately and elegant Fifth Ave mansion, the Neue showcases German and Austrian artists, with impressive works by Gustav Klimt and Egon Schiele. **Café Sabarsky**, on the ground floor, is alone worth a visit for its fin de siécle European vibe, rich desserts (apple strudel $8) and cabaret performances on Thursday nights ($45).

Whitney Museum of American Art MUSEUM

(Map p84; ☎212-570-3600; www.whitney.org; 945 Madison Ave, at 75th St; admission $18; ⏲11am-6pm Wed, Thu, Sat & Sun, to 9pm Fri) One of the few museums that concentrates on American works of art, specializing in 20th-century and contemporary art, with works by Hopper, Pollock and Rothko, as well as special shows, such as the much-ballyhooed Biennial. The Whitney is moving in 2015 to Gansevoort St in the Meatpacking District.

Jewish Museum MUSEUM

(Map p84; ☎212-423-3200; www.jewishmuseum.org; 1109 Fifth Ave at 92nd St; adult/child $12/free; ⏲11am-5:45pm Sat-Tue, to 8pm Thu, to 4pm Fri)

Central Park & Uptown

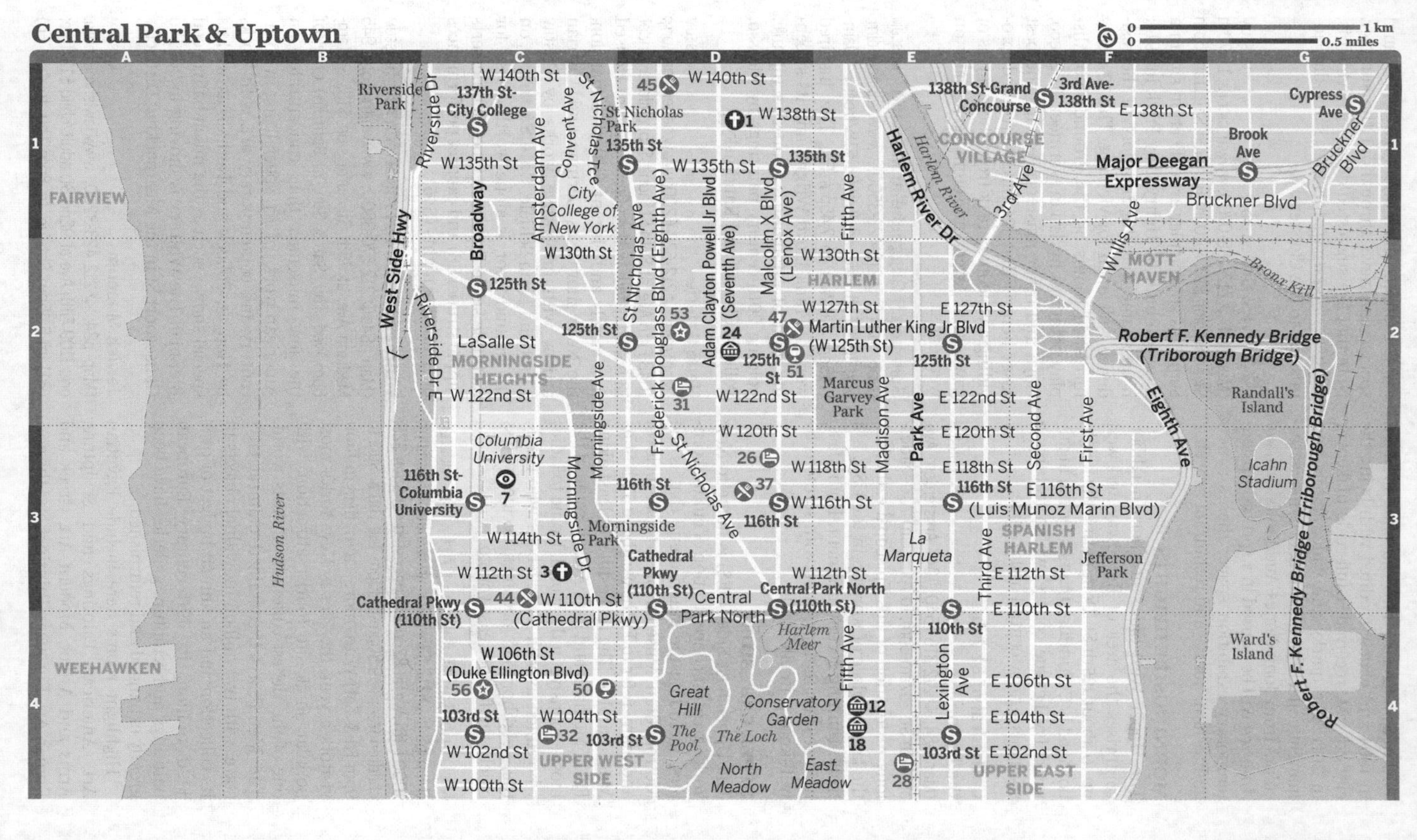

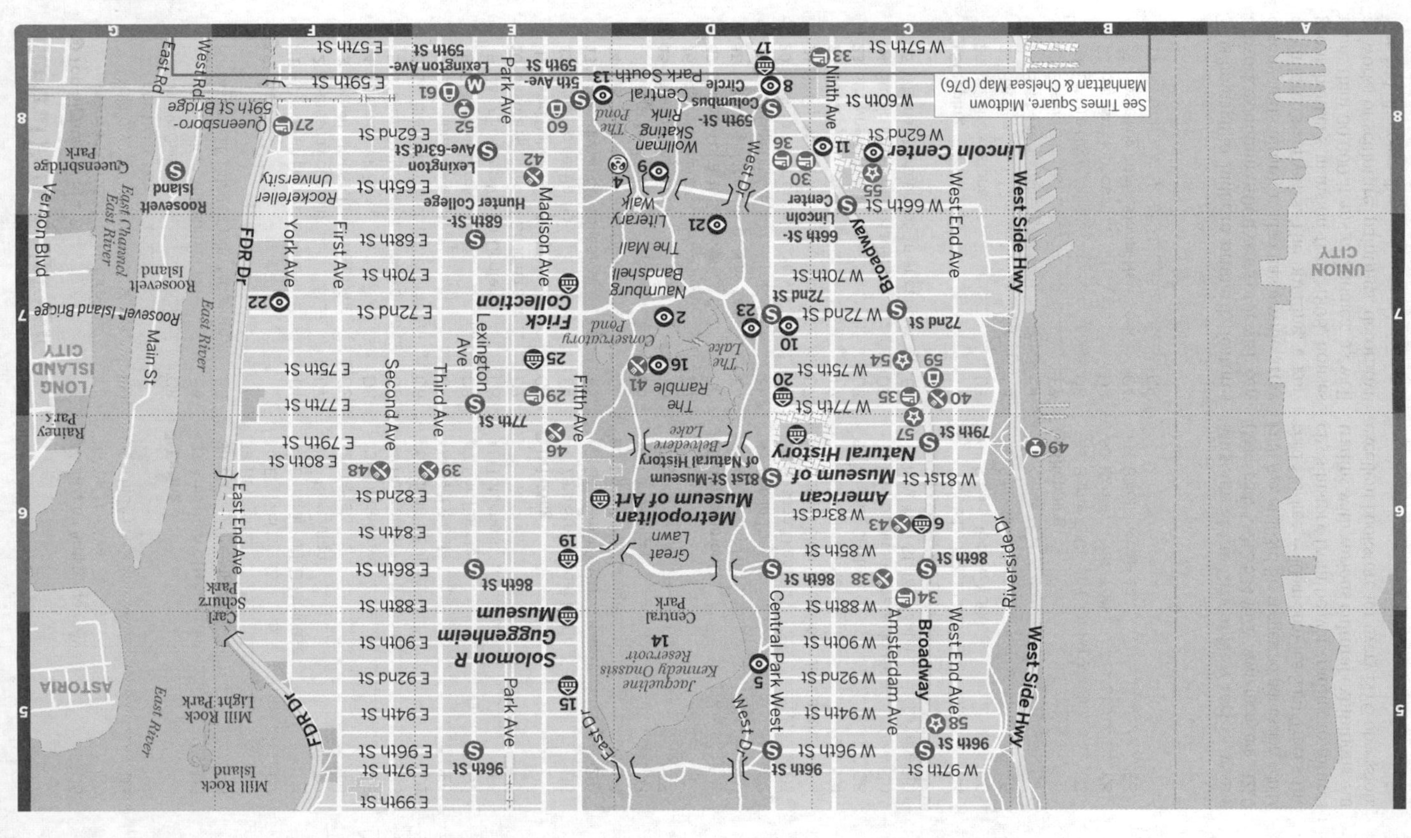

Solomon R Guggenheim Museum
Metropolitan Museum of Art
American Museum of Natural History
Frick Collection
Lincoln Center
Central Park
Jacqueline Kennedy Onassis Reservoir
Great Lawn
Belvedere Lake
The Ramble
The Lake
Conservatory Pond
Naumburg Bandshell
The Mall
Literary Walk
Wollman Skating Rink
The Pond
Columbus Circle
Central Park South
Central Park West
Broadway
Amsterdam Ave
West End Ave
Riverside Dr
West Side Hwy
Ninth Ave
Fifth Ave
Madison Ave
Park Ave
Lexington Ave
Third Ave
Second Ave
First Ave
York Ave
East End Ave
FDR Dr
East Dr
West Dr
Carl Schurz Park
Mill Rock Island
Mill Rock Light Park
East River
ASTORIA
LONG ISLAND CITY
Rainey Park
Vernon Blvd
Roosevelt Island
Main St
Roosevelt Island Bridge
East Channel East River
Queensbridge Park
Queensboro-59th St Bridge
Rockefeller University
Hunter College
West Rd
East Rd
UNION CITY
See Times Square, Midtown Manhattan & Chelsea Map (p76)

Central Park & Uptown

Top Sights

- American Museum of Natural History ... D6
- Frick Collection ... E7
- Lincoln Center ... C8
- Metropolitan Museum of Art ... E6
- Solomon R Guggenheim Museum ... E5

Sights

- **1** Abyssinian Baptist Church ... D1
- **2** Bethesda Fountain ... D7
- **3** Cathedral of St John the Divine ... C3
- **4** Central Park Zoo ... D8
- **5** Central Park's Safari Playground ... D5
- **6** Children's Museum of Manhattan ... C6
- **7** Columbia University ... C3
- **8** Columbus Circle ... D8
- **9** Dairy Building Visitor Center ... D8
- **10** Dakota Apartment Building ... D7
- **11** David Rubenstein Atrium ... C8
- **12** El Museo del Barrio ... E4
- **13** Horse-drawn Carriages ... E8
- **14** Jacqueline Kennedy Onassis Reservoir ... D5
- **15** Jewish Museum ... E5
- **16** Loeb Boathouse ... D7
- **17** Museum of Arts & Design ... D8
- **18** Museum of the City of New York ... E4
- **19** Neue Galerie ... E6
- **20** New York Historical Society ... D7
- **21** Sheep Meadow ... D7
- **22** Sotheby's ... F7
- **23** Strawberry Fields ... D7
- **24** Studio Museum in Harlem ... D2
- **25** Whitney Museum of American Art ... E7

Sleeping

- **26** 102 Brownstone ... D3
- **27** Bentley ... F8
- **28** Bubba & Bean Lodges ... E4
- **29** Carlyle ... E7
- **30** Empire Hotel ... D8
- **31** Harlem Flophouse ... D2
- **32** Hostelling International-New York ... C4
- **33** Hudson ... C8
- **34** Jazz on Amsterdam Ave ... C6
- **35** On The Ave ... C7
- **36** YMCA ... D8

Eating

- **37** Amy Ruth's Restaurant ... D3
- **38** Barney Greengrass ... C6
- **39** Beyoglu ... E6
- **40** Big Nick's ... C7
- **41** Central Park Boathouse Restaurant ... D7
- **42** Daniel ... E8
- **43** Flor de Mayo ... C6
- **44** Hungarian Pastry Shop ... C3
- **45** Londel's Supper Club ... D1
- **46** Nectar Café ... E6
- **47** Red Rooster ... D2
- **48** Totonno's ... F6

Drinking

- **49** 79th Street Boat Basin ... B6
- Bemelman's Bar ... (see 29)
- **50** Ding Dong Lounge ... C4
- **51** Lenox Lounge ... D2
- **52** Subway Inn ... E8

Entertainment

- Alice Tully Hall ... (see 55)
- **53** Apollo Theater ... D2
- **54** Beacon Theater ... C7
- Dizzy's Club Coca-Cola: Jazz at the Lincoln Center ... (see 55)
- **55** Lincoln Center ... C8
- Metropolitan Opera House ... (see 55)
- New York State Theater ... (see 55)
- **56** Smoke Jazz & Supper Club-Lounge ... C4
- **57** Stand-Up New York ... C6
- **58** Symphony Space ... C5

Shopping

- **59** Barney's Co-op (Uptown) ... C7
- **60** Barney's New York ... E8
- **61** Bloomingdale's ... E8

This homage to Judaism primarily features artwork examining 4000 years of Jewish ceremony and culture; it also has a wide array of children's activities. The building, a gorgeous banker's mansion from 1908, houses more than 30,000 items of Judaica, as well as works of sculpture, paintings, decorative arts and photography.

Museum of the City of New York MUSEUM
(Map p84; ☎212-534-1672; www.mcny.org; 1220 Fifth Ave, at 103rd St; suggested admission adult/child $10/free; ⏲10am-5pm Tue-Sun) Traces the city's history from beaver trading to futures trading with various cultural exhibitions. An excellent bookstore for every NYC obsession.

El Museo del Barrio MUSEUM
(☎212-831-7272; www.elmuseo.org; 1230 Fifth Ave, at 104th St; adult/child $9/free; ⊙11am-6pm Tue-Sun) The Latino cultural institution houses a collection of Latin American and Caribbean art with a special focus on the Puerto Rican and Dominican communities. There's also an attractive street-side cafe.

HARLEM

The heart of African American culture has been beating in Harlem since its emergence as a black enclave in the 1920s. This neighborhood north of Central Park has been the setting for extraordinary accomplishments in art, music, dance, education and letters from the likes of Frederick Douglass, Paul Robeson, Thurgood Marshall, James Baldwin, Alvin Ailey, Billie Holiday, Jessie Jackson and many other African American luminaries. After steady decline from the 1960s to early '90s, Harlem is today experiencing something of a second renaissance in the form of million-dollar brownstones and condos for sale next door to neglected tenement buildings and the presence of big box national chain stores all along 125th St.

For a traditional view of Harlem, visit on Sunday morning, when well-dressed locals flock to neighborhood churches. Just be respectful of the fact that these people are attending a religious service (rather than being on display for tourists). Unless you're invited by a member of a small congregation, stick to the bigger churches.

Abyssinian Baptist Church RELIGIOUS
(Map p84; ☎212-862-7474; www.abyssinian.org; 132 W 138th St) Has a superb choir and a charismatic pastor, Calvin O Butts, who welcomes tourists and prays for them. Sunday services start at 9am and 11am – the later one is *very* well attended.

Apollo Theater ARTS CENTER
(Map p84; ☎212-531-5300; www.apollotheater.com; 253 W 125th St) Not just a mythical legend but a living theater. Head here for concerts (Prince performed here in 2009) and its famous (if very touristy) amateur night ($19 to $29), 'where stars are born and legends are made.'

Studio Museum in Harlem MUSEUM
(Map p84; ☎212-864-4500; www.studiomuseum.org; 144 W 125th St; suggested donation $7; ⊙noon-9pm Thu & Fri, to 6pm Sat & Sun) One of the premier showcases for African American artists; look for excellent rotating exhibits from painters, sculptors, illustrators and other installation artists.

WASHINGTON HEIGHTS

Near the northern tip of Manhattan (above 155th St), Washington Heights takes its name from the first US president, who set up a Continental Army fort here during the Revolutionary War. An isolated spot until the end of the 19th century, it attracted lots of new blood as New Yorkers sniffed out affordable rents. Still, this neighborhood manages to retain its Latino – mainly Dominican – flavor, and is an interesting mix of blocks that alternate between former downtowners and longtime residents who operate within a tight, warm community.

TOP CHOICE **Cloisters** MUSEUM
(Map p64; ☎212-923-3700; www.metmuseum.org/cloisters; Fort Tryon Park, at 190th St; suggested admission adult/child $20/free; ⊙9:30am-4:45pm Tue-Sun Nov-Feb, to 5:15pm Mar-Oct) Most visitors to Washington Heights come here, a branch of the Metropolitan Museum of Art. Constructed in the 1930s using stones and fragments from several French and Spanish medieval monasteries, the romantic, castle-like creation houses medieval frescoes, tapestries, courtyards, gardens and paintings, and has commanding views of the Hudson. The walk from the subway stop to the museum through Fort Tryon Park offers stupendous **views** of the Hudson River; rock climbers head here for practice.

WORTH A TRIP

THE LITTLE RED LIGHTHOUSE

Manhattan's last remaining lighthouse acquired its affectionate nickname from the 1942 classic children's book, *The Little Red Lighthouse and the Great Grey Bridge*. Decommissioned after the construction of the GW Bridge, which looms massively overhead, the lighthouse was saved from demolition by an outpouring of public support. To visit, cross the pedestrian bridge over the Henry Hudson Parkway at the end of 181st St and follow the winding path down to the park at the edge of the water.

BROOKLYN

Brooklyn is a world in and of itself; residents sometimes don't go into Manhattan for days or even weeks at a time. With 2.5 million people and growing, from well-to-do new parents seeking stately brownstones in Carroll Gardens to young band members wanting cheap rents near gigs in Williamsburg, this outer borough has long succeeded Manhattan in the cool and livability factors in many people's minds. From sandy beaches and breezy boardwalks at one end to foodie destinations at the other, and with a massive range of ethnic enclaves, world-class entertainment, stately architecture and endless shopping strips in between, Brooklyn is a rival to Manhattan's attractions. The **Brooklyn Tourism & Visitors Center** (☎718-802-3846; www.brooklyntourism.org; 209 Borough Hall, Joralemon St; ⏰10am-6pm Mon-Fri), in Brooklyn Heights, is an informative place to begin.

TOP CHOICE Coney Island & Brighton Beach NEIGHBORHOOD

About 50 minutes by subway from Midtown, this popular pair of beach neighborhoods makes for a great day trip. The wide sandy beach of **Coney Island** has retained its nostalgic, kitschy and slightly sleazy charms, wood-plank boardwalk and famous 1927 Cyclone roller coaster despite the recent makeover of the amusement park area (a handful of adrenalin-pumping thrill rides are a recent addition) and plans for developers to transform the area into a sleek residential city complete with high-rise hotels. The **New York Aquarium** (☎718-741-1818; www.nyaquarium.com; Surf Ave, btwn 5th & W 8th Sts; adult/child $15/11; ⏰10am-6pm Mon-Fri, to 7pm Sat & Sun; 👪) is a big hit with kids, as is taking in an early evening baseball game at **KeySpan Park** (☎718-449-8497; 1904 Surf Ave), the waterfront stadium for the minor league Brooklyn Cyclones.

A five-minute stroll north along the boardwalk past handball courts where some of the best in the world compete brings you to **Brighton Beach** ('Little Odessa'), where old-timers play chess and locals enjoy pierogies (boiled dumplings filled with meat or vegetables) and vodka shots in the sun at several boardwalk eateries. Then head into the heart of the 'hood, busy Brighton Beach Ave, to hit the many Russian shops, bakeries and restaurants.

Park Slope & Prospect Heights NEIGHBORHOOD

The Park Slope neighborhood is known for its classic brownstones, tons of great eateries and boutiques (especially along Fifth Ave, which is more cutting edge than the other major strip, Seventh Ave), lesbian residents and stroller-pushing couples who resemble those on the Upper West Side (but have a backyard attached to their apartment). The 585-acre Prospect Park, created in 1866, is considered the greatest achievement of landscape designers Olmsted and Vaux, who also designed Central Park. Wander along its forested pathways, go for a run along its 3-plus-mile loop or jump on a boat that tours its 60-acre lake from May to October; a new skating rink is open in winter. Next door is the excellent 52-acre **Brooklyn Botanic Garden** (☎718-623-7200; www.bbg.org; 1000 Washington Ave; adult/child $8/free, free Tue; ⏰8am-6pm Tue-Fri, from 10am Sat & Sun), which features impressive cherry-tree blossoms in spring. Beside the garden is the **Brooklyn Museum** (☎718-638-5000; www.brooklynmuseum.org; 200 Eastern Pkwy; suggested admission $10; ⏰11am-6pm Wed, Sat & Sun, to 10pm Thu & Fri) with comprehensive collections of African, Islamic and Asian art, plus the Elizabeth A Sackler Center for Feminist Art.

Brooklyn Heights & Downtown Brooklyn NEIGHBORHOOD

When Robert Fulton's steam ferries started regular services across the East River in the early 19th century, well-to-do Manhattanites began building stellar houses – Victorian Gothic, Romanesque, neo-Greco, Italianate and others – in Brooklyn Heights. Strolling along the tree-lined streets to gaze at them now is a lovely afternoon activity; don't miss the 1881 Queen Anne–style landmark building that houses the **Brooklyn Historical Society** (☎718-222-4111; www.brooklynhistory.org; 128 Pierrepont St; admission $6; ⏰noon-5pm Wed-Fri & Sun, 10am-5pm Sat), which features a library (with some 33,000 grainy digitized photos from decades past), auditorium and museum devoted to the borough. The society also leads several walking tours.

Follow **Montague St**, the Heights' main commercial avenue, down to the waterfront until you hit the **Brooklyn Heights Promenade**, which juts out over the Brooklyn–Queens Expwy to offer stunning views of Lower Manhattan. Underneath the Expwy is the **Brooklyn Bridge Park**, an 85-acre development of landscaped green space and pathways, built on piers stretching from the Brooklyn Bridge south to Atlantic Ave.

The 1848 beaux-arts **Brooklyn Borough Hall** (209 Joralemon St) straddles both Brooklyn Heights and downtown Brooklyn, characterized by its various courts. The small but fascinating **New York Transit Museum** (☎718-694-1600; www.mta.info/mta/museum; Boerum Pl, at Schermerhorn St; adult/child $5/3; ⊙10am-4pm Tue-Fri, noon-5pm Sat & Sun) has an amazing collection of original subway cars and transit memorabilia dating back more than a century. Construction of the long-delayed and controversial **Barclay's Center**, future home to the NBA's New Jersey Nets, is finally progressing apace across the street from the Atlantic Center shopping mall in downtown Brooklyn. The surrounding neighborhoods expect change, as well as a worsening of the already terrible traffic, after the team moves here in 2012.

Dumbo NEIGHBORHOOD

Dumbo's nickname is an acronym for its location: 'Down Under the Manhattan–Brooklyn Bridge Overpass,' and while this north Brooklyn slice of waterfront used to be strictly for industry, it's now the domain of high-end condos, furniture shops and art galleries. Several highly regarded performing arts spaces are located in the cobblestone streets and the **Empire-Fulton Ferry State Park** hugs the waterfront and offers picture postcard Manhattan views.

Boerum Hill, Cobble Hill, Carroll Gardens & Red Hook NEIGHBORHOOD

These neighborhoods, home to a mix of families, mostly Italian, who have lived here for generations, and former Manhattanites looking for a real life after the city, are full of tree-lined streets with rows of attractively restored brownstones. **Smith St** and **Court St** are the two main arteries connecting to the most southerly area of the three, Carroll Gardens. The former is known as 'restaurant row,' while the latter has more of the old-school groceries, bakeries and red-sauce restaurants. A block west of here is **Cobble Hill Park**, a manicured patch of green with benches and picnic tables where locals hang. Even further west (and south) is **Red Hook**, a waterfront area with cobblestoned streets and hulking industrial buildings. Though it's a bit of a hike from the subway line, the formerly gritty area is now home to a handful of bars and eateries, as well as a massive waterfront branch of **Fairway** (☎718-694-6868; 480 Van Brunt St), a beloved gourmet grocery with breathtaking **views** of NY harbor and the Statue of Liberty. Also here is the Swedish furniture megastore Ikea (see p67 for information on the free water taxi to downtown Manhattan), which has transformed the neighboring waterfront into attractive green spaces and lounging areas.

Williamsburg, Greenpoint & Bushwick NEIGHBORHOOD

There is a definite Williamsburg look: skinny jeans, multiple tattoos, a discreet body piercing, shaggy hair for men, maybe some kind of retro head covering for a woman. Denizens of this raggedy and rowdy neighborhood across the East River on the L train seem to have time and money to slouch in cafes and party all night in bars; a fair share of older – early 30s – transplants from Manhattan and Europe qualify as elders. The main artery is **Bedford Ave** between N 10th St and Metropolitan Ave, where there are boutiques, cafes, bars and cheap eateries. But cool spots have also sprouted along N 6th St and Berry St, and perhaps a sign of the times is that the uber-hip consider Williamsburg over and have long-since moved on to colonizing next door **Greenpoint**, a traditionally Polish neighborhood as well as the former warehouse buildings further out in **Bushwick**. The **Brooklyn Brewery** (☎718-486-7422; www.brooklynbrewery.com; 79 N 11th St; admission free; ⊙6-11pm Fri, noon-5pm Sat) hosts weekend tours (on the hour from noon to 6pm), special events and pub nights.

Fort Greene NEIGHBORHOOD

This residential neighborhood of late-19th-century brownstones and gospel churches is home to a racially diverse group of young professionals and working-class families. Its gem is the **Brooklyn Academy of Music** (Map p70; ☎718-636-4100; www.bam.org; 30 Lafayette Ave), a highly respected performing arts complex and cinema. A well-regarded art and architecture school, the **Pratt Institute** calls the neighborhood home. Unbeknownst to the majority of dog walkers and sunbathers, over 11,000 prisoners of war from the Revolutionary War's Continental Army are buried underneath the grassy mounds of **Fort Greene Park**.

THE BRONX

Brooklyn's fierce northern rival is this 42-sq-mile borough, which has several claims to fame: the Yankees, fondly known as the

Bronx Bombers, who can be seen in all their pinstriped glory at the new **Yankee Stadium** (Map p64; www.yankees.com; 161st St, at River Ave) in spring and summer; the 'real' Little Italy, or **Belmont** (Map p64; www.arthuravenuebronx.com), bustling stretches of Arthur and Belmont Aves that burst with Italian gourmet markets and eateries; and a super-sized attitude that's been mythologized in Hollywood movies from *The Godfather* to *Rumble in the Bronx*.

But it's also got some cool surprises up its sleeve: a quarter of the Bronx is parkland, including the city beach of Pelham Bay Park.

Also up in these parts is the magical City Island, a little slice of New England in the Bronx.

TOP CHOICE **New York Botanical Garden** GARDENS
(Map p64; ☎718-817-8700; www.nybg.org; Bronx River Pkwy, at Fordham Rd; grounds only adult/child $6/3, all-gardens adult/child $20/8; ⏰10am-6pm Tue-Sun; 👪) There are 250 acres, with old-growth forest, a wetlands trail, nearly 3000 roses and tens of thousands of newly planted azalea plants.

Bronx Wildlife Conservation Park ZOO
(Map p64; ☎718-220-5100; www.bronxzoo.com; Bronx River Pkwy, at Fordham Rd; adult/child $16/12; ⏰10am-5pm Apr-Oct; 👪) Otherwise known as the Bronx Zoo, this is one of the biggest, best and most progressive zoos anywhere.

Woodlawn Cemetery CEMETERY
(Map p64; ☎718-920-0500; www.thewoodlawncemetery.org; Webster Ave, at 233rd St) Famous, historic and fascinating, 400-acre burial ground of many notable Americans, including Irving Berlin and Herman Melville.

QUEENS

There is no longer any typical Queens accent. Think Archie and Edith Bunker in *All in the Family* and you're as likely to hear Bengali and Spanish – 170 languages are spoken – in this, the largest (282 sq miles) and most ethnically diverse county in the country. There are few of the tree-lined brownstone streets you find in Brooklyn, and the majority of the neighborhoods, architecturally speaking at least, are unbefitting of this borough's grand name. However, because close to half its 2.3 million residents were born abroad, parts of Queens are endlessly reconstituting themselves, creating a vibrant and heady alternative universe to Manhattan. It's also home to two major airports, the Mets, a hip modern-art scene, miles of excellent beaches in the **Rockaways** and walking trails in the **Gateway National Recreation Area** (Map p64; www.nps.gov/gate), a wildlife refuge in Jamaica Bay only minutes from JFK airport. The **Queens Historical Society** (☎718-939-0647; www.queenshistoricalsociety.org) offers tours on many areas of the massive borough.

WORTH A TRIP

CITY ISLAND

Only 15 miles from midtown but a complete world away is the surprising neighborhood of **City Island**, a 1.5-mile-long fishing community that's filled with boat slips, yacht clubs, waterfront seafood eateries and windswept little spits of sand. Lovely Victorian clapboard houses look more New England than the Bronx.

Astoria NEIGHBORHOOD
Home to the largest Greek community outside of Greece, this is obviously the place to find amazing Greek bakeries, restaurants and gourmet shops, mainly along **Broadway**. An influx of Eastern European, Middle Eastern (Steinway Ave, known as 'Little Egypt,' is the place for falafel, kebabs and hookah pipes) and Latino immigrants have created a rich and diverse mix. Young bohemian types have also migrated here, making the area Queens' answer to Williamsburg. A reminder that moviemaking started in Astoria in the 1920s, the newly renovated **American Museum of the Moving Image** (☎718-777-6888; www.ammi.org; 36-01 35th Ave, at 36th St; admission $7; ⏰10am-5pm Tue-Fri) exposes some of the mysteries of the craft with amazing exhibits and screenings in its recently renovated ornate theater. In summer, cool off at the **Astoria Pool** (19th St, at 23rd Dr), the city's largest and oldest. Much of the neighborhood, as well as curious Manhattanites, can be found at the **Bohemian Hall & Beer Garden** (2919 24th Ave, Astoria; ⏰5pm-1am Mon-Thu, to 3am Fri & Sat) during warm afternoons and evenings.

Long Island City NEIGHBORHOOD
Neighboring Long Island City has several high-rise condominiums lining the riverfront with fantastic views of Manhattan. The area has also become a hub of art museums.

PS 1 Contemporary Art Center (718-784-2084; www.ps1.org; 22-25 Jackson Ave, at 46th Ave; suggested donation $10; noon-6pm Thu-Mon) is dedicated solely to new, cutting-edge works. On Saturdays (admission $15, open 2pm to 9pm) from early July through September, the center's outdoor courtyard is transformed into an installation art space and crammed with the highest concentration of hipsters this side of the Mississippi. If the weather is pleasant, don't miss the waterside **Socrates Sculpture Park** (718-956-1819; www.socratessculpturepark.org; Broadway, at Vernon Blvd; admission free; 10am-dusk) with its outdoor exhibits of massive, climbable sculptures by greats including Mark di Suvero, who founded the space.

Flushing & Corona NEIGHBORHOOD

The intersection of Main St and Roosevelt Ave, downtown Flushing, can feel like the Times Square of a city a world away from NYC. Immigrants from all over Asia, primarily Chinese and Korean, make up this neighborhood bursting at the seams with markets and restaurants filled with delicious and cheap delicacies. The Long Island Rail Road station and terminal for the 7 train see around 100,000 people pass through daily. **Flushing Meadows Corona Park**, meanwhile, is the home of **Citi Field**, the **USTA National Tennis Center** (the US Open is held here every August) and many lakes, ball fields, bike paths and grassy expanses, and was used for the 1939 and 1964 World's Fairs, of which there are quite a few faded leftovers – including Queens' most famous landmark, the stainless steel Unisphere, standing 120ft high and weighing 380 tons. Kids can learn about science and technology through fun hands-on exhibits at the **New York Hall of Science** (718-699-0005; www.nysci.org; adult/child $11/8; 9:30am-2pm Mon-Thu, to 5pm Fri, to 6pm Sat & Sun;); a quirky mini-golf course is on the site. Also within this massive park is the **Queens Museum of Art** (718-592-9700; www.queensmuseum.org; New York City Bldg, Flushing Meadows Corona Park; suggested donation $5; noon-6pm Wed-Sun).

Jackson Heights NEIGHBORHOOD

A fascinating mix of Indian (74th St) and South American (Roosevelt Ave) cultures, this is the place to purchase saris and 22-karat gold, dine on South Indian *masala dosas* – huge, paper-thin rice crepes folded around flavorful mixtures of masala potatoes, peas, cilantro and other earthy treats – and continue on with a plate of Colombian arepas (corn pancakes), a bite of Argentine empanadas and a cocktail at one of several Latin gay and lesbian bars, several of which line the main drag of Broadway.

STATEN ISLAND

While many New Yorkers will say that Staten Island has more in common with its neighbor, New Jersey, because of its suburban house and car cultures, there are some undoubtedly compelling reasons to count this borough in your urban explorations. First and foremost is the free **Staten Island Ferry** (718-876-8441; www.siferry.com; 24hr; 25min), which shuttles blasé commuters to work while offering breathtaking views of the Statue of Liberty and the Manhattan skyline. Not far from the ferry station on the Staten Island side is the **Richmond County Bank Ballpark** (Map p64; www.siyanks.com; Richmond Terrace), home to the minor-league Staten Island Yankees, as well as the hipper-than-ever neighborhood of St George.

Activities

Cycling

Hundreds of miles of designated bike lanes have been added throughout the city by Mayor Bloomberg's very pro-cycling City Hall, sometimes despite objections. However, unless you're an experienced urban cyclist, pedaling through the streets can be a high-risk activity, as bike lanes are often blocked by trucks, taxis and double-parked cars. More than 28-miles of mostly riverfront have been integrated into the **Manhattan Waterfront Greenway**, a patchwork of park pathways, overpasses and a few city streets that circle the entire island of Manhattan. The mostly uninterrupted 10-mile stretch from the GW Bridge to Battery Park, including **Hudson River Park**, is perhaps the most spectacular. Of course **Central Park** and Brooklyn's **Prospect Park** have lovely cycling paths and the beautiful **Franklin D Roosevelt Boardwalk** (cnr Father Capadanno Blvd & Sand Lane) along South Beach in Staten Island, hugs 4 miles of unspoiled beaches.

For cycling tips and weekend trips, contact **Five Borough Bicycle Club** (347-688-2925; www.5bbc.org). **Transportation Alternatives** (212-629-8080; www.transalt.org), a nonprofit bicycle-lobbying group, is also a good source of information. Gay cycling enthusiasts should check the website of **Fast & Fabulous** (www.fastnfab.org), a gay cycling club that organizes long weekend rides. For bike rentals, try Central Park's **Loeb Boathouse** or locate a rental shop on the comprehensive website **Bike New York** (www.bikenewyork.org). The Bloomberg administration is planning its own large-scale bike-sharing program throughout the city.

Water Sports

This is an island, after all, and as such there are plenty of opportunities for boating and kayaking. The **Downtown Boathouse** (Map p70; www.downtownboathouse.org; Pier 40, near Houston St; ⏲9am-6pm Sat & Sun May 15-Oct 15) offers free 20-minute kayaking (including equipment) in the protected embayment of the Hudson River. Other locations include Pier 96 and 72nd St.

In Central Park, **Loeb Boathouse** (Map p84; ☎212-517-2233; www.thecentralparkboathouse.com; Central Park, btwn 74th & 75th Sts; per hr $12; ⏲10am-dusk Mar-Oct) rents rowboats for romantic trysts, and even fills Venice-style gondolas in summer ($30 for 30 minutes). For a sailing adventure, hop aboard the *Schooner Adirondack* at **Chelsea Piers** (Map p76).

If you'd rather get all wet, check out the cool new **Floating Pool Lady** (www.floatingpool.org), a 25m swimming pool on top of a massive barge that moves around the Hudson and docks in various city locations. Admission is free but limited to 175 people, so expect to wait on hot days.

Surfers may be surprised to find a tight group of wave worshippers within city limits, at Queens' **Rockaway Beach** at 90th St, where you can hang ten after only a 45-minute ride on the A train from midtown.

New York for Children

Contrary to popular belief, New York can be a pretty child-friendly city. Cutting edge playgrounds have proliferated from Union Square to Battery Park and of course the city's major parks, including **Central Park's Safari Playground** (Map p84), have them in abundance. There are at least as many attractions that would appeal to toddlers and tweens as there are for adults, from the two children's museums – **Children's Museum of Manhattan** (Map p84; ☎212-721-1223; www.cmom.org; 212 W 83rd St, btwn Broadway & Amsterdam Ave; admission $10; ⏲10am-5pm Tue-Sun) and the **Brooklyn Children's Museum** (☎718-735-4400; www.brooklynkids.org; 145 Brooklyn Ave, Prospect Heights; admission $7.50; ⏲11am-5pm Wed-Fri, from 10am Sat & Sun) – to the Central Park and Bronx zoos to the Coney Island aquarium. Times Square's themed megastores and their neighboring kid-friendly restaurants are easy options. Check out the weekend Arts section of the *New York Times* for kid-themed events and performances.

 Tours

The following is just a sample:

Big Onion Walking Tours WALKING
(☎212-439-1090; www.bigonion.com; tours $15) Popular and quirky guided tours specializing in ethnic and neighborhood tours.

Circle Line BOAT
(Map p76; ☎212-563-3200; www.circleline42.com; Pier 83, W 42nd St; tickets $16-34) Ferry boat tours, from semicircle to a full island cruise with guided commentary.

Gray Line Sightseeing BUS
(☎212-445-0848; www.coachusa.com/newyorksights; 49 W 45th St; adult/child from $42/$32) Hop-on, hop-off double-decker multilingual guided bus tours of all the boroughs (except Staten Island).

Jetty Jumpers BOAT
(☎917-734-9919; www.jettyjumpers.com; tours $275) Offers guided jet-ski tours of NYC waterways.

Municipal Art Society WALKING
(☎212-935-3960; www.mas.org; 457 Madison Ave; tours adult $15) Various scheduled tours focusing on architecture and history.

New York City Audubon WALKING
(☎212-691-7483; www.nycaudubon.org; tours $8-100) Expert instructors and guides lead trips including birding in Central Park and the Bronx and ecology cruises of the Jamaica Bay Wildlife Refuge.

On Location Tours WALKING
(☎212-209-3370; www.screentours.com; tours $15-45) A *Gossip Girl* tour is the latest addition to the list of tours available for fulfilling your Carrie Bradshaw or Tony Soprano fantasies.

Festivals & Events

Festivities never cease in New York. From cultural street fairs to foodie events and outdoor concerts, you are bound to find something that will excite you, no matter the time of year. There's almost too much to digest in summer, when outdoor celebrations proliferate.

Restaurant Week FOOD
(☎212-484-1222; www.nycgo.com) Dine at top restaurants for $20 and $30 deals – first in February and again in July.

Armory Show CULTURAL
(☎212-645-6440; www.thearmoryshow.com; Piers 92 & 94, West Side Hwy at 52nd & 54th Sts) New York's biggest contemporary art fair sweeps the city in March, showcasing the new work of thousands of artists from around the world.

Tribeca Film Festival FILM
(☎212-941-2400; www.tribecafilmfestival.com) Robert De Niro co-organizes this local downtown film fest, held in late April and early May, that's quickly rising in prestige on the circuit.

Fleet Week NAVAL
(☎212-245-0072) Annual convocation of sailors and their naval ships and air rescue teams, who descend upon the city in their formal whites every May.

Lesbian, Gay, Bisexual & Transgender Pride CULTURAL
(☎212-807-7433; www.nycpride.org) Pride month, in June, with a packed calendar of parties and events, culminates with a major march down Fifth Ave on the last Sunday of the month.

Mermaid Parade CULTURAL
(www.coneyisland.com/mermaid) Something of Mardi Gras on the boardwalk, Surf Ave on Coney Island in Brooklyn turns into an artistic, crazy and fun free-expression zone in late June.

New York Film Festival FILM
(www.filmlinc.com) Major world premieres from prominent directors at this Lincoln Center event, held in late September.

New Yorker Festival CULTURAL
(www.newyorker.com) A mid-October line-up of interviews, talks and tours from some of the most prominent literary and cultural figures in the world.

Sleeping

Keep in mind that prices change depending on the value of the euro, yen and other worldwide currencies, as well as the general drift of the global economic climate, not to mention the day of the week and the season, with spring and fall being most expensive. Tax adds an additional 13.25% per night. For longer stays, an apartment rental or sublet can be the best option (there's no tax on rentals), secured with the help of an agency like **City Sonnet** (☎212-614-3034; www.westvillagebb.com; apt from $135 per night). A cluster of national chains, including Sheraton, Ramada and Holiday Inn, have affordably priced rooms in hotels within a few blocks of one another around 39th Ave in Long Island City, Queens, a quick N, Q or R train into midtown Manhattan directly across the river.

LOWER MANHATTAN

Gild Hall Wall Street BOUTIQUE HOTEL **$$$**
(Map p66; ☎212-232-7700; www.wallstreetdistrict.com; 15 Gold St; r from $225; ❄@📶) Part of the Thompson line of fabulous NYC hotels, Gild Hall sports a funky English-hunting-lodge lobby. All the rooms, including the small and simple standards, have oversized leather headboards and notably comfortable beds. Only a few blocks from Wall St and several subway lines, you won't feel stranded.

Wall Street Inn LUXURY HOTEL **$$$**
(Map p66; ☎212-747-1500; www.thewallstreetinn.com; 9 S William St; r incl breakfast from $275; ❄📶) Lehman Brothers, the failed bank, once occupied this classic limestone building and, while the mood of the hotel is very early American banker, there's little risk in a stay here. Old-fashioned and warm rather than stuffy, the rooms, with luxurious marble baths, are slightly over-furnished for their size.

TRIBECA & SOHO

Soho Grand Hotel BOUTIQUE HOTEL **$$$**
(Map p70; ☎212-965-3000; www.sohogrand.com; 310 W Broadway; d $195-450; ❄@📶) The original boutique hotel of the 'hood still reigns, with its striking glass-and-cast-iron lobby stairway, and 367 rooms with cool, clean lines plus Frette linens, plasma flat-screen TVs and Kiehl's grooming products. The lobby's Grand Lounge buzzes with action.

Sixty Thompson BOUTIQUE HOTEL **$$$**
(Map p70; ☎212-431-0400; www.60thompson.com; 60 Thompson St, btwn Broome & Spring Sts; s/d $360/425; ❄@📶) Another minimalist charmer. Rooms here have down duvets, flat-screen TVs and cozy tweed sofas. The rooftop Thom Bar is a stunning place to see and be seen.

Cosmopolitan Hotel HOTEL **$$$**
(Map p66; ☎212-566-1900; www.cosmohotel.com; 95 W Broadway, at Chambers St; d from $200; ❄📶) Don't let the name fool you – rather than being urbane and sophisticated, the Cosmopolitan is more akin to the average Main St USA hotel. Clean, carpeted, though decidedly cramped, it's an affordable downtown option with a cafe serving crepes attached.

TOP CHOICE **Lita SoHo** HOTEL $$$
(Map p70; ☎212-925-3600; www.solitasohohotel.com; 159 Grand St, at Lafayette St; r from $220;) Part of the Clarion chain, the SoLita is a clean, functional alternative with boutique-style furnishings close to Little Italy, Chinatown, Soho and the Lower East Side. Lower winter rates.

Hotel Azure HOTEL $$$
(Map p70; ☎212-925-4378; www.hotelazure.com; 120 Lafayette St; r from $220;) Another choice only a block away. Also good deals in winter.

LOWER EAST SIDE & EAST VILLAGE

Bowery Hotel BOUTIQUE HOTEL $$$
(Map p70; ☎212-505-9100; www.theboweryhotel.com; 335 Bowery, btwn E 2nd & 3rd Sts; r from $325;) Perhaps as far as you can get from the Bowery's gritty flophouse history, this stunningly stylish hotel is all 19th-century elegance. Rooms come equipped with lots of light and sleek furnishings mixed with antiques. The baroque-style lobby bar attracts the young and chic and on-site restaurant Gemma serves upscale Italian.

Hotel on Rivington BOUTIQUE HOTEL $$
(Map p70; ☎212-475-2600; www.hotelonrivington.com; 107 Rivington St, btwn Essex & Ludlow Sts; r from $160;) This shimmering 20-floor tower looms large over Lower East Side tenement buildings, its glass-enclosed rooms offering stunning views of the East River and downtown's spread. Rooms vary quite a bit – some have balconies, some have hanging flat-screen TVs – and the ground-floor restaurant is a scenester hot spot.

Gem Hotel BOUTIQUE HOTEL $$
(Map p70; ☎212-358-8844; www.thegemhotel.com; 135 Houston St, at Forsyth St; r from $180;) The Gem still has the plain, boxy exterior of the Howard Johnson hotel that once occupied the site, however the small cheerful rooms have plush bedding, small desks and flat-screen TVs. Expect some street noise.

East Village Bed & Coffee B&B $$
(Map p70; ☎212-533-4175; www.bedandcoffee.com; 110 Ave C, btwn 7th & 8th Sts; r with shared bath from $115;) The 10 airy rooms sport different well-executed themes – Mexican (with a bright-yellow wall and pressed-tin doodads), Zen (with a small Buddha and icy tones) and so on – and common areas are lovely, from the high-ceilinged kitchen to the leafy back garden.

WEST (GREENWICH) VILLAGE

Abingdon Guest House B&B $$
(Map p70; ☎212-243-5384; www.abingdonguesthouse.com; 21 Eighth Ave, at Jane St; r from $159;) Don't look out the window and you'll swear you've landed in a New England B&B. Elegant, comfortable rooms feature four-poster beds, (nonworking) fireplaces, scads of exposed brick, and billowing curtains. Plus a lovely little garden out back.

Larchmont Hotel HOTEL $$
(Map p70; ☎212-989-9333; www.larchmonthotel.com; 27 W 11th St, btwn Fifth & Sixth Aves; s/d with shared bath & breakfast from $90/119;) Housed in a prewar building that blends in with the other fine brownstones on the block, a stay at the Larchmont is about location. The carpeted rooms are basic and in need of updating, as are the communal baths, but it's not a bad deal for the price.

Jane Hotel HOTEL $$
(Map p70; ☎212-924-6700; www.thejanenyc.com; 113 Jane St; r with shared bath from $100;) Originally built for sailors (which is obvious after one look at the cabin-sized rooms), then a temporary refuge for survivors of the *Titanic,* a YMCA and rock-and-roll venue, the single bunk rooms feature flat-screen TVs and the communal showers are more than adequate.

MEATPACKING DISTRICT & CHELSEA

Hotel Gansevoort LUXURY HOTEL $$$
(Map p70; ☎212-206-6700; www.hotelgansevoort.com; 18 Ninth Ave, at 13th St; r from $395;) This 187-room luxury hotel in the trendy Meatpacking District has been a hit for its 400-thread-count linens, hypoallergenic down duvets, plasma TVs, chic basement spa and rooftop bar with fabulous views. Down-to-earth types, beware: it's on the nauseatingly trendy side of things.

Ace Hotel New York City BOUTIQUE HOTEL $$
(Map p76; ☎212-679-2222; www.acehotel.com/newyork; 20 W 29th St; r from $99-369;) This outpost of a hip Pacific northwest chain is on the northern edge of Chelsea. Clever touches such as vintage turntables and handwritten welcome notes elevate the Ace beyond the standard. However, prison-issued bunk beds in one of the room styles are missteps. Juice, coffee and croissants are available in the morning.

Chelsea Lodge B&B $$
(Map p76; ☎212-243-4499; www.chelsealodge.com; 318 W 20th St, at Eighth Ave; s/d $124/134;

❄) Housed in a landmark brownstone, the European-style 20-room Chelsea Lodge has homey, well-kept, though tight, rooms. There are showers and sinks in rooms, but toilets are down the hall. Six suite rooms have private bathrooms, and two come with private garden access. Wi-fi in the lobby.

Chelsea International Hostel HOSTEL $
(Map p76; ☎212-243-3700; www.chelseahostel.com; 222 W 20th St, btwn Seventh & Eighth Aves; dm with/without bath $70/65, s/d with shared bath $70/155; ❄@📶) This well-located hostel draws an international crowd accustomed to partying and bunking down for a few hours. No doubt you'll make friends in the communal kitchen.

UNION SQUARE, FLATIRON DISTRICT & GRAMERCY PARK

Marcel BOUTIQUE HOTEL $$
(Map p76; ☎212-696-3800; www.nychotels.com; 201 E 24th St, at Third Ave; d from $175; ❄📶) Minimalist with earth-tone touches, this 97-room inn is a poor-man's chic boutique and that's not a bad thing. Modernist rooms on the avenue have great views, and the sleek lounge is a great place to unwind from a day of touring. Visit its website for other classy affordable inns within the Amsterdam Hospitality group.

Chelsea Inn B&B $$
(Map p76; ☎212-645-8989; www.chelseainn.com; 46 W 17th St, near Sixth Ave; r from $100; ❄📶) This funky-charming hideaway made up of two adjoining 19th-century four-story walk-up townhouses has small but comfortable rooms that look like they were furnished entirely from flea markets or grandma's attic. Most of the rooms have private baths; the two rooms that go for the lowest prices share a bathroom.

Gershwin Hotel HOTEL $$
(Map p76; ☎212-545-8000; www.gershwinhotel.com; 7 E 27th St, at Fifth Ave; dm/d/ste from $45/109/299; ❄@📶) This popular and funky spot is half youth hostel, half hotel, and buzzes with original pop art, touring bands and a young and artsy European clientele.

MIDTOWN

Hudson HOTEL $$$
(Map p84; ☎212-554-6000; www.hudsonhotel.com; 356 W 58th St, btwn Eighth & Ninth Aves; r from $240; ❄@📶) This delicious marriage between designer Phillipe Starck and hotelier Ian Schrager is an absolute jewel – if you're not aching for quiet, that is. Part hotel and part nightclub, this beauty has several lounge bars that are always jammin', and the teensy rooms are highly stylized, with lots of glass, bright wood and gossamer scrims.

Room-Mate Grace BOUTIQUE HOTEL $$
(Map p76; ☎212-354-2323; www.room-matehotels.com; 125 W 45th St; r incl breakfast from $185; ❄📶🏊) Part of a Spanish chain, this ultra-hip hotel is good value when you consider you're steps from the midtown action. Like other hotels of the same genre, space is at a premium and sleekness is prized over warmth. A steam room, sauna and lively pool-bar are reasons to choose the Mate over others.

Pod Hotel HOTEL $$
(Map p76; ☎212-355-0300; www.thepodhotel.com; 230 E 51st St, btwn Second & Third Aves; r from $129; ❄@📶) A dream come true for folks who'd like to live inside their iPod – or at least curl up and sleep with it – this affordable hot spot has a range of room types, most barely big enough for the bed. 'Pods' have bright bedding, tight workspaces, flat-screen TVs, iPod docking stations and 'rain' showerheads.

414 Hotel HOTEL $$
(Map p76; ☎212-399-0006; www.414hotel.com; 414 W 46th St, btwn Ninth & Tenth Aves; r incl breakfast from $200; ❄📶) More like a guesthouse than a hotel and only a couple of blocks west of Times Square. All rooms are well-kept and attractively furnished and there's a small courtyard between the townhouse's two buildings; a small kitchen for guests to use.

Yotel HOTEL $$
(Map p76; ☎646-449-7700; www.yotel.com; 570 Tenth Ave, at 41st St; r from $150; ❄📶) Sci-fi meets boutique meets airport terminal at this newest outpost of an international chain. Super helpful staff (crew) and a cool bar, lounge and restaurant – plus a robot (mechanical arm) will store your luggage.

Broadway Rooms HOTEL $$
(Map p76; ☎212-397-9686; www.broadwayrooms.com; 337 W 55th St, btwn Eighth & Ninth Aves; r with shared bath $107-220; ❄@) Though the name has changed (formerly 1291 B&B), this hostel-hotel is still rough around the edges, with cramped private rooms and shared rooms with a bunk bed and two single beds, best for small groups.

Big Apple Hostel HOSTEL $
(Map p76; ☎212-302-2603; www.bigapplehostel.com; 119 W 45thSt, btwn Sixth & Seventh Aves; dm/r $44/135; ❄@☎) Dreary rooms with exposed pipes, windows open onto fire escapes, but at least there's a small outdoor patio for fresh air.

UPPER WEST SIDE

Empire Hotel HOTEL $$$
(Map p84; ☎212-265-7400; www.empirehotelnyc.com; 44 W 63rd St; r from $225; ❄@☎) An uptown version of the W, the Empire is a chic hotel directly across the street from the Lincoln Center. The decor is all classy earth tones and rooms are a decent size – for NYC. There's a rooftop pool deck with fabulous views and, when not closed for private functions, it's a nighttime hot spot.

On the Ave BOUTIQUE HOTEL $$$
(Map p84; ☎212-362-1100; www.ontheave.com; 2178 Broadway, at W 77th St; r from $225; ❄@☎) A more welcoming feel and larger rooms make On the Ave a cut above the average sleek boutique hotel. And it's a good deal considering the high-concept design, stainless steel and marble baths, featherbeds, flat-screen TVs and original artwork. It's near the Lincoln Center, Central Park and a slew of good eats.

YMCA HOSTEL $$
(Map p84; ☎212-912-2600; www.ymca.com; 5 W 63rd St at Central Park West; r from $100; ❄@) Just steps from Central Park, this grand art-deco building has several floors – 8th to the 13th – of basic, but clean, rooms. Guests have access to extensive, but old-school, gym, racquet ball courts, pool and sauna. Wi-fi on the ground floor. Other locations on the Upper East Side and Harlem.

Jazz on Amsterdam Ave HOSTEL $
(Map p84; ☎646-490-7348; www.jazzhostels.com; 201 W 87th St at Amsterdam Ave; dm $44, r $100; ❄@) Only a short walk to Central Park, this hostel chain's Upper West Side branch has clean rooms, both private and two- to six-bed dorms. Free wi-fi in the lobby. Other branches in Harlem and Chelsea.

Hostelling International-New York HOSTEL $
(Map p84; ☎212-932-2300; www.hinewyork.org; 891 Amsterdam Ave, at 103rd St; dm $32-40, d from $135; ❄@☎) It's got clean, safe and air-conditioned dorm rooms in a gorgeous landmark building, with a sprawling and shady patio and a super-friendly vibe.

UPPER EAST SIDE

Carlyle LUXURY HOTEL $$$
(Map p84; ☎212-744-1600; www.thecarlyle.com; 35 E 76th St, btwn Madison & Park Aves; r from $450; ❄☎) This legendary New York classic, the epitome of old-fashioned luxury hosts foreign dignitaries and celebrities alike. Opulence reigns from the hushed lobby with glossy marble floors to framed English country scenes or Audubon prints in the rooms; some have terraces and baby grand pianos.

Bentley BOUTIQUE HOTEL $$$
(Map p84; ☎888-664-6835; www.nychotels.com; 500 E 62nd St, at York Ave; r from $200; ❄☎) Featuring great East River views, the Bentley overlooks FDR Dr, as far east as you can go. Formerly an office building, the hotel has shed its utilitarian past in the form of chic boutique-hotel styling, a swanky lobby and sleek rooms.

Bubba & Bean Lodges B&B $$
(Map p84; ☎917-345-7914; www.bblodges.com; 1598 Lexington Ave, btwn 101st & 102nd Sts; r from $180; ❄☎) Hardwood floors, crisp white walls and pretty navy bedspreads make the rooms at this nifty B&B feel spacious, modern and youthful. The rooms are really more like full apartments (some fit up to six people). Good winter rates.

HARLEM

102 Brownstone HOTEL $$
(Map p84; ☎212-662-4223; www.102brownstone.com; 102 W 118th St, btwn Malcolm X & Adam Clayton Powell Blvds; r from $120; ❄☎) A wonderfully redone Greek Revival row house on a beautiful residential street; room styles, all with plush bedding, range from Zen to classy boudoir.

710 Guest Suites APARTMENT $$
(☎212-491-5622; www.710guestsuites.com; 710 St Nicholas Ave, at 146th St; ste from $174; ❄☎) Three fabulously chic suites with high ceilings, contemporary furnishings and wood floors in a brownstone. Three-night minimum and lower rates from January through March make this exceptional good value.

Harlem Flophouse INN $$
(Map p84; ☎347-632-1960; www.harlemflophouse.com; 242 W 123rd St, btwn Adam Clayton Powell & Frederick Douglass Blvds; r with shared bath from $125) The four attractive bedrooms have antique light fixtures, glossed-wood floors and big beds, plus classic tin ceilings and wooden shutters. Cat on the premises.

BROOKLYN

TOP CHOICE New York Loft Hostel HOSTEL $
(☎718-366-1351; 248 Varet St; dm/r incl breakfast $65/90; ❄📶) Live like a Williamsburg or more accurately Bushwick hipster in this renovated loft building. Brick walls, high ceilings, a beautiful kitchen and rooftop Jacuzzi make Manhattan hostels seem like tenements. Closest subway is Morgan Ave L stop.

Nu Hotel HOTEL $$$
(☎718-852-8585; www.nuhotelbrooklyn.com; 85 Smith St; d incl breakfast from $199; ❄@📶) This location, only blocks from Brooklyn Heights and a nexus of attractive brownstone neighborhoods, is absolutely ideal – except for the fact that it's across the street from the Brooklyn House of Detention. It has a chic minimalist vibe and the clean, all-white rooms are comfortable.

Hotel Le Bleu HOTEL $$
(☎718-625-1500; www.hotelbleu.com; 370 4th Ave; d incl breakfast $169-349; P❄@📶) On a busy avenue with belching trucks and auto body shops, however, welcoming and busy Park Slope is a short walk away. Boutique styling: sleek, white, minimalistic – king-sized beds and balconies with good views of Manhattan.

3B B&B $$
(☎347-762-2632; www.3bbrooklyn.com; 136 Lawrence St; dm/r incl breakfast $40/120; ❄📶) The 3rd floor unity of this downtown Brooklyn brownstone has been turned into a bright and contemporary four-room B&B.

Eating

In a city with nearly 19,000 restaurants, and new ones opening every single day, where are you supposed to begin? From Little Albania to Little Uzbekistan, your choice of ethnic eats is only a short subway ride away. A hotbed of buzz-worthy culinary invention and trends like artisanal doughnuts, farm-to-table pork sandwiches and *haute cuisine* reinterpretations of fried chicken, pizza and good ol' burgers and fries, NYC's restaurant scene, like the city is constantly reinventing itself. The latest foodie obsession is the flotilla of roving, tweeting food trucks, the 21st-century equivalent of the classic pushcart, selling gourmet cupcakes, dumplings and Jamaican curry goat and everything in between.

A, B, C

Those letter grades you see posted in the windows of every NYC restaurant aren't the report cards of the owner's kids. They're issued by the NYC health department after an inspection of each establishment's hygiene standards. A is best and C worst – anything lower, well, you probably wouldn't want to eat there anyway.

LOWER MANHATTAN

Bridge Café MODERN AMERICAN $$
(Map p66; 279 Water St; mains $23; ⊙11:45am-11pm) Serving downtown since 1794, this unassuming cozy restaurant is widely credited with being the oldest in the city. There's nothing stodgy or Revolutionary War-era about the modern meat and seafood menu sourced with seasonal ingredients and the banana chocolate bread-pudding dessert is a satisfying coda to the meal.

Smorgas Chef Wall St SCANDINAVIAN $$
(Map p66; 53 Stone St; mains $9-24; ⊙10:30am-10:30pm) Located on quaint and narrow Stone St (the colony of New Amsterdam's first paved roadway), this fine bistro serves Scandinavian fare such as Swedish meatballs as well as lighter fare like fish and salads. During the summer months, Smorgas Chef and neighboring restaurants put tables outside, turning the street into one big block party.

Table Tales SANDWICHES $
(Map p66; 243 Water St; mains $9; ⊙11:30am-10pm Mon-Sat) Take a break from the tourist mobbed, chain-saturated South St Seaport area at this precious and cozy nook, run by a catering company, where you'll find a chill vibe along with both filling cafe items and full-on dinner mains.

Ruben's Empanadas ARGENTINE, FAST FOOD $
(Map p66; 76 Nassau St, at John St; empanadas $4; ⊙9am-7pm) Refuel with one of this Argentine chain's filling, greaseless empanadas in endless varieties, from chicken to apple or spicy tofu. Two other locations in the neighborhood.

Zaitstaff BURGERS $
(Map p66; 72 Nassua St; mains $9; ⊙9:30am-9:30pm, 10:30am-1pm Sat & Sun) A loyal following packs this little restaurant amid blocks full of delis and fast-food chains for

its Kobe Beef burgers (turkey and veggie as well).

Alfanoose MIDDLE EASTERN $
(Map p66; 8 Maiden Lane, btwn Broadway & Nassau; mains $6; ⌚11:30am-9:30pm Mon-Sat) Syrian-Lebanese specialties, as many vegetarian as meat and a few not found on the typical falafel-joint menu.

TRIBECA, SOHO & NOHO

Mooncake Foods ASIAN, SANDWICHES $
(Map p70; 28 Watts St, at Broome; mains $8; ⌚10am-11pm Mon-Fri, 9am-11pm Sat & Sun) This unpretentious family-run restaurant serves some of the best sandwiches in the neighborhood, nay city. Try the smoked white-fish salad sandwich or Vietnamese pork meatball hero. Another location in Chelsea and uptown in Hell's Kitchen.

Edward's AMERICAN $$
(Map p66; 136 W Broadway, btwn Thomas & Duane Sts; mains $13; ⌚9am-midnight) Located on a busy block in Tribeca, Edward's has the feel of a casual European bistro – high ceilings, mirrored walls and darkwood booths. The menu offers everything from pasta to burgers.

La Esquina Taqueria MEXICAN $
(Map p70; 114 Kenmare St, at Cleveland Pl; mains $6; ⌚8am-1:45am, from noon Sat & Sun) This Mexican hot spot, whose only marking is a huge neon sign that blares 'The Corner' (hence *la esquina*), bustles night and day for good reason. Delectable, authentic treats are served at the counter or in the mellow cafe around the corner.

Bubby's Pie Company AMERICAN $$
(Map p66; 120 Hudson St, at N Moore St; mains $12-25; ⌚1am-noon Mon, 8am-midnight Tue, 24hr Wed-Sun) This kid-friendly Tribeca standby is *the* place for simple, big, delicious food: slow-cooked BBQ, grits, matzo-ball soup, buttermilk potato salad, fried okra and big fat breakfasts, all melt-in-your-mouth good.

CHINATOWN, LITTLE ITALY & NOLITA

Peasant ITALIAN $$$
(Map p70; ☎212-965-9511; 194 Elizabeth St, btwn Spring & Prince Sts; mains $20-30; ⌚6-11pm Tue-Sat, to 10pm Sun) A warm dining area of bare oak tables is structured around a brick hearth and open kitchen, which lovingly turns out hearty, pan-Italian, mostly meat-based fare. Solid stunners include gnocchi with wild mushrooms and oven-baked rabbit. After dinner, head downstairs to the dark and cozy cellar wine bar.

Ruby's AMERICAN $$
(Map p70; 219 Mulberry St; mains $12; ⌚10am-11pm) Tuck in those elbows for a seat at one of the picnic tables at this unpretentious tiny nook serving healthy salads, paninis and apparently Aussie burgers (ground beef mixed with onions and peppers and topped with fried eggs, beets and roasted pineapple).

Torrisi Italian Specialties ITALIAN $
(Map p70; 250 Mulberry St, at Prince; sandwiches $8; ⌚11am-10pm) By day, an unassuming grocery-restaurant with meat hanging in the windows and sandwiches like chicken parm and lasagna. At night, Torrisi serves a prix fixe feast ($45) of inventive, haute versions of Italian-American favorites with local and seasonal ingredients.

Focolare ITALIAN $$
(Map p70; 115 Mulberry St, btwn Canal & Hester; mains $15; ⌚11am-10pm) If you're bent on a Little Italy dinner experience, this is a fine choice, at least as much for its cozy interior as the classic dishes.

Bánh Mí Saigon Bakery VIETNAMESE $
(Map p70; 198 Grand St; mains $5; ⌚10am-7pm) This no-frills storefront doles out some of

EATING NYC: CHINATOWN

With hundreds of restaurants, from holes-in-the-wall to banquet-sized dining rooms, Chinatown is wonderful for exploring cheap eats on an empty stomach. One of the best places to lunch for Cantonese cuisine is **Amazing 66** (Map p66; 66 Mott St, at Canal St; mains $7; ⌚11am-11pm). The best of the dumpling joints is **Vanessa's Dumpling House** (Map p70; 118 Eldridge St, at Broome St; 4 dumplings $1; ⌚7:30am-10:30pm). Head to **Big Wong King** (Map p66; 67 Mott St, at Canal; mains $5-20; ⌚7am-9:30pm) for chopped meat over rice and reliable congee (sweet or savory soft rice soup). Always busy **Joe's Shanghai** (Map p66; 9 Pell St; mains $10; ⌚11am-11pm) is tourist-friendly and does good noodle and soup dishes. And finally, the **Egg Custard King** (Map p70; Natalie Bakery Inc; 271 Grand St; custards $1; ⌚7am-9:30pm) is the place for the eponymous dessert.

the best *bánh mì* – Vietnamese roast-pork sandwiches served on fat baguettes – in town.

Fonda Nolita MEXICAN **$**
(Map p70; 267 Elizabeth St, near Houston St, mains $4; ⏲8am-midnight) Hearty tacos (try the chorizo breakfast one) served out of a VW wagon parked inside.

LOWER EAST SIDE

Spitzer's Corner MODERN AMERICAN **$$**
(Map p70; ☎212-228-0027; 101 Rivington St; mains $9-19; ⏲noon-4am Mon-Sat, 10am-midnight Sun) The corner location offers an open-air gastropub experience with a concise menu designed by a Michelin-starred chef, and more than 40 different beers on tap. Large communal tables and a lengthy counter facing the street encourage socializing.

Katz's Delicatessen DELI **$$**
(Map p70; 205 E Houston St; sandwiches $13; ⏲8am-9:45pm Mon & Tue, to 10:45pm Wed, Thu & Sun, to 2:45am Fri & Sat) One of the few remaining Jewish delicatessens in the city, Katz's attracts locals, tourists and celebrities whose photos line the walls. Massive pastrami, corned beef, brisket and tongue sandwiches are throwbacks, as is the payment system: hold on to the ticket you're handed when you walk in and pay cash only.

Kuma Inn ASIAN **$$**
(Map p70; ☎212-353-8866; 113 Ludlow St, btwn Delancey & Rivington; mains $11; ⏲6-11pm) Reservations are a must at this strikingly popular spot, in a secretive 2nd-floor location that feels like a reconfigured apartment. Filipino- and Thai-inspired tapas rung the gamut, from vegetarian summer rolls to an oyster omelet and grilled salmon with mung beans and pickled onions.

Fat Radish MODERN AMERICAN **$$$**
(Map p70; 17 Orchard St; mains $21; ⏲8am-midnight, from 11am Sat & Sun, closed Mon) Young and fashionable pack in to this dimly lit dining room with exposed white brick and industrial touches. There's a loud buzz and people checking each other out but the entrees, typical of the local-seasonal-haute pub fare fad are worth your attention.

Economy Candy CANDY **$**
(Map p70; 108 Rivington St; candies from $4; ⏲9am-6pm Sun-Fri, 10am-5pm Sat) Fancy any of the myriad crazy, nostalgic candies you consumed as a kid? Whatever it is, as long as it contains sugar, it's probably crammed or stacked in this hole-in-the-wall candy purveyor.

Russ & Daughters DELI **$**
(Map p70; 179 E Houston St; mains $5; ⏲8am-8pm Mon-Fri, to 7pm Sat, to 5:30pm Sun) Evocative of a bygone era, this landmark establishment serves up Eastern European Jewish delicacies like caviar, herring and lox, and of course a smear of cream cheese on a bagel.

Souvlaki GR GREEK **$**
(Map p70; 116 Stanton St, near Essex St; mains $5; ⏲11am-midnight) Owners of a food truck have opened this little restaurant that looks like a soundstage for a film set on a Greek isle.

Donut Plant DESSERT **$**
(Map p70; 379 Grand St, at Norfolk; doughnuts $2.75; ⏲6:30am-6:30pm) Inventively flavored (eg peanut butter and jelly) doughnuts with all-natural ingredients. Another location in the Chelsea Hotel at 222 W 23rd St.

EAST VILLAGE

Every cuisine and style is represented in the East Village, though even the very best places are certainly more casual than stuffy. St Marks Place and around, from Third to Second Ave, has turned into a little Tokyo with loads of Japanese sushi and grill restaurants. Cookie-cutter Indian restaurants line Sixth St between First and Second Ave.

TOP CHOICE **Momofuku Noodle Bar** JAPANESE **$$**
(Map p70; 171 First Ave, at 11th St; mains $9-16; ⏲noon-4pm & 5:30-11pm Sun-Thu, to midnight Fri & Sat) Ramen and steamed buns are the name of the game at this infinitely creative Japanese eatery, part of the growing David Chang empire. Seating is on stools at a long bar or at communal tables. Momofuku's famous steamed chicken and pork buns ($9 for two) are recommended.

Counter VEGETARIAN **$$**
(Map p70; ☎212-982-5870; 105 First Ave, btwn E 6th & 7th Sts; mains $15-25; ⏲5pm-midnight Mon-Thu, to 1am Fri, 11am-1am Sat, to 4pm Sun; ✎) This unique eatery manages to mix infused-vodka martinis and organic vegetarian cuisine with outlandish success. Credit the futuristic, backlit dining room, fabulous large-scale artwork and innovative dishes like cauliflower 'risotto.'

Il Bagatto ITALIAN **$$**
(Map p70; ☎212-228-0977; 192 E 2nd St, near Ave B; mains $18; ⏲5:30pm-midnight, closed Mon) A

bustling yet romantic little nook, this spot has thoroughly delicious Italian creations at exceptionally reasonable prices – plus an excellent wine list.

Xi'an Famous Foods CHINESE $
(Map p70; 81 St Mark's Pl, at First Ave; mains $6; ⏲24hr) This Flushing, Queens, original is a sliver of a restaurant with an interesting menu specializing in spicy noodle and soup dishes. Two other locations in Chinatown.

Veselka EASTERN EUROPEAN $$
(Map p70; 144 Second Ave, at 9th St; mains $12; ⏲24hr) Generations of East Villagers have been coming to this bustling institution for blintzes and breakfast regardless of the late hour.

WEST (GREENWICH) VILLAGE

Blue Hill MODERN AMERICAN $$$
(Map p70; ☎212-539-1776; 75 Washington Pl, btwn Sixth Ave & MacDougal St; mains $22-50; ⏲5:30-11pm Mon-Sat, to 10pm Sun) A place for high-rolling Slow Food junkies, Blue Hill is a low-key, high-class dining spot where you can be certain that everything on your plate is fresh and seasonal. Expect barely seasoned veggies as centerpieces for dishes with poultry and fish. The below-street-level space is sophisticated and serene.

Buvette FRENCH $$
(Map p70; 42 Grove St; mains $12; ⏲8am-2am Mon-Fri, 11am-2am Sat & Sun) Cramped or cozy depending on your mood, this romantically lit bistro serves up miniaturized versions of inspired tapas-like dishes such as house-cured salt cod whipped with olive oil. Meat, cheeses and tartines on offer as well.

Snack Taverna GREEK $$
(Map p70; 63 Bedford St; mains $15-25; ⏲noon-11pm Mon-Sat, to 10pm Sun) If you can't make it out to the Greek restaurants in Astoria, Queens, try this West Village place. The menu goes beyond the standard gyro and moussaka – the small plates like the smoked trout with barley rusks, tomato, cheese and balsamic vinaigrette are excellent.

Perilla MODERN AMERICAN $$
(Map p70; ☎212-929-6868; 9 Jones St; mains $22-27; ⏲5:30-11pm Mon-Thu, to 11:30pm Fri & Sat, 11am-10pm Sun) Run by popular reality-TV show *Top Chef,* Perilla is an extremely creative yet well-grounded American bistro. The spicy duck meatballs and roasted main sardines are both good ways to start off a meal.

Thelewala INDIAN $$
(Map p70; 112 MacDougal St, near Minetta Lane; mains $5; ⏲11:30am-2am Sun-Thu, to 5am Fri & Sat) Located on a food strip with high turnover, the delicious 'Calcutta rolls' and 'street food' at this tiny and sleek eatery should guarantee a long stay.

Taïm MIDDLE EASTERN $
(Map p70; 222 Waverly Pl, btwn Perry & W 11th Sts; mains $7-9; ⏲noon-10pm) This tiny little falafel joint serves smoothies, salads and tasty falafel, which ranges from the traditional to those spiced up with roasted red pepper or hot harissa.

CHELSEA, UNION SQUARE, FLATIRON DISTRICT & GRAMERCY PARK

TOP CHOICE **The Breslin** MODERN AMERICAN $$
(Map p76; 16 West 29th St; mains $18; ⏲7am-midnight) It might be hard to hear yourself think and the hipster overflow from the attached uber-trendy Ace Hotel can rub some the wrong way... However, what really matters is the pub-influenced meat heavy menu by widely celebrated chef April Bloomfield's doesn't disappoint. Big groups can occupy the single large table fronting the open kitchen for the whole roasted suckling pig extravaganza (per person $65 with sides, salad and desserts). No reservations, so expect a wait.

Eataly ITALIAN $
(Map p76; www.eataly.com; 200 Fifth Ave at 23rd St; mains $7; ⏲noon-10pm) The Macy's of food courts, celebrity-chef Mario Batali's NYC empire now has a footprint to match his ambitions. With a handful of specialty dining halls, all with a different focus (pizza, fish, vegetables, meat, pasta) and the *pièce de résistance,* a rooftop beer garden, not to mention a coffee shop, gelateria and grocery, there's enough choice to overwhelm even a blogging gourmand.

Co. PIZZERIA $$
(Map p76; 230 Ninth Ave, at 24th St; pizza $16; ⏲5-11pm) Unsurprisingly, because the chef/owner of this contemporary pizzeria is first and foremost a baker, the paper-thin crust is arguably the best in the city. Go with a group to sample a number of pies with a combination of fresh and inventive toppings.

Chat N' Chew AMERICAN $$
(Map p66; 10 E 16th St; mains $12-20; ⏲11am-midnight Mon-Fri, 10am-midnight Sat, 10am-11pm Sun) It's all down-home comfort food, though of a generally high quality, like macaroni and cheese, mashed potatoes and fried chicken; the onion ring loaf should be divided by a minimum of four people – who don't suffer from heart disease.

Blossom VEGAN $$$
(Map p66; ☎212-627-1144; 187 Ninth Ave, btwn 21st & 22nd Sts; mains $25-35; ⏲noon-10:30pm Fri, Sat & Sun, 5-10pm Mon-Thu; ✎) A creative and elegant vegan spot, housed in a Chelsea town house, where menu items span the globe and enliven the taste buds. Try the flaky seitan empanada, mojo-marinated tempeh or portobello stuffed with cashew-tahini sauce.

The Highliner DINER $$
(Map p76; 210 Tenth Ave, at 22nd St; mains $12; ⏲11am-11pm) Former space of beloved Empire Diner, this new spot, regardless of the quality of its fancy diner fare, will draw in High Line roving crowds.

Shake Shack BURGERS $
(Map p76; Madison Ave, at E 23rd St; burgers from $4; ⏲11am-11pm) Tourists line up in droves for the hamburgers and shakes at this Madison Square Park counter-window-serving institution.

Chennai Garden INDIAN $$
(Map p76; 129 E 27th St, btwn Park & Lexington Aves; mains $9-15; ⏲noon-10pm) Come for South Indian faves such as paper-thin dosas (rice-flour pancakes) stuffed with spicy mixtures of potatoes and peas, and a range of more expected curries.

Chelsea Market MARKET $$
(Map p76; www.chelseamarket.com; 75 Ninth Ave, btwn W 15th & 16th Sts; ⏲7am-10pm Mon-Sat, 7am-10pm Mon-Sat, 8am-8pm Sun) Will thrill gourmet food fans with its 800ft-long shopping concourse.

MIDTOWN

TOP CHOICE **Kum Gang San** KOREAN $$
(Map p76; 49 W 32nd St, at Broadway; mains $12-26; ⏲24hr) One of Koreatown's larger and more extravagant restaurants, Kum Gang San serves standout barbecue – you do it at your table. As in most Korean restaurants, the side dishes that accompany the mains are delicious meals in themselves. Large, loud and kind of kitschy, it's still a reliable introduction to Koreatown.

Pietrasanta ITALIAN $$
(Map p76; ☎212-265 9471; 683 9th Ave, at 47th St; mains $16-24; ⏲noon-10:30pm Mon-Thu & Sun, to midnight Fri & Sat) The best of the many Italian restaurants within several blocks from here, Pietrasanta welcomes as many neighborhood regulars as tourists in the city for a night of theater. The pumpkin ravioli is a favorite, as are the hummus and flavored butter spreads.

Café Edison DELI $
(Map p76; 228 W 47th St, btwn Broadway & Eighth Ave; mains from $6; ⏲6am-9:30pm Mon-Sat, to 7:30pm Sun) Where else can you get a bologna sandwich? This landmark New York spot has been in business since the 1930s, serving up American diner classics like grilled cheese, hot corned beef, open-faced turkey sandwiches and cheese blintzes. Cash only.

Ellen's Stardust Diner DINER $$
(Map p76; 1650 Broadway, at 51st St; mains $15; ⏲7am-midnight Mon-Thu, to 1am Fri & Sat, to 11pm Sun) No New Yorker would be caught dead here, but this '50s theme diner/dinner theater is a super-fun place to head after a show. When the talented waitstaff belt out show tunes and pop songs while picking up your checks, you can't help but applaud.

44 & X MODERN AMERICAN $$
(Map p76; 622 Tenth Ave, at W 44th St; mains $16-30; ⏲5:30pm-midnight Mon-Fri, 11:30am-midnight Sat, to 10:30pm Sun) Worth venturing this far west for, this sleek and airy dining room serves a little something for everyone, from macaroni and cheese to grilled braised short ribs.

Mandoo Bar KOREAN $$
(Map p76; 2 W 32nd St, near Fifth Ave; mains $10; ⏲11:30am-11pm) Handmade in the street-side window, the Korean dumplings served at this narrow eatery are a nice change from all the BBQ places on the block.

Mechango Tei JAPANESE $$
(Map p76; 45th St, btwn Lexington & Third Aves; mains $11; ⏲11:30am-11:30pm) Slurp down a bowl of the signature dish at this bona fide noodle house. The photo-heavy menu helps put novices at ease. Another location on 55th St between Fifth and Sixth Aves.

Poseidon Bakery BAKERY $
(Map p76; 629 Ninth Ave, at W 44th St; pastries from $2; ⏲9am-7pm Tue-Sat). Family-owned Greek bakery serving handmade baklava (pastry made with walnuts and almonds) and spanakopita (feta cheese and spinach wrapped in phyllo pastry) are delicious.

Sophie's CUBAN $

(Map p76; 21 W 45th St, btwn Fifth & Sixth Ave; mains from $6; ⏲10am-8pm Mon-Fri, to 6pm Sat) Bustling lunchtime spot, beef and oxtail stew, grilled chicken, beans and rice, meat patties to go ($2); seven other locations throughout the city.

Daisy May's BBQ BARBECUE $$

(Map p76; 626 Eleventh Ave, at 46th St; mains $12; ⏲11am-10pm) A convenient stop on your way to the Intrepid or Hudson River Park and one of the better BBQ places in the city with Memphis-style ribs.

Patsy's ITALIAN $$$

(Map p76; 236 W 56th St, btwn Broadway & Eight Ave; mains $23; ⏲noon-9:30pm) Sinatra used to eat at this old-school Italian restaurant.

UPPER WEST SIDE & MORNINGSIDE HEIGHTS

Big Nick's DINER $

(Map p84; 2175 Broadway at 77th St; mains $8; ⏲24hr) Looking something like the mess hall of a Cold War-era submarine with a menu the size of the NYC phonebook (these still exist), a meal at Big Nick's is a nostalgia-filled trip down a greasy memory lane. That's not to say the food, including the 1lb sumo burger, gyros, hot dogs, quesadillas, ribs, tofu pizza, challah Monte Cristo, to name only a few choices, is not good. It is generally, but that you just don't find places like this any more.

Barney Greengrass DELI $$

(Map p84; 541 Amsterdam Ave, at W 86th St; mains $8-17; ⏲8:30am-4pm Tue-Fri, to 5pm Sat & Sun) Old-school Upper Westsiders and pilgrims from other neighborhoods crowd this century-old 'sturgeon king' on weekends. It serves a long list of traditional if pricey Jewish delicacies, from bagels and lox to sturgeon scrambled with eggs and onions.

Hungarian Pastry Shop BAKERY $

(Map p84; 1030 Amsterdam Ave, btwn W 110th & 111th Sts; pastries $2-4; ⏲7:30am-11:30pm, to 10:30pm Sun) Bring a dog-eared copy of Kierkegaard to blend in with the intensely serious Columbia University students working in front of steaming laptops and cooling coffee. Excellent pastries and cakes are available.

Flor de Mayo CHINESE, SOUTH AMERICAN $$

(Map p84; 484 Amsterdam Ave, at 83rd St; mains $9-14; ⏲noon-midnight) One of a handful of unpretentious NYC restaurants combining Peruvian and Chinese cuisine. It's somewhat hectic at dinnertime, but it's the place for choosing between egg foo young and *ceviche de pescado.*

UPPER EAST SIDE

Daniel FRENCH $$$

(Map p84; ☎212-288-0033; 60 E 65th St, btwn Madison & Park Aves; 3-course prix fixe dinners $105; ⏲Mon-Sat 5:30-11pm) This chichi French palace features floral arrangements and wide-eyed foodies who gawk over plates of peekytoe crab and celery-root salad, foie gras terrine with gala apples and black truffle-crusted lobster – and that's just the first course. There's an all-veggie menu, too.

Central Park Boathouse Restaurant AMERICAN $$$

(Map p84; ☎212-517-2233; Central Park Lake, enter Fifth Ave, at 72nd St; mains $15-40; ⏲noon-9:30pm) The historic Loeb Boathouse, perched on the shores of the park's lake, is one of the city's more incredible settings for a serene and romantic meal. Food is top-notch, too – reserve early and aim for an outdoor table.

Beyoglu TURKISH $$

(Map p84; ☎212-650-0850; 1431 Third Ave at 81st St; mains $15; ⏲noon-10:30pm) A loungey space that's just a short stroll away from the Met, serving traditional small plates, such as yogurt soup, doner kebabs and eggplant puree. Down a shot or two of the traditional, anisette-flavored raki as an after-meal spirit.

Totonno's ITALIAN $$

(Map p84; 1544 Second Ave; mains $14; ⏲noon-4pm Mon-Fri) The Manhattan branch of a Coney Island classic New York pizza joint.

Nectar Café DINER $$

(Map p84; 1022 Madison Ave at 79th St; mains $13; ⏲6am-9pm) Only a few blocks from several major museums, this standard diner's prices are only justified by its location – but still for this'hood it's not bad value.

HARLEM

Red Rooster MODERN AMERICAN $$$

(Map p84; ☎212-792-9001; 310 Lenox Ave, near 125th St; mains $14-32; ⏲11:30am-10:30pm) Something of a pioneer, chef Marcus Samuelson's sophisticated uptown venture steps from the 2 or 3 train stop has a downtown bistro vibe. A variety of southern, soul and new American cooking, the kitchen does blackened catfish, meatballs with mashed potatoes and ligonberries and creative sandwiches. The front bar area and breakfast nook has pastries, biscuits and coffee.

Amy Ruth's Restaurant SOUTHERN $$
(Map p84; 113 W 116th St, btwn Malcolm X & Adam Clayton Powell Jr Blvds; mains $10-16; ⏲11:30am-11pm Mon, from 8:30am Tue-Thu & Sun, to 5:30am Fri & Sat) Tourists flock here for the specialty waffles; choose from sweet (chocolate, strawberry, blueberry, smothered in sautéed apples) or savory (paired with fried chicken, rib-eye or catfish). Smoked ham, chicken and dumplings are favorites as well.

Londel's Supper Club CAJUN $$
(Map p84; ☎212-234-6114; 2620 Frederick Douglass Blvd; mains $12-24; ⏲11:30am-11pm Tue-Sat, to 5pm Sun) The wall photos of famous patrons are testament to this elegant restaurant's status and popularity. Londel's menu combines Cajun and continental flavors and live jazz Friday and Saturday nights.

BROOKLYN

Of course it's impossible to begin to do justice to Brooklyn's eating options – it's as much a foodie's paradise as Manhattan. Virtually every ethnic cuisine has a significant presence somewhere in this area. As far as neighborhoods close to Manhattan go: Williamsburg is chockablock with eateries, as are Fifth and Seventh Aves in Park Slope. Smith St is 'Restaurant Row' in the Carroll Gardens and Cobble Hill neighborhoods. Atlantic Ave, near Court St, has a number of excellent Middle Eastern restaurants and groceries.

TOP CHOICE **Frankies 457** ITALIAN $$
(457 Court St, Carroll Gardens; mains $15; ⏲11am-11pm Sun-Thu, to midnight Fri & Sat) A Carroll Garden's favorite packing in regulars night after night, Frankies feels both homey and romantic. Dark and candlelit at night, it has an attractive backyard garden for warm weather brunches. Small cheese plates, crostinis and veggie side dishes can be shared by the table.

Blue Ribbon Brasserie SEAFOOD, AMERICAN $$$
(☎718-840-0404; 280 5th Ave, btwn 1st St & Garfield Pl, Park Slope; mains $15-27; ⏲5pm-midnight Mon-Thu & Sun, to 2am Fri & Sat) This restaurant in the heart of Park Slope has something for everyone: an incredible raw bar, pork ribs, matzo-ball soup, paella, fried chicken and chocolate-chip bread pudding. It's open late but doesn't take reservations for parties fewer than six.

Farm on Adderly MODERN AMERICAN $$
(☎718-287-3101; 1108 Cortelyou Rd, Ditmas Park; dinner mains $18; ⏲11:30am-11pm) This is the sort of farm-to-table place where waiters know the life story of the fish, poultry and meat on your plate – if pressed they might be able to supply names. Dine in the patio out back but whatever you do try the Cascadia cocktail (pear brandy, gin, absinthe, honey and tonic) and the salted chocolate mousse for dessert.

Peter Luger STEAKHOUSE $$$
(☎718-387-7400; 178 Broadway, Williamsburg; lunch mains $5-20, dinner mains $30-32; ⏲11:45am-9:45pm Mon-Thu, to 10:45pm Fri & Sat, 12:45-9:45pm Sun) The aged porterhouse at this venerable 100-year-old German steakhouse at the foot of the Williamsburg Bridge is often regarded as one of the best steaks in the country. Reservations required and cash and debit cards only.

Tom's Restaurant DINER $
(782 Washington Ave, at Sterling Ave, Prospect Heights; mains $6; ⏲6am-4pm) Inspiration for the eponymously named Suzanne Vega song, this old-school soda fountain diner's specialty is its variety of pancakes (eg mango walnut). Coffee and cookies are served to those waiting in the line that invariably snakes out the door on weekend mornings.

Bar Tabac FRENCH $$
(128 Smith St, at Dean, Cobble Hill; mains $15; ⏲11am-2am) No better place for weekend brunch at one of this bistro's sidewalk tables while the jazz band plays inside.

Roberta's PIZZERIA $$
(261 Moore St, near Bogart, Bushwick; pizzas $14; ⏲noon-midnight) Worth the trip to a gritty Bushwick block, this pizzeria does Neapolitan pies with creative topping combinations.

Yemen Café MIDDLE EASTERN $$
(176 Atlantic Ave, Brooklyn Heights; mains $9; ⏲10am-10:30pm) This welcoming authentic Yemeni cafeteria-style place is above a barbershop.

Drinking

Watering holes come in many forms in this city: sleek lounges, cozy pubs and booze-soaked dives – no smoke, though, thanks to city law. The majority are open to 4am, though closing (and opening) times do vary. Here's a highly selective sampling.

DOWNTOWN

Decibel SAKE BAR
(Map p70; 240 E 9th St; 6pm-3am) Just nod your head and sip. Hearing is a challenge even when you're crammed in a corner touching knees. Nevertheless, this cozy and dark downstairs hideaway feels like an authentic Tokyo dive, from the sake varieties to the delicious snacks.

KGB Bar BAR
(Map p70; 212-505-3360; 85 E 4th St, at 2nd Ave; 7pm-3:30am) The East Village's own grungy Algonquin roundtable has been drawing literary types to its regular readings since the early 1990s. Even when there's no artist in residence the heavily worn wood bar is good for kicking back.

Mayahuel TEQUILA BAR
(Map p70; 304 E 6th St, at Second Ave; 6pm-2am) About as far from your typical spring break tequila bar as you can get – more like the cellar of a monastery. Devotees of the fermented agave can seriously indulge themselves experimenting with dozens of varieties (all cocktails $13).

McSorley's Old Ale House BAR
(Map p70; 15 E 7th St, btwn Second & Third Aves; 11am-1am) Around since 1854 – it has the cobwebs and sawdust floors to prove it McSorley's feels far removed from the East Village veneer of cool: you're more likely to drink with firefighters, Wall St refugees and a few tourists.

Fat Cat BAR
(Map p70; 75 Christopher St, at Seventh Ave; cover up to $3; 2pm-5am Mon-Thu, from noon Fri-Sun;) Evocative of a fantasy fraternity basement, this gaming paradise has Ping-Pong, billiards, chess, even shuffleboard, cheap beer and live music every night.

Fresh Salt BAR
(Map p66; 146 Beekman St; 10am-4am) Only steps from a beautiful pier on the East River, and close to the financial district, Fresh Salt manages to avoid the boisterous feel of the after-work Wall St crowd. This small and rustic bar has board games (Boggle, chess etc) and a great hummus plate.

Mulberry Project COCKTAIL BAR
(Map p70; 646-448-4536; 149 Mulberry St, near Grand St; 7pm-4am) This Little Italy bar has a 2nd floor outdoor patio, a great place to sip a custom-crafted cocktail made by mixologists – not bartenders.

Henrietta Hudson LESBIAN
(Map p70; 438 Hudson St, at Morton St; 5pm-4am Wed-Sun, to 2am Mon & Tue) All sorts of cute young women storm this long-running lesbian spot, a former pool-and-pint joint that's now a sleek lounge with varied DJs.

Welcome to the Johnsons BAR
(Map p70; 123 Rivington St; 3pm-4am) Looking like a set from *The Brady Bunch* or *That '70s Show,* this Lower East Side theme bar can be enjoyed with or without irony. Wash down the free Doritos with a Jack Daniel's and root beer.

Schiller's Liquor Bar BAR
(Map p70; 131 Rivington St, at Norfolk St; 11am-1am Mon-Wed, to 2am Thu, to 3am Fri, 10am-3am Sat, 10am-1am Sun) This trendy spot serves cocktails as delicious as its food (mains $12 to $25).

Ulysses COCKTAIL BAR
(Map p66; 58 Stone St; 11am-4am) Big with old-school financial types, Ulysses is an Irish-modern hybrid, with a long bar and a kitchen serving oysters and sandwiches and picnic tables out on cobbled Stone St.

MIDTOWN

TOP CHOICE **Russian Vodka Room** BAR
(Map p76; 265 W 52nd St, btwn 8th Ave & Broadway; 4pm-2am) Actual Russians aren't uncommon at this swanky and welcoming bar. The lighting is dark and the corner booths intimate, but more importantly the dozens of flavored vodkas, from cranberry to horseradish, are fun to experiment with. Eastern European dishes such as latkes, smoked fish and schnitzel can tame a rumbling stomach.

Rudy's Bar & Grill DIVE BAR
(Map p76; 627 Ninth Ave; 8am-4am) This semi-dive bar – neighborhood newcomers and professional types rub beer-soaked shoulders with hard-core drinkers – is a good place for cheap beer and even greasy hot dogs, if you don't mind not being able to hear yourself think. A backyard garden with makeshift furniture and artificial turf is open in the summer months.

Morrell Wine Bar & Café WINE BAR
(Map p76; 1 Rockefeller Plaza, W 48th St, btwn Fifth & Sixth Aves; 11:30am-midnight Mon-Sat, noon-6pm Sun) The list of vinos at this pioneering New York City wine bar is over 2000 long, with a whopping 150 available by the glass. And the airy, split-level room, right across

from the famous skating rink, is equally as intoxicating.

Therapy GAY
(Map p76; 348 W 52nd St, btwn Eighth & Ninth Aves; ⏲5pm-2am, to 4am Fri & Sat) Multileveled, airy and sleekly contemporary, Therapy is a longstanding gay Hell's Kitchen hot spot. Theme nights abound, from stand-up comedy to musical shows.

Réunion Surf Bar BAR
(Map p76; 357 W 44th St at Ninth Ave; ⏲5:30pm-2am, to 4am Thu-Sat) Swanky Tiki-themed bar and restaurant serving delicious French South Pacific cuisine, eg banana-leaf-steamed mahi mahi.

Mé Bar ROOFTOP BAR
(Map p76; 14th fl, 17 W 32nd St near Fifth Ave; ⏲5:30pm-2am Sun-Tue, to 4am Wed-Sat) The small rooftop deck of the budget La Quinta hotel in Koreatown feels like a secret, though one with great views of the Empire State Building.

On the Rocks COCKTAIL BAR
(Map p76; 696 Tenth Ave, btwn 48th & 49th Sts; ⏲5pm-4am) Whisky nerds will delight at this cubbyhole-sized space.

Rum House COCKTAIL BAR
(Map p76; 228 W 47th St, btwn Broadway & Eighth Ave; ⏲11am-4am) Once a no-frills regulars bar in the Edison Hotel, now renovated with wood-paneling, leather banquets and mixologists.

UPTOWN

79th Street Boat Basin BAR
(Map p84; W 79th St, in Riverside Park; ⏲noon-11pm) A covered, open-sided party spot under the ancient arches of a park overpass, this is an Upper West Side favorite once spring hits. Order a pitcher, some snacks and enjoy the sunset view over the Hudson River.

Subway Inn BAR
(Map p84; 143 E 60th St, btwn Lexington & Third Aves; ⏲11am-4am) An old-geezer watering hole with cheap drinks and loads of authenticity. The entire scene – from the vintage neon sign outside to the well-worn red booths and old guys huddled inside – is truly reminiscent of bygone days.

Lenox Lounge COCKTAIL BAR
(Map p84; ☎212-427-0253; 288 Malcolm X Blvd (Lenox Ave), btwn 124th & 125th Sts; ⏲noon-4am) The classic art-deco Lounge, which once hosted the likes of Billie Holiday and Miles Davis and is an old favorite of local jazz cats, is still going strong. The luxe Zebra Room in back is a beautiful and historic setting to hear top-flight musicians. Cover charge can be pricey.

Bemelman's Bar BAR
(Map p84; Carlyle Hotel, 35 E 76th St, at Madison Ave; ⏲11am-1am) Waiters wear white jackets, a baby grand piano is always being played and Ludwig Bemelman's *Madeline* murals surround you. It's a classic spot for a serious cocktail – the kind of place that could easily turn up in a Woody Allen film.

Ding Dong Lounge BAR
(Map p84; 929 Columbus Ave, btwn 105th & 106th Sts; ⏲4pm-4am) This former crack den turned punk bar is a small slice of downtown for streams of Columbia students and nearby hostel guests. There's a pool table and some cuckoo clocks, and the DJ dips into kept-real R&B.

BROOKLYN

Brooklyn Social BAR
(335 Smith St, at Carroll St, Carroll Gardens; ⏲5pm-2am, to 4am Fri & Sat) Typical of this genre of bar, signage is a no-no and discretion an asset. Young neighborhood types cozy up to the bar or one of the barely lit corner lounges.

Iona Bar BAR
(180 Grand St; ⏲1pm-4am) Hipsters infiltrate this Scottish-Irish bar on weekend nights; other nights it's a less American Apparel crowd enjoying happy hour (beer $4). Meat and veggie pies play second fiddle in summer when the barbecue in the backyard garden turns out hamburgers and hot dogs.

Turkey's Nest BAR
(94 Bedford Ave, at N 12th St; ⏲10am-4am) The eclectic crowd at the Nest in Williamsburg loves the huge Styrofoam containers of cheap beer and cocktails served in plastic cups. Watch the Yankees or the Mets or play the hunting video game in the back. Whatever you do, wear a hazmat suit when you use the toilet.

Union Hall BAR
(702 Union St, at Fifth Ave; ⏲4pm-4am, from noon Sat & Sun) In Park Slope, head to this creatively idiosyncratic bar – leather chairs à la a snooty London social club, walls lined with bookshelves and two bocce courts, plus live music downstairs and an outdoor patio.

Weather Up BAR
(589 Vanderbilt Ave; ⏲7pm-3am, closed Mon) No signage marks the exterior of this dark and shadowy Prospect Heights cocktail-centric speakeasy-like neighborhood favorite.

Radegast Hall & Biergarten BEER HALL
(113 N 3rd St; ⏲4pm-4am) Rowdy Williamsburg spot with excellent veal schnitzel.

Henry Public BAR
(329 Henry St, at Atlantic Ave; ⏲5pm-2am, Fri to 4am, from noon Sat & Sun) Part of the Brooklyn saloon-style revival, Henry Public has a handsome zinc-tipped bar and excellent turkey-leg sandwich.

☆ Entertainment

Those with unlimited fuel and appetites can gorge themselves on a seemingly infinite number of entertainments – from Broadway shows to performance art in someone's Brooklyn living room, and everything in between. *New York* magazine and the weekend editions of the *New York Times* are great guides for what's on once you arrive.

NIGHTCLUBS

Most nightclubs are open from 10pm to 4am but some open earlier.

SOBs CLUB
(Map p70; ☎212-243-4940; www.sobs.com; 204 Varick St, at W Houston) Brazilian bossa nova, samba and other Latin vibes draw a mix of those who know how to move smooth and sensually and those who like to watch.

Santos Party House CLUB
(Map p66; ☎212-584-5492; www.santosparty house; 96 Lafayette St; cover $5-15) Shaggy rocker Andrew WK created this bi-level 8000-sq-ft cavernous bare-bones dance club. Devoted to good times and good vibes, this place requires that you check your attitude at the door – funk to electronica, and WK spins some nights.

Beauty & Essex CLUB
(Map p70; ☎212-614-0146; www.beautyandessex.com; 146 Essex St) This newcomer's glamour is concealed behind a pawnshop front space and memories of its former incarnation as a furniture store. Now, there's 10,000-sq-ft of sleek lounge space filled with a mix of well-dressed twenty- and thirty-somethings.

Sullivan Room CLUB
(Map p70; ☎212-505-1703; www.sullivanroom.com; 218 Sullivan St, btwn Bleecker & W 3rd Sts; ⏲Wed-Sun) An eclectic downtown mix and top-flight DJs make Sullivan Room one of the best places to dance the night away. There's nothing pretentious – no need for high heels or cheesy leather jackets.

Cielo CLUB
(Map p70; ☎212-645-5700; www.cieloclub.com; 18 Little W 12th St, btwn Ninth Ave & Washington St; cover $5-20) Known for its intimate space and kick-ass sound system, this space-age-looking Meatpacking District staple packs in a fashionable, multiculti crowd nightly for its blend of tribal, old-school house and soulful grooves.

Pacha CLUB
(Map p76; ☎212-209-7500; www.pachanyc.com; 618 W 46th St, btwn Eleventh Ave & West Side Hwy) A massive and spectacular place, this is 30,000 sq ft and four levels of glowing, sleek spaces and cozy seating nooks that rise up to surround the main dance-floor atrium. Big-name DJs are always on tap.

M2 Ultra Lounge CLUB
(Map p76; ☎212-629-9000; www.m2ultralounge.com; 530 W 28th St, btwn Tenth & Eleventh Aves; admission $20; ⏲Thu-Sat) This megaclub will blow out your ear drums and your wallet – drinks are expensive ($15). In some ways this is the classic big club – long lines, opulent booths, bottle service and sexy go-go dancers.

LIVE MUSIC

Maybe less indie-dominated than music scenes in Austin or Seattle, NYC does of course still boast an enormous number of venues varying greatly in size, crowd and genre of music.

Le Poisson Rouge LIVE MUSIC
(Map p70; ☎212-796-0741; www.lepoissonrouge.com; 158 Bleecker St, at Sullivan St) This Bleecker St basement club is one of the premier venues for experimental contemporary, from classical to indie rock to electro-acoustic.

Joe's Pub LIVE MUSIC
(Map p70; ☎212-967-7555; www.joespub.com; Public Theater, 425 Lafayette St, btwn Astor Pl & E 4th St) Part cabaret theater, part rock and new-indie venue, this small and lovely supper club has hosts a wonderful variety of styles, voices and talent.

BB King Blues Club & Grill LIVE MUSIC
(Map p76; ☎212-997-4144; www.bbkingblues.com; 237 W 42nd St) In the heart of Times Square

JAZZ

Second only to New Orleans, Harlem was an early home to a flourishing jazz scene and one of its principal beating hearts. The neighborhood fostered greats like Duke Ellington, Charlie Parker, John Coltrane and Thelonius Monk. From bebop to free improvisation, in classic art-deco clubs and at intimate jam sessions, Harlem and other important venues scattered throughout the city, especially around the Village, continue to foster old-timers and talented newcomers alike. Tune in to **WKCR** (89.9 FM) for jazz and especially from 8:20am to 9:30am Monday through Friday for Phil Schaap's 27-year-old program in which he dazzles listeners with his encyclopedic knowledge and appreciation for the art form. The **National Jazz Museum in Harlem** (212-348-8300; www.jazzmuseuminharlem.org; 104 E 126th St, Suite 2D; admission free; 10am-4pm Mon-Fri) has a collection of books, CDs and photos for passionate fans.

Smalls (Map p70; 212-252-5091; www.smallsjazzclub.com; 183 W 4th St; cover $20) is a subterranean jazz dungeon that rivals the world-famous **Village Vanguard** (Map p70; 212-255-4037; www.villagevanguard.com; 178 Seventh Ave, at W 11th St) in terms of sheer talent. Of course, the latter has hosted every major star of the past 50 years; there's a two-drink minimum and a serious no-talking policy.

Heading uptown, **Dizzy's Club Coca-Cola: Jazz at the Lincoln Center** (Map p84; 212-258-9595; www.jalc.org/dccc; 5th fl, Time Warner Bldg, Broadway, at W 60th St), one of Lincoln Center's three jazz venues, has stunning views overlooking Central Park and nightly shows featuring top lineups. Further north on the Upper West Side, check out the **Smoke Jazz & Supper Club-Lounge** (Map p84; 212-864-6662; www.smokejazz.com; 2751 Broadway, btwn W 105th & 106th Sts), which gets crowded on weekends.

offers old-school blues along with rock, folk and reggae acts.

Barge Music CLASSICAL MUSIC
(718-624-2083; www.bargemusic.org; Fulton Ferry Landing) Exceptionally talented classical musicians perform in this intimate space, a decommissioned barge docked under the Brooklyn Bridge.

Highline Ballroom LIVE MUSIC
(Map p76; 212-414-5994; www.highlineballroom.com; 431 W 16th St, btwn Ninth & Tenth Aves) A classy Chelsea venue with an eclectic lineup, from Mandy Moore to Moby.

Beacon Theatre CONCERT VENUE
(Map p84; 212-465-6500; www.beacontheatre.com; 2124 Broadway, btwn W 74th & 75th Sts) This Upper West Side venue hosts big acts for folks who want to see shows in an environment that's more intimate than that of a big concert arena.

Madison Square Garden CONCERT VENUE
(Map p76; 212-465-5800; www.thegarden.com; Seventh Ave, btwn W 31st & W 33rd Sts) For the biggest acts like Green Day and Andrea Bocelli, this place draws stadium-sized crowds.

Radio City Music Hall CONCERT VENUE
(Map p76; 212-247-4777; www.radiocity.com; Sixth Ave, at W 50th St) In the middle of Midtown, the architecturally grand concert hall hosts the likes of Barry Manilow and Cirque de Soleil and of course the famous Christmas spectacular.

Mercury Lounge LIVE MUSIC
(Map p70; 212-260-4700; www.mercuryloungenyc.com; 217 E Houston St)

Delancey Lounge LIVE MUSIC
(Map p70; 212-254-9920; www.thedelancey.com; 168 Delancey St, at Clinton St) Great indie-band bookings.

Webster Hall CONCERT VENUE
(Map p70; 212-353-1600; www.websterhall.com; 125 E 11th St, at 3rd Ave)

Irving Plaza CONCERT VENUE
(Map p76; 212-777-6800; www.irvingplaza.com; 17 Irving Pl)

Terminal 5 CONCERT VENUE
(Map p76; 212-260-4700; www.terminal5nyc.com; 610 W 56th St, at 11th Ave) All book big and quality acts.

Southpaw LIVE MUSIC
(718-230-0236; www.spsounds.com; 125 5th Ave) In Park Slope, Brooklyn, head here for a nightly lineup.

THEATER

In general, 'Broadway' productions are staged in the lavish, early-20th-century theaters surrounding Times Square. You'll choose your theater based on its production – *The Book of Mormon, Spider-Man: Turn off the Dark, Lion King*. Evening performances begin at 8pm.

'Off Broadway' simply refers to shows performed in smaller spaces (500 seats or fewer), which is why you'll find many just around the corner from Broadway venues, as well as elsewhere in town. 'Off-off Broadway' events include readings, experimental and cutting-edge performances and improvisations held in spaces with fewer than 100 seats; these venues are primarily downtown. Some of the world's best theater happens in these more intimate venues before moving to Broadway. Some distinguished theaters include:

Public Theater THEATER
(Map p70; ☎212-539-8500; www.publictheater.org; 425 Lafayette St, btwn Astor Pl & E 4th St)

St Ann's Warehouse THEATER
(☎718-254-8779; www.stannswarehouse.org; 38 Water St)

PS 122 THEATER
(Map p70; ☎212-477-5288; www.ps122.org; 150 First Ave, at E 9th St)

Playwrights Horizon THEATER
(Map p76; ☎212-564-1235; www.playwrightshorizon.org; 416 W 42nd St, btwn Ninth & Tenth Aves)

New York Theater Workshop THEATER
(Map p70; ☎212-780-9037; www.nytw.org; 79 E 4th St, btwn Second & Third Aves)

Ontological Theater THEATER
(Map p70; ☎212-420-1916; www.ontological.com; 131 E 10th St)

Choose from current shows by checking print publications, or a website such as **Theater Mania** (www.theatermania.com). You can purchase tickets through **Telecharge** (☎212-239-6200; www.telecharge.com) and **Ticketmaster** (www.ticketmaster.com) for standard ticket sales, or **TKTS ticket booths** (www.tkts.com; Downtown Map p66; Front St, at John St, South St Seaport; ⊙11am-6pm; Midtown Map p76; under the red steps, 47th St, at Broadway; ⊙3-8pm) for same-day tickets to Broadway and off-Broadway musicals at up to 50% off regular prices.

COMEDY

From lowbrow prop comics to experimental conceptual humor, there's a venue for every taste and budget. More-established ones push the alcohol with drink minimums.

Upright Citizens Brigade Theatre COMEDY
(Map p76; ☎212-366-9176; www.ucbtheatre.com; 307 W 26th St) Improv venue featuring well-known, emerging and probably-won't-emerge comedians in this small basement theater nightly.

Village Lantern COMEDY
(Map p70; ☎212-260-7993; www.villagelantern.com; 167 Bleecker St) Nightly alternative comedy underneath a bar of the same name.

Caroline's on Broadway COMEDY
(Map p76; ☎212-956-0101; www.carolines.com; 1626 Broadway) One of the best-known places in the city, and host to the biggest names on the circuit.

Gotham Comedy Club COMEDY
(Map p76; ☎212-367-9000; www.gothamcomedyclub.com; 208 W 23rd St, btwn Seventh & Eighth Aves) A plush venue featuring mostly mainstream-style comedy.

Stand-Up New York COMEDY
(Map p84; ☎212-595-0850; www.standupny.com; 236 W 78th St; tickets $5-12) Gets surprise appearances from star comedians.

CINEMAS

Long lines in the evenings and on weekends are the norm. It's recommended that you call and buy your tickets in advance (unless it's midweek, midday or for a film that's been out for months already). Most cinemas are handled either through **Movie Fone** (☎212-777-3456; www.moviefone.com) or **Fandango** (www.fandango.com). You'll have to pay an extra $1.25 more per ticket, but it's worth it. Large chain theaters with stadium seating are scattered throughout the city including several in the Times Square and Union Square areas. During the summer months free outdoor screenings blossom throughout the city on rooftops and park spaces.

IFC Center CINEMA
(Map p70; ☎212-924-7771; www.ifccenter.com; 323 Sixth Ave, at 3rd St) Formerly the Waverly, is a three-screen art-house cinema showing new indies, cult classics and foreign films – and the popcorn is organic.

Landmark Sunshine Cinema CINEMA
(Map p70; ☎212-358-7709; www.landmarktheatres.com; 143 E Houston St) Housed in a former Yiddish theater; shows first-run indies.

Anthology Film Archives CINEMA
(Map p70; ☎212-505-5181; www.anthologyfilmarchives.org; 32 Second Ave, at E 2nd St) Film studies majors head to this schoolhouse-

like building, for independent and avant-garde cinema.

Brooklyn Academy of Music Rose Cinemas CINEMA
(BAM; ☎718-636-4100; www.bam.org; 30 Lafayette Ave) In Brooklyn, and comfortable as well as popular for its new-release indies and special festival screenings.

Film Forum CINEMA
(Map p70; ☎212-627-2035; www.filmforum.org; 209 W Houston St) Thc long and narrow theaters can't dent cineastes' love for this institution showing revivals, classics and documentaries.

Ziegfeld CINEMA
(Map p76; ☎212-307-1862; www.clearviewcinemas.com; 141 W 54th St) A regal old-school holdout with over a thousand seats, crystal chandeliers and Hollywood blockbusters on its single screen.

PERFORMING ARTS

World-class performers and venues mean the city is a year-round mecca for arts-lovers.

Every top-end genre has a stage at the massive Lincoln Center complex. Its Avery Fisher Hall is the showplace of the New York Philharmonic, while recently redesigned Alice Tully Hall houses the Chamber Music Society of Lincoln Center, and the New York State Theater is home to the New York City Ballet (the New York City Opera decided to decamp in 2011). Great drama is found at both the Mitzi E Newhouse and Vivian Beaumont theaters; and frequent concerts at the Juilliard School. But the biggest draw is the Metropolitan Opera House, home to the Metropolitan Opera and American Ballet Theater.

Carnegie Hall CONCERT VENUE
(Map p76; ☎212-247-7800; www.carnegiehall.org; 154 W 57th St, at Seventh Ave) Since 1891, the historic Carnegie Hall has hosted performances by the likes of Tchaikovsky, Mahler and Prokofiev and more recently Stevie Wonder, Sting and Tony Bennett. Today its three halls host visiting philharmonics, the New York Pops orchestra and various world-class musicians (mostly closed in July and August). Before or after a performance, check out the recently remade **Rose Museum** for a history of the institution.

Symphony Space PERFORMING ARTS
(Map p84; ☎212-864-5400; www.symphonyspace.org; 2537 Broadway, at W 95th St) A multigenre space with several facilities in one. This Upper West Side gem is home to many performance series as well as theater, cabaret, comedy, dance and world-music concerts throughout the week.

Brooklyn Academy of Music PERFORMING ARTS
(BAM; ☎718-636-4100; www.bam.org; 30 Lafayette Ave) Sort of a Brooklyn version of the Lincoln Center – in its all-inclusiveness rather than its vibe, which is much edgier – the spectacular academy also hosts everything from modern dance to opera, cutting-edge theater and music concerts.

SPORTS

In 2009 the city's two major-league baseball teams, the uber-successful **New York Yankees** (www.yankees.com), who play at **Yankee Stadium** (Map p64; cnr 161st St & River Ave, the Bronx), and the more historically beleaguered **New York Mets** (www.mets.com), who play at **Citi Field** (Map p64; 126th St, at Roosevelt Ave, Flushing, Queens), inaugurated long-anticipated brand-new stadiums. For less-grand settings but no-less-pleasant outings, check out the minor-league **Staten Island Yankees** (www.siyanks.com) at **Richmond County Bank Ballpark** (Map p64; 75 Richmond Terrace, Staten Island) or the **Brooklyn Cyclones** (www.brooklyncyclones.com) at **KeySpan Park** (Map p64; cnr Surf Ave & W 17th St, Coney Island).

For basketball, you can get courtside with the NBA's **New York Knicks** (www.nba.com/knicks) at **Madison Square Garden** (btwn Seventh Ave & 33rd St), called the 'mecca of basketball'; the Knicks have been rejuvenated by the acquisition of stars Carmelo Anthony and Amar'e Stoudemire. The cross-river rivals, **New Jersey Nets** (www.nba.com/nets) are scheduled to move to the Atlantic Yards, a large complex in downtown Brooklyn some time in 2012. Also playing at Madison Square Garden, the women's WNBA league team **New York Liberty** (www.wnba.com/liberty) provides a more laid-back time.

New York City's NFL (pro-football) teams, the **Giants** (www.giants.com) and **Jets** (www.newyorkjets.com), share the **New Meadowlands Stadium** in East Rutherford, New Jersey.

 Shopping

While chain stores have proliferated, turning once-idiosyncratic blocks into versions of generic strip malls, NYC is still the best

American city for shopping. It's not unusual for shops – especially downtown boutiques – to stay open until 10pm or 11pm.

DOWNTOWN

Lower Manhattan is where you'll find across-the-board bargains, as well as more of the small, stylish boutiques. Downtown's coolest offerings are in NoLita (just east of SoHo), the East Village and the Lower East Side. SoHo has more expensive though no less fashionable stores, while Broadway from Union Sq to Canal St is lined with big retailers like H&M and Urban Outfitters, as well as dozens of jeans and shoe stores – the museum-like Prada NYC flagship is also here. The streets of Chinatown are filled with knock-off designer handbags, jewelry, perfume and watches.

For coveted designer labels stroll through the Meatpacking District around 14th St and Ninth Ave.

TOP CHOICE **Strand Bookstore** BOOKS
(Map p70; 828 Broadway, at E 12th St; ⌚9:30am-10:30pm Mon-Sat, from 11am Sun) The city's preeminent bibliophile warehouse, selling new and used books.

Century 21 DEPARTMENT STORE
(Map p66; 22 Cortlandt St, at Church St) A four-level department store loved by New Yorkers of every income, is shorthand for designer bargains.

J&R Music & Computer World ELECTRONICS
(Map p66; 15-23 Park Row) Every electronic need, especially computer and camera related, can be satisfied here. Takes up a full city block.

Eastern Mountain Sports OUTDOOR EQUIPMENT
(Map p70; 530 Broadway, at Spring St) A high-quality outdoor emporium outfitting every imaginable adventure and the staff is extremely knowledgeable and friendly.

Bloomingdale's SoHo DEPARTMENT STORE
(Map p70; 504 Broadway) The smaller, younger outpost of the Upper East Side legend focuses on designer fashion.

Topshop WOMEN'S CLOTHING
(Map p70; 478 Broadway, at Broome St) The trendy British superstore for women; where to go for shiny spandex and disco tops.

Uniqlo CLOTHING
(Map p70; 546 Broadway) Japanese retailer with moderately priced men's and women's fashions.

McNally Jackson Books BOOKS
(Map p70; ☎212-274-1160; 52 Prince St; ⌚10am-10pm Mon-Sat, to 9pm Sun) A NoLita refuge containing a nice cafe and regular author readings.

Idlewild Books BOOKSTORE
(Map p76; ☎212-414-8888; 12 W 19th St; ⌚11:30am-8pm Mon-Fri, noon-7pm Sat & Sun) Near Union Square. Fiction and nonfiction are uniquely organized by country and regions of the world.

Apple Store ELECTRONICS
(Map p66; 401 W Fourteenth St, at Ninth Ave) Pilgrims flock here for shiny new gadgets.

MIDTOWN & UPTOWN

Midtown's Fifth Ave and the Upper East Side's Madison Ave have the famous high-end fashion and clothing by international designers. Times Square has many super-sized stores, though they're all chains. Chelsea has more unique boutiques, though it too has been colonized by banks, drugstores and big-box retailers.

Tiffany & Co JEWELRY
(Map p76; 727 Fifth Ave) Has become synonymous with NYC luxury. This famous jeweler, with the trademark clock-hoisting Atlas over the door, carries fine diamond rings, watches, necklaces etc, as well as crystal and glassware.

Macy's DEPARTMENT STORE
(Map p76; 151 W 34th St) The grande dame of midtown department stores sells everything from jeans to kitchen appliances.

Bloomingdale's DEPARTMENT STORE
(Map p84; 1000 3rd Ave, at E 59th St) Uptown, the sprawling, overwhelming Bloomingdale's is akin to the Metropolitan Museum of Art for shoppers.

Barney's Co-op CLOTHING
(Downtown Map p76; 236 W 18th St; Uptown Map p84; 2151 Broadway) Offers hipper, less-expensive versions of high-end fashion.

ℹ Information

Internet Access

There are many wi-fi access hot spots around the city, including Lincoln Center uptown, Bryant Park in midtown, Union Square downtown and the entire Dumbo neighborhood in Brooklyn; summer 2011 plans call for a total of 20 NYC parks to offer free wi-fi in the near future. The hourly fee for surfing the web at internet cafes ranges from $3 to $12. If you have a laptop, you won't have to go far to find a coffee shop or restaurant with free wi-fi and of course there are more than 200 Starbucks and a handful of Barnes & Nobles with free wi-fi as well.

Cybercafe Times Square (250 W 49th St, btwn Broadway & 8th Ave; per 30min $7; ⏲8am-11pm Mon-Fri, from 11am Sat & Sun)

Netzone Internet Cafe (28 W 32nd St, 5th fl; per hr $5; ⏲9am-5am)

New York Public Library (☎212-930-0800; www.nypl.org/branch/local; E 42nd St, at Fifth Ave) Offers free half-hour internet access; more than 80 other local branches also have free access.

Media

Daily News (www.nydailynews.com) A daily tabloid, leans toward the sensational – archrivals of the *New York Post*.

New York (www.newyorkmagazine.com) Weekly featuring nationally oriented reporting as well as NYC-centric news and listings for the arts and culture-oriented reader.

New York Post (www.nypost.com) Famous for spicy headlines, celebrity scandal-laden Page Six and good sports coverage.

New York Times (www.nytimes.com) The 'Gray Lady' is the newspaper of record for readers throughout the US and much of the English-speaking world.

NY1 An excellent source of local news, this is the city's all-day news station on Time Warner cable's Channel 1.

Onion (www.onion.com) Weekly fake news and satire website; the print edition has real and extensive listings for goings-on about town, especially comedy.

Village Voice (www.villagevoice.com) The weekly tabloid is still a good resource for events, clubs and music listings.

WFUV-90.7FM The area's best alternative-music radio station is run by the Bronx's Fordham University.

WNYC 820am or 93.9FM National Public Radio's local affiliate.

Medical Services

Big retail pharmacies are everywhere and some stay open late.

Interchurch Center Medical Office (☎212-870-3053; www.interchurch-center.org; 475 Riverside Dr) Upper West Side office open to general public. Recommended for reasonably priced travel immunizations; offers expert consultation as well.

New York University Langone Medical Center (☎212-263-7300; 550 First Ave; ⏲24hr)

Travel MD (☎212-737-1212; www.travelmd.com) A 24-hour house-call service for travelers and residents.

Telephone

There are thousands of pay telephones lining the streets, but many are out of order. Manhattan's telephone area codes are ☎212, ☎646, ☎917 and the newest ☎929; in the four other boroughs they're ☎718 and ☎347. You must dial 1 + the area code, even if you're calling from a borough that uses the same one you're calling to.

The city's wonderful ☎311 service allows you to dial from anywhere within the city for info or help with any city agency, from the parking-ticket bureau to the noise complaint department.

Tourist Information

New York City & Company (Map p76; ☎212-484-1222; www.nycgo.com; 810 Seventh Ave, at 53rd St; ⏲8:30am-6pm Mon-Fri, 9am-5pm Sat & Sun) The official information service of the Convention & Visitors Bureau, it has helpful multilingual staff. Other branches include Chinatown (Map p66; cnr Canal, Walker & Baxter Sts; ⏲10am-6pm Mon-Fri, to 7pm Sat); Harlem (Map p84; 144 W 125th St btwn Adam Clayton Powell & Malcolm X Blvds; ⏲noon-6pm Mon-Fri, 10am-6pm Sat & Sun); Lower Manhattan (Map p66; City Hall Park at Broadway; ⏲9am-6pm Mon-Fri, 10am-5pm Sat & Sun); Times Square (Map p76; 1560 Broadway, btwn 46th & 47th Sts; ⏲8am-8pm Mon-Sun).

ℹ Getting There & Away

Air

Three major airports serve New York City. The biggest is **John F Kennedy International Airport** (JFK; www.panynj.gov/aviation/jfk frame), in the borough of Queens, which is also home to **La Guardia Airport** (LGA; www.panynj.gov/aviation/lgaframe). **Newark Liberty International Airport** (EWR; www.panynj.com), across the Hudson River in Newark, NJ, is another option. While using online booking websites, search 'NYC' rather than a specific airport, which will allow most sites to search all three spots at once. **Long Island MacArthur Airport** (ISP; www.macarthurairport.com), in Islip, is a money-saving (though time-consuming) alternative, but may make sense if a visit to the Hamptons or other parts of Long Island are in your plans.

Bus

The massive and confusing **Port Authority Bus Terminal** (Map p76; 625 Eighth Ave, btwn 40th & 42nd St) is the gateway for buses into and out of Manhattan. **Short Line** (www.shortlinebus.com) runs numerous buses to towns in northern New Jersey and upstate New York, while **New Jersey Transit** (www.njtransit.state.nj.us) buses serve all of New Jersey.

A number of comfortable and reliably safe bus companies with midtown locations, including **Bolt Bus** (www.boltbus.com) and **Megabus** (www.megabus.com), link NYC to Philadelphia ($10, two hours), Boston ($25, four hours 15 minutes) and Washington, DC ($25, four hours 30 minutes); most offer free wi-fi. Those bus companies running from Chinatown have seriously spotty safety records.

Car & Motorcycle

See p1174 for information about vehicle rentals. Note that renting a car in the city is expensive, starting at about $75 a day for a midsize car – before extra charges like the 13.25% tax and various insurance costs.

Ferry

Seastreak (www.seastreak.com; round-trip $43) to Sandy Hook, New Jersey and **New York Waterway** (www.nywaterway.com) leave from Pier 11 on the East River near Wall St and the World Financial Center on the Hudson for Hoboken, Jersey City and other destinations.

Train

Penn Station (Map p76; 33rd St, btwn Seventh & Eighth Aves), not to be confused with the Penn Station in Newark, NJ, is the departure point for all **Amtrak** (www.amtrak.com) trains, including the speedy Acela Express service to Boston (three hours 45 minutes) and Washington, DC (two hours 52 minutes). All fares and durations vary based on the day of the week and the time of day you want to travel. Also arriving into Penn Station (NYC), as well as points in Brooklyn and Queens, is the **Long Island Rail Road** (LIRR; www.mta.nyc.ny.us/lirr), which serves several hundred-thousand commuters each day. **New Jersey Transit** (www.njtransit.com) also operates trains from Penn Station (NYC), with services to the suburbs and the Jersey Shore. Another option for getting into New Jersey, but strictly to points north of the city such as Hoboken and Newark, is the **New Jersey PATH** (www.pathrail.com), which runs trains on a separate-fare system ($1.75) along the length of Sixth Ave, with stops at 34th, 23rd, 14th, 9th and Christopher Sts, and the reopened World Trade Center station.

The only train line that still departs from Grand Central Station, Park Ave at 42nd St, is the **Metro-North Railroad** (www.mnr.org), which serves the northern city suburbs, Connecticut and locations throughout the Hudson Valley.

ℹ Getting Around

To & From the Airport

All major airports have on-site car-rental agencies. It's a hassle to drive into NYC, though, and many folks take taxis, shelling out the $45 taxi flat rate (plus toll and tip) from JFK and Newark or a metered fare of about $35 to Midtown from La Guardia.

A cheaper and pretty easy option to/from JFK is the **AirTrain** ($5 one way), which connects to subway lines into the city ($2.25; coming from the city, take the Far Rockaway-bound A train) or to the LIRR (about $7 one way) at Jamaica Station in Queens (this is probably the quickest route to Penn Station in the city).

To/from Newark, the AirTrain links all terminals to a New Jersey Transit train station, which connects to Penn Station in NYC ($12.50 one way combined NJ Transit/Airtrain ticket).

For La Guardia, a reliable option to consider if you allow plenty of time is the M60 bus ($2.25), which heads to/from Manhattan across 125th St in Harlem and makes stops along Broadway on the Upper West Side.

All three airports are also served by express buses ($12 to $15) and shuttle vans ($20); such companies include the **New York Airport Service Express Bus** (www.nyairportservice.com), which leaves every 15 minutes for Port Authority, Penn Station (NYC) and Grand Central Station; and **Super Shuttle Manhattan** (www.supershuttle.com), which picks you (and others) up anywhere, on demand, with a reservation.

Car & Motorcycle

Even for the most spiritually centered, road rage is an inevitable byproduct of driving within the city. Traffic is a perpetual problem and topic of conversation.

If you are driving out or in, however, know that the worst part is joining the masses as they try to squeeze through tunnels and over bridges to traverse the various waterways that surround Manhattan. Be aware of local laws, such as the fact that you can't make a right on red (like you can in the rest of the state) and also the fact that every other street is one way.

Ferry

An East River ferry service (one way $4, every 20 minutes) connecting spots in Brooklyn (Greenpoint, North and South Williamsburg and Dumbo) and Queens (Long Island City) with Manhattan (Pier 11 at Wall St and E 34th St) was inaugurated in June 2011.

Public Transportation

The **Metropolitan Transport Authority** (MTA; www.mta.info) runs both the subway and bus systems. Depending on the train line, time of day and whether the door slams in your face or not, New York City's 100-year-old round-the-clock subway system (per ride $2.25) is your best friend or worst enemy. The 656-mile system can be intimidating at first, but regardless of its faults it's an incredible resource and achievement, linking the most disparate neighborhoods in a continually pulsating network. Maps should be available for the taking at every stop. To board, you must purchase a MetroCard, available at windows and self-serve machines, which accept change, dollars or credit/debit cards; purchasing many rides at once works out cheaper per trip.

If you're not in a big hurry, consider taking the bus (per ride $2.25). You get to see the world go by, they run 24/7 and they're easy to navigate – going crosstown at all the major street byways (14th, 23rd, 34th, 42nd, 72nd Sts and all the others that are two-way roads) and uptown or downtown, depending which avenue they serve. You can pay with a MetroCard or exact change but not bills. Transfers from one line to another are free, as are transfers to or from the subway.

Taxi

The classic NYC yellow cab is no longer a boxy gas-guzzling behemoth but rather a streamlined hybrid model, outfitted with mini-TVs and credit-card machines. No matter the make or year of the car, however, expect a herky-jerky, somewhat out-of-control ride. Current fares are $2.50 for the initial charge (first one-fifth mile), 40¢ each additional one-fifth mile, as well as per 60 seconds of being stopped in traffic, $1 peak surcharge (weekdays 4pm to 8pm), and 50¢ night surcharge (8pm to 6am daily). Tips are expected to be 10% to 15%; minivan cabs can hold five to six passengers. You can only hail a cab that has a lit light on its roof. Also know that it can be difficult to score a taxi in the rain, at rush hour and at around 4pm, when many drivers end their shifts.

Pedicabs – human-powered taxis, basically cycle rickshaws – roam around Central Park South and other heavily touristy areas. Rides cost around $10 to $20 but fares are negotiable.

NEW YORK STATE

There's upstate and downstate and never the twain shall meet. The two have about as much in common as NYC's Upper East Side and the Bronx. And yet everyone shares the same governor and dysfunctional legislature in the capital, Albany. While this incompatibility produces legislative gridlock and downright operatic drama, it's a blessing for those who cherish quiet and pastoral idylls as much as Lower East Side bars and the subway. Defined largely by its inland waterways – the Hudson River, the 524-mile Erie Canal connecting Albany to Buffalo, and the St Lawrence River – New York stretches to the Canadian border at world-famous Niagara Falls and under-the-radar Thousand Islands. Buffalo is a cheap foodies' paradise and wine aficionados can pick their favorite vintage from around the state, but especially in the Finger Lakes region close to the college town of Ithaca. From wilderness trails with backcountry camping to small-town Americana and miles and miles of sandy beaches, from the historic, grand estates and artists colonies in the Hudson Valley and Catskills to the rugged and remote Adirondacks, it's easy to understand why so many people leave the city, never to return.

Information

New York State Office of Parks, Recreation and Historic Preservation (☎518-474-0456, 800-456-2267; www.nysparks.com) Camping,

NEW YORK FACTS

» **Nicknames** Empire State, Excelsior State, Knickerbocker State

» **Population** 19.5 million

» **Area** 47,214 sq miles

» **Capital city** Albany (population 94,000)

» **Other cities** Buffalo (population 261,000)

» **Sales tax** 4%, plus additional county and state taxes (total approximately 8%)

» **Birthplace of** Poet Walt Whitman (1819–92), President Theodore Roosevelt (1858–1919), President Franklin D Roosevelt (1882–1945), first lady Eleanor Roosevelt (1884–1962), painter Edward Hopper (1882–1967), movie star Humphrey Bogart (1899–1957), comic Lucille Ball (1911–89), filmmaker Woody Allen (b 1935), actor Tom Cruise (b 1962), pro athlete Michael Jordan (b 1963), pop star Jennifer Lopez (b 1969)

» **Home of** Six Nations of the Iroquois Confederacy, first US cattle ranch (1747, in Montauk, Long Island), US women's suffrage movement (1872), Erie Canal (1825)

» **Politics** popular Democratic governor Mario Cuomo, NYC overwhelmingly Democratic, upstate more conservative

» **Famous for** Niagara Falls (half of it), the Hamptons, Cornell University, Hudson River

» **Unusual river** Genesee River is one of the few rivers in the world that flows south–north, from south central New York into Lake Ontario at Rochester

» **Driving distances** NYC to Albany 160 miles, NYC to Buffalo 375 miles

lodging and general info on all state parks. Reservations can be made up to nine months in advance.

511 New York: Traffic, Travel & Transit Info (www.511ny.org) Weather advisories, road information and more.

Uncork New York (☎585-394-3620; www.newyorkwines.org) One-stop shop for statewide wine info.

Long Island

Private-school blazers, nightmare commutes, strip malls colonized by national chains, cookie-cutter suburbia, moneyed resorts, windswept dunes and magnificent beaches – and those accents. Long Island, a long peninsula contiguous with the boroughs of Brooklyn and Queens, has all of these things, which explains its somewhat complicated reputation. The site of small European whaling and fishing ports from as early as 1640, Levittown, just 25 miles east of Manhattan in Nassau County, is where builders first perfected the art of mass-producing homes. But visions of suburban dystopia aside, Long Island has wide ocean and bay beaches, important historic sites, renowned vineyards, rural regions and of course the Hamptons, in all their luxuriously sunbaked glory.

NORTH SHORE

Outside the suburban town of Port Washington, **Sands Point Preserve** (☎516-571-7900; www.sandspointpreserve.org; 127 Middleneck Rd; admission per car $5, free Thu; ⏲9am-4:30pm) includes forested trails and a beautiful sandy bayfront beach worth a stroll; it's also home to the 1923 **Falaise** (admission $6; ⏲tours hourly noon-3pm Thu-Sun Jun-Oct), one of the few remaining Gold Coast mansions and now a museum. East of there is the bucolic town of Oyster Bay, home to **Sagamore Hill** (☎516-922-4788; www.nps.gov/sahi; adult/child $5/free; ⏲10am-4pm Wed-Sun), where Theodore Roosevelt vacationed during his presidency. Spring and summer months mean long waits for guided tours. A nature trail leading from behind the excellent **museum** (admission free) ends at a picturesque waterfront beach.

SOUTH SHORE

Despite the periodic roar of over-flying jets, **Long Beach**, the closest beach to the city and most accessible by train, has a main town strip with ice-cream shops, bars and eateries, a lively surfers' scene and pale trendy city types mixing with suntanned locals.

On summer weekends the mob scene on the 6-mile stretch of pretty **Jones Beach** is a microcosm of the city's diversity, attracting surfers, wild city folk, local teens, nudists, staid families, gay and lesbian people and plenty of old-timers. The Long Island Rail Road (LIRR) service to Wantagh has a bus connection to Jones Beach.

Further east, just off the southern shore, is a separate barrier island. **Fire Island** includes **Fire Island National Seashore** (☎631-289-4810; www.nps.gov) and several summer-only villages accessible by ferry from Long Island. The Fire Island Pines and Cherry Grove (both car-free) comprise a historic, gay bacchanalia that attracts men and women in droves from New York City, while villages on the west end cater to straight singles and families. There are limited places to stay, and booking in advance is strongly advised (check www.fireisland.com for accommodations information). Beach camping is allowed in **Watch Hill** (☎631-567-6664; www.watchhillfi.com; campsites $25; ⏲early May-late Oct), though mosquitoes can be fierce and reservations are a must. At the western end of Fire Island, **Robert Moses State Park** is the only spot accessible by car. **Fire Island Ferries** (☎631-665-3600; www.fireislandferries.com) runs services to Fire Island beaches and the national seashore; the terminals are close to LIRR stations at Bayshore, Sayville and Patchogue (round-trip adult/child $17/7.50, May to November).

THE HAMPTONS

Attitudes about the Hamptons are about as varied as the number of Maseratis and Land Rovers cruising the perfectly landscaped streets, however no amount of attitudinizing can detract from the sheer beauty of the beaches and what's left of the picturesque farms and woodland. If you can bury the envy, a pleasurable day of sightseeing can be had simply driving past the homes of the extravagantly wealthy, ranging from cutting-edge modernist to faux-castle monstrosities. However, many summertime residents are partying the weekends away in much more modest group rentals and at the revolving doors of clubs. While each Hampton is not geographically far from every other, traffic can be a nightmare. Check out long-time

Hamptons resident and publisher of local paper Dan Rattiner's *In the Hamptons* for stories of the area's famous characters.

Southampton

Though the village of Southampton appears blemish-free as if it has been Botoxed, it gets a face-lift at night when raucous clubgoers let their hair down. Its beaches – only Coopers Beach (per day $40) and Road D (free) offer parking to non-residents May 31 to Sep 15 – are sweeping and gorgeous, and the **Parrish Art Museum** (☎631-283-2118; www.parrishart.org; 25 Jobs Lane; adult/child $5/3; ⏲11am-5pm, daily Jun–mid-Sep) is an impressive regional institution. At the edge of the village is a small Native American reservation, home to the Shinnecock Nation, which runs a tiny **museum** (☎631-287-4923; 45 Montauk Hwy; adult/child $5/3; ⏲11am-4pm Thu-Sat, from noon Sun); a decades-long effort to build a large casino on Shinnecock land continues to make its way through a jumble of legal and other obstacles. For a quick and reasonable meal try **Golden Pear** (99 Main St; sandwiches $9; ⏲7:30am- 5pm), which serves delicious soups, salads and wraps.

Bridgehampton & Sag Harbor

Moving east, Bridgehampton has a more modest-looking drag, but has its fair share of trendy boutiques and fine restaurants. The modest low-slung **Enclave Inn** (☎631-537-2900; www.enclaveinnn.com; 2668 Montauk Hwy; r from $99; ❄📶🚭), just a few blocks from the heart of the village, is one of the better value accommodation options; there are four other locations elsewhere in the Hamptons. Old-fashioned diner **Candy Kitchen** (☎646-537-9885; Main St; mains $5-12; ⏲7am-6pm) has a luncheonette counter serving filling breakfasts, burgers and sandwiches.

Seven miles north, on Peconic Bay, is the lovely old whaling town of Sag Harbor; ferries to Shelter Island leave a few miles north of here. Check out its **Whaling & Historical Museum** (☎631-725-0770; www.sagharborwhalingmuseum.org; adult/child $5/1; ⏲10am-5pm May-Oct), or simply stroll up and down its narrow, Cape Cod–like streets. Get gourmet sustenance at **Provisions** (☎631-725-3636; cnr Bay & Division Sts; sandwiches $9; ⏲8:30am-8pm), a natural foods market with delicious take-out wraps, burritos and sandwiches.

East Hampton

Don't be fooled by the oh-so-casual-looking summer attire, heavy on pastels and sweaters tied around the neck – the sunglasses alone are probably equal to a month's rent. Some of the highest profile boldface celebrities have homes here. Catch readings, theater and art exhibits at **Guild Hall** (☎631-324-0806; www.guildhall.org; 158 Main St). East of town on the way to Bridgehampton is the **Townline BBQ** (3593 Montauk Hwy; mains $9; ⏲11:30am-9pm Sun, Mon & Thu, to 10pm Fri & Sat), a down-to-earth roadside restaurant churning out smoky ribs and barbecue sandwiches. Just to the west toward Amagansett is **La Fondita** (74 Montauk Hwy; mains $9; ⏲11:30am-8pm Wed, Thu & Sun, to 9pm Fri & Sat), the place to go for reasonably priced Mexican fare. Nightclubs come and go with the seasons. A word to the wise: strike the phrase 'bottle service' from your vocabulary.

Montauk & Around

More Jersey Shore, less polo club, Montauk is the humble stepsister of the Hamptons, though its beaches are equally beautiful. There's a slew of relatively reasonable restaurants and a louder bar scene. At the very eastern, wind-whipped tip of the South Fork is **Montauk Point State Park**, with its impressive, 1796 **Montauk Point Lighthouse** (www.montauklighthouse.com; adult/child $9/4; ⏲10:30am-5:30pm, hours vary), the fourth oldest still-active lighthouse in the US. You can camp a few miles west of town at the dune-swept **Hither Hills State Park** (☎631-668-2554; www.nysparks.com; New York residents/nonresidents Mon-Fri $28/56, higher prices Sat & Sun; ⏲Apr-Nov), right on the beach; just reserve early during summer months. Several miles to the north is the Montauk harbor, with dockside restaurants and hundreds of boats in the marinas.

You'll find a string of standard motels near the entrance to the town beach, including the **Ocean Resort Inn** (☎631-668-2300; www.oceanresortinn.com; 96 S Emerson Ave; r $105-165; ❄📶). A few miles west, just across the street from the beach, is **Sunrise Guesthouse** (☎631-668-7286; www.sunrisebnb.com; 681 Old Montauk Hwy; r $115-145; ❄), a modest and comfortable B&B.

Two great places to wind down the day (from May to October) with drinks and hearty, fresh seafood are the roadside restaurants **Clam Bar** (2025 Montauk Hwy; mains 7-$22; ⏲noon-8pm) and **Lobster Roll** (1980 Montauk Hwy; mains $11-26; ⏲11:30am-9:30pm) aka 'Lunch', now in its fifth decade, both on the highway between Amagansett and Montauk.

NORTH FORK & SHELTER ISLAND

Mainly, the North Fork is known for its unspoiled farmland and wineries – there are close to 30 vineyards, clustered mainly around the towns of Jamesport, Cutchogue and Southold – and the **Long Island Wine Council** (☎631-722-2220; www.liwines.com) provides details of the local wine trail, which runs along Rte 25 north of Peconic Bay. One of the nicer outdoor settings for a tasting is the **Peconic Bay Winery** (☎631-734-7361; www.peconicbaywinery.com; 31320 Main Rd/Rte 25, Cutchogue); this also means it's popular with bus and limo-loads of partiers. Beforehand, stop at popular **Love Lane Kitchen** (240 Love Lane; mains $10; ⏲7am-9:30pm, to 6pm Mon-Tue) in Matituck for a meal, especially weekend brunch.

The main North Fork town and the place for ferries to Shelter Island, **Greenport** is a charming laid-back place lined with restaurants and cafes, including family-owned **Claudio's Clam Bar** (111 Main St; mains $15; ⏲11:30am-9pm) with a wraparound deck perched over the marina. Or grab sandwiches and a cupcake at **Butta' Cakes Café** (119 Main St; sandwiches $9; ⏲8am-9:30pm) for a picnic at the **Harbor Front Park** where you can take a spin on the historic carousel.

Between the North and South Forks, **Shelter Island**, accessible by ferry from North Haven to the south and Greenport to the north (vehicle and driver $9, 10 minutes, every 15 to 20 minutes), is a low-key microcosm of beautiful Hamptons real estate and the **Mashomack Nature Preserve** (☎631-749-1001; www.nature.org/mashomack; ⏲9am-5pm, closed Tue except Jul & Aug) covering over 2000 acres of the southern part of the island. It's a great spot for hiking or kayaking (no cycling).

On Shelter Island, just down the road from **Crescent Beach** and nestled on a prime piece of property surrounded by woods fronting the bay, **Pridwin Beach Hotel & Cottages** (☎631-749-0476; www.pridwin.com; r & cottages from $159-199; P ❄ 📶) has standard hotel rooms as well as private water-view cottages, some in high-designer style.

ℹ Getting There & Around

The most direct driving route is along the I-495, aka the LIE (Long Island Expwy), though be sure to avoid rush hour, when it's commuter hell. Once in the Hamptons, there is one main road to the end, Montauk Hwy. The **Long Island Rail Road** (LIRR; www.mta.nyc.ny.us/lirr) serves all regions of Long Island, including the Hamptons ($25 one way, two hours 45 minutes), from Penn Station (NYC), Brooklyn and Queens. The **Hampton Jitney** (www.hamptonjitney.com; one way Tue-Thu $26, Fri-Mon $30) and **Hampton Luxury Liner** (www.hamptonluxuryliner.com; one way $40) bus services connect Manhattan's midtown and Upper East Side to various Hamptons villages; the former also has services to/from various spots in Brooklyn.

Hudson Valley

Immediately north of New York City, green becomes the dominant color and the vistas of the Hudson River and the mountains breathe life into your urban-weary body. The region was home to the Hudson River School of painting in the 19th century and its history is preserved in the many grand estates and picturesque villages. The Lower Valley and Middle Valley are more populated and suburban, while the Upper Valley has a rural feel, with hills leading into the Catskills mountain region. For area-wide information, check out the **Hudson Valley Network** (www.hvnet.com).

LOWER HUDSON VALLEY

A pristine forested wilderness with miles of hiking trails is available just 40 miles north of New York City: **Harriman State Park** (☎845-786-2701) covers 72 sq miles and offers swimming, hiking and camping; adjacent **Bear Mountain State Park** (☎845-786-2701; ⏲8am-dusk) offers great views from its 1305ft peak, with the Manhattan skyline looming beyond the river and surrounding greenery; and there's a restaurant and lodging at the inn on Hessian Lake. In both parks there are several scenic roads snaking their way past secluded lakes with gorgeous vistas.

Several magnificent homes and gardens can be found near Tarrytown and Sleepy Hollow, on the east side of the Hudson. **Kykuit**, one of the properties of the Rockefeller family, has an impressive array of Asian and European artwork and immaculately kept gardens with breathtaking views. **Lyndhurst** is the estate of railroad tycoon Jay Gould and **Sunnyside** is the home of author Washington Irving. Go to the **Historic Hudson Valley** (www.hudsonvalley.org) website for info on these and other historic attractions.

West of Rte 9W and 50 miles north of New York City, the **Storm King Art Center** (☎845-534-3115; www.stormking.org; Old Pleasant

Rd, Mountainville; adult/child $12/free; ⏲10am-5:30pm Wed-Sun Apr-Nov) is a 500-acre outdoor sculpture park with rolling hills that showcases stunning avant-garde sculpture by well-known artists; a free tram gives tours of the grounds. Nearby **West Point** (☎845-938-2638; ⏲9am-5pm), open to visitors on **guided tours** (☎845-446-4724; www.westpointtours.com; adult/child $12/9), was a strategic fort before becoming the US Military Academy in 1802. Not far from here, the large, strip mall filled town of Newburgh is the site of **Washington's Headquarters State Historic Site** (☎845-562-1195; Liberty St, at Washington St; donations accepted; ⏲10am-5pm Wed-Sat, from 1pm Sun, Apr-Oct), General George's longest-lasting base during the Revolutionary War; there's a museum, galleries and maps.

Across the river, near the town of Cold Spring, the **Hudson Valley Shakespeare Festival** (☎845-265-9575; www.hvshakespeare.org) takes place between mid-June and early September, staging impressive open-air productions at the Boscobel estate, a magnificent piece of property.

At Beacon, a fairly nondescript town east of Rte 9W, fashionable regulars of the international art scene stop for **Dia Beacon** (☎845-440-0100; www.diaart.org; adult/child $10/free; ⏲11am-6pm Thu-Mon mid-Apr–mid-Oct, call for other hr), which features a renowned collection from 1960 to the present, and enormous sculptures and installation pieces.

MIDDLE & UPPER HUDSON VALLEY

On the western side of the Hudson is **New Paltz**, home of a campus of the State University of New York, natural food stores and a liberal ecofriendly vibe. In the distance behind the town the ridge of the Shawangunk (Shon-gum or just the 'Gunks') mountains rises more than 2000ft above sea level. More than two-dozen miles of nature trails and some of the best rock climbing in the Eastern US is found in the **Mohonk Mountain Preserve** (☎845-255-0919; www.mohonkpreserve.org; day pass for hikers/climbers & cyclists $12/17). Nearby **Minnewaska State Park Preserve** has 12,000 acres of wild landscape, the centerpiece of which is a usually ice-cold mountain lake. Contact **Alpine Adventures** (☎877-486-5769; www.alpineendeavors.com) for climbing instruction and equipment.

The iconic **Mohonk Mountain House** (☎845-255-1000; www.mohonk.com; 1000 Mountain Rest Rd; r $320-2500; ❄📶🏊) looks like it's straight out of a fairy tale: a rustic castle perched magnificently over a dark lake. It's an all-inclusive resort where guests can gorge on elaborate five-course meals, stroll through gardens, hike miles of trails, canoe, swim etc. A luxury spa center is there to work out the kinks. Nonovernight guests can visit the grounds (adult/child per day $25/20, less on weekdays) – well worth the price of admission.

On the eastern side of the river is **Hudson** – a beautiful town with a hip, gay-friendly community of artists, writers and performers who fled the city. Warren St, the main roadway through town, is lined with antiques shops, high-end furniture stores, galleries and cafes. A historic Greek Revival home c 1830, the **Union Street Guest House** (☎518-828-0958; www.unionstreetguesthouse; 345-349 Union St; r from $125; ❄📶) has been transformed into a cozy boutique-style inn.

Further south is **Rhinebeck**, with a charming main street, inns, farms and wineries. There's also an **Aerodrome Museum** (☎845-752-3200; www.oldrhinebeck.org; ⏲10am-5pm mid-Jun–mid-Oct) and the destination bistro, worth the trip in itself, **Terrapin** (☎845-876-3330; 6426 Montgomery St; lunch sandwiches $7, dinner mains from $19; ⏲11:30am-11:30pm). Another good choice is the **Bread Alone Bakery** (45 E Market St; mains $9; ⏲7am-7pm, 8am-3pm), which serves lunch specialties like a brisket panini and spinach and feta quiche.

Just south of Rhinebeck is **Hyde Park**, long associated with the Roosevelts, a prominent family since the 19th century. The estate of 1520 acres, formerly a working farm, includes the **Franklin D Roosevelt Library & Museum** (☎800-337-8474; www.fdrlibrary.marist.edu; 511 Albany Post Rd/Rte 9; admission $14; ⏲9am-6pm May-Oct, to 5pm Nov-Apr), which details important achievements in FDR's presidency; a visit usually includes a guided tour of FDR's lifelong home where he delivered his fireside chats. First Lady Eleanor Roosevelt's peaceful cottage, **Val-Kill** (☎877-444-6777; www.nps.gov/elro; admission $8; ⏲9am-5pm), was her retreat from Hyde Park, FDR's mother and FDR himself. Across the street from the entrance to the library and museum is the **Hyde Park Drive-In Movie Theater** (☎845-229-4738; 4114 Albany Post Rd/Rte 9). Just north of here is the 54-room **Vanderbilt Mansion** (☎877-559-6777; www.nps.gov/vama; Rte 9; admission $8; ⏲9am-5pm), a Gilded Age spectacle of lavish beaux-arts design; nearly all of the original furnishings imported from European castles and villas remain in this country house – the smallest of any of the Vanderbilt family's! Hudson River views are best from the gardens and the Bard Rock trail on the property.

Hyde Park's famous **Culinary Institute of America** (☎845-471-6608; www.ciachef.edu; 1964 Campus Dr) trains future chefs and can satisfy absolutely anyone's gastronomic cravings; the **Apple Pie Café** (mains $10; ⏲7:30am-5pm), one of the student-staffed eateries looks out onto a tranquil courtyard and serves up gourmet sandwiches as well as specialty pastries (these go fast and the selection is slim at the end of the day). If you're between tours in Hyde Park, the **Eveready Diner** (4189 Albany Post Rd/Rte 9; mains $10; ⏲5am-1am Sun-Thu, 24hr Fri & Sat), a modernized version of the classic soda fountain restaurant might be more convenient.

A little further south of here is **Poughkeepsie** (puh-*kip*-see), the largest town on the Hudson's east bank famous for **Vassar**, a private liberal-arts college that until 1969 only admitted women. Worth a stroll for its breathtaking views is the **Walkway Over the Hudson** (www.walkway.org; ⏲7am-sunset); formerly the Highland-Poughkeepsie railroad bridge and since 2009 the world's longest pedestrian bridge and the state's newest park. Cheap motel chains are clustered along Rte 9, south of the Mid-Hudson Bridge, but try the **Copper Penny Inn** (☎845-452-3045; www.copperpennyinn.com; 2406 Hackensack Rd; r incl breakfast $140-230; ❄), a charming and cheerful B&B set on 12 wooded acres.

Catskills

The introduction of fine cuisine and cute boutiques has yet to overwhelm the pastoral atmosphere and small-town charm of the Catskills. For some out-of-staters this bucolic region of undulating, forest-covered mountains and picturesque farmland is still synonymous with Borscht-belt family resorts. However, that era is long past, and after some economically tough times the Catskills, though having a lower profile than the Hamptons, have become a popular choice for sophisticated city dwellers seeking second-home getaways.

WOODSTOCK & AROUND

Shorthand for free love, free expression and the political ferment of the 1960s, world-famous **Woodstock** today still wears its counterculture tie-dye in the form of healing centers, art galleries, cafes and an eclectic mix of aging hippies and young Phish-fan types. The famous 1969 Woodstock music festival, though, actually occurred in Bethel, a town over 40 miles southwest. Overlooking Woodstock's town square, actually in front of the bus stop, is the **Village Green B&B** (☎845-679-0313; 12 Tinker St; r incl breakfast $135; ❄📶), a three-story Victorian with comfortable rooms. Housed in an elegantly-restored farmhouse half a mile southeast of the town square, **Cucina** (☎845-679-9800; 109 Mill Hill Rd; mains $18; ⏲5am-late, from 11am Sat & Sun) does sophisticated seasonal Italian fare and thin crust pizzas.

Saugerties, just 7 miles east of Woodstock, is not nearly as quaint and feels by comparison like the big city, but the **Saugerties Lighthouse** (☎845-247-0656; www.saugertieslighthouse.com; r incl breakfast $200; ⏲Thu-Sun, closed Feb) offers a truly romantic and unique place to lay your head. The picturesque 1869 landmark is located on a small island in the Esopus Creek, accessible by boat or more commonly by a half-mile-long trail from the parking lot. Rooms are booked far in advance but a walk to the lighthouse is highly recommended regardless.

Having a car is near essential in these parts. **Adirondack Trailways** (www.trailwaysny.com) operates daily buses from NYC to Kingston (one way $25, two hours), the Catskills' gateway town, as well as to Catskills and Woodstock (one way $27, two hours 30 minutes). Buses leave from NYC's Port Authority. The commuter rail line **Metro-North** (www.mta.info/mnr) makes stops through the Lower and Middle Hudson Valleys.

Finger Lakes Region

A bird's-eye view of this region of rolling hills and 11 long narrow lakes – the eponymous fingers – reveals an outdoor paradise stretching all the way from Albany to far-western New York. Of course there's boating, fishing, cycling, hiking and cross-country skiing, but this is also the state's premier wine-growing region, with more than 65 vineyards, enough for the most discerning oenophile.

SCENIC DRIVE: ROUTE 28 & AROUND

One sign that you've crossed into the Catskills is when the unending asphalt gives way to dense greenery crowding the snaking roadway as you exit the I-87 and turn onto Rte 28. As you drive through the heart of the region, the vistas open up and the mountains (around 35 peaks are above 3500ft) take on stunning coloring depending on the season and time of day. Esopus Creek winds its way through the area and **Ashokan Reservoir** is a nice place for a walk or drive.

Emerson Spa Resort (877-688-2828; www.emersonresort.com; 5340 Rte 28, Mt Tremper; r at lodge/inn from $159/199;) offers a full-service base for Catskills adventures whatever time of year. From luxurious Asian-inspired suites to rustic-chic rooms in the log-cabin-style lodge, Emerson aims to please; staff can help arrange trips from skiing to kayaking. The Phoenix restaurant (mains $15 to $30) is probably the best in the region and the Catamount, popular with locals, has pub fare (mains $10) including burgers and BBQ ribs and live music and dancing Monday nights. The world's largest kaleidoscope and kaleidoscope boutique, selling sculpture quality pieces, is attached, as well as a coffee-sandwich shop.

Only a few miles further west is the one-lane town of **Phoenicia**. It's a pleasant place to stop for a meal and a tube – **Town Tinker Tube Rental** (845-688-5553; www.towntinker.com; 10 Bridge St; tubes per day $15) can hook you up for repeated forays down the Esopus rapids. The refreshing water of Pine Hill Lake at nearby **Belleayre Beach** (845-254-5600; www.belleayre.com;) is the summertime place to cool off (or ski in the winter). Continuing on Rte 28 takes you past the town of Fleischmann's, where you can stop for the night at the **River Run B&B** (845-254-4884; www.riverrunbedandbreakfast.com; 882 Main St; r from $89-135;), a professionally run Victorian inn.

In nearby Arkville, you can take a scenic ride on the historic **Delaware & Ulster Rail Line** (845-586-3877; www.durr.org; Hwy 28; adult/child $12/7; 11am & 2pm, Sat & Sun Jun-Nov, additional trips Thu & Fri Jul-Sep;). In the winter, skiers should head further north, where Rtes 23 and 23A lead you to **Hunter Mountain Ski Bowl** (518-263-4223; www.huntermtn.com), a year-round resort with challenging runs and a 1600ft vertical drop.

From here you can carry on to the **Roxbury** (607-326-7200; www.theroxburymotel.com; 2258 County Hwy 41; r $100-335;), in the tiny village of the same name, a wonderfully creative gem of a place with luxuriously designed and whimsically named rooms, each inspired by a particular '60s- or '70s-era TV show; a spa is attached and a cool cocktail lounge is across the street (open Wednesday to Sunday).

West of Roxbury is the 26-mile-long **Catskill Scenic Trail** (a good map is available at www.catskillscenictrail.org), a mostly flat path built on top of a former rail bed, ideal for cycling, hiking and cross-country skiing in the winter. For rougher hikes through dense forest, the **Utsayantha Trail System** intersects at several points around the town of Stamford.

ITHACA & AROUND

An idyllic home for college students and older generations of hippies who cherish elements of the traditional collegiate lifestyle – laid-back vibe, cafe poetry readings, art-house cinemas, green quads, good eats – Ithaca is perched above Cayuga Lake. Besides being a destination in itself, it is also a convenient halfway point between New York City and Niagara Falls. For tourist information, head to the **Visit Ithaca Information Center** (607-272-1313; www.visitithaca.com; 904 E Shore Dr; 9am-5pm Mon-Fri, from 10am Sat).

Founded in 1865, **Cornell University** boasts a lovely campus, mixing traditional and contemporary architecture, and sits high on a hill overlooking the picturesque town below. The modern **Herbert F Johnson Museum of Fine Art** (607-255-6464; www.museum.cornell.edu; University Ave; admission free; 10am-5pm Tue- Sun), designed by IM Pei, has a major Asian collection, plus pre-Columbian, American and European exhibits. Just east of the center of the campus is **Cornell Plantations** (607-255-2400; www.cornellplantations.org; Plantations Rd; admission free; dawn-dusk), an expertly curated herb and flower garden, arboretum. Kids can go interactive-wild at the extremely hands-on **Sciencenter** (☎607-272-0600; www.sciencecenter.org; 601 First St; adult/child $7/5; ⏰10am-5pm Tue-Sat, from noon Sun; 👪). On several weekends from July through August Tony Simons, a professor at Cornell's School of Hotel Administration turns his attention to teaching beginners how to **firewalk** (www.ithacafirewalks.com; per person $75) – in the very least it's an exercise in motivation.

The area around Ithaca is known for its waterfalls, gorges and gorgeous parks. However, downtown has its very own, **Cascadilla Gorge**, starting several blocks from Ithaca Commons and ending, after a steep and stunning vertical climb, at the Performing Arts Center of Cornell. Eight miles north on Rte 89, the spectacular **Taughannock Falls** spills 215ft into the steep gorge below; **Taughannock Falls State Park** (☎607-387-6739; www.taughannock.com; Rte 89) has two major hiking trails, craggy gorges, tent-trailer sites and cabins. **Buttermilk Falls Park** (☎summer 607-273-5761, winter 607-273-3440; Rte 13) has a popular swimming hole at the foot of the falls, as does **Robert Treman Park** (☎607-273-3440; 105 Enfield Falls Rd), a few miles further out of town. **Filmore Glen Park** (☎315-497-0130; 1686 Rte 38) 20 miles to the northeast of Ithaca outside the town of Moravia offers more wooded hiking trails.

Dozens of wineries line the shores of Cayuga Lake, Lake Seneca and Lake Keuka. Two recommended Cayuga Lake wineries are **Sheldrake Point** (☎607-532-9401; www.sheldrakeppoint.com; 7448 County Rd), which has lake views and award-winning whites and **Americana Vineyards** (☎607-387-6801; www.americanavineyards.com; 4367 E Covert Rd) whose **Crystal Lake Café** (mains $11; ⏰noon-8pm Thu-Sun) farm-to-table menu is highly recommended by locals. Also on Rte 89 near the village of Interlaken is the **Creamery** (⏰11am-8pm), a roadside restaurant that in addition to conventional ice-cream sundaes serves buzz-inducing wine-infused sorbet ($4).

Around 44 miles to the southwest is the charming town of Corning, home to Corning Glass Works and the hugely popular **Corning Museum of Glass** (☎800-732-6845; www.cmog.org; adult/child $14/free; ⏰9am-8pm; 👪). The massive complex is home to fascinating exhibits on glassmaking arts, complete with demonstrations and interactive items for kids.

Sleeping

TOP CHOICE William Henry Miller Inn B&B **$$**
(☎607-256-4553; www.millerinn.com; 303 N Aurora St, Ithaca; r incl breakfast $115-215; ❄📶) Gracious and grand, only a few steps from the commons, is a completely restored historic home with luxuriously designed rooms – three have Jacuzzis – and a gourmet breakfast.

Inn on Columbia INN **$$**
(☎607-272-0204; www.columbiabb.com; 228 Columbia St, Ithaca; d $150; ❄📶) Also recommended; a modern, contemporary home on a quiet residential street.

Climbing Vine Cottage HUT **$$**
(☎607-564-7410; www.climbingvinecottage.com; 257 Piper Rd, Newfield; d $150; ❄📶) Rather a fully furnished yurt with mod-cons in a beautifully landscaped garden setting off Rte 34 south of Ithaca.

Buttonwood Grove Winery CABIN **$$**
(☎607-869-9760; www.buttonwoodgrove.com; 5986 Rte 89; r $135) Has four fully furnished log cabins nestled in the hills above Lake Cayuga (open April to December); free wine tasting included.

Eating

A half-dozen restaurants, including Japanese, Middle Eastern, Mexican and Spanish tapas, with outdoor seating line North Aurora St between East State and East Seneca Sts at the east end of the Commons. Relatively upscale **Mercato** (108 N Aurora St; mains $20; ⏰5-9pm Mon-Thu, to 10pm Fri & Sat) is one of the best. **Ithaca's Farmers Market** (Third St; www.ithacamarket.com; ⏰Apr-Dec) is considered one of the region's best; local wines and cheeses are highlights; check the website for operating hours.

Glenwood Pines BURGERS **$**
(burgers $5; ⏰11am-9:30pm Sun-Thu, to 10:30pm Fri & Sat) According to locals in the know this modest roadside restaurant, overlooking Lake Cayuga on Rte 89 and 4 miles north of Ithaca, serves the best burger.

Moosewood Restaurant VEGETARIAN **$$**
(215 N Cayuga St; mains $8-18; ⏰11:30am-8:30pm) Famous for its creative and constantly changing vegetarian menu and recipe books by founder Mollie Katzen.

Yerba Maté Factor Café & Juice Bar SANDWICHES **$**
(143 The Commons; mains $8; ⏰9am-9pm Mon-Thu, to 3pm Fri, from noon Sun) Run by

members of a fairly obscure religious organization, this large restaurant, housed in a converted historic building on the Ithaca commons, is good for Belgian waffles, sandwiches and coffee.

Hazelnut Kitchen AMERICAN **$$**
(☎607-387-4433; 53 East Main St, Trumansburg; ⏱dinner only) The menu here is inspired by local ingredients and changes monthly. It is 12 miles north of Ithaca.

ℹ Getting There & Away

Shortline Bus (www.coachusa.com) has frequent departures to New York City ($53, four hours). Delta Airlines has direct flights from the **Ithaca Tompkins Regional Airport** (ITH; www.flyithaca.com) to Detroit, Newark and Philadelphia.

Capital Region

ALBANY

Synonymous with legislative dysfunction as much as legislative power, Albany (or 'Smallbany' to jaded locals) remains a tourism backwater. It became New York State's capital in 1797 because of its geographic centrality to local colonies and its strategic importance in the fur trade. Several blocks from the city center and the ostentatiously modern government buildings in the 98-acre Empire State Plaza, stately brownstones give way to derelict and neglected streets and a general feeling of malaise. **Lark St**, north and uphill of downtown, has several restaurants and bars popular with university students when school is in session.

East of the plaza is the **Albany Institute of History & Art** (☎518-463-4478; www.albanyinstitute.org; 125 Washington Ave; adult/child $10/6; ⏱10am-5pm Wed-Sat, noon-5pm Sun), which houses decorative arts and works by Hudson River School painters.

There are a handful of chain hotels downtown, however **74 State** (☎518-434-7410; www.74state.com; 74 State St; r incl breakfast from $180; ❄📶), a high-end boutique hotel in the heart of downtown is a better choice.

A number of restaurants are located along Pearl St and Lark St and a strip of bars and clubs on North Pearl St downtown gets hopping when workers spill out of the nearby government buildings. To experience Albany in all its elegant and back-room-dealing clubby glory try **Jack's Oyster House** (☎518-465-8854; 42 State St; mains $19-25; ⏱11:30am-10pm), serving porterhouse steaks and seafood with a French twist; its lunchtime menu has burgers and sandwiches ($10). **Albany Pump Station** (19 Quackenbush Sq; mains $12; ⏱11:30am-10pm) has its own microbrewery and large varied menu while **Justin's** (☎518-436-7008; www.justinsonlark.com; 301 Lark St; ⏱11am-1am) has live jazz every night of the week, dinner and drinks.

SARATOGA SPRINGS

When 'taking the waters' was equivalent to a trip to the hospital, this settlement north of Albany was world famous in its heyday in the early 1800s – Joseph Bonaparte, Napoleon's older brother and King of Spain, took his medicine here once. Despite the encroachment of large-scale retail chains, Saratoga Springs' main commercial street retains something of the artsy, laid-back feel of a college town and it's rightly famous for its performing arts, horse racing and the liberal-arts Skidmore College.

The only remaining bathhouse – the first was built in 1784 – is the **Roosevelt Baths and Spa** (☎866-925-0622; www.rooseveltbathsandspa.com; 40min spa $25; ⏱9am-7pm) in the 2300-acre **Saratoga Spa State Park** (☎518-584-2535; www.saratogaspastatepark.org; 19 Roosevelt Dr; per car $4; ⏱sunrise-sunset). The mineral- and gas-infused waters are pumped underground from Lincoln Springs over a mile away. These days very hot tap water is added to the mix, though purists insist on going cold. Park grounds include golf courses, picnic areas, an Olympic-sized pool complex, multiuse trails, ice rinks and world-famous **Saratoga Performing Arts Center** (☎518-587-3330; www.spac.org; 108 Ave of the Pines), with orchestra, jazz, pop, rock and dance performances. From late July to September, horse-racing fans flock to **Saratoga Race Course** (☎518-584-6200; www.saratogaracetrack.com; 267 Union Ave; admission/clubhouse $3/5), the country's oldest thoroughbred track.

There are more campsites around Lake George further north; however, the **Rustic Barn Campground** (☎518-654-6588; www.rusticbarncampground.com; 4748 Rte 9; campsites/cabins $26/160), on a wooded property with a pond and hiking trails about 9 miles north in Corinth, is an option. There are plenty of inns and B&Bs in town; impossible to overlook is the four-story ornately designed facade of the landmark 19th-century **Adelphi Hotel** (☎518-587-4688; www.adelphihotel.

com; 365 Broadway; r/ste incl breakfast from $130/170;); rooms are individually and idiosyncratically decorated (open May to October).

Restaurants and cafes line Broadway and the intimate side streets, including cozy **Mrs London's** (464 Broadway; mains $10; 7am-6pm, to 9pm Fri & Sat, closed Mon),which serves satisfying pastries as well as vegetarian paninis, soups and salads. With prices and decor from a bygone era, there's no more old-school place than the basic diner **Compton's** (457 Broadway; mains $4; 4am-2:45pm). A few miles south of town is **PJ's Bar-B-Q** (Rte 9; mains $6; 11am-9pm), a honky-tonk style roadhouse eatery that serves up slow-cooked ribs (six for $12) and smoked brisket, chicken and pork sandwiches.

Getting There & Around

Adirondacks Trailways (www.trailwaysny.com) and **Greyhound** (www.greyhound.com) head to/from New York City (one way $45, four hours). Amtrak stops out of New York City ($52 one way, four hours), and several major airlines fly into **Albany International Airport** (ALB; www.albanyairport.com) about 10 miles north from downtown.

COOPERSTOWN

For sports fans, **Cooperstown**, 50 miles west of Albany, is instantly recognized as the home of the shrine for the national sport (baseball). But the small-town atmosphere and stunning views of the countryside around beautiful Ostego Lake make it worth visiting even for those who don't know the difference between ERA and RBI.

The **National Baseball Hall of Fame & Museum** (888-425-5633; 25 Main St; www.baseballhall.org; adult/child $19.50/7; 9am-5pm, to 9pm summer;) has exhibits, a theater, a library and an interactive statistical database. The old stone **Fenimore Art Museum** (888-547-1450; www.fenimoreartmuseum.org; 5798 Lake Rd/Hwy 80; adult/child $12/free; 10am-5pm) has an outstanding collection of Americana.

Several affordable low-slung motels line Rte 80 alongside the lake outside of town. The **Inn at Cooperstown** (607-547-5756; www.innatcooperstown.com; 16 Chestnut St; r incl breakfast from $110;) is a beautifully restored country home located just blocks from Main St. The tiny **Cooperstown Diner** (136½ Main St; mains $8; 6am-8pm) does burgers and comfort food.

The Adirondacks

Majestic and wild, the Adirondacks, a mountain range with 42 peaks over 4000ft high, rival any of the nation's wilderness areas for sheer awe-inspiring beauty. The 9375 sq miles of park and forest preserve that climb from central New York State to the Canadian border include towns, mountains, lakes, rivers and more than 2000 miles of hiking trails. There's good trout, salmon and pike fishing, along with excellent camping spots. The Adirondack Forest Preserve covers 40% of the park, preserving the area's pristine integrity. In colonial times settlers exploited the forests for beaver fur, timber and hemlock bark, but by the 19th century 'log cabin' wilderness retreats, both in the form of hotels and grand estates, became fashionable.

LAKE GEORGE, LAKE PLACID & SARANAC LAKE

Maybe it's a blessing that the primary gateway to the Adirondacks, the village of **Lake George**, is a kitsch tourist town full of cotton candy, arcades and cheap souvenirs. The real reason for coming is the 32-mile-long lake itself, with its crystalline waters and forested shoreline, and once you leave the town behind the contrast is only more striking. Paddlewheel boat cruises, parasailing, kayaking and fishing trips are popular.

The state maintains wonderfully remote **campgrounds** (800-456-2267; www.dec.ny.gov/outdoor; tent sites $25) on Lake George's islands, and one of several places for wilderness information is the **Adirondack Mountain Club** (518-668-4447; www.adk.org; 814 Goggins Rd). Small motels line the main street of Lake George toward the northern end of town. Two with lake views that can be recommended are **Georgian Lakeside Resort** (518-668-5401; www.georgianresort.com; r incl breakfast from $99;) and newly renovated **Surfside on the Lake** (518-668-2442; www.surfsideonthelake.com; r from $50;). Dozens more hotels, inns and cabins extend north on either side of Rte 9 to the village of **Bolton Landing**.

It's something of a stretch to imagine this small mountain resort was once at the center of the world's attention – well, twice. In 1932 and 1980, **Lake Placid** hosted the Winter Olympics and the facilities and infrastructure remain; elite athletes still train here. Parts of the **Olympic sports centers** (518-523-1420; www.whitefacelakeplacid.com) are open to visitors, including ice arenas, a

BUGS

Come May swarms of black flies can be enough of a scourge to discourage some people from traveling to the Adirondacks. Through much of June the problem of these gnat-like flying insects can be such a sanity-challenging nuisance that residents stay indoors and when outdoors experiment with all manner of home remedies to keep the bites at bay.

ski-jumping complex and a chance to **bobsled** (per day $70, ⌚10am-4pm Thu-Mon Jun-Jul) with a professional driver. Hotels, restaurants, bookstores and shops line the frontier-like main street in town, which actually fronts Mirror Lake. Skiers should head to nearby **Whiteface Mountain** (www.whiteface.com), with 80 trails and a serious 3400ft vertical drop.

South of Lake Placid town, **Adirondack Loj** (☎518-523-3441; www.adk.org; dm/r incl breakfast $55/160), run by the Adirondack Mountain Club (ADK), is a rustic retreat surrounded by mountains on the shore of peaceful Heart Lake. Wilderness campsites, lean-tos and cabins are also available.

Further north is the **Saranac Lake** region, where you'll find even more secluded wilderness areas – small lakes and ponds, ancient forests and wetlands. The town of Saranac Lake itself, once a center for tuberculosis treatments, feels a little down on its luck. However, the nearby **Porcupine Inn** (☎518-891-5160; www.theporcupine.com; 350 Park Ave; r incl breakfast $155-252; ❄📶), housed in a classic Adirondacks-style lodge house, is run with loving care and perfection. A hike up to nearby Moody Pond and Baker Mountain affords excellent views of the area.

Getting There & Around

Both **Greyhound** (www.greyhound.com) and **Adirondack Trailways** (www.trailwaysny.com) serve various towns in the region. A car is really essential for exploring the region.

Thousand Islands Region

Virtually unknown to downstate New Yorkers, in part because of its relative inaccessibility, this region of over 1800 islands – from tiny outcroppings just large enough to lie down on to larger islands with roads and towns – is a scenic wonderland separating the US from Canada. From its source in the Atlantic Ocean far to the north, the wide and deceptively fast-moving St Lawrence River East empties into Lake Ontario at Cape Vincent. This portion of the river was once a summer playground for the very rich, who built large, stately homes here. It is still a popular vacation area known for its boating, camping and even shipwreck scuba diving.

Sackets Harbor was the site of a major battle during the War of 1812. While it is on Lake Ontario and not technically part of the Thousand Islands, it is a convenient starting point for touring the region. Several inviting restaurants line the street that runs down to the harbor front with waterside patio seating.

The relaxing, French-heritage village of **Cape Vincent** is at the western end of the river where it meets the lake. Drive out to the **Tibbetts Point Lighthouse** for stunning lake views; an attractive **hostel** (☎315-654-3450; www.hihostels.com; dm/r $18/40) shares the property. Nearby **Burnham Point State Park** (☎315-654-2522; Rte 12E; campsites $25) has wooded, lakeside campsites.

Clayton, 15 miles to the east along the Seaway Trail (Rte 12), has more than a dozen marinas and a few good eating choices in an area generally bereft of them. **TI Adventures** (☎315-686-2500; www.tiadventures.com; 1011 State St; half-day kayak rental $30) rents kayaks and runs white-water rafting trips down the Black River. Such activities are also organized by several companies in Watertown, a sizable city half an hour's drive to the south.

Lyric Coffee House (246 James St, Clayton; ⌚8am-8pm, 9am-4pm Sun; 📶), surprisingly contemporary for this town, serves specialty coffee drinks, gelato, pastries and specials such as lasagna for lunch.

Further east, **Alexandria Bay** (Alex Bay), an early-20th-century resort town, is still the center of tourism on the American side – its sister city is Gananoque in Canada. While it is run-down and tacky, there's enough around to keep you occupied: go-karts, minigolf and a **drive-in movie theater** (www.baydrivein.com; adult/child $5/2; 👪) are only minutes away. It's also the departure point for ferries to Heart Island, where **Boldt Castle** (☎315-482-2501; www.boldtcastle.com; adult/child $6.50/4; ⌚10am-6:30pm mid-May–mid-Oct) marks the love story of a rags-to-riches New York hotelier who built the castle for his beloved wife. Sadly, she died before its completion. The same hotelier once asked his chef to create a new salad dressing, which was popularized as 'Thousand Island' – an unfortunate blend of ketchup, mayonnaise and relish. **Uncle Sam's Boat Tours** (☎315-482-2611; www.usboattours.com, 45 James St; 2-nation tour adult/child $18.50/9.25;) has several departures daily for its recommended two-nation cruise (visiting both the US and Canadian sides of the river), which allows you to stop at Boldt Castle and ride back on one of its half-hourly ferries for free.

Wellesley Island State Park (☎518-482-2722; www.nysparks.com; campsites from $15) offers camping, which is probably the best accommodations option even for the raccoon-averse. Many sites are almost directly on the riverfront and some have their own 'private' beaches. The island is only accessible by crossing a toll portion ($2.50) of the Thousand Islands Bridge.

There are several supposedly upscale resorts around Alex Bay, though none is especially good value. Probably the best midrange choice is **Capt Thomson's Resort** (☎315-482-9961; www.captthomsons.com; 45 James St; d from $80;) on the waterfront next to the office for Uncle Sam's Boat Tours.

Jet Blue (www.jetblue.com) has regular daily flights to Hancock International Airport (SYR) in Syracuse, an hour and a half south. Several major car-rental agencies have offices in the airport. Cyclists will enjoy the mostly flat Scenic Byway Trail.

Western New York

Still trying to find their feet after hemorrhaging industries and population for over a decade, most of the cities in this region live in the shadow of Niagara Falls, a natural wonder that attracts upward of 12 million visitors from around the world per year. Buffalo was once a booming industrial center and the terminus of the Erie Canal, which used to serve as the transportation lifeline connecting the Great Lakes and the Atlantic Ocean; it now boasts an indigenous culinary scene and Bohemian enclaves. Syracuse and Rochester are both home to big universities.

BUFFALO

This often maligned working-class city does have long, cold winters and its fair share of abandoned industrial buildings, but Buffalo also has a vibrant community of college students and thirty-somethings living well in cheap real estate and gorging on this city's unique and tasty cuisine. Settled by the French in 1758 – its name is believed to derive from *beau fleuve* (beautiful river) – the city's illustrious past as a former trading post and later a booming manufacturing center and terminus of the Erie Canal means there's a certain nostalgia and hopefulness to the continuing limbo of ambitious revitalization plans (the latest calls for a massive expansion and relocation of the University of Buffalo medical school to downtown). Buffalo is about an eight-hour trip from New York City and less than an hour south of Niagara Falls.

The helpful **Buffalo Niagara Convention & Visitors Bureau** (☎716-218-2922; www.visitbuffaloniagara.com; 617 Main St; ⏲10am-4pm Mon-Fri, 10am-2pm Sat) has good walking-tour pamphlets and a great website.

Sights & Activities

Architecture buffs will enjoy the city (for details check out www.walkbuffalo.com). North of downtown, sprawling Delaware Park was designed by Frederick Law Olmsted. The **Elmwood** neighborhood, stretching along Elmwood Ave between Allen St and Delaware Park, is dotted with hip cafes, restaurants, boutiques and bookstores. Hertle Ave, designated as 'Little Italy' in North Buffalo also has several good restaurants and cafes.

This is a hard-core sports town and locals live and die with the **NFL Buffalo Bills** (www.buffalobills.com) football team and the **Buffalo Sabres** (www.sabres.com), the city's NHL ice-hockey team. A lower-key, but no less recommended, option to rub elbow's with local sports fanatics is to catch the **Buffalo Bisons** (www.bisons.com), the AAA affiliate of the major-league baseball team, the New York Mets, in their trendy-traditional downtown ballpark.

Albright-Knox Art Gallery MUSEUM
(☎716-882-8700; www.albrightknox.org; 1285 Elmwood Ave; adult/child $12/5; ⏲10am-5pm Tue-Sun, to 10pm first Fri) A sizable museum, including some of the best French Impressionists and American masters.

Burchfield Penney MUSEUM
(☎716-878-6011; www.burchfieldpenney.org; 1300 Elmwood Ave; adult/child $9/5; ⏲10am-5pm Tue, Wed, Fri & Sat, to 9pm Thu, 11am-5pm Sun) Modern building housing works, mostly American and western New York artists, from the late 19th century to contemporary.

Frank Lloyd Wright Darwin Martin House TOUR
(☎716-856-3858; www.darwinmartinhouse.org; 125 Jewett Pkwy; tours $15-40) Tours of the 1904 Prairie-style home and neighboring **Barton House** (118 Summit Ave) begin with a video and exhibits at the next-door visitor center. The $50 million restoration, which began in 1992, is nearing completion; the iconic pergola was only rebuilt in 2007.

Theodore Roosevelt Inaugural National Historic Site MUSEUM
(☎716-884-0095; www.trsite.org; 641 Delaware Ave; adult/child $10/5; ⏲9am-5pm Mon-Fri, noon-5pm Sat & Sun) Partly guided tours of the Ansley-Wilcox house examine the tale of Teddy's emergency swearing-in here following the assassination of William McKinley in 1901. Interactive exhibits for the attention deficient.

Sleeping

Standard chains line the highways around the city. Depending on the weather and time of day, downtown can feel like a ghost town. However, it's a geographically convenient base and the **Hamptons Inn & Suites** (☎716-855-2223; www.hamptoninn.com; 220 Delaware Ave; r incl breakfast from $150; P❄@🛜≋) can be recommended for its large rooms and excellent breakfast.

Mansion on Delaware Avenue B&B $$
(☎716-886-3300; www.mansionondelaware.com; 414 Delaware Ave; r incl breakfast from $175; ❄🛜) For truly luxurious accommodations and flawless service, head to this very special and grand mansion.

Beau Fleuve B&B $$
(☎800-278-0245; www.beaufleuve.com; 242 Linwood Ave; s/d incl breakfast from $120/135; ❄) A historic B&B in the Linwood neighborhood.

Hostelling International – Buffalo Niagara HOSTEL $
(☎716-852-5222; www.hostelbuffalo.com; 667 Main St; dm/r $25/60; ❄@) For budget travelers.

Eating

Buffalo is curiously blessed with an abundance of eateries serving unique, tasty and cheap dishes.

TOP CHOICE **Anchor Bar** PUB $$
(☎716-883-1134; 1047 Main St; 10 wings $11; ⏲10am-11pm Mon-Thu, 10am-1am Fri & Sat) For the famous deep-fried chicken wings covered in a spicy sauce, head to this landmark bar, which claims credit for inventing the 'delicacy.' Sandwiches, burgers, seafood, pizza and pasta are also on the menu. Motorcycles and other random paraphernalia line the walls and live music Thursday through Saturday nights.

Ulrich's GERMAN $$
(☎716-8; 674 Ellicott St; mains $15; ⏲11:15am-late Mon-Sat) One of Buffalo's oldest taverns has warped floors and dark wood walls. Try the gut-busting German fish fry, which comes with red cabbage, sauerkraut, potatoes and vegetables. Homemade potato pancakes ($7), liverwurst and red onions on rye ($11) are also recommended.

Left Bank FRENCH $$
(☎716-882-3509; 511 Rhode Island St; mains $10-19; ⏲5-11pm Mon-Thu, to midnight Fri & Sat, 11am-10pm Sun) Housed in an attractive 100-year-old building, Left Bank is an atmospheric restaurant serving large portions of homemade ravioli, grilled meat and good wine.

Betty's MODERN AMERICAN $$
(☎716-362-0633; 370 Virginia St; mains $12; ⏲8am-9pm Tue, 8am-10pm Wed-Fri, 9am-10pm Sat, 9am-3pm Sun) For slightly more upscale eats. In the neighborhood of Allentown, Betty's does interpretations of American comfort food.

Also recommended:

Duff's PUB $
(☎716-834-6234; 3651 Sheridan Dr, Amherst; 10 wings $8; ⏲11am-11pm) Locals in the know say the wings here are the best.

Bob & John's La Hacienda SANDWICHES, PIZZA $
(☎716-836-5411; 1545 Hertel Ave; sandwiches $5, 10 wings $9; ⏲11am-11pm) Serves sandwiches, buffalo wings and, according to some, the best pizza in Buffalo.

Ted's FAST FOOD $
(☎716-834-6287; Sheridan Ave; hot dogs $2; ⏲10:30am-11pm Mon-Sun) Fast-food specialty is hot dogs, foot-longs, any way you like 'em.

Chef's ITALIAN $$
(☎716-856-9187; 291 Seneca St; mains $15; ⏲11am-9pm Mon-Sat) In business for 85 years, this is a Buffalo landmark doling out classic red-sauce Italian dishes.

Drinking & Entertainment

Bars along Chippewa St (aka Chip Strip) are open until 4am and cater primarily to the frat-boy crowd. More eclectic neighborhoods such as Elmwood, Linwood and Allentown have more than their fair share of late-night options. From June through August a **summer concert series** (☎716-856-3150; www.buffaloplace.com) draws an eclectic mix of new and established artists to outdoor spaces in downtown.

Several gay bars are clustered around the south end of Elmwood.

Nietzches DIVE BAR
(☎716-886-8539; 248 Allen St; ⏲1pm-2am) A legendary dive bar with live music.

Allen Street Hardware Cafe LIVE MUSIC
(☎716-882-8843; 245 Allen St; ⏲5pm-midnight, to 1am Fri & Sat) Where the best local musicians play to regularly packed houses. Full food menu as well.

Eddie Brady's BAR
(97 Genesee St; ⏲5pm-2am) Neighborhood tavern in a rehabilitated downtown building (c 1863).

Getting There & Around

Buffalo Niagara International Airport (BUF; www.buffaloairport.com), about 16 miles east of downtown, is a regional hub. Jet Blue Airways offers affordable round-trip fares from New York City. Buses arrive and depart from the **Greyhound terminal** (181 Ellicott St). **NFTA** (www.nfta.com) local bus 40 goes to the transit center on the American side of Niagara Falls ($1.75, one hour). From the downtown **Amtrak train station** (75 Exchange St), you can catch trains to major cities (to NYC is $55, eight hours; to Albany $43, six hours; to Syracuse $24, 2½ hours). The Exchange Street station can feel dodgy, especially at night; locals recommend the Buffalo-Depew station (55 Dick Rd), 6 miles east.

NIAGARA FALLS & AROUND

It's a tale of two cities and two falls, though either side of this international border affords views of an undeniably dramatic natural wonder. There are honeymooners and heart-shaped Jacuzzis, arcades, tacky shops and kitsch boardwalk-like sights, but as long as your attention is focused nothing can detract from the majestic sight. The closer to the falls you get the more impressive they seem and the wetter you become. For good reason, the Canadian side is where almost everyone visits, though it's easy to stroll back and forth between the two. The New York side is dominated by the purple, glass-covered Seneca Niagara Casino & Hotel, which towers over the surrounding derelict blocks.

Sights & Activities

The falls are in two separate towns: Niagara Falls, New York (USA) and Niagara Falls, Ontario (Canada). The towns face each other across the Niagara River, spanned by the Rainbow Bridge, which is accessible for cars and pedestrians. Famous landscape architect Frederick Law Olmstead helped rescue and preserve the New York side which by the 1870s was dominated by industry and gaudy signs. You can see views of the **American Falls** and their western portion, the **Bridal Veil Falls**, which drop 180ft from the **Prospect Point Observation Tower** (admission $1, ⏲9:30am-5pm Mon-Thu, to 7pm Fri & Sat, to 6pm Sun). Cross the small bridge to **Goat Island** for close-up viewpoints, including Terrapin Point, which has a fine view of Horseshoe Falls and pedestrian bridges to the Three Sisters Islands in the upper rapids. From the north corner of Goat Island, an elevator descends to the **Cave of the Winds** (☎716-278-1730; adult/child $6/4; ⏲9am-5pm), where walkways go within 25ft of the cataracts (raincoats provided). The **Maid of the Mist** (☎716-284-8897; www.maidofthemist.com; tours adult/child $13.50/8; ⏲10am-5pm Mon-Fri, to 6pm Sat & Sun May-Sep; 👪) boat trip around the bottom of the falls has been a major attraction since 1846 and is highly recommended. Boats leave from the base of the Prospect Park Observation Tower on the US side and from the bottom of Clifton Hill on the Canadian side.

For those seeking more of an adrenaline rush, check out **Whirlpool Jet Boat Tours** (☎888-438-4444; www.whirlpooljet.com; 1 hr adult/child $50/42), which leave from **Lewiston**, a charming town with several good eateries 8 miles north of Niagara Falls. Shoppers can head to the **Tanger Outlet stores** a few miles west of town for designer-wear deals.

Northeast of Niagara Falls is the town of **Lockport**, the western terminus of the Erie Canal. There's an excellent visitors center and **museum** and **boat tours** during the summer months.

Sleeping & Eating

Some of the national hotel chains are represented – Ramada Inn, Howard Johnson, Holiday Inn, however the pickings are slim compared to the Canadian side. There are a few restaurants near the bridge area, including several Indian takeaway places.

TOP CHOICE **The Giacomo** BOUTIQUE HOTEL **$$**
(☎716-299-0200; www.thegiacomo.com; 220 First St; r from $150; P❄📶) The equal of any Canadi-

an-side lodging in terms of stylish comfort, the Giacomo occupies a renovated 1929 art-deco office tower. While the majority of floors are taken up by high-end condos, the three dozen spacious rooms are luxuriously appointed and the 19th-floor lounge offers spectacular falls views. Considering the fact that it sleeps eight comfortably, the platinum suite, suitable for a season of *Real Life Niagara Falls,* is a good deal ($500, two-night minimum).

Information

On the US side, the **Niagara Tourism & Convention Corporation** (☎716-282-8992; www.niagara-usa.com; 10 Rainbow Blvd; ⏰9am-7pm Jun-Sep 15, to 5pm Sep 16-May 31) has all sorts of guides; its Canadian counterpart is located near the base of the **Skylon Tower** (☎905-356-6061; www.niagarafallstourism.com; 5400 Robinson St; ⏰9am-5pm).

Getting There & Around

NFTA (Niagara Frontier Transportation Authority; www.nfta.com) has seven daily buses from the Buffalo Airport to Niagara Falls; look for the 210 Metro Link Express ($3, 50 minutes). The stop in Niagara Falls is at First and Rainbow Blvd (there's no reason to go to the terminal at Main and Pine Sts). Taxis run around $75. For downtown Buffalo bus 40 leaves from Third St and Old Falls Blvd ($1.75, one hour). The **Amtrak train station** (27th St, at Lockport Rd) is about 2 miles northeast of downtown. From Niagara Falls, daily trains go to Buffalo ($12, 35 minutes), Toronto ($38, three hours) and New York City ($60, nine hours). **Greyhound** (303 Rainbow Blvd) buses are run out of the Daredevil Museum.

Parking costs $5 to $10 a day on either side of the falls. Most of the midrange hotels offer complimentary parking to guests, while upscale hotels (on the Canadian side) tend to charge $10 to $20 a day for the privilege.

Crossing the Rainbow Bridge to Canada and return costs US$3.25/1 per car/pedestrian. There are customs and immigration stations at each end – US citizens are required to have their passport or an enhanced driver's license (see p1168). Driving a rental car from the US over the border should not be a problem (see p1165 and p1169) but check with your rental company before you depart.

NEW JERSEY

There are McMansions, à la the *Real Housewives of New Jersey* (NJ), guys who speak with thick Jersey accents like characters from a TV crime drama, and guidos and guidettes who spend their days GTL'ing (gym, tan and laundry) on the Shore. However, the state is at least as well defined by high-tech and banking headquarters and sophisticated, progressive people living in charming towns. Get off the exits, flee the malls and you are privy to a beautiful side of the state: a quarter is farmland and it has 127 miles of beautiful beaches and charming and fun beachside towns, as well, of course, as two of New York City's greatest icons: the Statue of Liberty and Ellis Island.

Information

NJ.com (www.nj.com) Statewide news from all the major dailies including the Newark Star-Ledger and Hudson County's Jersey Journal.

New Jersey Monthly (www.njmonthly.com) Monthly glossy with features on attractions and other stories relevant to visitors.

NEW JERSEY FACTS

» **Nickname** Garden State

» **Population** 8.8 million

» **Area** 8722 sq miles

» **Capital city** Trenton (population 85,000)

» **Other cities** Newark (population 277,000)

» **Sales tax** 7%

» **Birthplace of** musician Count Basie (1904–84), singer Frank Sinatra (1915–98), actor Meryl Streep (b 1949), musician Bruce Springsteen (b 1949), actor John Travolta (b 1954), musician Jon Bon Jovi (b 1962), rapper Queen Latifah (b 1970), pop band Jonas Brothers: Kevin (b 1987), Joseph (b 1989), Nicolas (b 1992)

» **Home of** the first movie (1889), first professional baseball game (1896), first drive-in theater (1933), the Statue of Liberty

» **Politics** Republican governor Chris Christie though strong traditionally Democratic legislature

» **Famous for** *The Jersey Shore* (the real thing and MTV reality show), the setting for *The Sopranos*, Bruce Springsteen's musical beginnings

» **Number of** wineries 36

» **Driving distances** Newark to NYC 11 miles, Atlantic City to NYC 135 miles

New Jersey Department of Environmental Protection (www.state.nj.us/dep/parksandforests) Comprehensive information on all state parks, including camping and historic sites.

Getting There & Away

Though NJ is made up of folks who love their cars, there are other transportation options:

New Jersey PATH train (www.panynj.gov/path) Connects lower Manhattan to Hoboken, Jersey City and Newark.

New Jersey Transit (www.njtransit.com) Operates buses out of NYC's Port Authority and trains out of Penn Station, NYC.

New York Waterway (www.nywaterway.com) Ferries to northern New Jersey.

Northern New Jersey

Stay east and you'll experience the Jersey urban jungle. Go west to find its opposite: the peaceful, refreshing landscape of the Delaware Water Gap and rolling Kittatinny Mountains.

HOBOKEN & JERSEY CITY

A sort of TV-land version of a cityscape, Hoboken is a cute little urban pocket just across the Hudson River from New York City – and, because of cheaper rents that lured pioneers over a decade ago, a sort of sixth city borough, too. On weekends the bars and live-music venues come alive – especially the legendary **Maxwell's** (☎201-653-1703; www.maxwellsnj.com; 1039 Washington St), which has featured up-and-coming rock bands since 1978. But the town also has loads of restaurants lining commercial Washington St, some lovely residential lanes and a leafy, revitalized waterfront – a far cry from when the gritty *On the Waterfront* was filmed here.

Perhaps there's no clearer symbol for this transformation than the crowds that line up every morning to glimpse the spectacular confections made by Bartolo Jr 'Buddy' Valastro of reality TV show *Cake Boss* at **Carlo's City Hall Bake Shop** (☎201-659-3671; www.carlosbakery.com; 95 Washington St; ⏲7am-7:30pm Mon-Wed & Sun, to 9pm Thu-Sat).

High-rise buildings housing condominiums and the offices of financial firms seeking lower rents have transformed **Jersey City** for better or worse from a primarily blue-collar and immigrant neighborhood into a 'restored' area for the upwardly mobile. Its biggest draw is the 1200-acre **Liberty State Park** (☎201-915-3440; www.libertystatepark.org; ⏲6am-10pm), which hosts outdoor concerts with the Manhattan skyline as a backdrop and has a great bike trail, and also operates **ferries** (☎877-523-9849; www.statuecruises.com) to Ellis Island and the Statue of Liberty. Also in the park and great for kids – virtually every exhibit is interactive – is the expansive and modern **Liberty Science Center** (☎201-200-1000; www.lsc.org; adult/child $15.75/11.50, extra for IMAX & special exhibits; ⏲9am-5pm; 👪).

BORDER CROSSING: CANADIAN NIAGARA FALLS

When people say they are visiting the falls they usually mean the Canadian side, which is naturally blessed with superior views. Canada's **Horseshoe Falls** are wider and especially photogenic from Queen Victoria Park; at night they're illuminated with a colored light show. The **Journey Behind the Falls** (adult/child US$15/7; ⏲9am-8:30pm Mon-Fri) gives access to a spray-soaked viewing area beneath the falls. **Niagara on the Lake**, 15km to the north, is a small town full of elegant B&Bs and a famous summertime theater festival.

Virtually every major hotel chain has at least several locations on the Canadian side of the falls. Backpackers can head to the somewhat messy **HI Niagara Falls Hostel** (☎905-357-0770; www.hostellingniagara.com; 4549 Cataract Ave; dm/r incl breakfast US$30/60; ❄📶). **Skyline Inn** (☎905-374-4444; www.skylineinnniagarafalls.com; 4800 Bender St; r from US$70; P❄@📶) is a good choice if you're seeking a budget place away from the noise and there's a walkway to the **indoor waterpark** across the street. River Rd is lined with B&Bs but **Chestnut Inn** (☎905-374-7623; www.chestnutinnbb.com; 4983 River Rd; r from US$90; ❄), a tastefully decorated colonial home with a wrap-around porch, stands above the rest.

Obvious tourist-trap restaurants are a dime a dozen in and around Clifton Hill. American fare and chains dominate the culinary scene. The Lundy's Lane area has tons of cheap eats.

NEWARK

Though many NYC-bound travelers fly into Newark Liberty International Airport, few stick around to see the city they've landed in. Long mired in images of the 1960s race riots that made it off-limits to many for so long, Newark has been on a long road to recovery. Cory Booker, the city's young, high-profile ambitious mayor, who took office in 2006, is only the city's third mayor since 1970. Crime, endemic poverty and dwindling finances all continue to mar the city's reputation though downtown streets bustle with shoppers and office workers during the daytime in warmer months.

Brazilian, Portuguese and Spanish restaurants line the streets of the thriving **Ironbound District** (www.goironbound.com) only a few blocks from the city's neoclassic **Penn Station** (accessible from NYC's same-named station via NJ Transit). Down some sangria and the seafood combo for two ($41) at the fortress-like **Iberia Peninsula** (63-69 Ferry St; mains $15; 11am-2am). Not far from here is the **Newark Museum** (973-596-6550; www.newarkmuseum.org; 49 Washington St; suggested donation $10; noon-5pm Wed-Fri, 10am-5pm Sat & Sun), which has a renowned Tibetan collection and hosts the annual Newark Black Film Festival in June. Some 2700 cherry trees blossom in April in the 400-acre Frederick Law Olmstead-designed **Branch Brook Park**. The **New Jersey Performing Arts Center** (888-466-5722; www.njpac.org; 1 Center St) is the city's crowning jewel, hosting national orchestras, operas, dance, jazz and other performances. The **Prudential Center** (www.prucenter.com), aka 'The Rock' has become the focal point for sports, home to the New Jersey Devils hockey team, plus basketball games and concerts.

DELAWARE WATER GAP

The Delaware River meanders in a tight S-curve through the ridge of NJ's Kittatinny Mountains, and its beauteous image turned this region into a resort area, beginning in the 19th century. The **Delaware Water Gap National Recreation Area** (570-426-2452; www.nps.gov/dewa), which comprises land in both New Jersey and Pennsylvania, was established as a protected area in 1965, and today it's still an unspoiled place to swim, boat, fish, camp, hike and see wildlife – just 70 miles east of New York City.

The 3348-acre **Kittatinny Valley State Park** (973-786-6445; admission free) is home to lakes with boat launches, lime outcroppings and campsites, plus former railroads that have been converted into hiking and cycling trails. North of here, **High Point State Park** (973-875-1471; vehicle weekdays/weekends $5/10), which is also great for camping and hiking, has a monument that, at 1803ft above sea level, affords wonderful views of surrounding lakes, hills and farmland. The nearby town of **Milford** across the border in Pennsylvania is a charming place with several good restaurants.

Princeton & Around

Central New Jersey, otherwise known as 'the armpit' (only for how it looks on a map, of course), is home to a string of beautiful, wealthy communities including Princeton, at the eastern border of Pennsylvania as well as the state capital of Trenton.

Settled by an English Quaker missionary, the tiny town of Princeton is filled with lovely architecture and several noteworthy sites, number one of which is its Ivy League **Princeton University** (www.princeton.edu), which was built in the mid-1700s and soon became one of the largest structures in the early colonies. The town's **Palmer Square**, built in 1936, is a lovely place to shop and stroll. The **Historical Society of Princeton** (609-921-6748; www.princetonhistory.org; 158 Nassau St; tours adult/child $7/4) leads historical walking tours of the town on Sundays at 2pm, and the **Orange Key Guide Service & Campus Information Office** (609-258-3060; www.princeton.edu/orangekey) offers free university tours.

Accommodations are expensive and hard to find during graduation time in May and June, but beyond that it should be easy to arrange for a stay at one of several atmospheric inns, including the traditionally furnished **Nassau Inn** (609-921-7500; www.nassauinn.com; 10 Palmer Sq; r incl breakfast from $169; @) and the **Inn at Glencairn** (609-497-1737; www.innatglencairn.com; 3301 Lawrenceville Rd; r incl breakfast from $195;), a renovated Georgian manor with old-world style and modern amenities.

It may not be the most beautiful place, but New Jersey's capital, **Trenton**, has several historic sites, a museum and farmers market worth stopping in on – especially if you can pair it up with a trip to Philly or Atlantic City.

Jersey Shore

Perhaps the most famous and revered feature of New Jersey is its sparkling shore, stretching from Sandy Hook to Cape May and studded with resort towns from tacky to classy (www.visitthejerseyshore.com). You'll find as many mothers pushing strollers as throngs proudly clutching souvenir beer bongs. Though it's mobbed during summer weekends, you could find yourself wonderfully alone on the sand come early fall. Beach access varies across communities, though the majority charge reasonably priced fees for the day. Putting up a tent in a state park or private campground is a low cost alternative during the summer months when finding good-value accommodations is nearly as difficult as locating un-tattooed skin.

SANDY HOOK & AROUND

At the northernmost tip of the Jersey Shore is the **Sandy Hook Gateway National Recreation Area** (☎732-872-5970; www.nps.gov/gate; off Rte 36; parking per car $10; ⏰7am-10pm), a 7-mile-long sandy barrier beach at the entrance to New York Harbor. You can see the city skyline from your beach blanket on clear days, which only heightens the sense of pleasure and feeling of dislocation. The ocean side of the peninsula has wide, sandy beaches (including a nude beach, the only legal one in NJ, at Gunnison Beach) edged by an extensive system of bike trails, while the bay side is great for fishing or wading. The brick buildings of the abandoned coastguard station, **Fort Hancock** (⏰1-5pm Sat & Sun) houses a small museum. The **Sandy Hook Lighthouse**, which offers guided tours, is the oldest in the country. Bug spray is recommended as biting flies can be a nuisance at dusk.

The town next door, the **Highlands**, has a few seafood restaurants on the water and an outpost of the famous Brooklyn pizzeria **Grimaldi's** (☎732-291-1711; 123 Bay Ave; small pizza $14; ⏰3-10pm, from noon Sat & Sun), whose coal-fired brick-oven pies are the equal of the original. A fast ferry service **Seastreak** (☎800-262-8743; www.seastreak.com; round-trip adult/child $43/16, 1hr), runs between Sandy Hook (and the Highlands) and Pier 11 in downtown Manhattan or East 35th St, NYC.

About 10 miles inland is the artsy town of **Red Bank**, with a hoppin' main strip of shops, galleries and cafes, plus a sizable Mexican population (and plenty of authentic Mexican-food eateries. New Jersey Transit stops here.

LONG BRANCH, ASBURY PARK & OCEAN GROVE

Sanitized and slightly generic compared to other shore locations, **Long Branch** is the first major beach town south of the Highlands. A mall-like food-and-shopping complex by the ocean packs 'em in for everything from Greek dinners to swimwear shopping. Just a bit inland from here is the famed **Monmouth Park Race Track** (☎732-222-5100; www.monmouthpark.com; grandstand/clubhouse $3/5; ⏰11:30am-6pm May-Aug), where you can see thoroughbred racing in a gracious, historic setting.

Just south of Long Branch massive homes the size of museums in the community of **Deal** are worth a look simply to gawk at. However, once you cross over Deal Lake into **Asbury Park**, luxury gives way to abandoned row houses and potholed streets. The town though, which experienced passing prominence in the 1970s when Bruce Springsteen 'arrived' at the **Stone Pony** (☎732-502-0600; www.stoneponyonline.com; 913 Ocean Ave) nightclub and then a major decline, is being revitalized. Led by wealthy gay men from NYC who snapped up blocks of forgotten Victorian homes and storefronts to refurbish, the downtown (one of the liveliest on the shore), which includes several blocks of Cookman Ave, is lined with charming shops, cafes and restaurants. The sprawling **Antique Emporium of Asbury Park** (☎732-774-8230; 646 Cookman Ave; ⏰11am-5pm Mon-Sat & noon-5pm Sun) has two levels of amazing finds, while trendy **Restaurant Plan B** (☎732-807-4710; 705 Cookman Ave; mains $10-25; ⏰4:30-9pm Tue-Thu & Sun, to 10pm Fri, to 11pm Sat) serves excellent weekend brunch. On the southern end of the boardwalk, the grand looking renovated art-deco **Paramount Theatre** (☎732-897-8810; www.apboardwalk.com/venues; 1300 Ocean Ave) hosts live theater and music performances.

The town immediately to the south, **Ocean Grove**, is a fascinating place to wander. Founded by Methodists in the 19th century, the place retains what's left of a post-Civil War **Tent City** revival camp – now a historic site with 114 cottage-like canvas tents clustered together that are used for summer homes. The town has dazzling ornate well-preserved Victorian architecture and a 6500-seat wooden auditorium, and there are many beautiful, big-porched **Victorian inns** to choose from for a stay; visit www.oceangrovenj.com for guidance. A few miles inland just off the Garden State Pkwy is a very utilitarian-looking **Premium outlet** store mall.

BRADLEY BEACH TO SPRING LAKE

Bradley Beach has row after row of adorable summer cottages and a beautiful stretch of shore. **Belmar's beach** is equally inviting and has a boardwalk with a few food shacks and a handful of restaurants and busy bars on the oceanfront road. The **New Jersey Sandcastle Contest** (www.njsandcastle.com) is held here in mid-July.

South of here is **Spring Lake**, a wealthy community once known as the 'Irish Riviera,' with meticulously manicured lawns, grand oceanfront Victorian houses, a gorgeous beach and elegant accommodations. If you're interested in a low-key quiet base – a stay here is about as far from the typical shore boardwalk experience as you can get – try the bright and airy **Grand Victorian at Spring Lake** (449-5327; www.grandvictorianspringlake.com; 1505 Ocean Ave; r from $79;).

Only 5 miles inland from Spring Lake is quirky **Historic Village at Allaire** (732-919-3500; www.allairevillage.org; adult/child $3/2; noon-4pm Wed-Sun late May-early Sep, check for other times), the remains of what was a thriving 19th-century village called Howell Works. You can still visit various 'shops,' all run by folks in period costume.

OCEAN COUNTY BEACHES

Just south of the Manasquan River is **Point Pleasant**, whose northern end of the boardwalk is backed by small, idiosyncratic vacation homes only feet from the beach-going hordes. The southern half, called **Jenkinson's Boardwalk** has the usual salt-water taffy shops, eateries, amusement rides, as well as an aquarium good for kids and an enormous bar and restaurant for adults jutting out over the beach. A few seafood restaurants with outdoor patios built over the water can be found on a marina and inlet of the river – one worth a try is the **Shrimp Box** (75 Inlet Dr; sandwiches $10, mains $17; noon-10:30pm). Just north of here in Manasquan, **Inlet Beach** has the Shore's most reliable year-round waves for surfers.

Just below there, the narrow **Barnegat Peninsula** barrier island extends some 22 miles south from Point Pleasant. In its center, **Seaside Heights** of MTV reality-show *Jersey Shore* fame sucks in the raucous twenty-something summer crowds with two amusement piers and an above-average number of boardwalk bars. Because the beach is relatively narrow, this is not the place to go for privacy or quiet. Grab a seat – and a drink and tortilla chips – at the 2nd floor terrace of **Spicy Cantina** (500 Boardwalk; mains $11; 11am-midnight) for a front-row seat of the human parade below. Or better yet ride the **chair lift** running from the Casino Pier to the northern end of the boardwalk. If the ocean is not to your taste, beat the heat on the lazy river at the **Breakwater Beach Waterpark** (www.casinopiernj.com/breakwaterbeach; admission $25; 10am-7pm May-Aug;). To witness guidos and guidettes in all of their fist-bumping glory check out **Karma** (401 Blvd; Thu-Sun), the nightclub of choice for Snooki, Sitch and the gang. There isn't much to recommend about a stay at one of the crash pads on the neglected sun-baked streets inland from the boardwalk. Camping at **Surf & Stream Campground** (732-349-8919; www.surfnstream.com; 1801 Ridgeway Rd/Rte 571, Toms River; campsites $45) is a convenient option.

Occupying the southern third of Barnegat Peninsula is **Island Beach State Park** (732-793-0506; www.islandbeachnj.org; per car weekday/weekend $6/10; 8am-dusk), a 10-mile barrier island that's pure, untouched dunes and wetlands. Although the very southern tip of the park is within throwing distance of **Long Beach Island** just across a narrow inlet to the bay south of here, to reach this long sliver of an island with beautiful beaches and impressive summer homes you have to backtrack all the way to Seaside Heights and travel along Rte 9 or the Garden State Pkwy. The landmark **Barnegat Lighthouse State Park** (609-494-2016; www.njparksandforests.org; off Long Beach Blvd; 8am-4pm) offers panoramic views at the top and fishermen cast off from a jetty extending 2000ft along the Atlantic Ocean. A few miles south of Rte 72 that bisects Long Beach Island is **Daddy O** (609-361-5100; www.daddyohotel.com; 4401 Long Beach Blvd; r $195-375;), a sleek boutique hotel and restaurant near the ocean.

South Jersey

When folks from Philly say they're heading to the Shore, they're more often than not referring to this slice of the coastline. A mixture of kitsch and country, the state's southern region – represents the best of New Jersey's extremes.

PINE BARRENS

Locals call this region the Pinelands – and like to carry on the lore about the one million acres of pine forest being home to a mythical beast known as the 'Jersey Devil.' Containing several state parks and forests, the area is a haven for bird-watchers, hikers, campers, canoeists and all-round nature enthusiasts. Inland is the **Wharton State Forest** (☎609-561-0024; www.state.nj.us), one of the good places to canoe – as well as hike and picnic. A good outfitter is **Micks Pine Barrens Canoe and Kayak Rental** (☎609-726-1515; www.mickscanoerental.com; 3107 Rte 563, Chatsworth; per day kayak $43, canoe $55), which has maps and other details about boating trips in the area. Further south along the coast is the **Edwin B Forsythe National Wildlife Refuge** (☎609-652-1665; www.forsythe.fws.gov; per vehicle $4), 40,000 acres of bays, coves, forests, marshes, swamps, and barrier beaches and a paradise for bird-watchers.

ATLANTIC CITY

It's not exactly Vegas, but for many a trip to AC conjures *Hangover*-like scenes of debauchery. And while you might spot bachelors and bachelorettes, gray-haired retirees and vacationing families are at least as accurate as a cross section of typical visitors. Inside the casinos that never see the light of day, it's easy to forget there's a wide white-sand beach just outside and boarded-up shop windows a few blocks in the other direction. The 'AC', known throughout the late 19th and early 20th century for its grand boardwalk and Oceanside amusement pier and the glamorously corrupt one of the HBO series *Boardwalk Empire* set in 1920 Prohibition-era AC, has been thoroughly overturned. Since 1977 when the state approved gambling casinos in the hope of revitalizing this fading resort, it has been on a bumpy ride. An ever expanding number of mostly Native American–owned casinos throughout Pennsylvania and New York are challenging AC's gambling hegemony and raison d'être. A slew of nightclubs and hotel-casinos like the massive Borgata have brought glitz and glamour, the **Pier at Caesars**, a spiffy shopping mall jutting out into the Atlantic, a steady stream of overseas visitors and an express train service from NYC have kept AC from hemorrhaging too many visitors. If gambling isn't your thing, the boardwalk offers up an all-star roster of summer indulgence, from funnel cakes to go-karts to cheesy gift shops. The small **Atlantic City Historical Museum** (☎609-347-5839; www.acmuseum.org; cnr Boardwalk & New Jersey Aves; admission free; ⏱10am-4pm) provides a quirky look at AC's past.

Sleeping & Eating

A handful of motor inns and cheap motels line Pacific Ave, a block inland from the boardwalk. The best in-casino dining is to be had at the Borgata. Good (and more affordable) food can be found in the 'real' part of downtown, too.

Chelsea BOUTIQUE HOTEL **$**
(☎800-548-3030; www.thechelsea-ac.com; 111 S Chelsea Ave; r from $80; P❄@📶🏊) Non-casino, trendy with art-deco-style furnishings. Rooms in the attached annex are less expensive. Also houses a retro diner, steakhouse and cabana club.

Water Club & Spa BOUTIQUE HOTEL **$$**
(☎609-317-8888; www.thewaterclubhotel.com; 1 Renaissance Way; r from $119; P❄@📶🏊) This club is 43-story boutique-style chic.

Borgata CASINO **$$**
(☎866-692-6742; www.theborgata.com; r $149-400; P❄📶🏊) An enormous Las Vegas-like resort with high-style rooms, a full-service spa, major concert hall, four five-star restaurants and, of course, a grand casino in the Marina District.

Reddings SOUTHERN **$**
(1545 Pacific Ave; mains $10; ⏱11am-10pm Mon-Thu, 7am-midnight Fri & Sat) One of the most satisfying noncasino meals in AC. The chef-owner, a Harlem transplant, serves fine Southern-style cooking, like chicken dumplings and turkey chops, in a large and comfortable dining room.

Kelsey & Kim's Café BARBECUE **$**
(201 Melrose Ave; mains $9; ⏱7am-10pm) Excellent southern comfort food like fried whiting, pulled BBQ beef brisket sandwich and fried chicken.

Drinking & Entertainment

It's the casinos, as you may have guessed, that are the biggest draw here. Inside they're all basically the same: nonstop clanging, flashing and miles of blackjack, poker, baccarat and craps tables.

Beyond the casino walls you'll find the wide, oceanfront **boardwalk**, the first in the world; enjoy a walk or a hand-pushed rolling-chair ride (there's a price chart posted inside each chair).

Check out the calendar at the Borgata, which has a comedy club, an intimate concert hall and a massive music venue that hosts big acts.

Information

The **Atlantic City Convention & Visitors Bureau** (☎609-348 7100; www.atlanticcitynj.com; 2314 Pacific Ave; ⏱9am-5pm) has a location in the middle of the Atlantic City Expwy and another right on the boardwalk at Mississippi Ave. **Atlantic City Weekly** (www.atlanticcity weekly.com) has useful info on events, clubs and eateries.

Getting There & Away

Air Tran and Spirit Airlines fly into the small **Atlantic City International Airport** (ACY; www.acairport.com), a 20-minute drive from the center of Atlantic City and a great option for reaching any part of South Jersey or Philadelphia.

There are a busload of bus options to AC, including NJ Transit (one way $36, 2½ hours) and Greyhound (one way $25, 2½ hours), both leaving from New York's Port Authority. A casino will often refund much of the fare (in chips, coins or coupons) if you get a bus directly to its door.

New Jersey Transit (www.njtransit.com) trains only go to Atlantic City from Philadelphia (one way $10, 1½ hours). A double-decker train service, **ACES** (Atlantic City Express Train Service; www.acestrain.com; ⏱Fri-Sun) connects AC to Penn Station, NYC (from $29, two hours 40 minutes).

OCEAN CITY & THE WILDWOODS

South of Atlantic City, Ocean City is an old-fashioned family holiday spot, home to dune-swept beaches and a number of child-centric arcades and themed playlands along its lively boardwalk. Motels are plentiful, relatively cheap and old-fashioned, as are the myriad crab shacks and seafood joints. Around 25 miles southwest of Ocean City down a long country road is the family-run **Frontier Campground** (☎609-390-3649; www.frontiercampground.com; campsites $35); sites are surrounded by blossoming pink and white mountain laurel flowers.

Further south on the way to Cape May, the three towns of **North Wildwood**, **Wildwood** and **Wildwood Crest** are an archaeological find – whitewashed motels with flashing neon signs, turquoise curtains and pink doors, especially in Wildwood Crest, a kitsch slice of 1950s Americana. Check out eye-catching motel signs like the **Lollipop** at 23rd and Atlantic Aves. Wildwood, a party town popular with teens, twenty-somethings and the young primarily Eastern Europeans who staff the restaurants and shops, is the main social focus. The width of the beach (all three beaches are free), more than 1000ft in parts making it the widest in NJ, means there's never a lack of space. Several massive piers are host to **water parks** and **amusement parks** – easily the rival of any Six Flags Great Adventure – with roller coasters and rides best suited to aspiring astronauts anchoring the 2 mile-long Grand Daddy of Jersey Shore boardwalks. Glow-in-the-dark 3D mini-golf is a good example of the Wildwood boardwalk ethos – take it far, then one step further. Maybe the best ride of all, and one that doesn't induce nausea, is the **tram** (one way $2.50; ⏱9am-1am) running the length of the boardwalk from Wildwood Crest to North Wildwood. There's always a line for a table at Jersey Shore staple pizzeria **Mack & Manco's** on the boardwalk (it has other shore boardwalk locations).

About 250 small motels – no corporate chains here – offer rooms for $50 to $250, however, it makes sense to narrow your search to the more salubrious area of Wildwood Crest. The Day Glo-colored ultra-retro **Caribbean Motel** (☎609-522-8292; www.caribbeanmotel.com; 5600 Ocean Ave; r from $65; ❄📶🏊) has been painstakingly and lovingly renovated – think of a cross between the TV shows *Happy Days* and *The Jetsons*. Another recommended place is the **Pan American Hotel** (☎609-522-6936; www.panamericanhotel.com; 5901 Ocean Ave; r from $100; ❄📶🏊).

CAPE MAY

Founded in 1620, Cape May – the only place in the state where the sun both rises and sets over the water – is on the state's southern tip and is the country's oldest seashore resort. Its sweeping beaches get crowded in summer, but the stunning Victorian architecture is attractive year-round.

In addition to 600 gingerbread-style houses, the city boasts antique shops and places for dolphin-, whale- (May to December) and bird-watching, and is just outside the **Cape May Point State Park** and its 157ft **Cape May Lighthouse** (☎609-884-5404; www.capemaymac.org; adult/child $7/3; ⏱10am-8pm Jun-Sep); there's an excellent visitors center and museum with exhibits on wildlife in the area. A mile-long loop of the nearby **Cape May Bird Observatory** (☎609-884-2736; www.birdcapemay.org; Sunset Blvd; admission $5; ⏱9:30am-4:30pm, closed Tue) is a pleasant stroll through preserved wetlands. The wide sandy **beach** at the park (free) or the one in town is the main attraction in summer months. **Aqua Trails** (☎609-884-5600;

www.aquatrails.com) offers kayak tours of the coastal wetlands.

Cape May's B&B options are endless, though the majority lean toward overstuffed and chintzy; check out www.capemaytimes for an up-to-date listing. The classic, sprawling **Congress Hall** (609-884-8422; www.congresshall.com; 251 Beach Ave; r $100-465;) has a range of beautiful quarters overlooking the ocean, plus there's a cool on-site restaurant and bar; the affiliated **Beach Shack** (www.beachshack.com) and **Star Inn** (www.thestarinn.net) offer a variety of accommodations for various budgets.

The size (and decor) of a high-school cafeteria from the 1950s, **Uncle Bill's Pancake House** (Beach Ave at Perry St; mains $7; 6:30am-2pm) has been drawing in crowds for its flapjacks for 50 years. Otherwise head to the Washington Street Mall, a cobblestone street lined with shops and more than a half-dozen restaurants.

To continue your journey further south without having to backtrack north and far inland, the **Cape May-Lewes Ferry** (www.cmlf.com; car/passenger $44/8; 1½hr) crosses the bay to Lewes, Delaware near Rehoboth Beach.

PENNSYLVANIA

In a state so large it's unsurprising that geography in part determines identity. The further west you go the closer you are to the rest of America. Philadelphia, once the heart of the British colonial empire and the intellectual and spiritual motor of its demise, is firmly ensconced culturally in the East Coast. Residents of Pittsburgh and western Pennsylvania (PA), on the other hand, are proud to identify themselves as part of the city or immediate region, relishing their distinctiveness from East Coasters and their blue-collar reputation. Moving east to west, the terrain becomes more rugged and you begin to appreciate the sheer size and diversity of this one state. Philly's Independence Park and historic district offer an ideal opportunity to come to some understanding of this nation's origins. Nearby, the battle sites of Gettysburg and Valley Forge provide another chance to travel back in time. But the city and state offer more than the clichés associated with school field trips. Stunning natural forests and mountain areas including the Poconos and Allegheny National Forest provide endless outdoor adventures. Both Philly and Pittsburgh are vibrant university cities with thriving music, performance and art scenes. Frank Lloyd Wright's architectural masterpiece, Fallingwater, and Amish country, not to mention the region's small, artsy towns, are perfect for weekend getaways.

History

William Penn, a Quaker, founded his colony in 1681, making Philadelphia its capital. His 'holy experiment' respected religious freedom (a stance that attracted other minority religious sects, including the well-known Mennonite and Amish communities), liberal government and even indigenous inhabitants. But it didn't take long for European settlers to displace those communities, thus giving rise to Pennsylvania's status as the richest and most populous British colony in North America. It had great influence on the independence movement and, much later, became an economic leader through its major supply of coal, iron and timber, followed by raw materials and labor during WWI and WWII. In the postwar period its industrial importance gradually declined. Urban-renewal programs and the growth of service, high-tech and health-care industries have boosted the economy, most notably in Philadelphia and Pittsburgh.

Philadelphia

Although it may seem like a little sibling to NYC, which is less than 90 miles away, Philadelphia is more representative of what East Coast city living is like. And in the minds of many, it offers every upside of urban life – burgeoning food, music and art scenes, neighborhoods with distinct personalities, copious parkland and maybe equally importantly, relatively affordable real estate. The older, preserved buildings in historic Philadelphia provide a picture of what colonial American cities once looked like – based on a grid with wide streets and public squares.

For a time the second-largest city in the British Empire (after London), Philadelphia became a center for opposition to British colonial policy. It was the new nation's capital at the start of the Revolutionary War and again after the war until 1790, when Washington, DC, took over. By the 19th century, New York City had superseded Philadelphia as the nation's cultural, commercial and industrial center. Though urban renewal has been going on for decades, some parts of the city formerly populated by industrial work-

PENNSYLVANIA FACTS

» **Nicknames** Keystone State, Quaker State

» **Population** 12.4 million

» **Area** 46,058 sq miles

» **Capital city** Harrisburg (population 53,000)

» **Other cities** Philadelphia (population 1.45 million), Pittsburgh (population 313,000), Erie (population 102,000)

» **Sales tax** 6%

» **Birthplace of** Writer Louisa May Alcott (1832–88), dancer Martha Graham (1878–1948), artist Andy Warhol (1928–87), movie star Grace Kelly (1929–82), comic Bill Cosby (b 1937)

» **Home of** US Constitution, the Liberty Bell, first daily newspaper (1784), first auto service station (1913), first computer (1946)

» **Politics** 'Swing state,' Republican Governor, progressive Philly and blue collar Democrats elsewhere

» **Famous for** soft pretzels, Amish people, Philadelphia cheesesteak, Pittsburgh steel mills

» **Wildlife** home of the largest herd of wild elk east of the Mississippi

» **Driving distances** Philadelphia to NYC 100 miles, Philadelphia to Pittsburgh 306 miles

ers are blighted and worlds away from the carefully manicured lawns and park-service-glutted historic district around the Liberty Bell and Independence Hall.

Sights & Activities

Philadelphia is easy to navigate. Most sights and accommodations are within walking distance of each other, or a short bus ride away. East–west streets are named; north–south streets are numbered, except for Broad and Front Sts.

Historic Philadelphia includes Independence National Historic Park and Old City, which extends east to the waterfront. West of the historic district is Center City, home to Penn Sq and City Hall. The Delaware and Schuylkill (*skoo*-kill) Rivers border South Philadelphia, which features the colorful Italian Market, restaurants and bars. West of the Schuylkill, University City has two important campuses as well as a major museum. Northwest Philadelphia includes the genteel suburbs of Chestnut Hill and Germantown, plus Manayunk, with plenty of bustling pubs and hip eateries. The South St area, between S 2nd, 10th, Pine and Fitzwater Sts, has Bohemian boutiques, bars, eateries and music venues. Northern Liberties is a burgeoning neighborhood with eclectic cafes and restaurants.

Independence National Historic Park HISTORIC SITE
(☎215-597-1785; www.nps.gov/inde) This L-shaped 45-acre park, along with Old City, has been dubbed 'America's most historic square mile.' Once the backbone of the United States government, today it is the backbone of Philadelphia's tourist trade. Stroll around and you'll see storied buildings in which the seeds for the Revolutionary War were planted and the US government came into bloom. You'll also find beautiful, shaded urban lawns dotted with large groups of schoolchildren and costumed actors. Most sites are open every day from 9am to 5pm, and some are closed Monday. Note that you must call or stop in to the **Independence Visitor Center** to make a timed reservation before visiting the high-volume Independence Hall, and beware that lines for the Liberty Bell can be extremely long.

Liberty Bell Center
(Map p140; 6th & Market Sts) Philadelphia's top tourist attraction was commissioned to commemorate the 50th anniversary of the Charter of Privileges (Pennsylvania's constitution, enacted in 1701 by William Penn). The 2080lb bronze bell was made in London's East End by the Whitechapel Bell Foundry in 1751. The bell's inscription, from Leviticus 25:10, reads: 'Proclaim liberty through all the land, to all the inhabitants thereof.' The bell was secured in the belfry of the Pennsylvania State House (now Independence Hall) and tolled on important occasions, most notably the first public reading of the Declaration of Independence in Independence Sq. The bell became badly cracked during the 19th century; despite initial repairs it became unusable in 1846 after tolling for George Washington's birthday.

National Constitution Center
(Map p140; ☎215-409-6700; www.constitutioncenter.org; 525 Arch St; adult/child $12/8; ⏲9:30am-5pm Mon-Fri, to 6pm Sat, noon-5pm

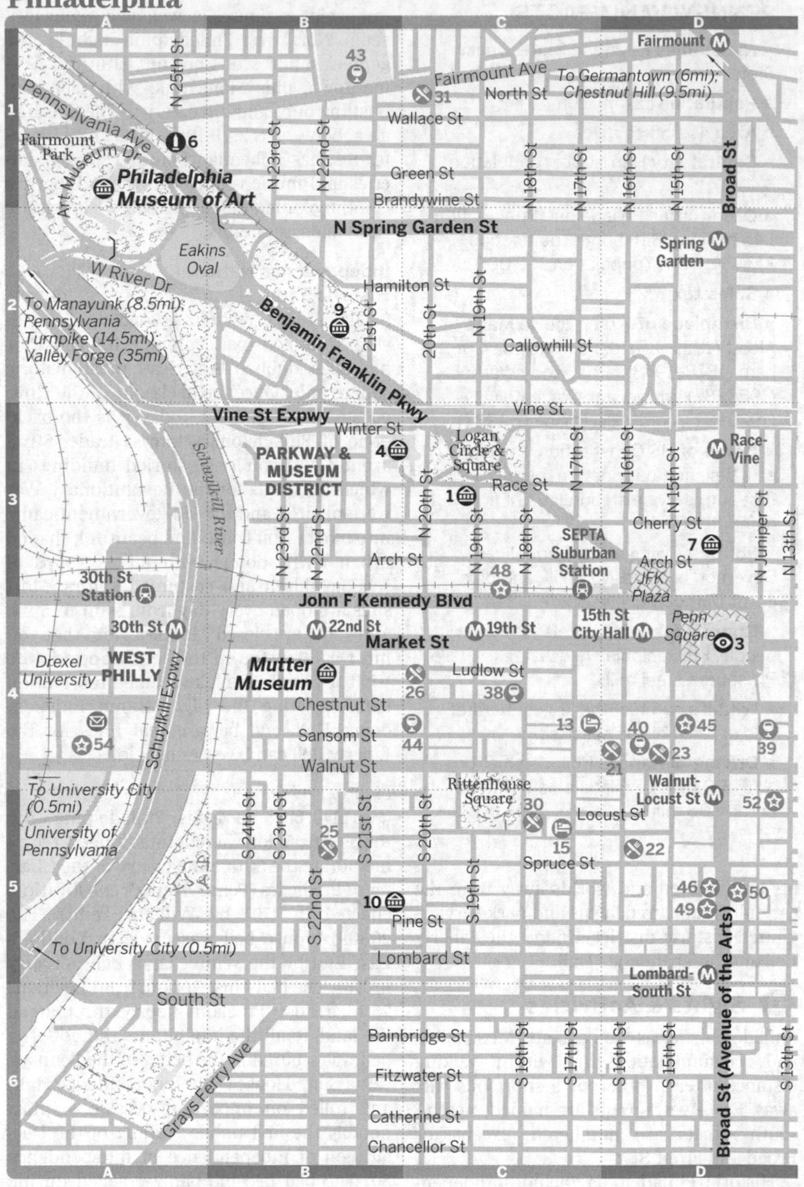

Sun;) Highly recommended, next to the visitor center, makes the United States Constitution interesting for a general audience through theater-in-the-round reenactments. There are exhibits, including interactive voting booths and Signer's Hall, which contains lifelike bronze statues of the signers in action.

Independence Hall

(Map p140; Chestnut St, btwn 5th & 6th Sts) The 'birthplace of American government,' where

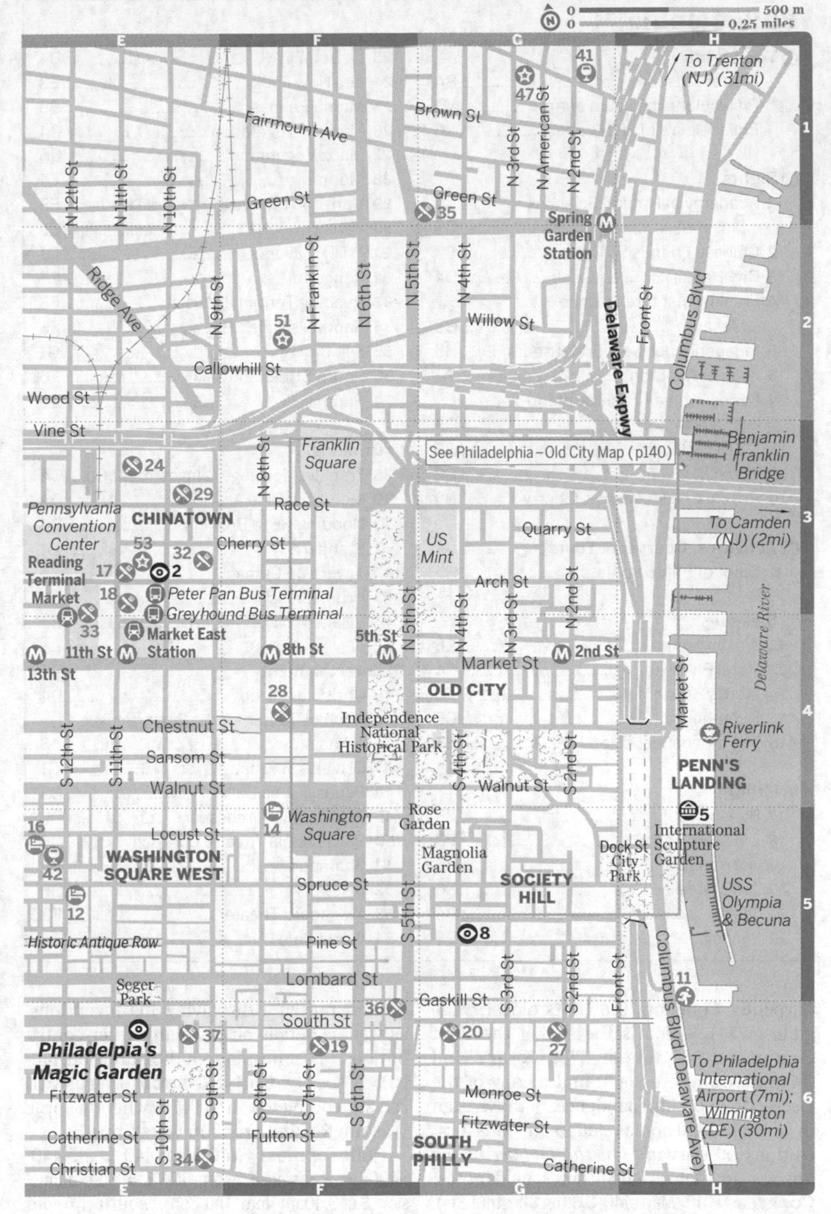

delegates from the 13 colonies approved the Declaration of Independence on July 4, 1776. A great example of Georgian architecture, it sports understated lines that reveal Philadelphia's Quaker heritage. Behind is **Independence Square**, where the Declaration of Independence was first read in public.

Other Attractions

Other attractions in this historic park include: **Carpenters' Hall**, owned by the

Philadelphia

Top Sights

Mutter Museum B4
Philadelphia Museum of Art A1
Philadelpia's Magic Garden E6

Sights

1 Academy of Natural Sciences Museum C3
2 Chinese Friendship Gate E3
3 City Hall D4
4 Franklin Institute Science Museum B3
5 Independence Seaport Museum H5
6 Joan of Arc Statue A1
7 Pennsylvania Academy of the Fine Arts D3
8 Physick House G5
9 Rodin Museum B2
10 Rosenbach Museum & Library B5

Activities, Courses & Tours

11 Spirit of Philadelphia H5

Sleeping

12 Alexander Inn E5
13 Hotel Palomar C4
14 Morris House Hotel F5
15 Rittenhouse 1715 .... C5
16 The Independent Hotel E5

Eating

17 Banana Leaf E3
18 Dim Sum Garden E3
19 Horizons F6
20 Jim's Steaks G6
21 Joe's D4
22 La Viola D5
23 Le Bec-Fin D4
24 Lee How Fook E3
25 Mama Palmas B5
26 Mama's Vegetarian C4
27 Maoz Vegetarian G6
28 Morimoto F4
29 Nanzhou Handdrawn Noodle House E3
30 Parc Brasserie C5
31 Philly Flavors C1
32 Rangoon E3
33 Reading Terminal Market E3
34 Sabrina's Cafe E6
35 Silk City Diner G1
36 South Street Souvlaki F6
37 Supper E6

Drinking

38 Franklin Mortgage & Investment Co. C4
39 McGillin's Olde Ale House D4
40 Nodding Head Brewery D4
41 Standard Tap G1
42 Tavern on Camac E5
43 Urban Saloon B1
44 Village Whiskey C4

Entertainment

45 Chris' Jazz Club D4
46 Kimmel Center for the Performing Arts D5
47 Ortlieb's Jazzhaus G1
48 Pennsylvania Ballet C3
49 Philadelphia Orchestra D5
50 Philadelphia Theatre Company D5
51 Shampoo F2
52 Sisters D5
53 Trocadero Theater E3
54 World Cafe Live A4

Carpenter Company, the USA's oldest trade guild (1724), which is the site of the First Continental Congress in 1774; **Library Hall** (Map p140), where you'll find a copy of the Declaration of Independence, handwritten in a letter by Thomas Jefferson, plus first editions of Darwin's *On the Origin of the Species* and Lewis and Clark's field notes; **Congress Hall** (Map p140; S 6th & Chestnut Sts), the meeting place for US Congress when Philly was the nation's capital; and **Old City Hall** (Map p140), finished in 1791, which was home to the US Supreme Court until 1800. The **Franklin Court** (Map p140) complex, a row of restored tenements, pays tribute to Benjamin Franklin with a clever underground museum displaying his inventions, as well as details on his many other contributions (as statesman, author and journalist) to society. **Christ Church** (Map p140; N 2nd St), completed in 1744, is where George Washington and Franklin worshipped.

Philosophical Hall (Map p140; ☎215-440-3400; www.apsmuseum.org; 104 S 5th St; admission $1; ⏲10am-4pm Thu-Sun), south of Old City Hall, is the headquarters of the American Philosophical Society, founded in 1743 by Benjamin Franklin. Past members have included Thomas Jefferson, Marie Curie, Thomas Edison, Charles Darwin and Albert Einstein.

Second Bank of the US (Map p140; Chestnut St, btwn 4th & 5th Sts), modeled after the Greek Parthenon, is an 1824 marble-faced Greek Revival masterpiece that was home to the world's most powerful financial institution until President Andrew Jackson dissolved its charter in 1836. The building then became the Philadelphia Customs House until 1935, when it became a museum. Today it's home to the **National Portrait Gallery** (Map p140; Chestnut St; admission free; 30min free guided tours noon, 3pm & 4pm Sat & Sun), housing many paintings by Charles Willson Peale, America's top portrait artist at the time of the American Revolution.

OLD CITY

Old City – the area bounded by Walnut, Vine, Front and 6th Sts – picks up where Independence National Historical Park leaves off. And, along with Society Hill, Old City was early Philadelphia. The 1970s saw revitalization, with many warehouses converted into apartments, galleries and small businesses. Today it's a quaint and fascinating place for a stroll. Check out the 9ft-tall **Ben Franklin sculpture** at Fourth and Arch Sts.

Elfreth's Alley STREET

(Map p140; off 2nd St, btwn Arch & Race Sts) The tiny, cobblestoned alley is believed to be the oldest continuously occupied street in the USA. Its 32 well-preserved brick row houses are still inhabited with real live Philadelphians, so be considerate as you stroll along, and be sure to stop into **Elfreth's Alley Museum** (Map p140; ☎215-574-0560; www.elfrethsalley.org; No 126; guided tours $5; ⏲10am-5pm Tue-Sat, from noon Sun), which was built in 1755 by blacksmith and alley namesake Jeremiah Elfreth; it's been restored and furnished to its 1790 appearance.

National Museum of American Jewish History MUSEUM

(Map p140; ☎215-923-3811; www.nmajh.org; 55 N 5th St; adult/child $12/free; ⏲10am-5pm Tue-Fri, to 5:30pm Sat & Sun) The distinctly translucent facade of the museum houses state-of-the-art exhibits that examine the historical role of Jews in the USA.

Betsy Ross House HISTORIC BUILDING

(Map p140; ☎215-686-1252; www.betsyrosshouse.org; 239 Arch St; suggested donation adult/child $4/3; ⏲10am-5pm) Where it is believed that Betsy Griscom Ross (1752–1836), upholsterer and seamstress, may have sewn the first US flag.

FREE **Clay Studio** GALLERY

(Map p140; ☎215-925-3453; www.theclaystudio.org; 139 N 2nd St; ⏲11am-7pm Tue-Sat, noon-6pm Sun) Staid exhibits as well as oddball works in ceramic; it's been in Old City since 1974 and is partially responsible for the development of the area's burgeoning gallery scene.

FREE **US Mint** TOUR

(Map p140; ☎215-408-0110; www.usmint.gov; Arch St, btwn 4th & 5th Sts; ⏲tours 9am-3pm Mon-Fri) You can line up for same-day, self-guided tours that last about 45 minutes.

Arch Street Meeting House RELIGIOUS

(Map p140; ☎215-627-2667; www.archstreetfriends.org; 320 Arch St; ⏲9am-5pm Mon-Sat, 1-5pm Sun) The USA's largest Quaker meeting house.

SOCIETY HILL

Architecture from the 18th and 19th centuries dominates the lovely residential neighborhood of Society Hill, bound by Front and 8th Sts from east to west, and Walnut and Lombard Sts north and south. Along the cobblestoned streets you'll see mainly 18th- and 19th-century brick row houses, mixed in with the occasional modern high-rise, like the **Society Hill Towers** designed by IM Pei, but **Washington Square** was conceived as part of William Penn's original city plan, and offers a peaceful respite from sightseeing.

Physick House HISTORIC BUILDING

(Map p136; ☎215-925-7866; 321 S 4th St, at Delancey St; adult/child $5/free; ⏲noon-4pm Thu-Sat, 1-4pm Sun) The home of surgeon Philip Syng Physick was built in 1786 by Henry Hill – a wine importer who kept City Tavern well stocked – and is the only freestanding, Federal-style mansion remaining in Society Hill.

Powel House HISTORIC BUILDING

(Map p140; ☎215-627-0364; 244 S 3rd St; adult/child $5/free; ⏲noon-4pm Thu-Sat, 1-4pm Sun) The 18th-century house was home to Samuel Powel, a mayor of Philadelphia during colonial times.

CENTER CITY, RITTENHOUSE SQUARE & AROUND

Philadelphia's center of creativity, commerce, culture and just about everything else, this region is the engine that drives the city. It contains the city's tallest buildings,

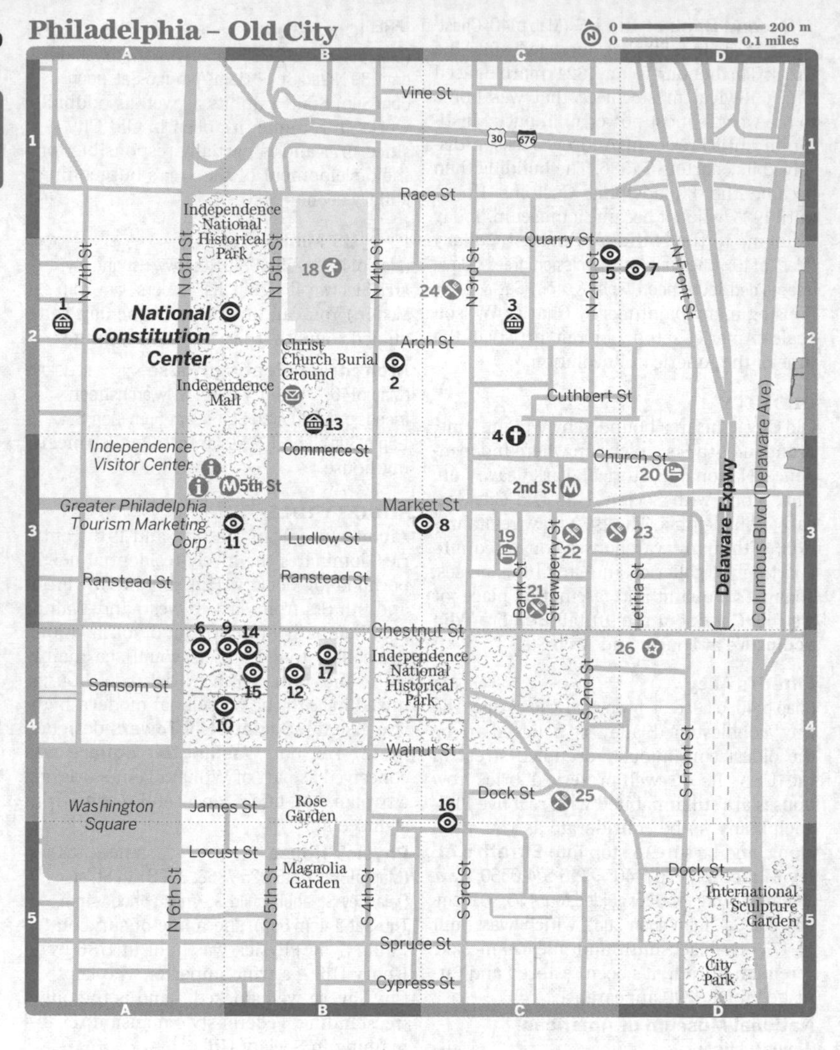

the financial district, big hotels, museums, concert halls, shops and restaurants.

The leafy **Rittenhouse Square**, with its wading pool and fine statues, is the best known of William Penn's city squares.

City Hall HISTORIC BUILDING

(Map p136; ☎215-686-2840; www.phila.gov; cnr Broad & Market Sts) The majestic City Hall, completed in 1901, stands 548ft tall in Penn Sq. It's the world's tallest masonry construction without a steel frame, and it's topped by a 27-ton bronze statue of William Penn. Just below that is an **observation deck** (admission $5; ⏲9:30am-4:15pm), where you can get a bird's-eye view of the city.

Mutter Museum MUSEUM

(Map p136; ☎215-563-3737; www.collphyphil.org; 19 S 22nd St; adult/child $14/10; ⏲10am-5pm) Skip med school and visit the seriously twisted to learn all about the history of medicine in the US.

Rosenbach Museum & Library MUSEUM

(Map p136; ☎215-732-1600; www.rosenbach.org; 2010 Delancey Pl; adult/child $10/5; ⏲noon-5pm Tue & Fri, to 8pm Wed & Thu, to 6pm Sat & Sun) For bibliophiles, as it features rare

Philadelphia – Old City

Top Sights

	National Constitution Center	B2

Sights

1	African American Museum in Philadelphia	A2
2	Arch St Meeting House	B2
3	Betsy Ross House	C2
4	Christ Church	C3
5	Clay Studio	C2
6	Congress Hall	A4
7	Elfreth's Alley	D2
	Elfreth's Alley Museum	(see 7)
8	Franklin Court	C3
9	Independence Hall	B4
10	Independence Square	A4
11	Liberty Bell Center	B3
12	Library Hall	B4
13	National Museum of American Jewish History	B2
	National Portrait Gallery	(see 17)
14	Old City Hall	B4
15	Philosophical Hall	B4
16	Powel House	C4
17	Second Bank of the US	B4

Activities, Courses & Tours

	Riverboat Queen	(see 7)
18	US Mint	B2

Sleeping

19	Apple Hostels of Philadelphia	C3
20	Penn's View Hotel	D3

Eating

21	Amada	C3
	Continental	(see 23)
22	Cuba Libre	C3
23	Franklin Fountain	C3
	Han Dynasty	(see 26)
24	La Locanda del Ghiottone	C2
25	Zahav	C4

Entertainment

26	Brasil's	D4

books and manuscripts, including James Joyce's *Ulysses*, and special exhibits.

BENJAMIN FRANKLIN PARKWAY & MUSEUM DISTRICT

Modeled after the Champs Elysées in Paris, the parkway is a center of museums and other landmarks.

TOP CHOICE Philadelphia Museum of Art MUSEUM

(Map p136; ☎215-763-8100; www.philamuseum.org; cnr Benjamin Franklin Pkwy & 26th St; adult/child $16/free; ⏱10am-5pm Tue-Sun, to 8:45pm Fri) This is the area's highlight and is one of the nation's largest and most important museums, featuring some excellent collections of Asian art, Renaissance masterpieces, postimpressionist works and modern pieces by Picasso, Duchamp and Matisse. The grand stairway at its entrance was immortalized when Sylvester Stallone ran up the steps in the 1976 flick *Rocky*. You can enjoy music, food and wine on Friday nights.

Pennsylvania Academy of the Fine Arts MUSEUM

(Map p136; ☎215-972-7600; www.pafa.org; 118 N Broad St; adult/child $15/free; ⏱10am-5pm Tue-Sat, from 11am Sun) A prestigious academy that has a museum with works by American painters, including Charles Willson Peale and Thomas Eakins.

Franklin Institute Science Museum MUSEUM

(Map p136; ☎215-448-1200; www2.fi.edu; 222 N 20th St; adult/child $15.50/12; ⏱9:30am-5pm; 👪) Where hands-on science displays were pioneered; a highlight is the kids-oriented interactive sports center.

Academy of Natural Sciences Museum MUSEUM

(Map p136; ☎215-299-1000; www.ansp.org; 1900 Benjamin Franklin Pkwy; adult/child $12/10; ⏱10am-4:30pm Mon-Fri, to 5pm Sat & Sun) Features a terrific dinosaur exhibition where you can dig for fossils on weekends.

Rodin Museum MUSEUM

(Map p136; ☎215-568-6026; www.rodinmuseum.org; Benjamin Franklin Pkwy & N 22nd St; suggested donation $5; ⏱10am-5pm Tue-Sun) You'll find Rodin's great works *The Thinker* and *Burghers of Calais* here.

SOUTH STREET

Sort of a Greenwich Village of Philly, **South Street** is where one goes to find record shops, art-supply stores, tiny cheapskate eateries and college favorites such as head shops, T-shirt stores and the teenage goth chicks who populate them.

Philadelphia's Magic Garden GARDENS
(Map p136; ☎215-733-0390; www.philadelphiasmagicgardens.org; 1020 South St; adult/child $5/2; ⏱11am-6pm, to 8pm Fri & Sat) A hidden gem worth seeking out is this mystical, art-filled pocket of land that's the passion of mosaic muralist Isaiah Zagar.

SOUTH PHILADELPHIA

Italian Market MARKET
(www.italianmarketphilly.org; S 9th St, btwn Wharton & Fitzwater Sts; ⏱9am-5pm Tue-Sat, to 2pm Sun) A highlight of South Philadelphia. One of the country's largest outdoor markets, it's where butchers and artisans hawk produce and cheese, homemade pastas, incredible pastries and freshly slaughtered fish and meats, from lamb to pheasant. A great time to experience it in all its glory is in mid-May, for the annual **South Ninth Street Italian Market Festival**.

Mummers Museum MUSEUM
(☎215-336-3050; www.mummersmuseum.com; 1100 S 2nd St; adult/child $3.50/2.50; ⏱9:30am-4:30pm Wed, Fri & Sat, to 9:30pm Thu) Celebrating the tradition of disguise and masquerade. It has an integral role in the famed Mummers Parade, which takes place here every New Year's Day.

CHINATOWN & AROUND

The fourth-largest Chinatown in the USA, Philly's version has existed since the 1860s. Chinese immigrants who built America's transcontinental railroads started out west and worked their way here. Today's Chinatown remains a center for immigrants, though now many of the neighborhood's residents come from Malaysia, Thailand and Vietnam in addition to every province in China. Though it does hold a few residents, the tone of Chinatown is thoroughly commercial.

African American Museum in Philadelphia MUSEUM
(Map p140; ☎215-574-0380; www.aampmuseum.org; 701 Arch St; adult/child $10/8; ⏱10am-5pm Tue-Sat, from noon Sun) Housed in a foreboding concrete building, it contains excellent collections on African American history and culture.

Chinese Friendship Gate LANDMARK
(Map p136; N 10th St, btwn Cherry & Arch Sts) A decorative arch built in 1984 as a joint project between Philadelphia and its Chinese sister city, Tianjin. The multicolored, four-story gate is Chinatown's most conspicuous landmark.

PENN'S LANDING

Back in its heyday Penn's Landing – the waterfront area along the Delaware River between Market and Lombard Sts – was a very active port area. Eventually those transactions moved further south down the Delaware, and today most of the excitement is about boarding boats, like the **Riverboat Queen** (Map p140; ☎215-923-2628; www.riverboatqueenfleet.com; tours from $15) or **Spirit of Philadelphia** (Map p136; ☎866-394-8439; www.spiritcruises.com; tours from $40), for booze cruises, or simply strolling along the water's edge. The 1.8-mile **Benjamin Franklin Bridge**, the world's largest suspension bridge when completed in 1926, spans the Delaware River and dominates the view.

Independence Seaport Museum MUSEUM
(Map p136; ☎215-413-8655; www.phillyseaport.org; 211 S Columbus Blvd; adult/child $12/7; ⏱10am-5pm) The museum highlights Philadelphia's role as an immigration hub; its shipyard closed in 1995 after 200 years. Nearby is a grassy sculpture garden.

UNIVERSITY CITY

This neighborhood, separated from downtown Philly by the Schuylkill River, feels like one big college town. That's because it's home to both Drexel University and the Ivy League **University of Pennsylvania** (commonly called 'U Penn'), founded in 1740. The leafy, bustling campus makes for a pleasant afternoon stroll, and it's got two museums definitely worth a visit.

University Museum of Archaeology & Anthropology MUSEUM
(☎215-898-4000; www.pennmuseum.org; 3260 South St; adult/child $10/6; ⏱10am-5pm Tue & Thu-Sun, to 8pm Wed) Contains archaeological treasures from ancient Egypt, Mesopotamia, Mesoamerica, Greece, Rome and North America.

FREE **Institute of Contemporary Art** MUSEUM
(☎215-898-7108; www.icaphila.org; 118 S 36th St; ⏱11am-8pm Wed, to 6pm Thu & Fri, to 5pm Sat & Sun) An excellent place to catch shows by folks making a big splash at the cutting edge of the art world.

30th St Station LANDMARK
(☎215-349-2153; 30th St, at Market St) Whether you're catching a train or not, be sure to pop your head into this romantic, neoclassical station while you're in the 'hood.

FAIRMOUNT PARK

The snaking Schuylkill River bisects this 9200-acre green space that's bigger than New York's Central Park and, in fact, the largest city park in the country. From the earliest days of spring every corner is thrumming with activity – ball games, runners, picnickers, you name it. Runners will love the tree-lined, riverside trails, which range from 2 miles to 10 miles in length. Park trails are also great for cycling. Stop by **Fairmount Bicycles** (☎267-507-9370; www.fairmountbicycles.com; 2015 Fairmount Ave) for rentals (full/half-day $18/30) and information.

Boathouse Row HOUSE

On the east bank, Boathouse Row has Victorian-era rowing-club buildings that lend a lovely old-fashioned flavor to this stretch. Across the park are a number of **early American houses** (adult/child $5/2) that are open to the public.

Shofuso Japanese House and Garden HOUSE, GARDEN

(☎215-878-5097; www.shofuso.com; adult/child $6/3; ⏲10am-4pm Wed-Fri, 11am-5pm Sat & Sun May-Sep) A picturesque home and teahouse constructed in the traditional 16th-century style. Scattered all throughout the park are some notable monuments, including one, at the far east end, for **Joan of Arc**.

Philadelphia Zoo ZOO

(☎215-243-1100; www.philadelphiazoo.org; 3400 Girard Ave; adult/child $18/15; ⏲9:30am-5pm) The country's oldest zoo, which has tigers, pumas, polar bears – you name it – in naturalistic habitats.

MANAYUNK

A compact residential neighborhood northwest of the city, with steep hills and Victorian row houses, Manayunk, from a Native American expression meaning 'where we go to drink,' is a lovely place for an afternoon and evening. Just be aware that thousands of others have the same idea on weekend nights, when this otherwise peaceful area overlooking the Schuylkill River has the feel of a raucous frat party. As well as drinking, visitors are also permitted to eat and shop. Parking is near impossible to come by here on weekends, so cycling is a good option – there's a towpath that runs alongside the neighborhood.

GERMANTOWN & CHESTNUT HILL

An odd mix of blight and preserved grandeur, the Germantown historic district – a good 20-minute drive or ride north on the Septa 23 from central downtown Philly – has a handful of tiny museums and notable homes worth checking out.

Wissahickon Valley Park PARK

(☎215-247-0417; www.fow.org) One of the best places to go for a run in the city is this long and narrow park, part of the Fairmount Park system; essentially a steep forested gorge with 57 miles of trails.

Cliveden of the National Trust HISTORIC BUILDING

(☎215-848-1777; www.cliveden1767.wordpress.com; 6401 Germantown Ave; admission $10; ⏲noon-4pm Thu-Sun) The summer home of wealthy Benjamin Chew was built in 1760 and was used as a de facto stronghold in the Battle of Germantown during the Revolutionary War in 1777.

Chestnut Hill NEIGHBORHOOD

(www.chestnuthillpa.com) Located just north of Germantown, with its quaint, small-town-like main strip of shops and eateries, and huge and historic residential homes and mansions.

Johnson House HISTORIC BUILDING

(☎215-438-1768; www.johnsonhouse.org; 6306 Germantown Ave; adult/child $8/4; ⏲10am-4pm Thu & Fri, from 1pm Sat) Tours of the site of a 1768 station house for the Underground Railroad.

Tours

Ed Mauger's Philadelphia on Foot WALKING

(☎215-627-8680; www.ushistory.org/more/mauger; per person $20) Historian and author Ed Mauger offers walking tours with a wide variety of themes, including Exercise Your Rights (Conservatives Tour), Exercise Your Lefts (Liberals Tour) and Women in the Colony.

Mural Tours TROLLEY

(☎215-389-8687; www.muralarts.org/tours; tours free to $30) Guided trolley tour of the city's diverse and colorful outdoor murals, the largest collection in the country.

Philadelphia Trolley Works & 76 Carriage Company TROLLEY

(☎215-389-8687; www.phillytour.com; adult/child from $25/10) Tour part of the city or just about every last corner, either on a narrated trolley ride or quieter horse-drawn carriage.

Festivals & Events

Mummers' Parade CULTURAL
(www.mummers.com) A very Philly parade, this is an elaborate celebration of costumes every New Year's Day (January 1).

Manayunk Arts Festival CULTURAL
(www.manayunk.com) It's the largest outdoor arts and crafts show in the Delaware Valley, with more than 250 artists from across the country each June.

Philadelphia Live Arts Festival & Philly Fringe CULTURAL
(www.livearts-fringe.org) Catch the latest in cutting-edge performance each September.

Sleeping

Though the majority of places are found in and around Center City, alternatives are sprinkled throughout other neighborhoods. There's certainly no shortage of places to stay, but it's primarily national chains or B&Bs. The Lowes, Sofitel and Westin can all be recommended. Note that most hotels offer some kind of parking service, usually costing about $20 to $45 per day.

Morris House Hotel BOUTIQUE HOTEL **$$$**
(Map p136; 215-922-2446; www.morrishousehotel.com; 225 S 8th St; r incl breakfast from $189;) If Benjamin Franklin were a hotelier he would have designed a place exactly like the Morris House Hotel. Upscale colonial-era boutique, this Federal-era building has the friendly charm and intimacy of an elegant B&B and the professionalism and good taste of a designer-run 21st-century establishment.

Hotel Palomar BOUTIQUE HOTEL **$$**
(Map p136; 888-725-1778; www.hotelpalomar-philadelphia.com; 117 S 17th St; r from $149;) Part of the Kimpton chain, the Palomar, occupying a former office building a few blocks from Rittenhouse Square is the new kid on Philly's boutique block. Marble and dark wood accents add warmth to the hip and stylish room furnishings. On offer are wine and snacks, hot chocolate (in winter), a gym and an attached restaurant.

The Independent Philadelphia BOUTIQUE HOTEL **$$**
(Map p136; 215-772-1440; www.theindependenthotel.com; 1234 Locust St; r incl breakfast from $150;) Another good Center City option housed in a handsome brick Georgian-Revival building with a four-story atrium. The wood-floored rooms are cozy and bright and the complimentary off-site gym pass and wine and cheese every evening sweeten the deal.

Rittenhouse 1715 BOUTIQUE HOTEL **$$$**
(Map p136; 215-546-6500; www.rittenhouse1715.com; 1715 Rittenhouse Sq; r from $206;) Just steps from Rittenhouse Sq, this is an elegant, top-notch choice. Housed in a 1911 mansion and infused with old-world sophistication, it's brimming with modern amenities – iPod docking stations, plasma TVs and rain showerheads. The friendly and efficient staff is also worth noting.

Penn's View Hotel HOTEL **$$**
(Map p140; 215-922-7600; www.pennsviewhotel.com; 14 N Front St, at Market St; r from $155;) Housed in three early-19th-century buildings overlooking the Delaware waterfront, Penn's View is ideal for exploring the Old City district. Quaint and full of character, but not overly nostalgic, the rooms have marble baths and modern conveniences.

Alexander Inn HOTEL **$$**
(Map p136; 215-923-1004; www.alexanderinn.com; 12th & Spruce Sts; s/d incl breakfast from $120/130; @) Exceptionally good value for its Center City location and for the professionalism and helpfulness of its staff. While the room decor is fairly standard you wouldn't expect a fitness room or breakfast at this price.

Apple Hostels of Philadelphia HOSTEL **$**
(Map p140; 215-922-0222; www.applehostels.com; 32 S Bank St; dm $37, r from $90; @) Sparkling clean and in a safe neighborhood just a short walk from major sights, there's no competition in this price bracket. Everything looks like it's straight out of an Ikea catalogue – not a bad thing. Friendly and helpful staff and events such as walking tours and movie nights with free beer (Tuesday).

Chamounix Mansion Hostel HOSTEL **$**
(215-878-3676; www.philahostel.org; 3250 Chamounix Dr, West Fairmount Park; dm $23; @) Looking more like a B&B than hostel, the Chamounix really should only be considered by those with use of a car. It's in a lovely wooded area in Fairmount Park north of the city on the way to Manayunk. Despite the 19th-century-style parlor and large communal rooms, the dorms themselves are basic but clean.

Eating

Philly is deservedly known for its cheesesteaks – you shouldn't leave without a sampling – the city's dining scene has grown exponentially, in part due to the contributions of the Starr and Garces groups, which have added a range of quality international eateries. Because of Pennsylvania's arcane liquor laws, many restaurants are Bring Your Own Bottle (BYOB).

OLD CITY

Amada SPANISH $$

(Map p140; ☎215-625-2450; 217 Chestnut St; tapas $6-20; ⏰11:30am-10pm Mon-Thu, to midnight Fri, 5pm-midnight Sat, 4-10pm Sun) Weekend dinner reservations at this Spanish tapas place, the first of renowned restaurateur Jose Garce's Philly eateries, are still hard to come by. The long communal tables foster a happening and loud atmosphere and the combination of bold and traditionally flavored dishes are phenomenal.

Cuba Libre CUBAN $$

(Map p140; ☎215-627-0666; 10 S 2nd St; dinner $13-31; ⏰11:30am-10pm Mon-Fri, from 10:30am Sat & Sun, to 11:30pm Fri & Sat) Colonial America couldn't feel further away at this festive, multistoried Cuban eatery and rum bar. The creative and inspired menu includes Cuban sandwiches, guava-spiced BBQ, and savory black beans and salads tossed with smoked fish.

La Locanda del Ghiottone ITALIAN $$

(Map p140; ☎215-829-1465; 130 N Third St; mains $17; ⏰5-11pm Tue-Sun) The name means 'the Place of the Glutton,' and Chef Giussepe and Joe the head waiter encourage overeating. Unlike other nearby trendy spots, this place is small and modestly designed. The gnocchi, mushroom crepes and mussels are recommended. BYOB.

Silk City Diner DINER $$

(Map p136; 435 Spring Garden St; mains $13; ⏰4pm-1am, from 10am Sat & Sun) Cocktails have replaced milkshakes at this classic-looking diner on the edge of the Old City and Northern Liberties. It's worth noting Silk City is as much a late night dance spot – Jerseyites come in for Saturday DJ nights. Outdoor beer garden in summer.

Franklin Fountain DESSERTS $

(Map p140; 116 Market St; ⏰11am-midnight) One of the more romantic date spots in the city, especially on weekend nights, this very-old-school ice-cream parlor features locally grown fruit and top-flight sundaes.

Zahav MIDDLE EASTERN $$

(Map p140; ☎215-625-8800; 237 St James Pl; mains $11; ⏰5-10pm Sun-Thu, to 11pm Fri & Sat) Small plates of sophisticated and modern Israeli and North African cuisine on Society Hill towers grounds.

CENTER CITY & AROUND

TOP CHOICE Morimoto JAPANESE $$$

(Map p136; ☎215-413-9070; 723 Chestnut St; mains $25; ⏰11:30am-10pm Mon-Fri, to midnight Fri & Sat) High concept and heavily stylized from the dining room that looks like a futuristic aquarium to a menu of globe-spanning influence and eclectic combinations, a meal at this *Iron Chef* regular's restaurant is a theatrical experience.

Le Bec-Fin FRENCH $$$

(Map p136; ☎215-567-1000; 1523 Walnut St; prix fixe dinners $80-185; ⏰11:30am-10:30pm Mon-Fri, from 5:30pm Sat) Totally over-the-top in its old-world snooty splendor, Le Bec-Fin is rated by many gourmets as the country's best restaurant for its setting, service and superb French food. Expect top-notch service, stuffy diners and rich and sophisticated meat and seafood dishes. The five-course lunch menu at $55 is good value.

Reading Terminal Market MARKET $

(Map p136; cnr 12th & Arch Sts; dishes $3-10; ⏰8am-6pm Mon-Sat, 9am-5pm Sun) At the budget end, this huge indoor market is the best you'll find. Take your pick, from fresh Amish cheeses and Thai desserts, to falafel, cheesesteaks, salad bars, sushi, Peking duck, great Mexican and cups of fresh-roasted java.

Supper MODERN AMERICAN $$

(Map p136; ☎215-592-8180; South St; mains $24; ⏰6pm-11:30pm) Truly farm-to-table, supplied with fresh seasonal produce by its very own farm, Supper epitomizes the current culinary spirit which weds the rural with the urban. Entrees are inventive and tasty creations like crispy confit duck leg with pecan waffles.

La Viola ITALIAN $$

(Map p136; ☎215-735-8630; 253 S 16th St, at Spruce St; mains $13; ⏰11am-10pm Tue-Sat, 4-10pm Sun) Facing off across the street from one another are the old and new La Violas – both BYOB. The former is a cramped and unpretentious dining room, while the latter is larger and more modern; the cuisine at both, however, is fresh and reasonably priced.

Parc Brasserie FRENCH $$$
(Map p136; ☎215-545-2262; 227 S 18th St; mains from $23; ⏰7:30am-11pm, to midnight Fri & Sat) This enormous polished Rittenhouse Sq prime people-watching bistro hits all the right notes. Brunch and lunch menus are good value.

Mama Palmas PIZZERIA $$
(Map p136; ☎215-735-7357; 2229 Spruce St; pizzas $10; ⏰4-10pm Tue-Fri, 11am-11pm Sat, 2-10pm Sun) Just off Rittenhouse Sq, this small BYOB place serves up some of the best thin-slice brick-oven pizza in the city.

Continental DINER $$
(Map p140; 138 Market St; mains $15; ⏰11:30am-11pm, to midnight Thu-Sat, from 10am Sat & Sun) Stylish Stephen Starr joint housed in the shell of a classic diner – Korean pork tacos and tofu tempura mean the cuisine is not stuck in the past.

Mama's Vegetarian FALAFEL $
(Map p136; 18 S 20th St; sandwiches $6; ⏰11am-9pm Mon-Thu, to 3pm Fri, noon-7pm Sun; ☑) An always bustling kosher Middle Eastern eatery, serves heaping falafel north of the city center.

Joe's PIZZERIA $
(Map p136; 122 S 16th St; slices $2.25) Some of the best pizza by the slice in the whole neighborhood.

Philly Flavors ICE CREAM $
(Map p136; 2004 Fairmount Ave, at 20th St; ices $2.50; ⏰11am-11pm Sun-Thu, to midnight Fri & Sat) Some say this is the best place for Italian ices in the city.

SOUTH STREET

Jim's Steaks SANDWICHES $
(Map p136; 400 South St, at 4th St; steak sandwiches $6-8; ⏰10am-1am Mon-Thu, to 3am Fri & Sat, 11am-10pm Sun) If you can brave the long lines you'll be in for a treat at this Philly institution, which serves mouthwatering cheesesteaks and hoagies (plus soups, salads and breakfasts).

Horizons VEGAN $$
(Map p136; ☎215-923-6117; 611 S 7th St; mains $15-20; ⏰6-10pm Tue-Thu, 6-11pm Fri & Sat; ☑) One of the few restaurants in Philly to satisfy the vegan gourmand, Horizons serves healthy, guilt-free dishes made of soy and veggies.

Maoz Vegetarian FALAFEL $
(Map p136; 248 South St; dishes $6; ⏰11am-10pm Sun-Thu, to 3am Fri & Sat) This tiny storefront, an outpost of an international chain is always packed and known for its fresh falafel sandwiches.

CHINATOWN

Rangoon ASIAN $$
(Map p136; 112 N 9th St; mains $6-15; ⏰11:30am-9pm Sun-Thu, to 10pm Fri & Sat) Try this Burmese spot in Chinatown, offering a huge array of tantalizing specialties from spicy red-bean shrimp and curried chicken with egg noodles to coconut tofu.

Han Dynasty CHINESE $$
(Map p140; 108 Chestnut St; mains $15; ⏰11:30am-11:30pm) Innovative and burn-your-tongue spicy soups and noodle dishes in a more upscale dining room.

Dim Sum Garden CHINESE $
(Map p136; 59 N 11th St, mains $6; ⏰11:30am-10pm) Overall, not the most salubrious looking hole-in-the-wall near the bus station but some of the tastiest steamed buns in the city.

Nanzhou Handdrawn Noodle House CHINESE $
(Map p136; 927 Race St; mains $6; ⏰11:30am-10pm) Serves satisfying and inexpensive meat noodle soups.

Banana Leaf ASIAN $
(Map p136; 1009 Arch St; mains $8; ⏰11am-1am) Specializes in Malaysian and Japanese cuisine.

Lee How Fook CHINESE $$
(Map p136; 219 N 11th St; mains $9-13; ⏰11:30am-10pm Tue-Sun) Has excellent contemporary Chinese.

SOUTH PHILADELPHIA & ITALIAN MARKET

Local aficionados debate the relative merits of this city's legendary cheesesteak shops as if they are biblical scholars parsing the meaning of Deuteronomy.

The area around the corner of Washington and 11th Sts is chockablock with tasty family-owned Vietnamese restaurants.

Paradiso ITALIAN $$$
(☎215-271-2066; 1627 E Passyunk Ave; mains $18-26; ⏰11:30am-10pm Mon-Thu, Fri & Sat to midnight) An elegant airy part of South Philly's Restaurant Row, Paradiso turns out upscale Italian feasts such as pistachio-crusted lamb chops, homemade gnocchi and New York strip steak glazed with anchovy butter.

Fond AMERICAN **$$$**
(212-551-5000; 1617 E Passyunk Ave; mains $25; 5:30-10pm) Tired of the neighborhood sandwich shops? Head to this upscale fine dining restaurant whose young chefs turn out creatively conceived fish, meat and chicken dishes with French accents and seasonal ingredients.

Pat's King of Steaks SANDWICHES **$**
(1237 E Passyunk Ave, at S 9th St; sandwiches $7; 24hr) Considered classic Philly, frequented as much by tourists and inebriated patrons, possibly unaware of the level of grease they're ingesting, as diehard locals.

Tony Luke's Old Philly Style Sandwiches SANDWICHES **$**
(39 E Oregon Ave; sandwiches $7; 6am-midnight Mon-Thu, to 2am Fri & Sat) Some swear by Tony Luke's, especially the roast pork or roast beef with hot peppers; it's by the sports stadiums with picnic tables and an ordering window.

South Street Souvlaki GREEK **$**
(Map p136; 507 South St; mains $9; noon-9:30pm Tue-Thu, to 10pm Fri & Sat, to 9pm Sun) One of the best places for Greek food in the city.

Sabrina's Cafe AMERICAN **$**
(Map p136; 910 Christian St; mains $9; 8am-10pm Tue-Sat, to 4pm Sun & Mon) An extremely popular brunch spot.

UNIVERSITY CITY

White Dog Cafe MODERN AMERICAN **$$$**
(215-386-9224; 3420 Sansom St; dinner mains $27; 11:30am-9:15pm Mon-Thu, to 10pm Fri & Sat, from 10:30am Sat & Sun) This 27-year-old institution is the kind of funky-yet-upscale place that college students get their visiting parents to take them to for special dinners or brunch ($11). The local, largely organic menu offers creative interpretations of meat and fish dishes.

Pod ASIAN **$$$**
(215-387-1803; 3636 Sansom St; dinner mains $14-29; 11:30am-11pm Mon-Thu, to midnight Fri, 5pm-midnight Sat, to 10pm Sun) Part of restaurateur Stephen Starr's empire, this space-age-looking theme restaurant has pan-Asian treats including dumplings and some of the best sushi in Philly, plus plenty of quirky cocktails and original desserts.

Satellite Coffee Shop CAFE **$**
(701 S 50th St; sandwiches $5; 7am-10pm) This Cedar Park vegetarian-friendly cafe is a boho meeting ground – try the kale smoothie and vegan wraps.

Abyssinia Ethiopian Restaurant ETHIOPIAN **$**
(229 S 45th St; mains $9; 9am-midnight) Excellent foul madamas (bean dip) and good brunch with a recommended bar upstairs.

Fu-Wah Mini Market SANDWICHES **$**
(819 S 47th St; mains $4.50; 9am-9pm) Serves up tofu hoagies and Vietnamese chicken sandwiches.

Lee's Hoagie House SANDWICHES **$**
(4034 Walnut St; sandwiches $7; 10am-10pm Mon-Sat, 10:30am-9pm Sun) For meat and chicken sandwiches, definitely the best in area.

Koreana KOREAN **$**
(3801 Chestnut St; mains $7; 11:30am-10pm, closed Mon) Satisfies students and others interested in good, inexpensive Korean fare; enter from the parking lot in the back of the shopping plaza.

Distrito MEXICAN **$$**
(3945 Chestnut St; mains $9-30; 11:30am-11pm Mon-Fri, 5-11pm Sat, to 10pm Sun) The vibrant pink and lime decor doesn't drown out the taste of the contemporary Mexican fare.

Green Line Café CAFE **$**
(4239 Baltimore Ave; mains $4; 7am-11pm, 8am-8pm Sun) One of the better spots for coffee.

MANAYUNK & AROUND

Trolley Car Diner DINER **$$**
(7619 Germantown Ave; dinner mains $9-20; 7am-9pm Mon-Thu, to 10pm Fri & Sat) Housed in a classic art-deco diner, this old-fashioned, family-style diner serves all the comfort food: club sandwiches, patty melts, fried shrimp, salads and a homemade, white-bean 'peanut butter' sandwich.

Dalessandro's Steaks SANDWICHES **$**
(600 Wendover St, Roxborough; mains $6.50; 11am-midnight Mon-Sat, to 9pm Sun) Cheesesteak snobs rave about this place.

Chubby's SANDWICHES **$**
(5826 Henry Ave; mains $6.50; 11am-1am Mon-Thu, to 2am Fri & Sat, to 11pm Sun) Has the better chicken sandwiches.

Mama's Pizzeria PIZZA, SANDWICHES **$**
(426 Belmont Ave, Bala Cynwyd; sandwiches $10; 11am-9pm) Another contestant in the cheesesteaks sweepstakes – certainly Mama's are right up there in size.

Kildare's Irish Pub PUB **$**
(4417 Main St; mains $9; 11am-2am Mon-Sat, from 10am Sun) The place for chicken wings – grilled, fried and baked.

Drinking & Entertainment

Bars & Nightclubs

McGillin's Olde Ale House PUB
(Map p136; 1310 Drury St; ⏲11am-2am) Philadelphia's oldest continually operated tavern (since 1860) has great buffalo wings (Tuesday is a special wing night) and karaoke on Wednesdays and Fridays.

Standard Tap PUB
(Map p136; cnr 2nd & Poplar Sts; ⏲4pm-2am) One of the pioneers in the gastropub movement, this Northern Liberties bar offers a great selection of local brews on tap, as well as burgers and steaks.

Urban Saloon PUB
(Map p136; 2120 Fairmount Ave; ⏲5pm-2am Mon-Fri, 11am-2am Sat & Sun) This Fairmount bar has a neighborhood feel. Dancing Friday nights, and a kid-friendly brunch Sundays (the peanut burger is recommended).

Shampoo NIGHTCLUB
(Map p136; ☎215-922-7500; www.shampooonline.com; Willow St, btwn N 7th & 8th Sts; cover $7-12; ⏲9pm-2am) Home to foam parties, hot tubs and velvet seating, this giant nightclub's weekly repertoire includes an immensely popular gay night on Fridays and a conventional free-for-all on Saturdays.

Fiume BAR
(45th & Locust St; ⏲6pm-2am) Tiny spot above the Abyssinia Ethiopian restaurant in West Philly. Live music Thursday through Sunday.

Brasil's NIGHTCLUB
(Map p140; ☎215-413-1700; www.brasilsnightclub-philly.com; 112 Chestnut St; cover $10; ⏲10pm-2am Wed-Sat) The place to bump and grind to Latin, Brazilian and Caribbean sounds, with DJ John Rockwell.

Elena's Soul BAR, LIVE MUSIC
(⏲215-724-3043; 4912 Baltimore Ave; ⏲3pm-2am) Live blues, jazz, drinks, food, place to dance – all rolled into one West Philly spot.

Village Whiskey BAR
(Map p136; 118 S 20th St; ⏲11:30am-11:30pm, to 1am Fri & Sat) Cool vibe, long whiskey menu and creative cuisine.

Franklin Mortgage & Investment Co COCKTAIL BAR
(Map p136; 112 S 18th St; ⏲5pm-2am) Expertly made rye, whiskey and gin drinks in a classy setting.

Local 44 BAR
(4333 Spruce St; ⏲11:30am-midnight) Good pub grub and beer selection.

Gojjo Bar & Restaurant BAR
(4540 Baltimore Ave; ⏲4pm-2am) Great back patio at this Ethiopian place.

Other places to recommend in the burgeoning brewpub scene:

Earth Bread & Brewery BREWERY
(7136 Germantown Ave; ⏲4:30pm-midnight, closed Mon)

Nodding Head Brewery BREWERY
(Map p136; 1516 Sansom St; ⏲11:30am-2am)

An area that lies between Broad and 12th Sts and Walnut and Pine Sts, unofficially called 'gayborhood,' was dubbed Midtown Village and permanently decked out with rainbow-flag-festooned street signs during a special ceremony. Because nights and venues change frequently, check out www.phillygaycalendar.com.

Tavern on Camac GAY
(Map p136; ☎215-545-0900; 243 S Camac St; ☎4pm-2am) Show tunes and other old-school fun reign in the downstairs piano bar; one of the older gay bars in Philly, while a small upstairs dance floor gets packed with dance-happy folks.

Sisters LESBIAN
(Map p136; ☎215-735-0735; www.sistersnightclub.com; 1320 Chancellor St; ⏲5pm-2am Tue-Sat, from noon Sun) A huge nightclub and restaurant for the ladies.

Dock Street Brewery & Restaurant BREWERY
(701 S 50th St; ⏲3pm-11pm, to 1am Fri & Sat) Artisan beer and brick oven pizza in West Philly.

Live Music

Chris' Jazz Club JAZZ
(Map p136; ☎215-568-3131; www.chrisjazzcafe.com; 1421 Sansom St; cover $10-20) Showcasing local talent along with national greats, this intimate space features a four o'clock piano happy-hour Tuesday through Friday and good bands Monday through Saturday nights.

Ortlieb's Jazzhaus JAZZ
(Map p136; ☎215-922-1035; www.ortliebsjazzhaus.com; 847 N 3rd St; cover Tue-Thu, $10 Fri, $15 Sat, $3 Sun) A respectable jazz lineup with a house band jamming every Tuesday night and Cajun cuisine on the menu (mains $20).

World Cafe Live LIVE MUSIC
(Map p136; ☎215-222-1400; www.worldcafelive.com; 3025 Walnut St; cover $10-40) Located on the eastern edge of University City, World Cafe Live has upstairs and downstairs performance spaces featuring a restaurant and bar and is home to the radio station WXPN. It hosts an eclectic variety of live acts.

Theater & Culture

Kimmel Center for the Performing Arts PERFORMING ARTS
(Map p136; ☎215-790-5800; www.kimmelcenter.org; cnr Broad & Spruce Sts) Philadelphia's most active center for fine music, the Kimmel Center organizes a vast array of performances, including those for many of the companies following.

Philadelphia Theatre Company THEATER
(Map p136; ☎215-985-0420; www.philadelphiatheatrecompany.org; Suzanne Roberts Theatre, 480 S Broad St, at Lombard St) This company, which produces quality contemporary plays by regional actors, has a high-end home in the heart of the arts district.

Pennsylvania Ballet DANCE
(Map p136; ☎215-551-7000; www.paballet.org; 1819 John F Kennedy Blvd) An excellent dance company that performs in the beautiful Academy of Music and the next-door Merriam Theater.

Philadelphia Dance Company DANCE
(☎215-387-8200; www.philadanco.org; 9 N Preston St) For almost 40 years this company has been providing top-shelf exhibitions of dance, blending ballet and modern as the resident company at the Kimmel Center.

Philadelphia Orchestra CLASSICAL MUSIC
(Map p136; ☎215-893-1999; www.philorch.org; cnr Broad & Spruce Sts) The city's orchestra, founded in 1900, is going through tough financial times. After filing for bankruptcy in April, 2011 its future is in flux.

Trocadero Theater PERFORMING ARTS
(Map p136; ☎215-922-6888; www.thetroc.com; 1003 Arch St; cover up to $12) An arts and culture showcase in Chinatown housed in a 19th- century Victorian theater. Monday night is movie night with a hodgepodge of musicians, spoken-word artists and comedians other nights.

Sports

Football is all about the **Philadelphia Eagles** (www.philadelphiaeagles.com), who play at state-of-the-art **Lincoln Financial Field** (S 11th St) from August through January, usually twice a month, on Sunday. The baseball team is the National League **Philadelphia Phillies** (www.phillies.mlb.com), who play 81 home games at **Citizen's Bank Park** from April to October. Finally, basketball comes courtesy of the **Philadelphia 76ers** (www.nba.com/sixers) at **Wells Fargo Center** (3601 S Broad St).

Information

Media

Philadelphia Daily News (www.philly.com/dailynews) A tabloid-style daily.

Philadelphia Magazine (www.phillymag.com) A monthly glossy.

Philadelphia Weekly (www.philadelphiaweekly.com) Free alternative available at street boxes around town.

Philly.com (www.philly.com) News, listings and more, courtesy of the *Philadelphia Inquirer*.

WHYY 91-FM (www.whyy.org) Local National Public Radio affiliate.

Medical Services

Pennsylvania Hospital (☎215-829-3000; www.pennhealth.com/hup; 800 Spruce St; ⊙24hr)

Tourist Information

Greater Philadelphia Tourism Marketing Corp (www.visitphilly.com; 6th St, at Market St) The highly developed, nonprofit visitors bureau has comprehensive visitor information. Its welcome center shares space with the NPS center.

Independence Visitor Center (☎800-537-7676; www.independencevisitorcenter.com; 6th St, at Market St; ⊙8:30am-5:30pm) Run by the NPS, the center distributes useful visitor guides and maps, and sells tickets for the various official tours that depart from nearby locations.

Getting There & Away

Air

Philadelphia International Airport (PHL; www.phl.org; 8000 Essington Ave), 7 miles south of Center City, is served by direct international flights; domestically, it has flights to over 100 destinations in the USA.

Bus

Greyhound (www.greyhound.com; 1001 Filbert St) and **Peter Pan Bus Lines** (www.peterpanbus.com; 1001 Filbert St) are the major bus carriers; **Bolt Bus** (www.boltbus.com) and **Mega Bus** (www.us.megabus.com) are popular and comfortable competitors. Greyhound connects Philadelphia with hundreds of cities nationwide, while Peter Pan and the others concentrate on the northeast. When booked online a round-trip fare to New York City can be as low as $18 (2½ hours one way), to Atlantic City it's $20 (1½ hours) and to Washington, DC, it's $28 (4½ hours). **NJ Transit** (www.njtransit.com) carries you from Philly to various points in New Jersey.

Car

Several interstate highways lead through and around Philadelphia. From the north and south, the I-95 (Delaware Expwy) follows the eastern edge of the city beside the Delaware River, with several exits for Center City. The I-276 (Pennsylvania Turnpike) runs east across the northern part of the city and over the river to connect with the New Jersey Turnpike.

Train

Beautiful 30th St Station is one of the biggest train hubs in the country. **Amtrak** (www.amtrak.com) provides service from here to Boston (regional and Acela express service one way $87 to $206, five to 5¾ hours) and Pittsburgh (regional service from $47, 7¼ hours). A cheaper (not compared to the bus) but longer and more complicated way to get to NYC is to take the Septa R7 suburban train to Trenton in New Jersey. From there you can connect with **NJ Transit** (www.njtransit.state.nj.us) to Newark's Penn Station, then continue on NJ Transit to New York City's Penn Station.

Getting Around

The fare for a taxi to Center City from the airport is a flat fee of $25. The airport is also served by Septa's regional service using the R1 line. The R1 ($7) will drop you off in University City or in numerous stops in Center City.

Downtown distances are short enough to let you see most places on foot, and a train, bus or taxi can get you to places further out relatively easily.

Septa (www.septa.org) operates Philadelphia's municipal buses, plus two subway lines and a trolley service. Though extensive and reliable, the web of bus lines (120 routes servicing 159 sq miles) is difficult to make sense of. The one-way fare on most routes is $2, for which you'll need exact change or a token. Many subway stations and transit stores sell discounted packages of two tokens for $3.10.

Cabs, especially around City Center, are easy to hail. The flag drop or fare upon entry is $2.70, then $2.30 per mile or portion thereof. All licensed taxis have GPS and most accept credit cards.

The **Phlash** (www.phillyphlash.com; 9:30am-6pm) shuttle bus looks like an old-school trolley and loops between Penn's Landing and the Philadelphia Museum of Art (one way/all day $2/5). It runs approximately every 15 minutes.

Around Philadelphia

BRANDYWINE VALLEY

Straddling the Pennsylvania–Delaware border southwest of Philadelphia, the Brandywine Valley is a patchwork of rolling, wooded countryside, historic villages, gardens, mansions and museums. The spectacular **Longwood Gardens** (610-388-1000; www.longwoodgardens.org; Rte 1; adult/child $18/free; 9am-5pm, to 6pm Apr-Aug;) near Kennett Sq has 1050 acres, 20 indoor gardens and 11,000 kinds of plants, with something always in bloom. There's also a Children's Garden with a maze, fireworks and illuminated fountains in summer, and festive lights at Christmas. The **Brandywine Valley Wine Trail** (www.bvwinetrail.com), meanwhile, is a lovely conduit between a handful of vineyards, all with tasting rooms.

A showcase of American artwork, the **Brandywine River Museum** (610-388-2700; www.brandywinemuseum.org; cnr Hwy 1 & Rte 100; adult/child $10/6; 9:30am-4:30pm), at Chadd's Ford, includes the work of the Brandywine School – Howard Pyle, NC Wyeths and Maxfield Parrish. One of the valley's most famous attractions, though, is **Winterthur** (302-888-4600; www.winterthur.org; 5105 Kennett Pike/Rte 52, Winterthur, DE; adult/child $18/5; 10am-5pm Tue-Sun), actually in Delaware, an important museum of American furniture and decorative arts that was the country estate of Henry Francis du Pont until he opened it to the public in 1951.

VALLEY FORGE

After being defeated at the Battle of Brandywine Creek and the British occupation of Philadelphia in 1777, General Washington and 12,000 continental troops withdrew to Valley Forge. Today, Valley Forge symbolizes Washington's endurance and leadership. The **Valley Forge National Historic Park** (610-783-1099; www.nps.gov/vafo; cnr N Gulph Rd & Rte 23; admission free; park grounds 7am-dark, welcome center & Washington's Headquarters 9am-5pm) contains 5½ sq miles of scenic beauty and open space 20 miles northwest of downtown Philadelphia – a remembrance of where 2000 of George Washington's 12,000 troops perished from freezing temperatures, hunger and disease, while many others returned home. A 22-mile cycling path along the Schuylkill River connects Valley Forge to Philadelphia.

NEW HOPE & LAMBERTVILLE

New Hope, about 40 miles north of Philadelphia and its sister town Lambertville, across the Delaware River in NJ, sit equidistant from Philadelphia and New York City, and are a pair of quaint, artsy little towns. Both are edged with long and peaceful towpaths, perfect for runners, cyclists and strollers, and a bridge with a walking lane lets you crisscross between the two with ease. The towns draw a large number of gay folk; rainbow flags hanging outside various businesses demonstrate the town's gay-friendliness.

The **Golden Nugget Antique Market** (609-397-0811; www.gnmarket.com; 1850 River Rd; 6am-4pm Wed, Sat & Sun), 1 mile south of Lambertville, has all sorts of finds, from furniture to clothing, from a variety of dealers. Or spend a few picturesque hours gliding downstream in a canoe, kayak, raft or tube, courtesy of **Bucks County River Country** (215-297-5000; www.rivercountry.net; 2 Walters Lane, Point Pleasant; rental 9am-2:30pm, return by 5pm), about 8 miles north of New Hope on Rte 32.

Both towns have a plethora of cute B&Bs, if you decide to make a weekend out of it. Try the **York Street House Bed & Breakfast** (609-397-3007; www.yorkstreethouse.com; 42 York St, Lambertville; r incl breakfast $125-260;), a 1909 mansion with cozy rooms and big breakfasts.

For a meal in a divinely renovated former church try the **Marsha Brown Creole Kitchen and Lounge** (15 S Main St, New Hope; mains $15-22; 5-10pm) in New Hope serving catfish, steaks and lobster. Or head 4 miles north to the town of Stockton to **Meil's Restaurant** (cnr Main & Bridge Sts; mains $10-15; 8am-9pm Sun-Thu, to 10pm Fri & Sat) for large portions of satisfying comfort food.

Pennsylvania Dutch Country

The core of Pennsylvania Dutch Country lies in the southeast region of Pennsylvania, in an area about 20 miles by 15 miles, east of Lancaster. The Amish (*ah*-mish), Mennonite and Brethren religious communities are collectively known as the 'Plain People.' All are Anabaptist sects, who were persecuted in their native Switzerland, and from the early 1700s settled in tolerant Pennsylvania. Speaking German dialects, they became known as 'Dutch' (from 'Deutsch'). Most Pennsylvania Dutch live on farms and their beliefs vary from sect to sect. Many do not use electricity, and most opt for horse-drawn buggies – a delightful sight, and sound, in the area. The strictest believers, the Old Order Amish, wear dark, plain clothing, and live a simple, Bible-centered life – but have, ironically, become a major tourist attraction, thus bringing busloads of gawkers and the requisite strip malls, chain restaurants and hotels that lend this entire area an oxymoronic quality, to say the least. Because there is so much commercial development – fast-food restaurants, mini-malls, big-box chain stores, tract housing – continually encroaching on multigenerational family farms, it takes some doing to appreciate the unique nature of the area. Try to find your way through a series of back roads snaking their way through rural countryside between Intercourse and Strasburg.

Sights & Activities

On the western edge of Amish country, the city of **Lancaster** – a mix of art galleries, well-preserved brick row houses and somewhat

IF YOU HAVE A FEW MORE DAYS

The town of **Bethlehem**, from its initial founding by a small religious community to heavy industry center to its current incarnation as a gambling destination, retains a charming historic quality. The massive **casino** built on the site of the former Bethlehem Steel factory takes design cues from its utilitarian past.

The town of Easton, home to Lafayette College, is in the Lehigh Valley, just over the New Jersey border and on the banks of the Delaware River, only 70 miles or so from both Philadelphia and New York City. Kids can get silly with the hands-on exhibits at the **Crayola Factory** (610-515-8000; www.crayola.com/factory; 30 Centre Sq; admission incl National Canal Museum $9.75; 11am-5pm Memorial Day-Labor Day;). If you want to make an evening of it, grab a cozy room at the **Lafayette Inn** (610-253-4500; www.lafayetteinn.com; 525 W Monroe St; r incl breakfast $125-175;) and dinner at sophisticated Tuscan trattoria **Sette Luna** (219 Ferry St; mains $15; 11:30am-10pm) a few blocks from the center of town.

derelict blocks – was briefly the US capital in September 1777, when Congress stopped here overnight. The monthly **First Friday** (www.lancasterarts.com) celebration brings out a friendly local crowd for gallery hops along artsy Prince St.

Probably named for its crossroads location, **Intercourse** has heavily touristy shops selling clothing, quilts, candles, furniture, fudge and, of course, souvenirs with off-color jokes. The **Tanger Outlet stores** on Rte 30 draw tourists with their 21st-century designer clothes.

FREE **Heritage Center Museum** MUSEUM
(☎717-299-6440; www.lancasterheritage.com; 13 W King St, Lancaster; ⊙9am-5pm Mon-Sat, 10am-3pm Sun) Has a collection of 18th- and 19th-century paintings and period furniture, and gives an excellent overview of Amish culture.

Aaron & Jessica's Buggy Rides TOUR
(☎717-768-8828; 3121 Old Philadelphia Pike; ⊙9am-5pm Mon-Sat; adult/child $10/6;) Does a fun 2-mile tour narrated by an Amish driver.

Turkey Hill Experience TOUR
(☎888-986-8784; www.turkeyhillexperience.com; 301 Linden St, Columbia; adult/child $14/11; ⊙10am-5pm) This brand name's interactive homage to cows and ice cream a la Hershey's Chocolate World.

Sturgis Pretzel House TOUR
(☎717-626-4354; www.juliussturgis.com; 219 E Main St, Lititz; admission $3; ⊙9am-5pm Mon-Sat) Twist your own dough at the USA's first pretzel factory.

Ephrata Cloister HISTORIC SITE
(☎717-733-6600; www.ephratacloister.org; 632 W Main St, Ephrata; adult/child $9/6; ⊙9am-5pm Mon-Sat, from noon Sun) Gives tours of its collection of surviving restored buildings at one of the country's earliest religious communities.

Sleeping

There's a slew of inns and B&Bs in Amish country, and you will find cheap motels along the southeastern portion of Rte 462/Rte 30. Farm homes rent rooms for $50 to $100 – they welcome kids, provide home-cooked meals and offer a unique opportunity to experience farm life.

Fulton Steamboat Inn HOTEL $$
(☎717-299-9999; 1 Hartman Bridge Rd; r from $100;) A nautically themed hotel in land-locked Amish country seems like a gimmick even if the inventor of the steamboat was born nearby. The slight kitsch works however – from shiny brass old-timey light fixtures and painterly wall-paper – the hotel's interior is rather elegant and rooms are spacious and comfy. It's located at a crossroads convenient for trips to farm country or Lancaster.

Red Caboose Motel & Restaurant MOTEL $$
(☎888-687-5005; www.redcaboosemotel.com; 312 Paradise Lane, Ronks; r from $120;) There's nothing very hobo-esque about a night's sleep in one of these 25-ton cabooses – TVs and mini-fridges included – though the basic furnishings aren't the draw. Even if spaces are narrow – the width of a train car – the novelty appeals to adults as well as kids. Set on a beautiful rural lane surrounded by picturesque countryside with a small petting zoo and silo to climb with views.

Cork Factory BOUTIQUE HOTEL $$
(☎717-735-2075; www.corkfactoryhotel.com; 480 New Holland Ave; r incl breakfast from $125;) An abandoned brick behemoth now houses a stylishly up-to-date hotel only a few miles northeast of the Lancaster city center. Sunday brunch at the hotel's restaurant is a fusion of seasonal new American and down-home comfort cooking.

Beacon Hollow Farm HOMESTAY $
(☎717-768-8218; 130 Centreville Rd; r incl breakfast $95) A dairy farm in Gordonville, has a cozy cottage with two bedrooms, provides a country breakfast and lets you milk the cows.

Landis Farm HOMESTAY $$
(☎717-898-7028; www.landisfarm.com; 2048 Gochlan Rd, Manheim; r incl breakfast $100) A slightly more upscale and modern (complete with cable TV) experience can be had at this 200-year-old stone home with pinewood floors.

Eating

To sample one of the famous family-style restaurants and hearty dishes of Amish country, get prepared to rub elbows with lots of tourists. Stop by the **Dutch Haven** (2857 Lincoln Hwy/Rte 30, Ronks; 6-inch pies $7) for a sticky-sweet shoofly pie.

TOP CHOICE **Bird-in-Hand Farmers Market** MARKET $
(☎717-393-9674; 2710 Old Philadelphia Pike, Bird-in-Hand; ⊙8:30am-5:30pm Wed-Sat Jul-Oct, call for

other times of year) Great deals on tasty locally made jams, cheeses, pretzels, beef jerky and more; two lunch counters serve meals.

Good 'N Plenty Restaurant AMERICAN **$$**
(Rte 896, Smoketown; mains $11; ⌚11:30am-8pm Mon-Sat, closed Jan) Sure, you'll be dining with busloads of tourists and your cardiologist might not approve, but hunkering down at one of the picnic tables for a family-style meal ($21) is a lot of fun. Besides the main dining room, which is the size of a football field, there are a couple of other mini-areas where you can order from an à la carte menu.

Miller's BUFFET **$$**
(Rte 30, Ronks; mains $11; ⌚7am-8pm Mon-Sat) To smorgasbord ($23) or not to smorgasbord there's no question. Otherwise, the alternative menu of diner-style dishes is fairly ordinary. The anchor of a touristy complex of shops, this pavilion-size restaurant draws crowds for the buffet featuring Amish-style entrees and desserts.

Family Cupboard Restaurant & Buffet BUFFET **$$**
(3029 Old Philadelphia Pike; mains $11; ⌚11am-8pm Mon-Thu, 7am-8pm Fri & Sat) To avoid the tour-bus crush, try this place in Bird-in-Hand, for mouthwatering specials such as ham loaf (yes, that's right) and chicken in gravy over waffles.

Lancaster Brewing Co PUB **$$**
(302 N Plum St, Lancaster; mains $9-22; ⌚11:30am-10pm) Just down the street from the Cork Factory Hotel in Lancaster, the bar here draws young neighborhood regulars and the menu is a big step-up from standard pub fare – rack of wild boar and cranberry sausage is an example – but you can't beat specials like 35¢-wing night.

Central Market MARKET **$**
(23 N Market St, Lancaster; ⌚6am-4pm Tue & Fri, to 2pm Sat) The bustling market offers local produce, cheese, meats and Amish baked goods and crafts.

ℹ Information

Use a map to navigate the back roads, avoiding main Rtes 30 and 340, or simply visit in winter when tourism is down. Even better, rent a bicycle from **Rails to Trail Bicycle Shop** (☎717-367-7000; www.railstotrail.com; 1010 Hershey Rd, Elizabethtown; rental per day $25; ⌚10am-6pm) between Hershey and Lancaster, pack some food and hit the road. The **Dutch Country Visitors Center** (☎800-723-8824; www.padutchcountry.com; ⌚9am-6pm Mon-Sat, to 4pm Sun), off Rte 30 in Lancaster, offers comprehensive information.

ℹ Getting There & Around

RRTA (www.redrosetransit.com) local buses link the main towns, but a car is much more convenient for sightseeing. The **Capitol Trailways & Greyhound terminal** (Lancaster train station) has buses to Philadelphia ($15, two hours 40 minutes) and Pittsburgh ($71, eight hours). The **Amtrak train station** (53 McGovern Ave, Lancaster) has trains to and from Philadelphia ($15, 70 minutes) and Pittsburgh ($48, six hours).

South Central Pennsylvania

HERSHEY

Less than two hours from Philly is the fabled kids' favorite **Hershey** (www.hersheypa.com), home to a collection of attractions that detail, hype and, of course, hawk, the many trappings of Milton Hershey's chocolate empire. The pièce de résistance is **Hershey Park** (☎800-437-7439; www.hersheypark.com; 100 W Hersheypark Dr; adult/child $54/33; ⌚10am-10pm Jun-Aug, days & times vary other months; 👪), an amusement park with more than 60 thrill rides, a zoo, water park plus various performances and frequent fireworks displays. Don a hairnet and apron and punch in a few choices on a computer screen and then *voilà*, watch your very own chocolate bar roll down a conveyor belt at the **Create Your Own Candy Bar** ($15) attraction, part of **Hershey's Chocolate World**, a mock factory and massive candy store with overstimulating features like singing characters and free chocolate galore. For a more low-key informational visit, try the **Hershey Story, The Museum on Chocolate Avenue** (☎717-534-3439; www.hersheymuseum.org; 111 W Chocolate Ave; adult/child $10/7.50; ⌚9am-7pm summer, to 5:30pm other times), which explores the life and fascinating legacy of Mr Hershey through interactive history exhibits; try molding your own candy in the hands-on 'Chocolate Lab.'

GETTYSBURG

This tranquil, compact and history-laden town, 145 miles west of Philadelphia, saw one of the Civil War's most decisive and bloody battles. It's also where Lincoln delivered his Gettysburg Address. The area is anchored by the 8-sq-mile **Gettysburg National Military**

Park (☎717-334-1124; www.nps.gov/gett; 1195 Baltimore Pike (Rte 97); park admission free; ⏲6am-10pm Apr-Oct, to 7pm Nov-Mar), with a great **museum and visitor center** (☎877-874-2578; www.gettysburgfoundation.org; adult/child $10.50/6.50 ⏲8am-6pm). Here you can pick up a map that details a self-guided auto tour, with somber sights including the Wheatfield, which was strewn with more than 4000 dead and wounded after battle.

The annual **Civil War Battle Reenactment** (☎717-338-1525; www.gettysburgreenactment.com), a festival taking place the first weekend of July, features living-history encampments and battle reenactments drawing aficionados from near and wide.

For accommodations, try the stately three-story Victorian **Brickhouse Inn** (☎717-338-9337; www.brickhouseinn.com; 452 Baltimore St; r $115-165; ❄📶), built c 1898, a wonderful B&B with charming rooms and an outdoor patio. For a meal in Gettysburg's oldest home, built in 1776, head to **Dobbin House Tavern** (☎717-334-2100; 89 Steinwehr Ave; mains $8-25; ⏲11:30am-9pm), which serves heaping sandwiches and more elaborate meat and fish meals in kitschy themed dining rooms.

Northeastern Pennsylvania

Occupying the northeast corner of Pennsylvania is the famed **Poconos** (☎800-762-6667; www.800poconos.com) region, containing 2400 sq miles of mountains, streams, waterfalls, lakes and forests, making it a beautifully natural getaway at any time during the four seasons. Among the quaint (as well as tacky) towns is adorable **Milford**, home to the lovingly and luxuriously restored **Hotel Fauchere** (☎570-409-1212; www.hotelfauchere.com; 401 Broad St; r incl breakfast from $215; ❄📶); the hotel's stylish **Bar Louis** (mains $21, sandwiches $11) has seasonally inspired fare. The menu at **Muir House** (☎570-296-6373; 102 State St; mains $21; ⏲from 5:30pm Wed-Sun) includes a stuffed lamburger ($19) and bulgogi in a lettuce wrap ($12).

For river fun, contact **Adventure Sports** (☎570-223-0505; www.adventuresport.com; Rte 209; per day canoe/kayak $40/44; ⏲9am-6pm May-Oct) in Marshalls Creek, Pennsylvania. There are several different put-in and take-out points that allow a variety of itineraries, from quick half-day trips to leisurely multi-day adventures. Camping is allowed at many points along the way and is a great way to experience the beauty of the area.

A little further west in a tucked-away valley is **Jim Thorpe** (named for an athletic hero of the early 1900s who was buried here – but likely never visited – after town officials decided they needed a signature tourism sight; one of Thorpe's sons recently sued the town to have the remains moved to Oklahoma, his father's home state), which offers a slew of **mountain-biking** trails and **rafting** runs (as well as the requisite outfitters).

North of here, where the Delaware River swings west, marking the border between Pennsylvania and New York, and not far from the Catskills, are a number of small, primarily blue-collar towns with the occasional bistro that caters to weekending downstaters. **Lander's River Trips** (☎800-252-3925; www.landersrivertrips.com; per day canoe/kayak/tube $39/45/26) in Callicoon, NY, and in Narrowsburg, NY, further down the river, rents canoes, kayaks and tubes. The rocks at nearby **Skinners Falls** is a great place to spend the day.

> **WORTH A TRIP**
>
> **PENNSYLVANIA WILDS**
>
> Commonly and appropriately referred to as the Pennsylvania Wilds, this little-visited part of Central Pennsylvania includes the largest free-roaming elk herd east of the Mississippi – **Elk State Forest** (www.elkcountryvisitorscenter.com); an official dark sky park and the best place in the northeastern US for stargazing – **Cherry Springs State Park** (www.dcnr.state.pa.us/stateparks/parks/cheerysprings); the **Kizua Bridge Skywalk** (www.visitanf.com) part of the Allegheny National Forest; and overlooks and waterfalls around **Pine Creek Gorge** (www.visittiogapa.com/canyon) in the Tioga State Forest.

Pittsburgh

Famous as an industrial center during the 19th century, to many Americans Pittsburgh still conjures stark images of billowing clouds emanating from steel and coal factories. Today's city, however, despite continuing economic challenges, has a well-earned reputation for being one of the more livable metropolitan areas in the country. The city sits at the point where the Monongahela and Allegheny Rivers join the Ohio River, spreads out over the waterways and has hilly neighborhoods connected by picturesque bridges (all with footpaths), more than any other city in the US. Teeming with students from the many universities in town, it's a surprisingly hip and cultured city with top-notch museums, abundant greenery and several bustling neighborhoods with lively restaurant and bar scenes.

Scottish-born immigrant Andrew Carnegie made his fortune here by modernizing steel production, and his legacy is still synonymous with the city and its many cultural and educational institutions. Production dipped during the Great Depression but rose again because of mass-produced automobiles in the 1930s. When the economy and local steel industry took another major hit in the 1970s, the city's pride was buoyed by its local NFL football team: the Steelers achieved a remarkable run of four Super Bowl championships, a feat whose importance to the continuing psyche of some Pittsburghers can't be underestimated. After the steel industry's demise, Pittsburgh's economy has refocused on health care, technology and education and the city is home to several notable Fortune 500 companies, including Alcoa and Heinz.

Sights & Activities

Points of interest in Pittsburgh are scattered everywhere, and the city's spread-out nature makes it a difficult place to cover thoroughly on foot. Driving can also be troublesome, due to the oddly laid-out streets, which confuse even locals. Public buses, luckily, are quite reliable. University of Pittsburgh, Carnegie-Mellon University, Duquesne University and several other smaller colleges are all large presences in town, with sprawling campuses and bustling academic crowds.

The mystical-sounding **Golden Triangle**, between the converging Monongahela and Allegheny Rivers, is Pittsburgh's renovated downtown. Just northeast of here, the **Strip** offers warehouses, ethnic food stores and nightclubs and a little further north is gallery-filled up-and-coming **Lawrenceville**. Across the Allegheny River, the **North Side** has big sports stadiums plus several museums. Across the Monongahela River is the **South Side**, whose Slopes rise up to Mt Washington; at the **Flats**, E Carson St bustles with clubs and restaurants. East of downtown is **Oakland**, the university area, and beyond that **Squirrel Hill** and **Shadyside**, residential neighborhoods with an elegant, small-town feel.

Pittsburgh Parks Conservancy PARK
(☎412-682-7275; www.pittsburghparks.org) For pretty much any outdoor pursuit, the best option is the elaborate, 1700-acre system of the Pittsburgh Parks Conservancy, which comprises **Schenley Park** (with ball fields, a public swimming pool and golf course), **Highland Park** (with swimming pool, tennis courts and cycling track), **Riverview Park** (sporting ball fields and horseback riding trails) and **Frick Park** (with hiking trails, clay courts and a bowling green), all with beautiful running, cycling and in-line skating trails. Check out **Golden Triangle Bike Rental** (☎412-600-0675; www.goldentrianglebikenblade.com; 600 First Ave; rental per hr/day $8/30) for rentals and tours of the city; there's even a continuous trail all the way to Washington, DC called the **Great Allegheny Passage** (www.gaptrail.org). Another prime source for info on cycling, hiking and kayaking in the city's parks and around the area is **Venture Outdoors** (☎412-255-0564; www.wpfi.org; 304 Forbes Ave).

DOWNTOWN

This area is referred to as the 'Golden Triangle' only in official tourist brochures.

Point State Park PARK
At the triangle's tip is the renovated and beautified waterfront, which is popular during summer with strollers, cyclists, loungers and runners; for a longer run, head to the 11-mile gravel-paved **Montour Trail** (www.montourtrail.org), accessible by crossing the 6th St Bridge and catching the paved path at the Carnegie Science Center. The park's renovated **Fort Pitt Museum** (☎412-281-9285; www.heinzhistorycenter.org; 101 Commonwealth Pl; adult/child $5/free; ⏲10am-5pm) commemorates the historic heritage of the French and Indian War.

Senator John Heinz Pittsburgh Regional History Center MUSEUM
(☎412-454-6000; www.heinzhistorycenter.org; 1212 Smallman St; adult/child incl Sports Museum $10/5; ⏲10am-5pm) The remodeled brick warehouse offers a good take on the region's past, with exhibits on the French and Indian War, early settlers, immigrants, steel and the glass industry; it's also home to the **Western Pennsylvania Sports Museum** (⏲10am-5pm; 👪), focusing on champs from

Pittsburgh. Fun interactive exhibits for kids and adults who refuse to admit their shot at professional sports has passed them by.

August Wilson Center for African American Culture ARTS CENTER
(☎412-258-2700; www.augustwilsoncenter.org; 980 Liberty Ave) Named after an award-winning playwright and Pittsburgh native son, this contemporary institution focuses on African American arts, performance and culture.

SOUTH SIDE & MT WASHINGTON

Youthful, funky and bustling like NYC's East Village, the South Side is bursting with shops, eateries and drinking spots. In the 10 blocks between the 10th St Bridge and Birmingham Bridge there are dozens of bars, including a bunch of hole-in-the-wall joints.

TOP CHOICE **Monongahela & Duquesne Incline** TRAM
(one way adult/child $2.25/1.10; ⏲5:30am-12:45am Mon-Sat, from 7am Sun) The historic funicular railroads (c 1877) that run up and down **Mt Washington**'s steep slopes afford great city views, especially at night. At the start of the Duquesne Incline is **Station Square** (Station Sq Dr, at Fort Pitt Bridge), a group of beautiful, renovated railway buildings that now comprise what is essentially a big ol' mall. Rising up from the bustling South Side valley is the neighborhood called the **South Side Slopes**, a fascinating community of houses that seem perilously perched on the edge of cliffs, accessible via steep, winding roads and hundreds of stairs.

FREE **Society for Contemporary Art** ARTS CENTER
(☎412-261-7003; www.contemporarycraft.org; 2100 Smallman St; ⏲10am-5pm Mon-Sat) For cutting-edge crafts and other art exhibitions.

NORTH SIDE

While this part of town feels most populated when its PNC Park is filled with sports fans for a Pittsburgh Steelers game, rest assured that its many museums are hopping, too.

TOP CHOICE **Andy Warhol Museum** MUSEUM
(☎412-237-8300; www.warhol.org; 117 Sandusky St; adult/child $15/8; ⏲10am-5pm Tue-Thu, Sat & Sun, to 10pm Fri) Celebrates Pittsburgh's coolest native son, who became famous for his pop art, avant-garde movies, celebrity connections and Velvet Underground spectaculars. Exhibits include celebrity portraits, while the museum's theater hosts frequent film screenings and quirky performers. Friday-night cocktails at the museum are popular with Pittsburgh's gay community.

Carnegie Science Center MUSEUM
(☎412-237-3400; www.carnegiesciencecenter.org; 1 Allegheny Ave; adult/child $18/10, IMAX & special exhibits extra; ⏲10am-5pm Sun-Fri, to 7pm Sat; 👪) Great for kids and a cut above the average hands-on science museum, with innovative exhibits on subjects ranging from outer space to candy.

Children's Museum of Pittsburgh MUSEUM
(☎412-322-5058; www.pittsburghkids.org; Allegheny Sq; adult/child $11/10; ⏲10am-5pm Mon-Sat, noon-5pm Sun; 👪) Features loads of interactive exhibits, including a chance for kids to get under the hood of real cars and some child-friendly Warhol works.

Mexican War Streets NEIGHBORHOOD
Nearby in the northwest is the Mexican War Streets neighborhood, named after battles and soldiers of the 1846 Mexican War. The carefully restored row houses, with Greek Revival doorways and Gothic turrets lining the quiet streets, make for a peaceful, post museum stroll.

National Aviary ZOO
(☎412-323-7235; www.aviary.org; 700 Arch St, Allegheny Sq; adult/child $13/11; ⏲10am-5pm; 👪) Another treat, with more than 600 exotic and endangered birds.

Mattress Factory ARTS CENTER
(☎412-231-3169; www.mattress.org; 500 Sampsonia Way; adult/child $10/free; ⏲10am-5pm Tue-Sat, 1-5pm Sun) Hosting unique large-scale installation art and frequent performances.

OAKLAND & AROUND

The University of Pittsburgh and Carnegie Mellon University are here, and the surrounding streets are packed with cheap eateries, cafes, shops and student homes.

Carnegie Museums MUSEUM
(☎412-622-3131; www.carnegiemuseums.org; 4400 Forbes Ave; adult/child to both $15/11; ⏲10am-5pm Tue-Sat, from noon Sun) The **Carnegie Museum of Art** (www.cmoa.org), with terrific exhibits of architecture, impressionist, postimpressionist and modern American paintings; and the **Carnegie Museum of Natural History** (www.carnegiemnh.org) featuring a complete Tyrannosaurus skeleton and exhibits on Pennsylvania geology and Inuit prehistory.

FREE **Frick Art & Historical Center** MUSEUM
(☎412-371-0600; www.frickart.org; 7227 Reynolds St; ⏰10am-5pm, closed Mon) East of Oakland, in Point Breeze, is this wonderful center, which displays some of Henry Clay Frick's Flemish, French and Italian paintings in its Art Museum; assorted classics in the Car & Carriage Museum; more than five acres of grounds and gardens; and Clayton (tours $10), the restored 1872 Frick mansion.

Phipps Conservatory GARDENS
(☎412-622-6914; www.phipps.conservatory.org; One Schenley Park; adult/child $12/9; ⏰9:30am-5pm, to 10pm Fri) An impressive steel and glass greenhouse with beautifully designed and curated gardens.

FREE **Cathedral of Learning** TOWER
(☎412-624-6000; 4200 Fifth Ave; tours $3; ⏰9am-3pm Mon-Sat, from 11am Sun) Rising up from the center of the U Pitt campus, a grand, 42-story Gothic tower which, at 535ft, is the second-tallest education building in the world. It houses the elegant **Nationality Classrooms**, each representing a different style and period; most are accessible only with a guided tour.

SQUIRREL HILL & SHADYSIDE

These upscale neighborhoods feature wide streets, excellent restaurants, chain stores and independent boutiques and bakeries (try the burnt-almond tortes, a classic Pittsburgh dessert). Squirrel Hill is home to Pittsburgh's large Jewish community, the city's best kosher eateries, butchers and Judaica shops; apartment buildings, duplexes and more modest housing are almost as common as the grand mansions the neighborhood is known for.

In Shadyside, Walnut St is the bustling main strip. The leafy campus of **Chatham University**, located between the two neighborhoods, is a nice place to stroll.

GREATER PITTSBURGH

Formerly gritty **Lawrenceville** has become the city's **Interior Design District**, comprising the stretch on and around Butler St from 16th to 62nd Sts. It's a long and spotty strip of shops, galleries, studios, bars and eateries that's on every hipster's radar, and runs into the gentrifying **Garfield** neighborhood, a good place for cheap ethnic eats. **Bloomfield**, a really little Little Italy, is a strip of groceries, Italian eateries and, of all things, a landmark Polish restaurant, the Bloomfield Bridge Tavern. The Pittsburgh zoo and aquarium and a waterpark are nearby.

Tour-Ed Mine MINE
(☎724-224-4720; www.tour-edmine.com; 748 Bull Creek Rd, Tarentum; adult/child $7.50/6.50; ⏰10am-4pm, closed Tue, Jun-Sep) To experience something of the claustrophobia and learn about the working lives of coal miners, take this tour 160ft below the earth's surface.

Kennywood Amusement Park AMUSEMENT PARK
(☎412-461-0500; 4800 Kennywood Blvd, West Mifflin; www.kennywood.com; adult/child $37/24; ⏰10:30am-10pm Jun-Aug) A nationally historic landmarked amusement park 12 miles southeast of downtown with four old wooden roller coasters.

Tours

TOP CHOICE **Alan Irvine Storyteller Tours** WALKING
(☎412-521-6406; www.alanirvine.com; tours $10-15) This historian brings the city's past to life in a journey through several different neighborhoods.

'Burgh Bits & Bites Food Tour WALKING
(☎800-979-3370; www.burghfoodtour.com; tours $35) Wonderful way to discover the city's unique ethnic eats.

Pittsburgh History & Landmarks Foundation WALKING
(☎412-471-5808; www.phlf.org; Station Sq; some tours free, others from $5) Specialized historic, architectural or cultural tours by foot or motor coach.

Festivals & Events

Hothouse CULTURAL
(www.sproutfund.org/hothouse) Annual summertime night of eclectic performance, art and music supports Pittsburgh's creative side.

Three Rivers Art Festival CULTURAL
(www.3riversartsfes.org) Showcasing the city's cultural credentials, this 10-day blowout in June features free concerts and outdoor visual and performance arts in Point State Park.

Sleeping

Straight-up chain hotels, especially around Oakland, dominate the city's lodging options. The Omni Penn Hotel towers over the downtown district. For more character, check in with the **Pittsburgh Bed & Breakfast Association** (www.pittsburghbnb.com).

Inn on Negley INN $$
(☎412-661-0631; www.innonnegley.com; 703 Negley Ave; r $180-240; P❄📶) Formerly a pair of Shadyside inns, these two Victorian houses have been combined into one newly refurbished gem with a clean-line aesthetic that still bursts with romance. It features four-poster beds, handsome furniture and fireplaces, large windows and, in some rooms, hot tubs.

The Priory INN $$
(☎412-231-3338; www.thepriory.com; 614 Pressley St; r incl breakfast from $140; P❄📶) Housed in a former Catholic monastery on the North Side just over the Veterans Bridge, the Priory is a mix of old-fashion furnishings with contemporary design touches. There's a parlor with a fireplace and interior courtyard good for drinks in warm months. A new wing with rooms was added in 2011. Attached is the magnificent Grand Hall, a former church, now host to weddings and events.

Inn on the Mexican War Streets INN $$
(☎412-231-6544; www.innonthemexicanwarstreets.com; 604 W North Ave; r incl breakfast $139-189; P❄📶) This historic, gay-owned mansion on the North Side is near the museums and right on the bus line that takes you downtown. Expect hearty homemade breakfasts, charming hosts, stunning antique furnishings and an elegant porch, plus a martini lounge and the four-star restaurant Acanthus.

The Parador Inn B&B $$
(☎412-231-4800; www.theparadorinn.com; 939 Western Ave; r incl breakfast $150; P❄📶) This lovingly restored mansion on the North Side not far from the National Aviary and Heinz Field is a charming hodgepodge of aesthetic influence – from Victorian to Caribbean and everything in between. The owner is on hand to answer any questions and there are public rooms and a garden to relax in.

Sunnyledge HOTEL $$$
(☎412-683-5014; www.sunnyledge.com; 5124 Fifth Ave; r/ste $189/275; ❄) Though it refers to itself as a 'boutique hotel,' it would be more accurate to describe the Sunnyledge as a 'historic' one. Housed in an 1886 mansion in Shadyside, the atmosphere is one of traditional elegance that's overwrought at times.

Morning Glory Inn INN $$$
(☎412-431-1707; www.gloryinn.com; 2119 Sarah St; r incl breakfast $145-190, ste $175-450; ❄📶) An Italianate-style Victorian brick townhouse in the heart of the busy South Side. The overall decor is slightly chintzy but you can relax in the charming backyard patio, and delicious breakfasts are a major plus.

Eating

The highest concentration and majority of restaurants are located on the South Side on and around Carson St. The Italian shops in the Strip district are where local chefs go to shop for meat and cheese.

Southside

Cafe du Jour MEDITERRANEAN $$$
(1107 E Carson St; mains $15-35; ⏲11:30am-10pm Mon-Sat) Part of the raucous South Side 'hood, Cafe du Jour has a constantly changing menu of Mediterranean dishes. It does especially good soups and salads for lunch; try to get a seat in the small outside courtyard. It's BYOB.

Dish Osteria Bar MEDITERRANEAN $$
(☎412-390-2012; 128 S 17th St; mains $18; ⏲5pm-2am Mon-Sat) A tucked-away, intimate locals' fave. The simple wood tables and floors belie the at-times extravagant Mediterranean creations, which range from fresh sardines with caramelized onions to fettuccine with lamb *ragù*.

Gypsy Café MEDITERRANEAN $$
(☎412-381-4977; 1330 Bingham St; mains $15; ⏲11:30am-midnight) The purple floors and walls and brightly colored rugs make loyal patrons here as happy as the fresh, seasonal fare. Sample menu items include a smoked trout plate and a stew of shrimp, scallop and feta. Hours are changeable so call ahead.

Café Zenith VEGETARIAN $$
(86 S 26th St; mains $10; ⏲11am-9pm Thu-Sat, 11am-3pm Sun) A meal at this Southside restaurant is like eating in an antique shop and everything from the formica tables and up, is for sale. Regardless, the Sunday brunch ($10) and lengthy tea menu are up to date.

City Grill AMERICAN $$
(2019 E Carson St; mains $10-25; ⏲11am-11pm Mon-Thu, to midnight Fri & Sat, 4-10pm Sun) On the South Side; known for mouthwatering burgers, considered one of the best in the city.

Kessab's MIDDLE EASTERN **$**
(1207 Carson St; mains $6; ⊙10:30am-10pm Mon-Thu, to 11pm Fri & Sat) This Lebanese restaurant on the South Side serves splendid baba ghanoush.

Double Wide Grill AMERICAN **$$**
(2339 E Carson St; mains $16; ⊙11am-10pm Mon-Wed, to midnight Thu-Sat, 10am-10pm Sun) Does barbecue as well as interesting veggie options like pulled seitan and coconut tofu.

Other Neighborhoods

Dinette PIZZERIA **$$**
(☎412-362-0202; 5996 Penn Circle South; pizzas $14; ⊙6-11ppm, to midnight Fri & Sat) James Beard award-semi finalist two years running, Sonja Finn has elevated this casual Shadyside eatery into a destination for Yinzer foodies. The individual gourmet thin-crust pizzas are topped with locally sourced meat and produce and an excellent wine selection.

Primanti Bros SANDWICHES **$**
(18th St, at Smallman St; sandwiches $6; ⊙24hr) A Pittsburgh institution on the Strip, this always packed place specializes in greasy and delicious hot sandwiches – from knockwurst and cheese to the 'Pitts-burger cheesesteak.' Other outlets are in Oakland, downtown and South Side.

Essie's Original Hot Dog Shop FAST FOOD **$**
(3901 Forbes Ave; meals $3; ⊙10am-3:30am Mon-Thu, to 5am Fri & Sat) Affectionately nicknamed 'dirty Os' or 'the O' by locals, this Oakland favorite is known for its cheap dogs and mounds of crispy fries – especially after a night at the bars.

Quiet Storm Coffeehouse & Restaurant VEGETARIAN **$**
(5430 Penn Ave; mains $8; ⊙8am-7pm Mon-Thu, to 10pm Fri, 10am-10pm Sat, 10am-4pm Sun; ✎) This hipster-filled, multiuse cafe in Garfield specializes in veggie and vegan cuisine and hosts frequent readings and musical performances.

Pamela's Diner DINER **$**
(3703 Forbes Ave; mains $6; ⊙7:30am-4pm) Locals – and President Obama, who said the crepe-style pancakes were his favorite – swear by the breakfast at this Oakland spot. Other locations in the Strip, Shadyside and Squirrel Hill.

Ritter's Diner DINER **$**
(5221 Baum Blvd; mains $7; ⊙24hr) A classic greasy spoon where locals of the Bloomfield neighborhood head for a pierogi after a long night out. Each table has its own jukebox.

Pho Minh VIETNAMESE **$**
(4917 Penn Ave; mains $7; ⊙noon-9pm Wed, Thu & Sun, to 10pm Fri & Sat) Tiny and popular in Bloomfield; does excellent Vietnamese noodle, soup and tofu dishes.

Drinking & Entertainment

BARS & NIGHTCLUBS

Most nightlife is centered on the South Side and the Strip. Carson St is ground zero for bar-hopping. You'll find several big, frenzied dance clubs, known 'meatmarkets,' clustered at the edge of the Strip district. Most gay bars are in a concentrated stretch of Liberty Ave downtown. They're hoppin' and plentiful.

Bloomfield Bridge Tavern PUB
(4412 Liberty Ave; ⊙5:30pm-2am Tue-Sat) The only Polish restaurant in Lil' Italy, is a gritty pub that serves beers with excellent sides of pierogi and the occasional indie rock band.

Church Brew Works BREWERY
(3525 Liberty Ave; ⊙10:30am-10pm) Serving handcrafted beers in a massive former church space, this brewery is a standout in Lawrenceville.

Hofbräuhaus BEER HALL
(2705 S Water St; ⊙11am-11pm, to 2am Fri & Sat) An imitation of the famous Munich beer hall and only a block off Carson.

Gooski BAR
(3117 Brereton St; ⊙3pm-2am) Hipster bar in Polish Hill neighborhood with cheap drinks and jukebox.

Brillo Box Bar BAR
(4104 Penn Ave; ⊙11am-2am Tue-Sat, from 6pm Sun) Live music, excellent menu and a good Sunday brunch at this popular spot in Lawrenceville.

Dee's Cafe BAR
(1314 E Carson St; ⊙noon-2am Mon-Sat, from 2pm Sun) The Southside bar for billiards with Pabst on tap.

Smokin' Joe's BAR
(2001 E Carson St; ⊙11am-2am) Good for its huge beer selection.

LIVE MUSIC

Shadow Lounge LIVE MUSIC
(☎412-363-8277; www.shadowlounge.net; 5972 Baum Blvd) Two venues for catching hot

hip-hop and house DJs, plus indie bands, readings and open-mic nights.

Rex Theater CONCERT VENUE
(☎412-381-6811; www.rextheater.com; 1602 E Carson St) This is a favorite South Side venue, a converted movie theater, for touring jazz, rock and indie bands; everyone from Edgar Winter to Ani DiFranco.

Manchester Craftsman Guild LIVE MUSIC
(☎412-322-0800; www.mcgjazz.org; 1815 Metropolitan St) Live concerts and recordings of top jazz musicians are held here, on the north side of the city.

Club Café LIVE MUSIC
(☎412-431-4950; www.clubcafelive.com; 56-58 S 12th St) On the South Side, has live music nightly, mostly of the singer-songwriter type.

THEATER & CULTURE

Pittsburgh Cultural Trust PERFORMING ARTS
(☎412-471-6070; www.pgharts.org; 803 Liberty Ave) Promotes all downtown arts, from the Pittsburgh Dance Council and PNC Broadway in Pittsburgh to visual art and opera; the website has links to all main arts venues.

Gist Street Readings PERFORMING ARTS
(www.giststreet.org; 3rd fl, 305 Gist St; readings $10) Holds monthly readings from local and well-known national literary figures. Best to get there when doors open at 7:15pm, since turnout is typically large. Bring your own refreshments.

Harris Theater CINEMA
(☎412-682-4111; www.pghfilmmakers.org; 809 Liberty Ave) The restored theater screens a wide variety of art-house films, often part of film festivals. Operated by the Pittsburgh Filmmakers organization.

SPORTS

Pittsburgh is a big-time sports city. Fans will tell you they bleed black and gold, the colors of the hometown NFL franchise the **Steelers** who play at **Heinz Field** (www.pittsburghsteelers.com). Also on the North Side, just by the Allegheny River, is **PNC Park** (www.pirateball.com), where the Pittsburgh Pirates major-league baseball team bases itself. **Mellon Arena** (www.penguins.nhl.com), just east of downtown, is where the NHL Pittsburgh Penguins drop the puck. The University of Pittsburgh basketball team, the **Pitt Panthers** (www.pittsburghpanthers.com), is a perennial top-ranked team with a rabid fan base.

Information

Media

Pittsburgh City Paper (www.pghcitypaper.com) Free alternative weekly with extensive arts listings.

Pittsburgh Post-Gazette (www.post-gazette.com) A major daily.

Pittsburgh Tribune-Review (www.pittsburghlive.com) Another major daily.

Pittsburgh's Out (www.outonline.com) Free monthly gay newspaper.

WQED-FM: 90.5 Local National Public Radio affiliate.

WYEP-FM: 91.3 Local independent station with eclectic music.

Medical Services

Allegheny County Health Department (☎412-687-2243; 3333 Forbes Ave) Has a walk-in medical center.

University of Pittsburgh Medical Center (☎412-647-8762; 200 Lothrop St; ⏲24hr) Emergency, high-ranking medical care.

Tourist Information

Greater Pittsburgh Convention & Visitors Bureau Main Branch (☎412-281-7711; www.visitpittsburgh.com; Suite 2800, 120 Fifth Ave; ⏲10am-6pm Mon-Fri, to 4pm Sat, to 3pm Sun) Publishes the *Official Visitors Guide* and provides maps and tourist advice.

Websites

Citysearch (pittsburgh.citysearch.com) Nightlife, restaurant and shopping listings.

Pittsburgh.net (www.pittsburgh.net) Listings, neighborhoods and events.

Pop City (www.popcitymedia.com) Weekly e-magazine highlighting arts and cultural events.

Getting There & Away

Air

Pittsburgh International Airport (PIT; www.pitairport.com), 18 miles west from downtown, has direct connections to Europe, Canada and major US cities via a slew of airlines.

Bus

Arriving in its station near the Strip, **Greyhound** (cnr 11th St & Liberty Ave) has frequent buses to Philadelphia ($46, seven hours), New York ($54, 11 hours) and Chicago, IL ($62, 10 to 14 hours).

Car

Pittsburgh is easily accessible via major highways, from the north or south on the I-76 or I-79, from the west on Rte 22 and from the east on the I-70. It's about an eight-hour drive from New York City and about three hours from Buffalo.

Train

Amtrak (1100 Liberty Ave) is behind the magnificent original train station, with trains heading to cities including Philadelphia (from $47, seven to eight hours) and New York (from $63, nine to 11 hours).

Getting Around

The excellent **28X Airport Flyer** (www.portauthority.org/PAAC.com; one way $2.60) public bus makes runs from the airport to Oakland and downtown every 20 minutes. Taxis are readily available and cost about $40 (not including tip) to downtown. Various shuttles also make downtown runs and cost $15 to $20 per person one way.

Driving around Pittsburgh can be extremely frustrating – roads end with no warning, one-way streets can take you in circles and there are various bridges to contend with.

Port Authority Transit (www.portauthority.org) operates an extensive bus system and a limited light-rail system, the 'T,' which is useful for going from downtown to the South Side. Bus and T fares range from free to $3, depending on the zone in which you're traveling.

For taxis, call **Yellow Cab Co of Pittsburgh** (☎412-321-8100), which charges by zone.

Around Pittsburgh

A Frank Lloyd Wright masterpiece, **Fallingwater** (☎724-329-8501; www.fallingwater.org; adult/child $18/12; ⏰10am-4pm, closed Wed, check for detailed schedule) is south of Pittsburgh on Rte 381. Completed in 1939 as a weekend retreat for the Kaufmanns, owners of the Pittsburgh department store, the building blends seamlessly with its natural setting. To see inside you must take one of the hourly guided tours, and reservations are recommended. A more intensive two-hour tour, with photography permitted, is offered ($55; times vary depending on day and month, reservations required). The rather attractive forested grounds open at 8:30am.

Much less visited is **Kentuck Knob** (☎724-329-1901; www.kentuckknob.com; adult/child $16/10; ⏰10am-5pm Tue-Sun, from noon Wed), another Frank Lloyd Wright house (designed in 1953), built into the side of a rolling hill. It's noted for its natural materials, hexagonal design and honeycomb skylights. House tours last about an hour and include a jaunt through the onsite sculpture garden, with works by Andy Goldsworthy, Ray Smith and others.

To spend a night or two in the area, opt for the historic mountaintop **Summit Inn** (☎724-438-8594; www.summitinnresort.com; 101 Skyline Dr; r from $120; ❄📶🏊) or the swank **Nemacolin Woodlands Resort & Spa** (☎724-329-8555; www.nemacolin.com; 1001 Lafayette Dr; r from $200), with a spa, golf course and dining rooms. Both are in Farmington.

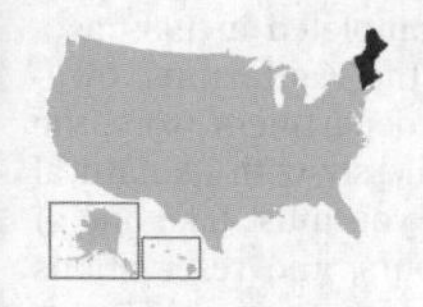

New England

Includes »

Massachusetts..............167
Boston..........................167
Cape Cod...................... 185
Nantucket..................... 194
Martha's Vineyard........ 195
Rhode Island 201
Providence 201
Newport........................203
Connecticut..................207
Vermont.........................212
New Hampshire............ 222
Maine............................230

Best Places to Eat

» Simon Pearce (p217)

» Mezze Bistro + Bar (p200)

» Frank Pepe's (p208)

» Costantino's Venda Ravioli (p202)

» Black Trumpet Bistro (p223)

Best Places to Stay

» Omni Parker House (p175)

» Carpe Diem (p192)

» Willard Street Inn (p220)

» Ale House Inn (p223)

» Providence Biltmore (p202)

Why Go?

New England may look small on a map, but don't let that fool you. Yes, you could drive from one end to the other in a day but really, why would you want to? There are simply too many enticements along the way. The cities offer a vibrant mix of historical sites, chef-driven restaurants and Ivy League campuses. On the coast you'll find age-old fishing villages and sandy beaches begging a dip. Or head inland, where the northern states are as rural and rugged as the mountains that run up their spines. So take it slow. Crack open a lobster and let the sweet juices run down your fingers. Hike quiet trails. Or just get lost on a scenic back road and count the covered bridges. And if you're lucky enough to be here in autumn, you'll be rewarded with the most brilliant fall foliage you'll ever see.

When to Go

Boston

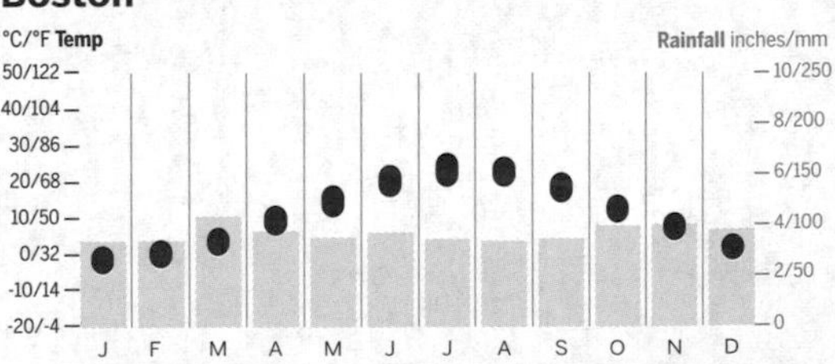

May–Jun Uncrowded sights and lightly trodden trails. Whale-watching begins.

Jul–Aug Top tourist season with summer festivals, warm ocean water and beach parties.

Fall New England's blazing foliage peaks from mid-September to mid-October.

Getting There & Around

Getting to New England is easy, but once you arrive you'll need a car if you want to explore the region thoroughly. The coastal I-95 and the inland I-91, the main north–south highways, transverse New England from Connecticut to Canada. Public transportation is fine between major cities but scarce in the countryside. **Greyhound** (www.greyhound.com) operates the most extensive bus service.

Amtrak's (www.amtrak.com) Northeast Corridor service connects Boston, Providence, Hartford and New Haven with New York City; smaller regional services operate elsewhere in New England.

Boston's **Logan International Airport** (BOS) is New England's main hub. **TF Green Airport** (PVD) in Providence, Rhode Island, and **Manchester Airport** (MHT) in New Hampshire – both about an hour's drive from Boston – are growing 'minihubs' boasting less congestion and cheaper fares.

NEW ENGLAND PARKS

Acadia National Park (p239), on the rugged, northeastern coast of Maine, is the region's only national park but numerous other large tracts of New England's forest, mountains and shoreline are set aside for preservation and recreation.

The **White Mountain National Forest** (p226), a vast 800,000-acre expanse of New Hampshire and Maine, offers a wonderland of scenic drives, hiking trails, campgrounds and ski slopes. Vermont's **Green Mountain National Forest** (p215) covers 400,000 acres of unspoiled forest that's crossed by the Appalachian Trail. Another gem of nationally preserved lands is the **Cape Cod National Seashore** (p190), a 44,600-acre stretch of rolling dunes and stunning beaches that's perfect for swimming, cycling and seaside hikes.

State parks are plentiful throughout New England, ranging from green niches in urban locations to the remote, untamed wilderness of **Baxter State Park** (p243) in northern Maine.

Seafood Specialties

» **Clam chowder** Or, as Bostonians say, *chow-dah*, combines chopped clams, potatoes and clam juice in a milk base

» **Oysters** Served raw on the half-shell or, for the less intrepid, broiled; sweetest are Wellfleet oysters from Cape Cod

» **Steamers** Soft-shelled clams steamed and served in a bucket of briny broth

» **Clambake** A meal of steamed lobster, clams and corn on the cob

DON'T MISS

You can't leave New England without cracking open a steamed lobster at a beachside seafood shack, such as the Lobster Dock in Boothbay Harbor.

Fast Facts

» Hub cities: Boston (population 617,600), Providence (population 178,000)

» Boston to Acadia National Park: 310 miles

» Time zone: Eastern

» States covered in this chapter: Massachusetts, Rhode Island, Connecticut, Vermont, New Hampshire, Maine

Did You Know?

Four of the six US states that have legalized gay marriage are in New England.

Resources

» Discover New England (www.discovernewengland.org) links to destinations throughout New England.

» Yankee Magazine's fall foliage guide (www.yankeefoliage.com) gives foliage forecasts and scenic drives.

New England Highlights

1. Following in the footsteps of Colonial rebel rousers along **Boston's Freedom Trail** (p174)
2. Romping across the dunes at **Cape Cod National Seashore** (p190)
3. Ogling the palatial mansions and basking in music at folk and jazz festivals in **Newport** (p203)
4. Wandering the cobbled Moby Dick–era streets of **Nantucket** (p194)
5. Driving the scenic **Kancamagus Highway** (p225) across the craggy White Mountains
6. Hiking and cycling the carriage roads of **Acadia National Park** (p239)

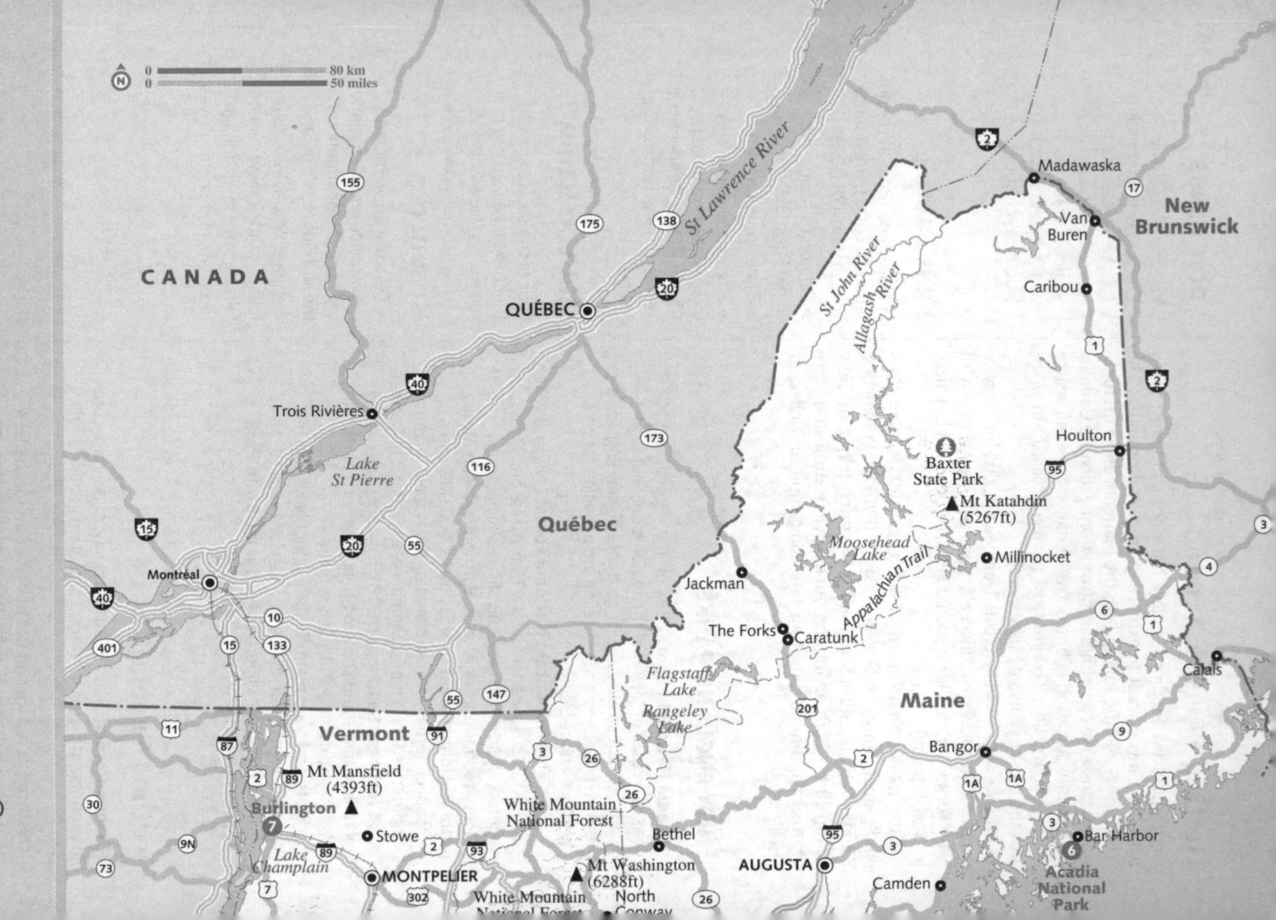

7 Working off an organic lunch at one of **Burlington's** (p219) green cafes with a paddle around Lake Champlain

8 Stretching your quads on a hike in the **Green Mountains** (p215)

9 Treating yourself to dazzling fall foliage in the **Berkshires** (p199) and **Litchfield Hills** (p211)

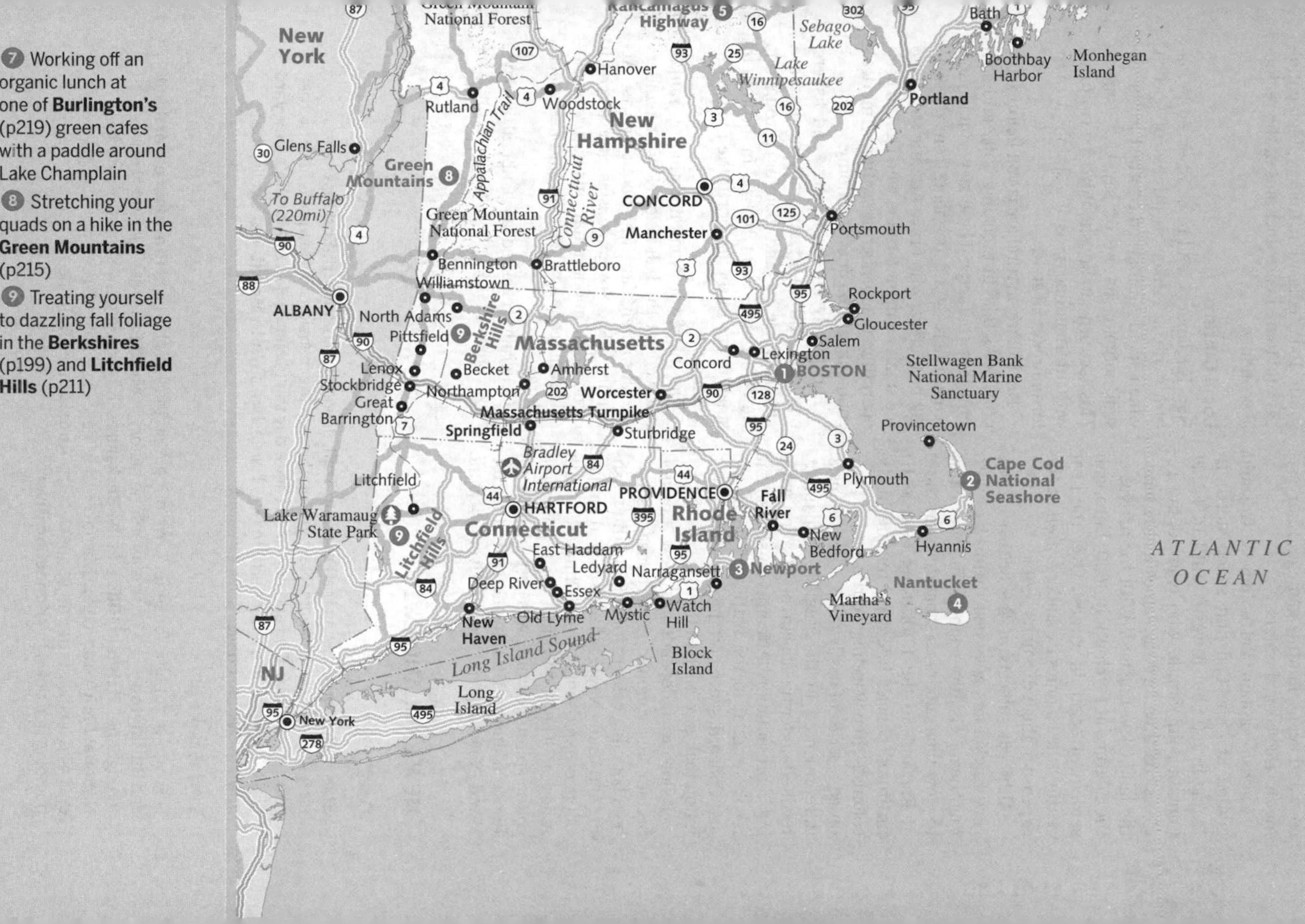

History

When the first European settlers arrived, New England was inhabited by native Algonquians who lived in small tribes, raising corn and beans, hunting game and harvesting the rich coastal waters.

English captain Bartholomew Gosnold landed at Cape Cod and sailed north to Maine in 1602 but it wasn't until 1614 that Captain John Smith, who charted the region's coastline for King James I, christened the land 'New England.' With the arrival of the Pilgrims at Plymouth in 1620, European settlement began in earnest. Over the next century the colonies expanded, often at the expense of the indigenous people.

Although subjects of the British crown, New Englanders governed themselves with their own legislative councils and they came to view their affairs as separate from those of England. In the 1770s King George III instituted policies intent on reining in the colonists' free-wheeling spirits and he imposed a series of costly taxes. The colonists, unrepresented in the English Parliament, revolted under the slogan 'no taxation without representation.' Attempts to squash the revolt resulted in the battles of Lexington and Concord, setting off the American Revolution that gave birth to the USA in 1776.

Following independence, New England became an economic powerhouse, its harbors booming centers for shipbuilding, fishing and trade. New England's famed Yankee Clippers plied ports from China to South America. The USA's first water-powered cotton-spinning mill was established in Rhode Island in 1793. In the years that followed New England's swift rivers became the engines of vast mills turning out clothing, shoes and machinery.

But no boom lasts forever. By the early 20th century many of the mills had moved south. Today education, finance, biotechnology and tourism are linchpins of the regional economy.

Local Culture

New Englanders tend to be reserved by nature, with a Yankee thriftiness of speech, which stands in marked contrast to the casual outgoing nature of, say, Californians. This taciturn quality shouldn't be confused with unfriendliness, as it's simply a more formal regional style.

Particularly in rural areas you'll notice the pride folks take in their ingenuity and self-sufficient character. These New Englanders remain fiercely independent, from the fishing boat crews who brave Atlantic storms to the small Vermont farmers who fight to keep operating independently within America's gobble-up agribusiness economy.

Fortunately for the farmers and fishers, buy-local and go-organic movements have grown by leaps and bounds throughout New England. From bistros in Boston to small towns in the far north the menus are greening.

One place you won't find that ol' Yankee reserve is at the ball field. New Englanders are absolutely fanatical about sports. Attending a Red Sox game is as close as you'll come to a modern-day gladiators-at-the-coliseum scene – wild cheers and nasty jeers galore.

Generally regarded as a liberal enclave, New England's in the forefront on pro-

NEW ENGLAND IN...

One Week

Start in **Boston**, cruising the **Freedom Trail**, dining at a cozy **North End bistro** and exploring the city's highlights. Next, tramp through the mansions in **Newport**, then hit the beaches on **Cape Cod** and hop a ferry for a day trip to **Nantucket** or **Martha's Vineyard**. End the week with a jaunt north to New Hampshire's **White Mountains**, circling back down the **Maine coast**.

Two Weeks

Now you've got time for serious exploring. Visit the lively burgs of **Providence**, **Portland** and **Burlington**, get a taste of maritime history in **Mystic** and take a leisurely drive through the **Litchfield Hills** and the **Berkshires**. Kayak along the shores of **Acadia National Park**. Wrap it up in Maine's vast wilderness, where you can work up a sweat on a hike up the northernmost peak of the **Appalachian Trail** and take an adrenaline-pumping ride down the **Kennebec River**.

gressive political issues from gay rights to health-care reform. Indeed the universal health insurance program in Massachusetts became the model for President Obama's national plan.

MASSACHUSETTS

New England's most populous state packs in appealing variety from the woodsy hills of the Berkshires to the sandy beaches of Cape Cod. Massachusetts' rich history oozes from almost every quarter: you can explore Plymouth, 'America's hometown;' walk the Freedom Trail in Boston, where the first shots of the American Revolution rang out; and hit the cobbled streets of the old whaling village of Nantucket. University-laden Boston offers all the accoutrements – from world-class museums to edgy nightlife – you'd expect of a great college town. Provincetown's a gay-extravaganza whirl like no other, Northampton's got the coolest cafe scene this side of New York, and Martha's Vineyard offers the perfect family vacation – just ask the Obamas and Clintons.

History

Massachusetts has played a leading role in American politics since the arrival of the first colonists. In the 18th century, spurred by a booming maritime trade, Massachusetts colonists revolted against trade restrictions imposed by Great Britain. British attempts to put down the revolt resulted in the 1770 Boston Massacre, which became a rallying cry to action. In 1773, angered by a new British-imposed tax on tea, colonists raided three British merchant ships and dumped their cargo of tea into Boston Harbor. Known as the Boston Tea Party, this tax revolt against the crown set the stage for the battles that started the American Revolution.

In the 19th century Massachusetts became the center of the world's whaling industry, bringing unprecedented wealth to the islands of Nantucket and Martha's Vineyard, whose ports are still lined with grand sea captains' homes.

MASSACHUSETTS FACTS

» **Nickname** Bay State

» **Population** 6.5 million

» **Area** 7840 sq miles

» **Capital city** Boston (population 617,600)

» **Other cities** Worcester (population 181,000), Springfield (population 153,000)

» **Sales tax** 6.25%

» **Birthplace of** inventor Benjamin Franklin (1706–90), five presidents including John F Kennedy (1917–63), authors Jack Kerouac (1922–69) and Henry David Thoreau (1817–62)

» **Home of** Harvard University, Boston Marathon, Plymouth Rock

» **Politics** New England's most liberal state

» **Famous for** Boston Tea Party, first state to legalize gay marriage

» **Most parodied accent** Bostonians' pahk the cah in Hahvahd Yahd

» **Driving distances** Boston to Provincetown 145 miles, Boston to Northampton 98 miles

Information

Boston Globe (www.boston.com) The region's main newspaper has a great online site.

Massachusetts Dept of Conservation and Recreation (☎877-422-6762; www.mass.gov/dcr/recreate/camping.htm) Offers camping in 29 state parks.

Massachusetts Office of Travel & Tourism (☎617-973-8500; www.massvacation.com) Provides information on the entire state.

Boston

One of America's oldest cities is also one of its youngest. A score of colleges and universities add a fresh face to this historic capital and feed a thriving arts and entertainment scene. But don't think for a minute that Boston is all about the literati. Grab a seat in the bleachers at Fenway Park and join the fanatical fans cheering on the Red Sox. Wicked pissah (super cool), as they say here in the Hub.

History

When the Massachusetts Bay Colony was established by England in 1630, Boston became its capital. It's a city of firsts: Boston Latin School, the first public school in the USA, was founded in 1635, followed a year later by Harvard, the nation's first university. The first newspaper in the colonies was printed here in 1704, America's first labor union organized here in 1795 and the country's first subway system opened in Boston in 1897.

Not only were the first battles of the American Revolution fought here, but Boston was also home to the first African American regiment to fight in the US Civil War. Waves of immigrants, especially Irish in the mid-18th century and Italians in the early 20th, have infused the city with European influences.

Today Boston remains at the forefront of higher learning and its universities have spawned world-renowned industries in biotechnology, medicine and finance.

Sights & Activities

Boston retains an intimate scale that's best experienced on foot. Most of Boston's main attractions are found in or near the city center, making it easy to ramble from one to the next.

Begin at Boston Common, where you'll find the tourist office and the start of the Freedom Trail. Everything radiates out from the Common, with historic sites, graceful parks and promenades around every corner.

BOSTON COMMON & PUBLIC GARDEN

Boston Common PARK

(Map p176) The heart of Boston since 1634, the 50-acre common, bordered by Tremont, Beacon and Charles Sts, was the nation's first public park. In years past it was a pasture for cattle grazing, a staging ground for soldiers of the American Revolution and the site of chastising pillory-and-stocks for those who dared defy Puritan mores. These days it's a gloriously carefree scene, especially at the **Frog Pond**, where waders cool off on hot summer days and ice-skaters frolic in winter.

Public Garden GARDENS

(Map p176) Adjoining the Common, the 24-acre Public Garden provides an inviting oasis of bountiful flowers and shady trees. Its centerpiece, a tranquil lagoon with old-fashioned pedal-powered **Swan Boats** (www.swanboats.com; adult/child $2.75/1.50; 10am-4pm or 5pm mid-Apr–mid-Sep;), has been delighting children for generations.

BEACON HILL & DOWNTOWN

Rising above Boston Common is Beacon Hill, Boston's most historic and affluent neighborhood. To the east is the city's downtown, with a curious mix of Colonial-era sights and modern office buildings.

FREE **State House** HISTORIC BUILDING

(Map p176; 617-727-3676; Beacon St, at Park St; 8am-5pm Mon-Fri) Crowning Beacon Hill is the golden-domed capitol building, the seat of Massachusetts' government since 1798. Volunteers lead free 40-minute tours from 10am to 3:30pm.

Granary Burying Ground CEMETERY

(Map p176; cnr Tremont & Park Sts) Tons of history lie buried at this Colonial graveyard, which dates to 1660 and holds the bones of influential Bostonians, including Revolutionary heroes Paul Revere, Samuel Adams and John Hancock.

BOSTON IN...

Two Days

Follow in the footsteps of America's revolutionary founders on the **Freedom Trail**, stopping to imbibe a little history at the **Bell in Hand Tavern**, the oldest tavern in the USA. Wrap up your first day with a scrumptious meal in the **North End**, Boston's 'Little Italy.'

Your mother always wanted you to go to Harvard, right? Begin day two in **Cambridge** poking around Harvard Sq and cruising the campus sights. End the day gallery browsing and schmoozing with the beautiful people on **Newbury St**.

Four Days

Start day three at one of the city's stellar museums – for classic American art, head to the **Museum of Fine Arts** or for cutting edge, the **Institute of Contemporary Art**. For a sumptuous city view, take an elevator up 50 floors to the **Prudential Center Skywalk**.

On your final day, head west to **Lexington** and **Concord** if you have a literary inclination, or spend the day at kid-friendly **Plimoth Plantation**. When you get back into town, take in a **play** at one of Boston's renowned theaters or head to Fenway Park to catch a **Red Sox** game.

Faneuil Hall HISTORIC SITE
(Map p176; Congress St) This landmark red-brick hall, topped with its famed grasshopper weathervane, has been a market and public meeting place since 1740. Today the hall, Quincy Market and North and South Market buildings make up the Faneuil Hall Marketplace chock-full of small shops and eateries.

Museum of Afro-American History MUSEUM
(Map p176; www.afroammuseum.org; 46 Joy St; adult/child $5/3; ⌚10am-4pm Mon-Sat) Illustrating the accomplishments of Boston's African American community, this museum includes the adjacent **African Meeting House**, where former slave Frederick Douglass recruited African American soldiers to fight in the Civil War.

Old South Meeting House HISTORIC BUILDING
(Map p176; www.oldsouthmeetinghouse.org; 310 Washington St; adult/child $6/1; ⌚9:30am-5pm) In 1773 Colonists met here for a rousing debate on taxation before throwing the Boston Tea Party.

Old State House HISTORIC BUILDING
(Map p176; www.bostonhistory.org; 206 Washington St; adult/child $7.50/3; ⌚9am-5pm) Boston's oldest public building, erected in 1713, has simple displays depicting the American Revolution.

NORTH END & CHARLESTOWN

An old-world warren of narrow streets, the Italian North End offers visitors an irresistible mix of colorful period buildings and mouthwatering eateries. Colonial sights spill across the river into Charlestown, home to America's oldest battleship.

Paul Revere House HISTORIC BUILDING
(Map p176; www.paulreverehouse.org; 19 North Sq; adult/child $3.50/1; ⌚9:30am-5:15pm) The oldest (1680) house still standing in Boston. Even more significantly, it's the former home of Paul Revere, a leader of the colonial militia the Minutemen, so named for their ability to deploy rapidly. It was Revere who jumped on his horse and rode through the streets shouting the warning 'the British are coming.'

Old North Church CHURCH
(Map p176; www.oldnorth.com; 193 Salem St; ⌚9am-6pm Jun-Oct, 9am-5pm Nov-May) It was at this church, built c 1723, that two lanterns were hung in the steeple on that pivotal night of April 18, 1775, signaling to a waiting Paul Revere that British forces were setting out by sea ('one if by land, two if by sea').

> **BOSTON GOES GREEN**
>
> The hulking highway that once tore across the center of the city has morphed into a ribbon of green stretching from Chinatown to the North End. Known as the Rose Kennedy Greenway in honor of JFK's mother, this meandering green space reclaims land that was until a few years back the elevated section of I-93.
>
> Completed in late 2008, the interconnecting pocket parks that comprise the greenway offer shady respites from the city bustle, replete with water fountains, artwork and sculpture gardens.
>
> Incidentally, if you're wondering what happened to the highway, it's now buried in tunnels running beneath the city, thanks to the 'Big Dig,' the costliest highway project in US history.

FREE **USS Constitution** BATTLESHIP
(Map p170; www.history.navy.mil/ussconstitution; Charlestown Navy Yard; ⌚10am-6pm Tue-Sun Apr-Oct, 10am-4pm Thu-Sun Nov-Mar; 🚸) Clamber the decks of this legendary warship, built in 1797. Its oak-timbered hull is so thick that cannonballs literally bounced off it, earning it the nickname 'Old Ironsides.' Families: don't miss the museum, which has sailor garb that kids can don for photo ops.

FREE **Bunker Hill Monument** MONUMENT
(Map p170; www.nps.gov/bost; Monument Sq; ⌚9am-5pm) This 221ft granite obelisk commemorates the American Revolution's first major battle and offers a fine vista for those willing to climb 294 stairs (huff, huff).

BACK BAY

Extending west from Boston Common this well-groomed neighborhood boasts graceful brownstone residences, grand edifices and the tony shopping mecca of Newbury St.

Copley Square PLAZA
(Map p170) Here you'll find a cluster of handsome historic buildings, including the ornate French-Romanesque **Trinity Church** (www.trinitychurchboston.org; cnr Boylston & Clarendon Sts; adult/child $7/free; ⌚9am-5pm Mon-Sat, 1-6pm Sun), the masterwork of architect

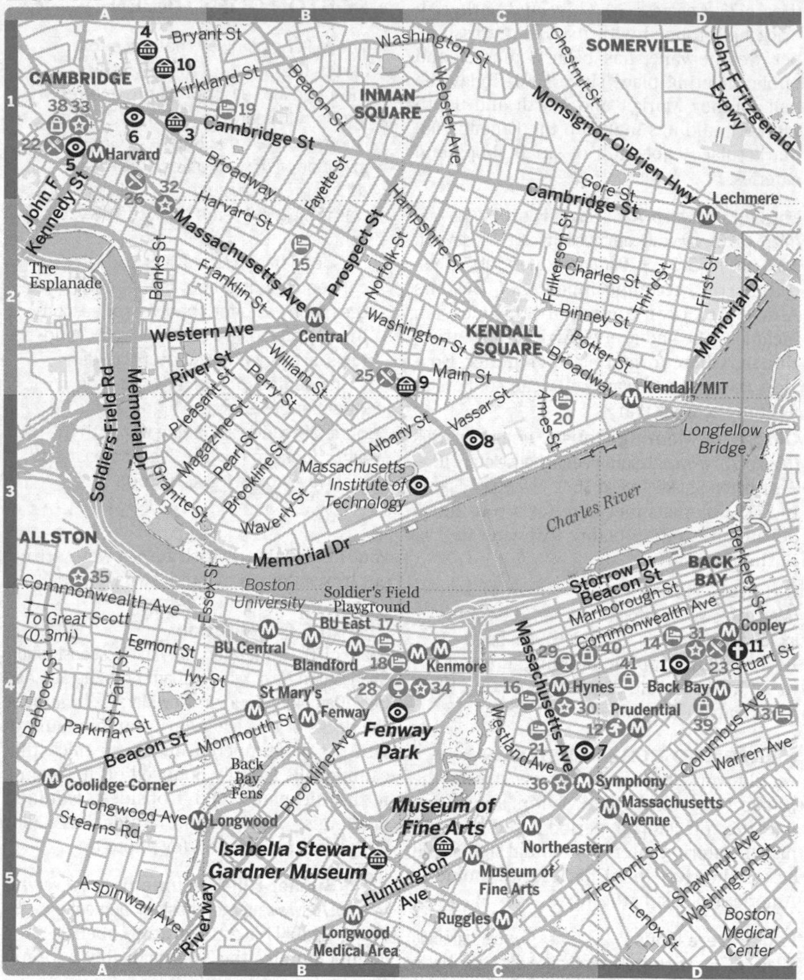

HH Richardson. Across the street, the classic **Boston Public Library** (www.blp.org; 700 Boylston St; ⏲9am-9pm Mon-Thu, 9am-5pm Fri & Sat; 📶), America's first municipal library, lends credence to Boston's reputation as the 'Athens of America.' Pick up a self-guided tour brochure and wander around, noting gems like the murals by John Singer Sargent and sculpture by Augustus Saint-Gaudens.

Prudential Center Skywalk VIEWPOINT
(Map p170; ☎617-859-0648; 800 Boylston St; adult/child $12/8; ⏲10am-10pm) For a stunning 360-degree bird's-eye view of the city, head to this tower's 50th-floor observation deck.

WATERFRONT & SEAPORT DISTRICT

Boston's waterfront offers an ever-growing list of attractions, all connected by the Harborwalk, a dedicated pedestrian path.

Institute of Contemporary Art MUSEUM
(off Map p176; ☎617-478-3100; www.icaboston.org; 100 Northern Ave; adult/child $15/free; ⏲10am-5pm Tue, Wed, Sat & Sun, 10am-9pm Thu & Fri) This dazzling museum snags rave exhibits by the likes of street artist Shepard Fairey. The building's striking cantilevered architecture defines modern, and its floor-to-ceiling glass walls pop with Boston's most dramatic harbor view. Admission's free after 5pm Thursday.

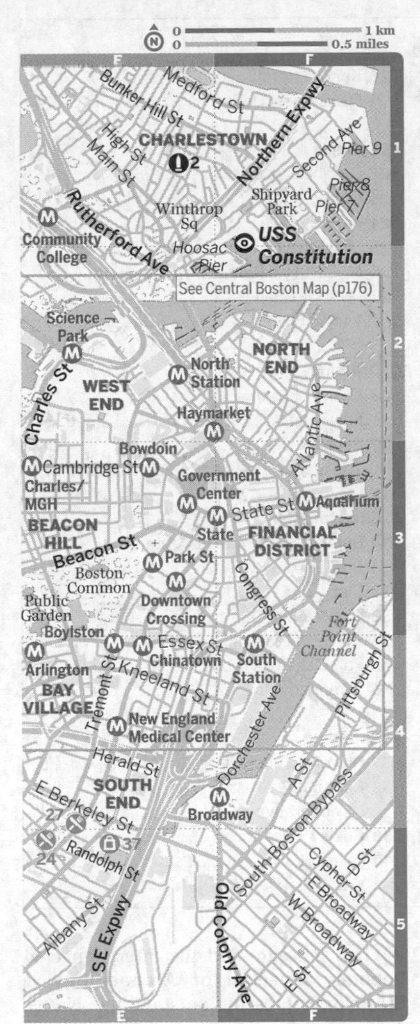

New England Aquarium

AQUARIUM

(Map p176; ☎617-973-5200; www.neaq.org; Central Wharf; adult/child $22/14; ⏰9am-5pm Mon-Fri, 9am-6pm Sat & Sun; 🚸) Centering on a four-story tank teeming with sharks and tropical fish, this aquarium is a magnet for kids. The cool penguin pool is a big hit. Also popular are the aquarium's **whale-watching cruises** (adult/child $40/32; ⏰Apr-Oct), led by naturalists. The cruises head 30 miles out to Stellwagen Bank National Marine Sanctuary, a massive underwater plateau off Cape Cod's northern point, where you can see humpback whales doing their acrobatics.

CHINATOWN, THEATER DISTRICT & SOUTH END

Compact and easy to stroll, Chinatown offers up enticing Asian eateries cheek-by-jowl, while the adjacent Theater District is clustered with performing-arts venues. The sprawling South End boasts one of America's largest concentrations of Victorian row houses, a burgeoning art scene and terrific neighborhood cafes.

FENWAY & KENMORE SQUARE

With world-class museums and America's oldest ballpark, the Fenway neighborhood is a destination in itself.

Museum of Fine Arts

MUSEUM

(MFA; Map p170; ☎617-267-9300; www.mfa.org; 465 Huntington Ave; adult/child $20/7.50; ⏰10am-4:45pm Sat-Tue, 10am-9:45pm Wed-Fri) One of the country's finest art museums just got better with the opening of its spectacular new Art of the Americas wing, whose 53 galleries showcase everything from pre-Columbian art to Paul Revere silver and Winslow Homer paintings. The MFA also has a solid French Impressionist collection, Egyptian mummies and much more. Admission is free for everyone after 4pm on Wednesdays and for children after 3pm weekdays, all day weekends and daily in summer.

Isabella Stewart Gardner Museum

MUSEUM

(Map p170; ☎617-566-1401; www.gardnermuseum.org; 280 The Fenway; adult/child $12/free; ⏰11am-5pm Tue-Sun) Gardner assembled her vast collection – which ranges from Rembrandts to portraits by Bostonian John Singer Sargent – a century ago and lived in the magnificent Venetian-style palazzo that houses it all. Seeing the mansion itself, with its garden courtyard, is alone worth the price of admission. And if your name's Isabella, the ticket is free!

CAMBRIDGE

On the north side of the Charles River lies politically progressive Cambridge, home to academic heavyweights Harvard University and Massachusetts Institute of Technology (MIT). Some 30,000 students make for a diverse, lively scene. Its central **Harvard Square** (Map p170) overflows with cafes, bookstores and street performers.

Harvard University

COLLEGE CAMPUS

(Map p170) Along Massachusetts Ave, opposite the Harvard T station, lies the leafy campus of Harvard University. Dozens of Nobel laureates and eight US presidents

Top Sights

Fenway Park B4
Isabella Stewart Gardner Museum B5
Museum of Fine Arts C5
USS Constitution F1

Sights

1 Boston Public Library D4
2 Bunker Hill Monument E1
3 Harvard Art Museums A1
4 Harvard Museum of Natural History A1
5 Harvard Square A1
6 Harvard University A1
7 Mapparium C4
8 MIT Information Center C3
9 MIT Museum C2
10 Peabody Museum of Archaeology & Ethnology A1
Prudential Center Skywalk .... (see 41)
11 Trinity Church D4

Activities, Courses & Tours

12 Boston Duck Tours D4

Sleeping

13 Chandler Inn D4
14 Charlesmark Hotel D4
15 Harding House B2
16 HI Boston Hostel C4
17 HI Fenway Summer Hostel B4
18 Hotel Buckminster B4
19 Irving House B1
20 Kendall Hotel C3
21 Oasis Guest House C4

Eating

22 Casablanca A1
23 Copley Square Farmers Market D4
24 Franklin Café E5
25 Miracle of Science Bar & Grill B2
26 Mr Bartley's Burger Cottage A1
27 Myers + Chang E4
Veggie Planet .... (see 33)

Drinking

28 Cask 'n' Flagon B4
Fritz .... (see 13)
29 Sonsie C4
Top of the Hub .... (see 41)

Entertainment

30 Berklee Performance Center C4
31 BosTix D4
32 Club Oberon A2
33 Club Passim A1
34 House of Blues C4
35 Paradise Rock Club A3
36 Symphony Hall C4

Shopping

37 Bromfield Art Gallery E5
38 Cambridge Artists Cooperative A1
39 Copley Place D4
40 Jake's House C4
41 Prudential Center D4

are among its graduates – for other chewy tidbits join a free student-led campus tour at the **Harvard University Information Center** (617-495-1573; www.harvard.edu/visitors; 1350 Massachusetts Ave; 1hr tours 10am, noon & 2pm Mon-Sat).

Harvard Art Museums MUSEUM

(Map p170; 617-495-9400; www.harvardartmuseum.org; 485 Broadway; adult/child $9/free; 10am-5pm Tue-Sat) It should come as no surprise that the nation's oldest (1636) and wealthiest university has amassed incredible art collections, with works covering a broad gamut from Picasso to Islamic art.

Harvard Museum of Natural History MUSEUM

(Map p170; 617-495-3045; www.hmnh.harvard.edu; 26 Oxford St; adult/child $9/6; 9am-5pm;) This museum and the interconnected **Peabody Museum of Archaeology & Ethnology** present outstanding Native American exhibits and an exquisite collection of 4000 hand-blown glass flowers. The admission price gets you through the doors of both attractions.

Massachusetts Institute of Technology COLLEGE CAMPUS

(MIT; Map p170) Nerds rule ever so proudly at America's foremost tech campus. Stop at the **MIT Information Center** (Map p170; 617-253-4795; www.mit.edu; 77 Massachusetts Ave; free 90min tours 11am & 3pm Mon-Fri) for the scoop on where to see campus art, including Henry Moore bronzes and cutting-edge architecture by the likes of Frank Gehry.

MIT Museum MUSEUM
(Map p170; www.mit.edu/museum; 265 Massachusetts Ave, adult/child $7.50/3; ⏲10am-5pm) Packed with wow-'em exhibits like the world's largest holography collection, robots from MIT's Artificial Intelligence Laboratory and cool kinetic sculptures. Swing by between 10am and noon on Sundays and admission is free.

GREATER BOSTON

Museum of Science MUSEUM
(Map p176; ☎617-723-2500; www.mos.org; Charles River Dam; adult/child $21/18; ⏲9am-5pm Sat-Thu, 9am-9pm Fri, longer hr Jul-Aug; 👪) At this state-of-the-art museum, a short hop from MIT, hundreds of interactive displays explore the latest tech trends. Clamber around a full-scale space capsule, explore nanotechnology and more. Kids will find plenty of hands-on fun. A fresh multimillion-dollar upgrade of the museum's **planetarium** adds another dimension.

John F Kennedy Library & Museum MUSEUM
(off Map p170; ☎617-514-1600; www.jfklibrary.org; Columbia Point; adult/child $12/free; ⏲9am-5pm) In a striking IM Pei–designed building overlooking Boston Harbor, this museum provides an ode to all things Kennedy. Theaters and multimedia displays replay key historical events such as the Cuban missile crisis. Take the T's Red Line to JFK/UMass, then hop on a free 'JFK' shuttle bus.

Tours

Boston Duck Tours ADVENTURE
(Map p170; ☎617-723-3825; www.bostonducktours.com; adult/child $32/22; ⏲9am-dusk mid-Mar–mid-Nov; 👪) Ridiculously popular tours using WWII amphibious vehicles that cruise the downtown streets before splashing into the Charles River. Tours leave from the Prudential Center and the Museum of Science.

Boston By Foot WALKING
(☎617-367-2345; www.bostonbyfoot.org; adult/child $12/8; ⏲May-Oct) Knowledgeable guides lead a variety of city tours, including Freedom Trail walks that uncover fun tidbits like the hidden crypts under the King's Chapel. Other tours focus on architecture, literary landmarks and the Italian-centric North End. Departure points vary.

Freedom Trail Foundation WALKING
(Map p176; ☎617-357-8300; www.thefreedomtrail.org; adult/child $12/6; ⏲10:30am-5pm; 👪) Guides dressed in Colonial garb – think Ben Franklin – lead 90-minute walking tours of the Freedom Trail, departing from the visitor center on the Boston Common. They also do a Freedom Trail pub crawl on Tuesday evenings.

Segway Experience SEGWAY
(Map p176; ☎617-723-2500; www.mos.org; 1hr tour $65; ⏲10am-1pm) Satisfy your inner geek on a Segway tour from the Museum of Science to the MIT campus, taking in lots of cool sights. Participants must be aged 14 or older and weigh 100 pounds to 260 pounds.

Urban Adventours BICYCLE
(Map p176; ☎617-670-0637; www.urbanadventours.com; 103 Atlantic Ave; tour $50; ⏲9:30am-4:30pm) Cyclists can pedal the Freedom Trail, take in a brewery or bike Boston at night.

FREE **Boston National Historical Park Visitors Center** WALKING
(Map p176; ☎617-242-5642; www.nps.gov/bost; 15 State St; ⏲9am-5pm) Park rangers lead walking tours of the Freedom Trail.

Festivals & Events

Boston Marathon RUNNING EVENT
(www.baa.org) One of the country's most prestigious marathons takes runners on a 26.2-mile course ending at Copley Sq on Patriots Day, a Massachusetts holiday on the third Monday in April.

Fourth of July PATRIOTIC FESTIVAL
(www.july4th.org) Boston hosts one of the biggest Independence Day bashes in the USA, with a free Boston Pops concert on the Esplanade and a fireworks display that's televised nationally.

Patron Saints' Feasts RELIGIOUS FESTIVAL
(www.northendboston.com) In the North End, Italian patron saints are celebrated with food and music events on weekends in July and August.

WHAT THE...?

Ever had a hankering to walk across the entire planet? The Christian Science Church's **Mapparium** (Map p170; www.marybakereddylibrary.org; 200 Massachusetts Ave; adult/child $6/4; ⏲10am-4pm Tue-Sun; 👪), an enormous stained-glass globe with a bridge through its center, provides the easiest route.

START BOSTON COMMON
FINISH BUNKER HILL MONUMENT
DISTANCE 2.5 MILES
DURATION THREE HOURS

Walking Tour
Freedom Trail

Trace America's revolutionary birth along the Freedom Trail, which covers Boston's key Colonial sites. The well-trodden route, marked by a double row of red bricks, starts at the 1 **Boston Common**, America's oldest public park. Follow the trail north to the gold-domed 2 **State House**, designed by Charles Bulfinch, Colonial Boston's best-known architect. Rounding Park St onto Tremont St takes you past the Colonial-era 3 **Park Street Church**; the 4 **Granary Burying Ground**, where victims of the Boston Massacre lie buried; and 5 **King's Chapel**, topped with one of Paul Revere's bells. Continue down School St, past the site of 6 **Boston's first public school**, built in 1635, and the 7 **Old Corner Bookstore**, a 19th-century haunt of literary geniuses Hawthorne and Emerson.

A minute's detour south from the corner of School and Washington Sts leads to the 8 **Old South Meeting House**, where the nitty-gritty on the Boston Tea Party is proudly displayed. True diehards will find more Revolutionary exhibits at the 9 **Old State House**. Nearby, a ring of cobblestones at the intersection of State, Devonshire and Congress Sts marks the 10 **Boston Massacre site**, where the first victims of the American Revolution died. Next up is 11 **Faneuil Hall**, a public market since Colonial times.

Walk north on Union St and up Hanover St, the trattoria-rich heart of Boston's Italian enclave. Treat yourself to lunch before continuing to North Sq, where you can tour the 12 **Paul Revere House**, the Revolutionary hero's former home. Follow the trail to the 13 **Old North Church**, where a lookout in the steeple signaled to Revere that the British were coming, setting off his famous midnight gallop.

Continue northwest on Hull St, where you'll find more Colonial graves at 14 **Copp's Hill Burying Ground** before crossing the Charlestown Bridge to reach the 15 **USS Constitution**, the world's oldest commissioned warship. To the north lies 16 **Bunker Hill Monument**, the site of the first battle fought in the American Revolution.

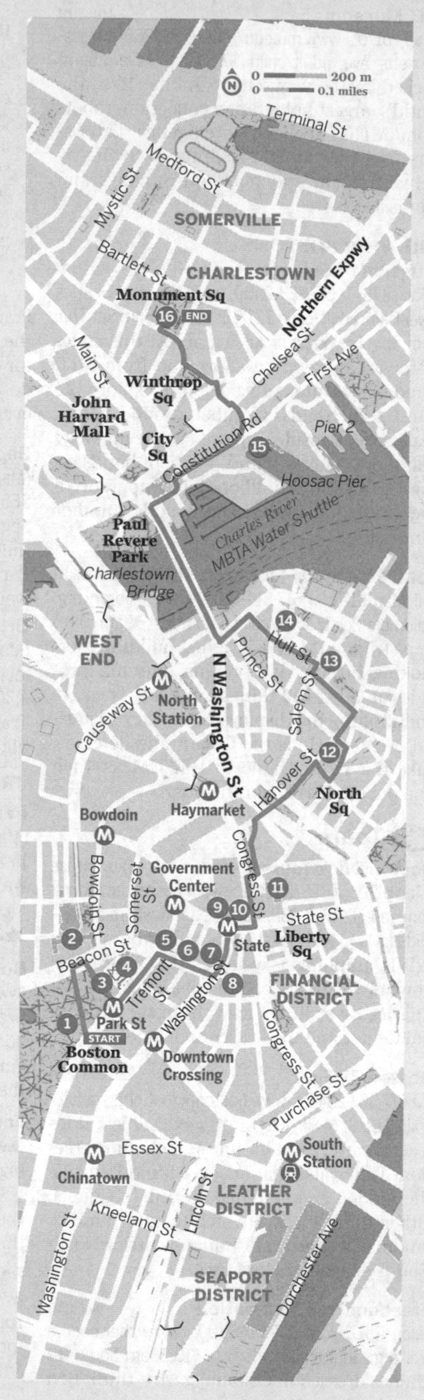

Head of the Charles Regatta ROWING RACE
(www.hocr.org) Spectators line the banks of the Charles River on a weekend in mid-October to watch the world's largest rowing event.

Sleeping

Boston has a reputation for high hotel prices, but online discounts can lessen the sting at even high-end places. You'll typically find the best deals on weekends. The majority of hotels are in the downtown area and the Back Bay, both convenient to public transportation and sightseeing.

For places that book solely through agencies, try **Bed & Breakfast Associates Bay Colony** (617-720-0522, www.bnbboston.com; r from $100), which handles B&Bs, rooms and apartments.

TOP CHOICE **Omni Parker House** HISTORIC HOTEL $$
(Map p176; 617-227-8600; www.omniparkerhouse.com; 60 School St; r $219-419;) If the walls could talk, this historic hotel overlooking the Freedom Trail would fill volumes. Employees have included Malcolm X and Ho Chi Minh, the guest list Charles Dickens and JFK. Despite its well-polished elegance, dark woods and chandeliers, there's nothing stodgy about the place – you can be as comfortable here in a T-shirt as in a suit and tie. And you couldn't be more in the thick of things; it's just a stroll to many of Boston's top sights.

Harding House B&B $
(Map p170; 617-876-2888; www.cambridgeinns.com/harding; 288 Harvard St; r incl breakfast $165-265;) A classic Victorian, blending comfort and artistry in spacious, bright rooms. Old wooden floors toss back a warm glow and lovely antique furnishings complete the inviting atmosphere. Perks include museum passes and a breakfast table replete with organic delights.

Charlesmark Hotel BOUTIQUE HOTEL $$
(Map p170; 617-247-1212; www.thecharlesmark.com; 655 Boylston St; r incl breakfast $189-219; @) This smart boutique hotel packs it all from an unbeatable Copley Sq location to cheery rooms graced with artwork, Italian tile and high-tech amenities. Runners, take note: the Boston Marathon finish line is just outside the front door.

Harborside Inn HOTEL $$$
(Map p176; 617-723-7500; www.harborsideinnboston.com; 185 State St; r $189-269; @)

DOWNLOADABLE WALKING TOURS

If you're traveling with an MP3 player, you can be your own guide by downloading a free walking tour of Cambridge at www.cambridge-usa.org and of the Harborwalk at www.bostonharborwalk.com.

This renovated 19th-century warehouse-turned-inn offers cozy rooms just steps from Faneuil Hall and Boston's waterfront. No two rooms are alike but period ambience, from the exposed brick walls to the hardwood floors, prevails throughout. Light sleepers should request an inside atrium room.

Chandler Inn BOUTIQUE HOTEL $$
(Map p170; 617-482-3450; www.chandlerinn.com; 26 Chandler St; r $149-179;) For a delectable taste of the hip South End, book a room at this European-style boutique hotel within roaming range of some of Boston's hottest nightspots. The staff is friendly, the rooms small but tidy, and the price a fraction of any faceless chain hotel.

Hotel Buckminster HOTEL $$
(Map p170; 617-236-7050; www.bostonhotelbuckminster.com; 645 Beacon St; r $149-189;) Built in 1897 by renowned architect Stanford White, this Kenmore Sq hotel is a mere baseball's toss from Fenway Park. Don't expect anything fancy – it's a faded dame, but the rooms are adequate and sport money-saving conveniences such as microwaves and refrigerators.

HI Boston Hostel HOSTEL $
(Map p170; 617-536-9455; www.bostonhostel.org; 12 Hemenway St; dm incl breakfast $31-48, r incl breakfast $73-132; @) This terrific year-round Back Bay hostel offers dorm rooms with just four to six beds and lots of perks, from free use of linens to organized tours. It fills quickly, especially in summer, so book early.

Kendall Hotel BOUTIQUE HOTEL $$
(Map p170; 617-577-1300; www.kendallhotel.com; 350 Main St; r incl breakfast $129-199;) Unique, reasonably priced and on the doorstep of the MIT campus, this former brick firehouse retains a firefighter riff, without a whiff of 'cutesy.'

Central Boston

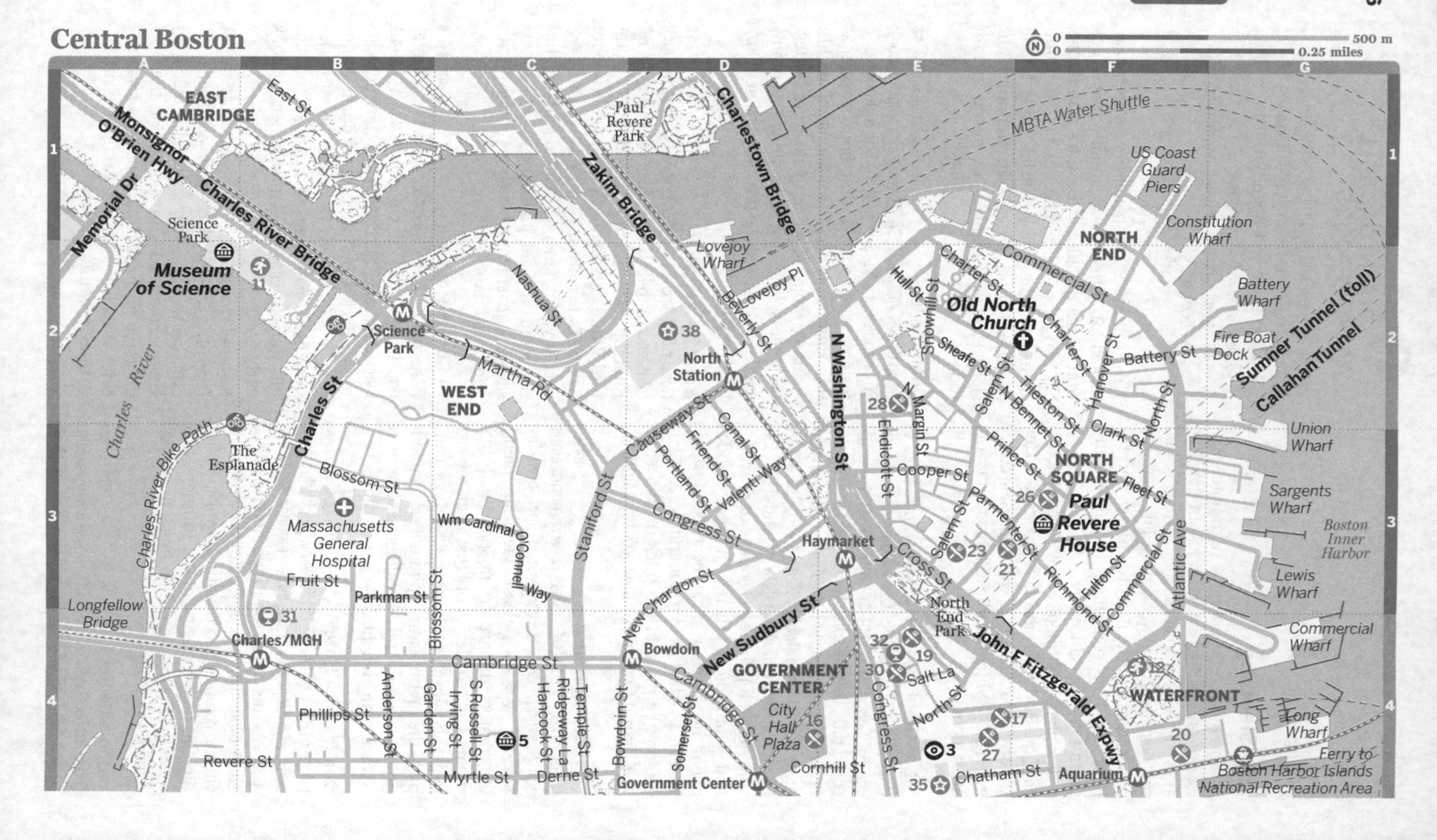

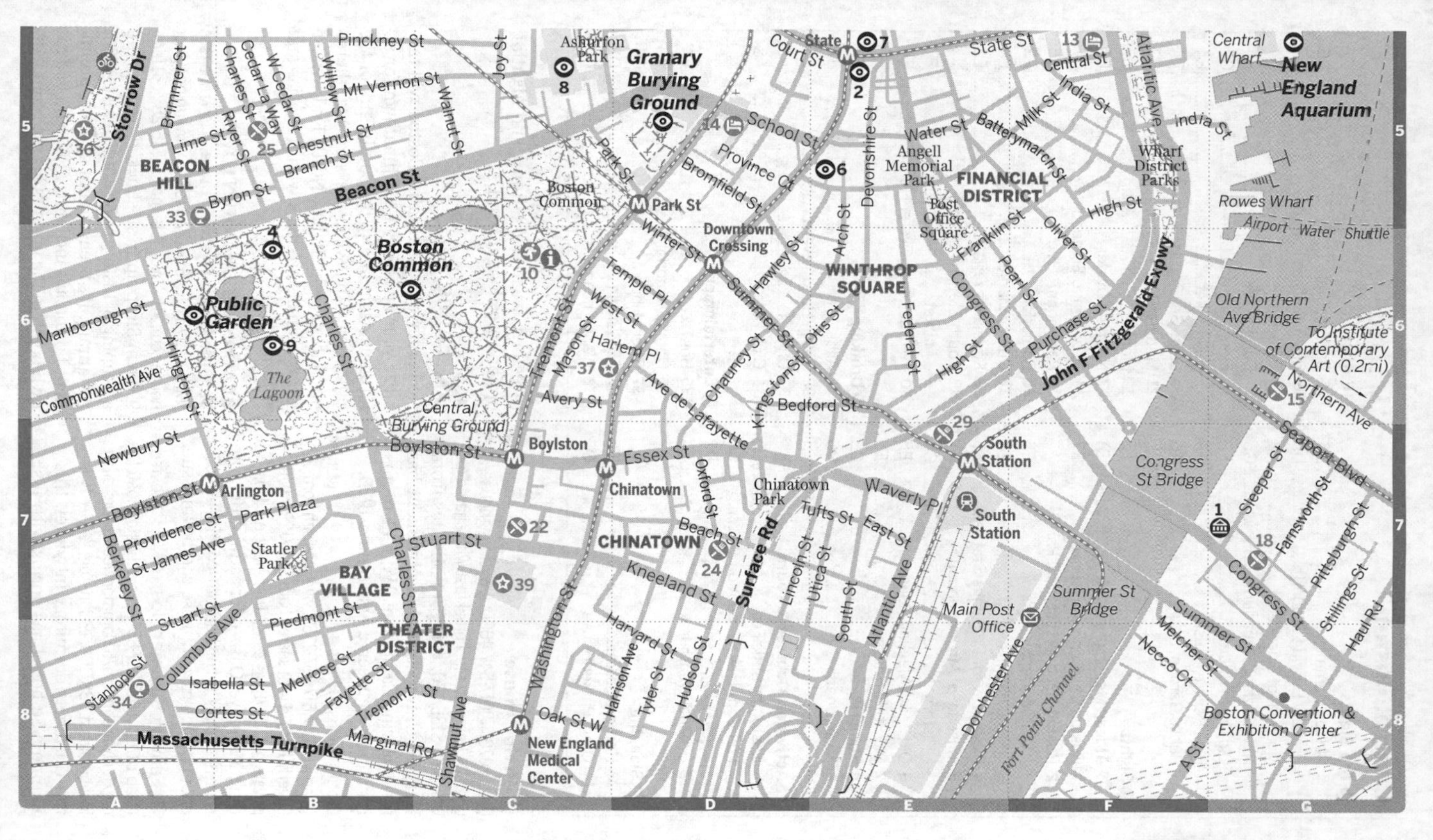
Storrow Dr
36
Brimmer St
Pinckney St
Charles St
Cedar La Way
W Cedar St
Willow St
Mt Vernon St
Joy St
Walnut St
Ashburton Park
8
Granary Burying Ground
Lime St
River St
25
Chestnut St
Branch St
BEACON HILL
Byron St
33
Beacon St
4
Boston Common
Park St
School St
14
Province Ct
Bromfield St
Court St
State
7
2
State St
13
Central St
India St
Milk St
Water St
Batterymarch St
Devonshire St
6
Angell Memorial Park
FINANCIAL DISTRICT
Post Office Square
Franklin St
Oliver St
High St
Atlantic Ave
India St
Wharf District Parks
Central Wharf
New England Aquarium
Rowes Wharf
Airport Water Shuttle
Public Garden
9
The Lagoon
Marlborough St
Arlington St
Commonwealth Ave
Charles St
10
Tremont St
Mason St
Temple Pl
West St
Winter St
Downtown Crossing
Hawley St
Arch St
WINTHROP SQUARE
Summer St
Otis St
Chauncy St
Kingston St
Harlem Pl
37
Ave de Lafayette
Avery St
Federal St
Congress St
Pearl St
High St
Purchase St
John F Fitzgerald Expwy
Old Northern Ave Bridge
To Institute of Contemporary Art (0.2mi)
15
Northern Ave
Seaport Blvd
Central Burying Ground
Bedford St
Newbury St
Boylston St
Boylston
Essex St
Chinatown
Oxford St
Chinatown Park
29
South Station
Waverly Pl
Congress St Bridge
Sleeper St
Farnsworth St
Pittsburgh St
Arlington
Park Plaza
Providence St
St James Ave
Berkeley St
Statler Park
22
Stuart St
Charles St S
CHINATOWN
Beach St
24
Surface Rd
Tufts St
East St
Lincoln St
Utica St
1
18
BAY VILLAGE
39
Kneeland St
South St
Atlantic Ave
Main Post Office
Summer St Bridge
Congress St
Stillings St
Haul Rd
Stuart St
Columbus Ave
Piedmont St
THEATER DISTRICT
Washington St
Harvard St
Harrison Ave
Tyler St
Hudson St
Dorchester Ave
Fort Point Channel
Summer St
Melcher St
Necco Ct
Stanhope St
34
Isabella St
Melrose St
Fayette St
Tremont St
Cortes St
Shawmut Ave
Oak St W
New England Medical Center
Boston Convention & Exhibition Center
A St
Massachusetts Turnpike
Marginal Rd

Central Boston

Top Sights
- Boston Common ... B6
- Granary Burying Ground ... D5
- Museum of Science ... A2
- New England Aquarium ... G5
- Old North Church ... F2
- Paul Revere House ... F3
- Public Garden ... A6

Sights
- African Meeting House ... (see 5)
- 1 Boston Children's Museum ... G7
- 2 Boston National Historical Park Visitors Center ... E5
- 3 Faneuil Hall ... E4
- 4 Make Way for Ducklings Statue ... B6
- 5 Museum of Afro-American History ... C4
- 6 Old South Meeting House ... E5
- 7 Old State House ... E5
- 8 State House ... C5
- 9 Swan Boats ... B6

Activities, Courses & Tours
- Boston by Little Feet ... (see 3)
- 10 Freedom Trail Foundation ... C6
- 11 Segway Experience ... B2
- 12 Urban Adventours ... F4

Sleeping
- 13 Harborside Inn ... F5
- 14 Omni Parker House ... D5

Eating
- 15 Barking Crab ... G6
- 16 City Hall Plaza Farmers Market ... D4
- 17 Durgin Park ... E4
- 18 Flour Bakery & Cafe ... G7
- 19 Haymarket ... E4
- 20 Legal Sea Foods ... F4
- 21 Modern Pastry Shop ... E3
- 22 Montien ... C7
- 23 Neptune Oyster ... E3
- 24 New Jumbo Seafood ... D7
- 25 Paramount ... B5
- 26 Pomodoro ... F3
- 27 Quincy Market ... E4
- 28 Regina Pizzeria ... E2
- 29 South Station Farmers Market ... E7
- 30 Ye Olde Union Oyster House ... E4

Drinking
- 31 Alibi ... B4
- 32 Bell in Hand Tavern ... E4
- 33 Cheers ... A5
- 34 Club Café ... A8

Entertainment
- 35 BosTix ... E4
- 36 Hatch Memorial Shell ... A5
- 37 Opera House ... C6
- 38 TD Garden ... D2
- 39 Wang Theatre ... C7

Irving House B&B **$$**
(Map p170; ☎617-547-4600; www.irvinghouse.com; 24 Irving St; r incl breakfast with shared/private bath $135/170;) Minutes from Harvard University and a convenient base for exploring Cambridge. With 44 rooms it's a cross between a hotel and a B&B.

Oasis Guest House B&B **$$**
(Map p170; ☎617-267-2262; www.oasisgh.com; 22 Edgerly Rd; s/d with shared bath $99/129, r with private bath $179;) Just beyond bustling Mass Ave, Oasis offers straightforward rooms simply furnished but comfortable enough. One caveat: noise can be an issue.

HI Fenway Summer Hostel HOSTEL **$**
(Map p170; ☎617-267-8599; www.bostonhostel.org/fenway.shtml; 575 Commonwealth Ave; dm/r incl breakfast $38/100; Jun-Aug;) A Boston University dormitory in winter, this Kenmore Sq hostel has dorms with just three beds each. Good dining and nightlife options are close at hand.

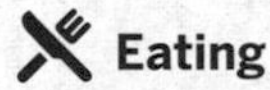

Eating

No matter what your taste, Boston will tantalize your buds. Head to Chinatown for affordable Asian fare, to the South End for the cafe scene. And when the sun sets, there's no place like the Italian North End, whose narrow streets are thick with trattorias and ristorantes.

BEACON HILL & DOWNTOWN

Ye Olde Union Oyster House SEAFOOD **$$$**
(Map p176; ☎617-227-2750; www.unionoysterhouse.com; 41 Union St; mains $16-28; 11am-9:30pm) Slurp up fresh-shucked oysters and a heaping of history at Boston's oldest (1826) restaurant. It's been a haunt of many prominent Bostonians including JFK, who had his own booth in the upstairs dining room. For-

get the meat dishes – this place is all about seafood.

Durgin Park AMERICAN $$
(Map p176; ☎617-227-2038; 340 Faneuil Hall Marketplace; lunch mains $9-30; ⏰11:30am-10pm Mon-Sat, 11:30am-9pm Sun; 👪) Climb the stairs to this storied eatery for a taste of good ole Colonial fare. Durgin Park's been dishing out New England staples like Yankee pot roast, Indian pudding and slow-cooked Boston baked beans since 1827.

Paramount AMERICAN $
(Map p176; www.paramountboston.com; 44 Charles St; mains $5-18; ⏰8am-10pm) Beacon Hill's top neighborhood eatery, with fruity pancakes, meaty sandwiches and a loyal following.

Quincy Market FOOD COURT $
(Map p176; off Congress & North Sts; ⏰10am-9pm Mon-Sat, noon-6pm Sun; 📶👪) For a quick eat along the Freedom Trail, stop at this storied market lined with stalls selling everything from Chinese food to New England clam chowder.

NORTH END

TOP CHOICE **Pomodoro** ITALIAN $$
(Map p176; ☎617-367-4348; www.pomodoroboston.com; 319 Hanover St; mains $15-25; ⏰3-11pm Tue-Fri, 11am-11pm Sat & Sun) This cozy place is one romantic setting for homestyle Italian cuisine. The food is simply but perfectly prepared: snag a table and order the most delectable seafood *fra diavolo* in the entire North End. Reserve ahead or be prepared to wait.

Modern Pastry Shop BAKERY $
(Map p176; www.modernpastry.com; 257 Hanover St; snacks $2-4; ⏰8am-10pm Sun-Fri, 7am-midnight Sat) Not the biggest bakery on Hanover St, but certainly the best. Chocolate ganache and decadent cannoli filled to order in front of your eyes…oh so sweet!

Neptune Oyster SEAFOOD $$$
(Map p176; ☎617-742-3474; www.neptuneoyster.com; 63 Salem St; mains $20-32; ⏰11:30am-11pm) Barely bigger than a clam, this snappy place has the North End's best raw bar and good Italian-style seafood. You *will* want to start with the oysters.

Regina Pizzeria PIZZA $$
(Map p176; www.pizzeriaregina.com; 11 Thatcher St; pizzas $12-18; ⏰11:30am-11:30pm) The North End's finest thin-crust pizza by the slice or pie.

WATERFRONT & SEAPORT DISTRICT

Flour Bakery & Cafe BAKERY $
(Map p176; www.flourbakery.com; 12 Farnsworth St; light eats $3-10; ⏰7am-7pm Mon-Fri, 8am-6pm Sat, 9am-4pm Sun; 👪) Certified green and scrumptiously affordable, this bakery makes awesome pecan sticky buns and wildly innovative sandwiches and pizzas. Their motto is 'make life sweeter…eat dessert first.' No argument here.

BOSTON FOR CHILDREN

Boston is a family-friendly destination. Changing stations are ubiquitous in public restrooms and many restaurants offer children's menus and high chairs.

You'll have no trouble taking your kid's stroller on the T. Boston's crowded old streets and sidewalks present more of a challenge. Curbs are not always cut for easy rolling, so keep this in mind if you'll be pushing a stroller.

Boston's small scale makes it easy for families to explore. A good place to start is the **Public Garden**, where fans of Robert McCloskey's classic Boston tale *Make Way for Ducklings* can visit bronze **statues** (Map p176) of the famous mallards and paddle the lagoon in one of the Swan Boats. Across the street at the **Boston Common** (p168), kids can cool their toes in the Frog Pond and romp on playground swings and jungle gyms.

Boston Children's Museum (Map p176; ☎617-426-6500; www.bostonchildrensmuseum.org; 300 Congress St; admission $12; ⏰10am-5pm Sat-Thu, 10am-9pm Fri) offers oodles of fun for the younger ones, while the **Museum of Science** (p173) thrills kids of all ages. Hits at the **New England Aquarium** (p171) include petting cool creatures at the touch pool, watching seals being fed and hopping aboard a whale-watching tour.

Boston By Little Feet (Map p176; ☎617-367-2345; www.bostonbyfoot.org; 1hr tour $8), departing from Faneuil Hall and designed for kids aged six to 12, offers a fun slice of the Freedom Trail from a child's perspective. And those quirky, quacky **Boston Duck Tours** (p173) are always a hit.

FARMERS MARKETS

Boston has several neighborhood farmers markets that truck seasonal fruits and vegetables into the city from mid-May to November. The ultimate bonanza of ripe and ready produce is the **Haymarket** (Map p176; Blackstone & Hanover Sts; ⏲7am-5pm Fri & Sat), where more than 100 vendors line up along the street.

Other markets:

City Hall Plaza (Map p176; City Hall Plaza; ⏲11am-6pm Mon & Wed)

Copley Square (Map p170; St James Ave; ⏲11am-6pm Tue & Fri)

South Station (Map p176; Dewey Sq; ⏲11:30am-6:30pm Tue & Thu)

Barking Crab SEAFOOD **$$**
(Map p176; ☎617-426-2722; www.thebarkingcrab.com; 88 Sleeper St; mains $12-34; ⏲11:30am-10pm; 👪) A waterfront landmark, this brightly painted and ever-bustling seafood shack serves big buckets of steaming crabs, authentic New England clambakes and good ol' beer-battered fish and chips.

Legal Sea Foods SEAFOOD **$$$**
(Map p176; ☎617-227-3115; www.legalseafoods.com; 255 State St; mains $15-32; ⏲11am-10:30pm Mon-Sat, 11am-10pm Sun) Running with the motto 'If it isn't fresh, it isn't Legal,' this waterfront establishment indeed serves top-of-the-line seafood – broiled, grilled or fried – and invariably draws a satisfied crowd.

CHINATOWN, THEATER DISTRICT & SOUTH END

TOP CHOICE **Myers + Chang** ASIAN FUSION **$$**
(Map p170; ☎617-542-5200; www.myersandchang.com; 1145 Washington St; mains $10-18; ⏲11:30am-10pm Sun-Wed, 11:30am-11pm Thu-Sat) A marriage of two South End top chefs, this smokin' multi-ethnic joint dishes up eclectic taste treats, blending Thai, Chinese and Vietnamese influences with an urban New England tweak. Think shiitake-basil spring rolls, wok-roasted mussels and tea-smoked spareribs. No matter what you order, the spicy, fresh herbs carry the day. The food's local whenever possible, the scene's hip and casual.

New Jumbo Seafood CHINESE **$$**
(Map p176; www.newjumboseafoodrestaurant.com; 5 Hudson St; mains $6-30; ⏲11am-1am Sun-Thu, 11am-4am Fri & Sat) A wall of tanks crawling with lobster, crabs and eels constitute the decor at this Chinatown classic renowned for its fresh seafood and Cantonese cuisine. Lunch specials ($5) offered weekdays until 3pm are a bargain.

Montien THAI **$$**
(Map p176; ☎617-338-5600; www.montien-boston.com; 63 Stuart St; mains $10-16; ⏲11:30am-10:30pm Mon-Sat, 4:30-10pm Sun; ✎) For a tasty meal before the opening curtain, head to this Thai restaurant in the midst of the theater district. Montien has wonderfully fragrant curries and other spicy counterparts, including scores of vegetarian options. The food's the real deal, so let the server know how much heat you can handle.

Franklin Café AMERICAN **$$**
(Map p170; ☎617-350-0010; www.franklincafe.com; 278 Shawmut Ave; mains $16-20; ⏲5:30pm-1:30am) Search out this tiny South End haunt for New American comfort food with a gourmet twist. Everyone orders the roasted turkey meatloaf with cinnamon fig gravy and chive mashed potatoes – arguably the most famous meal in the South End. Just a half-dozen booths and a line of bar stools, so get there early.

CAMBRIDGE

Veggie Planet VEGETARIAN **$**
(☎617-661-1513; www.veggieplanet.net; Club Passim, 47 Palmer St; mains $6-12; ⏲11:30am-10:30pm; ✎👪) The crunchy granola crowd gravitates to this cafe, a block northwest of Harvard Square, for all things vegetarian. Creativity knows no bounds – vegans favor the coconut curry tofu pizza. Big organic salads and delicious homemade soups too.

Mr Bartley's Burger Cottage BURGERS **$**
(Map p170; www.mrbartley.com; 1246 Massachusetts Ave; burgers $10-12; ⏲11am-9pm Mon-Sat; 👪) Join the Ivy Leaguers at this landmark joint serving juicy hamburgers with quirky names, like the Yuppie Burger topped with boursin cheese and bacon. The onion rings and sweet potato fries score an A-plus too.

Casablanca MEDITERRANEAN **$$**
(☎617-876-0999; www.casablanca-restaurant.com; 40 Brattle St; mains $10-24; ⏲11:30am-11:30pm) A colorful mural depicting Rick's Café sets the stage for innovative Mediterranean delights at this Harvard Sq hangout of film fans and other arty types.

Miracle of Science Bar & Grill PUB $$
(Map p170; www.miracleofscience.us; 321 Massachusetts Ave; mains $6-14; ⏲7am-1am Mon-Fri, 9am-1pm Sat & Sun) With all the decor of your high-school science lab, this bar and grill is still pretty hip, and is popular among MIT students.

Drinking

Alibi LOUNGE
(Map p176; www.alibiboston.com; 215 Charles St) The quirkiest place to have a drink in Boston is in the former Charles Street Jail, now renovated into the upscale Liberty Hotel. The lounge decor features slammin' remnants of its former life, such as iron cell bars.

Cask 'n' Flagon SPORTS BAR
(Map p170; www.casknflagon.com; 62 Brookline Ave) Sports bars pepper the neighborhood around Fenway Park, including this venerable place, which is wallpapered with classic Red Sox memorabilia and frenzied fans.

Bell in Hand Tavern PUB
(Map p176; www.bellinhand.com; 45 Union St) A gaggle of bars lines historic Union St, just north of Faneuil Hall, including this one, which opened in 1795, making it the oldest tavern in the USA.

Cheers BAR
(Map p176; www.cheersboston.com; 84 Beacon St) Only the exterior of this landmark bar appeared in the opening scenes of the *Cheers* sitcom and it serves so many tourists that nobody knows anybody's name, but what the heck.

Top of the Hub LOUNGE
(Map p170; www.topofthehub.net; 800 Boylston St) A head-spinning city view is on tap at this chic restaurant-lounge on the 52nd floor of the Prudential Center.

Sonsie CAFE
(Map p170; www.sonsieboston.com; 327 Newbury St) Overlooking the action on trendy Newbury St, Sonsie is where the beautiful people go to see and be seen. Lemontini, anyone?

Shays PUB
(www.shayspubandwinebar.com; 58 John F Kennedy St, Cambridge) Harvard's favorite student bar, three blocks south of Harvard Sq. It's crowded, cozy and cheap – what's not to love?

☆ Entertainment

Boston's entertainment scene offers something for everyone. For up-to-the-minute listings, grab a copy of the free *Boston Phoenix*.

Nightclubs & Live Music

Club Passim FOLK
(☎617-492-7679; www.clubpassim.org; 47 Palmer St) Folkies flock to this venerable Cambridge club, which has been a haunt of up-and-coming folk singers since the days of Dylan and Baez. It's just a couple of minutes walk northwest of the Harvard Sq metro stop.

Paradise Rock Club ROCK
(off Map p170; ☎617-562-8800; www.thedise.com; 967 Commonwealth Ave) Top bands – like U2, whose first gig in the USA was on this stage – rock at this edgy landmark club.

Great Scott ROCK
(off Map p170; ☎617-566-9014; www.greatscottboston.com; 1222 Commonwealth Ave) The 'it' place for rock and indie, this cavernous club rarely gets uncomfortably crowded.

House of Blues ROCK
(Map p170; ☎888-693-2583; www.hob.com/boston; 15 Lansdowne St) Big venue with big-name regional acts like J Geils Band, the Cars and My Chemical Romance.

GAY & LESBIAN BOSTON

Naturally, the hub city of the first state to legalize gay marriage embraces gay travelers. You'll find openly gay communities throughout Boston and Cambridge, but the pulse of the action beats from Boston's South End.

The stalwart of the gay and lesbian scene is **Club Café** (Map p176; www.clubcafe.com; 209 Columbus Ave), a convivial South End bar and entertainment venue. Another gay landmark is **Fritz** (Map p170; www.fritzboston.com; 26 Chandler St), a bustling, hustling watering hole in the South End that proudly proclaims itself 'Boston's gay sports bar.'

You'll find other LGBT gathering spots, as well as events and entertainment listings, at **Bay Windows** (www.baywindows.com), a weekly serving the gay and lesbian community, and **Edge Boston** (www.edgeboston.com). The city's biggest gay and lesbian event, **Boston Pride** (www.bostonpride.org), includes a parade, a festival and block parties in mid-June.

Berklee Performance Center ECLECTIC
(Map p170; ☎617-747-2261; www.berkleebpc.com; 136 Massachusetts Ave) One of America's premier music schools hosts concerts by famed alumni and other renowned artists.

Theater & Culture

Hatch Memorial Shell BANDSTAND
(Map p176; Charles River Esplanade;) Free summer concerts take place at this outdoor bandstand on the banks of the Charles River. The highlight is the Boston Pops' July 4 concert and fireworks, the biggest annual music event in Boston.

Club Oberon EXPERIMENTAL THEATER
(Map p170; ☎866-811-4111; www.cluboberon.com; 2 Arrow St, Cambridge) Part theater, part nightclub, with a versatile space that allows the stage to be anywhere and everywhere as the actors interact with the audience.

Wang Theatre THEATER, DANCE
(Map p176; ☎617-482-9393; www.citicenter.org; 270 Tremont St) One of New England's largest theaters, this lavish 1925 landmark hosts top dance and theater performances.

Symphony Hall MUSIC
(Map p170; ☎888-266-1200; www.bso.org; 301 Massachusetts Ave) The celebrated Boston Symphony Orchestra and Boston Pops perform here.

Opera House THEATER
(Map p176; ☎617-880-2442; http://bostonoperahouseonline.com; 539 Washington St) Restored to its 1920s grandeur, this extravagant theater hosts Broadway productions.

Sports

Boston is a huge sports city with top-rated pro teams. From April to September join the fans cheering on the **Boston Red Sox** (☎617-267-1700; www.redsox.com), at **Fenway Park** (Map p170), major-league baseball's oldest (1912) and most storied ballpark.

CHEAP SEATS

Half-price tickets to same-day theater and concerts in Boston are sold at the **BosTix kiosks** (www.bostix.org; ⏰10am-6pm Tue-Sat, 11am-4pm Sun) Faneuil Hall (Map p176; Congress St); Copley Sq (Map p170; cnr Dartmouth & Boylston Sts). No plastic– these deals are cash only.

TD Garden BASKETBALL, HOCKEY
(Map p176; 150 Causeway St) From October to April, the NBA **Boston Celtics** (☎617-523-3030; www.celtics.com) play basketball, and the 2011 Stanley Cup–winning **Boston Bruins** (☎617-624-2327; www.bostonbruins.com) play ice hockey here.

Gillette Stadium FOOTBALL, SOCCER
In Foxboro, 25 miles south of Boston, the NFL **New England Patriots** (☎800-543-1776; www.patriots.com) play football from August to January and the MLS **New England Revolution** (☎877-438-7387; www.revolutionsoccer.net) plays soccer from April to October.

Shopping

Head to Newbury St for the most interesting shopping stroll. Starting on its highbrow east end it's all Armani, Brooks Brothers and Cartier, but by the time you reach the west end you'll find offbeat shops and funky bookstores.

Copley Place (Map p170; www.shopcopleyplace.com; 100 Huntington Ave) and the **Prudential Center** (Map p170; www.prudentialcenter.com; 800 Boylston St), both in Back Bay, are the city's main indoor malls.

Jake's House CLOTHING
(Map p170; www.lifeisgood.com; 285 Newbury St;) Life *is* good for this locally designed brand of T-shirts and backpacks in fun-loving styles.

Coop CLOTHING
(thecoop.com; 1400 Massachusetts Ave, Cambridge) Harvard Sq institution selling sweatshirts and all sorts of souvenirs emblazoned with the Harvard logo, as well as regional books and music.

Cambridge Artists' Cooperative ARTS & CRAFTS
(Map p170; www.cambridgeartistscoop.com; 59a Church St, Cambridge) Wide range of arts and crafts at this multifloor Harvard Sq gallery operated by Cambridge artists.

Bromfield Art Gallery ARTS & CRAFTS
(Map p170; www.bromfieldgallery.com; 450 Harrison Ave) Browse for arts and crafts at Boston's oldest cooperative.

Information

Internet Access

Boston Public Library (Map p170; www.bpl.org; 700 Boylston St; ⏰9am-9pm Mon-Thu, 9am-5pm Fri & Sat) Free for 15 minutes, or get a visitor card at the circulation desk and sign up for longer terminal time.

Tech Superpowers & Internet Café (www.techsuperpowers.com; 252 Newbury St; per 15min/1hr $3/5; ⏰9am-7pm Mon-Fri, 11am-4pm Sat & Sun) Provides online computers, but if you have your own device wi-fi access is free throughout Newbury St.

Media

Boston Globe (www.boston.com) New England's major daily newspaper provides a wealth of information online.

Boston Phoenix (www.thephoenix.com) Free alternative weekly with solid arts and entertainment coverage.

Improper Bostonian (www.improper.com) A sassy biweekly distributed free from sidewalk dispenser boxes.

Medical Services

CVS Pharmacy (☎617-437-8414; www.cvs.com; 587 Boylston St; ⏰24hr) Opposite the public library.

Massachusetts General Hospital (☎617-726-2000; www.mgh.org; 55 Fruit St; ⏰24hr) At the west side of the city center.

Money

You'll find ATMs throughout the city, including at most subway stations. Foreign currency can be exchanged at **Citizens Bank** (www.citizensbank.com); State St (53 State St); Boylston St (607 Boylston St).

Post

Main post office (Map p176; www.usps.com; 25 Dorchester Ave; ⏰6am-midnight) One block southeast of South Station. There are other post offices around central Boston and near Harvard Sq.

Tourist Information

Cambridge Visitor Information Booth (☎617-497-1630; www.cambridge-usa.org; Harvard Sq; ⏰9am-5pm) This kiosk right on the square has the nitty-gritty on Cambridge.

Greater Boston Convention & Visitors Bureau (www.bostonusa.com) Has visitor centers at Boston Common (Map p176; ☎617-426-3115; 148 Tremont St; ⏰8:30am-5pm Mon-Fri, 9am-5pm Sat & Sun) and the Prudential Center (Map p170; 800 Boylston St; ⏰9am-5pm).

Websites

www.bostoncentral.com A solid resource for families, with listings for activities good for kids.

www.cityofboston.gov Official website of Boston city government with links to visitor services.

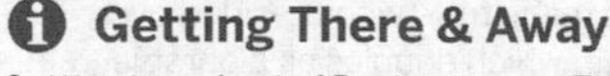

Getting There & Away

Getting in and out of Boston is easy. The train and bus stations are conveniently side by side, and the airport is a short subway ride away.

AIR Logan International Airport (BOS; www.massport.com/logan), just across Boston Harbor from the city center, is served by major US and foreign airlines and has full services.

BUS South Station (Map p176; 700 Atlantic Ave) is the terminal for an extensive network of long-distance buses operated by **Greyhound** (www.greyhound.com). In addition, **Fung Wah Bus Company** (www.fungwahbus.com) runs buses between South Station and New York City for just $15 each way.

TRAIN MBTA Commuter Rail (www.mbta.com) trains connect Boston's North Station (Map p176) with Concord and Salem and Boston's South Station (Map p176) with Plymouth and Providence; fares vary with the distance, maxing out at $8.25.

The **Amtrak** (www.amtrak.com) terminal is at South Station; trains to New York cost $67 (4¼ hours) or $99 on the speedier *Acela Express* (3½ hours).

Getting Around

TO/FROM THE AIRPORT Downtown Boston is just a few miles from Logan International Airport and is accessible by subway.

CAR Major car-rental companies have offices at the airport, and many have locations around the city. Bear in mind that driving in Boston is utterly confusing with lots of one-way streets and archaic traffic patterns. It's best to stick to public transportation within the city. If you're traveling onward by rental car, pick up your car at the end of your Boston visit.

SUBWAY The **MBTA** (www.mbta.com; single ride $2, day/week pass $9/15; ⏰5:30am-12:30am) operates the USA's oldest subway (the 'T'), built in 1897. Five color-coded lines – Red, Blue, Green, Orange and Silver – radiate from the downtown stations of Park St, Downtown Crossing and Government Center. 'Inbound' trains are headed for one of these stations, 'outbound' trains away from them.

GRAB A BIKE

In the summer of 2011 Boston launched **Hubway** (www.thehubway.com), a new bike sharing program with 600 bicycles stationed at 60 kiosks throughout the city. The program is expected to grow tenfold in the next couple of years. The good: it's cheap and convenient – $5 unlocks a bike for you to use all day; you can pick it up at one kiosk and drop it back at another. The bad: roads are narrow, bike lanes few and Boston traffic aggressive. Want to test the waters? The first 30 minutes are free.

TAXI Taxis are plentiful; expect to pay between $10 and $25 between two points within the city limits. Flag taxis on the street, find them at major hotels or call **Metro Cab** (☎617-242-8000) or **Independent** (☎617-426-8700).

Around Boston

The historic towns rimming Boston make for fine day-tripping. If you don't have your own transportation, you can reach these places by MBTA (p183) buses and rail.

LEXINGTON & CONCORD

In 1775 the Colonial town of Lexington, 15 miles northwest of Boston, was the site of the first battle of the American Revolution. Following the battle, the British redcoats marched 10 miles west to Concord where they fought the American Minutemen at the town's North Bridge – the first American victory. You can revisit this momentous bit of history at **Minute Man National Historic Park** (☎978-369-6993; www.nps.gov/mima; 174 Liberty St, Concord; admission free; ⏲9am-5pm) and along the 5.5-mile **Battle Road Trail**, which is open to cyclists as well as hikers.

In the 19th century, Concord harbored a vibrant literary community. Next to the **Old North Bridge** is the **Old Manse** (☎978-369-3909; 269 Monument St; adult/child $8/5), former home of author Nathaniel Hawthorne. Within a mile of the town center are the **Ralph Waldo Emerson house** (☎978-369-2236; 28 Cambridge Turnpike; adult/child $8/6), Louisa May Alcott's **Orchard House** (☎978-369-4118; 399 Lexington Rd; adult/child $9/5) and the **Wayside** (☎978-369-6993; 455 Lexington Rd; adult/child $5/free), where Alcott's *Little Women* was set.

Walden Pond, where Henry David Thoreau lived and wrote *Walden,* is 3 miles south of the town center; you can visit his cabin site and take an inspiring hike around the pond. All these authors are laid to rest in **Sleepy Hollow Cemetery** (Bedford St) in the town center. Admission is free to Walden Pond and the cemetery. **Concord Chamber of Commerce** (☎978-369-3120; www.concordchamberofcommerce.org; 58 Main St; ⏲10am-4pm) has full details on sites, including opening hours for the homes, which vary with the season.

SALEM

Salem, 20 miles northeast of Boston, burned itself an infamous place in history with the 1692 hysteria that put innocent people to death for witchcraft. The tragedy has proven a boon for operators of numerous Salem witch attractions, some serious, others just milking witchy-wacky-woo for all it's worth. **Destination Salem** (☎877-725-3662; www.salem.org; 2 New Liberty St; ⏲9am-5pm) has full information on town sights.

The exceptional **Peabody Essex Museum** (☎978-745-9500; www.pem.org; East India Sq; adult/child $15/free; ⏲10am-5pm Tue-Sun) reflects Salem's rich maritime history. The museum was founded upon the art, artifacts and curios collected by Salem traders during their early expeditions to the Far East. As the exhibits attest, they had deep pockets and refined taste. In addition to world-class Chinese and Pacific Island displays, the museum boasts an excellent Native American collection.

Salem was the center of a thriving clipper-ship trade with China and its preeminent trader, Elias Derby, became America's first millionaire. For a sense of those glory days,

WITCH HUNTS

In early 1692 a group of Salem girls began to act strangely. The work of the devil? The girls, pressured to blame someone, accused a slave named Tituba of witchcraft. Under torture, Tituba accused others and soon accusations were flying thick and fast. By September, 55 had pleaded guilty and 19 who wouldn't 'confess' to witchcraft were hanged. The frenzy finally died down when the accusers pointed at the governor's wife.

The most poignant site in Salem is the **Witch Trials Memorial** (Charter St), a quiet park behind the Peabody Essex Museum, where simple stones are inscribed with the names and final words of the victims, decrying the injustice befallen them.

Best of Salem's other 'witchy' sites is the **Witch House** (www.witchhouse.info; 310 Essex St; adult/child $10.25/6.25; ⏲10am-5pm), the home of the magistrate who presided over the trials. To dig deeper, read Arthur Miller's *The Crucible,* which doubles as a parable to the 1950s anticommunist 'witch hunts' in the US Senate that resulted in Miller's own blacklisting.

WORTH A TRIP

NEW BEDFORD, 'THE WHALING CITY'

At the height of the whaling era, New Bedford was the largest whaling port on earth. Among the thousands finding work on the ships was author Herman Melville, who roamed the harborfront before setting off on the adventure that inspired *Moby-Dick*. Indeed, the opening scenes of the novel are set in New Bedford. With its gas lamps and cobbled stone streets, the town center looks much as it did in 1841 when Melville crewed up on the whaler *Acushnet*. The old port, which extends four blocks inland from the harbor, is now preserved as **New Bedford National Historical Park**. Start at the **Park Visitor Center** (☎508-996-4095; www.nps.gpv/nebe; 33 Williams St; ⏰9am-5pm), where you can pick up a map and watch a short film that'll make the perfect introduction to your sightseeing.

Within a stone's throw of the visitor center lies the **Seaman's Bethel**, the chapel where Melville and crewmates attended services before setting sail for the Pacific whaling grounds. Nearby at the terrific **New Bedford Whaling Museum** (☎508-997-0046; www.whalingmuseum.org; 18 Johnny Cake Hill; adult/child $10/6; ⏰9am-5pm) you'll gape at full-size whale skeletons, clamber aboard a half-size replica of a whaling schooner and find evocative exhibits. Search for the one on Frederick Douglass, the former slave who landed a job as a dockworker here at age 21 and left three years later as one of America's leading abolitionists. (New Bedford in the 19th century was one of the most integrated places in America.)

Today New Bedford still looks to the sea and lays claim to being New England's largest fishing port. For the best briny delights in town make your way to **Antonio's** (☎508-990-3636; www.antoniosnewbedford.com; 267 Coggeshall St; meals $10-18; ⏰11:30am-9:30pm), where fresh catch melds with New Bedford's Portuguese heritage; the delicious paella, brimming with lobster and shellfish, will sate any appetite.

To get to New Bedford take I-195 to MA 18 south; take the Elm St exit. Park at the municipal parking garage, a block up Elm St. The national park visitor center is one short block to the south.

take a walk along Derby St and out to Derby Wharf, now the center of the **Salem Maritime National Historic Site**.

PLYMOUTH

Proclaiming itself 'America's hometown,' Plymouth celebrates its heritage as the region's first permanent European settlement. **Plymouth Rock**, a weather-worn chunk of granite on the harborfront, is said to mark the place the Pilgrims came ashore in 1620. Don't expect anything monumental; the rock upon which America was built is indeed small – so diminutive that most visitors have to take a second look.

These days, people make their pilgrimage to **Plimoth Plantation** (☎508-746-1622; www.plimoth.org; MA 3A; adult/child $29.50/19; ⏰9am-5pm mid-Mar–Nov; 👪), an authentically recreated 1627 Pilgrim village. Everything – the houses, the crops, the food cooked over wood stoves and even the vocabulary used by the costumed interpreters – is meticulously true to the period. Equally insightful are the home sites of the Wampanoag tribe, who helped the Pilgrims through their first difficult winter. If you're traveling with kids, or you're a history buff, don't miss it. The admission price includes entry to the *Mayflower II*, a replica of the Pilgrims' ship, at Plymouth Harbor.

Destination Plymouth (☎508-747-7533; www.visit-plymouth.com; 134 Court St; ⏰8am-4pm), has details on all sights. When hunger strikes, you'll find good seafood restaurants right at the harbor.

Cape Cod

Clambering across the National Seashore dunes, cycling the Cape Cod Rail Trail, eating oysters at Wellfleet Harbor – this sandy peninsula serves up a bounty of local flavor. Fringed with 400 miles of sparkling shoreline, 'the Cape,' as it's called by Cape Codders, rates as New England's top beach destination. But there's a lot more than just beaches here. When you've had your fill of sun and sand, get out and explore artist enclaves, take a cruise, or join the free-spirited street scene in Provincetown.

Cape Cod, Martha's Vineyard & Nantucket

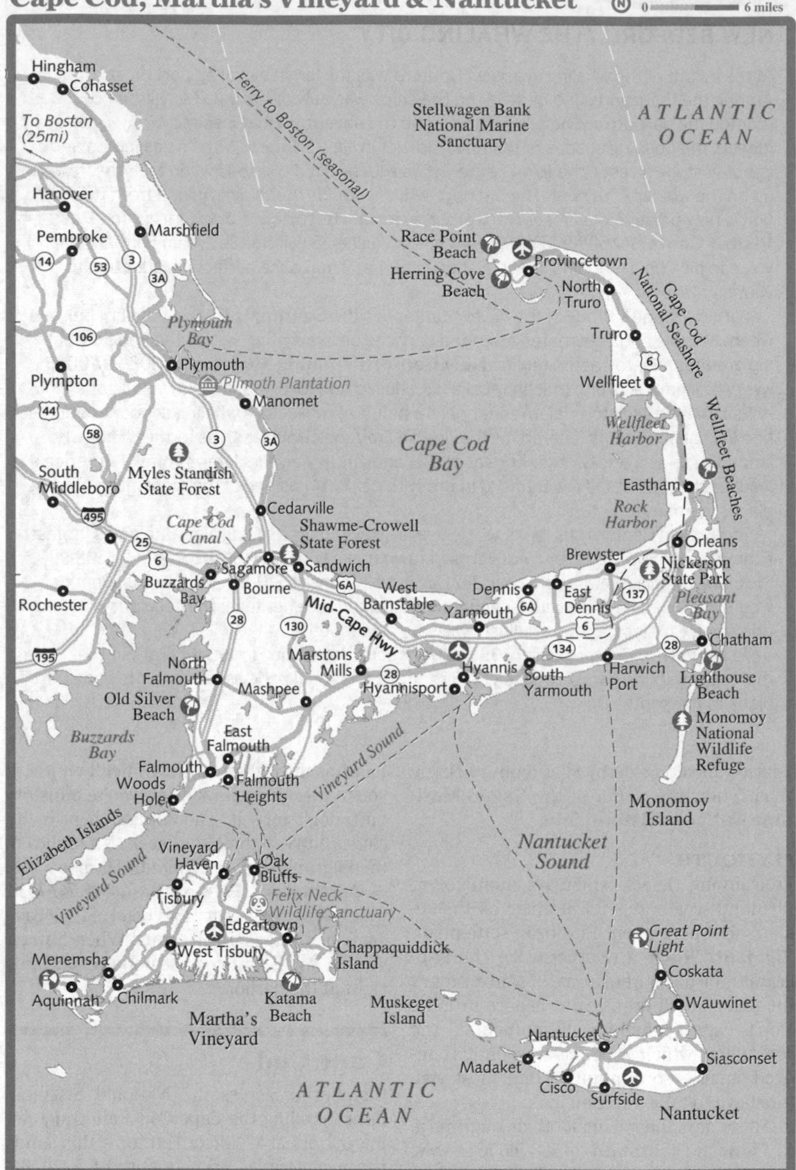

Cape Cod Chamber of Commerce (☎508-362-3225; www.capecodchamber.org; MA 132 at US 6, Hyannis; ⏲10am-5pm) has info.

SANDWICH

The Cape's oldest village wraps its historic center around a picturesque swan pond with a grist mill (c 1654) and several small museums.

Sights & Activities

If you're ready for salt spray, head to **Sandy Neck Beach** (Sandy Neck Rd), off MA 6A, a 6-mile dune-backed strand (parking $15) ideal for beachcombing and a bracing swim.

Sandwich Glass Museum MUSEUM
(☎508-888-0251; www.sandwichglassmuseum.org; 129 Main St; adult/child $5/1.25; ⏰9:30am-5pm) Artfully displayed here is the town's 19th-century glass-making heritage. Glass-blowing demonstrations are given on the hour.

Heritage Museums & Gardens MUSEUM
(☎508-888-3300; www.heritagemuseumsandgardens.org; cnr Grove & Pine Sts; adult/child $12/6; ⏰10am-5pm;) The 76-acre site sports a terrific **vintage automobile collection**, folk-art exhibits and one of the finest **rhododendron gardens** in America. Kids will love riding the classic 1912 **carousel**.

Hoxie House HISTORIC HOUSE
(☎508-888-1173; 18 Water St; adult/child $3/2; ⏰10am-5pm Mon-Sat, 1-5pm Sun) The Cape's oldest house (c 1640).

Cape Cod Canal BIKE PATH
A 6-mile path perfect for cycling and in-line skating runs along the south side of the Cape Cod Canal starting at Sandwich Harbor.

Sleeping & Eating

Belfry Inne & Bistro B&B $$
(☎508-888-8550; www.belfryinn.com; 8 Jarves St; r incl breakfast $189-255;) Ever fall asleep in church? Then you'll love the rooms, some with the original stained-glass windows, in this creatively restored former church, now an upmarket B&B. If, however, having the angel Gabriel watching over you in bed seems a bit too quirky, Belfry has two adjacent inns with more conventional rooms.

Shawme-Crowell State Forest CAMPGROUND $
(☎508-888-0351; www.reserveamerica.com; MA 130; campsites $14) You'll find 285 shady campsites in this 700-acre woodland, near MA 6A.

Brown Jug CAFE $
(www.thebrownjug.com; 155 Main St; mains $6-10; ⏰9am-5pm Tue-Sat, noon-4pm Sun) A great sandwich in Sandwich? Natch. This smart wine shop/cafe makes fab salads, sandwiches and cheese plates. Or step up to the deli and stock your picnic basket with truffle mousse pâté, caviar and artisanal breads for a romantic outing.

Seafood Sam's SEAFOOD $$
(www.seafoodsams.com; 6 Coast Guard Rd; mains $10-20; ⏰11am-9pm;) Sam's is a good family choice for fish and chips, clams and lobster. Dine at picnic tables overlooking Cape Cod Canal and watch the fishing boats sail by.

FALMOUTH

Fantastic beaches and a seaside bike trail highlight the Cape's second-largest town.

Sights & Activities

TOP CHOICE **Shining Sea Bikeway** BIKE TRAIL
Cyclists won't want to miss this 10.7-mile beaut that runs along the entire west coast of Falmouth, offering unspoiled views of salt ponds and seascapes. The route is flat, making it well suited as a family outing. **Corner Cycle** (☎508-540-4195; www.cyclecorner.com; 115 Palmer Ave; per day $17; ⏰9am-6pm) rents bicycles near the trail.

Old Silver Beach BEACH
(off MA 28A, North Falmouth; parking $20;) Deeply indented Falmouth has 70 miles of coastline, none finer than this long, sandy stretch with calm water. A rock jetty, sandbars and tidal pools provide lots of fun diversions for kids.

Sleeping & Eating

Falmouth Heights Motor Lodge MOTEL $$
(☎508-548-3623; www.falmouthheightsresort.com; 146 Falmouth Heights Rd; r incl breakfast from $149;) Don't be fooled by the name. This tidy family-run operation is no drive-up motor lodge – it's not even on the highway. All 28 rooms are a cut above the competition. The beach and Vineyard ferry are minutes away.

Casino Wharf FX SEAFOOD $$
(☎508-540-6160; www.casinowharf.weebly.com; 286 Grand Ave; mains $10-30; ⏰11:30am-10:30pm) This place is so close to the water that you could cast a fishing pole from the deck. But

WHAT THE...?

Lobster mania takes a new twist at **Ben & Bill's Chocolate Emporium** (209 Main St, Falmouth; cones $5; ⏰9am-11pm) where the crustacean has crawled onto the ice-cream menu. Forget plain vanilla. Step up to the counter and order a scoop of lobster ice cream. Now there's one you won't find with the old 31 flavors folks.

why bother? Just grab a deck table and let the feast begin. Music, often live and lively, on weekends.

Clam Shack SEAFOOD $
(227 Clinton Ave; items $5-15; ⏲11:30am-7:30pm) A classic of the genre, right on Falmouth Harbor. It's tiny, with picnic tables on the back deck and lots of fried seafood. The clams, huge juicy bellies cooked to a perfect crisp, are the place to start.

HYANNIS

Cape Cod's commercial hub, Hyannis is best known to visitors as the summer home of the Kennedy clan and a jumping-off point for ferries to Nantucket and Martha's Vineyard.

Sights & Activities

The town's mile-long Main St is fun to stroll and the place for dining, drinking and shopping. **Kalmus Beach** (Ocean St) is popular for windsurfing, while **Craigville Beach** (Craigville Beach Rd) is where the college set goes; parking at either costs $15.

John F Kennedy Hyannis Museum MUSEUM
(☎508-790-3077; http://jfkhyannismuseum.org; 397 Main St; adult/child $5/2.50; ⏲9am-5pm Mon-Sat, noon-5pm Sun) Celebrates the USA's 35th president with photos, videos and exhibits.

Hy-Line Cruises HARBOR CRUISE
(☎508-790-0696; www.hylinecruises.com; Ocean St Dock; adult/child $16/8; ⏲mid-Apr–Oct) Offers an hour-long harbor cruise aboard an old-fashioned steamer that circles past the compound of Kennedy family homes.

Sleeping

TOP CHOICE **Anchor-In** HOTEL $$
(☎508-775-0357; www.anchorin.com; 1 South St; r incl breakfast $139-259; ❄@🛜≋) Bright airy rooms with harbor-view balconies separate this family-run, boutique hotel from all the chains back on the highway. And if you're planning a day trip to Nantucket, the ferry is just a stroll away.

HI-Hyannis HOSTEL $
(☎508-775-7990; http://capecod.hiusa.org; 111 Ocean St; dm/private r incl breakfast $32/99; @🛜) Overlooking the harbor, this shiny new hostel is within walking distance of the Main St scene, beaches and ferries. Just 44 beds, so book early.

SeaCoast Inn MOTEL $$
(☎508-775-3828; www.seacoastcapecod.com; 33 Ocean St; r incl breakfast $108-158; ❄@🛜) The rates are a bargain, but it's no Plain Jane. Rooms are spacious with perks aplenty, from free wi-fi to kitchenettes, and the central location is just minutes from everything in town.

Eating

Raw Bar SEAFOOD $$
(www.therawbar.com; 230 Ocean St; lobster rolls $18-25; ⏲11am-7pm) Come here for the mother of all lobster rolls – it's like eating an entire lobster in a bun. The view overlooking Hyannis Harbor isn't hard to swallow either.

Brazilian Grill BRAZILIAN $$
(680 Main St; lunch/dinner buffet $15/28; ⏲11:30am-10pm) Celebrate Hyannis' Brazil-

WORTH A TRIP

WOODS HOLE

The tiny village of Woods Hole is home to the largest oceanographic institution in the US. Research at the Woods Hole Oceanographic Institution (WHOI, pronounced 'hooey') has covered the gamut from exploring the sunken *Titanic* to global warming studies.

For the skinny, join one of the free tours departing from the **WHOI information office** (☎508-289-2252; www.whoi.edu; 93 Water St; ⏲75-min tours 10:30am & 1:30pm Mon-Fri Jul & Aug). You'll also gain insights into scientists' work at the **WHOI Ocean Science Exhibit Center** (15 School St; admission free; ⏲10am-4:30pm Mon-Sat).

Woods Hole Science Aquarium (http://aquarium.nefsc.noaa.gov; 166 Water St; admission free; ⏲11am-4pm Tue-Sat; 👪) has little flash and dazzle, but you'll find unusual sea life specimens, local fish and the *Homarus americanus* (aka lobster). Kids will enjoy the touch-tank creatures. Coolest time to come is at 11am or 4pm when the seals are fed.

Keeping with the nautical theme, head over to the drawbridge where you'll find **Fishmonger Café** (56 Water St; mains $10-25; ⏲7am-9:30pm), with water views in every direction and an eclectic menu emphasizing fresh seafood.

To get to Woods Hole from Falmouth center take Woods Hole Rd south from MA28.

SCENIC DRIVE: MA 6A

When exploring the Cape, eschew the speedy Mid-Cape Hwy (US 6) and follow instead the Old King's Hwy (MA 6A), which snakes along Cape Cod Bay. The longest continuous stretch of historic district in the USA, it's lined with gracious period homes, antique shops and art galleries, all of which makes for good browsing en route.

ian side at this real-deal *rodízio,* a feast that pairs a splendid buffet with *churrasco* (barbecued meats on skewers) brought to your table by hunky gauchos in traditional garb.

La Petite France Café CAFE $
(www.lapetitefrancecafe.com; 349 Main St; sandwiches $7; ⏲7am-3pm Mon-Sat) The star of the Hyannis cafe scene makes flaky croissants, superb baguette sandwiches and homemade soups.

BREWSTER

Woodsy Brewster, on the Cape's bay side, makes a good base for outdoorsy types. The Cape Cod Rail Trail cuts clear across town and there are excellent options for camping, hiking and water activities.

Sights & Activities

FREE **Nickerson State Park** STATE PARK
(☎508-896-3491; 3488 MA 6A; ⏲dawn-dusk) Miles of cycling and walking trails and eight ponds with sandy beaches highlight this 2000-acre oasis.

Jack's Boat Rental
(☎508-349-9808; www.jacksboatrental.com; rentals per hr $20-40; ⏲9am-6pm) Rents canoes, kayaks, stand-up paddleboards and sailboats in the park.

Barbara's Bike
(☎508-896-7231; www.barbsbikeshop.com; rental per day $24; ⏲9am-6pm) Rents bicycles by the park entrance.

Cape Cod Museum of Natural History MUSEUM
(☎508-896-3867; www.ccmnh.org; 869 MA 6A; adult/child $8/3.50; ⏲9:30am-4pm; 👪) Come here for exhibits on the Cape's creatures and a cool boardwalk trail that tromps across a saltmarsh to a remote beach.

Sleeping

Old Sea Pines Inn B&B $$
(☎508-896-6114; www.oldseapinesinn.com; 2553 MA 6A; r incl breakfast $85-165; @📶) A former girls' school dating to 1840, the inn's 21 rooms retain a simple yesteryear look. It's a bit like staying at grandma's house: antique fittings, sepia photographs, clawfoot bathtubs. No TV, but rocking chairs await on the porch.

Nickerson State Park CAMPGROUND $
(☎877-422-6762; www.reserveamerica.com; campsites $17) Head here for Cape Cod's best camping with 418 wooded campsites; it often fills, so reserve your spot early.

Eating

TOP CHOICE **Brewster Fish House** SEAFOOD $$
(www.brewsterfish.com; 2208 MA 6A; mains $12-30; ⏲11:30am-3pm & 5-9:30pm) Not an eye-catcher from the outside but inside you'll find some of the best seafood on the Cape. Start with the lobster bisque, naturally sweet with chunks of fresh lobster. From there it's safe to cast your net in any direction. Just 11 tables, and no reservations, so think lunch or early dinner to avoid long waits.

Cobie's CLAM SHACK $$
(3256 MA 6A; takeout $8-23; ⏲10:30am-9pm) Conveniently located near Nickerson State Park, this roadside clam shack dishes out fried seafood that you can crunch and munch at outdoor picnic tables.

CHATHAM

Upscale inns and tony shops are a hallmark of the Cape's most genteel town, but some of Chatham's finest pleasures come free for the taking. Start your exploring on Main St, with its old sea captains' houses and cool art galleries.

At **Chatham Fish Pier** (Shore Rd) watch fishermen unload their catch and spot seals basking on nearby shoals. A mile south on Shore Rd is **Lighthouse Beach**, an endless expanse of sea and sandbars that offers some of the finest beach strolling on Cape Cod. The 7600-acre **Monomoy National Wildlife Refuge** (www.fws.gov/northeast/monomoy) covers two uninhabited islands thick with shorebirds; to see it up close take the 1½-hour boat tour with **Monomoy Island Excursions** (☎508-430-7772; www.monomoyseacruise.com; 702 MA 28, Harwich Port; adult/child $35/30).

Sleeping & Eating

Bow Roof House B&B $$
(☎508-945-1346; 59 Queen Anne Rd; r incl breakfast $100-115) This homey, six-room, c 1780 house is delightfully old-fashioned in price and offerings, and within walking distance of the town center and beach. Except for a few later-day conveniences like the addition of private bathrooms, the house looks nearly the same as it did in colonial times.

Chatham Squire PUB $$
(www.thesquire.com; 487 Main St; mains $8-22; ⌚11:30am-10pm) This perky pub is the busiest place in town. The menu's piled high with Monomoy steamers, raw oysters and other briny local delights. How fresh is the seafood? Just take one look at the fishermen hanging at the bar.

CAPE COD NATIONAL SEASHORE

Cape Cod National Seashore (www.nps.gov/caco) extends some 40 miles around the curve of the Outer Cape and encompasses most of the shoreline from Eastham to Provincetown. It's a treasure-trove of unspoiled beaches, dunes, salt marshes and forests. Thanks to President John F Kennedy, this vast area was set aside for preservation in the 1960s, just before a building boom hit the rest of his native Cape Cod. The **Salt Pond Visitor Center** (☎508-255-3421; cnr US 6 & Nauset Rd, Eastham; admission free; ⌚9am-5pm) is the place to start and has a great view to boot. Here you will find exhibits and films about the area's ecology and the scoop on the park's numerous cycling and hiking trails, some of which begin right at the center.

You brought your board, didn't you? **Coast Guard Beach**, just down the road from the visitor center, is a stunner that attracts everyone from surfers to beachcombers. And the view of untouched Nauset Marsh from the dunes above the beach is nothing short of spectacular. **Nauset Light Beach**, running north from Coast Guard Beach, takes its name from the lighthouse perched above it; three other classic lighthouses are nearby. Summertime beach parking passes cost $15/45 per day/season and are valid at all Cape Cod National Seashore beaches including Provincetown.

WELLFLEET

Art galleries, primo beaches and those famous Wellfleet oysters lure visitors to this little seaside town.

Sights & Activities

Wellfleet Beaches BEACHES
Marconi Beach has a monument to Guglielmo Marconi, who sent the first wireless transmission across the Atlantic from this site, and a beach backed by undulating dunes. The adjacent **White Crest Beach** and **Cahoon Hollow Beach** offer high-octane surfing. **SickDay Surf Shop** (☎508-214-4158; www.sickdaysurf.com; 361 Main St; half-/full day $18/25; ⌚9am-9pm Mon-Sat) rents surfboards.

Wellfleet Bay Wildlife Sanctuary WILDLIFE SANCTUARY
(☎508-349-2615; www.massaudubon.org; West Rd, off US 6; adult/child $5/3; ⌚8:30am-dusk; 👪) Birders flock to Mass Audubon's 1100-acre sanctuary, where trails cross tidal creeks, salt marshes and sandy beaches.

Festivals & Events

Wellfleet OysterFest FOOD
(www.wellfleetoysterfest.org) Held in mid-October the town hall parking lot morphs into a wildly popular festival with a beer garden, oyster shucking contest and, of course, belly-busters of the blessed bivalves.

Sleeping & Eating

Stone Lion Inn of Cape Cod B&B $$
(☎508-349-9565; www.stonelioncapecod.com; 130 Commercial St; r incl breakfast $150-220; ❄📶) Historic without being cloying, this 1871 Victorian is the finest place in Wellfleet to tuck

CYCLING THE RAIL TRAIL

A poster child for the rails-to-trail movement, the **Cape Cod Rail Trail** follows a former railroad track for 22 glorious miles past cranberry bogs and along sandy ponds ideal for a dip. It's one of the finest cycling trails in all New England. There's a hefty dose of Olde Cape Cod scenery en route and you can detour into quiet villages for lunch or sightseeing. The path begins in Dennis on MA 134 and continues all the way to South Wellfleet. If you have time to do only part of the trail, begin at Nickerson State Park in Brewster and head for the Cape Cod National Seashore in Eastham. Bicycle rentals are available at the trailhead in Dennis, at Nickerson State Park and opposite the National Seashore's Salt Pond Visitor Center.

in. Pine floors, antique decor and handcrafted furnishings set the tone. The location is handy for exploring town on foot.

Mac's Seafood Market CLAM SHACK $$
(www.macsseafood.com; Wellfleet Town Pier, takeout $6-20; ⌚7:30am-11pm) Head here for market-fresh seafood at bargain prices. Fried-fish standards are paired with snappy-fresh oysters harvested from nearby flats. Order at a window and chow down at picnic tables overlooking Wellfleet Harbor.

Mac's Shack SEAFOOD $$
(☎508-349-6333; 91 Commercial St; mains $15-30; ⌚4:30-9:45pm) Fancier, full-service version of Mac's Seafood Market.

PB Boulangerie & Bistro FRENCH BAKERY $
(www.pbboulangeriebistro.com; 15 Lecount Hollow Rd; ⌚7am-7pm Wed-Sun) Incredible pastries and artisanal breads.

Drinking & Entertainment

TOP CHOICE **Beachcomber** DANCE CLUB
(☎508-349-6055; www.thebeachcomber.com; 1120 Cahoon Hollow Rd) 'Da Coma' is the coolest summertime hangout on the entire Cape. Set in a former lifesaving station right on Cahoon Hollow Beach, you can enjoy the surf action till the sun goes down. And at night some really hot bands – like the Wailers and the Lemonheads – take to the stage.

Wellfleet Harbor Actors Theater THEATER
(WHAT; ☎508-349-9428; www.what.org; 2357 US 6) This acclaimed theater produces edgy contemporary plays.

Wellfleet Drive-In DRIVE-IN
(☎508-349-7176; www.wellfleetcinemas.com; US 6; 👪) Enjoy an evening of nostalgia at this old-fashioned drive-in theater.

TRURO

Squeezed between Cape Cod Bay on the west and the open Atlantic on the east, narrow Truro abounds with water views and beaches.

Sights

Cape Cod Highland Light LIGHTHOUSE
(www.capecodlight.org; Light House Rd; admission $4; ⌚10am-5:30pm) Dating to 1797, this lighthouse casts the brightest light on the New England coastline and offers a sweeping view.

Sleeping

Hostelling International Truro HOSTEL $
(☎508-349-3889; http://capecod.hiusa.org; N Pamet Rd; dm incl breakfast $32-42; @) Budget digs don't get more atmospheric than at this former coast guard station dramatically sited amid beach dunes. Book early.

PROVINCETOWN

This is it: as far as you can go on the Cape, and more than just geographically. The draw is irresistible. Fringe writers and artists began making a summer haven in Provincetown a century ago. Today this sandy outpost has morphed into the hottest gay and lesbian destination in the Northeast. Flamboyant street scenes, brilliant art galleries and unbridled nightlife paint the town center. But that's only half the show. Provincetown's untamed coastline and vast beaches also beg exploring. Sail off on a whale-watch, cruise the night away, get lost in the dunes – but whatever you do, don't miss this unique corner of New England.

Sights & Activities

Cape Cod National Seashore NATIONAL SEASHORE
The **Province Lands Visitor Center** (www.nps.gov/caco; Race Point Rd; admission free; ⌚9am-5pm) has displays on dune ecology and a rooftop observation deck with a 360-degree view of the outermost reaches of Cape Cod. The deck stays open to midnight, offering stellar stargazing.

The nearby **Race Point Beach** is a breathtaking stretch of sand with crashing surf and undulating dunes as far as the eye can see. Swimmers favor the calmer though equally brisk waters of **Herring Cove Beach**; nude (though illegal) sunbathers head to the left, families to the right. Herring Cove faces west, making for spectacular sunsets.

TOP CHOICE **Whale-Watching** WHALE-WATCHING
Provincetown is the perfect launch point for whale-watching, since it's the closest port to Stellwagen Bank National Marine Sanctuary, a summer feeding ground for humpback whales. These awesome creatures with a flair for acrobatic breaching come surprisingly close to the boats, offering great photo ops. Many of the 300 remaining North Atlantic right whales, the world's most endangered whale species, also frequent these waters.

Dolphin Fleet Whale Watch WHALE-WATCHING
(☎508-240-3636; www.whalewatch.com; MacMillan Wharf; adult/child $39/31; ⌚Apr-Oct; 👪) Offers up to nine tours daily in peak season, each lasting three to four hours.

Pilgrim Monument MUSEUM
(www.pilgrim-monument.org; High Pole Rd; adult/child $7/3.50; ⏲9am-5pm) Climb to the top of the USA's tallest all-granite structure, 253ft high, for a sweeping view of town and the surrounding coast. The monument and its interesting museum commemorate the *Mayflower* Pilgrims, who landed in Provincetown in 1620 before moving on to Plymouth.

Provincetown Art Association & Museum MUSEUM
(PAAM; www.paam.org; 460 Commercial St; adult/child $7/free; ⏲11am-8pm Mon-Thu, 11am-10pm Fri, 11am-5pm Sat & Sun) Established in 1914 to celebrate the town's thriving art community, this superb museum displays the works of artists who have found inspiration in Provincetown over the past century. On Friday evenings, admission is free.

Cycling CYCLING
Eight exhilarating miles of bike trails crisscross the forest and undulating dunes of the Cape Cod National Seashore and lead to Herring Cove and Race Point Beaches.

The best place to rent bicycles is at **Ptown Bikes** (☎508-487-8735; www.ptownbikes.com; 42 Bradford St; per day $22; ⏲9am-6pm) though you'll also find rental shops in the center of town on Commercial St.

Art's Dune Tours TOURS
(☎508-487-1950; www.artsdunetours.com; 4 Standish St; adult/child $26/17) Hour-long 4WD tours through the dunes.

Whydah Pirate Museum MUSEUM
(www.whydah.org; MacMillan Wharf; adult/child $10/8; ⏲10am-5pm) See the salvaged booty from a pirate ship that sank off Cape Cod in 1717.

Festivals & Events

Carnival Week CARNIVAL PARADE
(www.ptown.org/carnival.asp; mid-Aug) Mardi Gras, drag queens, flowery floats – this is the ultimate gay party event in this gay party town, attracting tens of thousands of revelers.

Sleeping

Provincetown offers nearly 100 guesthouses without a single chain hotel to mar the view. In summer it's wise to book ahead, doubly so on weekends. If you arrive without a booking, the chamber of commerce keeps tabs on available rooms.

GALLERY BROWSING

Provincetown hosts scores of art galleries. For the best browsing begin at PAAM and walk southwest along waterfront Commercial St. Over the next few blocks every second storefront harbors a gallery worth a peek.

TOP CHOICE **Carpe Diem** INN $$$
(☎508-487-4242; www.carpediemguesthouse.com; 12 Johnson St; r incl breakfast $175-359; ❄@📶) Sophisticated and relaxed, with smiling buddhas, orchid sprays and a European-style spa. Each room's decor is inspired by a different gay literary genius; the room themed on poet Raj Rao, for example, has sumptuous embroidered fabrics and hand-carved Native American furniture.

Christopher's by the Bay B&B $$
(☎508-487-9263; www.christophersbythebay.com; 8 Johnson St; r with shared/private bath from $105/155; ❄📶) Tucked away on a quiet side street, this welcoming inn is top value. The 2nd-floor rooms are the largest and snazziest, but the 3rd-floor rooms, which share a bathroom, get the ocean view.

Cape Codder GUESTHOUSE $
(☎508-487-0131; www.capecodderguests.com; 570 Commercial St; r with shared bath $60-85; 📶) The cheaper rooms are small, there are no TVs or phones, but it's clean, and heck, for these prices in this town it's a deal. The 14 rooms share just four baths, so time yourself accordingly.

Race Point Lighthouse LIGHTHOUSE INN $$
(☎508-487-9930; www.racepointlighthouse.net; Race Point; r $155-185) Shack up at a 19th-century lighthouse amid the dunes.

Moffett House GUESTHOUSE $$
(☎508-487-6615; www.moffetthouse.com; 296a Commercial St; r with shared bath $90-174; ❄📶) A quiet guesthouse with a bonus: free bicycles for your entire stay.

Pilgrim House Hotel BOUTIQUE HOTEL $$
(☎508-487-6424; www.thepilgrimhouse.com; 336 Commercial St; r $159-250; ❄📶) Fresh arty decor and a party-central location directly above Vixen nightclub.

Dunes' Edge Campground CAMPGROUND $
(☎508-487-9815; www.dunes-edge.com; 386 US 6; campsites $40; 👪) Camp amid the dunes at this family-friendly place.

Eating

Every third building on Commercial St houses some sort of eatery, so that's the place to start.

Mews Restaurant & Café BISTRO $$
(☎508-487-1500; www.mews.com; 429 Commercial St; mains $12-18; ⏲6-10pm) Want affordable gourmet? Skip the excellent but pricey restaurant and go upstairs to the bar for a fab view, great martinis and scrumptious bistro fare. Perhaps the Angus gorgonzola burger?

Fanizzi's by the Sea FAMILY RESTAURANT $$
(☎508-487-1964; www.fanizzisrestaurant.com; 539 Commercial St; mains $10-25; ⏲11:30am-10pm; 👪) Consistent food, an amazing water view and reasonable prices make this restaurant at the east end of Provincetown a sure winner. The extensive menu has something for everyone, from fresh seafood to salads and fajitas.

Purple Feather CAFE $
(www.thepurplefeather.com; 334 Commercial St; snacks $3-10; ⏲8am-midnight; 📶) Head to this stylish cafe for killer panini sandwiches, blueberry gelato and decadent desserts all made from scratch. No better place in town for light eats.

Lobster Pot SEAFOOD $$$
(☎508-487-0842; www.ptownlobsterpot.com; 321 Commercial St; mains $20-35; ⏲11:30am-10pm) True to its name, this bustling fish house overlooking the ocean is *the* place for lobster. Service can be s-l-o-w. Best way to beat the crowd is to come in mid-afternoon.

Portuguese Bakery BAKERY $
(299 Commercial St; snacks $2-5; ⏲7am-11pm) Old-school bakery serving up linguica sandwiches and Portuguese pastries.

Karoo Kafe SOUTH AFRICAN $$
(www.karookafe.com; 338 Commercial St; mains $8-16; ⏲11am-9pm; 🌱) Authentic home-style cooking from South Africa. The ostrich satay's a favorite.

Spiritus Pizza PIZZERIA $
(www.spirituspizza.com; 190 Commercial St; pizza slice $3; ⏲11:30am-2am) A favorite spot for a late-night bite and cruising after the clubs close.

Drinking & Entertainment

BARS

Patio CAFE
(www.ptownpatio.com; 328 Commercial St) Grab yourself a sidewalk table and order up a ginger-lime cosmo at this umbrella-shaded cafe hugging the pulsating center of Commercial St.

Ross' Grill BISTRO
(www.rossgrille.com; 237 Commercial St) A fab water view and 75 different wines by the glass.

NIGHTCLUBS

Provincetown is awash with gay clubs, drag shows and cabarets. And don't be shy if you're straight – everyone's welcome.

Crown & Anchor NIGHTCLUB
(www.onlyatthecrown.com; 247 Commercial St) The queen of the scene, this multiwing complex has a nightclub, a leather bar and a steamy cabaret that takes it to the limit.

Vixen NIGHTCLUB
(www.ptownvixen.com; 336 Commercial St) A favorite lesbian hangout, with everything from an intimate wine bar to comedy shows and dancing.

A-House DANCE CLUB
(www.ahouse.com; 4 Masonic Pl) A hot weekend dance spot for gay men.

THEATER

Provincetown boasts a rich theater history. Eugene O'Neill began his writing career here and several stars including Marlon Brando and Richard Gere performed on Provincetown stages before they hit the big screen.

Provincetown Theater THEATER
(☎508-487-7487; www.provincetowntheater.org; 238 Bradford St) Provincetown's leading theater

WHAT THE...?

In a town of quirky attractions the **Provincetown Public Library** (356 Commercial St; 📶) might be the last place you'd expect to find a hidden treasure. Erected in 1860 as a church, it was turned into a museum a century later, complete with a replica of Provincetown's race-winning schooner *Rose Dorothea*. When the museum went bust, the town converted the building to a library. One catch: the boat, which occupies the building's upper deck, was too big to remove. So it's still there, with bookshelves built around it. Pop upstairs and take a look.

troupe, the New Provincetown Players, takes the stage here.

Shopping

Shops lining Commercial St sell everything from kitsch and tourist T-shirts to quality crafts and edgy clothing.

Shop Therapy SEX TOYS
(www.shoptherapy.com; 346 Commercial St) Downstairs it's tie-dye clothing and X-rated bumper stickers. But everyone gravitates upstairs, where the sex toys are wild enough to make an Amsterdam madam blush. Parents, use discretion: your teenagers *will* want to go inside.

Womencrafts CRAFTS
(www.womencrafts.com; 376 Commercial St) The name says it all: jewelry, pottery, books and music by female artists from across America.

Information

Post office (www.usps.com; 219 Commercial St)

Provincetown Business Guild (www.ptown.org) Website that is oriented towards the gay community.

Provincetown Chamber of Commerce (☎508-487-3424; www.ptownchamber.com; 307 Commercial St; ⏰9am-5pm) The town's helpful tourist office is located at MacMillan Wharf.

Provincetown on the Web (www.provincetown.com) Online guide with the entertainment scoop.

Seamen's Bank (221 Commercial St) Has a 24-hour ATM.

Wired Puppy (www.wiredpuppy.com; 379 Commercial St; ⏰6:30am-10pm; 📶) Free online computers for the price of an espresso.

Getting There & Away

Plymouth & Brockton buses (www.p-b.com) connect Boston and Provincetown ($35, 3½ hours). From mid-May to mid-October, **Bay State Cruise Company** (☎877-783-3779; www.baystatecruises.com) runs a ferry (round-trip $79, 1½ hours) between Boston's World Trade Center Pier and MacMillan Wharf.

Nantucket

Once home port to the world's largest whaling fleet, Nantucket's storied past is reflected in its period homes and cobbled streets. When whaling went bust in the mid-19th century the town plunged from riches to rags. The population dwindled, and its grand old houses sat idle until wealthy urbanites discovered Nantucket made a fine place to summer. High-end tourism has been Nantucket's mainstay ever since.

Sights & Activities

Step off the boat and you're in the only place in the USA where the entire town is a National Historic Landmark. It's a bit like stepping into a museum – wander around, soak up the atmosphere. Start your explorations by strolling up Main St, where you'll find the grandest whaling-era mansions lined up in a row.

Nantucket Whaling Museum MUSEUM
(www.nha.org; 13 Broad St; adult/child $17/8; ⏰10am-5pm) A top sight is this evocative museum in a former spermaceti (whale-oil) candle factory.

Nantucket Beaches BEACHES
If you have young 'uns head to **Children's Beach**, right in Nantucket town, where the water's calm and there's a playground. **Surfside Beach**, 2 miles to the south, is where the college crowd heads for an active scene and bodysurfing waves. The best place to catch the sunset is **Madaket Beach**, 5.5 miles west of town.

Cycling CYCLING
No destination on the island is more than 8 miles from town and thanks to Nantucket's relatively flat terrain and dedicated bike trails, cycling is an easy way to explore. For a fun outing, cycle to the picturesque village of **Siasconset** ('Sconset), known for its rose-covered cottages. A couple of companies rent bikes ($30 a day) right at the ferry docks.

Sleeping

Pineapple Inn B&B **$$$**
(☎508-228-9992; www.pineappleinn.com; 10 Hussey St; r incl breakfast $200-375; ❄@📶) The 12 guest rooms at this 1838 whaling captain's house have been completely restored with understated elegance. Run by restaurateurs, the inn is justifiably famous for its breakfast. Everything, including the oversized beds with goose-down comforters, spells complete romance.

Nesbitt Inn B&B **$$**
(☎508-228-0156; nesbittinn@comcast.net; 21 Broad St; s incl breakfast $105, d $125-170) Operating as an inn since 1872, Nesbitt's a bit faded

but it has damn good prices and plenty of old-fashioned character. The finest room, the Captain's Quarters, has a bay window overlooking bustling Broad St and a cavernous bathroom with a real-deal clawfoot tub. Most other guest rooms share bathrooms.

HI Nantucket HOSTEL $
(☎508-228-0433; http://capecod.hiusa.org; 31 Western Ave; dm incl breakfast $32-42; @) Known locally as Star of the Sea, this atmospheric hostel in an 1873 lifesaving station has a million-dollar setting at Surfside Beach. As Nantucket's sole nod to the budget traveler, it books up well in advance.

Eating

Centre Street Bistro CAFE $$
(www.nantucketbistro.com; 29 Centre St; lunch $7-12, dinner $20-30; ⊙11:30am-9:30pm; ✎) Settle in at a parasol-shaded sidewalk table and watch the traffic trickle by at this relaxed cafe. The chef-owners make everything from scratch from the breakfast granola to the warm goat's cheese tarts.

Brotherhood of Thieves PUB $$
(www.brotherhoodofthieves.com; 23 Broad St; mains $7-25; ⊙11:30am-1am) Nantucketers come here for the friendly tavern atmosphere – all brick and dark woods – and the island's best burgers. Good fresh seafood too, including sweet Nantucket scallops.

Black-Eyed Susan's CAFE $$
(www.black-eyedsusans.com; 10 India St; mains $8-30; ⊙7am-1pm daily & 6-10pm Mon-Sat) Snag a seat on the back patio and try the sourdough French toast topped with caramelized pecans and Jack Daniels butter. At dinner the fish of the day with black-eyed peas takes top honors.

Information

Visitor Services (☎508-228-0925; www.nantucket-ma.gov/visitor; 25 Federal St; ⊙9am-5pm) has tourist information and maintains a kiosk at the ferry dock.

Getting There & Around

AIR **Cape Air** (www.flycapeair.com) flies from Boston, Hyannis, Martha's Vineyard and Providence to Nantucket Memorial Airport (ACK).

BOAT The **Steamship Authority** (☎508-477-8600; www.steamshipauthority.com; round-trip adult/child slow ferry $35/18, fast ferry $67/34) runs ferries throughout the day between Hyannis and Nantucket. The fast ferry takes an hour; the slow ferry 2¼ hours. The slow ferry takes cars, but the $400 round-trip fare aims to discourage visitors from adding to traffic congestion on Nantucket's narrow streets.

BUS Getting around Nantucket is a snap. The **NRTA Shuttle** (www.shuttlenantucket.com; rides $1-2, day pass $7; ⊙late May-Sep) operates buses around town and to 'Sconset, Madaket and the beaches. Buses have bike racks, so cyclists can bus one way and pedal back.

Martha's Vineyard

New England's largest island is a world unto itself. Home to 15,500 year-round residents, its population swells to 100,000 in summer. The towns are charming, the beaches good, the restaurants chef-driven. And there's something for every mood here – fine-dine in gentrified Edgartown one day and hit the cotton candy and carousel scene in Oak Bluffs the next.

Martha's Vineyard Chamber of Commerce (☎508-693-0085; www.mvy.com; 24 Beach Rd, Vineyard Haven; ⊙9am-5pm Mon-Fri) has visitor information. There are also summertime visitor kiosks at the ferry terminals.

OAK BLUFFS

Odds are this ferry-port town, where the lion's share of boats arrive, will be your introduction to the island. Welcome to the Vineyard's summer fun mecca – a place to wander with an ice-cream cone in hand, poke around honky-tonk sights and go clubbing into the night.

Sights & Activities

Campgrounds & Tabernacle GINGERBREAD HOUSES
Oak Bluffs started out in the mid-19th century as a summer retreat by a revivalist church, whose members enjoyed a day at the beach as much as a gospel service. They built around 300 cottages, each adorned with whimsical gingerbread trim. These brightly painted cottages – known today as the Campgrounds – surround **Trinity Park** and its open-air **Tabernacle** (1879), a venue for community sing-alongs, festivals and concerts.

Flying Horses Carousel HISTORIC SITE
(www.mvpreservation.org; cnr Lake & Circuit Aves; rides $2; ⊙10am-10pm; 👪) Take a nostalgic ride on the USA's oldest merry-go-round, which has been captivating kids of all ages since 1876. The antique horses have manes of real horse hair and if you stare into their

glass eyes you'll see neat little silver animals inside.

Bike Trail CYCLING

A scenic bike trail runs along the coast connecting Oak Bluffs, Vineyard Haven and Edgartown – it's largely flat so makes a good pedal for families. Rent bicycles at **Anderson's Bike Rental** (☎508-693-9346; 1 Circuit Ave Extension; per day $18; ⏲9am-6pm) near the ferry terminal.

Sleeping

Nashua House HOTEL $$

(☎508-693-0043; www.nashuahouse.com; 30 Kennebec Ave; r with shared bath $69-219;) The Vineyard the way it used to be – no phones, no TV, no in-room bath. Instead you'll find suitably simple and spotlessly clean accommodations at this small inn right in the center of town.

Narragansett House B&B $$

(☎508-693-3627; www.narragansetthouse.com; 46 Narragansett Ave; r incl breakfast $140-275;) On a quiet residential street, this B&B occupies two adjacent Victorian gingerbread-trimmed houses. It's old-fashioned without being cloying and unlike other places in this price range all rooms have private baths.

Eating

Slice of Life CAFE $$

(www.sliceoflifemv.com; 50 Circuit Ave; mains $8-20; ⏲8am-9pm Tue-Sat;) The look is casual, the fare is gourmet: portobello mushroom omelets, roasted cod with sun-dried tomatoes and luscious desserts.

Giordano's ITALIAN $$

(www.giosmv.com; cnr Circuit & Lake Aves; mains $10-20; ⏲11:30am-10:30pm) Established in 1930, this family-friendly eatery is famous for its fried clams and also serves good hand-tossed pizzas.

MV Bakery BAKERY $

(5 Post Office Sq; baked goods $1-3; ⏲7am-5pm) Inexpensive coffee, famous apple fritters and cannoli are served all day, but best time to swing by is from 9pm to midnight, when folks line up at the back door to buy hot doughnuts straight from the baker.

Drinking & Entertainment

Offshore Ale Co MICROBREWERY

(www.offshoreale.com; 30 Kennebec Ave) This popular microbrewery is the place to enjoy a pint of Vineyard ale while soaking up live jazz and Irish music on weekday nights.

Lampost DANCE CLUB

(www.lampostmv.com; Circuit Ave) Head to this combo bar and nightclub for the hottest dance scene on the island. In the unlikely event you don't find what you're looking for here, keep cruising Circuit Ave where you'll stumble across several dive bars (one actually named the Dive Bar, another the Ritz), both dirty and nice.

VINEYARD HAVEN

A harbor full of classic wooden sailboats, and streets lined with eye-catching restaurants and shops, lures visitors to this appealing town.

Sleeping & Eating

HI Martha's Vineyard HOSTEL $

(☎508-693-2665; http://capecod.hiusa.org; Edgartown-West Tisbury Rd, West Tisbury; dm $32-42; @) Reserve early for one of the 72 beds at this popular purpose-built hostel 8 miles from Vineyard Haven. The public bus stops out front and it's right on the bike path.

Art Cliff Diner CAFE $$

(☎508-693-1224; 39 Beach Rd; mains $7-15; ⏲7am-2pm Thu-Tue) *The* place for breakfast and lunch. Chef-owner Gina Stanley, a grad of the prestigious Culinary Institute of America, adds flair to everything she touches from the lemon crepes to the fresh-fish tacos. Expect a line – it's worth the wait.

EDGARTOWN

Perched on a fine natural harbor, Edgartown has a rich maritime history and a patrician air. At the height of the whaling era it was home to more than 100 sea captains whose fortunes built the grand old homes that line the streets today.

Stroll along Main St where you'll find several historic buildings, some of which open to visitors during the summer.

Sights

Katama Beach BEACH

(Katama Rd) One of the Vineyard's best beaches is just 4 miles south of Edgartown center. Also called South Beach, Katama stretches for three magnificent miles. Rough surf is the norm on the ocean side but there are protected salt ponds on the inland side.

Sleeping & Eating

Edgartown Inn GUESTHOUSE $$

(☎508-627-4794; www.edgartowninn.com; 56 N Water St; r with shared bath $100-125, with private bath $150-300;) The inn's the best bargain

IF YOU HAVE A FEW MORE DAYS

Known as **Up-Island**, the rural western half of Martha's Vineyard is a patchwork of rolling hills, small farms and open fields frequented by wild turkeys and deer. Feast your eyes and your belly at the picturesque fishing village of **Menemsha**, where you'll find seafood shacks with food so fresh the boats unload their catch at the back door. They'll shuck you an oyster and steam you a lobster while you watch and you can eat al fresco on a harbor-side bench.

The coastal **Aquinnah Cliffs**, also known as the Gay Head Cliffs, are so special they're a National Natural Landmark. These 150ft-high cliffs glow with an amazing array of colors that can be best appreciated in the late-afternoon light. You can hang out at **Aquinnah Beach**, just below the multihued cliffs, or walk a mile north along the shore to an area that's popular with nude sunbathers.

Cedar Tree Neck Sanctuary (www.sheriffsmeadow.org; Indian Hill Rd, West Tisbury; admission free; ⌚8:30am-5:30pm), off State Rd, has an inviting 2.5-mile hike across native bogs and forest to a coastal bluff with views of Cape Cod. The Massachusetts Audubon Society's **Felix Neck Wildlife Sanctuary** (www.massaudubon.org; Edgartown-Vineyard Haven Rd; adult/child $4/3; ⌚dawn-dusk) is a birder's paradise with 4 miles of trails skirting marshes and ponds.

in town with straightforward rooms spread across three adjacent buildings. The oldest dates to 1798 and claims Nathaniel Hawthorne and Daniel Webster among its early guests!

Détente FRENCH **$$$**
(☎508-627-8810; www.detentemv.com; 3 Nevin Sq; mains $28-40; ⌚5-10pm) Détente's French-inspired fare includes a rave rendition of ahi tuna tartare served with vanilla-lychee puree. Local organic greens, island-raised chicken and Nantucket bay scallops get plenty of billing on the innovative menu.

Among the Flowers Café CAFE **$$**
(17 Mayhew Lane; mains $7-20; ⌚8am-4pm; ☑) Join the townies on the garden patio for crepes, homemade soups and sandwiches. Although everything's served on paper plates, it's still kinda chichi. In July and August it also serves dinner.

Getting There & Around

Boat

Frequent ferries operated by the **Steamship Authority** (☎508-477-8600; www.steamshipauthority.com; round-trip adult/child/car $16/8.50/135) link Woods Hole to both Vineyard Haven and Oak Bluffs, a 45-minute voyage. If you're bringing a car, book well in advance.

From Falmouth Harbor, the passenger-only ferry **Island Queen** (☎508-548-4800; www.islandqueen.com; 75 Falmouth Heights Rd; round-trip adult/child $18/9) sails to Oak Bluffs several times daily in summer.

From Hyannis, **Hy-Line Cruises** (☎508-778-2600; www.hylinecruises.com; Ocean St Dock; round-trip adult/child slow ferry $45/free, fast ferry $71/48) operates a slow ferry (1½ hours) once daily to Oak Bluffs and a high-speed ferry (55 minutes) five times daily.

Bus

Martha's Vineyard Regional Transit Authority (www.vineyardtransit.com; 1-/3-day pass $7/15) operates a bus network with frequent service between towns. It's a practical way to get around and you can even reach out-of-the-way destinations like the Aquinnah Cliffs.

Central Massachusetts

Poking around this central swath of Massachusetts, between big-city Boston and the fashionable Berkshires, provides a taste of the less-touristed stretch of the state. But it's no sleeper, thanks largely to a score of colleges that infuse a youthful spirit to the region.

The **Central Massachusetts Convention & Visitors Bureau** (☎508-755-7400; www.centralmass.org) and the **Greater Springfield Convention & Visitors Bureau** (☎413-787-1548; www.valleyvisitor.com) provide regional visitor information.

WORCESTER

The state's second-largest city had its glory days in the 19th century. The industries that made the town rich went bust but the old barons left a legacy in Worcester's fine museums. The first-rate **Worcester Art Museum**

DON'T MISS

WORCESTER DINERS

Worcester nurtured a great American icon: the diner. Here, in this rustbelt city, you'll find a dozen of them tucked behind warehouses, underneath old train trestles, or steps from dicey bars. **Miss Worcester Diner** (300 Southbridge St; meals $5-8; ⏲6am-2pm) is a classic of the genre. Built in 1948, it was a showroom diner of Worcester Lunch Car Company, who produced 650 diners at its factory right across the street. Harleys parked on the sidewalk and Red Sox paraphernalia on the walls set the tone. Enticing selections like banana bread French toast compete with the usual greasy spoon menu of chili dogs and biscuits with gravy. It's one tasty slice of Americana.

(☎508-799-4406; www.worcesterart.org; 55 Salisbury St; adult/child $14/free; ⏲11am-5pm Wed-Fr & Sun, 10am-5pm Sat) showcases works by luminary French Impressionists and American masters like Whistler. The amazing **Higgins Armory Museum** (☎508-853-6015; www.higgins.org; 100 Barber Ave; adult/child $10/7; ⏲10am-4pm Tue-Sat, noon-4pm Sun) is a military buff's heaven. It started as the private collection of a local steel tycoon who built a fanciful art-deco armory to house thousands of military collectibles including Corinthian helmets from ancient Greece and more than 100 full suits of armor.

SPRINGFIELD

Workaday Springfield's top claim to fame is as the birthplace of the all-American game of basketball. The **Naismith Basketball Hall of Fame** (☎413-781-6500, www.hoophall.com; 1000 W Columbus Ave; adult/child $17/12; ⏲10am-5pm;), south of I-91, celebrates the sport with exhibits and memorabilia from all the big hoop stars.

It's also the hometown of Theodor Seuss Geisel, aka children's author Dr Seuss. You'll find life-size bronze sculpture of the Cat in the Hat and other wonky characters at the **Dr Seuss National Memorial Sculpture Garden** (cnr State & Chestnut Sts; admission free).

NORTHAMPTON

The region's best dining, hottest nightlife and most interesting street scenes all await in this uber-hip burg known for its liberal politics and outspoken lesbian community. Easy to explore on foot, the eclectic town center is chockablock with cafes, funky shops and art galleries. **Greater Northampton Chamber of Commerce** (☎413-584-1900; www.explorenorthampton.com; 99 Pleasant St; ⏲9am-5pm Mon-Fri) is information central.

The **Smith College** (www.smith.edu) campus, covering 127 acres with lovely gardens, is well worth a stroll. Don't miss the **Smith College Museum of Art** (☎413-585-2760; Elm St at Bedford Tce; adult/child $5/2; ⏲10am-4pm Tue-Sat, noon-4pm Sun), which boasts an impressive collection of 19th- and 20th-century European and North American paintings, including works by John Singleton Copley, Eastman Johnson and Claude Monet.

Sleeping

Hotel Northampton HISTORIC HOTEL $$
(☎413-584-3100; www.hotelnorthampton.com; 36 King St; r from $180;) Northampton's most upscale sleep since 1927, this 100-room hotel in the town center features period decor and well-appointed rooms.

Autumn Inn MOTEL $$
(☎413-584-7660; www.hampshirehospitality.com; 259 Elm St/MA 9; r incl breakfast $99-169; @) Despite its motel-like layout, this two-story place near Smith College sports an agreeable inn-like ambience and large, comfy rooms.

Eating

Sylvester's FAMILY DINING $
(www.sylvestersrestaurant.com; 111 Pleasant St; mains $5-10; ⏲7am-3pm) Follow the locals to this unassuming eatery for the best breakfast in town. Forget mixes – everything is from scratch, real maple syrup tops the pancakes, the home fries are loaded with sautéed onions and the omelets are however you like them.

Paul & Elizabeth's CAFE $$
(www.paulandelizabeths.com; 150 Main St; mains $8-16; ⏲11:30am-9:15pm;) Fresh, local and organic ingredients highlight the menu at this stellar natural food cafe serving innovative vegetarian fare and Japanese-style fish dishes.

Green Bean CAFE $
(241 Main St; mains $6-8; ⏲7am-3pm) Pioneer Valley farmers stock the kitchen at this cute eatery that dishes up organic eggs at breakfast and juicy hormone-free beef burgers at lunch.

Drinking & Entertainment

Northampton Brewery BREWPUB
(www.northamptonbrewery.com; 11 Brewster Ct) On a sunny day you'll find half of Northampton chugging ales on the rooftop beer garden at New England's oldest microbrewery.

Calvin Theatre CONCERT VENUE
(413-584-0610; www.iheg.com; 19 King St) The venue for big-name performances for everything from hot rock and indie bands to comedy shows.

Diva's CLUB
(www.divasofnoho.com; 492 Pleasant St) The city's main gay-centric dance club keeps patrons sweaty with a steady diet of thumping house music.

Iron Horse Music Hall CONCERT VENUE
(413-584-0610; www.iheg.com; 20 Center St) Nationally acclaimed folk and jazz artists line up to play in this intimate setting.

Haymarket Café CAFE
(www.haymarketcafe.com; 185 Main St;) Northampton's coolest hangout for bohemians and caffeine addicts.

AMHERST

This college town, a short drive from Northampton, is built around the mega **University of Massachusetts** (www.umass.edu) and two small colleges, the liberal **Hampshire College** (www.hampshire.edu) and the prestigious **Amherst College** (www.amherst.edu). Contact them for campus tours and event information; there's always something happening. If hunger strikes, you'll find the usual bevy of college-town eateries radiating out from Main St in the town center.

The lifelong home of poet Emily Dickinson (1830–86), the 'belle of Amherst,' is open to the public as the **Emily Dickinson Museum** (413-542-8161; www.emilydickinsonmuseum.org; 280 Main St; adult/child $8/4; 11am-4pm Wed-Sun). Admission includes a 40-minute tour.

The Berkshires

Tranquil towns and a wealth of cultural attractions are nestled in these cool green hills. For more than a century the Berkshires have been a favored retreat for wealthy Bostonians and New Yorkers. And we're not just talking Rockefellers – the entire Boston symphony summers here as well. The **Berkshire Visitors Bureau** (413-743-4500; www.berkshires.org; 3 Hoosac St, Adams; 10am-5pm) can provide information on the entire region.

GREAT BARRINGTON

Hands-down the best place in the Berkshires to be at mealtime. Head straight to the intersection of Main (US 7) and Railroad Sts in the town center where you'll find an artful mix of galleries and eateries serving mouth-watering food – everything from bakeries to ethnic cuisines.

For wholesome Berkshire-grown meals on a budget, go to **Eastern Mountain Cafe** (www.berkshire.coop; 42 Bridge St; meals $6-10; 8am-7pm Mon-Sat, 10am-5pm Sun;) inside the Berkshire Co-op Market. Families will love **Baba Louie's** (www.babalouiespizza.com; 286 Main St; pizzas $12-18; 11:30am-9:30pm;) for its organic wood-fired pizzas and $6 kids specials. For fine dining, **Allium** (413-528-2118; www.alliumberkshires.com; 42 Railroad St; mains $15-28; 5-9:30pm) offers innovative New American cuisine in a stylish setting.

STOCKBRIDGE

This timeless New England town, sans even a single traffic light, looks like something straight out of a Norman Rockwell drawing. Oh wait…it is! Rockwell (1894–1978), the most popular illustrator in US history, lived on Main St and used the town and its residents as subjects. At the evocative **Norman Rockwell Museum** (413-298-4100; www.nrm.org; 9 Glendale Rd/MA 183; adult/child $15/5; 10am-5pm), Rockwell's slice-of-Americana paintings come to life when examined up close.

LENOX

The cultural heart of the Berkshires, the refined village of Lenox hosts one of the country's premier music series, the open-air **Tanglewood Music Festival** (413-637-5165; www.tanglewood.org; late Jun-early Sep), featuring the Boston Symphony Orchestra and guest artists like James Taylor and Yo-Yo Ma. Buy a lawn ticket, spread a blanket, uncork a bottle of wine and enjoy the quintessential Berkshires experience.

Shakespeare & Company (413-637-1199; www.shakespeare.org; 70 Kemble St) performs the Bard's work throughout the summer. The renowned **Jacob's Pillow Dance Festival** (413-243-9919; www.jacobspillow.org; 385 George Carter Rd; Jun-Aug), 10 miles east of Lenox in Becket, stages contemporary dance performances.

The **Mount** (413-551-5111; www.edithwharton.org; 2 Plunkett St, at US 7; adult/child $16/free; 10am-5pm May-Oct), novelist Edith Wharton's former estate, offers hour-long tours of her mansion and inspirational gardens.

Charming period inns abound in Lenox. The senior of them, **Birchwood Inn** (413-637-2600; www.birchwood-inn.com; 7 Hubbard St; r incl breakfast $175-335;), registered its first guest in 1767 and continues to offer warm hospitality today.

Spread across three historic houses, **Cornell in Lenox** (413-637-4800; www.cornellbandb.com; 203 Main St; r incl breakfast $150-200;) offers good value in a high-priced town.

You'll find stylish bistros along Church St in the town center, including **Bistro Zinc** (413-637-8800; www.bistrozinc.com; 56 Church St; mains $15-30; 11:30am-3pm & 5:30-10pm) with hot postmodern decor and French-inspired New American fare. For family fare at honest prices visit **Olde Heritage Tavern** (12 Housatonic St; mains $6-15; 8am-10pm), an upbeat pub whose menu ranges from waffles to steaks.

PITTSFIELD

Just west of the town of Pittsfield is **Hancock Shaker Village** (413-443-0188; www.hancockshakervillage.org; US 20; adult/child $17/4; 10am-5pm May-Oct), a fascinating museum illustrating the lives of the Shakers, the religious sect that founded the village in 1783. The Shakers believed in communal ownership, the sanctity of work and celibacy, the latter of which proved to be their demise. Their handiwork – graceful in its simplicity – includes wooden furnishings and 20 buildings, the most famous of which is the round stone barn.

WILLIAMSTOWN & NORTH ADAMS

Cradled by the Berkshire's rolling hills, Williamstown is a picture-perfect New England college town revolving around the leafy campus of Williams College. Williamstown and neighboring North Adams boast three outstanding art museums, each a worthy destination in itself.

Sights & Activities

TOP CHOICE Clark Art Institute MUSEUM
(413-458-2303; www.clarkart.edu; 225 South St, Williamstown; adult/child Jun-Oct $15/free, Nov-May free to all; 10am-5pm, closed Mon Sep-Jun) Focuses on 19th-century paintings with oodles of Renoirs and other French impressionists as well as a solid collection of American paintings by Winslow Homer, John Singer Sargent and others.

FREE Williams College Museum of Art MUSEUM
(413-597-2429; www.wcma.org; 15 Lawrence Hall Dr, Williamstown; 10am-5pm Tue-Sat, 1-5pm Sun) Showcases works by American luminaries such as Mary Cassett, Edward Hopper and Georgia O'Keeffe.

Mass MoCA MUSEUM
(413-662-2111; www.massmoca.org; 87 Marshall St, North Adams; adult/child $15/5; 10am-6pm Jul & Aug, 11am-5pm Wed-Mon Sep-Jun;) This contemporary art museum sprawls across an amazing 222,000 sq ft, making it the USA's largest. Bring your walking shoes! In addition to description-defying installation pieces, MoCA is a venue for cutting-edge theater and dance.

Mt Greylock State Reservation PARK
(413-499-4262; www.mass.gov/dcr/parks/mtGreylock; 30 Rockwell Rd, Lanesborough) Just south of North Adams, this park has trails up to Massachusetts' highest peak (3491ft), where there's a panoramic view of several ranges and, on a clear day, five different states. The park offers camping, backpack shelters and a rustic lodge; see its website for details.

Festivals & Events

Williamstown Theatre Festival THEATER
(413-597-3400; www.wtfestival.org; 1000 Main St, Williamstown) This first-rate festival stages contemporary and classic plays in July and August, often with notable casts.

Sleeping & Eating

River Bend Farm B&B $$
(413-458-3121; www.windsorsofstonington.com/RBF; 643 US 7; r incl breakfast with shared bath $120) Step back to the 18th century in this Georgian Colonial B&B furnished with real-deal antiques and boasting five fireplaces.

Porches B&B $$
(413-664-0400; www.porches.com; 231 River St; r incl breakfast $180-250;) Across the street from MASS MoCA, the artsy rooms here combine well-considered color palettes, ample lighting and French doors.

TOP CHOICE Mezze Bistro + Bar FUSION $$$
(413-458-0123; www.mezzerestaurant.com; 777 US 7; mains $18-27; 5-10pm) East meets West

at this chic restaurant where chef Joji Sumi masterfully blends contemporary American cuisine with classic French and Japanese influences. The seasonal farm-to-table menu, utilizes organic meats, cheeses and produce.

Tunnel City Coffee CAFE $
(www.tunnelcitycoffee.com; 100 Spring St; snacks $2-6; 6am-6pm;) Come to this student haunt near Williams College campus for potent espressos, light eats and sugar-laced desserts.

RHODE ISLAND

America's smallest state packs a lot into a compact package, more than making up for its lack of land with 400 miles of craggy coastline, deeply indented bays and lovely beaches. The state's engaging capital, Providence, is small enough to be friendly but big enough to offer top-notch dining and attractions. Newport, a summer haunt of the well-heeled, brims with opulent mansions, pretty yachts and world-class music festivals. Should you want to take it further afield, hopping on a ferry to Block Island makes a perfect day-trip.

RHODE ISLAND FACTS

» **Nicknames** Ocean State, Little Rhody

» **Population** 1,053,000

» **Area** 1045 sq miles

» **Capital city** Providence (population 178,000)

» **Other city** Newport (population 24,700)

» **Sales tax** 7%

» **Birthplace of** Broadway composer George M Cohan (1878–1942) and toy icon Mr Potato Head (b 1952)

» **Home of** the first US tennis championships

» **Politics** majority vote Democrat

» **Famous for** being the smallest state

» **Official state bird** A chicken? Why not? The Rhode Island Red revolutionized the poultry industry

» **Driving distances** Providence to Newport 37 miles, Providence to Boston 50 miles

History

The name Roger Williams (1603–83) gave to the community he founded in 1636 – nothing less than Providence! – spoke to the optimism his followers shared. A religious outcast from Puritanical Boston, Williams established the colony on the principle that all people were entitled to freedom of conscience. He was an early advocate of separation of religion and government, a concept that later became a foundation of the US Constitution. Progressive little Rhode Island became the first American colony to abolish slavery (1774) and the first to declare independence from Britain in 1776.

Information

Providence Journal (www.projo.com) The state's largest daily newspaper.

Rhode Island Parks (www.riparks.com) Offers camping in five state parks.

Rhode Island Tourism Division (800-250-7384; www.visitrhodeisland.com) Distributes visitor information on the whole state.

Providence

The revitalization of Providence has turned this once-dreary capital into one of the finest small cities in the Northeast. Not only has it been infused with an artsy edge, but it's the only city in the USA to have its entire downtown on the National Register of Historic Places. From the period buildings in the city center to the cafe-laden streets embracing Brown University, everything about this town invites a closer look.

Sights & Activities

Exit 22 off I-95 deposits you downtown. The university area is a short walk to the east. The colorful Italian enclave of Federal Hill centers on Atwells Ave, a mile west of the city center.

Museum of Art MUSEUM
(401-454-6500; www.risdmuseum.org; 224 Benefit St; adult/child $10/3; 10am-5pm Tue-Sun) Wonderfully eclectic, the Rhode Island School of Design's art museum showcases everything from ancient Greek art to 20th-century American paintings and decorative arts. Pop in before 1pm Sunday and admission is free.

FREE **State House** HISTORIC BUILDING
(401-222-3983; 82 Smith St; 8:30am-4:30pm Mon-Fri, free tours 9am, 10am & 11am) Providence's

WHAT THE...?

Move over, Christo. Providence has blazed onto the public art installation scene with **WaterFire** (www.waterfire.org), set on the river that meanders through the city center. Nearly 100 braziers poke above the water, each supporting a bonfire that roars after dark. Flames dance off the water, music plays, black-clad gondoliers glide by, and party-goers pack the riverbanks. A captivating blend of art and entertainment, WaterFire takes place about a dozen times between May and September, mostly on Saturday, from sunset to 1am.

focal point is crowned with one of the world's largest self-supporting marble domes. Check out the Gilbert Stuart portrait of George Washington, then compare it to the $1 bill in your wallet.

FREE **Roger Williams Park** PARK
(1000 Elmwood Ave;) With so many Victorian-era touches, such as its classic carousel, it's been cited by the National Trust for Historic Preservation as one of America's top urban parks. Among its varied sights are flowery **botanical gardens** and a **zoo** (401-785-3510; www.rogerwilliamsparkzoo.org; adult/child $12/8; 9am-4pm;) with snow leopards and elephants. From downtown, take I-95 south to exit 17.

Culinary Archives & Museum MUSEUM
(401-598-2805; www.culinary.org; 315 Harborside Blvd; adult/child $7/2; 10am-5pm Tue-Sun) This offbeat museum contains half-a-million items devoted to the history of dining – everything from ancient cookbooks to early-20th-century dining cars. It's at Johnson & Wales University; take I-95 exit 18, turn right on Allens Ave and follow the signs.

Brown University COLLEGE CAMPUS
(www.brown.edu; 71 George St) On the hillside above the Rhode Island School of Design lies the eminently strollable Brown University campus awash in Ivy League charm.

Sleeping

TOP CHOICE **Providence Biltmore** HISTORIC HOTEL $$
(401-421-0700; www.providencebiltmore.com; 11 Dorrance St; r/ste from $159/199;) Entering the chandeliered lobby of this historic downtown hotel is like stepping back into the 1920s. The classic appeal continues in the rooms fitted with damask upholstered chairs, gilt mirrors and king beds.

Edgewood Manor INN $$
(401-781-0099; www.providence-lodging.com; 232 Norwood Ave; r incl breakfast $139-299;) If you're in the mood for pampering, book a room in this elegant Greek Revival B&B bordering Roger Williams Park. The lavish lobby drips with museum-quality antiques, while the rooms boast four-poster mahogany beds and marble baths.

Christopher Dodge House B&B $$
(401-351-6111; www.providence-hotel.com; 11 W Park St; r incl breakfast $149-190; @) Cozy quilts and gas fireplaces add a warm glow at this inviting B&B overlooking the State House. If it's full, ask about its sister inn, the Mowry-Nicholson House, just a block away.

Eating

Providence abounds with superb eateries. For the 'Little Italy' immersion, stroll the trattorias lining Atwells Ave on Federal Hill. For the cafe scene head to Thayer St, on the hill above Brown University.

TOP CHOICE **Costantino's Venda Ravioli** DELI $
(www.vendaravioli.com; 265 Atwells Ave; meals $6-14; 8:30am-6pm Mon-Sat, 8:30am-5pm Sun) Grab one of the small tables lining this bustling deli for the most amazing dining experience on Federal Hill. Hanging salamis, crispy breads, every imaginable antipasto, real gelato – you'll think you're in Italy.

Meeting Street Café CAFE $$
(www.meetingstreetcafe.com; 220 Meeting St; mains $8-15; 8am-11pm) For thick sandwiches and luscious desserts head to this perky cafe near Brown University. The meats are hormone-free, the veggies fresh and the servings so big that most everything feeds two.

Cassarino's ITALIAN $$
(401-751-3333; www.cassarinosri.com; 177 Atwells Ave; mains $15-20; 11:30am-10pm Mon-Fri, noon-11pm Sat) Good Italian fare at moderate prices in a Federal Hill setting that would make Tony Soprano feel at home. Excellent $10 lunch deals before 3pm Monday to Friday.

Caserta Pizzeria PIZZERIA $$
(401-621-3618; www.casertapizzeria.com; 121 Spruce St; pizza $7-19; 9:30am-10:30pm)

Spartan eatery on the back side of Federal Hill serving the best Sicilian pizza in all Rhode Island. The secret: a sauce so spicy it'll make your mouth sing.

East Side Pockets MEDITERRANEAN $
(www.eastsidepocket.com; 278 Thayer St; mains $4-7; ⌚10am-1am Mon-Sat, 10am-10pm Sun; ✎) Fabulous falafels and baklava at student-friendly prices.

Drinking & Entertainment

Providence Performing Arts Center PERFORMING ARTS
(☎401-421-2787; www.ppacri.org; 220 Weybosset St) Concerts, comedy and Broadway musicals take the stage at this beautifully restored 1928 art-deco theater.

Lupo's Heartbreak Hotel MUSIC
(☎401-331-5876; www.lupos.com; 79 Washington St) Providence's legendary music venue features top rock bands and indie acts.

Trinity Brewhouse MICROBREWERY
(☎401-453-2337; www.trinitybrewhouse.com; 186 Fountain St; ⌚11:30am-1am Sun-Thu, noon-2am Fri & Sat) This microbrewery in the entertainment district brews terrific British-style beers. Don't miss the stouts.

AS220 CLUB
(☎401-831-9327; www.as220.org; 115 Empire St; ⌚5pm-1am) An alternative space abuzz with experimental bands, offbeat films, poetry slams – you never know what you'll find here.

Shopping

Boutiques and funky collegian shops can be found along Thayer St near Brown University. For urban shopping, **Providence Place** (www.providenceplace.com; 1 Providence Place) in the city center is Rhode Island's largest mall.

Information

Post office (www.usps.com; 2 Exchange Tce)

Providence Visitor Information Center (☎401-751-1177; www.goprovidence.com; Rhode Island Convention Center, 1 Sabin St; ⌚9am-5pm Mon-Sat)

Getting There & Away

TF Green Airport (PVD; www.pvdairport.com; I-95, exit 13, Warwick), 20 minutes south of downtown Providence, is served by major US airlines and car-rental companies.

Peter Pan Bus Lines (www.peterpanbus.com) connects Providence with Boston ($8, 1¼ hours) and New York ($37, 3½ hours). **Amtrak** (www.amtrak.com) trains also link cities in the Northeast with Providence.

The **Rhode Island Public Transit Authority** (RIPTA; www.ripta.com; one way $2, day pass $6) runs old-fashioned, trolley-style buses throughout the city from its downtown Kennedy Plaza hub; other RIPTA buses link Providence with Newport.

Newport

The town's very name conjures up images of Great Gatsby mansions and unbridled wealth. In the 1890s Newport became *the* place for rich New Yorkers to summer. They built opulent seaside mansions, each successive one attempting to outdo the neighbors. These mansions – dubbed 'summer cottages' – are so dazzling that people still flock to Newport today just to ogle them. Newport is also famous for its legendary music festivals and its active yachting scene.

Sights & Activities

Preservation Society of Newport County MANSIONS
(☎401-847-1000; www.newportmansions.org; 424 Bellevue Ave; all 5 sites adult/child $31/10, Breakers alone $16.50/4, Breakers plus 1 other mansion $24/6) Five of Newport's grandest mansions are managed by this society. Each mansion takes about 90 minutes to tour. From April to mid-October, the Breakers is open from 9am to 5pm and the other mansions from 10am to 5pm. Off-season hours vary – call ahead.

Breakers
(44 Ochre Point Ave) If you have time for only one Newport mansion, make it this extravagant 70-room, 1895 Italian Renaissance mega-palace built for Cornelius Vanderbilt II, patriarch of America's then-richest family.

Rosecliff
(548 Bellevue Ave) A 1902 masterpiece of architect Stanford White, Rosecliff resembles the Grand Trianon at Versailles. Its immense ballroom had a starring role in Robert Redford's *The Great Gatsby*.

Marble House
(596 Bellevue Ave) The Palace of Versailles also inspired this 1892 mansion, posh with Louis XIV–style furnishings.

Elms
(367 Bellevue Ave) Built in 1901, the Elms is nearly identical to the Château d'Asnières near Paris.

Newport Area

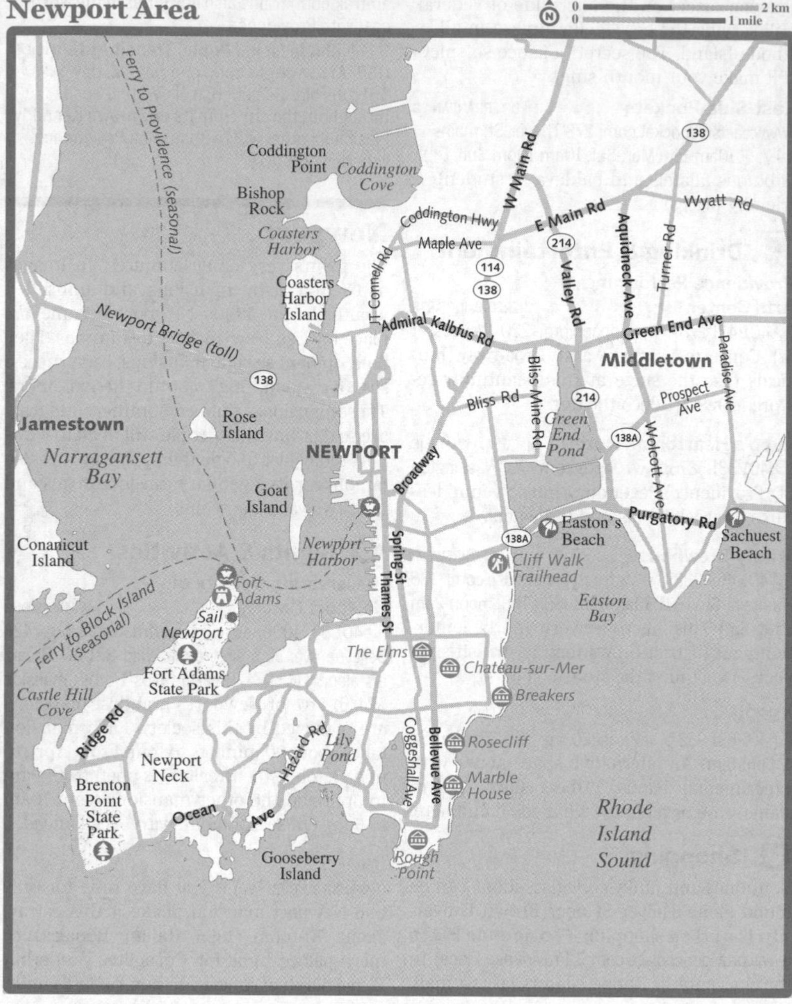

Chateau-sur-Mer
(474 Bellevue Ave) This Victorian mansion, built in 1852, was the first of Newport's palatial 'summer cottages.'

Rough Point MANSION
(www.newportrestoration.com; 680 Bellevue Ave; admission $25; ⌚9:45am-5pm Tue-Sat) Once called the 'richest little girl in the world,' Doris Duke (1912–1993) was just 13 years old when she inherited this English manor estate from her father. Duke had a passion for travel and art collecting; Rough Point houses many of her holdings, from Ming dynasty ceramics to Renoir paintings. The grounds are equally impressive.

FREE **Cliff Walk** WALKING
For a glorious hike take the 3.5-mile Cliff Walk, which hugs the coast along the back side of the mansions. You will not only enjoy the same dramatic ocean views that were once reserved for the filthy rich, but you will get to gawk at their mansions along the way. The Cliff Walk stretches from Memorial Blvd to Bailey's Beach; a scenic place to start is at Ruggles Ave near the Breakers.

International Tennis Hall of Fame MUSEUM
(401-849-3990; www.tennisfame.com; 194 Bellevue Ave; adult/child $11/free; 9:30am-5pm) The world's largest tennis museum is housed in the club where America's first tennis championships took place in 1881. For $90 you can jump into your whites and play a game on those classic grass courts.

FREE **Fort Adams State Park** PARK
(www.riparks.com; Harrison Ave; sunrise-sunset) Site of the largest coastal fortification (c 1824) in the USA, Fort Adams borders Newport Harbor with expansive lawns ideal for picnicking. Swimming is OK at Fort Adams, but **Easton's Beach** (Memorial Blvd), also known as 'First Beach,' and **Sachuest (Second) Beach** (Purgatory Rd) are better.

Touro Synagogue National Historic Site SYNAGOGUE
(401-847-4794; www.tourosynagogue.org; 85 Touro St; adult/child $5/free; noon-2pm Sun-Fri) Tour the oldest synagogue (c 1763) in the USA, an architectural gem that treads the line between austere and lavish.

Sail Newport SAILING
(401-846-1983; www.sailnewport.org; 60 Fort Adams Rd; sailboat rental per 3hr $64-121; 9am-7pm) As you'd expect in the hometown of the prestigious America's Cup, the sailing in breezy Newport is phenomenal.

Adirondack II CRUISE
(401-847-0000; www.sail-newport.com; 1½hr cruise $27-35; 11am-7pm) This schooner sails from Bowen's Wharf five times a day.

Festivals & Events

Newport's summer music events draw large crowds, so plan ahead.

TOP CHOICE **Newport Folk Festival** MUSIC
(www.newportfolkfest.com; Fort Adams State Park; admission $69-77) Everybody who's anybody in the folk world has taken the stage at this hallmark festival, held the last weekend in July.

Newport Jazz Festival MUSIC
(www.newportjazzfest.net; Fort Adams State Park; admission $40-100) The roster reads like a who's who of jazz, with the likes of Dave Brubeck and Wynton Marsalis, on a weekend in early August.

Newport Music Festival MUSIC
(www.newportmusic.org; admission $20-40) A class act, with 17 days of chamber music held at various mansions in July.

Sleeping

Stella Maris Inn INN $$
(401-849-2862; www.stellamarisinn.com; 91 Washington St; r incl breakfast $125-195;) Grab a rocking chair on the porch and watch the sailboats breeze by at this comfortably old-fashioned inn occupying a former convent. High ceilings and heaps of dark wood set the mood. In a quiet neighborhood and just a stroll to the city center.

Ivy Lodge INN $$$
(401-849-6865; www.ivylodge.com; 12 Clay St; r incl breakfast $169-379;) Treat yourself to the good life at this grand Victorian inn mere steps from Newport's sumptuous mansions. All rooms have antique furnishings, most have fireplaces, and if you need more romance, some have Jacuzzis.

Admiral Fitzroy Inn INN $$
(401-848-8000; www.admiralfitzroy.com; 398 Thames St; r $145-300;) Named for the admiral who sailed with Darwin, the atmosphere is fittingly nautical. The inn fronts bustling Thames St near the harbor. While noise from emptying bars can be disruptive, the rooftop terrace makes up for it with sweeping water views.

Newport International Hostel HOSTEL $
(401-369-0243; www.newporthostel.com; 16 Howard St; dm with shared bath incl breakfast $35-89; @) This central hostel in a period home has just a handful of beds, so book ahead. The friendly manager has tips aplenty for having a great time in Newport without breaking the bank.

Eating

TOP CHOICE **Mooring** SEAFOOD $$
(401-846-2260; www.mooringrestaurant.com; Sayer's Wharf; mains $10-36; 11:30am-10pm) A harborfront setting and a menu brimming with fresh seafood make this an unbeatable combination for seaside dining. Tip: if it's packed, take the side entrance to the bar, grab a stool and order the meaty clam chowder and a 'bag of doughnuts' (tangy lobster fritters).

Salvation Café CAFE $$
(401-847-2620; www.salvationcafe.com; 140 Broadway; mains $14-25; 5-10pm) A funky, eclectic decor and brilliant food are in store at this bohemian cafe. The multiethnic menu ranges far and wide, from pad Thai to Moroccan spiced lamb, but seldom misses the mark.

Mamma Luisa ITALIAN **$$**
(☎401-848-5257; www.mammaluisa.com; 673 Thames St; mains $14-25; ⏲5-10pm Thu-Tue) Escape the Newport crowds at this cozy restaurant serving classic pasta dishes (cheese ravioli with fava beans, spaghetti *alle vongole*), as well as meat and fish entrees. Upstairs feels like eating at grandma's house.

Gary's Handy Lunch DINER **$**
(462 Thames St; mains $4-8; ⏲5am-3pm, to 8pm Fri) Newport's working folk kick-start their day over coffee and simple breakfast fare at this old-school diner.

Wharf Pub PUB **$$**
(☎401-846-9233; Bowen's Wharf; mains $10-18; ⏲11:30am-11pm) Reasonable prices, good portions and fast service. Think sandwiches, fried calamari and burgers. Wash it down with a Newport Storm ale.

Drinking & Entertainment

Newport Blues Café CLUB
(☎401-841-5510; www.newportblues.com; 286 Thames St) Intimate atmosphere and one of the best blues and R&B scenes this side of New York City.

Fastnet BAR
(www.thefastnetpub.com; 1 Broadway) This friendly pub serves a fine selection of Irish beers on tap, decent pub grub and live-feed rugby.

Information

Citizens Bank (☎401-847-4411; 8 Washington Sq)

Newport Gateway Transportation & Visitors Center (☎800-976-5122; www.gonewport.com; 23 America's Cup Ave; ⏲9am-5pm) Newport's tourist office distributes a handy guide and tracks accommodation vacancies.

Post office (www.usps.com; 320 Thames St)

Getting There & Away

Peter Pan Bus Lines (www.peterpanbus.com) has several buses daily to Boston ($27, 1¾ hours). State-run **RIPTA** (www.ripta.com) operates frequent buses (one way $2, day pass $6) from the visitor bureau to the mansions, beaches and Providence.

Scooter World (☎401-619-1349; Christie's Landing; per day $30; ⏲9am-7pm) rents bicycles.

Rhode Island Beaches

If you're up for a day at the beach, Rhode Island's southwestern coastal towns fit the bill. It is the Ocean State, after all.

The mile-long **Narragansett Town Beach** in Narragansett is the place to go for surfing. The nearby **Scarborough State Beach** is among Rhode Island's finest, with a wide beach, a glorious pavilion and inviting boardwalks. **Watch Hill** at the state's

IF YOU HAVE A FEW MORE DAYS

Unspoiled **Block Island**, separated from the rest of Rhode Island by 12 miles of open ocean, offers simple pleasures: rolling farms, uncrowded beaches and miles of quiet hiking and cycling trails.

Ferries dock at Old Harbor, the main town, which has changed little since its gingerbread houses were built in the late 19th century. The beaches begin right at the north side of town. If you continue north 2 miles you'll come to the **Clay Head Nature Trail**, which follows high clay bluffs above the beach offering good bird-watching along the way. **Rodman Hollow**, a 100-acre wildlife refuge at the island's south end, is also laced with interesting trails.

A mere 7 miles long, Block Island begs to be explored by bicycle; several places near the ferry dock rent them for $25 a day. The **Block Island Chamber of Commerce** (☎800-383-2474; www.blockislandchamber.com), at the ferry dock, can help with accommodations, but be aware the island's four-dozen inns typically book out in summer and many require minimum stays.

The **Block Island Ferry** (☎866-783-7996; www.blockislandferry.com; adult round-trip slow/high-speed $26/36) operates high-speed (30 minutes) and slow-speed (55 minutes) ferries from Galilee State Pier in Point Judith, each four to eight times a day, as well as once-daily slow ferries (two hours, July and August) from Fort Adams State Park in Newport. Children pay half price; bring a bicycle along for $6 round-trip. Schedules are convenient for day-trippers, thanks to morning departures and late-afternoon returns.

southwestern tip is a wonderful place to turn back the clock, with its Flying Horse Carousel and Victorian setting. The **South County Tourism Council** (☎800-548-4662; www.southcountyri.com) has details on the entire area.

CONNECTICUT

Sandwiched between sexy New York City and northerly New England's quainter quarters, Connecticut typically gets short shrift by travelers. Sure the brawny I-95 coastal corridor is largely industrial, but take a closer look and you're in for pleasant surprises. Seaside Mystic, with its nautical attractions, and the time-honored towns bordering the Connecticut River are a whole other world, and the Litchfield Hills, in the state's northwestern corner, are as charmingly rural as any place in New England.

Incidentally, the Connecticut River, which slices clear across Connecticut, gives the state its name. The word comes from the Mohegan mouthful *quinnehtukqut*, which means 'place of the long river.'

History

In 1633 the Dutch built a small settlement at current-day Hartford, but it was the English, arriving en masse in the following years, that shaped Connecticut.

Thanks to the industriousness of the citizenry, the Connecticut Yankee peddler became a fixture in early American society, traveling by wagon from town to town selling clocks and other manufactured gadgets. Connecticut etched a leading role in the Industrial Revolution when Eli Whitney built a New Haven factory in 1798 to produce firearms with interchangeable parts – the beginning of modern mass production.

In 1810 America's first insurance company opened in Hartford and by the 1870s the city boasted the highest per capita income in the USA. Two of America's leading literary figures, Harriet Beecher Stowe (1811–96) and Mark Twain (1835–1910), were Hartford neighbors for 17 years.

Information

There are welcome centers at the Hartford airport and on I-95 and I-84 when entering the state by car.

Connecticut Tourism Division (www.ctvisit.com) Distributes visitor information for the entire state.

Hartford Courant (www.courant.com) The state's largest newspaper with online entertainment listings.

CONNECTICUT FACTS

» **Nicknames** Constitution State, Nutmeg State

» **Population** 3.6 million

» **Area** 4845 sq miles

» **Capital city** Hartford (population 124,775)

» **Sales tax** 6%

» **Birthplace of** abolitionist John Brown (1800–59), circus man PT Barnum (1810–91), actress Katharine Hepburn (1909–2003)

» **Home of** the first written constitution in the US; the first lollipop, Frisbee and helicopter

» **Politics** Democrat-leaning state

» **Famous for** starting the US insurance biz and building the first nuclear submarine

» **Quirkiest state song lyrics** *Yankee Doodle*, which entwines patriotism with doodles, feathers and macaroni

» **Driving distances** Hartford to New Haven 40 miles, Hartford to Providence 75 miles

Connecticut Coast

The Connecticut coast is not all of a piece. The western end is largely a bedroom community connected by commuter rail to New York City. By the time you get to New Haven, Connecticut's artsier side shines through. Maritime Mystic, at the eastern end of the state, spotlights tall ships and the siren call of the sea.

NEW HAVEN

For visitors New Haven is all about Yale. Head straight to New Haven Green, graced by old Colonial churches and Yale's hallowed ivy-covered walls. The city's top museums and best restaurants are all within a few blocks of the Green. The oldest planned city in America (1638), New Haven (population 129,800) is laid out in orderly blocks spreading out from the Green, making it a cinch to get around. **INFO New Haven** (☎203-773-9494; www.infonewhaven.com; 1000 Chapel

St; ⏲10am-9pm Mon-Sat, noon-5pm Sun) is the city's helpful tourist office.

Sights & Activities

Yale University COLLEGE CAMPUS

Not only is it the prestigious alma mater of five US presidents but it's one cool campus thick with Gothic buildings. Most impressive of the spires is **Harkness Tower**, from which a carillon peals at measured moments throughout the day. For campus tours or to pick up a campus map, drop by Yale's **visitor center** (☎203-432-2300; www.yale.edu/visitor; 149 Elm St; ⏲9am-4:30pm Mon-Fri, 11am-4pm Sat & Sun) on the north side of the Green. There are free one-hour tours at 10:30am and 2pm weekdays, and at 1:30pm on weekends.

FREE **Yale University Art Gallery** MUSEUM

(☎203-432-0600; artgallery.yale.edu; 1111 Chapel St; ⏲10am-5pm Tue-Sat, 1-6pm Sun) America's oldest university art museum boasts American masterworks by Winslow Homer, Edward Hopper and Jackson Pollock, as well as a superb European collection that includes Vincent van Gogh's *The Night Café*.

Peabody Museum of Natural History MUSEUM

(☎203-432-5050; www.yale.edu/peabody; 170 Whitney Ave; adult/child $9/5; ⏲10am-5pm Mon-Sat, noon-5pm Sun; 👪) Wannabe paleontologists will be thrilled by the dinosaurs here.

FREE **Yale Center for British Art** MUSEUM

(☎203-432-2800; ycba.yale.edu; 1080 Chapel St; ⏲10am-5pm Tue-Sat, noon-5pm Sun) The most comprehensive British art collection outside the UK.

Sleeping

Study at Yale HOTEL $$$

(☎203-503-3900; www.studyhotels.com; 1157 Chapel St; r from $219; ❄📶) Ready for an Ivy League splurge? This sleek boutique hotel right in the midst of the campus offers 124 ultra-mod rooms with featherbeds, soft leather chairs, flat-screen TVs and iPod docking stations.

Touch of Ireland Guest House B&B $$

(☎203-787-7997; www.touchofirelandguesthouse.com; 670 Whitney Ave; r incl breakfast $135-150; ❄📶) Share tips with fellow travelers in the fireplaced den at this friendly B&B on the north side of the city. The four guest rooms sport an Irish theme and comfy down-home decor.

Eating

TOP CHOICE **Frank Pepe's** PIZZERIA $$

(☎203-865-5762; www.pepespizzeria.com; 157 Wooster St; pizza $7-20; ⏲11:30am-10pm) New Haven's most famous eatery takes its name from the Italian immigrant who tossed America's first pizza a century ago. You'd best believe they've got the recipe down pat. For the ultimate, order Pepe's signature white pizza topped with garlicky fresh clams.

Miya's Sushi JAPANESE $$

(☎203-777-9760; www.miyassushi.com; 68 Howe St; meals $18-40; ⏲Tue-Sat 12:30-11pm; ✎) Tokyo meets Yale at this fun restaurant serving superb sushi, an amazing sake selection and tasty vegetarian offerings. Miya's menu focuses on sustainable species, earning it a top award from the Monterey Bay Aquarium. The menu is broad and inventive – start with the pumpkin miso soup.

Louis' Lunch BURGERS $

(www.louislunch.com; 261 Crown St; hamburgers $5.25; ⏲11am-3:45pm Tue & Wed, noon-2am Thu-Sat) New Haven's classic hamburger joint invented America's iconic fast food in 1900 and it still broils burgers in the original cast-iron vertical grills. Some things have changed over the century – but you won't find them here. Don't even think of asking for ketchup.

Sally's Apizza PIZZERIA $$

(☎203-624-5271; www.sallysapizza.com; 237 Wooster St; pizza $7-16; ⏲5-10:30pm Tue-Sun) If Pepe's is packed, as it often is, try this place nearby, a breakaway started by a relative of Pepe's in 1938. Like Pepe's, Sally's also specializes in terrific wood-fired thin-crust pizza.

Entertainment

New Haven has a first-rate theater scene. The free weekly *New Haven Advocate* (www.newhavenadvocate.com) lists current entertainment happenings.

Toad's Place MUSIC

(☎203-624-8623; www.toadsplace.com; 300 York St) The hottest music scene this side of New York City. Everyone from Count Basie to Bob Dylan and U2 have taken the stage at this legendary venue.

Shubert Theater THEATER

(☎203-562-5666; www.shubert.com; 247 College St) Catch a hit before it happens at the venerable Shubert, which has been hosting Broadway musicals on their trial runs since 1914.

Yale Repertory Theatre THEATER
(☎203-432-1234; www.yale.edu/yalerep; 1120 Chapel St)

Long Wharf Theatre THEATER
(☎203-787-4282; www.longwharf.org; 222 Sargent Dr)

Getting There & Away

By train from New York City skip Amtrak and take **Metro North** (www.mta.info; one way $14-19), which has near-hourly services and the lowest fares. **Greyhound Bus Lines** (www.greyhound.com) connects New Haven to scores of cities including Hartford ($18, one hour) and Boston ($37, four hours).

MYSTIC & AROUND

A centuries-old seaport, Mystic boasts a top-notch nautical museum, a stellar aquarium and attractive period accommodations. Yes, it gets inundated with summer tourists, but there's a good reason why everyone stops here (including fans of the 1988 film *Mystic Pizza*), so get off the highway and check it out. Swing by on a weekday to avoid the worst of the crowds. The **Greater Mystic Chamber of Commerce** (☎860-572-1102; www.mysticchamber.org; 2 Roosevelt Ave; ⏲9am-4:30pm), at the old train station, has visitor information.

Sights & Activities

Mystic Seaport MUSEUM
(☎860-572-5315; www.mysticseaport.org; 75 Greenmanville Ave/CT 27; adult/child $24/15; ⏲9am-5pm; 👪) America's maritime history springs to life as costumed interpreters ply their trades at this sprawling re-created 19th-century seaport village. You can scurry aboard several historic sailing vessels, including the *Charles W Morgan* (built in 1841), the last surviving wooden whaling ship in the world. If you want to experience a little voyage yourself, the **Sabino**, a 1908 steamboat, departs hourly ($5.50) on jaunts up the Mystic River.

Mystic Aquarium AQUARIUM
(☎860-572-5955; www.mysticaquarium.org; 55 Coogan Blvd; adult/child $26/19; ⏲9am-6pm; 👪) Home to all manner of interesting sea creatures, and we're not talking just fish. The residents include penguins, sea lions and even a beluga whale! And where else can a kid pet a cownose ray?

Foxwoods Resort & Casino CASINO
(☎800-369-9663; www.foxwoods.com; CT 2, Ledyard) Feeling lucky? In nearby Ledyard, the Mashantucket Pequot tribe operates this mega-splash casino, the largest gambling venue this side of Vegas.

Mashantucket Pequot Museum & Research Center MUSEUM
(☎800-411-9671; www.pequotmuseum.org; 110 Pequot Trail, off CT 214, Mashantucket; adult/child $15/10; ⏲10am-4pm Wed-Sat) This extensive center, funded by the casino, features a reconstructed 16th-century Native American village.

Sleeping

Old Mystic Inn B&B $$
(☎860-572-9422; www.oldmysticinn.com; 52 Main St, Old Mystic; r incl breakfast $165-215; 📶) Canopy beds, cozy fireplaces and gourmet breakfasts set the tone at this romantic 1784 Colonial inn near the head of the Mystic River. Formerly a bookstore, its rooms are themed after American authors like Henry David Thoreau and Mark Twain.

Whaler's Inn INN $$
(☎860-536-1506; www.whalersinnmystic.com; 20 E Main St; r $139-259; ❄@📶) By the drawbridge in the center of Mystic, this place offers a variety of comfy accommodations from traditionally decorated rooms in an 1865 Victorian house to modern rooms in motel-style buildings. It's an ideal location for walking to just about everything.

Eating & Drinking

S&P Oyster Co SEAFOOD $$
(☎860-536-2674; www.sp-oyster.com; 1 Holmes St; mains $10-25; ⏲11:30am-10pm) On a summer day, there's nothing better than dining on the waterfront. This reliable seafood eatery, famous for oysters on the half shell and hefty portions of fish and chips, is in the town center at the east side of the drawbridge.

Harp & Hound PUB $$
(☎860-572-7778; www.harpandhound.com; 4 Pearl St; mains $8-15; ⏲11:30am-1pm) This pub, in a historic building on the west side of the drawbridge, is the late-night place to grab a pint of Irish ale; decent pub grub and English football on the telly too.

Mystic Drawbridge Ice Cream ICE CREAM $
(www.mysticdrawbridgeicecream.com; 2 W Main St; cones $4; ⏲9am-11pm) Strolling through town is best done with an ice-cream cone in your hand. In addition to cool flavors of

homemade ice cream, this perpetually buzzing parlor also serves sandwiches, salads and baked goods.

Lower Connecticut River Valley

Several Colonial-era towns grace the banks of the Connecticut River, offering up their rural charm at an unhurried pace. The **River Valley Tourism District** (☎860-787-9640; www.visitctriver.com) provides information on the region.

ESSEX

The genteel riverside town of Essex, established in 1635, makes a good starting point for exploring the valley. The streets are lined with handsome Federal-period houses, the legacy of rum and tobacco fortunes made in the 19th century.

The **Connecticut River Museum** (☎860-767-8269; www.ctrivermuseum.org; 67 Main St; adult/child $8/5; ⏲10am-5pm Tue-Sun) exhibits regional history and includes a reproduction of the world's first submarine, a hand-propelled vessel built at this site in 1776.

The best way to see the river valley is hopping aboard the **Essex Steam Train & Riverboat** (☎860-767-0103; www.essexsteamtrain.com; 1 Railroad Ave; adult/child $17/9, with cruise $26/17; ⏲departure times vary;), an antique steam locomotive that runs 6 scenic miles to Deep River, where you can cruise on a Mississippi-style riverboat before returning by train.

The landmark **Griswold Inn** (☎860-767-1776; www.griswoldinn.com; 36 Main St; r incl breakfast $110-305;), in the town center, has been providing cozy Colonial comfort since 1776, making it one of the oldest inns in America. It's also a favorite place to dine on traditional New England cuisine in a historic setting.

OLD LYME

Set near the mouth of the Connecticut River, Old Lyme was home to some 60 sea captains in the 19th century. Today its claim to fame is its art community. In the early 1900s art patron Florence Griswold opened her estate to visiting artists, many of whom offered paintings in lieu of rent. Her Georgian mansion, now the **Florence Griswold Museum** (☎860-434-5542; www.flogris.org; 96 Lyme St; adult/child $9/free; ⏲10am-5pm Tue-Sat, 1-5pm Sun), exhibits 6000 works with solid collections of American Impressionist paintings, sculpture and decorative arts.

The prettiest place to lay your head is the classy **Bee & Thistle Inn** (☎860-434-1667; www.beeandthistleinn.com; 100 Lyme St; r $180-275;), a 1756 Dutch Colonial farmhouse with antique-filled rooms and four-poster beds.

EAST HADDAM

Two intriguing attractions mark this small town on the east bank of the Connecticut River. The medieval-style **Gillette Castle** (☎860-526-2336; 67 River Rd; adult/child $10/4; ⏲10am-4:30pm late May–mid-Oct) is a wildly eccentric stone-turreted mansion built in 1919 by actor William Hooker Gillette, who made his fortune playing Sherlock Holmes. The classic **Goodspeed Opera House** (☎860-873-8668; www.goodspeed.org; 6 Main St), an 1876 Victorian music hall known as 'the birthplace of the American musical,' still produces a full schedule of musicals.

Hartford

Connecticut's capital is best known as the hometown of America's insurance industry – not exactly a 'let's-rush-to-see-the-place' endorsement. But look beyond its backbone of office buildings and you'll find some worthwhile sights offering unique slices of Americana. The **Greater Hartford Welcome**

WHAT THE...?

Jaded museum browsers, don't turn your nose up at this one. Garbage goes green at the curious **Trash Museum** (☎860-757-7765, 211 Murphy Rd, Hartford; admission free; ⏲noon-4pm Wed-Fri Sep-Jun, 10am-2pm Tue, 10am-4pm Wed-Fri Jul-Aug) smack in the midst of a trash facility. Run by the Connecticut Resources Recovery Authority (CRRA), it enlightens visitors on earth-friendly recycling techniques. A viewing platform overlooking the sorting operation takes center stage while cool sculptures made from trash and wormy composting displays plug the green side of it all. You'll also get the scoop on CRRA's trash-to-energy program that fuels a billion kilowatts of green electric power annually. To get to the museum take I-91 to exit 27, which dumps you right at the site.

Center (☎860-244-0253; www.enjoyhartford.com; 31 Pratt St; ⏲9am-5pm Mon-Fri) distributes tourist information.

Sights & Activities

Mark Twain House & Museum MUSEUM
(☎860-247-0998; www.marktwainhouse.org; 351 Farmington Ave; adult/child $16/10; ⏲9:30am-5:30pm Mon-Sat, noon-5:30pm Sun) It was at this former home of Samuel Langhorne Clemens, aka Mark Twain, that the legendary author penned many of his greatest works, including *A Connecticut Yankee in King Arthur's Court*. The house itself, a Victorian Gothic with fanciful turrets and gables, reflects Twain's quirky character.

Harriet Beecher Stowe House MUSEUM
(☎860-522-9258; www.harrietbeecherstowe.org; 77 Forest St; adult/child $9/6; ⏲9:30am-4:30pm Tue-Sat, noon-4:30pm Sun) Next door to the Twain house is the former home of Harriet Beecher Stowe, who wrote *Uncle Tom's Cabin*. The book so rallied Americans against slavery that Abraham Lincoln once credited Stowe with starting the US Civil War.

Wadsworth Atheneum MUSEUM
(☎860-278-2670; www.wadsworthatheneum.org; 600 Main St; adult/child $10/free; ⏲11am-5pm Wed-Fri, 10am-5pm Sat & Sun) America's oldest art museum showcases outstanding collections of Hudson River School paintings and sculptures by renowned Connecticut artist Alexander Calder (1898–1976).

FREE **State Capitol** HISTORIC BUILDING
(☎860-240-0222; cnr Capitol Ave & Trinity St; ⏲9am-3pm Mon-Fri) You can tour the state capitol, built in 1879 in such a hodgepodge of styles that it's sometimes dubbed 'the most beautiful ugly building in the world.' Below the capitol grounds, the 37-acre **Bushnell Park** features a working 1914 carousel, lovely gardens and summer concerts.

Old State House HISTORIC BUILDING
(☎860-522-6766; www.ctosh.org; 800 Main St; adult/child $6/3; ⏲10am-5pm Tue-Sat) The real prize of Connecticut's public buildings, designed by famed Colonial architect Charles Bulfinch. Erected in 1796, it's one of the oldest capitol buildings in the USA.

Sleeping & Eating

Hilton Hartford HOTEL $$
(☎860-728-5151; www.hilton.com; 315 Trumbull St; r $100-189; ❄@≋) Within walking distance of the city's central sights, this is Hartford's most conveniently located hotel. The rooms are dated but comfortable, and amenities include state-of-the-art fitness facilities. On weekends, when the lowest rates are offered, it's a deal.

Vaughan's Public House PUB $$
(☎860-882-1560; www.irishpublichouse.com; 59 Pratt St; pub fare $9-16; ⏲11:30am-1am) This friendly Irish pub serves a full menu ranging from hearty sandwiches and salads to perfect beer-battered cod and chips. A river of Guinness flows, with good happy hour deals from 3pm to 7pm.

Mo's Midtown Restaurant DINER $
(☎860-236-7741; 25 Whitney St; meals $3-7; ⏲7am-2:30pm Mon-Fri, 8am-1:30pm Sat & Sun) Head to this classic diner for fab breakfast fare on a shoestring. The grill is heaped with home-fried potatoes, served alongside stacks of whole-wheat pancakes loaded with seasonal fruit. Awesome huevos rancheros too.

Getting There & Away

The conveniently central **Union Station** (www.amtrak.com; 1 Union Pl) links Hartford by train to cities throughout the Northeast, including New Haven (one way $17, one hour) and New York City (one way $52, three hours).

Litchfield Hills

Laced with lakes, woodlands and vineyards, the rolling hill country of northwestern Connecticut provides rich opportunities for quiet escapes. The **Litchfield Hills Connecticut Visitors Bureau** (www.litchfieldhills.com) has information on the entire region.

LITCHFIELD

Founded in 1719, Litchfield prospered from the commerce brought by stagecoaches traveling between Hartford and Albany, and its many handsome period buildings are a testimony to that era. Stroll along North and South Sts to see the finest homes, including the 1773 **Tapping Reeve House & Law School** (☎860-567-4501; www.litchfieldhistoricalsociety.org; 82 South St; adult/child $5/free; ⏲11am-5pm Tue-Sat, 1-5pm Sun), the USA's first law school, which trained 129 members of Congress. Included in the admission fee is the **Litchfield History Museum** (7 South St).

Haight-Brown Vineyard (☎860-567-4045; www.haightvineyards.com; 29 Chestnut Hill Rd, off CT 118; ⏲noon-5pm), the state's first winery, offers tours, tastings and self-guided vineyard walks.

If you're ready for a hike, Connecticut's largest wildlife preserve, the **White Memorial Conservation Center** (☎860-567-0857; www.whitememorialcc.org; US 202; admission free; ⊙sunrise-sunset), 2.5 miles west of town, has 35 miles of inviting trails with good bird-watching.

LAKE WARAMAUG

The most beautiful of the dozens of lakes and ponds in the Litchfield Hills is Lake Waramaug. As you make your way around the northern shore on North Shore Rd, stop at **Hopkins Vineyard** (☎860-868-7954; www.hopkinsvineyard.com; 25 Hopkins Rd; ⊙10am-5pm Mon-Sat, 11am-5pm Sun) for wine tastings. It's next to the 19th-century **Hopkins Inn** (☎860-868-7295; www.thehopkinsinn.com; 22 Hopkins Rd, Warren; r from $130; ❄📶), which has lake-view accommodations and a well-regarded restaurant with Austrian-influenced country fare. **Lake Waramaug State Park** (☎860-868-0220; 30 Lake Waramaug Rd; sites $17-$27) has lakeside campsites, but book well in advance.

VERMONT

Artisanal cheeses, buckets of maple syrup, Ben & Jerry's ice cream...just try to get out of this state without gaining 10 pounds. Fortunately, there are plenty of ways to work it off: hike the trails of the Green Mountains, paddle a kayak on Lake Champlain or hit Vermont's snowy slopes.

Vermont gives true meaning to the word rural. Its capital would barely rate as a small town in other states and even its largest city, Burlington, has just 42,500 content souls. The countryside is a blanket of rolling green, with 80% of the state forested and most of the rest given over to some of the prettiest farms you'll ever see. So take your time, meander down quiet side roads, stop in those picturesque villages, and sample a taste of the good life.

History

Frenchman Samuel de Champlain explored Vermont in 1609 and in his ever-humble manner lent his name to Vermont's largest lake.

Vermont played a key role in the American Revolution in 1775 when Ethan Allen led a local militia, the Green Mountain Boys, to Fort Ticonderoga, capturing it from the British. In later years Allen took a friendlier stance toward the British, and considered petitioning the crown to make Vermont an independent British state. In 1791, two years after Allen's death, Vermont was finally admitted to the USA.

The state's independent streak is as long and deep as a vein of Vermont marble. Long a land of dairy farmers, Vermont is still largely agricultural and has the lowest population of any New England state.

VERMONT FACTS

» **Nickname** Green Mountain State

» **Population** 625,740

» **Area** 9250 sq miles

» **Capital city** Montpelier (population 8050)

» **Other cities** Burlington (population 42,500)

» **Sales tax** 6%

» **Birthplace of** Mormon leader Brigham Young (1801–77), President Calvin Coolidge (1872–1933)

» **Home of** more than 100 covered bridges

» **Politics** independent streak, leaning Democrat

» **Famous for** Ben & Jerry's ice cream

» **Sudsiest state** most microbreweries per capita in the USA

» **Driving distances** Burlington to Bennington 116 miles, Burlington to Portland, Maine 194 miles

ℹ Information

Vermont Dept of Tourism (www.vermontvacation.com) Online information by region, season and other user-friendly categories.

Vermont State Parks (www.vtstateparks.com) Operates 40 state parks with camping.

Southern Vermont

The southern swath of Vermont holds its oldest towns, the cool trails of the Green Mountain National Forest and plenty of scenic back roads just aching to be explored.

BRATTLEBORO

Ever wonder where the 1960s counter-culture went? It's alive and well in this riverside burg overflowing with craft shops and more tie-dye per capita than any other place in New England.

Sights & Activities

Begin at Main St, which is lined with period buildings, including the handsome art-deco Latchis Building, which houses a hotel and theater.

Windham County, surrounding Brattleboro, boasts several **covered bridges**. Pick up a driving guide to them at the **Brattleboro Area Chamber of Commerce** (☎802-254-4565; www.brattleborochamber.org; 180 Main St; ⊙9am-5pm Mon-Fri).

Brattleboro Museum & Art Center MUSEUM
(www.brattleboromuseum.org; 10 Vernon St; adult/child $6/free; ⊙11am-5pm Thu-Mon) Showcases the multimedia works of regional artists.

Sleeping

Forty Putney Road B&B B&B $$
(☎802-254-6268; www.fortyputneyroad.com; 192 Putney Rd; r incl breakfast $179-269; @📶) This estate-home-turned-B&B is one sweet spot: classy rooms, beautiful grounds, river views, hot tub, billiards and a gourmet breakfast. The 'beer geek' owners even have a pint-size pub perfect for sampling Vermont brews.

Vermont & New Hampshire

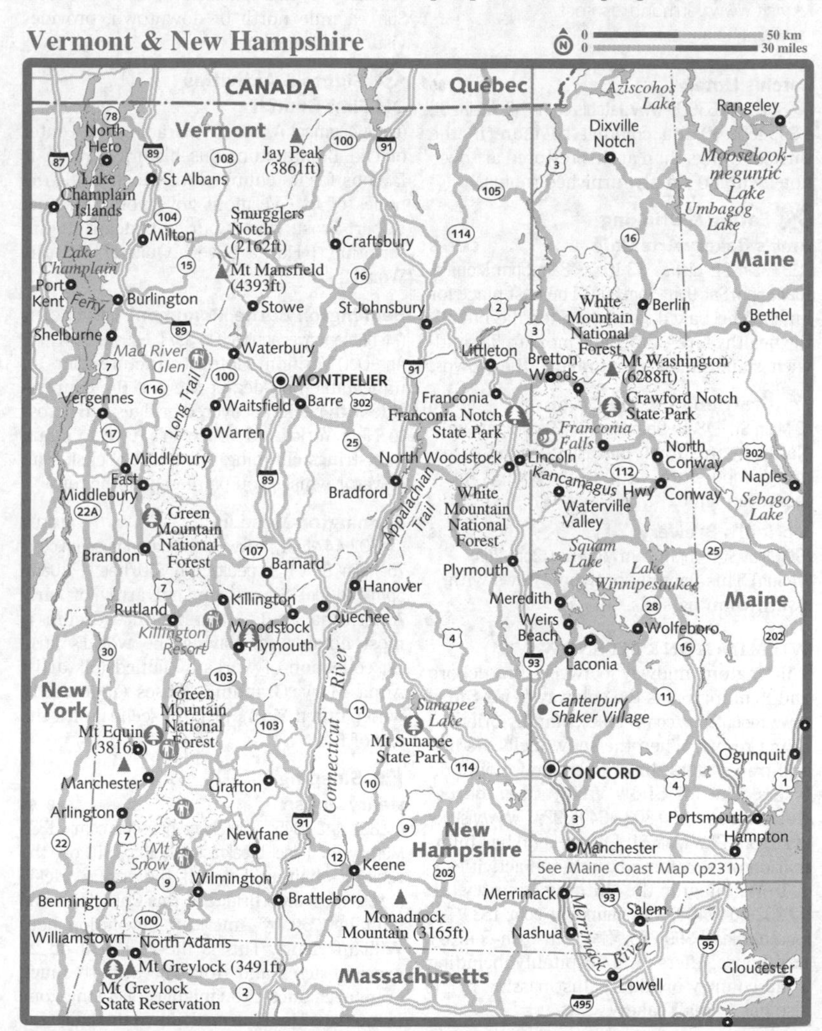

VERMONT FRESH NETWORK

Locavore food dominates in Vermont, and the state has its own label: the farm and chef partnership **Vermont Fresh Network** identifies restaurants that focus on sustainable, locally sourced food. Just look for the green-and-white square sticker with a plate and silverware drawn in it – it's an easy way of knowing that the eatery probably got its eggs from a neighboring farm. For a full listing of restaurants with this label, visit www.vermontfresh.net.

Latchis Hotel HOTEL $$
(☎802-254-6300; www.latchis.com; 50 Main St; r $95-160;) You couldn't be more in the thick of things than at this restored art-deco hotel with 30 simply furnished rooms.

Eating & Drinking

Amy's Bakery Arts Café CAFE $
(113 Main St; dishes $3-10; ⏲8am-5pm Mon-Fri, 10am-5pm Sat, 9am-5pm Sun) The best place for lunch. The baked goods are terrific but it's the healthy fare – tapenade mozzarella sandwiches and salads – that rake in the crowds.

Brattleboro Food Co-op DELI $
(2 Main St; ⏲8am-9pm Mon-Sat, 9am-9pm Sun) Naturally this town has a big-league health-food store, with all the fixings for a locavore picnic.

McNeill's Brewery PUB $
(90 Elliot St; ⏲5pm-2am Mon-Thu, 2pm-2am Fri-Sun) This friendly brewpub flows with award-winning suds.

WILMINGTON & MT SNOW

Wilmington, midway between Brattleboro and Bennington, is the gateway to **Mt Snow** (www.mountsnow.com; VT100), a family-oriented skiing resort. When the snow melts, its lifts and trail system draw hikers and mountain bikers. The **Mt Snow Valley Chamber of Commerce** (☎802-464-8092; www.visitvermont.com; 21 W Main St; ⏲10am-5pm) has information on accommodations and activities.

In Wilmington the **Nutmeg Country Inn** (☎802-464-7400; www.nutmeginn.com; 153 VT 9; r incl breakfast $99-205;), an 18th-century farmhouse, offers local hospitality including a full country breakfast. Just passing by? It also has a small bakery.

BENNINGTON

A measure of how rural southern Vermont really is, cozy Bennington, with just 15,000 inhabitants, ranks as the region's largest town. You'll find an interesting mix of cafes and shops downtown along Main St, while the hillside area known as Old Bennington boasts age-old Colonial homes and a trio of covered bridges. A hilltop granite obelisk commemorating the 1777 Battle of Bennington towers above it all, making Bennington visible from miles around.

The **Bennington Area Chamber of Commerce** (☎802-447-3311; www.bennington.com; US 7; ⏲9am-5pm Mon-Fri, 10am-4pm Sat & Sun), a mile north of downtown, provides visitor information.

Sights & Activities

Old First Church HISTORIC SITE
(cnr Monument Ave & VT 9) Gracing the center of Old Bennington, this historic church is famous for its churchyard, which holds the bones of five Vermont governors and poet Robert Frost, who is buried beneath the inscription 'I Had a Lover's Quarrel with the World.'

Bennington Battle Monument HISTORIC SITE
(Monument Ave; adult/child $3/1; ⏲9am-5pm mid-Apr–Oct) Vermont's loftiest structure offers an unbeatable 360-degree view of the countryside with peeks at covered bridges and across to New York. And you won't have to strain hamstrings climbing this 306ft obelisk – an elevator whisks you painlessly to the top.

Bennington Museum MUSEUM
(☎802-447-1571; www.benningtonmuseum.com; 75 Main St/VT 9; adult/child $10/free; ⏲10am-5pm Thu-Tue) Showcasing an array of early Americana crafts, Bennington Museum is most notable for having the world's largest collection of works by famed folk artist Anna Mary 'Grandma' Moses (1860–1961), who painted Vermont farm scenes until the age of 100.

Sleeping

Henry House B&B $$
(☎802-442-7045; www.henryhouseinn.com; 1338 Murphy Rd; r incl breakfast $90-145) Sit on the rocking chair and watch the traffic trickle across a covered bridge at this Colonial home built in 1769 by American Revolution hero William Henry. This is the real deal on 25 peaceful acres and dripping with so much original character you might expect long-gone Lieutenant Henry to walk down the hall.

Paradise Inn MOTEL **$$**
(☎802-442-8351; www.theparadisemotorinn.com; 141 W Main St; r $85-145;) Attractive rooms, a quiet yet central setting and a heated outdoor pool add up to good bang for the buck. Spend the extra for a premier room and enjoy your own little sauna and a Jacuzzi.

Eating & Drinking

TOP CHOICE **Blue Benn Diner** DINER **$**
(☎802-442-5140; 314 North St; mains $5-12; ⊙6am-4:45pm Mon-Fri, 7am-3:45pm Sat & Sun) It may be a classic 1950s-era diner, but it's no greasy spoon. The extensive menu includes breakfast all day and a healthy mix of American, Asian and Mexican fare – even vegetarian. Scrambled tofu with shiitake mushrooms, or perhaps the chocolate chip raspberry pancakes?

Izabella's CAFE **$**
(☎802-447-4949; 351 W Main St; mains $6-10; ⊙8:30am-3pm Tue-Fri, 8:30am-4pm Sat) This hip cafe in the center of town adds an innovative twist to American standards. The locavore menu changes with the season. If you're lucky, the baked apple and cheddar scones or the zesty Senegalese peanut soup will be on offer.

Madison Brewing Co PUB **$$**
(☎802-442-7397; www.madisonbrewingco.com; 428 Main St; mains $9-20; ⊙11:30am-9:30pm;) A family-style microbrewery? Yep, this perky pub-restaurant brews homemade root beer as well as heady malt ales. The food ranges from veggie burgers to juicy steaks and there's even a kids menu.

Shopping

Bennington Potters POTTERY
(www.benningtonpotters.com; 324 County St) Bennington pottery is a popular souvenir. Tour the workshop where the distinctively mottled-design stoneware has been made for more than a half-century, and follow with a visit to the on-site shop.

MANCHESTER

Sitting in the shadow of Mt Equinox, Manchester's been a fashionable summer retreat since the 19th century. The mountain scenery, the agreeable climate and the Batten Kill River – Vermont's best trout stream – continue to draw vacationers today.

The town has two faces, both likable. Manchester Center, at the north end, sports cafes and upscale outlet stores. To the south lies dignified Manchester Village, lined with marble sidewalks, stately homes and the posh Equinox hotel.

The **Manchester & the Mountains Regional Chamber of Commerce** (☎800-362-4144; www.manchestervermont.net; 5046 Main St, Manchester Center; ⊙9am-5pm Mon-Fri, 10am-5pm Sat) provides visitor information.

Sights & Activities

The **Appalachian Trail**, which overlaps the **Long Trail** in Vermont, passes just east of Manchester. For trail maps as well as details on shorter day hikes, stop by the **Green Mountain National Forest office** (☎802-362-2307; 2538 Depot St, Manchester Center; ⊙8am-4:30pm Mon-Fri).

For a view from the top, drive to the summit of **Mt Equinox** (3816ft). Take VT 7A south of Manchester to **Skyline Drive** (☎802-362-1114; car & driver $12, additional passenger $2; ⊙9am-sunset May-Oct), a private 5-mile toll road.

Hildene HISTORIC SITE
(☎802-362-1788; www.hildene.org; 1005 Hildene Rd/VT 7A; adult/child $13/5; ⊙9:30am-4:30pm) Just south of Manchester, this 24-room Georgian Revival mansion was the country estate

SCENIC DRIVE: COVERED BRIDGES

A 30-minute detour from Bennington takes you across three picture-perfect covered bridges spanning the Wallomsac River at the rural north side of town. To get started turn west onto VT 67A just north of the tourist office and continue 3.5 miles, turning left on Murphy Rd at the **Burt Henry Covered Bridge**. Exhale, slow down: you're back in horse and buggy days. As you pop out the back side of this 117ft-long bridge dating to 1840, curve to the left. Murphy Rd soon loops through the **Paper Mill Bridge**, which takes its name from the 1790 mill that once sat beneath the bridge (look along the river for the old gear works). Next turn right onto VT 67A, go half a mile and turn right onto Silk Rd where you'll soon cross the **Silk Road Bridge** (c 1840). If you continue along Silk Rd for 2 miles, bearing to the left at each turn, you'll reach the **Bennington Battle Monument**.

of Robert Todd Lincoln, son of President Abraham Lincoln. You can tour the mansion decorated with original Lincoln family furnishings and stroll its lovely gardens, though don't expect much to be in bloom before June.

American Museum of Fly Fishing MUSEUM
(www.amff.com; 4104 VT 7A; adult/child $5/3; ⌚10am-4pm Tue-Sat) Anglers make pilgrimages to Manchester to visit this museum, where rods used by Ernest Hemingway and other famed fishers are displayed; to shop at the adjacent **Orvis** flagship store, which is dedicated to outfitting fisher-folk; and to fly-fish for trout in the **Batten Kill River**.

BattenKill Canoe BOATING
(☎802-362-2800; www.battenkill.com; 6328 VT 7A, Arlington; rentals per day $40-70; ⌚9:30am-5:30pm May-Oct) Located 5 miles south of Manchester, rents canoes and kayaks for paddling the Batten Kill River.

Sleeping

Aspen Motel MOTEL $
(☎802-362-2450; www.theaspenatmanchester.com, 5669 Main St/VT 7A; r $80-115;) An affordable standout, this family-run hotel set back serenely from the road has 25 comfortable rooms and a convenient location within walking distance of Manchester Center.

Equinox RESORT $$$
(☎802-362-4700; www.equinoxresort.com; 3567 Main St; r $289-689;) Manchester's grande dame since 1769 boasts 195 rooms, its own 18-hole golf course, two pools, restaurants and a luxury spa. Despite modern upgrades its handsome period character prevails.

Eating

TOP CHOICE **Up for Breakfast** BREAKFAST $
(☎802-362-4204; 4935 Main St; mains $6-14; ⌚7am-12:30pm Mon-Fri, 7am-1:30pm Sat & Sun) Search out this hole-in-the-wall 2nd-floor restaurant in Manchester Center for the best breakfast in town, anything from good ol' blueberry pancakes to smoked-salmon-and-caper omelets.

Ye Olde Tavern AMERICAN $$$
(☎802-362-0611; www.yeoldetavern.net; 5183 Main St; mains $17-28; ⌚5-9:30pm) Hearthside dining enhances the experience at this gracious 1790s inn. The menu ranges from colonial favorites like Yankee pot roast to a delectable roast duck in a port wine reduction sauce.

Spiral Press Café CAFE $
(cnr VT 11 & 7A; mains $6-10; ⌚7am-6:30pm;) Stop at this Manchester Center cafe attached to Northshire Bookstore for flaky croissants and delicious panini sandwiches. Good lattes too.

Central Vermont

Nestled in the Green Mountains, central Vermont is classic small-town, big-countryside New England. Its time-honored villages and ski resorts have been luring travelers for generations.

WOODSTOCK & QUECHEE

The archetypal Vermont town, Woodstock has streets lined with graceful Federal- and Georgian-style houses. The Ottauquechee River, spanned by a covered bridge, meanders right through the heart of town. Quechee (*kwee*-chee), Woodstock's smaller cousin 7 miles to the northeast, abounds in rural scenery. The whole area invites you to slow down. The **Woodstock Area Chamber of Commerce** (☎802-457-3555; www.woodstockvt.com; 61 Central St; ⌚8:30am-4:30pm Mon-Fri) provides visitor information.

Sights & Activities

Quechee Gorge, an impressive 170ft-deep gash cut by the Ottauquechee River, can be viewed from above or along walking trails that skirt the 3000ft-long chasm. Begin at the **Quechee Gorge Visitor Center** (☎802-295-6852; US 4, Quechee; ⌚9am-5pm May-Oct, 10am-4pm Nov-Apr), at the east side of the gorge, where you can pick up a trail map.

FREE **Marsh-Billings-Rockefeller National Historical Park** PARK
(☎802-457-3368; www.nps.gov/mabi) Occupying a former Rockefeller family estate, this is the only national park to tell the story of America's conservation history and land stewardship. The 550-acre park is crisscrossed with shady trails that beg a stroll and it's just a mile north of Woodstock center.

VINS Nature Center RAPTOR CENTER
(☎802-359-5000; www.vinsweb.org; US 4, Quechee; adult/child $10.50/8.50; ⌚10am-5:30pm;) A mile west of the gorge, rehabilitates injured bald eagles and other raptors. Get a close-up look at these magnificent birds, then enjoy a nature walk on the center's 47 acres.

Billings Farm & Museum FARM
(☎802-457-2355; www.billingsfarm.org; VT 12, at River Rd; adult/child $12/6; ⏱10am-5pm May-Oct;) See what 19th-century farm life was all about at this living-history museum and functioning dairy farm adjacent to the Marsh-Billings-Rockefeller National Historical Park.

Sleeping

Ardmore Inn B&B $$
(☎802-457-3887; www.ardmoreinn.com; 23 Pleasant St, Woodstock; r incl breakfast $130-205;) This congenial inn, just a five-minute walk from Woodstock town center, occupies a stately 1867 Greek Revival building and features five antique-laden rooms with marble baths. The home-cooked multicourse breakfast seals the deal.

Shire Riverview Motel MOTEL $$
(☎802-457-2211; www.shiremotel.com; 46 Pleasant St/US 4; r $98-188;) The best motel value in Woodstock center. The colonial decor's agreeable, the manager helpful and the view of the Ottauquechee River, which runs along the motel's back side, is second to none.

Quechee State Park CAMPGROUND $
(☎888-409-7579; www.vtstateparks.com; 5800 US 4, Quechee; campsites/lean-tos $20/27) Campers will find 45 pine-shaded campsites and seven lean-tos in this 600-acre park bordering Quechee Gorge.

Eating

TOP CHOICE **Simon Pearce** NEW AMERICAN $$
(☎802-295-1470; www.simonpearce.com; 1760 Main St, Quechee; lunch mains $13-17, dinner mains $25-32; ⏱11:30am-2:45pm & 6-9pm) Not only is Simon Pearce an unbeatable choice for an upscale meal but lunch is surprisingly affordable. Start by watching the artisans hand-blowing glass and throwing pottery in the basement workshops, then go upstairs and enjoy creative New American fare served on their handiwork. Very cool place – it even generates its own electricity from the waterfall the restaurant overlooks.

Prince & the Pauper AMERICAN $$$
(☎802-457-1818; www.princeandpauper.com; 24 Elm St; bistro mains $14-22, prix-fixe menu $49; ⏱6-9pm) The boneless lamb in puff pastry is a rave at this classic New England restaurant in the center of Woodstock. If you're not up for the hearty three-course fixed-price dinner, there's also a bistro menu with lighter fare and enticing options.

Osteria Pane e Salute ITALIAN $$
(☎802-457-4882; www.osteriapaneesalute.com; 61 Central St; mains $14-21; ⏱6-10pm Thu-Mon) Come here for superb thin-crust Tuscan-style pizzas and traditional Italian fare the way mama used to make it...well, if your mama was Italian. Think slow food, boutique Italian wines and aromatic spices.

KILLINGTON

An hour's drive west of Woodstock, **Killington Resort** (www.killington.com) is New England's answer to Vail, boasting 200 runs on seven mountains, a vertical drop of 3150ft and more than 30 lifts. And thanks to the world's most extensive snowmaking system, Killington has one of the longest seasons in the east. Come summer when the snow melts, mountain bikers and hikers claim the slopes.

There are more than a hundred places to stay in the Killington area, from cozy ski lodges to chain hotels. Most are along Killington Rd, the 6-mile road that heads up the mountain from US 4. The **Killington Chamber of Commerce** (☎802-773-4181; www.killingtonchamber.com; US 4; ⏱10am-4:30pm Mon-Sat) has all the nitty-gritty.

MIDDLEBURY

This former factory town has converted its old water-driven mills into enticing riverside restaurants and galleries. Add the verdant campus of Middlebury College and you've got yourself a fine place to while away an afternoon. The small but diverse **Middlebury College Museum of Art** (☎802-443-5007; S Main St; admission free; ⏱10am-5pm Tue-Fri, noon-5pm Sat & Sun) takes you on a world twirl beginning with an Egyptian sarcophagus and ending with Andy Warhol. The **Addison County Chamber of Commerce** (☎802-388-7951; www.addisoncounty.com; 93 Court St; ⏱9am-5pm Mon-Fri) has area information.

On the National Register of Historic Places, the gracious, 1803 Federal-style **Inn on the Green** (☎802-388-7512; www.innonthegreen.com; 71 S Pleasant St; r incl breakfast $149-269; @) has 11 attractive rooms that overlook the town green. Talk about pampering – they'll even serve you breakfast in bed.

For a slice of retro Americana, stop at the **A&W Drive-In** (1557 US 7; mains $3-6; ⏱11am-8pm) where carhops – some on roller skates – deliver root beer floats, cheeseburgers, onion rings and other artery-clogging goodness directly to your car window.

For a fine river view and good food at honest prices make your way to **Storm Cafe** (www.thestormcafe.com; 3 Mill St; mains $5-22; ⊙11am-6pm Tue-Sat), which serves up a standard cafe menu of soups, salads and sandwiches at lunch and fancier fare at dinner.

WARREN & WAITSFIELD

The towns of Warren and Waitsfield boast two significant ski areas: **Sugarbush** (www.sugarbush.com) and **Mad River Glen** (madriver.glen.com), in the mountains west of VT 100. Opportunities abound for cycling, canoeing, horseback riding, kayaking, gliding and other activities. Stop at the **Mad River Valley Chamber of Commerce** (☎802-496-3409; www.madrivervalley.com; VT 100, Waitsfield; ⊙9am-5pm Mon-Fri) for a mountain of details; brochures and restrooms are available 24/7 in the chamber's lobby.

Northern Vermont

The lushly green northern region of Vermont cradles the fetching state capital of Montpelier, the ski mecca of Stowe, the vibrant college town of Burlington and the state's highest mountains. It has some of the prettiest landscapes in the Northeast.

MONTPELIER

America's smallest capital, Montpelier is a thoroughly likable town full of period buildings and backed by verdant hills. It speaks to its village nature that you can walk in the front door of the gold-domed **State House** (www.vtstatehouse.org; 115 State St; admission free; ⊙tours 10am-3:30pm Mon-Fri, 11am-2:30pm Sat Jul–mid-Oct), built c 1836, and exit out the back onto a forested trail. Tours run on the half hour. The **Central Vermont Chamber of Commerce** (www.centralvt.com) has tourist information on Montpelier.

If you come through at mealtime, head for the intersection of State and Main Sts, where you'll find several restaurants. Don't even think junk food – Montpelier prides itself on being the only state capital in the USA without a McDonald's! The bakery-cafe **La Brioche** (89 Main St; snacks $2-7; ⊙6:30am-5pm Mon-Fri, 7am-5pm Sat), run by students from Montpelier's New England Culinary Institute, gets an A-plus for its innovative sandwiches and flaky French pastries. Or make your way over to **Hunger Mountain Co-op** (☎802-223-8000; 623 Stone Cutters Way; buffet $8; ⊙8am-7:30pm), a terrific health-food store and deli with cafe tables perched above a river.

SCENIC DRIVE: VT 100

Running up the rugged backbone of Vermont, VT 100 meanders through the rural heart of the state. This quintessential country road rambles past rolling pastures speckled with cows, through tiny villages with white-steepled churches and along green mountains crossed with hiking trails and ski slopes. It's the perfect sidetrip for those who want to slow down, inhale pine-scented air and soak up the bucolic country life that forms the very soul of Vermont. Think farm stands, century-old farmhouses converted to small inns, pottery shops, country stores and home-style cafes. The road runs north to south all the way from Massachusetts to Canada. It has some tranquil moments but never a dull one – jump on for a taste of it at any point.

STOWE & AROUND

With Vermont's highest peak, Mt Mansfield (4393ft), as its backdrop, Stowe ranks as Vermont's classiest ski destination. It packs all the Alpine thrills you could ask for – both cross-country and downhill skiing, with gentle runs for novices and challenging drops for pros. Cycling, hiking and kayaking take center stage in the summer. Lodgings and eateries are thick along VT 108 (Mountain Rd), which continues northwest from Stowe center to the ski resorts. The **Stowe Visitors Center** (☎802-253-7321; www.gostowe.com; 51 Main St; ⊙9am-5pm Mon-Sat) provides information.

Sights & Activities

The 5.5-mile **Stowe Recreation Path**, a greenway running along the West Branch River northwest from the village center, is a great place for walking, jogging, cycling and skating.

Vermont's **Long Trail**, which passes through Stowe, follows the crest of the Green Mountains and runs the entire length of Vermont with rustic cabins, lean-tos and campsites along the way. Its caretaker, the **Green Mountain Club** (☎802-244-7037; www.greenmountainclub.org; 4711 Waterbury-Stowe Rd, VT 100), has full details on the Long Trail and shorter day hikes around Stowe.

If the snow has cleared, be sure to take a drive through dramatic **Smugglers Notch**, northwest of Stowe on VT 108 (the road's closed in winter). This narrow pass slices through mountains with 1000ft cliffs on either side, and there are plenty of places where you can stop along the way to ooh and aah or take a short walk.

Ben & Jerry's Ice Cream Factory TOUR
(☎802-882-1240; www.benjerrys.com; 1281 VT 100, Waterbury; adult/child $3/free; ⏱9am-5:30pm, with longer summer hr; 👪) Get the inside scoop, where tours and a moo-vie about the hippie founders are topped off with a taste tease of the latest flavor.

Stowe Mountain Resort SKIING
(☎802-253-3000; www.stowe.com; 5781 Mountain Rd) Wintertime's action-central, this twin-peak resort has a variety of terrains with ski runs suitable for all levels.

AJ's Ski & Sports SPORTS RENTALS
(☎802-253-4593; www.ajssportinggoods.com; 350 Mountain Rd; ⏱10am-6pm) Next to the Stowe Recreation Path, rents skis and snowboards for $29 per day and bikes for $27 per day.

Umiak Outdoor Outfitters BOATING
(☎802-253-2317; www.umiak.com; 849 S Main St; ⏱9am-6pm) Rents canoes ($50 per day) and kayaks ($40) and offers two-hour guided river trips ($45).

Sleeping

Fiddler's Green Inn INN $$
(☎802-253-8124; www.fiddlersgreeninn.com; 4859 Mountain Rd; r incl breakfast $125; ❄) This 1820s farmhouse near Stowe's ski lifts has rustic appeal with a fieldstone fireplace that roars on nippy nights and seven straightforward guest rooms geared to outdoor enthusiasts.

Trapp Family Lodge LODGE $$$
(☎802-253-8511; www.trappfamily.com; 700 Trapp Hill Rd; r from $270; @📶🏊) If the *Sound of Music* is one of your favorite things, then you'll love this Austrian-style mountain lodge built by the Von Trapp family and offering cross-country skiing, snowshoeing and hiking.

Best Western Waterbury-Stowe MOTEL $$
(☎802-244-7822; www.bestwesternwaterburystowe.com; VT 100, I-89 exit 10; r incl breakfast $109-149; ❄@📶🏊👪) Family-friendly, this convenient hotel has a playground, a sunny atrium pool and fitness facilities a notch above the usual standards. And it's just a short drive from Ben & Jerry's.

Smugglers Notch State Park CAMPGROUND $
(☎802-253-4014; 6443 Mountain Rd; campsites/lean-tos $20/27; ⏱mid-May–mid-Oct) Camp at the base of Mt Mansfield, 9 miles northwest of downtown Stowe on VT 108.

Eating

TOP CHOICE Hen of the Wood AMERICAN $$$
(☎802-244-7300; www.henofthewood.com; 92 Stowe St, Woodbury; mains $18-32; ⏱5-10pm Tue-Sat) Arguably the finest dining in northern Vermont, this chef-driven restaurant gets rave reviews for its innovative farm-to-table cuisine. Set in a historic grist mill, the ambience is as fine as the food, which features densely flavored dishes like smoked duck breast and sheep's milk gnocchi.

Pie-casso PIZZERIA $$
(☎802-253-4411; www.piecasso.com; 1899 Mountain Rd; mains $9-22; ⏱11am-9pm) This pizzeria goes far beyond the simple pie: organic arugula chicken salad, portobello paninis and hand-tossed pesto pizzas are just part of the menu. There's a bar and live music too.

Harvest Market MARKET $
(1031 Mountain Rd; ⏱7am-5:30pm) Stop at this gourmet market for morning coffee and delicious pastries, Vermont cheeses and sandwiches before you head for the hills.

Burlington

This hip college town on the shores of scenic Lake Champlain is one of those places that makes you think, wouldn't it be great to live here? The cafe and club scene is on par with a much bigger city, while the slow, friendly pace is pure small town. And where else can you walk to the end of Main St and paddle off in a kayak?

Sights

Vermont's largest city is a manageable place with most of its cafes and pubs on or near Church St Marketplace, a brick-lined pedestrian mall, where half of Burlington hangs on a sunny day. The mall sits midway between the University of Vermont and Lake Champlain.

Fleming Museum MUSEUM
(☎802-656-2090; www.uvm.edu/~fleming; 61 Colchester Ave; adult/child $5/3; ⏱noon-4pm Tue-Fri, 1-5pm Sat & Sun May-Aug, longer hr Sep-Apr) The

WHAT THE...?

Packrats, take note. The **world's tallest filing cabinet** – a 50ft-high shrine to dead letters – sits in a roadside field midway between downtown and Magic Hat Brewery. Turn west onto Flynn Ave off US 7/Shelburne Rd and go 700 yards; it's on the right, adjacent to 208 Flynn Ave.

University of Vermont's (UVM) beautiful beaux-arts-style museum houses a 2000-item Native American gallery and works by American artists ranging from John James Audubon to Andy Warhol.

Magic Hat Brewery BREWERY
(802-658-2739; www.magichat.net; 5 Bartlett Bay Rd, South Burlington; 10am-6pm Mon-Sat, noon-5pm Sun) This insanely popular brewery, off US 7, offers free tours of its brew operation – and of course they'll tip the tap to let you sample the art. Perhaps the coolest brewery you'll ever see.

Shelburne Museum MUSEUM
(802-985-3346; www.shelburnemuseum.org; US 7, Shelburne; adult/child $20/10; 10am-5pm Mon-Sat, noon-5pm Sun mid-May–Oct) On a 45-acre estate, 7 miles south of Burlington in Shelburne, this museum boasts a stellar collection of American folk art, New England architecture and, well, just about everything. The wildly eclectic collection ranges from an early American sawmill to the Lake Champlain side-wheeler steamship *Ticonderoga*. How's that for lawn decor?

Shelburne Farms FARM
(802-985-8686; www.shelburnefarms.org; 1611 Harbor Rd, Shelburne; adult/child $8/5; 9am-5pm) You can get a taste of Vermont farm life at this classic 1400-acre farm laid out by Frederick Law Olmsted, America's premier 19th-century landscape architect. Try your hand at milking a cow, feed the chickens, or hike the extensive nature trails through pastures and along Lake Champlain.

ECHO Lake Aquarium & Science Center AQUARIUM
(802-864-1848; www.echovermont.org; 1 College St; adult/child $10.50/8.50; 10am-5pm;) On the waterfront, ECHO will delight youngsters with its aquatic habitats wriggling with creatures and hands-on interactive exhibits illuminating Lake Champlain's ecological wonders.

Oakledge Park PARK
(Flynn Ave) Near the south end of the Burlington Bike Path, this park has a **beach**, an awesome **tree house** at its south end and the **Burlington Earth Clock**, a cool Stonehenge-wannabe sun clock, at its north end.

Activities

Ready for outdoor adventures? Head to the waterfront, where options include boating on **Lake Champlain** and cycling, in-line skating and walking on the 9-mile shorefront **Burlington Bike Path**. Jump-off points and equipment rentals for all these activities are within a block of each other near the waterfront end of Main St.

Local Motion BICYCLE RENTAL
(802-652-2453; www.localmotion.org; 1 Steele St; bikes per day $30; 10am-6pm) Rents quality bikes.

Waterfront Boat Rentals BOAT RENTAL
(802-864-4858; www.waterfrontboatrentals.com; Perkins Pier; rentals per hr $10-16; 10am-6pm) Rents canoes, kayaks and rowboats.

Lake Champlain Cruises CRUISE
(802-864-7669; www.lakechamplaincruises.com; 1 King St; 1½-hr trip adult/child $15/6) For an inexpensive cruise of the lake, hop aboard the 115ft *Northern Lights*, a replicated 19th-century steamboat.

Sleeping

TOP CHOICE **Willard Street Inn** INN $$
(802-651-8710; www.willardstreetinn.com; 349 S Willard St; r incl breakfast $145-235;) With marble floors and a solarium dining room, this gracious inn, a short walk from UVM, is a class act. The 14 rooms are comfy, some with lake views and gas fireplaces, and the gourmet breakfast will start your day in style.

Inn at Shelburne Farms INN $$$
(802-985-8498; www.shelburnefarms.org; 1611 Harbor Rd, Shelburne; r with shared bath $155, private bath $260-465) Vacation like a millionaire at this lakefront manor-house-turned-inn at Shelburne Farms. On the National Register of Historic Places, this former summer residence of the Vanderbilts has 24 antique-filled bedrooms and the air of a bygone era.

Lang House B&B $$
(☎802-652-2500; www.langhouse.com; 360 Main St; r incl breakfast $145-245; ❄📶) Little extras like cozy bathrobes and a home-cooked breakfast add to the appeal of this friendly Victorian inn. Situated between downtown and the university, it makes an ideal base for exploring Burlington.

Burlington Hostel HOSTEL $
(☎802-540-3043; www.theburlingtonhostel.com; 53 Main St; dm incl breakfast $30; ❄@📶) Just minutes from the action centers of Church St and Lake Champlain, Burlington's hostel accommodates up to 48 guests and offers both mixed and women-only dorms.

North Beach Campground CAMPGROUND $
(☎802-862-0942; www.enjoyburlington.com; 60 Institute Rd; campsites $26; 📶) This choice lakeside campground skirts the Burlington Bike Path and has a sandy beach with kayak and canoe rentals.

Eating

Magnolia Bistro CAFE $$
(☎802-846-7446; www.magnoliabistro.com; 1 Lawson Lane; mains $7-12; ⏲7am-3pm Mon-Fri, 8am-3pm Sat & Sun; 📶) Magnolia utilizes sustainable local ingredients from range-fed beef to leafy green salads, and is certified by the Green Restaurant Association. Specialties include the house-cured organic salmon and the Vermont maple sausage omelet.

Penny Cluse Café CAFE $
(www.pennycluse.com; 169 Cherry St; mains $7-10; ⏲6:45am-3pm Mon-Fri, 8am-3pm Sat & Sun) One block east of Church St Marketplace, Penny Cluse packs a perky college crowd with its southwestern accented dishes like ranchero-style omelets, fish tacos and freshly squeezed juices. Forget weekends, however, when the wait just for a table can be more than an hour.

L'Amante ITALIAN $$$
(☎802-863-5200; www.lamante.com; 126 College St; mains $23-30; ⏲5-10pm Mon-Sat) Sleek yet engagingly informal, L'Amante serves upscale northern Italian cuisine such as squash-blossom fritters with truffle oil, and swordfish with saffron-encrusted risotto. Perfect for a memorable night out.

Stone Soup CAFE $
(www.stonesoupvt.com; 211 College St; mains $5-10; ⏲7am-9pm Mon-Fri, 9am-9pm Sat; 🖉📶) Don't let the bargain prices fool you. The food at this laid-back cafe is hearty and healthy, most of it vegetarian, much of it organic. Sandwiches, soups and a buffet bar of fresh salads and hot dishes shore up the menu.

August First Bakery & Cafe BAKERY $
(www.augustfirstvt.com; 149 S Champlain St; sandwiches $5-9; ⏲7:30am-5pm Mon-Fri, 8am-3pm Sat) Thickly stacked sandwiches on homebaked organic bread and sinful pastries are in store at this bakery-cafe a block from the waterfront.

Muddy Waters CAFE $
(184 Main St; snacks $3-6; ⏲7:30am-6pm Mon, 7:30am-11pm Tue-Sun; 🖉) As much a chill-out spot as eatery, this arty student haunt offers light eats like vegan chili and a full array of drinks from espressos and smoothies to Vermont-brewed beers.

Burlington Farmers Market MARKET $
(www.burlingtonfarmersmarket.org; cnr St Paul & Cottage Sts; ⏲8:30am-2pm Sat) Fruits and veggies don't get any fresher than at this outdoor market a block south of Church St Marketplace that's run by local farmers.

Drinking & Entertainment

Nectar's CLUB
(www.liveatnectars.com; 188 Main St) This is the place where the jam band Phish got its start; aspiring bands still take the stage at Nectar's hoping to be the next big thing. Maybe you'll catch a rising star.

Radio Bean COFFEEHOUSE
(www.radiobean.com; 8 N Winooski Ave; ⏲8am-2am; 📶) A social hub for the music scene, this bohemian coffeehouse serves fair-trade coffee by day and transforms after dark into an intimate venue for jazz and indie bands.

Vermont Pub & Brewery MICROBREWERY
(www.vermontbrewery.com; 144 College St; ⏲11:30am-1am Sun-Wed, 11:30am-2am Thu-Sat) Vermont's oldest microbrewery attracts a crowd with its bustling outdoor beer garden and burly ales. Try the Dogbite Bitter and howl at the moon.

Red Square CLUB
(www.redsquarevt.com; 136 Church St) With a stylish Soho-like ambience, this is where the club crowd hangs to listen to Burlington's best roadhouse music, which spills onto the outdoor patio on warm nights.

Splash at the Boathouse BAR
(0 College St; ⏲11:30am-2am) Head to this floating boathouse at the foot of College

St for a fabulous view of Lake Champlain. *The* place to enjoy a sunset drink.

Shopping

You'll find boutiques and smart craft shops along Church St Marketplace. Don't miss the **Frog Hollow Craft Center** (www.froghollow.org; 85 Church St), a collective featuring some of the finest work in Burlington.

Information

Fletcher Allen Health Care (802-847-0000; 111 Colchester Ave; 24hr) Vermont's largest hospital.

Lake Champlain Regional Chamber of Commerce (802-863-3489; www.vermont.org; 60 Main St; 8am-5pm Mon-Fri) Also maintains a 24-hour visitor kiosk on Church St Marketplace.

Post office (www.usps.com; 11 Elmwood Ave)

Seven Days (www.7dvt.com) Free weekly with event and entertainment listings.

Getting There & Away

Lake Champlain Ferries (802-864-9804; www.ferries.com; King St Dock; adult/child/car $4.95/2.20/17.50) runs ferries several times a day from mid-June to mid-October across the lake to Port Kent, NY (one hour).

NEW HAMPSHIRE

You're gonna like the scale of things in the Granite State: the towns are small and personable, the mountains majestic and rugged. The heart of New Hampshire is unquestionably the granite peaks of the White Mountain National Forest. Outdoor enthusiasts of all stripes flock to New England's highest range (6288ft at Mt Washington) for cold-weather skiing, summer hiking and brilliant fall foliage scenery. Oh, and don't be fooled by that politically conservative label that people stick on the state. The state mantra, 'Live Free or Die,' indeed rings from every automobile license plate, but truth be told residents here pride themselves on their independent spirit more than right-wing politics.

History

Named in 1629 after the English county of Hampshire, New Hampshire was one of the first American colonies to declare its independence from England in 1776. During the 19th-century industrialization boom, the state's leading city, Manchester, became such a powerhouse that its textile mills were the world's largest.

New Hampshire played a high-profile role in 1944 when president Franklin D Roosevelt gathered leaders from 44 Allied nations to remote Bretton Woods for a conference to rebuild global capitalism. It was at the Bretton Woods Conference that the World Bank and the International Monetary Fund emerged.

In 1963 New Hampshire, long famed for its antitax sentiments, found another way to raise revenue – by becoming the first state in the USA to have a legal lottery.

Information

Welcome centers are situated at major state border crossings, including one at the south end of I-93 that's open 24/7.

New Hampshire Division of Parks and Recreation (877-647-2757; www.nhstateparks.org) Offers camping in 19 state parks.

New Hampshire Division of Travel & Tourism Development (603-271-2665; www.visitnh.gov) Distributes visitor information on the state, as do the welcome centers.

Union Leader (www.unionleader.com) The state's largest newspaper.

NEW HAMPSHIRE FACTS

» **Nicknames** Granite State, White Mountain State

» **Population** 1.3 million

» **Area** 8968 sq miles

» **Capital city** Concord (population 42,700)

» **Other cities** Manchester (population 109,600)

» **Sales tax** none

» **Birthplace of** America's first astronaut Alan Shepard (1923–98), *The Da Vinci Code* author Dan Brown (b 1964)

» **Home of** the highest mountains in northeastern USA

» **Politics** New England's most Republican state

» **Famous for** being the first to vote in US presidential primaries, which gives the state enormous political influence for its size

» **Most extreme state motto** 'Live Free or Die'

» **Driving distances** Boston to Portsmouth 60 miles, Concord to Hanover 66 miles

Portsmouth

America's third-oldest city (1623), Portsmouth wears its history on its sleeve. Its roots are in shipbuilding, but New Hampshire's sole coastal city also has a hip, youthful energy. The old maritime warehouses along the harbor now house cafes and boutiques. Elegant period homes built by shipbuilding tycoons have been converted into B&Bs.

Sights & Activities

Strawbery Banke Museum MUSEUM

(☎603-433-1100; www.strawberybanke.org; cnr Hancock & Marcy Sts; adult/child $15/10; ⏰10am-5pm May-Oct) Encompassing an entire neighborhood of 40 period buildings, Strawbery Banke is an eclectic living-history museum depicting the town's multilayered past. Visit the old general store, watch the potter throw his clay then treat yourself to a scoop of homemade ice cream.

USS Albacore MUSEUM

(☎603-436-3680; http://ussalbacore.org; 600 Market St; adult/child $5/3; ⏰9:30am-5pm Jun–mid-Oct, 9:30am-4pm Thu-Mon mid-Oct–May) Like a fish out of water, this 205ft-long submarine is now a beached museum on a grassy lawn. Launched from Portsmouth Naval Shipyard in 1953, the Albacore was once the world's fastest submarine.

Isles of Shoals Steamship Company CRUISE

(☎603-431-5500; www.islesofshoals.com; 315 Market St; adult/child $28/18; 👪) From May to September you can hop aboard a replica 1900s ferry for a leisurely harbor cruise that takes in three lighthouses, nine islands and countless harbor sights. On Fridays the cruise includes a lobster clambake (adult/child $58/27).

Sleeping

TOP CHOICE **Ale House Inn** INN $$

(☎603-431-7760; www.alehouseinn.com; 121 Bow St; r $140-239, ❄📶) Portsmouth's snazziest boutique inn occupies an atmospheric brewery (c 1880). The building's period character of brick and wood fuses flawlessly with the rooms' clean contemporary design. Perks like in-room iPads, guest bicycles and free tickets to the adjacent repertory theater add to the appeal.

Inn at Strawbery Banke B&B $$

(☎603-436-7242; www.innatstrawberybanke.com; 314 Court St; r incl breakfast $160-170) Friendly innkeepers, cozy rooms and a delicious homemade breakfast are the hallmarks of this Colonial-era B&B convenient to both the Strawbery Banke Museum and the city center.

Eating & Drinking

Head to the intersection of Market and Congress Sts, where restaurants and cafes are thick on the ground.

TOP CHOICE **Black Trumpet Bistro** INTERNATIONAL $$$

(☎603-431-0887; www.blacktrumpetbistro.com; 29 Ceres St; mains $17-35; ⏰5:30-9pm) Chef-driven and oozing sophisticated ambience, Portsmouth's top bistro whips up inventive dishes like baharat-crusted dayboat scallops over whipped parsnips and olive oil cake with tiramisu and brandy espresso. Fab food, high energy and high-decibel levels.

Jumpin' Jay's Fish Café SEAFOOD $$$

(☎603-766-3474; www.jumpinjays.com; 150 Congress St; mains $20-26; ⏰5:30-10pm) Fish-fanciers book tables at this sleek contemporary seafooder, which features a wide range of fresh pan-seared fish spiced with delicious sauces. Other briny delights include a raw bar with regional oysters.

Breaking New Grounds CAFE $

(14 Market St; snacks $2-5; ⏰6:30am-11pm; 📶) Get your caffeine fix at this cafe smack in the heart of town. Plump muffins, crispy croissants and outdoor tables perfect for people-watching.

Friendly Toast DINER $

(113 Congress St; mains $7-10; ⏰7am-10pm Sun-Thu, 7am-2am Fri & Sat; 📶🥬) Whimsical furnishings set the scene for filling omelets, Tex-Mex and vegetarian fare at this retro diner serving breakfast all day.

Portsmouth Brewery MICROBREWERY $

(www.portsmouthbrewery.com; 56 Market St; light eats $7-12; 📶) This lively microbrewery serves specialty beers like Smuttynose Portsmouth Lager along with light eats, including the best fish sandwich in town.

Information

Greater Portsmouth Chamber of Commerce (☎603-436-3988; www.portsmouthchamber.org; 500 Market St; ⏰8:30am-5pm Mon-Fri, lobby 24hr) Provides visitor information.

Monadnock State Park

The 3165ft **Mt Monadnock** (www.nhstateparks.org; NH 124; adult/child $4/2), in the southwestern corner of the state, is the most hiked summit in New England. 'Mountain That Stands Alone' in Algonquian, Monadnock is relatively isolated from other peaks, which means hikers who make the 5-mile round-trip to the summit are rewarded with unspoiled views of three states.

Manchester

A couple of colleges and an art school give this old mill town fresh vitality. New Hampshire's largest city, Manchester became a manufacturing powerhouse in the 19th century by harnessing the ripping Merrimack River. The brick **Amoskeag Mills** (1838), which stretch along the Commercial St riverbanks for more than a mile, now house software companies and other 21st-century backbones of the city's economy.

Head to Elm St near the town green where you'll find the tourist office and the lion's share of eateries and pubs. The **Greater Manchester Chamber of Commerce** (☎603-666-6600; www.manchester-chamber.org; 889 Elm St; ⊙9am-5pm) has visitor information.

The city's highlight, the **Currier Museum of Art** (☎603-669-6144; www.currier.org; 201 Myrtle Way; adult/child $10/free, Sat morning free; ⊙11am-5pm Sun, Mon & Wed-Fri, 10am-5pm Sat), showcases works by American artists Georgia O'Keeffe and Andrew Wyeth. It also operates the 1950 **Zimmerman House** (tours $15), the only home in New England designed by famed American architect Frank Lloyd Wright (1867–1959) open to the public.

I-93, US 3 and NH 101 all pass through Manchester. The **Manchester Airport** (MHT; www.flymanchester.com) is served by major US airlines, including discounter Southwest Airlines. **Greyhound** (www.greyhound.com) provides bus services between Manchester and other New England cities.

Concord

History-laden Concord makes a refreshing break. Don't let the fact that it's a state capital throw you – think of it as a laid-back little town that just happens to have a capitol building gracing Main St, the way other communities this size would have a town hall. Everything radiates out from the State House – you'll find several delis and restaurants nearby.

The gold-domed, eagle-topped **State House** (107 N Main St; admission free; ⊙8am-4:30pm Mon-Fri), built in 1819 of New Hampshire granite, houses the oldest legislative chamber in the US. Forget heavy-handed security, this is a remarkably relaxed affair – you can walk right in, check out the intriguing lobby display of battle-tattered Civil War flags, then head up to the 2nd floor to visit the chamber. The **Museum of New Hampshire History** (☎603-228-6688; www.nhhistory.org; 6 Eagle Sq; adult/child $5.50/3; ⊙9:30am-5pm Mon-Sat, noon-5pm Sun, closed Mon Jan-Jun), opposite the State House, chronicles the history of the Granite State in more depth. **Pierce Manse** (☎603-225-4555; www.piercemanse.org; 14 Horseshoe Pond Lane; adult/child $7/3; ⊙11am-3pm Tue-Sat mid-Jun–mid-Sep), the home of Franklin Pierce (1804–69), the only

WORTH A TRIP

CANTERBURY SHAKER VILLAGE

A traditional Shaker community from 1792, **Canterbury Shaker Village** (☎603-783-9511; www.shakers.org; 288 Shaker Rd, Canterbury; adult/child $17/8; ⊙10am-5pm mid-May–Oct) maintains the Shaker heritage as a living-history museum. Interpreters demonstrate the Shakers' daily lives, artisans create Shaker crafts, and walking trails invite pond-side strolls. The greening of America has deep roots here – for more than two centuries the Shakers' abundant gardens have been turning out vegetables, medicinal herbs and bountiful flowers the organic way. If you're ready for a soulful diversion you could easily spend half a day here on the farm, which covers nearly 700 acres. Take a little wholesomeness home with you – there's a store selling Shaker handicrafts, a farm stand and a superb restaurant serving the kind of food grandma used to make using heirloom veggies fresh picked from the garden. The village is 15 miles north of Concord; take I-93 to exit 18 and follow the signs.

SCENIC DRIVE: KANCAMAGUS HIGHWAY

One of New England's finest, the 35-mile Kancamagus Hwy (NH 112) is a beauty of a road cutting through the **White Mountain National Forest** between Conway and Lincoln. Laced with excellent hiking trails, scenic lookouts and swimmable streams, this is as natural as it gets. There's absolutely no development along the entire highway, which reaches its highest point at **Kancamagus Pass** (2868ft).

You can pick up brochures and hiking maps at the **Saco Ranger District Office** (603-447-5448; 33 Kancamagus Hwy; 8am-4:30pm) at the eastern end of the highway near Conway.

Coming from Conway, 6.5 miles west of the Saco ranger station, you'll see **Lower Falls** on the north side of the road – stop here for the view and a swim. No trip along this highway is complete without taking the 20-minute hike to the breathtaking cascade of **Sabbaday Falls**; the trail begins at Mile 15 on the south side of the road. The best place to spot moose is along the shores of **Lily Pond**; stop at the roadside overview at Mile 18. At the Lincoln Woods ranger station, which is near the Mile 29 marker, cross the suspension footbridge over the river and hike 3 miles to **Franconia Falls**, the finest swimming hole in the entire national forest, complete with a natural rock slide. Parking anywhere along the highway costs $3 per day (honor system) or $5 per week; just fill out an envelope at any of the parking areas.

The White Mountain National Forest is ideal for campers, and you'll find several campgrounds run by the forest service accessible from the Kancamagus Hwy. Most are on a first-come, first-served basis; pick up a list at the Saco ranger station.

US president to hail from New Hampshire, can be toured in summer. The **Greater Concord Chamber of Commerce** (603-224-2508; www.concordnhchamber.com; 40 Commercial St; 9am-5pm Mon-Fri, 9am-3pm Sat) maintains a tourist information kiosk on the sidewalk in front of the State House.

Lake Winnipesaukee

A popular summer retreat for families looking for a break from the city, New Hampshire's largest lake stretches 28 miles in length, contains 274 islands and offers abundant opportunities for swimming, boating and fishing.

WEIRS BEACH

This lakeside town dishes up a curious slice of honky-tonk Americana with its celebrated video arcades, mini-golf courses and go-cart tracks. The **Lakes Region Chamber of Commerce** (603-524-5531; www.lakesregionchamber.org; 383 S Main St, Laconia; 8:30am-4:30pm Mon-Fri) supplies information on the area.

Mount Washington Cruises (603-366-5531; www.cruisenh.com; cruises $27-43) operates scenic lake cruises, the pricier ones with champagne brunch, from Weirs Beach aboard the old-fashioned MS *Mount Washington*. For a unique experience hop aboard the MV *Sophie C*, the oldest floating post office in the USA, on its two-hour **cruise** (adult/child $24/12) to deliver mail to the lake islands.

Winnipesaukee Scenic Railroad (603-279-5253; www.hoborr.com; adult/child $15/11) offers train rides along the shore of Lake Winnipesaukee.

WOLFEBORO

On the opposite side of Lake Winnipesaukee, and a world away from the ticky-tacky commercialism of Weirs Beach, sits genteel Wolfeboro. Anointing itself 'the oldest summer resort in America,' the town's awash with graceful period buildings, including several that are open to the public. The **Wolfeboro Chamber of Commerce** (603-569-2200; www.wolfeborochamber.com; 32 Central Ave; 10am-5pm Mon-Sat, 11am-2pm Sun), in the old train station, has the scoop on everything from boat rentals to lakeside beaches.

Wolfeboro is home to the **Great Waters Music Festival** (603-569-7710; www.greatwaters.org; Brewster Academy, NH 28; Jul & Aug), featuring folk, jazz and blues artists at venues throughout town.

Off NH 28, about 4 miles north of town, is lakeside **Wolfeboro Campground** (603-569-9881; www.wolfeborocampground.com; 61 Haines Hill Rd; campsites $30) with 50 wooded campsites.

The classic stay is the **Wolfeboro Inn** (☎603-569-3016; www.wolfeboroinn.com; 90 N Main St; r incl breakfast $179-259), the town's principal lodging since 1812. Some of the rooms have balconies overlooking the lake. The inn's cozy pub, **Wolfe's Tavern** (90 N Main St; mains $10-24; ⏰8am-10pm), offers a varied menu ranging from pizza to seafood. The old-school **Wolfeboro Diner** (5 N Main St; mains $5-10; ⏰7am-2pm) hits the mark with juicy cheeseburgers and straightforward breakfast fare at honest prices.

White Mountains

What the Rockies are to Colorado the White Mountains are to New Hampshire. New England's loftiest mountain range is a magnet for adventurers, with boundless opportunities for everything from hiking and kayaking to skiing. Those who prefer to take it in from the comfort of a car seat won't be disappointed either, as scenic drives wind over rugged mountains ripping with waterfalls, sheer rock faces and sharply cut gorges.

You'll find information on the White Mountains at ranger stations throughout the **White Mountain National Forest** (www.fs.fed.us/r9/white) and chambers of commerce in the towns along the way.

WATERVILLE VALLEY

In the shadow of Mt Tecumseh, Waterville Valley was developed as a resort community during the latter half of the 20th century, when hotels, condos, golf courses and ski trails were all laid out. It's very much a planned community and arguably a bit too groomed but there's plenty to do, including tennis, indoor ice skating, cycling and other family fun. The **Waterville Valley Region Chamber of Commerce** (☎603-726-3804; www.watervillevalleyregion.com; 12 Vintinner Rd, Campton; ⏰9am-5pm), off I-93 exit 28, has all the details.

Like many New England ski mountains, the **Waterville Valley ski area** (www.waterville.com) is open in the summer for mountain biking and hiking.

MT WASHINGTON VALLEY

Stretching north from the eastern terminus of the Kancamagus Hwy, Mt Washington Valley includes the towns of Conway, North Conway, Intervale, Glen, Jackson and Bartlett. Every conceivable outdoor activity is available. The area's hub and biggest town, North Conway, is also a center for outlet shopping, including some earthy stores like LL Bean.

Sights & Activities

Conway Scenic Railroad RAILROAD
(☎603-356-5251; www.conwayscenic.com; NH 16, North Conway; adult $15-65, child $10-50; ⏰daily May-Oct, Sat & Sun Apr & Nov; 👪) Nostalgia at its finest, this antique steam train operates a variety of excursions from North Conway through Mt Washington Valley and dramatic Crawford Notch. It's a real stunner, especially during the fall foliage season.

Echo Lake State Park PARK
(www.nhstateparks.org; River Rd; adult/child $4/2) Two miles west of North Conway off US 302, this park rests at the foot of a sheer rock wall called White Horse Ledge. Come here for lakeside hiking, swimming and the road up to 700ft-high Cathedral Ledge for panoramic views.

Saco Bound BOATING
(☎603-447-2177; www.sacobound.com; 2561 E Main/US 302, Conway; rental per day $26) If you're up for a water adventure, Saco Bound rents canoes and kayaks and also offers guided tours ranging from placid lake paddles to day-long white-water outings.

Attitash SKI RESORT
(☎603-374-2368; www.attitash.com; US 302, Bartlett) This ski resort 5 miles west of Glen also operates America's longest alpine slide in summer.

Black Mountain Ski Area SKI RESORT
(☎603-383-4490; www.blackmt.com; NH 16B, Jackson) Cross-country skiing mecca with summertime horseback riding.

Sleeping

North Conway in particular is thick with sleeping options from resort hotels to cozy inns.

TOP CHOICE **Wildflowers Inn** B&B $$
(☎603-356-7567; www.wildflowersinn.com; 3486 White Mountain Hwy, North Conway; r incl breakfast $99-269; ❄📶) Start your day with a three-course gourmet breakfast at this elegant Victorian-style inn. Other pluses: pretty rooms with comfy beds and fireplaces, a living room with a pool table and a huge deck with huge views. The higher-priced rooms are large suites with two-person Jacuzzis.

Cranmore Inn B&B $$
(☎603-356-5502; www.cranmoreinn.com; 80 Kearsarge St, North Conway; r incl breakfast $89-149;

) With a convenient location, this North Conway landmark has been operating as a country inn since 1863 and good-value, home-style comfort is its key to success.

North Conway Grand Hotel HOTEL $$
(603-356-9300; www.northconwaygrand.com; NH 16, Settlers' Green, North Conway; r $99-229;) If you're looking for all the trappings of a resort hotel, this family-friendly place has commodious rooms with full amenities and extras like a free DVD library and children's programs.

White Mountains Hostel HOSTEL $
(603-447-1001; www.whitemountainshostel.com; 36 Washington St, Conway; dm/r $23/58;) Perched on the edge of the White Mountain National Forest, off NH 16, this 45-bed hostel in a converted farmhouse is well situated for outdoor adventurers.

Saco River Camping Area CAMPGROUND $
(603-356-3360; www.sacorivercampingarea.com; 1550 NH 16, North Conway; campsites $32;) On the Saco River, with canoe and kayak rentals and a heated pool.

Eating & Drinking

TOP CHOICE **Peach's** CAFE $
(www.peachesnorthconway.com; 2506 White Mountain Hwy, North Conway; mains $6-10; 7am-2:30pm) This peachy place, a half-mile south of the chamber of commerce, really captures a small-town feel. Who can resist fruit-smothered waffles, hearty omelets and homemade soups served in somebody's cozy living room?

Flatbread Company PIZZERIA $$
(603-356-4470; www.flatbreadcompany.com; 2760 White Mountain Hwy, North Conway; pizzas $11-20; 11:30am-10pm) A socially conscious pizzeria, Flatbread uses organic veggies and nitrate-free meats, and dishes up a portion of its profits to local environmental causes. The deliciously crispy pizzas are cooked in front of your eyes in a wood-fired clay oven built into the dining room.

Moat Mountain Smoke House & Brewing Co PUB $$
(603-356-6381; www.moatmountain.com; 3378 White Mountain Hwy; mains $8-22; 11:30am-11pm) Barbecued ribs and juicy burgers are mainstays at this watering hole restaurant, which brews its own ales on site.

Café Noche MEXICAN $$
(www.cafenoche.net; 147 Main St, Conway; meals $10-15; 11:30am-9pm) Tex-Mex fare topped with real-deal salsas at this festive central Conway spot. The margaritas, in a head spinning variety of flavors, will rev up the appetite.

Information

Mt Washington Valley Chamber of Commerce (603-356-5701; www.mtwashingtonvalley.org; 2617 White Mountain Hwy, North Conway; 9am-5pm) Information on the entire region.

NORTH WOODSTOCK & LINCOLN

You'll pass right through the twin towns of Lincoln and North Woodstock on your way between the Kancamagus Hwy and Franconia Notch State Park, so it's a handy place to break for a bite or a bed. The towns straddle the Pemigewasset River at the intersection of NH 112 and US 3. If you're ready for some action, **Loon Mountain** (603-745-8111; www.loonmtn.com; Kancamagus Hwy, Lincoln) offers winter skiing and snowboarding, and in summer has mountain-bike trails, climbing walls and New Hampshire's longest gondola ride. Or ratchet the adrenaline up a notch by zipping 2000ft down a hillside while strapped to just a cable with **Alpine Adventures** (603-745-9911; www.alpinezipline.com; 41 Main St, Lincoln; zips $89; 9am-4pm) treetop zip line.

Sleeping

Woodstock Inn INN $$
(603-745-3951; www.woodstockinnnh.com; US 3, North Woodstock; r incl breakfast with shared bath $78-129, with private bath $99-229;) Spread across five historic houses in the heart of North Woodstock, this inn offers a variety of comfortable rooms, many furnished with antiques, some with fireplaces and Jacuzzi baths.

Wilderness Inn B&B $$
(603-745-3890; www.thewildernessinn.com; cnr US 3 & NH 112; r incl breakfast $85-165;) Gather round the fireplace with other guests at this century-old B&B with hardwood floors and country-style decor. Or if you want your own private space, swing for the cottage ($175) with a gas fireplace and oversized Jacuzzi tub. The multicourse breakfasts are marvelous.

Eating

TOP CHOICE **Cascade Coffee House** CAFE $
(115 Main St, North Woodstock; mains $4-9; 7am-3pm Mon-Fri, 7am-5pm Sat & Sun;) This creative place in the center of town serves

up luscious pastries, fresh smoothies and micro-roaster coffees. At lunch, you'll also find crispy panini sandwiches and innovative salads.

Woodstock Inn Station & Brewery PUB **$$**
(603-745-3951; US 3, North Woodstock; mains $9-23; 11:30am-10pm) If your family can't settle on what to eat, this brewpub satisfies an amazing range of food cravings with pub grub, steaks, pizza and Mexican fare. There's live entertainment on weekends in summer and frothy microbrewed ales year-round.

Information

Lincoln-Woodstock Chamber of Commerce
(603-745-6621; www.lincolnwoodstock.com; Main St/NH 112, Lincoln; 9am-5pm Mon-Fri)

FRANCONIA NOTCH STATE PARK

Franconia Notch is the most celebrated mountain pass in New England, a narrow gorge shaped over the eons by a rushing stream slicing through the craggy granite. I-93, in places feeling more like a country road than a highway, runs straight through the state park. The **Franconia Notch State Park visitor center** (603-745-8391; www.franconianotchstatepark.com; I-93, exit 34A), 4 miles north of North Woodstock, can give you details on hikes in the park, which range from short nature walks to day-long treks.

Sights & Activities

Flume Gorge HIKING
(www.flumegorge.com; adult/child $13/10; 9am-5pm May-Oct) A 2-mile self-guided walk beginning at the park visitor center takes you right through this awesome cleft in the granite bedrock, which narrows to a mere 12ft, as water rushes at your feet. The rock walls tower 90ft above you. One cool walk on a hot day.

Frost Place HISTORIC SITE
(603-823-5510; www.frostplace.org; 158 Ridge Rd, Franconia; adult/child $5/3; 1-5pm Sat & Sun late May-Jun, 1-5pm Wed-Mon Jul–mid-Oct) A few miles north of Franconia Notch lies the farm where poet Robert Frost (1874–1963) wrote his most famous poems, 'The Road Not Taken' and 'Stopping by Woods on a Snowy Evening.' The farmhouse retains the simplicity and inspiration of Frost's day.

Cannon Mountain Aerial Tramway TRAM
(603-823-8800; www.cannonmt.com; I-93, exit 34B; round-trip adult/child $13/10; 9am-5pm late May–mid-Oct;) This tram whisks you to a 4080ft summit, where you're rewarded with breathtaking views of Franconia Notch and the White Mountains.

Basin Trail HIKING
For an enjoyable 20-minute stroll, stop at the Basin pull-off, between exits 34A and 34B, where a half-mile trail runs along a pretty stream to a glacier-carved granite pool.

Echo Lake BEACH
(603-823-8800; I-93, exit 34C; adult/child $4/2; 10am-5:30pm) A swimming lake just off the highway where you can also rent kayaks and canoes.

Sleeping

Lafayette Place Campground CAMPGROUND **$**
(603-271-3628; www.reserveamerica.com; campsites $25) Franconia Notch State Park's popular campground is a hub for hikers. The 97 wooded campsites fill up early in summer, so it's best to reserve in advance.

BRETTON WOODS & CRAWFORD NOTCH

Before 1944, Bretton Woods was known primarily as a low-key retreat for wealthy visitors who patronized the majestic Mt Washington Hotel. After President Roosevelt chose the hotel for the historic conference that established a new post-WWII economic order, the town's name took on worldwide recognition. The countryside, with Mt Washington looming above it, is as magnificent today as it was back then. The **Twin Mountain-Bretton Woods Chamber of Commerce** (800-245-8946; www.twin-mountain.org; cnr US 302 & US 3, Twin Mountain) has details on the area.

The region's largest ski area, **Bretton Woods ski station** (603-278-3320; www.brettonwoods.com; US 302) offers downhill and cross-country skiing as well as a zipline.

US 302 heads south from Bretton Woods to Crawford Notch (1773ft) through stunning mountain scenery ripe with towering cascades. **Crawford Notch State Park** (603-374-2272; www.nhstateparks.org; adult/child $4/2) maintains an extensive system of hiking trails, including short hikes around a pond and to a waterfall, and a longer trek up Mt Washington.

Sleeping

Mt Washington Hotel HOTEL **$$$**
(603-278-1000; www.mountwashingtonresort.com; US 302; r $149-600;) If walls could

talk, the ones here could spin quite a tale. Opened in 1902, this grande dame of New England mountain resorts boasts 2600 acres of grounds, 27 holes of golf, 12 clay tennis courts, a pair of heated pools and an equestrian center.

Dry River Campground CAMPGROUND $
(☎603-271-3628; www.reserveamerica.org; US 302; campsites $25; ⊙late May-Sep) Inside Crawford Notch State Park, this campground has 33 quiet sites and good facilities.

MT WASHINGTON

From Pinkham Notch (2032ft), on NH 16 about 11 miles north of North Conway, a system of hiking trails provides access to the natural beauties of the Presidential Range, including lofty **Mt Washington** (6288ft), the highest mountain east of the Mississippi and north of the Smoky Mountains. Hikers need to be prepared: Mt Washington's weather is notoriously severe and can turn on a dime. Dress warmly – not only does the mountain register New England's coldest temperatures (in summer, the average at the summit is 45°F) but unrelenting winds make it feel colder than the thermometer reading. In fact, Mt Washington holds the record for the USA's strongest wind gust – 231mph!

One of the most popular trails up Mt Washington begins at the AMC's Pinkham Notch Visitor Center and runs 4.2 strenuous miles to the summit, taking four to five hours to reach the top and a bit less on the way down.

If your quads aren't up for a workout, the **Mt Washington Auto Road** (☎603-466-3988; www.mountwashingtonautoroad.com; car & driver $25, extra adult/child $8/6; ⊙mid-May–mid-Oct) offers easier summit access, weather permitting.

While purists walk, and the out-of-shape drive, the quaintest way to reach the summit is to take the **Mt Washington Cog Railway** (☎603-278-5404; www.thecog.com; adult/child $62/39, ⊙May-Oct). Since 1869, coal-fired steam-powered locomotives have followed a 3.5-mile track up a steep mountainside trestle for a jaw-dropping excursion.

The **Pinkham Notch Visitor Center** (☎603-466-2727; www.outdoors.org; NH 16; ⊙6:30am-10pm), run by the Appalachian Mountain Club (AMC), is the area's informational nexus for like-minded adventurers and a good place to buy hiking necessities, including topographic trail maps and the handy *AMC White Mountain Guide.*

The AMC runs the adjacent **Joe Dodge Lodge** (☎603-466 2727; r incl breakfast & dinner $75). **Dolly Copp Campground** (☎603-466-2713; www.campsnh.com; NH 16; campsites $20), a USFS campground 6 miles north of the AMC's Pinkham Notch facilities, has 176 simple campsites.

Hanover

The archetypal New England college town, Hanover has a town green that is bordered on all four sides by the handsome brick edifices of Dartmouth College. Virtually the whole town is given over to this Ivy League school; chartered in 1769, Dartmouth is the nation's ninth-oldest college.

Main St, rolling down from the green, is surrounded by perky pubs, shops and cafes that cater to the collegian crowd.

Sights & Activities

Dartmouth College COLLEGE CAMPUS
Hanover is all about Dartmouth College, so hit the campus. Join a free student-guided **campus walking tour** (☎603-646-2875; www.dartmouth.edu) or just pick up a map at the admissions office and head off on your own. Don't miss the **Baker-Berry Library**, splashed with the grand *Epic of American Civilization,* painted by the outspoken Mexican muralist José Clemente Orozco (1883–1949), who taught at Dartmouth in the 1930s.

FREE **Hood Museum of Art** MUSEUM
(☎603-646-2808; Wheelock St; ⊙10am-5pm Tue-Sat, to 9pm Wed, noon-5pm Sun) The collections here cover a wide swath from Assyrian stone reliefs that date back to 883 BC to contemporary American art by heavyweights Jackson Pollock and Edward Hopper.

Sleeping & Eating

Chieftain Motor Inn MOTEL $$
(☎603-643-2550; www.chieftaininn.com; 84 Lyme Rd/NH 10; r $119-140;) In a riverfront setting on the north side of town, this rustic inn offers complimentary use of canoes, making it a good spot to combine an outing with a night's sleep.

Canoe Club Bistro CAFE $$
(☎603-643-9660; www.canoeclub.us; 27 S Main St; mains $10-23; ⊙11:30am-11:30pm) This smart cafe does a fine job with grilled food – not

just burgers and steaks, but also tasty treats like duck breast with fig port glaze. There's also live entertainment nightly – anything from acoustic to jazz.

Lou's DINER **$**
(lousrestaurant.net; 30 S Main St; mains $5-10; 6am-3pm Mon-Fri, 7am-3pm Sat & Sun) A student haunt since 1947, Lou's has good sandwiches and pastries, but everybody comes to this simple diner for the hearty breakfasts served until closing.

Drinking & Entertainment

Murphy's on the Green PUB
(www.murphysonthegreen.com; 11 S Main St) At this classic Irish pub, students and faculty discuss weighty matters over pints of Irish ale.

Hopkins Center for the Arts PERFORMING ARTS
(603-646-2422; www.hop.dartmouth.edu; Lebanon St) The 'Hop' is Dartmouth's refined venue for string quartets, modern dance and plays.

Information

Hanover Area Chamber of Commerce (603-643-3115; www.hanoverchamber.org; 53 S Main St; 9am-4pm Mon-Fri) Good place to start your visit.

MAINE

Maine is New England's frontier – a land so vast it could swallow the region's five other states with scarcely a gulp. The sea looms large with mile after mile of sandy beaches, craggy sea cliffs and quiet harbors. While time-honored fishing villages and seaside lobster joints are the fame of Maine, inland travel also offers ample reward. Maine's rugged interior is given over to rushing rivers, dense forests and lofty mountains just aching to be explored.

As a traveler in Maine, your choices are as spectacularly varied as the landscape. You can opt to sail serenely along the coast on a graceful schooner or rip through white-water rapids on a river raft, spend the night in an old sea captain's home-turned-B&B, or camp among the moose on a backwoods lake.

History

It's estimated that 20,000 Native Americans from tribes known collectively as Wabanaki ('People of the Dawn') inhabited Maine when the first Europeans arrived. The French and English vied to establish colonies in Maine during the 1600s, but, deterred by the harsh winters, these settlements failed.

In 1652 Massachusetts annexed the territory of Maine to provide a front line of defense against potential attacks during the French and Indian Wars. And indeed Maine at times did become a battlefield between English colonists in New England and French forces in Canada. In the early 19th century, in an attempt to settle sparsely populated Maine, 100-acre homesteads were offered free to settlers willing to farm the land. In 1820 Maine broke from Massachusetts and entered the Union as a state.

In 1851 Maine became the first state to ban the sale of alcoholic beverages, the start of a temperance movement that eventually took hold throughout the United States. It wasn't until 1934 that Prohibition was finally lifted.

MAINE FACTS

» **Nickname** Pine Tree State

» **Population** 1.3 million

» **Area** 35,387 sq miles

» **Capital city** Augusta (population 18,600)

» **Other cities** Portland (population 66,200)

» **Sales tax** 5%

» **Birthplace of** poet Henry Wadsworth Longfellow (1807–82)

» **Home of** horror novelist Stephen King

» **Politics** split between Democrats and Republicans

» **Famous for** lobster, moose, blueberries, LL Bean

» **State drink** Maine gave the world Moxie, America's first (1884) and spunkiest soft drink

» **Driving distances** Portland to Acadia National Park 160 miles, Portland to Boston 150 miles

Information

If you're entering the state on I-95 heading north, stop at the well-stocked visitor information center on the highway.

Maine Bureau of Parks and Land (800-332-1501; www.maine.gov/doc/parks) Offers camping in 12 state parks.

Maine Coast

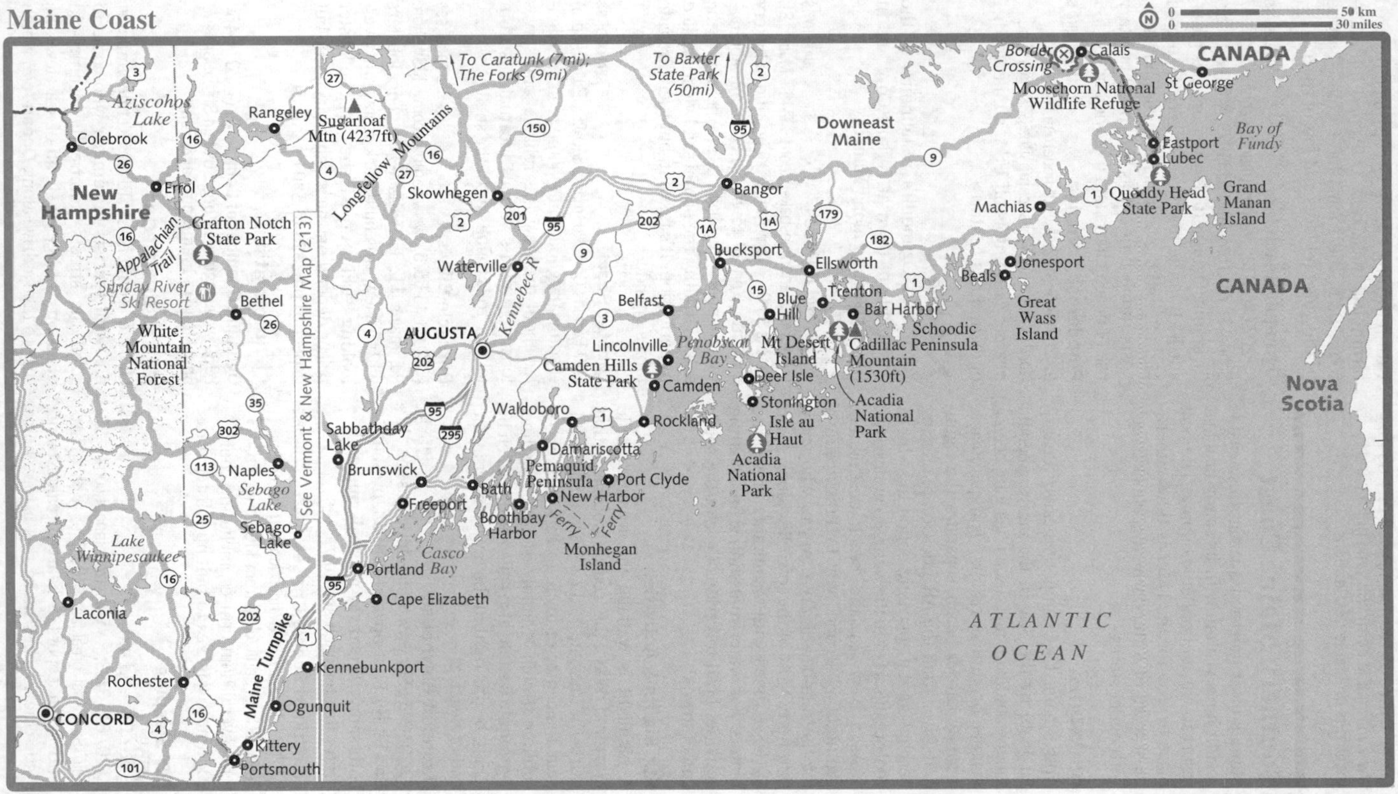

0 – 50 km
0 – 30 miles

CANADA
St George
Calais
Border Crossing
Moosehorn National Wildlife Refuge
Bay of Fundy
Eastport
Lubec
Quoddy Head State Park
Grand Manan Island
Machias
Downeast Maine
Jonesport
Beals
Great Wass Island
CANADA
Nova Scotia
To Baxter State Park (50mi)
To Caratunk (7mi); The Forks (9mi)
Bangor
Bucksport
Ellsworth
Trenton
Bar Harbor
Schoodic Peninsula
Blue Hill
Mt Desert Island
Cadillac Mountain (1530ft)
Acadia National Park
Deer Isle
Stonington
Isle au Haut
Acadia National Park
Penobscot Bay
Belfast
Lincolnville
Camden Hills State Park
Camden
Rockland
Waldoboro
Damariscotta
Pemaquid Peninsula
Port Clyde
New Harbor
Ferry
Ferry
Monhegan Island
Boothbay Harbor
Bath
Brunswick
Freeport
Casco Bay
Portland
Cape Elizabeth
Sabbathday Lake
AUGUSTA
Kennebec R
Waterville
Skowhegen
Longfellow Mountains
Sugarloaf Mtn (4237ft)
Rangeley
See Vermont & New Hampshire Map (213)
Kennebunkport
Ogunquit
Kittery
Portsmouth
Maine Turnpike
Naples
Sebago Lake
Sebago Lake
Bethel
Grafton Notch State Park
Appalachian Trail
Sunday River Ski Resort
White Mountain National Forest
Errol
Colebrook
Aziscohos Lake
New Hampshire
Lake Winnipesaukee
Laconia
Rochester
CONCORD
ATLANTIC OCEAN

Maine Office of Tourism (☎888-624-6345; www.visitmaine.com) Will send out a handy magazine on Maine destinations.

Southern Maine Coast

Maine's most touristed quarter, this seaside region lures visitors with its sandy beaches, resort towns and outlet shopping. The best place to stop for the latter is the southernmost town of Kittery, which is chockablock with outlet stores.

OGUNQUIT

Aptly named, Ogunquit means 'Beautiful Place by the Sea' in the native Abenaki tongue, and its 3-mile beach has long been a magnet for summer visitors. Ogunquit Beach, a sandy barrier beach, separates the Ogunquit River from the Atlantic Ocean, offering beachgoers the appealing option to swim in cool ocean surf or in the warmer, calmer cove.

As a New England beach destination, Ogunquit is second only to Provincetown for the number of gay travelers who vacation here. Most of the town lies along Main St (US 1), lined with restaurants, shops and motels. For waterfront dining and boating activities head to Perkins Cove at the south end of town.

Sights & Activities

A highlight is walking the scenic 1.5-mile **Marginal Way**, the coastal footpath that skirts the 'margin' of the sea from Shore Rd, near the center of town, to Perkins Cove. A sublime stretch of family-friendly coastline, **Ogunquit Beach**, also called Main Beach by locals, begins right in the town center at the end of Beach St.

Ogunquit Playhouse THEATER
(☎207-646-5511; www.ogunquitplayhouse.org; 10 Main St; 👪) First opened in 1933, presents both showy Broadway musicals and children's theater each summer.

Finestkind Scenic Cruises CRUISE
(☎207-646-5227; www.finestkindcruises.com; Perkins Cove; adult/child from $16/8; 👪) Offers several boat cruises, including cool 50-minute voyages to pull up lobster traps.

Sleeping

TOP CHOICE **Gazebo Inn** B&B $$
(☎207-646-3733; www.gazeboinnogt.com; 572 Main St; r incl breakfast $109-239; ❄📶🏊) Attentive innkeepers, a hearty breakfast and rustic-chic touches make this a top choice with returning guests. Occupying a restored farmhouse that's been converted into a 14-room B&B, the rooms have exposed wood beams, gas fireplaces and lots of space.

Ogunquit Beach Inn B&B $$
(☎207-646-1112; www.ogunquitbeachinn.com; 67 School St; r incl breakfast $139-179; ❄📶) A favorite among Ogunquit's gay visitors, this pleasant B&B in the town center is close to both Main St and the beach. The accommodating hosts supply little extras like complimentary use of beach chairs and a movie library.

Pinederosa Camping CAMPGROUND $
(☎207-646-2492; www.pinederosa.com; 128 North Village Rd, Wells; campsites $30; 🏊) The nearest camping is off US 1, a mile north of Ogunquit's center.

Eating

You'll find Ogunquit's restaurants on the south side of town at Perkins Cove and in the town center along Main St.

Bread & Roses BAKERY $
(www.breadandrosesbakery.com; 246 Main St; snacks $3-9; ⊙7am-7pm; 🌿) The kind of bakery that most small towns only dream about – the raspberry croissants are heavenly, the salads healthy, the panini sandwiches grilled to perfection. It's takeout, but there are cafe tables outside.

Lobster Shack SEAFOOD $$
(110 Perkins Cove Rd; mains $10-25; ⊙11am-8pm) If you want good seafood and aren't particular about the view, this reliable joint serves lobster in all its various incarnations from lobster rolls to lobster in the shell.

Barnacle Billy's SEAFOOD $$$
(☎207-646-5575; www.barnbilly.com; 183 Shore Rd; mains $12-35; ⊙11am-9pm) For lobsters with a view, this landmark restaurant overlooking Perkins Cove is the one. The lobster prices depend on the weight you choose but expect to pay $25 to $30 on average.

Information

Ogunquit Chamber of Commerce (☎207-646-2939; www.ogunquit.org; 36 Main St; ⊙9am-5pm Mon-Fri, 10am-3pm Sat & Sun)

KENNEBUNKPORT

On the Kennebunk River, Kennebunkport fills with tourists in summer who come to stroll the streets, admire the century-old mansions and get their fill of sea views. Be sure to take a drive along **Ocean Ave**, which runs along the east side of the Kennebunk River and then follows a scenic stretch of the Atlantic that holds some of Kennebunkport's finest estates, including the summer home of former president George Bush Snr.

Three public beaches extend along the west side of the Kennebunk River and are known collectively as **Kennebunk Beach**. The center of town spreads out from Dock Sq, which is along ME 9 (Western Ave) at the east side of the Kennebunk River bridge. The **Kennebunk/Kennebunkport Chamber of Commerce** (207-967-0857; www.visitthekennebunks.com; 17 Western Ave; 10am-5pm Mon-Fri year-round, 10am-3pm Sat & Sun Jun-Sep) has tourist information.

Sleeping

Franciscan Guest House GUESTHOUSE $$
(207-967-4865; www.franciscanguesthouse.com; 26 Beach Ave; r incl breakfast $89-159;) Serenity awaits at this suitably simple, but perfectly comfortable, 50-room guesthouse on the grounds of St Anthony's Monastery. Enjoy the outdoor saltwater pool and 60 acres of wooded walking trails.

Colony Hotel HOTEL $$
(207-967-3331; www.thecolonyhotel.com; 140 Ocean Ave; r incl breakfast $129-299;) Built in 1914, this grand dame of a summer resort evokes the splendor of bygone days. The 124 old-fashioned rooms have vintage cabbage-rose wallpaper and authentically creaky floors. Be aware they're anything but soundproof – upper floor rooms are quietest.

Green Heron Inn INN $$$
(207-967-3315; www.greenheroninn.com; 126 Ocean Ave; r incl breakfast $190-225;) In a fine neighborhood, overlooking a picturesque cove, this engaging inn has 10 cozy rooms and is within walking distance of a sandy beach and several restaurants. Breakfast is a multicourse event.

Eating

Bandaloop BISTRO $$$
(207-967-4994; www.bandaloop.biz; 2 Dock Sq; mains $17-27; 5-9:30pm;) Local, organic and deliciously innovative, running the gamut from grilled ribeye steak to baked tofu with hemp-seed crust. For the perfect starter order the skillet steamed Casco Bay mussels and a Peak's organic ale.

Hurricane AMERICAN $$$
(207-967-9111; www.hurricanerestaurant.com; 29 Dock Sq; mains $10-45; 11:30am-9:30pm) Right on the water with good food and a wonderful sense of place. If you're not whizzing through and have time for a leisurely lunch, order the handpicked Maine crabmeat sandwich on sourdough, a glass of wine and enjoy the view.

Clam Shack SEAFOOD $$
(2 Western Ave; mains $7-20; 11am-9:30pm) By the bridge at the west side of the Kennebunk River, this simple joint is justifiably famous for its fried clams, but the lobster roll overflowing with succulent chunks of lobster is the ultimate prize here.

Portland

The 18th-century poet Henry Wadsworth Longfellow referred to his childhood city as the 'jewel by the sea,' and thanks to a hefty revitalization effort, Portland once again sparkles. Its lively waterfront, burgeoning gallery scene and manageable size add up to great exploring. Foodies, rev up your taste buds: cutting-edge cafes and chef-driven restaurants have turned Portland into the hottest dining scene north of Boston.

Portland sits on a hilly peninsula surrounded on three sides by water: Back Cove, Casco Bay and the Fore River. It's easy to find your way around. Commercial St (US 1A) runs along the waterfront through the Old Port, while the parallel Congress St is the main thoroughfare through downtown.

Sights

Old Port NEIGHBORHOOD
Portland's heart thumps from the Old Port, where salt-scented breezes, brick sidewalks and gas-lamp-lit streets just beg for poking about. This restored waterfront district centers on the handsome 19th-century buildings lining Commercial St and the narrow side streets extending a few blocks inland. Once home to the brawny warehouses and merchant quarters of a bustling port, the focus has shifted from shipping to shopping. What to do here? Eat some wicked fresh seafood, down a local microbrew and peruse the numerous galleries.

Portland Museum of Art MUSEUM
(207-775-6148; www.portlandmuseum.org; 7 Congress Sq; adult/child $10/4, 5-9pm Fri free; 10am-5pm Sat-Thu, 10am-9pm Fri, closed Mon mid-Oct–May) Works of Maine painters Winslow Homer, Edward Hopper and Andrew Wyeth are showcased here. Maine's finest art

museum also boasts solid contemporary collections; post-Impressionist works by Picasso, Monet and Renoir; and a brilliant collection of Portland art glass. If you enjoy period homes, be sure to stroll through the restored 1801 **McLellan House**, entered through the museum and included in the ticket price.

Fort Williams Park LIGHTHOUSE
(admission free; sunrise-sunset) Up for a picnic in an unbeatable setting? Head 4 miles south of central Portland to Cape Elizabeth and this 90-acre park where you'll find **Portland Head Light** (207-799-2661; www.portlandheadlight.com; 1000 Shore Rd, Cape Elizabeth; lighthouse museum adult/child $2/1; 10am-4pm Jun-Oct), New England's most photographed lighthouse and the oldest (1791) of Maine's more than 60 lighthouses.

Portland Observatory Museum HISTORIC SITE
(207-774-5561; www.portlandlandmarks.org; 138 Congress St; adult/child $8/5; 10am-5pm late May-early Oct) History buffs won't want to miss this hilltop museum, built in 1807 as a maritime signal station to direct ships entering the bustling harbor. Its function was roughly on par with that of an airport traffic control tower today. From the top of this observatory, the last of its kind remaining in the USA, you'll be rewarded with a sweeping view of Casco Bay.

Longfellow House HISTORIC BUILDING
(207-879-0427; www.mainehistory.org; 489 Congress St; adult/child $12/3; 10am-5pm Mon-Sat, noon-5pm Sun May-Oct) The childhood home of Henry Wadsworth Longfellow (1807–82) retains its original character, complete with the poet's family furnishings. Admission includes entry to the adjacent **Maine Historical Society Museum**, which has exhibits on the state's history.

Children's Museum of Maine MUSEUM
(207-828-1234; www.childrensmuseumofme.org; 142 Free St; admission $9; 10am-5pm Mon-Sat, noon-5pm Sun, closed Mon Sep-May;) Folks with children in tow should head to this house of fun, next to the Portland Museum of Art.

Maine Narrow Gauge Railroad Co & Museum RAILROAD
(207-828-0814; www.mngrr.org; 58 Fore St; adult/child $10/6; 10am-4pm mid-May–Oct, shorter hr off-season;) Ride antique steam trains along Casco Bay; journeys depart on the hour.

Activities

For a whole different angle on Portland and Casco Bay, hop one of the boats offering narrated scenic cruises out of Portland Harbor.

Casco Bay Lines CRUISE
(207-774-7871; www.cascobaylines.com; 56 Commercial St; adult $13-24, child $7-11) This outfit tours the Portland coast and Casco Bay islands on a variety of cruises that last from 1¾ to six hours.

Maine Island Kayak Company KAYAKING
(207-766-2373; www.maineislandkayak.com; 70 Luther St, Peaks Island; tour $70; May-Nov) You can have Casco Bay Lines drop you off at Peaks Island and then hook up with this outfit for a half-day kayak tour of the bay.

Portland Schooner Company CRUISE
(207-776-2500; www.portlandschooner.com; 56 Commercial St; adult/child $35/10; May-Oct) Let the wind carry you away on a two-hour sail aboard an elegant century-old wooden schooner.

Sleeping

In addition to in-town choices, there are several chain hotels south of the city near the airport.

Morrill Mansion B&B $$
(207-774-6900; www.morrillmansion.com; 249 Vaughan St; r incl breakfast $149-239;) The former home of Charles Morrill, who founded B&M baked beans, this B&B has seven handsome guest rooms furnished in a trim, classic style. Little extras like a generous home-cooked breakfast and afternoon cookies add a welcoming touch. Ask about last-minute discounts.

Inn at St John INN $$
(207-773-6481; www.innatstjohn.com; 939 Congress St; r incl breakfast $79-169; @) Built in 1897 to accommodate train passengers arriving at the old Union Station, this Victorian hotel retains its period character with style. One caveat: the location opposite the bus station and hospital can be noisy. Light sleepers should request a room away from Congress St.

La Quinta Inn HOTEL $$
(207-871-0611; www.laquinta.com; 340 Park St; r incl breakfast $75-149; @) Best value among the chains, La Quinta has well-maintained rooms and a convenient location opposite the ballpark of the Portland Sea Dogs, a Boston Red Sox–affiliate team.

Portland Harbor Hotel HOTEL $$$
(207-775-9090; www.portlandharborhotel.com; 468 Fore St; r from $269;) Portland's finest hotel radiates period appeal from the coiffed lobby to the classically fitted rooms with sunny gold walls and pert blue toile bedspreads.

Eating

TOP CHOICE **Green Elephant** VEGETARIAN $$
(207-347-3111; www.greenelephantmaine.com; 608 Congress St; mains $9-13; 11:30am-2:30pm Tue-Sat & 5-9:30pm Tue-Sun;) Even carnivores shouldn't miss the brilliant vegetarian fare at this Zen-chic, Thai-inspired cafe. Start with the crispy spinach wontons, then move on to one of the exotic soy creations like gingered 'duck' with shiitake mushrooms. Save room for the incredible chocolate orange mousse pie.

Hugo's FUSION $$$
(207-774-8538; www.hugos.net; 88 Middle St; mains $24-30; 5:30-9pm Tue-Sat) James Beard award-winning chef Rob Evans presides over this temple of molecular gastronomy. Trained at Napa Valley's elite restaurant French Laundry, Evans masterfully fuses California influences with fresh New England ingredients. Pistachio-encrusted lobster anyone?

Great Lost Bear PUB $$
(www.greatlostbear.com; 540 Forest Ave; mains $8-16; noon-11pm;) Decked out in flea-market kitsch, this boisterous cave of a bar and restaurant is a Portland institution. You'll find dozens of regional brews on tap, big juicy burgers and all the usual pub grub. Skip the bland Tex-Mex offerings.

Standard Baking Co BAKERY $
(75 Commercial St; snacks $2-4; 7am-6pm Mon-Fri, 7am-5pm Sat & Sun) For a sweet breakfast treat, wander around to this Old Port bakery and order a blueberry cream scone and a chocolate croissant. Portland's best organic rustic breads are also made here.

Portland Lobster Co SEAFOOD $$
(www.portlandlobstercompany.com; 180 Commercial St; mains $10-23; 11am-9pm) Lobster stew, lobster rolls and lobster dinners shore up the menu at this harborfront shack. Take your meal to the deck and watch the boats pull up as you get crackin'.

J's Oyster SEAFOOD $$
(www.jsoyster.com; 5 Portland Pier; mains $6-24; 11:30am-11:30pm Mon-Sat, noon-10:30pm Sun) This well-loved joint has the cheapest raw oysters in town. Eat 'em on the deck overlooking the pier. The oyster-averse have sandwiches and seafood mains to choose from.

Drinking & Entertainment

Gritty McDuff's BREWPUB
(www.grittys.com; 396 Fore St; 11am-1am) This Old Port brewpub has it all: harbor views, high energy, good pub grub and award-winning ales. Order up a robust pint of Black Fly stout and join the crowd.

Big Easy Blues Club CLUB
(www.bigeasyportland.com; 55 Market St) There's live music nightly at this intimate music club featuring a lineup of rock, jazz and blues bands.

Blackstone's BAR
(www.blackstones.com; 6 Pine St) Portland's oldest gay bar is still a fine place for a drink.

Shopping

Go to Exchange and Fore Sts for gallery row.

Edgecomb Potters FINE ART
(www.edgecombpotters.com; 49 Exchange St) Where contemporary pottery, glass and sculpture rules.

Abacus CRAFTS
(www.abacusgallery.com; 44 Exchange St) For jewelry, glass and colorful gift items.

Maine Potters Market POTTERY
(www.mainepottermarket.com; 376 Fore St) A collective of top Maine potters.

Information

Greater Portland Convention & Visitors Bureau (207-772-5800; www.visitportland.com; 14 Ocean Gateway Pier; 9am-5pm Mon-Fri year-round, 9am-4pm Sat & Sun Jul & Aug) Pick up a free Portland guide here.

Maine Medical Center (207-662-0111; 22 Bramhall St; 24hr)

Portland Phoenix (www.thephoenix.com/portland) Free alternative weekly newspaper, covering events and entertainment.

Portland Public Library (www.portlandlibrary.com; 5 Monument Sq; 10am-7pm Mon-Thu, 10am-6pm Fri, 10am-5pm Sat;) Free internet access.

Post office (www.usps.com; 400 Congress St; 8am-7pm Mon-Fri, 9am-1pm Sat)

Getting There & Around

Portland International Jetport (PWM; www.portlandjetport.org) has nonstop flights to cities in the eastern US.

Greyhound (www.greyhound.com) buses and **Amtrak** (800-872-7245; www.amtrak.com) trains connect Portland and Boston; both take about 2½ hours and charge $20 to $24 one way.

The local bus **Metro** (www.gpmetrobus.com; fares $1.50), which runs throughout the city, has its main terminus at Monument Sq, the intersection of Elm and Congress Sts.

Central Maine Coast

Midcoast Maine is where the mountains meet the sea. You'll find craggy peninsulas jutting deep into the Atlantic, alluring seaside villages and endless opportunities for hiking, sailing and kayaking.

FREEPORT

The fame and fortune of Freeport, 16 miles northeast of Portland, began a century ago when Leon Leonwood Bean opened a shop to sell equipment to hunters and fishers heading north into the Maine wilderness. Bean's good value earned him loyal customers, and over the years the **LL Bean store** (www.llbean.com; Main St; 24hr) has expanded to add sportswear to its outdoor gear. Although a hundred other stores have joined the pack, the wildly popular LL Bean is still the epicenter of town.

Ironically, this former stopover for hardy outdoor types is now devoted entirely to city-style shopping, consisting of a mile-long Main St (US 1) lined with outlet stores that sell everything from dinnerware to shoes. **Freeport Merchants Association** (207-865-1212; www.freeportusa.com; 23 Depot St; 9am-5pm Mon-Fri) provides information.

Although 'shop till you drop' may be the town's motto, there's no need to stay on your feet all night – this town has some two dozen inns.

The Victorian-era **White Cedar Inn** (207-865-9099; www.whitecedarinn.com; 178 Main St; r incl breakfast $150-185;) is conveniently located within walking distance of the shops. The former home of Arctic explorer Donald MacMillan, it has seven atmospheric rooms, with brass beds and working fireplaces.

A favorite with shoppers, **Lobster Cooker** (207-865-4349; www.lobstercooker.net; 39 Main St; mains $9-22; 11am-7pm), just south of LL Bean, has generous fish sandwiches, homemade chowders and steamed lobsters.

For the best atmosphere, head to the casual, harbor-side **Harraseeket Lunch & Lobster Co** (207-865-4888; www.harraseeketlunchandlobster.com; 36 Main St, South Freeport; mains $10-25; 11am-7:45pm, to 8:45pm Jul & Aug), 3 miles south of Freeport center, for its popular lobster dinners, steamers and fried seafood. Feast at picnic tables within spitting distance of the bay.

BATH

Bath has been renowned for shipbuilding since Colonial times and that remains the raison d'être for the town today. **Bath Iron Works**, one of the largest shipyards in the USA, builds steel frigates and other ships for the US Navy. The substantial **Maine Maritime Museum** (207-443-1316; www.mainemaritimemuseum.org; 243 Washington St; adult/child $12/9; 9:30am-5pm), south of the ironworks on the Kennebec River, showcases the town's centuries-old maritime history, which included construction of the six-mast schooner *Wyoming*, the largest wooden vessel ever built in the USA.

BOOTHBAY HARBOR

On a fjord-like harbor, this achingly picturesque fishing village with narrow, winding streets is thick with tourists in the summer. Other than eating lobster, the main activity here is hopping on boats. **Balmy Days Cruises** (207-633-2284; www.balmydayscruises.com; Pier 8) runs one-hour harbor tours (adult/child $15/8) and day trips to Monhegan Island (adult/child $32/18). **Cap'n Fish's Boat Trips** (207-633-3244; www.mainewhales.com; Pier 1;) offers four-hour whale-watching trips (adult/child $38/25). **Tidal Transit** (207-633-7140; www.kayakboothbay.com; 18 Granary Way) leads three-hour kayak tours ($45 to $50) up coastal waters where wildlife abounds. The **Boothbay Harbor Region Chamber of Commerce** (207-633-2353; www.boothbayharbor.com; 192 Townsend Ave; 8am-5pm Mon-Fri) provides visitor information.

Sleeping & Eating

Tugboat Inn HOTEL $$
(207-633-4434; www.tugboatinn.com; 80 Commercial St; r incl breakfast $100-240;) Wings of this hotel, literally hanging over the water, are on piers, offering the most amazing water views you'll ever experience without being on a boat. You could cast a fishing pole from your front door. The rooms themselves are straightforward, nothing fancy – this is all about the setting.

PEMAQUID PENINSULA

Adorning the southernmost tip of the Pemaquid Peninsula, **Pemaquid Point** is one of the most wildly beautiful places in Maine, with its tortured igneous rock formations pounded by treacherous seas. Perched atop the rocks in the 7-acre **Lighthouse Park** (☎207-677-2494; www.bristolparks.org; Pemaquid Point; adult/child $2/free; ⏲sunrise-sunset) is the 11,000 candle power Pemaquid Light, built in 1827. A climb to the top will reward you with a fine coastal view. A star of the 61 surviving lighthouses along the Maine coast, you may well be carrying an image of Pemaquid Light in your pocket without knowing it – it's the beauty featured on the back of the Maine state quarter. The keeper's house now serves as the **Fishermen's Museum** (⏲9am-5:15pm mid-May–mid-Oct) displaying period photos, old fishing gear and lighthouse paraphernalia. Admission is included in the park fee. Pemaquid Peninsula is 15 miles south of US 1 via ME 130.

Topside Inn B&B **$$**
(☎207-633-5404; www.topsideinn.com; 60 McKown St; r incl breakfast $155-275) Perched on a hilltop, this 19th-century sea captain's house turned B&B has 21 comfortable rooms, hospitable owners and a quiet location. Request an upper-floor room in the main house for a stunning panorama.

Gray Homestead CAMPGROUND **$**
(☎207-633-4612; www.graysoceancamping.com; 21 Homestead Rd, Southport; campsites $37) Fall asleep to the lull of the surf at this oceanside campground 4 miles south of Boothbay Harbor via ME 27 and 238.

Lobster Dock SEAFOOD **$$**
(www.thelobsterdock.com; 49 Atlantic Ave; mains $10-25; ⏲11:30am-8:30pm) Boothbay Harbor crawls with lobster eateries. This is one of the best and cheapest. From chunky lobster stew to boiled lobster in the shell, this seaside place perfects everything that can be done with Maine's signature shellfish.

Blue Moon Cafe CAFE **$**
(54 Commercial St; mains $5-8 ⏲7:30am-2:30pm) Get a $5 breakfast with a million-dollar view on the waterfront deck of this family-run cafe serving omelets, blueberry pancakes and sandwiches.

MONHEGAN ISLAND

This small granite island with high cliffs and crashing surf, 9 miles off the Maine coast, attracts summer day-trippers, artists and nature-lovers who find inspiration in the dramatic views and agreeable isolation. Tidy and manageable, Monhegan is just 1.5 miles long and a half-mile wide. The online **Monhegan Island Visitor's Guide** (www.monheganwelcome.com) has information and accommodation links. Rooms typically book out in summer, so plan ahead if you're not just visiting on a day trip.

In addition to its 17 miles of walking trails, there's an 1824 **lighthouse** with a small museum in the former keeper's house and several artists' studios that you can poke your head into.

The 28 rooms in the 1870 **Monhegan House** (☎207-594-7983; www.monheganhouse.com; s/d incl breakfast $87/155;) have shared baths but offer cheery ocean and lighthouse views. The cafe at the Monhegan House sells pizza, sandwiches and ice cream.

Departing from Port Clyde, the **Monhegan Boat Line** (☎207-372-8848; www.monheganboat.com; round-trip adult/child $32/18) runs three trips daily to Monhegan from late May to mid-October, once a day for the rest of the year. The **MV Hardy III** (☎800-278-3346; www.hardyboat.com; round-trip adult/child $32/18; ⏲mid-Jun–Sep) departs for Monhegan twice daily from New Harbor, on the east side of the Pemaquid Peninsula. Both boats take approximately one hour and both have early morning departures and late-afternoon returns, perfect for day-tripping.

CAMDEN

With rolling hills as a backdrop and a harbor full of sailboats, Camden is a gem. Home to Maine's justly famed fleet of windjammers, it attracts nautical-minded souls.

You can get a superb view of pretty Camden and its surroundings by taking the 45-minute climb up Mt Battie in **Camden Hills State Park** (☎207-236-3109; 280 Belfast Rd/US 1; adult/child $4.50/1; ⏲7am-sunset) at the north side of Camden.

Lobster fanatics (and who isn't!) won't want to miss the **Maine Lobster Festival** (www.mainelobsterfestival.com), New England's ultimate homage to the crusty crustacean,

HOIST THE SAILS

Feel the wind in your hair and history at your side aboard the gracious, multimasted sailing ships known as windjammers. The sailing ships, both historic and replicas, gather in the harbors at Camden and neighboring Rockland to take passengers out on day trips and overnight sails.

Day sails cruise for two hours in Penobscot Bay from June to October for around $35 and you can usually book your place on the day. On the Camden waterfront, look for the 86ft wooden tall-ship **Appledore** (207-236-8353; www.appledore2.com) and the two-masted schooner **Olad** (207-236-2323; www.maineschooners.com).

Other schooners make two- to six-day cruises, offer memorable wildlife viewing (seals, whales and puffins) and typically include stops at Acadia National Park, small coastal towns and offshore islands for a lobster picnic.

You can get full details on several glorious options in one fell swoop through the **Maine Windjammer Association** (800-807-9463; www.sailmainecoast.com), which represents 13 traditional tall ships, several of which have been designated National Historic Landmarks. Among them is the granddaddy of the schooner trade, the *Lewis R French*, America's oldest (1871) windjammer. Rates range from $400 for a two-day cruise to $1000 for a six-day voyage and are a bargain when you consider they include meals and accommodation. Reservations for the overnight sails are a must. Prices are highest in midsummer. June offers long days, uncrowded harbors and lower rates, though the weather can be cool. Late September, when the foliage takes on autumn colors, captures the scenery at its finest.

held near the beginning of August in nearby Rockland.

The **Camden-Rockport-Lincolnville Chamber of Commerce** (207-236-4404; www.camdenme.org; 2 Public Landing; 9am-5pm), near the harbor, provides visitor information on the region.

Sleeping

Camden Maine Stay Inn B&B $$
(207-236-9636; www.camdenmainestay.com; 22 High St; r incl breakfast $135-270;) This stately 1802 home has lovely gardens, an agreeable period ambience and a fine location, just a couple blocks from restaurants and the waterfront. The friendly owners offer eight nicely appointed rooms and can share a wealth of insights on the area.

Whitehall Inn INN $$
(207-236-3391; www.whitehall-inn.com; 52 High St; r incl breakfast $119-219; May-Oct;) Camden-raised poet Edna St Vincent Millay got her start reciting poetry to guests at this century-old summer hotel. The 45 rooms have a vintage boarding-house character, some with in-room pedestal sinks and claw-foot tubs.

Captain Swift Inn B&B $$
(207-236-8113; www.swiftinn.com; 72 Elm St; r incl breakfast $119-245;) Crème brûlée French toast? That gives you just a taste of what you're in for at this pampering B&B. Occupying an 1810 Federal-style home, the eight comfortable rooms vary, but think hardwood floors, four-poster beds and a warm fireplace.

Camden Hills State Park CAMPGROUND $
(207-624-9950; www.campwithme.com; 280 Belfast Rd/US 1; campsites $27; mid-May–mid-Oct) This popular park has 107 forested campsites and 30 miles of scenic hiking trails; reservations advised in midsummer.

Eating

Camden Deli DELI $
(www.camdendeli.com; 37 Main St; mains $6-10; 7am-10pm) Family-run Camden Deli has a rooftop deck overlooking Camden Harbor and everything from Maine blueberry pancakes to Italian sub sandwiches piled high with salami and hot peppers. Come between 4pm and 7pm for free appetizers and $3 draft beers.

Cappy's SEAFOOD $$
(www.cappyschowder.com; 1 Main St; mains $8-15; 11am-11pm;) The star of Cappy's is the award-winning clam chowder, sold by the cup, bowl or pint. You can also order burgers, fresh fish sandwiches and lobster rolls but definitely start off with the rich, creamy chowder. Good bakery items too.

Waterfront SEAFOOD $$
(207-236-3747; www.waterfrontcamden.com; 40 Bayview St; mains $10-28; 11:30am-9pm) Perched smack on the water, this harborfront eatery specializes in seafood with a twist. Local rock crab and artichoke fondue, blackened haddock, lobster risotto – yowza!

BLUE HILL

Graced with period houses, Blue Hill is a charming coastal town that's home to artists and craftspeople. Start your exploration at Main St and the adjoining Union St, where you'll find several quality galleries selling Blue Hill pottery, sculptures and paintings.

Since 1902 the **Kneisel Hall Chamber Music Festival** (207-374-2203; www.kneisel.org; Pleasant St/ME 15; tickets $20-30; Fri-Sun late Jun-Aug) has attracted visitors from far and wide to its summer concert series. The **Blue Hill Peninsula Chamber of Commerce** (207-374-3242; www.bluehillpeninsula.org; 107 Main St; 10am-4pm Mon-Fri) has visitor information.

Evening hors d'oeuvres by the fireplace and a gourmet breakfast are just two of the perks at **Blue Hill Inn** (207-374-2844; www.bluehillinn.com; 40 Union St; r incl breakfast $145-225;), the town's landmark B&B since 1840.

Every artists' enclave needs a top-notch natural food store, and in these hills it's the **Blue Hill Co-op** (http://bluehill.coop; 4 Ellsworth Rd; mains $5-8; 7am-7pm), which also serves good cafe fare including crunchy granola, falafels and organic coffee.

Acadia National Park

The only national park in New England, Acadia encompasses an unspoiled wilderness of undulating coastal mountains, towering sea cliffs, surf-pounded beaches and quiet ponds. The dramatic landscape offers a plethora of activities for both leisurely hikers and adrenaline junkies.

The park was established in 1919 on land that John D Rockefeller donated to the national parks system to save from encroaching lumber interests. Today you can hike and bike along the same carriage roads that Rockefeller once rode his horse and buggy on. The park covers over 62 sq miles, including most of mountainous Mount Desert Island and tracts of land on the Schoodic Peninsula and Isle au Haut, and holds a wide diversity of wildlife including moose, puffins and bald eagles.

Information

Granite mountains and coastal vistas greet you upon entering **Acadia National Park** (www.nps.gov/acad). The park is open year-round, though Park Loop Rd and most facilities are closed in winter. An admission fee is charged from May 1 to October 31. The fee, which is valid for seven consecutive days, is $20 per vehicle between mid-June and early October, $10 at other times, and $5 on bike or foot.

Start your exploration at **Hulls Cove Visitor Center** (207-288-3338; ME 3; 8am-4:30pm mid-Apr–mid-Jun & Oct, 8am-6pm mid-Jun–Aug, 8am-5pm Sep), from where the 20-mile **Park Loop Rd** circumnavigates the eastern portion of the park.

Sights & Activities

PARK LOOP ROAD

Park Loop Rd, the main sightseeing jaunt through the park, takes you to several of Acadia's highlights. If you're up for a bracing swim or just want to stroll Acadia's longest beach, stop at **Sand Beach**. About a mile beyond Sand Beach you'll come to **Thunder Hole**, where wild Atlantic waves crash into a deep narrow chasm with such force that it creates a thundering boom, loudest during incoming tides. Look to the south to see **Otter Cliffs**, a favorite rock-climbing spot that rises vertically from the sea. At **Jordan Pond** choose from a 1-mile nature trail loop around the south side of the pond or a 3.5-mile trail that skirts the entire pond perimeter. After you've worked up an appetite, reward yourself with a relaxing afternoon tea on the lawn of Jordan Pond House. Near the end of Park Loop Rd a side road leads up to Cadillac Mountain.

CADILLAC MOUNTAIN

The majestic centerpiece of Acadia National Park is Cadillac Mountain (1530ft), the highest coastal peak in the eastern US, reached by a 3.5-mile spur road off Park Loop Rd. Four **trails** lead to the summit from four directions should you prefer hiking boots to rubber tires. The panoramic 360-degree view of ocean, islands and mountains is a winner any time of the day, but it's truly magical at dawn when hardy souls flock to the top to watch the sun rise over Frenchman Bay.

OTHER ACTIVITIES

Some 125 miles of **hiking trails** crisscross Acadia National Park, from easy half-mile nature walks and level rambles to mountain treks up steep and rocky terrain. A standout is the 3-mile round-trip **Ocean Trail**, which runs between Sand Beach and Otter Cliffs and takes in the most interesting coastal scenery in the park. Pick up a guide describing all the trails at the visitor center.

The park's 45 miles of carriage roads are the prime attraction for **cycling**. You can rent quality mountain bikes, replaced new at the start of each season, at **Acadia Bike** (☎207-288-9605; www.acadiabike.com; 48 Cottage St, Bar Harbor; per day $22; ⏱8am-8pm).

Rock climbing on the park's sea cliffs and mountains is breathtaking. Gear up with **Acadia Mountain Guides** (☎207-288-8186; www.acadiamountainguides.com; 228 Main St, Bar Harbor; half-day outing $75-140; ⏱May-Oct); rates include a guide, instruction and equipment.

Scores of **ranger-led programs**, including nature walks, birding talks and kids' field trips, are available in the park. Check the schedule at the visitor center. For information on kayaking and other activities see Bar Harbor.

Sleeping & Eating

The park has two campgrounds, both wooded and with running water, showers and barbecue pits. If these are full several commercial campgrounds can be found just outside Acadia National Park.

There are scores of restaurants, inns and hotels in Bar Harbor, just a mile beyond the park.

Blackwoods Campground CAMPGROUND **$**
(☎877-444-6777; www.recreation.gov; ME 3; campsites $20; ⏱year-round) This 279-site campground, 5 miles south of Bar Harbor, accepts advance reservations for all its sites.

Seawall Campground CAMPGROUND **$**
(www.recreation.gov; ME 102A; campsites $14-20; ⏱late May-Sep) This 210-site campground, 4 miles south of Southwest Harbor, operates mostly on a first-come, first-served basis but accepts some advance reservations.

Jordan Pond House AMERICAN **$$**
(☎207-276-3316; www.thejordanpondhouse.com; afternoon tea $9, mains $10-25; ⏱11:30am-9pm mid-May–Oct) For a memorable afternoon break sit on the lawn overlooking the pond and order afternoon tea served with warm popovers and homemade strawberry jam. The park's sole restaurant also has lobster rolls at lunchtime and prime rib dinners.

Getting There & Around

The convenient **Island Explorer** (www.exploreacadia.com; rides free; ⏱late Jun-early Oct) runs eight shuttle bus routes throughout Acadia National Park and to adjacent Bar Harbor, linking trailheads, campgrounds and accommodations.

Bar Harbor

Set on the doorstep of Acadia National Park, this alluring coastal town once rivaled Newport, RI, as a trendy summer destination for wealthy Americans. Today many of the old mansions have been turned into inviting inns and the town has become a magnet for outdoor enthusiasts. The **Bar Harbor Chamber of Commerce** (☎207-288-5103; www.barharbormaine.com; 1201 Bar Harbor Rd/ME 3, Trenton; ⏱8am-6pm late May–mid-Oct, 8am-5pm Mon-Fri mid-Oct–late May) has a convenient welcome center just before the bridge onto Mount Desert Island.

Sights & Activities

Abbe Museum MUSEUM
(☎207-288-3519; www.abbemuseum.com; 26 Mount Desert St; adult/child $6/2; ⏱10am-5pm) Abbe has fascinating presentations on the Native American tribes that hail from this region and thousands of artifacts ranging from pottery dating back more than a millennium to contemporary woodcarvings and baskets.

Bar Harbor Whale Watch CRUISE
(☎207-288-2386; www.barharborwhales.com; 1 West St; adult $32-62, child $20-32; ⏱mid-May–Oct;) This outfit has a wide variety of sightseeing cruises, including whale-watching and puffin trips. It also offers a ranger-led tour to Baker Island, a 130-acre island that's part of Acadia National Park but reachable only by boat.

Coastal Kayaking Tours KAYAKING
(☎207-288-9605; www.acadiafun.com; 48 Cottage St; 2½/4hr tours $38/48; ⏱8am-8pm) Kayaking tours generally go to the islands in Frenchman Bay or the west side of Mount Desert Island, depending on which way the wind's blowing. This outfit offers personalized tours, taking out a maximum of six kayaks at a time.

Downeast Windjammer Cruises CRUISE
(☎207-288-4585; www.downeastwindjammer.com; 27 Main St; adult/child $38/28) For a cruise in style, hop aboard the four-mast

schooner *Margaret Todd,* which sets sail three times a day.

Acadian Nature Cruises CRUISE
(☎207-288-2386; www.acadiannaturecruises.com; 1 West St; adult/child $27/16; ⊙mid-May–Oct) See bald eagles, seals and coastal sights on these narrated two-hour nature cruises.

Sleeping

There's no shortage of sleeping options in Bar Harbor, ranging from period B&Bs to the usual chain hotels.

Holland Inn B&B $$
(☎207-288-4804; www.hollandinn.com; 35 Holland Ave; r incl breakfast $95-175; ❄📶) Nine cheery rooms with frill-free decor, a hearty breakfast and innkeepers who make you feel at home are in store at this inn just a short stroll from the town center and waterfront.

Anne's White Columns Inn B&B $$
(☎207-288-5357; www.anneswhitecolumns.com; 57 Mount Desert St; r incl breakfast $75-165; ❄) Once a Christian Scientist church, this B&B's name refers to its dramatic columned entrance. Rooms have a quirky Victorian charm, with plenty of florals and bric-a-brac. Get here in time for the afternoon wine and cheese reception.

Aysgarth Station Inn B&B $$
(☎207-288-9655; 20 Roberts Ave; www.aysgarth.com; r incl breakfast $115-155; ❄) On a quiet side street, this 1895 B&B has six cozy rooms with homey touches. Request the Tan Hill room, which is on the 3rd floor, for a view of Cadillac Mountain.

Acadia Park Inn MOTEL $$
(☎207-288-5823; www.acadiaparkinn.com; ME 3; r incl breakfast $109-169; ❄📶) A good base for exploring the national park, this motel has comfy renovated rooms just 2 miles north of the park's main entrance.

Aurora Inn MOTEL $$
(☎207-288-3771; www.aurorainn.com; 51 Holland Ave; r $89-169; ❄📶) Retro motor lodge with 10 simple rooms and a convenient in-town location.

Eating & Drinking

TOP CHOICE **Cafe This Way** AMERICAN $$
(☎207-288-4483; www.cafethisway.com; 14½ Mount Desert St; mains breakfast $6-9, dinner $15-24; ⊙7-11:30am Mon-Sat, 8am-1pm Sun, 5:30-9pm nightly; 🖉) *The* place in Bar Harbor for breakfast. Vegans will love the scrambled tofu chock-full of veggies, old-schoolers the eggs Benedict with smoked salmon. Solid seafood menu at dinner.

McKays AMERICAN $$
(☎207-288-2002; www.mckayspublichouse.com; 231 Main St; mains $10-20; ⊙4:30-9:30pm Tue-Sun) One of Maine's buy-local and organic-when-possible restaurants, this pub-style eatery dishes up Maine crab cakes, farm-raised chicken and good ol' beer-battered fish and chips.

Trenton Bridge Lobster Pound SEAFOOD $$
(ME 3, Ellsworth; lobsters $10-15; ⊙10:30am-8pm Mon-Sat) Sit at a picnic table and crack open a boiled lobster at this traditional lobster pound bordering the causeway that connects Mount Desert Island to mainland Maine.

Finback Alehouse BISTRO $$
(☎207-288-0233; www.finbackalehouseme.com; 30 Cottage St; mains $10-20; ⊙11am-1am) Creative Maine-centric fare featuring locally caught seafood and juicy grass-fed sirloin burgers. Live music on weekends.

2 Cats CAFE $$
(☎207-288-2808; www.2catsbarharbor.com; 130 Cottage St; mains $8-17; ⊙7am-1pm; 🖉) The perfect place for scones and tea on drizzly day. Awesome lobster omelets too

Havana LATIN $$$
(☎207-288-2822; www.havanamaine.com; 318 Main St; mains $19-29; ⊙5-10pm) Maine goes Latin at this elegant dinner restaurant presenting seafood with a Cuban twist. Award-winning wine list.

Downeast Maine

The 900-plus miles of coastline running northeast from Bar Harbor are sparsely populated, slower-paced and foggier than southern and western Maine. Highlights include the **Schoodic Peninsula**, whose tip is a noncontiguous part of Acadia National Park; the lobster fishing villages of **Jonesport** and **Beals**; and **Great Wass Island**, a nature preserve with walking paths and good bird-watching, including the chance to see puffins.

Machias, with a branch of the University of Maine, is the center of commerce along this stretch of coast. **Lubec** is about as far east as you can go and still be in the USA;

folks like to watch the sun rise at nearby **Quoddy Head State Park** so they can say they were the first in the country to catch the sun's rays.

Calais (*ka*-lus), at the northern end of US 1, is a twin town to St Stephen in New Brunswick, Canada. Southwest of Calais is the **Moosehorn National Wildlife Refuge** (moosehorn.fws.gov; US 1, Baring; admission free; ⏲sunrise-sunset), which has hiking trails and offers opportunities to spot bald eagles, America's national bird.

Interior Maine

Sparsely populated northern and western Maine is rugged outdoor country. River rafting, hiking trails up Maine's highest mountain and the ski town of Bethel make the region a magnet for adventurers.

AUGUSTA

In 1827 Augusta became Maine's capital, but it's small and, truth be told, not terribly interesting. The **Kennebec Valley Chamber of Commerce** (☎207-623-4559; www.augustamaine.com; 21 University Dr; ⏲8:30am-5pm Mon-Fri) provides information on Augusta. If you're passing through, take a gander at the granite **State House** (1829), then stop at the adjacent **Maine State Museum** (☎207-287-2301; www.mainestatemuseum.org; State House Complex, State St; adult/child $2/1; ⏲9am-5pm Tue-Fri, 10am-4pm Sat; 👪), a treasure trove of fascinating exhibits tracing the state's natural and cultural history.

BANGOR

A boomtown during Maine's 19th-century lumbering prosperity, Bangor was destroyed by a sweeping fire in 1911. Today it's a modern, workaday town, perhaps most famous as the hometown of horror novelist Stephen King (look for his mansion – complete with bat-and-spider-web gate – among the grand houses along West Broadway). Can't miss the **Bangor Region Chamber of Commerce** (☎207-947-0307; www.bangorregion.com; 519 Main St; ⏲9am-5pm Mon-Fri) in the shadow of a 31-foot-tall (yikes!) Paul Bunyan statue.

SABBATHDAY LAKE

The nation's only active Shaker community is at Sabbathday Lake, 25 miles north of Portland. Founded in the early 18th century, a handful of devotees keep the Shaker tradition of simple living, hard work and fine artistry alive. You can tour several of their buildings on a visit to the **Shaker Museum** (☎207-926-4597; www.shaker.lib.me.us; adult/child $6.50/2; ⏲10am-4:30pm Mon-Sat late May–mid-Oct). To get there, take exit 63 off the Maine Turnpike and continue north for 8 miles on ME 26.

BETHEL

The rural community of Bethel, nestled in the rolling Maine woods 12 miles east of New Hampshire on ME 26, offers an engaging combination of mountain scenery, outdoor escapades and good-value accommodations. **Bethel Area Chamber of Commerce** (☎207-824-2282; www.bethelmaine.com; 8 Station Pl; ⏲9am-5pm Mon-Fri) provides information for visitors.

Activities

Bethel Outdoor Adventure KAYAKING
(☎207-824-4224; www.betheloutdooradventure.com; 121 Mayville Rd/US 2; per day kayak/canoe $45/65; ⏲8am-6pm) Right beside the banks of the Androscoggin River, this outfitter rents canoes and kayaks; rates include a shuttle upriver allowing you to paddle back at your own pace. It also rents bicycles, can set you up for fly-fishing and offers on-site camping.

Grafton Notch State Park HIKING
(☎207-824-2912; ME 26) If you're ready for a hike, head to this park north of Bethel for pretty mountain scenery, waterfalls and lots of trails of varying lengths.

Sunday River Ski Resort SKIING
(☎800-543-2754; www.sundayriver.com; ME 26; 👪) Located 6 miles north of Bethel, Sunday River is one of the best family-oriented ski centers in the region, with eight interconnected mountain peaks and 120 trails.

Sleeping & Eating

Chapman Inn B&B **$**
(☎207-824-2657; www.chapmaninn.com; 2 Church St; incl breakfast dm $35, r $89-129; ❄@📶) A great place to share notes with fellow travelers, this friendly, central 1865 B&B has 10 country-style rooms as well as hostel-style dorm beds. A gourmet breakfast, billiards, two saunas and free bicycles add to the fun.

Sudbury Inn & Suds Pub INN **$$**
(☎207-824-2174; www.sudburyinn.com; 151 Main St; r incl breakfast $99-159; ❄) The choice place to stay in downtown Bethel, this historic inn has 17 rooms, a pub with 29 beers on tap, pizza and live weekend entertainment. It

also has an excellent dinner restaurant serving Maine-centric fare (mains $18 to $26).

White Mountain National Forest CAMPGROUND **$**
(☎877-444-6777; www.recreation.gov; campsites $18) The Maine portion of this national forest has several basic campgrounds near Bethel.

CARATUNK & THE FORKS

For white-water rafting at its best, head to the **Kennebec River**, below the Harris Dam, where the water shoots through a dramatic 12-mile gorge. With rapid names like Whitewasher and Magic Falls, you know you're in for an adrenaline rush.

The adjoining villages of Caratunk and The Forks, on US 201 south of Jackman, are at the center of the Kennebec River rafting operations. The options range from rolling rapids and heart-stopping drops to calmer waters where children as young as seven can join in. Rates range from $75 to $130 per person for a day-long outing. Multiday packages, with camping or cabin accommodations, can also be arranged.

Reliable operators include the following:

Crab Apple Whitewater RAFTING
(☎800-553-7238; www.crabapplewhitewater.com)

Three Rivers Whitewater RAFTING
(☎877-846-7238; www.threeriverswhitewater.com)

Northern Outdoors RAFTING
(☎800-765-7238; www.northernoutdoors.com)

BAXTER STATE PARK

Set in the remote forests of northern Maine, **Baxter State Park** (☎207-723-5140; www.baxterstateparkauthority.com; per car $14) centers on Mt Katahdin (5267ft), Maine's tallest mountain and the northern terminus of the 2175-mile **Appalachian Trail** (www.nps.gov/appa). This vast 209,500-acre park is maintained in a wilderness state – no electricity and no running water (bring your own or plan on purifying stream water) – and there's a good chance you'll see moose, deer and black bear. Baxter has extensive hiking trails, several leading to the top of Mt Katahdin, which can be hiked round-trip in a day as long as you're in good shape and get an early start.

Baxter's 10 campgrounds contain 1200 campsites ($30 per day) but they do fill up, so it's best to book in advance.

At Millinocket, south of Baxter State Park, there are motels, campgrounds, restaurants and outfitters that specialize in white-water rafting and kayaking on the Penobscot River. Get information from the **Katahdin Area Chamber of Commerce** (☎207-723-4443; www.katahdinmaine.com; 1029 Central St, Millinocket).

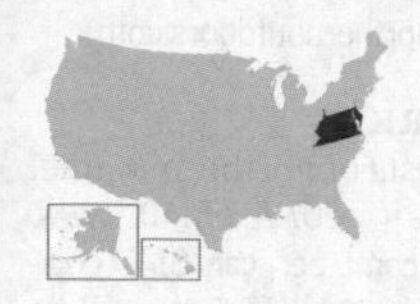

Washington, DC & the Capital Region

Includes »

Washington, DC 248
Maryland 270
Baltimore 271
Annapolis 281
Delaware 287
Virginia 291
Fredericksburg 295
Richmond 296
Petersburg 299
West Virginia 315
Eastern Panhandle 315

Best Places to Eat

» Minibar at Café Atlantico (p264)

» Blue Hill Tavern (p278)

» Robert Morris Inn (p284)

» Fat Canary (p301)

» Local (p308)

Best Places to Stay

» Hay-Adams (p261)

» Bellmoor Inn & Spa (p289)

» Colonial Williamsburg Historic Lodging (p300)

» Martha Washington Inn (p314)

» Greenbrier (p319)

Why Go?

No matter your politics, it's hard not to fall for the nation's capital. Iconic monuments, vast (and free) museums and venerable restaurants serving cuisine from around the globe: this is just the beginning of the great DC experience. There's much to discover: leafy cobblestoned neighborhoods, sprawling markets, heady multicultural nightspots and verdant parks – not to mention the corridors of power where visionaries and demagogues still roam.

Beyond the Beltway, the diverse landscapes of Maryland, Virginia, West Virginia and Delaware offer potent enticement to travel beyond the marble city. Craggy mountains, rushing rivers, vast nature reserves (including islands where wild horses run), sparkling beaches, historic villages and the magnificent Chesapeake Bay form the backdrop to memorable adventures: sailing, hiking, rafting, camping or simply sitting on a pretty stretch of shoreline, planning the next seafood feast. It's a place where traditions run deep – from the nation's birthplace to Virginia's still-thriving bluegrass scene.

When to Go

Washington, DC

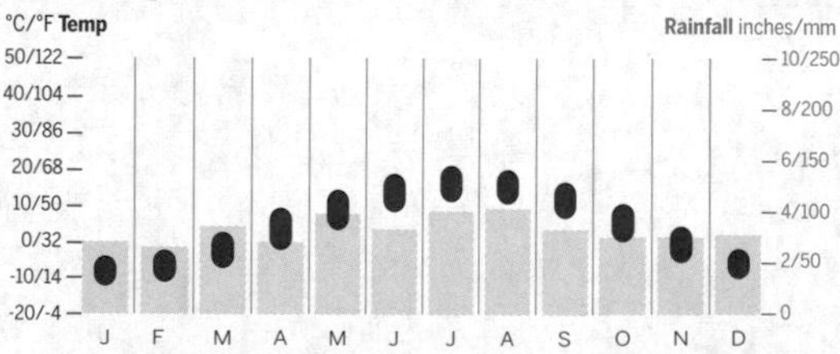

Mar-Apr Cherry blossoms bring crowds to the city in bloom during DC's most popular festival.

Jun-Aug Beaches and resorts heave; prices high and accommodations scarce.

Sep-Oct Fewer crowds and lower prices, but pleasant temperatures and fiery fall scenery.

Transportation

The region is served by three major airports: Washington Dulles International Airport (IAD), Ronald Reagan Washington National Airport (DCA) and Baltimore/Washington International Thurgood Marshall Airport (BWI). Norfolk International Airport (ORF) and Richmond International Airport (RIC) are smaller regional hubs.

Traveling by train is possible in some areas, with service provided by **Amtrak** (www.amtrak.com). Key towns connected by rail from DC include Baltimore, MD; Wilmington, DE; Harpers Ferry, WV; and in VA: Manassas, Fredericksburg, Richmond, Williamsburg, Newport News and Charlottesville.

TIPS ON VISITING WASHINGTON, DC

DC has a lot of great museums, but there's no way to see them all – even if you spend two weeks in the capital. Some sights – like the Washington Monument, US Holocaust Memorial Museum and Ford's Theatre – have limited admittance; if they're high on your list, go early to ensure you get a spot.

Aside from the Museum of the American Indian, which has a great restaurant, dining is limited along the Mall. One strategy: hit Eastern Market first to assemble a picnic for later in the day (on the Mall or around the Tidal Basin).

If possible, leave the car at home. The Metro is excellent, and driving in the city can get pricey – with overnight lots charging upward of $25 a night.

Best National Parks

» The New River Gorge National River (p318) is utterly Eden-like and home to white-tailed deer and black bears. It also has world-class white-water rafting.

» Shenandoah National Park (p309) provides spectacular scenery along the Blue Ridge Mountains, with great hiking and camping, including along the Appalachian Trail.

» Assateague Island National Seashore (p285) and Chincoteague (p306) are beautiful coastal environments with great blue herons, ospreys, blue crabs and wild horses.

» George Washington and Jefferson national forests (p310) protect more than 1500 sq miles of forests and alpine scenery bordering the Shenandoah Valley.

» Virginia's famous battlefields are also part of the park system. Good places to reconnect with America's darkest hours are Antietam (p286) and Manassas (p295).

DON'T MISS

With Chesapeake Bay at its doorstep, this region is pure heaven for seafood-lovers. The Maine Avenue Fish Market (p264) in DC is legendary. In Baltimore, Annapolis and all along Maryland's Eastern Shore, you'll also find top-notch seafood.

Fast Facts

» Population: 622,000 (Baltimore), 602,000 (Washington, DC), 440,000 (Virginia Beach)

» Distances from DC: Baltimore (40 miles), Williamsburg (152 miles), Abingdon (362 miles)

» Time Zone: Eastern

» States covered in this chapter: Washington, DC, Maryland, Delaware, Virginia, West Virginia

Did You Know?

» Thomas Jefferson was one of many Virginians to make wine in the state in the past 400 years. Now, Virginia has over 192 wineries and earns high marks at international awards shows.

Resources

» Washington (www.washington.org) lists upcoming events and loads of DC details.

» The Crooked Road (www.thecrookedroad.org) is the gateway to Virginia's heritage music trail.

» Virginia Wine (www.virginiawine.org) is essential for planning a route through wine country.

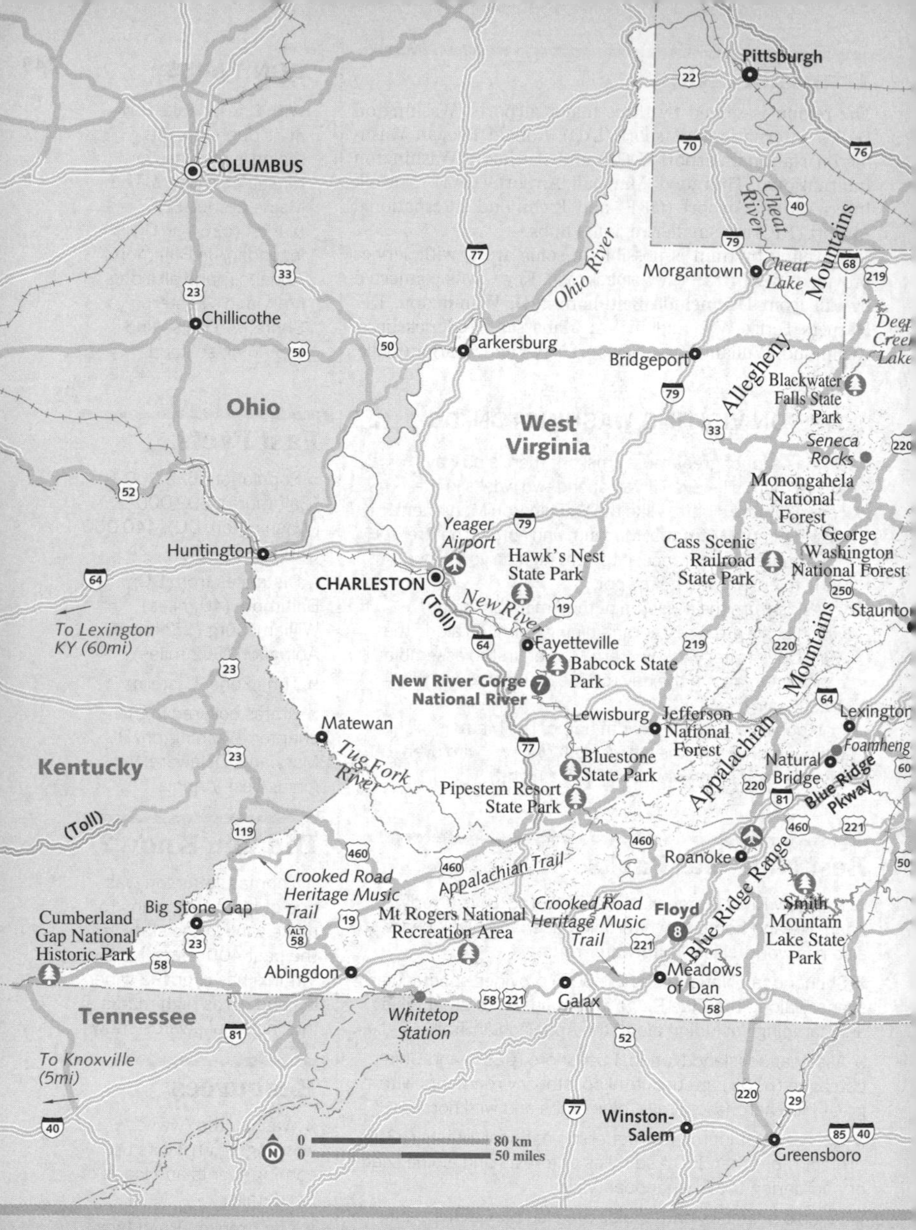

Washington, DC & the Capital Region Highlights

1. Visit Washington's **Smithsonian Institution museums** (p252), then watch the sunset over **Lincoln Memorial** (p255).
2. Trace America's roots at the living-history museum of **Colonial Williamsburg** (p299).
3. Explore the region's nautical past with a pub crawl through the cobblestoned port-town neighborhood of **Fells Point** (p276), Baltimore.
4. Take a Sunday drive along **Skyline Drive** (p309), followed by hiking and camping under

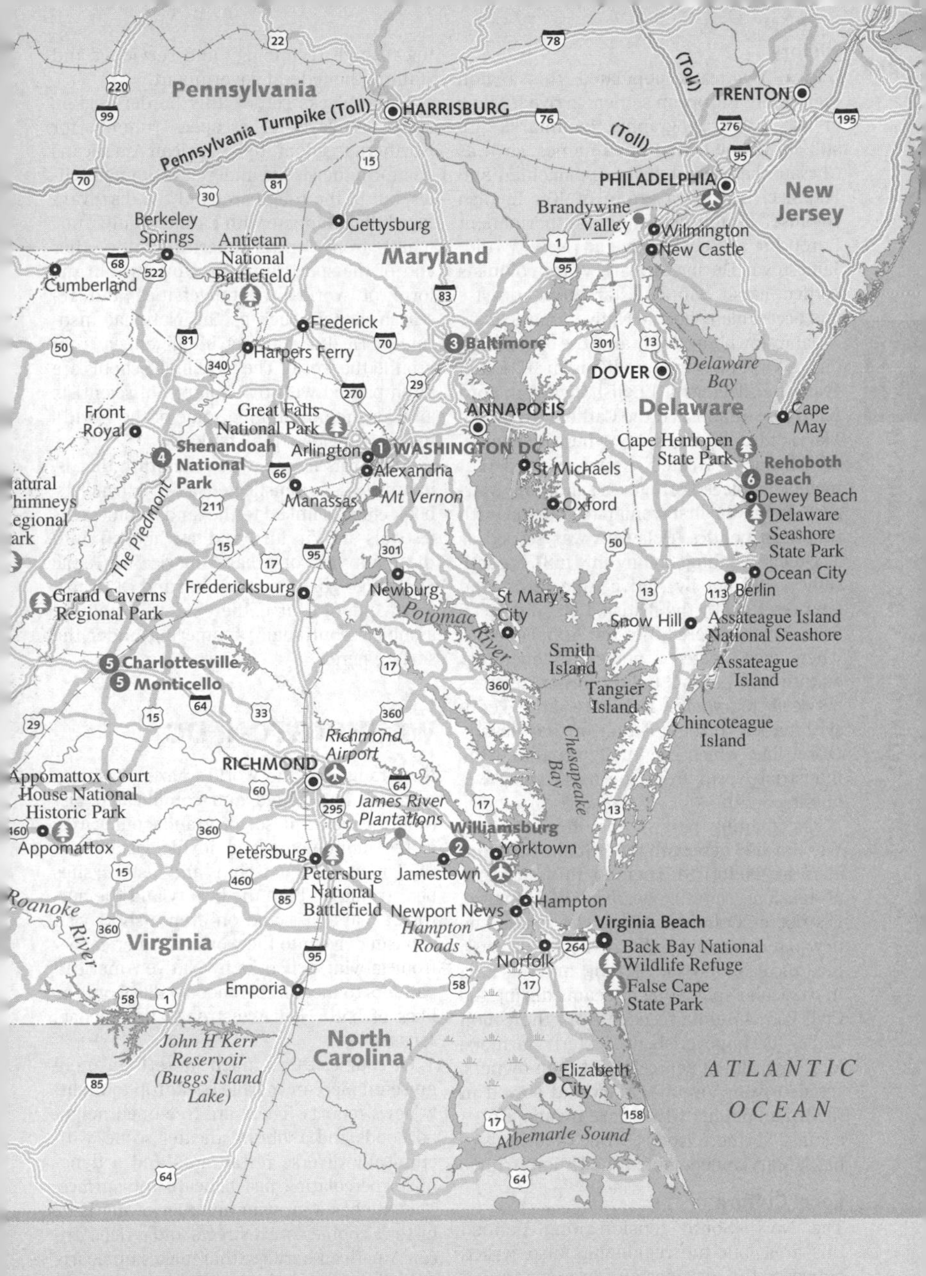

the stars in **Shenandoah National Park** (p309).

5 Marvel at Thomas Jefferson's masterpieces of **Monticello** (p306) and the **University of Virginia** (p307) in historic Charlottesville.

6 Stroll the boardwalk in the family- and gay-friendly resort of **Rehoboth Beach** (p288).

7 Tackle the rapids of **New River Gorge National River** (p318) in Fayetteville.

8 Feel the beat of the clog dancers at a jamboree in **Floyd, VA** (p314).

History

Native Americans populated this region long before European settlers arrived. Many of the area's geographic landmarks are still known by their Indian names, such as Chesapeake, Shenandoah, Appalachian and Potomac. In 1607 a group of 108 English colonists established the first permanent European settlement in the New World: Jamestown. During the early years, colonists battled harsh winters, starvation, disease and occasionally hostile Native Americans.

Jamestown survived, and the Royal Colony of Virginia came into being in 1624. Ten years later, fleeing the English Civil War, Lord Baltimore established the Catholic colony of Maryland at St Mary's City, where a Spanish-Jewish doctor treated a town council that included a black Portuguese sailor and Margaret Brent, the first woman to vote in North American politics. Delaware was settled as a Dutch whaling colony in 1631, practically wiped out by Native Americans, and later resettled by the British. Celts displaced from Britain filtered into the Appalachians, where they created a fiercely independent culture that persists today. Border disputes between Maryland, Delaware and Pennsylvania led to the creation of the Mason-Dixon line, which eventually separated the industrial North from the agrarian, slave-holding South.

The fighting part of the Revolutionary War finished here with the British surrender at Yorktown in 1781. Then, to diffuse regional tension, central, swampy Washington, District of Columbia (DC), was made the new nation's capital. But divisions of class, race and economy were strong, and this area in particular split along its seams during the Civil War: Virginia seceded from the Union while its impoverished western farmers, long resentful of genteel plantation owners, seceded from Virginia. Maryland stayed in the Union but her white slave-owners rioted against Northern troops, while thousands of black Marylanders joined the Union Army.

Local Culture

The North-South tension long defined this area, but the region has also jerked between the aristocratic pretensions of upper-class Virginia, miners and watermen, immigrant boroughs and the ever-changing rulers of Washington, DC. Since the Civil War, local economies have made the shift from agriculture and manufacturing to high technology and servicing and staffing the federal government.

Many blacks settled this border region, either as slaves or escapees running for Northern freedom. Today African Americans still form the visible underclass of major cities, but in the rough arena of the disadvantaged they compete with Latino immigrants, mainly from Central America. At the other end of the spectrum, ivory towers – in the form of world-class universities and research centers such as the National Institute of Health – attract intelligentsia from around the world. The local high schools are often packed with the children of scientists and consultants staffing some of the world's most prestigious think tanks.

All of this has spawned a culture that is, in turns, as sophisticated as a journalists' book club, as linked to the land as bluegrass festivals in Virginia and as hooked into the main vein of urban America as Tupac Shakur, go-go, Baltimore Club and DC Hardcore. And, of course, there's always politics, a subject continually simmering under the surface here.

WASHINGTON, DC

No stranger to the world's gaze, Washington, DC, is a proud and complicated city (politics makes it so) of grand boulevards, iconic monuments and idyllic vistas over the Potomac. Its museums and historic sites bear tribute to both the beauty and the horror of years past, and on even a short visit you can delve into the world of Americana – from moving artworks by Native American painters to memorable moonwalks from the likes of both Neil Armstrong and Michael Jackson.

Of course, DC is much more than mere museum piece or marble backdrop to nightly news reports. There are tree-lined neighborhoods and a vibrant theater scene, with ethnically diverse restaurants and a dynamism percolating just beneath the surface. The city has a growing number of markets, historic cobblestoned streets and a rich African American heritage that makes up nearly 50% of the population.

More than just a city of politicos, DC is home to folks who've passed homes through the family over generations, and new immigrants from El Salvador. Artists and creative types are drawn to Washington's undeniable intellectual energy, laboring alongside more

WASHINGTON, DC FACTS

» **Nicknames** DC, Chocolate City

» **Population** 602,000

» **Area** 68.3 sq miles

» **Capital city** Exactly!

» **Sales tax** 5.75%

» **Birthplace of** Duke Ellington (1899–1974), Marvin Gaye (1939–84), Dave Chappelle (b 1973)

» **Home of** The Redskins, cherry blossoms, all three branches of American government

» **Politics** Overwhelmingly democrat

» **Famous for** National symbols, crime, partying interns, struggle for Congressional recognition

» **Unofficial motto and license plate slogan** Taxation Without Representation

» **Driving distances** Washington, DC, to Baltimore 40 miles, Washington, DC, to Virginia Beach 210 miles

over-achieving and talented types than any city of this size deserves.

History

Like a lot of American history, the District of Columbia (DC) story is one of compromise. In this case, the balance was struck between Northern and Southern politicians who wanted to plant a federal city between their power bases. As potential capitals such as Boston, Philadelphia and Baltimore were rejected as too urban-industrial by Southern plantation owners, it was decided a new city would be carved at the 13 colonies' midway point, along the banks of the Potomac River. Maryland and Virginia donated the land (which Virginia took back in the 19th century).

DC was originally run by Congress, was torched by the British during the War of 1812, and lost the south-bank slave port of Alexandria to Virginia in 1846 (when abolition talk was buzzing in the capital). Over the years, DC evolved along diverging tracks; as a marbled temple to federal government and residential city for federal employees on the one hand, and an urban ghetto for northbound African Americans and overseas immigrants on the other.

The city finally got its own mayor in 1973 (Walter Washington, among the first African American mayors of a major American city). Ever under-funded, today DC residents are taxed like other American citizens, yet lack a voting seat in Congress. The educated upper class is leagues away from the neglected destitute; almost half the population has a university degree, yet a third are functionally illiterate.

With the election of Barack Obama in 2008, Washington, DC, has gained a bit of cool cachet – New Yorkers are coming here now, instead of the other way around! President Obama's habit of playing pickup basketball and patronizing local restaurants makes him the rarest of breeds: a president who doesn't just live in Washington, but is also a Washingtonian.

Sights

The capital was designed by two planners to be perfectly navigable. Unfortunately, their urban visions have mashed up against each other. Pierre L'Enfant's diagonal state-named streets share space with Andrew Ellicott's grid (remember: letters go east–west, numbers north–south). On top of that the city is divided into four quadrants with identical addresses in different divisions – F and 14th NW puts you near the White House, while F and 14th NE puts you near Rosedale Playground.

The majority of sites lie in the Northwest (NW) quadrant, while the most run-down neighborhoods tend to be in the Southeast (SE). Keep your urban wits about you at night, and be prepared for crowds during events such as the Cherry Blossom Festival. The Potomac River is to your south and west; Maryland lies to the north and east; and the Beltway, the capital ring road, encircles the entire package.

NATIONAL MALL

Marble buildings that resemble Greek temples, Abe Lincoln and a reflecting pool, memorials commemorating tragic conflicts of the past – the Mall is all this and more. It is America's great public space, where citizens come to protest their government, go for scenic runs, visit museums and commune with America's most revered icons. The 1.9-mile-long lawn is anchored at one end by the Lincoln Memorial, at the other by Capitol Hill, intersected by the reflecting pool and WWII memorial, and centered by the Washington Monument.

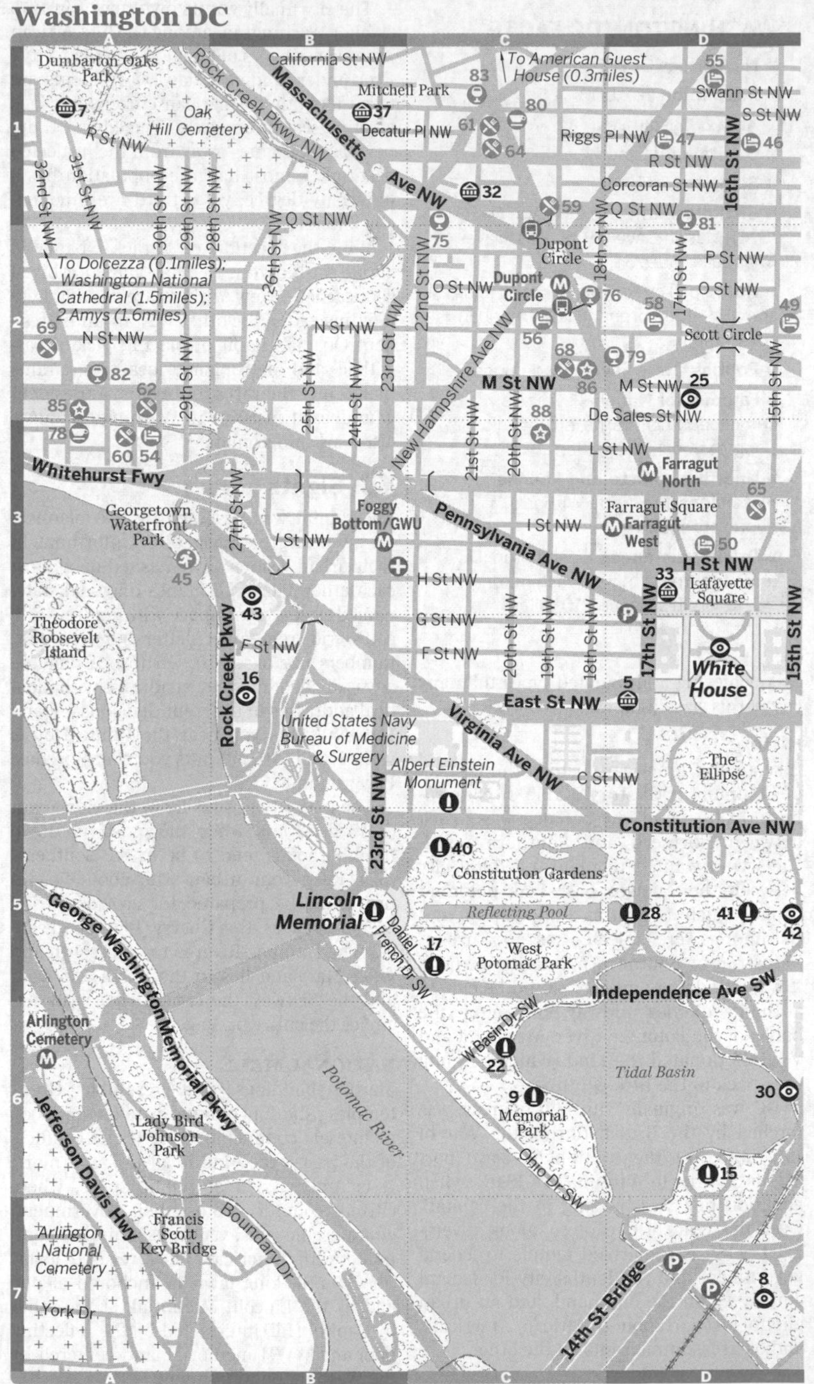
Dumbarton Oaks Park
Oak Hill Cemetery
Rock Creek Pkwy NW
California St NW
Massachusetts Ave NW
Mitchell Park
Decatur Pl NW
To American Guest House (0.3miles)
Swann St NW
S St NW
Riggs Pl NW
R St NW
16th St NW
Corcoran St NW
Q St NW
Dupont Circle
18th St NW
17th St NW
P St NW
O St NW
To Dolcezza (0.1miles); Washington National Cathedral (1.5miles); 2 Amys (1.6miles)
32nd St NW
31st St NW
30th St NW
29th St NW
28th St NW
26th St NW
22nd St NW
23rd St NW
25th St NW
24th St NW
N St NW
New Hampshire Ave NW
Scott Circle
M St NW
De Sales St NW
L St NW
15th St NW
Farragut North
Whitehurst Fwy
21st St NW
20th St NW
Georgetown Waterfront Park
27th St NW
Foggy Bottom/GWU
Pennsylvania Ave NW
I St NW
Farragut Square
Farragut West
H St NW
Lafayette Square
Theodore Roosevelt Island
Rock Creek Pkwy
G St NW
F St NW
19th St NW
White House
East St NW
Virginia Ave NW
United States Navy Bureau of Medicine & Surgery
Albert Einstein Monument
C St NW
The Ellipse
Constitution Ave NW
Constitution Gardens
Lincoln Memorial
Daniel French Dr SW
Reflecting Pool
West Potomac Park
George Washington Memorial Pkwy
Independence Ave SW
Arlington Cemetery
W Basin Dr SW
Tidal Basin
Potomac River
Memorial Park
Jefferson Davis Hwy
Lady Bird Johnson Park
Ohio Dr SW
Boundary Dr
Arlington National Cemetery
Francis Scott Key Bridge
York Dr
14th St Bridge
A
B
C
D
1
2
3
4
5
6
7
7
37
83
80
55
61
64
47
46
32
59
81
75
76
58
49
56
69
68
79
82
86
25
62
88
85
78
60
54
65
50
45
33
43
16
5
40
28
41
42
17
22
9
30
15
8

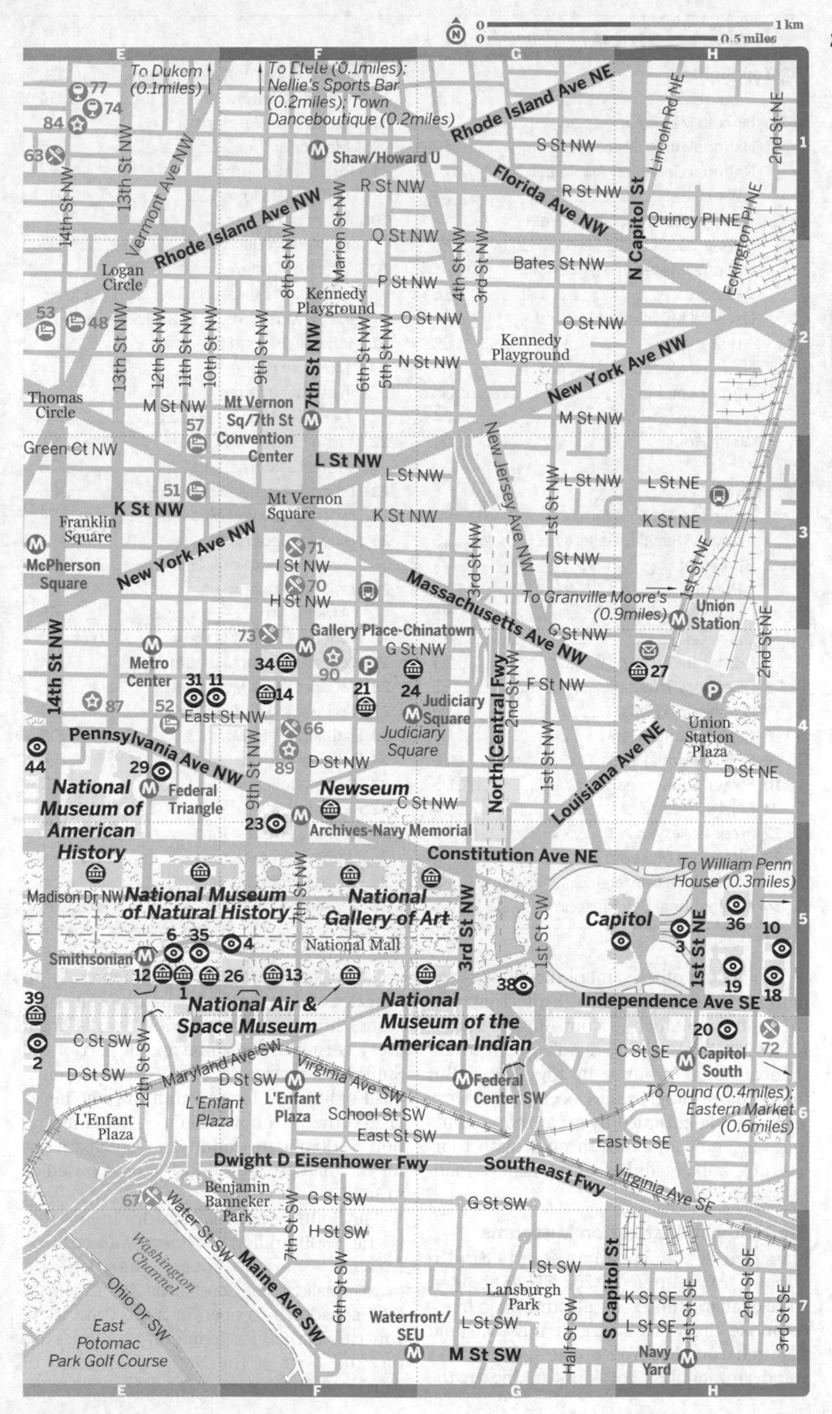

0 1 km
0 0.5 miles
E
F
G
H
1
2
3
4
5
6
7
To Dukem (0.1miles)
To Etete (0.1miles); Nellie's Sports Bar (0.2miles); Town Danceboutique (0.2miles)
Rhode Island Ave NE
S St NW
Shaw/Howard U
Florida Ave NW
R St NW
Q St NW
Quincy Pl NE
Bates St NW
P St NW
O St NW
N St NW
M St NW
L St NW
L St NE
K St NW
K St NE
I St NW
H St NW
G St NW
F St NW
East St NW
D St NW
D St NE
C St NW
14th St NW
13th St NW
12th St NW
11th St NW
10th St NW
9th St NW
8th St NW
7th St NW
6th St NW
5th St NW
4th St NW
3rd St NW
2nd St NW
1st St NW
Marion St NW
Vermont Ave NW
Lincoln Rd NE
2nd St NE
1st St NE
Eckington Pl NE
N Capitol St
Rhode Island Ave NW
Logan Circle
Kennedy Playground
New York Ave NW
Thomas Circle
Mt Vernon Sq/7th St Convention Center
Green Ct NW
Mt Vernon Square
Franklin Square
McPherson Square
Massachusetts Ave NW
New Jersey Ave NW
To Granville Moore's (0.9miles)
Union Station
Gallery Place-Chinatown
Metro Center
Judiciary Square
North Central Fwy
Union Station Plaza
Louisiana Ave NE
Pennsylvania Ave NW
National Museum of American History
Federal Triangle
Newseum
Archives-Navy Memorial
Constitution Ave NE
To William Penn House (0.3miles)
Madison Dr NW
National Museum of Natural History
National Gallery of Art
Capitol
National Mall
Smithsonian
3rd St NW
1st St SW
National Air & Space Museum
National Museum of the American Indian
Independence Ave SE
C St SW
C St SE
Capitol South
D St SW
Maryland Ave SW
Virginia Ave SW
L'Enfant Plaza
Federal Center SW
To Pound (0.4miles); Eastern Market (0.6miles)
School St SW
East St SW
East St SE
Dwight D Eisenhower Fwy
Southeast Fwy
Virginia Ave SE
Benjamin Banneker Park
G St SW
H St SW
Water St SW
Maine Ave SW
Washington Channel
Ohio Dr SW
East Potomac Park Golf Course
I St SW
Lansburgh Park
K St SE
L St SE
L St SW
M St SW
Waterfront/SEU
Navy Yard
Half St SW
S Capitol St
2nd St SE
3rd St SE
1st St SE
12th St SW
6th St SW
7th St SW
77 74 84 63 53 48 57 51 71 70 73 34 90 14 21 24 27 31 11 87 52 66 89 44 29 23 6 35 4 12 1 26 13 38 36 10 3 19 18 39 2 20 72 67

Washington DC

Top Sights

Capitol	H5
Lincoln Memorial	B5
National Air & Space Museum	F5
National Gallery of Art – East Wing	G5
National Gallery of Art – West Wing	F5
National Museum of American History	E5
National Museum of Natural History	E5
National Museum of the American Indian	G5
Newseum	F4
White House	D4

Sights

	American Art Museum	(see 34)
1	Arthur M Sackler Gallery	E5
2	Bureau of Engraving & Printing	E6
3	Capitol Visitor Center	H5
4	Carousel	F5
5	Corcoran Gallery	D4
6	Discovery Theater	E5
7	Dumbarton Oaks	A1
8	East Potomac Park	D7
9	FDR Memorial	C6
10	Folger Shakespeare Library	H5
11	Ford's Theatre	E4
12	Freer Gallery of Art	E5
13	Hirshhorn Museum & Sculpture Garden	F5
14	International Spy Museum	F4
15	Jefferson Memorial	D6
16	Kennedy Center	B4
17	Korean War Veterans Memorial	C5
18	Library of Congress (Adams Building)	H5
19	Library of Congress (Jefferson Building)	H5
20	Library of Congress (Madison Building)	H6
	Lincoln Museum	(see 11)
21	Marian Koshland Science Museum of the National Academy of Sciences	F4
22	Martin Luther King Jr National Memorial	C6
23	National Archives	F5
24	National Building Museum	F4
25	National Geographic Society's Explorer Hall	D2
26	National Museum of African Art	E5
	National Portrait Gallery	(see 34)
27	National Postal Museum	H4
28	National WWII Memorial	D5
29	Old Post Office Pavilion	E4
30	Paddleboat Rentals	D6
31	Peterson House	E4
32	Phillips Collection	C1
33	Renwick Gallery	D3
34	Reynolds Center for American Art	F4
35	Smithsonian Castle	E5
36	Supreme Court	H5

Perhaps no other symbol has housed the national ideal of massed voice affecting radical change so much – from Martin Luther King's 1963 'I Have a Dream' speech to antiglobalization protests in the 1990s. But hundreds of other rallies occur here every year; the Mall, framed by great monuments and museums and shot through with tourists, dog-walkers and idealists, acts as loudspeaker for any cause.

Smithsonian Institution Museums

Massive in size and ambition, the 19 **Smithsonian museums** (☎202-633-1000; www.si.edu), galleries and zoo – all admission free – comprise the world's largest museum and research complex. You could spend weeks wandering endless corridors taking in the great treasures, artifacts and ephemera from America and beyond. Massive dinosaur skeletons, lunar modules and artworks from every corner of the globe are all part of the Smithsonian largesse. Thanks go to the curious Englishman James Smithson, who never visited the USA but willed the fledgling nation $500,000 to found an 'establishment for the increase and diffusion of knowledge' in 1826.

The Smithsonian's latest work in progress is the $500-million **National Museum of African American History and Culture** (www.nmaahc.si.edu; Constitution Ave & 14th St NW), scheduled to open in 2015. Until then, you can peruse its temporary galleries on the 2nd floor of the National Museum of American History.

37	Textile Museum	B1
38	US Botanic Garden	G5
39	US Holocaust Memorial Museum	E6
40	Vietnam Veterans Memorial	C5
41	Washington Monument	D5
42	Washington Monument Kiosk	D5
43	Watergate Complex	B3
44	White House Visitor Center	E4

Activities, Courses & Tours

45	Thompson Boat Center	A3

Sleeping

46	Akwaaba	D1
47	Carlyle Suites	D1
48	Chester Arthur House	E2
49	District Hotel	D2
50	Hay-Adams	D3
51	HI-Washington, DC	E3
52	Hotel Harrington	E4
53	Hotel Helix	E2
54	Hotel Monticello	A3
55	Inn at Dupont Circle (North)	D1
56	Inn at Dupont Circle (South)	C2
57	Morrison-Clark Inn	E3
58	Tabard Inn	D2

Eating

59	Afterwords	C1
60	Baked & Wired	A3
61	Bistro Du Coin	C1
62	Citronelle	A2
63	Cork	E1
64	Dolcezza	C1
65	Georgia Brown's	D3
	Hill Country	(see 66)
66	Jaleo	F4
67	Maine Avenue Fish Market	E6
68	Malaysia Kopitiam	C2
69	Martin's Tavern	A2
70	Matchbox Pizza	F3
	Minibar at Café Atlantico	(see 89)
71	Ping Pong	F3
72	Sonoma	H6
73	Zaytinya	F4

Drinking

74	Bar Pilar	E1
75	Bier Baron	C1
76	Cafe Citron	C2
77	Cafe Saint-Ex	E1
78	Ching Ching Cha	A3
79	Current Sushi	D2
80	Filter	C1
81	JR's	D1
82	Mie N Yu Lounge	A2
83	Russia House	C1

Entertainment

84	Black Cat	E1
85	Blues Alley	A2
	Cobalt	(see 63)
86	Eighteenth Street Lounge	C2
	Kennedy Center	(see 16)
87	National Theatre	E4
88	Science Club	C3
89	Shakespeare Theatre	F4
	Ticketplace	(see 29)
90	Verizon Center	F4

All museums are open daily (except Christmas Day) 10am to 5:30pm unless noted. Some have extended hours in summer. Be prepared for lines and bag checks.

FREE National Air & Space Museum MUSEUM

(cnr 6th St & Independence Ave SW) The Air & Space Museum is the most popular Smithsonian museum; everyone flocks to see the Wright brothers' flyer, Chuck Yeager's *Bell X-1*, Charles Lindbergh's *Spirit of St Louis* and the *Apollo 11* command module. An IMAX theater, planetarium and ride simulator are all here (adult/child $9/7.50 each). More avionic pieces reside in Virginia at the Steven F Udvar-Hazy Center (p294), an annex to hold this museum's leftovers.

FREE National Museum of Natural History MUSEUM

(cnr 10th St & Constitution Ave SW) A favorite of the kids, the Museum of Natural History showcases dinosaur skeletons, an archaeology/anthropology collection, wonders from the ocean, and unusual gems and minerals, including the 45-carat Hope Diamond.

FREE National Museum of American History MUSEUM

(cnr Constitution Ave & 14th St NW) The Museum of American History is accented with the daily bric-a-brac of the American experience – synagogue shawls, protest signs and cotton gins – plus an enormous display of the original Star-Spangled Banner and icons such as Dorothy's slippers and Kermit the Frog.

FREE **National Museum of the American Indian** MUSEUM
(cnr 4th St & Independence Ave SW) The Museum of the American Indian provides a fine introduction to the indigenous people of the Americas, with an array of costumes, video and audio recordings, and cultural artifacts. Don't miss the regionally specialized menu of Native-inspired dishes at Café Mitsitam on the ground floor.

FREE **Hirshhorn Museum & Sculpture Garden** MUSEUM
(cnr 7th St & Independence Ave SW; ⌚museum 10am-5:30pm, garden 7:30am-dusk) The doughnut-shaped Hirshhorn Museum & Sculpture Garden houses a huge collection of modern sculpture, rotated regularly. It includes works by Rodin, Henry Moore and Ron Mueck, as well as paintings by O'Keeffe, Warhol, Man Ray and de Kooning.

FREE **National Museum of African Art** MUSEUM
(950 Independence Ave SW) The National Museum of African Art showcases masks, textiles and ceramics from the sub-Sahara, as well as ancient and contemporary art from all over the continent.

FREE **Arthur M Sackler Gallery** GALLERY
(1050 Independence Ave SW) Poring over ancient manuscripts and Japanese silk screens is a peaceful way to spend an afternoon at this quiet gallery and the adjoining **Freer Gallery of Art** (cnr Jefferson Dr & 12th St SW). Together they comprise the National Museum of Asian Art. The Freer, rather incongruously, also houses more than 1300 works by the American painter James Whistler.

Smithsonian Castle VISITOR CENTER
(1000 Jefferson Dr SW; ⌚8:30am-5pm) The red-turreted Smithsonian Castle is the visitor center for all museums, but is not that interesting in and of itself.

Other Museums & Monuments

FREE **National Gallery of Art** MUSEUM
(www.nga.gov; Constitution Ave NE, btwn 3rd & 4th Sts NW; ⌚10am-5pm Mon-Sat, 11am-6pm Sun) Set in two massive buildings, the National Gallery of Art houses a staggering art collection (over 100,000 objects), spanning the Middle Ages to the present. The neoclassical **west wing** houses European art through the 1800s, with an excellent range of Italian Renaissance works (including the continent's only da Vinci); the geometric **east wing**, designed by IM Pei, showcases modern art, with works by Picasso, Matisse, Pollock and a massive Calder mobile over the entrance lobby. An underground passage connects the two buildings.

FREE **US Holocaust Memorial Museum** MUSEUM
(www.ushmm.org; 100 Raoul Wallenberg Pl; ⌚10am-5:20pm) For a deep understanding of the Holocaust – its victims, perpetrators and bystanders – this harrowing museum

THE CAPITAL REGION IN...

One Week

Follow a version of the two-day DC itinerary and spend a day exploring underrated **Baltimore** or historic **Annapolis** before heading to Maryland's gorgeous **Eastern Shore** and the **Delaware beaches**. Head south to cross over the Chesapeake Bay bridge-tunnel and time-warp through Virginia's history: visit the nation's birthplace at **Jamestown** and take a wander through the 18th century at **Williamsburg**, followed by the nation's post–Civil War reconciliation at **Appomattox Court House**. Swing north through **Richmond**, where students, Dixie aristocracy and African American neighborhoods combine to form a fascinating whole, before rolling back into DC.

Two Weeks

Head to **Charlottesville** to experience Virginia's aristocratic soul (and good dining and B&B scene), then drive down her mountainous backbone through **Staunton**, **Lexington** and **Roanoke**. Follow the **Crooked Road** on a weekend to hear some of the nation's best bluegrass. Truck through West Virginia, stopping to hike, mountain bike or ski in the **Monongahela National Forest**, then go rafting in **New River Gorge** before returning to Washington via the hallowed battlefields of **Antietam**.

WASHINGTON, DC IN...

Two Days

Start your DC adventure at the Mall's much loved **Air & Space Museum** and **National Museum of Natural History**. Around lunchtime visit the **National Museum of the American Indian**, for aboriginal lore and a great meal. Wander down the **Mall** to the **Lincoln Memorial** and **Vietnam Veterans Memorial**. Before exhaustion creeps in, go to **U Street** for dining and drinks.

Next day, head to the **US Holocaust Memorial Museum**, **Arthur M Sackler Gallery** and **Freer Gallery of Art**. Catch the illuminated **White House** and the new **Martin Luther King Jr National Memorial** at night. For dinner, browse the restaurant-lined **Penn Quarter**.

Four Days

On day three, go to **Georgetown** for a morning stroll along the Potomac, followed by window-shopping and lunch at **Martin's Tavern**. Afterwards, visit the lovely **Dumbarton Oaks** gardens, then take a hike in **Rock Creek Park**. Head to **Dupont Circle** for dinner, followed by drinks at **Eighteenth Street Lounge**.

On the fourth day, visit the **Newseum**, **Capitol** and **Library of Congress**, then walk to **Eastern Market** for a meal. That evening, go to bohemian H Street NE; **Granville Moore's** is a good place to start off the night.

is a must-see. The main exhibit (not recommended for under-11s, who can go to a separate on-site exhibit that's also free) gives visitors the identity card of a single Holocaust victim, whom visitors can ponder while taking a winding route into a hellish past amid footage of ghettos, rail cars and death camps where so many were murdered. Only a limited number of visitors are admitted each day, so go early.

FREE Washington Monument MONUMENT

(⌚9am-10pm Jun-Aug, to 5pm Sep-May) Just peaking at 555ft (and 5in), the Washington Monument is the tallest building in the district. It took two phases of construction to complete; note the different hues of the stone. Tickets are free but must be reserved from the **kiosk** (15th St, btwn Madison St & Jefferson Dr SW; ⌚8:30am-4:30pm), or you can order them in advance by calling the **National Park Service** (☎877-444-6777; www.recreation.gov; tickets $1.50).

FREE Bureau of Engraving & Printing LANDMARK

(www.moneyfactory.gov; cnr 14th & C Sts SW; ⌚8:30am-3pm Mon-Fri) The Bureau of Engraving & Printing, aka the most glorified print shop in the world, is where all the US paper currency is designed. Some $32 million of it rolls off the presses daily. Get in line early at the ticket kiosk on Raoul Wallenberg Pl.

FREE Lincoln Memorial MONUMENT

(⌚24hr) Anchoring the Mall's west end is the hallowed shrine to Abraham Lincoln, who gazes peacefully across the reflecting pool beneath his neoclassical Doric-columned abode. To the left of Lincoln you can read the words of the Gettysburg Address, and the hall below highlights other great Lincolnisms; on the steps, Martin Luther King Jr delivered his famed 'I Have a Dream' speech.

FREE Vietnam Veterans Memorial MONUMENT

(Constitution Gardens; ⌚24hr) The opposite of DC's white, gleaming marble is this black, low-lying 'V,' an expression of the psychic scar wrought by the Vietnam War. The monument follows a descent deeper into the earth, with the names of the 58,267 dead soldiers – listed in the order in which they died – chiseled into the dark wall. It's a subtle, but profound monument – and all the more surprising as it was designed by 21-year-old undergraduate student Maya Lin in 1981.

FREE Korean War Veterans Memorial MONUMENT

(Constitution Gardens; ⌚24hr) The elaborate memorial depicts a patrol of ghostly steel soldiers marching by a wall of etched faces from that conflict; seen from a distance, the images on the wall form the outline of the Korean mountains.

FREE **National WWII Memorial** MONUMENT
(17th St, btwn Constitution & Independence Aves; ⏲24hr) Occupying one end of the reflecting pool (and controversially, the center of the Mall, the only war memorial to have that distinction), the National WWII Memorial honors the 400,000 Americans who died in the war, along with the 16 million US soldiers who served during the conflict. Stirring quotes are sprinkled about the monument.

Corcoran Gallery MUSEUM
(www.corcoran.org; cnr 17th St & New York Ave NW; adult/child $10/free; ⏲10am-5pm Wed-Sun, to 9pm Thu) DC's oldest art museum, the Corcoran Gallery, has had a tough time standing up to the free, federal competition around the block, but this hasn't stopped it from maintaining one of the most eclectic exhibitions in the country.

Newseum MUSEUM
(www.newseum.org; 555 Pennsylvania Ave NW; adult/child $22/13) Although you'll have to pay up, this massive, highly interactive news museum is well worth the admission price. You can delve inside the major events of recent years (the fall of the Berlin Wall, September 11, Hurricane Katrina), and spend hours watching moving film footage, perusing Pulitzer Prize–winning photographs and reading moving works by journalists killed in the line of duty.

CAPITOL HILL

The Capitol, appropriately, sits atop Capitol Hill (what L'Enfant called 'a pedestal waiting for a monument') across a plaza from the almost-as-regal Supreme Court and Library of Congress. Congressional office buildings surround the plaza. A pleasant residential district stretches from E Capitol St to Lincoln Park. Union Station, Capitol South and Eastern Market Metro stations serve this area.

Capitol LANDMARK
Since 1800, this is where the legislative branch of American government – ie Congress – has met to write the country's laws. The lower House of Representatives (435 members) and upper Senate (100) meet respectively in the south and north wings of the building.

A **visitor center** (www.visitthecapitol.gov; 1st & E Capitol Sts NE; ⏲8:30am-4:30pm Mon-Sat) showcases the exhaustive background of a building that fairly sweats history. If you book in advance (through http://tours.visitthecapitol.gov) you can go on a free tour of the building, which is as daunting as the exterior, if a little cluttered with the busts, statues and personal mementos of generations of Congress members.

To watch Congress in action, US citizens can request visitor passes from their representatives or senators (☎202-224-3121); foreign visitors show passports at the House gallery. Congressional committee hearings are actually more interesting (and substantive) if you care about what's being debated; check for a schedule, locations and to see if they're open to the public (they often are) at www.house.gov and www.senate.gov.

FREE **Library of Congress** LANDMARK
(www.loc.gov; 1st St SE; ⏲8:30am-4:30pm Mon-Sat) To prove to Europeans that America was cultured, John Adams plunked the world's largest library on Capitol Hill. The LOC's motivation is simple: 'universality,' the idea that all knowledge is useful. Stunning in scope and design, the building's baroque interior and neoclassical flourishes are set off by a Main Reading Room that looks like an ant colony constantly harvesting 29 million books. The visitor center and tours of the reading rooms are both located in the **Jefferson Building**, just behind the Capitol building.

FREE **Supreme Court** LANDMARK
(www.supremecourt.gov; 1 1st St NE; ⏲9am-4:30pm Mon-Fri) Even nonlaw students are impressed by the highest court in America. Arrive early to watch arguments (periodic Mondays through Wednesdays October to April). You can visit the permanent exhibits and the building's seven-spiral staircase year-round.

FREE **Folger Shakespeare Library** LIBRARY
(www.folger.edu; 201 E Capitol St SE; ⏲10am-5pm Mon-Sat) Houses the world's largest collection of Shakespeare materials.

FREE **National Postal Museum** MUSEUM
(www.postalmuseum.si.edu; 2 Massachusetts Ave NE; ⏲10am-5:30pm) Has the planet's largest stamp collection, plus an antique mail plane and touching war letters. A decent microbrewery sits above the museum.

FREE **US Botanic Garden** GARDENS
(www.usbg.gov; 100 Maryland Ave SW; ⏲10am-5pm) Hot, sticky and green with over 4000 different plant species on display.

TIDAL BASIN

It's magnificent to stroll around this man-made inlet and watch the monument lights wink across the Potomac. The blooms are loveliest during the Cherry Blossom Festival (p261), the city's annual spring rejuvenation, when the basin bursts into a pink and white floral collage. The original trees were a gift from the city of Tokyo, and planted in 1912. **Paddleboat rentals** (1501 Maine Ave SW; 2-person boat per hr $12) are available at the boathouse.

FREE Jefferson Memorial MONUMENT
(900 Ohio Dr SW; ⏲24hr) The domed memorial is etched with the Founding Father's most famous writings – although historians criticize some of the textual alterations (edited, allegedly, for space considerations).

FREE DR Memorial MONUMENT
(Memorial Park; ⏲24hr) A 7.5-acre tribute to the longest-serving president in US history and the era he governed. In a thoughtful, well-laid-out path, visitors are taken through the Depression, the New Deal era and WWII. It's best visited at night, when the interplay of rock, fountains and the lights of the Mall are enchanting.

FREE Martin Luther King Jr National Memorial MONUMENT
(www.mlkmemorial.org) After 25 years of planning and fundraising, the Martin Luther King Jr National Memorial opened in August 2011, on the banks of the Tidal Basin. It is the Mall's first memorial dedicated to both a nonpresident and an African American, and pays moving tribute (through quotes taken from a dozen speeches) to one of the world's great peace advocates.

DOWNTOWN

Downtown Washington began in what is now called Federal Triangle, but has since spread north and east, encompassing the area east of the White House to Judiciary Sq at 4th St, and from the Mall north to roughly M St. Hours of operation for the attractions listed here are 10am to 5:30pm daily, unless otherwise noted.

FREE National Archives LANDMARK
(www.archives.gov; 700 Constitution Ave NW; ⏲10am-7pm mid-Mar–early Sep, to 5:30pm Sep–mid-Mar) It's hard not to feel a little in awe of the big three documents in the National Archives. The Declaration of Independence, the Constitution and the Bill of Rights, plus one of four copies of the Magna Carta: taken together, it becomes clear just how radical the American experiment was for its time. The Public Vaults, a bare scratching of archival bric-a-brac, are a flashy rejoinder to the main exhibit.

FREE Reynolds Center for American Art MUSEUM
(cnr F & 8th Sts NW) Don't miss the Reynolds Center for American Art, which combines the **National Portrait Gallery** (www.npg.si.edu) with the **American Art Museum** (http://americanart.si.edu). From haunting depictions of the inner city and rural heartland to the self-taught visions of itinerant wanderers, the center has dedicated itself to capturing the optimism and critical self-appraisal of American art, and succeeds.

International Spy Museum MUSEUM
(www.spymuseum.org; 800 F St NW; adult/child $18/15; ⏲10am-6pm Sep–mid-Apr, 9am-7pm mid-Apr–Aug) You like those bits in the Bond movies with Q? Then you'll like the immensely popular International Spy Museum. All the undercover tools of the trade on display make this place great for (secret) history buffs. Get there early.

National Building Museum MUSEUM
(www.nbm.org; 401 F St NW; adult/child $8/5; ⏲10am-5pm Mon-Sat, from 11am Sun) Devoted to architecture and urban design, this under-appreciated museum is appropriately housed in a magnificent 19th-century edifice modeled after the Renaissance-era Palazzo Farnese in Rome. Four stories of ornamented balconies flank the dramatic 316ft-wide atrium, and the gold Corinthian columns rise 75ft high. Rotating exhibits on different aspects of the built environment are hidden in rooms off the atrium.

FREE Renwick Gallery MUSEUM
(cnr 17th St & Pennsylvania Ave NW) Near the White House, the Renwick Gallery is set in a stately 1859 mansion and exhibits a superb collection of American crafts and decorative art pieces. Highlights include over-the-top works like Larry Fuente's extravagantly kitsch *Game Fish* and Beth Lipman's ethereal *Bancketje (Banquet)*.

FREE Old Post Office Pavilion LOOKOUT
(www.oldpostofficedc.com; 1100 Pennsylvania Ave NW; ⏲10am-8pm Mon-Sat, noon-7pm Sun Apr-Aug,

10am-7pm Mon-Sat, noon-6pm Sun Sep-Mar) If you don't want to hassle with the lines at the Washington Monument, head to this little-visited 1899 Romanesque Revival building, where its 315ft observation tower gives great downtown panoramas. Down below, there's a floodlit atrium and international food court.

FREE **Ford's Theatre** HISTORIC SITE

(www.fordstheater.org; 511 10th St NW; ⏲9am-4pm) On April 14, 1865, John Wilkes Booth assassinated Abraham Lincoln in his box seat here. The theater still operates today; you can also take a tour of the theater, and learn about the events that transpired on that fateful April night. There's also a newly restored **Lincoln Museum** devoted to Lincoln's presidency that you can see as part of the tour. Arrive early to get a ticket, as limited numbers are admitted each day.

FREE **Peterson House** HISTORIC SITE

(www.fordstheater.org; 516 10th St NW; ⏲9am-5pm) Where Lincoln gave up the ghost the next morning. Closed indefinitely in 2010 for major renovations.

Marian Koshland Science Museum of the National Academy of Sciences MUSEUM

(www.koshland-science-museum.org; cnr 6th & E Sts NW; adult/child $5/3; ⏲10am-6pm Wed-Mon) A big, kid-friendly complex of hands-on, educational fun.

WHITE HOUSE & FOGGY BOTTOM

An expansive park called the Ellipse borders the Mall; on the east side is the powerbroker block of Pennsylvania Ave. Foggy Bottom was named for the mists that belched out of a local gasworks; now, as the home of the State Department and George Washington University, it's an upscale (if not terribly lively) neighborhood crawling with students and professionals.

White House LANDMARK

The White House has survived both fire (the Brits torched it in 1814 – only a thunderstorm saved its complete destruction) and insults (Jefferson groused that it was 'big enough for two emperors, one Pope and the grand Lama'). Although its facade has changed little since 1924, its interior has seen frequent renovations. Franklin Roosevelt added a pool; Truman gutted the whole place (and simply discarded many of its historical features – today's rooms are thus historical replicas); Jacqueline Kennedy brought back antique furnishings and historic details; Nixon added a bowling alley; Carter installed solar roof panels, which Reagan then removed; Clinton added a jogging track; and George W Bush included a T-ball field. Cars can no longer pass the White House on Pennsylvania Ave, clearing the area for posing school groups and round-the-clock peace activists.

A self-guided **tour** (☎202-456-7041; ⏲7:30am-11am Tue-Sat) will lead you through the ground and 1st floors, but the 2nd and 3rd floors are off-limits. These tours must be arranged (up to six months) in advance. Americans must apply via one of their state's members of Congress, and non-Americans must apply through either the US consulate in their home country or their country's consulate in DC. If that sounds like too much work, pop into the **White House visitor center** (www.whitehouse.gov; cnr 15th & E Sts NW; ⏲7:30am-4pm); it's not the real deal, but hey, there's executive paraphernalia scattered about.

The riverfront **Watergate complex** (2650 Virginia Ave NW) encompasses apartments, boutiques and the office towers that made 'Watergate' a byword for political scandal after it broke that President Nixon's 'plumbers' had bugged the headquarters of the 1972 Democratic National Committee.

ADAMS MORGAN, SHAW & U STREET

If it's not party time in Adams Morgan, it's time to get a hangover-cure lunch from an Ethiopian or Central American diner. This multiethnic neighborhood (especially 18th St) becomes sin central on weekend nights. The area isn't easily Metro-accessible; try to catch bus 98, which runs between Adams Morgan and U St stations.

To the east, Shaw stretches from around Thomas Circle to Meridian Hill Park and from N Capitol St to 15th St NW.

Lincoln Theatre LANDMARK

(☎202-328-6000; 1215 U St NW) The historic Lincoln Theatre was an early cornerstone of the nation's African American renaissance when it was founded in 1922. Luminaries such as DC native Duke Ellington as well as Louis Armstrong, Ella Fitzgerald, Billie Holiday and Sarah Vaughn and many others have all lit up the stage here. Following the 1968 assassination of Dr Martin Luther King Jr, riots devastated the commercial district. This area has since undergone a second renaissance; there are lots of excellent restaurants and bars around.

DUPONT CIRCLE

A well-heeled splice of gay community and DC diplomatic scene, this is city life at its best. Great restaurants, bars, bookstores and cafes, captivating architecture and the electric energy of a lived-in, happening neighborhood make Dupont worth a linger. The historic mansions have largely been converted into embassies, and Embassy Row (on Massachusetts Ave) runs through DC's thumping gay heart.

Phillips Collection MUSEUM
(www.phillipscollection.org; 1600 21st St NW; permanent collection admission free, special exhibitions adult/child $12/free; ⏲10am-5pm Tue-Sat, to 8:30pm Thu summer, 11am-6pm Sun) The first modern-art museum in the country (opened in 1921) houses a small but exquisite collection of European and American works – including pieces by Gauguin, van Gogh, Matisse, Picasso, O'Keefe, Hopper and many other greats. It's partially set in a beautifully restored Georgian Revival mansion.

Textile Museum MUSEUM
(www.textilemuseum.org; 2320 S St NW; suggested donation $8; ⏲10am-5pm Tue-Sat, from 1pm Sun) Set in two historic mansions in the Kalorama neighborhood, the oft-overlooked Textile Museum showcases beautifully wrought creations from across the globe, including pre-Columbian weavings, American quilts and Ottoman embroidery.

FREE **National Geographic Society's Explorer Hall** GALLERY
(1145 17 St NW; ⏲9am-5pm Mon-Sat, from 10am Sun) Rotating exhibits on worldwide expeditions are found here.

GEORGETOWN

Thousands of the bright and beautiful, from Georgetown students to ivory-tower academics and diplomats, call this leafy, aristocratic neighborhood home. At night, shop-a-block M St becomes congested with traffic, turning into a weird mix of high-school cruising and high-street boutique.

Get a historical overview from the **visitor center** (☎202-653-5190; 1057 Thomas Jefferson St NW; ⏲9am-4:30pm Wed-Sun), or join costumed guides on a history-intensive, hour-long, mule-driven barge trip along the **C&O Canal towpath** (adult/child $8/5; ⏲Apr–mid-Aug).

Dumbarton Oaks GARDENS
(www.doaks.org; cnr R & 31st Sts NW) A free museum featuring exquisite Byzantine and pre-Columbian art is housed within this historic mansion. More impressive, are the 10 acres of beautifully designed formal **gardens** (adult/child $8/5 Apr-Oct, free Nov-Mar; ⏲2-6pm Tue-Sun), which are simply stunning during the springtime blooms. Visit on weekdays to beat the crowds.

Georgetown University UNIVERSITY
(www.georgetown.edu; 37th & O Sts NW) Bill Clinton went to school here, which should give you an idea of the student body: smart, hard-working party people.

UPPER NORTHWEST DC

FREE **National Zoological Park** ZOO
(http://nationalzoo.si.edu; 3000 Connecticut Ave NW; ⏲10am-6pm Apr-Oct, to 4:30pm Nov-Mar) Home to over 2000 individual animals (400 different species) in natural habitats, this 163-acre zoo is famed for its giant pandas Mei Xiang and Tian Tian. Other highlights include the African lion pride, Asian elephants and dangling orangutans swinging 50ft overhead from steel cables and interconnected towers (the 'O Line').

Washington National Cathedral CHURCH
(☎202-537-6200; www.nationalcathedral.org; 3101 Wisconsin Ave NW; suggested donation $5; ⏲10am-5:30pm Mon-Fri, to 4:30pm Sat, 8am-5pm Sun) This Gothic cathedral, as dramatic as its European counterparts, blends both the spiritual and the profane in its architectural treasures. The stained-glass windows are stunning (check out the 'Space Window' with an imbedded lunar rock); you'll need binoculars to spy the Darth Vader gargoyle on the exterior. Specialized tours delve deeper into the esoteric; call or go online for the schedule.

ANACOSTIA

The drive from Georgetown to Anacostia takes about 30 minutes and the patience to endure a world of income disparity. The neighborhood's smack-, crack- and brick row houses sitting mere miles from the Mall form one of DC's great contradictory panoramas, yet strong communities persist. More tourists started arriving on the first day of the baseball season in 2008, when Nationals Stadium opened, bringing with it double-edged gentrification. The impact of renovation dollars can already be seen at some spruced-up intersections.

Frederick Douglass National Historic Site LANDMARK
(www.nps.gov/frdo; 1411 W St SE; ⌚9am-4pm) Freedom fighter, author and statesman Frederick Douglass occupied this beautifully sited hilltop house from 1878 until his death in 1895. Original furnishings, books, photographs and other personal belongings paint a compelling portrait of both the private and public life of this great man. Visits into the home are by organized tour only; call ☎877-444-6777 for times and to reserve a space ($1.50 reservation fee per ticket).

FREE **Anacostia Community Museum** MUSEUM
(☎202-633-4820; http://anacostia.si.edu; 1901 Fort Pl SE; ⌚10am-5pm) This Smithsonian museum is surrounded by the community that is the subject of its educational mission, and houses good rotating exhibits on the African American experience in the USA. Call ahead, as the museum closes for about a month between installations.

Activities

Under the auspices of the National Park Service (NPS), the 1754 acres of **Rock Creek Park** follow Rock Creek as it winds through the northwest of the city. There are miles of bicycling, hiking and horseback-riding trails, and even a few coyotes. The C&O Canal offers bicycling and hiking trails in canalside parks, and the lovely 11-mile **Capital Crescent Trail** (www.cctrail.org) connects Georgetown north to Silver Spring, MD, via some splendid Potomac River views. Fifteen miles north of DC, **Great Falls National Park** (www.nps.gov/grfa; per vehicle $5) is an outstanding slice of wilderness, great for rafting or rock climbing some of the beautiful cliffs that hang over the Potomac.

The **Potomac Heritage National Scenic Trail** (www.nps.gov/pohe) connects Chesapeake Bay to the Allegheny Highlands along an 830-mile network that includes the C&O Canal towpath, the 17-mile Mt Vernon Trail (Virginia) and the 75-mile Laurel Highlands Trail (Pennsylvania).

Thompson Boat Center BOAT RENTAL
(☎202-333-9543; www.thompsonboatcenter.com; cnr Virginia Ave & Rock Creek Pkwy NW; ⌚8am-5pm) At the Potomac River end of Rock Creek Park, it rents canoes (per hour $12), kayaks (per hour single/double $10/17) and bikes (per hour/day $7/28).

Big Wheel Bikes BICYCLE RENTAL
(☎202-337-0254; www.bigwheelbikes.com; 1034 33rd St NW; per hr/day $7/35; ⌚11am-7pm Tue-Fri, 10am-6pm Sat & Sun) A good bike-rental outfitter.

Capitol Bikeshare BICYCLE RENTAL
(☎877-430-2453; www.capitolbikeshare.com) Modeled on bike-sharing schemes in Europe, Capitol Bikeshare has a network of 1000-plus bicycles scattered at 100-odd stations around DC. To check out a bike, select the membership (24 hours is $5, five days is $15), insert credit card, and off you go. The first 30 minutes are free; after that, rates rise exponentially ($1.50/3/6 per extra 30/60/90 minutes). Call or go online for complete details.

Washington, DC for Children

Top destination for families is undoubtedly the (free!) zoo (p259). Museums around the city will entertain and educate children of all ages. But if you – or they – tire of indoor attractions, there are plenty of enticing green spaces, such as the 328-acre **East Potomac Park** (Ohio Dr SW), with playground, outdoor swimming pool, mini-golf and picnic facilities; it runs southeast of the Tidal Basin.

The DC-area **Our Kids** (www.our-kids.com) website has loads of listings for kid-centric shows and events, family-friendly restaurants and loads of activity ideas.

Many hotels offer babysitting services, but you can also book through the reputable organization **Mothers' Aides** (☎703-250-0700; www.mothersaides.com), with rates from $15 to $20 per hour.

THE MALL

The wide-open spaces of the Mall are perfect for outdoor family fun, whether you want to throw a Frisbee, have a picnic, ride the old-fashioned **carousel** (tickets $2.50) or stroll through museums.

Kids like things that go squish and/or make other things go squish; they can find both in the dinosaurs and insects of the National Museum of Natural History (p253). The Kennedy Center (p268) puts on entertaining shows for tots, and the National Air & Space Museum (p253) has moon rocks, IMAX films and a wild simulation ride.

The National Theatre (p268) offers free Saturday-morning performances, from puppet shows to tap dancers (reservations required).

Discovery Theater THEATER
(☎202-633-8700; www.discoverytheater.org; 1100 Jefferson Dr SW; adult/child $6/5) In the basement of the Ripley Center, stages entertaining shows for young audiences.

GREATER DC

National Children's Museum MUSEUM
(☎301-686-0225; www.ncm.museum; 112 Waterfront St, National Harbor, MD) Will reopen its expanded doors in 2013 in the National Harbor Complex, 10 miles south of the Mall.

Six Flags America AMUSEMENT PARK
(☎301-249-1500; www.sixflags.com/america; adult/child over 2yr $50/35; May-Oct) Located about 15 miles east of downtown in Largo, MD; offers a full array of roller coasters and tamer kiddie rides.

Tours

DC Metro Food Tours WALKING
(☎800-979-3370; www.dcmetrofoodtours.com; per person $27-60) These walking tours take in the culinary riches of DC, exploring various neighborhoods and stopping for bites along the way. Offerings include Eastern Market, U Street, Little Ethiopia, Georgetown and Alexandria, VA.

DC by Foot WALKING
(www.dcbyfoot.com) Guides for this free, tip-based walking tour dispense intriguing stories and historical details on different walks covering the National Mall, Arlington Cemetery and Lincoln's assassination.

Old Town Trolley Tours BUS
(☎888-910-8687; www.trolleytours.com; adult/child $35/25) This open-sided bus offers hop-on, hop-off exploring of the major sights of DC. The outfit also offers a 'monuments by moonlight' tour and the DC Ducks tour, via amphibious vehicle that plunges into the Potomac.

Bike and Roll BICYCLE
(☎202-842-2453; www.bikethesites.com; adult/child from $40/30; Mar-Nov) Offers a handful of day and evening bike tours around the city (plus combo boat–bike trips to Mt Vernon).

City Segway Tours SEGWAY
(☎202-626-0017; http://citysegwaytours.com/washington-dc) Extremely popular and relaxing way of seeing the major sites along the Mall and in Penn Quarter ($70).

Festivals & Events

National Cherry Blossom Festival CULTURAL
(www.nationalcherryblossomfestival.org) Held late March to early April. DC at her prettiest.

Smithsonian's Folklife Festival CULTURAL
(www.festival.si.edu) This fun family event, held over two weekends in June and July, features distinctive regional folk art, crafts, food and music.

Independence Day CULTURAL
Not surprisingly, a big deal here, celebrated on July 4 with a parade, an open-air concert and fireworks over the Mall.

Sleeping

For B&Bs and private apartments citywide, contact **Bed & Breakfast Accommodations** (☎877-893-3233; www.bedandbreakfastdc.com).

If you bring a car to DC, plan on $20 and up per day for in-and-out privileges (or stay in Arlington or Alexandria, where some hotels have free parking). Rates below don't include DC's hefty 14.5% hotel tax.

CAPITOL HILL

William Penn House HOSTEL $
(☎202-543-5560; www.williampennhouse.org; 515 E Capitol St SE; dm incl breakfast from $40;) On a peaceful street five blocks east of the Capitol, this friendly Quaker-run guesthouse with garden offers clean, well-maintained dorms, but it could use more bathrooms. The curious and spiritually minded can rise for the 7:30am worship service.

DOWNTOWN & WHITE HOUSE AREA

Hay-Adams LUXURY HOTEL $$$
(☎202-638-6600; www.hayadams-dc.com; 800 16th St NW; r from $379; P) One of the city's great heritage hotels, the Hay is a beautiful old building, where 'nothing is overlooked but the White House.' It's named for two mansions that once stood on the site (owned by secretary of state John Hay and historian Henry Adams) that were the nexus of Washington's political and intellectual elite. Today the hotel has a palazzo-style lobby and probably the best rooms of the old-school luxury genre in the city, all puffy mattresses like clouds shaded by four-poster canopies and gold braid tassels.

Morrison-Clark Inn BOUTIQUE HOTEL $$$
(☎202-898-1200; www.morrisonclark.com; 1015 L St NW; r from $220; P) Listed on the Register of Historic Places, this elegant inn

comprises two 1864 residences filled with fine antiques, chandeliers, richly hued drapes and other features evocative of the antebellum South. Some rooms come with private balconies or decorative marble fireplaces. Doting staff and a super central location.

Chester Arthur House B&B $$
(☎877-893-3233; www.chesterarthurhouse.com; 1339 14th St NW; r $175-250; ❄📶) Run by a delightful couple with serious travel experience under their belts – they both have National Geographic credentials – this is a good option for those wanting to explore beneath Washington's surface. Accommodations are in one of three rooms in a beautiful Logan Circle row house that's filled with antiques and collected ephemera from the hosts' global expeditions.

HI-Washington, DC HOSTEL $
(☎202-737-2333; 1009 11th St NW, at K St; dm incl breakfast from $35; ❄@📶) Top of the budget picks, this large, friendly hostel attracts a laid-back international crowd and has loads of amenities – lounge rooms, pool table, free tours and movie nights, kitchen and laundry.

Hotel Harrington HOTEL $$
(☎202-628-8140; www.hotel-harrington.com; 436 11th St NW; s/d from $125/145; ❄📶) One of the most affordable options near the Mall, this aging, family-run hotel has small basic rooms that are clean but in definite need of an update. Helpful service and a great location make the Harrington a great value for travelers who don't mind roughing it a bit.

District Hotel HOTEL $$
(☎202-232-7800; www.thedistricthotel.com; 1440 Rhode Island Ave NW; r $120-140; 📶) Home to some of the smallest rooms in DC, the District Hotel has Spartan quarters that are comfy enough if you're low maintenance. It's in a decent location within walking distance to downtown and Dupont.

ADAMS MORGAN

American Guest House B&B $$
(☎202-588-1180; www.americanguesthouse.com; 2005 Columbia Rd NW; r $160-220; ❄📶) This 12-room B&B earns high marks for its warm, friendly service, good breakfasts and elegantly furnished rooms. Decor runs the gamut from Victorian vibe (room 203) to New England cottage (room 304) to colonial love nest (room 303). Some quarters are rather small.

Adam's Inn B&B $$
(☎202-745-3600; www.adamsinn.com; 1746 Lanier Pl NW; r with shared/private bath from $109/139; P❄@) On a pretty, tree-lined street near Adams Morgan, this town house has small but nicely decorated rooms; thin walls mean you might hear your neighbor.

DUPONT CIRCLE

Carlyle Suites HOTEL $$$
(☎202-234-3200; www.carlylesuites.com; 1731 New Hampshire Ave NW; r from $220; ❄@📶) Inside this all-suites art-deco gem, you'll find sizable, handsomely furnished rooms with crisp white linens, luxury mattresses and full kitchens. The friendly staff is first-rate, and the added extras include free use of laptops and complimentary access to the Washington Sports Club.

Akwaaba B&B $$
(☎877-893-3233; www.akwaaba.com; 1708 16th St NW; r $150-265; ❄) Part of a small chain of B&Bs that emphasize African American heritage in its properties, the well-located Dupont branch has uniquely furnished rooms set in a late-19th-century mansion. Expect a friendly welcome and excellent cooked breakfasts.

Dupont Collection B&B $$
(☎202-467-6777; http://thedupontcollection.com; r $100-260; P❄📶) Brookland Inn (3742 12th St NE); Inn at Dupont Circle North (1620 T St NW); Inn at Dupont Circle South (1312 19th St NW) If you're craving a good range of B&B coziness in the heart of the capital, check out these three excellent heritage properties. Most centrally located are the inns at Dupont North and South; the former feels like the modern home of a wealthy friend, while the latter evokes much more of a chintz-and-lacy-linen sensibility. The Brookland is in the far northeast (but Metro accessible).

Tabard Inn HOTEL $$
(☎202-785-1277; www.tabardinn.com; 1739 N St NW; r with shared/private bath from $120/165; P❄📶) Set in a trio of 19th-century row houses, the Tabard Inn has attractive, antique-filled guest rooms sprinkled with unique flourishes – iron bedframes, wing-backed chairs, decorative fireplaces. There's an excellent restaurant here, with garden.

Hotel Helix BOUTIQUE HOTEL $$$
(☎202-462-9001; www.hotelhelix.com; 1430 Rhode Island Ave NW; r from $240; P❄@📶) Modish and highlighter bright, the Helix is playfully

TOP CAFES

Tryst CAFE $

(2459 18th St NW; 6:30am-late; wi-fi) In Adams Morgan, stylish Tryst with its smattering of tables and sofas attracts the laptop crowd by day (free wi-fi) and a more garrulous gathering by night; there's live jazz Monday to Wednesday (from 8pm), an early happy hour (3pm to 5:30pm) and decent coffees, small plates and desserts.

Baked & Wired CAFE $

(1052 Thomas Jefferson St NW; mains $3; 7am-8pm Mon-Fri, from 8am Sat & Sun; wi-fi) Baked & Wired is a cheery little Georgetown cafe that whips up beautifully made coffees and delectable desserts; it's a fine spot to join students in both real and virtual chatter (free wi-fi, of course).

Ching Ching Cha TEAHOUSE $$

(1063 Wisconsin Ave NW; teas $6-12; 11am-9pm) This airy, Zen-like teahouse feels a world away from the shopping mayhem of Georgetown's M Street. Stop in for a pot of rare tea (over 70 varieties). CCC also serves steamed dumplings, sweets and simple but flavorful three-course lunches ($14).

Pound CAFE $

(621 Pennsylvania Ave SE; mains $5-8; 7am-9:30pm Mon-Sat, 8am-8pm Sun; wi-fi) In Capitol Hill, Pound serves high-quality coffees amid an elegant rustic interior (exposed brick and timber, original plaster ceilings, wood floors and nicely lit artwork). Breakfast quesadillas, panini and daily lunch specials are tops – as is the Nutella latte.

Filter CAFE $

(1726 20th St NW; 7am-7pm Mon-Fri, from 8am Sat & Sun; wi-fi) On a quiet street in Dupont, Filter is a jewel-box-sized cafe with a tiny front patio, a hipsterish laptop-toting crowd and, most importantly, great coffee. Aussies and those who seek caffeinated perfection can get a decent flat white here.

cool – the perfect hotel for the bouncy international set that makes up the surrounding neighborhood of Dupont Circle.

GEORGETOWN

Hotel Monticello HOTEL $$$

(202-337-0900; www.monticellohotel.com; 1075 Thomas Jefferson St NW; r from $220; P ❄ wi-fi) In the heart of Georgetown, the Hotel Monticello has spacious rooms, with brass-and-crystal chandeliers, colonial-reproduction furniture, comfortable high-end mattresses and tasteful flower arrangements. Helpful staff.

Eating

As you might expect of one of the world's most international cities, DC has an eclectic palate, with a superb array of restaurants serving Ethiopian, Indian, Southeast Asian, French, Italian and more, plus good old-fashioned Southern fare.

CAPITOL HILL

Sonoma INTERNATIONAL $$$

(202-544-8088; 223 Pennsylvania Ave SE; mains $12-38; 11:30am-2:30pm Mon-Fri, 5-10pm Mon-Sat, 5-9pm Sun) Warmly lit Sonoma is an elegant spot for enjoying high-end bistro fare with some great wines (more than 50 by the glass). In addition to seasonal fish, roast duck breast, pizzas and pastas, diners can linger over tasty small plates, charcuterie and rich cheese plates. True to name, California varietals predominate. Service receives mixed reviews.

Granville Moore's MODERN AMERICAN $$

(1238 H St NE; mains $12-16; 5pm-midnight Sun-Thu, to 3am Fri & Sat) One of the anchors of the bohemian Atlas District (which runs along H St NE), Granville Moore's bills itself as a gastropub with a Belgian fetish. Indeed you'll find more than 70 Belgian beers by the bottle and at least seven on tap. There's also good pub fare (and recommended mussels), a lively happy hour, and fun crowds most nights.

Eastern Market MARKET $

(225 7th St SE; 7am-7pm Tue-Fri, to 6pm Sat, 9am-5pm Sun) One of the icons of Capitol Hill, this covered arcade sprawls with delectable produce and good cheer on the weekends.

The crab cakes at the Market Lunch stall are divine.

Jimmy T's Place DINER $

(501 E Capitol St SE; mains $6-10; ⏲7am-3pm Tue-Sun) Jimmy's is a neighborhood joint of the old school, where folks cram in to read the *Post,* have a burger or an omelet or some coffee and banter with staff behind the counter.

DOWNTOWN & WHITE HOUSE AREA

TOP CHOICE **Minibar at Café Atlantico** LATIN AMERICAN $$$

(☎202-393-0812; www.cafeatlantico.com; 405 8th St NW; tasting menu $150; ⏲6pm & 8:30pm, Tue-Sat) Atlantico's Minibar is foodie nirvana, where the lucky six (just six seats, folks) get wowed by animal bits spun into cotton candy and cocktails frothed into clouds. The tasting menu, entirely determined by the chef, is often delicious, and never dull. Reserve exactly one month in advance.

Maine Avenue Fish Market SEAFOOD $

(1100 Maine Ave SW; ⏲8am-9pm) If you're a seafood-lover, this sprawling and bustling fish market should take high priority on your itinerary. Over a dozen vendors sell some of America's freshest, tastiest seafood – we're talking fresh-off-the-boat fresh. Big plump oysters ($7 for six), crab cakes, soft-shell crabs, steamed crabs and peel-and-eat shrimp are just the beginning…

Hill Country BARBECUE $$

(www.hillcountrywdc.com; 410 7th St NW; mains $10-20; ⏲8am-9pm; 👪) Straight from Texas by way of, uh, Manhattan, Hill Country made fast friends following its opening in 2011. The ribs, chicken and sausage are all respectable, but the brisket (order it 'moist') is phenomenal. The barn-sized space fills with noisy chatter most nights, and it's all very informal – order your sides and meat by the pound from the smokemasters in back. There's live music (downstairs) from Tuesday to Saturday.

Zaytinya MEDITERRANEAN $$

(☎202-638-0800; 701 9th St NW; mezze $7-11; ⏲11:30am-11:30pm Tue-Sat, to 10pm Sun & Mon) One of the culinary crown jewels of chef José Andrés, ever-popular Zaytinya serves superb Greek, Turkish and Lebanese mezze (small plates) in a long narrow dining room with soaring ceilings and all-glass walls. Stop in for $4 happy hour specials (4:30pm to 6:30pm).

Ping Pong ASIAN $$

(☎202-506-3740; 900 7th St NW; dim sum $5-7; ⏲11:30am-11pm Mon-Sat, 11am-10pm Sun) At Ping Pong you can enjoy delectable dim sum anytime, but the stylish and open dining room gathers the liveliest crowds at night. The pan-Asian menu features delicate steamed dumplings, honey-roasted pork buns, seafood clay pots and other hits, plus tasty libations like plum wine and elderflower saketini cocktails.

Matchbox Pizza PIZZA $$

(☎202-289-4441; 713 H St NW; pizzas $14-21; ⏲11am-10:30pm Sun-Thu, to 1am Fri & Sat) One of the most popular pizzerias in DC serves celebrated thin-crust pies (like the spicy roasted pepper and smoked gouda 'fire & smoke'), plus much-lauded sliders (mini burgers; order them with gorgonzola). Prepare for big crowds on weekends.

Jaleo SPANISH $$

(☎202-628-7949; 480 7th St NW; tapas $7-12, dinner mains $16; ⏲11:30am-11:30pm Tue-Sat, to 10pm Sun & Mon) Amid vintage murals and buzzing ambience, Jaleo serves some of DC's best tapas. Garlicky gambas al ajillo (garlic shrimps), beet salad with pistachios and house-made pork sausage with white beans are top choices. The bar has a great happy hour ($4 tapas and sangria).

Georgia Brown's SOUTHERN $$

(☎202-393-4499; 950 15th St NW; mains $16-32; ⏲11:30am-10pm Mon-Thu, noon-11pm Fri & Sat, 10am-2:30pm & 5-10pm Sun) Georgia Brown's elevates the humble ingredients of the South (shrimp, cornmeal, catfish, grits and sausage) to high art in dishes like fried green tomatoes stuffed with herbed goat's cheese, and fried chicken marinated in sweet tea. The jazz brunch with a jaw-dropping buffet is probably DC's best.

ADAMS MORGAN, SHAW & U STREET

Busboys & Poets INTERNATIONAL $$

(☎203-387-7638; www.busboysandpoets.com; 2021 14th St NW; mains $8-16; ⏲8am-midnight Mon-Fri, from 9am Sat & Sun; 📶) A cultural icon, Busboys (named for a Langston Hughes poem) attracts an eclectic crowd who gather for coffee, bistro fare (pizzas, burgers, crab cakes) and a progressive line-up of events – book signings, poetry readings, film screenings.

Etete ETHIOPIAN $$

(☎202-232-7600; 1942 9th St NW; mains $10-20; ⏲11:30am-11pm; 🍷) In the small ethnic enclave sometimes called 'Little Ethiopia,' Etete serves authentic and high-quality food – fiery *yebeg wat* (spicy lamb stew), tender golden tibs (marinated short beef ribs), bountiful vegetarian platters and tangy *injera* (spongy flatbread) for soaking it all up. Culinary archrival **Dukem** (1114 U St NW) is up the street.

Cork MODERN AMERICAN **$$**
(1720 14th St NW; small plates $7-15; ⏲5pm-1am) This dark 'n' cozy wine bar manages to come off as foodie magnet and friendly neighborhood hangout all at once. You'll find over 50 wines by the glass, which go nicely with the small plates and cheese selection.

Pasta Mia ITALIAN **$$**
(1790 Columbia Rd NW; mains $10-15; ⏲6:30-10pm Mon-Sat) Even cold weather doesn't deter the faithful from lining up for their turn at affordable, monstrously portioned Italian on checkered tablecloths. No reservations, credit cards or line-jumping bribes accepted.

Diner AMERICAN **$$**
(2453 18th St NW; mains $8-16; ⏲24hr; 👪) The Diner is the ideal spot for late-night breakfast, (crowded) weekend bloody Mary brunches or anytime you want unfussy, well-prepared American fare (omelets, stuffed pancakes, mac 'n' cheese, grilled Portobello sandwiches, burgers and the like). It's a good spot for kids too (they'll even hang their Diner-made colorings on the wall).

Ben's Chili Bowl FAST FOOD **$**
(1213 U St NW; mains $4-9; ⏲11am-2am Mon-Thu, to 4am Fri & Sat, to 11pm Sun) One of DC's landmarks, Ben's has been going strong for over 50 years, doling out burgers, fries and the well-loved chili-smothered half-smokes (pork and beef sausages) from its old-school U St storefront.

DUPONT CIRCLE

TOP CHOICE **Bistro Du Coin** FRENCH **$$**
(☎202-234-6969; 1738 Connecticut Ave NW; mains $12-27; ⏲11:30am-11pm Sun-Wed, to 1am Thu-Sat) For a quick culinary journey across the Atlantic, the lively and much-loved Bistro Du Coin delivers the goods. You'll find consistently good onion soup, classic *steak-frites* (grilled steak and French fries), cassoulet, open-faced sandwiches and nine varieties of its famous *moules* (mussels). Try the *moules bretonnes* (with lobster) for pure decadence.

Malaysia Kopitiam MALAYSIAN **$$**
(1827 M St NW; mains $10-15; ⏲noon-10pm) This hole-in-the-wall restaurant is a good spot to get your Malaysian fix. Standouts include the *laksas* (curry noodle soups), *roti canai* (flatbread served with chicken curry) and crispy squid salad. The big picture menu helps with ordering.

Afterwords AMERICAN **$$**
(☎202-387-3825; 1517 Connecticut Ave NW; mains $12-20; ⏲7:30am-1am Sun-Thu, 24hr Fri & Sat; 📶) Not your average bookstore cafe, this buzzing spot overflows with good cheer at its packed cafe tables and outdoor patio. The menu features tasty bistro fare and an ample beer selection, making it a prime spot for happy hour, brunch and at all hours on weekends.

Dolcezza ICE CREAM **$**
(1704 Connecticut Ave NW; ice cream $4-7; ⏲8am-11pm Mon-Sat, to 8pm Sun; 📶) DC's best gelateria spreads over a dozen unique, delectable flavors (like Thai coconut milk, wildflower honey and champagne mango). Good coffees, vintage-chic decor and free wi-fi. There's also a Georgetown branch.

GEORGETOWN

Citronelle MODERN AMERICAN **$$$**
(☎202-625-2150; 3000 M St NW; tasting menu from $105; ⏲6-10pm Tue-Sat) Celebrated chef Michel Richard started this Georgetown dining destination, earning high marks for tender rack of lamb brushed with jalapeno-cumin sauce, wild salmon in lobster-saffron broth and other culinary gems. If you prefer not to shell out for the 10-course prix-fixe menu, you can dine à la carte in the more casual lounge.

Martin's Tavern AMERICAN **$$**
(☎202-333-7370; 1264 Wisconsin Ave NW; lunch mains $12-15, dinner $13-30; ⏲from 11:30am) Martin's is a favorite with Georgetown students and US presidents, who all enjoy the tavern's old-fashioned dining room and unfussy classics like thick burgers, crab cakes and prime rib.

Dolcezza ICE CREAM **$**
(1560 Wisconsin Ave NW; ice cream $4-7; ⏲noon-10pm Mon-Sat, to 9pm Sun) Serves amazingly good gelato from a menu that changes weekly. Recent hits include lime cilantro, Mexican coffee and lemon ricotta cardamom.

UPPER NORTHWEST DC

2 Amys PIZZA **$**
(3715 Macomb St NW; mains $3-7.25; ⏲noon-2:30pm Tue-Sun, 5-11pm daily; 👪) A bit out of

the way (but a stone's throw from Washington National Cathedral), 2 Amys serves some of DC's best thin-crust pizzas. Pies are sprinkled with market-fresh ingredients and baked to perfection in a wood-burning oven. Avoid the weekend crowds.

COLUMBIA HEIGHTS & AROUND

More and more restaurants and bars are opening in Columbia Heights and Petworth, north on the Green Line.

W Domku INTERNATIONAL **$$**
(☎202-722-7475; 821 Upshur St NW; mains $12-18; ⏲6-11pm Tue-Thu, noon-midnight Fri, 10am-midnight Sat, 10am-10pm Sun) A gem in the midst of an uninspiring stretch of Petworth, W Domku spreads a broad mix of Polish, Russian and Scandinavian fare – from goulash, fish stew and gravlax to house-infused aquavit. Retro furnishings and an easy-going vibe add to the appeal.

Palena MODERN AMERICAN **$$$**
(☎202-537-9250; 3529 Connecticut Ave NW; fixed-price menu from $75; ⏲11:30am-2pm & 5:30-10pm Tue-Sat, 10:30am-2pm Sun) Tucked away in Cleveland Park, northwest on the Red Line, Palena is one of DC's food-loving heavyweights. Red snapper with ramps (wild leeks) and oyster mushrooms, artichoke risotto and celery root soup with shrimp and almonds are recent favorites. Reserve ahead or eat in the more casual cafe (mains $14 to $26).

Drinking & Entertainment

See the weekly *Washington City Paper* (www.washingtoncitypaper.com) or *Washington Post* (www.washingtonpost.com) weekend section for comprehensive listings. Conveniently located at the Old Post Office Pavilion, **Ticketplace** (http://culturecapital.tix.com; 407 7th St NW; ⏲11am-6pm Wed-Fri, 10am-5pm Sat) sells same-day concert and show tickets at half-price (no phone sales).

Bars & Nightclubs

CAPITOL HILL & DOWNTOWN

Hawk & Dove BAR
(329 Pennsylvania Ave SE; ⏲from 10am) The quintessential Capitol Hill bar is a hot spot for political junkies, with intimate corner booths perfect for sipping pints and creating the next District scandal.

Red Palace LIVE MUSIC
(☎202-399-3201; http://redpalacedc.com; 1212 H St NE; ⏲from 5pm) A pillar of the frenzied H St scene, Red Palace has three bars and decent craft beer selections. The multiroom space books a mix of live bands and burlesque shows, with an abundance of indie rock and experimental sounds.

ADAMS MORGAN, SHAW & U STREET

Marvin LOUNGE
(2007 14th St NW; ⏲5:30pm-2am) Stylish but unpretentious, Marvin has a low-lit lounge with vaulted ceilings where DJs spin soul and rare grooves to a mixed 14th St crowd. The upstairs roof deck is a draw both on summer nights and in winter, when folks huddle under roaring heat lamps sipping cocktails and Belgian beers. Good bistro fare too.

Cafe Saint-Ex BAR
(1847 14th St NW; ⏲11am-1:30am) Amid framed drawings of *Le Petit Price* and wooden propellers (the place is named after French flyer and children's book author Antoine de Saint-Exupéry), this comfy classic serves up hearty bistro fare, a fine beer selection at the bar and DJs spinning fine grooves in the downstairs lounge, Gate 54. Head for the outdoor tables on warm nights.

Bar Pilar BAR
(1833 14th St NW; ⏲from 5pm Mon-Fri, from 11am Sat & Sun) Friendly neighborhood favorite Bar Pilar serves seasonal organic tapas dishes and excellent cocktails in a small, nicely designed space. The mustard-colored walls and curious collections (hats, Hemingway regalia) give it an old-fashioned feel.

Chi-Cha Lounge LOUNGE
(1624 U St NW; ⏲from 5pm) Slip through the double-sided mirror door, settle into a low settee and order up a hookah of fruit-flavored tobacco. Amid glowing candles and a backlit bar, the trendy clientele sip tropical cocktails and nosh on Andean-inspired tapas.

Madam's Organ LIVE MUSIC
(www.madamsorgan.com; 2461 18th St NW; cover $3-7; ⏲5pm-2am Sun-Thu, to 3am Fri & Sat) The Organ is a well-loved standby, with lively crowds, cheap drinks, a rambling interior and roof deck, free pool and bands playing nightly.

Dan's Café BAR
(2315 18th St NW; ⏲from 7:30pm Sun-Thu) Dan's dive is all the more grotty for its location: smack in the middle of the 18th St skimpy skirt parade. Inside this barely signed bar

GAY & LESBIAN BARS & CLUBS

One of Washington's gay bar scenes is concentrated around Dupont Circle.

Cobalt BAR

(http://cobaltdc.com; 1639 R St NW; admission Sun-Thu free, Fri & Sat $5-8) Featuring lots of hair product and faux-tanned gym bodies, Cobalt tends to gather a better-dressed late-20s to 30-something crowd who come for fun (but loud!) dance parties throughout the week. Attractive bartenders, good DJs and daily drink specials add to the allure.

Nellie's Sports Bar BAR

(www.nelliessportsbar.com; 900 U St NW) The vibe here is low-key, and Nellie's is a good place to hunker down among a friendly crowd for tasty bar bites, events' nights (including drag Bingo Tuesdays) or early drink specials. Twelve plasma screens show sporting events; there's also a roof deck and board games on hand.

Town Danceboutique BAR

(www.towndc.com; 2009 8th St NW; admission Sun-Thu free, Fri & Sat $5-12) With a great sound system and fine DJs, Town is the go-to spot for dancing, with two floors, various rooms (including an outdoor smoking area) and hilarious drag shows on weekends.

JR's BAR

(www.myjrsdc.com; 1519 17th St NW) This popular gay hangout is a great spot for happy hour, and is packed more often than not. Embarrassing show tunes karaoke is great fun on Monday nights.

is dim lighting, old locals, J Crew–looking types slumming it and cheap booze.

DUPONT CIRCLE

TOP CHOICE **Eighteenth Street Lounge** LOUNGE

(www.eighteenthstreetlounge.com; 1212 18th St NW; cover $5-15; from 9:30pm Sat & Sun, from 5:30pm Tue-Fri) Chandeliers, velvet sofas, antique wallpaper and an attractive dance-loving crowd adorn this multifloored mansion. The DJs here – spinning funk, soul, Brazilian beats – are phenomenal, which is not surprising given Eric Hilton (of Thievery Corporation) is co-owner.

Russia House LOUNGE

(1800 Connecticut Ave NW; from 5pm Mon-Fri, from 6pm Sat & Sun) Russophiles flock to this faded, elegant Dupont gem, with brassy chandeliers, candlelit chambers and stupefying vodka selection. A great spot for conversation and caviar – or heartier classics like pelmeni (dumplings), braised stuffed rabbit and shashlik (shish kabob).

Cafe Citron LOUNGE

(1343 Connecticut Ave NW; from 4pm Mon-Sat) Citron is a festive, Latin-loving lounge with dance-happy crowds who come for salsa, world beats, and ever-flowing pitchers of *mojitos* and margaritas. With never a cover, there are free salsa lessons on Wednesdays and flamenco shows on Mondays.

Bier Baron BAR

(1523 22nd St NW; from 11:30am Thu-Sun, from 4:30pm Mon-Wed) Since changing name and ownership, the former Brickskeller serves better food and has better service, with the same dark, pubby ambience and venerable selection of bottled and draft beer (over 500 brews!).

Current Sushi LOUNGE

(1215 Connecticut Ave NW; cover $10-15; from 10pm Thu-Sat) Above a sleek, modern sushi restaurant, this ethereal, tent-like club becomes dance central on Thursday through Saturday night, with well-dressed crowds packing the dance floor.

Science Club BAR

(www.scienceclubdc.com; 1136 19th St NW; from 5pm) In a warren of rooms scattered about a town house, the Science Club attracts a varied crowd of interns, transplants and young geeky types.

GEORGETOWN

Tombs BAR

(1226 36 St, at P St NW; from 11:30am Mon-Sat, from 9:30am Sun) If it looks familiar, think back to the '80s; this was the setting for *St Elmo's Fire*. Today this cozy, windowless bar is a favorite with Georgetown students and teaching assistants boozing under crew regalia.

Mie N Yu Lounge LOUNGE
(3125 M St NW; ⏲from 4pm) Mie N Yu (pronounced 'Me an you' – ugh) lays snob appeal and the Asian-fusion lounge thing on pretty thick, and the drink prices are equally excessive. But the wild decor – including themed rooms like the Tibetan Lounge, Turkish tent and Moroccan Bazaar – makes a colorful setting for a drink.

COLUMBIA HEIGHTS & AROUND

Red Derby BAR
(3718 14th St NW; ⏲5pm-2am Mon-Thu, to 3am Fri, 11am-3am Sat & Sun) The unsigned Red Derby draws a fun eclectic crowd with its satisfying food and drinks menu (thick burgers, sweet-potato fries and dozens of exotic beers served in the can). There's an open-air deck up top (with heat lamps), films screening on the wall and riotous brunch crowds ($2 mimosas and bloody Marys keep things lively). Order the $5 shot-and-Schlitz combo to start the night off with a bang.

Wonderland BAR
(1101 Kenyon St NW; ⏲5pm-2am Mon-Fri, from 11am Sat & Sun) In a residential stretch of Columbia Heights, Wonderland is friendly but divey with a spacious patio in front with outsize wooden benches just right on warm evenings. The upstairs dance floor sees a mix of DJs and bands, and gets packed on weekends.

Looking Glass Lounge BAR
(3634 Georgia Ave NW; ⏲from 5pm) Petworth's best nightspot is an artfully designed neighborhood dive with a great jukebox, DJs on weekends and a fine outdoor patio.

Raven BAR
(3125 Mt Pleasant Ave NW; ⏲from noon) The tattoo-loving Raven has cheap drinks, graffiti-stained bathrooms and more attitude than a pissed-off Ramone. Give it some respect and you may find this is DC's best spot for a $2 Schlitz.

Live Music

Black Cat LIVE MUSIC
(www.blackcatdc.com; 1811 14th St NW; ⏲8pm-2am Sun-Thu, 7pm-3am Fri & Sat) A pillar of DC's music scene since the 1990s, the battered Black Cat has hosted all the greats of years past (White Stripes, the Strokes, Arcade Fire among others). If you don't want to pony up for $20-a-ticket bands on the upstairs main stage (or the smaller Backstage below), head to the Red Room for jukebox, pool and strong cocktails.

9:30 Club LIVE MUSIC
(www.930.com; 815 V St NW) This spacious dive features two floors and a midsize stage (watch the action from the balcony or join the dancey mayhem below), with an excellent lineup of bands. Arrive early for a prime spot.

Blues Alley LIVE MUSIC
(www.bluesalley.com; 1073 Wisconsin Ave NW; ⏲from 8pm) The classy Georgetown jazz supper club attracts some big-name players, as well as some forgettable proponents of smooth jazz. Enter through the alley just off M, south of Wisconsin.

Verizon Center CONCERT VENUE
(☎202-628-3200; www.verizoncenter.com; 601 F St NW) DC's great big sports arena-cum-big-name-band venue.

Performing Arts

Kennedy Center PERFORMING ARTS
(☎800-434-1324; www.kennedy-center.org; 2700 F St NW) Perched on 17 acres along the Potomac, the magnificent Kennedy Center hosts a staggering array of performances – more than 2000 each year among its multiple venues – including the Concert Hall (home to the National Symphony), the Opera House and Eisenhower Theater. The Millennium Stage puts on free performances at 6pm daily.

Wolf Trap Farm Park for the Performing Arts PERFORMING ARTS
(☎703-255-1900; www.wolftrap.org; 1645 Trap Rd, Vienna, VA) This outdoor park some 40 minutes from downtown DC hosts summer performances by the National Symphony and other highly regarded musical and theatrical troupes.

National Theatre THEATER
(☎202-628-6161; www.nationaltheatre.org; 1321 Pennsylvania Ave NW) Washington's oldest continuously operating theater.

Shakespeare Theatre THEATER
(☎202-547-1122; www.shakespearedc.org; 450 7th St NW) The nation's foremost Shakespeare company presents masterfully staged pieces by the bard as well as works by George Bernard Shaw, Oscar Wilde, Ibsen, Eugene O'Neill and other greats.

Carter Barron Amphitheatre PERFORMING ARTS
(☎202-426-0486; www.nps.gov/rocr; cnr 16th St & Colorado Ave NW) In a lovely wooded setting (inside Rock Creek Park), you can

catch a mix of theater, dance and music (jazz, salsa, classical, reggae). Some events are free.

Sports

Washington Redskins FOOTBALL
(☎301-276-6800; www.redskins.com) The city's football team plays at **FedEx Field** (1600 Fedex Way, Landover, MD; tickets $40-500), east of DC in Maryland. The season runs from September to February.

Washington Nationals BASEBALL
(☎202-675-6287; http://washington.nationals.mlb.com) DC's baseball team plays at **Nationals Park** (1500 S Capitol St SE), along the Anacostia riverfront in southeast DC. The season runs from April through October.

DC United SOCCER
(☎202-587-5000; www.dcunited.com) DC United play at **Robert F Kennedy (RFK) Memorial Stadium** (2400 E Capitol St SE). The season runs from March through October.

Washington Capitals HOCKEY
(☎202-397-7328; http://capitals.nhl.com) DC's rough-and-tumble hockey team plays from October through April at the **Verizon Center** (601 F St NW).

Washington Wizards BASKETBALL
(☎202-661-5050; www.nba.com/wizards) NBA season runs from October through April, with home games played at the **Verizon Center** (601 F St NW). DC's WNBA team, the **Washington Mystics** (☎877-324-6671; www.wnba.com/mystics), also play here May to September.

Information

Internet Access

Kramerbooks (1517 Connecticut Ave NW, Dupont Circle; ⏲7:30am-1am Sun-Thu, 24hr Fri & Sat) One computer with free access in the bar.

Medical Services

CVS Pharmacy (☎202-785-1466; 6 Dupont Circle NW; ⏲24hr)

George Washington University Hospital (☎202-715-4000; 900 23rd St NW)

Post

Post office (2 Massachusetts Ave NE; ⏲9am-7pm Mon-Fri, to 5pm Sat & Sun)

Tourist Information

Destination DC (☎202-789-7000; www.washington.org; 901 7th St NW, 4th fl) Doles out loads of information online, over the phone or in person at a handy downtown location.

Disability Guide (☎301-528-8664; www.disabilityguide.org) Has useful info on museums, hotels and getting around; also publishes an annual accessibility guide ($5 available online).

International Visitors Information Desk (⏲9am-5pm Mon-Fri) At the Arrivals Terminal at Washington Dulles Airport, you'll find helpful multilingual staff at this post run by the Meridian International Center.

Websites

Online visitor information (www.washington.org, www.thedistrict.com)

Washington City Paper (www.washingtoncitypaper.com) Free edgy weekly with entertainment and dining listings.

Washington Post (www.washingtonpost.com) Respected daily city (and national) paper. Its tabloid-format daily *Express* is free. Check online for events listings.

Getting There & Away

Air

Washington Dulles International Airport (IAD; ☎703-572-2700), 26 miles west of the city center, and **Ronald Reagan Washington National Airport** (DCA; ☎703-417-8000), 4.5 miles south, are the main airports serving DC, although **Baltimore/Washington International Thurgood Marshall Airport** (BWI; ☎410-859-7111), 30 miles to the northeast, is also an option. All three airports, particularly Dulles and National, are major hubs for flights from around the world.

Bus

In addition to Greyhound, there are numerous cheap bus services to New York, Philadelphia and Richmond. Most charge around $20 for a one-way trip to NYC (it takes four to five hours). Pick-up locations are scattered around town, but are always Metro-accessible. Tickets usually need to be bought online, but can also be purchased on the bus itself if there is room.

Bolt Bus (☎877-265-8287; www.boltbus.com; 📶) The best of the budget options, Bolt Bus leaves from the upper level of Union Station.

DC2NY (☎202-332-2691; www.dc2ny.com; 20th St & Massachusetts Ave NW)

Greyhound (☎202-589-5141; www.greyhound.com; 1005 1st St NE) Provides nationwide service. The terminal is a few blocks north of Union Station; take a cab after dark.

Megabus (☎877-462-6342; www.us.megabus.com; 📶) Temporarily leaves from K & N Capitol Sts NW. Call to verify location.

New Century (☎202-789-8222; www.2001bus.com; 513 St NW)

Peter Pan Bus Lines (☎800-343-9999; www.peterpanbus.com) Travels to northeastern US; uses a terminal just opposite Greyhound's.

WashNY (☎866-287-6932; www.washny.com; 1333 19th St NW)

Train

Amtrak (☎800-872-7245; www.amtrak.com) Set inside the magnificent beaux-arts Union Station. Trains depart for nationwide destinations, including New York City (from $76, 3½ hours), Chicago (from $106, 18 hours), Miami (from $163, 24 hours) and Richmond, VA ($31, three hours).

MARC train (Maryland Rail Commuter; ☎866-743-3682; www.mtamaryland.com) This regional rail service for the Washington, DC–Baltimore metro area runs trains frequently to Baltimore ($7, 71 minutes) and other Maryland towns ($4 to $12); also goes to Harpers Ferry, WV ($15, 80 minutes).

Getting Around

To/From the Airport

If you're using Baltimore/Washington International Airport, you can travel between Union Station and the BWI terminal stop on either MARC train ($6, 40 minutes) or Amtrak ($14, 40 minutes).

Metrobus 5A (www.wmata.com) Runs from Dulles to Rosslyn Metro station (35 minutes) and central DC (L'Enfant Plaza, 48 minutes); it departs every 30 to 40 minutes. The combo bus/Metro fare is about $8.

Metrorail (www.wmata.com) National airport has its own Metro rail station, which is fast and cheap (around $2.50).

Supershuttle (☎800-258-3826; www.supershuttle.com) A door-to-door shuttle that connects downtown DC with Dulles ($29), National ($14) and BWI ($37).

Washington Flyer (www.washfly.com) Runs every 30 minutes from Dulles to West Falls Church Metro ($10).

Public Transportation

Metrorail (☎202-637-7000; www.wmata.com) One of the best transportation systems in the country will get you to most sights, hotel and business districts, and to the Maryland and Virginia suburbs. Trains start running at 5am Monday through Friday (from 7am on weekends); the last service is around midnight Sunday through Thursday and 3am on Fridays and Saturdays. Machines inside stations sell computerized fare cards; fares cost from $1.60 (children under five ride free). Unlimited travel passes are also available (one day/seven days from $9/33).

Circulator (www.dccirculator.com) Buses run along handy routes – including Union Station to/from Georgetown. One-way fare is $1.

Metrobus (www.wmata.com) Operates buses throughout the city and suburbs; have exact change handy (currently $1.70).

Taxi

For a cab, try **Capitol Cab** (☎202-636-1600), **Diamond** (☎202-387-6200) or **Yellow Cab** (☎202-544-1212).

MARYLAND

Maryland is often described as 'America in Miniature,' and for good reason. This small state has the best bits of the country, from the Appalachian Mountains in the west to sandy white beaches in the east. A blend of Northern streetwise and Southern down-home gives this most osmotic of border states an appealing identity crisis. Her main city, Baltimore, is a sharp, demanding port town; the Eastern Shore jumbles art-and-antique-minded city refugees and working fishermen; while the DC suburbs are packed with government and office workers seeking green space, and the poor seeking lower rents. Yet it all somehow works – scrumptious blue crabs, Natty Boh beer and

MARYLAND FACTS

- **Nickname** The Old Line State, the Free State
- **Population** 5.8 million
- **Area** 12,407 sq miles
- **Capital city** Annapolis (population 36,600)
- **Sales tax** 6%
- **Birthplace of** Abolitionist Frederick Douglass (1818–95), baseball great Babe Ruth (1895–1948), actor David Hasselhoff (b 1952), author Tom Clancy (b 1947), swimmer Michael Phelps (b 1985)
- **Home of** 'The Star-Spangled Banner,' Baltimore Orioles, TV crime shows *The Wire* and *Homicide: Life on the Street*
- **Politics** Staunch democrats
- **Famous for** Blue crabs, lacrosse, Chesapeake Bay
- **State sport** jousting
- **Driving distances** Baltimore to Annapolis 29 miles, Baltimore to Ocean City 147 miles

lovely Chesapeake country being the glue that binds all.

History

George Calvert established Maryland as a refuge for persecuted English Catholics in 1634 when he purchased St Mary's City from the local Piscataway, with whom he initially tried to coexist. Puritan refugees drove both Piscataway and Catholics from control and shifted power to Annapolis; their harassment of Catholics produced the Tolerance Act, a flawed but progressive law that allowed freedom of any (Christian) worship in Maryland – a North American first.

That commitment to diversity has always characterized this state, despite a mixed record on slavery. Although her loyalties were split during the Civil War, a Confederate invasion was halted here in 1862 at Antietam. Following the war, Maryland harnessed its black, white and immigrant work force, splitting the economy between Baltimore's industry and shipping, and the later need for services in Washington, DC. Today the answer to 'What makes a Marylander?' is 'all of the above': the state mixes rich, poor, the foreign-born, urban sophisticates and rural villages like few others.

Baltimore

Once one of the most important port towns in America, Baltimore – or 'Bawlmer' to locals – is a city of contradictions. On one hand she retains something of the ugly duckling – a defiant, working-class, somewhat gritty city still tied to her nautical past. But in recent years Baltimore has grown into a swan, filled with world-class museums, trendy shops, ethnic restaurants, boutique hotels, culture and sports. She does this all with a twinkle in the eye and a wisecrack on the lips. After all, this is a quirky city that spawned Billie Holiday and John Waters. Yet she remains intrinsically tied to the water, from the Disney-fied Inner Harbor and cobblestoned streets of portside Fells Point to the shores of Fort McHenry, birthplace of America's national anthem, 'The Star-Spangled Banner.' Baltimore lives up to her nickname, 'Charm City.'

Sights & Activities

HARBORPLACE & INNER HARBOR

This is where most tourists start and, unfortunately, end their Baltimore sightseeing. The Inner Harbor is a big, gleaming waterfront renewal project of shiny glass, air-conditioned malls and flashy bars that manages to capture the maritime heart of this city, albeit in a safe-for-the-family kinda way. But it's also just the tip of Baltimore's iceberg.

TOP CHOICE National Aquarium of Baltimore AQUARIUM
(www.aqua.org; 501 E Pratt St; adult/child $25/20; ⌚9am-5pm Sun-Thu, to 8pm Fri, to 6pm Sat) Standing seven-stories high and capped by a glass pyramid, this is widely considered to be the best aquarium in America. It houses 16,500 specimens of 660 species, a rooftop rainforest, a central ray pool and multistory shark tank. There's also a reconstruction of the Umbrawarra Gorge in Australia's Northern Territory, complete with 35ft waterfall, rocky cliffs and free-roaming birds and lizards. Kids will love the dolphin show and new 4D Immersion Theater (together an additional $5). Go on weekdays to beat the crowds.

Baltimore Maritime Museum MUSEUM
(www.baltomaritimemuseum.org; Piers 1, 3 & 5, off E Pratt St; 1/2/4 ships $11/14/18; ⌚10am-5:30pm) Ship-lovers can take a tour through four historic ships: a Coast Guard cutter, lightship, submarine and the **USS Constellation**, one of the last sail-powered warships built (in 1797) by the US Navy. Admission to the 1856 Seven Foot Knoll Lighthouse on Pier 5 is free.

Top of the World Observation Deck LOOKOUT
(www.viewbaltimore.org; 401 E Pratt St; adult/child $5/4; ⌚10am-6pm Wed-Thu, to 7pm Fri & Sat, 11am-6pm Sun) For a bird's-eye view of Baltimore, head to the observation deck at the World Trade Center.

DOWNTOWN & LITTLE ITALY

You can easily walk from downtown to Little Italy, but follow the delineated path as there's a rough housing project along the way.

National Great Blacks in Wax Museum MUSEUM
(www.greatblacksinwax.org; 1601 E North Ave; adult/child $12/10; ⌚9am-5pm Tue-Sat, noon-5pm Sun) In East Baltimore stands one of the country's best African American history museums, with exhibits on Frederick Douglass, Jackie Robinson, Martin Luther King Jr and Barack Obama, as well as lesser-known figures like explorer Matthew Henson. The

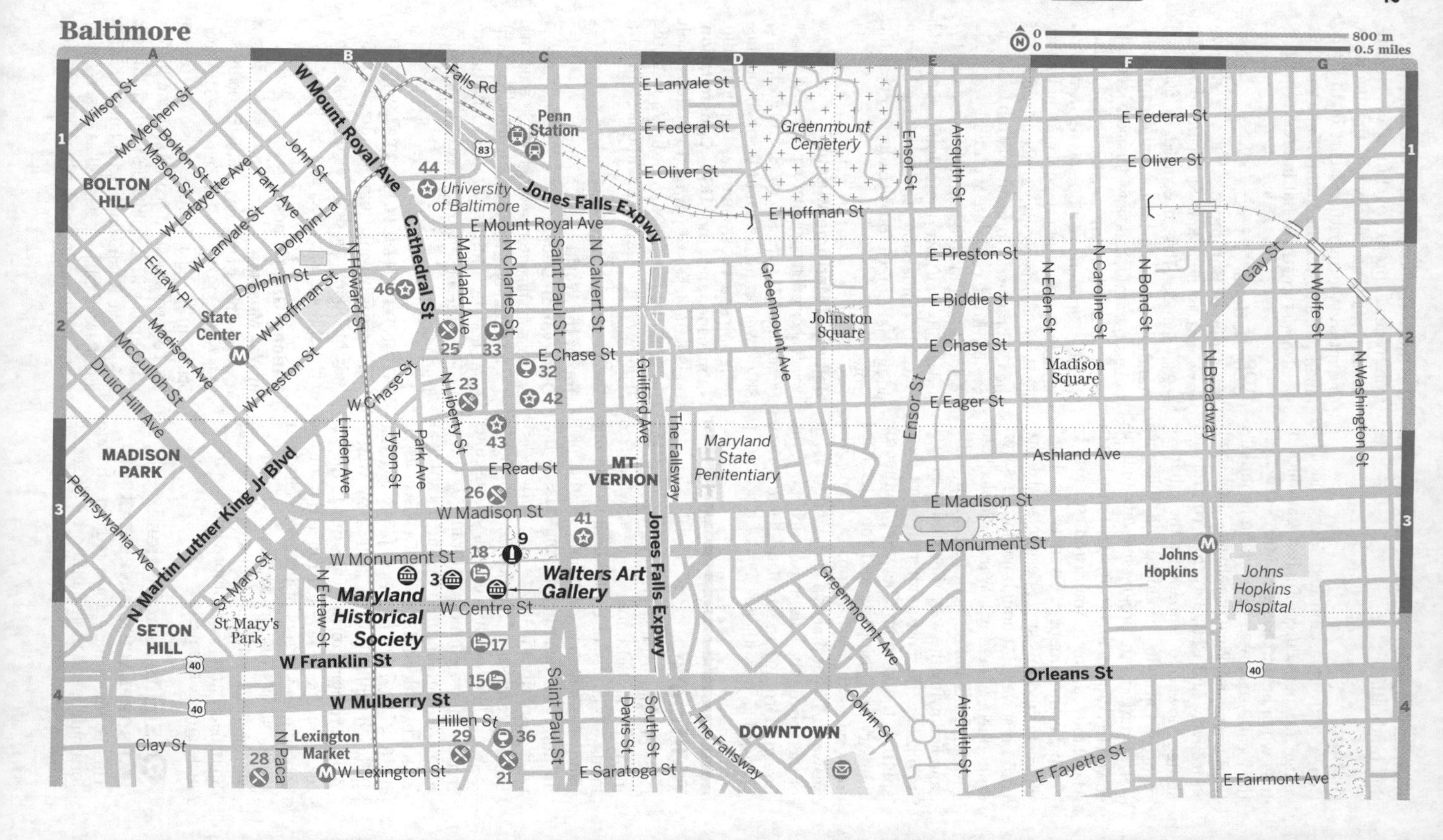
Baltimore
800 m
0.5 miles
Wilson St
McMechen St
Bolton St
Mason St
BOLTON HILL
W Lafayette Ave
Park Ave
John St
W Lanvale St
Dolphin La
Eutaw Pl
Dolphin St
W Hoffman St
State Center
Madison Ave
McCulloh St
Druid Hill Ave
W Preston St
MADISON PARK
Pennsylvania Ave
N Martin Luther King Jr Blvd
W Mount Royal Ave
Falls Rd
Penn Station
University of Baltimore
Jones Falls Expwy
E Mount Royal Ave
N Howard St
Cathedral St
Maryland Ave
N Charles St
Saint Paul St
N Calvert St
W Chase St
E Chase St
N Liberty St
Linden Ave
Tyson St
Park Ave
E Read St
MT VERNON
Guilford Ave
The Fallsway
W Madison St
W Monument St
Walters Art Gallery
Maryland Historical Society
N Eutaw St
W Centre St
St Mary St
St Mary's Park
SETON HILL
W Franklin St
W Mulberry St
Hillen St
Lexington Market
N Paca
W Lexington St
Clay St
Davis St
South St
E Saratoga St
DOWNTOWN
Colvin St
E Lanvale St
E Federal St
E Oliver St
E Hoffman St
Greenmount Cemetery
Ensor St
Aisquith St
E Preston St
E Biddle St
E Eager St
Greenmount Ave
Johnston Square
Maryland State Penitentiary
N Eden St
N Caroline St
N Bond St
Madison Square
Ashland Ave
Gay St
N Wolfe St
N Broadway
N Washington St
E Madison St
E Monument St
Johns Hopkins
Johns Hopkins Hospital
Orleans St
E Fayette St
E Fairmont Ave
40
83
3
9
15
17
18
21
23
25
26
28
29
32
33
36
41
42
43
44
46

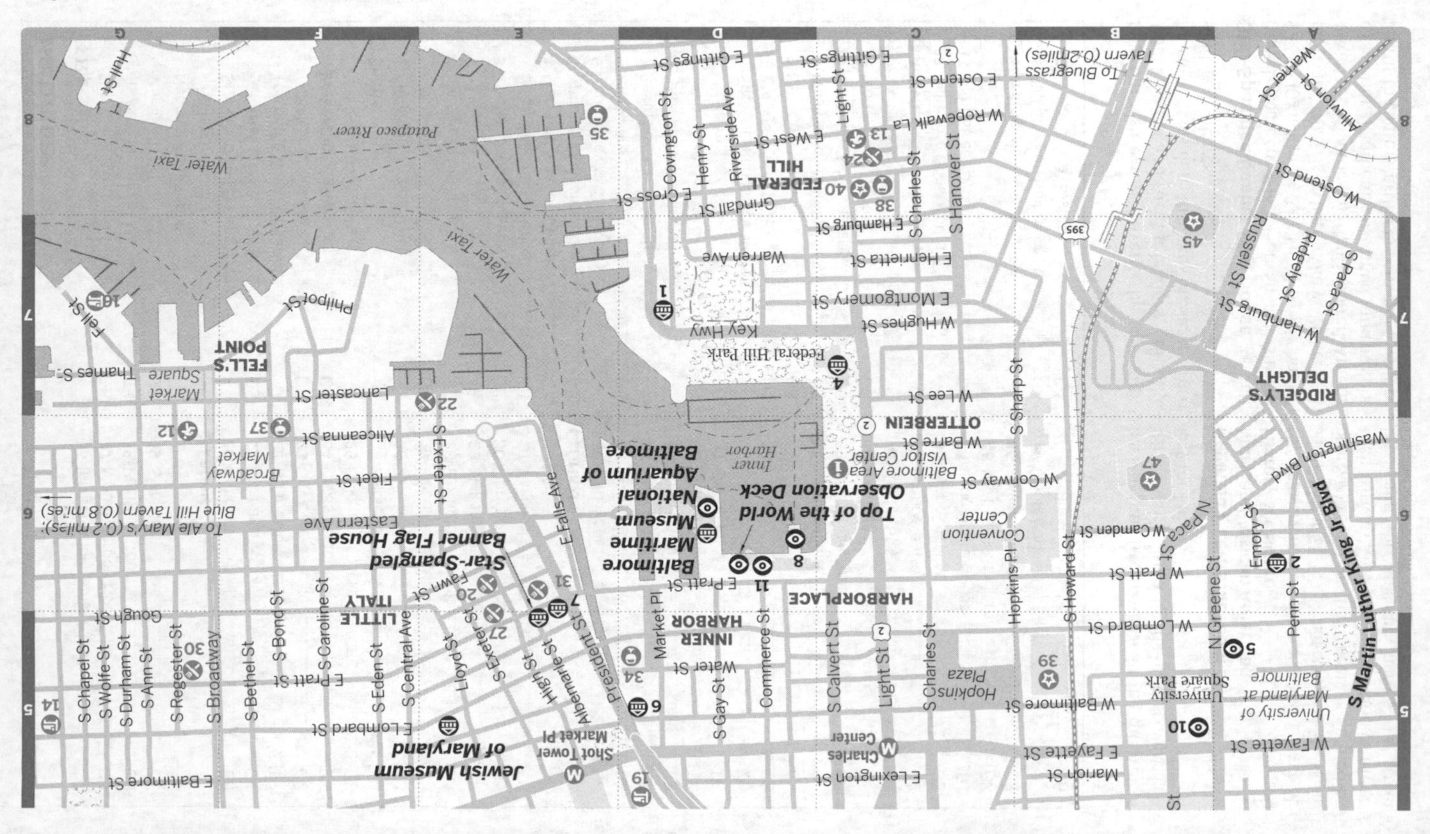
Jewish Museum of Maryland
Star-Spangled Banner Flag House
Baltimore Maritime Museum
National Aquarium of Baltimore
Top of the World Observation Deck
Baltimore Area Visitor Center
Inner Harbor
Federal Hill Park
LITTLE ITALY
INNER HARBOR
HARBORPLACE
FELL'S POINT
FEDERAL HILL
OTTERBEIN
RIDGELY'S DELIGHT
Shot Tower Market Pl
Charles Center
To Ale Mary's (0.2 miles); Blue Hill Tavern (0.8 miles)
To Bluegrass Tavern (0.2miles)
Broadway Market
Market Square
Convention Center
Hopkins Plaza
University Square Park
University of Maryland at Baltimore
Patapsco River
Water Taxi
E Baltimore St
S Chapel St
S Wolfe St
S Durham St
S Ann St
S Regester St
S Broadway
S Bethel St
S Bond St
S Caroline St
S Eden St
S Central Ave
Lloyd St
S Exeter St
High St
Albemarle St
President St
E Falls Ave
Eastern Ave
Fleet St
Aliceanna St
Lancaster St
Thames St
Fell St
Philpot St
Gough St
E Pratt St
E Lombard St
Fawn St
Market Pl
Water St
S Gay St
Commerce St
S Calvert St
Light St
S Charles St
E Lexington St
Hopkins Pl
S Howard St
S Sharp St
W Conway St
W Barre St
W Lee St
W Hughes St
E Montgomery St
E Henrietta St
E Hamburg St
S Hanover St
W Ropewalk La
E Ostend St
E Gittings St
E West St
Grindall St
Warren Ave
Key Hwy
E Cross St
Covington St
Henry St
Riverside Ave
Hull St
Marion St
E Fayette St
W Baltimore St
W Lombard St
W Pratt St
W Camden St
N Paca St
N Greene St
Emory St
Penn St
W Fayette St
S Martin Luther King Jr Blvd
Washington Blvd
W Hamburg St
Russell St
Ridgely St
S Paca St
W Ostend St
Alluvion St
Warner St

Baltimore

Top Sights
- Baltimore Maritime Museum ... D6
- Jewish Museum of Maryland ... E5
- Maryland Historical Society ... B3
- National Aquarium of Baltimore ... D6
- Star-Spangled Banner Flag House ... E5
- Top of the World Observation Deck ... D6
- Walters Art Gallery ... C3

Sights
- 1 American Visionary Art Museum ... D7
- 2 Babe Ruth Birthplace & Museum ... A6
- 3 Contemporary Museum ... C3
- Edgar Allan Poe's Grave ... (see 10)
- 4 Maryland Science Center ... C7
- 5 National Museum of Dentistry ... A5
- 6 Port Discovery Children's Museum ... D5
- 7 Reginald F Lewis Museum of Maryland African American History & Culture ... E6
- Sports Legends at Camden Yards ... (see 47)
- 8 USS Constellation ... D6
- 9 Washington Monument ... C3
- 10 Westminster Cemetery ... B5
- 11 World Trade Center ... D6

Activities, Courses & Tours
- 12 Baltimore Ghost Tours ... G6
- 13 Light Street Cycles ... C8

Sleeping
- 14 Blue Door on Baltimore ... G5
- 15 HI-Baltimore Hostel ... C4
- 16 Inn at Henderson's Wharf ... G7
- 17 Mount Vernon Hotel ... C4
- 18 Peabody Court ... C3
- 19 Sleep Inn ... D5

Eating
- 20 Amicci's ... E6
- 21 Cazbar ... C4
- 22 Charleston ... E7
- 23 City Cafe ... C2
- 24 Cross Street Market ... C8
- 25 Dukem ... C2
- Faidley's ... (see 28)
- 26 Helmand ... C3
- 27 Isabella's ... E5
- 28 Lexington Market ... B4
- 29 Mekong ... C4
- 30 Obrycki's ... G5
- 31 Vaccaro's Pastry ... E6

Drinking
- 32 13th Floor ... C2
- 33 Brewer's Art ... C2
- 34 Howl at the Moon ... D5
- 35 Little Havana ... E8
- 36 Mick O'Shea's ... C4
- 37 One-Eyed Mike's ... F6
- Owl Bar ... (see 32)
- 38 Pub Dog ... C8

Entertainment
- 39 1st Mariner Arena ... B5
- 40 8x10 ... C8
- 41 Center Stage ... C3
- 42 Grand Central ... C2
- 43 Hippo ... C3
- 44 Lyric Opera House ... B1
- 45 M&T Bank Stadium ... B7
- 46 Meyerhoff Symphony Hall ... B2
- 47 Oriole Park at Camden Yards ... B6

museum also covers slavery, the sickening Jim Crow era and African leaders – all told in surreal fashion through Madame Tussaud–style figures.

Star-Spangled Banner Flag House MUSEUM
(www.flaghouse.org; 844 E Pratt St; adult/student $7/5; ⏲10am-4pm Tue-Sat) This historic home, built in 1793, is where Mary Pickersgill sewed the gigantic flag that inspired America's national anthem. Costumed interpreters and 19th-century artifacts transport visitors back in time to dark days during the War of 1812; there's also a hands-on discovery gallery for kids.

Reginald F Lewis Museum of Maryland African American History & Culture MUSEUM
(www.africanamericanculture.org; 830 E Pratt St; adult/student $8/6; ⏲10am-5pm Wed-Sat, noon-5pm Sun) Few states have been as defined by their African American population as Maryland, and the museum, across the street

from a pre–Civil War slave market, effectively tells their complex tale.

Jewish Museum of Maryland MUSEUM
(www.jewishmuseummd.org; 15 Lloyd St; adult/student/child $8/4/3; ⊙noon-4pm Tue-Thu & Sun) Maryland has traditionally been home to one of the largest, most active Jewish communities in the country, and this is a fine place to explore the Jewish experience in America. It also houses two of the best-preserved historical synagogues in America.

Babe Ruth Birthplace & Museum MUSEUM
(www.baberuthmuseum.com; 216 Emory St; adult/child $6/3; ⊙10am-5pm, to 7pm during Orioles home games) Celebrates the Baltimore native son who happens to be the greatest baseball player in history. Four blocks east, **Sports Legends at Camden Yards** (Camden Station, cnr Camden & Sharp Sts; adult/child $8/4) honors more Maryland athletes. The museums share hours; combo tickets are $12/5.

B&O Railroad Museum MUSEUM
(☎410-752-2490; www.borail.org; 901 W Pratt St; adult/child $14/8; ⊙10am-4pm Mon-Sat, from 11am Sun) The Baltimore & Ohio railway was (arguably) the first passenger train in America, and the museum is a loving testament to both that line and American railroading in general. Train spotters will be in heaven among more than 150 different locomotives. Train rides cost an extra $3; call for the schedule.

Edgar Allan Poe House & Museum MUSEUM
(☎410-396-7932; 203 N Amity St; adult/child $4/free; ⊙noon-3:30pm Wed-Sat Apr-Nov) Home to Baltimore's most famous adopted son from 1832 to 1835, it was here that the macabre poet and writer first found fame after winning a $50 short-story contest. After moving around, Poe later returned to Baltimore in 1849, where he died in mysterious circumstances. His grave can be found in nearby **Westminster Cemetery** (cnr W Fayette & Greene Sts; admission free). The Poe House is located in a crime-ridden neighborhood, so it's best to drive or take a taxi; call to verify opening times before visiting.

National Museum of Dentistry MUSEUM
(☎410-706-0600; www.dentalmuseum.org; 31 S Greene St; adult/student/child $7/5/3; ⊙10am-4pm Wed-Sat, 1-4pm Sun) One of America's most unusual museums, this interactive museum traces the history of dental care from ancient Egypt to today. See George Washington's dentures (ivory, not wood) and old toothpaste, and check out Queen Victoria's 'toothbrush.'

Light Street Cycles BICYCLE RENTAL
(☎410-685-2234; 1124 Light St; rental per day $25-50; ⊙10am-8pm Mon-Fri, to 6pm Sat, 11am-3pm Sun) Rents out hybrids, mountain bikes and road bikes.

MT VERNON

FREE **Walters Art Gallery** MUSEUM
(www.thewalters.org; 600 N Charles St; ⊙10am-5pm Wed-Sun) Don't pass up this gallery, which spans over 55 centuries, from ancient to contemporary, with excellent displays of Asian treasures, rare and ornate manuscripts and books, and a comprehensive French paintings collection.

FREE **Contemporary Museum** MUSEUM
(www.contemporary.org; 100 W Centre St; ⊙noon-5pm Wed-Sun) So modern it's probably 'post,' this museum loves to ride the cutting edge of art. Auxiliary to the on-site exhibits is the museum's mission of bringing art to unexpected spots around the city.

Maryland Historical Society MUSEUM
(www.mdhs.org; 201 W Monument St; adult/child $6/4; ⊙10am-5pm Wed-Sat, noon-5pm Sun) With more than 5.4 million artifacts, this is one of the largest collections of Americana in the world, including Francis Scott Key's original manuscript of the 'Star-Spangled Banner.' There are often excellent temporary exhibits, as well as a fascinating permanent ones tracing Maryland's maritime history.

Washington Monument MONUMENT
(699 Washington Pl; suggested donation $5; ⊙10am-5pm Wed-Sun) For the best views of Baltimore, climb the 228 steps of the 178ft-tall Doric column dedicated to America's Founding Father, George Washington. It was designed by Robert Mills, who also created DC's Washington Monument. The ground floor contains a museum about Washington's life.

FEDERAL HILL & AROUND

On a bluff overlooking the harbor, **Federal Hill Park** lends its name to the comfortable neighborhood that's set around Cross St Market and comes alive after sundown.

TOP CHOICE **Fort McHenry National Monument & Historic Shrine** HISTORIC SITE
(www.nps.gov/fomc; 2400 E Fort Ave; adult/child $7/free; ⊙8am-4:45pm, to 7:45pm summer) On September 13 and 14, 1814, the star-shaped

fort successfully repelled a British navy attack during the Battle of Baltimore. After a long night of bombs bursting in the air, prisoner Francis Scott Key saw, 'by dawn's early light,' the tattered flag still waving, inspiring him to pen 'The Star-Spangled Banner' (set to the tune of a popular drinking song).

American Visionary Art Museum MUSEUM
(AVAM; www.avam.org; 800 Key Hwy; adult/child $16/10; ⏲10am-6pm Tue-Sun) AVAM is a showcase for self-taught (or 'outsider' art), a celebration of unbridled creativity utterly free of arts-scene pretension. Some of the work comes from asylums, others are created by self-inspired visionaries, but it's all rather captivating and well worth a long afternoon.

FELL'S POINT & CANTON

Once the center of Baltimore's shipbuilding industry, the historic cobblestoned neighborhood is now a gentrified mix of 18th-century homes and restaurants, bars and shops. The neighborhood has been the setting for several films and TV series, most notably *Homicide: Life on the Street*. Further east, the slightly more sophisticated streets of Canton fan out, with its grassy square surrounded by great restaurants and bars. On weekends, both neighborhoods can get quite crowded with bar-hoppers.

NORTH BALTIMORE

The 'Hon' expression of affection, an oft-imitated, but never quite duplicated, 'Bawlmerese' peculiarity, was born from **Hampden**, an urban neighborhood at the pinnacle of hipness. Spend a lazy afternoon browsing kitsch, antiques and eclectic clothing along the **Avenue** (aka W 36th St).

To get to Hampden, take the I-83 N, merge onto Falls Rd (northbound) and take a right onto the Avenue. The prestigious **Johns Hopkins University** (3400 N Charles St) is nearby.

Baltimore Museum of Art MUSEUM
(www.artbma.org; 10 Art Museum Dr, at 31st & N Charles Sts; permanent collection free; ⏲10am-5pm Wed-Fri, 11am-6pm Sat & Sun) With a massive collection (the early American, Asian and African galleries are particularly impressive) and a lovely sculpture garden, this museum easily competes with its Smithsonian cousins to the south.

Baltimore for Children

This city loves kids, and proves it with amazing museums, stroll-worthy waterfront promenades and family-friendly restaurants. Most attractions are centered on the Inner Harbor, including the National Aquarium of Baltimore (p271), perfect for pint-sized visitors. Kids can run wild o'er the ramparts of historic Fort McHenry National Monument & Historic Shrine (p275) too.

Port Discovery Children's Museum MUSEUM
(www.portdiscovery.org; Power Plant Live complex, 35 Market Pl; admission $13; ⏲10am-5pm Mon-Sat, noon-5pm Sun) Swinging into a three-level jungle tree house, producing a TV show and solving riddles in the Mystery House are a few ways to spend a fun-filled afternoon at this sprawling kids' museum.

Maryland Zoo in Baltimore ZOO
(www.marylandzoo.org; Druid Hill Park; adult/child $16/11; ⏲10am-4pm) Lily-pad hopping, adventures with Billy the Bog Turtle and grooming live animals are all in a day's play here. Prices are slightly cheaper on weekdays.

Maryland Science Center MUSEUM
(www.mdsci.org; 601 Light St; adult/child $15/12; ⏲10am-5pm Mon-Fri, to 6pm Sat, 11am-5pm Sun) This awesome center features a three-story atrium, tons of interactive exhibits on dinosaurs, outer space and the human body, and the requisite IMAX theater ($4 extra). Hours change seasonally so it's best to check online or call ahead first.

Tours

Baltimore Ghost Tours GHOST
(☎410-357-1186; www.baltimoreghosttours.com; adult/child $15/10; ⏲7pm Fri & Sat Mar-Nov) Offers several walking tours exploring the spooky and bizarre side of Baltimore. The popular Fells Point ghost walk departs from Max's on Broadway, 731 S Broadway. There's also a Fell's Point Haunted pub crawl ($20, must be over 21) and a walk around Mt Vernon.

Festivals & Events

Preakness HORSE RACING
(www.preakness.com) Held on the third Sunday of every May, the 'Freakness' is the second leg of the Triple Crown horse race.

Honfest CULTURAL
(www.honfest.net) Put on your best 'Bawlmerese' accent and head to Hampden for this June celebration of kitsch, beehive hairdos, rhinestone glasses and other Baltimore eccentricities.

Artscape CULTURAL
(www.artscape.org) America's largest free arts festival takes place in mid-July and features art displays, live music, theater and dance performances, international food vendors and more.

Sleeping

Stylish and affordable B&Bs are mostly found in the downtown burbs of Canton, Fell's Point and Federal Hill.

Inn at Henderson's Wharf HOTEL $$$
(☎410-522-7777; www.hendersonswharf.com; 1000 Fell St; r from $209; P ❄ ☎) A complimentary bottle of wine upon arrival sets the tone at this marvelously situated Fell's Point hotel, which began life as an 18th-century tobacco warehouse. Consistently rated one of the city's best lodges.

Inn at 2920 B&B $$
(☎410-342-4450, 877-774-2920; www.theinnat2920.com; 2920 Elliott St; r incl breakfast $175-235; ❄ @ ☎) Housed in a former bordello, this boutique B&B has five individual rooms, high-thread-count sheets, sleek, avant-garde decor and the nightlife-charged neighborhood of Canton right outside your door. The Jacuzzi bathtubs and green sensibility of the owners are a nice touch.

Blue Door on Baltimore B&B $$
(☎410-732-0191; www.bluedoorbaltimore.com; 2023 E Baltimore St; r $140-180; ❄ @ ☎) In an early 1900s row house, this spotless inn has three elegantly furnished rooms, each with a king-sized bed, claw-foot bathtub (and separate shower) and thoughtful extras like an in-room fountain and fresh flowers. It lies just north of Fells Point.

Peabody Court HOTEL $$
(☎410-727-7101; www.peabodycourthotel.com; 612 Cathedral St; r from $120; P ❄ ☎) Right in the middle of Mt Vernon, this upscale 104-room hotel has large, handsomely appointed guest rooms with all-marble bathrooms and top-notch service. Often has great deals online.

Sleep Inn HOTEL $$
(☎410-779-6166; www.sleepinn.com; 301 Fallsway; d/ste from $130/150; P ❄ @ ☎) Although it's part of a chain, this attractive, new (opened in 2011) hotel aims for a boutique feel with spacious rooms, high-end mattresses, big windows and artful details (like the B&W framed prints in the rooms, and a working vintage typewriter in the lobby). It's in a decent location, 10-minutes' walk to the Inner Harbor.

Mount Vernon Hotel HOTEL $$
(☎410-727-2000; www.mountvernonbaltimore.com; 24 W Franklin St; d $150; P ❄ ☎) The historic 1907 Mount Vernon Hotel is a good value for its comfortable, heritage-style rooms in a good location near the restaurant scene along Charles St. Hearty cooked breakfasts sweeten the deal.

HI-Baltimore Hostel HOSTEL $
(☎410-576-8880; www.hiusa.org/baltimore; 17 W Mulberry St; dm/d incl breakfast $25/65; ❄ @ ☎) Located in a beautifully restored 1857 mansion, the HI-Baltimore has four-, eight- and 12-bed dorms, plus a private double room. Helpful management, nice location and filigreed classical chic make this one of the region's best hostels.

Eating

Baltimore is an ethnically rich town that sits on top of the greatest seafood repository in the world, not to mention the fault line between the down-home South and cutting-edge innovation of the Northeast.

DOWNTOWN & LITTLE ITALY

Charleston SOUTHERN $$$
(☎410-332-7373; 1000 Lancaster St; 3-/6-courses $74/109; ⏰5:30-10pm Mon-Sat) One of Baltimore's most celebrated restaurants, Charleston serves beautifully prepared Southern-accented fare in a plush setting. Extensive wine list and superb desserts (always included).

Vaccaro's Pastry ITALIAN $
(222 Albemarle St; desserts $7; ⏰9am-10pm Sun-Thu, to midnight Fri & Sat) Vacarro's serves some of the best desserts and coffee in town. The cannoli are legendary, and the gelato and tiramisu are also quite good.

Isabella's PIZZA $$
(221 S High St; sandwiches $7-9, pizzas $13-15; ⏰11am-9pm Mon-Sat, to 5pm Sun) This casual neighborhood place has only a few tables, but it's worth crowding in to sample the excellent Italian pies and gourmet sandwiches, made from high-quality market-fresh ingredients.

Amicci's ITALIAN $$
(☎410-528-1096; 231 S High St; lunch mains $8-10, dinner $14-18; ⏰11am-10pm Sun-Thu, to midnight Fri & Sat; 🖉) This local icon serves up traditional Italian comfort food at reasonable

prices. Seafood-lovers and vegetarians will be especially pleased.

MT VERNON

Helmand AFGHAN $$
(☎410-752-0311; 806 N Charles St; mains $13-15; ⏰5-10pm Sun-Thu, to 11pm Fri & Sat) The Helmand is a longtime favorite for its *kaddo borawni* (pumpkin in yogurt-garlic sauce), vegetable platters and flavorful beef and lamb meatballs followed by cardamom ice cream. Good prices, but it's a dressy affair.

Cazbar TURKISH $$
(☎410-528-1222; 316 N Charles St; lunch mains $8-10, dinner $16-20; ⏰11am-midnight Mon-Thu, to 2am Fri & Sat, 4pm-midnight Sun) Along a restaurant-sprinkled stretch of Charles St, Cazbar spreads tasty Turkish fare (including creamy hummus and char-grilled lamb and other meats) amid bold colors, multihued lamps and a belly dancer on weekends. Upstairs becomes a lounge on Friday and Saturday with DJs, hookahs and a small dance floor.

City Cafe CAFE $$
(1001 Cathedral St; mains lunch $10-14, dinner $15-29; ⏰7:30am-10pm Mon-Fri, 10am-10pm Sat, 10am-8pm Sun; 📶) Bright, inviting cafe with floor-to-ceiling windows, desserts and gourmet sandwiches; dining room in back serves high-end bistro fare.

Dukem ETHIOPIAN $$
(☎410-385-0318; 1100 Maryland Ave; mains $12-16; ⏰11am-10:30pm) Delicious Ethiopian cooking, including spicy chicken, lamb and vegetarian dishes, all sopped up with spongy flatbread. There's live music some evenings.

Mekong VIETNAMESE $
(105 W Saratoga St; mains $8-10; ⏰11am-9pm Tue-Sat) Much loved hole-on-the-wall place serving first-rate pho (beef and rice noodle soup).

Lexington Market FAST FOOD $
(400 W Lexington St; ⏰9am-5pm Mon-Sat) Around since 1782, Lexington Market is famous but rather run-down. Don't miss the crab cakes at **Faidley's** (www.faidleyscrabcakes.com) seafood stall.

FEDERAL HILL & AROUND

Centro Tapas Bar SPANISH $
(☎443-869-6871; 1444 Light St; small plates $4-10; ⏰6-10pm Tue-Sat) An elegant neighborhood favorite for tasty sharing plates (lobster croquettes, roasted pork belly, wild sautéed mushrooms) and good wines by the glass. Warm nights offer dining on the backyard patio. Tuesday's $3 tapas menu is a draw.

Bluegrass Tavern MODERN AMERICAN $$
(☎410-244-5101; 1500 S Hanover St; mains $12-28; ⏰5-10pm Tue-Wed, to 11pm Thu-Sat, 10am-10pm Sun) Warm woods and boutique bourbons set the scene at this welcoming bar and upscale eatery. You'll find house-made charcuterie, unique beers and cocktails, and market fresh fare with Southern accents. Superb Sunday brunches (fresh doughnuts).

Cross Street Market MARKET $
(1065 Cross St, btwn Light & Charles Sts; ⏰7am-7pm Mon-Sat) This well-located food emporium has tempting stalls hawking oysters, crab cakes, sushi, fresh baked goodies, rotisserie chicken, and plenty of fruit, veg and picnic fare – plus beer (big ones) near the Charles St entrance.

FELL'S POINT & CANTON

TOP CHOICE **Blue Hill Tavern** MODERN AMERICAN $$$
(☎443-388-9363; 938 S Conkling St; mains $25-31; ⏰11:30am-2:30pm & 5-10pm Mon-Thu, to 11pm Fri, 5-11pm Sat, 4-9pm Sun) The dining room has blue shimmery fabrics and dark wood furnishings, a subtle backdrop to the bold and flavorful dishes at this award-winning spot. Recent hits include grilled octopus on endive with cloves, and tender slow-cooked lamb loin. Good service (and wine recommendations) and an outdoor rooftop bar in summer.

Obrycki's SEAFOOD $$$
(☎410-732-6399; 1727 E Pratt St; mains $19-30; ⏰11:30am-10pm Mon-Thu, to 11pm Fri & Sat, to 9:30pm Sun Mar-Nov) Despite its somewhat touristy reputation, Obrycki's is the go-to spot for crab-lovers, with crab soup, crab balls, crab cakes, steamed crabs and soft-shelled crabs.

HAMPDEN & NORTH BALITMORE

Cafe Hon DINER $$
(1002 W 36th St; mains $7-17; ⏰7am-9pm Mon-Fri, 9am-9pm Sat & Sun) You don't have to be sporting rhinestone-studded glasses and a bouffant hairdo to eat here, but you'll earn serious brownie points. The American comfort food at this veggie-friendly diner is as hearty as the cafe's attitude. After dinner, slide over to adjacent Hon Bar.

PaperMoon Diner DINER $$
(227 W 29th St; mains $7-16; ⏰7am-midnight Sun-Thu, to 2am Fri & Sat) Like a kaleidoscope

dream, this brightly colored, quintessential Baltimore diner is decorated with thousands of old toys, creepy mannequins and other quirky knickknacks. The real draw here is the anytime breakfast – fluffy French toast, crispy bacon and bagels with lox.

Drinking & Entertainment

On weekends, Fell's Point and Canton turn into temples of alcoholic excess that would make a Roman emperor blush. Mt Vernon and North Baltimore are a little more civilized, but any one of Baltimore's neighborhoods houses a cozy local pub. The Power Plant Live complex is filled with chain-brand clubs. In Federal Hill, Cross St is sprinkled with eat-and-drink spots. Unless otherwise noted, closing time is 2am.

Bars & Nightclubs

DOWNTOWN & LITTLE ITALY

Mick O'Shea's PUB

(328 N Charles St; from 11:30am) Your standard paraphernalia-festooned Irish pub, with live Irish music Friday and Saturday.

Howl at the Moon LIVE MUSIC

(22 Market Pl, Power Plant Live complex; cover Thu/Fri & Sat $5/7; from 7pm Wed-Sat) Howl stands out from the cookie-cutter clubs of Power Plant Live with its innovative theme: dueling pianos and a back-up band play audience requests, and everyone sings along.

MT VERNON

TOP CHOICE **Brewer's Art** BAR

(1106 N Charles St; from 4pm Mon-Sat, from 5pm Sun) This subterranean cave mesmerizes the senses with an overwhelming selection of beers. Its upstairs embodiment serves respectable dinners in its classy dining room.

Club Charles BAR

(1724 N Charles St; from 6pm) Hipsters adorned in the usual skinny jeans/vintage T-shirt uniform, as well as characters from other walks of life, flock to this 1940s art-deco cocktail lounge to enjoy good tunes and cheap drinks.

13th Floor COCKTAIL BAR

(1 E Chase St; from 5pm Wed-Fri, from 6pm Sat) Atop the Gothic Belvedere Hotel, this iconic but dated spot has fantastic views over Baltimore. Also in the Belvedere, the **Owl Bar** is a nostalgic throwback to '50s Baltimore, with a long wooden bar that attracts a martini-sipping crowd.

FEDERAL HILL

Little Havana BAR

(1325 Key Hwy; from 11:30am) A good after-work spot and a great place to sip *mojitos* on the waterfront deck, this converted brick warehouse is a major draw on warm, sunny days (especially around weekend brunch time).

8x10 LIVE MUSIC

(www.the8x10.com; 10 E Cross St; cover $10-20; from 7pm) Baltimore's premiere live music venue since 1983 mixes big-name acts with strong local talent in a funky concert hall that feels intimate and expansive all at once.

Pub Dog PUB

(20 E Cross St; 5pm-2am) Pictures of beloved canines adorn this cozy space (though their live compatriots are no longer allowed), which serves delicious brew (or two for $4), and tasty pizzas and bistro fare.

FELL'S POINT & CANTON

One-Eyed Mike's PUB

(708 S Bond St; 11am-2am) Handshakes and a hearty welcome will make you feel right at home at this popular pirate-themed spot. With tin ceilings and old-world details, it's also one of Baltimore's oldest taverns. There's gourmet grub and a handy outdoor patio/smoking space.

Ale Mary's BAR

(1939 Fleet St; from 4pm Mon-Thu, from 11:30am Fri-Sun) Its name and decor pay homage to Maryland's Catholic roots, with crosses, rosaries and nun things scattered about. Aside from the kitsch factor, Ale Mary's brings in a fun festive crowd and serves satisfying food (crab cakes, tater tots, bread pudding).

Gay & Lesbian Venues

Baltimore has a remarkably vibrant, multiracial gay scene. Club admission ranges from $5 to $10.

Grand Central GAY & LESBIAN

(www.centralstationpub.com; 1001 N Charles St; 9pm-2am Wed-Sun) More of a complex than a club, Central spreads a fancy to suit all moods – dance floor, pub and Sappho's (free admission for the ladies). Probably boasts B's best dance floors.

Hippo GAY

(www.clubhippo.com; 1 W Eager St; from 4pm) The Hippo has been around forever and is still one of the city's largest gay clubs (though some nights the dance floor is dead), with themed nights (gay bingo, karaoke, hip-hop).

Performing Arts & Theater

The Baltimore Symphony Orchestra performs at the **Meyerhoff Symphony Hall** (☎410-783-8000; www.bsomusic.org; 1212 Cathedral St), while the Baltimore Opera performs at the **Lyric Opera House** (☎410-685-5086; www.lyricoperahouse.com; 140 W Mt Royal Ave).

Theater options include **Center Stage** (☎410-332-0033; www.centerstage.org; 700 N Calvert St), which stages Shakespeare, Wilde, Miller and contemporary works; and **Charles Theatre** (☎410-727-3456; www.thecharles.com; 1711 N Charles St), screening the best art-house films in the city.

Sports

Whether it's touchdowns, home runs, goals or monster-truck shows, Baltimoreans love their sports. The town plays hard and parties even harder, with tailgating parties in parking lots and games showing on numerous televisions.

Baltimore Orioles BASEBALL
(☎888-848-2473; www.orioles.com) The Orioles play at **Oriole Park at Camden Yards** (333 W Camden St), arguably the best ballpark in America. Daily tours (admission $9) of the stadium are offered during regular season (April to October).

Baltimore Ravens FOOTBALL
(☎410-261-7283; www.baltimoreravens.com) The Ravens play at **M&T Bank Stadium** (1101 Russell St) from September to January.

Homewood Field LACROSSE
(☎410-516-7490; hopkinssports.cstv.com; Homewood Field on University Pkwy) Maryland is lacrosse heartland, and its residents are arguably the sport's most fanatic followers. The best place to watch 'lax' is at Johns Hopkins University's Homewood Field.

Baltimore Blast INDOOR SOCCER
(☎410-732-5278; www.baltimoreblast.com) The National Indoor Soccer League team plays at the **1st Mariner Arena** (☎410-347-2020; 201 W Baltimore St) from October to April.

Pimlico HORSE RACING
(www.pimlico.com; 5201 Park Heights Ave) Horse racing is huge from April to late May, especially at Pimlico, which hosts the Preakness (p276). The track is roughly 7 miles north of downtown.

Information

Internet Access

Enoch Pratt Free Library (400 Cathedral St; ⏲10am-8pm Mon-Wed, to 5pm Thu-Sat, 1-5pm Sun; wi-fi)

Media

Baltimore Sun (www.baltimoresun.com) Daily city newspaper.

City Paper (www.citypaper.com) Free alt-weekly.

Medical Services

University of Maryland Medical Center (☎410-328-8667; 22 S Greene St) Has a 24-hour emergency room.

Post

Post office (900 E Fayette St)

Tourist Information

Baltimore Area Visitor Center (☎877-225-8466; http://baltimore.org; 401 Light St; ⏲9am-6pm Mon-Fri) Located on the Inner Harbor. Sells the Harbor Pass (adult/child $60/45), which gives admission to six major area attractions.

Getting There & Away

The **Baltimore/Washington International Thurgood Marshall Airport** (BWI; ☎410-859-7111, www.bwiairport.com) is 10 miles south of downtown via I-295.

Greyhound and **Peter Pan Bus Lines** (☎410-752-7682; 2110 Haines St) have numerous buses from Washington, DC (roughly every 45 minutes, one hour, $11 to $16); from New York they cost $14 to $35 (12 to 15 per day, 4½ hours). The **BoltBus** (☎877-265-8287; www.boltbus.com; 1610 St Paul St; wi-fi) has seven buses a day to/from NYC (3½ hours, $13 to $19).

Penn Station (1500 N Charles St) is in north Baltimore. MARC operates weekday commuter trains to/from Washington, DC ($7, 71 minutes). **Amtrak** (☎800-872-7245; www.amtrak.com) trains serve the East Coast and beyond.

Getting Around

Light Rail (tickets $1.60; ⏲6am-11pm) runs from BWI airport to Lexington Market and Penn Station. Train frequency is every five to 10 minutes. MARC trains run hourly between Penn Station and BWI airport on weekdays for $4. **SuperShuttle** (☎800-258-3826; www.supershuttle.com) provides a BWI-van service to the Inner Harbor for $14. Check **Maryland Transit Administration** (MTA; www.mtamaryland.com) for all local transportation schedules and fares.

Baltimore Water Taxi (☎410-563-3901; www.baltimorewatertaxi.com; Inner Harbor; daily pass adult/child $10/5) docks at all harborside attractions and neighborhoods.

Annapolis

Annapolis is as charming as state capitals get. The Colonial architecture, cobblestones, flickering lamps and brick row houses are worthy of Dickens, but the effect isn't artificial; this city has preserved, rather than created, its heritage.

Perched on Chesapeake Bay, life in Annapolis (motto: 'Come Sail Away') revolves around the city's rich maritime traditions. It's home to the US Naval Academy, whose 'middies' (midshipmen students) stroll through town in their starched white uniforms. Sailing is not just a hobby, it's a way of life, and the city docks are crammed with vessels of all shapes and sizes. For landlubbers, the food is great, and a beer on the pier cooled by a salty headwind is even better.

There's a **visitor center** (www.visitannapolis.org; 26 West St; ⌚9am-5pm) and a seasonal information booth at City Dock. A **Maryland Welcome Center** (☎410-974-3400; 350 Rowe Blvd; ⌚9am-5pm) is inside the State House, and runs free tours of the building.

Sights & Activities

Annapolis has more 18th-century buildings than any other city in America, including the homes of all four Marylanders who signed the Declaration of Independence.

Think of the State House as a wheel hub from which most attractions fan out, leading to the City Dock and historic waterfront.

US Naval Academy UNIVERSITY

The undergraduate college of the US Navy is one of the most selective universities in America. The **Armel-Leftwich visitor center** (Gate 1, City Dock entrance; tours adult/child $9.50/7.50; ⌚9am-5pm) is the place to book tours and immerse yourself in all things Academy. Come for the formation weekdays at 12:05pm sharp, when the 4000 midshipmen and midshipwomen conduct a 20-minute military marching display in the yard. Photo ID is required for entry. If you've got a thing for American naval history, go on and revel in the **Naval Academy Museum** (118 Maryland Ave; admission free; ⌚9am-5pm Mon-Sat, from 11am Sun).

FREE **Maryland State House** HISTORIC SITE

(25 State Circle; ⌚9am-5pm Mon-Fri, 10am-4pm Sat & Sun) The country's oldest state capitol in continuous legislative use, the stately 1772 State House also served as national capital from 1733 to 1734. The Maryland Senate is in action here from January to April. The upside-down giant acorn atop the dome stands for wisdom. Photo ID is required for entry.

Hammond-Harwood House HISTORIC SITE

(www.hammondharwoodhouse.org; 19 Maryland Ave; adult/child $6/3; ⌚noon-5pm Tue-Sun Apr-Oct) Of the many historical homes in town, the 1774 HHH is the one to visit. It has a superb collection of decorative arts, including furniture, paintings and ephemera dating to the 18th century, and is one of the finest existing British Colonial homes in America.

St John's College UNIVERSITY

(www.stjohnscollege.edu; cnr College Ave & King George St) Take a self-guided tour through the grounds. Originally founded in 1696 as the King William's preparatory school, it's one of the oldest institutions of higher learning in the country.

Kunta Kinte–Alex Haley Memorial MONUMENT

At the City Dock, the Kunta Kinte–Alex Haley Memorial marks the spot where Kunta Kinte – ancestor of *Roots* author Alex Haley – was brought in chains from Africa. Haley received a 1977 special Pulitzer Prize Letters award for his epic.

William Paca House & Garden HISTORIC SITE

(annapolis.org; adult/child $8/5; ⌚10am-5pm Mon-Sat, noon-5pm Sun) An Annapolis highlight, founded in the 18th-century.

Tours

Four Centuries Walking Tour WALKING

(www.watermarkcruises.com; adult/child $16/10) A costumed docent will lead you on this great introduction to all things Annapolis. The 10:30am tour leaves from the visitor center and the 1:30pm tour leaves from the information booth at the City Dock; there's a slight variation in sights visited by each, but both cover the country's largest concentration of 18th-century buildings, influential African Americans and colonial spirits who don't want to leave. The associated one-hour **Pirates of the Chesapeake Cruise** (adult/child $16/13; ⌚late May-early Sep) is good 'yar'-worthy fun, especially for the kids.

Watermark Cruises CRUISE

(www.watermarkcruises.com; City Dock; 40min adult/child $13/5) The best way to explore the city's maritime heritage is on the water. Watermark, which operates the Four Centuries Walking Tour, offers a variety of cruise options, with frequent departures.

Woodwind CRUISE
(☎410-263-7837; www.schoonerwoodwind.com; 80 Compromise St; sunset cruise adult/child $39/25; ⊙May-Oct) This beautiful 74ft schooner offers two-hour day and sunset cruises. Or splurge for the Woodwind 'boat & breakfast' package (rooms $295, including breakfast), one of the more unique lodging options in town.

Sleeping

Historic Inns of Annapolis INN $$
(☎410-263-2641; www.historicinnsofannapolis.com; 58 State Circle; r $100-170; ❄📶) The Historic Inns comprise three different boutique guesthouses, each set in a heritage building in the heart of old Annapolis: the Maryland Inn, the Governor Calvert House and the Robert Johnson House. Common areas are packed with period details, and the best rooms boast antiques, a fireplace and attractive views (the cheapest are small and could use an update).

1908 William Page Inn B&B $$$
(☎410-263-1506; www.1908-williampageinn.com; 8 Martin St; r incl breakfast $175-235; P❄📶) For a romantic getaway, nothing beats this Victorian B&B. Beautifully decorated, comfortable rooms are capped with wonderful hospitality and delicious breakfast.

ScotLaur Inn B&B $$
(☎410-268-5665; www.scotlaurinn.com; 165 Main St; r $95-140; P❄📶) The folks from Chick & Ruth's Delly offer 10 simple pink-and-blue rooms with private bath at their B&B (bed and bagel) above the deli.

Country Inn & Suites HOTEL $
(☎410-571-6700; www.countryinns.com; 2600 Housley Rd, at Hwy 450; r from $86; P❄📶🏊) As charming as chains get, plus it has free shuttles to the historic district.

Eating & Drinking

With the Chesapeake at its doorstep, Annapolis has superb seafood.

Middleton Tavern SEAFOOD $$
(2 Market Space; mains $10-33; ⊙11:30am-1:30am Mon-Sat, from 10am Sun) One of the oldest continuously operating pubs in the country. As you'd expect from a waterside pub, the menu features some of the freshest seafood around. Live music most nights.

49 West CAFE $$
(☎410-626-9796; 49 West St; mains lunch $8-10, dinner $15-23; ⊙8am-11pm) This art-filled hideaway in Annapolis serves eclectic cuisine – breakfast standards, gourmet sandwiches and salads for lunch, seafood and bistro fare by night (seared tuna with pesto, *mojito*-glazed chicken), and good wines and cocktails. Live music most nights.

Galway Bay PUB $$
(☎410-263-8333; 63 Maryland Ave; mains $8-15; ⊙11am-midnight Mon-Sat, from 10:30am Sun) The epitome of a power-broker bar, this Irish-owned and -operated pub is the dark sort of hideaway where political deals go down over Jameson, stouts and mouth-watering seafood specials.

Chick & Ruth's Delly DINER $
(165 Main St; mains $6-10; ⊙6:30am-10pm Sun-Thu, to 11:30pm Fri & Sat) A cornerstone of Annapolis, the Delly is bursting with affable quirkiness and a big menu, heavy on sandwiches and breakfast fare. Patriots can relive grade-school days reciting the Pledge of Allegiance, weekdays at 8:30am (9:30am on weekends).

Annapolis Ice Cream Company ICE CREAM $
(196 Main St; ice cream $4-5; ⊙11am-10pm) Creamy ice cream made in-house from organic ingredients – good variety including seasonal flavors. Huge servings.

City Dock Cafe CAFE $
(18 Market Space; ⊙6:30am-10pm; 📶) A local favorite with excellent coffees and free wi-fi.

Rams Head Tavern PUB $$$
(www.ramsheadtavern.com; 33 West St; mains $10-30; ⊙from 11am) Serves pub fare and refreshing microbrews in an attractive oak-paneled setting, with live bands (tickets $15 to $55) onstage.

Getting There & Around

Greyhound runs buses to Washington, DC (once daily, $16). **Dillon's Bus** (www.dillonbus.com; tickets $5) has 26 weekday-only commuter buses between Annapolis and Washington, DC, connecting with various DC Metro lines. **Annapolis Transit** (☎410-263-7964) provides local transport.

Inexpensive **bikes** (per day $5; ⊙9am-8pm) are available for hire from the Harbormaster's office at the City Dock.

Eastern Shore

Just across the Chesapeake Bay Bridge, a short drive from the urban sprawl of the Baltimore–Washington corridor, Maryland's landscape makes a dramatic about-face. Nondescript suburbs and jammed highways give way to unbroken miles of bird-dotted wetlands, serene waterscapes, endless cornfields, sandy beaches and friendly little villages. The coastal flat plains are ideal for cycling. For the most part, the Eastern Shore retains its charm despite the growing influx of city-dwelling yuppies and day-trippers. This area revolves around the water: working waterfront communities still survive off Chesapeake Bay and its tributaries, and boating, fishing, crabbing and kayaking are a part of local life. This is America at its most genuine.

ST MICHAELS, TILGHMAN ISLAND & OXFORD

St Michaels, the prettiest little village on the Eastern Shore, lives up to its motto as 'the Heart & Soul of Chesapeake Bay.' It's a mix of old Victorian homes, quaint B&Bs, boutique shops and working docks, where escape artists from Washington mix with salty-dog crabbers. On weekends the village can get crowded with out-of-town boaters. During the War of 1812, inhabitants rigged up lanterns in a nearby forest and blacked out the town. British naval gunners shelled the trees, allowing St Michaels to escape destruction. The building now known as the **Cannonball House** (Mulberry St) was the only structure to have been hit.

At the lighthouse, the **Chesapeake Bay Maritime Museum** (www.cbmm.org; 213 N Talbot St; adult/child $13/6; ⌚9am-6pm summer) delves into the deep ties between Shore folk and America's largest estuary. Narrated 60-minute cruises aboard the **Patriot** (☎410-745-3100; www.patriotcruises.com; Navy Point; adult/child $25/13) leave from the dock near the Crab Claw several times a day.

The Victorian red-brick **Parsonage Inn** (☎410-745-8383; www.parsonage-inn.com; 210 N Talbot St; r incl breakfast $150-210; P❄) offers floral decadence (curtains, duvets) and brass beds, plus a friendly welcome by its hospitable innkeepers.

Next door to the Maritime Museum the **Crab Claw** (☎410-745-2900; 304 Burns St; mains $15-30; ⌚11am-10pm) has a splendid open-air setting at the water's edge. Get messy eating delicious steamed crabs ($36 to $60 per dozen) at picnic tables, or head upstairs for more refined seafood feasting.

At the end of the road over the Hwy 33 drawbridge, tiny **Tilghman Island** still runs a working waterfront where local captains take visitors out on graceful oyster skipjacks; the historic **Rebecca T Ruark** (☎410-829-3976; www.skipjack.org; 2hr cruises adult/child $30/15), built in 1886, is the oldest certified vessel of its kind.

Oxford is a small village with a history dating back to the 1600s and a fine spread

WORTH A TRIP

SCENIC DRIVE: MARITIME MARYLAND

Maryland and Chesapeake Bay have always been inextricable, but there are some places where the old-fashioned way of life on the bay seems to have changed little over the passing centuries.

About 150 miles south of Baltimore, at the edge of the Eastern Shore, is **Crisfield**, the top working water town in Maryland. Get visiting details at the **visitor center** (☎410-968-2501; 3 9th St; ⌚10am-4pm Mon-Sat). Any seafood you eat here will be first-rate, but for a true Shore experience, **Watermen's Inn** (☎410-968-2119; 901 W Main St; mains $12-20; ⌚11am-9pm Wed-Fri, from 8am Sat & Sun) is legendary. In a simple, unpretentious setting, you can feast on local catch from an ever-changing menu.

From here you can leave your car and take a boat to **Smith Island** (www.visitsmithisland.com), the only offshore settlement in the state. Several small vessels make the journey, including the **Captain Jason II** (☎410-425-2771; www.smithislandcruises.com; adult/child round-trip $25/13; ⌚12:30pm mid-Jun–Sep); call for schedule off season. Settled by fisherfolk from the English West Country some 400 years ago, the island's tiny population still speak with what linguists reckon is the closest thing to a 17th-century Cornish accent. The island's website has information on island B&Bs, restaurants and activities. Ferries will take you back to the mainland and the present day at 3:45pm.

EATING MARYLAND: BLUE CRABS

Eating at a crab shack, where the dress code stops at shorts and flip-flops, is the quintessential Chesapeake Bay experience. Folks in these parts take their crabs seriously and can spend hours debating the intricacies of how to crack a crab, the proper way to prepare them and where to find the best crabs. There is one thing Marylanders can agree on: they must be blue crabs (scientific name: *Callinectes sapidus*), a critter indigenous to these parts and one of the bay's most important economic products.

Steamed crabs are prepared very simply, using beer and Old Bay seasoning. One of the best crab shacks in the state is **Jimmy Cantler's Riverside Inn** (458 Forest Beach Rd, Annapolis; ⏲11am-11pm Sun-Thu, to midnight Sun), where eating a steamed crab has been elevated to an art form – a hands-on, messy endeavor, normally accompanied by corn on the cob and ice-cold beer. Another fine spot is across the bay at the Crab Claw (p283).

Although the blue crab numbers are down from historical levels – due to overfishing and water pollution – recent studies are showing they may be on a comeback. In 2009, 223 million adult blue crabs were estimated to be living in the bay – a 70% increase over 2008 and the first time in nearly two decades that adult blue crab abundance exceeded the interim goal of 200 million crabs.

of leafy streets and waterfront homes. Although you can drive there via US-333, it's well worth taking the old-fashioned **ferry** (☎410-745-9023; www.oxfordbellevueferry.com; 1 way car/additional passenger/pedestrian $11/1/3; ⏲9am-sunset Apr-Nov) from Bellevue. Try to turn up around sunset for memorable views.

Once in Oxford, don't miss the chance to dine at the celebrated **Robert Morris Inn** (☎410-226-5111; www.robertmorrisinn.com; 314 N Morris St; mains $17-29; ⏲7:30am-10am, noon-2:30pm & 5:30-9:30pm) near the ferry dock. Award-winning crab cakes, grilled local rockfish and medallions of spring lamb are nicely matched by wines and best followed by pavlova with berries and other desserts. You can also overnight in one of the inn's heritage-style rooms (from $200).

BERLIN & SNOW HILL

Imagine 'small-town, main street Americana,' cute that vision up by a few points, and you've come close to these Eastern Shore villages. Most of the buildings here are preserved or renovated to look preserved. Antiquity hunters will have to budget extra time to browse the antique shops littering this area.

In Berlin, the **Globe Theater** (☎410-641-0784; www.globetheater.com; 12 Broad St; lunch mains $6-12, dinner $11-25; ⏲11am-10pm; 📶) is a lovingly restored main stage that serves as a restaurant, bar, art gallery and theater for nightly live music; the kitchen serves eclectic American fare with global accents (seafood burritos, jerk chicken wraps). The nearby, still-functioning **Hair Shop** (17 N Main St) was used as a location in the 1999 film *Runaway Bride*.

There are B&Bs galore, but if you need an alternative try the **Atlantic Hotel** (☎410-641-3589; www.atlantichotel.com; 2 N Main St; r $115-245; P❄). This handsome, Gilded-era lodger gives guests the time-warp experience with all the modern amenities, and the attached **Drummer's Cafe** (lunch mains $9-14, dinner $17-34; ⏲11am-3pm & 5-10pm Mon-Sat, 10am-3pm Sun) serves up local favorites.

A few miles from Berlin, Snow Hill has a splendid location along the idyllic Pocomoke River. Get on the water with the **Pocomoke River Canoe Company** (☎410-632-3971; 312 N Washington St; canoe per hr/day $15/40). They'll even take you upriver so you can have a leisurely paddle downstream. Nearby **Furnace Town** (☎410-632-2032; www.furnacetown.com; Old Furnace Rd; adult/child $5/3; ⏲10am-5pm Apr-Oct), off Rte 12, is a living-history museum that marks the old location of a 19th-century iron-smelting town. In Snow Hill itself, while away an odd, rewarding half-hour in the **Julia A Purnell Museum** (☎410-632-0515; 208 W Market St; adult/child $2/50¢; ⏲10am-4pm Tue-Sat, from 1pm Sun Apr-Oct), a tiny structure that feels like an attic for the entire Eastern Shore.

Staying in town? Check out Snow Hill's **River House Inn** (☎410-632-2722; 201 E Market St; www.riverhouseinn.com; r $160-190, cottage $250-300; P❄📶🐾), with a lush backyard that overlooks a scenic bend of the river.

Palette (☎410-632-0055; 104 W Market St; mains $18-2; ⏰11am-3pm Tue-Wed, to 9pm Thu-Sat, 10am-2pm Sun) serves a changing menu of contemporary American fare, using organic locally sourced ingredients.

Ocean City

'The OC' is where you'll experience the American seaside resort at its tackiest. Here you can take a spin on nausea-inducing thrill rides, buy a T-shirt with obscene slogans and drink to excess at cheesy theme bars. The center of action is the 2.5-mile-long boardwalk, which stretches from the inlet to 27th St. The beach is attractive, but you'll have to contend with packs of horny teenagers and noisy crowds; the beaches north of the boardwalk are much quieter.

The **visitor center** (☎800-626-2326; www.ococean.com; ⏰9am-5pm), in the convention center on Coastal Hwy at 40th St, can help you find lodging. In summer, the town's tiny year-round population of 7100 swells to over 150,000; traffic is jammed and parking scarce.

Sleeping

King Charles Hotel GUESTHOUSE $$
(☎410-289-6141; www.kingcharleshotel.com; 1209 N Baltimore Ave, at 12th St; r $115-170; P ❄ 📶) This place could be a quaint summer cottage, except it happens to be a short stroll to the heart of the boardwalk action. It has aging but clean rooms with small porches attached, and it's quiet (owners discourage young partiers).

Spinnaker Motel HOTEL $$$
(☎410-289-5444; http://ocmotels.com/spinnaker; cnr 18th St & Baltimore Ave; r $160-250; P ❄ 📶 🏊) Cheaper than most beachfront hotels, the Spinnaker has friendly staff, comfortable beds, and balconies with ocean views. It's in the thick of things, so it could get noisy.

Eating & Drinking

Surf 'n' turf and all-you-can-eat deals are the order of the day. Dance clubs cluster around the boardwalk's southern tip.

TOP CHOICE **Liquid Assets** MODERN AMERICAN $$
(☎410-524-7037; www.la94.com; 94th St & Coastal Hwy; mains $10-26; ⏰11:30am-11pm) Like a diamond in the rough, this bistro gem and wine shop complex is hidden in a strip mall in north OC. The menu is a refreshing mix of innovative seafood, grilled meats and regional classics (Carolina pork BBQ, 'ahi tuna burger).

Fager's Island MODERN AMERICAN $$$
(☎410-524-5500; www.fagers.com; 60th St; mains $19-36; ⏰from 11am) The food is hit-and-miss, but it's a great place for a drink, with enviable views over Isle of Wight Bay. Live bands and DJs keep the bachelorettes rolling on weekends.

Seacrets BAR
(www.seacrets.com; cnr W 49th St & the Bay; ⏰8am-2am) A water-laced, Jamaican-themed, rum-soaked bar straight out of MTV's *Spring Break*. You can drift around in an inner tube while sipping a drink and people-watching at OC's most famous meet-market.

Getting There & Around

Greyhound (☎410-289-9307; 12848 Ocean Gateway) buses run daily to and from Washington, DC ($62, four hours) and Baltimore ($55, 3½ hours).

WORTH A TRIP

ASSATEAGUE ISLAND

Just 8 miles south but a world away from Ocean City is Assateague Island seashore, a perfectly barren landscape of sand dunes and beautiful, secluded beaches. This undeveloped barrier island is populated by the only herd of wild horses on the East Coast, made famous in the book *Misty of Chincoteague*.

The island is divided into three sections. In Maryland there's **Assateague State Park** (☎410-641-2918; Rte 611; admission/campsites $4/31; ⏰campground open late Apr-Oct) and federally administered **Assateague Island National Seashore** (☎410-641-1441; www.nps.gov/asis; Rte 611; admission/vehicles/campsites $3/15/20; ⏰visitors center 9am-5pm). Chincoteague National Wildlife Refuge (see p306) is in Virginia.

As well as swimming and sunbathing, recreational activities include birding, kayaking, canoeing, crabbing and fishing. There are no services on the Maryland side of the island, so you must bring all your own food and drink. Don't forget insect repellent; the mosquitoes and biting horseflies can be ferocious!

Ocean City Coastal Highway Bus (day pass $3) runs up and down the length of the beach, from 6am to 3am.

Western Maryland

The western spine of Maryland is mountain country. The Appalachian peaks soar to 3000ft above sea level, and the surrounding valleys are packed with rugged scenery and Civil War battlefields. This is Maryland's outdoor playground, where hiking, skiing, rock climbing and white-water rafting are just a short drive from Baltimore.

FREDERICK

Halfway between the battlefields of Gettysburg, PA, and Antietam, Frederick is a popular stop along the Civil War trail. Its 50-square-block historic district is filled with 18th- and 19th-century buildings in various states of renovation. The **visitor center** (☎301-600-2888; 151 S East St), across from the MARC train station, is a 10-minute walk to the historic district.

The **National Museum of Civil War Medicine** (www.civilwarmed.org; 48 E Patrick St; adult/child $6.50/4.50; ⏰10am-5pm Mon-Sat, from 11am Sun) gives a fascinating, sometimes gruesome look at the health conditions soldiers and doctors faced during the war, as well as important medical advances that resulted from the conflict.

Hollerstown Hill B&B (☎301-228-3630; www.hollerstownhill.com; 4 Clarke Pl; r $135-145; P❄📶) has four pattern-heavy rooms, an elegant billiards room and friendly, knowledgeable hosts.

On restaurant-lined Market St, **Volt** (☎301-696-3658; 228 N Market St; mains $29-40; ⏰noon-10pm) is one of Frederick's finest, with a seasonal, locally sourced menu, first-rate service and a loyal following who come from DC and beyond. It's set in a beautifully restored 19th-century mansion. Reserve months ahead for the Table 21 experience (21 courses for $121 served inside the kitchen). The three-course lunch for $25 is a great value.

Frederick is accessible via **Greyhound** (☎301-663-3311) and **MARC trains** (☎301-682-9716) located across from the visitor center at 100 S East St.

ANTIETAM NATIONAL BATTLEFIELD

The site of the bloodiest day in American history is, ironically, supremely peaceful, quiet and haunting, uncluttered save for plaques and statues. On September 17, 1862, General Robert E Lee's first invasion of the North was stalled here in a tactical stalemate that left over 23,000 dead, wounded or missing – more casualties than America had suffered in all her previous wars combined. Poignantly, many of the battlefield graves are inscribed with German and Irish names, a roll call of immigrants who died fighting for their new homeland.

The **visitor center** (☎301-432-5124; State Rd 65; 3-day individual/family pass $4/6; ⏰8:30am-6pm, to 5pm low season) sells a range of books and materials, including self-guided driving and walking tours of the battlefield.

Ten miles southeast of Antietam, off I-67 in **Burkittsville**, is **Gathland State Park** (☎301-791-4767; admission free; ⏰8am-sunset), with access to the Appalachian Trail. Burkittsville is also famous as the setting of *The Blair Witch Project*.

CUMBERLAND

At the Potomac River, the frontier outpost of Fort Cumberland (not to be confused with the Cumberland Gap between Virginia and Kentucky) was the pioneer gateway across the Alleghenies to Pittsburgh and the Ohio River. Today Cumberland has expanded into the outdoor recreation trade to guide visitors to the region's rivers, forests and mountains. The sights below are a short stroll from the pedestrian-friendly streets of downtown Cumberland.

Sights & Activities

C&O Canal National Historic Park TRAIL

A marvel of engineering, the C&O Canal was designed to stretch alongside the Potomac River from Chesapeake Bay to the Ohio River. Construction on the canal began in 1828 but was halted here in 1850 by the Appalachian Mountains. The park's protected 185-mile corridor includes a 12ft-wide towpath/hiking and bicycling trail, which goes all the way from here to Georgetown in DC. The **C&O Canal Museum** (☎301-739-4200; 15 Canal Pl; ⏰9am-5pm Mon-Fri) has displays chronicling the importance of river trade in eastern seaboard history.

Great Allegheny Passage TRAIL

(GAP; www.atatrail.org) Another great walking/cycling track is along this rail trail, which travels through valleys, along rivers and by small towns en route 135 miles northwest to Duquesne, PA. Still under construction, the GAP will eventually go all the way to Pittsburgh. The trail starts near Baltimore St and the canal, and from here links with the C&O Canal path, 200m to the south.

Western Maryland Scenic Railroad TRAIN
(☎800-872-4650; www.wmsr.com; 13 Canal St; adult/child $30/16; ⊙11:30am Fri-Sun May-Oct, Sat & Sun Nov-Dec) Outside the Allegheny County visitor center, near the start of the C&O Canal, passengers can catch steam-locomotive rides, traversing forests and steep ravines to Frostburg, a 3½-hour round-trip.

Cumberland Trail Connection CYCLING
(☎301-777-8724; www.ctcbikes.com; 14 Howard St, Canal Pl; half-day/day/week from $15/25/120; ⊙10am-6pm) Conveniently located near the start of the C&O Canal, this outfit rents out bikes (cruisers, touring bikes and mountain bikes), and also arranges shuttle service anywhere from Pittsburgh to DC. Canoe rentals were in the works.

Allegany Expeditions ADVENTURE TOUR
(☎301-722-5170; www.alleganyexpeditions.com; 10310 Columbus Ave/Rte 2) Leads adventure tours, including rock-climbing, canoeing, cross-country skiing and fly-fishing.

Eating

Queen City Creamery & Deli DINER $
(☎301-777-0011; 108 Harrison St; mains $6-8; ⊙7am-9pm) This retro soda fountain is like a 1940s time warp, with creamy shakes and homemade frozen custard, thick sandwiches and belly-filling breakfasts.

DEEP CREEK LAKE

In the extreme west of the panhandle, Maryland's largest freshwater lake is an all-seasons playground. The crimson and copper glow of the Alleghenies attracts thousands during the annual **Autumn Glory Festival** (www.autumngloryfestival.com) in October, rivaling New England's leaf-turning backdrops. In McHenry, the **Garrett County visitor center** (☎301-387-4386; www.visitdeepcreek.com; 15 Visitor Center Dr), off US 219 on the north end, has information on all outdoor activities, including the nearby ski resort, **Wisp** (☎301-387-4911; www.wispresort.com).

DELAWARE

Diminutive, delectable Delaware, the nation's second-smallest state (96 miles long and less than 35 miles across at its widest point) is overshadowed by her neighbors and overlooked by visitors to the Capital Region. And that's too bad, because Delaware has a lot more on offer than just tax-free shopping and chicken farms.

You may be pleasantly surprised to learn that Delaware is home to long white sandy beaches, cute colonial villages, a cozy countryside and small-town charm. A whole state just waiting to be explored, Delaware still rides on her reputation as being the first state to ratify the US Constitution, hence her new slogan: 'It's Good Being First.'

History

In colonial days Delaware was the subject of an aggressive land feud between Dutch, Swedish and British settlers. The former imported classically northern European middle-class concepts, the latter a plantation-based aristocracy, which is partly why Delaware remains a typically mid-Atlantic cultural hybrid today.

The little state's big moment came on December 7, 1787, when Delaware became the first state to ratify the US Constitution and thus the first state in the Union. It remained in that union throughout the Civil War, despite supporting slavery. During this period, as throughout much of the state's history, the economy drew on its chemical industry. DuPont, the world's second-largest chemical company, was founded here in 1802 as

DELAWARE FACTS

» **Nickname** The First State

» **Population** 900,000

» **Area** 1982 sq miles

» **Capital city** Dover (population 36,000)

» **Sales tax** none

» **Birthplace of** Rock musician George Thorogood (b 1952), actress Valerie Bertinelli (b 1960), actor Ryan Phillippe (b 1974)

» **Home of** Vice President Joe Biden, the Du Pont family, DuPont chemicals, credit-card companies, lots of chickens

» **Politics** usually democrat

» **Famous for** tax-free shopping, beautiful beaches

» **State bird** blue hen chicken

» **Driving distances** Wilmington to Dover 52 miles, Dover to Rehoboth Beach 43 miles a gunpowder factory by French Immigrant Eleuthère Irénée du Pont. Low taxes drew other firms (particularly credit-card companies) in the 20th century, boosting the state's prosperity.

Delaware Beaches

Delaware's 28 miles of sandy Atlantic beaches are the best reason to linger. All businesses and services listed here are open year-round unless otherwise noted, and all prices are for the high season (June to August). Low-season bargains abound.

LEWES

In 1631 the Dutch gave this whaling settlement the pretty name of Zwaanendael, or valley of the swans, before promptly getting massacred by local Nanticokes. The name was changed to Lewes (pronounced LOO-iss) when William Penn gained control of the area. Today it's an attractive seaside gem with a mix of English and Dutch architecture.

The **visitor center** (www.leweschamber.com; 120 Kings Hwy; ⌚9am-5pm Mon-Fri) directs you to sights such as the **Zwaanendael Museum** (102 Kings Hwy; admission free; ⌚10am-4:30pm Tue-Sat, 1:30-4:30pm Sun), where the friendly staff explains the Dutch roots of this first state settlement.

At **Fisherman's Wharf** (☎302-645-8862; www.fishlewes.com; 7 Anglers Rd) you can book boat trips on the water for sunset cruises (adult/child $15/10), dolphin-watching (adult/child $35/20) and fishing trips (half-day/day $45/85).

For more aquatic action, you can rent kayaks from **Quest Fitness Kayak** (☎302-745-2925; www.questfitnesskayak.com; Savannah Rd; kayak per 2/8hr $25/50), which operates a rental stand next to the Beacon Motel. It also runs scenic paddle tours around the Cape (adult/child $65/35).

You'll find restaurant and hotel options in the small historic downtown, including **Hotel Rodney** (☎302-645-6466; www.hotelrodneydelaware.com; 142 2nd St; r $140-250; P❄📶🚭), a charming boutique hotel with exquisite bedding and antique furniture. On the other side of the canal, **Beacon Motel** (☎302-645-4888; www.beaconmotel.com; 514 Savannah Rd; r $95-190; P❄📶🚭) has large, quiet rooms within a 10-minute walk to the beach.

There are charming restaurants and cafes sprinkled along 2nd St. Located by the drawbridge over the canal, the clapboard **Striper Bites Bistro** (☎302-645-4657; 107 Savannah Rd; lunch mains $10-12, dinner $16-24; ⌚11:30am-late Mon-Sat) specializes in innovative seafood dishes like Lewes rockfish and fish tacos. Across the drawbridge, the **Wharf** (☎302-645-7846; 7 Anglers Rd; mains $10-24; ⌚7am-1am) has a relaxing waterfront location (facing the canal), and serves a big selection of seafood and pub grub. Live music throughout the week.

The **Cape May–Lewes Ferry** (☎800-643-3779; www.capemaylewesferry.com; 43 Cape Henlopen Dr; per vehicle $36-44, plus per adult/child passenger $10/5) runs daily 90-minute ferries across Delaware Bay to New Jersey from the terminal, 1 mile from downtown Lewes. For foot passengers, a seasonal shuttle bus ($4) operates between the ferry terminal and Lewes and Rehoboth Beach. Fares are lower Sunday through Thursday. Reservations are recommended.

BIKING THE JUNCTION & BREAKWATER TRAIL

For a fantastic ride between Rehoboth and Lewes, rent a bike and hit the 6-mile Junction and Breakwater Trail. Named after the former rail line, which operated here in the 1800s, this smooth, graded greenway travels through wooded and open terrain, over coastal marshes and past farmland. Pick up a map from the Rehoboth visitor center or from **Atlantic Cycles** (www.atlanticcycles.net; 18 Wilmington Ave) in Rehoboth, which offers inexpensive rentals (half-day/day from $12/18). In Lewes, try **Ocean Cycles** (www.oceancylces.com; 514 E Savannah Rd) at the Beacon Motel.

CAPE HENLOPEN STATE PARK

One mile east of Lewes, more than 4000 acres of dune bluffs, pine forests and wetlands are preserved at this lovely **state park** (☎302-645-8983) that's popular with birdwatchers and beachgoers ($6 per out-of-state car). You can see clear to Cape May from the observation tower. **North Shores beach** draws many gay and lesbian couples. **Camping** (☎877-987-2757; campsites $30-32; ⌚Mar-Nov) includes oceanfront or wooded sites.

REHOBOTH BEACH & DEWEY BEACH

As the closest beach to Washington, DC (121 miles), Rehoboth is often dubbed 'the Nation's Summer Capital.' Founded in 1873 as a Christian seaside resort camp, Rehoboth is today a shining example of tolerance. It is both a family-friendly and gay-friendly destination, and has a particularly large lesbian community. There's even a gay beach – aka Poodle Beach – located, appropriately, at the end of Queen St.

Downtown Rehoboth is a mix of grand Victorian and gingerbread houses, tree-lined streets, boutique B&Bs and shops, posh restaurants, kiddie amusements and wide beaches fronted by a mile-long boardwalk. Rehoboth Ave, the main drag, is lined with restaurants and the usual tacky souvenir shops; it stretches from the **visitor center** (☎302-227-2233; www.beach-fun.com; 501 Rehoboth Ave; ⏰9am-5pm Mon-Fri, to 1pm Sat & Sun) at the traffic circle to the boardwalk. Outside of town, Rte 1 is a busy highway crammed with chain restaurants, hotels and outlet malls, where bargain-hunters take advantage of Delaware's tax-free shopping.

Less than 2 miles south on Hwy 1 is the tiny hamlet of Dewey Beach. Unapologetically known as 'Do Me' beach for its hook-up scene (straight) and hedonistic nightlife, Dewey is a major party beach.

Sleeping

As elsewhere on the coast, prices sky rocket in high season (June to August). Cheaper lodging options are located on Rte 1.

TOP CHOICE Bellmoor Inn & Spa BOUTIQUE HOTEL **$$$**
(☎800-425-2355; www.thebellmoor.com; 6 Christian St; r from $260; P❄@🛜) If money were no object, we'd splurge for a room at Rehoboth's most luxurious inn. With its English country decor, fireplaces, quiet garden and secluded setting, this is not your usual seaside resort. A full-service day spa caps the amenities.

Hotel Rehoboth BOUTIQUE HOTEL **$$$**
(☎302-227-4300; www.hotelrehoboth.com; 247 Rehoboth Ave; r $290-390; P❄@🛜🏊) Rehoboth's newest boutique hotel has gained a reputation for great service and luxurious amenities, including a free shuttle to the beach.

Crosswinds Motel MOTEL **$$$**
(☎302-227-7997; www.crosswindsmotel.com; 312 Rehoboth Ave; r $150-250; P❄🛜) Located in the heart of Rehoboth Ave, this simple motel offers great value for your dollar, with welcome amenities (minifridge, coffeemaker, flat-screen TV). Walk to the beach in 12 minutes.

Walls Apartments APARTMENT **$**
(☎302-227-2999; www.crosswindsmotel.com; cnr Christian St & Rehoboth Ave; r from $97; P) This aging complex of cabins and rustically furnished apartments sits in a great location a few blocks from the beach. The price is unbeatable, but the battered furniture and tattered carpets discourage most – plus some apartments have tubs but lack showers (there are outdoor showers, however). Cash only.

Eating & Drinking

Cheap eats are available on the boardwalk, with favorites like Thrasher's fries, Grotto's pizza and Dolle's saltwater taffy. For classier dining, browse the inviting restaurants sprinkled along Wilmington Ave.

TOP CHOICE Planet X FUSION **$$$**
(☎302-226-1928; 35 Wilmington Ave; mains $16-33; ⏰from 5pm; 🌱) This stylish spot shows its Asian influence in menu and decor – red paper lanterns and Buddhas adorn the walls, while diners feast on red Thai curry with jumbo shrimp and crab cakes with spicy Asian sesame noodles. There's al fresco dining on the open-sided front porch.

Henlopen City Oyster House SEAFOOD **$$$**
(50 Wilmington Ave; mains $21-26; ⏰from 3pm) Oyster- and seafood-lovers won't want to miss this elegant spot, where an enticing raw bar and beautifully prepared plates (soft-shell crabs, bouillabaisse, lobster mac 'n' cheese) draw crowds (arrive early; no reservations). Good microbrews, cocktails and wine selections make it an ideal early-evening drink-eat spot.

Cultured Pearl JAPANESE **$$$**
(☎302-227-8493; 301 Rehoboth Ave; mains $16-33; ⏰4:30pm-late) A longtime locals' favorite, this Asian restaurant has a Zen feel, with koi pond at the entrance and a pleasant rooftop deck. The sushi and appetizers are first-rate. Live music most nights.

Royal Treat ICE CREAM **$**
(4 Wilmington Ave; ice cream $3.50; ⏰8am-11:30pm) There's always a line outside this landmark ice-cream parlor, with giant servings of creamy rich concoctions. Breakfast is also popular.

Starboard RESTAURANT, BAR **$$**
(2009 Hwy 1, Dewey Beach; mains $6-18; ⏰9am-late Apr-Oct) A Dewey Beach tradition since 1960, the Starboard is the region's best bet

for brunch. Order the Eggs Del Marva – eggs Benedict topped with crab meat. At night, Starboard transforms into the area's biggest beach party with wall-to-wall drunks and live entertainment.

Dogfish Head MICROBREWERY **$$**
(www.dogfish.com; 320 Rehoboth Ave; mains $9-23; ⏲noon-late) When a place mixes its own brewery with some of the best live music on the Eastern Shore, you know you've got a winning combination.

ℹ Getting There & Around

The **Jolly Trolley** (one way $2.50; ⏲8am-2am summer) connects Rehoboth and Dewey, and makes frequent stops along the way. Unfortunately, long-distance buses no longer serve Rehoboth.

BETHANY BEACH & FENWICK ISLAND

Want to get away from it all? The seaside towns of Bethany and Fenwick, about halfway between Rehoboth and Ocean City, are known as 'the Quiet Resorts.' They share a tranquil, almost boring, family-friendly scene.

There are only a few restaurants and even fewer hotels here; most visitors stay in rented apartments and beach houses. For a nice change of pace from the usual seafood fare, **Bethany Blues BBQ** (☎302-537-1500; www.bethanyblues.com; 6 N Pennsylvania Ave; mains $14-24; ⏲4:30-9pm) has falling-off-the-bone ribs and pulled-pork sandwiches.

Northern & Central Delaware

The grit of Wilmington is balanced by the rolling hills and palatial residences of the Brandywine Valley, particularly the soaring estate of Winterthur. Dover is cute, friendly and gets a little lively after hours.

WILMINGTON

A unique cultural milieu (African Americans, Jews, Caribbean etc) and an energetic arts scene make this a town worth a visit. The central commercial district is along Market St, while Riverfront's old warehouses and other industrial sites have been transformed into shops, restaurants and museums. The **visitor center** (☎800-489-6664; www.visitwilmingtonde.com; 100 W 10th St; ⏲9am-5pm Mon-Fri) is downtown.

The **Delaware Art Museum** (www.delart.org; 800 S Madison St; adult/child $12/6, Sun free; ⏲10am-4pm Wed-Sat, from noon Sun) exhibits work of the local Brandywine School, including Edward Hopper, John Sloan and three generations of Wyeths. The **Delaware Center for the Contemporary Arts** (☎302-656-6466; www.thedcca.org; 200 S Madison St; admission free; ⏲10am-5pm Tue & Thu-Sat, from noon Wed & Sun) is bringing some mind-expanding culture to the Riverfront district. Located in an art-deco Woolworth's building, the **Delaware History Museum** (www.hsd.org; 200 S Madison St; adult/child $6/4; ⏲11am-4pm Wed-Sat) proves the First State has done loads more than earn its nickname.

The premier hotel in the state, the **Hotel du Pont** (☎302-594-3100; www.hoteldupont.com; cnr Market & 11th Sts, r $230-460; P❄📶) is luxurious and classy enough to satisfy its namesake (ie one of America's most successful industrialist families). On the riverfront, **Iron Hill Brewery** (☎302-472-2739; 710 South Madison St; mains $10-24; ⏲11am-11pm) is a spacious and airy multilevel space set in a converted brick warehouse. Satisfying microbrews (try the seasonal Belgian ale) match nicely with hearty pub grub (pizzas, sandwiches, pan-roasted chicken, barbecued shrimp).

Wilmington is accessible by Greyhound or Peter Pan Bus Lines, which run to DC ($20, three hours) and New York ($30, 2½ hours). Both bus lines serve the **Wilmington Transportation Center** (101 N French St). **Amtrak trains** (100 S French St) connect Wilmington with DC ($45, 1½ hours), Baltimore ($37, 45 minutes) and New York ($56, 1¾ hours).

BRANDYWINE VALLEY

After making their fortune, the French-descended Du Ponts turned the Brandywine Valley into a sort of American Loire Valley, and it remains a nesting ground for the wealthy and ostentatious to this day. The **Brandywine Valley Tourist Information Center** (☎610-719-1730; www.brandywinevalley.com), outside Longwood Gardens in Kennett Square, PA, distributes information on the region's triple crown of chateaux and gardens: Winterthur, Longwood Gardens and Nemours.

👁 Sights

Winterthur HISTORIC SITE
(☎302-888-4600; www.winterthur.org; Hwy 52; adult/child $18/5; ⏲10am-5pm Tue-Sun) Six miles northwest of Wilmington is the 175-room country estate of industrialist Henry

Francis du Pont and his collection of antiques and American arts, one of the world's largest.

Hagley Museum MUSEUM
(☎302-658-2400; www.hagley.org; Hwy 141; adult/child $11/4; ⏲9:30am-4:30pm) Another fascinating shrine to the Du Pont legacy, the sprawling outdoor museum includes the ruins of the original DuPont company mills, craftsmith demonstrations and exhibits on some of the DuPont company inventions such as nylon.

NEW CASTLE

New Castle is a web of cobblestoned streets and beautifully preserved 18th-century buildings, lying near the riverfront. The surrounding area, however, is a bit of an urban wasteland. Sights include the **Old Court House** (⏲closed Mon), the arsenal on the Green, churches and cemeteries dating back to the 17th century, and historic houses.

The five-room **Terry House B&B** (☎302-322-2505; www.terryhouse.com; 130 Delaware St; r $90-110; P 📶) is idyllically set in the historic district. The owner will play the piano for you while you enjoy a full breakfast.

A few doors down, **Jessop's Tavern** (114 Delaware St; mains $12-22; ⏲11:30am-9pm) serves up Dutch pot roast, Pilgrim's feast (oven-roasted turkey with all the fixings) plus fish-and-chips and other pub grub in a colonial atmosphere – complete with costumed waitstaff, creaky wooden floors and antique decorations.

DOVER

Central Dover has stately brick buildings and shady, tree-lined boulevards that make for an intriguing half-day's exploration.

Walk beside the **State House** (25 The Green) to find the **visitor center** (☎302-739-4266; 406 Federal St; ⏲8:30am-4:30pm Mon-Sat, from 1:30pm Sun) and history exhibits at the foot of a long plaza. Ask here about free walking tours in the area led by costumed interpreters. Free tours of the State House are also given.

The **Johnson Victrola Museum** (cnr Bank & New Sts; admission free; ⏲9am-4:30pm Wed-Sat) honors 'talking machine' pioneer Eldridge Johnson, including an exhibit on the RCA Records trademark dog, Nipper. The **Delaware Agriculture Museum and Village** (☎302-734-1618; www.agriculturalmuseum.org; 866 N Dupont Hwy; adult/child $5/3; ⏲10am-3pm Tue-Sat) is a living-history museum featuring a re-creation of an 1890s farming community.

Southeast of town, Dover Air Force Base is the country's largest air base and the first stop for America's returning war dead. There are no public ceremonies to mark their homecoming, but you can visit the **Air Mobility Command Museum** (☎302-677-5938; www.amcmuseum.org; cnr Hwys 9 & 1; admission free; ⏲9am-4pm Tue-Sun), filled with vintage planes and other aviation artifacts.

NASCAR fans worldwide know of **Dover International Speedway** (☎302-883-6500; doverspeedway.com; 1131 N Dupont Hwy), considered one of the best tracks in the country. See its website for current race schedules and ticket information. At the same location is Dover's other major attraction, **Dover Downs Casino** (☎302-674-4600; doverdowns.com; ⏲8am-4am Mon-Sat, from noon Sun), an enormous entertainment complex with slot machines, horse racing, hotel, spa and concert venue.

The **State Street Inn** (☎302-734-2294; 228 N State St; r $110-135) is a well-located inn near the State House, with four bright rooms with wood floors and period furnishings.

A short stroll from the State House, **Frazier's** (☎302-674-8875; 9 E Lockerman St; mains $8-19; ⏲from 11am) is a wood-paneled eatery with outdoor tables facing the river, and decent burgers, sandwiches and seafood.

Neighborhood bar **WT Smithers** (☎302-674-8875; 140 S State St; mains $8-16; ⏲from 11am Mon-Sat) attracts a mix of students and State House staff sharing buffalo wings and excellent beer on tap.

VIRGINIA

Beautiful, passionate, lovely Virginia is a state steeped in history. It's the birthplace of America, where English settlers established the first permanent colony in the New World in 1607. From there, the Commonwealth of Virginia has played a lead role in nearly every major American drama, from the Revolutionary and Civil wars to the Civil Rights movement and September 11, 2001.

Virginia's natural beauty is as diverse as her history and people. Chesapeake Bay and the wide sandy beaches kiss the Atlantic Ocean. Pine forests, marshes and rolling green hills form the soft curves of the central Piedmont region, while the rugged Appalachian Mountains and stunning Shenandoah Valley line her back.

The nation's invisible line between North and South is drawn here, somewhere around Richmond; you'll know it as soon as you hear the sweet southern drawl offering plates of biscuits and Virginia ham. With something for everyone, it's easy to appreciate the state's motto: 'Virginia is for Lovers.'

History

Humans have occupied Virginia for at least 5000 years. Several thousand Native Americans were already here in May 1607 when Captain James Smith and his crew sailed up Chesapeake Bay and founded Jamestown, the first permanent English colony in the New World. Named for the 'Virgin Queen' Elizabeth I, the territory originally occupied most of America's eastern seaboard. By 1610 most of the colonists had died from starvation in their quest for gold, until colonist John Rolfe (husband of Pocahontas) discovered Virginia's real riches: tobacco.

A feudal aristocracy grew out of tobacco farming, and many gentry scions became Founding Fathers, including native son George Washington. In the 19th century the slave-based plantation system grew in size and incompatibility with the industrializing North; Virginia seceded in 1861 and became the epicenter of the Civil War. Following its defeat the state walked a tense cultural tightrope, accruing a layered identity that included older aristocrats, a rural and urban working class, waves of immigrants and today, the burgeoning tech-heavy suburbs of DC. The state revels in its history, yet still wants to pioneer the American experiment; thus, while Virginia only reluctantly desegregated in the 1960s, today it houses one of the most ethnically diverse populations of the New South.

VIRGINIA FACTS

» **Nickname** Old Dominion

» **Population** 8 million

» **Area** 42,774 sq miles

» **Capital city** Richmond (population 202,000)

» **Sales tax** 5%

» **Birthplace of** eight US presidents including George Washington (1732–99), Confederate General Robert E Lee (1807-70), tennis ace Arthur Ashe (1943–93), author Tom Wolfe (b 1931), actress Sandra Bullock (b 1964)

» **Home of** the Pentagon, the CIA, more technology workers than any other state

» **Politics** Republican

» **Famous for** American history, tobacco, apples, Shenandoah National Park

» **State beverage** milk

» **Driving distances** Arlington to Shenandoah 113 miles, Richmond to Virginia Beach 108 miles

Northern Virginia

Hidden within its suburban sprawl exterior, 'NOVA' mixes small-town charm with metropolitan chic. Colonial villages and battlefields bump up against skyscrapers, shopping malls and world-class arts venues.

You'll discover unexpected green spaces like **Great Falls National Park** (☎703-285-2965; www.nps.gov/grfa; ⊙7am-sunset), a wilderness space that somehow survives despite being mere minutes from a major urban nexus. The park is a gorgeous, well-maintained forest cut through by the Potomac River, which surges over a series of white-water rapids. Kayaking (experienced paddlers only), rock climbing, hiking and fishing are all popular activities.

ARLINGTON

Just across the Potomac River from DC, Arlington County was once part of Washington until it was returned to Virginia in 1847. In recent years the gentrified neighborhoods of Arlington have spawned some tempting dining and nightlife options.

Sights & Activities

FREE **Arlington National Cemetery** HISTORIC SITE
(www.arlingtoncemetery.org; ⊙8am-7pm Apr-Sep, to 5pm Oct-Mar) The county's best-known attraction is the somber final resting place for more than 300,000 military personnel and their dependents, with veterans of every US war from the Revolution to Iraq. The cemetery is spread over 612 hilly acres. Departing from the visitor center, **Tourmobiles** (☎202-554-5100; www.tourmobile.com; adult/child $8.50/4.25) are a handy way to visit the cemetery's memorials.

Much of the cemetery was built on the grounds of **Arlington House**, the former

SCENIC DRIVE: VIRGINIA'S HORSE COUNTRY

About 40 miles west of Washington, DC, suburban sprawl gives way to endless green farms, vineyards, quaint villages and palatial estates and ponies. This is 'Horse Country,' where wealthy Washingtonians pursue their equestrian pastimes.

The following route is the most scenic drive to Shenandoah National Park. From DC, take Rte 50 West to **Middleburg**, a too-cute-for-words town of B&Bs, taverns, wine shops and boutiques. The **National Sporting Library** (☎540-687-6542; www.nsl.org; 102 The Plains Rd; ⊙10am-4pm Tue-Fri, from 1pm Sat) is a museum and research center devoted to horse and field sports like foxhunting, dressage, steeplechase and polo.

Griffin Tavern (☎540-675-3227; 659 Zachary Taylor Hwy; mains $9-20; ⊙11:30am-9pm) is a quintessential British pub with English and Irish food and beer; head southwest on Rte 522 and 211 to Flint Hill.

Six miles down Rte 211 is **Little Washington**, another cute town that's home to one of the finest B&B restaurants in America, the **Inn at Little Washington** (☎540-675-3800; www.theinnatlittlewashington.com; cnr Middle & Main Sts; r from $425). Further down the road at the foothills of the Blue Ridge Mountains is **Sperryville** and its many galleries and shops, a must-stop for antique-lovers. Continue 9 miles west to reach the Thornton Gap entrance of Skyline Dr in Shenandoah National Park (p309).

home of Robert E Lee and his wife Mary Anna Custis Lee, a descendant of Martha Washington. When Lee left to lead Virginia's army in the Civil War, Union troops confiscated the property to bury their dead. The **Tomb of the Unknowns** contains the remains of unidentified American servicemen from both World Wars and the Korean War; military guards retain a round-the-clock vigil and the changing of the guard (every half-hour March to September, every hour October to February) is one of Arlington's most moving sights. An eternal flame marks the **grave of John F Kennedy**, next to those of Jacqueline Kennedy Onassis and two of her infant children. The **Women in Military Service for America Memorial** (☎800-222-2294; www.womensmemorial.org) honors the two million women who have served in America's armed forces. Other points of interest include the **Pan Am Flight 103 cairn** and the **Space Shuttle Challenger memorial**.

Just north of the cemetery, the **Marine Corps Memorial** (N Meade & 14th Sts) depicts six soldiers raising the American flag on Iwo Jima. The Felix de Weldon–designed sculpture is based on an iconic photo by Associated Press photographer Joe Rosenthal.

Artisphere ARTS CENTER
(www.artisphere.com; 1101 Wilson Blvd; 📶) For something completely different, check out the excellent exhibits at this sleek, modern, multistory arts complex, which opened in 2011. Its several theaters host live performances (many free) – world music, film, experimental theater – and there's a cafe, restaurant and bar. It's a short stroll from Rosslyn Metro station.

Pentagon BUILDING
South of Arlington Cemetery is the Pentagon, the largest office building in the world. It's not open to the public, but outside you may visit the **Pentagon Memorial** (www.whs.mil/memorial; admission free; ⊙24hr); 184 illuminated benches honor each person killed in the September 11, 2001, terrorist attack on the Pentagon. Nearby, the three soaring arcs of the **Air Force Memorial** (☎703-247-5805; www.airforcememorial.org) invoke the contrails of jets.

Sleeping & Eating

Dozens of hotels, chic restaurants and bars are located along Clarendon and Wilson Blvds, clustered near Rosslyn and Clarendon Metro stations.

Whitlow's on Wilson AMERICAN **$$**
(☎703-276-9693; 2854 Clarendon Blvd; mains $8-21; ⊙11am-2am Mon-Fri, from 9am Sat & Sun) The neighborhood's best Sunday-brunch menu, plus weekday happy hour specials and live bands on weekends.

Ray's Hell-Burger BURGERS **$**
(1713 Wilson Blvd; burgers from $7; ⊙noon-10pm Tue-Sun, from 5pm Mon) In a nondescript strip mall, amid wooden benches and minimal ambience, Ray's is famed for its 10-ounce burgers, served with an array of fixings.

WORTH A TRIP

STEVEN F UDVAR-HAZY CENTER

The Smithsonian National Air & Space Museum's **Steven F Udvar-Hazy Center** (703-572-4118; 10am-5:30pm), located in Chantilly near Dulles airport, is a huge hangar filled with surplus planes and spacecraft that wouldn't fit at the museum's DC location. Highlights include the space shuttle *Enterprise*, the B-29 *Enola Gay*, SR-71 *Blackbird* and a Concorde supersonic airliner. While the museum is free, parking costs $15.

Order it with sweet potato fries. Obama took Russian pres Medvedev here (they apparently had cheddar cheese burgers).

Iota LIVE MUSIC
(703-522-8340; www.iotaclubandcafe.com; 2832 Wilson Blvd; cover free-$15; 7am-2am Mon-Fri, from 9am Sat & Sun;) Arlington's top spot to catch live local and national musicians nightly, with good food too; Norah Jones and John Mayer have performed here.

ALEXANDRIA

The charming colonial village of Alexandria is just 5 miles and 250 years away from Washington. Once a salty port town, Alexandria – known as 'Old Town' to locals – is today a posh collection of red-bricked colonial homes, cobblestoned streets, flickering gas lamps and a waterfront promenade. King St is packed with boutiques, outdoor cafes, and neighborhood bars and restaurants. The **visitor center** (703-838-5005; www.visitalexandriava.com; 221 King St; 9am-5pm) issues parking permits and discount tickets to historic sites.

The 333ft-tall **George Washington Masonic National Memorial** (www.gwmemorial.org; 101 Callahan Dr & King St; admission free; 9am-5pm) is an imposing tower modeled after Egypt's Lighthouse of Alexandria and dedicated to America's first president, who was a member of the shadowy Freemasons. **Gadsby's Tavern Museum** (www.gadsbystavernmuseum.us; 134 N Royal St; adult/child $5/3; 10am-5pm Tue-Sat, from 1pm Sun & Mon) has exhibits on colonial life and is still a working pub and restaurant; past guests included George Washington and Thomas Jefferson. Near the waterfront, the **Torpedo Factory Art Center** (www.torpedofactory.org; 105 N Union St; admission free; 10am-6pm Fri-Wed, to 9pm Thu) is a former munitions factory that today houses dozens of galleries and studios.

A stylish new addition to Alexandria, the inviting and sunlit **Brabo Tasting Room** (1600 King St; mains around $15; 11:30am-11pm Mon-Sat, to 10pm Sun) serves its signature mussels, tasty wood-fired tarts and gourmet sandwiches (like slow-roasted Angus beef with caramelized mushrooms), with a good beer and wine selection. Next door, high-end **Brabo** (703-894-3440; mains $28-38; from 5:30pm) serves superb seasonal fare.

One of Alexandria's best seafood spots is small, casual **Hank's Oyster Bar** (1026 King St; mains $6-28; 5:30-9:30pm Tue-Thu, 11:30am-midnight Fri & Sat, 11am-9:30pm Sun), serving up daily fish specials, seared scallops, lobster rolls, crab cakes and its famous oysters. **Momo Sushi & Cafe** (703-299-9092; 212 Queen St; sushi $10-23; 11:30am-2:30pm & 4-10pm Mon-Fri, noon-10pm Sat, 4pm-10pm Sun) has just 13 seats but serves excellent sushi.

The food is mediocre and beer selection weak, but the live bluegrass (from 8:30pm Friday and Saturday) hits the spot at the well-worn **Tiffany Tavern** (703-836-8844; 1116 King St; mains $10-20; 5pm-midnight Mon-Thu, to 2am Fri & Sat).

Just north of Old Town by the Braddock Rd Metro station is one of America's premier music halls, the **Birchmere** (703-549-7500; www.birchmere.com; 3701 Mt Vernon Ave; tickets $25-70). The legendary venue stages an eclectic range of acts, from Shawn Colvin to Eric Benét, plus past legends like Doc Watson and America.

To get to Alexandria from downtown DC, get off at the King St Metro station. A free trolley makes the one-mile journey between the Metro station and the waterfront (every 20 minutes, 11:30am to 10pm).

MOUNT VERNON

One of the most visited historic shrines in the nation, **Mount Vernon** (703-780-2000; www.mountvernon.org; adult/child $15/7; 9am-5pm, to 4pm Nov-Feb) was the beloved home of George and Martha Washington, who lived here from their marriage in 1759 until Washington's death in 1799. Now owned and operated by the Mount Vernon Ladies Association, the estate offers glimpses of 18th-century farm life and the first president's life as a country planter. Mount Vernon does not gloss over the Founding Father's slave ownership; visitors can tour the slave quarters and burial ground.

Other sights include Washington's **Distillery and Gristmill** (www.tourmobile.com; adult/child $4/2; incl Mount Vernon adult/child $30/15), 3 miles south of the estate. During warmer months, you can take a 40-minute **Sightseeing Cruise** (adult/child $9/5; ⏲Tue-Sun May-Aug, Sat & Sun Apr & Sep).

Mount Vernon is 16 miles south of DC off the Mount Vernon Memorial Hwy. By public transportation, take the Metro to Huntington, then switch to Fairfax Connector bus 101. **Tourmobile** (☎202-554-5100; www.tourmobile.com; adult/child incl admission $32/16; ⏲mid-Jun–Aug) offers one trip a day to Mount Vernon from Arlington National Cemetery. **Grayline** (☎202-289-1995; www.grayline.com; adult/child incl admission from $55/30) departs daily from DC's Union Station year-round.

Several companies offer seasonal boat trips from DC and Alexandria; the cheapest is **Potomac Riverboat Company** (☎703-684-0580; www.potomacriverboatco.com; adult/child incl admission $40/20). A healthy alternative is to take a lovely bike ride along the Potomac River from DC (18 miles from Roosevelt Island).

MANASSAS

On July 21, 1861, Union and Confederate soldiers clashed in the first major land battle of the Civil War. Expecting a quick victory, Union fans flocked here to picnic and watch the First Battle of Bull Run (known in the South as First Manassas). The surprise Southern victory erased any hopes of a quick end to the war. Union and Confederate soldiers again met on the same ground for the larger Second Battle of Manassas in August 1862; again the South was victorious. Today **Manassas National Battlefield Park** is a curving green hillscape, sectioned into fuzzy fields of tall grass and wildflowers by split-rail wood fences. Start your tour at the **Henry Hill Visitor Center** (☎703-361-1339; www.nps.gov/mana; adult/child $3/free; ⏲8:30am-5pm) to watch the orientation film and pick up park and trail maps.

Daily **Amtrak** (www.amtrak.com; one way $15-21) and **Virginia Railway Express** (VRE; www.vre.org; one way $9; ⏲Mon-Fri) trains make the 50-minute journey between DC's Union Station and the historic Old Town Manassas Railroad Station on 9431 West St; from there it's a 6-mile taxi ride to the park. There are several restaurants and bars around the Manassas train station, but the rest of the city is a mess of strip malls and suburban sprawl.

Fredericksburg

Fredericksburg is a pretty town with a historical district that is almost a cliché of small-town Americana. George Washington grew up here, and the Civil War exploded in the streets and surrounding fields. Today the main street is a pleasant amble of bookstores, gastropubs and cafes.

Sights

Fredericksburg & Spotsylvania National Military Park HISTORIC SITE

More than 13,000 Americans were killed during the Civil War in four battles fought in a 17-mile radius covered by this park and maintained by the NPS. Don't miss the burial site of Stonewall Jackson's amputated arm near the **Fredericksburg Battlefield visitor center** (1013 Lafayette Blvd; admission free, film $2; ⏲9am-5pm).

The **visitor center** (www.visitfred.com; 706 Caroline St; ⏲9am-5pm) offers a 'Timeless Fredericksburg' pass, which includes admission to nine local sights (adult/child $32/10).

James Monroe Museum & Memorial Library HISTORIC SITE

(908 Charles St; adult/child $5/1; ⏲10am-5pm Mon-Sat, from 1pm Sun) The museum's namesake was the nation's fifth president.

Mary Washington House HISTORIC SITE

(1200 Charles St; adult/child $5/2; ⏲11am-5pm Mon-Sat, noon-4pm Sun) The 18th-century home of George Washington's mother.

Rising Sun Tavern HISTORIC SITE

(1304 Caroline St; adult/child $5/2; ⏲10am-5pm Mon-Sat, noon-4pm Sun) A museum with tavern wenches.

Sleeping & Eating

You'll find dozens of restaurants and cafes along historic Caroline and William Sts.

Richard Johnston Inn B&B **$$**

(☎540-899-7606; www.therichardjohnstoninn.com; 711 Caroline St; r $115-225; P❄📶) In an 18th-century brick mansion, this cozy B&B scores points for location, comfort and friendliness (especially from the two resident Scottie dogs). Guests get full breakfast on weekends.

Griffin Bookshop & Cafe CAFE **$**

(106 Hanover St; ⏲10am-6pm Mon-Sat, to 5pm Sun; 📶) The Griffin is a great spot for booklovers, with friendly staff, free wi-fi, good coffees and pastries, an outdoor patio and great reading selections.

Kybecca Wine Bar TAPAS **$$**
(☎540-373-3338; 400 William St; tapas $6-21; ⊙5-11pm Mon-Thu, 3pm-midnight Fri & Sat, 11am-8pm Sun) Kybecca adds verve to Fredericksburg's dining scene, with tasty sharing plates (sherry-braised short ribs, bison-and-blue-cheese sliders, seared tuna) and an excellent beer and wine selection. Sidewalk seating and live music (acoustic) on Thursday through Saturday nights.

Getting There & Away

VRE ($11, 1½ hours) and **Amtrak** ($23 to $33, 1¼ hours) trains depart from the Fredericksburg train station (200 Lafayette Blvd) with service to DC. **Greyhound** has buses to/from DC ($15, five per day, 1½ hours) and Richmond ($18, three per day, one hour). The **Greyhound station** (☎540-373-2103; 1400 Jefferson Davis Hwy) is roughly 1.5 miles west of the historic district.

Richmond

Richmond has been the capital of the Commonwealth of Virginia since 1780. It was here during the American Revolution that patriot Patrick Henry gave his famous 'Give me Liberty, or give me Death!' speech. But Richmond is most notable for serving as the capital of the secessionist Confederate States of America during the Civil War from 1861 to 1865. Ironically, Richmond is now an ethnically diverse city, with a vibrant African American community. Of course, the attractive veneer of diversity cracks soon enough into ugly income disparities; most African American neighborhoods seem depressed compared with upmarket areas on the East and West ends of the center. This town also grapples with memorializing its controversial history. But in the end Richmond is a welcoming, warm traditional Southern city that is slowly being absorbed into the international milieu of the Northeast Corridor.

Sights

The James River bisects Richmond, with most attractions to its north. Uptown residential neighborhoods include the Fan district, south of Monument Ave, and Carytown, in the west end. Downtown, Court End holds the capitol and several museums. On E Cary St between 12th and 15th Sts, converted warehouses in Shockoe Slip house shops and restaurants. Once you pass under the trestle-like freeway overpass, you're in Shockoe Bottom. Just north of Court End is the historic African American neighborhood of Jackson Ward. Keep in mind that Cary St is more than 5 miles long; E Cary St is downtown, while W Cary St is in Carytown.

Monument Avenue, a tree-lined boulevard in northeast Richmond, holds **statues** of such revered Southern heroes as JEB Stuart, Robert E Lee, Matthew Fontaine Maury, Jefferson Davis, Stonewall Jackson and, controversially, African American tennis champion Arthur Ashe.

Jackson Ward, an African American neighborhood that was known as Little Africa in the late 19th century, is now a national historic landmark district. It comes off as a tough neighborhood (which it is), but there's a deep cultural legacy here as well.

The 1.25-mile waterfront **Canal Walk** between the James River and the Kanawha (ka-naw) and Haxall Canals is a lovely way of seeing a dozen highlights of Richmond history.

TOP CHOICE **Museum & White House of the Confederacy** HISTORIC SITE
(www.moc.org; cnr 12th & Clay Sts; adult/child $12/7; ⊙10am-5pm Mon-Sat, from noon Sun) Traces the history of the Confederate States of America with the country's largest collection of Confederate civilian and military artifacts. It's a must-see for any history and Civil War buff. The adjacent 1818 White House mansion was the home of CSA President Jefferson Davis.

American Civil War Center at Historic Tredegar MUSEUM
(www.tredegar.org; 500 Tredegar St; adult/child $8/2; ⊙9am-5pm) Located in an 1861 gun foundry, this fascinating site explores the causes and course of the Civil War from the perspectives of Union, Confederate and African American experiences. The center is one of 13 protected area sites that make up **Richmond National Battlefield Park** (www.nps.gov/rich).

FREE **Virginia State Capitol** BUILDING
(www.virginiacapitol.gov; cnr 9th & Grace Sts, Capitol Sq; ⊙9am-5pm Mon-Sat, 1-4pm Sun) Designed by Thomas Jefferson, the capitol building was completed in 1788 and houses the oldest legislative body in the Western Hemisphere, the Virginia General Assembly, established in 1619. Free tours.

Virginia Historical Society MUSEUM
(www.vahistorical.org; 428 N Blvd; adult/student $6/4; ⊙10am-5pm Tue-Sat, from 1pm Sat) Chang-

ing and permanent exhibits trace the history of the Commonwealth from prehistoric to present times.

St John's Episcopal Church CHURCH
(www.historicstjohnschurch.org; 2401 E Broad St; tours adult/child $7/5; ⏲10am-4pm, from 1pm Sun) It was here that firebrand Patrick Henry uttered his famous battle cry, 'Give me Liberty, or give me Death!' during the rebellious 1775 Second Virginia Convention. His speech is reenacted at 2pm on Sunday in summer.

FREE **Virginia Holocaust Museum** MUSEUM
(www.va-holocaust.com; 2000 E Cary St; ⏲9am-5pm Mon-Fri, from 11am Sat & Sun) The museum is structured like an attic/diorama of the Holocaust survivors who settled here after WWII. It's occasionally kitschy but still powerful, due to the personalized nature of the exhibits. Not recommended for children under 11.

Black History Museum & Cultural Center of Virginia MUSEUM
(www.blackhistorymuseum.org; 3 E Clay St; adult/child $5/3; ⏲10am-5pm Tue-Sat) Highlights the achievements of African American Virginians and displays collections of African arts, textiles and artifacts.

FREE **Virginia Museum of Fine Arts** MUSEUM
(VMFA; www.vmfa.state.va.us; 2800 Grove Ave; ⏲10am-5pm Sat-Wed, to 9pm Thu & Fri) Has a remarkable collection of European works, sacred Himalayan art and one of the largest Fabergé egg collections on display outside Russia. Also hosts excellent temporary exhibitions (admission free to $20).

Science Museum of Virginia MUSEUM
(www.smv.org; 2500 W Broad St; adult/child $11/10, incl IMAX adult/child $16/15; ⏲9:30am-5pm Mon-Sat, from 11:30am Sun) An interactive, educational, entertaining way to distract the kids.

Poe Museum MUSEUM
(www.poemuseum.org; 1914-16 E Main St; adult/student $6/5; ⏲10am-5pm Tue-Sat, from 11am Sun) Contains the world's largest collection of manuscripts and memorabilia of macabre poet Edgar Allan Poe, who lived and worked in Richmond.

FREE **Hollywood Cemetery** CEMETERY
(hollywoodcemetery.org; entrance cnr Albemarle & Cherry Sts; ⏲8am-5pm, to 6pm summer) This tranquil cemetery, perched above the James River rapids, contains the gravesites of two US presidents (James Monroe and John Tyler), the only Confederate president (Jefferson Davis) and 18,000 Confederate soldiers. Free walking tours are given at 10am, Monday through Saturday.

Sleeping

TOP CHOICE **Jefferson Hotel** LUXURY HOTEL $$$
(☎804-788-8000; www.jeffersonhotel.com; 101 W Franklin St; r from $250; P❄📶🏊) The Jefferson is Richmond's grandest hotel and one of the finest in America. The vision of tobacco tycoon and Confederate Major Lewis Ginter, the beaux-arts-style hotel was completed in 1895. Today it offers luxurious rooms, top-notch service and one of Richmond's finest restaurants. According to rumor, the magnificent grand staircase in the lobby served as the model for the famed stairs in *Gone with the Wind*.

Linden Row Inn BOUTIQUE HOTEL $$
(☎804-783-7000; www.lindenrowinn.com; 100 E Franklin St; r incl breakfast $109-159, ste $239; P❄@📶) This antebellum gem has 70 attractive rooms (with period Victorian furnishings) spread among neighboring Greek Revival town houses in an excellent downtown location. Friendly southern hospitality and thoughtful extras (free passes to the YMCA, free around-town shuttle service) sweeten the deal.

Museum District B&B B&B $$
(☎804-359-2332; www.museumdistrictbb.com; 2811 Grove Ave; r $100-195; P❄📶) In a fine location near the dining and drinking of Carytown, this stately 1920s brick B&B has earned many admirers for its warm welcome. Rooms are comfortably set and guests can enjoy the wide front porch, cozy parlor with fireplace, and excellent cooked breakfasts – plus wine and cheese in the evenings.

Berkeley Hotel HOTEL $$
(☎804-780-1300; www.berkeleyhotel.com; 1200 E Cary St; d from $175; P❄📶) Located in Shockoe Slip, this European-style, four-star hotel has spacious rooms with cherry furnishings and gracious staff. Many rooms have fine views over downtown, and there's a good restaurant on-site.

Omni Hotel HOTEL $$$
(☎804-344-7000; www.omnihotels.com; 100 S 12th St; r from $250; P❄📶🏊) In a 19-story building overlooking the James River, this

high-end hotel has comfortable rooms and loads of amenities (including a heated indoor pool). It's in a great location in the heart of Shockoe Slip.

Holiday Inn Express HOTEL $$
(☎804-788-1600; www.hiexpress.com; 201 E Cary St; r from $103; P@) The Holiday Inn is one of the cheapest options for staying in downtown Richmond, and earns decent marks for clean rooms and helpful staff.

Eating

You'll find dozens of restaurants along the cobbled streets of Shockoe Slip and Shockoe Bottom. Further west in Carytown (W Cary St between S Blvd and N Thompson St), you'll find even more dining options.

TOP CHOICE **Millie's Diner** MODERN AMERICAN $$$
(2603 E Main St; breakfast & lunch $7-10, dinner $20-32; 11am-2:30pm & 5:30-10:30pm Tue-Fri, 10am-3pm & 5:30-10:30pm Sat & Sun) Breakfast, lunch or dinner, Millie's does it all, and does it well. But where this Richmond icon really shines is Sunday brunch: the Devil's Mess – an open-faced omelet with spicy sausage, curry, veg, cheese and avocado – is quite legendary.

Julep's MODERN AMERICAN $$$
(☎804-377-3968; 1719 E Franklin St; mains $18-32; 5:30-10pm Mon-Sat) One of Richmond's finest restaurants serves decadent New Southern cuisine in a classy old-fashioned dining room that's cinematically set inside a restored 1817 building. Start with a mint julep, fried green tomatoes or jumbo lump crab soup, followed by Julep's signature shrimp and grits with grilled andouille sausage.

Tarrants MODERN AMERICAN $$$
(☎804-225-0035; 1 W Broad St; mains $9-24; 11am-10pm Sun-Thu, to midnight Fri & Sat) With old-fashioned wooden booths, antique fixtures and a copper ceiling, Tarrants is a warm and inviting spot to linger over a meal. Top picks from the extensive menu include fish tacos, pizzas and crab cakes, plus nicely made cocktails.

Ipanema Café AMERICAN $$
(917 W Grace St; mains $8-17; 11am-11pm Mon-Fri, from 5:30pm Sat & Sun;) This underground den is much loved by the bohemian and art-student crowd, with a tempting selection of vegan and vegetarian fare (tempeh 'bacon' sandwich, curried vegetables, changing specials), plus *moules-frites,* tuna melts and a few other nonveg options. Vegan desserts are outstanding.

Edo's Squid ITALIAN $$$
(☎804-864-5488; 411 N Harrison St; mains $12-30) Easily the best Italian restaurant in Richmond, Edo's serves up mouthwatering, authentic cuisine such as eggplant parmesan, spicy shrimp diavolo pasta, daily specials and, of course, squid. This place can get very crowded and noisy.

17th Street Farmers Market MARKET $
(cnr 17th & E Main Sts; 10am-7pm Thu, 5-9pm Fri, 10am-4pm Sat, 9am-4pm Sun) For cheap eats and fresh produce, check out the bustling market, which runs from early May through October. On Sundays, the market sells antiques.

Drinking & Entertainment

Lift CAFE
(218 W Broad St; 7am-7pm Mon-Fri, 8am-8pm Sat, 9am-7pm Sun;) Part coffeehouse, part art gallery, Lift serves stiff lattes and tasty sandwiches and salads. Sidewalk seating.

Tobacco Company Restaurant BAR
(☎804-782-9555; www.thetobaccocompany.com; 1201 E Cary St; from 11:30am) An embodiment of the era when tobacco was king, the atmosphere of this three-story, brothel-like restaurant-bar is more of a draw than the food. Come instead for drinks and live music (from 9:30pm Wednesday through Saturday).

Capital Ale House BAR
(623 E Main St; 11am-1:30am) Popular with political wonks from the nearby state capitol, this downtown pub has a superb beer selection (over 50 on tap and 250 bottled) and decent pub grub. The frozen trough on the bar keeps your drink ice-cold.

Byrd Theater CINEMA
(☎804-353-9911; www.byrdtheatre.com; 2908 W Cary St; tickets $2) You can't beat the price at this classic 1928 cinema, which shows second-run films. Wurlitzer-organ concerts precede the Saturday-night shows.

Richmond Centerstage THEATER
(☎804-592-3400; www.richmondcenterstage.com; 600 E Grace St) In 2009 Richmond raised the curtain on the area's premier venue for concerts, dance and theater, including touring Broadway productions.

Information

Media

Richmond-Times Dispatch (www2.timesdispatch.com) Daily newspaper.

Medical Services

Johnston-Willis Hospital (☎804-330-2000; 1401 Johnston-Willis Dr)

Richmond Community Hospital (☎804-225-1700; 1500 N 28th St)

Post

Post office (700 E Main St; ⏰7:30am-5pm Mon-Fri)

Tourist Information

Richmond visitor center (☎804-783-7450; www.visitrichmondva.com; 405 N 3rd St; ⏰9am-5pm)

Getting There & Around

The cab fare from **Richmond International Airport** (RIC; ☎804-226-3000), 10 miles east of town, is about $26.

Amtrak (☎800-872-7245) Trains stop at the main station at 7519 Staples Mill Rd, 7 miles north of town (accessible to downtown on bus 27). More convenient but less frequent trains stop downtown at the Main Street Station (1500 E Main St).

Greater Richmond Transit Company (GRTC; ☎804-358-4782; www.ridegrtc.com) Runs local buses (base fare $1.50, exact change only).

Greyhound/Trailways bus station (☎804-254-5910; www.greyhound.com; 2910 N Blvd)

Petersburg

About 25 miles south of Richmond, the little town of Petersburg played a big role in the Civil War as a major railway junction, providing Confederate troops and supplies. Union troops laid a 10-month siege of Petersburg in 1864–65, the longest on American soil. The **Siege Museum** (☎804-733-2404; 15 W Bank St; adult/child $5/4, with Old Blandford Church $11/9; ⏰10am-5pm) relates the plight of civilians during the siege. Several miles east of town, **Petersburg National Battlefield** (US 36; vehicle/pedestrian $5/3; ⏰9am-5pm) is where Union soldiers planted explosives underneath a Confederate breastwork, leading to the Battle of the Crater (novelized and cinematized in *Cold Mountain*). West of downtown in Pamplin Historical Park, the excellent **National Museum of the Civil War Soldier** (☎804-861-2408; adult/child 6-12yr $10/5; ⏰9am-5pm) illustrates the hardships faced by soldiers on both sides of the conflict. South of town, **Old Blandford Church** (☎804-733-2396; 319 S Crater St; adult/child $5/4; ⏰10am-5pm) has the largest collection of Tiffany glass windows in one place. Each exquisite pane is dedicated to one Confederate state and its war dead. More than 30,000 Confederate soldiers are buried on the church grounds.

Historic Triangle

This is America's birthplace. Nowhere else in the country has such a small area played such a pivotal role in the course of the nation's history. The nation's roots were planted in Jamestown, the first permanent English settlement in the New World. The flames of the American Revolution were fanned at the colonial capital of Williamsburg, and America finally won her independence from Britain at Yorktown.

You'll need at least two days to give the Triangle any justice. A daily free shuttle travels between the Williamsburg visitor center, Yorktown and Jamestown.

WILLIAMSBURG

If you visit only one historical town in Virginia, make it Williamsburg, home to Colonial Williamsburg, one of the most astounding and authentic living-history museums in the world. If any place is going to get kids into history, this is it, but it's plenty of fun for adults too.

The actual town of Williamsburg, Virginia's capital from 1699 to 1780, is a stately place. The prestigious campus of the College of William & Mary adds a decent dash of youth culture, with coffee shops, cheap pubs and fashion boutiques.

Sights & Activities

TOP CHOICE **Colonial Williamsburg** HISTORIC SITE

(www.colonialwilliamsburg.org; adult/child $38/19; ⏰9am-5pm) The restored capital of England's largest colony in the New World is a must-see attraction for visitors of all ages. This is not some cheesy, fenced-in theme park; Colonial Williamsburg is a living, breathing, working history museum that transports visitors back to the 1700s. The 301-acre historic area contains 88 original 18th-century buildings and several hundred faithful reproductions, including homes, taverns, shops and public buildings. The British Union Jack flutters everywhere. Costumed townsfolk and 'interpreters' in period dress go about their colonial jobs as blacksmiths, apothecaries, printers, barmaids, soldiers and patriots, breaking character only long enough to pose for a snapshot. Costumed patriots like Patrick Henry and Thomas Jefferson stand on their soapbox outside taverns, delivering impassioned speeches for freedom and democracy. Children will love the interactive, hands-on exhibits and activities, and hilarious skits such as witch trials, and tar and featherings.

Highlight buildings of Colonial Williamsburg include the reconstructed **Capitol Building** and **Governor's Palace**, the **Bruton Parish Church** and **Raleigh Tavern**. Walking around the historic district and patronizing the shops and taverns is free, but entry to building tours and most exhibits is restricted to ticket holders. Expect crowds, lines and petulant children, especially in summer.

To park and to purchase tickets, follow signs to the **visitor center** (757-229-1000; 8:45am-5pm), north of the historic district between Hwy 132 and Colonial Pkwy, where kids can hire out period costumes for $25 per day. Start off with a 30-minute film about Williamsburg, and peruse a copy of *Williamsburg This Week*, listing the day's programs and events. Most day activities are included with the admission price. Evening events (ghost walks, witch trials, chamber recitals) cost extra, typically $12.

Parking is free; shuttle buses run frequently to and from the historic district, or walk along the tree-lined footpath. You can also buy tickets at the **Merchants Square information booth** (9am-5pm) at the west end of Duke of Gloucester St.

Chartered in 1693, the **College of William & Mary** (www.wm.edu) is the second-oldest college in the country and retains the oldest academic building in continued use in the USA, the Sir Christopher Wren Building. The school's alumni include Thomas Jefferson, James Monroe and comedian Jon Stewart.

FREE **Williamsburg Winery** WINERY
(757-229-0999; www.williamsburgwinery.com; 5800 Wessex Hundred; tasting tours $10; 11am-6pm) Four miles southwest of downtown, the largest winery in Virginia cranks out 60,000 cases a year and 25 varieties of the sweet nectar of the gods. Stay for lunch at the on-site Gabriel Archer Tavern, serving up tasty sandwich and wrap plates; or book a table at the high-end Cafe Provencal for dinner (lunch/dinner mains from $10/25, restaurants open 11am to 4pm and 6pm to 9pm).

Sleeping

The **Williamsburg Hotel & Motel Association** (800-446-9244; www.gowilliamsburg.com) at the visitor center will help find and book accommodations at no cost. If you stay in Colonial Williamsburg, guesthouses can provide discount admission tickets (adult/child $30/15).

Colonial Williamsburg Historic Lodging GUESTHOUSE $$$
(757-253-2277; www.history.org; r $150-270) For true 18th-century immersion, guests can stay in one of 26 original colonial houses inside the historic district. Accommodations range in size and style, though the best have period furnishings, canopy beds and wood-burning fireplaces.

Williamsburg White House B&B $$
(757-229-8580; www.awilliamsburgwhitehouse.com; 718 Jamestown Rd; r $150-200; P) This romantic, beautifully furnished B&B decorated with red, white and blue bunting is located across the campus of William & Mary, just a few blocks' walk from Colonial Williamsburg.

Williamsburg Inn INN $$$
(757-253-2277; www.colonialwilliamsburg.com; 136 E Francis St; r from $320; P) Queen Elizabeth II has stayed here twice, so you know this place is palatial. Williamsburg's premier property is noted by its not-so-colonial price tag, but the pampering is nonstop at this prestigious resort.

Woodlands Hotel HOTEL $$
(757-253-2277; www.colonialwilliamsburgresorts.com; 105 Visitor Center Dr; r $110-210; P) Next door to the visitor center, this huge complex has bright, well-equipped rooms and excellent facilities. With two pools, mini-golf and kid's play areas, it's a popular choice with families. It's a peaceful tree-lined stroll (a half-mile) to the colonial area.

Governor's Inn HOTEL $
(757-253-2277; www.colonialwilliamsburgresorts.com; 506 N Henry St; r $60-110; P) Williamsburg's official 'economy' choice is a big box by any other name, but rooms are clean, and guests can use the pool and facilities of the Woodlands Hotel. It's in a great location three blocks from the historic district.

Williamsburg & Colonial KOA Resorts CAMPGROUND $
(☎800-562-1733; www.williamsburgkoa.com; 4000 Newman Rd, I-64 exit 234; campsites $22-37, cabins $52-70;) With two campgrounds rolled into one, you'll find superb amenities such as a pool, games rooms, movies and laundry facilities.

Eating

You will find many restaurants, cafes and pubs in Merchants Sq, adjacent to Colonial Williamsburg.

Fat Canary MODERN AMERICAN $$$
(☎757-229-3333; 410 Duke of Gloucester St, Merchants Sq; mains $28-36; ⊙5-10pm) For a splurge, there's no better place in the historic triangle. Top-notch service, excellent wines and heavenly desserts are only slightly upstaged by the magnificent seasonal cuisine (recent favorites: pan-seared sea scallops with oyster mushrooms; crispy quail with goat's cheese tamales; and heritage breed pork chop with gruyere bread pudding, Swiss chard, apples and bacon). You can dine on the elegant outdoor patio, or in the subdued dining room.

Cheese Shop DELI $
(410 Duke of Gloucester St, Merchants Sq; mains $6-7; ⊙10am-8pm Mon-Sat, 11am-6pm Sun) Adjoining Fat Canary, this gourmet deli showcases some flavorful sandwiches and antipasti, plus baguettes, pastries, wine, beer and wonderful cheeses.

King's Arms Tavern MODERN AMERICAN $$
(☎757-229-2141; 416 E Duke of Gloucester St; lunch mains $13-15, dinner $31-37; ⊙11:30am-2:30pm & 5-9pm) Of the four restaurants located within Colonial Williamsburg, this is the most elegant, serving early American cuisine like game pie – venison, rabbit and duck braised in port wine sauce.

Aromas CAFE $
(431 Prince George St; mains $5-15; ⊙7am-10pm Mon-Sat, 8am-8pm Sun;) One block north of Merchants Sq, Aromas is an inviting coffeehouse serving a wide range of fare, plus wine and beer. Outdoor seating and occasional live music.

Getting There & Around

Williamsburg Transportation Center (☎757-229-8750, cnr Boundary & Lafayette Sts) Amtrak trains run from here twice a day to Washington, DC ($40, four hours), Richmond ($20, 50 minutes) and New York ($84, eight hours). Greyhound buses run to Richmond ($18, one hour) five times daily. Buses to other destinations require a transfer in Richmond.

TRIANGLE THEME PARKS

Three miles east of Williamsburg on Hwy 60, **Busch Gardens** (☎800-343-7946; www.buschgardens.com; adult/child $64/54; ⊙Apr-Oct) is a European-themed park with some of the best roller coasters on the East Coast. Just down the road, off Hwy 199 east of Williamsburg, **Water Country USA** (☎800-343-7946; www.watercountryusa.com; adult/child $47/40; ⊙May-Sep) is a kids' paradise, with twisty slides, raging rapids and wave pools. A three-day combo ticket for both parks is $75. Parking is $13 at both places.

JAMESTOWN

The first permanent English settlement in North America was a horrific struggle that for many ended in tragedy. On May 14, 1607, a group of 104 English men and boys settled on this swampy island with a charter from the Virginia Company of London to search for gold and other riches. Instead, they found starvation and disease. By January of 1608, only about 40 colonists were still alive. The colony survived the 'Starving Time' with the leadership of Captain James Smith and help from local Powhatan. In 1619 the elected House of Burgesses convened, forming the first democratic government in the Americas.

Historic Jamestowne (☎757-856-1200; www.historicjamestowne.org; adult/child $10/free; ⊙8:30am-4:30pm), run by the NPS, is the original Jamestown site. Start your visit at the on-site museum and check out the statues of John Smith and Pocahontas. The original Jamestown ruins were rediscovered in 1994; visitors can watch the ongoing archaeological work at the site.

More child-friendly, the state-run **Jamestown Settlement** (☎757-253-4838; www.historyisfun.org; adult/child $16/8, incl Yorktown Victory Center $20/10; ⊙9am-5pm) reconstructs the 1607 James Fort, a Native American village and full-scale replicas of the first ships that brought the settlers to Jamestown, along with multimedia exhibits and costumed interpreters portraying life in the 17th century.

YORKTOWN

On October 19, 1781, British General Cornwallis surrendered to George Washington here, effectively ending the American Revolution. Overpowered by massive American guns on land and cut off from the sea by the

French, the British were in a hopeless position. Although Washington anticipated a much longer siege, the devastating barrage quickly overwhelmed Cornwallis, who surrendered within days.

Yorktown Battlefield (☎757-898-3400; incl Historic Jamestowne adult/child $10/free; ⊙9am-5pm), run by the NPS, is the site of the last major battle of the American Revolution. Start your tour at the visitor center and check out the orientation film and the display of Washington's original tent. The 7-mile Battlefield Rd Tour takes you past the major highlights. Don't miss a walk through the last British defensive sites, Redoubts 9 and 10.

The state-run **Yorktown Victory Center** (☎757-253-4838; www.historyisfun.org; adult/child $10/5; ⊙9am-5pm) is an interactive, living-history museum that focuses on reconstruction, reenactment and the Revolution's impact on the people who lived through it. At the re-created encampment, costumed Continental soldiers fire cannons and discuss food preparation and field medicine of the day.

The actual town of Yorktown is a pleasant waterfront village overlooking the York River with a nice range of shops, restaurants and pubs. Set in an atmospheric 1720 house, the **Carrot Tree** (☎757-988-1999; 411 Main St; mains $10-16; ⊙11am-3:30pm daily, 5-8:30pm Thu-Sat) is a good, affordable spot serving playfully named dishes like Lord Nelson's BBQ and Battlefield beef stroganoff. Afterwards, grab a beer at the **Yorktown Pub** (112 Water St; mains $8-22; ⊙11am-midnight), which hosts live music on weekends. For a more upscale option, **Nick's Riverwalk Restaurant** (☎757-875-1522; 323 Water St; lunch mains $10-16, dinner $18-32; ⊙11:30am-2:30pm & 5-9pm) offers waterfront dining and modern American cuisine.

JAMES RIVER PLANTATIONS

The grand homes of Virginia's slaveholding aristocracy were a clear sign of the era's class divisions. A string of them line scenic Hwy 5 on the north side of the river, though only a few are open to the public. The ones listed here run from east to west.

Sherwood Forest (☎804-829-5377; sherwoodforest.org; 14501 John Tyler Memorial Hwy), the longest frame house in the country, was the home of 10th US president John Tyler. Tours are available by appointment for $35 per person. The grounds (and a touching pet cemetery) are open to **self-guided tours** (adult/child $10/free; ⊙9am-5pm).

Berkeley (☎804-829-6018; www.berkeleyplantation.com; 12602 Harrison Landing Rd; adult/child $11/7.50; ⊙9:30am-4:30pm) was the site of the first official Thanksgiving in 1619. It was the birthplace and home of Benjamin Harrison V, a signer of the Declaration of Independence, and his son William Henry Harrison, ninth US president.

Shirley (☎800-232-1613; www.shirleyplantation.com; 501 Shirley Plantation Rd; adult/child $11/7.50; ⊙9am-5pm), situated picturesquely on the river, is Virginia's oldest plantation (1613) and perhaps the best example of how a British-model plantation actually appeared, with its tidy row of brick service and trade houses – tool barn, ice house, laundry etc – leading up to the big house.

Hampton Roads

The Hampton Roads (named not for asphalt, but the confluence of the James, Nansemond and Elizabeth Rivers and Chesapeake Bay) have always been prime real estate. The Powhatan Confederacy fished these waters and hunted the fingerlike protrusions of the Virginia coast for thousands of years before John Smith arrived in 1607. The pirate Blackbeard was killed here and had his head popped onto a pike, while navies from two continents littered the area with wreckage during the Revolutionary and Civil wars. Today Hampton Roads is known for its horribly congested roads, as well as its cultural mishmash of history, the military and the arts.

NORFOLK

Home to the world's largest naval base, it's not surprising that Norfolk had a reputation as a rowdy port town filled with drunken sailors. In recent years, the city has worked hard to clean up its image through development, gentrification and focusing on its burgeoning arts scene. Norfolk is now the state's second-largest city, with a diverse population of 243,000. But at the end of the day, it still revolves around the US Navy, as evident by the frequent sights of mammoth warships offshore and sounds of screaming fighter jets above.

There are two visitor centers: **Interstate** (I-64 exit 273; ⊙9am-5pm; 📶) and **Downtown** (www.visitnorfolktoday.com; 232 E Main St; ⊙9am-5pm Mon-Fri). The historic Ghent district, west of the city center, is where this town's refugee population of artsy types, foodies and cappuccino-lovers flocks.

Sights

Naval Station Norfolk NAVY BASE
(757-444-7955; www.cnic.navy.mil/norfolksta; 9079 Hampton Blvd; adult/child $10/5) The world's largest navy base, and one of the busiest airfields in the country, this is a must-see. Depending on what ships are in port, you might see aircraft carriers, destroyers, frigates, amphibious assault ships and submarines. The 45-minute bus tours are conducted by naval personnel and must be booked in advance (hours vary). Photo ID is required for adults. Alternatively, view the docks from a narrated, two-hour cruise aboard the **Victory Rover** (757-627-7406; www.navalbasecruises.com; adult/child $18/10; Mar-Dec).

Nauticus MUSEUM
(www.nauticus.org; 1 Waterside Dr; adult/child $12/10; 10am-5pm May-Aug, 10am-5pm Tue-Sat, from noon Sun Sep-Apr) This massive interactive maritime-themed museum has exhibits on undersea exploration, aquatic life of the Chesapeake Bay and US Naval lore. The museum's highlight is clambering around the decks and inner corridors of the **USS Wisconsin**. Built in 1943, it was the largest (887ft long) and last battleship built by the US Navy.

FREE **Chrysler Museum of Art** MUSEUM
(www.chrysler.org; 245 W Olney Rd; 10am-9pm Wed, to 5pm Thu-Sat, noon-5pm Sun) A glorious setting for a spectacular and eclectic collection of artifacts from ancient Egypt to the present day, including works by Monet, Matisse, Renoir, Warhol and a world-class collection of Tiffany blown glass.

FREE **MacArthur Memorial** MUSEUM
(www.macarthurmemorial.org; MacArthur Sq; 10am-5pm Mon-Sat, from 11am Sun) Houses the final resting place of WWII hero General Douglas MacArthur and his wife, Jean. The complex includes a museum, theater and exhibits of the general's military and personal artifacts.

Sleeping

For waterfront digs, there are tons of budget to midrange options lining Ocean View Ave (which actually borders the bay).

Page House Inn B&B $$$
(757-625-5033; www.pagehouseinn.com; 323 Fairfax Ave; r $150-230; P) Opposite the Chrysler Museum of Art, this luxurious B&B is a cornerstone of Norfolk elegance.

Residence Inn HOTEL $$
(757-842-6216; 227 W Brambleton Ave; r $140-160; P) A short stroll to Granby St, this friendly chain hotel has a boutique feel, with stylish, spacious rooms with small kitchenettes and excellent amenities.

Tazewell Hotel HOTEL $$
(757-623-6200; www.thetazewell.com; 245 Granby St; r $100-200;) Set in a heritage 1906 building, the Tazewell overlooks the heart of the Granby St pub and restaurant district. Rooms are small and basic – some could use an update.

Best Western MOTEL $$
(757-583-2621; 1330 E Ocean Ave; r from $120; P) Overlooking Chesapeake Bay, this place is a reliable and comfortable option.

Eating

Two of the best dining strips are downtown's Granby St and Ghent's Colley Ave.

Luna Maya LATIN AMERICAN $$
(757-622-6986; 2010 Colley Ave, Ghent; mains $13-19; 4:30-10pm Tue-Sat;) On Ghent's restaurant-lined Colley Ave, Luna Maya serves up delectable pan-Latin fare and ever-flowing *mojitos* in a stylish but somewhat rustic open dining room. It's run by two Bolivian sisters, and standouts include the *pastel de choclo con chorizo,* a Bolivian corn casserole with spicy chicken sausage.

Press 626 Cafe & Wine Bar MODERN AMERICAN $$$
(757-282-6234; 150 W Main St; mains $19-35; 11am-11pm Mon-Fri, from 5pm Sat, 10:30am-2:30pm Sun;) Embracing the slow food movement, Press 626 has a small high-end menu (pan-seared swordfish with sun-dried tomato polenta, for example), plus delectable cheeses and sharing plates. It's set in an elegant converted house, with tables scattered among warmly lit rooms and on the front porch. Great wine selection.

Todd Jurich's Bistro MODERN AMERICAN $$$
(757-622-3210; Boush & W Main St; mains $19-35; 11:30am-2:30pm Mon-Fri, 5:30-10pm Mon-Sat) This award-winning bistro serves innovative regional fare, like Virginia sea bass and

lump crab Norfolk with wilted greens and lemon confit.

Cutty Sark Marina SEAFOOD **$$**
(☎757-362-2942; 4707 Pretty Lake Ave; mains $8-15; ⏰11:30am-2:30pm Mon-Fri, 5:30-10pm Mon-Sat) For an authentic slice of old-school Maryland, head to this waterside seafood shack serving steamed shrimp, homemade crab cakes and deep-fried seafood platters. It's set in a boatyard, with old salts hunkering over the bar and no-nonsense service. It's four blocks south of East Ocean View Ave near Shore Dr (US 60).

Doumar's DINER **$**
(1919 Monticello Ave, at E 20th St, Ghent; mains $2-4; ⏰8am-11pm Mon-Sat) Since 1904 this slice of Americana has been the drive-up home of the world's original ice-cream-cone machine, plus great BBQ.

Drinking & Entertainment

Elliot's Fair Grounds CAFE
(806 Baldwin Ave, Ghent; ⏰7am-10pm Mon-Sat, from 8am Sun; 📶✍) This tiny, funky coffeehouse attracts everyone from students to sailors. The menu also includes vegan and kosher items such as Boca burgers.

Taphouse Grill at Ghent PUB
(931 W 21st St, Ghent) Good microbrews are served and good local bands jam at this warm little pub.

Getting There & Around

The region is served by **Norfolk International Airport** (NIA; ☎757-857-3351), 7 miles northeast of downtown Norfolk. **Greyhound** (☎757-625-7500; www.greyhound.com; 701 Monticello Ave) runs buses to Virginia Beach ($14, 35 minutes), Richmond ($28, 2¾ hours) and Washington, DC ($45, 6½ hours).

Hampton Roads Transit (☎757-222-6100; www.hrtransit.org) serves the entire Hampton Roads region. Buses ($1.50) run from downtown throughout the city and to Newport News and Virginia Beach. **Norfolk Electronic Transit** (NET; ⏰6:30am-11pm Mon-Fri, noon-midnight Sat, noon-8pm Sun) is a free bus service that connects Norfolk's major downtown sites, including Nauticus and the Chrysler Museum.

NEWPORT NEWS & HAMPTON

The city of Newport News comes off as a giant example of suburban sprawl, but there are several attractions here, notably the amazing **Mariners' Museum** (☎757-596-2222; www.marinersmuseum.org; 100 Museum Dr; adult/child $12/7; ⏰10am-5pm Wed-Sat, from noon Sun), one of the biggest, most comprehensive maritime museums in the world. The on-site **USS Monitor Center** houses the dredged carcass of the Civil War–era *Monitor,* one of the world's first ironclad warships, as well as a life-size replica of the real deal.

The **Virginia Living Museum** (☎757-595-1900; thevlm.org; 524 J Clyde Morris Blvd; adult/child $17/13; ⏰9am-5pm) is a fine introduction to Virginia's terrestrial and aquatic life set in naturalistic ecosystems. The complex comprises open-air animal enclosures, an aviary, gardens and a planetarium.

In nearby Hampton, the **Virginia Air & Space Center** (☎757-727-0900; www.vasc.org; 600 Settlers Landing Rd; adult/child $12/10; ⏰10am-5pm Mon-Wed, to 7pm Thu-Sun) will fascinate budding aeronautic geeks with exhibits like the *Apollo 11* command module and a DC-9 passenger plane. IMAX films cost extra.

Virginia Beach

With 35 miles of sandy beaches, a 3-mile concrete oceanfront boardwalk and nearby outdoor activities, it's no surprise that Virginia Beach is the largest city in the state (population 438,000) and a prime tourist destination. In recent years the city has worked hard to shed its unfortunate reputation as a rowdy 'Redneck Riviera.' With a $300 million facelift, the beach is wider and cleaner than ever, with dolphins frolicking offshore, and a heightened police presence (and antiprofanity signs!) aimed at keeping loutish drunken crowds in check. The town's appeal, however, is limited: uninspiring high-rise hotels dominate the horizon, while the crowded beachfront and traffic-choked streets leave much to be desired.

The I-264 runs straight to the **visitor center** (☎800-822-3224; www.visitvirginiabeach.com; 2100 Parks Ave; ⏰9am-5pm) and the beach. Surfing is permitted at the beach's southern end near Rudee Inlet and alongside the 14th St pier.

Sights

Virginia Aquarium & Marine Science Center AQUARIUM
(www.virginiaaquarium.com; 717 General Booth Blvd; adult/child $21/15; ⏰9am-6pm) If you want to see an aquarium done right, this is one of the country's best. Get up close and personal with marine life on one of the aquarium's dolphin- (adult/child $21/15, April to Octo-

ber) or whale-watching (adult/child $28/24, January to March) boat trips.

FREE **Mt Trashmore** PARK
(310 Edwin Dr; ⏲7:30am-dusk) Off I-64 exit 17B, Virginia Beach's only verticality was the creative solution to a landfill problem. Today the 165-acre park serves as a prime picnicking and kite-flying venue, with two lakes, playgrounds, a skate park and other recreational areas.

Fort Story HISTORIC SITE
(cnr 89th St & Pacific Ave) This active army base at Cape Henry is home to the 1791 **Old Cape Henry Lighthouse** (adult/child $5/3), offering spectacular views of the surrounding area from its observation deck. On summer Saturdays, the fort stages a re-created Native American village and 17th-century colonial outpost at the **Historic Villages at Cape Henry** (www.firstlandingfoundation.com; adult/child $8/5; ⏲2-6pm Jun-Aug). All adults must have a photo ID to enter the base.

First Landing State Park NATURE RESERVE
(☎800-933-7275; 2500 Shore Dr; admission per vehicle $4-5) Virginia's most-visited state park is a vast 2888-acre woodland with 20 miles of hiking trails, plus camping, biking, fishing, kayaking and swimming.

FREE **Edgar Cayce Association for Research & Enlightenment** SPIRITUAL
(☎800-333-4499; www.edgarcayce.org; 215 67th St; ⏲10am-8pm Mon-Sat, noon-6pm Sun) Founded by the self-proclaimed psychic of the early 20th century, the center has an extensive library and bookstore (with shelving categories like 'Life after Life' and 'Intuitive Arts'), a full schedule of drop-in lectures, and therapies such as massages, acupuncture, meditation and colonics.

Contemporary Arts Center of Virginia MUSEUM
(www.cacv.org; 2200 Parks Ave; adult/child $7/5; ⏲10am-5pm Tue-Fri, to 4pm Sat, noon-4pm Sun) Has excellent rotating exhibitions housed in a fresh, ultramodern building that lovingly focuses natural light onto an outstanding collection of local and international artwork.

Back Bay National Wildlife Refuge NATURE RESERVE
(www.fws.gov/backbay; per vehicle/pedestrian $5/2 Apr-Oct, free Nov-Mar; ⏲sunrise-sunset) This 9250-acre wildlife and migratory bird marshland habitat is most stunning during the December migration season.

FREE **Great Dismal Swamp National Wildlife Refuge** NATURE RESERVE
(⏲sunrise-sunset) Some 30 miles southwest of Virginia Beach, this 112,000-acre refuge, which straddles the North Carolina border, is rich in flora and fauna, including black bears, bobcats and more than 200 species of bird.

Sleeping

Angie's Guest Cottage & Hostel GUESTHOUSE $
(☎757-491-1830; www.angiescottage.com; 302 24th St; dm $23-31, s/d $52/64, cottages per week from $650; P❄) Located just one block from the beach, Angie's HI-USA-affiliated hostel offers five dormitories, two private rooms and a communal kitchen.

First Landing State Park CAMPGROUND $
(☎800-933-7275; dcr.virginia.gov; Cape Henry; campsites $24-30, cabins from $75) You couldn't ask for a prettier campground than the one at this bayfront state park, though cabins have no water view.

Cutty Sark Motel MOTEL $$
(☎757-428-2116; www.cuttysarkvb.com; 3614 Atlantic Ave; r $140-160, apt per week from $1000; P❄) Rooms at Cutty Sark have private balconies and kitchenettes, but check that the view you're promised doesn't look out onto a parking lot.

Eating & Drinking

There is no shortage of restaurants along the boardwalk and Atlantic Ave, most geared toward local seafood. A bevy of interchangeable clubs and bars sit between 17th and 23rd Sts around Pacific and Atlantic Aves.

Catch 31 SEAFOOD $$$
(☎757-213-3474; 3001 Atlantic Ave; mains $18-35; ⏲7am-11pm) One of the top seafood restaurants on the boardwalk has a sleek interior and a popular deck that's great for people-watching and catching a bit of an ocean breeze. Find it in the Hilton.

Mahi Mah's SEAFOOD $$$
(☎757-437-8030; www.mahimahs; 615 Atlantic Ave; mains $18-30; ⏲5pm-late Mon-Fri, from 7am Sat & Sun) Located in the Ramada Inn, this oceanfront local has some fantastic sushi, which makes up for the snail-paced service. After

SCENIC DRIVE: VIRGINIA'S EASTERN SHORE

Across the 17-mile Chesapeake Bay bridge-tunnel (fee $12), Virginia's isolated Eastern Shore has the feel of a remote, maritime escape, dotted with fishing villages and serene, low-lying natural refuges. A drive up or down the peninsula takes a little over an hour.

Tucked behind windswept Assateague Island (p285), the town of **Chincoteague** (shink-o-teeg), on the island of the same name, is Virginia's principal Eastern Shore destination. Chincoteague is famous for its oysters and late-July wild pony swim, when the small horses that inhabit Assateague are led across the channel for annual herd-thinning foal auctions.

The **chamber of commerce** (757-336-6161; www.chincoteaguechamber.com; 6733 Maddox Blvd; 9am-4:30pm Mon-Sat) has maps of hiking and bicycling trails up to and into the incredibly relaxing **Chincoteague National Wildlife Refuge** (per vehicle $8; 6am-8pm), a lovely wetland repose for migratory waterfowl. Five miles west of Chincoteague, stop by **NASA Wallops Flight Facility** (757-824-1344; admission free; 10am-4pm Thu-Mon), where you can watch occasional rocket launches and enjoy exhibits of the facility's work.

dark, this is one of the most popular nightspots on the beach.

Mary's Restaurant DINER **$**
(616 Virginia Beach Blvd; mains $4-9; 6am-3pm) A local institution for more than 40 years, Mary's is a great place to start the day with a tasty, filling, cheap breakfast. Fluffy, gooey, chocolate chip waffles have earned many fans.

Getting There & Around

Greyhound (757-422-2998; www.greyhound.com; 971 Virginia Beach Blvd) has several buses a day to Richmond ($33, 3½ hours), which also stop in Norfolk and Newport News; transfer in Richmond for services to Washington, DC, Wilmington, NYC and beyond. Buses depart from Circle D Food Mart, 1 mile west of the boardwalk. **Hampton Roads Transit** runs the Virginia Beach Wave trolley (tickets $1), which plies Atlantic Ave in summer.

The Piedmont

Central Virginia's rolling green landscape separates the coastal lowlands from the mountainous frontier. The fertile valley gives way to dozens of wineries, country villages and grand colonial estates.

CHARLOTTESVILLE

Set in the shadow of the Blue Ridge Mountains, Charlottesville is regularly ranked as one of the country's best places to live. This culturally rich town of 45,000 is home to the University of Virginia, which attracts Southern aristocracy and artsy lefties in equal proportion. With the UVA grounds and pedestrian downtown area overflowing with students, couples, professors and the occasional celebrity under a blanket of blue skies, 'C-ville' is practically perfect.

Charlottesville Visitor Center (877-386-1103; www.visitcharlottesville.org; 610 E Main St; 9am-5pm) is a helpful office in the heart of downtown.

MONTICELLO & AROUND

Monticello (434-984-9822; www.monticello.org; adult/child $22/8; 9am-6pm Mar-Oct, 10am-5pm Nov-Feb) is an architectural masterpiece designed and inhabited by Thomas Jefferson, Founding Father and third US president. 'I am as happy nowhere else and in no other society, and all my wishes end, where I hope my days will end, at Monticello,' wrote Jefferson, who spent 40 years building his dream home, finally completed in 1809. Today it is the only home in America designated a UN World Heritage site. Built in Roman neoclassical style, the house was the centerpiece of a 5000-acre plantation tended by 150 slaves. Monticello today does not gloss over Jefferson's role as a slave owner nor the likelihood that he fathered children with slave Sally Hemings, the complicated past of the man who declared that 'all men are created equal' in the Declaration of Independence. Jefferson and his family are buried in a small wooded plot near the home.

Visits to the house are conducted by guided tours only; you can take self-guided tours of the plantation grounds, gardens and cemetery. A high-tech exhibition center that opened in 2009 delves deeper into Jefferson's world – including exhibits on architecture, enlightenment through education and the complicated idea of liberty. The **Griffin Discovery Room** allows kids to put their hands on models of clever Jeffersonian inventions – like the duplicating polygraph machine. Frequent shuttles run from the visitor center to the hilltop house, or you can take the wooded footpath.

Tours are also offered of the nearby 1784 **Michie Tavern** (☎434-977-1234; www.michietavern.com; 683 Thomas Jefferson Pkwy; adult/child $9/7; ⊙9am-4:20pm) and James Monroe's estate, **Ash Lawn-Highland** (☎434-293-8000; www.ashlawnhighland.org; adult/child $12/6; ⊙9am-6pm Apr-Oct, 11am-5pm Nov-Mar), 2.5 miles east of Monticello. A combo ticket for all three is $36. Visit the Michie Tavern during lunchtime, when its dining room, the **Ordinary** (meals $17; ⊙11:15am-3:30pm), serves lunch buffets of Southern delights like fried chicken with biscuits.

UNIVERSITY OF VIRGINIA

One of the most beautiful college campuses in America, Thomas Jefferson's **University of Virginia** is a must-see. The classically designed buildings and grounds embody the spirit of communal living and learning that Jefferson envisioned. The centerpiece is the Jefferson-designed **Rotunda** (☎434-924-7969), a scale replica of Rome's Pantheon. Free, student-led tours of the Rotunda meet inside the main entrance daily at 10am, 11am, 2pm, 3pm and 4pm. The UVA **Art Museum** (155 Rugby Rd; admission free; ⊙noon-5pm Tue-Sun) has an eclectic and interesting collection of American, European and Asian arts.

Sleeping

There's a good selection of budget and midrange chain motels lining Emmet St/US 29 north of town. If you're after a reservation service, try **Guesthouses** (☎434-979-7264; www.va-guesthouses.com; r from $150), which provides cottages and B&B rooms in private homes. Two-night minimum stays are common on weekends.

Inn at Monticello B&B **$$$**
(☎434-979-3593; www.innatmonticello.com; 1188 Scottsville Rd; r $215; P❄🛜) Located across from Monticello, this Victorian B&B is set off against the Piedmont's rolling hillscape. Every one of the lodge's five rooms are cozy little testaments to colonial grandeur. Excellent cooked breakfasts.

South Street Inn B&B **$$$**
(☎434-979-0200; www.southstreetinn.com; 200 South St; r incl breakfast $160-255; P❄) In the heart of downtown, this elegant 1856 building went through previous incarnations as a girl's finishing school, boarding house and brothel. Now, it houses heritage-style rooms, some with antiques and working fireplaces. There's wine and cheese in the evenings.

Alexander House GUESTHOUSE **$**
(☎434-327-6447; www.alexanderhouse.us; 1205 Monticello Rd; dm/r $30/75; P@🛜) This friendly, laid-back guesthouse has three comfortable rooms as well as a separate six-bed bunkhouse for budget travelers. Those staying in the house share a bathroom but have free rein of the kitchen, living room and common areas. It's located in peaceful Belmont, home to an up-and-coming dining and cafe scene, a 15-minute walk to the downtown mall.

VIRGINIA VINEYARDS

Now the fifth-biggest wine producer in the USA, Virginia has 192 vineyards around the state, many located in the pretty hills around Charlottesville. Particularly notable is the Virginia Viognier. For more information on Virginia wine, visit www.virginiawine.org.

Jefferson Vineyards WINERY
(☎434-977-3042; www.jeffersonvineyards.com; 1353 Thomas Jefferson Pkwy, Charlottesville) Known for consistent quality vintage, this winery harvests from its namesake's original 1774 vineyard site.

Keswick Vineyards WINERY
(☎434-244-3341; www.keswickvineyards.com; 1575 Keswick Winery Dr, Keswick) Keswick won a wave of awards for its first vintage and has since been distilling a big range of grapes. It's off Rte 231.

Kluge Estate WINERY
(☎434-977-3895; www.klugeestateonline.com; 100 Grand Cru Dr, Charlottesville) Oenophiles regularly rate Kluge wine as the best in the state.

English Inn HOTEL **$$**
(434-971-9900; www.englishinncharlottesville.com; 2000 Morton Dr; r incl breakfast $100-160; P) British hospitality and furnishings and a Tudor facade accent this unique hotel. It's 1.5 miles north of UVA. Cheaper rates on weekdays.

White Pig B&B **$$**
(434-831-1416; www.thewhitepig.com; 5120 Irish Rd, Schuyler; r $160-185; P) Vegans and vegetarians should make a pilgrimage to the White Pig, about 22 miles southwest of Monticello. Located on the 170-acre Briar Creek Farm, this B&B/animal sanctuary has one of the most innovative vegan menus in the state. Rooms have pleasant meadow and garden views, and there's a hot tub for guests.

Eating & Drinking

The Downtown Mall, a pedestrian zone lined with dozens of shops and restaurants, is great for people-watching and outdoor dining on warm days. At night the bars along University Ave attract students and 20-somethings.

Local MODERN AMERICAN **$$**
(434-984-9749; 824 Hinton Ave; mains $11-25; 5:30-10pm Sun-Thu, to 11pm Fri & Sat) Amid Belmont's growing restaurant scene, the Local has earned many fans for its locavore-loving menu (black truffle mac 'n' cheese, roast duck with blood orange gastrique) and the elegant, warmly lit interior (exposed brick trimmed with colorful oil paintings). There's sidewalk and rooftop dining in warmer months, plus great cocktails.

Blue Moon Diner AMERICAN **$$**
(512 W Main St; mains $10-20; 8am-10pm Mon-Fri, from 9am Sat, 9am-3pm Sun) One of Charlottesville's best breakfast and weekend brunch spots is a festive retro-style diner that serves up delicious fare using locally sourced ingredients. You'll also find Virginia beers on tap, old-school rock on the radio, and the occasional live band.

Continental Divide MEXICAN **$$**
(811 W Main St; mains $10-15; 5:30-10pm) This fun, easy-going spot has no sign (look for the neon 'Get in Here' in the window) but is well worth seeking out for its Mexican fusion fare – tacos with slow-cooked pork, tuna tostadas, nachos with bison chili – and C-ville's best margaritas.

Zocalo FUSION **$$$**
(434-977-4944; 201 E Main St; mains $19-26; 5:30pm-2am Tue-Sun) This sleek and stylish restaurant-bar serves nicely turned-out Latin-inspired dishes (spicy tuna tartar, chili-dusted sea scallops, achiote-rubbed grilled pork). There's an outdoor patio for warm nights and a crackling fireplace in winter.

Mudhouse CAFE **$**
(213 W Main St; 7am-10pm Mon-Thu, to 11pm Fri & Sat, to 7pm Sun;) Do as the cool kids do and come here for bracing espresso, wi-fi and daily artsy happenings.

Splendora's Gelato Cafe ICE CREAM **$**
(317 E Main St; 9am-10pm Mon-Sat, from noon Sun;) Splendora's prepares creamy rich gelato, including flavors like pistachio, hazelnut, dulce de leche and gianduia.

Christian's Pizza PIZZA **$$**
(118 W Main St; slices $2-4, pies $10-16; 11am-9pm) A C-ville institution in the Downtown Mall, Christian's serves up tasty slices with a thin, crispy crust.

South Street Brewery SOUTHERN **$$**
(106 W South St; mains $9-18; from 5pm Mon-Sat) In a restored 1800s brick warehouse, you'll find tasty craft brews, good Southern bistro fare (barbecue pulled pork, crawfish-and-mushroom-stuffed trout) and occasional live bands (currently Wednesday nights from 10pm). It's a short stroll from the downtown mall.

Backyard BAR
(20 Elliewood Ave; 11am-2am Mon-Sat) The Backyard is a lively collegiate bar with a spacious outdoor space that gets packed on weekends. It's on a narrow lane sprinkled with restaurants and cafes, just off University Ave.

Getting There & Around

Amtrak (www.amtrak.com; 810 W Main St) Two daily trains to Washington, DC ($30, three hours).

Charlottesville Albemarle Airport (CHO; 434-973-8342; www.gocho.com) Ten miles north of downtown; offers regional flights.

Greyhound/Trailways terminal (434-295-5131; 310 W Main St) Runs three daily buses to both Richmond ($20, 1¼ hours) and Washington, DC ($23, three hours).

Trolley (6:40am-11:30pm Mon-Sat, 8am-5pm Sun) A free trolley connects W Main St with UVA.

APPOMATTOX COURT HOUSE & AROUND

At the McLean House in the town of Appomattox Court House, General Robert E Lee surrendered the Army of Northern Virginia to General Ulysses S Grant, in effect ending the Civil War. Instead of coming straight here, follow **Lee's retreat** (☎800-673-8732; www.varetreat.com) on a winding 25-stop tour that starts in Petersburg at Southside Railroad Station (River St and Cockade Alley) and cuts through some of the most attractive countryside in Virginia. Best take a detailed road map, as the trail is not always clearly marked. You'll finish at the 1700-acre **Appomattox Court House National Historic Park** (☎434-352-8987; www.nps.gov/apco; summer $4, Sep-May $3; ⊙8:30am-5pm). Most of the 27 restored buildings are open to visitors.

Shenandoah Valley

Local lore says Shenandoah was named for a Native American word meaning 'Daughter of the Stars.' True or not, there's no question that this is God's country, one of the most beautiful places in America. The 200-mile-long valley and its Blue Ridge Mountains hold amazing wonders at every turn, from small towns and wineries to battlefields and caverns. This was once the western border of colonial America, settled by Scotch-Irish frontiersmen who were Highland Clearance refugees. The area offers an array of outdoor activities including hiking, camping, fishing, horseback riding and canoeing.

SHENANDOAH NATIONAL PARK

One of the most spectacular national parks in the country, **Shenandoah** (☎540-999-3500; www.nps.gov/shen; week pass per car Mar-Nov $15, Dec-Feb $10) is like a new smile from nature: in spring and summer the wildflowers explode, in fall the leaves burn bright red and orange, and in winter a cold, starkly beautiful hibernation period sets in. White-tailed deer are a common sight and, if you're lucky, you might spot a black bear, bobcat or wild turkey. The park lies just 75 miles west of Washington, DC. Whatever your agenda, don't miss a visit to this amazing wonderland.

Sights & Activities

There are two visitor centers in the park, **Dickey Ridge** (Mile 4.6; ⊙8:30am-5pm mid-Apr–Oct) in the north and **Harry F Byrd** (Mile 51; ⊙8:30am-5pm Mar 31-Oct 27) in the south. Both have maps, backcountry permits and information on horseback riding, hang gliding, cycling (only on public roads) and other wholesome goodness. Shenandoah has more than 500 miles of hiking trails, including 101 miles of the Appalachian Trail. The trails described in this section are listed from north to south.

TOP CHOICE **Skyline Drive** SCENIC ROUTE

A 105-mile-long road running down the spine of the Blue Ridge Mountains, the Skyline Drive redefines the definition of 'Scenic Route.' You're constantly treated to an impressive view, but keep in mind the road is bendy, slow-going (35mph limit) and (in peak season) congested.

Old Rag Mountain HIKING

This is a tough, 8-mile circuit trail that culminates in a rocky scramble only suitable for the physically fit. Your reward is the summit of Old Rag Mountain and, along the way, some of the best views in Virginia.

Skyland HIKING

There are four easy trails here, none exceeding 1.6 miles, with a few steep sections throughout. Stony Man Trail gives great views for not-too-strenuous trekking.

Big Meadows HIKING

A very popular area with four easy-to-mid-level difficulty hikes. The Lewis Falls and Rose River trails run by the park's most spectacular waterfalls, and the former accesses the Appalachian Trail.

Bearfence Mountain HIKING

A short trail leads to a spectacular 360-degree viewpoint. The circuit hike is only 1.2 miles, but it involves a strenuous scramble over rocks.

Riprap HIKING

Three trails of varying difficulty. Blackrock Trail is an easy 1-mile loop that yields fantastic views. You can either hike the moderate 3.4-mile Riprap Trail to Chimney Rock, or detour and make a fairly strenuous 9.8-mile circuit that connects with the Appalachian Trail.

Sleeping & Eating

Camping is at four **NPS campgrounds** (☎877-444-6777; www.recreation.gov): **Mathews Arm** (Mile 22.1; campsites $15), **Big Meadows** (Mile 51.3; campsites $20), **Lewis Mountain** (Mile 57.5; campsites $15; no reservations) and **Loft Mountain** (Mile 79.5; campsites $15). Most are open mid-May to October. Camping elsewhere requires a free backcountry permit, available from any visitor center.

For not-so-rough lodging, stay at **Skyland Lodge** (Mile 41.7; r $87-200), **Big Meadows** (Mile 51.2; r $99-159) or **Lewis Mountain** (Mile 57.5; cabins from $76), all open from early March to mid-November. Reservations can be made by calling ☎800-999-4714 or booking online at www.visitshenandoah.com.

Skyland and Big Meadows both have restaurants and taverns with nightly live music. Big Meadows is the prettiest and largest resort in the park and offers the most services, including gas, laundry and camp store. It's best to bring your own food into the park if you're going camping or on extended hikes.

ℹ Getting There & Around

Amtrak trains run to Staunton, in the Shenandoah Valley, once a day from Washington, DC ($66, four hours). You'll really need your own wheels to explore the length and breadth of the park, which can be easily accessed from several exits off I-81.

FRONT ROYAL & AROUND

The northernmost tip of Skyline Dr initially comes off as a drab strip of gas stations, but there's a friendly enough main street and some cool caverns nearby. Stop in at the **visitor center** (☎800-338-2576; 414 E Main St; ⊙9am-5pm) and the **Shenandoah Valley Travel Association** (☎800-847-4878; www.visitshenandoah.org; US 211 W, I-81 exit 264; ⊙9am-5pm) before heading 'up' (a reference to altitude, not direction) the valley.

Front Royal's claim to fame is **Skyline Caverns** (☎540-635-4545; www.skylinecaverns.com; US 340; adult/child $16/8; ⊙9am-5pm Mon-Fri, to 6pm Sat, Sun & summer), which boast rare white-spiked anthodites – delicate mineral formations that resemble sea urchins. Kids may enjoy mini train rides ($3) and the mirror maze ($5).

Woodward House on Manor Grade (☎540-635-7010; www.acountryhome.com; 413 S Royal Ave/US 320; r $110-155, cottage $225; P ☎) is a cluttered B&B with seven cheerful rooms and two separate cottages (with wood-burning fireplaces). Sip your coffee from the deck and don't let the busy street below distract from the Blue Ridge Mountain vista.

Element (☎540-636-9293; jsgourmet.com; 206 S Royal Ave; mains $12-18; ⊙11am-3pm & 5-10pm Tue-Sat) is a foodie favorite for its quality bistro fare. The small dinner menu features changing specials like horseradish-crusted red snapper; for lunch, come for gourmet sandwiches ($8 to $10), soups and salads.

Upstairs from Element, **Apartment 2G** (☎540-636-9293; jsgourmet.com; 206 S Royal Ave; 5 courses $50; ⊙from 6:30pm Sat) serves decadent five-course dinners on Saturday evening in a cozy space (like dining at a friend's place). Reservations essential. Check the website for other culinary happenings.

Soul Mountain Cafe (☎540-636-0070; 1303 117 E Main St; mains $12-24; ⊙noon-9pm Mon-Sat, to 4pm Sun) serves tasty eclectic fare (pan-seared tuna, barbecue pulled pork) beneath a large portrait of Bob Marley.

Some 25 miles north, in the town of Winchester, is the **Museum of the Shenandoah Valley** (☎888-556-5799; www.shenandoahmuseum.org; 901 Amherst St; adult/student $12/10; ⊙10am-4pm Tue-Sun), which comprises an 18th-century period-filled house museum, 6-acre garden and a multimedia museum that delves into the valley's history. There's also a cafe.

If you can only fit one cavern into your itinerary, head 25 miles south from Front Royal to the world-class **Luray Caverns** (☎540-743-6551; www.luraycaverns.com; I-81 exit 264; adult/child $23/11; ⊙9am-6pm, to 7pm summer, to 4pm winter) and hear the 'Stalacpipe Organ,' hyped as the largest musical instrument on earth.

GEORGE WASHINGTON & JEFFERSON NATIONAL FORESTS

Stretching along the entire western edge of Virginia, these two mammoth **forests** (www.fs.fed.us/r8/gwj; campsites around $12, primitive camping free) comprise more than 1562 sq miles of mountainous terrain bordering the Shenandoah Valley. They contain challenging to easy trail networks, which include 330 miles of the **Appalachian Trail** (www.appalachiantrail.org) and mountain-biking routes. Hundreds of developed campgrounds are scattered throughout (most open mid-May to mid-September). **USDA Forest Service headquarters** (☎540-265-5100; 5162 Valleypointe Pkwy; ⊙8am-4:30pm Mon-Fri), off the Blue Ridge Pkwy in Roanoke, oversees a dozen ranger stations along the ranges.

STAUNTON & AROUND

This pretty little town jumps out of the mountains with its cozy college (Mary Baldwin), old time-y avenues and, oddly enough, one of America's premier Shakespeare companies. The **visitor center** (www.visitstaunton.com; 35 S New St; ⏲9am-6pm) is in the small historic downtown.

The excellent **Frontier Culture Museum** (☎540-332-7850; overlooking I-81 exit 222; adult/student/child $10/9/6; ⏲9am-5pm mid-Mar–Nov, 10am-4pm Dec–mid-Mar) has authentic historic buildings from Germany, Ireland and England, plus re-created West African dwellings and a separate area of American frontier dwellings on the site's 100-plus acres. Costumed interpreters (aided by bleating livestock) do an excellent job showing what life was like for the disparate ancestors of today's Virginians.

Woodrow Wilson Presidential Library (www.woodrowwilson.org; 18-24 N Coalter St; adult/student/child $14/7/5; ⏲9am-5pm Mon-Sat, from noon Sun) is a scholarly peek into the life of the 28th president and founder of the League of Nations, as well as the pre- and post-WWI era he emerged from.

Don't leave without catching a show at the 300-seat **Blackfriars Playhouse** (☎540-851-1733; www.americanshakespearecenter.com; 10 S Market St; tickets $20-42), where the American Shakespeare Center company performs in a stunning re-creation of Shakespeare's original indoor theater.

To stay right downtown, the thoroughly mauve and immensely welcoming **Frederick House** (☎540-885-4220; www.frederickhouse.com; 28 N New St; r incl breakfast $130-240; P❄📶) consists of five historical residences with 25 varied rooms and suites, all with private bathrooms and some with antique furnishings and decks.

Nearby, the **Miller House** (☎540-886-3186; www.millerhousebandb.com; 210 N New St; r incl breakfast $155-175; P❄) offers beautiful guestrooms with chandeliers, four-poster beds and decorative fireplaces in a beautifully restored Victorian.

Howard Johnson Express (☎540-886-5330; www.hojo.com; 268 N Central Ave; r $58; P❄📶🏊) is a clean, good-value cheapie, a short stroll to the historic district.

West Beverley St is sprinkled with restaurants and cafes. Leading Staunton's culinary renaissance, **Zynodoa** (☎540-885-7775; 115 E Beverley St; mains $21-28; ⏲5-11:30pm Wed-Sat, noon-8pm Sun) serves delectable seasonal fare, sustainably sourced. Recent hits: Ayrshire roasted pork with spicy black beans and Southern fried soft-shell crabs.

Another farm-to-table favorite, the **Staunton Grocery** (☎540 886 6880; 105 W Beverley St; lunch/dinner mains from $9/18; ⏲11am-2pm Wed-Sat, 5:30-9pm Tue-Sat) serves innovative fare with Southern accents (like roasted catfish with beluga lentils and bacon vinaigrette).

Split Banana (7 W Beverley St; ice cream from $3.15; ⏲11am-11pm; 👪) is an inviting, retro-style ice-cream parlor with 18 or so gelato-style flavors, all made on-site.

A valley tradition since 1947, **Mrs Rowe's** (☎540-886-1833; I-81 exit 222; mains $5-16; ⏲7am-8pm Mon-Sat, to 7pm Sun) offers home-cooked Southern fare and hospitality.

LEXINGTON & AROUND

This is the place to see Southern gentry at their stately best, as cadets from the Virginia Military Institute jog past the prestigious academics of Washington & Lee University. The **visitor center** (☎540-463-3777; 106 E Washington St; ⏲9am-5pm) has free parking.

You can learn about one of Lexington's favorite former residents at the **Stonewall Jackson House** (8 E Washington St; adult/child $8/6; ⏲9am-5pm Mon-Sat, from 1pm Sun). The future Confederate general lived (and did the polka) in the house from 1851 to 1861 before going off to war and into history.

You'll either feel admiration or pity for the disciplined cadets at **Virginia Military Institute** (VMI; Letcher Ave; ⏲9am-5pm when campus & museums open), the only university to have sent its entire graduating class into combat (plaques to student war dead are touching and ubiquitous). A full-dress parade takes place most Fridays at 4:30pm during the school year. The school's **George C Marshall Museum** (☎540-463-7103; adult/student $5/2; ⏲9am-5pm Tue-Sat, from 1pm Sun) honors the creator of the Marshall Plan for post-WWII European reconstruction. The **VMI Cadet Museum** (☎540-464-7334; admission free; ⏲9am-5pm) houses the stuffed carcass of Stonewall Jackson's horse, a homemade American flag made by an alumnus prisoner of war in Vietnam, and a tribute to VMI students killed in the War on Terror. Contact the museum for a free guided tour of the campus offered at noon.

Founded in 1749, colonnaded Washington & Lee University is one of the top small colleges in America. The **Lee Chapel & Museum** (☎540-458-8768; ⏲9am-4pm, from 1pm Sun) inters Robert E Lee, while his horse Traveller is buried outside. One of the four Confederate banners surrounding Lee's tomb is set in an original flagpole, a branch a rebel soldier turned into a makeshift standard.

Historic Country Inns (☎877-283-9680; 11 N Main St; r $110-145, ste $170-190; P❄) operates two inns downtown and one outside town. All of the buildings have some historical significance to Lexington, and most of the rooms are individually decorated with period antiques. The charming, eco-minded **Applewood Inn & Llama Trekking** (☎800-463-1902; www.applewoodbb.com; 242 Tarn Beck Lane; r $155-165; P❄) offers a slew of outdoorsy activities on a farm 12-minutes' drive southeast of Lexington.

Reserve well ahead for a memorable meal at **Red Hen** (☎540-464-4401; 11 E Washington St; mains $17-25; ⏰5:30-9pm Tue-Sat), with a creative menu that showcases the fine local produce (roasted pork loin with savory beer bread pudding and oyster mushrooms).

Bistro on Main (8 N Main St; mains $9-24; ⏰11:30am-2:30pm & 5-9pm Tue-Sat) is a bright, welcoming spot with big windows onto the main street, tasty bistro fare and a bar.

For old-fashioned amusement, catch a movie at **Hull's Drive-in** (☎540-463-2621; http://hullsdrivein.com; 2367 N Lee Hwy/US 11; per person $6; ⏰7pm Thu-Sun May-Oct), 5.5 miles north of town.

NATURAL BRIDGE & FOAMHENGE

Yes, it's a kitschy tourist trap, and yes, vocal creationists who insist it was made by the hand of God are dominating the site, but the 215ft-high **Natural Bridge** (www.naturalbridgeva.com; bridge adult/child $18/10, bridge & caverns $24/14; ⏰9am-dusk), 15 miles from Lexington, is still pretty cool. It was surveyed by 16-year-old George Washington, who supposedly carved his initials into the wall, and was once owned by Thomas Jefferson. You can also take a tour of some exceptionally deep caverns here.

Just up the road, check out **Foamhenge** (Hwy 11; admission free), a marvelous full-size replica of Stonehenge made entirely of Styrofoam. There are fine views – and even an onsite wizard. It's a mile north of Natural Bridge.

Blue Ridge Highlands & Southwest Virginia

The southwestern tip of Virginia is the most rugged part of the state. Turn onto the Blue Ridge Pkwy or any side road and you'll immediately plunge into dark strands of dogwood and fir, fast streams and white waterfalls. You're bound to see Confederate flags in the small towns, but there's a proud hospitality behind the fierce veneer of independence.

BLUE RIDGE PARKWAY

Where Skyline Dr ends, the **Blue Ridge Parkway** (www.blueridgeparkway.org, www.nps.gov/blri) picks up. The road is just as pretty and runs from the southern Appalachian ridge in Shenandoah National Park at Mile 0 to North Carolina's Great Smoky Mountains National Park at Mile 469. Wildflowers bloom in spring, and fall colors are spectacular, but watch out for foggy days; no guardrails can make for hairy driving. There are a dozen visitor centers scattered over the Pkwy, and any of them make a good kick-off point to start your trip. For more details, see p335.

Sights & Activities

There are all kinds of sights running along the Pkwy; these are a handful, listed from north to south:

Humpback Rocks HIKING
(Mile 5.8) Tour 19th-century farm buildings or take the steep trail to Humpback Rocks, offering spectacular 360-degree views.

Sherando Lake Recreation Area SWIMMING
(Off Mile 16; ☎540-291-2188) In George Washington National Forest (p310), you'll find two pretty lakes (one for swimming, one for fishing), with hiking trails and campsites. To get there, take Rte 664 W.

James River & Kanawha Canal HISTORIC SITE
(Mile 64) A footpath here leads to the 19th-century canal locks and, if you have time, a pleasant amble over river bluffs.

Peaks of Otter HIKING
(Mile 86) There are trails to the tops of these mountains: Sharp Top, Flat Top and Harkening Hill. Shuttles run to the top of Sharp Top or you can try a fairly challenging hike (3 miles return) to the summit.

Mabry Mill HISTORIC SITE
(Mile 176) One of the most photographed buildings in the state, the mill nests in such a fuzzy green vale you'll think you've entered the opening chapter of a Tolkien novel.

Sleeping

There are nine local **campgrounds** (☎877-444-6777; www.recreation.gov; campsites $16; ⏰May-Oct), four in Virginia. Every year the staggered opening date of facilities changes, but sites are generally accessible from April to November. Two NPS approved indoor facilities are on the Pkwy in Virginia.

Peaks of Otter LODGE $$
(☎540-586-1081; www.peaksofotter.com; Mile 86, 85554 Blue Ridge Pkwy; r $110-140; ❄) A pretty, split-rail-surrounded lodge on a small lake that's nestled between two of its namesake mountains. There's a restaurant, but no public phones and no cellphone reception.

Rocky Knob Cabins CABINS $
(☎540-593-3503; Mile 174, 256 Mabry Mill Rd; cabin with shared bath $65; ⏲May-Oct) Rustic cabins set in a secluded stretch of forest. Bring food, as eating options are limited along the Pkwy.

ROANOKE & AROUND

Illuminated by the giant star atop Mill Mountain, Roanoke is the largest city in the valley and is the self-proclaimed 'Capital of the Blue Ridge.' It has a compact set of attractions based around the bustling indoor-outdoor **Historic City Market** (213 Market St; ⏲7:30am-4:30pm Mon-Sat), a sumptuous farmers market loaded with temptations. For local information, check out the **Roanoke Valley Visitor Information Center** (☎540-342-6025; www.visitroanokeva.com; 101 Shenandoah Ave NE; ⏲9am-5pm) in the old Norfolk & Western train station.

The striking **Taubman Museum of Art** (www.taubmanmuseum.org; 110 Salem Ave SE; adult/child $7/4; ⏲10am-5pm Tue-Sat, to 8pm Fri, noon-5pm Sun), opened in 2008, is set in a sculptural steel-and-glass edifice that's reminiscent of the Guggenheim Bilbao (it's no coincidence, as architect Randall Stout was a one-time associate of Frank Gehry). Inside, you'll find a superb collection of artworks spanning 3500 years (particularly strong in 19th- and 20th-century American works).

Currently undergoing a massive $27 million renewal project, **Center in the Square** (☎540-342-5700; www.centerinthesquare.org; 1 Market Sq; ⏲10am-5pm Tue-Sat, from 1pm Sun) is the city's cultural heartbeat, with a science museum and planetarium (adult/child $8/6), local history museum (adult/child $3/2) and theater. The site of the **Harrison Museum of African American Culture** (admission free) was the first public high school for African Americans in America. It showcases local African American culture, and traditional and contemporary African art.

About 30 miles east of Roanoke, the tiny town of Bedford suffered the most casualties per capita during WWII, and hence was chosen to host the moving **National D-Day Memorial** (☎540-586-3329; US 460 & Hwy 122; adult/child $7/5; ⏲10am-5pm). Among its towering arch and flower garden is a cast of bronze figures re-enacting the storming of the beach, complete with bursts of water symbolizing the hail of bullets the soldiers faced. Walking tours ($3) leave hourly between 10:30am and 3:30pm.

Rose Hill (☎540-400-7785; www.bandbrosehill.com; 521 Washington Ave; r $100-125) is a charming and welcoming three-room B&B in Roanoke's historic district.

Market St is dotted with eateries, including much-loved, family-owned **Thelma's Chicken & Waffles** (315 Market St; mains $4-10; ⏲7am-10pm Tue-Sat, 10am-9pm Sun & Mon), serving tasty Southern classics like baby-back ribs, mac 'n' cheese, meatloaf and, of course, fried chicken and waffles.

MT ROGERS NATIONAL RECREATION AREA

This seriously beautiful district is well worth a visit from outdoor enthusiasts. Hike, fish or cross-country ski among ancient hardwood trees and the state's tallest peak. The **park headquarters** (☎276-783-5196; Hwy 16, Marion) offers maps and recreation directories. The NPS operates five campgrounds in the area; contact park headquarters for details.

ABINGDON

One of the most photogenic towns in Virginia, Abingdon retains fine Federal and Victorian architecture in its historic district, and hosts the bluegrass **Virginia Highlands Festival** over the first half of August. The **visitor center** (☎800-435-3440; 335 Cummings St; ⏲9am-5pm) has exhibits on local history.

Fields-Penn 1860 House Museum (208 W Main St; adult/child $3/2; ⏲11am-4pm Wed, from 1pm Thu-Sat) has exhibits on 19th-century life in southwest Virginia. Founded during the Depression, **Barter Theatre** (☎276-628-3991; www.bartertheatre.com; 133 W Main St; performances from $20) earned its name from audiences trading food for performances. Actors Gregory Peck and Ernest Borgnine (and uh, Wayne Knight, *Seinfeld*'s 'Newman') cut their teeth on Barter's stage.

The **Virginia Creeper Trail** (www.vacreepertrail.org), named for the railroad that once ran this route, travels 33 miles between Whitetop Station near the North Carolina border and downtown Abingdon. Several outfitters rent bikes, organize outings and run shuttles, including **Virginia Creeper Trail Bike Shop** (☎276-676-2552; www.vacreepertrailbikeshop.com; 201 Pecan St; per 2hr/day $10/20; ⏲9am-6pm Sun-Fri, from 8am Sat) near the trailhead.

Martha Washington Inn (☎276-628-3161; www.marthawashingtoninn.com; 150 W Main St; r from $225; P❄@📶≋), opposite the Barter, is the region's premier historic hotel, a Victorian sprawl of elegant rooms and excellent amenities (wood-paneled library, outdoor Jacuzzi, saltwater pool, tennis courts).

Step back in time at **Pop Ellis Soda Shoppe** (217 W Main St; mains $8-11; ⏲11am-4pm Mon, to 9pm Tue-Sat) with a beautifully restored interior reminiscent of 1920s-era soda fountains. Thick burgers, wraps and nachos are a fine accompaniment to hand-jerked sodas and milkshakes.

Equal parts cafe and bookstore, **Zazzy'z** (380 E Main St; mains around $5; ⏲8am-6pm Mon-Sat, 9am-3pm Sun) serves inexpensive quiches, lasagnas and panini, plus decent coffee.

THE CROOKED ROAD

When Scotch–Irish fiddle-and-reel married African American banjo-and-percussion, American mountain or 'old-time' music was born, with such genres as country and bluegrass. The latter genre still dominates the Blue Ridge, and Virginia's Heritage Music Trail, the 250-mile-long **Crooked Road** (www.thecrookedroad.org), takes you through nine sites associated with that history, along with some eye-stretching mountain scenery. It's well worth taking a detour and joining the music-loving fans of all ages who kick up their heels (many arrive with tap shoes) at these festive jamborees. During a live show you'll witness elders connecting to deep cultural roots and a new generation of musicians keeping that heritage alive and evolving.

FLOYD

Tiny, cute-as-a-postcard Floyd is nothing more than an intersection between Hwy 8 and 221, but life explodes on Friday nights at the **Floyd Country Store** (☎540-745-4563; www.floydcountrystore.com; 206 S Locust St; ⏲10am-11pm Fri, to 5:30pm Sat). Every Friday starting at 6:30pm, $5 gets you four bluegrass bands in four hours and the chance to watch happy crowds jam along to regional heritage. No smokin', no drinkin', but there's plenty of dancin' (of the jig-and-tap style) and good cheer. On weekends, there's lots of live music happening nearby.

Built in 2007 with ecofriendly materials and furnishings, **Hotel Floyd** (☎540-745-6080; www.hotelfloyd.com; 120 Wilson St; r $100-160; P❄📶) is one of the most 'green' hotels in Virginia, and is a model of sustainability. Each of the 14 unique rooms were decorated by local artisans. Eight miles west of Floyd, **Miracle Farm B&B** (☎540-789-2214; www.miraclefarmbnb.com; 179 Ida Rose Lane; r $125-155; P❄📶) has lovely ecofriendly cabins amid lush scenery.

When you're all jigged out, head for **Oddfella's** (110 N Locust St; lunch mains $7-14, dinner $8-21; ⏲11am-2:30pm Wed-Sat, 5-9pm Thu-Sun, 10am-3pm Sun), which has a woodsy, organic mostly Tex-Mex menu – and satisfying locally produced microbrews from the Shooting Creek Brewery.

Above the Harvest Moon health-food store, **Natasha's Market Cafe** (☎540-745-2450; 227 N Locust St; lunch/dinner mains from $8/16; ⏲11am-3pm Tue-Sat, 5:30-9pm Thu-Sat) is a bright and cheery spot serving organic local produce.

GALAX

Galax claims to be the world capital of mountain music, although it feels like anywhere-else-ville outside of the immediate downtown area, which is on the National Register of Historic Places. The main attraction is the **Rex Theater** (☎276-236-0329; www.rextheatergalax.com; 113 E Grayson St), a musty, red-curtained belle of yore. Frequent bluegrass acts cross its stage, but the easiest one to catch is the free Friday-night live WBRF 98.1 show, which pulls in crowds from across the mountains.

For a touch of the great outdoors, go for a hike or bike ride along the **New River Trail**, a 57-mile-long greenway along an abandoned railroad track north to Pulaski. It parallels the New River for 39 miles.

Tom Barr of **Barr's Fiddle Shop** (105 S Main St) is the Stradivarius of the mountains, a master craftsman sought out by fiddle and mandolin aficionados from across the world. The **Old Fiddler's Convention** (www.oldfiddlersconvention.com) is held on the second weekend in August in Galax; it's one of the premier mountain music festivals in the world.

Doctor's Inn (☎276-238-9998; thedoctorsinnvirginia.com; 406 W Stuart Dr; r $140-150; P❄📶) is a welcoming guesthouse with antique-filled chambers and excellent breakfasts.

The **Galax Smokehouse** (101 N Main St; mains $5-14; ⏲11am-9pm Mon-Sat, to 3pm Sun) serves platters of sweetly sauced Memphis-style BBQ.

CARTER FAMILY FOLD

In a tiny hamlet of SW Virginia, formerly known as Maces Spring (today part of Hiltons), you'll find one of the hallowed birthplaces of mountain music. The **Carter Family Fold** (☎276-386-6054; www.carterfamilyfold.org; AP Carter Hwy/Rte 614; adult/child $7/1; ⏲7:30pm Sat) continues the musical legacy begun by the talented Carter family back in 1927. Every Saturday night, the 900-person arena hosts first-rate bluegrass and gospel bands; there's also a museum with family memorabilia and the original mid-1800s log cabin where AP Carter was born. With no nearby lodging, your best bet is to stay in Abingdon (30 miles east), Kingsport, TN (12 miles southwest) or Bristol (25 miles southeast).

WEST VIRGINIA

Wild and wonderful West Virginia is often overlooked by American and foreign travelers. It doesn't help that the state can't seem to shake its negative stereotypes. That's too bad, because West Virginia is one of the prettiest states in the Union. With its line of unbroken green mountains, raging whitewater rivers and snowcapped ski resorts, this is an outdoor-lovers' paradise.

Created by secessionists from secession, the people here still think of themselves as hardscrabble sons of miners, and that perception isn't entirely off. But the Mountain State is also gentrifying and, occasionally, that's a good thing: the arts are flourishing in the valleys, where some towns offer a welcome break from the state's constantly evolving outdoor activities.

History

Virginia was once the biggest state in America, divided between the plantation aristocracy of the Tidewater and the mountains of what is now West Virginia. The latter were settled by tough farmers who staked out independent freeholds across the Appalachians. Always resentful of their Eastern brethren and their reliance on cheap (ie slave) labor, the mountaineers of West Virginia declared their independence from Virginia when the latter tried to break off from America during the Civil War.

Yet the scrappy, independent-at-all-costs stereotype was challenged in the late 19th and early 20th centuries, when miners here formed into cooperative unions and fought employers in some of the bloodiest battles in American labor history. That mix of chip-on-the-shoulder resentment toward authority and look-out-for-your-neighbor community values continues to characterize West Virginia today, although the creeping blandness of suburbia threatens this regional culture.

WEST VIRGINIA FACTS

- » **Nickname** Mountain State
- » **Population** 1.9 million
- » **Area** 24,230 sq miles
- » **Capital city** Charleston (population 52,000)
- » **Sales tax** 6%
- » **Birthplace of** Olympic gymnast Mary Lou Retton (b 1968), writer Pearl S Buck (1892–1973), pioneer aviator Chuck Yeager (b 1923), actor Don Knotts (1924–2006)
- » **Home of** The National Radio Astronomy Observatory, much of the American coal industry
- » **Politics** Republican
- » **Famous for** mountains, John Denver's 'Take Me Home, Country Roads,' the Hatfield–McCoy feud
- » **State slogan** 'Wild and Wonderful'
- » **Driving distances** Harpers Ferry to Fayetteville 280 miles, Fayetteville to Morgantown 148 miles

ℹ Information

West Virginia Division of Tourism (☎800-225-5982; www.wvtourism.com) operates welcome centers at interstate borders and in **Harpers Ferry** (☎304-535-2482). Check www.adventuresinwv.com for info on the state's myriad adventure tourism opportunities.

Many hotels and motels tack on a $1 'safe' fee, refundable upon request at checkout. So if you didn't use that room safe, get your dollar back.

Eastern Panhandle

The most accessible part of the state has always been a mountain getaway for DC types.

HARPERS FERRY

History lives on in this attractive town, set with steep cobblestoned streets framed by the Shenandoah Mountains and the confluence of the rushing Potomac and Shenandoah Rivers. The lower town functions as an open-air museum, with over a dozen buildings that you can wander through to get a taste of 19th-century life in the small town. Exhibits narrate the town's role at the forefront of westward expansion, American industry and, most famously, the slavery debate. In 1859 old John Brown tried to spark a slave uprising here and was hanged for his efforts; the incident rubbed friction between North and South into the fires of Civil War.

Pick up a pass to visit the historic buildings at the **Harpers Ferry National Historic Park Visitor Center** (☎304-535-6029; www.nps.gov/hafe; 171 Shoreline Dr; vehicle/pedestrian $6/4; ⊙8am-5pm) off Hwy 340. You can also park and take a free shuttle from here. Parking is extremely limited in Harpers Ferry proper.

Sights & Activities

There are great hikes in the area, from three-hour scrambles to the scenic overlook from the Maryland Heights Trail, past Civil War fortifications on the Loudoun Heights Trail or along the Appalachian Trail. You can also bike or walk along the C&O Canal towpath.

Master Armorer's House BUILDING
Among the free sites in the historic district, this 1858 house explains how rifle technology developed here revolutionized the firearms industry.

Appalachian Trail Conservancy HIKING
(☎304-535-6331; www.appalachiantrail.org; cnr Washington & Jackson Sts; ⊙9am-5pm Mon-Fri Apr-Oct) The 2160-mile Appalachian Trail is headquartered at this tremendous resource for hikers.

Storer College building MUSEUM
Long ago a teachers' college for freed slaves, it now traces the town's African American history.

John Brown Museum MUSEUM
(http://johnbrownwaxmuseum.com; 168 High St; adult/child $7/5; ⊙9am-4:30pm) This laughably tacky museum tells the story of Brown's life through music, voice recordings and life-size wax figures.

River Riders ADVENTURE SPORTS
(☎800-326-7238; www.riverriders.com; 408 Alstadts Hill Rd) The go-to place for rafting, canoeing, tubing, kayaking and multiday biking trips, plus bike rental (four hours $20).

O Be Joyfull WALKING TOURS
(☎732-801-0381; www.obejoyfull.com; 175 High St; adult/child from $8/5) Offers a variety of historical walking tours around Harpers Ferry, including a spooky 90-minute evening tour.

Sleeping & Eating

Jackson Rose B&B $$
(☎304-535-1528; www.thejacksonrose.com; 1167 W Washington St; r weekday/weekend $135/150; ❄📶) This marvelous brick 18th-century residence with stately gardens has three attractive guestrooms, including a room where Stonewall Jackson briefly lodged during the Civil War. Antique furnishings and vintage curios are sprinkled about the house, and the cooked breakfast is excellent. It's a 600m walk downhill to the historic district. No children under 12.

Town's Inn B&B $$
(☎304-702-1872, 877-489-2447; www.thetownsinn.com; 175 & 179 High St; r $70-140; ❄) Spread between two neighboring pre–Civil War residences, the Town's Inn has rooms ranging from small and minimalist to charming heritage-style quarters. It's set in the middle of the historic district with an indoor-outdoor restaurant as well.

HI-Harpers Ferry Hostel HOSTEL $
(☎301-834-7652; www.hiusa.org; 19123 Sandy Hook Rd, Knoxville, MD; dm $20; ⊙mid-Apr–mid-Oct; P❄@📶) Located 2 miles from downtown on the Maryland side of the Potomac River, this friendly hostel has plenty of amenities including a kitchen, laundry and lounge area with games and books.

Canal House AMERICAN $$
(1226 Washington St; mains $7-14; ⊙11am-3pm Wed-Sat, 5:30-8:30pm Thu-Sat, noon-6pm Sun; 👪) Roughly 1 mile west (and uphill) from the historic district, Canal House is a perennial favorite for delicious sandwiches and friendly service in a flower-trimmed stone house. Outdoor seating.

Anvil AMERICAN $$
(☎304-535-2582; 1270 Washington St; lunch mains $8-12, dinner $15-24; ⊙11am-9pm Wed-Sun) Local trout melting in honey-pecan butter and an elegant Federal dining room equals excellence at Anvil, in next-door Bolivar.

TOP CHOICE **Beans in the Belfry** AMERICAN $$
(☎301-834-7178; 122 W Potomac St, Brunswick, MD; ⏱9am-9pm Mon-Sat, to 7pm Sun; @📶👪) Across the river in Brunswick (roughly 10 miles east), you'll find this converted red-brick church, sheltering mismatched couches and kitsch-laden walls, light fare (chili, sandwiches, quiche) and a tiny stage where live folk, blues and bluegrass bands strike up most nights. Sunday jazz brunch ($16) is a hit.

ℹ Getting There & Around

Amtrak (www.amtrak.com) trains run to Washington's Union Station (one daily, 71 minutes, $14). **MARC trains** (mta.maryland.gov) run three times daily, Monday to Friday ($11).

BERKELEY SPRINGS

America's first spa town (George Washington relaxed here) is an odd jumble of spiritualism, artistic expression and pampering spa centers. Farmers in pickups sporting Confederate flags and acupuncturists in tie-dye smocks regard each other with bemusement on the roads of Bath (still the official name).

The Berkeley Springs State Park's **Roman Baths** (☎304-258-2711; 2 S Washington St; bath $22; ⏱10am-6pm) are uninspiring (soaks are in dimly lit individual tile-lined rooms), but it's the cheapest spa deal in town. (Fill your water bottle with some of the magic stuff at the fountain outside the door.) For a more indulgent experience, book a treatment (massages, facials, aromatherapy) across the green at the **Bath House** (☎800-431-4698; www.bathhouse.com; 21 Fairfax St; 1hr massage $75; ⏱10am-5pm).

Inn & Spa at Berkeley Springs (☎304-258-2210; thecountryinnatberkeleysprings.com; r from $110; P📶), right next to the park, has a wide range of accommodations, from bright, comfortable rooms with wood floors to more elegant suites. There's a good spa on-site.

Cacapon State Park (☎304-258-1022; 818 Cacapon Lodge Dr; lodge/cabins from $85/91) has simple lodge accommodations plus modern and rustic cabins (with fireplaces) in a peaceful wooded setting, 9 miles south of Berkeley Springs (off US 522). There's hiking, lake swimming and a golf course.

Tari's (33 N Washington St; lunch $8-10, dinner $15-2; ⏱11am-9pm) is a casual spot serving gourmet sandwiches and salads by day, and heartier fare (seafood, ribs, thyme-crusted lamb) by night. Reserve ahead for high-end cuisine at the elegant, award-winning **Lot 12 Public House** (☎304-258-6264; 117 Warren St; mains $23-30; ⏱from 5pm Thu-Sun), halfway up the hill.

Monongahela National Forest

Almost the entire eastern half of West Virginia is marked green parkland on the map, and all that goodness falls under the auspices of this stunning national forest. Within its 1400 sq miles are wild rivers, caves and the highest peak in the state (Spruce Knob). More than 850 miles of trails include the 124-mile **Allegheny Trail**, for hiking and backpacking, and the 75-mile rails-to-trails **Greenbrier River Trail**, popular with bicyclists.

Elkins, at the forest's western boundary, is a good base of operations. The **National Forest Service Headquarters** (☎304-636-1800; 200 Sycamore St; campsites $5-30, primitive camping free) distributes recreation directories for hiking, bicycling and camping. Stock up on trail mix, energy bars and hippie auras at **Good Energy Foods** (214 3rd St; ⏱9am-5:30pm Mon-Sat).

In the southern end of the forest, **Cranberry Mountain Nature Center** (☎304-653-4826; cnr Hwys 150 & 39/55; ⏱9am-4:30pm Thu-Mon May-Oct) has scientific information on the forest.

The surreal landscapes at **Seneca Rocks**, 35 miles southeast of Elkins, attract rock climbers up the 900ft-tall sandstone strata. **Seneca Shadows Campground** (☎877-444-6777; campsites $11-30; ⏱Apr-Oct) is 1 mile east.

An 8-mile portion of the Allegheny Trail links two full-service state parks 30 miles northeast of Elkins: **Canaan Valley Resort** (☎304-866-4121; www.canaanresort.com), a downhill ski resort, and **Blackwater Falls State Park** (☎304-259-5216; www.blackwaterfalls.com), with backcountry ski touring. Further south, **Snowshoe Mountain** (☎877-441-4386; www.snowshoemtn.com; lift tickets adult/student/child $79/76/66) is the state's largest downhill ski and snowboard resort, with a beautiful alpine-inspired, pedestrian village. Snowshoe is a popular mountain-biking center from spring to fall.

Nearby, the **Cass Scenic Railroad State Park** (☎304-456-4300; www.cassrailroad.com; train rides from $18) runs steam trains, from an old logging town to mountaintop overlooks, daily in summer and for peak fall foliage. Accommodations include cottages ($103 to $122) and cabooses ($85 to $119).

ROADSIDE MYSTERIES

See gravity and the known limits of tackiness defied at the **Mystery Hole** (☎304-658-9101; 16724 Midland Trail, Ansted, WV; adult/child $6/5; ⊙10:30am-6pm), one of the great attractions of roadside America. Everything inside this madhouse *tilts at an angle!* It's located 1 mile west of Hawks Nest State Park. Call ahead to check open days.

The **National Radio Astronomy Observatory** (☎304-456-2150; www.gb.nrao.edu; Green Bank; admission & tour free; ⊙9am-6pm summer, from 10am Thu-Mon rest of year) is home to the 328ft Green Bank Telescope, the largest movable radio dish in the world. The center lies within the country's only federal radio-free zone, which is why your car won't pick up any stations within 25 miles of the center.

Southern West Virginia

This part of the state has carved out a viable stake as adventure-sports capital of the eastern seaboard.

NEW RIVER GORGE NATIONAL RIVER

The New River is actually one of the oldest in the world, and the primeval forest gorge it runs through is one of the most breathtaking in the Appalachians. The NPS protects a stretch of the New River that falls 750ft over 50 miles, with a compact set of rapids up to Class V concentrated at the northernmost end.

Canyon Rim visitor center (☎304-574-2115; ⊙9am-5pm), just north of the impressive gorge bridge, is only one of five NPS visitor centers along the river, with information on scenic drives, river outfitters, gorge climbing, hiking and mountain biking, as well as white-water rafting to the north on the Gauley River. Rim and gorge trails offer beautiful views. There are several free basic camping areas.

Nearby **Hawks Nest State Park** offers views from its rim-top **lodge** (☎304-658-5212; www.hawksnestsp.com; r $77-84; ❄📶); from June through October it operates an aerial tram (closed Wednesday) to the river, where you can catch a cruising boat ride.

Babcock State Park (☎304-438-3004; www.babcocksp.com; cabins $77-88, campsites $20-23) has hiking, canoeing, horseback riding, camping and cabin accommodations. The park's highlight is its photogenic Glade Creek Grist Mill.

FAYETTEVILLE & AROUND

Dubbed one of the coolest small towns in America, pint-sized Fayetteville acts as the jumping-off point for New River thrill-seekers. On the third Saturday in October, hundreds of base jumpers parachute from the 876ft-high New River Gorge Bridge for the **Bridge Day Festival**.

Among the many state-licensed rafting outfitters in the area, **Cantrell Ultimate Rafting** (☎800-470-7238; www.ultimaterafting.com; packages from $60) stands out for its white-water rafting trips. For rock climbers, **Hard Rock** (☎304-574-0735; www.hardrockclimbing.com; 131 South Court St; half-day/day from $75/140) offers trips and training courses.

The **Beckley Exhibition Coal Mine** (☎304-256-1747; www.beckleymine.org; adult/child $20/12; ⊙10am-6pm Apr-Oct) in nearby Beckley is a museum on the region's coal heritage. Visitors can descend 1500ft to a former coal mine. Bring a jacket, as it's cold underground!

River Rock Retreat Hostel (☎304-574-0394; www.riverrockretreatandhostel.com; Lansing-Edmond Rd; dm $23; P❄), located less than 1 mile north of the New River Gorge Bridge, has basic, clean rooms and plenty of common space. Owner Joy Marr is a wealth of local information. Two miles south of the bridge, **Rifrafters Campground** (☎304-574-1065; www.rifrafters.com; Laurel Creek Rd; campsites per person $12, cabins d/q $40/80) has primitive campsites, comfy cabins and hot-shower and bathroom facilities.

TOP CHOICE **Pies & Pints** (219 W Maple Ave; pizza small/large $13/22; ⊙11:30am-9pm; 🖉) has delicious and innovative pizzas (like Cuban pork pie or eggplant and roasted red peppers), plus a huge beer selection (try the local Bridge Brew Works lager on draft).

Start the day with breakfast and coffee under stained-glass windows at **Cathedral Café & Bookstore** (134 S Court St; mains $5-8; ⊙8am-4pm; @📶).

GREENBRIER VALLEY

Tucked between the Allegheny Mountains, the eclectic Greenbrier Valley is home to breathtaking natural beauty and hot-spring spa towns, all anchored by the sophisticated artsy town of Lewisburg. The valley's star attraction is **Greenbrier** (800-453-4858; www.greenbrier.com; 300 W Main St, White Sulphur Springs; r from $279; P❄@), an unparalleled, luxurious hotel and spa resort. Dubbed the Queen of the Southern Spas, it was originally built in 1778 to pamper wealthy Southerners. In the 20th century, the Greenbrier housed a more covert amenity: a **nuclear bunker**. In the 1950s during the height of the Cold War, the government built this massive bunker under Greenbrier to house Congress in the event of a nuclear holocaust. It remained a secret until 1992, when *The Washington Post* spilled the beans; the bunker shut down three years later. Today visitors can take a guided **bunker tour** (adult/child $30/15, closed Jan-Mar) of this unique and fascinating bit of American lore.

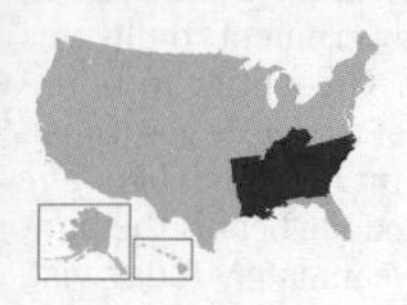

The South

Includes »

North Carolina.............324
South Carolina.............339
Tennessee.....................350
Kentucky.......................370
Georgia..........................378
Alabama........................397
Mississippi....................402
Louisiana......................409
Arkansas.......................433

Best Places to Stay

» Ansonborough Inn (p342)
» Music City Hostel (p364)
» 21c (p372)
» Kate Shepard House (p401)
» Shack Up Inn (p404)

Best Places to Eat

» Husk (p343)
» Prince's Hot Chicken (p364)
» Cochon (p422)
» Doe's Eat Place (p320)
» Commander's Palace (p423)

Why Go?

More than any other part of the country, the South has an identity all its own – a musical way of speaking, a complicated political history and a pride in a shared culture that cuts across state lines.

Nurtured by deep roots yet shaped by hardship, the South has produced some of America's most important culture, from novelists like William Faulkner and Flannery O'Connor, to foodstuffs like barbecue, bourbon and Coca-Cola, to music like blues and rock and roll. The cities of the South are some of the country's most fascinating, from antebellum beauties like New Orleans and Savannah to New South powerhouses like Atlanta and Charlotte.

But it's the legendary Southern hospitality that makes travel in the region such a pleasure. People round here *love* to talk. Stay long enough and you'll no doubt be invited for dinner.

When to Go

New Orleans

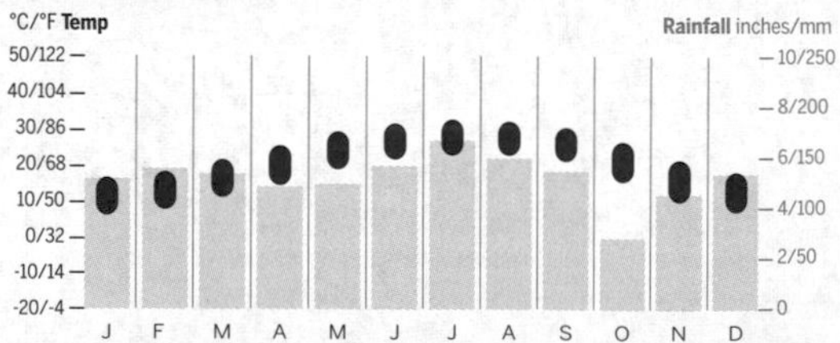

Nov–Feb Winter is generally mild here, and Christmas is a capital-E Event.

Apr–Jun Springs are lush and warm, abloom with fragrant jasmine, gardenia and tuberose.

Jul–Sep Summer is steamy, often unpleasantly so, and locals hit the beaches.

Understanding Southern Culture

Southerners have long been the butt of their fellow countrymen's jokes. They're slow-moving, hard-drinking, funny-talking and spend all their time fixing their pickup trucks and marrying their cousins. Or so the line goes. Well, while Southerners do tend to be relatively friendly and laid-back, the drawling country bumpkin is more the exception than the norm. Today's Southerner is just as likely to be a Mumbai-born motel owner in rural Arkansas, a fast-talking Atlanta investment banker with a glitzy high-rise condo, or a 20-something gay hipster in trendy Midtown Memphis.

Southerners do love sports, especially football, college basketball and NASCAR, while fine arts thrive in historic cities like Charleston and Savannah, and college towns like Chapel Hill, Knoxville and Athens are famed for their indie-music scenes. Religion is hugely important here – the so-called Bible belt runs smack through the South, with about half of all Southerners identifying as Evangelical Christians.

THE SOUTH FOR MUSIC LOVERS

The history of American music is the history of Southern music: the blues, bluegrass, jazz, gospel, country and rock and roll were all born here. Music hot spots include: Nashville, the birthplace of country music and home to more boot-stompin' honky-tonks than anywhere in the world; Memphis, where bluesmen still groove in the clubs of Beale St; and New Orleans, where you can hear world-class jazz, blues and zydeco every night of the week. Asheville, NC, is an emerging center of Appalachian revival music, while Kentucky claims bluegrass as its own.

Must-Eat Southern Foods

» Barbecue (region-wide, especially in North Carolina and Tennessee)

» Fried chicken (region-wide)

» Cornbread (region-wide)

» Shrimp and grits (South Carolina and Georgia coasts)

» Boudin (Cajun pork and rice sausage; Southern Louisiana)

» Gumbo/jambalaya/étouffée (rice and seafood or meat stew or mixture; Southern Louisiana)

» Po'boy (sandwich, traditionally with fried seafood or meat; Southern Louisiana)

» Hot tamales (cornmeal stuffed with spiced beef or pork; Mississippi Delta)

» Collards (a leafy green, often cooked with ham; region-wide)

» Pecan pie, coconut cake, red velvet cake, sweet-potato pie (region-wide)

» Bourbon (Kentucky)

DID YOU KNOW?

The South is America's fastest-growing region, with 14.3% of the country's population.

Fast Facts

» Nickname: Dixie

» Top three biggest cities: Atlanta, Charlotte, Memphis

» Time zones: Eastern, Central

Best Scenic Drives

» Blue Ridge Parkway – North Carolina to Virginia (www.blueridgeparkway.org)

» Natchez Trace – Tennessee to Mississippi (www.nps.gov/natr)

» Hwy 12 – North Carolina's Outer Banks

» Country Music Hwy/US 23 – Kentucky (countrymusichighway.com)

» Cherokee Foothills Scenic Hwy/SC 11 – South Carolina (www.discoversouthcarolina.com)

» Great River Road – Louisiana to Minnesota, including parts of Mississippi, Tennessee, Arkansas and Kentucky (www.experiencemississippiriver.com)

Resources

» www.visitsouth.com

» www.discoversouthcarolina.com

» www.visitnc.com

» www.tnvacation.com

» www.louisianatravel.com

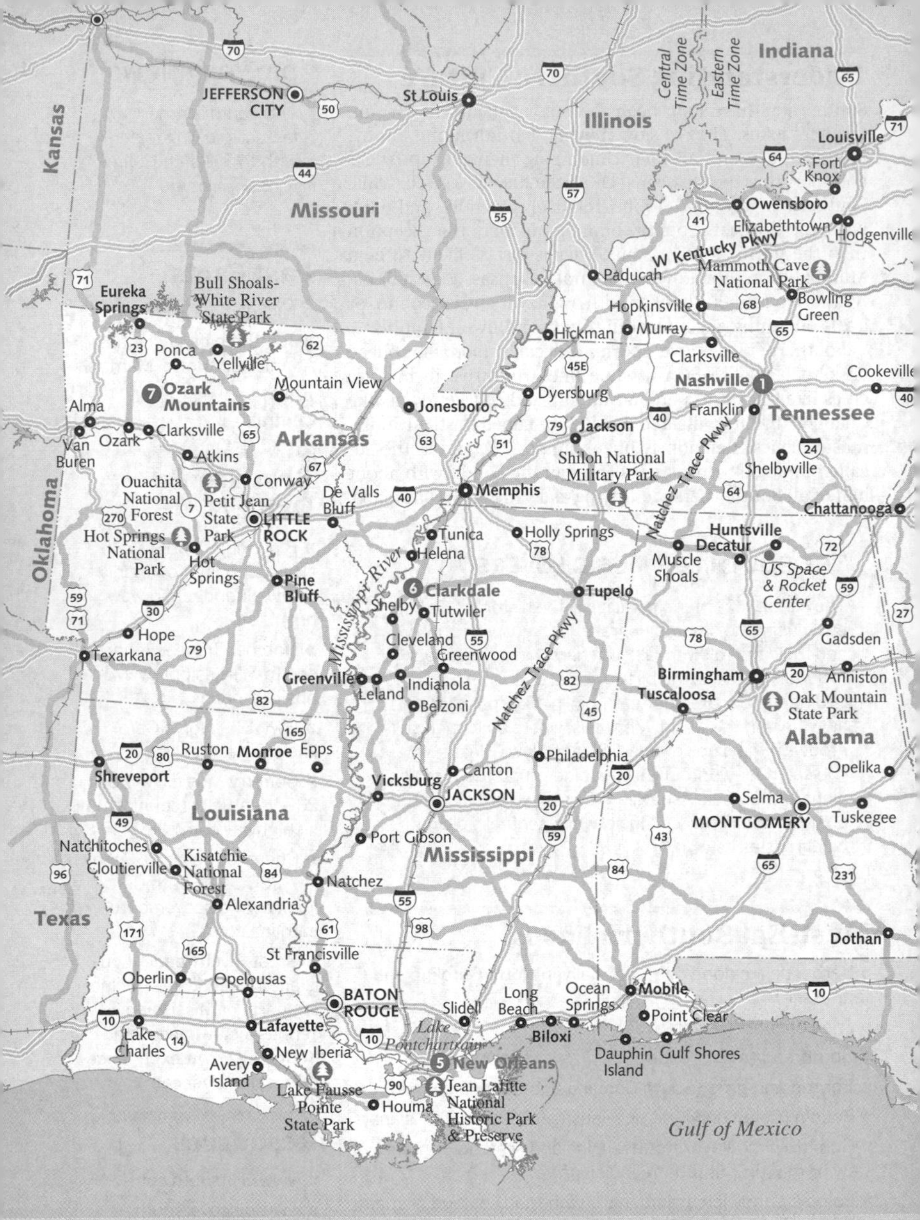

The South Highlights

❶ Stomping your boots at **Tootsie's Orchid Lounge** (p366) on Nashville's honky-tonk-lined Lower Broadway

❷ Hiking and camping in the magnificent **Great Smoky Mountains National Park** (p338)

❸ Driving windswept Hwy 12 the length of North Carolina's **Outer Banks** (p325) and riding the ferry to Ocracoke Island

❹ Touring the grand antebellum homes and cotton plantations of **Charleston** (p340)

❺ Putting yourself into a Cajun-Creole food-induced

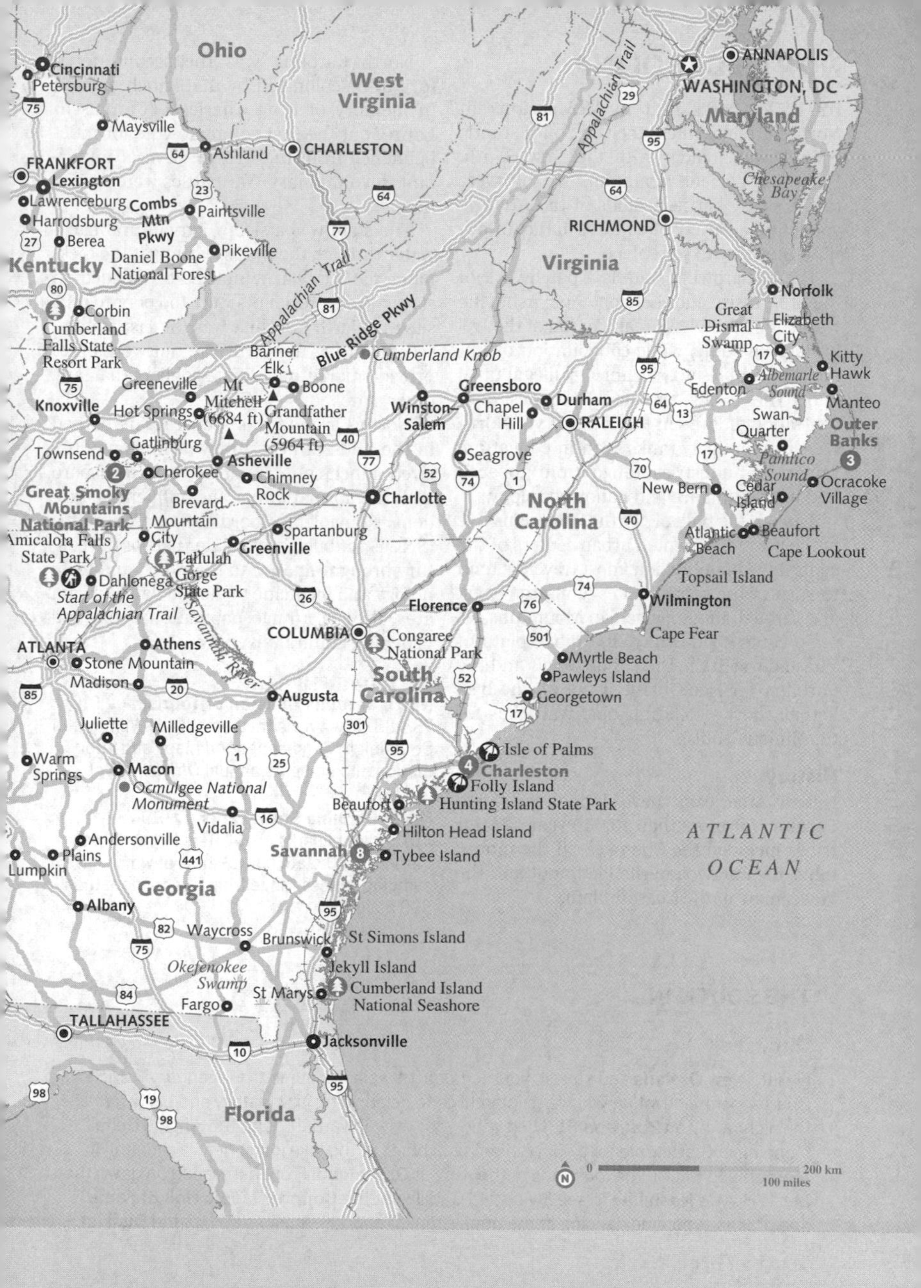

coma in **New Orleans** (p421), one of America's most treasured foodie havens.

6 Immersing yourself in the soul, rhythm, history and perseverance of the **Delta blues** (p404) in Clarksdale, MS

7 Exploring the caverns, mountains, rivers and forests of Arkansas' **Ozark Mountains** (p437), where folk music reigns

8 Falling for the hauntings, murderous tales and Southern hospitality in Georgia's living romance novel, the architecturally pristine **Savannah** (p391)

NORTH CAROLINA

It's trailer parks next to McMansions in North Carolina, where the Old South stands shoulder-to-shoulder with the New South. From the ancient mountains in the west to the sandy barrier islands of the Atlantic you'll find a variety of cultures and communities not easy to stereotype.

The fast-growing state is a patchwork of the progressive and the Stone Age: Asheville was named the 'New Freak Capital of the US' by *Rolling Stone,* while cohabitation of unmarried couples was technically illegal until 2006. The Raleigh area has the highest concentration of PhDs in the country, yet North Carolina routinely ranks 48th in education. Important industries range from tobacco and hogs to finance and nanotechnology.

Though the bulk of North Carolinians live in the business-oriented urban centers of the central Piedmont region, most travelers tend to stick to the scenic routes along the coast and through the Appalachian Mountains.

So come on down, ya'll, grab a plate of 'cue and watch the Duke Blue Devils and the Carolina Tar Heels battle it out on the basketball court – college hoops rival Jesus for Carolinians' souls.

History

Native Americans have inhabited North Carolina for more than 10,000 years. Major tribes included the Cherokee, in the mountains, the Catawba in the Piedmont and the Waccamaw in the Coastal Plain.

North Carolina was the second territory to be colonized by the British, named in memory of King Charles I (Carolus in Latin), but the first colony to vote for independence from the Crown. Several important Revolutionary War battles were fought here.

The state was a sleepy agricultural backwater through the 1800s, earning it the nickname the 'Rip Van Winkle State.' Divided on slavery (most residents were too poor to own slaves), North Carolina was the last state to secede during the Civil War, but went on to provide more Confederate soldiers than any other state.

North Carolina was a civil rights hotbed in the mid-20th century, with highly publicized lunch-counter sit-ins in Greensboro and the formation of the influential Student Nonviolent Coordinating Committee (SNCC) in Raleigh. The later part of the century brought finance to Charlotte, and technology and medicine to the Raleigh-Durham area, driving a huge population boom and widening cultural diversity.

Information

North Carolina Division of Tourism (919-733-8372; www.visitnc.com; 301 N Wilmington St, Raleigh) Sends out good maps and information, including its annual *Official Travel Guide*.

North Carolina State Parks (919-733-4181; www.ncparks.gov) Offers info on North Carolina's 40 state parks, some of which have camping (prices range from free to more than $20 a night).

THE SOUTH IN...

One Week

Fly into **New Orelans** and stretch your legs with a walking tour in the legendary French Quarter before devoting your remaining time to celebrating jazz history and partying the night away on **Bourbon St**. Then wind your way upward through the languid Delta, stopping in **Clarksdale** for a sultry evening of blues at the juke joints before alighting in **Memphis** to walk in the footsteps of the King at **Graceland**. From here, head on down the Music Hwy to **Nashville** to see Elvis' gold Cadillac at the **Country Music Hall of Fame** and practice your line dancing at the honky-tonks (country-music clubs) of the **District**.

Two to Three Weeks

Head east to hike amid the craggy peaks and waterfalls of **Great Smoky Mountains National Park** before a revitalizing overnight in the arty mountain town of **Asheville** and a tour of the scandalously opulent **Biltmore Estate**, America's largest private home. Plow straight through to the coast to loll on the sandy barrier islands of the isolated **Outer Banks**, then head down the coast to finish up in **Charleston**, with decadent food and postcard-pretty architecture.

North Carolina Coast

Which one of the following does not belong? A) windswept barrier islands; B) dignified Colonial villages once frequented by pirates; C) laid-back beach towns full of locally owned ice-cream shops and mom 'n' pop motels; D) flashy resort areas with mega-malls and beach-themed chain restaurants. If you answered 'D,' buy yourself a celebratory shrimp sandwich. The North Carolina coast is relatively undeveloped, so even the most touristy beaches still have a small-town vibe. If it's solitude you seek, head to the isolated Outer Banks (OBX), where fishermen still make their living hauling in shrimp and the older locals speak in an archaic British-tinged brogue. Further south, Wilmington is known as a center of film and TV production and its surrounding beaches are popular with local spring breakers and tourists.

OUTER BANKS

These fragile ribbons of sand trace the coastline for 100 miles, cut off from the mainland by various sounds and waterways. From north to south, the barrier islands of Bodie (pronounced 'Body'), Roanoke, Hatteras and Ocracoke, essentially large sandbars, are linked by bridges and ferries. The far-northern communities of **Corolla** (pronounced kur-*all*-ah, not like the car), **Duck** and **Southern Shores** are former duck-hunting grounds for the northeastern rich, and are quiet and upscale. The nearly contiguous Bodie Island towns of **Kitty Hawk**, **Kill Devil Hills** and **Nags Head** are heavily developed and more populist in nature, with fried-fish joints, outdoor bars, motels and dozens of sandals 'n' sunblock shops. **Roanoke Island**, west of Bodie Island, is home to tons of Colonial history and the quaint waterfront town of **Manteo**. Further south, **Hatteras Island** is a protected national seashore with a few teeny villages and a wild, windswept beauty. At the tail end of the banks, wild ponies run free and salty old Bankers shuck oysters and weave hammocks on **Ocracoke Island**, accessible only by ferry.

A meandering drive down Hwy 12, which connects much of the Outer Banks, is one of the truly great American road trips, whether you come during the stunningly desolate winter months or the sunny summer.

Sights

The following places are listed from north to south.

NORTH CAROLINA FACTS

» **Nickname** Tar Heel State

» **Population** 9.4 million

» **Area** 48,711 sq miles

» **Capital city** Raleigh (population 400,000)

» **Other cities** Charlotte (population 730,000)

» **Sales tax** 7%, plus an additional hotel-occupancy tax of up to 6%

» **Birthplace of** President James K Polk (1795–1849), jazzman John Coltrane (1926–67), NASCAR driver Richard Petty (b 1937), singer-songwriter Tori Amos (b 1963)

» **Home of** America's first state university, the Biltmore House, Krispy Kreme doughnuts

» **Politics** conservative in rural areas, increasingly liberal in urban ones

» **Famous for** *The Andy Griffith Show*, first airplane flight, college basketball

» **Pet name** natives are called 'tar heels,' a nickname of uncertain origin but said to be related to their pine tar production and their legendary stubbornness

» **Driving distances** Asheville to Raleigh 247 miles, Raleigh to Wilmington 131 miles

Currituck Heritage Park HISTORIC BUILDINGS
The sunflower-yellow, art-nouveau-style **Whalehead Club** (www.whaleheadclub.org; Corolla; tours $9; ⏲sunrise-sunset), built in the 1920s as a hunting 'cottage' for a Philadelphia industrialist, is the centerpiece of this manicured park in the village of Corolla. You can also climb the **Currituck Beach Lighthouse** (www.currituckbeachlight.com; adult/child $7/free) and visit the Victorian lighthouse-keeper's home, or check out the modern **Outer Banks Center for Wildlife Education** (admission free; ⏲9am-5pm) for an interesting film on area history, info on local hiking trails and duck-decoy carving classes.

Wright Brothers National Memorial PARK, MUSEUM
(www.nps.gov/wrbr; Kitty Hawk; admission $4; ⏲9am-5pm, to 6pm summer) This historic site is located among the same windswept Kitty Hawk dunes where self-taught engineers Wilbur and Orville Wright launched the

world's first successful airplane flight on December 17, 1903 (it lasted 12 seconds). A boulder now marks the take-off spot. Climb a nearby hill where the brothers conducted earlier glider experiments for fantastic views of sea and sound. The on-site **Wright Brothers Visitor Center** has a reproduction of the 1903 flyer and offers exhibits and lectures on aviation history.

Fort Raleigh National Historic Site HISTORIC BUILDINGS

In the late 1580s, three decades before the Pilgrims landed at Plymouth Rock, a group of 116 British colonists disappeared without a trace from their Roanoke Island settlement. Were they killed off by drought? Did they run away with a Native American tribe? Did they try to sail home and capsize? The fate of the 'Lost Colony' remains one of America's greatest mysteries, and the **visitor center** (www.nps.gov/fora; 1401 National Park Dr, Manteo; ⌚9am-5pm, to 6pm summer) has exhibits, artifacts, maps and a free film to fuel the imagination.

Attractions at the site include the **Lost Colony Outdoor Drama** (www.thelostcolony.org; adult/child $20/10; ⌚8pm Mon-Sat Jun-Aug). This beloved long-running musical from Pulitzer Prize–winning North Carolina playwright Paul Green dramatizes the fate of the colonists. It plays at the Waterside Theater throughout summer.

The 16th-century-style **Elizabethan Gardens** (www.elizabethangardens.org; adult/child $8/5; ⌚9am-8pm daily summer, shorter hr fall-spring) include a Shakespearian herb garden and rows of beautifully manicured flower beds.

North Carolina Aquarium AQUARIUM

(www.ncaquariums.com/roanoke-island; 374 Airport Rd, Roanoke Island; adult/child $8/6; ⌚9am-5pm; 👪) Watch tiger sharks glide through the gloomy depths, chill by the gator pond or stroke the slimy bellies of (de-barbed) stingrays in the touch tank. Great for kids.

Cape Hatteras National Seashore ISLANDS

Extending some 70 miles from south of Nags Head to the south end of Okracoke Island, this fragile necklace of islands remains blissfully free of overdevelopment. Natural attractions include local and migratory water birds, marshes, woodlands, dunes and miles of empty beaches. Don't miss the 156ft striped **Bodie Island Lighthouse**, south of Nags Head. You can't climb it, but it's darn photogenic. The following other attractions are listed north to south.

Pea Island National Wildlife Refuge

(www.fws.gov/peaisland; ⌚9am-4pm, to 5pm summer) At the northern end of Hatteras Island, this 5834-acre preserve is a birdwatcher's heaven, with nature trails and 13 miles of unspoiled beach.

Chicamacomico Lifesaving Station

(www.chicamacomico.net; Rodanthe village; admission $6; ⌚10am-5pm Mon-Fri Apr-Oct) Built in 1874, this was the first lifesaving station in the state, now a museum filled with pre-Coast Guard artifacts.

Cape Hatteras Lighthouse

(www.nps.gov/caha; climbing tours adult/child $7/3.50; ⌚9am-4:30pm, to 5:30pm Apr-Oct) At 208ft, this striking black-and-white-striped edifice is the tallest brick lighthouse in the US and is one of North Carolina's most iconic images. Climb the 248 steps and check out the visitor center (open year-round).

Graveyard of the Atlantic Museum

(www.graveyardoftheatlantic.com; Hatteras; admission by donation; ⌚10am-4pm) This museum is all about preserving the Outer Banks' maritime history, with exhibits about shipwrecks, piracy and salvaged cargo.

Ocracoke Island ISLAND

Accessed via the free Hatteras–Ocracoke ferry, **Ocracoke Village** (www.ocracokevillage.com) sits at the south end of 14-mile-long Ocracoke Island. It's a funky little village that's crowded in summer and desolate in winter, where the older residents still speak in the 17th-century British dialect known as 'Hoi Toide' (their pronunciation of 'high tide') and refer to nonislanders as 'dingbatters.' Edward Teach, aka Blackbeard the pirate, used to hide out in the area and was killed here in 1718. You can camp by the beach where the wild ponies run, have a fish sandwich in a local pub, ride a rented scooter or bike around the village's narrow streets or visit the 1823 **Ocracoke Lighthouse**, the oldest one still operating in North Carolina.

The island makes a terrific day trip from Hatteras Island, or you can stay the night. The island has a handful of B&Bs, an NPS (National Parks Service) campground and tons of rental cottages. Or try the **Island Inn** (☎252-928-4351, 877-456-3466; www.ocracokeislandinn.com; 25 Lighthouse Rd, Ocracoke; r from $99, villas from $199; P❄📶🏊), a grand

> ### OUTER BANKS ORIENTATION
>
> Hwy 12, also called Virginia Dare Trail or 'the coast road,' runs close to the Atlantic for the length of the Outer Banks. US 158, usually called 'the Bypass,' begins just north of Kitty Hawk and merges with US 64 as it crosses onto Roanoke Island. Locations are usually given in terms of 'mile posts' (Mile or MP), beginning with Mile 0 at the foot of the Wright Memorial Bridge at Kitty Hawk.

old turn-of-the-century clapboard inn built entirely from shipwrecked wood. Shabby-chic inn rooms come with mismatched bedspreads, spooky oil portraits and pedestal sinks, while two-story modern 'villas' across the street are bright and beachy.

For eats, grab a slice of the island's famous fig cake at the **Fig Tree Bakery** (Ocracoke Village; mains $2-6; ⌚8am-9pm summer, off-season hr vary), or head to **Howard's Pub** (Ocracoke Village; mains $6-16; ⌚11am-10pm Mon-Thu, to midnight Fri & Sat), a big old wooden pub that's been an island tradition for beer and fried seafood since the 1850s.

Activities

The same strong wind that helped the Wright brothers launch their biplane today propels windsurfers, sailors and hang gliders. Other popular activities include kayaking, fishing, cycling, horse tours and scuba diving – all well catered for in the northern resort areas. The usually calm coastal waters kick up between August and October, creating perfect conditions for bodysurfing.

TOP CHOICE **Kitty Hawk Kites** ADVENTURE SPORTS
(☎252-441-4124, 877-359-2447; www.kittyhawk.com; 3933 Croatan Hwy, Nags Head; bike/kayak rental per day $25/39) Has locations all over the Banks offering beginners' kiteboarding lessons (three hours $200) and hang-gliding lessons at Jockey's Ridge State Park (from $89). It also rents kayaks, sailboats, bikes and in-line skates and has a variety of tours and courses.

Wild Horse Adventure Tours DRIVING TOURS
(☎252-489-2020; wildhorsetour.com; 2hr tour adult/child $44/29) Offers guided 4WD tours over the dunes and through the maritime forest to see the unique wild mustang ponies that roam the Outer Banks.

Outer Banks Dive Center DIVING
(☎252-449-8349; www.obxdive.com; 3917 S Croatan Hwy, Nags Head; wreck dives $120) Has NAUI-certified instructors who run everything from basic classes to guided dives of the shipwrecks of the Graveyard of the Atlantic.

Sleeping

Crowds swarm the Outer Banks in summer, so reserve in advance. The area has few massive chain hotels, but hundreds of small motels, efficiencies and B&Bs; the visitor centers offer referrals. Also check www.outer-banks.com.

TOP CHOICE **Roanoke Island Inn** B&B **$$$**
(☎252-473-5511; www.roanokeislandinn.com; 305 Fernando St, Manteo; r from $198; P❄📶; ⌚Apr-Nov) One of historic downtown Manteo's sweetest inns, this sprawling white cottage wraps around a hidden garden and koi pond. Guests are welcome to lounge on the many porches, or borrow bikes to ride around the island. When evenings grow cool, retreat to your rustic-chic, warmly lit guest room and snuggle under the handmade quilt.

Sanderling Resort & Spa RESORT **$$$**
(☎252-261-4111, 877-650-4812; www.thesanderling.com; 1461 Duck Rd, Duck; r $349-459; P❄📶🏊) The poshest digs in the Outer Banks has impeccably tasteful neutral-toned rooms with decks and flat-screen TVs, several restaurants and bars, and a spa offering luxe oceanside massage.

Buccaneer Motel MOTEL **$$**
(☎252-261-2030, 800-442-4412; www.buccaneermotelouterbanks.com; Mile 5 Kitty Hawk; r from $99; P❄📶🏊) One of many deliciously retro motor motels lining the Coast Rd, the Buccaneer has clean, tile-floor rooms with wooden pirate swords on the doors, at bargain-basement rates.

Campgrounds CAMPGROUND **$**
(☎800-365-2267; www.nps.gov/caha/planyourvisit/campgrounds.htm; tent sites $20-23) The National Park Service runs four summer-only campgrounds on the islands, which feature cold-water showers and flush toilets. They are located at Oregon Inlet, near Bodie Island Lighthouse, Cape Point and Frisco near Cape Hatteras Lighthouse and **Ocracoke** (☎800-365-2267; www.recreation.gov) at Oregon Inlet (near Bodie Island Lighthouse), Cape Point and Frisco (both near Cape Hatteras Lighthouse), and Ocracoke Island. Only sites

at Ocracoke can be reserved; the others are first-come, first-served.

Eating & Drinking

The main tourist strip on Bodie Island has the most restaurants and nightlife, but many are only open Memorial Day through early fall.

Awful Arthur's Oyster Bar SEAFOOD **$$$**
(www.awfularthursobx.com; Mile 6; mains $6-23; 11am-10:30pm) Oysters go down easy at this friendly restaurant and raw bar (emphasis on the 'bar'), as do the excellent soft-shell crab sandwiches and sky-high, homemade key lime pie. Don't be shy about ordering a beer before noon; the locals aren't.

John's Drive-In SEAFOOD, AMERICAN **$$**
(3716 Virginia Dare Trail, Kitty Hawk; mains $5-13; 11am-6pm summer, shorter hr spring & fall, closed winter) A Kitty Hawk institution for perfectly fried baskets of 'dolphin' (mahimahi) and rockfish, to be eaten at outdoor picnic tables and washed down with one of hundreds of possible milkshake varieties.

Jolly Roger ITALIAN, AMERICAN **$$$**
(www.jollyrogerobx.com; Mile 6.5, Kill Devil Hills; mains $10-24; 6am-late) The atmosphere in this OBX institution could be described as 'pirate bordello,' with Christmas lights, mermaid murals and evening karaoke contests. Come for huuuuge Southern breakfasts, groaning platters of shrimp fettuccine, or late-night burgers at the bar.

Rundown Cafe CARIBBEAN, INTERNATIONAL **$**
(MP1, Kitty Hawk; mains $6-11; 11:30am-9pm, shorter hr fall-spring) Kiteboarders and surfers slurp up rundown (a Jamaican stew) and nibble on conch fritters, nachos, wontons and other global munchies at this big blue beach shack.

Information

The best sources of information are at the main visitor centers. Many smaller centers are open seasonally. Also useful is www.outerbanks.org. The entire Manteo waterfront has free wi-fi.

Corolla public library (1123 Ocean Trail/Hwy 12) Free internet access.

Visitor centers (9am-5pm) Hatteras (252-441-5711; Apr-Oct); Kitty Hawk (252-261-4644); Manteo (252-473-2138, 877-629-4386); Ocracoke (252-928-4531)

Getting There & Away

No public transportation exists to or on the Outer Banks. However, the **North Carolina Ferry System** (800-293-3779; www.outer-banks.com/ferry) operates several routes, including the free 40-minute Hatteras–Ocracoke car ferry, which runs at least hourly from 5am to 10pm; reservations aren't necessary. North Carolina ferries also run between Ocracoke and Cedar Island (one way $15, 2¼ hours) and Ocracoke and Swan Quarter on the mainland ($15, 2½ hours) every two hours or so; reservations are recommended in summer.

CRYSTAL COAST

The southern Outer Banks are collectively called the 'Crystal Coast,' at least for tourist offices' promotional purposes. Less rugged than the northern beaches, they include several historic coastal towns, a number of sparsely populated islands, and some vacation-friendly beaches.

A rather unappealing industrial and commercial stretch of US 70 goes through **Morehead City**, with plenty of chain hotels and restaurants. Stop here for shrimp burgers at **El's Drive-In** (3706 Arendell St; mains $3-6; 10:30am-10pm), a legendary seafood spot where your food is brought to you by carhop.

Down the road, postcard-pretty **Beaufort** (*bow*-fort), the third-oldest town in the state, has a charming boardwalk and mountains of B&Bs. The pirate Blackbeard was a frequent visitor to the area in the early 1700s – in 1996 the wreckage of his flagship, the *Queen Anne's Revenge,* was discovered at the bottom of Beaufort Inlet. See artifacts from the ship and meet modern shipbuilders at the **North Carolina Maritime Museum** (www.ncmaritimemuseum.org; 315 Front St; admission free; 9am-5pm Mon-Sat, from 1-5pm Sun). Blackbeard himself is said to have lived in the Hammock House off Front St. You can't go inside, but some claim you can still hear the screams of the pirate's murdered wife at night.

Small ferries leave regularly from the Beaufort boardwalk for the isolated islands of the **Cape Lookout National Seashore** (www.nps.gov/calo; ferries $14-25). Highlights include **Shackleford Banks**, an uninhabited sandbar with spectacular seashells and herds of wild ponies, and the diamond-patterned **Cape Lookout Lighthouse**. Primitive camping is allowed in some areas – the coolest place to sleep is on **Portsmouth Island**, where you can wander an abandoned 18th-century settlement and sleep on the beach. Hire a private ferry from Beaufort or Ocracoke and bring plenty of bug spray – the mosquitoes are absolutely notorious. There are also rustic multiroom

cabins (☎South Core 252-241-6783, North Core 252-732-4424; www.nps.gov/calo; from $73) popular with fishermen.

The **Bogue Banks**, across the Sound from Morehead City via the Atlantic Beach Causeway, have several well-trafficked beach communities – try Atlantic Beach if you like the smell of coconut suntan oil and doughnuts. Pine Knoll Shores is home to the **North Carolina Aquarium** (www.ncaquariums.com; 1 Roosevelt Blvd; adult/child $8/6; ⏲9am-5pm;), with an ultracool exhibit re-creating local shipwrecks. In Atlantic Beach, **Fort Macon State Park** (www.ncparks.gov; admission free; ⏲8am-9pm in summer, shorter hr in winter) draws crowds to its reconstructed Civil War fort.

WILMINGTON

Wilmington may not have the name recognition of other antebellum tourist destinations like Charleston and Savannah, but eastern North Carolina's largest city has historic neighborhoods, azalea-choked gardens and cute cafes aplenty. All that plus reasonable hotel prices and a lack of crowds make Wilmington a hidden gem, in our book. At night the historic riverfront downtown becomes the playground for local college students, tourists and the occasional Hollywood type – there are so many movie studios here the town has earned the nickname 'Wilmywood'.

Sights

Wilmington sits at the mouth of the Cape Fear River, about 8 miles from the beach. The historic **riverfront** is perhaps the city's most important sight, abounding with boutiques and boardwalks.

A **free trolley** runs through the historic district from morning through evening.

TOP CHOICE **Cape Fear Serpentarium** SNAKE ZOO

(www.capefearserpentarium.com; 20 Orange St; admission $8; ⏲11am-5pm Mon-Fri, to 6pm Sat & Sun) The place to go if you don't mind keeping reptilian company. You can gawk at yellow eyelash vipers, read about how it feels to die from the bite of the deadly bushmaster, and, at 3pm on Saturday and Sunday, watch gonzo herpetologist/ringmaster Dean Ripa hand-feed mice to his 100-plus species of beasties.

Battleship North Carolina HISTORIC SHIP

(www.battleshipnc.com; adult/child $12/6; ⏲8am-5pm, to 8pm summer) Take a river taxi ($5 round-trip) or cross the Cape Fear Bridge to get here. Self-guided tours take you through the decks of this 45,000-ton megaship, which earned 15 battle stars in the Pacific theater in WWII before being decommissioned in 1947.

Screen Gems Studios MOVIE STUDIO

(☎910-343-3433; www.screengemsstudios.com; 1223 N 23rd St; adult/child $12/5; ⏲noon & 2pm Sat & Sun summer) Offers a fun, one-hour, behind-the-scenes tour of the working studio where shows such as *Dawson's Creek* and *One Tree Hill* were filmed.

Airlie Gardens GARDEN

(www.airliegardens.org; 300 Airlie Rd; adult/child $5/3; ⏲9am-5pm, closed Sun winter) Wander

WILMINGTON-AREA BEACHES

While riverfront Wilmington doesn't have its own beach, there are plenty of sandy stretches just a few minutes away. These are listed from north to south.

» Surf City: a low-key beach town with good waves.

» Topsail Beach: a clean, white-sand beach, home to a sea-turtle rehab center.

» Wrightsville Beach: the closest to Wilmington, with plenty of fried-fish joints, sunglass shops and summer crowds.

» Carolina Beach: warm water and boardwalk equal row upon row of beach umbrellas.

» Kure Beach: a popular fishing beach and home to the North Carolina Aquarium at Fort Fisher.

» Southport: not a swimming beach, but a quaint town with tons of antique stores.

» Bald Head Island: accessible by ferry from Southport. This secluded sea-turtle sanctuary forbids cars, making travel difficult for those for who don't rent a golf cart.

» Caswell Beach: a quiet beach with nearby golf course.

» Oak Island: the largest beach community in North Carolina, with three piers.

beneath the wisteria, with 67 acres of bewitching formal flower beds, lakes and trails.

Sleeping & Eating

There are numerous budget hotels on Market St, just north of downtown. Restaurants directly on the waterfront can be crowded and mediocre; head a block or two inland for the best eats and nightlife.

Graystone Inn B&B $$$
(☎910-763-2000; www.graystoneinn.com; 100 S 3rd St; r incl breakfast $169-379; P) Built as the home of a turn-of-the-century railroad magnate, this imposing Renaissance-style mansion has nine splendiferous guest rooms with period furnishings such as claw-foot tubs, all walking distance from the downtown action.

Clarendon Inn HOTEL $$
(☎910-343-1990; www.clarendoninn.com; 117 S Second St; r from $99; P) Hovering in the gray zone between hotel and B&B, the friendly 11-room Clarendon offers an excellent location, comfy beds and a plethora of angel statues on every surface. Good value.

Crow Hill MODERN AMERICAN $$
(☎910-228-5332; www.crowhillnc.com; 9 Front St; mains $13-20; 5-10pm Tue-Sun, late night to 1am Fri & Sat; brunch 10am-2pm Sun) The city's current foodie darling for its local, seasonal approach to Southern fare – NC soft-shell crabs with sweet-pea custard, local pork cheeks with fried green tomatoes. Decor is very 'haute farm' – reclaimed wood tables, vintage hoes on the wall. Great brunch.

Front Street Brewery PUB $
(www.frontstreetbrewery.com; 9 N Front St; mains $7-14; 11:30am-10pm Sun-Wed, to 2am Thu-Sat) This two-story downtown pub is madly popular for simple grub, like drippy burgers and crab cakes, and for its microbrews. There are free beer tastings and brewery tours daily from 3pm to 5pm.

THE BARBECUE TRAIL

North Carolina pulled-pork BBQ is practically a religion in these parts, and the rivalry between Eastern Style (with a thin vinegar sauce) and Western Style (with a sweeter, tomato-based sauce) occasionally comes to blows. The North Carolina Barbecue Society has an interactive **Barbecue Trail map** (www.ncbbqsociety.com), directing 'cue pilgrims to the best spots. So try both styles, then take sides (hint: Eastern style is better. Just kidding! Sort of).

Information

The **visitor center** (☎910-341-4030, 800-222-4757; 505 Nutt St; 8:30am-5pm Mon-Fri, 9am-4pm Sat, from 1-4pm Sun), an 1800s freight warehouse, has a walking-tour map.

The Triangle

In the central North Carolina region known as the Piedmont, the cities of Raleigh, Durham and Chapel Hill form a rough triangle. Three top research universities – Duke, University of North Carolina and North Carolina State – are located here, as is the 7000-acre computer and biotech-office campus known as Research Triangle Park. Swarming with egghead computer programmers, bearded peace activists and hip young families, each town has its own unique personality, despite being only a few miles apart. Come here in March to see everyone – we mean *everyone* – go crazy for college basketball.

Getting There & Around

Raleigh-Durham International Airport (RDU; ☎919-840-2123; www.rdu.com), a significant hub, is a 25-minute (15 mile) drive northwest of downtown Raleigh. **Carolina Trailways/Greyhound** Raleigh (☎919-834-8275; 314 W Jones St); Durham (☎919-687-4800; 820 W Morgan St) serve Raleigh and Durham. The **Triangle Transit Authority** (☎919-549-9999; www.triangletransit.org; adult $2) operates buses linking Raleigh, Durham and Chapel Hill to each other and the airport.

RALEIGH

Founded in 1792 specifically to serve as the state capital, Raleigh remains a rather staid government town with some major sprawl issues. Still, the handsome downtown has some neat (and free!) museums and galleries, and the food and music scene is on the upswing.

Sights

Check out the handsome 1840 **state capitol** on Edenton St, one of the best examples of Greek Revival architecture. It's open for tours.

TOP CHOICE **North Carolina Museum of Art** MUSEUM
(www.ncartmuseum.org; 2110 Blue Ridge Rd; admission free; 9am-5pm Tue-Thu & Sat, 9am-9pm

Fri, 10am-5pm Sun) Worth the trip for the building alone – the light-filled glass-and-anodized-steel West Building won praise from architecture critics nationwide when it opened in 2010. The fine and wide-ranging collection, with everything from ancient Roman sculpture to Raphael to graffiti artists, is worthy as well, of course, as is the winding outdoor sculpture trail. A few miles west of downtown.

FREE **North Carolina Museum of Natural Sciences** MUSEUM
(www.naturalsciences.org; 11 W Jones St; ⏲9am-5pm Mon-Sat, noon-5pm Sun) See Willo, the world's only dinosaur with a heart (it's fossilized), at this modern, airy museum. There's also a unique and scary Acrocanthosaurus skeleton, five habitat dioramas and lots of well-done taxidermy.

FREE **North Carolina Museum of History** MUSEUM
(www.ncmuseumofhistory.org; 5 E Edenton St; ⏲9am-5pm Mon-Sat, noon-5pm Sun) Has all kinds of artifacts, such as Civil War photos, Cherokee crafts, 19th-century costumes and a special exhibit on stock-car racing.

Sleeping & Eating

Downtown is pretty quiet on nights and weekends, except for the City Market area at E Martin and S Person Sts. Just to the northwest, the Glenwood South neighborhood hops with cafes, bars and clubs. You'll find plenty of moderately priced chain hotels around Exit 10 off I-440 and off I-40 near the airport.

Umstead Hotel & Spa HOTEL $$$
(☎919-447-4000; www.theumstead.com; 100 Woodland Pond, Cary; r from $279; P❄@☜≋) Computer chips embedded in the silver room-service trays alert bellhops to whisk away leftovers post haste at this lavish new boutique hotel. How's that for taking care of details? In a wooded suburban office park, the Umstead caters to visiting biotech CEOs with simple, sumptuous rooms and a Zen-like spa.

Poole's Downtown Diner MODERN AMERICAN $$
(www.poolesdowntowndiner.com; 426 S McDowell St; mains $9-15; ⏲6pm-midnight Wed-Sat, brunch 10:30am-3pm Sat) Chef Ashley Christensen sautés burgers in duck fat and bakes the world's most exquisitely creamy mac 'n' cheese at this Southern diner-meets-Parisian bistro, the toast of the local food scene. Don't miss the haute takes on classic American pies like banana cream.

Raleigh Times PUB $
(www.raleightimesbar.com; 14 E Hargett St; mains $8-11; ⏲11:30am-2am) Chase plates of BBQ nachos with pints of North Carolina craft brews at this popular downtown pub.

Information

The **Raleigh Convention & Visitors Bureau** (☎866-724-8687; www.visitraleigh.com; 220 Fayetteville St; ⏲10am-5pm Mon-Sat) hands out maps and other info.

DURHAM & CHAPEL HILL

Ten miles apart, these two university towns are twinned by their rival basketball teams and left-leaning cultures. Most similarities end here, though. Chapel Hill is a postcard-pretty Southern college town whose culture revolves around the 30,000 students at the prestigious University of North Carolina, founded in 1789 as the nation's first state university. A funky, forward-thinking place, Chapel Hill is renowned for its indie rock scene and loud 'n' proud hippie culture. Down the road, Durham is a once-gritty tobacco-and-railroad town whose fortunes collapsed in the 1960s and have only recently begun to revive. Though still fundamentally a working-class Southern city, the presence of top-ranking Duke University has long drawn progressive types to the area and Durham is now making its name as hot spot for foodies, artists and gays and lesbians.

The hip former mill town of **Carrboro** is to the west. Here, the big lawn at **Weaver Street Market** (www.weaverstreetmarket.com) grocery co-op serves as an informal town square, with live music and free wi-fi.

In Durham, activity centers around the renovated brick tobacco warehouses of the handsome downtown: check out Brightleaf Sq and the American Tobacco Campus for shopping and outdoor dining.

Sights

TOP CHOICE **Duke Lemur Center** ZOO
(☎919-489-3364; www.lemur.duke.edu; 👪) Perhaps the coolest, least-known sight in Durham, the Lemur Center has the largest collection of endangered prosimian primates outside their native Madagascar. Only a robot could fail to melt at the sight of these big-eyed fuzzy-wuzzies. Call well in advance for tours, held Monday to Saturday by appointment only.

Duke University UNIVERSITY, GALLERY
(www.duke.edu) Endowed by the Duke family's cigarette fortune, the university has a Georgian-style East Campus and a neo-Gothic West Campus notable for its towering 1930s chapel. The **Nasher Museum of Art** (2001 Campus Dr; admission $5) is also worth a gander, as is the heavenly 55-acre **Sarah P Duke Gardens** (426 Anderson St; admission free).

University of North Carolina UNIVERSITY
(www.unc.edu) America's oldest public university has a classic quad lined with flowering pear trees and gracious antebellum buildings. Don't miss the Old Well, said to give good luck to students who drink from it.

Durham Bulls Athletic Park SPECTATOR SPORT
(www.dbulls.com; 409 Blackwell St; tickets $7-9;) Have a quintessentially American afternoon of beer and baseball watching the minor-league Durham Bulls (of 1988 Kevin Costner film *Bull Durham* fame), who play from April to September.

Sleeping

There are plenty of cheap chain motels off I-85 in north Durham.

TOP CHOICE **Inn at Celebrity Dairy** B&B **$$**
(919-742-5176; www.celebritydairy.com; 144 Celebrity Dairy Way; r incl breakfast $90-150;) Thirty miles west of Chapel Hill in rural Chatham County, this working goat dairy offers B&B accommodations in a Greek Revival farmhouse. Savor goat's-cheese omelets for breakfast then head out to the barn to pet the goat who provided the milk.

King's Daughters Inn INN **$$**
(919-354-7000; thekingsdaughtersinn.com; 204 N Buchanan Blvd; r incl breakfast from $165;) Once a charity home for elderly women, this 1926 Colonial Revival has been newly renovated into an ecofriendly inn with 11 elegant guest rooms and a yummy sun porch. On the edge of Duke campus, it's a fave with visiting professors.

Duke Tower HOTEL **$**
(919-687-4444, 866-385-3869; www.duketower.com; 807 W Trinity Ave; ste $85;) For less than most local hotel rooms you can have a contemporary condo with hardwood floors, full kitchen and flat-screen TV, in Durham's historic downtown tobacco-mill district.

Eating

Durham and Chapel Hill were recently named 'America's Foodiest Small Town' by *Bon Appétit*, and with good reason: the area abounds with top-notch restaurants of all stripes. Downtown Durham has scads of great restaurants, coffee shops and bars. Most of Chapel Hill's better restaurants are found along Franklin St.

TOP CHOICE **Scratch** BAKERY **$**
(www.piefantasy.com; 111 Orange St, Durham; mains $5-10; 7:30am-4pm Tue-Fri, 9am-3pm Sat & Sun) Baker Phoebe Lawless shoots sunshine and rainbows out of her fingertips at this nationally praised nook of a bakery, famed for its hyper-seasonal pies (fresh lavender in spring, local muscadine grape in fall) and delectable sandwiches and salads (try the pickled-egg salad).

Allen & Son's Barbecue BARBECUE **$**
(6203 Millhouse Rd, Chapel Hill; mains $7-10; 10am-5pm Tue-Wed, to 8pm Thu-Sat) Owner Keith Allen splits his own hickory wood behind this cinder-block cabin to smoke what many consider the best pork BBQ in the state. Try it topped with slaw on a soft bun with a side of hush puppies (balls of fried cornmeal) and a slice of frozen peanut butter pie.

Watts Grocery NEW SOUTHERN **$$$**
(919-416-5040; 1116 Broad St, Durham; mains $16-23; 11am-2:30pm & 5:30-10pm) Durham's hippest 'farm-to-table' joint serves upscale takes on local bounty (think bourbon-glazed pork belly, hand-cut buttermilk onion rings) in an airy renovated storefront. Sausage- and avocado-laden bowls of grits might just well be the best weekend brunch in town.

Lantern ASIAN **$$$**
(919-969-8846; www.lanternrestaurant.com; 243 W Franklin St, Chapel Hill; mains $17-26; 5:30-10pm Mon-Sat) Tea-smoked chicken and roll-your-own bento boxes have earned this modern Asian spot a shower of James Beard Awards.

Sunrise Biscuit Kitchen BREAKFAST, SOUTHERN **$**
(1305 E Franklin St, Chapel Hill; mains $2-4; 6am-2pm) Fried chicken biscuits washed down with sweet tea are one of America's truly great breakfasts, and the reason this venerable drive-thru is always jam-packed at 7am.

Drinking & Entertainment

Chapel Hill has an excellent music scene, with shows nearly every night of the week. For entertainment listings, pick up the free weekly *Independent* (www.indyweek.com).

Fullsteam Brewery BREWPUB
(www.fullsteam.ag; 726 Rigsbee Ave, Durham) Calling itself a 'plow-to-pint' brewery, Fullsteam has gained national attention for pushing the boundaries of beer with wild, super-Southern concoctions like sweet-potato lager and persimmon ale. Mixed-age crowds.

Top of the Hill PUB
(100 E Franklin St, Chapel Hill) The 2nd-story patio of this downtown restaurant and microbrewery is *the* place for the Chapel Hill preppy set to see and be seen after football games.

Cat's Cradle MUSIC
(www.catscradle.com; 300 E Main St, Carrboro) Everyone from Nirvana to Arcade Fire has played the Cradle, hosting the cream of the indie-music world for three decades. Most shows all-ages.

Information

Visitor center Durham (919-687-0288, 800-446-8604; www.durham-nc.com; 101 E Morgan St; 8:30am-5pm Mon-Fri, 10am-2pm Sat); Chapel Hill (501 W Franklin St; www.visitchapelhill.org) For information and maps.

Charlotte

The largest city in North Carolina and the biggest US banking center after New York, Charlotte has the sprawling, sometimes faceless look of many New South suburban megalopolises. But although the Queen City, as it's known, is primarily a business town, it's got a few good museums, stately old neighborhoods and lots of fine food.

Busy Tryon St cuts through skyscraper-filled 'uptown' Charlotte, home to banks, hotels, museums and restaurants. The renovated textile mills of the NoDa neighborhood (named for its location on N Davidson St) and the funky mix of boutiques and restaurants in the Plaza-Midwood area, just northeast of uptown, have a hipper vibe.

Sights & Activities

FREE **Billy Graham Library** RELIGIOUS
(www.billygrahamlibrary.org; 4330 Westmont Dr; 9:30am-5pm Mon-Sat) Those interested in the phenomenon of Christian evangelism in America will be fascinated (or annoyed) by this multimedia 'library,' a tribute to the life of superstar evangelist and 'pastor to the presidents' Billy Graham, a Charlotte native. The 90-minute tour starts with a gospel-preaching animatronic cow and ends with a paper questionnaire asking whether or not you've been moved to accept Christ today.

Mint Museum of Art MUSEUM
(www.mintmuseum.org; 2730 Randolph Rd; adult/child $10/5; 10am-9pm Tue, 10am-5pm Wed-Sat, noon-5pm Sun) Housed in the imposing 19th-century US mint building. The hushed halls display historic maps, American paintings and an impressive number of gruesome Spanish Colonial bleeding-saint statues.

Levine Museum of the New South MUSEUM
(www.museumofthenewsouth.org; 200 E 7th St; adult/child $6/5; 10am-5pm Mon-Sat, noon-5pm Sun) This slick museum has an informative permanent exhibit on post–Civil War Southern history and culture, from sharecropping to sit-ins.

TOP CHOICE **US National Whitewater Center** ADVENTURE SPORTS
(www.usnwc.org; 500 Whitewater Center Pkwy; all-sport day pass adult/child $49/39, individual activities $15-25, 3hr canopy tour $89; 10am-6pm, later in summer) A beyond-awesome hybrid of nature center and waterpark, this 400-acre facility is home to the largest manmade white-water river in the world, whose rapids serve as training grounds for Olympic canoe and kayak teams. Paddle it yourself as part of a guided rafting trip, or try one of the center's other high-octane activities: zip-lines, an outdoor rock climbing wall, multiple ropes courses, paddleboarding, aerial canopy tours of the surrounding forest, miles of wooded hiking and mountain-biking trails.

Charlotte Motor Speedway SPEEDWAY
(www.charlottemotorspeedway.com; tours $9; tours 9:30am-3:30pm Mon-Sat, 1:30-3:30pm Sun) NASCAR races, a homegrown Southeastern obsession, are held at the visible-from-outer-space speedway, 12 miles northeast of town. For the ultimate thrill/near-death experience, ride shotgun at up to 165 miles per hour in a real stock car with the **Richard Petty Driving Experience** (800-237-3889; www.1800bepetty.com; rides from $149).

Sleeping & Eating

Because so many uptown hotels cater to the business traveler, rates are often lower on weekends. Cheaper chains cluster off I-85 and I-77. Uptown eating and drinking options cater to the preppy young banker set; you'll see more tattoos at the laid-back pubs and bistros of NoDa.

Duke Mansion B&B $$
(704-714-4400; www.dukemansion.com; 400 Hermitage Rd; r from $179; P❄@) Tucked away in an oak-shaded residential neighborhood, this stately white-columned inn was the residence of 19th-century tobacco millionaire James B Duke and still retains the quiet, discreet feel of a posh private home. Most rooms have high ceilings and their own screened-in sleeping porches.

Hotel Sierra HOTEL $$
(704-373-9700; www.hotel-sierra.com; 435 E Trade St; r from $148; P❄@) With a space-agey lime-and-charcoal color scheme and a gleaming lobby full of business travelers typing frantically into their BlackBerrys, the brand-new Sierra is *very* Charlotte.

TOP CHOICE **Price's Chicken Coop** SOUTHERN $
(1614 Camden Rd; mains $5-10; 10am-6pm Tue-Sat) A Charlotte institution, scruffy Price's regularly makes 'Best Fried Chicken in America' lists. Line up to order your 'dark quarter' or 'white half' from the army of white-jacketed cooks, then take your bounty outside – there's no seating.

Bar-B-Q King BARBECUE $
(2900 Wilkinson Blvd; mains $4-9; 10:30am-10:30pm Tue-Thu, 10am-11:30pm Fri & Sat) A venerable retro drive-in, where carhops deliver minced-pork platters and perfectly fried trout sandwiches to your driver's side window.

Rí Rá PUB $$
(www.rira.com; 208 N Tryon St; mains $11-19; 11am-2am) A friendly mixed-age crowd downs Guinness and nibbles fish-and-chips at this Victorian-style uptown Irish pub.

Information

The downtown **visitor center** (704-331-2700, 800-231-4636; www.charlottesgotalot.com; 330 S Tryon St; 8:30am-5pm Mon-Fri, 9am-3pm Sat) publishes maps and a visitor's guide. The **public library** (College St) has 90 terminals with free internet. Check out the alt-weekly *Creative Loafing* (charlotte.creativeloafting.com) for entertainment listings.

Getting There & Around

Charlotte Douglas International Airport (CLT; 704-359-4027; www.charmeck.org/departments/airport; 5501 Josh Birmingham Pkwy) is a US Airways hub with direct flights from Europe and the UK. Both the **Greyhound station** (601 W Trade St) and **Amtrak** (1914 N Tryon St) are handy to Uptown. **Charlotte Area Transit** (www.charmeck.org) runs local bus and light-rail services; its main station is at 310 E Trade St.

North Carolina Mountains

Seekers of all sorts have been drawn to these ancient mountains for hundreds of years. The Cherokee came to hunt, Scots-Irish immigrants came in the 1700s looking for a better life, fugitives hid from the law in the deep forests, the ill came to take in the fresh air, and naturalists came to hike the craggy trails.

The Appalachians in the western part of the state include the Great Smoky, Blue Ridge, Pisgah and Black Mountain subranges. Carpeted in blue-green hemlock, pine and oak trees, these cool hills are home to cougars, deer, black bears, wild turkeys and great horned owls. Hiking, camping, climbing and rafting adventures abound, and there's another jaw-dropping photo opportunity around every bend.

HIGH COUNTRY

The northwestern corner of the state is known as 'High Country.' Its main towns are Boone, Blowing Rock and Banner Elk, all short drives from the Blue Ridge Pkwy. **Boone** is a lively college town, home to Appalachian State University (ASU). **Blowing Rock** and **Banner Elk** are quaint tourist centers near the winter ski areas.

Sights & Activities

Hwy 321 from Blowing Rock to Boone is studded with gem-panning mines and other tourist traps.

Tweetsie Railroad AMUSEMENT PARK
(www.tweetsie.com; adult/child $34/22;) A much-loved Wild West–themed amusement park. Opening hours vary by season.

Grandfather Mountain HIKING
(www.grandfather.com; Blue Ridge Pkwy Mile 305; adult/child $15/7; 8am-6pm) This place rakes in car tourists who tiptoe across its vertigo-

SCENIC DRIVE: THE BLUE RIDGE PARKWAY

Commissioned by President Franklin D Roosevelt as a Depression-era public-works project, the glorious Blue Ridge Pkwy traverses the southern Appalachians from Virginia's Shenandoah National Park at Mile 0 to the Great Smoky Mountains National Park at Mile 469. North Carolina's piece of the parkway twists and turns for 262 miles of killer alpine vistas. The National Park Service **campgrounds and visitor centers** (☎877-444-6777; www.blueridgeparkway.org; tent sites $16) are open May to October. Parkway entrance is free; be aware that restrooms and gas stations are few and far between.

Parkway highlights and campgrounds include the following:

Cumberland Knob (Mile 217.5) NPS visitor center, easy walk to the knob.

Doughton Park (Mile 241.1) Gas, food, trails and camping.

Blowing Rock (Mile 291.8) Small tourist town, named for a craggy, commercialized cliff that offers great views, occasional updrafts and a Native American love story.

Moses H Cone Memorial Park (Mile 294.1) A lovely old estate with pleasant walks and a craft shop.

Julian Price Memorial Park (Mile 296.9) Camping.

Grandfather Mountain (Mile 305.1) Hugely popular for its mile-high pedestrian 'swinging bridge.'

Linville Falls (Mile 316.4) Short hiking trails to the falls, campsites.

Linville Caverns (Mile 317) Limestone cave with neat formations and underground streams; tours $7.

Little Switzerland (Mile 334) Old-style mountain resort.

Crabtree Meadows (Mile 339.5) Camping.

Mt Mitchell State Park (Mile 355.5) Highest peak east of the Mississippi (6684ft); hiking and camping.

Craggy Gardens (Mile 364) Hiking trails explode with rhododendron blossoms in summer.

Folk Art Center (Mile 382) Local crafts for sale.

Mount Pisgah (Mile 408.8) Hiking and camping.

inducing mile-high suspension bridge. Lose the crowds on one of 11 hiking trails, the most difficult of which include steep hands-and-knees scrambles.

River and Earth Adventures OUTDOORS
(☎828-963-5491; www.raftcavehike.com; 1655 Hwy 105, Boone; half-/full-day rafting from $65/100) Offers everything from family-friendly caving trips to rafting Class V rapids at Watauga Gorge. Ecoconscious guides even pack organic lunches. Bike and kayak rentals.

Sleeping & Eating

Chain motels abound in Boone. You'll find private campgrounds and B&Bs scattered throughout the hills.

Mast Farm Inn B&B **$$**
(☎828-963-5857, 888-963-5857; www.mastfarminn.com; 2543 Broadstone Rd, Blowing Rock; r/cottages from $99/149; P❄📶) In the achingly beautiful hamlet of Valle Crucis, this restored farmhouse defines rustic chic with worn hardwood floors, claw-foot tubs and handmade toffees on your bedside table. The upscale mountain cuisine at the inn's restaurant, Simplicity, is worth a trip in itself.

Hob Nob Farm Cafe CAFE **$$**
(www.hobnobfarmcafe.com; 506 West King St, Boone; mains $7-14; ⏰10am-10pm Wed-Sun) Inside a wildly painted cottage, mountain town hippie types gobble up avocado-tempeh melts, Thai curry bowls and sloppy burgers made from local beef. Brunch is served until 5pm.

Knights on Main SOUTHERN **$$**
(www.knightsonmainrestaurant.com; 870 Main St, Blowing Rock; mains $7-17; ⏰7am-8:30pm, to 2:30pm Sun) This wood-paneled family diner

is *the* place to try livermush, a mountain specialty consisting of…well, you can guess.

Information

The High Country **visitor center** (☎828-264-1299, 800-438-7500; www.highcountryhost.com; 1700 Blowing Rock Rd, Boone; ⏲9am-5pm) has info on accommodations and outdoors outfitters.

ASHEVILLE

This Jazz Age gem of a city appears like a mirage out of the mists of the Blue Ridge Mountains. Long a vacation destination for moneyed East Coasters (F Scott Fitzgerald was a fan), the city now has a huge artist population and a highly visible contingent of hard-core hippies. The art-deco buildings of downtown remain much the same as they were in 1930, though the area is now hopping with decidedly modern boutiques, restaurants, vintage stores and record shops. Visit Asheville once and you'll likely find yourself perusing local real-estate listings on the sly once you've returned home.

Sights

Downtown is compact and easy to negotiate on foot. The shopping's fantastic, with everything from hippie-dippy candle shops to vintage shops to high-end local art. West Ashville is an up-and-coming area, still gritty but very cool.

TOP CHOICE **Biltmore Estate** HOUSE, GARDENS
(www.biltmore.com; adult/child under 17 $59/5; ⏲9am-4:30pm) With 43 bathrooms, 65 fireplaces and a private bowling alley, the Gilded Age estate is a veritable American Versailles. The country's largest private home and Asheville's number-one tourist attraction, it was built in 1895 for shipping and railroad heir George Washington Vanderbilt II, who modeled it after the grand chateaux he'd seen on his various European jaunts. Viewing the estate and its 250 acres of gorgeously manicured grounds and gardens takes several hours. There are numerous cafes, a gift shop the size of a small supermarket, a hoity-toity hotel, and an award-winning winery that offers free tastings.

Chimney Rock Park PARK
(www.chimneyrockpark.com; adult/child $14/6; ⏲8:30am-4:30pm) A 20-mile drive southeast of Asheville, the American flag flaps in the breeze atop this popular park's namesake 315ft granite monolith. An elevator takes visitors up to the chimney, but the real draw is the exciting hike around the cliffs to a 404ft waterfall.

Thomas Wolfe Memorial HOUSE
(www.wolfememorial.com; 52 N Market St; admission $1; ⏲9am-5pm Tue-Sat, 1-5pm Sun) Downtown, this is *Look Homeward Angel* author Thomas Wolfe's childhood home, displaying artifacts from his brief life.

Sleeping

The **Asheville Bed & Breakfast Association** (☎877-262-6867; www.ashevillebba.com) handles bookings for numerous area B&Bs, from gingerbread cottages to alpine cabins.

Sweet Peas HOSTEL $
(☎828-285-8488; www.sweetpeashostel.com; 23 Rankin Ave; dm/pod/r $28/35/60; P❄@📶) Asheville's newest hostel looks as if it tumbled out of the IKEA catalog, with shipshape steel bunk beds and blond wood sleeping 'pods' with retractable curtains and reading lamps. The loftlike space is very open and can be noisy (a downstairs pub adds to the ruckus) – what you lose in privacy and quiet, you gain in style, cleanliness, sociability and an unbeatable downtown location.

Grove Park Inn Resort & Spa RESORT $$
(☎828-252-2711; www.groveparkinn.com; 290 Macon Ave; r from $135; P❄📶≋) Built in 1913, this titanic arts-and-crafts-style stone lodge clings to the side of the mountain like the castle of a goblin king. Inside is a mini-village of 510 richly appointed rooms, four restaurants, numerous shops and an underground grotto of a spa, complete with stone pools and an indoor waterfall.

Campfire Lodgings CAMPGROUND $$
(☎828-658-8012; www.campfirelodgings.com; 116 Appalachian Village Rd; tent sites $38, yurts from $115; P❄📶) All yurts should have flat-screen TVs, don't you think? Sleep like the world's most stylish Mongolian nomad in one of these furnished multiroom tents, on the side of a hill with stunning valley views. Cabins and tent sites are also available.

Lion and the Rose B&B $$$
(☎828-546-6988; www.lion-rose.com; 276 Montford Ave; r $135-225; P❄📶) The recipe for a perfect B&B: a grand Queen Anne in a historic neighborhood, with a gorgeous English garden, grand but unfussy decor, friendly owners and an even friendlier little fox terrier.

Bon Paul & Sharky's Hostel HOSTEL $
(☎828-350-9929; www.bonpaulandsharkys.com; 816 Haywood Rd; tent sites per person $15, dm/r $24/65; P❄@📶) In the hip West Asheville residential neighborhood, this cottage has a friendly college-dorm vibe and sweet amenities including foosball, communal bikes and backyard tent space.

Eating

Asheville is a great foodie town – many visitors come here just to eat!

TOP CHOICE **Admiral** MODERN AMERICAN $$$
(☎828-252-2541; www.theadmiralnc.com; 400 Haywood Rd; mains $17-26; ⏲5pm-11pm Mon-Sat) Walking by, you might guess this little concrete bunker was a dive bar. That's what they want you to think. This purposefully inconspicuous West Asheville spot is one of the state's – perhaps the country's – finest New American restaurants, serving wildly creative and irreverent dishes like duck breast with pimento cheese, steak tartare with Sriracha (hot chili sauce) aioli, and banana-Nutella-marshmallow cake with tempura apples. Phone a week ahead for reservations and *maybe* you'll get lucky and score a table.

French Broad Chocolate Lounge BAKERY, DESSERTS $
(frenchbroadchocolates.com; 10 S Lexington; snacks $2-6; ⏲11am-11pm, to midnight Fri & Sat) Small-batch organic chocolates in flavors like masala chai and orange-fennel, fat slices of maple cake with smoked salt, shot glasses full of 'liquid truffles,' pints of local stout served á la mode with vanilla ice cream... hey, where'd you go?

Salsa's CARIBBEAN $$
(www.salsas-asheville.com; 6 Patton Ave; mains $9-17; ⏲11:30am-2:30pm & 5:30-9pm) This tiny, brightly painted joint serves amazing, mutant Latin-fusion cuisine – think lamb empanadas with goat's cheese and banana salsa or crab-jalapeño-saffron-fennel egg rolls.

Rosetta's Kitchen VEGETARIAN $
(rosettaskitchen.com; 116 N Lexington Ave; mains $7-10; ⏲11am-11pm Mon-Thu, to 3am Fri & Sat, to 9pm Sun; 🖉) An institution among Asheville's dreadlocked set, where you can belly up to the counter for a bowl of peanut-butter tofu (looks awful, tastes heavenly) at 2am.

Tupelo Honey NEW SOUTHERN $$
(☎828-255-4863, www.tupelohoney.com; 12 College St; mains $9-22; ⏲9am-10pm) A longtime favorite for New Southern fare like pork chops with peach salsa. We especially like this cozy bistro for breakfast – try the sweet-potato pancakes.

Grove Arcade SELF-CATERING
(Page Ave) Try this massive Gothic-style building for fancy groceries and produce.

Drinking & Entertainment

Downtown Asheville has all types of bars and cafes, from frat-boy beer halls to hookah-n-sprout hippie holes-in-the-wall. West Asheville has a more laid-back townie vibe.

TOP CHOICE **Southern** BAR
(www.southernkitchenandbar.com; 41 N Lexington Ave) Fantastic new spot with upscale Southern pub grub (truffled deviled eggs, chicken 'n' waffles), a breezy patio and a long bar slinging fancy retro cocktails and local brews.

Jack of the Wood PUB
(jackofthewood.com; 95 Patton Ave) This Celtic pub is a good place to bond with local 20- and 30-somethings over a bottle of organic ale.

Asheville Pizza & Brewing Company BREWERY, CINEMA
(www.ashevillebrewing.com; 675 Merrimon Ave; movies $3; ⏲movies 1pm, 4pm, 7pm & 10pm) Catch a flick at the small theater inside this one-of-a-kind spot.

Orange Peel LIVE MUSIC
(www.theorangepeel.net; 101 Biltmore Ave; tickets $10-25) For live music, try this warehouse-sized place for big-name indie and punk.

Grey Eagle LIVE MUSIC
(www.thegreyeagle.com; 185 Clingman Ave; tickets $8-15) For bluegrass and jazz.

Information

The shiny new **visitor center** (☎828-258-6129; www.exploreasheville.com; 36 Montford Ave; ⏲9am-5pm) is at I-240 exit 4C.

The **public library** (67 Haywood Ave) has computers with free internet.

Getting There & Around

Asheville Transit (www.ashevilletransit.com; tickets $1) has 24 local bus routes running from 6am to 11:30pm Monday to Saturday. Twenty minutes south of town, **Asheville Regional Airport** (AVL; ☎828-684-2226; www.flyavl.com) has a handful of direct flights, including to/from

Atlanta, Charlotte and New York. **Greyhound** (2 Tunnel Rd) is just northeast of downtown.

GREAT SMOKY MOUNTAINS NATIONAL PARK

More than 10 million visitors a year come through this majestic park, one of the world's most biodiverse areas. Landscapes range from deep, dim spruce forest to sunny meadows carpeted with daisies and Queen Anne's lace to wide, coffee-brown rivers. There's ample hiking and camping, and opportunities for horseback riding, bike rental and fly-fishing. The North Carolina side has less traffic than the Tennessee side, so even at the height of summer tourist season you'll still have room to roam. For more information about the Tennessee section of this park, see p369.

Newfound Gap Rd/Hwy 441 is the only thoroughfare that crosses Great Smoky Mountains National Park, winding through the mountains from Gatlinburg, TN, to the town of Cherokee and the busy **Oconaluftee Visitor Center** (☎865-436-1200; Hwy 441), in the southeast. Pick up your backcountry camping permits here. The Oconaluftee River Trail, one of only two in the park that allows leashed pets, leaves from the visitor center and follows the river for 1.5 miles.

Nearby attractions include the 1886 **Mingus Mill** (self-guided tours free; ⏰9am-5pm 15 Mar-1 Dec), 2 miles west of Cherokee, a turbine-powered mill that still grinds wheat and corn much as it always has. The onsite **Mountain Farm Museum** is a restored 19th-century farmstead, complete with barn, blacksmith shop and smokehouse (with real pig heads!), assembled from original buildings from different parts of the park. A few miles away the **Smokemont Campground** (www.nps.gov/grsm; tent & RV sites $20) is the only North Carolina campground open year-round.

To the east, remote **Cataloochee Valley** has several historic buildings to wander through and is a prime location for elk and black bears.

SMOKY MOUNTAIN DAY HIKES

These are a few of our favorite short hikes in the North Carolina side of the park:

Big Creek Trail Hike an easy 2 miles to Mouse Creek Falls or go another 3 miles to backcountry campground; the trailhead's near I-40 on the park's northeastern edge.

Boogerman Trail Moderate 7-mile loop passing old farmsteads; access via Cove Creek Rd.

Chasteen Creek Falls From Smokemont campground, this 4-mile round-trip passes a small waterfall.

Shustack Tower Starting at massive Fontana Dam, climb 3.5 miles for killer views from an old fire tower.

SOUTHWESTERN NORTH CAROLINA

The state's westernmost tip is blanketed in parkland and sprinkled with tiny mountain towns. The area has a rich but sad Native American history – many of the original Cherokee inhabitants were forced off their lands during the 1830s and marched to Oklahoma on the Trail of Tears. Descendants of those who escaped are known as the Eastern Band of the Cherokee, about 12,000 of whom now occupy the 56,000-acre Qualla Boundary territory at the edge of Great Smoky Mountains National Park.

The unlovely town of **Cherokee** anchors the Qualla Boundary with ersatz Native American souvenir shops, fast-food joints and **Harrah's Cherokee Casino** (www.harrahs.com). The best sight is the modern **Museum of the Cherokee Indian** (www.cherokeemuseum.org; cnr Hwy 441 & Drama Rd; adult/child $10/6; ⏰9am-5pm), with an informative exhibit on the Trail of Tears and eerily realistic dioramas.

South of Cherokee, the contiguous **Pisgah** and **Nantahala National Forests** have more than a million acres of dense hardwood trees, windswept mountain balds and some of the country's best white water. Both contain portions of the Appalachian Trail. Pisgah highlights include the bubbling baths in the village of **Hot Springs** (www.hotspringsnc.org), the natural waterslide at **Sliding Rock**, and the 30-mile **Art Loeb Trail**, which skirts Cold Mountain of book and movie fame. Nantahala has several recreational lakes and dozens of roaring waterfalls, several of which can be easily accessed via the **Mountain Waters Scenic Byway**.

For plush accommodations try **Brevard**, a cute mountain town with tons of B&Bs on the east edge of Pisgah. Or head just north of Nantahala to quaint **Bryson City**, an ideal jumping-off point for outdoor adventures. It's home to the huge and highly recommended **Nantahala Outdoor Center** (☎828-488-2176, 828-586-8811; www.noc.com; 13077 Hwy 19/74; guided rafting trips $37-177), which specializes in wet and wild rafting trips down the Nantahala, French Broad, Pigeon and Ocoee Rivers, and rents out bikes, kayaks and more. It even has its own lodge and restaurant. From the Bryson City depot, the **Great Smoky Mountain Railroad** (☎800-872-4681; www.gsmr.com; Nantahala Gorge trip adult/child $53/31) runs scenic train excursions through the dramatic river valley.

SOUTH CAROLINA

Cross the border of South Carolina and plunge back in time. For a traveler heading down the eastern seaboard, venturing into South Carolina marks the beginning of the Deep South, where the air is hotter, the accents are thicker and traditions are clung to with even more fervor.

Starting at the silvery sands of the Atlantic Coast, the state climbs westward from the Coastal Plain and up through the Piedmont and into the Blue Ridge Mountains. Most travelers stick to the coast, with its splendid antebellum cities and palm-tree-studded beaches. But the interior has a wealth of sleepy old towns, wild and undeveloped state parks and spooky black-water swamps just waiting to be explored by canoe. Along the sea islands you hear the sweet songs of the Gullah, a culture and language created by former slaves who held onto many West African traditions through the ravages of time.

Whether you're looking for a romantic weekend in genteel, gardenia-scented Charleston or a week of riotous fun at bright, tacky Myrtle Beach, South Carolina is a lovely, affordable destination.

SOUTH CAROLINA FACTS

» **Nickname** Palmetto State

» **Population** 4.5 million

» **Area** 30,109 sq miles

» **Capital city** Columbia (population 130,000)

» **Other cities** Charleston (120,000)

» **Sales tax** 5%, plus up to 10% extra tax on accommodations

» **Birthplace of** jazzman Dizzy Gillespie (1917–93), political activist Jesse Jackson (b 1941), boxer Joe Frazier (b 1944), Wheel of Fortune hostess Vanna White (b 1957)

» **Home of** first US public library (1698), museum (1773) and steam railroad (1833)

» **Politics** one of America's top 10 most conservative states

» **Famous for** firing the first shot of the Civil War, from Charleston's Fort Sumter

» **Smelliest festival** Chitlin' Strut festival in Salley, a celebration of the odiferous stuffed pig's intestine dish chitterlings, or chitlins, a dubious Southern delicacy

» **Driving distances** Columbia to Charleston 115 miles, Charleston to Myrtle Beach 97 miles

History

More than 28 separate tribes of Native Americans have lived in what is now South Carolina, many of them Cherokee who were later forcibly removed during the Trail of Tears era.

The English founded the Carolina colony in 1670, with settlers pouring in from the royal outpost of Barbados, giving the port city known as Charles Towne a Caribbean flavor. West African slaves were brought over to turn the thick coastal swamps into rice paddies and by the mid-1700s the area was deeply divided between the slave-owning aristocrats of the Lowcountry and the poor Scots-Irish and German farmers of the rural backcountry.

South Carolina was the first state to secede from the Union, and the first battle of the Civil War occurred at Fort Sumter in Charleston Harbor. The end of the war left much of the state in ruins.

South Carolina traded in cotton and textiles for most of the 20th century. It remains a relatively poor agricultural state, though with a thriving coastal tourism business.

Information

South Carolina Department of Parks, Recreation & Tourism (☎803-734-1700 www.discoversouthcarolina.com; 1205 Pendleton St, Room 505, Columbia) Sends out *South Carolina Smiles*, the state's official vacation guide.

South Carolina State Parks (☎888-887-2757; www.southcarolinaparks.com) This helpful website lists activities, hiking trails and allows online reservations for campsites (prices vary).

Charleston

Put on your twinset and pearls or your seersucker suit, have a fortifying sip of sherry, and prepare to be thoroughly drenched in Southern charm. Charleston is a city for strolling, for admiring antebellum architecture, stopping to smell the blooming jasmine and long dinners on the verandah. A tooth-achingly romantic place, everywhere you turn another blushing bride is standing on the steps of yet another charming church.

Named the 'Best-Mannered City in America' 11 years in a row, Charleston is one of the most popular tourist destinations in the Southeast. In the high season the scent of gardenia and honeysuckle mixes with the tang of horse from the innumerable carriage tours that clip-clop down the cobblestones day and night. In winter the weather is milder and the crowds thinner, making Charleston a great bet for off-season travel.

History

Well before the Revolutionary War, Charles Towne (named for Charles II) was one of the busiest ports on the eastern seaboard, the center of a prosperous rice-growing and trading colony. With influences from the West Indies and Africa, France and other European countries, it became a cosmopolitan city, often compared to New Orleans.

The first shots of the Civil War rang out at Fort Sumter, in Charleston's harbor. After the war, as the labor-intensive rice plantations became uneconomical without slave labor, the city's importance declined. But much of the town's historic fabric remains, to the delight of four million tourists every year.

DON'T MISS

CHARLESTON'S SPECIAL CHARMS

» Eating fried shrimp in an old bait warehouse at the **Wreck of the Richard & Charlene** (p344)

» Ogling the oh-so-photogenic painted town houses of **Rainbow Row** (p341)

» Strolling past ancient churchyards abloom with flowers on the **Gateway Walk** (p340)

» Peeking into the lives of the 19th-century Southern aristocracy at **Middleton Place** (p346)

» Watching the sun set in a blaze of orange over the river at the **Rooftop at Vendue Inn** (p345)

Sights & Activities

HISTORIC DISTRICT

The quarter south of Beaufain and Hasell Sts has the bulk of the antebellum mansions, shops, bars and cafes. At the southernmost tip of the peninsula are the antebellum mansions of the Battery.

Gateway Walk CHURCHES

Long a culturally diverse city, Charleston gave refuge to persecuted French Protestants, Baptists and Jews over the years and earned the nickname the 'Holy City' for its abundance of houses of worship. The Gateway Walk, a little-known garden path between Archdale St and Philadelphia Alley, connects four of the city's most beautiful historic churches: the white-columned **St John's Lutheran Church**; the Gothic Revival **Unitarian Church**; the striking Romanesque **Circular Congregational Church**, originally founded in 1681; and **St Philip's Church**, with its picturesque steeple and 17th-century graveyard, parts of which were once reserved for 'strangers and transient white persons.'

Gibbes Museum of Art GALLERY

(www.gibbesmuseum.org; 135 Meeting St; adult/child $9/7; ⌚10am-5pm Tue-Sat, 1-5pm Sun) Houses a decent collection of American and Southern works; the most interesting way to visit is in conjunction with a two-hour **walking tour** (www.oldcharlestontours.com; tours $20) that combines the museum with various artistically significant city sights.

Old Slave Mart Museum MUSEUM

(www.nps.gov/nr/travel/charleston/osm.htm; 6 Chalmers St; adult/child $7/5; ⌚9am-5pm Mon-Sat) African men, women and children were once auctioned off here, now a museum of South Carolina's shameful past. Text-heavy exhibits illuminate the slave experience; the few artifacts, such as leg shackles, are especially chilling.

Old Exchange & Provost Dungeon HISTORIC BUILDING

(www.oldexchange.com; 122 E Bay St; adult/child $8/4; ⌚9am-5pm; 👪) Kids love this dungeon, built in 1771 as a customs house and later used as a prison for pirates. Costumed guides lead tours.

Kahal Kadosh Beth Elohim SYNAGOGUE
(www.kkbe.org; 90 Hasell St; tours 10am-noon & 1:30-3:30pm Mon-Thu, 10am-noon Fri) The oldest continuously used synagogue in the country. There are free tours by appointment.

City Market MARKET
(Market St) The historic market is the crowded center of the district, with vendors hawking junky souvenirs from open-air stalls.

White Point Park GARDEN
Take a seat in this shady park and ponder whether 'filthy-rich merchant seaman' is still a viable career.

Rainbow Row NEIGHBORHOOD
Around the corner from White Point Park, a stretch of lower E Bay St known as Rainbow Row is one of the most photographed areas of town for its candy-colored houses.

HISTORIC HOMES

About half a dozen majestic historic homes are open to visitors. Discounted combination tickets may tempt you to see more, but one or two will be enough for most people. Most houses are open from 10am to 5pm Monday to Saturday, 1pm to 5pm Sunday and run guided tours every half-hour. Admission is $10.

Heyward-Washington House HISTORIC BUILDING
(www.charlestonmuseum.org; 87 Church St), Built in 1772, this house belonged to Thomas Heyward Jr, a signer of the Declaration of Independence, and contains some lovely examples of Charleston-made mahogany furniture and the city's only preserved historic kitchen.

Nathaniel Russell House HISTORIC BUILDING
(www.historiccharleston.org; 51 Meeting St) Built by a Rhode Islander, known in Charleston as 'the king of the Yankees,' the 1808 Federal-style house is noted especially for its spectacular, self-supporting spiral staircase and lush English garden.

Joseph Manigault House HISTORIC BUILDING
(www.charlestonmuseum.org; 350 Meeting St) The three-story house was once the showpiece of a French Huguenot rice planter. Don't miss the tiny neoclassical temple in the garden.

Aiken-Rhett House HISTORIC BUILDING
(www.historiccharleston.org; 48 Elizabeth St) The only surviving urban plantation; it gives a fascinating look into antebellum life, including the role of slaves.

CHARLESTON FESTIVALS

Lowcountry Oyster Festival In January oyster-lovers in Mt Pleasant feast on 65,000lb of the salty bivalves.

Charleston Food & Wine Festival This newish March event draws celebrity chefs and well-heeled foodies.

Spoleto USA This 17-day performing arts festival in May is Charleston's biggest event, with operas, dramas and musicals staged across the city, and artisans and food vendors lining the streets.

Charleston Harbor Fest In June antique tall ships sail into town; visitors can take tours and sailing lessons.

MOJA Arts Festival Spirited poetry jams and gospel concerts mark this two-week September celebration of African American culture.

MARION SQUARE

Formerly home to the state weapons arsenal, this 10-acre park is Charleston's living room, with various monuments and an excellent Saturday farmers market.

Charleston Museum MUSEUM
(www.charlestonmuseum.org; 360 Meeting St; adult/child $10/5; ⏲9am-5pm Mon-Sat, from 1pm Sun) Founded in 1773, this claims to be the country's oldest museum, with exhibits from various periods of Charleston's long and storied history, from prehistoric whale skeletons to slave tags and Civil War weapons.

Children's Museum of the Lowcountry MUSEUM
(www.explorecml.org; 25 Ann St; admission $7; ⏲10am-5pm Tue-Sat, 1-5pm Sun; 👪) Has eight interactive exhibit areas, including a 30ft replica shrimp boat where kids can play captain.

AQUARIUM WHARF

Aquarium Wharf surrounds pretty Liberty Sq and is a great place to stroll around and watch the tugboats guiding ships into the seventh-largest container port in the US. The wharf is the embarkation point for tours to Fort Sumter.

Fort Sumter HISTORIC SITE
The first shots of the Civil War rang out at Fort Sumter, on a pentagon-shaped island in the harbor. A Confederate stronghold, the fort was shelled to bits by Union forces from 1863 to 1865. A few original guns and fortifications give a feel for the momentous history. The only way to get here is by boat tour (☎843-883-3123; www.nps.gov/fosu; adult/child $17/10; ⏱tours 9:30am, noon & 2:30pm summer, fewer winter), which also depart from Patriot's Point in Mt Pleasant, across the river.

South Carolina Aquarium AQUARIUM
(www.scaquarium.org; 100 Aquarium Wharf; adult/child $20/13; ⏱9am-5pm; 👪) The massive, excellent aquarium showcases the state's diverse aquatic life, from the otters of the Blue Ridge Mountains to the loggerhead turtles of the Atlantic. The highlight is the 42ft Great Ocean Tank, which teems with sharks and alien-looking puffer fish.

Arthur Ravenel Jr Bridge BRIDGE
Stretching across the Cooper River like some massive stringed instrument, the 3-mile-long Arthur Ravenel Jr Bridge is a triumph of contemporary engineering. Cycling or jogging across the protected no-car lane is one of active Charlestonians' go-to weekend activities. Rent a cruiser at **Charleston Bicycle Company** (☎843-407-0482; www.charlestonbicyclecompany.com; 334 M E Bay St; bikes per day $27).

Tours

Listing all of Charleston's walking, horse-carriage, bus and boat tours could take up this entire book. Ask at the visitor center for the gamut.

Culinary Tours of Charleston CULINARY TOUR
(☎800-918-0701; www.culinarytoursofcharleston.com; 2½hr tour $42) Sample grits, pralines, BBQ and more on this walking tour of Charleston's restaurants and markets.

Adventure Harbor Tours BOAT TOUR
(☎843-442-9455; www.adventureharbortours.com; Morris Island tour adult/child $55/25, off-the-beaten path tour adult/child $75/40) Runs fun trips to uninhabited Morris Island, great for shelling, and a quirky 'off-the-beaten-path' history tour of the harbor.

Charleston Footprints WALKING TOUR
(☎843-478-4718; www.charlestonfootprintss.com; 2hr tour $20) A highly rated walking tour of historical Charleston sights.

Olde Towne Carriage Company CARRIAGE TOUR
(☎843-722-1315; www.oldetownecarriage.com; 20 Anson St; 45min tour adult/child $20/12) Guides on this popular horse-drawn-carriage tour offer colorful commentary as you clip-clop around town.

Sleeping

Staying in the historic downtown is the most attractive option, but it's the most expensive, especially on weekends and in high season. The rates below are for high season (spring and early summer). The chain hotels on the highways offer significantly lower rates. Hotel parking in central downtown is usually between $15 and $20 a night; accommodations on the fringes of downtown often have free parking.

The city is bursting with charming B&Bs serving up Southern breakfasts and Southern hospitality. They fill up fast, so try using an agency such as **Historic Charleston B&B** (☎843-722-6606; www.historiccharlestonbedandbreakfast.com; 57 Broad St).

TOP CHOICE **Ansonborough Inn** HOTEL **$$$**
(☎800-522-2073; www.ansonboroughinn.com; 1 Maiden Ln; r $149-290; ❄📶) A central atrium done up with burnished pine, exposed beams and nautical-themed oil paintings makes this intimate Historic District hotel feel like being inside an antique sailing ship. Droll neo-Victorian touches like the Persian-carpeted glass elevator and the closet-sized British pub add a sense of fun. Huge guest rooms mix old and new, with worn leather couches, high ceilings and flat-screen TVs.

Battery Carriage House Inn B&B **$$$**
(☎843-727-3100; www.batterycarriagehouse.com; 20 S Battery; r from $219; P❄📶) Step through the iron gates and into this secluded 11-room treasure, where an interior garden filled with roses and whimsically trimmed topiary hedges begs you to sit down for a cup of tea. A 'gentleman ghost' is said to wander the Victorian-style rooms at night.

Restoration on King HOTEL **$$$**
(☎843-518-5100; www.restorationonking.com; 75 Wentworth St; r $299-499; ❄📶) Charleston's newest sleeping spot is an antidote to the city's traditional antiques-and-pineapples hotel decor. The 16 ultramodern luxury suites are more like private apartments, with exposed brick, sleek stainless steel and

gorgeous spa-style bathrooms. Splash out for one with a balcony.

Vendue Inn INN **$$$**
(843-577-7970; www.vendueinn.com; 19 Vendue Range; r incl breakfast $145-255;) This teeny boutique hotel, in the part of downtown known as the French Quarter, is decked out in a trendy mix of exposed brick and eccentric antiques. Rooms have cool amenities like deep soaking tubs and gas fireplaces. Even cooler is the aptly named Rooftop bar.

NotSo Hostel HOSTEL **$**
(843-722-8383; www.notsohostel.com; 156 Spring St; dm/r $23/60; P@) On the north edge of downtown, three tottering old houses have been carved into dorms and private rooms, the verandahs decked with hammocks. Get local tips from friendly staff members during the shared morning breakfast. A new nearby annex offers queen beds and a quieter vibe, good for couples.

Mills House Hotel HOTEL **$$**
(843-577-2400; www.millshouse.com; 115 Meeting St; r from $189;) This grand old dame (150 years young, *merci*) has had an $11-million facelift, and is now one of the most opulent choices in the area. Gilded elevators lead from an enormous marble lobby to 214 lushly upholstered rooms. The sun has still not set on the British Empire inside the clubby, wood-paneled Barbados Room restaurant.

1837 Bed & Breakfast B&B **$$**
(843-723-7166, 877-723-1837; www.1837bb.com; 126 Wentworth St; r incl breakfast $109-195; P) Like staying at the home of your eccentric, antique-loving aunt, 1837 has nine charmingly overdecorated rooms, including three in the old brick carriage house.

Palmer Pinckney Inn INN **$$$**
(843-722-1733; www.pinckneyinn.com; 19 Pinckney St; r $150-300; P) This bubblegum-pink 'single house' (a narrow building style characteristic of Charleston) has five twee guest rooms tucked away on a Historic District side street.

James Island County Park CAMPGROUND **$**
(843-795-7275; www.ccprc.com; 871 Riverland Dr; tent sites from $25, 8-person cottages $159) Southwest of town, this park offers shuttle services downtown. Reservations are highly recommended.

Anchorage Inn INN **$$**
(843-723-8300; www.anchoragecharleston.com; 26 Vendue Range; r from $99;) One of the best-value of Charleston's intimate Historic District inns, its rooms have the dark and small feel of ship's quarters but they're plenty plush.

Eating

Charleston is one of America's finest eating cities, and there are enough fabulous restaurants here for a town three times its size. The 'classic' Charleston establishments stick to fancy seafood with a French flair, while many of the trendy up-and-comers are reinventing Southern cuisine with a focus on the area's copious local bounty, from oysters to heirloom rice to heritage pork. On Saturday, stop by the terrific **farmers market** (Marion Sq; 8am-1pm Sat Apr-Oct).

TOP CHOICE **Husk** NEW SOUTHERN **$$$**
(843-577-2500; www.huskrestaurant.com; 76 Queen St; mains $22-26; 11:30am-2:30pm Mon-Sat, 5:30-10pm daily, brunch 10am-2:30pm Sun) The brain child of chef Sean Brock, the current toast of the foodie world, Husk was the South's most buzzed-about restaurant when it burst onto the scene in late 2010, and for damn good reason. Everything – *everything* – on the menu is grown or raised in the South, from the jalapeño marmalade-topped

LOWCOUNTRY CUISINE

The traditional cooking style of the South Carolina and Georgia coasts, Lowcountry cuisine is seafood-centric Southern fare with a heavy dash of West African influence. Dishes to look for:

» She-crab soup: cream-based crab soup fortified with sherry

» Lowcountry boil/Frogmore stew: crabs, shrimp, oysters and other local seafood boiled in a pot with corn and potatoes, generally eaten at picnics

» Country Captain: curried chicken stew, brought to the city via India by British sea captains

» Perlau: a rice-and-meat dish, cousin to rice pilaf

» Shrimp and grits: a classic Charleston fisherman's breakfast, now a ubiquitous main course

» Hoppin' John: a rice and bean dish, sometimes spicy

» Benne wafers: sesame-seed cookies

Georgia corn soup to the yuzu-scented Cooper River oysters, to the local lard featured in the 'pork butter' brought out with the restaurant's addictive sesame-seed rolls. The setting, in a two-story mansion, is elegant but unfussy, and the adjacent speakeasy-style bar (see Drinking) is straight-up terrific.

Wreck of the Richard & Charlene SEAFOOD $$$

(www.wreckrc.com; 106 Haddrell St; mains $12-25; ⏲5:30-8:30pm Sun-Thu, to 9:30pm Fri & Sat) It's practically impossible to find, but don't give up! This unmarked warehouse, down a dirt road overlooking Shem Creek in suburban Mt Pleasant, has what many consider the best fried seafood in the state. Kick back in a plastic chair with a free bowl of boiled peanuts while you wait; finish with the key lime bread pudding. No credit cards.

O-Ku JAPANESE $$$

(☎843-737-0112; www.o-kusushi.com; 463 King St; mains $16-29; ⏲11:30am-2pm Mon-Fri, 5-10:30pm Sun-Thu, to midnight Fri & Sat) Scenesters dine on irreverent sushi (try the fried potato-wrapped roll), Japanese street food (try Kurobuta pork sliders with grapefruit puree) and lavish seafood dishes at this new rock star of a restaurant, a big high-ceilinged space with a glammy black paint-and-mirrors decor. The lunchtime bento box ($10) is a steal.

FIG NEW SOUTHERN $$$

(☎843-805-5900; www.eatatfig.com; 232 Meeting St; mains $28-32; ⏲5:30-10:30pm Mon-Thu, to 11pm Fri-Sun) Foodies swoon over inspired nouvelle-Southern fare like crispy pig's trotters (that means 'feet' – local and hormone-free, of course) with celery-root remoulade in this rustic-chic dining room.

Glass Onion NEW SOUTHERN $$

(☎843-225-1717; www.ilovetheglassonion.com; 1219 Savannah Hwy; mains $12-19; ⏲11am-9pm Mon-Sat) In-the-know foodies flock across the bridge to West Ashley for Tuesday-night fried-chicken suppers at this funky art-filled diner, Charleston's newest spot for creative takes on Southern classics. The perfect stop for lunch on the way to visit the Ashley River plantations.

S.N.O.B. NEW SOUTHERN $$$

(☎843-723-3424; www.mavericksouthernkitchens.com; 192 E Bay St; mains $18-34; ⏲11:30am-3pm Mon-Fri, 5:30pm-late nightly) The cheeky name (it stands for 'slightly north of Broad,' as in Broad St) reflects the anything-goes spirit of this upscale-casual spot, which draws raves for its eclectic menu, filled with treats such as house-smoked salmon or sautéed squab breast over cheese grits.

Gullah Cuisine SOUTHERN $

(1717 Hwy 17 N, Mt Pleasant; mains $7-11; ⏲9am-3pm & 5-9:30pm) It's not much to look at,

CHARLESTON'S BEST BAKERIES

Ever the European-style city, Charleston has some of the finest bakeries outside the Continent.

Wildflour Pastry BAKERY $

(73 Spring St; pastries $1-3; ⏲6:30am-4pm Tue-Fri, 8am-3pm Sat, 8am-1pm Sun) On rapidly gentrifying Spring St, this sweet slip of a bakery turns out glorious Nutella-raspberry turnovers, jam scones and coffee cake muffins.

Sugar Bakeshop BAKERY $

(59 Cannon St; pastries $1-3; ⏲11am-6pm Mon-Fri, noon-5pm Sat) Pop into this teensy space on Thursdays for the Lady Baltimore cupcake, a retro Southern specialty with dried fruit and white frosting.

Baked BAKERY $

(160 E Bay St; pastries $1-5; ⏲7:30am-7pm; wi-fi) Salty caramel cake, red velvet whoopie pies and homemade marshmallows (and lots of table space with free wi-fi) make this Historic District spot a winner.

Macaroon Boutique BAKERY $

(45 John St; bags of macarons $7; ⏲8:30am-6pm Tue-Sat, to 4pm Sun) With perfect golden croissants and baggies of crisp, chewy macaroons, you might as well be in Paris. No seating.

but this dowdy suburban cafe is the best place to taste South Carolina's West African-influenced Gullah cooking. Go for the lunch buffet, groaning with red rice, okra gumbo (roux-based stew), oxtail stew and fried fish, and skip the dinner.

Hominy Grill NEW SOUTHERN **$$**
(www.hominygrill.com; 207 Rutledge Ave; mains $7-18; ⏲7:30am-9pm Mon-Fri, 9am-3pm Sat & Sun) Slightly off the beaten path, this neighborhood cafe serves modern, vegetarian-friendly Lowcountry cuisine in an old barbershop. The shady patio is tops for brunch.

Gaulart & Maliclet FRENCH **$$**
(www.fastandfrench.org; 98 Broad St; mains $8-15; ⏲8am-4pm Mon, 8am-10pm Tue-Thu, to 10:30pm Fri-Sun) Locals crowd around the shared tables at this tiny spot, known as 'Fast & French,' to nibble on Gallic cheeses and sausages or nightly specials ($15) that include bread, soup, a main dish and wine.

Drinking

Balmy Charleston evenings are perfect for lifting a cool cocktail or dancing to live blues. Check out the weekly *Charleston City Paper* and the 'Preview' section of Friday's *Post & Courier*.

TOP CHOICE **Husk Bar** BAR
(462 King St) Adjacent to the excellent new Husk restaurant (see Eating), this intimate brick-and-worn-wood spot recalls a speakeasy, with historic cocktails such as the Monkey Gland (gin, OJ, raspberry syrup). Very cool.

Rooftop at Vendue Inn BAR
(23 Vendue Range) This two-level rooftop bar has the best views of downtown, and the crowds to prove it. Enjoy afternoon nachos or late-night live blues.

Belmont BAR
(511 King St) Young hipsters mellow out with small-batch bourbon at this low-key new lounge, in a narrow 1930s-style King St storefront.

Blind Tiger PUB
(36-38 Broad St) A cozy and atmospheric dive, with stamped tin ceilings, a worn wood bar and good pub grub.

Closed for Business PUB
(535 King St) Charleston's best beer selection and a raucous neighborhood pub vibe.

Shopping

The historic district is clogged with overpriced souvenir shops and junk markets. Heading to King St is a better bet: hit lower King for antiques, middle King for scads of cool boutiques, and upper King for trendy design and gift shops. The main stretch of Broad St is known as 'Gallery Row' for its many art galleries.

Shops of Historic Charleston Foundation GIFTS
(108 Meeting St) This place showcases jewelry, home furnishings and furniture inspired by the city's historic homes, like earrings based on the cast-iron railings at the Aiken-Rhett House. Pick up a 'Charleston' candle, scented with hyacinth, white jasmine and tuberose.

Carolina Antique Maps & Prints MAPS, ART
(91 Church St) Buy a vintage map of Charleston or a magnolia-blossom botanical print at this crowded little shop, tucked away on a residential street.

Charleston Crafts Cooperative CRAFT
(161 Church St) A pricey, well-edited selection of contemporary South Carolina-made crafts such as sweetgrass baskets, hand-dyed silks and wood carvings.

Blue Bicycle Books BOOKS
(420 King St) Excellent local bookshop with a great selection of Southern history and culture.

Information

The City of Charleston maintains free public internet (wi-fi) access throughout the downtown area.

Charleston City Paper (www.charlestoncitypaper.com) Published each Wednesday, this alt-weekly has good entertainment and restaurant listings.

Main police station (☎843-577-7434; 180 Lockwood Blvd)

Post & Courier (www.charleston.net) Charleston's daily newspaper.

Post office (83 Broad St)

Public library (68 Calhoun St) Free internet access.

University Hospital (MUSC; ☎843-792-2300; 171 Ashley Ave; ⏲24hr) Emergency room.

Visitor center (☎843-853-8000; www.charlestoncvb.com; 375 Meeting St; ⏲8:30am-5pm) Find help with accommodations and tours or watch a half-hour video on Charleston history in this spacious renovated warehouse.

Getting There & Around

Charleston International Airport (CHS; 843-767-7009; www.chs-airport.com; 5500 International Blvd) is 12 miles outside of town in North Charleston, with 124 daily flights to 17 destinations.

The **Greyhound station** (3610 Dorchester Rd) and the **Amtrak train station** (4565 Gaynor Ave) are both in North Charleston.

CARTA (www.ridecarta.com; fare $1.75) runs city-wide buses; the free DASH streetcars do four loop routes from the visitor center.

Around Charleston

MT PLEASANT

Across the Cooper River is the residential and vacation community of Mt Pleasant, originally a summer retreat for early Charlestonians, along with the slim barrier resort islands of **Isle of Palms** and **Sullivan's Island**. Though increasingly glutted with traffic and strip malls, the area still has some charm, especially in the historic downtown, called the **Old Village**. Some good seafood restaurants sit overlooking the water at **Shem Creek**, where it's fun to dine creekside at sunset and watch the incoming fishing-boat crews unload their catch. This is also a good place to rent kayaks to tour the estuary.

Patriot's Point Naval & Maritime Museum (www.patriotspoint.org; 40 Patriots Point Rd; adult/child $18/11; 9am-6:30pm) is home to the USS *Yorktown,* a giant aircraft carrier used extensively in WWII. You can tour the ship's flight deck, bridge and ready rooms and get a glimpse of what life was like for its sailors. Also on site are a small museum, submarine, naval destroyer, Coast Guard cutter and a re-created 'fire base' from Vietnam. You can also catch the Fort Sumter boat tour from here.

Just 7 miles from Charleston on Hwy 17 N, **Boone Hall Plantation** (www.boonehallplantation.com; 1235 Long Point Rd; adult/child $19.50/9.50; 9am-5pm Mon-Sat, noon-5pm Sun) claims to be America's most photographed plantation. It's famous for its magical Avenue of Oaks, planted by Thomas Boone in 1743. Boone Hall is still a working plantation, though strawberries, tomatoes and Christmas trees long ago replaced cotton as the primary crop.

Near Boone Hall, the **Charles Pinckney National Historic Site** (1254 Long Point Rd; admission free; 9am-5pm) sits on the remaining 28 acres of Snee Farm, once the expansive plantation of statesman Charles Pinckney. There are archaeological and historical exhibits in the 1820s cottage turned museum, and several walking trails meandering through the magnolias.

ASHLEY RIVER PLANTATIONS

Only 20 minutes' drive from Charleston, three spectacular plantations are worthy of a detour. You'll be hard-pressed for time to visit all three in one outing, but you could squeeze in two (allow at least a couple of hours for each). Ashley River Rd is also known as SC 61, which can be reached from downtown Charleston via Hwy 17.

TOP CHOICE **Middleton Place** PLANTATION

(www.middletonplace.org; 4300 Ashley River Rd; gardens adult/child $22/10, house tour add $12; 9am-5pm) Designed in 1741, this plantation's vast gardens are the oldest in the US. One hundred slaves spent a decade terracing the land and digging the precise geometric canals for the owner, wealthy South Carolina politician Henry Middleton. The grounds are truly bewitching, a mix of classic formal French gardens and romantic woodland settings, bounded by real flooded rice paddies and fields full of rare breed farm animals (horse-drawn carriage tours are $15). In contrast to the antebellum plantation house, the very cool on-site **inn** (r incl plantation admission from $209) is a series of ecofriendly modernist glass boxes overlooking the Ashley River. Even if you don't stay the night, don't miss a traditional Lowcountry plantation lunch of she-crab soup and pole beans at the highly regarded **cafe** (lunch $11-13, dinner $23-32; 11am-3pm daily & 6-8pm Tue-Sun).

Magnolia Plantation HOUSE, GARDENS

(www.magnoliaplantation.com; 3550 Ashley River Rd; adult/child $15/10, house tour add $8; 8am-5:30pm) Sitting on 500 acres owned by the Drayton family since 1676, Magnolia Plantation is enjoyable even for those who disdain 'boring historical stuff.' It's a veritable plantation theme park, complete with a tram tour of the flora and fauna, boat tours, a swamp walk, a petting zoo, and an outdoor cafe full of wandering peacocks, in addition to the guided house tour. Don't miss the reconstructed cabins of the slaves who once tended the indigo, cotton, corn and sugarcane.

Drayton Hall HISTORIC BUILDING

(www.draytonhall.org; 3380 Ashley River Rd; adult/child $18/8; 9am-4:30pm, shorter hr in winter)

This 1738 Palladian brick mansion was the only structure on the Ashley River to survive the Revolutionary and Civil Wars and the great earthquake of 1886. Guided tours through the empty house will appeal to history and architecture buffs.

DON'T MISS

BOWEN'S ISLAND RESTAURANT

Down a long dirt road through Lowcountry marshland near Folly Beach, this unpainted wooden shack is one of the South's most venerable seafood dives – grab an oyster knife and start shucking! Cool beer and friendly locals give the place its soul. You'll find the restaurant at 1870 Bowen's Island Rd, open Tuesday to Saturday, 5pm to 10pm.

Lowcountry

From just north of Charleston, the southern half of the South Carolina coast is a tangle of islands cut off from the mainland by inlets and tidal marshes. Here, descendants of West African slaves known as the Gullah maintain small communities in the face of resort and golf-course development. The landscape ranges from tidy stretches of shimmery, oyster-gray sand, to wild, moss-shrouded maritime forests.

CHARLESTON COUNTY SEA ISLANDS

The following islands are all within an hour's drive from Charleston.

About 8 miles south of Charleston, **Folly Beach** is good for a day of sun and sand. **Folly Beach County Park** (cars/pedestrians $7/free; ⏲10am-6pm), on the west side, has public changing areas and beach-chair rentals. The other end of the island is popular with surfers.

Upscale rental homes and golf courses abound on **Kiawah Island**, just southeast of Charleston, while nearby **Edisto Island** (*ed-is-tow*) is a homespun family vacation spot without a single traffic light. At its southern tip, **Edisto Beach State Park** (admission $5; tent sites from $17, furnished cabins from $70) has a gorgeous, uncrowded beach and oak-shaded hiking trails and campgrounds.

Between Kiawah and Edisto, agricultural **Wadmalaw Island** is home to **Charleston Tea Plantation** (www.charlestonteaplantation.com; 6617 Maybank Hwy; trolley tours/factory tours $10/free; ⏲10am-4pm, noon-4pm Sun), America's only working tea farm. Ride a trolley through the fields, or buy prettily packaged Plantation Peach and Island Green teas in the gift shop.

BEAUFORT & HILTON HEAD

The southernmost stretch of South Carolina's coast is popular with a mostly upscale set of golfers and B&B aficionados, but the area's got quirky charms aplenty for everyone.

On Port Royal Island, the darling colonial town of **Beaufort** (byoo-furt) is often used as a set for Hollywood films about the South. The streets of the historic district are lined with antebellum homes and magnolias dripping with Spanish moss, and the riverfront downtown has gobs of linger-worthy cafes and galleries. The most romantic of the city's handful of B&Bs is the **Cuthbert House** (☎843-521-1315; www.cuthberthouseinn.com; 1203 Bay St; r from $169; 📶), a sumptuously grand white-columned mansion straight out of *Gone With the Wind II*. Bay St has the bulk of the cute bistros, but for some hardcore local flavor head inland to **Sgt White's** (1908 Boundary St; mains $6-12; ⏲11am-3pm Mon-Fri), where a retired Marine sergeant serves up juicy BBQ ribs, collards and cornbread.

South of Beaufort, some 20,000 young men and women go through boot camp each year at the **Marine Corps Recruit Depot** on Parris Island, made notorious by Stanley Kubrick's *Full Metal Jacket*. The fascinating base **museum** (admission free; ⏲10am-4:30pm) has antique uniforms and weaponry. Come for Friday graduations to see newly minted marines parade proudly in front of weeping family and friends.

East of Beaufort, the Sea Island Pkwy/Hwy 21 connects a series of marshy, rural islands, including **St Helena Island**, considered the heart of Gullah country. Once one of the nation's first schools for freed slaves, the **Penn Center** (www.penncenter.com; adult/child $5/2; ⏲11am-4pm Mon-Sat) has a small museum of Gullah culture and is a good place to get info for further exploration. Further down the road, **Hunting Island State Park** (☎843-838-2011; www.huntingisland.com; adult/child $5/3; tent sites/cabins from $17/107) has acres of spooky maritime forest, tidal lagoons, and empty, bone-white beach. The Vietnam War scenes from *Forrest Gump* were filmed in the marsh, a nature-lover's dream. Campgrounds fill up quickly in summer.

GULLAH CULTURE

Many parts of the US resemble the European cities from which the founding settlers emigrated, but only on remote islands along the Georgia and South Carolina coast can the same claim be given to Africa. From the region known as the Rice Coast (Sierra Leone, Senegal, the Gambia and Angola), African slaves were transported across the Atlantic to a landscape that was shockingly similar – swampy coastlines, tropical vegetation and hot, humid summers.

These new African Americans were able to retain many of their homeland traditions, even after the fall of slavery and well into the 20th century. The resulting Gullah (also known as Geechee) culture has its own language, an English-based Creole with many African words and sentence structures, and many traditions, including fantastic storytelling, art, music and crafts. The Gullah culture is celebrated annually with the energetic **Gullah Festival** (www.gullahfestival.org) in Beaufort. As many as 70,000 people gather on the last weekend in May to enjoy music, dance and crafts, including the famous Gullah sweetgrass baskets, and to eat traditional foods such as fried whiting, candied yams and okra gumbo.

Across Port Royal Sound, tony **Hilton Head Island** is South Carolina's largest barrier island and one of America's top golf spots. There are literally dozens of courses, many enclosed in posh private residential communities called 'plantations.' Though summer traffic and miles of stoplights make it hard to see the forest (or a tree) along Hwy 278, there are some lush nature preserves and wide white beaches hard enough to ride a bike on. At the entrance to the island is the **visitor center** (9:30am-5pm), with a small museum and info on accommodations and, well, golf.

North Coast

The coastline from the North Carolina border to the city of Georgetown is known as the Grand Strand, with some 60 miles of fast-food joints, beach resorts and three-story souvenir shops. What was once a laid-back summer destination for working-class people from across the Southeast has become some of the most overdeveloped real estate in the country. Whether you're ensconced in a behemoth resort or sleeping in a tent at a state park, all you need to enjoy your stay is a pair of flip-flops, a margarita and some quarters for the pinball machine.

MYRTLE BEACH

Love it or hate it, Myrtle Beach means summer vacation, American-style.

Bikers take advantage of the lack of helmet laws to let their graying ponytails fly in the wind, bikini-clad teenagers play Pac-Man and eat hot dogs in smoky arcades, and whole families roast like chickens on the white sand.

North Myrtle Beach, actually a separate town, is slightly lower-key, with a thriving culture based on the 'shag' (no, not that kind of shag) – a jitterbug-like dance invented here in the 1940s.

It ain't for nature-lovers, but with enormous outlet malls and innumerable mini-golf courses, water parks, daiquiri bars and T-shirt shops, it's a rowdy good time.

Sights & Activities

The beach itself is pleasant enough – wide, hot and crowded with umbrellas. Beachfront Ocean Blvd has the bulk of the hamburger stands and seedy gift shops. Hwy 17 is utterly choked with **mini-golf** courses, boasting everything from animatronic dinosaurs to faux volcanoes spewing lurid-pink water.

Several amusement park–shopping mall hybrids teem with people at all hours.

Brookgreen Gardens GARDENS
(www.brookgreen.org; adult/child $12/6; 9:30am-5pm) These magical gardens, 16 miles south of town on Hwy 17 S, are home to the largest collection of American sculpture in the country, set amid 9000 acres of rice plantation turned subtropical garden paradise.

Wonderworks MUSEUM
(www.wonderworksonline.com; tickets adult/child from $23/15; 10am-10pm;) In a fake upside-down building, this new interactive museum/amusement zone perfectly encapsulates Myrtle Beach's fun-but-migraine-inducing spirit, with ropes courses,

laser tag and various beeping, flashing 'science exhibits' such as an 'anti-gravity chamber.'

Broadway at the Beach MALL, LANDMARK
(www.broadwayatthebeach.com; 1325 Celebrity Circle) With shops, restaurants, nightclubs, rides and an IMAX theater, this is Myrtle Beach's nerve center.

Family Kingdom AMUSEMENT PARK
(www.family-kingdom.com; combo pass $35;) An old-fashioned amusement-and-water-park combo overlooking the ocean. Hours vary by season; it's closed in winter.

Sleeping

Hundreds of hotels, ranging from retro family-run motor inns to vast resort complexes, have prices that vary widely by season; a room might cost $30 in January and more than $150 in July. The following are high-season rates.

Serendipity Inn INN $$
(800-762-3229; www.serendipityinn.com; 407 71st Ave N; r incl breakfast $89-109; P) The closest thing to a B&B in resort-crazed Myrtle Beach, this intimate Spanish-style inn hides from the city's buzz on a quiet side street. Rooms, done up with florals and knickknacks, are comfy but not fancy.

Myrtle Beach State Park CAMPGROUND $$
(843-238-5325; www.southcarolinaparks.com; tent & RV sites $21-25, cabins & apts $65-176; P) Most campgrounds are veritable parking lots catering to families with RVs, but the best camping is found in the shady sites of this state park, 3 miles south of central Myrtle Beach.

Breakers RESORT $$
(800-952-4507; www.breakers.com; 2006 N Ocean Blvd; r $112-195; P) This long-standing megaresort has three towers of crisp, summery-yellow suites, with only-in-Myrtle-Beach amenities like a pirate-ship swimming pool and a pirate-themed bar.

Eating

The thousands of restaurants are mostly high-volume and middlebrow – think buffets longer than bowling alleys and 24-hour doughnut shops. Ironically, good seafood is hard to come by; locals go to the nearby fishing village of **Murrells Inlet**.

Prosser's BBQ SOUTHERN $$
(3750 Business Hwy 17; buffet lunch/dinner $7.50/13; 6am-8:30pm;) Your best bet on Murrells Inlet's 'restaurant row,' homey Prosser's has a gut-busting buffet of fried fish and chicken, sweet potatoes, mac 'n' cheese, and vinegary pulled pork. Hours vary by season. Worth the drive.

Duffy Street Seafood Shack SEAFOOD $$
(www.duffyst.com; 202 Main St, North Myrtle Beach; mains $8-20; 4pm-late) This place has a divey, peanut-shells-on-the-floor ambience and a raw bar 'happy hour' with 30¢ shrimp.

Drinking & Entertainment

TOP CHOICE **Fat Harold's Beach Club** DANCE
(www.fatharolds.com; 212 Main St, North Myrtle Beach) It's a gas to watch the graying beach bums groove to doo-wop and old-time rock and roll at this North Myrtle institution, which calls itself 'Home of the Shag.' The dance, that is. Free shag lessons are offered at 7pm every Tuesday.

Carolina Opry MUSICAL THEATER
(843-913-1400; www.thecarolinaopry.com; 8901a Business 17 N; 8pm Mon-Sat) Has glittery musicals and variety shows. Tickets from $35.

Information

Chapin Memorial Library (400 14th Ave N) Internet access.

Visitor center (843-626-7444, 800-496-8250; www.myrtlebeachinfo.com; 1200 N Oak St; 8:30am-5pm Mon-Fri, 10am-2pm Sat) Has loads of maps and brochures.

Getting There & Around

The traffic coming and going on Hwy 17 Business/Kings Hwy can be infuriating. To avoid 'the

MEXICAN HAT DANCE

Yes, that's a giant sombrero rising above I-95 on the North Carolina–South Carolina state line. *Bienvenidos* to **South of the Border**, a Mexican-flavored monument to American kitsch. Begun in the 1950s as a fireworks stand – pyrotechnics are illegal in North Carolina – it's since morphed into a combo rest stop, souvenir mall, motel and (mostly defunct) amusement park, promoted on hundreds of billboards by a wildly stereotypical Mexican cartoon character named Pedro. Stop for a photo, some taffy, and a key chain that pees when you squeeze it.

Strand' altogether, stay on the Hwy 17 bypass, or take Hwy 31/Carolina Bays Pkwy, which parallels Hwy 17 between Hwy 501 and Hwy 9.

Myrtle Beach International Airport (MYR; ☎843-448-1589; 1100 Jetport Rd) is located within the city limits, as is the **Greyhound** (511 7th Ave N) station.

AROUND MYRTLE BEACH

Fifteen minutes down I-17 is **Pawleys Island**, a narrow strip of pastel sea cottages that's worlds away from the neon of Myrtle Beach. There's not much to do here but kayak and fish, but that's just fine. Another 15 minutes will bring you to mellow **Georgetown**, South Carolina's third-oldest city. Have lunch on Front St, with photogenic 19th-century storefronts overlooking the water, or use it as a quiet jumping-off point for exploring the Francis Marion National Forest.

Columbia

South Carolina's state capital is a quiet place, with wide, shady streets and the kind of old-fashioned downtown where pillbox hats are still on display in the windows of family-run department stores. The University of South Carolina adds a youthful vibe, and college students whoop it up over basketball wins in campus-side bars. Though Columbia is a pleasant stop, most visitors, like General Sherman's troops, charge on through to the coast.

The grand, Corinthian-columned **State House** (www.scstatehouse.gov; 1100 Gervais St; admission free; ⏲9am-5pm Mon-Fri, 10am-5pm Sat) has bronze stars on its west side to mark the impacts from Northern troops' cannonballs.

The **South Carolina State Museum** (www.museum.state.sc.us; 301 Gervais St; adult/child $7/3; ⏲10am-5pm Tue-Sat, 1-5pm Sun) is housed in an 1894 textile factory building, one of the world's first electrically powered mills. Exhibits on science, technology and the state's cultural and natural history make a nice activity for a rainy day.

For eating and entertainment, head down Gervais St to the Vista, a hip renovated warehouse district popular with young professionals. For coffee and cheap ethnic food, mingle with USC students in Five Points, where Harden, Greene and Devine Sts meet Saluda Ave. Stop at popular new **Pawley's Front Porch** (www.pawleys5pts.com; 827 Harden St; mains $7-10; ⏲11:30am-10pm) to try a pimento cheeseburger (a burger topped with a cheese, mayonnaise and red pepper mixture), Columbia's answer to New York's pizza slice or Chicago's hot dog.

There are plenty of chain hotels off I-26. In Five Points, the 28-room **Inn at Claussen's** (☎803-765-0440; www.theinnatclaussens.com; 2003 Greene St; r $112-154; 📶) gamely attempts a boutique art-deco look, with modest success.

TENNESSEE

Most states have one official state song. Tennessee has seven. And that's not just a random fact – Tennessee has music deep within its soul. Here, the folk music of the Scots-Irish in the eastern mountains com-

EXPLORING SOUTH CAROLINA SWAMPS

Inky-black water, dyed with tannic acid leached from decaying plant matter. Bone-white cypress stumps like the femurs of long-dead giants. Spanish moss as dry and gray as witches' hair. There's nothing like hiking or canoeing through one of South Carolina's unearthly swamps to make you feel like a character in a Southern Gothic novel.

About 45 minutes from Charleston, **Beidler Forest** (www.beidlerforest.com; 336 Sanctuary Rd, Harleyville; ⏲9am-5pm Tue-Sun; adult/child $8/4) is a spooky 1800 acres of cypress swamp managed by the Audubon Society, who lead springtime weekend canoe trips (adult/child $30/15).

Near Columbia, the 22,000-acre **Congaree National Park** (www.nps.gov/cong; 100 National Park Rd, Hopkins; ⏲8:30am-5pm), America's largest contiguous, old-growth floodplain forest, has camping and free ranger-led canoe trips (reserve in advance; ☎803-776-4396). Casual day-trippers can wander the 2.4-mile elevated boardwalk.

Between Charleston and Myrtle Beach, **Francis Marion National Forest** (5821 Hwy 17 N, Awendaw) has 259,000 acres of black-water creeks, camping, and hiking trails, including the 42-mile Palmetto Trail, which runs along old logging routes. Charleston-based **Nature Adventures Outfitters** (☎843-568-3222; www.natureadventuresoutfitters.com; adult/child half-day $55/39) leads kayak and canoe trips.

bined with the bluesy rhythms of the African Americans in the western Delta to give birth to the modern country music that makes Nashville famous.

These three geographic regions, represented by the three stars on the Tennessee flag, have their own unique beauty: the heather-colored peaks of the Great Smoky Mountains descend into lush green valleys in the central plateau around Nashville and then onto the hot, sultry lowlands near Memphis.

In Tennessee you can hike shady mountain trails in the morning, and by evening whoop it up in a Nashville honky-tonk or walk the streets of Memphis with Elvis' ghost.

From country churches where snake handlers still speak in tongues, to modern cities where record execs wear their sunglasses even at night, Tennesseans are a zesty lot.

History

Spanish settlers first explored Tennessee in 1539 and French traders were plying the rivers by the 17th century. Virginian pioneers soon established their own settlement and fought the British in the American Revolution. Tennessee joined the United States as the 16th state in 1796, taking its named from the Cherokee town of Tanasi.

The Cherokee themselves were brutally booted from their homes, along with many other Tennessee tribes, in the mid-1800s and marched west along the Trail of Tears.

Tennessee was the second-to-last Southern state to secede during the Civil War, and many important battles were fought here. Immediately following the war, six Confederate veterans from the town of Pulaski formed the infamous Ku Klux Klan to disenfranchise and terrorize the newly free blacks.

Major industries today are textiles, tobacco, cattle and chemicals, with tourism, especially in Nashville and Memphis, raking in hundreds of millions of dollars a year.

Information

Department of Environment & Conservation (☎888-867-2757; www.state.tn.us/environment/parks) Check out this well-organized website for camping (prices range from free to $27 or more), hiking and fishing info for Tennessee's more than 50 state parks.

Department of Tourist Development (☎615-741-2159, 800-462-8366; www.tnvacation.com; 312 8th Ave N, Nashville) Has welcome centers at the state borders.

TENNESSEE FACTS

» **Nickname** Volunteer State

» **Population** 6.3 million

» **Area** 41,217 sq miles

» **Capital city** Nashville (population 630,000)

» **Other cities** Memphis (population 650,000)

» **Sales tax** 7%, plus local taxes of up to about 15%

» **Birthplace of** frontiersman Davy Crockett (1786–1836), soul diva Aretha Franklin (b 1942), singer Dolly Parton (b 1946)

» **Home of** Graceland, Grand Ole Opry, Jack Daniel's distillery

» **Politics** pretty darn conservative, with liberal hot spots in urban areas

» **Famous for** 'Tennessee Waltz,' country music, Tennessee walking horses

» **Odd law** in Tennessee, it's illegal to fire a gun at any wild game, other than whales, from a moving vehicle

» **Driving distances** Memphis to Nashville 213 miles, Nashville to Great Smoky Mountains National Park 223 miles

Memphis

Memphis doesn't just attract tourists. It draws pilgrims. Music-lovers come to lose themselves amid the throb of blues guitar on Beale St. Barbecue connoisseurs come to stuff themselves sick on smoky pulled pork and dry-rubbed ribs. Elvis fanatics fly in from London and Reykjavik and Osaka to worship at the altar of the King at Graceland. You could spend days hopping from one museum or historic site to another, stopping only for a spot o' barbecue, and leave happy.

But once you get away from the lights and the tourist buses, Memphis is a different place entirely. Named after the capital of ancient Egypt, it has a certain baroquely ruined quality that's both sad and beguiling. Poverty is rampant – Victorian mansions sit beside tumbledown shotgun shacks (a narrow style of house popular in the South), college campuses lie in the shadow of eerie abandoned factories, and whole neighborhoods seem to have been almost reclaimed by kudzu and honeysuckle vines.

But Memphis' wild river-town spirit reveals itself to visitors willing to look. Keep your eyes open and you'll find some of the country's strangest museums, most deliciously oddball restaurants (barbecued spaghetti, anyone?), spookiest cemeteries and craziest dive bars.

History

Union troops occupied Memphis during the Civil War, but the postwar collapse of the port city's cotton trade was far more devastating. After a yellow fever outbreak caused most whites to flee the city, Memphis was forced to declare bankruptcy. The African American community revived the town, led by Robert Church, a former slave. By the early 1900s Beale St was the hub of black social and civic activity, becoming an early center for what was to be known as blues music. In the '50s and '60s, local recording companies cut tracks for blues, soul, R & B and rockabilly artists such as Al Green, Johnny Cash and Elvis, cementing Memphis' place in the American music firmament.

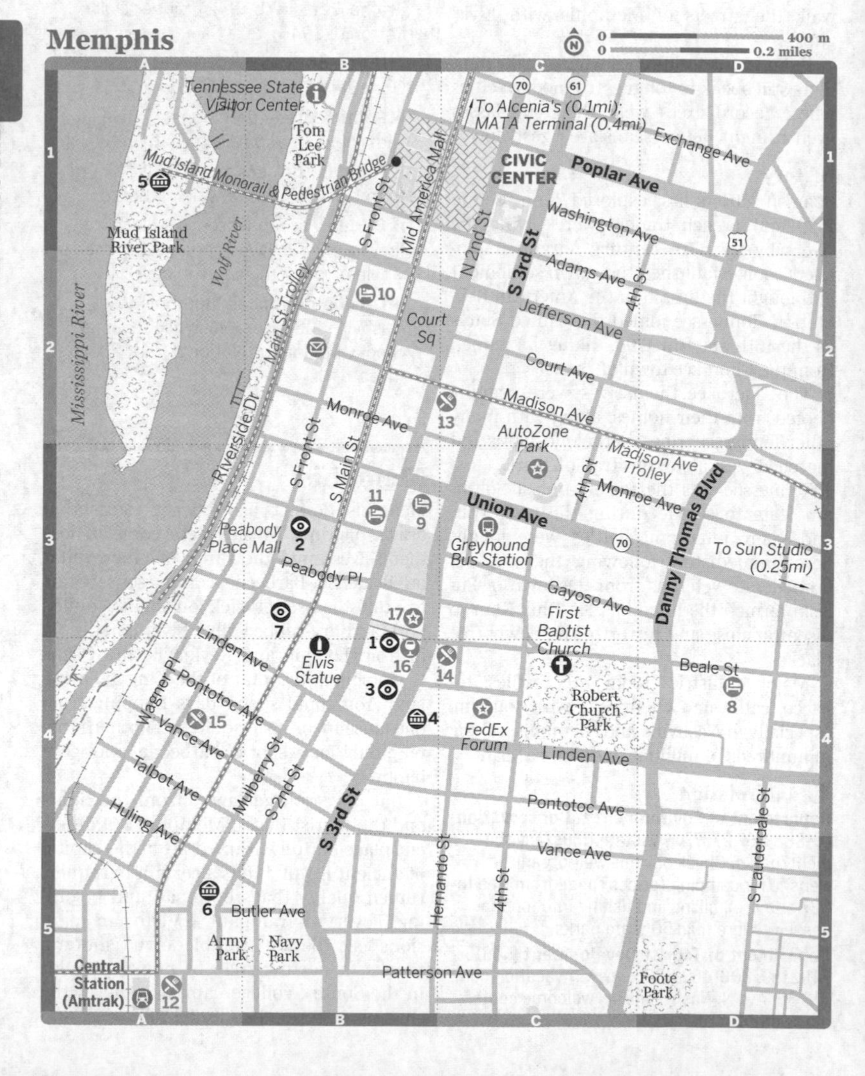

Sights & Activities

DOWNTOWN

TOP CHOICE **National Civil Rights Museum** MUSEUM

(www.civilrightsmuseum.org; 450 Mulberry St; adult/child $13/9.50; ⏲9am-5pm Mon & Wed-Sat, 1-5pm Sun Sep-May, to 6pm Jun-Aug) Housed in the Lorraine Motel, where the Reverend Dr Martin Luther King Jr was fatally shot on April 4, 1968, is the gut-wrenching National Civil Rights Museum. Five blocks south of Beale St, this museum's extensive exhibits, detailed timeline and accompanying audio-guide chronicle the ongoing struggles for African American freedom and equality in the US. Both Dr King's cultural contribution and his assassination serve as prisms for looking at the Civil Rights movement, its precursors and its indelible and continuing impact on American life. The turquoise exterior of the 1950s motel and two preserved interior rooms remain much as they were at the time of King's death, and serve as pilgrimage points in their own right.

FREE **Peabody Ducks** MARCHING DUCKS

(www.peabodymemphis.com; 11am & 5pm daily;) Every day at 11am sharp, five ducks file from the Peabody Hotel's gilded elevator, waddle across the red-carpeted lobby, and decamp in the marble lobby fountain for a day of happy splashing. The ducks make the reverse march at 5pm, when they retire to their penthouse accompanied by their red-coated Duckmaster. The march of the ducks, which dates back to a 1930s-era drunken prank, is a quintessential Memphis tradition. It always draws major crowds – get here early to secure your spot (the mezzanine has the best views).

Mud Island PARK, MUSEUM

(www.mudisland.com; park free; 125 N Front St; ⏲10am-5pm Tue-Sun Apr-Oct, later Jun-Aug;) A small peninsula jutting into the Mississippi, Mud Island is downtown Memphis' best-loved green space. The top part of the peninsula is a residential subdivision, while the bottom is home to the delightful **Mud Island River Park**. Hop the monorail ($4, or free with museum admission) or walk across the bridge to the park, where you can jog, rent bikes, or wade through a super-cool scale model of the Mississippi, which empties into a 1.3-million-gallon 'Gulf of Mexico' where visitors tool around in pedal boats. The park's **Mississippi River Museum** (adult/child $8/5; ⏲10am-5pm Apr-May & Sep-Oct, to 6pm Jun-Aug, closed Mon) has a cool full-size replica of a packet boat and other historical displays.

FREE **Center for Southern Folklore** ARTS CENTER

(☎901-525-3655; www.southernfolklore.com; 119 S Main St; ⏲11am-6pm Mon-Sat, to 5pm winter) A well-tended community space with a cafe, craft gallery and frequent (free!) local music performances and film screenings.

BEALE STREET

The pedestrian-only stretch of Beale St is a 24-hour carnival zone, where you'll find deep-fried funnel cakes, to-go beer counters, and music, music, music. Although locals don't hang out here much, visitors tend to get a kick out of the ribald, party-happy atmosphere.

Memphis

Sights

1 A Schwab's ... B4
2 Center for Southern Folklore ... B3
3 Gibson Beale Street Showcase ... B4
4 Memphis Rock 'n' Soul Museum ... B4
5 Mississippi River Museum ... A1
6 National Civil Rights Museum ... A5
7 Orpheum Theater ... B3
Peabody Ducks ... (see 9)

Sleeping

8 Inn at Hunt Phelan ... D4
9 Peabody Hotel ... B3
10 Sleep Inn at Court Square ... B2
11 Talbot Heirs ... B3

Eating

12 Arcade ... A5
13 Charlie Vergos' Rendezvous ... C2
14 Dyer's ... C4
15 Gus's World Famous Fried Chicken ... A4

Drinking

16 Silky O'Sullivan's ... B4

Entertainment

17 Rum Boogie ... B3

Shopping

Lansky Brothers ... (see 9)

Memphis Rock 'n' Soul Museum MUSEUM
(www.memphisrocknsoul.org; cnr Lt George W Lee Ave & 3rd St; adult/child $11/8; ⏲10am-7pm) The Smithsonian's museum, next to FedEx Forum, examines how African American and white music mingled in the Mississippi Delta to create modern sound. The audio tour has more than 100 songs.

Gibson Beale Street Showcase FACTORY TOUR
(www.gibson.com; 145 Lt George W Lee Ave; admission $10, no children under 5; ⏲tours 11am-4pm Mon-Sat, noon-4pm Sun) Take the fascinating 45-minute tour of this enormous place to see master craftspeople transform solid blocks of wood into legendary Gibson guitars. Tours leave on the hour.

Orpheum Theatre THEATER
(www.orpheum-memphis.com; 203 S Main St) Originally built for vaudeville, the Orpheum has been restored to its glittering 1928 glory. Today you can catch big comedy and Broadway shows; but beware – the ghost of a pigtailed little girl named Mary is said to giggle eerily between acts. Tours available – call ahead (☎901-525-7800).

A Schwab's HISTORIC STORE
(163 Beale St; ☎9am-5pm Mon-Sat) The original dry-goods store has three floors of voodoo powders, $1 neckties and Elvis shot glasses.

EAST OF DOWNTOWN

TOP CHOICE Sun Studio STUDIO TOUR
(www.sunstudio.com; 706 Union Ave; adult/child $12/free; ⏲10am-6pm) It doesn't look like much from outside, but this dusty storefront is ground zero for American rock and roll music. Starting in the early 1950s, Sun's Sam Phillips recorded blues artists such as Howlin' Wolf, BB King and Ike Turner, followed by the rockabilly dynasty of Jerry Lee Lewis, Johnny Cash, Roy Orbison and, of course, the King himself (who started here in 1953). Today packed 40-minute guided tours through the tiny studio offer a chance to hear original tapes of historic recording sessions. Guides are witty and full of anecdotes; many are musicians themselves. Pose for photos in the old recording studio on the 'X' where Elvis once stood, or buy a CD of the 'Million Dollar Quartet,' Sun's spontaneous 1956 jam session between Elvis, Johnny Cash, Carl Perkins and Jerry Lee Lewis.

From here, you can hop on the studio's free shuttle (hourly, starting at 11:15am), which does a loop between Sun Studio, Beale St and Graceland.

Pink Palace Museum & Planetarium MUSEUM, PLANETARIUM
(www.memphismuseums.org; 3050 Central Ave; adult/child $9.75/6.25, ⏲9am-5pm Mon-Sat, noon-5pm Sun) The 1923 building was built as a residence for Piggly Wiggly founder Clarence Saunders and opened in 1996 as a natural- and cultural-history museum. It mixes fossils, Civil War exhibits and a replica of the original 1916 Piggly Wiggly, the world's first self-service grocery store.

Children's Museum of Memphis MUSEUM
(www.cmom.com; 2525 Central Ave; admission $10; ⏲9am-5pm; 👪) Gives the kids a chance to let loose and play in, on and with exhibits such as an airplane cockpit, tornado generator and waterwheel.

OVERTON PARK

Off Poplar Ave in Midtown, stately homes surround Overton Park, a 342-acre rolling green oasis in the middle of this often gritty city. If Beale St is Memphis' heart, then Overton Park is its lungs.

Memphis Zoo ZOO
(www.memphiszoo.org; 2000 Prentiss Pl; adult/child $15/10; ⏲9am-4pm Mar-Oct, to 4pm Nov-Feb; 👪) At the park's northwestern corner, this world-class zoo hosts two giant panda stars, Ya Ya and Le Le, in a $16-million exhibit on native Chinese wildlife and habitat. Other residents include the full gamut of monkeys, polar bears, penguins, eagles, sea lions and so on. Imagine an animal, the zoo probably has it.

Brooks Museum of Art GALLERY
(www.brooksmuseum.org; 1934 Poplar Ave; adult/child $7/3; ⏲10am-4pm Wed-Sat, to 8pm Thu, 11am-5pm Sun) At the park's western fringe, this well-regarded art museum has an excellent permanent collection encompassing everything from Renaissance sculpture to Impressionists (eg Renoir) to abstract expressionists (eg Robert Motherwell).

Levitt Shell AMPHITHEATER
(www.levittshell.org) This historic band shell was the site of Elvis' first concert, in 1954. Today the mod-looking white shell hosts free concerts all summer.

SOUTH OF DOWNTOWN

TOP CHOICE Graceland ELVIS' HOUSE
(☎901-332-3322, 800-238-2000; www.elvis.com; Elvis Presley Blvd/US 51; tours adult/child house-

only $31/14, full $35/17; ⊙9am-5pm Mon-Sat, to 4pm Sun, shorter hr & closed Tue winter) If you only make one stop in Memphis, it ought to be here: the sublimely kitschy, gloriously bizarre home of the King of Rock and Roll.

Though born in Mississippi, Elvis Presley was a true son of Memphis, raised in the Lauderdale Courts public housing projects, inspired by the blues in the Beale St clubs, and discovered at Sun Studio on Union Ave. In the spring of 1957, the already-famous 22-year-old spent $100,000 on a Colonial-style mansion, named Graceland by its previous owners. Priscilla Presley (who divorced Elvis in 1973) opened Graceland to tours in 1982, and now millions come here to pay homage to the King and gawk at the infamous decor. The King himself had the place redecorated in 1974; with a 15ft couch, fake waterfall, yellow vinyl walls and green shag-carpet ceiling – it's a virtual textbook of ostentatious '70s style. Elvis died here (in the upstairs bathroom) from heart failure in 1977. Throngs of fans still weep at his grave, next to the swimming pool out back.

You begin your tour at the high-tech visitor plaza on the other side of seedy Elvis Presley Blvd. Book ahead in the busy season to ensure a prompt tour time. The basic self-guided mansion tour comes with a headset audio narration with the voices of Elvis, Priscilla and Lisa Marie. Buy a package to see the entire estate, or pay extra for additional attractions: several clothing museums, the car museum, and two custom airplanes (check out the blue-and-gold private bathroom on the *Lisa Marie*, a Convair 880 Jet). Parking costs $10.

Graceland is 9 miles south of downtown on US 51, also called 'Elvis Presley Blvd.' Nondrivers can take bus 43 from downtown, or hop on the free Sun Studio shuttle.

Stax Museum of American Soul Music MUSEUM
(www.staxmuseum.com; 926 E McLemore Ave; adult/child $12/9; ⊙10am-5pm Mon-Sat, 1-5pm Sun Mar-Oct, closed Mon Nov-Mar) Wanna get funky? Head directly to Soulsville USA, where this 17,000-sq-ft museum sits on the site of the old Stax recording studio. This venerable spot was soul music's epicenter in the 1960s, when Otis Redding, Booker T and the MGs and Wilson Pickett recorded here. Dive into soul-music history with photos, displays of '60s and '70s peacock clothing and, above all, Isaac Hayes' 1972 Superfly Cadillac outfitted with shag-fur carpeting and 24-carat-gold exterior trim.

Full Gospel Tabernacle Church CHURCH
(www.algreenmusic.com; 787 Hale Rd; ⊙services 11:30am & 4pm Sun) If you're in town on a Sunday, put on your least-wrinkled pants and head to services at South Memphis, where soul music legend turned reverend Al Green presides over a powerful choir. Visitors are welcome, and usually take up about half the pews. Join in the whooping 'hallelujahs,' but don't forget the tithe (about $1 is fine). Green is not around every single weekend, but the services are a fascinating cultural experience nonetheless.

Tours

TOP CHOICE **American Dream Safari** DRIVING TOUR
(☎901-527-8870; www.americandreamsafari.com; walking tour per person $15, driving tours per vehicle from $125) Southern culture junkie Tad Pierson shows you the quirky, personal side of Memphis – juke joints, gospel churches, eerie decaying buildings – on foot or by car (in his pink Cadillac). Ask about day trips to the Delta and special photography tours.

Memphis Rock Tours DRIVING TOUR
(☎901-359-3102; www.shangrilaprojects.com; 2-person tour $75) Quirky custom tours of music sites and local restaurants.

Blues City Tours BUS TOUR
(☎901-522-9229; www.bluescitytours.com; adult/child from $24/16) A variety of bus tours, including an Elvis tour.

Memphis Riverboats BOAT TOUR
(☎901-527-5694, 800-221-6197; www.memphisriverboats.net; adult/child from $20/10) Sightseeing and dinner cruises on the Mississippi.

Festivals & Events

International Blues Challenge MUSIC
(www.blues.org) Sponsored by the Blues Foundation, each January/February blues acts do battle in front of a panel of judges.

Memphis in May CULTURAL
(www.memphisinmay.org) Every Friday, Saturday and Sunday in May something's cookin', whether it's the Beale St Music Festival, the barbecue contest or the grand finale sunset symphony.

Mid-South Fair FAIR
(www.midsouthfair.org) Since 1856, folks come out each September to this combo amusement park and agricultural fair.

Sleeping

Cheap and ultracheap chain motels lie off I-40, exit 279, across the river in West Memphis, AR. Prices jump during the Memphis in May festival.

DOWNTOWN

TOP CHOICE **Talbot Heirs** GUESTHOUSE $$
(901-527-9772, 800-955-3956; www.talbothouse.com; 99 S 2nd St; ste from $130;) Inconspicuously located on the 2nd floor of a busy downtown street, this cheerful guesthouse is one of Memphis' best kept and most unique secrets. Suites are more like studio apartments than hotel rooms, with Oriental rugs and funky local artwork, and kitchens stocked with snacks. Innkeepers Tom and Sandy know all the best local restaurants and bars – just ask. Parking costs $10.

Peabody Hotel HOTEL $$$
(901-529-4000; www.peabodymemphis.com; 149 Union Ave; r from $209;) The Mississippi Delta's most storied hotel, the Peabody has been catering to a Who's Who of Southern gentry since the 1860s. The hotel's current incarnation, a 13-story Italian Renaissance Revival-style building, dates to the 1920s. The Peabody continues to be a social center, with a spa, shops, various restaurants and a fabulously atmospheric marble-and-gold lobby bar. The daily march of the lobby fountain's resident mallard ducks (p353) is a legendary Memphis tradition.

Inn at Hunt Phelan B&B $$
(901-525-8225; www.huntphelan.com; 533 Beale St; r from $155; P) Outside the gates are dystopian warehouses and vacant lots. But inside the gates it's still 1828, the year this aristocratic mansion was built. Sip complimentary evening cocktails by the courtyard fountain and wander the 4.5-acre gardens before retiring to your four-poster bed (or heading to the Beale St bars, just down the road).

Sleep Inn at Court Square HOTEL $$
(901-522-9700; www.sleepinn.com; 400 N Front St; r from $110;) Our pick of the cheaper downtown digs, this stubby stucco box has pleasant, airy rooms with flat screen TVs. Parking is $12.

MIDTOWN

TOP CHOICE **Pilgrim House Hostel** HOSTEL $
(901-273-8341; 1000 S Cooper St; dm/r $15/30; P@) Yes, it's in a church. No, no one will try to convert you but the chatty young live-in staff may well invite you for a beer down the street, in Midtown's trendy Cooper-Young neighborhood. An international crowd plays cards and chats (no alcohol) in a sunny, open common area resembling an IKEA catalog. Dorms and private rooms are clean and spare. All guests must do a brief daily chore, like taking out the trash.

GRACELAND AREA

Heartbreak Hotel HOTEL $$
(901-332-1000, 877-777-0606; www.elvis.com/epheartbreakhotel/; 3677 Elvis Presley Blvd; d from $112; P@) At the end of Lonely St (seriously) across from Graceland, this basic hotel is tarted up with all things Elvis. Ramp up the kitsch with one of the themed suites, such as the red-velvet monstrosity that is the Burnin' Love room.

Memphis Graceland RV Park & Campground CAMPGROUND $
(901-396-7125; www.elvis.com; 3691 Elvis Presley Blvd; tent sites/cabins from $23/42; P) Next to Graceland and owned by Elvis Presley Enterprises. Keep Lisa Marie in business when you camp out or sleep in the no-frills log cabins (with shared bathrooms).

Days Inn Graceland MOTEL $
(901-346-5500; www.daysinn.com; 3839, Elvis Presley Blvd; r from $85; P) With a guitar-shaped pool, 24-hour Elvis channel, and neon Cadillacs on the roof, the Days Inn manages to out-Elvis the neighboring Heartbreak Hotel. Guest rooms themselves are clean but nothing special.

Eating

Locals come to blows over which of the city's chopped-pork sandwiches or dry-rubbed ribs are the best. Barbecue joints are scattered across the city; the ugliest exteriors often yield the tastiest goods. Beale St is lined with corporate barbecue and soul-food joints; few are worth the crowds or the price. Hip young locals head to the South Main Arts District or Midtown's Cooper-Young neighborhood for dinner and drinks.

DOWNTOWN

TOP CHOICE **Gus's World Famous Fried Chicken** CHICKEN $
(901-527-4877; 310 S Front St; mains $5-9; 11am-9pm Sun-Thu, to 10pm Fri & Sat) Fried-chicken connoisseurs across the globe twitch in their sleep at night, dreaming about the gossamer-light fried chicken at this down-

town concrete bunker. On busy nights, waits can top an hour. So worth it.

Alcenia's SOUTHERN $

(alcenias.com; 317 N Main St; mains $6-9; ⏲11am-5pm Tue-Fri, 9am-3pm Sat) The only thing sweeter than Alcenia's famous 'ghetto juice' (a diabetes-inducing fruit drink) is owner Betty-Joyce 'BJ' Chester-Tamayo – don't be surprised to receive a kiss on the top of the head as soon as you sit down. The lunch menu at this funky little gold- and purple-painted cafe rotates daily – look for killer fried chicken and catfish, melt-in-your-mouth spiced cabbage and an exquisite eggy custard pie.

Charlie Vergos' Rendezvous BARBECUE $$

(☎901-523-2746; www.hogsfly.com; 52 S 2nd St; mains $7-18; ⏲4:30-10:30pm Tue-Thu, 11am-11pm Fri & Sat) Tucked in an alleyway off Union Ave, this subterranean institution sells an astonishing 5 tons of its exquisite dry-rubbed ribs weekly. Friendly service and walls plastered with historic memorabilia make eating here an event. Expect a wait.

Arcade DINER $

(www.arcaderestaurant.com; 540 S Main St; mains $6-8; ⏲7am-3pm, plus dinner Fri) Elvis used to eat at this ultra-retro diner, Memphis' oldest. Crowds still pack in for sweet-potato pancakes and cheeseburgers.

Dyer's FAST FOOD $

(www.dyersonbeale.com; 205 Beale St; mains $6-8; ⏲11am-1am Sun-Thu, to 5am Fri & Sat) Dyer's legendary deep-fried burgers, fried using the same (continuously filtered) cooking grease since 1912, will sound far less disgusting when it's 3am and you've been sucking back beers on Beale St all night.

EAST OF DOWNTOWN

TOP CHOICE **Cozy Corner** BARBECUE $$

(www.cozycornerbbq.com; 745 N Pkwy; mains $5-16; ⏲10:30am-5pm Tue-Sat, later in summer) Slouch in a torn vinyl booth and devour an entire barbecued Cornish game hen, the house specialty at this pug-ugly cult favorite. Ribs and wings are spectacular too, and the fluffy, silken sweet-potato pie is an A-plus specimen of the classic Southern dessert.

Restaurant Iris NEW SOUTHERN $$$

(☎901-590-2828; www.restaurantiris.com; 2146 Monroe Ave; mains $23-34; ⏲5-10pm Mon-Sat, Sun brunch 3rd Sun each month) Chef Kelly English richly deserved his recent James Beard Award nomination, one of a pile of accolades he's accumulated since opening Iris in 2008. His avant-garde Creole menu sends foodies into paroxysms of delight, with playful dishes like a 'knuckle sandwich' of tarragon-flecked lobster, or an oyster-stuffed steak 'surf 'n' turf.' The setting, in a turreted cottage on a residential Midtown block, is so low-profile it feels like a speakeasy.

Sweet Grass SOUTHERN $$

(☎901-278-0278; www.sweetgrassmemphis.com; 937 S Cooper St; mains $16-23; ⏲5:30pm-late Tue-Sun, 11am-2pm Sun) Contemporary Low County cuisine (the seafood-heavy cooking of the South Carolina and Georgia coasts) wins raves at this sleek new Midtown bistro. Shrimp and grits, a classic fisherman's breakfast, is a crowd-pleaser.

Bar-B-Q Shop BARBECUE $$

(www.dancingpigs.com; 1782 Madison Ave; mains $9-16; ⏲11am-8:45pm) Chopped pork on grilled Texas toast and barbecued spaghetti (just try it) are house favorites at this friendly neighborhood spot, whose spacious wooden booths are popular with families.

Payne's Bar-B-Q BARBECUE $

(1762 Lamar Ave; mains $4-6; ⏲11am-6:30pm Tue-Sat) We'd say this converted gas station has the best chopped-pork sandwich in town, but we don't want to have to fight anyone. Decide for yourself.

Drinking & Entertainment

Many Memphis restaurants and bars mix food, drinks and music, so it's easy to turn a meal into a party. Beale St is the obvious spot for live blues, country, rock and jazz. Cover for most clubs is free or only a few bucks. Beale St warms up early, and its bars are open all day, while neighborhood clubs tend to start filling up around 10pm. Last call for alcohol is 3am, but bars sometimes close earlier on quiet nights. Hip locals head to the Cooper-Young neighborhood for everything from margarita bars to Irish pubs. To find out what's up tonight, check the Memphis Flyer's online calendar (www.memphisflyer.com).

Bars

TOP CHOICE **Earnestine & Hazel's** BAR

(531 S Main St) One of the great dive bars has a 2nd floor full of rusty bedsprings and claw-foot tubs, remnants of its brothel past. Climb the creaky stairs to shoot the breeze with Nate, a courtly gentleman who regales you with tales of Memphis past as he pours you a Miller Lite – he works the upstairs bar

on weekends. The Soul Burger, the bar's only food, is the stuff of legend. Watch out for ghosts. Things heat up after midnight.

Cove BAR
(www.thecovememphis.com; 2559 Broad Ave) Far from the Beale St crowds, this hipster-ish new dive rocks a nautical theme while serving retro cocktails (sidecars, Singapore Slings) and upscale bar snacks (oysters on the half shell, chips with fresh anchovies). A good place to meet locals.

Silky O'Sullivan's BAR
(silkyosullivans.com; 183 Beale St) Party-happy youth swill 'divers' out of yellow plastic buckets while goats graze in the courtyard of this massive bizarro Beale St tavern.

Live Music

Wild Bill's BLUES
(1580 Vollentine Ave; ⌚10pm-late Fri & Sat) Don't even think of showing up at this gritty, hole-in-the-wall juke joint before midnight. Order a 40oz beer and a basket of wings then sit back to watch some of the greatest blues acts in Memphis. Expect some stares from the locals; it's worth it for the kickass, ultra-authentic jams.

TOP CHOICE **Hi-Tone Cafe** LIVE MUSIC
(www.hitonememphis.com; 1913 Poplar Ave) Near Overton Park, this unassuming little dive is one of the city's best places to hear live local bands and touring indie acts.

Young Avenue Deli LIVE MUSIC
(www.youngavenuedeli.com; 2119 Young Ave) This Midtown favorite has food, pool, live music and a hip, laid-back young crowd.

Rum Boogie BLUES
(www.rumboogie.com; 182 Beale St) Huge, popular and noisy, this Cajun-themed Beale club hops every night to the tunes of the house blues band.

Minglewood Hall CONCERT VENUE
(www.minglewoodhall.com; 1555 Madison) In a former bread factory, this new space is part concert venue, part tattoo studio, part cafe.

Shopping

Beale St abounds with cheesy souvenir shops, while Cooper-Young is the place for boutiques and bookshops.

Lanksy Brothers CLOTHING
(149 Union Ave) The 'Clothier to the King,' this mid-century men's shop once outfitted Elvis with his two-tone shirts. Today it has a retro line of menswear, plus gifts and women's clothes. In the Peabody Hotel.

Burke's Book Store BOOKS
(936 S Cooper St) A delightfully disorganized 122-year-old bookshop, with an emphasis on Southern literature.

Memphis Flea Market MARKET
(777 Walnut Grove Rd, at The Agricenter) Nicknamed 'The Big One,' this 1000-plus vendor junque and antiques extravaganza is held on the third Saturday and Sunday of each month.

Information

Almost all hotels, and many restaurants, have free wi-fi.

Commercial Appeal (www.commercialappeal.com) Daily newspaper.

Main post office (555 S 3rd St)

Memphis Flyer (www.memphisflyer.com) Free weekly distributed on Thursday; has entertainment listings.

Police station (☎901-545-2677; 545 S Main St)

Public library (33 S Front St; ⌚10am-5pm Mon-Fri) Computers with free internet access.

Regional Medical Center (☎901-545-7100; 877 Jefferson Ave) Has the only level-one trauma center in the region.

Tennessee State Visitor Center (☎901-543-5333, 888-633-9099; www.memphistravel.com; 119 N Riverside Dr; ⌚9am-5pm Nov-Mar, to 6pm Apr-Oct) Brochures for the whole state.

Getting There & Around

Memphis International Airport (MEM; ☎901-922-8000; www.memphisairport.org; 2491 Winchester Rd) is 12 miles southeast of downtown via I-55; taxis to downtown cost about $30.

Memphis Area Transit Authority (www.matatransit.com; 444 N Main St; fares $1.50) operates local buses; 2A and 32A go to the airport.

MATA's vintage **trolleys** ($1, every 12 minutes) ply Main St and Front St downtown. **Greyhound** (www.greyhound.com; 203 Union Ave) is right downtown, as is **Central Station** (www.amtrak.com; 545 S Main St), the Amtrak terminal.

Shiloh National Military Park

'No soldier who took part in the two days' engagement at Shiloh ever spoiled for a fight again,' said one veteran of the bloody 1862 battle, which took place among these lovely fields and forests. During the fight 3400 soldiers died, and the Confederate forces were eventually repelled by the Union.

The **Shiloh National Military Park** (www.nps.gov/shil; per vehicle $5; ⌚park dawn-dusk, visitor center 8am-5pm) is located just north of the Mississippi border near the town of Crump, TN. The visitor center gives out maps and shows a video about the battle, and sells an audio tour.

The vast park can only be seen by car. Sights along the route include the Shiloh National Cemetery, an overlook of the Cumberland River where Union reinforcement troops arrived by ship, and various markers and monuments.

Nashville

Imagine you're an aspiring country singer arriving in downtown Nashville after days of hitchhiking, with nothing but your battered guitar on your back. Gaze up at the neon lights of Lower Broadway, take a deep breath of smoky, beer-perfumed air, feel the boot-stompin' rumble from deep inside the crowded honky-tonks, and say to yourself 'I've made it.'

For country-music fans and wannabe songwriters all over the world, a trip to Nashville is the ultimate pilgrimage. Think of any song involving a pickup truck, a bottle of booze, a no-good woman or a late, lamented hound dog, and chances are it came from Nashville. Since the 1920s the city has been attracting musicians who have taken the country genre from the 'hillbilly music' of the early 20th century to the slick 'Nashville sound' of the 1960s to the punk-tinged alt-country of the 1990s.

Nashville has many attractions to keep you busy, from the Country Music Hall of Fame and the revered Grand Ole Opry House to rough blues bars, historic buildings and big-name sports. It also has friendly people, a lively university community, excellent fried chicken and an unrivaled assortment of tacky souvenirs.

History

In 1925, this river port became known for its live-music radio program *Barn Dance,* later nicknamed the *Grand Ole Opry.* Its popularity soared, the city proclaimed itself the 'country-music capital of the world' and recording studios sprang up in Music Row.

Today Nashville is the second most populous city in Tennessee, with more than a dozen colleges and universities and an economy based on music, tourism, health care and publishing.

DON'T MISS

NASHVILLE'S TOP EXPERIENCES

» Watching the singin', stompin', fiddlin' extravaganza at the venerable **Grand Ole Opry** (p362)

» Feasting on diabolically spicy fried chicken at 3am at **Prince's Hot Chicken** (p364)

» Whooping it up at **Tootsie's Orchid Lounge** (p366), the grandmama of all honky-tonks

» Shopping for vintage cowboy boots at **Katy K's Ranch Dressing** (p363)

» Admiring Elvis' gold Caddy and other treasures at the vast **Country Music Hall of Fame** (p359)

Sights & Activities

Nashville sits on a rise beside the Cumberland River, with the state capitol situated at the highest point.

DOWNTOWN

The historic 2nd Ave N business area was the center of the cotton trade in the 1870s and 1880s, when most of the Victorian warehouses were built; note the cast-iron and masonry facades. Today it's the heart of the **District**, with shops, restaurants, underground saloons and nightclubs. Two blocks west, **Printers Alley** is a narrow cobblestoned lane known for its nightlife since the 1940s. Along the Cumberland River, Riverfront Park is a landscaped promenade featuring **Fort Nashborough**, a 1930s replica of the city's original outpost.

TOP CHOICE **Country Music Hall of Fame & Museum** MUSEUM

(www.countrymusichalloffame.com; 222 5th Ave S; adult/child $22/15; ⌚9am-5pm) 'Honor Thy Music' is the catchphrase of this monumental museum, reflecting the near-biblical importance of country music to Nashville's soul. See case upon case of artifacts including Patsy Cline's cocktail gown, Johnny Cash's guitar, Elvis' gold Cadillac and Conway Twitty's yearbook picture (back when he was Harold Jenkins). There are written

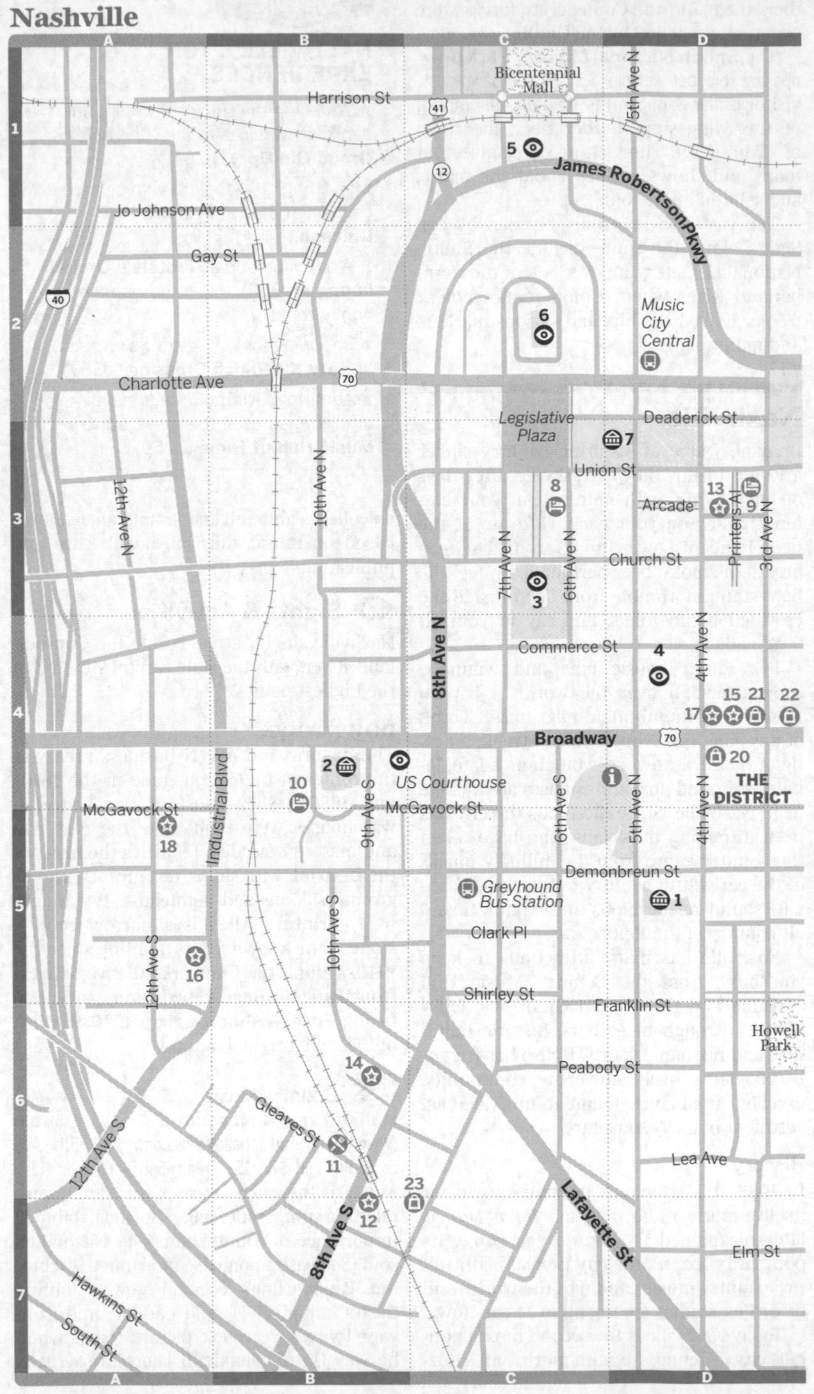

Bicentennial Mall
Harrison St
5th Ave N
5
James Robertson Pkwy
Jo Johnson Ave
Gay St
6
Music City Central
Charlotte Ave
Legislative Plaza
Deaderick St
7
Union St
8
13
9
Arcade
Printers Al
3rd Ave N
12th Ave N
10th Ave N
7th Ave N
6th Ave N
Church St
3
Commerce St
4
8th Ave N
4th Ave N
15
21
22
17
Broadway
2
US Courthouse
20
THE DISTRICT
10
McGavock St
18
Industrial Blvd
9th Ave S
6th Ave S
5th Ave N
Demonbreun St
Greyhound Bus Station
1
10th Ave S
Clark Pl
16
12th Ave S
Shirley St
Franklin St
Howell Park
14
Peabody St
Gleaves St
11
12th Ave S
Lea Ave
23
12
8th Ave S
Lafayette St
Elm St
Hawkins St
South St

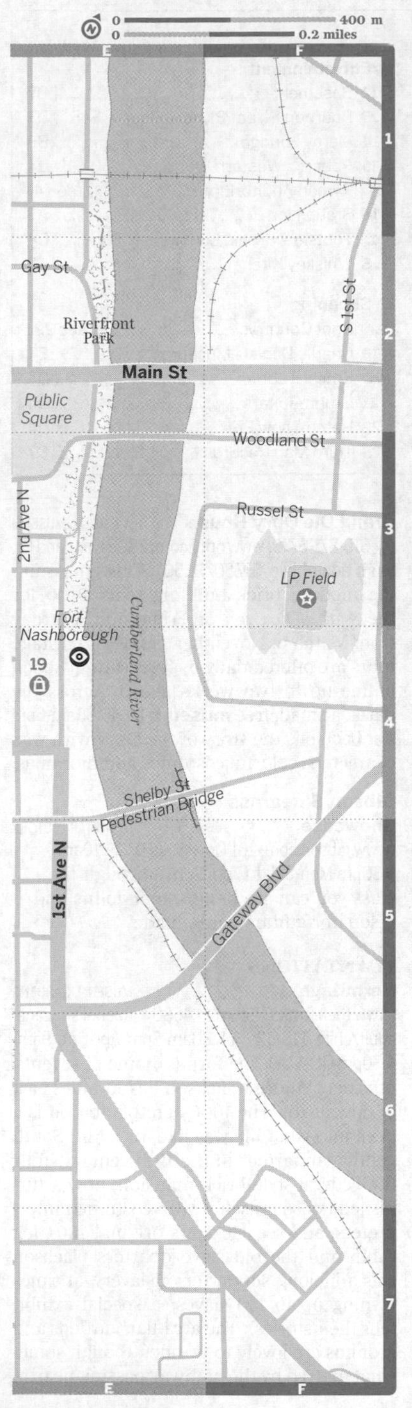

exhibits tracing country's roots, computer touch screens to allow access to recordings and photos from the Country Music Foundation's enormous archives and walk-in listening booths. The fact- and music-filled **audio tour** (additional $5) is narrated by contemporary country musicians. From here you can also take the **Studio B Tour** (1hr tour adult/child $13/11), which shuttles you to Radio Corporation of America's (RCA's) famed Music Row studio, where Elvis recorded 'Are You Lonesome Tonight?' and Dolly Parton cut 'I Will Always Love You.'

Ryman Auditorium HISTORIC BUILDING
(www.ryman.com; 116 5th Ave N; self-guided tour adult/child $13/6.50, backstage tour $17/10.50; ⏲9am-4pm) The so-called 'Mother Church of Country Music' has hosted a laundry list of 20th-century performers, from Martha Graham to Elvis to Katherine Hepburn to Bob Dylan. The soaring brick tabernacle was built in 1890 by wealthy riverboat captain Thomas Ryman to house religious revivals, and watching a show from one of its 2000 seats can still be described as a spiritual experience. The *Grand Ole Opry* took place here for 31 years, until it moved out to the Opryland complex in Music Valley in 1974. Today the *Opry* returns to the Ryman during winter.

Tennessee State Capitol HISTORIC BUILDING
(Charlotte Ave; tours free; ⏲tours 9am-4pm Mon-Fri) At the northeast edge of downtown, this 1845 Greek Revival building was built from local limestone and marble by slaves and prison inmates working alongside European artisans. Around back, steep stairs lead down to the **Tennessee Bicentennial Mall**, whose outdoor walls are covered with historical facts about Tennessee's history, and the wonderful daily **Farmers Market**.

FREE **Tennessee State Museum** MUSEUM
(www.tnmuseum.org; 5th Ave, btwn Union & Deaderick Sts; ⏲10am-5pm Tue-Sat, 1-5pm Sun) For history buffs, this engaging but not flashy museum offers a worthy look at the state's past, with Native American handicrafts, a life-size log cabin and quirky historical artifacts such as President Andrew Jackson's inaugural hat.

Frist Center for the Visual Arts GALLERY
(www.fristcenter.org; 919 Broadway; adult/child $10/free; ⏲10am-5:30pm Mon, Tue, Wed & Sat, to 9pm Thu & Fri, 1-5pm Sun) Hosts traveling exhibitions of everything from American folk

Nashville

Sights

1 Country Music Hall of Fame & Museum ... D5
2 Frist Center for the Visual Arts ... B4
3 Public Library ... C3
4 Ryman Auditorium ... D4
5 Tennessee Bicentennial Mall ... C1
6 Tennessee State Capitol ... C2
7 Tennessee State Museum ... D3

Sleeping

8 Hermitage Hotel ... C3
9 Indigo Nashville Downtown ... D3
10 Union Station Hotel ... B4

Eating

11 Arnold's ... B6

Entertainment

12 Basement ... B7
13 Bourbon Street Blues & Boogie Bar ... D3
14 Mercy Lounge ... B6
15 Robert's Western World ... D4
Ryman Auditorium ... (see 4)
16 Station Inn ... A5
17 Tootsie's Orchid Lounge ... D4
18 Whiskey Kitchen ... A5

Shopping

Boot Country ... (see 22)
19 Charlie Daniels Museum ... E4
20 Ernest Tubb ... D4
21 Gruhn Guitars ... D4
22 Hatch Show Print ... D4
23 Third Man Records ... C7

art to Picasso in the grand, refurbished post office building.

MIDTOWN

Along West End Ave, starting at 21st Ave, sits prestigious **Vanderbilt University**, founded in 1883 by railway magnate Cornelius Vanderbilt. The 330-acre campus buzzes with some 12,000 students, and student culture influences much of Midtown's vibe.

Parthenon PARK, GALLERY
(www.parthenon.org; 2600 West End Ave; adult/child $6/4; 9am-4:30pm Tue-Sat, plus Sun in summer) Yes, that is indeed a reproduction Athenian parthenon sitting in **Centennial Park**. Originally built in 1897 for Tennessee's Centennial Exposition and rebuilt in 1930 due to popular demand, the full-scale plaster copy of the 438-BC original now houses an art museum with a collection of American paintings and a 42ft statue of the Greek goddess Athena.

Music Row NEIGHBORHOOD
Just west of downtown, a stretch of 16th and 17th Aves are home to the production companies, agents, managers and promoters who run Nashville's country-music industry. There's not much to see, but you can pay to cut your own record at some of the smaller studios (about $25 to $100 an hour). 'World's Greatest Love Songs on the Kazoo,' anyone?

MUSIC VALLEY

This suburban tourist zone is about 10 miles northeast of downtown at Hwy 155/Briley Pkwy exits 11 and 12B, and reachable by bus.

Grand Ole Opry House TOUR, MUSEUM
(615-871-6779; www.opry.com; 2802 Opryland Dr; tours adult/child $17.50/12.50) This unassuming modern brick building seats 4400 for the *Grand Ole Opry* on Friday and Saturday from March to November. Guided backstage tours are offered daily by reservation – book online up to two weeks ahead. Across the plaza, a small, free **museum** (10:30am-6pm Mar-Dec) tells the story of the Opry with wax characters, colorful costumes and dioramas.

Gibson Bluegrass Showcase GUITAR FACTORY
(www.gibson.com; 161 Opry Mills Dr; 10am-9:30pm Mon-Sat, to 7pm Sun) Through the glass you can see banjos, mandolins and resonator guitars being made.

PLANTATIONS

Hermitage MUSEUM, GARDENS
(www.thehermitage.com; 4580 Rachel's Lane; adult/child $18/12; 8:30am-5pm Apr-Oct, 9am-4:30pm Oct-Mar) The former home of seventh president Andrew Jackson lies 15 miles east of downtown. The 1000-acre plantation is a peek into what life was like for a Mid-South gentleman farmer in the 19th century. Tour the Federal-style brick mansion, now a furnished house museum with costumed interpreters, and see Jackson's original 1804 log cabin and the old slave quarters (Jackson was a lifelong supporter of slavery, at times owning up to 150 slaves; a special exhibit tells their stories). The arcadian gardens and grounds are lovely to wander, though somewhat marred by the highway passing nearby.

Belle Meade Plantation HISTORIC BUILDING (www.bellemeadeplantation.com; 5025 Harding Pike; adult/child $16/8; ⏲9am-5pm Mon-Sat, 11am-5pm Sun) The Harding-Jackson family began raising thoroughbreds here (6 miles west of Nashville) in the early 1800s. Every horse entered in the Kentucky Derby in the past five years is a descendant of Belle Meade's studly sire, Bonnie Scotland, who died in 1880. The 1853 mansion is open to visitors, as are various interesting outbuildings, including a model slave cabin.

Tours

Ask at the visitor center for a list of the many theme tours available in Nashville.

TOP CHOICE **NashTrash** BUS TOUR (☎615-226-7300; www.nashtrash.com; 900 8th Ave N; 1½hr tours $32) The big-haired 'Jugg Sisters' lead a campy frolic through the risqué side of Nashville history while guests sip BYO booze. Buy in advance: tours can sell out *months* in advance.

Tommy's Tours BUS TOUR (☎615-335-2863; www.tommystours.com; tours from $40) Joke-cracking local Tommy Garmon leads highly entertaining three-hour tours of country music sights.

General Jackson Showboat BOAT TOUR (☎615-458-3900; www.generaljackson.com; tours from $46) Paddleboat sightseeing cruises of varying length on the Cumberland River, some with music and food.

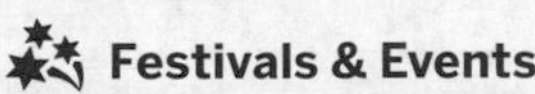

Festivals & Events

CMA Music Festival MUSIC (www.cmafest.com) Draws tens of thousands of country-music fans to town each June.

Tennessee State Fair FAIR (www.tennesseestatefair.org) Nine days of racing pigs, mule-pulls and cake bake-offs every September.

Sleeping

Bargain-bin chain motels cluster on all sides of downtown, along I-40 and I-65. Music Valley has a glut of family-friendly midprice chains.

DOWNTOWN

TOP CHOICE **Union Station Hotel** HOTEL $$$ (☎615-726-1001; www.unionstationhotelnashville.com; 1001 Broadway; r from $209; P❄📶) This soaring Romanesque stone castle was Nashville's train station back in the days when travel was a grand affair; today's it's downtown's most iconic hotel. The vaulted lobby is dressed in peach and gold with inlaid marble floors and a stained-glass ceiling. Rooms are tastefully modern, with flat-screen TVs and deep soaking tubs. Parking costs $20.

Hermitage Hotel HOTEL $$$ (☎615-244-3121, 888-888-9414; www.thehermitagehotel.com; 231 6th Ave N; r from $259; P❄📶) Nashville's first million-dollar hotel was a hit with the socialites when it opened in 1910.

VIVA NASHVEGAS!

Brash, glittery Nashville is proud to have earned the nickname NashVegas. So put on your rhinestone cowboy boots and explore the weird and wild side of town.

'Outlaw Country' star Willie Nelson sold all his worldly goods to pay off $16.7 million in unpaid taxes in the early 1990s. You can see them at the **Willie Nelson Museum** (www.willienelsongeneralstore; McGavock Pike, Music Valley; admission $10; ⏲8:30am-9pm), which might as well be called the Everything-But-Willie-Nelson's-Used-Toothbrush Museum. Up the street is the **Music City Wax Museum** (2515 McGavock Pike; admission $3; ⏲8am-10pm), with eerie, corpse-like statues of country stars dead and alive.

The Tuesday-night **Doyle and Debbie** show at the Station Inn (p366) is a cult-hit parody of a washed-up country-music duo.

Printer's Alley, once the epicenter of NashVegas vice, has cleaned up but still has at least one bar advertising **nude karaoke**. That's all we have to say about that.

Also downtown, the **Charlie Daniels Museum** (110 2nd Ave N; admission free; ⏲9am-late) is less museum and more gift shop, hawking everything from bacon-scented air fresheners to T-shirts bearing the likeness of 'Devil Went Down to Georgia' singer Daniels, who looks like a chicken-fried Santa Claus.

In the quirky 12th Ave S neighborhood, a former stylist to New York City's drag queens stocks bouffant wigs, vintage cowboy boots and handmade bolo ties at **Katy K's Ranch Dressing** (2407 12th Ave S).

WORTH A TRIP

JACK DANIEL'S DISTILLERY

The irony of the **Jack Daniel's Distillery** (www.jackdaniels.com; Rte 1, Lynchburg; tours free; ⏲9am-4:30pm) being in a 'dry county' is lost on no one – local liquor laws dictate that no hard stuff can be sold within county lines, thus the distillery cannot give out samples of its famous whiskey. But it can give hour-long free tours, where visitors are encouraged to take long sniffs of the golden brew. It's the oldest registered distillery in the US: the folks at Jack Daniels have been dripping whiskey through layers of charcoal then aging it in oak barrels since 1866. The distillery is located off Hwy 55 in the diminutive town of Lynchburg, which freely admits that all visitors are either here to see the distillery or they are lost.

The lobby feels like a Czar's palace, every surface covered in rich tapestries and ornate carvings. Rooms are generic upscale, with plush beds and mahogany furniture. Parking costs $20.

Indigo Nashville Downtown HOTEL **$$**
(☎877-846-3446; www.ichotelsgroup.com; 301 Union St; r from $139; P❄📶) Most of downtown's midprice hotels are corporate behemoths catering to conventioneers. Not so the newly opened Indigo, with its mod high-ceiling lobby, space age violet-and-lime color schemes, and arty floor-to-ceiling photomurals of Nashville landmarks. Parking is $20.

WEST END

TOP CHOICE **Music City Hostel** HOSTEL **$**
(☎615-692-1277; www.musiccityhostel.com; 1809 Patterson St; dm/r $25/70; P❄@📶) These squat brick bungalows are less than scenic, but Nashville's only hostel is lively and welcoming, with bike rental, common kitchen, a computer and free wi-fi. The crowd is young, international and fun – you can almost guarantee an evening jam session in the courtyard. Many kickin' West End bars are within walking distance.

Hutton Hotel HOTEL **$$$**
(☎615-340-9333; www.huttonhotel.com; 1808 West End Ave; r from $189; P❄@📶) Nashville's newest hotel is also its slickest, riffing on mid-Century Modern design with bamboo-paneled walls and grown-up beanbags in the lobby. Rust- and chocolate-colored rooms have miniature cactus gardens and a number of ecofriendly touches.

1501 Linden Manor B&B **$$**
(☎615-298-2701; www.nashville-bed-breakfast.com; 1501 Linden Ave; r from $125; P❄📶🏊) The husband-and-wife owners have filled this yellow Victorian cottage with antiques collected through their world travels – Persian rugs, Asian carvings, old Victrolas. Have homemade egg soufflés for breakfast in the sunny dining room, or dip your hand into the 'bottomless cookie jar' anytime.

MUSIC VALLEY

Gaylord Opryland Hotel RESORT **$$$**
(☎615-889-1000, 866-972-6779; www.gaylordhotels.com; 2800 Opryland Dr; r from $199; P❄@📶🏊) This whopping 2881-room hotel is a universe unto itself. Why set foot outdoors when you could ride a paddleboat along an artificial river, eat sushi beneath a faux waterfall in an indoor garden, shop for bolo ties in a model 19th-century town, or sip Scotch in an antebellum-style mansion, all *inside* the hotel's three massive glass atriums.

Nashville KOA Kampground CAMPGROUND **$**
(☎615-889-0282, 800-562-7789; www.koa.com; 2626 Music Valley Dr; campsites $39, cabins from $60, lodges $129; P📶🏊) Popular with RVers, this well-manicured, wholesome campground also has tent sites, cabins, and lodges with kitchenettes, all set back from the road. Amenities include a pool, game room, and snack bar.

Eating

The classic Nashville meal is the 'meat-and-three' – a heaping portion of fried chicken, meatloaf etc with your choice of three homestyle sides. Many of the restaurants in the District are high-volume tourist traps and are best avoided.

TOP CHOICE **Prince's Hot Chicken** CHICKEN **$**
(123 Ewing Dr; mains $4-8; ⏲noon-10pm Tue-Thu, noon-4am Fri & Sat) Cayenne-rubbed 'hot chicken,' fried to succulent perfection and served on a piece of white bread with a side

of pickles, is Nashville's unique contribution to the culinary universe. Tiny, faded Prince's, in a northside strip mall, is a local legend that's gotten shout-outs everywhere from the *New York Times* to *Bon Appétit*. In mild, medium, hot and death-defying extra hot, its chicken will burn a hole in your stomach and you'll come back begging for more.

City House NEW SOUTHERN **$$$**
(615-736-5838; cityhousenashville.com; 1222 4th Ave N; mains $9-24; 5pm-10pm Wed-Mon) This signless brick building in Nashville's gentrifying Germantown neighborhood hides one of the South's best new restaurants. The food, cooked in an open kitchen in the warehouselike space, is a crackling bang-up of Italy-meets-New South – local chicken livers with red-onion jam, pizza with house-cured pork belly, root-beer layer cake with buttermilk buttercream. Cocktails are a high art here: try a Kubric (Tennessee whiskey, artisan pear brandy, ginger ale).

Arnold's SOUTHERN **$**
(605 8th Ave S; mains $5-8; 6am-2:30pm Mon-Fri) Grab a tray and line up with college students, garbage collectors and country-music stars at Arnold's, king of the meat-and-three. Slabs of drippy roast beef are the house specialty, along with fried green tomatoes, cornbread two ways, and big gooey wedges of chocolate cream pie. This is Southern food at its finest.

Family Wash PUB **$$**
(www.familywash.com; 2038 Greenwood Ave; mains $9-15; 6pm-midnight Tue-Sat) This East Nashville neighborhood gastropub is the kind of place where you can eat a sublime roast garlic shepherd's pie and nurse a microbrew while watching the bartender shoot the breeze with the regulars and kids play with toy cars on the floor. Live music gets rolling on the small stage around 9pm most nights.

WORTH A TRIP

FRANKLIN

About 20 miles south of Nashville off I-65, the historic town of **Franklin** (www.historicfranklin.com) has a charming downtown and beautiful B&Bs. Stop off at **Puckett's Grocery** (www.puckettsgrocery.com; 120 4th Ave S; mains $10-20; 6am-6pm Sun-Thu, to late Fri & Sat) for a fried-catfish sandwich and some bluegrass.

Monell's SOUTHERN **$$**
(www.monellstn.com; 1235 6th Ave N; all-you-can-eat $16; 10:30am-2pm Mon, 10:30am-2pm & 5-8:30pm Tue-Fri, 8:30am-1pm & 5-8:30pm Sat, 8:30am-4pm Sun) In an old brick house just north of the District, Monell's is beloved for down-home Southern food served communally, meaning you sit with strangers and pass the food around the table yourselves. This being Nashville, you'll all be friends before you're done with your fried catfish.

Marché Artisan Foods BISTRO **$$**
(www.marcheartisanfoods.com; 1000 Main St; mains $9-16; 8am-9pm Tue-Sat, to 4pm Sun) In rapidly gentrifying East Nashville, this airy bistro has a veggie-friendly menu of light French- and Italian-inflected fare, made with seasonal local ingredients. Drop in for a cinnamon brioche at breakfast, or a plate of homemade gnocchi with sweet corn for dinner.

Pancake Pantry BREAKFAST **$**
(www.pancakepantry.com; 1796 21st Ave S; mains $5-9; 6am-3pm) For 50-plus years, crowds have been lining up for tall stacks of pancakes every-which-way at this iconic breakfast joint. Try the sweet-potato kind.

Elliston Place Soda Shop DINER **$**
(2111 Elliston Pl; mains $3-6; 7am-7pm Mon-Sat) This venerable eatery has served fountain Cokes and meat-and-threes to Vandy students since the 1930s, and the decor hasn't changed much since.

Drinking & Entertainment

Nashville has the nightlife of a city three times its size, and you'll be hard-pressed to find a place that *doesn't* have live music. College students, bachelor-party-goers, Danish backpackers and conventioneers all rock out downtown, where neon-lit Broadway looks like a country-fried Las Vegas. Bars and venues west and south of downtown tend to attract more locals, with many places clustered near Vanderbilt University. Last call is at 3am, so many bars stay open until then when it's busy.

Bars & Nightclubs

Cafe Coco CAFE, BAR
(www.cafecoco.com; 210 Louise Ave; 24hr) In a ramshackle old cottage just off Elliston Pl, Cafe Coco is like an especially groovy frat house, with a 24-hour whirl of action. Twenty-somethings snack on sandwiches and cake in the front parlor, smoke on the

BEST POPSICLES EVER

Locals know just where to head on steamy Tennessee afternoons: **Las Paletas Gourmet Popsicles** (2907 12th Ave S; Tue-Sat noon-7pm, to 5pm Sun), a groovy little popsicle shop selling icy treats in wild flavors such as chocolate-wasabi, hibiscus and olive oil.

large patio, drink at the bar and tap away on laptops in the old bedrooms (there's free wi-fi).

Whiskey Kitchen PUB
(www.whiskeykitchen.com; 118 12th Ave S) In the Gulch, an up-and-coming patch of rehabbed warehouses adjacent to downtown, this neo-Southern gastropub with a mile-long whiskey menu is one of Nashville's trendiest spots. Expect crowds.

Rumours Wine and Art Bar BAR
(www.rumourswinebar.com; 2404 12th Ave S) In the hip but low-key 12th Ave S neighborhood, this arty hangout is good for a chilling with a glass of Malbec.

Tribe BAR
(www.tribenashville.com; 1517 Church St) Ultra-friendly Tribe caters to a largely gay male crowd, though everyone is welcome to sip martinis, watch music videos and dance the night away.

Live Music

Nashville's opportunities for hearing live music are unparalleled. As well as the big venues, many talented country, folk, bluegrass, Southern-rock and blues performers play smoky honky-tonks, college bars, coffee shops and organic cafes for tips. Many places are free Monday to Friday or if you arrive early enough.

TOP CHOICE **Tootsie's Orchid Lounge** HONKY-TONK
(615-726-7937; www.tootsies.net; 422 Broadway) The most venerated of the downtown honky-tonks, Tootsie's vibrates with boot-stompin' every night of the week. In the 1960s club owner and den mother 'Tootsie' Bess nurtured the likes of Willie Nelson, Kris Kristofferson and Waylon Jennings. Now up-and-coming country musicians play the two tiny stages and it's not unusual for big stars to stop by for an impromptu jam session.

Grand Ole Opry MUSICAL THEATER
(615-871-6779; www.opry.com; 2802 Opryland Dr, Music Valley; adult $28-88, child $18-53) Though you'll find a variety of country shows throughout the week, the performance to see is the *Grand Ole Opry,* a lavish tribute to classic Nashville country music, every Tuesday, Friday and Saturday night. Shows return to the Ryman from November to February.

Bluebird Cafe CLUB
(615-383-1461; www.bluebirdcafe.com; 4104 Hillsboro Rd; cover free-$15; shows 6pm & 9:30pm) It's in a strip mall in suburban South Nashville, but don't let that fool you: some of the best original singer-songwriters in country music have graced this tiny stage. Steve Earle, Emmylou Harris and the Cowboy Junkies have all played the Bluebird, which was the setting for the 1993 Sandra Bullock and River Phoenix movie *The Thing Called Love*. Try your luck at Monday open mike nights.

Robert's Western World HONKY-TONK
(www.robertswesternworld.com; 416 Broadway) Buy a pair of boots, a beer or a burger at Robert's, a longtime favorite on the strip. Music starts at 11am and goes all night; Brazilbilly, the house band, rocks it after 10pm on weekends.

Station Inn CLUB
(615-255-3307; www.stationinn.com; 402 12th Ave S) South of downtown, this unassuming stone building is the best place in town for serious bluegrass. Don't miss the Tuesday-night Doyle and Debbie show (see p363).

Ryman Auditorium CONCERT VENUE
(tickets 615-458-8700, info 615-889-3060; www.ryman.com; 116 5th Ave) The Ryman's excellent acoustics, historic charm and large seating capacity have kept it the premier venue in town. The *Opry* returns for winter runs.

Bourbon Street Blues & Boogie Bar BLUES
(www.bourbonstreetblues.com; 220 Printer's Alley) A Printer's Alley standby, with low ceilings, sweet blues and Mardi Gras beads everywhere.

Tired of country?

Basement CLUB
(www.thebasementnashville.com; 1604 8th Ave S) Beneath Grimey's Records, has intimate alt-rock and folk shows.

Mercy Lounge CLUB
(www.mercylounge.com; 1 Cannery Row) Up the street, with arty rock-and-roll shows in an old brick cannery.

Exit/In CLUB
(www.exitin.com; 2208 Elliston Pl) On Elliston Pl, opened in 1971, does indie rock, hip-hop and more.

Shopping

Lower Broadway has tons of record shops, boot stores and souvenir stalls, but you can generally get better prices elsewhere. The 12th Ave South neighborhood is the spot for ultra-trendy boutiques and vintage stores. Don't miss the iconic Katy K's Ranch Dressing (p363).

TOP CHOICE **Hatch Show Print** ART, SOUVENIRS
(316 Broadway) One of the oldest letterpress print shops in the US, Hatch has been using old-school cut blocks to print its bright, iconic posters since the early days of Vaudeville. The company has produced graphic ads and posters for almost every country star since.

Ernest Tubb MUSIC
(417 Broadway) Marked by a giant neon guitar sign, this is the best place to shop for country and bluegrass records. Open late.

Third Man Records MUSIC
(623 7th Ave S) Music geeks freak out over this tiny new record shop and recording studio, owned by White Stripes frontman Jack White.

Elder's Bookstore BOOKS
(2115 Elliston Pl) This excellent used-book shop has been around since the 1930s.

Gruhn Guitars MUSIC
(400 Broadway) This renowned vintage instrument store has expert staff.

Opry Mills Mall MALL
(10am-9:30pm Mon-Sat, to 7pm Sun) Next door to the Opry, this sprawling outlet mall houses an IMAX theater, theme restaurants and dozens of big name retailers.

THREE-FOR-ONE COWBOY BOOTS

Embroidered leather cowboy boots, the unofficial Nashville uniform, are the city's quintessential souvenir and dozens of shops along Lower Broadway hawk overpriced pairs to tourists. But in-the-know shoppers will head to **Boot Country** (304 Broadway) for their legendary 'buy one, get two free' deal on everything from flashy alligator to rough 'n' ready riding boots.

Information

Downtown Nashville and Centennial Park have free wi-fi, as do nearly all hotels and many restaurants and coffee shops.

InsideOut (www.insideoutnashville.com) A weekly covering the local gay and lesbian scene.

Main police station (615-862-8600; 310 1st Ave S)

Nashville Scene (www.nashvillescene.com) Free alternative weekly with entertainment listings.

Nashville Visitors Information Center (615-259-4747; www.visitmusiccity.com; 501 Broadway, Sommet Center; 8:30am-5:30pm) Pick up free city maps here at the glass tower. Great online resource.

Post office (1718 Church St)

Public library (www.library.nashville.org; 615 Church St) Free internet access.

Tennessean (www.tennessean.com) Nashville's daily newspaper.

Vanderbilt University Medical Center (615-322-5000; 1211 22nd Ave S)

Getting There & Around

Nashville International Airport (BNS; 615-275-1675; www.nashintl.com), 8 miles east of town, is not a major air hub. MTA bus 18 links the airport and downtown; the **Gray Line Airport Express** (www.graylinenashville.com; one way/return $12/20; 5am-11pm) serves major downtown and West End hotels. Taxis charge a flat rate of $25 to downtown or Opryland.

Greyhound (1030 Charlotte Ave) is downtown. The **Metropolitan Transit Authority** (www.nashvillemta.org; fares $1.60) operates city bus services based downtown at **Music City Central** (400 Charlotte Ave). Express buses go to Music Valley.

Eastern Tennessee

Dolly Parton, Eastern Tennessee's most famous native, loves her home region so much she has made a successful career out of singing about girls who leave the honeysuckle-scented embrace of the Smoky Mountains for the false glitter of the city. They're always sorry.

Largely a rural region of small towns, rolling hills and river valleys, the eastern third of the state has friendly folks, hearty country food and pastoral charm to make most anyone feel at home.

The lush, heather-tinted Great Smoky Mountains are great for hiking, camping and rafting, while the region's two main

SCENIC DRIVE: NATCHEZ TRACE PARKWAY

About 25 miles southwest of Nashville off Hwy 100, drivers pick up the Natchez Trace Pkwy, which leads 444 miles southwest to Natchez, MS. This northern section is one of the most attractive stretches of the entire route, with broad-leafed trees leaning together to form an arch over the winding road. There are three primitive campsites along the way, free and available on a first-come, first-served basis. Near the parkway entrance, stop at the landmark **Loveless Cafe**, a 1950s roadhouse famous for its biscuits with homemade preserves, country ham and ample portions of Southern fried chicken.

urban areas, Knoxville and Chattanooga, are easygoing riverside cities with lively college populations and kicking music scenes.

CHATTANOOGA

Named 'the dirtiest city in America' in the 1960s, Chattanooga was shamed into cleaning up rampant industrial pollution and focusing on downtown revitalization. Today the city is recognized as being one of the country's greenest, with miles of well-used waterfront trails, free electric buses and pedestrian bridges crossing the Tennessee River. With world-class rock-climbing, hiking, biking and water-sports opportunities, it's one of the South's best cities for outdoorsy types.

The city was once a major railway hub throughout the 19th and 20th centuries, hence the 'Chattanooga Choo-Choo,' which was originally a reference to the Cincinnati Southern Railroad's passenger service from Cincinnati to Chattanooga and later the title of a 1941 Glen Miller song.

The Bluff View Art District at High and E 2nd Sts has upscale shops and restaurants overlooking the river.

Sights & Activities

On the North Shore, **Coolidge Park** is a good place to start a riverfront stroll. There's a carousel, well-used playing fields and a 50ft climbing wall attached to one of the columns supporting the **Walnut Street Bridge**.

Lookout Mountain OUTDOORS
(www.lookoutmtnattractions.com; 827 East Brow Rd; adult/child $46/24;) Some of Chattanooga's oldest and best-loved attractions are 6 miles outside the city. Admission price includes: the Incline Railway, which chugs up a steep incline to the top of the mountain; the world's longest underground waterfall, Ruby Falls; and Rock City, a garden with a dramatic cliff-top overlook. Opening hours vary by season. The mountain is also a popular hang-gliding location. The folks at **Lookout Mountain Flight Park** (800-688-5637; www.hanglide.com; 7201 Scenic Hwy, Rising Fawn, GA; intro tandem flight $199) give lessons.

Tennessee Aquarium AQUARIUM
(www.tnaqua.org; 1 Broad St; adult/child $25/15; 10am-6pm;) That glass pyramid looming over the riverside bluffs is the world's largest freshwater aquarium. Climb aboard the aquarium's high-speed catamaran for two-hour excursions through the Tennessee River Gorge (adult/child $29/22). While here, check out a show at the attached **IMAX theater** (adult/child $8.50/7).

Outdoor Chattanooga OUTDOORS
(423-643-6888; www.outdoorchattanooga.com) Hop on the pedestrian-only bridge to cross into downtown. Below you you'll notice the grass-covered 'living roof' of this city-run agency promoting active recreation. It leads hiking, kayaking and biking trips – call or check the website for schedules. It's also a good resource for outdoor info and trail suggestions.

Hunter Museum of American Art GALLERY
(www.huntermuseum.org; 10 Bluff View; adult/child $10/5; 10am-5pm Mon, Tue & Thu-Sat, noon-5pm Wed & Sun) East of the aquarium is the equally striking glass lobby of this museum, which has a fantastic 19th- and 20th-century collection. Check out the vertigo-inducing glass pedestrian bridge.

Sleeping & Eating

You can find plenty of budget motels around I-24 and I-75.

Chattanooga Choo-Choo Holiday Inn HOTEL $$
(423-266-5000; www.choochoo.com; 1400 Market St; r/railcars from $145/179;) The city's grand old railway terminal has been transformed into a bustling hotel, complete with 48 authentic Victorian railcar rooms, a retro Gilded Age bar and numerous shops.

Standard rooms and suites, in separate buildings, are clean but ordinary.

Stone Fort Inn B&B $$
(☎423-267-7866; www.stonefortinn.com; 120 E 10th St; r from $120; P ❄ ☎) Exposed brick and a stylish mix of antiques, vintage Coke art and kitschy-cool mounted deer heads make this downtown boutique hotel the hippest digs in town.

Raccoon Mountain Campground CAMPGROUND $
(☎423-821-9403; www.raccoonmountain.com; 319 W Hills Dr; tent sites from $18) The closest campsite to downtown has shady tent sites and well-maintained facilities, at the base of the nifty tour-able caverns of the same name.

TOP CHOICE **Zarzour's** SOUTHERN $
(1627 Rossville Ave; mains $5-8; ⊙11am-3:30pm Mon-Fri) 'We treat you like family here,' says the waitress at this tiny wood-paneled slip of a diner, Chattanooga's oldest restaurant. 'We just don't like our family very much!' She's kidding (we think), but that kind of salty banter is what makes Zarzour's such an experience: that, and the just-like-grammy-used-to-make hamburger steak, baked spaghetti and lemon ice box pie (a true classic of the genre).

Big River Grille & Brewing Works PUB $$
(222 Broad St; mains $9-20; ⊙11am-midnight Sun-Thu, to 2am Fri & Sat) A lively crowd drinks beer and chows down on crowd-pleasing upmarket pub grub – burgers, calamari, barbecue chicken pizza – in a warehouse-y downtown space with a big front patio.

Information

The **visitor center** (☎423-756-8687, 800-322-3344; www.chattanoogafun.com; 215 Broad St; ⊙8:30am-5:30pm) is huge and modern, with friendly staff.

Getting There & Around

Chattanooga's modest **airport** (CHA; ☎423-855-2202; www.chattairport.com; 1001 Airport Rd) is just east of the city. The **Greyhound station** (960 Airport Rd) is just down the road.

For access to most downtown sites, ride the free electric **shuttle buses** that ply the center. The visitor center has a route map.

KNOXVILLE

Once known as the 'underwear capital of the world' for its numerous textile mills, Knoxville is now home to the University of Tennessee and a vibrant arts and music scene. Downtown's **Market Square** is full of ornate, slightly crumbling 19th-century buildings and lovely outdoor cafes shaded by pear trees, while **Old Town**, an arty, renovated warehouse district centered on Gay St, is a food and nightlife hot spot.

The **visitor center** (☎865-523-7263, 800-727-8045; www.knoxville.org; 301 S Gay St; ⊙9am-5pm Mon-Sat, 1-5pm Sun) is downtown. If you're here at lunchtime, don't miss the hallowed **Blue Plate Special** (www.wdvx.com; admission free; ⊙noon Mon-Sat), a daily live concert put on at the visitor center by WDVX, Knoxville's venerable country and roots music radio station.

The city's visual centerpiece is the **Sunsphere**, a gold orb atop a tower that's the main remnant of the 1982 World Fair. You can take the elevator up to the (usually deserted) viewing deck to see the skyline and a dated exhibit on Knoxville's civic virtues.

You can't miss the massive orange basketball that marks the **Women's Basketball Hall of Fame** (www.wbhof.com; 700 Hall of Fame Dr; adult/child $8/6; ⊙10am-5pm Mon-Sat summer, 11am-5pm Tue-Sat winter), a nifty look at the sport from the time when women were forced to play in full-length dresses.

GREAT SMOKY MOUNTAINS NATIONAL PARK

The Cherokee called this territory Shaconage (shah-*cone*-ah-jey), meaning roughly 'land of the blue smoke,' for the heather-colored mist that hangs over the ancient peaks. The Southern Appalachians are the world's oldest mountain range, with mile upon mile of cool, humid deciduous forest.

The 815-sq-mile park is the country's most visited and, while the main arteries and attractions can get crowded, studies have shown that 95% of visitors never venture further than 100yd from their cars, so it's easy to leave the teeming masses behind.

Unlike most other national parks, Great Smoky charges no admission fee, nor will it ever; this proviso was written into the park's original charter as a stipulation for a $5-million Rockefeller family grant. Stop by a visitor center to pick up a park map and the free park newspaper, *Smokies Guide*. For more information about the North Carolina section of this park, see p338.

The remains of the 19th-century settlement at **Cades Cove** are some of the park's most popular sights, as evidenced by the teeth-grinding summer traffic jams on the loop road.

Mt LeConte has some of the park's best hikes, as well as the only non-camping accommodations, **LeConte Lodge** (☎865-429-5704; www.leconte-lodge.com; cabins per person $79). Though the only way to get to the lodge's rustic, electricity-free cabins is via an 8-mile uphill hike, it's so popular you need to reserve up to a year in advance. Dinner and breakfast are available for $37. You can drive right up to the dizzying heights of **Clingmans Dome**, the third-highest mountain east of the Mississippi, with a futuristic observation tower.

With 10 developed campgrounds offering about 1000 campsites, you'd think finding a place to pitch would be easy. Not so in the busy summer season: your best bet is to plan ahead. You can make **reservations** (☎800-365-2267; www.nps.gov/grsm) for some sites; others are first-come, first-served. Camping fees are $14 to $23 per night. Of the park's 10 campgrounds, only Cades Cove and Smokemont are open year-round; others are open March to October.

Backcountry camping (☎reservations 865-436-1231) is an excellent option. A (free) permit is required; you can make reservations and get permits at the ranger stations or visitor centers.

Information

The park's three interior visitor centers are **Sugarlands Visitor Center** (☎865-436-1291; ⏲8am-4:30pm, to later spring & summer), at the park's northern entrance near Gatlinburg; **Cades Cove Visitor Center** (☎877-444-6777; ⏲9am-4:30pm, to later spring & summer), halfway up Cades Cove Loop Rd, off Hwy 441 near the Gatlinburg entrance; and Oconaluftee Visitor Center (p338), at the park's southern entrance near Cherokee, NC.

GATLINBURG

Wildly kitschy Gatlinburg hunkers at the entrance of the Great Smoky Mountains National Park, waiting to stun hikers with the scent of fudge and cotton candy. Tourists flock here to ride the ski lifts, shop for Confederate-flag undershorts, get married at the many wedding chapels and play hillbilly-themed minigolf. Love it or hate it, the entire village is a gin-u-wine American roadside attraction.

Amuse yourself Gatlinburg-style at the city's various Ripley's franchise attractions (a 'Believe it or Not!' museum of oddities, a mirror maze, a haunted house, a massive aquarium), at the one-of-a-kind **Salt and Pepper Shaker Museum** (www.thesaltandpeppershakermuseum.com; Winery Sq; adult/child $3/free; ⏲10am-4pm), or by riding the scenic 2-mile aerial **tramway** (adult/child $11/8.50) to the Bavarian-themed Ober Gatlinburg ski resort. Afterwards, suck down free samples of white lightnin' at the **Ole Smoky Moonshine Distillery** (www.olesmokymoonshine.com; 903 Parkway; ⏲10am-10pm), the country's first licensed moonshine maker (sounds like an oxymoron to us!). Cap your day off with a frolic inside a giant hamster ball (yes, seriously) at **Zorb** (www.zorb.com; 203 Sugar Hollow Rd, Pigeon Forge; rides $37). It's all in day's fun in Gatlinburg.

Pigeon Forge (www.mypigeonforge.com), 10 miles north of Gatlinburg, is a tacky complex of motels, outlet malls and country-music theaters and restaurants, all of which have grown up in the shadow of **Dollywood**.

DOLLYWOOD

Dollywood (www.dollywood.com; 1020 Dollywood Lane; adult/child $57/46; ⏲Apr-Dec) is a self-created ode to the patron saint of East Tennessee, the big-haired, bigger-bosomed country singer Dolly Parton. The park features Appalachian-themed rides and attractions, from the Mystery Mine roller coaster to the bald-eagle sanctuary, to the faux one-room chapel named after the doctor who delivered Dolly.

KENTUCKY

With an economy based on bourbon, horse racing and tobacco, you might think Kentucky would rival Las Vegas as Sin Central. Well, yes and no. For every whiskey-soaked Louisville bar there's a dry county where you can't get anything stronger than ginger ale. For every racetrack there's a Catholic monastery or a Southern Baptist church.

Kentucky's full of strange juxtapositions like that. A geographic and cultural crossroads, the state combines the friendliness of the South, the rural frontier history of the West, the industry of the North and the aristocratic charm of the East.

Every corner of the state is easy on the eye. In spring the pastures of central Kentucky bloom with tiny azure buds, earning it the moniker 'Bluegrass State.' There are few sights more heartbreakingly beautiful than the rolling limestone hills of horse country, where thoroughbred breeding is a multimillion-dollar industry. Even the mountains, often maligned as 'hillbilly country,' blaze with color and culture.

History

British and French forces battled for control of Kentucky in the mid-1700s, recognizing the value of the fertile land that was once used by Native Americans as a hunting ground.

Legendary frontiersman Daniel Boone blazed a trail through the Cumberland Gap and the British began pouring over the Appalachians in 1775. The state became a battleground during the Revolutionary War, with local Shawnee allying with the crown.

Though a slave state, Kentucky was bitterly divided during the Civil War, with 30,000 fighting for the Confederacy and 64,000 for the Union. Both the Union president Abraham Lincoln and Confederacy president Jefferson Davis were Kentucky-born.

After the war, Kentucky built up its economy on railways, tobacco and coal-mining. Today its motto, 'Unbridled Spirit,' reflects the dominance of scenic horse country.

KENTUCKY FACTS

» **Nickname** Bluegrass State

» **Population** 4.3 million

» **Area** 39,728 sq miles

» **Capital city** Frankfort (pop 28,000)

» **Other cities** Louisville (pop 600,000), Lexington (pop 300,000)

» **Sales tax** 6%

» **Birthplace of** 16th US president Abraham Lincoln (1809–65), 'gonzo' journalist Hunter S Thompson (1937–2005), boxer Muhammad Ali (b 1942), actress Ashley Judd (b 1968)

» **Home of** Kentucky Derby, Louisville Slugger, bourbon

» **Politics** generally conservative; extremely conservative in rural areas

» **Famous for** horses, bluegrass music, fried chicken, caves

» **Interesting place names** Monkeys Eyebrow, Chicken Bristle, Shoulderblade, Hippo, Petroleum

» **Driving distances** Louisville to Lexington 77 miles, Lexington to Mammoth Cave National Park 135 miles

Information

The boundary between Eastern and Central time goes through the middle of Kentucky.

Kentucky State Parks (☎800-255-7275; www.parks.ky.gov) Offers info on hiking, caving, fishing, camping and more in Kentucky's 52 state parks. So-called 'Resort Parks' have more upscale options, like lodges, while 'Recreation Parks' are all about roughin' it.

Kentucky Travel (☎502-564-4930, 800-225-8747; www.kentuckytourism.com) Sends out a detailed booklet on the state's attractions.

Louisville

Best known as the home of the Kentucky Derby, Louisville (or Louahvul, as the locals say) is a handsome, underrated city. A major Ohio River shipping center during the days of westward expansion, Kentucky's largest city now has a lively working-class vibe, with corner pool halls, punk-rock bars and drive-through chili restaurants. It's a fun place to spend a day or two, checking out the museums, wandering the old neighborhoods, drinking a little bourbon.

Sights

The Victorian-era **Old Louisville** neighborhood, just south of downtown, is well worth a drive or stroll. Don't miss **St James Court**, just off Magnolia Ave, with its utterly charming gas lamp-lit park. There are several wonderful **historic homes** (www.historichomes.org) in the area open for tours, including Thomas Edison's old shotgun cottage.

TOP CHOICE **Churchill Downs** RACETRACK
(www.churchilldowns.com; 700 Central Ave) On the first Saturday in May, a who's who of uppercrust America puts on their pinstripe suits and most flamboyant hats and descends for the 'greatest two minutes in sports,' the Kentucky Derby. After the race, the crowd sings 'My Old Kentucky Home' and watches as the winning horse is covered in a blanket of roses. Then they party.

To be honest, they've been partying for a while. The **Kentucky Derby Festival** (www.kdf.org), which includes a balloon race and the largest fireworks display in North America, starts two weeks before the big event.

Most seats at the derby are by invitation only or they've been reserved years in advance. On Derby Day, $40 gets you into the paddock party scene (no seat) if you arrive early, but it's so crowded you won't see much of the race. Don't fret, though. From April through to November, you can get a $3 seat at the Downs for many exciting races, often warm-ups for the big events.

Kentucky Derby Museum
(www.derbymuseum.org; Gate 1, Central Ave; adult/child $13/5; ⊙8am-5pm Mon-Sat, 11am-5pm Sun) On the grounds, the museum has exhibits on derby history, including a peek into the life of jockeys and a roundup of the most illustrious horses. There is a 360-degree audiovisual about the race, and a behind-the-scenes track tour ($10) that leads you through the jockey's quarters and posh VIP seating areas.

Louisville Slugger Museum MUSEUM
(www.sluggermuseum.org; 800 W Main St; adult/child $10/5; ⊙9am-5pm Mon-Sat, noon-5pm Sun; 👪) Look for the 120ft baseball bat leaning against the museum – ya can't miss it. Hillerich & Bradsby Co have been making the famous Louisville Slugger here since 1884. The admission fee includes a plant tour, a hall of baseball memorabilia such as Babe Ruth's bat, a batting cage and a free mini slugger. Customized bats are sold in the lobby. Note: bat production halts on Sunday, as well as on Saturday in the winter.

Muhammad Ali Center CULTURAL CENTER
(www.alicenter.org; 144 N 6th St; adult/child $9/4; ⊙9:30am-5pm Mon-Sat, noon-5pm Sun) A love offering to the city from its most famous native. Self-guided tours include a stirring film on Ali's life and video projections of his most famous fights, as well as exhibits about the racial segregation and humanitarian issues that so vexed the outspoken man once known as the 'Louisville Lip.'

WORTH A TRIP

INTERNATIONAL BLUEGRASS MUSIC MUSEUM

Kentuckian Bill Monroe is considered the founding father of bluegrass music; his band, the Blue Grass Boys, gave the genre its name. Bluegrass has its roots in the old-time mountain music, mixed with the fast tempo of African songs and spiced with lashings of jazz. Any banjo picker or fiddle fan will appreciate the historic exhibits at the **International Bluegrass Music Museum** (www.bluegrass-museum.org; 107 Daviess St; admission $5; ⊙10am-5pm Tue-Sat, 1-4pm Sun) in Owensboro. The pretty Ohio River town, about 100 miles west of Louisville, also hosts the **ROMP Bluegrass Festival** (www.bluegrass-museum.org/riverofmusic) in June.

Frazier International History Museum MUSEUM
(www.fraziermuseum.org; 829 W Main St; adult/child $12/9; ⊙9am-5pm Mon-Sat, noon-5pm Sun) Surprisingly ambitious for a midsized city, this state-of-the-art museum covers 1000 years of history with grisly battle dioramas and costumed interpreters demonstrating swordplay and staging mock debates.

Speed Art Museum MUSEUM
(www.speedmuseum.org; 2035 S 3rd St; adult/child $10/5; ⊙10am-5pm Tue, Wed & Fri, to 9pm Thu, noon-5pm Sun) A handsome Greek Revival-style building with more than 12,000 pieces of art, from classical sculptures to Kentucky mint julep cups.

Sleeping

Chain hotels cluster near the airport off I-264. Check out www.louisvillebedandbreakfast.org for the lowdown on the city's many reasonably priced, historic B&Bs.

TOP CHOICE **21c** HOTEL $$$
(☎502-217-6300; www.21chotel.com; 700 W Main St; r from $240; P❄📶) This contemporary art-museum–hotel would be edgy anywhere; in laid-back Louisville, it's practically in a different dimension. Video screens project your distorted image on the wall as you wait for the elevator. Chandeliers made from scissors dangle weirdly in the hallways. Sexually suggestive sculptures in the lobby make even normally unflappable guidebook authors blush. Urban-loftlike rooms have iPod docks and mint julep kits in the mini-fridge. The hotel restaurant, Proof on Main, is one of the city's hippest New Southern bistros. Parking is $18.

Central Park B&B B&B $$
(☎502-638-1505, www.centralparkbandb.com; 1353 S 4th St; r incl breakfast $135-195; P❄📶) Sleep in Gilded Age style at this 1884 stone mansion, overlooking Old Louisville's Central Park. The decor is very 'Victorian maximalist' – chandeliers, stained glass everywhere and huge flower arrangements on every surface.

THE HAUNTED HOSPITAL

Towering over Louisville like a mad king's castle, the abandoned Waverly Hills Sanatorium once housed victims of an early 20th-century tuberculosis epidemic. When patients died, workers dumped their bodies down a chute into the basement. No wonder the place is said to be one of America's most haunted buildings. Search for spooks with a nighttime ghost-hunting **tour** (☎502-933-2142; www.therealwaverlyhills.com; 2hr tours/2hr ghost hunts/overnights $22/50/100; ⊙Mar-Aug); the genuinely fearless can even spend the night! Many claim it's the scariest place they've ever been.

Brown Hotel HOTEL **$$$**
(☎502-583-1234; www.brownhotel.com; 335 West Broadway; r from $250; P❄@🛜) Opera stars, queens and prime ministers have trod the marble floors of this storied downtown hotel, now restored to all its 1920s gilded glamour with 293 comfy rooms and a swank bar. Parking is $18.

Eating

The Highlands area around Bardstown and Baxter Rds is the spot for locally owned cafes and bars. Downtown's 'Fourth Street Live' is a rather contrived 'entertainment district' of casual shopping and dining; there are better pickings in the area, so don't be afraid to wander.

610 Magnolia NEW SOUTHERN **$$$**
(☎502-636-0783; www.610magnolia.com; 610 W Magnolia Ave; 3-/4-course prix fixe menu $50/60; ⊙6pm-10pm Thu-Sat) Only open three evenings a week, this sleek Scandinavia-meets-Kentucky bistro is Louisville's hottest-ticket restaurant (and the hardest to find – there's no sign, just look for the numbers '610' on the front). Local seasonal ingredients get a global treatment – chili-rubbed crispy pork belly, sashimi with bourbon-soy sauce, sweet-potato bread pudding – to jaw-dropping effect.

Lynn's Paradise Cafe DINER **$$**
(www.lynnsparadisecafe.com; 984 Barret Ave; mains $7-15; ⊙7am-10pm Mon-Fri, 8am-10pm Sat & Sun; 👪) It's breakfast anytime at this psychedelic diner, marked by the 10ft-tall teapot outside. Don't miss the homemade biscuits with sorghum butter, or the Hot Brown sandwich, a Louisville classic invented in the 1920s at the Brown Hotel.

Doc Crow's Southern Smokehouse & Raw Bar SOUTHERN, BARBECUE **$$**
(doccrows.com; 127 W Main St; mains $7-18; ⊙11am-10pm Mon-Thu, to 11pm Fri & Sat) In an 1880s-era distillery trendily rehabbed with exposed brick and reclaimed wood, Louisville hipsters sip bourbon, slurp oysters and munch on house-smoked BBQ ribs.

Drinking & Entertainment

The free weekly *Leo* (www.leoweekly.com) lists gigs and entertainment. You'll have no problem finding a watering hole in the Highlands area.

Old Seelbach Bar BAR
(www.seelbachhilton.com; 500 4th St) In the Gilded Era Seelbach Hilton, this is the city's top spot for elegant bourbon-sipping.

Holy Grale PUB
(www.holygralelouisville.com; 1034 Bardstown Rd) One of Bardstown's newest and most interesting bars is housed in an old church, with a menu of funked-up pub grub (Scotch quail eggs, kimchee hot dogs) and a dozen rare German, Belgian and Japanese brews on tap.

Rudyard Kipling BAR, MUSIC
(www.therudyardkipling.com; 422 W Oak St) In Old Louisville, this place is loved by arty locals for its intimate indie-bluegrass shows and Kentucky bar food (try the 'snappy cheese').

Actors Theatre of Louisville THEATER
(www.actorstheatre.org; 504 W Main St) This highly regarded theater performs everything from Shakespeare to contemporary musicals and has premiered several Pulitzer Prize–winning plays.

Information

Public library (301 York St) Surf the web free, downtown.

Visitor center (☎502-582-3732, 888-568-4784; www.gotolouisville.com; 301 S 4th St; ⊙10am-6pm Mon-Sat, noon-5pm Sun) Has a free exhibit about that great Kentucky icon, KFC founder Colonel Sanders.

Getting There & Around

Louisville's International Airport (SDF; ☎502-367-4636; www.flylouisville.com) is 5 miles south of town on I-65. Get there by cab (around

$18) or local bus 2. The **Greyhound station** (720 W Muhammad Ali Blvd) is just west of downtown. **TARC** (www.ridetarc.org; 1000 W Broadway) runs local buses ($1.50) from the Union Station depot.

Bluegrass Country

Drive through northeast Kentucky's Bluegrass Country on a sunny day and you'll get an idea of what the ancient Greeks were imagining when they wrote about the Elysian fields of paradise. Horses graze in the brilliant-green hills dotted with ponds, poplar trees and handsome estate houses. These once-wild woodlands and meadows have been a center of horse breeding for almost 250 years – the region's natural limestone deposits are said to produce especially nutritious grass. The area's principal city, Lexington, is known as the 'Horse Capital of the World.'

LEXINGTON

Even the prison looks like a country club in Lexington, home of million-dollar houses and multimillion-dollar horses. Once the wealthiest and most cultured city west of the Allegheny Mountains, it was called 'the Athens of the West' and today is home to the University of Kentucky and the heart of the thoroughbred-racehorse industry. The small downtown has some pretty Victorian neighborhoods, but most of the attractions are in the countryside outside the metro area.

WORTH A TRIP

NATIONAL CORVETTE MUSEUM

All hail America's favorite sports car, the made-in-Kentucky Chevrolet Corvette! Auto fans should not miss the pilgrimage to Bowling Green's space-agey **National Corvette Museum** (www.corvettemuseum.com; I-65, exit 28, Bowling Green; adult/child $10/5; ⏲8am-5pm), home to 80 Corvette models and walk-through dioramas filled with memorabilia (check out the 'Main Street,' a mockup of Corvette-loving 1950s America). The nearby **Bowling Green Assembly Plant** (www.bowlinggreenassemblyplant.com; ⏲tours 8:30am, 11:30am, 12:45pm & 2pm Mon-Thu) gives guided factory tours – book online at least nine days in advance, or show up 45 minutes early and hope for a walk-in spot.

Sights & Activities

Most of Lexington's sights are horse-related, or involve the city's many historic homes and estates.

TOP CHOICE **Headley-Whitney Museum** MUSEUM
(www.headley-whitney.org; 4435 Old Frankfort Pike; adult/child $10/7; ⏲10am-5pm Tue-Fri, noon-5pm Sat & Sun) This marvelously old place holds the private collection of the late George Headley, a jewelry designer whose gemstone trinkets and handmade dollhouses are on display, along with a truly bizarre garage turned 'seashell grotto.'

Kentucky Horse Park MUSEUM, PARK
(www.kyhorsepark.com; 4089 Iron Works Pkwy; adult/child $16/8; ⏲9am-5pm daily mid-Mar–Oct, Wed-Sun Nov–mid-Mar; 👪) An educational theme park and equestrian sports center sits on 1200 acres just north of Lexington. Horses representing 50 different breeds live in the park and participate in special live shows. Also included, the international **Museum of the Horse** has neat dioramas of the horse through history, from the tiny prehistoric 'eohippus' to the pony express mail carriers. Seasonal **horseback riding** costs $22. The adjacent **American Saddlebred Museum** focuses on America's first registered horse breed – for hard-core enthusiasts only.

Keeneland Race Course RACETRACK
(www.keeneland.com; 4201 Versailles Rd; tickets $5) Watch 'em run, with races in April and October and horse sales throughout the year. From March to November you can watch the champions train from sunrise to 10am.

Red Mile RACETRACK
(www.theredmile.com; 1200 Red Mile Rd) Head here to see harness racing, where jockeys are pulled behind horses in special two-wheeled carts. Live races are in the fall, but you can watch and wager on simulcasts of races from around the world year-round.

Thoroughbred Center TOUR
(www.thethoroughbredcenter.com; 3380 Paris Pike; adult/child $15/8; ⏲tours 9am Mon-Sat Apr-Oct, Mon-Fri Nov-Mar) Most farms are closed to the public, but you can see working racehorses up close here, with tours of the stables, practice tracks and paddocks.

BELIEVE IT OR NOT

Fact: nearly half of Americans don't believe in evolution. Hence the popularity of Petersburg, Kentucky's new multimillion-dollar **Creation Museum** (www.creationmuseum.org; 2800 Bullittsburg Church Rd; adult/child $25/15; ⏲10am-6pm Mon-Sat, noon-6pm Sun), an interactive tour through a biblical interpretation of history. The scientific-minded will fume at what may be seen as an antirational message. But that doesn't mean they won't enjoy the walk-through Noah's Ark, animatronic dinosaurs (creationists believe they coexisted with humans) and the zonkeys (zebra-donkey hybrids) in the petting zoo.

Mary Todd-Lincoln House HISTORIC BUILDING
(www.mtlhouse.org; 578 W Main St; adult/child $9/4; ⏲10am-3pm Mon-Sat) The 1806 house has articles from the first lady's childhood and her years as Abe's wife.

Waveland HISTORIC BUILDING
(http://parks.ky.gov/findparks/histparks/wl; 225 Waveland Museum Lane; ⏲9am-4pm) A 19th-century plantation.

Ashland HISTORIC BUILDING
(www.henryclay.org; 120 Sycamore Rd; adult/child $9/4; ⏲10am-4pm Tue-Sat, 1-4pm Sun) Just 1.5 miles east of downtown, it was the Italianate estate of statesman Henry Clay (1777–1852).

Whispering Woods HORSEBACK RIDING
(☎502-570-9663; www.whisperingwoodstrails.com; 265 Wright Lane; trail rides per hr $25; ⏲Mar-Nov) Call to arrange guided trail rides; in bucolic Georgetown.

Sleeping & Eating

There are several downtown cafes and bars with outdoor seating around Main and Limestone Sts. S Limestone, across from the UK campus, has student-friendly nightlife.

Kentucky Horse Park CAMPGROUND $
(☎859-259-4257, 800-370-6416; www.kyhorsepark.com; 4089 Iron Works Pkwy; electric/primitive campsites from $29/19;) The 260 paved sites are open year-round. There are showers, laundry, a grocery, playgrounds and more. Primitive camping is also available.

Gratz Park Inn HOTEL $$
(☎859-231-1777; www.gratzparkinn.com; 120 W 2nd St; r from $179;) On a quiet downtown street, this 40-room hotel feels like a genteel hunt club, with mahogany furnishings and Old World oil paintings in heavy frames. The attached restaurant, Jonathan's, serves fine regional cuisine.

TOP CHOICE **Holly Hill Inn** NEW SOUTHERN $$$
(☎859-846-4732; www.hollyhillinn.com; 426 N Winter St, Midway; 3-/5-course dinner menu $35-55; ⏲5:30-10pm Thu-Sat, 11am-2pm Sun year-round, plus 11am-2pm Fri & Sat spring & summer) Guests dine in the converted bedrooms and parlors of an elegant old farmhouse, just west of Lexington in the town of Midway. The husband-and-wife owners serve local bounty with a deft touch – lamb with scallion ravioli, farmstead egg custard with fiddlehead ferns – earning scads of foodie praise.

Horse & Barrel PUB $$
(101 N Broadway; mains $10-15; ⏲from 5pm) Part of DeSha's restaurant, this is a local favorite for bourbon sipping – there are more than 70 varieties on offer.

Information

Pick up maps and area information from the **visitor center** (☎859-233-7299, 800-845-3959; www.visitlex.com; 301 E Vine St; ⏲8:30am-5pm Mon-Fri, 10am-4pm Sat). The **public library** (140 E Main St; ⏲10am-5pm Tue-Fri, noon-5pm Sat & Sun;) has free internet access and free wi-fi for those with laptops.

Getting There & Around

Blue Grass Airport (LEX; ☎859-425-3114; www.bluegrassairport.com; 4000 Terminal Dr) is west of town, with about a dozen domestic nonstops. **Greyhound** (477 W New Circle Rd) is 2 miles from downtown. **Lex-Tran** (www.lextranonthemove.org) runs local buses (bus 6 goes to the Greyhound station).

FRANKFORT

A pretty little postcard of a town, all red brick and gingerbread trim, Kentucky's diminutive capital lies 26 miles west of Lexington on the banks of the Kentucky River. There are some notable historic buildings, including the **old state capitol** (admission free; ⏲10am-5pm Tue-Sat), which functioned from 1827 to 1910. Nearby is the handsome **Kentucky History Center** (www.history.ky.gov; 100 W Broadway St; admission free; ⏲8am-4pm Tue-Sat), for those truly interested in state history. Daniel Boone is buried in the **Frankfort Cemetery** (E Main St).

Central Kentucky

The Bluegrass Pkwy runs from I-65 in the west to Rte 60 in the east, passing through some of the most luscious pasturelands in Kentucky.

About 40 miles south of Louisville is **Bardstown**, the 'Bourbon Capital of the World'. The historic downtown comes alive in September for the **Kentucky Bourbon Festival** (www.kybourbonfestival.com). Have a meal, some bourbon and a good night's sleep in the dim limestone environs of **Old Talbott Tavern** (502-348-3494; www.talbotts.com; 107 W Stephen Foster Ave; r from $59; P ❄), which has been welcoming likes of Abraham Lincoln and Daniel Boone since the late 1700s.

Follow Hwy 31 southwest and turn left at Monks Rd to visit the ascetically beautiful **Abbey of Gethsemani**, a Trappist monastery once home to famed Catholic thinker Thomas Merton. You can buy monk-made fudge at the **gift shop** (9am-5pm Mon-Fri). Continue on Hwy 31 to **Hodgenville** and the **Abraham Lincoln Birthplace** (www.nps.

THE BOURBON TRAIL

Silky, caramel-colored bourbon whiskey was likely first distilled in Bourbon County, north of Lexington, around 1789. Today 90% of all bourbon is produced here in Kentucky (no other state is allowed to put its own name on the bottle). Good bourbon must contain at least 51% corn, and must also be stored in charred oak barrels for a minimum of two years. While most connoisseurs drink it straight or with water, you must try a mint julep, the archetypal Southern drink made with bourbon, sugar syrup and crushed mint.

The **Oscar Getz Museum of Whiskey History** (www.whiskeymuseum.com; 114 N 5th St; donations appreciated; 10am-4pm Mon-Sat, noon-4pm Sun), in Bardstown, tells the bourbon story with old moonshine stills and other artifacts.

Most of Kentucky's distilleries, which are centered on Bardstown and Frankfort, offer free tours. Check out Kentucky's official **Bourbon Trail website** (wwwkybourbontrail.com) – though note that it doesn't include every distillery.

Distilleries near Bardstown:

Heaven Hill (www.bourbonheritagecenter.com; 1311 Gilkey Run Rd, Bardstown) Not a distillery tour, but an interactive Bourbon Heritage Center, with a tasting room inside a giant barrel.

Jim Beam (www.jimbean.com; 149 Happy Hollow Rd, Clermont) Watch a film about the Beam family and sample small-batch bourbons at the country's largest bourbon distillery.

Maker's Mark (www.makersmark.com; 3350 Burks Spring Rd, Loretto) This restored Vic-torian distillery is like a bourbon theme park, with an old gristmill and a gift shop where you can seal your own bottle in red wax.

Tom Moore (www.1792bourbon.com; 300 Barton Rd, Bardstown) Connoisseur-quality 1792 Ridgemont Reserve is produced at this small distillery, the only one within Bards-town city limits.

Distilleries near Frankfort/Lawrenceburg:

Buffalo Trace (www.buffalotrace.com; 1001 Wilkinson Blvd, Frankfort) The nation's oldest continuously operating distillery has highly regarded tours and free tastings.

Four Roses (www.fourroses.us; 1224 Bonds Mills Rd, Lawrenceburg) One of the most scenic distilleries, in a riverside Spanish Mission-style building. Free tastings.

Wild Turkey (www.wildturkey.com; Hwy 62 E, Lawrenceburg) Master distiller Jimmy Russell has been making this extra-dark bourbon since 1954. The factory is more industrial than scenic.

Woodford Reserve (www.woodfordreserve.com; 7855 McCracken Pike, Versailles) The historic site along a creek is restored to its 1800s glory; the distillery still uses old-fashioned copper pots.

WORTH A TRIP

OTHER 'CAVE COUNTRY' CAVES

By the early-20th century Mammoth Cave had become such a popular attraction that owners of smaller local caves began diverting travelers heading to Mammoth by claiming it was flooded or quarantined. The inevitable conflicts became known as the 'Cave Wars.' Today you'll still see plenty of billboards beseeching you to visit other caves around Mammoth. Here are a few that are actually worth the drive:

Cub Run Cave (www.cubruncave.net; admission $14; ⏲9:30am-4:30pm, shorter hr winter) One of the 'newest' caves, discovered in 1950, with tons of colorful formations.

Diamond Caverns (1hr guided tours adult/child $16/8) Has guided tours of its vast cathedrals dripping stalactites and draped in pearly flowstone.

Hidden River Cave (www.cavern.org; admission $15; ⏲9am-5pm) A cave museum and a one-hour tour that takes you by the ruins of a turn-of-the-20th-century hydroelectric system. Special off-trail adventure tours can be arranged in advance during summer.

Lost River Cave (www.lostrivercave.com; admission $15; ⏲9am-6pm, shorter hr winter) Offers a family-friendly 25-minute boat ride through an underground river. There are 2 miles of hiking trails on-site.

gov/abli; admission free; ⏲8am-4:45pm, to 6:45pm summer), a faux-Greek temple constructed around an old log cabin. Ten minutes away is Honest Abe's boyhood home at Knob Creek, with hiking trails.

About 25 miles (30 minutes) southwest of Lexington is **Shaker Village at Pleasant Hill** (www.shakervillageky.org; 3501 Lexington Rd, Harrodsburg; adult/child $15/5; ⏲10am-5pm), home to a community of the Shaker religious sect until the early 1900s. Tour 14 impeccably restored buildings, set amid buttercup meadows and winding stone paths. There's an inn and restaurant, and a gift shop selling the Shakers' famous handicrafts.

Forty miles south of Lexington is **Berea**, famed for its folk art. The **Kentucky Artisan Center** (www.kentuckyartisancenter.ky.gov; Exit 77, off Hwy 75; ⏲8am-8pm) has a large variety of handcrafts and food.

DANIEL BOONE NATIONAL FOREST

These 707,000 acres of rugged ravines and gravity-defying sandstone arches cover much of the Appalachian foothills of eastern Kentucky. The forest has numerous state- and federal-run areas; the main **ranger station** (☎859-745-3100; www.fs.fed.us/r8/boone) is in Winchester.

An hour southeast of Lexington is the **Red River Gorge** area, whose cliffs and natural arches make for some of the best rock climbing in the country. **Red River Outdoors** (☎859-230-3567; www.redriveroutdoors.com; 415 Natural Bridge Rd, Slade; full-day guided climb from $115) offers guided climbing trips. Climbers can also pay $2 to camp out behind **Miguel's Pizza** (1890 Natural Bridge Rd, Slade; mains $10-14; ⏲7am-10pm Mon-Thu, to 11pm Fri & Sat) in the hamlet of Slade. Bordering Red River Gorge is the **Natural Bridge State Resort Park** (☎606-663-2214; www.parks.ky.gov; 2135 Natural Bridge Rd, Slade), notable for its gravity-defying 78ft-high sandstone arch. It's a family-friendly park, with camping, a variety of short hiking trails, and a lake with an island known as 'hoedown island' for its occasional clogging performances.

Further south, the **Cumberland Falls State Resort Park** (☎606-528-4121; admission free; tent sites $22, lodge r from $69) is one of the few places in the world to see a moonbow, a rainbow that sometimes forms in the fall's mist at night. The park has a rustic lodge and campgrounds. While you're there, head over to the adjacent **Natural Arch Scenic Area** to see the 90ft sandstone arch and hike the half-dozen trails. The nearby town of **Corbin** has the original Kentucky Fried Chicken restaurant, with a rather disturbing life-size statue of the Colonel.

MAMMOTH CAVE NATIONAL PARK

With the longest cave system on earth, **Mammoth Cave National Park** (www.nps.gov/maca; Exit 53, off I-65; ⏲8:45am-5:15pm) has some 300 miles of surveyed passageways. Mammoth is at least three times bigger than any other known cave, with vast interior cathedrals, bottomless pits and strange, undulating rock formations. The caves have been used for prehistoric mineral-gathering, as a source of saltpeter for gunpowder and as a tuberculosis hospital. Tourists started visiting around 1810 and guided tours have been offered since the 1830s. The area became a national park in 1926 and now brings nearly two million visitors each year.

The only way to see the caves is on the excellent **ranger-guided tours** (☎800-967-2283; adult $5-48) and it's wise to book ahead, especially in summer. Tours range from subterranean strolls to strenuous, day-long spelunking adventures. The history tour is especially interesting.

In addition to the caves, the park contains 70 miles of trails for hiking, horseback riding and mountain biking. There are also three campsites with restrooms, but no electricity or water hookups ($12 to $30), 12 free backcountry campsites, and the **Mammoth Cave Hotel** (☎270-758-2225; www.mammothcavehotel.com; r $89, cottages from $79; P❄), next to the visitor center, which has standard hotel rooms and, in spring and summer, rustic cottages. There is a gas station and convenience store near the visitor center. But to be honest, we prefer to drive down to shabby Cave City to sleep in the giant concrete tipis at the **Wigwam Village Inn** (☎270-773-3381; www.wigwamvillage.com; 601 N Dixie Hwy, Cave City; wigwams $40-70; P❄), a 1937 chunk of pure American kitsch.

GEORGIA

Vastly different at each of its edges, Georgia – the largest state east of the Mississippi River – is in many ways the perfect distillation of everything the South has to offer. It's a state of wild geographic and cultural extremes: right-leaning Republican politics rub against liberal idealism, small towns merge with gaping cities, northern mountains rise to the clouds and produce roaring rivers, while coastal marshlands teem with fiddler crabs and swaying cordgrass.

Atlanta is the state capital and the region's transportation hub, a sprawling metropolis with friendly neighborhoods alongside multinational corporations such as UPS and Coca-Cola. So start your trip in the city known as 'the ATL' then road-trip across the state to fall under the spell of Savannah's live oaks, seafood, antebellum homes and humid nights. From here you're close to the coastal barrier islands – bring your tuxedo to Jekyll Island and your hiking boots to Cumberland Island.

GEORGIA FACTS

» **Nickname** Peach State

» **Population** 9.7 million

» **Area** 59,425 sq miles

» **Capital city** Atlanta (population metro area 5.2 million)

» **Other cities** Savannah (population 136,286)

» **Sales tax** 7%

» **Birthplace of** baseball legend Ty Cobb (1886–1961), president Jimmy Carter (b 1924), civil rights leader Martin Luther King Jr (1929–68), singer Ray Charles (1930–2004)

» **Home of** Coca-Cola, the world's busiest airport, the world's biggest aquarium

» **Politics** socially conservative as a whole; Atlanta has been known to swing both ways

» **Famous for** peaches

» **Odd Law** donkeys may not be kept in bathtubs. Seriously, don't do it.

» **Driving distances** Atlanta to St Marys 343 miles, Atlanta to Dahlonega 75 miles

History

Permanent English settlement dates from 1733, when James Edward Oglethorpe founded Savannah. By the time of the Revolutionary War almost half the population was made up of slaves. Georgia held two crucial battlefronts in the latter part of the Civil War: Chickamauga, where Union troops were defeated, and Atlanta, which they conquered and burned.

In the 20th century the state vaulted to national prominence on the back of an eclectic group of events: the wildly popular novel and film *Gone With the Wind;* Reverend Martin Luther King Jr and civil rights protests; 39th US President Jimmy Carter; and Atlanta's rise as a global media and business center, culminating in the 1996 Summer Olympics.

ℹ Information

For statewide tourism information, contact the **Georgia Department of Economic Development** (☎800-847-4842; www.exploregeorgia.org). For information on state parks, contact the **Georgia Department of Natural Resources**

(☎800-864-7275; www.gastateparks.org), where you can find information on camping and activities in parks statewide. Forty-one parks offer tent-only and RV-site camping for around $25 to $28 per night. Most parks have laundry facilities.

Cars are the most convenient way to move around Georgia. (Atlanta has a citywide train system called MARTA, but service is limited. Some cyclists brave the city streets.) I-75 bisects the state running north-south; I-20 runs east-west.

You can expect to pay an additional 6% tax on hotel accommodations in Georgia.

Atlanta

With five million residents in the metro and outlying areas, the so-called capital of the South continues to experience explosive growth thanks to southbound Yankees and international immigrants alike. It's also booming as a tourist destination thanks to two glitzy 21st-century attractions – the Georgia Aquarium and the World of Coca-Cola – plus giant panda exhibits at Zoo Atlanta. Beyond the attractions you'll find a constellation of superlative restaurants, ample Civil War lore, miles of walking trails and a plethora of African American history.

Without natural boundaries to control development, Atlanta keeps growing – sometimes up, but mostly out. Suburban sprawl has turned Atlanta into an almost endless city. Increased car dependence creates horrendous traffic and pollution.

For all this suburbanization, Atlanta is a pretty city covered with trees and elegant homes. Distinct neighborhoods are like friendly small towns. Racial tensions are minimal in 'the city too busy to hate,' which prides itself as hometown to the civil rights titan Martin Luther King Jr.

History

Born as a railroad junction in 1837, Atlanta became a major Confederate transportation and munitions center for General William T Sherman, whose Union forces blazed through Georgia in 1864, leaving more than 90% of Atlanta's buildings in ruins.

After the war, Atlanta became the epitome of the 'New South,' a concept that entailed reconciliation with the North, the promotion of industrialized agriculture and a progressive business outlook. Segregation ended relatively painlessly here compared with other Southern cities, and President John F Kennedy lauded this transition as a model for other communities facing integration.

For the 1996 Summer Olympic Games the city put on her prettiest debutante gown and CNN beamed her picture worldwide. People took notice, the moving trucks came rolling down the freeways and, like summer weeds, condos sprouted everywhere. Since then, the city has focused its development energy on the downtown and midtown neighborhoods, both of which have flourished in recent years. Georgia's capital has also become known as the 'Motown of the South' thanks to its sizzling hip-hop and R & B scene.

Sights & Activities

DOWNTOWN

In recent years developers and politicians have been focusing on making the urban core more vibrant and livable. Big attractions in the city have contributed to the success.

TOP CHOICE Georgia Aquarium AQUARIUM

(www.georgiaaquarium.com; 225 Baker St; adult/child $25/19, with Dolphin combo $38/26; ⏲10am-5pm Sun-Fri, 9am-6pm Sat; 👪) The world's largest aquarium is Atlanta's showstopper. It's crowded, like Venice, but it's awesomeness is hard to deny: whale sharks, beluga whales and the new $110 million AT&T Dolphin Tales gallery, theater and show ($13.50 add-on), where human actors/trainers and majestic bottlenose dolphins perform together in a Vegas-meets-Broadway production of spectacle and cheese (think more *Pirates of the Caribbean* than underwater Cirque du Soleil).

World of Coca-Cola MUSEUM

(www.woccatlanta.com; 121 Baker St; adult/child $15/10; ⏲10am-6:30pm Sun-Thu, 9am-6:30pm Fri & Sat) Next door to the Georgia Aquarium, this self-congratulatory museum might prove entertaining to fans of the fizzy beverage and rash commercialization. The climactic moment comes when guests sample Coke products from around the world – a taste-bud-twisting good time! But there are also Andy Warhol pieces to view, a 4-D film to catch, company history to learn, and what seems like 20 billion promotional materials to behold.

CNN Center TV LOCATION

(☎404-827-2300; www.cnn.com/tour/atlanta; 1 CNN Center; 50min tour adult/child $15/10; ⏲9am-5pm) The headquarters of the cable-TV news

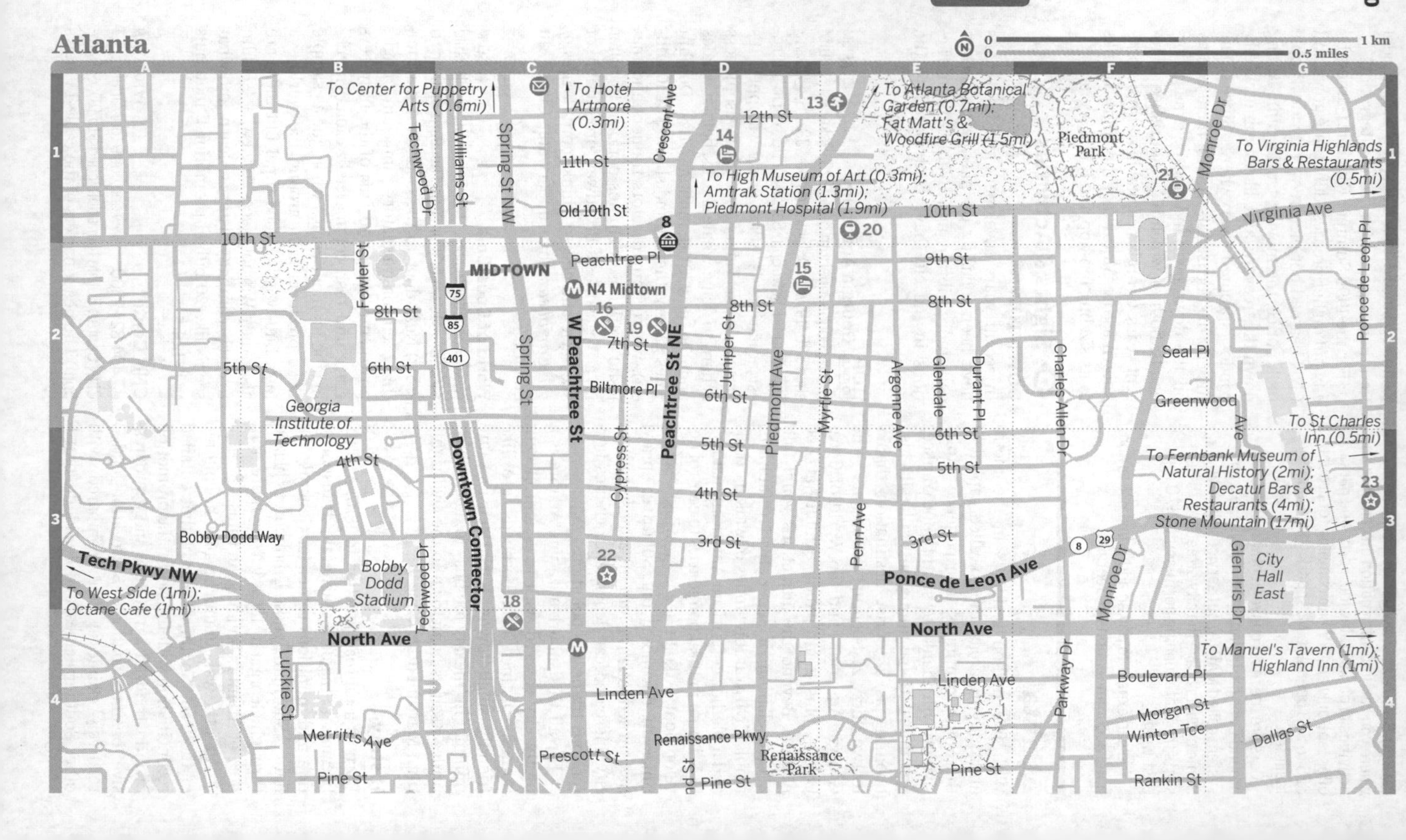
Atlanta
0 1 km
0 0.5 miles
To Center for Puppetry Arts (0.6mi)
To Hotel Artmore (0.3mi)
To Atlanta Botanical Garden (0.7mi); Fat Matt's & Woodfire Grill (1.5mi)
Piedmont Park
To Virginia Highlands Bars & Restaurants (0.5mi)
To High Museum of Art (0.3mi); Amtrak Station (1.3mi); Piedmont Hospital (1.9mi)
12th St
11th St
Old 10th St
10th St
Crescent Ave
Virginia Ave
Monroe Dr
Ponce de Leon Pl
Techwood Dr
Williams St
Spring St NW
Peachtree Pl
MIDTOWN
N4 Midtown
9th St
8th St
7th St
6th St
5th St
4th St
3rd St
Fowler St
Biltmore Pl
Spring St
W Peachtree St
Peachtree St NE
Juniper St
Piedmont Ave
Myrtle St
Argonne Ave
Glendale
Durant Pl
Charles Allen Dr
Seal Pl
Greenwood Ave
To St Charles Inn (0.5mi)
To Fernbank Museum of Natural History (2mi); Decatur Bars & Restaurants (4mi); Stone Mountain (17mi)
Georgia Institute of Technology
Downtown Connector
Cypress St
Penn Ave
Bobby Dodd Way
Tech Pkwy NW
To West Side (1mi); Octane Cafe (1mi)
Bobby Dodd Stadium
Ponce de Leon Ave
Glen Iris Dr
City Hall East
North Ave
To Manuel's Tavern (1mi); Highland Inn (1mi)
Luckie St
Linden Ave
Parkway Dr
Boulevard Pl
Morgan St
Winton Tce
Dallas St
Merritts Ave
Renaissance Pkwy
Renaissance Park
Prescott St
Pine St
Rankin St
75
85
401
8
29
8
13
14
15
16
18
19
20
21
22
23
A
B
C
D
E
F
G
1
2
3
4

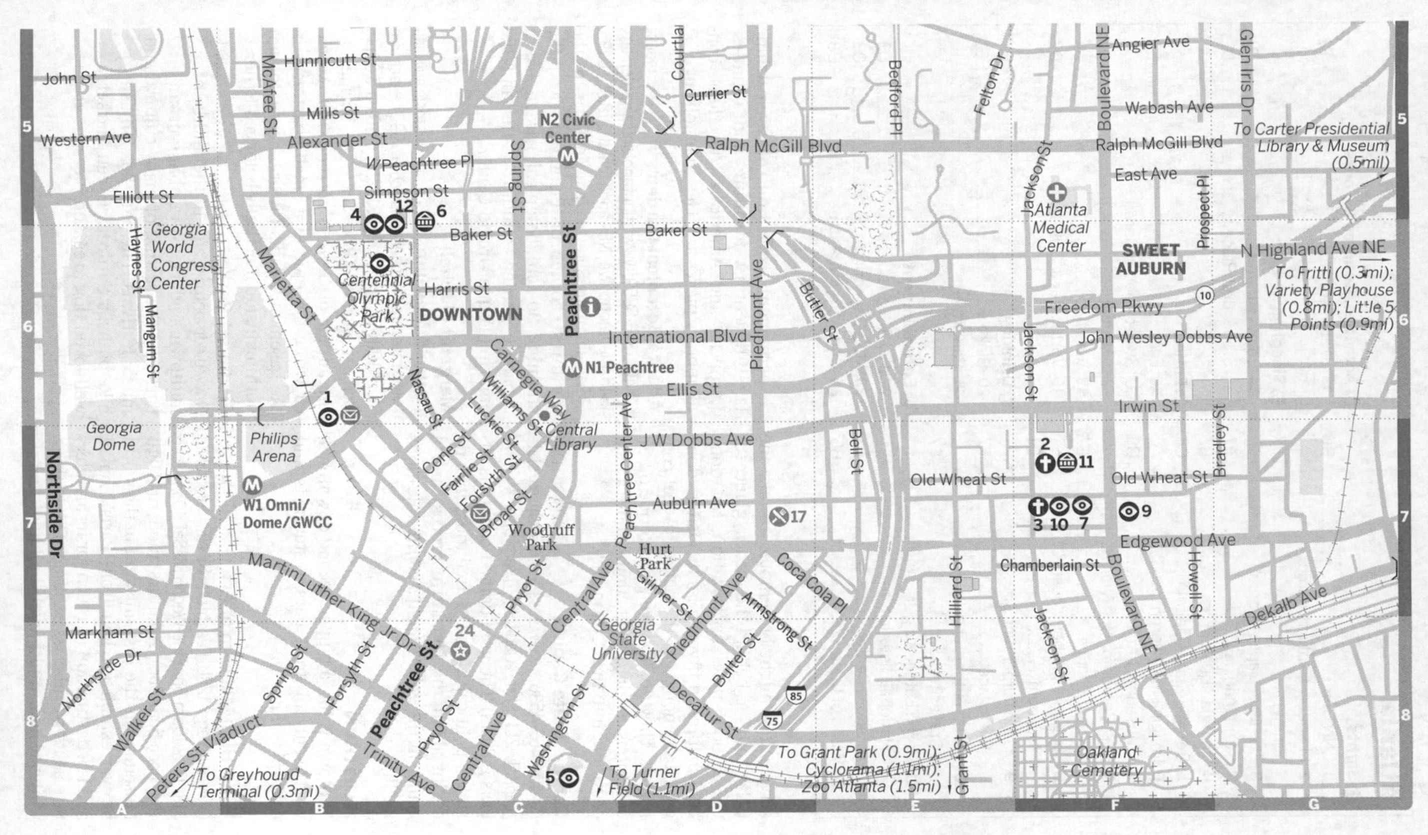
John St
Hunnicutt St
McAfee St
Mills St
Western Ave
Alexander St
W Peachtree Pl
Elliott St
Simpson St
Haynes St
Georgia World Congress Center
Mangum St
Marietta St
Baker St
Centennial Olympic Park
Harris St
DOWNTOWN
Spring St
N2 Civic Center
Peachtree St
International Blvd
N1 Peachtree
Carnegie Way
Williams St
Luckie St
Nassau St
Cone St
Fairlie St
Forsyth St
Broad St
Central Library
Ellis St
J W Dobbs Ave
Peachtree Center Ave
Auburn Ave
Woodruff Park
Hurt Park
Georgia Dome
Philips Arena
W1 Omni/ Dome/GWCC
Northside Dr
Martin Luther King Jr Dr
Markham St
Northside Dr
Walker St
Spring St
Forsyth St
Peachtree St
Pryor St
Central Ave
Washington St
Peters St Viaduct
To Greyhound Terminal (0.3mi)
Trinity Ave
Pryor St
Central Ave
Georgia State University
Gilmer St
Piedmont Ave
Armstrong St
Butler St
Coca Cola Pl
Decatur St
To Turner Field (1.1mi)
To Grant Park (0.9mi); Cyclorama (1.1mi); Zoo Atlanta (1.5mi)
Grant St
Courtland
Currier St
Ralph McGill Blvd
Baker St
Piedmont Ave
Butler St
Bell St
Bedford Pl
Felton Dr
Hilliard St
Old Wheat St
Jackson St
Atlanta Medical Center
Jackson St
Chamberlain St
Jackson St
Boulevard NE
Angier Ave
Wabash Ave
Ralph McGill Blvd
East Ave
Prospect Pl
SWEET AUBURN
Freedom Pkwy
John Wesley Dobbs Ave
Irwin St
Bradley St
Old Wheat St
Edgewood Ave
Howell St
Boulevard NE
Dekalb Ave
Oakland Cemetery
Glen Iris Dr
N Highland Ave NE
To Carter Presidential Library & Museum (0.5mil)
To Fritti (0.3mi); Variety Playhouse (0.8mi); Little 5 Points (0.9mi)

Atlanta

Sights

1 CNN Center ... B6
2 Ebenezer Baptist Church (new) ... F7
3 Ebenezer Baptist Church (original) ... F7
4 Georgia Aquarium ... B5
5 Georgia State Capitol ... C8
6 Imagine It! Children's Museum of Atlanta ... C5
7 King Center for Non-Violent Social Change ... F7
8 Margaret Mitchell House & Museum ... D1
9 Martin Luther King Jr Birthplace ... F7
10 Martin Luther King Jr Gravesite ... F7
11 Martin Luther King Jr National Historic Site Visitors Center ... F7
12 World of Coca-Cola ... B6

Activities, Courses & Tours

13 Skate Escape ... E1

Sleeping

14 Loews Atlanta ... D1
15 Stonehurst Place ... D2

Eating

16 Ecco ... C2
17 Sweet Auburn Curb Market ... D7
18 Varsity ... C4
19 Vortex Bar & Grill ... D2

Drinking

20 Blake's ... E1
21 Park Tavern ... F1

Entertainment

22 Fox Theatre ... C3
23 MJQ Concourse ... G3
24 Underground Atlanta ... C8

service. You might be tempted to take the CNN tour, a behind-the-scenes glance at the 24-hour news organization, but don't be heartbroken if you miss it. Visitors don't get close enough to the action to feel connected. They do, however, get to ride on an enormous escalator that climbs above a food court and into the CNN facility.

Georgia State Capitol HISTORIC BUILDING
(☎404-463-4536; www.sos.ga.gov/archives/state_capitol; 214 State Capitol; ⊙8am-5pm Mon-Fri, tours 11:30am) The gold-domed capitol is Atlanta's political hub. The free tours include a film about the legislative process and a glance at the government's communications facility.

MIDTOWN

Midtown is like a hipper, second downtown, with plenty of great bars, restaurants and cultural venues.

TOP CHOICE **High Museum of Art** GALLERY
(www.high.org; 1280 Peachtree St NE; adult/child $18/11; ⊙10am-5pm Tue-Wed, Fri & Sat, 10am-8pm Thu, noon-5pm Sun) Atlanta's modern High Museum was the first museum in the world to ever exhibit art lent from Paris' Louvre and is a destination as much for its architecture as its world-class exhibits. The striking whitewashed multi-level building houses a permanent collection of eye-catching late-19th-century furniture and countless European and American collections, contemporary pieces and Georgian folk art.

Atlanta Botanical Garden GARDENS
(☎404-876-5859; www.atlantabotanicalgarden.org; 1345 Piedmont Ave NE; adult/child $18.95/12.95; ⊙9am-5pm Tue-Sun, to 7pm Apr-Oct) In the northwest corner of Piedmont Park, the stunning 30-acre botanical garden has a Japanese garden, winding paths and the amazing Fuqua Orchid Center.

Margaret Mitchell House & Museum HISTORIC BUILDING
(www.margaretmitchellhouse.com; 990 Peachtree St, at 10th St; adult/child $13/10; ⊙10am-5:30pm Mon-Sat, noon-5:30pm Sun) A shrine to the author of *Gone With the Wind*. Mitchell wrote her epic in a small apartment in the basement of this historic house, though nothing inside it actually belonged to her.

Piedmont Park PARK
(www.piedmontpark.org) In the middle of midtown, a glorious, rambling urban park and the setting of many cultural and music festivals. The park has fantastic bike paths, a Saturday Green Market, a well-loved dog area and pleasant green spaces.

Skate Escape CYCLING
(☎404-892-1292; www.skateescape.com; 1086 Piedmont Ave NE) Rents out bicycles (from $6 per hour) and in-line skates ($6 per hour). It also has tandems ($12 per hour) and mountain bikes ($25 for three hours).

SWEET AUBURN

Auburn Ave was the thumping commercial and cultural heart of African American culture in the 1900s. Today a collection of sights is associated with Sweet Auburn's most famous son, Martin Luther King Jr, who was born and preached here and whose grave now looks onto the street.

All of the King sites are a few blocks' walk from the MARTA (Metropolitan Atlanta Rapid Transit Authority) King Memorial station.

Martin Luther King Jr National Historic Site HISTORIC SITE
The historic site commemorates the life, work and legacy of the civil rights lodestar. The center takes up several blocks. A stop by the excellent bustling **visitor center** (www.nps.gov/malu; 450 Auburn Ave NE; admission free; ⏰9am-5pm, to 6pm in summer) will help you get oriented with a map and brochure of area sites and exhibits.

King Center for Non-Violent Social Change MUSEUM
(www.thekingcenter.org; 449 Auburn Ave NE; ⏰9am-5pm, to 6pm summer) Across from the visitor center, it has more information on King's life and work and a few of his personal effects, including his Nobel Peace Prize. His **gravesite**, between the church and center, is surrounded by a long reflecting pool and can be viewed any time. From here, sign up for 30-minute first-come, first-served guided tours for the **Martin Luther King Jr Birthplace** (501 Auburn Ave; admission free).

FREE **Ebenezer Baptist Church** CHURCH
(www.historicebenezer.org; 407 Auburn Ave NE; ⏰tours 9am-6pm Mon-Sat, 1:30-6pm Sun) The preaching ground for King Jr, his father and grandfather, who were all pastors here, is also where King Jr's mother was murdered in 1974. A multimillion-dollar restoration of the church's balcony, hardwood flooring, pews, pulpit, altar furniture, stained-glass windows and baptismal pool to the 1960–68 period when King Jr served as co-pastor with his father, was completed in 2011. Tours are self-guided. Sunday services are now held at a new Ebenezer across the street.

GRANT PARK

Grant Park PARK
(www.grantpark.org) A large oasis of green situated on the edge of the city center, the park is home to **Zoo Atlanta** (www.zooatlanta.org; adult/child $20/16; ⏰9:30am-5:30pm Mon-Fri, to 6:30pm Sat & Sun; 👪), which features flamingos, elephants, kangaroos and the odd tiger. But the zoo's pride and joy are the giant pandas. They tend to have cubs that slaughter you with cuteness. Be prepared to wait to see the cubs.

For history buffs, on the south side of Grant Park is the **Cyclorama** building that houses the gigantic mural *Battle of Atlanta,* which visually recounts the history of the fight.

THE SHORT LIFE OF A CIVIL RIGHTS GIANT

Martin Luther King Jr, the quintessential figure of the American Civil Rights movement, was born in 1929, the son of an Atlanta preacher. His lineage was significant not only because he followed his father to the pulpit of Ebenezer Baptist Church, but also because his political speeches rang out with a preacher's inflections.

In 1955 King led the 'bus boycott' in Montgomery, AL. After a year of boycotting, the US Supreme Court removed laws that enforced segregated buses. From this successful beginning King emerged as an inspiring moral voice in civil rights.

His nonviolent approach to racial equality and peace makes his death all the more ironic: he was assassinated on a Memphis hotel balcony in 1968, four years after receiving the Nobel Peace Prize and five years after giving his legendary 'I Have a Dream' speech in Washington, DC.

King remains one of the most recognized and respected figures of the 20th century. Over 10 years he led a movement that essentially ended a system of statutory discrimination in existence since the country's founding. The Martin Luther King Jr National Historic Site and the King Center for Non-Violent Social Change in Atlanta are testaments to his moral vision, his ability to inspire others and his lasting impact on the fundamental fabric of American society.

GAY & LESBIAN ATLANTA

Atlanta – or 'Hotlanta' as some might call it – is one of the few places in Georgia, perhaps in the South, with a noticeable and active gay and lesbian population. Midtown is the center of gay life; the epicenter is around Piedmont Park and the intersection of 10th St and Piedmont Ave. The town of Decatur, east of downtown Atlanta, has a significant lesbian community. For news and information, grab a copy of the *Southern Voice* newspaper (www.sovo.com); also check out www.gayatlanta.com.

Atlanta Pride Festival (www.atlantapride.org) is a massive annual celebration of the city's gay and lesbian community. Held at the end of June in and around Piedmont Park, it attracts people from all over the country.

LITTLE FIVE POINTS & EAST ATLANTA

These two bohemian neighborhoods are close to one another, but miles away from mainstream Atlanta's genteel sensibilities. They're young, hipster neighborhoods with a definite alternative edge. Both are dominated by a main drag – **Euclid Ave** in L5P and **Flat Shoals Ave** in East Atlanta – and both are anchored by popular music venues, Variety Playhouse and the EARL, respectively. These neighborhoods offer Atlanta's most dense concentration of funky local boutiques; the stretch of Moreland Ave separating the two 'hoods is equally dense with big chain stores. Both neighborhoods can be explored well on foot, and both are jammed with restaurants.

VIRGINIA-HIGHLAND

Atlanta's preppiest neighborhood is populated by adorable homes (with big price tags) and beautiful boutiques (with big price tags). Highland Ave, running through the heart of the neighborhood, makes for a pleasant stroll.

POINTS EAST & DECATUR

TOP CHOICE **Carter Presidential Library & Museum** LIBRARY, MUSEUM
(☎404-865-7100; www.jimmycarterlibrary.org; 441 Freedom Pkwy; adult/child $8/free; ⏲9am-4:45pm Mon-Sat, noon-4:45pm Sun) Located on a hilltop overlooking downtown, it features exhibits highlighting Jimmy Carter's 1977–81 presidency, including a replica of the Oval Office. Carter's Nobel Prize is also on display. Don't miss the tranquil Japanese garden out back.

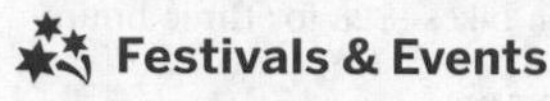

Festivals & Events

Atlanta Jazz Festival MUSIC
(www.atlantafestivals.com) A city-sponsored month-long event culminating in live concerts in Piedmont Park on Memorial Day weekend in late May.

Atlanta Pride Festival CULTURAL
(www.atlantapride.org) End of June.

National Black Arts Festival CULTURAL
(☎404-730-7315; www.nbaf.org) Artists from across the country converge on Atlanta for this festival celebrating African American music, theater, literature and film. Held in July at various locations.

Sleeping

Rates at downtown hotels tend to fluctuate wildly depending on whether there is a large convention in town. At weekends rates often go down away from downtown and rise in the city. A cheap option is to stay in one of the many chain hotels along the MARTA line outside downtown and take the train into the city for sightseeing.

St Charles Inn B&B $$
(☎404-875-1001; www.thesaintcharlesinn.com; 1001 St Charles Ave NE; r incl breakfast $115-215; P❄@📶) Ideally located steps from the shops and restaurants of Highland Ave and 15 minutes from everything else, this homey B&B – the friendliest we encountered – does all things right and cozy. There are seven fireplaces and some rooms have Jacuzzi tubs. The friendly innkeepers are a young hipster couple that can point you down the gastro/libation path of choice.

Hotel Artmore BOUTIQUE HOTEL $$
(☎404-876-6100; www.artmorehotel.com; 1302 W Peachtree St; r $99-209; ❄@📶) This funky art-deco gem wins all sorts of accolades: Excellent service, a wonderful, wine-inviting courtyard with fire pit and a superb location across the street from Arts Center MARTA station. The 1924 Spanish-Mediterranean architectural landmark was completely revamped in 2009 resulting in an artistic boutique hotel that's become an urban sanctuary for those who appreciate their trendiness with a dollop of discretion. Parking is $18.

Stonehurst Place B&B **$$$**
(☎404-881-0722; www.stonehurstplace.com; 923 Piedmont Ave NE; r $159-399; P❄@📶) Built in 1896 by the Hinman family, this elegant, almost Parisian B&B has all the modern amenities one could ask for and is fully updated with ecofriendly water treatment and heating systems. Smack in the middle of midtown, this is truly an exceptional place to stay in Atlanta if you have the budget.

Highland Inn INN **$$**
(☎404-874-5756; www.thehighlandinn.com; 644 N Highland Ave; s/d/ste incl breakfast $100/121/130; P❄📶) This aged European-style inn has a great location in the middle of Virginia-Highland. Appealing to touring musicians over the years and with its own casual music venue, the Ballroom Lounge, on the bottom floor, this ragged but clean hotel has lyrical personality.

Loews Atlanta BUSINESS HOTEL **$$**
(☎404-745-5000; ww.loewshotels.com; 1065 Peachtree St; r from $189; ❄@📶) Smart and modern, Atlanta's newest boutique business hotel is part of the Loews chain and offers luxury with all the fixings smack-dab in the heart of the arts in Midtown, walking distance from the Woodruff Arts Center and Fox Theatre. The attached Exhale Spa will soothe your weary heart after the board meetings and contemporary art – studio soundboard paintings, etc – add a bit of hi-tech artistic flair.

Eating

After New Orleans, Atlanta is the best city in the South to eat and food culture here is nothing short of obsessive. At time of writing, the gourmet burger, craft beer and mixology cultures were approaching fetish levels and the farm-to-table trend was a near given. Some of the most iconic eats of the USA were also born here: Krispy Kreme and Waffle House among them.

DOWNTOWN, MIDTOWN & NORTH

Woodfire Grill MODERN AMERICAN **$$$**
(☎404-347-9055; www.woodfiregrill.com; 1782 Cheshire Bridge Rd; mains $28-36; ⊙5:30-10pm Tue-Thu, till 11pm Fri & Sat) Fiercely bearded *Top Chef* Season 6 finalist Kevin Gillespie is at the helm at this superb choice, offering one of the city's most memorable foodie bangs for the buck and sublime service. À la carte is limited, but five-course ($65) and

ATLANTA FOR CHILDREN

Atlanta has plenty of activities to keep children entertained, delighted and – perhaps against their will – educated.

Fernbank Museum of Natural History MUSEUM
(☎404-929-6300; www.fernbankmuseum.org; 767 Clifton Rd NE; adult/child $17.50/15.50; ⊙10am-5pm Mon-Sat, noon-5pm Sun; 👪) There are better natural history museums, but Fernbank is especially kid-friendly with its new Naturequest exhibit. The museum covers the natural world from seashells to giant lizards, and it has an **IMAX theater** (adult/child $13/12).

Center for Puppetry Arts MUSEUM
(www.puppet.org; 1404 Spring St NW; museum $8.25; ⊙9am-3pm Tue-Fri, 9am-5pm Sat, 11am-5pm Sun; 👪) A wonderland for visitors of all ages and, hands-down, one of Atlanta's most unique attractions, the museum houses a treasury of puppets, some of which you get to operate yourself. Separate tickets are required for the performances.

Stone Summit ROCK CLIMBING
(www.ssclimbing.com; 3701 Presidential Pkwy; adult/child $12/10; ⊙6am-10pm Mon & Wed, 11am-10pm Tue & Thu-Fri, 10am-8pm Sat, noon-6pm Sun; 👪) The nation's largest climbing gym is especially welcoming for beginners and kids, so grab the whole family and get up those walls!

Imagine It! Children's Museum of Atlanta MUSEUM
(www.childrensmuseumatlanta.org; 275 Olympic Centennial Park Dr NW; admission $12.50; ⊙10am-4pm Mon-Fri, to 5pm Sat & Sun; 👪) A hands-on museum geared toward kids aged eight and under. Adults aren't allowed in without a youngster in tow.

seven-course ($85) tasting menus are given the attention of a *Top Chef* challenge with a Slow Food mentality: a stunning fried green tomato with bacon-hot sauce aioli, chili-rubbed Angus strip-loin in cumin-orange vinaigrette, wood-grilled honey-lacquered local quail – everything sourced, prepared and served according to all the sustainable buzz words.

Ecco EUROPEAN **$$$**
(404-347-9555; www.ecco-atlanta.com; 40 7th St NE; mains $19-25; 5:30-10pm Sun-Thu, till 11pm Fri & Sat) The vehemently sustainable Ecco was named America's best new restaurant in 2006 by *Esquire* magazine, and you can certainly have a blowout meal here. But you can also go the tapas/small bite route ($4 to $14) and leave floored with some change in your pocket. The fried goat's cheese with honey and black pepper and the chili-braised pork with garlic and homemade pappardelle are both extraordinary.

Fat Matt's Rib Shack BARBECUE **$$**
(www.fatmattsribshack.com; 1811 Piedmont Ave NE; sandwiches from $3.95; 11:30am-11:30pm Mon-Fri, to 12:30am Sat, 1-11:30pm Sun) A classic shrine to two great Southern traditions: barbecue and the blues. Take special note of the Brunswick stew, a delicious side dish best described as barbecue soup.

Varsity FAST FOOD **$**
(www.thevarsity.com; 61 North Ave, at Spring St; dogs from $1.35; 10am-11:30pm Mon-Thu, to 12:30am Fri & Sat) This drive-in restaurant on steroids (it's the world's largest) has been an Atlanta institution since 1928. It's little more than a glorified fast-food joint, but it's always packed.

WEST SIDE

Miller Union NEW SOUTHERN **$$$**
(404-685-3191; www.millerunion.com; 999 Brady Ave; mains $19-26; 11:30am-2:30pm Tue-Sat & 5-10pm Mon-Thu, 5-11pm Fri & Sat) Former stockyards have been transformed into Atlanta's most exciting newcomer, a lesson in restrained subtlety disguised as sustainable New Southern gastro-science in a city obsessed with both. Chef Steven Satterfield has wooed everyone from us to Martha Stewart with his appetizer egg cooked in celery cream.

Bocado AMERICAN **$$**
(www.bocadoatlanta.com; 887 Howell Mill Rd; lunch mains $8-11; 11am-2pm Mon-Fri, 5-10pm Mon-Sat) The name loosely translates as mouthful/morsel/bite from Spanish/Portuguese/Italian, but there's nothing little about the flavor packed into the viciously creative sandwiches and salads on offer at this West Side farm-to-table newcomer. Hello roasted poblano (a type of chili) and pimento cheese sandwich with bacon and fried green tomatoes, it's a pleasure to meet you.

SWEET AUBURN

Sweet Auburn Curb Market MARKET **$**
(www.sweetauburncurbmarket.com; 209 Edgewood Ave SE; mains $5-9; 8am-6pm Mon-Sat) This small market allows foodies to browse countless stalls for cooking ingredients or hot meals served on the premises, from organic coffee to Italian deli fare. Bell Street Burritos is particularly worthy of a trip here, serving up the sort of fresh, fat burritos that evoke San Francisco's Mission District.

LITTLE FIVE POINTS

Vortex Bar & Grill BURGERS **$**
(www.thevortexbarandgrill.com; 438 Moreland Ave; burgers from $6.45; 11am-midnight Sun-Thu, to 3am Fri & Sat) A scrappy joint where alterna-hispters mingle alongside Texas tourists and Morehouse College steppers. The snarky menu boasts loads of gourmet burgers, but don't discount the sublime black bean veggie melt. There's also a branch in Midtown (878 Peachtree St). No kids.

VIRGINIA-HIGHLAND & INMAN PARK

TOP CHOICE **Goin' Coastal** SEAFOOD **$$$**
(www.goincoastalseafood.com; 1021 Virginia Ave NE; mains $18-26; 5-10pm Mon-Thu, 10am-10pm Fri, 11:30am-11pm Sat & Sun) Atlanta needs another holy ethics-toting restaurant like it needs more traffic; but great seafood is still pretty off the radar here. That changes with this casual neighborhood seafood place in the heart of the Highlands run by a bunch of good ol' fishing buddies. Fresh blackboard catches of the day supplement stunning staples such as lobster tacos ($18), coastal trout ($24) and a heap of delicious sides (creamy grits, jalapeño corn-bread pudding). It only serves eco-acceptable fish and uses hydroponic greens grown with reclaimed water from high-tech urban farms inside reused shipping containers. Futuristic, fun and fabulous.

Fritti PIZZERIA **$$**
(www.frittirestaurant.com; 309 N Highland Ave NE; pizza $10-15; 11:30-3pm & 5:30-11pm, till

midnight Fri & Sat, 12:30-10pm Sun) Staunchly traditional pizza Napoletana emerges from an $18,000, 13,000lb, 1100°F (593°C) Uno Forno brick oven, hand-built brick-by-brick by *the* Stefano Ferrara – Naples' pizza God – with 100% Italian materials including volcanic ash from Mount Vesuvius. Fritti is not messing around. Cooking time: 45 seconds.

DECATUR

Independent Decatur, 6 miles east of downtown, has grown into a bohemian enclave of counterculture over the years and is now a bonafide foodie destination.

TOP CHOICE **Leon's Full Service** FUSION $$
(www.leonsfullservice.com; 131 E Ponce de Leon Ave; mains $11-19; ⏲5pm-1am Mon, 11:30am-1am Tue-Thu & Sun, till 2am Fri & Sat) If your indie rock friends got together and dreamed up a holier-than-thou menu and beer list, this is it. Everyone here thinks they are cooler than you, but the food excels: slow-roasted beef brisket in black peppercorn gravy, killer pub frites with specialty sauces, etc. It's all the rage in Decatur rightfully so.

Farm Burger BURGERS $
(www.farmburger.net; 410b W Ponce de Leon Ave; burgers from $6; ⏲11:30am-10pm Sun-Thu, 11:30am-10pm Fri & Sat) Southeastern sweetgrass-fed, locally farm-raised beef is the calling at this gourmet farm-to-table burger joint, the current trailblazer in an ongoing Atlanta burger war. Build your own from $6 from an unorthodox list that includes oxtail marmalade, roasted bone marrow and pimento and cheese (a Southern staple); or go for the daily-changing chalkboard special.

Taqueria del Sol MEXICAN $
(359 W. Ponce de Leon Ave; tacos $2.39; ⏲11am-2pm Mon-Fri & 5:30-9pm Tue-Thu, 12-3pm Sat & 5:30-10pm Fri & Sat) Smoked pork or fried chicken tacos and to-die-for shrimp corn chowder are highlights of this Mexican–Southern marriage, a great value in a city that can overwhelm with both sides of that culinary coin otherwise.

Drinking

Brick Store Pub BAR
(www.brickstorepub.com; 125 E Court Sq) Beer hounds geek out on Atlanta's best beer selection, with some 17 meticulously chosen draughts (so underground, they're striking oil) and a separate Belgian beer bar upstairs. In total, nearly 200 by the bottle and a cool quotient approaching exhausting.

Park Tavern BAR
(www.parktavern.com; 500 10th Street NE) This microbrewery/restaurant may not be on the modster It List, but its outdoor patio on the edge of Piedmont Park is one of the most beautiful spots in Atlanta to sit back and drink away a weekend afternoon.

Euclid Avenue Yacht Club BAR
(1136 Euclid Ave) A divey bar ideal for grabbing a drink before a show at the nearby Variety Playhouse.

Octane CAFE
(www.octanecoffee.com; 1009-B Marietta St; sandwiches $4-6; ⏲7am-11pm Mon-Thu, to midnight Fri, 8am-11pm Sat & Sun; wi-fi) This industrial-hip coffeehouse near Georgia Tech's campus brews the joe of choice for severe caffeine junkies, following a 'direct trade' philosophy.

Manuel's Tavern BAR
(www.manuelstavern.com; 602 N Highland Ave) A longtime political hangout that draws a good, conversational beer-drinking crowd.

Blake's GAY & LESBIAN
(www.blakesontheparkatlanta.com; 227 10th St NE) Right on Piedmont Park, Blake's bills itself as 'Atlanta's favorite gay bar since 1987.'

Entertainment

Atlanta has big-city nightlife with lots of live music and cultural events. Check out **Atlanta Coalition of Performing Arts** (www.atlantaperforms.com), which has info and links about the city's music, film, dance and theater scene. The **Atlanta Music Guide** (www.atlantamusicguide.com) maintains a live-music schedule, plus a directory of local venues and links to online ticketing.

Theater

Woodruff Arts Center ARTS CENTER
(www.woodruffcenter.org; 1280 Peachtree St NE, at 15th St) An arts campus hosting the High Museum, the Atlanta Symphony Orchestra and the Alliance Theatre.

Fox Theatre THEATER
(www.foxtheatre.org; 660 Peachtree St NE) A spectacular 1929 movie palace with fanciful Moorish and Egyptian designs. It hosts Broadway shows, and concerts in an auditorium holding more than 4500 people.

Live Music & Nightclubs

Cover charges at the following vary nightly. Check their respective websites for music calendars and ticket prices.

EARL LIVE MUSIC
(www.badearl.com; 488 Flat Shoals Ave) The indie rocker's pub of choice – a smoky restaurant with surprisingly good food; it's also a bar and a busy live-music venue.

Eddie's Attic LIVE MUSIC
(www.eddiesattic.com; 515b N McDonough St, Decatur) One of the city's best venues to hear live folk and acoustic music, renowned for breaking local artists, in a nonsmoking atmosphere seven nights a week.

MJQ Concourse CLUB
(☎404-870-0575; 736 Ponce de Leon Place NE) This club inside a former underground parking garage is now all the young indie scenester rage – you enter through a small retractable garage door in what looks like an indiscreet tool shed behind a Chipotle – I mean, where else?

Variety Playhouse LIVE MUSIC
(www.variety-playhouse.com; 1099 Euclid Ave NE) A smartly booked and well-run concert venue for a variety of touring artists.

Sports

Order tickets to sporting events through **Ticketmaster** (☎404-249-6400; www.ticketmaster.com).

Atlanta Braves BASEBALL
(☎404-522-7630; www.atlantabraves.com; tickets $8-90) The Major League Baseball (MLB) team plays at Turner Field. The MARTA/Braves shuttles to the games leave from **Underground Atlanta** (www.underground-atlanta.com; cnr Peachtree & Alabama Sts; ⏲10am-9pm Mon-Sat, 11am-6pm Sun) at Steve Polk Plaza beginning 90 minutes before the first pitch.

ℹ Information

Emergency & Medical Services

Atlanta Medical Center (www.atlantamedcenter.com; 303 Pkwy Dr NE)

Atlanta Police Department (☎404-614-6544; www.atlantapd.org)

Emory University Hospital (www.emoryhealthcare.org; 1364 Clifton Rd NE)

Piedmont Hospital (www.piedmonthospital.org; 1968 Peachtree Rd NW)

Internet Access

Central Library (www.afpls.org; 1 Margaret Mitchell Sq; ⏲9am-9pm Mon-Sat, 2-6pm Sun) Many branches of the public library offer two free 15-minute internet sessions daily, including this main branch.

Internet Resources

Access Atlanta (www.accessatlanta.com) A great place to find out about Atlanta news and upcoming events.

Atlanta Travel Guide (www.atlanta.net) Official site of the Atlanta Convention & Visitors Bureau with excellent links to shops, restaurants, hotels and upcoming events.

Media

Atlanta (www.atlantamagazine.com) A monthly general-interest magazine covering local issues, arts and dining.

Atlanta Daily World (www.atlantadailyworld.com) The nation's oldest continuously running African American newspaper (since 1928).

Atlanta Journal-Constitution (www.ajc.com) Atlanta's major daily newspaper, with a good travel section on Sunday.

Creative Loafing (www.clatl.com) For hip tips on music, arts and theater, this free alternative weekly comes out every Wednesday.

Post

For general postal information call ☎800-275-8777.

Post office CNN Center (190 Marietta St NW); Little Five Points (455 Moreland Ave NE); North Highland (1190 N Highland Ave NE); Phoenix Station (41 Marietta St NW)

Tourist Information

Atlanta Convention & Visitors Bureau (☎404-521- 6600; www.atlanta.net; 233 Peachtree St; ⏲9am-5pm Mon-Fri) Has an online neighborhood guide, a restaurant guide and a link to info for gay and lesbian travelers – in six languages. Its website also lets you buy a CityPass, a tremendous money saver that bundles admission to five attractions for the discounted price of $69.

ℹ Getting There & Away

Atlanta's huge **Hartsfield-Jackson International Airport** (ATL; www.atlanta-airport.com), 12 miles south of downtown, is a major regional hub and an international gateway. It's the busiest airport in the world in overall passenger traffic.

The **Greyhound terminal** (232 Forsyth St) is next to the MARTA Garnett station. Some destinations include Nashville, TN (five hours), New Orleans, LA (10½ hours), New York (20 hours), Miami, FL (16 hours) and Savannah, GA (4¾ hours).

The **Amtrak station** (1688 Peachtree St NW, at Deering Rd) is just north of downtown.

Getting Around

The **Metropolitan Atlanta Rapid Transit Authority** (MARTA; www.itsmarta.com; fares $2.50) rail line travels to/from the airport to downtown, along with a few less-useful routes used mostly by commuters. Individual tokens are no longer sold – every customer must purchase a Breeze card ($1), which can be loaded and reloaded as necessary.

The shuttle and car-rental agencies have desks in the airport situated at the baggage-claim level.

Driving in Atlanta can be infuriating. You'll often find yourself sitting in traffic jams, and it's easy to get disoriented – a road map is invaluable.

North Georgia

The southern end of the great Appalachian Range extends some 40 miles into Georgia's far north, providing some superb mountain scenery and wild white-water rivers. The landscape is unlike anywhere else in Georgia. The fall colors emerge late here, peaking in October.

A few days are warranted to see sites like the 1200ft-deep **Tallulah Gorge** (www.gastateparks.org/TallulahGorge), the mountain scenery and hiking trails at **Vogel State Park** (www.gastateparks.org/Vogel) and **Unicoi State Park** (www.gastateparks.org/Unicoi), and the interesting collection of Appalachian folk arts at the **Foxfire Museum** (www.foxfire.org; adult/child $6/3; ⌚8:30am-4:30pm Mon-Sat) in Mountain City.

DAHLONEGA

In 1828 Dahlonega was the site of the first gold rush in the USA. The boom these days, though, is in tourism. It's an easy day excursion from Atlanta and is a fantastic destination if you want to get away to the mountains.

Walking around the historic main square is an event in itself. Many offbeat shops compete for tourist dollars. The **visitor center** (☎706-864-3513; www.dahlonega.org; 13 S Park St; ⌚9am-5:30pm Mon-Fri, 10am-5pm Sat) has plenty of information on area sites and activities (including hiking, canoeing, kayaking, rafting and mountain biking).

Amicalola Falls State Park (☎706-265-4703; www.amicalolafalls.com), 18 miles west of Dahlonega on Hwy 52, features the 729ft **Amicalola Falls**, the highest waterfall in Georgia. The park offers spectacular scenery, a lodge, and excellent hiking and mountain-biking trails.

The **cycling** (www.cyclenorthgeorgia.com) was fantastic enough for Lance Armstrong to train here. **Dalhonega Wheelworks** (www.wheelworksga.com; 24 Alicia Lane; ⌚11am-6pm Mon, Tue, Thu, Fri, 1:30-6pm Wed, 9am-5pm Sat) is a nice bike shop in town with mountain and road bike rentals, bike guides and daily rides offered at the shop. The 35-mile **Three Gap** cycling loop is spectacular, but bring your climbing legs.

A number of wineries near Dahlonega actually produce some tasty products, but it's especially worth going to hang out at the gorgeous vineyards. **Frogtown Cellars** (www.frogtownwine.com; 700 Ridge Point Dr; ⌚noon-5pm Sun-Fri, to 6pm Sat, 12:30-5pm Sun) is a beautiful winery with a killer deck on which to sip libations and enjoy a panini lunch. It's one of the East Coast's most award-winning producers.

Crimson Moon Café (24 N Park St; mains $8-15; ⌚11am-3pm Mon, till 9pm Wed, till 10pm Thu-Fri, 8am-1pm Sat, 8am-8pm Sun) is an organic coffeehouse offering great Southern comfort food and an intimate live music venue.

Hiker Hostel (☎770-312-7342; www.hikerhostel.com; 7693 Hwy 19N; dm/r $17/40; P❄@📶), on Hwy 19N near the Three Gap Loop, is owned by an avid couple of cycling and outdoors enthusiasts. The hostel is new-ish, wonderfully kept with extra-cool dorm-bed drapes for privacy, and provides hearty breakfasts. The only downside is the blurred lines between staff and guest regarding bed maintenance in private rooms.

Central Georgia

Central Georgia is a kind of catch-all for everything that's not metro Atlanta, mountainous north Georgia or swampy Savannah-centric south Georgia. The remaining area feels rustic and Southern.

ATHENS

A beery, artsy and laid-back college town roughly 70 miles east of Atlanta, Athens has an extremely popular football team (the University of Georgia Bulldogs), a world-famous music scene (which has launched artists including the B-52s, R.E.M. and Widespread Panic) and a burgeoning restaurant culture. The university drives the culture of Athens and ensures an ever-replenishing supply of young bar-hoppers and concertgoers. The pleasant, walkable downtown offers a plethora of funky choices for eating, drinking and shopping.

For a more detailed music sites tour, pick up a copy of Lonely Planet's *The Carolinas, Georgia & the South Trips*.

Sights & Activities

State Botanical Garden of Georgia GARDENS
(www.uga.edu/~botgarden; 2450 S Milledge Ave; suggested donation $2; 8am-6pm, to 8pm summer) Truly gorgeous, with winding outdoor paths and a socio-historical edge to boot, Athens' gardens rivals Atlanta's. Signs provide smart context for its amazing collection of plants, which runs the gamut from rare and threatened species to nearly 5 miles of top-notch woodland walking trails.

Georgia Museum of Art MUSEUM
(www.georgiamuseum.org; 90 Carlton St; suggested donation $3; 10am-5pm Tue-Wed, Fri & Sat, to 9pm Thu, 1-5pm Sun) Fresh off a $20 million expansion, the state's modern, excellent art museum now boasts 16,000 sq ft of new galleries and an outdoor sculpture garden.

Sleeping & Eating

Athens does not have an awesome variety of places to stay. There are standard chains just out of town on W Broad St.

TOP CHOICE **Hotel Indigo** BOUTIQUE HOTEL $$
(706-546-0430; www.indigoathens.com; 500 College Ave; r weekend/weekday from $159/139; P) Athens' first – and desperately needed – boutique hotel is part of the Indigo chain, but here is a LEED Gold-certified sustainable standout (the first of InterContinental's 4500 hotels worldwide). Green elements throughout (regenerative elevators, priority parking for hybrid vehicles, 30% of the building constructed from recycled content) means it's environmentally sound, and the 130-room eco-chic hotel is steeped in local color (Jittery Joe's coffee instead of Starbucks, reclaimed barn-wood-framed posters of R.E.M. and the like).

Foundry Park Inn & Spa INN $$
(706-549-7020; www.foundryparkinn.com; 295 E Dougherty St; r $130-150; P) An upscale, non-corporate choice on pleasant grounds, including the restored Confederate iron foundry. In addition to its on-site spa the hotel campus includes a restaurant and the Melting Point, a cozy music venue.

TOP CHOICE **Five & Ten** AMERICAN $$$
(706-546-7300; www.fiveandten.com; 1653 S Lumpkin St; mains $18-29; 5:30-10pm Sun-Thu, to 11pm Fri & Sat, 10:30am-2:30pm Sun) Driven by sustainable ingredients, Five & Ten ranks among the South's best restaurants. Its menu is earthy and slightly gamey: sweetbreads, hand-cut pasta and Frogmore stew (stewed corn, sausage and potato). Reservations mandatory.

Farm 255 AMERICAN $$
(www.farm255.com; 255 W Washington St; mains $12-21; 5:30-10pm Tue-Thu, to 10:30pm Fri & Sat, 11am-2pm & 5:30-9:30pm Sun) This stylish, light-filled bistro gets much of its meat and vegetables from its own 5-acre, organic/biodynamic Blue Moon Farms outside of Athens. The operative word here is *fresh*.

Grit VEGETARIAN $
(www.thegrit.com; 199 Prince Ave; mains $5-8; 11am-10pm Mon-Fri 10am-3pm & 5-10pm Sat & Sun;) Get your tofu Reuben (grilled rye sandwich) or black-eyed pea burger on at this pioneering vegetarian spot whose landlord is R.E.M.'s Michael Stipe.

Grill DINER $
(www.thegrit.com; 171 College Ave; mains $5-8; 24hr) Downtown diner that's an Athens institution for curing late-night, drunken munches. It's all about the fries dipped in feta cheese.

Drinking & Entertainment

Nearly 100 bars and restaurants dot Athens' compact downtown area, so it's not hard to find a good time. Pick up a free *Flagpole* (www.flagpole.com) weekly to find out what's on.

Trappeze Pub PUB
(www.trappezepub.com; 269 W Washington St; draft beers $4-8; 11am-2am Mon-Sat, to midnight Sun) Those 'beer weirdos,' as one local put it, flock

BUCK MANOR

For a glimpse of a classic Athens musical legend, do a drive-by of 748 Cobb St, a Second Empire Victorian home painted 12 different colors and known as **Buck Manor**. R.E.M. guitarist Peter Buck lived here until his divorce from his wife, Barrie; and R.E.M. filmed the *Nightswimming* video here as well as a prerelease promotional video for *Out of Time*. Nirvana spent the night here when they played the 40 Watt Club in 1991.

here to enjoy a choice of 35 beers on tap and 260 by the bottle, with bartenders who wax poetic about suds like sommeliers talk Château d'Yquem. The above-average pub menu takes full advantage of the stock – pulled pork marinated in Unibroue Ephemere? Don't mind if I do.

40 Watt Club LIVE MUSIC
(www.40watt.com; 285 W Washington St) It has lounges, a tiki bar, $2 PBR beers, and indie rock on stage. It's where the big hitters in town play. No wonder it's legendary.

Manhattan Cafe BAR
(337 N Hull St) The antithesis of most downtown Athens bars, this dive is the spot to tie one on if you don't have an 8am Psych class to concern you. It's all funky lighting, mismatched reclaimed furniture and townie attitude.

Information

The **Athens Welcome Center** (706-353-1820; www.athenswelcomecenter.com; 280 E Dougherty St; 10am-5pm Mon-Sat, noon-5pm Sun), in a historic antebellum house at the corner of Thomas St, provides maps and information on local tours – these include a Civil War tour and the 'Walking Tour of Athens Music History.'

Savannah

Like a Southern belle who wears hot pants under her skirt, this grand historic town revolves around formal antebellum architecture and the revelry of local students from Savannah College of Art & Design. It sits alongside the Savannah River, about 18 miles from the coast, amid Lowcountry swamps and mammoth live oak trees dripping with Spanish moss. With its gorgeous mansions, cotton warehouses, wonderfully beautiful squares and Colonial public buildings, Savannah preserves its past with pride and grace. However, unlike its sister city of Charleston, SC, which retains its reputation as a dignified and refined cultural center, Savannah isn't clean-cut – the town has been described as 'a beautiful lady with a dirty face.'

Sights & Activities

The Central Park of Savannah is a sprawling rectangular green space called **Forsyth Park**. The park's beautiful fountain is a quintessential photo op.

Owens-Thomas House HISTORIC BUILDING
(www.telfair.org; 124 Abercorn St; adult/child $15/5; noon-5pm Mon, 10am-5pm Tue-Sat, 1-5pm Sun) Completed in 1819 by British architect William Jay, this gorgeous villa exemplifies English Regency-style architecture, which is known for its symmetry. The guided tour is fussy, but it delivers interesting trivia about the spooky 'haint blue' ceiling paint in the slave's quarters (made from crushed indigo, buttermilk and crushed oyster shells) and the number of years by which this mansion preceded the White House in getting running water (nearly 20).

Jepson Center for the Arts GALLERY
(JCA; www.telfair.org; 207 W York St; multivenue ticket adult/child $20/5; 10am-5pm Mon, Wed, Fri & Sat, 10am-8pm Thu, noon-5pm Sun;) Now over five years old but still looking pretty darn space-age by Savannah's standards, the JCA focuses on 20th- and 21st-century art. Its contents are modest in size but intriguing. There's also a neat interactive area for kids. The $20 multivenue ticket allows discounted admission to two affiliated museums, the Telfair and the Owens-Thomas House.

Mercer-Williams House HISTORIC BUILDING
(www.mercerhouse.com; 429 Bull St; adult/child $12.50/8) Although Jim Williams, the Savannah art dealer portrayed by Kevin Spacey in the film version of *Midnight in the Garden of Good and Evil,* died back in 1990, his infamous mansion didn't become a museum until 2004. You're not allowed to see the upstairs, where Williams' family still lives, but the downstairs is an interior decorator's fantasy.

Telfair Museum of Art MUSEUM
(www.telfair.org; 121 Barnard St; multi-venue ticket adult/child $20/5; noon-5pm Mon, 10am-5pm Tue-Sat, 1-5pm Sun) Along with silver from the 1800s and a colossal oil painting depicting a scene from the Hundred Years War, Sylvia Shaw's famous 1936 *Bird Girl* sculpture – the one on the cover of *Midnight in the Garden of Good and Evil* – stands inside this museum.

Cathedral of St John the Baptist CHURCH
Completed in 1896 but destroyed by fire two years later, this impressive cathedral, reopened in 1912, features stunning stained-glass transept windows from Austria depicting Christ's ascension into heaven as well as

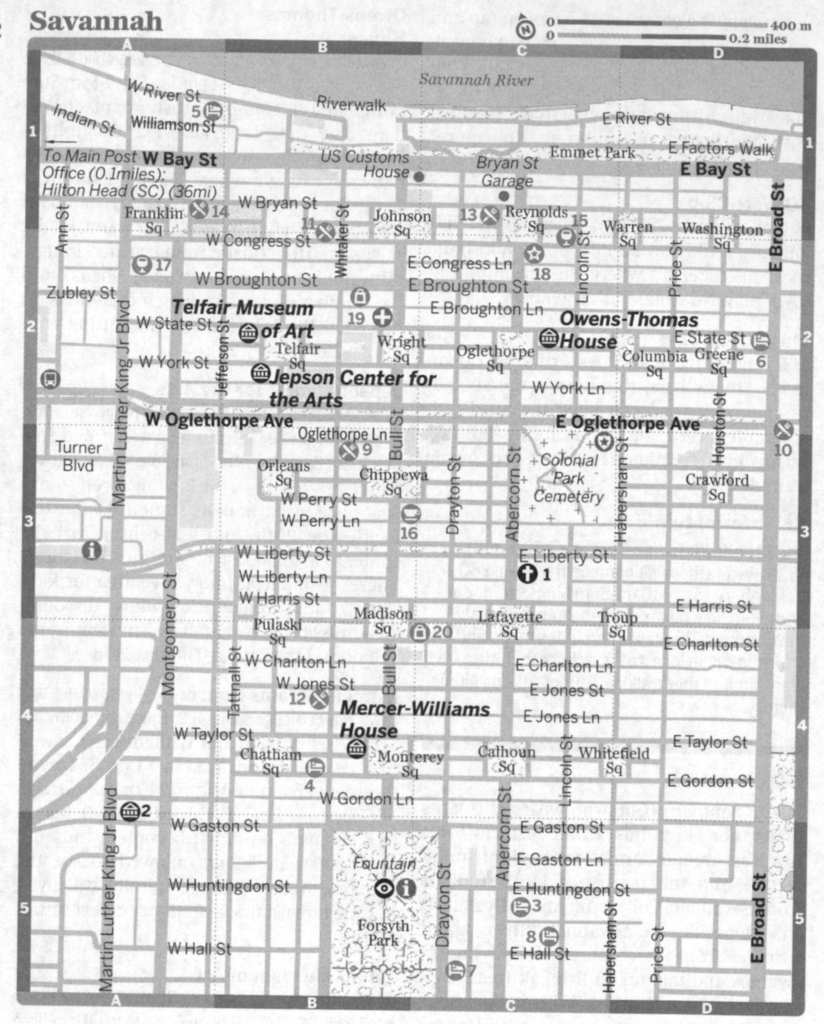

ornate Station of the Cross woodcarvings from Bavaria.

Ralph Mark Gilbert Civil Rights Museum MUSEUM
(460 Martin Luther King Jr Blvd; adult/child $8/4; ⏲9am-5pm Tue-Sat) Focuses on the local history of segregated schools, hotels, hospitals, jobs and lunch counters. Push the buttons at the Levy's lunch counter – a dramatization, but no less stinging.

Sleeping

Luckily for travelers, it's become stylish for Savannah hotels and B&Bs to serve hors d'oeuvres and wine to guests in the evening. Accommodations by the river have lots of hype and make your wallet quiver.

Bohemian Hotel BOUTIQUE HOTEL $$$
(☎912-721-3800; www.bohemianhotelsavannah.com; 102 West Bay St; r weekend/weekday $319/229; P❄@☎) Though it was meant to evoke a maritime theme (how awful?), thankfully it didn't take – stunning hot Gothic hallways and dark, dungeon-chic art are better adjectives to describe Savannah's new waterfront hotel. Staying here feels almost medieval, which is really kind of sinister and

Savannah

Top Sights

	Jepson Center for the Arts	B2
	Mercer-Williams House	B4
	Owens-Thomas House	C2
	Telfair Museum of Art	B2

Sights

1	Cathedral of St John the Baptist	C3
2	Ralph Mark Gilbert Civil Rights Museum	A4

Sleeping

3	Azalea Inn	C5
4	Bed & Breakfast Inn	B4
5	Bohemian Hotel	A1
6	Green Palm Inn	D2
7	Mansion on Forsyth Park	C5
8	Savannah Pensione	C5

Eating

9	Angel's BBQ	B3
10	Cha Bella	D2
11	Lady & Sons	B1
12	Mrs Wilkes'	B4
13	Olde Pink House	C1
14	Vinnie Van GoGo's	A1

Drinking

15	Abe's on Lincoln	C2
16	Gallery Espresso	B3
17	Lulu's Chocolate Bar	A2

Entertainment

18	Lucas Theatre for the Arts	C2

Shopping

19	Savannah Bee Company	B2
20	ShopSCAD	C4

great save the low-lit guest rooms – the one outright flaw. Small touches like driftwood and oyster chandeliers are fabulous and personalized service makes it feel far more intimate than its 75 rooms indicate. The views, especially from the Rocks rooftop bar, are exemplary. Parking is $21.

Thunderbird Inn MOTEL **$**

(912-232-2661; www.thethunderbirdinn.com; 611 W Oglethorpe Ave; r $99; P❄📶) A little dab of Palm Springs, a little dip of Vegas best describes this renovated vintage-chic 1964 motel that wins its own popularity contest – a 'Hippest hotel in Savannah' proclamation greets guests in the '60s-soundtracked lobby. But in a land of stuffy B&Bs this groovy place is an oasis, made all the better by a fresh coat of soothing paints and local SCAD (Savannah College of Art and Design) student art. The hotel is just outside the tourist area, across from the Greyhound station. Krispy Kreme donuts for breakfast!

Mansion on Forsyth Park HOTEL **$$$**

(912-238-5158; www.mansiononforsythpark.com; 700 Drayton St; r weekend/weekday $249/199; ❄@📶≋) A choice location and chic design highlight the luxe accommodations on offer at the 18,000-sq-ft Mansion – the sexy bathrooms alone are practically worth the money. The best part of the hotel-spa is the amazing local and international art that crowds its walls and hallways, over 400 original pieces in all. Parking costs $20 per day.

Green Palm Inn B&B **$$**

(912-447-8901; www.greenpalminn.com; 548 E President St; r from $149-189; P❄📶) With the capacity to host up to nine people, this cute B&B off Green Sq provides an intimate B&B experience. The rooms are meticulously cared for and staff is helpful and friendly.

Bed & Breakfast Inn B&B **$$**

(912-238-0518; www.savannahbnb.com; 117 W Gordon St; r weekday/weekend from $159/179; P❄📶) Spittin' distance from Savannah's most architecturally diverse square (Monterrey), this is a well-loved, well-worn establishment, but the rooms are crisp, unique and tidy. Easy to walk right by on a uniform street of 1850 row houses, the rooms are scattered about six buildings along the street.

Savannah Pensione GUESTHOUSE **$**

(912-236-7744; www.savannahpensione.com; 304 E Hall St; dm $23, r $45-60; ❄📶) It was run as a hostel for some 15 years but the owner of this basic neighborhood crash-pad got tired of backpackers traipsing up and down the historic steps in his 1894 Italianate mansion. Fair enough. Now a bare-bones pensione, it still has a vaguely hostel-like vibe and fills a definite niche in the market: dorms bed can be had for $23, but only for groups of three or more who know each other.

Azalea Inn B&B **$$$**

(912-236-2707; www.azaleainn.com; 217 E Huntingdon St; r from $200; P❄📶≋) Located on a quiet street, the Azalea has lovely rooms and a little pool in the back. The mural in the dining room, created by art students, is a highlight.

Eating

TOP CHOICE Mrs Wilkes' SOUTHERN $$
(www.mrswilkes.com; 107 W Jones St; lunch $16; 11am-2pm Mon-Fri) The line outside can begin as early as 8am at this first-come, first served, Southern comfort food institution. Once the lunch bell rings and you are seated family-style, the kitchen unloads on you: fried chicken, beef stew, meatloaf, cheese potatoes, collard greens, black-eyed peas, mac 'n' cheese, rutabaga, candied yams, squash casserole, creamed corn *and* biscuits. It's like Thanksgiving and the Last Supper rolled into one massive feast chased with sweet tea.

Olde Pink House NEW SOUTHERN $$$
(912-232-4286; 23 Abercorn St; mains $25-31; 5-10:30pm Sun-Mon, 11am-10:30pm Tue-Thu, 11am-11pm Fri & Sat) There are fancier and trendier restaurants in Savannah but this 1771 National Landmark on Reynolds Sq is rarely trumped for food or experience. The whole place epitomizes antebellum romance and you'll fall in love with the signature crispy scored flounder (though the menu is chock-full of irresistible Southern-bent delights). The service is casually flawless; the dark and cozy downstairs bar is also worthy of a cocktail pop-in. Damn near perfect.

Angel's BBQ BARBECUE $
(www.angels-bbq.com; 21 West Oglethorpe Lane; pulled-pork sandwich $6; 11:30am-3pm Tue, till 6pm Wed-Sat) Utterly low-brow and hidden down a uneventful lane, Angel's pulled-pork sandwich and sea-salted fries will leave you humbled and thoroughly satisfied – and that's before you tear through the impressive list of housemade sauces, one made with scary-hot ghost and Chiltepin chilies.

Cha Bella AMERICAN $$$
(102 E Broad St; brunch $15.95, dinner mains $17-32; 5:30-9pm Tue-Thu, till 10pm Fri & Sat, 5:30-9pm Sun) With a commitment to organic, local and well-presented vittles, this welcoming restaurant leaves pretension behind: swings hang on the lovely patio. The Georgia white-shrimp risotto or fish-market special will not leave you unpleased.

Lady & Sons SOUTHERN $$
(912-233-2600; www.ladyandsons.com; 102 W Congress St; buffets $14-18; 11am-9pm Mon-Thu, to 10pm Sat & Sun) Savannah's irrepressible culinary doyenne Paula Deen has created a monster – and, some say, lost the magic in the process. Her country cookin' is indeed delicious, but showing up at 9:30am for lunch or 3:30pm for dinner to put your name on the list means the whole thing has gotten a bit out of hand. Perhaps Deen might consider putting the soul back into her South?

Vinnie Van GoGo's PIZZERIA $
(www.vinnievangogo.com; 317 W Bryan St; pizza slices from $2.50; 4-11pm Mon-Thu, noon-midnight Fri & Sat, noon-11:30pm Sun) This locally owned pizzeria draws legions of locals for its Neapolitan brick-oven pizza.

Drinking

Rocks on the Roof BAR
(102 West Bay St; from 11am) The expansive rooftop bar at the new Bohemian Hotel is just what Savannah needed: a breezy, lipstick-red wrap-around rooftop set to an indie-cred soundtrack with lovely river views – best seen from seats on the northwest corner. There's live music Thursday to Saturday – prepare to rub elbows with the velvet rope.

Lulu's Chocolate Bar CAFE
(www.luluschocolatebar.net; 42 Martin Luther King Jr Blvd) More a place to sink yourself into a sugar coma than catch a buzz, Lulu's is an adorable yet chic neighborhood martini and dessert bar. The heavenly signature Lulutini here is pure chocolate decadence.

Gallery Espresso CAFE
(www.galleryespresso.com; 234 Bull St; 7:30am-10pm Mon-Fri, 8am-11pm Sat & Sun) Savannah's best coffee shop; this and the Sentient are two of the South's best as well. Gallery is cozier, more conveniently located and is near-fiendish regarding its teas. There's also light fare and scrumptious desserts.

Sentient Bean CAFE
(www.sentientbean.com; 13 E Park Ave; 7am-10pm;) This green coffeehouse cares about coffee and community. It has vegan treats, organic cafe fare and live music or performance art on its stage.

Abe's on Lincoln BAR
(17 Lincoln St) Ditch the tourists – drink with the locals.

☆ Entertainment

Wormhole LIVE MUSIC
(www.wormholebar.com; 2307 Bull St;) Embracing a broad scope of the alternative-music scene, this dive bar and venue is in the seedier part of town but will let you experience how alternative Savannah kicks it.

Lucas Theatre for the Arts THEATER
(912-525-5040; www.scad.edu/venues/lucas; 32 Abercorn St) Hosting concerts (guitarist Jonny Lang), plays *(Guys and Dolls)* and films *(The Day the Earth Stood Still)* in a historic building dating from 1921.

Shopping

TOP CHOICE **Savannah Bee Company** FOOD
(www.savannahbee.com; 104 W Broughton St) This internationally renowned honey dreamland is one of Savannah's must-stops: artisanal honey of infinitesimal varieties (free tastings) dots the wonderful store, as well as soaps, honey coffee and unique art and homewares.

ShopSCAD ARTS & CRAFTS
(www.shopscadonline.com; 340 Bull St; 9-5:30pm Mon-Wed, till 8pm Thu-Fri, 10am-8pm Sat, noon-5pm Sun) All the wares at this funky, kitschy boutique were designed by students, faculty and alumni of Savannah's prestigious art college.

E Shaver, Bookseller BOOKSHOP
(326 Bull St; 9:30am-5pm Mon-Sat) Shelves are stocked with tomes on local and regional history.

Information

Candler Hospital (www.sjchs.org; 5353 Reynolds St)

CVS Pharmacy (cnr Bull & W Broughton Sts)

Main Library (www.liveoakpl.org; 2002 Bull St; 9am-8pm Mon-Tue, to 6pm Wed-Fri, 2-6pm Sun;) Offers free internet and wi-fi access.

Post office Historic District (118 Barnard Street; 8am-5pm Mon-Fri); Main (1 E Bay St; 8am-5:30pm Mon-Fri, 9am-1pm Sat)

Savannah Chatham Metropolitan Police (912 651-6675; www.scmpd.org; cnr E Oglethorpe Ave & Habersham St)

Visitor center (912-944-0455; www.savannahvisit.com; 301 Martin Luther King Jr Blvd; 8:30am-5pm Mon-Fri, 9am-5pm Sat & Sun) Excellent resources and services are available in this center, based in a restored 1860s train station. Many privately operated city tours start here and there's tons of information about various city tours, from carriage to bus. There is also a small interactive tourist info kiosk in the new Visitor Center at Forsyth Park.

Getting There & Around

The **Savannah/Hilton Head International Airport** (SAV; www.savannahairport.com) is about 5 miles west of downtown off I-16. The visitor center runs shuttles from the airport to Historic District hotels for $25 round-trip.

Greyhound (610 W Oglethorpe Ave) has connections to Atlanta (about five hours), Charleston, SC (about two hours) and Jacksonville, FL (2½ hours).

The **Amtrak station** (2611 Seaboard Coastline Dr) is just a few miles west of the Historic District.

You won't need a car. It's best to park it and walk or take tours. Another Earth-friendly and entertaining way to get around is by bike taxi with **Savannah Pedicab** (912-232-7900; www.savannahpedicab.com; 30/60min $25/45, full day $150).

Chatham Area Transit (CAT; www.catchacat.org) operates local hybrid buses that run on used cooking oil, including a free shuttle that makes its way around the Historic District and stops within a couple of blocks of nearly every major site.

Brunswick & the Golden Isles

Georgia has a coast? Oh yes, a righteously beautiful one, blessed with a string of picturesque islands. The islands have very different characters and provide experiences ranging from the rustic to the spoiled rotten.

With its large shrimp-boat fleet and downtown historic district shaded beneath lush live oaks, **Brunswick** dates from 1733 and has charms you might miss when sailing by on I-95 or the Golden Isle Pkwy (US Hwy 17). During WWII Brunswick shipyards constructed 99 Liberty transport ships for the navy. Today a new 23ft scale model at **Mary Ross Waterfront Park** (Bay St) stands as a memorial to those ships and their builders.

Forest Hostel (912-264-9738; www.foresthostel.com; Hwy 82; per person $25; P), an International Youth Hostel, is worth checking out if you're up for staying in little nature-loving tree houses (sans air or heat) on an ecofriendly, sustainable campus. It's 10 miles outside Brunswick; phone reservations only.

Brunswick-Golden Isles Visitors Bureau (☎912-265-0620; www.bgivb.com; Hwy 17, St Simons Causeway; ⊙8:30am-5pm Mon-Fri) has loads of practical information about all the Golden Isles.

ST SIMONS ISLAND

Famous for its golf courses, resorts and majestic live oaks, St Simons Island is the largest and most developed of the Golden Isles. It lies 75 miles south of Savannah and just 5 miles from Brunswick. While the southern half of the island is a thickly settled residential and resort area, the northern half and adjacent **Sea Island** (www.explorestsimonsisland.com) and **Little St Simons** offer tracts of coastal wilderness amid a tidewater estuary.

JEKYLL ISLAND

An exclusive refuge for millionaires in the late 19th and early 20th centuries, Jekyll Island is a 4000-year-old barrier island with 10 miles of beaches. Today it's an unusual clash of wilderness, historically preserved buildings, modern hotels and a massive campground (complete with wi-fi). It's an easily navigable place – you can get around by car, horse or bicycle, but there's a $5 parking fee per day. The posh **Jekyll Island Club Hotel** (☎800-535-9547; www.jekyllclub.com; 371 Riverview Dr; d/ste from $209/319; P❄@📶🏊) looms large on this island. It's a great place for a drink after a sunset seafood dinner at nearby waterfront restaurant **Latitude 31** (www.latitude31andrahbar.com; mains $14-23; ⊙from 11:30am Tue-Sun), located right on the wharf. An endearing attraction is the **Georgia Sea Turtle Center** (www.georgiaseaturtlecenter.org; Hopkins Rd; adult/child $6/4; ⊙9am-5pm Sun-Tue, 10am-2pm Mon; 👪), a conservation center and turtle hospital where patients are on view for the public.

CUMBERLAND ISLAND & ST MARYS

An unspoiled paradise, a backpacker's fantasy, a site for day trips or extended stays – it's clear why the Carnegie family used Cumberland as a retreat long ago. Most of this southernmost barrier island is now occupied by the **Cumberland Island National Seashore** (www.nps.gov/cuis; admission $4). Almost half of its 36,415 acres consists of marsh, mudflats and tidal creeks. On the ocean side are 16 miles of wide, sandy beach that you might have all to yourself. The island's interior is characterized by a maritime forest. Ruins from the Carnegie estate **Dungeness** are astounding, as are the wild turkeys, tiny fiddler crabs and beautiful butterflies. Feral horses roam the island and are a common sight.

The only public access to the island is via boat to/from the quirky, lazy town of **St Marys** (www.stmaryswelcome.com). A convenient and pleasant **ferry** (☎912-882-4335; adult/child $20/14; ⊙departures 9am & 11:45am) leaves from the mainland at the St Marys dock. Reservations are staunchly recommended well before you arrive, and visitors are required to check in at the **Visitor's Center** (☎912-882-4336; ⊙8am-4:30pm) at the dock at least 30 minutes prior to departure. December through February, the ferry does not operate on Tuesday or Wednesday.

St Marys caters to tourists visiting Cumberland. This tiny, lush one-horse town has a number of comfortable B&Bs, including the lovely **Emma's Bed and Breakfast** (☎912-822-4199; www.emmasbedandbreakfast.com; 300 W Conyers St; r from $129; P❄📶), which is right off the main street on a quiet road. The decorations are thankfully not of the common Southern frilly variety and the staff is helpful. Ask for a midweek special. For something cheap and in the 'action' by the dock, the tattered **Riverview Hotel** (☎912-882-3242; www.riverviewhotelstmarys.com; 105 Osborne St; r from $79; P❄📶) might be worth braving to save a dime.

On Cumberland Island, the only private accommodations are at the **Greyfield Inn** (☎904261-6408; www.greyfieldinn.com; r incl meals $395-595), a mansion built in 1900, with a two-night minimum stay. Camping is available at **Sea Camp Beach** (☎912-882-4335; tent sites per person $4), a campground set among magnificent live oaks.

Note: there are no stores or waste bins on the island. Eat before arriving or bring lunch, and keep your trash with you.

OKEFENOKEE NATIONAL WILDLIFE REFUGE

Established in 1937, the **Okefenokee National Wildlife Refuge** (www.fws.gov/okefenokee) is a national gem, encompassing 396,000 acres of bog in a giant saucer-shaped depression that was once part of the ocean floor. The swamp is home to an estimated 9000 to 15,000 alligators, 234 bird species, 49 types of mammal and 60 amphibian species. The **Okefenokee Swamp Park** (www.okeswamp.com; US 1 South, Waycross; adult/child $12/11; ⊙9am-5:30pm) maintains around 3000 acres of the refuge and captive bears and gators on-site, or you can explore the swamp in a canoe or on a boat tour. The ultimate experience is a multiday canoe trip on the swamp's 120 miles of waterways. Call the US Fish & Wildlife Service's **Okefenokee National Wildlife Refuge Wilderness Canoe Guide** (☎912-496-7836; www.fws.gov/okefenokee) if you're considering a trip. Guided boat trips are also available if the water levels are high enough.

ALABAMA

Obsessed with football and race – two things Southerners never stop discussing – Alabama has been home to one of gridiron's most legendary coaches, Paul 'Bear' Bryant, and Jefferson Davis, the first president of the Confederacy in 1861 (the year the Civil War began).

In the 1950s and '60s, Alabama led the way for civil rights triumphs throughout the country and it continues to deal with its reputation and legacy of rebels, segregation, discrimination and wayward politicians – in the face of both progress and setbacks. Exploring Alabama provides a powerful insight into the racial dynamic and history in the USA.

Geographically, Alabama has a surprising diversity of landscapes, from foothills in the north and a gritty city in the middle to the subtropical Gulf Coast down south. Visitors come to see the heritage of antebellum architecture, to celebrate the country's oldest Mardi Gras, in Mobile, and to learn about the civil rights struggle. Every fall the University of Alabama Crimson Tide and the Auburn University Tigers continue one of college football's greatest rivalries.

ALABAMA FACTS

» **Nickname** The Heart of Dixie

» **Population** 4.7 million

» **Area** 52,419 sq miles

» **Capital city** Montgomery (population 224,119)

» **Other cities** Birmingham (population 212,237)

» **Sales tax** 4%, but up to 11% with local taxes

» **Birthplace of** Author Helen Keller (1880–1968), civil rights activist Rosa Parks (1913–2005), musician Hank Williams (1923–53)

» **Home of** US Space & Rocket Center

» **Politics** GOP stronghold – Alabama hasn't voted democratic since 1976

» **Famous for** Rosa Parks and the Civil Rights movement

» **Bitterest rivalry** University of Alabama vs Auburn University

» **Driving distances** Montgomery to Birmingham 91 miles, Mobile to Dauphin Island 38 miles

History

Alabama was among the first states to secede in the Civil War. Montgomery was the first Confederate capital. Alabama lost around 25,000 soldiers in the war, and reconstruction came slowly and painfully.

Racial segregation and Jim Crow laws survived into the mid-20th century, when the Civil Rights movement campaigned for desegregation of everything from public buses to private universities, a notion that Governor George Wallace opposed. In perhaps the most famous moment in civil rights history, an African American woman named Rosa Parks refused to give up her bus seat to a white passenger and was arrested; the ensuing uproar began to turn the tide in favor of racial equality. Alabama saw brutal repression and hostility, but federal civil rights and voting laws eventually prevailed. At a political level, reform has seen the election of dozens of African American mayors and representatives.

ℹ Information

Alabama Bureau of Tourism & Travel (☎334-242-4169, 800-252-2262; www.alabama.travel) Sends out a vacation guide and has a website with extensive tourism options. Foodies will definitely want to pick up a copy of *100 Dishes To Eat in Alabama Before You Die*.

Alabama State Parks (☎888-252-7272; www.alapark.com) There are 23 parks statewide with camping facilities ranging from primitive ($12) to RV hookups ($26). Advanced reservations are suggested for weekends and holidays.

Birmingham

No one can ignore Birmingham's checkered past – civil rights violence earned it the nickname 'Bombingham.' Even though that was decades ago, invisible racial boundaries are still evident and smack of the city's history. Yet this midsize, blue-collar city has made progress, can show you a good time, has a surprising amount of culture to offer and has integrated its civil rights struggle into the tourist experience.

Sights & Activities

Art-deco buildings in trendy **Five Points South** house shops, restaurants and nightspots. Equally noteworthy is the **Homewood** community's quaint commercial drag on 18th St S.

TOP CHOICE **Birmingham Civil Rights Institute** MUSEUM
(www.bcri.org; 520 16th St N; adult/child $12/3, Sun free; ⏲10am-5pm Tue-Sat, 1-5pm Sun) A maze of moving audio, video and photography exhibits tell the story of racial segregation in the USA, from WWI and the Civil Rights movement to racial and human-rights issues around the world today, and it reveals the complicated and shocking layers of Birmingham's history. A new $2.5-million renovation has spruced up displays and added an extensive exhibit on the 16th Street Baptist Church bombing in 1963.

16th Street Baptist Church CHURCH
(www.16thstreetbaptist.org; cnr 16th St & 6th Ave N; donation $5; ⏲ministry tours 10am-4pm Tue-Fri, 10am-1pm Sat) This became a gathering place for meetings and protests in the 1950s and '60s. When Ku Klux Klan members bombed the church in 1963, killing four girls, the city was flung into a whirlwind of social change. Today the rebuilt church is a memorial and a house of worship (services 10:45am Sunday).

Vulcan Park PARK
(www.visitvulcan.com; 1701 Valley View Dr; ⏲7am-10pm) Visible from all over the city thanks to the world's largest cast-iron statue, the park offers fantastic views for free, and an **observation tower** (adult/child $6/4; ⏲from 10am Mon-Sat, from 1pm Sun).

FREE **Birmingham Museum of Art** GALLERY
(www.artsbma.org; 2000 Rev Abraham Woods Jr Blvd; ⏲10am-5pm Tue-Sat, noon-5pm Sun) Collects work from Asia, Africa, Europe and the Americas. Don't miss the work of Rodin, Botero and Dalí in the sculpture garden.

Sleeping

Redmont Hotel HISTORIC HOTEL $$
(☎205-324-2101; www.theredmont.com; 2101 5th Ave N; r from $129; ❄@🛜) It's a toss up between here and Tutwiler for Birmingham's best, but the Redmont, born in the roaring '20s, wins since it's not a Hampton Inn. The hotel's piano and chandelier in the lobby lend a certain historical, old-world feel throughout and all deluxe rooms were just renovated giving it modern edge. The spacious rooftop bar doesn't hurt, either.

Hotel Highland HOTEL $$
(☎205-271-5800; www.thehotelhighland.com; 1023 20th St S; r from $119; P❄@🛜) Nuzzled right up next to the lively Five Points district, this colorful, slightly trippy, modern hotel manages to be very comfortable and a good deal. The rooms are a bit less bright and funky than the lobby, eliminating the need for sunglasses at night. Rates include a continental breakfast.

Cobb Lane Bed and Breakfast B&B $
(☎205-918-9090; www.cobblanebandb.com; 1309 19th St S; r from $89; P❄🛜) Aims for the traditional debutante-esque of Southern B&Bs, but ends up with a giant stuffed peacock in the fireplace, numerous porcelain dolls and the gaudy frilliness of an underage Southern beauty pageant.

Eating & Drinking

For such a small Southern city, student-tilted Birmingham has a wide variety of eateries and cafes, from ethnic to local, for all budgets.

TOP CHOICE **Hot & Hot Fish Club** SEAFOOD $$$
(www.hotandhotfishclub.com; 2180 11th Court South; mains $29-36; ⏲5:30-10:30pm Tue-Sat) This crazy-awesome Southside Birmingham restaurant – one of the South's best – will bring you to your knees hollerin' Gastro-Hallelujah's! Chef Chris Hastings was a James Beard Best Chef in the South finalist three years in a row – his daily-changing seasonal menu (including cocktails) is a knockout (the vanilla bean-infused lemonade with sweet tea vodka might be the best cocktail ever). Best seat in the house? The lengthy chef's counter, where Hastings chats up the guests while his unbelievably diverse and chill sous chefs work his creations into culinary genius.

Rib-It-Up BARBECUE $
(830 1st Ave North; mains $4-11; ⏲10:30am-9pm Mon-Thu, till midnight Fri & Sat) Barbecue rib *sandwich* – an absolute hot mess. What else do you need to know? OK, the neighborhood isn't the best, but there is no such thing as authentic barbecue next door to a Pottery Barn!

Garage Café CAFE $
(www.garagecafe.us; 2304 10th Ter S; sandwiches $7; 3pm-midnight Sun-Mon, 11-2am Tue-Sat) By day it's a great soup and create-your-own-sandwich spot; by night eclectic crowds knock back myriad beer choices while tapping their toes to live music in a courtyard full of junk, antiques, ceramic statues *and* the kitchen sink.

J Clyde BEER HALL $$
(www.jclyde.com; 1312 Cobb Lane S; mains $8 to $18; 3pm-midnight Mon, to 2am Tue-Thu & Sun, to 4am Fri) Over 40 beers on draft, hundreds in bottles and an additional one to three cask-conditioned ales with traditional British Beer Engines – the only Alabama bar to boast such devotion to suds. It sits on charming Cobb Lane in Five Points and there's plenty of good late-night pub grub to wash down the beer.

Lucy's Coffee and Tea CAFE
(www.lucyscoffeeandtea.com; 2007 University Blvd; mains $6-10; 7am-5pm Mon-Fri) Next door to the University of Alabama-Birmingham not far from Five Points, this artsy coffee shop is good for an espresso fix and solid paninis for lunch.

☆ Entertainment

TOP CHOICE **Gip's Place** LIVE MUSIC
(www.myspace.com/gipsjukejoint; 3101 Ave C, Bessemer) You'll need to ask a local for directions to this tin-roof makeshift backyard shack in a dicey neighborhood in Bessemer, one of the only truly authentic juke joints left outside Mississippi. Gip, a gravedigger by day, opens the doors on Saturday only, when the place is shoulder-to-shoulder with blues fans come one come all. It's BYOB but there's no need – *free* moonshine is passed around in Mason jars, permitted by a legal loophole in Alabama that says it must be given away, not sold.

Information

Greater Birmingham Convention & Visitors Bureau (205-458-8000, 800-458-8085; www.sweetbirmingham.com; 2200 9th Ave N; 8:30am-5pm Mon-Fri) Tourist information.

Getting There & Around

The **Birmingham International Airport** (BHM; www.flybirmingham.com) is about 5 miles northeast of downtown.

Greyhound (205-253-7190; 618 19th St N), north of downtown, serves cities including Huntsville, Montgomery, Atlanta, GA, Jackson, MS, and New Orleans, LA (10 hours). **Amtrak** (205-324-3033; 1819 Morris Ave), downtown, has trains daily to New York and New Orleans.

Birmingham Transit Authority (www.bjcta.org; adult $1.25) runs local buses.

Around Birmingham

North of Birmingham, the aerospace community of Huntsville hosts thc US space program that took off and attracted international aerospace-related companies.

US Space & Rocket Center (www.spacecamp.com/museum; I-565, exit 15; adult/child museum $20/15, with IMAX $28/22; 9am-5pm) is a combination science museum and theme park. It's a great place to take a kid, or to become one again. The center has IMAX films, exhibits, rides and video presentations.

East of Huntsville, in Scottsboro, you'll find the infamous **Unclaimed Baggage Center** (256-259-1525; www.unclaimedbaggage.com; 509 W Willow St; 9am-6pm Mon-Fri, 8am-6pm Sat), which draws pilgrims from far and wide who peruse the now-for-sale belongings of unfortunate air travelers who have lost their baggage irrevocably down the dark annals of fate. Finders keepers.

The area receives some acclaim for music history, and the cheesy-cool **Alabama Music Hall of Fame** (www.alamhof.org; 617 Hwy 72 W, Tuscumbia; adult/child $8/5; 9am-5pm Mon-Sat, 1-5pm Sun summer) immortalizes both Hank Williams and Lionel Richie.

WORTH A TRIP

AVE MARIA GROTTO

Located 50 miles north of Birmingham on the grounds of the only Benedictine monastery in Alabama, the amazing **Ave Maria Grotto** (www.avemaria-grotto.com; 1600 St. Bernard Dr, Cullman; adult/child $7/4.50; 9am-6pm) is more or less the work of one man, Brother Joseph Zoettl, who spent the better part of 35 years hand-sculpting stone and cement miniatures of the world's most prominent religious buildings. The attention to detail and level of skill in the 125 pieces is amazing, regardless of your personal views on religion. From an art perspective, it's even more miraculous yet – after all, this was just Brother Joseph's hobby.

Montgomery

In 1955 Rosa Parks refused to give up her seat to a white man on a Montgomery bus, launching a bus boycott and galvanizing the Civil Rights movement nationwide. The city has commemorated that incident with a museum, which (along with an excellent Shakespeare program) is the main reason to visit.

Although it's Alabama's capital city, Montgomery feels more like a sleepy little city with a dead downtown. To its credit, it covers both fine and folk arts well, with a terrific Shakespeare festival and a museum devoted to country-music legend Hank Williams.

Sights & Activities

Civil Rights Memorial Center MEMORIAL
(www.civilrightsmemorialcenter.org; 400 Washington Ave; adult/child $2/free; ⌚9am-4:30pm Mon-Fri, 10am-4pm Sat) With its circular design crafted by Maya Lin, this haunting memorial focuses on 40 martyrs of the Civil Rights movement, all murdered for countless senseless reasons, many of which have never been solved. MLK Jr was the most famous, but there were many 'faceless' deaths along the way, white and African American alike, that here provide some of the most somber moments in American history.

Rosa Parks Museum MUSEUM
(http://montgomery.troy.edu/rosaparks/museum; 251 Montgomery St; adult/child $6/4; ⌚9am-5pm Mon-Fri, 9am-3pm Sat; 👪) A tribute to Mrs Parks (who died in October 2005), the mu-seum features a sophisticated and wacky video re-creation of Montgomery's history of racial conflict and also the bus-seat protest.

Scott & Zelda Fitzgerald Museum MUSEUM
(919 Felder Ave; donation adult/child $5/2; ⌚10am-2pm Wed-Fri, 1-5pm Sat & Sun) The writers' home from 1931 to '32 now houses first editions, translations and original artwork including a mysterious self-portrait of Zelda in pencil.

Hank Williams Museum MUSEUM
(www.thehankwilliamsmuseum.com; 118 Commerce St; adult/child $8/3; ⌚9am-4:30pm Mon-Fri, 10am-4pm Sat, 1-4pm Sun) Pays homage to the country-music giant and Alabama native, a pioneer who effortlessly fused hillbilly music with African American blues.

Sleeping & Eating

Montgomery may not be known for its restaurants and accommodations but there are a couple of finds. The opening of the Alley, a new dining and entertainment district, shows great promise for revitalizing downtown.

Lattice Inn B&B $
(☎334-262-3388; www.thelatticeinn.com; 1414 S Hull St; r from $90; P❄@🛜≈) Most definitely this cute little B&B in the Garden District is a lovely alternative to chain hotels in Montgomery's downtown and outskirts. It's not fancy-pants, but well executed and homey with a consummate host.

Butterfly Inn B&B $$
(☎334-230-9708; www.butterflyinn.net; 135 Mildred St; r $96-126; P❄) Montgomery's first African American-owned B&B is cool and comfortable, but Isaiah's restaurant on site is the real coup, famous for its lemon pepper catfish ($8.75), peach cobbler and other soul food favorites.

Dreamland BBQ BARBECUE $
(www.dreamlandbbq.com; 101 Tallapoosa St; mains $8-11; ⌚11am-9pm Sun-Thu, till 10pm Sat) It's a chain but, before you poo-poo it, it's an Alabama chain and the ribs, chopped pork sandwich and traditional banana pudding are all extraordinary. It's the culinary cradle of the Alley, the focal point of Montgomery's downtown makeover.

Farmer's Market Cafe SOUTHERN $
(315 N McDonough St; meals without/with tea from $7.50/6.75; ⌚5:30am-2pm Mon-Fri) This oversized downtown cafeteria serves up God-fearing Southern home cooking at recession-friendly prices according to the meat/veggie combo of your choice. Don't skip the grits casserole.

Chris' Hot Dog FAST FOOD $
(www.chrishotdogs.com; 138 Dexter Ave; hot dogs $2.15; ⌚10am-7pm Mon-Thu & Sat, till 8pm Fri) This funky hot-dog dive has been a Montgomery institution since 1917 and was a favorite drinking den of Hank Williams.

Information

Montgomery Area Visitor Center (☎334-262-0013; www.visitingmontgomery.com; 300 Water St; ⌚8:30am-5pm Mon-Sat) Has tourist information and a helpful website.

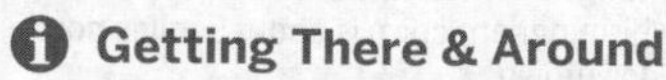

Getting There & Around

Montgomery Regional Airport (MGM; www.montgomeryairport.org; 4445 Selma Hwy) is about 15 miles from downtown and is served by daily flights from Atlanta, Charlotte, Cincinnati, Houston and Memphis. **Greyhound** (☎334-286-0658; 950 W South Blvd) also serves the city. The **Montgomery Area Transit System** (www.montgomerytransit.com; tickets $1) operates the city buses.

Selma

On Bloody Sunday, March 7, 1965, the media captured state troopers and deputies beating and gassing African Americans and white sympathizers near the Edmund Pettus Bridge. Led by Martin Luther King Jr, the crowd was marching to the state capital (Montgomery) to demonstrate for voting rights. This was the culmination of two years of violence, which ended when President Johnson signed the *Voting Rights Act* of 1965. Today Selma is a quiet town and though its attractions are few they do provide an excellent insight into the voting rights protests that were at the crux of the Civil Rights movement.

Selma's key attraction, the **National Voting Rights Museum** (www.nvrm.org; 1012 Water Ave; adult/senior & student $6/4; ⌚9am-5pm Mon-Fri, 10am-3pm Sat), near the Edmund Pettus Bridge, is an important stop as it honors the movement's 'foot soldiers' – the unsung heroes who marched for freedom.

Mobile

Wedged between Mississippi and Florida, the only real Alabama coastal town is Mobile (mo-*beel*), a seaport with green spaces, shady boulevards and four historic districts. It's ablaze with azaleas in early spring, and festivities are held throughout February for **Mardi Gras** (www.mobilemardigras.com), which has been celebrated here for nearly 200 years. Mobile can be fun like New Orleans, only the volume and brightness are turned way down. The Dauphin St historic district is where you'll find many bars and restaurants, and it's where much of the Mardi Gras action takes place.

Government St, near downtown, makes for a lovely drive thanks to its mansions and tree canopy. The **Leinkauf Historic District** has more great homes.

USS Alabama (www.ussalabama.com; 2703 Battleship Pkwy; adult/child $12/6; ⌚8am-6pm Apr-Sep, 8am-4pm Oct-Mar) is a 690ft behemoth famous for escaping nine major WWII battles unscathed. It's a worthwhile self-guided tour for its awesome size and might. While there, you can also tour a submarine and get up close and personal with military aircraft. Parking's $2.

Kate Shepard House (☎251-479-7048; www.kateshepardhouse.com; 1552 Monterrey Pl; r $160; P❄📶) is an adorable, meticulously restored 1897 Queen Anne–style B&B run by gracious host Wendy James. Everything in this charmer is perfect, personified most memorably in the pecan praline French toast. Foodgasm!

Home to Mobile's best burgers and consistently voted one of America's best bars, the ramshackle **Callaghan's Irish Social Club** (www.callaghansirishsocialclub.com; 916 Charleston St; burgers $7-9; ⌚11am-9pm Mon, 11am-10pm Tue & Wed, 11am-11pm Thu-Sat) in a 1920s-era building that used to house a meat market in the Oakleigh District, is unmissable.

WORTH A TRIP

DAUPHIN ISLAND

Alabama has an island? Yes, but many write it off because oil rigs grace its horizon. However unsung it may be, it's a worthwhile destination. The whole 14-mile-long, 1¾-mile-wide island is a designated bird sanctuary, with 6 miles for public use and 8 miles of private property. Though it has its fair share of traditional beach-vacation kitsch and the water is not sparkly turquoise, it's still pretty nice. The white-blonde beaches are stellar and prices reasonable. The island is accessed from the north by Hwy 193 and from the east by **ferry** (☎251-861-3000; www.mobilebayferry.com) shuttling from Fort Morgan.

For helpful maps and information, contact the **Dauphin Island Chamber of Commerce** (☎251-861-5524; www.dauphinislandcoc.com).

The biggest highlight is the **Dauphin Island Bird Sanctuary** (☎251-861-2120; www.coastalbirding.org), where you'll find what many people consider to be some of the best birding in the southeast. In addition, you'll encounter uncrowded beaches accessed only by hiking paths, placards explaining the flora and fauna, and several miles of winding trails.

MISSISSIPPI

One of the USA's most misunderstood (and yet most mythologized) states, Mississippi is home to gorgeous country roads, shabby juke joints, crispy catfish, hallowed authors and acres of cotton. Most people feel content to malign Mississippi, long scorned for its lamentable civil rights history and its low ranking on the list of nearly every national marker of economy and education, without ever experiencing it firsthand. But unpack your bags for a moment and you'll glimpse the real South. It lies somewhere amid the Confederate defeat at Vicksburg, the literary legacy of William Faulkner in bookish Oxford, the birthplace of the blues in the Mississippi Delta and the humble origins of Elvis Presley in Tupelo.

History

Stay in Mississippi long enough and you'll hear folks refer to a time 'when cotton was king.' That time dates back at least to 1860, when Mississippi was the country's leading cotton producer and one of the 10 wealthiest states. The Civil War wrecked Mississippi's economy, and reconstruction was traumatic.

MISSISSIPPI FACTS

» **Nickname** The Magnolia State

» **Population** 2.9 million

» **Area** 48,430 sq miles

» **Capital city** Jackson (population 173,514)

» **Other cities** Biloxi 45,670

» **Sales tax** 7%

» **Birthplace of** Author Eudora Welty (1909–2001), musicians Robert Johnson (1911–38) and Elvis Presley (1935–77), puppeteer Jim Henson (1936–90)

» **Home of** the blues

» **Politics** traditionally conservative, but has voted for third-party candidates more than any other state since WWII.

» **Famous for** cotton fields

» **Kitschiest souvenir** Elvis lunchbox in Tupelo

» **Driving distances** Jackson to Clarksdale 187 miles, Jackson to Ocean Springs 176 miles

And the state's racist history – from slavery through the civil rights era – has left deep scars. (One of the most famous incidents came in 1962, when violence erupted as student James Meredith became the first African American to attend the University of Mississippi.)

Today, though Mississippi is still a poor state, people have come to realize that the blues of the Delta – one of America's richest and most distinctive art forms – is worth celebrating. And that Mississippi has been disproportionately blessed with literary luminaries. Therefore, the state has developed a tourist industry revolving around its proud cultural history, as well as its waterfront casinos.

Information

Mississippi Division of Tourism Development (601-359-3297; www.visitmississippi.org) Has a directory of visitor bureaus.

Mississippi Wildlife, Fisheries, & Parks (1-800-467-2757; www.mississippistateparks.reserveamerica.com) Camping costs $11 to $22, depending on the facilities, and some parks have cabins for rent.

Tupelo

Unless you have an unhealthy Elvis obsession or want to pick up the Natchez Trace Pkwy, you probably shouldn't plan to spend a long time in Tupelo. But an afternoon pop-in is rewarding indeed if you are a fan of the King.

Elvis Presley's Birthplace (www.elvispresleybirthplace.com; 306 Elvis Presley Blvd; adult/child $12/6; 9am-5:30pm Mon-Sat, 1-5pm Sun) is east of downtown off Hwy 78. The 15-acre park complex contains the two-room shack Elvis lived in as a boy, a museum displaying personal items, a modest chapel and a massive gift shop.

Oxford

A refreshingly sophisticated little town that's bustling and prosperous, Oxford was named after the English city by colonists who hoped it would open a school as revered as its namesake. The University of Mississippi (Ole Miss) opened in 1848 and provides Oxford's heartbeat. (You know a town has an intellectual bent when its favorite native son is a literary lion like William Faulkner. But former Ole Miss quarterback Archie Manning runs a close second; the speed limit here on campus is 18mph, in deference to his old uniform number.)

Social life in Oxford revolves around 'the Square' (Courthouse Sq), a series of downtown blocks dotted with shops and eateries.

Sights & Activities

Rowan Oak HISTORIC BUILDING
(off Old Taylor Rd; www.rowanoak.com; adult/child $5/free; 10am-4pm Tue-Sat, 1-4pm Sun) Literary pilgrims head directly here, to the graceful 1840s home of William Faulkner, who authored so many brilliant and dense novels set in Mississippi, and whose work is celebrated in Oxford with an annual conference in July. Tours of Rowan Oak – where Faulkner lived from 1930 until he died in 1962 – are self-guided. The staff can also provide directions to **Faulkner's grave**, which is located in St Peter's Cemetery, northeast of the Square.

Square Books CULTURAL BUILDING
(www.squarebooks.com; 160 Courthouse Sq; 9am-9pm Mon-Thu, to 10pm Fri & Sat, 9am-6pm Sun) One of America's great independent bookstores is the epicenter of Oxford's lively literary scene and a frequent stop for traveling authors. There's a cafe and balcony upstairs, along with an immense section devoted to Faulkner.

FREE **University of Mississippi Museum** MUSEUM
(University Ave, at 5th St; www.museum.olemiss.edu; 10am-6 Tue-Sat) This museum has fine arts, folk arts, a Confederate uniform and a plethora of science-related marvels, including a microscope and electromagnet from the 19th century.

Sleeping & Eating

The cheapest accommodations are on the outskirts of town at chain hotels. But there are some other choices with more personality. A number of high-quality restaurants dot the Square.

Inn at Ravine B&B $$
(662-234-4555; www.oxfordravine.com; 53 County Rd 321; r from $100; P ❄ ≋) For those wanting a peaceful stay on Oxford's green fringes, there are two B&B-style guest rooms above the lovely restaurant Ravine, as well as a cabin.

(5) Twelve B&B $$
(662-234-8043; www.the512oxford.com; 512 Van Buren Ave; r from $115; P ❄ ≋) Formerly the Oliver Britt House (now under new management), this six-room B&B has an antebellum-style exterior, modern interior and Southern breakfasts to order. It's an easy walk from shops and restaurants at the Square.

TOP CHOICE **Ravine** AMERICAN $$$
(662-234-4555; www.oxfordravine.com; 53 County Rd 321; mains $16-32; Wed-Thu 6-9pm, Fri & Sat til 10pm, 10:30am-2pm & 6-9pm Sun; ≋) About 3 miles outside the city, this unpretentious, cozily elegant restaurant nuzzles up to the forest. Chef Joel Miller picks and pulls much of the produce and herbs from his garden outside and buys locally and organically when he can. The result is simply wonderful food and a delicious experience.

Taylor Grocery SEAFOOD $$
(www.taylorgrocery.com; 4 County Rd 338 A, Taylor; dishes $9-15; 5-10pm Thu-Sat, till 9pm Sun) Be prepared to wait – and to tailgate in the parking lot – at this splendidly rusticated catfish haunt. Get your cat fried or grilled, and bring a marker to sign your name on the wall. The joint is about 7 miles from downtown Oxford, south on Old Taylor Rd.

Bottletree Bakery BAKERY $
(923 Van Buren; cinnamon rolls $3.75; 7am-4pm Tue-Fri, 9am-4pm Sat, 9am-2pm Sun; ≋) Saucer-sized, sweet, sticky cinnamon rolls are the source of this bakery's acclaim. But it also has sandwiches, espresso drinks and 'humble pie.'

Entertainment

Proud Larry's LIVE MUSIC
(www.proudlarrys.com; 211 S Lamar Blvd) On the Square, this iconic music venue hosts some of the bigger names passing through town.

Rooster's Blues House BLUES
(www.roostersblueshouse.com; 114 Courthouse Sq) Also on the Square, this is where you'll find that soulful crooning on the weekends.

Mississippi Delta

One of the most mythical places in the USA, the Delta is a panoramic agricultural expanse that thrums with historic significance. Its vernacular food culture ranks as one of America's great folk arts, but even the grub is trumped by the Delta's other great cultural export: blues music. David L Cohn, Greenville native and author of *God Shakes Creation*, devised a geo-cultural definition of the region. He wrote that 'the Delta begins in the lobby of the Peabody Hotel in Memphis and ends on Catfish Row in Vicksburg.'

CLARKSDALE

If you come here for anything, come for the love of music. Clarksdale is the real deal. It hosts a healthy blues-lovin' tourist industry and also caters to moneyed patrons, but what keeps Clarksdale genuine is its residents: they adore music. It's no surprise that big-name blues bands still honor Clarksdale on the weekends and that music museums sprinkle the area. Over the twists and turns of its intriguing past, this little juke-jointed Delta town continues to navigate contradictions: wealth, poverty, white culture, black culture and blues culture.

Sights & Activities

Delta Blues Museum MUSEUM
(www.deltabluesmuseum.org; 1 Blues Alley; adult/child $7/5; ⏲9am-5pm Mon-Sat) A small but exciting and well-presented collection of memorabilia is on display, including Charlie Musselwhite's harmonica and BB King's guitar, Lucille. The shrine to Delta legend Muddy Waters is being expanded into a new 7000-sq-ft annex by 2012; local art exhibits and a gift shop round out the revelry.

Rock N' Roll & Blues Heritage Museum MUSEUM
(☎901-605-8662; www.blues2rock.com; 113 E Second St; admission $5; ⏲11am-5pm Fri-Sun) Theo, a jovial Dutch transplant and blues fanatic, has on display an impressive personal collection of records, memorabilia, and artifacts that traces the roots of rock and roll from blues through the '70s. His collection features all sorts of rare and interesting items (check out one of Muddy Waters' riders) and if he's not too busy, he's all too enthusiastic to compliment the display with loads of fascinating historical rhetoric. Open by appointment outside posted hours.

Festivals & Events

Clarksdale has two bluesy throw-downs.

Juke Joint Festival MUSIC
(www.jukejointfestival.com) Held in April, it's more about the venues than the headliners.

Sunflower River Blues & Gospel Festival MUSIC
(www.sunflowerfest.org) In August. Draws bigger names than Juke.

Sleeping & Eating

TOP CHOICE **Shack Up Inn** INN $$
(☎662-624-8329; www.shackupinn.com; r $65-165; P❄📶) At the cheeky Hopson Plantation, this self-titled 'bed and beer' 2 miles south on the west side of Hwy 49 evokes the blues like no other. Guests stay in refurbished sharecropper cabins or the creatively renovated cotton gin. The cabins have covered porches and are filled with old furniture and musical instruments. The old commissary, the Juke Joint Chapel (equipped with pews), is an atmospheric venue inside the cotton gin for live-music performances. The whole place reeks of down home dirty blues and

A WHOLE LOTTA JUKIN' GOING ON

It's believed that 'juke' is a West African word that survived in the Gullah language, the Creole–English hybrid spoken by isolated African Americans in the US. The Gullah 'juke' means 'wicked and disorderly.' Little wonder, then, that the term was applied to the roadside sweatboxes of the Mississippi Delta, where secular music, suggestive dancing, drinking and, in some cases, prostitution were the norm. The term 'jukebox' came into vogue when recorded music, spun on automated record-changing machines, began to supplant live musicians in such places, as well as in cafes and bars.

Most bona-fide juke joints are African American neighborhood clubs, and outside visitors can be a rarity. Many are mostly male hangouts. There are very few places that local women, even in groups, would turn up without a male chaperone. Otherwise, women can expect a lot of persistent, suggestive attention.

For a taste of the juke-joint scene, we recommend **Ground Zero** (www.groundzerobluesclub.com; 0 Blues Alley, Clarksdale; ⏲11am-2pm Mon-Tue, to 11pm Wed & Thu, to 2am Fri & Sat), a huge and friendly (read: somewhat sugar-coated) hall graffitied to death and owned by Morgan Freeman. By contrast, **Red's** (☎662-627-3166; 395 Sunflower Ave, Clarksdale), which is usually open on Friday and Saturday nights, looks a little scary to first-timers, but it is one of Clarksdale's best jukes. If the pit's smoking, order whatever's cooking.

Deep South character – possibly the coolest place you'll ever stay.

Riverside Hotel HISTORIC HOTEL **$**
(☎662-624-9163; ratfrankblues@yahoo.com; 615 Sunflower Ave; r with/without bath $70/65; ❄) Don't let a well-worn exterior put you off: this hotel, soaked in blues history – Bessie Smith died here when it was a hospital, everyone else has stayed here – offers clean and tidy rooms wrought with the spirits of the blues. It's family-run since 1944, when it was 'the black hotel' in town. The original proprietor's son, Rat, will charm your socks off with history, hospitality and prices.

Rust SOUTHERN **$$**
(218 Delta Ave; mains $12-26; ⏲6-9pm Wed-Thu, till 10pm Fri & Sat) A beacon of culinary cool in an otherwise downtrodden downtown, the souped-up Southern comfort food served here (blackened rib eye with red chili mustard, fried green tomatoes with citrus cream sauce) amid junkyard chic decor is hopefully the shape of things to come.

Madidi SOUTHERN **$$$**
(☎662-627-7770; www.madidires.com; 164 Delta Ave; mains $24-36; ⏲6-9pm Tue-Sat) Handsome and refined, just like cofounder Morgan Freeman, this upscale eatery has a menu including buttermilk fried quail, braised beef short ribs and wild-mushroom risotto. Reservations requested.

Hick's FAST FOOD **$**
(305 S State St; mains $2-8.50; ⏲11am-6pm Mon-Thu, to 10pm Fri & Sat) A don't-miss dive that's been here forever on the outskirts of town. It has the best Delta hot tamales in town (half a dozen for $5), as well as the best pulled pork.

Shopping

Cat Head Delta Blues & Folk Art ARTS & CRAFTS
(252 Delta Ave; ⏲10am-5pm Mon-Sat) Friendly St Louis carpetbagger Roger Stolle runs a colorful, all-purpose, blues emporium. The shelves are jammed with books, face jugs, local art and blues records. Stolle seems to know everyone in the Delta; skip the Chamber of Commerce and stop here for the lowdown.

AROUND CLARKSDALE

For such a poor, flat part of the country, the Delta has a surprisingly deep list of funky little towns with food, gambling and history to offer.

WORTH A TRIP

DOE'S EAT PLACE

James Beard Award–winning **Doe's Eat Place** (☎662-334-3315; www.doeseatplace.com; 502 Nelson St, Greenville; steaks $35-55; ⏲5:30-9pm Mon-Sat) is the priciest dive you're likely to ever come across, but the world-class steaks served here, in the middle of a poor neighborhood, are unforgettable, as is the experience in general, with the open kitchen smack-dab in the middle of the old-school family restaurant. It used to be you paid a kid a dollar to 'watch your car,' ie not break into it. Now there's a security guard outside. The family's third generation runs the show, one that began in 1941 with an African American–only honky-tonk (bar) in the front of the house and a restaurant serving steaks for whites in the back. Come early or make a reservation – this is the American dream on a plate.

The Delta's largest city, **Greenville** is roughly midway between Clarksdale and Vicksburg. It was here that the levee broke during the catastrophic Great Flood of 1927. Today it has some riverboat gambling and not much else. But in September, Greenville hosts the **Mississippi Delta Blues & Heritage Festival** (www.deltablues.org) near the intersection of Hwys 454 and 1.

East of Greenville, Hwy 82 heads out of the Delta. The **Highway 61 Blues Museum** (www.highway61blues.com; 307 N Broad St; ⏲10am-4pm Tue-Sat Nov-Feb, 10am-5pm Mon-Sat Mar-Oct), packs a mighty wallop in a condensed, six-room space venerating local bluesman from the Delta. The best part of a visit here is the presence, music and impromptu cat sketches of Pat Thomas, son of legendary local bluesman James 'Son Ford' Thomas, a real character you won't soon forget. **Leland** (www.lelandms.org) hosts the **Highway 61 Blues Festival** in June as well as the **Crawfish Festival** (crayfish) at the beginning of May.

Stopping in the tiny Delta town of **Indianola** is well worthwhile, to visit the incredible, modern **BB King Museum and Delta Interpretive Center** (www.bbkingmuseum.org; 400 Second St; adult/student/child $10/5/free; ⏲10am-5pm Tue-Sat, noon-5pm Sun-Mon, closed

Mon Nov-Mar). Situated in between Greenville and Greenwood on Hwy 82, this center, filled with interactive displays, video exhibits and an amazing array of blues and BB King artifacts, effectively communicates the history and legacy of the blues while shedding light on the soul of the Delta.

Greenwood is a poor Delta town furnished with one block of opulence due to Viking Range Corporation's investment (its headquarters is here). Visitors are usually wealthy patrons or splurging travelers who want to take advantage of the tourist beacon of Greenwood, the **Alluvian** (☎662-453-2114; www.thealluvian.com; 318 Howard St; r incl breakfast $195-340; P❄@📶), owned by Viking. This shockingly luxurious boutique hotel is equipped with a high-class spa, gourmet restaurant, Giardina's (locally pronounced 'Gardinia's'), and an unbelievably outfitted cooking school. If you feel like splurging, this might be the place, though some find the oasis of wealth a disturbing contrast to the poverty of the surrounding town.

As an alternative to the Alluvian, 3 miles north of Greenwood **Tallahatchie Flats** (☎662-453-1854; www.tallahatchieflats.com; 58458 County Rd 518; shacks $65-85; P❄) is a compound of shacks simulating rural homes called 'tenant houses' that once dotted the area. They're now outfitted for guests. Each sleeps two to four.

VICKSBURG

Vicksburg is famous for its strategic location in the Civil War, thanks to its position on a high bluff overlooking the Mississippi River, and history buffs dig it. General Ulysses S Grant besieged the city for 47 days, until its surrender on July 4, 1863, at which point the North gained dominance over North America's greatest river.

Sights & Activities

The major sights are readily accessible from I-20 exit 4B (Clay St). The old, slow downtown stretches along several cobblestoned blocks of Washington St, and **historic-house museums** cluster in the Garden District. Vicksburg's stretch of the **Mississippi River** has casinos. Down by the water is a block of murals depicting the history of the area, and a **Children's Art Park**.

National Military Park (www.nps.gov/vick; Clay St; per car/individual $8/4; ⌚8am-5pm Oct-Mar, til 7pm Apr-Sep), north of I-20 is a massive battlefield, Vicksburg's main attraction for Civil War buffs. A 16-mile driving tour passes historic markers explaining battle scenarios and key events. You can buy an audiotape tour on cassette or CD in the visitor center gift shop, or drive through on your own using the free map distributed on-site (but plan for at least two hours to do it justice). If you have your bike, cycling is a fantastic way to tour the place. Locals use the scenic park for walking and running, too. The cemetery contains some 17,000 Union graves, and a museum houses the ironclad gunboat USS *Cairo*. **Civil War reenactments** are held in May and July.

Sleeping & Eating

Corners Mansion B&B $$
(☎601-636-7421; www.thecorners.com; 601 Klein St; r incl breakfast $125-170; P❄📶) The best part of this Old South 1873 B&B could be looking over the Yazoo and Mississippi Rivers from your porch-swing vantage point. The gardens and Southern breakfast don't hurt either.

Battlefield Inn HOTEL $
(☎601-638-5811; www.battlefieldinn.org; 4137 N I-20 Frontage Rd; r incl breakfast from $85; P❄📶🏊) Shouting distance from the National Military Park and next door to the Battlefield Museum, there's a karaoke bar inside the hotel, a wet bar by the swimming pool and cannons on the property, but other than the vague 'Robert E Lee meets *Gone with the Wind*' theme, there is little reason to stay here over the surrounding chain hotels.

Walnut Hills SOUTHERN $$
(www.walnuthillsms.net; 1214 Adams St; mains $8-25; ⌚11am-9pm Mon-Sat, 11am-2pm Sun) For a dining experience that brings you back in time, head to this eatery where you can enjoy the utterly delectable, down-home Southern food elbow-to-elbow, family-style at a round table from 11am to 2pm. Try the blue-plate special ($9).

Highway 61 Coffeehouse CAFE $
(www.61coffee.blogspot.com; 1101 Washington St; ⌚7am-5pm Mon-Fri, 9am-5pm Sat; 📶) This surprisingly awesome coffee shop has occasional live music on Saturday afternoons, serves Fair Trade coffee and is a minuscule epicenter of artsy-ness.

Information

Visitor center (☎601-636-9421; www.visitvicksburg.com; 3300 Clay St; ⌚8am-5pm Mon-Sat & 10am-5pm Sun Mar-Oct, till 7pm

Mon-Sat & 10am-5pm Sun Nov-Feb) Hands out indispensable free maps that mark color-coded scenic driving paths into and out of the city.

Jackson

Mississippi's capital and largest city is victim to the common car-culture phenomenon of a latent (though stately and gentrifying) downtown surrounded by plush suburbs – sitting on top of an extinct volcano (most locals don't know that). However, interesting areas like the funky Fondren District, along with a cluster of well-done museums, historic sites and bars and restaurants, give insight into the culture of Mississippi and are elevating Jackson to a definite good time.

Sights

FREE **Mississippi Museum of Art** GALLERY

(www.msmuseumart.org; 380 South Lamar St; 10am-5pm Tue-Sat, noon-5pm Sun) This is the one fantastic attraction in Jackson. The collection of Mississippi art – a permanent exhibit dubbed 'The Mississippi Story' – is nothing less than superb. A new downtown green space called the Art Garden, with a symphony stage and live music, was underway at the time of writing.

FREE **Old Capitol Museum** MUSEUM

(http://mdah.state.ms.us/museum; 100 State St; 9am-5pm Tue-Sati, 1-5pm Sun) The state's Greek Revival capitol building from 1839 to 1903 received a stellar renovation in 2009. It now houses an extremely well-done museum that covers Mississippi's history from prehistoric to modern times.

Eudora Welty House HISTORIC BUILDING

(601-353-7762; www.mdah.state.ms.us/welty; 1119 Pinehurst St; tours 9am, 11am, 1pm & 3pm Tue-Fri) Southern-literature buffs should make a reservation to tour the Welty. The Pulitzer Prize–winning author lived in this Tudor Revival house for more than 75 years. It's now a true historical preservation down to the most minute details.

Smith Robertson Museum MUSEUM

(www.jacksonms.gov/visitors/museums/smithrobertson; 528 Bloom St; adult/child $4.50/1.50; 9am-5pm Mon-Fri, 10am-1pm Sat, 2-5pm Sun) Housed in Mississippi's first public school for African American kids, is the alma mater of author Richard Wright. It offers insight and explanation into the pain and perseverance of the African American legacy in Mississippi.

Mississippi Children's Museum MUSEUM

(www.mississippichildrensmuseum.com; 2148 Riverside Dr; admission $8; 9am-5pm Tue-Sat, 1-6pm Sun;) Jackson's brand new children's museum, opened in December 2010, was quickly recognized as one of the country's best. Many of the exhibits have a sustainable or Mississippi slant, and all are aimed educating the youngsters – the digestive-tract jungle gym that ends in a toilet might have gone too far, though.

Sleeping & Eating

Fondren District is the budding artsy, boho area of town, ie fun restaurants, art galleries and cafes dot a strip of traffic-heavy road. Farish St, a dilapidated downtown street thoroughly soaked in blues history, was being gutted and revitalized at the time of writing, with a BB King blues club on the way.

Old Capitol Inn BOUTIQUE HOTEL $$

(601-359-9000; www.oldcapitolinn.com; 226 N State St; r incl breakfast from $99;) A heck of a deal, this 24-room boutique hotel, near museums and restaurants, has up-to-date rooms that are comfortably and uniquely furnished. The rooftop deck, complete with hot tub, overlooks a courtyard and pool. A full Southern breakfast (and early-evening wine and cheese) are included and the thoughtful service is exemplified by details such as handwritten weather reports brought to your room.

Fairview Inn INN $$

(601-948-3429; www.fairviewinn.com; 734 Fairview St; s/d incl breakfast from $139/154;) For a colonial estate experience, the 18-room Fairview Inn will not let you down when it comes to Southern formality and traditions, including a grits-and-bacon kind of breakfast. It also has a full spa.

Two Sisters Kitchen SOUTHERN $$

(707 N Congress St; buffet weekends/weekdays $14.80/12.50; 11am-2pm Sun-Fri) Some serious Southern business is happening at this down-home buffet in a historical 1903 home: fried okra, cheese grits and legendary *skinless* fried chicken among the highlights. The line stretches out the door pretty much always and the all-you-can-eat price includes salad and dessert as well.

Walker's Drive-In SOUTHERN **$$$**
(www.walkersdrivein.com; 3016 N State St; dinner mains $28-32; ⏲11am-2pm Mon-Fri & from 5:30pm Tue-Sat) This truly outstanding restaurant calls itself a drive-in, but it's really a gussied-up diner that serves lusciously tweaked Southern staples. And it serves things like heavenly barbecued oysters dolloped with brie, and incredible fish dishes. There's an excellent wine list and service is impeccable.

High Noon Cafe VEGETARIAN
(2807 Old Canton Rd; mains $9-11; ⏲11:30am-2pm;) Tired of fried green pulled-pork-covered catfish? This organic vegetarian grill, inside the Rainbow Co-op grocery store in the Fondren District (which also has a free internet cafe, incidentally), does beet burgers, portabello Reubens and other healthy delights. Stock up on healthy groceries, too.

☆ Entertainment

TOP CHOICE **F Jones Corner** BLUES
(www.fjonescorner.com; 303 N Farish St; ⏲Tue-Fri 11am-2pm, Thu-Sat 10am-late) The real deal. All shapes and sizes descend on this down-home club when everywhere else closes; a race, color and creed potpourri on Farish St that hosts some seriously authentic Delta musicians who have been known to play until sunrise. Don't show up before 1am.

119 Underground BLUES
(www.underground119.com; 119 S President St; ⏲4pm-midnight Wed-Thu, 4pm-2am Fri, Sat 6pm-2am Sat) A funky, supremely cool supper club throwback serving up blues, jazz and bluegrass alongside excellent eats (the chef's Southern fusion comes from his extended travels and backyard urban garden) and juiced up creative cocktails (try the Robert Johnson – sweet tea vodka with fresh lemon juice).

ℹ Information

Convention & visitors bureau (☎601-960-1891; www.visitjackson.com; 111 E Capitol St, Suite 102; ⏲8am-5pm Mon-Fri) Free information.

ℹ Getting There & Away

At the junction of I-20 and I-55, it's easy to get in and out of Jackson. Its international **airport** (JAN; www.jmaa.com) is 10 miles east of downtown. **Greyhound** (☎601-353-6342; 300 W Capitol St) buses serve Birmingham, AL, Memphis, TN, and New Orleans, LA. Amtrak's *City of New Orleans* stops at the station.

Natchez

A tiny dollop of cosmopolitan in Mississippi, adorable Natchez stews together a wide variety of folks, from gay log-cabin republicans to intellectual liberals, to down-home folks. Perched on a bluff overlooking the Mississippi, it's the oldest town on the river and attracts tourists in search of antebellum history and architecture – 668 antebellum homes pepper the oldest civilized settlement on the Mississippi River (beating New Orleans by two years). It's also the end (or the beginning!) of the scenic 444-mile Natchez Trace Pkwy (p368), the state's cycling and recreational jewel.

The **visitor and welcome center** (☎601-446-6345; www.visitnatchez.org; 640 S Canal St; tours adult/child $12/8; ⏲8:30am-5pm Mon-Sat, 9am-4pm Sun) is a large, well-organized tourist resource with little exhibits of area history and a ton of information on local sites. Tours of the historic downtown and antebellum mansions leave here. During the 'pilgrimage' seasons in spring and fall, local mansions are opened to visitors.

Ever wish you could sleep in one of those historic homes with every room roped off? At the **Historic Oak Hill Inn** (☎601-446-2500; www.historicoakhill.com; 409 S Rankin St; r incl breakfast from $125; P❄📶), you can sleep in an original 1835 bed and dine on pre-Civil War Old Paris porcelain under 1850 Waterford crystal gasoliers – it's all about purist antebellum aristocratic living at this classic Natchez B&B. A high-strung staff makes for an immaculate experience and it's gay-friendly. The **Sunset View Guest Cottages** (☎601-870-2662; www.asunsetview.com; 26 Cemetery Rd; cottages $165-195; P❄📶) are warmly decorated cottages with private, stunning views of the Mississippi River. You can skip rocks into the Mississippi from the **Mark Twain Guesthouse** (☎601-446-8023; www.underthehillsaloon.com; 33 Silver St; r without bath $65-85; ❄📶) where three rooms (two with views) sit on top of a good local watering hole, the **Under the Hill Saloon**.

Economy options are limited here, but there is camping at **Natchez State Park** (www.mississippistateparks.reserveamerica.com; 230 Wickcliff Rd B; tent sites $13-24, RV sites $18, cabins $77-87). It's 1 mile east of the parkway on Hwy 61, 10 miles north of Natchez. Within the park is Emerald Mound, the second-largest Native American ceremonial mound of its type in the United States.

To get your fill of Southern eats, follow your nose to the **Pig Out Inn** (www.pigoutinnbq.com; 116 S Canal St; pulled-pork sandwich $4.75; 11am-9pm Mon-Sat, to 3pm Sun), where some people say you'll find the best ribs in town. **Natchez Coffee Co.** (509 Franklin St; mains $5-8; 7am-6pm Mon-Fri, 8am-5pm Sat & Sun;) is the spot for a latte or nicely done light bites.

Gulf Coast

In the backyard of New Orleans, the Gulf Coast's economy, traditionally based on the seafood industry, got a shot of adrenaline in the 1990s when big Vegas-style casinos muscled in alongside the sleepy fishing villages. And then a double whammy of disasters: just when the casinos in Biloxi had been rebuilt following Hurricane Katrina in 2005, the Deepwater Horizon oil spill in the Gulf in 2010 dealt the coast another unexpected blow. However, Mississippi's barrier islands help divert much of the oil problems toward New Orleans and Alabama, so Biloxi and Gulfport were largely spared and tourism had returned to 75% pre-spill levels at time of writing. The appeal? The manmade beaches are pleasant, and if you're a gambler you can jostle at the blackjack tables alongside Southern-speaking Vietnamese, Irish fishermen and bigwigs and environmentalists who have jetted in from big cities – all collaborating to rebuild a hard-luck area.

Keep track of what's open for business through the **Mississippi Gulf Coast Convention & Visitors Bureau** (228-896-6699; www.gulfcoast.org; 2350 Beach Blvd, Biloxi), which has a website that lists openings and reopenings.

Ocean Springs is one of the coolest, non-destroyed places on the Mississippi coast. Its **visitor center** (228-875-4424; www.oceanspringschamber.com; 1000 Washington St; 9am-4pm Mon-Fri) is at the head of Washington St, where you'll find a slew of cute shops, restaurants and coffeehouses.

Walter Anderson Museum (www.walterandersonmuseum.org; 510 Washington St; adult/child $10/5; 9:30am-4:30pm Mon-Sat, 12:30-4:30pm Sun) is a highlight of the city (and probably the state). A consummate artist and lover of Gulf Coast nature, Anderson had his fair share of turmoil and love that spurred his talent to great heights. After he died, the beachside shack where he lived was found to be completely covered in mind-blowing murals, which are now transplanted to the museum.

Hotels line the highway, or stay at **Oak Shade B&B** (888-875-4711; www.oakshade.net; 1017 La Fontaine Ave; r $95-140;). A visit here is very similar to just being a guest in a friend's home: comfy and relaxed. There's a lovely courtyard too. Marian, the owner, is laid-back and loves to help you do whatever you want to do in the area. Nice camping (and a visitor center) can be found at **Gulf Islands National Seashore Park** (www.nps.gov/guis; camping $16-20), which is a little bit out of town.

LOUISIANA

In the words of William Faulkner: 'The past is never dead. It's not even past.' Nowhere is that as true in the US as it is in Louisiana. Nostalgia for times long gone and recognition of hardships endured are found at every turn. This leads to a dynamic sense of place – natives are rooted here, and embrace what makes them unique. This is a state where African American cowboys strap washboards to their chests and strum the distinctive clicking sound of zydeco, and where gators lurk in swamps and are hunted by French-speaking Cajuns. Different cultures coexist – after all, don't we all just want to eat well and dance?

In the rolling hills and pine forests of northern Louisiana, the mostly Protestant population shares similar traits with other Southern states. But the world becomes a different place amid the swamps of southern Louisiana and the debauched streets of New Orleans – where jazz and Afro-Caribbean sounds are thick in the sultry air and make you unable to resist the urge to let loose.

History

The lower Mississippi River area was dominated by the Mississippian mound-building culture until around 1592 when Europeans arrived and decimated the Native Americans with the usual combination of disease, unfavorable treaties and outright hostility.

The land was then passed back and forth between France, Spain and England. After the American Revolution the whole area passed to the USA in the 1803 Louisiana Purchase, and Louisiana became a state in 1812.

LOUISIANA FACTS

» **Nicknames** Bayou State, Pelican State, Sportsman's Paradise

» **Population** 4.5 million

» **Area** 51,843 sq miles

» **Capital city** Baton Rouge (population 229,553)

» **Other cities** New Orleans (population 343,829)

» **Sales tax** 4%, plus local city and county taxes

» **Birthplace of** jazz, naturalist John James Audubon (1785–1851), trumpeter Louis 'Satchmo' Armstrong (1901–71), author Truman Capote (1924–84), musician Antoine 'Fats' Domino (b 1928), pop star Britney Spears (b 1981)

» **Home of** Tabasco sauce, chef Emeril Lagasse

» **Politics** normally a Republican stronghold but isn't afraid to veer left on occasion

» **Famous for** drive-thru margaritas

» **Official state reptile** alligator

» **Driving distances** New Orleans to Lafayette 137 miles, New Orleans to St Francisville 112 miles

Steamboats opened a vital trade network across the continent. New Orleans became a major port, and Louisiana's slave-based plantation economy kept up a flowing export of rice, tobacco, indigo, sugarcane and especially cotton. After the Civil War, Louisiana was readmitted to the Union in 1868, and the next 30 years saw political wrangling, economic stagnation and renewed discrimination against African Americans.

In the 1920s, industry and tourism developed, but the tradition of unorthodox and sometimes ruthless politics continues today. Race and economics are ongoing sources of struggle: witness the post-Katrina rebuilding process (p411). The 2005 hurricane and the flooding in its aftermath have reshaped southern Louisiana. Locals have negotiated the tricky path through redevelopment, the return of displaced peoples, wetland restoration and outsider involvement. Though revitalization has been more successful in some places, progress has been painfully slow in others, especially the poorer areas.

Information

Sixteen welcome centers dot freeways throughout the state, or contact the **Louisiana Office of Tourism** (225-342-8119; www.louisianatravel.com).

Louisiana State Parks (877-226-7652; www.crt.state.la.us/parks; primitive/premium sites $1/18) Louisiana has 22 state parks that offer camping. Some parks offer lodge accommodations and cabins. Reservations can be made on the **internet** (www.reserveamerica.com), by phone, or on a drop-in basis if there's availability.

New Orleans

New Orleans gets called the 'Big Easy' in all its promotional material, and this city does take it easy, to some degree. It's rare in America to see folks hold up traffic for the sake of pulling over and calling out, 'Yo Dante, wassup,' and rarer still for the people behind them to accept this nonchalantly and find another way around.

But when it comes to having a good time, New Orleanians are kind of like Manhattanites on a deadline. Just one more beer? Nah son, have a shot with that. You want a burger? How's about we put peanut butter and bacon on top? And throw in a huge baked potato with sour cream on the side. And hell, some crawfish (crayfish).

At the mouth of the Mississippi, remember the three 'I's. The first two, indulgence and immersion, are easy to pick up on. It's brown sugar on bacon instead of oatmeal for breakfast; a double served neat instead of light beer; sex in the morning instead of being early for work ('My streetcar was down'). But the biggest 'I' here is *intermixing*. Tolerating everything and learning from it is the soul of this city. Social tensions and divisions of race and income keep New Orleans jittery, but when its citizens aspire to that great Creole ideal – a mix of all influences into something better – we get: jazz; Nouveau Louisiana cuisine; storytellers from African *griots* (West African storyteller) to Seventh Ward rappers to Tennessee Williams; French town houses a few blocks from Foghorn Leghorn mansions groaning under sweet myrtle and bougainvillea; Mardi Gras celebrations that mix pagan mysticism with Catholic pageantry. Just don't forget the indulgence and immersion, because that Creole-ization gets watered down when folks don't live life to its intellectual and epicurean hilt.

New Orleans may take it easy, but it takes it. The whole hog.

History

The town of Nouvelle Orléans was founded as a French outpost in 1718 by Jean-Baptiste Le Moyne de Bienville. Early settlers arrived from France, Canada and Germany, and the French imported thousands of African slaves. The city became a central port in the slave trade; due to local laws some slaves were allowed to earn their freedom and assume an established place in the Creole community as *les gens de couleur libres* (free people of color).

The Spanish were largely responsible for building the French Quarter as it still looks today because fires in 1788 and 1794 decimated the earlier French architecture. The influx of Anglo-Americans after the Louisiana Purchase led to an expansion of the city into the Central Business District (CBD), Garden District and Uptown. By 1840 New Orleans was the nation's fourth-largest city, with more than 100,000 people.

New Orleans survived the Civil War intact after an early surrender to Union forces, but the economy languished with the end of the slavery-based plantations. In the early 1900s, New Orleans was the birthplace of jazz music. Many of the speakeasies and homes of the jazz originators have been destroyed through neglect, but the cultural claim was canonized in 1994 when the NPS established the New Orleans Jazz National Historical Park to celebrate the origins and evolution of America's most widely recognized indigenous musical art form. Oil and petrochemical industries developed in the 1950s, and today tourism is the other lifeblood of the local economy.

In 2005 Katrina, a relatively weak Category 3 hurricane, overwhelmed New Orleans' federal flood protection system in over 50 places. Some 80% of the city was flooded, over 1800 people lost their lives and the entire city was evacuated. Today the population stands at 70% of pre-Katrina levels. Although much has rebuilt and tourists are back with a bead-throwing vengeance, the city has irrevocably changed.

Sights & Activities

FRENCH QUARTER

Elegant, Caribbean-colonial architecture, lush gardens and wrought-iron accents are the visual norm in the French Quarter. But this is also the heart of New Orleans' tourism scene. Bourbon St generates a loutish membrane that sometimes makes the rest of the Quarter difficult to appreciate. Look past this. The 'Vieux Carré' (Old Quarter, first laid out in 1722) is the focal point of much of this

RENEWED ORLEANS

New Orleans is back. The 'Katrina Tattoo,' the line on thousands of buildings that marked the top elevation of 2005's Hurricane Katrina floodwaters, has faded, and talk of 'The Storm' is slowly but surely fading into the history books. The city has survived floods, fires, epidemics, oil spills and the Indianapolis Colts, so it's no surprise that Katrina would be any different. Sure, there are still buildings left scarred with international rescue codes and plenty of rebuilding to do, but it's business as usual in the 'Who Dat' Nation, especially on the 'sliver by the River' extending from the blocks of Riverbend down in a curve along Uptown and Magazine St, up into the CBD, French Quarter and Faubourg Marigny.

There are new hot spots as well, from art gallery row on St Claude Ave, recently made-over Oak St in Riverbend and the Tremé neighborhood of HBO fame. Thanks to the thousands of new arrivals, affectionately nicknamed YURPs – Young, Urban Rebuilding Professionals (they've even got a website: www.nolayurp.com) – who came to carve the city back to life from the sludge and muck, as well as returnees. There are also signs of renewed life in the embattled Ninth Ward, Gentilly, Lakeview and Broadmoor neighborhoods, where Idealistic 20- and 30-somethings are buying property and starting new businesses.

New Orleans has always been a beacon for the misfits of America. Now add entrepreneurs, techies and actors to that list. The newly coined 'Silicon Bayou' and 'Hollywood South' – at least four flicks are being shot on location here at any given time lately – are also becoming a litmus test for new frontiers of urban planning. Brad Pitt's Make It Right campaign (p416) has turned much of the Lower Ninth Ward into a model sustainable neighborhood with a retro futuristic vibe so cool that it's worth a visit just to gawk at the homes.

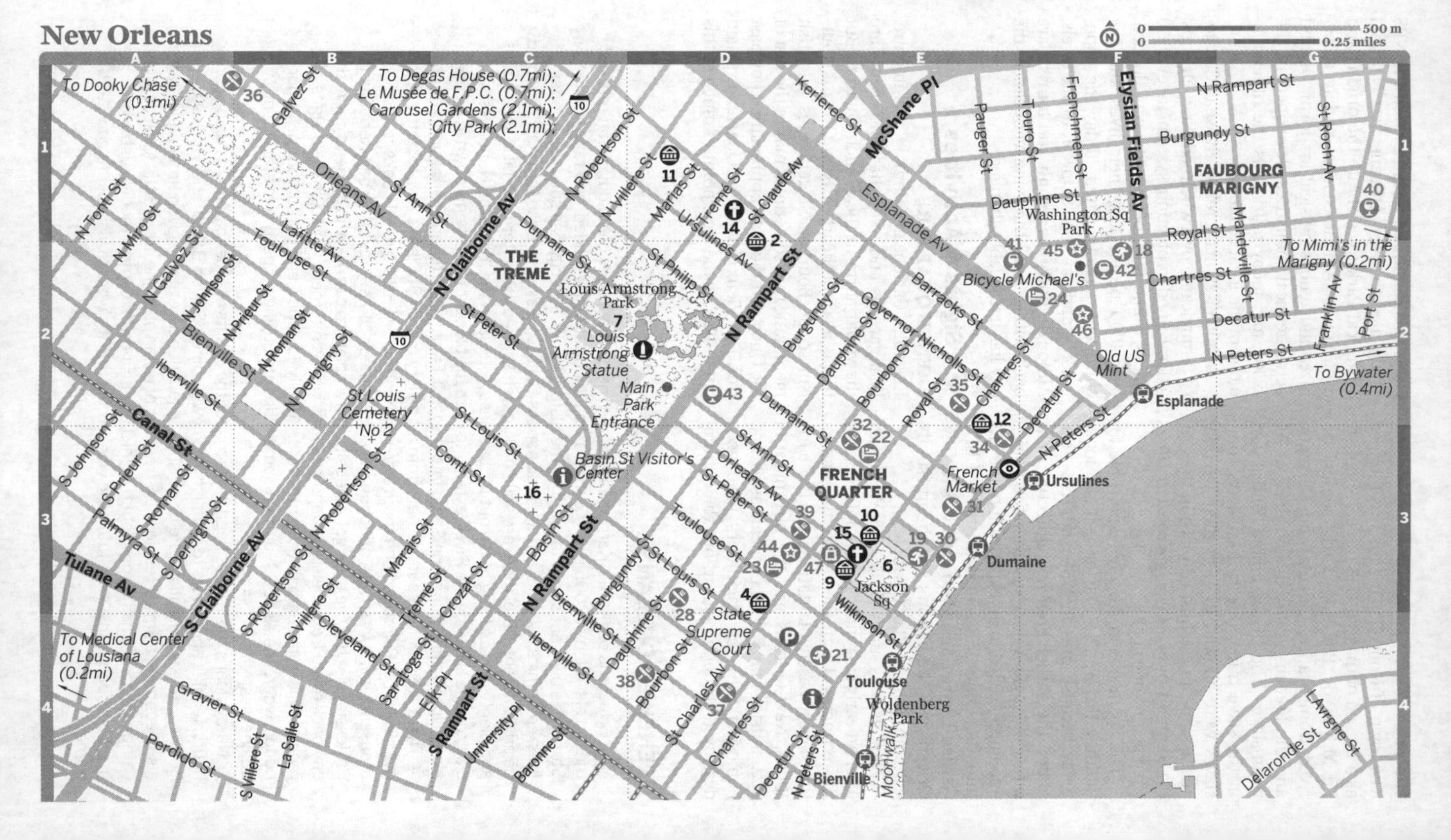
New Orleans
0 500 m
0 0.25 miles
To Dooky Chase (0.1mi)
To Degas House (0.7mi); Le Musée de F.P.C. (0.7mi); Carousel Gardens (2.1mi); City Park (2.1mi);
To Mimi's in the Marigny (0.2mi)
To Bywater (0.4mi)
To Medical Center of Lousiana (0.2mi)
FAUBOURG MARIGNY
THE TREMÉ
FRENCH QUARTER
Louis Armstrong Park
Louis Armstrong Statue
Main Park Entrance
Basin St Visitor's Center
St Louis Cemetery No 2
Washington Sq Park
Bicycle Michael's
Old US Mint
French Market
Jackson Sq
State Supreme Court
Woldenberg Park
Moonwalk
Esplanade
Ursulines
Dumaine
Toulouse
Bienville
Elysian Fields Av
McShane Pl
Esplanade Av
N Rampart St
S Rampart St
N Claiborne Av
S Claiborne Av
Canal St
Tulane Av
N Rampart St
Burgundy St
Royal St
Chartres St
Decatur St
N Peters St
St Roch Av
Mandeville St
Franklin Av
Port St
Pauger St
Touro St
Frenchmen St
Dauphine St
Kerlerec St
Barracks St
Governor Nicholls St
Bourbon St
St Claude Av
Ursulines Av
St Philip St
Dumaine St
St Ann St
Orleans Av
St Peter St
Toulouse St
St Louis St
Conti St
Bienville St
Iberville St
Wilkinson St
Basin St
Treme St
Marais St
N Villere St
N Robertson St
Crozat St
Galvez St
Lafitte Av
Elk Pl
Saratoga St
Cleveland St
University Pl
Baronne St
St Charles Av
Gravier St
Perdido St
La Salle St
S Villere St
S Robertson St
S Derbigny St
S Roman St
S Prieur St
S Johnson St
Palmyra St
N Derbigny St
N Roman St
N Prieur St
N Johnson St
N Galvez St
N Miro St
N Tonti St
Delaronde St
LAvrgne St

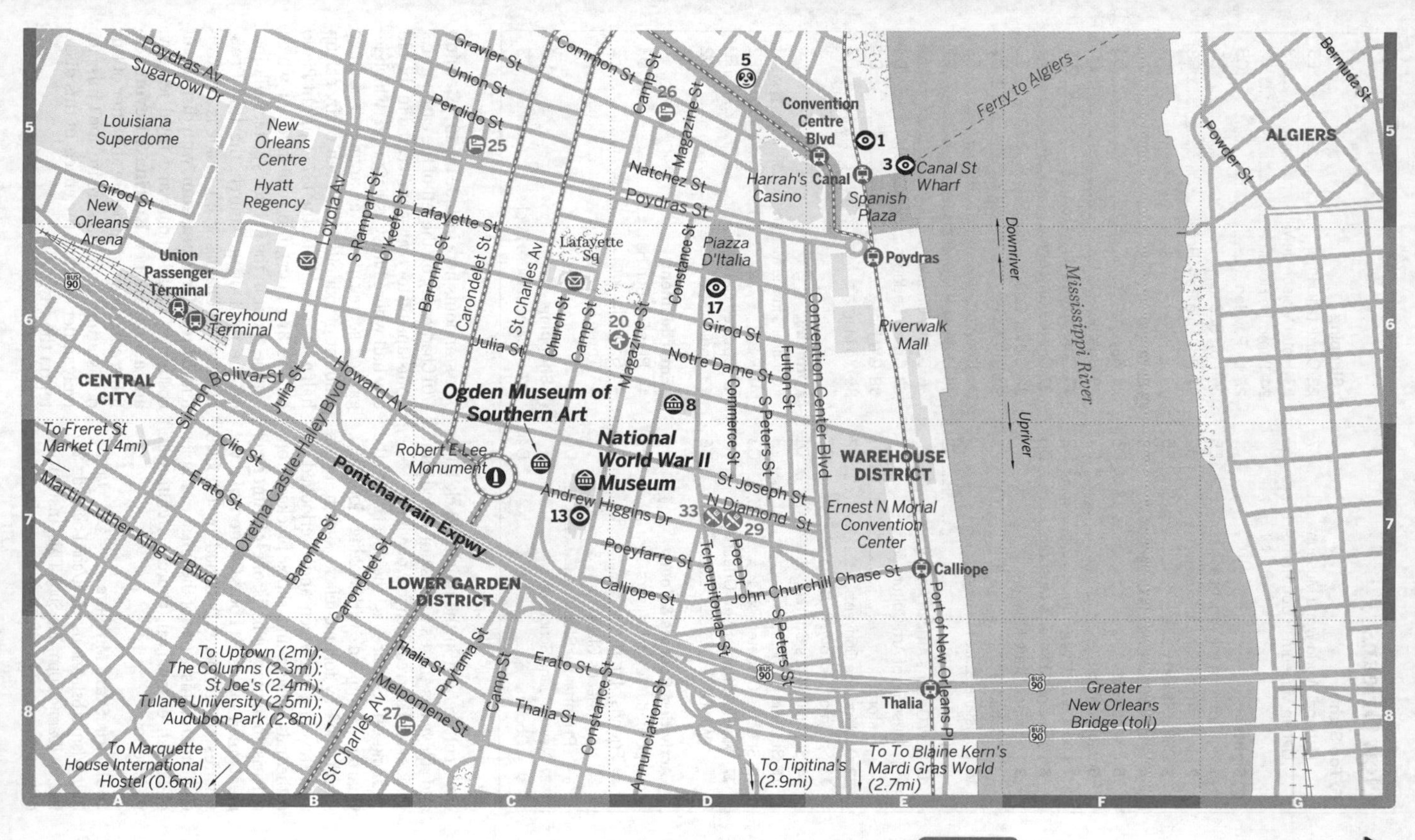

Poydras Av
Sugarbowl Dr
Louisiana Superdome
New Orleans Centre
Hyatt Regency
Girod St
New Orleans Arena
Union Passenger Terminal
Greyhound Terminal
CENTRAL CITY
To Freret St Market (1.4mi)
Martin Luther King Jr Blvd
Simon Bolivar St
Julia St
Oretha Castle-Haley Blvd
Howard Av
Clio St
Erato St
Baronne St
Carondelet St
Pontchartrain Expwy
LOWER GARDEN DISTRICT
To Uptown (2mi); The Columns (2.3mi); St Joe's (2.4mi); Tulane University (2.5mi); Audubon Park (2.8mi)
To Marquette House International Hostel (0.6mi)
St Charles Av
Melpomene St
Thalia St
Prytania St
Camp St
Gravier St
Union St
Perdido St
Common St
Loyola Av
S Rampart St
O'Keefe St
Lafayette St
St Charles Av
Lafayette Sq
Church St
Robert E Lee Monument
Ogden Museum of Southern Art
National World War II Museum
Andrew Higgins Dr
Poeyfarre St
Calliope St
Erato St
Thalia St
Constance St
Annunciation St
Magazine St
Natchez St
Poydras St
Constance St
Piazza D'Italia
Girod St
Notre Dame St
Commerce St
S Peters St
Fulton St
St Joseph St
N Diamond St
Tchoupitoulas St
Poe Dr
John Churchill Chase St
S Peters St
Convention Center Blvd
Convention Centre Blvd
Harrah's Casino
Canal
Spanish Plaza
Canal St Wharf
Poydras
Riverwalk Mall
WAREHOUSE DISTRICT
Ernest N Morial Convention Center
Calliope
Port of New Orleans Pl
Thalia
To Tipitina's (2.9mi)
To To Blaine Kern's Mardi Gras World (2.7mi)
Ferry to Algiers
Downriver
Upriver
Mississippi River
Greater New Orleans Bridge (toll)
ALGIERS
Powder St
Bermuda St

New Orleans

Top Sights

National World War II Museum C7
Ogden Museum of Southern Art C7

Sights

1 Aquarium of the Americas..................... E5
2 Backstreet Cultural Museum................ D2
3 Canal St Ferry.. E5
4 Historic New Orleans Collection........... D3
5 Insectarium.. D5
6 Jackson Sq E3
7 Louis Armstrong Park.......................... D2
8 Louisiana Children's Museum.............. D6
9 Louisiana State Museum (Cabildo) E3
10 Louisiana State Museum (Presbytère)... E3
11 New Orleans African American Museum of Art, Culture & History D1
12 Old Ursuline Convent E2
13 Solomon Victory Theater C7
14 St Augustine's Church D1
15 St Louis Cathedral................................ E3
16 St Louis Cemetery No 1 .... C3
17 Wine Institute of New Orleans (WINO) D6

Activities, Courses & Tours

18 Confederacy of Cruisers....................... F2
19 Friends of the Cabildo........................... E3
20 New Orleans GlassWorks & Printmaking Studio............................. D6
21 New Orleans School of Cooking D4

Sleeping

22 Cornstalk Hotel.. E3
23 Hotel Maison de Ville D3
24 Lamothe House F2
25 Le Pavillon C5
26 Loft 523.. D5
27 Prytania Park Hotel................................... B8

Eating

28 Bayona... D3
29 Butcher.. D7
30 Café du Monde.. E3
31 Central Grocery E3
32 Clover Grill.. E3
33 Cochon... D7
34 Coop's.. E3
35 Croissant d'Or Patisserie E2
36 Dooky Chase A1
37 Green Goddess D4
38 GW Fins.. D4
39 Yo Mama's... D3

Drinking

40 Mimi's in the Marigny................................ G1
41 R Bar.. E2
42 Spotted Cat... F2
43 Tonique.. D2

Entertainment

44 Preservation Hall.. D3
45 Snug Harbor.. F2
46 Three Muses F2

Shopping

47 Faulkner House Books............................... E3

city's culture and in the quieter back lanes and alleyways there's a sense of faded time shaken and stirred with joie de vivre.

Jackson Square is the heart of the Quarter. Sprinkled with lazing loungers, surrounded by fortune-tellers, sketch artists and traveling showmen and overlooked by cathedrals, offices and shops plucked from a Parisian fantasy, this is one of America's great green spaces. **St Louis Cathedral** is the square's masterpiece. Designed by Gilberto Guillemard, this is one of the finest examples of French ecumenical (church) architecture in America.

Louisiana State Museum MUSEUM
(http://lsm.crt.state.la.us; adult/child per bldg $6/free; 10am-4:30pm Tue-Sun) This institution operates several institutions across the state. The standouts here include the 1911 **Cabildo** (701 Chartres St), on the left of the cathedral, a Louisiana history museum located in the old city hall where Plessy vs Ferguson (which legalized segregation) was argued. The huge amount of exhibits inside can easily eat up half a day (don't miss the 1875 Upright Piano on the 3rd floor), the remainder of which can be spent in the Cabildo's sister building, on the right of the church, the 1813 **Presbytère** (751 Chartres St;). Inside is an excellent **Mardi Gras museum**, with displays of costumes, parade floats and royal jewelry; and a poignant new **Katrina & Beyond** exhibit, chronicling the before and after of this devastating storm – a surefire don't miss for truly understanding the effects of this disaster on the city.

Historic New Orleans Collection MUSEUM
(www.hnoc.org; 533 Royal St; admission free, tours $5; ⌚9:30am-4:30pm Tue-Sat, 10:30am-4:30pm Sun) In several exquisitely restored buildings are thoughtfully curated exhibits with an emphasis on archival materials, such as the original transfer documents of the Louisiana Purchase. Separate home, architecture/courtyard and history tours also run at 10am, 11am, 2pm and 3pm, the home being the most interesting.

Old Ursuline Convent HISTORIC BUILDING
(1112 Chartres St; adult/child $5/3; ⌚tours 10am-4pm Mon-Sat) In 1727, 12 Ursuline nuns arrived in New Orleans to care for the French garrison's 'miserable little hospital' and to educate the young girls of the colony. Between 1745 and 1752 the French colonial army built what is now the oldest structure in the Mississippi River Valley and the only remaining French building in the Quarter. The self-guided tour takes in various rotating exhibits and the beautiful St Mary's chapel.

THE TREMÉ

The oldest African American neighborhood in the city is obviously steeped in a lot of history.

Louis Armstrong Park (⌚9am-10pm) encompasses **Congo Square**, an American cultural landmark. Now a brick open space, it was the one place where enslaved people were allowed to congregate and play the music they had carried over the seas – a practice outlawed in most other slave-holding societies. The preservation of this musical heritage helped lay the groundwork for rhythms that would eventually become jazz. It was cordoned off and under a controversial facelift on our visit.

Backstreet Cultural Museum MUSEUM
(www.backstreetmuseum.org; 1116 St Claude Ave; admission $8; ⌚10am-5pm Tue-Sat) This is the place to see one facet of this town's distinctive customs – its African American side – and how they're expressed in daily life. The term 'backstreet' refers to New Orleans' 'back o' town,' or the poor African American neighborhoods. If you have any interest in Mardi Gras Indian suits (African Americans who dress up in Carnival-esque Native American costume), second lines and the activities of social aid and pleasure clubs (the local African American community version of civic associations), you need to stop by.

Le Musée de FPC MUSEUM
(Free People of Color Museum; www.lemuseedefpc.com; 2336 Esplanade Ave; adult/child $10/5; ⌚11am-4pm Wed-Sat or by appt) Inside a lovely 1859 Greek Revival mansion in the Upper Tremé, this newcomer showcases a 30-year collection of artifacts, documents, furniture and art telling the story of a forgotten subculture: the 'free people of color' before the Civil War. The small but fascinating collection includes original documentation of slaves who became free, either by *coartación* (buying their own freedom) or as a reward for particularly good service.

St Louis Cemetery No 1 CEMETERY
(Basin St; ⌚9am-3pm Mon-Sat, til noon Sun; 👪) This cemetery received the remains of most early Creoles. The shallow water table necessitated aboveground burials, with bodies placed in the family tombs you see to this day. The supposed grave of voodoo queen Marie Laveau is here, scratched with 'XXX's from spellbound devotees – this is graffiti you shouldn't add to, per the request of the family that owns the tomb.

New Orleans African American Museum of Art, Culture & History MUSEUM
(www.thenoaam.org; 1418 Governor Nicholls St; adult/student/child $7/5/3; ⌚11am-4pm Wed-Sat) Well-presented museum exhibiting rotating displays of local artists and more semipermanent installations on slavery and African American history in a series of tidy Creole homes.

St Augustine's Church CHURCH
(☎504-525-5934; www.staugustinecatholic church-neworleans.org; 1210 Governor Nicholls St) The 1824 church is the second-oldest African American Catholic church in the US; many jazz funeral processions originate here. It has Sunday services but you'll need to call ahead for a tour – it's still understaffed post-Katrina and usually closed.

FAUBOURG MARIGNY, THE BYWATER & THE NINTH WARD

North of the French Quarter are the Creole suburbs ('faubourgs,' which more accurately means 'neighborhoods') of the Marigny and the Bywater. The Marigny is the heart of the local gay scene. **Frenchman St**, which runs through the center of the 'hood, is a fantastic strip of live-music goodness – what Bourbon St used to be before the strip clubs and daiquiri factories took over. The Bywater is an edgier area, where a good mix of white, African American working class and artists are straddling the edge of urban cool. A lot of new New Orleanians have moved into this area, bringing a bit of gentrification along with some decent funkiness to the pretty rows of shotgun shacks.

Make It Right NEIGHBORHOOD
(www.makeitrightnola.org; N Clairborne at Tennessee St) Brad Pitt's futuristic green building project in the Lower Ninth Ward, Make It Right, dots the former devastated landscape like *Jetsons*-style living quarters. Some 75 sustainable, storm-resistant homes had been built at time of writing (45 of which are LEED-certified platinum), giving the neighborhood a beautiful kaleidoscopic aura that is in striking contrast to the despairing images beamed around the world during Katrina. The US Green Building Council has named the neighborhood the 'largest, greenest neighborhood of single family homes in America.'

Musicians' Village NEIGHBORHOOD
(www.nolamusiciansvillage.com; btwn North Roman, Alvar & North Johnson Sts) An 8-acre tract of some 81 houses, built primarily for musicians, a vital component of the city's cultural and economic landscape. If you visit, please bear in mind this is a living neighborhood; folks can get understandably tetchy if you take pictures of them or their property without asking permission or even getting out of your car. The brightly painted houses brighten up the surrounding neighborhood.

CBD & WAREHOUSE DISTRICT

The CBD and Warehouse District comprise the commercial section established after the Louisiana Purchase. Several outstanding museums anchor the Warehouse District and local art galleries cluster along Julia St, holding openings on the first Saturday evening of each month.

TOP CHOICE **National World War II Museum** MUSEUM
(www.nationalww2museum.org; 945 Magazine St; adult/student/child $18/9/free, with film $23/12/5; ⌚9am-5pm) The extensive, heart-wrenching museum should satisfy the historical curiosity of anyone with even a passing interest in WWII. The museum presents an admirably nuanced and thorough analysis of the biggest war of the 20th century. Of particular note is the **D-Day exhibition**, arguably the most in-depth of its type in the country. The new 4-D *Beyond All Boundaries* film, narrated by Tom Hanks and shown on a 120ft-wide immersive screen in the new **Solomon Victory Theater**, is a loud, proud and awesome extravaganza well worth the extra $5. Chef John Besh's casual American diner, the **American Sector** (mains $9.50-18) has also been added here – make it a day.

Ogden Museum of Southern Art MUSEUM
(www.ogdenmuseum.org; 925 Camp St; adult/student/child $10/8/5; ⌚10am-5pm Wed-Mon, 6-8pm Thu) One of our favorite museums in the city manages to be beautiful, educating and unpretentious all at once. New Orleans entrepreneur Roger Houston Ogden has assembled one of the finest collections of Southern art anywhere – far too large to keep to himself – which includes huge galleries ranging from Impressionist landscapes to outsider folk-art quirkiness, to contemporary installation work. There's live music from 6pm to 8pm Thursday for $10.

Blaine Kern's Mardi Gras World MUSEUM
(www.mardigrasworld.com; 1380 Port of New Orleans Pl; adult/child $19.95/12.95; ⌚tours 9:30am-4:30pm; 👪) This garish and good-fun place houses (and constructs) many of the greatest floats used in Mardi Gras parades. You can see them being built or on display any time of the year by popping by the facilities. After an outdated film on Mardi Gras history and a sample of King Cake, the tour takes you through the giant workshops where artists create elaborate floats for New Orleans krewes (marching clubs), Universal Studios and Disney World.

Aquarium of the Americas AQUARIUM
(www.audubooninstitute.org; 1 Canal St; adult/child $19.95/12.95; ⌚10am-5pm; 👪) Simulates an eclectic selection of watery habitats – look for the rare white alligator. You can buy combination tickets to the IMAX theater next door or the Audubon Zoo in Uptown.

Insectarium MUSEUM, GARDEN
(www.auduboninstitute.org; 423 Canal St; adult/child $15.95/10.95; ⌚10am-5pm; 👪) A supremely kid-friendly learning center that's a joy for budding entomologists. The Japanese garden dotted with whispering butterflies is particularly beautiful.

Canal Street Ferry RIVER
(pedestrian & cyclist/car free/$1; ⌚6:15am-12:15am) Departing from the foot of Canal St is a fast and fabulous ride across the

Mississippi to Algiers, an attractive historic neighborhood just across the river, and back.

GARDEN DISTRICT & UPTOWN

The main architectural division in New Orleans is between the elegant town houses of the Creole and French northeast and the magnificent mansions of the American district, settled after the Louisiana Purchase. These huge structures, plantationesque in their appearance, are most commonly found in the Garden District and Uptown. Magnificent oak trees arch over St Charles Ave, which cuts through the heart of this sector and where the supremely picturesque **St Charles Avenue streetcar** (per ride $1.25; 👪) runs. The boutiques and galleries of **Magazine St** form the best shopping strip in the city.

Further west, **Tulane and Loyola universities** occupy adjacent campuses alongside expansive **Audubon Park**. Tulane was founded in 1834 as a medical college in an attempt to control repeated cholera and yellow fever epidemics. Today the verdant campuses offer a welcome respite from city streets, while the universities host plenty of concerts and lectures.

Audubon Zoological Gardens ZOO
(www.auduboninstitute.org; 6500 Magazine St; adult/child $15/10; ⏲10am-5pm Tue-Sun) Among the country's best zoos. It contains the ultra-cool **Louisiana Swamp** exhibit, full of alligators, bobcats, foxes, bears and snapping turtles.

CITY PARK & MID-CITY

New Orleans Museum of Art MUSEUM
(www.noma.org; 1 Collins Diboll Circle; adult/child $10/6; ⏲10am-5pm Tue-Thu, Sat & Sun, to 9pm Fri) Inside the park, the elegant museum was opened in 1911 and is well worth a visit both for its special exhibitions and top-floor galleries of African, Asian (don't miss the outstanding Qing dynasty snuff-bottle collection), Native American and Oceanic art. Its **sculpture garden** (admission free; ⏲10am-4:30pm Sat-Thu, til 8:45pm Fri) contains a cutting-edge collection in lush, meticulously planned grounds.

City Park PARK
(www.neworleanscitypark.com) The **Canal streetcar** makes the run from the CBD to City Park. Three miles long, 1 mile wide, stroked by weeping willows and Spanish moss and dotted with museums, gardens, waterways, bridges, birds and the occasional alligator, City Park is the nation's fifth-largest urban park (bigger than Central Park in NYC) and New Orleans' prettiest green lung.

Fair Grounds PARK
(1751 Gentilly Blvd, btwn Gentilly Blvd & Fortin St) Besides hosting the regular horse-racing season, the fair grounds are also home to the huge springtime New Orleans Jazz & Heritage Festival.

Courses

New Orleans School of Cooking COOKING
(☎504-525-2665; www.neworleansschoolofcooking.com; 524 St Louis St; $23–27) A food demonstration – not a hands-on class. Menus rotate daily, but rest assured you'll be snacking on creations such as gumbo, jambalaya and pralines at the end of class, all the while learning about the history of the city as told by the charismatic chefs.

Wine Institute of New Orleans (WINO) COOKING
(☎504-324-8000; www.winoschool.com; 610 Tchoupitoulas St; classes from $35) The 'institute'

NEW ORLEANS FOR CHILDREN

Many of New Orleans' daytime attractions are well suited for kids: the Audubon Zoological Gardens, Aquarium of the Americas (p416) and Mardi Gras World (p416), for example.

Carousel Gardens AMUSEMENT PARK
(www.neworleanscitypark.com; admission $3; ⏲11am-6pm spring & fall, 10am-4pm Thu, 10am-10pm Fri, 11am-10pm Sat, 11am-6pm summer; 👪) The 1906 carousel is a gem of vintage carny-ride happiness inside City Park.

Louisiana Children's Museum MUSEUM
(www.lcm.org; 420 Julia St; admission $8; ⏲9:30am-4:30pm Tue-Sat, noon-4:30pm Sun, 9:30-4:30pm Mon in summer; 👪) Great hands-on exploratory exhibits and toddler area. Children under 16 must be accompanied by an adult.

runs classes on wine tasting, food pairing and the like, aimed at both amateur enthusiasts and folks looking to get professionally employed in the wine and spirit industry. It's also a wine bar and shop with 120 wines on tap for tasting.

New Orleans GlassWorks & Printmaking Studio ART
(☎504-529-7279; www.neworleansglassworks.com; 727 Magazine St; classes $75-125) Try your hand at glassblowing (really!) or printmaking or both: you can design your own wine glasses and labels in the two-hour Wine and Design combo. Prices fluctuate with natural gas prices.

Tours

Tours, tours everywhere! Check the *New Orleans Official Visitors Guide* for a full selection of the myriad offerings. Some companies now give post-Katrina devastation/rebuilding tours. The Jean Lafitte National Historic Park and Preserve Visitor Center (p425) leads free walking tours of the French Quarter at 9:30am (get tickets at 9am).

Confederacy of Cruisers CYCLING
(☎504-400-5468; www.confederacyofcruisers.com; tour $45) Get yourself out of the Quarter and on two wheels – this super informative, laid-back bike tour takes you through Nola's non-Disneyland neighborhoods – Faubourg Marigny, Esplanade Ridge, the Tremé – often with a bar stop and the occasional jazz funeral pop-in along the way.

Friends of the Cabildo WALKING
(☎504-523-3939; 1850 House Museum Store, 523 St Ann St; adult/student/child $15/10/free; ⊙tours 10am & 1:30pm Tue-Sun) Volunteers lead the best available walking tours of the Quarter.

Festivals & Events

New Orleans never needs an excuse to party – whether in commemoration of shrimp and petroleum or the mighty mirliton (a kind of squash), there's almost always some celebration in town. Just a few listings follow; check www.neworleanscvb.com for more.

Mardi Gras CULTURAL
In February or early March, Fat Tuesday marks the orgasmic finale of the Carnival season.

St Patrick's Day CULTURAL
March 17 and its closest weekend see parades of cabbage-wielding Irishfolk.

St Joseph's Day – Super Sunday CULTURAL
March 19 and its nearest Sunday bring 'gangs' of Mardi Gras Indians out into the streets in all their feathered, drumming glory. The Super Sunday parade usually begins around noon at Bayou St John and Orleans Ave, but follows no fixed route.

Tennessee Williams Literary Festival LITERARY
(www.tennesseewilliams.net) In March, five days of literary panels, plays and parties celebrate the author's work.

French Quarter Festival MUSIC
(www.fqfi.org) The second weekend of April; free music on multiple stages.

Jazz Fest MUSIC
The last weekend of April and the first weekend of May; a world-renowned extravaganza of music, food, crafts and good living.

Southern Decadence GAY & LESBIAN
(www.southerndecadence.net) A huge gay, lesbian and transgender festival, including a leather block party, on Labor Day weekend (first weekend in September).

Sleeping

Rates peak during Mardi Gras and Jazz Fest, and fall in the hot summer months. Book early and call or check the internet for special deals. Hotel sales tax is 13%, plus $1 to $3 per person per night. Parking in the Quarter costs $15 to $25 per day.

TOP CHOICE **Columns** HISTORIC HOTEL $$
(☎504-899-9308; www.thecolumns.com; 3811 St Charles Ave; r incl breakfast weekend/weekday from $160/120; ❄📶) A steal in low season (from $99), still a deal in high, this stately 1883 Italianate mansion in the Garden District is both elegant and relaxed, boasting all sorts of extraordinary original features: a stained-glass-topped staircase, elaborate marble fireplaces, richly carved woodwork throughout etc. To top it off, there's a lovely 2nd-floor porch overlooking oak-draped St Charles Ave and a damn inviting bar. It's everything that's wonderful about Nola.

Loft 523 BOUTIQUE HOTEL $$$
(☎504-200-6523; www.loft523.com; 523 Gravier St; r low/high season $79/299; @📶) The hip industrial-minimalist style of Loft 523's 16 lodgings is a jarring change of pace for New Orleans (that's a compliment). Those are $5000 Fortuny lamps, for Godsakes.

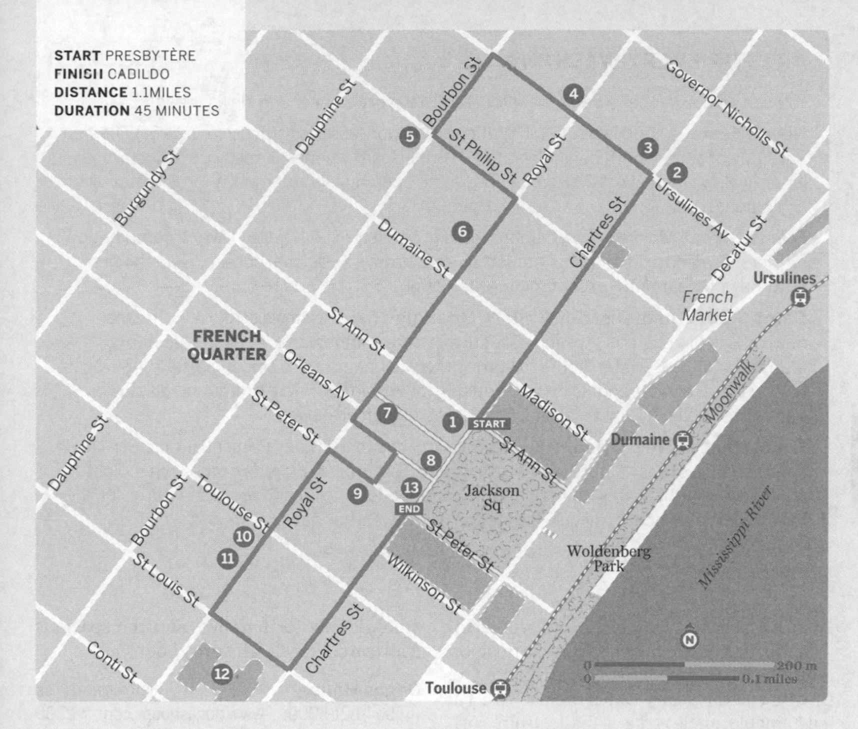

Walking Tour

French Quarter

Begin your walk at the 1 **Presbytère** on Jackson Sq and head down Chartres St to the corner of Ursulines Ave and the 2 **Old Ursuline Convent**.

Directly across Chartres St, at No 1113, the 1826 3 **Beauregard-Keyes House** combines Creole and American-style design. Walk along Ursulines Ave to Royal St – the soda fountain at the 4 **Royal Pharmacy** is a preserved relic from halcyon malt-shop days.

Continue up Ursulines Ave and then turn left onto Bourbon St. The ramshackle one-story structure on the corner of St Philip St is a salty little tavern and National Historic Landmark called 5 **Lafitte's Blacksmith Shop**. Head down St Philip back to Royal St and take a right.

When it comes to quintessential New Orleans postcard images, Royal St takes the prize. Cast-iron galleries grace the buildings and a profusion of flowers garland the facades.

At No 915 the 6 **Cornstalk Hotel** stands behind one of the most frequently photographed fences anywhere. At Orleans Ave, stately magnolia trees and lush tropical plants fill 7 **St Anthony's Garden**, behind 8 **St Louis Cathedral**.

Alongside the garden, take the inviting Pirate's Alley and turn right down Cabildo Alley and then right up St Peter St toward Royal St. Tennessee Williams shacked up at No 632 St Peter, the 9 **Avart-Peretti House** in 1946–47 while he wrote *A Streetcar Named Desire*.

Turn left on Royal St. At the corner of Royal and Toulouse Sts stands a pair of houses built by Jean François Merieult in the 1790s. The 10 **Court of Two Lions**, at 541 Royal St, opens onto Toulouse St and next door is the 11 **Historic New Orleans Collection**.

On the next block, the massive 1909 12 **State Supreme Court Building** was the setting for many scenes in director Oliver Stone's movie *JFK*.

Head down St Louis St to Chartres St and turn left. As Jackson Sq comes into view, you'll reach the Presbytère's near-identical twin, the 13 **Cabildo**.

ART FOR EVERY WEEKEND

You can discover local art and meet local artists every weekend in New Orleans.

New Orleans Arts District Art Walk (www.neworleansartsdistrict.com; Julia St) The first Saturday of each month beginning at 6pm until close (whenever, really), the fine art galleries in New Orleans Art District celebrate the opening night of month-long feature artist exhibitions.

Freret Street Market (www.freretmarket.org; cnr Freret St & Napoleon Ave) A combination farmers, flea and art show, this market offers a great mix of local culture. Held the first Saturday of the month (except for July and August) from noon to 5pm.

Saint Claude Arts District Gallery Openings (www.scadnola.com) New Orleans' newest arts district, this growing collective of art exhibition spaces spans Faubourg Marigny and the Bywater, home to some of New Orleans' more eclectic artists. Ask locals for weekend recommendations and you may be rewarded with a fire-eating display or impromptu collective installations at a secret, hidden art space.

Art Market of New Orleans (www.artscouncilofneworleans.org; Palmer Park, cnr Carrolton & Claiborne Aves) Last Saturday of every month. Featuring hundreds of the area's most creative local artists, this monthly market is juried for quality and always features local food, music and kids' activities. Perfect on warm-weather days.

With thanks to Lindsay Glatz, Arts Council of New Orleans.

Whirligig-shaped fans circle over low-lying Mondo beds and polished concrete floors and that half-egg-shaped tub is about as inviting as the Pearly Gates themselves. The sustainable angle – keys made from corn, partially-used toiletries being shipped off to countries in need – are mere bonuses. In summer, the $79 rate is downright theft.

Prytania Park Hotel HOTEL **$**
(☎504-524-0427; www.prytaniaparkhotel.com; 1525 Prytania St; r from $49-69; P❄📶) This great-value complex of three separate hotels offers friendly, well-located bang-for-the-buck. The Prytania Park's offers clean-cut, smallish rooms with flat-screen TVs for budget travelers. The **Prytania Oaks** (r $79-109) is sleeker and the **Queen Anne** (rooms $99-119) is an exquisite boutique hotel, newly renovated and bedecked with antiques. It's a perfect spot for folks of all budgets bouncing between the Quarter and the Garden District and/or Uptown. Parking is free and so is access to St Charles Ave Atheltic Club.

Lamothe House HISTORIC B&B **$$$**
(☎504-947-1161; www.lamothehouse.com; 621 Esplanade Ave; r incl breakfast $109-189, ste incl breakfast $209-399; ❄📶🏊) Splashes of blue or green have lightened up the grand rooms in this 1839 mansion complete with gilt accents, rococo carvings and delicate oil paintings. Starker rooms in the outbuildings adjoin easily for families, and the spacious courtyard lets you all spread out.

Degas House HISTORIC HOTEL **$$**
(☎504-821-5009; www.degashouse.com; 2306 Esplanade Ave; r incl breakfast from $199; P❄📶) Edgar Degas, the famed French Impressionist, lived in this 1852 Italianate house when visiting his mother's family in the early 1870s. Arty rooms recall the painter's stay with reproductions of his work and period furnishings. The suites have balconies and fireplaces, while the less-expensive garret rooms are the cramped top-floor quarters that once offered resident artist's some much-need respite.

Cornstalk Hotel B&B **$$$**
(☎504-523-1515; www.cornstalkhotel.com; 915 Royal St; r $115-250; ❄📶) Pass through the famous cast-iron fence and into a plush, antiqued B&B where the serenity sweeps away the whirl of the busy streets outside. Gemlike rooms are all luxurious and clean – carpets are given the once-over monthly! Limited parking.

Hotel Maison de Ville HISTORIC HOTEL **$$$**
(☎504-561-5858; www.hotelmaisondeville.com; 727 Toulouse St; ❄📶🏊) New owners were redoing the courtyard, renovating the slave quarter suites, the facade, balconies etc at time of writing. The one- and two-bedroom Audubon Cottage suites (where artist John J Audubon

stayed and painted while in town) surround a lushly landscaped courtyard; the pool is rumored to be the oldest in the Quarter (from the late 1700s). It's all scheduled to reopen in the fall of 2011 so if genteel Southern comfort and polished charm are what you're after, it's worth looking into when it does.

Le Pavillon HISTORIC HOTEL **$$$**
(504-581-3111; www.lepavillon.com; 833 Poydras Ave; r $129-299, ste $199-499;) Built in 1907, this elegant European-style hotel's opulent marble lobby, plush, classic rooms and rooftop pool are a steal. Decadent suites might prevent you from ever leaving the building. If booking a queen room, request a bay window. Parking costs $25.

India House Hostel HOSTEL **$**
(504-821-1904; www.indiahousehostel.com; 124 S Lopez St; dm/d $20/55;) In Mid-City, this place has a free-spirited party atmosphere. A large aboveground swimming pool and cabana-like patio add ambience to the three well-used old houses that serve as sparse but nice dorms. As for staff, Dutch trainees and Dutch management are lovely and helpful, others are is a bit off-putting. Many of the private rooms are little more than private dorms, so ask ahead if you want an actual double bed.

Marquette House International Hostel HOSTEL **$**
(504-523-3014; www.neworleansinternationalhostel.com; 2249 Carondelet St; dm $17-25, s/d from $53/66; office 7am-noon & 5-10pm;) A sprawling compound of both dorms and private rooms (with refrigerators and microwaves) near the Garden District. Serviceable, but certainly not luxurious, the rooms are upstaged by the lush garden area, perfect for hanging out and meeting fellow travelers.

Eating

Louisiana may have the greatest native culinary tradition in the USA – not necessarily by dint of the quality of food (although quality is very high) but from the long history that lies behind dishes that are older than most American states; and, while the rest of us eat to live, New Orleanians live to eat – despite the post-Katrina drop in population, there are 15% more restaurants now!

FRENCH QUARTER

GW Fins SEAFOOD, CAJUN **$$$**
(504-581-3467; www.gwfins.com; 808 Bienville St; mains $26-36; 5-10pm Sun-Thu, to 10:30pm Fri & Sat) Fins focuses almost entirely on fish: fresh caught and prepped so the flavor of the sea is always accented and never overwhelmed. And it's not your average dishes, either: wood-grilled mangrove snapper, parmesan-crusted sheep's head, and hell, why not go for the bourbon-and-vanilla mashed potatoes to round it all out? For New Orleans this is light, almost delicate dining – a refreshing breath of salty air if you're getting jambalaya-ed out.

Bayona MODERN AMERICAN **$$$**
(504-525-4455; www.bayona.com; 430 Dauphine St; mains $27-32; 11:30am-2pm Mon-Fri & 6-10pm Mon-Thu, 6-11pm Fri & Sat) Bayona is a great splurge in the Quarter. It's rich but not overwhelming, classy but unpretentious, innovative without being precocious. Expect fish, fowl and game on the daily-changing menu divided between long-time classics and daily specials (about four of each), all done up in a way that makes you raise an eyebrow, then smile like you've discovered comfort food gone classy.

Green Goddess FUSION **$$**
(www.greengoddessnola.com; 307 Exchange Pl; mains $7-17; 11:30am-3:30pm Mon & Wed, 11am-3:30pm & 6pm-late Thu-Sun) Down a quiet alley off the Quarter, the Green Goddess is not only part of Nola's current mixologist craze (blueberry, basil, black pepper and jalapeño martini, anyone?) but is a global fusion godsend when you just can't bear another plate of red beans and rice. Not that an Irish porter cheddar grilled cheese melted with pear butter is any healthier, but it sure does send your taste buds on a welcomed journey elsewhere.

Coop's CAJUN, CREOLE **$$**
(1109 Decatur St; mains $8-17.50; 11am-3am) For a cheap but thoroughly satisfying meal in the Quarter, this Cajun country shack disguised as a divey bar is as good as it gets: try the rabbit and sausage jambalaya or the red beans and rice for a taste of Cajun heaven. You can get out of here stuffed to a Creole stupor for under $15.

Central Grocery ITALIAN **$$**
(923 Decatur St; half/full muffuletta $7.50/14.50; 9am-5pm Mon-Sat) Here, in 1906, a Sicilian immigrant invented the world-famous *muffuletta* sandwich – a round, seeded loaf of bread stuffed with ham, salami, provolone and marinated olive salad that's roughly the size of a manhole cover. This is still the best place in town to get one.

Yo Mama's BURGERS $

(www.yomamasbarandgrill.com; 727 St Peters St; burgers $6.50-10.50; ⌚11am-3am) Let us lay it on the line: peanut butter and bacon burger. That's right: looks like a cheeseburger, but that ain't melted cheddar on top. Honestly, it's great: somehow the stickiness of the peanut butter compliments the char-grilled edge of the meat. New Orleans: peanut butter and bacon burger.

Croissant D'Or Patisserie CAFE $

(617 Ursulines Ave; items $1.50-5.75; ⌚6:30am-3pm Mon & Wed-Sun) This ancient and spotlessly clean pastry shop is where many Quarter locals start their day. Bring a paper, order coffee and a croissant and bliss out. On your way in, check out the tiled sign on the threshold that says 'ladies entrance' – a holdover from pre-feminist days that is no longer enforced.

Clover Grill DINER $

(900 Bourbon St; mains $3-8; ⌚24hr) Gay greasy spoon? Yup. It's all slightly surreal, given this place otherwise totally resembles a '50s diner, but nothing adds to the Americana like a prima-donna-style argument between an out-of-makeup drag queen and a drunk club kid, all likely set to blaring disco music.

Café du Monde CAFE $

(800 Decatur St; beignets $2.14; ⌚24hr; 👪) Du Monde is overrated, but you're probably gonna go there, so here goes: the coffee is decent and the beignets (square, sugar-coated fritters) are inconsistent. The atmosphere is off-putting: you're a number forced through the wringer, trying to shout over Bob and Fran while they mispronounce 'jambalaya' and a street musician badly mangles John Lennon's 'Imagine.' At least it's open 24 hours.

THE TREMÉ

Willie Mae's Scotch House SOUTHERN $$

(2401 St Ann St; fried chicken $10; ⌚11am-7pm Mon-Sat) The fried chicken at Willie Mae's is good. Very good. But it's not the best in the world, despite being named an 'American Classic' by the James Beard foundation in 2005.

Dooky Chase SOUTHERN $$

(2301 Orleans Ave; buffet $17.95; ⌚11am-3pm Tue-Fri) Ray Charles wrote 'Early in the Morning' about Dooky's, local civil rights leaders used the spot as an informal headquarters in the 1960s and Bush and Barack have tucked into the refined soul food at this overpriced Tremé backbone.

FAUBOURG MARIGNY & THE BYWATER

Bacchanal CAFE $$

(www.bacchanalwine.com; 600 Poland Ave; mains $8-14, cheese per piece from $5; ⌚11am-midnight) Grab a bottle of wine, let the folks behind the counter prep your *fromage* into a work of art, then kick back in a backyard of overgrown garden green scattered with rusted-out lawn chairs and tatty foldouts set to whoever showed up to play live that day. Or order from the limited but inventive full menu. It's a sort of high-end hillbilly wine and cheese hangout – and it's great.

Elizabeth's CAJUN, CREOLE $$$

(www.elizabeths-restaurant.com; 601 Gallier St; mains $16-26; ⌚8am-2:30pm & 6-10pm Tue-Sat, 8am-2:30pm Sun) Elizabeth's is deceptively divey, way too dark and probably too laid-back. The food is overly simplistic at times, startlingly out-of-the-box at others. But it tastes as good as the best haute New Orleans chefs can offer. Be sure to order some praline bacon, no matter the time of day: fried up in brown sugar and, as far as we can tell, God's own cooking oil.

CBD & WAREHOUSE DISTRICT

TOP CHOICE **Cochon** CONTEMPORARY CAJUN $$$

(☎504-588-2123; www.cochonrestaurant.com; 930 Tchoupitoulas St; mains $19-25; ⌚11am-10pm Mon-Fri, 5:30-10pm Sat) James Beard Award–winning chef Donald Link's fabulous brasserie serves up gourmet Southern comfort food in such curious and intriguing ways, you won't know what to do with yourself. The housemade Louisiana *cochon* – moist, pulled-pork heaven on the inside, crusty, pan-seared perfection on the outside – is probably the best swine you will ever have, unless you eat here twice. The mac 'n' cheese? It's laced with bacon fat – end of story. Link's fearless willingness to pair the simply succulent with the exceptionally extravagant catapult this cultishly loved spot into the echelons of truly unique cuisine – and there's moonshine to wash it all down. Reservations essential.

Butcher CAJUN, SOUTHERN $$

(www.cochonbutcher.com; 930 Tchoupitoulas St; sandwiches $9-12; ⌚10am-10pm Mon-Thu, til 11pm Fri & Sat, til 4pm Sun) Around the corner from Cochon, Chef Donald Link makes his in-house cured meat philosophy accessible to all budgets at this don't-miss butcher shop-deli and bar. Sandwich highlights here include milk-fed pork Cubans, Carolina-style pulled pork, the Cochon muffaletta and the Buckboard bacon melt. Pair it with pancetta mac 'n' cheese and bacon pralines. This is an empire in the making.

GARDEN DISTRICT & UPTOWN

TOP CHOICE Commander's Palace CONTEMPORARY CREOLE $$$
(☎504-899-8221; www.commanderspalace.com; 1403 Washington Ave; dinner mains $28-45; ⏱11:30am-2pm Mon-Fri, to 1pm Sat, 10:30am-1:30pm Sun & 6:30-10pm Mon-Sat) It's no small coincidence that some of the most famous Nola chefs – check that, US chefs – got their start in this kitchen (Paul Prudhomme, Emeril Lagasse); this New Orleans grand dame is outstanding across the board. Chef Tory McPhail's (remember that name!) shrimp-and-tasso appetizer swimming in Louisiana hot sauce and the hickory-grilled pork are two of the most explosively satisfying dishes you will ever encounter. It's an impeccable mainstay of Creole cooking and knowledgeable, friendly service, in the heart of the gorgeous Garden District. Pop in for the lunchtime 25¢ martinis and a cup of the signature turtle soup ($8), or a *prix fixe* extravaganza. No shorts allowed.

Boucherie NEW SOUTHERN $$
(☎504-862-5514; www.boucherie-nola.com; 8115 Jeannette St; large plates $12-15; ⏱11am-3pm & 5:30-9pm Tue-Sat) Just when you thought a Krispy Kreme doughnut was already perfection personified, Boucherie comes along and turns it into a bread pudding. When married to a honey-glazed, drowning in syrup, that heavy bread pudding becomes airy yet drool-tastically unforgettable! For dinner, blackened shrimp-and-grits cakes are darkly sweet and savory, garlic parmesan fries are gloriously stinky and gooey and the smoked Wagyu beef brisket just melts in your mouth. And it's all so reasonably priced.

Mat and Naddie's CONTEMPORARY CREOLE $$$
(☎504-861-9600; www.matandnaddies.com; 937 Leonidas St; mains $22-29; ⏱11am-2pm Mon-Fri, 5:30-9:30pm Thu-Sat & Mon) Set in a beautiful riverfront shotgun house with a Christmas-light-bedecked patio in the back, M&N's is rich, innovative, even outlandish: artichoke, sun-dried tomato and roasted garlic cheesecake (oh yes!), sherry-marinated grilled quail with waffles, pecan sweet-potato pie – all crazy delicious. It's high quality topped with quirkiness and a great indicator of what chefs can do when they think outside the gastro box around here.

Cowbell AMERICAN $$
(www.cowbell-nola.com; 8801 Oak St; mains $10-14; ⏱11:30am-3pm Tue-Sat & 5-10pm Tue-Thu, till 11pm Fri & Sat) This hipster farm-to-table hangout in a former gas station dishes out simple, sustainable comfort food free of horrible stuff like hormones, pesticides and other crap that makes food taste like cardboard – so says the owner. The natural, grass-fed burger is indeed great and the limited menu features Gulf fish tacos, adult-style grilled cheese and organic lime chicken, which is gobbled down by Riverbend's cooler-than-thou set in an aluminum-sided, silo-chic gourmet shack.

Domilise's Po-Boys CREOLE $$
(5240 Annunciation St; po'boys $9-13; ⏱10am-7pm Mon-Wed & Fri, 10:30am-7pm Sat) A dilapidated white shack by the river serving Dixie beer (brewed in Wisconsin!), staffed by folks who've worked here for decades and dressing one of the most legendary po' boys (traditional Louisiana submarine sandwich) in the city. It's cash only and prepare to hurry up and wait on weekends.

Drinking

New Orleans is a drinking town. Heads up: Bourbon St sucks. Get into the neighborhoods and experience some of the best bars in America. The kinder, gentler strip runs along Frenchmen St in Faubourg Marigny.

Most bars open every day, often by noon, get hopping around 10pm, and can stay open all night. There's no cover charge unless there's live music. It's illegal to have open glass liquor containers in the street, so all bars dispense plastic 'go cups' when you're ready to wander.

Spotted Cat LIVE MUSIC
(www.spottedcatmusicclub.com; 623 Frenchmen St) A throwback retro cool permeates through this excellent Frenchman staple you might recognize from numerous episodes of *Tremé*. Hipster jazz is on nightly and there's never a cover unless a special event is on.

Mimi's in the Marigny BAR
(2601 Royal St; ⏱til 5am) Great bi-level bar (pool downstairs, music upstairs) serving up excellent Spanish tapas ($5 to $8), casual neighborhood jazz (most nights) and DJs on

the weekend (Swamp Pop every other Friday, Retro Soul otherwise).

Tonique BAR
(www.bartonique.com; 820 Rampart St) If you're going to drink in the Quarter (on the edge of it, anyway), this serious cocktail bar is the place, where cool folks who appreciate an excellent concoction gather over the best Sazerac we had in town. And we had many.

St Joe's BAR
(5535 Magazine St) Good-time Uptown pious-themed bar with great blueberry mojitos (praise the Lord!), a cool back courtyard and friendly ambience.

R Bar BAR
(1431 Royal St) Somewhere between a dive and a neighborhood joint; a beer and a shot runs you $5.

☆ Entertainment

What's New Orleans without live local music? Almost any weekend night you can find something for every taste: jazz, blues, brass band, country, Dixieland, zydeco, rock or Cajun. Free shows in the daytime abound. Check *Gambit* (www.bestofneworleans.com), *Offbeat* (www.offbeat.com) or www.nolafunguide.com for schedules.

Three Muses JAZZ
(www.thethreemuses.com; 536 Frenchman St; ⏲4-10pm Wed-Thu & Sun-Mon, til 2am Fri & Sat) This newcomer was an instant hit with both musicians and foodies – they've managed to happily marry an excellent soundtrack with gourmet cuisine in a more intimate room than most on Frenchman. There's loads of great local art to peruse between acts and courses. Start here.

Preservation Hall JAZZ
(www.preservationhall.com; 726 St Peter St; ⏲8-11pm) A veritable museum of traditional and Dixieland jazz, Preservation Hall is a pilgrimage. But like many religious obligations, it ain't necessarily easy, with no air-conditioning, limited seating and no refreshments (you can bring your own water, that's it).

Snug Harbor JAZZ
(www.snugjazz.com; 626 Frenchmen St) In the Marigny, the city's best contemporary jazz venue is all about world-class music and a good variety of acts. If you can't spring for the show (cover $15 to $25), sit downstairs at the bar and watch on close-circuit.

Maple Leaf Bar LIVE MUSIC
(☎504-866-9359; 8316 Oak St) Riverbend's pride and joy, its pressed-tin ceiling and close atmosphere get especially heated late. Big nights are Papa Grows Funk on Mondays and Rebirth Brass Band on Tuesdays.

Tipitina's LIVE MUSIC
(www.tipitinas.com; 501 Napoleon Ave) Always drawing a lively crowd, this legendary Uptown club rocks out like the musical mecca it is: local jazz, blues, soul and funk stop in, as well as national touring bands.

Vaughan's LIVE MUSIC
(800 Lesseps St) A great Bywater neighborhood bar that hosts local favorite and awesome trumpeter Kermit Ruffins on Thursday nights.

Shopping

Faulkner House Books BOOKSHOP
(www.faulknerhousebooks.net; 624 Pirate's Alley; ⏲10am-5:30pm) The erudite owner of this former residence of author William Faulkner sells rare first editions and new titles.

Maple Street Book Shop BOOKSHOP
(www.maplestreetbookshop.com; 7523 Maple St; ⏲9am-7pm Mon-Sat, 11am-5pm Sun) A mainstay independent bookstore in Uptown, with a used bookstore affiliate next door.

ℹ Information

Dangers & Annoyances

New Orleans has a high violent-crime rate, and neighborhoods go from good to ghetto very quickly. Be careful walking too far north of Faubourg Marigny and the Bywater (St Claude Ave is a good place to stop), south of Magazine St (things get dodgier past Laurel St) and too far north of Rampart St (Lakeside) from the French Quarter into Tremé without a specific destination in mind. Stick to places that are well peopled, particularly at night, and spring for a cab to avoid dark walks. In the Quarter, street hustlers frequently approach tourists – just walk away. With all that said, don't be paranoid. Crime here, as in most of America, tends to be between people who already know each other.

Emergency & Medical Services

Medical Center of Louisiana (www.mclno.org; 2021 Perdido St; ⏲24hr) Has an emergency room.

Internet Access

There's pretty good wi-fi coverage in the CBD, French Quarter, Garden and Lower Garden Districts and Uptown. Almost every coffee shop in the city has wi-fi coverage. Libraries have free internet access for cardholders.

Zotz (8210 Oak St; per 30min $4; ⏲7m-1am; 📶) Appropriately funky coffee shop in Riverbend neighborhood, popular with Tulane types. Coffee is here is organic/Fair Trade.

Internet Resources & Media

Gambit Weekly (www.bestofneworleans.com) Free weekly hot sheet of music, culture, politics and classifieds.

NOLA Fun Guide (www.nolafunguide.com) Great website for up-to-date info on gigs, gallery openings and the like.

Offbeat Magazine (www.offbeat.com) Free monthly specializing in music.

Times-Picayune (www.nola.com) New Orleans' daily newspaper has an entertainment calendar, and 'Lagniappe,' a more extensive guide, is included every Friday.

WWOZ 90.7 FM (www.wwoz.org) Tune in here for Louisiana music and more.

Post

Post office Lafayette Sq (610 S Maestri Pl; ⏲8:30am-4:30pm Mon-Fri); Main branch (701 Loyola Ave; ⏲7am-7pm Mon-Fri, 8am-4pm Sat) Mail sent General Delivery, New Orleans, LA 70112, goes to the main branch. Postboxes in outlying areas are not necessarily reliable since Katrina.

Tourist Information

The city's official visitor website is www.neworleansonline.com.

Jean Lafitte National Historic Park and Preserve Visitor Center (☎504-589-2636; www.nps.gov/jela; 419 Decatur St; ⏲9am-5pm) Operated by the NPS, with exhibits on local history, guided walks and daily live music. There's not much in the park office itself, but educational musical programs are held on most days of the week. Many of the park rangers are musicians and knowledgeable lecturers, and their presentations discuss musical developments, cultural changes, regional styles, myths, legends and musical techniques in relation to the broad subject of jazz.

Basin St Visitor's Center (☎504-293-2600; www.neworleanscvb.com; 501 Bason St; ⏲9am-5pm) Affiliated with the New Orleans CVB, this interactive tourist info center inside the former freight administration building of the Southern Railway has loads of helpful info and maps as well as an historical overview film and a small rail museum component. It's next door to St Louis Cemetery No 1.

Louisiana Visitor's Center (☎504-566-5661; www.louisianatravel.com; 529 St Ann St; ⏲8:30am-5pm) Provides lots of free information and maps for Nola and the state.

ℹ Getting There & Away

Louis Armstrong New Orleans International Airport (MSY; www.flymsy.com; 900 Airline Hwy), 11 miles west of the city, handles primarily domestic flights.

The **Union Passenger Terminal** (☎504-299-1880; 1001 Loyola Ave) is home to **Greyhound** (☎504-525-6075; ⏲5:15am-1pm & 2:30-6pm), which has regular buses to Baton Rouge ($18 to $23, two hours), Memphis, TN ($63 to $79, 11 hours) and Atlanta, GA ($84 to $106, 12 hours). **Amtrak** (☎504-528-1610; ⏲ticketing 5:45am-10pm) trains also operate from the Union Passenger Terminal, running to Jackson, MS; Memphis, TN; Chicago, IL. Birmingham, AL; Atlanta, GA; Washington, DC; New York City; Los Angeles, CA; and Miami, FL.

ℹ Getting Around

To/From the Airport

There's an information booth at the airport's A&B concourse. The **Airport Shuttle** (☎866-596-2699; www.airportshuttleneworleans.com; one way per person $20) runs to downtown hotels. The **Jefferson Transit** (☎504-364-3450; www.jeffersontransit.org; adult $2) airport route E2 picks up outside entrance 7 on the airport's upper level; it stops along Airline Hwy (Hwy 61) on its way into town (final stop Tulane and Loyola Aves). After 7pm it only goes to Tulane and Carrollton Aves in Mid-City; a solid 5 miles through a dreary neighborhood to get to the CBD, from here you must transfer to a Regional Transit Authority (RTA) bus – a haphazard transfer at best, especially with luggage.

Taxis downtown cost $33 for one or two people, $14 more for each additional passenger.

Car & Motorcycle

Bringing a car is a useful way of exploring beyond the Quarter; just be aware that parking in the Quarter is a hassle. Garages charge about $13 for the first three hours and $30 to $35 for 24 hours.

BIG EASY PARKING

It's not a hard and fast rule, but New Orleans lost numerous bus lines post-Katrina, especially in the French Quarter, where buses no longer go. Locals in the know often park in now-unused bus lanes regardless of the outdated signage banning parking there. It's still a risk if a particular parking enforcement officer is having a bad day, but locals report that you will almost always be OK.

Public Transportation

The **Regional Transit Authority** (RTA; www.norta.com) runs the local bus service. Bus and streetcar fares are $1.25, plus 25¢ for transfers; express buses cost $1.50. Exact change is required. RTA Visitor Passes for one/three days cost $5/12.

The RTA also operates three **streetcar** lines. The historic St Charles streetcar is running only a short loop in the CBD due to hurricane damage to the Uptown tracks. The Canal streetcar makes a long journey up Canal St to City Park, with a spur on Carrollton Ave. The Riverfront line runs 2 miles along the levee from the Old US Mint, past Canal St, to the upriver convention center and back.

For a taxi, call **United Cabs** (504-522-9771; www.unitedcabs.com) or **White Fleet Cabs** (504-822-3800).

Rent bicycles at **Bicycle Michael's** (504-945-9505; www.bicyclemichaels.com; 622 Frenchmen St; rentals per day $35; 10am-7pm Mon, Tue & Thu-Sat, to 5pm Sun), in Faubourg Marigny.

SWAMP TOURS

You haven't experienced Louisiana unless you've been out on its waterways, and the easiest way to do it is to join a swamp tour. Arrange them from New Orleans or go on your own and contract directly with a bayou-side company.

Annie Miller's Son's Swamp & Marsh Tours TOUR
(985-868-4758; www.annie-miller.com; 3718 Southdown Mandalay Rd, Houma; adult/child $15/10;) The son of legendary swamp guide Annie Miller has taken up his mom's tracks.

Westwego Swamp Adventures TOUR
(504-581-4501; www.westwegoswampadventures.com; 501 Laroussini St, Westwego; adult/child with transport $49/24;) One of the closest to New Orleans, it can pick you up in the Quarter.

Around New Orleans

Leaving gritty, colorful New Orleans quickly catapults you into a world of swamps, bayous, antebellum plantation homes and laid-back small communities. A foray into these lesser-known environs makes for an off-the-beaten-path adventure.

THE NORTH SHORE

Bedroom communities sprawl along **Lake Ponchartrain's** north shore, but head north of Mandeville and you'll reach the bucolic village of **Abita Springs**, which was popular in the late 1800s for its curative waters. Today the spring water still flows from a fountain in the center of the village, but the primary liquid attraction here is the **Abita Brew Pub** (www.abitabrewpub.com; 7201 Holly St; tours free; 11am-9pm Tue-Fri, to 10pm Sat), where you can choose from 10 Abita beers on tap that are made a mile west of town at **Abita Brewery** (www.abita.com; 166 Barbee Rd; tours free; tours 2pm Wed-Fri, 11am, noon, 1pm & 2pm Sat).

Other local libations can be found on Hwy 1082, where you'll encounter Louisiana's finest wines at **Ponchartrain Vineyards** (www.pontchartrainvineyards.com; 81250 Old Military Rd; tasting room noon-5pm Wed-Sun). It's a pleasant surprise that tends to diverge from the syrupy sweet wines usually produced down South. To the south, **Covington** has a worthwhile downtown with funky antique shops.

The 31-mile **Tammany Trace trail** (www.tammanytrace.org) connects north shore towns, beginning in Covington, passing through Abita Springs and **Fontainebleau State Park**, on the lakeshore near Mandeville, and terminating in Slidell. This converted railroad makes for a lovely bike ride that drops you into each town's center. In Mandeville you can rent bikes at the **Old Mandeville Café and Kickstand Bike Rental** (www.kickstand.bz; 690 Lafitte St; 8am-4pm Mon-Sat, 10am-4pm Sun).

BARATARIA PRESERVE

This section of the **Jean Lafitte National Historical Park & Preserve**, south of New Orleans near the town of Marrero, provides the easiest access to the dense swamplands that ring New Orleans. The 8 miles of platform trails are a stunning way to tread lightly through the fecund, thriving swamp where you can check out gators and other fascinating plant life and creatures. The preserve is home to alligators, nutrias, tree frogs and hundreds of species of birds. It is well worth taking a ranger-led walk to learn about the many ecosystems that make up what are often lumped together as 'wetlands.'

Start at the **NPS Visitors Center** (504-589-2330; www.nps.gov/jela; Hwy 3134; admission free; 9am-5pm;), 1 mile west of Hwy 45 off the Barataria Blvd exit, where you can pick up a map or join a guided walk or canoe trip (most Saturday mornings and monthly on full-moon nights; call to reserve a spot). The center has informational exhibits and a 25-minute documentary on swampland habitats. To rent canoes or kayaks for a tour or an independent paddle, go to **Bayou Barn** (☎504-689-2663; www.bayoubarn.net; canoes per person $20, 1-person kayak per day $25; ⊙10am-6pm Thu-Sun) on the Bayou de Familles just outside the park entrance.

RIVER ROAD

Elaborate plantation homes dot the east and west banks of the Mississippi River between New Orleans and Baton Rouge. First indigo, then cotton and sugarcane, brought great wealth to these plantations, many of which are open to the public. Most tours focus on the lives of the plantation owners, the restored architecture and the ornate gardens of antebellum Louisiana, and they skip over the story of plantation slaves who made up the majority of the plantations' population. It's easy to explore the area by car or organized tour.

Laura Plantation (www.lauraplantation.com; 2247 Hwy 18; adult/child $18/5; ⊙10am-4pm), in Vacherie on the west bank, offers the most dynamic and informative tour. This ever-evolving and popular tour teases out the distinctions between Creole, Anglo and African American antebellum life via meticulous research and the written records of the Creole women who ran the place for generations.

Also in Vacherie, the most impressive aspect of **Oak Alley Plantation** (www.oakalleyplantation.com; 3645 Hwy 18; adult/child $18/4.50; ⊙9am-4:40pm) is its canopy of 28 majestic live oaks lining the entry to the grandiose Greek Revival-style house – even better with a fresh mint julep ($6). The tour is relatively staid, but there are guest cottages ($130 to $170) and a restaurant on-site.

Be sure to flesh out any plantation tour with a visit to the **River Road African American Museum** (www.africanamericanmuseum.org; 406 Charles St; museum $4; ⊙10am-5pm Wed-Sat, 1-5pm Sun), 25 miles further along in Donaldsonville. This excellent museum preserves the important history of African Americans in the rural communities along the Mississippi.

BATON ROUGE

In 1699 French explorers named this area *baton rouge* (red stick) when they came upon a reddened cypress pole that Bayagoulas and Houma Native Americans had staked in the ground to mark the boundaries of their respective hunting territories. An industrial town with a bustling port and the state capital, formerly lethargic Baton Rouge has swollen in size as relocated New Orleanians settle post-Katrina. Visitors are mostly drawn to Baton Rouge for Louisiana State University (LSU) and Southern University (the largest historically African American university in the country).

Sights & Activities

FREE **Louisiana State Capitol** HISTORIC BUILDING
(⊙9am-4pm Tue-Sat) The art-deco skyscraper looming over town is a must-visit. Built at the height of the Great Depression to the tune of $5 million, it's populist governor 'Kingfish' Huey Long's most visible legacy. The 27th-floor **observation deck** offers stunning views and the ornate lobby is equally impressive. There are hourly free tours.

Louisiana Arts & Science Museum MUSEUM
(www.lasm.org; 100 S River Rd; adult/child $7/6, with planetarium show $9/8; ⊙10am-3pm Tue-Fri, 10am-5pm Sat, 1-4pm Sun;) Interesting arts and natural-history installations, and planetarium shows. If you just want a good stretch of the legs, there's a pleasant **pedestrian/bike path** along the Mississippi River, stretching 2.5 miles from the downtown promenade to LSU.

FREE **Old State Capitol** HISTORIC BUILDING
(www.crt.state.la.us/tourism/capitol; 100 North Blvd; ⊙9am-4pm Tue-Sat) The Gothic Revival, pink fairytale-castlelike building makes you think Governor Bobby Jindal is going to 'throw down his long hair' to Louisianans. It houses exhibits about the state's colorful political history.

LSU Museum of Art MUSEUM
(www.lsumoa.com; 100 Lafayette St; adult/child $5/free; ⊙10am-5pm Tue-Sat, to 8pm Thu, 1-5pm Sun) Across the street it holds a small exhibit, the highlight being about Louisiana 'Old and New.'

Dixie Landin & Blue Bayou AMUSEMENT PARK
(www.bluebayou.com; adult/child $35/28;) Just east of town at I-10 and Highland Rd. Kids will love the respective amusement and water park; check the online calendar for opening hours.

Sleeping & Eating

Stockade Bed & Breakfast B&B **$$$**
(☎225-769-7358; www.thestockade.com; 8860 Highland Rd; r incl breakfast $135-215; P)

DON'T MISS

PO'BOY PERFECTION

Louisiana's best po'boy ain't in N'Awlins, you'll find it under an I-10 overpass in Baton Rouge. How legit is *that?* **Georges** (www.georgesbr.com; 2943 Perkins Rd; meals $5-12; ⌚11am-10:30pm Sun-Thu, till 11pm Fri & Sat) is a divey bar with dollar bills stapled to the ceiling and a chalkboard menu that is cause for genuflecting. The menu, among other things, boasts 13 po' boys, from exotic choices like spicy BBQ pork to the classic shrimp – a perfectly seasoned, crispy, batter-fried pile of heavenly goodness on Louisiana French bread. Can't decide between that and the equally killer cheeseburgers? Go for the cheeseburger po' boy. Done deal.

Chain hotels line the sides of I-10, but for a more intimate stay, try this wonderful B&B with five spacious, comfortable and elegant rooms just 3½ miles southeast of LSU and within earshot of several standout neighborhood restaurants. Book ahead on weekends, especially during football season.

Schlittz & Giggles BAR, PIZZERIA **$$**
(www.schlittz.com; 301 3rd St; pizzas $10-22; ⌚11am-midnight Mon-Thu, to 3am Fri-Sun; 📶) The food stands up to the awesomely named downtown late-night bar and pizzeria. Bubbly coeds serve up thin-as-black-ice pizza slices ($3 to $3.50) and fabulous paninis to a student crowd, while a gaggle of old-timer locals tend to belly up at the bar.

Buzz Café CAFE **$**
(www.thebuzzcafe.org; 340 Florida St; meals $7-9; ⌚7:30am-2pm Mon-Fri; 📶) For an awesome cup of joe and a plethora of creative wraps and sandwiches at a funky coffee shop in a historic building, try the Buzz.

☆ Entertainment

Varsity Theatre LIVE MUSIC
(www.varsitytheatre.com; 3353 Highland Rd; ⌚8pm-2am) At the gates of LSU, you'll find live music here, often on weeknights. The attached restaurant boasts an extensive beer selection and a raucous college crowd.

Boudreaux and Thiboudeux LIVE MUSIC
(www.bandtlive.com; 214 3rd St) Try this place downtown for live music Thursday to Saturday and a great upstairs balcony bar.

ℹ Information

Visitor center (☎800-527-6843; www.visitbatonrouge.com; 358 3rd St; ⌚8am-5pm) The downtown city branch has maps, brochures of local attractions, and festival schedules.

Capital Park Visitor Center (☎225-219-1200; www.louisianatravel.com; 702 River Rd N; ⌚8am-4:30pm) Near the visitor center, it's even more extensive.

ℹ Getting There & Around

Baton Rouge lies 80 miles west of New Orleans on I-10. **Baton Rouge Metropolitan Airport** (BTR; www.flybtr.com) is north of town off I-110. **Greyhound** (☎225-383-3811; 1253 Florida Blvd, at N 12th St) has regular buses to New Orleans, Lafayette and Atlanta, GA. **Capitol Area Transit System** (CATS; www.brcats.com) operates buses around town.

ST FRANCISVILLE

North of Baton Rouge, the lush town of St Francisville and its neighboring plantations have historically been, and continue to be, a lovely respite from the heat of the Delta. During the antebellum decade it was home to plantation millionaires, and much of their architecture is still intact. Its lazy tree-lined streets and plethora of historic homes and churches, as well as galleries and antique shops, are well worth a visit.

Sights & Activities

In town, stroll down historic **Royal St** to catch a glimpse of antebellum homes and buildings-turned-homes. The visitor center has pamphlets that lead you on self-guided tours.

Myrtles Plantation HISTORIC BUILDING
(☎225-635-6277, 800-809-0565; www.myrtlesplantation.com; 7747 US Hwy 61 N; ⌚9am-4:30pm, tours 6pm, 7pm & 8pm Fri & Sat) An especially notable B&B because supposedly it's haunted, and it has night mystery tours (by reservation) on the weekend. We heard secondhand corroboration of the supernatural presence, so it might be fun to stay overnight (rooms from $115) to commune with the other world.

Sleeping & Eating

TOP CHOICE **3-V Tourist Court** HISTORIC INN **$$**
(☎225-721-7003; 5689 Commerce St; 1-/2-bed cabins $80/130; P❄📶) One of the oldest motor inns in the United States (started in the 1930s and on the National Register of Historic Places), these five units bring you back to simpler times. Rooms have period decorations and fixtures, though a recent

renovation upgraded the beds, hardwood floors and flat-screen TVs into borderline trendy territory.

Shadetree Inn Bed and Breakfast B&B **$$**
(☎225-635-6116; www.shadetreeinn.com; cnr Royal St & Ferdinand St; r from $175; P❄📶) Sidled up against the historic district and a bird sanctuary, this super cozy B&B has a gorgeous flower-strewn, hammock-hung courtyard and spacious, upscale rustic rooms. A deluxe continental breakfast can be served in your room and is included along with a bottle of wine or champagne.

Magnolia Café CAFE **$$**
(www.themagnoliacafe.com; 5687 Commerce St; mains $7-12; ⏲10am-4pm Sun-Wed, to 9pm Thu-Sat) The nucleus of what's happening in St Francisville, the Magnolia Café used to be a health-food store/VW bus repair shop. Now it's where people go to eat, socialize and dance to live music on Friday night. Try the cheesy shrimp po'boy.

Birdman Coffee and Books CAFE **$**
(Commerce St; mains $5-6.50; ⏲7-5pm Mon-Fri, 8am-5pm Sat & Sun; 📶) Right in front of the Magnolia Café lies the Birdman, *the* spot for a local breakfast (old-fashioned yellow grits, sweet-potato pancakes etc) and local art.

ℹ Information

Tourist information (☎225-635-4224; www.stfrancisville.us; 11757 Ferdinand St) Provides helpful information about the numerous plantations open for view in the area, many of which offer B&B services.

Cajun Country

One of the truly unique parts of the US, Acadiana is named for French settlers exiled from L'Acadie (now Nova Scotia, Canada) by the British in 1755. As they lived alongside Native Americans and Creoles, 'Acadian' eventually morphed into 'Cajun.' The harrowing journey to Louisiana and the fight for survival in its swamplands are points of cultural pride for modern-day Cajuns, and do a lot to explain their combination of toughness and absolute ease.

Cajuns are the largest French-speaking minority in the US – prepare to hear it on radios and in the sing-song lilt of their English. While Lafayette is the nexus of Acadiana, getting out and around the waterways, villages and ramshackle roadside taverns really drops you straight into Cajun living. It's hard to find a bad meal here; jambalaya (rice-based dish with tomatoes, sausage and shrimp) and crawfish étouffée (a thick Cajun stew) are prepared slowly with pride (and cayenne!), and if folks aren't fishing, then they are probably dancing. Don't expect to sit on the sidelines…*allons danson* (let's dance).

LAFAYETTE

At its edges Lafayette looks like Anytown USA, but venture into its nucleus and you'll find an unsung jewel, especially if you like to shake your moneymaker. Surprisingly, its incredibly vibrant music scene remains relatively under the radar. Around the university town, bands are rocking most any night, and you'll drink a beer next to genuine, life-lovin', laid-back folks looking for a dance or to kick back and appreciate the show. Between venues, there are some of the best restaurants and bars in Louisiana outside New Orleans, all nicely organized for your eating and drinking pleasure in the compact and cool historic downtown, and a fascinating hipster retro bike culture.

👁 Sights & Activities

Acadiana Center for the Arts GALLERY
(☎337-233-7060; www.acadianacenterforthearts.org; 101 W Vermilion St; adult/child/student $5/2/3; ⏲10am-5pm Tue-Fri, to 6pm Sat) This arts center in the heart of downtown maintains three chic galleries and hosts dynamic theater, lectures and special events.

University Art Museum MUSEUM
(museum.louisi ana.edu; 710 E St Mary Blvd; adult/youth $5/3; ⏲9am-5pm Tue-Thu, 9am-noon Fri, 10am-5pm Sat) Just south of Girard Park, the sleek museum hosts beautifully curated exhibits, often leaning toward an educational slant.

Vermilionville CULTURAL BUILDING
(www.vermilionville.org; 300 Fisher Rd; adult/student $8/5; ⏲10am-4pm Tue-Sun; 👪) A tranquil restored/re-created 19th-century Cajun village wends along the bayou near the airport. Friendly costumed docents explain Cajun, Creole and Native American history; local bands perform on Sundays. They also offer guided **boat tours** (☎337-233-4077; adult/students $12/8; ⏲10:30am Tue-Sat Mar-May & Sep-Nov) of Bayou Vermilion.

FREE **Acadian Cultural Center** MUSEUM
(www.nps.gov/jela; 501 Fisher Rd; ⏲8am-5pm) The best NPS museum in Cajun Country, next door to Vermilionville.

Festivals & Events

At the fabulous, free **Festival International de Louisiane** (www.festivalinternational.com), hundreds of local and international artists rock out for five days in April – the largest *free* music festival of its caliber in the US.

Sleeping & Eating

Chains clump near exits 101 and 103, off I-10 (doubles from $65). Head to Jefferson St mid downtown to take your choice of bars and restaurants, from sushi to Mexican.

TOP CHOICE Blue Moon Guest House GUESTHOUSE $
(☎337-234-2422, 877-766-2583; www.bluemoonguesthouse.com; 215 E Convent St; dm $18, r $73-94; P❄@📶) This tidy old home is one of Louisiana's travel gems, an upscale hostel-like hangout, walking distance from downtown. Snag a bed and you'll be on the guest list for Lafayette's most popular down-home music venue, located in the backyard. The friendly owners, full kitchen, and camaraderie among guests create a unique music-meets-migration environment catering to backpackers, flashpackers and those in transition (flashbackpackers?). Prices skyrocket during festival time.

Buchanan Lofts BOUTIQUE APARTMENTS $$
(☎337-534-4922; www.buchananlofts.com; 403 S Buchanan; r per night/week from $100/600; P❄@📶) These tragically hip lofts could be in New York City if they weren't so big: Doused in contemporary cool art and design – all fruits of the friendly owner's globetrotting – the extra spacious units all come with kitchenettes and are awash in exposed brick and hardwoods, with small knickknacks such as steel drums livening up the industrial motif.

TOP CHOICE Johnson's Boucanière CAJUN $
(1111 St John St; mains $5-8; ⏲10am-5pm Thu-Fri, 7am-3pm Sat) This resurrected 70-year-old family prairie smoker business turns out detour-worthy *boudin* (Cajun-style pork and rice sausage) and an unstoppable smoked pork-brisket sandwich topped with smoked sausage. You can smell it from a block away and can't miss the chic aluminum-sided shack with wraparound porch.

French Press BREAKFAST $$
(www.thefrenchpresslafayette.com; 214 E Vermillion; breakfast $6-$10.50; ⏲7am-2pm Tue-Thu, 7am-2pm & 5:30-9pm Fri, 9am-2pm & 5:30-9pm Sat, 9am-2pm Sun; 📶) This new French-Cajun hybrid is a breakfast pleaser, with an outstanding breakfast sandwich, cheddar grits (that will kill you dead), organic granola (offset the grits) and black bean and crab cake eggs benedict, served in a modern cafe atmosphere with excellent French press coffee.

Pamplona Tapas Bar TAPAS $$
(www.pamplonatapas.com; 631 Jefferson St; tapas from $4; ⏲11am-2pm & 5-20pm Tue-Thu, to 11pm Fri, 5-11pm Sat; 📶) A bit more upscale, this place does a robust trade in excellent Spanish tapas (eg bacon-wrapped dates on a bed of blue cheese; chorizo-stuffed mushrooms) and a fabulous Spanish wine selection (by the glass $6 to $11).

Old Tyme Grocery CAJUN $
(218 W St Mary St; po'boys $6-10; ⏲9am-10pm Mon-Fri, 9am-7pm Sat) Famous po'boys.

Entertainment

To find out what's playing around town, pick up the free weekly *Times* (www.thetimesofacadiana.com) or *Independent* (www.theind.com).

Blue Moon Saloon LIVE MUSIC
(www.bluemoonpresents.com; 215 E Convent St; cover $5-8) This intimate venue on the back porch of the accompanying guesthouse is what Louisiana is all about: good music, good people and good beer. What's not to love?

Lafayette specializes in big ol' dance halls that offer one-stop entertainment, dancing and local cuisine. Some standout Cajun music and dance joints:

Mulate's DANCE
(325 Mills Ave, Breaux Bridge) On the way to Breaux Bridge.

Randol's DANCE
(www.randols.com; 2320 Kaliste Saloom Rd, Lafayette; ⏲5-10pm Sun-Thu, to 11pm Fri & Sat) South of town.

Prejean's DANCE
(www.prejeans.com; 3480 NE Evangeline Thruway/I-49, North Lafayette) Two miles north of town.

Information

Visitor center (☎337-232-3737, 800-346-1958; www.lafayettetravel.com; 1400 NW Evangeline Thruway; ⏲8:30am-5pm Mon-Fri, 9am-5pm Sat & Sun)

Getting There & Away

From I-10, exit 103A, the Evangeline Thruway (Hwy 167) goes to the center of town. **Grey-**

hound (☎337-235-1541; 315 Lee Ave) operates from a hub beside the central commercial district, making several runs daily to New Orleans (3½ hours) and Baton Rouge (one hour). **Amtrak's** (133 E Grant St) *Sunset Limited* goes to New Orleans three times a week.

CAJUN WETLANDS

In 1755, *le Grande Dérangement,* the British expulsion of the rural French settlers from Acadiana, created a homeless population of Acadians who searched for decades for a place to settle. In 1785, seven boatloads of exiles arrived in New Orleans. By the early 19th century, 3000 to 4000 Acadians occupied the swamplands southwest of New Orleans. Native American tribes such as the Attakapas helped them learn to eke out a living based upon fishing and trapping, and the aquatic way of life is still the backdrop to modern living.

East and south of Lafayette, the **Atchafalaya Basin** is the preternatural heart of the Cajun wetlands. Stop in to the **Atchafalaya Welcome Center** (☎337-228-1094; Butte La Rose; ⌚8:30am-5pm), at Exit 121 from I-10, to learn how to penetrate the dense jungle protecting these swamps, lakes and bayous from the casual visitor. They'll fill you in on camping in **Indian Bayou** and exploring the **Sherburne Wildlife Management Area**, as well as the exquisitely situated **Lake Fausse Pointe State Park**.

Eleven miles east of Lafayette in the sleepy, crawfish-lovin' town of **Breaux Bridge**, you'll find sophisticated **Café des Amis** (www.cafedesamis.com; 140 E Bridge St; mains $14-24; ⌚11am-2pm Tue, to 9pm Wed & Thu, 7:30am-9:30pm Fri & Sat, 8am-2pm Sun), where you can relax amid funky local art as waiters trot out sumptuous weekend breakfasts, sometimes set to a zydeco jam. If you just want good coffee, friendly folks and wi-fi, **Fly's Coffee House** (109 N Main St; ⌚7am-6pm Sun-Thu, to 7pm Fri & Sat; 📶) is your place.

Check out the friendly **Tourist Center** (☎337-332-8500; www.breauxbridgelive.com; 318 E Bridge St; ⌚8am-4pm Mon-Fri, to noon Sat), who can hook you up with one of numerous B&Bs in town, like tidy **Maison des Amis** (☎337-507-3399; www.maisondesamis.com; 111 Washington St; r $100-125; P❄📶) right along Bayou Teche. If you're in town the first week of May, don't miss the gluttony of music, dancing and Cajun food at the **Crawfish Festival** (www.bbcrawfest.com).

Tiny **St Martinville** (www.stmartinville.org), 15 miles southeast of Lafayette, packs a mighty punch. Within one block of the bayou in the town center, visit the **African American Museum & Acadian Memorial** (www.acadianmemorial.org; adult/child $3/free; ⌚10am-4pm) to learn about the diasporas of both Cajuns and African Americans.

One mile north of the town center, **Longfellow-Evangeline State Historic Site** (www.lastateparks.com; 1200 N Main St; adult/child $4/free; ⌚9am-5pm) explains the nuances of Creole and Acadian history, and gives tours of its restored Raised Creole Cottage and replica Acadian farmstead.

WORTH A TRIP

SPICE ISLAND

Drive southwest of New Iberia along Hwy 329 through cane fields to lush and lovely **Avery Island** (admission per vehicle $1), home of **McIlhenny Tabasco** (☎337-365-8173; tours free; ⌚9am-4pm) and its excellent **wildlife sanctuary** (adult/child $8/5; ⌚9am-5:30pm). The beautiful, manicured paths around the island actually cover a salt dome that extends 8 miles below the surface. Even though the air smells lightly of Tabasco, alligators and egrets bask in the protected sunshine – bring a lunch and mosquito repellent.

At the Tabasco store, you can sample Tabasco-laced grub, including sweet and spicy ice cream and jalapeño soda.

CAJUN PRAIRIE

Think: dancing cowboys! Cajun and African American settlers to the higher, drier terrain north of Lafayette developed a culture based around animal husbandry and farming, and the ten-gallon hat still rules. It's also the hotbed of Cajun and zydeco music (and thus accordions) and crawfish farming.

Opelousas squats sleepily alongside Hwy 49, and its historic downtown is home to the esoteric **Museum & Interpretive Center** (315 N Main St; admission free; ⌚9am-5pm Mon-Sat); check out the doll collection.

The top zydeco joints in Acadiana, **Slim's Y-Ki-Ki** (www.slimsykiki.com; Hwy 182 N), a few miles north on Main St, across from the Piggly Wiggly, and the **Zydeco Hall of Fame** (11154 Hwy 190), 4 miles west in Lawtell, strike it up most weekends. Wear your dancing shoes and don't be afraid to sweat!

Plaisance, northwest of Opelousas, hosts the grassroots, fun-for-the-family **Southwest**

Louisiana Zydeco Festival (www.zydeco.org) in August.

In **Eunice** (www.eunice-la.com) there's the Saturday-night 'Rendez-Vous des Cajuns' at the **Liberty Theater** (200 Park Ave; admission $5), which is broadcast on local radio. In fact, visitors are welcome all day at **KBON** (www.kbon.com; 109 S 2nd St), 101.1FM. Browse the capacious Wall of Fame, signed by visiting musicians. Two blocks away, the **Cajun Music Hall of Fame & Museum** (www.cajunfrenchmusic.org; 230 S CC Duson Dr; admission free; 9am-5pm Tue-Sat) caters to the die-hard music buff, and the NPS runs the **Prairie Acadian Cultural Center** (cnr 3rd St & Park Ave; admission free; 8am-5pm Tue-Fri, to 6pm Sat) with interesting exhibits on swamp life and Cajun culture, and showing a variety of documentaries explaining the history of the area.

If all this leaves you in need of a respite, try centrally located **Potier's Cajun Inn** (337-457-0440; 110 W Park Ave; r from $55; P) for spacious, down-home-Cajun-style cozy apartments with kitchenettes. **Ruby's Café** (221 W Walnut Ave; meals $7; 6am-2pm Mon-Fri) does popular plate lunches in a 1950s diner setting and **Café Mosiac** (202 S 2nd St; meals $3-4.50;) is a smart coffeehouse with waffles and grilled sandwiches.

Though **Mamou** has a great name, the main thing the town's got going for it is **Fred's Lounge** (420 6th St; 8am-1:30pm Sat), with its Saturday-morning live Cajun band and charming country waltzes.

Cane River Country

The central part of the state is a crossroads of Louisiana's distinct cultures, politics and religions, with bilingual French Catholic and Franco African people along the Cane River, and monolingual, chiefly Protestant residents to the north. Hwy 119 meanders alongside the Cane River. You'll pass locals dipping fishing poles into the lazy water or whiling away the day on front-porch rockers.

Melrose Plantation (318-379-0055; I-49, exit 119; adult/child $10/4; noon-4pm Tue-Sun) is a complex of interesting buildings built by a family of 'free people of color' headed by Marie Therese Coincoin. The early-20th-century owner, Cammie Henry, housed artists and writers such as William Faulkner and Sherwood Anderson in the 1796 Yucca House. Congo-style Africa House contains a vivid 50ft mural depicting plantation life by Clementine Hunter, the renowned folk artist. Hunter had been a field-hand and cook at Melrose before picking up a paintbrush at age 50. The nearby **Kate Chopin House** (243 Hwy 495, Cloutierville) was the author's residence while she wrote *The Awakening*.

NATCHITOCHES

A bit further north you'll find French architecture in historic Natchitoches (mysteriously pronounced *nak*-id-esh), which is split scenically by the Cane River and is the oldest permanent settlement in the Louisiana Purchase. It gained significant notoriety after Hollywood filmmakers arrived in 1988 to film the blockbuster movie *Steel Magnolias*. Head to the **Visitor Bureau** (800-259-1714; www.natchitoches.net; 781 Front St; 9am-5pm) for information about the tours of Creole plantation estates and the numerous B&Bs in town.

Not to be missed is the Natchitoches meat pie famously served by **Lasyone's** (www.lasyones.com; 622 Second St; meat pies $4; 7am-3pm Mon-Sat). The meat pie's heritage dates back to the 1800s when African American youngsters sold them from street corners. Today this crispy fried savory remains ever-popular, with Lasyone's at the epicenter.

If you don't want to stay in a B&B, the 20-room **Church Street Inn** (318-238-8890; www.churchstinn.com; 120 Church St; r incl breakfast from $99; P) is a solid option. From here, you can stroll to downtown eateries and shops then cozy up in your room or do yoga on the communal balcony.

Right in the thick of this densely forested and sparsely populated part of Louisiana, just a short drive from Natchitoches, is the gorgeous **Kisatchie National Forest** (318-473-7160; www.fs.fed.us/r8/kisatchie), 937 sq miles of hilly Southern yellow pine and hardwood. Trails aren't incredibly well maintained, as they are mostly used by hunters in the hunting season, but there are opportunities to mountain bike, hike, swim and go on scenic drives. It's especially splendid during the shoulder seasons. Bring repellent in summer.

Northern Louisiana

Make no mistake: the rural, oil-industry towns along the Baptist Bible belt make northern Louisiana as far removed from New Orleans as Paris, TX, is from Paris, France. Even in the commercial center of

Shreveport, in the far northwest corner of Louisiana, this is a region battling to find self-definition after decades of decline.

Captain Henry Shreve cleared a 165-mile logjam on the Red River and founded the river-port town of **Shreveport**, in 1839. The city boomed with oil discoveries in the early 1900s, but declined after WWII. Some revitalization came in the form of huge Vegas-sized casinos and a riverfront entertainment complex. The **visitor center** (☎318-222-9391, 800-458-4748; www.shreveport-bossier.org; 629 Spring St; ⏲8am-5pm Mon-Fri, 10am-2pm Sat) is downtown. If you're a rose-lover, it would be a shame to miss the **Gardens of the American Rose Center** (www.ars.org; 8877 Jefferson Paige Rd; adult/child $5.50/4.50; ⏲9am-5pm Mon-Sat, 1-5pm Sun), which contains more than 65 individual gardens designed to show how roses can be grown in a home garden – take Exit 5 off the I-20. **Columbia Cafe** (www.columbiacafe.com; 3030 Creswell St; mains $8-17; ⏲7am-10pm Tue-Fri, 10am-10pm Sat, 10am-2pm Sun) might entice you to stop and grab a bite. Eat outside on the patio or inside among local art. The New American fusion is uncomplicated and surprisingly progressive, as in buffalo burgers instead of beef. Tasty!

About 50 miles northeast of Monroe on Hwy 557 near the town of Epps, the **Poverty Point State Historic Site** (www.crt.state.la.us; 6859 Hwy 577, Pioneer; adult/child $4/free; ⏲9am-5pm) has a remarkable series of earthworks and mounds along what was once the Mississippi River. A two-story observation tower gives a view of the site's six concentric ridges. Around 1000 BC this was the hub of a civilization comprising hundreds of communities, with trading links as far north as the Great Lakes.

ARKANSAS

Tucked smack in the center of the US, hiding out between the Midwest and the Deep South, Arkansas is America's overlooked treasure. The natural areas are off the charts: the worn slopes of the Ozarks and the Ouachita (wash-*ee*-tah) mountains; clean, gushing rivers; and lakes bridged by crenelated granite and limestone outcroppings. The entire state is dotted with exceptionally well-presented state parks and tiny, empty roads crisscrossing dense forests that let out onto surprising, sweeping vistas and gentle pastures dotted with grazing horses. The rural towns of Mountain View and Eureka Springs hold quirky charm. Don't be fooled by talk of Wal-Mart or backwoods culture. As one local put it, 'Say what you want about Arkansas, but it's a outdoor paradise.'

History

Caddo, Osage and Quapaw Native Americans had permanent settlements here when Spaniard Hernando de Soto visited in the mid-1500s. Frenchman Henri de Tonti founded the first white settlement in 1686. After the 1803 Louisiana Purchase, Arkansas became a US territory, and slave-holding planters moved into the Delta to grow cotton. Poorer immigrants from Appalachia settled in the Ozark and Ouachita plateaus.

On the edge of the frontier, lawlessness persisted until the Civil War. Reconstruction was difficult, and development only came after 1870 with the expansion of railroads. Racial tension peaked in 1957, with the incident at Central High School in Little Rock.

The state has one of the lowest per-capita incomes in the US, with many poor African Americans in the Delta and poor whites in the Ozarks.

ARKANSAS FACTS

» **Nickname** Natural State

» **Population** 2.9 million

» **Area** 52,068 sq miles

» **Capital city** Little Rock (population 193,524)

» **Other cities** Fayetteville (population 77,143)

» **Sales tax** 6%, plus 2% visitors tax and local taxes

» **Birthplace of** General Douglas MacArthur (1880–1964), musician Johnny Cash (1932–2003), former President Bill Clinton (b 1946), author John Grisham (b 1955), actor Billy Bob Thornton (b 1955)

» **Home of** Wal-Mart

» **Politics** like most Southern states, opposition to Civil Rights turned the state Republican in the '60's

» **Famous for** football fans 'calling the Hogs'

» **Official state instrument** fiddle

» **Driving distances** Little Rock to Eureka Springs 182 miles, Eureka Springs to Mountain View 123 miles

Information

Arkansas State Parks (☎888-287-2757; www.arkansasstateparks.com) Arkansas' well-reputed park system has 52 state parks, 30 offering camping (tent and RV sites $13 to $30, depending on amenities). A number of the parks offer lodge and cabin accommodations. Due to popularity, reservations on weekends and holidays often require multiday stays.

Department of Parks & Tourism (☎501-682-7777; www.arkansas.com; 1 Capitol Mall, Little Rock) Sends out a vacation planning kit; ask for the excellent annual *State Parks Guide* and *Adventure Guide*.

Little Rock

Downtown Little Rock, strangled in the last several decades by parking lots and bad city planning, is now perking up a bit with the burgeoning River Market district. Across the river, North Little Rock, with a growing enclave of shops and restaurants, stretches alongside the extensive riverfront park. This conservative city definitely has some worthwhile things going on, but you just have to know where to look or it all might blur in strip-mall whiplash.

Sights

The best stroll is in the **River Market district** (www.rivermarket.info), an area of shops, galleries, restaurants and pubs on W Markham St and President Clinton Ave along the riverbank. **Ottenheimer Market Hall** (btwn S Commerce & S Rock Sts; ⏲7am-6pm Mon-Sat) houses an eclectic collection of food stalls and shops.

The **Hillcrest Neighborhood** toward west Little Rock is a tiny epicenter of cafes and funky shops and is a communing ground for minority strains of counterculture in the city.

FREE Little Rock Central High School HISTORIC SITE
(www.nps.gov/chsc; 2125 Daisy Bates Dr; ⏲9:30am-4:30pm, tours 9am & 1:15pm Mon-Fri mid-Aug–early Jun) Little Rock's most riveting attraction is the site of the 1957 desegregation crisis that changed the country forever. It was here that a group of African American students known as the Little Rock Nine were first denied entry inside the then all-white high school (despite a 1954 Supreme Court ruling forcing the integration of public schools) then escorted by the 1200-man 101st Airborne Battle Group, a pivotal moment in the American Civil Rights Movement. Today it's both a National Historic Site and a working high school – the most beautiful one you will ever see. There's a spiffy new visitor center airing all the dirty laundry and putting the crisis into perspective alongside the greater Civil Rights Movement. The guides are fantastic, including Spirit Trickey, the daughter of one of the nine.

William J Clinton Presidential Center LIBRARY
(www.clintonlibrary.gov; 1200 President Clinton Ave; adult/child $7/3, with audio $10/6; ⏲9am-5pm Mon-Sat, 1-5pm Sun) Houses the largest archival collection in presidential history, including 80 million pages of documents and two million photographs. Peruse the full-scale replica of the Oval Office, the exhibits on all stages of Clinton's life or the gifts from visiting dignitaries (such as Lance Armstrong's yellow jersey). The entire complex is built to environmentally friendly 'green' standards.

FREE Old State House Museum MUSEUM
(www.oldstatehouse.com; 300 W Markham St; ⏲9am-5pm Mon-Sat, 1-5pm Sun) The state capitol from 1836 to 1911 now holds impressively restored legislative chambers and displays on Arkansas history and culture.

Riverfront Park PARK
Just northwest of downtown, Riverfront Park rolls pleasantly along the Arkansas River and both pedestrians and cyclists take advantage of this fantastic city park daily. You can't miss the **Big Dam Bridge** (www.bigdambridge.com; 🚸), which is the largest bridge built specifically for pedestrians and cyclists in the United States; it connects 17 miles of multiuse trails in Little Rock and North Little Rock that form a complete loop thanks to the renovation of the Rock Island railroad bridge – now renamed the Clinton Presidential Park Bridge – by the Clinton Foundation. For a proper perusal of Riverfront Park rent a bike (or tandem) from **River Trail Rentals** (☎501-374-5505; www.rivertrailrentals.com; 200 S Olive St; per 4-hr/day from $16/30; ⏲by appt Mon-Tue, 10-7pm Wed-Fri, 7am-7pm Sat, 11-6pm Sun) – outside opening hours you can call for a reservation. Otherwise **Chainwheel** (☎501-224-7651; www.chainwheel.com; 10300 Rodney Parham Rd; ⏲10am-6pm Mon-Fri, to 5pm Sat) is the best bike shop in town and can rent higher-end road or mountain bikes, depending on availability.

Sleeping & Eating

Because of government and convention-center traffic, it's difficult to find inexpensive hotels in downtown, and rates fluctuate wildly. Budget motels lie off the interstates.

Capital Hotel BOUTIQUE HOTEL **$$**
(501-374-7474, 888-293-4121; www.capitalhotel.com; 111 W Markham St; r from $160; P ❄ @ 📶) Renovated into the stately Capital Hotel, this 1872 former bank building with a cast-iron facade – a near-extinct architectural feature – is top digs in Little Rock. There is a wonderful outdoor mezzanine for cocktails (and, unfortunately, smokers) and massive elevators, the largest hydraulic lifts in Arkansas, to whisk you away all of four floors. The chef at Ashley's, one of two restaurants on the premises, won *Food & Wine*'s People's Choice Best New Chef for the Midwest in 2011 (except this ain't the Midwest, though it's no fault of the food).

Rosemont HISTORIC B&B **$$**
(501-374-7456; www.rosemontoflittlerock.com; 515 W 15th St; r incl breakfast from $99; P ❄ 📶) In an 1880s restored farmhouse near the Governor's mansion, this place oozes cozy Southern charms. The proprietors have also opened some historic cottages a block away (from $160).

House PUB **$$**
(www.facebook.com/TheHouseInHillcrest; 722 N Palm St; mains $9-14; 7am-6pm Mon-Sat; 11am-2pm Mon-Fri; 📶) Arkansas' first gastropub is run by Hillcrest hipsters who know their way around an eclectic menu that traverses from burgers and BBQ to Thai and Greek (and maybe the best sweet-potato fries – ever).

Homer's DINER **$**
(www.homersrestaurant.com; 2001 East Roosevelt; mains $2-7; 7am-2pm Mon-Fri) It's a schlep out by the airport in the industrial district, but businessmen smoking stogies rubbing elbows with hunters in overalls and Air Force officers on break and high-ranking politicos hatching plans make a visit to this country-cooking classic worth it for local theater alone.

Acadia SOUTHERN **$$$**
(www.acadiahillcrest.com; 3000 Kavanaugh Blvd; dinner mains from $18-24; 11am-2pm Mon-Fri & 5:30-10pm Mon-Sat; 📶) Another Hillcrest standout, Acadia's multilevel patio with twinkling lights is a fabulous place to enjoy fancy-shmancy Southern dishes like smoked Gouda mac 'n' cheese. Lunch is a steal here (mains $9 to $12).

Flying Fish SEAFOOD **$$**
(511 President Clinton Ave; meals $5.50-17; 11am-10pm) The idea was hatched out of East Texas, but the catfish at this down-home seafood place walkable from Clinton library is classic: you *can* get it grilled, but you know deep down fried is the only way to go, served with (fried) fries and (fried) hush puppies. When in Rome, folks, when in Rome...

River City CAFE **$**
(www.rivercityteacoffeeandcream.com; 2715 Kavanaugh Blvd; 5:30-10pm Mon-Sat) Killer Hillcrest tea and coffeehouse. Espresso: 75¢!

Information

Visitor center (501-371-0076, 877-220-2568; www.littlerock.com; 615 E Capitol Ave; 9am-5pm Mon-Sat, 1-5pm Sun) Housed in 1842 Curran Hall.

Getting There & Around

Little Rock National Airport (LIT; 501-372-3439; www.lrn-airport.com) lies just east of downtown. The **Greyhound station** (501-372-3007; 118 E Washington St), in North Little Rock, serves Hot Springs (one to two hours), Memphis, TN (2½ hours), and New Orleans, LA (18 hours). Amtrak occupies **Union Station** (501-372-6841; 1400 W Markham St). **Central Arkansas Transit** (CAT; 501-375-6717; www.cat.org) runs local buses; a trolley makes a loop on W Markham St and President Clinton Ave (adult/child $1.35/60¢).

Hot Springs

It's a wonder that the little city of Hot Springs, with its strip malls, mini-golf suburbs and gasping downtown, hosted the vacationing elite of New York City's organized crime. At full throttle in the 1930s, the city was a hotbed of gambling, bootlegging, prostitution, opulence and dangerous thugs. Yet it was also a spot of truce between warring gangs, a place where it was decreed that all criminals could be gluttonous hedonists in peace. When gambling was squelched, so was the city's economy.

Though it still hasn't recovered from that blow, the healing waters have always drawn people, everyone from the Native American populations to present-day pilgrims. Elaborate restored bathhouses, where you can still get old-school spa treatments, line

Bathhouse Row behind shady magnolias on the east side of Central Ave.

Sights & Activities

A promenade runs through the park around the hillside behind Bathhouse Row, where some springs survive intact, and a network of trails covers Hot Springs' mountains. Unfortunately, only two of the historic Bathhouse Row bathhouses are in operation, but bids were being evaluated by the NPS at time of writing to rechristen the others, including one as a microbrewery.

Gangster Museum of America MUSEUM
(www.tgmoa.com; 510 Central Ave; adult/child $10/4; ⌚10am-6pm Sun-Thu, to 7pm Fri & Sat) See the intriguing underbelly of Hot Springs' history, which explains the sin-filled glory days of Hot Springs when this small town in the middle of nowhere turned into a pinpoint of lavish wealth. Highlights include original slots – that still spew money! – and other gambling tables and equipment.

Que Paw Baths SPA
(www.quapawbaths.com; 413 Central Ave; thermal bath $18, with 25min massage $50; ⌚10am-6pm Mon & Wed, 10am-7pm Thu-Sat,10am-3pm Sun) If the traditional 'wham, bam, thank you, ma'am' approach at the Buckstaff Bathhouse isn't your thing, the newly remodeled Qua Paw offers a more 21st-century approach, with lovely restored thermal baths, green treatments and a sustainable-minded outlook throughout.

FREE **NPS Visitor Center** MUSEUM
(☎501-620-6715; 369 Central Ave; ⌚9am-5pm) On Bathhouse Row in the 1915 Fordyce bathhouse, the NPS visitor center and **museum** have exhibits about the park's history first as a Native American free-trade zone, and later as a turn-of-the-19th-century European spa.

Hot Springs Mountain Tower OUTDOORS
(adult/child $7/4; ⌚9am-5pm Nov-Feb, til 6pm Mar-May 15 & Labor Day-Oct, til 9pm May 16-Labor Day) On the top of Hot Springs Mountain, the 216ft tower has spectacular views of the surrounding mountains covered with dogwood, hickory, oak and pine – lovely in the spring and fall.

Sleeping & Eating

Chain motels line highways around town; the visitor center has a list of lakeside rental properties and area B&Bs. Some restaurants congregate along the Central Ave tourist strip and offer ho-hum food.

Alpine Inn INN $
(☎501-624-9164; www.alpine-inn-hot-springs.com; 741 Park Ave/Hwy 7 N; r $55-90; P❄📶≋) The friendly Scottish owners of this inn, less than a mile from Bathhouse Row, have spent a few years upgrading this old motor court hotel. The tidily maintained row of somewhat-themed, impeccable rooms include new flat-screen TVs and scrumptious beds; and some offer kitchenettes. The Mackintosh room, a nod to Scotland's architectural son, is our favorite.

Arlington Resort Hotel & Spa HISTORIC HOTEL $
(☎501-623-7771; www.arlingtonhotel.com; 239 Central Ave; s/d from $79/89, with mineral baths $139; P❄📶≋) This imposing historic hotel tops Bathhouse Row and constantly references its glory days. The grand lobby tries to set the tone for the antique in-house spa and aging rooms and there's a half-hearted Starbucks if you're looking for decent coffee. Catch a foxtrot on the weekend when there might be a live band.

Cajun Boilers CAJUN, SEAFOOD $$
(www.cajunboilers.com; 2806 Albert Pike Rd; mains $8-20; ⌚11am-10pm Mon-Sat to 9pm Sun; 👪) A loud and boisterous seafood spot right on Lake Hamilton, a few miles from Bathhouse Row. The outdoor patio is a fabulous setting to tear into the famous crawfish boil, catfish fried or blackened, or shrimp étouffée. You can boat up or drive up.

McClard's BARBECUE $$
(www.mcclards.com; 505 Albert Pike; mains $4-15; ⌚11am-8pm Tue-Sat) Southwest of the center, it may be Bill Clinton's favorite boyhood BBQ but reviews are seriously mixed about whether the ribs, slow-cooked beans and creamy slaw here are truly up to snuff.

Information

Visitor center (☎501-321-2277, 800-772-2489; www.hotsprings.org; 629 Central Ave; ⌚9am-5pm, until 7pm Jun-Aug) For city information or to pick up a map of Clinton-related sites.

Getting There & Away

Greyhound (☎501-623-5574; 1001 Central Ave) has buses heading to Little Rock (1½ hours, three daily).

Around Hot Springs

The wild, pretty **Ouachita National Forest** (☎501-321-5202; welcome center 100 Reserve St, Hot Springs; ⊙8am-4:30pm) is studded with lakes and draws hunters, fisherfolk, mountain bikers and boaters. The small roads through the mountains unfailingly bring hidden nooks and wonderful views. The Ouachita boasts two designated National Forest Scenic Byways: Arkansas Scenic Hwy 7 and Talimena Scenic Byway, navigating mountain ranges from Arkansas into Oklahoma. If you stop in the welcome center, leave your camera behind – it's a federal building.

Hot Springs National Park (www.nps.gov/hosp), a tiny preserve nearby, has thermal waters in and around town from which spew a collected 700,000 gallons of 143°F (62°C) water daily from 47 natural springs, and attract modern-day pilgrims who bathe in or sip its waters.

Clinton buffs might stop at **Hope**, where the ex-pres spent his first seven years, but there's not much to see other than the spiffy **Hope Visitor Center & Museum** (www.hopearkansas.net; 100 E Division St; ⊙8:30am-5pm Mon-Fri, from 9am Sat, 1-4pm Sun), in the old depot, and the **President Bill Clinton First Home Museum** (www.clintonchildhoodhomemuseum.com; 117. S. Hervey St; admission free; ⊙8:30am-4:30pm), now part of the National Park Service.

If you want to test your luck and diamond-spotting skills, head to **Crater of Diamonds State Park** (www.craterofdiamondsstatepark.com; 209 State Park Rd; ⊙8am-5pm), where you can scour the **diamond field** (adult/child $7/4) in which three- to 40-carat diamonds have been found, and where valuable diamonds continue to be found today.

Arkansas River Valley

The Arkansas River cuts a swath across the state from Oklahoma to Mississippi. Folks come to fish, canoe and camp along its banks and tributaries.

The excellently maintained trails of **Petit Jean State Park** (☎501-727-5441; www.petitjeanstatepark.com; 👪), west of Morrilton, wind past a lush 95ft waterfall, romantic grottoes, expansive vistas, and dense forests. There's a rustic stone lodge, reasonable **cabins** (per night $100-175) and campgrounds. Another stellar state park is **Mount Magazine** (☎479-963-8502; www.mountmagazinestatepark.com; 16878 Hwy 309 S, Paris), which maintains 14 miles of trails around Arkansas' highest point. Outdoor enthusiasts enjoy great hang gliding and rock climbing here as well as hiking.

The spectacular **Highway 23/Pig Trail Byway**, lined with wild echinacea and lilies, climbs up through **Ozark National Forest** and into the mountains; an excellent way to reach Eureka Springs in the Ozark Mountains.

The **Arkansas and Missouri Railway** (www.arkansasmissouri-rr.com; adult/child from $35/18; ⊙Fri & Sat Apr-Sep) offers a 70-mile trip through the Boston Mountain Range from **Van Buren** to **Winslow** and back.

Ozark Mountains

Stretching from northwest and central Arkansas into Missouri, the **Ozark Mountains** (☎870-404-2741; www.ozarkmountainregion.com) are an ancient range, once surrounded by sea and now well worn by time. Verdant rolling mountains give way to misty fields, and dramatic karst formations line sparkling lakes, meandering rivers and scenic back roads. Though some of the towns bank on kitschy hillbilly culture, scratch below the surface to find the unique cultural traditions, such as acoustic folk music and home-cooked hush puppies and catfish.

MOUNTAIN VIEW

Detour east of US 65 or along Hwy 5 to this wacky Ozark town, known for its tradition of informal music-making at Courtsquare. Creeping commercialism is taking its toll, as the **Visitor Information Center** (☎870-269-8068; www.yourplaceinthemountains.com; 107 N Peabody Ave; ⊙9am-4:30pm Mon-Sat) promotes the place as the 'Folk Music Capital of the World,' but loads of live folk-music and bizarre festivals keep it real, including the **Championship Outhouse Races**, where crowds cheer on their favorite 'people-powered potty' racing to the finish line – it usually takes place around the last week in October. Cutesy sandstone architecture downtown, one of Arkansas' last standing drive-in movie theaters, and the pickin' parks and impromptu hill music, gospel and bluegrass hootenannies (jam sessions and folk music parties) in the **Courtsquare** by the Stone County Courthouse (especially on Saturday night) – and on porches all around town anytime – make a visit here quirky and fun.

DON'T MISS

A LOVELY LOOP

Downtown Eureka Springs is beautiful in and of itself, but the town's real coup is its easily overlooked **Historic Loop**, a 3.5-mile ring of history through downtown and around neighboring residential neighborhoods that will blow your mind. The route is dotted with over 300 Victorian homes, all built before 1910, each and every one of them a jaw-dropper and on par with any preserved historic district in the USA.

There are several ways to enjoy the route if you don't have your own wheels. Pick up a *Six Scenic Walking Tours* brochure from the visitor center in Eureka Springs; rent a bike from **Adventure Mountain Outfitters** (☎479-253-0900; www.adventuremountainoutfitters.com; 151 Spring St, Eureka Springs; half day $50; ⊙9am-5pm Wed-Sat); or catch the Red Line of the **Eureka Trolley** (www.eurekatrolley.org; adult/child $5/1; ⊙9am-5pm Jan-Apr & Nov-Dec, til 8pm Sun May-Oct).

Ozark Folk Center State Park (www.ozarkfolkcenter.com; auditorium adult/child $10/6; ⊙10am-5pm Wed-Sat), just north of town, hosts ongoing craft demonstrations and a traditional herb garden, as well as nightly live music from 7pm that brings in an avid, older crowd.

The spectacular **Blanchard Springs Caverns** (☎888-757-2246; off Hwy 14; adult/child $10.50/5.50, wild cave tour $75; ⊙9am-6pm Apr-Sep; 👪), located 15 miles northwest of Mountain View, were carved by an underground river and rival those at Carlsbad Caverns National Park, Southeastern New Mexico. It's another little-known, mind-blowing spot in Arkansas. Three Forest Service guided tours range from disabled-accessible to adventurous three- to four-hour spelunking sessions. The welcoming and historic 1918 **Wildflower B&B** (☎870-269-4383; www.wildflowerbb.com; 100 Washington; r incl breakfast from $89; P❄📶) is right on the Courtsquare with a rocking chair-equipped wraparound porch, cozy down-home trappings and a $20 midweek discount. Breakfast connoisseurs will be particularly pleased, especially if they get the guava puff pastry or baked hash browns. **Tommy's Famous Pizza and BBQ** (cnr Carpenter & W Main Sts; pizza $5.50-24, mains $6.40-13.20; ⊙from 3pm) is run by the friendliest bunch of backwoods hippies you could ask for. The pulled-pork BBQ pizza marries Tommy's specialties indulgently.

EUREKA SPRINGS

Artsy, quirky and drop-dead gorgeous, Eureka Springs, near Arkansas' Northwestern corner, perches in a steep valley and is one of the coolest towns in the South. Victorian buildings line crooked streets and a crunchy local population welcomes all – it's one of the most explicitly gay-friendly towns in the Ozarks and an island of Democratic blue in an absolute sea of Republican red. On the surface, art galleries and kitschy shops compete with commercialized country music and the 70ft **Christ of the Ozarks** statue for your attention. But bend a local's ear and find out who's playing at the nearest pub or the location of their favorite swimming hole and this idiosyncratic village will take on new dimensions. Furthermore, hiking, biking, and horseback-riding opportunities abound. Adding to its appeal, there are no red lights or perpendicular cross streets, so zipping around its historical beauty is a breeze.

The **visitor center** (☎479-253-8737; www.eurekaspringschamber.com; 516 Village Circle, Hwy 62 E; ⊙9am-5pm) has information about lodging, activities, tours and local attractions, such as the rockin' **Blues Festival** (www.eurekaspringsblues.com) at the end of May. The old **ES & NA Railway** (www.esnarailway.com; 299 N Main St; adult/child $13.50/6.75; ⊙Tue-Sat Apr-Oct) puffs through the Ozark hills on an hour-long tour three times a day (four times on Saturday).

Thorncrown Chapel (☎479-253-7401; www.thorncrown.com; 12968 Hwy 62 West; donation suggested; ⊙9am-5pm Apr-Nov, 11am-4pm Mar & Dec) is a magnificent sanctuary made of glass, with its 48ft-tall wooden skeleton holding 425 windows. There's not much between your prayers and God's green earth here. It's just outside of town in the woods. The exquisite **Queen Anne Mansion** (www.thequeenannemansion.com; 115 W Van Buren; tours adult/child $15/9, guided $25/15), originally built in Carthage, Missouri in 1891, debuted in 2010 after a five-year, multimillion-dollar restoration. Original period pieces dot the gorgeously furnished home, a non-negotiable stop for architecture and antique buffs.

If your budget can stand it, bypass the cheap motels on the rim of the canyon and splurge on lodging in the town center. Right in the historic downtown is the super-comfortable and historic **New Orleans Hotel and Suchness Spa** (479-253-8630; www.neworleanshotelandspa.com; 63 Spring St; r $84-204; P ❄ 📶), which sends you reeling back in time, except that it houses a spa with a menu fully loaded for your body and chakra needs. **Treehouse Cottages** (479-253-8667; www.treehousecottages.com; 165 W Van Buren St; from $145; P ❄ 📶) offers gorgeous sunlit, Jacuzzi-equipped tree houses (that are more like cottages on stilts) in the woods.

Right across the street is **Bubba's BBQ** (www.bubbasbarbecueeurekasprings.com; 166 W Van Buren St; mains $5.50-13; 11am-9pm Mon-Sat), which is a genuine Southern meat joint in a town that has its fair share of tourist contrivance. At **Mud Street Café** (www.mudstreetcafe.com; 22 G S Main St; mains $9-13; 8am-3pm Thu-Tue) in downtown, the coffee drinks and breakfasts are renowned. The cheese plate menu reads like a work of art at the sophisticated wine and cheese bar, the **Stone House** (www.eurekastonehouse.com; 89 S Main St; cheese plates $25-47; 1-10pm Wed-Sat), which serves captivating European and artisan Stateside cheese paired with some 30 wines by the glass ($8 to $15).

BUFFALO NATIONAL RIVER

Yet another under-acknowledged Arkansas gem, this 135-mile river flows beneath dramatic bluffs through unspoiled Ozark forest. The upriver section tends to have most of the white water, while the lower reaches ease lazily along – perfect for a float. The **Buffalo National River** (870-741-5443; www.nps.gov/buff) has 10 **campgrounds** (877-444-6777; www.recreation.gov; tent/RV sites $10/20) and three designated wilderness areas; the most accessible is through the **Tyler Bend visitor center** (870-439-2502; 8:30am-4:30pm), 11 miles north of Marshall on Hwy 65, where you call also pick up a list of approved outfitters for self-guided rafting or canoe trips, the best way to tour the park and see the gargantuan limestone bluffs.

Evidence of human occupation here dates back some 10,000 years, but this wild and naturally bountiful area kept even modern Ozark settlers isolated and self-sufficient. They developed a distinct dialect, along with unique craftsmanship and musical traits. Thanks to its National River designation in 1972, the Buffalo is one of the few remaining unpolluted, free-flowing rivers in the country.

Arkansas Delta

Roughly 120 miles east of Little Rock, the Great River Rd follows the west bank of the Mississippi River through the Arkansas Delta. Blues town of yesteryear, **Helena** is now a depressed little Arkansas town. However, it explodes for its annual **Arkansas Blues & Heritage Festival** (www.bluesandheritagefest.com; admission free) when blues musicians and 100,000 fans take over downtown for three days in early October. Food stalls sell home-cooked soul food and BBQ.

Year-round, blues fans and history buffs should visit the **Delta Cultural Center** (870-338-4350; www.deltaculturalcenter.com; 141 Cherry St; admission free; 9am-5pm Tue-Sat), which is in two buildings: the Train Depot and the Visitor Center. The museum displays all manner of blues memorabilia such as Albert King's and Sister Rosetta Tharpe's guitars, and John Lee Hooker's signed handkerchief.

The world's longest-running blues radio program, *King Biscuit Time,* is broadcast here (12:15pm Monday to Friday), and *Delta Sounds* (1pm Monday to Friday) often has live musicians. Other than that, music in Helena is not to be found.

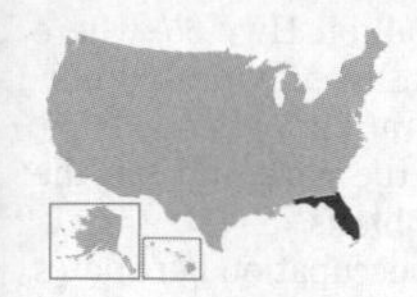

Florida

Includes »

South Florida 445
Miami 445
Fort Lauderdale 459
The Everglades 463
Florida Keys 466
Atlantic Coast 474
Daytona Beach 476
West Coast 481
Tampa 481
Central Florida 489
Orlando 489
Walt Disney World Resort 493
Florida Panhandle......... 495

Best Places to Eat

» Senora Martinez (p456)

» Sustain (p457)

» Café Solé (p473)

» Floridian (p479)

» Refinery (p483)

Best Places to Stay

» Pelican Hotel (p455)

» Biltmore Hotel (p455)

» Dickens House (p485)

» Pillars (p460)

» Everglades International Hostel (p465)

Why Go?

Blessed with almost year-round sunshine, Florida is a hothouse orchid – a bold, sexy, semitropical peninsula edged with bone-white beaches, caressed by teal waters and clad in lurid neon sunsets. Surreal, garish, wacky and perpetually self-amused, Florida is a fantasy-filled swampy wonderland of giddy delights, from alligators, mermaids and Mickey Mouse to Miami's hedonistic, art-fueled, celebrity playground.

Florida's gorgeous beaches are its calling card, and you could visit one every day of the year and still not see them all. But the state offers much more: the prehistoric Everglades, Orlando's phantasmagorical theme parks, the pastel-colored eye candy of South Beach, Key West's nightly carnival, Key Largo's coral reefs. In ways natural and unnatural, Florida's perpetual promise is of escape, both from mundane life and the reasoned constraints of polite society.

When to Go

Miami

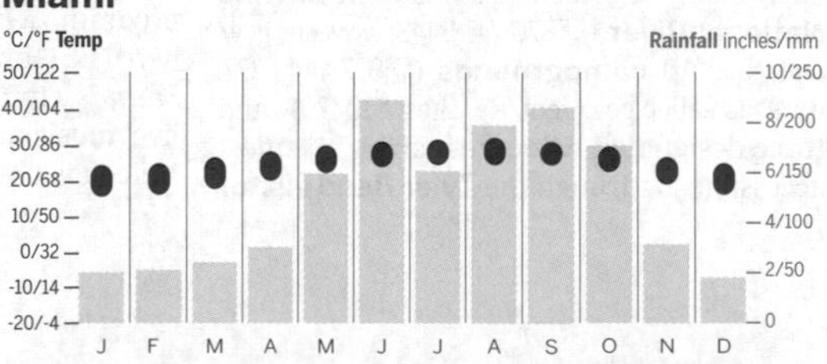

Feb-Apr During the last of the winter dry period, the south Florida high season coincides with spring break.

Jun-Aug The hot, humid wet months are peak season for northern Florida beaches and theme parks.

Sep-Oct The ideal shoulder season with fewer crowds, cooler temperatures and warm waters.

Spring Training

Every March, 13 major league baseball teams hold their spring training in stadiums across central and south Florida. That's around 240 exhibition games in 30 days, and it's a pilgrimage for many fans, since the intimate stadiums put you within spitting and signing distance of big leaguers and future hall of famers. For information, visit www.floridagrapefruitleague.com.

AMERICA'S BEST STATE PARKS

Encountering Florida's bizarre, beautiful terrain and its wealth of ancient critters, migratory seabirds and imposing wildlife is unquestionably a highlight. Thankfully, Florida makes it easy for travelers with one of the nation's best state park systems. It is the first and only state to be a two-time recipient of the National Gold Medal Award for Excellence (in 1999 and 2005), and was a finalist once again in 2011.

The state's 160 state parks span an overwhelming array of environments, home to epic coral reefs (John Pennekamp), thousands of alligators (Myakka River), otherworldly limestone karst terrain (Paynes Prairie) and crystal springs (Wakulla Springs). Of course, Florida is also legendary for the quality of its beaches, including such top beach parks as Grayton Beach, Fort DeSoto, Honeymoon Island and St Joseph Peninsula.

For the full list, visit **Florida State Parks** (www.floridastateparks.org). For advice on wildlife watching (what, when and how), visit the **Florida Fish & Wildlife Commission** (http://myfwc.com), which also facilitates boating, hunting and fishing.

Green Florida

Until recently, Florida wasn't known for conservation and ecotourism, but that's changing fast. Here are some resources for local issues and sustainable travel.

» Department of Environmental Protection (DEP; www.dep.state.fl.us) State-run agency tackles ecological and sustainability issues.

» Green Lodging Program (www.dep.state.fl.us/greenlodging) DEP-run program recognizes lodgings committed to conservation and sustainability.

» Florida Sierra Club (http://florida.sierraclub.org) Venerable outdoors and advocacy group.

» Florida Surfrider (http://florida.surfrider.org) Grassroots surfer-run nonprofit dedicated to protecting America's beaches; 11 Florida chapters.

» Greenopia (www.greenopia.com) Rates ecofriendly businesses in six major Florida cities.

HIAASEN'S FLORIDA

Writer Carl Hiaasen's unique, black-comic vision of Florida is a hilarious gumbo of misfits and murderous developers. Try *Skinny Dip* (for adults), *Hoot* (for kids) and *Paradise Screwed* (for his selected columns).

Fast Facts

» Population: Miami 399,460, Miami-Dade County 2.5 million

» Distances from Miami: Key West (160 miles), Orlando (235 miles)

» Time zones: Eastern (eastern Florida), Central Time Zone (western Panhandle)

Kid Stuff

Need to rent baby gear? Want formula and diapers shipped ahead to your hotel? Need a babysitter?

» Baby's Away (www.babysawayrentals.com)

» Babies Travel Lite (www.babiestravellite.com)

» Kids' Nite Out (www.kidsniteout.com)

Resources

» Visit Florida (www.visitflorida.com) is the official state tourism website.

» My Florida (www.myflorida.com) is the official government portal.

» Florida Smart (www.floridasmart.com) provides comprehensive Florida links.

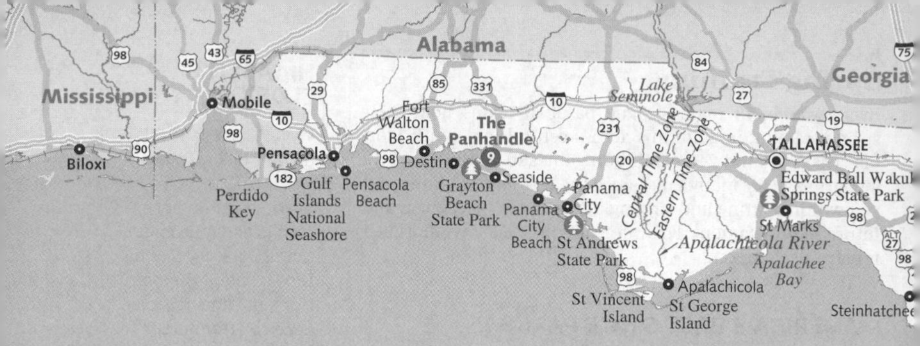

Gulf of Mexico

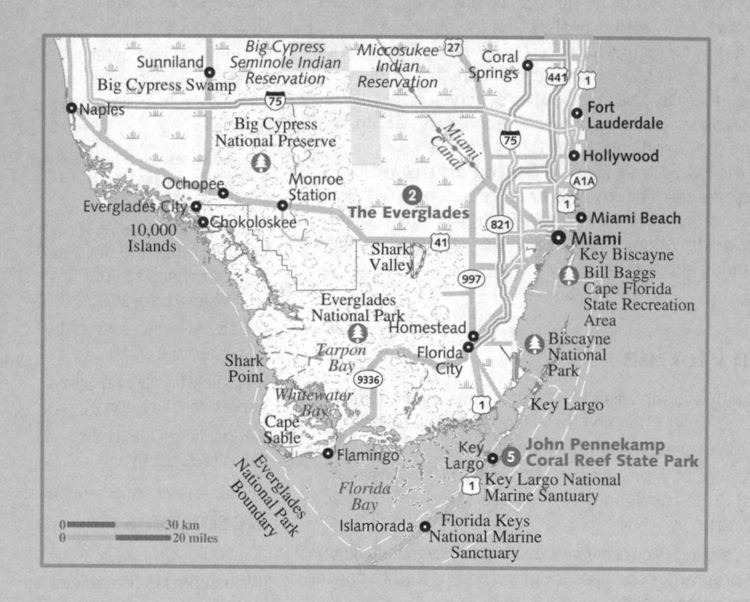

Florida Highlights

1. Marvel at the bright-painted works of art in **Miami's museums and galleries** (p445)
2. Paddle among the alligators and saw grass of the **Everglades** (p463)
3. Be swept up in the nostalgia and thrill rides of **Walt Disney World** (p493)
4. Join Mallory Square's sunset bacchanal in **Key West** (p470)
5. Snorkel and dive the USA's most extensive coral reef at **John Pennekamp** (p467)

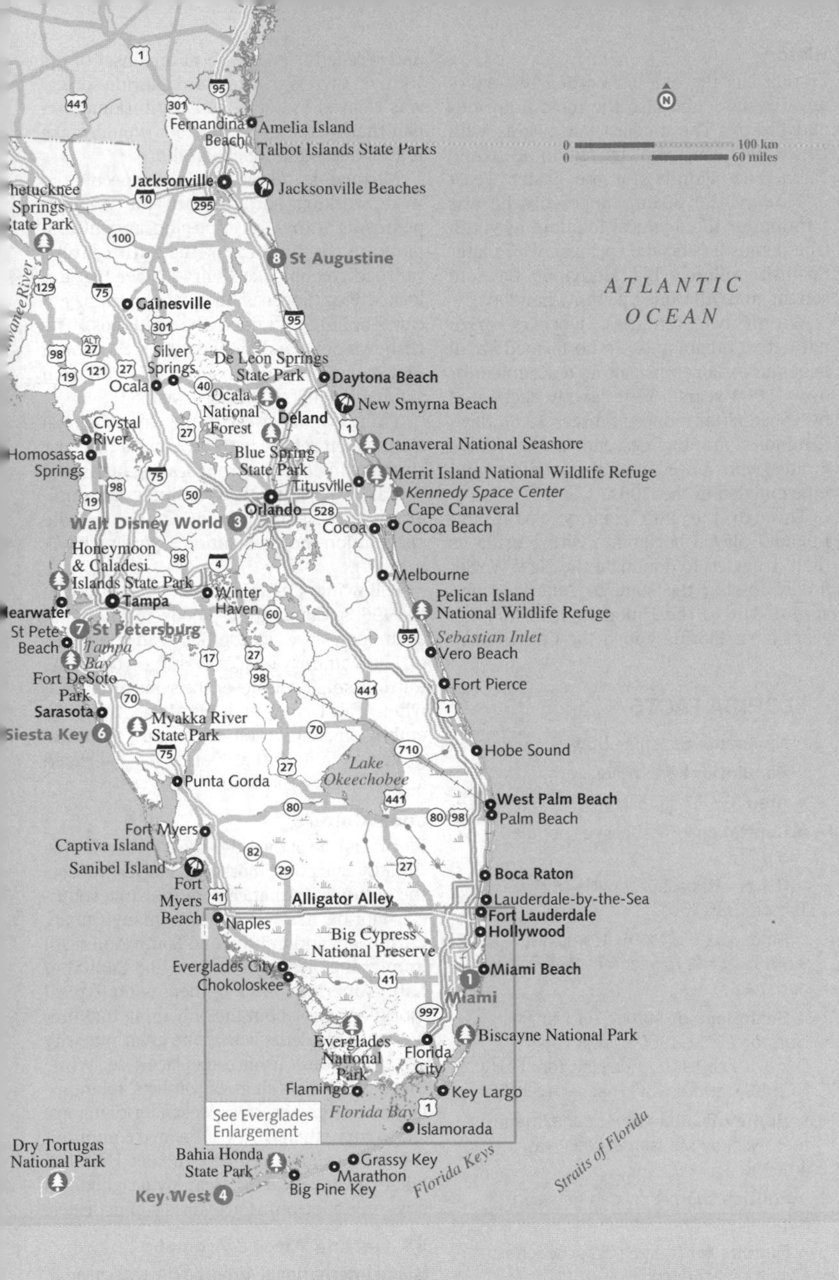

6 Relax on the sugar sand beaches of Sarasota's **Siesta Key** (p486)

7 Ponder the symbolism of the Hallucinogenic Toreador at St Petersburg's **Salvador Dalí Museum** (p485)

8 Growl like a pirate among the historic Spanish buildings of **St Augustine** (p478)

9 Road-trip through the fun-loving beach towns and quiet silken sands of the **Panhandle** (p497)

History

Florida has the oldest recorded history of any US state, and also the most notorious and bizarre. The modern tale begins with Ponce de León, who arrived in 1513 and claimed La Florida (for the Easter 'Feast of Flowers') for Spain. Supposedly, he was hunting for the mythical fountain of youth (the peninsula's crystal springs), while later Spanish explorers like Hernando de Soto sought gold. All came up empty handed.

Within two centuries, Florida's original native inhabitants – who formed small tribes across a peninsula they'd occupied for over 11,000 years – were largely decimated by Spanish-introduced diseases. Today's Seminoles are the descendents of native groups who moved into the territory and intermingled in the 1700s.

Through the 18th century, Spain and England played hot potato with Florida as they struggled to dominate the New World, finally tossing the state to America, who admitted it to the Union in 1845. Sixteen years later, Florida joined the Confederacy and seceded from the US at the onset of the 1861–65 Civil War. Afterward, Florida society was cleaved by social and institutional racism that by the 1950s and '60s would make it a battleground for civil rights.

Meanwhile, developers and speculators were working hard to turn the swampy peninsula into a vacation and agricultural paradise. By the turn of the 20th century, railroad tycoons like Henry Flagler had unlocked Florida's coastlines, while a frenzy of canal-building drained the wetlands. The rush was on, and in the 1920s the South Florida land boom transformed Miami from sandbar to metropolis in 10 years.

Things went bust with the Great Depression, which set the pattern: Florida has ever since swung between intoxicating highs and brutal lows, riding the vicissitudes of immigration, tourism, hurricanes and real estate speculation (not to mention a thriving black market).

Following Castro's Cuban revolution in the 1960s, Cuban exiles flooded Miami, and each successive decade has seen the ranks of Latin immigrants grow and diversify. As for tourism, it was never the same after 1971, when Walt Disney built his Magic Kingdom, embodying the vision of eternal youth and perfected fantasy that Florida has packaged and sold since the beginning.

FLORIDA FACTS

» **Nickname** Sunshine State

» **Population** 18.8 million

» **Area** 53,927 sq miles

» **Capital city** Tallahassee (population 168,979)

» **Other cities** Jacksonville (821,780), Tampa (335,700)

» **Sales tax** 6% (some towns add 9.5% to 11.5% to accommodations and meals)

» **Birthplace of** Author Zora Neale Hurston (1891–1960), actor Faye Dunaway (b 1941), musician Tom Petty (b 1950), author Carl Hiaasen (b 1953)

» **Home of** Cuban Americans, manatees, Mickey Mouse, retirees, key lime pie

» **Politics** sharply divided between Republicans and Democrats

» **Famous for** theme parks, beaches, alligators, art deco

» **Notable local invention** frozen concentrated orange juice (1946)

» **Driving distances** Miami to Key West 160 miles, Miami to Orlando 235 miles

Local Culture

Florida is one of the USA's most diverse states. Broadly speaking, northern Florida reflects the culture of America's South, while southern Florida has welcomed so many Cuban, Caribbean, and Central and South American immigrants, it's been dubbed 'the Capital of Latin America.' As such, there is no 'typical Floridian,' and about the only thing that unifies state residents is that the great majority are transplants from someplace else. While this has led to its share of conflicts, tolerance is more often the rule. Most Floridians are left to carve their own self-defined communities, be they gays, retirees, Cubans, Haitians, bikers, evangelicals, Nascar-loving good old boys or globetrotting art-world sophisticates.

Getting There & Around

Miami International Airport (MIA; www.miami-airport.com) is an international gateway, as are Orlando, Tampa and Fort Lauderdale. The Fort Lauderdale and Miami airports are about 30 minutes apart; it's almost always cheaper to fly into Fort Lauderdale. Miami is also home to the world's busiest cruise port.

FLORIDA IN...

One Week

Start in **Miami** and plan on spending three full days exploring the museums and galleries, the art-deco district, Little Havana and the South Beach scene. Take a day to hike and kayak the **Everglades**, and don't miss **Coral Castle**. Then spend three days in the Keys: snorkel at **John Pennekamp Coral Reef State Park**, go tarpon fishing in **Islamorada** and let yourself get loose in **Key West**.

Two Weeks

Spend one or two days at the theme parks of **Orlando**, then scoot over to **Tampa** for fine cuisine and Ybor City nightlife. Get surreal in **St Petersburg** at the Salvador Dalí Museum, and visit a few **Tampa Bay Area beaches**. Finally, save a couple of days for **Sarasota**, with its jaw-dropping Ringling Museum Complex and the dreamy sands of **Siesta Key**.

Greyhound (www.greyhound.com) has widespread service throughout the state. **Amtrak** (www.amtrak.com) *Silver Meteor* and *Silver Star* trains run daily between New York and Miami.

Car-rental rates in Florida tend to fluctuate, but expect to pay at least $300 to $350 a week for a typical economy car.

SOUTH FLORIDA

Exemplifying the state's diversity, South Florida is a vivid pastiche of all that makes Florida wicked and wild. First is the multicultural entrepôt of Miami, and the sophisticated, rich beach communities stretching north from Fort Lauderdale to Palm Beach. In striking contrast, the beaches are bordered by the subtropical wilderness of the Everglades, while the tip of the state peters out in an ellipsis of fun-loving islands, culminating in anything-goes Key West.

Miami

Miami moves to a different rhythm from anywhere else in the USA. Pastel-hued, subtropical beauty and Latin sexiness are everywhere: from the cigar-filled dance halls where Havana expats dance to *son* and boleros to the exclusive nightclubs where stiletto-heeled Brazilian models shake to Latin hip-hop. Whether you're meeting avant-garde gallery hipsters or passing the buffed, perfect bodies recumbent along South Beach, everyone can seem oh-so-artfully posed. Meanwhile, street vendors and restaurants dish out flavors of the Caribbean, Cuba, Argentina and Haiti. For travelers, the city can be as intoxicating as a sweaty-glassed *mojito*.

Miami is its own world, an international city whose tempos, concerns and inspirations often arrive from distant shores. Over half the population is Latino and over 60% speak predominantly Spanish. In fact, many northern Floridians don't consider immigrant-rich Miami to be part of the state, and many Miamians, particularly Cubans, feel the same way.

Sights

Greater Miami is a sprawling metropolis that includes suburbs such as Coral Gables and Coconut Grove, and neighborhoods such as Little Havana and Little Haiti. Miami is on the mainland, while Miami Beach lies 4 miles east across Biscayne Bay.

Downtown Miami operates on a fairly normal grid system, with Flagler St as the main east–west drag, and 2nd Ave as the main north–south conduit. North of downtown (along NE 2nd Ave from about 17th St to 41st St), Wynwood and the Design District are focal points for art, food and nightlife. Just north again is Little Haiti.

To reach Little Havana, head west on SW 8th St, or Calle Ocho, which pierces the heart of the neighborhood (and becomes the Tamiami Trail/Hwy 41). Just south of Little Havana are Coconut Grove and Coral Gables.

South Beach is actually the southern part of Miami Beach, extending from 5th St north to 21st St. Washington Ave is the main commercial artery.

For more on South Florida, pick up a copy of Lonely Planet's guide to *Miami & the Keys*.

Greater Miami

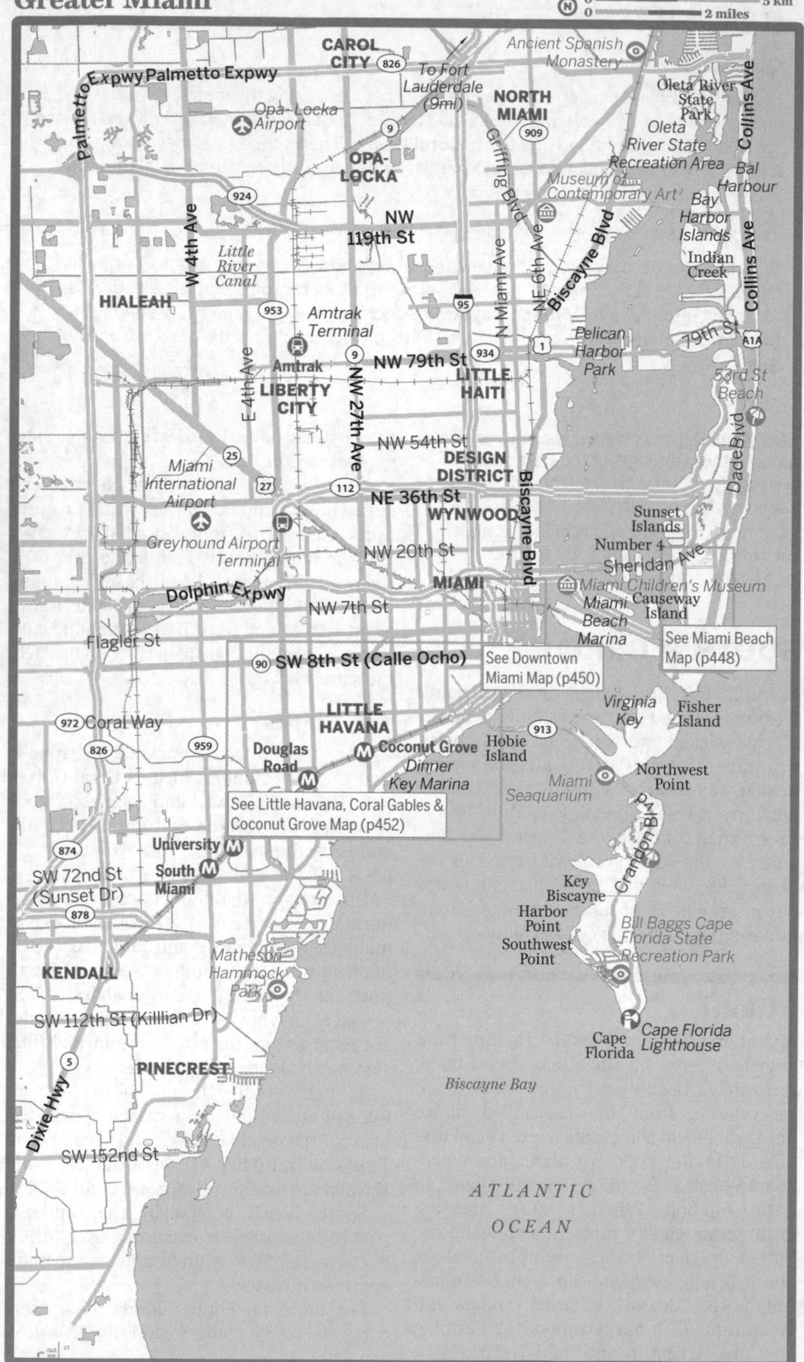

MIAMI BEACH

Miami Beach has some of the best beaches in the country, with white sand and warm aquamarine water that rivals the Bahamas. That movie in your head of art-deco hotels, in-line-skating models, preening young studs and cruising cars? That's **Ocean Drive** (from 1st to 11th Sts), with the beach merely a backdrop for strutting peacocks. This confluence of waves, sunshine and exhibitionist beauty is what made South Beach (or 'SoBe') world-famous.

In the evening, stroll down **Española Way**, a *trés* European strip lined with restaurants and cafes. Just a few blocks north, **Lincoln Road** (between Alton Rd and Washington Ave) becomes a pedestrian mall, or outdoor fashion runway, so all may admire SoBe's fabulously gorgeous creatures.

TOP CHOICE Art Deco Historic District NEIGHBORHOOD

The well-preserved, pastel-hued Art Deco Historic District verily screams 'Miami.' It's the largest concentration of deco anywhere in the world, with approximately 1200 buildings lining the streets around Ocean Dr and Collins Ave. For tours and info, make your first stop the **Art Deco Welcome Center** (Map p448; ☎305-531-3484; www.mdpl.org; 1200 Ocean Dr; ⏲9:30am-7pm).

Wolfsonian-FIU MUSEUM

(Map p448; www.wolfsonian.org; 1001 Washington Ave; adult/child $5/3.50; ⏲11am-9pm Thu, to 6pm Fri & Sat, noon-5pm Sun) A fascinating collection that spans transportation, urbanism, industrial design, advertising and political propaganda from the late 19th to mid-20th century.

Bass Museum of Art MUSEUM

(off Map p448; www.bassmuseum.org; 2121 Park Ave; adult/child $8/6; ⏲noon-5pm Wed-Sun) The best art museum in Miami Beach has a playfully futurist facade, and the collection isn't shabby either, ranging from 16th-century European religious works to Renaissance paintings.

World Erotic Art Museum MUSEUM

(Map p448; www.weam.com; 1205 Washington Ave; adult over 18yr $15; ⏲11am-10pm, to midnight Fri & Sat) Unfazed by SoBe's bare flesh? Something will get your attention here, with an amazingly extensive collection of naughty and erotic art, and even furniture depicting all sorts of parts and acts.

DOWNTOWN MIAMI

Downtown isn't a tourist magnet, outside of the Arsht performing arts center and sports arena. Still the **Metro-Dade Cultural Center Plaza** (Map p450; 101 W Flagler St) is home to two worthwhile museums; a $10 combo ticket is good for both.

History Miami MUSEUM

(Map p450; www.historymiami.org; adult/child $8/5; ⏲10am-5pm Tue-Fri, from noon Sat & Sun) South Florida's complex, excitable history of Seminole warriors, rumrunners, pirates, land grabbers, tourists and Latin American immigrants is succinctly and vividly told.

MIAMI IN...

Two Days

Focus your first day on South Beach. Bookend an afternoon of sunning and swimming with a walking tour through the **Art Deco Historic District** and a visit to **Wolfsonian-FIU**, which explains it all. That evening, sample some Haitian cuisine at **Tap Tap**, while away the evening with swanky cocktails at **Skybar** or, for a low-key brew, head to **Room**. For a late jolt, stop by the **World Erotic Art Museum**, open to midnight on weekends. Next morning, shop for Cuban music along Calle Ocho in **Little Havana**, followed by classic Cuban cuisine at **Versailles**. Go for a stroll at **Vizcaya Museum & Gardens**, cool off with a dip at the **Venetian Pool**, then end the day with dinner and cocktails at **Senora Martinez**.

Four Days

Follow the two-day itinerary, then head to the **Everglades** on day three and jump in a kayak. For your last day, immerse yourself in art and design in **Wynwood** and the **Design District**, followed by a visit to the **Miami Art Museum** or **Museum of Contemporary Art**. In the evening, party with the hipsters at the **Electric Pickle** or check out some live music: enjoy rock at **Tobacco Road** or Latin grooves at **La Covacha**.

Miami Beach

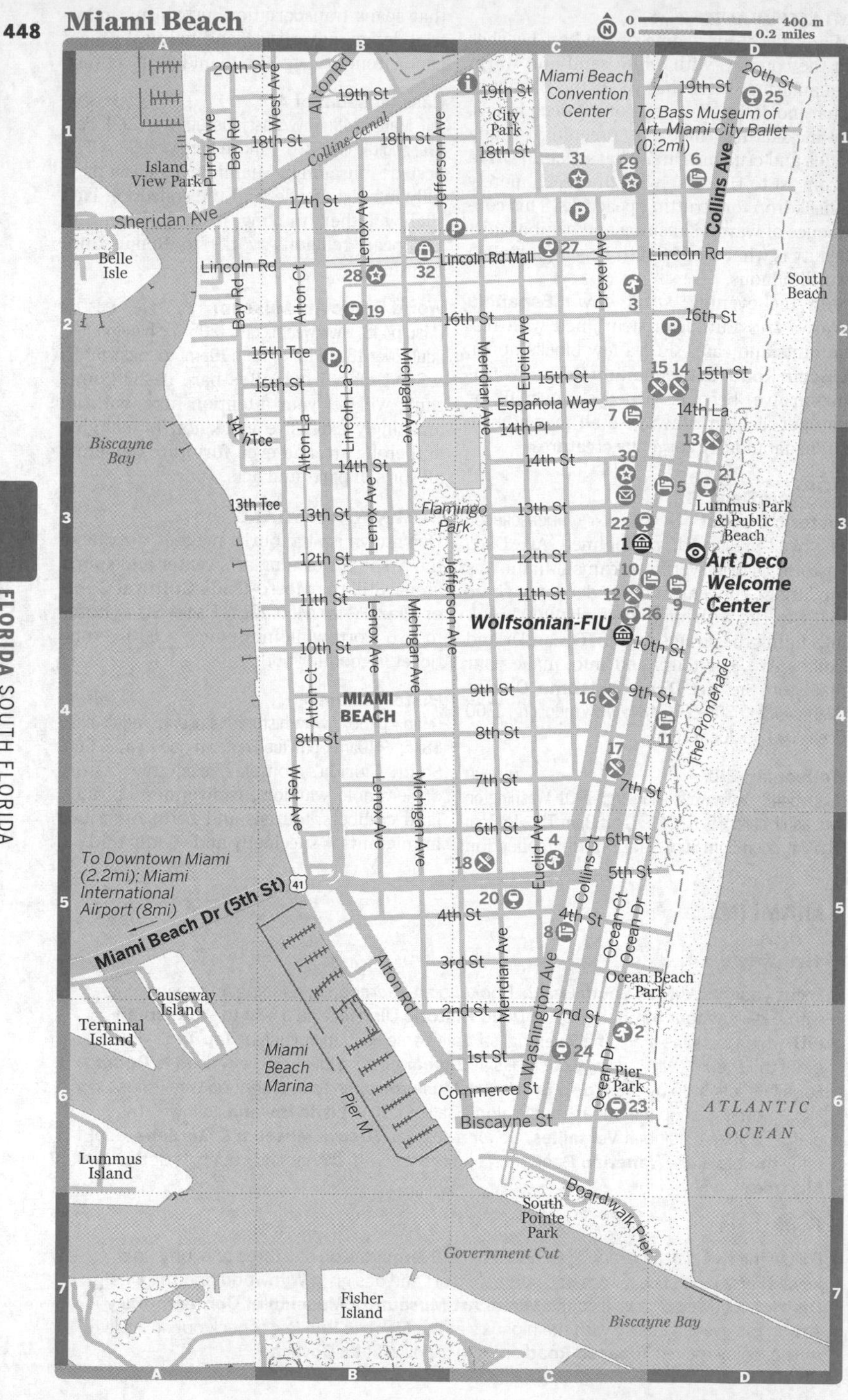

0 400 m
0 0.2 miles
20th St
19th St
18th St
17th St
Sheridan Ave
Collins Canal
Alton Rd
West Ave
Purdy Ave
Bay Rd
Island View Park
Belle Isle
Jefferson Ave
City Park
Miami Beach Convention Center
To Bass Museum of Art, Miami City Ballet (0.2mi)
Collins Ave
Lincoln Rd
Lincoln Rd Mall
Lenox Ave
Alton Ct
Drexel Ave
South Beach
16th St
15th Tce
15th St
Lincoln La S
Michigan Ave
Meridian Ave
Euclid Ave
Española Way
14th Pl
14th La
14th Tce
14th St
Biscayne Bay
Alton La
13th Tce
13th St
Flamingo Park
Lummus Park & Public Beach
12th St
11th St
Art Deco Welcome Center
Wolfsonian-FIU
10th St
9th St
MIAMI BEACH
8th St
The Promenade
7th St
6th St
5th St
4th St
3rd St
2nd St
1st St
Commerce St
Biscayne St
To Downtown Miami (2.2mi); Miami International Airport (8mi)
Miami Beach Dr (5th St)
41
Causeway Island
Terminal Island
Miami Beach Marina
Pier M
Washington Ave
Collins Ct
Ocean Ct
Ocean Dr
Ocean Beach Park
Pier Park
ATLANTIC OCEAN
Lummus Island
South Pointe Park
Boardwalk Pier
Government Cut
Fisher Island
Biscayne Bay

Miami Art Museum MUSEUM
(MAM; Map p450; www.miamiartmuseum.org; adult/child $8/free, 2nd Sat free; ⌚10am-5pm Tue-Fri, from noon Sat & Sun) Philip Johnson–designed building features rotating exhibits on post-WWII international art. It is scheduled to move to Bicentennial Park in 2013.

LITTLE HAVANA

As SW 8th St heads away from downtown, it becomes **Calle Ocho** (pronounced *kah*-yeh *oh*-cho, Spanish for 'Eighth Street'). That's when you know you've arrived in Little Havana, the most prominent community of Cuban Americans in the US. Despite the cultural monuments, this is no Cuban theme park. The district remains a living, breathing immigrant enclave, though one whose residents have become, admittedly, more broadly Central American. One of the best times to come is the last Friday of the month during **Viernes Culturales** (www.viernesculturales.com; ⌚6-11pm), or 'Cultural Fridays,' a street fair showcasing Latino artists and musicians.

TOP CHOICE **Máximo Gómez Park** PARK
(Map p452; cnr Calle Ocho & SW 15th Ave) Get a sensory-filled taste of old Cuba. It's also known as 'Domino Park,' and you'll understand why when you see the old-timers throwing bones.

Cuba Ocho GALLERY
(Map p452; ☎305-285-5880; cubaocho.com; 1465 SW 8th St; ⌚9am-6pm) The jewel of the Little Havana Art District, Cuba Ocho functions as a Cuban community center, art gallery and research outpost. Check for events and performances.

El Crédito Cigars CIGARS
(Map p452; ☎305-858-4162; 1106 SW 8th St) One of Miami's most popular cigar stores; watch *tabaqueros* hand-roll them.

FREE **Bay of Pigs Museum & Library** LIBRARY
(Map p452; www.bayofpigsmuseum.org; 1821 SW 9th St; ⌚9am-4pm Mon-Sat) History buffs can stop by to learn more about the ill-fated Cuban invasion and pay tribute to the 2506 Brigade.

DESIGN DISTRICT, WYNWOOD & LITTLE HAITI

Proving that SoBe doesn't hold the lease on hip, these two trendy areas north of downtown – all but deserted 25 years ago – have

Miami Beach

Top Sights
- Art Deco Welcome Center ... D3
- Wolfsonian-FIU ... C4

Sights
- 1 World Erotic Art Museum ... C3

Activities, Courses & Tours
- 2 Boucher Brothers Watersports ... C6
- 3 Fritz's Skate Shop ... C2
- 4 Miami Beach Bicycle Center ... C5

Sleeping
- 5 Beachcomber Hotel ... D3
- 6 Cadet Hotel ... D1
- 7 Clay Hotel & Miami Beach International Hostel ... C2
- 8 Hotel St Augustine ... C5
- 9 Kent Hotel ... D3
- 10 Lords Hotel ... C3
- 11 Pelican Hotel ... D4

Eating
- 12 11th Street Diner ... C3
- 13 Front Porch Cafe ... D3
- 14 Jerry's Famous Deli ... D2
- 15 Osteria del Teatro ... D2
- 16 Pizza Rustica ... C4
- 17 Puerto Sagua ... C4
- 18 Tap Tap ... C5

Drinking
- 19 Abbey Brewery ... B2
- 20 Abraxas ... C5
- 21 B Bar ... D3
- 22 Mansion ... C3
- 23 Nikki Beach Club ... C6
- 24 Room ... C6
- 25 Skybar ... D1
- 26 Twist ... C3
- 27 Zeke's Roadhouse ... C2

Entertainment
- 28 Colony Theatre ... B2
- 29 Fillmore Miami Beach at Jackie Gleason Theater ... C1
- 30 Jazid ... C3
- 31 New World Center ... C1

Shopping
- 32 Books & Books ... B2

Downtown Miami

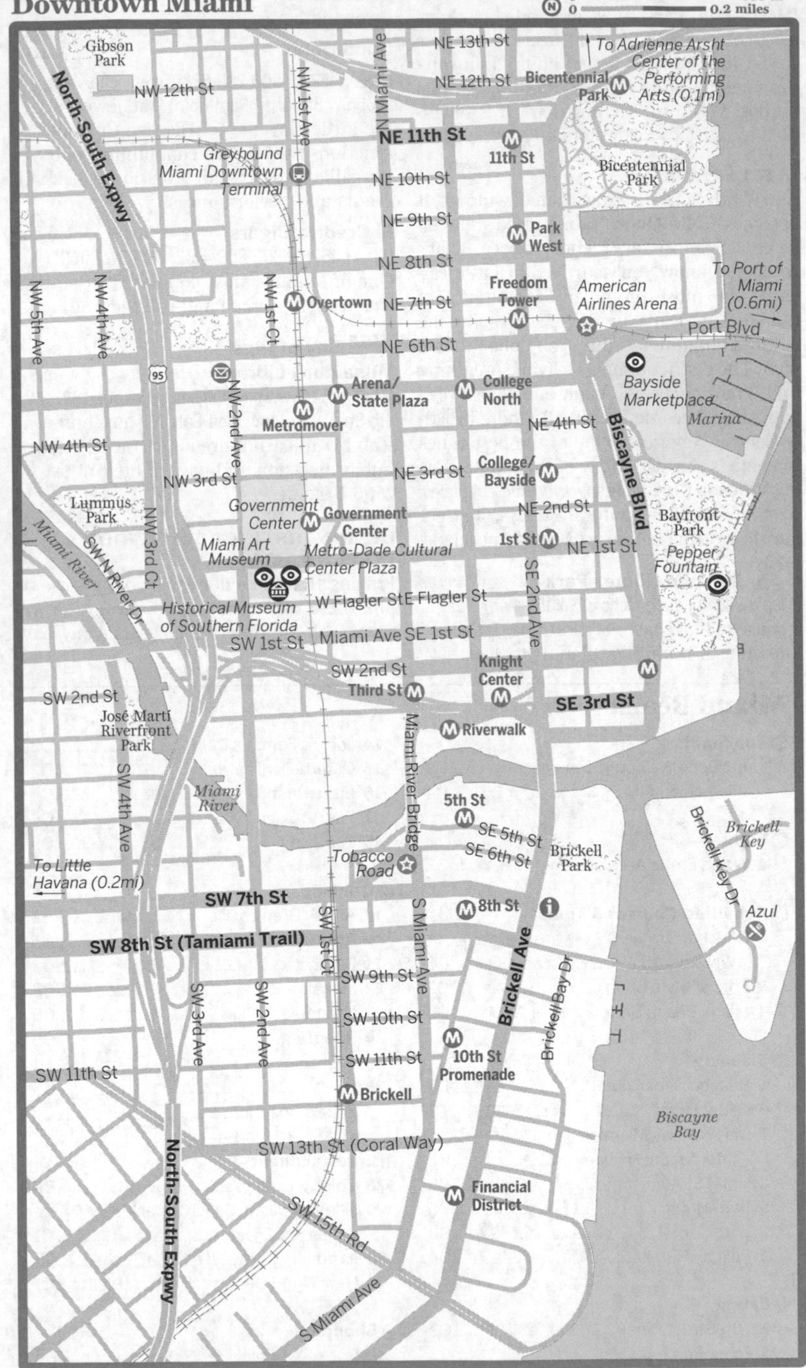

ensconced themselves as bastions of art and design. The **Design District** (Map p446; www.miamidesigndistrict.net) is a mecca for interior designers, home to dozens of galleries and contemporary furniture, fixture and design showrooms. Just south of the Design District, **Wynwood** is a notable arts district, with myriad galleries and art studios housed in abandoned factories and warehouses.

The home of Miami's Haitian refugees, **Little Haiti** is defined by brightly painted homes, markets and *botanicas* (voodoo shops).

Little Haiti Cultural Center GALLERY
(☎305-960-2969; www.miamigov.com/LHCulturalcenter; 212 NE 59th Tce; ⏲9am-5pm) Miami has the largest community of *Ayisens* (Haitians) in the world outside Haiti, and this cultural center is the place to learn about their story. Time your visit for **Big Night in Little Haiti** (www.bignightlittlehaiti.com), a monthly street celebration on the third Friday from 6pm to 10pm.

CORAL GABLES & COCONUT GROVE

For a slower pace and a more European feel, head inland. Designed as a 'model suburb' by George Merrick in the early 1920s, Coral Gables is a Mediterranean-style village that's centered around the shops and restaurants of the **Miracle Mile** (Map p452), a four-block section of Coral Way between Douglas and LeJeune Rds.

TOP CHOICE **Vizcaya Museum & Gardens** HISTORIC BUILDING
(Map p452; www.vizcayamuseum.org; 3251 S Miami Ave; adult/child $12/5; ⏲9:30am-4:30pm Wed-Mon) In Coconut Grove, this Italian Renaissance-style villa, the housing equivalent of a Fabergé egg, is Miami's most fairy-tale residence. The 70 rooms are stuffed with centuries-old furnishings and art, and the 30-acre grounds contain splendid formal gardens and Florentine gazebos.

Biltmore Hotel HISTORIC BUILDING
(Map p452; www.biltmorehotel.com; 1200 Anastasia Ave) Architecturally speaking, the crown jewel of Coral Gables is this magnificent edifice that once housed a speakeasy run by Al Capone. Even if you don't stay, drop by for afternoon tea or a drink at the bar and gawk at the pool.

Venetian Pool SWIMMING POOL
(Map p452; www.coralgablesvenetianpool.com; 2701 DeSoto Blvd; adult/child $11/7.35; ⏲10am-4:30pm) 'Swimming pool' doesn't even begin to describe this spring-fed goblet, made by filling in the limestone quarry used to build Coral Gables. With waterfalls, grottos and an Italianate feel, it looks like a vacation home for rich mermaids. Don't settle for a peek through wrought-iron fences – best to dive right in.

Lowe Art Museum MUSEUM
(Map p452; www.lowemuseum.org, 1301 Stanford Dr; adult/student $10/5; ⏲10am-4pm Tue-Sat, from noon Sun) The Lowe's tremendous collection satisfies a wide range of tastes, but it's particularly strong in Asian, African and South Pacific art and archaeology, and its pre-Columbian and Mesoamerican collection is stunning.

WYNWOOD GALLERIES

In Wynwood, Miami's hip proving ground for avant-garde art, 'Wypsters' (Wynwood hipsters) stock dozens of galleries with 'guerrilla' installations, new murals, graffiti and other inscrutableness. The neighborhood is roughly bound by NW 20th and NW 37th streets on the south and north, and N Miami Ave and NW 3rd Ave east and west.

The best way to experience the scene is to attend the **Wynwood and Design District Arts Walks** (www.artcircuits.com), with music, food and wine on the second Saturday of the month from 7pm to 10pm.

» **PanAmerican Art Projects** (www.panamericanart.com; 2450 NW 2nd Ave; ⏲9:30am-5:30pm Tue-Fri, from noon Sat) Showcases work from European and Chinese artists as well as those from the Americas.

» **Art Modern Gallery** (www.artmoderngallery.com; 175 NW 23rd St; ⏲noon-4:30pm Mon-Sat) Surprise! Focuses on modern, contemporary and pop art.

» **Curator's Voice Art Projects** (www.curatorsvoiceartprojects.com; 2509 NW 2nd Ave; ⏲9:30am-5:30pm Mon-Fri, from noon Sat) A large and elegant showplace for the avant-garde.

Little Havana, Coral Gables & Coconut Grove

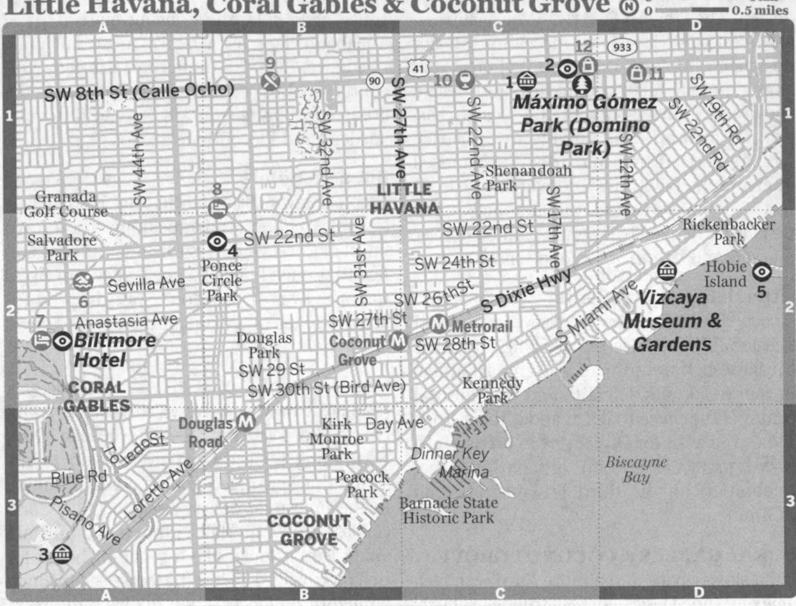

Little Havana

Top Sights
- Biltmore Hotel A2
- Máximo Gómez Park (Domino Park) C1
- Vizcaya Museum & Gardens D2

Sights
- 1 Bay of Pigs Museum & Library C1
- 2 Cuba Ocho C1
- 3 Lowe Art Museum A3
- 4 Miracle Mile B2
- 5 Sailboards Miami D2

Activities, Courses & Tours
- 6 Venetian Pool A2

Sleeping
- 7 Biltmore Hotel A2
- 8 Hotel St Michel B1

Eating
- 9 Versailles B1

Drinking
- 10 Hoy Como Ayer C1

Shopping
- Books & Books .... (see 4)
- 11 El Crédito Cigars D1
- 12 Little-Havana-To-Go C1

GREATER MIAMI

Museum of Contemporary Art MUSEUM
(MoCA; Map p446; www.mocanomi.org; 770 NE 125th St; adult/student $5/3; ⏲11am-5pm Tue & Thu-Sat, 1-9pm Wed, noon-5pm Sun) North of downtown, MoCA has frequently changing exhibitions focusing on international, national and emerging artists.

Ancient Spanish Monastery CHURCH
(Map p446; ☎305-945-1461; www.spanishmonastery.com; 16711 W Dixie Hwy; adult/child $8/4; ⏲10am-4pm Mon-Sat, from 11am Sun) Said to be the oldest building in the Western Hemisphere, this monastery was built in Segovia, Spain, in 1141 and shipped here by William Randolph Hearst. Call to confirm hours.

KEY BISCAYNE

Bill Baggs Cape Florida State Recreation Park PARK
(Map p446; www.floridastateparks.org/capeflorida; 1200 S Crandon Blvd; car/bicycle $8/2; ⏲8am-dusk) Serene beaches and stunning sunsets are just across the Rickenbacker Causeway (toll $1) at Key Biscayne, where you'll find the boardwalks and bike trails of this beachfront park. From the park's southern shore you can catch a glimpse of **Stiltsville**, seven colorful houses hovering on pilings in the shallow waters of Biscayne Bay.

Activities

Cycling & In-Line Skating

Skating or cycling the strip along Ocean Dr in South Beach is pure Miami; also try the Rickenbacker Causeway to Key Biscayne.

Fritz's Skate Shop CYCLING
(Map p448; ☎305-532-1954; www.fritzmiamibeach.com; 1620 Washington Ave; ⊙10am-10pm) Rentals and free in-line skate lessons (10:30am Sunday).

Miami Beach Bicycle Center CYCLING
(Map p448; www.bikemiamibeach.com; 601 5th St; per hr/day $8/24; ⊙10am-7pm Mon-Sat, to 5pm Sun) Convenient bike rentals in the heart of SoBe.

Water Sports

Boucher Brothers Watersports WATER SPORTS
(Map p448; www.boucherbrothers.com; 161 Ocean Dr; ⊙10:30am-4:30pm) Rentals and lessons for all sorts of water-related activities: kayaking, waterskiing, windsurfing, parasailing, waverunners and boats.

Sailboards Miami WATER SPORTS
(Map p452; www.sailboardsmiami.com; 1 Rickenbacker Causeway; ⊙10am-6pm Fri-Tue) The waters off Key Biscayne are perfect for windsurfing, kayaking and kiteboarding; get your gear and lessons here.

Miami for Children

The best beaches for kids are in Miami Beach north of 21st St, especially at 53rd St, which has a playground and public toilets, and the dune-packed beach around 73rd St. Also head south to Matheson Hammock Park (Map p446), which has calm artificial lagoons.

Miami Seaquarium AQUARIUM
(Map p446; ☎305-361-5705; www.miamiseaquarium.com; 4400 Rickenbacker Causeway; adult/child $38.95/29.95; ⊙9:30am-6pm, last entry 4:30pm) On Key Biscayne, this 38-acre marine-life park is more extensive than the usual aquarium; it also rehabilitates dolphins, manatees and sea turtles, and presents great animal shows. You can also swim with the dolphins.

Miami Children's Museum MUSEUM
(www.miamichildrensmuseum.org; 980 MacArthur Causeway; admission $15; ⊙10am-6pm) On Watson Island, between downtown Miami and Miami Beach, this hands-on museum has fun music and art studios, as well as some branded 'work' experiences that make it feel a tad corporate.

Jungle Island ZOO
(www.jungleisland.com; 1111 Parrot Jungle Trail, off MacArthur Causeway; adult/child $33/25; ⊙10am-5pm) Also on Watson Island, Jungle Island is packed with tropical birds, alligators, orangutans, chimps and (wait for it, *Napoleon Dynamite* fans) a liger, a cross between a lion and a tiger.

Miami Metrozoo ZOO
(www.miamimetrozoo.com; 12400 SW 152nd St; adult/child $16/12; ⊙9:30am-5:30pm, last entry 4pm) A huge zoo in far south Miami with all the exotic Asian and African species.

Monkey Jungle ZOO
(www.monkeyjungle.com; 14805 SW 216th St; adult/child $30/24; ⊙9:30am-5pm, last entry 4pm) The tagline – 'Where humans are caged and monkeys run free' – tells you all you need to know. Unforgettable fun, also in south Miami.

Tours

Miami Design Preservation League WALKING
(☎305-531-3484; guided tours adult/child $20/free; ⊙10:30am Fri-Wed, 6:30pm Thu) Learn about art deco and its icons on a 90-minute walking tour departing from the Art Deco Welcome Center (Map p448) at 1200 Ocean Dr, Miami Beach.

Dr Paul George WALKING, CYCLING
(☎305-375-1621; www.hmsf.org/programs-adult.htm; tours $25-42) Historian extraordinaire Dr Paul George leads fascinating bike, boat, coach and walking tours, including those that focus on Stiltsville. Get the full menu online.

South Beach Bike Tours CYCLING
(☎305-673-2002; www.southbeachbiketours.com; half-day tour per person $59) Three-hour, two-wheel tours of South Beach.

Festivals & Events

Calle Ocho Festival CULTURAL
(www.carnavalmiami.com) This massive street party in March is the culmination of Carnaval Miami, a 10-day celebration of Latin culture.

Winter Music Conference MUSIC
(www.wmcon.com) The SXSW of dance music and electronica takes place every March.

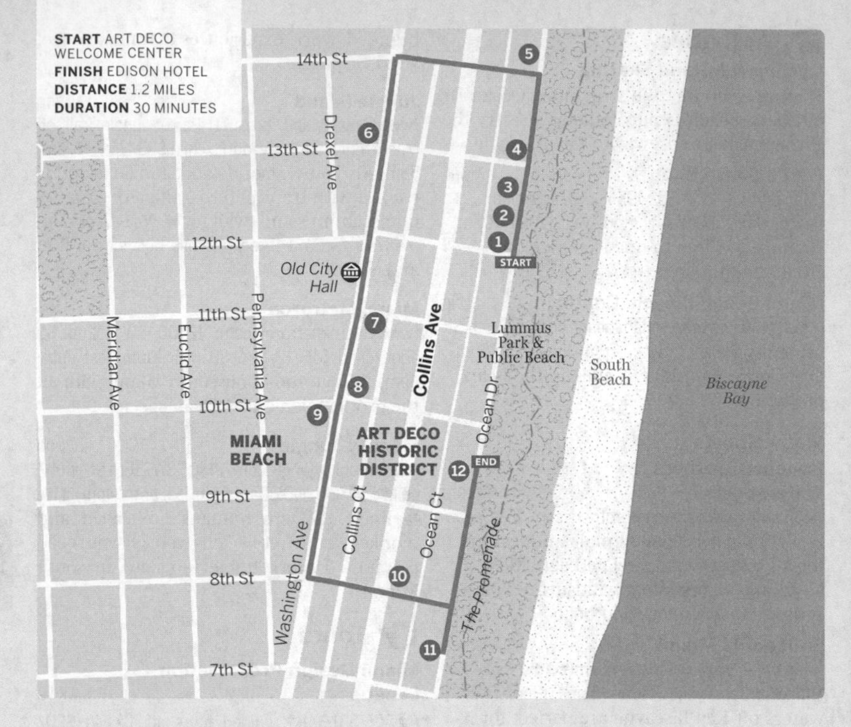

Walking Tour

Art Deco Magic

There are excellent walking tours available for the Art Deco Historic District – both guided and self-guided – but if you just want to hit the highlights, follow this quick and easy path.

Start at the 1 **Art Deco Welcome Center** at the corner of Ocean Dr and 12th St, and head inside for a taste of deco style. Next, go north on Ocean Dr. Between 12th and 14th Sts, you'll see three classic examples of deco hotels: the 2 **Leslie**, with classic 'eyebrows' and a typically boxy shape; the 3 **Carlyle**, which was featured in the film *The Birdcage;* and the graceful 4 **Cardozo Hotel**, with sleek, rounded edges. At 14th St, peek inside the 5 **Winter Haven Hotel** to see its fabulous terrazzo floors.

Turn left and head along 14th St to Washington Ave, and turn left again to find the 6 **US Post Office** at 13th St. Step inside to admire the domed ceiling and marble stamp tables, and try whispering into the domed ceiling. Two blocks down on your left is the 7 **11th St Diner**, a gleaming aluminum deco-style Pullman car where you can also stop for lunch. At 10th St, you'll find the 8 **Wolfsonian-FIU**, an excellent museum with many deco-era treasures, and across the street is the beautifully restored 9 **Hotel Astor**.

Turn left on 8th St and head east to Collins Ave. On the corner, you'll see 10 **Hotel** – originally the Tiffany Hotel and still topped by a deco-style neon spire bearing that name. Continue to Ocean Dr and turn right to see the 11 **Colony Hotel** and its famous neon sign, then double back to find the 1935 12 **Edison Hotel**, another creation of deco legend Henry Hohauser, half a block past 9th St.

Goombay Festival CULTURE
(www.goombayfestivalcoconutgrove.com) This massive fest, held in Coconut Grove on the first week of June, celebrates Bahamian culture.

White Party MUSIC
(www.whiteparty.net) This weeklong extravaganza in November draws more than 15,000 gay men and women for nonstop partying all over town.

Art Basel Miami Beach ART
(www.artbaselmiamibeach.com) An internationally important art show held each December – a sister event to Art Basel Switzerland.

Sleeping

Miami Beach is the well-hyped mecca for stylish boutique hotels in renovated art-deco buildings. To find them and other chic options, check out www.miamiboutiquehotels.com. Rates vary widely by season and all bets are off during spring break, when rates can quintuple; the summer months are slowest. For hotel parking, expect to pay $20 to $35 a night.

SOUTH BEACH

TOP CHOICE **Pelican Hotel** BOUTIQUE HOTEL $$$
(Map p448; ☎305-673-3373; www.pelicanhotel.com; 826 Ocean Dr; r $225-345;) The name and deco facade don't hint at anything unusual, but the decorators went wild inside with great themes such as 'Best Whorehouse,' 'Executive Zebra' and 'Me Tarzan, You Vain.'

TOP CHOICE **Hotel St Augustine** BOUTIQUE HOTEL $$$
(Map p448; ☎305-532-0570; www.hotelstaugustine.com; 347 Washington Ave; r $180-280;) Wood that's blonder than Barbie and a crisp-and-clean deco theme combine to create one of South Beach's most elegant yet stunningly modern sleeps. A hip-and-homey standout.

Lords Hotel BOUTIQUE HOTEL $$
(Map p448; ☎877-448-4754; www.lordsouthbeach.com; 1120 Collins Ave; r $120-240, ste $330-540;) The epicenter of South Beach's gay scene is this cream puff of a hotel, with rooms decked out in lemony yellow and offset by pop art. Lords is hip, yet doesn't affect an attitude.

Kent Hotel BOUTIQUE HOTEL $$
(Map p448; ☎305-604-5068; www.thekenthotel.com; 1131 Collins Ave; r $79-220;) The lobby is a kick, filled with fuchsia and electric-orange geometric furniture plus bright Lucite toy blocks. Rooms continue the playfulness. One of South Beach's better deals.

Cadet Hotel BOUTIQUE HOTEL $$$
(Map p448; ☎305-672-6688; www.cadethotel.com; 1701 James Ave; r $170-280;) This unassuming little boutique hotel has the perfect deco aesthetic, with creative embellishments everywhere and a shaded verandah that's an oasis of calm.

Miami Beach International Hostel HOSTEL $
(Map p448; ☎305-534-2988; www.clayhotel.com; 1438 Washington Ave; dm $25-29, r $60-120;) Nestled off Española Way and just blocks from the beach, this century-old Spanish-style building has an illustrious history and clean, affordable rooms.

Beachcomber Hotel HOTEL $$
(Map p448; ☎305-531-3755; www.beachcombermiami.com; 1340 Collins Ave; r $89-189;) Inside the green-banana-colored exterior, the Beachcomber has 29 cozy rooms.

NORTHERN MIAMI BEACH

TOP CHOICE **Circa 39** BOUTIQUE HOTEL $$
(☎305-538-3900; www.circa39.com; 3900 Collins Ave; r $90-150;) If you love South Beach style but loathe the South Beach attitude, Circa has got your back. Combines one of the funkiest lobbies in Miami, hip icy-blue-and-white rooms and a welcoming attitude. Web rates are phenomenal.

CORAL GABLES

TOP CHOICE **Biltmore Hotel** HOTEL $$$
(Map p452; ☎305-913-3158; www.biltmorehotel.com; 1200 Anastasia Ave; r $240-400;) This 1926 hotel is a National Historic Landmark and an icon of luxury. Standard rooms may be small, but public spaces are palatial; its fabulous pool is the largest hotel pool in the country.

Hotel St Michel HOTEL $$
(Map p452; ☎305-444-1666; www.hotelstmichel.com; 162 Alcazar Ave; r $125-220;) You could conceivably think you're in Europe in this vaulted place at Coral Gables, with inlaid floors, old-world charm and just 28 rooms.

Eating

Florida's most international city has an international-level food scene.

SOUTH BEACH

TOP CHOICE **Tap Tap** HAITIAN $$
(Map p448; ☎305-672-2898; www.taptaprestaurant.com; 819 5th St; mains $9-20; ⏰noon-11pm Mon-Thu, to midnight Fri & Sat) In this tropi-psychedelic Haitian eatery, you dine under bright murals of Papa Legba, enjoying cuisine that's a happy marriage of West Africa, France and the Caribbean: try spicy pumpkin soup, curried goat and *mayi moulen*, a signature side of cornmeal.

TOP CHOICE **Osteria del Teatro** ITALIAN $$
(Map p448; ☎305-538-7850; http://osteriadelteatromiami.com; 1443 Washington Ave; mains $16-31; ⏰6-11pm Mon-Thu, to 1am Fri-Sun) Stick to the specials of one of Miami's oldest and best Italian restaurants, and you can't go wrong. Better yet, let the gracious Italian waiters coddle and order for you. They never pick wrong.

Puerto Sagua CUBAN $
(Map p448; ☎305-673-1115; 700 Collins Ave; mains $6-17; ⏰7:30am-2am) Pull up to the counter for authentic, tasty and inexpensive *ropa vieja* (shredded beef), black beans and *arroz con pollo* (rice with chicken) – plus some of the best Cuban coffee in town – at this beloved Cuban diner.

11th St Diner DINER $
(Map p448; www.eleventhstreetdiner.com; 1065 Washington Ave; mains $8-16; ⏰24hr) This deco diner housed inside a gleaming Pullman train car sees round-the-clock activity and is especially popular with people staggering home from clubs.

Pizza Rustica PIZZERIA $
(Map p448; www.pizza-rustica.com; 863 Washington Ave; slices $3-5; ⏰11am-6pm) Big square slices that are a meal in themselves – when you're wandering around hungry, there's nothing better. Also at 1447 Washington Ave and 667 Lincoln Rd.

Jerry's Famous Deli DELI $$
(Map p448; www.jerrysfamousdeli.com; 1450 Collins Ave; mains $9-18; ⏰24hr) Jerry's does it all – from pastrami melts to Chinese chicken salad to fettuccine Alfredo – and does it all day long. It also does it big, with huge portions served in a large, open, deco space.

Front Porch Cafe AMERICAN $$
(Map p448; ☎305-531-8300; 1418 Ocean Dr; mains $10-18; ⏰7am-11pm) Pull up a chair on the front porch of the Penguin Hotel for great breakfasts, huge portions and reasonable prices, all overlooking the ocean.

DOWNTOWN MIAMI

Azul FUSION $$$
(Map p450; ☎305-913-8288; 500 Brickell Key Dr; mains $30-72; ⏰7-11pm Mon-Sat) Be pampered at this terrific restaurant on Brickell Key with a stellar Asian fusion menu. In addition to a massive wine list and waterfront views of downtown, Azul offers some of the best service in Miami.

LITTLE HAVANA

Versailles CUBAN $
(Map p452; ☎305-444-0240; 3555 SW 8th St; mains $5-20; ⏰8am-2am) *The* Cuban restaurant in town is not to be missed. It finds room for everybody in the large, cafeteria-style dining rooms.

DESIGN DISTRICT & WYNWOOD

TOP CHOICE **Senora Martinez** FUSION $$$
(☎305-573-5474; www.sramartinez.com; 4000 NE 2nd Ave; mains $13-30; ⏰noon-3pm Tue-Sun, 6-11pm

EATING MIAMI: LATIN AMERICAN SPICE

Thanks to its immigrant heritage, Miami is legendary for its authentic Cuban, Haitian, Brazilian and other Latin American cuisines. Cuban food is a mix of Caribbean, African and Latin American influences, and the fertile cross-pollination of these traditions has given rise to endlessly creative, tasty gourmet fusions, sometimes dubbed 'nuevo Latino,' 'nouvelle Floridian' or 'Floribbean' cuisine.

For a good introduction to Cuban food, sidle up to a Cuban *loncheria* (snack bar) and order a *pan cubano:* a buttered, grilled baguette stuffed with ham, roast pork, cheese, mustard and pickles. For dinner, order the classic *ropa vieja:* shredded flank steak cooked in tomatoes and peppers, and accompanied by fried plantains, black beans and yellow rice.

Other treats to look for include Haitian *griots* (marinated fried pork), Jamaican jerk chicken, Brazilian BBQ, Central American *gallo pinto* (red beans and rice) and *batidos*, a milky, refreshing Latin American fruit smoothie.

Tue-Thu, to midnight Fri-Sat, to 10pm Sun;) One of Miami's most exciting top-end restaurants, Senora Martinez pushes the boundaries of experimentation and plain good food. The menu is eclectic – exemplifying Miami itself.

Sustain AMERICAN **$$$**
(305-424-9079; www.sustainmiami.com; 3252 NE 1st Ave; mains $13-30; 11:30am-3pm & 5-10:30pm;) Sustain is one of Miami's leading – and more affordable – purveyors of locally sourced, organically grown food. The lovely dining room and fantastic cuisine make a meal both carnivores and vegetarians adore.

Drinking & Entertainment

Miami truly comes alive at night. There is always something going on, and usually till the wee hours, with many bars staying open till 3am or 5am. For events calendars and gallery, bar and club reviews, check out www.cooljunkie.com, www.miaminights.com and www.beachedmiami.com.

Bars

There are tons of bars along Ocean Dr; a happy-hour meander unearths half-price drinks.

TOP CHOICE **Room** BAR
(Map p448; www.theotheroom.com; 100 Collins Ave) This dark, atmospheric, boutique beer bar is a gem: hip and sexy as hell but with a low-key attitude. Per the name, it's small and gets crowded.

Abraxas BAR
(Map p448; 407 Meridian Ave) In a classic deco building, Abraxas couldn't be friendlier. Uncrowded and serving fantastic beer from around the world, it's tucked away in a residential part of South Beach.

Zeke's Roadhouse BAR
(Map p448; 625 Lincoln Rd) Great beer selection, and lots of it, cheaply priced; the outdoor seating on Lincoln Rd doesn't hurt either.

Electric Pickle BAR
(www.electricpicklemiami.com; 2826 N Miami Ave) Wynwood's arty hipsters become glamorous club kids in this two-story hepcat hot spot. The Pickle is sexy, gorgeous and literate.

Abbey Brewery BAR
(Map p448; www.abbeybrewinginc.com; 1115 16th St) The only brewpub in South Beach is packed with friendly folks listening to the Grateful Dead and slinging back the excellent homebrew.

B Bar BAR
(Map p448; Betsy Hotel, 1440 Ocean Ave) This basement bar, under the Betsy Hotel, draws the usual crowd of beautiful, in-the-know, SoBe-tastic types and has some unusual entertainment: an odd, low-hanging reflective ceiling that ripples when touched.

Nightclubs

To increase your chances of getting into the major nightclubs, call ahead to get on the guest list. Having gorgeous, well-dressed females in your group doesn't hurt either (unless you're going to a gay bar). In South Beach clubs and live music venues, covers range from $20 to $25, and half that elsewhere.

Bardot CLUB
(305-576-5570; www.bardotmiami.com; 3456 N Miami Ave) In Wynwood, Bardot is a saucy vision of decadent excess, yet the glam local scene is more laid-back than SoBe.

Skybar CLUB
(Map p448; 305-695-3900; Shore Club, 1901 Collins Ave) Sip chic cocktails on the alfresco terrace – they're too expensive to guzzle. Or, if you're 'somebody,' head for the indoor A-list Red Room. Both have a luxurious Moroccan theme and beautiful people-watching.

Twist CLUB
(Map p448; 305-538-9478; www.twistsobe.com; 1057 Washington Ave) This (free) gay hangout has serious staying power and a little bit of something for everyone, including dancing, drag shows and go-go dancers.

Nikki Beach Club CLUB
(Map p448; 305-538-1111; www.nikkibeach.com; 1 Ocean Dr; cover from $25) Lounge on beds or inside your own tipi in this beach-chic outdoor space that's right on the sand.

Mansion CLUB
(Map p448; 305-532-1525; www.mansionmiami.com; 1235 Washington Ave; cover from $20; Thu-Sun) *Was that Lindsay Lohan?* Prepare for some quality time with the velvet rope and wear fly duds to enter this grandiose, exclusive megaclub, which lives up to its name.

Live Music

La Covacha LIVE MUSIC
(305-594-3717; www.lacovacha.com; 10730 NW 25th St, Doral) Well-loved, tourist-free, very

hip Latin club for up-and-coming bands and DJs. A long drive.

Tobacco Road BAR
(Map p450; ☎305-374-1198; www.tobacco-road.com; 626 S Miami Ave) Old-school roadhouse around since 1912; blues, jazz and occasional impromptu jams by well-known rockers.

Hoy Como Ayer LIVE MUSIC
(Map p452; ☎305-541-2631; www.hoycomoayer.us; 2212 SW 8th St) Authentic Cuban music.

Jazid LOUNGE
(Map p448; ☎305-673-9372; www.jazid.net; 1342 Washington Ave) Jazz in a candlelit lounge; upstairs, DJ-fueled soul and hip-hop.

Churchill's BAR
(☎305-757-1807; www.churchillspub.com; 5501 NE 2nd Ave) The best of indie/punk music – as well as UK football broadcasts.

Theater & Culture

Adrienne Arsht Center for the Performing Arts PERFORMING ARTS
(off Map p450; ☎305-949-6722; www.arshtcenter.org; 1300 Biscayne Blvd) Showcases jazz from around the world, as well as theater, dance, music, comedy and more.

New World Center CLASSICAL MUSIC
(Map p448; ☎305-673-3330; www.nws.edu; 500 17th St) The new home of the acclaimed New World Symphony is one of the most beautiful buildings in Miami.

Colony Theater PERFORMING ARTS
(Map p448; ☎305-674-1040; www.mbculture.com; 1040 Lincoln Rd) Everything – from off-Broadway productions to ballet and movies – plays in this renovated 1934 art-deco showpiece.

Miami City Ballet DANCE
(off Map p448; ☎305-929-7000; www.miamicityballet.org; 2200 Liberty Ave) One of the USA's premier Ballanchine companies.

Fillmore Miami Beach at Jackie Gleason Theater PERFORMING ARTS
(Map p448; ☎305-673-7300; www.gleasontheater.com; 1700 Washington Ave) Miami Beach's premier showcase for Broadway shows, headliners and the Miami City Ballet.

Sports

Miami hosts pro teams in all four major US team sports.

Miami Dolphins FOOTBALL
(www.miamidolphins.com; Sun Life Stadium, 2269 Dan Marino Blvd; tickets from $35) NFL football season runs from August to December.

Florida Marlins BASEBALL
(www.marlins.mlb.com; Sun Life Stadium, 2269 Dan Marino Blvd; tickets from $15) MLB baseball season is May to September.

Miami Heat BASKETBALL
(Map p450; www.nba.com/heat; American Airlines Arena, 601 Biscayne Blvd; tickets from $20) NBA basketball season is November to April.

Florida Panthers HOCKEY
(☎954-835-7000; http://panthers.nhl.com; Bank Atlantic Center, 1 Panther Pkwy, Sunrise; tickets from $15) NHL hockey season runs mid-October to mid-April.

Shopping

Browse for one-of-a-kind and designer items at the South Beach boutiques around Collins Ave between 6th and 9th Sts and along Lincoln Rd mall. For unique items, try Little Havana and the Design District.

Bal Harbour Shops MALL
(www.balharbourshops.com; 9700 Collins Ave) Miami's most elegant mall.

Bayside Marketplace MALL
(Map p450; www.baysidemarketplace.com; 401 Biscayne Blvd) Near the marina, a buzzy if touristy shopping and entertainment hub.

Little-Havana-to-Go CUBAN
(Map p452; www.littlehavanatogo.com; 1442 SW 8th St/Calle Ocho) Stocks authentic Cuban goods and clothing.

Books & Books BOOKS
(www.booksandbooks.com; 927 Lincoln Rd) Best indie bookstore in South Florida; the original location is at 265 Aragon Ave and there's another in Bal Harbour Shops.

Information

Dangers & Annoyances

Miami has a few areas considered dangerous at night: Little Haiti, stretches of the Miami riverfront and Biscayne Blvd, and areas below 5th St in South Beach. Downtown, use caution near the Greyhound station and shantytowns around causeways, bridges and overpasses.

Emergency

Beach Patrol (☎305-673-7714)

Internet Access

Most hotels offer wi-fi access (as do Starbucks), and libraries also have free internet terminals.

Internet Resources

Art Circuits (www.artcircuits.com) Insider info on art events; neighborhood-by-neighborhood gallery maps.

Mango & Lime (www.mangoandlime.net) The best local food blog.

Miami Beach 411 (www.miamibeach411.com) A great general guide for Miami Beach visitors.

Media

El Nuevo Herald (www.elnuevoherald.com) Spanish-language daily published by the *Miami Herald*.

Miami Herald (www.miamiherald.com) The city's major English-language daily.

Miami New Times (www.miaminewtimes.com) Edgy, alternative weekly.

Medical Services

Mount Sinai Medical Center (☎305-674-2121, 24hr visitors medical line 305-674-2222; 4300 Alton Rd) The area's best emergency room.

Money

Bank of America has branch offices all over Miami and Miami Beach. To get currency exchanged, go to **Amex** (www.amex.com; 100 N Biscayne Blvd; ⏲9am-5pm Mon-Fri) in downtown Miami.

Tourist Information

Greater Miami & the Beaches Convention & Visitors Bureau (☎305-539-3000; www.miamiandbeaches.com; 701 Brickell Ave, 27th fl; ⏲8:30am-5pm Mon-Fri)

Miami Beach Chamber of Commerce (☎305-672-1300; www.miamibeachchamber.com; 1920 Meridian Ave; ⏲9am-5pm Mon-Fri)

Getting There & Away

Miami International Airport (MIA; www.miami-airport.com) is about 6 miles west of downtown and is accessible by **SuperShuttle** (☎305-871-8210; www.supershuttle.com), which costs about $26 to South Beach.

Greyhound goes to all major cities in Florida. Main terminals are the **Airport terminal** (☎305-871-1810; 4111 NW 27th St) and **Miami Downtown terminal** (☎305-374-6160; 1012 NW 1st Ave).

Amtrak (☎305-835-1222; 8303 NW 37th Ave) has a main Miami terminal. The **Tri-Rail** (☎800-874-7245; www.tri-rail.com) commuter system serves Miami (with a free transfer to Miami's transit system) and MIA, Fort Lauderdale and its airport, and West Palm Beach and its airport ($11.55 round-trip).

Getting Around

Metro-Dade Transit (☎305-891-3131; www.miami dade.gov/transit) runs the local Metrobus and Metrorail ($2), as well as the free **Metromover** monorail serving downtown.

Fort Lauderdale

Fort Lauderdale was once known as spring break party central, but like the drunken teens who once littered the beach, the town has grown up and moved on. It's now a stylish, sophisticated city known more for museums, Venice-style waterways, yachting and open-air cafes than wet T-shirt contests and beer bongs. It's also a very popular gay and lesbian destination, along with most of South Florida. Of course, the beach is as lovely as always.

For local information, head to the **visitor bureau** (☎954-765-4466; www.sunny.org; 100 E Broward Blvd, Suite 200).

Sights & Activities

Fort Lauderdale Beach & Promenade BEACH

Fort Lauderdale's promenade – a wide, brick, palm-tree-dotted pathway swooping along the beach and A1A – is a magnet for runners, in-line skaters, walkers and cyclists. The white-sand beach, meanwhile, is one of the nation's cleanest and best, stretching 7 miles to Lauderdale-by-the-Sea, with dedicated family-, gay- and dog-friendly sections. Boating, diving, snorkeling and fishing are all extremely popular.

Museum of Art MUSEUM

(www.moaflnsu.org; 1 E Las Olas Blvd; adult/child $10/7; ⏲11am-6pm, to 8pm Wed, noon-5pm Sun) A curvaceous Florida standout with an impressive collection of modern masters (Picasso, Matisse, Warhol), plus Cuban, African and South American art.

Museum of Discovery & Science MUSEUM

(www.mods.org; 401 SW 2nd St; adult/child $11/9; ⏲10am-5pm Mon-Sat, noon-6pm Sun) A 52ft kinetic-energy sculpture greets you, and fun exhibits include Gizmo City and Runways to Rockets – where it actually *is* rocket science. Plus there's an Everglades exhibit and IMAX theater.

Fort Lauderdale Antique Car Museum MUSEUM

(www.antiquecarmuseum.org; 1527 Packard Ave; adult/child $8/5; ⏲9am-3pm Mon-Fri) Nostalgic car-lovers should motor here; it features 22 vintage Packards and auto memorabilia.

Bonnet House HISTORIC HOME

(www.bonnethouse.org; 900 N Birch Rd; adult/child $20/16, grounds only $10; ⏲10am-4pm Tue-Sat,

GAY & LESBIAN FORT LAUDERDALE

Sure, Miami's South Beach is a mecca for gay travelers, but Fort Lauderdale has long been nipping at the high heels of its southern neighbor. Plus, compared to South Beach, Lauderdale's scene is less exclusive and more rainbow-flag oriented.

Fort Lauderdale is home to several dozen gay bars and clubs, as many gay guesthouses, and a couple of way-gay residential hubs, including **Victoria Park**, the established gay ghetto, and **Wilton Manors**, more recently gay-gentrified and boasting endless nightlife options.

Two places catering exclusively to gay male clients, and that just happen to be clothing optional, are the stylish **Schubert Resort** (954-763-7434; www.schubertresort.com; 855 NE 20th Ave; ste $99-309;) and **Pineapple Point** (888-844-7295; www.pineapplepoint.com; 315 NE 16th Tce; r $199-279, ste $299-399;), an intimate guesthouse tucked away in a quiet residential neighborhood.

For more information on local gay life, visit www.gayftlauderdale.com. Other resources that cover South Florida include the glossy weekly *Hot Spots* (www.hotspotsmagazine.com), the insanely comprehensive www.jumponmarkslist.com, and www.sunny.org/glbt.

from 11am Sun) Wandering the 35 acres of lush, subtropical gardens, you might just spot the resident Brazilian squirrel monkeys. The art-filled house is open to guided tours only.

Gondola Man GONDOLA RIDE
(877-926-2467; www.gondolaman.com; ride $125) Explore the 'Venice of America' with a romantic ride that takes you up and down the canals of the rich and famous.

Water Taxi WATER TAXI
(www.watertaxi.com; all-day pass adult/child $20/12) For the best unofficial tour of the city, hop on the water taxi, whose drivers offer a lively narration as they ply Fort Lauderdale's canals and waterways. Check online for locations.

Sleeping

The area from Rio Mar St in the south to Vistamar St in the north, and from Hwy A1A in the east to Bayshore Dr in the west, offers the highest concentration of accommodations in all price ranges. Check out **Superior Small Lodgings** (www.sunny.org/ssl).

TOP CHOICE **Pillars** B&B $$$
(954-467-9639; www.pillarshotel.com; 111 N Birch Rd; r $179-520;) From the harp in the sitting area to the private balconies and the intimate prearranged dinners for two, this tiny boutique B&B radiates hushed good taste. A block from the beach, facing one of the best sunsets in town.

Riverside Hotel HOTEL $$
(954-467-0671; www.riversidehotel.com; 620 E Las Olas Blvd; r $143-200;) This Fort Lauderdale landmark – fabulously located downtown on Las Olas – has three room types: more modern rooms in the newer tower, restored rooms in the original property and the more old-fashioned 'classic' rooms.

Shell Motel MOTEL $
(954-463-1723; www.sableresorts.com; 330 Bayshore Dr; r/ste from $85/150;) One of six modest motels owned by the same company, this sweet Old Florida–style spot has bright, clean rooms surrounding a small pool. Splash out for a roomy suite.

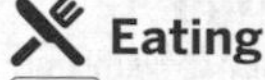

Eating

TOP CHOICE **Gran Forno** ITALIAN $
(www.granforno.com; 1235 E Las Olas Blvd; mains $6-12; 7:30am-7pm Tue-Sun) The best lunch spot in downtown Fort Lauderdale is this delightfully old-school Milanese-style bakery and cafe: warm crusty pastries, bubbling pizzas, and fat golden loaves of ciabatta, sliced and stuffed with ham, roast peppers, pesto and other delicacies.

Rustic Inn SEAFOOD $$$
(954-584-1637; www.rusticinn.com; 4331 Ravenswood Rd; mains $14-45; 10:30am-10:45pm, to 9pm Sun) Hungry locals at this messy, noisy crab house use wooden mallets at long, newspaper-covered tables to get at the Dungeness, blue and golden crabs drenched in garlic.

Casablanca Cafe MEDITERRANEAN $$$
(954-764-3500; 3049 Alhambra St; mains $10-38; 11:30am-1am Sun-Tue, to 2am Wed-Sat) Try

to score a seat on the upstairs balcony of this Moroccan-style home where Mediterranean-inspired food and Florida-style ocean views are served. Live music Wednesdays through Sundays.

11th Street Annex AMERICAN $
(http://twouglysisters.com; 14 SW 11th St; lunch $9; ⏲11:30am-2pm Mon-Fri) In this off-the-beaten-path peach cottage, the 'two ugly sisters' serve whatever strikes their fancy: perhaps brie mac 'n' cheese, chicken confit and sour cream chocolate cake. Most of the vegetables are grown from the cottage's garden.

Cafe Sharaku ASIAN FUSION $$$
(☎954-563-2888; www.cafesharaku.com; 2736 N Federal Hwy; mains $25-32; ⏲11:30am-3pm Tue-Fri, 5:30-10pm Tue-Sun) Local foodies whisper to one another about this exquisite 18-seat bistro, but the cat's out of the bag: Sharaku is a fabulous temple of gemlike fish and seafood creations.

Drinking & Entertainment

Bars generally stay open until 4am on weekends and 2am during the week. Meander the **Riverwalk** (www.goriverwalk.com) along the New River, where you'll find the alfresco mall **Las Olas Riverfront** (SW 1st Ave at Las Olas Blvd), with stores, restaurants, a movie theater and entertainment.

Elbo Room BAR
(www.elboroom.com; 241 S Fort Lauderdale Beach Blvd) Featured in the movie *Where the Boys Are,* Elbo Room hangs onto its somewhat seedy reputation as one of the oldest and diviest bars around.

Lulu's Bait Shack BAR
(www.lulusbaitshack.com; 17 S Fort Lauderdale Beach Blvd) Lures 'em in with buckets of beer, bowls of mussels and fishbowl drinks at the ocean's edge.

Voodoo Lounge NIGHTCLUB
(www.voodooloungeflorida.com; 111 SW 2nd Ave; ⏲10pm-4am Wed-Sun) A massive nightclub – look for Sunday drag nights, Latin nights and other themed events.

Getting There & Around

The **Fort Lauderdale-Hollywood International Airport** (FLL; www.fll.net) is served by more than 35 airlines, some with nonstop flights from Europe. A taxi from the airport to downtown costs around $20.

The **Greyhound station** (☎954-764-6551; 515 NE 3rd St at Federal Hwy) is four blocks from Broward Central Terminal, with multiple daily services. The **train station** (200 SW 21st Tce) serves **Amtrak** (☎800-872-7245; www.amtrak.com), and the **Tri-Rail** (www.tri-rail.com) has services to Miami and Palm Beach.

Hail a **Sun Trolley** (www.suntrolley.com; per ride 50¢) for rides between downtown, the beach, Las Olas and the Riverfront.

Palm Beach & Around

Palm Beach isn't all yachts and mansions – but just about. This area, 45 miles north of Fort Lauderdale, is where railroad baron Henry Flagler built his winter retreat, and it's also home to Donald Trump's **Mar-a-Lago** (cnr Southern & S Ocean Blvds). In other words, if you're looking for middle-class tourism or Florida kitsch, keep driving. Contact the Palm Beach County **Convention & Visitor Bureau** (☎800-544-2756; www.palmbeachfl.com; 1555 Palm Beach Lakes Blvd) in West Palm Beach for area information and maps.

BOCA RATON

Halfway between Fort Lauderdale and Palm Beach is this largely residential stretch of picturesque coast that's been preserved from major development. For a great taste, hike the elevated boardwalks of the **Gumbo Limbo Nature Center** (www.gumbolimbo.

FLORIDA'S SEMINOLES

If you want to learn about Florida's Seminole people, the best place is the **Ah-Tah-Thi-Ki Museum** (☎877-902-1113; www.ahtahthiki.com; Big Cypress Seminole Indian Reservation, Clewiston; adult/child & senior $9/6; ⏲9am-5pm), 17 miles north of I-75, west of Fort Lauderdale. The museum is set within a cypress dome cut through with an interpretive boardwalk, so from the start it strikes a balance between environmentalism and education. Permanent exhibits include dioramas depicting scenes of traditional Seminole life, an old school 'living village' and re-created ceremonial grounds. Temporary exhibits have even more academic polish, and overall the museum does an excellent job of presenting Seminole history and tribal life today.

org; 1801 N Ocean Blvd; admission by donation; ⏲9am-4pm Mon-Sat, from noon Sun), a beautiful wetlands preserve; also visit its sea turtle rehabilitation center. Another good reason to stop is the outstanding **Boca Raton Museum of Art** (www.bocamuseum.org; 501 Plaza Real, Mizner Park; adult/child $8/4; ⏲10am-5pm Tue-Fri, from noon Sat & Sun), with a permanent collection of contemporary works by Picasso, Matisse, Warhol and more. The museum is in **Mizner Park** (www.miznerpark.org; cnr US 1 & Mizner Blvd), a ritzy outdoor mall with stores, restaurants and regular free concerts.

PALM BEACH

About 30 miles north of Boca Raton are Palm Beach and West Palm Beach. The two towns have flip-flopped the traditional coastal hierarchy: Palm Beach, the beach town, is more upscale, while West Palm Beach on the mainland is younger and livelier. Because Palm Beach is an enclave of the ultrawealthy, especially during its winter 'social season,' most travelers just window-shop the oceanfront mansions and boutiques lining the aptly named **Worth Avenue** (www.worth-avenue.com).

One of the country's most fascinating museums is the resplendent **Flagler Museum** (www.flagler.org; 1 Whitehall Way; adult/child $18/10; ⏲10am-5pm Tue-Sat, from noon Sun), housed in the railroad magnate's 1902 winter estate, Whitehall Mansion. The elaborate 55-room palace is an evocative immersion in Gilded Age opulence.

Modeled after Rome's Villa Medici, Flagler's opulent oceanfront 1896 hotel, the **Breakers** (☎561-655-6611; www.thebreakers.com; 1 S County Rd; r $270-1250; P❄@📶🏊), is a super-luxurious world unto itself, encompassing two golf courses, 10 tennis courts, a three-pool Mediterranean beach club and a trove of restaurants.

In the trendy Omphoy Hotel, **Michelle Bernstein's** (☎561-540-6440; www.omphoy.com; 2842 S Ocean Blvd; mains $29-38; ⏲5:30-10pm) is the latest outpost for this Miami celebrity chef. Come for gourmet riffs on Nouvelle Floridian cuisine, emphasizing South Florida produce. Or, kick it Formica-style with an egg cream and a low-cal platter at the lunch counter in **Green's Pharmacy** (151 N County Rd; mains $4-13; ⏲7am-3pm Mon-Sat, to 2pm Sun).

WEST PALM BEACH

Henry Flagler initially developed West Palm Beach as a working-class community to support Palm Beach, and indeed, West Palm today works harder, plays harder and is simply cooler and more relaxed. It's a groovy place to explore.

Florida's largest museum, the **Norton Museum of Art** (www.norton.org; 1451 S Olive Ave; adult/child $12/5; ⏲10am-5pm Tue-Sat, to 9pm Thu, from 11am Sun) houses an enormous collection of American and European modern masters and Impressionists, along with a large Buddha head presiding over an impressive Asian art collection. If you like that, you'll love the outdoor **Ann Norton Sculpture Garden** (www.ansg.org; 253 Barcelona Rd; admission $7; ⏲10am-4pm Wed-Sun). This serene collection of sculptures sprinkled among verdant gardens is a real West Palm gem.

If you have children, take them to **Lion Country Safari** (www.lioncountrysafari.com; 2003 Lion Country Safari Rd; adult/child $26.50/19.50; ⏲9:30am-5:30pm), the country's first cageless drive-through safari, where around 900 creatures roam freely around 500 acres.

The coolest lodging in town is **Hotel Biba** (☎561-832-0094; www.hotelbiba.com; 320 Belvedere Rd; r summer/winter $79/129; P❄📶🏊). The retro-funky exterior looks like a cute, 1950s motel in honeydew-melon green, but the rooms have a modern boutique style that would be right at home in Miami's SoBe.

Much of the action centers around **CityPlace** (www.cityplace.com; 700 S Rosemary Ave), a European village-style outdoor mall with splashing fountains and a slew of dining and entertainment options. Clematis St also has several worthy bars, live-music clubs and restaurants, and every Thursday **Clematis by Night** (www.clematisbynight.net; ⏲6-9:30pm Thu) hosts friendly outdoor concerts. If you're hungry, try **Rocco's Tacos & Tequila Bar** (www.roccostacos.com; 224 Clematis St; mains $12-19; ⏲11:30am-11pm, to midnight Tue-Wed, to 1am Thu-Sat), a saucy *nuevo* Mexican restaurant with funky decor, tableside guacamole and 175 different kinds of tequila – no wonder it's so loud in here!

Admirably servicing its migration of snowbirds is **Palm Beach International Airport** (PBI; www.pbia.org), 2.5 miles west of downtown West Palm Beach. The downtown **Tri-Rail station** (☎800-875-7245; 201 S Tamarind Ave) also serves as the **Amtrak station** (☎561-832-6169).

The Everglades

Contrary to what you may have heard, the Everglades is not a swamp. Or at least, it's not *only* a swamp. Its complex taxonomy of environments is most accurately characterized as a wet prairie – grasslands that happen to be flooded most of the year. Nor is it stagnant. In the wet season, a horizon-wide river creeps ever-so-slowly beneath the rustling saw grass and around the subtly raised cypress and hardwood hammocks toward the ocean. The Everglades are indeed filled with alligators – and perhaps a few dead bodies, as *CSI: Miami* would have it. Yet its beauty is not measured in fear or geological drama, but in the timeless, slow Jurassic flap of a great blue heron as it glides over its vast and shockingly gentle domain.

Which is one reason that exploring the Everglades by foot, bicycle, canoe and kayak (or camping) is so much more satisfying than by noisy, vibrating airboat. There is an incredible variety of wonderful creatures to see within this unique, subtropical wilderness: all those alligators, bottlenose dolphins, manatees, snowy egrets, herons, anhingas, bald eagles and ospreys. And there are accessible entrances that, at the cost of a few hours, get you easily into the Everglades' soft heart.

The Everglades has two seasons: the summer wet season and the winter dry season. Winter – from December to April – is the prime time to visit: the weather is mild and pleasant, and the wildlife is out in abundance. In summer – May through October – it's stiflingly hot, humid and buggy, with frequently afternoon thunderstorms. In addition, as water sources spread out, the animals disperse.

EVERGLADES NATIONAL PARK

While the Everglades have a history dating back to prehistoric times, the park wasn't founded until 1947. It's considered the most endangered national park in the USA, but the Comprehensive Everglades Restoration Plan has been enacted to undo some of the damage done by draining and development.

The park has three main entrances and areas: in the south along Rte 9336 through Homestead and Florida City to Ernest Coe Visitor Center and, at road's end, Flamingo; along the Tamiami Trail/Hwy 41 in the north to Shark Valley; and on the Gulf Coast near Everglades City.

The main park entry points have visitor centers where you can get maps, camping permits and ranger information. You only need to pay the entrance fee (per car/pedestrian $10/5 for seven days) once to access all points.

Even in winter it's almost impossible to avoid mosquitoes, but they're ferocious in summer: bring *strong* repellent. Alligators are also prevalent. As obvious as it sounds,

SAVING THE EVERGLADES

For most of human history, the Everglades were an utter and almost entirely uninhabited wilderness. But by 1900 the desire to settle South Florida led Florida governor Napoleon Bonaparte Broward to envision an 'Empire of the Everglades.' Broward set in motion 70 years of canal building that drained about half the swamp and effectively cut off what had been a vibrant 100-mile-long river from its source, Lake Okeechobee.

South Florida's burgeoning cities, suburbs and agriculture then did two things: thirstily sucked up the fresh water while dumping pollutants into what is, essentially, the peninsula's kidney – vital wetlands that help cleanse the Florida Aquifer. If allowed to continue unabated, this process would eventually kill the Everglades and leave South Florida uninhabitable.

Marjory Stoneman Douglas, who famously dubbed the Everglades a 'river of grass,' almost single-handedly raised the alarm in the 1940s, and in 1947 the Everglades were protected as a national park, the first for reasons of conservation, not natural beauty. This, however, was only a first step.

Fast forward to today: in 2000 the **Comprehensive Everglades Restoration Plan** (CERP; www.evergladesplan.org) was approved, a 30-year proposal to fill in canals, remove levees and restore the water flow. Yet political battles and the high estimated price tag ($15 billion and counting) have slowed progress. And as funding has fallen to a fraction of what's needed, some wonder about the future viability of one of the USA's biggest, most ambitious environmental projects.

For an overview of Everglades history, visit www.theevergladesstory.org.

never, ever feed them: it's illegal and is a sure way to provoke attacks. Four types of poisonous snakes call the Everglades home; avoid all snakes, just in case, and wear long, thick socks and lace-up boots.

Sights & Activities

Shark Valley Visitor Center PARK
(☎305-221-8776; Tamiami Trail; ⏲8:30am-6pm) For a quick peek from Miami, come here. On the excellent two-hour **tram tour** (☎305-221-8455; www.sharkvalleytramtours.com; adult/child $18.25/11.50) along the 15-mile asphalt road, you'll see copious numbers of alligators and lots of migratory herons and ibis in winter. The narration by park rangers is both knowledgeable and witty, providing an ideal overview of the Everglades and its inhabitants. Halfway along the trail is the 50ft-high observation tower, an ugly concrete structure that offers a dramatic panorama of the 'river of grass.' The pancake-flat road is also perfect for **cycling** (rental per hr $7.50); stop and gawk as long and often as you wish. Bring water.

Ernest Coe Visitor Center PARK
(☎305-242-7700; www.nps.gov/ever; Hwy 9336; ⏲8am-5pm) Those with a day to give the Glades could start with this visitor center in the south. It has excellent, museum-quality exhibits and tons of activity info: the road accesses numerous short trails and lots of top-drawer canoeing opportunities. Call for a schedule of fun ranger-led programs, such as the two-hour 'slough slog.' Most programs start at the nearby **Royal Palm Visitor Center** (☎305-242-7700; Hwy 9336; ⏲8am-4:15pm), where you can catch two short trails. The Anhinga Trail is great for wildlife spotting, especially alligators in winter, and the Gumbo-Limbo showcases plants and trees.

Flamingo Visitor Center PARK
(☎239-695-2945; ⏲8am-4:15pm) From Royal Palm, Hwy 9336 cuts through the belly of the park for 38 miles until it reaches the isolated Flamingo Visitor Center, which has maps of canoeing and hiking trails. Call ahead about the status of facilities: the former Flamingo Lodge was wiped out by hurricanes in 2005, and at the time of research **Flamingo Marina** (☎239-695-3101) was closed for renovations. It should reopen again and offer backcountry boat tours and kayak/canoe rentals for self-guided trips along the coast.

Gulf Coast Visitor Center PARK
(☎239-695-3311; 815 Oyster Bar Lane, off Hwy 29, Everglades City; ⏲9am-4:30pm) Those with more time should also consider visiting the northwestern edge of the Everglades, where the mangroves and waterways of the **10,000 Islands** offer incredible canoeing and kayaking opportunities, and great boat tours with a chance to spot dolphins. The visitor center is next to the marina, with rentals (from $13 per hour) and various guided boat trips (from $25). Everglades City also has other private tour operators who can get you camping in the 10,000 Islands.

Sleeping

Everglades National Park has two developed **campgrounds** (☎877-444-6777; www.recreation.gov; campsites Nov-Apr $16, low season free). The best are the first-come, first-served sites at **Long Pine Key** (☎305-242-7873); reserve ahead for campsites at **Flamingo**. They both have water, toilets and grills; Flamingo adds cold-water showers and electricity. Camping is free in summer because it's brutally hot and wet.

Backcountry camping (permit $10, plus per person per night $2) is throughout the park and includes beach sites, ground sites and chickees (covered wooden platforms above the water). A permit from the visitor center is required.

Around the Everglades

Coming from Miami, the gateway town of Homestead on the east side of the park can make a good base, especially if you're headed for the Keys.

BISCAYNE NATIONAL PARK

Just south of Miami (and east of Homestead), this national park is only 5% land. The 95% that's water is **Biscayne National Underwater Park** (☎305-230-1100; www.nps.gov/bisc, www.biscayneunderwater.com), containing a portion of the world's third-largest coral reef, where manatees, dolphins and sea turtles highlight a vibrant, diverse ecosystem. Get general park information from **Dante Fascell Visitor Center** (☎305-230-7275; 9700 SW 328th St, Homestead; ⏲8:30am-5pm). The park offers canoe/kayak rentals, snorkel and dive trips, and popular three-hour glass-bottom boat tours; all require reservations.

HOMESTEAD & FLORIDA CITY

Homestead and Florida City don't look like much, but they have some true Everglades highlights. Without question the most heart-warming is the **Everglades Outpost** (☎305-247-8000; www.evergladesoutpost.org; 35601 SW 192nd Ave, Homestead; admission $20; ⏰10am-4pm Sat & Sun, by appointment Mon-Fri), which cares for neglected and abused wild animals; residents include gibbons, wolves, cobras and a pair of majestic tigers.

Much more than a farmer's stand, **Robert Is Here** (☎305-246-1592; www.robertishere.com; 19200 SW 344th St, Homestead; ⏰8am-7pm Nov-Aug) is a kitschy Old Florida institution with a petting zoo, live music and crazy-good milk shakes.

The Homestead–Florida City area has no shortage of chain motels; try Rt 1 Krome Ave. If you don't mind hostel living, seriously consider the **Everglades International Hostel** (☎305-248-1122; www.evergladeshostel.com; 20 SW 2nd Ave, Florida City; camping/dm/r $18/28/75; P❄@☎). Rooms are good value, the vibe is very friendly, but the back gardens – wow. It's a fantasia of natural delights, and the hostel conducts some of the best Everglades tours around. For a more pampered, personal touch than the chain hotels, book a room at the historic **Redland Hotel** (☎305-246-1904; www.redlandhotel.com; 5 S Flagler Ave, Homestead; r $83-150; P☎). Homestead's modestly quaint main street, along Krome Ave, is the central restaurant and shopping district.

TAMIAMI TRAIL

The Tamiami Trail/Hwy 41 starts in Miami and beelines to Naples along the north edge of Everglades National Park.

The first sign you've left the city behind is **Pit BBQ** (16400 SW 8th St; mains $4-9; ⏰11am-11:30pm), between Shark Valley and Miami. A bastion of country music and Confederate flags, it's as cheesy as a dairy.

At the entrance to the Everglades' Shark Valley is **Miccosukee Village** (☎305-552-8365; www.miccosukee.com; village/airboat ride $8/10; ⏰9am-5pm), an informative, entertaining open-air museum showcasing Miccosukee culture. Tour traditional homes, attend performances (from dance to gator wrestling), take an airboat ride and peruse handmade crafts in the gift store.

About 20 miles west of Shark Valley, you reach the **Oasis Visitor Center** (☎239-695-1201; ⏰9am-4:30pm) for 1139-sq-mile **Big Cypress National Preserve** (www.nps.gov/bicy). Good exhibits and short trails bring the region's ecology to life, though the adventurous might consider tackling a portion of the **Florida National Scenic Trail** (www.floridatrail.org); 31 miles cut through Big Cypress.

Half a mile east of the visitor center, drop into the **Big Cypress Gallery** (☎941-695-2428; www.clydebutcher.com; 52388 Tamiami Trail; ⏰10am-5pm Wed-Mon), displaying Clyde Butcher's work; his large-scale B&W landscape photographs spotlight the region's unusual beauty.

The tiny town of **Ochopee** is home to the country's smallest post office. If that's not enough to make you pull over, then stop into the eccentric **Skunk Ape Research Headquarters** (☎239-695-2275; www.skunkape.info; 40904 Tamiami Trail E; ⏰7am-7pm), dedicated to tracking Bigfoot's legendary, if stinky, Everglades kin. They're goofy but sincere. Based out of Skunk Ape HQ, **Everglades Adventure Tours** (☎800-504-6554; www.evergladesadventuretours.com; tours from $69) offers knowledgeable swamp hikes, 'safaris,' airboats and, best of all, trips being poled around in a canoe or skiff.

Finally, just east of Ochopee, is the quintessential 1950s-style swamp shack, **Joanie's Blue Crab Cafe** (☎239-695-2682; 39395 Tamiami Trail; mains $9-15; ⏰10am-5pm Wed-Mon), with open rafters, colorful, shellacked picnic tables and a swamp dinner of gator nuggets and fritters.

EVERGLADES CITY

This small town at the edge of the park makes a good base for exploring the 10,000 Islands region. With large renovated rooms, **Everglades City Motel** (☎239-695-4244; www.evergladescitymotel.com; 310 Collier Ave; r from $80; ❄☎) is an exceptionally good value, and the fantastically friendly staff can hook

WHAT THE...?

'You will be seeing unusual accomplishment' reads the inscription on the rough-hewn quarried wall. That's an understatement. Exemplifying all that is weird and wacky about South Florida, **Coral Castle** (www.coralcastle.com; 28655 S Dixie Hwy, Homestead; adult/child $12/7; ⏰8am-6pm, to 8pm Sat & Sun) is a unique monument to unrequited love. Of course, what's an altar-jilted Latvian to do, except move to Florida and hand carve, unseen, in the dead of night, a rock compound that includes a 'throne room,' a sun dial, a stone stockade and a revolving boulder gate that engineers, to this day, cannot explain?

A KINDER, GENTLER WILDERNESS ENCOUNTER

As you explore Florida's outdoors and encounter its wildlife, keep in mind the following guidelines.

» **Airboats and swamp buggies** For exploring wetlands, airboats are better than big-wheeled buggies, but nonmotorized (and silent) canoes and kayaks are least-damaging and disruptive.

» **Wild dolphins** Captive dolphins are typically rescued animals already acclimated to humans. However, federal law makes it illegal to feed, pursue or touch wild dolphins in the ocean.

» **Manatee swims** When swimming near manatees, a federally protected endangered species, look but don't touch. 'Passive observation' is the standard.

» **Feeding wild animals** In a word, don't. Acclimating wild animals to humans usually leads to the animal's death, whether because of accidents or aggression.

» **Sea-turtle nesting sites** It's a federal crime to approach nesting sea turtles or hatchling runs. Observe beach warning signs. If you encounter nesting turtles, keep your distance and no flash photos.

» **Coral-reef etiquette** Never touch the coral reef. It's that simple. Coral polyps are living organisms. Touching or breaking coral creates openings for infection and disease.

you up with any kind of tour. The same can be said for the **Ivey House Bed & Breakfast** (239-695-3299; www.iveyhouse.com; 107 Camellia St; lodge $74-120, inn $99-209;). Choose between basic lodge accommodations or somewhat sprucer inn rooms, then book some of the region's best nature trips with the on-site **North American Canoe Tours** (941-695-3299/4666; www.evergladesadventures.com; tours $25-65; Nov–mid-Apr). Ask about room/tour packages.

A mile or so south, **JT's Island Grill & Gallery** (239-695-3633; 238 Mamie St, Chokoloskee; mains $5-16; 11am-3pm late Oct-May) serves up delicious lunches in a restored 1890 general store with retro kitsch and charm to spare.

For dinner, try the **Seafood Depot** (239-695-0075; 102 Collier Ave; mains $14-33; 10:30am-9pm), a haven of fried seafood and a great place to sample gator and frog's legs; just douse with Tabasco and devour.

Florida Keys

Before Henry Flagler completed his railroad in 1912, which connected the Keys to the mainland, this 126-mile string of islands was just a series of untethered bumps of land accessible only by boat. (Little surprise, then, that their early economies were built on piracy, smuggling, ship salvaging and fishing.) Flagler's railroad was destroyed by a hurricane in 1935, but what remained of its bridges allowed the Overseas Hwy to be completed in 1938. Now, streams of travelers swarm down from the mainland to indulge in the alluring jade-green waters, laid-back island lifestyle, great fishing, and idyllic snorkeling and diving.

The islands are typically divided into the Upper Keys (Key Largo to Islamorada), Middle Keys and Lower Keys (from Little Duck Key). Yet far from petering out, they crescendo at highway's end, reaching their grand finale in Key West – the Keys' gloriously unkempt, bawdy, freak-loving exclamation point.

Many addresses in the Keys are noted by their proximity to mile markers (indicated as MM), which start at MM126 in Florida City and count down to MM0 in Key West. They also might indicate whether they're 'oceanside' (the south side of the highway) or 'bayside' (which is north).

The **Florida Keys & Key West Visitors Bureau** (800-352-5397; www.fla-keys.com) has information; also check www.keysnews.com.

KEY LARGO

Stretching from Key Largo to Islamorada, the Upper Keys are cluttered with touristy shops and motels. At first you can't even see the water from the highway, then – bam – you're in Islamorada and water is everywhere.

Key Largo has long been romanticized in movies and song, so it can be a shock to arrive and find…no Bogart, no Bacall, no lovesick Sade. Yes, Key Largo is underwhelming, a sleepy island and town with middling views. That is, if all you do is stick to the highway and keep your head above water. Root down side roads for those legendary island idiosyncracies, and dive underwater for the most amazing coral reef in the continental US.

For maps and brochures, visit the **chamber of commerce** (☎305-451-4747; www.keylargo.org; MM 106 bayside; ⊙9am-6pm).

Sights & Activities

John Pennekamp Coral Reef State Park
PARK

(☎305-451-6300; www.pennekamppark.com; MM 102.5 oceanside; car/pedestrian or bicycle $8/2; ⊙8am-sunset) This park has boardwalk trails through mangroves and a cute aquarium, but as the USA's first underwater park, it's true jewel box is beneath the sea, a vast living coral reef that's home to a panoply of sea life (and the oft-photographed statue *Christ of the Deep*).

Your options for seeing the reef are many: take a 2½-hour **glass-bottom boat tour** (adult/child $24/17; ⊙9:15am, 12:15pm & 3pm) on a thoroughly modern 38ft catamaran. Dive in with a **snorkeling trip** (adult/child $30/25) or two-tank **diving trip** (☎305-451-6322; $60); half-day trips leave twice daily, usually around 9am and 1pm. Or go DIY and rent a **canoe or kayak** (per hr single/double $12/17) and journey through a 3-mile network of water trails. Call the park for boat-rental information.

Florida Bay Outfitters
KAYAKING

(☎305-451-3018; www.kayakfloridakeys.com; MM 104 bayside; kayak rental per half-day $40) All sorts of guided kayak trips and rentals.

Horizon Divers
DIVING

(☎305-453-3535; www.horizondivers.com; 100 Ocean Dr, off MM 100 oceanside; snorkel/scuba trips $50/80) Friendly crew; offers rentals, dive trips and scuba instruction.

Sleeping

In addition to luxe resorts, Key Largo has loads of bright, cheery motels and camping.

Largo Lodge
HOTEL $$

(☎305-451-0424; www.largolodge.com; MM 102 bayside; cottages $125-195; P) These six charming, sunny cottages with their own private beach – family owned since the '50s – are surrounded by palm trees, tropical flowers and lots of roaming birds, for a taste of Florida in the good old days.

Key Largo House Boatel
HOUSEBOAT $$

(☎305-766-0871; www.keylargohouseboatel.com; Shoreland Dr, MM 103.5 oceanside; houseboats from $75-150) These five houseboats are a steal. The largest is incredibly spacious, sleeping six people comfortably. The boats are right on the docks, so no possibility of being isolated from land (or booze). Call for directions.

Kona Kai Resort & Gallery
HOTEL $$$

(☎305-852-7200; www.konakairesort.com; MM 97.8 bayside; r $199-369; P❄📶🏊) This intimate hideaway features 11 airy rooms and suites (with full kitchens). They're all bright and comfortable, but some feel a little too old-fashioned. Tons of activities, plus its own beach.

John Pennekamp Coral Reef State Park
CAMPGROUND $

(☎800-326-3521; www.pennekamppark.com; campsites $32) Sleep near the fishes at one of the 47 coral-reef-adjacent sites here. Camping's popular; reserve well in advance.

Eating & Drinking

TOP CHOICE Key Largo Conch House
FUSION $$

(☎305-453-4844; www.keylargocoffeehouse.com; MM 100.2 oceanside; mains $8-25; ⊙7am-10pm) Now *this* feels like the islands: conch architecture, tropical foliage, a parrot, and crab and conch dishes that ease you off the mainland.

Mrs Mac's Kitchen
AMERICAN $$

(MM 99.4 bayside; mains $7-18; ⊙7am-9:30pm Mon-Sat) This cute roadside diner bedecked with rusty license plates serves classic highway food such as burgers and fish baskets.

Fish House
SEAFOOD $$

(☎305-451-4665; www.fishhouse.com; MM 102.4 oceanside; mains $12-28; ⊙11:30am-10pm) Delivers on its name, serving fish, fish and more fish that's as fresh as it gets. Your main decision: fried, broiled, jerked, blackened or grilled?

Alabama Jack's
BAR

(http://alabamajacks.com; 58000 Card Sound Rd; mains $5-25; ⊙11am-7pm) On the back road between Key Largo and Florida City, this funky open-air joint draws an eclectic booze-hungry crowd of genuine Keys characters. Try the rave-worthy conch fritters.

ISLAMORADA

Things finally get pretty around Islamorada, which is actually a long string of several islands (from MM90 to MM74); the epicenter is Upper Matecumbe Key. Several little nooks of beach are easily accessible, providing scenic rest stops. Housed in an old red caboose, the **chamber of commerce** (☎305-664-4503; www.islamoradachamber.com; MM 83.2 bayside; ⊙9am-5pm Mon-Fri, 10am-3pm Sat & Sun) has area information.

Sights & Activities

Billed as 'the Sportfishing Capital of the World,' Islamorada is an angler's paradise. Indeed, most of its highlights involve getting on or in the sea.

TOP CHOICE Robbie's Marina MARINA
(☎305-664-9814; www.robbies.com; MM 77.5 bayside; ⊙8am-6pm) This marina/roadside attraction offers the buffet of boating options: fishing charters, jet skiing, party boats, ecotours, snorkeling trips, kayak rentals and more (come here to visit the area's island parks). At a minimum, stop to feed the freakishly large tarpon from the dock ($3 per bucket, $1 to watch), and sift the flea market/tourist shop for tacky seaside trinkets.

Indian Key Historic State Park ISLAND
(☎305-664-2540; www.floridastateparks.org/indiankey; ⊙8am-sunset) A few hundred yards offshore, this peaceful little island contains the derelict, crumbling foundations of a 19th-century settlement that was wiped out by Native Americans during the Second Seminole War. It's a moody ramble, accessible only by kayak or boat.

Lignumvitae Key State Botanical Park ISLAND
(☎305-664-2540; www.floridastateparks.org/lignumvitaekey; ⊙9am-5pm Thu-Mon) It'll feel like just you and about a jillion mosquitoes on this bayside island park, with virgin tropical forests and the 1919 Matheson House. Come for the shipwrecked isolation. Robbie's Marina offers boat rentals and tours.

Florida Keys History of Diving Museum MUSEUM
(www.divingmuseum.org; MM 83; adult/child $12/6; ⊙10am-5pm, to 7pm Wed) Don't miss this collection of diving paraphernalia from around the world, including diving 'suits' and technology from the 19th century. This charmingly eccentric museum embodies the quirky Keys.

Theater of the Sea DOLPHIN ENCOUNTER
(☎305-664-2431; www.theaterofthesea.com; MM 84.5 bayside; adult/child $27/19.45; ⊙9:30am-4pm) Dolphins and sea lions perform in an intimate, close-up setting, and for an extra fee you can meet or swim with them.

Windley Key Fossil Reef Geological State Site PARK
(☎305-664-2540; www.floridastateparks.org/windleykey; MM 85.5 oceanside) Check out layer after layer of geological history in the quarry, with 8ft walls of fossilized coral.

FREE Anne's Beach BEACH
(MM 73.5 oceanside) The area's best public beach; shaded picnic tables and a bright ribbon of sand.

Sleeping & Eating

Casa Morada BOUTIQUE HOTEL $$$
(☎305-664-0044; www.casamorada.com; 136 Madeira Rd, off MM 82.2; ste summer $239-459, winter $299-659; P❄️📶🏊) Come for a welcome dash of South Beach sophistication mixed with laid-back Keys style. The slick bar is a great oceanside sunset perch.

Ragged Edge Resort RESORT $$
(☎305-852-5389; www.ragged-edge.com; 243 Treasure Harbor Rd; apt $69-259; P❄️🏊) Swim off the docks at this happily unpretentious oceanfront complex off MM 86.5. It has 10 spotless and popular efficiencies and apartments, and a happily comatose vibe.

Long Key State Recreation Area CAMPGROUND $
(☎305-664-4815, 305-326-3521; www.floridastateparks.org/longkey; MM 67.5; campsites $38.50) Book as far ahead as possible for the 60 coveted oceanfront campsites in this shady, 965-acre park.

Midway Cafe CAFE $
(80499 Overseas Hwy; mains under $5; ⊙7am-3pm Thu-Tue, to 2pm Sun) The lovely folks who run this art-filled cafe roast their own beans and make destination-worthy baked goods. Celebrate your Keys adventure with a friendly cup of joe.

Morada Bay AMERICAN $$$
(☎305-664-0604; www.moradabay-restaurant.com; MM 81.6 bayside; lunch $10-15, dinner $21-29; ⊙11:30am-10pm) Grab a table under a palm tree on the white-sand beach and sip a rum drink with your fresh seafood for a lovely, easygoing Caribbean experience. Don't miss the monthly full-moon party.

Hog Heaven BAR $$
(☎305-664-9669; MM 83 oceanside; mains $10-18; ⊙11am-3:30am) From sandwiches and salads

to seafood nachos and T-bone steaks, the diverse menu rocks. Come during happy hour (4pm to 8pm) and bring a designated driver; the drinks are practically free.

GRASSY KEY

To reach Grassy Key in the Middle Keys, you enjoy a vivid sensation of island-hopping, ending with the biggest hop, the **Seven Mile Bridge**, one of the world's longest causeways.

Sedate Grassy Key was once the village-like heart of the Keys. Today, the main reason for travelers to pause is the **Dolphin Research Center** (305-289-1121; www.dolphins.org; MM 59 bayside; adult/child $20/15, swim program $180-650; 9am-4pm). Of all the dolphin swimming spots in the Keys, this is preferred simply because the dolphins are free to leave the grounds and a lot of marine-biology research goes on behind the scenes.

MARATHON

Halfway between Key Largo and Key West, Marathon is the most sizable town between them; it's a good base and a hub for commercial fishing and lobster boats. Get local information at the **visitor center** (305-743-5417; www.floridakeysmarathon.com; MM 53.5 bayside; 9am-5pm).

Sights & Activities

Crane Point Museum MUSEUM
(www.cranepoint.net; MM 50.5 bayside; adult/child $12.50/8.50; 9am-5pm Mon-Sat, from noon Sun) Escape all the development at this 63-acre reserve, where you'll find a vast system of nature trails and mangroves, a raised boardwalk and a rare early-20th-century Bahamian-style house. Kids will enjoy pirate and wreck exhibits, a walk-through coral reef tunnel and the bird hospital.

Turtle Hospital ANIMAL SANCTUARY
(305-743-2552; www.theturtlehospital.org; 2396 Overseas Hwy; adult/child $15/7.50; 9am-6pm) Call ahead to make sure hospital staff are around. This labor of love is a heart-warming encounter with injured and diseased sea turtles, who are sweetly cared for.

Pigeon Key National Historic District ISLAND
(305-743-5999; www.pigeonkey.net; adult/child $12/9; tours 10am, 11:30am, 1pm & 2:30pm) On the Marathon side of Seven Mile Bridge, this tiny key served as a camp for the workers who toiled to build the Overseas Hwy in the 1930s. You can tour the historic structures or just sun and snorkel on the beach. Reach it by ferry, included in admission. Also here, the **Old Seven Mile Bridge** is closed to traffic and serves as the 'World's Longest Fishing Bridge.'

Sombrero Beach BEACH
(Sombrero Beach Rd, off MM 50 oceanside) One of the few white-sand, mangrove-free beaches in the Keys; good swimming.

Marathon Kayak KAYAKING
(305-395-0355; www.marathonkayak.com; 6363 Overseas Hwy/MM 50 oceanside) Kayak instruction and three-hour guided eco-tours (from $45 per person).

Sleeping & Eating

Seascape MOTEL $$
(305-743-6212; 1275 76th St, btwn MM 51 & 52; r from $125; P) The classy, understated luxury in this B&B manifests in the nine rooms, which all have a different feel, from old-fashioned cottage to sleek boutique. Seascape also has a waterfront pool, kayaks for guest use and includes breakfast.

Siesta Motel MOTEL $
(305-743-5671; www.siestamotel.net; MM 51 oceanside; r $75-105; P) Head here for one of the cheapest, cleanest flops in the Keys, located in a friendly cluster of cute Marathon homes – with great service, to boot.

Keys Fisheries SEAFOOD $
(305-743-4353; 35th St, off MM 49 bayside; mains $7-16; 11:30am-9pm) Shoo the seagulls from your picnic table on the deck and dig in to fresh seafood in a down-and-dirty dockside atmosphere. The lobster reuben is the stuff of legend.

Hurricane AMERICAN $$
(www.hurricaneblues.com; MM 49.5 bayside; mains $12-19; 11am-midnight) As well as being a favorite Marathon bar, the Hurricane also serves an excellent menu of creative South Florida–inspired goodness, like snapper stuffed with crabmeat and conch sliders jerked in Caribbean seasoning.

Wooden Spoon AMERICAN $
(MM 51 oceanside; mains $3-9; 7am-3pm) It's the best breakfast around, served by sweet Southern women who know their way around a diner. The biscuits are fluffy, the sausage gravy is delicious, and the grits buttery and creamy.

LOWER KEYS

The Lower Keys (MM 46 to MM 0) are fierce bastions of conch culture in all its variety. The **chamber of commerce** (☎305-872-2411; www.lowerkeyschamber.com; MM 31 oceanside; ⏰9am-5pm Mon-Fri, to 3pm Sat) is on Big Pine Key.

One of Florida's most acclaimed beaches – and certainly the best in the Keys for its shallow, warm water – is at **Bahia Honda State Park** (www.bahiahondapark.com; MM 36.8 oceanside; per car/bicycle $5/2; ⏰8am-sunset), a 524-acre park with nature trails, ranger-led programs and water-sports rentals. Snorkel some of the best coral reefs outside Key Largo.

Drive slowly: along the highway in Big Pine Key is the 84,000-acre **National Key Deer Refuge**. Stop by or contact the **visitor center** (☎305-872-2239; www.fws.gov/nationalkeydeer; MM30.5 bayside; ⏰8am-5pm Mon-Fri) at Big Pine Shopping Center to learn more about these endangered, miniature deer and the trails where you can view them; Key Deer are easiest to spot at dusk and dawn.

Looe Key (floridakeys.noaa.gov) is actually an offshore marine sanctuary teeming with colorful tropical fish and coral; try **Looe Key Dive Center** (☎305-872-2215; www.diveflakeys.com; MM 27.5 oceanside; snorkel/dive $44/84) on Ramrod Key for snorkeling and diving day trips; the sanctuary contains wreck dives as well.

To spend the night, camping at **Bahia Honda State Park** (☎800-326-3521; campsites/cabins $36/160) is sublime; it'd be perfect except for the sandflies. There are also six popular waterfront cabins. Reserve far ahead for all. For a completely different experience, book one of the four cozily scrumptious rooms at **Deer Run Bed & Breakfast** (☎305-872-2015; www.deerunfloridabb.com; 1997 Long Beach Dr, Big Pine Key, off MM 33 oceanside; r $235-355; ❄🏊). This state-certified green lodge and vegetarian B&B is a garden of quirky delights, and the owners are extremely helpful and decidedly not self-righteous.

It's hard to miss the jumbo shrimp statue that marks your arrival at the **Good Food Conspiracy** (☎305-872-3945; MM 30 oceanside; mains $7-10; ⏰9:30am-7pm Mon-Sat, 11am-5pm Sun), where you'll find healthy hippie food along with your classic Keys photo op.

The proprietors at the **No Name Pub** (☎305-872-9115; N Watson Blvd, off MM 30.5 bayside; mains $8-20; ⏰11am-11pm), 1.5 miles north of US 1 on Big Pine Key, know where their retirement is coming from: the approximately $60,000 in $1 bills stapled to the walls by customers; stop by for pizza, beer and kooky ambience.

KEY WEST

While parts of Big Pine Key would fit easily in Florida's rural Panhandle, crazy, cultured, gay-friendly Key West would fit nowhere else. It's an eccentric frontier town that fosters and promotes its own brand of funky insanity. Perhaps this is a quirk of geography: Key West is the literal end of the road on the map of the continental US, closer to Cuba than the rest of America and a welcoming port for all sorts of global wayfarers. Or perhaps, as a local saying goes, 'They shook the United States and all the nuts fell to the bottom.'

Artists, renegades, homosexuals and free spirits have long made Key West their own. It's impossible to tease apart high and low culture: on one side are expensive art galleries, literary festivals, Caribbean villas and Hemingway's legacy. On the other are S&M fetish parades, frat boys toppling black-out drunk and 30-something women tossing their bras to the rafters.

Originally called 'Cayo Hueso' – Spanish for 'Bone Island' – Key West was named for all the skeletons that early explorers found littering the beach. These days, people flock to Key West to soak up the sun, the mellow atmosphere, more than a little booze, and to reset their internal clocks to 'island time.'

Sights

Key West has more than its fair share of historic homes, buildings and districts (like the colorful Bahama Village); it's a walkable town that rewards exploring. Naturally, you'll snap a pic at the USA's much ballyhooed **Southernmost Point Marker**; just know that the red-and-black buoy isn't even the proper southernmost point on Key West.

TOP CHOICE Mallory Square SQUARE

Sunset at Mallory Sq, at the end of Duval St, is a bizzaro attraction of the highest order. It takes all those energies, subcultures and oddities of Keys life – the hippies, the rednecks, the foreigners and the tourists – and focuses them into one torchlit, playfully edgy (but family-friendly) street party. Come for the jugglers, fire-eaters, sassy acrobats and tightrope-walking dogs, and stay for the after-dark madness.

Duval Street STREET

Key West locals have a love–hate relationship with their island's most famous road. Duval, Old Town Key West's main drag, is a miracle mile of booze, tacky everything and awful behavior that still manages, somehow, to be fun. At the end of the night, the 'Duval Crawl' is one of the best pub crawls in the country.

Hemingway House HOUSE

(☎305-294-1136; www.hemingwayhome.com; 907 Whitehead St; adult/child $12.50/6; ⏲9am-5pm) Ernest Hemingway lived in this Spanish-Colonial house from 1931 to 1940 – to write, drink and fish, if not always in that order. Tours run every half-hour, and as you listen to docent-spun yarns of Papa, you'll see his studio, his unusual pool, and the descendents of his six-toed cats languishing in the sun, on furniture and pretty much wherever they feel like.

FREE **Florida Keys Eco-Discovery Center** MUSEUM

(☎305-809-4750; http://eco-discovery.com/ecokw.html; 35 East Quay Rd; ⏲9am-4pm Tue-Sat) This excellent nature center pulls together all the plants, animals and habitats that make up the Keys' unique ecosystem and presents them in fresh, accessible ways. A great place for kids and the big picture.

Key West Cemetery CEMETERY

(cnr Margaret & Angela Sts) This dark, alluring Gothic labyrinth is in the center of town. Livening up the mausoleums are famous epitaphs like 'I told you I was sick.'

Key West Butterfly & Nature Conservatory ANIMAL SANCTUARY

(☎305-296-2988; www.keywestbutterfly.com; 1316 Duval St; adult/child $12/8.50; ⏲9am-5pm) Even if you have only the faintest interest in butterflies, you'll find yourself entranced by the sheer quantity flittering around you here.

Museum of Art & History at the Custom House MUSEUM

(☎305-295-6616; www.kwahs.com/customhouse; 281 Front St; adult/child $7/5; ⏲9:30am-4:30pm) Offering a more low-key, less swashbuckling version of Key West history, this is an interesting collection of folklore, international art and historical exhibits housed in the impressive former Customs House.

Fort East Martello Museum & Gardens MUSEUM

(☎305-296-3913; www.kwahs.com/martello.htm; 3501 S Roosevelt Blvd; adult/child $7/5; ⏲9:30am-4:30pm) This fortress preserves interesting historical artifacts and some fabulous folk art by Mario Sanchez and 'junk' sculptures by Stanley Papio. Yet Martello's most famous resident – Robert the Doll – is a genuinely creepy, supposedly haunted, 19th-century doll that's kept in a glass case to keep him from making mischief.

WORTH A TRIP

DRY TORTUGAS

Seventy miles west of the Keys in the middle of the Gulf, **Dry Tortugas National Park** (☎305-242-7700; www.nps.gov/drto) is America's most inaccessible national park. Reachable only by boat or plane, it rewards your efforts to get there with amazing snorkeling, diving, bird-watching and stargazing.

Ponce de León christened the area *Las Tortugas* (the Turtles) after the abundant sea turtles; a lack of fresh water led sailors to add 'dry.' But this is more than just a pretty cluster of islands with no drinking water. The never-completed Civil War–era **Fort Jefferson** provides a striking hexagonal centerpiece of red brick rising up from the emerald waters on **Garden Key** – which has a visitor center and 13 first-come, first-served **campsites** (per person per night $3). Reserve far ahead, and bring everything you need, including water, though you might be able to barter with the Cuban-American fishing boats for lobster.

To get there, the **Yankee Freedom II** (☎305-294-7009; www.yankeefreedom.com) operates a fast ferry between Garden Key and the Historic Seaport (north end of Margaret St). Round-trip fares cost $165/120 per adult/child. Reserve ahead; includes breakfast, a picnic lunch, snorkeling gear and tour of the fort.

Key West Seaplanes (☎305-294-0709; www.seaplanesofkeywest.com) can take up to 10 passengers. A four-hour trip costs $250/190 per adult/child; an eight-hour trip costs $515/365. Reserve a week ahead.

Activities

Fort Zachary Taylor BEACH
(www.floridastateparks.org/forttaylor; per car/pedestrian $6/2; ⌚8am-sunset) Key West has three city beaches, but they aren't special; most head to Bahia Honda. That said, Fort Zachary Taylor has the best beach on Key West, with white sand, decent swimming and some near-shore snorkeling; it's great for sunsets and picnics.

Dive Key West DIVING
(☎305-296-3823; www.divekeywest.com) Key West generally doesn't have great reefs for snorkeling, but it has some wreck diving, such as a massive WWII ship sunk purposefully in 2009. Dive Key West arranges trips.

Subtropic Dive Center DIVING
(☎305-296-9914; www.subtropic.com) Arranges wreck-diving trips.

Charter Boat Key West FISHING
(www.charterboatkeywest.com) Fishing and cruising charters.

Reelax Charters KAYAKING
(☎305-304-1392; www.keyskayaking.com; MM 17 Sugarloaf Key Marina; kayak trips $200) Runs guided kayaks from nearby Sugarloaf Key.

Jolly II Rover CRUISE
(☎305-304-2235; www.schoonerjollyrover.com; cnr Greene & Elizabeth Sts, Schooner Wharf; cruise $39) Book a sunset cruise on a pirate ship.

Tours

Both the **Conch Tour Train** (☎305-294-5161; adult/child $29/26; ⌚9am-4:30pm) and **Old Town Trolley** (☎305-296-6688; adult/child $29/26; ⌚9am-4:30pm) offer tours leaving from Mallory Sq. The train offers a 90-minute narrated tour in a breezy, open car, while the hop-on/hop-off trolley makes 12 stops around town.

Original Ghost Tours GHOST
(☎305-294-9255; www.hauntedtours.com; 423 Fleming St; adult/child $15/10; ⌚8pm & 9pm) Is your guesthouse haunted? Probably. Why should you fear Robert the Doll in East Martello? Don't ask.

Festivals & Events

Key West hosts a party every sunset, but residents don't need an excuse to go crazy.

Conch Republic Independence Celebration CULTURE
(www.conchrepublic.com) A 10-day tribute to Conch Independence, held every April; vie for (made-up) public offices and watch a drag queens footrace.

Hemingway Days Festival CULTURE
(www.hemingwaydays.net) Includes a bull run, marlin tournament and look-alike contest, as well as literary events, in late July.

Fantasy Fest CULTURE
(www.fantasyfest.net) Room rates get hiked to the hilt for this raucous, 10-day Halloween-meets-Carnivale event in late October.

Sleeping

Key West lodging is generally pretty expensive – especially in the wintertime and even *more* especially during special events, when room rates can triple. Book ahead, or you may well end up joining the long traffic jam headed back to the mainland.

You can find chain motels in New Town, but you've got to stay in Old Town to truly experience Key West. Visit the **Key West Innkeepers Association** (www.keywestinns.com) for more guesthouses; pretty much all are gay-friendly.

Curry Mansion Inn HOTEL **$$$**
(☎305-294-5349; http://currymansion.com; 511 Caroline St; r winter $240-365, summer $195-285; P❄📶🏊) In a city full of stately 19th-century homes, the Curry Mansion is especially handsome. It's a pleasing mix of aristocratic American elements, but especially the bright Floridian rooms with canopied beds. Enjoy bougainvillea and breezes on the verandah.

Mermaid & the Alligator GUESTHOUSE **$$$**
(☎305-294-1894; www.kwmermaid.com; 729 Truman Ave; r winter $218-298, summer $148-198; P❄@📶🏊) Book way ahead: with only nine rooms, this place's charm exceeds its capacity. It's chock-a-block with treasures collected from the owners' travels, giving it a worldly flair that's simultaneously European and Zen.

L'Habitation GUESTHOUSE **$$**
(☎305-293-9203; www.lhabitation.com; 408 Eaton St; r $109-179; ❄📶) At this beautiful classic Keys cottage, the friendly, bilingual owners welcome guests in English or French. The cute rooms come kitted out in light tropical shades, with lamps that look like contemporary art pieces and skittles-bright quilts.

Big Ruby's Guesthouse HOTEL **$$$**
(☎305-296-2323; www.bigrubys.com; 409 Apelrouth Lane; r $195-305; P❄📶🏊) Catering exclusively to a gay clientele, the hotel's exterior is all refined Conch mansion, while

inside, the rooms are sleekly contemporary. The capper is the clothing-optional lagoon pool. Breakfast is included.

Caribbean House GUESTHOUSE $
(☎305-296-0999; www.geocities.com/caribbeanhousekw; 226 Petronia St; r from $85; P❄@) In the heart of Bahama Village, rooms are tiny, but they're clean, cozy and cheery. Add free breakfast and welcoming hosts and you get a rare find in Key West: a bargain.

Key Lime Inn HOTEL $$
(☎800-559-4430; www.historickeywestinns.com; 725 Truman Ave; r $99-229; P) These cozy cottages are scattered around a tropical hardwood backdrop. Inside, the blissfully cool rooms are greener than a jade mine, with wicker furniture and tiny flat-screens to keep you from ever leaving.

Eating

You aren't technically allowed to leave the island without sampling the conch fritters – like hushpuppies, but made with conch – or the key lime pie, made with key limes, sweetened condensed milk, eggs and sugar on a Graham-cracker crust.

TOP CHOICE **Café Solé** FRENCH $$$
(☎305-294-0230; www.cafesole.com; 1029 Southard St; lunch $5-11, dinner $25-32; ⏰5:30-10pm) Conch carpaccio with capers? Yellowtail fillet and foie gras? Oh yes. This locally and critically acclaimed venue is known for its cozy back-porch ambience and innovative menus, the result of a French-trained chef exploring island ingredients.

Mo's Restaurant CARIBBEAN $$
(http://salsalocakeywest.com; 1116 White St; mains $11-16; ⏰11am-10pm Mon-Sat) If the phrase 'Caribbean home cooking' causes drool to form in the corners of your mouth, don't hesitate. The dishes are mainly Haitian, and they're delicious.

Blue Heaven AMERICAN $$$
(☎305-296-8666; http://blueheavenkw.homestead.com; 729 Thomas St; dinner $19-38; ⏰8am-3pm & 5-10pm) One of the island's quirkiest venues (and it's a high bar), where you dine in an outdoor courtyard with a flock of chickens. Customers gladly wait, bemusedly, for Blue Heaven's well-executed, Southern-fried interpretation of Keys cuisine.

Camille's FUSION $$
(☎305-296-4811; 1202 Simonton St; lunch $4-13, dinner $14-25; ⏰8am-10pm;) This healthy and tasty neighborhood joint is where local families go for a casual meal. Still, homey Camille's keeps its knives sharp, and the inventive menu ranges from French toast with Godiva liqueur to tasty chicken salad.

El Siboney CUBAN $$
(900 Catherine St; mains $10-16; ⏰11am-9:30pm) Key West is only 90 miles from Cuba, so this awesome rough-and-ready corner establishment is quite literally the closest you can get to real Cuban food in the US. Cash only.

Conch Town Café SEAFOOD $
(801 Thomas St; mains $5-18; ⏰11:30am-7:30pm) Many bypass this walk-up/carry-out, with its plastic patio furniture and scruffy island vibe. It's a shame, as it serves deliciously 'cracked' (deep-fried) conch with a lip-puckeringly sour-lime marinade.

Drinking

Another way to think of Key West is as a floating bar. You can crawl your way along Duval St till about 3am, when most bars close.

TOP CHOICE **Green Parrot** BAR
(www.greenparrot.com; 601 Whitehead St) This rogue's cantina has the longest tenure of any bar on the island (since 1890). It's a fabulous dive drawing a lively mix of locals and out-of-towners, with a century's worth of strange decor. Men, don't miss the urinal.

La Te Da CABARET
(www.lateda.com; 1125 Duval St) Look for drag queens to mark your arrival at this complex that has three bars and a cabaret space famous for its drag shows.

Porch BAR
(429 Caroline St) Escape the Duval St frat boy bars at the Porch, where knowledgeable bartenders dispense artisan beers. It sounds civilized, and almost is, by Key West standards.

Garden of Eden BAR
(224 Duval St) You can make like Adam and Eve at this clothing-optional rooftop bar; the fig leaf is also optional.

Captain Tony's Saloon BAR
(www.capttonyssaloon.com; 428 Greene St) This former icehouse, morgue and Hemingway haunt is built around the town's old hanging tree. The eclectic decor includes emancipated bras and signed dollar bills.

Virgilio's JAZZ
(www.virgilioskeywest.com; 524 Duval St) Thank God for a little variety. This town needs a dark, candlelit martini lounge where you can chill to jazz and salsa. Enter on Appelrouth Lane.

801 Bourbon Bar GAY
(www.801bourbon.com; 801 Duval St) Boys will be boys.

Aqua GAY & LESBIAN
(www.aquakeywest.com; 711 Duval St) All genders.

Pearl's Rainbow LESBIAN
(www.pearlsrainbow.com; 525 United St) Lesbian pool bar.

Information

A great trip-planning resource is www.fla-keys.com/keywest. In town, get maps and brochures at **Key West Chamber of Commerce** (305-294-2587; www.keywestchamber.org; 510 Greene St; 8am-6:30pm Mon-Sat, to 6pm Sun).

Gay and lesbian visitors can get information at the **Gay & Lesbian Community Center** (305-292-3223; http://lgbtcenter.com; 513 Truman Ave).

Getting There & Around

The easiest way to travel around Key West and the Keys is by car, though traffic along the one major route, US 1, can be maddening during the winter high season. **Greyhound** (305-296-9072; www.greyhound.com; 3535 S Roosevelt Blvd) serves the Keys along US Hwy 1 from downtown Miami.

You can fly into **Key West International Airport** (EYW; www.keywestinternationalairport.com) with frequent flights from major cities, most going through Miami. Or, take a fast catamaran from Fort Myers or Miami; call the **Key West Express** (888-539-2628; www.seakeywestexpress.com) for schedules and fares.

Within Key West, bicycles are the preferred mode of travel (rentals along Duval St run $10 a day). **City Transit System** (www.kwtransit.com; tickets $2) runs color-coded buses through downtown and the Lower Keys.

ATLANTIC COAST

Florida's East Coast is a study in contrasts: there are the astronaut training and (now-ended) space shuttle launches of Kennedy Space Center, and the cobblestone streets of the nation's oldest city, St Augustine. There are Daytona's screaming, oval Nascar racetrack and the undeveloped beaches and intercoastal waterways of Canaveral National Seashore. There's rocking out in Jacksonville, skimming stones on Amelia Island, and catching waves on Cocoa Beach.

Space Coast

They call the Titusville–Cocoa Beach–Melbourne area the Space Coast because it's home to NASA, but it could just as easily be referring to the miles of undeveloped beaches and protected national parkland, where space is plentiful. Once the setting for the iconic 1960s TV series *I Dream of Jeannie*, the Space Coast is the real-life home to the Kennedy Space Center, with its massive visitor complex. Cocoa Beach is also a magnet for surfers, with Florida's best waves. Visitor information is available through **Florida's Space Coast Office of Tourism** (321-433-4470; www.space-coast.com; 430 Brevard Ave, Cocoa Village; 8am-5pm Mon-Sat).

Sights & Activities

Kennedy Space Center Visitor Complex MUSEUM
(321-449-4444; www.kennedyspacecenter.com; adult/child $41/31; 9am-5:30pm) Houston, we have an attraction. It was perhaps inevitable that, considering its proximity to Orlando, the space center would develop a ride, and thus **Shuttle Launch Experience** officially achieved lift-off. Reaching a top 'speed' of 17,500mph – vertically – this realistic simulator ride was designed by astronauts to feel just like a space-shuttle takeoff, but without the teary goodbyes.

Your ticket to the complex includes a two-hour bus tour, a 45-minute IMAX film, live-action stage shows, exhibits on subjects such as early space exploration and encounters with astronauts. It also includes the **Astronaut Hall of Fame**, where you'll experience the G-Force Trainer and other simulator rides.

Add-on options abound, depending on how serious you are about your astronaut experience (they're popular – book in advance). **Discover KSC** (adult/child $21/15) includes a visit to the massive Vehicle Assembly Building, while **Cape Canaveral: Then & Now** (adult/child $21/15) is an extended guided tour that includes the Air Force Space & Missile Museum. Hungry space enthusiasts can have **Lunch with an Astronaut** (adult/child $44/33), and the action-oriented **Astronaut Training Experience** (ticket $145) prepares you for spaceflight, should the opportunity arise.

As of 2011, NASA ended its space shuttle program indefinitely, which means an end to watching shuttle launches at Kennedy. However, because of this you can expect changes, both with exhibits and visitor facilities as well as with Kennedy's role in the next phase of the US space program.

FREE **Merritt Island National Wildlife Refuge** WILDLIFE RESERVE
(www.merrittisland.com; SR 402, Titusville; ⏲visitor center 8am-4:30pm Mon-Fri, 9am-5pm Sat & Sun, closed Sun Apr-Oct) This unspoiled 140,000-acre refuge is one of the country's best birding spots, especially from October to May (early morning and after 4pm). More endangered and threatened species of wildlife inhabit the swamps, marshes and hardwood hammocks here than at any other site in the continental US. The best viewing is on Black Point Wildlife Dr.

Canaveral National Seashore PARK
(☎386-428-3384; www.nps.gov/cana; adult/child $3/free; ⏲6am-6pm Oct-Mar, to 8pm Apr-Sep) The 24 miles of pristine, windswept beaches comprise the longest stretch of undeveloped beach on Florida's east coast. They include family-friendly **Apollo Beach** on the north end with its gentle surf, untrammeled **Klondike Beach** in the middle – a favorite of campers and nature lovers – and **Playalinda Beach** at the south end, which is surfer central.

Mosquito Lagoon, with islands and mangroves teeming with wildlife, hugs the west side of the barrier island. Rent kayaks in Cocoa Beach. Rangers offer **pontoon boat tours** (per person $20) from the visitor information center on most Sundays. From June through August, rangers lead groups on nightly **sea turtle nesting tours** (adult/child 8-16yr $14/free; ⏲7am-11:30pm); reservations required.

Water Sports

In addition to surfing the region's beaches, the Banana River, Indian River Lagoon and Mosquito Lagoon lure folks into all kinds of watercraft.

Island Watercraft Rental BOATING
(☎321-454-7661; www.islandwatercraftrentals.com; 1872 E 520 Causeway, Cocoa Beach) Offers pontoons (half-day $250), fishing boats (two hours $90) and motorboats (half-day $225), as well as inner-tubes and skis.

SURF'S UP ON THE SPACE COAST

For surfers, the 70 miles of Space Coast beaches from New Smyrna to Sebastian Inlet get the state's best waves. Ten-time world champion surfer Kelly Slater was born in Cocoa Beach, which remains the epicenter of the surf community. For the local scene and surf reports, visit **Florida Surfing** (www.floridasurfing.com) and **Surf Guru** (www.surfguru.com).

In Cocoa Beach, the long-running **Ron Jon Surf School** (☎321-868-1980; www.cocoabeachsurfingschool.com; 3901 N Atlantic Ave; per hr $50-65) offers lessons for all ages and levels, and sponsors the Ron Jon Easter Surf Festival, Florida's largest.

Ron Jon's Surf Shop SURFING, BOATING
(☎321-799-8888; www.ronjons.com; 4151 N Atlantic Ave, Cocoa Beach) Local icon rents just about anything water-related, from fat-tired beach bikes ($15 daily) to surfboards ($30 daily); also a huge store.

Sleeping

Charming Cocoa Beach has the most options, as well as the most chains. For a quieter stay, Vero Beach is also attractive.

Beach Place Guesthouses APARTMENT **$$$**
(☎321-783-4045; www.beachplaceguesthouses.com; 1445 S Atlantic Ave, Cocoa Beach; ste $195-350;) A slice of heavenly relaxation in Cocoa Beach's partying beach scene, this laid-back two-story guesthouse in a residential neighborhood has roomy suites with hammocks and a lovely deck, all just steps from the dunes and beach.

Fawlty Towers MOTEL **$**
(☎321-784-3870; www.fawltytowersresort.com; 100 E Cocoa Beach Causeway, Cocoa Beach; r $90-114; P) Beneath this motel's gloriously garish and extremely pink exterior lie fairly straightforward rooms with an unbeatable beachside location; quiet pool and tiki bar.

South Beach Place MOTEL **$$**
(☎772-231-5366; www.southbeachplacevero.com; 1705 S Ocean Dr, Vero Beach; ste per day $125-175, per week $700-1050;) Old Florida with a facelift, this tasteful and bright two-story motel in Vero Beach sits in a particularly

quiet stretch across from the beach. One-bedroom suites have a full kitchen.

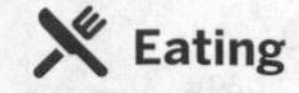

Eating

Fat Snook SEAFOOD **$$$**
(☎321-784-1190; http://thefatsnook.com; 2464 S Atlantic Ave, Cocoa Beach; mains $21-34; ⏰5-10pm) Hidden inside an uninspired building, yet sporting cool, minimalist decor, tiny Fat Snook stands out as an oasis of fine cooking. Yes, there's a distinct air of food snobbery here, but it's so tasty, no one seems to mind.

Slow and Low Barbecue BARBECUE **$$**
(306 N Orlando Ave, Cocoa Beach; mains $8-20; ⏰11am-midnight) After a day on the beach, nothing satisfies better than a plate overflowing with barbecue ribs, fried okra, turnip greens and sweet fried potatoes. There's a daily happy hour and live music Thursday through Sunday.

Simply Delicious CAFE **$**
(125 N Orlando Ave, Cocoa Beach; mains $6-12; ⏰8am-3pm Tue-Sat, to 2pm Sun) You can't miss this little yellow house on the southbound stretch of A1A. It's a homey Americana place – nothing fancy, nothing trendy, just simply delicious.

Maison Martinique FRENCH **$$$**
(☎772-231-5366; Caribbean Court Boutique Hotel, 1601 S Ocean Dr, Vero Beach; mains $18-35; ⏰5-10pm) In Vero Beach, outstanding French cuisine with first-rate service and intimate surrounds. On warm evenings, eat by the little pool; for something more casual, head to the piano bar upstairs.

Getting There & Away

From Orlando take Hwy 528 east, which connects with Hwy A1A. **Greyhound** (www.greyhound.com) has services from West Palm Beach and Orlando to Titusville. **Vero Beach Shuttle** (☎772-267-0550; www.verobeachshuttle.com) provides airport shuttle service.

Daytona Beach

With typical Floridian hype, Daytona bills itself as 'the World's Most Famous Beach.' Well, not really, and anyway, its fame is less about quality than the size of the parties this expansive beach has witnessed. To wit: spring break and Nascar.

Daytona has long been, and remains, a family destination, and it preserves some retro '50s carnival attractions. Until recently, it also hosted the quintessential *Girls Gone Wild* spring break madness. However, the town has cracked down on drunken loutishness and wardrobe malfunctions, and spring break here isn't what it used to be, though it still draws crowds.

What hasn't slowed down (pun intended) is Nascar, which was born here in 1947. As early as 1902, pioneers in the auto industry would drag race down the beach's hard-packed sands to test their inventions. That gave way to stock-car racing, which was eventually formalized and moved to the Daytona International Speedway.

Today the population quintuples during February's **Speed Weeks**, and half a million bikers roar into town for motorcycle events in spring and fall. Be aware that traffic police, cognizant of the local need for speed, are vigilant.

The **Daytona Beach Convention & Visitors Bureau** (☎386-255-0415; www.daytonabeach.com; 126 E Orange Ave; ⏰9am-5pm Mon-Fri) has great lodging listings. Gay and lesbian travelers can visit www.gaydaytona.com.

Sights & Activities

Daytona Beach BEACH
(per car $5) This perfectly planar stretch of sand was once the city's raceway. You can still drive sections at a strictly enforced top speed of 10mph. Or rent an ATV, fat-tired cruiser or recumbent trike. Water sports rentals are ubiquitous.

Daytona International Speedway RACETRACK
(☎800-748-7467; www.daytonaintlspeedway.com; 1801 W International Speedway Blvd; tickets from $20) The Holy Grail of raceways has a diverse race schedule. Ticket prices accelerate rapidly for the big races, headlined by the **Daytona 500** in February, but you can wander the massive stands for free on nonrace days. Two first-come, first-served **tram tours** (tickets $15-22) take in the track, pits and behind-the-scenes areas. Real fanatics can indulge in the **Richard Petty Driving Experience** (☎800-237-3889; www.drivepetty.com), where you can either ride shotgun ($135) around the track or take a day to become the driver ($2200); check schedule online.

Museum of Arts & Sciences MUSEUM
(www.moas.org; 1040 Museum Blvd; adult/student $13/7; ⏰9am-5pm Tue-Sat, from 11am Sun) A wonderful mishmash of everything from

Cuban art to Coca-Cola relics to a 13ft giant sloth skeleton.

Marine Science Center AQUARIUM
(www.marinesciencecenter.com; 100 Lighthouse Dr; adult/child $5/2; ⏲10am-4pm Tue-Sat, from noon Sun) Sea turtles nest on Daytona's beaches, and this rehab center cares for the sick and injured. Lots of seabirds too.

Ponce de León Inlet Lighthouse LIGHTHOUSE
(www.ponceinlet.org; 4931 S Peninsula Dr; adult/child $5/1.50; ⏲10am-6pm winter, to 9pm summer) About 6 miles south of Daytona Beach, it's 203 steps up to the top of Florida's tallest lighthouse.

Daytona Beach Drive-In Church CHURCH
(www.driveinchurch.net; 3140 S Atlantic Ave; ⏲services 8:30am & 10am Sun) In auto-obsessed Daytona, cars are a religion, and in this former drive-in movie theater you can get religion in your car.

Sleeping

Daytona lodging is plentiful and spans all budgets and styles. Prices soar during events; book well ahead.

TOP CHOICE **August Seven Inn** B&B $$
(☎386-248-8420; www.jpaugust.net; 1209 S Peninsula Dr; r $99-155; P❄📶≋) The friendly innkeepers of this gorgeous B&B have stocked it with period antiques and stylish deco, creating a soothing haven from Daytona's typical Nascar-and-spring-break carnival.

Tropical Manor RESORT $$
(☎386-252-4920; www.tropicalmanor.com; 2237 S Atlantic Ave; r $88-315; P❄📶≋) This immaculate beachfront property is like a playful pastel vision of Candy Land. Every room type is available, from motel rooms to efficiencies, large suites to cottages.

Sun Viking Lodge RESORT $$
(☎386-252-6252; www.sunviking.com; 2411 S Atlantic Ave; r $80-285; P❄📶≋👪) Most rooms have kitchenettes, but they could stand a reno – oh never mind. For families, it's ideal: two pools, a 60ft waterslide, beach access, shuffleboard, endless activities and a Viking theme!

Shores RESORT $$$
(☎386-767-7350; www.shoresresort.com; 2637 N Atlantic Ave; r $120-320; P❄📶≋) One of Daytona's most elegant offerings, this chic, beachfront boutique has hand-striped walls, a full-service spa and sophisticated color palette.

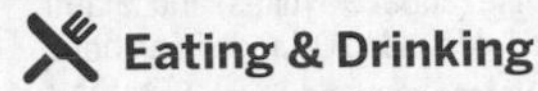

Eating & Drinking

Dancing Avocado Kitchen MEXICAN $
(110 S Beach St; mains $6-11; ⏲8am-4pm Mon-Sat; 🥬) Fresh, healthful, yummy Mexican dishes like extreme burritos and quesadillas dominate the menu at this vegetarian-oriented cafe, but the signature dancing avocado melt is tops.

Rose Villa CONTINENTAL $$$
(☎386-615-7673; www.rosevillaormond.com; 43 West Granada Blvd, Ormond Beach; mains $18-32; ⏲5-10pm Tue-Thu, to 11pm Fri & Sat) This lovely new under-the-radar bistro is in a renovated Victorian house a few miles north of Daytona. The menu is charmingly old-fashioned 'Continental' – veal chop in cream sauce, Scottish salmon with caper butter – and the vintage setting enchanting.

Pasha Middle East Cafe MIDDLE EASTERN $
(www.pashacafedaytona.com; 919 W International Speedway Blvd; mains $5-14; ⏲10am-7pm Mon-Sat, noon-6pm Sun) Chow on falafel, kabob, hummus, tabbouleh – and of course baklava – in a casual, family-run cafe and deli.

Aunt Catfish's on the River SOUTHERN $$
(☎386-767-4768; www.auntcatfishontheriver.com; 4009 Halifax Dr, Port Orange; mains $8-25; ⏲11:30am-9pm) Southern-style seafood lolling in butter and Cajun-spice catfish make this place insanely popular.

Entertainment

Daytona's entertainment scene skews to rocking biker bars (mostly along Main St) and high-octane dance clubs (on or near Seabreeze Blvd).

Razzles CLUB
(www.razzlesnightclub.com; 611 Seabreeze Blvd) The reigning dance club, permanently thumping.

Froggy's Saloon BAR
(www.froggyssaloon.com; 800 Main St) It's bike week all year long; check your liver at the door.

Getting There & Around

Daytona Beach International Airport (DAB; www.flydaytonafirst.com) is just east of the Speedway, and the **Greyhound bus station** (www.greyhound.com; 138 S Ridgewood Ave) is the starting point for services around Florida.

Daytona is close to the intersection of two of Florida's major interstates: I-95 is the quickest way to Jacksonville (about 90 miles) and Miami (260 miles), and I-4 leads to Orlando in an hour.

Votran (www.votran.com; adult/child $1.25/free) runs buses and trolleys throughout the city.

St Augustine

The first this, the oldest that...St Augustine was founded by the Spanish in 1565, which means it's chock-full of age-related superlatives. Tourists flock here to stroll the ancient streets, and horse-drawn carriages clip-clop past townsfolk dressed in period costume around the National Historic Landmark District, aka the oldest permanent settlement in the US.

At times St Augustine screams, 'Hey, everyone, look how quaint we are!' but it stops just short of theme park plastic-ness because, well, the buildings and monuments are real, and the narrow, cafe-strewn lanes are genuinely charming. Walk the cobblestoned streets or stand where Juan Ponce de León landed in 1513, and the historical distance occasionally collapses into present-moment chills.

The main **visitor center** (☎904-825-1000; www.floridashistoriccoast.com; 10 Castillo Dr; ⌚8:30am-5:30pm) screens a 45-minute film on the town's history. Also visit the city website, www.ci.st-augustine.fl.us.

Sights & Activities

The town's two Henry Flagler buildings shouldn't be missed.

Lightner Museum MUSEUM
(☎904-824-2874; www.lightnermuseum.org; 75 King St; adult/child $10/5; ⌚9am-5pm) Flagler's former Hotel Alcazar is now home to this wonderful museum, with a little bit of everything from ornate Gilded Age furnishings to collections of marbles and cigar-box labels.

Hotel Ponce de León HISTORIC BUILDING
(74 King St; tours adult/child $7/1; ⌚tours hourly 10am-3pm) Across the street is this gorgeous former hotel, which was built in the 1880s and is now the world's most gorgeous dormitory, belonging to Flagler College. Take a guided tour (summer only) – or at least step inside to gawk at the lobby for free.

Spanish Quarter Museum HISTORIC BUILDINGS
(☎904-825-6830; 53 St George St; adult/child $7/4; ⌚9am-4:45pm) See how they did things back in the 18th century at this re-creation of Spanish-colonial St Augustine, complete with craftspeople demonstrating blacksmithing, leather working and other trades.

Pirate & Treasure Museum MUSEUM
(www.thepiratemuseum.com; 12 S Castillo Dr; adult/child $12/7; ⌚9am-8pm) A mash-up of theme park and museum, this celebration of all things pirate has real historical treasures (and genuine gold) as well as animatronic pirates, blasting cannons and a kid-friendly treasure hunt.

Castillo de San Marcos National Monument FORT
(www.nps.gov/casa; btwn San Marcos Ave & Matanzas River; adult/child $6/free; ⌚8:45am-5:15pm) This incredibly photogenic fort is another atmospheric monument to longevity: it's the country's oldest masonry fort, completed by the Spanish in 1695. Park rangers lead programs hourly and shoot off cannons most weekends.

Oldest Houses HISTORIC BUILDINGS
The **González-Alvarez House** (www.oldesthouse.com; 14 St Francis St; adult/student $8/4; ⌚9am-5pm) is the oldest house in the US, on a site occupied since the 1600s. The **Oldest Wooden School House** (www.oldestwoodenschoolhouse.com; 14 St George St; adult/child $3/2; ⌚10am-4:30pm Mon-Sat, from 11am Sun) is peopled by animatronic teachers and pupils, and includes a dungeon!

Fountain of Youth HISTORIC SITE
(www.fountainofyouthflorida.com; 11 Magnolia Ave; adult/child $10/6; ⌚9am-5pm) Insert tongue firmly in cheek and step right up for an acrid cup of eternal youth at this 'archaeological park.' As the story goes, Spanish explorer Juan Ponce de León came ashore here in 1513, and he considered this freshwater stream the possible legendary Fountain of Youth.

Anastasia State Recreation Area PARK
(☎904-461-2033; 1340 Hwy A1A; car $8) Locals escape the tourist hordes here, with a terrific beach, a campground (campsites $28) and rentals for all kinds of water sports.

Tours

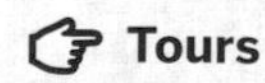

St Augustine City Walks WALKING
(☎904-540-3476; www.staugustinecitywalks.com; tours $14-45) Extremely fun walking tours of all kinds, from silly to serious.

Old Town Trolley Tours TROLLEY
(☎904-829-3800; www.trolleytours.com; 167 San Marco Ave; adult/child $23/10) Hop-on/hop-off narrated trolley tours.

St Augustine Sightseeing Trains TRAIN
(☎904-829-6545; www.redtrains.com; 170 San Marco Ave; adult/child $22/9) Hop-on/hop-off narrated train tours.

Sleeping

St Augustine is a popular weekend escape; expect room rates to rise about 30% on Friday and Saturday. Inexpensive motels and chain hotels line San Marco Ave, near where it meets US Hwy 1. More than two dozen atmospheric B&Bs can be found at www.staugustineinns.com.

TOP CHOICE **At Journey's End** B&B $$
(☎904-829-0076; www.atjourneysend.com; 89 Cedar St; r $129-219; P❄📶👪) Free from the granny-ish decor that haunts many St Augustine B&Bs, this pet-friendly, kid-friendly and gay-friendly spot is outfitted in a chic mix of antiques and modern furniture, and run by some affable hosts. Breakfast is included.

Casa Monica HOTEL $$$
(☎904-827-1888; www.casamonica.com; 95 Cordova St; r $179-779; P❄📶🏊) Built in 1888, this is *the* luxe hotel in town, with turrets and fountains adding to the Spanish-Moorish castle atmosphere. Rooms are also richly appointed, with wrought-iron beds and every amenity.

Casa de Solana B&B $$
(☎877-824-3555; www.casadesolana.com; 21 Aviles St; r $129-249; P📶) Just off pedestrian-only Aviles St in the oldest part of town, this utterly charming little inn remains faithful to its early-1800s period decor. Rooms are a bit small, but price and location make it a great deal.

Pirate Haus Inn HOSTEL $
(☎904-808-1999; www.piratehaus.com; 32 Treasury St; dm $20, r $50-95; P❄📶) It's not fancy, but this family-friendly European-style guesthouse-hostel has an unbeatable location. Includes 'pirate pancake' breakfast.

Eating & Drinking

St Augustine has a notable dining scene, though it's also rife with overpriced tourist traps.

TOP CHOICE **Floridian** NEW AMERICAN $$
(☎904-829-0655; www.thefloridianstaug.com; 39 Cordova St; mains $12-20; ⏰11am-3pm & 5-9pm Wed-Mon, to 10pm Fri & Sat) Though it oozes with hipster-locavore earnestness, this new farm-to-table restaurant is so friggin' fabulous you won't mind. The chef-owners serve whimsical neo-Southern creations in an oh-so-cool dining room.

Spanish Bakery BAKERY $
(www.thespanishbakery.com; 42½ St George St; mains $3-5.50; ⏰9:30am-3pm) Through an arched gate in a table-filled courtyard, this diminutive stucco bakeshop serves empanadas, sausage rolls and other conquistador-era favorites. Don't hesitate; they sell out quick.

Casa Maya MEXICAN $$
(17 Hypolita St; mains $6-18; ⏰10am-3:30pm daily, 5:30-9pm Wed-Sun; 🖉) Snappy jazz wafts through the jasmine-shaded patio of this tasty vegetarian-friendly Mayan (or Northern Central American) restaurant. Don't miss the hibiscus sangria!

Collage INTERNATIONAL $$$
(☎904-829-0055; www.collagestaug.com; 60 Hypolita St; mains $26-36; ⏰from 5:30pm) This upscale spot feels a world away from the bustling touristy downtown. The seafood-heavy menu wins raves for its subtle touch with global flavors.

Scarlett O'Hara's PUB $
(www.scarlettoharas.net; 70 Hypolita St; mains $5-14; ⏰11am-1am) Leave your hoop skirt at home. This rowdy place is a fine spot for beer and pub grub.

Taberna del Gallo BAR
(53 St George St; ⏰2-9:30pm Thu-Sat, noon-7pm Sun) Flickering candles provide the only light at this 1736 stone tavern. Sing sea shanties on weekends.

AIA Ale Works PUB
(www.a1aaleworks.com; 1 King St; ⏰11am-11:30pm Sun-Thu, to midnight Fri & Sat) Who needs historical ambience with fine-crafted beer like this?

Getting There & Around

The **Greyhound bus station** (☎904-829-6401; 1711 Dobbs Rd) is a few miles from the heart of things. Once you're in Old Town, you can get almost everywhere on foot.

Jacksonville

Are we there yet? Have we left yet? It's hard to tell, because Jacksonville sprawls out over a whopping 840 sq miles, making it the largest city by area in the continental US (eclipsed only by Anchorage, AK). Jacksonville Beach, known locally as 'Jax Beach,' is about 17 miles east of the city center and is where you'll find white sand and most of the action. For information, peruse www.visit jacksonville.com.

Sights & Activities

TOP CHOICE **Cummer Museum of Art & Gardens** MUSEUM
(www.cummer.org; 829 Riverside Ave; adult/student $10/6; 10am-9pm Tue, to 5pm Wed-Sat, noon-5pm Sun) This handsome museum, Jacksonville's premier cultural space, has a genuinely excellent collection of American and European paintings, Asian decorative art and antiquities.

Museum of Science & History MUSEUM
(www.themosh.org; 1025 Museum Circle; adult/child $10/8; 10am-5pm Mon-Fri, to 6pm Sat, 1-6pm Sun) Packing kids? This museum offers dinosaurs, a planetarium and educational exhibits on Jacksonville's cultural and natural history.

FREE **Anheuser-Busch Brewery** BREWERY TOUR
(www.budweisertours.com; 111 Busch Dr; 10am-4pm Mon-Sat) Enjoy a free tour (and free beer if you're over 21).

Jacksonville Museum of Modern Art MUSEUM
(www.mocajacksonville.org; 333 N Laura St; adult/child $8/5; 10am-4pm Tue-Sat, to 9pm Thu, from noon Sun) The focus of this ultra-modern space extends beyond painting: get lost among contemporary sculpture, prints, photography and film.

Sleeping & Eating

The cheapest rooms are along I-95 and I-10, where the lower-priced chains congregate. Beach lodging rates often rise in summer.

Inn at Oak Street B&B $$
(904-379-5525; www.innatoakstreet.com; 2114 Oak St; r $120-165; P) This gabled three-story 1902 house, with views of the St Johns River, is a peaceful B&B with loads of upscale touches. Handsome, unfussy and includes gourmet breakfast.

Riverdale Inn B&B $$
(904-354-5080; www.riverdaleinn.com; 1521 Riverside Ave; r $120-220; P) In the early 1900s this was one of 50 or so mansions lining Riverside. Now there are only two left, and you're invited to enjoy its lovely rooms with full breakfast.

TOP CHOICE **Clark's Fish Camp** SOUTHERN $$
(www.clarksfishcamp.com; 12903 Hood Landing Rd; mains $13-22; 5:30-9:30pm Mon-Fri, from 11:30am Sat & Sun) Sample Florida's Southern 'Cracker' cuisine of gator, snake, catfish and frog's legs while surrounded by the surreal animal menagerie of 'America's largest private taxidermy collection.' This swamp shack is unforgettable. It's far south of downtown Jacksonville.

Aix MEDITERRANEAN $$$
(904-398-1949; www.bistrox.com; 1440 San Marco Blvd; mains $14-28; 11am-10pm Mon-Thu, to 11pm Fri, 5-11pm Sat, 5-9pm Sun) Dine with the fashionable food mavens on fusion-y Mediterranean dishes at Aix, whose menu bursts with global flavors. Reservations recommended.

River City Brewing Company SEAFOOD $$$
(904-398-2299; www.rivercitybrew.com; 835 Museum Circle; mains $18-30; 10am-3pm & 5-10pm Mon-Sat, 10:30am-2:30pm Sun) The perfect place to quaff a microbrew and enjoy some upscale seafood overlooking the water.

Entertainment

Jacksonville Landing MALL
(www.jacksonvillelanding.com; 2 Independent Dr) Downtown, has restaurants, shops, bars and free outdoor entertainment.

Freebird Live LIVE MUSIC
(904-246-2473; www.freebirdlive.com; 200 N 1st St; 8pm-2am) At the beach, a rocking music venue and home of the band Lynyrd Skynyrd.

Getting There & Around

North of the city, **Jacksonville International Airport** (JAX; www.jia.aero) has rental cars. **Greyhound** (www.greyhound.com; 10 N Pearl St) serves numerous cities, and **Amtrak** (904-766-5110; www.amtrak.com; 3570 Clifford Lane) has trains from the north and south. The **Jacksonville Transportation Authority** (www.jtafla.com) runs a monorail and **city buses** (fare $1).

Amelia Island & Around

Residents are quick to tell you: Amelia Island is just as old as that braggart St Augustine – they just can't prove it. Unfortunately, no Ponce de León, no plaque, so they have to content themselves with being a pretty little island of moss-draped Southern charm and home to **Fernandina Beach**, a shrimping village with 40 blocks of historic buildings and romantic B&Bs. Pick up walking-tour maps and information at the **visitor center** (904-261-3248; www.ameliaisland.org; 102 Centre St; 11am-4pm Mon-Sat, from noon Sun).

To learn about Amelia Island's intricate history, which has seen it ruled under eight different flags starting with the French in 1562, check out the **Amelia Island Museum of History** (www.ameliamuseum.org; 233 S 3rd St; adult/student $7/4; 10am-4pm Mon-Sat, from 1pm Sun). Admission includes tours at 11am and 2pm.

Take a half-hour horse-drawn carriage tour with the **Old Towne Carriage Co** (904-556-2662; www.ameliacarriagetours.com; adult/child $15/7.50) or **Amelia Island Carriages** (904-556-2662; adult/child $15/7). If you'd rather a carriage didn't come between you and your horse, **Kelly's Seahorse Ranch** (904-491-5166; www.kellyranchinc.com; ride per hr $60) offers beachfront trail rides for riders aged 13 and over.

Capping the north end of the island, the Spanish moss–draped **Fort Clinch State Park** (904-277-7274; 2601 Atlantic Ave; pedestrian/car $2/6; 8am-dusk) has beaches, camping ($26), bike trails and a commanding Civil War–era **fort** (9am-5pm), with reenactments taking place the first full weekend of every month.

Amelia Island is part of the **Talbot Islands State Parks** (904-251-2320; 8am-dusk), which includes the pristine shoreline at **Little Talbot Island** (car $5) and the 'boneyard beach' at **Big Talbot Island State Park** (car $3), where silvered tree skeletons create a dramatic landscape. Both are south of Amelia Island down the First Coast Hwy.

From fall through spring, surfable beach breaks can be common, especially at Main Beach. **Pipeline Surf Shop** (904-277-3717; 2022 1st Ave) rents boards and wetsuits, and gives lessons.

At Fernandina Beach, **Elizabeth Pointe Lodge** (904-277-4851; www.elizabethpointelodge.com; 98 S Fletcher Ave; r $215-460; P) looks like an old Nantucket-style sea captain's house with wraparound porches, gracious service and beautifully appointed rooms. Also at the beach is the Victorian Gothic **Fairbanks House** (904-277-0500; www.fairbankshouse.com; 227 S 7th St; r $175-265; P), an atmospheric mansion where Indiana Jones might retire, as well as **Hoyt House** (904-277-4300; www.hoythouse.com; 804 Atlantic Ave; r $185-240; P), another lovely inn with lavish breakfasts and a pool (a rarity among Amelia B&Bs).

Downtown Fernandina Beach is the place to eat. Small plates and mains link arms happily at the tiny, stylish **29 South** (904-277-7919; www.29southrestaurant.com; 29 S 3rd St; mains $18-28; 11:30am-2:30pm Tue-Sat, 5:30-9:30pm Mon-Sat, 10am-2pm Sun), a neo-Southern gourmet bistro. Another foodie destination is **Merge** (904-277-8797; 510 S 8th St; meals $20-26; from 5pm), featuring exquisite seafood dishes using local ingredients. For something more low-key and funky, try **Café Karibo & Karibrew** (www.cafekaribo.com; 27 N 3rd St; mains $8-24; 11am-9pm Tue-Sun, to 3pm Mon), with a two-story cafe on one side and a down-home brewpub on the other.

Fernandina does beat out St Augustine in one 'oldest' category: Florida's oldest bar, the **Palace Saloon** (www.thepalacesaloon.com; 113 Centre St), with swinging doors, draped velvet and a deadly Pirate's Punch.

WEST COAST

Every evening along the seemingly endless powdery white-sand beaches of the Gulf Coast, the tangerine sun kisses the silver-mantled indigo waters before slipping off to bed. The west coast's barrier islands are a Florida promoter's dream – not only are they less commercially cluttered than their Atlantic counterparts, they remain equally rich in cultural sophistication, gourmet cuisine and natural beauty. Searching for mermaids and flamenco dancers, manatees and open-mouthed alligators, the circus and Salvador Dalí? Look no further.

Tampa

From the outside, Florida's third-largest city seems all business, even generically so. But Tampa surprises: its revitalized riverfront is a sparkling green swathe dotted with intriguing cultural institutions, and its historic Ybor City district preserves the city's Cuban cigar-industry past while, at night, transforming into the Gulf Coast's hottest bar and nightclub scene. South Tampa, meanwhile, has a cutting-edge dining scene that's drawing food mavens from Orlando and Miami.

Sights

DOWNTOWN TAMPA

Aside from the zoo, downtown's sights are in or along Tampa's attractive green space, **Riverwalk** (www.thetampariverwalk.com).

TOP CHOICE **Florida Aquarium** AQUARIUM
(☎813-273-4000; www.flaquarium.org; 701 Channelside Dr; adult/child $20/15; ⊙9:30am-5pm) Tampa's excellent aquarium is among the state's best. Cleverly designed, the re-created swamp lets you walk among herons and ibis as they prowl the mangroves. Programs let you swim with the fishes (and the sharks) or take a catamaran ecotour in Tampa Bay.

Lowry Park Zoo ZOO
(www.lowryparkzoo.com; 1101 W Sligh Ave; adult/child $24/19; ⊙9:30am-5pm) North of downtown, Tampa's zoo gets you as close to the animals as possible, with several free-flight aviaries, a camel ride, giraffe feeding, wallaby enclosure and rhino 'encounter.'

Tampa Museum of Art MUSEUM
(www.tampamuseum.org; 120 W Gasparilla Plaza; adult/child $10/5; ⊙11am-7pm Mon-Thu, to 8pm Fri, to 5pm Sat & Sun) In 2010 the museum christened its dramatically cantilevered new home. Six galleries balance Greek and Roman antiquities, contemporary photography and new media with major traveling exhibitions.

Tampa Bay History Center MUSEUM
(www.tampabayhistorycenter.org; 801 Old Water St; adult/child $12/7; ⊙10am-5pm) This first-rate history museum presents the region's Seminole people, Cracker pioneers and Tampa's Cuban community and cigar industry. The cartography collection dazzles.

Henry B Plant Museum MUSEUM
(www.plantmuseum.com; 401 W Kennedy Blvd; admission $10; ⊙10am-5pm Tue-Sat, from noon Sun) The silver minarets of Henry B Plant's 1891 Tampa Bay Hotel glint majestically. Now part of the University of Tampa, one section re-creates the original hotel's luxurious, gilded late-Victorian world.

Glazer Children's Museum CHILDREN'S MUSEUM
(www.glazermuseum.org; 110 W Gasparilla Plaza; adult/child 1-12yr $15/9.50; ⊙10am-5pm Mon-Fri, to 6pm Sat, 1-6pm Sun) Creative play spaces for kids don't get any better than this crayon-bright, inventive museum. Eager staff and tons of coolio fun; adjacent Curtis Hixon Park is picnic-and-playground friendly.

YBOR CITY

Like the illicit love child of Key West and Miami's Little Havana, Ybor City's cobblestoned 19th-century historic district is a redolent mix of wrought-iron balconies, globe streetlamps, immigrant history, ethnic cuisine, cigars and hip, happening nightlife. Diverse and youthful, Ybor (ee-bore) City oozes rakish, scruffy charm.

The **visitor center** (www.ybor.org; 1600 E 8th Ave; ⊙9am-5pm Mon-Sat, from noon Sun) is itself an excellent small museum. The main drag – along 7th Ave (La Septima) between 14th

MANATEES & MERMAIDS

Apparently, Florida's Spanish discoverers confused manatees with mermaids, but it's not hard to tell them apart. Mermaids are those beautiful long-haired women with the spangly tails swimming in the underwater theater at **Weeki Wachee Springs** (www.weekiwachee.com; 6131 Commercial Way, Weeki Wachee; adult/child $25/17; ⊙10am-4pm). Their graceful adagios and *The Little Mermaid* show (three times daily) are Florida's most delightfully kitschy entertainment (just 45 minutes north of Tampa).

Lovable, ponderous, 1000lb manatees are the ones nibbling lettuce in the crystal bathtub of **Homosassa Springs Wildlife State Park** (www.floridastateparks.org/homosassasprings; adult/child $13/5; ⊙9am-5:30pm, last entry 4pm), with its own underwater observatory (20 minutes north of Weeki Wachee).

Sadly, you can't swim with the mermaids, but you can with the manatees. Head a few miles north to King's Bay, within the **Crystal River National Wildlife Refuge** (www.fws.gov/crystalriver; 1502 SE Kings Bay Dr; ⊙visitor center 8am-4pm Mon-Fri), where the visitor center can guide you to nearly 40 commercial operators that, had they existed, would have spared the Spaniards lots of heartache.

and 21st Sts – is packed with eats, drinks, shops and cigar stores.

Ybor City Museum State Park MUSEUM
(www.ybormuseum.org; 1818 E 9th Ave; admission $4; 9am-5pm) This dusty, old-school history museum preserves a bygone era, with cigar-worker houses and wonderful photos. Best is the museum store; get expert cigar advice and join its **walking tour** (813-428-0854; tour $8; 10:30am Sat), run by a cigar-maker with a PhD.

BUSCH GARDENS & ADVENTURE ISLAND

No, it's not as thematically immersive as Orlando's Disney World or Universal, but Tampa's big theme park, **Busch Gardens** (www.buschgardens.com; 10000 McKinley Dr; adult/child $80/70), will satisfy your adrenaline craving with epic roller coasters and flume rides that weave through an African-theme wildlife park. Music, performances and interactive 4D movies round out a full day. Check the website for opening hours, which vary seasonally.

Adjacent **Adventure Island** (www.adventureisland.com; 10001 McKinley Dr; adult/child $43/39; daily mid-Mar–Aug, weekends only Sep-Oct) is a massive water park with slides and rides galore. Discounts and combination tickets are available online.

Sleeping

Chains abound along Fowler Ave and Busch Blvd (Hwy 580), near Busch Gardens.

TOP CHOICE **Gram's Place** HOSTEL $
(813-221-0596; www.grams-inn-tampa.com; 3109 N Ola Ave; dm $23, r $25-70;) As charismatic as an aging rock star, Gram's is a tiny, welcoming hostel for international travelers who prefer personality over perfect linens. Dig the in-ground hot tub and Saturday night jams.

Tahitian Inn HOTEL $$
(813-877-6721; www.tahitianinn.com; 601 S Dale Mabry Hwy; r $100-170;) This family-owned, full-service hotel offers fresh, boutique stylings at midrange prices. Nice pool, and airport transportation.

Don Vicente de Ybor Historic Inn HISTORIC HOTEL $$
(813-241-4545; www.donvicenteinn.com; 1915 Republica de Cuba; r $130-200;) Slightly faded, the 1895 Don Vicente recalls Ybor City's glory days. Unfortunately, rooms are less warmly dramatic than the atmospheric Old World public spaces. Breakfast included.

Eating

At mealtime, focus on Ybor City, South Tampa's SoHo area (South Howard Ave) and up-and-coming Seminole Heights.

TOP CHOICE **Columbia Restaurant** SPANISH $$$
(813-248-4961; www.columbiarestaurant.com; 2117 E 7th Ave; mains $17-28; 11am-10pm Mon-Thu, to 11pm Fri & Sat, noon-9pm Sun) Definitely reserve ahead for the exuberant, twice-nightly flamenco shows, and enjoy robust, classic Spanish cuisine and heady *mojitos* and sangria. It's an Old World Iberian time warp.

Refinery FUSION $$
(813-237-2000; www.thetamparefinery.com; 5137 N Florida Ave; mains $12-18; 5-10pm Tue-Thu, to 11pm Fri & Sat, 11am-3pm Sun;) This blue-collar gourmet joint promises chipped plates and no pretensions, just playful, delicious hyperlocal cuisine that cleverly mixes a sustainability ethic with a punk attitude.

La Teresita SPANISH $
(www.lateresitarestaurant.com; 3246 W Columbus Dr; mains $5-7; 5am-midnight Mon-Wed, 24hr Thu-Sat, to 10pm Sun) Experience 'real' Tampa at the horseshoe-shaped counters of this Cuban cafeteria (skip the restaurant): order Spanish comfort food of grilled steak, plantains, neon-yellow rice and black beans.

Bern's Steak House STEAKHOUSE $$$
(813-251-2421; www.bernssteakhouse.com; 1208 S Howard Ave; mains $25-60; from 5pm) This legendary, nationally renowned steakhouse is an event as much as a meal. Dress up, order caviar and on-premises dry-aged beef, ask to tour the wine cellar and kitchens, and *don't* skip dessert.

Sidebern's FUSION $$$
(813-258-2233; www.sideberns.com; 2208 W Morrison Ave; mains $29-40; 5-10pm Mon-Thu, to 11pm Fri & Sat;) Don't feel like steak? This trendy alternative to Bern's offers inventive, big-city gourmet cuisine, locally sourced. Impeccable service.

Restaurant BT FUSION $$$
(813-258-1916; www.restaurantbt.com; 2507 S MacDill Ave; lunch $10-13, dinner $23-34; 11:30am-2:30pm & 5:30-10pm Mon-Sat, to 11pm Fri & Sat) Chef Trina Nguyan-Batley has

TAMPA BAY AREA BEACHES

The barrier islands of the Tampa Bay Area are graced with some of Florida's best beaches, whether you define 'best' as 'gorgeous untrammeled solitude' or 'family fun and thumping beach parties.' For more information, visit www.tampabaybeaches.com and www.visitstpeteclearwater.com. North to south, some highlights:

» **Honeymoon & Caladesi Islands** Two of Florida's most beautiful beaches; unspoiled, lightly visited Caladesi Island is only reachable by ferry.

» **Clearwater Beach** Idyllic soft white sand hosts raucous spring-break-style parties; huge resorts cater to the masses.

» **St Pete Beach** Double-wide strand is epicenter of activities and all-ages fun; packed with hotels, bars and restaurants.

» **Pass-a-Grille Beach** Most popular with city-based day-trippers; extremely long and backed by houses (not resorts); cute-as-a-button village for eats.

» **Fort DeSoto Park** North Beach is one of Florida's finest white-sand beaches; ideal for families. Extensive park includes bike and kayak rentals, fishing piers and a cafe.

combined her high-fashion background and Vietnamese upbringing to create this ultrachic temple to sustainable, locavore gastronomy.

Drinking & Entertainment

For nightlife, Ybor City is party central, though SoHo and Seminole Heights are also hip and happening. Tampa Bay's alternative weekly, **Creative Loafing** (www.cltampa.com), lists events and bars. Ybor City is also the center of Tampa's GLBT life; check out the **GaYbor District Coalition** (www.gaybor.com) and **Gay Tampa** (www.gaytampa.com).

TOP CHOICE **Skipper's Smokehouse** LIVE MUSIC
(www.skipperssmokehouse.com; cnr Skipper Rd & Nebraska Ave; cover $5-25; ⊙11am-midnight Tue-Sun) Feeling like it blew in from the Keys, Skipper's is a beloved, unpretentious open-air venue for blues, folk, reggae and gator-swamp rockabilly. Get directions online.

Straz Center for the Performing Arts PERFORMING ARTS
(☎813-229-7827; www.strazcenter.org; 1010 MacInnes Pl) This enormous, multivenue complex draws the gamut of fine arts performances: touring Broadway shows, pop concerts, opera, ballet, drama and more.

Information

Media

The Tampa Bay area has two major daily newspapers.

St Petersburg Times (www.tampabay.com)
Tampa Tribune (www.tampatrib.com)

Tourist Information

Tampa Bay Convention & Visitors Bureau (☎813-223-1111; www.visittampabay.com; 615 Channelside Dr; ⊙9:30am-5:30pm Mon-Sat, 11am-5pm Sun) The visitor center has good free maps and lots of information. Book hotels directly through the website.

Getting There & Around

Tampa International Airport (TPA; www.tampaairport.com; 5503 W Spruce St) has car-rental agencies. **Greyhound** (www.greyhound.com; 610 E Polk St) has numerous services. Trains run south to Miami and north through Jacksonville from the **Amtrak station** (www.amtrak.com; 601 Nebraska Ave). **Hillsborough Area Regional Transit** (HART; www.gohart.org; single/day pass $1.75/3.75) connects downtown and Ybor City with buses, trolleys and old-style streetcars.

St Petersburg

In the bay area, St Petersburg is the more arty, youthful sibling. It also has a more compact and walkable tourist district along its attractive harbor. For a cultural city base within easy striking distance of the region's excellent beaches, St Pete is a great choice.

For maps and info, visit the **chamber of commerce** (☎727-821-4069; http://pleasure.stpete.com; 100 2nd Ave N; ⊙9am-5pm Mon-Fri).

Sights

Most of the action is around and along Central Ave, from 8th Ave to Bayshore Dr, which fronts the harbor and tourist pier.

St Petersburg Museum of Fine Arts MUSEUM
(www.fine-arts.org; 255 Beach Dr NE; adult/child $17/10; ⏲10am-5pm Mon-Sat, from noon Sun) The Museum of Fine Arts collection is as broad as the Dalí's is deep, traversing the world's antiquities and following art's progression through nearly every era.

Florida Holocaust Museum MUSEUM
(www.flholocaustmuseum.org; 55 5th St S; adult/child $14/8; ⏲10am-5pm, to 8pm Thu) The understated exhibits of this Holocaust museum, one of the country's largest, present these mid-20th-century events with moving directness.

Chihuly Collection GALLERY
(www.chihulycollectionstpete.com; 400 Beach Dr; adult/child $15/12; ⏲10am-6pm Mon-Sat, from noon Sun) A paean to Chihuly's glass artistry, with galleries designed to hold the dramatic installations.

Sleeping

TOP CHOICE **Dickens House** B&B $$
(☎727-822-8622; www.dickenshouse.com; 335 8th Ave NE; r $130-230; P❄@📶) Five lushly designed rooms await in this passionately restored arts-and-crafts-style home. The gregarious, gay-friendly owner whips up a gourmet breakfast.

Ponce de Leon BOUTIQUE HOTEL $$
(☎727-550-9300; www.poncedeleonhotel.com; 95 Central Ave; r $110-150; P❄@📶) A boutique hotel with Spanish flair in the heart of downtown. Splashy murals, designer-cool decor, and the hot restaurant and bar are highlights; off-site parking is not.

Renaissance Vinoy Resort LUXURY HOTEL $$$
(☎727-894-1000; www.vinoyrenaissanceresort.com; 501 5th Ave NE; r $250-310; P❄@📶🏊) St Pete's coral pink grande dame, the newly renovated 1925 Vinoy is a sumptuous concoction with take-notice off-season and online deals. It's worth it just for the gorgeous pool.

Eating & Drinking

At night, focus on Central Ave between 2nd and 3rd Sts, and along the harborfront. Many restaurants have lively, late bar scenes.

TOP CHOICE **Ceviche** TAPAS $$
(☎727-209-2302; www.ceviche.com/1828; 95 Central Ave; tapas $5-13, mains $15-23; ⏲5-10pm Sun & Mon, to midnight Tue-Sat) Panache counts and Ceviche has it in spades, with an upbeat Spanish atmosphere and flavorful, creative, generously portioned tapas. End the evening in the sexy, cavernlike Flamenco Room below, with live flamenco Thursday and Saturday nights.

Bella Brava ITALIAN $$
(☎727-895-5515; www.bellabrava.com; 204 Beach Dr NE; lunch $7-10, dinner $14-20; ⏲11:30am-10pm, to 11pm Fri & Sat, 3-9pm Sun) Anchoring the prime waterfront intersection, Bella Brava specializes in contemporary northern Italian cooking and breezy, sidewalk dining.

DON'T MISS

SALVADOR DALÍ MUSEUM

Unveiled in 2011, the theatrical exterior of the new **Dalí Museum** (☎727-823-3767; www.thedali.org; 1 Dali Blvd; adult/child 6-12yr $21/7, after 5pm Thu $10; ⏲10am-5pm Mon-Wed, to 8pm Thu, to 5:30pm Fri & Sat, noon-5:30pm Sun) augurs great things: out of a wound in the towering white shoebox oozes the 75ft geodesic atrium Glass Enigma. Even better, what unfolds inside is a blueprint of what a modern art museum should be, or at least one that's devoted to understanding the life, art and impact of a revolutionary artist.

The new Dalí Museum is designed specifically to display all 96 oil paintings in the collection, along with 'key works from every moment and in every medium': drawings, prints, sculptures, photos, manuscripts, even movies, everything arranged chronologically and explained in context. Free docent tours and audioguides help unlock the rich symbolism of Dalí's monumental works, and the museum is so popular it's been known to draw 3000 people in a day.

Even if you dismiss his dripping clocks and curlicue mustache, this stunning museum – a crown jewel among Florida cultural institutions – makes a convincing case for Salvador Dalí's passionate, daring intellectualism and his visionary, even prescient 'surrealism.'

Garden MEDITERRANEAN $$
(☎727-896-3800; www.thegardendtsp.com; 217 Central Ave; lunch $7-10, dinner $14-20; ⏰11am-10pm Mon-Sat, to 2am Fri & Sat, 10am-2pm Sun) In a pretty hidden courtyard, Garden emphasizes Mediterranean-influenced salads and pastas. There's live jazz and DJs on weekends.

AnnaStella Cajun Bistro CAJUN $
(☎727-498-8978; www.annastellacajunbistro.com; 300 Beach Dr N; dishes $6-15; ⏰8am-10pm Sun-Thu, to 11pm Fri & Sat; 📶) Enjoy a Cajun-spiced breakfast or lunch and harbor views; great gumbo and fresh beignets.

☆ Entertainment

Jannus Live CONCERT VENUE
(www.jannuslive.com; 16 2nd St N; tickets $15-30) Well-loved outdoor concert venue inside an intimate courtyard; national and local bands reverberate downtown.

ℹ Getting There & Around

St Petersburg-Clearwater International Airport (PIE; www.fly2pie.com) is served by several major carriers. **Greyhound** (☎727-898-1496; www.greyhound.com; 180 9th St N) services include Tampa.

Pinellas Suncoast Transit Authority (PSTA; www.psta.net; fare $2) operates buses citywide and the Suncoast Beach Trolley that links the beaches from Clearwater to Pass-a-Grille. The **Looper trolley** (www.loopertrolley.com; fare 25¢) links downtown sights on a 30-minute narrated loop.

Sarasota

Sarasota is a welcoming, well-to-do bastion of the arts, with a performer's weakness for the theater's sodium lights. John Ringling set it on this course in 1911, when he made the town the winter home of his famous circus. Today the Ringling Museum Complex is a regional highlight, and Sarasota spills over with opera, theater and art. Stop by the **Visitor Information Center** (☎941-957-1877; www.sarasotafl.org; 701 N Tamiami Trail; ⏰10am-5pm Mon-Sat) for info and maps.

Yet Sarasota wouldn't be half as popular if it didn't have such luscious white-sand beaches. **Lido Beach** is closest and has free parking, but 5 miles away **Siesta Key** (www.siestakeychamber.com) has sand like confectioner's sugar and is one of Florida's best and most popular strands; Siesta Village is also a lively, family-friendly beach town.

Mote Aquarium (☎941-388-4441; www.mote.org; 1600 Ken Thompson Pkwy; adult/child $17/12; ⏰10am-5pm) is a leading shark research center providing intimate encounters with sharks, manatees, sea turtles, rays and more, plus marine biologist-led sea-life cruises.

Boasting the world's largest scientific collection of orchids and bromeliads, **Marie Selby Botanical Gardens** (www.selby.org; 811 S Palm Ave; adult/child $17/6; ⏰10am-5pm) is a relaxing yet fascinating botanical encounter.

About a half-hour from downtown, visit **Myakka River State Park** (www.myakkariver.org; per car $6; ⏰8am-sunset) to kayak or air-

RINGLING'S LEGACY: ART, ARCHITECTURE & THE CIRCUS

Circus impresario John Ringling was an avid fine art collector with upper-class aspirations who died flat broke. Rather than sell his art and estate, however, he willed both to the state of Florida.

Today the 66-acre **Ringling Museum Complex** (☎941-359-5700; www.ringling.org; 5401 Bayshore Rd; adult/child $25/10; ⏰10am-5:30pm, to 8pm Thu) is one of the Gulf Coast's premier attractions; it's worth a day and more. A good introduction is the 30-minute film in the historic 18th-century **Asolo Theater**, then tour Ringling's Venetian Gothic mansion, **Ca d'Zan**. Theatrically over-the-top Renaissance and Baroque decor includes masterful painted ceilings; guided tours grant access to the extravagant 2nd-floor living quarters.

Even more impressive, the **John & Mabel Ringling Museum of Art** is packed with imposing, passionate religious and mythological works from the 14th to 18th centuries. One wing presents contemporary exhibits and, in 2012, a new James Turrell–designed 'Sky Space.'

Finally, there's the one-of-a-kind **Circus Museum**. Really several museums, it displays ephemera from Ringling's traveling show, a history of the circus from sideshow to Cirque du Soleil, and in the center ring, a truly epic scale re-creation of the entire Ringling Bros circus in action. It's as thrilling as the circus itself.

boat among hundreds of alligators, and for the area's best hiking and camping; get directions and tour times online.

For arts and performance information, check out the **Arts and Cultural Alliance** (www.sarasotaarts.org). The all-encompassing **Van Wezel Performing Arts Hall** (941-953-3368; www.vanwezel.org; 777 N Tamiami Trail) showcases all types of performances, while the **Asolo Repertory Theatre** (941-351-8000; www.asolorep.org; 5555 N Tamiami Trail) is a lauded regional theater company.

Sleeping & Eating

In addition to downtown Sarasota and Siesta Village, **St Armands Circle** on Lido Key is an evening social hub, with a proliferation of stylish shops and restaurants.

TOP CHOICE **Hotel Ranola** BOUTIQUE HOTEL $$
(941-951-0111; www.hotelranola.com; 118 Indian Pl; r $180-190; P ❄ @) The nine rooms feel like a designer's brownstone apartment: free-spirited and effortlessly artful, but with real working kitchens. It's urban funk, walkable to downtown Sarasota.

Sunsets on the Key APARTMENT $$$
(941-312-9797; www.sunsetsonthekey.com; 5203 Avenida Navarre; apt $230-340; P ❄) In Siesta Village, eight well-kept, rigorously clean condo apartments are run like a hotel.

Owen's Fish Camp SOUTHERN $$
(941-951-6936; www.owensfishcamp.com; 516 Burns Lane; mains $9-20; 4-10pm, to 11pm Fri & Sat) This ironically hip swamp shack downtown serves upscale versions of Florida-style Southern cuisine. The emphasis is on seafood, and the energy is high.

Broken Egg BREAKFAST $
(www.thebrokenegg.com; 140 Avenida Messina; mains $7-14; 7:30am-2:30pm) This diner-style breakfast institution on Siesta Key, known for huge pancakes and cheddary home fries, is a social hub each morning.

Fort Myers

Workaday, sprawling Fort Myers is overshadowed by the region's pretty beaches and upscale, sophisticated towns. However, a recent facelift has spruced up the historic riverfront district (along 1st St between Broadway and Lee St) into an attractive, brick-lined collection of restaurants and bars. Visit www.fortmyers.org for information.

Fort Myers' main claim to fame is the **Edison & Ford Winter Estates** (www.edisonfordwinterestates.org; 2350 McGregor Blvd; adult/child $20/11; 9am-5:30pm). Famous inventor Thomas Edison built a winter home and lab here in 1885, and automaker Henry Ford became his neighbor in 1916. The excellent museum focuses mainly on the overwhelming scope of Edison's genius, and their homes are genteel, landscaped delights.

From November through March, one of the easiest ways to encounter wintering manatees is at **Lee County Manatee Park** (www.leeparks.org; 10901 State Rd 80; parking per hr/day $1/5; park 8am-sunset year-round, visitorscenter 9am-4pm Nov-Mar), a warm-water power-plant discharge canal that's now a protected sanctuary. The park is signed off Hwy 80, about 6.5 miles from downtown.

For an easily accessible taste of South Florida wetlands, meander the 1.2-mile boardwalk trail of the **Six Mile Cypress Slough Preserve** (www.leeparks.org/sixmile; 7791 Penzance Blvd; parking per hr/day $1/5; dawn-dusk).

Fort Myers Beach

Fifteen miles south of Fort Myers, Fort Myers Beach is 7 miles of talcum powder-fine sand along Estero Island, presided over by one of Florida's quintessential activity-and-party-fueled beach towns. Families often prefer Fort Myers Beach because it's more affordable than neighboring coastal towns, and coeds like it because its bars are louder and more raucous. For town information, visit www.fortmyersbeachchamber.org.

The only draw, and it's a good one, is the beachy fun, but nearby **Lovers Key State Park** (www.floridastateparks.org/loverskey; car/bike $8/2; sunrise-sunset) adds great shelling as well as hiking and kayaking among quiet islands and canals (frequented by manatees).

Impeccably clean and well maintained, **Edison Beach House** (239-463-1530; www.edisonbeachhouse.com; 830 Estero Blvd; r $200-335; ❄) is perfectly situated near action central (the so-called Times Sq area), yet soothingly comfortable, with full kitchens. For funky charm in a more low-key beach section, nab one of the six rooms at **Mango Street Inn** (239-233-8542; www.mangostreetinn.com; 126 Mango St; r $145-165; ❄), an idiosyncratic B&B serving delectable breakfasts by a Cajun-trained chef.

Sanibel & Captiva Islands

Shaped like a fish hook trying to lure Fort Myers, these two slivers of barrier island lie across a 2-mile causeway (toll $6). Upscale but unpretentious, with a carefully managed shoreline that feels remarkably lush and undeveloped, the islands are idyllic, cushy getaways, where bikes are the preferred mode of travel, the shelling is legendary and romantic meals are a reservation away. The **Sanibel & Captiva Islands Chamber of Commerce** (239-472-1080; www.sanibel-captiva.org; 1159 Causeway Rd, Sanibel; 9am-5pm;) is one of the most helpful VCs around and can help with accommodations.

In addition to its fabulous beaches, Sanibel's 6300-acre **JN 'Ding' Darling National Wildlife Refuge** (www.fws.gov/dingdarling; MM2 Sanibel-Captiva Rd, Sanibel; car/bike $5/1; visitor center 9am-5pm, refuge 7am-7pm Sat-Thu) is a splendid refuge that's home to an abundance of seabirds and wildlife. It has an excellent nature center, a 5-mile Wildlife Drive, narrated tram tours and easy kayaking in Tarpon Bay. For tours and boat rentals, contact **Tarpon Bay Explorers** (239-472-8900; www.tarponbayexplorers.com; 900 Tarpon Bay Rd, Sanibel).

Like a mermaid's jewel box, the **Bailey-Matthews Shell Museum** (www.shellmuseum.org; 3075 Sanibel-Captiva Rd, Sanibel; adult/child $7/4; 10am-5pm) is a natural history of the sea, with covetous displays of shells worldwide. To rent bikes or any other wheeled contrivance, visit **Billy's Rentals** (239-472-5248; www.billysrentals.com; 1470 Periwinkle Way, Sanibel; bikes per 2hr/day from $5/15; 8:30am-5pm).

On Captiva, the **'Tween Waters Inn** (239-472-5161; www.tween-waters.com; 15951 Captiva Dr, Captiva; r $160-215, ste $220-405;) is a full-service yet low-key resort with a variety of good-value lodging choices; ask for a renovated room. In addition to a big pool, tennis courts and spa, its marina offers various kayak rentals, guided trips and boat cruises.

For a more personal experience, stay in the five-room **Tarpon Tale Inn** (239-472-0939; www.tarpontale.com; 367 Periwinkle Way, Sanibel; r $150-260;), which does a nice imitation of a charming, hammock-strung B&B, but without breakfast.

Instead, start your day at the **Over Easy Cafe** (www.overeasycafesanibel.com; 630 Tarpon Rd, Sanibel; mains $8-13; 7am-2:30pm), which is where everyone goes for a top-quality, diner-style breakfast. For romantic gourmet, one excellent choice is **Sweet Melissa's Cafe** (239-472-1956; www.sweetmelissascafe.net; 1625 Periwinkle Way, Sanibel; tapas $11-14, mains $26-34; 11:30am-2:30pm Mon-Fri, from 5pm nightly), which offers creative, relaxed refinement.

If you have kids, prepare yourself for the spectacularly kitschy **Bubble Room** (www.bubbleroomrestaurant.com; 15001 Captiva Dr, Captiva; lunch $10-15, dinner $20-30; 11:30am-3pm & 4:30-9pm), a riotous pastiche of retro cartoons, superheroes, Christmas and Golden Era movie stars.

Naples

The Gulf Coast's answer to Palm Beach, Naples is a perfectly manicured, rich town with an adult sense of self and one of the most pristine, relaxed city beaches in the state. While it is certainly family friendly, it appeals most to romance-minded travelers seeking fine art and fine dining, trendy cocktails, fashion-conscious shopping and luscious sunsets. Visit www.napleschamber.org for city information.

For contemporary art, the sophisticated **Naples Museum of Art** (www.thephil.org; 5833 Pelican Bay Blvd; adult/child $8/4; 10am-4pm Tue-Sat, from noon Sun Oct-Jun) is a rewarding collection with cleverly designed exhibits. Meanwhile, one of the state's best nature conservancies and rehabilitation centers is **Naples Nature Center** (www.conservancy.org; 14th Ave N & Goodlette-Frank Rd; adult/child $10/5; 9am-4:30pm Mon-Sat), recently renovated into a LEED-certified campus with fantastic exhibits.

For well-polished, Mediterranean-style luxury in the heart of downtown's 5th Ave corridor, stay at the historic **Inn on 5th** (239-403-8777; www.innonfifth.com; 699 5th Ave S; r $320-500;). For a well-located, good-value midrange motel, the **Lemon Tree Inn** (239-262-1414; www.lemontreeinn.com; 250 9th St S, at 3rd Ave S; r $130-200;) is a pretty, bright choice.

Good eats are abundant. Top choices for a special meal include **Cafe Lurcat** (239-213-3357; www.cafelurcat.com; 494 5th Ave; lunch $14-18, dinner $25-40; 5-9:30pm Sun-Thu, to 10pm Fri & Sat), a sexy, multilevel restaurant and lively bar (open to 11pm or midnight nightly), and the off-the-beaten-path **IM Tapas** (239-403-8272; http://imtapas.com; 965 4th Ave N; tapas $9-21; from 5:30pm), where a mother-and-daughter team serves Madrid-worthy Spanish tapas.

CENTRAL FLORIDA

For a century, tourists came to Florida for, in essence, two things: its white-sand beaches and teal waters (and the resorts serving them), and to peek inside the alligator-infested Everglades. Walt Disney changed all that when he opened the Magic Kingdom in 1971. Today Orlando is the theme park capital of the world, and Walt Disney World is Florida's number one attraction.

Orlando

Like Las Vegas, Orlando is almost entirely given over to fantasy. It's a place to come when you want to imagine you're somewhere else: Hogwarts, perhaps, or Cinderella's Castle, or ancient Jerusalem, or Dr Seuss' world, or an African safari. And like Vegas' casinos, Orlando's theme parks work hard to be constantly entertaining thrill rides where the only concern is your pleasure. Even outside the theme parks, Orlando can exhibit a hyper atmosphere of fiberglass-modeled, cartoon-costumed pop culture amusement.

Yet there is, in fact, a real city to explore, one with tree-shaded parks of the natural variety, art museums, orchestras, and dinners that don't involve high-fiving Goofy. And just outside the city, Florida's wilderness and wildlife, particularly its crystal springs, can be as memorably bizarre as anything Ripley ever dreamed up.

Sights & Activities

DOWNTOWN & LOCH HAVEN PARK

Fashionable Thornton Park has several good restaurants and bars, while Loch Haven Park is home to a cluster of cultural institutions.

Orlando Museum of Art MUSEUM
(407-896-4231; www.omart.org; 2416 N Mills Ave; adult/child $8/5; 10am-4pm Tue-Fri, from noon Sat & Sun) Spotlighting American and African art as well as unique traveling exhibits.

Mennello Museum of American Art MUSEUM
(407-246-4278; www.mennellomuseum.org; 900 E Princeton St; adult/child $4/free; 10:30am-4:30pm Tue-Sat, from noon Sun) Features the bright folk art of Earl Cunningham, plus traveling exhibitions.

Orlando Science Center MUSEUM
(407-514-2000; www.osc.org; 777 E Princeton St; adult/child $15/10; 10am-5pm Thu-Tue) Candy-coated hands-on science for the whole family.

Harry P Leu Gardens PARK
(www.leugardens.org; 1920 N Forest Ave; adult/child $7/2; 9am-5pm) One mile east of Loch Haven Park is this 50-acre tranquil escape from all the gloss.

INTERNATIONAL DRIVE

Like a theme park itself, International Dr (I-Dr) is shoulder to shoulder with high-energy amusements: sprinkled among the major theme, wildlife and water parks, smaller attractions shout for attention: Ripley's Believe It or Not, the upside-down WonderWorks and an indoor skydiving experience. Chain restaurants and hotels also crowd the thoroughfare.

Universal Orlando Resort THEME PARK
(407-363-8000;www.universalorlando.com;1000 Universal Studios Plaza; 1-day ticket 1/2 parks $82/112, 4 days $140/150; from 9am) Smaller, easier to navigate and more pedestrian-friendly than Walt Disney World, Universal Orlando is everything you wish Disney could be. Universal features two theme parks, a water park, three hotels and an entertainment district. The megaplex is as absorbingly themed as Disney, but it replaces Snow White and the Seven Dwarves with Spider-Man, the Simpsons and – to widespread acclaim in 2010 – Harry Potter.

For good ol' scream-it-from-the-rooftops, no-holds-barred, laugh-out-loud fun, explore the multiple worlds within **Islands of Adventure**, which is packed with adrenaline rides. Marvel Super Hero Island is a sensory overload of comic book characters; there's dino-happy Jurassic Park; the ersatz-mystical Lost Continent; and the kid-friendly Toon Lagoon and Seuss Landing. But most famously of all, there is now the Wizarding World of Harry Potter, which brings to life Hogwarts and Hogsmeade in exquisite, rib-tickling detail.

At **Universal Studios**, the central question is: would you like to live the movies? Do battle with the Terminator? Go *Back to the Future?* Escape Jaws, Beetlejuice, the Mummy, *Men in Black* aliens and a *Twister* tornado? Do Lucille Ball, Curious George,

Greater Orlando & Theme Parks

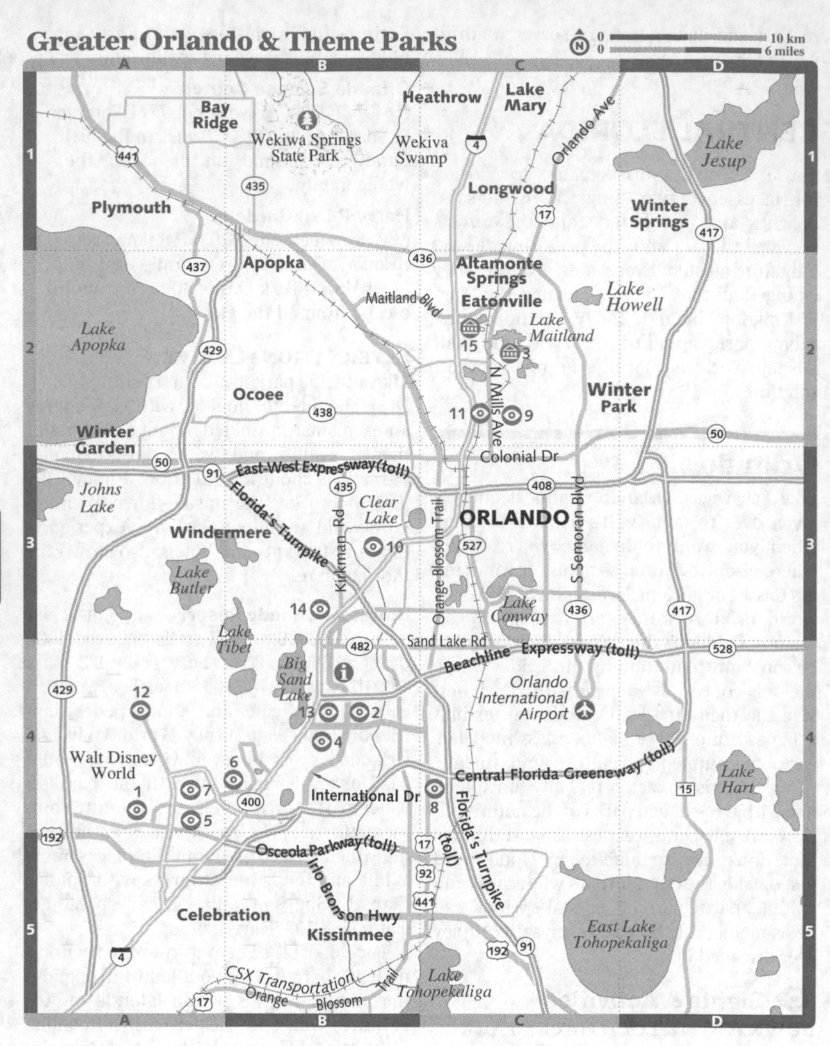

Shrek and the Simpsons amuse you? With a Hollywood backlot feel, Universal Studios' simulation-heavy rides are dedicated to silver screen and TV icons.

Review multiple ticket options online, which can include add-ons like Express Plus line skipping and a dining plan; resort hotel guests also get nice park perks.

SeaWorld AMUSEMENT PARK
(☎407-351-3600; www.seaworld.com; 7007 SeaWorld Dr; 2-day ticket $72; ⊙from 9am) A peculiarly Floridian blend of marine animal shows and thrill rides, SeaWorld is home to both Shamu the killer whale and Kraken the floorless roller coaster. While the rides provide jolts of adrenaline, the real draws are the up-close sea life encounters (with manta rays, sharks, penguins, beluga whales) and the excellent dolphin, sea lion and killer whale shows. Make sure to check show and feeding times online before visiting, and plan your day accordingly.

Check online for combo tickets with Discovery Cove and Aquatica.

Discovery Cove WATER PARK
(☎407-370-1280; www.discoverycove.com; 6000 Discovery Cove Way; admission $129-169, incl dolphin swim $199-319; ⊙8:30am-5:30pm) Attendance is

Greater Orlando & Theme Parks

Sights
1 Animal Kingdom........A4
2 Aquatica........B4
3 Charles Hosmer Morse Museum........C2
4 Discovery Cove........B4
5 Disney Hollywood Studios........A4
6 Downtown Disney........B4
7 Epcot........A4
8 Gatorland........C4
9 Harry P Leu Gardens........C2
10 Holy Land Experience........B3
11 Loch Haven Park........C2
12 Magic Kingdom........A4
Mennello Museum of American Art........(see 9)
Orlando Museum of Art........(see 9)
Orlando Science Center........(see 9)
13 SeaWorld........B4
14 Universal Studios Orlando........B3
15 Zora Neale Hurston National Museum of Fine Arts........C2

limited, ensuring Discovery Cove retains the feel of an exclusive tropical resort, complete with beaches, a fish-filled reef and an aviary. No high-speed thrills or frantic screaming, just blessed relaxation and the chance to swim with dolphins. The price is steep, but everything is included: buffet lunch, beer, towels, parking, even a day pass to SeaWorld.

Aquatica WATER PARK
(☎407-351-3600; www.aquaticabyseaworld.com; admission $42) Orlando's latest water park is newer, cleaner and prettier than the others, but in the end, it's the same combination of lazy rivers, splash zones, wave pools and slippery slides that everyone looks for.

Holy Land Experience THEME PARK
(☎407-872-2272; www.holylandexperience.com; 4655 Vineland Rd; adult/child 6-12yr $35/20; ⊙10am-6pm Mon-Sat) Just north of I-Dr, this is an earnest re-creation of ancient Jerusalem and biblical times, which makes it a theme park, but without roller coasters and pop culture sarcasm.

WINTER PARK

On the northern edge of Orlando, Winter Park is a friendly college town with some outstanding museums and a relaxing downtown.

Charles Hosmer Morse Museum of American Art MUSEUM
(www.morsemuseum.org; 445 N Park Ave; adult/child $5/free; ⊙9:30am-4pm Tue-Sat, from 1pm Sun) Internationally famous, with the world's most comprehensive collection of Tiffany glass; stunning centerpiece is a chapel interior.

FREE **Zora Neale Hurston National Museum of Fine Arts** MUSEUM
(www.zoranealehurstonmuseum.com; 227 E Kennedy Blvd, Eatonville; ⊙9am-4pm Mon-Fri, 11am-1pm Sat) In neighboring Eatonville (get directions online), this museum is dedicated to Florida novelist Zora Neale Hurston; changing exhibits of African American artists.

GREATER ORLANDO

Gatorland AMUSEMENT PARK
(www.gatorland.com; 14501 S Orange Blossom Trail/Hwy 17; adult/child $23/15; ⊙9am-5pm) This Old Florida throwback is small, silly and kitschy. It's all about alligators, with gator wrestling, gators jumping, feeding gators hot dogs and other great squeal-worthy moments.

Legoland THEME PARK
(http://florida.legoland.com; 1 Legoland Way, Winter Haven; adult/child $65/55; ⊙10am-5pm) In Winter Haven, Florida's newest theme park was not yet open at the time of research. Like its California cousin, Legoland rebuilds the world brick by brick, but to scale, with rides and build-your-own fun that are heaven for the 12-and-under set.

Sleeping

In addition to the Walt Disney World resorts, Orlando has countless lodging options. Most are clustered around I-Dr, US 192 in Kissimmee and I-4. **Reserve Orlando** (www.reserveorlando.com) is a central booking agency. **Universal Orlando Resort** (☎407-363-8000; r & ste from $270) has three recommended hotels.

EO Inn & Spa BOUTIQUE HOTEL $$
(☎407-481-8485; www.eoinn.com; 227 N Eola Dr; r $139-229; P❄📶🏊) Sleek and understated, this downtown boutique inn overlooks Lake Eola near Thornton Park, with neutral-toned rooms that are elegant in their simplicity.

Courtyard at Lake Lucerne B&B $$
(☎407-648-5188; www.orlandohistoricinn.com; 211 N Lucerne Circle E; r $99-225; P❄📶👪) This lovely

historic inn, with enchanting gardens and genteel breakfast, has roomy art-deco suites and handsome antiques throughout. Unfortunately, it sits directly under two highway overpasses.

Veranda Bed & Breakfast B&B $$
(407-849-0321; www.theverandabandb.com; 115 N Summerlin Ave; r $110-270;) Ideal for wandering Thornton Park and Lake Eola, this European-style B&B has big antique beds and is a lovely retreat from all the bustle.

Barefoot'n in the Keys MOTEL $$
(407-397-1144; www.barefootn.com; 2750 Florida Plaza Blvd; ste $80-300;) Clean, bright and spacious suites in a yellow six-story building. Low-key, friendly and close to Disney, this makes an excellent alternative to generic chains.

Eating

On and around I-Dr you'll find an explosion of chains; a half-mile stretch of Sand Lake Rd has been dubbed 'restaurant row' for its upscale dining.

Dessert Lady Café CAFE $
(407-999-5696; 120 W Church St; mains $5-10; 11:30am-11pm Tue-Thu, to midnight Fri, 4pm-midnight Sat) There's a bordello atmosphere and a bistro menu of pulled-pork sliders, chicken salad, soups and quiches to go with the sinful desserts, from fruit cobbler to bourbon pecan pie.

Graffiti Junktion American Burger Bar BURGERS $$
(900 E Washington St, Thornton Park; mains $12-25; 11pm-1am, to midnight Sun) This neon graffiti-covered happenin' hangout is all about massive burgers with attitude. Top yours with a fried egg, artichoke hearts, chili, avocado and more.

Ravenous Pig AMERICAN $$$
(407-628-2333; 1234 Orange Ave, Winter Park; mains $14-29; 11:30am-2pm & 5:30-9:30pm Tue-Thu, to 10:30pm Fri & Sat) One of Orlando's most talked-about foodie destinations, this bustling hot spot serves designer cocktails and creative, delicious versions of shrimp and grits, and lobster tacos. Reservations recommended.

Yellow Dog Eats BARBECUE $$
(407-296-0609; www.yellowdogeats.com; 1236 Hempel Ave, Windermere; mains $10-20; 11am-9pm) Housed in an old, tin-roof general store, and quirky to the extreme, it's not your typical barbecue. Try the excellent Cuban-style black beans and the Florida Cracker (pulled pork with gouda, bacon and fried onions). It's a drive; get directions online.

Dandelion Communitea Café VEGETARIAN $
(407-362-1864; http://dandelioncommunitea.com; 618 N Thornton Ave; mains $5-10; 11am-10pm Mon-Sat, to 5pm Sun;) Unabashedly crunchy and definitively organic, this pillar of creative, sustainable, locavore vegetarianism is genuinely delicious, with tons of community spirit. Look for events.

Drinking & Entertainment

Orlando Weekly (www.orlandoweekly.com) is the best source for entertainment listings. There's plenty to do downtown, where there's a happening bar district around Orange Ave between Church St and Jefferson St.

Universal Studio's **CityWalk** (www.citywalkorlando.com) has a concentration of cinemas, restaurants, clubs and big-name shows.

Social LIVE MUSIC
(www.thesocial.org; 54 N Orange Ave) Check out great live music.

Latitudes BAR
(www.churchstreetbars.com; 33 W Church St) Island-inspired rooftop bar, with two more bars below.

Wall St Plaza BAR
(www.wallstplaza.net; 25 Wall St Plaza) Eight theme bars, with live music, all in one plaza.

Parliament House GAY
(www.parliamenthouse.com; 410 N Orange Blossom Trail) Legendary gay resort and drag shows; six bars.

Information

For city information, good multilingual guides and maps, visit Orlando's **Official Visitor Center** (407-363-5872; www.visitorlando.com; 8723 International Dr; 8:30am-6:30pm). Gay travelers can peruse www.orlandogaycities.com. For theme park advice, visit www.themeparkinsider.com.

Getting There & Around

Orlando International Airport (MCO; www.orlandoairports.net) has buses and taxis to major tourist areas. **Mears Transportation** (407-423-5566; www.mearstransportation.com) provides shuttles for $20 to $30 per person.

Greyhound (www.greyhound.com; 555 N John Young Pkwy) serves numerous cities. **Amtrak** (www.amtrak.com; 1400 Sligh Blvd) has daily trains south to Miami and north to New York City.

Orlando's bus network is operated by **Lynx** (www.golynx.com; ride/day pass $2/4.50). **I-Ride Trolley** (www.iridetrolley.com; adult/child $1/free; ⏲8am-10:30pm) buses run along I-Dr.

When driving, note that I-4 is the main north–south connector, though it's confusingly labeled east–west. To go north, take I-4 east (toward Daytona); to go south, get on I-4 west (toward Tampa). The main east–west roads are Hwy 50 and Hwy 528 (the Bee Line Expwy), which accesses Orlando International Airport.

Walt Disney World Resort

Covering 40 sq miles, **Walt Disney World** (WDW; http://disneyworld.disney.go.com) is the largest theme park resort in the world. It includes four separate theme parks, two water parks, a sports complex, five golf courses, two dozen hotels, 100 restaurants and two shopping and nightlife districts – proving that it's not such a small world, after all. At times it feels ridiculously crowded and corporate, but with or without kids, you won't be able to inoculate yourself against Disney's highly infectious enthusiasm and warm-hearted nostalgia. Naturally, expectations run high, and even the self-proclaimed 'happiest place on earth' doesn't always live up to its billing. Still, it always happens: Cinderella curtsies to your little Belle, your own Jedi knight vanquishes Darth Maul, or you tear up on that corny ride about our tiny planet, and you're swept up in the magic.

Sights & Activities

Anytime schools are out – during summer and holidays – WDW will be the most crowded. The least crowded times are January to February, mid-September through October and early December. Late fall tends to have the best weather; frequent downpours accompany the hot, humid summer months.

Magic Kingdom THEME PARK

When people think of WDW, they picture the Magic Kingdom, from the iconic Cinderella's Castle to Space Mountain, the Haunted Mansion and Pirates of the Caribbean (now including Johnny Depp's Jack Sparrow). This is where the fireworks and nighttime light parade illuminate **Main Street, USA**. For Disney mythology, it doesn't get better, and rides and shows aim squarely at young kids and their parents and grandparents.

Disney Hollywood Studios THEME PARK

Formerly Disney-MGM Studios, this is the least-charming of Disney's parks. However, it does have two of WDW's most exciting rides: the unpredictable elevator in the **Twilight Zone Tower of Terror** and the Aerosmith-themed **Rock 'n' Roller Coaster**. Wannabe singers can audition for the American Idol Experience, kids can join the Jedi Training Academy, and various programs present Walt Disney himself and how Disney's movies are made.

Epcot THEME PARK

An acronym for 'Experimental Prototype Community of Tomorrow,' Epcot was Disney's vision of a high-tech city when it opened in 1982. It's divided into two halves: **Future World**, with rides and corporate-sponsored interactive exhibits, and **World Showcase**, providing an interesting toe-dip into the cultures of 11 countries. Epcot is much more soothingly low-key than other parks, and it has some of the best food and shopping. Plus, a few rides are WDW highlights, like Soarin' and Mission: Space. The interactive Turtle Talk with Crush is delightful.

Animal Kingdom THEME PARK

This sometimes surreal blend of African safari, zoo, rides, costumed characters, shows and dinosaurs establishes its own distinct tone. It's best at animal encounters and shows, with the 110-acre **Kilimanjaro Safaris** as its centerpiece. The iconic **Tree of Life** houses the fun It's Tough to Be a Bug! show, and **Expedition Everest** and **Kali River Rapids** are the top thrill rides.

Tickets

The simple logic behind ticket options is the longer you stay, the less you pay (per day). Tickets allow entrance to one park per day, and can range from one to 10 days: adults from $82 to $262, and children aged three to nine from $74 to $239. By day six, the per day cost is 50% the single-day ticket, and so on. Buy in advance to avoid lines at the gate.

Options you can add (for extra cost) are discount passes to other Disney areas, a no-expiration option (for unused days) and, the most recommended, Park Hopper ($56), allowing entrance to all four WDW parks in a day. Check online for packages.

For discounts, check out www.mousesavers.com and www.undercovertourist.com.

Sleeping

WDW has 24 family-friendly sleeping options, from camping to deluxe resorts, and Disney guests receive great perks (extended park hours, discount dining plans, free transportation, airport shuttles). Rates vary by season, and there are 20 seasons! Disney's thorough website outlines rates and amenities for every property. Approximate rates given below are for peak season.

For the most amenities, choose a roomy **Deluxe Villa** (villas $540-1600), the only properties with full kitchen and in-room washer/dryer. At the other end of the scale, the **campground** (campsites $70-100, cabins $360) is meticulously maintained, with lots of activities. **Value Resorts** (r $120-150) are the least-expensive option (besides camping); quality is equivalent to basic chain hotels, and (fair warning) they are favored by school groups.

When evaluating properties, the main thing to consider is their location to the parks you want to visit; room quality is uniformly average except at the handful of top deluxe properties. Many visitors prefer the Deluxe Resort hotels in Epcot (Boardwalk Inn, Beach Club and Yacht Club, Swan and Dolphin); these are walkable to Epcot, Hollywood Studios and Disney's Boardwalk.

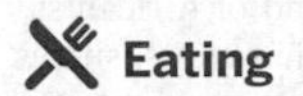

Eating

Theme park food ranges from OK to awful; the most interesting is served in Epcot's World Showcase. Sit-down meals are best, but *always* make reservations; seats can be impossible to get without one. For any dining, you can call **central reservations** (☎407-939-3463) up to 180 days in advance.

Disney has three dinner shows (a luau, country-style BBQ and vaudeville show) and about 15 character meals, and these are insanely popular (see website for details). Book them the minute your 180-day window opens. The most sought-after meal is **Cinderella's Royal Table** (adult $33-45, child $24-28) inside the Magic Kingdom's castle, where you dine with Disney princesses.

Sci-Fi Dine-In Theater AMERICAN
(Hollywood Studios; mains $11-21) Dine in Cadillacs and watch classic sci-fi flicks.

California Grill AMERICAN
(Contemporary Resort; mains $15-38) Coveted seats with great views of the Magic Kingdom fireworks.

O'Hana HAWAIIAN
(Polynesian Resort; mains $15-30) Great South Pacific decor and interactive Polynesian-themed luau shenanigans.

Boma BUFFET
(Animal Kingdom Lodge; adult/child breakfast $17/10, dinner $27/13) African-inspired eatery with pleasant surroundings and a buffet several notches above the rest.

Victoria and Albert AMERICAN
(Grand Floridian; prix fixe $125-200) A true jacket-and-tie, crystal goblet romantic gourmet restaurant – no kidding, and no kids (under 10).

Entertainment

In addition to theme park events like Magic Kingdom parades and fireworks and Epcot's Illuminations, Disney has two entertainment districts – Downtown Disney and Disney's Boardwalk – with eats, bars, music, movies, shops and shows.

Cirque du Soleil CIRCUS
(☎407-939-7600; www.cirquedusoleil.com; adult $76-132, child $61-105; ⏲6pm & 9pm Tue-Sat) The best live show in Disney World; exquisite theatrical acrobatics.

House of Blues LIVE MUSIC
(☎407-934-2583; www.houseofblues.com) Top acts visit this national chain; Sunday's Gospel Brunch truly rocks.

DisneyQuest ARCADE
(1 day $36-42; ⏲11:30am-10pm Sun-Thu, to 11pm Fri & Sat) Five floors of virtual reality and arcade games.

ESPN's Wide World of Sports Complex SPECTATOR SPORT
(www.espnwwos.disney.go.com) This 220-acre sports facility hosts hundreds of amateur and professional sporting events.

Getting There & Around

Most hotels in Kissimmee and Orlando – and all Disney properties – offer free transportation to WDW. Disney-owned resorts also offer free transportation from the airport. Drivers can reach all four parks via I-4 and park for $14. The Magic Kingdom lot is huge; trams get you to the entrance.

Within WDW, a complex network of monorails, boats and buses get you between the parks, resorts and entertainment districts. Pick up a transportation map at your resort or at Guest Relations; Disney's official **phone apps** (http://m.disneyworld.go.com) can also be helpful.

Around Orlando

Just north of Orlando await some of Florida's best outdoor adventures, particularly swimming, snorkeling and kayaking in its crystal-clear, 72°F (22°C) natural springs. Closest is **Wekiwa Springs State Park** (☎407-884-2008; www.floridastateparks.org/wekiwasprings; car/campsites $6/24), with 13 miles of hiking trails, a spring-fed swimming hole, nice campground and the tranquil 'Wild and Scenic' Wekiva River; rent kayaks from **Nature Adventures** (☎407-884-4311; www.canoewekiva.com; kayak rental $15-20).

Blue Spring State Park (☎386-775-3663; www.floridastateparks.org/bluespring; car/campsites $6/24) is a favorite of wintering manatees, and two-hour cruises ply the St John's River. Just north of Deland, **De Leon Springs State Park** (☎386-985-4212; www.floridastateparks.org/deleonsprings; car $6; ⏲8am-dusk) has a huge swimming area, more kayaking and tours of the Ponce de León's alleged fountain of youth.

Connoisseurs of Old Florida shouldn't miss **Silver Springs** (www.silversprings.com; adult/child under 10yr $30/25; ⏲10am-5pm), near Ocala, which invented the glass-bottom boat and remains a delightfully old-fashioned nature theme park.

To really escape into raw wilderness, head for the **Ocala National Forest** (http://fs.usda.gov/ocala), which has dozens of campgrounds, hundreds of miles of trails and 600 lakes. The hiking, biking, canoeing and camping are some of the state's best. See the website for visitor centers and descriptions.

FLORIDA PANHANDLE

Take all the things that are great about the Deep South – friendly people, molasses-slow pace, oak-lined country roads, fried food galore – and then add several hundred miles of sugar-white beaches, dozens of gin-clear natural springs and all the fresh oysters you can suck down, and there you have it: the fantastic, highly underrated Florida Panhandle.

Tallahassee

Florida's capital, cradled between gently rising hills and beneath tree-canopied roadways, is a calm and gracious city. Geographically and culturally, it's closer to Atlanta than it is to Miami, and far more Southern than the majority of the state it administrates. Despite the city's two major universities (Florida State and Florida Agricultural and Mechanical University) and its status as a government center, there's not much to detain a visitor for more than a day or two.

Get information from the **visitor center** (☎850-413-9200; www.visittallahassee.com; 106 E Jefferson St; ⏲8am-5pm Mon-Fri).

Sights & Activities

Mary Brogan Museum of Art & Science MUSEUM
(www.thebrogan.org; 350 S Duval St; adult/child $7.50/5; ⏲10am-5pm Mon-Sat, from 1pm Sun) Affiliated with the Smithsonian, this museum mixes a kid-friendly, hands-on science center with the Tallahassee art museum to good effect.

FREE **Museum of Florida History** MUSEUM
(www.museumoffloridahistory.com; 500 S Bronough St; ⏲9am-4:30pm Mon-Fri, from 10am Sat, from noon Sun) Here it is, Florida's history splayed out in fun, crisp exhibits: from mastodon skeletons to Florida's Paleo-Indians and Spanish shipwrecks, the Civil War to 'tin-can tourism.'

Mission San Luis HISTORIC SITE
(www.missionsanluis.org; 2020 W Mission Rd; adult/child $5/2; ⏲10am-4pm Tue-Sun) The 60-acre site of a 17th-century Spanish and Apalachee mission that's been wonderfully reconstructed, especially the soaring Council House. Good tours included with admission provide a fascinating taste of 300 years ago.

FREE **Florida Capitol Buildings** HISTORIC BUILDING
Old and new, side by side. The current **Florida State Capitol** (cnr Pensacola & Duval Sts; ⏲8am-5pm Mon-Fri) is, in a word, ugly, but its observation deck is worth seeing. Next door, the **Historic Capitol** (www.flhistoriccapitol.gov; 400 S Monroe St; ⏲9am-4:30pm Mon-Fri, from 10am Sat, from noon Sun) is the more charming 1902 predecessor. Inside, the **Florida Legislative Research Center and Museum** (www.flrcm.com) has intriguing government and cultural exhibits, including one on the infamous 2000 US presidential election.

Sleeping & Eating

Chains are clumped at exits along I-10 and along Monroe St between I-10 and downtown.

Hotel Duval HOTEL $$
(☎850-224-6000; www.hotelduval.com; 415 N Monroe St; r from $119; P❄≋🛜) Tallahassee's slickest digs. This new 117-room hotel goes in for a neo-mod look. A rooftop bar and lounge is open until 2am most nights, and Shula's, a fancy chain steakhouse, is off the lobby.

Governor's Inn HOTEL $$
(☎850-681-6855; www.thegovinn.com; 209 S Adams St; r $129-149; P❄🛜) In a stellar downtown location, this warm, inviting inn has everything from single rooms to two-level loft suites, plus a daily cocktail hour.

Catfish Pad SEAFOOD $
(www.catfishpad.com; 4229 W Pensacola St; mains $4-11; ⊙11am-3pm & 5-9pm Mon-Sat) There's no doubt you're in the South at this home-style seafood joint. Go for a plate of cornmeal-battered catfish with a side of grits, chased down with a cup of sweet tea. Yum.

Reangthai THAI $$
(☎850-386-7898; reangthai.com; 2740 Capital Circle NE; mains $13-20; ⊙11am-2pm Tue-Fri, 5-10pm Mon-Sat) The real deal, and elegant despite its strip mall setting, Reangthai serves the kind of spicy, fish sauce-y, explode-in-your-mouth cuisine so many American Thai restaurants shy away from.

Andrew's Downtown ITALIAN $$
(☎850-222-3444; www.andrewsdowntown.com; 228 S Adams St; mains $9-36; ⊙11:30am-10pm) Downtown's see-and-be-seen political hot spot. At this split-level place, the downstairs grill serves casual burgers and beer, while upstairs serves upscale neo-Tuscan dishes.

☆ Entertainment

Bradfordville Blues Club LIVE MUSIC
(☎850-906-0766; www.bradfordvilleblues.com; 7152 Moses Lane, off Bradfordville Rd; tickets $15-20; ⊙8pm-2am Fri & Sat) Down the end of a dirt road lit by tiki torches, you'll find a bonfire raging under the live oaks at this hidden-away juke joint that hosts excellent national blues acts.

ℹ Getting There & Around

The **Tallahassee Regional Airport** (TLH; www.talgov.com/airport) is about 5 miles southwest of downtown, off Hwy 263. The **Greyhound station** (www.greyhound.com; 112 W Tennessee St, at Duval St) is right downtown. **Star Metro** (www.talgov.com/starmetro; fare $1.25) provides local bus service.

Apalachicola & Around

Slow, mellow and perfectly preserved, Apalachicola is one of the Panhandle's most irresistible, romantic villages. Perched on the edge of a broad bay famous for its oysters, the oak-shaded town is a hugely popular getaway, with a new wave of bistros, art galleries, eclectic boutiques and historic B&Bs.

For town information, visit www.apalachicolabay.org. For nature, the pristine **St Vincent Island** (www.fws.gov/saintvincent) holds pearly dunes, pine forests and wetlands teeming with wildlife. Neighboring **St George Island State Park** (www.floridastateparks.org/stgeorgeisland; car $6) offers 9 miles of glorious, undeveloped beaches. In town, seek out fishing charters and wildlife cruises.

Ensure romance with a night's stay at **Coombs House Inn** (☎850-653-9199; www.coombshouseinn.com; 80 6th St; r $129-269; P❄🛜), a stunning Victorian home transformed into a luscious, luxury B&B. Sample the town's famous bivalve, freshly shucked, baked or fried, at **Papa Joe's Oyster Bar & Grill** (www.papajoesoysterbar.com; 301b Market St; mains $8-18; ⊙11:30am-10pm).

Panama City Beach

There's no mistaking Panama City Beach for anything other than it is: a quintessentially Floridian, carnival-esqe beach town. Spring breakers and summer vacationers flock here for the beautiful white-sand beaches and the hurdy-gurdy of amusements, while mile after mile of high-rise condos insist on disrupting the view. Stop by the **visitor bureau** (☎850-233-5070; www.visitpanamacitybeach.com, www.pcbeach.org; 17001 Panama City Beach Pkwy; ⊙8am-5pm) for information.

A renowned wreck-diving site, the area around Panama City Beach has dozens of natural, historic and artificial reefs. **Dive Locker** (☎850-230-8006; www.divelocker.net; 106 Thomas Dr; ⊙8am-6pm Mon-Sat) has dives from $90, gear included. Get inspiration at the **Museum of Man in the Sea** (www.manthesea.org; 17314 Panama City Beach Pkwy; adult/child $5/free; ⊙10am-4pm Tue-Sun), showcasing the history of diving.

St Andrews State Park (www.floridastateparks.org/standrews; car $8) is a peaceful escape with nature trails, swimming beaches and wildlife. Just offshore, **Shell Island** has fantastic snorkeling, and **shuttles** (www.

SCENIC DRIVE: HIGHWAY 30A

Along the Panhandle coast between Panama City Beach and Destin, skip the main highway (Hwy 98) in favor of one of the most enchanting drives in Florida: Scenic Hwy 30A. This 18-mile stretch of road hugs what's referred to as the Emerald Coast for its almost fluorescent, gem-colored waters lapping brilliant white beaches of ground-quartz crystal.

Leading off Scenic Hwy 30A are pristine, wild parklands like **Grayton Beach State Park** (www.floridastateparks.org/graytonbeach; 357 Main Park Rd, Santa Rosa Beach; car $5), considered one of Florida's prettiest, most pristine strands. About 15 quaint communities hug the coast, some arty and funky, and some master-planned resorts with matchy-matchy architectural perfection. Of these, the most intriguing and surreal is the little village of **Seaside** (www.seasidefl.com), a Necco Wafer–colored town that was hailed as a model of New Urbanism in the 1980s.

Seaside is such an idealized vision that, unaltered, it formed the setting for the 1998 film *The Truman Show*, about a man whose 'perfect life' is nothing but a TV show. Other variations on this theme are WaterColor, Alys Beach and Rosemary Beach.

Good online resources are www.30a.com and www.visitsouthwalton.com.

shellislandshuttle.com; trip plus gear $22) depart every 30 minutes in summer.

Sleeping

Summer is the high season for Panhandle beaches. Panama City doesn't lack for choice; to avoid spring breakers, look for the code phrase 'family-friendly.'

Wisteria Inn MOTEL $$
(☎850-234-0557; www.wisteria-inn.com; 20404 Front Beach Rd; r from $109; P ❄ ≋) This sweet little 15-room motel has a bright, Caribbean theme, poolside mimosa hours and an 'adults only' policy that discourages spring breakers.

Beachbreak by the Sea MOTEL $
(☎850-234-3870; www.beachbreakbythesea.com; 15405 Front Beach Rd; d $79-169; P ❄ ≋) A refreshing four-story spot in a sea of high-rises, this place offers basic motel-style rooms, a central beachfront location and continental breakfast.

Eating & Drinking

Pineapple Willy's CARIBBEAN $$
(www.pwillys.com; 9875 S Thomas Dr; mains $15-22; ⏲11am-late) Ask for a table on the restaurant pier for breezy beachside dining. Famed for its signature drinks and its house special: Jack Daniels BBQ ribs.

Firefly NOUVELLE CUISINE $$$
(☎850-249-3359; www.fireflypcb.com; 535 Beckrich Rd; mains $22-36; ⏲5-10pm) This uber atmospheric, fine dining establishment beckons with clever seafood dishes and its cool Library Lounge. It's good enough for the US president – Obama ate here in 2010.

Tootsie's Orchid Lounge HONKY TONK
(www.tootsies.net; Pier Park; ⏲10am-late) Lacks the dusty character of the Nashville original, but the nonstop live country music is still plenty boot stompin'.

Getting There & Around

The **Panama City International Airport** (PFN; www.iflybeaches.com) is served by a few major airlines. The **Greyhound Station** (www.greyhound.com; 917 Harrison Ave) is in Panama City, and the limited **Bay Town Trolley** (www.baytowntrolley.org; fare $1.50) runs only weekdays from 6am to 8pm.

Pensacola & Pensacola Beach

Neighbors with Alabama, Pensacola and its adjacent beach town welcome visitors driving in from the west. Its gorgeous snow-white beaches and tolerance of the annual spring break bacchanal ensure Pensacola's popularity. There is also a thrumming military culture and a sultry, Spanish-style downtown. The **visitor bureau** (☎850-434-1234; www.visitpensacola.com, www.visitpensacolabeach.com; 1401 E Gregory St; ⏲8am-5pm; @) has maps.

The region has taken its licks in recent years. In 2004 Hurricane Ivan did its best to smash the place, and in 2010 the Deepwater Horizon oil spill in the Gulf of Mexico tainted beaches with tar balls. However, today, all Panhandle beaches are clean of oil, Pensacola's buildings and roads are repaired, and the region is eager to welcome travelers back.

Sights & Activities

In 2007 a 910ft-long aircraft carrier was intentionally sunk off the coast of Pensacola to make the world's largest artificial reef. Now dubbed 'the Great Carrier Reef,' the **USS Oriskany** sits in the sand 210ft below the surface. One of many outfitters, **MBT Divers** (☎850-455-7702; www.mbtdivers.com; 3920 Barrancas Ave) offers two-tank Oriskany dives for $150, plus various other charters.

Historic Pensacola Village HISTORIC BUILDINGS
(www.historicpensacola.org; Zaragoza St, btwn Tarragona & Adams Sts; adult/child $6/3; ⊙10am-4pm Tue-Sat, tours 11am, 1pm & 2:30pm) Pensacola says 'take that, St Augustine!' with this village, a self-contained enclave of historic homes and museums. Admission is good for one week and includes a guided tour and entrance to each building.

FREE **National Museum of Naval Aviation** MUSEUM
(www.navalaviationmuseum.org; 1750 Radford Blvd; ⊙9am-5pm) The Pensacola Naval Air Station (NAS) is home to both the museum – a don't-miss collection of jaw-dropping military aircraft – and the elite **Blue Angels** (www.blueangels.navy.mil) squadron. You can watch the Blue Angels practice their death-defying air show at 8:30am most Tuesdays and Wednesdays between March and November.

Pensacola Museum of Art ART MUSEUM
(www.pensacolamuseumofart.org; 407 S Jefferson St; adult/child $5/free; ⊙10am-5pm Tue-Fri, from noon Sat) In the city's old jail (1908), this lovely art museum features an impressive, growing collection of major 20th- and 21st-century artists, spanning cubism, realism, pop art and folk art.

Gulf Islands National Seashore PARK
(www.nps.gov/guis; 7-day pedestrian & cyclist/car $3/8; ⊙sunrise-sunset) To enjoy the area's lovely white sands, head to the easy-access Pensacola Beach or the neighboring Gulf Islands National Seashore, part of a 150-mile stretch of undeveloped beach. Aim for the **Naval Live Oaks** section for a calm, family-friendly beach, and drive out to **Fort Pickens** to poke around this crumbling wreck of a 19th-century fort.

WHAT THE...?

Every April, locals gather along the Florida–Alabama state line on Perdido Key for a time-honored tradition: the **Interstate Mullet Toss**. The idea – apart from a great excuse for a party – is to see who can throw their (dead) mullet the furthest into Alabama (we're talking fish, not the unfortunate '80s hairstyle). The event is organized by the **Flora-Bama Lounge, Package and Oyster Bar** (www.florabama.com; 17395 Perdido Key Dr; ⊙10am-10pm Mon-Thu, to late Fri-Sun), a legendary roadhouse that's worth visiting even when the fish aren't flying.

Sleeping

Pensacola Victorian B&B B&B $$
(☎850-434-2818; www.pensacolavictorian.com; 203 W Gregory St; r $85-125; P❄️📶) This stately 1892 Queen Anne building offers four lovingly maintained guest rooms – we especially like Suzanne's Room, with its hardwood floors, blue toile prints and clawfoot tub. It's about a mile north of downtown Pensacola.

New World Inn HOTEL $$
(☎850-432-4111; www.newworldlanding.com; 600 S Palafox St; r from $109; P❄️📶) Peek under the lid of this former box factory and you'll find surprisingly lovely rooms with luxe bedding and real carpeting (a beach-town luxury).

Paradise Inn MOTEL $$
(☎850-932-2319; www.paradiseinn-pb.com; 21 Via de Luna Dr; r $100-200; P❄️📶🏊) Across from the beach, this sherbet-colored motel is a lively, cheery place thanks to its popular bar and grill (for quiet, ask for rooms on the parking lot's far side). Rooms are small and clean, with tiled floors and brightly painted walls.

Eating & Drinking

TOP CHOICE **Joe Patti's** SEAFOOD $
(www.joepattis.com; 534 South B St, at Main St; ⊙7am-6pm Mon-Thu & Sat, to 7pm Fri) At this beloved seafood emporium, get dock-fresh fish and seafood, prepared picnic food and sushi.

Dharma Blue INTERNATIONAL $$
(☎850-433-1275; www.dharmablue.com; 300 S Alcaniz St; mains $9-21; ⊙11am-4pm & 5-9:30pm Mon-Sat) Many locals consider this the area's

best restaurant. The eclectic menu goes from fried green tomatoes to luscious sushi rolls.

Jerry's Drive-In AMERICAN **$**
(2815 E Cervantes St; mains $7-12; ⌚10am-10pm Mon-Fri, from 7am Sat) No longer a drive-in or owned by Jerry, but this greasy spoon is always packed – possibly because you can hardly eat for less. Cash only.

Peg Leg Pete's SEAFOOD **$$**
(☎850-932-4139; 1010 Fort Pickens Rd; mains $8-20; ⌚11am-10pm) Raw? Rockefeller? Casino? Get your oysters any way you like 'em at this popular beach hangout with live music and pirate decor.

McGuire's Irish Pub IRISH **$$**
(www.mcguiresirishpub.com; 600 E Gregory St; mains $11-30; ⌚11am-late) Promising 'feasting, imbibery and debauchery,' this barnlike spot delivers all three. Stick to steaks and burgers, and don't mind the animal heads or dollar-bill-adorned walls. Stay late, and be prepared to sing along.

TOP CHOICE **Seville Quarter** CLUB
(www.sevillequarter.com; 130 E Government St; ⌚11am-late) Taking up an entire city block, this massive entertainment complex contains seven separate eating, drinking and music venues, along with an HG Wells-ian 1890s decor.

Getting There & Around

Five miles northeast of downtown, **Pensacola Regional Airport** (PNS; www.flypensacola.com) is served by major airlines. The **Greyhound station** (www.greyhound.com; 505 W Burgess Rd) is 9 miles north of downtown.

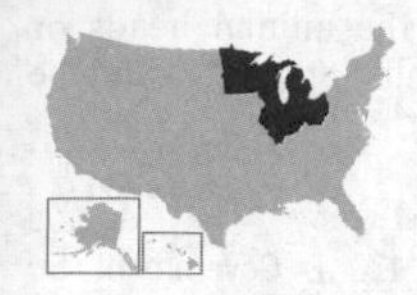

Great Lakes

Includes »

Illinois....505
Chicago....505
Indiana....535
Indianapolis....536
Ohio....542
Cleveland....542
Amish Country....548
Cincinnati....551
Michigan....555
Detroit....555
Wisconsin....572
Milwaukee....572
Minnesota....582
Minneapolis....582

Best Places to Eat

» Zingerman's Roadhouse (p563)

» Terry's Turf Club (p553)

» Slows Bar BQ (p560)

» Next (p526)

» Bryant-Lake Bowl (p587)

Best Places to Stay

» Inn on Ferry Street (p559)

» Hotel Burnham (p522)

» Arbor House (p577)

» Lighthouse B&B (p595)

» Inn Serendipity (p579)

Why Go?

Don't be fooled by all the corn. Behind it lurks surfing beaches and Tibetan temples, car-free islands and the green-draped night-lights of the aurora borealis. The Midwest takes its knocks for being middle-of-nowhere boring. So consider the moose-filled national parks, urban five-ways and Hemingway, Dylan and Vonnegut sites its little secret.

Roll call for the Midwest's cities starts with Chicago, which unfurls what is arguably the country's mightiest skyline. Milwaukee keeps the beer-and-Harley flame burning, while Minneapolis shines a hipster beacon out over the fields. Detroit rocks, plain and simple.

The Great Lakes themselves are huge, like inland seas, offering beaches, dunes, resort towns and lots of lighthouse-dotted scenery. Dairy farms and fruit orchards blanket the region, meaning that fresh pie and ice cream awaits road trippers. And when the Midwest does flatten out? There's always a goofball roadside attraction, like the meaty Spam museum or world's biggest ball of twine, to revive imaginations.

When to Go

Chicago

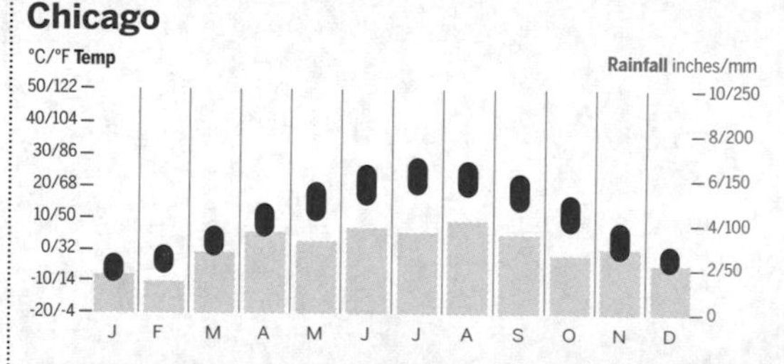

Jan & Feb Skiers and snowmobilers hit the trails.

Jul & Aug Ah, finally, it's warm! Beer gardens hop, beaches splash, and festivals rock most weekends.

Sep & Oct Fair weather, bountiful farm and orchard harvests, and shoulder-season bargains.

Getting There & Around

Chicago's O'Hare International Airport (ORD) is the main air hub for the region. Detroit (DTW), Cleveland (CLE) and Minneapolis (MSP) also have busy airports.

A car is the easiest way to get around, especially if you want to head down Route 66 or dawdle on scenic backroads. Small change is useful for tollways such as the I-80 and I-90 through northern Illinois, Indiana and Ohio.

Greyhound (www.greyhound.com) connects many local cities and towns. Upstart **Megabus** (www.megabus.com/us) provides an efficient alternative between major Great Lakes cities. Note that Megabus has no terminals (drop-off and pick-up are at various street corners), and all purchases must be made in advance online (you cannot buy a ticket from the driver).

Amtrak's national rail network centers on Chicago. Trains depart at least once daily for San Francisco *(California Zephyr)*, Seattle *(Empire Builder)*, New York City *(Lake Shore Limited)*, New Orleans *(City of New Orleans)* and San Antonio *(Texas Eagle)*. Regional trains chug to Milwaukee (seven daily) and Detroit (three daily).

Two car/passenger ferries sail across Lake Michigan, providing a shortcut between Wisconsin and Michigan. The **Lake Express** (www.lake-express.com) crosses between Milwaukee and Muskegon. The older **SS Badger** (www.ssbadger.com) crosses between Manitowoc and Ludington.

TOP FIVE ACTIVITY HOT SPOTS

» Boundary Waters (p596) Canoe where wolves and moose roam

» Wisconsin's Rails to Trails (p573) Pedal through cow-dotted farmland

» Apostle Islands (p581) Kayak through sea caves

» New Buffalo (p565) Learn to surf in Harbor Country

» Isle Royale (p571) Hike and camp in pristine backcountry

Pre-Planning

A couple of things to know before you go: pre-booking accommodation during summer is a good idea, especially in resort-orientated places such as Mackinac Island in Michigan, and the North Shore in Minnesota. It's also advised for festival-packed cities such as Milwaukee and Chicago.

Chowhounds who crave dinner at top-end restaurants such as Chicago's Alinea, Next or Frontera Grill/Topolobampo should make reservations six to eight weeks in advance.

Eyeing a nice beachfront campsite at one of the state parks? Better nab it early on; most parks take online reservations for a small fee.

Bring insect repellent, especially if you're heading to the Northwoods. The blackflies in spring and mosquitoes in summer can be brutal.

DON'T MISS

Only in the Midwest can you fork into proper cheese curds (Wisconsin), deep-dish pizza (Chicago) and sugar cream pie (Indiana).

Fast Facts

» Hub cities: Chicago (population 2.8 million), Minneapolis (population 372,800)

» Chicago to Minneapolis: 400 miles

» Chicago to Detroit: 285 miles

» Time zone: Eastern (IN, OH, MI), Central (IL, WI, MN)

» States covered in this chapter: Illinois, Indiana, Ohio, Michigan, Wisconsin, Minnesota

Did You Know?

The Great Lakes possess about 20% of the earth's and 95% of America's fresh water.

Resources

» Midwest Microbrews (www.midwestmicrobrews.com) The sudsy lowdown

» Great Lakes Information Network (www.great-lakes.net) Environmental news

» Changing Gears (www.changinggears.info) Rust Belt reinvention stories

Great Lakes Highlights

1. Absorbing the skyscrapers, museums, festivals and foodie bounty of **Chicago** (p505)
2. Beach lounging, berry eating and surfing on Michigan's **Gold Coast** (p565)
3. Slowing down for clip-clopping horses and buggies in **Amish Country** (p542and p548)
4. Polka dancing at a Friday-night fish fry in **Milwaukee** (p572)
5. Paddling the **Boundary Waters** (p596) and sleeping under a blanket of stars
6. Cycling along the river against the urban backdrop of **Detroit** (p555)
7. Taking the slowpoke, pie-filled route through Illinois on **Route 66** (p534)

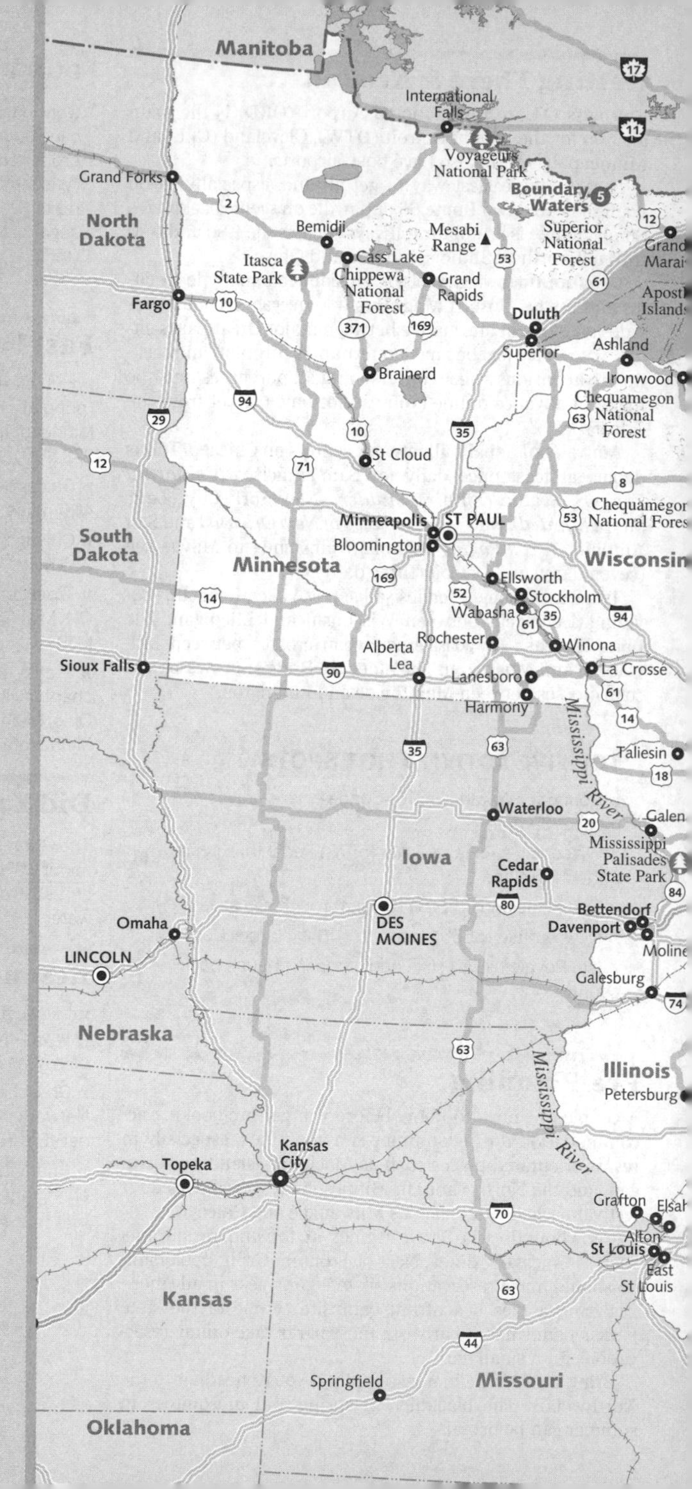

0 200 km
0 100 miles
Québec
CANADA
Ontario
Thunder Bay
Isle Royale National Park
Grand Portage
Lake Superior
Copper Harbor
Keweenaw Peninsula
Porcupine Mountains Wilderness State Park
Houghton
Pictured Rocks National Lakeshore
Tahquamenon Falls
Sault Ste Marie
Lake Nipissing
Ottawa National Forest
Marquette
Naubinway
Iron Mountain
St Ignace
Mackinaw City
Mackinac Island
Manitoulin Island
Georgian Bay
Lake Michigan
Washington Island
Leelanau Peninsula
Petoskey
Boyne City
Charlevoix
Nicolet National Forest
Manitou Islands
Leland
Empire
Frankfort
Traverse City
Huron National Forest
Lake Huron
Lake Simcoe
Wausau
Door Peninsula
Central Time Zone
Eastern Time Zone
Green Bay
Sleeping Bear Dunes National Lakeshore
Saginaw Bay
TORONTO
Oshkosh
Ludington
Michigan
Hamilton
Muskegon
Grand Rapids
Port Huron
Milwaukee
Flint
London
MADISON
Gold Coast
Holland
LANSING
Saugatuck/Douglas
Detroit
New York
Monroe
Racine
Dearborn
Erie
Kalamazoo
Ann Arbor
Lake Erie
Madison
Pelee Island
Bass Islands
Kelleys Island
Chicago
Middlebury
Toledo
Pennsylvania
East Chicago
South Bend
Cleveland
Indiana Dunes State Park
Auburn
Akron
Canton
Indiana
Marion
Peoria
Fairmount
Ohio
Bloomington
Atlanta
COLUMBUS
Champaign
Yellow Springs
Lancaster
SPRINGFIELD
INDIANAPOLIS
Dayton
Marietta
Terre Haute
Athens
Nashville
Columbus
Chillicothe
Cincinnati
Route 66
Bloomington
Covington
West Virginia
Wabash River
Madison
Vincennes
Ohio River
Huntington
Charleston
FRANKFORT
Louisville
Lexington
New Harmony
Harmonie State Park
Kentucky
Shawnee National Forest
Cypress Creek National Wildlife Refuge
Cairo
Paducah
Virginia

History

The region's first residents included the Hopewell (around 200 BC) and Mississippi River mound builders (around AD 700). Both left behind mysterious piles of earth that were tombs for their leaders and possibly tributes to their deities. You can see remnants at Cahokia in southern Illinois, and Mound City in southeastern Ohio.

The mound-building cultures began to decline around AD 1000, and over the next centuries the Miami, Shawnee and Winnebago moved in.

French voyageurs (fur traders) arrived in the early 17th century and established missions and forts. The British turned up soon after that, with the rivalry spilling over into the French and Indian Wars (Seven Years' War, 1754–61), after which Britain took control of all of the land east of the Mississippi. Following the Revolutionary War, the Great Lakes area became the new USA's Northwest Territory, which soon was divided into states and locked to the region after it developed its impressive canal and railroad network. But conflicts soon erupted between the newcomers and the Native Americans, including the 1811 Battle of Tippecanoe in Indiana; the bloody 1832 Black Hawk War in Wisconsin, Illinois and around, which forced indigenous people to move west of the Mississippi; and the 1862 Sioux uprising in Minnesota.

Throughout the late 19th and early 20th centuries, industries sprang up and grew quickly, fueled by resources of coal and iron, and cheap transport on the lakes. The work available brought huge influxes of immigrants from Ireland, Germany, Scandinavia and southern and eastern Europe. For decades after the Civil War, a great number of African Americans also migrated to the region's urban centers from the South.

The area prospered during WWII and throughout the 1950s, but was followed by 20 years of social turmoil and economic stagnation. Manufacturing industries declined, which walloped Rust Belt cities such as Detroit and Cleveland with high unemployment and 'white flight' (ie white middle-class families who fled to the suburbs).

The 1980s and '90s brought urban revitalization. The region's population increased, notably with newcomers from Asia and Mexico. Growth in the service and high-tech sectors resulted in economic balance, although manufacturing industries such as car making and steel still played a big role, meaning that when the economic crisis hit in 2008, Great Lakes towns felt the pinch first and foremost.

Local Culture

The Great Lakes region – aka the Midwest – is the USA's solid, sensible heartland. Folks here shrug at the brash glitz of the East Coast and flaky sex appeal of the West Coast, happy instead to be in the plain-speaking middle. It's no surprise that novelist Ernest Hemingway hailed from this part of the country, where words are seldom wasted.

If the Midwest had a mantra, it might be to work hard, go to church, and stick to the straight and narrow...unless there's a sports game happening, and then it's OK to slather on the body paint and dye your hair purple (or whatever team colors dictate). Baseball, football, basketball and ice hockey are all hugely popular, with the big cities sponsoring pro teams for each sport.

Music has always been a big part of local culture. Muddy Waters and Chess Re-

GREAT LAKES IN...

Five Days

Spend the first two days in **Chicago**. On your third day, make the 1½-hour trip to Milwaukee for culture, both high- and lowbrow. Take the ferry over to Michigan and spend your fourth day beaching in **Saugatuck**. Circle back via **Indiana Dunes** or **Indiana's Amish Country**.

10 Days

After two days in **Chicago**, on day three make for **Madison** and its surrounding quirky sights. Spend your fourth and fifth days at the **Apostle Islands**, and then head into the Upper Peninsula to visit **Marquette** and **Pictured Rocks** for a few days, followed by **Sleeping Bear Dunes** and the wineries around **Traverse City**. Return via the galleries, pies and beaches of **Saugatuck**.

cords spawned the electric blues in Chicago. Motown Records started the soul sound in Detroit. Alt rock shakes both cities (think Wilco in Chicago, White Stripes in Detroit), and has come out of Minneapolis (the Replacements, Hüsker Dü), and Dayton, Ohio (Guided By Voices, the Breeders), as well.

The region is more diverse than outsiders might expect. Immigrants from Mexico, Africa, the Middle East and Asia have established communities throughout the Midwest, mostly in the cities, where they are making welcomed contributions, especially to local dining scenes.

ILLINOIS FACTS

» **Nicknames** Prairie State, Land of Lincoln

» **Population** 12.9 million

» **Area** 57,900 sq miles

» **Capital city** Springfield (population 116,500)

» **Other cities** Chicago (population 2.8 million)

» **Sales tax** 6.25%

» **Birthplace of** author Ernest Hemingway (1899–1961), animator Walt Disney (1901–66), jazz musician Miles Davis (1926–91), actor Bill Murray (b 1950)

» **Home of** cornfields, Route 66 starting point

» **Politics** Democratic in Chicago, Republican downstate

» **Famous for** skyscrapers, corn dogs, Abe Lincoln sights

» **Official snack food** popcorn

» **Driving distances** Chicago to Milwaukee 92 miles, Chicago to Springfield 200 miles

ILLINOIS

Chicago dominates the state with its sky-high architecture and superlative museums, restaurants and music clubs. But venturing further afield reveals Hemingway's hometown of 'wide lawns and narrow minds,' scattered shrines to local hero Abe Lincoln, and a trail of corn dogs, pies and drive-in movie theaters down Route 66. A cypress swamp and a prehistoric World Heritage site make appearances in Illinois too.

Information

Illinois Bureau of Tourism (www.enjoyillinois.com)

Illinois Highway Conditions (www.gettingaroundillinois.com)

Illinois State Park Information (www.dnr.illinois.gov) State parks are free to visit. Campsites cost $6 to $35; some accept reservations (www.reserveamerica.com; $5).

Chicago

Loving Chicago is 'like loving a woman with a broken nose: you may well find lovelier lovelies, but never a lovely so real.' Writer Nelson Algren summed it up well in *Chicago: City on the Make*. There's something about this cloud-scraping city that bewitches. Well, maybe not during the six-month winter, when the 'Windy City' gets slapped by snowy blasts; however, come May, when the weather warms and everyone dashes for the outdoor festivals, ballparks, lakefront beaches and beer gardens – ahh, nowhere tops Chicago. Literally: the Willis Tower is here, the USA's tallest building.

Beyond its mighty architecture, Chicago is a city of Mexican, Polish, Vietnamese and other ethnic neighborhoods in which to wander. It's a city of blues, jazz and rock clubs any night of the week. And it's a chowhound's town, where the queues for hot dogs equal those of North America's top restaurant.

Forgive us, but it has to be said: the Windy City will blow you away with its low-key, cultured awesomeness.

History

In the late 17th century, the Potawatomi gave the name Checagou – meaning wild onions – to the once-swampy environs. The new city's pivotal moment happened on October 8, 1871, when (so the story goes) Mrs O'Leary's cow kicked over the lantern that started the Great Chicago Fire. It torched the entire inner city and left 90,000 people homeless.

'Damn,' said the city planners. 'Guess we shouldn't have built everything from wood. It's flammable.' So they rebuilt with steel and created space for bold new structures, such as the world's first skyscraper, which popped up in 1885.

Al Capone's gang more or less ran things during the 1920s and corrupted the city's political system. Local government has had issues ever since, with 30 city council members going to jail since 1970.

Metro Chicago Area

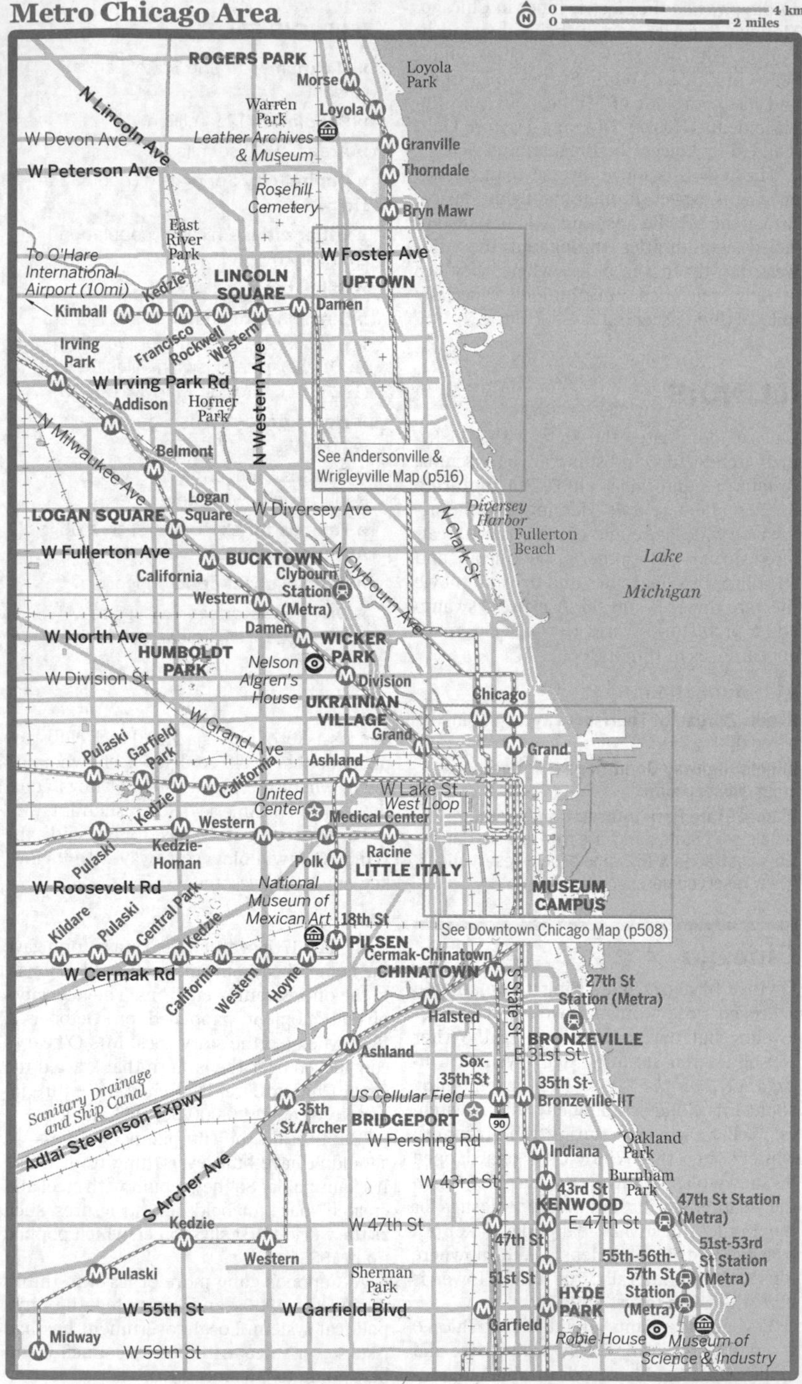

For the last half-century, the biggest name in Chicago has been Daley: Richard J Daley, mayor from 1955 to 1976; and son Richard M Daley, who governed from 1989 to 2011.

Sights

Chicago's main attractions are found mostly in or near the city center, though visits to distant neighborhoods, like Pilsen and Hyde Park, can also be rewarding.

The city's streets are laid out on a grid and numbered. Madison and State Sts in the Loop are the grid's center. As you go north, south, east or west from here, each increase of 800 in street numbers corresponds to 1 mile. For instance, Chicago Ave (800 N) is followed by North Ave (1600 N) and Fullerton Ave (2400 N), at which point you're 3 miles north of downtown.

For more in-depth city explorations, pick up Lonely Planet's *Chicago* guide or *Chicago Encounter* guide.

THE LOOP

The city center and financial district is named for the elevated train tracks that lasso its streets. It's busy all day, though not much happens at night other than in Millennium Park and the Theater District, near the intersection of N State and W Randolph Sts.

FREE Millennium Park PARK

(Map p508; www.millenniumpark.org; Welcome Center, 201 E Randolph St; ⏲6am-11pm; 👪) Rising boldly by the lakefront, Millennium Park is a treasure trove of free and arty sights. Frank Gehry's 120ft-high swooping silver band shell anchors what is, in essence, an outdoor modern design gallery. It includes Jaume Plensa's 50ft-high **Crown Fountain**, which projects video images of locals spitting water, gargoyle style; the Gehry-designed **BP Bridge** that spans Columbus Dr and offers great skyline views; and the **McCormick Tribune Ice Rink** that fills with skaters in winter (and alfresco diners in summer). The newest installment is the **Nichols Bridgeway** that arches from the park up to the Art Institute's 3rd-floor contemporary sculpture garden (free to view).

However, the thing that has become the park's biggest draw is 'the Bean' – officially titled **Cloud Gate** – Anish Kapoor's ridiculously smooth, 110-ton, silver-drop sculpture. Locals and visitors alike find it hard to resist such playful art, as you'll see from all the folks splashing around in Crown Fountain and touching the sculpture.

In summer, Millennium's acoustically awesome band shell – **Pritzker Pavilion** – hosts free concerts at lunchtime and at 6:30pm. For the latter, bring a picnic and bottle of wine and tune in to new music on Mondays, jazz and world music on Thursdays, and classical music on most other days. Each Saturday free exercise classes (yoga at 8am, Pilates at 9am and dance at 10am) take place on the Great Lawn. And

CHICAGO IN...

Two Days

On your first day, take an **architectural tour** and gaze up at the city's skyscrapers. Look down from the **John Hancock Center**, one of the world's tallest buildings. See 'the Bean' reflect the skyline, and splash with Crown Fountain's human gargoyles at **Millennium Park**. Hungry after all that walking? Chow down on a deep-dish pizza at **Giordano's**.

Make the second day a cultural one: explore the **Art Institute of Chicago** or **Field Museum of Natural History**. Browse boutiques and grab a stylish dinner in **Wicker Park**. Then head north to Al Capone's gin joint, the **Green Mill**, for an evening of jazz.

Four Days

Follow the two-day itinerary and, on your third day, rent a bicycle, dip your toes in Lake Michigan at **North Avenue Beach** and cruise through **Lincoln Park**, making stops at the zoo and conservatory. If it's baseball season, head to **Wrigley Field** for a Cubs game. A smoky blues club, such as **Buddy Guy's Legends**, is a fine way to finish the day (or start the morning).

Pick a neighborhood on your fourth day, and eat, shop and soak up the culture: murals and mole sauce in **Pilsen**, pagodas and Vietnamese sandwiches in **Uptown**, or Obama and the Nuclear Energy sculpture in **Hyde Park**. Then see a play at one of Chicago's 200 theaters, or a comedy at **Second City**.

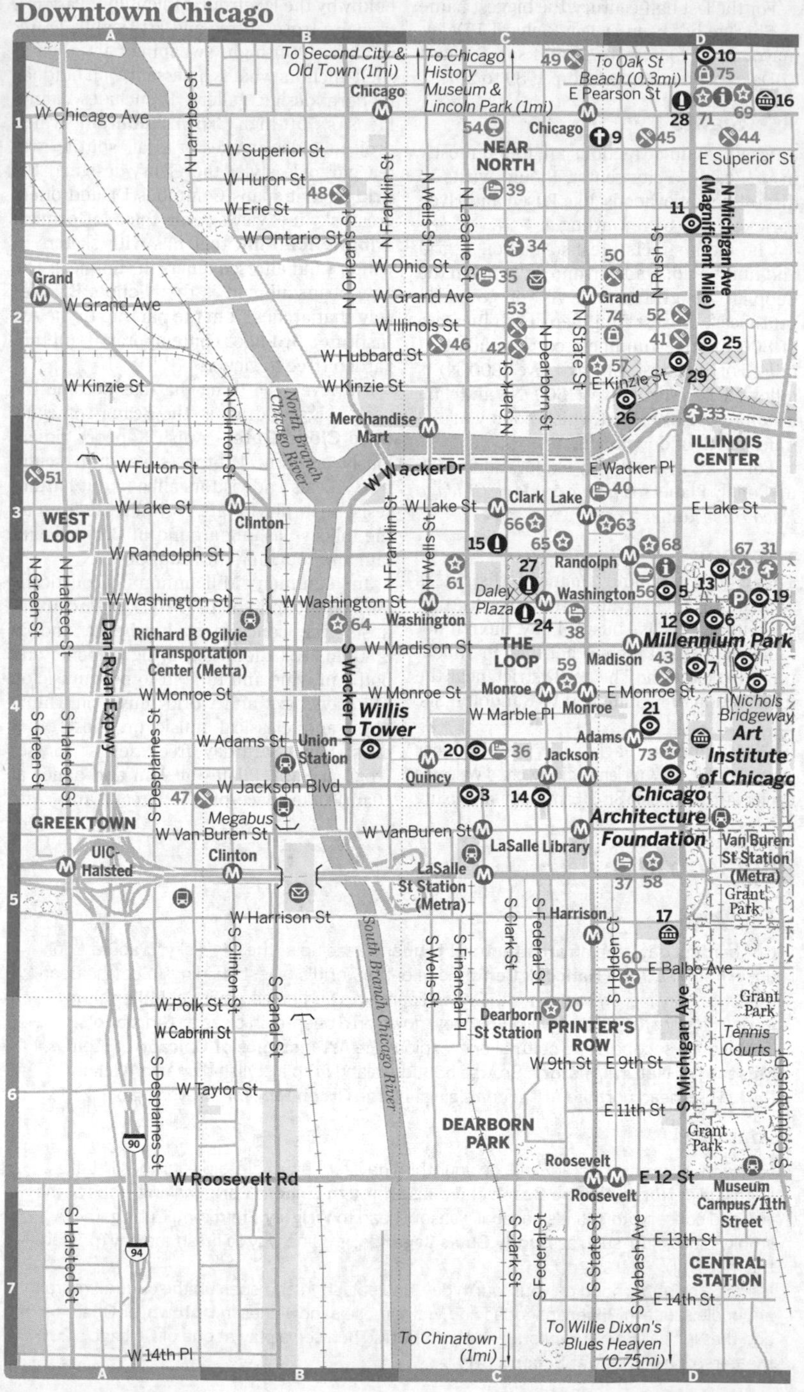
To Second City & Old Town (1mi)
To Chicago History Museum & Lincoln Park (1mi)
To Oak St Beach (0.3mi)
W Chicago Ave
E Pearson St
Chicago
NEAR NORTH
W Superior St
E Superior St
W Huron St
W Erie St
W Ontario St
W Ohio St
W Grand Ave
W Illinois St
W Hubbard St
W Kinzie St
E Kinzie St
N Larrabee St
N Orleans St
N Franklin St
N Wells St
N LaSalle St
N Clark St
N Dearborn St
N State St
N Rush St
N Michigan Ave (Magnificent Mile)
Grand
North Branch Chicago River
Merchandise Mart
ILLINOIS CENTER
W Fulton St
W Wacker Dr
E Wacker Pl
W Lake St
E Lake St
Clinton
Clark Lake
WEST LOOP
W Randolph St
Randolph
W Washington St
Washington
Daley Plaza
N Green St
N Halsted St
Dan Ryan Expwy
Richard B Ogilvie Transportation Center (Metra)
W Madison St
Madison
THE LOOP
Millennium Park
W Monroe St
E Monroe St
Monroe
W Marble Pl
Nichols Bridgeway
S Wacker Dr
Willis Tower
S Green St
S Halsted St
S Desplaines St
W Adams St
Union Station
Adams
Art Institute of Chicago
Quincy
Jackson
W Jackson Blvd
Chicago Architecture Foundation
GREEKTOWN
Megabus
W Van Buren St
W VanBuren St
LaSalle Library
Van Buren St Station (Metra)
UIC-Halsted
LaSalle St Station (Metra)
Grant Park
W Harrison St
Harrison
S Clinton St
S Canal St
South Branch Chicago River
S Wells St
S Financial Pl
S Clark St
S Federal St
S Holden Ct
E Balbo Ave
S Michigan Ave
W Polk St
W Cabrini St
Dearborn St Station
PRINTER'S ROW
Grant Park Tennis Courts
W 9th St
E 9th St
W Taylor St
E 11th St
DEARBORN PARK
S Columbus Dr
90
Roosevelt
W Roosevelt Rd
E 12 St
Museum Campus/11th Street
S State St
S Wabash Ave
E 13th St
94
CENTRAL STATION
E 14th St
W 14th Pl
To Chinatown (1mi)
To Willie Dixon's Blues Heaven (0.75mi)

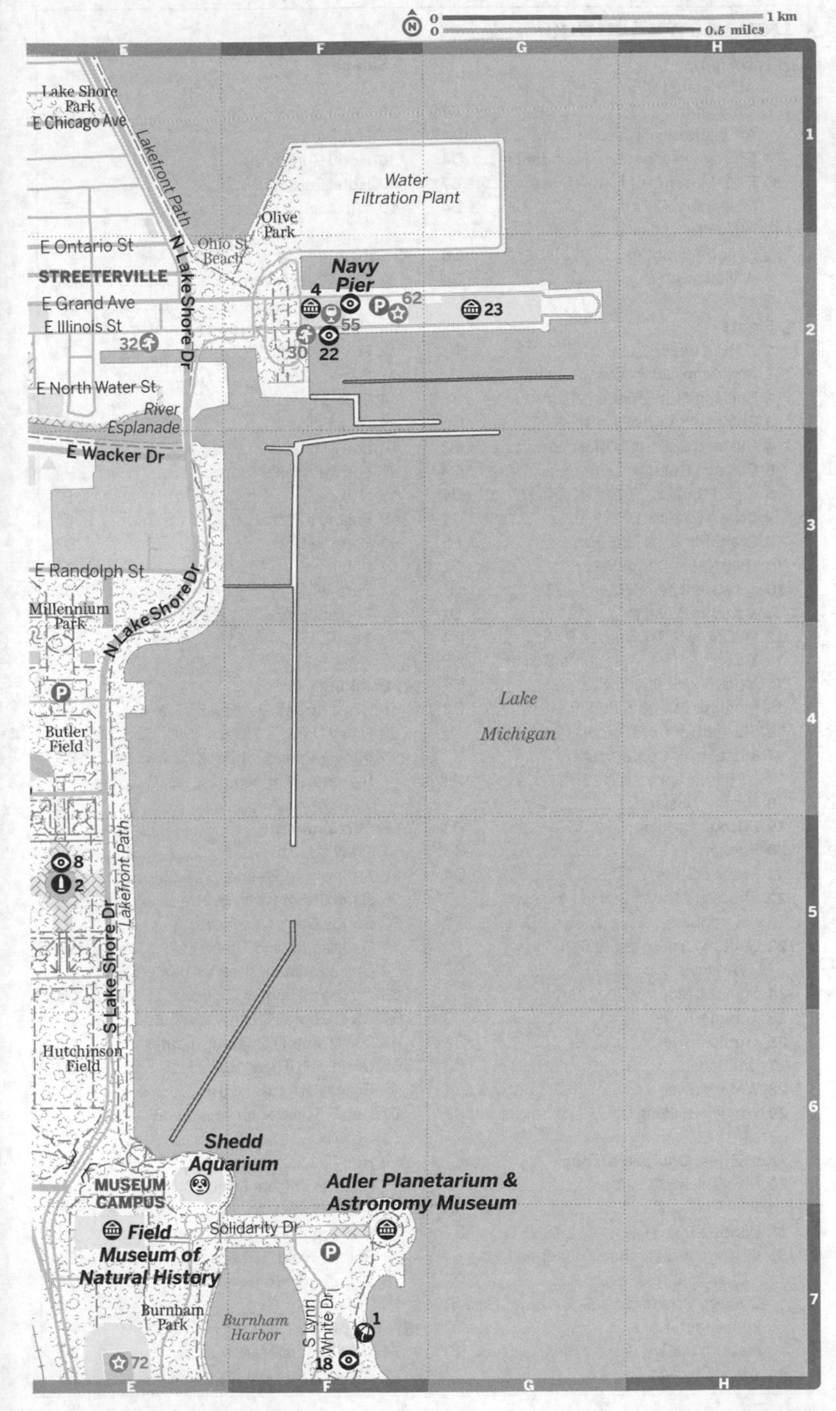
0 1 km
0 0.5 miles
Lake Shore Park
E Chicago Ave
Lakefront Path
Water Filtration Plant
Olive Park
E Ontario St
Ohio St Beach
N Lake Shore Dr
STREETERVILLE
Navy Pier
E Grand Ave
E Illinois St
E North Water St
River Esplanade
E Wacker Dr
E Randolph St
Millennium Park
N Lake Shore Dr
Butler Field
Lake Michigan
S Lake Shore Dr
Lakefront Path
Hutchinson Field
Shedd Aquarium
MUSEUM CAMPUS
Adler Planetarium & Astronomy Museum
Field Museum of Natural History
Solidarity Dr
Burnham Park
Burnham Harbor
S Lynn White Dr

Downtown Chicago

Top Sights
Adler Planetarium & Astronomy Museum ... F7
Art Institute of Chicago ... D4
Chicago Architecture Foundation ... D4
Field Museum of Natural History ... E7
Millennium Park ... D4
Navy Pier ... F2
Shedd Aquarium ... E6
Willis Tower ... B4

Sights
1 12th St Beach ... F7
American Girl Place ... (see 75)
2 Buckingham Fountain ... E5
3 Chicago Board of Trade ... C4
4 Chicago Children's Museum ... F2
5 Chicago Cultural Center ... D3
6 Cloud Gate ... D4
7 Crown Fountain ... D4
8 Grant Park ... E5
9 Holy Name Cathedral ... C1
10 John Hancock Center ... D1
11 Magnificent Mile ... D1
12 McCormick Tribune Ice Rink ... D4
13 Millennium Park Welcome Center ... D3
14 Monadnock Building ... C4
15 Monument with Standing Beast ... C3
16 Museum of Contemporary Art ... D1
17 Museum of Contemporary Photography ... D5
18 Northerly Island ... F7
19 Pritzker Pavilion ... D3
20 Rookery ... C4
21 Route 66 Sign ... D4
22 Shoreline Water Taxi to Museum Campus ... F2
23 Smith Museum of Stained Glass Windows ... G2
24 Sun, the Moon & One Star ... C4
25 Tribune Tower ... D2
26 Trump Tower ... D2
27 Untitled ... C3
28 Water Tower ... D1
29 Wrigley Building ... D2

Activities, Courses & Tours
30 Bike Chicago ... F2
31 Bike Chicago ... D3
32 Bobby's Bike Hike ... E2
33 Chicago Architecture Foundation Boat Tour Dock ... D2
Chicago Greeter ... (see 5)
InstaGreeter ... (see 5)
McCormick Tribune Ice Rink ... (see 12)
34 Weird Chicago Tours ... C2

Sleeping
35 Best Western River North ... C2
36 Central Loop Hotel ... C4
37 HI-Chicago ... D5
38 Hotel Burnham ... C3
39 Hotel Felix ... C1
40 Wit ... C3

Eating
41 Billy Goat Tavern ... D2
Cafecito ... (see 37)
Chicago's Downtown Farmstand (see 68)
42 Frontera Grill ... C2
43 Gage ... D4
44 Gino's East ... D1
45 Giordano's ... D1
46 Lou Malnati's ... C2
47 Lou Mitchell's ... B4
48 Mr Beef ... B1
49 Pizano's Pizza ... C1
50 Pizzeria Uno ... D2
51 Publican ... A3
52 Purple Pig ... D2
Topolobampo ... (see 42)
53 Xoco ... C2

Drinking
54 Clark Street Ale House ... C1
55 Harry Caray's Tavern ... F2
56 Intelligentsia Coffee ... D3
Signature Lounge ... (see 10)

Entertainment
57 Andy's ... C2
58 Auditorium Theater ... D5
59 Bank of America Theatre ... C4
60 Buddy Guy's Legends ... D5
61 Cadillac Palace Theater ... C3
62 Chicago Shakespeare Theater ... F2
63 Chicago Theater ... D3
64 Civic Opera House ... B4
65 Ford Center/Oriental Theater ... C3
66 Goodman Theatre ... C3
Grant Park Orchestra ... (see 13)
67 Harris Theater for Music and Dance ... D3
68 Hot Tix ... D3
69 Hot Tix ... D1
Hubbard Street Dance Chicago .. (see 67)
70 Jazz Showcase ... C6
71 Lookingglass Theatre Company ... D1
72 Soldier Field ... E7
73 Symphony Center ... D4

Shopping
74 Jazz Record Mart ... D2
75 Water Tower Place ... D1

the Family Fun Tent provides free kids' activities daily between 10am and 3pm. Free walking tours (Welcome Center; ⌚11:30am and 1pm) take place daily, or do it yourself with a downloadable tour from the website.

Technically, Millennium is part of the northwest corner of Grant Park (see p511).

Art Institute of Chicago MUSEUM
(Map p508; ☎312-443-3600; www.artic.edu/aic; 111 S Michigan Ave; adult/child $18/free; ⌚10:30am-5pm, to 8pm Thu;) The second-largest art museum in the country, the Art Institute houses treasures and masterpieces from around the globe, including a fabulous selection of both impressionist and post-impressionist paintings. The Modern Wing dazzles with natural light, and hangs Picassos and Mirós on its 3rd floor.

Allow two hours to browse the museum's highlights; art buffs should allocate much longer. Ask at the front desk about free talks and tours once you're inside. Note that the 3rd-floor contemporary sculpture garden is always free. It has great city views and connects to Millennium Park via the mod, pedestrian-only Nichols Bridgeway.

Willis Tower TOWER
(Map p508; ☎312-875-9696; www.the-skydeck.com; 233 S Wacker Dr; adult/child $17/11; ⌚9am-10pm Apr-Sep, 10am-8pm Oct-Mar) Yes, you're at the right place. Willis Tower was the Sears Tower until mid-2009, when insurance broker Willis Group Holdings bought the naming rights. No matter what you call it, it's still the USA's tallest building (1454ft), and its 103rd-floor Skydeck puts visitors way up in the clouds.

Enter via Jackson Blvd, then take the elevator down to the waiting area, where you go through security and pay admission. Queues can be up to an hour on busy days (peak times are in summer, between 11am to 4pm Friday through Sunday). There's a factoid-filled film to watch, and then the ear-popping, 70-second ride to the top. Step onto the glass-floored Ledge for a feeling of mid-air suspension and knee-buckling view straight down. For those who prefer a drink with their vista, the Gold Coast's John Hancock Center (p513) is a better choice.

FREE **Chicago Cultural Center** CULTURAL BUILDING
(Map p508; ☎312-744-6630; www.chicagoculturalcenter.org; 78 E Washington St; ⌚8am-7pm Mon-Thu, 8am-6pm Fri, 9am-6pm Sat, 10am-6pm Sun;) The block-long, beaux arts building houses art exhibitions, foreign films, and jazz and world music concerts at 12:15pm on weekdays. It also contains the world's largest Tiffany stained-glass dome, Chicago's main visitor center and a local authors' gallery, in which you can browse Nelson Algren and Studs Terkel books.

Grant Park PARK
(Map p508; Michigan Ave btwn 12th & Randolph Sts; ⌚6am-11pm) Grant Park hosts the city's mega-events, such as Taste of Chicago, Blues Fest and Lollapalooza. **Buckingham Fountain** (cnr Congress Pkwy & Columbus Dr) is Grant's centerpiece. The fountain is one of the world's largest, with a 1.5-million-gallon capacity. It lets loose on the hour every hour between 10am and 11pm mid-April to mid-October, accompanied at night by multicolored lights and music.

Public Artworks MONUMENTS
(Map p508) Chicago has commissioned several head-scratching public sculptures

ONLINE TICKETS & DISCOUNT CARDS

Most major sights, including the Art Institute, Shedd Aquarium and Willis Tower, allow you to buy tickets online. The advantage is that you're assured entry and you get to skip the regular ticket lines. The disadvantage is that you have to pay a service fee of $1.50 to $4 per ticket (sometimes it's just per order), and at times the prepay line is almost as long as the regular one. Our suggestion: consider buying online in summer and for big exhibits; otherwise, there's no need.

Chicago offers a couple of discount cards that also let you skip the regular queues:

» **Go Chicago Card** (www.gochicagocard.com) Allows you to visit an unlimited number of attractions for a flat fee; good for one, two, three, five or seven consecutive days.

» **CityPass** (www.citypass.com) Gives access to five of the city's top draws, including Shedd Aquarium and Willis Tower, over nine days; a better option if you prefer a more leisurely sightseeing pace.

FAMOUS LOOP ARCHITECTURE

Ever since it presented the world with the first skyscraper, Chicago has thought big with its architecture and pushed the envelope of modern design. The Loop is a fantastic place to roam and gawk at these ambitious structures.

The **Chicago Architecture Foundation** (Map p508; www.architecture.org) runs tours that explain the following buildings and more:

» **Chicago Board of Trade** (Map p508; 141 W Jackson Blvd) A 1930 art deco gem. Inside, manic traders swap futures and options. Outside, check out the giant statue of Ceres, the goddess of agriculture, that tops the building.

» **Rookery** (Map p508; 209 S LaSalle St) The 1888 Rookery looks fortresslike outside, but the inside of this office building is light and airy thanks to Frank Lloyd Wright's atrium overhaul. Pigeons used to roost here, hence the name.

» **Monadnock Building** (Map p508; 53 W Jackson Blvd) Architectural pilgrims get weak-kneed when they see the Monadnock Building, which is two buildings in one. The north is the older, traditional design from 1891, while the south is the newer, mod half from 1893. See the difference? The Monadnock remains true to its original purpose as an office building.

throughout the decades. The Loop's triumvirate of puzzlement includes:

Untitled (50 W Washington St) Pablo Picasso's work, which everyone just calls 'the Picasso.'

Sun, the Moon and One Star (69 W Washington St) Joan Miró's work, which everyone just calls 'Miró's Chicago.'

Monument with Standing Beast (100 W Randolph St) Jean Dubuffet's creation, which everyone calls 'Snoopy in a Blender.'

Route 66 Sign (Adams St btwn Michigan & Wabash Aves) Attention Route 66 buffs: the Mother Road's starting point is here. Look for the marker on Adams St's north side as you head west toward Wabash Ave.

SOUTH LOOP

The South Loop, which includes the lower ends of downtown and Grant Park, has soared recently, from dereliction to development central. The Museum Campus is the lakefront area south of Grant Park, where three top attractions huddle.

Field Museum of Natural History MUSEUM
(Map p508; ☎312-922-9410; www.fieldmuseum.org; 1400 S Lake Shore Dr; adult/child $15/10; ⏲9am-5pm; 👪) The mammoth Field Museum houses everything but the kitchen sink – beetles, mummies, gemstones, Bushman the stuffed ape. The collection's rockstar is Sue, the largest *Tyrannosaurus rex* yet discovered. She even gets her own gift shop. Special exhibits, like the 3D movie, cost extra.

Shedd Aquarium AQUARIUM
(Map p508; ☎312-939-2438; www.sheddaquarium.org; 1200 S Lake Shore Dr; adult/child $29/20; ⏲9am-6pm Jun-Aug, to 5pm Sep-May; 👪) Top draws at the kiddie-mobbed Shedd Aquarium include the Oceanarium, with its beluga whales and frolicking white-sided dolphins, and the shark exhibit, where there's just 5in of Plexiglas between you and two dozen fierce-looking swimmers. The 4D theater and the odd aquatic show cost extra (around $4 each).

Adler Planetarium & Astronomy Museum MUSEUM
(Map p508; ☎312-922-7827; www.adlerplanetarium.org; 1300 S Lake Shore Dr; adult/child $12/8; ⏲9:30am-6pm Jun-Aug, 10am-4pm Sep-May; 👪) Space enthusiasts will get a big bang (pun!) out of the Adler. There are public telescopes from which to view the stars, 3D lectures where you can learn about supernovas, and the Planet Explorers exhibit where kids can 'launch' a rocket. The Adler's front steps offer Chicago's primo skyline view (and are a renowned spot for the adults to smooch).

Other sights around the Museum Campus:

12th Street Beach BEACH
(Map p508) A path runs south from the planetarium to this handsome, secluded crescent of sand.

Northerly Island PARK
(Map p508; 1400 S Lynn White Dr) Hosts big-name summer concerts (which you can hear from 12th St Beach), trails and birdwatching.

FREE **Museum of Contemporary Photography** MUSEUM

(Map p508; ☎312-663-5554; www.mocp.org; Columbia College, 600 S Michigan Ave; ⊙10am-5pm Mon-Sat, to 8pm Thu, noon-5pm Sun) A small museum worth exploring.

NEAR NORTH

The Loop may be where Chicago fortunes are made, but the Near North is where those fortunes are spent. Shops, restaurants and amusements abound.

FREE **Navy Pier** WATERFRONT

(Map p508; ☎312-595-7437; www.navypier.com; 600 E Grand Ave; ⊙10am-10pm, to midnight Fri & Sat; 👪) Half-mile-long Navy Pier is Chicago's most-visited attraction, sporting a 150ft Ferris wheel (per ride $6), an IMAX theater, a beer garden and gimmicky chain restaurants. Locals groan over its commercialization, but its lakefront view and cool breezes can't be beat. The fireworks displays on summer Wednesdays (9:30pm) and Saturdays (10:15pm) are a treat too.

The Chicago Children's Museum (p520) and gorgeous **Smith Museum of Stained Glass Windows** (Map p508; ☎312-595-5024; Festival Hall; admission free; ⊙10am-10pm, to midnight Fri & Sat) are also on the pier, as are several boat-cruise operators. Try the **Shoreline water taxi** (Map p508; www.shorelinesightseeing.com; ⊙10am-7pm late May–early Sep) for a fun ride to the Museum Campus (adult/child $7/4).

Magnificent Mile STREET

(Map p508; www.themagnificentmile.com; N Michigan Ave) Spanning Michigan Ave between the river and Oak St, the Mag Mile is the much-touted upscale shopping strip, where Bloomingdales, Neiman's and Saks will lighten your wallet.

Tribune Tower TOWER

(Map p508; 435 N Michigan Ave) Take a close look when passing by the gothic tower to see chunks of the Taj Mahal, Parthenon and other famous structures embedded in the lower walls.

Trump Tower TOWER

(Map p508; 401 N Wabash Ave) The Donald's 1360ft tower is now Chicago's second-tallest building, though architecture critics have mocked its 'toothpick' look.

Wrigley Building TOWER

(Map p508; 400 N Wabash Ave) Built by the chewing-gum maker, the white terra-cotta exterior glows as white as the Doublemint Twins' teeth.

GOLD COAST

The Gold Coast has been the address of Chicago's wealthiest residents for more than 125 years.

John Hancock Center TOWER

(off Map p508; ☎888-875-8439; www.hancockobservatory.com; 875 N Michigan Ave; adult/child $15/10; ⊙9am-11pm) Get high in Chicago's third-tallest skyscraper. In many ways the

CAPONE'S CHICAGO

The city would rather not discuss its gangster past; consequently there are no brochures or exhibits about infamous sites. So you'll need to use your imagination when visiting the following as most are not designated as notorious.

Two murders took place near **Holy Name Cathedral** (Map p508; 735 N State St). In 1924 North Side boss Dion O'Banion was gunned down in his florist shop (738 N State St) after he crossed Al Capone. O'Banion's replacement, Hymie Weiss, fared no better. In 1926 he was killed on his way to church by bullets flying from a window at 740 N State St.

The **St Valentine's Day Massacre Site** (2122 N Clark St, Lincoln Park) is where Capone's goons, dressed as cops, lined up seven members of Bugs Moran's gang against the garage wall that used to be here and sprayed them with bullets. The garage was torn down in 1967.

In 1934, the 'lady in red' betrayed John Dillinger at the **Biograph Theater** (2433 N Lincoln Ave, Lincoln Park). Dillinger was shot by the FBI outside it.

The speakeasy in the basement of the glamorous jazz bar **Green Mill** (p528) was a Capone favorite.

Capone's Chicago Home (7244 S Prairie Ave) is deep on the South Side in a sketchy area, so use caution. The residence was used mostly by Capone's wife, Mae, his mom and other relatives.

view here surpasses the one at Willis Tower, as the Hancock is closer to the lake and a little further north. Those needing a city history lesson should ascend to the 94th-floor observatory, and listen to the archaic audio tour that comes with admission. Those secure in their knowledge should shoot up to the 96th-floor Signature Lounge, where the view is free if you buy a drink ($6 to $14).

Museum of Contemporary Art MUSEUM
(Map p508; ☎312-280-2660; www.mcachicago.org; 220 E Chicago Ave; adult/student $12/7; ⌚10am-8pm Tue, 10am-5pm Wed-Sun) Consider it the Art Institute's brash, rebellious sibling, with especially strong minimalist, surrealist and book arts collections, and permanent works by Franz Kline, Rene Magritté, Cindy Sherman and Andy Warhol.

Original Playboy Mansion BUILDING
(1340 N State St) Hugh Hefner began wearing his all-day jammies here, when the rigors of magazine production and heavy partying prevented him from getting dressed. The building contains condos now, but a visit still allows you to boast, 'I've been to the Playboy Mansion.' Head east a block to Astor St and ogle more manors between the 1300 and 1500 blocks.

Water Tower LANDMARK
(Map p508; cnr Chicago & Michigan Aves) The 154ft-tall, turreted tower is a defining city landmark: it was the sole downtown survivor of the 1871 Great Fire.

DON'T MISS

MIDWESTERN BEERS

The Midwest is ready to pour you a cold one thanks to its German heritage. Yes, Budweiser and Miller are based here, but that's not what we're talking about. Far more exciting is the region's cache of craft brewers. Keep an eye on the taps for these slurpable suds-makers, available throughout the area:

» **Bell's** Kalamazoo, MI
» **Capital** Madison, WI
» **Founder's** Grand Rapids, MI
» **Goose Island** Chicago, IL
» **Great Lakes** Cleveland, OH
» **Lakefront** Milwaukee, WI
» **New Holland** Holland, MI
» **Summit** St Paul, MN
» **Three Floyds** Munster, IN
» **Two Brothers** Warrenville, IL

Oak Street Beach BEACH
(off Map p508; 1000 N Lake Shore Dr) Packs in bodies beautiful at the edge of downtown.

LINCOLN PARK & OLD TOWN

Lincoln Park (off Map p508) is Chicago's largest green space, an urban oasis spanning 1200 leafy acres along the lakefront. 'Lincoln Park' is also the name for the abutting neighborhood. Both are alive day and night with people jogging, walking dogs, pushing strollers and driving in circles looking for a place to park.

Old Town rests at the southwest foot of Lincoln Park. The intersection of North Ave and Wells St is the epicenter, with saucy restaurants, bars and the Second City improv club fanning out from here.

FREE **Lincoln Park Zoo** ZOO
(☎312-742-2000; www.lpzoo.org; 2200 N Cannon Dr; ⌚10am-4:30pm Nov-Mar, to 5pm Apr-Oct, to 6:30pm Sat & Sun Jun-Aug; 👪) It's a local family favorite, filled with gorillas, lions, tigers and other exotic creatures in the shadow of downtown. Check out the Regenstein African Journey, Primate House and Nature Boardwalk for the cream of the crop.

FREE **Lincoln Park Conservatory** GARDENS
(☎312-742-7736; 2391 N Stockton Dr; ⌚9am-5pm) Near the zoo's north entrance, the magnificent 1891 hothouse coaxes palms, ferns and orchids to flourish. In winter, it becomes a soothing, 75-degree escape from the icy winds raging outside.

North Avenue Beach BEACH
(1600 N Lake Shore Dr; 👪) Chicago's most popular and amenity-laden stretch of sand wafts a southern California vibe. You can rent bikes, kayaks, volleyballs and lounge chairs, as well as eat and drink at the party-orientated beach house. It's 2 miles north of the Loop.

Chicago History Museum MUSEUM
(off Map p508; ☎312-642-4600; www.chicagohistory.org; 1601 N Clark St; adult/child $14/free; ⌚9:30am-4:30pm Mon-Sat, noon-5pm Sun) Multimedia displays cover it all, from the Great Fire to the 1968 Democratic Convention. President Lincoln's deathbed is here; so is the chance to 'become' a Chicago hot dog covered in condiments (in the kids' area, but adults are welcome for the photo op).

LAKE VIEW & WRIGLEYVILLE

North of Lincoln Park, these neighborhoods can be enjoyed by ambling along Halsted St, Clark St, Belmont Ave or Southport Ave, which are well supplied with restaurants, bars and shops. Ivy-covered **Wrigley Field** (Map p516; 1060 W Addison St) is named after the chewing-gum guy and is home to the much-loved but perpetually losing Chicago Cubs. If they're playing a game, you can peep through the 'knothole,' a garage door-sized opening on Sheffield Ave, to watch the action for free. For ticket information, see p529.

ANDERSONVILLE & UPTOWN

These northern neighborhoods (Map p516) are good for a delicious browse. Andersonville is an old Swedish enclave centered on Clark St, where timeworn, European-tinged businesses mix with new foodie restaurants, funky boutiques, vintage shops and gay and lesbian bars. Take the CTA Red Line to the Berwyn stop, and walk west for about a mile.

Around the corner to the south, Uptown is a whole different scene. Take the Red Line to the Argyle stop, and you're in the heart of 'Little Saigon' and its pho-serving storefronts.

WICKER PARK, BUCKTOWN & UKRAINIAN VILLAGE

West of Lincoln Park, these three neighborhoods (Map p506) – once havens for working-class, central European immigrants and bohemian writers – are hot property. Heaps of fashion boutiques, hipster record stores, thrift shops and cocktail lounges have shot up, especially near the Milwaukee-North-Damen Aves intersection. Division St is also prime wandering territory. It used to be called 'Polish Broadway' for all the polka bars that lined it, but now the requisite cafes and crafty businesses have taken over. There aren't many actual sights here, aside from **Nelson Algren's House** (Map p506; 1958 W Evergreen Ave), where he wrote several gritty, Chicago-based novels. Alas, it's a private residence, so you can only admire it from the sidewalk. Take the CTA Blue Line to Damen (for Algren) or Division.

LOGAN SQUARE & HUMBOLDT PARK

When artists and hipsters got priced out of Wicker Park, they moved west to the Latino communities of Logan Square and Humboldt Park (Map p506). For visitors, these are places for small, cool-cat eateries, brewpubs and music clubs. Take the CTA Blue Line to Logan Square or California.

BLUES FANS' PILGRIMAGE

From 1957 to 1967, the humble building at 2120 S Michigan Ave was Chess Records, the seminal electric blues label. Muddy Waters, Howlin' Wolf and Bo Diddley cut tracks here, and paved the way for rock 'n' roll with their sick licks and amped-up sound. Chuck Berry and the Rolling Stones arrived soon after. The studio is now called **Willie Dixon's Blues Heaven** (☎312-808-1286; www.bluesheaven.com; 2120 S Michigan Ave; tours $10; ⏰11am-4pm Mon-Fri, noon-2pm Sat), named for the bassist who wrote most of Chess' hits. Staff give tours that take in the reception area (Minnie Ripperton worked the desk) and main studio. Free blues concerts rock the side garden on summer Thursdays at 6pm. The building is near Chinatown, and about a mile south of the Museum Campus.

NEAR WEST SIDE & PILSEN

Just west of the Loop is, well, the **West Loop** (Map p508). It's akin to New York City's Meatpacking District, with chic restaurants, clubs and galleries poking out between meat-processing plants. W Randolph St and W Fulton Market are the main veins. Nearby **Greektown** (off Map p508) runs along S Halsted St near W Jackson Blvd. The areas are about 1.25 miles west of the Loop and most easily reached by taxi.

Southwest lies the enclave of **Pilsen** (Map p506), a festive mix of art galleries, Mexican bakeries, hipster cafes and murals on the buildings. The CTA Pink Line to 18th St drops you in the midst.

FREE National Museum of Mexican Art MUSEUM

(Map p506; ☎312-738-1503; www.nationalmuseumofmexicanart.org; 1852 W 19th St; ⏰10am-5pm Tue-Sun) The largest Latino arts institution in the US, this museum's vivid permanent collection includes classical paintings, shining gold altars, skeleton-rich folk art and colorful beadwork.

Pilsen Mural Tours WALKING TOUR

(☎773-342-4191; per group 1½hr tour $100) Local artist Jose Guerrero leads the highly recommended tours, during which you can learn more about this traditional art form; call to arrange an excursion.

Andersonville & Wrigleyville

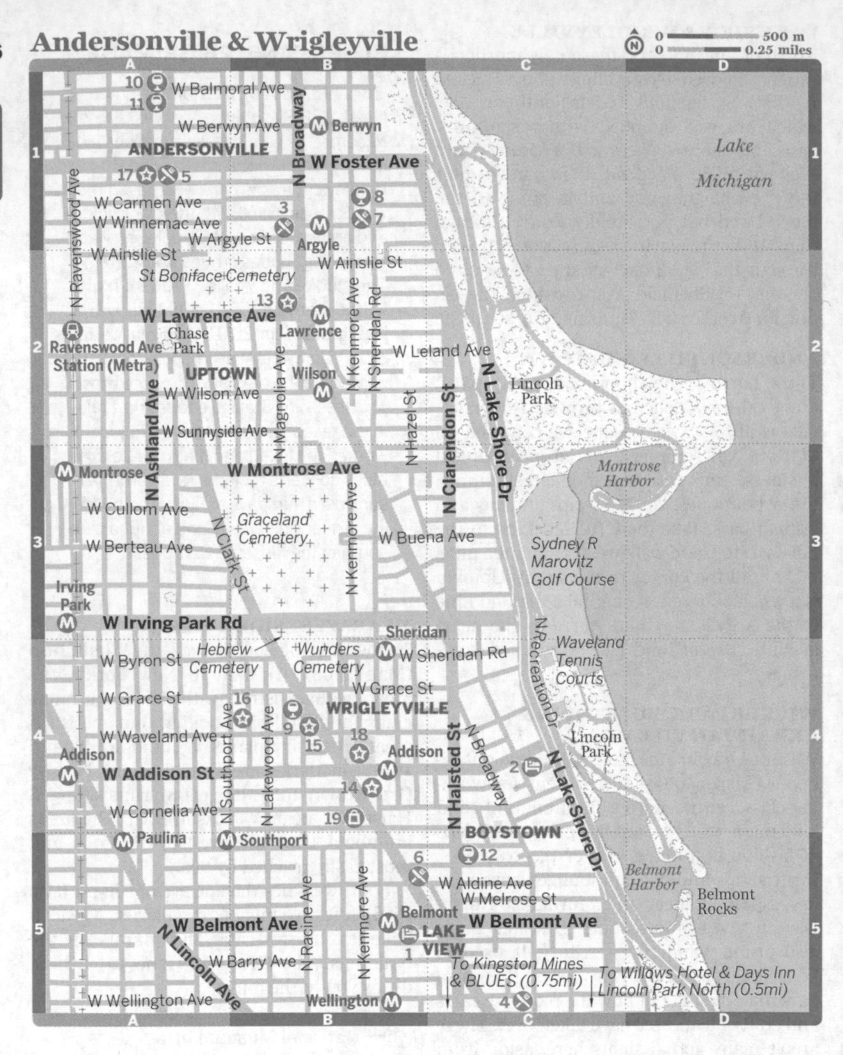

CHINATOWN

Chinatown's (off Map p508) charm is best enjoyed by going bakery to bakery, nibbling chestnut cakes and almond cookies, and shopping for Hello Kitty items. Wentworth Ave, south of Cermak Rd, is the retail heart of old Chinatown; Chinatown Sq, along Archer Ave north of Cermak, is the newer commerce district. It's an easy 10-minute train ride from the Loop. Take the CTA Red Line to the Cermak-Chinatown stop.

HYDE PARK & SOUTH SIDE

The South Side is the generic term applied to Chicago's myriad neighborhoods, including some of its most impoverished, that lie south of 25th St. Hyde Park and abutting Kenwood are the South Side's stars, catapulted into the spotlight by local boy Barack Obama. Unless stated otherwise, sights are reached via Metra Electric Line trains from Millennium Station downtown to the 55th-56th-57th St stop.

InstaGreeter (www.chicagogreeter.com/instagreeter) offers free one-hour walking tours from the **Hyde Park Art Center** (5020 S Cornell Ave; ⌚10am-3pm Sat Jun-early Oct). Several bicycle tours (p517) also cruise by all the highlights.

Andersonville & Wrigleyville

Sights
Wrigley Field .... (see 18)

Sleeping
1 City Suites Hotel B5
2 Majestic Hotel C4

Eating
3 Ba Le Bakery B1
4 Crisp C5
5 Hopleaf A1
6 Mia Francesca B5
7 Tweet B1

Drinking
8 Big Chicks B1
9 Ginger Man B4
10 Hamburger Mary's A1
11 Marty's A1
12 Sidetrack C5

Entertainment
13 Green Mill B2
14 iO Improv B4
15 Metro B4
16 Music Box Theatre B4
17 Neo-Futurists A1
Smart Bar .... (see 15)
18 Wrigley Field B4

Shopping
19 Strange Cargo B4

Obama Sights BUILDINGS
Hefty security means you can't get close to **Obama's house** (5046 S Greenwood Ave), but you can stand across the street on Hyde Park Blvd and try to glimpse the red-brick Georgian-style manor. Better yet, visit his barber Zariff and the bulletproof glass-encased presidential barber chair at the **Hyde Park Hair Salon** (5234 S Blackstone Ave). Take the Metra Electric Line to 51st-53rd St.

University of Chicago UNIVERSITY
(5801 S Ellis Ave) Faculty and students have racked up more than 80 Nobel prizes within U of C's hallowed halls. The economics and physics departments lay claim to most. It's also where the nuclear age began: Enrico Fermi and his Manhattan Project cronies built a reactor and carried out the world's first controlled atomic reaction on December 2, 1942. The **Nuclear Energy sculpture** (S Ellis Ave btwn E 56th & E 57th Sts), by Henry Moore, marks the spot where it blew its stack.

Museum of Science & Industry MUSEUM
(Map p506; ☎773-684-1414; www.msichicago.org; 5700 S Lake Shore Dr; adult/child $15/10; ⏲9:30am-5:30pm Jun-Aug, reduced Sep-May) This colossal play-palace will overstimulate the serenest of souls with its flashy exhibits. Highlights include a WWII German U-boat nestled in an underground display ($8 extra to tour it) and the 'Science Storms' exhibit with a mock tornado.

Robie House ARCHITECTURE
(Map p506; ☎708-848-1976; www.gowright.org; 5757 S Woodlawn Ave; adult/child $15/12; ⏲11am-4pm Thu-Mon) Of the numerous buildings that Frank Lloyd Wright designed around Chicago, none is more famous or influential than Robie House. The resemblance of its horizontal lines to the flat landscape of the Midwestern prairie became known as the Prairie style. Inside are 174 stained-glass windows and doors, which you'll see on the hour-long tours (frequency varies by season).

Activities

Tucked away among Chicago's 552 parks are public golf courses, ice rinks, swimming pools and more. Activities are free or low cost, and the necessary equipment is usually available for rent. The **Chicago Park District** (www.chicagoparkdistrict.com) runs the show; **golf information** (☎312-245-0909; www.cpdgolf.com) is separate.

Cycling

Riding along the 18.5-mile lakefront path is a fantastic way to see the city. Two companies rent wheels. The cost is roughly $10 per hour, or $35 per day (helmet and lock included). Both companies also offer two- to four-hour tours ($35 to $60, including bikes) that cover themes like the lakefront, beer and pizza munching, or Obama sights (highly recommended!). The **Active Transportation Alliance** (www.activetrans.org) lists bike events around town.

Bike Chicago CYCLING
(Map p508; ☎888-245-3929; www.bikechicago.com; 239 E Randolph St; ⏲6:30am-8pm Mon-Fri, from 8am Sat & Sun, closed Sat & Sun Nov-Mar) This one's quite corporate, and has multiple locations. The main one is at Millennium Park; there's another at Navy Pier.

Bobby's Bike Hike CYCLING

(Map p508; ☎312-915-0995; www.bobbysbikehike.com; 465 N McClurg Ct; ⏲8:30am-7pm Jun-Aug, closed Dec-Feb) The eager upstart; located at the River East Docks' Ogden Slip.

Water Sports

Take a dip, build a sand castle or laze in the sun at any of Chicago's 30-plus beaches. Lifeguards patrol the shores in summer; check with the **Chicago Park District** (www.chicagoparkdistrict.com) for water-quality advisories before embarking. **North Avenue Beach** (p514) and **Oak Street Beach** (off Map p508), both close to downtown, are particularly body-filled. Brace yourself as the water remains butt-numbing well into July.

Ice Skating

Millennium Park's **McCormick Tribune Ice Rink** (Map p508; ☎312-742-5222; www.millenniumpark.org; 55 N Michigan Ave; skate rental $10; ⏲late Nov-Feb) heats up when the temperature plummets.

Offbeat Chicago

Sure, your friends will listen politely as you describe your trip to the Willis Tower's tip, but you'll stop them mid-yawn when you unleash stories of how you boozed with roller babes and honed your cornhole strategy (see p518). Chicago has a fine collection of unusual sights and activities to supplement its standard attractions.

Cornhole GAME

(www.chicagoleaguesports.com) Get your mind out of the gutter; we're not talking dirty here. We mean an activity in which small corn-filled bags (aka beanbags) are tossed into a sloped box with a hole in it. Cornhole is a game! Several bars have leagues and tournaments.

International Museum of Surgical Science MUSEUM

(☎312-642-6502; www.imss.org; 1524 N Lake Shore Dr; adult/child $15/7, admission free Tue; ⏲10am-5pm Tue-Sat, noon-5pm Sun) A blood-letting exhibit and fine collection of 'stones' (as in kidney stones and gallstones) are among the offerings at this museum, and the hemorrhoid surgery toolkit serves as a reminder to eat lots of fiber. It's in the Gold Coast, about a mile north of the Water Tower area.

Windy City Rollers SPECTATOR SPORT

(www.windycityrollers.com; UIC Pavilion, 525 S Racine Ave; tickets $20-40) The bang-'em-up sport of roller derby was born in Chicago in 1935, and the battlin' babes here will show you how it's played, bruises and all. Matches take place monthly at UIC Pavilion, west of the Loop (take the Blue Line to Racine).

Leather Archives & Museum MUSEUM

(Map p506; ☎773-761-9200; www.leatherarchives.org; 6418 N Greenview Ave; admission $10; ⏲11am-7pm Thu & Fri, to 5pm Sat & Sun) Who knew Ben Franklin liked to be flogged and Egypt's Queen Hatshepsut had a foot fetish? This museum reveals these facts and more in its displays of leather, fetish and S&M subcultures. It's 8 miles north of the Loop, and 1.5 miles north of Andersonville.

Weird Chicago Tours BUS TOUR

(www.weirdchicago.com) Drives by kinky and spooky spots.

Chic-A-Go-Go TV SHOW

(www.roctober.com/chicagogo) The cable-access show's live dance audience isn't just kids: adults, too, can shake it on the dancefloor with Miss Mia and Ratso.

☞ Tours

Tours get you out on the water and into further-flung neighborhoods, and many companies offer discounts if you book online. Outdoor-oriented tours operate from April to November only, unless specified otherwise. For cycling jaunts, see p517.

If guided tours aren't your thing, you can always do it yourself with free downloadable audio tours, such as the Buddy Guy–narrated **Chicago Blues Tour** (www.downloadchicagotours.com/bluesmedia), or the **Chicago Movie Tour** (www.onscreenillinois.com), providing a peek at sites from *The Untouchables* and other famous flicks.

FREE **Chicago Greeter** WALKING TOUR

(Map p508; ☎312-744-8000; www.chicagogreeter.com; ⏲year-round) This outfit pairs you with a local city dweller who will take you on a personal two- to four-hour tour customized by theme (architecture, history, gay and lesbian and more) or neighborhood. Travel is by foot and/or public transportation; reserve seven business days in advance.

FREE **InstaGreeter** WALKING TOUR

(Map p508; www.chicagogreeter.com/instagreeter; 77 E Randolph St; ⏲10am-4pm Fri-Sun year-round) The quicker version of Chicago Greeter, offering on-the-spot one-hour tours from the

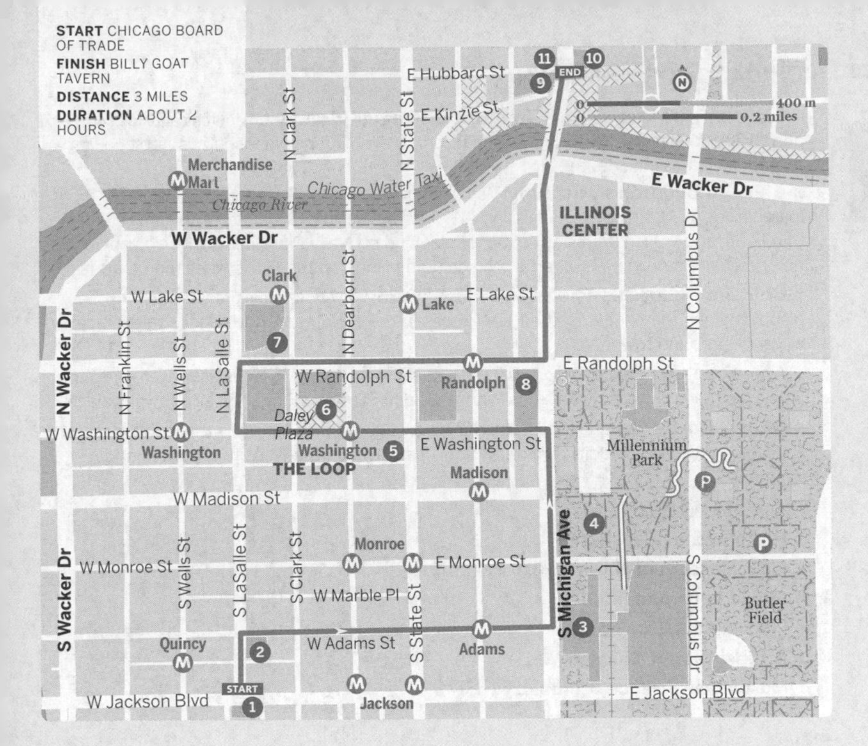

Walking Tour

The Loop

This tour swoops through the Loop, highlighting Chicago's revered art and architecture, with a visit to Al Capone's dentist thrown in for good measure.

Start at the 1 **Chicago Board of Trade**, where guys in Technicolor coats swap corn (or something like that) inside a cool art deco building. Step into the nearby 2 **Rookery** to see Frank Lloyd Wright's handiwork in the atrium.

Head east on Adams St to the 3 **Art Institute**, one of the city's most-visited attractions. The lion statues out front make a classic keepsake photo. Walk a few blocks north to avant-garde 4 **Millennium Park**, and saunter in to explore 'the Bean' sculpture, human-gargoyle fountains and other contemporary designs.

Leave Millennium Park and head west on Washington St to 5 **Hotel Burnham**. It's housed in the Reliance Building, which was the precursor to modern skyscraper design; Capone's dentist drilled teeth in what's now room 809. Just west, Picasso's 6 **Untitled**, created by Mr Abstract himself, is ensconced in Daley Plaza. Bird, dog, woman? You decide. Then go north on Clark St to 7 **Monument with Standing Beast**, another head-scratching sculpture.

Walk east on Randolph St through the theater district. Pop into the 8 **Cultural Center** to get a soda in the cafe and maybe catch a free concert. Refreshed? Now go north on Michigan Ave and cross the Chicago River. Just north of the bridge you'll pass the 9 **Wrigley Building**, shining bright and white, and the nearby Gothic, eye-popping 10 **Tribune Tower**.

To finish your tour, visit 11 **Billy Goat Tavern**, a vintage Chicago dive that spawned the Curse of the Cubs. Just look around at the walls and you'll get the details, but in short: the tavern's owner, Billy Sianis, once tried to enter Wrigley Field with his pet goat. The smelly creature was denied entry, so Sianis called down a mighty curse on the baseball team in retaliation. They've stunk ever since.

CHICAGO FOR CHILDREN

Chicago is a kid's kind of town. **Time Out Chicago Kids** (www.timeoutchicagokids.com) and **Chicago Parent** (www.chicagoparent.com) are indispensible resources. Top choices for toddlin' times include:

» **Chicago Children's Museum** (Map p508; ☎312-527-1000; www.chicagochildrensmuseum.org; 700 E Grand Ave; admission $12, free Thu evening; ⏱10am-5pm, to 8pm Thu) Climb, dig and splash in this educational playland on Navy Pier; follow with an expedition down the carnival-like wharf itself, including spins on the Ferris wheel and carousel.

» **Chicago Children's Theatre** (☎773-227-0180; www.chicagochildrenstheatre.org) See a show by one the best kids' theater troupes in the country. Performances take place at venues around town.

» **American Girl Place** (Map p508; www.americangirl.com; 835 N Michigan Ave; 👪) Young ladies sip tea and get new hair-dos with their dolls at this multistory, girl-power palace.

» **Chic-A-Go-Go** (www.roctober.com/chicagogo) Groove at a taping of this cable-access TV show that's like a kiddie version of *Soul Train*. Check the website for dates and locations.

Other kid-friendly activities:

» **North Avenue Beach** (p514)

» **Field Museum of Natural History** (p512)

» **Shedd Aquarium** (p512)

» **Lincoln Park Zoo** (p514)

» **Art Institute of Chicago** (p511)

» **Museum of Science & Industry** (p517)

Chicago Cultural Center visitor center. InstaGreeter also has outlets open on summer Saturdays at Second City and the Hyde Park Art Center (p516).

TOP CHOICE Chicago Architecture Foundation BOAT TOUR, WALKING TOUR
(Map p508; ☎312-922-3432; www.architecture.org; 224 S Michigan Ave; tours $5-40) The gold-standard boat tours ($35) sail from Michigan Ave's river dock, while the popular Rise of the Skyscraper walking tours ($16) leave from the downtown Michigan Ave address. Weekday lunchtime tours ($5) explore individual landmark buildings.

Wateriders KAYAKING
(☎312-953-9287; www.wateriders.com; 950 N Kingsbury St; 2½hr tours $50-60) Slither through a canyon of glass and steel while kayaking the Chicago River. The daily 'Ghost and Gangster' trips glide by notorious downtown venues. The launch site is west of downtown, near where Chicago Ave meets the river.

Chicago History Museum BOAT TOUR, WALKING TOUR
(off Map p508; ☎312-642-4600; www.chicagohistory.org; tours $15-45) It counts pub crawls, kayak jaunts and cemetery walks among its tour arsenal. Departure points and times vary.

Weird Chicago Tours BUS TOUR
(Map p508; ☎888-446-7859; www.weirdchicago.com; cnr Clark & Ontario Sts; 3hr tours $30; ⏱7pm Thu-Sat, 3pm Sat & Sun) Drives by ghost, gangster and red-light sites. Departs from outside the Hard Rock Cafe.

Chicago Food Planet Tours WALKING TOUR
(☎212-209-3370; www.chicagofoodplanet.com; 3hr tours $45) Graze through Wicker Park, Near North or Chinatown. Departure points and times vary.

Chicago Rocks Tour BUS TOUR
(www.chicagorockstour.com; 3½hr tours $28) For the music fans in the crowd: sites, sounds and stories of the Smashing Pumpkins, Wilco and other Chicago bands from the 1980s onward. Departure points and times vary.

Festivals & Events

Chicago has a full events calendar all year, but the biggies take place in the summer. The following events are held downtown on a weekend, unless noted otherwise. **Explore**

Chicago (www.explorechicago.org/specialevents) has exact dates and other details.

FREE **St Patrick's Day Parade** CULTURAL
(www.chicagostpatsparade.com; ⌚mid-Mar) The local plumbers union dyes the Chicago River shamrock green; a big parade follows.

FREE **Blues Festival** MUSIC
(www.chicagobluesfestival.us; ⌚early Jun) It's the biggest free blues fest in the world, with three days of the music that made Chicago famous.

FREE **Taste of Chicago** FOOD
(www.tasteofchicago.us; ⌚late Jun–early Jul) The 10-day bash in Grant Park includes bands and lots of food on a stick.

FREE **SummerDance** MUSIC
(www.chicagosummerdance.org; 601 S Michigan Ave; ⌚6pm Thu-Sat, 4pm Sun early Jul–mid-Sep) Bands play rumba, samba and other world music preceded by fun dance lessons; held at the Spirit of Music Garden in Grant Park.

Pitchfork Music Festival MUSIC
(www.pitchforkmusicfestival.com; day pass $45; ⌚mid-Jul) Indie bands strum for three days in Union Park.

Lollapalooza MUSIC
(www.lollapalooza.com; day pass around $100; ⌚early Aug) Up to 130 bands spill off eight stages at Grant Park's three-day mega-gig.

FREE **Jazz Festival** MUSIC
(www.chicagojazzfestival.us; ⌚early Sep) Top names on the national jazz scene play over Labor Day weekend.

Sleeping

Chicago lodging doesn't come cheap. The best way to cut costs is to use a bidding site like Priceline or Hotwire (look for 'River North' or 'Mag Mile' locations). On weekends and when the frequent big conventions

GAY & LESBIAN CHICAGO

Chicago has a flourishing gay and lesbian scene. **Gay Chicago** (www.gaychicagonews.com), the **Windy City Times** (www.windycitymediagroup.com) and **Pink magazine** (www.pinkmag.com) provide the local lowdown.

The **Chicago Area Gay & Lesbian Chamber of Commerce** (www.glchamber.org) has an online tourism directory. Chicago Greeter (see p518) offers personalized sightseeing trips.

The biggest concentration of bars and clubs is in Wrigleyville on N Halsted St between Belmont Ave and Grace St, an area known as Boystown. Andersonville, aka Girls' Town, is another area with many choices. Top picks:

Big Chicks BAR
(Map p516; www.bigchicks.com; 5024 N Sheridan Rd; 📶) Despite the name, both men and women frequent Big Chicks, with its weekend DJs, art displays and next-door organic restaurant **Tweet** (www.tweet.biz; 5020 N Sheridan Ave; ⌚9am-3pm Wed-Mon; 📶), where weekend brunch packs 'em in.

Sidetrack CLUB
(Map p516; www.sidetrackchicago.com; 3349 N Halsted St) Massive Sidetrack thumps dance music and show tunes and is prime for people watching.

Hamburger Mary's BAR
(Map p516; www.hamburgermarys.com/chicago; 5400 N Clark St) Cabaret, karaoke, burgers and a booze-soaked outdoor patio make for good times at this hot spot.

Chance's Dances DANCE
(www.chancesdances.org) Organizes queer dance parties at clubs around town.

Pride Parade FESTIVAL
(www.chicagopridecalendar.org; ⌚late Jun) Pride winds through Boystown and attracts more than 450,000 revelers.

North Halsted Street Market Days FESTIVAL
(www.northalsted.com; ⌚early Aug) Another raucous event on the Boystown calendar, featuring a street fair and wild costumes.

trample through town, your options become much slimmer, so plan ahead to avoid unpleasant surprises. The prices we've listed are normal midweek rates in summer, the high season. Taxes add 15.4%.

B&Bs give a nice bang for the midrange buck. Contact the **Chicago Bed & Breakfast Association** (www.chicago-bed-breakfast.com; r $125-250), which represents 18 guesthouses. Many properties have two- to three-night minimum stays. Vacation rentals in local apartments are also a good deal here. Try **Vacation Rental By Owner** (www.vrbo.com) or **Craigslist** (www.chicago.craigslist.org).

Hotels in the Loop are convenient to Grant Park, the museums and business district, but the area is pretty dead come nightfall. Accommodations in the Near North and Gold Coast are most popular, given their proximity to eating, shopping and entertainment venues. Rooms in Lincoln Park, Lake View and Wicker Park entice because they're often cheaper than rooms downtown; they are also near swingin' nightlife.

Wi-fi is free unless noted otherwise. You pay dearly for parking in Chicago, around $45 per night downtown, and $22 in outlying neighborhoods.

LOOP & NEAR NORTH

TOP CHOICE Hotel Burnham HOTEL $$$

(Map p508; ☎312-782-1111; www.burnhamhotel.com; 1 W Washington St; r from $189; P ⊖ ❄ @ ☜) The proprietors brag that the Burnham has the highest guest return rates in Chicago; it's easy to see why. Housed in the Loop's landmark 1890s Reliance Building (precedent for the modern skyscraper), its super-slick decor woos architecture buffs. The bright, butter-colored rooms are furnished with mahogany writing desks and chaise lounges. The hotel also hosts a complimentary wine happy hour each evening.

Hotel Felix HOTEL $$

(Map p508; ☎312-447-3440; www.hotelfelixchicago.com; 111 W Huron St; r $139-189; P ⊖ ❄ @ ☜) Opened in 2009 in the Near North, the 225-room, 12-story Felix is downtown's first hotel to earn ecofriendly LEED certification (Silver status, to be exact). The earth-toned, mod-furnished rooms are small but efficiently and comfortably designed. Parking is free if you drive a hybrid.

HI-Chicago HOSTEL $

(Map p508; ☎312-360-0300; www.hichicago.org; 24 E Congress Pkwy; dm incl breakfast $29-38; P ⊖ ❄ @ ☜) Chicago's best hostel is immaculate, conveniently placed in the Loop, and offers bonuses like a staffed information desk, free volunteer-led tours and discount passes to museums and shows. The simple dorm rooms have six to 12 beds, and most have attached baths.

Best Western River North HOTEL $$

(Map p508; ☎312-467-0800; www.rivernorthhotel.com; 125 W Ohio St; r $159-219; P ⊖ ❄ ☜ ≋ ♿) Well-maintained rooms with maple veneer beds and desks, together with free parking (!), an indoor pool and sundeck overlooking the city, make this Near North value.

Wit HOTEL $$$

(Map p508; ☎312-467-0200; www.thewithotel.com; 201 N State St; r from $229; P ⊖ ❄ @ ☜) Viewtastic rooms, a rooftop bar and an on-site movie theater draw holidaying hipsters and business travelers to the design-savvy, green-glass Wit. Wi-fi costs $10 per day (though it's free in the lobby).

Central Loop Hotel HOTEL $$

(Map p508; ☎312-601-3525; www.centralloophotel.com; 111 W Adams St; r $119-179; P ❄ @ ☜) This small business hotel has good prices if you're stuck paying rack rates. The owners have a similar property called Club Quarters at 75 E Wacker Dr.

LAKEVIEW & WICKER PARK/ BUCKTOWN

Willows Hotel HOTEL $$

(off Map p516; ☎773-528-8400; www.willowshotelchicago.com; 555 W Surf St; r incl breakfast $169-229; P ⊖ ❄ ☜) Small and stylish, the Willows wins an architectural gold star. The chic little lobby provides a swell refuge of overstuffed chairs by the fireplace, while the 55 rooms, done up in shades of peach, cream and soft green, evoke a 19th-century French countryside feel. It's a block north of the commercial hub where Broadway, Clark and Diversey streets intersect.

Wicker Park Inn B&B $$

(☎773-486-2743; www.wickerparkinn.com; 1329 N Wicker Park Ave; r incl breakfast $149-199; ⊖ ❄ ☜) This brick row house is steps away from Chicago's most rockin' bar-restaurant scene. The sunny rooms aren't huge, but have hardwood floors, pastel colors and small desk spaces. Across the street, two apartments with kitchens provide a self-contained experience. The inn is about a half-mile southeast of the CTA Blue Line stop at Damen.

Days Inn Lincoln Park North HOTEL **$$**
(off Map p516; 773-525-7010; www.lpndaysinn.com; 644 W Diversey Pkwy; r incl breakfast $120-180; P) This well-maintained chain hotel in Lincoln Park is a favorite of both families and touring indie bands, providing good service and perks like free health club access. It's an easy amble to the lakefront's parks and beaches, and a 15-minute bus ride to downtown. It's right at the hustle-bustle intersection of Broadway, Clark and Diversey streets.

Longman & Eagle INN **$$**
(773-276-7110; www.longmanandeagle.com; 2657 N Kedzie Ave; r $75-200;) Check in at the Michelin-starred gastropub downstairs, then head to your wood-floored, vintage-stylish accommodation on the floor above. The six rooms aren't particularly soundproofed, but after using your whiskey tokens in the bar, you probably won't care. Take the Blue Line to Logan Sq and walk a block north on Kedzie Ave.

The owners of the Willows Hotel have two other similarly styled and priced properties in the Lake View neighborhood:

City Suites Hotel HOTEL **$$**
(Map p516; 773-404-3400; www.chicagocitysuites.com; 933 W Belmont Ave) Located near the CTA Red/Brown Line Belmont station, City Suites is a bit noisier than its counterparts.

Majestic Hotel HOTEL **$$**
(Map p516; 773-404-3499; www.majestic-chicago.com; 528 W Brompton Ave) The Majestic lies east toward the lake and is more remote than its counterparts.

Eating

For years epicures wrote off Chicago as a meaty backwater. Then a funny thing happened: the city won a heap of James Beard awards, and foodie magazines like *Saveur* ranked it as the nation's top restaurant scene. The beauty here is even the buzziest restaurants are accessible: they're visionary yet traditional, pubby at the core and decently priced. You can also fork into a superb range of ethnic eats, especially if you break out of downtown and head for neighborhoods such as Pilsen or Uptown.

Need help deciding where to eat? Check these local resources: **LTH Forum** (www.lthforum.com) and **Chicago Gluttons** (www.chicagogluttons.com).

THE LOOP & SOUTH LOOP

Most Loop eateries are geared to lunch crowds of office workers.

Cafecito CUBAN **$**
(Map p508; www.cafecitochicago.com; 26 E Congress Pkwy; sandwiches $4-6; 6am-9pm Mon-Fri, 10am-6pm Sat & Sun;) Attached to the hostel and perfect for the hungry, thrifty traveler,

EATING CHICAGO: THE HOLY TRINITY

Chicago cooks up three beloved specialties. Foremost is deep-dish pizza, a hulking mass of crust that rises two or three inches above the plate and cradles a molten pile of toppings. One gooey piece is practically a meal. A large pizza averages $20 at the following places (all open from 11am to 10pm or so daily):

» **Pizzeria Uno** (Map p508; www.unos.com; 29 E Ohio St) The deep-dish concept originated here in 1943; sister outlet Due is one block north.

» **Gino's East** (Map p508; www.ginoseast.com; 162 E Superior St) Write on the walls while you wait for your pie.

» **Lou Malnati's** (Map p508; www.loumalnatis.com; 439 N Wells St) Famous for its butter crust.

» **Giordano's** (Map p508; www.giordanos.com; 730 N Rush St) Perfectly tangy tomato sauce.

» **Pizano's** (Map p508; www.pizanoschicago.com; 864 N State St) Oprah's favorite.

No less iconic is the Chicago hot dog – a wiener that's been 'dragged through the garden' (ie topped with onions, tomatoes, shredded lettuce, bell peppers, pepperoncini and sweet relish, or variations thereof, but *never* ketchup), and then cushioned on a poppy-seed bun. Hot Doug's (p526) does it right.

The city is also revered for its spicy, drippy, only-in-Chicago Italian beef sandwiches. Mr Beef (p524) serves the gold standard.

FARM TO FORK FARE

These entities provide unique ways to eat local, sustainable foods:

» The outdoor **Green City Market** (www.chicagogreencitymarket.org; 1790 N Clark St; ⌚7am-1pm Wed & Sat mid-May–late Oct) offers heirloom veggies, homemade pies, chef demos and much more at Lincoln Park's south end.

» **Chicago's Downtown Farmstand** (Map p508; www.chicagofarmstand.com; 66 E Randolph St; ⌚11am-7pm Tue-Fri, to 4pm Sat) sells locally made honey, pastries and produce. Farmers come in to share stories on Fridays at noon.

» **Clandestino** (www.clandestinodining.com; multicourse meals $65-100) is an underground, 'community dining project,' where chef Efrain Cuevas serves sustainable meals in changing locations, such as galleries or lofts. Sign up for the online mailing list, and grab a spot when he sends out event invitations.

Cafecito serves killer Cuban sandwiches layered with citrus-garlic-marinated roasted pork and ham. Strong coffee and hearty egg sandwiches make a fine breakfast.

Gage PUB $$$
(Map p508; ☎312-372-4243; www.thegagechicago.com; 24 S Michigan Ave; mains $16-32; ⌚11am-11pm, to midnight Fri) This gastropub dishes up Irish-tinged grub with a fanciful twist, such as Guinness-battered fish and chips, and fries smothered in curry gravy. The booze rocks, too, including a solid whiskey list and small-batch beers that pair with the food.

Lou Mitchell's BREAKFAST $
(www.loumitchellsrestaurant.com; 565 W Jackson Blvd; mains $6-11; ⌚5:30am-3pm Mon-Sat, 7am-3pm Sun) A relic of Route 66, Lou's old-school waitresses deliver double-yoked eggs and thick-cut French toast just west of the Loop by Union Station. There's usually a queue, but free doughnut holes and Milk Duds help ease the wait.

NEAR NORTH

This is where you'll find Chicago's mother lode of restaurants.

Frontera Grill MEXICAN $$$
(Map p508; ☎312-661-1434; www.rickbayless.com; 445 N Clark St; mains $18-30; ⌚lunch Tue-Fri, dinner Tue-Sat, brunch Sat) Perhaps you've seen chef Rick Bayless on TV, stirring up pepper sauces and other jump-off-the-tongue Mexican creations. His isn't your typical taco menu: Bayless uses seasonal, sustainable ingredients for flavor-packed fare. No wonder it's a fave of President Obama. Sister restaurant **Topolobampo**, in an adjoining room, is sleeker and pricier, with similar hours.

Xoco MEXICAN $$
(Map p508; www.rickbayless.com; 449 N Clark St; mains $8-13; ⌚8am-9pm Tue-Thu, 8am-10pm Fri & Sat) Next door to Frontera Grill, crunch into warm *churros* (spiraled dough fritters) for breakfast, meaty *tortas* (sandwiches) for lunch and rich *caldos* (soups) for dinner at Rick Bayless' Mexican street-food joint.

Billy Goat Tavern BURGERS $
(Map p508; www.billygoattavern.com; lower level, 430 N Michigan Ave; burgers $4-6; ⌚6am-2am Mon-Fri, 10am-2am Sat & Sun) *Tribune* and *Sun-Times* reporters have guzzled in the subterranean Billy Goat for decades. Order a 'cheezborger' and Schlitz, then look around at the newspapered walls to get the scoop on infamous local stories, such as the Cubs Curse.

Purple Pig MEDITERRANEAN $
(Map p508; ☎312-464-1744; www.thepurplepigchicago.com; 500 N Michigan Ave; small plates $7-9; ⌚11:30am-midnight Sun-Thu, to 1am Fri & Sat; ✎) The Pig's Magnificent Mile location, wide-ranging meat and veggie menu, long list of affordable vinos, and late-night serving hours make it a crowd pleaser. Milk-braised pork shoulder is the hamtastic specialty.

Mr Beef SANDWICHES $
(666 N Orleans St; sandwiches $4-7; ⌚8am-7pm Mon-Thu, to 5am Fri, 10:30am-3:30pm & 10:30pm-5am Sat) A Chicago specialty, the Italian beef sandwich stacks up like this: thin-sliced, slow-cooked roast beef that's sopped in natural gravy and *giardiniera* (spicy, pickled vegetables), and then heaped on a hoagie roll. Mr Beef serves the best at its picnic-style tables. It's about four blocks west of Hotel Felix.

LINCOLN PARK & OLD TOWN

Halsted, Lincoln and Clark Sts are the main veins teeming with restaurants and bars. Parking is frightful, but the CTA Red Line to North or Fullerton will put you in their midst.

Alinea NEW AMERICAN **$$$**
(☎312-867-0110; www.alinea-restaurant.com; 1723 N Halsted St; multicourse tastings $150-225; ⌚5:30-9:30pm Wed-Sun) Superstar chef Grant Achatz is the guy behind Alinea's 'molecular gastronomy.' If you secure a coveted reservation, prepare for roughly 12 to 24 courses of mind-bending, space-age cuisine. Dishes may emanate from a centrifuge or be pressed into a capsule. *Restaurant Magazine* has named it North America's number-one restaurant; reserve as far ahead as possible.

Wiener's Circle AMERICAN **$**
(☎773-477-7444; 2622 N Clark St; items $3-6; ⌚10:30am-4am Sun-Thu, to 5am Fri & Sat) As famous for its unruly, foul-mouthed ambience as its char-dogs and cheddar fries, the Wiener Circle is *the* place for late-night munchies. It helps to be shnockered before entering.

LAKE VIEW & WRIGLEYVILLE

Clark, Halsted, Belmont and Southport are fertile streets. Parking stinks, so take the CTA Red Line to Addison (for Wrigleyville) or the Brown Line to the Belmont or Southport stops.

Crisp ASIAN **$**
(Map p516; www.crisponline.com; 2940 N Broadway; mains $7-12; ⌚11:30am-9pm Tue-Thu & Sun, to 10:30pm Fri & Sat) Music pours from the stereo, and cheap, delicious Korean fusions arrive from the kitchen at this cheerful cafe. The 'Bad Boy Buddha' bowl, a variation on *bi bim bop* (mixed vegetables with rice), is one of the best cheap lunches in town.

ROLLING WITH FOOD TRUCKS

Chicago is finally getting in on the food truck action. Perhaps you'd like tortilla soup ladled by gentlemen in Mexican wrestling masks? The Tamale Spaceship can deliver. Other popular purveyors include the Gaztro-Wagon (Indian-style 'naan-wiches') and Meatyballs Mobile ('globes of goodness'). Most trucks tweet their location; the **Tribune's food blog** (www.twitter.com/@tribstew/chicago-food-trucks) amalgamates them.

Mia Francesca ITALIAN **$$**
(Map p516; ☎773-281-3310; www.miafrancesca.com; 3311 N Clark St; mains $13-27; ⌚5-10pm Sun-Thu, to 11pm Fri & Sat) Local chain Mia's buzzes with regulars who come for the trattoria's Italian standards, such as seafood linguine, spinach ravioli and mushroom-sauced veal medallions, all prepared with simple flair.

ANDERSONVILLE & UPTOWN

For 'Little Saigon' take the CTA Red Line to Argyle. For the European cafes in Andersonville, go one stop further to Berwyn.

Hopleaf EUROPEAN **$$**
(Map p516; ☎773-334-9851; www.hopleaf.com; 5148 N Clark St; mains $10-17; ⌚5-11pm Mon-Thu, to midnight Fri & Sat, 4-10pm Sun) A cozy, European-style tavern, Hopleaf draws crowds for its Montréal-style smoked brisket, cashew-butter-and-fig-jam sandwich and the house-specialty – *frites* and ale-soaked mussels. It also pours 200 types of brew. Prepare to queue.

Ba Le Bakery VIETNAMESE **$**
(Map p516; ☎773-561-4424; 5016 N Broadway; sandwiches $3-5; ⌚7:30am-8pm) Ba Le serves Saigon-style *banh mi* sandwiches, with steamed pork, shrimp cakes or meatballs on fresh baguettes made right here.

WICKER PARK, BUCKTOWN & UKRAINIAN VILLAGE

Trendy restaurants open almost every day in these 'hoods. Take the CTA Blue Line to Damen.

Handlebar Bar & Grill INTERNATIONAL **$$**
(☎773-384-9546; www.handlebarchicago.com; 2311 W North Ave; mains $9-14; ⌚10am-midnight Mon-Thu, to 2am Fri & Sat, to 11pm Sun; ☑) Local cyclists congregate around the eclectic, vegetarian-friendly menu (ie West African groundnut stew) and summertime patio to quaff from the well-curated beer list.

Big Star Taqueria MEXICAN **$**
(www.bigstarchicago.com; 1531 N Damen Ave; tacos $3-4; ⌚11:30am-2am) This honky-tonk gets packed, but damn, the tacos are worth the wait – pork belly in tomato-*guajillo* (chili) sauce and lamb shoulder with *queso fresco* (white cheese) accompany the specialty whiskey list. Cash only.

DIY: HOW TO FIND A REAL CHICAGO BAR

Unfortunately, we can't list every watering hole in town, but we can give you the tools to go out and discover classic, character-filled bars on your own. Look for the following:

» an 'Old Style' beer sign swinging out front

» a well-worn dart board and/or pool table inside

» patrons wearing Cubs-, White Sox- or Bears-logoed ballcaps

» bottles of brew served in buckets of ice

» sports on TV (with the latter being a 1974 Zenith, not some fancy flat-screen thing).

LOGAN SQUARE & HUMBOLDT PARK

Eats and drinks ring the intersection of Milwaukee, Logan and Kedzie Blvds. Get the CTA Blue Line to Logan Square or California.

TOP CHOICE Hot Doug's AMERICAN $

(☎773-279-9550; www.hotdougs.com; 3324 N California Ave; mains $3-8; ⏲10:30am-4pm Mon-Sat) Doug's the man to fulfill all your hot-dog fantasies. He serves multiple dog styles (Polish, bratwursts, Chicago) cooked multiple dog ways (char-grilled, deep-fried, steamed). Confused? He'll explain it all. Doug also makes gourmet 'haute dogs,' such as blue-cheese pork with cherry cream sauce. It's sublime, but a heck of a haul unless you're traveling by car. Cash only.

Bonsoiree NEW AMERICAN $$$

(☎773-486-7511; www.bonsoireechicago.com; 2728 W Armitage Ave; multicourse meal $60-90; ⏲5-10pm Tue-Sat, to 9pm Sun) It started as an underground supper club, and Saturdays are still an invitation-only event (go to the website to get on the mailing list). Otherwise, dinner at Bonsoiree is a leisurely, multicourse affair where the chefs whip up inspired comfort foods (often with a Japanese bent). It's unusually casual for such fine dining, right up to being BYOB.

NEAR WEST SIDE & PILSEN

Greektown extends along S Halsted St (take the Blue Line to UIC-Halsted), and the Mexican Pilsen enclave centers around W 18th St (take the Pink Line to 18th). The West Loop holds several stylish eateries along Randolph and Fulton Market Sts (taxi from downtown $10).

Next ECLECTIC $$$

(☎312-226-0858; www.nextrestaurant.com; 953 W Fulton Market; multicourse meal $100; ⏲5:30-9:30pm Wed-Sun) Grant Achatz's West Loop restaurant, which opened in 2011, is the hottest ticket in town. And we mean it literally – you need a ticket to dine at Next, which operates like a time machine. It started by serving an eight-course French meal from 1906 Paris, but every three months the whole thing changes: new era, new menu, new decor. Sign up for tickets at the website as early as possible. Prices vary by date, time and menu (early weekdays cost less than prime-time weekends), and you pay when you book. Check the Twitter feed (@nextrestaraunt) for possible last-minute seats.

Don Pedro Carnitas MEXICAN $

(1113 W 18th St; tacos $1.50-2; ⏲6am-6pm Mon-Fri, 5am-5pm Sat, to 3pm Sun) At this no-frills Pilsen meat hive, a man with a machete salutes you at the front counter. He awaits your command to hack off pork pieces, and then wraps the thick chunks with onion and cilantro in a fresh tortilla. Cash only.

Publican AMERICAN $$$

(☎312-733-9555; www.thepublicanrestaurant.com; 837 W Fulton Market; mains $16-30; ⏲3:30-10:30pm Mon-Thu, to 11:30pm Fri & Sat, 10am-2pm & 5-10pm Sun) Set up like a swanky beer hall, Publican specializes in oysters, hams and fine suds – all from small family farms and microbrewers.

Drinking

During the long winters, Chicagoans count on bars for warmth. The usual closing time is 2am, but some places stay open until 4am or 5am. In summer many bars boast beer gardens.

THE LOOP & NEAR NORTH

Restaurants such as the Gage, Billy Goat Tavern and Purple Pig (see Eating) make fine drinking destinations, too.

Signature Lounge LOUNGE

(Map p508; www.signatureroom.com; John Hancock Center, 875 N Michigan Ave; ⏲from 11am) Have the Hancock Observatory view without the Hancock Observatory admission price. Grab the elevator up to the 96th floor and order a beverage while looking out over the city. Ladies: don't miss the bathroom view.

Clark Street Ale House BAR
(Map p508; 742 N Clark St; from 4pm) Do as the retro sign advises and 'Stop & Drink Liquor.' Midwestern microbrews are the main draw; order a three-beer sampler for $5.

Intelligentsia Coffee CAFE
(Map p508; www.intelligentsia.com; 53 E Randolph St; from 6am Mon-Fri, 7am Sat & Sun) The local chain roasts its own beans and percolates strong stuff. Staff recently won the US Barista Championship.

Harry Caray's Tavern BAR
(Map p508; www.harrycaraystavern.com; 700 E Grand Ave; from 11am) Relieves thirst on Navy Pier; it has decent brews and a small sports memorabilia 'museum.'

OLD TOWN & WRIGLEYVILLE

TOP CHOICE **Old Town Ale House** BAR
(www.oldtownalehouse.net; 219 W North Ave; from 8am Mon-Sat, from noon Sun) This unpretentious favorite lets you mingle with beautiful people and grizzled regulars, seated pint by pint under the nude-politician paintings. It's across the street from Second City.

Gingerman Tavern BAR
(Map p516; 3740 N Clark St; from 3pm Mon-Fri, from noon Sat & Sun) The pool tables, good beer selection and pierced-and-tattooed patrons make Gingerman wonderfully different from the surrounding Wrigleyville sports bars.

WICKER PARK, BUCKTOWN & UKRAINIAN VILLAGE

Map Room PUB
(www.maproom.com; 1949 N Hoyne Ave; from 6:30am Mon-Fri, 7:30am Sat, 11am Sun;) At this map-and-globe-filled 'travelers' tavern' artsy types sip coffee by day and suds from the 200-strong beer list by night. There's free ethnic food on Tuesdays at 7pm.

Danny's BAR
(1951 W Dickens Ave) Danny's comfortably dim and dog-eared ambience is perfect for conversations over a pint. A poetry-reading series and occasional DJs add to the scruffy artiness.

Matchbox BAR
(770 N Milwaukee Ave; from 4pm) Lawyers, artists and bums all squeeze in for retro cocktails. It's small as – you got it – a matchbox, with about 10 barstools; everyone else stands against the back wall. Matchbox sits by its lonesome northwest of downtown, near the Blue Line stop at Chicago.

WEST LOOP

Aviary COCKTAIL BAR
(www.twitter.com/@aviarycocktails; 955 W Fulton Market; from 6pm Wed-Sun) Grant Achatz's bar beside Next (see p526) is more in spirit (pun!) with his other restaurant, Alinea. The lounge shakes and stirs one-of-a-kind drinks such as Buttered Popcorn, which tastes as advertised. The selection changes frequently, as do the 19 different types of ice. Drinks cost around $16 each.

☆ Entertainment

Check the **Reader** (www.chicagoreader.com) and **Time Out Chicago** (www.timeoutchicago.com) for listings.

Live Music

Blues and jazz have deep roots in Chicago, and indie rock clubs slouch on almost every corner. Cover charges range from $5 to $20.

BLUES

Buddy Guy's Legends BLUES
(Map p508; www.buddyguys.com; 700 S Wabash Ave) Top local and national acts wail on the stage of local icon Buddy Guy. The man himself usually plugs in his axe in January.

Kingston Mines BLUES
(www.kingstonmines.com; 2548 N Halsted St) Two stages, seven nights a week, ensure somebody's always on. It's noisy, hot, sweaty, crowded and conveniently located in Lincoln Park.

DISCOUNT TICKETS

National ticket broker **Goldstar** (www.goldstar.com) sells half-price tickets to all sorts of Chicago entertainment, including theater performances, sports events and concerts. You'll fare best if you sign up at least three weeks ahead of time, as Goldstar typically releases its seats well in advance of shows.

For same-day theater seats at half-price, try **Hot Tix** (www.hottix.org). You can buy them online, or in person at booths in the **Chicago Tourism Center** (Map p508; 72 E Randolph St) and **Water Works Visitor Center** (Map p508; 163 E Pearson St).

BLUES BLUES
(www.chicagobluesbar.com; 2519 N Halsted St) Across the street from Kingston Mines, this veteran club draws a slightly older crowd that soaks up every crackling, electrified moment.

Rosa's BLUES
(www.rosaslounge.com; 3420 W Armitage Ave; ⏲closed Sun, Mon & Wed) Rosa's is a real-deal venue that brings in local talent and dedicated fans to a somewhat dodgy Logan Sq block.

Lee's Unleaded Blues BLUES
(www.leesunleadedblues.com; 7401 S South Chicago Ave; ⏲closed Mon-Thu) Buried deep on the South Side, Lee's is a genuine juke joint. The crowd dresses in their finest threads, and everyone jams until dawn.

JAZZ

Green Mill JAZZ
(Map p516; www.greenmilljazz.com; 4802 N Broadway) The timeless Green Mill earned its notoriety as Al Capone's favorite speakeasy (the tunnels where he hid the booze are still underneath the bar), and you can feel his ghost urging you on to another martini. Local and national artists perform six nights per week; Sundays are for the nationally acclaimed poetry slam.

Jazz Showcase JAZZ
(Map p508; www.jazzshowcase.com; 806 S Plymouth Court) The gorgeous room is the top spot for national acts to blow their horns.

Andy's JAZZ
(Map p508; www.andysjazzclub.com; 11 E Hubbard St) Andy's is affordable and mixed, from its multiage clientele to its fusion of swing, bop and Afro-pop.

ROCK & FOLK

Hideout LIVE MUSIC
(www.hideoutchicago.com; 1354 W Wabansia Ave) Hidden behind a factory at the edge of Bucktown, this two-room lodge of indie rock and alt-country is well worth seeking out. The owners have nursed an outsider, underground vibe, and the place feels like the downstairs of your grandma's rumpus room. Music and other events (bingo, literary readings etc) take place nightly.

Metro LIVE MUSIC
(Map p516; www.metrochicago.com; 3730 N Clark St) The Metro is legendary for loud rock. Local bands on the verge of stardom and national names looking for an 'intimate' venue turn up the volume.

Empty Bottle LIVE MUSIC
(www.emptybottle.com; 1035 N Western Ave) The scruffy, go-to club for edgy indie rock and jazz; Monday's show is always free (and there's $1.50 Pabst).

Double Door LIVE MUSIC
(www.doubledoor.com; 1572 N Milwaukee Ave) Alternative rock that is *just* under the radar finds a home a this former liquor store.

Theater

Chicago's reputation for stage drama is well deserved. Many productions export to Broadway. The city's top troupes:

Steppenwolf Theatre THEATER
(☎312-335-1650; www.steppenwolf.org; 1650 N Halsted St) Drama club of Malkovich, Sinise and other Hollywood stars; 2 miles north of the Loop in Lincoln Park.

Goodman Theatre THEATER
(Map p508; ☎312-443-3800; www.goodmantheatre.org; 170 N Dearborn St) Known for new and classic American works.

Other first-rate companies:

Chicago Shakespeare Theater THEATER
(Map p508; ☎312-595-5600; www.chicagoshakes.com; 800 E Grand Ave) Will's comedies and tragedies at Navy Pier.

Lookingglass Theatre Company THEATER
(Map p508; ☎312-337-0665; www.lookingglasstheatre.org; 821 N Michigan Ave) Improv-based works, often incorporating acrobatics.

Neo-Futurists THEATER
(Map p516; ☎773-275-5255; www.neofuturists.org; 5153 N Ashland Ave) Original works that make you ponder and laugh simultaneously.

Dreamboat old theaters that host touring shows cluster at State and Randolph Sts. **Broadway in Chicago** (☎800-775-2000; www.broadwayinchicago.com) handles tickets for most:

Auditorium Theater THEATER
(Map p508; 50 E Congress Pkwy)

Bank of America Theatre THEATER
(Map p508; 18 W Monroe St)

Cadillac Palace Theater THEATER
(Map p508; 151 W Randolph St)

Chicago Theater THEATER
(Map p508; 175 N State St)

Ford Center/Oriental Theatre THEATER
(Map p508; 24 W Randolph St)

Comedy

Improv comedy began in Chicago, and the city still nurtures the best in the business.

Second City COMEDY
(off Map p508; ☎312-337-3992; www.secondcity.com; 1616 N Wells St) It's the cream of the crop, where Bill Murray, Stephen Colbert, Tina Fey and many more honed their sharp, biting wit. Bargain: turn up after the evening's last show (Friday excluded), and watch the comics improv a performance for free.

iO Improv COMEDY
(Map p516; ☎773-880-0199; www.ioimprov.com; 3541 N Clark St) Chicago's other major improv house.

Sports

Chicago Cubs BASEBALL
(www.cubs.com) The Cubs last won the World Series in 1908, but their fans still pack baseball's most charming stadium, **Wrigley Field** (Map p516; 1060 W Addison St), which dates from 1914 and is known for its ivy-walled field and classic neon entrance sign. For tickets, check the website for deals, or try the box office two to three hours before game time. Take the CTA Red Line to Addison; it's 4.5 miles north of the Loop.

Chicago White Sox BASEBALL
(www.whitesox.com) The Sox are the Cubs' South Side rivals and play in the more modern 'Cell,' aka **US Cellular Field** (Map p506; 333 W 35th St). Tickets are usually cheaper and easier to get than at Wrigley; Monday is half-price night. Take the CTA Red Line to the Sox-35th St station; it's 4.5 miles south of the Loop.

Chicago Bulls BASKETBALL
(www.nba.com/bulls) Is Derrick Rose the new Michael Jordan? Find out at the **United Center** (Map p506; 1901 W Madison St), where the Bulls shoot hoops. It's about 2 miles west of the Loop. CTA runs special buses (No 19) on game days; it's best not to walk here.

Chicago Blackhawks HOCKEY
(www.chicagoblackhawks.com) The 2010 Stanley Cup winners skate in front of big crowds. They share the United Center with the Bulls.

Chicago Bears FOOTBALL
(www.chicagobears.com) Da Bears, Chicago's NFL team, tackle at **Soldier Field** (Map p508; 425 E McFetridge Dr), recognizable by its classical-meets-flying-saucer architecture. Expect beery tailgate parties, sleet and snow.

Clubs

Clubs in the Near North and West Loop tend to be cavernous and luxurious (with dress codes). Clubs in Wicker Park-Ukrainian Village are usually more casual.

Late Bar CLUB
(www.latebarchicago.com; 3534 W Belmont Ave; ⌚Tue-Sat) Owned by a couple of DJs, Late Bar's weird, new wave vibe draws fans of all stripes. It's off the beaten path in a forlorn stretch of Logan Sq, though easily reachable via the Blue Line train to Belmont.

Smart Bar CLUB
(Map p516; www.smartbarchicago.com; ⌚Wed-Sat) Long-standing, unpretentious favorite for dancing, attached to the Metro rock club.

Darkroom CLUB
(www.darkroombar.com; 2210 W Chicago Ave) Welcomes everyone from goths to reggae-heads with its eclectic spins in Ukrainian Village.

Performing Arts

FREE **Grant Park Orchestra** CLASSICAL MUSIC
(Map p508; ☎312-742-7638; www.grantparkmusicfestival.com) The beloved group puts on free classical concerts in Millennium Park throughout the summer.

Symphony Center CLASSICAL MUSIC
(Map p508; ☎312-294-3000; www.cso.org; 220 S Michigan Ave) The Chicago Symphony Orchestra plays in the Daniel Burnham–designed hall.

Civic Opera House OPERA
(☎312-332-2244; www.lyricopera.org; 20 N Wacker Dr) The renowned Lyric Opera of Chicago high C's in this chandeliered venue. It's a few blocks west of the Loop.

Hubbard Street Dance Chicago DANCE
(☎312-850-9744; www.hubbardstreetdance.com) Chicago's preeminent dance company performs at the **Harris Theater for Music and Dance** (Map p508; www.harristheaterchicago.org; 205 E Randolph St).

Shopping

The shoppers' siren song emanates from N Michigan Ave, along the Magnificent Mile. **Water Tower Place** (Map p508; 835 N Michigan Ave) is among the large vertical malls here. Moving onward, boutiques fill Wicker Park/Bucktown (indie and vintage), Lincoln Park (posh), Lake View (countercultural) and Andersonville (all of the above).

FREEBIES

The city's official portal, **Explore Chicago** (www.explorechicago.org), provides a Twitter feed (twitter.com/explorechicago) of free events each day, as well as excellent free neighborhood maps and guides.

Chicago Architecture Foundation Shop SOUVENIRS
(Map p508; www.architecture.org/shop; 224 S Michigan Ave) Skyline posters, Frank Lloyd Wright note cards, skyscraper models and more for those with an edifice complex.

Strange Cargo CLOTHING
(Map p516; www.strangecargo.com; 3448 N Clark St) The retro store stocks kitschy iron-on T-shirts featuring Ditka, Obama and other renowned Chicagoans.

Jazz Record Mart MUSIC
(Map p508; www.jazzmart.com; 27 E Illinois St) One-stop shop for Chicago jazz and blues CDs and vinyl.

Quimby's BOOKS
(www.quimbys.com; 1854 W North Ave) Ground Zero for comics, zines and underground culture; in Wicker Park.

Information

Emergency & Medical Services

Northwestern Memorial Hospital (312-926-5188; 251 E Erie St) Well-respected hospital downtown.

Stroger Cook County Hospital (312-864-1300; 1969 W Ogden Ave) Public hospital serving low-income patients; 2.5 miles west of the Loop.

Walgreens (312-664-8686; 757 N Michigan Ave; 24hr) On the Mag Mile.

Internet Access

Many bars and restaurants have free wi-fi, as does the Chicago Cultural Center. Or try:

Harold Washington Library Center (www.chipublib.org; 400 S State St; 9am-9pm Mon-Thu, to 5pm Fri & Sat, 1-5pm Sun) A grand, art-filled building with free wi-fi throughout and 3rd-floor internet terminals (get a day pass at the counter).

Media

Chicago Reader (www.chicagoreader.com) Free alternative newspaper with comprehensive arts and entertainment listings.

Chicago Sun-Times (www.suntimes.com) The *Tribune's* daily, tabloidesque competitor.

Chicago Tribune (www.chicagotribune.com) The city's stalwart daily newspaper; its younger, trimmed-down, freebie version is *RedEye*.

Time Out Chicago (www.timeoutchicago.com) Weekly magazine with all-encompassing listings.

Money

ATMs are plentiful downtown, with many near Chicago and Michigan Aves. To change money, try Terminal 5 at O'Hare International or the following places in the Loop:

Travelex (312-807-4941; 19 S LaSalle St; Mon-Fri)

World's Money Exchange (312-641-2151; 203 N LaSalle St; Mon-Fri)

Post

Post office Fort Dearborn (540 N Dearborn St); Main (433 W Harrison St; 7:30am-midnight)

Tourist Information

The **Chicago Office of Tourism** (312-744-2400; www.explorechicago.org) operates two well-stocked visitor centers, each with a staffed information desk, ticket outlet, cafe and free wi-fi:

Chicago Cultural Center Visitors Center (77 E Randolph St; 8am-7pm Mon-Thu, 8am-6pm Fri, 9am-6pm Sat, 10am-6pm Sun)

Water Works Visitors Center (163 E Pearson St; 8am-7pm Mon-Thu, 8am-6pm Fri, 10am-6pm Sat, 10am-4pm Sun)

Websites

Chicagoist (www.chicagoist.com) Quirky take on news, food, arts and events.

Gaper's Block (www.gapersblock.com) News and events site with Chicago attitude.

Huffington Post Chicago (www.huffingtonpost.com/chicago) Amalgamates news from major local sources.

Getting There & Away

Air

Chicago Midway Airport (MDW; off Map p506; www.flychicago.com) The smaller airport used mostly by domestic carriers, such as Southwest; often has cheaper flights than from O'Hare.

O'Hare International Airport (ORD; off Map p506; www.flychicago.com) Chicago's larger airport, and among the world's busiest. Headquarters for United Airlines and a hub for American. Most non-US airlines and international flights use Terminal 5 (except Lufthansa and flights from Canada).

Bus

Greyhound (☎312-408-5800; www.greyhound.com; 630 W Harrison St) Main station is two blocks southwest from the CTA Blue Line Clinton stop. Buses run frequently to Cleveland (7½ hours), Detroit (seven hours) and Minneapolis (nine hours), as well as to small towns throughout the USA.

Megabus (Map p508; www.megabus.com/us; southeast cnr Canal St & Jackson Blvd) Travels only to major Midwestern cities. Prices are often less, and quality and efficiency are better than Greyhound on these routes. The bus stop is adjacent to Union Station.

Train

Chicago's classic **Union Station** (Map p508; 225 S Canal St) is the hub for **Amtrak's** (☎800-872-7245; www.amtrak.com) national and regional service. Routes include:

DETROIT (5½ hours, three trains daily)

MILWAUKEE (1½ hours, seven trains daily)

MINNEAPOLIS/ST PAUL (eight hours, one train daily)

NEW YORK (20½ hours, one train daily)

SAN FRANCISCO (EMERYVILLE) (53 hours, one train daily)

ST LOUIS (5½ hours, five trains daily)

Getting Around

To/From the Airport

CHICAGO MIDWAY AIRPORT 11 miles southwest of the Loop, connected via the CTA Orange Line ($2.25). Other options include shuttles (per person $24) and cabs ($30 to $40).

O'HARE INTERNATIONAL AIRPORT 17 miles northwest of the Loop. The cheapest, and often the quickest, way to/from O'Hare is by the CTA Blue Line ($2.25), but the station is a long walk from the flight terminals. Airport Express shuttles run between the airport and downtown hotels (per person $29). Cabs to/from downtown cost about $45.

Bicycle

Chicago has 120 miles of bike lanes. Get free maps from the city's **transportation department** (www.chicagobikes.org). Bike racks are plentiful; the biggest, with showers, is at the **McDonalds Cycle Center** (www.chicagobikestation.com; 239 E Randolph St) in Millennium Park. Lock it or lose it. For bike-rental information, see p517.

Car & Motorcycle

Be warned: street and garage/lot parking is expensive. If you must, try **East Monroe Garage** (www.millenniumgarages.com; Columbus Dr btwn Randolph & Monroe Sts; per day $24). Chicago's rush-hour traffic is abysmal.

Public Transportation

The **Chicago Transit Authority** (CTA; www.transitchicago.com) operates the city's buses and the elevated/subway train system (aka the El). CTA buses go everywhere from early morning until late evening. Two of the eight color-coded train lines – the Red Line, and the Blue Line to O'Hare International Airport – operate 24 hours a day. The other lines run from about 5am to midnight daily. During the day, you shouldn't have to wait more than 15 minutes for a train. Get free maps at any station.

The standard fare per train is $2.25; per bus, it is $2. Transfers cost 25¢. On buses, you can use a fare card (called a Transit Card) or pay with exact change (in which case the price goes up to $2.25). On the train, you must use a Transit Card, which is sold from vending machines at train stations. Day passes (one-/three-day pass $5.75/14) provide excellent savings, but they can be purchased only at airports and various drug stores and currency exchanges.

Metra commuter trains (www.metrarail.com) have 12 routes serving the suburbs from four terminals ringing the Loop: LaSalle St Station, Millennium Station, Union Station and Richard B Ogilvie Transportation Center (a few blocks north of Union Station). Some lines run daily, while others operate only during weekday rush hours. Metra fares cost $2.25 to $8.50. An all-weekend pass costs $7.

PACE (www.pacebus.com) runs the suburban bus system that connects with city transport.

Taxi

Cabs are plentiful in the Loop, north to Andersonville and northwest to Wicker Park/Bucktown. Flagfall is $2.25, plus $1.80 per mile and $1 per extra passenger; a 15% tip is expected. Venture outside city limits and you'll pay one and a half times the fare. Recommended companies:

Flash Cab (☎773-561-1444)

Yellow Cab (☎312-829-4222)

Around Chicago

OAK PARK

Located 10 miles west of the Loop and easily reached via CTA train, Oak Park has spawned two famous sons: novelist Ernest Hemingway was born here, and architect Frank Lloyd Wright lived and worked here from 1889 to 1909.

During Wright's 20 years in Oak Park, he designed many houses. Stop at the **visitor center** (☎888-625-7275; www.visitoakpark.com; 158 N Forest Ave; ⊙10am-5pm) and buy an architectural site map ($4), which gives their locations. To actually get inside a Wright-designed dwelling, you'll need to visit the

Frank Lloyd Wright Home & Studio (☎708-848-1976; www.gowright.org; 951 Chicago Ave; adult/child $15/12; ⏰11am-4pm). Tour frequency varies, from every 20 minutes on summer weekends to every hour in winter. The Studio also offers guided neighborhood walking tours, as well as a self-guided audio version.

Despite Hemingway calling Oak Park a 'village of wide lawns and narrow minds,' the town still pays homage to him at the **Ernest Hemingway Museum** (☎708-848-2222; www.ehfop.org; 200 N Oak Park Ave; adult/child $10/8; ⏰1-5pm Sun-Fri, 10am-5pm Sat). Admission also includes access to **Hemingway's Birthplace** (339 N Oak Park Ave) across the street.

From downtown Chicago, take the CTA Green Line to its terminus at the Harlem stop, which lands you about four blocks from the visitor center. The train traverses some bleak neighborhoods before emerging into Oak Park's wide-lawn splendor.

EVANSTON & NORTH SHORE

Evanston, 14 miles north of the Loop and reached via the CTA Purple Line, combines sprawling old houses with a compact downtown. It's home to Northwestern University.

Beyond are Chicago's northern lakeshore suburbs, which became popular with the wealthy in the late 19th century. A classic 30-mile drive follows Sheridan Rd through various well-off towns to the socioeconomic apex of Lake Forest. Attractions include the **Baha'i House of Worship** (www.bahai.us/bahai-temple; 100 Linden Ave, Wilmette; admission free; ⏰6am-10pm), a glistening white architectural marvel, and the **Chicago Botanic Garden** (☎847-835-5440; www.chicagobotanic.org; 1000 Lake Cook Rd, Glencoe; admission free; ⏰8am-sunset), with hiking trails, 255 bird species and weekend cooking demos by well-known chefs. Parking costs $20.

Inland lies the **Illinois Holocaust Museum** (☎847-967-4800; www.ilholocaustmuseum.org; 9603 Woods Dr, Skokie; adult/child $12/6; ⏰10am-5pm Mon-Fri, to 8pm Thu, 11am-4pm Sat & Sun). Besides its excellent videos of survivors' stories from WWII, the museum contains thought-provoking art about genocides in Armenia, Rwanda, Cambodia and others.

Galena & Northern Illinois

The highlight is the hilly northwest, where cottonwood trees, grazing horses and twisty roads over old stagecoach trails fill the pocket around Galena.

En route is Union, where the **Illinois Railway Museum** (☎815-923-4000; www.irm.org; US 20 to Union Rd; adult $8-12, child $4-8 depending upon season; ⏰hours vary Apr-Oct) sends trainspotters into fits of ecstasy with 200 acres of locomotives.

GALENA

Galena, spread across wooded hillsides near the Mississippi River, amid rolling, barn-dotted farmland, draws hordes of Chicagoans to its perfectly preserved, Civil War–era streets. While it sometimes gets chided as a place for the 'newly wed and nearly dead,' thanks to all the tourist-oriented B&Bs, fudge and antique shops, there's no denying the little town's beauty. Red-brick mansions in Greek Revival, Gothic Revival and Queen Anne styles fill the streets, left over from Galena's heyday in the mid-1800s, when local lead mines made it rich. Throw in cool kayak trips, foodie farm tours and winding backroad drives, and you've got a lovely, slowpoke getaway.

The **visitor center** (☎877-464-2536; www.galena.org; 101 Bouthillier St; ⏰9am-5pm), in the 1857 train depot as you enter from the east, is a good place to start. Get a map, leave your car in the lot ($5 per day) and explore on foot.

Elegant old Main St curves around the hillside and the historic heart of town. Among numerous sights is the **Ulysses S Grant Home** (☎815-777-3310; www.granthome.com; 500 Bouthillier St; adult/child $4/2; ⏰9am-4:45pm Wed-Sun, reduced hrs Nov-Mar), which was a gift from local Republicans to the victorious general at the Civil War's end. Grant lived here until he became the country's 18th president. The elaborate Italianate **Belvedere Mansion** (☎815-777-0747; www.belvederemansionandgardens.com; 1008 Park Ave; adult/child $13/free; ⏰11am-4pm Sun-Fri, to 5pm Sat, closed mid-Nov–mid-May) hangs the green drapes from *Gone With the Wind*.

Outdoors enthusiasts should head to **Fever River Outfitters** (☎815-776-9425; www.feverriveroutfitters.com; 525 S Main St; ⏰10am-5pm, closed Tue-Thu early Sep-late May), which rents canoes, kayaks, stand up paddleboards, bicycles and snowshoes. It also offers guided tours, such as two-hour kayak trips ($45 per person, equipment included) on the Mississippi River's backwaters. Or visit local bison ranches, artisan cheesemakers and herb farms on a culinary tour with **Learn Great Foods** (☎866-240-1650; www.learngreatfoods.com; tours $50-125).

Excursions vary; check online for the schedule and locations.

Galena brims with quilt-laden B&Bs. Most cost $100 to $200 nightly and fill up during weekends. The visitor center website provides contact information. Presidential types can be like Grant and Lincoln and stay in the well-furnished rooms at **DeSoto House Hotel** (815-777-0090; www.desotohouse.com; 230 S Main St; r $128-200;), which dates from 1855. **Grant Hills Motel** (877-421-0924; www.granthills.com; 9372 US 20; r $70-90;) is a no-frills option 1.5 miles east of town, with countryside views and a horseshoe pitch.

111 Main (815-777-8030; www.oneelevenmain.com; 111 N Main St; mains $16-24; 11am-10pm) makes meatloaf, pork-and-mashed-potatoes and other Midwestern favorites using ingredients sourced from local farms. **Victory Cafe** (www.victorycafes.com; 200 N Main St; mains $5-11; 6am-3pm) is ideal for biscuit-and-gravy breakfasts or lunchtime sandwiches. The **VFW Hall** (100 S Main St) provides a sublime opportunity to sip cheap beers and watch TV alongside veterans of long-ago wars. Don't be shy: as the sign out front says, the public is welcome.

QUAD CITIES

South of Galena along a pretty stretch of the **Great River Road** (www.greatriverroad-illinois.org) is scenic **Mississippi Palisades State Park** (815-273-2731), a popular rock-climbing, hiking and camping area; pick up trail maps at the north entrance park office.

Further downstream, the **Quad Cities** (www.visitquadcities.com) – Moline and Rock Island in Illinois, and Davenport and Bettendorf across the river in Iowa – make a surprisingly good stop. Rock Island has an appealing downtown (based at 2nd Ave and 18th St), with a couple of cafes and a lively pub and music scene. On the edge of town, **Black Hawk State Historic Site** (www.blackhawkpark.org; 1510 46th Ave; sunrise-10pm) is a huge park with trails by the Rock River. Its **Hauberg Indian Museum** (309-788-9536; Watch Tower Lodge; admission free; 9am-noon & 1-5pm Wed-Sun) outlines the story of Sauk leader Black Hawk and his people.

Out in the Mississippi River, the actual island of **Rock Island** once held a Civil War–era arsenal and POW camp. It now maintains an impressive arms **museum** (Tue-Sun), Civil War cemetery, national cemetery and visitor center for barge viewing. All are free, but bring photo ID as the island is still an active army facility.

Moline is the home of John Deere, the international farm machinery manufacturer. Downtown holds the **John Deere Pavilion** (www.johndeerepavilion.com; admission free; 1400 River Dr; 9am-5pm Mon-Fri, 10am-5pm Sat, noon-4pm Sun;), a kiddie-beloved museum/showroom. For Iowa-side attractions, see p618.

Springfield & Central Illinois

Abraham Lincoln and Route 66 sights are sprinkled liberally throughout central Illinois, which is otherwise farmland plain. East of Decatur, Arthur and Arcola are Amish centers.

SPRINGFIELD

The small state capital has a serious obsession with Abraham Lincoln, who practiced law here from 1837 to 1861. Many of the attractions are walkable downtown and cost little or nothing.

Sights & Activities

FREE Lincoln Home & Visitor Center HISTORIC SITE
(217-492-4150; www.nps.gov/liho; 426 S 7th St; 8:30am-5pm) Start at the National Park Service visitor center, where you must pick up a ticket to enter Lincoln's 12-room abode, located directly across the street. You can then walk through the house where Abe and Mary Lincoln lived from 1844 until they moved to the White House in 1861; rangers are stationed throughout to provide background information and answer questions.

Lincoln Presidential Library & Museum MUSEUM
(217-558-8844; www.presidentlincoln.org; 212 N 6th St; adult/child $12/6; 9am-5pm;) It contains the most complete Lincoln collection in the world. Real-deal artifacts like Abe's shaving mirror and briefcase join whiz-bang exhibits and Disneyesque holograms that keep the kids agog.

FREE Lincoln's Tomb CEMETERY
(1441 Monument Ave; 9am-5pm, closed Sun & Mon Sep-May) After his assassination, Lincoln's body was returned to Springfield, where it lies in an impressive tomb in Oak Ridge Cemetery, 1.5 miles north of downtown. The gleam on the nose of Lincoln's

WORTH A TRIP

ROUTE 66: GET YOUR KICKS IN ILLINOIS

America's 'Mother Road' kicks off in Chicago on Adams St, just west of Michigan Ave. Before embarking, fuel up at Lou Mitchell's (p524) diner near Union Station. After all, it's 300 miles from here to the Missouri state line.

Sadly, most of the original Route 66 has been superseded by I-55 in Illinois, though the old road still exists in scattered sections often paralleling the interstate. Keep an eye out for brown 'Historic Route 66' signs, which pop up at crucial junctions to mark the way.

Our first stop rises from the cornfields 60 miles south in Wilmington. Here the Gemini Giant – a 28ft fiberglass spaceman – stands guard outside the **Launching Pad Drive In** (810 E Baltimore St; burgers $2-6; ⏲11am-7:30pm). To reach it, exit I-55 at Joliet Rd, and follow it south as it becomes Hwy 53 into town.

Motor 45 miles onward to Pontiac and the tchotchke-and-photo-filled **Route 66 Hall of Fame** (☎815-844-4566; 110 W Howard St; admission free; ⏲9am-5pm Mon-Fri, 10am-4pm Sat). Cruise another 50 miles to Shirley and **Funk's Grove** (☎309-874-3360; www.funksmaplesirup.com; ⏲call for seasonal hrs), a pretty 19th-century maple syrup farm and nature preserve (exit 154 off I-55).

Ten miles later you'll reach the throwback hamlet of Atlanta. Pull up a chair at the **Palms Grill Cafe** (☎217-648-2233; 110 SW Arch St; mains $4-9; ⏲8am-5pm Sun-Thu, to 8pm Fri & Sat), where thick slabs of gooseberry, sour cream raisin and other retro pies tempt from the glass case. Then walk across the street to snap a photo with **Tall Paul**, a sky-high statue of Paul Bunyan clutching a hot dog.

The state capital of Springfield, 50 miles further on, harbors a trio of sights: **Shea's Gas Station Museum** (p534), the **Cozy Dog Drive In** (p535) and **Route 66 Drive In** (p534).

Further south, a good section of old Route 66 parallels I-55 through Litchfield, where you can fork into chicken fried steak while chatting up locals at the 1924 **Ariston Cafe** (www.ariston-cafe.com; S Old Rte 66; mains $7-15; ⏲11am-9pm Tue-Fri, 4-10pm Sat, 11am-8pm Sun). Finally, before driving into Missouri, detour off I-270 at exit 3. Follow Hwy 203 south, turn right at the first stoplight and drive west to the 1929 **Chain of Rocks Bridge** (⏲9am-sunset). Only open to pedestrians and cyclists these days, the mile-long span over the Mississippi River has a 22-degree angled bend (cause of many a crash, hence the ban on cars).

For more information, visit the **Route 66 Association of Illinois** (www.il66assoc.org) or **Illinois Route 66 Scenic Byway** (www.illinoisroute66.org). Detailed driving directions are at www.historic66.com/illinois.

bust, created by visitors' light touches, indicates the numbers of those who pay their respects here.

FREE **Old State Capitol** HISTORIC SITE
(☎217-785-9363; www.oldstatecapitol.org; cnr 5th & Adams Sts; ⏲9am-5pm, closed Sun & Mon Sep-May) Chatterbox docents will take you through the building and regale you with more Lincoln stories, such as how he gave his famous 'House Divided' speech here in 1858. Suggested donation is $4.

Springfield's Lincoln-free attractions are:

Shea's Gas Station Museum MUSEUM
(☎217-522-0475; 2075 Peoria Rd; admission $2; ⏲8am-4pm Tue-Fri, to noon Sat) Octogenarian Bill Shea shares his famed collection of Route 66 pumps and signs.

Route 66 Drive In CINEMA
(☎217-698-0066; www.route66-drivein.com; 1700 Recreation Dr; adult/child $7/4; ⏲nightly Jun-Aug, weekends mid-Apr–May & Sep) It screens first-run flicks under the stars.

Sleeping & Eating

Statehouse Inn HOTEL $$
(☎217-528-5100; www.thestatehouseinn.com; 101 E Adams St; r incl breakfast $95-155; P❄@📶) It looks concrete-drab outside, but inside, the Statehouse shows its style. Comfy beds and large baths fill the rooms; a retro bar fills the lobby.

Inn at 835 B&B $$
(☎217-523-4466; www.innat835.com; 835 S 2nd St; r incl breakfast $130-200; P❄📶) The historic, arts and crafts–style manor offers 10

rooms of the four-post bed, claw-foot bathtub variety.

Cozy Dog Drive In DINER **$**
(www.cozydogdrivein.com; 2935 S 6th St; mains $2-4; ⊙8am-8pm Mon-Sat) It's a Route 66 legend – the reputed birthplace of the corn dog! – with memorabilia and souvenirs in addition to the deeply fried main course on a stick.

D'Arcy's Pint PUB **$**
(www.darcyspintonline.com; 661 W Stanford Ave; mains $6-12; ⊙11am-10pm Mon-Thu, to 11pm Fri & Sat) D'Arcy's piles up Springfield's best 'horseshoe,' a local sandwich of fried meat on toasted bread, mounded with french fries and smothered in melted cheese. It's 4 miles south of downtown.

Information

Springfield Convention & Visitors Bureau (www.visitspringfieldillinois.com) Produces a useful visitors' guide.

Getting There & Around

The downtown **Amtrak station** (☎217-753-2013; cnr 3rd & Washington Sts) has five trains daily to/from St Louis (two hours) and Chicago (3½ hours).

PETERSBURG

When Lincoln first arrived in Illinois in 1831, he worked variously as a clerk, storekeeper and postmaster in the frontier village of New Salem before studying law and moving to Springfield. In Petersburg, 20 miles northwest of Springfield, **Lincoln's New Salem State Historic Site** (☎217-632-4000; www.lincolnsnewsalem.com; Hwy 97; suggested donation adult/child $4/2; ⊙9am-5pm, closed Mon & Tue mid-Sep–mid-Apr) reconstructs the village with building replicas, historical displays and costumed performances – a pretty informative and entertaining package.

Southern Illinois

A surprise awaits near Collinsville, 8 miles east of East St Louis: classified as a Unesco World Heritage site with the likes of Stonehenge, the Acropolis and the Egyptian pyramids is **Cahokia Mounds State Historic Site** (☎618-346-5160; www.cahokiamounds.org; Collinsville Rd; suggested donation adult/child $4/2; ⊙visitor center 9am-5pm, grounds 8am-dusk). Cahokia protects the remnants of North America's largest prehistoric city (20,000 people, with suburbs), dating from AD 1200. While the 65 earthen mounds, including the enormous Monk's Mound and the 'Woodhenge' sun calendar, are not overwhelmingly impressive in themselves, the whole site is worth seeing. If you're approaching from the north, take exit 24 off I-255 S; if approaching from St Louis, take exit 6 off I-55/70.

A short distance north of St Louis, Hwy 100 between **Grafton** and **Alton** is perhaps the most scenic 15 miles of the entire Great River Road. As you slip under wind-hewn bluffs, keep an eye out for the turnoff to itty-bitty **Elsah** (www.elsah.org), a hidden hamlet of 19th-century stone cottages, wood buggy shops and farmhouses.

An exception to the state's flat farmland is the green southernmost section, punctuated by rolling **Shawnee National Forest** (☎618-253-7114; www.fs.usda.gov/shawnee) and its rocky outcroppings. The area has numerous state parks and recreation areas good for hiking, climbing, swimming, fishing and canoeing, particularly around **Little Grassy Lake** and **Devil's Kitchen**. And who would think that Florida-like swampland, complete with bald cypress trees and croaking bullfrogs, would be here? But it is, at **Cypress Creek National Wildlife Refuge** (☎618-634-2231; www.fws.gov/midwest/cypresscreek).

Union County, near the state's southern tip, has wineries and orchards. Sample the wares on the 35-mile **Shawnee Hills Wine Trail** (www.shawneewinetrail.com), which connects 12 vineyards.

INDIANA

The state revs up around the Indy 500 race, but otherwise it's about slow-paced pleasures in corn-stubbled Indiana: pie-eating in Amish Country, meditating in Bloomington's Tibetan temples and admiring the big architecture in small Columbus. For the record, folks have called Indianans 'Hoosiers' since the 1830s, but the word's origin is unknown. One theory is that early settlers knocking on a door were met with 'Who's here?' which soon became 'Hoosier.' It's certainly something to discuss with locals, perhaps over a traditional pork tenderloin sandwich.

Information

Indiana Highway Conditions (☎800-261-7623; www.trafficwise.in.gov)

Indiana State Park Information (☎800-622-4931; www.in.gov/dnr/parklake) Park entry costs $2 per day by foot or bicycle, $5 to $10 by vehicle. Campsites cost $6 to $39;

reservations accepted (☎866-622-6746; www.camp.in.gov).

Indiana Tourism (☎888-365-6946; www.visitindiana.com)

Indianapolis

Clean-cut Indy is the state capital and a perfectly pleasant place to ogle racecars and take a spin around the renowned speedway. The art museum and White River State Park have their merits, as do the Mass Ave and Broad Ripple 'hoods for eating and drinking. And Kurt Vonnegut fans are in for a treat.

Many early carmakers opened shop in the city, but were eclipsed by the Detroit giants. They did leave a lasting legacy – a 2.5-mile test track, which became the site for the first Indianapolis 500 race in 1911 (won at an average speed of 75mph).

Sights & Activities

Downtown's bulls-eye is Monument Circle. White River State Park and its many attractions lie about three-quarters of a mile west. The Broad Ripple neighborhood is 7 miles north at College Ave and 62nd St.

Indianapolis Motor Speedway MUSEUM
(☎317-492-6784; www.indianapolismotorspeedway.com; 4790 W 16th St) The Speedway, home of the Indianapolis 500 motor race, is Indy's supersight. The **Hall of Fame Museum** (adult/child $5/3; ⏲9am-5pm) features 75 racing cars (including former winners), a 500lb Tiffany trophy and a track tour ($5 extra). OK, so you're on a bus for the latter and not even beginning to burn rubber at 37mph, but it's still fun to pretend.

The big race itself is held on Memorial Day weekend (last weekend of May) and attended by 450,000 crazed fans. **Tickets** (☎317-484-6700, 800-822-4639; www.imstix.com; $30-150) can be hard to come by. Try the prerace trials and practices for easier access and cheaper prices.

Other races at the Speedway are the NASCAR **Brickyard 400** in late July and the **Motorcycle Grand Prix** in late August. The track is about 6 miles northwest of downtown.

White River State Park PARK
(http://inwhiteriver.wrsp.in.gov) The expansive park, located at the edge of downtown, contains several worthwhile sights. The adobe **Eiteljorg Museum of American Indians & Western Art** (☎317-636-9378; www.eiteljorg.org; 500 W Washington St; adult/child $8/5; ⏲10am-5pm Mon-Sat, noon-5pm Sun) features Native American basketry, pots and masks, as well as a realistic/romantic Western painting collection with works by Frederic Remington and Georgia O'Keeffe.

The **NCAA Hall of Champions** (☎800-735-6222; www.ncaahallofchampions.org; 700 W Washington St; adult/child $5/3; ⏲10am-5pm Tue-Sat, noon-5pm Sun) reveals the country's fascination with college sports. The interactive exhibits let you shoot free throws or climb onto a swimming platform à la Michael Phelps. You'll probably find most Hoosiers hovering around the basketball exhibits, as locals are renowned hoop-ball fanatics.

Other park highlights include an atmospheric **minor-league baseball stadium**, a **zoo**, a **canal walk**, **gardens**, a **science museum** and a military **Medal of Honor Memorial**.

FREE **Indianapolis Museum of Art** MUSEUM
(☎317-920-2660; www.imamuseum.org; 4000 Michigan Rd; ⏲11am-5pm Tue-Sat, to 9pm Thu & Fri, noon-5pm Sun; 📶) The museum has a terrific collection of European art (especially Turner and some post-Impressionists), African tribal art, South Pacific art and Chinese

INDIANA FACTS

- **Nickname** Hoosier State
- **Population** 6.4 million
- **Area** 36,420 sq miles
- **Capital city** Indianapolis (population 785,600)
- **Sales tax** 7%
- **Birthplace of** Author Kurt Vonnegut (1922–2007), actor James Dean (1931–55), TV host David Letterman (b 1947), rocker John Mellencamp (b 1951), King of Pop Michael Jackson (1958–2009)
- **Home of** farmers, corn
- **Politics** typically Republican
- **Famous for** Indy 500 motor race, basketball fanaticism, pork tenderloin sandwich
- **Official pie** sugar cream
- **Driving distances** Indianapolis to Chicago 185 miles, Indianapolis to Bloomington 53 miles

works. The venue is linked to **Oldfields – Lilly House & Gardens** (⌚11am-5pm Tue-Sat, noon-5pm Sun), the 26-acre estate of the Lilly pharmaceutical family, and **Fairbanks Art & Nature Park** (⌚sunrise-sunset), which features sculptures and audio installations amid 100 acres of woodlands.

FREE **Kurt Vonnegut Memorial Library** MUSEUM
(www.vonnegutlibrary.org; 340 N Senate Ave; ⌚noon-5pm Thu-Tue) Author Kurt Vonnegut was born and raised in Indy, and this humble museum pays homage with displays including his typewriter, Pall Mall cigarettes and Purple Heart medal from WWII. Don't miss the painting of the Tralfamadorians (from *Slaughterhouse-Five*) and his raft of rejection letters from publishers. Vonnegut's children donated most of the artifacts.

Monument Circle MONUMENT, MUSEUM
(1 Monument Circle) At Monument Circle, the city center is marked by the jaw-dropping 284ft **Soldiers & Sailors Monument**. For a bizarre (and cramped) experience, take the elevator ($2) to the top. Beneath is the **Civil War Museum** (admission free; ⌚10:30am-5:30pm Wed-Sun), which neatly outlines the conflict and Indiana's abolition position. A few blocks north, the **World War Memorial** (cnr Vermont & Meridian Sts) is another impressively beefy monument.

Indiana Medical History Museum MUSEUM
(☎317-635-7329; www.imhm.org; 3045 W Vermont St; adult/child $5/1; ⌚10am-4pm Thu-Sat) A guide leads you through century-old pathology labs. The highlight, especially for zombies, is the room full of brains in jars. There's also a healing herb garden to walk through. It's a few miles west of White River park.

FREE **Indianapolis Hiking Club** HIKING
(www.indyhike.org) Who knew you could hike in Indy? Join free, 5- to 8-mile jaunts around downtown, Broad Ripple, rugged Eagle Creek Park and elsewhere. Check the website for times and departure points.

Festivals

The city celebrates the Indy 500 throughout May with the **500 Festival** (www.500festival.com; tickets from $7). Events include a racecar drivers' parade and a community shindig at the racetrack.

Sleeping

Hotels cost more and are usually full during race weeks in May, July and August. Add 17% tax to the prices listed here. Look for low-cost motels off I-465, the freeway that circles Indianapolis.

Indy Hostel HOSTEL $
(☎317-727-1696; www.indyhostel.us; 4903 Winthrop Ave; weekday/weekend dm $26/29, r $58/64; P❄@📶) This small, friendly hostel has four dorm rooms in configurations from four to six beds. One room is for females only, while the others are mixed. There are also a couple of private rooms. The Monon Trail hiking/cycling path runs beside the property. It's located by Broad Ripple, so a bit of a haul from downtown (though on bus 17).

Conrad Indianapolis HOTEL $$$
(☎317-713-5000; www.conradindianapolis.com; 50 W Washington St; r from $250; P❄@📶≋) The Conrad is Indy's top address: a 241-room beauty near the sports venues. Spa services, 42-inch plasma screen TVs and bath telephones are part of the package. Wi-fi costs $14, and parking is $33.

Stone Soup B&B $$
(☎866-639-9550; www.stonesoupinn.com; 1304 N Central Ave; r incl breakfast $85-145; P⊖❄📶) The nine rooms sprawl throughout a rambling house filled with antiques and stained glass. The less-expensive rooms share a bath.

Hampton Inn HOTEL $$
(☎317-261-1200; www.hamptondt.com; 105 S Meridian St; r incl breakfast $139-169; P❄@📶) Handsome-looking public areas, plush beds and the prime downtown location make this a fine chain hotel choice. Parking is $15.

Eating

Massachusetts Ave (www.discovermassave.com), by downtown, is bounteous when the stomach growls. **Broad Ripple** (www.discoverbroadripple.com), 7 miles north, has pubs, cafes and ethnic eateries.

Mug 'N' Bun AMERICAN $
(www.mug-n-bun.com; 5211 W 10th St; mains $3-5; ⌚10am-9pm Sun-Thu, to 10pm Fri & Sat) The mugs are frosted and filled with a wonderful home-brewed root beer. The buns contain burgers, chili dogs and juicy pork tenderloins. And don't forget the fried macaroni-and-cheese wedges. At this vintage drive-in near the Speedway, you are served – where else? – in your car.

INDIANA FOODWAYS

Which restaurants serve the best pork tenderloin and sugar cream pie? Where are the local farmers markets and rib fests? What's the recipe for corn pudding? The **Indiana Foodways Alliance** (www.indianafoodways.com) is your one-stop shop for Hoosier cuisine information.

Shapiro's Deli DELI **$$**
(☎317-631-4041; www.shapiros.com; 808 S Meridian St; mains $8-15; ⏲6:45am-8pm; 📶) Chomp into a towering corned beef or peppery pastrami sandwich on homemade bread, and then chase it with fat slices of chocolate cake or fruit pie.

Bazbeaux PIZZERIA **$$$**
(www.bazbeaux.com; 329 Massachusetts Ave; large pizza $19-23; ⏲11am-10pm Sun-Thu, to 11pm Fri & Sat) A local favorite, Bazbeaux offers an eclectic pizza selection, like the 'Tchoupitoulas,' topped with Cajun shrimp and andouille sausage. Muffaletta sandwiches, stromboli and Belgian beer are some of the other unusual offerings.

City Market MARKET **$**
(www.indycm.com; 222 E Market St; ⏲6am-3pm Mon-Fri, 10am-4pm Sat) Ethnic food stalls and local produce vendors fill the city's old marketplace, which dates from 1886. It's ideal for lunchtime grazing.

Drinking & Entertainment

Downtown and Mass Ave have some good watering holes; Broad Ripple has several.

Bars & Nightclubs

Slippery Noodle Inn BAR
(www.slipperynoodle.com; 372 S Meridian St) Downtown's Noodle is the oldest bar in the state, and has seen action as a whorehouse, slaughterhouse, gangster hangout and Underground Railroad station; currently, it's one of the best blues clubs in the country. There's live music nightly, and it's cheap.

Rathskeller BEER HALL
(www.rathskeller.com; 401 E Michigan St) Quaff German brews at the outdoor beer garden's picnic tables in summer, or at the deer-head-lined indoor beer hall once winter strikes. The six-beer sampler gets you acquainted with the wares. It is located in the historic Athenaeum building near Mass Ave.

Plump's Last Shot BAR
(6416 Cornell Ave) Bobby Plump inspired the iconic movie *Hoosiers*. He's the kid who swished in the last-second shot, so his tiny school beat the 'big city' school in the 1950s state basketball championship. There's sports memorabilia everywhere, and sometimes Bobby himself is on-site. It's located in a big house in Broad Ripple – great for people-watching and sipping a cold one on the dog-friendly patio.

Sports

The motor races aren't the only coveted spectator events. The NFL's Colts win football games under a huge retractable roof at **Lucas Oil Stadium** (☎317-262-3389; www.colts.com; 500 S Capitol Ave). The NBA's Pacers shoot hoops at **Conseco Fieldhouse** (☎317-917-2500; www.pacers.com; 125 S Pennsylvania St).

Shopping

You could buy a speedway flag or Colts jersey as your Indy souvenir. Or you could purchase a bottle of mead made by a couple of enthusiastic former beekeepers at **New Day Meadery** (www.newdaymeadery.com; 1102 E Prospect St; ⏲2-9pm Tue-Fri, noon-9pm Sat, noon-4pm Sun). Sip the honeyed wares in the tasting room (eight samples for $5) before making your selection.

Information

Emergency & Medical Services

Indiana University Medical Center (☎317-274-4705; 550 N University Blvd)

Media

Gay Indy (www.gayindy.org) Gay and lesbian news and entertainment listings.

Indianapolis Star (www.indystar.com) The city's daily newspaper.

Nuvo (www.nuvo.net) Free, weekly alternative paper with the arts and music low-down.

Tourist Information

Indianapolis Convention & Visitors Bureau (☎800-323-4639; www.visitindy.com) Download a free city app and print out coupons from the website.

Getting There & Around

The fancy **Indianapolis International Airport** (IND; www.indianapolisairport.com; 7800 Col H Weir Cook Memorial Dr) is 16 miles southwest of town. The Washington bus (8) runs between the airport and downtown ($1.75, 50 minutes); the Green Line bus does it quicker ($7, 20 minutes). A cab to downtown costs about $35.

Greyhound (☎317-267-3076; www.greyhound.com) shares **Union Station** (350 S Illinois St) with Amtrak. Buses go frequently to Cincinnati (two hours) and Chicago (3½ hours). **Megabus** (www.megabus.com/us) stops at 200 E Washington St, and is often cheaper. Amtrak travels these routes but takes almost twice as long and (nonsensically) costs more.

IndyGo (www.indygo.net; fare $1.75) runs the local buses. Bus 17 goes to Broad Ripple. Service is minimal during weekends.

For a taxi, call **Yellow Cab** (☎317-487-7777).

Bloomington & Central Indiana

Bluegrass music, architectural hot spots, Tibetan temples and James Dean all furrow into the farmland around here.

FAIRMOUNT

This small town, north on Hwy 9, is the birthplace of James Dean, one of the original icons of cool. Fans should head directly to the **Historical Museum** (☎765-948-4555; www.jamesdeanartifacts.com; 203 E Washington St; admission free; ⏲10am-5pm Mon-Sat, noon-5pm Sun Mar-Nov) to see Dean's bongo drums, among other artifacts. This is also the place to pick up a free map that will guide you to sites like the farmhouse where Jimmy grew up and his red-lipstick-kissed grave site. The museum sells Dean posters, zippo lighters and other memorabilia, and sponsors the annual **James Dean Festival** (admission free; ⏲late Sep), when as many as 50,000 fans pour in for four days of music and revelry. The privately owned **James Dean Gallery** (☎765-948-3326; www.jamesdeangallery.com; 425 N Main St; admission free; ⏲9am-6pm) has more memorabilia a few blocks away.

COLUMBUS

When you think of the USA's great architectural cities – Chicago, New York, Washington, DC – Columbus, Indiana, doesn't quite leap to mind, but it should. Located 40 miles south of Indianapolis on I-65, Columbus is a remarkable gallery of physical design. Since the 1940s the city and its leading corporations have commissioned some of the world's best architects, including Eero Saarinen, Richard Meier and IM Pei, to create both public and private buildings. Stop at the **visitor center** (☎812-378-2622; www.columbus.in.us; 506 5th St; ⏲9am-5pm Mon-Sat, noon-5pm Sun Mar-Nov, closed Sun Dec-Feb) to pick up a self-guided tour map ($3) or join a two-hour bus tour (adult/child $20/10); they depart at 10am Monday to Friday, 10am and 2pm Saturday, and 3pm Sunday. Over 70 notable buildings and pieces of public art are spread over a wide area (car required), but about 15 diverse works can be seen on foot downtown.

Hotel Indigo (☎812-375-9100; www.hotelindigo.com; 400 Brown St; r from $135-180; ❄📶🏊), also downtown, offers the chain's trademark mod, cheery rooms, plus a fluffy white dog who works as the lobby ambassador (he even has his own email address). A few blocks away you can grab a counter stool, chat up Wilma and her fellow servers, and let the sugar buzz begin at retro **Zaharakos** (www.zaharakos.com; 329 Washington St; ⏲8am-8pm Mon-Fri, 9am-8pm Sat & Sun), a 1909 soda fountain.

NASHVILLE

Gentrified and antique-filled, this 19th-century town west of Columbus on Hwy 46 is now a bustling tourist center, at its busiest in fall when leaf-peepers pour in. The **visitor center** (☎800-753-3255; www.browncounty.com; 10 N Van Buren St; ⏲10am-5pm Mon-Thu, to 6pm Fri & Sat, 10:30am-4pm Sun; 📶) provides maps and online coupons.

Beyond gallery browsing, Nashville is the jump-off point to **Brown County State Park** (☎812-988-6406; www.browncountystatepark.us; tent & RV sites $13-26, cabins from $72), a 15,700-acre stand of oak, hickory and birch trees, where trails give hikers, mountain bikers and horseback riders access to the area's green hill country.

Among several B&Bs, central **Artists Colony Inn** (☎812-988-0600; www.artistscolonyinn.com; 105 S Van Buren St; r incl breakfast $112-170; 🚭📶) stands out for its spiffy, Shaker-style rooms. The **dining room** (mains $9-17; ⏲7:30am-8pm Sun-Thu, to 9pm Fri & Sat) offers traditional Hoosier fare, such as catfish and pork tenderloins.

As with Nashville, Tennessee, Nashville, Indiana enjoys country music, and bands play regularly at several venues. To shake a leg, mosey into **Mike's Music & Dance Barn** (☎812-988-8636; www.thedancebarn.com; 2277 Hwy 46; ⏲Thu-Mon). The **Bill Monroe Museum** (☎812-988-6422; 5163 Rte 135 N, Bean Blossom; adult/child $4/free; ⏲9am-5pm, closed Tue & Wed Nov-Apr), 5 miles north of town, hails the bluegrass hero.

BLOOMINGTON

Lively and lovely Bloomington, 53 miles south of Indianapolis via Hwy 37, is the home of Indiana University. The town centers on Courthouse Sq, surrounded by restaurants, bars, bookshops and the historic facade of Fountain Sq Mall. Nearly everything is walkable. The **Bloomington CVB** (www.visitbloomington.com) has a downloadable guide.

On the expansive campus, the **Art Museum** (☎812-855-5445; www.indiana.edu/~iuam; 1133 E 7th St; admission free; ⏰10am-5pm Tue-Sat, noon-5pm Sun, reduced hr summer), designed by IM Pei, contains an excellent collection of African art, as well as European and US paintings.

The colorful, prayer flag-covered **Tibetan Mongolian Buddhist Cultural Center** (☎812-336-6807.tibetancc.com; 3655 Snoddy Rd; admission free; ⏰sunrise-sunset) and stupa, as well as the **Dagom Gaden Tensung Ling Monastery** (☎812-339-0857; www.dgtlmonastery.org; 102 Clubhouse Dr; admission free; ⏰9am-6pm), indicate Bloomington's significant Tibetan presence. Both offer free teachings and meditation sessions; check the websites for weekly schedules.

If you arrive in mid-April and wonder why an extra 20,000 people are hanging out in town, it's for the **Little 500** (www.iusf.indiana.edu; tickets $25). Lance Armstrong called the bike race, where amateurs ride one-speed Schwinns for 200 laps around a quarter-mile track, 'the coolest event I ever attended.'

Look for cheap lodgings along N Walnut St near Hwy 46. **Grant Street Inn** (☎800-328-4350; www.grantstinn.com; 310 N Grant St; r incl breakfast $149-229; @) fluffs up 24 rooms in a Victorian house and annex near campus.

For a town of its size, Bloomington offers a mind-blowing array of ethnic restaurants – everything from Burmese to Eritrean to Mexican. Browse Kirkwood Ave and E 4th St. **Anyetsang's Little Tibet** (☎812-331-0122; www.anyetsangs.com; 415 E 4th St; mains $9-13; ⏰11am-9:30pm Wed-Mon) offers specialties from the Himalayan homeland. Pubs on Kirkwood Ave, close to the university, cater to the student crowd. **Nick's English Hut** (www.nicksenglishhut.com; 423 E Kirkwood Ave) pours not only for students and professors, but has filled the cups of Kurt Vonnegut, Dylan Thomas and Barack Obama, as well.

Southern Indiana

The pretty hills, caves, rivers and utopian history of southern Indiana mark it as a completely different region from the flat and industrialized north.

OHIO RIVER

The Indiana segment of the 981-mile Ohio River marks the state's southern border. From tiny Aurora, in the southeastern corner of the state, Hwys 56, 156, 62 and 66, known collectively as the **Ohio River Scenic Route**, wind through a varied landscape.

Coming from the east, a perfect place to stop is little **Madison**, a well-preserved river settlement from the mid-19th century where architectural beauties beckon genteelly from the streets. At the **visitor center** (☎812-265-2956; www.visitmadison.org; 601 W First St; ⏰9am-5pm Mon-Fri, 10am-3pm Sat, 11am-5pm Sun), pick up a walking tour brochure, which will lead you by notable landmarks.

Madison has motels around its edges, as well as several B&Bs. Main St lines up numerous places for a bite, interspersed with antique stores. Large, wooded **Clifty Falls State Park** (☎812-273-8885; tent & RV sites $10-26), off Hwy 56 and a couple of miles west of town, has camping, hiking trails, views and waterfalls.

In Clarksville, **Falls of the Ohio State Park** (☎812-280-9970; www.fallsoftheohio.org; 201 W Riverside Dr) has only rapids, no falls, but is of interest for its 386-million-year-old fossil beds. The **interpretive center** (adult/child $5/2; ⏰9am-5pm Mon-Sat, 1-5pm Sun) explains it all. Quench your thirst in adjacent New Albany, home to **New Albanian Brewing Company Public House & Pizzeria** (www.newalbanian.com; 3312 Plaza Dr; ⏰11am-midnight Mon-Sat). Or cross the bridge to Louisville, Kentucky, where the tonsil-singeing native bourbon awaits....

Scenic Hwy 62 heads west and leads to the Lincoln Hills and southern Indiana's limestone caves. A plunge into **Marengo Cave** (☎812-365-2705; www.marengocave.com; ⏰9am-6pm, to 5pm Sep-May), north on Hwy 66, is highly recommended. It offers a 40-minute tour (adult/child $13.50/7), 70-minute tour ($15/7.50) or combination tour ($21/11) walking past stalagmites and other ancient formations. The same group operates **Cave Country Canoes** (www.cavecountrycanoes.com; ⏰May-Oct) in nearby Milltown, with half-day ($23), full-day ($26) or longer trips on the scenic Blue River; keep an eye out for river otters and rare hellbender salamanders.

Four miles south of Dale, off I-64, is the **Lincoln Boyhood National Memorial** (☎812-937-4541; www.nps.gov/libo; adult/child $3/free; ⊙8am-5pm), where young Abe lived from age seven to 21. This isolated site also includes admission to a working **pioneer farm** (⊙8am-5pm mid-Apr–Sep).

NEW HARMONY

In southwest Indiana, the Wabash River forms the border with Illinois. Beside it, south of I-64, captivating **New Harmony** is the site of two early communal-living experiments and is worth a visit. In the early 19th century a German Christian sect, the Harmonists, developed a sophisticated town here while awaiting the Second Coming. Later, the British utopian Robert Owen acquired the town. Learn more and pick up a walking-tour map at the angular **Atheneum Visitors Center** (☎812-682-4474; www.usi.edu/hnh; 401 N Arthur St; ⊙9:30am-5pm).

Today New Harmony retains an air of contemplation, if not otherworldliness, which you can experience at its newer attractions, such as the templelike Roofless Church and the Labyrinth, a maze symbolizing the spirit's quest. The town has a couple of guesthouses and camping at **Harmonie State Park** (☎812-682-4821; campsites $11-27). Pop into **Main Cafe** (508 Main St; mains $4-7; ⊙5:30am-1pm Mon-Fri) for a ham-bean-and-cornbread lunch, but save room for the coconut cream pie.

Northern Indiana

The truck-laden I-80/I-90 tollways cut across Indiana's northern section. Parallel US 20 is slower and cheaper, but not much more attractive.

INDIANA DUNES

Hugely popular on summer days with sunbathers from Chicago and South Bend, **Indiana Dunes National Lakeshore** (☎219-926-7561; www.nps.gov/indu; admission free, tent & RV sites $15) stretches along 21 miles of Lake Michigan shoreline. In addition to its beaches, the area is noted for its plant variety: everything from cacti to pine trees sprouts here. Hiking trails crisscross the dunes and woodlands, winding by a peat bog, a still-operating 1870s farm and a blue heron rookery, among other payoffs. Mt Baldy is the top dune to climb. Oddly, all this natural bounty lies smack-dab next to smoke-belching factories, which you'll also see at various vantage points. Stop at the **Dorothy Buell Visitor Center** (☎219-926-7561; Hwy 49; ⊙8:30am-6:30pm Jun-Aug, to 4:30pm Sep-May) for beach details, a schedule of ranger-guided walks and activities, and to pick up hiking, biking and birding maps. Or get guides in advance via the **Porter County Convention & Visitors Bureau** (www.indianadunes.com).

Indiana Dunes State Park (☎219-926-1952; www.dnr.in.gov/parklake; per car $10, tent & RV sites $17-28) is a 2100-acre, shoreside pocket within the national lakeshore; it's located at the end of Hwy 49, near Chesterton. It has more amenities, but also more regulation and more crowds (plus the vehicle entry fee). Wintertime brings out the cross-country skiers; summertime brings out the hikers. Seven trails zigzag over the landscape; No 4 up Mt Tom rewards with Chicago skyline views.

Other than a couple of beachfront snack bars, you won't find much to eat in the parks, so stop at homey, Italian **Lucrezia** (☎219-926-5829; www.lucreziacafe.com; 428 S Calumet Rd; mains $17-27; ⊙11am-10pm Sun-Thu, to 11pm Fri & Sat) in Chesterton.

The Dunes are an easy day trip from Chicago. Driving takes one hour. The **South Shore Metra train** (www.nictd.com) makes the journey from Millennium Station downtown, and it's about 1¼ hours to the Dune Park or Beverly Shores stops (note both stations are a 1½-mile walk from the beach). Those who want to make a night of it can camp (national lakeshore campsites $15, state park tent and RV sites $17 to $28).

Near Illinois, the steel cities of **Gary** and **East Chicago** present some of the bleakest urban landscapes anywhere. Taking the train (Amtrak or South Shore line) through here will get you up close and personal with the industrial underbelly.

SOUTH BEND

South Bend is home to the **University of Notre Dame**. You know how people in certain towns say, 'football is a religion here'? They mean it at Notre Dame, where *Touchdown Jesus* lords over the 80,000-capacity stadium (it's a mural of the resurrected Christ with arms raised, though the pose bears a striking resemblance to a referee signaling a touchdown). Tours of the pretty campus, including the Lourdes Grotto replica, start at the **visitor center** (www.nd.edu/

visitors; 111 Eck Center). Less visited but worth a stop is the **Studebaker National Museum** (☎574-235-9714; www.studebakermuseum.org; 201 S Chapin St; adult/child $8/5; ⏲10am-5pm Mon-Sat, noon-5pm Sun) near downtown, where you can gaze at a gorgeous 1956 Packard and other classic beauties.

AMISH COUNTRY

East of South Bend, around **Shipshewana** and **Middlebury**, is the USA's third-largest Amish community. Horses and buggies clip-clop by, and long-bearded men hand-plow the tidy fields. Get situated with maps from the **Elkhart County CVB** (☎800-517-9739; www.amishcountry.org). Better yet, pick a backroad between the two towns and head down it. Often you'll see families selling beeswax candles, quilts and fresh produce on their porch, which beats the often-touristy shops and restaurants on the main roads. Note most places close on Sunday.

Village Inn (☎574-825-2043; 105 S Main St; mains $3-7; ⏲5am-8pm Mon-Fri, to 2pm Sat), in Middlebury, sells real-deal pies; bonneted women in pastel dresses come in at 4:30am to bake the flaky wares. Arrive before noon, or you'll be looking at crumbs.

AUBURN

Just before reaching the Ohio border, classic car connoisseurs should dip south on I-69 to the town of Auburn, where the Cord Company produced the USA's favorite cars in the 1920s and '30s. The **Auburn Cord Duesenberg Museum** (☎260-925-1444; www.automobilemuseum.org; 1600 S Wayne St; adult/child $10/6; ⏲9am-5pm, to 8pm Thu) has a wonderful display of early roadsters in a beautiful art deco setting. Next door are the vintage rigs of the **National Automotive and Truck Museum** (☎260-925-9100; www.natmus.org; 1000 Gordon Buehrig Pl; adult/child $7/4; ⏲9am-5pm).

OHIO

All right, time for your Ohio quiz. In the Buckeye State you can 1) watch butter churn on an Amish farm; 2) party your ass off at an island resort; 3) lose your stomach on one of the world's fastest roller coasters; 4) suck down a dreamy creamy milk shake fresh from a working dairy; or 5) examine a mondo, mysterious snake sculpture built into the earth. And the answer is...all of these. It hurts locals' feelings when visitors think the only thing to do here is tip over cows. C'mon, give Ohio a chance. Besides these activities, you can partake in a five-way in Cincinnati (see p553) and rock out in Cleveland.

OHIO FACTS

- **Nickname** Buckeye State
- **Population** 11.5 million
- **Area** 44,825 sq miles
- **Capital city** Columbus (population 733,200)
- **Other cities** Cleveland (population 444,300), Cincinnati (population 332,250)
- **Sales tax** 5.5%
- **Birthplace of** inventor Thomas Edison (1847–1931), author Toni Morrison (b 1931), entrepreneur Ted Turner (b 1938), filmmaker Steven Spielberg (b 1947)
- **Home of** sows, roller coasters, aviation pioneers Wright Brothers
- **Politics** swing state
- **Famous for** first airplane, first pro baseball team, birthplace of seven US presidents
- **State rock song** 'Hang On Sloopy'
- **Driving distances** Cleveland to Columbus 142 miles, Columbus to Cincinnati 108 miles

Information

Ohio Division of Travel and Tourism (☎800-282-5393; www.discoverohio.com)

Ohio Highway Conditions (www.buckeyetraffic.org)

Ohio State Park Information (☎614-265-6561; www.ohiodnr.com/parks) State parks are free to visit; some have free wi-fi. Tent and RV sites cost $10 to $36; reservations accepted (☎866-644-6727; www.ohio.reserveworld.com; fee $8.25).

Cleveland

Does it or does it not rock? That is the question. Drawing from its roots as a working man's town, Cleveland has toiled hard in recent years to prove it does. Step one was to control the urban decay/river-on-fire thing – the Cuyahoga River was once so polluted that it actually burned. Check. Step two was to bring a worthy attraction to town, say the Rock and Roll Hall of Fame. Check. Step three was to get grub beyond steak-and potatoes. Check. So can Cleveland finally wipe the sweat from its brow? More or less. Much of the downtown area remains bleak, though there are definite pockets of freshness.

Sights & Activities

Cleveland's center is Public Sq, dominated by the conspicuous Terminal Tower. Most attractions are downtown on the lakefront or at University Circle (the area around Case Western Reserve University, Cleveland Clinic and other institutions).

DOWNTOWN

Keep an eye out for the **Greater Cleveland Aquarium** (www.greaterclevelandaquarium.com), slated to open by 2012 in the Flats.

Rock and Roll Hall of Fame & Museum MUSEUM
(☎216-781-7625; www.rockhall.com; 1 Key Plaza; adult/child $22/13; ⏰10am-5:30pm, to 9pm Wed year-round, to 9pm Sat Jun-Aug) Cleveland's top attraction is more than a collection of memorabilia, though it does have Jimi Hendrix's Stratocaster, Keith Moon's platform shoes and Ray Charles' sunglasses. Interactive multimedia exhibits trace the history and social context of rock music and the performers who created it. Why is the museum in Cleveland? Because this is the hometown of Alan Freed, the disk jockey who popularized the term 'rock 'n' roll' in the early 1950s, and because the city lobbied hard and paid big. Be prepared for crowds (especially thick until 1pm or so). In summer, Johnny Cash's tour bus parks outside; climb aboard to see how the Man in Black lived.

Great Lakes Science Center MUSEUM
(☎216-694-2000; www.glsc.org; 601 Erieside Ave; adult/child $11/9; ⏰10am-5pm; 👪) One of 10 museums in the country with a NASA affiliation, Great Lakes goes deep in space with rockets and moon stones, as well as exhibits on the lakes' environmental problems. The wind turbine and solar panels out front provide 6% of the museum's energy.

William G Mather MUSEUM
(☎216-574-6262; http://wgmather.nhlink.net; 305 Mather Way; adult/child $7/5; ⏰11am-5pm daily Jun-Aug, Fri-Sun only May, Sep & Oct, closed Nov-Apr) Take a self-guided walk-about on this humungous freighter incarnated as a steamship museum. It's docked beside the Science Center, which manages it.

USS Cod MUSEUM
(☎216-566-8770; www.usscod.org; 1089 E 9th St; adult/child $7/4; ⏰10am-5pm May-Sep) The storied submarine *USS Cod* saw action in WWII. You're free to climb through it, tight spaces, ladders and all, while listening to audio stories about life on board.

OHIO CITY & TREMONT

West Side Market MARKET
(www.westsidemarket.org; cnr W 25th St & Lorain Ave; ⏰7am-4pm Mon & Wed, to 6pm Fri & Sat) The European-style market overflows with greengrocers and their fruit and vegetable pyramids, as well as purveyors of Hungarian sausage, Mexican flat breads and Polish pierogi.

Christmas Story House & Museum FILM LOCATION
(☎216-298-4919; www.achristmasstoryhouse.com; 3159 W 11th St; adult/child $8/6; ⏰10am-5pm Thu-Sat, noon-5pm Sun) Remember the beloved 1983 film *A Christmas Story,* in which Ralphie yearns for a Red Ryder BB gun? The original house sits in Tremont, complete with leg lamp. This attraction's for true fans only.

UNIVERSITY CIRCLE

Several museums and attractions are within walking distance of each other at University Circle, 5 miles east of downtown. Carless? Take the HealthLine bus to Adelbert.

FREE **Cleveland Museum of Art** MUSEUM
(☎216-421-7340; www.clevelandart.org; 11150 East Blvd; ⏰10am-5pm Tue-Sun, to 9pm Wed & Fri) The gem of the group, the art museum houses an excellent collection of European paintings, as well as African, Asian and American art. It's undergoing a whopping expansion, to be completed in 2013. Head to the 2nd floor for rock star works from Impressionists, Picasso and surrealists.

Cleveland Botanical Garden GARDENS
(☎216-721-1600; www.cbgarden.org; 11030 East Blvd; adult/child $8.50/3; ⏰10am-5pm Tue-Sat, noon-5pm Sun, to 9pm Wed Jun-Aug) Has a Costa Rican cloud forest and Madagascan desert exhibits. An ice-skating rink opens nearby in winter; skate rentals cost $3. Parking costs $5 to $10 per day and gives access to all the museums here.

Lakeview Cemetery GARDENS
(☎216-421-2665; www.lakeviewcemetery.com; 12316 Euclid Ave; ⏲7:30am-7:30pm) Beyond the circle further east, don't forget this eclectic 'outdoor museum' where President Garfield and John Rockefeller rest, or more intriguingly, local comic book hero Harvey Pekar and crimefighter Eliot Ness.

Sleeping

Prices listed are for summer, which is high season, and do not include the 16.25% tax. Modest motels are southwest of Cleveland's center, near the airport. The W 150th exit off I-71 (exit 240) has several options for less than $100.

Brownstone Inn B&B $$
(☎216-426-1753; www.brownstoneinndowntown.com; 3649 Prospect Ave; r incl breakfast $89-139; P❄@📶) This Victorian townhouse B&B has a whole lotta personality. All five rooms have a private bath, and each comes equipped with robes to lounge in and an invitation for evening aperitifs. It's between downtown and University Circle, though in a bit of a no-man's-land for walkable entertainment.

University Circle B&B B&B $$
(☎866-735-5960; www.ucbnb.com; 1575 E 108th St; r incl breakfast $110-145; P❄📶) Located in the heart of University Circle and within walking distance of its museums, this four-room B&B gets lots of academic visitors. Two rooms share a bath.

Hilton Garden Inn HOTEL $$
(☎216-658-6400; www.hiltongardeninn.com; 1100 Carnegie Ave; r $110-169; P❄@📶🏊) While nothing fancy, the Hilton's rooms are good value with comfy beds, wi-fi-rigged workstations and mini refrigerators. It's right by the baseball park. Parking costs $16.

Holiday Inn Express HOTEL $$
(☎216-443-1000; www.hiexpress.com; 629 Euclid Ave; r incl breakfast $115-180; P❄@📶) Another OK chain option, in an old bank building that's conveniently located near the E 4th St entertainment strip. Parking costs $14.

Eating

There's more range than you might expect in a Rust Belt town. TV food dudes from Anthony Bourdain to Guy Fieri have filmed shows here and raved over the offerings.

DOWNTOWN

The Warehouse District, between W 6th and W 9th Sts, jumps with trendy restaurants. Off the beaten path and east of the city center, Asiatown (bounded by Payne and St Clair Aves, and E 30th and 40ths Sts) has several Chinese, Vietnamese and Korean eateries.

Lola AMERICAN $$$
(☎216-621-5652; www.lolabistro.com; 2058 E 4th St; mains $22-31; ⏲11:30am-2:30pm Mon-Fri, 5-10pm Mon-Thu, to 11pm Fri & Sat) Famous for his piercings, Food Channel TV appearances and multiple national awards, local boy Michael Symon has put Cleveland on the foodie map with Lola. The lower-priced lunch dishes are the most fun; say, coconut-and-lime-tinged scallop ceviche, or the show-stopper – an egg-and-cheese-topped fried bologna sandwich.

OHIO CITY & TREMONT

Ohio City and Tremont, which straddle I-90 south of downtown, are areas that have lots of new establishments popping up. Buzzworthy, sustainably focused **Crop Bistro** (www.cropbistro.com) should open by the West Side Market by the time you're reading this.

West Side Market Cafe CAFE $
(☎216-579-6800; 1995 W 25th St; mains $6-9; ⏲7am-4pm Mon-Thu, to 6pm Fri & Sat, 9am-3pm Sun) This is a smart stop if you're craving well-made breakfast and lunch fare, and cheap fish and chicken mains. The cafe is inside West Side Market itself, which overflows with prepared foods that are handy for picnicking or road-tripping.

Sokolowski's University Inn EASTERN EUROPEAN $$
(☎216-771-9236; www.sokolowskis.com; 1201 University Rd; mains $7-15; ⏲11am-3pm Mon-Fri, 5-9pm Fri, 4-9pm Sat) The portions are huge, enough to fuel the hungriest steelworker. It's cafeteria style, so grab a tray and fill it with plump pierogi, cabbage rolls and other rib-sticking Polish fare.

Lolita AMERICAN $$
(☎216-771-5652; www.lolitarestaurant.com; 900 Literary Rd; mains $9-17; ⏲5-11pm Tue-Thu, to 1am Fri & Sat, 4-9pm Sun) It's the lighter-fare sister of Lola (downtown). Munch on Iowa prosciutto, mussels and Neapolitan-style pizzas with cold local beer. Five-dollar food specials rock happy hour (5pm to 6:30pm, and after 9:30pm or so).

South Side AMERICAN $$
(☎216-937-2288; 2207 W 11 St; sandwiches $9-11, mains $14-19; ⊙11am-2am; 📶) Local athletes, blue-collar electricians and everyone in between pile into this sleek Tremont establishment to drink at the winding granite bar. They come for the late-night food too, like the grouper sandwich, veggie Reuben and Kobe burger.

LITTLE ITALY & COVENTRY

These two neighborhoods make prime stops for refueling after hanging out in University Circle. Little Italy is closest: it's along Mayfield Rd, near Lake View Cemetery (look out for the Rte 322 sign). Alternatively, relaxed Coventry Village is a bit further east off Mayfield Rd.

Presti's Bakery BAKERY $
(www.prestisbakery.com; 12101 Mayfield Rd; items $2-6; ⊙6am-9pm Mon-Thu, to 10pm Fri & Sat, to 6pm Sun) Try Presti's for its popular sandwiches, stromboli and divine pastries.

Tommy's INTERNATIONAL $
(☎216-321-7757; www.tommyscoventry.com; 1823 Coventry Rd; mains $6-10; ⊙9am-9pm Sun-Thu, to 10pm Fri, 7:30am-10pm Sat; 🌿) Tofu, seitan and other old-school veggie dishes emerge from the kitchen, though carnivores have multiple options, too.

Drinking

The downtown action centers on the young, testosterone-fueled Warehouse District (around W 6th St), and around E 4th St's entertainment venues. Tremont is also chockablock with chic bars. Most places stay open until 2am.

Great Lakes Brewing Company BREWERY
(www.greatlakesbrewing.com; 2516 Market Ave; ⊙Mon-Sat) Great Lakes wins numerous prizes for its brewed-on-the-premises beers. Added historical bonus: Eliot Ness got into a shootout with criminals here; ask the bartender to show you the bullet holes.

Major Hoopples BAR
(1930 Columbus Rd; ⊙Mon-Sat) Look over the bar for Cleveland's best skyline view from this friendly, eclectic watering hole. They project films and sports games on the bridge abutment out back.

Johnny's Little Bar BAR
(www.johnnyscleveland.com; 614 Frankfort Ave) One of the Warehouse District's more casual, compact offerings. The hard-to-find entrance is on Frankfort Ave, a side street.

Entertainment

Gordon Square Arts District (www.gordonsquare.org) has a fun pocket of theaters, live music venues and cafes along Detroit Ave between W 56th and W 69th Sts, a few miles west of downtown.

Live Music

Check *Scene* (www.clevescene.com) and Friday's *Plain Dealer* (www.cleveland.com) for listings.

TOP CHOICE **Happy Dog** LIVE MUSIC
(www.happydogcleveland.com; 5801 Detroit Ave) Listen to scrappy bands while munching on a wienie, for which you can choose from among 50 toppings, from gourmet (black truffle) to, er, less gourmet (peanut butter and jelly); in the Gordon Sq district.

Grog Shop LIVE MUSIC
(☎216-321-5588; www.grogshop.gs; 2785 Euclid Hts Blvd) Up-and-coming rockers thrash at Coventry's long-established music house.

Beachland Ballroom LIVE MUSIC
(www.beachlandballroom.com; 15711 Waterloo Rd) Hip young bands play at this venue east of downtown.

Sports

Cleveland is a serious jock town with three modern downtown venues. Whatever you do, don't mention the name 'LeBron' (the basketball player who famously defected to Miami).

Progressive Field BASEBALL
(www.indians.com; 2401 Ontario St) The Indians (aka 'the Tribe') hit here; great sightlines make it a good park to see a game.

Quicken Loans Arena BASKETBALL
(www.nba.com/cavaliers; 1 Center Ct) The Cavaliers play basketball at 'the Q,' which doubles as an entertainment venue.

Cleveland Browns Stadium FOOTBALL
(www.clevelandbrowns.com; 1085 W 3rd St) The NFL's Browns pass the football and score touchdowns on the lakefront.

Performing Arts

Severance Hall CLASSICAL MUSIC
(☎216-231-1111; www.clevelandorchestra.com; 11001 Euclid Ave) The acclaimed Cleveland Symphony Orchestra holds its season (August

to May) at Severance Hall, located by the University Circle museums. The orchestra's summer home is Blossom Music Center in Cuyahoga Valley National Park, about 22 miles south.

Playhouse Square Center THEATER
(☎216-771-4444; www.playhousesquare.com; 1501 Euclid Ave) This elegant center hosts theater, opera and ballet. Check the website for $10 'Smart Seats.'

Information

Emergency & Medical Services

MetroHealth Medical Center (☎216-778-7800; 2500 MetroHealth Dr)

Internet Access

Many of Cleveland's public places have free wi-fi, such as Tower City and University Circle.

Media

Gay People's Chronicle (www.gaypeopleschronicle.com) Free weekly publication with entertainment listings.

Plain Dealer (www.cleveland.com) The city's daily newspaper.

Scene (www.clevescene.com) A weekly entertainment paper.

Tourist Information

Cleveland Convention & Visitors Bureau (www.positivelycleveland.com) Official website; the Twitter feed lists daily deals.

Visitor center (☎216-875-6680; 100 Public Sq, Suite 100; ⏲9am-5pm Mon-Fri, plus 10am-3pm Sat Jun-Aug) Staffed desk, coupons and computers to make reservations; in the Higbee Building.

Websites

Cool Cleveland (www.coolcleveland.com) Hip arts and cultural happenings.

Ohio City (www.ohiocity.org) Eats and drinks in the neighborhood.

Tremont (www.restoretremont.com) Eats, drinks and gallery hops in the neighborhood.

Getting There & Around

Eleven miles southwest of downtown, **Cleveland Hopkins International Airport** (CLE; www.clevelandairport.com; 5300 Riverside Dr) is linked by the Red Line train ($2.25). A cab to downtown costs about $30.

From downtown, **Greyhound** (☎216-781-0520; 1465 Chester Ave) offers frequent departures to Chicago (7½ hours) and New York City (13 hours). **Megabus** (www.megabus.com/us) also goes to Chicago, often for lower fares; check the website for the departure point.

WORTH A TRIP

ICE WINE VINEYARDS

Canada may grab all the glory for its ice wines, but Ohio has some chilled grapes up its sleeve, too. Tour and try sips at **Debonne Vineyards** (☎440-466-3485; www.debonne.com; 7743 Doty Rd; 8-sample tasting $6; ⏲noon-6pm Mon & Tue, to 11pm Wed & Fri, to 8pm Thu & Sat, 1-6pm Sun) in Madison, 40 miles northeast of Cleveland, which reaps praise for its sweet concoctions with hints of melon and apricot. Several other ice wine makers are also in the area, thanks to the local climate of long autumns, followed by winters cold enough to freeze grapes but not so cold that the vines die. Check the **Wine Growers of the Grand River Valley** (www.wggrv.com) for thirst-quenching locations.

Amtrak (☎216-696-5115; 200 Cleveland Memorial Shoreway) runs once daily to Chicago (seven hours) and New York City (13 hours).

The **Regional Transit Authority** (RTA; www.riderta.com; fare $2.25) operates the Red Line train that goes to both the airport and Ohio City. It also runs the HealthLine bus that motors along Euclid Ave from downtown to University Circle's museums. Day passes are $5.

For cab service, try phoning **Americab** (☎216-429-1111).

Around Cleveland

Sixty miles south of Cleveland, **Canton** is the birthplace of the NFL and home to the **Pro Football Hall of Fame** (☎330-456-8207; www.profootballhof.com; 2121 George Halas Dr; adult/child $21/15; ⏲9am-8pm, to 5pm Sep-May), a shrine for the gridiron-obsessed. Look for the football-shaped tower off I-77.

West of Cleveland, attractive **Oberlin** is an old-fashioned college town, with noteworthy architecture by Cass Gilbert, Frank Lloyd Wright and Robert Venturi. Further west, just south of I-90, the tiny town of **Milan** is the birthplace of Thomas Edison. His home, restored to its 1847 likeness, is now a small **museum** (☎419-499-2135; www.tomedison.org; 9 Edison Dr; adult/child $7/4; ⏲10am-5pm Tue-Sat, 1-5pm Sun, reduced hrs winter, closed Jan) outlining his inventions, like the light bulb and phonograph.

Still further west, on US 20 and surrounded by farmland, is **Clyde**, which bills itself as the USA's most famous small town. It got that way when native son Sherwood Anderson published *Winesburg, Ohio* in 1919. It didn't take long for the unimpressed residents to figure out where the fictitious town really was. Stop at the **Clyde Museum** (☎419-547-7946; www.clydeheritageleague.org; 124 W Buckeye St; admission free; ⏰1-4pm Thu Apr-Sep & by appointment) in the old church for Anderson tidbits or at the library, a few doors down.

Erie Lakeshore & Islands

In summer this good-time resort area is one of the busiest – and most expensive – places in Ohio. The season lasts from mid-May to mid-September, and then just about everything shuts down. Make sure you prebook your accommodations.

Sandusky, long a port, now serves as the jump-off point to the Erie Islands and a mighty group of roller coasters (see boxed text, p547). The **visitor center** (☎419-625-2984; www.shoresandislands.com; 4424 Milan Rd; ⏰8am-8pm Mon-Fri, 9am-6pm Sat, 9am-3pm Sun) provides lodging and ferry information. Loads of chain motels line the highways heading into town.

BASS ISLANDS

In the war of 1812's Battle of Lake Erie, Admiral Perry met the enemy English fleet near **South Bass Island**. His victory ensured that all the lands south of the Great Lakes became US, not Canadian, territory. But history is all but forgotten on a summer weekend in packed Put In Bay, the island's main town and a party place full of boaters, restaurants and shops. Move beyond it, and you'll find a winery and opportunities for camping, fishing, kayaking and swimming.

A singular attraction is the 352ft Doric column known as **Perry's Victory and International Peace Memorial** (www.nps.gov/pevi; admission $3; ⏰10am-7pm). Climb to the observation deck for views of the battle site and, on a good day, Canada.

The **Chamber of Commerce** (☎419-285-2832; www.visitputinbay.com; 148 Delaware Ave; ⏰10am-4pm Mon-Fri, to 5pm Sat & Sun) has information on activities and lodging. **Ashley's Island House** (☎419-285-2844; www.ashleysislandhouse.com; 557 Catawba Ave; r with shared/private bath from $70/100; ❄📶) is a 13-room B&B, where naval officers stayed in the late 1800s. The **Beer Barrel Saloon** (www.beerbarrelpib.com; Delaware Ave; ⏰11am-1am) has plenty of space for imbibing – its bar is 406ft long.

Cabs and tour buses serve the island, though cycling is a fine way to get around. Two ferry companies make the 20-minute trip regularly from the mainland. **Jet Express** (☎800-245-1538; www.jet-express.com) runs passenger-only boats direct to Put In Bay from Port Clinton (one way adult/child $14/2) almost hourly. It also departs from Sandusky ($18/5), stopping at Kelleys Island en route. Leave your car in the lot (per day $10) at either dock. **Miller Boatline** (☎800-500-2421; www.millerferry.com) operates a vehicle ferry that is the cheapest option, departing from further-flung Catawba (one way adult/child $6.50/1.50, car $15) every 30 minutes. It also cruises to **Middle Bass Island**, a good day trip from South Bass, offering nature and quiet.

KELLEYS ISLAND

Peaceful and green, Kelleys Island is a popular weekend escape, especially for families. It has pretty 19th-century buildings, Native

DON'T MISS

CEDAR POINT'S RAGING ROLLER COASTERS

Cedar Point Amusement Park (☎419-627-2350; www.cedarpoint.com; adult/child $47/21; ⏰10am-10pm, closed Nov–mid-May) regularly wins the 'world's best amusement park' award, chosen each year by the public, which goes wild for the venue's 17 adrenaline-pumping roller coasters. Stomach droppers include the Top Thrill Dragster, one of the globe's tallest and fastest rides. It climbs 420ft into the air before plunging and whipping around at 120mph. Meanwhile, the Maverick drops at a 95-degree angle (that's steeper than straight down) and blasts over eight hills. If those and the 15 other coasters aren't enough to keep you occupied, the surrounding area has a nice beach, a water park and a slew of old-fashioned, cotton-candy-fueled attractions. It's about 6 miles from Sandusky. Parking costs $10.

American pictographs, a good beach and glacial grooves raked through its landscape. Even its old limestone quarries are scenic.

The **Chamber of Commerce** (☎419-746-2360; www.kelleysislandchamber.com; Seaway Marina Bldg; ⏲9:30am-4pm), by the ferry dock, has information on accommodations and activities – hiking, camping, kayaking and fishing are popular. The Village, the island's small commercial center, has places to eat, drink, shop and rent bicycles – the recommended way to sightsee.

Kelleys Island Ferry (☎419-798-9763; www.kelleysislandferry.com) departs from the wee village of Marblehead (one way adult/child $9.50/6, car $15). The crossing takes about 20 minutes and leaves hourly (more frequently in summer). **Jet Express** (☎800-245-1538; www.jet-express.com) departs from Sandusky (one way adult/child $14/4, no cars) and also goes onward to Put In Bay on South Bass Island (island-hopping one way $20/6, no cars).

PELEE ISLAND

Pelee, the largest Erie island, is a ridiculously green, quiet wine-producing and bird-watching destination that belongs to Canada. **Pelee Island Transportation** (☎800-661-2220; www.ontarioferries.com) runs a ferry (one way adult/child $13.75/6.75, car $30) from Sandusky to Pelee and onward to Ontario's mainland. Check www.pelee.org for lodging and trip planning information.

Amish Country

Rural Wayne and Holmes counties are home to the USA's largest Amish community. They're only 80 miles south of Cleveland, but visiting here is like entering a pre-industrial time warp.

Descendants of conservative Dutch-Swiss religious factions who migrated to the USA during the 18th century, the Amish continue to follow the *ordnung* (way of life), in varying degrees. Many adhere to rules prohibiting the use of electricity, telephones and motorized vehicles. They wear traditional clothing, farm the land with plow and mule, and go to church in horse-drawn buggies. Others are not so strict.

Unfortunately, what would surely be a peaceful country scene is often disturbed by behemoth tour buses. Many Amish are happy to profit from this influx of outside dollars, but don't equate this with free photographic access – the Amish typically view photographs as taboo. Drive carefully as roads are narrow and curvy, and there's always the chance of pulling up on a slow-moving buggy just around the bend. Many places are closed Sunday.

Sights & Activities

Kidron, on Rte 52, makes a good starting point. A short distance south, **Berlin** is the area's tchotchke-shop-filled core, while **Millersburg** is the region's largest town, more antique-y than Amish; US 62 connects these two 'busy' spots.

To get further off the beaten path, take Rte 557 or County Rd 70, both of which twist through the countryside to wee **Charm**, about 5 miles south of Berlin.

Lehman's DEPARTMENT STORE

(www.lehmans.com; 4779 Kidron Rd, Kidron; ⏲8am-6pm Mon-Sat) Lehman's is an absolute must-see. It is the Amish community's main purveyor of modern-looking products that use no electricity, housed in a 32,000-sq-ft barn. Stroll through to ogle wind-up flashlights, wood-burning stoves and hand-cranked meat grinders.

FREE **Kidron Auction** MARKET

(www.kidronauction.com; 4885 Kidron Rd, Kidron; ⏲from 10am Thu) If it's Thursday, follow the buggy line-up down the road from Lehman's to the livestock barn. Hay gets auctioned at 10am, cows at 11am and pigs at 1pm. A flea market rings the barn for folks seeking nonmooing merchandise. Similar auctions take place in Sugarcreek (Monday and Friday), Farmerstown (Tuesday) and Mt Hope (Wednesday).

FREE **Heini's Cheese Chalet** CHEESEMAKING FACTORY

(☎800-253-6636; www.heinis.com; 6005 Hwy 77, Berlin; tours free; ⏲8:30am-5pm Mon-Sat) Heini's whips up more than 70 cheeses. Learn how Amish farmers hand-milk their cows and spring-cool (versus machine-refrigerate) the output before delivering it each day. Then grab abundant samples and peruse the kitschy 'History of Cheesemaking' mural. To see the curd-cutting in action, come before 11am weekdays (except on Wednesdays).

Hershberger's Farm & Bakery FARM

(☎330-674-6096; 5452 Hwy 557, Millersburg; ⏲bakery 8am-5pm Mon-Sat year-round, farm from 10am mid-Apr–Oct; 👪) Gorge on 25 kinds of pie, homemade ice cream cones and seasonal produce from the market inside. Pet the farmyard animals (free) and take pony rides ($3) outside.

Yoder's Amish Home FARM
(☎330-893-2541; www.yodersamishhome.com; 6050 Rte 515, Walnut Creek; tours adult/child $11/7; ⌚10am-5pm Mon-Sat mid-Apr–late Oct; 🚸) Peek into a local home and one-room schoolhouse, and take a buggy ride through a field at this Amish farm that's open to visitors.

Sleeping & Eating

Hotel Millersburg HISTORIC HOTEL **$$**
(☎330-674-1457; www.hotelmillersburg.com; 35 W Jackson St, Millersburg; r $79-149; ❄📶) Built in 1847 as a stagecoach inn, the property still provides lodging in its 26 casual rooms, which sit above a modern dining room and tavern (one of the few places to get a beer in Amish Country).

Guggisberg Swiss Inn HOTEL **$$**
(☎330-893-3600; www.guggisbergswissinn.com; 5025 Rte 557, Charm; r incl breakfast $100-150; ❄📶🚸) The 24 tidy, compact rooms are bright with quilts and light-wood furnishings. A cheesemaking facility and horseback riding stable are on the grounds, too.

Boyd & Wurthmann Restaurant AMERICAN **$**
(☎330-893-3287; Main St, Berlin; mains $5-10; ⌚5:30am-8pm Mon-Sat) Hubcap-sized pancakes, 23 pie flavors, fat sandwiches and Amish specialties such as country-fried steak draw locals and tourists alike. Cash only.

Information

Holmes County Chamber of Commerce (www.visitamishcountry.com)

Columbus

Ohio's capital city is like the blind date your mom arranges – average looking, restrained personality, but solid and affable. Better yet, she's easy on the wallet, an influence from Ohio State University's 55,000 students (the uni is the nation's second largest). A substantial gay population has taken up residence in Columbus in recent years.

Sights & Activities

German Village NEIGHBORHOOD
(www.germanvillage.com) The remarkably large, all-brick German Village, a half mile south of downtown, is a restored 19th-century neighborhood with beer halls, cobbled streets and Italianate and Queen Anne architecture.

Short North NEIGHBORHOOD
(www.shortnorth.org) Just north of downtown, the browse-worthy Short North is a redeveloped strip of High St that holds contemporary art galleries, restaurants and jazz bars.

Wexner Center for the Arts ARTS CENTER
(☎614-292-3535; www.wexarts.org; cnr 15th & N High Sts; admission $5; ⌚11am-6pm Tue, Wed & Sun, to 8pm Thu-Sat) The campus' arts center offers cutting-edge art exhibits, films and performances.

Sleeping & Eating

German Village and the Short North provide fertile grazing and guzzling grounds. The **Arena District** (www.arenadistrict.com) bursts with midrange chains and brewpubs. Around the university and along N High St from 15th Ave onward, you'll find everything from Mexican to Ethiopian to sushi.

Short North B&B B&B **$$**
(☎614-299-5050; www.columbus-bed-breakfast.com; 50 E Lincoln St; r incl breakfast $129-149; P❄📶) The seven well-maintained rooms are steps away from the eponymous neighborhood's scene.

Red Roof Inn HOTEL **$$**
(☎614-224-6539; www.redroof.com; 111 E Nationwide Blvd; r incl breakfast $85-139; P⊖❄📶) Located in the Arena District, it's not bad as far as the chain goes. Parking is $10.

Schmidt's GERMAN **$$**
(☎614-444-6808; www.schmidthaus.com; 240 E Kossuth St; mains $8-15; ⌚11am 9pm Sun & Mon, to 10pm Tue-Thu, to 11pm Fri & Sat) In German Village, shovel in Old Country staples like sausage and schnitzel, but save room for the whopping half-pound cream puffs. Oompah bands play Wednesday to Saturday.

Skillet AMERICAN **$$**
(☎614-443-2266; www.skilletruf.com; 410 E Whittier St) A teeny restaurant in German Village serving rustic, locally sourced fare.

North Market MARKET **$**
(www.northmarket.com; 59 Spruce St; ⌚9am-5pm Mon, to 7pm Tue-Fri, 8am-5pm Sat, noon-5pm Sun) Local farmers' produce and prepared foods; renowned ice cream by Jeni.

★ Entertainment

Spectator sports rule the city.

Ohio Stadium FOOTBALL
(☎800-462-8257; www.ohiostatebuckeyes.com; 411 Woody Hayes Dr) The Ohio State Buckeyes pack a rabid crowd into legendary, horseshoe-shaped Ohio Stadium for their games, held on Saturdays in the fall. Expect 102,000 extra partiers in town.

Nationwide Arena HOCKEY
(☎614-246-2000; www.bluejackets.com; 200 W Nationwide Blvd) The pro Columbus Blue Jackets slap the puck at downtown's big arena.

Crew Stadium SOCCER
(☎614-447-2739; www.thecrew.com) The popular Columbus Crew pro soccer team kicks north off I-71 and 17th Ave, from March to October.

ℹ Information

Media

Alive (www.columbusalive.com) Free weekly entertainment newspaper.

Columbus Dispatch (www.dispatch.com) The daily newspaper.

Outlook (www.outlookmedia.com) Monthly gay and lesbian publication.

Tourist Information

Columbus Convention & Visitors Bureau (☎866-397-2657; www.experiencecolumbus.com)

ℹ Getting There & Away

The **Port Columbus Airport** (CMH; www.port-columbus.com) is 10 miles east of town. A cab to downtown costs about $25.

Greyhound (☎614-221-4642; www.greyhound.com; 111 E Town St) buses run at least six times daily to Cincinnati (two hours) and Cleveland (2½ hours). Often cheaper, **Megabus** (www.megabus.com/us) runs a couple times daily to Cincinnati and Chicago. Check the website for locations.

Athens & Southeastern Ohio

Ohio's southeastern corner cradles most of its forested areas, as well as the rolling foothills of the Appalachian Mountains and scattered farms.

Around Lancaster, southeast of Columbus, the hills lead gently into **Hocking County**, a region of streams and waterfalls, sandstone cliffs and cavelike formations. It's splendid to explore in any season, with miles of trails for hiking and rivers for canoeing, as well as abundant campgrounds and cabins at **Hocking Hills State Park** (☎740-385-6165; www.hockinghills.com; 20160 Hwy 664; campsites/cottages from $24/130). **Old Man's Cave** is a scenic winner for hiking. **Hocking Valley Canoe Livery** (☎740-385-8685; www.hockinghillscanoeing.com; 31251 Chieftain Dr; 2hr tours $42; ⏲Apr-Oct) lets you paddle by moonlight and tiki torch from nearby Logan. **Earth-Water-Rock: Outdoor Adventures** (☎740-664-5220; www.ewroutdoors.com; half-day tour $85-110) provides thrills with guided rock climbing and rappelling trips; beginners are welcome.

Athens (www.athensohio.com) makes a lovely base for seeing the region. Situated where US 50 crosses US 33, it's set among wooded hills and built around the Ohio University campus (which comprises half the town). Student cafes and pubs line Court St, Athens' main road. The **Village Bakery & Cafe** (www.dellazona.com; 268 E State St; mains $4-8; ⏲7:30am-8pm Tue-Sat, 9am-2pm Sun) uses organic veggies, grass-fed meat and farmstead cheeses in its pizzas, soups and sandwiches.

The area south of Columbus was a center for the fascinating ancient Hopewell people, who left behind huge geometric earthworks and burial mounds from around 200 BC to AD 600. For a fine introduction visit the **Hopewell Culture National Historical Park** (☎740-774-1126; www.nps.gov/hocu; Hwy 104 north of I-35; admission free; ⏲8:30am-6pm Jun-Aug, to 4:30pm Sep-May), 3 miles north of Chillicothe. Stop in the visitor center, and then wander about the variously shaped ceremonial mounds spread over 13-acre **Mound City**, a mysterious town of the dead. **Serpent Mound** (☎937-587-2796; www.ohiohistory.org; 3850 Hwy 73; per vehicle $7; ⏲10am-5pm Fri-Sun Jun-Aug), southwest of Chillicothe and 4 miles northwest of Locust Grove, is perhaps the most captivating site of all. The giant, uncoiling snake stretches over a quarter of a mile and is the largest effigy mound in the USA.

Dayton & Yellow Springs

Dayton has the aviation sights, but little Yellow Springs (18 miles northeast on US 68) has much more to offer in terms of accommodations and places to eat.

Sights & Activities

FREE National Museum of the US Air Force MUSEUM
(937-255-3286; www.nationalmuseum.af.mil; 1100 Spaatz St; 9am-5pm) Located at the Wright-Patterson Air Force Base, 6 miles northeast of Dayton, the museum has everything from a Wright Brothers exhibit and Sopwith Camel (WWI biplane) to a Stealth bomber. Don't miss the annex with its collection of presidential planes; a free shuttle bus takes you over to the hangar (which you'll need a passport or driver's license to enter). Expect your visit to take three or more hours.

Carillon Historical Park HISTORIC SITE
(937-293-2841; www.daytonhistory.org; 1000 Carillon Blvd; adult/child $8/5; 9:30am-5pm Mon-Sat, noon-5pm Sun) The many heritage attractions include the 1905 Wright Flyer III biplane and a replica of the Wright workshop.

FREE Dayton Aviation Heritage National Historical Park HISTORIC SITE
(937-225-7705; www.nps.gov/daav; 16 S Williams St; 8:30am-5pm) Includes the Wright Cycle Company Complex, where the brothers developed bikes and aviation ideas.

Sleeping & Eating

The following listings are located in Yellow Springs, a top-notch place to experience down-home Ohio.

Morgan House B&B $$
(937-767-1761; www.arthurmorganhouse.com; 120 W Limestone St; r incl breakfast $90-125;) The six comfy rooms have super-soft linens and private baths. Breakfasts are organic, with free-trade African coffee.

TOP CHOICE Young's Jersey Dairy AMERICAN $$
(937-325-0629; www.youngsdairy.com; 6880 Springfield-Xenia Rd) Young's is a working dairy farm with two restaurants: the **Golden Jersey Inn** (mains $9-15; lunch & dinner Mon-Fri, plus breakfast Sat & Sun), serving dishes like buttermilk chicken; and the **Dairy Store** (sandwiches $3.50-6.50; 7am-11pm Sun-Thu, to midnight Fri & Sat), serving sandwiches, dreamy ice cream and Ohio's best milk shakes. There's also minigolf, batting cages and opportunities to watch the cows get milked.

Winds Cafe AMERICAN $$$
(937-767-1144; www.windscafe.com; 215 Xenia Ave; mains $18-25; 11:30am-2pm & 5-10pm Tue-Sat, 10am-3pm Sun) A hippie co-op 30 years ago, the Winds has grown up to become a sophisticated foodie favorite plating seasonal dishes like fig-sauced asparagus crepes and rhubarb halibut.

Cincinnati

Cincinnati splashes up the Ohio River's banks. Its prettiness surprises, as do its haunted music-club mansions, its twisting streets to hilltop Mt Adams, and the locals' unashamed ardor for a five-way (see boxed text, p553). Amid all that action, don't forget to catch a baseball game, stroll the riverfront and gape at some serious neon.

Sights & Activities

Many attractions are closed on Monday.

DOWNTOWN

National Underground Railroad Freedom Center MUSEUM
(513-333-7500; www.freedomcenter.org; 50 E Freedom Way; adult/child $12/8; 11am-5pm Tue-Sat) Cincinnati was a prominent stop on the Underground Railroad and a center for abolitionist activities led by residents, such as Harriet Beecher Stowe. The Freedom Center tells their stories. Exhibits show how slaves escaped to the north, and the ways in which slavery still exists today. Download the free iPhone app for extra insight while touring.

Findlay Market MARKET
(www.findlaymarket.org; 1801 Race St; 9am-6pm Tue-Fri, 8am-6pm Sat, 10am-4pm Sun) Indoor-outdoor Findlay Market greens the somewhat blighted area at downtown's northern edge. It's a good stop for fresh produce, meats, cheeses and baked goods. The Belgian waffle guy will wow your taste buds.

Rosenthal Center for Contemporary Arts MUSEUM
(513-721-0390; www.contemporaryartscenter.org; 44 E 6th St; adult/child $7.50/4.50, admission free Mon evening; 10am-9pm Mon, 10am-6pm Wed-Fri, 11am-6pm Sat & Sun) This center displays modern art in an avant-garde building designed by Iraqi architect Zaha Hadid. The structure and its artworks are a pretty big deal for traditionalist Cincy.

DON'T MISS

AMERICAN SIGN MUSEUM

The **American Sign Museum** (☎513-258-4020; www.signmuseum.net; 2515 Essex Pl; adult/child $10/free; ⏰10am-4pm Sat or by appointment) is a bit out of the way and challenging to find, but the cache of flashing, lightbulb-studded beacons offers a mighty reward. Passionate proprietor Tod Swormstedt likely will show you around the warehouse, where you'll burn your retinas staring at vintage neon drive-in signs, hulking genies and the Frisch's Big Boy, among many other nostalgic novelties. It's a one-of-a-kind horde for people who treasure the past. Located in the Essex building of artists' studios, 3 miles north of downtown, just west of I-71.

Fountain Square PLAZA
(www.myfountainsquare.com; cnr 5th & Vine Sts; 📶) Fountain Square is the city's centerpiece, a public space with a seasonal ice rink, chess tables, concerts, a Reds ticket kiosk and the fancy old 'Spirit of the Waters' fountain.

An amble along the riverfront is well worthwhile, taking you past several parks and bridges:

Roebling Suspension Bridge BRIDGE
(www.roeblingbridge.org) The elegant 1876 spanner was a forerunner of John Roebling's famous Brooklyn Bridge in New York. It's cool to walk across while passing cars make it 'sing' around you. It links to Covington, Kentucky (see p552).

Purple People Bridge BRIDGE
(www.purplepeoplebridge.com) This pedestrian-only bridge provides a unique crossing from Sawyer Point (a nifty park dotted by whimsical monuments and flying pigs) to Newport, Kentucky (see p552).

COVINGTON & NEWPORT

Covington and Newport, Kentucky, are sort of suburbs of Cincinnati, just over the river from downtown. Newport is to the east and known for its massive **Newport on the Levee** (www.newportonthelevee.com) restaurant and shopping complex. Covington lies to the west and has the **MainStrasse** (www.mainstrasse.org) quarter, filled with funky restaurants and bars in the neighborhood's 19th-century brick row houses. Antebellum mansions fringe Riverside Dr, and old paddle-wheel boats tie up along the water's edge.

Newport Aquarium AQUARIUM
(☎859-491-3467; www.newportaquarium.com; One Aquarium Way; adult/child $22/15; ⏰9am-7pm Jun-Aug, 10am-6pm Sep-May) Meet parading penguins, Sweet Pea the shark ray and lots of other razor-toothed fish at Newport's large, well-regarded facility.

MT ADAMS

It might be a bit of a stretch to compare Mt Adams, immediately east of downtown, to Paris' Montmartre, but this hilly 19th-century enclave of narrow, twisting streets, Victorian town houses, galleries, bars and restaurants is certainly a pleasurable surprise. Most visitors ascend for a quick look around and a drink.

To get here, follow 7th St east of downtown to Gilbert Ave, bear northwest to Elsinore Ave, and head up the hill to reach the lakes, paths and cultural offerings in Eden Park. The yard at nearby **Immacula Church** (30 Guido St) is worth a stop for its killer views over the city.

FREE **Cincinnati Art Museum** MUSEUM
(☎513-721-5204; www.cincinnatiartmuseum.org; 953 Eden Park Dr; ⏰11am-5pm Tue-Sun) The collection spans 6000 years, with an emphasis on ancient Middle Eastern art and European old masters, plus a wing devoted to local works. Parking costs $4.

FREE **Krohn Conservatory** GARDENS
(☎513-421-4086; www.cincinnatiparks.com/krohn-conservatory; 1501 Eden Park Dr; ⏰10am-5pm Tue-Sun) The vast greenhouse sprouts a rainforest, desert flora and glorious seasonal flower shows (separate admission $3 to $6).

WEST END

Cincinnati Museum Center MUSEUM
(☎513-287-7000; www.cincymuseum.org; 1301 Western Ave; adult/child $12.50/8.50; ⏰10am-5pm Mon-Sat, 11am-6pm Sun; 👪) Two miles northwest of downtown, this museum complex occupies the 1933 Union Terminal, an art deco jewel still used by Amtrak. The interior has fantastic murals made of Rookwood tiles. The Museum of Natural History & Science is mostly geared to kids, but it does have a limestone cave with real bats inside. A history museum, children's museum and Omnimax theater round out the offerings; the admission fee provides entry to all. Parking costs $6.

Tours

Architreks WALKING
(☎513-421-4469; www.cincinnati-walks.org; tours adult/child $15/5; ⊙May-Oct) Guided walking tours of various neighborhoods, including downtown, Mt Adams and Northside. Departure points and days/times vary.

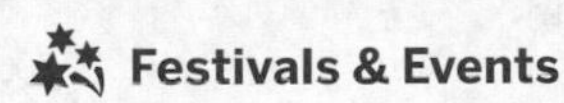

Festivals & Events

Oktoberfest FOOD
(www.oktoberfestzinzinnati.com; ⊙mid-Sep) German beer, brats and mania.

Midpoint Music Festival MUSIC
(www.mpmf.com; ⊙late Sep) Indie bands flood various venues; three-day passes cost $49.

Sleeping

Hotel tax is cheaper on the Kentucky side at 11.3%, versus the 17% charged in Cincinnati. Tax is not included in the following prices.

Several midrange chain options line up on the Kentucky riverfront. You'll save money (less tax, free parking), but be prepared either to walk a few miles or take a short bus ride to reach downtown Cincy.

The **Greater Cincinnati B&B Network** (www.cincinnatibb.com) has links to Kentucky-side properties.

Cincinnatian Hotel HOTEL $$$
(☎513-381-3000; www.cincinnatianhotel.com; 601 Vine St; r $160-260; P⊖❄☰) The Cincinnatian is in a magnificent 1882 Victorian building; the spacious rooms have fluffy towels, silk-soft sheets and huge round bathtubs. Rates drop to the lower end of the price range during weekends. Parking costs $28.

Best Western Mariemont Inn HOTEL $$
(☎513-271-2100; www.mariemontinn.com; 6880 Wooster Pike; r $150-209; P⊖❄☰) If you're looking for something unusual and out of the rat race, try this Tudor-style lodge with massive beamed ceilings and a fireplace in every room. It sits on the town square in a quiet neighborhood 10 miles northeast of downtown.

Residence Inn Cincinnati Downtown HOTEL $$$
(☎513-651-1234; www.marriott.com; 506 E 4th St; r incl breakfast $199-299; P⊖❄@☰) Welcome to Cincy's first new downtown hotel in 30 years. The glistening rooms are suites with full kitchens. Parking costs $20.

Holiday Inn Express HOTEL $$
(☎859-957-2320; www.hiexpress.com; 109 Landmark Dr; r incl breakfast $125-180; P❄@☰≋) It's a good pick among the riverfront chains; located about three-quarters of a mile east of Newport on the Levee.

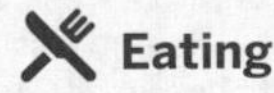

Eating

In addition to downtown, dining options concentrate along the Kentucky riverfront and in the Northside neighborhood (north of where I-74 and I-75 intersect, 5 miles north of downtown).

TOP CHOICE **Terry's Turf Club** BURGERS $$
(☎513-533-4222; 4618 Eastern Ave; mains $8-15; ⊙4pm-midnight Mon-Wed, from 11am Thu, 11am-2:30am Fri & Sat, noon-10pm Sun) Burger aficionados practically pee in their pants waiting for Terry's fat patties. The wine-with-wild-mushroom sauce is the epic topper, though other concoctions (rosemary garlic, wasabi red curry ginger) will blow your mind, too. And fear not, vegetarians: the mushroom burger gets plaudits. Terry's eccentricity reflects in his decor, with enough neon and cra-zee signs to light up Vegas. Located 7 miles east of downtown via Columbia Pkwy.

Hathaway's DINER $
(☎513-621-1332; Carew Tower, 441 Vine St; mains $5-8; ⊙6:30am-4pm Mon-Fri, 8am-3pm Sat) Hathaway's hasn't changed its retro dinette

> **DON'T MISS**
>
> **CHILI FIVE-WAY**
>
> Don't worry – you can keep your clothes on for this experience, though you may want to loosen your belt. A 'five-way' in Cincinnati has to do with chili, which is a local specialty. It comprises meat sauce (spiced with chocolate and cinnamon) ladled over spaghetti and beans, then garnished with cheese and onions. Although you can get it three-way (minus onions and beans) or four-way (minus onions *or* beans), you should go the whole way – after all, life's an adventure. **Skyline Chili** (www.skylinechili.com; 643 Vine St; items $3.50-7.50; ⊙10:30am-8pm Mon-Fri, 11am-4pm Sat) has a cultlike following devoted to its version. There are outlets throughout town; this one is downtown near Fountain Sq.

tables, or apron-wearing waitresses, since it started feeding hungry businesspeople 30-plus years ago. Try the goetta (pork, oats, onions and herbs) for breakfast – it's a Cincy specialty. The milk shakes will please sweet tooths.

Honey AMERICAN **$$**
(513-541-4300; www.honeynorthside.com; 4034 Hamilton Ave; mains $15-23; 5-9pm Tue-Thu, to 10pm Fri & Sat, 11am-2pm Sun;) Seasonal comfort food – maybe Creole meatloaf or sweet pea ravioli – fills the plates on Honey's low-lit, sturdy wood tables. Brunch is a fan favorite, offering a special gift to herbivores: vegan goetta.

Otto's CAFE **$$$**
(859-491-6678; www.ottosonmain.com; 521 Main St; sandwiches $8-11, mains $19-23; 11am-3pm Mon, to 10pm Tue-Sat, 10am-9pm Sun) Fork into 'hot brown' (a local meat-and-cheese specialty) and thick-cut sandwiches for lunch, or shrimp and grits with wine for dinner at this Covington bistro.

Graeter's Ice Cream ICE CREAM **$**
(www.graeters.com; 511 Walnut St; scoops $2.50-5; 6:30am-9pm Mon-Fri, 7am-9pm Sat, 11am-7pm Sun) It's a local delicacy, with scoop shops around the city. The flavors that mix in the gargantuan, chunky chocolate chips top the list.

Drinking

Both Mt Adams and Northside are busy nightspots.

Blind Lemon BAR
(www.theblindlemon.com; 936 Hatch St) Head down the passageway to enter this atmospheric old speakeasy in Mt Adams. It has an outdoor courtyard in summer, with a fire pit added in winter, and there's live music nightly.

Motr Pub BAR
(www.motrpub.com; 1345 Main St) Located in the on again, off again – currently on again – gritty Over-the-Rhine neighborhood on downtown's northern edge, Motr lets arty types congregate around their Hudepohls (local beer) and rockumentary movie nights.

Comet BAR
(www.cometbar.com; 4579 Hamilton Ave;) The casual Comet, in Northside, has the city's best jukebox and bar food; try the burrito.

City View Tavern BAR
(www.cityviewtavern.com; 403 Oregon St) From atop Mt Adams, the city sparkles out in front of you at this unassuming boozer.

Entertainment

Scope for free publications like *CityBeat* for current listings.

Sports

Great American Ballpark BASEBALL
(513-765-7000; www.cincinnatireds.com; 100 Main St) Home to the Reds – pro baseball's first team – Cincy is a great place to catch a game thanks to its bells-and-whistles riverside ballpark.

Paul Brown Stadium FOOTBALL
(513-621-3550; www.bengals.com; 1 Paul Brown Stadium) The Bengals pro football team scrimmages a few blocks west of the ballpark.

Live Music

Southgate House LIVE MUSIC
(859-431-2201; www.southgatehouse.com; 24 E 3rd St) Big and small, touring and local bands alike play in this 1814 haunted mansion in Newport, which also happens to be the birthplace of the tommy gun.

Northside Tavern LIVE MUSIC
(513-542-3603; www.northside-tavern.com; 4163 Hamilton Ave) Local bands plug in their amps here, and it's always free.

Performing Arts

Music Hall CLASSICAL MUSIC
(513-721-8222; www.cincinnatiarts.org; 1241 Elm St) The acoustically pristine Music Hall is where the symphony orchestra, pops orchestra, opera and ballet hold their seasons. This is not the best neighborhood, so be cautious and park nearby.

Aronoff Center THEATER
(513-621-2787; www.cincinnatiarts.org; 650 Walnut St) The mod Aronoff hosts touring shows.

Information

Media

Cincinnati Enquirer (www.cincinnati.com) Daily newspaper.

CityBeat (www.citybeat.com) Free alternative weekly paper with good entertainment listings.

Rainbow Cincinnati (www.gaycincinnati.com) GLBT news and business listings.

Tourist Information

Cincinnati USA Regional Tourism Network (☎800-344-3445; www.cincinnatiusa.com) Call or go online for a visitor's guide.

Getting There & Around

The **Cincinnati/Northern Kentucky International Airport** (CVG; www.cvgairport.com) is actually in Kentucky, 13 miles south. To get downtown, take the TANK bus ($1.75) from near Terminal 3; a cab costs about $30.

Greyhound (☎513-352-6012; www.greyhound.com; 1005 Gilbert Ave) buses travel daily to Indianapolis (2½ hours) and Columbus (two hours). Often cheaper and quicker, **Megabus** (www.megabus.com/us) travels the same routes, and goes to Chicago (six hours). It departs from downtown Cincy at 4th and Race Sts.

Amtrak (☎513-651-3337; www.amtrak.com) choo-choos into **Union Terminal** (1301 Western Ave) thrice weekly en route to Chicago (9½ hours) and Washington, DC (14½ hours), departing in the middle of the night.

Metro (www.go-metro.com; fare $1.75) runs the local buses and links with the **Transit Authority of Northern Kentucky** (TANK; www.tankbus.org; fare $1-1.75).

MICHIGAN

More, more, more – Michigan is the Midwest state that cranks it up. It sports more beaches than the Atlantic seaboard. More than half the state is covered by forests. And more cherries and berries get shoveled into pies here than anywhere else in the USA. Plus its gritty city Detroit is the Midwest's rawest of all – and we mean that in a good way. Of course, there's more unemployment in Michigan than any other state, but we digress…

Michigan occupies prime real estate, surrounded by four of the five Great Lakes – Superior, Michigan, Huron and Erie. Islands freckle its coast – Mackinac, Beaver and Isle Royale – and make top touring destinations. Surfing beaches, colored sandstone cliffs and trekkable sand dunes also woo visitors.

The state consists of two parts split by water: the larger Lower Peninsula, shaped like a mitten; and the smaller, lightly populated Upper Peninsula, shaped like a slipper. They are linked by the gasp-worthy Mackinac Bridge, which spans the Straits of Mackinac (pronounced *mac*-in-aw).

MICHIGAN FACTS

» **Nicknames** Great Lakes State, Wolverine State

» **Population** 10 million

» **Area** 96,720 sq miles

» **Capital city** Lansing (population 114,300)

» **Other cities** Detroit (population 871,100)

» **Sales tax** 6%

» **Birthplace of** industrialist Henry Ford (1863–1947), filmmaker Francis Ford Coppola (b 1939), musician Stevie Wonder (b 1950), singer Madonna (b 1958), Google co-founder Larry Page (b 1973)

» **Home of** auto assembly plants, freshwater beaches

» **Politics** leans Democratic

» **Famous for** cars, Cornflakes, tart cherries, Motown music

» **State reptile** painted turtle

» **Driving distances** Detroit to Traverse City 255 miles, Detroit to Cleveland 168 miles

Information

Michigan Highway Conditions (☎800-381-8477; www.michigan.gov/mdot)

Michigan State Park Information (☎800-447-2757; www.michigan.gov/stateparks) Park entry requires a vehicle permit (per day/year $8/29). Campsites cost $16 to $33; reservations accepted (www.midnrreservations.com; fee $8). Some parks have wi-fi.

Travel Michigan (☎800-644-2489; www.michigan.org)

Detroit

Tell any American that you're planning to visit Detroit, and then watch their eyebrows shoot up quizzically. They'll ask 'Why?' and warn you about the off-the-chart homicide rates, boarded-up buildings with trash swirling at their bases, and whoppingly high foreclosure rates where homes sell for $1. 'Detroit's a crap-hole. You'll get killed there.'

While the aforementioned attributes are true, and although the city does waft a sort of bombed-out, apocalyptic vibe, it's these same qualities that fuel a raw urban energy you won't find anywhere else. Artists, entrepreneurs and young people are moving in, and a DIY spirit pervades. They're converting

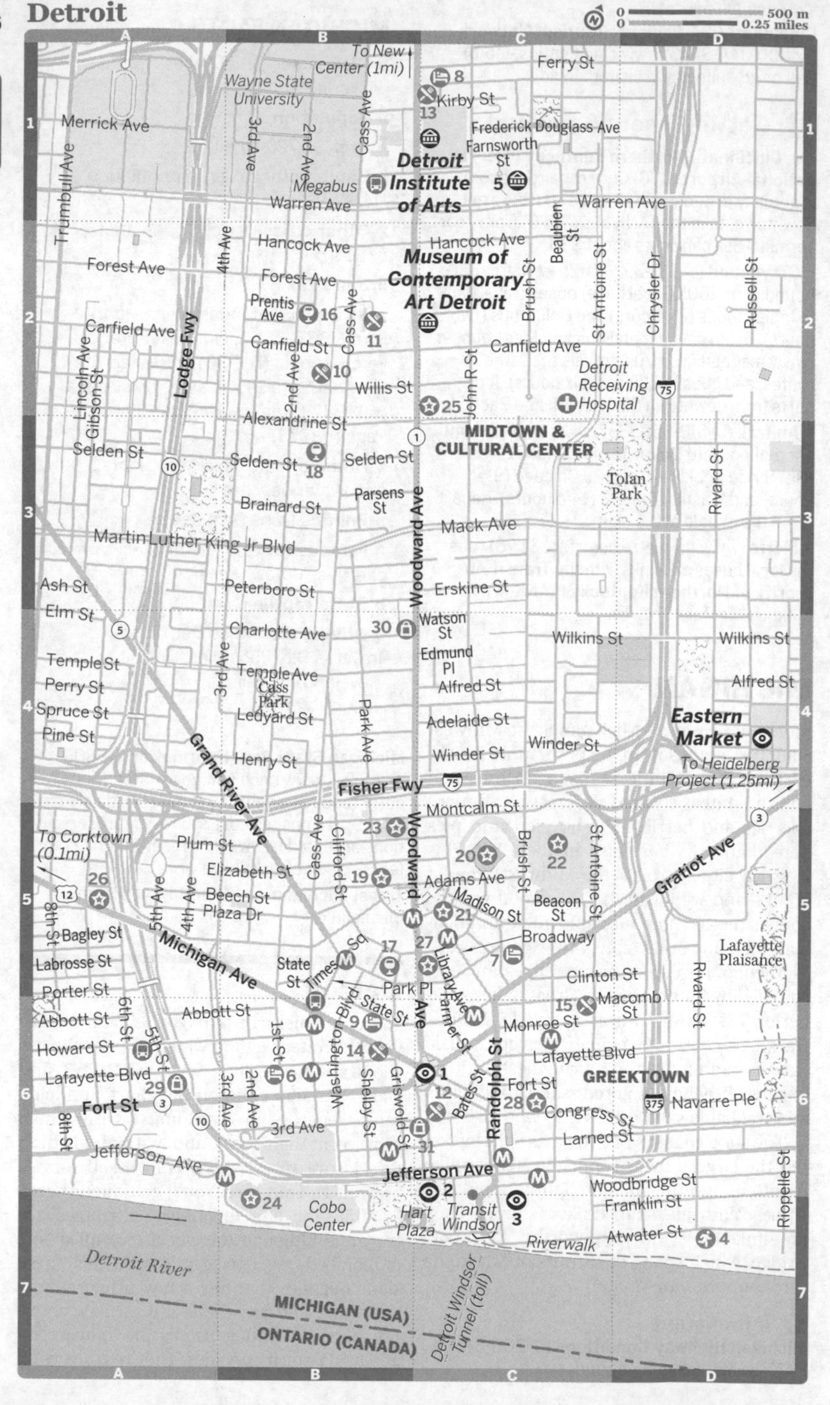

Detroit Institute of Arts
Museum of Contemporary Art Detroit
MIDTOWN & CULTURAL CENTER
Eastern Market
GREEKTOWN
Wayne State University
Detroit Receiving Hospital
Tolan Park
Cass Park
Lafayette Plaisance
Cobo Center
Hart Plaza
Transit Windsor
Detroit River
MICHIGAN (USA)
ONTARIO (CANADA)
Detroit Windsor Tunnel (toll)
To New Center (1mi)
To Corktown (0.1mi)
To Heidelberg Project (1.25mi)
Megabus
Woodward Ave
Lodge Fwy
Fisher Fwy
Grand River Ave
Michigan Ave
Gratiot Ave
Jefferson Ave
Riverwalk

Detroit

Top Sights
Detroit Institute of Arts ... C1
Eastern Market ... D4
Museum of Contemporary Art Detroit ... C2

Sights
1 Campus Martius ... C6
2 Hart Plaza ... C6
3 Renaissance Center ... C7
4 Wright Museum of African American History ... C1

Activities, Courses & Tours
5 Wheelhouse Bikes ... D7

Sleeping
6 Ft Shelby Doubletree Hotel ... B6
7 Hilton Garden Inn ... C5
8 Inn on Ferry Street ... C1
9 Westin Book Cadillac ... B6

Eating
10 Avalon International Breads ... B2
11 Cass Cafe ... B2
12 Foran's Grand Trunk Pub ... C6
13 Good Girls Go to Paris Crepes ... C1
14 Lafayette Coney Island ... B6
15 Laikon Cafe ... C6

Drinking
16 Bronx ... B2
17 D'Mongo's ... B5
18 Honest John's ... B3

Entertainment
19 Cliff Bell's Jazz Club ... B5
20 Comerica Park ... C5
21 Detroit Opera House ... C5
22 Ford Field ... C5
23 Fox Theatre ... B5
24 Joe Louis Arena ... B7
25 Magic Stick ... C2
Majestic Theater ... (see 25)
26 PJ's Lager House ... A5
27 Puppet ART/Detroit Puppet Theater ... C5
28 St Andrew's Hall ... C6

Shopping
29 John King Books ... A6
30 People's Records ... B4
31 Pure Detroit ... C6

vacant lots into urban farms and abandoned buildings into hostels and museums. Plus, they shred a mean guitar in 'the D.' Very mean.

History

French explorer Antoine de La Mothe Cadillac founded Detroit in 1701. Sweet fortune arrived in the 1920s, when Henry Ford began churning out cars. He didn't invent the automobile, as so many mistakenly believe, but he did perfect assembly-line manufacturing and mass-production techniques. The result was the Model T, the first car the USA's middle class could afford to own.

Detroit quickly became the motor capital of the world. General Motors (GM), Chrysler and Ford were all headquartered in or near Detroit (and still are). The 1950s were the city's heyday, when the population exceeded two million and Motown music hit the airwaves. But racial tensions in 1967 and Japanese car competitors in the 1970s shook the city and its industry. Detroit entered an era of deep decline, losing about two-thirds of its population.

The D resurged somewhat in the mid-2000s, only to see the global economic crisis of 2008–09 crush the auto industry. GM and Chrysler filed for bankruptcy, and thousands of blue- and white-collar workers lost their jobs. The city continues to 'restructure.'

Sights & Activities

Downtown revolves around the riverfront Renaissance Center and nearby Hart Plaza. Woodward Ave, the city's main boulevard, heads north from here to Midtown (containing the Cultural Center and its museums, plus Wayne State University) and on to architecturally rich New Center (a mile beyond). Bar-filled Corktown sits west of downtown. The Mile Roads are Detroit's major east-west arteries; 8 Mile forms the city-suburbs boundary. Across the Detroit River lies Windsor, Canada.

Sights are commonly closed on Monday and Tuesday.

MIDTOWN & CULTURAL CENTER

Detroit Institute of Arts MUSEUM
(313-833-7900; www.dia.org; 5200 Woodward Ave; adult/child $8/4; 10am-4pm Wed & Thu, 10am-10pm Fri, 10am-5pm Sat & Sun) It's the cream of the local museum crop, lauded

for its American collection. The centerpiece is Diego Rivera's mural *Detroit Industry,* which fills an entire room and reflects the city's blue-collar labor history.

FREE Museum of Contemporary Art Detroit MUSEUM
(MOCAD; ☎313-832-6622; www.mocadetroit.org; 4454 Woodward Ave; ⏲11am-5pm Wed-Sun, to 8pm Thu & Fri) MOCAD opened in 2006 in an abandoned, graffiti-slathered auto dealership. Heat lamps hang from the ceiling over peculiar exhibits that change every few months.

Wright Museum of African American History MUSEUM
(☎313-494-5800; www.maah-detroit.org; 315 E Warren Ave; adult/child $8/5; ⏲9am-5pm Tue-Sat, 1-5pm Sun) It holds less than it appears to from the impressive exterior, though it's worth a look inside. The full-scale model of slaves chained up on a dark, creaking slave ship will leave you chilled.

NEW CENTER

Motown Historical Museum MUSEUM
(☎313-875-2264; www.motownmuseum.com; 2648 W Grand Blvd; adult/child $10/8; ⏲10am-6pm Tue-Sat, plus Mon Jul & Aug) In this row of modest houses Berry Gordy launched Motown Records – and the careers of Stevie Wonder, Diana Ross, Marvin Gaye and Michael Jackson – with an $800 loan in 1959. Gordy and Motown split for Los Angeles in 1972, but you can still step into humble Studio A and see where the famed names recorded their first hits. A tour takes about 1½ hours, and consists mostly of looking at old photos and listening to guides' stories. The museum is 2 miles northwest of Midtown.

Model T Automotive Heritage Complex MUSEUM
(☎313-872-8759; www.tplex.org; 461 Piquette Ave; adult/child $10/free; ⏲10am-4pm Wed-Fri, 9am-4pm Sat, noon-4pm Sun Apr-Nov) Henry Ford cranked out the first Model T in this landmark factory. Admission includes a tour into the workshop and 'experimental room,' plus loads of classic cars to view. It's about 1 mile northeast of the Detroit Institute of Arts.

DOWNTOWN & AROUND

Busy **Greektown** (centered on Monroe St) has restaurants, bakeries and a casino.

Riverwalk & Dequindre Cut WALKING, CYCLING
(www.detroitriverfront.org) The city's swell riverfront path runs for 3 miles along the churning Detroit River west from Hart Plaza east to Mt Elliott St, passing several parks, outdoor theaters, riverboats and fishing spots en route. Eventually it will extend all the way to beachy **Belle Isle** (detour onto Jefferson Ave to get there now). About halfway along the Riverwalk, near Orleans St, the 1.5-mile Dequindre Cut Greenway path juts north, offering a convenient passageway to Eastern Market.

Wheelhouse Bikes BICYCLE RENTAL
(☎313-656-2453; www.wheelhousedetroit.com; 1340 E Atwater St; per 2hr $15; ⏲11am-8pm Mon-Sat, to 5pm Sun) Cycling is a great way to explore the city. Wheelhouse rents sturdy two-wheelers (helmet and lock included) on the Riverwalk at Rivard Plaza. Tours ($35 including bike rental) on weekends roll by various neighborhoods and architectural sites.

Eastern Market MARKET
(www.detroiteasternmarket.com; Gratiot Ave & Russell St) Produce, cheese, spice and flower vendors fill the large halls on Saturday, but you also can turn up Monday through Friday to browse the specialty shops (props to the peanut roaster), cafes and ethnic eats that flank the market on Russell and Market Sts.

Renaissance Center BUILDING
(RenCen; www.gmrencen.com; 330 E Jefferson Ave; 📶) GM's glossy, cloud-poking headquarters is a fine place to grab a bite (in the Wintergarden), take a free hour-long tour (Monday through Friday at noon and 2pm) or embark on the riverfront walkway.

Hart Plaza PLAZA
(cnr Jefferson & Woodward Aves) This is the site of many free, summer weekend festivals and concerts. While there, check out the sculpture of Joe Louis' mighty fist.

Campus Martius PLAZA
(www.campusmartiuspark.org; 800 Woodward Ave) It's another communal hot spot downtown, with an outdoor ice rink in winter, and eating areas, concerts and films in summer.

People Mover MONORAIL
(www.thepeoplemover.com; fare $0.50) As mass transit, the monorail's 3-mile loop on elevated tracks around downtown won't get you very far. As a tourist attraction, it's a sweet ride providing great views of the city and riverfront.

FREE Heidelberg Project ART INSTALLATION
(www.heidelberg.org; 3600 Heidelberg St; ⏲sunrise-sunset) Polka-dotted streets, houses

covered in Technicolor paint blobs, strange sculptures in yards – this is no acid trip, but rather an art installation that covers an entire neighborhood. It's the brainchild of street artist Tyree Guyton, who wanted to beautify his run-down community (which has the dubious distinction of being the USA's most economically depressed 'hood). Get here by taking Gratiot Ave northwest to Heidelberg St; the project spans from Ellery to Mt Elliott Sts.

Tours

Preservation Wayne WALKING
(313-577-7674; www.preservationwayne.org; 2.5hr tours $10-15; 5:30pm Tue & 10am Sat May-Sep) offers architectural walking tours through downtown, Midtown and other neighborhoods; departure points vary.

Festivals & Events

North American International Auto Show CARS
(www.naias.com; tickets $12; mid-Jan) It's autos galore for two weeks in mid-January at the Cobo Center.

Movement Electronic Music Festival MUSIC
(www.movement.us; day pass $40; late May) The world's largest electronic music festival congregates in Hart Plaza over Memorial Day weekend.

Sleeping

Add 9% to 15% tax (it varies by lodging size and location) to the rates listed here, unless stated otherwise.

Affordable motels abound in Detroit's suburbs. If you're arriving from Metro Airport, follow the signs for Merriman Rd when leaving the airport and take your pick.

TOP CHOICE **Inn on Ferry Street** INN $$
(313-871-6000; www.innonferrystreet.com; 84 E Ferry St; r incl breakfast from $149; P) Forty guest rooms fill a row of Victorian mansions right by the art museum. The lower-cost rooms are small but have deliciously soft bedding; the larger rooms feature plenty of antique wood furnishings. The healthy hot breakfast and shuttle to downtown are nice touches.

Detroit Hostel HOSTEL $
(248-807-2131; www.hosteldetroit.com; 2700 Vermont St; dm $18-27, r $40-45; P) Volunteers rehabbed this old building, gathered up recycled materials and donations for the patchwork furnishings, and opened it to the public in 2011. There's a 10-bed dorm, two two-bed dorms and five private rooms; everyone shares the four bathrooms, three kitchens and backyard herb garden. Bookings are taken online only (and must be done at least 24 hours in advance). Parking costs $10 per day, as do bicycle rentals. The hostel is located in Corktown on a desolate street, but near several good bars and restaurants.

Ft Shelby Doubletree Hotel HOTEL $$
(313-963-5600, 800-222-8733; http://doubletree1.hilton.com; 525 W Lafayette Blvd; ste $126-169; P) This new hotel fills a historic beaux arts building downtown. All rooms are suites, with both the sitting area and bedroom equipped with HDTV and free wi-fi. Parking costs $20, and there's free shuttle service around downtown.

Westin Book Cadillac HOTEL $$$
(313-442-1600; www.bookcadillacwestin.com; 1114 Washington Blvd; r weekend/weekday from $179/299; P) Opened in 2008, 'the Book' swooped into a 1924 landmark building and took over as the top address in town. It has all the amenities you'd expect at a swanky, 453-room hotel. In-room wi-fi costs $8 per day; parking costs $25.

Eating

Two nearby suburbs also have caches of hip restaurants and bars: walkable, gay-oriented Ferndale at 9 Mile Rd and Woodward Ave, and Royal Oak just north of Ferndale between 12 and 13 Mile Rds.

MIDTOWN & CULTURAL CENTER

Good Girls Go to Paris Crepes CREPERIE $
(877-727-4727; www.goodgirlsgotopariscrepes.com; 15 E Kirby St; mains $5-8; 9am-4pm Mon-Wed, to 8pm Thu, to 10pm Fri & Sat, to 5pm Sun) This red-walled, French-style cafe transports diners across the pond via its sweet (Heath Bar and ricotta) and savory (goat cheese and fig) pancakes.

Cass Cafe CAFE $$
(313-831-1400; www.casscafe.com; 4620 Cass Ave; mains $8-15; 11am-11pm Mon-Thu, 11am-1am Fri & Sat, 5-10pm Sun;) The Cass is a bohemian art gallery fused with a bar and restaurant that serves soups, sandwiches and veggie beauties, like the lentil-walnut burger. Service can be fickle.

Avalon International Breads BAKERY $
(☎313-832-0008; www.avalonbreads.net; 422 W Willis St; mains $5-9; ⏲6am-6pm Tue-Sat, 8am-4pm Sun) Detroit's earthy types huddle round the hearth at Avalon, where its fresh-baked bread (like scallion dill or country Italian) makes an excellent base for the sandwiches it serves.

DOWNTOWN

Foran's Grand Trunk Pub PUB $$
(☎313-961-3043; www.grandtrunkpub.com; 612 Woodward Ave; mains $7-12; ⏲11am-2am) If the high vaulted ceiling and long narrow space make you feel like you're in an old railroad ticket station, that's because you are. The food is pub grub – sandwiches, burgers and shepherd's pie – but made with local ingredients such as Avalon bread and Eastern Market produce. The taps pour 18 Michigan craft brews.

Lafayette Coney Island AMERICAN $
(☎313-964-8198; 118 Lafayette Blvd; items $2.50-4; ⏲7:30am-4am Mon-Thu, to 5am Fri & Sat, 9:30am-4am Sun) The 'coney' – a hot dog smothered with chili and onions – is a Detroit specialty. When the craving strikes (and it will), take care of business at Lafayette. The minimalist menu consists of burgers, fries and beer, in addition to the signature item. Cash only.

Laikon Cafe GREEK $$
(☎313-963-7058; 569 Monroe St; mains $9-14; ⏲11am-10pm Sun-Thu, to midnight Fri & Sat, closed Tue) Chef-owner Kostas has cooked staples like lamb and flaming cheese in his homey, old-school Greek restaurant for decades.

CORKTOWN & MEXICANTOWN

Mexicantown, along Bagley St 3 miles west of downtown, offers several inexpensive Mexican restaurants.

TOP CHOICE **Slows Bar BQ** BARBECUE $$
(☎313-962-9828; www.slowsbarbq.com; 2138 Michigan Ave; mains $10-18, half-rack ribs $19; ⏲11am-10pm Sun & Mon, to 11pm Tue-Thu, to midnight Fri & Sat; Wi-Fi) Mmm, slow-cooked southern-style barbecue in Corktown. Carnivores can carve into the three-meat combo plate (brisket, pulled pork and chicken). Vegetarians have options from okra fritters to a faux-meat chicken sandwich. The taps yield 21 quality beers.

Drinking

TOP CHOICE **Bronx** BAR
(4476 2nd Ave; Wi-Fi) There's not much inside Detroit's best boozer besides a pool table, dim lighting and a couple of jukeboxes filled with ballsy rock and soul. But that's the way the hipsters, slackers and rockers (the White Stripes used to hang here) like their dive bars. They're also fond of the beefy burgers served late at night and the cheap beer selection.

Honest John's BAR
(www.honestjohnsdetroit.com; 488 Selden St; ⏲7am-2am; Wi-Fi) There really is a John and he's a Detroit classic, as is his unassuming bar where cops, nurses and other local workers toss back a cold one postshift.

D'Mongo's BAR
(www.cafedmongos.com; 1439 Griswold St; ⏲6pm-2am Fri) With its retro ambience, ribs cookin' on the outdoor smoker, and jazz or country bands croonin', it's a pity this secret hideaway is open on Fridays only.

Entertainment

Live Music

Cover charges hover between $5 and $15.

FROM MOTOWN TO ROCK CITY

Motown Records and soul music put Detroit on the map in the 1960s, while the thrashing punk rock of the Stooges and MC5 was the 1970s response to that smooth sound. By 1976, Detroit was dubbed 'Rock City' by a Kiss song (though – just Detroit's luck – the tune was eclipsed by its B-side, 'Beth'). In recent years it has been hard-edged rock – aka whiplash rock 'n' roll – that has pushed the city to the music scene forefront. Homegrown stars include the White Stripes, Von Bondies and Dirtbombs. Rap (thank you, Eminem) and techno are Detroit's other renowned genres. Many music aficionados say the city's blight is what produces such a beautifully angry explosion of sound, and who's to argue? Scope free publications like the *Metro Times* and *Real Detroit Weekly*, or blogs like 'Motor City Rocks' (www.motorcityrocks.com), for current show and club listings.

Magic Stick & Majestic Theater LIVE MUSIC
(www.majesticdetroit.com; 4120-4140 Woodward Ave) The White Stripes and Von Bondies are rockers who've risen from the beer-splattered ranks at the Magic Stick. The Majestic Theater next door hosts larger shows. There's bowling, billiards, a pizza joint and cafe. Something cool rocks here nightly.

PJ's Lager House LIVE MUSIC
(www.pjslagerhouse.com; 1254 Michigan Ave) This Corktown punk-underground club is dingy in an atmospheric way, with scrappy bands or DJs playing most nights.

Cliff Bell's Jazz Club LIVE MUSIC
(www.cliffbells.com; 2030 Park Ave; Tue-Sun) With its dark wood, candlelight and art deco decor, Bell's evokes 1930s elegance. Local jazz bands and poetry readings attract a diverse young audience nightly.

Baker's Keyboard Lounge LIVE MUSIC
(www.bakerskeyboardlounge.com; 20510 Livernois Ave; Tue-Sun) Everyone from Miles Davis to Thelonious Monk to Nina Simone has let loose at the self-proclaimed 'world's oldest jazz club' on Detroit's far northwest side.

St Andrew's Hall LIVE MUSIC
(www.facebook.com/standrewshall; 431 E Congress St) St Andrew's is a well-known alternative band venue in an old church. Downstairs is Shelter, a smaller music/dance club.

Performing Arts

Puppet ART/Detroit Puppet Theater THEATER
(313-961-7777; www.puppetart.org; 25 E Grand River Ave; adult/child $10/5;) Soviet-trained puppeteers perform beautiful shows in this 70-person theater; a small museum displays puppets from different cultures. Shows are typically held on Saturday afternoons.

Detroit Opera House OPERA
(313-237-7464; www.motopera.com; 1526 Broadway) Gorgeous interior, top-tier company and nurturer of many renowned African American performers.

Fox Theatre THEATER
(313-983-6611; 2211 Woodward Ave) This is a gloriously restored 1928 venue that large touring shows occupy.

Sports

Comerica Park BASEBALL
(www.detroittigers.com; 2100 Woodward Ave;) The Detroit Tigers play pro baseball at Comerica, one of the league's most decked-out stadiums. The park is particularly kid friendly, with a small Ferris wheel and carousel inside (per ride $2 each).

Joe Louis Arena HOCKEY
(www.detroitredwings.com; 600 Civic Center Dr) The much-loved Red Wings play pro ice hockey at this arena where, if you can wrangle tickets, you might witness the strange octopus-throwing custom.

Ford Field FOOTBALL
(www.detroitlions.com; 2000 Brush St) The struggling Lions toss the pigskin at this indoor stadium next to Comerica Park.

Palace of Auburn Hills BASKETBALL
(www.nba.com/pistons; 5 Championship Dr) The Palace hosts the Pistons pro basketball team. It's about 30 miles northwest of downtown; take I-75 to exit 81.

Shopping

Pure Detroit SOUVENIRS
(www.puredetroit.com; 500 Griswold St; 10:30am-5:30pm Mon-Sat) Local artists create stylish products for Pure Detroit that celebrate the city's fast-cars-and-rock-music culture. Pick up handbags made from recycled seatbelts, groovy hoodies and local Pewabic pottery. Located in the landmark, mosaic-strewn Guardian Building (worth a peek in its own right).

People's Records MUSIC
(3161 Woodward Ave; 10am-6pm Mon-Sat) Calling all crate-diggers: DJ-owned People's Records is your vinyl Valhalla. Used 45s are the specialty, with more than 80,000 jazz, soul and R & B titles filling bins.

John King Books BOOKS
(www.rarebooklink.com; 901 W Lafayette Blvd; 9:30am-5:30pm Mon-Sat) Set aside some time to browse this insanely massive, musty warren of secondhand books.

Information

The area between the sports arenas north to around Willis Rd is pretty deserted and best avoided on foot come nighttime.

Emergency & Medical Services

Detroit Receiving Hospital (313-745-3000; 4201 St Antoine St)

Internet Access

You'll find free wi-fi in many cafes and bars, as well as the Renaissance Center lobby.

Media

Between the Lines (www.pridesource.com) Free, weekly gay and lesbian paper.

Detroit Free Press (www.freep.com) Daily.

Detroit News (www.detnews.com) Daily.

Metro Times (www.metrotimes.com) Free alternative weekly that is the best guide to the entertainment scene.

Real Detroit Weekly (www.realdetroitweekly.com) Another free weekly for entertainment listings.

Tourist Information

Detroit Convention & Visitors Bureau (☎800-338-7648; www.visitdetroit.com)

Websites

DetroitYES (www.detroityes.com) Images organized as 'tours' reveal the city's soul.

Forgotten Detroit (www.forgottendetroit.com) A website devoted to Detroit's 'ruins' (ie decaying buildings).

Model D (www.modeldmedia.com) Weekly e-zine about local developments and food/entertainment options, broken down by neighborhood.

Getting There & Around

Detroit Metro Airport (DTW; www.metroairport.com), a Delta Airlines hub, is about 20 miles southwest of Detroit. Transport options from the airport to the city are few: you can take a cab for about $45; or you can take the 125 SMART bus ($2), but it takes one to 1½ hours to get downtown.

Greyhound (☎313-961-8005; 1001 Howard St) runs to various cities in Michigan and beyond. **Megabus** (www.megabus.com/us) runs to/from Chicago (5½ hours) daily; departures are from downtown (corner of Cass and Michigan) and Wayne State University (corner off Cass and Warren Aves).

Amtrak (☎313-873-3442; 11 W Baltimore Ave) trains go thrice daily to Chicago (5½ hours). You can also head east – to New York (16½ hours) or destinations en route – but you'll first be bused to Toledo.

Transit Windsor (☎519-944-4111; www.citywindsor.ca/001209.asp) operates the Tunnel Bus to Windsor, Canada. It costs $3.75 (American or Canadian) and departs by Mariner's Church (corner of Randolph St and Jefferson Ave) near the Detroit-Windsor Tunnel entrance, as well as other spots downtown. Bring your passport.

For information on the People Mover city-rail line, see p558.

For taxi service, call **Checker Cab** (☎313-963-7000).

Around Detroit

Stunning Americana and good eatin' lie just down the road from Detroit.

DEARBORN

Dearborn is 10 miles west of downtown Detroit and home to two of the USA's finest museums. The indoor **Henry Ford Museum** (☎313-982-6001; www.thehenryford.org; 20900 Oakwood Blvd; adult/child $15/11; ⌚9:30am-5pm) contains a fascinating wealth of American culture, such as the chair Lincoln was sitting in when he was assassinated, the presidential limo in which Kennedy was killed, the hot-dog-shaped Oscar Mayer Wienermobile (photo op!) and the bus on which Rosa Parks refused to give up her seat. Don't worry: you'll get your vintage car fix here too. Parking is $5. The adjacent, outdoor **Greenfield Village** (adult/child $22/16; ⌚9:30am-5pm daily mid-Apr–Oct, 9:30am-5pm Fri-Sun Nov & Dec) features historic buildings shipped in from all over the country, reconstructed and restored, such as Thomas Edison's laboratory from Menlo Park and the Wright Brothers' airplane workshop. Plus you can add on the **Rouge Factory Tour** (adult/child $15/11; ⌚9:30am-3pm Mon-Sat) and see F-150 trucks roll off the assembly line where Ford first perfected his self-sufficient, mass-production techniques.

The three attractions are separate, but you can get a **combination ticket** (adult/child $32/24) for Henry Ford and Greenfield Village. Plan on at least one very full day at the complex.

Dearborn has the nation's greatest concentration of people of Arab descent, so it's no surprise that the **Arab American National Museum** (☎313-582-2266; www.arabamericanmuseum.org; 13624 Michigan Ave; adult/child $6/3; ⌚10am-6pm Wed-Sat, noon-5pm Sun) popped up here. It's a noble concept, located in a pretty, bright-tiled building, but it's not terribly exciting unless actor Jamie Farr's *M*A*S*H* TV-show script wows you. The thousand-and-one Arabian eateries lining Michigan Ave provide a more engaging feel for the culture. Cavernous **La Pita** (www.lapitadearborn.com; 22681 Newman St; sandwiches $4-5, mains $10-19; ⌚10am-11pm Mon-Sat, 11am-10pm Sun) is a classic; it's a block south of Michigan Ave, tucked into one of the many strip malls along the road.

ANN ARBOR

Forty-odd miles west of Detroit, liberal and bookish Ann Arbor is home to the Univer-

CLASSIC CARS IN MICHIGAN

More than sand dunes, beaches and Mackinac Island fudge, Michigan is synonymous with cars. While the connection hasn't been so positive in recent years, the state commemorates its glory days via several auto museums. The following fleets are within a few hours' drive from the Motor City.

Henry Ford Museum (p562) This Dearborn museum is loaded with vintage cars, including the first one Henry Ford ever built. In adjacent Greenfield Village you can ride in a Model T that rolled off the assembly line in 1923.

Automotive Hall of Fame (☎313-240-4000; www.automotivehalloffame.org; 21400 Oakwood Blvd, Dearborn; adult/child $8/4; ⊙9am-5pm Wed-Sun) Next door to the Henry Ford Museum, the interactive Auto Hall focuses on the people behind famed cars, such as Mr Ferdinand Porsche and Mr Soichiro Honda.

Walter P Chrysler Museum (☎248-944-0001; www.chryslerheritage.com; 1 Chrysler Dr, Auburn Hills; adult/child $8/4; ⊙10am-5pm Tue-Sat, noon-5pm Sun) This museum at Chrysler's headquarters (take exit 78 off I-75) has 70 beauties on display, including rare Dodge, DeSoto, Nash and Hudson models.

Gilmore Car Museum (☎269-671-5089; www.gilmorecarmuseum.org; 6865 Hickory Rd, Hickory Corners; adult/child $10/8; ⊙9am-5pm Mon-Fri, to 6pm Sat & Sun, closed Nov-Apr) North of Kalamazoo along Hwy 43, this museum complex offers 22 barns filled with 120 vintage autos, including 15 Rolls Royces dating back to a 1910 Silver Ghost.

RE Olds Transportation Museum (☎517-372-0529; www.reoldsmuseum.org; 240 Museum Dr, Lansing; adult/child $5/3; ⊙10am-5pm Tue-Sat year-round, noon-5pm Sun Apr-Oct) Twenty vintage cars sit in the old Lansing City Bus Garage, including the first Oldsmobile, which was built in 1897.

sity of Michigan. The walkable downtown, which abuts the campus, is loaded with free-trade coffee shops, bookstores, brewpubs and independent record stores. It's also a mecca for chowhounds; follow the drool trail toward anything named 'Zingerman's.'

Sights & Activities

FREE **University of Michigan Museum of Art** MUSEUM
(☎734-764-0395; www.umma.umich.edu; 525 S State St; ⊙10am-5pm Tue-Sat, noon-5pm Sun) The campus' big, bold, massively expanded art museum impresses with its collections of Asian ceramics, Tiffany glass and German expressionist works.

Ann Arbor Farmers Market MARKET
(www.a2gov.org/market; 315 Detroit St; ⊙7am-3pm Wed & Sat May-Dec, Sat only Jan-Apr) Given the surrounding bounty of orchards and farms, it's no surprise this place is stuffed to the rafters with everything from spicy pickles to cider to mushroom-growing kits; located downtown near Zingerman's Deli.

Zingerman's Bakehouse COOKING COURSE
(www.bakewithzing.com; 3723 Plaza Dr) Part of Zingerman's epicurean empire, the Bakehouse offers popular 'bake-cations,' from two-hour cookie-making classes to week-long pastry courses.

Eating & Drinking

TOP CHOICE **Zingerman's Roadhouse** AMERICAN $$
(☎734-663-3663; www.zingermansroadhouse.com; 2501 Jackson Ave; burgers $12-15, mains $17-27; ⊙7am-10pm Mon-Thu, to 11pm Fri, 9am-11pm Sat, 9am-9pm Sun) Two words: doughnut sundae. The bourbon-caramel-sauced dessert is pure genius, as are the traditional American dishes like Carolina grits, Iowa pork chops and Massachusetts oysters using sustainably produced ingredients. It's 2 miles west of downtown.

Zingerman's Delicatessen DELI $$
(☎734-663-3354; www.zingermansdeli.com; 422 Detroit St; sandwiches $10-16; ⊙7am-10pm) The shop that launched the foodie frenzy, Z's deli piles local, organic and specialty ingredients onto towering sandwiches in a downtown location.

Arbor Brewing Company BREWERY
(www.arborbrewing.com; 114 E Washington St) Swig handcrafted beer, like the crisp Sacred Cow IPA.

☆ Entertainment

If you happen to arrive on a fall weekend and wonder why 110,000 people – the size of Ann Arbor's entire population, more or less – are crowding into the school's stadium, the answer is football. Tickets are nearly impossible to purchase, especially when nemesis Ohio State is in town. You can try by contacting the **U of M Ticket Office** (☎734-764-0247; www.mgoblue.com/ticketoffice).

Blind Pig LIVE MUSIC
(www.blindpigmusic.com; 208 S 1st St) Everyone from John Lennon to Nirvana to the Circle Jerks has rocked the storied stage.

Ark LIVE MUSIC
(www.a2ark.org; 316 S Main St) The Ark hosts acoustic and folk-oriented tunesmiths.

ℹ Information

There are several B&Bs within walking distance of downtown. Hotels tend to be about 5 miles out, with several clustered south on State St. The CVB website has contact details.

Ann Arbor Convention & Visitors Bureau (www.annarbor.org)

Lansing & Central Michigan

Michigan's heartland, plunked in the center of the Lower Peninsula, alternates between fertile farms and highway-crossed urban areas.

LANSING

Smallish Lansing is the state capital; a few miles east lies East Lansing, home of Michigan State University. The **Greater Lansing CVB** (www.lansing.org) has information on both.

Between Lansing's downtown and the university is the **River Trail** (www.lansingrivertrail.org), which extends 8-plus miles along the shores of Michigan's longest river, the Grand. The paved path is popular with cyclists, joggers and inline skaters, and links a number of attractions, including a children's museum, zoo and fish ladder.

Downtown, the **Michigan Historical Museum** (☎517-373-3559; www.michigan.gov/museum; 702 W Kalamazoo St; admission free; ⏲9am-4:30pm Mon-Fri, 10am-4pm Sat, 1-5pm Sun) features 26 permanent galleries, including a replica UP copper mine you can walk through. The **RE Olds Transportation Museum** (see the boxed text, p563) will please car buffs.

Lansing's downtown hotels feed off politicians and lobbyists, so they're fairly expensive. It's best to head to East Lansing's **Wild Goose Inn** (☎517-333-3334; www.wildgooseinn.com; 512 Albert St; r incl breakfast $139-159; ⊜📶), a six-room B&B one block from Michigan State's campus. All rooms have fireplaces and most have Jacuzzis.

Kewpee's (www.kewpees.com; 118 S Washington Sq; mains $3-7; ⏲8am-6pm Mon-Fri, 11am-2pm Sat) has been feeding folks olive burgers and crisp onion rings by the capitol for more than 85 years. For breakfast, **Golden Harvest** (☎517-485-3663; 1625 Turner St; mains $7-9; ⏲7am-2:30pm Mon-Fri, from 8am Sat & Sun) is a loud, punk-rock-meets-hippie diner serving the sausage-and-French-toast Bubba Sandwich and hearty omelets; cash only. Abundant restaurants, pubs and nightclubs also fill Michigan State's northern campus area.

GRAND RAPIDS

The second-largest city in Michigan, Grand Rapids is known for office-furniture manufacturing, a conservative Dutch Reform attitude and the fact that it's only 30 miles from Lake Michigan's Gold Coast. The **Grand Rapids CVB** (www.visitgrandrapids.org) provides maps, coupons and any other information you'll need.

The downtown **Gerald R Ford Museum** (☎616-254-0400; www.fordlibrarymuseum.gov; 303 Pearl St NW; adult/child $7/3; ⏲9am-5pm) is dedicated to the only Michigander president (he was born with a different name in Nebraska). Ford stepped into the Oval Office after Richard Nixon and his vice president, Spiro Agnew, resigned in disgrace. It's an intriguing period in US history, and the museum does an excellent job of covering it, down to displaying the burglary tools used in the Watergate break-in. Ford died in 2006 and is buried on the museum's grounds.

The 118-acre **Frederik Meijer Gardens** (☎616-957-1580; www.meijergardens.org; 1000 E Beltline NE; adult/child $12/6; ⏲9am-5pm Mon-Sat, to 9pm Tue, 11am-5pm Sun) features impressive blooms and sculptures by Auguste Rodin, Henry Moore and others. It is 5 miles east of downtown via I-196.

If you're whizzing through Grand Rapids with time for only one stop, make it **Founders Brewing Company** (www.foundersbrewing.com; 235 Grandville Ave SW; sandwiches $6-8; ⏲11am-2am Mon-Sat, 3pm-2am Sun; 🖉). The ruby-tinged Dirty Bastard Ale is good swillin', and there's meaty (or vegetable-y, for vegetarians) deli sandwiches to soak it up.

Lake Michigan Shore

They don't call it the Gold Coast for nothing. Michigan's 300-mile western shoreline features seemingly endless stretches of beaches, dunes, wineries, orchards and B&B-filled towns that boom during the summer – and shiver during the snow-packed winter. Note all state parks listed here take **campsite reservations** (☎800-447-2757; www.midnrreservations.com; fee $8) and require a vehicle permit (day/year $8/29), unless specified otherwise.

HARBOR COUNTRY

Harbor Country refers to a group of eight small, lake-hugging towns just over the Michigan border (an easy day trip from Chicago). Yep, they've got your requisite beaches, wineries and antique shops; they've got a couple of big surprises too. The **Harbor Country Chamber of Commerce** (www.harborcountry.org) has the basics.

First up, surfing. Believe it, people: you can surf Lake Michigan, and the VW-bus-driving dudes at **Third Coast Surf Shop** (☎269-932-4575; www.thirdcoastsurfshop.com; 22 S Smith St; ⊙10am-6pm mid-May–mid-Sep) will show you how. They provide wetsuits and boards for surfing, skim boarding and paddle boarding (rentals per day $20 to $35). For novices, they offer 1½-hour **lessons** (incl equipment $55-75) right on the public beach June through mid-September. The surf shop is in New Buffalo, Harbor Country's biggest town.

Three Oaks is the only Harbor community that's inland (6 miles in, via US 12). Here Green Acres meets Greenwich Village in a funky farm-and-arts blend. By day, rent bikes at **Dewey Cannon Trading Company** (☎269-756-3361; www.applecidercentury.com; 3 Dewey Cannon Ave; bike per day $15; ⊙10am-4pm Sun-Fri, to 9pm Sat) and cycle lightly used rural roads past orchards and wineries. By eve, catch a provocative play or art-house flick at Three Oaks' theaters.

Hungry? Get a wax paper-wrapped cheeseburger, spicy curly fries and cold beer at **Redamak's** (www.redamaks.com; 616 E Buffalo St; burgers $5-10; ⊙noon-10:30pm Mar-Oct) in New Buffalo.

SAUGATUCK & DOUGLAS

Saugatuck is one of the Gold Coast's most popular resort areas, known for its strong arts community, numerous B&Bs and gay-friendly vibe. Douglas is its twin city a mile or so south, and they've pretty much sprawled into one. The **Saugatuck/Douglas CVB** (www.saugatuck.com) provides maps and more.

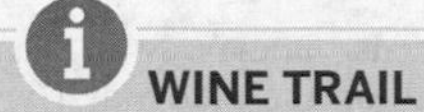

WINE TRAIL

A dozen wineries cluster between New Buffalo and Saugatuck. The **Lake Michigan Shore Wine Trail** (www.lakemichiganshorewinetrail.com) provides a downloadable map of vineyards and tasting rooms. Most are signposted off the highway.

The best thing to do in Saugatuck is also the most affordable. Jump aboard the clackety **Saugatuck Chain Ferry** (foot of Mary St; one way $1; ⊙9am-9pm late May-early Sep) and the operator will pull you across the Kalamazoo River. On the other side, walk to the dock's left and soon you'll come to **Mt Baldhead**, a 200ft-high sand dune. Huff up the stairs to see the grand view, and then race down the north side to beautiful **Oval Beach**.

Galleries and shops proliferate downtown on Water and Butler Sts. Antiquing prevails on the Blue Star Hwy running south for 20 miles. Blueberry U-pick farms share this stretch of road and make a juicy stop, too.

Several frilly B&Bs are tucked into the Saugatuck's century-old Victorian homes, with most ranging from $125 to $300 per night. Try the **Bayside Inn** (☎269-857-4321; www.baysideinn.net; 618 Water St; r incl breakfast $150-280; 📶), a 10-room former boathouse on Saugatuck's waterfront, or the retro-cool **Pines Motorlodge** (☎269-857-5211; www.thepinesmotorlodge.com; 56 Blue Star Hwy; r incl breakfast $129-189; 📶), with rooms amid the firs in Douglas.

For eats, **Wicks Park Bar & Grill** (☎269-857-2888; www.wickspark.com; 449 Water St; mains $11-25; ⊙11:30am-10pm), by the chain ferry, gets props for its lake perch and live music. Locals like to hang out and sip the house-made suds at **Saugatuck Brewing Company** (www.saugatuckbrewing.com; 2948 Blue Star Hwy; ⊙11am-11pm Sun-Thu, to midnight Fri & Sat). For dessert, buy a bulging slice at **Crane's Pie Pantry** (☎269-561-2297; www.cranespiepantry.com; 6054 124th Ave; ⊙9am-8pm Mon-Sat, 11am-8pm Sun May-Oct, reduced hr Nov-Apr), or pick apples and peaches in the surrounding orchards. Crane's is in Fennville, 3 miles south on the Blue Star Hwy, then 4 miles inland on Hwy 89.

HOLLAND

Holland (www.holland.org) lies 11 miles north of Saugatuck via US 31. Yes, there's plenty of kitschy tulips, windmills and clogs. But there's also an excellent brewery and eco-hotel hiding in town. They sit a block apart, making it way too easy to raise another Dragon's Milk ale at the **New Holland Brewing Company Pub** (www.newhollandbrew.com; 66 E 8th St; from 11am) before stumbling into your bamboo sheets at the Gold-LEED-certified **City Flats Hotel** (616-796-2100; www.cityflatshotel.com; 61 E 7th St; r $119-219;).

MUSKEGON & LUDINGTON

These towns are jump-off points for the two ferries that sail across the lake, providing a shortcut between Michigan and Wisconsin. The **Lake Express** (866-914-1010; www.lake-express.com; May-Oct) crosses between Muskegon and Milwaukee (one way adult/child/car $95/28/101, 2½ hours). The older **SS Badger** (888-337-7948; www.ssbadger.com; mid-May–mid-Oct) crosses from Ludington to Manitowoc (one way adult/child/car $70/24/59, four hours).

The towns themselves aren't much, but the **Muskegon Luge & Sports Complex** (231-744-9629; www.msports.org; 442 Scenic Dr) kicks butt with its full-on luge track (usable during summer, too) and cross-country ski trails. And lakeside **Ludington State Park** (231-843-8671; tent & RV sites $16-29, cabins $45; year-round), beyond the city limits on M-116, is one of Michigan's largest and most popular playlots. It has a top-notch trail system, a renovated lighthouse to visit (or live in, as a volunteer lighthouse keeper) and miles of beach.

HIKING TRAIL MAPS

Plot out your walk in the woods with **Michigan Trail Maps** (www.michigantrailmaps.com), a free resource with more than 100 trail guides. Search by county, trail length or activity (ie birding), then download and print the high-quality maps as pdfs. So far the trails covered are on the Lower Peninsula, but Upper Peninsula treks are reportedly in the works.

SLEEPING BEAR DUNES NATIONAL LAKESHORE

This national park stretches from north of Frankfort to just before Leland, on the Leelanau Peninsula. Stop at the park's **visitor center** (231-326-5134; www.nps.gov/slbe; 9922 Front St; 8:30am-6pm Jun-Aug, to 4pm Sep-May) in Empire for information, trail maps and vehicle entry permits (week/annual $10/20).

Attractions include the famous **dune climb** along Hwy 109, where you trudge up the 200ft-high dune and then run or roll down. Gluttons for leg-muscle punishment can keep slogging all the way to Lake Michigan, a strenuous 1½-hour trek one way; bring water. There are also plenty of easier hikes; ask at the visitor center. Short on time or stamina? Take the 7-mile, one-lane, picnic-grove-studded **Pierce Stocking Scenic Drive**, perhaps the best way to absorb the stunning lake vistas.

After you leave the park, swing into little **Leland** (www.lelandmi.com). Grab a bite at a waterfront restaurant downtown, and poke around atmospheric Fishtown with its weather-beaten shacks-cum-shops. Boats depart from here for the Manitou Islands (see the boxed text, p567).

TRAVERSE CITY

Michigan's 'cherry capital' is the largest city in the northern half of the Lower Peninsula. It's got a bit of urban sprawl, but it's still a happenin' base from which to see the Sleeping Bear Dunes, Mission Peninsula wineries, U-pick orchards and other area attractions.

Stop at the downtown **visitor center** (231-947-1120; www.traversecity.com; 101 W Grandview Pkwy; 9am-5pm Mon-Fri, 9am-3pm Sat) for maps and the do-it-yourself foodie tour brochure (also available online; click 'Things to Do' on the website). Or see what **Learn Great Foods** (866-240-1650; www.learngreatfoods.com; tours $50-125) has on its guided tour schedule; there's usually a weekly jaunt to farms and fisheries on the Leelanau Peninsula, including alfresco dinner among the greens.

Road tripping out to the wineries is a must. Head north from Traverse City on Hwy 37 for 20 miles to the end of the grape- and cherry-planted Old Mission Peninsula. You'll be spoiled for choice: **Chateau Grand Traverse** (www.cgtwines.com; 10am-7pm Mon-Sat, to 6pm Sun) and **Chateau Chantal** (www.chateauchantal.com; 11am-8pm Mon-Sat, to 5pm Sun) pour crowd-pleasing Chardonnay and Pinot Noir. **Peninsula Cellars** (www.peninsulacellars.com; ⏲10am-6pm), in an old schoolhouse, makes fine whites and is often less crowded. Whatever bottle you buy, take it out to Lighthouse Park beach, at the peninsula's tip, and enjoy it with the waves chilling your toes. The wineries stay open year-round, though they reduce their hours in winter.

The town goes all Hollywood during the **Traverse City Film Festival** (www.traversecityfilmfest.org; ⏲late Jul), when founder (and native Michigander) Michael Moore comes in and unspools a six-day slate of documentaries, international flicks and 'just great movies.'

Dozens of beaches, resorts, motels and water sports operators line US 31 around Traverse City. Lodgings are often full – and more expensive – during weekends; the visitor center website has contact details. Most resorts overlooking the bay cost $150 to $250 per night. The aforementioned Chantal and Grand Traverse wineries also double as B&Bs and fit into this price range.

Guests can rent jet skis and enjoy nightly bonfires at **Park Shore Resort** (☎877-349-8898; www.parkshoreresort.com; 1401 US 31 N; r incl breakfast weekday/weekend from $150/190; ❄📶🏊). Motels on the other side of US 31 (away from the water) are more moderately priced, such as **Mitchell Creek Inn** (☎231-947-9330; www.mitchellcreek.com; 894 Munson Ave; r/cottages from $60/125; 📶), near the state park beach.

After a day of fun in the sun, refresh with sandwiches at gastronome favorite **Folgarelli's** (☎231-941-7651; www.folgarellis.net; 424 W Front St; sandwiches $6-9; ⏲9:30am-6:30pm Mon-Fri, to 5:30pm Sat, 11am-4pm Sun) and Belgian and Michigan craft beers at **7 Monks Taproom** (www.7monkstap.com; 128 S Union St).

CHARLEVOIX & PETOSKEY

These two towns hold several Hemingway sights. They're also where Michigan's upper-crusters maintain summer homes. The downtown areas of both places have gourmet restaurants and high-class shops, and the marinas are filled with yachts.

In Petoskey, **Stafford's Perry Hotel** (☎231-347-4000; www.staffords.com; Bay at Lewis St; r $129-259; ❄@📶) is a grand historic place in which to stay. **Petoskey State Park** (☎231-347-2311; 2475 Hwy 119; tent & RV sites $27-29; ⏲year-round) is north along Hwy 119 and has a beautiful beach. Look for indigenous Petoskey stones, which are honeycomb-patterned fragments of ancient coral. From here, Hwy 119 – aka the **Tunnel of Trees scenic route** – dips and curves through thick forest as it rolls north along a sublime bluff, en route to the Straits of Mackinac.

WORTH A TRIP

MANITOU ISLANDS

If you're looking for a wilderness adventure, the Manitou Islands – part of Sleeping Bear Dunes National Lakeshore – deliver. **Manitou Island Transit** (☎231-256-9061; www.manitoutransit.com) can help plan overnight camping trips on North Manitou, or day trips to South Manitou. Kayaking and hiking are popular activities, especially the 7-mile trek to the Valley of the Giants, a mystical stand of cedar trees on South Manitou. **Ferries** (round-trip adult/child $32/18, 1½hr) sail from Leland two to seven times per week from May to mid-October.

Straits of Mackinac

This region, between the Upper and Lower Peninsulas, features a long history of forts and fudge shops. Car-free Mackinac Island is Michigan's premier tourist draw.

One of the most spectacular sights in the area is the 5-mile-long **Mackinac Bridge** (known locally as 'Big Mac'), which spans the Straits of Mackinac. The $3.50 toll is worth every penny as the views from the bridge, which include two Great Lakes, two peninsulas and hundreds of islands, are second to none in Michigan.

And remember: despite the spelling, it's pronounced *mac*-in-aw.

MACKINAW CITY

At the south end of Mackinac Bridge, bordering I-75, is touristy Mackinaw City. It serves mainly as a jump-off point to Mackinac Island, but it does have a couple of interesting sights.

Next to the bridge (its visitor center is actually beneath the bridge) is **Colonial Michilimackinac** (☎231-436-5564; www.mackinacparks.com; adult/child $10.50/6.50; ⏲9:30am-7pm Jun-Aug, to 5pm May & Sep–mid-Oct), a National Historic Landmark that features a reconstructed stockade first built in 1715 by the French. Some 3 miles southeast of the city on US 23 is **Historic Mill Creek** (☎231-436-4226; www.mackinacparks.com; adult/child

HEMINGWAY'S HAUNTS

A number of writers have ties to northwest Michigan, but none are as famous as Ernest Hemingway, who spent the summers of his youth at his family's cottage on Walloon Lake. Hemingway buffs often tour the area to view the places that made their way into his writing.

First up: Horton Bay. As you head north on US 31, past yacht-filled Charlevoix, look for Boyne City Rd veering off to the east. It skirts Lake Charlevoix and eventually arrives at the **Horton Bay General Store** (☎231-582-7827; www.hortonbaygeneralstore.com; 05115 Boyne City Rd; ⏲late May-early Sep). Hemingway fans will recognize the building, with its 'high false front,' from his short story 'Up in Michigan.' For the mother lode of Hemingway books and souvenirs, pop into the **Red Fox Inn Bookstore** (05156 Boyne City Rd; ⏲late May–early Sep) next door.

Further up Hwy 31 in Petoskey, you can see the Hemingway collection at the **Little Traverse History Museum** (☎231-347-2620; www.petoskeymuseum.org; 100 Depot Ct; adult/child $2/1; ⏲10am-4pm Mon-Fri, 1-4pm Sat Jun–mid-Oct), including rare first-edition books that the author autographed for a friend when he visited in 1947. Afterward, toss back a drink at **City Park Grill** (☎231-347-0101; www.cityparkgrill.com; 432 E Lake St; ⏲11:30am-11pm Mon-Fri, to midnight Sat & Sun), where Hemingway was a regular.

The **Michigan Hemingway Society** (www.michiganhemingwaysociety.org) provides further information for self-guided tours. It also hosts the weekend-long **Hemingway festival** (⏲mid-Oct).

$8/4.75; ⏲9am-5:30pm Jun-Aug, to 4:30pm May & Sep–mid-Oct), which has an 18th-century sawmill, historic displays and nature trails. A combination ticket for both sights, along with Fort Mackinac (p569), is available at a discount.

If you can't find lodging on Mackinac Island – which should be your first choice – motels line I-75 and US 23 in Mackinaw City. Most cost $100-plus per night. Try **Days Inn** (☎231-436-8961; www.daysinnbridgeview.com; 206 N Nicolet St; r incl breakfast $115-170; ❄📶🏊).

ST IGNACE

At the north end of Mackinac Bridge is St Ignace, the other departure point for Mackinac Island and the second-oldest settlement in Michigan – Père Jacques Marquette founded a mission here in 1671. As soon as you've paid your bridge toll, you'll pass a huge **visitor center** (☎906-643-6979; I-75N; ⏲8am-6pm summer, 9am-5pm rest of year) which has racks of statewide information.

MACKINAC ISLAND

From either Mackinaw City or St Ignace you can catch a ferry to Mackinac Island, Michigan's top crowd-puller. The island's location in the straits between Lake Michigan and Lake Huron made it a prized port in the North American fur trade, and a site the British and Americans battled over many times.

The most important date on this 3.8-sq-mile island was 1898 – the year cars were banned in order to encourage tourism. Today all travel is by horse or bicycle; even the police use bikes to patrol the town. The crowds of tourists – called Fudgies by the islanders – can be crushing at times, particularly during summer weekends. But when the last ferry leaves in the evening and clears out the day-trippers, Mackinac's real charm emerges and you drift back into another, slower era.

The **visitor center** (☎800-454-5227; www.mackinacisland.org; Main St; ⏲9am-5pm), by the Arnold Line ferry dock, has maps for hiking and cycling. Eighty percent of the island is state parkland. Not much stays open between November and April.

Sights & Activities

Edging the island's shoreline is Hwy 185, the only Michigan highway that doesn't permit cars. The best way to view the incredible scenery along this 8-mile road is by bicycle; bring your own or rent one in town for $8 per hour at one of the many businesses. You can loop around the flat road in about an hour.

The two best attractions – **Arch Rock** (a huge limestone arch that sits 150ft above Lake Huron) and **Fort Holmes** (the island's other fort) – are both free. You can also ride past the **Grand Hotel**, which boasts a porch stretching halfway to Detroit. Unfortunately, if you're not staying at the Grand (minimum $235 per night per person), it costs $10 to stroll its long porch. Best to admire from afar.

Fort Mackinac HISTORIC SITE
(906-847-3328; www.mackinacparks.com; adult/child $10.50/6.50; 9:30am-6pm Jun-Aug, 9:30am-4:30pm May & Sep–mid-Oct;) Fort Mackinac sits atop limestone cliffs near downtown. Built by the British in 1780, it's one of the best-preserved military forts in the country. Costumed interpreters and cannon and rifle firings (every half-hour) entertain the kids. Stop into the tearoom for a bite and million-dollar view of downtown and the Straits of Mackinac from the outdoor tables.

The fort admission price also allows you entry to five other museums in town along Market St, including the Dr Beaumont Museum (where the doctor performed his famous digestive tract experiments) and Benjamin Blacksmith Shop. The **Mackinac Art Museum** (adult/child $5/3.50), housing Native American and other arts by the fort, is the newest member of the fold.

Sleeping

Rooms are booked far in advance during summer weekends; July to mid-August is peak season. The visitor center website has lodging contacts. Camping is not permitted anywhere on the island.

Most hotels and B&Bs charge at least $180 for two people. Exceptions (all are walkable from downtown) include:

Bogan Lane Inn B&B $$
(906-847-3439; www.boganlaneinn.com; Bogan Lane; r incl breakfast $85-125; year-round;) Four rooms, shared bath.

Cloghaun B&B B&B $$
(906-847-3885; www.cloghaun.com; Market St; r incl breakfast $110-195; mid-May–late Oct;) Eleven rooms, some with shared bath.

Hart's B&B B&B $$
(906-847-3854; www.hartsmackinac.com; Market St; r incl breakfast $150-180; mid-May–late Oct;) Eight rooms, all with private bath.

Eating & Drinking

Fudge shops are the island's best-known eateries; resistance is futile when they use fans to blow the aroma out onto Huron St. Hamburger and sandwich shops abound downtown.

JL Beanery Coffeehouse CAFE $
(906-847-6533; Huron St; mains $6-13; 7am-7pm;) Read the newspaper, sip a steaming cup of joe and gaze at the lake at this waterside cafe. It serves dandy breakfasts, sandwiches and soups.

Horn's Bar BURGERS, MEXICAN $$
(906-847-6154; www.hornsbar.com; Main St; mains $10-19; 11am-2am) Horn's saloon serves American burgers and south-of-the-border fare, and there's live entertainment nightly.

Village Inn AMERICAN $$$
(906-847-3542; www.viofmackinac.com; Hoban St; mains $18-23; 8am-10pm) Planked whitefish, pan-fried perch and other fresh-from-the-lake fish, meat and pasta dishes stuff diners at this year-round local hangout with a bar and outdoor seating.

Getting There & Around

Three ferry companies – **Arnold Line** (800-542-8528; www.arnoldline.com), **Shepler's** (800-828-6157; www.sheplersferry.com) and **Star Line** (800-638-9892; www.mackinacferry.com) – operate out of Mackinaw City and St Ignace, and charge the same rates: round-trip adult/child/bicycle $22/11/8. Book online and you'll save a few bucks. The ferries run several times daily from May to October; Arnold Line runs longer, weather permitting. The trip takes about 15 minutes, and once on the island, horse-drawn cabs will take you anywhere, or rent a bicycle.

Upper Peninsula

Rugged and isolated, with hardwood forests blanketing 90% of its land, the Upper Peninsula (UP) is a Midwest highlight. Only 45 miles of interstate highway slice through the trees, punctuated by a handful of cities, of which Marquette (population 20,000) is the largest. Between the small towns lie miles of undeveloped shoreline on Lakes Huron, Michigan and Superior; scenic two-lane roads; and pasties, the local meat-and-vegetable pot pies brought over by Cornish miners 150 years ago.

You'll find it's a different world up north. Residents of the UP, aka 'Yoopers,' consider themselves distinct from the rest of the state – they've even threatened to secede in the past.

SAULT STE MARIE & TAHQUAMENON FALLS

Founded in 1668, Sault Ste Marie (Sault is pronounced 'soo') is Michigan's oldest city and the third oldest in the USA. The town is best known for its locks that raise and lower 1000ft-long freighters between the different lake levels. **Soo Locks Park & Visitors Center** (admission free; ⏲9am-9pm mid-May–mid-Oct) is on Portage Ave downtown (take exit 394 off I-75 and go left). It features displays, videos and observation decks from which you can watch the boats leap 21ft from Lake Superior to Lake Huron. Pubs and cafes line Portage Ave. The **Sault CVB** (www.saultstemarie.com) has all the lowdown.

An hour's drive west of Sault Ste Marie, via Hwy 28 and Hwy 123, is eastern UP's top attraction: lovely **Tahquamenon Falls**, with tea-colored waters tinted so by upstream hemlock leaves. The Upper Falls in **Tahquamenon Falls State Park** (☎906-492-3415; per vehicle $8), 200ft across with a 50ft drop, wow onlookers – including Henry Wadsworth Longfellow, who mentioned them in his *Song of Hiawatha*. The Lower Falls are a series of small cascades that swirl around an island; many visitors rent a rowboat and paddle out to it. The large state park also has camping (tent & RV sites $16 to $23), great hiking and – bonus – a brewpub near the park entrance.

North of the park, beyond the little town of Paradise, is the fascinating **Great Lakes Shipwreck Museum** (☎888-492-3747; www.shipwreckmuseum.com; 18335 N Whitefish Point Rd; adult/child $13/9; ⏲10am-6pm May-Oct), whose intriguing displays include items trawled up from sunken ships. Dozens of vessels – including the *Edmund Fitzgerald* that Gordon Lightfoot crooned about – have sunk in the area's congested sea lanes and storm-tossed weather, earning it such nicknames as the 'Shipwreck Coast' and 'Graveyard of the Great Lakes.' The grounds also include a lighthouse President Lincoln commissioned and a bird observatory that 300 species fly by. To have the foggy place to yourself, spend the night at **Whitefish Point Light Station B&B** (☎888-492-3747; r $150; ⏲Apr–mid-Nov), which offers five rooms in the old Coast Guard crew quarters on-site.

PICTURED ROCKS NATIONAL LAKESHORE

Stretching along prime Lake Superior real estate, **Pictured Rocks National Lakeshore** (www.nps.gov/piro) is a series of wild cliffs and caves where blue and green minerals have streaked the red and yellow sandstone into a kaleidoscope of color. Rte 58 (Alger County Rd) spans the park for 52 slow miles from **Grand Marais** in the east to **Munising** in the west. Top sights (from east to west) include **Au Sable Point Lighthouse** (reached via a 3-mile round-trip walk beside shipwreck skeletons), agate-strewn **Twelvemile Beach**, hike-rich **Chapel Falls** and view-worthy **Miners Castle Overlook**.

Several boat tours launch from Munising. **Pictured Rock Cruises** (☎906-387-2379; www.picturedrocks.com; 100 W City Park Dr; 2½hr tours adult/child $35/10) departs from the city pier downtown and glides along the shore to Miners Castle. **Shipwreck Tours** (☎906-387-4477; www.shipwrecktours.com; 1204 Commercial St; 2hr tours adult/child $30/12) sails in glass-bottom boats to see sunken schooners.

Grand Island (www.grandislandmi.com), part of Hiawatha National Forest, is also a quick jaunt from Munising. Hop aboard the **Grand Island Ferry** (☎906-387-3503; round-trip adult/child $15/10; ⏲late May–mid-Oct) to get there and rent a mountain bike (per day $25) to zip around. There's also a ferry/bus tour package ($22). The ferry dock is on Hwy 28, which is about 4 miles west of Munising.

Munising has lots of motels, such as tidy **Alger Falls Motel** (☎906-387-3536; www.algerfallsmotel.com; E9427 Hwy 28; r $50-70; ❄📶). **Falling Rock Cafe & Bookstore** (☎906-387-3008; www.fallingrockcafe.com; 104 E Munising Ave; mains $5-9; ⏲9am-8pm Sun-Fri, to 10pm Sat; 📶) provides sandwiches and live music.

Staying in wee Grand Marais, on the park's east side, is also recommended. Turn in at **Hilltop Cabins and Motel** (☎906-494-2331; www.hilltopcabins.net; N14176 Ellen St; r & cabins $75-150; 📶) after a meal of whitefish sandwiches and brewskis at rustic **Lake Superior Brewing Company** (☎906-494-2337; N14283 Lake Ave; mains $7-13; ⏲noon-11pm).

MARQUETTE

From Munising, Hwy 28 heads west and hugs Lake Superior. This beautiful stretch of highway has lots of beaches, roadside parks and rest areas where you can pull over and enjoy the scenery. Within 45 miles you'll reach outdoorsy, oft-snowy Marquette.

Stop at the log-lodge **visitor center** (☎906-249-9066; www.marquettecountry.org; 2201 US 41; ⏲9am-5pm) as you enter the city for brochures on local hiking trails and waterfalls.

The easy **Sugarloaf Mountain Trail** and the harder, wildernesslike **Hogsback Mountain Trail** offer panoramic views. Both are reached from County Rd 550, just north

WHAT THE...?

Behold Big Gus, the world's largest chainsaw. And Big Ernie, the world's largest rifle. Kitsch runs rampant at **Da Yoopers Tourist Trap and Museum** (☎800-628-9978; www.dayoopers.com; admission free; ⏲9am-7pm Mon-Sat, 11am-6pm Sun, with seasonal variations), 15 miles west of Marquette on Hwy 28/41, past Ishpeming. Browse the store for only-in-the-UP gifts, say, a polyester moose tie or beer-can wind chimes.

of Marquette. In the city, the high bluffs of **Presque Isle Park** make a great place to catch the sunset. The **Noquemanon Trail Network** (www.noquetrails.org) is highly recommended for mountain biking and cross-country skiing.

Marquette is the perfect place to stay put for a few days to explore the central UP. Budgeteers can bunk at **Value Host Motor Inn** (☎906-225-5000; www.valuehostmotorinn.com; 1101 US 41 W; r incl breakfast $55-65; ❄📶) a few miles west of town. Downtown's **Landmark Inn** (☎906-228-2580; www.thelandmarkinn.com; 230 N Front St; r $139-229; ❄📶) fills a historic lakefront building and has a couple of resident ghosts.

Sample the local meat-veggie pie specialty at **Jean Kay's Pasties & Subs** (www.jeankayspasties.com; 1635 Presque Isle Ave; items $4-6; ⏲11am-9pm Mon-Fri, to 8pm Sat & Sun). In a quonset hut at Main St's foot, **Thill's Fish House** (☎906-226-9851; 250 E Main St; items $4-9; ⏲8am-5:30pm Mon-Fri, to 4pm Sat) is Marquette's last commercial fishing operation, and it hauls in fat catches daily; try the smoked whitefish sausage. **UpFront and Company** (www.upfrontandcompany.com; 102 E Main St; mains $13-19; ⏲11am-10pm Mon-Fri, 2-10pm Sat, closed Mon in winter) fires up the wood oven for pizzas, the taps for hearty beers and the amps for live music.

ISLE ROYALE NATIONAL PARK

Totally free of vehicles and roads, **Isle Royale National Park** (www.nps.gov/isro; fee per day $4; ⏲mid-May–Oct), a 210-sq-mile island in Lake Superior, is certainly the place to go for peace and quiet. It gets fewer visitors in a year than Yellowstone National Park gets in a day, which means the packs of wolves and moose creeping through the forest are all yours.

The island is laced with 165 miles of hiking trails that connect dozens of campgrounds along Superior and inland lakes. You must be totally prepared for this wilderness adventure, with a tent, camping stove, sleeping bags, food and water filter. Otherwise, be a softie and bunk at the **Rock Harbor Lodge** (☎906-337-4993; www.isleroyaleresort.com; cottages $229-254; ⏲late May-early Sep).

From the dock outside the **park headquarters** (800 E Lakeshore Dr) in Houghton, the **Ranger III** (☎906-482-0984) departs at 9am on Tuesday and Friday for the six-hour boat trip (round trip adult/child $120/40) to Rock Harbor, at the east end of the island. **Royale Air Service** (☎877-359-4753; www.royaleairservice.com) offers a quicker trip, flying from Houghton County Airport to Rock Harbor in 30 minutes (round trip $290). Or head 50 miles up the Keweenaw Peninsula to Copper Harbor (a beautiful drive) and jump on the **Isle Royale Queen** (☎906-289-4437; www.isleroyale.com) for the 8am three-hour crossing (round-trip adult/child $130/65). It usually runs daily during peak season from late July to mid-August. Bringing a kayak or canoe on the ferries costs an additional $40 to $50 round-trip, and ensure you make reservations well in advance. You can also access Isle Royale from Grand Portage, Minnesota (p595).

PORCUPINE MOUNTAINS WILDERNESS STATE PARK

Michigan's largest state park, with 90 miles of trails, is another UP winner, and it's a heck of a lot easier to reach than Isle Royale. 'The Porkies,' as they're called, are so rugged that loggers bypassed most of the range in the early 19th century, leaving the park with the largest tract of virgin forest between the Rocky Mountains and Adirondacks.

From Silver City, head west on Hwy 107 to reach the **Porcupine Mountains visitors center** (☎906-885-5275; www.porcupinemountains.com; 412 S Boundary Rd; ⏲10am-6pm mid-May–mid-Oct), where you buy vehicle entry permits (per day/year $8/29) and backcountry permits (one to four people per night $14). Continue to the end of Hwy 107 and climb 300ft for the stunning view of **Lake of the Clouds**.

Winter is also a busy time at the Porkies, with downhill skiing (a 787ft vertical drop) and 26 miles of cross-country trails on offer; check with the **ski area** (☎906-289-4105; www.skitheporkies.com) for conditions and costs.

The park rents **rustic cabins** (☎906-885-5275; www.mi.gov/porkies; cabins $60) perfect for wilderness adventurers, as you have to hike in 1 to 4 miles, boil your own water and use a privy. **Sunshine Motel & Cabins** (☎906-884-2187; www.ontonagon.net/sunshinemotel; 24077 Hwy 64; r $60, cabins $66-104), 3 miles west of Ontonagon, provides another good base.

WISCONSIN

Wisconsin is cheesy and proud of it. The state pumps out 2.4 billion pounds of cheddar, Gouda and other smelly goodness – a quarter of America's hunks – from its cow-speckled farmland per year. Local license plates read 'The Dairy State' with udder dignity. Folks here even refer to themselves as 'cheeseheads' and emphasize it by wearing novelty foam rubber cheese-wedge hats for special occasions (most notably during Green Bay Packers football games).

So embrace the cheese thing, because there's a good chance you'll be here for a while. Wisconsin has heaps to offer: exploring the craggy cliffs and lighthouses of Door County, kayaking through sea caves at Apostle Islands National Lakeshore, cow chip throwing along US 12 and soaking up beer, art and festivals in Milwaukee and Madison.

WISCONSIN FACTS

» **Nicknames** Badger State, America's Dairyland

» **Population** 5.7 million

» **Area** 65,500 sq miles

» **Capital city** Madison (population 223,400)

» **Other cities** Milwaukee (population 573,360)

» **Sales tax** 5%

» **Birthplace of** author Laura Ingalls Wilder (1867–1957), architect Frank Lloyd Wright (1867–1959), painter Georgia O'Keeffe (1887–1986), actor Orson Welles (1915–85), guitar maker Les Paul (1915–2009)

» **Home of** 'Cheesehead' Packer fans, dairy farms, water parks

» **Politics** leans Democratic

» **Famous for** breweries, artisanal cheese, first state to legislate gay rights

» **Official dance** polka

» **Driving distances** Milwaukee to Minneapolis 336 miles, Milwaukee to Madison 80 miles

Information

Travel Green Wisconsin (www.travelgreenwisconsin.com) Certifies businesses as ecofriendly by grading them on waste reduction, energy efficiency and seven other categories.

Wisconsin B&B Association (www.wbba.org)

Wisconsin Department of Tourism (☎800-432-8747; www.travelwisconsin.com) Produces loads of free guides on subjects like bird-watching, biking, golf and rustic roads; also a free app.

Wisconsin Highway Conditions (☎511; www.511wi.gov)

Wisconsin Milk Marketing Board (www.eatwisconsincheese.com) Provides a free statewide map of cheesemakers titled *A Traveler's Guide to America's Dairyland.*

Wisconsin State Park Information (☎608-266-2181; www.wiparks.net) Park entry requires a vehicle permit (per day/year $10/35). Campsites cost from $12 to $25; **reservations** (☎888-947-2757; www.wisconsinstateparks.reserveamerica.com; fee $10) accepted.

Milwaukee

Here's the thing about Milwaukee: it's cool, but for some reason everyone refuses to admit it. Yes, the reputation lingers as a working man's town of brewskis, bowling alleys and polka halls. But attractions like the Calatrava-designed art museum, badass Harley-Davidson Museum and stylish eating and shopping 'hoods have turned Wisconsin's largest city into a surprisingly groovy place. In summertime, festivals let loose with revelry by the lake almost every weekend. And where else on the planet will you see racing sausages?

History

Milwaukee was first settled by Germans in the 1840s. Many started small breweries, but a few decades later the introduction of bulk brewing technology turned beer production into a major industry here. Milwaukee earned its 'Brew City' and 'Nation's Watering Hole' nicknames in the 1880s when Pabst, Schlitz, Blatz, Miller and 80 other breweries made suds here. Today, only Miller and a few microbreweries remain.

TWO-WHEELING WISCONSIN

Wisconsin has converted an impressive number of abandoned railroad lines into paved, bike-only paths. They go up hills, through old tunnels, over bridges and alongside pastures. Wherever you are in the state, there's likely a sweet ride nearby; check the **Department of Tourism's Bike Path Directory** (www.travelwisconsin.com/bike_path_and_touring_directory.aspx). The **400 State Trail** (www.400statetrail.org) and **Elroy-Sparta Trail** (www.elroy-sparta-trail.com) top the list.

Bike rentals are available in gateway towns, and you can buy trail passes (per day/year $4/20) at area businesses or trailhead drop-boxes.

Sights & Activities

Lake Michigan sits to the east of the city, and is rimmed by parkland. The Riverwalk path runs along both sides of the Milwaukee River downtown.

Harley-Davidson Museum & Plant MUSEUM, TOUR

(☎877-436-8738; www.h-dmuseum.com; 400 W Canal St; adult/child $16/10; ⏰9am-6pm, to 8pm Thu May-Oct, reduced rest of year) In 1903 local schoolmates William Harley and Arthur Davidson built and sold their first Harley-Davidson motorcycle. A century later the big bikes are a symbol of American manufacturing pride. The Harley-Davidson Museum pays homage in a sprawling industrial building just south of downtown. Hundreds of bikes show the styles through the decades, including the flashy rides of Elvis and Evel Knievel. Plus you get to sit in the saddle of various bikes (on the bottom floor, behind the Design Lab), as well as get a minilesson on how to ride (by the front entrance). Even nonbikers will enjoy the place.

Hog-heads can get another fix at the **Harley-Davidson plant** (☎877-883-1450; www.harley-davidson.com; W156 N9000 Pilgrim Rd; 30min tours free; ⏰9am-2pm Mon), in the suburb of Menomonee Falls, a 25-minute drive northwest of downtown. This is where the engines are built. Longer tours also take place on Wednesday and Friday, but only as part of a package deal you buy from the museum (per person $38, including tour, museum admission, and a bus ride between the two venues). No open shoes are permitted.

Milwaukee Art Museum MUSEUM

(☎414-224-3200; www.mam.org; 700 N Art Museum Dr; adult/child $14/12; ⏰10am-5pm, to 8pm Thu, closed Mon Sep-May; 📶) Even those who aren't usually museum-goers will be struck by this lakeside museum, which features a stunning winglike addition by Santiago Calatrava. It soars open and closed every day at 10am, noon and at closing time, which is wild to see. There are fabulous folk and outsider art galleries, and a sizeable collection of Georgia O'Keeffe paintings.

FREE **Miller Brewing Company** TOUR

(☎414-931-2337; www.millercoors.com; 4251 W State St; ⏰10:30am-3:30pm Mon-Sat, to 4:30pm in summer) Pabst and Schlitz have moved on, but Miller preserves Milwaukee's beer legacy. Join the legions of drinkers lined up for the free tours. Though the mass-produced beer may not be your favorite, the factory impresses with its sheer scale: you'll visit the packaging plant where 2000 cans are filled each minute, and the warehouse where a half-million cases await shipment. And then there's the generous tasting session at the tour's end, where you can down three full-size samples. Don't forget your ID.

Lakefront Brewery TOUR

(☎414-372-8800; www.lakefrontbrewery.com; 1872 N Commerce St; 1hr tours $7; ⏰Mon-Sun) Well-loved Lakefront Brewery, across the river from Brady St, has afternoon tours, but the swellest time to visit is on Friday nights when there's a fish fry, 16 beers to try and a polka band letting loose. Tour times vary throughout the week, but there's usually at least a 2pm and 3pm walk-through.

Sprecher Brewing Company TOUR

(☎414-964-2739; www.sprecherbrewery.com; 701 W Glendale Ave; tours $4; ⏰4pm Mon-Fri, noon-2pm Sat & Sun) The small microbrewery's tour includes a museum of memorabilia from long-gone Milwaukee suds-makers and a beer garden replete with oompah music. It's 6 miles north of downtown; reservations are required.

Discovery World at Pier Wisconsin MUSEUM

(☎414-765-9966; www.discoveryworld.org; 500 N Harbor Dr; adult/child $17/13; ⏰9am-5pm Tue-Fri, 10am-5pm Sat & Sun; 👪) The city's lakefront science and technology museum is primarily a kid-pleaser, with freshwater and saltwater

WHAT THE...?

Rumor has it the **Bronze Fonz** (east side of the Riverwalk, just south of Wells St downtown) is the most photographed sight in Milwaukee. Fonz, aka Arthur Fonzarelli, was a character from the 1970s TV show *Happy Days*, which was set in the city. What do you think – do the blue pants get an 'Aaay' or 'Whoa!'?

aquariums (where you can touch sharks and sturgeon) and a dockside, triple-masted Great Lakes schooner to climb aboard ($5 extra). Adults will appreciate the Les Paul exhibit, showcasing the Wisconsin native's pioneering guitars and sound equipment.

Lakefront Park PARK
The parkland edging Lake Michigan is prime for walking, cycling and in-line skating. Also here is Bradford Beach, which is good for swimming and lounging.

Festivals & Events

Summerfest MUSIC
(www.summerfest.com; day pass $15; ⌚late Jun-early Jul) It's dubbed 'the world's largest music festival,' and indeed hundreds of rock, blues, jazz, country and alternative bands swarm its 10 stages over 11 days. The scene totally rocks; it is held at downtown's lakefront festival grounds.

Other popular parties, held downtown during various summer weekends:

PrideFest CULTURAL
(www.pridefest.com; ⌚mid-Jun)

Polish Fest CULTURAL
(www.polishfest.org; ⌚late Jun)

German Fest CULTURAL
(www.germanfest.com; ⌚late Jul)

Irish Fest CULTURAL
(www.irishfest.com; ⌚mid-Aug)

Sleeping

Rates in this section are for summer, the peak season, when you should book in advance. Tax (15.1%) is not included. For cheap chain lodging, try Howell Ave, south near the airport.

Comfort Inn & Suites Downtown Lakeshore HOTEL $$
(☎414-276-8800; www.choicehotels.com; 916 E State St; r incl breakfast $110-170; P⊖❄☎) Check in here and you'll be laying low in the same digs as touring indie bands who come to town. The breakfast buffet, location near the lakefront and shuttle bus to local sights supplement the contemporary rooms. Parking costs $10.

County Clare Irish Inn INN $$
(☎414-272-5273; www.countyclare-inn.com; 1234 N Astor St; r incl breakfast $129-179; P⊖❄☎) It's another winner near the lakefront. Rooms have that snug Irish-cottage feel, with four-post beds, white wainscot walls and whirlpool baths. There's free parking and an on-site Guinness-pouring pub, of course.

Iron Horse Hotel HOTEL $$$
(☎888-543-4766; www.theironhorsehotel.com; 500 W Florida St; r from $189-259; P❄☎) This boutique hotel near the Harley Museum is geared toward motorcycle enthusiasts, with covered parking for bikes. Most of the loft-style rooms retain the post-and-beam, exposed-brick interior of what was once a bedding factory. Parking costs $25.

Aloft HOTEL $$
(☎414-226-0122; www.aloftmilwaukeedowntown.com; 1230 Old World Third St; r $129-179; P⊖❄☎) The chain's Milwaukee property has the usual compact, industrial-looking tone. It's inland and not as convenient for festival-goers, though it is near sausagey Old World Third St and Water St's bar action (thus a bit noisy). Parking costs $23.

Eating

Good places to scope for eats include Germanic N Old World 3rd St downtown; the fashionable East Side by the University of Wisconsin-Milwaukee; hip, Italian-based Brady St by its intersection with N Farwell Ave; and the gastropub-filled Third Ward, anchored along N Milwaukee St south of I-94.

The Friday night fish fry is a highly social tradition observed throughout Wisconsin and all over Milwaukee. Try it at Lakefront Brewery (see p573), which complements its fish with microbrews and a polka band.

Another Milwaukee specialty is frozen custard, which is like ice cream only smoother and richer. **Leon's** (www.leonsfrozencustard.us; 3131 S 27th St; ⌚11am-midnight) and **Kopp's** (www.kopps.com; 5373 N Port Washington Rd, Glendale; ⌚10:30am-11:30pm) are popular purveyors.

Roots Restaurant and Cellar AMERICAN $$$
(☎414-374-8480; www.rootsmilwaukee.com; 1818 N Hubbard St; small plates $8-15, mains $19-36;

⌚5-9pm Mon-Thu, to 10pm Fri & Sat, 10am-2pm & 5-9pm Sun; 🖉) The Slow Food chefs host two options for dining. Upstairs is the sleek, pricier main room with mains like soy-grilled tilapia. The funky downstairs offers small plates, like the seafood sausage corn dog. The outdoor patio with views is prime for cocktails. It is located across the river from Brady St.

Distil AMERICAN $$
(☎414-220-9411; www.distilmilwaukee.com; 722 N Milwaukee St; mains $10-20; ⌚from 5pm Mon-Sat) It's all about artisanal fare at dark, coppery Distil. The menu focuses on cheese and charcuterie (burgers, too). Heck, the beef comes from the owner's cow. Mixologists stir up Corpse Revivers and Sidecars to accompany the food.

Milwaukee Public Market MARKET $
(www.milwaukeepublicmarket.org; 400 N Water St; ⌚10am-8pm Mon-Fri, 8am-7pm Sat, 10am-6pm Sun; 📶) This Third Ward market stocks mostly prepared foods – cheese, chocolate, beer, frozen custard. Take them upstairs where there are tables, free wi-fi and $1 used books.

Drinking & Entertainment

Bars

Several bars tap kegs around N Water and E State Sts downtown, in the Third Ward and along Brady St between Astor and Farwell Sts. Drinkeries stay open to 2am.

TOP CHOICE **Palm Tavern** BAR
(2989 S Kinnickinnic Ave; ⌚from 5pm Mon-Sat, from 7pm Sun) Located in the fresh south-side neighborhood of Bay View, this warm, jazzy little bar has a mammoth selection of beer (heavy on the Belgians) and single-malt Scotches.

Von Trier BAR
(www.vontriers.com; 2235 N Farwell Ave) The German Von Trier is a long-standing, real-deal favorite, with plenty of good stuff on tap, a *biergarten* and the famed free popcorn.

Kochanski's Concertina Beer Hall BAR
(www.beer-hall.com; 1920 S 37th St; ⌚Wed-Sun; 📶) Live polka music rules at kitschy Kochanski's, with beers from Schlitz to Polish drafts to Wisconsin craft labels. It's 5 miles southwest of downtown.

Sports

Miller Park BASEBALL
(www.milwaukeebrewers.com; 1 Brewers Way) The Brewers play baseball at fab Miller Park, which has a retractable roof, real grass and racing sausages (see the boxed text, p571). It's located near S 46th St.

Bradley Center BASKETBALL
(www.nba.com/bucks; 1001 N 4th St) The NBA's Milwaukee Bucks dunk here.

AMERICA'S BOWLING CAPITAL

You're in Milwaukee, so you probably should just do it: bowl. The city once had more than 200 bowling alleys, and many retro lanes still hide in timeworn dives. To get your game on try **Landmark Lanes** (www.landmarklanes.com; 2220 N Farwell Ave; per game $2.50-3.50; ⌚5pm-1:30am Mon-Thu, noon-1:30am Fri-Sun; 📶), offering 16 beat-up alleys in the historic 1927 Oriental Theater. An arcade, three bars and butt-cheap beer round out the atmosphere.

Information

Emergency & Medical Services

Froedtert Hospital (☎414-805-3000; 9200 W Wisconsin Ave)

Internet Access

The East Side neighborhood near the University of Wisconsin-Milwaukee has several coffee shops with free wi-fi.

Media

Milwaukee Journal Sentinel (www.jsonline.com) The city's daily newspaper.

Quest (www.quest-online.com) GLBT entertainment magazine.

Shepherd Express (www.expressmilwaukee.com) Free alternative weekly paper.

Tourist Information

Milwaukee Convention & Visitors Bureau (☎800-554-1448; www.visitmilwaukee.org)

Websites

On Milwaukee (www.onmilwaukee.com) Site for traffic and weather updates, plus restaurant and entertainment reviews.

Getting There & Around

General Mitchell International Airport (MKE; www.mitchellairport.com) is 8 miles south of downtown. Take public bus 80 ($2.25) or a cab ($30).

WHAT THE...?

It's common to see strange things after too many stadium beers. But a group of giant sausages sprinting around Miller Park's perimeter – is that for *real*? It is if it's the middle of the 6th inning. That's when the famous 'Racing Sausages' (actually five people in costumes) waddle onto the field to give the fans a thrill. If you don't know your encased meats, that's Brat, Polish, Italian, Hot Dog and Chorizo vying for supremacy.

The **Lake Express ferry** (☎866-914-1010; www.lake-express.com) sails from downtown (the terminal is located a few miles south of the city center) to Muskegon, Michigan, providing easy access to Michigan's beach-lined Gold Coast. See p566 for details.

Greyhound (☎414-272-2156; 433 W St Paul Ave) runs frequent buses to Chicago (two hours) and Minneapolis (seven hours). **Badger Bus** (☎414-276-7490; www.badgerbus.com; 635 N James Lovell St) goes to Madison ($19, two hours). **Megabus** (www.megabus.com/us) runs express to Chicago (two hours) and Minneapolis (six hours), often for lower fares than Greyhound.

Amtrak (☎414-271-0840; 433 W St Paul Ave) runs the *Hiawatha* train seven times a day to/from Chicago ($22, 1½ hours); catch it downtown (it shares the station with Greyhound) or at the airport.

The **Milwaukee County Transit System** (www.ridemcts.com; fare $2.25) provides the local bus service. Bus 31 goes to Miller Brewery; bus 90 goes to Miller Park.

For taxi service, try phoning **Yellow Cab** (☎414-271-1800).

Madison

Madison reaps a lot of kudos – most walkable city, best road-biking city, most vegetarian friendly, gay friendly, environmentally friendly and just plain all-round friendliest city in the USA. Ensconced on a narrow isthmus between Mendota and Monona Lakes, it's a pretty combination of small, grassy state capital and liberal, bookish college town. An impressive foodie/locavore scene has been cooking here for years.

Sights & Activities

State St runs from the capitol west to the University of Wisconsin. The lengthy avenue is lined with free-trade coffee shops, parked bicycles and incense-wafting stores selling hacky sacks and flowy Indian skirts.

Dane County Farmers Market MARKET
(www.dcfm.org; Capitol Sq; ⏲6am-2pm Sat, late Apr-early Nov) On Saturdays, a food bazaar takes over Capitol Sq. It's one of the nation's most expansive markets, famed for its artisanal cheeses. All the cheese, veggies, flowers and breads are made by the folks behind the 150 vendor tables.

FREE **State Capitol** BUILDING
(☎608-266-0382; ⏲8am-6pm Mon-Fri, to 4pm Sat & Sun) The X-shaped capitol is the largest outside Washington, DC, and marks the heart of downtown. Tours are available on the hour most days, or you can go up to the observation deck on your own for a view. Recently the capitol has been the site of big-time protests pitting state Democrats against Republicans.

FREE **Museum of Contemporary Art** MUSEUM
(☎608-257-0158; www.mmoca.org; 227 State St; ⏲noon-5pm Tue-Thu, to 8pm Fri, 10am-8pm Sat, noon-5pm Sun) The glassy museum holds works by Diego Rivera, Claes Oldenburg, Cindy Sherman and others. Exhibits change several times a year, so you never know what you'll see. There's also a rooftop garden and martini lounge. The museum connects to the **Overture Center for the Arts** (www.overturecenter.com; 201 State St), home to jazz, opera, dance and other performing arts.

Machinery Row CYCLING
(☎608-442-5974; www.machineryrowbicycles.com; 601 Williamson St; rental per day $20; ⏲9am-9pm Mon-Fri, to 7pm Sat, 10am-7pm Sun) It'd be a shame to leave town without taking advantage of the city's 120 miles of bike trails. Get wheels and maps at this shop, located near the hostel and by various trailheads.

Rutabaga Paddlesports WATER SPORTS
(☎608-223-9300; www.rutabaga.com; 220 W Broadway; rental per half-/full day $25/40; ⏲10am-8pm Mon-Fri, to 6pm Sat, 11am-5pm Sun) Rent a canoe or kayak to paddle the lakes; it's 5 miles southeast of Capitol Sq and right on the water.

FREE **Arboretum** GARDENS
(☎608-263-7888; http://uwarboretum.org; 1207 Seminole Hwy; ⏲7am-10pm) The campus' 1260-acre arboretum is dense with lilac.

Festivals & Events

FREE World's Largest Brat Fest FOOD

(www.bratfest.com; late May) At this Memorial Day weekend festival, 208,000 bratwursts go down the hatch, accompanied by rides and bands.

Great Taste of the Midwest Beer Festival FOOD

(www.mhtg.org; tickets $50; early Aug) Tickets sell out fast for this festival where 120 craft brewers pour their elixirs.

Sleeping

Moderately priced motels can be found off I-90/I-94 (about 6 miles from the town center), off Hwy 12/18 and also along Washington Ave.

TOP CHOICE Arbor House B&B $$

(608-238-2981; www.arbor-house.com; 3402 Monroe St; r incl breakfast weekday $110-175, weekend $150-230;) Arbor House was an old tavern back in the mid-1800s. Now it's a wind-powered, energy-efficient-appliance-using, vegetarian-breakfast-serving B&B. It's located about 3 miles southwest of the State Capitol but accessible to public transportation. The owners will lend you mountain bikes, too.

HI Madison Hostel HOSTEL $

(608-441-0144; www.hiusa.org/madison; 141 S Butler St; dm $22-27, r $57; P@) The brightly painted, 33-bed brick house is located on a quiet street a short walk from the State Capitol. Dorms are gender segregated; linens are free. A Costa Rican restaurant cooks below the hostel, which is handy for dinner. Parking is $7.

University Inn HOTEL $$

(608-285-8040, 800-279-4881; www.universityinn.org; 441 N Frances St; r $89-129; P@) The rooms are fine, though nothing special; the inn's greatest asset is its handy location right by State St and university action. Rates are highest at weekends.

Eating & Drinking

A global smorgasbord of restaurants peppers State St amid the pizza, sandwich and cheap-beer joints; many places have inviting patios. Cruising Williamson ('Willy') St turns up cafes, dumpling bars and Lao and Thai joints. Bars stay open to 2am. **Isthmus** (www.thedailypage.com) is the free entertainment paper.

TOP CHOICE The Old Fashioned AMERICAN $$

(608-310-4545; www.theoldfashioned.com; 23 N Pinckney St; mains $8-16; 7:30am-10:30pm Mon & Tue, 7:30am-2am Wed-Fri, 9am-2am Sat, 9am-10pm Sun) With its dark, woodsy decor, the Old Fashioned evokes a supper club, a type of time-warped eatery common in the upper Midwest. The menu is all Wisconsin specialties, including walleye, cheese soup and sausages. There's even a relish tray, for those who know their supper club staples. It's hard to choose among the 150 types of state-brewed suds in bottles, so opt for a sampler (four or eight little glasses) from the 30 Wisconsin tap beers.

Graze & L'Etoile AMERICAN $$$

(608-251-0500; www.letoile-restaurant.com; 1 S Pinckney St; pub mains $16-22, restaurant mains $29-42; pub breakfast, lunch & dinner Mon-Sat, brunch Sun, restaurant dinner Mon-Sat) Slow Food pioneer Odessa Piper offered farm-to-table dinners at L'Etoile for 30 years. These days, chef Tory Miller does the cooking with seasonal ingredients sourced at the farmers market. He also helms Graze, the gastropub next door, that dishes up sustainable comfort foods such as fried chicken and waffles, mussels and *frites,* and burgers.

Food Trucks ECLECTIC $

(mains $1-8;) Madison's fleet impresses. The more traditional ones, serving barbecue, burritos, southwestern-style fare and Chinese food, ring the Capitol. The corner of King St is well endowed. Trucks ladling out more adventurous dishes – ie East African, Jamaican, Indonesian, vegan – huddle at the foot of State St by campus.

Himal Chuli ASIAN $$

(608-251-9225; 318 State St; mains $8-15; 11am-9pm Mon-Thu, to 10pm Fri & Sat, noon-8pm Sun;) Cheerful and cozy Himal Chuli serves up homemade Nepali fare, including lots of vegetarian dishes.

Ian's Pizza PIZZERIA $

(608-257-9248; www.ianspizza.com; 115 State St; slices $3.50; 11am-2am) Crazy slices topped by macaroni and cheese (most popular), guacamole taco, barbecue chicken and about 20 other items are in high demand, especially late at night.

WORTH A TRIP

WORTH A TRIP: ODDBALL US 12

Unusual sights huddle around US 12, all easy to experience on a northerly day trip from Madison.

Heading west out of town (take University Ave), stop first at the **National Mustard Museum** (☎800-438-6878; www.mustardmuseum.com; 7477 Hubbard Ave; admission free; ⊙10am-5pm) in suburban Middleton. Born of one man's ridiculously intense passion, the building houses 5200 mustards and kooky condiment memorabilia. Tongue-in-cheek humor abounds, especially if CMO (chief mustard officer) Barry Levenson is there to give you the shtick.

About 20 miles further on US 12 is the town of Prairie du Sac. It hosts the annual **Cow Chip Throw** (www.wiscowchip.com; admission free; ⊙1st weekend Sep), where 800 competitors fling dried manure patties as far as the eye can see; the record is 248ft.

Seven miles onward is **Dr Evermor's Sculpture Park** (www.worldofevermor.com; admission free; ⊙9am-5pm Mon & Thu-Sat, noon-5pm Sun). The doc welds old pipes, carburetors and other salvaged metal into a hallucinatory world of futuristic birds, dragons and other bizarre structures. The crowning glory is the giant, egg-domed Forevertron, once cited by *Guinness World Records* as the globe's largest scrap metal sculpture. Finding the park entrance is tricky. Look for the Badger Army Ammunition Plant, and then a small sign leading you into a driveway across the street.

Baraboo, about 45 miles northwest of Madison, was once the winter home of the Ringling Brothers Circus. **Circus World Museum** (☎608-356-8341; www.wisconsinhistory.org/circusworld; 550 Water St; adult/child summer $15/8, winter $7/3.50; ⊙9am-6pm summer, reduced hr winter; 👪) preserves a nostalgic collection of wagons, posters and equipment from the touring big-top heyday. In summer, admission includes clowns, animals and acrobats doing the three-ring thing.

Continue north another 12 miles to the **Wisconsin Dells** (☎800-223-3557; www.wisdells.com; 👪), a megacenter of kitschy diversions, including 21 water parks, water-skiing thrill shows and super-minigolf courses. It's a jolting contrast to the natural appeal of the area, with its scenic limestone formations carved by the Wisconsin River. To appreciate the original attraction, take a boat tour or walk the trails at Mirror Lake or Devil's Lake state parks.

Memorial Union AMERICAN
(www.union.wisc.edu/venue-muterrace.htm; 800 Langdon St) The campus Union is Madison's gathering spot. The festive lakeside terrace pours microbrews and hosts free live music and free Monday night films, while the indoor ice cream shop scoops hulking cones from the university dairy.

Shopping

Fromagination (☎608-255-2430; www.fromagination.com; 12 S Carroll St; ⊙9:30am-6pm Mon-Fri, 9am-4pm Sat) specializes in small-batch and hard-to-find local cheese. If you miss the Saturday farmers market, you can find many of the same cheeses here. Be sure to pick up some cheese curds to experience their squeaky bite.

Information

Madison Convention & Visitors Bureau (www.visitmadison.com)

Getting There & Around

Badger Bus (www.badgerbus.com) uses Memorial Union as its pick-up/drop-off point for trips to Milwaukee ($19, two hours), as does **Megabus** (www.megabus.com/us) for trips to Chicago (four hours) and Minneapolis (4½ hours).

Taliesin & Southern Wisconsin

This part of Wisconsin has some of the prettiest landscapes in the state, particularly the hilly southwest. Architecture fans can be unleashed at Taliesin, the Frank Lloyd Wright ubersight, and Racine, where two of his other works stand. Dairies around here cut a lot of cheese.

RACINE

Racine is an unremarkable industrial town 30 miles south of Milwaukee, but it has two key Frank Lloyd Wright sights, both of which offer 45-minute tours that must be prebooked. The first, the **Johnson Wax Company Administration Building** (☎262-260-2154; 1525 Howe St; admission free; ⊙tours 11:45am & 12:45pm Fri, noon Sat), dates from 1939 and is a magnificent space with tall, flared columns. The second is the lakeside **Wingspread** (☎262-681-3353; www.johnsonfdn.org; 33 E Four Mile Rd; admission free; ⊙9:30am-2:30pm Tue-Fri), the last and largest of Wright's Prairie houses.

GREEN COUNTY

This pastoral area holds the nation's greatest concentration of cheesemakers, and **Green County Tourism** (www.greencounty.org) will introduce you to them. Monroe is a fine place to start sniffing. Follow your nose to **Roth Käse** (657 Second St; ⊙9am-6pm Mon-Fri, 10am-5pm Sat & Sun), a store and factory where you can watch cheesemakers in action from the observation deck (weekday mornings only) and delve into the 'bargain bin' for hunks. Bite into a fresh limburger-and-raw-onion sandwich at **Baumgartner's** (www.baumgartnercheese.com; 1023 Sixteenth Ave; sandwiches $4-7; ⊙8am-11pm), an old Swiss tavern on the town square. At night, catch a flick at the local drive-in movie theater, and then climb into bed at **Inn Serendipity** (☎608-329-7056; www.innserendipity.com; 7843 County Rd P; r incl breakfast $110-125), a two-room, wind-and-solar-powered B&B on a 5-acre organic farm in Browntown, about 10 miles west of Monroe.

For more on local dairy producers and plant tours, pick up **A Traveler's Guide to America's Dairyland** (www.eatwisconsincheese.com) map.

SPRING GREEN

Forty miles west of Madison and 3 miles south of the small town of Spring Green, **Taliesin** was the home of Frank Lloyd Wright for most of his life and is the site of his architectural school. It's now a major pilgrimage destination for fans and followers. The house was built in 1903, the Hillside Home School in 1932, and the **visitor center** (☎608-588-7900; www.taliesinpreservation.org; Hwy 23; ⊙9am-5:30pm May-Oct) in 1953. A wide range of guided tours ($16 to $80) cover various parts of the complex; reserve in advance for the lengthier ones. The one-hour Hillside Tour ($16) provides a nice introduction to Wright's work.

A few miles south of Taliesin is the **House on the Rock** (☎608-935-3639; www.thehouseontherock.com; 5754 Hwy 23; adult/child $12.50/7.50; ⊙9am-6pm May-Aug, to 5pm rest of year, closed Tue-Thu Nov-Apr), one of Wisconsin's busiest attractions. Alex Jordan built the structure atop a rock column in 1959 (some say as an 'up yours' to neighbor Frank Lloyd Wright). He then stuffed the house to mind-blowing proportions with wonderments, including the world's largest carousel, whirring music machines, freaky dolls and crazed folk art. The house is broken into three parts, each with its own tour. Visitors with stamina (and about four hours to kill) can experience the whole shebang for adult/child $28.50/15.50.

Spring Green has a B&B in town and six motels strung along Hwy 14, north of town. Small **Usonian Inn** (☎877-876-6426; www.usonianinn.com; E 5116 Hwy 14; r $85-135; ⊖❄⊜) was designed by a Wright student. Check www.springgreen.com for more options.

Chomp sandwiches or inventive specials like sweet potato stew at **Spring Green General Store** (www.springgreengeneralstore.com; 137 S Albany St; mains $5-7; ⊙9am-6pm Mon-Fri, 8am-6pm Sat, 8am-4pm Sun).

The **American Players Theatre** (☎608-588-2361; www.playinthewoods.org) stages classical productions at an outdoor amphitheater by the Wisconsin River.

Along the Mississippi River

The Mississippi River forms most of Wisconsin's western border, and alongside it run some of the most scenic sections of the **Great River Road** (www.wigreatriverroad.org) – the designated route that follows Old Man River from Minnesota to the Gulf of Mexico.

From Madison, head west on US 18. You'll hit the River Road (aka Hwy 35) at **Prairie du Chien**. North of town, the hilly riverside wends through the scene of the final battle in the bloody Black Hawk War. Historic markers tell part of the story, which finished at the Battle of Bad Ax when Native American men, women and children were massacred trying to flee across the Mississippi.

At Genoa, Hwy 56 leads inland for 20 miles to the trout-fishing mecca of **Viroqua** (www.viroquatourism.com), a pretty little town surrounded by organic farms and distinctive round barns. Pop into **Viroqua Food Cooperative** (www.viroquafood.coop; 609 Main St; ⊙7am-9pm Mon-Sat, 9am-8pm Sun) to meet farmers and munch their wares.

Back riverside and 18 miles upstream, **La Crosse** (www.explorelacrosse.com) has a historic center nestling restaurants and pubs. Grandad Bluff offers grand views of the river. It's east of town along Main St (which becomes Bliss Rd); follow Bliss Rd up the hill and then turn right on Grandad Bluff Rd. The **World's Largest Six-Pack** (3rd St S) is also in town. The 'cans' are actually storage tanks for City Brewery and hold enough beer to provide one person with a six-pack a day for 3351 years (or so the sign says).

For destinations on up the road, see Southern Minnesota (p592).

Door County & Eastern Wisconsin

Rocky, lighthouse-dotted Door County draws crowds in summer, while Green Bay draws crazed football fans in the freakin' freezing winter.

GREEN BAY

Green Bay (www.greenbay.com) is a modest industrial town best known as the fabled 'frozen tundra' where the Green Bay Packers win Super Bowls. The franchise is unique as the only community-owned nonprofit team in the NFL; perhaps pride in ownership is what makes the fans so die-hard (and wear foam-rubber cheese wedges on their head).

While tickets are nearly impossible to obtain, you can always get into the spirit by joining a pregame tailgate party. The generous flow of alcohol has led to Green Bay's reputation as a 'drinking town with a football problem.' On nongame days, visit the **Green Bay Packer Hall of Fame** (☎920-569-7512; www.lambeaufield.com; adult/child $10/5; ⏱9am-6pm Mon-Sat, 10am-5pm Sun) at Lambeau Field, which is indeed packed with memorabilia and movies that'll intrigue any pigskin fan.

The **National Railroad Museum** (☎920-437-7623; www.nationalrrmuseum.org; 2285 S Broadway; adult/child $9/6.50 May-Sep; ⏱9am-5pm Mon-Sat, 11am-5pm Sun, closed Mon Jan-Apr) features some of the biggest locomotives ever to haul freight into Green Bay's vast yards; train rides ($2) are offered in summer.

Bare-bones **Bay Motel** (☎920-494-3441; www.baymotelgreenbay.com; 1301 S Military Ave; r $52-75; 📶) is a mile from Lambeau Field. **Hinterland** (☎920-438-8050; www.hinterlandbeer.com; 313 Dousman St) gastropub brings a touch of rustic swankiness to beer drinkers.

DOOR COUNTY

With its rocky coastline, picturesque lighthouses, cherry orchards and small 19th-century villages, you have to admit Door County is pretty damn lovely. The area spreads across a narrow peninsula jutting 75 miles into Lake Michigan, and visitors usually loop around on the county's two highways. Hwy 57 runs beside Lake Michigan and goes through Jacksonport and Baileys Harbor; this is known as the more scenic 'quiet side.' Hwy 42 borders Green Bay and passes through (from south to north) Egg Harbor, Fish Creek, Ephraim and Sister Bay; this side is more action oriented. Only about half the businesses stay open from November to April.

Sights & Activities

Parkland blankets the county. Bayside **Peninsula State Park** is the largest, with bluff-side hiking and biking trails and a beach for kayaking and sailing. In winter, cross-country skiers and snowshoers take over the trails. On the lake side, secluded **Newport State Park** offers trails, backcountry camping and solitude. **Whitefish Dunes State Park** has sandscapes and a wide beach (beware of riptides). Adjacent **Cave Point Park** is known for its sea caves and kayaking. Multiactivity outfitters include:

Bayshore Outdoor Store (☎920-854-9220; www.kayakdoorcounty.com; Sister Bay)

Nor Door Sport & Cyclery (☎920-868-2275; www.nordoorsports.com; Fish Creek)

Sleeping & Eating

The bay side has the most lodging. Prices listed are for July and August, the peak season; many places have minimum-stay requirements. Local restaurants often host a 'fish boil,' a regional specialty started by

TALK LIKE A LOCAL

Admit it: you're puzzled by how to pronounce town names like Prairie du Chien and Lac du Flambeau. Lucky for you, **Miss Pronouncer** (www.misspronouncer.com) provides recordings of how to say it in Wisconsinese. She covers 190 cities, 1260 towns and heaps of famous locals' names. Soon you'll be chattering on about your visit to Rio *(rye-o)* or Chequamegon *(sheh wom again)* with confidence.

Scandinavian lumberjacks, in which whitefish, potatoes and onions are cooked in a fiery cauldron. Finish with Door's famous cherry pie.

Egg Harbor Lodge INN $$
(920-868-3115; www.eggharborlodge.com; Egg Harbor; r $159-199;) All rooms have a water view and free bike use.

Julie's Park Cafe and Motel MOTEL $
(920-868-2999; www.juliesmotel.com; Fish Creek; r $82-106;) It's tidy and relatively low cost; located beside Peninsula State Park.

Peninsula State Park CAMPGROUND $
(920-868-3258; tent & RV sites $17-25; Fish Creek) Peninsula holds nearly 500 amenity-laden campsites.

JJ's PUB $$
(920-854-4513; jjslapuerta.com; Sister Bay; mains $9-16; 11am-2am, closed Sun-Tue in winter) Hang with the young boater types at this good-time pub attached to a Mexican restaurant.

Village Cafe AMERICAN $
(920-868-3342; www.villagecafe-doorcounty.com; Egg Harbor; sandwiches $6.50-8.50, mains $14-16; 7am-8pm) Delicious breakfast, lunch and dinner platters.

Information

Door County Visitors Bureau (800-527-3529; www.doorcounty.com) Special-interest brochures on art galleries, biking and lighthouses.

Apostle Islands & Northern Wisconsin

The north is a thinly populated region of forests and lakes, where folks paddle and fish in summer, and ski and snowmobile in winter. The cliffy, windswept Apostle Islands steal the show.

NORTHWOODS & LAKELANDS

Nicolet National Forest is a vast, wooded district ideal for outdoor activities. The simple crossroads of **Langlade** is a center for white-water river adventures. **Wolf River Guides** (715-882-3002; www.wolfriverguides.com) provides half-day kayak-paddling classes followed by a half-day trip on the water (per person $110), while **Wolf River Lodge** (715-882-2182; www.wolfriverlodge.com; r incl breakfast $100;) provides accommodation where you can dry off, get warm and celebrate your accomplishments in the on-site bar.

North on Hwy 13, folk artist and retired lumberjack Fred Smith's **Concrete Park** (www.friendsoffredsmith.org; admission free; sunrise-sunset) in Phillips is extraordinary, with 200-plus whimsical, life-size sculptures.

West on Hwy 70, **Chequamegon National Forest** offers exceptional mountain biking with 300 miles of off-road trails. The **Chequamegon Area Mountain Bike Association** (www.cambatrails.org) has trail maps and bike rental information. The season culminates in mid-September with the **Chequamegon Fat Tire Festival** (www.cheqfattire.com), when 1700 strong-legged men and women peddle 40 grueling miles through the woods. The town of **Hayward** (www.haywardareachamber.com) makes a good base.

> **SCENIC DRIVE: HIGHWAY 13**
>
> After departing Bayfield, Hwy 13 takes a fine route around the Lake Superior shore, past the Ojibwa community of **Red Cliff** and the Apostle Islands' mainland segment, which has a beach. Tiny **Cornucopia**, looking every bit like a seaside village, has great sunsets. The road runs on through a timeless countryside of forest and farm reaching US 2 for the final miles back to civilization at Superior.

APOSTLE ISLANDS

The 21 rugged Apostle Islands, floating in Lake Superior and freckling Wisconsin's northern tip, are a state highlight. Jump off from **Bayfield** (www.bayfield.org), a humming resort town with hilly streets, Victorian-era buildings, apple orchards and nary a fast-food restaurant in sight.

The **Apostle Islands National Lakeshore visitors center** (715-779-3397; www.nps.gov/apis; 410 Washington Ave; 8am-4:30pm Jun-Sep, closed Sat & Sun Oct-May) has camping permits (per night $10) and paddling and hiking information. The forested islands have no facilities, and walking is the only way to get around.

Various companies offer seasonal boat trips around the islands, and kayaking is very popular. Try **Living Adventure** (715-779-9503; www.livingadventure.com; Hwy 13; half-/full-day tour $59/99; Jun-Sep) for a guided paddle through arches and sea caves; beginners are welcome. If you prefer a motor to power your explorations, climb aboard the **Apostle Islands Cruise Service** (☎715-779-3925; www.apostleisland.com; ⊙mid-May–mid-Oct) boat. It departs at 10am from Bayfield's City Dock for a three-hour narrated trip past sea caves and lighthouses (adult/child $40/24).

Inhabited **Madeline Island** (www.madelineisland.com), a fine day trip, is reached by a 20-minute **ferry** (☎715-747-2051; www.madferry.com) from Bayfield (round-trip adult/child/bicycle/car $12/6/6/24). Its walkable village of La Pointe has some mid-priced places to stay, and restaurants. Bus tours are available, and you can rent bikes and mopeds – everything is near the ferry dock. **Big Bay State Park** (☎715-747-6425; tent & RV sites $15-17, vehicle $10) has a beach and trails.

Back in Bayfield, there are loads of B&Bs and inns, but reserve ahead in summer; see www.bayfield.org for options. Most rooms at no-frills **Seagull Bay Motel** (☎715-779-5558; www.seagullbay.com; 325 S 7th St; r $75-105; ⊜☜) have decks; ask for a lake view. Going upscale: **Pinehurst Inn** (☎877-499-7651; www.pinehurstinn.com; 83645 Hwy 13; r incl breakfast $119-199; ⊜☜) is a carbon-neutral, solar-heated, eight-room B&B.

Ecoconscious **Big Water Cafe** (www.bigwatercoffee.com; 117 Rittenhouse Ave; mains $5-10; ⊙7am-8pm summer, to 4pm winter) serves sandwiches, local farmstead cheeses and area microbrews. Kitschy, flamingo-themed **Maggie's** (☎715-779-5641; www.maggies-bayfield.com; 257 Manypenny Ave; mains $7-16; ⊙11:30am-9pm Sun-Thu, to 10pm Fri & Sat) is the place to sample local lake trout and whitefish; there are pizza and burgers too.

The **Big Top Chautauqua** (☎888-244-8368; www.bigtop.org) is a major regional summer event with big-name concerts and musical theater; call for schedule and prices.

MINNESOTA

Is Minnesota really the land of 10,000 lakes, as so often advertised? You betcha. Actually, in typically modest style, the state has undermarketed itself – there are 11,842 lakes. Which is great news for travelers. Intrepid outdoorsfolk can wet their paddles in the Boundary Waters, where nighttime brings a blanket of stars and the lullaby of wolf howls. Those wanting to get further off the beaten path can journey to Voyageurs National Park, where there's more water than roadway. If that all seems too far-flung, stick to the Twin Cities of Minneapolis and St Paul, where you can't swing a moose without hitting something cool or cultural. And for those looking for middle ground – a cross between the big city and big woods – the dramatic, freighter-filled port of Duluth beckons.

MINNESOTA FACTS

» **Nicknames** North Star State, Gopher State

» **Population** 5.3 million

» **Area** 86,940 sq miles

» **Capital city** St Paul (population 273,500)

» **Other cities** Minneapolis (population 372,800)

» **Sales tax** 6.88%

» **Birthplace of** author F Scott Fitzgerald (1896–1940), songwriter Bob Dylan (b 1941), filmmakers Joel Coen (b 1954) and Ethan Coen (b 1957)

» **Home of** lumberjack legend Paul Bunyan, Spam, walleye fish, Hmong and Somali immigrants

» **Politics** leans Democratic

» **Famous for** niceness, funny accents, snowy weather, 10,000 lakes

» **Official muffin** blueberry

» **Driving distances** Minneapolis to Duluth 153 miles, Minneapolis to Boundary Waters 245 miles

ℹ Information

Minnesota Highway Conditions (☎511; www.511mn.org)

Minnesota Office of Tourism (☎888-868-7476; www.exploreminnesota.com)

Minnesota State Park Information (☎888-646-6367; www.mnstateparks.info) Park entry requires a vehicle permit (per day/year $5/25). Campsites cost $12 to $25; **reservations** (☎866-857-2757; www.stayatmnparks.com; fee $8.50) accepted.

Minneapolis

Minneapolis is the biggest and artiest town on the prairie, with all the trimmings of progressive prosperity – swank art museums, rowdy rock clubs, organic and ethnic eateries, and enough theaters to be nicknamed Mini-Apple (second only to the

Big Apple). It's always happenin', even in winter. But there's no attitude to go along with the abundance. It's the kind of place where homeless people are treated kindly at the coffee shops, where the buses are kept immaculately clean, and where the public workers tell everyone to 'Have a nice day,' rain or shine (or snow). The city is 'Minnesota Nice' in action.

History

Timber was the city's first boom industry, and water-powered sawmills rose along the Mississippi River in the mid-1800s. Wheat from the prairies also needed to be processed, so flour mills churned into the next big business. The population boomed in the late 19th century with mass immigration, especially from Scandinavia and Germany. Today Minneapolis' Nordic heritage is evident, whereas twin city St Paul is more German and Irish-Catholic.

Sights & Activities

The Mississippi River flows northeast of downtown. Despite the name, Uptown is actually southwest of downtown, with Hennepin Ave as its main axis. Minneapolis' twin city, St Paul, is 10 miles east.

Most attractions are closed Monday; many stay open late Thursday.

DOWNTOWN & LORING PARK

Nicollet Mall STREET

Nicollet Mall is the pedestrian-friendly portion of Nicollet Ave in the heart of downtown, dense with stores, bars and restaurants. It's perhaps most famous as the spot where Mary Tyler Moore (of '70s TV fame) threw her hat into the air during the show's opening sequence. A cheesy **MTM statue** (8th St S & Nicollet Mall) depicts our girl doing just that. A **farmers market** (www.mplsfarmersmarket.com; 6am-6pm) takes over the mall on Thursdays from May to November.

FREE **Minneapolis Sculpture Garden** GARDENS

(726 Vineland Pl; 6am-midnight) The 11-acre garden, studded with contemporary works such as the oft-photographed *Spoonbridge & Cherry* by Claes Oldenburg, sits beside the Walker Art Center. The Cowles Conservatory, abloom with exotic hothouse flowers, is also on the grounds. The garden connects to attractive Loring Park by a sculptural pedestrian bridge over I-94.

Walker Art Center MUSEUM

(612-375-7622; www.walkerart.org; 725 Vineland Pl; adult/child $10/free, admission free Thu evening; 11am-5pm Tue-Sun, to 9pm Thu) The first-class center has a strong permanent collection of 20th-century art and photography, including big-name US painters and great US pop art.

RIVERFRONT DISTRICT

At the north edge of downtown at the foot of Portland Ave is the **St Anthony Falls Heritage Trail**, a recommended 2-mile path that provides both interesting history (placards dot the route) and the city's best access to the banks of the Mississippi River. View the cascading **St Anthony Falls** from the car-free **Stone Arch Bridge**. On the north side of the river, Main St SE has a stretch of redeveloped buildings housing restaurants and bars. From here you can walk down to **Water Power Park** and feel the river's frothy spray. Pick up a free trail map at the Mill City Museum.

Definitely head next door to the cobalt-blue Guthrie Theater (see p588) and make your way up to its '**Endless Bridge**,' a cantilevered walkway overlooking the river. You don't need a theater ticket – it's intended as a public space – though see a show if you can as the Guthrie is one of the Midwest's finest companies. **Gold Medal Park** spirals next door.

Mill City Museum MUSEUM

(612-341-7555; www.millcitymuseum.org; 704 2nd St S; adult/child $10/5; 10am-5pm Tue-Sat, noon-5pm Sun, open Mon Jul & Aug) The building is indeed a former mill, and highlights include a ride inside an eight-story grain elevator ('the Flour Tower'), Betty Crocker exhibits and a baking lab. It's not terribly exciting unless you're really into milling history. The **Mill City Farmer's Market** (www.millcityfarmersmarket.org; 8am-1pm Sat mid-May–mid-Oct) takes place in the museum's attached train shed; cooking demos fire up at 10am.

NORTHEAST

Once a working-class Eastern European neighborhood, Northeast (so named because of its position to the river) is where urbanites and artists now work and play. They appreciate the dive bars pouring microbrews along with Pabst, and boutiques selling ecogifts next to companies grinding sausage. Hundreds of craftsfolk and galleries fill historic industrial buildings. They fling open their doors the first Thursday of each month when

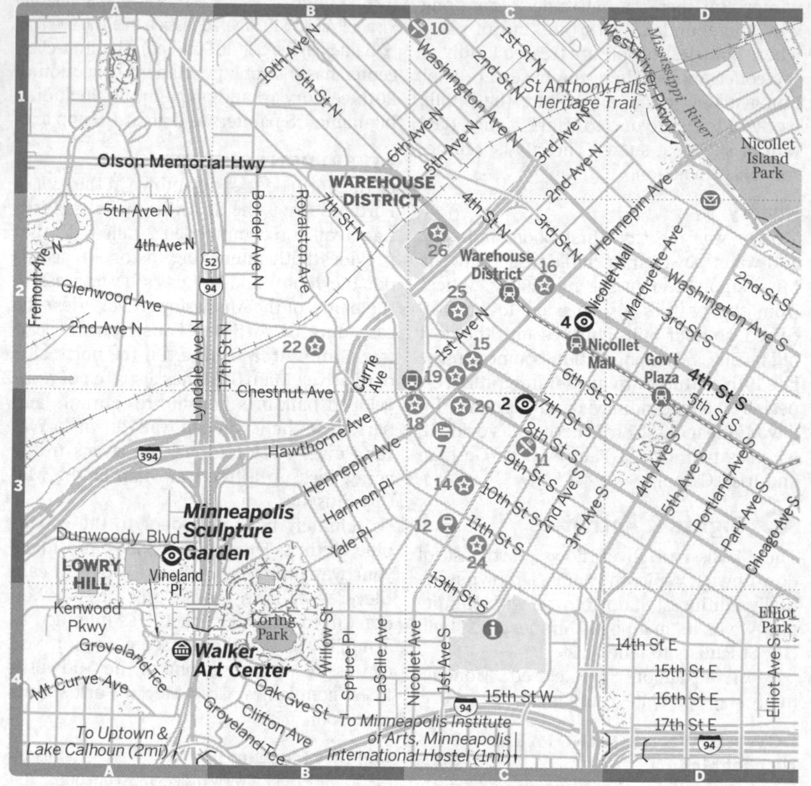

the **Northeast Minneapolis Arts Association** (www.nemaa.org) sponsors a gallery walk. Heady streets include 4th St NE and 13th Ave NE.

UNIVERSITY AREA

The **University of Minnesota**, by the river southeast of Minneapolis' center, is one of the USA's largest campuses, with over 50,000 students. Most of the campus is in the **East Bank** neighborhood.

Dinkytown, based at 14th Ave SE and 4th St SE, is dense with student cafes and bookshops. A small part of the university is on the **West Bank** of the Mississippi River, near the intersection of 4th St S and Riverside Ave. This area has a few restaurants, some student hangouts and a big Somali community.

FREE **Weisman Art Museum** MUSEUM
(☎612-625-9494; www.weisman.umn.edu; 333 E River Rd; ⏲10am-5pm Tue-Fri, to 8pm Thu, 11am-5pm Sat & Sun) The Weisman, which occupies a swooping silver structure by architect Frank Gehry, is a uni (and city) highlight. It was in expansion mode at the time of writing, set to reopen with double the space and five new galleries for American art, ceramics and works on paper.

UPTOWN, LYN-LAKE & WHITTIER

These three neighborhoods are south of downtown.

Uptown, based around the intersection of Hennepin Ave S and Lake St, is a punk-yuppie collision of shops and restaurants that stays lively until late. **Lyn-Lake** abuts Uptown to the east and sports a similar urban-cool vibe; it's centered on Lyndale and Lake Sts. (Get the name?)

Uptown is a convenient jump-off point to the '**Chain of Lakes**' – Lake Calhoun, Lake of the Isles, Lake Harriet, Cedar Lake and Brownie Lake. It seems all of Minneapolis is out frolicking by the water – not surpris-

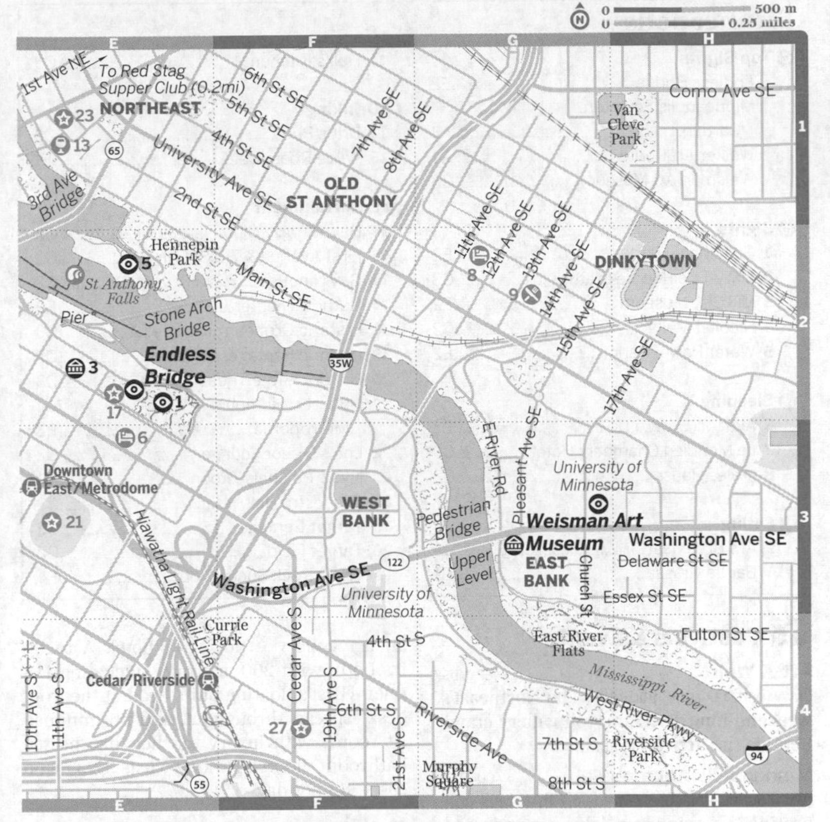

ing, really, since this is known as the 'city of lakes.' Paved cycling paths (which double as cross-country ski trails in winter) meander around the five lakes, where you can go boating in summer or ice skating in winter.

Lake Calhoun sits at the foot of Lake St, where there are amenities galore. Further around Lake Calhoun, Thomas Beach is popular for swimming. Cedar Lake's freewheeling Hidden Beach (aka East Cedar Beach) used to bring out the nudists, though it's mostly clothed folks lolling about these days.

FREE **Minneapolis Institute of Arts** MUSEUM
(612-870-3131; www.artsmia.org; 2400 3rd Ave S; 10am-5pm Tue-Sat, to 9pm Thu, 11am-5pm Sun) This museum is a huge treasure trove housing a veritable history of art. The modern and contemporary collections astonish, while the Prairie School and Asian galleries are also highlights. Brochures at the front desk can help you winnow it down to the must-sees if you're short on time. The museum is 1 mile due south of the convention center via 3rd Ave S.

Calhoun Rental CYCLING
(612-827-8231; www.calhounbikerental.com; 1622 W Lake St; per half-/full day $25/35; 10am-7pm Mon-Fri, 9am-8pm Sat, 10am-8pm Sun Apr-Oct) In Uptown, a couple blocks west of Lake Calhoun, this shop rents bikes (helmet, lock and bike map included); credit card and driver's license are required. It also offers two- to four-hour cycling tours ($39 to $49) around the water Friday through Sunday; reserve in advance.

Lake Calhoun Kiosk WATER SPORTS
(612-823-5765; base of Lake St; per hr $11-17; 10am-8pm late May-Aug, weekends only Sep & Oct) The kiosk, at the foot of Lake St, rents canoes, kayaks and paddleboats. It's a busy spot as there's also a patio restaurant and sailing school here.

Minneapolis

Top Sights
- Endless Bridge E2
- Minneapolis Sculpture Garden A3
- Walker Art Center A4
- Weisman Art Museum G3

Sights
- 1 Gold Medal Park E2
- 2 Mary Tyler Moore Statue C3
- 3 Mill City Museum E2
- 4 Nicollet Mall C2
- 5 Water Power Park E2

Sleeping
- 6 Aloft E3
- 7 Le Meridien Chambers Hotel C3
- 8 Wales House G2

Eating
- 9 Al's Breakfast G2
- 10 Bar La Grassa C1
- 11 Hell's Kitchen C3

Drinking
- 12 Brit's Pub C3
- 13 Wilde Roast Cafe E1

Entertainment
- 14 Dakota Jazz Club C3
- 15 First Avenue & 7th St Entry C2
- 16 Gay Nineties C2
- 17 Guthrie Theater E2
- 18 Historic Orpheum Theatre C3
- 19 Historic Pantages Theatre C2
- 20 Historic State Theatre C3
- 21 Hubert H Humphrey Metrodome E3
- 22 Lee's Liquor Lounge B2
- 23 Nye's Polonaise Room E1
- 24 Orchestra Hall C3
- 25 Target Center C2
- 26 Target Field C2
- 27 Triple Rock Social Club F4

Festivals & Events

Art-A-Whirl MUSIC
(www.nemaa.org; mid-May) The Northeast's weekend-long, rock-and-roll gallery crawl heralds the arrival of spring.

Minneapolis Aquatennial CULTURAL
(www.aquatennial.org; mid-Jul) Ten days celebrating the ubiquitous lakes via parades, beach bashes and fireworks.

Holidazzle CULTURAL
(www.holidazzle.com; Dec) Parades, lights and lots of good cheer downtown throughout December.

Sleeping

B&Bs offer the best value – they've got budget prices but are solidly midrange in quality. Tax adds 13.4% to prices.

Wales House B&B $
(612-331-3931; www.waleshouse.com; 1115 5th St SE; r without/with shared bath, incl breakfast from $65/75; P) This cheery 10-bedroom B&B often houses scholars from the nearby University of Minnesota. Curl up with a book on the porch, or lounge by the fireplace. A two-night minimum stay is required.

Le Meridien Chambers Hotel HOTEL $$$
(612-767-6900; www.lemeridienchambers.com; 901 Hennepin Ave S; r $189-289; P) It's an art gallery – no, it's a hotel. Actually, it's both, with 200 artworks (including Damien Hirst's floating bull's head at the front desk) spread throughout, and 60 minimalist rooms with luxury touches, like heated bathroom floors. Parking costs $28, wi-fi costs $13 per day.

Aloft HOTEL $$
(612-455-8400; www.alofthotels.com/minneapolis; 900 Washington Ave S; r $109-149; P@) Aloft's compact, efficiently designed, industrial-toned rooms draw a younger clientele. The clubby lobby has board games, a cocktail lounge and 24-hour snacks. There's a tiny pool and decent fitness room. Parking costs $15.

Evelo's B&B B&B $
(612-374-9656; 2301 Bryant Ave S; r with shared bath, incl breakfast $75-95;) Evelo's three rooms creak and charm in this polished-wood-filled Victorian home. They're close quartered, but the B&B's strategic location between the Walker Art Center and Uptown compensates.

Minneapolis International Hostel HOSTEL $
(612-522-5000; www.minneapolishostel.com; 2400 Stevens Ave S; dm $28-34, r without/with bath $60/81; @) This homey hostel beside the Minneapolis Institute of Arts has antique furniture, wood floors and fluffy quilts

on the beds. The 48 beds come in a variety of configurations, from a 15-bed male dorm to private rooms with en suite bath. It's easy to miss, as there's no sign on the front (due to the building's historic designation). Reservations are recommended.

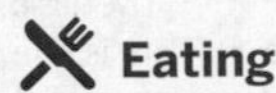

Eating

Minneapolis has ripened into a rich dining scene known for its many restaurants that use local, sustainable ingredients.

DOWNTOWN & NORTHEAST

Nicollet Mall is loaded with eateries.

Bar La Grassa ITALIAN **$$$**
(☎612-333-3837; www.barlagrassa.com; 800 Washington Ave N; pastas $12-24, mains $16-45; ⏰5pm-midnight Mon-Thu, to 1am Fri & Sat, to 10pm Sun) Chef Isaac Becker won the 2011 James Beard award for 'best in the midwest,' so expect great things from the small plates menu of fresh pastas, bruschetta and secondi. It is located about a mile northwest of downtown's core.

Hell's Kitchen AMERICAN **$$**
(☎612-332-4700; www.hellskitcheninc.com; 80 9th St S; mains $10-20; ⏰6:30am-9pm Mon-Wed, to 2am Thu & Fri, 7:30am-2am Sat, 7:30am-9pm Sun; 📶) Descend the stairs to Hell's devilish lair, where spirited waitstaff bring you uniquely Minnesotan foods, like the walleye bacon-lettuce-tomato sandwich, bison burger and lemon-ricotta hotcakes. Happy hour (3pm to 6pm) at the bar is a dandy deal. It morphs into a club with DJs late on weekend nights.

Red Stag Supper Club AMERICAN **$$$**
(☎612-767-7766; www.redstagsupperclub.com; 509 1st Ave NE; bar menu $8-13, mains $18-27; ⏰11am-2am Mon-Fri, 9am-2am Sat & Sun) The exposed-beam Northwoods lodge look belies Red Stag's LEED-certified architecture. The locally sourced arugula-and-pine-nut flatbread sandwiches, smelt fries, smoked trout and cassoulet soothe the stomach. There are good deals for Tuesday dinner.

UNIVERSITY AREA

Low-priced eateries cluster in the campus area by Washington Ave and Oak St.

Al's Breakfast BREAKFAST **$**
(☎612-331-9991; 413 14th Ave SE; mains $4-8; ⏰6am-1pm Mon-Sat, 9am-1pm Sun) It's the ultimate hole-in-the-wall: 14 stools at a tiny counter. Whenever a customer comes in, everyone picks up their plates and scoots down to make room for the newcomer. Fruitfull pancakes are the big crowd-pleaser. Cash only.

UPTOWN, LYN-LAKE & WHITTIER

Vietnamese, Greek, African and other ethnic restaurants line Nicollet Ave S between Franklin Ave (near the Minneapolis Institute of Arts) and 28th St – the stretch is known as 'Eat Street.' Lake St in Uptown is a rich vein for stylish bars and cafes.

TOP CHOICE **Bryant-Lake Bowl** AMERICAN **$$**
(☎612-825-3737; www.bryantlakebowl.com; 810 W Lake St; sandwiches $7-9, mains $11-16; ⏰8am-12:30am; 📶✍) A workingman's bowling alley meets epicurean food at the BLB. Artisanal cheese plates, mock duck rolls, cornmeal-crusted walleye strips and organic oatmeal melt in the mouth. A long list of local beers washes it all down. The on-site theater always has something intriguing and odd going on too.

MINNEAPOLIS FOR CHILDREN

Note that many of the top sights for wee ones are in St Paul, at the Mall of America and at Fort Snelling. Others include:

» **Minnesota Zoo** (☎952-431-9500; www.mnzoo.org; 13000 Zoo Blvd; adult/child $18/12; ⏰9am-6pm summer, 9am-4pm winter; 👪) You'll have to travel a way to get to the respected zoo in suburban Apple Valley, which is 20 miles south of town. It has naturalistic habitats for its 400-plus species, with an emphasis on cold-climate creatures. Parking is $5.

» **Valleyfair** (☎952-445-7600; www.valleyfair.com; 1 Valleyfair Dr; adult/child $42/10; ⏰from 10am mid-May–Aug, weekends only Sep & Oct, closing times vary; 👪) If the rides at the Mall of America aren't enough, drive out to this full-scale amusement park 25 miles southwest in Shakopee. Parking costs $10.

» **Children's Theatre Company** (☎612-874-0400; www.childrenstheatre.org; 2400 3rd Ave S; 👪) So good it won a Tony award for 'outstanding regional theater.'

Peninsula ASIAN **$$**
(☎612-871-8282; www.peninsulamalaysiancuisine.com; 2608 Nicollet Ave S; mains $9-15; ⏰11am-10pm Sun-Thu, to 11pm Fri & Sat; ✓) Malaysian dishes – including *achat* (tangy vegetable salad in peanut dressing), red curry hot pot, spicy crab and fish in banana leaves – rock the palate in this contemporary restaurant.

Uptown Cafeteria & Support Group AMERICAN **$$**
(☎612-877-7263; www.uptowncafeteria.com; 3001 Hennepin Ave; mains $13-22; ⏰11:30am-late Mon-Fri, 9am-late Sat & Sun; ✓) One of Uptown's concept-y hot spots, the Cafeteria features a great roof deck and pretty darn good comfort food along the lines of chicken pot pie and meatloaf.

Drinking

Bars stay open until 2am. Happy hour typically lasts from 3pm to 6pm.

Brit's Pub PUB
(www.britspub.com; 1110 Nicollet Mall) A lawn bowling green on the roof, plus Brit's sweeping selection of Scotch, port and beer, is sure to unleash skills you never knew you had.

Grumpy's BAR
(www.grumpys-bar.com/nordeast; 2200 4th St NE) Grumpy's is the Northeast's classic dive, with cheap (but good) beer and an outdoor patio. Sample the specialty 'hot dish' on Tuesdays for $1.

Entertainment

With its large student population and thriving performing-arts scene, Minneapolis has an active nightlife. Check *Vita.MN* (www.vita.mn) and *City Pages* (www.citypages.com) for current goings on.

Live Music

Minneapolis rocks; everyone's in a band, it seems. Acts such as Prince and post-punkers Hüsker Dü and the Replacements cut their teeth here.

First Avenue & 7th St Entry LIVE MUSIC
(www.first-avenue.com; 701 1st Ave N) This is the bedrock of Minneapolis' music scene, and it still pulls in top bands and big crowds. Check out the exterior stars; they're all bands that have graced the stage.

Nye's Polonaise Room LIVE MUSIC
(www.nyespolonaise.com; 112 E Hennepin Ave) The World's Most Dangerous Polka Band lets loose Friday and Saturday. It's smashing fun, and enhanced if you find yourself an old-timer to twirl you around the room.

Triple Rock Social Club LIVE MUSIC
(www.triplerocksocialclub.com; 629 Cedar Ave) Triple Rock is a popular punk-alternative club.

Lee's Liquor Lounge LIVE MUSIC
(www.leesliquorlounge.com; 101 Glenwood Ave) Rockabilly and country-tinged alt bands twang here.

Dakota Jazz Club LIVE MUSIC
(www.dakotacooks.com; 1010 Nicollet Mall) The Dakota is a classy venue that gets big-name jazz acts.

Theater & Performing Arts

They don't call it Mini-Apple for nothing, with 100-plus theater groups here. The Guthrie and other venues put unsold tickets on sale 15 minutes before showtime for $15 to $30.

Guthrie Theater THEATER
(☎612-377-2224; www.guthrietheater.org; 818 2nd St S) This is Minneapolis' top-gun theater troupe, with the jumbo facility to prove it.

GAY & LESBIAN MINNEAPOLIS

Minneapolis has one of the country's highest percentages of gay, lesbian, bisexual and transgender (GLBT) residents, and the city enjoys strong GLBT rights. The **Minneapolis Convention & Visitors Association** (www.glbtminneapolis.org) has a comprehensive website for events, nightlife, news and attractions. Or pick up the free, biweekly magazine *Lavender* (www.lavendermagazine.com) at coffee shops around town.

For nightlife, **Gay Nineties** (www.gay90s.com; 408 Hennepin Ave S) has dancing, dining and drag shows that attract both gay and straight clientele. **Wilde Roast Cafe** (www.wilderoastcafe.com; 65 Main St SE) features amazing baked goods, riverfront digs and a Victorian ambience worthy of its namesake, Oscar Wilde; it was ranked 'best cafe' by *Lavender*.

The **Pride Festival** (www.tcpride.com; ⏰late Jun), one of the USA's largest, draws about 400,000 revelers.

Historic Pantages, State & Orpheum Theatres THEATER
(☎612-339-7007; www.hennepintheatretrust.org) These classy palaces are main venues for Broadway shows and touring acts, all in a row on Hennepin Ave S at street Nos 710, 805 and 910, respectively.

Brave New Workshop Theatre THEATER
(☎612-332-6620; www.bravenewworkshop.com; 2605 Hennepin Ave S) An established venue for musical comedy, revue and satire; in Uptown.

Orchestra Hall CLASSICAL
(☎612-371-5656; www.minnesotaorchestra.org; 1111 Nicollet Mall) Superb acoustics for concerts by the acclaimed Minnesota Symphony Orchestra.

Sports

Minnesotans love their sports teams. Note that ice hockey happens in St Paul (see p591).

Target Field BASEBALL
(www.minnesotatwins.com; 3rd Ave N btwn 5th & 7th Sts N) The new stadium for the Twins pro baseball team is notable for its beyond-the-norm, locally focused food and drink.

Hubert H Humphrey Metrodome FOOTBALL
(www.vikings.com; 900 5th St S) The Vikings pro football team passes in the marshmallow-like 'Dome (notable for its roof crashing in 2010 under the weight of too much snow).

Target Center BASKETBALL
(www.nba.com/timberwolves; 600 1st Ave N) This is where the Timberwolves pro basketball team plays.

ℹ Information

Emergency & Medical Services

Fairview/University of Minnesota Medical Center (☎612-273-6402; 2450 Riverside Ave)

Internet Access

Minneapolis Public Library (www.hclib.org; 300 Nicollet Mall; ⏲10am-8pm Tue & Thu, to 6pm Wed, Fri & Sat, noon-5pm Sun) Mod facility with free internet and wi-fi.

Media

City Pages (www.citypages.com) Weekly entertainment freebie.

Pioneer Press (www.twincities.com) St Paul's daily.

Star Tribune (www.startribune.com) Minneapolis' daily.

Vita.MN (www.vita.mn) The *Star Tribune*'s weekly entertainment freebie.

Tourist Information

Minneapolis Convention & Visitors Association (☎612-767-8000; www.minneapolis.org) Coupons, maps, guides and bike-route info online.

Websites

Ask the Minneapolitan (www.asktheminneapolitan.wordpress.com) Scenesters' guide to art shows, concerts and festivals.

Minneapolis Bicycle Program (www.ci.minneapolis.mn.us/bicycles) Trail maps and anything else you want to know about local cycling.

ℹ Getting There & Around

Air

The **Minneapolis-St Paul International Airport** (MSP; www.mspairport.com) is between the two cities to the south. It's the home of Delta Airlines, which operates several direct flights to/from Europe.

The Hiawatha light-rail line (regular/rush-hour fare $1.75/2.25, 25 minutes) is the cheapest way into Minneapolis. Bus 54 (regular/rush-hour fare $1.75/2.25, 25 minutes) goes to St Paul. Taxis cost around $45.

Bicycle

Minneapolis hovers near the top of rankings for 'best bike city' in the US. It has 84 miles of off-street paths, plus a large bicycle-share program, à la Paris. **Nice Ride** (www.niceridemn.com; ⏲Apr-Oct) has 1000 bikes in 80 self-serve kiosks around the city. Users pay a subscription fee (per day/month $5/30) online or at the kiosk, plus a small fee per half-hour of use (with the first half-hour free). Bikes can be returned to any kiosk. For traditional rentals (which work better if you're riding for recreation versus transportation purposes), see p585.

Bus

Greyhound (☎612-371-3325; 950 Hawthorne Ave) Runs frequent buses to Milwaukee (seven hours), Chicago (nine hours) and Duluth (three hours).

Megabus (www.megabus.com/us) Runs express to Milwaukee (six hours) and Chicago (eight hours), often for lower fares than Greyhound. It departs from both downtown and the university; check the website for exact locations.

Public Transportation

Metro Transit (www.metrotransit.org; regular/rush-hr fare $1.75/2.25) runs frequent buses throughout the area, as well as the excellent Hiawatha light-rail line between downtown and the Mall of America. Express bus 94 (regular/rush-hour fare $2.25/3) connects Minneapolis to St Paul; it departs from 6th St N's south side, just west of Hennepin Ave. A day pass ($6) is available from any rail station or bus driver.

Taxi

Call **Yellow Cab** (☎612-824-4444).

Train

The **Amtrak station** (☎651-644-6012; 730 Transfer Rd), off University Ave SE, is between Minneapolis and St Paul. Trains go daily to Chicago (eight hours) and Seattle (37 hours). The ride east to La Crosse (three hours), Wisconsin, is beautiful, skirting the Mississippi River and offering multiple eagle sightings.

St Paul

Smaller and quieter than its twin city Minneapolis, St Paul has retained more of a historic character. Walk through F Scott Fitzgerald's old stomping grounds, trek the trails along the mighty Mississippi River, or slurp some Lao soup.

Sights & Activities

Downtown and Cathedral Hill hold most of the action. The latter features eccentric shops, Gilded Age Victorian mansions and, of course, the hulking church that gives the area its name. Downtown has the museums. An insider's tip: there's a shortcut between the two areas, a footpath that starts on the Hill House's west side and drops into downtown.

Revitalized **Harriet Island**, running south off Wabasha St downtown, is a lovely place to meander; it has a park, river walk, concert stages and fishing dock.

F Scott Fitzgerald Sights & Summit Avenue — STREET

Great Gatsby author F Scott Fitzgerald is St Paul's most celebrated literary son. The Pullman-style apartment at **481 Laurel Avenue** is his birthplace. Four blocks away, Fitzgerald lived in the brownstone at **599 Summit Avenue** when he published *This Side of Paradise*. Both are private residences. From here stroll along Summit Ave toward the cathedral and gape at the Victorian homes rising from the street. Literature buffs should grab the *Fitzgerald Homes and Haunts* map at the visitor center to see other footprints.

FREE Landmark Center — MUSEUM

(www.landmarkcenter.org; 75 W 5th St; 8am-5pm Mon-Fri, to 8pm Thu, 10am-5pm Sat, noon-5pm Sun) Downtown's turreted 1902 Landmark Center used to be the federal courthouse, where gangsters such as Alvin 'Creepy' Karpis were tried; plaques by the various rooms show who was brought to justice here. In addition to the city's visitor center, the building also contains a couple of small museums. On the 2nd floor the **Schubert Club Museum** (☎651-292-3267; www.schubert.org; noon-4pm Sun-Fri) has a brilliant collection of old pianos and harpsichords – some tickled by Mozart, Beethoven and the like – as well as old manuscripts and letters from famous composers. The club plays free chamber music concerts Thursdays at noon from October to April. A free wood-turning museum (it's a decorative form of woodworking) is also on the 2nd floor.

FREE Mississippi River Visitors Center — INTERPRETIVE CENTER

(☎651-293-0200; www.nps.gov/miss; 9:30am-5pm Sun-Thu, to 9pm Fri & Sat) The National Park Service visitor center occupies an alcove in the science museum's lobby. Definitely stop by to pick up trail maps and see what sort of free ranger-guided walks and bike rides are going on. Most take place at 10am on Wednesday, Thursday and Saturday in summer. In winter, the center hosts ice-fishing and snowshoeing jaunts.

Science Museum of Minnesota — MUSEUM

(☎651-221-9444; www.smm.org; 120 W Kellogg Blvd; adult/child $11/8.50; 9:30am-9:30pm, reduced hr in winter) Has the usual hands-on kids' exhibits and Omnimax theater ($5 extra). Adults will be entertained by the wacky quackery of the 4th floor's 'questionable medical devices.'

St Paul Curling Club — SNOW SPORTS

(www.stpaulcurlingclub.org; 470 Selby Ave; from 11am Oct-May) For those uninitiated in northern ways, curling is a winter sport that involves sliding a hubcap-sized 'puck' down the ice toward a bull's-eye. The friendly folks here don't mind if you stop in to watch the action. Heck, they might invite you to share a Labatt's from the upstairs bar.

Cathedral of St Paul — CHURCH

(www.cathedralsaintpaul.org; 239 Selby Ave; 7am-7pm Sun-Fri, to 9pm Sat) Modeled on St Peter's Basilica in Rome, the cathedral presides over the city from its hilltop perch.

James J Hill House — HISTORIC BUILDING

(☎651-297-2555; www.mnhs.org/hillhouse; 240 Summit Ave; adult/child $8/5; 10am-3:30pm

ST PAUL FOR CHILDREN

Add the Science Museum of Minnesota (see p590) to the list below. Kids love its laser show and Omnimax.

» **Minnesota Children's Museum** (651-225-6000; www.mcm.org; 10 W 7th St; admission $9; 9am-4pm Mon-Thu, to 8pm Fri & Sat, to 5pm Sun;) Has the usual gamut of hands-on activities, as well as a giant anthill to burrow through, and the 'One World' intercultural community where kids can shop and vote.

» **Minnesota History Center** (651-259-3000; www.minnesotahistorycenter.org; 345 W Kellogg Blvd; adult/child $10/5, admission free Tue evening; 10am-8pm Tue, 10am-5pm Wed-Sat, noon-5pm Sun;) Educates with its 'A to Z' treasure hunt and climbable boxcar.

Wed-Sat, 1-3:30pm Sun) Tour the palatial stone mansion of railroad magnate Hill. It's a Gilded Age beauty, with five floors and 22 fireplaces.

Tours

Down In History Tours WALKING
(651-292-1220; www.wabashastreetcaves.com; 215 S Wabasha St; 45min tours $6; 5pm Thu, 11am Sat & Sun) Explore St Paul's underground caves, which gangsters once used as a speakeasy. The fun ratchets up on Thursday nights, when a swing band plays in the caverns (admission $7).

Festivals & Events

St Paul Winter Carnival CULTURAL
(www.winter-carnival.com; late Jan) Ten days of ice sculptures, ice skating and ice fishing.

Sleeping

You'll find a bigger selection of accommodations in Minneapolis.

Covington Inn B&B $$
(651-292-1411; www.covingtoninn.com; 100 Harriet Island Rd; r incl breakfast $150-235;) This four-room, Harriet Island B&B is on a tugboat floating in the Mississippi River; watch the river traffic glide by while sipping your morning coffee.

Holiday Inn HOTEL $$
(651-225-1515; www.holiday-inn.com/stpaulmn; 175 W 7th St; r $99-169;) The rooms are the usual decent quality you expect from the Holiday Inn chain; the perks are the location adjacent to the RiverCentre (convention center), a small pool and an on-site Irish pub. Parking is $15.

Eating & Drinking

Grand Ave between Dale and Victoria Sts is a worthy browse, with cafes, foodie shops and ethnic eats in close proximity. Selby Ave by the intersection of Western Ave N also holds a quirky line-up.

Mickey's Dining Car DINER $
(www.mickeysdiningcar.com; 36 W 7th St; mains $4-9; 24hr) Mickey's is a downtown classic, the kind of place where the friendly waitress calls you 'honey' and satisfied regulars line the bar with their coffee cups and newspapers. The food has timeless appeal, too: burgers, malts and apple pie.

WA Frost & Company AMERICAN $$
(651-224-5715; www.wafrost.com; 374 Selby Ave; small plates $9-16, mains $18-34; 11am-1:30pm Mon-Fri, 10:30am-2pm Sat & Sun, 5-10pm daily) Frost's tree-shaded, ivy-covered, twinkling-light patio is right out of a Fitzgerald novel, perfect for a glass of wine, beer or gin. The restaurant locally sources many ingredients for dishes like the artisanal cheese plate, glazed tofu steak and cardamom-glazed duck.

Hmongtown Marketplace ASIAN $
(www.hmongtownmarketplace.com; 217 Como Ave; mains $5-8; 8am-8pm) The nation's largest enclave of Hmong immigrants lives in the Twin Cities, and this market delivers their favorite Vietnamese, Lao and Thai dishes at its humble food court. Find the West Building and head to the back where vendors ladle hot-spiced papaya salad, beef ribs, sticky rice and curry noodle soup. Then stroll the market, where you can fix your dentures or buy a cockatoo or brass gong.

Happy Gnome PUB
(www.thehappygnome.com; 498 Selby Ave; from 11:30am;) Seventy craft beers flow from the taps, best sipped on the fireplace-warmed outdoor patio. The pub sits across the parking lot from the St Paul Curling Club.

Entertainment

Fitzgerald Theater THEATER
(651-290-1221; www.fitzgeraldtheater.org; 10 E Exchange St) Where Garrison Keillor tapes his *Prairie Home Companion* radio show.

Ordway Center for Performing Arts CLASSICAL MUSIC
(☎651-224-4222; www.ordway.org; 345 Washington St) Chamber music and the Minnesota Opera fill the hall here.

Xcel Energy Center HOCKEY
(www.wild.com; 199 Kellogg Blvd) The Wild pro hockey team skates at Xcel.

Shopping

Common Good Books BOOKS
(www.commongoodbooks.com; 165 Western Ave N; ⏱10am-10pm, to 8pm Sun) Garrison Keillor owns this skylit, basement bookstore, tucked under a coffee shop. It stacks shelves of fiction and nature books by Midwest authors – many of whom may be in the upstairs cafe tapping away at their laptops (the list by the front door shows all the novels written by patrons at the tables).

Information

Visitor center (☎651-292-3225; www.visitstpaul.com; 75 W 5th St; ⏱10am-4pm Mon-Sat, noon-4pm Sun) In the Landmark Center; makes a good first stop for maps and DIY walking tour info.

Getting There & Around

St Paul is served by the same transit systems as Minneapolis; see p589 for details. Greyhound bus routes serving Minneapolis usually stop at the **St Paul station** (☎651-222-0507; 166 W University Ave) too.

Around Minneapolis-St Paul

Mall of America MALL, AMUSEMENT PARK
(www.mallofamerica.com; off I-494 at 24th Ave; ⏱10am-9:30pm Mon-Sat, 11am-7pm Sun; 👪) The Mall of America, located in suburban Bloomington near the airport, is the USA's largest shopping center. Yes, it's just a mall, filled with the usual stores, movie theaters and eateries. But there's also a wedding chapel inside. And an 18-hole **minigolf course** (☎952-883-8777; 3rd fl; admission $8). And an amusement park, aka **Nickelodeon Universe** (☎952-883-8600; www.nickelodeonuniverse.com), with 24 rides, including a couple of scream-inducing roller coasters. To walk through will cost you nothing; a one-day, unlimited-ride wristband is $30; or you can pay for rides individually ($3 to $6). What's more, the state's largest aquarium, **Minnesota Sea Life** (☎952-883-0202; www.sealifeus.com; adult/child $20/16) – where children can touch sharks and stingrays – is in the mall too. Combination passes are available to save dough. The Hiawatha light-rail runs to/from downtown.

Fort Snelling HISTORIC SITE
(☎612-726-1171; www.historicfortsnelling.org; cnr Hwys 5 & 55; adult/child $10/5; ⏱10am-5pm Tue-Sat, noon-5pm Sun Jun-Aug, Sat only Sep & Oct; 👪) East of the mall, Fort Snelling is the state's oldest structure, established in 1820 as a frontier outpost in the remote Northwest Territory. Guides in period dress show restored buildings and reenact pioneer life.

WHAT THE...?

Behold the **World's Largest Ball of Twine** (☎320-693-7544; www.darwintwineball.com; 1st St; admission free; ⏱24hr) in Darwin, 62 miles west of Minneapolis on US 12. To be specific, it's the 'Largest Built by One Person' – Francis A Johnson wrapped the 17,400lb whopper on his farm over the course of 29 years. Gawk at it in the town gazebo. Better yet, visit the **museum** (⏱1-4pm Apr-Sep, by appointment Oct-Mar) beside it and buy your own twine ball starter kit in the gift shop.

Southern Minnesota

Some of the scenic southeast can be seen on short drives from the Twin Cities. Better is a loop of a few days' duration, following the rivers and stopping in some of the historic towns and state parks.

Due east of St Paul, on Hwy 36, touristy **Stillwater** (www.ilovestillwater.com), on the lower St Croix River, is an old logging town with restored 19th-century buildings, river cruises and antique stores. It's also an official 'booktown,' an honor bestowed upon a few small towns worldwide that possess an extraordinary number of antiquarian bookshops. What's more, the town is filled with classy historic B&Bs.

Larger **Red Wing**, to the south on US 61, is a similar but less-interesting restored town, though it does offer its famous Red Wing Shoes – actually more like sturdy boots – and salt glaze pottery.

The prettiest part of the **Mississippi Valley** area begins south of here. To drive it and see the best bits, you'll need to flip-flop back and forth between Minnesota and Wisconsin on the Great River Road.

From Red Wing, cross the river on US 63. Before heading south along the water though, let's make a cheesy detour. Go north on US 63 in Wisconsin for 12 miles until you hit US 10. Turn right, and within a few miles, you're in Ellsworth, the 'Cheese Curd Capital.' Pull into **Ellsworth Cooperative Creamery** (☎715-273-4311; www.ellsworthcheesecurds.com; 232 N Wallace St; ⊙8am-5pm Mon-Fri, 8am-2pm Sat) – curd-maker for A&W and Dairy Queen – and savor squeaky goodness hot off the press (11am is prime time).

Back along the river on Wisconsin Hwy 35, a great stretch of road edges the bluffs beside **Maiden Rock**, **Stockholm** and **Pepin**. Follow your nose to local bakeries and cafes in the area.

Continuing south, cross back over the river to **Wabasha** in Minnesota, which has a historic downtown and large population of bald eagles that congregate in winter. To learn more, visit the **National Eagle Center** (☎651-565-4989; www.nationaleaglecenter.org; 50 Pembroke Ave; adult/child $8/5; ⊙10am-5pm Sun-Thu, 9am-6pm Fri & Sat).

Inland and south, the Bluff Country is dotted with limestone bluffs, southeast Minnesota's main geological feature. **Lanesboro** is a gem for rails-to-trails cycling and canoeing. Seven miles westward on County Rd 8 (call for directions) is **Old Barn Resort** (☎507-467-2512; www.barnresort.com; dm/r $25/50, camp/RV site $28/36; ⊙Apr–mid-Nov;), a pastoral hostel-cum-campground-restaurant-outfitter. **Harmony**, south of Lanesboro, is the center of an Amish community and another welcoming town.

SPAM MUSEUM

Sitting by its lonesome in Austin, near where I-35 and I-90 intersect in southern Minnesota, lies the **Spam Museum** (☎800-588-7726; www.spam.com; 1101 N Main St; admission free; ⊙10am-5pm Mon-Sat, noon-5pm Sun;), an entire institution devoted to the peculiar meat. It educates on how the blue tins have fed armies, become a Hawaiian food staple and inspired legions of haiku writers. What's more, you can chat up the staff (aka 'spambassadors'), indulge in free samples, and try your hand at canning the sweet pork magic.

Duluth & Northern Minnesota

Northern Minnesota is where you come to 'do some fishing, do some drinking,' as one resident summed it up.

DULUTH

At the Great Lakes' westernmost end, Duluth (with its neighbor, Superior, Wisconsin) is one of the busiest ports in the country. The town's dramatic location spliced into a cliff makes it a fab place to see changeable Lake Superior in action. The water, along with the area's trails and natural splendor, has earned Duluth a reputation as a hot spot for outdoors junkies.

Sights & Activities

The waterfront area is distinctive. Mosey along the Lakewalk trail and around Canal Park, where most of the sights cluster. Look for the Aerial Lift Bridge, which rises to let ships into the port; about 1000 ships a year pass through here.

Maritime Visitors Center MUSEUM
(☎218-720-5260; www.lsmma.com; 600 Lake Ave S; admission free; ⊙10am-9pm Jun-Aug, reduced hours Sep-May) Check the computer screens inside to learn what time the big ships will be sailing through port. The first-rate center also has exhibits on Great Lakes shipping and shipwrecks.

William A Irvin MUSEUM
(☎218-722-7876; www.williamairvin.com; 350 Harbor Dr; adult/child $10/8; ⊙9am-6pm Jun-Aug, 10am-4pm May, Sep & Oct) To continue the nautical theme, tour this mighty 610ft Great Lakes freighter.

Great Lakes Aquarium AQUARIUM
(☎218-740-3474; www.glaquarium.org; 353 Harbor Dr; adult/child $14.50/8.50; ⊙10am-6pm;) One of the country's few freshwater aquariums, the highlights here include the daily stingray feedings at 2pm, and the otter tanks.

Vista Fleet BOAT TOUR
(☎218-722-6218; www.vistafleet.com; 323 Harbor Dr; adult/child $16/8; ⊙mid-May–Oct) Ah, everyone loves a boat ride. Vista's two-hour harbor cruise is a favorite, departing from the dock beside the *William A Irvin* in Canal Park.

DYLAN IN DULUTH

While Hibbing and the Iron Range are most often associated with Bob Dylan, he was born in Duluth. You'll see brown-and-white signs on Superior and London streets for **Bob Dylan Way** (www.bobdylanway.com), pointing out places associated with the legend (like the armory where he saw Buddy Holly in concert, and decided to become a musician). But you're on your own to find **Dylan's birthplace** (519 3rd Ave E), up a hill a few blocks northeast of downtown. Dylan lived on the top floor until age six, when his family moved inland to Hibbing. It's a private residence (and unmarked), so all you can do is stare from the street.

Leif Erikson Park PARK
(cnr London Rd & 14th Ave E) This is a lakefront sweet spot with a rose garden, replica of Leif's Viking ship and free outdoor movies each Friday night in summer. Take the Lakewalk from Canal Park (about 1½ miles) and you can say you hiked the Superior Trail (p596), which traverses this stretch.

University of Minnesota Duluth's Outdoor Program OUTDOORS
(☎218-726-6134, 218-726-7128; www.umdrsop.org; 154 Sports & Health Center; rental per day $20-40) Rent kayaks, camping gear and other equipment from the university. It also offers rock climbing, paddleboarding and snow-kiting programs; beginners are welcome for all activities.

Spirit Mountain SKIING
(☎218-628-2891; www.spiritmt.com; 9500 Spirit Mountain Pl; per day adult/child $47/37; ⌚9am-8pm Sun-Thu, to 9pm Fri & Sat mid-Nov–Mar) Skiing and snowboarding are big pastimes come winter; a new zip line is in the works for summer. The mountain is 10 miles south of Duluth.

Enger Park PARK
(Skyline Pkwy) For a spectacular view of the city and harbor, climb the rock tower in Enger Park, located a couple miles southwest by the golf course.

Sleeping

Duluth has several B&Bs; rooms cost at least $125 in the summer. Check **Duluth Historic Inns** (www.duluthbandb.com) for listings. The town's accommodations fill up fast in summer, which may mean you'll have to try your luck across the border in Superior, Wisconsin (where it's cheaper too).

Fitger's Inn HOTEL $$
(☎218-722-8826; www.fitgers.com; 600 E Superior St; r incl breakfast $99-209;) Fitger's carved its 62 large rooms, each with slightly varied decor, from an old brewery. Located on the Lakewalk, the pricier rooms have great water views. The free shuttle to local sights is handy.

Willard Munger Inn INN $$
(☎218-624-4814, 800-982-2453; www.mungerinn.com; 7408 Grand Ave; r incl breakfast $70-136;) Family-owned Munger Inn offers a fine variety of rooms (budget to Jacuzzi suites), along with perks for outdoor enthusiasts, such as hiking and biking trails right outside the door, free use of bikes and canoes and a fire pit. It's near Spirit Mountain.

Eating & Drinking

Most restaurants and bars reduce their hours in winter. The Canal Park waterfront area has eateries in all price ranges.

DeWitt-Seitz Marketplace ECLECTIC $$
(www.dewittseitz.com; 394 Lake Ave S) This building in Canal Park holds several eateries, including vegetarian-friendly **Taste of Saigon** (⌚11am-8:30pm Sun-Thu, to 9:30pm Fri & Sat;), hippyish cafe **Amazing Grace** (⌚7am-10pm) and **Northern Waters Smokehaus** (⌚10am-9pm Mon-Sat, 11am-5pm Sun), with sustainably harvested salmon and whitefish (primo for picnics).

Chester Creek Cafe CAFE $$
(☎218-723-8569; www.astccc.net; 1902 E 8th St; mains $7-14; ⌚7am-9pm Mon-Sat, 7:30am-8pm Sun;) Earthy and pinewood-boothed, Chester Creek plates omelets, tempeh Reubens, Thai tofu curry, and fish and meat dishes. It's in the university area, about 2 miles from downtown.

Pizza Luce PIZZERIA $$
(☎218-727-7400; www.pizzaluce.com; 11 E Superior St; large pizza $20-22; ⌚8am-1:30am Sun-Thu, to 2:30am Fri & Sat;) It cooks locally sourced breakfasts and gourmet pizzas. It's also plugged into the local music scene and hosts bands. Fully licensed.

Fitger's Brewhouse BREWERY
(www.fitgersbrewhouse.net; 600 E Superior St; ⌚from 11am) In the hotel complex, the Brew-

house rocks with live music and fresh brews. Try them via the seven-beer sampler (3oz glasses $7).

TOP CHOICE **Thirsty Pagan** BREWERY (www.thirstypaganbrewing.com; 1623 Broadway St; ⊙from 4pm) This one's a bit of a trek, over the bridge in Superior, Wisconsin (a 10-minute drive), but worth it for the aggressive, spicy beers to wash down hand-tossed pizzas.

Shopping

Electric Fetus MUSIC (☎218-722-9970; www.electricfetus.com; 12 E Superior St; ⊙9am-9pm Mon-Fri, 9am-8pm Sat, 11am-6pm Sun) Sells a whopping selection of CDs, vinyl and local arts and crafts, including Dylan tunes and T-shirts. It sits across the street from Pizza Luce.

Information

Duluth Visitors Center (☎800-438-5884; www.visitduluth.com; Harbor Dr; ⊙9:30am-7:30pm summer) Seasonal center, opposite the Vista dock.

Getting There & Around

Greyhound (☎218-722-5591; 4426 Grand Ave) has a couple of buses daily to Minneapolis ($20 to $36, three hours).

NORTH SHORE

Hwy 61 (see p595) is the main vein through the North Shore. It edges Lake Superior and passes numerous state parks, waterfalls, hiking trails and mom-and-pop towns en route to Canada. Lots of weekend, summer and fall traffic makes reservations essential.

Two Harbors (www.twoharborschamber.com) has a museum, lighthouse and B&B. Actually, the latter two are one and the same, with the **Lighthouse B&B** (☎218-834-4814; www.lighthousebb.org; r incl breakfast $135-155) being a unique place to spend the night if you can snag one of its four rooms. Nearby, **Betty's Pies** (www.bettyspies.com; 1633 Hwy 61; sandwiches $5-9; ⊙7am-9pm, reduced Oct-May) wafts a five-layer chocolate tinful among its rackful of wares.

Route highlights north of Two Harbors are Gooseberry Falls, Split Rock Lighthouse and Palisade Head. About 110 miles from Duluth, artsy little **Grand Marais** (www.grandmarais.com) makes an excellent base for exploring the Boundary Waters and environs. For Boundary permits and information, visit the **Gunflint Ranger Station** (☎218-387-1750; ⊙7am-5pm May-Sep), just south of town.

Do-it-yourself enthusiasts can learn to build boats, tie flies or brew beer at the **North House Folk School** (☎218-387-9762; www.northhousefolkschool.com; 500 Hwy 61). The course list is phenomenal – as is the school's two-hour sailing trip aboard the Viking schooner *Hjordis* (adult/child $45/35). Reserve in advance.

Grand Marais' lodging options include camping, resorts and motels, like the **Harbor Inn** (☎218-387-1191; www.bytheharbor.com; 207 Wisconsin St; r $115-135;) in town or rustic, trail-encircled **Naniboujou Lodge** (☎218-387-2688; www.naniboujou.com; 20 Naniboujou; r $95-115), which is 14 miles north of town. **Sven and Ole's** (☎218-387-1713; www.svenandoles.com; 9 Wisconsin St; sandwiches $6-8; ⊙11am-8pm, to 9pm Thu-Sat) is a classic for sandwiches and pizza; beer flows from the attached Pickled Herring Pub. Ecofriendly **Angry Trout Cafe** (☎218-387-1265; www.angrytroutcafe.com; 416 Hwy 61; mains $19-25; ⊙11am-8:30pm May–mid-Oct) grills fresh-plucked lake fish in a converted fishing shanty.

Hwy 61 continues to **Grand Portage National Monument** (☎218-475-0123; www.nps.gov/grpo; admission free; ⊙hrs vary, mid-May–mid-Oct), beside Canada, where the early

SCENIC DRIVE: HIGHWAY 61

Hwy 61 conjures a headful of images. Local boy Bob Dylan mythologized it in his angry 1965 album *Highway 61 Revisited*. It's the fabled 'Blues Highway' clasping the Mississippi River en route to New Orleans (see p40). And in northern Minnesota, it evokes red-tinged cliffs and forested beaches as it follows Lake Superior's shoreline.

But let's back up and get a few things straight. The Blues Highway is actually US 61, and it starts just north of the Twin Cities. Hwy 61 is a state scenic road, and it starts in Duluth. To confuse matters more, there are two 61s between Duluth and Two Harbors: a four-lane expressway and a two-lane 'Old Hwy 61' (also called North Shore Scenic Drive, which morphs from London Rd in Duluth). Whatever the name, take it. After Two Harbors, it's one wondrous strip of pavement all the way to the Canadian border. For more information, check the North Shore Scenic Drive at www.superiorbyways.com.

voyageurs had to carry their canoes around the Pigeon River rapids. This was the center of a far-flung trading empire, and the reconstructed 1788 trading post and Ojibwe village is well worth seeing. **Isle Royale National Park** in Lake Superior is reached by daily **ferries** (☎218-475-0024; www.isleroyaleboats.com; day trip adult/child $53/30) from May to October. (The park is also accessible from Michigan; see p571.)

BOUNDARY WATERS

From Two Harbors, Hwy 2 runs inland to the legendary **Boundary Waters Canoe Area Wilderness (BWCAW)**. This pristine region has more than 1000 lakes and streams in which to dip a paddle. It's possible to go just for the day, but most people opt for at least one night of camping. If you're willing to dig in and canoe for a while, you'll lose the crowds. Camping then becomes a wonderfully remote experience where it will be you, the howling wolves, the moose who's nuzzling the tent and the aurora borealis' greenish light filling the night sky. Beginners are welcome, and everyone can get set up with gear from local lodges and outfitters. **Permits** (☎877-550-6777; www.recreation.gov; adult/child $16/8, plus $6 reservation fee) are required for overnight stays. Day permits, though free, are also required; get them at BWCAW entry point kiosks or ranger stations. Call **Superior National Forest** (☎218-626-4300; www.fs.fed.us/r9/forests/superior/bwcaw) for details; the website has a useful trip planning guide. Try to plan ahead, as permits are quota restricted and sometimes run out.

Many argue the best BWCAW access is via the engaging town of **Ely** (www.ely.org), northeast of the Iron Range area, which has accommodations, restaurants and scores of outfitters. The **International Wolf Center** (☎218-365-4695; www.wolf.org; 1369 Hwy 169; adult/child $8.50/4.50; ⏰10am-5pm, closed Sun-Thu mid-Oct–mid-May) offers intriguing exhibits and wolf-viewing trips. Across the highway from the center, **Kawishiwi Ranger Station** (☎218-365-7600; 1393 Hwy 169; ⏰7am-4:30pm May-Sep) provides expert BWCAW camping and canoeing details, trip suggestions and required permits.

In winter, Ely gets mushy – it's a renowned dogsledding town. Outfitters such as **Wintergreen Dogsled Lodge** (☎218-365-6022; www.dogsledding.com; 4hr tour $125) offer numerous packages.

IRON RANGE DISTRICT

An area of red-tinged scrubby hills rather than mountains, Minnesota's Iron Range District consists of the Mesabi and Vermilion Ranges, running north and south of Hwy 169 from roughly Grand Rapids northeast to Ely. Iron was discovered here in the 1850s, and at one time more than three-quarters of the nation's iron ore was extracted from these vast open-pit mines. Visitors can see working mines and the terrain's raw, sparse beauty all along Hwy 169.

In **Calumet**, a perfect introduction is the **Hill Annex Mine State Park** (☎218-247-7215; www.mnstateparks.info; 880 Gary St; tours adult/child $10/6; ⏰9am-5pm Wed-Sat), with its open-pit tours and exhibit center. Tours are held in summertime only, from Wednesday to Saturday at 12:30pm and 3pm; there's also a fossil tour at 10am.

An even bigger pit sprawls in **Hibbing**, where a must-see **viewpoint** (admission free; ⏰9am-5pm mid-May–mid-Sep) north of town overlooks the 3-mile Hull-Rust Mahoning Mine. Bob Dylan lived at 2425 E 7th Ave as a boy and teenager; the **Hibbing Public Library** (☎218-362-5959; www.hibbing.lib.mn.us; 2020 E 5th Ave; ⏰9am-8pm Mon-Thu, to 5pm Fri) has well-done Dylan displays and a free walking tour map (available online, too) that takes you past various sites, like the place

SUPERIOR HIKING TRAIL

The 205-mile **Superior Hiking Trail** (www.shta.org) follows the lake-hugging ridgeline between Two Harbors and the Canadian border. Along the way it passes dramatic red-rock overlooks and the occasional moose and black bear. Trailheads with parking lots pop up every 5 to 10 miles, making it ideal for day hikes. The **Superior Shuttle** (☎218-834-5511; www.superiorhikingshuttle.com; from $17; ⏰Fri-Sun mid-May–mid-Oct) makes life even easier, picking up trekkers from 17 stops along the route. Overnight hikers will find 81 backcountry campsites and several lodges to cushion the body come nightfall; the trail website has details. The whole footpath is free, with no reservations or permits required. Duluth also sports 39 miles of the trail, which should be connected to Two Harbors by 2012.

where Bobby had his bar mitzvah. **Zimmy's** (www.zimmys.com; 531 E Howard St; mains $14-20; ⏲11am-1am) has more memorabilia, plus drinks and pub grub. For a bed, try **Hibbing Park Hotel** (☎218-262-3481; www.hibbingparkhotel.com; 1402 E Howard St; r $60-95; ❄📶🏊).

Soudan sports the area's only **underground mine** (☎218-753-2245; www.soudan.umn.edu; 1379 Stuntz Bay Rd; tours adult/child $10/6; ⏲10am-4pm late May-early Sep); wear warm clothes. A fire halted tours in 2011, but they should be operating again by 2012.

GREEN & NATIVE-OWNED BUSINESSES

Green Routes (www.greenroutes.org) lists sustainable, community-oriented eateries, accommodations, shops and activity providers, including many that are Native American–owned. Most listings are in Minnesota, though there are a few from surrounding states such as Wisconsin and South Dakota, too.

VOYAGEURS NATIONAL PARK

In the 17th century, French-Canadian fur traders, or voyageurs, began exploring the Great Lakes and northern rivers by canoe. **Voyageurs National Park** (www.nps.gov/voya) covers part of their customary waterway, which became the border between the USA and Canada.

It's all about water up here. Most of the park is accessible only by hiking or motorboat – the waters are mostly too wide and too rough for canoeing, though kayaks are becoming popular. A few access roads lead to campgrounds and lodges on or near Lake Superior, but these are mostly used by people putting in their own boats.

The visitor centers are car accessible and good places to begin your visit. Twelve miles east of International Falls on Hwy 11 is **Rainy Lake Visitors Center** (☎218-286-5258; ⏲9am-5pm late May-Sep, closed Mon & Tue rest of year), the main park office. Ranger-guided walks and boat tours are available here. Seasonal visitor centers are at **Ash River** (☎218-374-3221; ⏲9am-5pm late May-Sep) and **Kabetogama Lake** (☎218-875-2111; ⏲9am-5pm late May-Sep). These areas have outfitters, rentals and services, plus some smaller bays for canoeing.

Houseboating is the region's rage. Outfitters such as **Ebel's** (☎888-883-2357; www.ebels.com; 10326 Ash River Trail, Orr) and **Voyagaire Houseboats** (☎800-882-6287; www.voyagaire.com; 7576 Gold Coast Rd, Crane Lake) can set you up. Rentals range from $275 to $700 per day, depending on boat size. Novice boaters are welcome and receive instruction on how to operate the vessels.

Otherwise, for sleeping, your choices are pretty much camping or resorts. The 12-room, shared-bath **Kettle Falls Hotel** (☎218-240-1724; www.kettlefallshotel.com; r/cottage incl breakfast $80/160; ⏲May–mid-Oct) is an exception, located in the park's midst and accessible only by boat; make arrangements with the owners for pick-up (per person round-trip $45). **Nelson's Resort** (☎800-433-0743; www.nelsonsresort.com; 7632 Nelson Rd; cabins from $180) at Crane Lake is a winner for hiking, fishing and relaxing under blue skies.

While this is certainly a remote and wild area, those seeking wildlife, canoeing and forest camping in all their glory are best off in the Boundary Waters.

BEMIDJI & CHIPPEWA NATIONAL FOREST

This area is synonymous with outdoor activities and summer fun. Campsites and cottages abound, and almost everybody is fishing-crazy.

Itasca State Park (☎218-266-2100; www.mnstateparks.info; off Hwy 71 N; per vehicle $5, tent & RV sites $16-25) is an area highlight. You can walk across the tiny headwaters of the mighty Mississippi River, rent canoes or bikes, hike the trails and camp. The log **HI Mississippi Headwaters Hostel** (☎218-266-3415; www.mississippiheadwatershostel.org; dm $24-27, r $80-130; 🚭📶) is in the park; winter hours vary, so call ahead. Or if you want a little rustic luxury, try the venerable **Douglas Lodge** (☎866-857-2757; r $75-130; 📶), run by the park, which also has cabins and two good dining rooms.

On the western edge of the forest, about 30 miles from Itasca, tidy **Bemidji** is an old lumber town with a well-preserved downtown and a giant statue of logger Paul Bunyan and his faithful blue ox, Babe. The **visitor center** (☎800-458-2223; www.visitbemidji.com; 300 Bemidji Ave N; ⏲8am-5pm Mon-Fri, 10am-4pm Sat, 11am-2pm Sun Jun-Aug, closed Sat & Sun Sep-May) displays Paul's toothbrush. Stay by the lake and fish at **Taber's Log Cabins** (☎218-751-5781; www.taberslogcabins.com; 2404 Bemidji Ave N; cabins $69-79; ⏲May-Oct; 📶).

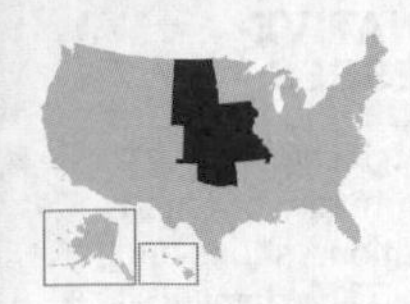

Great Plains

Includes »

Missouri....602
St Louis....603
Kansas City....612
Iowa....616
Des Moines....617
North Dakota....620
South Dakota....624
Nebraska....634
Omaha....634
Kansas....639
Wichita....639
Oklahoma....644
Oklahoma City....644
Tulsa....648

Best Places to Eat

» Oklahoma Joe's (p614)
» Arthur Bryant's (p614)
» Ted Drewes (p607)
» Cattlemen's Steakhouse (p645)

Best Places to Stay

» Hotel Fort Des Moines (p617)
» Alexis Park Inn & Suites (p619)
» Hotel Donaldson (p621)
» Hotel Alex Johnson (p630)

Why Go?

To best appreciate this vast and underappreciated region in the heart of the US, you need to split the name. The first word, 'great,' is easy. Great food, great scenery, great tornadoes, great people all apply. The problem is with 'plains.' 'Humdrum' and 'flat' are two words that come to mind. Neither applies. Amid the endless horizons and raw natural drama are surprises such as St Louis and Kansas City, the Alpine beauty of the Black Hills and the legacy of Route 66.

Great distances across the beguiling wide-open spaces are the biggest impediment to enjoying this enormous region. In this chapter, many sights are organized around the interstates and the more-intriguing two-laners, but more far-flung points of interest and scenic drives are also included.

From miles of sand dunes to lushly forested countryside, small towns to great cities, the majestic sweep of the continent's center is yours to explore.

When to Go

St Louis

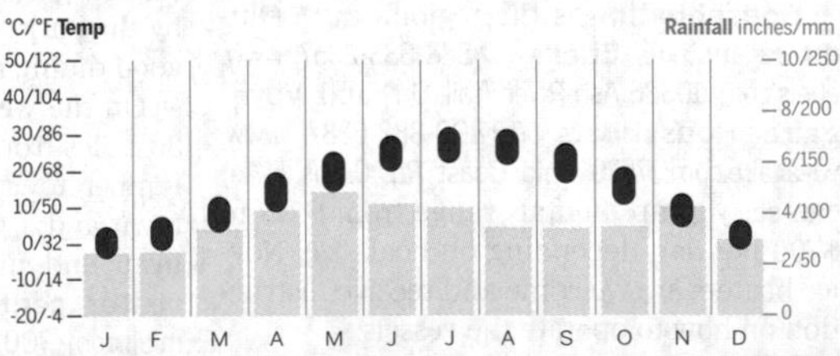

Nov-Mar Attractions cut back hours, or close. Blizzards shut down roads and trains for days.

Apr, May, Sep & Oct Average maximum of 55°F (13°C); uncrowded seasons to visit.

Jun-Aug Thunderstorms and even tornados add drama, sultry days and wildflowers bloom.

Getting There & Around

The main airport is **Lambert-St Louis International** (www.flystl.com), but visitors from abroad will be better off flying to Chicago, Denver or Dallas and connecting to one of the region's myriad airports or hitting the open roads.

Greyhound buses only cover some interstates, but **Jefferson Lines** (www.jeffersonlines.com) and **Burlington Trailways** (www.burlingtontrailways.com) take up some slack. They both honor Greyhound's Discovery Pass.

Amtrak (www.amtrak.com) routes across the Plains make getting here by train easy, but getting around impractical.

California Zephyr Between Chicago and San Francisco via Iowa (including Osceola, south of Des Moines) and Nebraska (including Omaha and Lincoln).

Empire Builder Between Chicago and Seattle via North Dakota.

Heartland Flyer Between Fort Worth and Oklahoma City.

Lincoln Service Between Chicago and St Louis.

Missouri River Runner Between St Louis and Kansas City.

Southwest Chief Between Chicago and Los Angeles via Missouri (including Kansas City) and Kansas (including Topeka and Dodge City).

Texas Eagle Between Chicago and San Antonio via St Louis.

GET YOUR KICKS

Unlike in the rest of the US, you can get somewhat of a feel for this region from the interstate, since the wide-open spaces know no bounds. But the real joy of the region is the many two-lane roads. Substantial stretches of Route 66 survive and are covered in the Missouri (p610), Kansas (p640) and Oklahoma (p647) sections. And don't overlook other roads like US 2, US 20 and US 50.

Top Five Great Plains Parks

» Theodore Roosevelt National Park (p623) Buffalo roam amid stunning canyons carved by rivers after the ice age.

» Badlands National Park (p626) Bizarrely eroded rocks and canyons offer an unforgettable spectacle.

» Wind Cave National Park (p633) Below ground is one of the world's largest cave formations; above ground deer, antelope and bison play.

» Homestead National Monument (p636) Farmland has hikes amid rivers and wildflowers.

» Tallgrass Prairie National Preserve (p643) Most of the prairie grasslands have gone by way of the farmer's plow: only 1% of the original tallgrass survives at places like this.

DON'T MISS

Local diners and cafes with fab home-cooked food are where locals gather to chew on all the news and gossip. Dozens are listed in this chapter.

Fast Facts

» Hub cities: Kansas City (population 460,000), Omaha (population 409,000)

» St Louis to Oklahoma City: 497 miles

» Omaha to Rapid City: 510 miles

» Time zones: Central (one hour behind NYC), Mountain (two hours behind NYC)

» States covered in this chapter: Missouri, Iowa, North Dakota, South Dakota, Nebraska, Kansas, Oklahoma

Did You Know?

The population density in North Dakota is 9.7 people per sq mile. In NYC it's 26,800 per sq mile.

Resources

» National Scenic Byways (www.byways.org) details scores of nationally designated scenic drives in the region.

» National Park Service (www.nps.gov) lists little-known sites.

» Tornado Tracker (www.tornadotracker.net) has links to myriad tornado tracking sites.

Great Plains Highlights

1. Immerse yourself in the blues rhythms of one of America's great old cities: **St Louis** (p603)
2. Go from mountain highs in the **Black Hills** (p627) to valley lows in **Badlands National Park** (p626)
3. Gape at the wildly striated, otherworldly landscapes of **Theodore Roosevelt National Park** (p623)
4. Eat yourself silly on the amazing barbecue in **Kansas City** (p614)
5. Find your own rhythms in quietly beautiful **Chase County, Kansas** (p643)

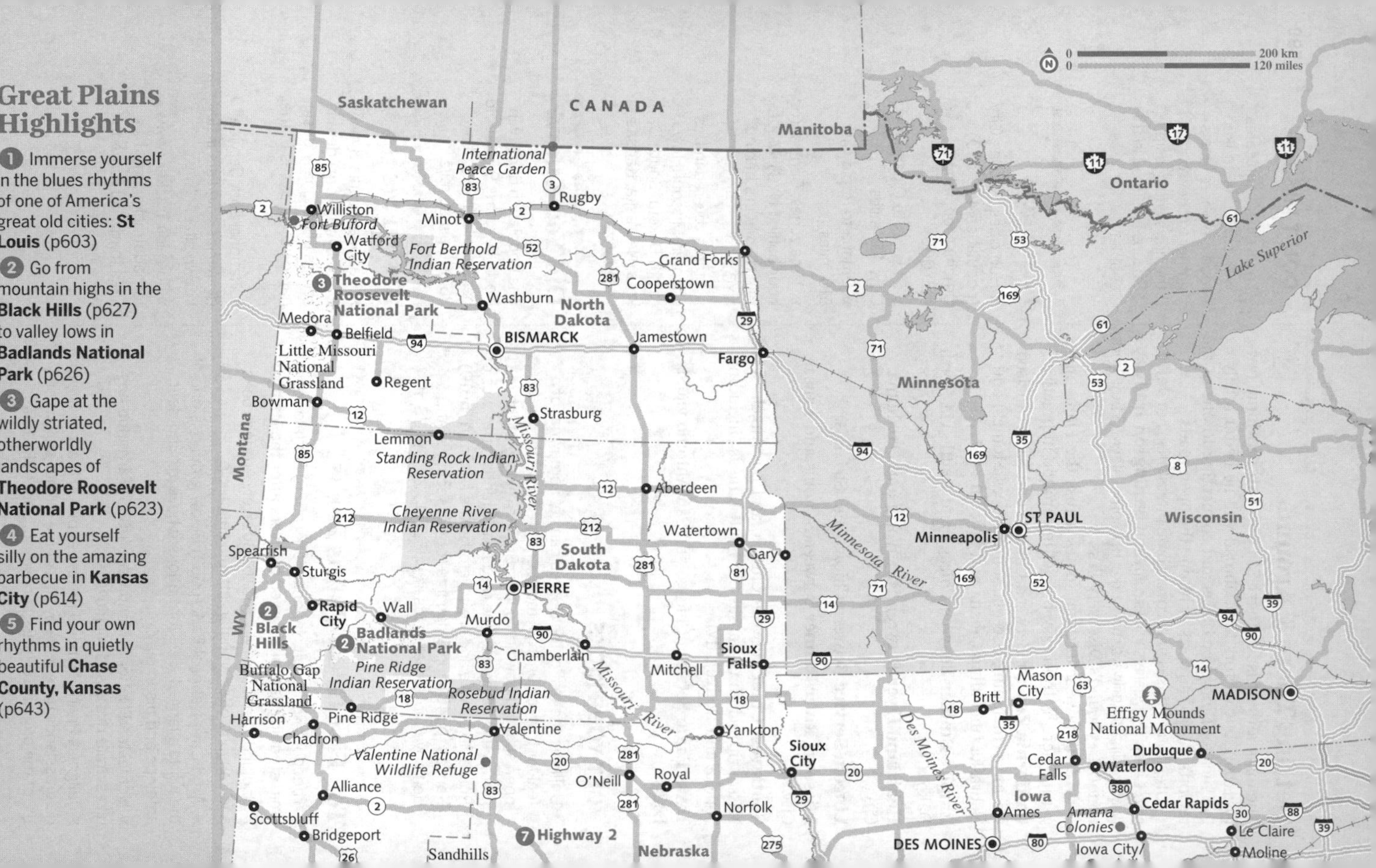

6 Veer off the interstates for beguiling alternate routes such as old **Route 66** through Missouri (p610), Kansas (p640) and Oklahoma (p647)

7 Put the pedal to the metal and your eyeballs on high through the entrancing rolling hills and inland dunes traversed by Nebraska's **Highway 2** (p637)

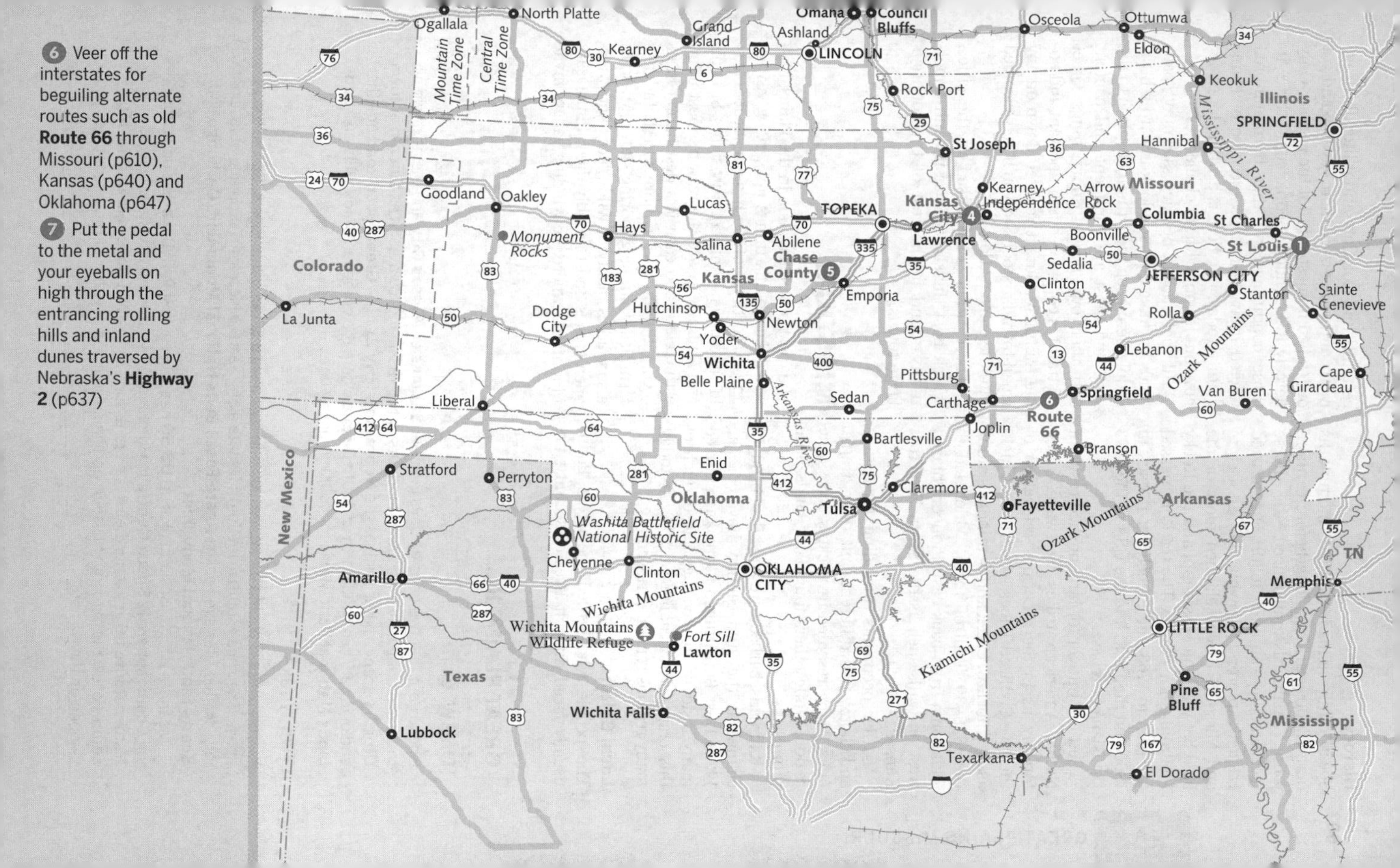

History

Spear-toting nomads hunted mammoths here 11,000 years ago, long before cannon-toting Spaniards introduced the horse (accidentally) around 1630. Fur-frenzied French explorers, following the Mississippi and Missouri Rivers, claimed most of the land between the Mississippi and the Rocky Mountains for France. The territory passed to Spain in 1763, the French got it back in 1800 and then sold it to the USA in the 1803 Louisiana Purchase.

Settlers' hunger for land pushed resident Native American tribes westward, often forcibly, as in the notorious relocation of the Five Civilized Tribes – Cherokee, Chickasaw, Choctaw, Creek and Seminole – along the 1838–39 'Trail of Tears,' which led to Oklahoma from back east. Pioneers blazed west on trails such as the Santa Fe across Kansas.

Earlier occupants, including the Osage and Sioux, had different, but often tragic, fates. Many resettled in pockets across the region, while others fought for lands once promised.

Railroads, barbed wire and oil all brought change as the 20th century hovered. The 1930s Dust Bowl ruined farms and spurred many residents to say: 'I've had enough of this crap – I'm heading west.' Even today, many regions remain eerily empty.

Local Culture

The people who settled the Great Plains usually faced difficult lives of scarcity, uncertainty and isolation; and it literally drove many of them crazy. Others gave up and got out (failed homesteads dot the region). Only fiercely independent people could thrive in those conditions and that born-and-bred rugged individualism is the core of Plains culture today. Life here is a whole lot easier now, but it's not without challenges.

All that staring out across empty space tends to make a person look inward a little. People here keep their thoughts close to the vest, and most are confident and content with their own way of doing things. Quiet restraint is considered an important and polite trait here. But sit yourself down on any small-town barstool and you'll be welcomed into the conversation.

These traits get diffused in the cities, which host the same diversity and opportunity found in the rest of the country's large towns.

MISSOURI

The most populated state in the Plains, Missouri likes to mix things up, serving visitors ample portions of both sophisticated city life and down-home country sights. St Louis and Kansas City are the region's most interesting cities and each is a destination in its own right. But, with more forest and less farm field than neighboring states, Missouri also cradles plenty of wild places and wide-open spaces, most notably the rolling Ozark Mountains, where the winding valleys invite

GREAT PLAINS IN...

One Week

Spend your first two or three days in either **St Louis** or **Kansas City** and the next two or three exploring the small-town standouts of Nebraska and Iowa, such as **Lincoln** or **Iowa City**. Try scenic routes such as the **Nebraska's Hwy 2** or the **Great River Road** at either end of Iowa. Then head north to South Dakota where the gorgeous **Black Hills** and **Badlands National Park** will vie for your remaining time.

Two Weeks

With two weeks behind the wheel, you can take a big bite out of the Plains. Do the trip as above. Then head south from South Dakota along eastern Nebraska, stopping at fascinating, isolated sites such as the **Agate Fossil Beds National Monument**, **Carhenge** and **Scotts Bluff National Monument**.

Meander into Kansas and pick up **US 50** heading east. Stop at the amazing, astonishing **Cosmosphere & Space Centre** in Hutchinson. Head south to Oklahoma and join historic **Route 66** going northeast for sights such as the **Will Rogers Memorial Museum**. Follow the road into Missouri and finish your trip at either of the major cities you skipped on the way out.

MISSOURI FACTS

» **Nickname** Show-Me State

» **Population** 6 million

» **Area** 69,710 sq miles

» **Capital city** Jefferson City (population 40,000)

» **Other cities** St Louis (population 320,000), Kansas City (population 460,000)

» **Sales tax** 4.23%

» **Birthplace of** author Samuel Clemens (Mark Twain; 1835–1910), scientist George Washington Carver (1864–1943), author William S Burroughs (1914–97), author Maya Angelou (b 1928), singer Sheryl Crow (b 1962)

» **Home of** Budweiser, Chuck Berry

» **Politics** split between Democrats and Republicans

» **Famous for** Gateway Arch, Branson

» **Official dance** square dance

» **Driving distances** St Louis to Kansas City 250 miles, St Louis to Chicago 300 miles

adventurous exploring or just some laid-back meandering behind the steering wheel. Maybe you'll find an adventure worthy of Hannibal native Mark Twain as you wander the state.

History

Claimed by France as part of the Louisiana Territory in 1682, Missouri had only a few small river towns by the start of the 19th century when the land passed to American hands and Lewis and Clark pushed up the Missouri River. Missouri was admitted to the Union as a slave state in 1821, per the Missouri Compromise (which permitted slavery in Missouri but prohibited it in any other part of the Louisiana Territory above the 36°30´ parallel), but abolitionists never compromised their ideals, and bitter feelings were stoked along the Missouri–Kansas border by Civil War time.

The state's 'Show-Me' nickname is attributed to Congressman Willard Duncan Vandiver, who said in an 1899 speech, 'I come from a state that raises corn and cotton and cockleburs and Democrats, and frothy eloquence neither convinces nor satisfies me. I am from Missouri. You have got to show me.' The name now implies a stalwart, not-easily-impressed character.

Information

Bed & Breakfast Inns of Missouri (www.bbim.org)

Missouri Division of Tourism (www.visitmo.com)

Missouri state parks (www.mostateparks.com) State parks are free to visit. Site fees range from $12 to $26 and some sites may be reserved in advance.

St Louis

Slide into St Louis and revel in the unique vibe of the largest city in the Great Plains. Beer, bowling and baseball are some of the top attractions, but history and culture, much of it linked to the Mississippi River, are a vital part of the fabric. And, of course, there's the iconic Gateway Arch that you have seen in a million pictures; it's even more impressive in reality. Many music legends, including Scott Joplin, Chuck Berry, Tina Turner and Miles Davis, got their start here and the bouncy live-music venues keep the flame burning.

History

Fur-trapper Pierre Laclede knew prime real estate when he saw it, so he put down stakes at the junction of the Mississippi and Missouri Rivers in 1764. The hustle picked up considerably when prospectors discovered gold in California in 1848 and St Louis became the jump-off point (aka 'Gateway to the West') for get-rich-quick dreamers.

St Louis became known as a center of innovation after hosting the 1904 World's Fair. Aviator Charles Lindbergh furthered the reputation in 1927 when he flew the first nonstop, solo transatlantic flight in the 'Spirit of St Louis,' named for the far-sighted town that funded the aircraft. Grand plans have always been part of the city's self-assurance and you'll find no chips on local shoulders.

Sights & Activities

The landmark Gateway Arch rises right along the Mississippi River. Downtown runs west of the arch. Begin a visit here and wander for half a day. Then explore the rest of the city.

The neighborhoods of most interest radiate out from this core. These include the following:

Downtown St Louis

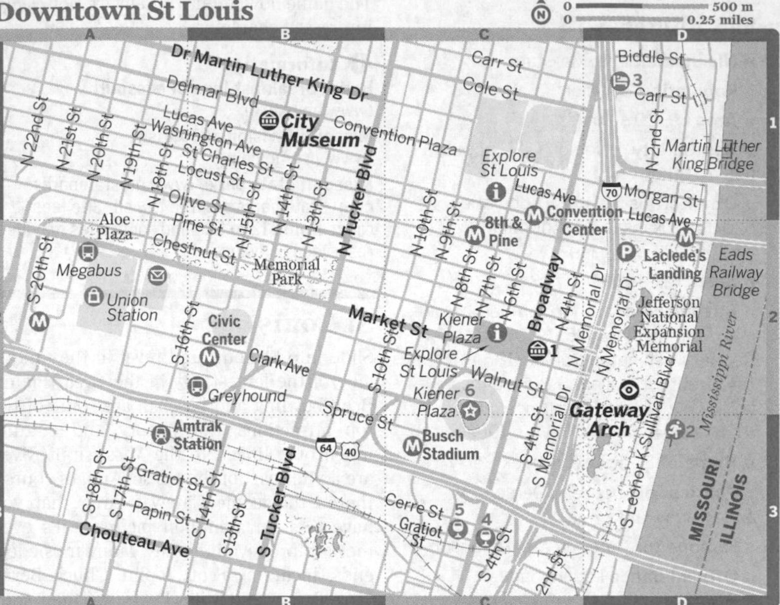

Downtown St Louis

Top Sights
- City Museum B1
- Gateway Arch D2

Sights
- 1 Old Courthouse & Museum C2

Activities, Courses & Tours
- 2 Gateway Arch Riverboats D3

Sleeping
- 3 America's Best Value Downtown St Louis D1

Drinking
- 4 BB's C3
- 5 Beale C3

Entertainment
- 6 Busch Stadium C2

Central West End Just east of Forest Park, a posh center for nightlife and shopping.

The Hill An Italian-American neighborhood with good delis and eateries.

Lafayette Square Historic, upscale and trendy.

The Loop Northwest of Forest Park, funky shops and nightlife line Delmar Blvd.

Soulard The city's oldest quarter, with good cafes, bars and blues.

South Grand Bohemian and gentrifying, surrounds beautiful Tower Grove Park and has a slew of ethnic restaurants.

Cross the river to see **Cahokia Mounds State Historic Site** (p535).

TOP CHOICE **Jefferson National Expansion Memorial/Gateway Arch** MONUMENT

(www.gatewayarch.com; ⏲8am-10pm Jun-Aug, 9am-6pm Sep-May) As a symbol for St Louis, the arch has soared above any expectations its backers could have had in 1965 when it opened. The centerpiece of this National Park Service property, the silvery, shimmering Gateway Arch is the Great Plains' own Eiffel Tower. It stands 630ft high and symbolizes St Louis' historical role as 'Gateway to the West.' The **tram ride** (adult/child $10/5) takes you to the tight confines at the top.

The grounds around the arch are bucolic but are something of an island. Unfortunately, well-founded fears of flooding mean that the arch site sits high atop levees and walls to the east while the west side is blocked by the noxious barriers of Memorial

Dr and I-70 (read about plans to massively improve the area here: www.cityarchrivercompetition.org). Download downtown walking tours at www.coreofdiscovery.com.

FREE Museum of Westward Expansion MUSEUM

(www.nps.gov/jeff; ⏲8am-10pm Jun-Aug, 9am-6pm Sep-May) This subterranean museum, under the Arch, chronicles the Lewis and Clark expedition. Two theaters here show **films** (adult/child $7/2.50) throughout the day.

FREE Old Courthouse & Museum HISTORIC BUILDING

(11 N 4th St; ⏲8am-4:30pm) Facing the Gateway Arch, this 1845 courthouse is where the famed Dred Scott slavery case was first tried. Galleries depict the trial's history, as well as that of the city.

TOP CHOICE Forest Park PARK, MUSEUMS

(www.stlouis.missouri.org/citygov/parks/forestpark; ⏲6am-10pm) New York City may have Central Park, but St Louis has the bigger (by 528 acres) Forest Park. The superb, 1371-acre spread was the setting of the 1904 World's Fair. It's a beautiful place to escape to and is dotted with attractions, many free. Two walkable neighborhoods, The Loop and Central West End, are close.

The **Visitor and Education Center** (www.forestparkforever.org; 5595 Grand Dr; ⏲8:30am-7pm Mon-Fri, 9am-4pm Sat & Sun) is in an old streetcar pavilion and has a cafe. Free walking tours leave from here, or you can borrow an iPod audio tour.

Missouri History Museum

(www.mohistory.org; 5700 Lindell Blvd; ⏲10am-6pm, to 8pm Tue) Presents the story of St Louis, starring such worthies as the World's Fair, Charles Lindbergh (look for the sales receipt for his first plane – he bought it at a variety store!) and a host of bluesmen. Oral histories from those who fought segregation are moving.

St Louis Art Museum

(www.slam.org; 1 Fine Arts Dr; ⏲10am-5pm Tue-Sun, to 9pm Fri) A grand beaux-arts palace originally built for the World's Fair. Now housing this storied institution, its collections span time and styles.

St Louis Zoo

(www.stlzoo.org; 1 Government Dr; fee for some exhibits; ⏲8am-5pm daily, to 7pm Fri-Sun Jun-Aug; 👪) Divided into themed zones, this vast zoo includes a fascinating River's Edge area with African critters.

St Louis Science Center

(www.slsc.org; 5050 Oakland Ave; ⏲9:30am-5:30pm Mon-Sat, from 11am Sun Jun-Aug, to 4:30pm rest of year; 👪) Live demonstrations, dinosaurs, a planetarium and an IMAX theater (additional fee).

Park Activities

In warm weather, sail over to the **Boathouse** (6101 Government Dr; boat rental per hr $15; ⏲10am-sunset) to paddle over Post-Dispatch Lake. In cooler weather, make for the **Steinberg Ice Skating Rink** (off N Kingshighway Blvd; admission $6, skates rental $4; ⏲10am-9pm Sun-Thu, 10am-midnight Fri & Sat Nov-Mar). **City Cycling Tours** (www.citycyclingtours.com; 3hr tour $30; ⏲daily year-round, call for times) offers narrated rides through the park (bicycles and helmets included) starting at the visitor center. Bike rental from the visitor center costs $10/25 per hour/half-day.

TOP CHOICE City Museum MUSEUM

(www.citymuseum.org; 701 N 15th St; admission $12; ⏲9am-5pm Mon-Thu, 9am-1am Fri & Sat, 11am-5pm Sun; 👪) Possibly the wildest highlight to any visit to St Louis is this frivolous, frilly fun house in a vast old shoe factory. The Museum of Mirth, Mystery and Mayhem sets the tone. Run, jump and explore all manner of exhibits. A rooftop Ferris wheel ($5) offers grand views of the city.

FREE Grant's Farm PARK

(www.grantsfarm.com; 10501 Gravois Rd; ⏲9am-3:30pm Tue-Fri, 9am-4pm Sat, 9:30am-4pm Sun mid-May–mid-Aug, reduced hr spring & fall, closed Nov–mid-Apr; 👪) A small-time theme park on the beer-brewing Busch family's rural retreat, Grant's Farm thrills kids with its Clydesdale horses and 1000 other animals from six continents; a tram takes you through the preserve where the beasts roam free. Parking costs $11.

Gateway Arch Riverboats BOAT TOUR

(1hr tour adult/child $14/8; ⏲10:30am-6pm) Churn up the Big Muddy on replica 19th-century steamboats. A park ranger narrates the midday cruises and those after 3pm sail subject to availability. There are also numerous dinner and drinking cruises. Various combo tickets are available.

Missouri Botanical Garden GARDENS
(www.mobot.org; 4344 Shaw Ave; adult/child $8/free; 9am-5pm) These 150-year-old gardens hold a 14-acre Japanese garden, carnivorous plant bog and Victorian-style hedge maze.

Museum of Transportation MUSEUM
(www.transportmuseumassociation.org; 3015 Barrett Station Rd, I-270, near exit 8; adult/student $6/4; 10am-5pm) Huge railroad locomotives, historic cars cooler than your rental and more that moves.

FREE **Pulitzer Foundation for the Arts** MUSEUM
(www.pulitzerarts.org; 3716 Washington Blvd; noon-5pm Wed & Sat) Grand Center landmark, has programs and exhibits across disciplines including architecture.

Festivals & Events

Big Muddy Blues Festival MUSIC
(www.bigmuddybluesfestival.com; admission free) Has five stages of riverfront blues at Laclede's Landing on the Labor Day weekend (September).

Sleeping

Just about every midrange and upscale chain has a hotel near the Gateway Arch in downtown. Indie cheapies are thin on the ground in interesting areas but you'll find plenty near the airport and you can ride the MetroLink light-rail into the city. Upscale Clayton on I-170 exit 1F also has rail access and a cluster of chains.

Parkway Hotel HOTEL $$
(314-256-7777; www.theparkwayhotel.com; 4550 Forest Park Blvd; r $105-200; P❄@) Right in the midst of the upscale fun of the Central West End, this indie eight-story hotel contains 220 modern rooms inside a grand limestone building. Standards are high, hot breakfasts are included and you simply can't beat the location right across from Forest Park.

Moonrise Hotel HOTEL $$$
(314-721-1111; www.moonrisehotel.com; 6177 Delmar Blvd; r $150-220; P❄@) Easily the city's most stylish hotel, the Moonrise has a high profile amid the high energy of the Loop neighborhood. Rooms are sleekly decorated with just enough whimsy to slow things down to comfy. Amenities include 24-hour room service.

Napoleon's Retreat B&B $$
(314-772-6979; www.napoleonsretreat.com; 1815 Lafayette Ave; r $110-180, 2-night min weekends; ❄@) A lovely Second French Empire home in historic Lafayette Sq, this B&B has five bold and beautiful rooms, each with private bath and antique furnishings. Michael and Jeff are excellent hosts.

Water Tower Inn HOTEL $
(314-977-7500; www.slu.edu/x27017.xml; Saint Louis University, 3545 Lafayette Ave; r $80-100; P❄) Right in the middle of Saint Louis University and near the interesting Central West End, the 62 rooms here are clean and functional; there's a laundry.

Huckleberry Finn Hostel HOSTEL $
(314-241-0076; www.huckfinnhostel.com; 1908 S 12th St, Soulard; dm $25; ❄) In two old town houses, this independent hostel is a bit ragged, but it's a friendly gathering spot with a piano in the lounge/kitchen, and free lockers. Its Soulard location is ideal. Be sure to reserve ahead.

America's Best Value Downtown St Louis MOTEL $
(314-421-6556; www.hoteldowntownstl.com; 1100 N 3rd St; r from $65; P❄) When you're sleeping in one of the bare-bones but clean rooms here, you can't see just what a charmless place this is. But the Laclede's Landing location is good, as are the prices.

Eating

St Louis boasts the region's most diverse selection of food. The magazine and website **Sauce** (www.saucemagazine.com) is full of reviews.

DOWNTOWN

Laclede's Landing, along the riverfront next to the historic Eads Railway Bridge, has several restaurants, though generally people pop down here for the atmosphere – cobblestoned streets, converted brick buildings and free-flowing beer – rather than the food.

TOP CHOICE **Crown Candy Kitchen** SODA FOUNTAIN $
(1401 St Louis Ave, North St Louis; mains $4-10; 10:30am-10pm Mon-Sat, to 6pm Sun) An authentic family-run soda fountain that's been making families smile since 1913. Malts (try the butterscotch) come with spoons, the floats, well, float, and you can snack on chili dogs where the wiener groans under

EATING ST LOUIS: LOCAL SPECIALTIES

Try these local specialties:

» **Frozen custard** Don't dare leave town without licking yourself silly on this super-creamy ice cream–like treat at historic **Ted Drewes** (6726 Chippewa St; cones 50c to $2.50; ⌚11am-11pm Feb-Dec). There's a smaller summer-only branch at 4224 S Grand Blvd. Rich and poor rub elbows enjoying a 'concrete,' a delectable stirred-up combination of flavors.

» **Toasted ravioli** They're filled with meat, coated in breadcrumbs, then deep-fried. **Charlie Gitto's** probably started it all, but practically every restaurant on the Hill serves them.

» **St Louis pizza** Its thin-crusted, square-cut pizzas are really addictive. They're made with Provel cheese, a locally beloved gooey concoction of processed cheddar, swiss and provolone. Local chain **Imo's** (www.imospizza.com; large specials $16), with over 70 locations across the metro area, bakes 'the square beyond compare.'

» **Schlafly beer** This sign in the window speaks well of the bar; the only St Louis brewery still locally owned produces more than 40 superb styles of beer through the year, including an excellent dry-hopped American Pale Ale.

the toppings. Homemade candies top it off. It's an oasis in the struggling North St Louis neighborhood.

SOULARD & LAFAYETTE SQUARE

Restaurants and pubs occupy most corners in Soulard, with plenty of live blues and Irish music. Just wander. Lafayette Sq, 1 mile northwest, has various trendy spots.

Joanie's Pizzeria PIZZERIA **$$**
(www.joanies.com; 2101 Menard St, Soulard; mains $10-15; ⌚11am-11pm) Long a favorite before a Cardinals game, this unassuming neighborhood bar and grill turns out beloved local-style pizza (although this version is Provel-free). The sauce wins kudos as does the toasted ravioli – another local fave.

1111 Mississippi MODERN AMERICAN **$$$**
(☎314-241-9999; www.1111-m.com; 1111 Mississippi Ave, Lafayette Sq; mains $9-22; ⌚11am-10pm Mon-Thu, to midnight Fri & Sat) This popular bistro and wine bar fills an old shoe factory. Dinner mains draw on regional specialties with an Italian accent. Other options on the seasonal menu include sandwiches, pizzas, steaks and many veggie options. Excellent wine bar.

John D McGurk's BAR & GRILL **$$**
(1200 Russell Blvd, Soulard; mains $7-20; ⌚11am-1:30am Mon-Sat, 3pm-midnight Sun) The city's favorite pub oozes charm inside, where there's live Irish music many nights, but you can't beat the backyard garden. The steaky menu is a cut above pub fare.

Soulard Farmers Market MARKET **$**
(www.soulardmarket.com; 7th St, Soulard; ⌚8am-5pm Wed-Sat) A local treasure with a range of vendors selling the best organic regional produce and foodstuffs. Picnic or nosh yourself silly.

SOUTH GRAND

Running along South Grand Blvd, this young, Bohemian area near beautiful Tower Grove Park has a slew of excellent ethnic restaurants, many with outside terraces.

MoKaBe's Coffeehouse CAFE **$**
(3606 Arsenal St; snacks $3; ⌚8am-midnight; 📶🌿) Overlooking Tower Grove Park, this hangout for neighborhood activists, hipsters and generally cool folk buzzes day and night. Grab a coffee, a baked treat or a veggie sandwich and ponder the views or jump online.

THE HILL

This tiny-housed Italian neighborhood has innumerable pasta joints. Stroll the tidy streets and stop for a coffee at an Italian cafe or deli.

TOP CHOICE **Milo's Bocce Garden** ITALIAN **$$**
(5201 Wilson Ave; mains $6-14; ⌚11am-1am) Enjoy sandwiches, pizzas and pastas out on the vast outdoor courtyard or inside the old-world bar. Watch and join the regulars on the busy bocce ball courts.

Charlie Gitto's ITALIAN **$$$**
(☎314-772-8898; www.charliegittos.com; 26 Shaw Ave; mains $16-40; ⌚5-10pm Mon-Thu, 5-11pm Fri

YOUR BELGIAN BUD

The world's largest beer plant, the historic **Anheuser-Busch Brewery** (www.budweisertours.com; cnr 12th & Lynch Sts; admission free; 9am-4pm Mon-Sat, 11:30am-4pm Sun, to 5pm Jun-Aug, from 10am Sep-Apr), gives the sort of marketing-driven tours you'd expect from the company with nearly half of the US market. View the bottling plant and famous Clydesdale horses. One thing to note: the purchase of this St Louis icon by the Belgian InBev in 2008 is a sore spot locally. And don't ask: 'How do you remove all the flavor?'

& Sat, 4-10pm Sun) Legendary Charlie Gitto's makes a strong claim to having invented St Louis' famous toasted ravioli. On any night the weather allows, dine under the huge tree on the patio. Classy but casual.

Adriana's ITALIAN **$**
(5101 Shaw Ave; mains $4-10; 10:30am-3pm Mon-Sat) This classic Italian deli serves up fresh salads and sandwiches (get the meaty Hill Boy) to ravenous lunching crowds. There's also good pizza and pasta.

CENTRAL WEST END & THE LOOP

Sidewalk cafes rule Euclid Ave in posh and trendy old Central West End. The Loop is near Washington University and runs along Delmar Blvd (embedded with the St Louis Walk of Fame) and has many bars and ethnic restaurants catering to a hipster crowd.

Duff's FUSION **$$**
(www.dineatduffs.com; 392 N Euclid Ave, Central West End; mains $8-18; 11am-10pm Sun-Thu, to midnight Fri & Sat) The hippies who once tossed back cheap Chablis here are now enjoying the many fine wines on the long list. Duff's has gentrified with the neighborhood and serves an eclectic fusion menu of sandwiches, salads and more ambitious fare. Score a sidewalk table outside under the trees.

Wild Flower AMERICAN **$$$**
(314-367-9888; www.wildflowerdining.com; 4590 Laclede Ave, Central West End; mains $10-30; 11am-10pm Wed-Mon, to 11pm Fri & Sat) One of the largest patios on the Euclid Ave strip is ideal for hours of people-watching. The menu is fresh and there are seasonal specials. Lots of appetizers are good for sharing, dinner mains include steaks, seafood and pasta. Brunch is a cut above the norm.

Ranoush MIDDLE EASTERN **$$**
(6501 Delmar Blvd, The Loop; mains $7-16; 11am-11pm; ) Hard-working brothers are always ready to greet you at the door of this inviting Middle Eastern restaurant, which gets a mix of customers from Syrians to scenesters. Everything is fresh and the hummus comes redolent with garlic. Great patio in summer.

Drinking & Entertainment

Check the **Riverfront Times** (www.riverfronttimes.com) for updates on entertainment options around town. Purchase tickets for most venues through **MetroTix** (www.metrotix.com).

Bars & Nightclubs

Laclede's Landing, Soulard and The Loop are loaded with pubs and bars, many with live music. Most bars close at 1:30am, though some have 3am licenses.

TOP CHOICE **Blueberry Hill** PUB, LIVE MUSIC
(www.blueberryhill.com; 6504 Delmar Blvd, The Loop) St Louis native Chuck Berry still rocks the small basement bar here at least one Wednesday a month. The $35 tickets sell out very quickly. The venue hosts smaller-tier bands on the other nights. It has good pub food, games, darts and more.

BB's BAR, BLUES
(www.bbsjazzbluessoups.com; 700 S Broadway, Downtown; 6pm-3am) Part blues club, part blues museum, there's good music most nights in this glossy two-level joint. Good bar food includes legendary sweet potato fries. **Beale** (www.bealeonbroadway.com; 701 S Broadway), right across the street, is also a great blues venue.

Pageant LIVE MUSIC
(314-726-6161; www.thepageant.com; 6161 Delmar Blvd, The Loop) A big venue for touring bands.

Shanti PUB, LIVE MUSIC
(www.soulardshanti.com; 825 Allen Ave, Soulard; 10am-1:30am Mon-Sat) Meaning 'peace' in Sanskrit, Shanti is the Bohemian heart of Soulard. It hosts a popular Tuesday open mike and folk-bluegrass-rock acts most other nights.

Performing Arts

Grand Center, west of downtown, is the heart of St Louis' theater scene and home of the **St Louis Symphony Orchestra** (www.

stlsymphony.org; 718 N Grand Blvd), which has 50 free tickets for most performances.

The **Municipal Opera** (Muny; www.muny.com) hosts nightly summer musicals outdoors in Forest Park; some of the 12,000 seats are free.

Gay & Lesbian Venues

The Central West End is the GLBT community's hub, but Soulard and South Grand also have hangouts. Peruse the **Vital Voice** (www.thevitalvoice.com) for more.

Loading Zone GAY, BAR
(16 S Euclid Ave; ⏲3:30pm-1:30am Mon-Sat) Cheery neighborhood gay bar packs 'em in for 'Showtunes Tuesdays,' which gets a huge, mixed crowd.

Sports

Busch Stadium BASEBALL
(www.stlcardinals.com; Broadway & Clark Ave) The Cardinals play in this fun, retro stadium, opened in 2006. They dramatically won the World Series in 2011 after falling behind and staging a historic comeback.

Shopping

The Loop and Euclid Ave in the Central West End have the best mix of local shops.

Cherokee Antique Row ANTIQUES
(Cherokee St, east of Jefferson Ave to Indiana Ave) Six blocks of antique-filled stores in the appropriately historic Cherokee-Lemp neighborhood.

Left Bank Books BOOKS
(www.left-bank.com; 399 North Euclid, Central West End; ⏲10am-10pm Mon-Sat, 11am-6pm Sun) A great indie bookstore stocking new and used titles. There are excellent recommendations of books by local authors and frequent author readings.

ℹ Information

Media

KDHX FM 88.1 (www.kdhx.org) Community-run radio playing folk, blues, odd rock and local arts reports.

Riverfront Times (www.riverfronttimes.com) The city's alternative weekly.

St Louis Post-Dispatch (www.stltoday.com) St Louis' daily newspaper.

St Louis Sinner A free, monthly paper with a radical and alternative slant.

Post

Post office (1720 Market St; ⏲8am-8pm Mon-Fri, 8am-1pm Sat)

Tourist Information

Explore St Louis (www.explorestlouis.com; America's Center, cnr 7th St & Washington Ave; ⏲8:30am-5pm Mon-Sat, 11am-4pm Sun) An excellent resource, with other branches in Kiener Plaza (corner of 6th and Chestnut), and at the airport.

Missouri Welcome Center (☎314-869-7100; www.visitmo.com; I-270 exit 34; ⏲8am-5pm, closed Sun Nov-Mar)

ℹ Getting There & Around

Lambert-St Louis International Airport (www.flystl.com) is the hub of the Great Plains, with flights to many US cities. The airport is 12 miles northwest of downtown and is connected by the light-rail MetroLink ($3.75), taxi (about $35) and **Go Best Express** (☎314-222-5300; www.gobestexpress.com; $21) shuttles, which can drop you off in the main areas of town.

Amtrak (www.amtrak.com; 551 S 16th St) *Lincoln Service* travels five times daily to Chicago (from $25, 5½ hours). Two daily *Missouri River Runner* trains go to/from Kansas City (from $26, 5½ hours). The daily *Texas Eagle* goes to Dallas (16 hours).

Greyhound (430 S 15th St) Buses depart several times daily to Chicago ($40, six to seven hours), Memphis ($55, six hours), Kansas City ($30, 4½ hours) and many more cities. The station is near Amtrak downtown.

Megabus (www.megabus.com) Runs services to Chicago and Kansas City from as little as $15 one way; it stops next to Union Station on 20th St.

Metro (www.metrostlouis.org; single/day pass $2.25/7.50) Runs local buses and the MetroLink light-rail system (which connects the airport, The Loop, Central West End and downtown). Buses 30 and 40 serve Soulard from downtown.

St Louis County Cabs (☎314-993-8294)

Around St Louis

Several appealing and historic river towns north and south of St Louis on the Mississippi and just west on the Missouri make popular weekend trips for St Louisans, including the historic pair of St Charles and Hannibal. If you're looking for some grand meeting of the two rivers however, don't. The two muddies meet in a swirl of silt and are surrounded by square miles of – you guessed it – muddy and inaccessible floodplains.

ST CHARLES

This Missouri River town, founded in 1769 by the French, is just 20 miles northwest

ROUTE 66: GET YOUR KICKS IN MISSOURI

The Show-Me State will show you a long swath of the Mother Road. Meet the route in **St Louis**, where **Ted Drewes Frozen Custard** (p607) has been serving generations of roadies from its Route 66 location on Chippewa St. There are a couple of well-signed historic routes through the city.

Follow I-44 (the interstate is built over most of Route 66 in Missouri) west to **Route 66 State Park** (www.mostateparks.com/route66.htm; I-44 exit 266; ⏲7am-30min after sunset), with its visitor center and **museum** (admission free; ⏲9am-4:30pm Mar-Nov) inside a 1935 roadhouse. Although the displays show vintage scenes from around St Louis, the real intrigue here concerns the town of Times Beach, which once stood on this very site. It was contaminated with dioxin and in the 1980s the government had to raze the entire area.

Speed southwest on I-44 to Stanton, then follow the signs to family-mobbed **Meramec Caverns** (www.americascave.com; adult/child $19/9.50; ⏲8:30am-7:30pm summer, reduced hr rest of year), as interesting for the Civil War history and hokey charm as for the stalactites; and the conspiracy-crazy **Jesse James Wax Museum** (adult/child $6/3; ⏲9am-6pm Jun-Aug, reduced hr rest of year), which posits that James faked his death and lived until 1951.

The **Route 66 Museum & Research Center** (www.lebanon-laclede.lib.mo.us; 915 S Jefferson St; admission free; ⏲8am-8pm Mon-Thu, 8am-5pm Fri & Sat) at the library in Lebanon has memorabilia past and present. Ready for a snooze? Head to the 1940s **Munger Moss Motel** (☎417-532-3111; www.mungermoss.com; 1336 E Rte 66; r from $45; ❄📶🏊). It's got a monster of a neon sign and Mother Road–loving owners.

Ditch the interstate west of **Springfield**, taking Hwy 96 to Civil War–era **Carthage** with its historic town square and **66 Drive-In Theatre** (www.66drivein.com; 17231 Old 66 Blvd; adult/child $7/3; ⏲Fri-Sun Apr-Oct). In **Joplin**, which is still recovering from its horrible 2011 tornado, get on State Hwy 66, turning onto old Route 66 (the pre-1940s route), before the Kansas state line.

The **Route 66 Association of Missouri** (www.missouri66.org) has loads of info.

of St Louis. The cobblestoned Main St anchors a well-preserved downtown where you can visit the **first state capitol** (200 S Main St; admission free, tours adult/child $4/free; ⏲10am-4pm Mon-Sat, noon-4pm Sun, closed Mon Nov-Mar). Ask at the **visitor center** (☎800-366-2427; www.historicstcharles.com; 230 S Main St; ⏲8am-5pm Mon-Fri, 10am-5pm Sat, noon-5pm Sun) about tours, which pass some rare French colonial architecture in the **Frenchtown neighborhood** just north.

Lewis and Clark began their epic journey in St Charles on May 21, 1804 and their encampment is reenacted annually on that date. The **Lewis & Clark Boathouse and Nature Center** (www.lewisandclarkcenter.org; 1050 Riverside Dr; adult/child $4/2; ⏲10am-5pm Mon-Sat, noon-5pm Sun) has a handful of displays about the duo.

Hotels are spread along St Charles' four I-70 exits. St Charles also has several historic B&Bs, including **Boone's Colonial Inn** (☎888-377-0003; www.boonescolonialinn.com; 322 S Main St; r $185-325; ❄📶). The three rooms in the 1820 stone row houses are posh.

HANNIBAL

When the air is sultry in this old river town, you almost expect to hear the whistle of a paddle steamer. Mark Twain's boyhood home, 100 miles northwest of St Louis, has some authentically vintage sections and plenty of sites where you can get a sense of the muse and his creations Tom Sawyer and Huck Finn.

The **Mark Twain Boyhood Home & Museum** (www.marktwainmuseum.org; 415 N Main St; adult/child $9/5; ⏲9am-5pm) presents eight buildings, including two homes Twain lived in and that of Laura Hawkins, the real-life inspiration for Becky Thatcher. Afterward, float down the Mississippi on the **Mark Twain Riverboat** (www.marktwainriverboat.com; Center St; 1hr sightseeing cruise adult/child $16/12; ⏲Apr-Nov, schedule varies). **National Tom Sawyer Days** (www.hannibaljaycees.org/NTSD.html; ⏲around Jul 4 weekend) features frog-jumping and fence-painting contests and much more.

Many of Hannibal's historic homes are now B&Bs. The **Hannibal Visitors Bureau** (☎866-263-4825; www.visithannibal.com;

505 N 3rd St; ⌚9am-5pm) keeps contacts for all forms of lodging. **Garden House B&B** (☎573-221-7800, 866-423-7800; www.gardenhousebedandbreakfast.com; 301 N 5th St; r $90-240; ❄📶), in a Victorian house, lives up to its name. Some rooms share bathrooms.

Along I-70

The main highway artery between St Louis and Kansas City, I-70, is a congested dud (with a surprising number of porn and sex shops); whenever possible, leave the interstate.

You'll find much to engage with on **US 50**, which meanders on a parallel path south of I-70. From Jefferson City, **Hwy 94** follows the Missouri River east toward St Louis and passes through a beautiful region of wineries and forests.

There are a couple of good excuses to exit if you are on I-70. **Columbia** is home to the much-lauded University of Missouri. The downtown is easily walkable and is a very attractive collection of old brick buildings that feature thriving cafes, bars, bookstores and more. Try **Uprise Bakery** (10 Hitt St; meals $3-10; ⌚7am-8pm Mon-Sat), renowned for its organic meals and baked goods.

Some 30 miles west of Columbia and 10 miles north of I-70, **Arrow Rock State Historic Site** (www.mostateparks.com/park/arrow-rock-state-historic-site; ⌚visitor center 10am-4pm Mar-Nov) is a small preserved town that feels little changed since the 1830s when it was on the main stagecoach route west.

The Ozarks

Ozark hill country spreads across southern Missouri and extends into northern Arkansas and eastern Oklahoma.

At massive **Johnson's Shut-Ins State Park** (www.mostateparks.com/jshutins.htm), 8 miles north of Lesterville on Hwy N, the swift Black River swirls through canyon-like gorges (shut-ins). The swimming is some of the most exciting you'll find outside a water park.

North of US 60, in the state's south-central region, the **Ozark National Scenic Riverways** (www.nps.gov/ozar) – the Current and Jack's Fork Rivers – boast 134 miles of splendid canoeing and inner-tubing (rental agencies abound). Weekends often get busy and boisterous. The headquarters, along with outfitters and motels, is in **Van Buren**. **Eminence** also makes a good base. There are many campgrounds along the rivers. Hwy 19 through here is a scenic gem.

BRANSON

Hokey Branson is a cheerfully shameless tourist resort in the tradition of Blackpool or Atlantic City. The main attractions are the more than 50 theaters hosting 100-plus country music, magic and comedy shows. The neon-lit '76 Strip' (Hwy 76) packs in miles of motels, restaurants, wax museums, shopping malls, fun parks and theaters. As Bart Simpson once said: 'It's like Vegas; if it were run by Ned Flanders.'

During the summer and again in November and December, the SUV-laden traffic often crawls. It's often faster to walk than drive, although few others have this idea.

The **Branson Lakes Area Convention & Visitors Bureau** (☎800-296-0463; www.explorebranson.com; junction Hwy 248 & US 65; ⌚8am-5pm Mon-Sat, 10am-4pm Sun), just west of the US 65 junction, has town and lodging information. The scores of 'Visitor Information' centers around town (even the 'official' ones) are fronts for time-share sales outfits. Sit through a pitch, however, and you can get free tickets to a show.

Popular **theater shows** feature performers you may have thought were dead (eg Andy Williams). However, Branson has been the salvation for scores of entertainers young and old whose careers collapsed after the death of variety shows on TV (who knew there were still bird acts?). Patriotic themes are a stock part of every show; the official singer of the Republican Party, Lee Greenwood, seems to have a lifetime contract. Fundamentalist Christian themes are also common; expect dancers wearing enough fabric to outfit all of their counterparts in Vegas for a year. And while fudge is available in copious quantities, irony is not: when we drove by a much-hyped Titanic attraction, the sign implored people to come in and 'renew your wedding vows.' Expect a lot of Elvis.

Theaters usually run afternoon and evening shows, and sometimes morning ones. Prices range from about $25 to $50 a head, but you rarely need to pay full price. Pick up any of the many coupon books around town or stop by **Branson 2 for 1 Tickets** (www.branson2for1tickets.com; 1100 W Hwy 76), which does business with, as the sign says, 'No Bull.' Reserve a week in advance during peak seasons.

Two attractions, opened in 1959 and 1960 respectively, spurred the Branson boom. The **Baldknobbers Jamboree** (www.baldknobbers.com; 2835 W Hwy 76; adult/child $30/16), a cornball country music and comedy show; and **Silver Dollar City** (www.silverdollarcity.com; adult/child $55/45; ⌚vary), a huge amusement park west of town.

Sleeping & Eating

There are dozens of indie and chain motels (starting at around $35) along Hwy 76 on the strip. **Meloday Lane Inn** (☎417-338-8598; www.melodylanebranson.com; 2821 W Hwy 76; r from $60;) is a large old property with good-sized rooms and pool and actual large trees with shade out front (a Strip rarity).

Nicer places are off the Strip in quieter locales. **Table Rock Lake**, snaking through the hills southwest of town, is a deservedly popular destination for boating, fishing, camping and other outdoor activities, and it also has good value lodging. Try unassuming **Indian Trails Resort** (☎417-338-2327; www.indiantrailsresort.com; Indian Point Rd; cottages $85-185;), on the lake 9 miles south of Branson.

Branson cuisine consists almost entirely of fast food, junk food and all-you-can-eat buffets (most priced $5 to $10). But for classic American diner fare that wins raves, try the family-run **Billy Gail's Cafe** (5291 Hwy 265; mains $5-8; ⌚7am-5pm). Housed in a shady old gas station, the pancakes, grits, omelets, burgers and more are literally hugely good.

Kansas City

Wide open and inviting, Kansas City (KC) is famed for its barbecues (100-plus joints smoke it up), fountains (more than 200; on par with Rome) and jazz. The latter serves as an anchor for a vibrant African American community. Attractive neighborhoods jostle for your attention and you can easily run aground for several days as you enjoy the local vibe, which ranges from buff to boho.

History

Kansas City began life in 1821 as a trading post but really came into its own once westward expansion began. The Oregon, California and Santa Fe trails all met steamboats loaded with pioneers here.

Jazz exploded in the early 1930s under Mayor Tom Pendergast's Prohibition-era tenure, when he allowed alcohol to flow freely. At its peak, KC had more than 100 nightclubs, dance halls and vaudeville houses swinging to the beat (and booze). The roaring good times ended with Pendergast's indictment on tax evasion (the same way they got Capone) and the scene had largely faded by the mid-1940s.

Sights & Activities

State Line Rd divides KC Missouri and KC Kansas (a conservative suburban sprawl with little to offer travelers). KC Missouri has some distinct areas, including the art-deco-filled downtown. **Quality Hill**, around W 10th St and Broadway, has grand, restored buildings from the 1920s.

Interesting neighborhoods include the following:

Country Club Plaza Often shortened to 'the Plaza,' this 1920s shopping district is an attraction in itself.

Crossroads Arts District Around Baltimore and 20th Sts, it lives up to its name.

Crown Plaza South of downtown, this 1970s development is anchored by several major hotels and Hallmark (yes, the greeting card company is located right here).

Historic Jazz District On the upswing, this old African American neighborhood is at 18th and Vine Sts.

River Market Historic and still home to a large farmers market; immediately north of downtown.

Westport On Westport Rd just west of Main St and filled with alluring locally owned restaurants and bars.

TOP CHOICE **National WWI Museum** MUSEUM
(www.theworldwar.org; 100 W 26th St; adult/child $12/6; ⌚10am-5pm, closed Mon Sep-May) You enter this impressive modern museum on a glass walkway over a field of red poppies, the symbol of the trench fighting. Through detailed and engaging displays you learn about a war that is almost forgotten by most Americans. The only quibble is that more effort is spent on the hardware and uniforms of the war as opposed to the actual horrific conditions. The museum is crowned by the historic **Liberty Memorial**, which has views over the city.

Museums at 18th & Vine MUSEUMS
(1616 E 18th St; adult/child $8/3; ⌚9am-6pm Tue-Sat, noon-6pm Sun) At the heart of KC's 1920s African American neighborhood is this mu-

seum complex. You'll learn about different styles, rhythms, instruments and musicians – including KC native Charlie Parker – at the interactive **American Jazz Museum** (www.americanjazzmuseum.com). The **Negro Leagues Baseball Museum** (www.nlbm.com) covers African American teams (such as the KC Monarchs and New York Black Yankees) that flourished until baseball became fully integrated.

Country Club Plaza NEIGHBORHOOD
(www.countryclubplaza.com) Built in the 1920s, this posh commercial district boasts finely detailed, sumptuous Spanish architecture. It's rich with public art and sculptures – look for the walking tour brochure and check out just two examples: the **Spanish Bullfight Mural** (Central St) and the **Fountain of Neptune** (47th St & Wornall Rd). The Plaza is centered on Broadway and 47th Sts.

FREE **Nelson-Atkins Museum of Art** MUSEUM
(www.nelson-atkins.org; 4525 Oak St; 10am-5pm Wed & Sat, 10am-9pm Thu-Fri, noon-5pm Sun) Giant badminton shuttlecocks (the building represents the net) surround this encyclopedic museum, which has standout European painting, photography and Asian art collections. Its luminescent Bloch Building, designed by Steven Holl, has earned rave reviews.

Arabia Steamboat Museum MUSEUM
(www.1856.com; 400 Grand Blvd; adult/child $15/6; 10am-5pm Mon-Sat, noon-5pm Sun) In River Market, this museum displays 200 tons of salvaged 'treasure' from a riverboat that sunk in 1856 (one of hundreds claimed by the river).

FREE **Kemper Museum of Contemporary Art** MUSEUM
(www.kemperart.org; 4420 Warwick Blvd; 10am-4pm Tue-Thu, 10am-9pm Fri & Sat, 11am-5pm Sun) Near the Nelson-Atkins and Country Club Plaza, this museum is small and edgy.

Toy and Miniature Museum of Kansas City MUSEUM
(www.toyandminiaturemuseum.org; 5235 Oak St; adult/child $7/5; 10am-4pm Wed-Sat, from 1pm Sun;) Over 100 years of toys spread over 38 rooms.

Festivals & Events

American Royal Barbecue FOOD
(www.americanroyal.com) The world's largest barbecue contest (500 teams); it takes place in the old stockyards the first weekend in October.

Sleeping

Downtown, Westport and the Plaza are good lodging options near the action. For something cheap, you'll need to head out on the interstate: north on I-35 and I-29 and east on I-70 are good places to look.

TOP CHOICE **Q Hotel** HOTEL $$
(816-931-0001; www.theqhotel.com; 560 Westport Rd, Westport; r incl breakfast from $110;) This environmentally conscious indie hotel is centrally located in Westport. All 125 rooms have a bright color scheme that seems as fresh as spring. Free breakfasts include fair-trade coffee and there are many other thoughtful extras including regular yoga classes.

Southmoreland on the Plaza B&B $$
(816-531-7979; www.southmoreland.com; 116 E 46th St, Country Club Plaza; r incl breakfast $110-200;) The 13 rooms at this posh B&B are furnished like the home of your rich country club friends. It's a big old mansion between the art museums and the Plaza. Extras include Jacuzzis, decks, sherry, fresh flowers and more.

Aladdin HOTEL $$
(816-421-8888; www.hialaddin.com; 1215 Wyandotte St, Downtown; r $80-200;) Affiliated with Holiday Inn, this 16-story hotel dates from 1925. It has been restored to its Italian Romanesque splendor and has 193 compact but entirely comfortable rooms. It was a legendary haunt of mobsters and Greta Garbo.

America's Best Value Inn MOTEL $
(816-531-9250; www.econolodge.com; 3240 Broadway; r from $60;) Ideally located and convenient to everything, this basic 52-room motel has inside corridors and a pool big enough for a small family.

Eating & Drinking

Westport and Country Club Plaza are your best bets for clusters of atmospheric local food and drink places. Don't leave town without hitting a few barbecue joints.

The heavily hyped new **Power & Light District** (www.powerandlightdistrict.com) is a vast urban development centered on Grand Blvd and W 12th St. It has dozens of chain restaurants, formula bars and live-performance venues. When there's no

EATING KANSAS CITY: BBQ

Savoring hickory-smoked brisket, pork, chicken or ribs at one of the barbecue joints around town is a must for any visitor. The local style is pit-smoked and slathered with heavily seasoned vinegar-based sauces. You may well swoon for 'burnt ends,' the crispy ends of smoked pork or beef brisket. Amazing.

Oklahoma Joe's BBQ **$$**

(www.oklahomajoesbbq.com; 3002 W 47th Ave, KC, KS; mains $6-14; ⌚11am-8:30pm Mon-Thu, to 9:30pm Fri & Sat) The best reason to cross the state border (it's actually not far from the Plaza), this legendary BBQ joint housed in a brightly lit old gas station makes grown men's voices crack with joyous emotion. The burnt ends are pleasure on a plate and the various sides like the potato salad are no slouches either.

Arthur Bryant's BBQ **$**

(www.arthurbryantsbbq.com; 1727 Brooklyn Ave; ⌚10am-9:30pm Mon-Thu, 10am-10pm Fri & Sat, 11am-8pm Sun) Not far from the Jazz District, this famous institution serves up piles of superb BBQ in a somewhat slick setting. The sauce is silky and fiery; service is sweet.

sporting event or convention in town it can seem rather bleak.

Be sure to try a locally brewed Boulevard Beer; bars close between 1:30am and 3am.

TOP CHOICE **City Market** MARKET **$**

(www.thecitymarket.org; cnr W 5th St & Grand Blvd) City Market is a haven for small local businesses selling an idiosyncratic range of foods and other items. Ethnic groceries abound and there is a farmers market for regional producers on weekends. Little cafes and greasy spoons do big business from breakfast through dinner.

Le Fou Frog FRENCH **$$$**

(www.lefoufrog.com; City Market, 400 E 5th St; mains $15-25; ⌚5-10pm Tue-Sun, 11am-2pm Thu) Take a trip to Paris without leaving the prairie at this small bistro that's authentic right down to the at-times brusque service. The food is superb, especially hearty stalwarts such as cassoulet. Tables outside are to be cherished.

Classic Cup AMERICAN **$$**

(www.classiccup.com; 301 W 47th St, Country Club Plaza; mains $8-20; ⌚7am-10pm) A long-running classic that has thrived even as upscale chains have muscled into the Plaza. Think upscale bistro fare (complex salads, sandwiches with cheeses from Europe, tender little steaks and the like) served with panache. Two tough scores you should try for: a table on the streetside terrace and brunch.

Foundry PUB **$$**

(www.foundrykc.com; 424 Westport Rd, Westport; mains $7-12; ⌚4pm-3am) From the vast terrace to the retro-industrial interior, the Foundry is a factory of fun. There's a huge drinks and beer selection plus an ever-intriguing menu of stylish pub vittles. On weekends it seems like half of KC is here, so order two drinks at a time – and two of the oddly addictive soft pretzels.

TOP CHOICE **Zoo Bar** BAR

(1220 McGee St, Downtown; ⌚11am-1:30pm) The raw-edged antidote to the artifice of the nearby Power & Light District. Shoot some pool, shoot off your mouth, write something stronger than 'shoot' on the highly entertaining bathroom walls. Characters are more common than bottlecaps on the floor and soon you'll be one of them.

Westport Coffeehouse CAFE **$**

(www.westportcoffeehouse.com; 4010 Pennsylvania St; sandwiches $6-7; ⌚8am-11pm Mon-Thu, to midnight Fri & Sat, 10am-10pm Sun; @📶) This laid-back place off the main drag has good coffee and specialty teas. Look for live music, comedy, art films and more at night.

☆ Entertainment

The free weekly **Pitch** (www.pitch.com) has the top cultural calendar. *Jam* magazine covers the local jazz scene. Live-music venues are scattered across the city.

TOP CHOICE **Mutual Musicians Foundation** JAZZ

(www.thefoundationjamson.org; 1823 Highland Ave; ⌚midnight-6am Fri & Sat) Near 18th and Vine, this little club has hosted after-hours jams since 1930. Veteran musicians jam with young hotshots in a large, pretension-free hall. A little bar serves cheap drinks in plastic cups, which makes up for the $10 cover. The friendly crowd spans the gamut and feels like the ultimate house party.

Riot Room LIVE MUSIC
(www.theriotroom.com; 4048 Broadway, Westport) Part dive, part cutting-edge live-music venue, the Riot Room always rocks – and has many good beers.

Jardine's BLUES, JAZZ
(www.jardines4jazz.com; 4536 Main St, Country Club Plaza) This mannered club has nightly jazz, plus Saturday afternoons.

Truman Sports Complex STADIUMS
(I-70 exit 9) Locals are passionate about Major League Baseball's **Royals** (www.kcroyals.com) and the NFL's **Chiefs** (www.kcchiefs.com). Both play at gleaming side-by-side stadiums in the Truman Sports Complex, east of the city near Independence.

Shopping

Historic Country Club Plaza is KC's top shopping destination (its lavish architecture is modeled on Seville, Spain and dates to 1923), though sadly it's mostly upscale national chains. Westport has more eclectic shops as does 39th St. More than 60 galleries call Crossroads Art District home.

Halls DEPARTMENT STORE
(www.halls.com; 211 Nichols Rd, Country Club Plaza) Founded in 1913 by the same family behind, you guessed it, Hallmark, this high end store is so gracious, you may wish you were wearing gloves. There's top merchandise in KC's answer to Nordstroms.

Prospero's Books BOOKS
(www.prosperosbookstore.com; 1800 W 39th St; ⌚10am-9pm) Funky used bookstore in a vibey part of town. Great recommendations, live poetry and even a few bands.

Zebedee's MUSIC
(www.zebedeesrpm.com; 1208 W 39th St; ⌚11am-8pm Mon & Wed-Sat, noon-5pm Sun) Has a great vinyl collection, including lots of old jazz.

Information

Media

Kansas City Star (www.kansascity.com) Daily paper.

Pitch (www.pitch.com) Free alt-weekly newspaper.

Post

Post office (300 W Pershing; ⌚7am-6pm Mon-Fri, 7:30am-3:30pm Sat) In Union Station.

Tourist Information

Greater Kansas City Visitor Center (☎800-767-7700; www.visitkc.com; 22nd fl, 1100 Main St, City Center Sq; ⌚8:30am-5pm Mon-Fri) A desk is also staffed daily in Union Station.

Missouri Welcome Center (☎816-889-3330; www.visitmo.com; I-70 exit 9; ⌚8am-5pm) Statewide maps and information.

Getting There & Around

KC International Airport (www.flykci.com) is a confusing array of circular terminals 16 miles northwest of downtown. A taxi to downtown/Plaza costs about $40/45. Or take the cheaper **Super Shuttle** (☎800-258-3826; downtown/Plaza $17/18).

Amtrak (www.amtrak.com) In majestic Union Station; has two daily *Missouri River Runner* trains to St Louis (from $26, 5½ hours). The *Southwest Chief* stops here on its daily runs between Chicago and LA.

Greyhound (www.greyhound.com; 1101 Troost St) Sends buses daily to St Louis ($30, 4½ hours) and Denver ($90, 11 hours) from the station poorly located east downtown.

Jefferson Lines (www.jeffersonlines.com) Heads to Omaha ($40, three to four hours), Minneapolis ($80, eight to 10 hours) via Des Moines and Oklahoma City ($65, seven hours) via Tulsa.

Megabus (www.megabus.com; 3rd St & Grand Blvd, Downtown) Serves St Louis and Chicago for as low as $15.

Metro (www.kcata.org; adult/child $1.50/75c) A one-day unlimited bus pass costs $3. Bus 57 runs regularly between downtown, Westport and Country Club Plaza.

Yellow Cab (☎888-471-6050)

MISSOURI: EXTRAS & DETOURS

Sixty-five miles south of St Louis, the petite, French-founded Mississippi River town of **Sainte Genevieve**, MO, oozes history. Many of the restored 18th- and 19th-century buildings are now B&Bs and gift shops.

The **George Washington Carver National Monument** (www.nps.gov/gwca; Diamond; admission free; ⌚9am-5pm) is at the birthplace of this African American renaissance man, who accomplished a lot more than just experimenting with peanuts. It's near Joplin. Take exit 11A off I-44, then follow US 71 4.5 miles south to Hwy V, then go east.

Around Kansas City

INDEPENDENCE

Just east of Kansas City, picture-perfect Independence is the perfect stereotype for an old Midwestern small town. It was the home of Harry S Truman, US president from 1945 to 1953.

Sights & Activities

Independence's attractions can easily fill a day.

TOP CHOICE **Truman Home** HISTORIC BUILDING
(www.nps.gov/hstr; 219 N Delaware St; tours adult/child $4/free) See the simple life Harry and Bess lived in this simple but charming wood house. It is furnished with their original belongings and you fully expect the couple to wander out and say hello. Truman lived here from 1919 to 1972 and in retirement entertained visiting dignitaries in his strictly pedestrian front room – he's said to have hoped none of the callers would linger more than 30 minutes.

Tour tickets are sold at the **visitor center** (223 N Main St; ⏲8:30am-5pm). Ask for directions to the Truman farm where the future president 'got his common sense.'

Truman Presidential Museum & Library MUSEUM
(www.trumanlibrary.org; 500 W US 24; adult/child $8/3; ⏲9am-5pm Mon-Sat, noon-5pm Sun year-round, to 9pm Thu summer) Thousands of objects, including the famous 'The BUCK STOPS here!' sign, from the man who led the US through one of its most tumultuous eras are displayed in this vast, modern building.

National Frontier Trails Museum MUSEUM
(www.ci.independence.mo.us/nftm; 318 W Pacific St; adult/child $6/3; ⏲9am-4:30pm Mon-Sat, 12:30-4:30pm Sun) Gives a good look at life for the pioneers along the Santa Fe, California and Oregon Trails; many began their journey in Independence.

Truman Historic Walking Trail WALKING TOUR
Starting at the visitor center, this 2.7-mile self-guiding route leads to dozens of Truman-related sites, including the courthouse where he began his political career.

Sleeping & Eating

Higher Ground Hotel HOTEL $
(☎816-836-0292; www.olivebranchinn.us; 200 N Delaware; r $65-90; ❄📶) Stay across from the Truman House at this modern place that looks like a school. The 30 rooms are commodious and comfortable.

Clinton's Soda Fountain SODA FOUNTAIN $
(100 W Maple Ave; mains $4-8; ⏲9am-6pm Mon-Sat) Little changed from when Truman got his first job here as a soda jerk.

ST JOSEPH

The first Pony Express set out, carrying mail from 'St Jo' 2000 miles west to California, in 1860. The service, making the trip in as little as eight days, lasted just 18 months before telegraph lines made the riders redundant. The **Pony Express National Museum** (www.ponyexpress.org; 914 Penn St; adult/child $5/free; ⏲9am-5pm Mon-Sat, 1-5pm Sun) tells the story of the Express and its riders, who were mostly orphans due to the dangers.

St Jo, 50 miles north of Kansas City, was also home to outlaw Jesse James. He was killed at what is now the **Jesse James Home Museum** (cnr 12th & Penn Sts; adult/child $3/1.50; ⏲10am-4pm Mon-Sat, 1-4pm Sun, Sat & Sun only Nov-Mar). The fateful bullet hole is still in the wall.

Housed in the former 'State Lunatic Asylum No 2,' the **Glore Psychiatric Museum** (www.stjosephmuseum.org; 3406 Frederick Ave; adult/child $5/free; ⏲10am-5pm Mon-Sat, 1-5pm Sun) gives a frightening and fascinating look at lobotomies, the 'bath of surprise' and other discredited treatments. Tickets also include entrance to several other museums.

Get details on the town's many museums at the **visitor center** (☎800-785-0360; www.stjomo.com; 109 S 4th St; ⏲9am-4pm Mon-Sat) right downtown.

IOWA

Instead of two girls for every boy, Iowa has eight pigs for every person. But there's a lot more to do here than roll in the mud. The towering bluffs on the Mississippi River and the soaring Loess Hills lining the Missouri River bookend the state; in between you'll find the writers' town of Iowa City, the commune-dwellers of the Amana Colonies and lots of little towns full of highlights.

In fact, Iowa surprises in many ways. It makes or breaks presidential-hopefuls: the Iowa Caucus opens the national election battle and wins by George W Bush in 2000 and Barrack Obama in 2008 stunned many pundits and launched their victorious campaigns. In 2009 the state shirked its staid image by allowing same-sex marriages.

IOWA FACTS

» **Nickname** Hawkeye State

» **Population** 3.1 million

» **Area** 56,275 sq miles

» **Capital city** Des Moines (population 203,500)

» **Sales tax** 6%

» **Birthplace of** painter Grant Wood (1891–1942), actor John Wayne (1907–79), author Bill Bryson (b 1951)

» **Home of** Madison County's bridges

» **Politics** center-right with flashes of liberalism

» **Famous for** Iowa Caucus that opens the presidential election season

» **Official flower** wild rose

» **Driving distances** Dubuque to Chicago 180 miles, Des Moines to Rapid City 625 miles

History

After the 1832 Black Hawk War pushed local Native Americans westward, immigrants flooded into Iowa from all parts of the world and hit the ground farming. Some established experimental communities such as the Germans of the Amana Colonies. Others spread out and kept coaxing the soil (95% of the land is fertile) until Iowa attained its current status as a leading grain producer (biofuel has caused a boomlet) and the US leader in hogs and corn (much of the latter ends up as syrup in junk food).

Information

Iowa Bed & Breakfast Guild (800-743-4692; www.ia-bednbreakfast-inns.com)

Iowa state parks (www.iowadnr.gov) State parks are free to visit. Half of the park campsites are reservable; fees range from $6 to $20 per night.

Iowa Tourism Office (www.traveliowa.com)

Iowa Wine & Beer (www.iowawineandbeer.com) Craft brewing and, yes, winemaking are booming in Iowa.

Des Moines

Des Moines, meaning 'of the monks' not 'in the corn' as the surrounding fields might suggest, is Iowa's snoozy capital. The town really is rather dull, but does have one of the nation's best state capitols and state fairs. Pause, but then get out and see the state.

Sights & Activities

The Des Moines River slices through downtown. The Court Ave Entertainment District sits just west, while East Village, at the foot of the capitol, and east of the river, is home to art and design galleries, eateries, clubs and a few gay bars.

State Capitol HISTORIC BUILDING
(cnr E 9th St & Grand Ave; 8am-4:30pm Mon-Fri, 9am-4pm Sat) The bling-heavy capitol (1886) must have been Liberace's favorite government building. Its every detail, from the sparkling gold dome to the spiral staircases and stained glass in the law library, seems to strive to outdo the other. Join a free tour and you can climb halfway up the dome.

FREE **State Historical Museum** MUSEUM
(www.iowahistory.org; 600 E Locust St; 9am-4:30pm Mon-Sat, noon-4:30pm Sun) This engaging museum, at the foot of the capitol, features first-person accounts from people who lived through a particular historical era or event.

Festivals & Events

Iowa State Fair STATE FAIR
(www.iowastatefair.org; cnr E 30th St & E University Ave; adult/child $10/4;) Much more than just country music and butter sculpture, this festival draws a million visitors over its 10-day mid-August run. They enjoy the award-winning farm critters and just about every food imaginable that can be shoved on a stick. It's the setting for the Rogers and Hammerstein musical *State Fair* and the 1945 film version.

Sleeping

Chains of all flavors congregate on I-80 at exits 121, 124, 131 and 136.

TOP CHOICE **Hotel Fort Des Moines** HOTEL $$
(515-243-1161; www.hotelfortdesmoines.com; 1000 Walnut St; r $90-180;) Everyone from Mae West to JFK has spent the night in this old-world hotel. It retains its 1917 elegance and the 204 rooms spread across 11 floors are well equipped.

Holiday Inn Express HOTEL $$
(515-255-4000; www.hiexpress.com; 1140 24th St; r $80-150;) Housed in a renovated old brick building, this 52-room hotel is

close to Drake University in an attractive old part of town with plenty of bars and restaurants within an easy walk (try the Drake Diner next door).

Eating & Drinking

Downtown's Court Ave, Ingersoll Ave in the west and East Village (Grand Ave and Locust St) are good for browsing restaurants.

TOP CHOICE **Jesse's Embers** STEAKHOUSE $$$
(www.theoriginaljessesembers.com; 3301 Ingersoll Ave; mains $8-22; ⏲11am-10pm Mon-Fri, from 5pm Sat) A classic with an original open kitchen before they were trendy. Succulent steaks (go for the prime sirloin) are perfectly grilled and come with sides such as garlic-laden bread. There's a tiny bar, frosted beer mugs and servers who know what you want first.

House of Bricks BAR $$
(www.thehouseofbricks.com; 525 E Grand Ave; meals $10-15; ⏲11am-late) A gritty live-music legend in the East Village, it serves up tasty, beer-absorbent chow.

Information

Visitor center (☎877-773-8821; www.seedesmoines.com; 400 Locust St, Suite 265; ⏲8:30am-5pm Mon-Fri) Downtown.

Madison County

This scenic county, about 30 miles southwest of Des Moines, slumbered for half a century until Robert James Waller's blockbuster, tear-jerking novel *The Bridges of Madison County* and its 1995 Clint Eastwood/Meryl Streep movie version brought in scores of fans to check out the covered bridges where Robert and Francesca fueled their affair. Pick up (or download) a map to all six surviving bridges and other movie sets at the **Chamber of Commerce** (☎800-298-6119; www.madisoncounty.com; 73 Jefferson St; ⏲9am-5pm Mon-Fri, 10am-4pm Sat, noon-4pm Sun) in Winterset.

The humble **birthplace of John Wayne** (www.johnwaynebirthplace.org; 216 S 2nd St, Winterset; adult/child $6/2; ⏲10am-4:30pm), aka Marion Robert Morrison, is now a small museum.

The farms and open land in this region are as bucolic as a painting. And that applies to the towns. Besides Winterset and it's silver-domed courthouse, **Adel**, 20 miles north on US 169, has its own beautiful courthouse square surrounded by shops and cafes.

WORTH A TRIP

GRANT WOOD'S ELDON

Grab a 'tool' out of your trunk and make your very own parody of Grant Wood's iconic painting *American Gothic* (1930) in tiny Eldon, about 90 miles southeast of Des Moines. The original house is across from the **American Gothic House Center** (www.americangothichouse.net; American Gothic St; admission free; ⏲10am-5pm Tue-Sat, 1-4pm Sun-Mon summer, 10am-4pm Tue-Fri, 1-4pm Sat-Mon rest of year), which does a swell job of interpreting the painting that sparked a million parodies. The actual painting is in the Art Institute of Chicago (p511).

Wood spent much of his time in tiny **Stone City**, a cute little burg 14 miles north of Mt Vernon, off Hwy 1. It's on the 68-mile-long **Grant Wood Scenic Byway**.

Along I-80

Many of Iowa's attractions are within an easy drive of bland I-80, which runs east-west across the state's center. Much more interesting alternatives are US 20 (p620) and US 30 (p620).

QUAD CITIES

Four cities straddle the Mississippi River by I-80: Davenport and Bettendorf in Iowa and Moline and Rock Island in Illinois. See p533 for Illinois-side details. The **visitor center** (☎800-747-7800; www.visitquadcities.com; 102 S Harrison St, Davenport; ⏲9am-5pm Mon-Sat, from noon Sun) has bike rentals ($10 per hour) for a ride along the Big Muddy.

You can cruise the gorgeous Mississippi on the Victorian-style riverboat **Twilight** (☎800-331-1467; www.riverboattwilight.com; $350 per person double, incl hotel & meals), which runs two-day round-trips to Dubuque from nearby Le Claire.

Motels are found at I-74 exit 2 and I-780 exit 295A.

IOWA CITY

The youthful, artsy vibe here is courtesy of the **University of Iowa campus** (www.uiowa.edu), home to good art and natural history museums. It spills across both sides of the Iowa River; to the east it mingles with charming downtown's restaurants and bars. In summer (when the student-to-townie ratio evens out) the city mellows somewhat, but there is always something happening. For a sharp parody of the town and school, read Jane Smiley's *Moo*.

The cute gold-domed building at the heart of campus is the **Old Capitol** (admission free; ⏲10am-3pm Tue-Wed & Fri, 10am-5pm Thu & Sat, 1-5pm Sun). Built in 1840, it was the seat of government until 1857 when Des Moines grabbed the reins. It's now a museum with galleries and furnishings from back in its heyday.

Sleeping

Chain motels line 1st Ave in Coralville (I-80 exit 242) like hogs at the trough. Beer and cheap chow abound downtown.

TOP CHOICE **Alexis Park Inn & Suites** MOTEL **$$**
(☎319-337-8665; www.alexisparkinn.com; 1165 S Riverside Dr; r $70-150; ❄@📶) Locally owned, this modest apartment complex has been converted into an extraordinary motel. The large rooms have kitchens and, reflecting the interests of the owners, each is decorated with an aerospace theme.

Brown Street Inn B&B **$$**
(☎319-338-0435; www.brownstreetinn.com; 430 Brown St; r $85-165; ❄@📶) Four-poster beds and other antiques adorn this six-room 1913 Dutch Colonial place that's an easy walk from downtown.

Eating & Drinking

Motley Cow Cafe AMERICAN **$$$**
(www.motleycowcafe.com; 160 N Linn St; mains $14-23; ⏲11:30am-2:30pm Mon-Fri, 5-10pm Mon-Sat, 9:30am-2pm Sun) Organic regional fare on a seasonal menu keeps the tables filled at this local favorite for dates and assignations.

Dave's Foxhead Tavern BAR
(402 E Market St) Popular with the writers' workshop crowd, who debate gerunds while slouched in booths. Pool is also big in this tiny boozer, which boasts a wonderfully eclectic jukebox.

Shopping

Prairie Lights BOOKS
(www.prairielights.com; 15 S Dubuque St; ⏲9am-6pm) A bookstore worthy of a university that runs the famous Iowa Writers' Workshop.

Information

The **visitor center** (☎800-283-6592; www.iowacitycoralville.org; 900 1st Ave; ⏲8am-5pm Mon-Fri) is in neighboring Coralville, an unfortunate town with all the chains and urban sprawl missing from Iowa City.

AMANA COLONIES

These seven villages, just northwest of Iowa City, are stretched along a 17-mile loop. All were established as German religious communes between 1855 and 1861 by inspirationists who, until the Great Depression, lived a utopian life with no wages paid and all assets communally owned. Unlike the Amish and Mennonite religions, inspirationists embrace modern technology (and tourism).

Today the seven well-preserved (and well-organized) villages offer a glimpse of this unique culture, and there are lots of arts, crafts, cheeses, baked goods and wines to buy. However they are not immune to commercial pressures as evidenced by establishments such as a 'Man Cave' amid the more traditional shops.

Six museums are sprinkled throughout the villages, including the insightful **Amana Heritage Museum** (4310 220th Trail, Amana; ⏲9am-5pm Mon-Sat, noon-4pm Sun Apr-Oct, Sat only Mar & Nov-Dec). The others are open in

IOWA: DETOURS & EXTRAS

Effigy Mounds National Monument (www.nps.gov/efmo; admission free; ⏲8am-6pm summer, to 4:30pm rest of year) commemorates hundreds of Native American burial mounds, which sit in the bluffs high above the Mississippi River in far northeast Iowa.

The only museum of its kind, **Hobo Museum** (☎641-843-9104; www.hobo.com; 51 Main Ave S, US 18; ⏲10am-5pm summer), located in north-central Britt, hosts the National Hobo Convention on the second weekend in August. Confirm hours in advance.

Great River Road (see also p40) has an Iowa route that hugs the Mississippi and passes through some isolated towns (**Bellevue** is a gem and lives up to its name with good river views) and some verdant, rural scenery. **Burlington** has an excellent visitor center and is good for a break. Download maps and info at www.byways.org and www.iowagreatriverroad.com.

summer only. An $8/free adult/child pass gets you into them all. Another popular stop is the privately owned **Barn Museum** (220th Trl, South Amana; adult/child $4/2; ⌚9am-5pm Apr-Oct), which has miniature versions of the hay-filled buildings found across rural America.

The villages have many good-value B&Bs and historic inns including **Zuber's Homestead Hotel** (☎319-622-3911; www.zubershomesteadhotel.com; 2206 44 Ave, Homestead; r $85-120; ❄📶), with 15 individually decorated rooms in an 1890s brick building.

One of the Amanas' top draws is the hefty-portioned, home-cooked German cuisine dished out at various humble dining spots. **Millstream Brewing** (835 48th Ave, Amana; ⌚9am-7pm summer, reduced hr rest of year) is an excellent microbrewer. It serves its own beer and brews from others in Iowa at its shop and beer garden.

Stop at the grain-elevator-shaped **visitor center** (☎800-579-2294; www.amanacolonies.com; 622 46th Ave, Amana; ⌚9am-5pm Mon-Sat, 10am-5pm Sun Apr-Oct, 10am-4pm rest of year) for the essential guide-map. It offers bike rental ($15 per day), an ideal way to tour the area.

Along US 30

Like a clichéd needlepoint come to life, US 30 passes through fertile fields dotted with whitewashed farmhouses and red-hued barns. It parallels I-80 an average of 20 to 30 miles to the north before dropping down to Nebraska near Omaha.

The real attraction here is just enjoying the succession of small towns. In a state blessed with pretty places, **Mt Vernon** is one of the loveliest. It may be only two blocks long but there's a lot here.

Lincoln Cafe (☎319-895-4041; www.foodisimportant.com; 117 1st St W, Mt Vernon; mains $6-20; ⌚11am-2pm & 5-9pm Tue-Sat, 10am-2pm Sun) is a foodie favorite; it serves amazing versions of local foods (try the burger with Maytag blue cheese).

Ames, 25 miles north of Des Moines, is home to Iowa State University and has lots of good motels and undergrad dives.

Along US 20

Stretching from Dubuque on the Mississippi River to Sioux City on the Missouri River, US 20 has offered up charms similar to those on US 30 to generations of travelers seeking new lives, adventure or just a new farm implement.

DUBUQUE

Dubuque makes a great entry to Iowa from Illinois: 19th-century Victorian homes line its narrow and lively streets between the Mississippi River and seven steep limestone hills.

The **4th Street Elevator** (www.dbq.com/fenplco/; cnr 4th St & Fenelon; adult/child round-trip $2/1; ⌚8am-10pm Apr-Nov), built in 1882, climbs a steep hill for huge views. Ring the bell to begin the ride. Learn about life (of all sorts) on the Mississippi at the impressive **National Mississippi River Museum & Aquarium** (www.rivermuseum.com; 350 E 3rd St; adult/child $15/10; ⌚9am-6pm summer, 10am-5pm rest of year). Nearby, the **Spirit of Dubuque** (☎563-583-8093; www.dubuqueriverrides.com; 3rd St, at Ice Harbor; adult/child from $21/15; ⌚May-Oct) offers a variety of Mississippi sightseeing and dining cruises on a mock-paddleboat.

The historic eight-story **Hotel Julien** (☎563-556-4200; www.hoteljuliendubuque.com; 200 Main St; r $110-230; ❄📶) was built in 1914 and was once owned by Al Capone. A lavish renovation has turned it upscale and it's a real antidote for chains.

Main St is lined with good eateries grand and humble.

Get information from the downtown **visitor center** (☎800-798-4748; www.traveldubuque.com; 300 Main St; ⌚9am-6pm Mon-Sat, 9am-3pm Sun summer, 9am-4pm Mon-Sat, 9am-1pm Sun rest of year).

WATERLOO & AROUND

Home to five **John Deere tractor factories**, Waterloo is the place to get one of those prized green-and-yellow caps you've seen across middle America. Fun and free tractor-driven **Tractor Assembly Tours** (☎319-292-7668; 3500 E Donald St; ⌚tours 8am, 10am & 1pm Mon-Fri) show how these vehicles are made. The minimum age is 13 years and reservations are required.

NORTH DAKOTA

'Magnificent desolation. Buzz Aldrin used it to describe the moon and it applies just as well in North Dakota. Fields of grain – green in the spring and summer, bronze in the fall and white in winter – stretch beyond every horizon. Except the rugged 'badlands' of the far west, geographic relief is subtle. More

NORTH DAKOTA FACTS

» **Nickname** Peace Garden State

» **Population** 675,000

» **Area** 70,705 sq miles

» **Capital city** Bismarck (population 63,000)

» **Sales tax** 5%

» **Birthplace of** legendary Shoshone woman Sacagawea (1788–1812), cream of wheat (1893), bandleader Lawrence Welk (1903–92), singer-writer of westerns Louis L'Amour (1908–88)

» **Home of** world's largest bison, turtle and Holstein statues

» **Politics** Conservative Republican

» **Famous for** the movie *Fargo*

» **Official fish** northern pike

» **Driving distances** Fargo to Bismarck 193 miles

often it is the collapsing remains of a failed homestead that break up the vistas.

Isolated in the far US north, North Dakota is the least visited state. But that just means that there's less traffic as you whiz along at the usual legal limit of 75mph. This is a place to get lost on remote two-lane routes and to appreciate the magnificence of raw land.

History

During their epic journey, Lewis and Clark spent more time in what is now North Dakota than any other state, meeting up with Shoshone guide Sacagawea on their way west. In the mid-19th century, smallpox epidemics came up the Missouri River, decimating the Arikara, Mandan and Hidatsa tribes, who affiliated and established the Like-a-Fishhook Village around 1845. When the railroad arrived in North Dakota in the 1870s, thousands of settlers flocked in to take up allotments under the Homestead Act. By 1889 the state population was more than 250,000, half foreign-born (one in eight were from Norway).

Young Theodore Roosevelt came here to ditch his city-slicker image. As president, inspired by his time in North Dakota, he earned the title 'The Father of Conservation' for his work creating national forests and parks.

Despite those seemingly endless summer fields of grain, the state's economy is tied to large oil deposits in the west. Soaring oil prices have turned once-moribund towns such as Watford City into boomtowns, with vast trailer encampments for oil-field workers and roads clogged – and battered – by huge trucks.

Information

North Dakota Bed & Breakfast Association (888-271-3380; www.ndbba.com)

North Dakota state parks (reservations 800-807-4723; www.parkrec.nd.gov) Vehicle permits cost $5/25 per day/year. Nearly half of the park campsites are reservable; fees range from $10 to $20 per night.

North Dakota Tourism Division (800-435-5663; www.ndtourism.com)

Along I-94

Arrowing across North Dakota, I-94 provides easy access to most of the state's top attractions, although it would not be the road of scenic choice (US 2 is more atmospheric).

FARGO

Named for the Fargo of Wells Fargo Bank, North Dakota's biggest city has been a fur-trading post, a frontier town, a quick-divorce capital and a haven for folks in the Federal Witness Protection Program; not to mention the namesake of the Coen Brothers' film *Fargo* – though the movie was set across the Red River in Minnesota. Still, expect to hear a lot of accents similar to Frances McDormand's unforgettable version in the film. Film fame aside, there's not a lot in Fargo worth more than a quick stop off the highway.

The modern, ambitious **Plains Art Museum** (www.plainsart.org; 704 1st Ave N; adult/child $5/free; 11am-5pm Tue-Sat, 1-5pm Sun, to 8pm Thu) features sophisticated programing in a renovated warehouse. The permanent collection includes contemporary work by Native American artists.

Sleeping & Eating

Chain motels cluster at exits 64 on I-29 and 348 on I-94.

TOP CHOICE **Hotel Donaldson** HOTEL $$
(701-478-1000; www.hoteldonaldson.com; 101 Broadway; r from $170;) A stylish and swank revamp of a flophouse, the 17 luxurious suites here are each decorated by a local artist.

LEWIS & CLARK IN NORTH DAKOTA

North of Bismarck are several worthwhile attractions near the spot where Lewis and Clark wintered with the Mandan in 1804–05. They offer an evocative look at the lives of the Native Americans and the explorers amid lands that even today seem little changed.

The **North Dakota Lewis & Clark Interpretive Center** (www.fortmandan.com; US 83, Washburn; adult/child $7.50/5; ⏲9am-5pm daily year-round, from noon Sun winter) is a big, modern center where you can learn about the duo's epic expedition and the Native Americans who helped them. Check out the beautiful drawings from George Catlin's Portfolio.

The same ticket gets you into **Fort Mandan** (CR 17), a replica of the fort built by Lewis and Clark, 2.5 miles west (10 miles downstream from the flooded original site). It sits on a lonely stretch of the Missouri River marked by a monument to Seaman, the expedition's dog. Inside the small but worthwhile info building, look for the display on period medicine, including 'Thunderclappers.'

At **Knife River Indian Villages National Historical Site** (www.nps.gov/knri; Stanton; admission free; ⏲8am-6pm, to 4:30pm winter) you can still see the mounds left by three earthen villages of the Hidastas, who lived on the Knife River, a narrow tributary of the Missouri, for more than 900 years. The National Park Service has re-created one of the earthen lodges. A stroll through the mostly wide-open and wild site leads to the village site where Lewis and Clark met Sacagawea. The historical site is just north of Stanton (22 miles west of Washburn) on Hwy 200, which runs through verdant rolling prairie for 110 miles between US 83 and US 85.

Fargo's most chic restaurant and rooftop bar (!) may lack competition but are still very cool.

Widman's Candy Shop SWEETS $
(4325 13th Ave S/I-29, near exit 64; snacks $1-5; ⏲9:30am-7pm Mon-Fri, to 5pm Sat) Widman's has been run by the same family since 1885. Ignore the current surrounds in a tatty strip mall and delight in the legendary chocolate-covered potato chips and flaxseed.

Information

The grain-elevator-shaped **visitor center** (☎800-235-7654; www.fargomoorhead.org; 2001 44th St; ⏲7:30am-6pm Mon-Fri, 10am-4pm Sat & Sun summer, 8am-5pm Mon-Fri rest of year) is off I-94 exit 348.

BISMARCK

Like the surrounding plains of wheat, Bismarck, North Dakota's capital, has a quick and bountiful summer. Otherwise, it's a compact place that hunkers down for the long winters where the low averages -4°F (-20°C).

The stark 1930s **State Capitol** (N 7th St; ⏲8am-4pm Mon-Fri, tours hourly except noon, plus 9am-4pm Sat & 1-4pm Sun summer) is often referred to as the 'skyscraper of the prairie' and looks something like a Stalinist school of dentistry from the outside, but has some art-deco flourishes inside. There's an observation deck on the 18th floor.

Behind the Sacagawea statue, the huge **North Dakota Heritage Center** (www.history.nd.gov; Capitol Hill; admission free; ⏲8am-5pm Mon-Fri, 10am-5pm Sat & Sun) has details on everything from Norwegian bachelor farmers to the scores of nuclear bombs perched on missiles in silos across the state.

Fort Abraham Lincoln State Park (www.parkrec.nd.gov; $5 per vehicle, plus adult/child to tour historical sites $6/4), 7 miles south of Mandan on SR 1806, is well worth the detour. Its **On-A-Slant Indian Village** has five re-created Mandan earth lodges, while the fort, with several replica buildings, is where Custer departed from for the Battle of Little Bighorn.

Sleeping & Eating

In Bismarck, chain motels congregate around I-94 exit 159.

Little Cottage Cafe DINER $$
(2513 E Main Ave; mains $5-12; ⏲6am-8pm) Down near the train tracks near the center, this is a classic diner with hearty local food (bring on the meatloaf!). Almost as many free newspapers lay about as the inert regulars; the timeless waitresses (honey!) never let coffee cups empty.

Best Western Ramkota Hotel MOTEL $$
(☎701-258-7700; www.bismarck.ramkota.com; 800 S Third St; r $80-140; ❄📶🏊) Big motel

near a mall; has 306 rooms around an indoor pool with a 150ft slide (whee!).

Information

Bismarck-Mandan Visitor Center (800-767-3555; www.discoverbismarckmandan.com; 1600 Burnt Boat Dr, Bismarck; 7:30am-7pm Mon-Fri, 8am-6pm Sat, 10am-5pm Sun summer, 8am-5pm Mon-Fri rest of year) off I-94 exit 157.

WEST OF BISMARK

West on I-94, stop and see **Sue, the World's Largest Holstein Cow** at New Salem (exit 127). At exit 72, there's a unique detour south along the Enchanted Hwy (p623). In Dickinson, an hour west of Sue, the **Dakota Dinosaur Museum** (701-225-3466; www.dakotadino.com; I-94 exit 61; adult/child $7/4; 9am-5pm May-Sep) has oodles of dinosaur fossils and statues, most found in the state.

MOUNTAIN TIME IN NORTH DAKOTA

The southwest quarter of North Dakota, including Medora, uses Mountain Time, which is one hour earlier than the rest of the state's Central Time.

Theodore Roosevelt National Park

A tortured land known as the 'badlands' and whose colors seem to change with the moods of nature, **Theodore Roosevelt National Park** (www.nps.gov/thro; 7-day pass per vehicle $10) is the state's natural highlight. Bizarre rock formations, streaked with a rainbow of red, yellow, brown, black and silver minerals, are framed by green prairie.

Roosevelt described this area as 'a land of vast, silent spaces, of lonely rivers, and of plains where the wild game stared at the passing horsemen,' and it's hard to describe the place better even today. Wildlife is still everywhere: mule deer, wild horses, bighorn sheep, elk, bison, around 200 bird species and, of course, sprawling subterranean prairie dog towns.

The park is divided into sections:

South Unit Most visitors opt for the 36-mile scenic drive that begins in Medora, an enjoyable town just off I-94. Prairie dogs are a highlight.

North Unit Gets few visitors but is well worth the journey for the 14-mile drive to the **Oxbow Overlook**, with its wide views into the vast and colorfully striated river canyon. The verdant surrounds are protected as the **Little Missouri National Grassland** and bison are everywhere. It is 68 miles north of I-94 on US 85.

The park has three visitor centers, including the **Medora visitor center** (8am-6pm summer, 8am-4:30pm rest of year), with Theodore Roosevelt's old cabin out back.

Hikers can explore 85 miles of backcountry trails. For a good adventure, hike or cycle the 96-mile **Maah Daah Hey Trail** between the park units. Driving, continue north on US 85 to Fort Buford (p624).

MEDORA

Medora (www.medora.com) is a somewhat re-created and restored pioneer town that

NORTH DAKOTA: DETOURS & EXTRAS

North Dakota still has underground nuclear missiles waiting for launch orders, however many more have been deactivated because of treaty agreements with the Russians. **Minuteman Missile State Historic Site** (www.history.nd.gov; adult/child $10/3; 10am-6pm mid-May–mid-Sep, reduced hr rest of year), near Cooperstown on Hwys 45 and 200, includes an underground command center from where missiles were launched. Visits are by tour. The other site, the missile silo, is actually more eerie. Often unattended, you can ponder the doors that hid a rocket with over 500 kilotons of nuclear explosive power (the Hiroshima bomb had 15 kilotons). It's surrounded by mundane farmland and a few distant farmhouses.

The **International Peace Garden** (www.peacegarden.com; per vehicle $10) provides a change of pace from nukes; some 150,000 flowers and several monuments sit symbolically on the North Dakota–Manitoba border on US 281.

The **Enchanted Highway** (www.enchantedhighway.net) has huge whimsical metal sculptures of local folks and critters by local artist Gary Greff. It runs for 32 miles straight south to Regent from I-94 exit 72.

is quite appealing and relatively uncommercialized. Accommodations include motels and B&Bs.

The most atmospheric choice is the **Rough Riders Hotel** (☎701-623-4444; www.medora.com/rough-riders; 301 3rd Ave; r $125-200; ❄📶), which dates back to 1885. Renovations made the eight original rooms dude-worthy and added 68 new ones.

The park itself has two simple **campgrounds** (campsites $10) and free backcountry camping (permit required).

Along US 2

US 2 is the more interesting alternative to I-94. The endless sky vistas stretch even further than the seas of golden grain. **Grand Forks** is a stolid city, while **Devils Lake** is one of the top waterfowl hunting destinations in the country. The entire area is subject to the flood-prone Red River.

RUGBY

Rugby is about halfway down the highway, but its more notable location identity is as the **geographical center of North America**. The **Prairie Village Museum** (www.prairievillagemuseum.com; 102 US 2 SE; adult/child $7/3; ⌚8am-6pm mid-May–mid-Sep) re-creates Great Plains life through the decades.

MINOT

North Dakota's fourth-largest city is home to military bases and markets itself with the slogan 'My Minot Means Fun.' It's not. But it does celebrate its Scandinavian roots during **Norsk Høstfest** (www.hostfest.com; ⌚early Oct), which is promoted as the world's largest Scandinavian festival.

Minot has a full range of modest chain motels along US 2, 52 and 83.

WEST TO MONTANA

West of Minot the land is dotted with forlorn little settlements slipping back into the prairie soil. However, the skyline is enlivened by the flames and bright lights of hundreds of oil drilling rigs. It's a huge boom fueled by the same high prices you curse when refilling your tank and the result is that small towns – and every motel – between Minot and Montana are swamped with workers.

Twenty-two miles southwest of Williston along SR 1804, **Fort Buford** (www.history.nd.gov; adult/child $5/2.50; ⌚9am-6pm mid-May–mid-Sep) is the bleak army outpost where Sitting Bull surrendered. The adjacent **Missouri-Yellowstone Confluence Interpretive Center** (⌚8am-6pm mid-May–mid-Sep, 9am-4pm Wed-Sun rest of year) includes the fort's visitor center. Swing by the boat landing in May to see anglers reeling in paddlefish.

About 2 miles west, on the Montana–North Dakota border, the more evocative **Fort Union Trading Post** (www.nps.gov/fous; admission free; ⌚8am-8pm Central Time summer, 9am-5:30pm rest of year) is a reconstruction of the American Fur Company post built in 1828.

SOUTH DAKOTA

Gently rolling prairies through shallow fertile valleys mark much of this endlessly attractive state. But head southwest and hell breaks loose – in a good way. The Badlands National Park is the geologic equivalent of fireworks. The Black Hills are like opera: majestic, challenging, intriguing and even frustrating. Mt Rushmore matches the Statue of Liberty for five-star icon status. Throughout the state are important Native American sites and interesting towns big and small.

ℹ Information

Bed & Breakfast Innkeepers of South Dakota (☎888-500-4667; www.southdakotabnb.com)

South Dakota Department of Tourism (☎800-732-5682; www.travelsd.com)

SOUTH DAKOTA FACTS

- **Nickname** Mt Rushmore State
- **Population** 805,000
- **Area** 77,125 sq miles
- **Capital city** Pierre (population 14,100)
- **Sales tax** 4%
- **Birthplace of** Sitting Bull (c 1831–90), Crazy Horse (c 1840–77) and Black Elk (c 1863–1950), all of Little Bighorn fame, and genial broadcaster Tom Brokaw (b 1940)
- **Home of** Mt Rushmore, the Sioux
- **Politics** increasingly Republican
- **Famous for** HBO TV show *Deadwood*, Wounded Knee Massacre
- **Official animal** coyote
- **Driving distances** Sioux Falls to Rapid City 341 miles, Sioux Falls to Des Moines 283 miles

WORTH A TRIP

LITTLE HOUSE(S) ON THE PRAIRIE

Fans of *Little House on the Prairie* should head to Laura Ingalls Wilder's former home, **De Smet**. The pint-sized author lived here from age 12 when her peripatetic Pa finally settled down (much of her famous book was based on her time in Independence, KS). The town is 40 miles west of I-29 (exit 133) on US 14.

Right in town, the fussy and frilly complex that's home to the **Laura Ingalls Wilder Memorial Society** (www.discoverlaura.org; 105 Olivet Ave; adult/child $8/4; 9am-5:30pm Mon-Sat & 11am-5:30pm Sun summer, reduced hr rest of year;) has tours inside two original Wilder homes (adult/child $8/4) – the one where the Wilders spent the first winter in 1879 and the home Michael Landon, er, 'Pa', later built.

Just outside town and down a dirt road, the actual **Ingalls Homestead** (www.ingallshomestead.com; 20812 Homestead Rd; admission $10; 9am-7pm summer;) has been much gussied up and includes all manner of attractions about 19th-century farm life and Laura herself. It's well done, with nary a fudge shop in sight.

Near the homestead, the long-running outdoor **Laura Ingalls Wilder Pageant** (www.desmetpageant.org; adult/child $8/5; July weekends) reenacts melodramatic scenes from Laura's books. Townfolk fill the roles, including one very lucky young girl.

South Dakota state parks (reservations 800-710-2267; www.gfp.sd.gov) Vehicle permits cost $6/28 per day/year. Most park campsites are reservable; fees range from $8 to $25 per night. Cabins start at $35.

Sioux Falls

South Dakota's largest city (population 154,000) lives up to its name at **Falls Park** just north of downtown where the Big Sioux River plunges through a long series of rock faces. The park has a **visitor center** (605-367-7430; www.siouxfallscvb.com; 10am-9pm daily Apr–mid-Oct, reduced hr winter) with city-wide information and an observation tower.

The huge pink quartzite **Old Courthouse Museum** (www.siouxlandmuseums.com; 200 W 6th St; admission free; 8am-5pm Mon-Fri, 9am-5pm Sat, noon-5pm Sun, to 8pm Thu), a restored 1890s building, has three floors of well-curated changing exhibits on the region.

Sioux Falls has motels at I-29 exits 77 to 83. For diner fare look for the brilliant sign outside otherwise humble **Bob's Cafe** (1312 W 12th St; mains $4-9; 7am-8pm). You'll find 11 stools and some of the best breakfasts, burgers, onion rings and chicken in the region.

Along I-90

Easily one of the least interesting stretches of interstate highway, I-90 across South Dakota does have some worthy stops along the way. For driving alternatives such as US 14, see p633.

MITCHELL

Every year, half a million people pull off I-90 (exit 332) to see the Taj Mahal of agriculture, the all-time-ultimate roadside attraction, the **Corn Palace** (www.cornpalace.org; 604 N Main St; admission free; 8am-9pm summer, reduced hr rest of year). Close to 300,000 ears of corn are used each year to create a tableaux of murals on the outside of the building. Ponder the scenes and you may find a kernel of truth or just say 'aw shucks.'

CHAMBERLAIN

In a picturesque site where I-90 crosses the Missouri River, Chamberlain (exit 263) is home to the excellent **Akta Lakota Museum & Cultural Center** (www.aktalakota.org; 1301 N Main St; admission free; 8am-6pm Mon-Sat, 9am-5pm Sun summer, 8am-5pm Mon-Sat rest of year) at St Joseph's Indian School. It has Lakota cultural displays and contemporary art from numerous tribes.

History buffs should pop into the hilltop rest stop, between exits 263 and 265, where the **Lewis & Clark Information Center** (admission free; 8am-6pm May-Oct) has exhibits on the intrepid band.

PIERRE

Pierre (pronounced *'peer'*) is just too small (population 14,100) and ordinary to feel like a seat of power. Small-town Victorian homes overlook the imposing 1910 **State Capitol** (500 E Capitol Ave; 8am-10pm) with its black copper dome.

The best reason to detour off I-90 here is because it lies along the **Native American**

MOUNTAIN TIME

Roughly the western one-third of South Dakota – including the Black Hills and everything west of I-90 exit 177 – use Mountain Time, which is one hour earlier than Central Time in the rest of the state.

Scenic Byway and lonely, stark **US 14** (for both, see p633).

Exhibits at the **South Dakota Cultural Heritage Center** (www.history.sd.gov; 900 Governor's Dr; adult/child $4/free; 9am-6:30pm Mon-Sat, 1-4:30pm Sun summer, to 4:30pm rest of year) include a bloody Ghost Dance shirt from Wounded Knee.

At a bend on the Missouri River, **Framboise Island** has several hiking trails and plentiful wildlife. It's across from where the Lewis and Clark expedition spent four days and was nearly derailed when they inadvertently offended members of the local Brule tribe.

Most hotels lie along US 83. The **Pierre Inn & Suites** (605-224-5981; www.pierreinnste.com; 200 W Pleasant Dr; r from $60;) has solid motel-style rooms with fridges and microwaves. It's close to the cute center of Pierre, with shops that include a bookstore.

The Pierre **visitor center** (800-962-2034; www.pierre.org; 800 W Dakota Ave; 8am-5pm Mon-Fri) is near Framboise Island.

MINUTEMAN MISSILE NATIONAL HISTORIC SITE

In the 1960s and 1970s, 450 Minutemen II intercontinental ballistic missiles, always at the ready in underground silos, were just 30 minutes from their targets in the Soviet Union. The missiles have since been retired (more modern ones are still lurking in silos across the northern Great Plains). The first national park dedicated to the Cold War preserves a silo and its underground launch facility.

At the small temporary **visitor contact station** (Map p628; 605-433-5552; www.nps.gov/mimi; I-90 exit 131; 8am-4:30pm), you can get tickets for the free tours of the nearby launch complex where two people stood ready around the clock to turn keys launching missiles from this part of South Dakota. Tours are given daily and are first-come, first-served. However, you can reserve Wednesday tours by phone up to seven days in advance.

The **silo** (I-90 exit 116; 8am-4pm) can be viewed without a tour through a glass cover.

WALL

Hyped for hundreds of miles, **Wall Drug** (www.walldrug.com; 510 Main St; 6:30am-6pm, extended hr summer;) is a surprisingly enjoyable stop. It really does have 5¢ coffee, free ice water and enough diversions and come-ons to warm the heart of schlock-lovers everywhere. But amid the fudge in the faux frontier complex is a superb bookstore with the best selection of regional titles we've seen.

The highly recommended **Story of Wounded Knee** (www.woundedkneemuseum.org; I-90 exit 110; adult/child $6/free; 8:30am-5:30pm Apr-Oct, extended hr summer) tells the story of the massacre from the Lakota perspective using photos and narratives. It's more insightful than anything at the actual site (see p627).

The namesake town of the drugstore is a good place for an overnight pause. It's compact and walkable, there are tasty and cheap cafes and bars, and several good indie motels, including **Sunshine Inn** (605-279-2178; www.sunshineinnatwallsd.com; 608 Main St; r $50-80;), which has a genial owner and 22 basic and sparkling rooms.

BADLANDS NATIONAL PARK

This otherworldly landscape, oddly softened by its fantastic rainbow hues, is a spectacle of sheer walls and spikes stabbing the dry air. It was understandably named *mako sica* (badland) by Native Americans. Looking over the bizarre formations from the corrugated walls surrounding Badlands is like seeing an ocean someone boiled dry.

The park's north unit gets the most visitors; the Hwy 240 loop road is easily reached from I-90 (exits 110 and 131) and you can drive it in an hour if you're in a hurry (and not stuck behind an RV). Lookouts and vistas abound.

Much less visited is the portion west of Hwy 240 along the gravel Sage Creek Rim Rd. There are stops at prairie dog towns and this is where most backcountry hikers and campers go. There is nearly no water or shade here, so don't strike out into the wilderness unprepared. The less-accessible south units are in the Pine Ridge Indian Reservation and see few visitors.

The **Ben Reifel Visitor Center** (www.nps.gov/badl; Hwy 240; 7am-7pm summer, 8am-5pm Apr-May & Sep-Oct, 8am-4pm rest of year) has good exhibits and advice for ways to ditch your car to appreciate the geologic wonders. The **White River Visitor Center** (Hwy 27; ⏲10am-4pm summer) is small. A seven-day pass costs $15 for cars and $7 for cyclists.

Neither the developed **Cedar Pass Campground** (campsites $15) or primitive **Sage Creek Campground** (campsites free) take reservations. Hotels can be found on I-90 in Kadoka and Wall, or stay at a cozy cabin inside the park at **Cedar Pass Lodge** (☎605-433-5460; www.cedarpasslodge.com; Hwy 240; cabins $85-115; ⏲mid-Apr–mid-Oct). There is a restaurant and shops.

The national park, along with the surrounding **Buffalo Gap National Grassland**, protects the country's largest prairie grasslands, several species of Plains mammal (including bison and black-footed ferret), prairie falcons and lots of snakes. The **National Grasslands Visitors Centre** (www.fs.fed.us/grasslands; 798 Main St, Wall; ⏲8am-5pm summer, to 4:30pm Mon-Fri rest of year) has good displays on this underappreciated and complex ecosystem. Rangers can map out back-road routes that will let you do looping tours of Badlands National Park and the grasslands without ever touching I-90. **Hwy 44** to Rapid City is also a fine alternative to the interstate.

Pine Ridge Indian Reservation

Home to the Lakota Oglala Sioux, the Pine Ridge reservation south of Badlands National Park is one of the nation's poorest 'counties,' with over half the population living below the poverty line. Despite being at times a jarring dose of reality, it is also a place welcoming to visitors.

In 1890 the new Ghost Dance religion, which the Lakota followers believed would bring back their ancestors and eliminate the white man, became wildly popular. This struck fear into the area's soldiers and settlers and the frenetic circle dances were outlawed. The 7th US Cavalry rounded up a band of Lakota under Chief Big Foot and brought them to the small village of Wounded Knee. On December 29, as the soldiers began to search for weapons, a shot was fired (nobody knows by who), leading to the massacre of more than 250 men, women and children, most of them unarmed. It's one of the most infamous atrocities in US history. Twenty-five soldiers also died.

The shabby **Wounded Knee Massacre Site** (Map p628), 16 miles northeast of Pine Ridge town, is bisected by new two-lane Hwy 27 and marked by a faded roadside sign. The mass grave, often frequented by people looking for handouts, sits atop the hill near a church. The nearby visitor center has little to offer: stop at the Story of Wounded Knee in Wall (p626) instead. Hwy 27 north of the site passes through some seldom-visited tracts of the badlands.

Four miles north of Pine Ridge town at the Red Cloud Indian School is the **Red Cloud Heritage Center** (www.redcloudschool.org; Hwy 18; admission free; ⏲8am-6pm Mon-Fri, 8am-5pm Sat, 11am-5pm Sun summer, 8am-5pm Mon-Fri rest of year), a well-curated art museum with traditional and contemporary work and a craft shop. Look for photos taken after the massacre showing the frozen bodies of the dead with their expressions of shock locked in place.

Tune in to what's happening on KILI (90.1 FM), 'the voice of the Lakota nation,' which broadcasts community events and often plays traditional music.

Black Hills

This stunning region on the Wyoming–South Dakota border lures oodles of visitors with its winding canyons and wildly eroded 7000ft peaks. The region's name – the 'Black' comes from the dark Ponderosa pine-covered slopes – was conferred by the Lakota Sioux. In the 1868 Fort Laramie Treaty, they were assured that the hills would be theirs for eternity, but the discovery of gold changed that and the Sioux were shoved out to low-value flatlands only six years later. *Dances with Wolves* covers some of this period.

You'll need several days to explore the area. Throughout are bucolic back-road drives, caves, bison herds, forests, Mt Rushmore and Crazy Horse monuments and outdoor activities (ballooning, cycling, rock climbing, boating, fishing, hiking, downhill skiing, gold-panning etc). Like fool's gold, gaudy tourist traps lurk in corners and keep things lively.

ℹ Information

There are hundreds of hotels and campgrounds across the hills; still, during summer, room rates shoot up like geysers and reservations are essential. Avoid visiting during the Sturgis motorcycle rally (August), when hogs rule the roads and fill the rooms. Much is closed October to April.

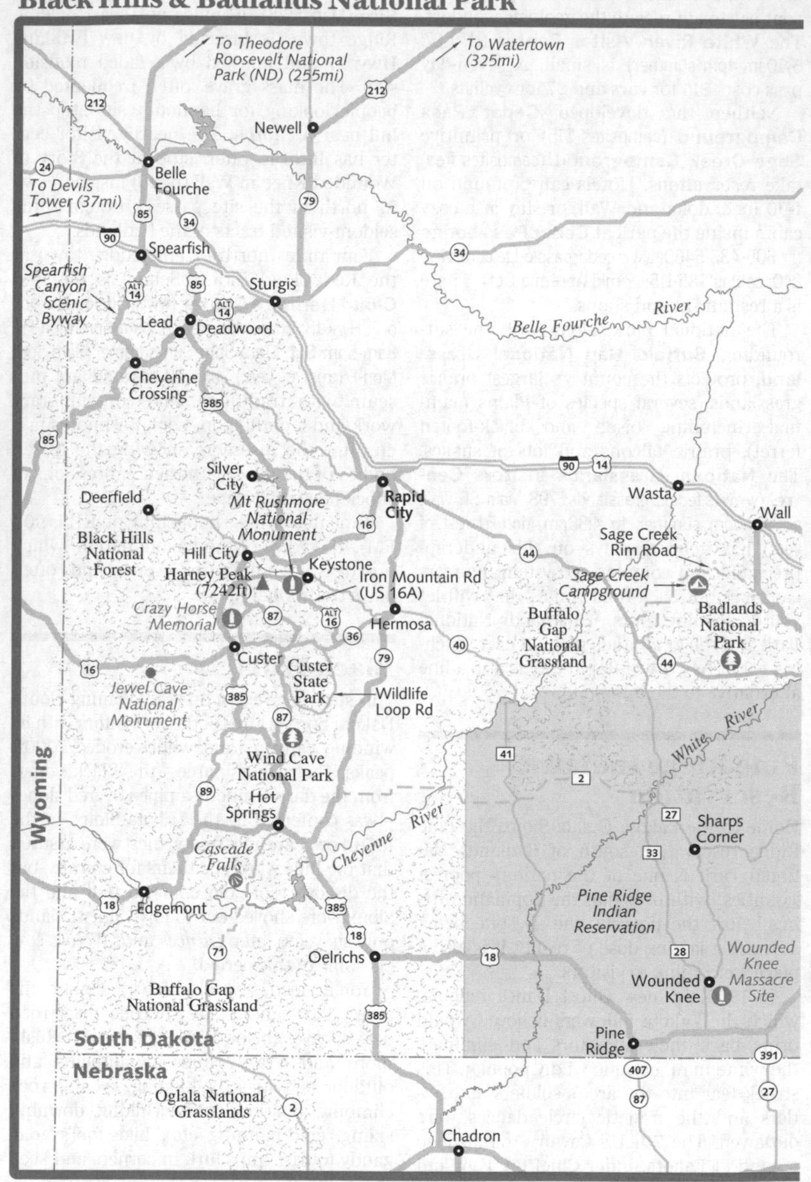

Visitor centers and reservations:

Black Hills Central Reservations (☎866-601-5103; www.blackhillsvacations.com) Accommodation reservations and last-minute deals.

Black Hills Visitor Center (☎605-355-3700; www.blackhillsbadlands.com; I-90 exit 61, Rapid City; ⏰8am-8pm summer, to 5pm rest of year) Tons of info including apps.

BLACK HILLS NATIONAL FOREST

The majority of the Black Hills lie within this 1875-sq-mile mixture of protected and logged forest, perforated by pockets of pri-

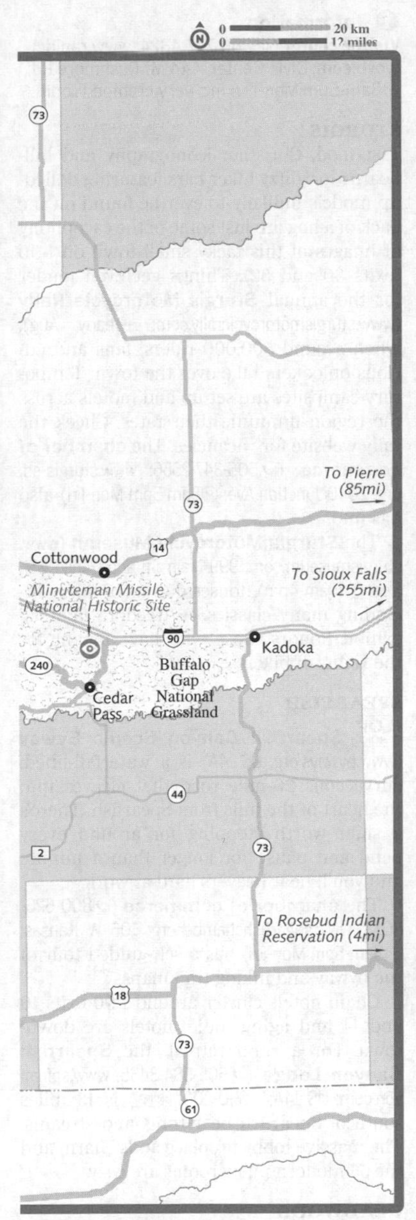

vate land on most roads. The scenery is fantastic, whether you get deep into it on the 450 miles of hiking trails or drive the byways and gravel fire roads. The 111-mile **Centennial Trail** meanders across the Black Hills linking Sturgis to Wind Cave National Park.

The 109-mile **George S Mickelson Trail** (www.mickelsontrail.com; daily/annual fee $3/15) cuts through much of the forest, running from Deadwood through Hill City and Custer to Edgemont on an abandoned railway line. There are bike rentals at various trailside towns.

The forest **headquarters** (605-673-9200; www.fs.fed.us/bhnf; 25041 US 16; 7:30am-5pm Mon-Fri) is in Custer and a modern **visitor center** (US 385, near Hwy 44; 8:30am-6pm summer) sits on the Pactola Reservoir between Hill City and Rapid City.

Good camping abounds in the forest. There are 30 basic (no showers or electricity) **campgrounds** (reservations 877-444-6777; www.recreation.gov; campsites free-$25) and backcountry camping is allowed just about anywhere (free; no open fires). Reserve in summer.

RAPID CITY

A worthy capital to the region, 'Rapid' has an intriguing, lively and walkable downtown. Well-preserved brick buildings, filled with quality shopping and dining, make it a good urban base.

Sights

Get a walking-tour brochure of Rapid's historic buildings and public art from the visitor center.

TOP CHOICE Statues of Presidents MONUMENTS

From a shifty-eyed Nixon in repose to a triumphant Harry Truman, lifelike statues dot corners throughout the center. Collect all 44.

FREE Museum of Geology MUSEUM

(museum.sdsmt.edu; 501 E St Joseph St, O'Harra Bldg; 9am-5pm Mon-Fri, 9am-6pm Sat, noon-5pm Sun summer, 9am-4pm Mon-Fri, 10am-4pm Sat rest of year) All that drama underground has produced some spectacular rocks. See these plus dinosaur bones and some stellar fossils here, at the South Dakota School of Mines & Technology.

Family friendly and wonderfully schlocky tourist attractions vie for dollars along Hwy 16 on the way to Mt Rushmore. Among them:

Bear Country USA WILDLIFE RESERVE

(www.bearcountryusa.com; Hwy 16, 8 miles south of Rapid City; adult/child $16/10; 8am-6pm summer, reduced hr rest of year, closed winter;) Oodles of bears big and small in this drive-through park live off the land and hope you'll do something forbidden like offering them a Big Mac, or your hand.

Reptile Gardens WILDLIFE RESERVE
(www.reptilegardens.com; Hwy 16, 5 miles south of Rapid City; adult/child $15/10; ⏲8am-7pm summer, reduced hr rest of year, closed winter; 👪) Reptiles, snakes, giant tortoises and many more critters inspire countless 'wows!' a day.

Sleeping & Eating

Motels, many indie, cluster at I-90 exits 57 and 60, downtown and US16 south of town. Main St has scores of eateries and bars.

TOP CHOICE **Hotel Alex Johnson** HOTEL $$$
(☎605-342-1210; www.alexjohnson.com; 523 6th St; r $60-250; ❄@📶) The design of this 1927 classic magically blends Germanic Tudor architecture and traditional Lakota Sioux symbols – note the lobby's painted ceiling and the chandelier made of war lances. The 127 rooms are modern and slightly posh but the real appeal here is that it hasn't been turned into a boutique hotel. Its timeless qualities include a portrait of guest Al Capone near the front desk.

TOP CHOICE **Tally's** AMERICAN $$
(530 6th St; mains $6-20; ⏲7am-11pm Mon-Sat) Carter or Reagan? Both statues are out front and you can ponder your preference while you savor the upscale diner fare at this stylish cafe and bar. Breakfasts are as good as ever, more creative regional fare is on offer at night.

Corn Exchange FRENCH $$$
(☎605-343-5070; www.cornexchange.com; 727 Main St; mains $15-25; ⏲5-9pm Tue-Sat) Seasonal menus, local and organic produce and a talented kitchen make this small bistro a standout. Dishes use simple preparations that emphasize the inherent flavors of the food. But don't get carried away: desserts are dreamy.

Town House Motel MOTEL $
(☎605-342-8143; www.blackhillsmotels.com; 210 St Joseph St; r $40-70; ❄📶🏊) A classic yet clean 40-room motel within walking distance of all the downtown joys. The exterior corridors overlook the parking area and pool.

Firehouse Brewing Co PUB $$
(www.firehousebrewing.com; 610 Main St; mains $6-18; ⏲4pm-midnight) Microbrews and plenty of tasty pub grub are served year-round. In summer there's live music in the beer garden.

Information

Visitor center (☎866-727-4324; www.rapidcitycvb.com; Civic Center, 444 Mt Rushmore Rd; ⏲8am-5pm Mon-Fri) In a very cramped room.

STURGIS

Fast food, Christian iconography and billboards for glitzy biker bars featuring dolled-up models unlikely to ever be found on the back of a hog are just some of the cacophony of images of this tacky small town on I-90 (exits 30 and 32). Things get even louder for the annual **Sturgis Motorcycle Rally** (www.sturgismotorcyclerally.com; ⏲early Aug), when around 500,000 riders, fans and curious onlookers take over the town. Temporary campsites are set up and motels across the region unmuffle their rates. Check the rally website for vacancies. The **chamber of commerce** (☎605-347-2556; www.sturgis-sd.org; 2040 Junction Ave; ⏲8am-5pm Mon-Fri) also has info.

The **Sturgis Motorcycle Museum** (www.sturgismuseum.com; 999 Main St; adult/child $5/free; ⏲10am-4pm) houses dozens of bikes, including many classics. A 'freedom fighters' exhibit honors those who have fought for the rights of bikers.

SPEARFISH

TOP CHOICE **Spearfish Canyon Scenic Byway** (www.byways.org; US 14A) is a waterfall-lined, curvaceous 20-mile road that cleaves into the heart of the hills from Spearfish. There's a sight worth stopping for around every bend and pause for longer than a minute and you'll hear beavers hard at work.

The **chamber of commerce** (☎800-626-8013; www.spearfishchamber.org; 106 W Kansas; ⏲8am-5pm Mon-Fri) has a self-guided tour of the byway and hiking trail maps.

Chain hotels cluster around I-90 exits 10 and 14 and aging indie motels are downtown. For a rural retreat, the **Spearfish Canyon Lodge** (☎605-584-3435; www.spfcanyon.com; US 14A; r $90-200; ❄📶) is 13 miles south of Spearfish near trails and streams. The massive lobby fireplace adds charm and the 55 modern piney rooms are cozy.

DEADWOOD

'No law at all in Deadwood, is that true?' So began the eponymous HBO TV series. Today things have changed, although the 80 gambling halls big and small would no doubt put a sly grin on the faces of the hard characters who founded the town.

Settled illegally by eager gold rushers in the 1870s, Deadwood is now a National Historic Landmark. Its atmospheric streets are lined with gold-rush-era buildings lavishly restored with casino dollars. Its storied past is easy to find (and surprisingly in line with the TV series). There's eternal devotion to Wild Bill Hickok, who was shot in the back of the head here in 1876 while gambling.

Sights

Actors reenact famous **shootouts** (4pm & 6pm daily) on Main St during summer. **Hickok's murder** (1pm, 3pm, 5pm & 7pm) is acted out in Saloon No 10. A **trial** (8pm) of the killer takes place in the Masonic Temple (Main St).

Downtown is walkable, but the fake **trolley** (per ride $1) can be handy for getting between attractions, hotels and parking lots.

Mount Moriah Cemetery HISTORIC SITE
(adult/child $1/50¢; 8am-8pm summer, 8am-5pm rest of year) Calamity Jane (born Martha Canary, 1850–1903) and Hickok (1847–76) rest side by side up on Boot Hill at the very steep cemetery. Entertaining bus tours ($9) leave hourly from Main St.

Deadwood History & Information Center MUSEUM
(800-999-1876; www.deadwood.org; Pine St; 8am-7pm summer, 9am-5pm rest of year) This splendid center, in the restored train depot, has tons of info, plus exhibits and photos of the town's history. Ask about tours led by local history buffs.

Adams Museum MUSEUM
(www.adamsmuseumandhouse.org; 54 Sherman St; adult/child $5/2; 9am-5pm daily summer, 10am-4pm Tue-Sat rest of year) Does an excellent job of capturing the town's colorful past.

Sleeping

Casinos offer up buffets with plenty of cheap chow. Wander the streets for better choices. There are scores of motels to stay right in the center. Many bars/casinos have dining rooms upstairs.

Deadwood Dick's HOTEL $$
(605-578-3224; www.deadwooddicks.com; 51 Sherman St; r $60-200) These home-style and idiosyncratic rooms feature furniture from the owner's antique shop and range in size from small doubles to large suites with kitchens. The characterful bar on the ground floor abuts the shop.

Bullock Hotel HOTEL $$
(605-578-1745; www.historicbullock.com; 633 Main St; r from $100;) Fans of the TV show will recall the conflicted but upstanding sheriff Seth Bullock. This hotel was opened by the real Bullock in 1895. The 36 rooms are modern and comfortable while retaining the period charm of the building.

Eating & Drinking

Thyme Bistro AMERICAN $$
(605-578-7566; 87 Sherman St; mains $10-20; 11am-2pm Tue-Sun, 5-9pm Thu-Sat) Away from the mob of casinos, this modest-looking restaurant serves up some of the best food in town. The seasonal menu ranges from sandwiches and lighter fare at lunch to meaty mains at night. Desserts are popular and the coffee is the best in town.

Saloon No 10 BAR
(www.saloon10.com; 657 Main St; 8am-2am) Dark paneled walls and sawdust on the floor are features of this storied bar. The original, where Hickok literally lost big time, stood across the street, but the building burned to the ground and the owners brought the bar over here.

LEAD

Just uphill from Deadwood, Lead (pronounced *leed*) has an unrestored charm and still bears plenty of scars from the mining era. Peek at the 1250ft-deep **Homestake gold mine** (160 W Main St; admission free; 24hr) to see what open-pit mining can do to a mountain. Nearby are the same mine's shafts, which plunge more than 1.5 miles below the surface and are now being used for physics research.

The **Main Street Manor Hostel** (605-717-2044; www.mainstreetmanorhostel.com; 515 W Main St; dm $15-25; closed Dec & Jan;) is a gem in its own right. Guests get use of the kitchen, garden and laundry at this very friendly place.

US 385

The scenic spine of the Black Hills, US 385 runs 90 miles from Deadwood to Hot Springs and beyond. Beautiful meadows and dark stands of conifers are interspersed with roadside attractions that include kangaroos, mistletoe and, of course, Elvis.

HILL CITY

One of the most appealing towns up in the hills, Hill City (www.hillcitysd.com) has a certain dignity not found at places such as Keystone. Its main drag has cafes and galleries.

TOP CHOICE **1880 Train** (www.1880train.com; 222 Railroad Ave; adult/child round-trip $24/12; ⌚May-Oct) is a classic steam train running through rugged country to Keystone. A train museum is next door.

Lantern Inn (☎605-574-2582; www.lanterninn.com; 580 E Main St; r $65-130;) is an 18-room motel-style place spread over two stories fronting attractive grounds.

MOUNT RUSHMORE

Fans of *North by Northwest* may remember the charmingly piney and low-key visitor center where Cary Grant gets plugged. That was then (1959). Today the public areas around Mt Rushmore seem devilishly designed to rob visitors of any enjoyment from their visit. Yes, the amazing mountainside sculpture is still there. George Washington, Thomas Jefferson, Abraham Lincoln and Theodore Roosevelt are each in their own 60ft-tall glory. But trying to appreciate one of the most iconic American images is just that: trying.

A bunkerlike multilevel parking garage greets visitors followed by bombastic entrances that obscure the memorial. You pass through an overwrought avenue of all 50 state flags before reaching a terrace, underneath which is the **visitor center** (www.nps.gov/moru; admission free, parking $11; ⌚8am-10pm summer, 8am-5pm rest of year). Displays here are aimed at short attention spans and give little feel for the massive physical effort of the team (led by sculptor Gutzon Borglum) who created the memorial between 1927 and 1941.

Fortunately, with a little walking, you can escape the crowds and commercialism and fully appreciate this magnificent work. The **Presidential Trail** loop leads near the monument for some fine nostril views and past the fascinating sculptors' studio. A **nature trail** to the right as you face the entrance connects the viewing and parking areas, passing through a pine forest.

KEYSTONE

The nearest lodging and restaurants to Mt Rushmore are in Keystone, a one-time mining town now solely devoted to milking the monument. Gaudy motels vie with fudgeries for your attention.

CRAZY HORSE MEMORIAL

The world's largest monument, the **Crazy Horse Memorial** (www.crazyhorsememorial.org; US 385; per person/car $10/27; ⌚7am-dusk summer, 8am-5pm rest of year) is, as author Ian Frazier describes, 'a ruin, only in reverse.' Onlookers at the 563ft-tall work-in-progress can gawk at what will be the Sioux leader astride his horse, pointing to the horizon saying, 'My lands are where my dead lie buried.'

Never photographed or persuaded to sign a meaningless treaty, Crazy Horse was chosen for a monument that Lakota Sioux elders hoped would balance the presidential focus of Mt Rushmore. In 1948 a Boston-born sculptor, the indefatigable Korczak Ziolkowski, started blasting granite. His family have continued the work since his death in 1982. (It should also be noted that many Native Americans oppose the monument as desecration of sacred land.)

No one is predicting when the sculpture will be complete (the face was dedicated in 1998). A rather thrilling **laser-light show** that tells the story of the monument and what it represents is splashed across the rock face on summer evenings.

The huge **visitor center** includes a Native American museum, a cultural center where you can see artisans at work and Ziolkowski's studio. A bus ($4) takes you to the base of the mountain.

WHAT THE...?

Only four presidents on Mt Rushmore right? Well, maybe not. Nature may have provided a fifth. Drive 1.4 miles northwest from the Mt Rushmore parking entrance (away from Keystone) on Hwy 244 and look for a sheer rock face that's the backside of Mt Rushmore. Pull over safely and then decide just which president might be honored by the rather lurid shape on the rock face. Which head of state it represents may depend on your politics.

CUSTER STATE PARK

The only reason 111-sq-mile **Custer State Park** (www.custerstatepark.info; 7-day pass per car $15) isn't a national park is that the state grabbed it first. It boasts one of the largest free-roaming bison herds in the world (about 1500), the famous 'begging burros' (donkeys seeking handouts) and more than 200 bird species. Other wildlife include elk, pronghorns, mountain goats, bighorn sheep, coyotes, prairie dogs, mountain lions and bobcats.

The **Peter Norbeck Visitor Center** (☎605-255-4464; US 16A; ⏲8am-8pm summer, 9am-5pm rest of year), situated on the eastern side of the park, contains good exhibits and offers activities such as gold-panning demonstrations and guided nature walks. The nearby **Black Hills Playhouse** (www.blackhillsplayhouse.com; tickets $32-37) hosts summer theater.

Meandering over awesome stone bridges and across sublime Alpine meadows, the 18-mile **Wildlife Loop Road** and the incredible 14-mile **Needles Highway** (SD 87) are two superb drives in the park. The latter links with US 385 at either end.

However, the real road star is **Iron Mountain Road** (Hwy 16A). It's a 16-mile roller coaster of wooden bridges, virtual loop-the-loops, narrow tunnels and stunning vistas on the section between the park's west entrance and Keystone.

Hiking through the pine-covered hills and prairie grassland (keep an eye out for rattlesnakes) is a great way to see wildlife and rock formations. The Sylvan Lake Shore, Sunday Gulch, Cathedral Spires and French Creek Natural Area trails are all highly recommended.

You can pitch a tent in eight **campgrounds** (☎800-710-2267; www.campsd.com; tent sites $18-27) around the park. At four, you can rent a well-equipped camping cabin for $47 per night. Reservations are vital in summer.

Backcountry camping ($6 per person per night) is allowed in the French Creek Natural Area. The park also has four impressive **resorts** (☎888-875-0001; www.custerresorts.com) with a mix of lodge rooms and cabins starting at $95 and going much higher. Book well ahead. The town of **Custer**, the main gateway into the park, has plenty of hotels and restaurants.

WIND CAVE NATIONAL PARK

This park, protecting 44 sq miles of grassland and forest, sits just south of Custer State Park. The central feature is, of course, the cave, which contains 132 miles of mapped passages. The cave's foremost feature is its 'boxwork' calcite formations (95% of all that are known exist here), which look like honeycomb and date back 60 to 100 million years. The strong gusts, which are felt at the entrance, but not inside, give the cave its name. The **visitor center** (www.nps.gov/wica; ⏲8am-7pm summer, reduced hr rest of year) has details on the variety of **tours** (adult $7-23, child $3.50-4.50) that are offered. The four-hour Wild Cave Tour offers an orgy of spelunking.

Hiking is a popular activity in the park, where you'll find the southern end of the 111-mile **Centennial Trail** to Sturgis. The **campground** (campsites $6-12) rarely fills and backcountry camping (free with permit) is allowed in limited areas.

JEWEL CAVE NATIONAL MONUMENT

Another of the Black Hills' many fascinating caves is Jewel Cave, 13 miles west of Custer on US 16, so named because calcite crystals line nearly all of its walls. Currently 145 miles have been surveyed, making it the second-longest known cave in the world, but it is presumed to be the longest. **Tours** (☎reservations 605-673-8300; adult $4-27, child free-$4) range in length and difficulty; reservations (seven days in advance max) are recommended. Make arrangements at the **visitor center** (www.nps.gov/jeca; ⏲8am-5:30pm). If you'll only visit one Black Hills cave, this would be a good choice.

SOUTH DAKOTA: DETOURS & EXTRAS

Large swaths of South Dakota are unchanged since the 19th century when the Native Americans and the US Army clashed. See the land as it was then along the **Native American Scenic Byway** (www.byways.org), which begins in Chamberlain on Hwy 50 and meanders 100 crooked miles northwest to Pierre along Hwy 1806, following the Missouri River through rolling, rugged countryside. This stretch makes a good detour off I-90.

Highway 14 runs across the middle of the state, crossing I-29 at Brookings (exit 133), then west through De Smet to Pierre and on to Wall. It meanders through a sea of grassland under big skies colored by long sunsets stretching across the broad horizon.

Way off in the northwest corner of the state, **Petrified Wood Park** (⏲park 24hr, museum 9am-5pm Jun-Aug) is a 1930s collection of geologic oddities covering an entire city block in the center of little **Lemmon**.

HOT SPRINGS

This surprisingly attractive town, south of the main Black Hills circuit, boasts ornate 1890s red sandstone buildings and warm mineral springs feeding the Fall River.

You can fill your water bottles at **Kidney Springs**, just south of the **visitor center** (800-325-6991; www.hotsprings-sd.com; 801 S 6th St; 9am-7pm summer) or swim at **Cascade Falls**, which is 71°F (22°C) all year, 11 miles south on US 71. The water at **Evans Plunge** (www.evansplunge.com; 1145 N River St; adult/child $12/10; 10am-9pm summer, reduced hr rest of year), a giant indoor geothermal springs waterpark, is always 87°F (30.5°C).

The remarkable **Mammoth Site** (www.mammothsite.com; 1800 US 18 bypass; adult/child $8/6; 8am-8pm May 15–Aug 15, reduced hr rest of year) is the country's largest left-as-found mammoth fossil display. Hundreds of animals perished in a sinkhole here about 26,000 years ago. In July you can join paleontologists digging for more bones.

TOP CHOICE **Red Rock River Resort** (605-745-4400; www.redrockriverresort.com; 603 N River St; r $85-170;) has cozy and stylish rooms in a beautiful 1891 downtown building, plus spa facilities (day passes for nonguests $25).

NEBRASKA

Those who just see Nebraska as 480 miles of blandness along I-80 are missing out on a lot. The Cornhusker State (they do grow a lot of the stuff) has beautiful river valleys and an often stark bleakness that is entrancing. Its links to the past – from vast fields of dinosaur remains to Native American culture to the toils of hardy settlers – provides a dramatic storyline. Dotted with cute little towns, Nebraska's two main cities, Omaha and Lincoln, are vibrant and artful.

The key to enjoying this long stoic stretch of country is to take the little roads, whether it's US 30 instead of I-80, US 20 to the Black Hills or the lonely and magnificent US 2.

Information

Nebraska Association of Bed & Breakfasts (877-223-6222; www.nebraskabb.com)

Nebraska state parks (reservations 402-471-1414; www.outdoornebraska.ne.gov) Vehicle permits cost $5/21 per day/year. Some campsites at popular parks are reservable; fees are $7 to $26 per night.

Nebraska Travel & Tourism Division (888-444-1867; www.visitnebraska.org)

NEBRASKA FACTS

- » **Nickname** Cornhusker State
- » **Population** 1.83 million
- » **Area** 77,360 sq miles
- » **Capital city** Lincoln (population 260,000)
- » **Other cities** Omaha (population 409,000)
- » **Sales tax** 5.5%
- » **Birthplace of** dancer Fred Astaire (1899–1987), actors Marlon Brando (1924–2004) and Hilary Swank (b 1974), civil rights leader Malcolm X (1925–65)
- » **Home of** Air Force generals
- » **Politics** center-right
- » **Famous for** only unicameral state legislature, corn
- » **Official beverage** milk
- » **Driving distances** Omaha to the Wyoming border on I-80 480 miles, Omaha to Kansas City 186 miles

Omaha

Be careful if you're planning a quick pit stop in Omaha. Home to the vibrant brick-and-cobblestoned Old Market neighborhood downtown, a lively music scene and several quality museums, this town can turn a few hours into a few days. After all, billionaire Warren Buffet lives here and when is he ever wrong?

Omaha grew to prominence as a transport hub. Its location on the Missouri River and proximity to the Platte made it an important stop on the Oregon, California and Mormon Trails, and later the Union Pacific Railroad stretched west from here. These days Omaha is in the nation's top 10 for billionaires and Fortune 500 companies per capita.

Sights & Activities

It's easy to spend much of your Omaha visit in **Old Market** on the river edge of downtown. This revitalized warehouse district, full of nightclubs, restaurants and funky shops, easily holds its own when it comes to aesthetics, energy and sophistication. Nearby parks boast fountains and waterside walks.

TOP CHOICE **Durham Museum** MUSEUM
(www.durhammuseum.org; 801 S 10th St; adult/child $7/5; ⌚10am-8pm Tue, 10am-5pm Wed-Sat, 1-5pm Sun) The soaring art-deco Union Station train depot houses a remarkable museum. Covering local history from the Lewis and Clark expedition to the Omaha stockyards to the trains that once called here, the Durham makes the most of its beautiful surrounds. The soda fountain still serves hot dogs and phosphates.

The museum offers themed **historic tours** of Omaha in summer several days per week ($15).

Joslyn Art Museum MUSEUM
(www.joslyn.org; 2200 Dodge St; adult/child $8/5; ⌚10am-4pm Tue-Sat, noon-4pm Sun, to 8pm Thu) The admired and architecturally imposing museum has a great collection of 19th- and 20th-century European and American art and has a good selection of Western-themed works plus an exciting sculpture garden.

TOP CHOICE **Union Pacific Railroad Museum** MUSEUM
(www.uprr.com; 200 Pearl St, Council Bluffs, IA; admission by donation; ⌚10am-4pm Tue-Sat) Just across the river in the cute little downtown area of Council Bluffs, Iowa; this grand museum tells the story of the world's most profitable railroad, the company that rammed the transcontinental railroad west from here in the 1860s. Look for the pictures of Ronald Reagan and his chimp-pal Bonzo aboard a train.

Sleeping

There is a good mix of midrange and budget hotels along US 275 near 60th St, at I-80 exits 445 and 449 and across the river in Council Bluffs, IA, at I-29 exit 51. Old Market has several midrange chains.

TOP CHOICE **Omaha Magnolia Hotel** HOTEL $$
(☎402-341-2500; www.magnoliahotelomaha.com; 1615 Howard St; r incl breakfast $110-200; ❄@🛜) Not far from Old Market, the Magnolia is a boutique hotel housed in a gorgeous restored 1923 Italianate high-rise. The 145 rooms have a vibrant, modern style. Rates include a full buffet breakfast and bedtime milk and cookies.

Courtyard by Marriott Old Market HOTEL $$
(☎402-346-2200; www.marriott.com; 101 S 10th St; r $120-200; P❄@🛜≋) Partly housed in an old 11-story warehouse on the edge of Old Market, the Courtyard breaks with the chain mold. Newly refurbished, it has thoughtful amenities throughout its 167 rooms, and there's an indoor pool.

Eating & Drinking

The best thing you can do is just wander Old Market and see what you find.

CHASING TORNADOES

Much of the Great Plains is prone to severe weather, including violent thunderstorms, hail the size of softballs, spectacular lightning storms and more. But the real stars of these meteorological nightmares are tornadoes. Far less benign than the cyclones that carried Dorothy off to Oz, tornadoes cause death and destruction from the Great Plains east across the central US. In 2011, a huge tornado killed more than 150 people and flattened Joplin, MO. With winds of 300mph or more, tornadoes are both awesome and terrifying. Still, each year many people visit the region hoping to spot a funnel cloud, drawn by the sheer spectacle and elemental drama.

Tour companies use gadget-filled vans to chase storms across multiple states, with no guarantee that you'll actually see a storm. Costs average $200 to $400 a day and May to August offer the best spotting. Operators include the following:

Cloud 9 Tours (☎405-323-1145; www.cloud9tours.com)

Silver Lining Tours (☎832-717-4712; www.silverliningtours.com)

Tempest Tours (☎817-274-9313; www.tempesttours.com)

For a completely overhyped look at the world of storm-spotters – in the best Hollywood tradition – check out the 1996 movie *Twister* or watch the reality show *Storm Chasers* on Discovery TV. Read the recollections of veteran tornado chaser Roger Hill in *Hunting Nature's Fury*.

DON'T MISS

AMERICA'S FIRST HOMESTEAD

Homestead National Monument (www.nps.gov/home; Hwy 4, Beatrice; admission free; ⏲heritage center 9am-5pm) is on the site of the very first homestead granted under the landmark *Homestead Act of 1862,* which opened much of the US to settlers who received land for free if they made it productive. The pioneering Freeman family is buried here and you can see their reconstructed log house and hike the site. The heritage center is a striking building with good displays. The site is 4 miles west of Beatrice, 35 miles south of Lincoln on Hwy 77. It's off Hwy 136, which is designated the 'Heritage Highway' scenic byway and passes through tumbledown yet evocative old towns such as Franklin.

TOP CHOICE **Urban Wine Company** WINE BAR **$$**
(www.urbanwinecompany.com; 1037 Jones St; small plates $6-11; ⏲4pm-late Tue-Sat, noon-9pm Sun) An Old Market gem. Sample glasses from a vast wine list and enjoy dishes such as a chef's choice cheese platter and prosciutto lavosh.

Omaha Prime STEAKHOUSE **$$$**
(☎402-341-7040; www.omaha-prime.com; 415 S 11th St; mains $20-35; ⏲8am-10pm) Billionaire Warren Buffet drops by this Old Market stalwart for steaks, which is a fine recommendation given this is a great steak town. House-aged beef dominates the menu and waiters bring hunks around to help you order.

Mister Toad's BAR
(1002 Howard St; ⏲noon-1am) Sit out front on benches under big trees or nab a corner table inside while you work through the beer and cocktail list. It's woodsy, worn and flirting with dive-bar status. There's live jazz Sunday nights.

Bronco's BURGERS **$**
(4540 Leavenworth St; mains $4-7; ⏲7am-11pm) Classic local burger joint with a great neon sign and a few tables scattered inside and out. Everything, including the burgers, is ultrafresh.

ℹ Information

City Weekly (www.omahacityweekly.com) Free weekly good entertainment listings.

Visitor center (☎866-937-6624; www.visitomaha.com; 1001 Farnam St; ⏲9am-6pm Mon-Sat, to 4pm Sun summer, reduced hr rest of year) Near the Old Market; contains a good coffee bar.

ℹ Getting There & Away

Amtrak's *California Zephyr* stops in Omaha on its run between Northern California and Chicago.

Around Omaha

If you see large military planes drifting across the sky slowly, they're likely headed for one of Omaha's large military air bases.

Strategic Air & Space Museum MUSEUM
(www.strategicairandspace.com; I-80 exit 426, Ashland; adult/child $12/6; ⏲10am-5pm, closed Wed winter) After WWII Omaha's Offutt Air Force Base was home to the US Air Force Strategic Air Command, the force of nuclear bombers detailed in Stanley Kubrick's *Dr Strangelove.* This legacy is documented at this cavernous museum, which boasts a huge collection of bombers, from the B-52 to the B-17. Don't expect exhibits looking at the wider implications of bombing. It's 30 miles southwest of Omaha, well within the kill radius of a 1-megaton bomb.

Lincoln

Home to the historic Haymarket District and a lively bar scene thanks to the huge downtown campus of the University of Nebraska, Lincoln makes a good overnight stop. Nebraska's capital city is a very livable place and has more parks per capita than any other similarly sized US city.

👁 Sights

The **University of Nebraska** (www.unl.edu) has its main campus in the middle of town. The complex is as practical as a farmer and lacks real highlights but is an interesting stroll. However, you'll have no end of excitement on one of the six fall Saturdays when the Cornhuskers football team plays at home. Passions run high, especially as the team adjusts to a controversial move from its traditional home, the Big 12 Conference, to the traditionally Midwestern Big 10. (There's also criticism that academics have faltered because in 2011 the university was the first ever booted out of the Association of American Universities.)

State Capitol LANDMARK
(www.capitol.org; 1445 K St; hourly tours free; ⏲8am-5pm Mon-Fri, 10am-5pm Sat, 1-5pm Sun) From the outside, Nebraska's remarkable 1932 400ft-high state capitol represents the apex of phallic architecture (like many tall buildings in the Plains, it's often called the penis on the prairie), while the symbolically rich interior curiously combines classical and art-deco motifs. A 14th-floor observation deck is open to the public.

Museum of Nebraska History MUSEUM
(www.nebraskahistory.org; 131 Centennial Mall N; admission by donation; ⏲9am-4:30pm Mon-Fri, 1-4:30pm Sat & Sun) Follows the Cornhusker State's story, starting with a large First Nebraskans room.

Sleeping

Most hotels are near I-80. Those around exit 403 are mostly midrange, while there are budget motels aplenty at exit 399.

Atwood House B&B B&B $$
(☎402-438-4567; www.atwoodhouse.com; 740 S 17th St; r $85-200; P❄📶) One of several elegant B&Bs in old mansions near downtown and the capitol, this one was constructed in 1894 and contains an opulent wood interior (sort of like a doll house; pretend your name is Barbie) and a grand colonnaded exterior.

Embassy Suites Hotel HOTEL $$
(☎402-474-1111; www.embassysuites.hilton.com; 1040 P St; ste incl breakfast from $129; P❄@📶🏊) This downtown Haymarket-handy hotel has 252 spacious rooms around a nine-story atrium. A full breakfast is included.

Eating & Drinking

Lincoln's Haymarket District, a browsing-friendly six-block warehouse area dating from the early 20th century, has numerous cafes, restaurants, coffeehouses and bars. If you're after falafel sandwiches followed by beer and body shots, follow the undergrads down O St to 14th St.

TOP CHOICE **Indigo Bridge** CAFE $
(701 P St, Haymarket; meals $0-5; ⏲8am-10pm; 📶) This fine cafe in a fantastic bookstore serves coffees and snacks through the day. At lunch on weekdays, enjoy hearty organic soup and bread and pay what you can afford.

Yia Yia's Pizza PIZZERIA $$
(1423 O St; mains $8-15; ⏲11am-11pm) Many a hangover has been chased away by the cheesy, gooey goodness here at this Lincoln legend. The pizzas are cracker-thin and made from scratch. Sit at a sidewalk table or inside amid the gregarious college crowd.

Information

The **visitor center** (☎800-423-8212; www.lincoln.org; 201 N 7th St, Haymarket; ⏲9am-8pm Mon-Fri, 8am-2pm Sat, noon-4pm Sun summer, reduced hr rest of year) is inside Lincoln Station, where Amtrak's *California Zephyr* stops.

Along I-80

Shortly after Lincoln, I-80 runs an almost razor-straight 83 miles before hugging the Platte River. Several towns along its route to Wyoming make up for its often monotonous stretches. Whenever possible, use US 30, which bounces from one interesting burg to the next (Gothenburg, exit 211, is especially attractive), following the busy Union Pacific (UP) mainline the entire way.

GRAND ISLAND

TOP CHOICE **Stuhr Museum of the Prairie Pioneer** (www.stuhrmuseum.org; I-80 exit 312; adult/child $8/6; ⏲9am-5pm Mon-Sat, noon-5pm Sun) is an amazing combination of museum exhibits with a vast outdoor living museum. Note how conditions dramatically improved from the homes in 1860 to 1890 thanks to riches made possible by the railroad.

Upstream of Grand Island, the Platte hosts 500,000 sandhill cranes (80% of the world population) and 15 million waterfowl during the spring migration (mid-February to early April). The **Nebraska Nature &**

SCENIC DRIVE: HIGHWAY 2

Nebraska's **Highway 2** branches northwest from I-80 and Grand Island through Broken Bow 272 miles to Alliance in the panhandle. It crosses the lonely and lovely **Sandhills** – 19,000 sq miles of sand dunes covered in grass – one of the country's most isolated areas. With the wind whistling in your ears, the distant call of a hawk and the biggest skies imaginable, this is pure iconic Great Plains travel.

NEBRASKA: DETOURS & EXTRAS

Carhenge (www.carhenge.com; Alliance) is a Stonehenge replica assembled from 38 discarded cars that lures 80,000 Desoto druids a year. This artful reproduction rises out of a field 3 miles north of Alliance along Hwy 87, east of US 385, the road to the Black Hills.

Scotts Bluff National Monument has been a beacon to travelers for centuries. Rising 800ft above the flat plains of western Nebraska, it was an important waypoint on the Oregon Trail in the mid-19th century. You can still see wagon ruts today in the park. The **visitor center** (www.nps.gov/scbl; Gering; per vehicle $5; ⌚8am-7pm summer, to 5pm rest of year) has displays and can guide you to walks and drives. It's off US 26 south of Scottsbluff town.

Visitor Center (www.nebraskanature.org; I-80 exit 305, Alda; ⌚9am-5pm Mon-Sat year-round, 8am-6pm daily Mar) is a good place to break out the binoculars.

KEARNEY

The **Great Platte River Road Archway Monument** (www.archway.org; adult/child $10/3; ⌚9am-6pm summer, reduced hr rest of year) arches unexpectedly over I-80 east of Kearney near exit 272. The multimedia exhibits tell an engaging story of the people who've passed this way, from those riding wagon trains to those zipping down the interstate.

Like all the I-80 towns, Kearney has no shortage of motels. A good indie choice near downtown is **Midtown Western Inn** (☎308-237-3153; www.midtownwesterninn.com; 1401 2nd Ave; r $45-90; ❄📶🏊), which has a vintage motel vibe with huge, clean rooms.

The compact downtown, near US 30 and the bust UP mainline, has good cafes and bars including **Thunderhead Brewing Co** (www.thunderheadbrewing.com; 18 E 21st St; mains $5-10; ⌚noon-1am), which makes a fine dark wheat beer and serves pizza and sandwiches.

NORTH PLATTE

North Platte, a rail-fan mecca, is home to the **Buffalo Bill Ranch State Historical Park** (www.outdoornebraska.ne.gov; per car $5; ⌚9am-5pm daily summer, 9am-4pm Mon-Fri Apr-May & Sep-Oct), 2 miles north of US 30. Once the home of Bill Cody, the father of rodeo and the famed Wild West Show, it's now a fun museum that reflects his colorful life.

Enjoy sweeping views of Union Pacific's **Bailey Yard**, the world's largest rail classification yard, from the **Golden Spike Tower** (www.goldenspiketower.com; 1249 N Homestead Rd; adult/child $7/5; ⌚9am-7pm Mon-Sat, from 1pm Sun summer, to 5pm rest of year), an eight-story observation tower with indoor and outdoor decks. From I-80, take exit 177.

Along US 20

The further west you go on US 20, the more space you'll see between towns, trees and pickup trucks. The western end of the road, known as the **Bridges to Buttes Byway**, traverses a Nebraska barely touched by time. Look for wild geologic features that pop out of the rolling green hills.

ROYAL

Watch paleontologists work at **Ashfall Fossil Beds** (www.ashfall.unl.edu; 86930 517th Ave; adult/child $5/3 plus vehicle permit $4; ⌚9am-5pm Mon-Sat, 11am-5pm Sun, reduced hr May & Sep–mid-Oct), 8 miles northwest of town. You can see unearthed prehistoric skeletons of hundreds of animals, including rhinoceroses, buried 12 million years ago by ash from a Pompeii-like explosion in what is now Idaho.

VALENTINE

Fortunately, 'America's Heart City' doesn't milk the schtick. It sits on the edge of the Sandhills and is a great base for canoeing, kayaking and inner-tubing the winding canyons of the federally protected **Niobrara River Scenic River** (www.nps.gov/niob). The river crosses the **Fort Niobrara National Wildlife Refuge** (www.fws.gov/fortniobrara; ⌚visitor center 8am-4:30pm daily Jun-Aug, closed weekends rest of year). Driving tours here take you past bison, elk and more.

Floating down the river draws scores of people through the summer. Sheer limestone bluffs, lush forests and spring-fed waterfalls along the banks shatter any 'flat Nebraska' stereotypes. The **visitor center** (☎402-376-2969; www.visitvalentine.com; 253 N Main St; ⌚9am-7pm Mon-Sat summer, 9am-5pm Mon-Fri rest of year) can steer you to one of many local outfitters for a river adventure via canoe, kayak or inner-tube (from $16).

Twenty miles south of town, the **Valentine National Wildlife Refuge** (www.fws.gov/valentine; Hwy 83) has some superb Sandhills scenery and lots of lakes.

The classic red-brick **Trade Winds Motel** (☎402-376-1600; www.tradewindslodge.com; US 20 & 83; r $50-100; ❄📶🏊) has 32 comfy and clean rooms with fridges and microwaves.

NORTHERN PANHANDLE

Get a feel for the tough lives led by early residents at the **Museum of the Fur Trade** (www.furtrade.org; adult/child $5/free; ⏰8am-5pm May-Oct), 3 miles east of Chadron, which includes the restored sod-roofed Bordeaux Trading Post, which swapped pelts for guns, blankets and whiskey from 1837 to 1876.

Fort Robinson State Park (www.outdoornebraska.ne.gov; admission per vehicle $5; ⏰sunrise-sunset), 4 miles west of Crawford, is where Crazy Horse was killed in 1877 while in captivity. It has camping and cabins.

At Harrison, detour 23 miles south on pastoral Hwy 29 to reach **Agate Fossil Beds National Monument** (☎308-668-2211; www.nps.gov/agfo; admission free; ⏰8am-6pm summer, 8am-4pm rest of year), a rich source of unusual fossils dating back 20 million years. The Native American artifact display is small but excellent.

KANSAS

Wicked witches and yellow-brick roads, pitched battles over slavery and tornadoes powerful enough to pulverize entire towns are some of the more lurid images of Kansas. But the common image – amber waves of grain from north to south and east to west is closer to reality.

There's a simple beauty to the green rolling hills and limitless horizons. Places such as Chase County beguile those who value understatement. Gems abound, from the amazing space museum in Hutchinson to the indie music clubs of Lawrence. Most importantly, follow the Great Plains credo of ditching the interstate for the two-laners and make your own discoveries. The website www.kansassampler.org is a brilliant resource for finding the best the state has to offer, as is the guidebook *8 Wonders of Kansas*.

Information

Kansas Bed & Breakfast Association (☎888-572-2632; www.kbba.com)

Kansas state parks (www.kdwp.state.ks.us) Per vehicle per day/year $4.20/24.70. Campsites cost $7.50 to $11.

Kansas Travel & Tourism (☎785-296-2009; www.travelks.com)

KANSAS FACTS

- **Nickname** Sunflower State
- **Population** 2.9 million
- **Area** 82,282 sq miles
- **Capital city** Topeka (population 128,000)
- **Other cities** Wichita (population 385,000)
- **Sales tax** 5.3%
- **Birthplace of** aviator Amelia Earhart (1897–1937), temperance crusader Carrie Nation (1846–1911), TV talker Dr Phil (b 1950), Pizza Hut (established 1958), singer-songwriter Melissa Etheridge (b 1961)
- **Home of** Dorothy and Toto (of *Wizard of Oz* fame)
- **Politics** very conservative, many tea-party adherents
- **Famous for** wheat
- **Official state song** 'Home on the Range'
- **Driving distances** Wichita to Kansas City 200 miles, Dodge City to Abilene 188 miles

Wichita

From its early cow-town days at the head of the Chisholm Trail in the 1870s to its current claim as Air Capital of the World (thanks to about half the world's general aviation aircraft being built here by the likes of Cessna and others), Kansas' largest city has always been a prosperous place. It's a worthwhile stopover but not at the expense of the rest of the state.

Sights

Wichita's historic, all-brick Old Town, good for shopping, eating and drinking, is on the east side of downtown, while the parklike Museums on the River district fills a triangle of green space between the Big and Little Arkansas Rivers to the west.

The Museums on the River district includes the first three sights listed here, plus

ROUTE 66: GET YOUR KICKS IN KANSAS

Only 13 miles of Route 66 pass through the southeast corner of Kansas, but it's a good drive.

The first town you hit after Joplin, **Galena**, has been on the decline since even before the last of the area's lead and zinc mines closed in the 1970s.

Three miles down the road is **Riverton**, where you might consider a detour 20 miles north to Pittsburg for some famous fried chicken (p643).

Cross US 400 and stay on old Route 66 to the 1923 **Marsh Rainbow Arch Bridge**, the last of its kind.

From the bridge, it's less than 3 miles south to **Baxter Springs**, the site of a Civil War massacre and numerous bank robberies. The multifaceted **Baxter Springs Heritage Center** (www.baxterspringsmuseum.org; 740 East Ave; admission free; ⏲10am-4:30pm Mon-Sat, 1-4:30pm Sun Apr-Oct, closed Mon-Wed Nov-Mar) has helped restore a 1939 Phillips 66 gas station into the **Kansas Route 66 Visitor Center** (☎620-856-2066; ⏲10am-5pm Mon-Sat). Military Ave (US 69A) takes you into Oklahoma.

botanical gardens and a science museum aimed at kids.

TOP CHOICE Old Cowtown MUSEUM
(www.oldcowtown.org; 1865 Museum Blvd; adult/child $8/5.50; ⏲9:30am-4:30pm Wed-Sun; 👪) An open-air museum that re-creates the Wild West (as seen on TV...). Pioneer-era buildings, staged gunfights and guides in cowboy costumes thrill kids. The river walks here are bucolic.

Mid-America All-Indian Center MUSEUM
(www.theindiancenter.org; 650 N Seneca St; adult/child $7/3; ⏲10am-4pm Tue-Sat) Guarded by Wichita artist Blackbear Bosin's 44ft statue 'Keeper of the Plains,' this museum has exhibits of Native American art and artifacts, as well as a traditional Wichita-style grass lodge.

Exploration Place MUSEUM
(www.exploration.org; 300 N McLean Blvd; adult/child from $8/6; ⏲10am-5pm Mon-Sat, noon-5pm Sun; 👪) Right on the river confluence, this striking modern museum has no end of cool exhibits including a tornado chamber where you can feel 75mph winds and a sublime erosion model where you can see water create a new little Kansas.

Museum of World Treasures MUSEUM
(www.worldtreasures.org; 835 E 1st St; adult/child $9/7; ⏲10am-5pm Mon-Sat, noon-5pm Sun) With a complete T-Rex, Egyptian mummies, Greek pottery, Abraham Lincoln's walking cane, military relics, a sports hall of fame and much more, this museum has something for everyone.

Sleeping

Hotbeds for chains include I-135 exit 1AB, I-35 exit 50 and the Hwy 96 Rock Rd and Webb Rd exits. Broadway north of the center offers a mixed bag of indie cheapies.

TOP CHOICE Hotel at Old Town HOTEL **$$**
(☎316-267-4800; www.hotelatoldtown.com; 830 1st St; r $100-200; P❄@📶) In the midst of Old Town nightlife, this restored hotel is housed in the 1906 factory of the Keen Kutter Corp, a maker of household goods. Rooms have high ceilings, fridges and microwaves and there's a good breakfast buffet. It's the pick compared with some nearby upscale chains.

Cambridge Suites HOTEL **$$**
(☎316-263-1061; www.cambridge-suites.com; 711 S Main St; r $80-180; P❄📶🏊) On the south edge of downtown, suites here range up to two-bedroom in size and have kitchens. It's modern and commodious, perfect for families or quarreling couples.

Eating & Drinking

Wichita is the home of Pizza Hut, but that's far from the pinnacle of the city's dining options. For some real-deal Mexican or Vietnamese, drive north on Broadway and take your pick. Old Town has a fruitful **farmers market** (⏲7am-noon Sat May-Oct).

TOP CHOICE Doc's Steak House STEAKHOUSE **$$**
(1515 N Broadway; mains $5-12; ⏲11am-10pm) Once owned by the brother of the genius that started Wall Drug (p626), this local institution is home to the wildly addictive garlic salad (trust us, plunge in, order a double).

Steaks, chicken fried steak and pork chops are amazing bargains.

Nu Way Cafe BURGERS $
(1416 W Douglas Ave; mains $3-5; ⌚11am-9pm) Frosty glasses of homemade root beer are among the highlights at this west-of-downtown outlet of a beloved Wichita chain. Old-style Formica is a backdrop for delicate onion rings, loose-meat sandwiches and much more.

Anchor BAR & GRILL $$
(www.anchorwichita.com; 1109 E Douglas Ave; mains $7-12; ⌚9pm-late) On the edge of Old Town, this vintage pub has high ceilings, a tiled floor, a great beer selection (try the hoppy draft Ska) and tasty food from breakfast to late at night. It totally outclasses the nearby chain and theme bars.

Information

The **visitor center** (☎800-288-9424; www.visitwichita.com; 515 S Main; ⌚8am-5pm Mon-Fri) is geared toward conventions.

Along I-70

What it lacks in glamour, Kansas' 420-mile 'Main Street' makes up for in efficiency, quickly shuttling you from Kansas City to the Colorado border. The scenery can be monotonous, but as always there are many interesting stops along the way. West of Salina, the landscape around I-70 stretches into rolling, wide-open plains, with winds sometimes strong enough to knock over 18-wheelers. US 50 (p643) and US 56 (p643) are intriguing alternatives.

LAWRENCE

Lawrence, 40 miles west of Kansas City, has been an island of progressive politics from the start. Founded by abolitionists in 1854 and an important stop on the Underground Railroad, it became a battlefield in the clash between pro- and antislavery factions. In 1863, the Missouri 'Bushwhackers' of William Clarke Quantrill raided Lawrence, killing nearly 200 people and burning much of it to the ground. The city survived, however, and so did its free-thinking spirit, which is fitting for the home of the **University of Kansas** (KU; www.ku.edu).

Sights

The appealing downtown, where townies and students merge, centers on **Massachusetts St**, one of the most pleasant streets in this part of the country for a stroll.

FREE **Spencer Museum of Art** ART GALLERY
(www.spencerart.ku.edu; 1301 Mississippi St; ⌚10am-4pm Tue-Sat, noon-4pm Sun, to 8pm Thu) It isn't large, but this museum has a collection encompassing work by Western artist Frederic Remington and many European masters.

Sleeping & Eating

Lawrence's motels cluster at the junction of US 40 and US 59 south of I-70. The choices downtown make Lawrence the state's best stop for the night.

Halcyon House B&B B&B $
(☎888-441-0314; www.thehalcyonhouse.com; 1000 Ohio St; r $60-100; P❄📶) The nine cute bedrooms here (some share bathrooms) have lots of natural light, and there's a landscaped garden and homemade baked goods for breakfast. Downtown is just a short walk away.

Eldridge Hotel HOTEL $$
(☎785-749-5011; www.eldridgehotel.com; 701 Massachusetts St; r from $140; P❄@📶) The 56 modern two-room suites at this historic 1926

WORTH A TRIP

AMERICA'S BEST SPACE MUSEUM

Possibly the most surprising sight in Kansas, the amazing **Cosmosphere & Space Center** (www.cosmo.org; 1100 N Plum St, Hutchinson; all-day pass adult/child $17/15, museum only $12/10; ⌚9am-7pm Mon-Sat, noon-7pm Sun summer, to 6pm Sun-Thu rest of year; 👪) captures the race to the moon better than any museum on the planet. Absorbing displays and artifacts such as the Apollo 13 command module will enthrall you for hours. The museum regularly is called in to build props for Hollywood movies portraying the space race, including *Apollo 13*.

All puns aside, the museum's isolated location in Hutchinson might as well be the moon, but if you're making a day trip from Wichita or just stopping off in this small city of huge grain elevators, savor the local BBQ at **Danny Boy's Smokehouse** (307 N Main St; meals $5-9; ⌚11am-8pm), a much-lauded smoked-meat purveyor in restaurant-filled downtown.

downtown hotel have antique-style furnishings. The bar and restaurant are stylish; the ghost misunderstood (rumors abound).

TOP CHOICE **Free State Brewing** PUB $$
(www.freestatebrewing.com; 636 Massachusetts St; mains $6-15; 11am-late) One of many good places on Mass downtown, this is the first brewery in Kansas since Carrie Nation got one closed in 1880. A cut above brewpub standards, the beers are excellent. The food is much-loved as well, leaning toward cheesy thirst-inducing classics.

Burger Stand at the Casbah BURGERS $
(803 Massachusetts St; mains $5-9; kitchen 11am-10pm;) In one of downtown's better bars, this upscale burger kitchen turns out some yummie numbers, including a tasty veggie burger. Most ingredients are sourced locally.

Entertainment

Bottleneck LIVE MUSIC
(www.bottlenecklive.com; 737 New Hampshire) The music scene in town is up to college-town standards and this joint usually has the best of the newest. Top bands often skip KC for the Bottleneck.

Information

Visitor information center (785-865-4499; www.visitlawrence.com; 402 N 2nd St; 8:30am-5pm Mon-Sat, 1-5pm Sun) Offers self-guided and iPod tours of Lawrence's anti-slavery heritage and sites.

TOPEKA

Kansas and its vital role in America's race relations is symbolized in the otherwise humdrum state capital of Topeka.

Sights

TOP CHOICE **Brown vs Board of Education National Historic Site** MUSEUM
(www.nps.gov/brvb; 1515 SE Monroe St; admission free; 9am-5pm) It took real guts to challenge the segregationist laws common in the US in the 1950s and the stories of these courageous men and women are here. Set in Monroe Elementary School, one of Topeka's African American schools at the time of the landmark 1954 Supreme Court decision that banned segregation in US schools, the displays cover the whole Civil Rights movement. Note the huge photo of the white woman screaming racial epitaphs – she looks like a rabid primate.

State Capitol LANDMARK
(300 SW 10th St; 8am-5pm daily, tours 9am-3pm Mon-Fri) Under the huge green dome, don't miss the fiery John Steuart Curry mural of abolitionist John Brown.

Kansas History Center MUSEUM
(www.kshs.org; 6425 SW 6th Ave; adult/child $6/4; 9am-5pm Tue-Sat, 1-5pm Sun) From a Cheyenne war lance to Carrie Nation's hammer, this engaging center is packed with Kansas stories.

Eating

Porubsky's Grocery DELI $
(508 NE Sardou Ave; 10am-7pm Mon-Sat) Hard by the old Santa Fe mainline close to downtown, this old Russian deli has been serving up simple sandwiches at it's Formica counters since 1947. The chili (only Monday to Thursday) is best with piles of crackers. Best here are the housemade pickles, which burst with horseradishy goodness.

ABILENE

In the late 19th century, Abilene was a rowdy cow town at the end of the Chisholm Trail. Today its compact core of historic brick buildings and well-preserved neighborhoods seems perfectly appropriate for the birthplace of Dwight D Eisenhower (1890–1969), president and WWII general.

Fittingly set against a backdrop of grain elevators, the rather regal **Eisenhower Center** (www.eisenhower.archives.gov; 200 SE 4th St; museum adult/child $8/1, house $2; 8am-5:45pm summer, 9am-4:45pm rest of year) includes Ike's boyhood home, a museum and library, and his and Mamie's graves. Displays cover the Eisenhower presidential era (1953–61) and his role as allied commander in WWII. However, his ability to forge agreement between the squabbling allies is not fully covered. A highlight is the original text of his speech warning about the military-industrial complex.

The **Brookville Hotel** (www.brookvillehotel.com; 105 E Lafayette; meals $15; 11am-2pm & 4-7:30pm Wed-Sun) has been serving fried chicken since Ike graduated from West Point (1915). Cream-style corn, fresh biscuits and much more come with every meal.

LUCAS

'Outsider art,' meaning works created outside the bounds of traditional culture, has blossomed in tiny Lucas. Samuel Dinsmoor began it all in 1907 by filling his yard with enormous concrete sculptures espousing his eccentric philosophies. His **Garden of Eden** (www.garden-of-eden lucas-kansas.com; 301 2nd St; adult/child $6/1; ⏲10am-5pm May-Oct, 1-4pm Mar-Apr, 1-4pm Sat & Sun Nov-Feb) is visible from the sidewalk, but paid admission lets you hear some wonderful stories and see his remains in a glass-topped coffin (!).

The phenomenal **Grassroots Art Center** (☎785-525-6118; www.grassrootsart.net; 213 S Main St; adult/child $6/2; ⏲10am-5pm Mon-Sat, 1-5pm Sun May-Sep, 10am-4pm Mon & Thu-Sat, 1-4pm Sun Oct-Apr) has gathered works made of materials such as buttons, barbed wire, pull-tabs and strange machines by self-taught, self-motivated artists from around Kansas.

The best way to reach Lucas is along the **Post Rock Scenic Byway**, a scenic 18-mile jaunt past Wilson Lake starting at I-70 exit 206.

HAYS

The town of Hays grew up around its namesake fort, built in the 1860s to protect railroad workers from Native Americans, but most people stop today for a look much further into the past at the domed **Sternberg Museum of Natural History** (www.fhsu.edu/sternberg; 3000 Sternberg Dr; adult/child $8/5; ⏲9am-6pm Tue-Sat, 1-6pm Sun). It houses many unusual fossils, including its famous fish-within-a-fish, and animated dinosaurs.

Along US 50

Fabled US 50 splits off from I-35 at Emporia and follows the old Santa Fe mainline west through classic Kansas vistas.

CHASE COUNTY

Nearly a perfect square, this is the county William Least Heat-Moon examined mile by mile in his best-selling *Prairyerth*.

The beautiful Flint Hills roll through here and are home to two-thirds of the nation's remaining tallgrass prairie. The 10,894-acre **Tallgrass Prairie National Preserve** (www.nps.gov/tapr; admission free; ⏲buildings 9am-4:30pm, trails 24hr), 2 miles northwest of Strong City and US 50, is a perfect place to hike the prairie and revel in its ever-changing colorful flowers. Rangers offer tours of the preserved ranch and **bus tours** (⏲tours 11am, 1pm & 3pm May-Oct) of the prairie.

The rangers also have maps of some evocative remote drives in the county, as well as a tour of sights from Moon's book. Don't miss the showstopping **County Courthouse** in Cottonwood Falls, 2 miles south of Strong City. Completed in 1873, it is a fantasy of French Renaissance style.

Along US 56

US 56 follows the old Santa Fe Trail to Dodge City through the heart of the heartland. Most sights along here are also easily reached from US 50.

The large Mennonite communities around **Hillsboro** are descendants of Russian immigrants who brought the 'Turkey Red' strain of wheat to the Plains, where it thrived despite harsh conditions.

A further 110 miles west in **Larned**, the **Santa Fe Trail Center Museum** (www.santafetrailcenter.org; 1349 Hwy 156; adult/child $4/1.50; ⏲9am-5pm, closed Mon Sep-May) details the vital route linking the US and Mexico for

KANSAS: DETOURS & EXTRAS

» **Nicodemus** is the only surviving town in the west built by emancipated slaves from the south after the Civil War. A national park **visitor center** (www.nps.gov/nico; admission free; ⏲9am-4:30pm) recounts the town's history and the experience of African Americans in the west. The town is on US 24 about 35 miles north of I-70 via US 183 or US 283.

» **Monument Rocks** are 80ft-tall pyramid-shaped chalk formations that look like a Jawa hangout in *Star Wars*. Go 25 miles southeast of Oakley via US 83 off I-70 exit 76.

» **Fort Scott** (www.nps.gov; admission $3; ⏲8am-5pm) is a restored fort near the Missouri border that dates to 1842. While the parade grounds and buildings in the heart of its namesake city are interesting, the real draw here is the story of the battles between pro- and antislavery forces that were fought here before the Civil War.

» **Legendary fried chicken** is a hallmark of six restaurants in far southeastern Crawford County. Try **Chicken Mary's** (1133 E 600th Ave, Pittsburg; meals from $6; ⏲11am-8pm), which isn't far from where Route 66 crosses into Kansas.

much of the 19th century. Six miles west of town on Hwy 156, **Fort Larned National Historic Site** (www.nps.gov/fols; admission free; ⌚8:30am-4:30pm) is a remarkably well-preserved Santa Fe Trail fort.

DODGE CITY

Dodge City, where famous lawmen Bat Masterson and Wyatt Earp tried, sometimes successfully, to keep law and order, had a notorious reputation during the 1870s and 1880s. The long-running TV series *Gunsmoke* (1955–75) spurred tourism and big crowds have got the heck *into* Dodge ever since. Geared toward families, historical authenticity here plays a distant second fiddle to fun and frolic.

Tours (adult/child $7/5; ⌚tours 9:30am, 10:45am, 1:30pm & 3pm summer) on fake trolleys start at the **visitor center** (☎800-653-9378; www.visitdodgecity.org; 400 W Wyatt Earp Blvd; ⌚8am-6:30pm summer, 8:30am-5pm Mon-Fri Sep-Apr). Expect to hear a lot of well-spun apocryphal yarns. Self-guided audio tours and free maps let you visit on your own schedule.

The studio-backlot-like **Boot Hill Museum** (www.boothill.org; adult/child summer $8/7.50, rest of year $10/8; ⌚8am-8pm summer, 9am-5pm Sep-Apr; 👪) includes a cemetery, jail and saloon, where gunslingers reenact high-noon shootouts while Miss Kitty and her dancing gals do the cancan.

Escape the schmaltz and view surviving **Santa Fe Trail wagon-wheel ruts** about 9 miles west of town on US 50. The site is well marked.

Chain and indie motels line Business US 50, aka Wyatt Earp Blvd.

OKLAHOMA

Oklahoma gets its name from the Choctaw name for 'Red People.' One look at the state's vividly red earth and you'll wonder if the name is more of a sartorial than an ethnic comment. Still, with 39 tribes located here, it is a place with deep Native American significance. Museums, cultural displays and more abound.

The other side of the Old West coin, cowboys, also figure prominently in the Sooner State. Although pickups have replaced horses, there's still a great sense of the open range, interrupted only by urban Oklahoma City and Tulsa. Oklahoma's share of Route 66 (see p647) links some of the Mother Road's iconic highlights and there are myriad atmospheric old towns. And just when it seems the vistas go on forever, mountains in the south and far west add texture.

OKLAHOMA FACTS

» **Nickname** Sooner State

» **Population** 3.65 million

» **Area** 69,900 sq miles

» **Capital city** Oklahoma City (population 580,000)

» **Other cities** Tulsa (population 392,000)

» **Sales tax** 4.5%

» **Birthplace of** humorist Will Rogers (1879–1935), athlete Jim Thorpe (1888–1953), folk musician Woody Guthrie (1912–67), parking meters (invented 1935), actor Brad Pitt (b 1963)

» **Home of** the band The Flaming Lips

» **Politics** deeply conservative

» **Famous for** 1930s dust bowl, Carrie Underwood

» **Official state meal** okra, chicken fried steak and 10 more dishes

» **Driving distances** Oklahoma City to Tulsa 104 miles, Kansas to Texas following historic Route 66 426 miles

ℹ Information

Oklahoma Bed & Breakfast Association (☎866-676-5522; www.okbba.com)

Oklahoma Department of Tourism (www.travelok.com)

Oklahoma state parks (www.touroklahoma.com) Most parks are free for day-use; campsites cost $12 to $28 per night, some are reservable.

Oklahoma City

Often abbreviated to OKC, Oklahoma City is nearly dead-center in the state and is the cultural and political capital. It has worked hard over the years to become more than just a cow town, all without turning its back on its cowboy heritage. It makes a good pause on your Route 66 travels and has numerous attractions plus good restaurants that offer more than just chicken fried steak.

The city is forever linked to the 1995 bombing of the Alfred P Murrah Federal Building and the memorials to this tragedy are moving and worthy stops.

Sights

You'll brush up against real cowboys in **Stockyards City** (www.stockyardscity.org; Agnew Ave & Exchange Ave), southwest of downtown, either in the shops and restaurants that cater to them or at the **Oklahoma National Stockyards** (auctions 9am Mon-Tue), the world's largest stocker and feeder cattle market.

TOP CHOICE **Oklahoma City National Memorial Museum** MEMORIAL, MUSEUM
(www.oklahomacitynationalmemorial.org; 620 N Harvey Ave; adult/student $10/8; 9am-6pm Mon-Sat, noon-6pm Sun) The story of America's worst incident of domestic terrorism is told at this poignant museum, which avoids becoming mawkish and lets the horrible events speak for themselves. The outdoor **Symbolic Memorial** (N Harvey Ave; admission free; 24hr) has 168 empty chair sculptures for each of the people killed in the attack (the 19 small ones are for the children who perished in the day-care center).

National Cowboy & Western Heritage Museum MUSEUM
(www.nationalcowboymuseum.org; 1700 NE 63rd St; adult/child $12.50/6; 10am-5pm) Only the smells are missing here, with both art and history covered. Even if you come for just one, you're sure to be enthralled by the other. The excellent collection of Western painting and sculpture features many works by Charles M Russell and Frederic Remington, while the historical galleries range from barbed wire to rodeos to cowboy hats.

Oklahoma History Center MUSEUM
(www.okhistorycenter.org; 2401 N Laird Ave; adult/child $5/3; 10am-5pm Mon-Sat) Makes people the focus as it tells the story of the Sooner State.

State Capitol LANDMARK
(2300 N Lincoln Blvd; 7am-7pm Mon-Fri, 9am-4pm Sat & Sun) Built in 1917, but only got its dome in 2002.

American Indian Cultural Center & Museum MUSEUM
(www.aiccm.org; Junction I-40 & I-35) When it's complete, this landmark center with its arresting design will be one of the top Native American institutions in the world. In the meantime, its construction proceeds with fits and starts while its budget is mired in state politics.

Festivals & Events

State Fair Park (www.okstatefairpark.com; I-44 & NW 10th St) hosts frequent horse- or rodeo-related events. (The state fair itself is a dud.)

Red Earth Native American Cultural Festival CULTURAL
(www.redearth.org) Native Americans come from across the nation to celebrate and compete in early June.

Sleeping

Many older motels line I-35 south of town; newer chain properties stack up along I-44 and the NW Expwy/Hwy 3. Staying near Bricktown puts you near nightlife action.

Grandison Inn at Maney Park B&B $$
(405-232-8778; www.grandisoninn.com; 1200 N Shartel St; r $140-190; P) In a genteel quarter of OKC just NW of downtown, this gracious 1904-vintage B&B welcomes guests to eight rooms with period charm and modern amenities such as DVD players. The house has amazing woodwork, including a show-stopping staircase.

Colcord Hotel HOTEL $$$
(405-601-4300; www.colcordhotel.com; 15 N Robinson Ave; r $170-350; P@) OKC's first skyscraper, built in 1910, is now a 12-story boutique hotel. Many original flourishes, like the marble-clad lobby, survive, while the 108 rooms have a stylish, contemporary touch. This luxurious hotel is walking distance to Bricktown.

Hampton Inn & Suites Bricktown HOTEL $$
(405-232-3600; www.hampton/hilton.com; 300 E Sheridan Ave; r $100-180; P) This brick-clad 200-room hotel in Bricktown is across from the ballpark. Built in a traditional style, the rooms are very comfortable and modern.

Eating

Bunches of eateries cluster in Bricktown, line Western Ave between 41st and 82nd Sts, and anchor the Asian district (around 23rd St and Classen Blvd) with reasonable Vietnamese, Chinese and Thai noodle houses.

TOP CHOICE **Cattlemen's Steakhouse** STEAKHOUSE $$$
(www.cattlemensrestaurant.com; 1309 S Agnew Ave, Stockyards City; breakfasts $4-7, lunches $4-25, dinners $10-25; 6am-10pm Sun-Thu, 6am-midnight

ROUTE 66: GET YOUR KICKS IN OKLAHOMA

Oklahoma's connection with America's Main Street runs deep: the road's chief proponent, Cyrus Avery, was a Sooner; John Steinbeck's *Grapes of Wrath* told of the plight of Depression-era Okie farmers fleeing west on Route 66; and Oklahoma has more miles of the original alignment than any other state. The **Oklahoma Route 66 Association** (www.oklahomaroute66.com) puts out an excellent booklet that you can pick up from most visitor centers along the road. It's vital because so many of the brown-and-white Historic Route 66 signs have been stolen for souvenirs and the original road goes by a variety of monikers, including OK 66, US 69, US 270 etc.

Shortly after you enter the state from Kansas on US 69A you'll come to **Miami**. Continue south through town on Main St and 2.5 miles after crossing the Neosho River turn right at the T-intersection. This will take you to the first of two original and very rough 9ft-wide alignments. The second, E 140 Rd (turn west) comes soon after the first, just before I-44.

You'll cross I-44 twice before rolling into **Vinita**. **Clanton's** (319 E Illinois Ave; mains $4-10; ⌚5:30am-8pm Mon-Fri, to 2pm Sat & Sun) dates back to 1927 and is the place for chicken fried steak and calf fries (don't ask).

Thirty miles further on, **Foyil** is worth a 4-mile detour on Hwy 28A to the massive and colorful concrete sculptures of **Totem Pole Park** (www.rchs1.org; admission free; ⌚24/7).

Another 10 miles brings you to **Claremore** (p650), former home of Will Rogers.

Next up at the port city of **Catoosa**, just before Tulsa, is one of the most photographed Route 66 landmarks, the 80ft-long **Blue Whale** (2680 N Hwy 66).

East 11th St takes you into and right through art deco-rich **Tulsa**; be sure to look for the iconic neon wonder of the restored **Meadow Gold sign** at S Quaker Ave. Southwest Blvd takes you across the river and out of town.

The rural route from Tulsa to Oklahoma City is one of the longest continuous stretches of Mother Road remaining (110 miles), a fine alternative to the I-44 tollway. At **Chandler**,

Fri & Sat) OKC's most storied restaurant, this Stockyards City institution has been feeding cowpokes and city slickers slabs of beef and lamb's fries (that's a polite way of saying gonads) since 1910. Deals are still cut at the counter (where you can jump the wait for tables) and back in the luxe booths.

Picasso's Cafe AMERICAN **$$**
(www.picassosonpaseo.com; 3009 Paseo; mains $10-20; ⌚11am-late) A hip fusion of bistro, bar and venue, Picasso has a full bar and is renowned for its Bloody Mary's at noon. It also has an artistic sensibility, with works by local artists on display. Live music leans to acoustic, while the food is fresh and inventive. Grab a table outside.

Ann's Chicken Fry House SOUTHERN **$$**
(4106 NW 39th St; mains $4-12; ⌚11am-8:30pm Tue-Sat) Part real diner, part tourist attraction, Ann's is a Route 66 veteran renowned for its – you guessed it – chicken fried steak. Okra and cream gravy also star. The fried chicken also lives up to the rep. Get the black-eyed peas.

Classen Grill TEX-MEX **$**
(5124 Classen Circle; mains $5-9; ⌚6am-3pm) A classic Tex-Mex diner that serves up vast plates of huevos rancheros to the waiting crowds. North-of-the-border fare such as pancakes also get nods but it's the piquant dishes that really shine.

Drinking & Entertainment

For listings, check out the free weekly **Oklahoma Gazette** (www.okgazette.com) or just head to the renovated warehouses in the **Bricktown District**, which contain a vast array of bars, some good, some purely chain. To make a complete night of it in the district, watch the Triple A Redhawks play at **Bricktown Ballpark** (www.oklahomaredhawks.com; 2 Mickey Mantle Dr).

The heart of gay Oklahoma is the **39th Street Strip** (west of Pennsylvania Ave).

Bricktown Brewery PUB
(www.bricktownbrewery.com; 1 N Oklahoma Ave; ⌚11am-1am) A large microbrewery in Bricktown, with revelers splayed out across large rooms enjoying pool, darts and just being spectators. Always hopping and has a decent food menu.

Red Rooster BAR
(3100 N Walker Ave, Paseo; mains $6-8; ⌚11am-late) They've been pouring pitchers of beer

60 miles southwest of Tulsa, the **Route 66 Interpretive Center** (www.route66interpretivecenter.org; 400 E Rte 66; adult/child $5/4; ⏲10am-5pm Tue-Sat, 1-5pm Sun) re-creates the experience of driving the road through the decades. It's housed in a magnificent 1936 armory.

Route 66 follows US 77 into **Oklahoma City** and beyond that, it's unmarked. Take Kelley Ave south, head over to Lincoln Blvd at 50th St and turn west on NW 23rd St at the capitol. You'll leave OKC by turning north on May Ave and west on NW 39th St past **Ann's Chicken Fry House**. Beyond this, the route follows Business I-40.

El Reno, 20 miles west of OKC, is home to the fried onion burger (average $3), a road-food classic. Among several historic drive-ins and dives, try **Johnnie's Grill** (301 S Rock Island) or **Sid's** (300 S Choctaw). Ground beef is combined with raw onions and then cooked and caramelized on the grill. Both are open 10am to 8pm (Sid's has outdoor tables, Johnnie's the bigger dining area).

Some 17 miles west of El Reno, take a stretch of US 281 that runs on the north side of I-40 between exits 108 and 101. Where it crosses the Canadian River on the 38-truss-long **Pony Bridge**, stop at the west end. Here's the spot they had to ditch gramps in the 1939 movie version of the *Grapes of Wrath.*

In **Clinton**, walk through six decades of history, memorabilia and music at the mid-sized **Route 66 Museum** (www.route66.org; 2229 W Gary Blvd; adult/child $4/1; ⏲9am-7pm Mon-Sat, 1-6pm Sun summer, reduced hr rest of year).

Thirty miles further west in **Elk City**, the **National Route 66 Museum** (adult/child $5/4; ⏲9am-7pm Mon-Sat, 1-5pm Sun summer, reduced hr rest of year) has the usual old cars, photos and is part of a re-created pioneer town and a farm museum.

Route 66 spills into Texas at **Texola**, which is just a dust devil away from being a ghost town.

at this neighborhood institution since 1939. Boy are their arms tired! Shoot some pool, try not to fall off the stool, meet the best collection of characters in OKC and have one of their famous cheeseburgers.

Shopping

The **Paseo Arts District** isn't much more than Paseo Dr itself, but there are several art galleries and boutiques in the Spanish colonial buildings. You can buy all forms of Western wear and gear in **Stockyards City**, which is the real deal for cowboys. Start at **Langston's** (2224 Exchange Ave), which has a vast selection.

Full Circle Bookstore BOOKS
(50 Penn Pl Mall, 1900 NW Expwy; ⏲10am-9pm Mon-Thu, 10am-10pm Fri & Sat, noon-5pm Sun;) A superb independent bookstore that stocks many Route 66 books and has a cafe.

Information

Oklahoma City Visitors Center (☎800-225-5652; www.visitokc.com; 123 Park Ave; ⏲8:30am-5pm Mon-Fri)

Oklahoma Welcome Center (☎405-478-4637; www.travelok.com; I-35 exit 137; ⏲8:30am-5pm) Has city info too.

Getting There & Around

Will Rogers World Airport (OKC; www.flyokc.com) is 5 miles southwest of downtown; a cab costs about $20 to downtown.

Amtrak (www.amtrak.com; 100 S EK Gaylord Blvd) The *Heartland Flyer* goes from OKC to Fort Worth ($35, 4¼ hours). Buy your ticket on the train.

Go Metro (www.gometro.org; fare $1.50) Runs city buses.

Greyhound (Union Bus Station, 427 W Sheridan Ave) Daily buses to Dallas ($40, five hours), Wichita ($30, 2¾ hours) and Tulsa ($23, two hours, five daily), among other destinations.

Yellow Cab (☎405-232-6161)

Western Oklahoma

West of Oklahoma City toward Texas the land opens into expansive prairie fields; nowhere as beautifully as in the Wichita Mountains, which, along with some Route 66 attractions and Native American sites, make this prime road-trip country.

Sixty miles southwest of OKC, **Anadarko** and the surrounding area are home to 64 Native American tribes. The town hosts powwows and other events almost monthly. Going north from town, US 281 runs through a beautiful area of multihued sandstone canyons and bluffs.

Tulsa

Self-billed as the 'Oil Capital of the World,' Tulsa has never dirtied its hands much on the black gold that oozes out elsewhere in the state. Rather, it is the home to scores of energy companies that make their living drilling for oil, selling it or supplying those who do. The steady wealth this provides once helped create Tulsa's richly detailed art-deco downtown. But today Tulsa (population 392,000) is not the most charming Great Plains town: suburban sprawl has dispersed its appeal and much life seems to center on the malls and chains gathered at highway interchanges.

Sights & Activities

Downtown Tulsa has so much art-deco architecture it was once known as the 'Terra-Cotta City.' The **Philcade Building** (511 S Boston), with its glorious T-shaped lobby, and **Boston Avenue United Methodist Church** (1301 S Boston; ⏲8:30am-5pm Mon-Fri, 8am-5pm Sun, guided tour noon Sun), rising at the end of downtown, are two exceptional examples. A free walking guide from the visitor center will lead you to dozens more.

TOP CHOICE **Oklahoma Jazz Hall of Fame** MUSEUM
(www.okjazz.org; 111 E 1st St; admission free; ⏲9am-5pm Mon-Fri, 4-7:30pm Sun) Tulsa's beautiful Union Station is filled with sound again, but now it's melodious as opposed to cacophonous. During the first half of the 20th century, Tulsa was at literally at the crossroads of American music with performers both homegrown and from afar. Learn about greats like Charlie Christian, Ernie Fields, Sr and Wallace Willis in detailed exhibits. For most of the year there are Sunday concerts – often featuring inductees and played in the once-segregated grand concourse at 4pm.

Gilcrease Museum MUSEUM
(www.gilcrease.org; 1400 Gilcrease Museum Rd; adult/child $8/free; ⏲10am-5pm Tue-Sun) Northwest of downtown, off Hwy 64, this superb American art museum sits on the manicured estate of a Native American who discovered oil on his allotment.

Philbrook Museum of Art MUSEUM
(www.philbrook.org; 2727 S Rockford Rd, east of Peoria Ave; adult/child $7.50/free; ⏲10am-5pm Tue-Sun, to 8pm Thu) South of town, another oil magnate's converted Italianate villa, also ringed by fabulous foliage, houses some fine Native American works.

FREE **Prayer Tower** LANDMARK
(7777 S Lewis Ave; ⏲2-5pm Mon-Fri) With a 200ft UFO-like tower at its heart, the campus of Oral Roberts University is as idiosyncratic as its late televangelist founder.

Sleeping

Chain motels aplenty line Hwy 244 and I-44, especially at the latter's exits 229 and 232.

Inn at Woodward Park B&B $$
(☎918-712-9770; www.innatwoodwardpark.com; 1521 E 21st St; r $100-140; P ❄ ☎) In a historic neighborhood south of the center, this elegant 1920s B&B has three themed rooms surrounded by lavish gardens. Rooms have DVD players and queen-size beds. The Philbrook Museum of Art is a short walk through a beautiful park.

Hotel Ambassador HOTEL $$$
(☎918-587-8200; www.hotelambassador-tulsa.com; 1324 S Main St; r from $200-300; P ❄ @ ☎) Look in the hallway for the photos of this 1929 nine-story hotel before its opulent renovation. Public spaces are suitably grand; the 55 rooms have a contemporary feel that helps the somewhat close quarters seem a tad larger. All nine stories are close to the center.

LEGACY OF A RIOT

On Memorial Day, May 30, 1921 an African American man and a white woman were alone on an elevator in downtown Tulsa and she screamed. The how and why have never been answered but it sparked three days of race riots in which 35 blocks of Tulsa's main African American neighborhood were destroyed by roving gangs and even by bombs lobbed from the airplanes. Thousands were left homeless, hundreds injured and scores killed.

OKLAHOMA: DETOURS & EXTRAS

Following Route 66 through Oklahoma can seem like one long detour and can offer days of exploration. But there are many more options in various corners of the state.

Brick-and-stone Victorian buildings line street after street of **Guthrie**, Oklahoma's first capital, 25 miles north of Oklahoma City. The well-preserved downtown contains shops, museums, B&Bs and eateries.

Washita Battlefield National Historic Site (www.nps.gov/waba; Hwy 47A, 2 miles west of Cheyenne; admission free; ⌚sunrise-sunset) is where George Custer's troops launched an 1868 attack on the peaceful village of Chief Black Kettle. The **visitor center** (admission free; ⌚8am-5pm) also contains a good museum. There's a self-guiding trail or you can opt to take a free ranger-led tour. It is located 25 miles north of Route 66/I-40.

The **Pioneer Woman Museum** (www.pioneerwomanmuseum.com; Ponca City; adult/child $3/2; ⌚10am-5pm Tue-Sat) honors the people who did the real work in the Old West, while the men hung around towns waiting for shoot-outs or getting liquored up in saloons. At least that's how it seems in the movies. It's 15 miles east of I-35 in northern Oklahoma.

Eating & Drinking

Look for dining options in the Brookside neighborhood, on Peoria Ave between 31st and 51st Sts; on Historic Cherry St (now 15th St) just east of Peoria Ave; and the artsy Brady District, centered on Brady and Main Sts immediately north of downtown.

Elmer's BBQ $
(www.elmersbbq.com; 4130 S Peoria St; mains $5-10; ⌚11am-8pm Tue-Sat) A legendary barbecue joint where the star of the menu is the potentially deadly 'Badwich,' a bun-crushing combo of superbly smoked sausages, ham, beef, pork and more. The dining room is bright and newly tiled. The meat may inspire you to play the house piano.

Coney I-Lander AMERICAN $
(5219 E 41st St; meals $4-6; ⌚10am-9pm) On Tulsa's close-in Southroads area on the east side you'll find a string of iconic old local fast-food places serving brilliant burgers and more. This small chain is especially beloved for its Coney Island hot dogs, which are laden with rich chili. Even better are the Frito pies, which take the namesake and bury it under chili, cheese and onions. Addictive.

Ri Le's VIETNAMESE $$
(4932 E 91st St; mains $5-12; ⌚noon-9pm) Tulsa has a vibrant Vietnamese community that dates back to the 1970s. Among the many fine eateries is this absolute gem. The namesake owner wanders the tables ensuring diners are having a pho-tastic time.

Entertainment

The **Urban Tulsa Weekly** (www.urbantulsa.com) has the scoop of what's going on.

TOP CHOICE **Cain's Ballroom** LIVE MUSIC
(www.cainsballroom.com; 423 N Main St) Rising rockers grace the boards where Bob Wills played Western swing in the '30s and the Sex Pistols caused confusion in 1978 (check the wall Sid Vicious punched a hole in).

Discoveryland! THEATER
(www.discoverylandusa.com; 19501 W 41st St, Sand Springs; adult/child $20/free; ⌚7pm Mon-Sat summer) Whether you're a boy or a girl you just can't say no to this high-energy outdoor production of *Oklahoma!* A Western musical revue and Native American dancers kick things off. It's 10 miles west of Tulsa.

Information

Tulsa Visitor Center (☎800-558-3311; www.visittulsa.com; William Center Towers II, 2 W 2nd St; ⌚8am-5pm Mon-Fri) With its pleading slogan 'please stay' it will help you find the city's elusive charms.

Getting There & Around

Tulsa International Airport (TUL; www.tulsaairports.com) is situated off Hwy 11 northeast of downtown.

Greyhound (317 S Detroit Ave) Buses include Oklahoma City ($23, two hours, five daily) and St Louis ($80, eight hours).

Tulsa Transit (www.tulsatransit.org; one-day pass $3.25) Buses originate downtown at 319 S Denver Ave.

Green Country

Subtle forested hills interspersed with iconic red dirt and lakes cover Oklahoma's northeast corner, aka **Green Country** (www.greencountryok.com), which includes Tulsa. The area has a strong Native American influence, as it is where several of the Five Civilized Tribes (Cherokee, Chickasaw, Choctaw, Creek and Seminole) were relocated in the 1820s and '30s.

BARTLESVILLE

Oklahoma's first commercial oil well was dug in Bartlesville, 50 miles north of Tulsa, and soon after in 1905 Frank Phillips, of Phillips 66 fame, arrived to dig more. You can relive these rough-and-tumble days at the slick-as-a-lube-job **Phillips Petroleum Company Museum** (www.phillips66museum.com; 410 S Keeler Ave; admission free; ⌚10am-4pm Mon-Sat) right in town.

Phillips' vast county estate, **Woolaroc** (www.woolaroc.org; Rte 123, 12 miles southwest of town; adult/child $8/free; ⌚10am-5pm Wed-Sun, open Tue summer), is now an excellent museum of southwestern art and culture, and a wildlife refuge with buffalo.

You can tour the only Frank Lloyd Wright–designed skyscraper ever built, the 1956, 221ft **Price Tower Arts Center** (www.pricetower.org; 510 Dewey Ave; adult/child $6/free, tours $12/10; ⌚10am-5pm Tue-Sat, noon-5pm Sun). Inside and out it is like *Architectural Digest* meets the *Jetsons*. Wright shopped the design around for 30 years before he found clients willing to build it here.

You can stay in one of 19 Wright-inspired rooms in the **Inn at Price Tower** (☎918-336-1000; r from $145; ❄). The 15th-floor bar, Cooper, has sweeping views of the prairie.

CLAREMORE

This was the setting for the 1931 play *Green Grow the Lilacs,* which became the hugely popular musical *Oklahoma!,* which chronicles *highly* fictionalized events in 1906.

Born in a log cabin just north of town in 1879, Will Rogers was a cowboy, a hilarious homespun philosopher, star of radio and movies, and part Cherokee. The hilltop **Will Rogers Memorial Museum** (www.willrogers.com; 1720 W Will Rogers Blvd; admission free; ⌚8am-5pm), 30 miles northeast of Tulsa off Route 66, is an entertaining tribute to a man good for quotes such as 'An ignorant person is one who doesn't know what you have just found out.'

TRAIL OF TEARS COUNTRY

The area southeast of present-day Tulsa was, and to some degree still is, Creek and Cherokee land. This is an excellent place to learn about Native American culture, especially before the 1800s.

Namesake of Merle Haggard's 1969 hit 'Okie from Muskogee?', **Muskogee** ('where even squares can have a ball') is 49 miles southeast of Tulsa, and is home to the **Five Civilized Tribes Museum** (www.fivetribes.org; Agency Hill, Honor Heights Dr; adult/student $4/2; ⌚10am-5pm Mon-Sat, 1-5pm Sun) inside an 1875 Union Indian Agency house. It recalls the cultures of the Native Americans forcibly moved here from America's southeast.

Twenty miles east on Hwy 62 is **Tahlequah** (tal-*ah*-quaw), the Cherokee capital since 1839. The excellent **Cherokee Heritage Center** (www.cherokeeheritage.org; 21192 Keeler Rd, Park Hill; adult/child $8.50/5; ⌚10am-5pm Mon-Sat, 1-5pm Sun, closed Jan) features Native American–led tours through a re-creation of a pre-European contact woodland village. The museum focuses on the Trail of Tears.

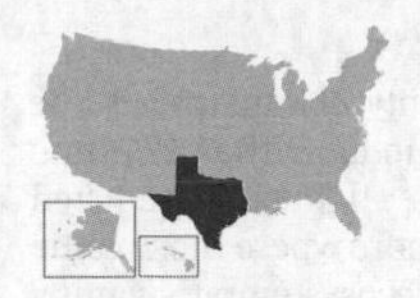

Texas

Includes »

South-Central Texas.....653
Austin.........................656
San Antonio.................666
Houston........................672
Southern Gulf Coast....680
Dallas-Fort Worth.........682
Dallas...........................682
Fort Worth....................689
West Texas....................694
Big Bend National Park................694
Central West Texas.......697
El Paso..........................699

Why Go?

Cue the theme music, and make it something epic: Texas is as big and sweeping a state as can be imagined. If it were a country, it would be the 40th largest. And as big as it is geographically, it is equally large in people's imaginations.

Cattle ranches, pick-up trucks, cowboy boots and thick Texas drawls – all of those are part of the culture, to be sure. But an Old West theme park it is not. With a state this big, there's room for Texas to be whatever you want it to be.

You can find beaches, theme parks, citified shopping and nightlife, historical monuments and a vibrant music scene. And the nearly year-round warm weather makes it ideal for outdoor activities like rock climbing, cycling, hiking and rowing. So saddle up for whatever adventure suits you best: the Lone Star state is ready to ride.

Best Places to Eat

» Hotel Limpia Dining Room (p697)

» Food Shark (p698)

» Güero's Taco Bar (p660)

» Love Shack (p692)

» Bread Winners (p686)

Best Places to Stay

» Gage Hotel (p699)

» Hotel San José (p657)

» Hotel Belmont (p685)

» Hotel ZaZa (p674)

» Stockyards Hotel (p691)

When to Go

Austin

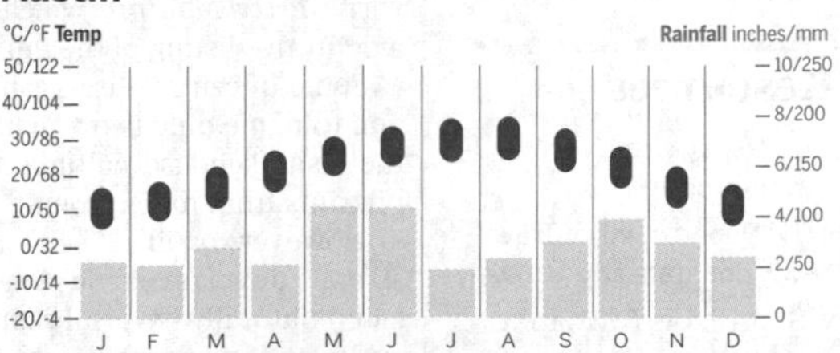

Mar Warm weather during spring break attracts college students and families with kids.

Apr-May Wildflowers line the roadsides, festivals are in full swing and summer is yet to swelter.

Oct The crowds have thinned, the heat has broken, but it's still warm enough for shorts.

DID YOU KNOW?

Texas is unique in the USA as the only state that was once its own republic (1836–45). It still sometimes threatens to secede.

Fast Facts

» Hub cities: Dallas (population 1.3 million), Houston, (population 2.3 million)

» Dallas to Houston: 242 miles

» Austin to San Antonio: 78 miles

» Time zone: Central, except El Paso, which is Mountain

Best Small Towns

» Marfa (p698) boasts minimalist art and mystery lights.

» Fredericksburg (p665) is lovely during wildflower season.

» Terlingua (p695) is a pretty happening ghost town.

» Under-the-radar Denton (p688) rocks.

» Find Texas' oldest dance hall in Gruene (p664).

Resources

» Texas Tourism (www.traveltex.com)

» TX Department of Travel (www.dot.state.tx.us/travel)

» State Parks (www.tpwd.state.tx.us)

Texas Parks

In a state as big as Texas, there's plenty of exploring to be done, and the wide, open spaces pack in more than 125 state parks, historic sites and natural areas. Highlights are listed in this chapter, but there's are plenty more where those came from. You could seek out the unique ecosystem at swampy Caddo Lake, watch bats fly out of the Devil's Sinkhole, or descend into a 120-mile-long chasm at Palo Duro Canyon, just to name a few. Some parks are remote and rustic; others are downright fancy. Create your own adventure using the free guide from **Texas Parks & Wildlife** (☎800-792-1112, central reservations 512-389-8900; www.tpwd.state.tx.us), available both in print and online.

GETTING AROUND

Texas is big, but it's easy to get around. The best way to travel is to rent a car or bring your own. Flying is another good option if time is short, especially with cut-rate carrier **Southwest Airlines** (☎800-435-9792; www.iflyswa.com), where short hops within Texas can cost as little as $49 one way if you book ahead.

There's also limited train service within Texas. Amtrak's Sunset Limited (Florida–California) passes through Houston, San Antonio and El Paso, and the Texas Eagle (San Antonio–Chicago) stops in Dallas-Fort Worth and Austin. Note that trains often have late-night arrivals or departures in Texas.

Greyhound and its partner **Kerrville Bus Lines** (☎800-231-2222; www.iridekbc.com) serve all but the tiniest towns, though it may take several transfers and twice as long as by car.

Barbecue Etiquette

Make no bones about it: Texas barbecue is an obsession. It's the subject of countless newspaper and magazine articles, from national press like the *New York Times* to regional favorite *Texas Monthly*, which publishes what many consider a definitive listing of the top barbecue joints in Texas.

Some of central Texas' smaller towns – Lockhart and Elgin, to name only two – maintain perennial reputations for their smokehouse cultures and routinely draw dedicated pilgrims from miles around.

However you like it best – sliced thick onto butcher paper, slapped down on picnic plates, doused with a tangy sauce or eaten naturally flavorful right out of the smokehouse barbecue pit – be sure to savor it, and then argue to the death that your way is the best way. Like a true Texan.

History

Texas hasn't always been Texas. Or Mexico, for that matter. Or the United States, or Spain, or France…or any of the six flags that once flew over this epic state in its eight changes of sovereignty.

Given that the conquerors' diseases wiped out much of the indigenous population, it seems a bit ironic that the Spaniards named the territory Tejas (*tay*-has) – a corruption of the Caddo word for 'friend.' Caddo, Apache and Karankawa were among the tribes that Spanish explorers encountered when they arrived to map the Gulf Coast in 1519.

Spain's rule of the territory continued until Mexico won its independence in 1821. That same year, Mexican general Antonio López de Santa Anna eliminated the state federation system, outlawed slavery and curtailed immigration. None of this sat well with independent-minded 'Texians' (US- and Mexico-born Texans) who had been given cheap land grants and Mexican citizenship. Clashes escalated into the Texas War for Independence (1835–36). A month after Santa Anna's forces massacred survivors of the siege in San Antonio, Sam Houston's rebels routed the Mexican troops at San Jacinto with the cry 'Remember the Alamo!'. And thus the Republic of Texas was born. The nation's short life ended nine years later when, by treaty, Texas opted to become the 28th state of the Union.

The last battle of the Civil War (Texas was on the Confederate side) was reputedly fought near Brownsville in May of 1865 – one month after the war had ended. Cattle-ranching formed the core of Texas' postwar economy, but it was the black gold that spewed up from Spindletop in 1910 that really changed everything. From then on, for better or worse, the state's economy has run on oil.

Local Culture

Trying to typify Texas culture is like tryin' to wrestle a pig in mud – it's awful slippery. In vast generalization, Austin is alternative Texas, where environmental integrity and quality of life are avidly discussed. Dallasites are the shoppers and society trendsetters; more is spent on silicone implants there than anywhere else in the US besides LA. In conservative, casual Houston, oil-and-gas industrialists dine at clubby steakhouses. And San Antonio is the most Tex-Mexican of the bunch – a showplace of Hispanic culture.

TEXAS FACTS

» **Nickname** Lone Star State

» **Population** 25.1 million

» **Area** 261,797 sq miles

» **Other cities** Houston (population 2,257,926), San Antonio (population 1,373,668), Dallas (population 1,299,542), El Paso (population 620,456)

» **Capital city** Austin (population 786,386)

» **Sales tax** 6.25%

» **Birthplace of** singer Buddy Holly (1936–59), entrepreneur Howard Hughes (1905–76), rocker Janis Joplin (1943–70), country singer George Strait (b 1952), actor Matthew McConaughey (b 1969)

» **Home of** Dr Pepper, corn dogs and two Presidents Bush

» **Politics** mostly leans Republican (but don't tell the Austinites)

» **Famous for** real cowboys and the football-playing Cowboys, great BBQ

» **Best souvenir** 'Don't mess with Texas' toilet paper

» **Driving distances** Fort Stockton to El Paso 240 miles, Houston to Dallas 240 miles, Abilene to El Paso 450 miles

SOUTH-CENTRAL TEXAS

So what if the hills are more mole-size than mountainous; they – and the rivers that flow through them – still define south-central Texas. To the north is the state capital of Austin, where music, music and more music are on the schedule, day or night. Eighty miles south, the major metropolitan center of San Antonio is home to the Alamo and the festive Riverwalk bars and restaurants. Between and to the west of the two towns is the Hill Country. Here you can eat great BBQ, dance across an old wooden floor or spend a lazy day floating on the river in small Texas-y towns that show the influence of early German and Czech settlers. If you want to get to the heart of Texas in a short time, south-central Texas is the way to go.

Texas Highlights

1 Scoot across a well-worn wooden floor at Texas' oldest dance hall in **Gruene** (p664).

2 Remember **The Alamo** (p667), a historical shrine to the men who fought for Texas independence.

3 State capital **Austin** (p656) beguiles with loads of live music and funky food trucks galore.

4 Ponder JFK conspiracy theories at the one-of-a-kind **Sixth Floor Museum** (p683).

5 Immerse yourself in cowboy culture at the **Stockyards Historic District** (p689).

6 Discover the rugged natural beauty of **Big Bend National Park** (p694).

7 Get a stellar view of the night sky at the **McDonald Observatory** (p697) star party.

8 Find the perfect pair of cowboy boots (or have them custom-made) in **El Paso** (p699).

9 Peeking at postmodern art is fascinating (and free!) at Houston's **Menil Collection** (p672).

10 Wander the shady trails through fragrant piney woods at **Big Thicket National Preserve** (p680).

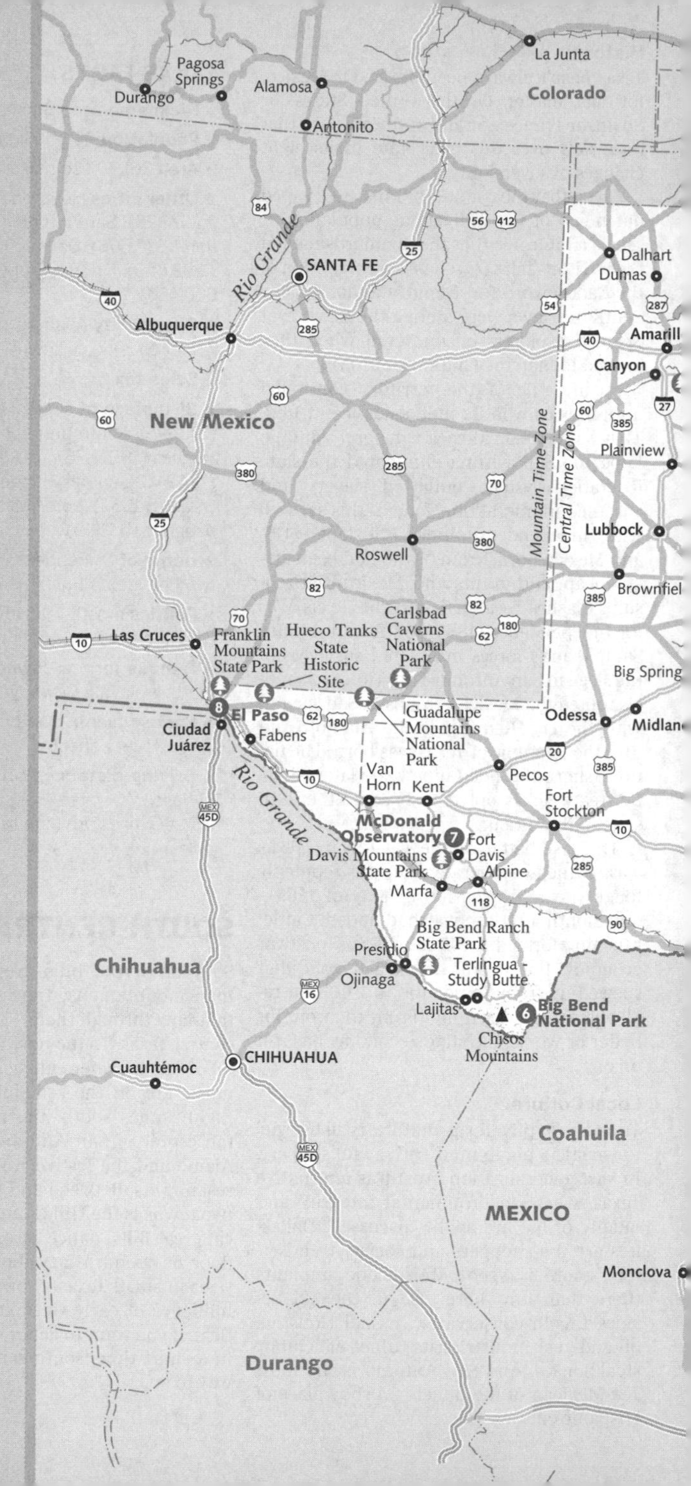

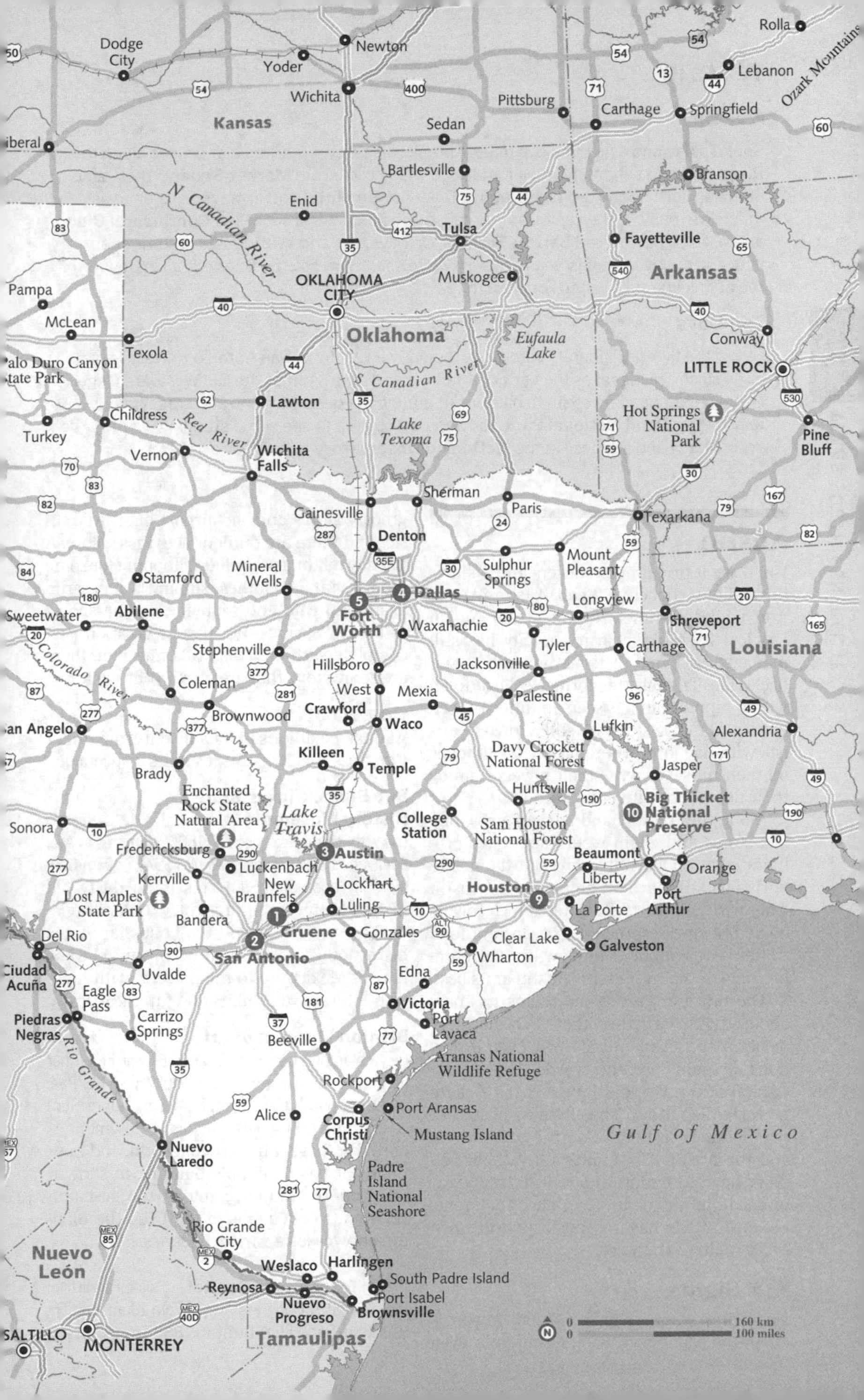
Dodge City
Newton
Yoder
Wichita
Kansas
Pittsburg
Carthage
Springfield
Rolla
Lebanon
Ozark Mountains
Sedan
Liberal
Bartlesville
Branson
N Canadian River
Enid
Tulsa
Fayetteville
Arkansas
Muskogee
OKLAHOMA CITY
Oklahoma
Pampa
McLean
Texola
Eufaula Lake
Conway
LITTLE ROCK
Palo Duro Canyon State Park
S Canadian River
Lawton
Childress
Red River
Turkey
Vernon
Wichita Falls
Lake Texoma
Hot Springs National Park
Pine Bluff
Sherman
Paris
Gainesville
Texarkana
Denton
Mineral Wells
Stamford
Sulphur Springs
Mount Pleasant
Dallas
Fort Worth
Abilene
Sweetwater
Longview
Shreveport
Waxahachie
Tyler
Carthage
Louisiana
Stephenville
Colorado River
Hillsboro
Jacksonville
Coleman
West
Mexia
Palestine
Brownwood
Crawford
Waco
San Angelo
Lufkin
Alexandria
Killeen
Temple
Davy Crockett National Forest
Jasper
Brady
Enchanted Rock State Natural Area
Lake Travis
Huntsville
Big Thicket National Preserve
College Station
Sam Houston National Forest
Sonora
Fredericksburg
Austin
Luckenbach
Beaumont
Orange
Kerrville
New Braunfels
Lockhart
Houston
Liberty
Port Arthur
Lost Maples State Park
Luling
La Porte
Bandera
Gruene
Gonzales
Clear Lake
Galveston
Del Rio
San Antonio
Wharton
Ciudad Acuña
Uvalde
Eagle Pass
Edna
Victoria
Piedras Negras
Carrizo Springs
Port Lavaca
Beeville
Rio Grande
Aransas National Wildlife Refuge
Rockport
Alice
Port Aransas
Corpus Christi
Mustang Island
Gulf of Mexico
Nuevo Laredo
Padre Island National Seashore
Rio Grande City
Nuevo León
Weslaco
Harlingen
South Padre Island
Reynosa
Port Isabel
Nuevo Progreso
Brownsville
SALTILLO
MONTERREY
Tamaulipas
0 160 km
0 100 miles
N

TEXAS IN...

Five Days

Spend a day and a night enjoying San Antonio, sipping margaritas in the cafes along the **Riverwalk** and bargain-hunting for Mexico-made trinkets in **Market Square**. Then head 80 miles north: book two nights at the funky **Austin Motel** and arrange to listen to as much live music in the capital as you can, maybe catching a set at the **Continental Club** and taking a dip in frigid **Barton Springs**. On days four and five, indulge in some shopping and dining in **Dallas** before moving on to see the western art and sights in Cowtown, the apt nickname given to **Fort Worth**.

Ten Days

Follow the five-day itinerary in reverse, then drive west from San Antonio to West Texas – or fly since driving takes the better part of a day. Stay a night at the Old West–era **Gage Hotel** before heading south to hike or raft among the deep canyons and craggy mountains of **Big Bend National Park**. You should also stop to see some stunning avant-garde art in **Marfa** and stargaze at the **McDonald Observatory** in Fort Davis.

Austin

You'll see it on bumper stickers and T-shirts throughout the city: 'Keep Austin Weird.' And while old-timers grumble that Austin has lost its funky charm, the city has still managed to hang on to its incredibly laid-back vibe. Though this former college town with a hippie soul has seen an influx of tech types and movie stars, it's still a town of artists with day jobs, where people try to focus on their music or write their novel or annoy their neighbors with crazy yard art.

Along the freeway and in the 'burbs, big-box stores and chain restaurants have proliferated at an alarming rate. But the neighborhoods still have an authentically Austin feel, with all sorts of interesting, locally owned businesses, including a flock of food trailers – a symbol of the low-key entrepreneurialism that represents Austin at its best.

The one thing everyone seems to know about Austin whether they've been there or not is that it's a music town, even if they don't actually use the words 'Live Music Capital of the World' (though that's a claim no one's disputing). The city now hosts two major music festivals, South by Southwest and the Austin City Limits festival, but you don't have to endure the crowds and exorbitant hotel prices to experience the scene, because Austin has live music all over town every night of the week.

Sights

Don't limit yourself to the sights; Austin is about the experience. Bars, restaurants, even grocery stores and the airport have live music. And there are outdoor activities galore. A full day might also include shopping for some groovy vintage clothes, sipping a margarita at a patio cafe and lounging on the shores of Barton Springs. But if your vacation isn't complete without a visit to a museum, there are some stops that are worth your while.

DOWNTOWN

At dusk bazillions of bats fly out from under Congress Ave Bridge – it's quite a spectacle.

Bob Bullock Texas State History Museum MUSEUM
(www.thestoryoftexas.com; 1800 Congress Ave; adult/child $9/6, Texas Spirit film $5/4; ⏲9am-6pm Mon-Sat, noon-6pm Sun) This is no dusty old historical museum. Big, glitzy and still relatively new, it shows off the Lone Star State's history, all the way from when it used to be part of Mexico up to the present, with high-tech interactive exhibits and fun theatrics.

Blanton Museum of Art MUSEUM
(www.blantonmuseum.org; 200 E Martin Luther King Blvd at Congress Ave; adult/child $9/free; ⏲10am-5pm Tue-Fri, 11am-5pm Sat, 1-5pm Sun) A big university with a big endowment is bound to have a big art collection, and now, finally, it has a suitable building to show it off properly. Ranking among the best university art collections in the USA, the Blanton showcases a variety of styles.

FREE **Texas State Capitol** HISTORIC BUILDING
(cnr 11th St & Congress Ave; ⏲7am-10pm Mon-Fri, 9am-8pm Sat & Sun) Built in 1888 from sunset-

red granite, this state capitol is the largest in the US, backing up the ubiquitous claim that everything is bigger in Texas. If nothing else, take a peek at the lovely rotunda and try out the whispering gallery created by its curved ceiling.

Austin Children's Museum MUSEUM
(www.austinkids.org; 201 Colorado St; adult & youth/under 2yr $6.50/4.50; ⏲10am-5pm Tue-Sat, 10am-8pm Wed, noon-5pm Sun) Kids can try their hand at running a ranch, ordering a meal at the Global Diner and hanging upside down beneath a bridge, just like the real Austin bats.

Activities

Barton Springs Pool SWIMMING
(2201 Barton Springs Rd; adult/child $3/2; ⏲9am-10pm Fri-Wed mid-Apr–Sep) Hot? Not for long. Even when the temperature hits 100, you'll be shivering in a jiff after you jump into this icy-cold natural spring pool. Draped with century-old pecan trees, the area around the pool is a social scene in itself, and the place gets packed on a hot summer day.

Lady Bird Lake OUTDOORS
Enjoy it from dry land on the hike-and-bike trail, or get out on the water at the **Rowing Dock** (☎512-459-0999; www.rowingdock.com; 2418 Stratford Dr; ⏲6:30am-8pm), which rents kayaks for $10 to $20 per hour and water cycles for slightly more.

Zilker Park PARK
(www.ci.austin.tx.us/zilker; 2200 Barton Springs Rd) Barton Springs forms the centerpiece of this 351-acre park, which has trails, a nature center and botanical gardens. Rent kayaks at **Zilker Park Boat Rentals** (2100 Barton Springs Rd; www.zilkerboats.com; per hr/day $12/40; ⏲10am-dark daily May-Oct) and paddle from the park out onto Lady Bird Lake.

Bicycle Sport Shop BICYCLE RENTAL
(☎512-477-3472; www.bicyclesportshop.com; 517 S Lamar Blvd; ⏲10am-7pm Mon-Fri, 9am-6pm Sat, 11am-5pm Sun) Reserve ahead and rent a bike (from $22 for a half-day). A free PDF map brochure of all bicycle routes in Austin is available online at www.cityofaustin.org/bicycle.

Festivals & Events

South by Southwest MULTIMEDIA
(SXSW; www.sxsw.com) One of the American music industry's biggest gatherings, held in mid-March, has now expanded to include film and interactive.

Austin City Limits Music Festival MUSIC
(www.aclfestival.com; 3-day pass $185) The locals' favorite: more than 130 bands play on eight stages for three days in September. Tickets can sell out months in advance, so plan ahead.

Sleeping

South Congress (SoCo) has some quirky and cool digs. Hotels downtown are high-rent, but you don't have to go far to find reasonable motels. Chain motels line up all along I-35; south of town, a whole slew of them congregate near the Oltorf St intersection.

TOP CHOICE **Hotel San José** HOTEL $$
(☎512-444-7322; www.sanjosehotel.com; 1316 S Congress Ave; r with shared bath $105, with bath $175-360; P❄📶🏊) Local hotelier Liz Lambert revamped a 1930s-vintage motel into a

MUSIC FESTIVALS

For five nights in mid-March tens of thousands of record-label reps, musicians, journalists and rabid fans from around the country descend on Austin for **South by Southwest** (SXSW; www.sxsw.com), a musical extravaganza that attracts a couple of thousand groups and solo artists from around the world to 90 different Austin venues.

Though SXSW started out as an opportunity for little-known bands and singers to catch the ear of a record-label rep, today it features bands that have already been signed, as well as big-name performers who haven't needed exposure in decades.

So that's where music lovers go in the spring, but what do they do in autumn? Now there's a second festival that, while not as big as SXSW, has been swiftly gaining on it in terms of popularity: the **Austin City Limits Festival** (ACL; ☎tickets 888-512-SHOW; www.aclfestival.com; 1-/3-day pass $85/185). The three-day festival held each October on eight stages in Zilker Park books more than 100 pretty impressive acts and sells out months in advance.

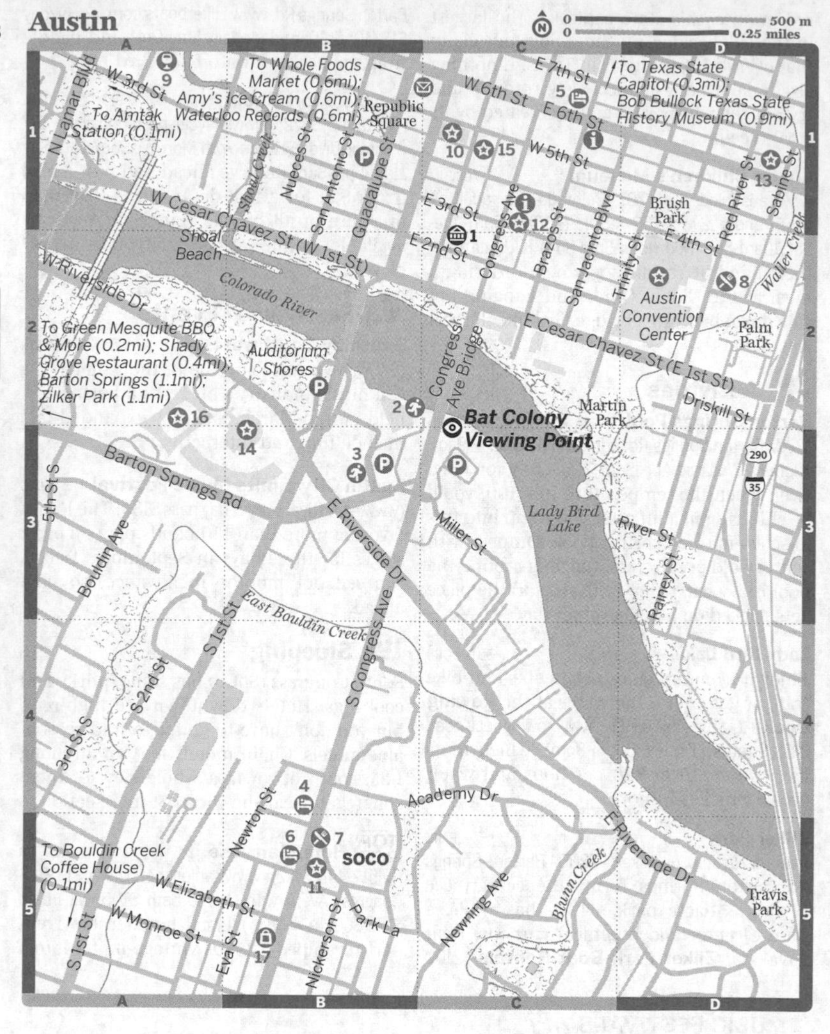

chic SoCo retreat with minimalist rooms, native Texas gardens and a very Austin-esque hotel bar in the courtyard that's known for its celebrity-spotting potential.

Austin Motel MOTEL **$$**
(☎512-441-1157; www.austinmotel.com; 1220 S Congress Ave; r $80-110, ste $137-178; P❄📶🏊) Decorated with a waterfall mural or retro polka dots, each room is individually fun or funky. Random, savvy-thrift-shopper furniture makes this old motor-court motel oddly appealing. Take your chances, or hand-pick your room from the website.

Driskill Hotel HISTORIC HOTEL **$$$**
(☎512-474-5911, 800-252-9367; www.driskillhotel.com; 604 Brazos St; r $185-275, ste $300-900; P📶) Built from native stone by a wealthy cattle baron in the 1800s, this hotel is pure Texas, from the leather couches to the mounted longhorn head on the wall. (Not to worry, the elegant rooms are taxidermy-free.)

Goodall Wooten DORM **$**
(☎512-472-1343; 2112 Guadalupe St; s & d $30-40; ❄@) A private dorm near the University of Texas, 'the Woo' generally has rooms available mid-May to mid-August, and some-

Austin

Top Sights

Bat Colony Viewing Point C2

Sights

1 Austin Children's Museum C2

Activities, Courses & Tours

2 Capital Cruises B2
3 Lone Star Riverboat B3

Sleeping

4 Austin Motel B4
5 Driskill Hotel C1
6 Hotel San José B5

Eating

7 Amy's Ice Cream B5
Güero's Taco Bar ..... (see 6)
8 Moonshine Patio Bar & Grill D2

Drinking

9 Tiniest Bar in Texas A1

Entertainment

10 Antone's C1
11 Continental Club B5
12 Elephant Room C1
13 Emo's D1
14 Long Center for the Performing Arts B3
15 Oilcan Harry's C1
16 Palmer Events Center A2

Shopping

17 Uncommon Objects B5

times has space for travelers at other times of the year. Each room has a small refrigerator. Stay six nights, get the seventh free.

HI Austin HOSTEL **$**
(☎512-444-2294; www.hiaustin.org; 2200 S Lakeshore Blvd; dm members/nonmembers $22/25; P❄@📶) Two-story views of the lake from the sunny great room – complete with fish tank, guitar and comfy couches – might make even nonhostelers consider a stay. Bus it or rent a bike ($10 a day) for the 2.5-mile trek to downtown.

Inn at Pearl Street B&B **$$**
(☎512-478-0051, 800-494-2261; www.innpearl.com; 1809 Pearl St; d $125-195; P❄📶) This is a preservationist's dream come true. The owners picked up this run-down property, dusted it off and – well, they more than dusted it off. They completely restored it and decorated it in a plush, European style that makes it a cozy place to shack up for a few days.

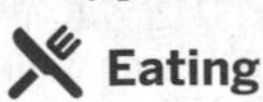

Eating

It's easy to find good, cheap food in Austin. South Congress provides a slew of options, but you'll be competing with lots of other hungry diners for a table. Those in the know go instead to S 1st St (1400 to 2100 blocks), where Mexican herbalists and tattoo parlors alternate with trailer-park food courts and organic cafes. Barton Springs Rd (east of Lamar Blvd) also has a number of interesting eateries, and Guadalupe St by UT is the place to look for cheap eats. Some great meat-market BBQ is available in nearby central Texas; for some mouth-watering suggestions, see the boxed text on p663.

DOWNTOWN

Moonshine Patio Bar & Grill AMERICAN **$$**
(☎512-236-9599; 303 Red River St; lunch $9-14, dinner $11-21; ⏰11am-10pm Mon-Thu, to 11pm Fri & Sat, 9:30am-2:30pm & 5-10pm Sun) Dating from the mid-1850s, this historic building is a remarkably well preserved homage to Austin's early days. Within its exposed limestone walls, you can enjoy upscale comfort food, half-price appetizers at happy hour or a lavish Sunday brunch buffet ($16.95).

Whole Foods Market MARKET **$**
(www.wholefoods.com; 525 N Lamar Blvd; sandwiches $6-9, mains $6-15; ⏰8am-10pm; 📶) The flagship of the Austin-founded Whole Foods Market is a gourmet grocery and cafe with restaurant counters and a staggering takeaway buffet, including self-made salads, global mains, deli sandwiches and more.

> **WHAT THE...?**
>
> Keep an eye out for Austin's **moonlight towers**. All the rage in the late 1800s, these 165ft-tall street lamps were designed to give off the light of a full moon. Austin is the only city in which these historic triangular metal towers topped by a halo of six large bulbs towers still operate. Fifteen burn bright around the city: how many can you spot?

DON'T MISS

MEALS ON WHEELS

Food trailers are here to stay – even if they can move around at whim. We haven't listed any of these rolling restaurants because of their transient nature, but instead invite you to explore some of the areas where they congregate. Wander from trailer to trailer till one strikes your fancy, or make a progressive dinner out of it. Look for clusters of airstreams and taco trucks in some of these likely spots:

» **South Congress** (btwn Elizabeth & Monroe Sts) At time of research, a parking lot across from the main drag of SoCo had several trailers, but there was talk of someone building a permanent structure there. If it's still there, look for the awesome **Mighty Cone**.

» **South Austin Trailer Park & Eatery** (1311 S First) This seems to be a rather settled trailer community, with a fence, an official name, a sign and picnic tables. Cross your fingers that there's still a **Torchy's Tacos** trailer.

» **South Lamar** (1219 S Lamar Blvd) If you're lucky, you'll find **Gourdoughs** in this parking lot cluster. The gourmet doughnuts are expensive but provide a full dessert for two.

» **Flip Happy Crepes** (10am-2:30pm Wed-Fri, 9am-3pm Sat, 10am-2pm Sun) There's only one trailer here, parked behind 400 Josephine St, but it was one of the (if not *the*) first, so we thought it deserved a mention.

Amy's Ice Cream ICE CREAM **$**
(www.amysicecreams.com; 1012 W Sixth St; 11:30am-midnight Sun-Thu, 11:30am-1am Fri & Sat) It's not just the ice cream we love; it's the toppings that get pounded and blended in, violently but lovingly, by the staff wielding a metal scoop in each hand. There's a branch on 1302 S Congress Ave.

SOUTH AUSTIN

TOP CHOICE **Güero's Taco Bar** TEX-MEX **$$**
(1412 S Congress Ave; mains $6-15; 11am-10pm Mon-Wed, to 11pm Thu & Fri, 8am-11pm Sat & Sun) Oh, Güero's, how we love you. Why must you make us wait? Well, clearly it's because of the three million other hungry people crammed into your bar area. Still, we'll try to be patient, because we love the atmosphere lent by the century-old former feed-and-seed store, and because we have an obsessive craving for your chicken tortilla soup.

Green Mesquite BBQ & More BARBECUE **$**
(1400 Barton Springs Rd; mains $6-10, kids' plates $4; 11am-10pm Sun-Thu, to 11pm Fri & Sat) As its T-shirts say, Green Mesquite has been 'horrifying vegetarians since 1988.' This inexpensive, low-key spot has lots of meat, pecan pie, cold beer and a shady outdoor area that's lovely on cool days.

Bouldin Creek Coffee House VEGETARIAN **$**
(1900 S 1st St; meals $5-7; 8am-midnight Mon-Fri, 9am-midnight Sat & Sun;) You can get your veggie chorizo scrambler or organic oatmeal with apples all day long at this eclectic vegan/vegetarian eatery that's got an earthy-crunchy vibe and plenty of good people-watching.

AROUND TOWN

Trudy's Texas Star TEX-MEX **$**
(409 W 30th; mains $7-12; 4pm-midnight Mon-Thu, 9am-2am Fri & Sat, 9am-midnight Sun) Get your Tex-Mex fix here; the menu is consistently good, with several healthier-than-usual options. But we'll let you in on a little secret: this place could serve beans and dirt and people would still line up for the margaritas, which might very well be the best in Austin.

Shady Grove Restaurant AMERICAN **$$**
(1624 Barton Springs Rd; mains $7-12; 11am-10:30pm Sun-Thu, to 11pm Fri & Sat) 'Do you want inside or out?' Really, what kind of question is that? We came for the shady patio, like everyone else. Outdoors under the pecan trees is prime real estate for enjoying everything from chili cheese fries to the vegetarian Hippie Sandwich.

Salt Lick Bar-B-Que BARBECUE **$$**
(512-858-4959; www.saltlickbbq.com; 18300 FM 1826, Driftwood; mains $12-21; 11am-10pm) It's worth the 20-mile drive just to see the massive outdoor barbecue pits at this park-like place off US 290. It's a bit of a tourist fave,

but the crowd-filled experience still gets our nod. BYOB.

Drinking

There are bejillions of bars in Austin, so what follows is only a very short list. The legendary 6th St bar scene has spilled onto nearby thoroughfares, especially on Red River St.

Many of the new places on Sixth St are shot bars aimed at party-hardy college students and tourists, while the Red River establishments retain a harder local edge. The lounges around the Warehouse District (near the intersection of W 4th and Colorado Sts) are a bit more upscale, while SoCo caters to the more offbeat in eclectic Austin.

Hotel San José BAR
(1316 S Congress Ave) Transcending the hotel-bar genre, this one is actually a cool, Zen-like outdoor patio that attracts a chill crowd, and it's a nice place to hang if you want to actually have a conversation.

Ginny's Little Longhorn Saloon BAR
(5434 Burnet Rd) This funky little cinder-block building is one of those dive bars that Austinites love so very much – and did even before it became nationally famous for Chicken-Shit Bingo on Sunday nights.

Contigo BAR
(2027 Anchor Lane) Big shade trees over a relaxed patio make this one of the nicest places in town to chill out with a cocktail.

Hula Hut THEME BAR
(3825 Lake Austin Blvd) Outdoor bar with a sprawling deck over Lake Austin.

Tiniest Bar in Texas BAR
(817 W 5th St) Tiny bar, huge patio, super-casual vibe.

DRUNK DIALING

If you plan to drive in Austin, and if you've been known to enjoy some adult beverages of the margarita persuasion, then quick, program ☎512-783-7865 into your phone and file it under **Square Patrol** (www.squarepatrol.org).

These designated drivers for hire pull up on a moped, which they fold up and toss in your trunk, then drive you safely home before scooting off into the night. A $20 donation is requested for the service, which seems like a small price to pay for not getting a ticket or not having to figure out where you left your car the next day.

Entertainment

We'll start with one venue that doesn't fall neatly into any one category:

Highball CLUB
(1142 S Lamar Blvd; ⌚4:30pm-2am Mon-Fri, 1pm-2am, from 10am Sun) Bar? Brunch spot? Bowling alley? Karaoke? Skee-ball? Retro-swanky amusement emporium? The Highball is all of those things. In other words, if you're not sure what you want to do, this is a good place to start. It's next door to (and owned by) the folks at Alamo Drafthouse, so you're sure to find something that amuses you.

Live Music

On any given Friday night there are several hundred acts playing in the town's 200 or so venues, and even on an off night (Monday and Tuesday are usually the slowest) you'll typically have your pick of more than two dozen performances.

THE SWARM

Looking very much like a special effect from a B movie, a funnel cloud of up to 1.5 million Mexican free-tailed bats swarms from under the **Congress Avenue Bridge** nightly from late March to early November. Turns out, Austin isn't just the live-music capital of the world; it's also home to the largest urban bat population in North America.

Austinites have embraced the winged mammals – figuratively speaking of course – and gather to watch the bats' nightly exodus right around dusk as they leave for their evening meal. (Not to worry, they're looking for insects, and they mostly stay out of your hair.)

There's lots of standing around parking lots and on the bridge itself, but if you want a more leisurely bat-watching experience, try the TGI Friday's restaurant by the Radisson Hotel on Lady Bird Lake, or the Lone Star Riverboat or Capital Cruises for **bat-watching tours**.

To plan your attack, check out the weekly *Austin Chronicle* or Thursday's *Austin American-Statesman.*

Continental Club LIVE MUSIC
(www.continentalclub.com; 1315 S Congress Ave) No passive toe-tapping here; this 1950s-era lounge has a dancefloor that's always swinging with some of the city's best local acts.

Broken Spoke LIVE MUSIC
(www.brokenspokeaustintx.com; 3201 S Lamar Blvd; ⏲11am-midnight Tue-Thu, to 1am Fri & Sat) With sand-covered wood floors and wagon-wheel chandeliers that George Strait once hung from, Broken Spoke is a true Texas honky-tonk.

Cactus Cafe LIVE MUSIC
(www.utexas.edu/universityunions; Texas Union, cnr 24th & Guadalupe Sts; ⏲varies by show) Listen to acoustic up close and personal at this intimate club on the UT campus.

Antone's LIVE MUSIC
(www.antones.net; 213 W 5th St) A key player in Austin's musical history, Antone's has attracted the best of the blues and other popular local acts since 1975. All ages, all the time.

Elephant Room LIVE MUSIC
(www.elephantroom.com; 315 Congress Ave) This intimate, subterranean jazz club has a cool vibe, and live music almost every night.

Emo's LIVE MUSIC
(www.emosaustin.com; 603 Red River St) Emo's leads the pack in the punk and indie scene along Red River St.

Theater & Cinema

Long Center for the Performing Arts PERFORMING ARTS
(www.longcenter.org; 701 W Riverside Dr) This state-of-the-art theater opened in late 2008 as part of a waterfront redevelopment along Lady Bird Lake. The multistage venue hosts drama, dance, concerts and comedians.

Alamo Drafthouse Cinema THEATER
(www.drafthouse.com; 1120 S Lamar Blvd; admission $9.50) Easily the most fun you can have at the movies: sing along with *Grease,* quote along with *Princess Bride,* or just enjoy food and drink delivered right to your seat during first-run films.

Sports

Get ready to rumble – it's roller-derby night and the Hellcat women skaters are expected to kick some Cherry Bomb ass. No matter who wins, the **TXRD Lonestar Rollergirls** (www.txrd.com) league always puts on a good show, usually at the **Palmer Events Center** (900 Barton Springs Rd).

 Shopping

Not many folks visit Austin just to shop. That said, music is a huge industry here and you'll find heaps of it in Austin's record stores. Vintage is a lifestyle, and the city's best hunting grounds for retro fashions and furnishings are South Austin and Guadalupe St near UT. Get a map at www.vintagearoundtownguide.com.

On the first Thursday of the month, S Congress Ave is definitely the place to be, when

GAY & LESBIAN AUSTIN

With a thriving gay population – not to mention pretty mellow straight people – Austin is arguably the most gay-friendly city in Texas. The **Austin Gay & Lesbian Chamber of Commerce** (www.aglcc.org) sponsors the Pride Parade in June, as well as smaller events throughout the year. The *Austin Chronicle* (www.austinchronicle.com) runs a gay event column among the weekly listings, and the glossy *L Style/G Style* (www.lstylegstyle.com) magazine has a dual gal/guy focus.

Austin's gay and lesbian club scene is mainly in the Warehouse District, though there are outposts elsewhere. Near the state capitol, **Charlie's** (1301 Lavaca St; ⏲2pm-2am) is the oldest gay bar in town. Friendly staff, a laid-back atmosphere, pool tables, $5 steak nights and free parking are just some of the perks. On some nights DJs spin progressive house music.

The dance floor is packed most nights at **Oilcan Harry's** (211 W 4th St). As much as the girls wish it were a mixed crowd, this scene is all about the boys. Sweaty ones.

Outside town, at Lake Travis, **Hippie Hollow** (www.hippiehollow.com; 7000 Comanche Trail; day pass $10; ⏲9am-dusk Sep-May, 8am-dusk Jun-Aug) is a clothing-optional, gay-friendly beach. First Splash and Last Splash parties (the first Sunday in May and September, respectively) draw big crowds.

WORTH A TRIP

LOCKHART BARBECUE

In 1999 the Texas Legislature adopted a resolution naming Lockhart the barbecue capital of Texas. Of course, that means it's the barbecue capital of the *world*. You can eat very well for under $10 at these places:

Black's Barbecue (215 N Main St; ⏱10am-8pm Sun-Thu, 10am-8:30pm Fri & Sat) A longtime Lockhart favorite since 1932, with sausage so good Lyndon Johnson had Black's cater a party at the nation's capital.

Kreuz Market (619 N Colorado St; ⏱10:30am-8pm Mon-Sat) Serving Lockhart since 1900, the barnlike Kreuz Market uses a dry rub, which means you shouldn't insult it by asking for barbecue sauce. Kreuz doesn't serve it, and the meat doesn't need it.

Chisholm Trail Bar-B-Q (1323 S Colorado St; ⏱11am-8:30pm) Like Black's and Kreuz Market, Chisholm Trail has been named one of the top 10 barbecue restaurants in the state by *Texas Monthly* magazine.

Smitty's Market (208 S Commerce St; ⏱7am-6pm Mon-Fri, 7am-6:30pm Sat, 9am-3pm Sun) The blackened pit room and homely dining room are all original (knives used to be chained to the tables). Ask to have the fat trimmed off the brisket if you're particular about that.

stores stay open until 10pm and there's live entertainment; visit www.firstthursday.info for upcoming events.

TOP CHOICE **Uncommon Objects** VINTAGE
(1512 S Congress Ave; ⏱11am-7pm Sun-Thu, 11am-8pm Fri & Sat) 'Curious oddities' is what they advertise at this quirky antique store that sells all manner of fabulous knickknackery, all displayed with an artful eye.

Waterloo Records MUSIC
(www.waterloorecords.com; 600 N Lamar Blvd; ⏱9am-10pm) If you want to stock up on music, this is the record store. There are sections reserved just for local bands, and listening stations featuring Texas, indie and alt-country acts.

University Coop SOUVENIRS
(2246 Guadalupe St; ⏱8:30am-7:30pm Mon-Fri, 9:30am-6pm Sat, 11am-5pm Sun) Stock up on souvenirs sporting the Longhorn logo at this store brimming with school spirit.

Book People Inc BOOKS
(603 N Lamar Blvd; ⏱9am-11pm) Grab a coffee and browse the shelves of this lively independent bookstore across the street from Waterloo Records.

Information

Austin indoors is nonsmoking, period (bars, too). A vast wi-fi network blankets downtown. For other hot spots check out www.austinwirelesscity.org. City of Austin libraries (www.ci.austin.tx.us) have free internet.

Austin American-Statesman (www.statesman.com) Daily newspaper.

Austin Chronicle (www.austinchronicle.com) Weekly newspaper, lots of entertainment info.

Austin Visitor Information Center (☎512-478-0098; www.austintexas.org; 209 E 6th St; ⏱9am-5pm Mon-Fri, to 9:30-5:30pm Sat & Sun) Helpful staff, free maps, extensive racks of information brochures and a sample of local souvenirs for sale.

FedEx Office (327 Congress Ave; ⏱7am-11pm Mon-Fri, 9am-9pm Sat & Sun) Internet access 30¢ a minute.

KLRU TV (www.klru.org) PBS affiliate with local programming that includes the popular music show *Austin City Limits*.

Getting There & Around

Austin-Bergstrom International Airport (AUS; www.ci.austin.tx.us/austinairport) is off Hwy 71, southeast of downtown. The Airport Flyer (bus 100, $1) runs to downtown (7th St and Congress Ave) and UT (Congress Ave and 18th St) every 40 minutes or so. **SuperShuttle** (☎512-258-3826; www.supershuttle.com) charges around $15 from the airport to downtown. A taxi between the airport and downtown costs from $25 to $30. Most of the national rental-car companies are represented at the airport.

The downtown **Amtrak station** (www.amtrak.com; 250 N Lamar Blvd) is served by the *Texas Eagle* that extends from Chicago to Los Angeles. The **Greyhound Bus Station** (www.greyhound.com; 916 E Koenig Lane) is on the north side of town off I-35; take bus 7-Duval ($1) to downtown.

Austin's handy public transit system is run by **Capital Metro** (CapMetro; ☎512-474-1200;

www.capmetro.org). Call for directions to anywhere or stop into the downtown **Capital Metro Transit Store** (323 Congress Ave; ⏲7:30am-5pm Mon-Fri) for information.

Around Austin

Northwest of Austin along the Colorado River are the six Highland Lakes. Though recent years have seen serious droughts, one of the most popular lakes for recreation – when there's water – is the 19,000-sq-acre **Lake Travis**. Rent boats and jet skis at the associated marina, or overnight in the posh digs at **Lakeway Resort and Spa** (☎512-261-6600; www.lakewayresortandspa.com; 101 Lakeway Dr; r from $189;), off Hwy 71. **Lake Austin Spa Resort** (☎512-372-7300; www.lakeaustin.com; 1705 S Quinlan Park Rd, off FM 2222; 3-night packages from $1600;) is the premier place to be pampered in the state. And Lake Travis has Texas' only official nude beach. **Hippie Hollow** (www.hippiehollow.com; day pass $10; ⏲9am-dusk Sep-May, 8am-dusk Jun-Aug) is a popular gay hangout with regular events – naked yoga, anyone? To get there from FM 2222, take Rte 620 south 1.5 miles to Comanche Trail and turn right. The entrance is 2 miles ahead on the left.

Hill Country

New York has the Hamptons, San Francisco has the wine country, and Texas has the Hill Country, whose natural beauty paired with its easygoing nature has inspired more than a few early retirements. Detour down dirt roads in search of fields of wildflowers, check into a dude ranch, float along the Guadalupe River or twirl around the floor of an old dance hall. Most of the small towns in the rolling hills and valleys west of Austin and San Antonio are easy day trips from either city.

GRUENE

False-front wood buildings and old German homes make this the quintessential rustic Texas town. All of Gruene (pronounced *green*) is on the National Historic Register – and boy, do day-trippers know it. You won't be alone wandering among the arts-and-crafts and knickknack shops in search of the perfect straw cowboy hat.

Sights & Activities

Gruene Hall DANCE HALL

(www.gruenehall.com; 1280 Gruene Rd; ⏲11am-11pm Mon-Wed, to midnight Thu & Fri, 10am-1am Sat, 10am-9pm Sun) Folks have been congregating here since 1878, making it one of Texas' oldest dancehalls and the oldest continually operating one. Toss back a longneck, two-step to live music on the well-worn wooden dance floor, or play horseshoes out in the yard. There's only a cover on weekend nights and when big acts are playing, so at least stroll through and soak up the vibe.

Rockin' R River Rides RIVER RIDES

(☎830-629-9999; www.rockinr.com; 1405 Gruene Rd; tubes per day $17; ⏲9am-2:30pm Sun-Fri, from 8am Sat) Floating down the Guadalupe in an inner tube is a Texas summer tradition. This outfitter buses you upstream and you float the three to four hours back to base. Put a plastic cooler full of beverages (no bottles) in a bottom-fortified tube next to you and you have a day.

Sleeping & Eating

Gruene Mansion Inn INN $$

(☎830-629-2641; www.gruenemansioninn.com; 1275 Gruene Rd; d $195-250) This cluster of buildings is practically its own village, with rooms in the mansion, a former carriage house and the old barns. Richly decorated in a style the owners call 'rustic Victorian elegance,' the rooms feature lots of wood, floral prints and pressed-tin ceiling tiles.

SCENIC DRIVE: WILDFLOWER TRAILS

You know spring has arrived in Texas when you see cars pulling up roadside and families climbing out to take the requisite picture of their kids surrounded by bluebonnets – the state flower. From March to April in Hill Country, orange Indian paintbrushes, deep-purple winecups and white-to-blue bluebonnets are at their peak. To see vast cultivated fields of color, there's **Wildseed Farms** (www.wildseedfarms.com; 100 Legacy Dr; admission free; ⏲9:30am-6:30pm), which is 7 miles east of Fredericksburg on US 290. Or for a more do-it-yourself experience, check with TXDOT's **Wildflower Hotline** (☎800-452-9292) to find out what's blooming where. Taking Rte 16 and FM 1323, north from Fredericksburg and east to Willow City, is usually a good route. Then again you might just set to wandering – most backroads host their own shows daily.

Gristmill Restaurant AMERICAN **$$**
(1287 Gruene Rd; mains $15-22; ⏰11am-10pm Sun-Thu, to 11pm Fri & Sat) Behind Gruene Hall and right under the water tower, this restaurant is located within the brick remnants of a long-gone gristmill. Indoor seating affords a rustic ambience, and outdoor tables get a view of the river.

Getting There & Away

Gruene is just off I-10 and Rte 46, 45 miles south of Austin and 25 miles northeast of San Antonio.

FREDERICKSBURG

With fields full of wildflowers, shops full of antiques and streets full of historic buildings and bed and breakfasts, Fredericksburg is the poster child for 'quaint,' serving as the region's largest old German-settled town (c 1870) and unofficial capital of the Hill Country.

It's more cute than cool, but it's not a bad place to linger a bit – especially during wildflower season. It also makes a good base of operations for exploring the surrounding areas. Stop by the **Fredericksburg Convention & Visitors Bureau** (☎830-997-6523; www.fredericksburg-texas.com; 302 E Austin St; ⏰8:30am-5pm Mon-Fri, from 9am Sat, 11am-3pm Sun) to get your bearings.

Sights & Activities

Spend an hour or two wandering Fredericksburg's historic district; despite having more than its share of touristy shops, it's retained the look (if not the feel) of 125 years ago.

Mid-May through June is peach-pickin' season around town. You can get them straight from the farm, and some will let you pick your own. For a list of more than 20 local **peach farms**, visit www.texaspeaches.com.

Thanks to its conducive *terroir*, the area is also becoming known for its prolific wineries. If winery-hopping is on the agenda, print up a map at www.texaswinetrail.com or www.wineroad290.com.

National Museum of the Pacific War MUSEUM
(www.nimitz-museum.org; 340 E Main St; adult/child $12/6; ⏰9am-5pm) Admiral Chester Nimitz was born in Fredericksburg, so a museum commemorating his life makes perfect sense – although the addition of a second building housing intimidating large artillery can seem a bit anachronistic in the peaceful Hill Country.

U-R-B-A-N P-L-A-N-N-I-N-G

Street names in Fredericksburg appear to be a mishmash of trees, Texas towns and former US presidents. But they were actually named so their initials spell out secret codes. The streets crossing Main St to the east of Courthouse Sq are Adams, Llano, Lincoln, Washington, Elk, Lee, Columbus, Olive, Mesquite and Eagle. And the streets to the west are Crockett, Orange, Milam, Edison, Bowie, Acorn, Cherry and Kay.

Enchanted Rock State Natural Area HIKING
(☎830-685-3636; www.tpwd.state.tx.us; 16710 Ranch Rd 965; adult/child $6/free; ⏰8am-10pm) North of town about 18 miles, you'll find a dome of pink granite dating from the Proterozoic era rising 425ft above ground – one of the largest batholiths in the US. If you want to climb it, go early; gates close when the daily attendance quota is reached.

Sleeping & Eating

Gastehaus Schmidt ACCOMMODATION SERVICES
(☎830-997-5612; www.fbglodging.com) Nearly 300 B&Bs do business in this county; this reservation service helps sort them out.

Roadrunner Inn INN **$$**
(☎830-997-8555; www.theroadrunnerinn.com; 306-B E Main St; d $169-189; ❄📶) If you want to ensure your lodging is doily-free, check out one of the three smartly retro rooms that feature kitchenettes, Jacuzzi tubs and flat-screen TVs.

Hill Top Café AMERICAN **$$**
(☎830-997-8922; 10661 US 87; mains $12-25; ⏰11am-2pm & 5-9pm Tue-Sun) Ten miles north of town inside a renovated 1950s gas station, this cozy roadhouse serves up satisfying meals and Hill Country ambience at its best. Reservations recommended.

Rather Sweet Bakery & Café BAKERY, CAFE **$**
(249 E Main St; sweets $2-5, sandwiches $6-9; ⏰8am-5pm Mon-Sat) Newsman Dan Rather came from Fredericksburg; his star-chef daughter Rebecca runs this shady patio cafe. Stop in front at **Rather Sweet, Too** for grab-and-go goodies.

Getting There & Away

Fredericksburg is 78 miles west of Austin on Hwy 281, and 70 miles north of San Antonio (via I-10 and US 87). **Kerrville Bus Co** (☎800-474-3352;

www.iridekbc.com; Golden Convenience Store, 1001 S Adams St) sends two daily buses to and from San Antonio (from $27, two hours); none to Austin.

LUCKENBACH

As small as Luckenbach is – three permanent residents, not counting the cat – it's big on Texas charm. You won't find a more laid-back place, where the main activity is sitting under an old oak tree with a bottle of Shiner Bock and listening to guitar pickers, who are often accompanied by roosters.

The heart of the, er, action is the old trading post established back in 1849 – now the **Luckenbach General Store** (⌚10am-9pm Mon-Sat, noon-9pm Sun), which also serves as the local post office, saloon and community center.

Check the website for the **music schedule** (www.luckenbachtexas.com). Sometimes the guitar picking starts at 1pm, sometimes 5pm, and weekends usually see live-music events in the old **dance hall** – a Texas classic. The 4th of July and Labor Day weekends are deluged with visitors for concerts.

We'd be remiss if we didn't mention that Luckenbach was made famous in a country song by Waylon Jennings – but we figured you either already knew that, or wouldn't really care.

From Fredericksburg, take US 290 east then take FM 1376 south for about 3 miles.

BANDERA

Bandera has the look and feel of an old Western movie set, and that's just the effect the locals want in order to support their claim as the Cowboy Capital of Texas. There are certainly lots of dude ranches around, and rodeos and horseback riding are easy to come by. At least stop for a beer and dance in one of the many hole-in-the-wall cowboy bars and honky-tonks, where you'll find friendly locals, good live music and a rich atmosphere.

Ready to saddle up? The friendly folks at **Bandera County Visitors Bureau** (☎800-364-3833; www.banderacowboycapital.com; ½ block south of Main St on Hwy 16 S; ⌚9am-5pm Mon-Fri, 10am-3pm Sat) know nearly a dozen places in and around town were you can go **horseback riding**. For overnights, they can also direct you to **dude ranch accommodations**, with packages that include lodging, meals and an equine excursion for an average of $95 to $150 per person, per night. There may also be hayrides, kids' programs, ropin' lessons and swimming, depending on the place.

During the summer, you can catch a **rodeo** at **Twin Elm Ranch** (www.twinelmranch.com; cnr Rte 470 & Hwy 16; rodeo adult/under 6 $6/free; ⌚8pm Fri May-Aug) on Friday nights.

Fuel up for your day with a steak-and-eggs breakfast at **OST Restaurant** (305 Main St; breakfast $4-7, mains $7-14; ⌚6am-9pm). For entertainment after the sun goes down, mosey over to the patio at **11th Street Cowboy Bar** (307 11th St; ⌚to midnight Sun-Thu, to 2am Fri & Sat). Hank Williams Sr used to play at **Arky Blue's Silver Dollar Saloon** (308 Main St; ⌚10am-2am); look for the table into which he carved his name. Both bars have live country crooners from Friday to Sunday.

Bandera is an hour or less from San Antonio on Rte 16 (Bandera Rd).

San Antonio

In most large cities, downtown is bustling with businesspeople dressed for office work hurrying to their meetings and luncheons. Not so in San Antonio. Instead, downtown is filled with tourists in shorts consulting their maps. In fact, many people are surprised to find that two of the state's most popular destinations – the Riverwalk and the Alamo – are right smack dab in the middle of downtown, surrounded by historical hotels, tourist attractions and souvenir shops. The volume of visitors is daunting (as is the amount of commercial crap that's developed around the Alamo – Davy Crockett's wild amusement ride?), but the lively Tex-Mex culture is worth experiencing.

Sights & Activities

In addition to what's listed here, there are flashy diversions downtown (rides, laser-tag mazes, believe-it-or-not freak shows…) and two amusement parks (Fiesta Texas and SeaWorld) on Loop 1604.

The intersection of Commerce and Losoya Sts is the very heart of downtown and the Riverwalk, which runs in a U shape below street level. Signs point out access stairways, but a 3-D map bought at the info center is the best way to get oriented. The artsy **Southtown** neighborhood and the **King William Historic District** lie south along the river.

FREE **The Alamo** MISSION
(www.thealamo.org; 300 Alamo Plaza; ⌚9am-5:30pm Mon-Sat, from 10am Sun) The folks who valiantly fought for Texas' independence

REMEMBERING THE ALAMO *Sarah Chandler*

'You may all go to hell, and I will go to Texas.' – Davy Crockett, in 1835

It's hard to tell the story of the Battle of the Alamo – there is hot debate about almost every fact. For instance, it's difficult to verify with exact certainty the number of defenders, of Mexican troops and of casualties, among many other details. This is a volatile issue because Texans are touchy about people challenging the legends of their heroes.

Objective accounts are hard to find. It is, however, generally agreed that on February 23, 1836, Mexican general Antonio López de Santa Anna led anywhere from 2500 to 5000 Mexican troops in an attack against the Alamo. The 160 or so men inside the fortress included James Bowie (of knife fame), who was in command of the Alamo until pneumonia rendered him too sick; William B Travis, who took command of the troops after Bowie's incapacity; and perhaps most famous of all, David Crockett, called 'Davy' by everyone who knew him. Crockett, a three-time US congressman from Tennessee with interesting taste in headgear, first gained fame as a frontiersman and then for his public arguments with President Andrew Jackson over the latter's murderous campaigns of Indian 'removal' in the southeastern USA. Less well known were Bowie's and Travis' black slaves, who fought alongside their masters during the battle and survived.

Travis dispatched a now-famous letter to other revolutionaries pleading for reinforcements, saying that his men would not stand down under any circumstances – his call was for 'Victory or Death.' Because of slow communications, the only reinforcements that arrived in time were a group of about 30 men from Gonzales, Texas, bringing the total number of Alamo defenders up to 189, according to literature from the Daughters of the Republic of Texas (DRT).

Santa Anna's troops pounded the Alamo for 13 days before retaking it. Mexican losses were devastating; estimates run as low as 1000 and as high as 2000. When the Alamo was finally recaptured, the advancing troops executed almost all of the surviving defenders. The few who were spared, mostly women, children and slaves, were interrogated and released.

The Battle of the Alamo was pivotal in the war: during the two weeks Santa Anna's army was distracted in San Antonio, Texas troops were gathering strength and advancing, fueled by what they called the wholesale slaughter of their brothers in arms, under the battle cry 'Remember the Alamo!'

from Mexico would never have imagined the Alamo as it is today, surrounded by tacky tourist attractions and having its picture taken every 17 seconds or so by people exclaiming how much smaller it looks in real life. But it's more than just a photo op. Go on in and find out why the story of the Alamo can rouse a Texan's sense of state pride like few other things. You might notice some of the visitors getting downright dewy-eyed at the description of how a few hundred revolutionaries died defending the fort against thousands of Mexican troops.

Riverwalk RIVERFRONT DEVELOPMENT

(www.thesanantonioriverwalk.com) An essential part of the San Antonio experience, this charming canal and pedestrian street is the main artery at the heart of San Antonio's tourism efforts. Restaurant after restaurant and bar after bar vie for your attention. In mid-2009, the first part of a $259 million expansion effort connected the commercial core with the developing Pearl Brewery shopping complex to the north.

Rio San Antonio Cruises BOAT TOUR

(www.riosanantonio.com; adult/child 5yr & under $8.25/2; ⏲9am-9pm) Narrated cruises ply the entire extended river length daily, offering a nice visual overview along with a light history lesson; plus, it's just a pleasant way to pass the time. Buy tickets across the water from the Hilton near Market and S Alamo Sts.

Museo Alameda MUSEUM

(www.thealameda.org; 101 S Santa Rosa St; adult/child $4/free; ⏲10am-6pm Tue-Sun) The largest Hispanic museum in the US is also a Smithsonian affiliate, which means it gets to draw on the Smithsonian's extensive collections for its rotating displays. Check out the

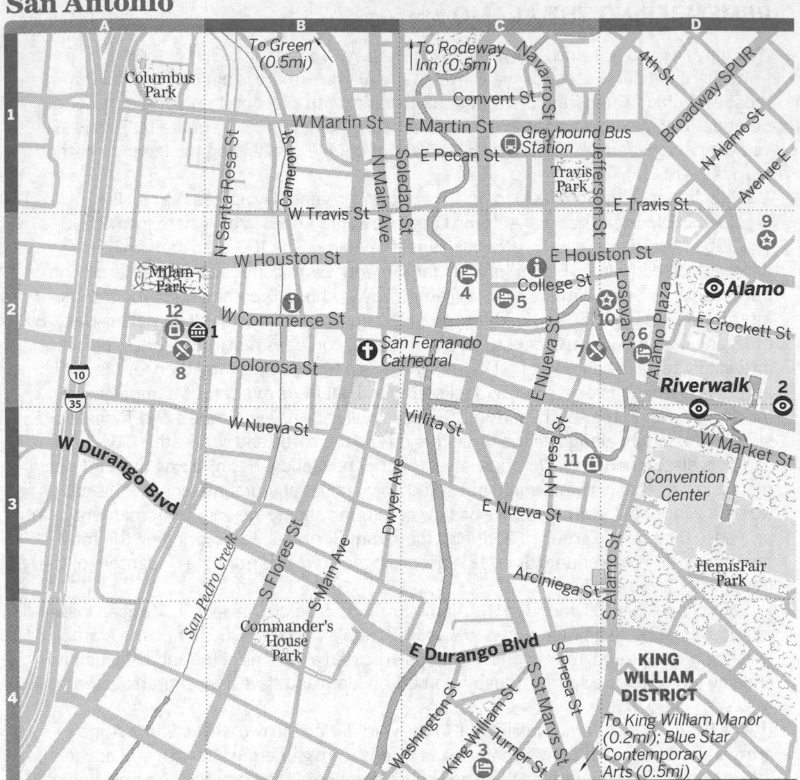

crazy-cool building: the surprisingly modern exterior (no adobe here) has hot-pink walls accented with metal panels that resemble a tin luminaria.

Mission Trail MISSION

Spain's missionary presence can best be felt at the ruins of the four missions south of town. Together, Missions Concepción (1731), San José (1720), San Juan (1731) and Espada (1745–56) make up **San Antonio Missions National Historical Park** (www.nps.gov/saan). Stop first at **Mission San José** (6701 San José Dr; admission free; 9am-5pm), which is also the location of the main **visitor center**. Known in its time as the Queen of the Missions, it's certainly the largest and arguably the most beautiful. And because it's a little more remote and pastoral, surrounded by thick stone walls, you can really get a sense of what life was like here in the 18th and 19th centuries.

AROUND DOWNTOWN

Brackenridge Park PARK

(3910 N St Mary's St; 5am-11pm) North of downtown near Trinity University, this 343-acre park is a great place to spend the day with your family. In addition to the **San Antonio Zoo** (www.sazoo-aq.org; 3903 N St Mary's St; adult/child $10.75/8; 9am-6pm), you'll find the Brackenridge Eagle **miniature train** (adult/child $3.25/2.70), an old-fashioned **carousel** (adult/child $2.50/2) and the **Japanese Tea Gardens**.

San Antonio Museum of Art MUSEUM

(SAMA; www.samuseum.org; 200 W Jones Ave; adult/child $8/3; 10am-9pm Tue, 10am-5pm Wed-Sat, noon-6pm Sun) Housed in the original 1880s Lone Star Brewery, SAMA reflects San Antonio's strong Hispanic influence with an one of the most comprehensive collections of Latin American art in the U.S.

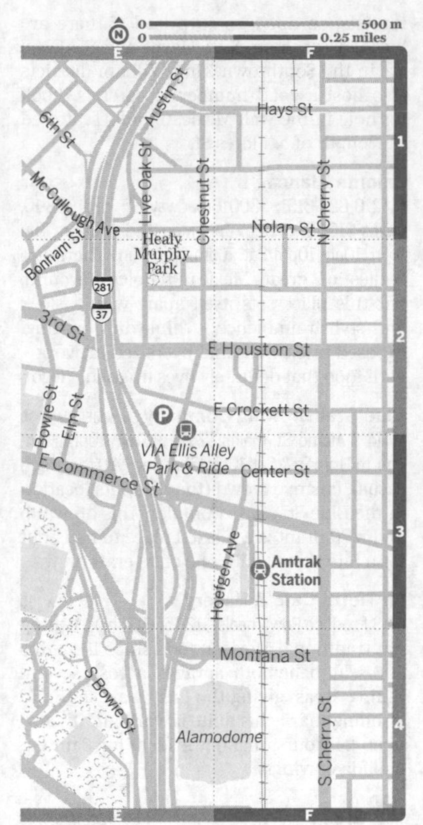

San Antonio

Top Sights
Alamo D2
Riverwalk D3

Sights
1 Museo Alameda A2
2 Rio San Antonio Cruises D3

Sleeping
3 A Yellow Rose Inn C4
4 Hotel Valencia C2
5 Omni La Mansión del Rio C2
6 Riverwalk Vista D2

Eating
7 Boudro's C2
8 Mi Tierra Café & Bakery A2

Entertainment
9 Bonham Exchange D2
10 Jim Cullum's Landing D2

Shopping
11 La Villita C3
12 Market Square A2

McNay Art Museum MUSEUM
(www.mcnayart.org; 600 N New Braunfels Ave; adult/child $8/free; 10am-5pm Tue-Sat, noon-5pm Sun) In addition to seeing paintings by household names such as Van Gogh, Picasso, Matisse, Renoir, O'Keeffe and Cézanne, half the fun is wandering the spectacular Spanish Colonial revival-style mansion that was the home of Marion Koogler McNay.

Festivals & Events

San Antonio Stock Show & Rodeo RODEO
(www.sarodeo.com) Big-name concerts follow each night's rodeo; 16 days in mid-February.

Fiesta San Antonio CULTURAL
(www.fiesta-sa.org) Over 10 days in mid-April there are river parades, carnivals, Tejano music, dancing and tons of food in a mammoth, citywide party.

Sleeping

San Antonio has at least 10 gazillion-trillion hotel rooms, so you have plenty of choices right downtown. Because of the tourist trade, rates are higher on weekends. San Antonio also has its fair share of B&Bs, and generally speaking they're good value, ensconced in fine old homes in the more historic areas of the city.

Riverwalk Vista B&B $$
(210-223-3200, 866-898-4782; 262 Losoya St; www.riverwalkvista.com; d incl breakfast $120-210, ste $180-270;) Soaring ceilings with enormous windows, exposed brick walls, crisp, white bedding – this is simplicity done right.

Hotel Valencia BOUTIQUE HOTEL $$$
(210-227-9700; www.hotelvalencia-riverwalk.com; 150 E Houston St; d $119-319;) Faux-mink throws, molded concrete, light shining through perforated metal – this place is all about texture. It could have been transported from New York City, both in its minimalist-chic style and in the size of some of the smaller rooms, but it's a hip option if you eschew chains and historic hotels.

Omni La Mansion del Rio HISTORIC HOTEL $$$
(210-518-1000; www.lamansion.com; 112 College St; d $219-399;) This fabulous

DITCH THE CAR

Parking-garage fees in San Antonio really add up. You can park free at the **VIA Ellis Alley Park & Ride** (btwn E Crockett & Center Sts), a quick two stops from the Alamo. Ask for a parking transfer on the bus and put it in the slot to 'pay' when you exit.

downtown property was born out of 19th-century religious school buildings in the Spanish-Mexican hacienda style. It's on a quiet stretch of the Riverwalk, and its discreet oasis attracts stars and other notables.

Rodeway Inn Downtown MOTEL $
(210-223-2951; www.rodewayinn.com; 900 N Main Ave; d $47-87; P❄📶🏊) The Alamo and Riverwalk are just 1 mile away, and the downtown trolley comes right to your door. Rooms are basic as can be, but you'll save some dollars, especially when you factor in free parking and continental breakfast.

Hill Country Inn & Suites HOTEL $
(210-599-4204, 866-729-7186; www.shellhospitality.com; 2383 NE Loop 410; d incl breakfast $59-99; P❄📶🏊👪) Just north of downtown, this anachronistic place feels like it belongs in the Hill Country than off an interstate, with ranch-style porches and country-style furnishings. It's great for families.

Kin William Manor B&B $$
(210-222-0144; www.kingwilliammanor.com; 1037 S Alamo St; d incl breakfast $135-199; P❄📶🏊) A grand, Greek Revival mansion with understatedly elegant rooms.

Noble Inns B&B $$
(210-223-2353, 800-242-2770; www.nobleinns.com; d incl breakfast from $149; P❄📶🏊) This collection of three inns has something for everyone – at least everyone who likes antiques and Victorian style.

A Yellow Rose Inn B&B $$
(210-229-9903, 800-950-9903; www.ayellowrose.com; 229 Madison St; d incl breakfast $89-200; P❄📶) We love the flexible breakfast policy: take your breakfast in your room, or skip it and pay a little less.

Eating & Drinking

The Riverwalk offers easy pickings for dinner and drinking, but they're there for the tourists, so don't be surprised if there are busloads of them. S St Marys and S Alamo Sts in the Southtown-King William districts also host a good number of eateries. Look for hole-in-the-wall Mexican joints scattered the length of N Flores St.

Paloma Blanca TEX-MEX $$
(210-822-6151; 5800 Broadway St; lunch $8-10, mains $10-18; 11am-9pm Mon-Wed, to 10pm Thu & Fri, 10am-10pm Sat, 10am-9pm Sun) There are oodles of great Mexican choices around, but this place sets itself apart with a sleek and stylish ambience – think dim lighting, exposed brick walls and oversized artwork – with food that definitely lives up to the decor.

Blue Star Brewing Company AMERICAN $$
(1414 S Alamo St; mains $7-13; 11am-10pm Mon-Thu, to 11pm Fri & Sat, 10am-9pm Sun) Attracting a casual, creative crowd (thanks to its location in the Blue Star Arts Complex) this brewpub and restaurant is a relaxed place to hang out for a bite served with one of its craft brews.

Mi Tierra Cafe & Bakery TEX-MEX $$
(218 Produce Row; meals $12-15; 24hr) Dishing out traditional Mexican food since 1941, this 500-seat behemoth sprawls across several dining areas, giving the busy wait staff and strolling mariachis quite a workout. It's also open 24 hours, making it ideal for 3am enchilada cravings.

Green VEGETARIAN $
(1017 N Flores St; meals $6-10; 8am-9pm Sun-Fri;) Vegetarians all around the city must've breathed a sigh of contentment when this cafe opened up. It's the only place in town

WORTH A TRIP

FLOORE'S COUNTRY STORE

This terrific old bar and dance hall first opened in 1942 as a store run by a friend of Willie Nelson. (Willie used to play here nightly; the sign still says so.) Today at **John T Floore's Country Store** (www.liveatfloores.com; 14492 Bandera Rd, Helotes; tickets $10-30; 11am-1am Fri & Sat, to 10pm Sun), whether in the outdoor stage yard or by the fire in the rustic building, this is the true way to hear Texas country music on a Friday or Saturday night. Bandera Rd is off Hwy 16. Sunday night is family dance night and there's no cover.

WORTH A TRIP

THE HOME OF SHINER BOCK

The highlight of any trip to Shiner, Texas, the self-proclaimed 'cleanest little city in Texas,' is a tour of the **Spoetzl Brewery** (www.shiner.com; 603 E Brewery St; tours free; ⏲tours usually 11am & 1:30pm Mon-Fri) where Shiner Bock beer is brewed. Czech and German settlers who began making beer under brewmaster Kosmos Spoetzl founded the brewery more than 90 years ago. Today the brewery still produces several types using the same methods, including bock, blonde, honey wheat, summer stock and winter ale. You can sample the beers for free after the tour in the little bar.

By car from San Antonio, take I-10 past Luling to US 95 and go south right to the very doors of Spoetzl Brewery. From Austin, take US 183 south through Luling to Gonzales, then turn east and follow US 90A, which brings you right into the center of town; cross the railroad tracks and make a left turn on US 95 to reach the brewery.

(at least at the time of research) that's 100% vegetarian, and it's 100% kosher to boot.

Guenther House CAFE $
(205 E Guenther St; meals $7-9; ⏲7am-3pm) Enjoy some of the sweetest, light waffles ever at the cafe in the historic home to former owners of the Pioneer Flour Mill (next door).

Boudro's AMERICAN $$$
(☎210-224-8484; 421 E Commerce St; lunch $8-12, dinner mains $20-32; ⏲11am-11pm Sun-Thu, to midnight Fri & Sat) Boudro's is the locals' riverside favorite for upscale Texas tastes. Try the quail stuffed with poblano peppers, apricots and corn.

☆ Entertainment

For listings of local music and cultural events, pick up the free weekly *San Antonio Current* (www.sacurrent.com).

Live Music & Nightclubs

The Riverwalk's many chain clubs blur together even before you've started drinking. Resist their glossy allure and opt for one of these San Antonio originals.

Cove LIVE MUSIC
(☎210-227-2683; http://thecove.us/cove; 606 W Cypress St; ⏲11am-10pm Tue-Thu, to 11pm Fri & Sat, noon-7pm Sun; 👪) Jazz, bluegrass, roots and rock – they play it all. The Cove is an incredibly unique combo of food stand/cafe/laundromat/car wash, with a kiddie playground (you read right).

Jim Cullum's Landing LIVE MUSIC
(☎210-223-7266; www.landing.com; 123 Losoya St) Jazz at the Landing is not just a San Antonio tradition; it's also a syndicated show on NPR (National Public Radio). Reservations recommended.

Bonham Exchange CLUB
(www.bonhamexchange.com; 411 Bonham St) A rather stalwart brick building conceals San Antonio's premier, multifloor gay dance club.

Sports

Four-time NBA champions the **San Antonio Spurs** (www.nba.com/spurs) shoot hoops at the **AT&T Center** (1 AT&T Center Pkwy & Walters St), off I-35. Purchase tickets through **Ticketmaster** (☎210-224-9600; www.ticketmaster.com).

Shopping

A few artisan craft shops exist among the tourist-T-shirt-filled Riverwalk. The old buildings of the city's first neighborhood, **La Villita** (www.lavillita.com; La Villita St), house the largest concentration of galleries and boutiques.

Blue Star Contemporary Art Center ARTS CENTER
(www.bluestarart.org; 116 Blue Star; ⏲noon-6pm Tue-Sat) A 1920s warehouse contains this center and its fiber arts, photography and contemporary studio spaces.

Market Square MARKET
(www.marketsquaresa.com; 514 W Commerce St; ⏲10am-8pm Jun-Aug, to 6pm Sep-May) A little bit of Mexico in downtown San Antonio, Market Square is a fair approximation of a trip south of the border, with Mexican food, mariachi bands, and store after store filled with Mexican wares.

ℹ Information

Visitor center 'amigos' (in turquoise shirts and straw hats) roam the downtown core offering direction.

Out in San Antonio (www.outinsanantonio.com) Local gay and lesbian info online.

San Antonio Public Library (www.mysapl.org) Branch locations provide free internet access across the city.

San Antonio Express-News (www.mysanantonio.com) Daily news and travel info on web.

Visitor Information Center (☎210-207-6748; www.sanantoniovisit.com; 317 Alamo Plaza; ⏰9am-5pm) Free coupon booklets and souvenirs for sale, but don't expect restaurant recommendations – they aren't allowed to make 'em.

Getting There & Away

You can reach 28 US and Mexican cities nonstop from **San Antonio International Airport** (SAT; www.sanantonio.gov/airport), 8 miles north of the Riverwalk off I-410, east of Hwy 281. VIA city bus 5 ($1) runs from the airport to downtown about every 30 minutes, or you can take a **SATrans** (☎210-281-9900; www.saairportshuttle.com) shuttle bus for $17. A taxicab ride will cost about $25. Major car-rental agencies all have offices at the airport.

From the **Greyhound Bus Station** (www.greyhound.com; 500 N St Marys St), you can get to all the big cities in the state (and lots of the small ones). The *Sunset Limited* (Florida–California) and *Texas Eagle* (San Antonio–Chicago) trains stop a few days a week (usually late at night) at the **Amtrak Station** (www.amtrak.com; 350 Hoefgen Ave).

Getting Around

The extremely tourist-friendly downtown trolleybus routes ($1.10 one way) are the best way to cover any distance around downtown. Buy a day pass ($4) at **VIA Downtown Information Center** (☎210-362-2020; www.viainfo.net; 211 W Commerce St; ⏰7am-6pm Mon-Fri, 9am-2pm Sat).

Houston

Concrete superhighways may blind you to Houston's good points when you first zoom into the sprawling town. But, look around. The nation's fourth-largest city (2.2 million in the city proper, 5.8 million in the metro area) is really a multicultural, zoning-free hodgepodge in which you see both world-class paintings and funky folk art. In one strip mall there might be a Vietnamese grocery, a Venezuelan empanada stand and a high-priced Texas meat market. And outside of town are Space Center Houston and the Gulf of Mexico beaches on Galveston Island. The interest's here; you just have to drive a little to get to it.

Sights & Activities

Museum-lovers, you've hit the jackpot in Houston, and the high-stakes action is hottest in the aptly named Museum District. As one of the most extensive arts districts in the country, this area seethes with big art, big money and big trees overhanging the streets. You'll find the major museums north and northeast of Hermann Park; to plan your route, pick up a copy of the essential *Houston Museum District* guide, available at the visitor bureau and some museums.

In addition to the sights listed here, there are small museums on the Holocaust, printing history, funerary tradition and firefighters. Don't miss the day trips (see p679).

FREE **Menil Collection** MUSEUM
(Map p674; www.menil.org; 1515 Sul Ross St; ⏰11am-7pm Wed-Sun) Local philanthropists John and Dominique de Menil's 15,000 artworks form the core of the impressive collection. The couple's taste ran from the medieval to the surreal – several rooms in the main building are devoted to the likes of René Magritte and Max Ernst. The **Cy Twombly Gallery** annex contains very abstract art. And Menil's importation of a complete 13th-century Cypriot fresco almost caused an international incident. But in the end Dominique custom-built the stun-

DON'T MISS

HOUSTON, WE HAVE AN ATTRACTION...

Dream of a landing on the moon? You can't get any closer (without years of training) than at **Space Center Houston** (www.spacecenter.org; 1601 NASA Rd 1, Clear Lake; adult/child $21/17; ⏰10am-5pm Mon-Fri, 10am-6pm Sat & Sun), off I-45 S, the official visitor center and museum of NASA's Johnson Space Center. Interactive exhibits let you try your hand at picking up an object in space or landing the shuttle. Be sure to enter the short theater films, because you exit past Apollo capsules and history exhibits. The free tram tour covers the center at work – shuttle training facilities, zero-gravity labs and the original mission control ('Houston, we have a problem').

ning **Byzantine Fresco Chapel Museum** to fit the ceiling art, which is to be held in trust for 99 years. Fourteen large abstract-expressionist Mark Rothko paintings anchor the much more modern sanctuary, **Rothko Chapel** (⌚10am-6pm daily).

Museum of Fine Arts, Houston MUSEUM
(Map p674; www.mfah.org; 1001 Bissonnet St; adult/child $7/3.50, free Thu; ⌚10am-5pm Tue & Wed, 10am-9pm Thu, 10am-7pm Fri & Sat, 12:15-7pm Sun) French impressionism and post-1945 European and American painting shine in this nationally renowned palace of art, which includes major works by Picasso and Rembrandt. Across the street, admire the talents of luminaries such as Rodin and Matisse in the tranquil **Cullen Sculpture Garden** (Map p674; cnr Montrose Blvd & Bissonnet St; admission free; ⌚dawn-dusk).

FREE **Art Car Museum** MUSEUM
(www.artcarmuseum.com; 140 Heights Blvd; ⌚11am-6pm Wed-Sun) The handful of art cars represented here are something to behold; some of them are straight out of *Mad Max*. But they're really just bait to lure you in to check out the quirky-cool rotating art exhibits, which have included subjects like road refuse and bone art. If you want to get your art-car fix, you'll have to attend the **Art Car Parade** in May, but, in the meantime, this free museum is definitely worth a stop.

Houston Museum of Natural Science MUSEUM
(Map p674; www.hmns.org; 5555 Hermann Park Dr; adult/child $15/10; ⌚9am-5pm Wed-Mon, to 8pm Tue) If you're over 16 and you find yourself thinking, 'Science museums are actually sorta cool!' you're not alone; this museum appeals to all ages. Delve into excellent traveling shows, and ooh and aah over permanent exhibits that include dinosaurs, fossils, gems and mineral exhibits, plus an IMAX, a planetarium and a butterfly conservatory.

Houston for Children

Discovery Green PARK
(Map p678; www.discoverygreen.com; 1500 McKinney St; ⌚6am-11pm) Young 'uns gettin' restless? Since mid-2008, there's been a new place to play right downtown. The 12-acre park has a lake, playground, play fountains, art, restaurants and an outdoor performance space. The entire park was constructed to strict Leadership in Energy and Environmental Design (LEED) 'gold level' standards.

Hermann Park PARK
(Map p674; www.hermannpark.org; Fannin St & Hermann Park Dr) This 445-acre park is home to playgrounds, a lake with paddleboats, the **Hermann Park Miniature Train** (per ride $3; ⌚10am-5:30pm Mon-Fri, to 6pm Sat & Sun) and the **Houston Zoo** (www.houstonzoo.org; 1513 6200 Hermann Park Dr; adult/child $12/8; ⌚9am-6pm, to 7pm Mar-Nov).

Children's Museum of Houston MUSEUM
(Map p674; www.cmhouston.org; 1500 Binz St; admission $8; ⌚9am-6pm Tue-Sat, to 8pm Thu, noon-6pm Sun) Walking distance from the park is this activity-filled museum, where little ones can make tortillas in a Mexican village or draw in an open-air art studio.

AND NOW FOR SOMETHING COMPLETELY DIFFERENT

Conservative Houston has a wacky creative streak, especially when it comes to its quirkiest museums. Follow up a visit to the Art Car Museum with a pilgrimage to the **Orange Show Center for Visionary Art** (www.orangeshow.org; 2402 Munger St; admission $1; ⌚noon-5pm Sat & Sun), a mazelike junk-art tribute to one man's favorite citrus fruit. The center fosters the folk-art vision by offering children's art education and keeping up the 50,000-strong **Beer Can House** (www.beercanhouse.org; 222 Malone St; grounds admission $2, guided tour $5; ⌚noon-5pm Sat & Sun), off Memorial Dr.

Festivals & Events

Houston Livestock Show & Rodeo RODEO
(www.hlsr.com) Twenty days in March of midway rides, prize bulls and a nightly rodeo, followed by a concert.

Art Car Parade & Festival FESTIVAL
(www.orangeshow.org; Allen Parkway) Wacky, arted-out vehicles hit the streets en masse the second Sunday in May.

Sleeping

Chain motels line all the major freeways. If you are visiting the Space Center and Galveston, consider staying on I-45 south.

Central Houston

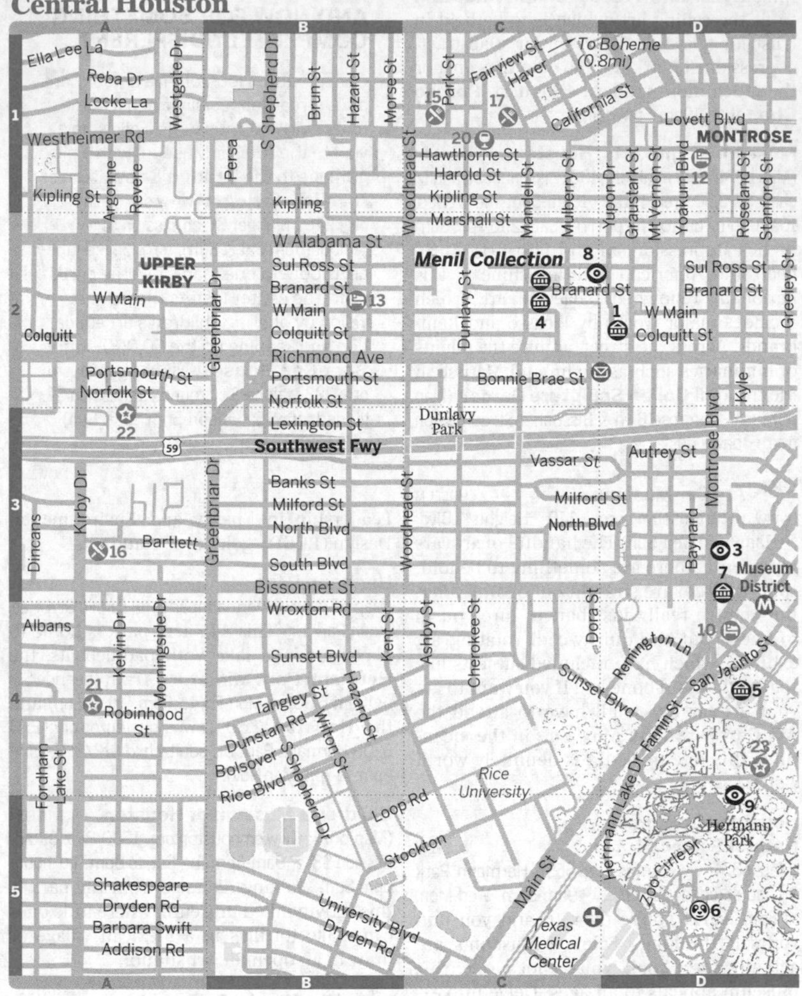

Modern B&B B&B **$$**

(Map p674; ☎832-279-6367; http://modernbb.com; 4003 Hazard St; r incl breakfast $100-200; P❄@📶) An architect's dream, this mod, solar-powered building is rife with airy decks, spiral staircases and sunlight. Slate showers, in-room Jacuzzi tubs, private decks and iPod docking stations.

Hotel ZaZa BOUTIQUE HOTEL **$$$**

(Map p674; ☎713-526-1991; www.hotelzaza.com; 5701 Main St; r $205-270; P❄@📶🏊) Why the drama? Why not! ZaZa is a flamboyant antidote to a world of chain hotels, from the stylish rooms to the over-the-top themed suites to the Vegas-style poolside bar. It also occupies a prime spot overlooking Hermann Park.

Sara's Bed & Breakfast Inn B&B **$$**

(☎713-868-1130; www.saras.com; 941 Heights Blvd; r incl breakfast $115-155, ste $155-175; P❄@📶) Traditional B&Bs aren't really Houston's style, but this Queen Anne mansion in the heart of the happenin' Heights is a lovely exception, with nine rooms and two suites named after Texas towns and tastefully furnished with antiques.

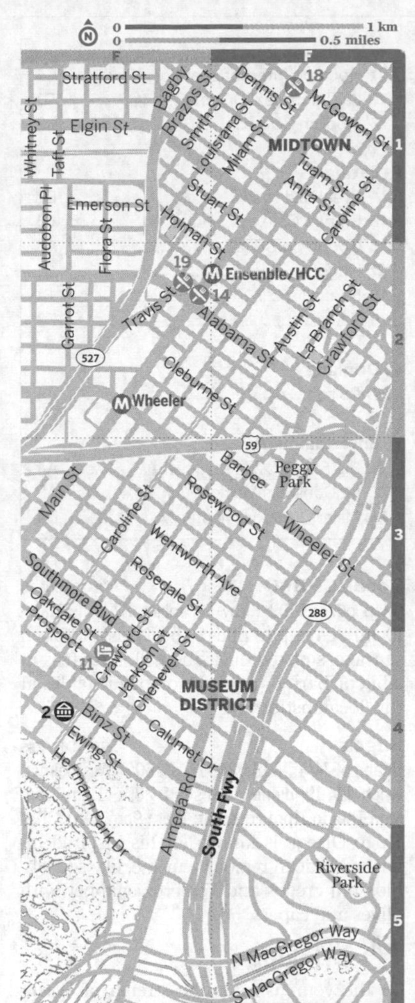

La Colombe d'Or Hotel HISTORIC HOTEL **$$$**
(Map p674; ☎713-524-7999; www.lacolombedor.com; 3410 Montrose Blvd; r $295-525; ❄) Sotheby-quality antiques and rare oil paintings fill the six suitelike rooms in this 1923 Montrose mansion.

Houston International Hostel HOSTEL **$**
(Map p674; ☎713-523-1009; www.houstonhostel.com; 5302 Crawford St; dm/s/d $15/25/40; P❄@) An easy walk to Houston's major museums and light rail makes this a steal. A mix of semipermanent residents and backpackers; friendly, eccentric staff and worn '70s furnishings lend a hippie tour-bus feel, though it's clean and safe.

Greenway Inn & Suites MOTEL **$**
(☎713-523-1009; www.greenwayinnste.com; 2929 I-59 S; r $58-100; P❄) Basic bed-and-desk motel, not far from Montrose.

Eating

Houstonians eat out more than residents of any other US city, and the *New York Times* called the foodie scene 'world class.' To keep abreast of what's hot and what's not, search online reviews and local food blogs. Montrose and Upper Kirby are two of the principal eating enclaves, but the downtown is improving; check out the restaurants clustered around Main and McKinney Sts and the new-in-2009 Pavillions complex at Fannin & Dallas Sts. Steak is huge in Houston; most all of the national heavy hitters – Ruth's Chris, the Palm etc – are on Westheimer near the Galleria.

DOWNTOWN

Treebeards CAJUN **$**
(Map p678; 315 Travis St; mains $7-10; 11am-2pm Mon-Fri) Treebeards spices up lunchtime (only) with Cajun specialties and Southern favorites like gumbo, jambalaya and étouffé, as well as daily lunch specials like blackened catfish and jerk chicken.

Original Ninfas MEXICAN **$$**
(2704 Navigation Blvd; mains $10-20; 11am-10pm, to 11pm Fri & Sat;) Don't be fooled by the countless imitations: this is the one and only original, where generations of Houstonians have been coming since the 1970s for 'shrimp diablo,' *tacos al carbon* (tacos cooked over charcoal) and handmade tamales, all crafted with a dash of hometown pride.

Kim Son VIETNAMESE **$$**
(off Map p678; 2001 Jefferson St; lunch specials $7-10, mains $10-18; 11am-11pm Sun-Thu, to midnight Fri & Sat;) This is not a place for the indecisive: the humongous menu has hundreds of choices. The good news is, you're likely to find whatever you're craving at this downtown institution, and there's a good variety of vegetarian options.

MIDTOWN

Breakfast Klub CAFE **$**
(Map p674; www.thebreakfastklub.com; 3711 Travis St; mains $8-12; 7am-2pm Mon-Fri, 8am-2pm Sat) Down-home cookin' with soul, whether

Central Houston

Top Sights

Menil Collection C2

Sights

1 Byzantine Fresco Chapel Museum D2
2 Children's Museum of Houston E4
3 Cullen Sculpture Garden D3
4 Cy Twombly Gallery C2
5 Houston Museum of Natural Science D4
6 Houston Zoo D5
7 Museum of Fine Arts, Houston D3
8 Rothko Chapel C2

Activities, Courses & Tours

9 Hermann Park Miniature Train D5

Sleeping

10 Hotel Za Za D4
11 Houston International Hostel E4
12 La Colombe d'Or Hotel D1
13 Modern B&B B2

Eating

14 Breakfast Klub E2
15 Empire Café C1
16 Goode Co BBQ A3
17 Hugo's C1
18 Reef F1
19 T'afia E2

Drinking

20 Poisen Girl C1

Entertainment

21 Big Easy A4
22 McGonigel's Mucky Duck A3
23 Miller Outdoor Theater D4

it's wings 'n' waffles or catfish 'n' grits. Expect a wait at this bustling place that's social central.

Reef SEAFOOD $$$
(Map p674; ☎713-526-8282; 2600 Travis St; lunch $11-21, dinner mains $19-29; ⊙11am-10pm Mon-Fri, 5-11pm Sat) The chef has won oodles of awards and the attention of countless foodies for the Gulf Coast seafood served in a sleek and sophisticated dining room with a skyline-view raw bar.

T'afia AMERICAN $$
(Map p674; ☎713-524-69922; 3701 Travis St; mains $17-24; ⊙5:30-10pm Tue-Thu, to 10:30pm Fri & Sat) Nationally renowned chef Monica Pope brings top-quality local and organic ingredients to life in her new American cuisine. There are lots of ways to nosh, including small plates, big plates, brunch, and fantabulous free appetizers (!) at happy hour Tuesday through Thursday.

MONTROSE & UPPER KIRBY

TOP CHOICE **Empire Café** AMERICAN $$
(Map p674; 1732 Westheimer Rd; mains $8-14; ⊙7:30am-10pm, to 11pm Fri & Sat;) A classic fixture of the Montrose neighborhood with a shady patio and one of the best all-day breakfasts in town, the Empire's a jack of all trades that manages to excel at everything: coffee, lunch, evening cocktails…

Goode Co BBQ BARBECUE $
(Map p674; 5109 Kirby Dr; mains $7-11; ⊙11am-10pm) Belly up to piles of beef brisket, Czech sausage, smoked duck and gallon ice teas in a big ol' barn or out back on picnic tables at this local institution.

Hugo's MEXICAN $$$
(Map p674; ☎713-524-7744; 1600 Westheimer; lunch $14-19, dinner mains $18-28; ⊙11am-10pm Mon-Thu, to 11pm Fri & Sat; 10am-9pm Sun) Chef Hugo Ortega is known for his inspired interior-Mexican regional cuisine, like squash-blossom crepes and Veracruz snapper with olives and capers.

Drinking

To the youngish set, the stretch of Washington Ave bars and clubs defines all that is hip and happening in Houston nightlife (although lately downtown is none too shabby in that department). The corner of White Oak and Studemont in the Heights has a few funky little bars, including a roadhouse, a tiki bar and a live music club in an old house.

La Carafe BAR
(Map p678; 813 Congress St) In an 1860 building, this intimate downtown place has one of the town's best jukeboxes, well-priced wines by the glass and an ancient wooden bar lit by candles.

Boheme CAFE
(Map p674; 307 Fairview St; ⏲8:30am-midnight Sun & Mon, to 2am Tue-Sat; 📶) Bewitching Boheme is part wine bar, part coffee shop and 100% bohemian. The frozen mojitos reign among our favorite drinks in town.

Poison Girl BAR
(Map p674; 1641 Westheimer Rd) Seductive pin-up girls, a killer back patio and some vintage pinball games add up to Houston's sexiest dive.

Onion Creek Cafe CAFE
(3106 White Oak; ⏲7am-2am) A great neighborhood hangout in the Heights with a big patio; open from early-morning coffee to late-night cocktails.

☆ Entertainment

There's a fair bit of nightlife around the Preston and Main Street Square stops downtown. Montrose and Midtown have clubs, but they're spread around. Look for listings in the independent weekly *Houston Press* (www.houstonpress.com) and in the Thursday edition of the *Houston Chronicle* (www.chron.com).

Live Music

When it's time to rock out, visit www.spacecityrock.com, the online version of a local music mag.

McGonigel's Mucky Duck LIVE MUSIC
(Map p674; ☎713-528-5999; www.mcgonigels.com; 2425 Norfolk St) Listen nightly to live acoustic, Irish, folk and country performers in pubby surrounds.

Big Easy LIVE MUSIC
(Map p674; ww.thebigeasyblues.com; 5731 Kirby Dr; ⏲6pm-2am Mon-Thu, 3pm-2am Fri, 6pm-1am Sun) This unpretentious place in the Village honors Houston's New Orleans connection with live blues and zydeco.

Sambuca Jazz Cafe LIVE MUSIC
(Map p678; www.sambucarestaurant.com; 909 Texas Ave) A swanky supper club, Sambuca serves live jazz accompanied by an eclectic menu.

Theater & Performing Arts

The Houston Grand Opera, the Society of the Performing Arts, Houston Ballet, Da Camera chamber orchestra and the Houston Symphony all perform downtown in the **Theater District** (www.houstontheaterdistrict.org). From the district's website, you can purchase tickets and view all schedules.

Miller Outdoor Theatre THEATER
(Map p674; ☎281-823-9103; ww.milleroutdoortheatre.com; 6000 Hermann Park Dr) Hermann Park's outdoor theater is a great place to lay out a blanket on a summer night and enjoy a free play, musical or concert.

Alley Theatre THEATER
(Map p678; ☎713-220-5700; www.alleytheatre.org; 615 Texas Ave) Houston's heavy-hitter theater is one of the last in the nation to keep a resident company of actors. From classics to modern plays, the magic of this ensemble is palpable.

Sports

Reliant Stadium (www.reliantpark.com; 1 Reliant Park) is home to the **Houston Texans** (www.houstontexans.com) football team. The **Houston Astros** (www.astros.com) play pro baseball downtown at **Minute Maid Park** (Map p678; 501 Crawford St). The **Toyota Center** (Map p678; www.houstontoyotacenter.com; 1510 Polk St) is home to the **Houston Rockets** (www.houstonrockets.com) NBA basketball team.

Shopping

Galleria MALL
(www.simon.com; 5085 Westheimer Rd) In a state full of big malls, this one's the biggest. A huge conglomeration of shops collide in and

IF YOU HAVE A FEW MORE DAYS

Just 15 miles west of downtown, you can see where Texas nationhood was won on April 21, 1836. The 570ft **San Jacinto Monument** (www.tpwd.state.tx.us; 3523 Hwy 134, La Porte; adult/child $12/8; ⏲9am-6pm) looks like the Washington Monument but has a cement star on top (which makes it 12ft taller). Tour the museum, watch the movie and then ride up to the observation deck to look over the 1000-acre battlefield, where Texan forces under General Sam Houston shouted 'Remember the Alamo' while whooping Mexican general Santa Anna's forces. You can tour the still-afloat 1912 **Battleship Texas** (adult/child $10/5; ⏲10am-5pm), also part of the park.

Downtown Houston

Sights

1 Discovery Green C4

Eating

2 Treebeards C2

Drinking

3 La Carafe C2

Entertainment

4 Alley Theatre B2
5 Minute Maid Park D3
6 Sambuca Jazz Cafe B2
7 Toyota Center B4

near this mazelike place, which is off I-610. Macy's, Foley's and Nordstrom anchor nearly 400 mall stores.

For browsing in more eclectic and locally owned stores, hit the neighborhoods:

Along 19th St (between Yale St and Shepherd Dr) in the **Heights** (www.heightsfirstsaturday.com), you'll find unique antiques, clever crafts and cafes. On the first Saturday of every month, the street takes on a carnival-like air with outdoor booths and entertainment.

In Montrose, **Westheimer St** is a dream for crafty fashionistas and antique-hunters alike. Start on Dunlavy Rd and work your way down the street, where you'll find a mix of used- and new-clothing stores running the gamut from vintage to punk rock to Tokyo mod, plus lots of funky old furniture.

For slightly less rebellious fashion terrain, stroll around **Rice Village** and let the window displays lure you in.

Information

Chase Bank (712 Main St) Currency exchange and ATM.

Greater Houston Convention & Visitors Bureau (Map p678; ☎713-437-5200; www.

visithoustontexas.com; cnr Walker & Bagby Sts; ⌚9am-4pm Mon-Sat) Free parking on Walker St.

Houston Public Library (www.hpl.lib.tx.us; 500 McKinney St; ⌚10am-8pm Mon-Thu, 10am-5pm Sat) Free internet computers and wi-fi.

KUHT 88.7 Classical music and NPR from the University of Houston.

Memorial Hermann Hospital (6411 Fannin St) Part of the Texas Medical Center megacomplex.

Police station (☎713-529-3100; 802 Westheimer Rd; ⌚24hr)

Post office (Map p678; 401 Franklin St)

ℹ Getting There & Around

Houston Airport System (www.fly2houston.com) has two airports. Twenty-two miles north of the city center, **George Bush Intercontinental** (IAH; btwn I-45 & I-59 N), home base for Continental Airlines, serves cities worldwide through many carriers. Twelve miles southeast of town, **William P Hobby Airport** (HOU), off I-45 S, is a major hub for Southwest Airlines and domestic travel. Read your ticket closely: some airlines, like Delta, fly out of both airports. Wi-fi is available at both facilities.

Cabs are readily available at both airports. Airport rates are determined by zone, and you'll pay either the flat zone rate or the meter rate, whatever's less. You'll shell out $60 to get from George Bush Intercontinental to downtown; from Hobby it's about $25.

The Hobby airport bus (88) connects to downtown (and to the Downtown Transit Center light-rail stop) from Monday to Saturday, 6am to 11pm ($1.25). The Airport Direct bus runs between downtown and Bush Intercontinental ($4.50) throughout the day. **SuperShuttle** (☎800-258-3826; www.supershuttle.com) provides service from both Bush ($23) and Hobby ($19) airports.

Long-distance buses arrive at the **Greyhound Bus Terminal** (off Map p678; www.greyhound.com; 2121 Main St), which is located between downtown and the Museum District, and two blocks from the Downtown Transit Center light-rail stop.

The *Sunset Limited* train stops at the **Amtrak Station** (Map p678; www.amtrak.com; 902 Washington Ave) three times a week.

Houston's **Metropolitan Transit Authority** (Metro; ☎713-635-4000; www.ridemetro.org) runs the convenient light-rail system; $1.25 gets you a one-way ride. Most of the in-town sights are along the Downtown–Museum District–Reliant Park light-rail corridor. If you want to venture further, you'll need to rent a car; the bus system is mostly inefficient for visitors' needs. Every major national car-rental agency can be found at either airport.

Around Houston

GALVESTON

Don't think of Galveston as just another beach town. What makes it irresistible is that it's actually a historic town that happens to have some beaches. An easy day trip from Houston, it's also a very popular cruise-ship port, which has been a vital boost to the economy.

In 2008, Galveston was ravaged by a direct hit from Hurricane Ike. Many of the gingerbread-covered Victorian homes in the historic districts have been restored, but missing is the canopy of mature trees that once graced the island.

👁 Sights & Activities

Nothing more than a sandy barrier island, Galveston stretches 30 miles in length and is no more than 3 miles wide. The center of activity on the island, the historic 'Strand' district (around the intersection of 22nd and Mechanic Sts) is best covered on foot so you can check out the many attractions, shops, restaurants and bars. Find loads more dining and activity info at **Galveston Island Visitors Center** (☎409-797-5145; www.galveston.com; Ashton Villa, 2328 Broadway; ⌚9am-5pm).

For quick and easy beach access, park anywhere along the seawall. Or, if you want more sand to spread out on, head to **East Beach** (parking $8, walk-ins free) at the eastern end of the island.

Great Storm Theatre THEATER
(www.galveston.com/pier21theatre; cnr Pier 21 & Harborside Dr; adult/child $5/4; ⌚11am-5pm Wed-Mon, to 6pm in summer) This 30-minute multimedia documentary avoids the maudlin as it recounts the 1900 hurricane through photos, special effects and eyewitness accounts of the deadliest natural disaster in US history.

Texas Seaport Museum MUSEUM
(www.tsm-elissa.org; cnr Harborside Dr & 21st St; adult/child $8/5; ⌚10am-5pm) This vast museum explains life around Galveston's port during its heyday in the 19th century. Outside, you can tour the *Elissa,* a beautiful 1877 Scottish tall ship.

Moody Gardens GARDENS
(www.moodygardens.com; 1 Hope Blvd; adult/child under 3yr $50/free; ⌚10am-6pm; 👪) Kids seem to love all the activity stuffed in and around the glass pyramids: aquariums, a penguin

encounter, a butterfly rainforest, theater rides... Entrance to individual attractions can also be purchased à la carte.

Sleeping & Eating

It's no surprise that the sea is the primary food source in Galveston; fish restaurants (mostly chains) line the bayside piers near the Strand.

Beachcomber Inn MOTEL **$**
(409-744-7133; www.galvestoninn.com; 2825 61st St; r $60-89;) A block from the beach, this indie motel is a neat and clean bargain.

Hotel Galvez HOTEL **$$$**
(409-765-7721; www.galveston.com/galvez; 2024 Seawall Blvd; r $179-300;) Bask in palm-fringed Spanish-colonial luxury in this historic hotel, where the pool deck has a lovely Gulf view and the full-service spa came back online mid-2009.

Shrimp N Stuff SEAFOOD **$$**
(3901 Ave O; mains $7-14; 10:30am-8:30pm Mon-Thu, to 9:30 Fri & Sat) Skip the big, expensive seafood emporiums and get your fried seafood fix at this beachy-casual fave.

Mosquito Cafe CAFE **$$**
(628 14 St; mains $7-20; 11am-9pm Tue-Fri, 8am-9pm Sat, 8am-3pm Sun) There's lots to love about this place, from the fresh ingredients to the wonderful baked goods to the ridiculously big sandwiches.

Spot CAFE **$$**
(3204 Seawall Blvd; mains $11-21; 11am-10pm Sun-Thu, to 11pm Sat & Sun) The three old houses containing the restaurant-tiki bar/ice-cream parlor are a favorite local hangout, with a great Gulf-view patio.

Getting There & Away

Kerrville Bus Company (800-335-3722; www.iridekbc.com; 3825 Broadway) runs a morning bus and an evening bus (from $20, one hour) to Houston. Ike knocked the around-town **Galveston Island Rail Trolley** (www.islandtransit.net) clear off its tracks; when (if?) it will be running again is uncertain.

PINEY WOODS

In Piney Woods, northeast Texas, 100ft-plus-tall trees outnumber people. Nature is the attraction, but don't expect breathtaking vistas; here you'll find quiet trails and varied ecosystems. At **Big Thicket National Preserve** (www.nps.gov/bith; cnr US 69 & Rte 420; admission free; visitor center 9am-5pm), coastal plains meet desert sand dunes, and cypress swamps stand next to pine and hardwood forests. If you're lucky, you may run across one of 20 species of small wild orchids while hiking the 45 miles of trail. The eight disparate park units are 100 miles northwest of Houston.

SOUTHERN GULF COAST

Images of rowdy spring breakers aside, the Gulf Coast is known for its sparkling bays, small harbors filled with shrimp boats and more than 60 miles of protected beaches. Some parts of the Gulf Coast – like Port Arthur or Brazosport – have shunned the tourist trade and embraced the steady income that refineries and oilrigs can provide. But tiny coastal communities and wandering coastal back roads are reason enough to visit.

Aransas National Wildlife Refuge

For bird-watchers, the premier site on the Texas coast is the 115,000-acre **Aransas National Wildlife Refuge** (www.fws.gov/southwest/refuges/texas/aransas; per person/carload $3/5; 6am-dusk, visitor center 8:30am-4:30pm). The scenery alone is spectacular, and close to 400 bird species have been documented here.

None are more famous than the extremely rare whooping cranes that summer in Canada and spend their winters in the refuge. These endangered white birds – the tallest in North America – can stand 5ft tall with a 7ft wingspan.

WORTH A TRIP

PORT ARANSAS

Driving north, Padre Island morphs imperceptibly into Mustang Island, at the tip of which (20 miles along) is **Port Aransas** (www.portaransas.org). This bustling little fishing and vacation village is worth a stop. From divey to divine, there are lots of places to eat seafood – look for names like Fin's, Hook's, Trout Street. Gulf fishing charters depart from here; **Fisherman's Wharf** (www.wharfcat.com; 900 N Tarpon St; 5hr trip adult/child $60/30) has regular deep-sea excursions and runs jetty boats to outer islands (adult/child $12/6).

From the observation tower you can usually spot one or two, but boats tour the estuaries from November to March, and this is easily the best way to get a good view of rare birds. Captain Tommy with **Rockport Birding & Kayak Adventures** (☎877-892-4737; www.whoopingcranetours.com; 3½hr tours $45; ⏰7:30am & 1pm Mar-Nov) has a relatively small, shallow-drafting boat, and so can get you into back bays that larger charters can't reach.

Corpus Christi & Around

The salt breezes and palm tree–lined bay are quite pleasant in this 'city by the sea' whose population numbers 285,000. Downtown has a waterfront promenade and a few museums, but there's not too much in town to entice visitors. Trip out to Padre Island and the National Seashore for a beachy break, though don't expect the windblown surf to be azure blue. To the north, Port Aransas is a bustling little fishing town with tons of restaurants and boat charters.

Shoreline Dr, in downtown Corpus, has a small beach; the street continues south as Ocean Dr, which has bayfront playgrounds and parks, as well as some serious mansions lining it. **Corpus Christi Convention & Visitors Bureau** (☎800-766-2322; www.corpuschristi-tx-cvb.org; 1823 N Chaparral; ⏰9am-5pm Thu-Mon) has helpful coupons online.

After the bay, the second sight you're likely to notice is the 900ft-long WWII aircraft carrier moored just north of the ship channel at the **USS Lexington Museum** (www.usslexington.com; 2914 N Shoreline Blvd; adult/child $14/9; ⏰9am-6pm Jun-Aug, to 5pm rest of year). A number of high-tech exhibits give visitors a chance to experience wartime experiences without enlisting.

Explore shipwrecks, see how Texas proved to be the doom for French explorer La Salle and see the moldering remains of reproductions of two of Columbus' ships at **Museum of Science & History** (www.ccmuseum.com; 1900 N Chaparral St; adult/child $12.50/6; ⏰10am-5pm Tue-Sat, noon-5pm Sun; 👪).

Twenty miles east of downtown, off Hwy 358 (SPID), the sugar-sand beaches of **Padre Island** beckon. (Technically, this is 'North' Padre Island, but locals just call it 'the island.') Public access is easy – you can drive and park on the packed sand at the water's edge. No environmental groups seem to be protesting, but there is also a parking lot at **Bob Hall Pier** (15820 Park Rd 22) that you can use instead.

Downtown, there are several waterfront hotels; **Bayfront Inn** (☎361-883-7271; www.bayfrontinncc.com; 601 N Shoreline Blvd; r $60-110; ❄🏊) has the best basic-motel deals with a view of the bay. Numerous condos are for short-term rent on the island (see the visitors bureau website), and **Holiday Inn Sunspree Resort** (☎361-949-8041; www.ichotelsgroup.com; 15202 Windward Dr; r from $90; ❄@📶🏊👪) sits right on the sand; plus it has a complimentary kids' club from Memorial Day through to Labor Day.

Bars and restaurants are clustered on the streets surrounding Chaparral and Water Sts downtown – there are few restaurants on the island. Eat a fried-shrimp wrap from a surfboard table at longtime fave **Executive Surf Club** (309 N Water St; mains $6-10; ⏰11am-11pm Sun-Wed, to midnight Thu-Sat). **Brewster Street Icehouse** (1724 N Tancahua St; mains $7-16; ⏰11am-2am; 👪) has country-fried everything, cold brews, live country music (Thursday to Saturday nights) and a playground for the kiddies.

PADRE ISLAND NATIONAL SEASHORE

The 60 southern miles of 'North' Padre Island that lie outside Corpus Christi city limits are all a protected part of the **Padre Island National Seashore** (www.nps.gov/pais; Park Rd 22; 7-day pass per car $10; ⏰visitor center 9am-5pm). Four-wheel drive is necessary to see the extent of the park, but if you hike even a short distance from the visitor center, you'll be free of the crowds. The constant wind not only creates and moves dunes, it also attracts kitesurfers and windsurfers to the inland-side Bird Island Basin area. Watch for the endangered Kemp Ridley sea turtles that nest in the park and are closely protected. If you're visiting in late summer, you might be able to take part in a turtle release; call the **Hatchling Hotline** (☎361-949-7163) for information. Camping is available at the semideveloped, paved **Malaquite Campground** ($8), or go primitive: beach camping is free with a permit.

South Padre Island

Want to parasail, bungee jump and drink yourself silly? This condo-crammed island has beach activities and bars galore. **South Padre Island Visitor Center** (☎956-761-6433, 800-767-2373; www.sopadre.com; 600 Padre

Blvd; ⏲8am-6pm Mon-Fri, 9am-5pm Sat & Sun) website has a comprehensive list of minigolf courses, rowdy restaurants, condo rentals and beachfront hotels. The tours and feeding presentations every 30 minutes at **Sea Turtle Inc** (www.seaturtleinc.com; 6617 Padre Blvd; suggested donation adult/child $3/2; ⏲10am-4pm Tue-Sun) rescue facility are refreshingly educational entertainment.

If you want to experience a hard-core fisherman's life, stop in Port Isabel (before you cross the bridge) to eat or stay at **Marchan's White Sands Motel, Marina & Restaurant** (☎956-943-2414; www.the-white-sands.com; 418 W Hwy 100; breakfast $4-8, mains $7-16, r $49-109; ⏲6am-9pm Tue-Sat, to 2pm Mon, reduced hr off season; ❄🏊).

The Valley

Way down here in the Rio Grande Valley (known simply as 'the Valley'), you're spittin' distance from Mexico. Citrus tree plantations are gradually giving way to new subdivisions, but there are enough remaining to supply the roadside stands at which you can pick up fresh local grapefruits and oranges (harvested November through May).

Nuevo Progreso (www.shop-progreso.com), Mexico, is the border shopping town that's probably been the least affected by drug-cartel violence. We have friends who still visit regularly; nonetheless, we're urging caution. See the boxed text, p699.

The closest US town to the crossing is **Weslaco** (www.weslaco.com), a farming community 58 miles west of South Padre Island known for its sweet onions. On the road to Mexico you'll find both the **Best Western Palm Aire** (☎956-969-2411; www.bestwesternpalmaire.com; 415 S International Blvd, Weslaco; r $59-72; ❄@📶🏊), with a tropical pool and hot tub, and the **Blue Onion** (423 S International Blvd, Weslaco; mains $5-11; ⏲11am-9pm Mon-Thu, to 10pm Fri & Sat), with locally loved homemade meals and flatbread.

Birders flock to the Valley's parks associated with the **World Birding Center** (www.worldbirdingcenter.org). Migrating avian masses, including thousands of hawks, pass through this natural corridor along the main north–south American fly route from March to April and September to October. Twenty miles or so west of Weslaco, the visitor and educational center at **Bentsen-Rio Grande Valley State Park** (2800 S Bentsen Palm Dr, Mission; adult/child $5/free; ⏲park 7am-10pm, center 8am-5pm) is a model of sustainable, green-driven architecture, including rainwater collection. Rent a bike (from $5 a day) or take the tram the 2 miles into the park. There, alligators and birds roam the wetlands, and you may spot a javelina (wild pig) or a horny toad on your way to the hawk-observation tower.

Twenty-seven miles southwest of South Padre in **Brownsville** (www.brownsville.org), the southernmost town in Texas, **Gladys Porter Zoo** (www.gpz.org; 500 Ringgold St; adult/child $9.50/6.50; ⏲9am-5:30pm Mon-Fri, to 6pm Sat & Sun; 👪) is a lush tropical botanical garden with a conservation bent. It specializes in breeding endangered animals like Komodo dragons and Philippine crocodiles.

Both Brownsville and Harlingen (30 miles east of Weslaco, 50 miles northwest of South Padre) have regional airports and national car rental.

DALLAS-FORT WORTH

Dallas and Fort Worth are as different as a Beemer-driving yuppie and a rancher in a Dodge dually pickup truck – the proverbial city slicker and his country cousin. Just 30 miles apart, the two towns anchor a giant megalopolis of six million people known as the Metroplex. Go see the excesses of the Big D and then day-trip to Fort Worth – the cowboy and Western sights and museums there might be the state's best-kept secret.

Dallas

Bright lights, big hair, shiny cars… In many ways, upscale Dallas is the belle of the Texas ball. From JR Ewing and the TV show Dallas to the Dallas Cowboys and their cheerleaders, Dallas has made a heavy mark on American popular culture, which seems fitting for a city whose ethos is image consciousness and conspicuous consumption.

With all that money, it's no surprise that there's an amazing dining scene. (You can tell which place is hot by the caliber of cars the valet leaves out front.) With more malls per capita than anywhere else in the US – not to mention the second-highest debt per resident – shopping is definitely this city's guiltiest pleasure. Just don't try to scratch too deep below the surface; you may be disappointed.

SOUTHFORK RANCH

Who shot JR? Locals certainly no longer care (the TV drama *Dallas* was canceled in 1992), but that doesn't stop interstate and international visitors from driving 20 miles north from Dallas to tour **Southfork Ranch** (☎972-442-7800; www.southfork.com; 3700 Hogge Rd/FM 2551, Plano; adult/child $9.50/7; ⏲9am-5pm). If you are expecting to see Miss Ellie's kitchen or JR's bedroom, don't. The ranch was used for exterior filming only; interior shots were filmed on a Hollywood set.

Sights

True to the theme that 'everything's bigger in Texas', downtown Dallas' arts district (www.thedallasartsdistrict.org) is the biggest (and one of the best) in the nation, with 68 acres of arts, entertainment and culture.

North of downtown, uptown has smart, trendy bars, restaurants and hotels; follow Harwood St (or St Paul St, if you're taking the trolley) to McKinney Ave. Bars also line Greenville Ave, northeast of downtown off Ross Ave. Deep Ellum, at the eastern end of Elm St, is a bit gritty, but it's the nucleus of Dallas' small live-music scene.

DOWNTOWN

TOP CHOICE Sixth Floor Museum MUSEUM
(Map p684; www.jfk.org; Book Depository, 411 Elm St; adult/child under 5yr $13.50/free; ⏲10am-6pm Tue-Sun, noon-6pm Mon) No city wants the distinction of being the site of a presidential assassination – especially if that president happens to be John F Kennedy. But rather than downplay the events that sent the city reeling in 1963, Dallas gives visitors a unique opportunity to delve into the shooting in this fascinating and memorable museum. And while any museum dedicated to the subject could have reconstructed the historical event using footage, audio clips and eyewitness accounts, this museum located in the former Book Depository can give you goosebumps when you see the exact window from which Lee Harvey Oswald fired upon the motorcade. (If that last statement raises your hackles, not to worry: the displays don't shy away from conspiracy theories, either.)

Dealey Plaza & the Grassy Knoll PARK
(Map p684) Now a National Historic Landmark, this rectangular park is south of the Book Depository. From Dealey Plaza, walk along Elm St beside the infamous grassy knoll, and look for the white 'X' in the road that marks the exact spot where the president was shot. Most days there are conspiracy theorists on hand who are more than happy to point out where additional gunmen might have hidden.

Dallas Museum of Art MUSEUM
(Map p684; www.dm-art.org; 1717 N Harwood St; adult/child $10/free; ⏲11am-5pm Tue-Sun, to 9pm Thu; 👪📶) This museum is a high-caliber world tour of decorative and fine art befitting a big city. Our faves include Edward Hopper's enigmatic *Lighthouse Hill* and Rodin's *Sculptor and his Muse*. The Spanish Colonial art section is extraordinary. Kids (and parents) will appreciate the Young Learners Gallery, with fun projects for young 'uns.

Nasher Sculpture Center MUSEUM
(Map p684; www.nashersculpturecenter.org; 2001 Flora St; adult/child $10/free; ⏲11am-5pm Tue-Sun) Modern-art installations shine both inside and out at the fabulous glass-and-steel Nasher Sculpture Center. The Nashers accumulated what might be one of the greatest privately held sculpture collections in the world, with works by Calder, de Kooning, Rodin, Serra and Miró, and the divine sculpture garden is one of the best in the country.

Fair Park MUSEUM
(www.fairpark.org; 1300 Robert B Cullum Blvd; all-access passport adult/child $27/16, museums also priced individually) The art deco buildings of Fair Park, which were created for the 1936 Texas Centennial Exposition, today contain seven museums that focus on science, railroads, African American and women's history. While the grounds are safe, the surrounding area is best avoided; luckily, on-site parking is plentiful and free (State Fair excepted).

Dallas World Aquarium AQUARIUM
(Map p684; 1801 N Griffin St; www.dwazoo.com; adult/child $21/13; ⏲10am-5pm; 👪) Among the flora and fauna of 14 countries, you can explore the watery Mayan world of a Central American jungle.

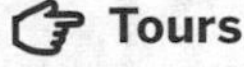

Tours

John Nagle WALKING
(☎214-674-6295; www.jfktours.com; tours $20; ⏲by appointment Sat & Sun) Dramatic and

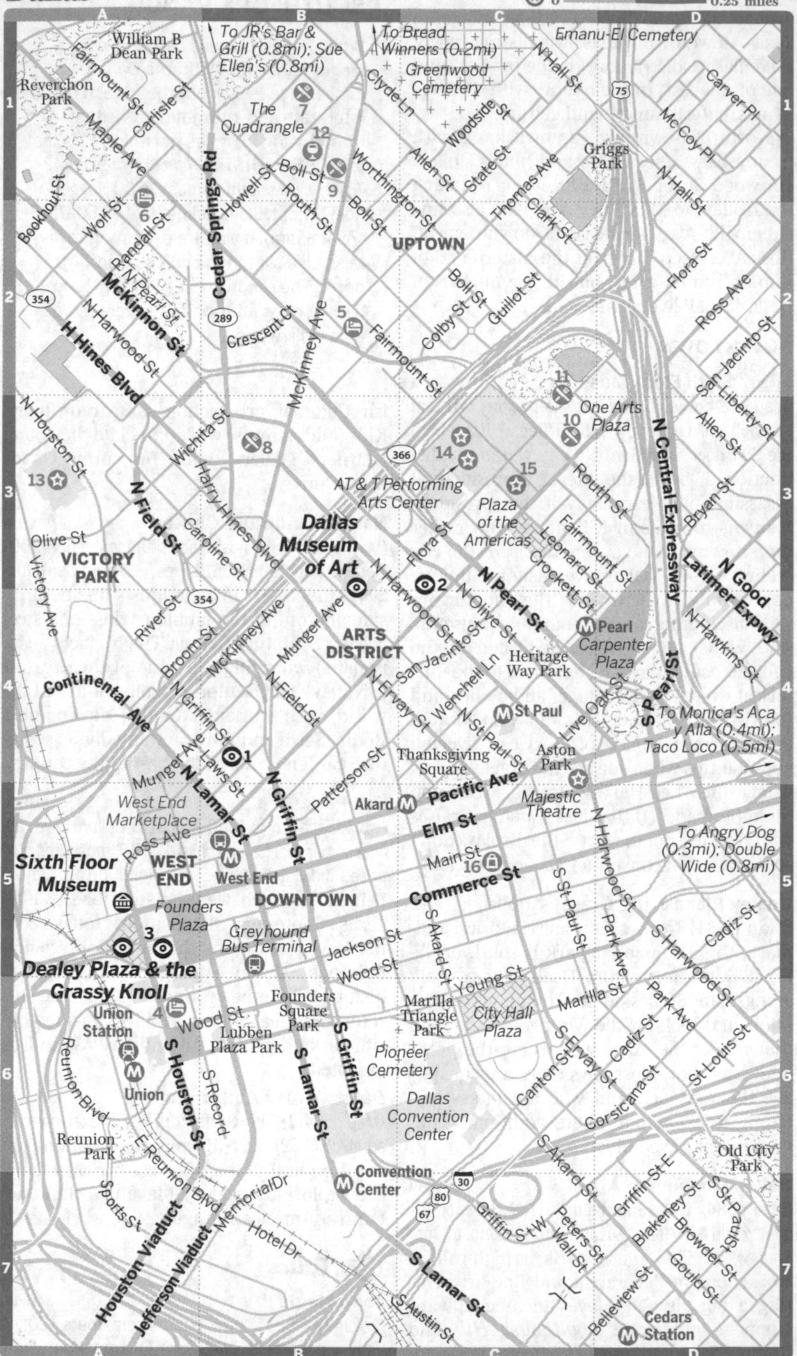
To JR's Bar & Grill (0.8mi); Sue Ellen's (0.8mi)
To Bread Winners (0.2mi)
Emanu-El Cemetery
Greenwood Cemetery
William B Dean Park
Reverchon Park
The Quadrangle
Griggs Park
UPTOWN
McKinney Ave
Cedar Springs Rd
McKinnon St
H Hines Blvd
One Arts Plaza
AT & T Performing Arts Center
Dallas Museum of Art
Plaza of the Americas
VICTORY PARK
ARTS DISTRICT
N Central Expressway
N Good Latimer Expwy
Pearl Carpenter Plaza
Heritage Way Park
St Paul
To Monica's Aca y Alla (0.4mi); Taco Loco (0.5mi)
Thanksgiving Square
Aston Park
Majestic Theatre
Akard
Pacific Ave
Elm St
To Angry Dog (0.3mi); Double Wide (0.8mi)
West End Marketplace
Sixth Floor Museum
WEST END
West End
DOWNTOWN
Commerce St
Founders Plaza
Greyhound Bus Terminal
Dealey Plaza & the Grassy Knoll
Union Station
Union
Founders Square Park
Lubben Plaza Park
Marilla Triangle Park
City Hall Plaza
Pioneer Cemetery
Dallas Convention Center
Reunion Park
Convention Center
Old City Park
Cedars Station
Houston Viaduct
Jefferson Viaduct
S Lamar St
S Griffin St
S Houston St
N Lamar St
N Griffin St
N Pearl St
S Pearl St
TEXAS DALLAS-FORT WORTH

Dallas

Top Sights

Dallas Museum of Art.......B3
Dealey Plaza & the Grassy Knoll.......A5
Sixth Floor Museum.......A5

Sights

1 Dallas World Aquarium.......B4
2 Nasher Sculpture Center.......C3
3 Old Red Courthouse.......A5

Sleeping

4 Hotel Lawrence.......A6
5 Hotel Za Za.......B2
6 Stoneleigh Hotel.......A1

Eating

7 Dream Cafe.......B1
8 Fearing's.......B3
9 S&D Oyster Company.......B1
10 Screen Door.......C3
11 Tei-An.......C2

Drinking

12 Ginger Man.......B1

Entertainment

13 American Airlines Center.......A3
14 Winspear Opera House.......C3
15 Wyly Theatre.......C3

Shopping

16 Neiman Marcus.......C5

committed conspiracy theorist-historian guides 1¼-hour walking tours of JFK assassination sights.

Festivals & Events

State Fair of Texas FAIR

(www.bigtex.com; Fair Park, 1300 Cullum Blvd) The 52ft Big Tex statue towers – and talks – over Fair Park from late September to October. Come ride one of the tallest Ferris wheels in North America, eat corny dogs (this is where they were invented), and browse among the prize-winning cows, sheep and quilts.

Sleeping

Staying uptown, you're closest to restaurants and nightlife, but hotels there can get pricey. The further you get from the center, the cheaper the highway chain motels get.

TOP CHOICE **Hotel Belmont** BOUTIQUE HOTEL $$

(☎866-870-8010; www.belmontdallas.com; 901 Fort Worth Ave; d $109-199; P ❄ @ ⓦ ≋) Just two miles west of downtown, this stylish 1940s bungalow hotel is a fabulously low-key antidote to Dallas' flashier digs, with a touch of mid-century modern design and more than its share of soul. The garden rooms – with soaking tubs, Moroccan-blue tile work, kilim rugs and some city views – are tops.

Abby Guesthouse GUESTHOUSE $

(☎214-264-4804; www.abbyguesthouse.com; 5417 Goodwin Ave; r $59-69; P ❄ @ ⓦ ♿) This bright and cheerful garden cottage is within walking distance of great cafes and bars on Upper Greenville Ave; with a full kitchen and sunny private patio, it's a total steal.

Hotel Lawrence HOTEL $$

(Map p684; ☎214-761-9090; www.hotellawrencedallas.com; 302 S Houston St; r $89-189; P ❄ @ ⓦ) One of the better deals among the midrange hotels (although the $17 valet parking isn't such a steal), Hotel Lawrence has a convenient downtown location in a 1925 building.

Hotel Palomar HOTEL $$

(☎214-520-7969; www.hotelpalomar-dallas.com; 5300 E Mockingbird Lane; r from $169; P ❄ @ ⓦ ≋) The Palomar combines dramatic flair – like zebra robes, a Hollywood-esque infinity pool and a chichi spa – with eco-conscious policies and enough freebies (like the nightly wine and cheese happy hour) to make you feel good about being spoiled.

Mansion on Turtle Creek LUXURY HOTEL $$$

(☎214-559-2100; www.rosewoodhotels.com; 2821 Turtle Creek Blvd; r $275-600; P ❄ @ ⓦ ≋) Step into a life of ease, where for every two guests there's one staff member attending. This is *the* definitive five-star Dallas hotel, and worth it if you've got it. Fresh flowers sit atop hand-carved European guest-room furnishings, and dinner is served in the original, 1925 marble-clad Italianate villa.

Stoneleigh Hotel HISTORIC HOTEL $$$

(Map p684; ☎800-921-8498; www.stoneleighhotel.com; 2927 Maple Ave; r $200-450; P ❄ @ ⓦ) A $36 million makeover in 2008 upped the art deco quotient.

Hotel ZaZa BOUTIQUE HOTEL $$$

(Map p684; ☎214-468-8399; www.hotelzaza.com; 2332 Leonard St; r $229-395; P ❄ @ ⓦ ≋) Hip, over-the-top eclectic rooms.

Eating

The stretch of Main near Akard St has some interesting food options, but downtown in

TASTES BORN IN TEXAS

» **Corny dogs** Cornbread-batter-dipped hot dogs on a stick were created in 1948 by Neil Fletcher for the State Fair of Texas; Fletcher's still sells 'em there; now available with jalapeño cornbread too.

» **Dr Pepper** A pharmacist in a Waco drugstore-soda shop invented this aromatic cola in the 1880s. Pay homage at the **Dr Pepper Museum** (☎254-757-1024; 300 S 5th St, Waco; museum free, tours adult/child $6/3; ⏰10am-4:15pm Mon-Sat, from noon on Sun) in Waco, about halfway between Austin and Dallas.

» **Shiner Bock** The state's favorite amber ale came to be when Kosmos Spoetzl brought Bavarian brewing to Shiner, Texas, in 1914. Available countrywide, it's still brewed at Spoetzl Brewery (p671).

general is pretty quiet. For those living in **uptown** (www.uptowndallas.net), dining out nightly is de rigueur, so there are plenty of options. You'll also do well eating just about anywhere along Knox-Henderson Sts, to the north.

UPTOWN & KNOX-HENDERSON

TOP CHOICE **Bread Winners** AMERICAN **$$**
(off Map p684; 3301 McKinney Ave; breakfast & lunch $9-12, dinner $11-19; ⏰breakfast & lunch 7am-4pm Mon-Sat, 8am-3pm Sun, dinner 5-10pm Tue-Thu, to 11pm Fri & Sat, to 9pm Sun; 👪✍) If sipping a peach Bellini in a lush courtyard atrium is the reward for the agony of choosing what to order for brunch, then bring on the pain. Veggie Benedict or breakfast casserole? Bananas Foster waffle or raspberry cream cheese–stuffed French toast? Lunch and dinner offer similar, though less tortuous, conundrums. In a pinch, at least stop in for something decadent from the bakery counter.

Fearing's AMERICAN **$$$**
(Map p684; ☎214-922-4848; Ritz-Carlton Hotel, 2121 McKinney Ave; lunch mains $16-22, dinner mains $32-50; ⏰11:30am-2:30pm & 6-10:30pm Mon-Sat, 11:15am-3pm & 6-10pm Sun) Press accolades keep pouring in for chef Dean Fearing's four-star, four-dining room restaurant in the Ritz-Carlton. No need to dress up to enjoy the upscale Texas cuisine. Choose to sup in the lively open-kitchen room, a glass-enclosed conservatory, a tropical courtyard or the white-tableclothed 'gallery.'

Gloria's MEXICAN **$$**
(3223 Lemmon Ave; mains $11-15; ⏰11am-10pm) Plantains, black beans and yucca are big players on the El Salvadorian Mexican menu. Gloria's has done so well that it's expanded to several local venues.

Dream Cafe CAFE **$$**
(Map p684; 2800 Routh St; lunch $8-11, dinner mains $10-19; ⏰7am-9pm Sun-Thu, to 10pm Fri & Sat; 👪) Start your day early with a fabulous breakfast or chill on its shady patio at lunchtime with some healthy, hearty fare. There's even a playground to keep the young 'uns amused.

S&D Oyster Company SEAFOOD **$$**
(Map p684; 2701 McKinney Ave; mains $12-18; ⏰11am-10pm) An uptown staple for ages – the no-frills decor and great fried seafood keep 'em coming back. Try the BBQ shrimp.

DEEP ELLUM

Monica's Aca y Alla MEXICAN **$**
(off Map p684; www.monicas.com; 2914 Main St; lunch $4-8, dinner $6-18; ⏰closed Mon; ✍) Try the Mexican lasagna at lunch or the tilapia Veracruz for dinner at this always-social Deep Ellum favorite that rocks a glam Mexico City vibe. One dollar mimosas at brunch? Sign us up.

Angry Dog BURGERS **$**
(off Map p684; 2726 Commerce St; mains $5-9; ⏰11am-midnight Mon-Thu, to 2am Fri & Sat, noon-10pm Sun) Workers crowd in at lunchtime for the unbeatable burgers at this saloon.

Taco Loco TEX-MEX **$**
(off Map p684; 3014 Main St; dishes $2-8; ⏰6am-10pm Mon-Thu, to 3am Fri & Sat) A fried catfish taco with avocado is $4.25, which is good, because it's 2am, the bars have just closed and you've got five bucks left. The breakfast tacos and tamales are addictive.

DOWNTOWN

One Arts Plaza, at 1722 Routh St, hosts five restaurants (Italian, Southern, Japanese and wine bars); **Tei-An** (Map p684; mains $12-20; ⏰11:30am-2pm & 6-10:30pm Tue-Sun) is most interesting because it specializes in laboriously handmade Japanese soba noodle dishes. **Screen Door** (Map p684; lunch $10-18, dinner mains $25-35; ⏰lunch 11am-2pm Mon-Fri, dinner 5-9:30pm Mon-Thu, to 11pm Fri & Sat) serves an artistic interpretation of Southern mainstays.

Drinking

Numerous pubs with outdoor patios are to be found in uptown along not only McKinney Ave (in the 2500 to 2800 blocks especially), but also Knox St near Willis Ave. Note that bars and clubs in Dallas (at least mostly) have succumbed to the indoor smoking ban.

TOP CHOICE Old Monk PUB
(2847 N Henderson Ave) The dimly lit patio on a starry night! The perfect cheese plate! The Belgian beers! We'll admit it – this is one of our favorite pubs in Texas.

Belmont Bar HOTEL BAR
(Hotel Belmont, 901 Fort Worth Ave) Sip your adult beverage on a stylish terrace overlooking the city. Sometimes the bar screens B-grade flicks on the white stucco wall in the garden.

Ginger Man PUB
(Map p684; 2718 Boll St) An appropriately spice-colored house is home to this always-busy neighborhood pub. The bar has multi-level patios and porches, out front and back.

Double Wide BAR
(off Map p684; 3510 Commerce St, Deep Ellum; ⌚7am-2am Mon-Sat, noon-2am Sun) Are these rednecks pretending to be hipsters or hipsters pretending to be rednecks? Live music keeps the irony from killing the fun.

Entertainment

For entertainment listings, check the weekly alternative newspaper *Dallas Observer* (www.dallasobserver.com) or *Guide Live* (www.guidelive.com), which appears in Friday's *Dallas Morning News*.

Live Music & Nightclubs

During lunch hour, office workers crowd into the bars and restaurants of downtown's **Deep Ellum** (www.deepellumtexas). The scene at night is definitely grittier, but this is still live-music central. Most of the clubs are hard-core, but you'll occasionally find country or jazz. The bars and clubs of Lower Greenville Ave (1500 to 2200 blocks) cater to a crowd temperament somewhere between the uptown yuppies and downtown grunge set.

Sports

Mesquite Rodeo RODEO
(www.mesquiterodeo.com; 1818 Rodeo Dr; tickets $15-30; ⌚8pm Fri & Sat May-Sep) Bronc-bustin', bull-ridin' cowboys square off at weekend rodeos broadcast nationwide. Take I-30 15 miles east to Hwy 80.

Dallas Cowboys FOOTBALL
The **Cowboys** (www.dallascowboys.com) got the nickname 'America's Team' after they won three US football championships in the 1990s. Their snazzy new, retractable-roof home, **Cowboys Stadium** (Map p690; 925 N Collins St, Arlington; stadium tours adult/child $18/15; ⌚10am-6pm Mon-Sat, 11am-5pm Sun), opened in mid-2009.

American Airlines Center STADIUM
(Map p684; www.americanairlinescenter.com; 2500 Victory Ave) Located in Victory Park, hosts mega-concerts and is home to the **Dallas Stars** (☎214-467-8277; www.dallasstars.com) ice-hockey team and the **Dallas Mavericks** (☎214-747-6287; www.dallasmavericks.com) pro basketball team.

GAY & LESBIAN DALLAS

Dallas' gay and lesbian scene centers on Cedar Springs Rd and Oak Lawn Ave, north of Uptown. There's also a good-sized gay enclave in Oak Cliff across town. Check the **Resource Center Dallas** (☎214-528-0144; www.resourcecenterdallas.org; 2701 Reagan St) for GLBT resources and info. The *Dallas Voice* newspaper (www.dallasvoice.com) is the town's gay and lesbian advocate.

You've got to love that the top gay and lesbian bars in Dallas are named JR's and Sue Ellen's, respectively, after the two lead (and presumably straight) characters in *Dallas*.

» **JR's Bar & Grill** (www.caven.com; 3923 Cedar Springs Rd, Uptown) One of the busiest bars in Texas, JR's serves lunch daily and boasts a variety of fun entertainment at night.

» **Sue Ellen's** (3014 Throckmorton St) Chill out in the 'lipstick lounge' or on the dancefloor at Dallas' favorite lesbian bar.

Theater & Culture

AT&T Performing Arts Center THEATER
(Map p684; www.attpac.org; 2403 Flora St) With the opening of this multibillion-dollar center in October 2009, Dallas now has four new, architecturally noteworthy performance venues including the 2000-seat Winspear Opera House, the 1500-seat Wyly Theatre and an open-air stage, Strauss Sq.

 Shopping

You can find some interesting gifts of arty housewares, like vintage Fiestaware plates, in the quirky, but small, **Bishop Arts District** (www.bishopartsdistrict.com). On the northern end of uptown (at Lemmon and McKinney Aves), the **West Village** (www.westvil.com) neighborhood has a collection of chain stores and individual boutiques, like 'Cowboy Cool.'

Neiman Marcus DEPARTMENT STORE
(Map p684; www.neimanmarcus.com; 1618 Main St) A downtown landmark, this six-story behemoth was the first Neiman Marcus store in the country.

NorthPark Center MALL
(Map p690; www.northparkcenter.com; 8687 N Central Expressway) Almost 2 million sq ft of retail space, Northpark is shopping nirvana for Dallasites.

Galleria MALL
(Map p690; www.galleriadallas.com; 13355 Noel Rd) The Galleria is another mega shopping mall, a favorite with out-of-towners – maybe it's the ice-skating rink in the center?

 Information

Bank of America (1401 Elm St) Foreign currency exchange.

Central Library (1515 Young St; ⏲10am-5pm Tue-Wed, noon-8pm Thu, 10am-5pm Fri & Sat, 1-5pm Sun) Get a free internet card at the desk.

Dallas CVB Visitor Center (Map p684; ☎214-571-1000; www.visitdallas.com; Old Red Courthouse, 100 S Houston St; ⏲9am-5pm) Free 20-minute internet access.

Dallas Morning News (www.dallasnews.com) The city's daily newspaper.

Parkland Memorial Hospital (☎214-590-8000; 5201 Harry Hines Blvd)

Police station (☎214-670-4413; 334 S Hall St)

 Getting There & Away

American Airlines' home port is **Dallas-Fort Worth International Airport** (DFW; Map p690; www.dfwairport.com), 16 miles northwest of the city via I-35 E. Great Britain and Mexico are among the nonstop international destinations. Southwest Airlines uses smaller **Dallas Love Field Airport** (DAL; Map p690; www.dallaslovefield.com), just northwest of downtown.

WORTH A TRIP

COOL SMALL TOWNS OUTSIDE THE METROPLEX

What? There's more to life in this part of Texas than shopping malls, suburbs and big-name attractions? Yes. Northeast Texas is full of small towns organized around courthouse squares, where spring and fall festivals and rodeos are big doggone deals. Check the **Texas Highways** (www.texashighways.com) listings to find one that suits you. For example, **Tyler** (www.tylertexas.com; cnr I-20 & US 69), 100 miles east of Dallas, is known for its October Rose Festival and its 14-acre municipal garden (in bloom April to November).

Here are a few more of our favorite small towns in the region:

» A bastion of college cool and indie cred, **Denton** has a great music scene (www.mydentonmusic.com). Rock out at **Dan's Silver Leaf** (☎940-320-2000; www.danssilverleaf.com; 103 Industrial St) or two-step with gay cowboys at perhaps the best-named bar in Texas, **Mable Peabody's Beauty Parlor and Chain Saw Repair** (☎940-566-9910; www.mablepeabodys.com; 1125 E University).

» Architecture fans dig south-of-Dallas **Waxahachie** (www.waxahachiechamber.com) for its Victorian, Greek Revival and Queen Anne architecture.

» Czech it out: stopping for kolaches off I-35 at the **Czech Stop** is a ritual for many on the drive between Dallas and Austin. It's in historic **West**, the Czech Heritage Capital of Texas.

» West of Waco, **Crawford** has become synonymous with ex-president George W Bush, whose **ranch** is about 8 miles from town. Just keep in mind that there's really nothing to see – and that the Secret Service doesn't look kindly on parked cars outside the ranch (don't even *think* about trespassing).

Greyhound buses make runs all over the country from the **Greyhound Bus Terminal** (Map p684; www.greyhound.com; 205 S Lamar St). Amtrak's San Antonio–Chicago *Texas Eagle* stops at downtown's **Union Station** (Map p684; www.amtrak.com; 401 S Houston St).

Getting Around

To/From the Airport

From Monday to Saturday you can ride the **Trinity Railway Express** (www.trinityrailwayexpress.org) between downtown's Union Station and the Center Port/DFW Airport stop ($3.50 one way), which is actually in a parking lot; free shuttle buses take you to the terminals. Daily, DART bus 39 ($1.75) travels between downtown's **West End Transit Station** (Map p684; 800 Pacific Ave) and Dallas Love Field, but service is limited on weekends.

It's often easiest to take a shared-ride shuttle like **SuperShuttle** (817-329-2000; www.supershuttle.com), which runs from DFW or Dallas Love Field to downtown for $17. A taxi from DFW to downtown will run you around $50; from Love Field it's only around $20.

Every major rental-car company has an office at DFW, and many are at Dallas Love Field too.

Bus & Light Rail

Travel to uptown from downtown on the free **McKinney Ave Trolley** (214-855-0006; www.mata.org; 7am-10pm Mon-Thu, to midnight Friday, 10am-midnight Sat, to 10pm Sun), which runs from the corner of Ross Ave and St Paul St, near the Dallas Museum of Art, and up McKinney Ave to Hall St.

Dallas Area Rapid Transit (DART; 214-979-1111; www.dart.org) operates buses and an extensive light-rail system that connects Union Station and other stops downtown with outlying areas (single trip local/systemwide $2.50/3.50). Day passes (local/systemwide $5/7) are available from the store at the **Akard Station** (Map p684; 1401 Pacific Ave; 7:30am-5:30pm Mon-Fri).

Car & Motorcycle

If you do rent a car, be warned that rush-hour freeway traffic is bad and there's little free parking downtown. Public garages cost from $12 per day.

Fort Worth

Often called 'Where the West Begins' – and more often referred to as 'Cowtown' – Fort Worth is one town that still has its twang.

The place first became famous during the great open-range cattle drives of the late 19th century, when more than 10 million head of cattle tramped through the city on the Chisholm Trail. Today you can see a mini-cattle drive in the morning and a rodeo on Saturday night.

Down in the Cultural District, tour the Cowgirl Museum and others, including three amazing art collections. Then, after you've meditated on minimalism, Sundance Sq's restaurants and bars call you to the kick-up-your-heels downtown.

Whatever you do, don't mistake Fort Worth for being Dallas' sidekick. This city's got a headstrong spirit of its own, and it's more user-friendly than Dallas (and greener and cleaner). Bottom line? There's a lot to do here – without a lot of pretense.

Sights

The Stockyards are cowboy central; most area museums call the leafy Cultural District home.

STOCKYARDS NATIONAL HISTORIC DISTRICT

Sure, you'll spot cowboys on horseback roaming around, but wander the dusty streets of the Stockyards and you'll be soon mingling with a mix of families, bikers, curious European tourists and novelty-seeking college kids. This place puts fun first, with equal parts authentic history and camera-ready tourism thrown into the pot.

Stockyards HISTORIC SITE

(Map p690; www.fortworthstockyards.org; Exchange Ave) Westernwear stores and knick-knack shops, saloons and steakhouses occupy the Old West–era buildings of the Stockyards. City-paid cowboys on horseback roam the district, answering questions and posing for photos. Twice a day, at 11:30am and 4pm, they drive a small herd (16 to 20 beasts) of Texas longhorns down the block in front of the visitor center. It's a *goll-dang* Kodak moment, pardner.

Cowtown Coliseum RODEO

(www.stockyardsrodeo.com; 121 E Exchange Ave; adult/child rodeo $15/10, Wild West Show $12/8) See a real live rodeo at 8pm on Friday and Saturday nights year-round. From June to August, horses and riders show off at Pawnee Bill's Wild West Show (2:30pm and 4:30pm on Saturday and Sunday).

CULTURAL DISTRICT

Five major museums and the Will Rogers Memorial Center are part of the parklike **Cultural District** (Map p690; www.fwculture.com).

Dallas–Fort Worth Metroplex

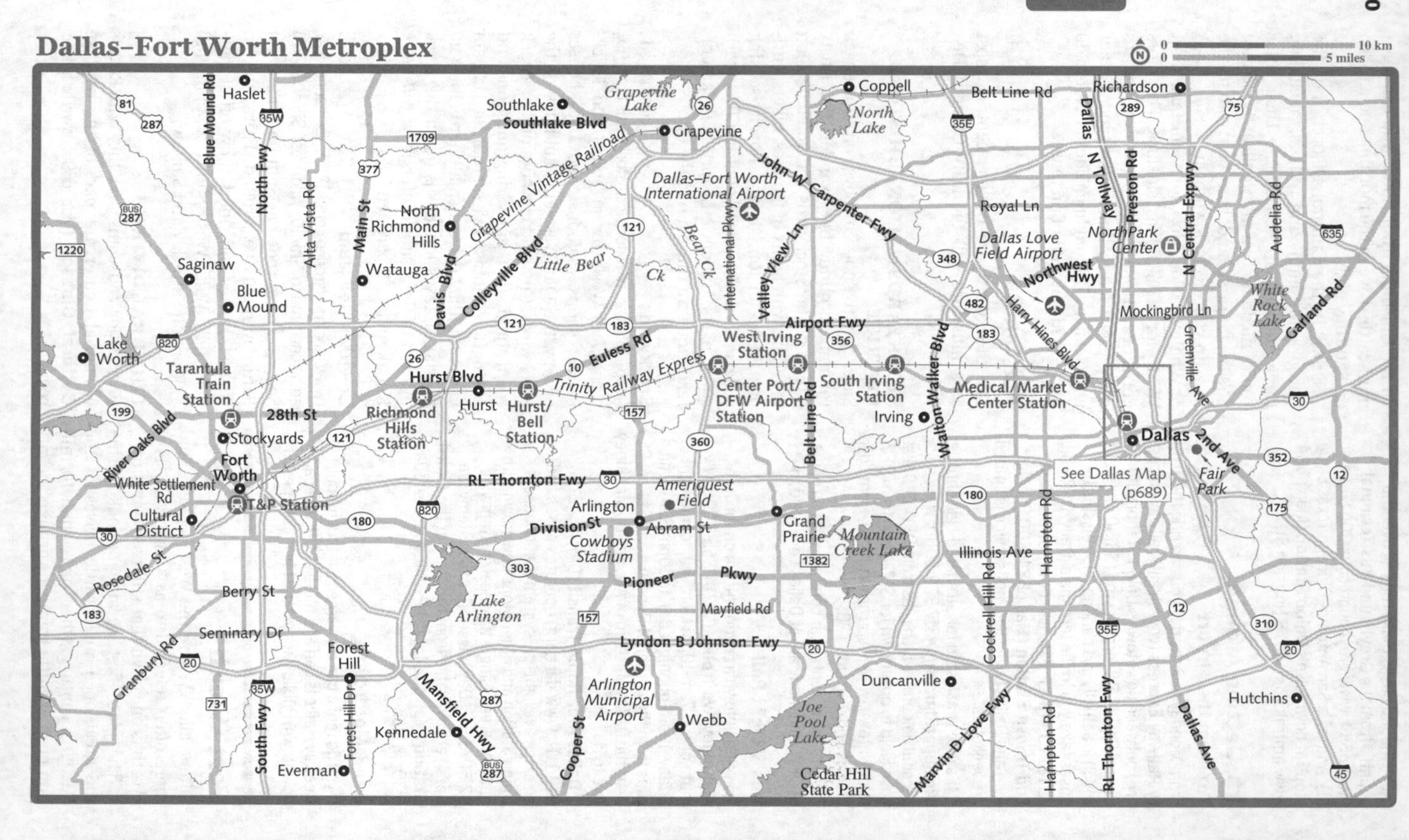

FREE **Kimbell Art Museum** MUSEUM
(www.kimbellart.org; 3333 Camp Bowie Blvd; ⏲10am-5pm Tue-Thu & Sat, noon-8pm Fri, noon-5pm Sun) Some art aficionados say this is the country's best 'small' art museum while some say it's one of the unqualified best. Take your time perusing: the stunning architecture lets in natural light that allows visitors to see paintings from antiquity to the 20th century the way the artists originally intended.

National Cowgirl Museum MUSEUM
(www.cowgirl.net; 1721 Gendy St; adult/child $10/8; ⏲10am-5pm) Not just for girls, this airy, impressive museum explores the myth and the reality of cowgirls in American culture. From rhinestone costumes to rare film footage, this is a fun and educational ride: by the time you walk out, you'll have a whole new appreciation for these tough and sassy ladies. If you're cowgirl enough, film yourself riding the bucking bronc.

FREE **Amon Carter Museum** MUSEUM
(www.cartermuseum.org; 3501 Camp Bowie Blvd; ⏲10am-5pm Tue-Sat, extended hr Thu, noon-5pm Sun) You can see displays of pre-1945 American art, including one of the country's best compilations of work by western artists Frederic Remington and Charles M Russell. There's also an extensive photography collection.

Modern Art Museum of Fort Worth MUSEUM
(www.themodern.org; 3200 Darnell St; adult/child $10/free; ⏲10am-5pm Tue-Sun, extended hr Thu) Entering this museum, you round a corner from womblike, concrete galleries to be confronted by a two-story wall of glass looking out at the city skyline. Noteworthy art in the collection includes work by Picasso and Mark Rothko.

Museum of Science & History MUSEUM
(www.fwmuseum.org; 1600 Gendy St; adult/child $14/10; ⏲10am-5pm; 👪) Your Cowgirl ticket also gets you in to this kid-friendly museum brimming with fossils, dinosaurs and fun things to do – like the planetarium and an Omni IMAX theater. A huge expansion, completed in late 2009, immerses you in today's cattle-breeding and cowboy industry.

DOWNTOWN

One of the best pedestrian downtowns in the nation? Seriously…in Texas? The point is, it's a passel of fun (and not much hassle)

FREE RIDE

Fort Worth's coolest transportation option is the free **Molly the Trolley** (☎817-215-8600; www.mollythetrolley.com; ⏲10am-10pm), a vintage trolley system that serves passengers traveling around downtown.

to hang out in the 14-block **Sundance Sq** (www.sundancesquare.com), near Main and 3rd Sts. Colorful architecture, art galleries and a host of bars and restaurants make this one supremely strollable, friendly 'hood. Bonus: parking garages are free after 5pm and on weekends.

FREE **Sid Richardson Collection of Western Art** MUSEUM
(www.sidrichardsonmuseum.org; 309 Main St; ⏲9am-5pm Mon-Thu, to 8pm Fri & Sat, noon-5pm Sun) If the Stockyards didn't sate your hunger for all things Western, pop in here for some art.

Festivals & Events

Fort Worth Stock Show & Rodeo RODEO
(www.fwstockshowrodeo.com) The town's biggest event, which is held in late January or early February each year at **Will Rogers Coliseum** (1 Amon Carter Sq) in the Cultural District.

Sleeping

It's also easy to do a day trip to Fort Worth from Dallas…

TOP CHOICE **Stockyards Hotel** HISTORIC HOTEL $$$
(☎817-625-6427; www.stockyardshotel.com; 109 E Exchange Ave; r $189-269; ste $219-489; ❄📶) First opened in 1907, this place clings to its cowboy past with Western-themed art, cowboyed-out rooms and a grand Old West lobby with lots of leather. Hide out in the Bonnie and Clyde room, actually occupied by Clyde Barrow during his 1932 Fort Worth stay (the faux bullet holes and boot jacks only add to the mystique).

Miss Molly's Hotel Bed & Breakfast B&B $$
(☎817-626-1522; www.missmollyshotel.com; 109 W Exchange Ave; r incl breakfast $50-$175; ❄📶) Set in the heart of the Stockyards, Miss Molly's occupies a former bordello. Its heavily atmospheric vibe will feel authentic to some,

eerie to others, but probably at least a little charming either way. At $50, rooms are a bargain during the week, and only the over-the-top madam's quarters fetches the $175 rate (and only on weekends).

Etta's Place B&B $$
(☎817-255-5760; www.ettas-place.com; 200 W 3rd St; r incl breakfast from $150, ste from $185; ❄📶) A grand piano, a comfy library and quilts galore are among the cozy pleasures at this Sundance Sq B&B. Breakfasts, like scrambled egg pizza with poblano pepper grits, can be taken on the airy patio.

Holiday Inn Express HOTEL $$
(☎817-698-9595; www.hiexpress.com; 1111 W Lancaster Ave; r $117-159; ❄@📶🏊) A retro vibe pervades this surprisingly stylish hotel, 1 mile southwest of downtown.

Ashton Hotel BOUTIQUE HOTEL $$$
(☎866-327-4866; www.theashtonhotel.com; 610 Main St; r $208-290; ❄📶) This small hotel in a turn-of-the-century building off Sundance Sq offers hush-hush elegance without an ounce of snootiness. Valet parking is $17.

Texas White House B&B B&B $$
(☎817-923-3597; www.texaswhitehouse.com; 1417 Eighth Ave; r incl breakfast $129-149, ste $219-249; ❄📶) Large historic home, contemporary Texas style – near downtown.

Eating

Put on the feed bag at the numerous cafes and restaurants in Sundance Sq and in the Stockyards (the latter is a tad touristy, but all good fun). Note that steak prices around town are weighty, but then so is the portion of beef.

TOP CHOICE **Love Shack** BURGERS $
(110 E Ex change Ave; burgers $5-7; ⏰11am-7pm Mon-Wed, to 9pm Thu, to 11pm Fri & Sat, to 9pm Sun) Hankering for a little red meat? Stop by for a gourmet burger at this joint owned by native son and Food Network iron chef Tim Love. Don't miss the home-cut fries or Parmesan chips – oh, and those double-thick milk shakes…yum. Live local music plays on Saturdays at 8pm.

Buffet at the Kimbell BUFFET $
(3333 Camp Bowie Blvd; small/large plate $8/10; ⏰lunch Tue-Sun, dinner Fri; 🖉) Fuel up for museum-hopping at the Kimbell; lunching in the tranquil courtyard remains one of Cowtown's not-so-secret pleasures (and deals). Pick your plate size, and then assemble your ideal meal. Instead of endless options, they make a reasonably sized and beautifully prepared spread of fresh salads, soups, quiches and sandwiches.

Nonna Tata ITALIAN $$
(☎817-332-0250; 1400 W Magnolia Ave; lunch $9-12, dinner $13-23; ⏰lunch 11am-3pm Tue-Fri, dinner 5:30-8:30pm Tue-Thu, to 9:30 Fri; 🖉) This tiny, unpretentious place is as authentic as Italian gets in Texas. Some ground rules: be prepared to wait – the pasta is worth it. Bring your own wine, as well as cash or euros because it doesn't take credit cards. And whatever you do, save room for dessert.

Joe T Garcia's MEXICAN $$
(2201 N Commerce St; mains $8-14; ⏰11am-2:30pm & 5-10pm Mon-Thu, 11am-11pm Fri & Sat, to 10pm Sun) The most famous restaurant in Fort Worth, this fourth-generation place takes up a city block. Dinners in the candlelit walled courtyard are magical, as Mexican-tile fountains bubble among the acres of tropical foliage. On weekends the line (no reservations!) often stretches around the block.

8.0 Restaurant & Bar AMERICAN $
(111 E 3rd St, Sundance Sq; mains $8-10; ⏰11am-11pm Tue-Sat, 3-10pm Sun) 'Mom's Meatloaf' and Mexican enchiladas are both on the mixed-up but lovable menu. A large patio under the trees with live music on Wednesdays and DJs on summer weekends makes this a favorite place to kick back.

Angelo's Barbecue BARBECUE $
(2533 White Settlement Rd; plates $6-12; ⏰11am-10pm Mon-Sat) They've been smokin' brisket, ribs and sausage at this BBQ joint north of the Cultural District since 1958.

Drinking

All the restaurants in and around Sundance Sq have popular bars attached.

Flying Saucer Draught Emporium BEER HALL
(111 E 4th St; ⏰11am-midnight Mon & Tue, to 1am Wed & Thu, to 2am Fri & Sat, noon-midnight Sun) You definitely won't go thirsty: the bar inside this old brick building is made for craft-beer lovers (80 brews on tap). How can you not love a bar whose jam-packed patio is called 'Half-Acre Hell?'

Booger Red's HOTEL BAR
(109 E Exchange Ave) Inside the Stockyards Hotel, you can straddle a saddle at the bar to sip your brew.

DON'T MISS

THE WORLD'S LARGEST HONKY-TONK

That's the claim to fame of **Billy Bob's Texas** (www.billybobstexas.com; 2520 Rodeo Plaza, Stockyards; cover $2-5 Sun-Thu, varies Fri & Sat; ⏲11am-2am Mon-Sat, noon-2am Sun). Here are a few things you should know to properly appreciate the behemoth:

» The 127,000 sq ft building – that's nearly 3 acres – can hold more than 6000 people.

» The building was originally an open-air barn that housed cattle during the Fort Worth Stock Show.

» The sloped floors were built to make it easier to wash away the runoff from the cows.

» Instead of a mechanical bull, Billy Bob's has a live bull-riding competition on Friday and Saturday nights (admission $2.50. open 9pm and 10pm) in its indoor arena.

» It's surprisingly family friendly, with arcade games and other attractions geared at kids.

The Usual BAR
(1408 W Magnolia Ave) Proof that the retro craft-cocktail craze has come to Fort Worth? This bar that serves up debonair drinks like 'Jimador's Revenge' and 'Taxation & Representation.'

☆ Entertainment

On weekend evenings, country music becomes common in the Stockyards District, and a variety of live bands play in and around Sundance Sq. Look for listings in *Fort Worth Weekly* (www.fwweekly.com).

Live Music

Pearls Dance Hall DANCE
(www.pearlsdancehall.com; 302 W Exchange Ave) On the edge of the stockyards, this raucous old brothel once owned by Buffalo Bill Cody is an atmospheric place to hear traditional country music with an edge. Texas luminaries like Dale Watson are known to rock out here.

White Elephant Saloon BAR
(www.whiteelephantsaloon.com; 106 E Exchange Ave; ⏲noon-midnight Sun-Thu, to 2am Fri & Sat) Stockyards cowboys have been bellying up to this bar since 1887 (now Tim Love owns it too). Local singers and songwriters are showcased nightly.

Theater & Performing Arts

Bass Performance Hall THEATER
(www.basshall.com; 555 Commerce St) The glittery Bass Hall's theaters host everything from Mingo Fishtrap to the Will Rogers Follies. The symphony, ballet and opera also make their home here.

ℹ Information

Central Library (500 W 3rd St; ⏲10am-6pm Mon, Wed, Fri & Sat, noon-8pm Tue & Thu, 1-5pm Sun) Free internet access.

Fort Worth Convention & Visitors Bureau (www.fortworth.com) Cultural District (☎817-882-8588; 3401 W Lancaster Ave; ⏲9am-5pm Mon-Sat); Downtown (☎817-698-3300; 508 N Main St; ⏲10am-6pm Mon-Sat); Stockyards (☎817-624-4741; 130 E Exchange Ave; ⏲9am-6pm Mon-Sat, 10am-4pm Sun) The most together tourist board in the state; ask for the spiffy free 3-D maps.

ℹ Getting There & Around

From Monday to Saturday you can ride the **Trinity Railway Express** (www.trinityrailwayexpress.org) between Fort Worth's **T&P Station** (Map p690; 221 W Lancaster Ave) and the Center Port/DFW Airport stop ($3.50 one way); free shuttle buses take you from the train parking lot to the terminals. If you're coming into Dallas Love Field, you'll have to transfer through in downtown Dallas.

Eleven buses a day make the one-hour trip (from $6.60) from the downtown Fort Worth **Greyhound Bus Terminal** (www.greyhound.com; 901 Commerce St) to Dallas.

For bus service, look to **Fort Worth Transit Authority** (The T; ☎817-215-8600; www.the-t.com; $1.50): bus 1 goes to the Stockyards and bus 2W goes to the Cultural District (depart from the ITC Transfer Center at Jones and 9th Sts).

The *Texas Eagle* stops at the **Amtrak Station** (www.amtrak.com; 1001 Jones St) en route to San Antonio or Chicago. Monday to Saturday the **Trinity Railway Express** (TRE; ☎817-215-8600; www.trinityrailwayexpress.com; T&P Station, 1600 Throckmorton St) connects downtown Fort Worth with downtown Dallas ($2.50, 1¼ hours).

WEST TEXAS

Tumbleweeds roll across dusty ground, cacti bloom in desert sands, endless skies contain shimmering heat: West Texas is the stuff of Hollywood screen-maker dreams. Drive west along I-10 and there's a whole lotta nothin' to see except scrub brush and open skies. Turn south off the interstate and it's a different story. Big Bend National Park is a moonscape of desert mountains and deep arroyos on the Mexican border – a river-running, mountain-hiking paradise. Around the park, more mountains and small-town surprises await.

Big Bend National Park

The Chisos Mountains rise up at the center of **Big Bend National Park** (www.nps.gov/bibe; 7-day pass per vehicle $20). To the west, the dramatic mesas and rock formations are the result of ancient volcanic activity. To the east stretches desert habitat. The diverse geography in the park's 800,000 acres supports mountain lions and black bears, though you're more likely to see some of the 56 species of reptiles and 100 bird types. The park runs along the Rio Grande, but there's no legal access to Mexico here. River-rafting and other outdoor outfitters are based outside the park (see the boxed text, p695). The **Panther Junction Visitors Center** (☎915-477-2251; ⏲8am-6pm) is along the main park road, 29 miles from the Persimmon Gap entrance gate, south of Marathon, and 26 miles from the Maverick entrance at Study Butte. Gasoline is sold nearby.

The park puts out pamphlets, but the best guide to Big Bend's 150-plus miles of hiking paths is *Hiking Big Bend* by Laurence Parent. Among the easier jaunts is the pleasant **Chisos Basin Loop Trail**, an easy 1.6-mile round-trip hike from the visitors center. This trail enjoys a relatively large amount of shade provided by the Mexican piñons and alligator junipers.

The 5.5-mile **Window Trail** is a bit more strenuous, but it has a great payoff: after descending into a shady canyon, the trail suddenly ends with a narrowed pass and a 200ft drop-off. This is a clear sign it's time to turn around, but not before admiring the Window, a narrow slot in the canyon that frames a dramatic view to the west.

The 4.8-mile **Lost Mine Trail** is all about views, which, as you climb over 1000ft in elevation, just get better and better. You'll be right up there with Casa Grande, Lost Mine Peak and, from the highest point, the Sierra del Carmen.

Many serious hikers say the **South Rim** is their favorite Big Bend trek, mainly because of the view at the end: from the South Rim at the southwestern edge of the High Chisos, the vista includes Santa Elena Canyon and the Sierra del Carmen. It's a 13-mile to 14.5-mile round-trip hike, so plan on either a very long day or an overnight outing. Check with the visitor center, as part of the trail is closed during peregrine falcon nesting season (February 1 to July 15).

Ten to 20°F hotter down on the desert floor, the 1.5-mile **Santa Elena Canyon Trail** (40 miles southwest of Panther Junction) is another popular trek because of the

ROUTE 66: GET YOUR KICKS IN TEXAS

The Texas Panhandle isn't exactly a hub of tourism, but it does get plenty of folks passing through as they pay homage to the Mother Road. If you find yourself up that-a-away, here are the top Texas stops on a Route 66 road trip, going from west to east:

Cadillac Ranch (I-40, btwn exits 60 & 62) This iconic roadside attraction features 10 Cadillacs buried headlights down and tailfins up.

Downtown Amarillo The San Jacinto District still has original Route 66 businesses, and W 6th St is a short, but entirely original, Mother Road segment.

Big Texan Steak Ranch (www.bigtexan.com; 7700 I-40 E, exit 74; mains $16-39; ❄🏨) A giant waving cowboy welcomes you to this roadside attraction/steakhouse that'll serve you a 72oz steak – free if you can eat it in under an hour.

Bug Ranch (Hwy 207 access road) In response to Cadillac Ranch, five stripped down VW bugs have sprouted 18 miles east of Amarillo.

Devil's Rope Museum (www.barbwiremuseum.com; 100 Kingsley St, McLean; admission free; ⏲10am-4pm Tue-Sat) Learn more about barbed wire than you ever thought possible.

OUTDOOR ACCESS

Most people see Big Bend from a road or a trail, but there are some captivating perspectives you can only get with an outfitter's help. Several companies based in Terlingua-Study Butte lead multihour to multiday, multisport trips in the region. River-rafting (in high enough water) or canoeing through the canyons are the most popular options. (The river flows principally in fall and winter; in the summer it can be just a trickle.) For a short trip, float through Santa Elena Canyon (half-day from $140). If you have four days, the remote, 33-mile Boquillas Canyon trip (from $685 with meals and tents) is a guider's favorite – no other people, just great rock formations and hiking.

The guides at **Big Bend River Tours** (432-371-3033; www.bigbendrivertours.com; Rte 170), just west of Hwy 118, have run the river more than a time or two themselves. They also combine rafting with horseback-riding expeditions. Active, do-it-yourself types should check out **Desert Sports** (432-371-2727; www.desertsportstx.com; Rte 170), 5 miles west of Hwy 118; the dedicated staff rents canoes ($50 per day), bikes ($35) and inflatable kayaks ($40) and will shuttle you in your car or theirs to river-launch and pick-up points ($45 to $200). Hike, bike and float tours are also available. **Far Flung Outdoor Center** (432-371-2633; www.farflungoutdoorcenter.com; Rte 170 at Hwy 118) is a bit more motor-oriented. Three-hour Jeep (from $65) and ATV (from $135) tours are on offer, in addition to the requisite rafting trips.

stunning rock and river views. It's rated easy, but you have to wade through a stream and climb stairs in the canyon wall.

Stone-and-wooden-beam cottages at **Chisos Mountains Lodge** (877-386-4383; http://chisosmountainslodge.com; lodge & motel r $113-117, cottages $141) are the most secluded of several lodging options, but the standard motel rooms present a convenient option. Restaurant food here is so-so; better to pack a cooler ahead of time. The complex has a **visitor center** (9am-4:30pm) and a **camp store** (9am-9pm) with basic supplies. The mountain climate at **Chisos Basin Campground** (877-444-6777; www.recreation.gov; campsites $14) attracts the most campers in the park.

The abundant cottonwood trees shading the desert **Rio Grande Village Campground** (877-444-6777; www.recreation.gov; campsites $14) are quite unexpected – unless you know that this was once part of a pioneer's farm and the irrigation canals are still in use.

West of Big Bend National Park

Small towns. Ghost towns. Towns that aren't even really towns. Throw in lots of dust and a scorching summer heat that dries out the stream of visitors until it's just a trickle. This isn't everyone's idea of a dream vacation. But if you can't relax out here, then you just plain can't relax. Whatever concerns you in your everyday life is likely to melt away along with anything you leave in your car. Speaking of cars, this is the land that public transportation forgot. You'll need a car out 'round these parts.

TERLINGUA-STUDY BUTTE

A former mining boomtown in the late 19th and early 20th centuries, Terlingua went bust when they closed down the mines in the 1940s. The town dried up and blew away like a tumbleweed, leaving buildings that fell into ruins and earning Terlingua a place in Texas folklore as a ghost town. But slowly the area has become repopulated, thanks in large part to the fact that it's only a few miles outside of Big Bend National Park.

By the way, you'll hear people talk about Terlingua, Study Butte, and Terlingua ghost town as if they're three different towns, but the only real town here is Terlingua; the other two are just areas of the town.

Sleeping & Eating

TOP CHOICE **La Posada Milagro** INN $$
(432-371-3044; www.laposadamilagro.net; 100 Milagro Rd, Terlingua ghost town; d $185-210;)
Built on top of and even incorporating some of the adobe ruins in the historic ghost town, this guesthouse pulls off an amazing feat of providing stylish rooms that blend in perfectly with the surroundings. The decor is west-Texas chic, and there's a nice patio for enjoying the cool evenings. Budget travelers can book a simpler room with four bunk beds for $145 a night.

SCENIC DRIVE: EL CAMINO DEL RIO

West of Lajitas, Rte 170 (also known as River Rd, or *El Camino Del Rio* in Spanish) hugs the Rio Grande through some of the most spectacular and remote scenery in Big Bend country. Relatively few Big Bend visitors experience this driving adventure, even though it can be navigated in any vehicle with good brakes. Strap in and hold on: you have the Rio Grande on one side and fanciful geological formations all around, and at one point there's a 15% grade – the maximum allowable. When you reach Presidio, head north on US 67 to get to Marfa. Or, if you plan to go back the way you came, at least travel as far as Colorado Canyon (20 miles from Lajitas) for the best scenery.

Chisos Mining Co Motel MOTEL **$**
(☎432-371-2430; www.cmcm.cc; FM 170; s/d $57/$76, cabins from $97; ❄) You'll recognize this quirky little place less than a mile west of Hwy 118 when you spot the oversized Easter eggs on the roof. The rooms are minimalist, but as cheap as you'll find.

TOP CHOICE **Starlight Theater** AMERICAN **$$**
(☎432-371-2326; 100 Ivey St; mains $9-18; ⏰5pm-midnight) You'd think a ghost town would be dead at night (pardon the pun) but the Starlight Theater keeps things lively. This former movie theater had fallen into roofless disrepair (thus the 'starlight' name) before being converted into a restaurant. There's live music nearly every night in spring and fall, and if there's no entertainment inside, there's usually someone strumming a guitar outside on the porch. To get there, take Hwy 170 to the ghost town turnoff and follow the road to the end.

Espresso...Y Poco Mas CAFE **$**
(☎432-371-3044; 100 Milagro Rd; food $2.50-6.50; ⏰8am-2pm, to 1pm in summer) This walkup counter at La Posada Milagro is a refreshing surprise, where you can find pastries, breakfast burritos, lunches and what might just be the best iced coffee in all of west Texas.

Kathy's Kosmic Kowgirl Kafe AMERICAN **$**
(☎432-371-2164; Hwy 170; barbecue & sandwiches $4-9; ⏰6:30am-3pm Thu-Mon) Part food stand, part roadside attraction, (and about a mile west of Hwy 118), this hot-pink trailer with hot pink lawn decor sometimes shows movies and has campfires at night.

Shopping

Terlingua Trading Co GIFTS
(100 Ivey St; ⏰11am-7pm) This store in the ghost town has great gifts, from hot sauces and wines to an impressive selection of books. Pick up a brochure on the walking tour of historic Terlingua, or buy a beer inside the store and hang out on the porch with locals at sunset.

LAJITAS TO PRESIDIO

About half an hour west from the junction in Terlingua, you can trade funky and dusty for trendy and upscale (but still dusty) at **Lajitas Golf Resort & Spa** (☎877-525-4827; www.lajitas.com; d from $149). What used to be small-town Texas got bought up and revamped into a swanky destination. The old Trading Post is gone and in its place is a new general store. (The former Trading Post was the stuff of folk legend, as it was the home of a beer-drinking goat who got elected mayor of the town. Alas, no more.)

The nine-hole course that included a shot over the river into Mexico has now moved to drier ground to escape flooding, and now it's the 18-hole **Black Jack's Crossing**. The **Lajitas Equestrian Center** offers horseback trail rides by the hour ($70) as well as full-day rides to the Buena Suerte Mine and Ghost Town.

Lajitas is the eastern gateway of the massive **Big Bend Ranch State Park** (☎432-358-4444; www.tpwd.state.tx.us; off Rte 170; adult/child $3/free). At 433 sq miles, it's more than 11 times larger than Texas' next biggest state park (Franklin Mountains in El Paso). Taking up almost all the desert between Lajitas and Presidio, Big Bend Ranch reaches north from the Rio Grande into some of the wildest country in North America. It is full of notable features, most prominently the Solitario, formed 36 million years ago in a volcanic explosion. The resulting caldera measures 8 miles east to west and 9 miles north to south. As massive as it is, this former ranch is one of the best-kept secrets in Big Bend country.

Access to the park is limited and a permit is required, even if you're just passing through. Stop for your day-use (adult/child $3/free) and camping permits (primitive campsites $8, backcountry $5) at one of the three park offices.

Barton Warnock Visitor Center (432-424-3327; FM 170; 8am-4:30pm) One mile east of Lajitas, this education center is staffed by some of the most knowledgeable folks in the region.

Sauceda Ranger Station (432-358-4444; 8am-4:30pm, 7am-4pm May-August) In the park interior, this outpost requires a 27-mile drive up a dirt road.

Fort Leaton State Historic Site (432-229-3613; FM 170; 8am-4:30pm) The park's eastern entrance, 3 miles east of Presidio.

Central West Texas

The small towns of west Texas have become more than just the gateway to Big Bend National Park. Fort Davis, Marfa, Alpine and Marathon have a sprawling, easy-going charm and plenty of ways to keep a road-tripper entertained.

FORT DAVIS

False-front wooden buildings, an old fort and a stellar observatory make Texas' tallest town (elevation 5000ft) a Big Bend must-see. Its altitudinal advantage makes it a popular oasis during the summer, when west Texans head towards the mountains to escape the searing desert heat.

McDonald Observatory OBSERVATORY
(432-426-3640; www.mcdonaldobservatory.org; daytime pass adult/child $8/7, star parties adult/child $10/8; visitor center 10am-5:30pm, tours 11am & 2pm) A day pass gets you a guided tour (including close-up peeks at – but not through – the 107-inch Harlan J Smith Telescope and the 430-inch Hobby-Eberly Telescope) as well as a solar viewing, where you get to stare at the sun without scorching your eyeballs. But that's nothing compared to the evening **star parties**.

Fort Davis National Historic Site HISTORIC SITE
(www.nps.gov/foda; Hwy 17; adult/child $3/free; 8am-5pm except major holidays) A remarkably well-preserved frontier military post with an impressive backdrop at the foot of Sleeping Lion Mountain, Fort Davis was established in 1854 and abandoned in 1891. More than 20 buildings remain – five of them restored with period furnishings – as well as 100 or so ruins.

Davis Mountains State Park PARK
(www.tpwd.state.tx.us; Hwy 118; adult/child $5/free) Hiking, mountain biking, horseback riding (BYO horse), bird-watching and stargazing are all big attractions here amid the most extensive mountain range in Texas.

Sleeping & Eating

Indian Lodge INN $
(512-389-8982; Davis Mountains State Park; d $90-110, ste $120-135;) Located in the Davis Mountains State Park, this historic 39-room inn has 18 inch-thick adobe walls, hand-carved cedar furniture and ceilings of pine viga and latilla that give it the look of a Southwestern pueblo.

Old Schoolhouse Bed & Breakfast B&B $
(432-426-2050; www.schoolhousebnb.com; 401 Front St; r incl breakfast s $79-89, d $93-101;) You can't really tell it used to be the town's schoolhouse, but you can tell the owners put a lot of work into being great hosts, from the comfy rooms to the wonderful homemade breakfasts.

TOP CHOICE **Hotel Limpia Dining Room** AMERICAN $$
(Main St; mains $10-20; dinner 5-9pm Tue-Sun) The house specialty is (and has been for years) the burgundy-marinated pot roast, and we're not saying everyone keeps eating the broth like soup even after the meat is gone, but you wouldn't blame us if we did, would you?

Murphy's Pizzeria & Café PIZZERIA $
(107 Musquiz Dr; mains $6-20; 11am-9pm Tue-Sat, to 8pm Sun) Plenty of choices make this casual cafe an easy sell when you need to grab a bite.

DON'T MISS

A STAR-STUDDED EVENT

On Tuesday, Friday and Saturday nights, about half an hour after sunset, **McDonald Observatory** shows off its favorite planets, galaxies and globular clusters at its popular **Star Parties**, where professional astronomers guide you in some heavy-duty stargazing. Using ridiculously powerful laser pointers, they give you a tour of the night sky, and you'll get to use some of the telescopes to play planetary peeping tom. (It gets surprisingly brisk up there at night so dress warm and bring blankets.)

MARFA

Founded in the 1880s Marfa got its first taste of fame when Rock Hudson, Elizabeth Taylor and James Dean came to town to film the 1956 Warner Brothers film *Giant*. It's also become a pilgrimage for art lovers, thanks to one of the world's largest installations of minimalist art. This, in turn, has attracted a disproportionate amount of art galleries, quirky lodging options and interesting restaurants.

Marfa is on its own schedule, which is pretty much made up according to whim. Plan on coming late in the week or on a weekend; half the town is closed early in the week.

Sights & Activities

Marfa has all sorts of art to explore, and you can pick up a list of galleries at the **Chamber of Commerce** (☎432-729-4942; www.marfacc.com; Hotel Paisano, 207 N Highland Ave; ⏲9am-6pm Mon-Fri, 10am-2pm Sat).

Chinati Foundation MUSEUM

(☎432-729-4406; www.chinati.org; 1 Calvary Row; adult/student $25/10; ⏲by guided tour only 10am & 2pm Wed-Sun) Minimalist artist Donald Judd single-handedly put Marfa on the art-world map when he created the Chinati Foundation on the site of a former army post, using the abandoned buildings to create and display one of the world's largest permanent installations of minimalist art.

Marfa Lights OUTDOORS

Ghost lights, mystery lights…call them what you want, but the real mystery of the lights that flicker on the horizon at night seems to be how many of the sightings are actually just car headlights. And because the Marfa Lights are one of West Texas' top tourist attractions, no one wants to be too specific about how to tell for sure. Decide for yourself at the **Marfa Lights Viewing Area** about 8 miles east of Marfa on Hwy 90/67.

WHAT THE…?

So you're driving along a two-lane highway in dusty west Texas, out in the middle of nowhere, when suddenly a small building appears up in the distance like a mirage. As you zip past it you glance over and see…a Prada store? Known as the **Marfa Prada** (although it's really closer to Valentine) this art installation doesn't sell $1700 handbags, but it does get your attention as a tongue-in-cheek commentary on consumerism.

Sleeping & Eating

Thunderbird BOUTIQUE HOTEL $$

(☎877-729-1984; www.thunderbirdmarfa.com; 601 West San Antonio St; d $120-150;) This classic 1950s motel was reopened in 2005 as a small boutique with a spiffy new look. The rooms are hip and minimalist, and the grounds and common areas are as cool as the desert air at night.

El Cosmico CAMPGROUND $

(☎432-729-1950; www.elcosmico.com; 802 S Highland Ave; tents $20, yurts $60, trailers $110-125;) One of the funkiest choices in all of Texas, El Cosmico lets you sleep in a stylishly converted travel trailer, a tepee or a yurt.

Hotel Paisano HOTEL $$

(☎866-729-3669; www.hotelpaisano.com; 207 N Highland Ave; d $99-149, ste $159-210; @) Marfa's historic hotel is where the cast of the movie *Giant* stayed. Some of the rooms could stand a little updating, but the place does have a dignified charm.

TOP CHOICE **Food Shark** AMERICAN $

(105 S Highland; meals $5-8; ⏲11:30am-3pm Tue-Fri) See that battered old food trailer pulled up under the open-air pavilion where the weekend farmers market is? You do? Lucky you! That means Food Shark is open for business. Daily specials are excellent, and sell out early.

Cochineal AMERICAN $$$

(☎432-729-3300; 107 W San Antonio St; breakfast $4-10, dinner $18-36; ⏲breakfast/lunch 8:30am-1pm Thu-Sun, dinner 6-10pm Thu-Tue) The menu changes regularly, due to a focus on local, organic ingredients, but Cochineal is where foodies get their fix at dinnertime. It's also one of the few places you can get a proper breakfast, which is a treat.

Padre's BAR $

(209 W El Paso St; meals $3-8; ⏲11:30am-10:00pm Mon-Sat) With the fickle schedules of so many local restaurants, you need a place that will actually stay open and feed you, even if it is bar food. On the plus side, it's also a bar.

ALPINE

Primarily a pit stop, this university town has no real attractions of note. But it is the most sizable population (5700) in Big Bend – and the only place with big-name chain motels, numerous restaurants, grocery stores and

HOT TOPIC: BORDERLANDS

Tex has always mixed well with Mex. But the flow of Texans casually crossing into Mexican border towns has slowed to a trickle due to violence. According to US State Department reports, more than 1800 people were killed in Ciudad Juárez from January 2008 to February 2009. In March 2009, Mexican president Filipe Calderon sent troops into that city to quell drug cartel–related violence. The state department urges caution when visiting *all* border towns in Mexico – as do we. Crime continues in border towns like Nuevo Laredo as well. Ciudad Juárez was not a stranger to violence before President Calderon started trying to clean up the cartels. An earlier wave of murders involved Mexican women disappearing (*The Daughters of Juarez* by Teresa Rodriguez, is a provocative read), but didn't affect travelers.

more than one gas station. You can get regionwide information at the **Alpine Chamber of Commerce** (☎432-837-2326; www.alpinetexas.com; 106 N 3rd St; ⏲8am-5pm Mon-Fri, 8am-4pm Sat).

Antelope Lodge (☎432-837-2451; www.antelopelodge.com; 2310 W Hwy 90; s $44-60, d $49-65, ste $85; ❄📶) may just be the best deal in the Big Bend area. Compact rooms in white-stucco-and-red-tile cottages circle around a grassy lawn in true (renovated) 1930s motor-court style.

Another retro motor court is the more upscale **Maverick Inn** (☎432-837-0628; www.themaverickinn.com; 1200 E Holland Ave; r $95-145; ❄📶🏊). We can't help but love the vibe of this place, from the west Texas-style furnishings to the cool neon-art sign.

Look for grocery stores along Holland Ave and Ave E in the town center. You can dig into super-fresh pizzas and pastas (and use the wi-fi) at the friendly **La Trattoria** (202 W Holland Ave; breakfasts $4-8, mains $8-16; ⏲7:30am-3:30pm & 5-9pm Tue-Thu, to 10pm Fri & Sat; 📶).

For serious dining, **Reata** (203 N 5th St; lunch $8-14, dinner $14-32; ⏲11:30am-2pm daily & 5-10pm Mon-Sat) turns on the ranch-style charm in the front dining room. Or, step back into the lively bar area where you can feel free to nibble your way around the menu and enjoy a margarita. (The tortilla soup brought us back the next day for seconds.)

MARATHON

The tiny town of Marathon (population 455) isn't much more than a main street with a few cafes and a historic hotel, 58 miles north of Big Bend National Park. Don't miss the historic **Gage Hotel** (☎432-386-4205; www.gagehotel.com; 102 NW First St [Hwy 90], Marathon; d $90-97, with private bath $115-198; ❄🏊). Built in 1927, it has a fabulous Old West style that's matched only by its love of taxidermy. Each room at this property is individually (though similarly) decorated with Indian blankets, cowboy gear and leather accents. The associated **12 Gage** (mains $21-38; ⏲from 6pm, seating till 8:45 Mon-Thu, 9:45pm Fri & Sat) whips up gourmet renditions of Texas faves, and the **White Buffalo Bar** invites you to enjoy a margarita while trying to ignore their namesake's glassy stare.

Before heading to Big Bend, stock up on picnic supplies at **French Co Grocer** (206 N Ave D; ⏲7:30am-9pm Mon-Fri, from 8am Sat, from 9am Sun), or enjoy them at the tables outside at this charming little grocery – formerly the WM French General Merchandise store, established in 1900.

The **Famous Burro** (100 NE First St; mains $7-12; ⏲restaurant 5-10pm Wed-Sun, bar 5pm-midnight Wed-Sat), a bar-restaurant in a funky old filling station, changes its upscale comfort food menu weekly. Sometimes there's live music; sometimes it's movie night.

El Paso

Well, you've made it. You're just about as far west in Texas as you can go. Surrounded mostly by New Mexico and Mexico, El Paso seems to have more in common with its non-Texas neighbors than it does with Texas itself.

Sadly, El Paso and its sister city – Ciudad Juárez, Mexico, which is right across the river – have had a bit of a falling out. At one time, the two cities were inextricably linked, with tourists streaming back and forth across the Good Neighbor International Bridge all day long. But with the rise in gang- and drug-related violence, Juárez has become so dangerous that there is now little traffic between the two sides.

Sights & Activities

TOP CHOICE El Paso Museum of Art MUSEUM
(www.elpasoartmuseum.org; 1 Arts Festival Plaza; admission free, special exhibits extra; ⏲9am-5pm Tue-Sat, 9am-9pm Thu, noon-5pm Sun) This thoroughly enjoyable museum is in a former Greyhound station. They'd want us to brag about their Madonna and Child (c 1200), but the Southwestern art is terrific, and the engaging modern pieces round out the collection nicely.

FREE El Paso Holocaust Museum MUSEUM
(www.elpasoholocaustmuseum.org; 715 N Oregon St; ⏲9am-4pm Tue-Fri, 1-5pm Sat & Sun) It may seem a little anachronistic in a predominately Hispanic town, but the Holocaust Museum is as much a surprise inside as out for its thoughtful and moving exhibits that are imaginatively presented for maximum impact.

Franklin Mountains State Park PARK
(www.tpwd.state.tx.us; Transmountain Rd; adult/child $4/free; ⏲8am-5pm Mon-Fri, 6:30am-8pm Sat & Sun) At 23,863 acres, this is the largest urban park in the US. The park has 118 miles of mountain-bike, hiking and equestrian trails, as well as 17 rock-climbing routes; the **visitor center** (1331 McKelligon Canyon Rd) can point you in the right direction.

Wyler Aerial Tramway TRAMWAY
(1700 McKinley Ave; adult/child $7/4; ⏲noon-6pm Mon, Thu & Sun, to 8pm Fri & Sat) Sure, you'd feel a sense of accomplishment if you hiked to the top of the Franklin Mountains. We're not suggesting you take the easy way out (or are we?) but it only takes about four minutes to take a gondola to the top.

WHAT TIME IS IT?

When it comes to time zones, El Paso sides with New Mexico, conforming to Mountain Time rather than Central Time like the rest of Texas. Confusing? Occasionally. If you're telling someone in neighboring Van Horn or Fort Stockton what time you'll meet them, be sure to add on the extra hour you'll lose just by leaving El Paso.

Sleeping

Most of El Paso's lodging is in characterless chain motels found along I-10; choose your desired location first – the places are pretty much the same.

TOP CHOICE Coral Motel MOTEL $
(☎915-772-3263; fax 915-779-6053; 6420 Montana Ave; s/d $45; ❄) Anyone who loves 1950s roadside nostalgia will feel right at home at this funky little motel that mixes genres wildly, from the Spanish-style barrel tile roof to the Jetsons-esque sign to the mishmash interiors.

Hilton Garden Inn HOTEL $$
(☎915-351-2121; www.hiltongardeninn.com; 111 W University Ave; r $89-169; ❄@🛜🏊) Opened at the edge of UTEP, the Garden Inn was built to blend with campus architecture. So, of course, it resembles a Bhutanese *dzong*, or religious fortress – what else? (Architects thought the style would fit the desert mountain landscape.) The interior is more nice-chain-hotel than exotic monastery.

Camino Real Hotel HOTEL $$
(☎915-534-3000, 800-769-4300; www.caminoreal.com; 101 S El Paso St; d $99-129; ❄@🛜🏊) The only US location of an upscale Mexican hotel chain, the Camino Real has a prime location steps from the convention center and downtown museums; a gorgeous bar with an art glass dome; large, comfortable rooms; and pretty friendly service, even when it's swamped.

Eating & Drinking

Mexican is the food of choice in El Paso: the town's known for a special bright-red chili-and-tomato sauce used on enchiladas. Tex-Mex in El Paso is cheap and abundant:

Crave AMERICAN $$$
(300 Cincinnati Ave; mains $9-30; ⏲7am-11pm Mon-Sat, 7am-6pm Sun) Winning extra points for style – from the cool sign to the forks hanging from the ceiling – this hip little eatery serves up comfort food and classics with a little extra flair. Although dinner goes up to $30, there's still plenty to munch on in the $12-and-under category.

Magic Pan Restaurant AMERICAN $$$
(Doniphan Dr; lunch $9-11, dinner $18-28; ⏲11am-2pm Tue-Sun, 5-10pm Wed-Sat) This cute little courtyard cafe is a treat. By day, enjoy ultrafresh soups, salads and sandwiches under the shade trees on the breezy patio. At night, it takes on more of a fine-dining tone, with an upscale menu ranging from paella to tenderloin.

Cattleman's Steakhouse STEAKHOUSE **$$$**
(☎915-544-3200; Indian Cliffs Ranch; mains $15-33; ⏲5pm-10pm Mon-Fri, 12:30-10pm Sat, 12:30-9pm Sun) It's 20 miles east, but some folks would drive 200 for the setting that's straight outta the movies. It's 4.5 miles north of the I-10 at Fabens.

Chicos Tacos TEX-MEX **$**
(5305 Montana Ave; tacos $1-4; ⏲9am-1:30am Sun-Thu, to 3am Fri & Sat) Indulge your late-night taco cravings.

H&H Car Wash TEX-MEX **$**
(701 E Yandell Ave; mains $4-7; ⏲7am-3pm) This tiny hole-in-the-wall Mexican diner is attached to a hand car wash.

L&J Café & Bar TEX-MEX **$**
(3622 E Missouri; mains $7-12; ⏲kitchen 10am-9pm, bar to 2am) Everything served at this friendly Tex-Mex bar is tasty.

☆ Entertainment

Bars come and go quickly in El Paso. Your best bet is to head to El Paso's mini-entertainment district near UTEP (around Cincinnati St between Mesa and Stanton) to see what's happening in the bars and restaurants that are clustered there. For cultural and music listings, pick up the free weekly *El Paso Scene* (www.epscene.com) or the Friday 'Tiempo' supplement to the *El Paso Times* (www.elpasotimes.com).

Plaza Theatre THEATER
(www.theplazatheatre.org; 125 Pioneer Plaza) This elaborate theater under the stars is all indoors: pinpoint lights replicate stars, and vines cling to faux Spanish courtyard walls. Plays, concerts and shows are staged at this 1930 downtown landmark.

Shopping

On I-10 east of town, several warehouselike shops sell all the goodies you can find in Mexico – pottery, blankets, silver – at similar prices.

El Paso Saddleblanket MEXICAN IMPORTS
(6926 Gateway East) One acre of Mexican imports.

Galeria San Ysidro ART, FURNITURE
(801 Texas Ave) About 62,000ft of art and furniture.

El Paso Connection FURNISHINGS
(14301 Gateway Blvd) A 12-room warehouse full of furnishings.

ℹ Information

Note that El Paso is in the Mountain time zone, one hour behind the rest of the state. **El Paso Public Library** (501 N Oregon; ⏲9am-8pm Mon-Thu, 11am-6pm Fri, 9am-6pm Sat, 1-5pm Sun) has free internet access.

The **El Paso Visitors Center** (☎915-534-0601; www.visitelpaso.com; 1 Civic Center Plaza; ⏲8am-5pm Mon-Fri, 10am-3pm Sat) stocks racks and racks of brochures, and the staff is quite helpful.

ℹ Getting There & Around

El Paso International Airport (ELP; www.elpasointernationalairport.com), 8 miles northeast of downtown off I-10, services 16 US and two

GET THE BOOT

Maybe you've always wanted a pair of cowboy boots. Or maybe it's just a side effect of your Texas travels. Sure you could pick up a pair of mass-produced boots, but nothing beats a custom-made pair for a mighty fine fit. Even if you can't round up the $800 to $3500 a custom pair costs, make an appointment to visit **Rocketbuster Boots** (☎915-541-1300; www.rocketbuster.com; 115 S Anthony St; ⏲by appointment) and you'll see what all the fuss is about.

As boot-maker to the stars, Rocketbuster has shod such celebrities as Julia Roberts, Dwight Yoakum, Emmylou Harris and Oprah Winfrey. The over-the-top designs include everything from wild floral prints to 1950s-era pin-up cowgirls to Day of the Dead skeletons. Owner-designer Nevena Christi will gladly show you around, and you can pick up leather pillows and boot-shaped Christmas stockings for just $75 to $300.

Numerous other custom boot-makers work around town, including **Caboots** (www.caboots.com; 2100 Wyoming St; ⏲9am-5pm Mon-Fri), which also sells a few pre-made pairs (about $300). Bargain shopping? Check out the local outlet centers along I-10, such as **Justin Boots Outlet** (7100 Gateway Blvd E; ⏲9am-8pm Mon-Fri, to 6pm Sat, noon-5pm Sun) and **Tony Lama Factory Store** (7156 Gateway Blvd E; ⏲9am-7pm Mon-Fri, to 6pm Sat, noon-5pm Sun).

Mexican cities. Numerous chain rental-car companies are on-site (you really need a car here).

Amtrak's Florida–California *Sunset Limited* stops at **Union Depot** (www.amtrak.com; 700 San Francisco Ave). The terminal for **Greyhound** (www.greyhound.com; 200 W San Antonio Ave) is four blocks from the center of downtown.

Hueco Tanks State Historic Site

About 32 miles east of El Paso is the 860-acre **Hueco Tanks State Historical Park** (www.tpwd.state.tx.us; 6900 Hueco Tanks Rd/FM 2775; adult/child $5/free; ⏲8am-6pm daily, 7am-7pm Fri-Sun in summer). Popular today among rock climbers, the area has attracted humans for as many as 10,000 years, and park staff estimates there are more than 2000 pictographs at the site, some dating back 5000 years.

To minimize human impact, a daily visitor quota is enforced; make reservations 24 hours in advance (☎central reservations 512-389-8900) to gain entry. You can explore the North Mountain area by yourself, but to hike deeper into the park – where the more interesting pictographs are – you have to reserve and join one of the free **pictograph** or **bouldering/hiking tours** (⏲Wed-Sun, times vary).

Guadalupe Mountains National Park

At 8749ft, remote Guadalupe Peak is the highest point in Texas. McKittrick Canyon has the state's best autumn foliage, and impressive spring wildflower displays in April. Winter vistas of snow-covered succulents seem incongruous and amazing. Though beautiful, this is one of the nation's least-visited national parks – it's not so easy to reach from Texas, and there aren't many services. You'll find the closest motels in Whites City, about 35 miles to the north in New Mexico, near Carlsbad Caverns National Park. El Paso is 120 miles to the west.

The **Headquarters Visitors Center** (☎915-828-3251; www.nps.gov/gumo; 7-day pass $5, campsites $8; ⏲8am-6pm Jun-Aug, to 4:30pm rest of year), off US 62/180 at Pine Springs, also has camping. Of the 80 miles of trails, the most rewarding trek is strenuous – from the visitor-center parking lot to **Guadalupe Peak**, it's an 8.5-mile round-trip that gains 3000ft in elevation. A fairly easy day hike is **McKittrick Canyon Trail** (⏲8am-4:30pm), a 6.8-mile round-trip. The trailhead is off US 62/180, 11 miles northeast of the visitor center.

To get to the park's even more remote northern segment, **Dog Canyon**, you have to take Hwy 137 into New Mexico. Ten back-country campsites (permit required) dot the section. No water is available in the back-country. No gasoline, food or beverages are sold anywhere in the park.

PALO DURO CANYON STATE PARK

While not strictly in West Texas, the Panhandle is West-ish, and we couldn't pass up the chance to mention **Palo Duro Canyon**, up near Amarillo. At 120 miles long and about 5 miles wide, Palo Duro Canyon is among the largest in the US, second only to the Grand Canyon. The cliffs striated in yellows, reds and oranges, rock towers and other geologic oddities are a refreshing surprise amongst the seemingly endless flatness of the plains, and are worth at least a gander.

The multihued canyon was created by the Prairie Dog Town Fork of the Red River, a long name for a little river. The great gorge has sheltered and inspired people for a long time. Prehistoric Indians lived in the canyon 12,000 years ago, and Coronado may have stopped by in 1541. Palo Duro was the site of an 1874 battle between Comanche and Kiowa warriors and the US Army. The over 26,000 acres that make up the park attract hikers, horseback riders and mountain bikers eager for recreation, and artists and photographers drawn by the magnificent blend of color and desert light.

The **park** (☎806-488-2227; www.tpwd.state.tx.us; adult/child $5/free; ⏲main gate 6am-8pm Mon-Thu, to 10pm Fri & Sat, shorter hr in winter) is at the end of TX 217, 12 miles east of Canyon. The best time to visit is in the fall or winter because it gets dang hot here in the summertime (carry lots of water!). A small but pretty 1934 visitors center overlooks the canyon, has interpretive exhibits on the area's geology and history, the region's best bookstore and good tourist info.

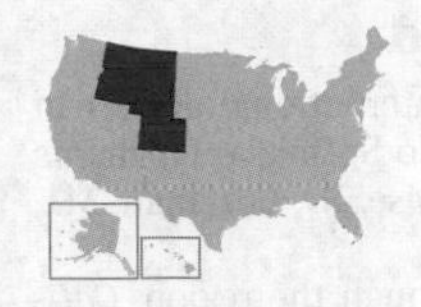

Rocky Mountains

Includes »

Colorado....................709
Denver....................709
Central & Northern Mountains....................725
Wyoming....................741
Yellowstone National Park....................744
Grand Teton National Park....................750
Montana....................754
Glacier National Park....761
Idaho....................763

Best Places to Eat

» Kitchen (p720)
» Root Down (p713)
» Silk Road (p759)
» Pine Creek Cookhouse (p732)
» Domo (p713)
» Cafe Diva (p727)

Best Places to Stay

» Queen Anne Bed & Breakfast Inn (p712)
» Modern Hotel (p764)
» Chautauqua Lodge (p720)
» Alpine House (p752)
» Old Faithful Inn (p749)

Why Go?

The high backbone of the lower 48, the Rockies are nature on steroids, with rows of snowcapped peaks, rugged canyons and wild rivers running buckshot all over the Western states. With their beauty and vitality, it's no wonder that 100 years ago ailing patients came here with last-ditch hopes to be cured.

The Rocky Mountains' healing powers persist. You can choose between tranquility (try Wyoming, the USA's most under-populated state) and adrenaline (measured in vertical drop). Locals love a good mud-spattered adventure and, with plenty of climbing, skiing and white-water paddling, it's easy to join in. Afterwards, relax by soaking in hot springs under a roof of stars, sipping pints of cold microbrews or feasting on farm-to-table food.

Lastly, don't miss the supersized charms of Yellowstone, Rocky Mountain, Grand Teton and Glacier National Parks, where the big five (grizzly bears, moose, bison, mountain lions and wolves) still roam wild.

When to Go

Denver

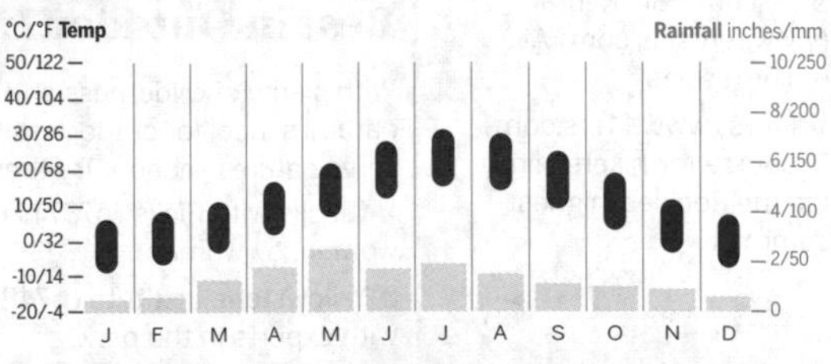

Jun-Aug Long days of sunshine ideal for biking, hiking, farmers markets and summer festivals.

Sep & Oct Fall foliage coincides with terrific lodging deals.

Jan & Feb Snow dusted peaks, powdery slopes, après-ski parties deluxe.

DON'T MISS

Don a Stetson and gallop the sagebrush wilderness of Wyoming or Montana.

Fast Facts

» Hub city: Denver (population 600,000)

» Denver to Yellowstone National Park: 595 miles

» Time zone: Mountain (two hours behind NYC)

» States covered in this chapter: Colorado, Idaho, Montana & Wyoming

Did You Know?

Pitch your tent in Yellowstone National Park and you'll be sleeping atop one of the world's largest supervolcanoes. It's active every 640,000 years: an eruption is due soon – give or take 10,000 years.

Resources

» Denver Post (www.denverpost.com) The region's top newspaper

» 5280 (www.5280.com) Denver's best monthly magazine

» Discount Ski Rental (www.rentskis.com) At major resorts

» 14ers (www.14ers.com) Resource for hikers climbing the Rockies' highest summits

Getting There & Around

Denver (DEN) has the only major international airport in the region. Both Denver and Colorado Springs offer flights on smaller planes to Jackson, WY, Boise, ID, Bozeman, MT, Aspen, CO, and other destinations.

Two Amtrak train routes pass through the region. *California Zephyr,* traveling daily between Emeryville, CA and Chicago, IL, has six stops in Colorado, including Denver, Fraser-Winter Park, Glenwood Springs and Grand Junction. *Empire Builder* runs daily from Seattle, WA, or Portland, OR, to Chicago, IL, with 12 stops in Montana (including Whitefish and East and West Glacier) and one stop in Idaho at Sandpoint.

Greyhound travels some parts of the Rocky Mountains. But to really get out and explore you'll need a car.

NATIONAL PARKS

The region is home to some of the USA's biggest national parks. In Colorado, **Rocky Mountain National Park** offers awesome hiking through alpine forests and tundra. There's also the Sahara-like wonder of **Great Sand Dunes National Park** and **Mesa Verde National Park**, an archaeological preserve with elaborate cliff-side dwellings.

Wyoming has **Grand Teton National Park**, with dramatic craggy peaks, and **Yellowstone National Park**, the country's first national park, a true wonderland of volcanic geysers, hot springs and forested mountains. In Montana, **Glacier National Park** features high sedimentary peaks, small glaciers and lots of wildlife, including grizzly bears. Idaho is home to **Hells Canyon National Recreation Area**, where the Snake River carves the deepest canyon in North America. The **National Park Service** (NPS; www.nps.gov) also manages over two dozen other historic sites, monuments, nature preserves and recreational areas statewide.

Best in Outdoor Instruction

With plenty of wilderness and tough terrain, the Rockies are a natural school for outdoor skills, and a perfect place to observe nature in action. Try these:

» Chicks with Picks (p737) Fun ice-climbing clinics for women, by women.

» Yellowstone Institute (p748) Study wolves, ecology or arts with experts in the park.

» Teton Science Schools (p752) Best for kids; both about nature and in it.

» Colorado Mountain School (p724) Climb a peak safely or learn belay skills.

History

Before the late 18th century, when French trappers and Spaniards stepped in, the Rocky Mountain area was a land of many tribes, including the Nez Percé, the Shoshone, the Crow, the Lakota and the Ute.

Meriwether Lewis and William Clark claimed their enduring fame after the USA bought almost all of present-day Montana, Wyoming and eastern Colorado in the Louisiana Purchase in 1803. The two explorers set out to survey the land, covering 8000 miles in three years. Their success urged on other adventurers, and soon the migration was in motion. Wagon trains voyaged to the mountainous lands right into the 20th century, only temporarily slowed by the completion of the Transcontinental Railroad across southern Wyoming in the late 1860s.

To accommodate settlers, the US purged the western frontier of the Spanish, British and, in a truly shameful era, most of the Native American population. The government signed endless treaties to defuse Native American objections to increasing settlement, but always reneged and shunted tribes onto smaller reservations. Gold-miners' incursions into Native American territory in Montana and the building of US Army forts along the Bozeman Trail ignited a series of wars with the Lakota, Cheyenne, Arapaho and others.

Gold and silver mania preceded Colorado's entry to statehood in 1876. Statehood

ROCKY MOUNTAINS IN...

Two Weeks

Start your Rocky Mountain odyssey in the **Denver** area. Go tubing, vintage-clothes shopping or biking in outdoor-mad, totally boho **Boulder**, then soak up the liberal rays eavesdropping at a sidewalk cafe. Enjoy the vistas of the **Rocky Mountain National Park** before heading west on I-70 to play in the mountains around **Breckenridge**, which also has the best beginner slopes in Colorado. Go to ski and mountain bike mecca **Steamboat Springs** before crossing the border into Wyoming.

Your first stop in the state should be **Lander,** rock-climbing destination extraordinaire. Continue north to chic **Jackson** and the majestic **Grand Teton National Park** before hitting iconic **Yellowstone National Park**. Save at least three days for exploring this geyser-packed wonderland.

Cross the state line into 'big sky country' and slowly make your way northwest through Montana, stopping in funky **Bozeman** and lively **Missoula** before visiting **Flathead Lake**. Wind up your trip in Idaho. If it's summer, you can paddle the wild white-water of **Hells Canyon National Recreation Area** before continuing to up-and-coming **Boise**. End your trip with a few days skiing **Sun Valley** and partying in **Ketchum**. The town and ski resort, despite being *the* winter playground du jour for today's Hollywood set, are refreshingly unpretentious and affordable.

One Month

With a month on your hands, you can really delve into the region's off-the-beaten-path treasures. Follow the two-week itinerary, but dip southwest in Colorado – an up-and-coming wine region – before visiting Wyoming. Ride the 4WD trails around **Ouray**. Be sure to visit **Mesa Verde National Park** and its ancient cliff dwellings.

In Montana, you'll want to get lost backpacking in the **Bob Marshall Wilderness Complex** and visit **Glacier National Park** before the glaciers disappear altogether. In Idaho, spend more time playing in **Sun Valley** and be sure to explore the shops, pubs and yummy organic restaurants in delightful little **Ketchum**. With a one-month trip, you also have time to drive along a few of Idaho's fantastically remote scenic byways. Make sure you cruise Hwy 75 from Sun Valley north to **Stanley**. Situated on the wide banks of the Salmon River, this stunning mountain hamlet is completely surrounded by national forest land and wilderness areas. Wild good looks withstanding, Stanley is also blessed with world-class trout fishing and mild to wild rafting. Take Hwy 21 from Stanley to Boise. This scenic drive takes you through miles of dense ponderosa forests, and past some excellent, solitary riverside camping spots – some of which come with their own natural hot-springs pools.

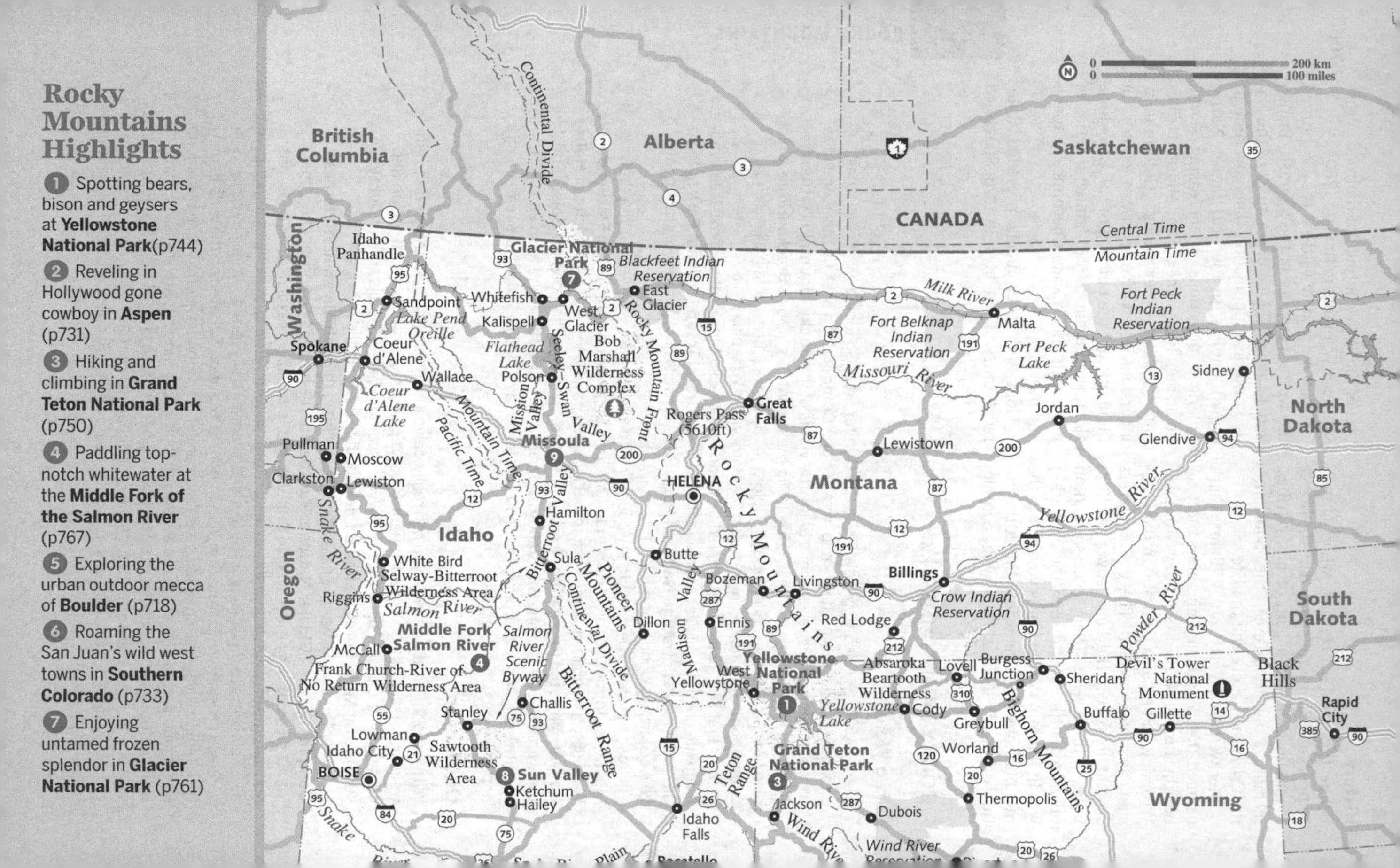

Rocky Mountains Highlights
1 Spotting bears, bison and geysers at Yellowstone National Park (p744)
2 Reveling in Hollywood gone cowboy in Aspen (p731)
3 Hiking and climbing in Grand Teton National Park (p750)
4 Paddling top-notch whitewater at the Middle Fork of the Salmon River (p767)
5 Exploring the urban outdoor mecca of Boulder (p718)
6 Roaming the San Juan's wild west towns in Southern Colorado (p733)
7 Enjoying untamed frozen splendor in Glacier National Park (p761)
200 km
100 miles
British Columbia
Alberta
Saskatchewan
CANADA
Continental Divide
Central Time
Mountain Time
Washington
Idaho Panhandle
Glacier National Park
Blackfeet Indian Reservation
East Glacier
Milk River
Fort Peck Indian Reservation
Sandpoint
Whitefish
West Glacier
Kalispell
Lake Pend Oreille
Rocky Mountain Front
Fort Belknap Indian Reservation
Malta
Fort Peck Lake
Spokane
Coeur d'Alene
Flathead Lake
Seeley
Bob Marshall Wilderness Complex
Missouri River
Sidney
Wallace
Polson
Swan Valley
Mission Valley
Great Falls
Rogers Pass (5610ft)
Jordan
North Dakota
Coeur d'Alene Lake
Mountain Time
Pacific Time
Missoula
Lewistown
Glendive
Pullman
Moscow
Clarkston
Lewiston
HELENA
Rocky Mountains
Montana
Yellowstone River
Snake River
Hamilton
Idaho
Bitterroot Valley
Oregon
White Bird
Selway-Bitterroot Wilderness Area
Sula
Butte
Pioneer Mountains
Billings
Riggins
Salmon River
Continental Divide
Bozeman
Valley
Livingston
Crow Indian Reservation
Powder River
South Dakota
Middle Fork Salmon River
Salmon River Scenic Byway
Dillon
Madison
Ennis
Red Lodge
McCall
Frank Church-River of No Return Wilderness Area
West Yellowstone
Yellowstone National Park
Absaroka Beartooth Wilderness
Lovell
Burgess Junction
Sheridan
Devil's Tower National Monument
Black Hills
Challis
Bitterroot Range
Yellowstone Lake
Cody
Greybull
Bighorn Mountains
Buffalo
Gillette
Rapid City
Stanley
Lowman
Idaho City
Sawtooth Wilderness Area
Grand Teton National Park
Teton Range
Worland
BOISE
Sun Valley
Ketchum
Hailey
Thermopolis
Wyoming
Snake
Idaho Falls
Jackson
Wind River
Dubois
Wind River Reservation

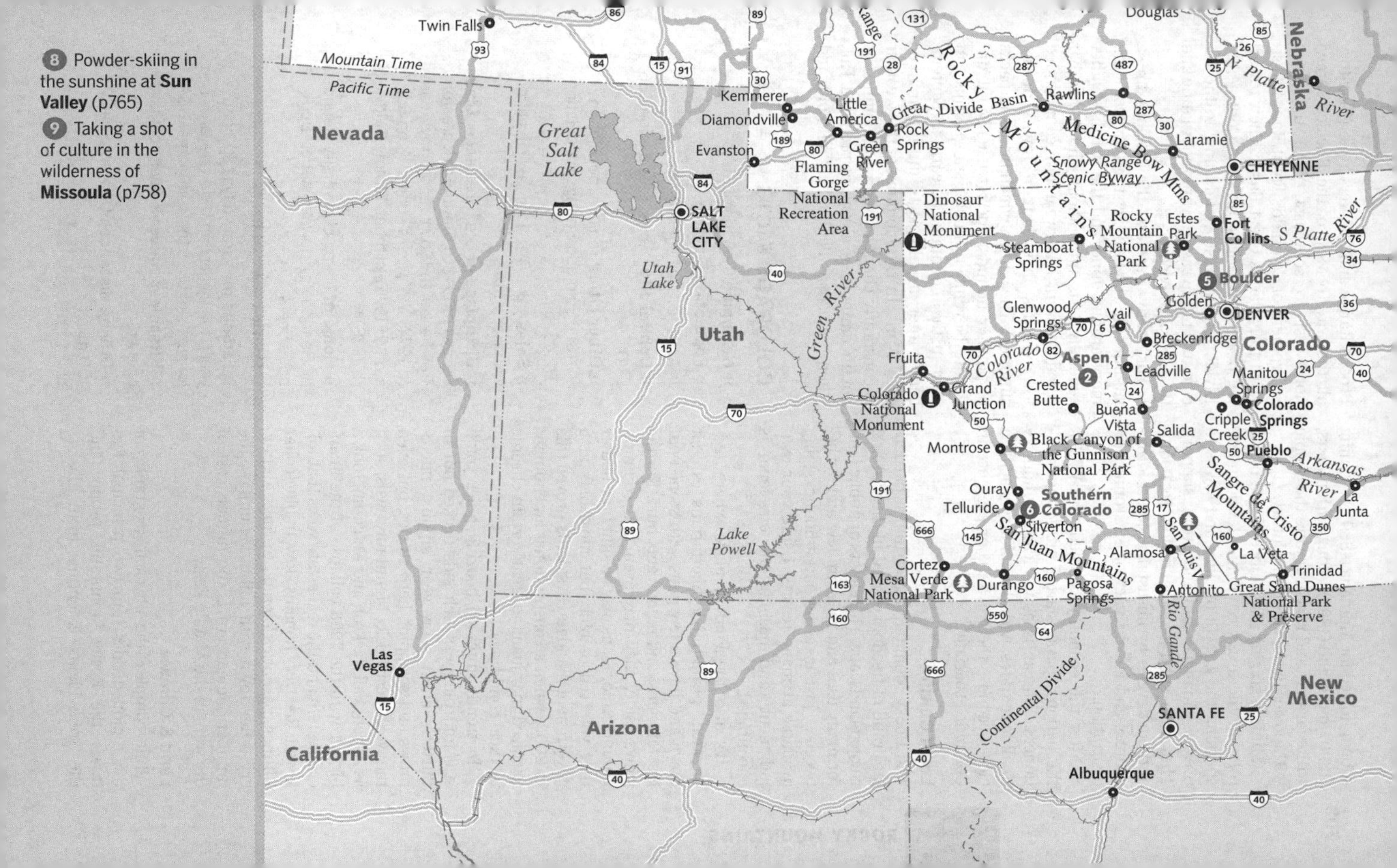

8 Powder-skiing in the sunshine at **Sun Valley** (p765)
9 Taking a shot of culture in the wilderness of **Missoula** (p758)
Twin Falls
Mountain Time
Pacific Time
Nevada
Great Salt Lake
SALT LAKE CITY
Utah Lake
Utah
Kemmerer
Diamondville
Evanston
Little America
Green River
Rock Springs
Flaming Gorge National Recreation Area
Rocky Mountains
Great Divide Basin
Rawlins
Medicine Bow Mtns
Snowy Range Scenic Byway
Laramie
CHEYENNE
Nebraska
N Platte River
Douglas
Dinosaur National Monument
Steamboat Springs
Rocky Mountain National Park
Estes Park
Fort Collins
S Platte River
Boulder
Golden
DENVER
Colorado
Glenwood Springs
Vail
Breckenridge
Aspen
Leadville
Fruita
Grand Junction
Colorado River
Colorado National Monument
Crested Butte
Buena Vista
Salida
Manitou Springs
Colorado Springs
Cripple Creek
Pueblo
Arkansas River
La Junta
Montrose
Black Canyon of the Gunnison National Park
Ouray
Telluride
Southern Colorado
Silverton
San Juan Mountains
Sangre de Cristo Mountains
San Luis V
La Veta
Trinidad
Alamosa
Antonito
Great Sand Dunes National Park & Preserve
Cortez
Mesa Verde National Park
Durango
Pagosa Springs
Rio Gande
Green River
Lake Powell
Las Vegas
California
Arizona
Continental Divide
New Mexico
SANTA FE
Albuquerque

soon followed for Montana (1889), Wyoming (1890) and Idaho (1890). Along with miners, white farmers and ranchers were the people with power in the late 19th century.

Mining, grazing and timber played major roles in the area's economic development, sparking the growth of cities and towns to provide financial and industrial support. They also subjected the region to boom-and-bust cycles by unsustainable use of resources and left a legacy of environmental disruption.

After the economy boomed post-WWII, the national parks started attracting vacationers. Tourism is now a leading industry in all four states, with the military placing a close second – there is a major presence in Colorado especially.

Local Culture

The Rocky Mountain states tout a particular brand of freedom echoed in the vast and rugged landscape. There's lots of public land for many uses and rules are few and far between – just take the out-of-bound skiing available at many resorts. Using your own judgment (and pushing the envelope) is encouraged.

It's also the kind of place where red-blooded, pistol-toting libertarians can sit down and have a few pints with stoned-out trustafarians, and no one gets hurt. Karmic views aside, they may even find common ground. Coloradans may be split on whether they vote red or blue, but most balk at a government mandate. Residents proved this in 2000, when a constitutional amendment legalized marijuana to treat certain chronic medical conditions.

In trendy après-ski boozing holes you'll still find plenty of rich kids decked out in Burton's latest snow gear, sipping microbrews and swapping hero stories, but even the wealthiest Rocky Mountain towns, such as Aspen, Vail, Jackson and Ketchum, took a big hit with the 2008 collapse of the financial system and the real-estate woes that followed. Recovery remains slow. In blue-collar Billings, patriotic Colorado Springs and every other town with military families, the number-one concern is the human cost of the wars in the Middle East.

Land & Climate

While complex, the physical geography of the region divides into two principal features: the Rocky Mountains proper and the Great Plains. Extending from Alaska's Brooks Range and Canada's Yukon Territory all the way to Mexico, the Rockies sprawl northwest to southeast, from the steep escarpment of Colorado's Front Range westward to Nevada's Great Basin. Their towering peaks and ridges form the Continental Divide: to the west, waters flow to the Pacific, and to the east, toward the Atlantic and the Gulf of Mexico.

For many travelers, the Rockies are a summer destination. It starts to feel summery around June, and the warm weather generally lasts until about mid-September (though warm outerwear is recommended for evenings in mountain towns during summer). The winter, which brings in packs of powder hounds, doesn't usually hit until late November, though snowstorms can start in the mountains as early as September. Winter usually lasts until March or early April. In the mountains, the weather is constantly changing (snow in summer is not uncommon), so always be prepared. Fall, when the aspens flaunt their fall gold, and

COLORADO FACTS

» **Nickname** Centennial State

» **Population** 5 million

» **Area** 104,247 sq miles

» **Capital city** Denver (population 566,974)

» **Other cities** Boulder (population 91,481), Colorado Springs (population 372,437)

» **Sales tax** 2.9% state tax, plus individual city taxes

» **Birthplace of** Ute tribal leader Chief Ouray (1833–80); South Park creator Trey Parker (b 1969); actor Amy Adams (b 1974); *127 Hours* subject Aron Ralston (b 1975), climber Tommy Caldwell (b 1978)

» **Home of** Naropa University (founded by Beat poets), powder slopes, boutique beers

» **Politics** swing state

» **Famous for** sunny days (300 per year), the highest altitude vineyards and longest ski run in the continental USA

» **Kitschiest souvenir** deer-hoof bottle openers

» **Driving distances** Denver to Vail 100 miles

early summer, when wildflowers bloom, are wonderful times to visit.

Getting There & Around

Travel here takes time. The Rockies are sparsely developed, with attractions spread across long distances and linked by roads that meander between mountains and canyons. With limited public transportation, touring in a private vehicle is best. After all, road-tripping is one of *the* reasons to explore this scenic region.

In rural areas services are few and far between – the I-80 across Wyoming is a notorious offender. It's not unusual to go more than 100 miles between gas stations. When in doubt, fill up.

The main travel hub is **Denver International Airport** (DIA; www.flydenver.com), although if you are coming on a domestic flight, check out **Colorado Springs Airport** (COS; www.springsgov.com/airportindex.aspx) as well: fares are often lower, it's quicker to navigate than DIA and it's nearly as convenient. Both Denver and Colorado Springs offer flights on smaller planes to cities and resort towns around the region – Jackson, WY, Boise, ID, Bozeman, MT, and Aspen, CO, are just a few options. Salt Lake City, UT, also has connections with destinations in all four states.

Greyhound (☎800-231-2222; www.greyhound.com) has fixed routes throughout the Rockies, and offers the most comprehensive bus service. The following **Amtrak** (☎800-872-7245; www.amtrak.com) services run to and around the region:

California Zephyr Daily between Emeryville, CA (in San Francisco Bay Area), and Chicago, IL, with six stops in Colorado, including Denver, Fraser-Winter Park, Glenwood Springs and Grand Junction.

Empire Builder Runs daily from Seattle, WA, or Portland, OR, to Chicago, IL, with 12 stops in Montana (including Whitefish and East and West Glacier) and one stop in Idaho at Sandpoint.

COLORADO

Graced with the greatest concentration of high peaks – dubbed 14ers for their height of 14000ft – Colorado is a burly state. From its double-diamond powder runs to the stout microbrews and stiff espresso drinks, all this sunny energy conspires to remind you of this. With universities and hopping high-tech, Coloradans do have a highly industrious side, though more than a few will call in sick to work when snow starts dumping in the high country.

It's no wonder that so many East Coasters, Californians and everyone in between have come to make their homes in this modern Shangri-La, propped up by Latin American workers meeting the endless needs of the hospitality industry. While much of the state is considered conservative, many Coloradans care deeply about environmental issues and have a friendly can-do ethos that is inspiring.

Information

Colorado Road Conditions (☎877-315-7623; www.state.co.us) Highway advisories.

Colorado State Parks (☎303-470-1144; www.parks.state.co.us) Tent and RV sites cost from $10 to $24 per night, depending on facilities. Rustic cabins and yurts are also available in some parks and those with wood-burning stoves may be available year-round. Advance reservations for specific campsites are taken, but subject to a $10 nonrefundable booking fee. Reservation changes cost $6.

Colorado Travel & Tourism Authority (☎800-265-6723; www.colorado.com) State-wide tourism information.

Denver Post (www.denverpost.com) Denver's major daily newspaper.

Denver

Spirited, urbane and self-aware, Denver is the region's cosmopolitan capital. The gleaming skyscrapers of Denver's Downtown and historic LoDo districts sit packed with breweries and the best culinary scene between Chicago and California – not to mention the 40ft blue bear and 60ft dancer sculptures. In the iconic sports arenas of Invesco Field at Mile High and Coors Field, home runs, high fives and mobs of rabid sports fans are nearly a nightly spectacle. Way off in the distance, rising though the high-altitude haze and all that thin air, is the jagged purple line of the Front Range, a gateway to some of the most spectacular wilderness on the continent. There's a whole lot to do in Denver.

The city is compact and friendly. Sitting at exactly 5280ft (1 mile) high – hence the nickname 'Mile High City' – this one-time Wild West railway town is a cool place to acclimatize, with low humidity and lots of Colorado sunshine.

Sights & Activities

16th Street Mall & LoDo NEIGHBORHOOD

The 16th Street Mall, a pedestrian-only strip of downtown, is lined with shops, restaurants and bars. The funkier **LoDo**, around Larimer Sq, is the best place to have a drink or browse the boutiques.

Denver Art Museum MUSEUM

(☎720-865-5000; www.denverartmuseum.org; 100 W 14th Ave; adult/student $13/10; 1st Sat of month free; ⏰10am-5pm Tue-Thu, Sat & Sun, 10am-8pm Fri) The DAM is home to one of the largest Native American art collections in the US and puts on special avant-garde multimedia exhibits. The Western American Art section of the permanent collection is justifiably famous.

Denver

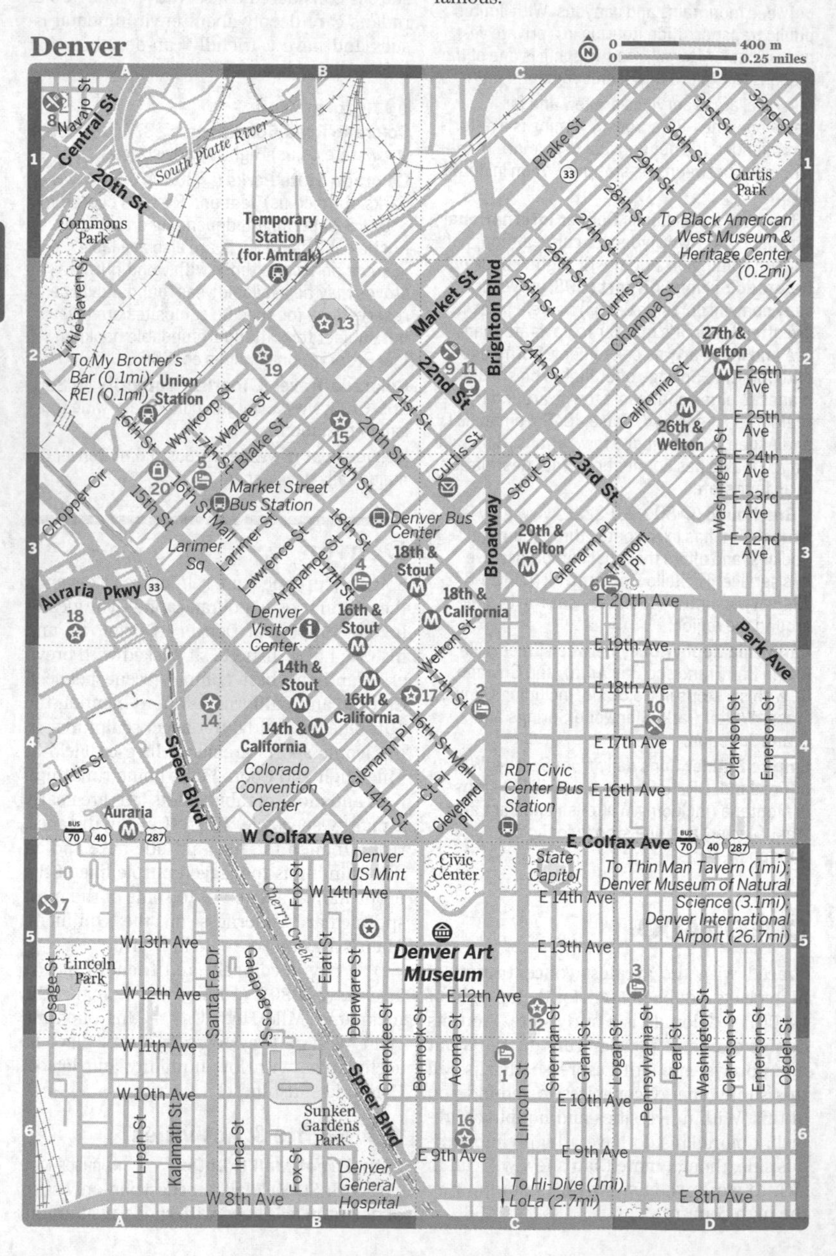

The $110-million Frederic C Hamilton wing, designed by Daniel Libeskind, is a strange, angular, fanlike edifice. It's inspired and mesmerizing. If you think the place looks weird from the outside, look inside: shapes shift with each turn, thanks to a combination of design and uncanny natural-light tricks.

Black American West Museum & Heritage Center MUSEUM
(☎303-482-2242; www.blackamericanwestmuseum.com; 3091 California St; adult/child $8/6; ⏰10am-2pm Tue-Sat) Denver is also home to the excellent Black American West Museum & Heritage Center, dedicated to 'telling history how it was.' It provides an intriguing look at the contributions of African Americans during the pioneer era – according to museum statistics, one in three Colorado cowboys were African American.

Red Rocks Park & Amphitheatre ARTS CENTER
(☎303-640-2637; www.redrocksonline.com; 16352 County Rd 93; park admission free; ⏰5am-11pm) Set between 400ft-high red sandstone rocks 15 miles southwest of Denver, this natural amphitheater was a Ute camping spot. Acoustics are so good, artists record live albums here. The 9000-seat theater offers stunning views and draws big-name bands.

Children's Museum MUSEUM
(☎303-433-7444; www.mychildsmuseum.org; 2121 Children's Museum Dr; admission $8; ⏰9am-4pm Mon-Fri, 10am-5pm Sat & Sun; 👪) If you've got kids, check out the Children's Museum, which is full of excellent interactive exhibits. A particularly well-regarded section is the kid-size grocery store, where your little consumers can push a shopping cart of their very own while learning about food and health. In the 'Arts à la carte' section kids can get creative with crafts that they can take home, using recycled materials.

Denver Museum of Nature & Science MUSEUM
(☎303-322-7009; www.dmns.org; 2001 Colorado Blvd; museum adult/child $12/6, IMAX $10/8; ⏰9am-5pm; 👪) Located 3.5 miles east of downtown, it has an IMAX theater, the Gates Planetarium and absorbing exhibits for all ages.

Festivals & Events

FREE **Cinco de Mayo** CULTURAL
(☎303-534-8342; www.cincodemayodenver.com; Civic Center Park) Enjoy salsa music and margaritas at one of the country's biggest Cinco de Mayo celebrations, held over two days on the first weekend in May. With three stages and more than 350 exhibitors and food vendors, it's huge fun.

Cherry Creek Arts Festival ARTS
(www.cherryarts.org; cnr Clayton St & E 3rd Ave) A sprawling celebration of visual, culinary and performing arts where a quarter of a million visitors browse the giant block party. The three-day event takes place around July 4.

Taste of Colorado FOOD
(☎303-295-6330; www.atasteofcolorado.com; Civic Center Park) Food stalls of over 50

Denver

Top Sights
Denver Art Museum C5

Sleeping
1 11th Avenue Hotel C6
2 Brown Palace Hotel C4
3 Capitol Hill Mansion B&B D5
4 Hotel Monaco B3
5 Jet Hotel A3
6 Queen Anne Bed & Breakfast Inn C3

Eating
7 Domo Restaurant A5
8 Root Down A1
9 Snooze C2
10 Steuben's Food Service D4

Drinking
11 Great Divide Brewing Company C2
Jet Lounge .... (see 5)

Entertainment
12 Church C5
13 Coors Field B2
14 Denver Center for the Performing Arts A4
15 El Chapultepec B2
16 La Rumba C6
17 Paramount Theatre B4
18 Pepsi Center A3
19 Sing Sing B2

Shopping
20 Tattered Cover Bookstore A3

restaurants; there's also booze, live music, and arts-and-crafts vendors at this Labor Day festival.

Great American Beer Festival BEER
(☎303-447-0816, 1888-822-627; www.greatamericanbeerfestival.com; 700 14th St) Colorado has more microbreweries than any other US state, and this hugely popular event in early September sells out in advance. More than 500 breweries are represented, from the big players to the home-brew enthusiasts.

Sleeping

Besides the places mentioned here, there are chain and independent motels throughout the city, with rooms starting at $75. Check out **Lonely Planet Hotels & Hostels** (www.lonelyplanet.com/hotels), with a range of sleeping options in the Denver 'burbs. Those on a budget should consider the very clean International Youth Hostel in nearby Boulder, as Denver's hostels were catering more to transients than backpackers when we dropped by.

TOP CHOICE Queen Anne Bed & Breakfast Inn B&B $$
(☎303-296-6666; www.queenannebnb.com; 2147 Tremont Pl; r incl breakfast $135-215; P❄📶) Earthy, cool and modern, this outstanding B&B is also cutting-edge sustainable. That means almost zero waste, a high standard of recycling and composting, locally sourced furnishings and gorgeous edible gardens. But the verve and romance comes mainly from its design. Four Denver artists have remade the suites with stunning results. Highlights include a forest mural that engulfs guests slumbering in organic bed sheets and a playful suite with oversized modern art in black-and-white motifs.

Chef-owner Milan Doshi keeps the kitchen on too. Guests get happy hour with Colorado wines and hors d'oeuvres. Breakfasts vary from waffles with blueberries and lavender to Indian-style potato pancakes. Free townie bikes let you ditch the car to explore Denver like a local

Hotel Monaco BOUTIQUE HOTEL $$$
(☎303-296-1717; www.monaco-denver.com; 1717 Champa St; r from $199; P❄@📶) This ultra-stylish boutique joint is a favorite with the celebrity set. Modern rooms blend French and art deco – think bold colors and fabulous European-style feather beds. Don't miss the evening 'Altitude Adjustment Hour,' when guests enjoy free wine and five-minute massages. The place is 100% pet-friendly; staff will even deliver a named goldfish to your room upon request. Discounts are routinely offered online.

Capitol Hill Mansion B&B B&B $$
(☎303-839-5221; www.capitolhillmansion.com; 1207 Pennsylvania St; r incl breakfast $119-219; P❄@📶) Stained-glass windows, original 1890s woodwork and turrets make this delightful, gay- and family-friendly Roman esque mansion a special place to stay. Rooms are elegant, uniquely decorated and come with different special features – one has a solarium, another boasts Jacuzzi tubs.

Brown Palace Hotel HISTORIC HOTEL $$$
(☎303-297-3111; www.brownpalace.com; 321 17th St; r from $299; P❄) Gaze up to the stained-glass crowned atrium and it's clear why this palace is shortlisted among the country's elite historic hotels. There's deco artwork, a four-star spa, imported marble, and staff who discretely float down the halls. The rooms, which have been hosting presidents since Teddy Roosevelt's days, have the elegance of a distant era.

One of the coolest features is the pianist playing Gershwin and ragtime favorites (we hear rooms on the 4th and 5th floors have an acoustically perfect perch).

If it's beyond your budget, ask a concierge for a free self-guided tour or check out tea time or a cocktail. The martini is predictably perfect and served with a sterling bowl of warm pecans.

Jet Hotel BOUTIQUE HOTEL $$
(☎303-572-3300; www.thejethotel.com; 1612 Wazee St; r $99-169; P❄@📶) Priced for partying, this slick (if slightly pretentious) boutique hotel in the heart of LoDo is all about fun, especially on weekends. That's when Denver's beautiful people come for the slumber-party-with-bottle-service experience – you can dance all night in the swank 1st-floor lounge, then stumble up to your bold lollipop-color quarters, burrow under the thick white comforters and sleep until brunch. Stay on a weekday if you want a posh central hotel room without the boozy party scene and accompanying noise. The healthy Asian fusion menu of the Swing Thai is perfect for kicking last night's hangover.

11th Avenue Hotel HOTEL $
(☎303-894-0529; www.11thavenuehotel.com; 1112 Broadway; dm $20, s/d $43/54, without bath

WHAT THE...?

So you just get into Denver and you have a few microbrews and suddenly your head is swirling. What's going on? Longstanding claims say that a person gets drunk quicker at high altitudes. Recent studies, including some conducted by the FAA, prove this to be untrue. However, don't say 'make mine a double' just yet. While altitude doesn't change how the body metabolizes alcohol, studies show it may exacerbate problems with acclimating, such as headaches and dizziness.

$37/48; ❄📶) Well located in the Golden Triangle district, this bare budget hotel may look vaguely like something from a Jim Jarmusch movie, but it's clean. Part of its MO is to assist people recovering from drug and alcohol problems (staff and residents) with affordable accommodations. It's safe, secure and a decent place for budget travelers.

Eating

Cheap street meals are found on the 16th St Mall. The pedestrian mall and LoDo are full of restaurants catering to all budgets and continents, and many of them have great sidewalk seating in the summer months.

TOP CHOICE **Steuben's Food Service** AMERICAN $$
(☎303-803-1001; www.steubens.com; 523 E 17th Ave; mains $8-21; ⏰11am-11pm Sun-Thu, 11am-midnight Fri & Sat; 👪) Although styled as a mid-century drive-in, the upscale treatment of comfort food (mac 'n' cheese, fried chicken, lobster rolls) and the solar-powered kitchen demonstrate Steuben's contemporary smarts. In summer, open garage doors lining the street create a breezy atmosphere and bargains come after 10pm with a burger, hand-cut fries and beer for $5.

Follow the restaurant on Facebook or Twitter to get details about Steuben's mobile truck, powered by recycled veggie oil and often seen at Civic Park.

Root Down MODERN AMERICAN $$$
(☎303-993-4200; www.rootdowndenver.com; 1600 W 33rd Ave; small plates $6-15; ⏰5-10pm Sun-Thu, 5-11pm Fri & Sat, brunch 10am-2:30pm Sat & Sun) In a converted gas station, chef Justin Cucci has undertaken one of the city's most ambitious culinary concepts, marrying sustainable 'field-to-fork' practices, high-concept culinary fusions and a low-impact, energy-efficient ethos. The menu changes seasonally, but consider yourself lucky if it includes the sweet-potato falafel or hoisin-duck confit sliders.

Root Down is largely wind-powered and decorated with reused and reclaimed materials, and it recycles *everything*. It's conceptually brilliant and one of Denver's most thrilling dining experiences.

Domo Restaurant JAPANESE $$
(☎303-595-3666; www.domorestaurant.com; 1365 Osage St; mains $10-22) Nestled in a beautiful Japanese garden, Denver's best Japanese restaurant is undeniably a romantic spot. This is Japanese country food and quality sushi too good to be served with heaps of soy. Each main is accompanied by seven traditional side dishes. The spicy *maguro* and *hamachi* combination *donburi* is an explosively flavorful combination of fresh fish, seaweed and chili-soy dressing.

Snooze CAFE $
(☎303-297-0700; www.snoozeeatery.com; 2262 Larimer St; mains $4-12; ⏰6:30am-2:30pm Mon-Fri, 7am-12:30pm Sat & Sun; 👪) Stomachs unite and grumble for this brick cafe's soft breakfast tacos with ranchero sauce, sweet potato pancakes with ginger sauce or salmon benedict. Creative and fresh, it's a strong start to any day. The restaurant also has a strong sustainability focus, which includes using local organic produce.

LoLa MEXICAN $
(☎720-570-8686; www.loladenver.com; 1575 Boulder St; mains $4-12; ⏰5pm-close Mon-Fri, 10am-2pm & 2:30-5pm Sat & Sun) Bringing costal Mexican to a landlocked town, LoLa pleases with fresh, smoky, chili-infused fare, best paired with a fantastic cocktail (try the hibiscus tea with citrus-infused tequila). Everybody loves the guacamole that's handmade at your table. To continue the party, check out the downstairs tequila bar. To get there, take 15th St past Confluence Park.

Drinking

Most bars and nightspots are in LoDo and around Coors Field. The biweekly gay newspaper *Out Front*, found in coffee shops and bars, has entertainment listings. Many of the venues listed in the Eating section of this book are also bars.

Great Divide Brewing Company BREWPUB
(www.greatdivide.com; 2201 Arapahoe St; ⏲2-8pm Mon & Tue, 2-10pm Wed-Sat) An excellent local brewery focused on crafting exquisite beer. Belly up to the bar and try the spectrum of seasonal brews.

Thin Man Tavern BAR
(www.thinmantavern.com; 2015 E 17th Ave) Considered among the best low-key singles' spots in the city, this neighborhood tavern is unexpectedly decked out with old Catholic paintings and ambient vintage lampshades. See free art films in the basement-level Ubisububi Room or classics flicks outside in the parking lot in summer.

Jet Lounge BAR
(www.thejethotel.com; 1612 Wazee St) This place to see and be seen in Denver has a bedroom-meets-house-party vibe: candles, cozy couches and a weekend DJ. Order bottle service, sit back and melt into the party.

My Brother's Bar BAR
(2376 15th St) Classic rock and roll, lacquered booths and tables made from old wood barrels greet you inside Denver's oldest bar. Grab a seat on the leafy patio if it's nice outside. The bar is on a popular cycle path, and has been a local institution since it opened.

☆ Entertainment

To find out what's happening with music, theater and other performing arts, pick up a free copy of *Westword*.

TOP CHOICE **Hi-Dive** LIVE MUSIC
(☎720-570-4500; www.hi-dive.com; 7 S Broadway) Local rock heroes and touring indie bands light up the stage at the Hi-Dive, a venue at the heart of Denver's local music scene. During big shows it gets deafeningly loud, cheek-to-jowl with hipsters and humid as an armpit. In other words, it's perfect.

El Chapultepec LIVE MUSIC
(☎303-295-9126; 1962 Market St; ⏲7am-2am, music from 9pm) This smoky little old-school joint is a dedicated jazz venue attracting a diverse clientele. Since it opened in 1951 Frank Sinatra, Tony Bennett and Ella Fitzgerald have played here, as have Jagger and Richards. Local jazz bands take the tiny stage nightly, but you never know who might drop by.

Grizzly Rose LIVE MUSIC
(www.grizzlyrose.com; 5450 N Valley Hwy; ⏲from 6pm Tue-Sun; 👪) This is one kick-ass honky-tonk – 40,000 sq ft of hot live music – attracting cowboys from as far away as Cheyenne. The Country Music Association called it the best country bar in America. If you've never experienced line dancing, then put on the boots, grab the Stetson and let loose.

Just north of the city limits off I-25 (you'll have to drive or cab it), the Grizzly is famous for bringing in huge industry stars – Willie Nelson, Lee Ann Rimes – for more than reasonable ticket prices.

La Rumba CLUB
(www.larumba-denver.com; 99 W 9th Ave; ⏲9pm-2am Fri-Sun) Though this place wobbles along as a salsa club the rest of the weekend, its Club Lip Gloss on Friday nights is a great party. Indie rock, garage and British pop bring an ultra-hip, gay-friendly vibe to the dance floor.

Church CLUB
(1160 Lincoln St) In a former cathedral, this club draws a large and diverse, though young, crowd. Lit by hundreds of altar candles and flashing blue strobe lights, it has three dance floors, a couple of lounges and even a sushi bar! Arrive before 10pm on weekends to avoid the $10 cover charge.

Sing Sing BAR
(☎303-291-0880; 1735 19th St) Very popular with bachelorette parties, this campy dueling piano bar fills quickly. Arrive around 6:30pm to score a table near the pianos. It's loud and the food is lackluster but the atmosphere is really fun. Song requests are taken (usually accompanied by $5).

Denver Performing Arts Complex PERFORMING ARTS
(☎720-865-4220; www.artscomplex.com; cnr 14th & Champa St) This massive complex – one of the largest of its kind – occupies four city blocks and houses several major theaters, the historic Ellie Caulkins Opera House and the Seawell Grand Ballroom. It's also home to the Colorado Ballet, Denver Center for the Performing Arts, Opera Colorado and the Colorado Symphony Orchestra.

Paramount Theatre CONCERT VENUE
(☎303-534-8336; www.denverparamount.com; 1621 Glenarm Pl) Music venue for national acts.

Invesco Field at Mile High STADIUM
(☎720-258-3000; www.invescofieldatmilehigh.com; 1805 S Bryant St; 👪) The much-lauded Denver Broncos football team and the Colorado Rapids soccer team play here, 1 mile

west of Downtown. It also plays host to big acts, like U2.

Coors Field BASEBALL
(800-388-7625; www.mlb.com/col/ballpark/; 2001 Blake St;) Denver is a city known for manic sports fans, and boasts five pro teams. The Colorado Rockies play baseball at the highly rated Coors Field.

Pepsi Center STADIUM
(303-405-1111; www.pepsicenter.com; 1000 Chopper Circle) The mammoth Pepsi Center hosts the Denver Nuggets basketball team, the Colorado Mammoth of the National Lacrosse League and the Colorado Avalanche hockey team. In off-season it's a mega concert venue.

Shopping

The pedestrian-only 16th St Mall and the boutiques of LoDo are the city's main downtown shopping areas.

TOP CHOICE **Tattered Cover Bookstore** BOOKS
(1628 16th St; 6:30am-9pm Mon-Fri, 9am-9pm Sat, 10am-6pm Sun) Denver's most loved bookstore is in this main shopping area. The armchair-travel section is wonderful – curl into the battered and comfy chairs scattered around the shop.

REI OUTDOOR EQUIPMENT, SPORTS
(Recreational Equipment Incorporated; 303-756-3100; www.rei.com; 1416 Platte St) The flagship store of this outdoor equipment supplier is an essential stop for those using Denver as a springboard into the great outdoors. In addition to top gear for camping, cycling, climbing and skiing, it has a rental department, maps and the Pinnacle, a 47ft indoor structure of simulated red sandstone for climbing and repelling.

There's also a desk of Colorado's Outdoor Recreation Information Center, where you can get information on state and national parks.

Information

In the event of a citywide emergency, radio station KOA (850 AM) is a designated point of information.

5280 Monthly glossy mag, has a comprehensive dining guide.

Denver Post (www.denverpost.com) The mainstream newspaper.

Denver Visitor Center (303-892-1505; www.denver.org; 918 16th St; 9am-5pm Mon-Fri)

ORIC Desk (Outdoor Recreation Information Center; REI main line 303-756-3100; www.oriconline.org; 1416 Platte St;) For outdoor trips, hit this desk inside the REI store, with maps and expert information. Hosts free Discover Colorado classes every Sunday at 3pm.

Police Headquarters (720-913-2000; 1331 Cherokee St)

Post office (951 20th St; 8am-6:30pm Mon-Fri, 9am-6:30pm Sat) Main branch.

University Hospital (303-399-1211; 4200 E 9th Ave; 24hr) Emergency services.

Westword (www.westword.com) This free weekly is the best source for local events.

Getting There & Away

Denver International Airport (DIA; www.flydenver.com; 8500 Peña Blvd) is served by around 20 airlines and offers flights to nearly every major US city. Located 24 miles east of downtown, DIA is connected with I-70 exit 238 by 12-mile-long Peña Blvd. Tourist and airport information is available at a **booth** (303-342-2000) in the terminal's central hall.

Greyhound buses stop at **Denver Bus Center** (303-293-6555; 1055 19th St), which runs services to Boise (from $151, 19 hours), Los Angeles (from $125, 22 hours) and other destinations.

Amtrak's *California Zephyr* runs daily between Chicago and San Francisco via Denver. Trains arrive and depart from a **Temporary Station** (1800 21st St) behind Coors Field until light-rail renovations at Union Station finish in 2014. For recorded information on arrival and departure times, call 303-534-2812. **Amtrak** (800-872-7245; www.amtrak.com) can also provide schedule information and train reservations.

Getting Around

To/From the Airport

All transportation companies have booths near the baggage-claim area. Public **Regional Transit District** (RTD; 303-299-6000; www.rtd-denver.com) runs a SkyRide service to the airport from downtown Denver hourly ($9 to $13, one hour). RTD also goes to Boulder ($13, 1½ hours) from the **Market Street Bus Station** (cnr 16th & Market Sts). **Shuttle King Limo** (303-363-8000; www.shuttlekinglimo.com) charges $20 to $35 for rides from DIA to destinations in and around Denver. **SuperShuttle** (303-370-1300) offers shared van services (from $22) between the Denver area and the airport.

Bicycle

For two-wheel transportation, **Denver B-Cycle** (denver.bcycle.com) is a new, citywide program that has townie bikes available at strategic locations, but riders must sign up online first (24 hours $6).

Car & Motorcycle

Street parking can be a pain, but there are slews of pay garages in downtown and LoDo. Nearly all the major car-rental agencies have counters at DIA, a few have offices in downtown Denver. Before you rent, check rates where you will be staying – it may be considerably cheaper than the airport.

Public Transportation

RTD provides public transportation throughout the Denver and Boulder area. Local buses cost $2.25 for local services, $4 for express services. Useful free shuttle buses run along the 16th St Mall.

RTD also operates a light-rail line serving 16 stations on a 12-mile route through downtown. Fares are the same as for local buses.

Taxi

For 24-hour cab service:

Metro Taxi (☎303-333-3333)

Zone Cab (☎303-444-8888)

Front Range

In addition to Denver, the Front Range is home to Colorado Springs, Boulder and Rocky Mountain National Park. Colorado's most populated region – and still growing – it's the launch pad for most Rocky Mountain adventures. I-25 is the north–south artery along the Front Range (which is just a name for this part of the Rocky Mountains), with Colorado Springs and Denver, 65 miles apart, both sitting on this highway.

COLORADO SPRINGS

The site of one of the country's first destination resorts, Colorado Springs sits at the foot of stunning Pikes Peak. You can summit this 14er by cars or cog railway or just lace up your boots and hike it. The city's craggy, striking red-rock vein that juts and runs for more than 10 miles is best admired at the Garden of the Gods.

Pinned down with four military bases, Colorado Springs is also a strange and sprawling quilt of neighborhoods of old (and new) money in Broadmoor, the evangelized planned community that is Briargate, the hippie stronghold of Manitou Springs, the pioneer sector of Old Colorado City, and finally the downtown district which mixes fine art, Olympic dreams and, yes, a touch of downbeat desperation.

Sights & Activities

TOP CHOICE **Pikes Peak** MOUNTAIN
(☎719-385-7325; www.springsgov.com; Pikes Peak; per adult/child/5-person car $12/5/40, cog railway round-trip adult/child $33/18; ⌚9am-3pm winter, 7:30am-8pm Memorial Day-Labor Day, 9am-5pm Oct 1-Memorial Day) At 14,110ft, Pikes Peak may not be one of the tallest of Colorado's 54 14ers, but it's certainly the most famous. Maybe because it's the only one with a road and a train to the top? That's where you'll find an observation platform and a kitschy gift shop.

FREE **Garden of the Gods** PARK
(☎719-634-6666; www.gardenofgods.com; 1805 N 30th St; ⌚8am-8pm Memorial Day-Labor Day, 9am-5pm Labor Day-Memorial Day) A compound

DON'T MISS

CLIMBING YOUR FIRST 14ER

Known as Colorado's easiest 14er, **Quandary Peak** (www.fs.usda.gov; County Rd 851; 👪), near Breckenridge, is the state's 15th highest peak at 14,265ft. Though you will see plenty of dogs and children, 'easiest' may be misleading – the summit remains three grueling miles from the trailhead. Go between June and September.

The trail ascends to the west; after about 10 minutes of moderate climbing, follow the right fork to a trail junction. Head left, avoiding the road, and almost immediately you will snatch some views of Mt Helen and Quandary (although the real summit is still hidden).

Just below timberline you'll meet the trail from Monte Cristo Gulch – note it so you don't take the wrong fork on your way back down. From here it's a steep haul to the top. Start early and aim to turn around by noon, as afternoon lightning is typical during summer. It's a 6-mile round-trip, taking roughly between seven and eight hours. To get here, take Colorado 9 to County Rd 850. Make a right and turn right again onto 851. Drive 1.1 miles to the unmarked trailhead. Park parallel on the fire road.

of 13 bouldered peaks and soaring red-rock pinnacles accessed by a network of concrete paths and trails. It's a great place for families.

FREE Barr Trail HIKING

You can also reach the Pike's Peak summit on foot, via the tough 12.5-mile Barr Trail. From the trailhead, just above the Manitou Springs depot, the path climbs 7300ft. Fit hikers should reach the top in about eight hours, but should leave very early to avoid dangerous afternoon thunderstorms. Many hikers split the trip into two days, stopping to acclimatize overnight at Barr Camp at the halfway point (10,200ft).

Colorado Springs Fine Arts Center MUSEUM

(FAC; ☎719-634-5583; www.csfineartscenter.org; 30 W Dale St; adult/senior & student $10/8.50; ⊙10am-5pm Tue-Sun) A sophisticated collection with terrific Latin American art, Mexican clay figures, Native American basketry and quilts, wood-cut prints from social justice artist Leopold Mendez, and abstract work from local artists. Recently and beautifully redone, it also houses a fine restaurant and cafe.

Festivals & Events

Colorado Balloon Classic BALLOONING

(☎719-471-4833; www.balloonclassic.com; 1605 E Pikes Peak Ave) For 35 years running, hot-air ballooners, both amateur and pro, have been launching Technicolor balloons just after sunrise for three straight days over the Labor Day weekend. You'll have to wake with the roosters to see it all, but it's definitely worth your while.

Emma Crawford Coffin Races RACE

(www.manitousprings.org; Manitou Ave) In 1929 the coffin of Emma Crawford was unearthed by erosion and slid down Red Mountain. Today, coffins are decked out with wheels and run down Manitou Ave for three hours on the Saturday before Halloween (October).

Sleeping

There are cheap 1950s-style independent motels on Nevada Ave about 1 mile north and 1 mile south of the central business district. For the more upscale chains, like Holiday Inn and Best Western, try the Fillmore, Garden of the Gods and Circle Ave exits off I-25.

TOP CHOICE Broadmoor RESORT $$$

(☎719-634-7711; www.broadmoor.com; 1 Lake Ave; r from $300; P❄@📶🏊) One of the top five-star resorts in the US, the 744-room Broadmoor sits before the blue-green slopes of Cheyenne Mountain. Hollywood stars, A-list pro athletes, and nearly every president since FDR have made it a point to visit (and that includes Obama). Everything here is exquisite: acres of lush grounds and a shimmering lake, pool, world-class golf, ornately decorated public spaces, myriad bars and restaurants, an incredible spa and ubercomfortable European-style guest rooms that invoke Marie Antoinette on a binge. Service is spectacular and dogs are welcome too. Check online for seasonal deals.

Two Sisters Inn B&B $$

(☎719-685-9684; www.twosisinn.com; 10 Otoe Pl; r without bath $79, with bath $135-155; P❄📶) A longtime favorite among B&B aficionados, this place has five rooms (including the honeymoon cottage out back) set in a rose-colored Victorian home, built in 1919 by two sisters. It was originally a boarding house for schoolteachers, and has been an inn since 1990. There's a magnificent stained-glass front door and an 1896 piano in the parlor; it has won awards for its breakfast recipes.

Hyatt Place HOTEL $

(☎719-265-9385; www.coloradosprings.place.hyatt.com; 503 West Garden of the Gods Rd; r $71-99; P❄@📶🏊👪) Even with its corporate sheen and IKEA-chic decor, we can dig this place. Okay, it's a chain and a bit close to Hwy 25, but rooms are sizable and super-clean with cushy linens, new beds, massive flat-screens and a comfy sitting area. Factor in the helpful staff and free continental breakfast, and it's a steal.

Barr Camp CAMPGROUND $

(www.barrcamp.com; Barr Trail; tents $12, lean-tos $17, cabin dm $28) At the halfway point on the Barr Trail, about 6.5 miles from the Pikes Peak summit, you can pitch a tent, shelter in a lean-to or reserve a bare-bones cabin. There's drinking water and showers; dinner ($8) is available Wednesday to Sunday. Reservations are essential and must be made online in advance. The camp is open year-round and gets fully booked up, even in winter.

Eating

The Tejon Strip downtown has the most offerings for dining.

La'au's MEXICAN $

(www.laaustacoshop.com; 830 N Tejon St; dishes $6-9; ⊙11am-9pm) Fresh, light and deeply

WORTH A TRIP

CRIPPLE CREEK CASINOS

Just an hour from Colorado Springs yet worlds away, Cripple Creek hurls you back into the Wild West of lore. This once lucky lady produced a staggering $413 million in gold by 1952.

The booze still flows and gambling still thrives, but yesteryear's saloons and brothels are now tasteful casinos.

It's 50 miles southwest of Colorado Springs on Hwy 67. Catch the **Ramblin' Express** (719-590-8687; www.ramblinexpress.com; round-trip tickets $25; departures 7am-10pm) from Colorado Springs' 8th St Depot.

flavorful, this modern taco hut hits the spot. If you've never had Hawaiian tacos before, think peanut chicken topped with fresh mango and Peruvian *ají* (hot peppers). Best for a quickie, it sits in the alley behind Tejon and Cache la Poudre.

Shugas CAFE **$**
(719-328-1412; www.shugas.com; 702 S Cascade St; dishes $6-9; 11am-midnight Mon-Sat;) If you thought Colorado Springs couldn't be hip, stroll to Shuga's, a southern-style cafe with a knack for knockout espresso drinks and hot cocktails. Cuter than buttons, this little white house is decked out in paper cranes and red vinyl chairs. There's also patio seating. The food – brie BLT on rosemary toast, Brazilian coconut shrimp soup – comforts and delights. Don't miss vintage-movie Saturdays.

Nosh MODERN AMERICAN **$$**
(719-635-6674; www.nosh121.com; 121 S Tejon St; small plates $9-21; 11am-10pm) Everyone's favorite downtown dining room and patio. Doused in color and artwork, this upscale cafe serves small plates of lentil or bison dumplings, scallop crudo, chili-glazed burgers and all manner of roasted veggies. These are the best downtown eats by far.

Adam's Mountain Cafe MODERN AMERICAN **$$**
(719-685-1430; www.adamsmountain.com; 934 Manitou Ave; mains $7-16; 8am-3pm & 5-9pm Tue-Sat, to 3pm Sun;) In Manitou Springs, this slow-food cafe makes a lovely stop. Breakfast includes orange-almond French toast and huevos rancheros (eggs and beans on a tortilla). Dinner gets eclectic with offerings such as Moroccan chicken with preserved lemons and Brazilian spiced barramundi. The interior is airy and attractive with marble floors and exposed rafters, and there's patio dining too.

Drinking

The downtown Tejon Strip, between Platte and Colorado Sts, is where most of the after-dark action happens, although it's relatively tame.

TOP CHOICE **Swirl** WINE BAR
(www.swirlwineemporium.com; 717 Manitou Ave; 4-10pm Sun-Thu, to midnight Fri & Sat) Behind a stylish bottle shop in Manitou Springs, this nook bar is intimate and cool. The garden patio has dangling lights and vines while inside there are antique armchairs and a fireplace. It's a superb spot to celebrate life, beauty and love.

Trinity Brewing Co BREWPUB
(www.trinitybrew.com; 1466 Garden of the Gods Rd; 11am-midnight Thu-Sat, 11am-10pm Sun-Wed) Inspired by Belgium's beer cafes, the eco-friendly Trinity Brewing Co serves potent artisanal beers made from rare ingredients. The slow food menu has vegan BBQ sandwiches and 10% discounts are bestowed if you arrive on foot or by bike.

Information

Colorado Springs Visitor Center (719-635-7506; www.visitcos.com; 515 S Cascade Ave; 8:30am-5pm;) Has all the usual tourist information.

Getting There & Around

Colorado Springs Municipal Airport (719-550-1972; www.springsgov.com/airportindex.aspx; 7770 Milton E Proby Parkway) is a viable alternative to Denver. The **Yellow Cab** (719-634-5000) fare from the airport to the city center is $30.

Buses between Cheyenne, WY, and Pueblo, CO, stop daily at **Greyhound** (719-635-1505; 120 S Weber St). **Mountain Metropolitan Transit** (719-385-7433; www.springsgov.com; adult $1.75) offers schedule information and route maps for all local buses; find information online.

BOULDER

Tucked up against its soaring signature Flatirons, this idyllic college town has a sweet location and a palpable ecosophistication that has attracted entrepreneurs, athletes, hippies and hard-bodies like moths to the moonlight.

Boulder's mad love of the outdoors was officially legislated in 1967, when it became the first US city to tax itself specifically to preserve open space. Thanks to such vision, packs of cyclists whip up and down the Boulder Creek corridor, which links city and county parks those taxpayer dollars have purchased. The pedestrian-only Pearl St Mall is lively and perfect for strolling, especially at night, when students from University of Colorado and Naropa University mingle into the wee hours.

In many ways it is Boulder, not Denver, that is the region's tourist hub. The city is about the same distance from Denver International Airport, and staying here puts you closer to local trails in the foothills, as well as the big ski resorts west on I-70 and Rocky Mountain National Park.

Sights & Activities

Boulder's two areas to see and be seen are the downtown Pearl St Mall and the University Hill district (next to campus), both off Broadway. Overlooking the city from the west are the Flatirons, an eye-catching rock formation.

TOP CHOICE Chautauqua Park PARK

(www.chautauqua.com; 900 Baseline Rd) This historic landmark park is the gateway to Boulder's most magnificent slab of open space (we're talking about the Flatirons), which also has a wide, lush lawn that attracts picnickers. It also gets copious hikers, climbers and trail runners. World-class musicians perform each summer at the auditorium.

Boulder Creek Bike Path CYCLING

(24 hr;) The most utilized commuter bike path in town, this fabulously smooth and mostly straight creekside concrete path follows Boulder Creek from Foothill Parkway all the way to the spilt of Boulder Canyon and Four Mile Canyon Rd west of downtown – a total distance of over 5 miles one-way. The path also feeds urban bike lanes that lead all over town.

Boulder Rock Club ROCK CLIMBING

(303-447-2804; www.totalclimbing.com; 2829 Mapleton Ave; day pass adult/child $15/8, private lessons $50, 3 2hr intro classes with gear rental $130; 8am-10pm Mon, 6am-11pm Tue-Thu, 8am-11pm Fri, 10am-8pm Sat & Sun;) Climb indoors at this massive warehouse full of artificial rock faces cragged with ledges and routes. The auto-belay system allows solo climbers an anchor. Staff is a great resource for local climbing routes and tips too.

Eldorado Canyon State Park OUTDOORS

(303-494-3943; visitor center 9am 5pm) One of the country's most favored rock-climbing areas, offering Class 5.5 to 5.12 climbs and some nice hiking trails. The park entrance is on Eldorado Springs Dr, west of Hwy 93. Information is available from Boulder Rock Club.

University Bicycles CYCLING

(www.ubikes.com; 839 Pearl St; 4hr rental $15; 10am-6pm Mon-Sat, 10am-5pm Sun) There are plenty of places to rent bicycles to cruise around town, but this has the widest range of rides and the most helpful staff.

Festivals & Events

FREE Boulder Creek Festival MUSIC, FOOD

(303-449-3137; www.bceproductions.com; Central Park, Canyon Blvd) Billed as the kick-off to summer and capped with the fabulous Bolder Boulder, this massive Memorial Day weekend (May) festival has 10 event areas featuring more than 30 live entertainers and 500 vendors. With food and drink, music and sunshine, what's not to love?

Bolder Boulder ATHLETICS

(303-444-7223; www.bolderboulder.com; adult $44-48) Held in a self-consciously hyper

WORTH A TRIP

SUSTAINABLE BREWS

New Belgium Brewing Co (800-622-4044; www.newbelgium.com; 500 Lined St; admission free; guided tours 10am-6pm, Tue-Sat) satisfies beer connoisseurs with its hearty Fat Tire Amber Ale, and diverse concoctions like 1554, Trippell and Sunshine Wheat. Recognized as one of the world's most environmentally conscious breweries, a 100,000kw turbine keeps it wind-powered. The brewery also sponsors cool events such as bike-in cinema and scavenger hunts on the ski slopes. It's in the college town of Fort Collins (home to Colorado State University), a worthwhile 46-mile drive north of Boulder on I-25 – especially if you're heading to Wyoming. Reserve tickets online – these popular tours include complimentary tasting of the flagship and specialty brews.

athletic town, this is the biggest foot race within the city limits. It doesn't take itself too seriously – spectators scream, there are runners in costume, and live music plays throughout the course. It's held on Memorial Day (May).

Sleeping

Boulder has dozens of options – drive down Broadway or Hwy 36 to take your pick. Booking online usually scores the best discounts.

TOP CHOICE Chautauqua Lodge HISTORIC HOTEL **$**
(☎303-442-3282; www.chautauqua.com; 900 Baseline Rd; r from $73, cottages from $139; P ❄ ᯤ ♿) Adjoining beautiful hiking trails to the Flatirons, this leafy neighborhood of cottages is our top pick. It has contemporary rooms and one- to three-bedroom cottages with porches and beds with patchwork quilts. It's perfect for families and pets. All have full kitchens, though the wraparound porch of the Chautauqua Dining Hall is a local favorite for breakfast.

Hotel Boulderado HISTORIC HOTEL **$$$**
(☎303-442-4344; www.boulderado.com; 2115 13th St; r from $224; P ❄ ᯤ) Celebrating a century of service in 2009, the charming Boulderado, full of Victorian elegance and wonderful public spaces, is a National Register landmark and a romantic place to spend the night. Each antique-filled room is uniquely decorated, and the stained-glass atrium and glacial water fountain accent the jazz-washed lobby.

Boulder International Youth Hostel HOSTEL **$**
(☎303-442-0522; www.boulderinternationalhostel.com; 1107 12th St; dm $27, s/d without bath $52/62; P ᯤ) A great deal in the raucous university frat-house neighborhood, this hostel has been meeting the needs of travelers since 1961. Single-sex dorms and private rooms are worn but clean. Bring bedding or rent linens for $7 per stay.

Alps B&B **$$$**
(☎303-444-5445; www.alpsinn.com; 38619 Boulder Canyon Dr; r $159-279; P ❄ @ ᯤ) Constructed in the 1870s, this inn charms with Mission furnishings, stained-glass windows and antique fireplaces. Many rooms feature a private whirlpool for two with French doors leading to a garden, patio or private porch with views of Boulder Creek and the canyon. The generous spa amenities may appeal to couples looking for a romantic stop.

St Julien Hotel & Spa HOTEL **$$$**
(☎720-406-9696, reservations 877-303-0900; www.stjulien.com; 900 Walnut St; r from $289; P ❄ @ ᯤ ≋ ♿) In the heart of downtown, Boulder's finest four-star is modern and refined, with photographs of local scenery and cork walls that warm the room ambience. With fabulous Flatiron views, the back patio hosts live world music, jazz concerts and wild salsa parties. Rooms are plush, and so are the robes.

Eating

Boulder's dining scene has dozens of great options. Most are centered on the Pearl Street Mall, while bargains are more likely to be found on the Hill. Between 3:30pm and 6:30pm nearly every restaurant in the city features a happy hour with some kind of amazing food and drink special. It's a great way to try fine dining on a budget – check websites for details.

TOP CHOICE Kitchen MODERN AMERICAN **$$$**
(☎303-544-5973; www.thekitchencafe.com; 1039 Pearl St; mains $11-25; ⊙11am-9pm Mon, to 10pm Tue-Fri, 9am-2pm & 5:30-10pm Sat, 9:30am-2pm & 5:30-9pm Sun; ᯤ) Clean lines, stacks of crusty bread, a daily menu and lots of light: Kitchen is one of the finest kitchens in town. Fresh farmers-market ingredients are crafted into rustic tapas: think roasted root vegetables, shaved prosciutto and mussels steamed in wine and cream. The pulled-pork sandwich rocks, but save room for the sticky toffee pudding. Check out community hour (daily 3pm to 5:30pm) – a good way to meet the neighbors. A younger crowd gathers at the more casual upstairs bar.

Boulder Dushanbe Teahouse FUSION **$$**
(☎303-442-4993; 1770 13th St; mains $8-20; ⊙8am-10pm) No visit to Boulder is complete without a meal at this incredible Tajik work of art, a gift from Boulder's sister city (Dushanbe, Tajikistan). Incredible craftsmanship and meticulous painting envelop the vibrant multicolored interior. The international fare ranges from Amazonian to Mediterranean to, of course, Tajik. Outside, in the quiet gardens, is a lovely, shaded full-service patio. It's an intimate place to grab cocktails or dinner with friends on a warm summer day.

EATING THE ROCKIES

Start by digging into regional *Edible* (www.edible.com) magazines online – a great resource for farmers markets and innovative eats.

Boulder is worth a stop since it is America's Foodiest Small Town, according to *Bon Appetit*. At **Kitchen** (☎303-544-5973; www.thekitchencafe.com; per person $35) Monday is community night, which means shared tables and a homegrown five-course meal served family-style, with 20% of proceeds going to charity. Go behind the scenes with **Local Table Tours** (☎303-909-5747; www.localtabletours.com; tours $20-70), a tour presenting a smattering of great local cuisine and inside knowledge on food and wine or coffee and pastries. The cocktail crawl is a hit.

For fine dining in a warehouse or an airplane hangar, Denver's **Hush** (www.hushdenver.com) sponsors fun pop-up dinners with top regional chefs, by invitation only – make contact online.

Our favorite farm dinner, **On the Farm** (☎307-413-3203; onthefarminidaho@gmail.com; Victor, ID; 6-course meal $75), in Idaho's Teton Valley, serves sumptuous and sustainable local food with the most spectacular backdrop.

Lucile's CAJUN **$**
(☎303-442-4743; www.luciles.com; 2142 14th St; mains $7-14; ⏲7am-2pm Mon-Fri, from 8am Sat & Sun; 👪) This New Orleans–style diner has perfected breakfast; the Creole egg dishes (served over creamy spinach alongside cheesy grits or perfectly blackened trout) are the thing to order. Start with a steaming mug of chai or chicory coffee and an order of beignets.

Zoe Ma Ma CHINESE **$**
(2010 10th St; mains $5-13; ⏲11am-10pm Sun-Thu, 11am-11pm Fri & Sat) At Boulder's hippest noodle bar you can slurp and munch fresh street food at a long outdoor counter. Mama, the Taiwanese matriarch, is on hand, cooking and chatting up customers in her Crocs. Organic noodles are made from scratch, as are the garlicky melt-in-your mouth pot stickers.

Sink PUB **$**
(www.thesink.com; 1165 13th St; mains $5-10; ⏲11am-2am, kitchen to 10pm) Dim and graffiti-scrawled, the Sink has been a Hill classic since 1923. Colorful characters cover the cavernous space – the scene alone is almost worth a visit. Almost. Once you've washed back the legendary Sink burger with a slug of a local microbrew, you'll be glad you stuck around.

Alfalfa's SELF-CATERING
(www.alfalfas.com; 1651 Broadway St; ⏲7:30am-10pm) A small, community-oriented natural market with a wonderful selection of prepared food and an inviting indoor-outdoor dining area to enjoy it in.

Drinking & Entertainment

Playboy didn't vote CU the best party school for nothing – the blocks around the Pearl St Mall and the Hill churn out fun, with many restaurants doubling as bars or turning into all-out dance clubs come 10pm.

Mountain Sun Pub & Brewery BREWERY
(1535 Pearl St) Boulder's favorite brewery serves a rainbow of brews from chocolaty to fruity, and packs in an eclectic crowd of yuppies, hippies and everyone in between. Walls are lined with tapestries, there are board games to amuse you and the pub grub (especially the burgers) is delicious. There's usually live music of the bluegrass and jam-band variety on Sunday and Monday nights.

Bitter Bar COCKTAIL BAR
(☎303-442-3050; www.happynoodlehouse.com; 835 Walnut St; cocktails $9-15) A chic Boulder speakeasy – think pan-Asian environs and killer cocktails, like the scrumptious lavender-infused Blue Velvet – that make the evening slip happily out of focus.

West End Tavern PUB
(www.thewestendtavern.com; 926 Pearl St) Nothing fancy, just loungy booths, a fantastic roof deck and tasty pub grub.

Boulder Theater CINEMA, MUSIC
(☎303-786-7030; www.bouldertheatre.com; 2032 14th St) This old movie-theater-turned-historic-venue brings in slightly under-the-radar acts like jazz great Charlie Hunter, the madmen rockers of Gogol Bordello and West African divas, Les Nubians. But it also screens classic films and short-film festivals

that can and should be enjoyed with a glass of beer.

Shopping

Boulder has great shopping and galleries. The outdoor 29th St Mall, with a movie theatre, just off 28th St between Canyon and Pearl St, is a recent addition.

Pearl Street Mall MALL

The main feature of downtown Boulder is the Pearl Street Mall, a vibrant pedestrian zone filled with kids' climbing boulders and splash fountains, bars, galleries and restaurants.

Momentum HANDICRAFTS

(www.ourmomentum.com; 1625 Pearl St; 10am-7pm Tue-Sat, 11am-6pm Sun) The kitchen sink of unique global gifts – Zulu wire baskets, fabulous scarves from India, Nepal and Ecuador – all handcrafted and purchased at fair value from disadvantaged artisans. Every item purchased provides a direct economic lifeline to the artists.

Common Threads CLOTHING

(www.commonthreadsboulder.com; 2707 Spruce St; 10am-6pm Mon-Sat, noon-5pm Sun) Vintage shopping at its most haute couture, this fun place is where to go for secondhand Choos and Prada purses. The shop is a pleasure to browse, with clothing organized by color and type on visually aesthetic racks, just like a big-city boutique.

Boulder Bookstore BOOKS

(www.boulderbookstore.indiebound.com; 1107 Pearl St) Boulder's favorite indie bookstore has a huge travel section downstairs and hosts readings and workshops.

Information

Boulder Visitor Center (303-442-2911; www.bouldercoloradousa.com; 2440 Pearl St; 8:30am-5pm Mon-Thu, 8:30am-4pm Fri) Offers information and internet access.

Getting There & Around

Boulder has fabulous public transportation, with services extending as far away as Denver and its airport. Ecofriendly buses are run by **RTD** (303-299-6000; www.rtd-denver.com; per ride $2-4.50). Maps are available at **Boulder Station** (cnr 14th & Walnut Sts). RTD buses (route B) operate between Boulder Station and Denver's Market St Bus Station ($3.50, one hour). RTD's SkyRide bus (route AB) heads to Denver International Airport ($13, 1½ hours, hourly). **SuperShuttle** (303-444-0808) provides hotel ($25) and door-to-door ($32) shuttle service from the airport.

For two-wheel transportation, **Boulder B-Cycle** (boulder.bcycle.com; 24-hr rental $5) is a new citywide program with townie bikes available at strategic locations, but riders must sign up online first.

ROCKY MOUNTAIN NATIONAL PARK

Rocky Mountain National Park showcases classic alpine scenery, with wildflower meadows and serene mountain lakes set under snowcapped peaks. There are over three million visitors annually, but many stay on the beaten path. Hike an extra mile and enjoy the incredible solitude. In winter the park becomes a great place to snowshoe or go backcountry skiing. Elk are the park's signature mammal – you will even see them grazing hotel lawns, but also keep an eye out for bighorn sheep, moose, marmots and black bears.

Activities

Trails OUTDOORS

The bustling Bear Lake Trailhead offers easy **hikes** to several lakes and beyond. Another busy area is Glacier Gorge Junction Trailhead. The free Glacier Basin–Bear Lake shuttle services both.

Forested Fern Lake, 4 miles from the Moraine Park Trailhead, is dominated by craggy Notchtop Peak. You can complete a loop to the Bear Lake shuttle stop in about 8.5 miles for a rewarding day hike. The strenuous **Flattop Mountain Trail** is the only cross-park trail, linking Bear Creek on the east side with either Tonahutu Creek Trail or the North Inlet Trail on the west side.

Families might consider the moderate hikes to **Calypso Cascades** in the Wild Basin or to **Gem Lake** in the Lumpy Ridge area.

Trail Ridge Rd crosses the Continental Divide at Milner Pass (10,759ft), where trails head 4 miles (and up 2000ft!) southeast to Mt Ida, which offers fantastic views.

Trails on the west side of the park are quieter and less trodden than those on the east side. Try the short and easy East Inlet Trail to **Adams Falls** (0.3 miles) or the more moderate 3.7-mile Colorado River Trail to the **Lulu City** site.

Before July, many of the trails are snowbound, and high water runoff makes passage difficult. On the east side, the Bear Lake and Glacier Gorge Junction Trailheads offer good routes for **cross-country skiing** and **snowshoeing**. **Backcountry skiing** is also possible; check with the visitor centers.

Sleeping & Eating

The only overnight accommodations in the park are at campgrounds. Dining options and the majority of motel or hotel accommodations are around Estes Park or Grand Lake, located on the other side of the Trail Ridge Road Pass.

The park's formal campgrounds provide campfire programs, have public telephones and a seven-day limit during summer months; all except Longs Peak take RVs (no hookups). The water supply is turned off during winter.

You will need a backcountry permit to stay outside developed park campgrounds. None of the campgrounds have showers, but they do have flush toilets in summer and outhouse facilities in winter. Sites include a fire ring, picnic table and one parking spot.

Olive Ridge Campground CAMPGROUND $
(☎303-541-2500; campsites $14; ⊙mid-May–Nov) Well-kept United States Forest Service (USFS) campground with access to four trailheads: St Vrain Mountain, Wild Basin, Longs Peak and Twin Sisters.

Moraine Park Campground CAMPGROUND $
(☎877-444-6777; www.recreation.gov; off Bear Lake Rd; summer campsites $20) Has 245 sites. Reserve via the website. Walk-in, tent-only sites in the D Loop are recommended if you want quiet. At night in the summer, there are numerous ranger-led programs in the amphitheater.

The campground is served by the shuttle buses on Bear Lake Rd through the summer.

Aspenglen Campground CAMPGROUND $
(☎877-444-6777; www.recreation.gov; State Hwy 34; campsites summer $20) With only 54 sites, this is the smallest of the park's bookable camping. There are many tent-only sites, including some walk-ins, and a limited number of trailers are allowed. This is the quietest park that's highly accessible (5 miles west of Estes Park on US 34).

Timber Creek Campground CAMPGROUND $
(Trail Ridge Rd, US Hwy 34; campsites $20) This campground has 100 sites and remains open through the winter. No reservations accepted. The only established campground on the west side of the park, it's 7 miles north of Grand Lake.

Glacier Basin Campground CAMPGROUND $
(☎877-444-6777; www.recreation.gov; off Bear Lake Rd; campsites summer $20) This developed campground has a large area for group camping and accommodates RVs. It is served by the shuttle buses on Bear Lake Rd throughout the summer. Reserve through the website.

Information

Entry to the park (vehicles $20, hikers and cyclists $10) is valid for seven days. Backcountry permits ($20) are required for overnight trips.

Alpine Visitor Center (www.nps.gov/romo; Fall River Pass; ⊙10:30am-4:30pm late May–mid-Jun, 9am-5pm late Jun-early Sep, 10:30am-4:30pm early Sep–mid-Oct) Right in the middle of the park at 11,796ft, with views, cafeteria and information.

Beaver Meadows Visitor Center (☎970-586-1206; www.nps.gov/romo; US Hwy 36; ⊙8am-9pm late Jun-late Aug, to 4:30pm or 5pm rest of year) The primary visitor center and best stop for park information, if you're approaching from Estes Park. You can see a film about the park, browse a small gift shop and reserve backcountry camping sites.

Kawuneeche Visitor Center (☎970-627-3471; 16018 US Hwy 34; ⊙8am-6pm last week May-Labor Day, 8am-5pm Labor Day-end of Sep, 8am-4:30pm Oct-end of May) On the west side of the park, with ranger-led walks and discussions, backcountry permits and family activities.

Getting There & Away

Trail Ridge Rd (US 34) is the only east–west route through the park and is closed in winter. The most direct route from Boulder follows US 36 through Lyons to the east entrances.

There are two entrance stations on the east side, Fall River (US 34) and Beaver Meadows (US 36). The Grand Lake Station (also US 34) is the only entry on the west side. Year-round access is available through Kawuneeche Valley along the Colorado River headwaters to Timber Creek Campground. The main centers of visitor activity on the park's east side are the Alpine Visitor Center, high on Trail Ridge Rd and Bear Lake Rd, which leads to campgrounds, trailheads and the Moraine Park Museum.

North of Estes Park, Devils Gulch Rd leads to several hiking trails. Further out on Devils Gulch Rd, you pass through the village of Glen Haven to reach the trailhead entry to the park along the North Fork of the Big Thompson River.

Getting Around

A majority of visitors enter the park in their own cars, using the long and winding Trail Ridge Rd (US 34) to cross the Continental Divide. In summer a free shuttle bus operates from the Estes Park Visitor Center multiple times daily, bringing hikers to a park-and-ride location where you can pick up other shuttles. The year-round option leaves the Glacier Basin parking area toward Bear Lake, in the parks lower elevations. During the summer peak, a second shuttle operates between Moraine Park campground and the Glacier Basin parking area. Shuttles run on weekends only from mid-August through September.

ESTES PARK

It's no small irony that becoming a nature-lovers hub has turned the gateway to one of the most pristine outdoor escapes in the US into the kind of place you'll need to escape from. T-shirt shops and ice-cream parlors, sidewalks jammed with tourists and streets plugged with RVs: welcome to Estes Park, the chaotic outpost at the edge of Rocky Mountain National Park.

Activities

Colorado Mountain School ROCK CLIMBING
(☎303-447-2804; www.totalclimbing.com; 341 Moraine Ave; half-day guided climbs per person from $125) The largest climbing operator in the region has world-class instructors. It's the only organization allowed to operate within Rocky Mountain National Park and offers basic courses such as Intro to Rock Climbing as well as dorm lodging at Total Climbing Lodge.

Sleeping

Estes Park's dozens of hotels fill up fast in summer. There are some passable budget options but the many lovely area campgrounds are the best-value. You can rent camping gear from **Estes Park Mountain Shop** (☎970-586-6548; www.estesparkmountainshop.com; 2050 Big Thompson Ave; 2-person camping set-up $32; ⏲8am-9pm).

Try the **Estes Park Visitor Center** (☎970-577-9900; www.estesparkresortcvb.com; 500 Big Thompson Ave; ⏲9am-8pm Jun-Aug, 8am-5pm Mon-Fri, 9am-5pm Sat, 10am-4pm Sun Sep-May), just east of the US 36 junction, for help with lodging; note that many places close in winter.

TOP CHOICE **Stanley Hotel** HOTEL $$$
(☎970-586-3371; www.stanleyhotel.com; 333 Wonderview Ave; r from $199; P) The inspiration for Stephen King's famous cult novel *The Shining,* this white Georgian Colonial Revival is the grand dame of Rocky Mountain resort hotels. Stately rooms evoke the Old West, with replica antiques and modernized amenities. Vast public spaces with plump leather couches are warmed with stone fireplaces. In addition to mountain views and splendid dining, there are even nighttime ghost hunts (they claim 17 haunted rooms).

YMCA of the Rockies – Estes Park Center RESORT $$
(☎970-586-3341; www.ymcarockies.org; 2515 Tunnel Rd; r & d from $109, cabins from $129; P) This very kid-friendly resort sits in a serene and ultra-pristine location in the mountains just outside town. The 860-acre plot is home to cabins and motel rooms along with lots of wide-open spaces dotted with forests and fields of wildflowers. Just a few minutes outside of Estes Park (but definitely away from the hustle of town), it offers a range of activities.

Mary's Lake Lodge LODGE $$$
(☎970-577-9495; www.maryslakelodge.com; 2625 Marys Lake Rd; r & d from $99, cabins from $199; P) This old wooden lodge reeks of Wild West ambience, down to the creaky front porch. Rooms and condo cabins are a blend of modern and historic. Both the saloon-style **Tavern** (mains $7-20; ⏲11am-11pm) and fine-dining **Chalet Room** (mains $12-20; ⏲5pm-10pm) have seating on the heated porch. A big hot tub under the stars, a fire pit and live music five nights per week nicely round out the amenities. Mary's is 3 miles south of Estes Park off Hwy 7.

Total Climbing Lodge HOSTEL $
(☎303-447-2804; www.totalclimbing.com; 341 Moraine Ave; dm $25; P@) Lodging at this bustling hub of climbers is the best dorm option in town, with sleeping bags, soap, pillow and towels included in the price. Expect simple pine bunks, a Ping-Pong table and a laid-back vibe.

Eating

Estes Park Brewery BREWPUB
(www.epbrewery.com; 470 Prospect Village Dr; ⏲11am-2am Mon-Sun) The town's brewpub serves pizza, burgers and wings, and at least eight different house beers, in a big, boxy room resembling a cross between a classroom and a country kitchen. Pool tables and outdoor seating keep the place rocking late into the night.

Ed's Cantina & Grill MEXICAN $$
(☎970-586-2919; www.edscantina.com; 390 E Elkhorn Ave; mains $9-15; ⏲11am-late daily, from 8am Sat & Sun) With an outdoor patio right on the river, Ed's is a great place to kick back with a margarita and one of the daily $3

blue-plate specials (think fried, rolled tortillas) with shredded pork and guacamole). Serving Mexican and American staples, the restaurant is in a retro-mod space with leather booth seating and a bold primary color scheme. The bar is in a separate room with light-wood stools featuring comfortable high backs.

Getting There & Away

From Denver International Airport, **Estes Park Shuttle** (970-586-5151; www.estesparkshuttle.com) runs four times daily to Estes Park (one-way/return $45/85).

Central & Northern Mountains

Colorado's central and northern mountains are well known for their plethora of ski resorts – including world-famous Aspen and Vail, family-friendly Breckenridge and never-summer A-Basin.

WINTER PARK

Less than two hours from Denver, unpretentious Winter Park is a favorite ski resort with Front Rangers, who flock here from as far away as Colorado Springs to ski fresh tracks each weekend. Beginners can frolic on miles of powdery groomers while experts test their skills on Mary Jane's world-class bumps. The congenial town is a wonderful base for year-round romping. Most services are along US 40 (the main drag), including the **visitor center** (970-726-4118; www.winterpark-info.com; 78841 Hwy 40; 8am-5pm Mon-Fri, 9am-5pm Sat & Sun).

South of town, **Winter Park Resort** (970-726-5514; www.winterparkresort.com; cnr Hwy 40 & Colorado 81; 2-day lift ticket adult $120-172, child $66-86) covers five mountains and has a vertical drop of more than 2600ft. Experts love it here because more than half of the runs are geared solely for highly skilled skiers. It also has 45 miles of lift-accessible **mountain-biking trails** connecting to a 600-mile trail system running through the valley. Other fine rides in the area include the road up to **Rollins Pass**.

Devil's Thumb Ranch (800-933-4339; www.devilsthumbranch.com; 3530 County Rd 83; r from $93, cabins from $165, trail passes adult/child & senior $18/8, rental packages $20/10, ice skating $10;), with a cowboy chic bunkhouse and cabins alongside a 65-mile network of trails, makes an ultra-romantic getaway for the active-minded. Geothermal heat, reclaimed wood and low-emission fireplaces make it green. Summer guests can go horseback riding ($90 to $170 per person) in the high country. It's north of Fraser.

The best deal around is the friendly **Rocky Mountain Chalet** (970-726-8256, 866-467-8351; www.therockymountainchalet.com; 15 Co Rd 72; dm $36, r $89-179;), with plush, comfortable doubles, dorm rooms and a sparkling kitchen.

For inspired dining, **Tavern at Tabernash** (970-726-4430; www.tabernashtavern.com; 72287 US Hwy 40; mains $17-32; 5-9pm Tue-Sat;) whets the appetite with barbecued pork chops served with grilled Palisades peaches or venison burgers. There are vegan and gluten-free options too. Reserve ahead. It's just north of Fraser.

STEAMBOAT SPRINGS

With luxuriant tree-skiing, top-notch trails for mountain-biking and a laid back Western feel, Steamboat beats out other ski towns in both real ambience and offerings. Its historic center is cool for rambling, hot springs top off a hard day of play, and locals couldn't be friendlier.

WORTH A TRIP

THE VAGABOND RANCH

Moose outnumber people at the remote **Vagabond Ranch** (303-242-5338; www.vagabondranch.com; per person $45;), a fine backcountry in Colorado's pristine Never Summer Range. By backcountry we mean a 3-mile dirt access road – it can be driven in summer but you'll need to park the car and ski or snowmobile in for winter fun.

Ringed by high peaks and ponderosa forest, this former stagecoach stop features a smattering of comfortable cabins – ranging from rustic to elegant – at 9000ft. Features include chef-worthy cooking facilities, firewood, a hot tub, solar power and composting toilets. Like any ski hut, lodgings may be shared, but couples or groups can book privates (we recommend the retro-gorgeous Parkview for couples). Dedicated trails are groomed in winter for cross-country skiing or snowmobiling and it also hosts yoga and meditation retreats.

It's 22 miles from Granby (near Winter Park).

Central & Northern Mountains

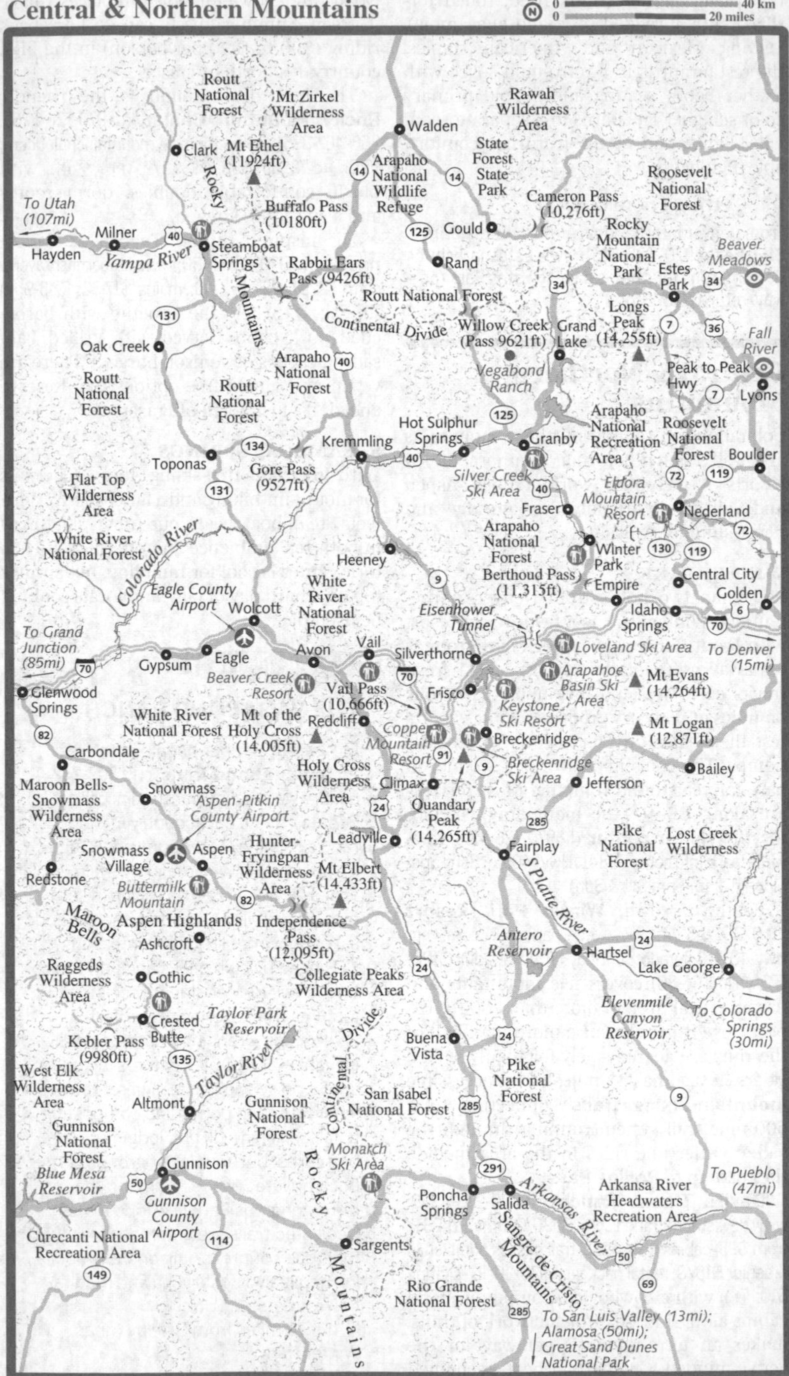

Sights & Activities

Steamboat Mountain Resort SNOW SPORTS
(Steamboat Mountain Resort; ☎ticket office 970-871-5252; www.steamboat.com; lift ticket adult/child $94/59; ⏲ticket office 8am-5pm) Known for a 3600ft vertical drop, excellent powder and trails for all levels, this is the main draw for winter visitors and some of the best skiing in the US. In the ski area there are (overpriced) food and equipment vendors galore.

TOP CHOICE **Strawberry Park Hot Springs** SPRING
(☎970-879-0342; www.strawberryhotsprings.com; 44200 County Rd; per day adult/child $10/5; ⏲10am-10:30pm Sun-Thu, to midnight Fri & Sat;) Steamboat's favorite hot springs are actually outside the city limits, but offer great back-to-basics relaxation. Water is 104°F in these tasteful stone pools formed by cascading drops. To stay over, choose from covered wagons ($65) with a double mattress on the floor (quite unique) or rustic cabins ($55). There's no electricity (you get gas lanterns) and you'll need your own linens.

Be sure to reserve. Weekend reservations require a two-night stay. Note that the thermal pools are clothing optional after dark.

Old Town Hot Springs SPRING
(☎970-879-1828; www.steamboathotsprings.org; 136 Lincoln Ave; adult/student & senior/child $15/10/7; ⏲5:30am-9:45pm Mon-Fri, 7am-8:45pm Sat, 8am-8:45pm Sun;) Right in the center of town, the mineral water here is warmer than most in the area. Kids will dig the 230ft-long waterslides and the aquatic climbing wall.

Sleeping & Eating

There are plenty of places to sleep; contact **Steamboat Central Reservations** (☎970-879-0740, www.steamboat.com; Mt Werner Circle, off Gondola Sq) for condos and other options near the ski area.

Hotel Bristol HOTEL $$
(☎970-879-3083; www.steamboathotelbristol.com; 917 Lincoln Ave; d $149;) The elegant Hotel Bristol has small, but sophisticated, Western digs, with dark-wood and brass furnishings and Pendleton wool blankets on the beds. There's a ski shuttle, a six-person indoor Jacuzzi and a cozy restaurant.

TOP CHOICE **Cafe Diva** FUSION $$$
(☎970-871-0508; www.cafediva.com; 1855 Ski Time Square Dr; mains $21-40; ⏲5:30-10pm) Locals love this romantic nook where every dish is worth savoring. Offerings change, but always fuse Asian, Italian and Latin flavors. Think duck tamales with avocado cream, and sweet-pea ravioli with homemade ricotta.

Backcountry Provisions DELI $
(www.backcountryprovisions.com; 635 Lincoln Ave; sandwiches $7-10; ⏲7am-5pm;) Efficient and delicious, this Colorado sandwich chain uses ultra-fresh ingredients. The curried turkey smothered in cranberry hits the spot. Take it to go if you're hiking or skiing for the day.

Slopeside Grill BAR
(www.slopesidegrill.com; 1855 Ski Time Sq; ⏲noon-midnight) The uncontested hub of après-ski activity, this ski-up bar also has excellent pizza and cooks a range of food well. In summer, kids can play on the lawn.

Information

Steamboat Springs Visitor Center (☎970-879-0880, 877-754-2269; www.steamboatchamber.com; 1255 S Lincoln Ave; ⏲8am-5pm Mon-Fri, 10am-3pm Sat)

Getting There & Away

Buses between Denver and Salt Lake City stop at the **Greyhound Terminal** (☎970-870-0504; 1505 Lincoln Ave), about half a mile west of town. **Steamboat Springs Transit** (☎970-879-3717, for pick-up in Mountain Area 970-846-1279; http://steamboatsprings.net) runs free buses between Old Town and the ski resort year-round. Steamboat is 166 miles northwest of Denver via US 40.

BRECKENRIDGE & AROUND

Set at 9600ft, at the foot of a marvelous range of treeless peaks, Breck is a sweetly surviving gold-mining town with a lovely national historic district. With down-to-earth grace, the town boasts family-friendly ski runs that don't disappoint and always draw a giddy crowd. If you should happen to grow restless, there are four great ski resorts and outlet shopping less than an hour away.

Activities

Breckenridge Ski Area SNOW SPORTS
(☎970-453-5000; www.breckenridge.snow.com; 150 Watson Ave; lift ticket adult/child/senior $63/44/53; ⏲lifts 8:30am-4pm, gondola 8am-5pm Nov-April;) Spans four mountains and features some of the best beginner and intermediate terrain in the state (the green runs are flatter than most in Colorado), as well as killer steeps and chutes for experts, and a renowned snowboard park.

Arapahoe Basin Ski Area SNOW SPORTS
(☎970-468-0718, 888-272-7246; www.arapahoebasin.com; lift adult/child/15-19yr/senior $54/29/49/51; ⌚9am-4pm Mon-Fri, from 8:30am Sat & Sun) North America's highest resort, about 12 miles from Breck, is smaller, less commercial and usually open until at least mid-June! Full of steeps, walls and backcountry terrain, it's a local favorite because it doesn't draw herds of package tourists. The outdoor bar is a great place to kick back with a cold microbrew, and people are always grilling burgers and socializing at impromptu tailgate parties in the parking lot (known as 'the beach').

Peak 8 Fun Park AMUSEMENT PARK
(☎970-453-5000; www.breckenridge.com/peak-8-fun-park.aspx; Peak 8; half-/full-day pass $50/65; ⌚8:30am-5pm Jun-Aug; 👪) With a laundry list of made-for-thrills activities, including a big-air trampoline ($10), climbing wall ($8), mountain-bike park (adult/child $30/20) with bike rentals (half-/full day $42/52) and the celebrated SuperSlide – a luge-like course taken on a sled at exhilarating speeds.

Festivals & Events

Ullr Fest CULTURAL
(www.gobreck.com) In early to mid-January, the Ullr Fest celebrates the Norse god of winter with a wild parade and four-day festival featuring a twisted version of the Dating Game, an ice-skating party and a bonfire.

FREE **International Snow Sculpture Championship** SNOW
(www.gobreck.com; 150 W Adams Ave; ⌚mid-Jan–early Feb; 👪) Sculptors from around the world descend on Breck to create meltable masterpieces. It starts in mid-January and lasts for three weeks on River walk.

Sleeping

For slope-side rentals, contact **Great Western Lodging** (☎888-333-4535; www.gwlodging.com; 322 N Main St) for mostly upscale options. Campers can look for USFS campgrounds outside of town.

TOP CHOICE **Fireside Inn** B&B, HOSTEL $
(☎970-453-6456; www.firesideinn.com; 114 N French St; dm $39, d $134-168; P❄@📶👪) The best deal for single travelers, this cozy hostel and B&B is a find. The bunks with extra blankets are probably a better deal than the private rooms, which, though charming, have seen a little wear. All guests can enjoy the chlorine-free barrel hot tub and resident snuggly dog. Niki, the English host, is a delight and very helpful with local information. It's a 10-minute walk to the gondola in ski boots.

Abbet Placer Inn B&B $$
(☎970-453-6489; www.abbettplacer.com; 205 S French St; r Jun-Aug $129-219, Dec-Feb $129-239; P❄📶👪) This violet house has five large, themed rooms well decked-out with wood furnishings, iPod docks and fluffy robes. It's very low key. The warm and welcoming hosts cook big breakfasts, and guests can enjoy a lovely outdoor Jacuzzi deck and use of a common kitchenette. Check-in is from 4pm to 7pm.

Eating & Drinking

TOP CHOICE **Hearthstone** MODERN AMERICAN $$$
(☎970-453-1148; www.stormrestaurants.com; 130 S Ridge St; mains $13-38; ⌚4pm-late) One of Breck's favorites, this restored 1886 Victorian churns out creative mountain fare such as house-smoked trout and chile relleno (stuffed chilies) with goat's cheese and honey. Fresh and delicious, it's worth a splurge, or hit happy hour (4pm to 6pm) for $5 plates paired with wine. If the weather cooperates, you can dine out on the three-tiered patios out front. Reservations are highly recommended.

Clint's Bakery & Coffee House SANDWICHES $
(131 S Main St; sandwiches from $5.95, coffee drinks from $2; ⌚7am-9pm Sun-Thu, to 10pm Fri & Sat; 📶👪) Brainy baristas steam up a chalkboard full of latte and mocha flavors and dozens of loose-leaf teas. If you're hungry, the downstairs bagelry stacks burly sandwiches and tasty breakfast bagels with egg and ham, lox, sausage and cheese. The bagelry closes at 3pm.

Downstairs at Eric's BAR
(www.downstairsaterics.com; 111 S Main St; ⌚11am-midnight; 👪) Downstairs at Eric's is a Breckenridge institution. Locals flock to this electric basement joint with a game room full of vintage pinball machines, for the pitchers, juicy burgers and delicious mashed potatoes (mains from $6). There are more than 120 beers, including several microbrews, to choose from.

THE ROCKIES FOR POWDER HOUNDS

Well worth the five-hour road trip from Denver, **Crested Butte** promises deep powder and lovely open terrain, next to a mining outpost re-tooled to be one of Colorado's coolest small towns.

If you're short on travel time, go directly to Summit County. Use lively **Breckenridge** as your base and conquer four areas on one combo lift ticket, including the mastodon resort of **Vail**, our favorite for remote back bowl terrain, and the ultra-local and laid-back **Arapahoe Basin Ski Area**. A-basin stays open into June, when spring skiing means tailgating with beer and barbecue between slush runs.

From Crested Butte, you can head a little further south and ski the slopes at **Telluride**; from Summit County and Vail, **Aspen** is nearby. Both are true old gold towns. Be sure to devote at least a few hours to exploring Aspen's glitzy shops and Telluride's down-to-earth bars for a real local vibe in a historic Wild West setting.

From Aspen, catch a local flight up to **Jackson Hole Mountain Resort** to do some real vertical powder riding in the Grand Tetons.

Shopping

Outlets at Silverthorne CLOTHING
(www.outletsatsilverthorne.com; Silverthorne; ⏲10am-8pm Mon-Sat, 11am-6pm Sun) Located 15 minutes from Breckenridge, just off I-70, are three shopping villages of designer brand stores with discount prices. Brands include Calvin Klein, Nike, Levi's, Gap and many others.

Information

Visitor center (☎970-453-6018, 888-251-2417; www.gobreck.com; 309 N Main St; ⏲9am-5pm) Has information on the myriad area activities.

Getting There & Around

Breckenridge is 9 miles south of I-70 on Hwy 9 and about 100 miles from Denver or Colorado Springs.

Colorado Mountain Express (☎970-926-9800; www.ridecme.com; per person $79) runs shuttles between Breckenridge and Denver International Airport.

For free rides within the city limits, **Free Ride** (Summit County Public Transport; ☎970-547-3140; www.townofbreckenridge.com) patrols the streets.

To get between Breckenridge, Keystone or Vail, hop on free **Summit Stages buses** (☎970-668-0999; www.summitstage.com; 150 Watson Ave; ⏲6:25am-1:45am), which run all day.

VAIL

Darling of the rich and sometime famous, Vail resembles an elaborate adult amusement park, with everything man-made from the golf greens down to the indoor waterfalls. It's compact and highly walkable, but the location (a highway runs through it) lacks the natural drama of most Rocky Mountain destinations. That said, no serious skier would dispute its status as the best ski resort in Colorado, with its powdery back bowls, chutes and wickedly fun terrain.

Sights & Activities

Vail Mountain SNOW SPORTS
(☎970-476-9090; www.vail.com; lift ticket adult/child $99/46; ⏲9am-4pm, longer hours in season; 👪) Vail Mountain is our favorite in the state, with 5289 skiable acres, 193 trails, three terrain parks and some of the highest lift-ticket prices in the country. If you're a Colorado ski virgin, it's worth paying the extra buck to pop your cherry here. Especially on a sunny, blue, fresh-powder day.

For deals, try City Market grocery stores, which often sell reduced-price tickets. The mountaintop Adventure Ridge has child-friendly winter and summer sports.

FREE **Colorado Ski Museum** MUSEUM
(☎970-476-1876; www.skimuseum.net; 231 S Frontage Rd E; ⏲10am-6pm) Humble but informative, this museum takes you from the invention of skiing to the trials of the Tenth Mountain Division, a decorated WWII alpine unit that trained in these mountains. There are also hilarious fashions from the past, as well as the fledgling Colorado Ski and Snowboard Hall of Fame.

TOP CHOICE **Mount Holy Cross Wilderness** HIKING
(☎] 970-328-8688; 125 West 5th St, Eagle; ⏲9am-5pm Mon-Fri) Consult rangers for hiking tips. There are six developed campgrounds in the region. The strenuous Notch Mountain Trail affords great views of Mt of the Holy Cross

(14,009ft), or very experienced hikers can climb the mountain itself (a class 2 scramble) via Half Moon Pass Trail.

Vail to Breckenridge Bike Path CYCLING
(www.vail.com; 24hr;) From the West Vail Market you can ride along N Frontage Rd, crossing I-70 at the pedestrian overpass to Lionshead. On the south side of the freeway, a paved bike route extends from W Gore Creek Dr through Cascade Village, Lionshead and Vail Village and continues east on the 10-Mile Canyon Trail through auto-free road-bike heaven over Vail Pass to Frisco.

Sleeping

Vail is expensive, but rates do drop during the off-season.

Sebastian LODGE $$$
(970-888-1540; www.thesebastianvail.com; 16 Vail Rd; r & condos from $450;) Deluxe and modern, this upscale lodging is the latest addition to the Vail scene and its list of amenities is impressive, including a mountainside ski valet, goddess spa and adventure concierge. Room rates dip to affordable in the summer, the perfect time to enjoy the farm-to-table restaurant and a spectacular pool area with hot tubs frothing and spilling over like champagne. Not bad at all.

Austria Haus LODGE $$
(970-754-7850; www.austriahaushotel.com; 242 E Meadow Dr; r incl breakfast $106-559;) With outstanding service, Austria Haus is a great value for Vail. Tasteful rooms are post and beam and a touch retro, while corner suites have gorgeous adobe fireplaces and oversized tubs. Guests can book their preferred tee-off times at the prestigious Red Sky Ranch golf course nearby.

Gore Creek Campground CAMPGROUND $
(970-945-2521; Bighorn Rd; tent sites $13; Memorial Day-Labor Day) With pit toilets at the end of Bighorn Rd, this campground has 25 first-come, first-served tent sites with picnic tables and fire grates nestled in the woods by Gore Creek. Try the Slate Creek or Deluge Lake trails; the latter leads to a fish-packed lake. It's 6 miles east of Vail Village via the East Vail exit off I-70.

Eating & Drinking

TOP CHOICE **Osaki's** JAPANESE $$
(970-476-0977; 100 E Meadow Dr; sushi $8-20; 6pm-late Tue-Sat) A star disciple of Nobu Matsuhisa (yes, *that* Nobu), Osaki opened this low-key hole-in-the-wall temple devoted to all that is sweet, tender and raw. For a splurge, try the $100 seven-course tasting menu. But don't leave without tasting the salmon – it's simply spectacular. In summer it's 30% off. Reserve ahead.

Westside Cafe BREAKFAST $
(970-476-7890; www.westsidecafe.net; 2211 N Frontage Rd; mains $6-14; 7am-10pm;) Set in a West Vail mini-mall off the freeway, this morning beacon sets up skiers and boarders for a long day in the back bowls. Terrific breakfast skillets, large steaming mugs of coffee and Bloody Marys get our thumbs up.

Tap Room SPORTS BAR
(970-479-0500; www.taproomvail.com; 333 Bridge St; 11am-late Mon-Fri, 10am-late Sat & Sun;) A favorite on the Vail bar-hopping circuit, this laid-back sports bar shows ballgames all day and has a giant selection of beers and day-long drink specials. The kitchen churns out middling pub grub, but the chipped-wood bar is a fine place to sip a Native Z draft, plus, it has views of the mountain from the back patio.

Bōl THEME BAR
(970-476-9300; www.bolvail.com; 141 E Meadow Dr; plates $12-24; 5pm-1.30am;) Only in Vail, this high-energy bowling alley (lanes per hour $50, shoe rental $5) has progressive rock pumping, a sleek neon bar and strobe lights on the lanes. It's a magnet for the hip and beautiful. Try the fusion menu featuring pork buns with ponzo sauce and balsamic-tossed arugula. Kids are welcome until 9pm.

Information

Vail Visitor Center (970-479-1385; www.visitvailvalley.com; Transportation Center; 9am-5pm)

Getting There & Around

From December to early April only, **Eagle County Airport** (EGE; 970-524-9490), 35 miles west of Vail, has direct jet services to destinations across the country and rental car counters.

Colorado Mountain Express (970-926-9800; www.cmex.com) shuttles to/from Denver International Airport ($89) and Eagle County Airport ($49). Greyhound buses stop at the **Vail Transportation Center** (970-476-5137; 241 S Frontage Rd) en route to Denver ($34, 2½ hours) or Grand Junction ($30, 3¼ hours).

Vail's **free buses** (☎970-328-8143; http://vailgov.com/transit) stop in West Vail, East Vail and Sandstone; most have bike racks. Regional buses to Avon, Beaver Creek and Edwards charge $4.

Compact Vail Village, filled with upscale restaurants, bars and boutiques, is traffic free. Motorists must park at the Vail Transportation Center & Public Parking garage before entering the pedestrian mall area near the chairlifts. Lionshead is a secondary parking lot about half a mile to the west. It has direct lift access and is usually less crowded.

ASPEN

Immodestly posh Aspen is Colorado's glitziest high-octane resort, playing host to some of the wealthiest skiers in the world. The handsome, historic red-brick downtown is as alluring as the glistening slopes, but Aspen's greatest asset is its magnificent scenery. The stunning alpine environment – especially during late September and October, when the aspen trees put on a spectacular display – just adds extra sugar to an already sweet cake.

Sights & Activities

Aspen Mountain SNOW SPORTS
(☎800-525-6200; www.aspensnowmass.com; E Durant Ave; Aspen Mountain day pass summer $24, Aspen & Snowmass summer $29, Four Mountain 2-day pass $158-192, 1-day pass adult/teen & senior/child $96/87/62; lift 9am-3.30pm Nov 25-Apr 10;) Forget beginner terrain. Intermediate and advanced skiers do best at this iconic resort. For gentler terrain, check out the nearby sister resorts of Buttermilk and Snowmass, which has the longest vertical drop in the US.

Aspen Highlands SNOW SPORTS
(☎970-925-1220; www.aspensnowmas.com; Prospector Rd; Aspen Mountain day pass summer $24, Aspen & Snowmass Mountain $29, Four Mountain 2-day pass $158-192; 9am-3.30pm) A favorite of expert skiers, with steep, deep, tree runs and bumps.

Ashcroft Ski Touring SNOW SPORTS
(☎970-925-1971; www.pinecreekcookhouse.com/ashcroft.html; 11399 Castle Creek Rd; half-/full-day pass $10/15, child & senior $10;) With 20 miles of groomed trails through 600 acres of subalpine country with a spectacular backdrop. Rent classic cross-country ski equipment (rental packages $20), ski gear or snowshoes. Individual and group lessons ($75), as well as snowshoe and ski tours, are available daily. Shuttles ($35) to and from Aspen are available.

FREE **Hunter-Fryingpan Wilderness Area** HIKING
(☎970-925-3445; www.fs.usda.gov;) From Lone Pine Rd in Aspen, the Hunter Valley Trail (USFS Trail 1992) follows Hunter Creek northeast about 3 miles through wildflower meadows to the Sunnyside and Hunter Creek Trails, which lead into the 82,026-acre Hunter-Fryingpan Wilderness Area. It's less visited than other slices of the Rockies, with stunning campsites and rugged peaks, as well as the headwaters to both Hunter Creek and the Fryingpan River.

Ute City Cycles CYCLING
(☎970-920-3325; www.utecitycycles.com; 231 E Main St; bike rental per 24hr $75; 9am-6pm) A high-end road- and mountain-bike retailer offering limited rentals from its demo fleet. Rentals have a two-day maximum; no reservations. Staff can also point you in the direction of Aspen's best cycling.

Festivals

Aspen Music Festival MUSIC
(☎970-925-3254; www.aspenmusicfestival.com; 2 Music School Rd) Every summer (in July and August) classical musicians from around the world come to play, perform and learn from the masters of their craft. Orchestras and smaller groups are led by world-famous conductors and perform at the Wheeler Opera House, the Benedict Music Tent or on Aspen street corners.

Sleeping

Book through an online consolidator for the best deals. Avoid the week between Christmas and New Year, when prices skyrocket.

DON'T MISS

CYCLING TO MAROON BELLS

According to the Aspen cycling gurus, the most iconic road-bike ride in Aspen is the one to the stunning Maroon Bells. The climb is 11 lung-wrenching miles to the foot of one of the most picturesque wilderness areas in the Rockies. Your other alternative is the bus – the Maroon Bells road is actually closed to incoming car traffic – but if you crave sweet, beautiful pain, let your quads sing.

St Moritz Lodge HOSTEL $
(☎970-925-3220; www.stmoritzlodge.com; 334 W Hyman Ave; dm $58, r incl breakfast $189; P❄@📶≋👪) St Moritz is the best no-frills deal in town. Perks include a heated outdoor pool and grill overlooking Aspen Mountain, and a lobby with games, books and a piano. The European-style lodge offers a wide variety of options, from quiet dorms to two-bedroom condos. The cheapest options share bathrooms.

Annabelle Inn HOTEL $$$
(☎877-266-2466; www.annabelleinn.com; 232 W Main St; r incl breakfast $159-229; P❄@📶👪) Personable and unpretentious, the cute and quirky Annabelle Inn resembles an old-school European-style ski lodge in a central location. Rooms are cozy and come with flat-screen TVs and warm duvets. You can also enjoy after-dark ski video screenings from the upper-deck hot tub (one of two on the property).

Little Nell HOTEL $$$
(☎970-920-4600; www.thelittlenell.com; 675 E Durant Ave; r from $545; P❄@📶≋👪) This is a long-time Aspen institution at the foot of Aspen Mountain. Gas-burning fireplaces, high-thread-count linens and rich color schemes make up the elegant modernist decor. An adventure concierge is on hand to help guests get the most from the outdoors. Dining is outstanding and its open air Ajax Tavern is the town hot-spot for some après-ski unwinding.

The **USFS White River National Forest's Aspen Ranger District** (☎970-925-3445; www.fs.fed.us; 806 W Hallam St; ⏲8am-4:30pm Mon-Fri winter, 8am-4:30pm Mon-Sat summer) operates nine **campgrounds** (campsites $15-20).

Eating & Drinking

Aspen has few deals but après-ski is an institution, and even the better spots have food and drink bargains during happy hour.

TOP CHOICE **Pine Creek Cookhouse** AMERICAN $$$
(☎970-925-1044; www.pinecreekcookhouse.com; 12700 Castle Creek Rd; mains $16-24; ⏲noon-8pm Jun-Sep, sittings at noon, 1:30pm & 6pm Nov-Apr; 👪) The best setting around – a gorgeous cross-country ski-in to a log-cabin restaurant serving outstanding, fresh fusion fare. It's 11 miles up Castle Creek Canyon past the old mining town of Ashcroft. Shrimp tikka masala, grilled quail served over greens and house-smoked trout are all outstanding.

It's closed in October and May, but stays open all summer and winter, when you can get here from Ashcroft skiing or aboard the cookhouse's horse-drawn sleigh, then warm up by the crackling fire.

BB's Kitchen MODERN AMERICAN $$$
(☎970-429-8284; 525 E Cooper Ave, 2nd fl; mains $11-27; ⏲8am-5pm, 6-10pm) A local darling and winner of the 2011 Diners' Choice award, this 2nd-floor patio is the best spot for a casual lunch or a leisurely gourmet breakfast (think lobster Benedict or wild morel omelet). This isn't show food – the chef-owners are committed to quality, down to curing their own meats. For dinner, slip into a red booth for delicious house sausage pizza or poached halibut served over a gorgeous mint pea puree.

Pitkin County Steakhouse STEAKHOUSE $$$
(☎970-544-6328; www.pitkincountysteakhouse.com; 305 E Hopkins Ave; mains $26-58; ⏲from 6pm) Down-home and the most popular place for prime dry-aged steaks with a great salad bar. Set in the basement of a Hopkins Ave complex, it has an open kitchen scattered with dim-lit tables. In low season the dining room is only open Thursday to Saturday, but its adjacent tavern is always open for business.

Aspen Brewing Co BREWERY
(☎970-920-2739; www.aspenbrewingcompany.com; 557 N Mill St; pints $2.75; ⏲noon-9pm Mon-Sat, noon-6pm Sun) Tibetan prayer flags fly and reggae grooves at this microbrewery with six flavors brewed behind the bar.

J-Bar BAR
(www.hoteljerome.com; 330 E Main St) Once Aspen's premier saloon, back when the word 'saloon' had its own unique meaning, this bar was built into the Hotel Jerome in 1889 and remains full of historic charm and packed with everyone from local shopkeepers to Hollywood stars.

Information

Aspen Visitor Center (☎970-925-1940; www.aspenchamber.org; 425 Rio Grande Pl; ⏲8am-5pm Mon-Fri) Has all the usual information.

Getting There & Around

Four miles north of Aspen on Hwy 82, **Aspen-Pitkin County Airport** (☎970-920-5380; www.aspenairport.com; 233 E Airport Rd; 📶) has commuter flights from Denver, and nonstops to Phoenix, Los Angeles, San Francisco, Minneapolis and Memphis. **Colorado Mountain Express** (☎970-947-0506; www.cmex.com) runs frequent shuttles to/from Denver International Airport ($100, three hours).

Roaring Fork Transit Agency (970-920-1905; www.rfta.com) buses connect Aspen with the ski areas and runs free trips to and from Aspen-Pitkin County Airport.

BUENA VISTA & SALIDA

Buena Vista and Salida's small-town charms complement the fun of shooting the Arkansas River's rapids or soaking in hot springs under the stars. There are plenty of cheap motels, campgrounds and public lands suited to camping.

For rafting, stop by **Buffalo Joe's Whitewater Rafting** (866-283-3563; www.buffalojoe.com; 113 N Railroad St; day trip adult $64-105, child $45-69, 2-day trip $179/139; 8am-7pm). You'll want to run Brown's Canyon (Class III to IV), the Narrows (III to IV) or the Numbers (IV to V), and the earlier in the season the better (try for May and June, when the river is bloated with snow runoff and the rapids are much more intense). The company also rents mountain bikes and can recommend some great trails in the area.

After a day on the river, forget the soreness with a soak at **Cottonwood Hot Springs Inn & Spa** (719-395-6434; www.cottonwood-hot-springs.com; 18999 Co Rd 306; adult/child 16yr & under Mon-Fri $15/12, Sat & Sun $20/17, towel rental $1; 8am-midnight). These renovated springs are set on leafy grounds with gushing fountains of hot water, dangling vines and wind chimes. The five pools range in temperature from 94° to 110°F (34° to 43°C). For those staying here, **rooms** (from $102) have floral bedspreads and cheap wood furnishings, but they're super-clean and you can use the natural springs all night.

You'll need a car to get to this area south of Leadville on US 24.

CRESTED BUTTE

Powder-bound Crested Butte has retained its rural character better than most Colorado ski resorts. Remote, and ringed by three wilderness areas, this former mining village is counted among Colorado's best ski resorts (some say it's *the* best). The old town center features beautifully preserved Victorian-era buildings refitted with shops and businesses. Strolling two-wheel traffic matches its laid-back, happy attitude.

Most everything in town is on Elk Ave, including the **visitor center** (970-349-6438; www.crestedbuttechamber.com; 601 Elk Ave; 9am-5pm).

Crested Butte Mountain Resort (970-349-2222; www.skicb.com; lift ticket adult/child $87/44) sits 2 miles north of the town at the base of the impressive mountain of the same name, surrounded by forests, rugged mountain peaks and the West Elk, Raggeds and Maroon Bells-Snowmass Wilderness Areas. The scenery is breathtakingly beautiful. It caters mostly to intermediate and expert riders.

Crested Butte is also a **mountain-biking** mecca, full of excellent high-altitude singletrack trails. For maps, information and mountain-bike rentals, visit the **Alpineer** (970-349-5210; www.alpineer.com; 419 6th St).

Crested Butte International Hostel (970-349-0588; www.crestedbuttehostel.com; 615 Tonally Ave; dm $25-31, r $65-110; @) is one of Colorado's nicest hostels. The best private rooms have their own baths. Dorm bunks come with reading lamps and lockable drawers. The communal area is mountain rustic with a stone fireplace and comfortable couches. Rates vary dramatically by season, with fall being cheapest.

With phenomenal food, the funky-casual **Secret Stash** (970-349-6245; www.thesecretstash.com; 21 Elk Ave; mains $8-20; 5-10pm) is adored by locals, who also like the original cocktails. The house specialty is pizza; its Notorious Fig (with prosciutto, fresh figs and truffle oil) won the 2007 World Pizza Championship.

Crested Butte has an interesting music scene year-round. Check out the lively **Eldo Brewpub** (970-349-6125; 215 Elk Ave), one of the town's most popular microbreweries, which doubles as the club where most out-of-town bands play. Check out the great outdoor deck.

Crested Butte's air link to the outside world is **Gunnison County Airport** (970-641-2304), 28 miles south of the town. Shuttle **Alpine Express** (970-641-5074; www.alpineexpressshuttle.com; per person $34) goes to Crested Butte; reserve ahead in summer.

The free **Mountain Express** (970-349-7318; www.mtnexp.org) connects Crested Butte with Mt Crested Butte every 15 minutes in winter, less often in other seasons; check times at bus stops.

Southern Colorado

Home to the dramatic San Juan and Sangre de Cristo mountain ranges, Colorado's bottom half is just as pretty as its top, has fewer people and is filled with stuff to see and do.

GREAT SAND DUNES NATIONAL PARK

Landscapes collide in a shifting sea of sand at **Great Sand Dunes National Park** (719-378-2312; www.nps.gov/grsa; 11999 Hwy 150; admission $3; visitor center 9am-5pm, longer hours in summer), making you wonder whether a spaceship has whisked you to another planet. The 55-sq-mile dune park – the tallest sand peak rises 700ft above the valley floor – is squeezed between the jagged 14,000ft peaks of the Sangre de Cristo and San Juan Mountains and flat, arid scrub-brush of the San Luis Valley.

Plan a visit to this excellent-value national park (at just $3, admission is a steal) around a full moon. Stock up on supplies, stop by the visitor center for your free backcountry camping permit and hike into the surreal landscape to set up camp in the middle of nowhere (bring plenty of water). You won't be disappointed.

There are numerous **hiking trails**, or the more adventuresome can try **sandboarding** (where you ride a snowboard down the dunes) or sledding. You can rent a sled or sandboard for some of the world's greatest dune riding from Great Sand Dunes Oasis just outside the park. Don't bother to bring a bike – they are useless in these conditions. Spring, when the dunes are at their most moist, is the best time for boarding. For the slickest boarding, arrive a few hours after it rains, when the dunes are wet underneath, but dry on top. Try riding down Star Dune, roughly 750ft high. It's a strenuous 3-mile hike from the Dunes parking lot. The High Dune, about 650ft tall, is another option. Be sure to bring lots of water. Walking in loose sand is difficult, and summer temperatures on the dunes can exceed 130°F (54°C).

Owned and operated by the Nature Conservancy, **Inn at Zapata Ranch** (719-378-2356; www.zranch.org; 5303 Hwy 150; d with full board $250;) is a working cattle and bison ranch set amid groves of cottonwood trees. Peaceful, it features historic buildings, including the main inn, a refurbished 19th-century log structure, with distant views of the sand dunes. Horseback riding, mountain-bike rentals and massage therapy are also on offer.

In the national park, **Pinyon Flats Campground** (www.recreation.gov; Great Sand Dunes National Park; campsites $14; year-round) has 88 sites and year-round water. The less appealing **Great Sand Dunes Oasis** (719-378-2222; www.greatdunes.com; 5400 Hwy 150; tent/RV sites $18/28, cabins $40) has spartan cabins, showers and a laundry service.

The national park is about 35 miles northeast of Alamosa and 250 miles south of Denver. From Denver, take I-25 south to Hwy 160 west and turn onto Hwy 150 north. There is no public transportation.

DURANGO

An archetypal old Colorado mining-town, Durango is a regional darling that is nothing short of delightful. Its graceful hotels, Victorian-era saloons and tree-lined streets of sleepy bungalows invite you to pedal around soaking up all the good vibes. There is plenty to do outdoors. Style-wise, Durango is torn between its ragtime past and a cool, cutting-edge future where townie bikes, caffeine and farmers markets rule.

The town's historic central precinct is home to boutiques, bars, restaurants and theater halls. Foodies will revel in the innovative organic and locavore fare that is making it the best place to eat in the state. But the interesting galleries and live music, combined with a relaxed and congenial local populace, also make it a great place to visit.

Sights & Activities

TOP CHOICE Durango & Silverton Narrow Gauge Railroad TRAIN TOUR

(970-247-2733, www.durangotrain.com; 479 Main Ave; adult/child return from $83/49; departures 8am, 8:30am, 9:15am & 10am) Riding the Durango & Silverton Narrow Gauge Railroad is a Durango must. These vintage steam locomotives have been making the scenic 45-mile trip north to Silverton (3½ hours each way) for over 125 years. The dazzling journey allows two hours for exploring Silverton. This trip operates only from May through October. Check online for different winter options.

Mountain Biking CYCLING

From steep single-track to scenic road rides, Durango is a national hub for mountain biking. The easy **Old Railroad Grade Trail** is a 12.2-mile loop that uses both US Hwy 160 and a dirt road following the old railway tracks. From Durango take Hwy 160 west through the town of Hesperus. Turn right into the Cherry Creek Picnic Area, where the trail starts.

For something a bit more technical, try **Dry Fork Loop**, accessible from Lightner Creek just west of town. It has some great drops, blind corners and vegetation. Cycling shops on Main or Second Ave rent out mountain bikes.

Durango Mountain Resort SNOW SPORTS
(☎970-247-9000; www.durangomountainresort.com; 1 Skier Pl; lift tickets adult/child from $65/36; ⏲mid-Nov–Mar; @📶👪) Also known as Purgatory, this resort, 25 miles north on US 550, offers 1200 skiable acres of varying difficulty and boasts 260in of snow per year. Two terrain parks offer plenty of opportunities for snowboarders to catch big air. Check local grocery stores and newspapers for promotions and two-for-one lift tickets.

Sleeping

TOP CHOICE **Strater Hotel** HOTEL $$
(☎970-247-4431; www.strater.com; 699 Main Ave; d $169-189; ❄@📶👪) The past lives large in this historical Durango hotel with walnut antiques, hand-stenciled wallpapers and relics ranging from a Stradivarius violin to a gold-plated Winchester. But we can boast about the friendly staff, who go out of their way to resolve guests' quiries. Rooms lean toward the romantic, with comfortable beds amid antiques, crystal and lace. The hot tub is a romantic plus (reserved by the hour) as is the summertime melodrama (theater) the hotel runs. In winter, rates drop by more than 50%, making it a virtual steal. Look online.

Rochester House HOTEL $$
(☎970-385-1920; www.rochesterhotel.com; 721 E 2nd Ave; d $169-219; ❄📶👪) Influenced by old Westerns (movie posters and marquee lights adorn the hallways), the Rochester is a little bit of old Hollywood in the new West. It's linked to smaller accommodations, Leland House, across the street, where all guests check in. Rooms in both are spacious but slightly worn, some with kitchenettes. Still, you can't beat the cool townie bikes, available for guests to take spins around town. Pet rooms come with direct access outside.

Hometown Hostel HOSTEL $
(☎970-385-4115; www.durangohometownhostel.com; 736 Goeglein Gulch Rd; dm $30; ⏲reception 3:30-8pm; P@📶👪) The bee's knees of hostels, this suburban-style house sits on the winding road up to the college, next to a convenient bike path. A better class of backpackers, it's all-inclusive, with linen, towels, lockers and wi-fi. There are two single-sex dorms and a larger mixed dorm, and a great common kitchen and lounge area. Room rates fall with extended stays.

Day's End MOTEL $
(☎970-259-3311; www.daysenddurango.com; 2202 N Main Ave; r from $55; P❄📶🏊👪) The best budget motel bet is on a small creek just north of town. Rooms are well maintained and many have king-size beds. Skiers get discounts at Durango Mountain Resort. There's an indoor hot tub and BBQ grill by the creek. Pets are welcome.

Eating & Drinking

Durango has a fantastic dining scene, especially strong on organic and locally sourced foods. Get a local dining guide for all the options. It's also home to a slew of breweries.

TOP CHOICE **East by Southwest** ASIAN $$
(☎970-247-5533; http://eastbysouthwest.com; 160 E College Dr; sushi $4-13, mains $12-24; ⏲11:30am-3pm Mon-Sat, 5-10pm daily; 🖉👪) Low-lit but vibrant, this is a worthy local favorite. Skip the standards for goosebump-good house favorites like sashimi with jalapeño and rolls with mango and wasabi honey. Fish is fresh and they don't serve endangered species. An extensive fusion menu also offers Thai, Vietnamese and Indonesian, well matched with creative martinis and sake cocktails. For a deal, check out the happy hour food specials (5pm to 6:30pm) for around $6.

Randy's STEAK, SEAFOOD $$$
(☎970-247-9083; www.randysrestaurant.com; 152 E College Dr; mains $20-25; ⏲5-10pm) A popular seafood and steak spot, with refreshing lighter fare and specialties such as garlic polenta fries. Between 5pm and 6pm early-birds score the same menu for $12 to $14. Happy hour runs from 5pm to 7pm.

Durango Diner DINER $
(☎970-247-9889; www.durangodiner.com; 957 Main Ave; mains $7-18; ⏲6am-2pm Mon-Sat, 6am-1pm Sun; 🖉👪) Enjoy the open view of the griddle at this lovable greasy spoon with button-cute waitresses and monstrous plates of eggs, smothered burritos or French toast. It's a local institution.

Jean Pierre Bakery SANDWICHES, BAKERY $$
(☎970-247-7700; www.jeanpierrebakery.com; 601 Main Ave; mains $5-16; ⏲8am-9pm; 🖉) This French patisserie has tempting delicacies made from scratch. Prices are dear, but at $15 the soup-and-sandwich lunch special,

with a sumptuous French pastry (we recommend the sticky pecan roll), is a deal.

Steamworks Brewing BREWERY
(☎970-259-9200; www.steamworksbrewing.com; 801 E 2nd Ave; mains $10-15; ⊙1pm-midnight Mon-Fri, 11am-2am Sat & Sun) DJs and live music pump up the volume at this industrial microbrewery with high sloping rafters and metal pipes. College kids fill the large bar area, but there's also a separate dining room with a Cajun-influenced menu.

Diamond Belle Saloon BAR
(☎970-376-7150; www.strater.com; 699 Main Ave) A rowdy corner of the historic Strater Hotel, this elegant old-time bar has waitresses dressed in vintage Victorian garb and flashing fishnets, and live ragtime that keeps out-of-town visitors packed in, standing room only, at happy hour. Half-price appetizers and drink specials run from 4pm to 6pm.

Information

Visitor center (☎800-525-8855; www.durango.org; 111 S Camino del Rio) South of town at the Santa Rita exit from US 550.

Getting There & Around

Durango-La Plata County Airport (DRO; ☎970-247-8143; www.flydurango.com; 1000 Airport Rd) is 18 miles southwest of Durango via US 160 and Hwy 172. Greyhound buses run daily from the **Durango Bus Center** (☎970-259-2755; 275 E 8th Ave), north to Grand Junction and south to Albuquerque, NM.

Check **Durango Transit** (☎970-259-5438; www.getarounddurango.com) for local travel information. Durango buses are fitted with bicycle racks. It's free to ride the red T shuttle bus that circulates Main St.

Durango is at the junction of US 160 and US 550, 42 miles east of Cortez, 49 miles west of Pagosa Springs and 190 miles north of Albuquerque.

SILVERTON

Ringed by snowy peaks and steeped in sooty tales of a tawdry mining town, Silverton seems more at home in Alaska than the lower 48. But here it is. Whether you're into snowmobiling, powder skiing, fly-fishing, beer on tap or just basking in some very high-altitude sunshine, Silverton delivers.

It's a two-street town, but only one is paved. The main drag, Greene St, is where you'll find most businesses. Notorious Blair St, still unpaved, runs parallel to Greene and is a blast from the past. During the silver rush, Blair St was home to thriving brothels and boozing establishments.

In summer, Silverton has some of the west's best 4WD trails. Traveling in modified Chevy Suburbans without the top, **San Juan Backcountry** (☎970-387-5565; www.sanjuanbackcountry.com; 1119 Greene St; 2hr tours adult/child $60/40; ⊙May-Oct; 👪) offers both tours and rental jeeps.

Campers can try **Red Mountain Motel & RV Park** (☎970-382-5512; www.redmtmotelrvpk.com; 664 Greene St; motel r from $78, cabins from $70, tent/RV sites $20/38; P📶👪), a pet-friendly place that stays open year-round. Or splurge for romance at **Inn of the Rockies at the Historic Alma House** (☎970-387-5336; www.innoftherockies.com; 220 E 10th St; r incl breakfast from $110; P❄) with an outdoor hot tub and New Orleans–inspired breakfasts.

The town has its share of Western-style saloons, but for something original seek out

SCENIC DRIVES: SAN JUAN MOUNTAIN PASSES

With rugged peaks and deep canyon drops, the scenery of the San Juan mountain range is hard to beat. Suitable for all vehicles, the **Million Dollar Highway** (US 550) takes its name from the valuable ore in the roadbed. But the scenery is also golden – the paved road clings to crumbly mountains, passing old mine-head frames and big alpine scenery.

A demanding but fantastic drive, the 65-mile **Alpine Loop Backcountry Byway** (www.alpineloop.com) begins in **Ouray** and travels east to **Lake City** – a wonderful mountain hamlet worth a visit – before looping back to its starting point. Along the way you'll cross two 12,000ft mountain passes and swap pavement and people for solitude, spectacular views and abandoned mining haunts. You'll need a high-clearance 4WD vehicle and some off-road driving skills to conquer this drive; allow six hours.

Spectacular during autumn for the splendor of its yellow aspens, **Ophir Pass** connects Ouray to Telluride via a former wagon road. The moderate 4WD route passes former mines, with a gradual ascent to 11,789ft. To get there, drive south of Ouray on Hwy 550 for 18.1 miles to the right-hand turnoff for National Forest Access, Ophir Pass.

As with all 4WD routes and mountain passes, check for road closures before going.

Montanya Distillers (www.montanyadistillers.com; 1332 Blair St; mains $8-20; 11:30am-7pm;) a smart and cozy bar with exotic cocktails crafted with homemade syrups and award-winning rum. Organic tamales and other yummy edibles are served.

Silverton is 50 miles north of Durango and 24 miles south of Ouray off US 550.

OURAY

With gorgeous ice falls draping the box canyon and soothing hot springs that dot the valley floor, Ouray is a privileged place for nature, even for Colorado. For ice-climbers it's a world-class destination, but hikers and 4WD fans can also appreciate its rugged (and sometimes stunning) charms. The town is a well-preserved quarter-mile mining village sandwiched between imposing peaks.

Between Silverton and Ouray, US 550 is known as the Million Dollar Hwy because the roadbed fill contains valuable ore. One of the state's most memorable drives, this breathtaking stretch passes old mine-head frames and larger-than-life alpine scenery. Though paved, the road is scary in rain or snow, so take extra care.

Sights & Activities

The visitor center is at the hot-springs pool. Check out their leaflet on an excellent walking tour that takes in two-dozen buildings and houses constructed between 1880 and 1904.

FREE **Ouray Ice Park** ICE CLIMBING
(970-325-4061; www.ourayicepark.com; Hwy 361; 7am-5pm mid-Dec-March) Enthusiasts from around the globe come to ice climb at the world's first public ice park, spanning a 2-mile stretch of the Uncompahgre Gorge. The sublime (if chilly) experience offers something for all skill levels.

TOP CHOICE **Chicks with Picks** ROCK, ICE CLIMBING
(cell 970-316-1403, office 970-626-4424; www.chickswithpicks.net; 163 County Rd 12, Ridgway; prices vary) Arming women with ice tools and crampons, this group of renowned women athletes gives excellent instruction for all-comers (beginners included) in rock-climbing, bouldering and ice-climbing. Programs are fun and change frequently, with multiday excursions or town-based courses. The climbing clinics also go on the road all over the US.

Ouray Hot Springs SPRING
(970-325-7073; www.ourayhotsprings.com; 1220 Main St; adult/child $10/8; 10am-10pm Jun-Aug, noon-9pm Mon-Fri & 11am-9pm Sat & Sun Dec-Feb;) For a healing soak, try the historic Ouray Hot Springs. The crystal-clear natural spring water is free of the sulfur smells plaguing other hot springs around here, and the giant pool features a variety of soaking areas at temperatures ranging from 96° to 106°F (35.5° to 41°C). The complex also offers a gym and massage service.

San Juan Mountain Guides OUTDOORS
(970-325-4925, 866-525-4925; www.ourayclimbing.com; 474 Main St) Ouray's own professional guiding and climbing group is certified with the International Federation of Mountain Guides Association (IFMGA). It specializes in ice- and rock-climbing and wilderness backcountry skiing.

Festivals & Events

Ouray Ice Festival ICE CLIMBING
(970-325-4288; www.ourayicefestival.com; Jan;) The Ouray Ice Festival features four days of climbing competitions, dinners, slide shows and clinics in January. There's even a climbing wall set up for kids. You can watch the competitions for free, but to check out the various evening events you will need to make a donation ($15) to the ice park. Once inside you'll get free brews from popular Colorado microbrewer New Belgium.

Sleeping & Eating

TOP CHOICE **Wiesbaden** HOTEL $$
(970-325-4347; www.wiesbadenhotsprings.com; 625 5th St; r from $132;) Few hotels can boast their own natural indoor vapor cave (and it's rumored that, long ago, Chief Ouray used this one). This quirky new-age inn charms with quilted bedcovers, free organic coffee and a spacious outdoor hot-spring pool (included). Guests can use the Aveda salon or book a private, clothing-optional soaking tub with a waterfall ($35 per hour).

Box Canyon Lodge & Hot Springs LODGE $$
(970-325-4981; www.boxcanyonouray.com; 45 3rd Ave; d $159;) With geothermal heat, these pine-board rooms are toasty and spacious. A set of outdoor spring-fed barrel hot tubs are perfect for a romantic stargazing soak. Book well ahead.

Amphitheater Forest Service Campground CAMPGROUND $
(☎877-444-6777; www.ouraycolorado.com/amphitheater; US Hwy 550; tent sites $16; ⊙Jun-Aug) With great tent sites under the trees, this high-altitude campground is a score. On holiday weekends a three-night minimum applies. South of town on Hwy 550, take a signposted left-hand turn.

TOP CHOICE **Buen Tiempo Mexican Restaurant & Cantina** MEXICAN $$
(☎970-325-4544; 515 Main St; mains $7-19; ⊙6-10pm; ⓥ) From the chili-rubbed sirloin to the posole (hearty hominy soup) served with warm tortillas, Buen Tiempo delivers. Start with one of its signature margaritas, served with chips and spicy homemade salsa.

Information

Visitor center (☎970-325-4746; www.ouraycolorado.com; 1220 Main St; ⊙9am-5pm)

Getting There & Around

Ouray is 24 miles north of Silverton along US 550 and best reached by private vehicle.

TELLURIDE

Surrounded on three sides by mastodon peaks, exclusive Telluride feels cut off from the hubbub of the outside world, and it often is. Once a rough mining town, today it's dirtbag-meets-diva – mixing the few who can afford the real estate with those scratching out a slope-side living for the sport of it. The town center still has palpable old-time charm and the surroundings are simply gorgeous.

Colorado Ave, also known as Main St, is where you'll find most businesses. From downtown you can reach the ski mountain via two lifts and the gondola. The latter also links Telluride with Mountain Village, the true base for the Telluride Ski Area. Located 7 miles from town along Hwy 145, Mountain Village is a 20-minute drive east, but is only 12 minutes away by gondola (free for foot passengers).

WORTH A TRIP

COLORADO HUT TO HUT

An exceptional way to enjoy hundreds of miles of single-track in summer or virgin powder slopes in winter, **San Juan Hut Systems** (☎970-626-3033; www.sanjuan-huts.com; per person $30) continues the European tradition of hut-to-hut adventures with five backcountry mountain huts. Bring just your food, flashlight (torch) and sleeping bag: amenities include padded bunks, propane stoves, wood stoves for heating and firewood.

Mountain-biking routes go from Durango or Telluride to Moab, winding through high alpine and desert regions. Or pick one hut as your base for a few days of backcountry skiing or riding. There's terrain for all levels, though skiers should have knowledge of snow and avalanche conditions. If not, go with a guide.

The website has helpful tips and information on rental skis, bikes and (optional) guides based in Ridgway or Ouray.

Sights & Activities

Telluride Ski Resort SNOW SPORTS
(☎970-728-7533, 888-288-7360; www.tellurideskiresort.com; 565 Mountain Village Blvd; lift tickets adult/child $98/61) Covering three distinct areas, Telluride Ski Resort is served by 16 lifts. Much of the terrain is for advanced and intermediate skiers, but there's still ample choice for beginners.

Paragon Ski & Sport OUTDOORS
(☎970-728-4525; www.paragontelluride.com; 213 W Colorado Ave) Has branches at three locations in town and a huge selection of rental bikes. It's a one-stop shop for outdoor activities in Telluride.

Festivals & Events

Mountainfilm FILM
(www.mountainfilm.org) A four-day screening of outdoor adventure and environmental films on Memorial Day weekend (May).

Telluride Bluegrass Festival MUSIC
(☎800-624-2422; www.planetbluegrass.com; 4-day pass $185) A wild frolic held in June, with all-day and evening music, food stalls and local microbrews. Camping is popular during the festival. Check out the website for info on sites, shuttle services and combo ticket-and-camping packages – it's all very organized!

Telluride Film Festival FILM
(☎603-433-9202; www.telluridefilmfestival.com; tickets $20-650) National and international films are premiered throughout town in early September, and the event attracts big-name stars. For more information on the relatively complicated pricing scheme, visit the film festival website.

DON'T MISS

TELLURIDE'S GREAT OUTDOORS

Sure, the festivals are great, but there's much more to a Telluride summer:

Mountain biking

Follow the River Trail from Town Park to Hwy 145 for 2 miles. Join **Mill Creek Trail** west of the Texaco gas station, it climbs and follows the contour of the mountain and ends at the Jud Wiebe Trail (hikers only).

Hiking

Just over 2 miles, **Bear Creek Trail** ascends 1040ft to a beautiful cascading waterfall. From here you can access the strenuous **Wasatch Trail**, a 12-mile loop that heads west across the mountains to **Bridal Veil Falls** – Telluride's most impressive waterfalls. The Bear Creek trailhead is at the south end of Pine St, across the San Miguel River.

Cycling

A 31-mile (one-way) trip, **Lizard Head Pass** features amazing mountain panoramas.

Sleeping

Telluride's lodgings can fill quickly, and for the best rates it's best to book online. Unless you're planning to camp, however, don't expect budget deals. Telluride's activities and festivals keep it busy year-round. For vacation rentals, the most reputable agency is **Telluride Alpine Lodging** (☎888-893-0158; www.telluridelodging.com; 324 W Colorado Ave).

TOP CHOICE **Hotel Columbia** HOTEL $$$
(☎970-728-0660; www.columbiatelluride.com; 300 W San Juan Ave; d $350; P❄📶🏊) Locally owned and operated, this stylish hotel pampers guests. The gondola is across the street, so leave your gear in the ski and boot storage and head directly to a room with espresso maker, fireplace and heated tile floors. With shampoo dispensers and recycling, it's also pretty ecofriendly. Other highlights include a rooftop hot tub and fitness room.

Victorian Inn LODGE $$
(☎970-728-6601; www.tellurideinn.com; 401 W Pacific Ave; r from $159; ❄📶👪) The smell of fresh cinnamon rolls greets visitors at one of Telluride's better deals, offering comfortable rooms (some with kitchenettes) and a hot tub and dry sauna in a nice garden area. Staff is friendly and guests get lift-ticket discounts. Kids aged 12 and under stay free, and you can't beat the downtown location.

Telluride Town Park Campground CAMPGROUND $
(☎970-728-2173; 500 W Colorado Ave; tent sites $20; ⊙mid-May–mid-Sep) Right in the center of town, these 20 sites have access to showers, swimming and tennis. It fills up quickly in the high season. For other campgrounds within 10 miles of town, check with the visitor center.

Eating & Drinking

For the best deals, look for a taco stand or hot dog truck on Colorado Ave.

Butcher & the Baker CAFE $$
(☎970-728-3334; 217 E Colorado Ave; mains $8-14; ⊙7am-7pm Mon-Sat, 8am-2pm Sun; 👪) Two veterans of upscale local catering started this heartbreakingly cute cafe, and no one beats it for breakfast. Organic ingredients and locally sourced meats make it a cut above. The to-go sandwiches are the best bet for a gourmet meal on the trail.

La Cocina de Luz MEXICAN $$
(www.lacocinatelluride.com; 123 E Colorado Ave; mains $9-19; ⊙9am-9pm) As they lovingly serve two Colorado favorites (organic and Mexican), it's no wonder that the lunch line is 10 people deep on a slow day at this healthy taqueria. There are delicious details too, such as handmade tortillas and margaritas with organic lime and agave nectar. Vegan, gluten-free options too.

There TAPAS $
(☎970-728-1213; www.therebars.com; 627 W Pacific Ave; appetizers from $4; ⊙3pm-late) A hip snack-and-drink alcove featuring yummy East-meets-West inventions. Think soy paper wraps with salmon, steamed pork buns and sashimi tostadas and the Very Special Ramen Soup, with crab, duck or pork. Pair it with an original cocktail – we liked the jalapeño kiss.

New Sheridan Bar BAR
(☎970-728-3911; www.newsheridan.com; 231 W Colorado Ave) Mixes real local flavor with the see-and-be-seen crowd. Most of this historic bar survived the waning mining fortunes even as the adjoining hotel sold off chandeliers

and fine furnishings to pay the heating bills. Look for the bullet holes in the wall.

☆ Entertainment

Fly Me to the Moon Saloon LIVE MUSIC
(☎970-728-6666; 132 E Colorado Ave) Let your hair down and kick up your heels to the tunes of live bands at this saloon, the best place in Telluride to groove to live music.

Sheridan Opera House THEATER
(☎970-728-4539; www.sheridanoperahouse.com; 110 N Oak St) This historic venue has a burlesque charm and is always the center of Telluride's cultural life.

Information

Visitor center (☎970-728-3041, 888-353-5473; www.telluride.com; 398 W Colorado Ave; ⌚9am-5pm)

Getting There & Around

Commuter aircraft serve the mesa-top **Telluride Airport** (☎970-778-5051; www.tellurideairport.com; Last Dollar Rd), 5 miles east of town on Hwy 145. If the weather is poor, flights may be diverted to Montrose, 65 miles north. For car rental, National and Budget both have airport locations.

In ski season Montrose Regional Airport, 66 miles north, has direct flights to and from Denver (on United), Houston, Phoenix and limited cities on the East Coast.

Shared shuttles by **Telluride Express** (☎970-728-6000; www.tellurideexpress.com) go from the Telluride Airport to town or Mountain Village for $15. Shuttles between the Montrose Airport and Telluride cost $48.

MESA VERDE NATIONAL PARK

Shrouded in mystery, Mesa Verde, with its cliff dwellings and verdant valley walls, is a fascinating, if slightly eerie, national park to explore. It is here that a civilization of Ancestral Puebloans appears to have vanished in AD 1300, leaving behind a complex civilization of cliff dwellings, some accessed by sheer climbs. Mesa Verde is unique among parks for its focus on preserving this civilization's cultural relics so that future generations may continue to interpret the puzzling settlement, and subsequent abandonment, of the area.

Mesa Verde rewards travelers who set aside a day or more to take the ranger-led tours of Cliff Palace and Balcony House, explore Wetherill Mesa or participate in one of the campfire programs. But if you only have time for a short visit, check out the Chapin Mesa Museum and walk through the Spruce Tree House, where you can climb down a wooden ladder into the cool chamber of a kiva (ceremonial structure, usually partly underground).

Sights & Activities

FREE **Chapin Mesa Museum** MUSEUM
(☎970-529-4631; ⌚8am-6:30pm, 8am-5pm winter) A good first stop, with detailed dioramas and exhibits pertaining to the park. When park headquarters are closed on weekends, staff at the museum provide information.

Chapin Mesa ARCHEOLOGICAL SITE
The largest concentration of Ancestral Puebloan sites is at Chapin Mesa, where you'll see the densely clustered **Far View Site** and the large **Spruce Tree House**, the most accessible of sites, with a paved half-mile round-trip path.

If you want to see **Cliff Palace** or **Balcony House**, the only way is through an hour-long ranger-led tour booked in advance at the visitor center ($3). These tours are extremely popular; go early in the morning or a day in advance to book. Balcony House requires climbing a 32ft and 60ft ladder – those with medical problems should skip it.

Wetherill Mesa ARCHEOLOGICAL SITE
This is the second-largest concentration. Visitors may enter stabilized surface sites and two cliff dwellings, including the **Long House**, open from late May through August. South from Park Headquarters, the 6-mile **Mesa Top Road** connects excavated mesa-top sites, accessible cliff dwellings and vantage points to view inaccessible dwellings from the mesa rim.

TOP CHOICE **Aramark Mesa Verde** HIKING
(☎970-529-4421; www.visitmesaverde.com; adult $20-40) Highly recommended, these backcountry ranger tours are run through the park concessionaire. Backcountry hikes sell out fast, since they provide exclusive access to **Square House** (via an exposed one-mile hike) and **Spring House** (an eight-hour, 8-mile hike), but make very personalized trips to excavated pit homes, cliff dwellings and the **Spruce Tree House** daily from May to mid-October. Tickets available only online.

Sleeping & Eating

The nearby towns of Cortez and Mancos have plenty of midrange places to stay; inside the park there's camping and a lodge.

Morefield Campground CAMPGROUND $
(☎970-529-4465; www.nps.gov/meve; N Rim Rd; tent sites $20, canvas tents from $40; ⊙May–mid-Oct) Deluxe campers will dig the big canvas tents kitted out with two cots and a lantern. The park's camping option, located 4 miles from the entrance gate, also has 445 regular tent sites on grassy grounds conveniently located near Morefield Village. The village has a general store, gas station, restaurant, free showers and laundry.

Free evening campfire programs take place nightly from Memorial Day (May) to Labor Day (September) at the Morefield Campground Amphitheater.

Far View Lodge LODGE $$
(☎970-529-4421; www.visitmesaverde.com; N Rim Rd; r from $119; ⊙mid-Apr–Oct; P❄📶👪) Perched on a mesa top 15 miles inside the park entrance, this tasteful Pueblo-style lodge has 150 rooms, some with kiva fireplaces. Standard rooms don't have air con (or TV) and summer daytimes can be hot. The Southwestern-style kiva rooms are a worthwhile upgrade, with balconies, pounded copper sinks and bright patterned blankets. You can even bring your dog for an extra $10 per night.

Mutate Room MODERN AMERICAN $$
(☎800-449-2288; www.visitmesaverde.com; N Rim Rd; mains $15-25; ⊙5-7:30pm year-round, 7-10am Apr–mid-Oct; 🖉👪) Featuring lovely views, this innovative restaurant in the Far View Lodge offers regional flavors with some innovation, serving dishes such as cinnamon chili pork, elk shepherd's pie and trout crusted in pine nuts. You can also get local Colorado beers.

Far View Terrace Café CAFE $
(N Rim Rd; dishes from $5; ⊙7-10am, 11am-3pm & 5-8pm May–mid-Oct; 🖉👪) Housed in Far View Lodge, this self-service place offers reasonably priced meals. Don't miss the house special – the Navajo Taco.

Information

The park entrance is off US 160, midway between Cortez and Mancos. New in 2012, the **Mesa Verde Visitor and Research Center** (VRC; ☎970-529-4461; www.nps.gov/meve; 7-day park entry per vehicle $15, bicyclists, hikers & motorcyclists $8), located near the entrance, has information and news on park closures (many areas are closed in winter). It also sells tickets for **tours** ($3) of the magnificent Cliff Palace or Balcony House. Before the new visitor center opens, use the **Far View Visitor Center** (☎970-529-5034; ⊙8am-5pm), 15 miles from the entrance.

WYOMING

With wind, restless grasses and wide blue skies, the most sparsely populated state offers solitude to spare. Called the 'Bunchgrass end of the World' by writer Annie Proulx, Wyoming may be nuzzled in the bosom of America, but it's emptiness that defines it.

Though steeped in ranching culture – just see the line of Stetsons at the local credit union – Wyoming is the number-one coal producer in the US, and is also big in natural gas, crude oil and diamonds. Deeply conservative, its propensity toward industry has sometimes made it an uneasy steward of the land.

But wilderness may be Wyoming's greatest bounty. Its northwestern corner is home to the magnificent national parks of Yellowstone and Grand Teton. Chic Jackson and progressive Lander make great bases for epic hiking, climbing and skiing. For a truer taste of Western life, check out the plain prairie towns of Laramie and Cheyenne.

Information

Even on highways, distances are long, with gas stations few and far between. Driving hazards include frequent high gusty winds and fast-moving snow squalls that can create whiteout

WYOMING FACTS

» **Nickname** Equality State

» **Population** 564,000

» **Area** 97,100 sq miles

» **Capital city** Cheyenne (population 55,314)

» **Sales tax** 4%

» **Birthplace of** artist Jackson Pollock (1912-1956)

» **Home of** women's suffrage, coal mining, geysers, wolves

» **Politics** Conservative to the core

» **Famous for** rodeo, ranches, former Vice President Dick Cheney

» **Kitschiest souvenir** fur jock strap from a Jackson boutique

» **Driving distances** Cheyenne to Jackson 440 miles

blizzard conditions. If the weather gets too rough, the highway patrol will shut the entire interstate until it clears.

Wyoming Road Conditions (☎307-772-0824, 888-996-7623; www.wyoroad.info)

Wyoming State Parks & Historic Sites (☎307-777-6323; www.wyo-park.com; admission $6, historic site $4, camping per person $17) Wyoming has 12 state parks. Camping reservations are taken online or over the phone.

Wyoming Travel & Tourism (☎800-225-5996; www.wyomingtourism.org; 1520 Etchepare Circle, Cheyenne)

Cheyenne

Many a country tune has been penned about Wyoming's state capital and largest city, though Cheyenne is more like the Hollywood Western *before* the shooting begins. That is, until Frontier Days festival, a raucous July celebration of cowboy fun. At the junction of I-25 and I-80, it's an obvious pit stop.

Sights & Activities

FREE **Cheyenne Gunslingers** WILD WEST SHOW
(☎800-426-5009; www.cheyennegunslingers.com; cnr W 15th at Pioneer Ave; ⊙shows 6pm daily plus noon Sat Jun & Jul; 👪) A nonprofit group of actors who puts on a lively, if not exactly accurate Old West show – from near hangings to slippery jailbreaks. Stars include corrupt judges, smiling good guys and, of course, the bad-ass villains.

Frontier Days Old West Museum MUSEUM
(☎307-778-7290; 4601 N Carey Ave; adult/child $7/free; ⊙8am-6pm Mon-Fri, 9am-5pm Sat & Sun summer, 9am-5pm Mon-Fri, 10am-5pm Sat & Sun winter) For a peek into the pioneer past, visit the lively Frontier Days Old West Museum at I-25 exit 12. It is chock-full of rodeo memorabilia – from saddles to trophies.

Festivals & Events

TOP CHOICE **Cheyenne Frontier Days** RODEO
(☎307-778-7222; www.cfdrodeo.com; 4501 N Carey Ave; admission $16-30; 👪) If you've never seen a steer wrestler leap into action, this very Western event is bound to brand an impression. Beginning in late July, this is Wyoming's largest celebration. Crowds come from around the Rockies for 10 days of rodeos, concerts, dances, air shows, chili cook-offs and other shindigs. If you tire of the dusty action, check out the art sale and 'Indian village.'

Sleeping & Eating

Reservations are a must during Frontier Days, when rates double and everything within 50 miles is booked. A string of cheap motels line noisy Lincolnway (I-25 exit 9).

Nagle Warren Mansion Bed & Breakfast B&B $$
(☎307-637-3333; www.naglewarrenmansion.com; 222 E 17th St; r incl breakfast from $155; ❄📶) This lavish spread is a fabulous find. In a quickly-going-hip neighborhood, this historic 1888 house is decked out with late-19th-century regional antiques. Spacious and elegant, the mansion also boasts a hot tub, a reading room tucked into a turret and classic 1954 Schwinn bikes for cruising. Jim, the owner, entertains with his deep knowledge of local history and you can pay a visit to the excellent art gallery next door.

TOP CHOICE **Tortilla Factory** MEXICAN $
(715 S Greeley Hwy; mains $3-7; ⊙6am-8pm Mon-Sat, 8am-5pm Sun) A delicious Mexican dive, serving homemade tamales for only $1.50, and a range of authentic classics such as shredded-beef tacos and huevos rancheros. Go to the front for take-out or traditional Mexican baked goods; the restaurant entrance and parking are in the back.

Sanford's Grub & Pub PUB $
(115 E 17th St; mains $8-16; ⊙11am-10pm) The walls at this fun place are aflutter with sports bric-a-brac and road signs, and gets consistently good reviews for its novella-length menu of tasty eats, including half-pound burgers, chicken and junkyard nachos. Beer is served in ice-cold glasses.

Information

Cheyenne Visitor Center (☎307-778-3133; www.cheyenne.org; 1 Depot Sq; ⊙8am-5pm Mon-Fri, 9am-5pm Sat, 11am-5pm Sun, closed Sat & Sun in winter) A great resource.

Getting There & Around

Cheyenne Airport (CYS; ☎307-634-7071; www.cheyenneairport.com; 200 E 8th Ave) has daily flights to Denver. Greyhound buses depart from the **Black Hills Stage Lines** (☎307-635-1327; 5401 Walker Rd) daily for Billings, MT ($97, 9½ hours), and Denver, CO ($38, 2¾ hours), among other destinations.

WYOMING'S EMPTY NEST SYNDROME

Today Wyoming remains a rural state where most folk either work on the family ranch or have jobs in the energy agency. One of the hottest issues in the state is about how to keep the younger generation from moving away following university – indeed, census numbers show Wyoming's under-50-years-old population is quickly declining. To entice people to stay, or to interest other twenty-somethings to move to the state, politicians are offering cheap plots of land if residents agree to live and work in small towns for a set number of years. The state is also concentrating on boosting tourism revenues.

On weekdays, the **Cheyenne Transit Program** (CTP; ☎307-637-6253; adult $1, 6-18yr 75¢; ⊙service 6am-7pm Mon-Fri, 10am-5pm Sat) operates six local bus routes. Also, **Cheyenne Street Railway Trolley** (☎800-426-5009; 121 W 15th St; adult/child $10/5; ⊙May-Sep) takes visitors on tours through downtown.

Laramie

Home to the state's only four-year university, Laramie can be both hip and boisterous, a vibe missing from most Wyoming prairie towns. Worth exploring is the small historic downtown, a lively five-block grid of attractive two-story brick buildings with hand-painted signs and murals pushed up against the railroad tracks.

For an infusion of culture, check out one of the museums on the **University of Wyoming** (UW; ☎307-766-4075) campus. If you're traveling with the kids (or just feel like one), stop by the **Wyoming Frontier Prison** (☎307-745-616; www.wyomingfrontierprison.org; 975 Snowy Range Rd; adult/child $7/6; ⊙8am-5pm; 👪), a curious restoration of an early prison and frontier town.

There are numerous cheap sleeps off I-80 at exit 313. With landscaped gardens and three country-style rooms, **Mad Carpenter Inn** (☎307-742-0870; www.madcarpenter.home.bresnan.net; 353 N 8th St; r incl breakfast $85-115; ❄📶) has warmth to spare, the serious game room featuring billiards and Ping-Pong. In town, the **Gas Lite Motel** (☎307-742-6616; 960 N 3rd St; r $58; ❄📶🏊) relies on an outrageously kitsch setup (think cowboy cutouts and plastic horses) to sell its well-priced and pet-friendly digs.

With superlative brews, **Coal Creek Coffee Co** (110 E Grand Ave; mains $3-6; ⊙6am-10pm; 📶) is modern and stylish, with Fair Trade roasts and tasty sandwiches (eg blue-cheese and portobello panini). Doubtless the healthiest food for miles, **Sweet Melissa's** (213 S 1st St; mains $9; ⊙11am-9pm Mon-Sat; 🌿) does good down-home vegetarian. It's packed at lunchtime.

For live country music and beer, **Old Buckhorn Bar** (☎307-742-3554; 114 Ivinson St) is Laramie's oldest standing bar and a fantastic dive – check out the hand-scratched graffiti and half-century-old condom dispenser in the bathroom.

Located 4 miles west of town via I-80 exit 311, **Laramie Regional Airport** (☎307-742-4164) has daily flights to Denver. **Greyhound** (☎307-742-5188) buses stop at the **Tumbleweed Express gas station** (4700 Bluebird Lane) at the east end of town (I-80 exit 316). Fill up your tank (and tummy) in Laramie; heading west on I-80, the next services aren't for 75 miles.

Lander

Lander just might be the coolest little one-street town in Wyoming – and there are many of those. Just a stone's throw from the Wind River Reservation, it's a rock-climbing and mountaineering mecca in a friendly and unpretentious foothills setting. It is also home to **NOLS** (www.nols.com), the National Outdoor Leadership School, a renowned outdoor school that leads trips around the world and locally into the Wind River Range.

The **Lander Visitor Center** (☎307-332-3892; www.landerchamber.org; 160 N 1st St; ⊙9am-5pm Mon-Fri) is a good source of general information. If you've come to hike, camp or climb, you're best popping into **Wild Iris Mountain Sports** (☎307-332-4541; 333 Main St), a gear shop offering good advice and rental climbing or snow shoes. Pick up their cheat sheet with local tips. If you want to check out the single-track trails outside town, head down the street to **Freewheel Ski & Cycle** (☎307-332-6616; 378 W Main St).

The beautiful **Sinks Canyon State Park** (☎307-332-3077; 3079 Sinks Canyon Rd; admission $6; ⊙visitor center 9am-6pm Jun-Aug), 6 miles south of Lander, features a curious underground river. Flowing through a narrow canyon, the Middle Fork of the Popo Agie River disappears into the soluble Madison limestone called the Sinks and returns warmer a quarter-mile downstream in a pool called the Rise. The scenic **campgrounds** (campsites $17) come highly recommended by locals.

Chain hotels line Main St, but for a deal try the locally owned **Holiday Lodge** (☎307-332-2511; www.holidaylodgelander.com; 210 McFarlane Dr; r incl breakfast from $50; ❄📶). The look might say 1961, but it's scrubbed shiny and friendly, with thoughtful extras like an iron, makeup remover and sewing kits.

Decompress from long hours of travel or adventure at the backyard patio of **Gannett Grill** (☎307-332-8227; 128 Main St; mains $6-9; ⏰11am-9pm), a local institution, where you take a microbrew from the Lander Bar next door and wander back to your shady picnic table to dine on local beef burgers, crisp waffle fries and stone-oven pizzas. If you're feeling fancy, try the adjoining **Cowfish**, a more upscale dinner offering from the same folks. There's live music many nights.

Grab your coffee at chic **Old Town Coffee** (300 Main St; ⏰7am-7pm) where each cup is ground to order, as stiff as you like it.

Wind River Transportation Authority (☎307-856-7118; www.wrtabuslines.com) provides bus service to Jackson ($110) and other destinations; check the website for schedules.

Cody

Raucous Cody revels in its Wild West image (it's named after legendary showman William 'Buffalo Bill' Cody). With a staged streak of yeehaw, the town happily relays yarns (not always the whole story, mind you) about its past. Summer is high season, and Cody puts on quite an Old West show for the throngs of visitors making their way to Yellowstone National Park, 52 miles to the west. From Cody, the approach to geyserland through the Wapiti Valley is dramatic to say the least. President Teddy Roosevelt once said this stretch of pavement was 'the most scenic 50 miles in the world.'

The **visitor center** (☎307-587-2777; www.codychamber.org; 836 Sheridan Ave; ⏰8am-6pm Mon-Sat, 10am-3pm Sun Jun-Aug, 8am-5pm Mon-Fri Sep-May) is the logical starting point.

Cody's major tourist attraction is the superb **Buffalo Bill Historical Center** (www.bbhc.org; 720 Sheridan Ave; adult/child $18/10; ⏰8am-6pm May-Oct, 10am-5pm Nov, Mar & Apr, 10am-5pm Thu-Sun Dec-Feb). A sprawling complex of five museums, it showcases everything Western: from posters, grainy films and other lore pertaining to Buffalo Bill's world-famous Wild West shows, to galleries showcasing frontier artwork and a museum dedicated to Native Americans. Its Draper Museum of Natural History is a great primer for the Yellowstone ecosystem, with information on everything from wolves to grizzlies.

Also popular is the **Cody Nite Rodeo** (www.codystampederodeo.com; 519 West Yellowstone Ave; adult/child 7-12 yr $18/8), which giddy-ups nightly from June to August.

Built by ol' Bill himself in 1902, **Irma Hotel** (☎307-587-4221; www.irmahotel.com; 1192 Sheridan Ave; r from $112; ❄) offers historic rooms in the main building or less charming but cheaper modern rooms. Don't miss grabbing a beer at the restaurant's ornate cherrywood, a gift from Queen Victoria. Gunfights break out nightly at 6pm in front of the hotel from June through September.

The **Silver Dollar Bar** (1313 Sheridan Ave; mains $7-12) is a historic watering hole with live music nightly out on the outdoor deck. It serves epic burgers and has pool tables. Thursdays are 25¢-beer nights.

Yellowstone Regional Airport (COD; www.flyyra.com) is 1 mile east of Cody and runs daily flights to Salt Lake City and Denver.

Yellowstone National Park

They grow their critters and geysers big up in Yellowstone, America's first national park and Wyoming's flagship attraction. From shaggy grizzlies to oversized bison and magnificent packs of wolves, this park boasts the lower 48's most enigmatic concentration of wildlife. Throw in half the world's geysers, the country's largest high-altitude lake and a plethora of blue-ribbon rivers and waterfalls, all sitting pretty atop a giant supervolcano, and you'll quickly realize you've stumbled across one of Mother Nature's most fabulous creations.

When John Colter became the first white man to visit the area in 1807, the only inhabitants were Tukadikas (aka Sheepeaters), a Shoshone Bannock people who hunted bighorn sheep. Colter's reports of exploding geysers and boiling mud holes (at first laughingly dismissed as tall tales) brought in expeditions and tourism interest eagerly funded by the railroads. The park was established in 1872 (as the world's first) to preserve Yellowstone's spectacular geography: the geothermal phenomena, the fossil forests and Yellowstone Lake.

The 3472-sq-mile park is divided into five distinct regions (clockwise from the north): Mammoth, Roosevelt, Canyon, Lake and Geyser Countries.

Of the park's five entrance stations, only the North Entrance, near Gardiner, MT, is open year-round. The others, typically open May to October, offer access from the northeast (Cooke City, MT), east (Cody, WY), south (Grand Teton National Park) and west (West Yellowstone, MT). The park's main road is the 142-mile Grand Loop Rd scenic drive.

BEAT THE CROWDS

Yellowstone's wonderland attracts up to 30,000 visitors daily in July and August and over three million gatecrashers annually. Avoid the worst of the crowds with the following advice:

» Visit in May, September or October for decent weather and few people, or even better in winter (late December to March).

» Ditch 95% of the crowds by hiking a backcountry trail. Lose an amazing 99% by backpacking and camping overnight in a backcountry site (permit required).

» Follow the wildlife's example and be most active in the golden hours after dawn and before dusk.

» Pack lunch for one of the park's many scenic picnic areas and eat lodge dinners late (after 9pm).

» Make reservations for park lodging months in advance and book concession campgrounds *at least* the day before.

Sights & Activities

Just sitting on the porch of the Old Faithful Inn with a cocktail in hand waiting for Old Faithful geyser to erupt could be considered enough activity by itself but there's plenty else to keep you busy here, from hiking and backpacking to kayaking and fly-fishing. Most park trails are not groomed, but unplowed roads and trails are open for cross-country skiing.

Yellowstone is split into five distinct regions, each with unique attractions. Upon entering the national park you'll be given a basic map and a park newspaper detailing the excellent ranger-led talks and walks (well worth attending). All the visitor centers have information desks staffed by park rangers who can help you tailor a hike to your tastes, from great photo spots to best chance of spotting a bear.

Geyser Country GEYSERS, HIKING

With the densest collection of geothermal features in the park, Upper Geyser Basin contains 180 of the park's 250-odd geysers. The most famous is **Old Faithful**, which spews from 3700 to 8400 gallons of water 100ft to 180ft into the air every 1½ hours or so. For an easy walk, check out the predicted eruption times at the brand new visitor center and then follow the easy boardwalk trail around the Upper Geyser Loop. The park's most beautiful thermal feature is **Grand Prismatic Spring** in the Midway Geyser Basin. The Firehole and Madison Rivers offer superb fly-fishing and wildlife viewing.

Mammoth Country SPRINGS, HIKING

Known for the geothermal terraces and elk herds of historic **Mammoth** and the hot springs of **Norris Geyser Basin**, Mammoth Country is North America's most volatile and oldest-known continuously active thermal area. The peaks of the Gallatin Range rise to the northwest, towering above the area's lakes, creeks and numerous hiking trails.

Roosevelt Country WILDLIFE, HIKING

Fossil forests, the commanding **Lamar River Valley** and its tributary trout streams, **Tower Falls** and the Absaroka Mountains' craggy peaks are the highlights of Roosevelt Country, the park's most remote, scenic and undeveloped region. Several good hikes begin near **Tower Junction**.

Canyon Country LOOKOUTS, HIKING

A series of scenic overlooks linked by hiking trails highlight the colorful beauty and grandeur of the Grand Canyon of the Yellowstone and its impressive **Lower Falls**. South Rim Dr leads to the canyon's most spectacular overlook, at Artist Point. **Mud Volcano** is Canyon Country's primary geothermal area.

Lake Country LAKES, BOATING

Yellowstone Lake, the centerpiece of Lake Country and one of the world's largest

Yellowstone & Grand Teton National Parks

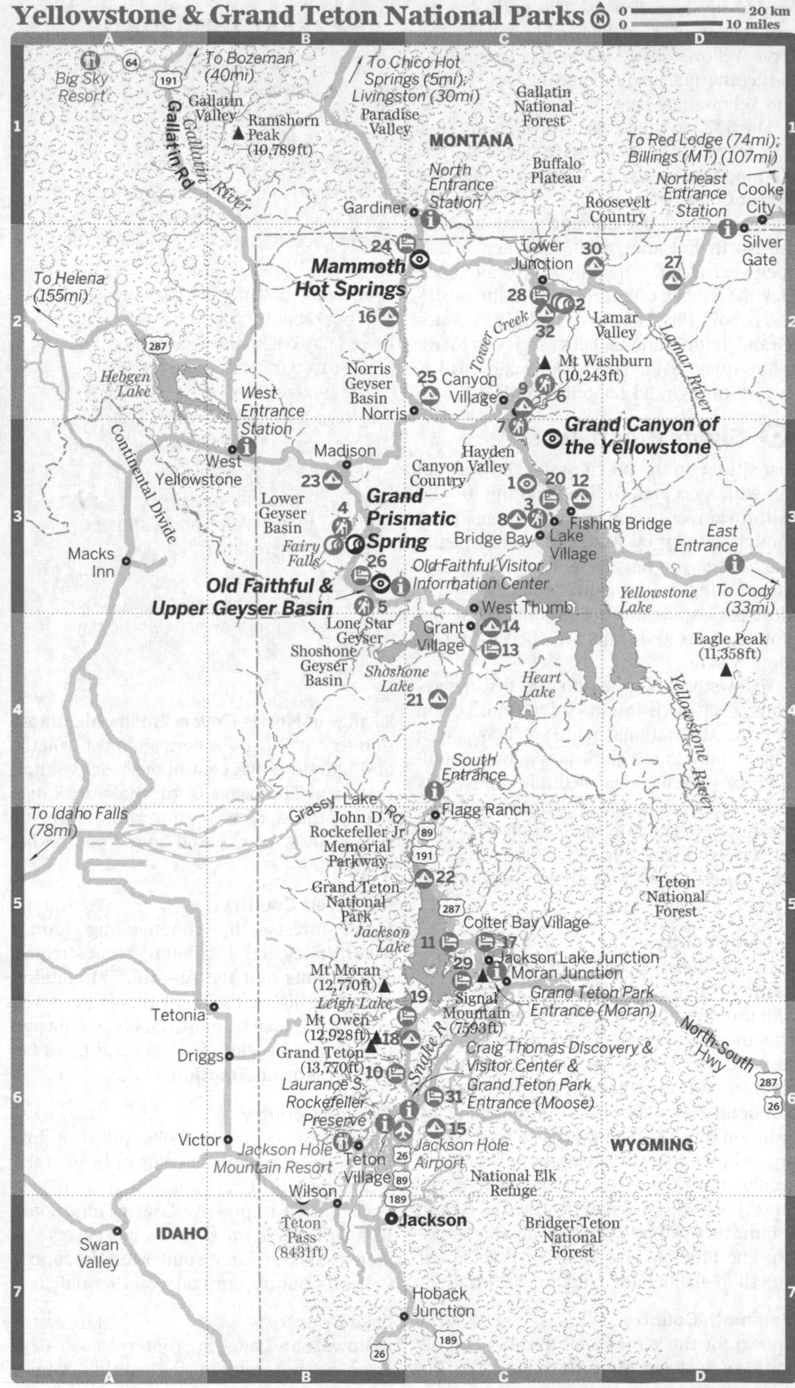

Yellowstone & Grand Teton National Parks

Top Sights
- Grand Canyon of the Yellowstone........C3
- Grand Prismatic Spring........B3
- Mammoth Hot Springs........C2
- Old Faithful & Upper Geyser Basin........B3

Sights
- 1 Mud Volcano........C3
- 2 Tower Falls........C2

Activities, Courses & Tours
- 3 Elephant Back Trailhead........C3
- 4 Fairy Falls HIking Trail........B3
- 5 Lone Star Geyser Tailhead........B3
- 6 Mt Washburn Trail........C2
- 7 South Rim Trail........C3

Sleeping
- 8 Bridge Bay Campground........C3
- 9 Canyon Campground........C2
- Canyon Lodge & Cabins........(see 9)
- 10 Climbers' Ranch........B6
- 11 Colter Bay Village........C5
- 12 Fishing Bridge RV Park........C3
- 13 Grant Village........C4
- 14 Grant Village Campground........C4
- 15 Gros Ventre Campground........C6
- 16 Indian Creek Campground........B2
- 17 Jackson Lake Lodge........C5
- 18 Jenny Lake Campground........C6
- 19 Jenny Lake Lodge........C6
- Lake Lodge Cabins........(see 20)
- 20 Lake Yellowstone Hotel........C3
- 21 Lewis Lake Campground........C4
- 22 Lizard Creek Campground........C5
- 23 Madison Campground........B3
- Mammoth Campground........(see 24)
- 24 Mammoth Hot Springs Hotel & Cabins........C2
- 25 Norris Campground........C2
- 26 Old Faithful Inn........B3
- Old Faithful Lodge Cabins........(see 26)
- Old Faithful Snow Lodge........(see 26)
- 27 Pebble Creek Campground........D2
- 28 Roosevelt Lodge Cabins........C2
- 29 Signal Mountain Lodge........C5
- 30 Slough Creek Campground........C2
- 31 Spur Ranch Log Cabins........C6
- 32 Tower Fall Campground........C2

Eating
- Jenny Lake Lodge........(see 19)
- Lake Yellowstone Hotel........(see 20)
- Mural Room........(see 17)
- Old Faithful Inn........(see 26)
- Peaks........(see 29)
- Pioneer Grill........(see 17)

alpine lakes, is a watery wilderness lined with volcanic beaches and best explored by boat or sea kayak. Rising east and southeast of the lakes, the wild and snowcapped Absaroka Range hides the wildest lands in the lower 48, perfect for epic backpacking or horseback trips.

Hiking Trails HIKING

Hikers can explore Yellowstone's backcountry from more than 92 trailheads that give access to 1100 miles of hiking trails. A free backcountry-use permit, which is available at visitor centers and ranger stations, is required for overnight trips. Backcountry camping is allowed in 300 designated sites, 60% of which can be reserved in advance by mail; a $20 fee applies to all bookings that are more than three days in advance.

After much heated debate and a narrowly avoided fistfight, we have settled on the following as our favorite five day hikes in the park.

Lone Star Geyser Trail

A good family hike or bike ride along an old service road to a geyser that erupts every three hours. Start at the Kepler Cascades parking area, southeast of the Old Faithful area (5 miles, easy).

South Rim Trail

A web of interconnected trails that follows the spectacular Yellowstone Canyon rim past the Lower Falls to scenic Artists Point then Lily Pad Lake, returning to Uncle Tom's trailhead via thermal areas and Clear Lake (3.5 miles, easy).

Mt Washburn

A fairly strenuous uphill hike from Dunraven Pass trailhead to a mountaintop fire tower, for 360-degree views over the park and nearby bighorn sheep (6.4 miles, moderate).

Elephant Back Mountain

An 800ft climb from near Lake Hotel to a panoramic viewpoint over Yellowstone Lake (3.5 miles, moderate).

WHERE THE BIG BEARS & BISON ROAM...

Along with the big mammals – grizzly, black bear, moose and bison – Yellowstone is home to elk, pronghorn antelope and bighorn sheep. Despite the grumblings of trigger-itchy ranchers just outside park boundaries, wolves (p1151) have been part of the national park since reintroduction in 1996. Both wolves and bison are native to the area, but by the end of the last century hunting and human habitation had sent their populations spiraling toward extinction. In the last decade, the numbers have once again risen, which has ecologists and rangers excited.

Hayden Valley, in Yellowstone's heart between Yellowstone Lake and Canyon Village, is your best all-round bet for wildlife viewing. For the best chances of seeing wildlife, head out at dawn or dusk, park at a turnout anywhere off the Grand Loop Rd and stage a stakeout. If you have patience and a pair of binoculars a grizzly just might wander into your viewfinder, or perhaps you'll spy a rutting elk or hear the bugle of a solitary moose before it dips its mighty head into the river for a drink.

Lamar Valley, in the north of the park, is ground zero for spotting wolves – it's where these magnificent beasts were first reintroduced. Ask rangers where packs are most active or attend a wolf-watching (or other) excursion with the recommended **Yellowstone Institute** (www.yellowstoneassociation.org). Hearing a wolf howl echoing across the valley at dusk is a magical, primeval experience that reminds us there are still places in the US wild enough to raise the hairs on the back of your neck.

Fairy Falls
Climb off trail to a viewpoint over spectacular Grand Prismatic Spring and then hike through lodgepole forest to the falls, before continuing on to beautiful Imperial Geyser (6 miles, easy).

Cycling CYCLING
Cyclists can ride on public roads and a few designated service roads, but not on the backcountry trails. The best season is April to October, when the roads are usually snow-free. From mid-March to mid-April the Mammoth–West Yellowstone park road is closed to cars but open to cyclists, offering a long but stress-free ride.

Yellowstone Raft Company ADVENTURE TOUR
(☎800-858-7781; www.yellowstoneraft.com) There is exhilarating white water through Yankee Jim Canyon on the Yellowstone River just north of the park boundary in Montana. This company offers a range of guided adventures out of Gardiner starting in late May.

Sleeping

NPS and private campgrounds, along with cabins, lodges and hotels, are all available in the park. Reservations are essential in summer. Contact the park concessionaire **Xanterra** (☎307-344-7311; www.yellowstonenationalparklodges.com) to reserve a spot at its campsites, cabins or lodges.

Plentiful accommodations can also be found in the gateway towns of Cody, Gardiner and West Yellowstone.

The best budget options are the seven NPS-run campgrounds (campsites $14) in **Mammoth** (year-round), **Tower Fall**, **Indian Creek**, **Pebble Creek**, **Slough Creek**, **Norris** and **Lewis Lake**, which are first-come, first-served. Xanterra runs five more campgrounds (listed here; reservations accepted, $20 per night), all with cold-water bathrooms, flush toilets and drinking water. RV sites with hookups are available at Fishing Bridge.

Xanterra-run cabins, hotels and lodges are spread around the park and are open from May or June to October. Mammoth Hot Springs Hotel and Old Faithful Snow Lodge are the exceptions; these are also open mid-December through March. All places are nonsmoking and none have air con, TV or internet connections.

Bridge Bay Campground CAMPGROUND $
(Lake Country) Near the west shore of Yellowstone Lake, popular with boaters, and with 425 sites.

Canyon Campground CAMPGROUND $
(Canyon Country) Centrally located, with pay showers and coin laundry nearby. There are 250 sites.

Fishing Bridge RV Park CAMPGROUND $
(Lake Country) Full hook-ups for hard-shell RVs only ($37). Pay showers and coin laundry. There are 325 sites.

Grant Village Campground CAMPGROUND $
(Lake Country) On Yellowstone Lake's southwest shore, it has 400 sites. Pay showers and coin laundry nearby.

Madison Campground CAMPGROUND $
(Geyser Country) The closest campground to Old Faithful, with 250 sites.

Roosevelt Lodge Cabins CABIN $
(Roosevelt Country; cabins $65-110) These cabins are good for families. With a cowboy vibe, the place offers nightly 'Old West dinner cookouts,' during which guests travel by horse or wagon to a large meadow 3 miles from the lodge for open-air buffets (book in advance).

Lake Lodge Cabins CABIN $$
(Lake Country; cabins $69-179) The main lodge boasts a large porch with lakeside mountain views and a cozy great room with two fireplaces. Choose from rustic 1920s wooden cabins or more modern motel-style modules.

Old Faithful Snow Lodge HOTEL $$
(Geyser Country; cabins $96-149, r $206) A stylish modern option that combines timber lodge style with modern fittings and park motifs.

TOP CHOICE **Old Faithful Inn** HOTEL $$
(Geyser Country; d without bath $96, with bath $126-236) It's little surprise Old Faithful Inn, built right next to the signature geyser, is the most requested lodging in the park. A national historic landmark, it embodies everything a national park lodge should. The immense timber lobby, with its huge stone fireplaces and sky-high knotted-pine ceilings, is the sort of place you'd imagine Teddy Roosevelt lingering. Rooms come in all price ranges, and many of the most interesting historic rooms share baths (hint: stay two nights, enjoy the atmosphere and get your money's worth). The public areas are alluring enough for cabin fever to not be an option!

Lake Yellowstone Hotel HOTEL $$
(Lake Country; cabins $130, r $149-223) Oozing grand 1920s Western ambience, this romantic, historic hotel is a classy option. It has Yellowstone's most divine lounge, which was made for daydreaming; it offers big picture windows with lake views, lots of natural light and a live string quartet serenading in the background. Rooms are well appointed, cabins more rustic.

Also recommended:

Old Faithful Lodge Cabins CABIN $
(Geyser Country; cabins 67-110) Views of Old Faithful; simple, rustic cabins.

Canyon Lodge & Cabins CABIN $$
(Canyon Country; cabins $96-179, r $170) Clean and tidy in a central locale.

Mammoth Hot Springs Hotel & Cabins HOTEL $$
(Mammoth Country; cabins $81-112, r with/without bath $87/120) Wide variety of sleeping options; elk are often seen grazing on the front lawn.

Grant Village HOTEL $$
(Lake Country; r $152) Near the southern edge of the park, it offers comfortable but dull motel-style rooms. Two nearby restaurants have fabulous lake views.

Eating

Snack bars, delis, burger counters and grocery stores are scattered around the park. In addition, most of the lodges offer breakfast buffets, salad bars, and lunch and dinner in formal dining rooms. Food, while not always exceptional, is quite good considering how many people the chef is cooking for, and not too overpriced for the exceptional views.

Old Faithful Inn AMERICAN $$
(☎307-545-4999; dinner mains $13-22) The buffets here will maximize your time spent geyser gazing but the à la carte options are more innovative, serving elk burgers, bison ravioli and the ever-popular pork osso bucco. Reservations recommended.

TOP CHOICE **Lake Yellowstone Hotel** AMERICAN $$
(☎307-344-7311; mains $13-33) Make sure you save your one unwrinkled outfit to dine in style at the dining room of the Lake Yellowstone Hotel, the best in the park. Lunch options include Idaho trout, salads and bison, antelope and elk sliders. Dinner consists of heavier fare and reservations are highly recommended.

Information

The park is technically open year-round, but most roads close during winter. Park entrance permits (hiker/vehicle $12/25) are valid for seven days for entry into both Yellowstone and Grand Teton National Parks. Summer-only visitor centers are evenly spaced every 20 to 30 miles along Grand Loop Rd.

Albright Visitors Center (☎307-344-2263; www.nps.gov/yell; Mammoth; ⊙8am-7pm Jun-Sep, 9am-5pm Oct-May) Serves as park headquarters. The park website is a fantastic resource.

Getting There & Away

The closest year-round airports are: Yellowstone Regional Airport (COD) in Cody (52 miles); Jackson Hole Airport (JAC) in Jackson (56 miles); Gallatin Field Airport (BZN) in Bozeman, MT (65 miles); and Idaho Falls Regional Airport (IDA) in Idaho Falls, ID (107 miles). The airport (WYS) in West Yellowstone, MT, is usually open June to September. It's often more affordable to fly into Billings, MT (170 miles), Salt Lake City, UT (390 miles) or Denver, CO (563 miles), then rent a car.

There is no public transportation to or within Yellowstone National Park.

Grand Teton National Park

With its jagged, rocky peaks, cool alpine lakes and fragrant forests, the Tetons rank among the finest scenery in America. Directly south of Yellowstone, Grand Teton National Park has 12 glacier-carved summits, which frame the singular Grand Teton (13,770ft). For mountain enthusiasts, this sublime and crazy terrain is thrilling. Less crowded than Yellowstone, the Tetons also have plenty of tranquility, along with wildlife such as bear, moose, grouse and marmot.

The park has two entrance stations: Moose (south), on Teton Park Rd west of Moose Junction; and Moran (east), on US 89/191/287 north of Moran Junction. The park is open year-round, although some roads and entrances close from around November to May 1, including part of Moose-Wilson Rd, restricting access to the park from Teton Village.

Activities

First up: there are 200 miles of **hiking trails** here, and you can't really go wrong with any of them. So pick up a map at the visitor center, and take a hike. A free backcountry-use permit, also available at visitor centers, is required for overnight trips. If that's not your style, fine. Climb a mountain instead. The Tetons are known for excellent short-route **rock climbs** as well as classic longer routes to summits like Grant Teton, Mt Moran and Mt Owen.

Fishing is another draw. Several species of whitefish and cutthroat, lake and brown trout thrive in local rivers and lakes. Get a license at the Moose Village store, Signal Mountain Lodge or Colter Bay Marina.

Cross-country skiing and **snowshoeing** are the best ways to take advantage of park winters. Pick up a brochure detailing routes at Craig Thomas Discovery & Visitor Center.

Jenny Lake Ranger Station ROCK CLIMBING
(☎307-739-3343; ⊙8am-6pm Jun-Aug) For climbing information.

Exum Mountain Guides ROCK CLIMBING
(☎307-733-2297; www.exumguides.com).For instruction and guided climbs.

Sleeping

Three different concessionaires run the park's six campgrounds. Demand is high from early July to Labor Day. Most campgrounds fill by 11am (Jenny Lake fills much earlier; Gros Ventre rarely fills up). Colter Bay and Jenny Lake have tent-only sites reserved for backpackers and cyclists.

Flagg Ranch Resorts CAMPGROUND $
(www.flaggranch.com; 2-person campsites $35) Accepts online reservations for Flagg Ranch campground, and also has cabins. Forever Resorts manages Signal Mountain and Lizard Creek campgrounds.

Grand Teton Lodge Company CAMPGROUND, LODGE $
(☎307-543-3111; www.gtlc.com; campsites $20) Runs most of the park's private lodges, cabins and the campgrounds of Colter Bay, Jenny Lake and Gros Ventre. Call for last-minute cancellations, though it's best to reserve ahead, as nearly everything is completely booked by early June. Each lodge has an activity desk.

TOP CHOICE **Jenny Lake Lodge** LODGE $$$
(☎307-543-3100; www.gtlc.com; cabins incl half board $620; ⊙Jun-Sep) Worn timbers, down comforters and colorful quilts imbue this elegant lodging off Teton Park Rd with a cozy atmosphere. The log cabins sport a deck but no TVs or radios (phones on request). Rainy days are for hunkering down at the fireplace in the main lodge with a game or book from the stacks. It doesn't come cheap, but includes breakfast, a five-course dinner, bicycle use and guided horseback riding.

Jackson Lake Lodge LODGE $$$
(☎307-543-3100; www.gtlc.com; r & cabins $229-320; ⊙Jun-Sep;) With soft sheets, meandering trails for long walks and enormous picture windows framing the luminous peaks, this lodge is the perfect place to woo that special someone. Yet the 348 cinder-block cottages are generally overpriced. Has a heated pool and pets are OK.

Spur Ranch Log Cabins CABIN **$$**
(☎307-733-2522; www.dornans.com; cabins $175-250; ⊙year-round) Gravel paths running through a broad wildflower meadow link these tranquil duplex cabins on the Snake River in Moose. Lodgepole pine furniture, Western styling and down bedding create a homey feel, but the views are what make it.

Climbers' Ranch CABIN **$**
(☎307-733-7271; www.americanalpineclub.org; Teton Park Rd; dm $22; ⊙Jun-Sep) Started as a refuge for serious climbers, this group of rustic log cabins run by the American Alpine Club is now available to hikers who want to take advantage of the spectacular in-park location. There is a bathhouse with showers and sheltered cook station with locking bins for coolers. Bring your own sleeping bag and pad (the bunks are bare, but it's still a great deal).

Signal Mountain Lodge LODGE **$$**
(☎307-543-2831; www.signalmtnlodge.com; r $175-228, cabins $132-198; campsites $21; ⊙May–mid-Oct) This spectacularly located place at the edge of Jackson Lake offers cozy, well-appointed cabins and rather posh rooms with stunning lake and mountain views.

Colter Bay Village CABIN **$**
(☎307-543-3100; www.gtlc.com; tent cabins $52, cabins with bath $119-165, without bath $65; ⊙Jun-Sep) Half a mile west of Colter Bay Junction, with two types of accommodations. Tent cabins (June to early September) are very basic structures with bare bunks and separate bathrooms. At these prices, you're better off camping. The log cabins, some original, are much more comfortable and a better deal; they're available late May to late September.

Eating

Colter Bay Village, Jackson Lake Lodge, Signal Mountain and Moose Junction have several reasonably priced cafes for breakfast and fast meals.

Mural Room MODERN AMERICAN **$$$**
(☎307-543-1911; Jackson Lake Lodge; mains $15-40; ⊙7am-9pm) With stirring views of the Tetons, gourmet selections include game dishes and imaginative creations like trout wrapped in sushi rice with sesame seeds. Breakfasts are very good; dinner reservations are recommended.

Peaks AMERICAN **$$$**
(☎307-543-2831; meals $18-28) Dine on selections of cheese and fruit, local free-range beef and organic polenta cakes. Small plates, like wild game sliders, are also available. While the indoor ambience is rather drab, the patio seating, starring sunsets over Jackson Lake and top-notch huckleberry margaritas, gets snapped up early.

Jenny Lake Lodge Dining Room MODERN AMERICAN **$$$**
(☎307-543-3352; breakfast dishes $19, lunch mains $10-30, dinner mains $60; ⊙7am-9pm) Leave your hiking boots in the car: men must wear jackets at the park's premier restaurant. Pasta, an excellent wine list and strip steak in soy glaze are some of the offerings. While we love the idea of a five-course meal in the wilderness, some diners report that the service and food need more attention. Dinner reservations are required.

Pioneer Grill DINER **$$**
(☎307-543-1911; Jackson Lake Lodge; mains $7-15; ⊙6am-10:30pm; 👪) A casual classic with leatherette stools lined up in a maze, the Pioneer serves up wraps, burgers and salads. Kids adore the hot fudge sundaes. A takeout window serves boxed lunches (order a day ahead) and room-service pizza for pooped hikers (5pm to 9pm).

Information

Park permits (hiker/vehicle $12/25) are valid for seven days for entry into both Yellowstone and Grand Teton National Parks. It's easy to stay in one park and explore the other in the same day.

Craig Thomas Discovery & Visitor Center (☎307-739-3399, backcountry permits 307-739-3309; Teton Park Rd; ⊙8am-7pm Jun-Aug, 8am-5pm rest of year), located in Moose.

Laurance S Rockefeller Preserve Center (☎307-739-3654; Moose-Wilson Rd; ⊙8am-6pm Jun-Aug, 9am-5pm rest of year) This recent addition gives information about the new and highly recommended Rockefeller Preserve, a less crowded option for hiking, located 4 miles south of Moose.

Park Headquarters (☎307-739-3600; www.nps.gov/grte; ⊙8am-7pm Jun-Aug, 8am-5pm rest of year) Shares a building with the Craig Thomas center.

Jackson

Technically this is Wyoming, but you'll have a hard time believing it. With a median age of 32, this Western town has evolved into a mecca for mountain lovers, hard-core climbers and skiers, easily recognizable as sunburned baristas.

The upswing of being posh and popular? Jackson is abuzz with life: trails and outdoor opportunities abound. Fresh sushi is flown in daily and generous purse-strings support a vigorous cultural life. Skip the souvenirs and remember why you came to Jackson in the first place: to visit its glorious backyard, Grand Teton National Park.

Sights

Downtown Jackson has a handful of historic buildings.

National Museum of Wildlife Art MUSEUM
(☎307-733-5771; www.wildlifeart.org; 2820 Rungius Rd; adult $10, child free with adult; ⏲9am-5pm) If you visit one area museum, make it this one. Major works by Bierstadt, Rungius, Remington and Russell that will make your skin prickle. The discovery gallery has a kids' studio for drawing and print rubbing that adults plainly envy. Check the website for summer film series and art-class schedules.

Center for the Arts ARTS CENTER
(☎307-734-8956; www.jhcenterforthearts.org; 240 S Glenwood S) One-stop shopping for culture, attracting big-name concert acts and featuring theater performances, classes, art exhibits and events. Check the calendar of events online.

FREE **National Elk Refuge** WILDLIFE RESERVE
(☎307-733-9212; www.nationalelkrefuge.fws.gov; Hwy 89; ⏲8am-5pm Sep-May, 8am-7pm Jun-Aug) Protects thousands of migrating wapiti from November to March. A 45-minute **horse-drawn sleigh ride** (adult/child $18/14; ⏲10am-4pm mid-Dec–Mar) is a highlight of a winter visit.

FREE **Town Square Shoot-out** WILD WEST SHOW
(⏲6.15pm Mon-Sat summer; 👪) In summer this hokey tourist draw takes place at 6:15pm Monday to Saturday.

Activities

Jackson Hole Mountain Resort SNOW SPORTS
(☎307-733-2292; www.jacksonhole.com; lift ticket adult/child from $59/32) One of the country's top ski destinations, Jackson Hole Mountain Resort, known as 'the Village,' boasts the USA's greatest continuous vertical rise – from the 6311ft base at Teton Village to the 10,450ft summit of Rendezvous Mountain. The terrain is mostly advanced, boasting lots of fluffy powder and rocky ledges made for jumping. When the snow melts, the resort runs a plethora of summertime activities; check the website for details.

Courses

TOP CHOICE **Teton Science Schools** ECOLOGY
(☎307-733-1313; www.tetonscience.org) No one beats this nonprofit for fun experiential education, with programs ranging from GPS scavenger hunts to ecology expeditions. Make inquiries through

Sleeping

Jackson has plenty of lodging options, both in town and around the ski hill. Reservations are essential in summer and winter.

TOP CHOICE **Alpine House** B&B $$$
(☎307-739-1570; www.alpinehouse.com; 285 N Glenwood St; d incl breakfast $185-225; @) Two former Olympic skiers have infused this downtown home with sunny Scandinavian style and personal touches like great service and a cozy mountaineering library. Amenities include plush robes, down comforters, a shared Finnish sauna and an outdoor Jacuzzi. Save your appetite for the creative breakfast options such as poached eggs over ricotta, with asparagus or multigrain French toast.

Buckrail Lodge MOTEL $
(☎307-733-2079; www.buckraillodge.com; 110 E Karnes Ave; r from $91; 📶❄) Spacious and charming log-cabin-style rooms, this steal is centrally located, with ample grounds and an outdoor Jacuzzi.

Hostel HOSTEL $
(☎307-733-3415; www.thehostel.us; 3315 Village Dr, Teton Village; dm/d $32/79; ⏲closed fall & spring shoulder seasons; @👪) Teton Village's only budget option, this old ski lodge offers private doubles and bunk-bed rooms with renovated showers for up to four. The spacious lounge with fireplace is ideal for movies or Scrabble tournaments and there's a playroom for tots. Guests can use a microwave and outdoor grill, coin laundry and a ski-waxing area.

Sundance Inn MOTEL $$
(☎307-733-3444, 888-478-6326; www.sundance-innjackson.com; 135 W Broadway; d $139; ❄) Simply a well-run motel, the Sundance distinguishes itself with good service and tidy rooms. Perks include an outdoor Jacuzzi and continental breakfast.

Golden Eagle Motor Inn MOTEL $$
(☎307-733-2042; 325 E Broadway; r $148;) Super-friendly and just far enough out of the fray, this refurbished motel with friendly hosts is a reliable choice in the center.

Eating & Drinking

Jackson is home to Wyoming's most sophisticated food. Many of our favorite restaurants here double as bars. For a deal, look for happy hour offers.

Pica's Mexican Taqueria MEXICAN $$
(1160 Alpine Lane; mains $7-15; ⏱11:30am-9pm Mon-Fri, 11am-4pm Sat & Sun) Cheap and supremely satisfying, with Baja tacos wrapped in homemade corn tortillas or *cochinita pibil* (chili-marinated pork), served with Mexican sodas. Locals love this place; it's the best value around.

Blue Lion FUSION $$$
(☎307-733-3912; 160 N Millward St; mains $15-34; ⏱from 6pm) In a precious cornflower-blue house, the Blue Lion offers outdoor dining under grand old trees on the deck. It creatively combines Thai and French influences in dishes such as beef tenderloin *au bleu* and green curry prawns.

Snake River Grill MODERN AMERICAN $$$
(☎307-733-0557; 84 E Broadway; mains $21-52 ⏱from 5:30pm) With a roaring stone fireplace and snappy white linens, this grill creates notable American haute cuisine. Grilled elk chops and wild mushroom pasta show a tendency toward the earthy. Sample the extensive wine list and the homemade ice cream or soufflé for dessert.

Bubba's Bar-B-Que BARBECUE $$
(☎307-733-2288; 100 Flat Creek Dr; mains $5-15; ⏱7am-10pm) Get the biggest, fluffiest breakfast biscuits for miles at this friendly and energetic bring-your-own-bottle (BYOB) eatery. Later on, it's got a decent salad bar, and serves up a ranch of ribs and racks.

Bunnery Bakery & Restaurant CAFE $
(☎307-733-5474; 130 N Cache St; mains $10; ⏱7am-3pm & 5-9pm summer) Lunch and breakfast at this buzzing cafe offer an assortment of hearty fare, including all-day eggs and great vegetarian options. The dessert case tempts with mammoth chocolate-cake slices, pecan pie and caramel cheesecake.

TOP CHOICE **Stagecoach Bar** BAR
(☎307-733-4407; 5755 W Hwy 22, Wilson) Jackson has no better place to shake your booty. 'Mon-day' means reggae, Thursday is disco night and every Sunday the house band croons country-and-western favorites until 10pm. Worth the short drive to Wilson (just past the Teton Village turnoff).

Snake River Brewing Co BREWPUB $$
(☎307-739-2337; 265 S Millward St; ⏱11:30am-midnight) With an arsenal of 22 microbrews made on the spot, some award-winning, it's no wonder that this is a favorite rendezvous spot. Food includes wood-fired pizzas and pasta (mains $6 to $15). Happy hour is from 4pm to 6pm.

IF YOU HAVE A FEW MORE DAYS

Wyoming is full of great places to get lost, sadly too many for us to elaborate on in this guide, but we'll prime you with a taster.

With vast grassy meadows, seas of wildflowers and peaceful conifer forests, the **Bighorn Mountains** in north-central Wyoming are truly awe-inspiring. Factor in gushing waterfalls and abundant wildlife and you've got a stupendous natural playground with hundreds of miles of marked trails.

Rising a dramatic 1267ft above the Belle Fourche River, the nearly vertical monolith of **Devil's Tower National Monument** is an awesome site. Known as Bears Lodge by some of the 20-plus Native American tribes who consider it sacred, it's a must-see if you are traveling between the Black Hills (on the Wyoming–South Dakota border) and the Tetons or Yellowstone.

West of Laramie, the lofty national forest stretching across **Medicine Bow Mountains** and **Snowy Range** is a wild and rugged place, perfect for multi-night hiking and camping trips.

Nestled in the shadow of the Bighorn Mountains, **Sheridan** boasts century-old buildings once home to Wyoming cattle barons. It's popular with adventure fanatics who come to play in the Bighorns.

Million Dollar Cowboy Bar BAR
(25 N Cache Dr) Most can't wait to plunk their hind quarters on a saddle stool in this dark chop house, an obligatory stop on the Western tour. Weekends get lively when the dance floor sparks up and karaoke drones.

Information

Jackson Hole Wyoming (www.jacksonholenet.com) A good website for information on the area.

Valley Bookstore (125 N Cache St) Sells regional maps.

Visitor center (307-733-3316; www.jacksonholechamber.com; 532 N Cache Dr; 9am-5pm)

Getting There & Around

Jackson Hole Airport (JAC; 307-733-7682) is 7 miles north of Jackson off US 26/89/189/191 within Grand Teton National Park. Daily flights serve Denver, Salt Lake City, Dallas and Houston, while weekend flights connect Jackson with Chicago.

Alltrans' Jackson Hole Express (307-733-1719; www.jacksonholebus.com) buses depart at 6:30am daily from Jackson's Exxon Station (cnr Hwy 89 S and S Park Loop Rd) for Salt Lake City (around $65, 5½ hours).

MONTANA

Montana should come with a note from the Surgeon General 'Warning: Montana is addictive, may cause mild euphoria and a slowing of the pulse.' Maybe it's the sky, which seems bigger and bluer here than anywhere else. Maybe it's the air, intoxicatingly crisp, fresh and scented with pine. Maybe it's the way the mountains melt into undulating ranchlands, or the sight of a shaggy grizzly sipping from an ice-blue glacier lake.

Maybe it's the independent frontier spirit, wild and free and oh-so-wonderfully American, that earned Montana its 'live and let live' state motto. Whatever the cause, Montana's the kind of place that remains with you long after you've left its beautiful spaces behind. And some of us never even go home.

Information

Montana Fish, Wildlife & Parks (406-444-2535; http://fwp.state.mt.us) Camping in Montana's 24 state parks costs around $15/23 per night for residents/nonresidents, while RV hookup sites (where available) cost an additional $5. Make reservations at 1-855-922-6768 or http://montanastateparks.reserveamerica.com.

MONTANA FACTS

» **Nickname** Treasure State, Big Sky Country

» **Population** 989,415

» **Area** 145,552 sq miles

» **Capital city** Helena (population 28,000)

» **Other cities** Billings (population 105,000), Missoula (67,000), Bozeman (37,000)

» **Sales tax** Montana has no state sales tax

» **Birthplace of** Hollywood movie star Gary Cooper (1901–61), legendary motorcycle daredevil Evel Knievel (1938–2007)

» **Home of** Crow, Blackfeet and Salish Native Americans

» **Politics** Republican ranchers and oilmen generally edge out the Democratic students and progressives of left-leaning Bozeman and Missoula

» **Famous for** big sky, fly-fishing, cowboys, grizzly bears

» **Random fact** Some Montana highways didn't have a set speed limit until the 1990s!

» **Driving distances** Bozeman to Denver 695 miles, Missoula to Whitefish 136 miles

Montana Road Conditions (800-226-7623, within Montana 511; www.mdt.mt.gov/travinfo)

Travel Montana (800-847-4868; www.visitmt.com)

Bozeman

In a gorgeous locale, surrounded by rolling green hills and pine forests and framed by snowcapped peaks, dog-friendly Bozeman is the coolest town in Montana (regardless of what Missoulans might tell you...). The historic Main St district is retro cowboy funky containing low brick buildings that house trendy boutiques, Bohemian wine bars and bustling sidewalk cafes serving global fare. The location, up against the Bridger and Gallatin mountains, makes it also one of the very best outdoor towns in the West.

Sights & Activities

Museum of the Rockies MUSEUM
(406-994-2251; www.museumoftherockies.org; 600 W Kagy Blvd; adult/child $10/7; 8am-8pm;) Montana State University's museum is the most entertaining in Montana and shouldn't be missed, with stellar dinosaur exhibits, early Native American art and laser planetarium shows.

Bridger Bowl Ski Area SNOW SPORTS
(406-587-2111; www.bridgerbowl.com; 15795 Bridger Canyon Rd; day lift ticket adult/child under 12yr $47/16; mid-Dec–Mar) Only in Bozeman would you find a nonprofit ski resort. But this excellent community-owned facility, 16 miles north of Bozeman, is just that. It's known for its fluffy, light powder and unbeatable prices – especially for children under 12.

Sleeping

The full gamut of chain motels lies north of downtown on 7th Ave, near I-90. There are more budget motels east of downtown on Main St, with rooms starting at around $50, depending on the season.

Bear Canyon Campground CAMPGROUND $
(800-438-1575; www.bearcanyoncampground.com; tent sites $20, RV sites $28-33; May–mid-Oct;) Three miles east of Bozeman off I-90 exit 313, Bear Canyon Campground is on top of a hill with great views of the surrounding valley. There's even a pool.

Bozeman Backpackers Hostel HOSTEL $
(406-586-4659; www.bozemanbackpackershostel.com; 405 W Olive St; dm/d $24/50) In a beautiful yellow-painted Victorian house built in 1890 (trivia: it was once home to actor Gary Cooper when he attended school in town), this Aussie-run independent hostel's casual approach means a relaxed vibe, friendly folk and no lockout. It's *the* place to rendezvous with active globe-stompers.

Lewis & Clark Motel MOTEL $$
(800-332-7666; www.lewisandclarkmotel.net; 824 W Main St; r $109-119;) For a drop of Vegas in your Montana, stay at this flashy, locally owned motel. The large rooms have floor-to-ceiling front windows and the piped 1950s music adds to the retro Rat Pack vibe.

Eating & Drinking

As a college town, Bozeman has no shortage of student-oriented cheap eats and enough watering holes to quench a college football team's thirst. Nearly everything is located on Main St.

La Tinga MEXICAN $
(12 E Main St; mains $1.50-7; 9am-2pm) Simple, cheap and authentic, La Tinga is no-frills dining at its tastiest. The tiny order-at-the-counter taco joint makes a delicious version of the Mexican pork dish it is named after, and lots of freshly made tacos starting at just $1.50, or choose the daily lunch combo deal for less than $7.

Community Co-Op SUPERMARKET $
(www.bozo.coop; 908 W Main; mains $5-10;) This beloved local is the best place to stock up on organic and bulk foods, as well as hot meals, salads and soups to eat in or take away. The W Main branch has a great organic coffeehouse upstairs.

John Bozeman's Bistro AMERICAN $$$
(406-587-4100; www.johnbozemansbistro.com; 125 W Main St; mains $14-30; closed Sun & Mon) Bozeman's best restaurant offers Thai, Creole and pan-Asian slants on the cowboy dinner steak, plus starters like lobster chowder and a weekly 'superfood' special, featuring especially nutritious seasonal vegetarian fare.

Plonk WINE BAR $$
(www.plonkwine.com; 29 E Main St; dinner mains $13-26; 11:30am-midnight) Where to go for a drawn-out three-martini, gossipy lunch? Plonk serves a wide-ranging menu from light snacks to full meals, mostly made from local organic products. In summer the entire front opens up and cool breezes enter the long building, which also has a shotgun bar and pressed-tin ceilings.

Molly Brown BAR
(www.mollybrownbozeman.com; 703 W Babcock) Popular with local MSU students, this noisy dive bar offers 20 beers on tap and eight pool tables for getting your game on.

Zebra Cocktail Lounge LOUNGE
(406-585-8851; 15 N Rouse St) Inside the Bozeman Hotel, this place is the epicenter of the local live music scene, strong on club and hip-hop.

Information

Visitor center (406-586-5421; www.bozemanchamber.com; 1003 N 7th Ave; 8am-5pm Mon-Fri) Can provide information on lodging and attractions in the area.

DON'T MISS

FLY-FISHING IN BIG SKY

Ever since Robert Redford and Brad Pitt made it look sexy in the 1992 classic, *A River Runs Through It*, Montana has been closely tied to fly-fishing cool. Whether you are just learning or a world-class trout wrangler, the wide, fast rivers are always spectacularly beautiful and filled with fish. Movie buffs: although the film – and book it is based on – is set in Missoula and the nearby Blackfoot River, the movie was actually shot around Livingston and the Yellowstone and Gallatin Rivers, which is the area we focus on here.

For DIY trout fishing, the Gallatin River, 8 miles southwest of Bozeman along Hwy 191, has the most accessible, consistent angling spots, closely followed by the beautiful Yellowstone River, 25 miles east of Bozeman in the Paradise Valley.

For the scoop on the difference between rainbow, brown and cutthroat trout – as well as flies, rods and a Montana fishing license – visit the **Bozeman Angler** (406-587-9111; www.bozemanangler.com; 23 E Main St, Bozeman; 9:30am-5:30pm Mon-Sat, 10am-3pm Sun). Owned by a local couple for over 15 years, the downtown shop runs a great introduction-to-fly-fishing class ($125 per person, casting lessons $40 per hour) on the second Saturday of the month between May and September. The day-long adventure teaches you the casting, lures and fish basics, feeds you, then sets you loose on the river (with a guide of course) to practice your newly minted skills. If you know what you're doing, but don't know where the best fishing holes are, contact the shop about a guided trip, which they'll customize to your experience and interest.

Getting There & Away

Gallatin Field Airport (BZN; 406-388-8321; www.bozemanairport.com) is 8 miles northwest of downtown. **Karst Stage** (406-556-3540; www.karststage.com) runs buses daily, December to April, from the airport to Big Sky ($51, one hour) and West Yellowstone (around $63.50, two hours); summer service is by reservation only.

Rimrock Stages buses depart from the **bus depot** (406-587-3110; www.rimrocktrailways.com; 1205 E Main St), half a mile from downtown, and service all Montana towns along I-90.

Gallatin & Paradise Valleys

Outdoor enthusiasts could explore the expansive beauty around the Gallatin and Paradise Valleys for days. **Big Sky Resort** (800-548-4486; www.bigskyresort.com; lift ticket adult $81), with multiple mountains, 400in of annual powder and Montana's longest vertical drop (4350ft), is one of the nation's premier downhill and cross-country ski destinations, especially now it has merged with neighboring Moonlight Basin. Lift lines are the shortest in the Rockies, and if you are traveling with kids then Big Sky is too good a deal to pass up – children under 10 ski free, while even your teenager saves $20 off the adult ticket price. In summer it offers gondola-served hiking and mountain-biking.

For backpacking and backcountry skiing, head to the Spanish Peaks section of the **Lee Metcalf Wilderness**. It covers 389 sq miles of Gallatin and Beaverhead National Forest land west of US 191. Numerous scenic USFS campgrounds snuggle up to the Gallatin Range on the east side of US 191.

Twenty miles south of Livingston, off US 89 en route to Yellowstone, unpretentious **Chico Hot Springs** (406-333-4933; www.chicohotsprings.com; r with bath $83-215, without bath $55-69; 8am-11pm;) has garnered quite a following in the last few years, even attracting celebrity residents from Hollywood. Some come to soak in the swimming-pool-sized open-air hot pools (admission for nonguests $6.50), others come for the lively bar hosting swinging country-and-western dance bands on weekends. The on-site restaurant (mains $20 to $30) is known for fine steak and seafood. It's not called Paradise for nothing.

Absaroka Beartooth Wilderness

The fabulous, vista-packed Absaroka Beartooth Wilderness covers more than 943,377 acres and is perfect for a solitary adventure. Thick forests, jagged peaks and marvelous, empty stretches of alpine tundra are all found in this wilderness, saddled between Paradise Valley in the west and Yellowstone National Park in the south. The thickly forested Absaroka Range dominates the area's west half and is most easily reached from Paradise Valley or the Boulder River Corridor. The Beartooth Range's high plateau and alpine lakes are best reached from the Beartooth Hwy south of Red Lodge. Because of its proximity to Yellowstone, the Beartooth portion gets two-thirds of the area's traffic.

A picturesque old mining town with fun bars and restaurants and a good range of places to stay, **Red Lodge** offers great day hikes, backpacking and, in winter, skiing right near town. The **Red Lodge Visitor Center** (406-446-1718; www.redlodge.com; 601 N Broadway Ave; 8am-6pm Mon-Fri, 9am-5pm Sat & Sun) has information on accommodations.

Billings

It's hard to believe laid-back little Billings is Montana's largest city. The friendly oil and ranching center is not a must-see but makes for a decent overnight pit stop. The historic downtown is hardly cosmopolitan, but emits a certain endearing charm.

Road-weary travelers will appreciate the convenient **Billings Hotel & Convention Center** (800-537-7286; www.billingshotel.net; 1223 Mullowney Lane; r from $103;). It has comfortable rooms, restaurant and bar on the premises and best of all – especially if you're road-tripping with the little ones – two huge waterslides at the indoor pool!

SCENIC DRIVE: THE ROOF OF THE ROCKIES

The awesome **Beartooth Highway** (US 212; www.beartoothhighway.com; Jun–mid-Oct) connects Red Lodge to Cooke City and Yellowstone's north entrance by an incredible 68-mile journey that passes at eye-level with 11,000ft peaks and wildflower-sprinkled alpine tundra. It's been called both American's most scenic drive and the premier motorcycle ride in the nation. We call it the most scenic route into Yellowstone Park. There are a dozen USFS campgrounds (reservations for some accepted at www.recreation.gov) along the highway, four of them within 12 miles of Red Lodge.

Fuel up at the chipper Downtown **McCormick Cafe** (2419 Montana Ave; meals $5-8; 7am-3pm Mon-Fri, 8am-3pm Sat, 8am-1pm Sun;), where you can get great breakfasts, lunchtime sandwiches, salads and crepes, all served on the hidden back patio.

The classiest dinner option in town is **Walkers Grill** (www.walkersgrill.com; 2700 1st Ave N; tapas $8-14, mains $17-33; 5-10pm), offering grills and fine tapas at the bar, with sophisticated Western decor.

Logan International Airport (BIL; www.flybillings.com), 2 miles north of downtown, has direct flights to Salt Lake City, Denver, Minneapolis, Seattle, Phoenix and destinations within Montana. The **bus depot** (406-245-5116; 2502 1st Ave N; 24hr) has services to Bozeman ($23, three hours) and Missoula ($48, eight hours).

Helena

With one foot in cowboy legend (Gary Cooper was born here) and the other in the more hip, less stereotypical lotus land of present-day Montana, diminutive Helena is one of the nation's smallest state capitals (population 28,000), a place where white-collared politicians draft legislation, while white-knuckle sportspeople disappear off into the Rocky Mountain foothills to indulge in that other Montana passion – outdoor adventure.

Back in town, half hidden among the Gore-tex and outdoor outfitters, Helena springs some subtler surprises: a Gallic-inspired neo-Gothic cathedral for one; an arty-farty pedestrian-only shopping quarter for another. Bring your bike helmet by all means; just don't forget to pack your cultural beret as well.

Sights & Activities

Many of Helena's sites are free, including the elegant old buildings along Last Chance Gulch (Helena's pedestrian shopping district), and the sights covered here.

State Capitol LANDMARK
(cnr Montana Ave & 6th St; 8am-6pm Mon-Fri) This grand neoclassical building was completed in 1902 and is known for its beacon-like dome that has been richly decorated with gold-rimmed paintings inside.

Cathedral of St Helena CHURCH
(530 N Ewing St) Rising like an apparition from old Europe over the town is this neo-Gothic

WORTH A TRIP

CUSTER'S LAST STAND

The best detour from Billings is to the **Little Bighorn Battlefield National Monument** (☎406-638-3224; www.nps.gov/libi; admission per car $10; ⏲8am-9pm), 65 miles outside town in the arid plains of the Crow (Apsaalooke) Indian Reservation. Home to one of the USA's best-known Native American battlefields, this is where General George Custer made his famous 'last stand.'

Custer, and 272 soldiers, messed one too many times with Native Americans (including Crazy Horse of the Lakota Sioux), who overwhelmed the force in a (frequently painted) massacre. A visitor center tells the tale or, better, take one of the five daily tours with a Crow guide through **Apsalooke Tours** (☎406-638-3114). The entrance is a mile east of I-90 on US 212. If you're here for the last weekend of June, the **Custer's Last Stand Reenactment** (www.custerslaststand.org; adult/child $20/8) is an annual hoot, 6 miles west of Hardin.

cathedral completed in 1914. Highlights include the baptistry, organ and intricate stained-glass windows.

Holter Museum of Art GALLERY
(www.holtermuseum.org; 12 E Lawrence St; ⏲10am-5.30pm Tue-Sat, noon-4pm Sun) Exhibits modern pieces by Montana artists.

Mt Helena City Park OUTDOORS
Nine hiking and mountain-biking trails wind through Mt Helena City Park, including one that takes you to the 5460ft-high summit of Mt Helena.

Sleeping & Eating

East of downtown near I-15 is a predictable string of chain motels. Most rooms are $60 to $85, and come with free continental breakfast, pool and Jacuzzi.

Sanders B&B **$$**
(☎406-442-3309; www.sandersbb.com; 328 N Ewing St; r incl breakfast $130-140; ❄) A historic B&B with seven elegant guest rooms, a wonderful old parlor and a breezy front porch. Each bedroom is unique and thoughtfully decorated.

Fire Tower Coffee House CAFE, BREAKFAST **$**
(www.firetowercoffee.com; 422 Last Chance Gulch; breakfast $4-7; ⏲6.30am-6pm Mon-Thu till 10pm Fri, 8am-5pm Sat, 8am-2pm Sun; 📶) is where to go for coffee, light meals and live music on Friday evening. Breakfast features a couple of types of egg-based burritos, while lunch has a wholesome sandwich selection.

Information

Helena Visitor Center (www.helenachamber.com; 225 Cruse Ave; ⏲8am-5pm Mon-Fri)

Getting There & Around

Two miles north of downtown, **Helena Regional Airport** (HNL; www.helenaairport.com) operates flights to most other airports in Montana, as well as to Salt Lake City, Seattle and Minneapolis. Rimrock Trailways leave from Helena's **Transit Center** (630 N Last Chance Gulch), where at least daily buses go to Missoula ($25, 2¼ hours), Billings ($42, 4¾ hours) and Bozeman ($22, two hours).

Missoula

Outsiders in Missoula usually spend the first 30 minutes wondering where they took a wrong turn; Austin, Texas? Portland, Oregon? Canada, perhaps? The confusion is understandable given the city's lack of standard Montana stereotypes. You'll find few Wild West saloons here and even fewer errant cowboys. Instead, Missoula is a refined university city with ample green space and an abundance of civic pride. Not surprisingly, the metro bounty is contagious. New arrivals have been flocking here for over a decade now, like greedy prospectors to a gold rush-era boomtown. Yet, despite it being one of the fastest growing cities in the US, sensible planning laws mean that Missoula rarely feels clamorous. The small traffic-calmed downtown core broadcasts an interesting array of historic buildings, and bicycles remain a popular method of urban transportation, particularly around the gorgeous university campus.

Sights

Missoula is a great city for walking, especially in the spring and summer, when enough people emerge onto the streets to give it a definable metro personality.

FREE **Smokejumper Visitor Center** MUSEUM
(W Broadway; ⏲10am-4pm Jun-Aug) Located seven miles west of downtown is this

active base for the heroic men and women who parachute into forests to combat raging wildfires. Its visitor center has thought-provoking audio and visual displays that do a great job illustrating the life of the Western firefighter.

FREE **Missoula Art Museum** MUSEUM
(www.missoulaartmuseum.org; 335 North Pattee; ⏲10am-5pm Mon-Thu, 10am-3pm Fri-Sun) All hail a city that encourages free-thinking art and then displays it free of charge in a plush new building that seamlessly grafts a sleek contemporary addition onto a 100-year-old library.

Activities

Clark Fork River Trail System CYCLING, HIKING
Sitting astride the Clark Fork River, Missoula has been bequeathed with an attractive riverside trail system punctuated by numerous parks. **Caras Park** is the most central and active green space with over a dozen annual festivals and a unique hard-carved **carousel.**

Mount Sentinel HIKING
A steep switchback trail from behind the football stadium, forged in the early 1900s by local university students, leads up to a concrete whitewashed 'M' (visible for miles around) on 5158ft Mt Sentinel. Tackle it on a warm summer's evening for glistening views of this much-loved city and its spectacular environs.

Adventure Cycling HQ CYCLING
(www.adventurecycling.org; 150 E Pine St; ⏲8am-5pm Mon-Fri, open Sat Jun-Aug) The HQ for America's premier nonprofit bicycle travel organization is something of a pilgrimage site for cross-continental cyclists, many of whom plan their route to pass through Missoula. They're always afforded a warm welcome and plenty of cycling info.

Fly-fishing FISHING
Montana and fly-fishing go together like ham and eggs. This is where Montana's most famous movie, *A River Runs Through It,* was set (although it was filmed outside Bozeman) and the area around Missoula has some of the best angling in the state. **Rock Creek**, 21 miles east of Missoula, is a designated blue-ribbon trout stream and the area's best year-round fishing spot.

Sleeping

Goldsmith's Bed & Breakfast B&B $$
(☎406-728-1585; www.goldsmithsinn.com; 809 E Front St; r $131-169; ❄@) This delightful B&B, with comfy rooms, is a pebble's toss from the river. The outdoor deck overlooking the water is the perfect place to kick back with a good novel. Rooms are attractive, featuring Victorian furniture. Some come with private sitting rooms, fireplaces and reading nooks.

Mountain Valley Inn MOTEL $
(☎800-249-9174; www.mountainvalleyinnmissoula.com; 420 W Broadway; d from $70; P❄🛜) Offering the best price for a downtown location, the Mountain Valley pulls few surprises, but delivers where it matters – clean rooms and a polite welcome.

Eating

TOP CHOICE **Silk Road** INTERNATIONAL $$
(www.silkroadcatering.com; 515 S Higgins; tapas $5-10; ⏲5-10pm) If Lonely Planet ever opened a restaurant, it would probably look something like this. Spanning global dishes from the Ivory Coast to Piedmont, Silk Road tackles a huge breadth of world cuisine and, more often than not, nails it. Dishes are tapas-sized, allowing you to mix and match. The Piedmontese risotto and cheese plate are highlights.

Liquid Planet CAFE $
(www.liquidplanet.com; 223 N Higgins) Started by a university professor in 2003, Liquid Planet is a coffeehouse that also positions itself as a wine-selling outlet and includes handwritten recommendations for every bottle. It also sells coffee beans (with more detailed explanations), smoothies, teas and pastries. Sustainability is the binding thread behind all its operations.

Depot STEAKHOUSE $$$
(201 W Railroad Ave; mains $13-35; ⏲11:30am-9pm) The Depot has a reputation for consistently good steaks served in upscale cowboy contemporary environs. The beef menu is almost as long as the wine list.

Iron Horse Brewpub BREWPUB $
(www.ironhorsebrewpub.com; 501 N Higgins St; ⏲11:30am-late) Rather swanky for a brewpub, the Iron Horse includes a plush upstairs bar complete with a saltwater aquarium. It's popular with students for its microbrews and traditional American pub grub.

Information

Visitor center (406-532-3250; www.missoulacvb.org; 101 E Main St; 8am-5pm Mon-Fri)

Getting There & Around

Missoula County International Airport (MSO; www.flymissoula.com) is 5 miles west of Missoula on US 12 W.

Greyhound buses serve most of the state and stop at the **depot** (1660 W Broadway), 1 mile west of town. **Rimrock Trailways** (www.rimrock-trailways.com) buses, connecting to Kalispell, Whitefish, Helena and Bozeman, also stop here.

Flathead Lake

The largest natural freshwater lake west of the Mississippi, sitting not an hour's drive from Glacier National Park, completes western Montana's embarrassment of natural lures. The lake's north shore is dominated by the nothing-to-write-home-about city of Kalispell; far more interesting is the southern end embellished by the small polished settlement of **Polson**, which sits on the Flathead Indian Reservation. There's a **visitor center** (www.polsonchamber.com; 418 Main St; 9am-5pm Mon-Fri) and a handful of accommodations here including the lakeside **Kwataqnuk Resort** (406-883-3636; www.kwataqnuk.com; 49708 US 93; r from $130; P), an above-average Best Western with a boat dock, indoor and outdoor pools and a relatively innocuous game room. Directly opposite, the lurid pink **Betty's Diner** (49779 US 93; meals $10-13) delivers salt-of-the-earth American food with customary Montana charm. From town you can walk 2 miles south along a trail starting on 7th Ave E to the mind-boggling **Miracle of America Museum** (www.miracleofamericamuseum.org; 58176 Hwy 93; admission $5; 8am-8pm Jun-Aug, 8:30am-5pm Mon-Sat Sep-May). At turns random and fascinating, it consists of 5 acres cluttered with the leftovers of American history. Wander past weird artifacts including the biggest buffalo (now stuffed) ever recorded in Montana.

Flathead Lake's eastern shore is kissed by the mysterious Mission Mountains while the west is a more pastoral land of apple orchards and grassy hills. To get the best all-round view, hit the water. Soloists can kayak or canoe the conceptual **Flathead Lake Marine Trail**, which links various state parks and **campsites** (406-751-4577; tent sites from $10) around the lake. The nearest site to Polson is Finley Point 5.5 miles away by water.

Lake cruises (www.kwataqnuk.com) are run out of the Kwataqnuk Resort in Polson. The 1½ hour Bay Cruise leaves daily at 10.30am and costs $17. There's also a three-hour excursion ($23) to **Wild Horse Island**, a day-use only state park where wild mares and steeds roam.

Bob Marshall Wilderness Complex

Away from the Pacific coast, America's northwest harbors some of the most lightly populated areas in the lower 48. Point in question: the Bob Marshall Wilderness Complex, an astounding 2344 sq miles of land strafed with 3200 miles of trails including sections that are a 40-mile slog from the nearest road. And you thought the US was car-obsessed.

Running roughly from the southern boundary of Glacier National Park in the north to Rogers Pass (on Hwy 200) in the south, there are actually three designated wilderness areas within the complex: Great Bear, Bob Marshall and Scapegoat. On the periphery the complex is buffered with national-forest lands offering campgrounds, road access to trailheads and quieter country when 'the Bob' (as locals and park rangers call it) hosts hunters in fall.

The main access point to the Bob from the south is from Hwy 200 via the **Monture Guard Station Cabin** (cabins $60), on the wilderness perimeter. To reach it you'll need to drive 7 miles north of Ovando and snowshoe or hike the last mile to your private abodes at the edge of the gorgeous Lewis and Clark Range. Contact the forest service about reservations.

Other Bob access points include the Seeley-Swan Valley in the west, Hungry Horse Reservoir in the north and the Rocky Mountain Front in the east. The easiest (and busiest) access routes are from the Benchmark and Gibson Reservoir trailheads in the Rocky Mountain Front.

Trails generally start steep, reaching the wilderness boundary after around 7 miles. It takes another 10 miles or so to really get into the Bob's heart. Good day-hikes run from all sides. Two USFS districts tend to the Bob, **Flathead National Forest Headquarters** (406-758-5208; www.fs.fed.us/r1/flathead; 650 Wolfpack Way, Kalispell; 8am-4:30pm Mon-Fri) and **Lewis & Clark National Forest Supervisors** (☎406-791-7700; www.fs.fed.us/r1/lewisclark; 1101 15th St N, Great Falls; ⏰8am-4:30pm Mon-Fri).

Whitefish

To be both 'rustic' and 'hip' within the same square mile is a hard act to pull off, but tiny Whitefish (population 8000) makes a good stab at it. Once sold as the main gateway to Glacier National Park, this charismatic New West town has earned enough kudos to merit a long-distance trip in its own right. Aside from grandiose Glacier (which is within an easy day's cycling distance), Whitefish is home to an attractive stash of restaurants, a historic railway station that doubles up as a **museum** (www.stumptownhistoricalsociety.org; 500 Depot St; admission free ⏰10am-4pm Mon-Sat) and underrated **Whitefish Mountain Resort** (www.bigmtn.com; lift ticket adult/child $56/27), which was known as Big Mountain until 2008, guards 3000 acres of varied ski terrain and offers night skiing at weekends.

Check with the **Whitefish Visitor Center** (www.whitefishvisit.com; 307 Spokane Ave; ⏰9am-5:30pm Mon-Fri) for more info on activities.

A string of chain motels lines US 93 south of Whitefish, but the savvy dock in town at the cheerful **Downtowner Inn** (☎406-862-2535; www.downtownermotel.cc; 224 Spokane Ave; r $67-117; ❄📶) with a gym, a Jacuzzi and an on-site cafe. Another option is the more upmarket **Pine Lodge** (☎406-862-7600; www.thepinelodge.com; 920 Spokane Ave; r $79-142; P❄📶🏊), which offers a handy free airport pick-up. Decent restaurants and bars abound, though most locals will point you in the direction of the **Buffalo Café** (www.buffalocafewhitefish.com; 514 3rd St E; breakfast $7-10), a breakfast and lunch hot spot.

Amtrak stops daily at Whitefish's **railroad depot** (500 Depot St) en route to West Glacier ($7) and East Glacier ($14). **Rimrock Trailways** (www.rimrocktrailways.com) runs daily buses to Kalispell and Missoula from the same location.

Glacier National Park

Few of the world's great natural wonders can emulate the US national park system, and few national parks are as magnificent and pristine as Glacier. Created in 1910 during the first flowering of the American conservationist movement, Glacier ranks among other national park classics such as Yellowstone, Yosemite and Grand Canyon. It is renowned for its historic 'parkitecture' lodges, spectacular arterial road (the Going-to-the-Sun Road), and intact pre-Columbian ecosystem. This is the only place in the lower 48 states where grizzly bears still roam in abundance and smart park management has kept the place accessible yet, at the same time, authentically wild (there is no populated town site à la Banff or Jasper). Among a slew of outdoor attractions, the park is particularly noted for its hiking, wildlife-spotting, and sparkling lakes, ideal for boating and fishing.

Although Glacier's tourist numbers are relatively high (two million a year), a large percentage of these people rarely stray far from the Going-to-the-Sun Road and almost all visit between June and September. Choose your moment and splendid isolation is yours for the taking. The park remains open year-round; however, most services are open only from mid-May to September.

Glacier's 1562 sq miles are divided into five regions, each centered on a ranger station: Polebridge (northwest); Lake McDonald (southwest), including the West Entrance and Apgar village; Two Medicine (southeast); St Mary (east); and Many Glacier (northeast). The 50-mile Going-to-the-Sun Road is the only paved road that traverses the park.

Sights & Activities

TOP CHOICE Going-to-the-Sun Road OUTDOORS

A strong contender for the most spectacular road in America, the 53-mile Going-to-the-Sun Road is a national historic landmark that skirts near shimmering Lake McDonald before angling sharply to the Garden Wall – the main dividing line between the west and east sides of the park. At Logan Pass you can stroll 1.5 miles to **Hidden Lake Overlook**; heartier hikers can try the 7.5-mile **Highline Trail**. The free shuttle stops on the western side of the road at the trailhead for **Avalanche Lake**, an easy 4-mile return hike to a stunning alpine lake in a cirque beautified with numerous weeping waterfalls.

Many Glacier HIKING

Anchored by the historic 1915 Many Glacier Lodge and sprinkled with more lakes than glaciers, this picturesque valley on the park's east side has some tremendous hikes, some of which link to the Going-to-the-Sun Road.

A favorite is the 9.4-mile (return) **Iceberg Lake Trail**, a steep but rewarding jaunt through flower meadows and pine forest to an iceberg infested lake.

Glacier Park Boat Co BOATING
(406-257-2426; www.glacierparkboats.com) Rents out kayaks and canoes, and runs popular guided tours (adult/child $23/11.50) from five locations in Glacier National Park.

Sleeping

There are 13 **NPS campgrounds** (406-888-7800; http://reservations.nps.gov; tent & RV sites $10-23) and seven historic lodges in the park, which operate between mid-May and the end of September. Of the sites, only Fish Creek and St Mary can be reserved in advance (up to five months). Sites fill by mid-morning, particularly in July and August.

Glacier also has seven historic lodges dating from the early 1900s.

TOP CHOICE **Many Glacier Hotel** HOTEL $$
(406-732-4411; www.glacierparkinc.com; Many Glacier Valley; r $145-189; mid-Jun–mid-Sep) Modeled after a Swiss chalet, this national historic landmark on Swiftcurrent Lake is the park's largest hotel, with 208 rooms featuring panoramic views. Evening entertainment, a lounge and fine-dining restaurant specializing in fondue all add to the appeal.

Lake McDonald Lodge HOTEL $$
(406-888-5431; www.glacierparkinc.com; Lake McDonald Valley; cabin/lodge r $128/182; May-Sep) Built in 1913, this old hunting lodge is adorned with stuffed-animal trophies and exudes relaxation. The 100 rooms are lodge, chalet or motel style. Nightly park-ranger talks and lake cruises add a rustic ambience. There's a restaurant and pizzeria.

Glacier Park Lodge HOTEL $$
(406-226-5600; www.glacierparkinc.com; East Glacier; r from $140; late May-Sep) The park's flagship lodge is a graceful, elegant place featuring interior balconies supported by Douglas fir timbers and a massive stone fireplace in the lobby. It's an aesthetically appealing, historically charming and very comfortable place to stay. Pluses include nine holes of golf and cozy reading nooks.

Rising Sun Motor Inn MOTEL $$
(406-732-5523; www.glacierparkinc.com; r $129-180; late May-early Sep) One of two classic 1940s-era wooden motels, the Rising Sun lies on the north shore of St Mary Lake in a small complex that includes a store, restaurant and boat launch. The rustic rooms and cabins offer everything an exhausted hiker could hope for.

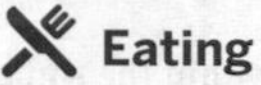

Eating

In summer there are grocery stores with limited camping supplies in Apgar, Lake McDonald Lodge, Rising Sun and at the Swiftcurrent Motor Inn. Most lodges have on-site restaurants. Dining options in West Glacier and St Mary offer mainly hearty hiking fare.

Park Café AMERCIAN $
(www.parkcafe.us; US 89, St Mary; breakfast $7-12; 7am-10pm Jun-Sep) In St Mary, and recommended for its dessert pies.

Ptarmigan Dining Room INTERNATIONAL $$$
(Many Glacier Lodge; mains $15-30; mid-Jun–early Sep) With its lakeside views, this is the most refined of the lodge restaurants.

Polebridge Mercantile BAKERY, SUPERMARKET $
(Polebridge Loop Rd; 7am-9pm May-Nov) In the North Fork Valley. Come here for cinnamon buns – known to pump a good couple of hours into tired hiking legs.

Information

Visitor centers and ranger stations in the park sell field guides and hand out hiking maps. Those at Apgar and St Mary are open daily May to October; the visitor center at Logan Pass is open when the Going-to-the-Sun Road is open. The Many Glacier, Two Medicine and Polebridge Ranger Stations close at the end of September. **Park headquarters** (406-888-7800; www.nps.gov/glac; 8am-4:30pm Mon-Fri), in West Glacier between US 2 and Apgar, is open year-round.

Entry to the park (hiker/vehicle $12/25) is valid for seven days. Day-hikers don't need permits, but overnight backpackers do (May to October only). Half of the permits are available on a first-come, first-served basis from the **Apgar Backcountry Permit Center** (permits per person per day $4; May 1-Oct 31), St Mary Visitor Center, and the Many Glacier, Two Medicine and Polebridge ranger stations.

The other half can be reserved at the Apgar Backcountry Permit Center, St Mary and Many Glacier visitor centers and Two Medicine and Polebridge ranger stations.

Getting There & Around

Amtrak's Empire Builder train stops daily at West Glacier (year round) and East Glacier Park (April to October) on its route between Seattle and Chicago. **Glacier National Park** (www.nps.gov/glac) runs free shuttles from Apgar Village to St Mary over Going-to-the-Sun Road from July 1 to Labor Day. **Glacier Park, Inc** (www.glacierparkinc.com) charges for its East Side Shuttle on the eastern side of the park with daily links to Waterton (Canada), Many Glacier, St Mary, Two Medicine and East Glacier.

IDAHO

Ascending Lemhi Pass in August 1805 just west of the headwaters of the Missouri River, American pathfinder, William Clarke of the Corps of Discovery expected to see a vast river plain stretching all the way to the Pacific. Instead he was confronted with range after range of uncharted mountains – the rugged, brutal landscape we now know as Idaho.

Famous for not being particularly famous, the nation's 43rd state is a pristine wilderness of Alaskan proportions that gets rudely ignored by most of the traffic heading west to Seattle or east to the more famous parks of Montana. In truth, much of this lightly trodden land is little changed since the days of Lewis and Clark including a vast 15,000-sq-km 'hole' that's in the middle of the state and bereft of roads, settlements, or any other form of human interference.

Flatter, dryer southern Idaho is dominated-by the Snake River, deployed as a transportation artery by early settlers on the Oregon Trail and tracked today by busy Hwy 84. But, outside of this narrow populated strip, the Idaho landscape is refreshingly free of the soulless strip-mall, fast food infestations so ubiquitous elsewhere in the US.

IDAHO FACTS

- » **Nickname** Gem State
- » **Population** 1,567,582
- » **Area** 83,570 sq miles
- » **Capital city** Boise (population 205,671)
- » **Other cities** Lewiston (population 31,293), Moscow (population 23,800), Idaho Falls (population 56,813).
- » **Sales tax** 6%
- » **Birthplace of** Lewis and Clark guide Sacagawea (1788–1812); politician and reality TV star Sarah Palin (b 1964); poet Ezra Pound (1885–1972); actress Lana Turner (1921–1995)
- » **Home of** Star garnet, Sun Valley ski resort
- » **Politics** reliably Republican with small pockets of Democrats, eg Sun Valley
- » **Famous for** potatoes, wilderness, clean air, the world's first chairlift
- » **State dance** square dance
- » **Driving distances** Boise to Idaho Falls 280 miles, Lewiston to Coeur d'Alene 116 miles

Boise

Understated, underrated and underappreciated, Idaho's state capital (and largest city) gets little name recognition from people outside the northwest. But, while rarely San Franciscan in its magnificence, Boise's affable downtown surprises blinkered outsiders with the modest spirit of an underdog. Who knew about the grandiose Idaho capitol building? Who dreamt of well-heeled wine bars and Parisian-style bistros? And what's the story with all that latent Basque culture? The city's highlights include all of the these, plus a salubrious university campus and a 'city of trees' moniker that is far more than just a marketing ploy. The result: Boise leaves a poignant and lasting impression – primarily because it's not supposed to.

Sights & Activities

Delve into the main business district, bounded by State, Grove, 4th and 9th Sts.

TOP CHOICE **Basque Block** NEIGHBORHOOD

(www.thebasqueblock.com) Unbeknownst to many, Boise harbors one of the largest Basque populations outside Spain. The European émigrés first arrived in Idaho in the 1910s to pursue jobs in shepherding and elements of their distinct culture can be glimpsed along Grove St between 6th St and Capitol Blvd. Sandwiched between the ethnic taverns, restaurants and bars is **Basque Museum & Cultural Center** (www.basquemuseum.com; 611 Grove St; adult/senior & student $5/4; ⏰10am-4pm Tue-Fri, 11am-3pm Sat) a commendable effort to unveil the intricacies of Basque culture and how it was transposed 6000 miles west to Idaho. Language lessons in Euskara, Europe's oldest language, are held here, while next door in the **Anduiza Fronton Building** (619 Grove St) there's a Basque handball court where aficionados play the traditional sport of pelota. The Boise club is affiliated to the US Federation of Pelota.

Idaho State Capitol LANDMARK

The joy of US state capitol buildings is that visitors can wander in spontaneously for free to admire some of the nation's best architecture. The Boise building, constructed from native sandstone, celebrates the neoclassical style in vogue when it was built in 1920. It was extensively refurbished in 2010 and is now heated with geothermal hot water.

Boise River & Greenbelt PARKS, MUSEUMS

Laid out in the 1960s, the tree-lined riverbanks of the Boise River protect 30 miles of vehicle-free trails and, in more recent times, have come to personify Boise's 'city of trees' credentials. In summer, the river is insanely popular for its floating and tubing. The put-in point is **Barber Park** (Eckert Rd; tube rental $12), 6 miles east of downtown from where you can float 5 miles downstream to the take-out point at Ann Morrison Park. There are four rest-stops en route and a shuttle bus ($3) runs from the take-out point.

The most central and action-packed space on the Greenbelt, 90-acre **Julia Davis Park** contains the **Idaho State Historical Museum** (610 N Julia Davis Dr, adult/reduced $5/4; ⌚9am-5pm Tue-Fri, 11am-5pm Sat) with well thought-out exhibits on Lewis and Clark; and the **Boise Art Museum** (www.boiseartmuseum.org; 670 N Julia Davis Dr, adult/senior & student $5/3; ⌚10am-5pm Tue-Sat, noon-5pm Sun) There's also a pretty outdoor **rose garden**.

Ridge to Rivers Trail System HIKING

(www.ridgetorivers.org) More rugged than the greenbelt are the scrub- and brush-covered foothills above town offering 75 miles of scenic, sometimes strenuous hiking and mountain-biking routes. The most immediate access from downtown is via Fort Boise Park on E Fort St, five blocks southeast of the state capitol building.

Sleeping

Here are three true gems.

TOP CHOICE **Modern Hotel** BOUTIQUE MOTEL $$

(208-424-8244; www.themodernhotel.com; 1314 W Grove St; d from $125; P) Making an oxymoron (a boutique motel!?) into a fashion statement, the Modern Hotel offers retro-trendy minimalist rooms and a slavishly hip bar slap-bang in the middle of downtown. The power showers are huge and the service is five-star.

Leku Ona BOUTIQUE HOTEL $

(208-345-6665; 117 S 6th St; www.lekuonaid.com; r $65-85;) A Basque boutique hotel, no less, styled à la 'the old country' and situated next door to a restaurant of the same name that serves delicious *pintxos* (Basque tapas). The operation is run by a Basque-born immigrant and is economical as well as authentic.

Hotel 43 BOUTIQUE HOTEL $$

(800-243-4622; www.hotel43.com; 981 Grove St; r $146-229;) Named after the latitude (Boise sits on the 43rd parallel) and in honor of Idaho being the 43rd state, this is an urban cozy boutique hotel in the heart of downtown. The 112 rooms and suites are artfully laid out and feature views of the state capitol and surrounding foothills. The swanky on-site Chandlers Restaurant and Martini Bar (mains from $15) is one of Boise's most popular watering and eating holes.

Eating & Drinking

Restaurants and nightspots are found downtown in the brick-lined pedestrian plaza of the Grove, and the gentrified former warehouse district between 8th St and Idaho Ave. The overall food scene is what you might call 'a turn up for the books.' Count on some exciting Basque specialties, an abundance of authentic French-style bistros and some exceptional wine bars.

Grape Escape WINE BAR $$

(800 W Idaho St; appetizers $7-11, mains $11-18) Sit alfresco and enjoy your Pinot Noir with light supper fare (bruschetta, salads and highly creative pizzas) logging the ubiquity of downtown cyclists, closet intellectuals and bright young things out for an early evening aperitif. The wine menu is almost as good as the people-watching.

La Vie en Rose BAKERY, BISTRO $

(www.lavieenrosebakery.com; 928 W Main St; mains $7-10; ⌚8am-5pm Tue-Sun) Have a European moment inside the turreted Idanha Hotel building at this authentic French bistro and bakery where the French-imbued menu includes *croque monsieur* (grilled cheese and ham sandwich), homemade *tarte* and Italian Illy coffee.

Bar Gernika PUB $
(www.bargernkia.com; 202 S Capitol Blvd; lunch $8-9; ⏲11am-midnight Mon-Thu till 1am Fri & Sat) *Ongi etorri* (welcome) to the Basque block's most accessible pub-tavern with a menu that leans heavily on old-country favorites such as lamb kabob, chorizo and beef tongue (on Saturdays only). It's a true only-in-Boise kind of place.

Bittercreek Ale House & Red Feather Lounge INTERNATIONAL $$
(www.justeatlocal.com; 246 N 8th St; mains $7-15; ⏲11:30am-late) These adjoining restaurants (owned by the same people) have lively sidewalk patios, intimate environs and lots of personality. They also serve wholesome, usually locally produced food with an emphasis on sustainable growth. The nouveau-American menu at Bittercreek features a good selection of vegetarian options (it does organic Idaho black bean burgers on request). Order one of the whiskey cocktails made using an old-fashioned pre-Prohibition-era recipe. The Red Feather is slightly more upscale, and does delicious wood-oven pizza and a set three-course menu for two ($23 per person).

Bardenay PUB $$
(www.bardenay.com; 610 Grove St; mains $8-18) Bardenay was the USA's very first 'distillery-pub,' and remains a one-of-a-kind watering hole. Today it serves its own home-brewed vodka, rum and gin in casual, airy environs. It gets consistently good reviews.

Information

Visitor center (☎208-344-5338; www.boise.org; 850 Front St; ⏲10am-5pm Mon-Fri, 10am-2pm Sat Jun-Aug, 9am-4pm Mon-Fri Sep-May)

Getting There & Around

Boise Municipal Airport (BOI; I-84 exit 53) has daily flights to Denver, Las Vegas, Phoenix, Portland, Salt Lake City, Seattle and Spokane. Greyhound services depart from the **bus station** (1212 W Bannock St) with routes fanning out to Lewiston and Spokane, Pendleton and Portland, and Twin Falls and Salt Lake City.

Ketchum & Sun Valley

In one of Idaho's most stunning natural locations sits a piece of ski history. Sun Valley was the first purpose-built ski resort in the US, hand-picked by Union Pacific Railroad scion William Averell Harriman (after an exhaustive search) in the 1930s and publicized by numerous members of the then glitterati such as Ernest Hemingway, Clark Gable and Gary Cooper. When Sun Valley opened in 1936 it sported the world's first chairlift and a showcase 'parkitecture' lodge that still acts as its premier resort.

In the years since, Sun Valley has kept its swanky Hollywood clientele and extended its facilities to include the legendary Bald Mountain, yet it remains a refined and pretty place (no fast-food joints or condo sprawl here). Highly rated nationwide, the resort is revered for its reliable high-quality snow, large elevation drop and almost windless weather. Backing it up is adjacent village Ketchum, 1 mile away, which predates Sun Valley and has held onto its authenticity and rustic beauty despite the skiing deluge. Ketchum is prime territory for fishing and hunting in summer, a fact borne out by its famous former resident, Ernest Hemingway.

Activities

Main St between 1st and 5th Sts is where you'll find nearly all the businesses. Sun Valley and its lodge is 1 mile to the north and easily walkable. Twelve miles south of Ketchum, also on Hwy 75, is Hailey, another delightful small town with a bar scene.

Wood River Trail HIKING, CYCLING
There are numerous hiking and mountain biking trails around Ketchum and Sun Valley, as well as excellent fishing spots. The Wood River Trail is the all-connecting artery linking Sun Valley with Ketchum and continuing 32 bucolic miles south down to Bellevue via Hailey. Bikes can be hired from **Pete Lane's** (per day $35) in the mall next to the Sun Valley Lodge.

Sun Valley Resort SNOW SPORTS
(www.sunvalley.com) Famous for its light, fluffy powder and celebrity guests, the dual-sited resort comprises advanced-terrain **Bald Mountain** (lift ticket $55-80) and easier-on-the-nerves **Dollar Mountain** (lift ticket adult $32-38, child $16-30), which also has a **tubing hill** (adult/child $10/5). In summer, take the chairlift to the top of either mountain, and hike or cycle down. Facilities are predictably plush.

Sleeping

Sun Valley Lodge HOTEL $$$
(☎208-622-2001; www.sunvalley.com; 1 Sun Valley Rd; r $229-329; ❄@🛜≋♿) Hemingway

HEMINGWAY: THE FINAL DAYS

Although Sun Valley and Ketchum never featured explicitly in the work of Ernest Miller Hemingway, the globe-trotting author had a deep affection for the area and became a frequent visitor following its development as a ski resort in the late 1930s. Legend has it that he completed his Spanish Civil War masterpiece *For Whom the Bell Tolls* in room 206 of the **Sun Valley Lodge** in between undertaking fishing and hunting excursions with well-heeled friends such as Gary Cooper and Clark Gable.

In the 1940s and '50s, Hemingway's Ketchum trips became more sporadic as he migrated south to Key West and Cuba but, following the Cuban revolution in 1959, and the subsequent expropriation of Hemingway's Havana house, the author moved permanently to Idaho in 1959. Increasingly paranoid and in declining physical and mental health, His final days weren't his happiest and on July 2, 1961, aged 61, he took his favorite gun, walked out onto the porch of his newly acquired home off Warm Springs Rd and blew his brains out.

There is a surprising (and refreshing) lack of hullaballoo surrounding Hemingway in Ketchum and you'll have to look hard to find the small, pretty **cemetery** half a mile north of the center on Hwy 75, where he is buried alongside his granddaughter Margaux. Pennies, cigars and the odd bottle of liquor furnish his simple grave. Hemingway's house is out of bounds to the public but there is a **monument** honoring him near Trail Creek, 1 mile beyond the Sun Valley Lodge. Downtown in Ketchum his favorite drinking holes were the **Casino Club** and the Alpine Club, now known as **Whiskey Jacques**.

completed *For Whom the Bell Tolls* in this swank 1930s-era beauty and the place has lost little of its luxurious pre-war sheen. Old-fashioned elegance is the lure in comfortable rooms that sometimes feel a little small by today's standards. Amenities include a fitness facility, game room, bowling alley and sauna. It also runs a ski shuttle and has a children's program.

Lift Tower Lodge MOTEL **$**
(208-726-5163; 703 S Main St; r $65-100; P) Lifelong members of the hoi polloi can hobnob with the millionaires of Ketchum and decamp afterwards to this friendly and economical small motel on the cusp of the ski village. The building is advertised with a landmark exhibition chairlift (c 1939) that is lit up after dark.

Tamarack Lodge HOTEL **$$**
(208-726-3344; www.tamaracksunvalley.com; 500 E Sun Valley Rd; r $109-139;) Tasteful rooms complete with fireplace, balcony and many amenities are offered at this well-maintained lodge. The Jacuzzi and indoor pool are definite assets. Discounts are often available midweek and off-season.

Eating & Drinking

TOP CHOICE **Roosevelt Grille** STEAKHOUSE, PUB **$$**
(www.rooseveltgrille.com; 280 N Main St; mains $9-19) What use is a classic ski town without the classic ski steakhouse and bar? An imperceptible amalgam of food (beef mostly), beer, sunny rooftop patio and congenial atmosphere make this the most popular vote in town – usually by a mile.

Rickshaw ASIAN **$$**
(www.eat-at-rickshaw.com; 460 Washington Ave N; small plates & mains $5-12; 5:30-10.30pm Tue-Sat, 5:30-9.30pm Sun) Sick of steak? This hippy-ish shack just off Main St does Asian fusion tapas – creative, fresh small plates inspired by the cuisine of Vietnam, Thailand, China and Indonesia, which the chef refers to as 'ethnic street food.'

Desperado's MEXICAN **$**
(208-726-3068; 211 4th St; mains $7-10; 11:30am-10pm Mon-Sat) You could eat steak seven nights a week in Ketchum but, to broaden your horizons a little, head metaphorically south to Desperado's for burritos, chimichangas (deep-fried burritos) and tacos washed down with a margarita.

Pioneer Saloon STEAKHOUSE **$$$**
(www.pioneersaloon.com; 320 N Main St; mains $12-25; 5:30pm-10pm) Around since the 1950s and originally an illicit gambling hall, the Pio is an unashamed Rocky Mountain restaurant decorated with deer heads, antique guns, bullet boards and – oh yes – some good food too, as long as you like beef and trout.

Casino Club BAR

(220 N Main St) In a ski resort less than 75 years old, this dive bar is the oldest thing still standing and has witnessed everything from gambling fist fights, to psychedelic hippies, to the rise and fall of Ernest Hemingway (yes, he downed a few in here), to tattooed men on Harleys riding through the front door. A survivor, if nothing else!

Information

Sun Valley/Ketchum Visitors Center (208-726-3423; www.visitsunvalley.com; 491 Sun Valley Rd; 9am-6pm)

Getting There & Around

The region's airport, **Friedman Memorial Airport** (www.flyfma.com) in Hailey is 12 miles south of Ketchum. **A-1 Taxi** (208-726-9351) offers rides to the airport from Ketchum ($22).

Sun Valley Express (www.sunvalleyexpress.com) operates a daily shuttle between Sun Valley and Boise Airport in both directions ($59 one-way).

Stanley

Tiny Stanley (population 100) might be the most scenic small town in America. Surrounded by protected wilderness and national-forest land, the remote outpost is nestled into the crook of Salmon River, miles from anywhere. It's the kind of place where peaceful high summer twilight stretches on past 10pm and you fall asleep to the river's melodic roar. The aptly named Sawtooth Mountains provide a dramatic backdrop.

Activities

Middle Fork of the Salmon RAFTING

Stanley is the jumping-off point for rafting the legendary Middle Fork of the Salmon. Billed as the 'last wild river' it's part of the longest undammed river system outside Alaska. Full trips last six days and allow you to float for 106 miles through the 300 or so rapids (class I to IV) of the 2.4-million-acre Frank Church–River of No Return Wilderness, miles from any form of civilization.

DON'T MISS

CENTRAL IDAHO'S SCENIC BYWAYS

Goodbye suburban strip malls, hello unblemished wilderness. All three roads into the remote Idahoan outpost of Stanley are designated National Scenic Byways (it's the only place in the US where this happens). Considering there are only 125 such roads in the country, it means 2.4% of American's prettiest pavement runs through bucolic Stanley.

Sawtooth Scenic Byway

Following the Salmon River along Hwy 75 north from Ketchum to Stanley this 60-mile drive is gorgeous, winding through a misty, thick ponderosa pine forest – where the air is crisp and fresh and smells like rain and nuts – before ascending the 8701ft **Galena Summit**. From the overlook at the top, there are views of the glacially carved Sawtooth Mountains.

Ponderosa Pine Scenic Byway

Hwy 21, between Stanley and Boise, is so beautiful it will be hard to reach your destination because you'll want to stop so much. From Stanley the trees increase in density, until you find yourself enveloped in a sweetly scented cloak of pine – an environment that seems more Pacific Northwest than classic Rockies. Fast-moving clouds bring frequent bursts of rain and the roadway can feel dangerous. Even in late May the snowfields stretch right down to the highway. Two of the road's many highlights are **Kikham Creek Hot Springs** (self-pay campsites $16), 6 miles east of Lowman, a primitive campground and natural hot springs boiling out of the creek; and the old restored gold rush town of **Idaho Falls**.

Salmon River Scenic Byway

Northeast of Stanley, Hwy 75 and US 93 make up another scenic road that runs beside the Salmon River for 161 miles to historic **Lost Trail Pass** on the Montana border, the point where Lewis and Clark first crossed the continental divide in 1805. Much of the surrounding scenery has changed little in over 200 years.

Camping is riverside and guides cook excellent food. Book through **Solitude River Trips** (www.rivertrips.com). Trips run June to August and cost approximately $1800 per person with transportation.

Main Fork of the Salmon RAFTING
For more affordable, albeit slightly less dramatic, white-water action than Middle Fork, do a DIY float trip down the Main Fork of the Salmon. There are 8 miles of quiet water, starting in Stanley, with views of the Sawtooth Mountains you can't see from the road. Bring fishing gear. Float trips in inflatable kayaks (single/double $30/40) can be arranged through **Sawtooth Rentals** (www.riversidemotel.biz; Hwy 75) at the Riverside Motel in Stanley.

Silver Creek Outfitters FISHING
(www.silver-creek.com; 1 Sun Valley Rd) There is epic trout fishing on the Salmon and in surrounding mountain lakes from March until November, with late June to early October the best time for dry fly-fishing. Silver Creek, run out of Sun Valley, does custom trips to remote river spots, only accessible via drift boat or float tube. There are no less than eight species of trout in these waters, including the mythical Steelhead. Measuring up to 40in, these fish swim east about 900 miles from the Pacific Ocean at the end of winter, arriving near Stanley in March and April.

Sleeping & Eating

There are about half a dozen hotels in Stanley, all done in traditional pioneer log-cabin style. During the short summer season a couple of restaurants open up.

Sawtooth Hotel HOTEL $
(☎208-721-2459; www.sawtoothhotel.com; 755 Ace of Diamonds St; d with/without bath $100/70;) This is what happens when the owners of the famous Stanley Baking Co open a hotel. Set in a nostalgic 1931 log motel, the Sawtooth updates the comforts of yesteryear, but keeps the hospitality effusively Stanley-esque. There are six rooms furnished old-country style, two of which have private bathrooms. Don't expect TVs or room phones, but count on home-spun dining that is exquisite.

TOP CHOICE **Stanley Baking Co** BAKERY, BREAKFAST $
(www.stanleybakingco.com; 250 Wall St; breakfast & lunch $6-9; ⏲7am-2pm May-Oct) After having lumbered the world with unhealthy delights of 'junk food,' the US claims culinary penance in more esoteric genres, such as the middle-of-nowhere bakery and brunch spot. Operating for five months of the year out of a small log cabin, Stanley Baking Co is the only place in town where you're likely to see a queue. The reason: off-the-ratings-scale homemade baked goods.

Idaho Panhandle

Borders are arbitrary in the long skinny spoon-handle of northern Idaho that brushes up against Canada. Historically this was never supposed to be Idaho anyway – a land dispute with Montana ended with the state claiming the panhandle in the 1880s – and, in both looks and attitude, the area has more in common with the Pacific Northwest than the Rockies. Tellingly, Spokane, a few miles west in Washington, acts as the regional hub and most of the panhandle observes Pacific Standard Time.

Near the Washington border, fast-growing **Coeur d'Alene** (population 44,000) is an extension of the Spokane metro area and the panhandle's largest town. However, it's overdeveloped with a rather tacky boardwalk waterfront and one of those Anywhere USA–type golf and spa resorts. The adjacent lake is ideal for water-based activities, in particular water-skiing. The **Coeur d'Alene Visitors Bureau** (☎877-782-9232; www.coeurdalene.org; 105 N 1st; ⏲10am-5pm Tue-Sat) has further information. It's not really worth stopping here unless it's late and you need to sleep, in which case go straight to the quirky pink-door **Flamingo Motel** (☎208-664-2159; www.flamingomotelidaho.com; 718 Sherman Ave; r $80-100; ❄), a retro 1950s throwback.

Sandpoint, on Lake Pend Oreille, is the nicest of the panhandle's towns. Set in a gorgeous wilderness locale surrounded by mountains, it also sports Idaho's only serviceable Amtrak **train station**, an attractive historic building dating from 1916. The *Empire Builder*, running daily between Seattle/Portland and Chicago, stops here.

You can soak up Idaho's largest lake from the **Pend Oreille Scenic Byway** (US 200), which hugs the north shore. Eleven miles northwest of town is highly rated **Schweitzer Mountain Resort** (www.schweitzer.com), lauded for its tree-skiing.

The best accommodation bargain for miles around is the clean, friendly mom-and-pop-run **Country Inn** (☎208-263-3333; www.countryinnsandpoint.com; 470700 Hwy 95; s/d $49/59), 3 miles south of Sandpoint.

USA's National Parks

Glacier National Park (p761)

Welcome to the Parks

National parks are America's big backyards. Every cross-country road trip connects the dots between the USA's big-shouldered cities, but not always its national parks. There you'll encounter remarkable places, rich in unspoiled wilderness, rare wildlife and rich history.

Some parks look much the same as they did centuries ago, when this nation was just starting out. From craggy islands off the Atlantic Coast, to prairie grasslands and buffalo herds across the Great Plains, to the Rocky Mountains raising their jagged teeth along the Continental Divide, and onward to the tallest trees on earth – coast redwoods – standing sentinel on Pacific shores, you'll be amazed by natural bounty.

Historically speaking, the USA's voracious appetite for land and material riches drove not only the false doctrine of Manifest Destiny, but a bonanza of building pioneer homesteads, farms, barrier fences, great dams, concrete roadways and train tracks from sea to shining sea. This artificial infrastructure quickly swallowed up vast wilderness tracts from the Appalachian Mountains to the mighty Mississippi River and far into the West.

That is, until the creation of a web of federally protected public lands, starting with the national parks, whose guiding mission is to 'preserve unimpaired the natural and cultural resources and values of the national park system for the enjoyment, education, and inspiration of this and future generations.'

1

WITOLD SKRYPCZAK/LONELY PLANET IMAGES ©

3

JOHN ELK III/LONELY PLANET IMAGES ©

Clockwise from top left

1. Canyonlands National Park (p850) **2.** Bryce Canyon National Park (p854) **3.** Olympic National Park (p1022).

Evolution of the Parks

During a trip to the Dakotas in 1831, artist George Catlin had a dream. As he watched the USA's rapid westward expansion damage the wilderness and Native American peoples, Catlin penned a call to action, to create 'a nation's park, containing man and beast, in all the wild and freshness of their nature's beauty!' Four decades later, Congress finally created Yellowstone National Park.

The late 19th century saw a rush of new parks – including Yosemite, Sequoia and Mount Rainier – as a nascent conservation movement fired up public enthusiasm. The Antiquities Act of 1906, signed by President Theodore Roosevelt, preserved a trove of archaeological sites from Native American cultures, including Mesa Verde and Devils Tower, and two years later the Grand Canyon.

The National Park Service (NPS) was created in 1916, with self-made millionaire and former ad man and tireless promoter Stephen Mather as its first director. In the 1930s, President Franklin Delano Roosevelt added 50 more historic sites and monuments to the NPS portfolio and hired Depression-era Civilian Conservation Corps (CCC) workers to build scenic byways and create recreational opportunities in the parks.

After WWII, the NPS kept expanding. The biggest growth spurt so far happened in 1980, when the Alaska National Interest Lands Conservation Act turned over 47 million acres of wilderness to the NPS, more than doubling the federal agency's holdings.

1

2

Right

1. Crater Lake National Park (p1052) **2.** Joshua Tree National Park (p930).

Early Park Heroes

In a country founded on the philosophy that individuals matter, the solo voices of artists, explorers, environmentalists and iconoclast presidents have given shape to the USA's national parks as much as government bureaucrats.

In the late 19th century, the herald of the Sierra Nevada, John Muir (1838-1914), galvanized the public while campaigning for a national park system, delivering open-air lectures and writing about the spiritual value of wilderness beyond just its economic advantages. He inspired President Theodore Roosevelt (1858-1919), a big-game hunter and rancher, to establish wildlife preserves, national forests and new national parks and monuments.

Women have also been pivotal in protecting parks, as narrated in Polly Kaufman's book *National Parks and the Woman's Voice: A History*. Western architect Mary Elizabeth Jane Colter (1869-1958), who built grand railway hotels for the Fred Harvey Company, helped create the rustic national-park architectural style, seen in her masterworks at Grand Canyon Village. Environmentalist Marjory Stoneman Douglas (1890–1998) penned the influential *The Everglades: River of Grass* (1947) while crusading for greater protections of Everglades National Park.

First lady during the 1960s, 'Lady Bird' Johnson (1912–2007) contributed to the groundbreaking report *With Heritage So Rich,* which led to the National Historic Preservation Act of 1966 that expanded the NPS system. Her parks advocacy also influenced her husband, President Lyndon B Johnson, who enacted more environmental-protection legislation than any administration since FDR.

Left

1. Yosemite Falls (p991), Yosemite National Park

2. Watchtower, Grand Canyon National Park (p823).

The Parks Today

Today the NPS protects almost 400 parklands and more than 80 million acres of land from coast to coast. Recent additions include noteworthy historical sites and memorials, including the Martin Luther King, Jr Memorial in Washington DC, NYC's African Burial Ground National Monument and Colorado's Sand Creek Massacre National Historic Site. Not all NPS growth has been without controversy, for example, when local residents protest added restrictions on public land use or when agency goals conflict with the self-determination rights of Native American nations.

Federal budget cuts and the enormous pressures of 280 million visitors every year together have also taken huge tolls on national parks, as has global warming, which leads to habitat loss and species extinction. Aiming to make major improvements in time for the NPS's 100th anniversary in 2016, ambitious centennial projects at parks across the country include restoring historic buildings, controlling invasive plant and animal species, and inventorying archaeological sites before they are lost forever.

Nonprofit partners such as the National Parks Conservation Association (www.npca.org) and Western National Parks Association (www.wnpa.org) are critical to national parks' survival. These organizations raise money, staff visitor centers, publish books and maps, and promote education and conservation in the parks. Recent media spotlights have also swayed public opinion about the importance of parks, including Ken Burns' inspiring documentary, *The National Parks: America's Best Idea* (www.pbs.org/nationalparks).

JOHN ELK III/LONELY PLANET IMAGES ©

2

CHRISTER FREDRIKSSON/LONELY PLANET IMAGES ©

Right

1. Grand Teton National Park (p750) **2.** Bear, Yellowstone National Park (p744).

Visiting the Parks

At any park entrance station, be ready to hand over some cash (credit cards may not be accepted). Entrance fees vary, from nothing at all to $25 per vehicle. Because ATMs are scarce in the parks, bring extra cash to pay for campsites, wilderness permits and guided tours. Ask at visitor centers about free (or low-cost) 'junior ranger' activity programs for kids.

National park lodges and campgrounds book up far in advance; for summer vacations, reserve six months to one year ahead. Some parks offer first-come, first-served campgrounds – if so, try to arrive between 10am and noon. For overnight backpacking and some day hikes, you'll need a wilderness permit; the number of permits is often subject to quotas, so apply in advance. Some park stores may sell or occasionally rent basic camping and outdoor supplies, but prices tend to be inflated and some items may be out of stock. Bring your own gear from home instead.

Do your utmost to preserve the park's wild and beautiful natural environment. Follow the principles of the Leave No Trace (www.lnt.org) outdoor ethics. National-park policies and regulations may seem restrictive, but they're intended to keep you safe and to protect natural and cultural resources. Pets are not allowed outside of the parks' developed areas, where they must be leashed and accompanied at all times.

Left

1. Geyser, Yellowstone National Park (p744) **2.** Angels Landing Trail (p855), Zion National Park.

Eastern USA

Roam from New England's rocky, wild and weather-beaten shores to the sugar-sand beaches shaded by palm trees of Florida. Or immerse yourself in the USA's wealth of historic sites starting with the nation's capital, then roll through the pastoral hills of old-timey Appalachia on the ridiculously scenic Blue Ridge Pkwy.

Great Smoky Mountains National Park

1 Receiving more visitors than any other US national park, this southern Appalachian woodland pocket protects thickly forested ridges where black bears, white-tailed deer, antlered elk, wild turkeys and over 1600 kinds of flowers all find sanctuary (p338).

Acadia National Park

2 Catch the first sunrise of the new year atop Cadillac Mountain, the highest point on the USA's eastern seaboard. Come back in summer to play on end-of-the-world islands tossed along rocky, wind-whipped Atlantic coastlines (p239).

Shenandoah National Park

3 Drive from the Great Smoky Mountains north along the historic Blue Ridge Parkway past Appalachian hill hamlets to Shenandoah, a pastoral preserve where waterfall and woodland paths await, just 75 miles from the nation's capital (p309).

Everglades National Park

4 Home to snaggle-toothed crocodiles, stealthy panthers, pink flamingos and mellow manatees, South Florida's Caribbean bays and 'rivers of grass' attract wildlife watchers, especially to unique hardwood hammock flood-plain islands (p463).

Mammoth Cave National Park

5 With hidden underground rivers and almost 400 miles explored, the world's longest cave system shows off sci-fi-looking stalactites and stalagmites up close (p377).

1

3

Clockwise from top left

1. Acadia National Park **2.** Cabin, Great Smoky Mountains National Park **3.** Alligator, Everglades National Park.

2

Great Plains & Rocky Mountains

Wildflower-strewn meadows, saw-toothed peaks and placid lakes along the spine of the Continental Divide are among America's most prized national parks. Equally rich in wildlife, Native American culture and Old West history, the Rocky Mountains and Great Plains embody the American frontier.

Yellowstone National Park

1 The country's oldest national park is full of geysers, hot springs and a wealth of megafauna – grizzly bears, bison, elk and more – that range across North America's largest intact natural ecosystem (p744).

Rocky Mountain National Park

2 At the top of the Continental Divide, jagged mountain peaks are just the tip of the iceberg at this park, speckled with more than 150 lakes and 450 miles of streams running through aromatic pine forests (p722).

Glacier National Park

3 Fly along the high-altitude Going-to-the-Sun Road, which appears to defy gravity as it winds for 50 miles through the mountain landscape of what Native Americans called 'The Backbone of the World' (p761).

Badlands National Park

4 In the midst of native prairie grasslands, where bison and bighorn sheep leave hoofprints, this alarmingly named park is an outdoor museum of ancient geology, with fossil beds that reveal traces of North America' prehistoric past (p626).

Mesa Verde National Park

5 Clamber onto the edge of the Colorado Plateau to visit the well-preserved Native American cliff dwellings of Ancestral Puebloans who inhabited the little-explored Four Corners area for generations (p740).

Clockwise from top left

1. St Mary's Lake, Glacier National Park **2.** Grand Prismatic Spring (p745), Yellowstone National Park **3.** Elk, Rocky Mountain National Park.

EMILY RIDDELL/LONELY PLANET IMAGES ©

HOLGER LEUE/LONELY PLANET IMAGES ©

2

Southwest USA

It takes time to explore the Southwest's meandering canyon country, epic deserts and Native American archaeological ruins. An ancient, colorful chasm carved by one of the USA's most powerful rivers is just the beginning. Meander down backcounty byways to uncover ancient sand dunes, twisting slot canyons, giant cacti and more.

Grand Canyon National Park

1 Arguably the USA's best-known natural attraction, the Grand Canyon is an incredible spectacle of colored rock strata, with many buttes and peaks spiring into a landscape that's always changing with the flow of the mighty Colorado River (p823).

Zion National Park

2 Pioneers almost believed they'd reached the promised land at this desert oasis, run through by a life-giving river. Get a thrill by rappelling down a slot canyon or pulling yourself up the cables to Angels Landing lookout (p855).

Bryce Canyon National Park

3 On of the same geological 'Grand Staircase' as the Grand Canyon, Bryce Canyon shows off a whimsical landscape of totem-shaped hoodoo rock formations, some rising as tall as a 10-story building! (p854)

Arches National Park

4 Just outside the four-seasons outdoor adventure hub of Moab, Utah, this iconic landscape of over 2000 naturally formed sandstone arches is mesmerizing at sunrise and sunset, when the gorgeously eroded desert rocks seem to glow (p850).

Saguaro National Park

5 An icon of the American West, spiky saguaro cacti stretch toward the sky in this Arizona desert park, where coyotes howl, Mexican spotted owls hoot and desert tortoises slowly make their way through the sere landscape (p832).

Clockwise from top left
1. Grand Canyon National Park **2.** Double Arch, Arches National Park **3.** Cactus, Saguaro National Park.

2

West Coast

Thunderous waterfalls, the sirens' call of glacier-carved peaks and the world's tallest, biggest *and* oldest trees are just some of the natural wonders that California offers. Meanwhile, smoking volcanic mountains, misty rain forests and untamed beaches meet in the Pacific Northwest.

Yosemite National Park

1 Explore the glaciated valleys, alpine wildflower meadows, groves of giant sequoias (the world's largest trees) and earth-shaking waterfalls that tumble over sheer granite cliffs in the USA's second-oldest national park (p989).

Olympic National Park

2 Lose yourself in the primeval rain forests, mist-clouded mountains carved by glaciers and lonely, wild Pacific Coast beaches, then watch salmon swim free in the recently restored Elwha River, site of the USA's largest dam removal (p1022).

Death Valley & Joshua Tree National Parks

3 Slide down sand dunes and stroll across salt flats at Badwater, the USA's lowest elevation, in hellishly hot Death Valley, then hop between boulders, native fan palm oases and forests of crooked Joshua trees in Southern California (p933 and p930).

Mt Rainier National Park

4 Meet a glacier-covered, rumbling giant that last erupted only 150 years ago and still reigns over the Pacific Northwest's volcanic Cascades Range. Day hike among wildflower meadows or tramp across high-elevation snow fields in mid-summer (p1031).

Redwood National Park

5 Be awed by towering ancient stands of coast redwoods, the tallest trees on earth, along the often foggy Northern California coast. Spot shaggy Roosevelt elk foraging in woodland prairies, then go tide-pooling along 40 miles of rugged beaches (p984).

JOHN MOCK/LONELY PLANET IMAGES ©

1

RICHARD CUMMINS/LONELY PLANET IMAGES ©

3

Clockwise from top left

1. Yosemite Valley (p991), Yosemite National Park
2. Death Valley National Park **3.** Mt Rainier National Park.

2

Beyond the Parks

The federal government protects so much more than just the USA's 58 national parks, although those usually leap to mind first.

Other NPS places for nature lovers include wilderness areas and national preserves. If it's scenery and adventure you're after, head for a national recreation area or national seashore. The NPS offers a lot for history buffs, too, from national memorials, monuments and battlefields to unique historic sites. Road trippers can drive national parkways, while hikers trek national scenic trails. Finally, there are a dozen or so miscellaneous NPS lands, including the White House in Washington, DC.

Thousands more natural areas are overseen by other federal land management agencies, including the US Forest Service (USFS; www.fs.fed.us), US Fish & Wildlife Service (USFWS; www.fws.gov) and Bureau of Land Management (BLM; www.blm.gov). Much like the NPS system, all of these public lands have uniquely valuable properties that justify putting them into the country's wilderness treasure chest.

FINAL FRONTIERS

Part of the USA for just more than 50 years, the far-flung states of Alaska and Hawaii offer some unforgettable wilderness experiences you just can't get in the 'Lower 48' or on 'da mainland.' You can trek volcanoes or possibly see lava flow at Hawaii's national parks. Meanwhile, Alaska's national parks give you a chance to watch glacial icebergs calve, witness majestic wildlife and summit the USA's highest peak, Mt McKinley (Denali).

Lava flow, Kilauea Volcano (p1091), Hawai'i Volcanoes National Park

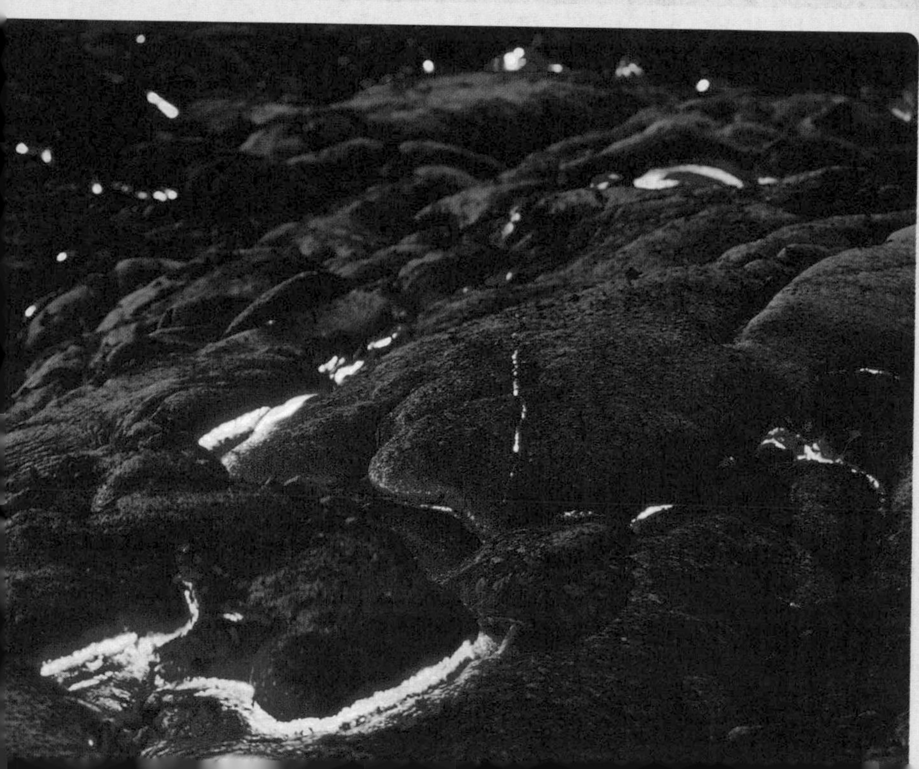

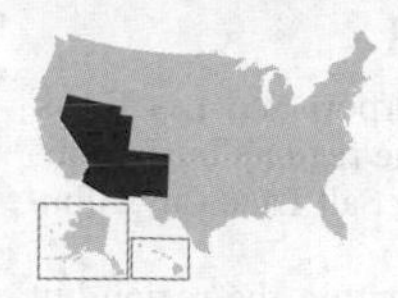

Southwest

Includes »

Nevada 790
Las Vegas 790
Arizona 808
Phoenix 809
Flagstaff 818
Grand Canyon National Park 823
Tucson 832
Utah 837
Salt Lake City 838
New Mexico 857
Albuquerque 858
Santa Fe 863
Taos 871

Best Places to Eat

» Café Diablo (p852)
» Elote Cafe (p821)
» Joël Robuchon (p797)
» Poco (p837)
» San Marcos Café (p867)

Best Places to Stay

» Cosmopolitan (p791)
» Earthship Rentals (p872)
» El Tovar Hotel (p826)
» Motor Lodge (p822)
» Sundance Resort (p847)

Why Go?

Breathtaking beauty and the allure of adventure merge seamlessly in the Southwest. This captivating mix has drawn dreamers and explorers for centuries. Pioneers staked their claims beside lush riverbanks, prospectors dug into mountains for untold riches, religious refugees built cities across empty deserts, while astronomers and rocket builders peered into star-filled skies. Today, artists and entrepreneurs flock to urban centers and quirky mining towns, energizing the entire region.

For travelers, beauty and adventure still loom large in this land of mountains, deserts and wide-open spaces sprawled across Nevada, Arizona, Utah and New Mexico. You can hike past red rocks, cycle beneath mountain skies, raft through canyons and roll the dice under the mesmerizing lights of Vegas. But remember: beauty and adventure here can also loom small. Study that saguaro up close. Ask a Hopi artist about his craft. Savor some green-chile stew. It's the tap-you-on-the-shoulder moments you may just cherish the most.

When to Go

Las Vegas

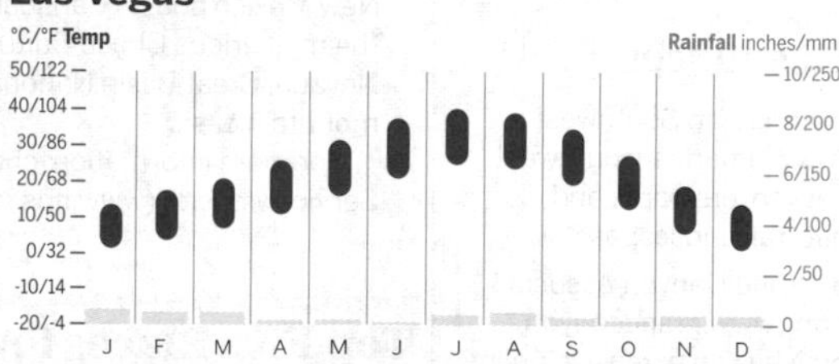

Jan Ski near Taos and Flagstaff. In Park City, hit the slopes and the Sundance Film Festival.

Jun-Aug High season for exploring national parks in New Mexico, Utah and northern Arizona.

Sep-Nov Hike to the bottom of the Grand Canyon or gaze at bright leaves in northern New Mexico.

DON'T MISS

A hike in the desert. Your choices? The Sonoran, Chihuahuan, Great Basin.

Fast Facts

» Hub cities: Las Vegas (population 553,000), Phoenix (population 1.4 million), Salt Lake City (population 181,743)

» Las Vegas to Grand Canyon National Park South Rim: 280 miles

» Los Angeles to Albuquerque: 670 miles

» Time zones: Nevada (Pacific), Arizona (Mountain, does not observe DST), Utah (Mountain), New Mexico (Mountain)

» States covered in this chapter: Nevada, Arizona, Utah, New Mexico

Did You Know?

Flash floods are most common from mid-July to early September. Avoid camping on sandy washes and canyon bottoms; don't drive across flooded roads. If hiking, move quickly to higher ground.

Resources

» American Southwest (www.americansouthwest.net) covers parks and natural landscapes.

» Grand Canyon Association (www.grandcanyon.org) has an extensive online bookstore for the park.

» Recreation.gov (www.recreation.gov) takes reservations for camping and other activities at nationally run outdoor areas.

Getting There & Around

Phoenix' Sky Harbor International Airport and Las Vegas' McCarran International Airport are the region's busiest airports, followed by the airports serving Salt Lake City, Albuquerque and Tucson.

Greyhound stops at major points within the region but doesn't serve all national parks or off-the-beaten-path tourist towns such as Moab. In larger cities, bus terminals can be in less-safe areas of town.

Private vehicles are often the only means to reach out-of-the-way towns, trailheads and swimming spots. For car rentals, see p1174.

Amtrak train service is much more limited than the bus system, although it does link many major Southwestern cities and offers bus connections to others (including Santa Fe and Phoenix). The *California Zephyr* crosses Utah and Nevada; the *Southwest Chief* stops in Arizona and New Mexico; and the *Sunset Limited* traverses southern Arizona and New Mexico.

NATIONAL & STATE PARKS

Containing 40 national parks and monuments, the Southwest is a scenic and cultural jackpot. Add some stunning state parks, and, well, you might need to extend your trip.

One of the most deservedly popular national parks is Arizona's Grand Canyon National Park. Other Arizona parks include Monument Valley Navajo Tribal Park, a desert basin with towering sandstone pillars and buttes; Canyon de Chelly National Monument, with ancient cliff dwellings; Petrified Forest National Park, with its odd mix of Painted Desert and fossilized logs; and Saguaro National Park, with pristine desert and giant cacti.

The southern red-rock Canyon Country in Utah includes five national parks: Arches, Canyonlands, Zion, Bryce Canyon and Capitol Reef, which offers exceptional wilderness solitude. Grand Staircase-Escalante National Monument is a mighty region of undeveloped desert. New Mexico boasts Carlsbad Caverns National Park and the mysterious Chaco Culture National Historic Park. In Nevada, Great Basin National Park is a rugged, remote mountain oasis.

For more information, check out the National Park Service website (www.nps.gov).

Top Five Places for Sunset Cocktails

» Asylum Restaurant, Jerome Grand Hotel (p822)

» Bell Tower Bar, La Fonda Hotel (p868)

» Grand Canyon Lodge's veranda (p827)

» Mix, Mandalay Bay (799)

» Parallel 88 (p856)

History

By about AD 100, three dominant cultures had emerged in the Southwest: the Hohokam, the Mogollon and the Ancestral Puebloans (formerly known as the Anasazi).

The Hohokam lived in the Arizona deserts from 300 BC to AD 1450, and created an incredible canal irrigation system, earthen pyramids and a rich heritage of pottery. Archaeological studies suggest that a cataclysmic event in the mid-15th century caused a dramatic decrease in the Hohokam's population, most notably in larger villages. Though it's not entirely clear what happened or where they went, the oral traditions of local tribes suggest that some Hohokam remained in the area and that members of these tribes are their descendants. From 200 BC to AD 1450 the Mogollon lived in the central mountains and valleys of the Southwest, and left behind what are now called the Gila Cliff Dwellings.

The Ancestral Puebloans left the richest heritage of archaeological sites, such as that at Chaco Culture National Historic Park. Today descendants of the Ancestral Puebloans are found in the Pueblo groups throughout New Mexico. The Hopi are descendants, too, and their village Old Oraibi (see the boxed text, p830) may be the oldest continuously inhabited settlement in North America.

In 1540 Francisco Vásquez de Coronado led an expedition from Mexico City to the Southwest. Instead of riches, his party found Native Americans, many of whom were then killed or displaced. More than 50 years later, Juan de Oñate established the first capital of New Mexico at San Gabriel. Great bloodshed resulted from Oñate's attempts to control Native American pueblos, and he left in failure in 1608. Santa Fe was established as the new capital around 1610.

Development in the Southwest expanded rapidly during the 19th century, mainly due to railroad and geological surveys. As the US pushed west, the army forcibly removed whole tribes of Native Americans in often horrifyingly brutal Indian Wars. Gold and silver mines drew fortune seekers, and practically overnight the lawless mining towns of the Wild West mushroomed. Capitalizing on the development, the Santa Fe Railroad lured an ocean of tourists to the West.

Modern settlement is closely linked to water use. Following the Reclamation Act of 1902, huge federally funded dams were built to control rivers, irrigate the desert and encourage development. Rancorous debates and disagreements over water rights are ongoing, especially with the phenomenal boom in residential development. Other big issues today are illegal immigration and fiscal solvency.

SOUTHWEST IN...

One Week

Museums and a burgeoning arts scene set an inspirational tone in **Phoenix**, an optimal springboard for exploring. In the morning, follow Camelback Rd into **Scottsdale** for top-notch shopping and gallery-hopping in Old Town. Drive north to **Sedona** for spiritual recharging before pondering the immensity of the **Grand Canyon**. From here, choose either bling or buttes. For bling, detour onto **Route 66**, cross the new bridge beside **Hoover Dam** then indulge your fantasies in **Las Vegas**. For buttes, drive east from the Grand Canyon into the Navajo country, cruising beneath the giant rock formations in **Monument Valley Navajo Tribal Park** then stepping back in time at stunning **Canyon de Chelly National Monument**.

Two Weeks

Start in glitzy **Las Vegas** before kicking back in funky **Flagstaff** and peering into the abyss at **Grand Canyon National Park**. Check out collegiate **Tucson** or frolic amongst cacti at **Saguaro National Park**. Watch the high-noon gunslinging in **Tombstone** before settling into Victorian **Bisbee**.

Secure your sunglasses for the blinding dunes of **White Sands National Monument** in nearby New Mexico then sink into **Santa Fe**, a magnet for art-lovers. Explore a pueblo in **Taos** and watch the sunrise at awesome **Monument Valley Navajo Tribal Park**. Head into Utah for the red-rock national parks, **Canyonlands** and **Arches**. Do the hoodoos at **Bryce Canyon** then pay your respects at glorious **Zion**.

Southwest Highlights

1. Ponder up to two billion years of geologic history at **Grand Canyon National Park** (p823)
2. Live your own John Wayne Western in northeastern Arizona's **Monument Valley** (p830)
3. Practice your fast draw in dusty **Tombstone** (p837)
4. Gallery-hop and jewelry-shop on the stylish streets of **Santa Fe** (p868)
5. Sled down a shimmering sand dune at **White Sands National Monument** (p878)
6. Wander a wonderland of stalactites at **Carlsbad Caverns National Park** (p881)
7. Live the high life on Las Vegas' **Strip** (p795)
8. Ogle towering spires of clay, silt and ash at **Cathedral Gorge State Park** (p808)
9. Snap a photo of graceful Delicate Arch at **Arches National Park** (p850)
10. Explore a majestic canyon and climb Angels Landing at **Zion National Park** (p855)

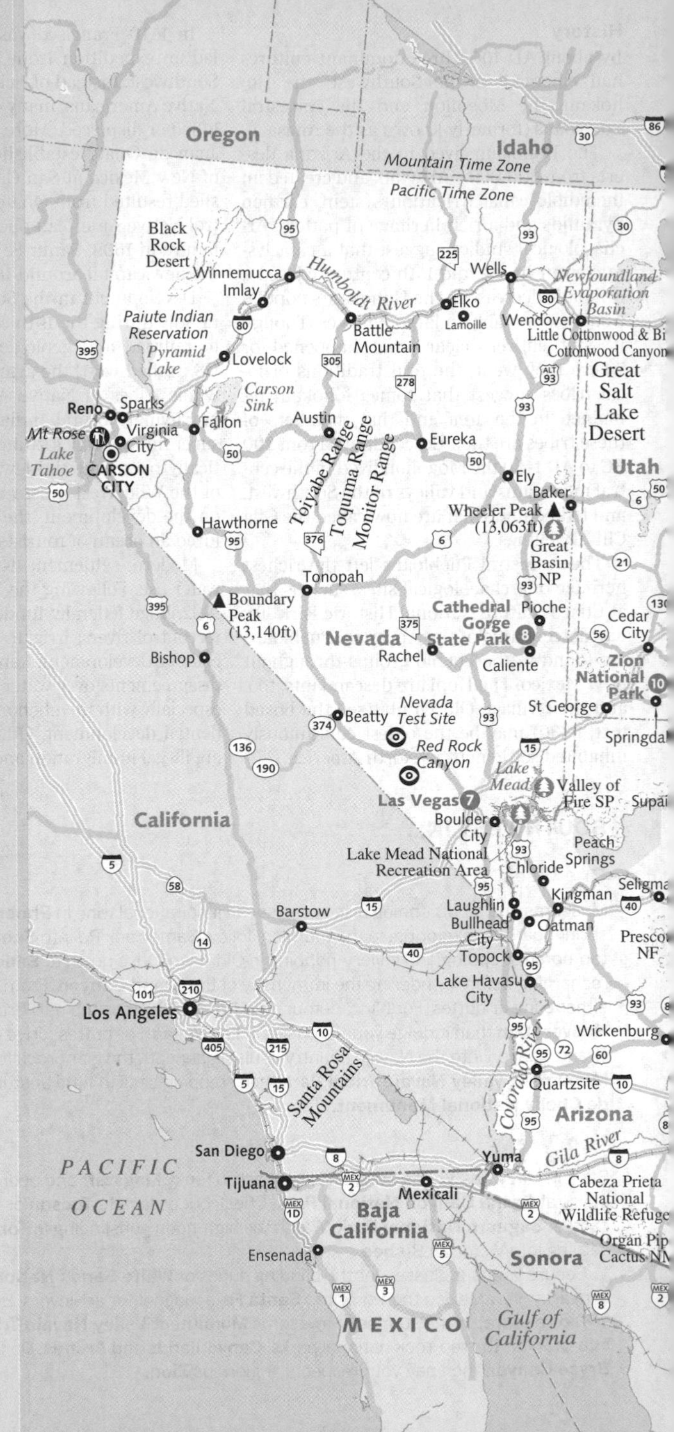

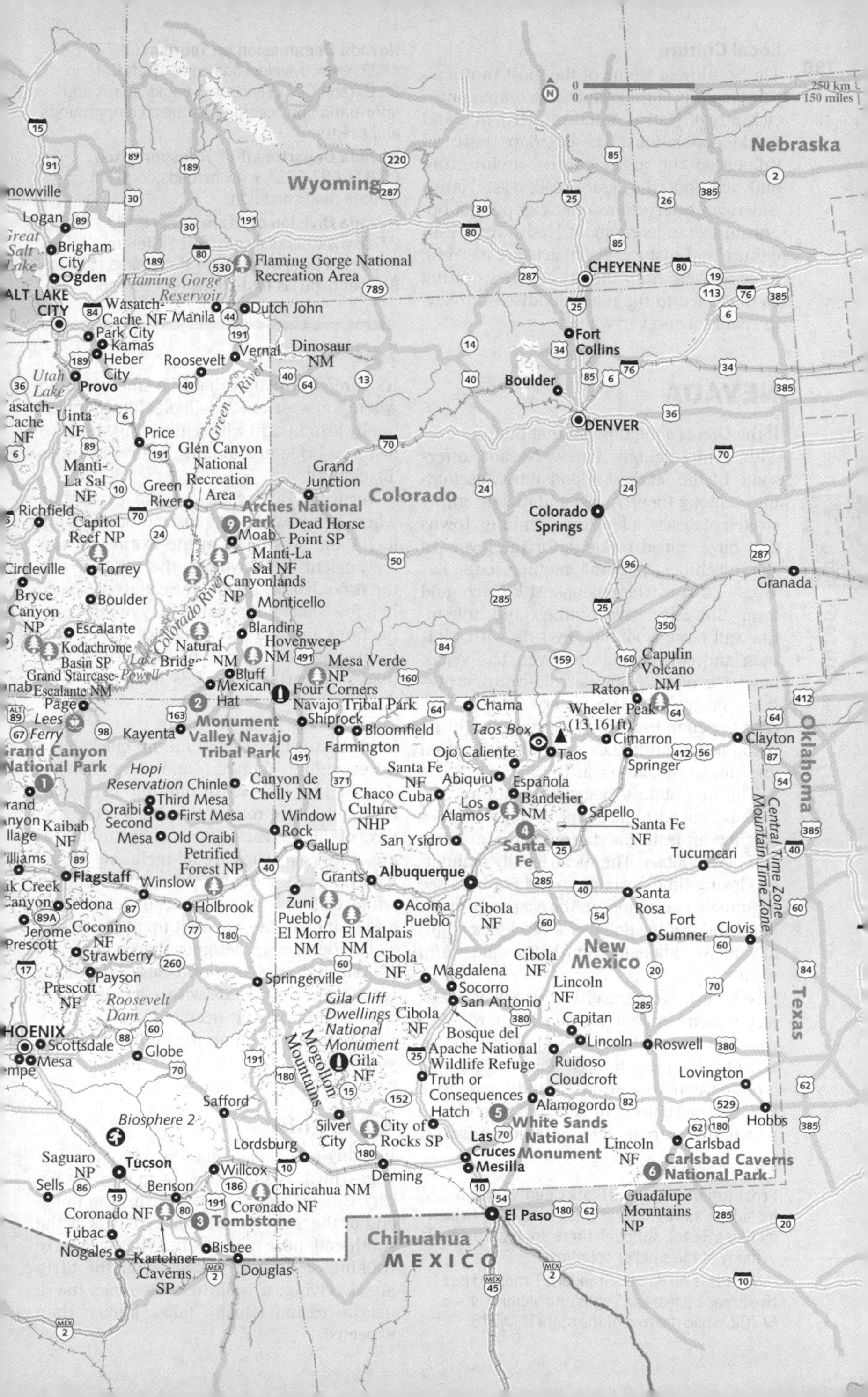

Wyoming
Colorado
Nebraska
New Mexico
Oklahoma
Texas
Chihuahua
MEXICO
Central Time Zone
Mountain Time Zone
250 km
150 miles
CHEYENNE
DENVER
Boulder
Fort Collins
Colorado Springs
Granada
Grand Junction
Flaming Gorge National Recreation Area
Flaming Gorge Reservoir
Dutch John
Manila
Vernal
Dinosaur NM
Roosevelt
SALT LAKE CITY
Logan
Brigham City
Ogden
Great Salt Lake
Wasatch-Cache NF
Park City
Kamas
Heber City
Provo
Utah Lake
Uinta NF
Price
Manti-La Sal NF
Green River
Glen Canyon National Recreation Area
Arches National Park
Dead Horse Point SP
Moab
Manti-La Sal NF
Canyonlands NP
Monticello
Blanding
Hovenweep NM
Mesa Verde NP
Richfield
Capitol Reef NP
Torrey
Circleville
Bryce Canyon NP
Boulder
Escalante
Kodachrome Basin SP
Grand Staircase-Escalante NM
Lake Powell
Natural Bridges NM
Bluff
Mexican Hat
Four Corners Navajo Tribal Park
Page
Lees Ferry
Kayenta
Monument Valley Navajo Tribal Park
Shiprock
Farmington
Bloomfield
Grand Canyon National Park
Hopi Reservation
Chinle
Canyon de Chelly NM
Third Mesa
Oraibi
Second Mesa
First Mesa
Old Oraibi
Kaibab NF
Window Rock
Gallup
Flagstaff
Winslow
Petrified Forest NP
Holbrook
Sedona
Jerome
Prescott
Coconino NF
Strawberry
Payson
Prescott NF
Roosevelt Dam
Scottsdale
Mesa
Globe
Springerville
Safford
Biosphere 2
Tucson
Saguaro NP
Sells
Willcox
Benson
Chiricahua NM
Coronado NF
Tombstone
Tubac
Nogales
Kartchner Caverns SP
Bisbee
Douglas
Lordsburg
Deming
Silver City
City of Rocks SP
Gila Cliff Dwellings National Monument
Mogollon Mountains
Gila NF
Chama
Taos Box
Taos
Wheeler Peak (13,161ft)
Raton
Capulin Volcano NM
Cimarron
Springer
Clayton
Ojo Caliente
Abiquiu
Española
Santa Fe NF
Cuba
Chaco Culture NHP
Los Alamos
Bandelier NM
Sapello
Santa Fe
San Ysidro
Grants
Albuquerque
Zuni Pueblo
El Morro NM
El Malpais NM
Acoma Pueblo
Cibola NF
Magdalena
Socorro
San Antonio
Bosque del Apache National Wildlife Refuge
Truth or Consequences
Hatch
Las Cruces
Mesilla
El Paso
Alamogordo
White Sands National Monument
Cloudcroft
Ruidoso
Capitan
Lincoln
Lincoln NF
Roswell
Tucumcari
Santa Rosa
Fort Sumner
Clovis
Lovington
Hobbs
Carlsbad
Carlsbad Caverns National Park
Guadalupe Mountains NP
Colorado River
Green River

Local Culture

The Southwest is one of the most multicultural regions of the country, encompassing a rich mix of Native American, Hispanic and Anglo populations. These groups have all influenced the area's cuisine, architecture and arts, but the Southwest's vast Native American reservations offer exceptional opportunities to learn about Native American culture and history. Visual arts are a strong force as well, from the art colonies dotting New Mexico to the roadside kitsch on view in small towns everywhere.

NEVADA

If the USA is a melting pot that bubbles over with contradictions, surely Nevada offers some of the starkest – and most fascinating – among them. A vast and mostly empty stretch of desert, a few former mining towns that have traded pickaxes for the levers of slot machines, and the mother lode, Las Vegas – this is where people still catch gold fever. Rural legalized brothels and hole-in-the-wall casinos sit side by side with Mormon and cowboy culture. Even Las Vegas, having evolved from its mid-century nostalgic beginnings, is a far cry from a postcard frozen in time. It's a constantly shifting paradox, a volatile cocktail of sophistication and smut, risk and reward.

The first state to legalize gambling, Nevada is loud with the chime of slot machines singing out from gas stations, supermarkets and hotel lobbies. There's no legally mandated closing time for bars, so get ready to see sequin-clad grandmas in the casino, beers in hand and trading dollars for blackjack chips, at 2am. Nevada banks on what people *really* want.

Wherever you travel in the Silver State, just remember that Nevada is weird. Witness the peaceful riot of self-expression at Burning Man, try to spot alien UFOs, visit atomic-weapons testing grounds and drive the 'Loneliest Road in America': they're all part of this surreal, unforgettable landscape.

Information

Prostitution is illegal in Clark County (which includes Las Vegas) and Washoe County (which includes Reno), although there are legal brothels in many of the smaller counties.

Nevada is on Pacific Standard Time and has two areas codes: Las Vegas and vicinity is ☎702, while the rest of the state is ☎775.

Nevada Commission on Tourism (☎775-687-4322; www.travelnevada.com; 401 N Carson St, Carson City) Sends free books, maps and information on accommodations, campgrounds and events.

Nevada Department of Transportation (☎877-687-6237; www.nvroads.com) For up-to-date road conditions.

Nevada Division of State Parks (☎775-684-2770; www.parks.nv.gov; 901 S Stewart St, 5th fl, Carson City) Camping in state parks ($10 to $15 per night) is first-come, first-served.

Las Vegas

It's three in the morning in a smoky casino when you spot an Elvis look-alike sauntering by arm in arm with a glittering showgirl just as a bride in a long white dress shrieks 'Blackjack!'

Vegas is Hollywood for the everyman, where you play the role instead of watching it. It's the only place in the world you can see ancient hieroglyphics, the Eiffel Tower, the Brooklyn Bridge and the canals of Venice in a few short hours. Sure, they're all reproductions, but in a slice of desert that's transformed itself into one of the most lavish places on earth, nothing is halfway – even the illusions.

Las Vegas is the ultimate escape. Time is irrelevant here. There are no clocks, just never-ending buffets and ever-flowing drinks. This is a city of multiple personalities, constantly reinventing itself since the days of the Rat Pack. Sin City aims to infatuate, and its reaches are all-inclusive. Hollywood bigwigs gyrate at A-list ultralounges, while college kids seek cheap debauchery and grandparents whoop it up at the penny slots. You can sip designer martinis as you sample the apex of world-class cuisine or wander the casino floor with a 3ft-high cocktail tied around your neck.

If you can dream up the kind of vacation you want, it's already a reality here. Welcome to the dream factory.

Sights

Roughly four miles long, the Strip, aka Las Vegas Blvd, is the center of gravity in Sin City. Circus Circus Las Vegas caps the north end of the Strip and Mandalay Bay is at the south end, near the airport. Whether you're walking or driving, distances on the Strip are deceiving; a walk to what looks like a nearby casino usually takes longer than expected.

NEVADA FACTS

» **Nickname** Silver State

» **Population** 2.76 million

» **Area** 109,800 sq miles

» **Capital city** Las Vegas (population 553,000)

» **Other cities** Reno (population 225,000)

» **Sales tax** 6.85%

» **Birthplace of** Patricia Nixon (b 1912), Andre Agassi (b 1970), Greg LeMond (b 1961)

» **Home of** the slot machine, Burning Man

» **Politics** Nevada has six electoral votes – the state swung Democratic in the 2008 presidential election, but it is split about evenly in sending elected officials to Washington; US Senate Majority Leader Harry Reid (D) is Nevada's most well-known politician

» **Famous for** the 1859 Comstock Lode (the country's richest known silver deposit), legalized gambling and prostitution (outlawed in certain counties), and liberal alcohol laws allowing 24-hour bars

» **Weirdest Nevada brothel name** Inez's Dancing and Diddling, Elko

» **Driving distances** Las Vegas to Reno: 452 miles, Great Basin National Park to Las Vegas: 313 miles

Downtown Las Vegas is the original town center and home to the city's oldest hotels and casinos: expect a retro feel, cheaper drinks and lower table limits. Its main drag is fun-loving Fremont St, four blocks of which are a covered pedestrian mall that runs a groovy light show every evening.

Major tourist areas are safe. However, Las Vegas Blvd between downtown and the Strip gets shabby, and Fremont St east of downtown is rather unsavory.

Casinos

TOP CHOICE **Cosmopolitan** CASINO

(www.cosmopolitanlasvegas.com; 3708 Las Vegas Blvd S) Hipsters who have long thought they were too cool for Vegas finally have a place to go where they don't need irony to endure – much less enjoy – the aesthetics. Like the new Hollywood 'It girl,' the Cosmo looks good at all times of the day or night, full of ingenues and entourages, plus regular folks who enjoy contemporary design. With a focus on pure fun, it avoids utter pretension, despite the constant wink-wink, retro moments: the Art-o-Matics (vintage cigarette machines hawking local art rather than nicotine), and possibly the best buffet in town, the **Wicked Spoon**.

TOP CHOICE **Encore** CASINO

(www.encorelasvegas.com; 3121 Las Vegas Blvd S) Steve Wynn has upped the wow factor, and the skyline, yet again with the Encore, a slice of the French Riviera in Las Vegas – and classy enough to entice any of the Riviera's regulars. Filled with indoor flower gardens, a butterfly motif and a dramatically luxe casino, it's an oasis of bright beauty. **Botero**, the restaurant headed by Mark LoRusso, is centered on a large sculpture by Fernando Botero himself. Encore is attached to its sister property, the $2.7-billion **Wynn Las Vegas** (www.wynnlasvegas.com; 3131 Las Vegas Blvd S). The entrance is obscured from the Strip by a $130-million artificial mountain, which rises 7 stories tall in some places. Inside, the Wynn resembles a natural paradise – with mountain views, tumbling waterfalls, fountains and other special effects.

TOP CHOICE **Hard Rock** CASINO

(www.hardrockhotel.com; 4455 Paradise Rd) Beloved by SoCal visitors, this très-hip casino hotel is home to one of the world's most impressive collections of rock and roll memorabilia, including Jim Morrison's handwritten lyrics to one of the Door's greatest hits and leather jackets from a who's who of famous rock stars. The Joint concert hall, Vanity Nightclub and 'Rehab' summer pool parties attract a pimped-out, sex-charged crowd flush with celebrities.

Bellagio CASINO

(www.bellagio.com; 3600 Las Vegas Blvd S) The Bellagio dazzles with Tuscan architecture and an 8-acre artificial lake, complete with don't-miss choreographed dancing fountains. Look up as you enter the lobby: the stunning ceiling adorned with a backlit glass sculpture composed of 2000 handblown flowers by renowned artist Dale Chihuly. The **Bellagio Gallery of Fine Art** (adult/child $13/free; ⌚10am-6pm Sun-Tue & Thu, to 7pm Wed, Fri & Sat) showcases temporary exhibits by

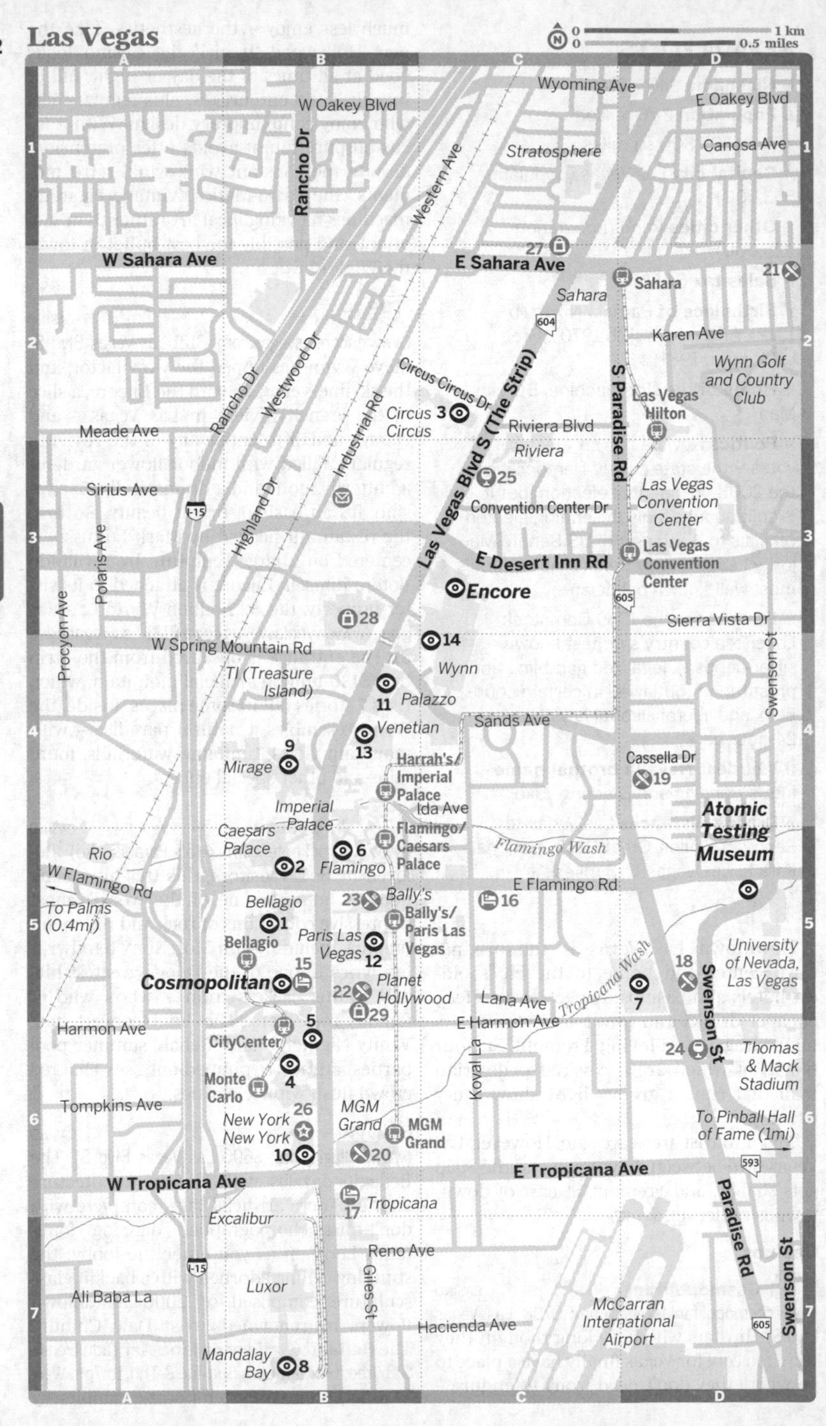

SOUTHWEST NEVADA

Las Vegas

Top Sights
Atomic Testing Museum D5
Cosmopolitan B5
Encore C3

Sights
Adventuredome .... (see 3)
Aria .... (see 5)
1 Bellagio B5
Bellagio Conservatory & Botanical Gardens .... (see 1)
Bellagio Gallery of Fine Art .... (see 1)
2 Caesars Palace B5
3 Circus Circus C2
4 CityCenter B6
5 Crystals B6
6 Flamingo B5
7 Hard Rock D5
8 Mandalay Bay B7
Mandarin Oriental .... (see 4)
Midway .... (see 3)
9 Mirage B4
10 New York New York B6
11 Palazzo B4
12 Paris Las Vegas B5
Shark Reef .... (see 8)
Vdara .... (see 4)
13 Venetian B4
Wildlife Habitat .... (see 6)
14 Wynn Las Vegas C4

Activities, Courses & Tours
Qua Baths & Spa .... (see 2)

Sleeping
Bill's Gamblin' Hall & Saloon .... (see 6)
Caesars Palace .... (see 2)
15 Cosmopolitan B5
Encore .... (see 14)
Hard Rock .... (see 7)
Mandalay Bay .... (see 8)
Paris Las Vegas .... (see 12)
16 Platinum Hotel & Spa C5
17 Tropicana B6

Eating
Buffet Bellagio .... (see 1)
DOCG Enoteca .... (see 15)
18 Ferraro's D5
Fiamma .... (see 20)
19 Firefly D4
House of Blues .... (see 8)
20 Joël Robuchon B6
L'Atelier de Joël Robuchon .... (see 20)
Le Village Buffet .... (see 12)
21 Lotus of Siam D2
Olives .... (see 1)
Pink Taco .... (see 7)
RM Seafood .... (see 8)
Sage .... (see 4)
Scarpetta .... (see 15)
Social House .... (see 5)
Society Café .... (see 14)
22 Spice Market Buffet B5
23 Sterling Brunch at Bally's B5
Sunday Gospel Brunch .... (see 7)
Todd English P.U.B. .... (see 4)
Victorian Room .... (see 6)
'wichcraft .... (see 20)
Wicked Spoon Buffet .... (see 15)

Drinking
Chandelier .... (see 15)
24 Double Down Saloon D6
25 Fireside Lounge C3
Gold Lounge .... (see 5)
LAVO .... (see 11)
Mix .... (see 8)
Parasol Up–Parasol Down .... (see 14)
Red Square .... (see 8)

Entertainment
Drai's .... (see 6)
Gold Lounge .... (see 4)
LOVE .... (see 9)
Marquee .... (see 15)
O .... (see 1)
Tix 4 Tonight .... (see 6)
Tryst .... (see 14)
26 Zumanity B6

Shopping
27 Bonanza Gifts C2
28 Fashion Show Mall B3
Forum Shops .... (see 2)
Grand Canal Shoppes .... (see 13)
29 Miracle Mile Shops B5
Shoppes at Palazzo .... (see 11)

top-notch artists. The **Bellagio Conservatory & Botanical Gardens** (admission free; ⏲daily) features changing exhibits throughout the year.

Venetian CASINO
(www.venetian.com; 3355 Las Vegas Blvd S) Hand-painted ceiling frescoes, roaming mimes, gondola rides and full-scale reproductions of famous Venice landmarks are found at the romantic Venetian. Next door, the **Palazzo** (www.palazzo.com; 3325 Las Vegas Blvd S) exploits a variation on the Italian theme to a less interesting effect: despite the caliber of the **Shoppes at the Palazzo** and the star-studded dining – including exhilarating ventures by culinary heavyweights Charlie Trotter, Emeril Legasse and Wolfgang Puck – the luxurious casino floor and common areas somehow exude a lackluster brand of excitement.

Caesars Palace CASINO
(www.caesarspalace.com; 3570 Las Vegas Blvd S) Quintessentially Las Vegas, Caesars Palace is a Greco-Roman fantasyland featuring marble reproductions of classical statuary, including a not-to-be-missed 4-ton Brahma shrine near the front entrance. Towering fountains, goddess-costumed cocktail waitresses and the swanky haute-couture **Forum Shops** all ante up the glitz.

Paris Las Vegas CASINO
(www.parislasvegas.com; 3655 Las Vegas Blvd S) Evoking the gaiety of the City of Light, Paris Las Vegas strives to capture the essence of the grand dame by re-creating her landmarks. Fine likenesses of the Opéra, the Arc de Triomphe, the Champs-Élysées, the soaring Eiffel Tower and even the Seine frame the property.

Mirage CASINO
(www.mirage.com; 3400 Las Vegas Blvd S) With a tropical setting replete with a huge atrium filled with jungle foliage and soothing cascades, the Mirage captures the imagination. Circling the atrium is a vast Polynesian-themed casino, which places gaming areas under separate roofs to evoke intimacy, including a popular high-limit poker room. Don't miss the 20,000-gallon saltwater aquarium, with 60 species of critters hailing from Fiji to the Red Sea. Out front in the lagoon, a fiery faux volcano erupts hourly after dark until midnight.

Flamingo CASINO
(www.flamingolasvegas.com; 3555 Las Vegas Blvd S) The Flamingo is quintessential vintage Vegas. Weave through the slot machines to the **Wildlife Habitat** (admission free; ⏲daily) to see the flock of Chilean flamingos that call these 15 tropical acres home.

New York New York CASINO
(www.nynyhotelcasino.com; 3790 Las Vegas Blvd S) A mini metropolis featuring scaled-down replicas of the Empire State Building, the Statue of Liberty, ringed by a September 11 memorial, and the Brooklyn Bridge.

Mandalay Bay CASINO
(M-Bay; www.mandalaybay.com; 3950 Las Vegas Blvd S) Not trying to be any one fantasy, the tropically themed Mandalay Bay is worth a walkthrough. Standout attractions include the multilevel **Shark Reef** (www.sharkreef.com; adult/child $18/12; ⏲10am-8pm Sun-Thu, 10am-10pm Fri & Sat; 👪), an aquarium home for thousands of marine beasties with a shallow pool where you can pet pint-sized sharks.

Palms CASINO
(www.palms.com; 4321 W Flamingo Rd) Equal parts sexy and downright sleazy, the Palms attracts loads of notorious celebrities (think Paris Hilton and Britney Spears) as well as a younger, mostly local crowd. Its restaurants and nightclubs are some of the hottest in town. Other highlights include a 14-screen cinema with IMAX capabilities and a live-music club, the **Pearl**. Just don't take the elevator to the **Playboy Club** expecting debauchery à la Hef's mansion: while a few bunny-eared, surgically enhanced ladies deal blackjack in a stylishly appointed lounge full of mostly men, the sexiest thing about it is the stunning skyline view.

Golden Nugget CASINO
(www.goldennugget.com; 129 E Fremont St) Looking like a million bucks, this casino hotel has set the downtown benchmark for extravagance since opening in 1946. No brass or cut glass was spared inside the swanky casino, known for its nonsmoking poker room; the RUSH Lounge, where live local bands play; the utterly lively casino and some of downtown's best restaurants. Don't miss the gigantic 61lb Hand of Faith, the world's largest gold nugget, around the corner from the hotel lobby.

Other Attractions

TOP CHOICE **Atomic Testing Museum** MUSEUM
(www.atomictestingmuseum.org; 755 E Flamingo Rd; adult/child $14/11; ⏲10am-5pm Mon-Sat, noon-5pm Sun) Recalling an era when the word 'atomic' conjured modernity and mystery, the Smithsonian-run Atomic Testing Museum remains an intriguing testament to the period when the fantastical – and destructive – power of nuclear energy was tested just outside of Las Vegas. Don't skip the deafening Ground Zero Theater, which mimics a concrete test bunker.

TOP CHOICE **Neon Museum** MUSEUM
(☎702-387-6366; www.neonmuseum.org; 821 Las Vegas Blvd N; displays free, guided tours $15; ⏲displays 24hr, guided tours noon & 2pm Tue-Sat) Experience the outdoor displays through a fascinating walking tour ($15) of the newly unveiled Neon Boneyard Park, where irreplaceable vintage neon signs – the original art form of Las Vegas – spend their retirement. At the time of going to print, the museum was expanding its digs and hoped to add a self-guided component in 2012; until then, be sure to reserve your tour at least a few weeks in advance.

Stroll around downtown come evening (when the neon comes out to play) to discover the free, self-guided component of the 'museum.' You'll find delightful al-fresco galleries of restored vintage neon signs, including sparkling genie lamps, glowing martini glasses and 1940s motel marquees. The biggest assemblages are found at the on the 3rd St cul-de-sac just north of Fremont St.

Fremont Street Experience STREET
(www.vegasexperience.com; Fremont St; ⏲hourly 7pm-midnight) A four-block pedestrian mall topped by an arched steel canopy and filled with computer-controlled lights, the Fremont Street Experience, between Main St and Las Vegas Blvd, has brought life back to downtown. Every evening, the canopy is transformed into a six-minute light-and-sound show enhanced by 550,000 watts of wraparound sound.

Downtown Arts District ARTS CENTER
On the **First Friday** (www.firstfriday-lasvegas.org) of each month, a carnival of 10,000 art-lovers, hipsters, indie musicians and hangers-on descend on Las Vegas' downtown arts district. These giant monthly block parties feature gallery openings, performance art, live bands and tattoo artists. The action revolves around the **Arts Factory** (101-109 E Charleston Blvd), **Commerce Street Studios** (1551 S Commerce St) and the **Funk House** (1228 S Casino Center Blvd).

CityCenter SHOPPING CENTER
(www.citycenter.com; 3780 Las Vegas Blvd S) We've seen this symbiotic relationship before (think giant hotel anchored by a mall 'concept') but the way that this futuristic-feeling complex places a small galaxy of hypermodern, chichi hotels in orbit around the glitzy **Crystals** (www.crystalsatcitycenter.com; 3720 Las Vegas Blvd S) shopping center is a first. The uber-upscale spread includes the subdued, stylish **Vdara** (www.vdara.com; 2600 W Harmon Ave), the hush-hush opulent **Mandarin Oriental** (www.mandarinoriental.com; 3752 Las Vegas Blvd) and the dramatic architectural showpiece **Aria** (www.arialasvegas.com; 3730 Las Vegas Blvd S), whose sophisticated casino provides a fitting backdrop to its many drop-dead gorgeous restaurants.

Activities

TOP CHOICE **Qua Baths & Spa** SPA
(☎702-731-7776; www.harrahs.com/qua; Caesars Palace, 3570 Las Vegas Blvd S; ⏲6am-8pm) Social spa going is encouraged in the tea lounge, herbal steam room and arctic ice room, where dry-ice snowflakes fall.

Desert Adventures KAYAKING, HIKING
(☎702-293-5026; www.kayaklasvegas.com; 1647 Nevada Hwy, Suite A, Boulder City; trips from $149) With Lake Mead and Hoover Dam just a few hours' drive away, would-be river rats should check out Desert Adventures for lots of half-, full- and multiday kayaking adventures. Hiking and horseback-riding trips, too.

Escape Adventures MOUNTAIN BIKING
(☎800-596-2953; www.escapeadventures.com; 8221 W Charleston Blvd; trips incl bike from $120) The source for guided mountain-bike tours of Red Rock Canyon State Park.

Sleeping

Rates rise and fall dramatically. Check hotel websites, which usually feature calendars listing day-by-day room rates.

THE STRIP

TOP CHOICE **Mandalay Bay** CASINO HOTEL $$
(☎702-632-7777; www.mandalaybay.com; 3950 Las Vegas Blvd S; r $100-380; ❄@🛜🏊) The ornately appointed rooms here have a South Seas theme, and the amenities include

LAS VEGAS FOR CHILDREN

State law prohibits people under 21 years of age from loitering in gaming areas.

The **Circus Circus** (www.circuscircus.com; 2880 Las Vegas Blvd S;) hotel complex is all about the kids, and its **Adventuredome** (adult/child $27/17; 10am-7pm Sun-Thu, 10am-midnight Fri & Sat;) is a 5-acre indoor theme park with fun ranging from laser tag to bumper cars and a roller coaster. The **Midway** (admission free; 11am-midnight;) features animals, acrobats and magicians performing on center stage.

The **Pinball Hall of Fame** (www.pinballmuseum.org; 1610 E Tropicana Ave; admission free, games 25-50¢; 11am-11pm Sun-Thu, to midnight Fri & Sat;) is an interactive museum that's more fun than any slot machine.

floor-to-ceiling windows and luxurious bathrooms. Swimmers will swoon over the pool complex, with a sand-and-surf beach.

TOP CHOICE Tropicana CASINO HOTEL **$**
(702-739-2222; www.troplv.com; 3801 Las Vegas Blvd S; r/ste from $40/140;) As once-celebrated retro properties go under, the Tropicana – keeping the Strip tropical vibe going since 1953 – just got (surprise!) cool again. The multimillion-dollar renovation shows, from the airy casino to the lush, relaxing gardens with their newly unveiled pool and beach club. The earth-toned, breezy rooms and bi-level suites are bargains

Cosmopolitan CASINO HOTEL **$$$**
(702-698-7000; www.cosmopolitanlasvegas.com; 3708 Las Vegas Blvd S; r $200-400;) Are the too-cool-for-school, hip rooms worth the price tag? The indie set seems to think so. The rooms are impressive exercises in mod design, but the real delight of staying here is to stumble out of your room at 1am to play some pool in the upper lobbies before going on a mission to find the 'secret' pizza joint.

Bill's Gamblin' Hall & Saloon CASINO HOTEL **$**
(702-737-2100; www.billslasvegas.com; 3595 Las Vegas Blvd S; r $70-200;) Set slap-bang mid-Strip with affordable rooms nice enough to sport plasma TVs, Bill's is great value, so book far ahead. Rooms feature Victorian-themed decor, and guests can use the pool next door at the Flamingo without charge.

Encore CASINO HOTEL **$$$**
(702-770-8000; www.encorelasvegas.com; 3121 Las Vegas Blvd S; r $199-850;) Classy and playful rather than overblown and opulent – even people cheering at the roulette table clap with a little more elegance. The rooms are studies in subdued luxury.

Caesars Palace CASINO HOTEL **$$**
(866-227-5938; www.caesarspalace.com; 3570 Las Vegas Blvd S; r from $99;) Send away the centurions and decamp in style – Caesars' standard rooms are some of the most luxurious you will find in town.

Paris Las Vegas CASINO HOTEL **$**
(702-946-7000; www.parislasvegas.com; 3655 Las Vegas Blvd S; r from $80;) Nice rooms with a nod to classic French design; the newer Red Rooms are a study in sumptuous class.

DOWNTOWN & OFF THE STRIP

Downtown hotels are generally less expensive than those on the Strip.

TOP CHOICE Hard Rock CASINO HOTEL **$$**
(702-693-5000; www.hardrockhotel.com; 4455 Paradise Rd; r $69-450;) Everything about this boutique hotel spells stardom. French doors reveal skyline and palm tree views, and brightly colored Euro-minimalist rooms feature souped-up stereos and plasma TVs. While we dig the jukeboxes in the HRH All-Suite Tower, the standard rooms are nearly as cool. The hottest action revolves around the lush Beach Club.

TOP CHOICE Artisan Hotel BOUTIQUE HOTEL **$**
(800-554-4092; www.artisanhotel.com; 1501 W Sahara Ave; r from $40;) A Gothic baroque fantasy with a decadent dash of rock and roll, each suite is themed around the work of a different artist. Yet with one of Vegas' best after-parties raging on weekend nights downstairs (a fave with the local alternative set), you may not spend much time in your room. The libidinous, mysterious vibe here isn't for everyone, but if you like it, you'll love it. Artisan's sister hotel,

Rumor (☎877-997-8667; www.rumorvegas.com; 455 E Harmon Ave; ste from $69) is across from the Hard Rock and features a carefree, Miami-cool atmosphere; its airy suites overlook a palm-shaded courtyard pool area dotted with daybeds and hammocks perfect for lounging.

El Cortez Cabana Suites BOUTIQUE HOTEL $
(☎800-634-6703; www.eccabana.com; 651 E Ogden Ave; ste $45-150) You probably won't recognize this sparkling little boutique hotel for its brief movie cameo in Scorcese's *Casino* (hint: Sharon Stone was murdered here) and that's a good thing, because a massive makeover has transformed it into a vintage oasis downtown. Mod suites decked out in mint green include iPod docking stations and retro tiled bathrooms. Plus the coolest vintage casino in town – the El Cortez – is right across the street.

Platinum Hotel BOUTIQUE HOTEL $$
(☎702-365-5000; www.theplatinumhotel.com; 211 E Flamingo Rd; r from $120) Just off the Strip, the coolly modern rooms at this spiffy, non-gaming property are comfortable and full of nice touches – many have fireplaces and they all have kitchens and Jacuzzi tubs.

Red Rock Resort RESORT $$$
(☎702-797-7878; www.redrocklasvegas.com; 11011 W Charleston Blvd; r $110-625) Red Rock touts itself as the first off-Strip billion-dollar gaming resort, and most people who stay here eschew the Strip forever more. There's free transportation between the Strip, and outings to the nearby Red Rocks State Park and beyond. Rooms are well appointed and comfy.

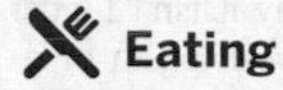

Eating

Sin City is an unmatched eating adventure. Reservations are a must for fancier restaurants; book in advance.

THE STRIP

On the Strip itself, cheap eats beyond fast-food joints are hard to find.

Sage AMERICAN $$$
(☎877-230-2742; www.arialasvegas.com; Aria, 3730 Las Vegas Blvd S; mains $25-42; ⊙5pm-11pm Mon-Sat) Acclaimed chef Shawn McClain meditates on the seasonally sublime with global inspiration and artisanal, farm-to-table ingredients in one of Vegas' most drop-dead gorgeous dining rooms. Don't miss the inspired seasonal cocktails doctored with housemade liqueurs, French absinthe, and fruit purees.

TOP CHOICE **Joël Robuchon** FRENCH $$$
(☎702-891-7925; MGM Grand, 3799 Las Vegas Blvd S; menus per person $120-420; ⊙5:30-10pm Sun-Thu, to 10:30pm Fri & Sat) A once-in-a-lifetime culinary experience; block off a solid three hours and get ready to eat your way through the multicourse seasonal menu of traditional French fare. **L'Atelier de Joël Robuchon**, next door, is where you can belly up to the counter for a slightly more economical but still delicious meal.

TOP CHOICE **DOCG Enoteca** ITALIAN $$
(☎702-698-7920; Cosmopolitan, 3708 Las Vegas Blvd S; mains $13-28; ⊙10am-5pm) Among the

DON'T MISS

COOL POOLS

Hard Rock (p791) Seasonal swim-up blackjack and killer 'Rehab' pool parties at the beautifully landscaped and uberhip Beach Club.

Mirage (p794) The lush tropical pool is a sight to behold, with waterfalls tumbling off cliffs, deep grottoes and palm-tree-studded islands for sunbathing.

Mandalay Bay (p794) Splash around an artificial sand-and-surf beach built from imported California sand and boasting a wave pool, lazy-river ride, casino and DJ-driven topless Moorea Beach Club.

Caesars Palace (p794) Corinthian columns, overflowing fountains, magnificent palms and marble-inlaid pools make the Garden of the Gods Oasis divine. Goddesses proffer frozen grapes in summer, including at the topless Venus pool lounge.

Golden Nugget (p794) Downtown's best pool offers lots of fun and zero attitude. Play poolside blackjack, or sip on a daiquiri in the Jacuzzi and watch the sharks frolic in the adjacent aquarium.

Cosmopolitan's alluring dining options, this is one of the least glitzy – but most authentic – choices. That's not to say it isn't loads of fun. Order up to-die-for fresh pasta or a wood-fired pizza in the stylish *enoteca* (wine shop)–inspired room that feels like you've joined a festive dinner party. Or head next door to sexy **Scarpetta**, which offers a more intimate, upscale experience by the same fantastic chef, Scott Conant.

Social House JAPANESE **$$$**
(☎702-736-1122; www.socialhouselv.com; Crystals at CityCenter, 3720 Las Vegas Blvd S; mains $24-44; ⊙5pm-10pm Mon-Thu, noon-11pm Fri & Sat, noon-10pm Sun) Nibble on creative dishes inspired by Japanese street food in one of the Strip's most serene yet sultry dining rooms. Watermarked scrolls, wooden screens, and loads of dramatic red and black conjure visions of Imperial Japan, while the sushi and steaks are totally contemporary.

RM Seafood SEAFOOD **$$$**
(☎702-632-9300; www.rmseafood.com; Mandalay Place, 3930 Las Vegas Blvd S; lunch $13-36, dinner $20-75; ⊙11:30am-11pm, restaurant 5pm-11pm) From ecoconscious chef Rick Moonen, modern American seafood dishes, such as Cajun popcorn and Maine lobster, come with comfort-food sides (like gourmet mac 'n' cheese), a raw shellfish and sushi bar, and a 'biscuit bar' serving savory salads.

Fiamma ITALIAN **$$$**
(☎702-891-7600; www.mgmgrand.com; MGM Grand, 3799 Las Vegas Blvd S; meals $50-60; ⊙5:30-10pm Sun & Mon, to 10:30pm Tue-Thu, to 11pm Fri & Sat) Fiamma is set in a row of outstanding restaurants at MGM Grand, but what sets it apart is that it's a top-tier dining experience you won't be paying off for the next decade. You haven't had spaghetti until you've had Fiamma's take on it, made with Kobe beef meatballs.

Victorian Room CAFE **$$**
(www.billslasvegas.com; Bill's Gamblin' Hall & Saloon, 3595 Las Vegas Blvd S; mains $8-25; ⊙24hr) A hokey old-fashioned San Francisco theme belies one of the best deals in sit-down restaurants in Las Vegas. The steak and eggs special ($7) is delicious around the clock.

Olives MEDITERRANEAN **$$$**
(☎702-693-8865; www.bellagio.com; Bellagio, 3600 Las Vegas Blvd S; mains $16-52; ⊙lunch & dinner) Bostonian chef Todd English dishes up homage to the life-giving fruit. Flatbread pizzas, housemade pastas and flame-licked meats get top billing, and patio tables overlook Lake Como. Try his rollicking new CityCenter venture, **Todd English PUB** (www.toddenglishpub.com; Crystals at CityCenter, 3720 Las Vegas Blvd S; mains $13-24; ⊙lunch & dinner), a strangely fun cross between a British pub and a frat party, with creative sliders, English pub classics, and an interesting promotion: if you drink your beer in less than seven seconds, it's on the house.

Society Café CAFE **$$**
(www.wynnlasvegas.com; Encore, 3121 Las Vegas Blvd S; mains $14-30; ⊙7am-midnight Sun-Thu, 7am-1am Fri & Sat) A slice of reasonably priced culinary heaven in the midst of Encore's loveliness. The basic cafe here is equal to fine dining at other joints.

'wichcraft SANDWICHES **$**
(www.mgmgrand.com; MGM Grand, 3799 Las Vegas Blvd S; sandwiches $8-11; ⊙10am-5pm) This designy little sandwich shop, the brainchild of celebrity chef Tom Colicchio, is one of the best places to taste gourmet on a budget.

DOWNTOWN & OFF THE STRIP

Traditionally off the culinary radar, downtown's restaurants offers better value than those on the Strip, whether a casino buffet or a retro steakhouse.

Just west of the Strip, the Asian restaurants on Spring Mountain Rd in Chinatown

WORTHY INDULGENCES: BEST BUFFETS

» **Wicked Spoon Buffet** (www.cosmopolitanlasvegas.com; Cosmopolitan, 3708 Las Vegas Blvd S)

» **Le Village Buffet** (www.parislasvegas.com; Paris Las Vegas, 3655 Las Vegas Blvd S)

» **Spice Market Buffet** (Planet Hollywood, 3667 Las Vegas Blvd S)

» **Sterling Brunch at Bally's** (☎702-967-7999; Bally's, 3645 Las Vegas Blvd S; ⊙Sun)

» **Buffet Bellagio** (☎702-693-7111; www.bellagio.com; Bellagio, 3600 Las Vegas Blvd S)

» **Sunday Gospel Brunch** (☎702-632-7600; www.hob.com; House of Blues, Mandalay Bay, 3950 Las Vegas Blvd S)

are also good budget options, with lots of vegetarian choices.

TOP CHOICE **Ferraro's** ITALIAN $$
(www.ferraroslasvegas.com, 4480 Paradise Rd; mains $10-39; ⏲11:30am-2am Mon-Fri, 4pm-2am Sat & Sun) The photos on the wall offer testimony to the fact that locals have been flocking to classy, family-owned Ferraro's for 85 years to devour savory Italian classics. These days, the fireplace patio and the amazing late night happy hour draw an eclectic crowd full of industry and foodie types at the friendly bar. To-die-for housemade pastas compete for attention with legendary osso buco, and a killer antipasti menu served until midnight.

TOP CHOICE **Firefly** TAPAS $$
(www.fireflylv.com; 3900 Paradise Rd; small dishes $4-10, large dishes $11-20; ⏲11:30am-2am Sun-Thu, to 3am Fri & Sat) Locals seem to agree on one thing about the Vegas food scene: a meal at Firefly can be twice as fun as an overdone Strip restaurant, and half the price. Is that why it's always hopping? Nosh on traditional Spanish tapas, while the bartender pours sangria and flavor-infused *mojitos*.

Lotus of Siam THAI $$
(www.saipinchutima.com; 953 E Sahara Ave; mains $9-29; ⏲11:30am-2pm Mon-Fri, 5:30-9:30pm Mon-Thu, 5:30-10pm Fr & Sat) The top Thai restaurant in the US? According to *Gourmet Magazine*, this is it. One bite of simple pad Thai – or any of the exotic northern Thai dishes – nearly proves it.

N9NE STEAKHOUSE $$$
(☎702-933-9900; www.palms.com; Palms, 4321 W Flamingo Rd; mains $26-43; ⏲dinner) At this hip steakhouse heavy with celebs, a dramatic dining room centers on a champagne-and-caviar bar. Chicago-style aged steaks and chops keep coming, along with everything from oysters Rockefeller to Pacific sashimi.

Pink Taco MEXICAN $$
(www.hardrockhotel.com; Hard Rock, 4455 Paradise Rd; mains $8-24; ⏲7am-11am Mon-Thu, to 3am Fri & Sat) Whether it's the 99¢ taco and margarita happy hour, the leafy poolside patio, or the friendly rock and roll clientele, Pink Taco always feels like a worthwhile party.

Golden Gate SEAFOOD $
(www.goldengatecasino.com; 1 E Fremont St; ⏲11am-3am) Famous $1.99 shrimp cocktails (super-size them for $3.99).

EMERGENCY ARTS

A coffee shop, an art gallery, studios, and a de facto community center of sorts, all under one roof and right smack downtown? The **Emergency Arts** (www.emergencyartslv.com; 520 Fremont St) building, also home to **Beat Coffeehouse** (www.thebeatlv.com; sandwiches $6-7; ⏲7am-midnight Mon-Fri, 9am-midnight Sat, 9am-3pm Sun) is a friendly bastion of laid-back cool and strong coffee where vintage vinyl spins on old turntables. If you're aching to meet some savvy locals who know their way around town, this is your hangout spot.

Drinking

For those who want to mingle with the locals and drink for free, check out **SpyOnVegas** (www.spyonvegas.com). It arranges an open bar at a different venue every weeknight.

THE STRIP

TOP CHOICE **Mix** LOUNGE
(www.mandalaybay.com; 64th fl, THEhotel at Mandalay Bay, 3950 Las Vegas Blvd S; cover after 10pm $20-25) THE place to grab sunset cocktails. The glassed-in elevator has amazing views, and that's before you even glimpse the mod interior design and soaring balcony.

TOP CHOICE **Gold Lounge** LOUNGE, CLUB
(www.arialasvegas.com; Aria, 3730 Las Vegas Blvd S; cover after 10pm $20-25) You won't find watered-down Top 40 at this luxurious ultralounge, but you will find gold, gold and more gold. It's a fitting homage to Elvis: make a toast in front of the giant portrait of the King himself.

Chandelier BAR
(www.cosmopolitanlasvegas.com; Cosmopolitan, 3708 Las Vegas Blvd S; ⏲5pm-2am) In a city full of lavish hotel lobby bars, this one pulls out all the stops. Kick back with the Cosmopolitan hipsters and enjoy the curiously thrilling feeling that you're tipsy inside a giant crystal chandelier.

LAVO LOUNGE, CLUB
(www.palazzo.com; Palazzo, 3325 Las Vegas Blvd S) One of the sexiest new restaurant-lounge-nightclub combos for the see-and-be-seen set, Lavo's terrace is the place to be at happy

hour. Sip a Bellini in the dramatically lit bar or stay to dance among reclining Renaissance nudes in the club upstairs.

Parasol Up – Parasol Down BAR, CAFE
(www.wynnlasvegas.com; Wynn Las Vegas, 3131 Las Vegas Blvd S; ⏲11am-4am Sun-Thu, to 5am Fri & Sat) Unwind with a fresh fruit *mojito* by the soothing waterfall at the Wynn to experience one of Vegas' most successful versions of paradise.

Red Square BAR
(www.mandalaybay.com; Mandalay Bay, 3950 Las Vegas Blvd S) Heaps of Russian caviar, a solid ice bar and over 200 frozen vodkas, infusions and cocktails. Don a Russian army coat to sip vodka in the subzero vault.

DOWNTOWN & OFF THE STRIP

Want to chill out with the locals? Head to one of their go-to favorites.

TOP CHOICE **Fireside Lounge** COCKTAIL BAR
(www.peppermilllasvegas.com; Peppermill, 2985 Las Vegas Blvd S; ⏲24hr) The Strip's most unlikely romantic hideaway is inside a retro coffee shop. Courting couples flock here for the low lighting, sunken fire pit and cozy nooks built for supping on multistrawed tiki drinks and for acting out your most inadvisable 'what happens in Vegas, stays in Vegas' moments.

TOP CHOICE **Double Down Saloon** BAR
(www.doubledownsaloon.com; 4640 Paradise Rd; no cover; ⏲24hr) You can't get more punk rock than a dive whose tangy, blood-red house drink is named 'Ass Juice' and where happy hour means everything in the bar is two bucks. (Ass Juice and a Twinkie for $5: one of Vegas' bizarrely badass bargains.) Killer Juke box, cash only.

Beauty Bar COCKTAIL BAR
(www.thebeautybar.com; 517 E Fremont St; cover $5-10) At the salvaged innards of a 1950s New Jersey beauty salon, swill a cocktail while you get a makeover demo or chill out with the hip DJs and live local bands. Then walk around the corner to the **Downtown Cocktail Room**, a speakeasy.

Frankie's Tiki Room THEME BAR
(www.frankiestikiroom.com; 1712 W Charleston Blvd; ⏲24hr) At the only round-the-clock tiki bar in the US, the drinks are rated in strength by skulls and the top tiki sculptors and painters in the world have their work on display.

☆ Entertainment

Las Vegas has no shortage of entertainment on any given night, and **Ticketmaster** (☎702-474-4000; www.ticketmaster.com) sells tickets for pretty much everything.

Tix 4 Tonight BOOKING SERVICE
(☎877-849-4868; www.tix4tonight.com; Bill's Gamblin' Hall & Saloon, 3595 Las Vegas Blvd S; ⏲10am-8pm) Offers half-price tix for a limited lineup of same-day shows and small discounts on 'always sold-out' shows.

Nightclubs & Live Music

Admission prices to nightclubs vary wildly based on the mood of door staff, male-to-female ratio, and how crowded the club is that night.

TOP CHOICE **Marquee** CLUB
(www.cosmopolitanlasvegas.com; Cosmopolitan, 3708 Las Vegas Blvd) When someone asks what the coolest club in Vegas is, Marquee is the undisputed answer. Celebrities (we spotted Macy Gray as we danced through the crowd), an outdoor beach club, hot DJs, and that certain *je ne sais quoi* that makes a club worth waiting in line for.

TOP CHOICE **Tryst** CLUB
(www.trystlasvegas.com; Wynn Las Vegas, 3131 Las Vegas Blvd S) All gimmicks aside, the flowing waterfall makes this place ridiculously (and literally) cool. Blood-red booths and plenty of space to dance ensure that you can have a killer time even without splurging for bottle service.

Drai's CLUB
(www.drais.net; Bill's Gamblin' Hall & Saloon, 3595 Las Vegas Blvd S; ⏲1am-8am Thu-Mon) Feel ready for an after-hours scene straight outta Hollywood? Things don't really get going here until 4am, when DJs spinning progressive discs keep the cool kids content. Dress to kill.

Stoney's Rockin' Country LIVE MUSIC
(www.stoneysrockincountry.com; 9151 Las Vegas Blvd S; cover $5-10; ⏲7pm-late Thu-Sun) An off-Strip place that's worth the trip. Friday and Saturday features all-you-can-drink draft beer specials and free line-dancing lessons. The mechanical bull is a blast.

Moon CLUB
(www.n9negroup.com; Palms, 4321 W Flamingo Rd; cover from $20; ⏲11pm-4am Tue & Thu-Sun) Stylishly outfitted like a nightclub in outer

VEGAS CLUBBING 101

Brave the velvet rope – or skip it altogether – with these nightlife survival tips we culled from the inner circle of Vegas doormen, VIP hosts, and concierges.

» Avoid waiting in that long line by booking ahead with the club VIP host. Most bigger clubs have someone working the door during the late afternoon and early evening hours.

» Ask the concierge of your hotel for clubbing suggestions – he or she will almost always have free passes for clubs, or be able to make you reservations with the VIP host.

» If you hit blackjack at the high-roller table or just want to splurge, think about bottle service. Yes, it's expensive (starting at around $300 to $400 and upwards for a bottle, including mixers, plus tax and tip), but it usually waives cover charge (and waiting in line) for your group, plus you get to chill out at a table – valuable 'real estate' in club speak.

space; the retractable roof opens for dancing to pulsating beats under the stars. Admission includes entry to the only Playboy Club in the world.

Production Shows

There are hundreds of shows to choose from in Vegas. Any Cirque du Soleil show tends to be an unforgettable experience.

TOP CHOICE Steel Panther LIVE MUSIC
(☎702-617-7777; www.greenvalleyranchresort.com; Green Valley Resort, 2300 Paseo Verde Pkwy, Henderson; admission free; ⏲11pm-late Thu) A hair-metal tribute band makes fun of the audience, themselves and the 1980s with sight gags, one-liners and many a drug and sex reference.

TOP CHOICE LOVE PERFORMING ARTS
(☎702-792-7777; www.cirquedusoleil.com; tickets $99-150) This show at the Mirage is a popular addition to the Cirque du Soleil lineup; locals who have seen many Cirque productions come and go say it's the best.

O PERFORMING ARTS
(☎702-796-9999; www.cirquedusoleil.com; tickets $99-200) Still a favorite is Cirque du Soleil's aquatic show, O, performed at the Bellagio.

Zumanity PERFORMING ARTS
(☎702-740-6815; www.cirquedusoleil.com; tickets $69-129) A Sensual and sexy adult-only show at New York New York.

Shopping

Bonanza Gifts GIFTS
(www.worldslargestgiftshop.com; 2440 Las Vegas Blvd S; ⏲11am-midnight) The best place for only-in-Vegas kitsch souvenirs.

The Attic VINTAGE
(www.atticvintage.com; 1018 S Main St; ⏲10am-6pm, closed Sun) Be mesmerized by fabulous hats and wigs, hippie-chic clubwear and lounge-lizard furnishings at Vegas' best vintage store.

Fashion Show Mall MALL
(www.thefashionshow.com; 3200 Las Vegas Blvd S) Nevada's biggest and flashiest mall.

Forum Shops MALL
(www.caesarspalace.com; Caesars Palace, 3570 Las Vegas Blvd S) Upscale stores in an air-conditioned version of Ancient Rome.

Grand Canal Shoppes MALL
(www.thegrandcanalshoppes.com; Venetian, 3355 Las Vegas Blvd S) Italianate indoor luxury mall with gondolas.

Shoppes at Palazzo MALL
(Palazzo, 3327 Las Vegas Blvd S) Sixty international designers, from Tory Burch to Jimmy Choo, flaunt their goodies.

Miracle Mile Shops MALL
(www.miraclemileshopslv.com; Planet Hollywood, 3663 Las Vegas Blvd S) A staggering 1.5 miles long; get a tattoo, a drink and duds.

Information

Emergency & Medical Services

Gamblers Anonymous (☎702-385-7732) Assistance with gambling concerns.

Police (☎702-828-3111)

Sunrise Hospital & Medical Center (☎702-731-8000; 3186 S Maryland Pkwy)

University Medical Center (☎702-383-2000; 1800 W Charleston Blvd)

Internet Access

Wi-fi is available in most hotel rooms (about $10 to $25 per day, sometimes included in the 'resort fee') and there are internet kiosks with attached printers in most hotel lobbies.

Internet Resources & Media

Cheapo Vegas (www.cheapovegas.com) Good for a run-down of casinos with low table limits and their insider's guide to cheap eating.

Las Vegas Review-Journal (www.lvrj.com) Daily paper with a weekend guide, *Neon*, on Friday.

Las Vegas Tourism (www.onlyinvegas.com) Official tourism website.

Las Vegas Weekly (www.lasvegasweekly.com) Free weekly with good entertainment and restaurant listings.

lasvegas.com (www.lasvegas.com) Travel services.

Lasvegaskids.net (www.lasvegaskids.net) The lowdown on what's up for the wee ones.

Vegas.com (www.vegas.com) Travel information with booking service.

Money

Every hotel-casino and bank and most convenience stores have an ATM. The ATM fee at most casinos is around $5. Best to stop at off-Strip banks if possible.

American Express (☎702-739-8474; Fashion Show Mall, 3200 Las Vegas Blvd S; ⊙10am-9pm Mon-Fri, 10am-8pm Sat, noon-6pm Sun) Changes currencies at competitive rates.

Post

Post office (☎702-382-5779; 201 Las Vegas Blvd S) Downtown.

Tourist Information

Las Vegas Visitor Information Center (☎702-847-4858; www.visitlasvegas.com; 3150 Paradise Rd; ⊙8am-5pm) Free local calls, internet access and maps galore.

ℹ Getting There & Around

Just south of the major Strip casinos and easily accessible from I-15, **McCarran International Airport** (www.mccarran.com) has direct flights from most US cities, and some from Canada and Europe. **Bell Trans** (☎702-739-7990; www.bell-trans.com) offers a shuttle service ($6.50) between the airport and the Strip. Fares to downtown destinations are slightly higher. At the airport, exit door 9 near baggage claim to find the Bell Trans booth.

All of the attractions in Vegas have free self-parking and valet parking available (tip $2). Fast, fun and fully wheelchair accessible, the **monorail** (☎702-699-8299; www.lvmonorail.com) connects the Sahara to the MGM Grand, stopping at major Strip megaresorts along the way, and operating from 7am to 2am Monday to Thursday and until 3am Friday through Sunday. A single ride is $5, a 24-hour pass is $12, and a three-day pass is $28. The **Deuce** (☎702-228-7433; www.rtcsouthernnevada.com), a local double-decker bus, runs frequently 24 hours daily between the Strip and downtown (two-/24-hour pass $5/7).

Around Las Vegas

Red Rock Canyon CANYON
(www.redrockcanyonlv.org; per car/bicycle $7/5; ⊙6am-dusk) This dramatic park is the perfect antidote to Vegas' artificial brightness. A 20-mile drive west of the Strip, the canyon is actually more like a valley, with the steep, rugged red-rock escarpment rising 3000ft on its western edge. There's a 13-mile scenic loop with access to hiking trails and first-come, first-served **camping** (tent sites $15) 2 miles east of the visitor center.

Lake Mead & Hoover Dam LAKE, HISTORIC SITE
Lake Mead and Hoover Dam are the most-visited sites within the **Lake Mead National Recreation Area** (www.nps.gov/lame), which encompasses 110-mile-long Lake Mead, 67-mile-long Lake Mohave and many miles of desert around the lakes. The excellent **Alan Bible Visitors Center** (☎702-293-8990; ⊙8:30am-4:30pm), on Hwy 93 halfway between Boulder City and Hoover Dam, has information on recreation and desert life. From there, North Shore Rd winds around the lake and makes a great scenic drive.

Straddling the Arizona–Nevada border, the graceful curve and art-deco style of the 726ft **Hoover Dam** (www.usbr.gov/lc/hooverdam) contrasts superbly with the stark landscape. Don't miss a stroll over the new **Mike O'Callaghan-Pat Tillman Memorial Bridge** (www.hooverdambypass.org) which features a pedestrian walkway with perfect

WORTH A TRIP

VALLEY OF FIRE STATE PARK

A masterpiece of desert scenery filled with psychedelically shaped sandstone outcroppings, this **park** (www.parks.nv.gov/vf.htm; admission $10) is a great escape 55 miles from Vegas. Hwy 169 runs right past the **visitor center** (☎702-397-2088; ⊙8:30am-4:30pm), which has hiking and **camping** (tent/RV sites $20/30) information and excellent desert-life exhibits.

views upstream of Hoover Dam. (Not recommended for anyone with vertigo.) Visitors can either take the 30-minute **power plant tour** (adult/child $11/9; ⏲9:15am-5:15pm, to 4:15pm Sep-Mar) or the more in-depth, one-hour **Hoover Dam tour** (no children under 8yr; tours $30).

Tickets for both tours are sold at the **visitor center** (⏲9am-6pm; exhibits adult/child $8/free). Tickets for the power plant tour only can be purchased online.

For a relaxing lunch or dinner break, head to nearby downtown Boulder City, where **Milo's** (538 Nevada Way; dishes $4.50-13; ⏲11am-10pm Sun-Thu, to midnight Fri & Sat) serves fresh sandwiches, salads and gourmet cheese plates at sidewalk tables outside the wine bar.

WORTH A TRIP

PYRAMID LAKE

A piercingly blue expanse in an otherwise barren landscape 25 miles north of Reno on the Paiute Indian Reservation, Pyramid Lake is popular for recreation and fishing. Permits for **camping** (primitive campsites per vehicle per night $9) and **fishing** (per person $9) are available at outdoor suppliers and CVS drugstore locations in Reno, and at the **ranger station** (☎775-476-1155; www.pyramidlake.us; ⏲8am-6pm) on SR 445 in Sutcliffe.

Western Nevada

A vast and mostly undeveloped sagebrush steppe, the western corner of the state is carved by mountain ranges and parched valleys. The place where modern Nevada began with the discovery of the famous Comstock silver lode in and around Virginia City, these days this part of the state lures visitors with outdoor adventure in the form of hiking, biking, and skiing on the many mountains. Contrasts here are as extreme as the weather: one moment you're driving through a quaint historic town full of grand homes built by silver barons, and the next you spot a tumbleweed blowing by a homely little bar that turns out to be the local (and legal) brothel. And then there's the casino lights and the kitschy mid-century wedding chapels that lure so many toward the gambling mecca of Reno.

For information about the Nevada side of Lake Tahoe, see p998.

RENO

A soothingly schizophrenic city of big-time gambling and top-notch outdoor adventures, Reno (population 225,000) resists pigeonholing. 'The Biggest Little City in the World' has something to raise the pulse of adrenaline junkies, hard-core gamblers and city people craving easy access to wide open spaces.

Sights

National Automobile Museum MUSEUM
(☎775-333-9300; www.automuseum.org; 10 S Lake St; adult/child/senior $10/4/8; ⏲9:30am-5:30pm Mon-Sat, 10am-4pm Sun; 👪) Stylized street scenes illustrate a century's worth of automobile history at this engaging car museum. The collection is enormous and impressive, with one-of-a-kind vehicles, including James Dean's 1949 Mercury from *Rebel Without a Cause,* a 1938 Phantom Corsair and a 24-karat gold-plated DeLorean, and rotating exhibits bringing in all kinds of souped-up or fabulously retro rides.

Nevada Museum of Art MUSEUM
(☎775-329-3333; www.nevadaart.org; 160 W Liberty St; adult/child/student & senior $10/1/8; ⏲10am-5pm Wed-Sun, 10am-8pm Thu) In a sparkling building inspired by the geologic formations of the Black Rock Desert north of town, a floating staircase leads to galleries showcasing temporary exhibits and images related to the American West. Great cafe for postcultural refueling.

University of Nevada UNIVERSITY
Pop into the flying saucer-shaped **Fleischmann Planetarium & Science Center** (☎775-784-4811; http://planetarium.unr.nevada.edu; 1650 N Virginia St; admission free; ⏲noon-5pm Mon & Tue, noon-9pm Fri, 10am-9pm Sat, 10am-5pm Sun) for a window on the universe during star shows and feature **presentations** (adult/child $6/4). Nearby is the **Nevada Historical Society Museum** (☎775-688-1190; www.museums.nevadaculture.org; 1650 N Virginia St; adult/under 17yr $4/free; ⏲10am-5pm Wed-Sat), which includes permanent exhibits on neon signs, local Native American culture and the presence of the federal government.

VIRGINIA STREET

Wedged between the I-80 and the Truckee River, downtown's N Virginia St is casino central. South of the river it continues as S Virginia St. All of the following hotel-casinos are open 24 hours.

Circus Circus CASINO
(www.circusreno.com; 500 N Sierra St;) The most family-friendly of the bunch, it has free circus acts to entertain kids beneath a giant, candy-striped big top, which also harbors a gazillion carnival and video games that look awfully similar to slot machines.

Silver Legacy CASINO
(www.silverlegacyreno.com; 407 N Virginia St) A Victorian-themed place, it's easily recognized by its white landmark dome, where a giant mock mining rig periodically erupts into a tame sound-and-light show.

Eldorado CASINO
(www.eldoradoreno.com; 345 N Virginia St) The Eldorado has a kitschy Fountain of Fortune that probably has Italian sculptor Bernini spinning in his grave.

Harrah's CASINO
(www.harrahsreno.com; 219 N Center St) Founded by Nevada gambling pioneer William Harrah in 1946, it's still one of the biggest and most popular casinos in town.

About 2 miles south of downtown are two of Reno's biggest casino hotels:

Peppermill CASINO
(www.peppermillreno.com; 2707 S Virginia St) Dazzles with a 17-story Tuscan-style tower.

Atlantis CASINO
(www.atlantiscasino.com; 3800 S Virginia St) Now more classy than zany, with an extensive spa, the remodeled casino retains a few tropical flourishes such as indoor waterfalls and palm trees.

Activities

Reno is a 30- to 60-minute drive from Tahoe ski resorts and many hotels and casinos offer special stay and ski packages.

RENO AREA TRAILS

For extensive information on regional hiking and biking trails, including the Mt Rose summit trail and the Tahoe-Pyramid Bikeway, download the **Truckee Meadows Trails guide** (www.reno.gov/Index.aspx?page=291).

Truckee River Whitewater Park WATER SPORTS
Mere steps from the casinos, the park's Class II and III rapids are gentle enough for kids riding inner tubes, yet sufficiently challenging for professional freestyle kayakers. Two courses wrap around Wingfield Park, a small river island that hosts free concerts in summertime. **Tahoe Whitewater Tours** (775-787-5000; www.gowhitewater.com) and **Wild Sierra Adventures** (866-323-8928; www.wildsierra.com) offer kayak trips and lessons.

Historic Reno Preservation Society WALKING TOUR
(775-747-4478; www.historicreno.org; tours $10) Dig deeper with a walking or cycling tour highlighting subjects including architecture, politics and literary history.

Sleeping

Lodging rates vary widely depending on the day of the week and local events. Sunday through Thursday are generally the best; Friday is more expensive and Saturday can be as much as triple the midweek rate.

In summer, there's gorgeous high-altitude camping at **Mt Rose** (877-444-6777; www.recreation.gov; Hwy 431; tent & RV sites $16).

Peppermill CASINO HOTEL $$
(775-826-2121; www.peppermillreno.com; 2707 S Virginia St; r Sun-Thu $50-140; Fri & Sat $70-200;) Now awash in Vegas-style opulence, the popular Peppermill boasts Tuscan-themed rooms in its newest 600-room tower, and has almost completed a plush remodel of its older rooms. The three sparkling pools (one indoor) are dreamy, with a full spa on hand. Geothermal energy powers the resort's hot water and heat.

Sands Regency CASINO HOTEL $
(775-348-2200; www.sandsregency.com; 345 N Arlington Ave; r Sun-Thu/Fri & Sat from $29/89;) Some of the largest standard digs in town, rooms here are decked out in a cheerful tropical palette of upbeat blues, reds and greens – a visual relief from standard-issue motel decor. The 17th-floor gym and Jacuzzi are perfectly positioned to capture your eyes with drop-dead panoramic mountain views. Empress Tower rooms are best.

Wildflower Village MOTEL $
(775-747-8848; www.wildflowervillage.com; 4395 W 4th St; r $50-75, B&B $100-125;) Perhaps more of a state of mind than a motel,

DON'T MISS

BURNING MAN

For one week at the end of August, **Burning Man** (www.burningman.com; admission $210-320) explodes onto the sunbaked Black Rock Desert, and Nevada sprouts a third major population center – Black Rock City. An experiential art party (and alternative universe) that climaxes in the immolation of a towering stick figure, Burning Man is a whirlwind of outlandish theme camps, dust-caked bicycles, bizarre bartering, costume-enhanced nudity and a general relinquishment of inhibitions.

this artists colony on the west edge of town has a tumbledown yet creative vibe. Murals decorate the facade of each room, and you can hear the freight trains rumble on by.

Eating

Reno's dining scene goes far beyond the casino buffets.

TOP CHOICE Old Granite Street Eatery AMERICAN $$
(☎775-622-3222; 243 S Sierra St; dishes $9-24; ⏲11am-10pm Mon-Thu, 11am-midnight Fri, 10am-midnight Sat, 10am-4pm Sun) A lovely well-lighted place for organic and local comfort food, old-school artisanal cocktails and seasonal craft beers, this antique-strewn hot spot enchants diners with its stately wooden bar, water served in old liquor bottles and its lengthy seasonal menu. Forgot to make a reservation? Check out the iconic rooster and pig murals and wait for seats at a community table fashioned from a barn door.

Pneumatic Diner VEGETARIAN $
(501 W 1st St, 2nd fl; dishes $6-9; ⏲noon-10pm Mon, 11am-10pm Tue-Thu, 11am-11pm Fri & Sat, 8am-10pm Sun; 🥕) Consume a garden of vegetarian delights under salvaged neon lights. This groovy little place near the river has meatless and vegan comfort food and desserts to tickle your inner two-year-old, such as the ice-cream-laden Cookie Bomb. It's attached to the Truckee River Terrace apartment complex; use the Ralston St entrance.

Silver Peak Restaurant & Brewery PUB $$
(124 Wonder St; mains lunch $8-10, dinner $9-21; ⏲11am-midnight) Casual and pretense-free, this place hums with the chatter of happy locals settling in for a night of microbrews and great eats, from pizza with roasted chicken to shrimp pasta and filet mignon.

Peg's Glorified Ham & Eggs DINER $
(420 S Sierra St; dishes $7-10; ⏲6:30am-2pm; 👪) Locally regarded as the best breakfast in town, Peg's offers tasty grill food that's not too greasy.

Drinking

Jungle Java & Jungle Vino CAFE, WINE BAR
(www.javajunglevino.com; 246 W 1st St; ⏲6am-midnight; 📶) A side-by-side coffee shop and wine bar with a cool mosaic floor and an internet cafe all rolled into one. The wine bar has weekly tastings, while the cafe serves breakfast bagels and lunchtime sandwiches ($8) and puts on diverse music shows.

Imperial Bar & Lounge BAR
(150 N Arlington Ave; ⏲11am-2am Thu-Sat, to midnight Sun-Wed) A classy bar inhabiting a relic of the past, this building was once an old bank, and in the middle of the wood floor you can see cement where the vault once stood. Sandwiches and pizzas go with 16 beers on tap and a buzzing weekend scene.

St James Infirmary BAR
(445 California Ave) With an eclectic menu of 120 bottled varieties and 18 on tap, beer aficionados will short-circuit with delight. Red lights blush over black-and-white retro banquettes and a wall of movie and music stills, and it hosts sporadic events including jazz and bluegrass performances.

Entertainment

The free weekly *Reno News & Review* (www.newsreview.com) is your best source for listings.

Edge CLUB
(www.edgeofreno.com; Peppermill, 2707 S Virginia St; admission $10-20; ⏲Thu-Sun) The Peppermill reels in the nighthounds with a big glitzy dance club, where go-go dancers, smoke machines and laser lights may cause sensory overload. If so, step outside to the view lounge patio and relax in front of cozy fire pits.

Knitting Factory LIVE MUSIC
(☎775-323-5648; http://re.knittingfactory.com; 211 N Virginia St) This mid-sized venue opened in 2010, filling a gap in Reno's music scene with mainstream and indie favorites.

Information

An **information center** sits near the baggage claim at Reno-Tahoe International Airport, which also has free wi-fi.

Java Jungle (246 W 1st St; per hr $2; ⏲6am-midnight; 📶) Great riverfront cafe with a few computers and free wi-fi.

Reno-Sparks Convention & Visitors Authority (☎800-367-7366; www.visitrenotahoe.com; 2nd fl, Reno Town Mall, 4001 S Virginia St; ⏲8am-5pm Mon-Fri)

Getting There & Away

About 5 miles southeast of downtown, **Reno-Tahoe International Airport** (www.renoairport.com; 📶) is served by most major airlines.

The **North Lake Tahoe Express** (☎866-216-5222; www.northlaketahoeexpress.com) operates a shuttle ($40, six to eight daily, 3:30am to midnight) to and from the airport to multiple North Shore Lake Tahoe locations including Truckee, Squaw Valley and Incline Village. Reserve in advance.

To reach South Lake Tahoe (weekdays only), take the wi-fi-equipped **RTC Intercity bus** (www.rtcwashoe.com) to the Nevada DOT stop in Carson City ($4, one hour, five per weekday) and then the **BlueGo** (www.bluego.org) 21X bus ($2 with RTC Intercity transfer, one hour, seven to eight daily) to the Stateline Transit Center.

Greyhound (☎775-322-2970; www.greyhound.com; 155 Stevenson St) buses run daily service to Truckee, Sacramento and San Francisco ($34, five to seven hours), as does the once-daily westbound California Zephyr route operated by **Amtrak** (☎775-329-8638; 280 N Center St). The train is slower and more expensive, but also more scenic and comfortable, with a bus connection from Emeryville for passengers to San Francisco ($46, 7½ hours).

Getting Around

The casino hotels offer frequent free airport shuttles for their guests (and don't ask to see reservations).

The local **RTC Ride buses** (☎775-348-7433; www.rtcwashoe.com; per ride/all day $2/4) blanket the city, and most routes converge at the RTC 4th St Station downtown. Useful routes include the RTC Rapid line for S Virginia St, 11 for Sparks and 19 for the airport. The free Sierra Spirit bus loops around all major downtown landmarks – including the casinos and the university – every 15 minutes from 7am to 7pm.

CARSON CITY

Is this the most underrated town in Nevada? We're going to double down and say that it is. An easy drive from Reno or Lake Tahoe, it's a perfect stop for lunch and a stroll around the quiet, old-fashioned downtown. Expect pretty historic buildings and pleasant tree-lined streets centered around the **1870 Nevada State Capitol** (cnr Musser & Carson; admission free), where you might spot the governor himself chatting with one of his constituents.

Train buffs shouldn't miss the **Nevada State Railroad Museum** (☎775-687-6953; 2180 S Carson St; adult/child $5/free; ⏲8:30am-4:30pm), which displays some 30 train cars and engines from the 1800s to the early 1900s.

Skip the sedate casinos and head to one of the worthwhile historical museums, or simply grab lunch at fetching **Comma Coffee** (www.commacoffee.com; 312 S Carson St; dishes $5-9) and eavesdrop on the conversation next to you – they're probably congresspersons or lobbyists discussing a new bill over lattes. Or spend the evening at the town's friendly, locally owned microbrewery, **High Sierra Brewing Company** (www.highsierrabrewco.com; 302 N Carson St; dishes $5-9; ⏲11am-midnight Sun-Thu, to 2am Fri & Sat), for great beer and burgers.

Hwy 395/Carson St is the main drag. The **visitor center** (www.visitcarsoncity.com; 1900 S Carson St; ⏲9am-4pm Mon-Fri, to 3pm Sat & Sun), a mile south of downtown, gives out a local map with interesting historical walking and driving tours. For hiking and camping information in the area, stop by the United States Forest Service (USFS) **Carson Ranger District Office** (☎775-882-2766; 1536 S Carson St; ⏲8am-4:30pm Mon-Fri).

VIRGINIA CITY

During the 1860s gold rush, Virginia City was a high-flying, rip-roaring Wild West boomtown. Newspaperman Samuel Clemens, alias Mark Twain, spent some time in this raucous place during its heyday; years later his eyewitness descriptions of mining life were published in a book called *Roughing It*.

The high-elevation town is a National Historic Landmark, with a main street of Victorian buildings, wooden sidewalks and some hokey but fun museums. To see how the mining elite lived, stop by the **Mackay Mansion** (D St) and the **Castle** (B St).

Locals agree that the best food in Virginia City is probably at **Cafe del Rio** (www.cafedelriovc.com; 394 S C St; mains $9-15; ⏲4:30-8pm Wed & Thu, 11:30am-8pm Fri & Sat, 10am-2pm Sun), serving a nice blend of *nuevo* Mexican and good cafe food, including breakfast.

LOCAL KNOWLEDGE

WHET THE WHISTLE

Drink like an old-time miner at one of the many Victorian-era watering holes that line Virginia City's C St. We like the longtime family-run **Bucket of Blood Saloon** (www.bucketofbloodsaloonvc.com; 1 S C St; ⌚2-7pm), which serves up beer and 'bar rules' at its antique wooden bar ('If the bartender doesn't laugh, you are not funny') and the **Palace Restaurant & Saloon** (www.palacerestaurant1875.com; 1 S C St; mains $6-10; ⌚vary), which is full of town memorabilia and serves up tasty breakfasts and lunches.

The main drag is C St; check out the **visitor center** (www.virginiacity-nv.org; 86 S C St; ⌚10am-4pm).

Nevada Great Basin

A trip across Nevada's Great Basin is a serene, almost haunting experience. But those on the quest for the 'Great American Road Trip' will relish the fascinating historic towns and quirky diversions tucked away along lonely desert highways.

ALONG I-80

Heading east from Reno, **Winnemucca**, 150 miles to the northeast, is the first worthwhile stop. It boasts a vintage downtown and a number of Basque restaurants, along with a yearly Basque festival. For information, stop by the **Winnemucca Convention & Visitors Authority** (☎775-623-5071; 50 W Winnemucca Blvd; ⌚8am-noon & 1-5pm Mon-Fri, 9am-noon Sat, 11am-4pm Sun). Check out the displays here, like a buckaroo (cowboy) hall of fame and big-game museum. Don't miss a stop at **The Griddle** (www.thegriddlecom; 460 W Winnemucca Blvd; mains $4-12; ⌚breakfast & lunch daily, dinner Thu-Sat), one of Nevada's best retro cafes, serving up fantastic breakfasts, diner classics and homemade desserts since 1948.

The culture of the American West is most diligently cultivated in **Elko**. Aspiring cowboys and cowgirls should visit the **Western Folklife Center** (www.westernfolklife.org; 501 Railroad St; exhibits adult/child $5/1; ⌚10am-5:30pm Tue-Fri, 10:30am-5:30pm Tue, 10am-5pm Sat), which offers art and history exhibits and also hosts the popular **Cowboy Poetry Gathering** each January. There's also a **National Basque Festival**, held every July 4, with games, traditional dancing and a 'Running of the Bulls' event. If you've never sampled Basque food, the best place in town for your inaugural experience is the **Star Hotel** (www.elkostarhotelcom; 246 Silver St; mains $15-32; ⌚lunch Mon-Fri, dinner Mon-Sat), a family-style supper club located in a circa-1910 boardinghouse for Basque sheepherders. The irrepressibly curious will not want to miss a peek behind the restaurant, where Elko's small 'red light' district of legal brothels sits, including 'Inez's Dancing and Diddling,' perhaps the most bizarrely named business – tawdry or not – in the state.

ALONG HIGHWAY 50

As you drive along Hwy 50, you'll soon understand why it's called the 'Loneliest Road in America.' Towns are few and far between, and the only sounds are the hum of the engine or the whisper of wind. Once part of the Lincoln Hwy, lonesome Hwy 50 follows the route of the Overland Stagecoach, the Pony Express and the first transcontinental telegraph line.

A fitting reward for surviving the west-east stretch of Highway 50 is the awesome, uncrowded **Great Basin National Park**. Near the Nevada–Utah border, it encompasses 13,063ft Wheeler Peak, rising abruptly from the desert. Hiking trails near the summit take in superb country with glacial lakes, ancient bristlecone pines and even a permanent ice field. Admission is free; the park **visitor center** (☎775-234-7331; www.nps.gov/grba; ⌚8am-5:30pm), just north of the town of **Baker**, is the place to get oriented.

For a 60- or 90-minute guided tour of the caves here that are richly decorated with rare limestone formations, head to the **Lehman Caves** (www.nps.gov/grba; admission $8-10; ⌚8:30am-4pm) five miles outside of Baker. There are first-come, first-served developed **campgrounds** (tent & RV sites $12) in the park.

ALONG HIGHWAY 95

Hwy 95 runs roughly north–south through the western part of the state; the southern section is starkly scenic as it passes the Nevada Test Site (where more than 720 nuclear weapons were exploded in the 1950s).

Five miles north of Beatty, **Bailey's Hot Springs & RV Park** (☎775-553-2395; tent/RV sites $18/21), a 1906 former railroad depot, has three private hot springs in antique bathhouses, open from 8am to 8pm daily. Overnight guests get complimentary usage, and day-trippers pay $5 per person for a 30-minute soak.

ALONG HIGHWAYS 375 & 93

Hwy 375 is dubbed the 'Extraterrestrial Hwy' because of the huge amount of UFO sightings along this stretch of concrete and because it intersects Hwy 93 near top-secret **Area 51**, part of Nellis Air Force Base and a supposed holding area for captured UFOs. In the tiny town of **Rachel**, on Hwy 375, **Little A'Le'Inn** (☎775-729-2515; www.aleinn.com; r from $45) accommodates earthlings and aliens alike, and sells extraterrestrial souvenirs. Probings not included.

ARIZONA

When it comes to travel, wise men say that you should enjoy the journey, not just the destination. It's ridiculously easy to follow this advice in Arizona. Yes, there's the Grand Canyon. Monument Valley. The red rocks of Sedona. Chiricahua National Monument. But it's the roads between these icons that breathe life and context into a trip. Route 66 was a highway for migrant workers heading west during the Depression. Hwy 89 channels Arizona's mining past as it carves past the sliding buildings of Jerome. Hwy 264 cuts across ancestral Hopi lands, unfurling below a village inhabited for the last 800 years.

Where to begin an Arizona road trip? One good place is Greater Phoenix. The region, ringed by mountains, is one of the biggest metro areas in the Southwest. It has the eating, sights and glorious spas you'd expect in a spot that stakes its claim on rest and renewal. Tucson is the funky, artsy gateway to southern Arizona's astronomical and historical sights. Only 60 miles from the Mexican border, it embraces its cross-border heritage.

Up north is Flagstaff, a cool mountain town where locals seek relief from the searing summer heat and people come to play on the nearby San Francisco Peaks all year long. On the northern edge of the state is the Grand Canyon, Arizona's star attraction. Carved over eons by the mighty Colorado River, the greatest hole on earth draws visitors from around the world.

WORTH A TRIP

CATHEDRAL GORGE STATE PARK

Awe, then *ahhh:* this is one of our favorite state parks not just in Nevada, but in the whole USA. **Cathedral Gorge State Park** (www.parks.nv.gov/cg.htm) really does feel like you've stepped into a magnificent, many-spired cathedral, albeit one whose dome is a view of the sky. Sleep under the stars at the first-come, first-served **tent & RV sites** ($17) set amid badlands-style cliffs.

History

Arizona was the last territory in the Lower 48 to become a state, and it celebrated its centennial in 2012. Why did it take so long for a territory filled with copper and ranchland to join the Union? Arizonans were seen as troublemakers by the federal government, and for years acquiring their riches wasn't worth the potential trouble.

Cynics might say that Arizonans are still making trouble. In 2010, Arizona's legislature passed the most restrictive anti-immigration law in the nation, garnering headlines and controversy. How severe was the illegal immigration problem? In 2009, 250,000 illegal immigrants crossed the state's 350-mile border with Mexico. The legislature wasn't spurred into action, however, until the mysterious shooting of a popular rancher near the border the following year. Today, the hot-button law, known as SB1070, winds through the court system.

The state was shaken in 2011 by the shooting of Democratic Congresswoman Gabrielle Giffords during a public appearance. She was critically injured and six bystanders and staff members were killed.

An ongoing statewide fiscal crisis has forced many state parks to operate on a five-day schedule, closing to visitors on Tuesdays and Wednesdays.

ℹ Information

Arizona is on Mountain Standard Time but is the only western state that does not observe daylight saving time from spring to early fall. The exception is the Navajo Reservation, which *does* observe daylight saving time.

Generally speaking, lodging rates in southern Arizona (including Phoenix, Tucson and Yuma) are

ARIZONA FACTS

» **Nickname** Grand Canyon State

» **Population** 6.39 million

» **Area** 113,637 sq miles

» **Capital city** Phoenix (population 1.4 million)

» **Other cities** Tucson (population 520,000), Flagstaff (population 65,800), Sedona (population 10,000)

» **Sales tax** 6.6%

» **Birthplace of** Apache chief Geronimo (1829–1909), political activist Cesar Chavez (1927–93), singer Linda Ronstadt (b 1946)

» **Home of** Sedona New Age movement, mining towns turned art colonies

» **Politics** majority vote Republican

» **Famous for** Grand Canyon, saguaro cacti

» **Best souvenir** pink cactus-shaped neon lamp from roadside stall

» **Driving distances** Phoenix to Grand Canyon Village: 235 miles, Tucson to Sedona: 230 miles

much higher in winter and spring, which are considered the state's 'high season.' Great deals are to be had in the hot areas in the height of summer.

Arizona Department of Transportation (www.az511.com) Updates on road conditions and traffic statewide with links to weather and safety information.

Arizona Office of Tourism (☎602-364-3700; www.arizonaguide.com) Free state information.

Arizona Public Lands Information Center (☎602-417-9300; www.publiclands.org) Information about USFS, NPS, Bureau of Land Management (BLM) and state lands and parks.

Arizona State Parks (☎602-542-4174; www.azstateparks.com) Fifteen of the state's parks have campgrounds. Online reservations will be available for 14 of them by the end of 2011. Camping in Lyman Lake State Park is first-come, first-served.

Phoenix

Anchoring nearly 2000 square miles of suburbs, strip malls and golf courses, Phoenix is the largest urban area in the Southwest. The beige sprawl does little to inspire travelers upon arrival, but if you look a little closer there's an interesting mix of upscale pampering and sunbaked weirdness.

Several 'towns' make up the region known as Greater Phoenix, which is comparable to a family. The City of Phoenix, with its downtown high-rises and top-notch museums, is the patriarch. Scottsdale is the stylish big sister who married up, Tempe the good-natured but occasionally rowdy college kid, and Mesa is the brother who wants a quiet life in the suburbs. And mom? She left for Flagstaff in June because it's just too darn hot.

How hot? In summer temperatures reach above 110°F (43°C). Resort rates drop dramatically, which is great for travelers on a budget, but the most popular time to visit is winter and spring, when pleasant days prevail.

Sights

Greater Phoenix, also known as the Valley of the Sun, is ringed by mountains that range from 2500ft to more than 7000ft in elevation. Central Ave runs north–south through Phoenix, dividing west addresses from east addresses; Washington St runs west–east, dividing north addresses from south addresses.

Scottsdale, Tempe and Mesa are east of the airport. Scottsdale Rd runs north–south between Scottsdale and Tempe. The airport is 3 miles southeast of downtown.

PHOENIX

TOP CHOICE **Heard Museum** MUSEUM

(Map p810; www.heard.org; 2301 N Central Ave; adult/6-12yr/student/senior $15/7.50/7.50/13.50; ⏲9:30am-5pm Mon-Sat, 11am-5pm Sun; 👪) This engaging museum houses one of the best Native American collections in the world. Check out the kachina (Hopi spirit doll) collection as well as the 'Boarding School Experience' gallery, a moving look at the controversial federal policy of removing Native American children from their families and sending them to remote boarding schools to Americanize them.

Desert Botanical Garden GARDENS

(Map p810; ☎480-941-1225; www.dbg.org; 1201 N Galvin Pkwy; adult/child/student/senior $18/8/10/15; ⏲8am-8pm Oct-Apr, 7am-8pm May-Sep) This inspirational garden is a refreshing place to reconnect with nature and offers a great introduction to desert plant life. Looping trails lead past an astonishing variety of desert denizens arranged by theme, including

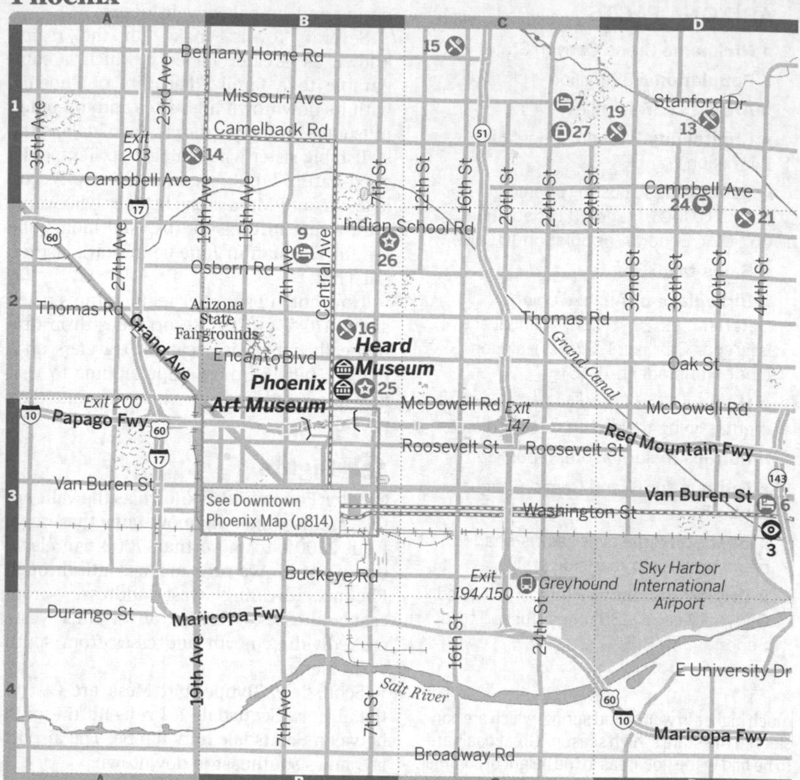

SOUTHWEST ARIZONA

a desert wildflower loop and a Sonoran Desert nature loop. Check for special seasonal events.

Phoenix Art Museum MUSEUM
(Map p810; ☎602-257-1222; www.phxart.org; 1625 N Central Ave; adult/child/student/senior $10/4/8/8, admission free Wed 3-9pm; ⏰10am-9pm Wed, 10am-5pm Thu-Sat, noon-5pm Sun) The Phoenix Art Museum is Arizona's premier repository of fine art. Galleries include works by Claude Monet, Diego Rivera and Georgia O'Keefe. Landscapes in the Western American gallery set the tone for adventure.

Pueblo Grande Museum & Archaeological Park MUSEUM
(Map p810; www.pueblogrande.com; 4619 E Washington St; adult/6-17yr/senior $6/5/3; ⏰9am-4:45pm Mon-Sat, 1-4:45pm Sun) Excavations at this fascinating Hohokam site, which dates back 1500 years, have yielded many clues about the daily lives of these ancient people famous for building a well-engineered 1000-mile network of irrigation canals.

SCOTTSDALE

Scottsdale's main draw is its popular shopping district, known as Old Town for its early-20th-century buildings (and others built to look old). The neighborhood is stuffed chockablock with art galleries, clothing stores for the modern cowgirl, and some of the best eating and drinking in the Valley of the Sun.

TOP CHOICE **Taliesin West** ARCHITECTURE
(☎480-860-2700; www.franklloydwright.org; 12621 Frank Lloyd Wright Blvd; ⏰9am-5pm) Taliesin West was Frank Lloyd Wright's desert home and studio, built between 1938 and 1940. Still home to an architecture school and open to the public for guided tours, it's a prime example of organic ar-

chitecture with buildings incorporating elements and structures found in surrounding nature. The 90-minute **Insights Tour** (adult/4-12yr/student & senior $32/17/28; ⌚half-hourly 9am-4pm Nov–mid-Apr, hourly 9am-4pm mid-Apr–Oct) is both informative and quick-moving.

TEMPE

Founded in 1885 and home to around 58,000 students, **Arizona State University** (ASU) is the heart and soul of Tempe. The **Gammage Auditorium** (cnr Mill Ave & Apache Blvd) was Frank Lloyd Wright's last major building.

Easily accessible by light-rail from downtown Phoenix, **Mill Avenue**, Tempe's main drag, is packed with chain restaurants, themed bars and other collegiate hangouts. While visiting, it's worth checking out **Tempe Town Lake**, an artificial lake with boat rides and paths perfect for strolling or biking its fringes. At **Cox Splash Playground** at the beach park, kids love to frolic under the oversized sprinklers.

FREE **Tempe Center for the Arts** ARTS CENTER
(Map p810; www.tempe.gov/tca; 700 W Rio Salado Pkwy; ⌚10am-6pm Tue-Fri, 11am-6pm Sat) On the lake, it has a sculpture garden and infinity pool, outside of the curved-steel building. Inside, there's a theater for the performing arts and a 3500-sq-ft gallery.

MESA

Founded by Mormons in 1877, low-key Mesa is one of the fastest-growing cities in the nation and is the third-largest city in Arizona, with a population of around 500,000.

Arizona Museum of Natural History MUSEUM
(off Map p810; ☎480-644-2230; www.azmnh.org; 53 N MacDonald St; adult/3-12yr/student/senior $10/6/8/9; ⌚10am-5pm Tue-Fri, 11am-5pm Sat, 1-5pm Sun; 👪) This captivating museum is worth a trip, especially if your kids are into dinosaurs (aren't they all?). In addition to the multilevel Dinosaur Mountain, there are loads of life-size casts of the giant beasts plus a touchable Apatosaurus thighbone. Other exhibits highlight Arizona's colorful past, from a prehistoric Hohokam village to an eight-cell territorial jail.

Activities

Piestewa Peak/Dreamy Draw Recreation Area HIKING
(☎602-261-8318; http://phoenix.gov/parks/; Squaw Peak Dr, Phoenix; ⌚6am-7pm) Previously known as Squaw Peak, this easy-to-access viewpoint was renamed for local Native

CACTUS LEAGUE SPRING TRAINING

Before the start of the major league baseball season, teams spend March in Arizona (Cactus League) and Florida (Grapefruit League) auditioning new players, practicing and playing games. Tickets are cheaper (from $6 to $8 depending on venue), the seats better, the lines shorter and the games more relaxed. Check www.cactusleague.com for schedules and links to tickets.

Phoenix

Top Sights
Desert Botanical Garden ... E3
Heard Museum ... B2
Old Town Scottsdale ... F2
Phoenix Art Museum ... B2

Sights
1 Arizona State University ... F4
Cox Splash Playground ... (see 5)
2 Gammage Auditorium ... F4
3 Pueblo Grande Museum ... D3
4 Tempe Center for the Arts ... E4
5 Tempe Town Lake ... E4

Activities, Courses & Tours
Tempe Boat Rentals ... (see 5)

Sleeping
6 Aloft Phoenix-Airport ... D3
7 Arizona Biltmore Resort & Spa ... C1
8 Best Western Inn of Tempe ... F3
9 Clarendon Hotel + Suites ... B2
10 Hotel Indigo Scottsdale ... F1
11 Hotel Valley Ho ... F2
12 Royal Palms Resort & Spa ... E1
Sanctuary on Camelback Mountain ... (see 22)

Eating
13 Chelsea's Kitchen ... D1
14 Da Vang ... A1
15 Dick's Hideaway ... C1
16 Durant's ... B2
17 Essence ... E4
18 Herb Box ... F2
19 Noca ... D1
20 Sugar Bowl ... F2
21 Tee Pee Mexican Food ... D2

Drinking
22 Edge/Jade Bar ... E1
23 Four Peaks Brewing Co ... F4
24 Postino Winecafé Arcadia ... D1

Entertainment
25 Phoenix Theatre ... B2
26 Rhythm Room ... B2

Shopping
27 Biltmore Fashion Park ... C1
28 Scottsdale Fashion Square ... F1

American soldier Lori Piestewa, killed in Iraq in 2003. The trek to the 2608ft summit is hugely popular and the saguaro-dotted park can get jammed on winter weekends. Dogs are allowed on some trails.

South Mountain Park HIKING, MOUNTAIN BIKING
(☎602-534-6324; http://phoenix.gov/parks/; 10919 Central Ave, Phoenix; ⏰5am-11pm) The 51-mile trail network (leashed dogs allowed) dips through canyons, over grassy hills and past granite walls, offering city views and access to Native American petroglyphs.

Cactus Adventures HIKING, MOUNTAIN BIKING
(☎480-688-9170; www.cactusadventures.com; 4747 Elliot Rd, Suite 21; half-day rentals from $30; ⏰9am-7pm Mon-Sat, 9am-5pm Sun) A quarter-mile pedal from South Mountain Park, Cactus Adventures rents bikes and offers guided hiking and biking tours.

Tempe Boat Rentals BOATING
(Map p810; ☎480-517-4050; http://boats4rent.com; 72 W Rio Salado Pkwy; pedal boats/kayaks/16ft pontoons $25/40/130 for 2hr) Rents watercraft at Tempe Town Lake.

Tours

Arizona Detours SIGHTSEEING
(☎866-438-6877; www.detoursaz.com) Offers day tours to far-flung locations such as Tombstone (adult/child $145/75) and the Grand Canyon (adult/child $155/90), and five-hour city tours (adult/child $80/45).

Arizona Outback Adventures HIKING
(☎480-945-2881; www.aoa-adventures.com; 16447 N 91st St, Scottsdale) Offers day trips for hiking ($95, minimum two people), mountain biking ($125, minimum two people), and other active outings.

Festivals & Events

Tostitos Fiesta Bowl SPORTS
(☎480-350-0911; www.fiestabowl.org) Held in early January at the University of Phoenix Stadium in Glendale, this football game is preceded by massive celebrations and parades.

Sleeping

Greater Phoenix is well stocked with hotels and resorts, but you won't find many B&Bs or cozy inns. Prices plummet in the super-hot summer, a time when Valley residents take advantage of super-low prices at their favorite resorts.

PHOENIX

Royal Palms Resort & Spa RESORT $$$
(Map p810; ☎602-840-3610; www.royalpalmsresortandspa.com; 5200 E Camelback Rd, Phoenix; r $329-429, ste from $366; P❄@📶≋) This posh boutique resort at the base of Camelback Mountain is a hushed and elegant place, dotted with Spanish Colonial villas, flower-lined walkways, and palms imported from Egypt. Pets can go Pavlovian for soft beds, personalized biscuits and walking services. There's a $28 daily resort fee.

Arizona Biltmore Resort & Spa RESORT $$$
(Map p810; ☎602-955-6600; www.arizonabiltmore.com; 2400 E Missouri Ave, Phoenix; r $300-459, ste from $489; P❄@📶≋👪) With architecture inspired by Frank Lloyd Wright, the Biltmore is perfect for connecting to the magic of yesterday. It boasts more than 700 discerning units, two golf courses, several pools, a spa, a kids club and more such luxe touches. Wi-fi can be spotty beyond the lobby and the main pool. Daily resort fee is $28.

Clarendon Hotel + Suites HOTEL $$
(Map p810; ☎602-252-7363; www.theclarendon.net; 401 W Clarendon Ave, Phoenix; r $160-199; P❄@📶≋) The Clarendon's finger-snapping, minimalist cool manages to be both welcoming and hip. In the standard rooms, look for 42-inch flat-screens, artsy prints and dark custom furniture. Ride up to the breezy skydeck for citywide views. The $20 daily fee covers wi-fi, parking and phone calls.

Aloft Phoenix-Airport HOTEL $$
(Map p810; ☎602-275-6300; www.aloftphoenixairport.com; 4450 E Washington St, Phoenix; r $129-160; P❄@📶≋) Rooms blend a pop-art sensibility with the cleanest edges of modern design. The hotel is near Tempe and across the street from the Pueblo Grand Museum. No extra fee for pets.

HI Phoenix Hostel HOSTEL $
(☎602-254-9803; www.phxhostel.org; 1026 N 9th St, Phoenix; dm $20-23, d $35-50; ❄@📶) A veritable UN of half-mad guests, this inviting 14-bed hostel sits in a working-class residential neighborhood and has relaxing garden nooks. The owners are fun, and they know Phoenix. Check-in is from 8am to 10am and 5pm to 10pm. Closed July and August. No credit cards.

Budget Lodge Downtown MOTEL $
(Map p814; ☎602-254-7247; www.blphx.com; 402 W Van Buren St, Phoenix; r incl breakfast $50-55; P❄📶) This no-nonsense workhorse is a clean, low-cost place to lay your head and provides the most important amenities: a microwave and fridge in every room, and complimentary breakfast.

SCOTTSDALE

TOP CHOICE **Boulders Resort** RESORT $$$
(☎480-488-9009; www.theboulders.com; 34631 N Tom Darlington Dr, Carefree; casitas $350-850, villas from $1050-1250; P❄@📶≋) This desert oasis blends nearly imperceptibly into a landscape of natural rock formations – and that's before you've enjoyed a session at the ultraposh on-site Golden Door Spa. Everything here is calculated to take the edge off travel, making it a perfect destination

PHOENIX FOR CHILDREN

Wet 'n Wild Phoenix (off Map p810; ☎623-201-2000; www.wetnwildphoenix.com; 4243 W Pinnacle Peak Rd, Glendale; over/under 48in tall $35/28, senior $28; ⏲10am-6pm Sun-Wed, 10am-10pm Thu-Sat, 11am-7pm Sun Jun-Jul, vary May, Aug & Sep; 👪) water park has pools, tube slides, wave pools, waterfalls and floating rivers. It's in Glendale, 2 miles west of I-17 at exit 217.

At the re-created 1880s frontier town **Rawhide Western Town & Steakhouse** (off Map p810; ☎480-502-5600; www.rawhide.com; 5700 W N Loop Rd, Chandler; admission free, per attraction or show $5, unlimited day pass $15; ⏲5-9pm Wed-Fri, noon-9:30pm Sat, noon-8:30pm Sun; 👪), about 20 miles south of Mesa, kids can enjoy all sorts of hokey-but-fun shenanigans. The steakhouse has rattlesnake for adventurous eaters. Opening hours vary seasonally.

Arizona Science Center (Map p814; ☎602-716-2000; www.azscience.org; 600 E Washington St; adult/3-17yr/senior $14/11/12; ⏲10am-5pm; 👪) is a high-tech temple of discovery, there are more than 300 hands-on exhibits and a planetarium.

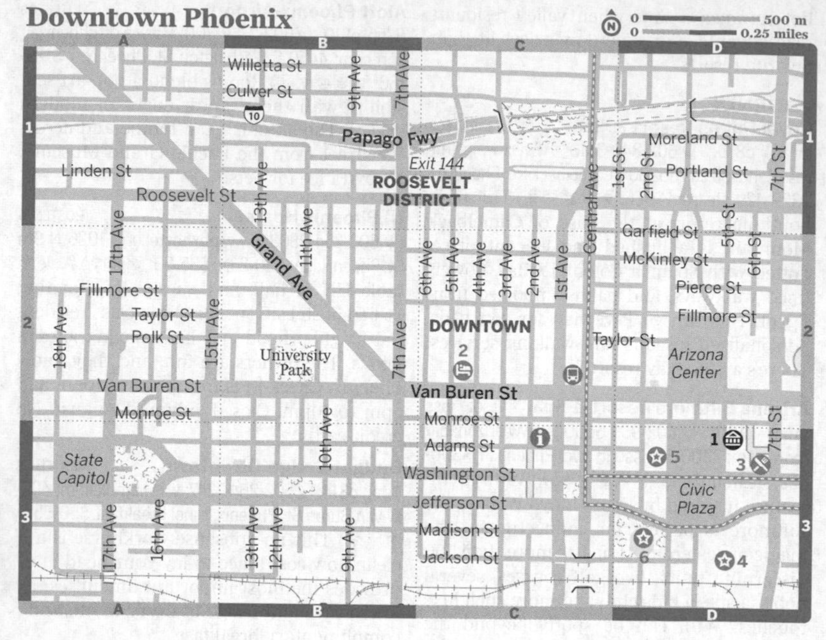

Downtown Phoenix

Sights
1 Arizona Science Center.......................D3

Sleeping
2 Budget Lodge Downtown...................C2

Eating
3 Pizzeria Bianco...................................D3

Entertainment
4 Chase Field D3
5 Symphony Hall.....................................D3
6 US Airways Center...............................D3

for recovering from jet lag or rediscovering your significant other. Daily resort fee is $30. Weekend rates can drop as low as $139 in summer.

TOP CHOICE Hotel Valley Ho BOUTIQUE HOTEL $$$
(Map p810; ☎480-248-2000; www.hotelvalleyho.com; 6850 E Main St, Scottsdale; r $289-339, ste $399-439;) Everything's swell at the Valley Ho, a jazzy joint that once bedded Bing Crosby, Natalie Wood and Janet Leigh. Today, bebop music, upbeat front staff and the 'ice fireplace' recapture the Rat Pack–era vibe, and the theme travels well to the balconied rooms. Pets stay free, but wi-fi is $10 per day.

Sanctuary on Camelback Mountain RESORT $$$
(Map p810; ☎480-948-2100; www.sanctuaryoncamelback.com; 5700 E McDonald Dr, Scottsdale; r $419-629, houses $1800-3500;) Mountain suites, spa casitas, private homes – chic lodgings are decorated with the beautiful warm tones of the desert and outfitted with whatever amenity your heart desires. Enjoy a sunset cocktail on the **Edge**, Sanctuary's swanky outdoor bar. Daily resort fee $18.

Hotel Indigo Scottsdale HOTEL $$
(Map p810; ☎480-941-9400; www.scottsdalehiphotel.com; 4415 N Civic Center Plaza; r $174-184, ste $204-224;) Hot-spot trappings include sumptuous bedding, outdoor fire pits, club music in the lobby, fancy toiletries and plasma TVs. Dogs welcome, at no extra charge.

Sleep Inn HOTEL $$
(off Map p814; ☎480-998-9211; www.sleepinnscottsdale.com; 16630 N Scottsdale Rd; r incl breakfast $99-114;) This outpost of the national chain in North Scottsdale wins points for its extensive breakfast,

friendly staff and proximity to Taliesin West.

TEMPE

TOP CHOICE Sheraton Wild Horse Pass Resort & Spa RESORT $$$
(☎602-225-0100; www.wildhorsepassresort.com; 5594 W Wild Horse Pass Blvd, Chandler; r $239-579; P❄@≋♿) Designed by the Gila River tribe as a luxurious place to soak up the best of Native American healing and wisdom, this oasis has comfortable rooms, spacious common areas, fine dining, two 18-hole golf courses, an equestrian center, tennis courts and a water slide modeled after Hohokam ruins. Wi-fi is available in the lobby.

Best Western Inn of Tempe HOTEL $
(Map p810; ☎480-784-2233; www.innoftempe.com; 670 N Scottsdale Rd; r incl breakfast $75-90; P❄@≋) This well-kept, helpful hotel is within walking distance of Tempe Town Lake and close to ASU and lively Mill Ave.

Eating

The Phoenix-Scottsdale area has the largest selection of restaurants in the Southwest.

TOP CHOICE Matt's Big Breakfast BREAKFAST $
(☎602-254-1074; www.mattsbigbreakfast.com; 801 N 1st St, at McKinley St; mains $5-8; ⊙6:30am-2:30pm Tue-Sun) Best. Breakfast. Ever. Every regular menu item is great, but daily specials, such as eggs scrambled with peppers and chorizo into fluffy-spicy-ohmygoodness on a bed of mouthwatering crispy homefries are supremely yummy. Sign in on the clipboard and bring quarters for the meter.

TOP CHOICE Dick's Hideaway MEXICAN $$
(Map p810; ☎602-265-5886; www.richardsonsnm.com; 6008 N 16th St; breakfast $8-16, lunch $12-16, dinner $17-37; ⊙7am-midnight) Grab a table beside the bar or join the communal table in the side room and settle in for hearty servings of savory, chile-slathered enchiladas, tamales and other New Mexican cuisine. We especially like the Hideaway for breakfast, when the Bloody Marys arrive with a shot of beer. The unmarked entrance is between the towering shrubs.

Durant's STEAKHOUSE $$$
(Map p810; ☎602-264-5967; www.durantsaz.com; 2611 N Central Ave; mains $17-34; ⊙lunch & dinner) This dark and manly place is a gloriously old-school steakhouse. You will get steak. It will be big and juicy. There will be a potato. The ambience is awesome too: red velvet cozy booths and the sense the Rat Pack is going to waltz in at any minute.

Pizzeria Bianco PIZZERIA $$
(Map p814; www.pizzeriabianco.com; 623 E Adams St; pizzas $12-16; ⊙11am-10pm Tue-Sat) James Beard winner Chris Bianco has stepped back from the ovens at his famous downtown pizza joint (allergies arc to blame), but the thin-crust gourmet pies remain as tasty as ever. The tiny restaurant is now open for lunch.

Da Vang VIETNAMESE $
(Map p810; 4538 N 19th Ave; mains $6-13; ⊙8am-8pm) Our favorite Vietnamese in the Valley is served in a Spartan dining room; it's as if the plainness of the location is in direct proportion to the awesomeness of the food. The pho is fantastic, and you'd be remiss not to try some of the lovely 'dry' rice noodle dishes.

Noca AMERICAN $$$
(Map p810; ☎602-956-6622; www.restaurantnoca.com; 3118 E Camelback Rd; mains $20-33; ⊙lunch & dinner Tue-Sun, open Mon Dec-Mar) Short for north of Camelback, Noca serves New American fare using American ingredients in the style of classical innovators such as the French Laundry. Think linguini with Maine lobster with shaved fennel in a spicy tomato broth.

Tee Pee Mexican Food MEXICAN $
(Map p810; www.teepeemexicanfood.com; 4144 E Indian School Rd; mains $8-11; ⊙11am-10pm Mon-Sat, to 9pm Sun) If you like piping-hot plates piled high with cheesy, messy American-style Mexican fare then grab a booth at this 40-year-old fave. George W Bush ate here in 2004 and ordered two enchiladas, rice and beans – now called the Presidential Special.

Chelsea's Kitchen AMERICAN $$
(Map p810; 5040 N 40th St; lunch $10-17, dinner $10-27; ⊙lunch & dinner daily, brunch Sun) The Western-inspired cuisine at this chic but casual place includes burgers, salad and tacos, but we're partial to the organic meats tanned to juicy perfection in the hardwood rotisserie. There's a nice patio too.

SCOTTSDALE

Fresh Mint VIETNAMESE, VEGETARIAN $
(off Map p810; www.freshmint.us.com; 13802 N Scottsdale Rd; mains $6-14; ⊙11am-9pm Mon-Sat; ✎) Never had kosher Vietnamese vegan? There's always a first time, and if it tastes like the food at Fresh Mint, you'd want to get

some more. If you're skeptical of soy chicken and tofu, we understand, but we respectfully submit that this stuff is as tasty as any bacon cheeseburger.

Mastro's Ocean Club SEAFOOD **$$$**
(off Map p810; ☎480-443-8555; www.mastrosrestaurants.com; 15045 N Kierland Blvd; mains $30-50; ⏲dinner) Mastro's is gunning for the title of best seafood in the Valley of the Sun, and it may just deserve the crown. It's part of an upscale chain, but don't hold that against it. The entire place screams class and affected atmosphere, but the real draw is incredibly rich decadent takes on everything that swims under the waves.

Herb Box AMERICAN **$$**
(Map p810; www.theherbbox.com; 7134 E Stetson Dr; lunches $10-15, dinners $14-25; ⏲lunch daily, dinner Mon-Sat) It's not just about sparkle and air kisses at this chichi bistro. It's also about fresh, regional ingredients, artful presentation and attentive service.

Sugar Bowl ICE CREAM **$**
(Map p810; 4005 N Scottsdale Rd; ice creams under $5, mains $6-9; ⏲11am-10pm Sun-Thu, 11am-midnight Fri & Sat;) This pink-and-white Valley institution has been working its ice-cream magic since the '50s. For more substantial fare, there's a whole menu of sandwiches and salads.

TEMPE

TOP CHOICE **Kai Restaurant** NATIVE AMERICAN **$$$**
(☎602-225-0100; www.wildhorsepassresort.com; 5594 W Wild Horse Pass Blvd, Chandler; mains $40-49, 8-course tasting menus $200; ⏲dinner Tue-Sat) Simple ingredients from mainly Native American farms and ranches are turned into something extraordinary. Dinners are like fine tapestries with dishes – such as the pecan-crusted Colorado lamb with native seeds mole – striking just the right balance between adventure and comfort. Dress nicely (no shorts or hats). It's at the Sheraton Wild Horse Pass Resort & Spa (p815) on the Gila River Indian Reservation. Kai closes for one month in August.

Essence CAFE **$**
(www.essencebakery.com; 825 W University Dr; breakfasts $5-7, lunches $8-9; ⏲7am-3pm Mon-Fri, 8am-3pm Sat, closed Sun) This breezy box of deliciousness serves egg dishes and French toast at breakfast, and salads, gourmet sandwiches and a few Mediterranean specialties at lunch. The ecominded cafe strives to use organic, locally grown fare.

Drinking

Scottsdale has the greatest concentration of trendy bars and clubs; Tempe attracts the student crowd; and Phoenix has a slew of long-standing dive bars that are in again.

TOP CHOICE **Postino Winecafé Arcadia** WINE BAR
(Map p810; www.postinowinecafe.com; 3939 E Campbell Ave, at 40th St, Phoenix; ⏲11am-11pm Mon-Thu, 11am-midnight Fri & Sat, 11am-10pm Sun) This convivial, indoor-outdoor wine bar is a perfect gathering spot for a few friends ready to enjoy the good life, but solos will do fine too. Highlights include the misting patio, rave-inducing bruschetta and $5 wines by the glass from 11am to 5pm.

Edge/Jade Bar BAR
(Map p810; 5700 E McDonald Dr, Sanctuary on Camelback Mountain, Scottsdale) Enjoy a sunset 'on the edge' at this stylish cocktail bar perched on the side of Camelback Mountain. No room outside? The equally posh, big-windowed Jade Bar should do just fine. Both are within the plush confines of the Sanctuary on Camelback Mountain resort. Complimentary valet.

Four Peaks Brewing Company BREWERY
(Map p810; www.fourpeaks.com; 1340 E 8th St, Tempe; ⏲11am-2am Mon-Sat, 10am-2am Sun) Beer-lovers rejoice: you're in for a treat at this quintessential neighborhood brewpub in a cool Mission Revival–style building.

Greasewood Flat BAR
(☎480-585-9430; www.greasewoodflat.net; 27375 N Alma School Pkwy, Scottsdale; ⏲11am-11pm) Cowboys, bikers and preppy golfers gather around the smoky barbecue and knock back the whiskey at this rustic ex-stagecoach stop, located 21 miles north of downtown Scottsdale. Cash only.

Entertainment

Both the **Arizona Opera** (☎602-266-7464; www.azopera.com) and the **Phoenix Symphony Orchestra** (☎602-495-1999; www.phoenixsymphony.org) perform at **Symphony Hall** (Map p814; 75 N 2nd St, Phoenix).

The men's basketball team, the **Phoenix Suns** (☎602-379-7900; www.nba.com/suns), and the women's team, the **Phoenix Mercury** (☎602-252-9622; www.wnba.com/mercury), play at the US Airways Center. The **Arizona**

Cardinals (☎602-379-0101; www.azcardinals.com) football team plays at the new University of Phoenix Stadium in Glendale. The **Arizona Diamondbacks** (☎602-462-6500; http://arizona.diamondbacks.mlb.com) play baseball at Chase Field (Map p814).

Rhythm Room LIVE MUSIC
(Map p810; ☎602-265-4842; www.rhythmroom.com; 1019 E Indian School Rd, Phoenix) Some of the Valley's best live acts take the stage at this small venue, where you pretty much feel like you're in the front row of every gig. It tends to attract more local and regional talent than the big names, which suits us just fine.

BS West GAY
(☎480-945-9028; www.bswest.com; 7125 E 5th Ave, Scottsdale; ⌚2pm-2am) A high-energy gay video bar and dance club in the Old Town Scottsdale area, this place has pool tables and a small dance floor, and hosts karaoke on Sundays.

Phoenix Theatre PERFORMING ARTS
(Map p810; ☎602-254-2151; www.phoenixtheatre.com; 100 E McDowell Rd) The city's main dramatic group puts on a good mix of mainstream and edgier performances. The attached cookie company does children's shows.

Shopping

The valley has several notable shopping malls. For more upscale shopping, visit the **Scottsdale Fashion Square** (Map p810; cnr Camelback & Scottsdale Rds) and the even more exclusive **Biltmore Fashion Park** (Map p810; cnr Camelback Rd & 24th St). In northern Scottsdale, the new and outdoor **Kierland Commons** (15205 N Kierland Blvd, Scottsdale) is pulling in crowds.

Heard Museum Bookshop ARTS & CRAFTS
(☎602-252-8344; www.heardmuseumshop.com; 2301 N Central Ave, Phoenix) Has the best range of books about Native Americans, and the most reliable and expansive selection of Native American arts and crafts.

Information

Emergency & Medical Services

Banner Good Samaritan Medical Center (☎602-839-2000; www.bannerhealth.com; 1111 E McDowell Rd, Phoenix) Has a 24-hour emergency room.

Police (☎602-262-6151; http://phoenix.gov/police; 620 W Washington St, Phoenix)

Internet Access

Burton Barr Central Library (☎602-262-4636; www.phoenixpubliclibrary.org; 1221 N Central Ave, Phoenix; ⌚9am-5pm Mon, 11am-9pm Tue-Thu, 9am-5pm Fri & Sat, 1-5pm Sun; @) Free internet access.

Internet Resources & Media

Arizona Republic (www.azcentral.com) Arizona's largest newspaper; publishes a free entertainment guide, *Calendar*, every Thursday.

KJZZ 91.5 fm (http://kjzz.org) National Public Radio (NPR).

Phoenix New Times (www.phoenixnewtimes.com) The major free weekly; lots of event and restaurant listings.

Post

Downtown post office (☎602-253-9648; 522 N Central Ave, Phoenix)

Tourist Information

Downtown Phoenix Visitor Information Center (Map p814; ☎602-254-6500; www.visitphoenix.com; 125 N 2nd St, Suite 120; ⌚8am-5pm Mon-Fri) The Valley's most complete source of tourist information.

Mesa Convention & Visitors Bureau (☎480-827-4700; www.mesacvb.com; 120 N Center St; ⌚8am-5pm Mon-Fri)

Scottsdale Convention & Visitors Bureau (☎480-421-1004; www.scottsdalecvb.com; 4343 N Scottsdale Rd, Suite 170; ⌚8am-5pm Mon-Fri) Inside the Galleria Corporate Center.

Tempe Convention & Visitors Bureau (Map p810; ☎480-894-8158; www.tempecvb.com; 51 W 3rd St, Suite 105; ⌚8:30am-5pm Mon-Fri)

Getting There & Around

Sky Harbor International Airport (www.skyharbor.com;) is 3 miles southeast of downtown Phoenix and served by 17 airlines, including United, American, Delta and British Airways. Its three terminals (Terminals 2, 3 and 4; Terminal 1 was demolished in 1990) and the parking lots are linked by the free 24-hour Airport Shuttle Bus.

Greyhound (Map p810; ☎602-389-4200; www.greyhound.com; 2115 E Buckeye Rd) runs buses to Tucson ($20 to $27, two hours, eight daily), Flagstaff ($32 to $42, three hours, five daily), Albuquerque ($71 to $89, 10 hours, five daily) and Los Angeles ($42 to $54, 7½ hours, 10 daily). Valley Metro's No 13 buses link the airport and the Greyhound station.

Valley Metro (☎602-253-5000; www.valleymetro.org) operates buses all over the Valley and a 20-mile light-rail line linking north Phoenix with downtown Phoenix, Tempe/ASU and downtown

Mesa. Fares for light-rail and bus are $1.75 per ride (no transfers) or $3.50 for a day pass. Buses run daily at intermittent times. **FLASH buses** (www.tempe.gov/tim/bus/flash.htm) operate daily around ASU and downtown Tempe, while the **Scottsdale Trolley** (www.scottsdaleaz.gov/trolley) loops around downtown Scottsdale, both at no charge.

Flagstaff

Flagstaff's laid-back charms are myriad, from its pedestrian-friendly historic downtown crammed with eclectic vernacular architecture and vintage neon to its high-altitude pursuits such as skiing and hiking. Locals are generally a happy, athletic bunch, skewing more toward granola than gunslinger. Northern Arizona University (NAU) gives Flagstaff its college-town flavor, while its railroad history still figures firmly in the town's identity. Throw in a healthy appreciation for craft beer, freshly roasted coffee beans and an all-round good time and you have the makings of a town you want to slow down and savor.

Sights

Museum of Northern Arizona MUSEUM
(www.musnaz.org; 3101 N Fort Valley Rd; adult/student $7/4; ⌚9am-5pm) If you have time for only one sight in Flagstaff, head to the Museum of Northern Arizona. It features exhibits on local Native American archaeology, history and customs, as well as geology, biology and the arts.

Lowell Observatory OBSERVATORY
(☎928-774-3358; www.lowell.edu; 1400 W Mars Hill Rd; adult/child $6/3; ⌚9am-5pm Mar-Oct, noon-5pm Nov-Feb, night hr vary) This observatory witnessed the first sighting of Pluto in 1920. Weather permitting, there's nightly stargazing, helped by the fact that Flagstaff is the first International Dark Sky city in the world. Day tours are offered from 10am to 4pm in summer, with reduced hours in winter.

Walnut Canyon National Monument PARK
(☎928-526-3367; www.nps.gov/waca; admission $5; ⌚8am-5pm May-Oct, 9am-5pm Nov-Apr) Sinagua cliff dwellings are set in the nearly vertical walls of a small limestone butte amid a forested canyon at this worth-a-trip monument. A short hiking trail descends past many cliff-dwelling rooms. The monument is 11 miles southeast of Flagstaff off I-40 exit 204.

Activities

Humphreys Peak HIKING
The state's highest mountain (12,663ft) is a reasonably straightforward, though strenuous, hike in summer. The trail, which begins in the Arizona Snowbowl, winds through forest, eventually coming out above the beautifully barren tree line. The total distance is 4.5 miles one-way; allow six to eight hours round-trip.

Arizona Snowbowl SKIING
(☎928-779-1951; www.arizonasnowbowl.com; Hwy 180 & Snowbowl Rd; lift ticket adult/child $49/26) Four lifts service 30 runs and a snowboarding park at elevations between 9200ft and 11,500ft. You can ride the chairlift (adult/child $12/8) in summer.

Sleeping

Flagstaff provides the widest variety of lodging choices in the region. Unlike in southern Arizona, summer is high season here.

Grand Canyon International Hostel HOSTEL $
(☎928-779-9421; www.grandcanyonhostel.com; 19½ S San Francisco St; dm incl breakfast $18-36, r without bath $43; ❄@📶) Run by friendly people in a historic building, dorms are clean and small. There's a kitchen, laundry facilities and a host of tours to the Grand Canyon and Sedona. Guests are fetched from the Greyhound bus for free.

Dubeau Hostel HOSTEL $
(☎928-774-6731; www.grandcanyonhostel.com; 19 W Phoenix Ave; dm incl breakfast $21-24, r $46-66; ❄@📶) Run by the Grand Canyon International Hostel folks. The private rooms are like basic hotel rooms, but at half the price. With a jukebox, things can get a little loud here.

Weatherford Hotel HISTORIC HOTEL $$
(☎928-779-1919; www.weatherfordhotel.com; 23 N Leroux St; r without bath $49-79, r with bath $89-139; ❄📶) This atmospheric hotel offers 11 charmingly decorated rooms with turn-of-the-20th-century feel. Three rooms also incorporate modern amenities such as TVs, phones and air-conditioning. Since the Weatherford's three bars often feature live music, it can get noisy.

Monte Vista Hotel HISTORIC HOTEL $$
(☎928-779-6971; www.hotelmontevista.com; 100 N San Francisco St; d $65-130, ste $120-175; ❄📶) Feather lampshades, vintage furniture, bold colors and eclectic decor – things are histori-

cally frisky in the 50 rooms and suites here, which are named for the film stars who slept in them. Ask for a quiet room if you're opposed to live music that may drift up from Monte Vista Lounge.

Eating

Wander around downtown and you'll stumble on plenty of eating options.

Criollo Latin Kitchen FUSION $$
(928-774-0541; www.criollolatinkitchen.com; 16 N San Francisco St; mains $13-30; 11am-10pm Mon-Thu, 11am-11pm Fri, 9am-11pm Sat, 9am-2pm & 4-10pm Sun) This Latin fusion spot has a romantic, industrial setting for cozy cocktail dates and delectable late-night small plates. The blue-corn blueberry pancakes make a strong argument for showing up for Sunday brunch. Food is sourced locally and sustainable when possible.

Beaver Street Brewery PUB $$
(www.beaverstreetbrewery.com; 11 S Beaver St; mains $8-12; 11am-11pm Sun-Thu, 11am-midnight Fri & Sat;) Beaver Street Brewery is a bustling place to go for a bite to eat with a pint of local microbrew. It usually has five handmade beers on tap and some seasonal brews. The menu is typical brewpub fare, with delicious pizzas, burgers and salads. Surprisingly, it's very family friendly.

Mountain Oasis INTERNATIONAL $$
(11 E Aspen; mains $9-19; 11am-9pm;) Vegetarians and vegans will find plenty of options on this internationally spiced menu. Tasty specialties include the TBLT (tempeh bacon, lettuce and tomato) and Thai veggies and tofu with peanut sauce and brown rice. Steak and chicken are also on the menu.

Drinking & Entertainment

TOP CHOICE **Museum Club** ROADHOUSE
(928-526-9434; 3404 E Rte 66; 11am-2am) Yee-haw! Kick up your heels at this honky-tonk roadhouse where the country dancing is nightly. Inside what looks like a huge log cabin you'll find a large wooden dance floor and a sumptuous elixir-filled mahogany bar. See their Facebook page for events.

Charly's Pub & Grill LIVE MUSIC
(928-779-1919; www.weatherfordhotel.com; 23 N Leroux St; 8am-10pm) This restaurant at the Weatherford Hotel has regular live music. Its fireplace and brick walls provide a cozy setting for the blues, jazz and folk played here. Upstairs, stroll the wraparound veranda outside the popular 3rd-floor Zane Grey Ballroom.

Macy's CAFE
(www.macyscoffee.net; 14 S Beaver St; 6am-8pm Mon-Wed, to 10pm Thu-Sun;) Macy's delicious house-roasted coffee has kept Flagstaff buzzing for over 30 years. Tasty vegetarian menu includes many vegan choices, with traditional cafe grub (mains $3 to $7). Cash only.

Cuvee 928 WINE BAR
(www.cuvee928winebar.com; 6 W Aspen Ave, Suite 110; 11:30am-9pm Mon-Tue, to 10pm Wed-Sat) With a central location on Heritage Sq, and patio seating, this wine bar is a pleasant venue for people-watching.

Information

Visitors center (928-774-9541; www.flagstaffarizona.org; 1 E Rte 66; 8am-5pm Mon-Sat, 9am-4pm Sun) Inside the historic Amtrak train station.

Getting There & Around

Flagstaff Pulliam Airport is 4 miles south of town off I-17. **US Airways** (www.usairways.com) offers several daily flights from Phoenix Sky Harbor International Airport. **Greyhound** (928-774-4573; www.greyhound.com; 399 S Malpais Ln) stops in Flagstaff en route to/from Albuquerque, Las Vegas, Los Angeles and Phoenix. **Arizona Shuttle** (928-226-8060; www.arizonashuttle.com) has shuttles that run to the park, Williams and Phoenix Sky Harbor Airport.

Operated by **Amtrak** (928-774-8679; www.amtrak.com; 1 E Route 66; 3am-10:45pm), the Southwest Chief stops at Flagstaff on its daily run between Chicago and Los Angeles.

Central Arizona

This part of Arizona draws people year-round for outdoor fun and is an oasis for summer visitors searching for cooler climes. After Phoenix, the land gains elevation, turning from high rolling desert to jagged hills covered in scrubby trees. Farther north still, mountains punctuate thick stands of pine.

WILLIAMS

Affable Williams, 60 miles south of Grand Canyon Village and 35 miles west of Flagstaff, is a gateway town with character. Classic motels and diners line Route 66, and the old-school homes and train station give a nod to simpler times.

Most tourists visit to ride the turn-of-the-19th-century **Grand Canyon Railway** (800-843-8724; www.thetrain.com; Railway Depot, 233 N

Grand Canyon Blvd; round-trip adult/child from $70/40; 🚸) to the South Rim (departs Williams 9:30am). Even if you're not a train buff, a trip is a scenic stress-free way to visit the Grand Canyon. Characters in period costumes provide historical and regional narration, and banjo folk music sets the tone. There's also a wildly popular Polar Express service (adult/child from $30/20) from November through January, ferrying pajama-clad kids to the 'North Pole' to visit Santa.

The **Red Garter Bed & Bakery** (☎928-635-1484; www.redgarter.com; 137 W Railroad Ave; r incl breakfast $120-145; ❄📶) is an 1897 bordello turned B&B where the ladies used to hang out the windows to flag down customers. The four rooms have nice period touches and the downstairs bakery has good coffee. The funky little **Grand Canyon Hotel** (☎928-635-1419; www.thegrandcanyonhotel.com; 145 W Rte 66; dm $28, r without bath $60, r with bath $70-125; ❄@📶) has small themed rooms and a six-bed dorm room.

Route 66 fans will dig the eclectic decor at **Cruiser's Cafe 66** (www.cruisers66.com; 233 W Rte 66; mains $10-20; ⏰3-10pm; 🚸). It's a fun place, serving tasty microbrews, BBQ and other American fare inside a 1930s filling station.

SEDONA

Sedona's a stunner, but it's intensely spiritual as well. Nestled amid majestic red sandstone formations at the southern end of Oak Creek Canyon, Sedona attracts spiritual seekers, artists and healers, and day-trippers from Phoenix fleeing the oppressive heat. Many New Age types believe that this area is the center of vortexes that radiate the earth's power, and Sedona's combination of scenic beauty and mysticism draws throngs of tourists year-round. New Age businesses dot downtown, along with galleries and gourmet restaurants, while the surrounding canyons offer excellent hiking and mountain biking.

In the middle of town, the 'Y' is the landmark junction of Hwys 89A and 179. Businesses are spread along both roads.

Sights & Activities

New Agers believe Sedona's rocks, cliffs and rivers radiate Mother Earth's mojo. The world's four best-known vortexes are here, and include **Bell Rock** near Village of Oak Creek east of Hwy 179, **Cathedral Rock** near Red Rock Crossing, **Airport Mesa** along Airport Rd, and **Boynton Canyon**. Airport Rd is also a great location for watching the Technicolor sunsets.

Coconino National Forest PARK
(USFS South Gateway Visitor Center ☎928-203-7500; www.redrockcountry.org/recreation; 8379 Hwy 179; ⏰8am-5pm) The best way to explore the area is by hiking, biking or horseback riding in the surrounding forest. Most day use and parking areas require a Red Rock Pass ($5/15 per day/week), which can be purchased at most area stores and lodging and at a number of self-serve kiosks at popular sites. The most scenic spots are along Hwy 89A north of Sedona, which snakes alongside Oak Creek through the heavily visited **Oak Creek Canyon**. The USFS visitor center is just south of the Village of Oak Creek.

FREE **Chapel of the Holy Cross** CHURCH
(www.chapeloftheholycross.com; 780 Chapel Rd; ⏰9am-5pm Mon-Sat, 10am-5pm Sun) Situated between spectacular, statuesque red-rock columns 3 miles south of town, this modern, nondenominational chapel was built in 1956 by Marguerite Brunwig Staude in the tradition of Frank Lloyd Wright.

Slide Rock State Park PARK
(☎928-282-3034; www.azstateparks.com; 6871 N Hwy 89A; per vehicle Jun-Aug $20, Sep-May $10; ⏰8am-7pm Jun-Aug, 8am-5pm Sep-May; 🚸) Swoosh down big rocks into cool creek water at Oak Creek Canyon's star attraction, or walk the hiking trails.

Pink Jeep Tours DRIVING TOUR
(☎928-282-5000; www.pinkjeep.com; 204 N Hwy 89A; tours from $72) Many companies offer 4WD tours, but Pink Jeep Tours has a great reputation and a vast variety of outings.

Fat Tire Bike Shop MOUNTAIN BIKING
(☎928-284-0210; www.bike-bean.com; 6020 Hwy 179; half-/full day from $30/40) A mountain-bike rental place with hiking, mellow biking and vortex-gazing.

Sleeping

Sedona hosts many beautiful B&Bs, creekside cabins, motels and full-service resorts. Dispersed camping is not permitted in Red Rock Canyon. The **USFS** (☎928-282-4119; www.recreation.gov) runs campgrounds (none with hookups) along Hwy Alt 89 in Oak Creek Canyon. All are nestled in the woods just off the road. It costs $20 to camp, but you don't need a Red Rock Pass. Reservations are accepted for all campgrounds except Pine Flat East. Six miles north of town, **Manzanita** has 18 sites, open year-round; 11.5 miles north, **Cave Springs** has 82 sites, and showers; **Pine Flat East and Pine Flat West**, 12.5 miles north, has 57 sites.

Cozy Cactus B&B **$$**
(928-284-0082; www.cozycactus.com; 80 Canyon Circle Dr, Village of Oak Creek; r $165-325;) This five-room B&B is particularly well suited for adventure-loving types ready to enjoy the great outdoors. The Southwest-style abode bumps up against a National Forest Trail and is just around the bend from cyclist-friendly Bell Rock Pathway.

Sedona Motel MOTEL **$**
(928-282-7187; www.thesedonamotel.com; 218 Hwy 179; r $79-89;) Directly south of the Y, this friendly little motel offers big value within walking distance of Tlaquepaque and uptown Sedona. Rooms are basic but clean, but the fantastic red-rock views may be all the luxury you need.

Eating & Drinking

TOP CHOICE **Elote Cafe** MEXICAN **$$**
(www.elotecafe.com; King's Ransom Hotel, 771 Hwy 179; mains $17-22; 5pm-late, Tue-Sat) Some of the best, most authentic Mexican food you'll find in the region, with unusual traditional dishes you won't find elsewhere, such as the fire-roasted corn with lime and cotija cheese, or tender, smoky pork cheeks. No reservations.

Dahl & DiLuca Ristorante ITALIAN **$$**
(928-282-5219; www.dahlanddiluca.com; 2321 Hwy Alt 89; mains $13-33; 5-10pm) Though this lovely Italian place fits perfectly into the groove and color scheme of Sedona, at the same time it feels like the kind of place you'd find in a small Italian seaside town. It's a bustling, welcoming spot serving excellent, authentic Italian food.

Coffee Pot Restaurant BREAKFAST **$**
(www.coffeepotsedona.com; 2050 W Hwy Alt 89; mains $4-11; 6am-2pm;) The go-to breakfast and lunch joint for decades, it's always busy. Meals are reasonably priced and the selection is huge – 101 types of omelet, for a start.

Sedona Memories DELI **$**
(928-282-0032; 321 Jordan Rd; mains $7; 10am-2pm Mon-Fri) This tiny local spot assembles gigantic sandwiches on slabs of homemade bread, with several vegetarian options. Cash only.

SCENIC DRIVES: ARIZONA'S BEST

» **Oak Creek Canyon** A thrilling plunge past swimming holes, rock-slides and crimson canyon walls on Hwy 89A between Flagstaff and Sedona.

» **Hwy89/89A Wickenburg to Sedona** The Old West meets the New West on this lazy drive past dude ranches, mining towns, art galleries and stylish wineries.

» **Patagonia-Sonoita Scenic Road** This one's for the birds, and those who like to track them, in Arizona's southern wine country on Hwys 82 and 83.

» **Kayenta-Monument Valley** Become the star of your own Western on an iconic loop past cinematic red rocks in Navajo country just off Hwy 163.

» **Vermilion Cliffs Scenic Road** A solitary drive on Hwy 89A through the Arizona Strip linking condor country, the North Rim and Mormon hideaways.

Information

Visitors center (928-282-7722; www.visitsedona.com; 331 Forest Rd; 8:30am-5pm Mon-Sat, 9am-3pm Sun) Has tourist information and last-minute hotel bookings.

Getting There & Around

The **Sedona-Phoenix Shuttle** (928-282-2066; www.sedona-phoenix-shuttle.com) runs between Phoenix Sky Harbor International Airport and Sedona eight times daily (one-way/round-trip $50/90). Try **Bob's Taxi** (928-282-1234) for local cab service.

JEROME

The childhood game Chutes and Ladders comes to mind on a stroll up and down the stairways of Jerome, a historic mining town clinging to the side of Cleopatra Hill – not always successfully as evidenced by the crumbling Sliding Jail. Shabbily chic, this resurrected ghost town has a romantic feel – especially once the weekend day-trippers clear out. It was known as the 'Wickedest Town in the West' during its late-1800s mining heyday, but today its historic buildings have been lovingly restored and turned into galleries, restaurants, B&Bs and, most recently, wine-tasting rooms.

DON'T MISS

VERDE VALLEY WINE TRAIL

Several new vineyards, wineries and tasting rooms have opened their doors along Hwy 89A and I-17, bringing a dash of style and energy to Cottonwood, Jerome and Cornville.

In Cottonwood, you can float to Verde River–adjacent **Alcantara Vineyards** (☎928-649-8463; 3445 S Grapevine Way) then stroll through Old Town where two new tasting rooms, **Arizona Stronghold** (☎928-639-2789; 1023 N Main St) and **Pillsbury Wine Company** (☎928-639-0646; 1012 N Main St), sit across from each other on Main St. Art, views and wine-sipping converge in Jerome, where there's a tasting room on every level of town, starting with **Bitter Creek Winery/Jerome Gallery** (☎928-634-7033; 240 Hull Ave) near the chamber of commerce visitor center. From there, stroll up to **Caduceus Cellars** (☎928-639-9463; www.cadeceus.org) then end with a final climb to **Jerome Winery** (☎928-639-9067; 403 Clark St), with its inviting patio.

Three wineries with tasting rooms hug a short stretch of Page Springs Rd east of Cornville: bistro-housing **Page Springs Cellars** (☎928-639-3004; 1500 N Page Springs Rd), welcoming **Oak Creek Vineyards** (☎928-649-0290; 1555 N Page Springs Rd) and mellow-rock-playing **Javelina Leap Vineyard** (☎928-649-2681; 1565 Page Springs Rd).

A community hospital during the town's mining years, the **Jerome Grand Hotel** (☎928-634-8200; www.jeromegrandhotel.com; 200 Hill St; r $120-205, ste $270-460; ❄📶) plays up its past with hospital relics in the hallways and an entertaining ghost tour that kids will enjoy. Wi-fi is available in the lobby only. The adjoining **Asylum Restaurant** (www.asylumrestaurant.com), with its valley and red-rock views, is a breathtaking spot for a cocktail. Downtown, the popular **Spirit Room Bar** (☎928-634-5006; 164 Main St; ⏲10am-2am), is the town's liveliest watering hole. For wine drinkers, there are three tasting rooms just a few steps away.

Even the quesadillas have personality at **15.Quince Grill & Cantina** (☎928-634-7087; www.15quincejerome.com; 363 Main St; mains $8-17; ⏲11am-8pm Mon & Wed, 11am-9pm Tue, Thu & Frid, 8am-9pm Sat, 8am-8pm Sun), a small but festive restaurant serving New Mexican–style dishes with a kick – the joint's known for its chile sauces. For a savory gourmet breakfast or lunch, step into the **Flatiron Café** (www.flatironcafejerome.com; 416 Main St; breakfast $7-13, lunch $9-13; ⏲7am-3pm Wed-Mon) at the Y intersection.

The **chamber of commerce** (☎928-634-2900; www.jeromechamber.com; Hull Ave, Hwy 89A north after the Flatiron Café split; ⏲11am-3pm), inside a small trailer, offers tourist information on the local attractions and art scene.

PRESCOTT

With a historic Victorian-era downtown and a colorful Wild West history, Prescott, Arizona's first territorial capital and home of the world's oldest rodeo, feels like the Midwest meets cowboy country. Residents are a diverse mix of retirees, artists and families looking for a taste of yesteryear's wholesomeness. The town boasts more than 500 buildings on the National Register of Historic Places. Along the plaza is **Whiskey Row**, an infamous strip of old saloons that still serve up their fair share of booze.

Just south of downtown, the fun-loving **Motor Lodge** (☎928-717-0157; www.themotorlodge.com; 503 S Montezuma St; r $89-139; P❄📶) welcomes guests with Fat Tire beers and 12 snazzy bungalows arranged around a central driveway – it's indie lodging at its best.

For breakfast, mosey into the friendly **Lone Spur Café** (106 W Gurley St; mains $7-16; ⏲8am-2pm), where you always order your breakfast with a biscuit and a side of sausage gravy – you can't count calories at a place this good. Portions are huge, and there are three bottles of hot sauce on every table. The cool, loftlike **Raven Café** (www.ravencafe.com; 142 N Cortez St; breakfast $5-9, lunch & dinner $8-18; ⏲7:30am-11pm Mon-Wed, 7:30am-midnight Thu-Sat, 8am-3pm Sun; 📶🥕) offers a mostly organic menu of sandwiches, burgers, salads and a few 'big plates.' And there are 30 beers on tap.

On Whiskey Row, the **Palace** (www.historicpalace.com; 120 S Montezuma St; ⏲11am-11pm) is an atmospheric place to drink; you enter through swinging saloon doors into a big room anchored by a Brunswick bar (saved during a 1900 fire). The divey **Bird Cage Saloon** (www.birdcagesaloon.com; 148 Whiskey Row;

⌚10am-2am) is filled with stuffed birds, and it merits a look-see.

The **chamber of commerce** (☎928-445-2000; www.visit-prescott.com; 117 W Goodwin; ⌚9am-5pm Mon-Fri, 10am-2pm Sat) has tourist information, including a handy walking tour pamphlet ($1) of historical Prescott.

Prescott Transit Authority (☎928-445-5470; www.prescotttransit.com; 820 E Sheldon St) runs buses to/from Phoenix airport (one-way adult/child $28/15, two hours, 16 daily) and Flagstaff ($22, 1½ hours, daily). Also offers a local taxi service.

Grand Canyon National Park

Why do folks become giddy when describing the Grand Canyon? One peek over the edge makes it clear. The canyon captivates travelers because of its sheer immensity; it's a tableau that reveals the earth's history layer by dramatic layer. Mother Nature adds artistic details – rugged plateaus, crumbly spires, shadowed ridges – that flirt and catch your eye as the sun crosses the sky.

Snaking along its floor are 277 miles of the Colorado River, which has carved the canyon over the past six million years and exposed rocks up to two billion years old – half the age of the earth.

The two rims of the Grand Canyon offer quite different experiences; they lie more than 200 miles apart by road and are rarely visited on the same trip. Most visitors choose the South Rim with its easy access, wealth of services and vistas that don't disappoint. The quieter North Rim has its own charms; at 8200ft elevation (1000ft higher than the South Rim), its cooler temperatures support wildflower meadows and tall, thick stands of aspen and spruce.

June is the driest month, July and August the wettest. January has average overnight lows of 13°F (-11°C) to 20°F (-7°C) and daytime highs around 40°F (4°C). Summer temperatures inside the canyon regularly soar above 100°F (38°C). While the South Rim is open year-round, most visitors come between late May and early September. The North Rim is open from mid-May to mid-October.

ℹ Information

The park's most developed area is Grand Canyon Village, 6 miles north of the South Rim Entrance Station. The only entrance to the North Rim lies 30 miles south of Jacob Lake on Hwy 67. The North Rim and South Rim are 215 miles apart by car, 21 miles on foot through the canyon, or 10 miles as the condor flies.

The **park entrance ticket** (vehicles/cyclists & pedestrians $25/12) is valid for seven days and can be used at both rims.

All overnight hikes and backcountry camping in the park require a permit. The **Backcountry Information Center** (☎928-638-7875; fax 928-638-7875; www.nps.gov/grca; Grand Canyon Village; ⌚8am-noon & 1-5pm, phone staffed 1-5pm Mon-Fri) accepts applications for backpacking permits ($10, plus $5 per person per night) for the current month and following four months only. Your chances are decent if you apply early (four months in advance for spring and fall) and provide alternative hiking itineraries. Reservations are accepted in person or by mail or fax. For more information see www.nps.gov/grca/planyourvisit/backcountry.htm.

If you arrive without a permit, head to the office, by Maswik Lodge, to join the waiting list.

SOUTH RIM In addition to the visitor centers listed below, information is available inside the park at Yavapai Observation Station, Verkamp's Visitor Center, El Tovar, Tusayan Ruins & Museum and Desert View Information Center.

Grand Canyon Visitor Center (☎928-638-7644; ⌚8am-5pm) Three hundred yards behind Mather Point, a large plaza encompasses this visitor center and the Books & More Store. On the plaza, bulletin boards display information about ranger programs, the weather, tours and hikes. The center's bright, spacious interior includes a ranger-staffed information desk and a lecture hall, where rangers offer daily talks.

TUSAYAN The **National Geographic Visitor Center** (☎928-638-2468; www.explorethecanyon.com; Hwy 64, Tusayan; adult/child $13/10; ⌚8am-10pm) is in Tusayan, 7 miles south of Grand Canyon Village; pay your $25 vehicle entrance fee here and spare yourself a potentially long wait at the park entrance, especially in summer. The IMAX theater screens the terrific 34-minute film *Grand Canyon – The Hidden Secrets*.

NORTH RIM **North Rim Visitor Center** (☎928-638-7864; www.nps.gov/grca; ⌚8am-6pm, closed mid-Oct–mid-May) Adjacent to the Grand Canyon Lodge, with maps, books, trail guides and current conditions.

SOUTH RIM

To escape the throngs, visit during fall or winter, especially on weekdays. You'll also gain some solitude by walking a short distance away from the viewpoints on the Rim Trail or by heading into the canyon itself.

Grand Canyon Region

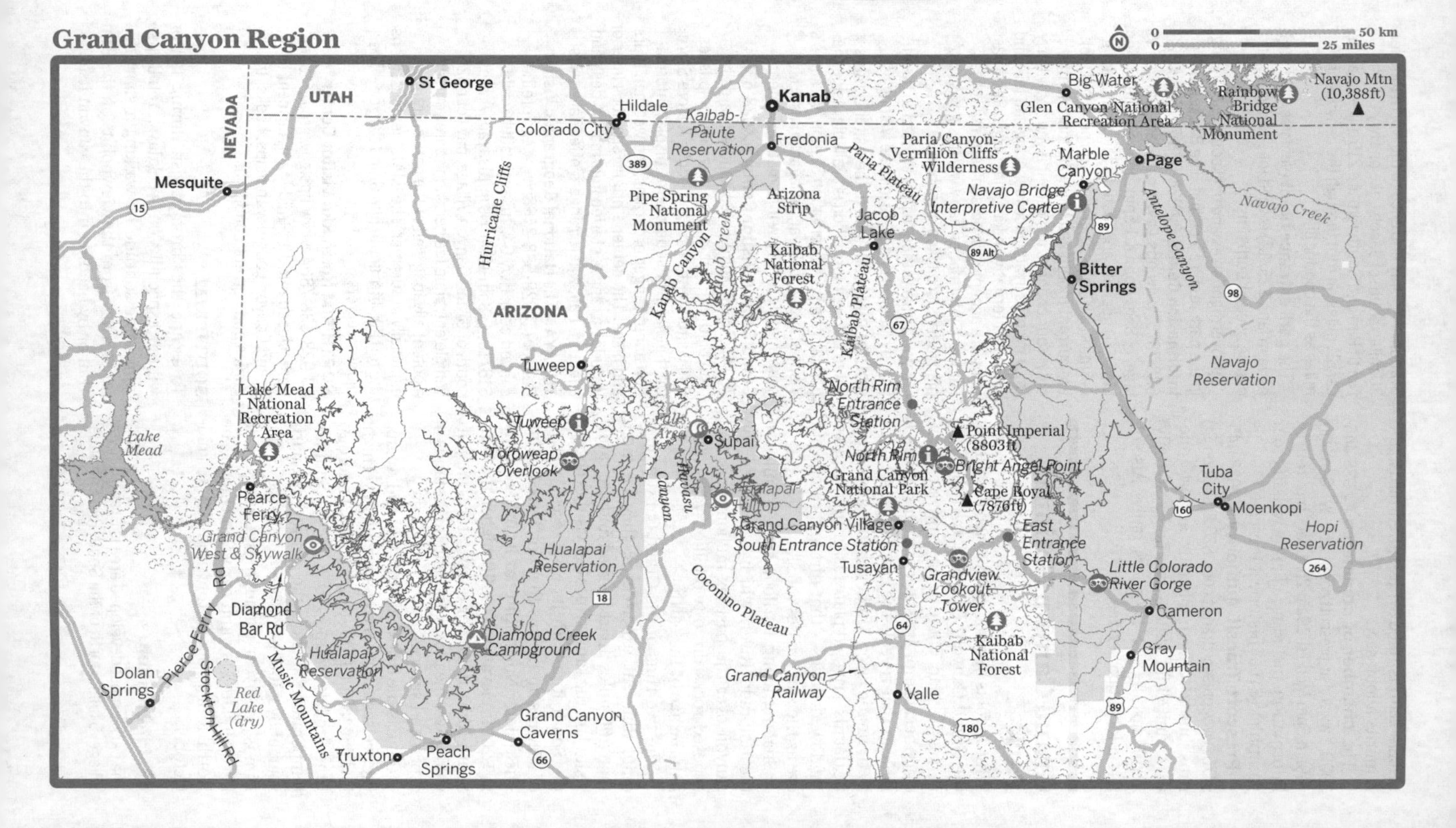

Sights & Activities

DRIVING & HIKING

A **scenic route** follows the rim on the west side of the village along Hermit Rd. Closed to private vehicles March through November, the road is serviced by the free park shuttle bus; cycling is encouraged because of the relatively light traffic. Stops offer spectacular views, and interpretive signs explain canyon features.

Hiking along the South Rim is among park visitors' favorite pastimes, with options for every skill level. The **Rim Trail** is the most popular, and easiest, walk in the park. It dips in and out of the scrubby pines of Kaibab National Forest and connects a series of scenic points and historical sights over 12 miles. Portions are paved, and every viewpoint is accessed by one of the three shuttle routes. The new **Trail of Time** exhibit borders the Rim Trail just west of Yavapai Observation Station. Here, every meter of the trail represents one million years of geologic history, with exhibits providing the details.

Desert View Drive starts to the east of Grand Canyon Village and follows the canyon rim for 26 miles to Desert View, the east entrance of the park. Pullouts offer spectacular views, and interpretive signs explain canyon features and geology.

The most popular of the corridor trails is the beautiful **Bright Angel Trail**. The steep and scenic 8-mile descent to the Colorado River is punctuated with four logical turnaround spots. Summer heat can be crippling; day hikers should either turn around at one of the two resthouses (a 3- to 6-mile round-trip) or hit the trail at dawn to safely make the longer hikes to Indian Garden and Plateau Point (9.2 and 12.2 miles round-trip respectively). Hiking to the river in one day should not be attempted. The trailhead is just wet of Bright Angel Lodge.

The **South Kaibab** is arguably one of the park's prettiest trails, combining stunning scenery and unobstructed 360-degree views with every step. Steep, rough and wholly exposed, summer ascents can be dangerous, and during this season rangers discourage all but the shortest day hikes – otherwise it's a 6-mile, grueling round-trip. Turn around at **Cedar Ridge**, perhaps the park's finest short day hike.

Individuals and groups who prefer a more in-depth experience while still giving something back can apply for various programs with **Grand Canyon Volunteers** (☎928-774-7488; www.gcvolunteers.org). One- and multiday programs include wildlife monitoring, native plant restoration and forest surveying.

CYCLING

Bright Angel Bicycles BICYCLE RENTAL
(☎928-814-8704; www.bikegrandcanyon.com; full day adult/child $35/25; ⊙8am-6pm May-Sep, 10am-4:30pm Mar-Apr & Oct-Nov, weather permitting) Renting 'comfort cruiser' bikes, the friendly folks here custom-fit each bike to the individual. Rates include helmet and bicycle-lock rental.

Tours

Xanterra HORSEBACK RIDING
(☎303-297-2757; www.grandcanyonlodges.com/mule-rides-716.html) Park tours are run by Xanterra, which has information desks at Bright Angel, Maswik and Yavapai Lodges. Various daily bus tours (tickets from $20) are offered.

Due to erosion concerns, the NPS has limited inner-canyon mule rides to those traveling all the way to Phantom Ranch. Rather than going below the rim, three-hour day trips ($119) now take riders along the rim, through the ponderosa, piñon and juniper forest to the Abyss overlook. Overnight trips (one/two people $482/850) and two-night trips (one/two people $701/1170) follow the Bright Angel Trail to the river, travel east on the River Trail and cross the river on the Kaibab Suspension Bridge. Riders spend the night at Phantom Ranch.

If you arrive at the park and want to join a mule trip the following day, ask about availability at the transportation desk at Bright Angel Lodge.

Sleeping

Advance or same-day reservations are required for the South Rim's six lodges, which are operated by **Xanterra** (☎888-297-2757; www.grandcanyonlodges.com). Use this phone number to make advance reservations (highly recommended) at any of the places (including Phantom Ranch) listed here. For same-day reservations or to reach a guest, call the **South Rim switchboard** (☎928-638-2631). If you can't find accommodations in the national park, try Tusayan (at South Rim Entrance Station), Valle (31 miles south), Cameron (53 miles east) or Williams (about 60 miles south).

The **National Park Service** (☎877-444-6777; www.recreation.gov) operates Mather and Desert View Campgrounds. All campgrounds and lodges are open year-round except Desert View, which closes from mid-October to mid-May.

TOP CHOICE **El Tovar Hotel** LODGE $$$
(d $178-273, ste $335-426;) Wide, inviting porches wreathe the rambling wooden structure, offering pleasant spots to people-watch and admire canyon views – even if you're not a guest. The public spaces show the lodgelike, genteel elegance of the park's heyday. The standard rooms are small but first-class. Suites are fantastic.

Bright Angel Lodge LODGE $
(d with/without private bath $92/81, cabins $113-178;) Built in 1935, the log-and-stone Bright Angel offers historic charm and refurbished rooms, the cheapest of which have shared bathrooms. Don't expect a TV in these very basic rooms (think university dorm room), but rim cabins have better views than TV.

Phantom Ranch LODGE $
(888-297-2757; dm $43;) It ain't the Four Seasons, but this summer-campy complex has its charms. Located at the bottom of the canyon, the ranch has basic cabins sleeping four to 10 people and segregated dorms. The ranch serves family-style meals (breakfast/dinner from $21/27) – reserve well in advance. No sleeping reservation? Show up at the Bright Angel Lodge transportation desk at 6am to snag a canceled bunk.

Mather Campground CAMPGROUND $
(877-444-6777; www.recreation.gov; Grand Canyon Village; tent & RV sites $18) Well-dispersed, relatively peaceful sites amid piñon and juniper trees. There are pay showers and laundry facilities nearby, drinking water, toilets, grills and a small general store. First-come, first-served during winter months.

Desert View Campground CAMPGROUND $
(tent & RV sites $12; mid-May–mid-Oct) Near the East Entrance Station, 26 miles east of Grand Canyon Village, this first-come, first-served campground is a quieter alternative to Mather. A small cafeteria-snack shop serves meals.

Also recommended:

Maswik Lodge LODGE $$
(d South/North $92/173, cabins $92;) Set away from the rim, but with a sports bar and cafeteria.

Kachina Lodge & Thunderbird Lodge LODGE $$
(d streetside/rimside $173/184;) Decent motel-style rooms in a central location. Some rooms have canyon views.

Yavapai Lodge LODGE $$
(d West/East $114/163; Apr-Oct;) Basic lodging amid peaceful piñon and juniper forest.

Trailer Village CAMPGROUND $
(Grand Canyon Village; tent & RV sites $32) Camp here if everywhere else is full. You can reserve well in advance or same day.

Eating & Drinking

El Tovar Dining Room INTERNATIONAL $$$
(928-638-2631, ext 6432; El Tovar; mains $18-31; 6:30-11am, 11:30am-2pm & 5-10pm) A stone's throw from the canyon's edge, it has the best views of any restaurant in the state, if not the country. The grand stone and dark-oak dining room warms the soul like an upscale lodge of yore, and the food, especially the steaks, makes the trip worthwhile. If you're not seated near a window, head to the verandah of the El Tovar Lounge afterward for a guaranteed Grand Canyon vista.

Bright Angel Lounge BAR $$
(Bright Angel Lodge; mains $10-26; 11:30am-3pm Mar-Oct & 4:30-10pm Mar-Dec) Perfect for those who want to unwind with a burger and a beer without cleaning up too much; a fun place to relax at night when the lack of windows and dark decor aren't such a big deal. It's beside the charmless Bright Angel Restaurant.

Arizona Room AMERICAN $$
(Bright Angel Lodge; mains $8-28; 11:30am-3pm Mar-Oct & 4:30-10pm Mar-Dec) Antler chandeliers hang from the ceiling and picture windows overlook the canyon. Mains include steak, chicken and fish dishes. No reservations; there's often a wait.

Also recommended:

Maswik Cafeteria CAFETERIA $
(Maswik Lodge; mains $4-10; 6am-10pm) Another cafeteria-style place.

Canyon Cafe at Yavapai Lodge CAFETERIA $
(Yavapai Lodge; mains $4-10; 6am-10pm) Cafeteria food, service and seating.

Canyon Village Marketplace MARKET $
(Market Plaza; 8am-8pm) Stock up on groceries or hit the deli.

Getting There & Around

Most people arrive at the canyon in private vehicles or on a tour. Parking can be a chore in Grand Canyon Village. Under the new Park-n-Ride program, summer visitors can buy a park ticket at the **National Geographic Visitor Center** (p835), park their vehicle at a designated lot, then hop aboard a free park shuttle that follows the **Tusayan Route** (8am-9:30pm mid-May–early Sep) to the Grand Canyon Visitor Center inside the park. Park passes are also okay for this option. The trip takes 20 minutes, and the first bus departs Tusayan at 8am. The last bus from the park leaves at 9:30pm.

Inside the park, free **park shuttles** operate along three routes: around Grand Canyon Village: west along Hermits Rest Route and east along Kaibab Trail Route. Buses typically run at least twice per hour, from one hour before sunset to one hour afterward.

A free shuttle from Bright Angel Lodge during the summer months, the **Hiker's Express** (4am, 5am, 6am Jun-Aug, 5am, 6am, 7am May & Sep) has pickups at the Backcountry Information Center and Grand Canyon Visitor Center, and then heads to the South Kaibab trailhead.

NORTH RIM

Head here for blessed solitude in nature's bountiful bosom; only 10% of park visitors make the trek. Meadows are thick with wildflowers and dense clusters of willowy aspen and spruce trees, and the air is often crisp, the skies big and blue.

Facilities on the North Rim are closed from mid-October to mid-May, although you can drive into the park and stay at the campground until the first snow closes the road from Jacob Lake.

Call the **North Rim Switchboard** (928-638-2612) to reach facilities on the North Rim.

Sights & Activities

The short and easy paved trail (0.5 miles) to **Bright Angel Point** is a canyon must. Beginning from the back porch of Grand Canyon Lodge, it goes to a narrow finger of an overlook with fabulous views.

The **North Kaibab Trail** is the North Rim's only maintained rim-to-river trail and connects with trails to the South Rim. The first 4.7 miles are the steepest, dropping 3050ft to **Roaring Springs** – a popular all-day hike. If you prefer a shorter day hike below the rim, walk just 0.75 miles down to **Coconino Overlook** or 2 miles to the **Supai Tunnel** to get a taste of steep inner-canyon hiking. The 28-mile round-trip to the Colorado River is a multiday affair.

Canyon Trail Rides (435-679-8665; www.canyonrides.com; Grand Canyon Lodge; mid-May–mid-Oct) offers one-hour ($40) and half-day ($75, minimum age 10 years) mule trips. Of the half-day trips, one is along the rim and the other drops into the Canyon on the North Kaibab Trail.

Sleeping

Accommodations are limited to one lodge and one campground. If these are booked, try your luck 80 miles north in Kanab, UT, or 84 miles northeast in Lees Ferry. There are also campgrounds in the Kaibab National Forest north of the park.

North Rim Campground CAMPGROUND $
(928-638-7814; www.recreation.gov; tent sites $6-18, RV sites $8-25) This campground, 1.5 miles north of Grand Canyon Lodge, offers pleasant sites on level ground blanketed in pine needles. There is water, a store, a snack bar and coin-operated showers and laundry facilities, but no hookups. Hikers and cross-country skiers can use the campground during winter months if they have a backcountry permit. Reservations accepted.

Grand Canyon Lodge HISTORIC HOTEL $$
(928-638-2611/12 same-day reservations, 480-337-1320 reservations outside the USA; www.grandcanyonlodgenorth.com; r $116, cabins $121-170; mid-May–mid-Oct;) Made of wood, stone and glass, the lodge is the kind of place you imagine should be perched on the rim. Rustic yet modern cabins make up the majority of accommodations. The most expensive cabins offer two rooms, a porch and beautiful rim views. The canyon views from the Sun Room are stunning, the lobby regal. Reserve far in advance.

Eating & Drinking

The lodge will also prepare sack lunches ($11), ready for pickup at 6:30am, for those wanting to picnic on the trail.

Grand Canyon Lodge Dining Room AMERICAN $$
(928-638-2611; mains $12-24; 6:30am-10am, 11:30am-2:30pm & 4:45-9:45pm mid-May–mid-Oct) The windows are so huge that you can sit anywhere and get a good view. The menu includes several vegetarian options and Western treats such as Utah Ruby trout and bison flank steak. Dinner reservations are required, and it's neighbors with the atmospheric Rough Rider Saloon, full of

memorabilia from the country's most adventurous president.

Grand Canyon Cookout Experience AMERICAN $$
(☎928-638-2611; adult/child $30-35/12-22; ⏰6-7:45pm Jun-Sep; 👪) This chuck-wagon-style cookout featuring barbecue and cornbread is more of an event than a meal. Kids love it. Make arrangements at the Grand Canyon Lodge.

ℹ Information

North Rim Visitor Center (☎928-638-7888; www.nps.gov/grca; ⏰8am-6pm, closed mid-Oct–mid-May) Beside Grand Canyon Lodge, this is the place to get information on the park, and the starting point for ranger-led nature walks and evening programs.

ℹ Getting There & Around

The **Transcanyon Shuttle** (☎928-638-2820; www.trans-canyonshuttle.com; one-way/round-trip $80/150; ⏰7am mid-May–mid-Oct) departs daily from Grand Canyon Lodge for the South Rim (five hours) and is perfect for rim-to-rim hikers. Reserve at least one or two weeks in advance. A complimentary **hikers' shuttle** to the North Kaibab Trail departs at both 5:45am and 7:10am from Grand Canyon Lodge. You must sign up for it at the front desk; if no one signs up the night before, it will not run.

Around the Grand Canyon

HAVASU CANYON

Even after the massive flooding that hit the area in August 2008 and closed it down for 10 months, Havasupai is still one of the most beautiful places in the canyon.

On the Havasupai Indian Reservation, about 195 miles west of the South Rim, the valley around Havasu Canyon has spring-fed waterfalls and sparkling swimming holes. The falls lie 10 miles below the rim, accessed via a moderately challenging hiking trail, and trips require an overnight stay in the nearby village of Supai.

Supai offers two sleeping options and reservations must be secured before starting out. There's a $35 entrance fee for all overnight guests. The **Havasupai Campground** (☎928-448-2121/2141; per night per person $17), 2 miles north of Supai, has primitive campsites along a creek. In addition, every camper must pay a $5 environmental fee, refunded if you pack out trash. The **Havasupai Lodge** (☎928-448-2111/2101; www.havasupaitribe.com/lodge.html; r $145; ❄) has motel rooms with canyon views but no phones or TVs. Check in by 5pm, when the lobby closes. A village cafe serves meals and accepts credit cards.

Continue through Havasu Canyon to the waterfalls and blue-green swimming holes. If you don't want to hike to Supai, call the lodge or campground to arrange for a mule or horse (round-trip to lodge/campground $120/187) to carry you there. Rides depart from Hualapai Hilltop, where the hiking trail begins. The road to Hualapai Hilltop is 7 miles east of Peach Springs off Route 66. Look for the marked turnoff and follow the road for 62 miles.

GRAND CANYON WEST

Grand Canyon West is not part of Grand Canyon National Park, which is about 215 driving miles to the east. Run by the Hualapai Nation, the remote site is 70 miles northeast of Kingman, and the last 9 miles are unpaved and unsuitable for RVs.

Grand Canyon Skywalk PARK
(☎928-769-2636; www.grandcanyonwest.com; per person $71; ⏰7am-7pm Apr-Sep, 8am-5pm Oct-Mar) A slender see-through glass horseshoe levitates over a 4000ft chasm of the Grand Canyon. The only way to visit is to purchase a package tour. A hop-on, hop-off shuttle travels the loop road to scenic points along the rim. Tours can include lunch, horse-drawn wagon rides from an ersatz Western town, and informal Native American performances.

Northeastern Arizona

Between the brooding buttes of Monument Valley, the blue waters of Lake Powell and the fossilized logs of the Petrified Forest National Park are photogenic lands locked in ancient history. Inhabited by Native Americans for centuries, this region is largely made up of reservation land called Navajo Nation, which spills into surrounding states. The Hopi reservation is here as well, completely surrounded by Navajo land.

LAKE POWELL

The country's second-largest artificial reservoir and part of the **Glen Canyon National Recreation Area**, Lake Powell stretches between Utah and Arizona. Set amid striking red-rock formations, sharply cut canyon and dramatic desert scenery, it's water-sports heaven. South of the lake and looking out over a pleasant stretch of the Colorado River is **Lee's Ferry** (tent & RV sites $12), a pleasant stopover with same-day and advance reservations.

The region's central town is **Page**, and Hwy 89 forms the main strip. The **Carl Hayden Visitor Center** (☎928-608-6404; www.nps.gov/glca; ⊙8am-6pm late May–early Sep, 8am-4:30pm early Sep–late May) is located at Glen Canyon Dam, 2.5 miles north of Page. **Tours** (☎928-608-6072; adult/child $5/2.50) run by the Glen Canyon Natural History Association take you inside the dam.

To visit photogenic **Antelope Canyon** (www.navajonationparks.org/htm/antelopecanyon.htm), a stunning sandstone slot canyon with two main parts, you must join a tour. **Upper Antelope Canyon** is easier to navigate and more touristed. Several tour companies offer trips into upper Antelope Canyon; try **Roger Ekis's Antelope Canyon Tours** (☎928-645-9102; www.antelopecanyon.com; 22 S Lake Powell Blvd; adult/child 5-12 $32/20). The more strenuous **Lower Antelope Canyon** sees much smaller crowds.

Chain hotels line Hwy 89 in Page and a number of independent places line 8th Ave. The owner encourages guests to feel right at home at **Debbie's Hide A Way** (☎928-645-1224; www.debbieshideaway.com; 117 8th Ave; ste $129-199; ❄@☎), where all accommodation is in basic suites. Suites include up to seven people, and there are free laundry facilities.

Six miles north of Page and with a direct view of the lake, **Lake Powell Resort** (☎928-645-2433; www.lakepowell.com; 100 Lake Shore Dr; RV sites $43, d $160-260, r $170-190, ste $250-280; ❄@☎≋) offers rooms, camping, houseboat rentals and a dining room with panoramic views. Wi-fi available in lobby only.

For breakfast in Page, the **Ranch House Grille** (819 N Navajo Dr; mains $6-13; ⊙6am-3pm) has good food, huge portions and fast service. A chalkboard menu includes excellent burgers and hot or cold submarines at **Slackers** (www.slackersqualitygrub.com; 810 N Navajo Dr; mains $6-12; ⊙11am-8pm Mon-Sat, vary seasonally), which gets crowded at lunch.

NAVAJO NATION

The wounds are healing but the scars remain on Arizona's Navajo lands, a testament to the uprooting and forced relocation of thousands of Native Americans to reservations.

Amid the isolation is some of North America's most spectacular scenery, including Monument Valley, cultural pride remain strong and many still speak Navajo as their first language. The Navajo rely heavily on tourism; visitors can help keep their heritage alive by staying on reservation land or purchasing their renowned crafts. Stopping at roadside stalls is a nice way to make purchases for personal interaction and making sure money goes straight into the artisan's pocket.

Unlike Arizona, the Navajo Nation observes Mountain daylight saving time. During summer, the reservation is one hour ahead of Arizona.

CAMERON

Cameron is the gateway to the east entrance of the Grand Canyon's South Rim, but the other reason people come here is for **Cameron Trading Post** (www.camerontradingpost.com), just north of the Hwy 64 turnoff to the Grand Canyon. Food, lodging, a gift shop and a post office are in this historic settlement. It's one of the few worthwhile places to stop on Hwy 89 between Flagstaff and Page.

CANYON DE CHELLY NATIONAL MONUMENT

This many-fingered canyon (pronounced *duh-shay*) contains several beautiful Ancestral Puebloan sites important to Navajo history, including ancient cliff dwellings. Families still farm the land, wintering on the rims, then moving to hogans on the canyon floor in spring and summer. The canyon is private Navajo property administered by the NPS. Enter hogans only with a guide and don't photograph people without their permission.

Most of the bottom of the canyon is off-limits to visitors unless you hire a guide. **Thunderbird Lodge** (☎928-674-5841; www.tbirdlodge.com; d Mar-Oct $115-171, Nov-Feb $66-95; ❄@☎) is the place to book a tour (from $46/35 per adult/child) into the canyon. The lodge also boasts comfortable rooms, an ATM and an inexpensive cafeteria serving tasty Navajo and American meals ($5 to $21).

The Canyon de Chelly **visitor center** (☎928-674-5500; www.nps.gov/cach; ⊙8am-5pm) is three miles from Rte 191 in the small village of Chinle. Near the visitor center, the **campground** has 96 large sites on a first-come, first-served basis, with water but no showers. At press time, the Navajo Nation was in the process of taking over campground management from the park service and implementing an overnight fee.

WORTH A TRIP

HOPI NATION

Descendants of the Ancestral Puebloans, the Hopi are one of the most untouched tribes in the United States. Their village of Old Oraibi may be the oldest continuously inhabited settlement in North America.

Hopi land is surrounded by the Navajo Nation. Hwy 264 runs past the three mesas (First, Second and Third Mesa) that form the heart of the Hopi reservation. On Second Mesa, some 10 miles west of First Mesa, the **Hopi Cultural Center Restaurant & Inn** (928-734-2401; www.hopiculturalcenter.com; breakfast & lunch $8-12, dinner $8-20; breakfast, lunch & dinner;) is as visitor-oriented as things get on the Hopiland reservation. It provides food and lodging (doubles $85 to $105), and there's the small **Hopi Museum** (928-734-6650; adult/child $3/1; 8am-5pm Mon-Fri, 9am-3pm Sat), filled with historic photographs and introductory cultural exhibits.

Photographs, sketching and recording are not allowed.

FOUR CORNERS NAVAJO TRIBAL PARK

Don't be shy: do a spread eagle at the **four corners marker** (928-871-6647; www.navajonationparks.org; admission $3; 7am-8pm May-Aug, 8am-5pm Sep-Apr), the middle-of-nowhere landmark that's looking spiffy after a 2010 renovation of the central plaza. The only spot in the US where you can straddle four states – Arizona, New Mexico, Colorado, Utah – it makes a good photograph, even if it's not 100% accurate. According to government surveyors, the marker is almost 2000ft east of where it should be (but it is the legally recognized border point, regardless).

MONUMENT VALLEY NAVAJO TRIBAL PARK

With flaming-red buttes and impossibly slender spires bursting to the heavens, the Monument Valley landscape off Hwy 163 has starred in countless Hollywood Westerns and looms large in many a road-trip daydream.

For up-close views of the towering formations, you'll need to visit the **Monument Valley Navajo Tribal Park** (435-727-5874; www.navajonationparks.org; per person $5; 6am-8pm May-Sep, 8am-4:30pm Oct-Apr), where a rough and unpaved scenic driving loop covers 17 miles of stunning valley views. You can drive it in your own vehicle or take a tour ($65, 2½ hours) through one of the kiosks in the parking lot (tours enter areas private vehicles can't).

Inside the tribal park is the **View Hotel at Monument Valley** (435-727-5555; www.monumentvalleyview.com; Hwy 163; r $219-229, ste $299-319; @). Built in harmony with the landscape, the sandstone-colored hotel blends naturally with its surroundings, and most of the 96 rooms have private balconies facing the monuments. The Navajo-based specialties at the adjoining restaurant (mains $13 to $23, no alcohol) are mediocre, but the red-rock panorama is stunning. Wi-fi is available in the lobby. A gift shop and small museum are within the hotel complex. Visitors can also overnight in the park's de facto **campground** (per vehicle $10). It's basically just a parking lot, but the awesome sunrise view makes up for the lack of amenities.

The historic **Goulding's Lodge** (435-727-3235; www.gouldings.com; r $185-205, tent sites $25, RV sites $25-44, cabins $79;), just across the border in Utah, offers lodge rooms, camping and small cabins. In Kayenta, 20 miles south, the two-story **Kayenta Monument Valley Inn** (928-697-3221; www.kayentamonumentvalleyinn.com; junction Hwys 160 & 163; r $229-249; @) doesn't look like much from the outside, but the rooms flash a little modern style and come with big flat-screen TVs.

WINSLOW

'Standing on a corner in Winslow, Arizona, such a fine sight to see...' Sound familiar? Thanks to the Eagles' twangy 1970s tune 'Take It Easy,' otherwise nondescript Winslow has earned its wings in pop-culture heaven. A small **park** (www.standinonthecorner.com; 2nd St) on Route 66 at Kinsley Ave pays homage to the band.

Just 50 miles east of Petrified Forest National Park, Winslow is a good regional base. Old motels border Route 66, and eateries sprinkle the downtown. The inviting 1929 **La Posada** (928-289-4366; www.laposada.org; 303 E 2nd; r $109-169;) is a restored hacienda designed by star architect du jour Mary Jane Colter. Elaborate tilework, glass-and-tin chandeliers, Navajo rugs and other details accent its palatial Western-style elegance. The on-site restaurant, the much-lauded **Turquoise Room** (928-289-2888; breakfast

$6-11, lunch $9-13, dinner $17-32; ⏲7am-9pm), serves the best meals between Flagstaff and Albuquerque; dishes have a neo-Southwestern flair.

PETRIFIED FOREST NATIONAL PARK

The multicolored Painted Desert here is strewn with fossilized logs predating the dinosaurs. This **national park** (☎928-524-6228; www.nps.gov/pefo; per vehicle $10; ⏲7am-7pm May-Aug, 7am-6pm Mar, Apr & Sep, 8am-5pm Oct-Feb) is an extraordinary site. The hard-to-miss **visitor center** is just half a mile north of I-40 and has maps and information on guided tours and science lectures.

The park straddles I-40 at exit 311, 25 miles east of Holbrook. From this exit, a 28-mile paved park road offers a splendid **scenic drive**. There are no campsites, but a number of short trails, ranging from less than a mile to two miles, pass through the best stands of petrified rock and ancient Native American dwellings in the park. Those prepared for rugged backcountry camping need to pick up a free permit at the visitor center.

Western Arizona

The Colorado River is alive with sun worshippers at Lake Havasu City, while Route 66 offers well-preserved stretches of classic highway near Kingman. South of the I-10, the wild, empty landscape is among the most barren in the West. If you're already here, there are some worthwhile sites, but there's nothing worth planning an itinerary around unless you're a Route 66 or boating fanatic.

KINGMAN & AROUND

Faded motels and gas stations galore grace Kingman's main drag, but several turn-of-the-19th-century buildings remain. If you're following the Route 66 trail (aka Andy Devine Ave here) or looking for cheap lodging, it's worth a stroll.

Pick up maps and brochures at the historic **Powerhouse Visitor Center** (☎928-753-6106; www.kingmantourism.org; 120 W Andy Devine Ave; ⏲8am-5pm), which has an impressive **Route 66 museum** (☎928-753-9889; adult/child/senior $4/free/3; ⏲9am-5pm).

A cool neon sign marks draws road-trippers to the **Hilltop Motel** (☎928-753-2198; www.hilltopmotelaz.com; 1901 E Andy Devine Ave; s/d $42/46; ❄@📶🏊) on Route 66. Rooms are a bit of a throwback, but are well kept, and the views are superb. Pets (dogs only) stay for $5. Just down the road, the **Dambar Steakhouse** (☎928-753-3523; 1960 E Andy Devine Ave; lunch $6-11, dinner $10-22; ⏲lunch & dinner; 👪) is a local landmark serving giant steaks in Old West bad-boy environs – but kiddies will be just fine at this spit-and-sawdust saloon with cowhide tablecloths.

ROADSIDE KITSCH ON ROUTE 66

Route 66 enthusiasts will find 400 miles of pavement stretching across Arizona, including the longest uninterrupted portion of old road left in the country, between Seligman and Topock. The Mother Road connects the dots between Winslow's windblown streets, Williams' 1940s-vintage downtown, Kingman's mining settlements and gun-slinging Oatman, with plenty of kitschy sights, listed here from west to east, along the way.

» **Wild Burros of Oatman** Mules beg for treats in the middle of the road.

» **Grand Canyon Caverns Tour & Underground Motel Room** A guided tour 21 stories underground loops past mummified bobcats, civil-defense supplies and a $700 motel room.

» **Burma Shave signs** Red-and-white ads from a bygone era between Grand Canyon Caverns and Seligman.

» **Seligman's Snow-Cap Drive In** Prankish burger and ice-cream joint open since 1953.

» **Meteor Crater** A 550ft-deep pockmark that's nearly 1 mile across, near Flagstaff.

» **Holbrook's Wigwam Motel** Concrete wigwams with hickory logpole furniture.

For more information, visit **Historic Route 66 Association of Arizona** (www.azrt66.com).

LAKE HAVASU CITY

When the city of London auctioned off its 1831 bridge in the late 1960s, developer Robert McCulloch bought it, took it apart, shipped it, and then reassembled it at Lake Havasu City, which sits along a dammed-up portion of the Colorado River. The place attracts hordes of young spring-breakers and weekend warriors who come to play in the water and party hard. An 'English Village' of pseudo-British pubs and tourist gift shops surrounds the bridge and houses the **visitor center** (☎928-855-5655; www.golakehavasu.com; 420 English Village; ⊙9am-5pm; @📶) where you can pick up tourist information and access the internet.

The hippest hotel in town is **Heat** (☎928-854-2833; www.heathotel.com; 1420 McCulloch Blvd; r $139-159, ste $191-256; ❄📶), a slick boutique property where the front desk doubles as a bar. Rooms are contemporary and most have private patios with views of London Bridge. For home-cooked Italian, head to **Angelina's Italian Kitchen** (☎928-680-3868; 2137 W Acoma Blvd; mains $8-27; ⊙dinner Tue-Sat), a very busy hole-in-the-wall on an industrial stretch east of downtown. For a hearty, open-air breakfast, rise and shine at the **Red Onion** (2013 N McCulloch Blvd; mains $7-11; ⊙8am-2pm daily, 4-8pm Thu & Fri), a popular eatery where the menu is loaded with omelets and diet-busting fare.

Tucson

Arizona's second-largest city is set in the Sonoran Desert, full of rolling, sandy hills and crowds of cacti. The vibe here is ramshackle-cool and cozy compared with the shiny vastness of Phoenix. A college town, Tucson (the 'c' is silent) is home turf to the 38,000-strong University of Arizona (U of A) and was an artsy, dress-down kind of place before that was the cool thing to be. Eclectic shops and scores of funky restaurants and bars flourish in this arid ground. Tucsonans are proud of the city's geographic and cultural proximity to Mexico (65 highway miles south); more than 35% of the population is of Mexican or Central American descent.

Sights & Activities

Downtown Tucson and the historic district are east of I-10 exit 258. About a mile northeast of downtown is the U of A campus; 4th Ave is the main drag here, packed with cafes, bars and interesting shops.

Saguaro National Park PARK

(www.nps.gov/sagu; 7-day pass per vehicle/bicycle $10/5; ⊙7am-sunset) This prickly canvas of green cacti and desert scrub is split in half by 30 miles of freeway and farms. Both sections sit at the edges of Tucson, but are still officially within the city.

You'll have a nice time exploring in either section, but if you want to make a day of it, head to **Saguaro West** (Tucson Mountain District), where you'll find several fun activities in and around the park. For maps and ranger-led programs, stop at the **Red Hills Visitor Center** (☎520-733-5158; 2700 N Kinney Rd; ⊙9am-5pm), which is also the starting point for the **Cactus Garden Trail**, a short, wheelchair-accessible path with interpretive signs for many of the park's cacti. The **Bajada Loop Drive**, an unpaved 6-mile loop that begins 1.5 miles west of the visitor center, provides fine views of cactus forests, several picnic spots and access to trailheads.

Saguaro East (Rincon Mountain District) is 15 miles east of downtown. The **visitor center** (☎520-733-5153; 3693 S Old Spanish Trail; ⊙9am-5pm) has information on day hikes, horseback riding and backcountry camping. Backcountry camping requires a permit ($6 per site per day) and must be obtained by noon on the day of your hike. This section of the park has about 130 miles of hiking (but only 2.5 miles of mountain-biking) trails. The meandering 8-mile **Cactus Forest Scenic Loop Drive**, a paved road open to cars and bicycles, provides access to picnic areas, trailheads and viewpoints.

TOP CHOICE **Arizona-Sonora Desert Museum** MUSEUM

(☎520-883-1380; www.desertmuseum.org; 2021 N Kinney Rd; adult/child Jun-Aug $12/3, Sep-May $14.50/4.50; ⊙8:30am-5pm Oct-Feb; 👪) This tribute to the Sonoran Desert is one part zoo, one part botanical garden and one part museum – a trifecta that'll keep young and old entertained for easily half a day. All sorts of desert denizens, from precocious coatis to playful prairie dogs, make their home in natural enclosures hemmed in by invisible fences. The grounds are thick with desert plants, and docents are on hand to answer questions and give demonstrations. Strollers and wheelchairs are available, and there's a gift shop, art gallery, restaurant and cafe. Hours vary seasonally.

Old Tucson Studios FILM LOCATION, AMUSEMENT PARK
(520-883-0100; www.oldtucson.com; 201 S Kinney Rd; adult/child $17/11; 10am-6pm Oct-May, 10am-6pm Fri-Sun Jun-Sep;) A few miles southeast of the Arizona-Sonora Desert Museum, Old Tucson Studios was an actual Western film set. Today it's a Western theme park with shootouts and stagecoach rides.

Pima Air & Space Museum MUSEUM
(520-574-0462; www.pimaair.org; 6000 E Valencia Rd; adult/child/senior & military Jun-Oct $13.75/8/11.75, Nov-May $15.50/9/12.75; 9am-5pm, last admission 4pm) An SR-71 Blackbird spy plane and JFK's Air Force One are among the stars at this private aircraft museum home to more than 300 'birds.' Hardcore plane-spotters should book ahead for the 90-minute bus tour of the nearby 309th **Aerospace Maintenance & Regeneration Center** (adult/child $7/4; Mon-Fri, departure times vary seasonally) – aka the 'boneyard' – where almost 4000 aircraft are mothballed.

FREE **Center for Creative Photography** MUSEUM
(CCP; 520-621-7968; www.creativephotography.org; 1030 N Olive Rd; donations appreciated; 9am-5pm Mon-Fri, 1-4pm Sat & Sun) The CCP is known for its ever-changing, high-caliber exhibits and for administering the archives of landscape photographer Ansel Adams. The museum closes between exhibits, so check the website before visiting.

Festivals & Events

Fiesta de los Vaqueros Rodeo RODEO
(520-741-2233; www.tucsonrodeo.com) Held during the last week of February, the huge nonmotorized parade is a locally famous spectacle.

Sleeping

Lodging prices vary considerably, with lower rates in summer and fall.

TOP CHOICE **Catalina Park Inn** B&B $$
(520-792-4541; www.catalinaparkinn.com; 309 E 1st St; r $139-149; ; closed Jul & Aug) Style, hospitality and comfort merge seamlessly at this inviting B&B just west of the University of Arizona. Hosts Mark Hall and Paul Richard have poured their hearts into restoring this 1927 Med-style villa, and their efforts are on display in the six guest rooms, from the oversized and over-the-top peacock-blue-and-gold Catalina Room to the white and uncluttered East Room with an iron canopy bed.

Arizona Inn RESORT $$$
(520-325-1541; www.arizonainn.com; 2200 E Elm St; r $259-333, ste $379-449;) The historic feel of this resort provides a sense of being one of the aristocracy. The mature gardens and old Arizona grace provide a respite not only from city life but also from the 21st century. Sip coffee on the porch, take high tea in the library, lounge by the small pool or join in a game of croquet, then retire to rooms furnished with antiques. The on-site spa is our favorite in town.

Hotel Congress HISTORIC HOTEL $$
(520-622-8848; www.hotelcongress.com; 311 E Congress St; r $90-120;) A groovy historic hotel with a hip rock-and-roll flavor, the Congress is a nonstop buzz of activity, mostly because of its popular bar, restaurant and nightclub downstairs. Infamous bank robber John Dillinger and his gang were captured here in 1934. Many rooms have period furnishings, rotary phones and wooden radios – but no TV. Ask for a room at the far end of the hotel if you're noise-sensitive. Pets stay for $10 per night.

Flamingo Hotel MOTEL $
(520-770-1910; www.flamingohoteltucson.com; 1300 N Stone Ave; r incl breakfast $60-105;) Though recently purchased by Quality Inn, this snazzy motel retains its great 1950s Rat Pack vibe. And the fact that Elvis slept here doesn't hurt. Rooms have stylish striped bedding, comfy beds, flat-screen plasma TVs and a good-sized desk. Pets stay for $20 per day.

Windmill Inn at St Philips Plaza HOTEL $$
(520-577-0007; www.windmillinns.com; 4250 N Campbell Ave; r incl breakfast $120-134;) Popular with University of Arizona fans during football season, this modern, friendly place wins kudos for spacious two-room suites (no charge for kids under 18 years of age), free continental breakfast, a lending library, a heated pool and free bike rentals. Pets stay free.

Roadrunner Hostel & Inn HOSTEL $
(520-940-7280; www.roadrunnerhostel.com; 346 E 12th St; dm/r incl breakfast $20/40;) This comfortable hostel within walking distance of the arts district has a large kitchen, free coffee and waffles in the morning, and

HOT DIGGETY DOG

Tucson's signature 'dish' is the Sonoran hot dog, a tasty example of what happens when Mexican ingredients meet American processed meat and penchant for excess. The ingredients? A bacon-wrapped hot dog layered with tomatillo salsa, pinto beans, shredded cheese, mayo, ketchup or mustard or both, chopped tomatoes and onions. We like 'em at **El Guero Canelo** (www.elguerocanelo.com; 5201 S 12th Ave, South Tucson).

a big-screen TV for watching movies. Dorms close between noon and 3pm for cleaning. Takes cash and traveler's checks only.

Eating

Your best bet for great food at good prices is 4th Ave; we've listed some of Tucson's standouts.

TOP CHOICE **Café Poca Cosa** SOUTH AMERICAN $$
(☎520-622-6400; www.cafepocacosa.com; 110 E Pennington St; lunch $13-15, dinner $19-26; ⊙lunch & dinner Tue-Sat) At this award-winning Nuevo-Mexican bistro, a Spanish-English chalkboard menu circulates between tables because dishes change twice daily. It's all freshly prepared, innovative and beautifully presented. The undecided can't go wrong by ordering the Plato Poca Cosa and letting chef Suzana D'avila decide. Great margaritas, too.

Pasco Kitchen & Lounge AMERICAN $$
(www.pascokitchen.com; 820 E University Blvd; lunch $9-14; dinner $9-14 ⊙11am-10pm Mon-Wed, 11am-11pm Thu, 11am-1am Fri & Sat, 11am-4pm Sun) The farmers market salad with yard bird is superb at this breezy new eatery near the university. The menu offers fresh, locally sourced homestyle favorites that are prepared with panache and a few tasty twists – think grass-fed all-natural burgers topped with braised pork belly and a fried egg, or grits with catfish and fried okra. The owners call it 'urban farm fare;' we call it delicious.

Mi Nidito MEXICAN $
(www.minidito.net; 1813 S 4th Ave; mains $6-13; ⊙lunch & dinner Wed-Sun) Bill Clinton's order at 'My Little Nest' has become the signature president's plate, a heaping mound of Mexican favorites – tacos, tostadas, burritos, enchiladas etc – groaning under melted cheese. Also give the prickly pear cactus chile or the *birria* (spicy, shredded beef) a whirl.

Lovin' Spoonfuls VEGAN $
(2990 N Campbell Ave; lunch $6-8, dinner $9-11; ⊙9:30am-9pm Mon-Sat, 10am-3pm Sun; ✎) Burgers, country-fried chicken, meatloaf, salads – the menu here reads like those at your typical cafe but there's one big difference: no animal products find their way into this vegan haven.

Hub Restaurant & Creamery AMERICAN $$
(☎520-207-8201; www.hubdowntown.com; 266 E Congress Ave; lunch $9-17, dinner $9-17 ⊙11am-2am) Upscale comfort food is the name of the game here, plus a few sandwiches and salads. If you don't want a meal, pop in for a scoop of flavor-packed gourmet ice cream – bacon scotch anyone?

El Charro Café MEXICAN $$
(☎520-622-1922; 311 N Court Ave; mains $7-18; ⊙lunch & dinner) The Flin family has been making innovative Mexican food at this buzzy hacienda since 1922. It's famous for the *carne seca,* sundried lean beef that's been reconstituted, shredded and grilled with green chile and onions.

Drinking & Entertainment

Downtown 4th Ave, near 6th St, is the happening bar-hop spot, and there are a number of nightclubs on downtown Congress St.

Club Congress LIVE MUSIC
(☎520-622-8848; www.hotelcongress.com; 311 E Congress St; cover $7-13) Live and DJ music are found at this very popular place that's sometimes a rock hangout and sometimes a dance club. The crowd depends on the night, but it's almost always a happening place.

Che's Lounge BAR
(☎520-623-2088; 350 N 4th Ave) A slightly skanky but hugely popular watering hole that rocks with live music Saturday nights. And it never charges a cover.

IBT's GAY CLUB
(☎520-882-3053; 616 N 4th Ave; no cover) Themes change nightly, from drag shows to techno dance mixes to karaoke.

Chocolate Iguana CAFE
(www.chocolateiguanaon4th.com; 500 N 4th Ave; ⊙8am-10pm Mon-Thu, 7am-10pm Fri, 8am-10pm Sat, 9am-6pm Sun) For coffee-lovers and chocoholics, this is the place.

Information

Emergency & Medical Services

Police (☎520-791-4444; http://cms3.tucsonaz.gov/; 270 S Stone Ave)

Tucson Medical Center (☎520-327-5461; www.tmcaz.com/TucsonMedicalCenter; 5301 E Grant Rd) Has 24-hour emergency services.

Internet Access

Joel D Valdez Main Library (☎520-594-5500; 101 N Stone Ave; ⌚9am-8pm Mon-Wed, 9am-6pm Thu, 9am-5pm Fri, 10am-5pm Sat, 1-5pm Sun; @📶) Free internet, including wi-fi.

Media

Arizona Daily Star (www.azstarnet.com) The Tucson region's daily newspaper.

Tucson Weekly (www.tucsonweekly.com) A free weekly full of entertainment and restaurant listings.

Money

ATMs are abundant. Foreign exchange is available at most banks; $5 is charged if you don't have an account. Tucson International Airport doesn't exchange currency.

Post

Post office (825 E University Blvd, Suite 111; ⌚8am-5pm Mon-Fri, 9am-12:30pm Sat)

Tourist Information

Tucson Convention & Visitors Bureau (☎520-624-1817; www.visittucson.org; 100 S Church Ave; ⌚9am-5pm Mon-Fri, to 4pm Sat & Sun) Ask for its free *Official Destination Guide*.

Getting There & Around

Tucson International Airport (☎520-573-8000; www.flytucsonairport.com) is 15 miles south of downtown. **Arizona Stagecoach** (☎877-782-4355; www.azstagecoach.com) runs shared van service with fares for about $29 between downtown and the airport. **Greyhound** (☎520-792-3475; www.greyhound.com; 471 W Congress St; ⌚7am-11pm) runs buses to Phoenix (from $21, two hours, daily) and Nogales (from $11, one hour, daily) and other destinations. The station is on the western end of Congress St, three miles from downtown. **Amtrak** (☎520-623-4442; www.amtrak.com; 400 E Toole Ave) is across from Hotel Congress and has train services to Los Angeles (from $38, 10 hours, three weekly) on the Sunset Limited.

The **Ronstadt Transit Center** (cnr Congress St & 6th Ave) is the major downtown transit hub. From here **Sun Tran** (☎520-792-9222; www.suntran.com) buses serve metropolitan Tucson (day pass $3.50).

Around Tucson

The places listed following are less than 1½ hours' drive from town and make great day trips.

NORTH OF TUCSON

About 35 miles away from downtown via backcountry roads, **Biosphere 2** (☎520-896-6200; www.b2science.org; 32540 S Biosphere Rd, Oracle; adult/child/senior $20/13/18; ⌚9am-4pm) is a 3-acre glassed dome housing seven separate microhabitats – a jungle, a desert, a swamp – designed to be self-sustaining. In 1991 eight bionauts entered Biosphere 2 for a two-year tour of duty, during which they were physically cut off from the outside world. They emerged thinner, but in fair shape. Although this experiment could be used as a prototype for future space stations, it was privately funded and controversial. The massive glass structure is now a University of Arizona–run earth science research institute. Visits are by guided tour.

WEST OF TUCSON

From Tucson, Hwy 86 heads west into some of the emptiest parts of the Sonoran Desert – except for the ubiquitous green-and-white border patrol trucks.

The lofty **Kitt Peak National Observatory** (☎520-318-8726; www.noao.edu/kpno; Hwy 86; visitor center admission by donation; ⌚9am-3:45pm) west of Sells features the largest collection of optical telescopes in the world. Guided tours (adult/child $7.75/4 November to May, $5.75/3 June to October, at 10am, 11:30am and 1:30pm) last about an hour. Book two to four weeks in advance for the worthwhile nightly observing program (adult/child $48/44; no programs from mid-July through August because of monsoon season) – clear, dry skies equal an awe-inspiring glimpse of the cosmos. Dress warmly, buy gas in Tucson (the nearest gas station is 30 miles from the observatory) and note that children under eight years of age are not allowed at the evening program for safety reasons. The picnic area draws amateur astronomers at night.

If you truly want to get away from it all, you can't get much further off the grid than the huge and exotic **Organ Pipe Cactus National Monument** (☎520-387-6849; www.nps.gov/orpi; Hwy 85; per vehicle $8) along the Mexican border. It's a gorgeous, forbidding land that supports an astonishing number of animals and plants, including 28 species of cacti, first and foremost its namesake organ-pipe. A giant columnar cactus, it differs from the more prevalent saguaro in that its branches radiate from the base. The 21-mile **Ajo Mountain Drive** takes you through a spectacular landscape of steep-sided, jagged cliffs and rock tinged a faintly hellish red. There are 208 first-come, first-served sites at **Twin Peaks Campground** (tent & RV sites $12) by the visitor center.

SOUTH OF TUCSON

South of Tucson, I-19 is the main route to Nogales and Mexico. Along the way are several interesting stops.

The striking **Mission San Xavier del Bac** (☎520-294-2624; www.sanxaviermission.org; 1950 W San Xavier Rd; donations appreciated; ⊙7am-5pm), nine miles south of downtown Tucson, is Arizona's oldest European building still in use. Dark and moody inside, it's a graceful blend of Moorish, Byzantine and late Mexican Renaissance architecture.

At exit 69, 16 miles south of the mission, the **Titan Missile Museum** (☎520-625-7736; www.titanmissilemuseum.org; 1580 W Duval Mine Rd, Suarita; adult/child/senior $9.50/6/8.50; ⊙8:45am-5:30pm Nov-Apr, 8:45am-5pm May-Oct) features an underground launch site for Cold War–era intercontinental ballistic missiles. Tours are chilling and informative.

If history and/or shopping for crafts interest you, head 48 miles south of Tucson to the small village of **Tubac** (www.tubacaz.com), with more than 100 galleries, studios and shops.

PATAGONIA & THE MOUNTAIN EMPIRE

Sandwiched in between the border, the Santa Rita Mountains and the Patagonia Mountains, this scenic region is one of the shiniest hidden gems in the Arizona jewel box. It's a lovely destination for bird-watching and wine tasting.

Bird-watchers and nature-lovers wander the gentle trails at the **Patagonia-Sonoita Creek Preserve** (☎520-394-2400; www.nature.org/arizona; 150 Blue Heaven Rd; admission $5; ⊙6:30am-4pm Wed-Sun Apr-Sep, from 7:30am Oct-Mar), an enchanting riparian willow forest managed by the Nature Conservancy. The peak migratory season is April through May, and late August to September. For a leisurely afternoon of wine tasting, head to the villages of **Sonoita** and **Elgin** north of Patagonia (see www.arizonavinesandwines.com). The big-sky views are terrific.

If you stick around for dinner, try the gourmet pizzas at **Velvet Elvis** (www.velvetelvispizza.com; 29 Naugle Ave, Patagonia; mains $8-26; ⊙5-9pm Thu, 3-9pm Fri & Sat, 10am-3pm Sun) – they're savory-licious. The photogenic **Duquesne House** (☎520-394-2732; www.theduquesnehouse.com; 357 Duquesne Ave, Patagonia; r $125; @) is an inviting, ranch-style B&B that once served as a boardinghouse for miners.

A small **visitor center** (☎520-394-9186; www.patagoniaaz.com; 307 McKeown Ave; ⊙10am-5pm Mon-Sat, 10am-4pm Sun) is tucked inside Mariposa Books & More in Patagonia.

Southeastern Arizona

Chockablock with places that loom large in the history of the Wild West, southern Arizona is home to the wonderfully preserved mining town of Bisbee, the OK Corral in Tombstone, and wonderland of stone spires at Chiricahua National Monument.

KARTCHNER CAVERNS STATE PARK

The emphasis is on education at **Kartchner Caverns State Park** (☎reservations 520-586-2283, information 520-586-4010; http://azstateparks.com; Hwy 90; park entrance per vehicle/bicycle $6/3, adult/child Rotunda Tour $23/13, Big Room Tour mid-Oct–mid-Apr $23/13; ⊙10am-3pm Mon-Fri Jun-Sep, to 3:40pm Sat & Sun, vary rest of year), a 2.5-mile-long wet limestone fantasia of rocks. Two guided tours explore different areas of the caverns, which were 'discovered' in 1974. The Rotunda/Throne Room Tour is open year-round; the Big Room Tour closes in mid-April for five months to protect the migratory bats that roost here. The park is 9 miles south of Benson, off I-10 at exit 302. The $6 entrance fee is waived for reserved tour tickets.

CHIRICAHUA NATIONAL MONUMENT

The towering rock spires at remote but mesmerizing **Chiricahua National Monument** (☎520-824-3560; www.nps.gov/chir; Hwy 181; adult/child $5/free) in the Chiricahua Mountains sometimes rise hundreds of feet high and often look like they're on the verge of tipping over. The **Bonita Canyon Scenic Drive** takes you 8 miles to Massai Point (6870ft) where you'll see thousands of spires positioned on the slopes like some petrified army. There are numerous hiking trails, but if you're short on time, hike the **Echo Canyon Trail** at least half a mile to the Grottoes, an amazing 'cathedral' of giant boulders where you can lie still and enjoy the wind-caressed silence. The monument is 36 miles southeast of Willcox off Hwy 186/181.

TOMBSTONE

In Tombstone's 19th-century heyday as a booming mining town the whiskey flowed and six-shooters blazed over disputes large and small, most famously at the OK Corral. Now a National Historic Landmark, it attracts hordes of tourists to its old Western buildings, stagecoach rides and nonstop gunfight reenactments.

And yes, you must visit the **OK Corral** (☎520-457-3456; www.ok-corral.com; Allen St, btwn 3rd & 4th Sts; admission $10, without gunfight $6; ⏰9am-5pm), site of the legendary gunfight between the Earps, Doc Holliday and the McLaurys and Billy Clanton on October 26, 1881. Also make time for the dusty **Bird Cage Theater** (☎520-457-3421; 517 E Allen St; adult/child/senior $10/7/9; ⏰8am-6pm), a one-time dance hall and saloon now crammed with historic odds and ends. And a merman.

The **Visitor & Information Center** (☎520-457-3929; www.tombstonechamber.com; cnr 395 E Allen & 4th Sts; ⏰9am-5pm) has walking maps and local recommendations.

BISBEE

Oozing old-fashioned ambience, Bisbee is a former copper-mining town that's now a delightful mix of aging Bohemians, elegant buildings, sumptuous restaurants and charming hotels. Most businesses are found in the Historic District (Old Bisbee), along Subway and Main Sts.

To burrow under the earth in a tour led by the retired miners who worked here, take the **Queen Mine Tour** (☎520-432-2071; www.queenminetour.com; 478 Dart Rd, off Hwy 80; adult/child $13/5.50; ⏰9am-3:30pm; 👪). Right outside of town, check out the **Lavender Pit**, an ugly yet impressive testament to strip mining.

Rest your head at **Shady Dell RV Park** (☎520-432-3567; www.theshadydell.com; 1 Douglas Rd; rates $50-145), a kitschy trailer park extraordinaire. Everything's done up with fun, retro furnishings. Swamp coolers provide cold air. **Copper Queen Hotel** (☎520-432-2216; www.copperqueen.com; 11 Howell; r $122-197; ❄@📶🏊), built in 1902, is still charming as heck and a number of rooms are themed after the famous personalities that stayed in them, including John Wayne. Rooms and hallways are bewitched by lovely copper lamps, and supposedly ghosts.

For good eats, stroll up Main St and pick a restaurant – you can't go wrong. A current hot spot is the fantastic **Poco** (☎520-432-3733; 15 Main St/Peddlar's Alley; mains $7.50-10; ⏰11am-8pm Wed-Sun; 🥕), a courtyard cafe that's earning kudos as far away as Patagonia for Mexican-inspired, mostly organic vegetarian fare. For fine American food continue up Main St to stylish **Cafe Roka** (☎520-432-5153; www.caferoka.com; 35 Main St; dinner $15-29; ⏰dinner Thu-Sat), where four-course dinners include salad, soup, sorbet and a rotating choice of crowd-pleasing mains.

The **visitor center** (☎520-432-3554; www.discoverbisbee.com; 2 Copper Queen Plaza; ⏰9am-5pm Mon-Fri, 10am-4pm Sat & Sun) is a good place to start.

UTAH

Shhhhh, don't tell. We wouldn't want word to get out that this oft-overlooked state is really one of nature's most perfect playgrounds. Utah's rugged terrain comes ready-made for hiking, biking, rafting, rappelling, rock climbing, skiing, snowboarding, snow riding, horseback riding, four-wheel driving… Need we go on? More than 65% of the state's lands are public, including 12 national parks and monuments – a dazzling display of haunting topography that leaves many awestruck.

Southern Utah red-rock country is defined by soaring Technicolor cliffs, spindles and spires that defy gravity, and seemingly endless expanses of sculpted sandstone desert. Northern Utah is dominated by the 11,000ft-high forest- and snow-covered peaks of the Wasatch Mountains. Interspersed throughout it all you'll find Native American rock-art sites and well-organized little towns with pioneer buildings dating back to the state's founding.

The enticing land was also what drew the first Mormon pioneers to the territory; still today, church members make up more than 50% of the wonderfully polite population. Rural towns can be quiet and conservative, but the rugged beauty has attracted outdoorsy, independent thinkers as well. Salt Lake and Park Cities especially have vibrant nightlife and foodie scenes.

So come wonder at the roadside geographic kaleidoscope, or go hiking where no one (literally) has hiked before. Just don't tell your friends: we'd like to keep this secret to ourselves.

UTAH FACTS

» **Nickname** Beehive State

» **Population** 2.9 million

» **Area** 84,900 sq miles

» **Capital city** Salt Lake City (population 181,743), metro area (1.2 million)

» **Other cities** St George (population 88,001)

» **Sales tax** 4.7%

» **Birthplace of** Entertainers Donny (b 1957) and Marie (b 1959) Osmond, beloved bandit Butch Cassidy (1866–1908)

» **Home of** 2002 Winter Olympic Games

» **Politics** mostly conservative

» **Famous for** Mormons, red-rock canyons, polygamy

» **Best souvenir** Wasatch Brewery T-shirt: 'Polygamy Porter – Why Have Just One?'

» **Driving distances** Salt Lake City to Moab 235 miles, St George to Salt Lake City 304 miles

History

Traces of the Ancestral Puebloan (or Anasazi) and Fremont people, this land's earliest human inhabitants, can today be seen in the rock art and ruins they left behind. But it was the modern Ute, Paiute and Navajo tribes who were living here when European-heritage settlers arrived in large numbers. Led by second church president, Brigham Young, Mormons fled to this territory to escape religious persecution starting in the late 1840s. They set about attempting to settle every inch of their new state, no matter how inhospitable, which resulted in skirmishes with Native Americans – and more than one abandoned ghost town.

For nearly 50 years after the United States acquired the Utah Territory from Mexico, petitions for statehood were rejected as a result of the Mormon practice of polygamy (taking multiple wives), which was illegal in the US. Tension and prosecutions grew until 1890, when Mormon leader Wilford Woodruff had a divine revelation and the church officially discontinued the practice. Utah became the 45th state in 1896. The modern Mormon church, now called the Church of Jesus Christ of Latter-Day Saints (LDS) continues to exert a strong influence here.

Information

Note that it can be difficult to change currency outside Salt Lake City, but ATMs are widespread.

Utah Office of Tourism (800-200-1160; www.utah.com) Publishes the free *Utah Travel Guide* and runs several visitor centers statewide. Website has links in six languages.

Utah State Parks & Recreation Department (877-887-2757; www.stateparks.utah.gov) Produces comprehensive guide to the 40-plus state parks; available online and at visitor centers.

Reserve America (801-322-3770, 800-322-3770; http://utahstateparks.reserveamerica.com) State park camping reservations.

Getting There & Away

Salt Lake City (SLC) has the state's only international airport. The much smaller St George airport has a couple domestic connections, but it's often cheaper to fly into Las Vegas (120 miles south) and rent a car. You will need a private vehicle to reach most places outside SLC and Park City.

Getting Around

Utah towns are typically laid out in a grid with streets aligned north–south or east–west. There's a zero point in the town center at the intersection of two major streets (often called Main St and Center St). Addresses and numerical street names radiate out from this point, rising by 100 with each city block. Thus, 500 South 400 East will be five blocks south and four blocks east of the zero point. The system is complicated to explain, but thankfully it's quite easy to use.

Salt Lake City

Snuggled up against the soaring peaks of the Wasatch Mountains, Salt Lake City is a small town with just enough edge to satisfy city slickers. Yes, it is the Mormon equivalent of Vatican City, but Utah's capital city is quite modern. A redeveloped downtown and local foodie scene balance out the city's charming anachronisms.

Sights

The second Mormon Church president and prophet, Brigham Young, declared 'This is the place!' when he first arrived with settlers in 1847. Salt Lake City remains the LDS church headquarters and most of the town's top sights are church related. The main LDS sights cluster near downtown's zero point for streets and addresses: the corner of S Temple (east–west) and Main St (north–south). Note that the 132ft-wide streets were originally built so that four oxen pulling a wagon could turn around. Just 45 minutes away, world-class hiking, climbing and snow sports await in the Wasatch Mountains.

TEMPLE SQUARE AREA

Temple Square PLAZA

(www.visittemplesquare.com; admission free; ⌚9am-9pm) The city's most famous sight, a 10-acre square filled with LDS buildings, flower gardens and fountains, is certainly awe-inspiring. Disarmingly nice LDS-member 'sister' and 'brother' volunteers answer questions and lead free 30-minute grounds tours from the visitor centers, inside the two entrances (on S and N Temple). Lording over the square, the 210ft-tall **Salt Lake Temple** is at its most ethereal when lit up at night. Atop the tallest spire stands a statue of the angel Moroni, who appeared to first LDS prophet, Joseph Smith, and led him to the Book of Mormon. The Temple and its ceremonies are private, open only to LDS members 'in good standing.' In addition to the noteworthy sights listed below, the square also contains a church history museum, Joseph Smith theatre and restaurants.

Tabernacle RELIGIOUS

(Temple Sq; admission free; ⌚9am-9pm) This domed, 1867 auditorium – with a massive 11,000-pipe organ – has incredible acoustics. A pin dropped in the front can be heard in the back, almost 200ft away. Free daily organ recitals are held at noon Monday through Saturday, 2pm Sunday. For more on choir performances, see Entertainment (p842).

Beehive House HISTORIC SITE

(67 E South Temple; tours free; ⌚9am-9pm Mon-Sat) The Beehive House was Brigham Young's main home during his tenure as governor and church president in Utah. The required tours, which begin on your arrival, vary in the amount of historic house detail provided versus religious education offered, depending on the particular LDS docent.

Family History Library LIBRARY

(www.familysearch.org; 35 N West Temple; admission free; ⌚8am-5pm Mon, 8am-9pm Tue-Sat) Investigating your ancestors? Start here. This incredible library contains more than 3.5 million genealogy-related microfilms, microfiches, books and other records gathered from more than 110 countries.

GREATER DOWNTOWN

State Capitol HISTORIC BUILDING

(www.utahstatecapitol.utah.gov; admission free; ⌚8am-8pm Mon-Fri, 8am-6pm Sat & Sun) The grand, 1916 State Capitol is set among 500 cherry trees on a hill north of Temple Sq. Inside, colorful Works Progress Administration (WPA) murals of pioneers, trappers and missionaries adorn part of the building's dome. Free hourly tours (from 9am to 4pm) start at the 1st-floor visitor center.

Pioneer Memorial Museum MUSEUM

(www.dupinternational.org; 300 N Main St; admission free; ⌚9am-5pm Mon-Sat year-round, 1-5pm Sun Jun-Aug) Vast, four-story treasure trove of pioneer artifacts.

City Creek PLAZA

(Social Hall Ave, btwn Regent & Richards Sts) This LDS-funded, 20-acre pedestrian plaza with fountains, restaurants and retail along City Creek was under construction at the time of research.

CAN I GET A DRINK IN UTAH?

Absolutely. Although there are still a few unusual liquor laws on the books, regulations have relaxed in recent years. Private club memberships are no more: a bar is now a bar (no minors allowed), and you don't have to order food to consume alcohol in one of them. As far as restaurants go, few have full liquor licenses, many more serve just beer and wine.

Remaining rules to remember:

» You must be dining at a full-license restaurant to order any alcoholic drink there. Mixed drinks and wine are available only after noon.

» In bars and restaurants, beer can be served from 10am.

» Packaged liquor can only be sold at state-run liquor stores (closed on Sundays), some beer is sold in convenience stores.

UNIVERSITY-FOOTHILL DISTRICT

This Is the Place Heritage Park HISTORIC SITE
(www.thisistheplace.org; 2601 E Sunnyside Ave; park admission free, village adult/child $10/7 Jun-Aug; ⏲9am-5pm Mon-Fri, 10am-5pm Sat;) A 450-acre park marks the spot where Brigham Young uttered the fateful words, 'This is the place.' The centerpiece is a living-history village where, June through August, costumed docents depict mid-19th-century life. Admission includes a tourist train ride and activities. During other seasons, guests can wander the village at various reduced rates, with varied to no interior-building access.

Utah Museum of Natural History MUSEUM
(http://umnh.utah.edu; Rio Tinto Center, Wakara Way; adult/child $7/5; ⏲10am-5pm Tue-Sun) The museum's prize Huntington Mammoth, one of the most complete of its kind, has a new home near the University of Utah campus. Find out more about area fossils, indigenous peoples and more at this modern center.

Red Butte Gardens GARDENS
(www.redbuttegarden.org; 300 Wakara Way; adult/child $8/6; ⏲9am-9pm May-Aug, 9am-5pm Sep-Apr) Both landscaped and natural gardens cover a lovely 150 acres, all accessible by trail, in the Wasatch foothills. Check online to see who's playing at the popular, outdoor summer concert series also held here.

Activities

Within easy reach on the east side of the Wasatch mountain range, Big and Little Cottonwood Canyons not only have excellent skiing but opportunities for hiking, mountain biking and camping. For more, see p843.

> WORTH A TRIP
>
> **KENNECOTT'S BINGHAM CANYON COPPER MINE**
>
> The view into the century-old **mine** (www.kennecott.com; Hwy 111; per vehicle $5; ⏲8am-8pm Apr-Oct), 20 miles southwest of SLC, is slightly unreal. Massive dump trucks (some more than 12ft tall) look no larger than toys as they wind up and down the world's largest excavation. The 2.5-mile-wide and 0.75-mile-deep gash, which is still growing, is visible from space – and there's a picture from *Apollo* 11 inside the museum to prove it. Overall, it's a fascinating stop.

Church Fork Trail HIKING
(Millcreek Canyon, off Wasatch Blvd; admission $3) Looking for the nearest workout with big views? Hike the 6-mile round-trip, pet-friendly trail up to Grandeur Peak (8299ft). Millcreek Canyon is 13.5 miles southwest of downtown.

Tours

Brochures for **Utah Heritage Foundation** (www.utahheritagefoundation.com) free self-guided walking tours are available online at the city visitor center.

Sleeping

Downtown rates vary greatly depending on local events and daily occupancy. Outside ski season, prices plunge at Wasatch Mountain resorts, about 45 minutes' from downtown. Cheaper chain motels cluster off I-80 near the airport and south in suburban Midvale.

Parish Place Bed & Breakfast B&B **$$**
(☎801-832-0970; www.parrishplace.com; 720 E Ashton Ave; r incl breakfast $99-139; P❄☎) 'Comfortably antique' well describes SLC's most reasonable, 19th-century mansion B&B. Rooms have both elegant and eclectic details – such as a commode that is behind a decorative screen instead of a door. Continental breakfast arrives in a basket at your door daily. Hot tub and complimentary beverage center on site.

Peery Hotel HOTEL **$$**
(☎801-521-4300; www.peeryhotel.com; 110 W 300 South; r $90-130; P❄@☎) This stately historic hotel (1910) stands smack in the center of the Broadway Ave entertainment district. Restaurants, bars and theaters are all within easy strolling distance. Expect upscale conveniences such as Egyptian-cotton robes, iPod docking stations and Tempurpedic mattresses. Parking $10 per day.

Hotel Monaco HOTEL **$$**
(☎801-595-0000; www.monaco-saltlakecity.com; 15 W 200 South; r $139-249; P❄@☎) Rich colors, sleek stripes and plush prints create a whimsical mix at this sassy boutique chain. Here pampered guest pets receive special treatment, and the front desk will loan you a goldfish if you need company. Evening wine receptions are free; parking ($15) and internet access ($10), extra.

Anniversary Inn B&B **$$$**
(☎801-363-4953; www.anniversaryinn.com; 678 E South Temple St; ste incl breakfast $129-249;

SALT LAKE CITY FOR CHILDREN

Young and old alike appreciate the University-Foothill District attractions, but there are also a couple kid-specific sights to see.

Discovery Gateway (www.discoverygateway.org; 444 W 100 South; admission $8.50; 10am-6pm Mon-Thu, 10am-8pm Fri & Sat, noon-6pm Sun;) is an enthusiastic, hands-on children's museum. The mock network-news desk in the media zone is particularly cool for budding journos.

More than 800 animals inhabit zones like the Asian Highlands on the landscaped 42-acre grounds of **Hogle Zoo** (www.hoglezoo.org; 2600 East Sunnyside Ave; adult/child $9/7; 9am-5pm;). Daily animal encounter programs help kids learn more about their favorite species.

P) Sleep among the tree trunks of an enchanted forest or inside an Egyptian pyramid: these 3-D themed suites are nothing if not over the top. The quiet Avenues location is near a few good restaurants, and not far from Temple Sq.

Grand America HOTEL $$$
(801-258-6000; www.grandamerica.com; 555 S Main St; r $189-289; P) Rooms in SLC's only true luxury hotel are decked out with Italian marble bathrooms, English wool carpeting, tasseled damask draperies and other cushy details. If that's not enough to spoil you, there's always afternoon high tea or the lavish Sunday brunch. Paid parking ($15).

Crystal Inn & Suites MOTEL $
(801-328-4466; www.crystalinnsaltlake.com; 230 W 500 South; r incl breakfast $75-95; P) Utah-owned, multistory motel with a superfriendly staff and loads of free amenities (including a huge, hot breakfast).

Avenues Hostel HOSTEL $
(801-359-3855; www.saltlakehostel.com; 107 F St; dm $18, s/d without bath $30/40, with bath $40/50;) Well-worn hostel; a bit halfway house–like with long-term residents, but a convenient location.

Eating

Many of Salt Lake City's bountiful assortment of ethnic and organically minded restaurants are within the downtown core.

TOP CHOICE **Red Iguana** MEXICAN $$
(736 W North Temple; mains $10-16; 11am-10pm Mon-Thu, 11am-11pm Fri, 10am-11pm Sat, 10am-9pm Sun) Ask for a plate of sample mole if you can't decide which of the seven chile- and chocolate-based sauces sounds best. Really, you can't go wrong with any of the thoughtfully flavored interior Mexican food at this always-packed, family-run restaurant. The incredibly tender *conchinita pibil* (shredded roast pork) tastes like it's been cooking for days.

Squatters Pub Brewery AMERICAN $$
(147 W Broadway; mains $9-15; 11am-midnight Sun-Thu, to 1am Fri & Sat) Come for an Emigration Pale Ale, stay for the blackened tilapia salad. In addition to great microbrews, Squatters does a wide range of American casual dishes well. The lively pub atmosphere is always fun.

Wild Grape AMERICAN $$$
(481 E South Temple; brunch & lunch mains $6-15, dinner mains $18-24; 8am-9:30pm Tue-Thu, 8am-10:30pm Fri, 9am-10:30pm Sat, 9am-9:30pm Sun) Billing itself as a 'new West' bistro, Wild Grape creates modern versions of country classics such as its wood-grilled pork chop with a sweetly sour blueberry sauce. Organic, locally sourced ingredients are a high priority here.

One World Everybody Eats ORGANIC $
(41 S 300 East; 11am-9pm Mon-Sat, 9am-5pm Sun) At this ecoconscious, community-oriented eatery, you get to decide what you pay and what your portion size will be (they'll provide suggestions). Daily changing menus of salads, stir-fries, pastas, Indian dishes and the like include great vegetarian options.

Curryer INDIAN $
(300 South, btwn S State & S Main Sts; dishes $4-6; 11am-2pm) This former hot-dog cart, modified with a tandoori oven, serves up a tasty range of regional Indian food from butter chicken to vegan-friendly *aloo matar* (spiced potatoes and peas).

Takashi JAPANESE $$$
(18 W Market St; rolls $8-14, mains $15-25; 11:30am-2pm & 5:30-10pm Mon-Sat) The best of a number of surprisingly good sushi restaurants in landlocked Salt Lake; even LA restaurant snobs rave about the excellent rolls at ever-so-chic Takashi.

Downtown Farmers Market MARKET $
(Pioneer Park, cnr 300 South & 300 West; 8am-1pm Sat mid-Jun–late Oct, 4pm-dusk Tue Aug-Sep) The town's summer outdoor market showcases locally grown produce, ready-to-eat baked goodies and local crafts.

Drinking

Pubs and bars that also serve food are mainstays of SLC's nightlife; no one minds if you just drink there.

Gracie's BAR
(326 S West Temple; 11am-2am) Even with two levels and four bars, Gracie's upscale bar-restaurant still gets crowded. The two sprawling patios are the best place to kick back. Live music or DJs most nights.

Green Pig PUB
(31 E 400 South; 11am-2am) Your friendly neighborhood watering hole hosts poker tournaments, has live jam sessions and plays sporting events on big screens. The roof patio is tops.

Café Marmalade GAY
(www.utahpridecenter.com; 361 N 300 West; 7am-9pm Mon-Fri, 8am-9pm Sat, 10am-9pm Sun) The upbeat coffee shop inside the Utah Pride Center has open mike nights, weekend BBQs and concerts, and the largest GLBT library in the state.

Tavernacle Social Club THEME BAR
(201 E Broadway; 5pm-1am Tue-Sat, 8pm-midnight Sun) Dueling pianos or karaoke nightly.

Coffee Garden CAFE
(895 E 900 South; 6am-11pm Sun-Thu, 6am-midnight Fri & Sat; wi-fi) Great, character-filled neighborhood, delicious coffee and baked goods.

Entertainment

Music

A complete list of local music is available online at www.cityweekly.net.

Mormon Tabernacle Choir LIVE MUSIC
(435-570-0080 for tickets; www.mormontabernaclechoir.org) Hearing the world-renown Mormon Tabernacle choir is must-do on any SLC visit. A live choir broadcast goes out every Sunday at 9:30am. September through November and January through May, attend in person at the **Tabernacle** (Temple Sq). Free public rehearsals are held there from 8pm to 9pm Thursdays. From June to August and in December, to accommodate larger crowds choir broadcasts and rehearsals are held at the 21,000-seat **LDS Conference Center** (cnr N Temple & Main Sts). Performance times stay the same, except that an extra Monday-to-Saturday organ recital takes place at 2pm.

Theater

The Salt Lake City Arts Council provides a complete cultural events calendar on its website (www.slcgov.com/arts/calendar.pdf). Reserve through **ArtTix** (801-355-2787; www.arttix.org).

Local venues include **Abravanel Hall** (123 W South Temple), **Capitol Theater** (50 W 200 South) and the **Rose Wagner Performing Arts Center** (138 W 300 South).

Sports

EnergySolutions Arena BASKETBALL
(www.nba.com/jazz; 301 W South Temple) Utah Jazz, the men's professional basketball team, play downtown.

E Center HOCKEY
(www.utahgrizzlies.com; 3200 S Decker Lake Dr, West Valley City) The International Hockey League's Utah Grizzlies play 8.5 miles outside of town.

Shopping

An interesting array of boutiques, antiques and cafes line up along **Broadway Avenue** (300 South), between 100 and 300 East. A few crafty shops and galleries can be found on in the 300 block of **W Pierpont Avenue**.

Sam Weller Books BOOKS
(801-328-2586; 254 S Main; 10am-7pm Mon-Sat) The city's biggest independent bookstore, with a noteworthy local rare book selection. At press time, Weller's was looking for a new location.

Information

Emergency & Medical Services

Police (801-799-3000; 315 E 200 South)

Salt Lake Regional Medical Center (801-350-4111; 1050 E South Temple; 24hr emergency)

Internet Access

Main Library (www.slcpl.org; 210 E 400 South; ⏲9am-9pm Mon-Thu, 9am-6pm Fri & Sat, 1-5pm Sun) Free wireless and internet access.

Media

City Weekly (www.cityweekly.net/utah) Free alternative weekly with good restaurant and entertainment listings.

Salt Lake Tribune (www.sltrib.com) Utah's largest-circulation paper.

Money

Wells Fargo (79 S Main St) Limited currency-exchange services.

Post

Downtown post office (200 W 200 South)

Tourist Information

Public Lands Information Center (☎801-466-6411; www.publiclands.org; 3285 E 3300 South; ⏲10:30am-5:30pm Mon-Fri, 9am-1pm Sat) Recreation information for the Wasatch-Cache National Forest; located inside the REI store.

Visitor Information Center (☎801-534-4900; Salt Palace Convention Center, 90 S West Temple; ⏲9am-6pm Mon-Fri, 9am-5pm Sat & Sun) Publishes free guide; on-site gift shop.

Websites

Downtown SLC (www.downtownslc.org) Arts, entertainment and business information about the downtown core.

Salt Lake Convention & Visitors Bureau (www.visitsaltlake.com) SLC's official tourist information website.

Getting There & Away

Air

Salt Lake City International Airport (www.slcairport.com; 776 N Terminal Dr), 5 miles northwest of downtown, has mostly domestic flights. But you can fly direct to Canada and Mexico. **Delta** (www.delta.com) is the main SLC carrier.

Bus

Greyhound (☎800-231-2222; www.greyhound.com; 300 S 600 West) connects SLC with Southwestern towns including the following:

St George, UT ($55, six hours)

Las Vegas, NV ($62, eight hours)

Denver, CO ($86, 10 hours)

Train

Traveling between Chicago and Oakland/Emeryville, the California Zephyr from **Amtrak** (☎801-322-3510; www.amtrak.com) stops daily at **Union Pacific Rail Depot** (340 S 600 West). Southwest destinations include Denver ($115, 15 hours) and Reno, NV ($64, 10 hours). Schedule delays can be substantial.

CONNECT PASS

Salt Lake City Convention & Visitors Bureau (www.visitsaltlake.com) sells a discount pass (one day, adult/child $24/20). But unless you plan to visit every child-friendly attraction in the town – and some outside of town – it likely isn't worth your while.

Getting Around

To/From the Airport

Utah Transit Authority (UTA; www.rideuta.com; one-way $2) Bus 550 travels downtown from the parking structure between terminals 1 and 2.

Xpress Shuttle (☎800-397-0773; www.expressshuttleutah.com) Shared van service; $16 to downtown.

Yellow Cab (☎801-521-2100) Private taxi, from $25 to downtown.

Public Transportation

UTA (www.rideuta.com) Trax, UTA's light-rail system, runs east from Central Station (600 W 250 South) to the University of Utah and south past Sandy. The center of downtown SLC is a free-fare zone. During ski season UTA buses serve the local ski resorts (all $7 round-trip).

Park City & the Wasatch Mountains

Utah has awesome skiing, some of the best anywhere in North America. Its fabulous low-density, low-moisture snow – between 300in and 500in annually – and thousands of acres of high-altitude terrain helped earn Utah the honor of hosting the 2002 Winter Olympics. The Wasatch Mountain Range that towers over SLC is home to numerous ski resorts, abundant hiking, camping and mountain biking – not to mention chichi Park City with its upscale amenities and world-class film festival.

SALT LAKE CITY RESORTS

Four world-class resorts in Little Cottonwood and Big Cottonwood Canyons, on the western side of the Wasatch mountain range, lie within 40 minutes' drive of downtown SLC. All have lodging and dining facilities. Day ski passes range from $55 to $75 per adult and $25 to $40 per child. A

Super Pass (www.visitsaltlakecity.com/ski/superpass; 2–6-day pass $114-336) requires reservations at one of the 80-plus area lodgings, but offers discounted ski access to all four resorts plus round-trip transportation from SLC. For a full list of summer hiking and biking trails, see www.utah.com/saltlake/hiking.htm.

BIG COTTONWOOD CANYON

Solitude Mountain Resort SNOW SPORTS
(☎801-534-1400; www.skisolitude.com) Exclusive, European-style village surrounded by excellent terrain. The Nordic Center has cross-country skiing in winter and nature trails in summer.

Brighton Resort SNOW SPORTS
(☎800-873-5512; www.brightonresort.com) Where all of SLC learned to ski; still an old-fashioned, family and first-timer favorite.

LITTLE COTTONWOOD CANYON

Snowbird Ski Area SNOW SPORTS
(☎800-385-2002; www.snowbird.com) The biggest and the busiest of them all, with all-round great snow riding – think steep and deep. Numerous lift-assist summer hiking trails; aerial tramway runs year-round.

Alta Ski Area SKIING
(☎800-258-2716; www.alta.com) A laid-back choice exclusive to skiers. No snowboarders affecting snow cover here.

PARK CITY

A mere 35 miles east of SLC via I-80, Park City (elevation 6900ft) skyrocketed to international fame when it hosted the downhill, jumping and sledding events at the 2002 Winter Olympics. The Southwest's most popular ski destination is still home to the US ski team. Come summer, residents (population 8100) gear up for hiking and mountain biking among the nearby peaks. The town itself – a silver-mining community during the 19th century – has an attractive and well-preserved main street lined with upscale galleries, shops, hotels, restaurants and bars. Despite the spread of prefab condos across the valley, the setting remains relatively charming. Winter (roughly late December through March) is busy season; during other months, businesses may close various days and resorts operate limited facilities.

Activities

In addition to snow sports (day lift tickets from $80/45 per adult/child), each area resort has posh lodging close to the slopes, numerous eateries and various summer activities, including mountain-bike rental and lift-assist hiking. More than 300 miles of hiking/biking trails crisscross area mountains; pick up maps at the visitor centers.

Park City Mountain Resort SNOW SPORTS
(☎435-649-8111; www.parkcitymountain.com) Family-friendly, supercentral Park City Mountain Resort has activities galore: more than 3300 acres of skiable terrain, snow-tubing, alpine coaster, year-round in-town lift, summer zip line...

Deer Valley Resort SKIING
(☎435-649-1000; www.deervalley.com) The area's most exclusive resort is known as much for its superb dining and hilltop St Regis Hotel as it is for the meticulously groomed, capacity-controlled slopes and ski valets. No snowboarding.

Canyons SNOW SPORTS
(☎435-649-5400; www.thecanyons.com) The Canyons is busy reinventing itself as part of a multimillion-dollar, multiyear expansion. Already it is the largest Utah resort, with several new lifts – including an enclosed, climate-controlled quad – and year-round gondola.

Utah Olympic Park ADVENTURE SPORTS
(www.olyparks.com/uop; 3419 Olympic Pkwy; admission free, guided tours adult/child $7/5; ⊙9am-

GREAT SALT LAKE

Once part of prehistoric Lake Bonneville, Great Salt Lake today covers 2000 sq miles and is far saltier than the ocean; you can easily float on its surface. The pretty, 15-mile-long **Antelope Island State Park** (www.stateparks.utah.gov; I-15 exit 332; per vehicle $9; ⊙7am-sunset), 40 miles northwest of SLC, has nice hiking and the best beaches for lake swimming (though they're occasionally stinky). It's also home to one of the largest bison herds in the country. A basic **campground** (tent & RV sites $13) operates year-round. Six of the 26 sites are available first-come, first-served, the rest by reservation.

6pm) Tour the 2002 Olympic ski-jumping, bobsledding, skeleton, Nordic combined and luge event facilities, check out the ski museum, and, if you're lucky, watch the pros practice (call for schedules). Paid activities include sports camps, freestyle shows and winter/summer bobsled rides (from $60).

Historic Union Pacific Rail Trail PARK
(http://stateparks.utah.gov; admission free; 24hr) A 28-mile multiuse trail that's also a state park. Pick it up at Bonanza Dr just south of Kearns Blvd.

Festivals & Events

Sundance Film Festival FILM
(www.sundance.org) Independent films and their makers, movie stars and fans fill the town to bursting for 10 days in late January. Passes, ticket packages and the few individual tickets sell out well in advance. Plan ahead.

Sleeping

More than 100 condos, hotels and resorts rent rooms in Park City. For complete listings, check www.visitparkcity.com. High-season winter rates are quoted below (minimum stays may be required); prices drop by half or more out of peak season.

Sky Lodge LUXURY HOTEL $$$
(435-658-2500; www.theskylodge.com; 201 Heber Ave; ste $285-495;) The urban-loft-like architecture containing the chic Sky Lodge suites both compliments and contrasts the three historic buildings that house the property's restaurants. You can't be more stylish, or more central, if you stay here.

Washington School House BOUTIQUE HOTEL $$$
(435-649-3800, 800-824-1672; http://washingtonschoolhouse.com; 543 Park Ave; ste incl breakfast $700;) Architect Trip Bennett oversaw the restoration that turned an 1898 limestone schoolhouse on a hill into a luxurious boutique hotel with 12 suites. How did the children ever concentrate when they could gaze out at the mountains through 9ft-tall windows instead?

Treasure Mountain Inn HOTEL $$$
(435-655-4501; www.treasuremountaininn.com; 255 Main St; ste $235-295;) Park City's first member of the Green Hotel Association utilizes wind energy and serves organic food in its breakfast restaurant. Some of the upscale condos have fireplaces, all have kitchens and are decorated in earthy tones.

WORTH A TRIP

MIRROR LAKE HIGHWAY

This alpine route, also known as Hwy 150, begins about 12 miles east of Park City in **Kamas** and climbs to elevations of more than 10,000ft as it covers the 65 miles into Wyoming. The highway provides breathtaking mountain vistas, passing by scores of lakes, campgrounds and trailheads in the **Uinta-Wasatch-Cache National Forest** (www.fs.fed.us). Note that sections may be closed to traffic well into spring due to heavy snowfall; check online.

Chateau Après Lodge MOTEL $
(435-649-9372; www.chateauapres.com; 1299 Norfolk Ave; dm/d/q $40/105/155;) The only budget-oriented accommodation in town is this basic, 1963 lodge – with a 1st-floor dorm – near the town ski lift. Reserve ahead.

Look for occasional deals at these lodge-like motels:

Best Western Landmark Inn MOTEL $$$
(435-649-7300; www.bwlandmarkinn.com; 6560 N Landmark Dr; r incl breakfast $219-239;)

Park City Peaks LODGE $$$
(435-649-5000; www.parkcitypeaks.com; 2121 Park Ave; r $189-249;)

Eating

Park City is well known for exceptional upscale eating; a reasonable meal is harder to find. In the spring and summer, look for half-off main-dish coupons in the *Park Record* newspaper. Note that from April through November restaurants reduce open hours variably, and may take extended breaks.

TOP CHOICE **Talisker** MODERN AMERICAN $$$
(435-658-5479; 515 Main St; mains $21-42; 5:30-10pm) Talisker elevates superb food to the sublime: lobster hush puppies, anyone? Settle into one of the four individually designed dining rooms and see what longtime resident and chef Jeff Murcko has to offer on his daily changing menu. Reservations required.

Maxwell's PIZZERIA $$
(1456 New Park Blvd; pizza slices $3, mains $10-20; 11am-9pm Sun-Thu, 11am-10pm Fri & Sat) Eat

with the locals at the pizza, pasta and beer joint tucked in a back corner of the stylish outdoor Redstone Mall, north of town. Huge, crispy-crusted 'Fat Boy' pizzas never linger long on the tables.

Zoom AMERICAN **$$$**
(☎435-649-9108; 660 Main St; mains $20-36; ⏰11:30am-2:30pm & 5-10pm) You're guaranteed to see co-owner Robert Redford at this all-American restaurant – if not in person, at least in his big artsy portrait and the Sundance Film Festival photos splashed across the walls of the rehabbed train depot. Reservations recommended.

Good Karma FUSION **$$**
(1782 Prospector Ave; breakfast $7-12, mains $10-20; ⏰7am-10pm) Whenever possible, local and organic ingredients are used in the Indo-Persian meals, with an Asian accent, at Good Karma. You'll recognize the place by the Tibetan prayer flags flapping out front.

Wasatch Brew Pub PUB **$$**
(250 Main St; lunch sandwiches $7-12, dinner mains $10-17; ⏰11am-10pm) Hearty pub grub goes down well with one of Wasatch Brewery's microbrewed drafts… say, First Amendment Lager. Don't forget to pick up a 'Polygamy Porter – Why Have Just One?' T-shirt on the way out.

In addition to any restaurant at Deer Valley Resort (p844), other top-end top picks (reservations advised) include the following:

Jean Louis Restaurant FRENCH **$$$**
(☎435-200-0602; 136 Heber Ave; mains $27-40; ⏰5:30-10pm) Classic French; only slightly snobby.

Wahso FUSION **$$$**
(☎435-615-0300; 577 Main St; mains $25-36; ⏰5-10pm) Sophisticated Indochine fusion.

☆ Entertainment

Main St is where it's at – with half a dozen or more bars, clubs and pubs. In winter, there's action nightly; weekends are most lively outside peak season. For listings, see www.thisweekinparkcity.com.

TOP CHOICE **High West Distillery & Saloon** BAR
(703 Park St; ⏰2pm-1am daily, closed Sun & Mon Apr-Jun & Sep-Dec) A former livery and Model A–era garage is now home to Park City's most happenin' nightspot. You can ski in for homemade rye whiskey at this microdistillery. What could be cooler?

No Name Saloon BAR
(447 Main St; ⏰11am-1am) There's a motorcycle hanging from the ceiling, Johnny Cash's 'Jackson' playing on the stereo and a waitress who might be lying about the history of this memorabilia-filled bar.

O'Shucks PUB
(427 Main St; ⏰10am-2am) A hard-partying dive bar, popular with a young snowboarder crowd, O'Shucks packs 'em in Tuesdays with $3 schooners (32oz beers).

Egyptian Theatre Company THEATER
(www.egyptiantheatrecompany.org; 328 Main St) The restored 1926 theater is a primary venue for Sundance; the rest of the year it hosts plays, musicals and concerts.

ℹ Information

Alpine Internet (638 Main St; internet acces per 15min $2.50; ⏰6:30am-6pm) Cyber coffeehouse.

Main Street Visitor Center (☎435-649-7457; 528 Main St; ⏰11am-6pm Mon-Sat, noon-6pm Sun) Small desk inside the Park City Museum downtown.

Visitor Information Center (☎435-649-6100; www.parkcityinfo.com; cnr Hwy 224 & Olympic Blvd; ⏰9am-7pm Mon-Sat, 11am-4pm Sun Jun-Sep, closes earlier Oct-May) Large office in the northern Kimball Junction area.

ℹ Getting There & Around

Park City Transportation (☎435-649-8567; www.parkcitytransportation.com) and **Powder for the People** (☎435-649-6648; www.powderforthepeople.com) both run shared van service ($39 one-way) and private-charter vans (from $99 for one to three people) from Salt Lake City airport. The latter also has Powder Chaser ski shuttles (from $45 round-trip) that will take you from Park City to Salt Lake City resorts.

The excellent **Park City Transit** (www.parkcity.org/citydepartments/transportation) system covers most of Park City, including the three ski resorts, and makes it easy not to need a car. Free trolleybuses run one to six times an hour from 8am to 11pm (reduced frequency in summer). There's a downloadable route map online.

HEBER CITY & AROUND

About 18 miles southeast of Park City, **Heber Valley** (www.gohebervalley.com) lies below Uinta National Forest in the Wasatch range. Heber City itself is fairly utilitarian, with basic motels and services. From here the 1904 **Heber Valley Historic Railroad** (☎435-654-5601; www.hebervalleyrr.org; 450 S 600 West; adult/child $30/25; ⏰late May–Oct) runs vari-

DON'T MISS

ROBERT REDFORD'S SUNDANCE RESORT

Wind your way up narrow and twisting Hwy 92, for a truly special experience at Robert Redford's **Sundance Resort** (☎801-225-4107; www.sundanceresort.com; 9521 Alpine Loop Rd, Provo; r $225-319; @📶). Even if a night's stay at this elegantly rustic, ecoconscious wilderness getaway is out of reach, you can have a great meal at the Treehouse restaurant or deli, attend an outdoor performance at the amphitheater or watch pottery being made (and sold) at the art shack. Skiing, hiking and spa services on site. The resort is 30 miles south of Park City, and 50 miles southeast of SLC.

ous family-friendly scenic trips through gorgeous **Provo Canyon**.

In nearby Midway, you can swim in **Homestead Crater** (☎435-654-1102; www.homesteadresort.com; Homestead Resort, 700 N Homestead Dr; admission $15; ⏲10am-7pm), a 65ft-deep geothermal pool (90°F) in a tall limestone cone open to the sky. This is way cool.

Northeastern Utah

Most people head northeast to explore Dinosaur National Monument, but this rural, oil-rich area also has some captivating wilderness terrain. All towns are a mile above sea level.

VERNAL

The capital of Utah's dinosaur country, Vernal welcomes visitors with a large pink dino-buddy and plenty of restaurants and motels with themed signs.

The informative film at the **Utah Field House of Natural History State Park Museum** (http://stateparks.utah.gov; 496 E Main St; ⏲9am-5pm Mon-Sat; 👪) is a great all-round introduction to Utah's dinosaurs. Interactive exhibits, video clips and, of course, giant fossils are wonderfully relevant to the area.

Don Hatch River Expeditions (☎435-789-4316; www.donhatchrivertrips.com; 221 N 400 East; ⏲May-Sep) offers rapid-riding and gentler float trips on the Green and Yampa Rivers.

Chain motels are numerous in town. For something different, try the luxe **Landmark Inn & Suites** (☎435-781-1800; Rte 149; r incl breakfast $69-109; 📶). All-American, down-home grub at **Naples Country Café** (1010 E Hwy 40; breakfast & sandwiches $4-8, mains $9-15; ⏲7am-10pm) includes mile-high meringue pies.

Dinosaurland Travel Board (☎800-477-5558; www.dinoland.com; 134 W Main; ⏲8am-5pm Mon-Fri) provides information on the entire region. Pick up driving-tour brochures for area rock art and dino tracks here.

DINOSAUR NATIONAL MONUMENT

One of the largest dinosaur fossil beds in North America was discovered here in 1909. The highlight of this **national monument** (www.nps.gov/dino; per vehicle $10; ⏲9am-5pm) is a dinosaur quarry, which was enclosed with hundreds of bones partially excavated but left in the rock. You can also hike up to touch still-embedded, 150-million-year-old fossils on the trail, and there's a scenic driving tour with Native American rock art. The monument straddles the Utah–Colorado state line. The Utah portion of the park, which contains all the fossils, is about 15 miles east of Vernal via Hwys 40 and 149.

FLAMING GORGE NATIONAL RECREATION AREA

Named for its fiery red sandstone, the **gorge area** (admission per vehicle $5) has boating along 375 miles of reservoir shoreline, fly-fishing and rafting on the Green River, trout-fishing, hiking and cross-country skiing. The lake's 6040ft elevation ensures pleasantly warm but not desperately hot summers – daytime highs average about 80°F. Get general information at www.flaminggorgecountry.com and contact the USFS **Flaming Gorge Headquarters** (☎435-784-3445; www.fs.fed.us/r4/ashley/recreation; 25 W Hwy 43; ⏲8am-5pm Mon-Fri) for the camping lowdown.

Activities at **Red Canyon Lodge** (☎435-889-3759; www.redcanyonlodge.com; 790 Red Canyon Rd, Dutch John; cabins $110; ⏲closed Mon-Thu Nov-Mar) include fishing, rowing, rafting and horseback riding, among others. Its pleasantly rustic cabins have no TVs. **Flaming Gorge Resort** (☎435-889-3773; www.flaminggorgeresort.com; 155 Greendale/Hwy 191, Dutch John; r $110, ste $150) has similar water-based fun, and rents motel rooms and suites. Both have decent restaurants.

Southeastern Utah

Snow-blanketed peaks in the distance provide stark contrast to the red-rock canyons that define this rugged corner of the Colorado Plateau. Over 65 million years, water has carved serpentine, sheer-walled gorges along the course of the Colorado and Green Rivers. Today these define the borders of expansive Canyonlands National Park. At nearby Arches National Park, erosion has sculpted thousands of arches and fin rock formations. Base yourself between the parks in Moab, aka activity central – a town built for mountain biking, river running and four-wheel driving. In the far southeastern corner of the state, Ancestral Puebloan sites are scattered among remote-and-rocky wilderness areas and parks. Most notable is Monument Valley, which extends into Arizona.

LOCAL PASSPORTS

Area national parks sell local passports (per vehicle $25) that are good for a year's entry to Arches and Canyonlands National Parks, plus Hovenweep and Natural Bridges National Monument. **Federal park passes** (www.nps.gov/findapark/passes.htm; per vehicle adult/senior $80/10), available online, allow year-long access to all federal recreation lands and are a great way to support the Southwest's amazing parks.

GREEN RIVER

The 'World's Watermelon Capital,' Green River offers a good base for river running on the Green and Colorado Rivers. The legendary one-armed Civil War veteran, geologist and ethnologist John Wesley Powell first explored these rivers in 1869 and 1871. Learn about his amazing travels at the extensive **John Wesley Powell River History Museum** (435-564-3427; www.jwprhm.com; 1765 E Main St; adult/child $4/1; 8am-7pm Sun-Sat), which also has exhibits on the Fremont Native Americans, geology and local history. The museum also serves as the local visitor center.

Local outfitters **Holiday Expeditions** (435-564-3273; www.holidayexpeditions.com) and **Moki Mac River Expeditions** (435-564-3361; www.mokimac.com) run day-long white-water-rafting trips (adult/child from $80/40), including lunch and transportation; ask about multiday excursions.

Family-owned, clean and cheerful, **Robbers Roost Motel** (435-564-3452; www.rrmotel.com; 325 W Main St; s $31-38, d $40-45;) is a great little motorcourt budget motel. At the much larger **River Terrace Inn** (435-564-3401; www.river-terrace.com; 1880 E Main St; r incl breakfast $110-106;), many of the motel rooms overlook the river. Noshing a burger with the post-rafting crowd at **Ray's Tavern** (25 S Broadway; mains $8-26; 11am-10pm) is far and away the best way in town to satisfy your hunger.

In southeastern Utah, Green River is the only stop on the daily *California Zephyr* train run by **Amtrak** (800-872-7245; www.amtrak.com; 250 S Broadway) to Denver, CO ($85, 10¾ hours). Green River is 182 miles southeast of Salt Lake City and 52 miles northwest of Moab.

MOAB

Southeastern Utah's largest community (population 5121) bills itself as the state's recreation capital, and… oh man, does it deliver. Scads of rafting and riding outfitters (mountain bike, horse, 4WD…) base here and take forays into surrounding public lands. And you can hike Arches or Canyonlands National Parks during the day, then come back to a comfy bed, a hot tub and your selection of surprisingly good restaurants at night. Do note that this alfresco adventure gateway is not a secret: the town is mobbed, especially during spring and fall festivals. If the traffic irritates you, remember that you can disappear into the vast surrounding desert in no time.

Activities

The Moab visitor center puts out several brochures on near-town rock art, hiking trails, driving tours, etc. Area outfitters offer half-day to multiday adventures (from $50 for four hours) that include transport, the activity, and sometimes, meals. Among the best are the following:

Sheri Griffith Expeditions RAFTING
(435-259-8229; www.griffithexp.com; 2231 S Hwy 191) Highly rated rafting outfitter; some multisport adventures.

Canyon Voyages ADVENTURE SPORTS
(435-259-6007; www.canyonvoyages.com; 211 N Main St) River running, raft-hike-bike-4WD combos available; kayak and canoe rentals too.

SOUTHWEST UTAH

Poison Spider Bicycles CYCLING, MOUNTAIN BIKING
(☎435-259-7882; www.poisonspiderbicycles.com; 497 N Main St) Mountain- and road-bike rentals and tours; superior service.

Farabee's Jeep Rental & Outlaw Tours EXTREME SPORTS
(☎435-259-7494; www.farabeesjeeprentals.com; 1125 S Highway 191) Four-wheel-drive rentals, self-drive and fully guided off-road 4WD tours.

Red Cliffs Lodge HORSEBACK RIDING
(☎435-259-2002; www.redcliffslodge.com/tours-activities; Mile 14, Hwy 128) Half-day trail rides.

Sleeping

Most lodgings in town have bike storage or facilities, plus hot tubs to soothe sore muscles. Despite having an incredible number of motels, the town does book up; reservations are highly recommended March through October.

Individual **BLM campsites** (www.blm.gov/utah/moab; tent & RV sites $8-12; ⏲year-round) in the area are first-come, first-served. In peak season, check with the Moab Information Center to see which sites are full.

Cali Cochitta B&B $$
(☎435-259-4961; www.moabdreaminn.com; 110 S 200 East; cottages incl breakfast $125-160; ❄📶) Make yourself at home in one of the charming brick cottages a short walk from downtown. A long wooden table on the patio provides a welcome setting for community breakfasts.

Sorrel River Ranch LODGE $$$
(☎435-259-4642; www.sorrelriver.com; Mile 17, Hwy 128; r $340-530; ❄@≋) Southeast Utah's only full-service luxury resort and restaurant was originally an 1803 homestead. The lodge and log cabins sit on 240, activity-filled acres along the banks of the Colorado River.

Redstone Inn MOTEL $
(☎435-259-3500; www.moabredstone.com; 535 S Main St; r $79-99; ❄📶) Great budget digs: simple, pine-paneled rooms have refrigerator, microwave, coffeemakers and free wired internet access. Walls are a bit thin though. Hot tub on-site, pool privileges at sister hotel across street.

Gonzo Inn MOTEL $$
(☎435-259-2515; www.gonzoinn.com; 100 W 200 South; r $159, ste $205-339, incl breakfast Apr-Oct; ❄@📶≋) Spruced-up standard motel with fun retro splashes of color; favored by cyclists.

Adventure Inn Moab MOTEL $
(☎435-259-6122; www.adventureinnmoab.com; 512 N Main St; s/d incl breakfast $65/80; ⏲closed Nov-Feb; ❄📶) Family-owned and friendly, single-story motel.

Eating

There's no shortage of places to fuel up in Moab, from backpacker coffeehouses to gourmet dining rooms. Pick up the *Moab Menu Guide* (www.moabmenuguide.com) at area lodgings. Some restaurants close earlier, or on variable days, from December through March.

TOP CHOICE **Love Muffin** CAFE $
(139 N Main St; mains $6-8; ⏲7am-2pm; 📶) Early-rising moms and adventure-hunting locals scarf up many of the homemade muffins – like the 'breakfast' with bacon and blueberries – before some people get out of bed. Not to worry; the largely organic menu at this vibrant cafe also includes creative sandwiches, breakfast burritos and inventive egg dishes such as 'Verde,' with brisket and slow-roasted salsa.

Jeffrey's Steakhouse STEAKHOUSE $$$
(☎435-259-3588; 218 N 100 West; mains $22-40; ⏲5pm-10pm) A historic sandstone building serves as home to one of the latest stars of the local dining scene. Jeffrey's is serious about beef, which comes grain-fed, Wagyu-style and in generous cuts. If the night is too good to end, head upstairs to the upscale Ghost Bar. Reservations advised.

Moab Brewery AMERICAN $$
(686 S Main St; mains $8-18; ⏲11:30am-10pm Mon-Thu, 11:30am-11pm Fri & Sat) A good bet for a group with diverse tastes. Choosing among the list of microbrews made in the vats just behind the bar area may be easier than deciding what to eat off the vast and varied menu.

Miguel's Baja Grill MEXICAN $$
(51 N Main St; dishes $12-20; ⏲5-10pm) Dine on Baja fish tacos and margaritas in the sky-lit breezeway patio lined with brightly painted walls. Fajitas, *chile rellenos* (stuffed peppers) and seafood mains are all ample sized.

Buck's Grill House SOUTHWESTERN $$$
(1394 N Hwy 191; mains $15-36; ⏲5:30-9:30pm; 👪) Think upscale-modern Southwest:

duck tamales with adobo, elk stew with horseradish cream…

Milt's BURGERS $

(356 Mill Creek Dr; mains $3-6; ⌚11am-8pm Mon-Sat) A classic 1954 burger stand with fresh-cut fries and oh-so-thick milkshakes.

Shopping

Look for art and photography galleries – along with T-shirt and Native American knickknacks – near the intersection of Center and Main Sts.

Arches Book Company & Back of Beyond BOOKS

(83 N Main St;) Excellent, adjacent indie bookstores with extensive regional selection. Also has coffee shop.

Information

Most businesses and services, including fuel and ATMs, are along Hwy 191, also called Main St in the center of town.

BLM (435-259-2100; www.blm.gov/utah/moab) Phone and internet assistance only.

Grand County Public Library (25 S 100 East; per hr free; ⌚9am-8pm Mon-Fri, to 5pm Sat) Easy 15-minute internet; register for longer access.

Moab Area Travel Council (435-259-8825; www.discovermoab.com; ⌚8am-5pm Mon-Fri) Excellent for pre-trip planning

Moab Information Center (cnr Main & Center Sts; ⌚8am-8pm) Excellent source of information on area parks, trails, activities, camping and weather. Extensive bookstore and knowledgeable staff. Walk-in only.

Getting There & Around

Great Lakes Airlines (800-554-5111; www.flygreatlakes.com) has regularly scheduled flights from **Canyonlands Airport** (www.moabairport.com), 16 miles north of town via Hwy 191, to Denver, CO, Las Vegas, NV and Page, AZ.

Moab Luxury Coach (435-940-4212; www.moabluxurycoach.com) operates a scheduled van service to and from SLC ($149 one-way, 4¾hr) and Green River ($119 one-way, 3¾hr). **Roadrunner Shuttle** (435-259-9402; www.roadrunnershuttle.com) and **Coyote Shuttle** (435-260-2097; www.coyoteshuttle.com) offer on-demand airport, hiker-biker and river shuttles.

Moab is 235 miles southeast of Salt Lake City, 150 miles northeast of Capital Reef National Park.

ARCHES NATIONAL PARK

One of the Southwest's most gorgeous parks, **Arches** (www.nps.gov/arch; 7-day pass per vehicle $10; ⌚24hr, visitor center 7:30am-6:30pm Apr-Oct, 8am-4:30pm Nov-Mar) boasts the world's greatest concentration of sandstone arches – more than 2000 ranging from 3ft to 300ft wide at last count. Nearly one million visitors make the pilgrimage here, just 5 miles north of Moab on Hwy 191, every year. Many noteworthy arches are easily reached by paved roads and relatively short hiking trails; much of the park can be covered in a day. To avoid crowds, consider a moonlight exploration, when it's cooler and the rocks feel ghostly.

Highlights include **Balanced Rock**, oft-photographed **Delicate Arch** (best captured in the late afternoon), spectacularly elongated **Landscape Arch** and popular **Windows Arches**. Reservations are necessary for the twice-daily ranger-led hikes into the fins of the **Fiery Furnace** (adult/child $10/5; ⌚Apr-Oct). Book in person or online at www.recreation.gov.

Because of water scarcity and heat, few visitors backpack, though it is allowed with free permits (available from the visitor center). The scenic **Devils Garden Campground** (518-885-3639; www.recreation.gov; Hwy 191; tent & RV sites $20) is 18 miles from the visitor center and fills up from March to October. Twenty-four sites are available on a first-come, first-served basis, 52 sites by reservation.

CANYONLANDS NATIONAL PARK

Red-rock fins, bridges, needles, spires, craters, mesas, buttes – **Canyonlands** (www.nps.gov/cany; 7-day per vehicle $10; ⌚24hr) is a crumbling, decaying beauty, a vision of ancient earth. Roads and rivers make inroads to this high-desert wilderness stretching 527 sq miles, but much of it is still an untamed environment. You can hike, raft (Cataract Canyon offers some of the wildest white water in the West) and 4WD here but be sure that you have plenty of gas, food and water.

The canyons of the Colorado and Green Rivers divide the park into three districts. **Island in the Sky** (435-259-4712; ⌚visitor center 9am-4:30pm Nov-Apr, 9am-6:30pm Mar-Oct) is most easily reached and offers amazing overlooks. Our favorite short hike is the half-mile loop to oft-photographed **Mesa Arch**, a slender, cliff-hugging span framing a picturesque view of Washer Woman Arch and Buck Canyon. Drive a bit further to reach the **Grand View Overlook** trailhead. The path follows the canyon's edge

DON'T MISS

NEWSPAPER ROCK RECREATION AREA

This tiny, free recreation area showcases a single large sandstone rock panel packed with more than 300 **petroglyphs** attributed to Ute and Ancestral Puebloan groups during a 2000-year period. The many red-rock figures etched out of a black 'desert varnish' surface make for great photos (evening sidelight is best). The site, about 12 miles along Hwy 211 from Hwy 191, is usually visited as a short stop on the way to the Needles section of Canyonlands National Park (8 miles further).

and ends at a praise-your-maker precipice. This park section is 32 miles from Moab; head north along Hwy 191 then southwest on Hwy 313.

Needles (☎435-259-4711; ⏲visitor center 9am-4:30pm Nov-Feb, 8am-6pm Mar-May, 8am-5pm Jun-Oct), the second district, is wilder and more far-flung, ideal for backpacking. Follow Hwy 191 south and Hwy 211 west, 40 miles from Moab.

And then there's the **Maze** (no services), a wild and remote area off Hwy 24 that is accessible by 4WD only. The Great Gallery within **Horseshoe Canyon** has superb life-size rock art left by prehistoric Native Americans. But you should not make this trip without adequate preparations in consultation with rangers in other sections.

In addition to normal entrance fees, permits ($5 to $30) are required for overnight backcountry and mountain-biking camping, 4WD trips and river trips. Reserve at least two weeks ahead, by fax or mail only, with the **NPS** (☎435-259-4351, fax 435-259-4285; www.nps.gov/cany/planyourvisit/backcountrypermits.htm). Some same- or next-day spots may be available where you pick up permits at the respective visitor center, but reservations are advised in spring and fall.

DEAD HORSE POINT STATE PARK

A tiny but stunning **state park** (www.stateparks.utah.gov; Hwy 313; admission per vehicle $10; ⏲6am-10pm, visitor center 8am-5pm), Dead Horse Point has been the setting for numerous movies, including the opening scene from *Mission Impossible II* and the finale of *Thelma & Louise*. Located just off Hwy 313 (the road to Canyonlands), the park has mesmerizing views atop red-rock canyons rimmed with white cliffs, of the Colorado River, Canyonlands National Park and the distant La Sal Mountains. The 21-site **Kayenta Campground** (☎801-322-3770; http://utahstateparks.reserveamerica.com; Hwy 313; tent & RV sites $20) provides limited water (bringing your own is highly recommended) and RV facilities. Four campsites are available, but it's first-come, first-served, the rest by reservation.

BLUFF

Surrounded by red rock, this tiny tot town (population 283) makes a comfortable, laid-back base for exploring the desolately beautiful southeastern corner of Utah. It sits along the San Juan River at the junction of Hwys 191 and 163, 100 miles south of Moab. Bluff was founded by Mormon pioneers in 1880; a few old buildings remain and some settlers' cabins have been reconstructed.

For up-close views of rock art and cliff dwellings, hire Vaughn Hadenfeldt at **Far Out Expeditions** (☎435-672-2294; www.faroutexpeditions.com; cnr 7th & Mulberry Sts; day trip from $165), to lead a single- or multiday hike into the desert surrounds. A rafting trip with **Wild Rivers Expeditions** (☎800-422-7654; www.riversandruins.com; 101 Main St; day trip adult/child $165/120; ⏲Mar-Oct), a history-and-geology-minded outfitter, also includes ancient sites.

The hospitable **Recapture Lodge** (☎435-672-2281; www.recapturelodge.com; Hwy 191; r incl breakfast $60-80; @📶🏊) is a rustic, cozy place to stay. Owners know the area inside and out and you can follow trails from here to the river. Also nice are the spacious log rooms at the **Desert Rose Inn** (☎435-672-2303; www.desertroseinn.com; 701 W Main St; r $99-119; ❄@📶).

Artsy **Comb Ridge Coffee** (Hwy 191; mains $2-6; ⏲7am-3pm Wed-Sun, vary Nov-Feb; 🌿) serves espresso, muffins and blue-corn pancakes inside a timber and adobe cafe. For lunch and dinner, the organic-minded **San Juan River Kitchen** (75 E Main St; lunch $8-13, dinner $9-20; ⏲11am-9pm Tue-Sun) offers regionally sourced, inspired Mexican American dishes.

NATURAL BRIDGES NATIONAL MONUMENT

Fifty-five miles northwest of Bluff and 40 miles west of Blanding, this really remote **monument** (www.nps.gov/nabr; Hwy 275; admission per vehicle $6; ⏲24hr, visitor center 8am-6pm Apr-Sep, 8am-5pm Oct-Mar) protects a white sandstone canyon (it's not red) containing three impressive and easily accessible natural bridges. The oldest, the Owachomo Bridge, spans 180ft but is only 9ft thick. The flat 9-mile Scenic Drive loop is ideal for overlooking. Thirteen basic **tent & RV sites** ($10) are available on a first-come, first-served basis; there is overflow camping space but no services (no food, no fuel... no businesses anywhere around).

HOVENWEEP NATIONAL MONUMENT

Beautiful, little-visited **Hovenweep** (Hwy 262; admission per vehicle $6; ⏲dusk-dawn, visitor center 8am-6pm Apr-Sep, 8am-5pm Oct-Mar), meaning 'deserted valley' in the Ute language, contains impressive towers and granaries that are part of prehistoric Ancestral Puebloan sites. The Square Tower Group is accessed near the visitor center, other sites require long hikes. The **campground** (tent & RV sites $10) has 31 basic, first-come, first-served sites (no food or fuel). The main access is east of Hwy 191 on Hwy 262 via Hatch Trading Post, more than 40 miles northeast of Bluff.

MONUMENT VALLEY

Twenty-five miles west from Bluff, after the village of **Mexican Hat** (named for an easy-to-spot sombrero-shaped rock), Hwy 163 winds southwest and enters the Navajo Indian reservation. Thirty miles south, the incredible mesas and buttes of **Monument Valley** rise up. Most of the area, including the tribal park with a 17-mile unpaved driving loop circling the massive formations, is in Arizona. For a complete listing of sights and services, see p830.

Southwestern Utah

Locals call it 'color country,' but the cutesy label hardly does justice to the eye-popping hues that saturate the landscape. The deep-crimson canyons of Zion, the delicate pink-and-orange minarets at Bryce Canyon, the swirling yellow-white domes of Capitol Reef – the land is so spectacular that it encompasses three national parks and the gigantic Grand Staircase-Escalante National Monument (GSENM).

This section is organized roughly northeast to southwest, following the highly scenic Hwy 12 and Hwy 89 from Capitol Reef National Park to Zion National Park and St George.

CAPITOL REEF NATIONAL PARK

Not as crowded as its fellow parks but equally scenic, **Capitol Reef** (www.nps.gov/care; cnr Hwy 24 & Scenic Dr; admission free, scenic drive per vehicle $5; ⏲24hr, visitor center & scenic drive 8am-6pm Apr-Oct, to 4:30pm Nov-Mar) contains much of the 100-mile Waterpocket Fold, created 65 million years ago when the earth's surface buckled up and folded, exposing a cross-section of geologic history that is downright painterly in its colorful intensity. Hwy 24 cuts grandly through the park, but make sure to take the **scenic drive** south, which passes through orchards – a legacy of Mormon settlement. In season, you can freely pick cherries, peaches and apples, as well as stop by the historic **Gifford Farmhouse** to see an old homestead and buy fruit-filled minipies. Grassy, first-come, first-served **tent & RV sites** ($10) fill fast spring through fall.

TORREY

Just 15 miles west of Capital Reef, the small pioneer town of Torrey serves as most visitors' base for sleeping and eating.

Ty Markham has done an exquisite job of bringing the spacious, 1914 **Torrey Schoolhouse** (☎435-633-4643; www.torreyschoolhouse.com; 150 N Center St; r incl breakfast $110-115; ⏲Apr-Oct; ❄📶) back to life as a B&B. Soaring ceilings hang over rooms decked out in dressed-down country elegance and gourmet breakfasts are organic. Western-themed **Austin's Chuck Wagon Lodge** (☎435-425-3335; www.austinschuckwagonmotel.com; 12 W Main St; r $75-85, cabins $135; ⏲mid-Mar–Oct; ❄📶🏊) motel rooms are clean but basic, with sturdy furniture and lots of space. Grab supplies at the on-site general store.

Highly stylized Southwestern food such as turkey *chimole* (a spicy stew), Mayan tamales and fire-roasted pork tenderloin on a cilantro waffle draws visitors to **Café Diablo** (☎435-425-3070; 599 W Main St; mains $22-30; ⏲11:30am-10pm mid-Apr–Oct) from across the state. Be sure to reserve ahead.

Wayne County Travel Council (☎435-425-3365; www.capitolreef.org; cnr Hwys 24 & 12; ⏲noon-7pm Apr-Oct) provides loads of information. Ask about area outfitters.

BOULDER

Though the tiny outpost of **Boulder** (www.boulderutah.com), population 188, is just 32 miles south of Torrey on Hwy 12, you have to cross Boulder Mountain to get there. The area is so rugged and isloated that a paved Hwy 12 didn't connect through until 1985. From here, the attractive **Burr Trail** heads east as a paved road across the northeastern corner of the Grand Staircase-Escalante National Monument, eventually winding up on a gravel road to Capital Reef's Waterpocket Fold and down to Bullfrog Marina on Lake Powell. To explore area canyons and rock art, consider a one-day trek (child-friendly) with knowledgeable **Earth Tours** (☎435-691-1241; www.earth-tours.com; half-/full-day tours $75/100).

The small-but-excellent **Anasazi State Park Museum** (www.stateparks.utah.gov; Main St/Hwy 12; admission $5; ⏲8am-6pm Jun-Aug, 9am-5pm Sep-May) curates artifacts and a Native American site inhabited from AD 1130 to 1175. Get information on area public lands inside the museum, at the GSENM Interagency Desk.

Plush rooms at **Boulder Mountain Lodge** (☎435-335-7460; www.boulder-utah.com; 20 N Hwy 12; r $110-175; ❄@📶) are nice enough, but it's the 15-acre wildlife sanctuary setting that's unsurpassed. An outdoor hot tub with mountain views is a particularly scenic spot to soak off trail-earned aches and bird-watch. The lodge's must-visit **Hell's Backbone Grill** (☎435-335-7464; Boulder Mountain Lodge, 20 N Hwy 12; breakfast $8-10, dinner $16-34; ⏲7-11:30am & 5:30-9:30pm Mar-Oct) serves soulful, earthy preparations of regionally inspired and sourced cuisine. Book ahead.

Organic vegetable tarts, eclectic burgers and scrumptious homemade desserts at **Burr Trail Grill & Outpost** (Hwy 12 & Burr Trail Rd; mains $7-18; ⏲11am-10pm Mar-Oct; 📶) rival dishes at the more famous restaurant next door. There's a coffee shop and gallery too.

GRAND STAIRCASE-ESCALANTE NATIONAL MONUMENT

The 2656-sq-mile **Grand Staircase-Escalante National Monument** (GSENM; www.ut.blm.gov/monument; admission free; ⏲24hr) covers more territory than Delaware and Rhode Island combined. It sprawls between Capitol Reef National Park, Glen Canyon National Recreation Area and Bryce Canyon National Park. The nearest services, and GSENM visitor centers, are in Boulder and Escalante on Hwy 12 in the north, and Kanab on US 89 in the south. Otherwise, infrastructure is minimal, leaving a vast, uninhabited canyonland full of 4WD roads that call to adventurous travelers who have the time and equipment to explore. Be warned: this waterless region was so inhospitable that it was the last to be mapped in the continental US.

A 6-mile, round-trip trail to **Lower Calf Creek Falls** (Mile 75, Hwy 12; admission per vehicle $2), between Boulder and Escalante, is the most accessible, and most used, trail in the park. The 13 creekside **tent & RV sites** ($7) fill fast (no reservations).

> **DON'T MISS**
>
> **HIGHWAY 12**
>
> Arguably Utah's most diverse and stunning route, **Highway 12 Scenic Byway** (http://scenicbyway12.com) winds through rugged canyonland on a 124-mile journey west of Bryce Canyon to near Capitol Reef. The section between Escalante and Torrey traverses a moonscape of sculpted slickrock, crosses narrow ridgebacks and climbs over an 11,000ft-tall mountain.

ESCALANTE

This gateway town of 750 people is the closest thing to a metropolis for miles and miles. It's a good place to base yourself – or to stock up and map it out – before venturing into the adjacent GSENM. The **Escalante Interagency Office** (☎435-826-5499; www.ut.blm.gov/monument; 775 W Main St; ⏲7:30am-5:30pm mid-Mar–Oct, 8am-4:30pm Nov–mid-Mar) is a superb resource center with complete information on all area monument and forest service lands surrounding. Escalante is 65 miles from Torrey, near Capital Reef National Park, and 30 slow and windy miles from Boulder.

Escalante Outfitters & Cafe (☎435-826-4266; www.escalanteoutfitters.com; 310 W Main St; ⏲8am-9pm; 📶) is a traveler's oasis, selling maps, books, camping supplies, liquor(!), espresso, breakfast and homemade pizza and salads. It also rents out tiny, rustic cabins ($45) and mountain bikes (from $35 per day). Outfitter **Excursions of Escalante** (☎800-839-7567; www.excursionsofescalante.com; 125 E Main St; full day trips from $145) leads area canyoneering, climbing and photo hikes; its cafe was under reconstruction at the time of research.

Recommended lodgings:

Canyons Bed & Breakfast B&B **$$**
(☎435-826-4747; www.canyonsbnb.com; 120 E Main St; r incl breakfast $125-135; ❄📶) Upscale, cabin-rooms surround a shady terrace.

Circle D Motel MOTEL **$**
(☎435-826-4297; www.escalantecircledmotel.com; 475 W Main St; r $65-75; ❄📶) Updated, older motel with a friendly proprietor and a full-service restaurant.

Rainbow Country Bed & Breakfast B&B **$**
(☎435-826-4567; www.bnbescalante.com; 586 E 300 S; r incl breakfast $69-109; ❄📶) Homey and relaxed B&B with a shared TV den.

KODACHROME BASIN STATE PARK

Dozens of red, pink and white sandstone chimneys highlight this colorful **state park** (www.stateparks.utah.gov; Cottonwood Canyon Rd; admission per vehicle $6), named for its photogenic landscape by the National Geographic Society. Twenty-four of the developed sites at the **campground** (☎801-322-3770; http://utahstateparks.reserveamerica.com; tent/RV sites with hookups $16/20) are available by reservation.

BRYCE CANYON NATIONAL PARK

The Grand Staircase, a series of steplike uplifted rock layers elevating north from the Grand Canyon, culminates at this rightly popular **national park** (www.nps.gov/brca; Hwy 63; 7-day pass per vehicle $25; ⊙24hr, visitor center 8am-8pm May-Sep, 8am-4:30pm Nov-Mar, 8am-6pm Oct & Apr) in the Pink Cliffs formation. It's full of wondrous sorbet-colored pinnacles and points, steeples and spires, and totem-pole-shaped 'hoodoo' formations. The canyon is actually an amphitheater eroded from the cliffs. From Hwy 12, turn south on Hwy 63; the park is 50 miles southwest of Escalante.

Rim Road Scenic Drive (8000ft) travels 18 miles one-way, roughly following the canyon rim past the visitor center, the lodge, incredible overlooks (don't miss **Inspiration Point**) and trailheads, ending at **Rainbow Point** (9115ft). From May through September, a free **shuttle bus** (⊙8am-6pm) runs from a staging area just north of the park to as far south as **Bryce Amphitheater**.

The two campgrounds, **North Campground** (☎877-444-6777; www.recreation.gov; tent & RV sites $15) and **Sunset Campground** (tent & RV sites $15; ⊙late spring–fall), both have toilets and water. Sunset is more wooded, but has fewer amenities and doesn't accept reservations. For laundry, showers and groceries, visit North Campground. During summer, sites fill before noon.

The 1920s **Bryce Canyon Lodge** (☎435-834-8700; www.brycecanyonforever.com; Hwy 63; r $135-180; ⊙Apr-Oct; @) exudes rustic mountain charm. Rooms are in modern hotel-style units, with up-to-date furnishings, and thin-walled duplex cabins with gas fireplaces and front porches. No TVs. The lodge **restaurant** (breakfast $6-10, lunch & dinner $12-40; ⊙6:30-10:30am, 11:30am-3pm & 5-10pm Apr-Oct) is excellent, if expensive.

Just north of the park boundaries, **Ruby's Inn** (☎435-834-5341; www.rubysinn.com; 1000 S Hwy 63; campsites $25-40, r $89-199; ❄@📶≋) is a town as much as it is a motel complex. Choose from several Best Western lodging options, plus a campground, before you take a helicopter ride, watch a rodeo, admire Western art, wash laundry, shop for groceries, fill up with gas, dine at one of several restaurants and then post a letter about it all.

Eleven miles east on Hwy 12, the small town of Tropic has additional food and lodging.

KANAB

At the southern edge of Grand Staircase-Escalante National Monument, vast expanses of rugged desert surround remote Kanab (population 3564). Western filmmakers made dozens of films here from the 1920s to the 1970s, and the town still has an Old West movie set feel to it.

The **Kanab GSENM Visitor Center** (www.ut.blm.gov/monument; 745 E Hwy 89; ⊙8am-5pm)

WORTH A TRIP

CEDAR CITY & BREAKS

At 10,000ft, the summer-only road to **Cedar Breaks National Monument** (www.nps.gov/cebr; admission $3; ⊙24hr Jun-Sep, visitor center 8am-6pm Jun-Sep) is one of the last to open after winter snow. But it's worth the wait the amazing amphitheater overlooks rival those of Bryce Canyon. Nearby **Cedar City** (www.scenicsouthernutah.com) is known for its four-month-long Shakespeare Festival and an abundance of adorable B&Bs. The town is on I-15, 52 miles north of St George and 90 miles west of Bryce Canyon; the national monument is 22 miles northeast of the town.

ELEVATION MATTERS

As elsewhere, southern Utah is generally warmer than northern Utah. But before you go making any assumptions about weather, check the elevation of your destination. Places less than an hour apart may have several thousand feet of elevation – and 20°F temperature – difference.

» St George (3000ft)

» Zion National Park – Springdale entrance (3900ft)

» Cedar Breaks National Monument (10,000ft)

» Bryce National Park Lodge (8100ft)

» Moab (4026ft)

» Salt Lake City (4226ft)

» Park City (7100ft)

provides monument information; **Kane County Office of Tourism** (☎435-644-5033; www.kaneutah.com; 78 S 100 E; ⏰10am-5pm, closed Sun Nov-May) focuses on town and movie sites.

John Wayne, Maureen O'Hara and Gregory Peck are a few Hollywood notables who slumbered at the somewhat-dated **Parry Lodge** (☎435-644-2601; 89 E Center St; r $60-80; ❄📶🏊). An old, brickfront building houses **Rocking V Cafe** (97 W Center St; mains 10-20; ⏰5-10pm), where fresh ingredients star in dishes such as buffalo tenderloin and curried quinoa.

ZION NATIONAL PARK

Entering **Zion** (www.nps.gov/zion; Hwy 9; 7-day pass per vehicle $25; ⏰24hr, Zion Canyon Visitor Center 8am-7pm May-Sep, 8am-6pm Apr & Oct, 8am-5pm Nov-Mar) from the east along Hwy 9, the route rolls past yellow sandstone and **Checkerboard Mesa** before reaching an impressive gallery-dotted tunnel and 3.5 miles of switchbacks going down in red-rock splendor. More than 100 miles of park trails here offer everything from leisurely strolls to wilderness backpacking and camping.

If you've time for only one activity, the 6-mile **Scenic Drive**, which pierces the heart of Zion Canyon, is it. From April through October, taking a free **shuttle** (⏰6:45am-10pm) from the visitor center is required, but you can hop off and on at any of the scenic stops and trailheads along the way. The famous **Angels Landing Trail** is a strenuous, 5.4-mile vertigo-inducer (1400ft elevation gain, with sheer drop-offs), but the views of Zion Canyon are phenomenal. Allow four hours round-trip.

For the 16-mile backpacking trip down through the **Narrows** (June to September only), you need a hiker shuttle and a backcountry permit from the visitor center, which usually requires advance reservation on the website. But you can get part of the experience by walking up from **Riverside Walk** 5 miles to **Big Springs**, where the canyon walls narrow and day trips end. Remember, in either direction, you're hiking *in* the Virgin River for most of the time.

Reserve far ahead and request a riverside site in the cottonwood-shaded **Watchman Campground** (☎800-365-2267; http://reservations.nps.gov; Hwy 9; tent sites $16, RV sites with hookups $18-30) by the canyon. Adjacent **South Campground** (tent & RV sites $16) is first-come, first-served only. Together these two campgrounds have almost 300 sites.

Smack in the middle of the scenic drive, rustic **Zion Lodge** (☎435-772-7700; www.zionlodge.com; r & cabins $160-180; ❄@📶) has 81 well-appointed motel rooms and 40 cabins with gas fireplaces. All have wooden porches with stellar red-rock cliff views, but no TVs. The lodge's full-service dining room, **Red Rock Grill** (breakfast $10-15, lunch $8-20, dinner $15-30; ⏰7am-10pm, hr vary Dec-Mar) has similarly amazing views. Just outside the park, the town of Springdale offers many more services.

Note that you must pay an entrance fee to drive on Hwy 9 through the park, even if you are just passing through. Motorhome drivers are also required to pay a $15 escort fee to cross through the 1.1-mile Zion-Mt Carmel tunnel at the east entrance.

SPRINGDALE

Positioned at the main south, entrance to Zion National Park, Springdale is a perfect little park town. Stunning red cliffs form the backdrop to eclectic cafes, restaurants are big on organic ingredients, and artist galleries are interspersed with indie motels and B&Bs. Many of the outdoorsy folk who live here moved from somewhere less beautiful, but you will occasionally run into a lifelong local.

In addition to hiking trails in the national park, you can take outfitter-led **climbing** and **canyoneering** trips (from $150 per half-day) on adjacent BLM lands. All the classes and trips with terrific **Zion Rock & Mountain Guides** (☎435-772-3303; www.zionrockguides.com; 1458 Zion Park Blvd) are private. Solo travelers can save money by joining an existing group with **Zion Adventure Company** (☎435-772-1001; www.zionadventures.com; 36 Lion Blvd). The latter also offers river tubing in summer; both have hiker/biker shuttles.

Springdale has an abundance of good restaurants and nice lodging options. The updated motorcourt rooms at **Canyon Ranch Motel** (☎435-772-3357; www.canyonranchmotel.com; 668 Zion Park Blvd; s $84-94, d $94-99, r with kitchenette $114-125;) ring a shady lawn with picnic tables and swings.

From colorful tractor reflectors to angel art, the owners' collections enliven every corner of the 1930s bungalow that is **Under-the-Eaves Bed & Breakfast** (☎435-772-3457; www.under-the-eaves.com; 980 Zion Park Blvd; r incl breakfast $95-185;). Five flower-filled acres spill down to the Virgin River bank at **Cliffrose Lodge** (☎435-772-3234; www.cliffroselodge.com; 281 Zion Park Blvd; r $129-259;).

Grab a coffee, breakfast burrito or turkey panini at **Mean Bean** (932 Zion Park Blvd; mains $4-10; ⌚7am-5pm Jun-Aug, 7am-2pm Sep-May;), a hiker-and-cyclist haven with a roof deck. Top-notch, seasonal meals at **Parallel 88** (☎435-772-3588; Driftwood Lodge, 1515 Zion Park Blvd; breakfasts $10-14, dinner mains $28-40; ⌚7:30-10:30am & 5-10pm) may include impossibly tender green-apple pork loin or a mile-high quiche. Gorgeous red-rock views are best appreciated at sunset; make a reservation.

> **POLYGAMY TODAY**
>
> Though the Mormon church eschewed plural marriage in 1890, there are those that still believe it is a divinely decreed practice. Most of the roughly 7000 residents in Hilldale-Colorado City on the Utah–Arizona border are polygamy-practicing members of the Fundamentalist Church of Jesus Christ of Latter-day Saints (FLDS). Walk into a Wal-Mart in Washington or Hurricane and the shoppers you see in pastel-colored, prairie-style dresses – with lengthy braids or elaborate up-dos – are likely sister wives. Other, less-conspicuous sects are active in the state as well.

The Mexican-tiled patio with twinkly lights at **Oscar's Café** (948 Zion Park Blvd; breakfast & sandwiches $5-10, mains $12-20; ⌚7:30am-10pm) and the **Bit & Spur Restaurant & Saloon** (1212 Zion Park Blvd; mains $13-18; ⌚5-10pm) are local-favored places to hang out, eat and drink at.

The **regional visitors bureau** (☎888-518-7070; www.zionpark.com) does not have a physical office. Request a travel planner by mail or check online. A Springdale menu guide, available at local lodgings, comes out every spring.

ST GEORGE

Nicknamed 'Dixie' for its warm weather and southern location, St George (population 88,001) is popular with retirees. This spacious Mormon town, with an eye-catching temple and pioneer buildings, makes a good stop between Las Vegas and Salt Lake City – or en route to Zion National Park.

St George's first residents weren't snowbirds from Idaho, but Jurassic-era dinosaurs. Entry to the **Dinosaur Discovery Site** (www.dinotrax.com; 2200 E Riverside Dr; adult/child $6/3; ⌚10am-6pm Mon-Sat) gets you an interpretive tour of a 15,000-sq-ft collection of in-situ dino tracks, beginning with a video. At 7400-acre **Snow Canyon State Park** (www.stateparks.utah.gov; Hwy 18; admission per vehicle $5), 9 miles north of town, short easy trails lead to tiny slot canyons, cinder cones, lava tubes and vast fields of undulating red slickrock.

Nearly every chain hotel known to humanity is represented somewhere in St George. When events aren't going on, lodging is plentiful and affordable; when they are, prices skyrocket. **Best Western Coral Hills** (☎435-673-4844; www.coralhills.com; 125 E St George Blvd; r incl breakfast $80-129;) is walking distance from downtown restaurants and historic buildings. Two lovely, late-1800 houses contain **Seven Wives Inn** (☎800-600-3737; www.sevenwivesinn.com; 217 N 100 West; r incl breakfast $99-185;), a charming B&B with manicured gardens and a small swimming pool.

Homemade cupcakes are not all **Twenty-five on Main** (25 N Main St; mains $6-14; ⌚8am-9pm Mon-Thu, to 10pm Fri & Sat) bakery-cafe does well. We also like the breakfast panini, a warm salmon salad and the veggie-filled pasta primavera. For something fancier, try the creative modern American mains at **Painted Pony** (2 W St George Blvd, Ancestor Sq;

lunch $12-20, dinner $21-38; ⏲11:30am-10pm Mon-Sat, 4-10pm Sun).

The **Chamber of Commerce** (☎435-628-1658; www.stgeorgechamber.com; 97 E St George Blvd; ⏲9am-5pm Mon-Fri) is the primary source for town info. **Utah Welcome Center** (☎435-673-4542; http://travel.utah.gov; Dixie Convention Center, 1835 Convention Center Dr; ⏲8:30am-5:30pm), off I-15, addresses statewide queries.

SGU Municipal Airport (www.flysgu.com; 4550 S Airport Parkway) has expanded service in recent years, with more to come. **Delta** (☎800-221-1212; www.delta.com) shuttles between Salt Lake City and St George several times daily; **United Express** (☎800-864-8331; www.united.com) has four weekly flights to-and-from Los Angeles. Taxis (downtown $15) and all the standard chain car rentals are available. Note that Las Vegas' McCarran International Airport, 120 miles south, often has better flight and car rental deals than Utah airports.

Greyhound (☎435-673-2933; www.greyhound.com; 1235 S Bluff St) departs from the local McDonald's, with buses to SLC ($65, 5½ hours) and Las Vegas, NV ($29, two hours). **St George Express** (☎435-652-1100; www.stgeorgeexpress.com; 1040 S Main St) has shuttle service to Las Vegas ($35, two hours) and Zion National Park ($25, 40 minutes).

NEW MEXICO

It's called the Land of Enchantment for a reason. The play of sunlight on juniper-speckled hills that roll to infinity; the traditional Hispanic mountain villages with pitched tin roofs atop old adobe homes; the gentle magnificence of the 13,000-foot Sangre de Cristo Mountains; plus volcanoes, river canyons and vast high desert plains beneath an even vaster sky – the beauty sneaks up on you, then casts a powerful spell. The culture, too, is alluring, with silhouetted crosses topping historic mud-brick missions, ancient and living Indian pueblos, chile-smothered enchiladas, real-life cowboys and a vibe of otherness that makes the state feel like it might be a foreign country.

The legend of Billy the Kid lurks around every corner. Miracle healings bring flocks of faithful pilgrims to Chimayo. Bats plumb the ethereal corners of Carlsbad Caverns. Something crashed near Roswell…

NEW MEXICO FACTS

- **Nickname** Land of Enchantment
- **Population** 2 million
- **Area** 121,599 sq miles
- **Capital city** Santa Fe (population 68,00)
- **Other cities** Albuquerque (population 545,800), Las Cruces (population 97,600)
- **Sales tax** 5% to 8%
- **Birthplace of** John Denver (1943–97), Smokey Bear (1950–76)
- **Home of** International UFO Museum & Research Center (Roswell), Julia Roberts
- **Politics** a 'purple' state, with a more liberal north and conservative south
- **Famous for** ancient pueblos, the first atomic bomb (1945), where Bugs Bunny should have turned left
- **State question** 'red or green?' (chile sauce, that is)
- **Driving distances** Albuquerque to Carlsbad 275 miles, Santa Fe to Taos 71 miles

Maybe New Mexico's indescribable charm is best expressed in the captivating paintings of Georgia O'Keeffe, the state's patron artist. She herself exclaimed, on her very first visit: 'Well! Well! Well!…This is wonderful! No one told me it was like this.'

But seriously, how could they?

History

People roamed the land here as far back as 10,500 BC, but by Coronado's arrival in the 16th century, Pueblos were the dominant communities. Santa Fe was crowned as the colonial capital in 1610, after which Spanish settlers and farmers fanned out across northern New Mexico and missionaries began their often violent efforts to convert the area's Puebloans to Catholicism. Following a successful revolt in 1680, Native Americans occupied Santa Fe until 1692, when Diego de Vargas recaptured the city.

In 1851 New Mexico became US territory. Native American wars, settlement by cowboys and miners and trade along the Santa Fe Trail further transformed the region, and the arrival of the railroad in the 1870s created an economic boom.

Painters and writers set up art colonies in Santa Fe and Taos in the early 20th century. In 1943 a scientific community descended on Los Alamos and developed the atomic bomb. Big issues include water rights (whoever owns the water has the power) and immigration.

Information

Where opening hours are listed by season (not month), readers should call first, as hours can fluctuate based on weather, budgets or for no reason at all.

New Mexico CultureNet (www.nmcn.org) A great overview of the state's contemporary cultural legacy.

New Mexico Magazine (www.nmmagazine.com) Good guide to the state with sections on destinations, diversions and comforts.

New Mexico Route 66 Association (www.rt66nm.org) Information on the famous path through the state.

New Mexico State Parks Division (www.emnrd.state.nm.us/prd; 1220 South St Francis Dr, Santa Fe) Info on state parks, with a link to camping reservations.

New Mexico Tourism Department (505-827-7400; www.newmexico.org) Order a free *Vacation Guide*, download a Scenic Byways map or research activities and accommodations.

Public Lands Information Center (877-851-8946; www.publiclands.org) Camping and recreation information.

Albuquerque

This bustling crossroads has a sneaky charm, one based more on its locals than big-city sparkle. The citizens here are proud of their city, and folks are more than happy to share history, highlights and must-try restaurants – which makes the state's most populous city much more than a dot on the Route 66 map.

Centuries-old adobes line the lively Old Town area, and the shops, restaurants and bars in the hip Nob Hill zone are all within easy walking distance of each other. Ancient petroglyphs cover rocks just outside town while modern museums explore space and nuclear energy. There's a distinctive and vibrant mix of university students, Native Americans, Hispanics, gays and lesbians. You'll find square dances and yoga classes flyered with equal enthusiasm, and ranch hands and real-estate brokers chow down at hole-in-the-wall taquerias and retro cafes.

Albuquerque's major boundaries are Paseo del Norte Dr to the north, Central Ave to the south, Rio Grande Blvd to the west and Tramway Blvd to the east. Central Ave is the main artery (aka old Route 66) – it passes through Old Town, downtown, the university and Nob Hill. The city is divided into four quadrants (NW, NE, SW and SE), and the intersection of Central Ave and the railroad tracks just east of downtown serves as the center point of the city.

Sights

OLD TOWN

From its foundation in 1706 until the arrival of the railroad in 1880, the plaza was the hub of Albuquerque; today Old Town is the city's most popular tourist area.

American International Rattlesnake Museum MUSEUM

(www.rattlesnakes.com; 202 San Felipe St NW; adult/child/senior $5/3/4; 11:30am-5:30pm Mon-Fri, 10am-6pm Sat, 1-5pm Sun) From eastern diamondback to rare tiger rattlers, you won't find more types of live rattlesnakes anywhere else in the world. Once you get over the freak-out factor, you'll be amazed not just by the variety of vipers but by the intricate beauty of their colors and patterns. Hopefully you'll never see them this close in the wild! Weekday hours are a little longer in summer.

Albuquerque Museum of Art & History MUSEUM

(www.cabq.gov/museum; 2000 Mountain Rd NW; adult/4-12yr/senior $4/1/2, admission free 1st Wed of month & 9am-1pm Sun; 9am-5pm Tue-Sun) Conquistador armor and weaponry are highlights at the Albuquerque Museum of Art & History, where visitors can study the city's tricultural Native American, Hispanic and Anglo past. Works by New Mexico artists also featured.

Also in the Old Town are **San Felipe de Neri Church** (built in 1793), **¡Explora! Children's Museum** (p860) and the **New Mexico Museum of Natural History & Science** (p860).

AROUND TOWN

The University of New Mexico (UNM) area has loads of good restaurants, casual bars, offbeat shops and hip college hangouts. The main drag is Central Ave between University and Carlisle Blvds. Just east is trendy Nob Hill, a pedestrian-friendly neighborhood

SCENIC DRIVES: NEW MEXICO'S BEST

» **Billy the Kid Scenic Byway** (www.billybyway.com) This mountain-and-valley loop in southeastern New Mexico swoops past Billy the Kid's stomping grounds, Smokey Bear's gravesite and the orchard-lined Hondo Valley. From Roswell, take Hwy 380 west.

» **High Road to Taos** The back road between Santa Fe and Taos passes through sculpted sandstone desert, fresh pine forests and rural villages with historic adobe churches and horse-filled pastures. The 13,000ft Truchas Peaks soar above. From Santa Fe, take Hwy 84/285 to Hwy 513 then follow the signs.

» **NM Highway 96** From Abiquiu to Cuba, this little road wends through the heart of Georgia O'Keeffe country, beneath the distinct profile of Cerro Pedernal, then passing Martian-red buttes and sandstone cliffs striped purple, yellow and ivory.

» **NM Highway 52** Head west from Truth or Consequences into the dramatic foothills of the Black Range, past the old mining towns of Winston and Chloride. Continue north, emerging onto the sweeping Plains of San Augustin before reaching the bizarre Very Large Array.

lined with indie coffee shops, stylish boutiques and patio-wrapped restaurants.

Indian Pueblo Cultural Center MUSEUM
(www.indianpueblo.org; 2401 12th St NW; adult/child & student/under 5yr $6/3/free; ⏲9am-5pm) Operated by New Mexico's 19 pueblos, the Indian Pueblo Cultural Center is a must for contextualizing the history of northern New Mexico. Appealing displays trace the development of Pueblo cultures, exhibit customs and crafts, and feature changing exhibits.

National Museum of Nuclear Science & History MUSEUM
(www.nuclearmuseum.org; 601 Eubank Blvd SE; adult/child & senior $8/7; ⏲9am-5pm) Exhibits examine the Manhattan Project, the history of arms control and the use of nuclear energy as an alternative energy source. Docents here are retired military, and they're very knowledgeable.

Petroglyph National Monument ARCHAEOLOGICAL SITE
(www.nps.gov/petr) More than 20,000 rock etchings are found inside the Petroglyph National Monument northwest of town. Stop by the visitor center (on Western Trail at Unser Blvd) to determine which of three viewing trails – in different sections of the park – best suits your interests. For a hike with great views but no rock art, hit the Volcanoes trail. Note: smash-and-grab thefts have been reported at some trailhead parking lots, so don't leave valuables in your vehicle. Head west on I-40 across the Rio Grande and take exit 154 north.

Sandia Peak Tramway CABLE CAR
(www.sandiapeak.com; Tramway Blvd; vehicle entrance fee $1, adult/13-20yr & senior/child/under 5yr $20/17/12/free; ⏲9am-8pm Wed-Mon, 5-8pm Tue Sep-May, 9am-9pm Jun-Aug) The 2.7-mile Sandia Peak Tramway starts in the desert realm of cholla cactus and soars to the pines atop 10,378ft Sandia Peak in about 15 minutes. The views are huge and that's what you're paying for at the restaurant at the top.

Activities

The omnipresent Sandia Mountains and the less crowded Manzano Mountains offer outdoor activities, including hiking, skiing (downhill and cross-country), mountain biking, rock climbing and camping. For information and maps, head to the **Cibola National Forest office** (☎505-346-3900; 2133 Osuna Rd NE, Albuquerque; ⏲8am-4:30pm Mon-Fri) or the **Sandia Ranger Station** (☎505-281-3304; 11776 Hwy 337, Tijeras; ⏲8am-4:30pm Mon-Fri), off I-40 exit 175 south, about 15 miles east of Albuquerque.

Sandia Crest National Scenic Byway DRIVING, HIKING
Reach the top of the Sandias via the eastern slope along the lovely Sandia Crest National Scenic Byway (I-40 exit 175 north), which passes numerous hiking trailheads. Alternatively, take the Sandia Peak Tramway or Hwy 165 from Placitas (I-25 exit 242), a dirt road through Las Huertas Canyon that passes the prehistoric dwelling of **Sandia Man Cave**.

ALBUQUERQUE FOR CHILDREN

The gung-ho **iExplora! Children's Museum** (www.explora.us; 1701 Mountain Rd NW; adult/under 12yr $8/4; ⏲10am-6pm Mon-Sat, noon-6pm Sun; 👪) will captivate your kiddies for hours. From the lofty high-wire bike to the leaping waters to the arts-and-crafts workshop, there's a hands-on exhibit for every type of child (don't miss the elevator). Not traveling with kids? Check the website to see if you're in town for the popular 'Adult Night.' Typically hosted by an acclaimed local scientist, it's become one of the hottest tickets in town.

The teen-friendly **New Mexico Museum of Natural History & Science** (www.nmnaturalhistory.org; 1801 Mountain Rd NW; adult/under 13yr $7/4; ⏲9am-5pm; 👪) features an Evolator (evolution elevator), which transports visitors through 38 million years of New Mexico's geologic and evolutionary history. The new Space Frontiers exhibit highlights the state's contribution to space exploration, from ancient Chaco observatories to an impressive, full-scale replica of the Mars Rover. The museum also contains a **Planetarium** (adult/child $7/4) and the newly 3-D IMAX-screened **DynaTheater** (adult/child $7/4).

Sandia Peak Ski Area SKIING, CYCLING

(☎505-242-9052; www.sandiapeak.com; half-/full-day lift tickets adult $35/50, teen, child & senior $30/40) Sometimes the snow here is great, other times it's lame, so check before heading up. The ski area opens on summer weekends and holidays (June to September) for mountain bikers. You can rent a bike at the base facility ($48 with $650 deposit) or ride the chairlift to the top of the peak with your own bike ($10). Drive here via Scenic Byway 536, or take the Sandia Peak Tramway (skis are allowed on the tram, but not bikes).

Discover Balloons BALLOONING

(☎505-842-1111; www.discoverballoons.com; 205c San Felipe NW; adult/under 12yr $160/125) Several companies will float you over the city and the Rio Grande, including Discover Balloons. Flights last about an hour, and many are offered early in the morning to catch optimal winds and the sunrise.

Tours

From mid-March to mid-December, the Albuquerque Museum of Art & History offers informative, guided **Old Town walking tours** (⏲11am Tue-Sun). They last 45 minutes to an hour and are free with museum admission.

Festivals & Events

Gathering of Nations CULTURAL

(www.gatheringofnations.com) The biggest Native American powwow in the world, with traditional music, dance, food, crafts and the crowning of Miss Indian World. Held each April.

Zia Regional Rodeo RODEO

The **New Mexico Gay Rodeo Association** (www.nmgra.com) hosts this event during the second weekend of August.

International Balloon Fiesta BALLOONING

(☎888-422-7277; www.balloonfiesta.com) In early October, some 800,000 spectators are drawn to this weeklong event. The highlight is the mass ascension, when more than 500 hot-air balloons launch nearly simultaneously.

Sleeping

Route 66 Hostel HOSTEL $

(☎505-247-1813; www.rt66hostel.com; 1012 Central Ave SW; dm $20, r from $25; P❄📶) Clean, fun and inexpensive, this place is simple and has a good travelers' vibe. A kitchen, library and outdoor patio are available for its guests to use.

TOP CHOICE **Andaluz** BOUTIQUE HOTEL $$

(☎505-242-9090; www.hotelandaluz.com; 125 2nd St NW; r $140-240; P❄@📶) Albuquerque's best hotel will wow you with style and attention to detail, from the dazzling lobby – where six arched nooks with tables and couches offer alluring spaces to talk and drink in public-privacy, to the Italian-made hypoallergenic bedding. The restaurant is one of the best in town, and there's a beautiful guest library and a rooftop bar. The hotel is so 'green' you can tour its solar water-heating system – the largest in the state. You'll get big discounts if you book online.

Mauger Estate B&B B&B $$
(505-242-8755; www.maugerbb.com; 701 Roma Ave NW; r incl breakfast $99-195, ste $160-205; P) This restored Queen Anne mansion (Mauger is pronounced 'major') has comfortable rooms with down comforters, stocked fridges and freshly cut flowers. Kids are welcome and there's one dog-friendly room complete with Wild West decor and a small yard ($20 extra).

Böttger Mansion B&B $$
(505-243-3639; www.bottger.com; 110 San Felipe St NW; r incl breakfast $104-179; P @) A friendly and informative proprietor gives this well-appointed Victorian-era B&B an edge over some tough competition. The eight-bedroom mansion, built in 1912, is close to Old Town Plaza, top-notch museums and several in-the-know New Mexican restaurants such as **Duran's Central Pharmacy** (1815 Central Ave; cash only). The honeysuckle-lined courtyard is a favorite with bird-watchers. Famous past guests include Elvis, Janis Joplin and Machine Gun Kelly.

Hotel Blue HOTEL $
(877-878-4868; www.thehotelblue.com; 717 Central Ave NW; r incl breakfast $60-99; P @) Well positioned beside a park and downtown, the art-deco 134-room Hotel Blue has Tempurpedic beds and a free airport shuttle. Bonus points awarded for the good-sized pool and 40in flat-screen TVs.

Eating

TOP CHOICE **Golden Crown Panaderia** BAKERY $
(505-243-2424; www.goldencrown.biz; 1103 Mountain Rd NW; mains $5-20; 7am-8pm Tue-Sat, 10am-8pm Sun) Who doesn't love a friendly neighborhood bakery? Especially one with gracious staff, fresh-from-the-oven bread and pizza, fruit-filled empanadas, smooth coffee and the frequent free cookie. Call ahead to reserve a loaf of quick-selling green-chile bread. Go to the website to check out the 'bread cam.'

Frontier CAFETERIA $
(2400 Central Ave SE; dishes $3-10; 5am-1pm;) An Albuquerque tradition, the Frontier boasts enormous cinnamon rolls, addictive green-chile stew, and the best huevos rancheros ever. The food and people-watching are outstanding, and students love the low prices on the breakfast, burgers and Mexican food.

Annapurna INDIAN $$
(www.chaishoppe.com; 2201 Silver Ave SE; mains $7-12; 7am-9pm Mon-Sat, 10am-8pm Sun;) For some of the freshest, tastiest health food in town, grab a seat within the bright, mural-covered walls of Annapurna. The delicately spiced ayurvedic dishes are all vegetarian or vegan, but they're so delicious that even carnivores will find something to love.

Flying Star Café DINER $
(www.flyingstarcafe.com; mains $8-11) Central Ave (3416 Central Ave SE; 6am-11pm Sun-Thu, 6am-midnight Fri & Sat) Juan Tabo Blvd (4501 Juan Tabo Blvd NE; 6am-10pm Sun-Thu, 6am-11pm Fri & Sat;) With seven constantly packed locations, this is the place to go for creative diner food made with regional ingredients, including homemade soups, main dishes from sandwiches to stir-fry, and yummy desserts. There's something here for everyone.

Artichoke Café MODERN AMERICAN $$$
(505-243-0200; www.artichokecafe.com; 424 Central Ave SE; lunch mains $8-16, dinner mains $19-30; 11am-2:30pm Mon-Fri, 5-9pm Mon & Sun, 5:30-10pm Tue-Sat) Voted an Albuquerque favorite many times over, this place takes the best from Italian, French and American cuisine and serves it with a touch of class.

Drinking & Entertainment

Popejoy Hall (www.popejoyhall.com; cnr Central Ave & Cornell St SE) and the historic **KiMo Theatre** (www.cabq.gov/kimo; 423 Central Ave NW) are the primary venues for big-name national acts, local opera, symphony and theater. To find out what's happening in town, grab a free copy of the weekly *Alibi* or visit www.alibi.com.

Satellite Coffee CAFE
(2300 Central Ave NE) Don't be put off by the hip, space-age appearance. The staff is welcoming and seats are filled with all manner of laptop-viewing, java-swilling locals. There are eight locations scattered across town; also try the one in Nob Hill (3513 Central Ave NE).

Copper Lounge LOUNGE
(1504 Central Ave SE, 2nd fl) If a parking lot filled with pickup trucks spells the word 'fun' in your party dictionary, then pull over for the red-brick Copper Lounge, where baseball caps and cowboy hats sip beer, play pool and scope the ladies.

Kelly's Brewery BREWERY

(3226 Central Ave SE) Grab a seat at a communal table then settle in for a convivial night of people-watching and beer-drinking at this former Ford dealership and gas station. On warm spring nights, it seems everyone in town is chilling on the sprawling patio.

Launch Pad LIVE MUSIC

(www.launchpadrocks.com; 618 Central Ave SW) Indie, reggae, punk and country bands rock the house most nights (though not at the same time). Look for the spaceship on Central Ave. Right next door is the **El Rey Theater** (www.elreytheater.com; 620 Central Ave SW), another longtime favorite for live music.

Shopping

For eclectic gifts, head to Nob Hill, east of the university. Park on Central Ave SE or one of the college-named side streets, then take a stroll past the inviting boutiques and specialty stores.

Palms Trading Post HANDICRAFTS

(1504 Lomas Blvd NW; 9am-5:30pm Mon-Sat) If you're looking for Native American crafts and informed salespeople who can give you advice, stop by the Palms Trading Post.

Silver Sun JEWELRY

(116 San Felipe St NW; 9am-4:30pm) Just south of the plaza, Silver Sun is a reputable spot for turquoise.

Mariposa Gallery ARTWORK

(www.mariposa-gallery.com; 3500 Central Ave SE) Beautiful and funky arts, crafts and jewelry, mostly by regional artists.

IMEC JEWELRY

(www.imecjewelry.net; 101 Amherst SE) Around the corner from Mariposa, you'll find more artistic fine jewelry at IMEC.

Information

Emergency & Medical Services

Police (505-764-1600; 400 Roma Ave NW)

Presbyterian Hospital (505-841-1234; 1100 Central Ave SE; 24hr emergency)

UNM Hospital (505-272-2411; 2211 Lomas Blvd NE; 24hr emergency) Head here if you don't have insurance.

Internet Access

Lots of restaurants and cafes have wi-fi.

Main Library (505-768-5141; 501 Copper Ave NW; 10am-6pm Mon & Thu-Sat, 10am-7pm Tue & Wed) Free internet access after purchasing a $3 SmartCard. Wi-fi available for free but must obtain access card.

Internet Resources

Albuquerque.com (www.albuquerque.com) Attractions, hotels and restaurants.

City of Albuquerque (www.cabq.gov) Information on public transportation, area attractions and more.

Post

Post office (505-346-1256; 201 5th St SW)

Tourist Information

The **Albuquerque Convention & Visitors Bureau** (www.itsatrip.org) has three visitor centers:

Downtown (505-842-9918; 20 First Plaza NW, cnr 2nd St & Copper Ave; 9am-4pm Mon- Fri)

Old Town (505-243-3215; 303 Romero St NW; 10am-5pm Oct-May, 10am-6pm Jun-Sep)

Sunport (Albuquerque International Airport) At the lower-level baggage claim.

Getting There & Around

Air

Albuquerque International Sunport (www.cabq.gov/airport; 2200 Sunport Blvd SE) is New Mexico's main airport and most major US airlines fly here. Cabs to downtown cost $20 to $25; try **Albuquerque Cab** (505-883-4888).

Bus

The **Alvarado Transportation Center** (100 1st St SW, cnr Central Ave) houses **ABQ RIDE** (505-243-4435; www.cabq.gov/transit; 8am-5pm), the public bus system. It covers most of Albuquerque from Monday to Friday and hits the major tourist spots daily (adult/child $1/35¢; one-day pass $2). Most lines run until 6pm. ABQ RIDE Route 50 connects the airport with downtown (last bus at 8pm Monday to Friday; limited service Saturday). Check the website for maps and exact schedules. Route 36 stops near Old Town and the Indian Pueblo Cultural Center.

Greyhound (505-243-4435; www.greyhound.com, 320 1st St SW) serves destinations throughout New Mexico.

Sandia Shuttle (888-775-5696; www.sandiashuttle.com) runs daily shuttles from Albuquerque to many Santa Fe hotels between 9am and 11pm (one-way/round-trip $25/45).

Twin Hearts Express (800-654-9456) runs a shuttle service from the airport to northern New Mexico destinations, including Santa Fe and Taos.

Train

The Southwest Chief stops daily at Albuquerque's **Amtrak station** (☎505-842-9650; www.amtrak.com; cnr 1st St & Central Ave), heading east to Chicago ($194, 26 hours) or west through Flagstaff, AZ ($90, five hours), to Los Angeles, CA (from $101, 16½ hours).

A commuter line, the **New Mexico Rail Runner Express** (www.nmrailrunner.com), shares the station, with eight departures for Santa Fe weekdays (one-way/day pass $7/8), four on Saturday and two on Sunday, though weekend service will likely be discontinued. The trip takes about 1½ hours.

Along I-40

Although you can zip between Albuquerque and Flagstaff, AZ, in less than five hours, the national monuments and pueblos along the way are well worth a visit. For a scenic loop, take Hwy 53 southwest from Grants, which leads to all the following sights, except Acoma. Hwy 602 brings you north to Gallup.

ACOMA PUEBLO

The dramatic mesa-top 'Sky City' sits 7000ft above sea level and 367ft above the surrounding plateau. One of the oldest continuously inhabited settlements in North America, this place has been home to pottery-making people since the later part of the 11th century. Guided **tours** (adult/senior/child $20/15/12; ⏰hourly 10am-3pm Fri-Sun mid-Oct–mid-Apr, 9am-3:30pm daily mid-Apr–mid-Oct) leave from the **visitor center** (☎800-747-0181; http://sccc.acomaskycity.org) at the bottom of the mesa and take two hours, or one hour just to tour the historic mission. From I-40, take exit 102, which is about 60 miles west of Albuquerque, then drive 12 miles south.

EL MORRO NATIONAL MONUMENT

The 200ft sandstone outcropping at this **monument** (www.nps.gov/elmo; adult/child $3/free; ⏰9am-6pm Jun-Aug, 9am-5pm Sep-Oct, 9am-4pm Nov-May), also known as 'Inscription Rock,' has been a travelers' oasis for millennia. Thousands of carvings – from petroglyphs in the pueblo at the top (c 1275) to elaborate inscriptions by the Spanish conquistadors and the Anglo pioneers – offer a unique means of tracing history. It's about 38 miles southwest of Grants via Hwy 53.

ZUNI PUEBLO

The Zuni are known worldwide for their delicately inlaid silverwork, which is sold in stores lining Hwy 53. Check in at the visitor center for information, photo permits and tours of the **pueblo** (☎505-782-7238; www.zunitourism.com; 1239 Hwy 53; tours $10; ⏰8:30am-5:30pm Mon-Fri, 10:30am-4pm Sat, noon-4pm Sun), which lead you among stone houses and beehive-shaped adobe ovens to the massive **Our Lady of Guadalupe Mission**, featuring impressive kachina murals. The **A:shiwi A:wan Museum & Heritage Center** (☎505-782-4403; www.ashiwi-museum.org; Ojo Caliente Rd; admission by donation; ⏰9am-5pm Mon-Fri) displays early photos and other tribal artifacts.

The friendly, eight-room **Inn at Halona** (☎505-782-4547; www.halona.com; Halona Plaza; r incl breakfast $79; ❄📶), decorated with local Zuni arts and crafts, is the only place to stay on the pueblo.

GALLUP

Because Gallup serves as the Navajo and Zuni peoples' major trading center, you'll find many trading posts, pawnshops, jewelry stores and crafts galleries in the historic district. It's arguably the best place in New Mexico for top-quality goods at fair prices. Gallup is another classic Route 66 town, with loads of vintage motels and businesses.

The town's lodging jewel is **El Rancho** (☎505-863-9311; www.elranchohotel.com; 1000 E Hwy 66; r from $76; P❄📶🏊). Many of the great actors of the 1940s and '50s stayed here. El Rancho features a superb Southwestern lobby, a restaurant, a bar and an eclectic selection of simple rooms. There's wi-fi in the lobby.

Visit the **chamber of commerce** (☎800-380-4989; www.thegallupchamber.com; 103 W Hwy 66; ⏰8:30am-5pm Mon-Fri) for details and events listings.

Santa Fe

Walking among the historic adobe neighborhoods or even around the tourist-filled plaza, there's no denying that Santa Fe has a timeless, earthy soul. Founded around 1610, Santa Fe is the second-oldest city and oldest state capital in the USA. It's got the oldest public building and throws the oldest party in the country (Fiesta). Yet the city is synonymous with contemporary chic, and boasts the second-largest art market in the nation, gourmet restaurants, great museums, spas and a world-class opera.

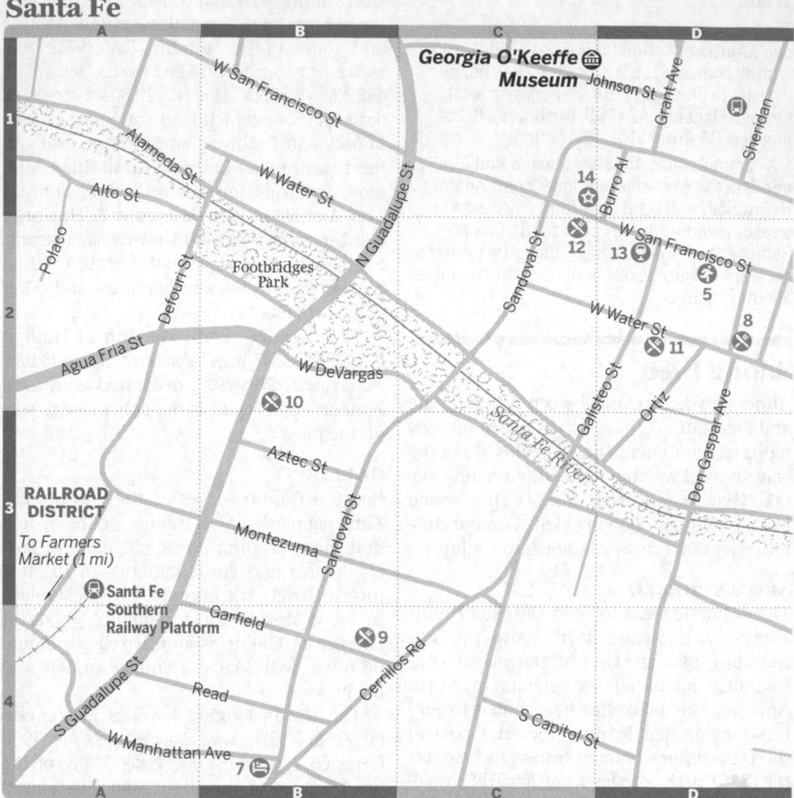

At 7000ft, it's also the highest state capital in the US, sitting at the base of the Sangre de Cristo range, a conveniently fantastic place to hike, mountain bike, backpack and ski.

Cerrillos Rd (I-25 exit 278), a 6-mile strip of hotels and fast-food restaurants, enters town from the south; Paseo de Peralta circles the center of town; St Francis Dr (I-25 exit 282) forms the western border of downtown and turns into Hwy 285, which heads north toward Los Alamos and Taos. Most downtown restaurants, galleries, museums and sights are within walking distance from the plaza, the historic center of town.

Sights

Art enthusiasts coming for the weekend may want to arrive early on Friday to take advantage of the evening's free admission policies at many museums.

Georgia O'Keeffe Museum MUSEUM

(☎505-946-1000; www.okeeffemuseum.org; 217 Johnson St; adult/senior/child $10/8/free; ⏲10am-5pm, to 8pm Fri) Possessing the world's largest collection of her work, the Georgia O'Keeffe Museum features the artist's paintings of flowers, bleached skulls and adobe architecture. Tours of O'Keeffe's house in Abiquiu (p870) require advance reservations.

Canyon Road NEIGHBORHOOD

(www.canyonroadarts.com) The epicenter of the city's upscale art scene. More than 100 galleries, studios, shops and restaurants line the narrow historic road. Look for Santa Fe School masterpieces, rare Native American antiquities and wild contemporary work. The area positively buzzes with activity during the early-evening art openings on Fridays, and especially on Christmas Eve.

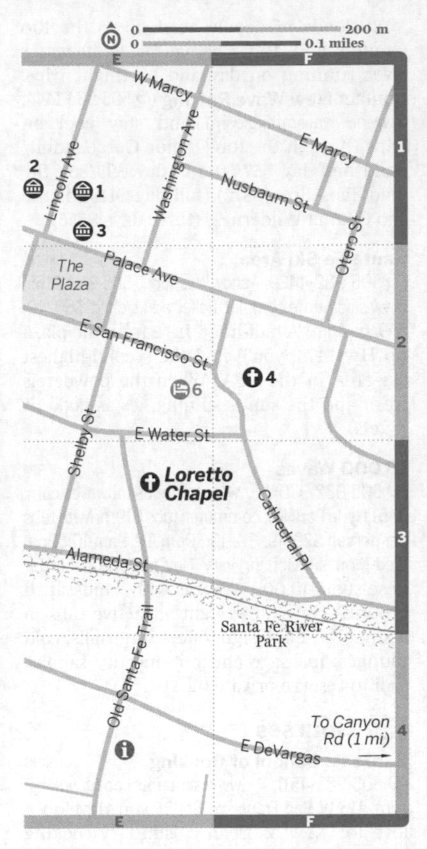

Santa Fe

Top Sights
Georgia O'Keeffe Museum C1
Loretto Chapel E3

Sights
1 New Mexico History Museum E1
2 New Mexico Museum of Art E1
3 Palace of the Governors E1
4 St Francis Cathedral F2

Activities, Courses & Tours
5 Santa Fe School of Cooking D2

Sleeping
6 La Fonda E2
7 Santa Fe Motel & Inn B4

Eating
8 Cafe Pasqual's D2
9 Cleopatra Café B4
10 Cowgirl Hall of Fame B2
11 Coyote Café D2
12 Tia Sophia's C2

Drinking
Bell Tower Bar .... (see 6)
13 Evangelo's D2

Entertainment
14 Lensic Performing Arts Center C1

FREE Wheelwright Museum of the American Indian MUSEUM
(www.wheelwright.org; 704 Camino Lejo; 10am-5pm Mon-Sat, 1-5pm Sun) In 1937, Mary Cabot established the Wheelwright Museum of the American Indian, part of Museum Hill, to showcase Navajo ceremonial art. While its strength continues to be Navajo exhibits, it now includes contemporary Native American art and historical artifacts as well.

Museum of New Mexico MUSEUM
(www.museumofnewmexico.org; 1 museum $9, 4-day pass to all 4 museums $20, under 16yr free; 10am-5pm Sat-Thu, 10am-8pm Fri, closed Mon winter) The Museum of New Mexico celebrated its centennial in 2009. It administers four museums around town:

Palace of the Governors HISTORIC BUILDING
(www.nmhistorymuseum.org; 105 W Palace Ave) On the plaza, this 400-year-old abode was once the seat of the Spanish colonial government. It displays a handful of regional relics, but most of its holdings are now shown in an adjacent exhibit space called the **New Mexico History Museum** (113 Lincoln Ave), a glossy, 96,000-sq-ft expansion that opened in 2009.

New Mexico Museum of Art MUSEUM
(www.nmartmuseum.org; 107 W Palace Ave) Just off the plaza, there are more than 20,000 piece of fine art here, mostly by Southwestern artists.

Museum of Indian Arts & Culture MUSEUM
(www.indianartsandculture.org; 710 Camino Lejo) On Museum Hill, this is one of the most complete collections of Native American arts and crafts – and a perfect companion to the nearby Wheelwright Museum.

Museum of International Folk Art MUSEUM
(www.internationalfolkart.org; 706 Camino Lejo;) Also on Museum Hill, the galleries here are at once whimsical and mind-blowing – featuring the world's largest collection of traditional folk art. Try to hit the incredible folk art market, held each June.

SANTA FE FOR CHILDREN

The newly expanded **Santa Fe Children's Museum** (www.santafechildrensmuseum.org; 1050 Old Pecos Trail; admission $9, $5 Sun; ⏲10am-6pm Tue-Sat, noon-5pm Sun; 🚸) features hands-on exhibits on science and art for young children. There are daily programs tackling subjects such as solar energy and printmaking.

Santa Fe Southern Railway (☎505-989-8600; www.thetraininsantafe.com; 410 S Guadalupe St; 🚸) runs excursions on restored railcars. Its four-hour trips (adult/child from $32/18), departing Saturdays at noon (with extra summer-only trains on Friday at 11am), venture through the high desert and are pulled by working freight trains. Shorter rides are offered on Sundays (year-round) and Wednesdays (summer). Reservations are recommended.

Also don't miss:

St Francis Cathedral CHURCH
(131 Cathedral Pl; ⏲8:30am-5pm) Houses the oldest Madonna statue in North America.

Shidoni Foundry GALLERY
(www.shidoni.com; 1508 Bishops Lodge Rd, Tesuque; ⏲10am-5pm Mon-Sat; 🚸) Five miles north of the plaza; outdoor sculpture garden, indoor gallery and on-site glass-blowing studio. On Saturdays, watch the artisans do huge bronze pours in the workshop ($2).

Loretto Chapel CHURCH
(207 Old Santa Fe Trail; admission $3; ⏲9am-5pm Mon-Sat, 10:30am-5pm Sun) Famous for its 'miraculous' spiral staircase that appears to be supported by thin air.

Activities

The **Pecos Wilderness** and **Santa Fe National Forest**, east of town, have more than 1000 miles of hiking trails, several of which lead to 12,000ft peaks. Summer storms are frequent, so prepare for hikes by checking weather reports. For maps and details, contact the Public Lands Information Center (p869). If mountain biking is your thing, drop into **Mellow Velo** (☎505-995-8356; www.mellowvelo.com; 621 Old Santa Fe Trail), which rents bikes and has loads of information about regional trails.

Busloads of people head up to the Rio Grande and Rio Chama for white-water river running on day and overnight trips. Contact **New Wave Rafting** (☎505-984-1444; www.newwaverafting.com) and stay cool on trips through the Rio Grande Gorge (adult/child half-day $57/50, full day $95/85), the wild Taos Box (p872) (full day $116) or the Rio Chama Wilderness (three days $525).

Santa Fe Ski Area SKIING
(☎505-982-4429, snow report 505-983-9155; www.skisantafe.com; lift ticket adult/child $60/40; ⏲9am-4pm) A half-hour drive from the plaza up Hwy 475, you'll find the second-highest ski area in the USA. When the powder is fresh and the sun is shining, it's as good as it gets.

10,000 Waves SPA
(☎505-982-9304; www.tenthousandwaves.com; 3451 Hyde Park Rd; communal tubs $19, private tubs per person $29-49; ⏲2-10:30pm Tue, 9am-10:30pm Wed-Mon Jul-Oct, hr vary Nov-Jun) The Japanese-style 10,000 Waves, with landscaped grounds concealing eight attractive tubs in a smooth Zen design, offers waterfalls, cold plunges, massage and hot and dry saunas. Call to reserve private tubs.

Courses

Santa Fe School of Cooking COOKING
(☎505-983-4511; www.santafeschoolofcooking.com; 116 W San Francisco St) If you develop a love for New Mexican cuisine, try cooking lessons here. Classes, including traditional New Mexican and Southwestern breakfast, are typically between 1½ and three hours long and cost $70 to $98. The family course is fun for kids.

Festivals & Events

Santa Fe's biggest festivals:

Spanish Market CULTURAL
(www.spanishmarket.org) In late July, traditional Spanish colonial arts, from *retablos* (paintings on wooden panels) and *bultos* (wooden carvings of religious figures), to handcrafted furniture and metalwork, make this juried show an artistic extravaganza.

Santa Fe Indian Market CULTURAL
(www.swaia.org) Typically held the weekend after the third Thursday in August, this event draws the country's finest Native American artisans to the plaza – and tens of thousands of visitors.

Santa Fe Fiesta CULTURAL
(www.santafefiesta.org) Two weeks of events in early September, including concerts, dances, parades and the burning of Zozobra (Old Man Gloom).

Sleeping

Cerrillos Rd is lined with chains and independent motels. There's camping in developed sites in Santa Fe National Forest and Hyde State Park on Hwy 475, the road to the ski basin.

Santa Fe Motel & Inn HOTEL $$
(505-982-1039; www.santafemotel.com; 510 Cerrillos Rd; r $89-155, casitas $119-169; P❄@) It's the aesthetic and technological attention to detail that make this downtown-adjacent motel a great pick. Bright tiles, clay sunbursts, LCD TVs and a welcoming chile pepper carefully placed atop your towels are just a few memorable pluses. Savor hot breakfasts on the kiva-anchored patio.

Silver Saddle Motel MOTEL $
(505-471-7663; www.silversaddlemotelllc.com; 2810 Cerrillos Rd; r incl continental breakfast from $45; P❄@) Shady wooden arcades outside and rustic cowboy-inspired decor inside, including some rooms with attractively tiled kitchenettes. For a bit of kitsch, request the Kenny Rogers or Wyatt Earp room. Probably the best value in town.

TOP CHOICE **La Fonda** HISTORIC HOTEL $$$
(505-982-5511; www.lafondasantafe.com; 100 E San Francisco St; r $210-400, ste $430-800; P❄@) Claiming to be the original 'Inn at the end of the Santa Fe Trail,' here since 1610, La Fonda has always offered some of the best lodging in town. The hotel today seamlessly blends modern luxury with folk-art touches; it's authentic, top-shelf Santa Fe style.

El Rey Inn HISTORIC HOTEL $$
(505-982-1931; www.elreyinnsantafe.com; 1862 Cerrillos Rd; r incl breakfast $99-165, ste from $150; P❄@) A highly recommended classic courtyard hotel, with super rooms, a great pool and hot tub, and even a kids' playground scattered around 5 acres of greenery. The inn recycles and takes a lot of green-friendly steps to conserve resources. Most rooms have air con.

Rancheros de Santa Fe Campground CAMPGROUND $
(505-466-3482; www.rancheros.com; 736 Old Las Vegas Hwy; tent/RV sites $23/39, cabins $48; mid-Mar–Oct;) Superfriendly, this wooded campground is seven miles southeast of town. Enjoy hot showers, cheap morning coffee and evening movies.

Eating

TOP CHOICE **San Marcos Café** NEW MEXICAN, AMERICAN $
(505-471-9298; www.sanmarcosfeed.com; 3877 Hwy 14; mains $7-10; 8am-2pm) About 10 minutes' drive south on Hwy 14, this spot is well worth the trip. Aside from the down-home feeling and the best red chile you'll ever taste, turkeys and peacocks strut and squabble outside and the whole place is connected to a feed store, giving it some genuine Western soul. The pastries and desserts – especially the bourbon apple pie – sate any sweet tooth. Make reservations on weekends.

Tune-Up Café INTERNATIONAL $$
(505-983-7060; www.tuneupcafe.com; 1115 Hickox St; mains $7-14; 7am-10pm Mon-Fri, 8am-10pm Sat & Sun) Santa Fe's newest favorite restaurant is casual, busy and does food right. The chef, from El Salvador, adds a few twists to classic New Mexican and American dishes, while also serving Salvadoran *pupusas* (stuffed corn tortillas), huevos and other specialties. The fish tacos and the *mole colorado enchiladas* (flavored with a red chile and a hint of chocolate) are especially tasty.

Horseman's Haven NEW MEXICAN $
(4354 Cerrillos Rd; mains $6-12; 8am-8pm Mon-Sat, 8:30am-2pm Sun) Hands down the hottest green chile in town! (The timid should order it on the side). Service is friendly and fast, and the enormous 3-D burrito might be the only thing you need to eat all day.

Cowgirl Hall of Fame BARBECUE $$
(www.cowgirlsantafe.com; 319 S Guadalupe St; mains $8-18; 11am-midnight Mon-Fri, 10am-midnight Sat, 10am-11pm Sun, bar open later) Two-step up to the cobblestoned courtyard and try the salmon tacos, butternut-squash casserole or the BBQ platter – all served with Western-style feminist flair. Youngsters are welcomed, with an outdoor play yard and buckets of coloring crayons to draw on the lengthy kids' menu. It also has a perennially popular bar with live music.

TOP CHOICE **Geronimo** MODERN AMERICAN $$$
(505-982-1500; 724 Canyon Rd; dishes $28-44; 5:45-10pm Mon-Thu, 5:45-11pm Fri & Sat)

Housed in a 1756 adobe, Geronimo is among the finest and most romantic restaurants in town. The short but diverse menu includes fiery sweet chile and honey-grilled prawns and peppery elk tenderloin with applewood-smoked bacon.

Other good choices:

Tia Sophia's NEW MEXICAN $
(210 W San Francisco St; mains $7-10; 7am-2pm Mon-Sat) Arguably the best New Mexican food around the plaza.

Café Pasqual's INTERNATIONAL $$$
(505-983-9340; www.pasquals.com; 121 Don Gaspar Ave; breakfast & lunch $9-17, dinner $20-30; 8am-3pm, 5:30-9pm) Sante Fe's most famous breakfast, for good reason.

Cleopatra Café MIDDLE EASTERN $
(418 Cerrillos Rd; mains $5-12; 6am-8pm Mon-Sat, 6am-6pm Sun;) Makes up for lack of ambience with taste and value – big platters of delicious kebabs, hummus, falafel and other Middle Eastern favorites. It's inside the Design Center.

Coyote Café MODERN AMERICAN $$$
(505-983-1615; www.coyotecafe.com; 132 W Water St; mains $28-56; 5:30-9:30pm) Simply legendary for its innovative cuisine and all-star kitchen.

Drinking & Entertainment

You'll also find live music and good drinking most nights at the Cowgirl Hall of Fame (p867).

Santa Fe Brewing Company BREWERY, LIVE MUSIC
(www.santafebrewing.com; 35 Fire Pl) Santa Fe's original microbrewery covers the full beer spectrum, from pilsner to porter to stout. Big-name bands perform here surprisingly often.

Evangelo's BAR, LIVE MUSIC
(200 W San Francisco St) There's foot-stompin' live music nightly at Evangelo's and the sounds of rock, blues, jazz and Latin combos spill into the street.

Lensic Performing Arts Center PERFORMING ARTS
(505-988-1234; www.lensic.org; 211 W San Francisco St) For live performances and movies, see what's doing at the Lensic Performing Arts Center. This beautifully renovated 1930s movie house is the city's premier venue for performing arts. Continuing its film history, it also holds $5 classic-movie screenings.

Santa Fe Opera OPERA
(800-280-4654; www.santafeopera.org; tickets $26-188; Jul & Aug) You can be a decked-out socialite or show up in cowboy boots and jeans; it doesn't matter. Opera fans (and those who've never attended an opera in their lives) come to Santa Fe for this alone: an architectural marvel, with views of wind-carved sandstone wilderness crowned with sunsets and moonrises, and at center stage internationally renowned vocal talent performing masterworks of aria and romance.

Bell Tower Bar BAR
(100 E San Francisco St) At La Fonda hotel, ascend five floors to the Bell Tower and watch one of those patented New Mexico sunsets.

El Farol BAR, LIVE MUSIC
(www.elfarolsf.com; 808 Canyon Rd) As much a restaurant as a bar; the specialties are tapas ($8), live music and the ambience of Santa Fe's oldest cantina.

Shopping

Offering carved howling coyotes, turquoise jewelry and fine art, Santa Fe attracts shoppers of all budgets. Head to the sidewalk outside the Palace of the Governors to buy Indian jewelry direct from the craftspeople who make it.

TOP CHOICE **Santa Fe Farmers Market** MARKET
(www.santafefarmersmarket; 1607 Paseo de Peralta; 7am-noon Sat mid-Apr–Oct, 9am-1pm Sat Nov–mid-Apr, 7am-noon Tue mid-May–Oct) Don't miss this market at the redeveloped rail yard. Free samples and a festive mood make for a very pleasant morning.

Pueblo of Tesuque Flea Market MARKET
(Hwy 84/285; 8am-4pm Fri-Sun Mar-Nov). This outdoor market a few minutes' drive north of Santa Fe at Tesuque Pueblo offers deals on high-quality rugs, jewelry, art and clothing.

Travel Bug MAPS, BOOKS
(www.mapsofnewmexico.com; 839 Paseo de Peralta; 7:30am-5:30pm Mon-Sat, 11am-4pm Sun;) A huge selection of guidebooks, maps and travel gear, plus travel slide shows on Saturdays.

Information

Emergency & Medical Services

Police (505-428-3700; 2515 Camino Entrada)

St Vincent's Hospital (☎505-983-3361; 455 St Michael's Dr; ⏱24hr emergency)

Internet Access

Santa Fe Public Library (☎505-955-6781; 145 Washington Ave) Reserve up to an hour of free access.

Travel Bug (☎505-992-0418; www.mapsofnewmexico.com; 839 Paseo de Peralta; @📶) Free wi-fi and internet access from on-site terminals.

Internet Resources

New Mexican (www.santafenewmexican.com) Daily paper with breaking news.

SantaFe.com (www.santafe.com) Listings for upcoming concerts, readings and openings in northern New Mexico.

Santa Fe Information (www.santafe.org) Official online visitors guide.

Santa Fe Reporter (www.sfreporter.com) Free alternative weekly; culture section has thorough listings of what's going on.

Post

Post office (120 S Federal Pl)

Tourist Information

New Mexico Tourism Department (☎505-827-7400; www.newmexico.org; 491 Old Santa Fe Trail; ⏱8:30am-5:30pm; 📶) Has brochures, a hotel reservation line, free coffee and free internet access.

Public Lands Information Center (☎505-438-7542; www.publiclands.org; 301 Dinosaur Trail; ⏱8:30am-4:30pm Mon-Fri) Tons of maps and information. Just south of the intersection of Cerillos Rd and I-25.

ℹ Getting There & Around

American Eagle (☎800-433-7300; www.aa.com) flies in and out of **Santa Fe Municipal Airport** (wwwsantafenm.gov; 121 Aviation Dr) with three daily flights to/from Dallas (DFW) and one daily flight to/from Los Angeles (LAX).

Sandia Shuttle Express (☎505-242-0302; www.sandiashuttle.com) runs between Santa Fe and the Albuquerque Sunport ($27). **North Central Regional Transit** (www.ncrtd.org) provides free shuttle bus service to Espanola, where you can transfer to shuttles to Taos, Los Alamos, Ojo Caliente and other northern destinations. Downtown pickup/drop-off is on Sheridan St, a block northwest of the plaza.

The **Rail Runner** (www.nmrailrunner.com) commuter train has multiple daily departures for Albuquerque – with connections to the airport and the zoo. The trip takes about 1½ hours. Weekend service may be discontinued. **Amtrak** (☎800-872-7245; www.amtrak.com) stops at Lamy; buses continue 17 miles to Santa Fe.

Santa Fe Trails (☎505-955-2001; www.santafenm.gov) provides local bus service (adult/senior & child $1/50¢ per ride, day pass $2/1). If you need a taxi, call **Capital City Cab** (☎505-438-0000).

If driving between Santa Fe and Albuquerque, try to take Hwy 14 – the **Turquoise Trail** – which passes through the old mining town (now art gallery town) of **Madrid**, 28 miles south of Santa Fe.

Around Santa Fe

Don't get too comfy in Santa Fe, because there's lots to see nearby.

PUEBLOS

North of Santa Fe is the heart of Puebloan lands. **Eight Northern Pueblos** (www.enipc.org) publishes the excellent and free *Eight Northern Indian Pueblos Visitors Guide,* available at area visitor centers. Its annual arts-and-crafts show is held in July; check the ENIPC website for exact dates and location.

Eight miles west of Pojoaque along Hwy 502, the ancient **San Ildefonso Pueblo** (☎505-455-3549; per vehicle $7, camera/video/sketching permits $10/20/25; ⏱8am-5pm daily, visitor center closed Sat & Sun winter) was the home of Maria Martinez, who in 1919 revived a distinctive traditional black-on-black pottery style. Several exceptional potters (including Maria's direct descendants) work in the pueblo; stop at the **Maria Poveka Martinez Museum** (admission free; ⏱8am-4pm Mon-Fri), which sells the pueblo's pottery.

Just north of San Ildefonso, on Hwy 30, **Santa Clara Pueblo** is home to the **Puye Cliff Dwellings** (☎888-320-5008; www.puyecliffs.com; tours adult/child $20/18; ⏱hourly 9am-5pm Apr-Sep, 10am-2pm Oct-Apr) where you can visit Ancestral Puebloan cliffside and mesa-top ruins.

LAS VEGAS

Not to be confused with the glittery city to the west in Nevada, this Vegas is one of the loveliest towns in New Mexico and one of the largest and oldest towns east of the Sangre de Cristo Mountains. Its eminently strollable downtown has a pretty Old Town Plaza and some 900 historic buildings listed in the National Register of Historic Places. Its architecture is a mix of Southwestern and Victorian.

Built in 1882 and carefully remodeled a century later, the recently expanded **Plaza Hotel** (☎505-425-3591, 800-328-1882; www.plazahotel-nm.com; 230 Plaza; r/ste incl breakfast

DON'T MISS

CHIMAYO

Twenty-eight miles north of Santa Fe is the so-called 'Lourdes of America' – **El Santuario de Chimayo** (www.elsantuariodechimayo.us; ⌚9am-5pm Oct-Apr, 9am-6pm May-Sep), one of the most important cultural sites in New Mexico. In 1816, this two-towered adobe chapel was built where the earth was said to have miraculous healing properties – even today, the faithful come to rub the *tierra bendita* – holy dirt – from a small pit inside the church on whatever hurts; some mix it with water and drink it. During holy week, about 30,000 pilgrims walk to Chimayo from Santa Fe, Albuquerque and beyond, in the largest Catholic pilgrimage in the USA. The artwork in the *santuario* is worth a trip on its own. Stop at **Rancho de Chimayo** (☎505-984-2100; www.ranchodechimayo.com; County Rd 98; mains $7-15; ⌚11:30am-9pm daily, 8:30am-10:30am Sat & Sun, closed Mon Nov-Apr) afterward for lunch or dinner.

from $79/139; ❄@🛜) is Las Vegas' most celebrated and historic lodging. The elegant building now offers 72 comfortable accommodations. Choose between Victorian-style, antique-filled rooms in the original building or bright, monochromatic rooms in the new adjoining wing.

Indulge in a good New Mexican meal at **Estella's Café** (148 Bridge St; mains $6-12; ⌚11am-3pm Mon-Wed, 11am-8pm Thu & Fri, 10am-3pm Sat). Estella's devoted patrons treasure the homemade red chile, *menudo* (tripe and grits) and scrumptious enchiladas.

From the plaza, Hot Springs Blvd leads 5 miles north to Gallinas Canyon and the massive **Montezuma Castle**; once a hotel, it's now the United World College of the West. Along the road there, you can soak in a series of natural **hot-spring pools**. Bring a swimsuit and test the water – some are scalding hot! Don't miss the **Dwan Light Sanctuary** (admission free; ⌚6am-10pm) on the school campus, a meditation chamber where prisms in the walls cast rainbows inside.

Ask for a walking-tour brochure from the **visitor center** (☎800-832-5947; www.lasvegasnewmexico.com; 500 Railroad Ave; ⌚10am-5pm Mon-Fri, 11am-4pm Sat & Sun Oct 15–Apr, longer hours May–Oct 14).

LOS ALAMOS

The top-secret Manhattan Project sprang to life in Los Alamos in 1943, turning a sleepy mesa-top village into a busy laboratory of secluded brainiacs. Here, in the 'town that didn't exist,' the first atomic bomb was developed in almost total secrecy. Today you'll encounter a fascinating dynamic in which souvenir T-shirts emblazoned with atomic explosions and 'La Bomba' wine are sold next to books on pueblo history and wilderness hiking.

You can't actually visit the **Los Alamos National Laboratory**, where lots of classified cutting-edge research still takes place, but you can visit the well-designed, interactive **Bradbury Science Museum** (www.lanl.gov/museum; cnr Central Ave & 15th; admission free; ⌚10am-5pm Tue-Sat, 1-5pm Sun & Mon; 👪), which covers atomic history. A short film traces the community's wartime history and reveals a few fascinating secrets. The small but interesting **Los Alamos Historical Museum** (www.losalamoshistory.org; 1050 Bathtub Row; admission free; ⌚10am-4pm Mon-Fri, 11am-4pm Sat, 1-4pm Sun) is on the nearby grounds of the former Los Alamos Ranch School – an outdoorsy school for boys that closed when the scientists arrived.

BANDELIER NATIONAL MONUMENT

Ancestral Puebloans dwelt in the cliffsides of beautiful Frijoles Canyon, now preserved within **Bandelier** (www.nps.gov/band; admission per vehicle $12; ⌚8am-6pm summer, 9am-5:30pm spring & fall, 9am-4:30pm winter). The adventurous can climb four ladders to reach ancient caves and kivas used until the mid-1500s. There are also almost 50 sq miles of canyon and mesalands offering scenic backpacking trails, plus camping at **Juniper Campground** (tent & RV sites $12), set among the pines near the monument entrance.

ABIQUIU

The tiny community of Abiquiu (sounds like 'barbecue'), on Hwy 84 about 45 minutes' drive northwest of Santa Fe, is famous because the renowned artist Georgia O'Keeffe lived and painted here from 1949 until her death in 1986. With the Chama River flowing through farmland and spectacular rock landscape, the ethereal setting continues to attract artists, and many live and work in Abiquiu. O'Keeffe's adobe house is open for limited visits, and the Georgia O'Keeffe Museum (p864) offers one-hour **tours** (☎505-685-4539; www.okeeffemuseum.org) on Tuesday, Thursday and Friday from March to November ($35), and also on Saturdays from June to October ($45), often booked months in advance.

A retreat center on 21,000 Technicolor acres that obviously inspired O'Keeffe's work (and was a shooting location for the movie *City Slickers*), **Ghost Ranch** (☎505-685-4333; www.ghostranch.org) has free hiking trails, a **dinosaur museum** (⏲9am-5pm Mon-Sat, 1-5pm Sun) and offers horseback rides (from $40), including instruction for kids as young as four years ($20). Basic **lodging** (tent sites $19, RV sites $22-29, dm incl breakfast $50, r without/with bath incl breakfast from $50/80) is available, too.

The lovely **Abiquiú Inn** (☎505-685-4378; www.abiquiuinn.com; Hwy 84; RV sites $18, r $140-200, ste $170, 4-person casitas $190; ❄📶) is a sprawling collection of shaded faux-adobes; spacious casitas have kitchenettes. Wi-fi is available in the lobby and the on-site restaurant, **Cafe Abiquiú** (breakfast mains $5-9, lunch & dinner mains $10-20; ⏲7am-9pm). The lunch and dinner menu includes numerous fish dishes, from chipotle honey-glazed salmon to trout tacos.

OJO CALIENTE

At 140 years old, **Ojo Caliente Mineral Springs Resort & Spa** (☎505-583-2233; www.ojospa.com; 50 Los Baños Rd; r $139-169, cottages $179-209, ste $229-349; 📶) is one of the country's oldest health resorts – and Pueblo Indians were using the springs long before then! Fifty miles north of Santa Fe on Hwy 285, the newly renovated resort offers 10 soaking pools with several combinations of minerals (shared/private pools from $18/40). In addition to the pleasant, if nothing special, historic hotel rooms, the resort has added 12 plush, boldly colored suites with kiva fireplaces and private soaking tubs, and 11 New Mexican–style cottages. Wi-fi is available in the lobby. The on-site **Artesian Restaurant** (breakfast mains $5-10, lunch $9-12, dinner $11-28; ⏲7:30am-10:30am, 11:30am-2:30pm & 5-9pm Sun-Thu, 5-9:30pm Fri & Sat) prepares organic and local ingredients with aplomb.

Taos

Taos is a place undeniably dominated by the power of its landscape: 12,300ft snow-capped peaks rise behind town; a sage-speckled plateau unrolls to the west before plunging 800ft straight down into the Rio Grande Gorge; the sky can be a searing sapphire blue or an ominous parade of rumbling thunderheads so big they dwarf the mountains. And then there are the sunsets...

Taos Pueblo, believed to be the oldest continuously inhabited community in the United States, roots the town in a long history with a rich cultural legacy – including conquistadors, Catholicism and cowboys. In the 20th century it became a magnet for artists, writers and creative thinkers, from DH Lawrence to Dennis Hopper. It remains a relaxed and eccentric place, with classic adobe architecture, fine-art galleries, quirky cafes and excellent restaurants. Its 5000 residents include Bohemians, alternative-energy aficionados and old-time Hispanic families. It's rural and worldly, and a little bit otherworldly.

Sights

The Museum Association of Taos offers a five-museum pass for $25 to the four museums listed below.

Harwood Museum of Art MUSEUM
(www.harwoodmuseum.org; 238 Ledoux St; adult/senior & student $8/7; ⏲10am-5pm Tue-Sat, noon-5pm Sun) Housed in a historic mid-19th-century adobe compound, the Harwood Museum of Art features paintings, drawings, prints, sculpture and photography by northern New Mexico artists, both historical and contemporary.

Taos Historic Museums MUSEUM
(www.taoshistoricmuseums.com; adult/child individual museums $8/4, both museums $12; ⏲10am-5pm Mon-Sat, noon-5pm Sun) Taos Historic Museum runs two houses: **Blumenschein Home** (222 Ledoux St), a trove of art from the 1920s by the Taos Society of Artists, and **Martínez Hacienda** (708 Lower Ranchitos Rd), a 21-room colonial trader's former home from 1804.

Millicent Rogers Museum MUSEUM
(www.millicentrogers.org; 1504 Millicent Rogers Museum Rd; adult/child $10/6; ⏲10am-5pm, closed Mon Nov-Mar) Filled with pottery, jewelry, baskets and textiles, this has one of the best collections of Native American and Spanish Colonial art in the US.

DON'T MISS

TAOS PUEBLO

Built around AD 1450 and continuously inhabited ever since, the streamside **Taos Pueblo** (☎575-758-1028; www.taospueblo.com; Taos Pueblo Rd; adult/child/under 11yr $10/5/free, photography or video permit $6; ⏲8am-4pm, closed for 6 weeks around Feb & Mar) is the largest existing multistoried pueblo structure in the US and one of the best surviving examples of traditional adobe construction.

Taos Art Museum & Fechin Institute MUSEUM
(www.fechin.com; 227 Paseo del Pueblo Norte; admission $8; ⏲10am-5pm Tue-Sun) The longtime home of Russian-born artist Nicolai Fechin, the house itself is worth just as much of a look as the collection of paintings, drawings and sculptures.

San Francisco de Asís Church CHURCH
(St Francis Plaza; ⏲9am-4pm Mon-Fri) Four miles south of Taos in Ranchos de Taos, the San Francisco de Asís Church, famed for the angles and curves of its adobe walls, was built in the mid-18th century but didn't open until 1815. It's been memorialized in Georgia O'Keeffe paintings and Ansel Adams photographs.

Rio Grande Gorge Bridge BRIDGE, CANYON
At 650ft above the Rio Grande, the steel Rio Grande Gorge Bridge is the second-highest suspension bridge in the US; the view down is eye-popping. For the best pictures of the bridge itself, park at the rest area on the western end of the span.

Earthships NEIGHBORHOOD
(www.earthship.net; Hwy 64; adult/under 12yr $5/free; ⏲10am-4pm) Just 1.5 miles west of the bridge is the fascinating community of Earthships, with self-sustaining, environmentally savvy houses built with recycled materials that are completely off the grid. You can also stay overnight in one.

Activities

During summer, **white-water rafting** is popular in the **Taos Box**, the steep-sided cliffs that frame the Rio Grande. Day-long trips begin at around $100 per person; contact the visitor center for local outfitters, where there's also good info about **hiking** and **mountain-biking** trails.

Taos Ski Valley SKIING
(☎866-968-7386; www.skitaos.org; lift ticket adult/teen 13-17 & senior/child $71/60/42) With a peak elevation of 11,819ft and a 2612ft vertical drop, Taos Ski Valley offers some of the most challenging skiing in the US and yet remains low-key and relaxed. The resort now allows snowboarders on its slopes.

Sleeping

TOP CHOICE **Earthship Rentals** BUNGALOW $$
(☎575-751-0462; www.earthship.net; Hwy 64; r $120-160) Experience an off-grid overnight in a boutique-chic, solar-powered dwelling. A cross between organic Gaudí architecture and space-age fantasy, these sustainable dwellings are put together using recycled tires, aluminum cans and sand, with rain catchment and gray-water systems to minimize their footprint. Half-buried in a valley surrounded by mountains, they *could* be hastily camouflaged alien vessels – you never know.

Historic Taos Inn HISTORIC HOTEL $$
(☎575-758-2233; www.taosinn.com; 125 Paseo del Pueblo Norte; r $75-275; P 📶) Even though it's not the plushest place in town, it's still fabulous, with a cozy lobby, a garden for the restaurant, heavy wooden furniture, a sunken fireplace and lots of live local music at its famed Adobe Bar. Parts of this landmark date to the 1800s – the older rooms are actually the nicest.

Abominable Snowmansion HOSTEL $
(☎575-776-8298; www.snowmansion.com; 476 State Hwy 150, Arroyo Seco; tent sites $15, dm $20, tipis $35, cabins $37, r with/without bath $59/45; P @ 📶) About 9 miles northeast of Taos, this well-worn and welcoming hostel is a cozy mountainside alternative to central Taos. A big, round fireplace warms guests in winter, and kitschy tipis are available in summer. There's a $3 discount on dorms and private rooms for Hostelling International (HI) members.

Sun God Lodge MOTEL $
(☎575-758-3162; www.sungodlodge.com; 919 Paseo del Pueblo Sur; r from $55; P ❄ 📶) The hospitable folks at this well-run two-story motel can fill you in on local history as well as the craziest bar in town. Rooms are clean – if a bit dark – and decorated with low-key

Southwestern flair. The highlight is the lush green courtyard dappled with twinkling lights, a scenic spot for a picnic or enjoying the sunset. Pets can stay for $20. Located 1.5 miles south of the plaza, the Sun God is a great budget choice.

Eating

TOP CHOICE Trading Post Cafe INTERNATIONAL $$$
(575-758-5089; www.tradingpostcafe.com; Hwy 68, Ranchos de Taos; lunch $8-14, dinner $16-32; 11:30am-9:30pm Tue-Sat, 5-9pm Sun) A longtime favorite, the Trading Post is a perfect blend of relaxed and refined. The food, from paella to pork chops, is always great. Portions of some dishes are so big, think about splitting a main course – or if you want to eat cheap but well, get a small salad and small soup. It'll be plenty!

TOP CHOICE Love Apple ORGANIC $$
(575-751-0050; www.theloveapple.net; 803 Paseo del Pueblo Norte; mains $13-18; 5-9pm Tue-Sun) Housed in the 19th century adobe Placitas Chapel, the understated rustic-sacred atmosphere is as much a part of this only-in-New-Mexico restaurant as the food is. From the posole with shepherd's lamb sausage to the grilled trout with chipotle cream, every dish is made from organic or free-range regional foods. Make reservations!

Taos Pizza Out Back PIZZERIA $$
(712 Paseo del Pueblo Norte; slices $3.50-7, whole pies $13-27; 11am-10pm daily May-Sep, 11am-9pm Sun-Thu, 11am-10pm Fri & Sat Oct-Apr) Warning: these pizza pies may be cruelly habit-forming. Located behind another business, this place uses organic ingredients and serves epicurean combos such as a Portabella Pie with sun-dried tomatoes and camembert. Slices are the size of a small country.

Taos Diner DINER $
(908 Paseo del Pueblo Norte; mains $4-12; 7am-2:30pm) It's with some reluctance that we share the existence of this marvelous place, a mountain-town diner with wood-paneled walls, tattooed waitresses, fresh-baked biscuits and coffee cups that are never less than half-full. This is diner grub at its finest, prepared with a Southwestern, organic spin. Mountain men, scruffy jocks, solo diners and happy tourists – everyone's welcome here. We like the Copper John's eggs with a side of green chile sauce.

Michael's Kitchen NEW MEXICAN $
(304 Paseo del Pueblo Norte; mains $7-16; 7am-2:30pm) Great breakfasts, freshly made pastries and tasty New Mexican fare.

El Gamal MIDDLE EASTERN $
(12 Dona Luz St; mains $6-10; 9am-5pm;) Vegetarians rejoice! Here's a great meatless Middle Eastern menu. There's a big kids' playroom in back, plus a pool table and free wi-fi.

Drinking & Entertainment

Adobe Bar BAR, LIVE MUSIC
(Historic Taos Inn, 125 Paseo del Pueblo Norte) Everybody's welcome in 'the living room of Taos.' And there's something about it: the chairs, the Taos Inn's history, the casualness, the tequila. The packed streetside patio has some of the state's finest margaritas, along with an eclectic lineup of great live music and never a cover.

KTAO Solar Center BAR, LIVE MUSIC
(www.ktao.com; 9 Ski Valley Rd; from 4pm) Watch the DJs at the 'world's most powerful solar radio station' while hitting happy hour at the solar center bar. It's also the home of the best live-music venue in town; you could catch a grooving local or big-name band.

Alley Cantina BAR, LIVE MUSIC
(121 Teresina Lane) It's a bit-cooler-than-thou, but maybe 'tude happens when you inhabit the oldest building in town. Catch live rock, blues, hip-hop or jazz almost nightly.

Shopping

Taos has historically been a mecca for artists, demonstrated by the huge number of galleries and studios in and around town. Indie stores and galleries line the **John Dunn Shops** (www.johndunnshops.com) pedestrian walkway linking Bent St to Taos Plaza. Here you'll find the well-stocked **Moby Dickens Bookshop** and the tiny but intriguing **G Robinson Old Prints & Maps** – a treat for cartography geeks.

Just east of the Plaza, pop into **El Rincón Trading Post** (114 Kit Carson Rd) and **Horse Feathers** (109 Kit Carson Rd) for classic Western memorabilia.

Information

Taos Vacation Guide (www.taosvacationguide.org) Great resource with lots of easy-to-navigate links.

Visitor center (☎575-758-3873; 1139 Paseo del Pueblo Sur; ⊙9am-5pm; @☎)

Wired? (705 Felicidad Lane; ⊙8am-6pm Mon-Fri, 8:30am-6pm Sat & Sun) Funky coffee shop with computers ($7 per hour). Free wi-fi for customers.

Getting There & Away

From Santa Fe, take either the scenic 'high road' along Hwys 76 and 518, with galleries, villages and sites worth exploring, or follow the lovely unfolding Rio Grande landscape on Hwy 68.

North Central Regional Transit (www.ncrtd.org) provides free shuttle-bus service to Espanola, where you can transfer to Santa Fe and other destinations. **Twin Hearts Express** (☎800-654-9456) will get you to Santa Fe ($40) and the Albuquerque airport ($50).

Northwestern New Mexico

Dubbed 'Indian Country' for good reason – huge swaths of land fall under the aegis of the Navajo, Pueblo, Zuni, Apache and Laguna tribes – this quadrant of New Mexico showcases remarkable ancient Indian sites alongside modern, solitary Native American settlements.

FARMINGTON & AROUND

The largest town in New Mexico's northwestern region, Farmington makes a convenient base from which to explore the Four Corners area. The **visitors bureau** (☎505-326-7602; www.farmingtonnm.org; Gateway Park, 3041 E Main St; ⊙8am-5pm Mon-Sat) has more information.

Shiprock, a 1700ft-high volcanic plug that rises eerily over the landscape to the west, was a landmark for the Anglo pioneers and is a sacred site to the Navajo.

An ancient pueblo, **Salmon Ruin & Heritage Park** (adult/child $3/1; ⊙8am-5pm Mon-Fri, 9am-5pm Sat & Sun) features a large village built by the Chaco people in the early 1100s. Abandoned, resettled by people from Mesa Verde and again abandoned before 1300, the site also includes the remains of a homestead, petroglyphs, a Navajo hogan and a wickiup (a rough brushwood shelter). Take Hwy 64 east 11 miles toward Bloomfield.

Fourteen miles northeast of Farmington, the 27-acre **Aztec Ruins National Monument** (www.nps.gov/azru; adult/under 16yr $5/free; ⊙8am-5pm Sep-May, 8am-6pm Jun-Aug) features the largest reconstructed kiva in the country, with an internal diameter of almost 50ft. A few steps away, let your imagination wander as you stoop through low doorways and dark rooms inside the West Ruin. In summer, rangers give early-afternoon talks at the c-1100 site about ancient architecture, trade routes and astronomy.

About 35 miles south of Farmington along Hwy 371, the undeveloped **Bisti Badlands & De-Na-Zin Wilderness** is a trippy, surreal landscape of strange, colorful rock formations, especially spectacular in the hours before sunset; desert enthusiasts shouldn't miss it. The Farmington **BLM office** (☎505-599-8900; www.nm.blm.gov; 1235 La Plata Hwy; ⊙8am-4:30pm Mon-Fri) has information.

The lovely, three-room **Silver River Adobe Inn B&B** (☎505-325-8219; www.silveradobe.com; 3151 W Main St, Farmington; r incl breakfast $115-175; ☎) offers a peaceful respite among the trees along the San Juan River.

Managing to be both trendy *and* kid-friendly, the hippish **Three Rivers Eatery & Brewhouse** (101 E Main St, Farmington; mains $8-26; ⊙11am-10pm; ☺) has good steaks and pub grub and its own microbrews.

CHACO CULTURE NATIONAL HISTORIC PARK

Featuring massive Ancestral Puebloan buildings set in an isolated high-desert environment, intriguing **Chaco** (www.nps.gov/chcu; admission per vehicle $8; ⊙7am-sunset, visitor center 8am-5pm) contains evidence of 5000 years of human occupation. In its prime, the community at Chaco Canyon was a major trading and ceremonial hub for the region – and the city the Puebloan people created here was masterly in its layout and design. Pueblo Bonito is four stories tall and may have had 600 to 800 rooms and kivas. As well as taking the self-guided loop tour, you can hike various **backcountry trails**. For stargazers, there's the **Night Skies** program offered Tuesday, Friday and Saturday evenings April through October.

The park is in a remote area approximately 80 miles south of Farmington. **Gallo Campground** (tent sites $10) is 1 mile east of the visitor center; no RV sites.

CHAMA

Nine miles south of the Colorado border, Chama's **Cumbres & Toltec Scenic Railway** (☎575-756-2151; www.cumbrestoltec.com; adult/child $91/50; ⊙late May–mid-Oct) is the longest (64 miles) and highest (over the 10,015ft-high Cumbres Pass) authentic narrow-gauge steam railroad in the US. It's a beautiful trip, particularly in September and October during the fall foliage, through mountains, canyons and high desert.

Northeastern New Mexico

East of Santa Fe, the lush Sangre de Cristo Mountains give way to vast rolling plains. Dusty grasslands stretch to infinity and further – to Texas. Cattle and dinosaur prints dot a landscape punctuated with volcanic cones. Ranching is an economic mainstay, and on many roads you'll see more cows than cars.

The Santa Fe Trail, along which pioneer settlers rolled in wagon trains, ran from New Mexico to Missouri. You can still see the wagon ruts in some places off I-25 between Santa Fe and Raton. For a bit of the Old West without a patina of consumer hype, this is the place.

CIMARRON

Cimarron once ranked among the rowdiest of Wild West towns; it's name even means 'wild' in Spanish. According to local lore, murder was such an everyday occurrence in the 1870s that peace-and-quiet was newsworthy, one paper going so far as to report: 'Everything is quiet in Cimarron. Nobody has been killed in three days.'

Today, the town is indeed quiet, luring nature-minded travelers who want to enjoy the great outdoors. Driving here to or from Taos, you'll pass through gorgeous **Cimarron Canyon State Park**, a steep-walled canyon with several hiking trails, excellent trout fishing and camping.

You can stay or dine (restaurant mains $5 to $20) at what's reputed to be one of the most haunted hotels in the USA, the 1872 **St James** (☎888-376-2664; www.exstjames.com; 617 S Collison St; r $70-120; ⏲7am-9pm) – one room is so spook-filled that it's never rented out! Many legends of the West stayed here, including Buffalo Bill, Annie Oakley, Wyatt Earp and Jesse James, and the front desk has a long list of who shot whom in the now-renovated hotel bar. The authentic period rooms make this one of the most historic-feeling hotels in New Mexico.

CAPULIN VOLCANO NATIONAL MONUMENT

Rising 1300ft above the surrounding plains, **Capulin** (www.nps.gov/cavo; admission per vehicle $5; ⏲8am-4pm) is the most accessible of several volcanoes in the area. From the visitor center, a 2-mile road spirals up the mountain to a parking lot at the crater rim (8182ft), where trails lead around and into the crater. The entrance is 3 miles north of Capulin village, which itself is 30 miles east of Raton on Hwy 87.

Southwestern New Mexico

The Rio Grande Valley unfurls from Albuquerque down to the bubbling hot springs of funky Truth or Consequences and beyond. Before the river hits the Texas line, it feeds one of New Mexico's agricultural treasures: Hatch, the so-called 'chile capital of the world.' The first atomic device was detonated at the Trinity Site, in the bone-dry desert east of the Rio known since Spanish times as the Jornada del Muerto – Journey of Death.

To the west, the rugged Gila National Forest is wild with backpacking and fishing adventures. The mountains' southern slopes descend into the Chihuahuan Desert that surrounds Las Cruces, the state's second-largest city.

TRUTH OR CONSEQUENCES & AROUND

An offbeat joie de vivre permeates the funky little town of Truth or Consequences, which was built on the site of natural hot springs in the 1880s. A bit of the quirkiness stems from the fact that the town changed its name from Hot Springs to Truth or Consequences (or 'T or C') in 1950, after a popular radio game show of the same name. Publicity these days comes courtesy of Virgin Galactic CEO Richard Branson and other space-travel visionaries driving the development of nearby **Spaceport America**, where wealthy tourists will launch into orbit sometime soon.

Spaceport tours (☎505-897-2886; www.ftstours.com; adult/under 12yr $59/29; ⏲9am & 1pm Fri-Sun) include a look at the launch site and mission control.

In T or C, wander around the hole-in-the-wall cafes, pop into a gallery, check out the engaging mishmash of exhibits at the **Geronimo Springs Museum** (www.geronimospringsmuseum.com; 211 Main St; adult/child $5/2.50; ⏲9am-5pm Mon-Sat, noon-5pm Sun) and definitely enjoy a soak in a hot-spring spa. The **visitor center** (☎575-894-1968; www.truthorconsequenceschamberofcommerce.org; 211 Main St; ⏲9am-4:30pm Mon-Fri, 9am-5pm Sat, noon-5pm Sun) has local listings.

About 60 miles north of town, sandhill cranes and Arctic geese winter in the 90 sq miles of fields and marshes at **Bosque del Apache National Wildlife Refuge** (www.fws.gov/southwest/refuges/newmex/bosque; admission per vehicle $5; State Hwy 1; ⊙refuge sunrise-sunset, visitor center 7:30am-4pm Mon-Fri, 8am-4:30pm Sat & Sun). There's a visitor center and driving tour. The Festival of the Cranes is held in mid-November.

Sleeping & Eating

Many local motels double as spas.

Riverbend Hot Springs BOUTIQUE HOTEL **$**
(☎575-894-7625; www.riverbendhotsprings.com; 100 Austin St; r from $70; ❄📶) Former hostel Riverbend Hot Springs now offers more traditional motel-style accommodations – no more tipis – from its fantastic perch beside the Rio Grande. Rooms exude a bright, quirky charm, and several units work well for groups. Private hot-spring tubs are available by the hour (guest/nonguest $10/15 for the first hour then $5/10 per additional hour), as is a public hot-spring pool (guest/nonguest free all day/$10 for the first hour then $5 per hour or $25 per day).

TOP CHOICE **Blackstone Hotsprings** BOUTIQUE HOTEL **$**
(☎575-894-0894; www.blackstonehotsprings.com; 410 Austin St; r $75-125; ❄📶) Blackstone embraces the T or C spirit with an upscale wink, decorating each of its seven rooms in the style of a classic TV show, from the *Jetsons* to the *Golden Girls* to *I Love Lucy*. Best part? Each room comes with its own hot-spring tub or waterfall. Worst part? If you like sleeping in darkness, quite a bit of courtyard light seeps into some rooms at night.

Happy Belly Deli DELI **$**
(313 N Broadway; mains $2-8; ⊙7am-3pm Mon-Fri, 8am-3pm Sat, 8am-noon Sun) Draws the morning crowd with fresh breakfast burritos.

Café BellaLuca ITALIAN **$$**
(www.cafebellaluca.com; 303 Jones St; lunch $6-15, dinner $10-34; ⊙11am-9pm Sun-Thu, 11am-10pm Fri & Sat) Earns raves for its Italian specialties; pizzas are amazing.

LAS CRUCES & AROUND

The second-largest city in New Mexico, Las Cruces is home to New Mexico State University (NMSU), but there's surprisingly little of real interest for visitors.

> **IF YOU HAVE A FEW MORE DAYS**
>
> Past the town of Magdalena on Hwy 60 is the **Very Large Array** (VLA; www.vla.nrao.edu; admission free; ⊙8:30am-dusk) radio telescope facility, a complex of 27 huge antenna dishes sprouting like giant mushrooms in the high plains. At the visitor center, watch a short film about the facility and take a self-guided walking tour with a window peek into the control building. It's 4 miles south of Hwy 60 off Hwy 52.

Sights

For many, a visit to neighboring **Mesilla** (aka Old Mesilla) is the highlight of their time in Las Cruces. Wander a few blocks off Old Mesilla's plaza in to gather the essence of a mid-19th-century Southwestern town of Hispanic heritage.

New Mexico Farm & Ranch Heritage Museum MUSEUM
(www.nmfarmandranchmuseum.org; 4100 Dripping Springs Rd, Las Cruces; adult/child $5/2; ⊙9am-5pm Mon-Sat, noon-5pm Sun) This terrific museum in Las Cruces has more than just engaging displays about the agricultural history of the state – it's got livestock! There are daily milking demonstrations and an occasional 'parade of breeds' of beef cattle, along with stalls of horses, donkeys, sheep and goats. Other demonstrations include blacksmithing (Friday to Sunday), spinning and weaving (Wednesday), and heritage cooking (call for schedule).

FREE **White Sands Missile Test Center Museum** MUSEUM
(www.wsmr-history.org; ⊙8am-4pm Mon-Fri, 10am-3pm Sat & Sun) About 25 miles east of Las Cruces along Hwy 70 (look for the White Sands Missile Range Headquarters sign), has been a major military testing site since 1945, and it still serves as an alternative landing site for the space shuttle. Look for the crazy outdoor missile park. Since it's on an army base, everyone entering over the age of 18 years must show ID, and the driver must present car registration and proof of insurance.

Sleeping

Lundeen Inn of the Arts B&B **$$**
(☎575-526-3326; www.innofthearts.com; 618 S Alameda Blvd, Las Cruces; r incl breakfast $79-125,

ste $99-155; ❄📶) In Las Cruces, Lundeen Inn of the Arts, a large turn-of-the-19th-century Mexican territorial-style inn, has seven guest rooms (all wildly different), genteel hosts, an airy living room with soaring ceilings (made of pressed tin) and a 300-piece fine-art gallery.

Eating

La Posta NEW MEXICAN **$$**
(www.laposta-de-mesilla.com; 2410 Calle de San Albino, Old Mesilla; mains $9-15; ⏱11am-9pm Sun-Thu, 11am-9:30pm Fri & Sat) The most famous restaurant in Old Mesilla, in a 200-year-old adobe, may at first raise your doubts with its fiesta-like decor and touristy feel. But the New Mexican dishes are consistently good, portions are huge, and service is prompt.

Nellie's Cafe NEW MEXICAN **$**
(1226 W Hadley Ave, Las Cruces; mains $6-10; ⏱8am-2pm) A favored local New Mexican restaurant, great for breakfast and lunch. Cash only.

Information

Las Cruces Visitors Bureau (☎575-541-2444; www.lascrucescvb.org; 211 N Water St, Las Cruces; ⏱8am-5pm Mon-Fri)

Getting There & Away

Greyhound (☎575-524-8518; www.greyhound.com; 390 S Valley Dr) has buses traversing the two interstate corridors (I-10 and I-25), as well as daily trips to Albuquerque ($27, 3½ hours), Roswell ($49, four hours) and El Paso ($11.25, one hour).

SILVER CITY & AROUND

The spirit of the Wild West still hangs in the air here, as if Billy the Kid himself – a former resident – might amble past at any moment. But things are changing, as the mountain-man/cowboy vibe succumbs to the charms of art galleries, coffeehouses and gelato. (One word of caution when strolling through downtown Silver City – look carefully before you step off the sidewalk. Because of monsoonal summer rains, curbs are higher than average, built to keep the Victorian and the brick and cast-iron buildings safe from quick-rising waters.)

Silver City is also the gateway to outdoor activities in the **Gila National Forest**, which is rugged country suitable for remote cross-country skiing, backpacking, camping, fishing and other activities.

Two hours north of Silver City, up a winding 42-mile road, is **Gila Cliff Dwellings National Monument** (www.nps.gov/gicl; admission $3; ⏱8:30am-5pm Jun-Aug, 9am-4pm Sep-May), occupied in the 13th century by Mogollons. Mysterious and relatively isolated, these remarkable cliff dwellings are easily accessed from a 1-mile loop trail and look very much as they would have at the turn of the first millennium. For **pictographs**, stop by the Lower Scorpion Campground and walk a short distance along the marked trail.

Weird rounded monoliths make the **City of Rocks State Park** (www.emnrd.state.nm.us/prd/cityrocks.htm; Hwy 61; day use $5, tent/RV sites $8/10) an intriguing playground, with great camping among the formations; there are tables and fire pits. For a rock-lined gem of a spot, check out campsite 43, the Lynx. Head 24 miles northwest of Deming along Hwy 180, then 3 miles northeast on Hwy 61.

For a smattering of Silver City's architectural history, overnight in the 22-room **Palace Hotel** (☎575-388-1811; www.silvercitypalacehotel.com; 106 W Broadway; r incl breakfast from $51; 📶). Exuding a low-key, turn-of-the-19th-century charm (no air con, older fixtures), the Palace is a great choice for those tired of cookie-cutter chains. On the corner, the lofty **Javalina** (201 N Bullard St; pastries $2-4; ⏱6am-9pm Mon-Thu, to 10pm Fri & Sat, to 7pm Sun; 📶) offers coffee, snacks and wi-fi in a comfy, come-as-you-are space.

Downtown offers a variey of restaurants, including the gourmet Mediterranean-themed **Shevek & Co Restaurant** (☎575-534-9168; www.silver-eats.com; 602 N Bullard St; mains $20-30; ⏱5-8:30pm Sun-Tue & Thu, 5-9pm Fri & Sat) and the vegetarian sandwich-and-salad shop **Peace Meal Cooperative** (601 N Bullard St; mains $5-8; ⏱9am-3pm Mon-Sat). For a real taste of local culture, head 7 miles north to Pinos Altos and the **Buckhorn Saloon** (☎575-538-9911; Main St, Pinos Altos; mains $10-35; ⏱4pm-10pm Mon-Sat), where the specialty is steak and there's live music most nights. Call for reservations.

Information

The **visitor center** (☎575-538-3785, www.silvercity.org; 201 N Hudson St; ⏱9am-5pm Mon-Fri, 10am-2pm Sat & Sun) and the **Gila National Forest Ranger Station** (☎575-388-8201; www.fs.fed.us/r3/gila; 3005 E Camino Del Bosque; ⏱8am-4:30pm Mon-Fri) have area information. To learn about the town's contentious mining history, watch the blacklisted 1954 movie *Salt of the Earth*.

Southeastern New Mexico

Two of New Mexico's greatest natural wonders are tucked down here in the arid southeast – mesmerizing White Sands National Monument and magnificent Carlsbad Caverns National Park. This region is also home to some of the state's most enduring legends: aliens in Roswell, Billy the Kid in Lincoln and Smokey Bear in Capitan. Most of the lowlands are covered by hot, rugged Chihuahuan Desert, but you can escape to cooler climes by driving up to higher altitudes around the popular forested resort towns such as Cloudcroft and Ruidoso.

WHITE SANDS NATIONAL MONUMENT

Slide, roll and slither through brilliant, towering sand hills. Sixteen miles southwest of Alamogordo (15 miles southwest of Hwy 82/70), gypsum covers 275 sq miles to create a dazzling white landscape at this crisp, stark **monument** (www.nps.gov/whsa; adult/under 16yr $3/free; ⌚7am-9pm Jun-Aug, 7am-sunset Sep-May). These captivating windswept dunes are a highlight of any trip to New Mexico. Don't forget your sunglasses – the sand is as bright as snow!

Spring for a $15 plastic saucer at the visitor center gift store then sled one of the back dunes. It's fun, and you can sell the disc back for $5 at day's end (no rentals to avoid liability). Check the park calendar for sunset strolls and occasional moonlight bicycle rides (adult/child under 16 years $5/2.50), the latter best reserved far in advance. Backcountry campsites, with no water or toilet facilities, are a mile from the scenic drive. Pick up one of the limited permits ($3, issued first-come, first-served) in person at the visitor center at least one hour before sunset.

ALAMOGORDO & AROUND

Alamogordo is the center of one of the most historically important space- and atomic-research programs in the country. The four-story **New Mexico Museum of Space History** (☎877-333-6589; www.nmspacemuseum.org; Hwy 2001; adult/senior/4-12yr $6/5/4; ⌚9am-5pm) has excellent exhibits on space research and flight. Its **Tombaugh IMAX Theater & Planetarium** (adult/senior/child $6/5.50/4.50) shows outstanding science-themed films on a huge wraparound screen.

Numerous motels stretch along White Sands Blvd, including **Best Western Desert Aire Motor Inn** (☎575-437-2110; www.bestwestern.com; 1021 S White Sands Blvd; r from $78; P ❄ @ 📶 ≋), with standard-issue rooms and suites (some with kitchenettes), along with a sauna. If you'd rather camp, hit **Oliver Lee State Park** (www.enmrd.state.nm.us/prd/oliverlee.htm; 409 Dog Canyon Rd; tent/RV sites $8/14), 12 miles south of Alamogordo. Grab some grub at the friendly **Pizza Patio & Pub** (2203 E 1st St; mains $7-15; ⌚11am-8pm Mon-Thu & Sat, to 9pm Fri) with pizzas, pastas, big salads and pitchers or pints of beer on tap.

CLOUDCROFT

Pleasant Cloudcroft, with turn-of-the-19th-century buildings, offers lots of outdoor recreation, a good base for exploration and a low-key feel. Situated high in the mountains, it provides welcome relief from the lowlands heat to the east. For good information on hiking trails, free maps of forest roads, and topo maps for sale, go to the **Lincoln National Forest Ranger Station** (4 Lost Lodge Rd; ⌚7:30am-4:30pm Mon-Fri). **High Altitude** (310 Burro St; rentals per day from $30; ⌚10am-5:30pm Mon-Thu, 10am-6pm Fri & Sat, 10am-5pm Sun) rents mountain bikes and has maps of local fat-tire routes.

The **Lodge Resort & Spa** (☎800-395-6343; www.thelodgeresort.com; 1 Corona Pl; r from $79; ❄ @ 📶 ≋) is one of the Southwest's best historic hotels. Rooms in the main Bavarian-style hotel are furnished with period and Victorian pieces. Within the lodge, **Rebecca's** (☎575-682-3131; breakfast & lunch $8-15, dinner $28-36; ⌚7-10:30am Mon-Sat, 7-10am Sun, 11:30am-2pm & 5:30-9pm, slightly longer hr summer), named after the resident ghost, offers by far the best food in town.

RUIDOSO

Downright bustling in summer and big with racetrack bettors, resorty Ruidoso (it means 'noisy' in Spanish) has an utterly pleasant climate thanks to its lofty and forested perch near Sierra Blanca (12,000ft). It's spread out along Hwy 48 (known as Mechem Dr or Sudderth Dr), the main drag.

👁 Sights & Activities

To stretch your legs, try the easily accessible **forest trails** on Cedar Creek Rd just west of **Smokey Bear Ranger Station** (901 Mechem Dr; ⌚7:30am-4:30pm Mon-Fri & Sat summer). Choose from the USFS Fitness Trail or the meandering paths at the Cedar Creek Picnic Area. Longer day hikes and backpacking routes abound in the White Mountain Wilderness, north of town. Always check fire restrictions around here – it's not unusual for the forest to close during dry spells.

Ski Apache SKIING
(☎575-464-3600, snow report 575-257-9001; www.skiapache.com; all-day lift ticket adult/child $39/25; ⏲9am-4pm) The best ski area south of Albuquerque, 18 miles northwest of Ruidoso on the slopes of beautiful Sierra Blanca Peak (about 12,000ft). To get there, take exit 532 off Hwy 48.

Flying J Ranch WILD WEST SHOW
(☎575-336-4330; www.flyingjranch.com; Hwy 48 N; adult/child $24/14; ⏲from 5:30pm Mon-Sat late May–early Sep, plus Sat Sep & early Oct; 👪) Circle the wagons and ride over about 1.5 miles north of Alto, for a meal. This 'Western village' stages gunfights and offers pony rides with its cowboy-style chuckwagon.

Ruidoso Downs Racetrack HORSE RACING
(☎575-378-4431; www.ruidownsracing.com; Hwy 70; grandstand seats free, boxes $35-55; ⏲races Fri-Mon late May–early Sep, casino 10am-midnight year-round) Serious horse racing happens here.

Hubbard Museum of the American West MUSEUM
(www.hubbardmuseum.org; 841 Hwy 70 W; adult/senior/child $6/5/2; ⏲9am-5pm; 👪) Displays Western-related items, with an emphasis on Old West stagecoaches, Native American artifacts and, well, all things horse.

Sleeping & Eating

Numerous motels, hotels and cute little cabin complexes line the streets. There's plenty of primitive camping along forest roads on the way to the ski area.

Sitzmark Chalet HOTEL $
(☎800-658-9694; www.sitzmark-chalet.com; 627 Sudderth Dr; r from $60; ❄📶) This ski-themed chalet offers 17 simple but nice rooms. Picnic tables, grills and an eight-person hot tub are welcome perks.

Upper Canyon Inn LODGE $$
(☎575-257-3005; www.uppercanyoninn.com; 215 Main Rd; r/cabins from $79/119; ❄📶) Rooms and cabins range from simple good values to rustic-chic luxury.

TOP CHOICE **Rickshaw** ASIAN $$
(☎575-257-2828; 601 Mechem Dr; www.rickshawnewmexico.com; lunch $7-9, dinner $11-22; ⏲11am-9pm Thu-Tue) The best Asian food south of Albuquerque, with selections inspired by but not slavish to the cuisines of Thailand, China and India. Finish with the ginger-pear crumble over homemade cinnamon ice cream.

Cornerstone Bakery BREAKFAST $
(359 Sudderth Dr; mains under $10; ⏲7:30am-2pm Mon-Sat, 7:30am-1pm Sun) Stay around long enough and this eatery may become your touchstone. Everything on the menu, from the omelets to croissant sandwiches, is worthy, and the piñon-flavored coffee is wonderful.

Café Rio PIZZERIA $$
(2547 Sudderth Dr; mains $5-25; ⏲11am-9pm) Friendly service isn't the first description that leaps to mind at this scruffy pizza joint, but oh…take one bite of a pillowy slice and all will be forgiven.

Information

The **chamber of commerce** (☎575-257-7395; www.ruidosonow.com; 720 Sudderth Dr; ⏲8am-4:30pm Mon-Fri, 9am-3pm Sat) has visitor information.

LINCOLN & CAPITAN

Fans of Western history won't want to miss little Lincoln. Twelve miles east of Capitan along the **Billy the Kid National Scenic Byway** (www.billybyway.com), this is where the gun battle that turned Billy the Kid into a legend took place. The whole town is beautifully preserved in close to original form and the main street has been designated the **Lincoln Town Monument**; modern influences (such as neon-lit motel signs, souvenir stands, fast-food joints) are not allowed.

Buy tickets to the most historic buildings at the **Anderson Freeman Visitors Center & Museum** (Hwy 380; admission to 5 sites adult/child $5/free; ⏲8:30am-4:30pm), where you'll also find exhibits on Buffalo soldiers, Apaches and the Lincoln County War. Make the fascinating **Courthouse Museum** your last stop; this is the well-marked site of Billy's most daring – and violent – escape. There's a plaque where one of his bullets slammed into the wall.

For overnighters, the **Ellis Store Country Inn** (☎575-653-4609; www.ellisstore.com; Mile 98, Hwy 380; r incl breakfast $89-119) offers three antique-filled rooms (complete with wood stove) in the main house; five additional rooms are located in a historic mill on the property. From Wednesday to Saturday the host offers an amazing six-course dinner ($75 per person), served in the lovely dining room. Perfect for special occasions; reservations recommended.

A few miles west on the road to Capitan, **Laughing Sheep Farm and Ranch** (575-653-4041; www.laughingsheepfarm.com; mains $11-36; 11am-3pm Wed-Sun, 5-8pm Fri & Sat) raises sheep, cows and bison – along with vegetables and fruits – then serves them for lunch and dinner. The dining room is comfortable and casual, with a play-dough table and an easel for kids and live fiddle music on weekend nights.

Like Lincoln, cozy Capitan is surrounded by the beautiful mountains of **Lincoln National Forest**. The main reason to come is so the kids can visit **Smokey Bear Historical State Park** (www.smokeybearpark.com; adult/7-12yr $2/1; 9am-5pm;), where Smokey (yes, there actually was a real Smokey Bear) is buried.

ROSWELL

If you believe 'The Truth Is Out There', then the Roswell Incident is already filed away in your memory banks. In 1947 a mysterious object crashed at a nearby ranch. No one would have skipped any sleep over it, but the military made a big to-do of hushing it up, and for a lot of folks, that sealed it: the aliens had landed! International curiosity and local ingenuity have transformed the city into a quirky extraterrestrial-wannabe zone. Bulbous white heads glow atop the downtown streetlamps and busloads of tourists come to find good souvenirs.

Believers and kitsch-seekers must check out the **International UFO Museum & Research Center** (www.roswellufomuseum.com; 114 N Main St; adult/child $5/2; 9am-5pm), displaying documents supporting the cover-up as well as lots of far-out art and exhibitions. The annual **Roswell UFO Festival** (www.roswellufofestival.com) beams down over the July 4 weekend, with an otherworldly costume parade, guest speakers, workshops and concerts.

Ho-hum chain motels line N Main St. About 36 miles south of Roswell, the **Heritage Inn** (575-748-2552; www.artesiaheritageinn.com; 209 W Main St, Artesia; r incl breakfast $104;) in Artesia offers 11 Old West–style rooms and is the nicest lodging in the area.

Superhero-themed **Farley's** (1315 N Main St; mains $7-13; 11am-11pm Sun-Thu, to 1am Fri & Sat) has 29 beers on tap as well as pub food and pizza in a huge industrial space. For simple, dependable Mexican fare downtown, try **Martin's Capitol Café** (110 W 4th St; mains $7-15; 6am-8:30pm Mon-Sat).

Pick up local information and have your picture snapped with an alien at the **visitors bureau** (575-624-0889; www.roswellmysteries.com; 912 N Main St; 8:30am-5:30pm Mon-Fri, 10am-3pm Sat & Sun;).

The **Greyhound Bus Depot** (575-622-2510; www.greyhound.com; 1100 N Virginia Ave) has buses to Carlsbad ($28, 1½ hours) and El Paso, TX, via Las Cruces ($54, five hours).

CARLSBAD

Travelers use Carlsbad as a base for visits to nearby Carlsbad Caverns National Park and the Guadalupe Mountains. The **Park Service office** (575-885-8884; 3225 National Parks Hwy; 8am-4:30pm Mon-Fri) on the south edge of town has information on both.

On the northwestern outskirts of town, off Hwy 285, **Living Desert State Park** (1504 Miehls Dr; adult/7-12yr $5/3; 8am-8pm late Jun–Aug, 9am-5pm Sep-May;) is a great place to see and learn about desert plants and wildlife. There's a good 1.3-mile trail that showcases different habitats of the Chihuahuan Desert, with live antelopes, wolves, roadrunners and more.

Most Carlsbad lodging consists of chain motels on S Canal St or National Parks Hwy. The top value is the **Stagecoach Inn** (575-887-1148; 1819 S Canal St; r from $40;), with clean rooms, a pool, and a good on-site playground for kids. The best accommodation in town is the new, luxurious **Trinity Hotel** (575-234-9891; www.thetrinityhotel.com; 201 S Canal St; r $129-199;), a historic building that was originally the First National Bank; the sitting room of one suite is inside the old vault! The restaurant here is Carlsbad's classiest.

The perky **Blue House Bakery & Cafe** (609 N Canyon St; mains under $10; breakfast 6am-noon Mon & Sat, breakfast & lunch 6am-2pm Tue-Fri) brews the best coffee in this quadrant of New Mexico. Get there before 10am for the full selection of pastries. Locals and visitors crowd **Lucy's** (701 S Canal St; mains $7-16; 11am-9pm Mon-Thu, 11am-9:30pm Fri & Sat), where you can scarf down cheap New Mexican meals.

For other in-the-know advice, visit the **chamber of commerce** (575-887-6516; www.carlsbadchamber.com; 302 S Canal St; 9am-5pm Mon, 8am-5pm Tue-Fri year-round, 9am-3pm Sat May-Sep).

Greyhound (575-628-0768; www.greyhound.com; 3102 National Parks Hwy) buses depart from the Shamrock gas station inside Food Jet South. Destinations include El Paso, TX ($49, three hours), and Albuquerque ($49, 4½ hours).

CARLSBAD CAVERNS NATIONAL PARK

Scores of wondrous caves hide under the hills at this unique **national park** (☎575-785-2232, bat info 505-785-3012; www.nps.gov/cave; 3225 National Parks Hwy; adult/child $6/free; ⏰caves 8:30am-4pm late May–early Sep, 8:30am-3:30pm early Sep–late May), which covers 73 sq miles. The cavern formations are an ethereal wonderland of stalactites and fantastical geological features. You can ride an elevator from the visitor center (which descends the length of the Empire State Building in under a minute) or take a 2-mile subterranean walk from the cave mouth to the Big Room, an underground chamber 1800ft long, 255ft high and more than 800ft below the surface. If you've got kids (or are just feeling goofy), plastic caving helmets with headlamps are sold in the gift shop.

Guided tours of additional caves are available (adult $7 to $20, child $3.50 to $10), and should be reserved well in advance (call ☎877-444-6777 or visit www.recreation.gov). Bring long sleeves and closed shoes; it gets chilly.

The cave's other claim to fame is the 300,000-plus Mexican free-tailed bat colony that roosts here from mid-May to mid-October. Be here by sunset, when they cyclone out for an all-evening insect feast.

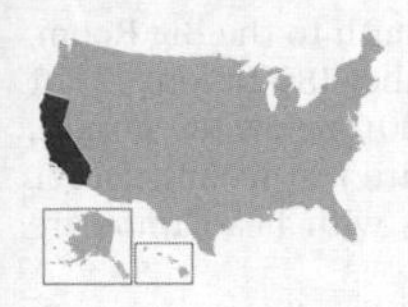

California

Includes »

Los Angeles 887
Southern California Coast 911
San Diego 916
Palm Springs & The Deserts 928
Joshua Tree National Park 930
Death Valley National Park 933
San Francisco & The Bay Area 947
Northern California 975
Yosemite National Park 989
Lake Tahoe 998

Best Places to Eat

» Benu (p964)

» Chez Panisse (p974)

» Zazu (p979)

» Bazaar (p905)

» Passionfish (p944)

Best Places to Stay

» Beverly Hills Hotel (p902)

» Hotel Del Coronado (p923)

» Ahwahnee Hotel (p993)

» Beltane Ranch (p978)

» Mar Vista Cottages (p981)

Why Go?

With bohemian spirit and high-tech savvy, not to mention a die-hard passion for the good life – whether that means cracking open a vintage bottle of Zinfandel, summiting a 14,000ft peak or surfing the Pacific – California soars beyond any expectations sold on Hollywood's silver screens.

More than anything, California is iconic. It was here that the hurly-burly gold rush kicked off in the mid-19th century. Naturalist John Muir rhapsodized about the Sierra Nevada's 'range of light,' and Jack Kerouac and the Beat Generation defined what it really means to hit the road.

California's multicultural melting pot has been cookin' since this bountiful promised land was staked out by Spain and Mexico. Today waves of immigrants still look to find their own American dream on these palm-tree-studded Pacific shores. It's time for you to join them.

When to Go

Los Angeles

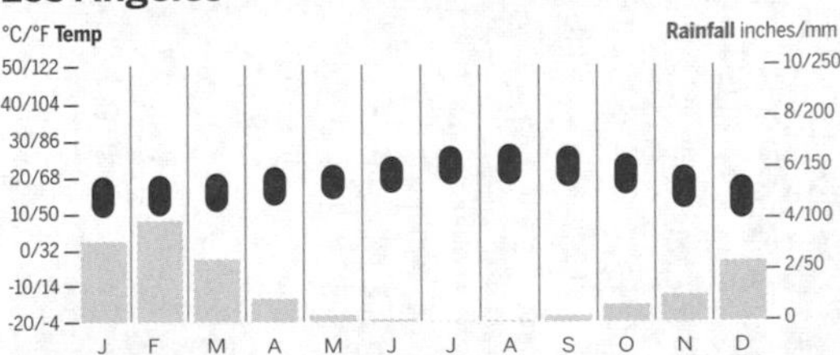

Jun-Aug Mostly sunny weather and crowded with families taking summer vacations.

Apr-May & Sep-Oct Cooler weather, but mostly cloudless days; travel bargains.

Nov-Mar Peak tourism at mountain ski resorts and in SoCal's dry, warm desert regions.

Transportation

Los Angeles (LAX) and San Francisco (SFO) are major international airports. Sacramento, Oakland, San Jose, Burbank, Orange County and San Diego handle primarily domestic flights.

Four main Amtrak routes connect California with the rest of the USA: *California Zephyr* (Chicago–San Francisco Bay Area), *Coast Starlight* (Seattle–Los Angeles), *Southwest Chief* (Chicago–LA) and *Sunset Limited* (New Orleans–LA). Amtrak's intrastate routes include the *Pacific Surfliner* (San Diego–LA–Santa Barbara–San Luis Obispo), *Capitol Corridor* (San Jose–Oakland–Berkeley–Sacramento) and *San Joaquin* (Bakersfield to Oakland or Sacramento, with Yosemite Valley buses from Merced).

Greyhound reaches into many corners of the state. But to really get out and explore, especially away from the coast, you'll need a car.

NATIONAL & STATE PARKS

Yosemite and Sequoia became California's first national parks in 1890, and today there are six more: Kings Canyon, Death Valley, Joshua Tree, Channel Islands, Redwood and Lassen Volcanic. The **National Park Service** (NPS; www.nps.gov) also manages almost 20 other historic sites, monuments, nature preserves and recreational areas statewide.

California's 278 **state parks** (☎916-653-6995; www.parks.ca.gov) are a diverse bunch: expect everything from marine preserves to redwood forests, protecting nearly a third of the coastline and offering 3000 miles of hiking, biking and equestrian trails.

For camping on federal lands, see p1154. Day-use parking fees are $4 to $15; campsites cost $10 to $65 nightly. **ReserveAmerica** (☎800-444-7275; www.reserveamerica.com) handles state-park camping reservations.

Warning! Check current park closures and reduced opening hours due to state-budget cutbacks – call ahead or check the park website.

Top Five California Beaches

» Coronado (p918) Sun yourself along San Diego's boundless Silver Strand.

» Huntington Beach (p915) Bonfires, beach volleyball and rolling waves in 'Surf City USA.'

» Zuma (p899) Crystal aquamarine waters, frothy surf and tawny sand, just north of Malibu.

» Santa Cruz (p944) Surf's up! And the beach boardwalk's carnival fun never stops.

» Point Reyes (p973) Wild, windy, end-of-the-world beaches, perfect for wildlife watching.

DON'T MISS

You can't leave California without hugging a tree! We suggest coast redwoods, which can live for 2000 years and grow to 379ft tall.

Fast Facts

» Population: Los Angeles (3,792,620), San Francisco (805,235)

» Driving distance: Los Angeles to San Francisco (380 miles)

» Time zone: Pacific Standard

Did You Know?

Just a few of California's inventions: the internet and the iPad, power yoga and reality TV, the space shuttle and Mickey Mouse, the Cobb salad and the fortune cookie.

Resources

» California Travel & Tourism Commission (www.visitcalifornia.com)

» California Highway Information (www.dot.ca.gov/hq/roadinfo)

» Department of Forestry and Fire Protection (www.fire.ca.gov)

» USGS Earthquake Hazards (http://quake.usgs.gov/recenteqs/latest.htm)

California Highlights

1. Chase waterfalls and climb granite domes in **Yosemite National Park** (p989)
2. Make the most of multicultural neighborhoods and Hollywood's red-carpet nightlife in **Los Angeles** (p887)
3. Cruise Hwy 1 above sculpted sea cliffs along the rocky coast of **Big Sur** (p940)
4. Taste seasonal, farm-fresh bounty at the Ferry Building Marketplace in **San Francisco** (p966)
5. Surf perfect waves off sunny **San Diego** (p923) and **Orange County** (p915) beaches
6. Wallow in a mud bath near Napa Valley vineyards in **Calistoga** (p976)

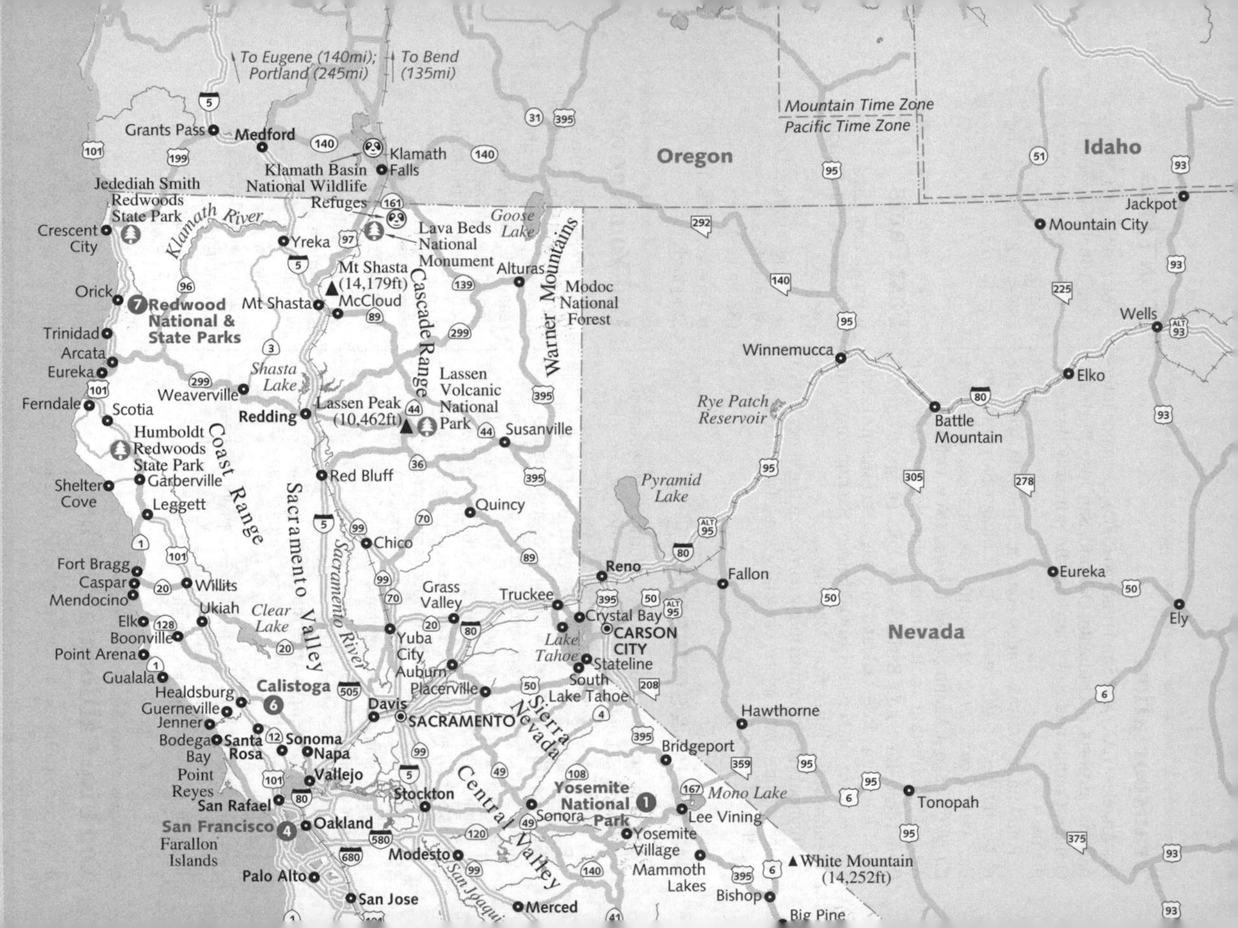

7 Crane your neck up at the world's tallest trees in **Redwood National & State Parks** (p983)

8 Trek across sand dunes and explore Old West ghost towns in **Death Valley National Park** (p933)

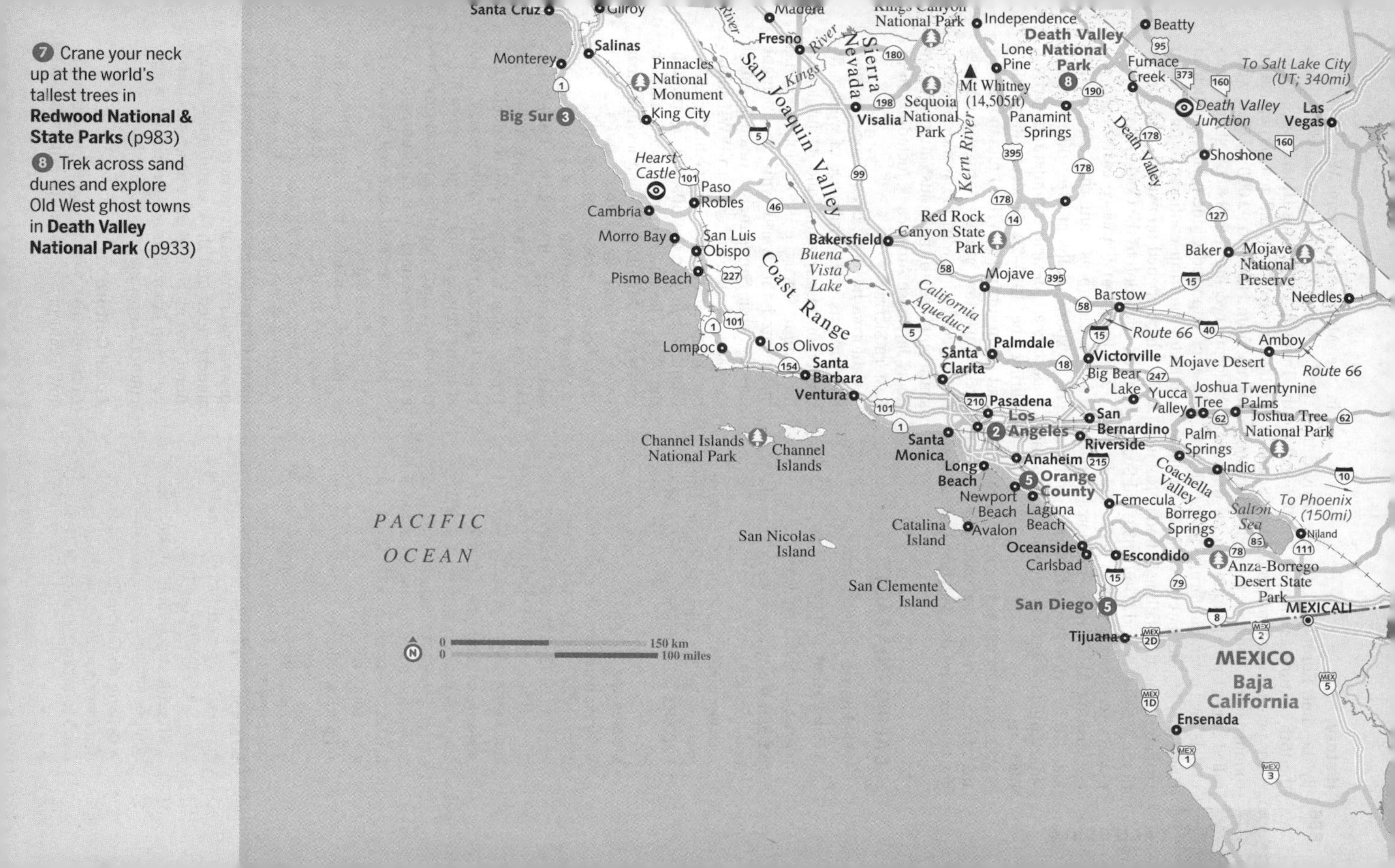

History

By the time European explorers arrived in the 16th century, as many as 300,000 indigenous people called this land home. Spanish conquistadors combed through what they called Alta (Upper) California (as opposed to Baja, or Lower, California) in search of a fabled 'city of gold,' but they left the territory virtually alone after failing to find it. Not until the Mission Period (1769–1833) did Spain make a serious attempt to settle the land, establishing 21 Catholic missions – many founded by priest Junípero Serra – and presidios (military forts) to keep out British and Russians.

After winning independence from Spain in 1821, Mexico briefly ruled California, but then got trounced by the fledgling United States in the Mexican-American War (1846–48). The discovery of gold just over a week before the Treaty of Guadalupe Hidalgo was signed sent the territory's nonindigenous population soaring from 14,000 to 92,000 by 1850, when California became the 31st US state. Thousands of imported Chinese laborers helped complete the transcontinental railroad in 1869, which opened up markets and further spurred migration to the Golden State.

The 1906 San Francisco earthquake was barely a hiccup as California continued to grow exponentially in size, diversity and importance. Mexican immigrants arrived during the 1910–20 Mexican Revolution, and again during WWII, to fill labor shortages. Important military-driven industries developed during wartime, while anti-Asian sentiments led to the unjust internment of many Japanese Americans, including in the Eastern Sierra.

California has long been a social pioneer thanks to its size, confluence of wealth, diversity of immigration and technological innovation. Since the 1930s, Hollywood has mesmerized the world with its cinematic dreams, while San Francisco reacted against the banal complacency of post-WWII suburbia by spreading Beat poetry in the 1950s, hippie free love in the '60s and gay pride in the '70s. The internet revolution, initially spurred by high-tech visionaries in Silicon Valley, rewired the country and led to a 1990s boom in overspeculated stocks.

When the bubble burst, plunging the state's economy into chaos, Californians blamed their Democratic governor, Gray Davis, and, in a controversial recall election, voted to give Arnold Schwarzenegger a shot at fixing things. Despite some early fumbles, the actor-turned-Republican-politician 'Governator' surprisingly put environmental issues and controversial stem-cell research at the top of his agenda.

Budget shortfalls have caused another staggering financial crisis that Sacramento lawmakers and once-again Governor Jerry Brown have yet to resolve. Meanwhile, the need for public education reform builds, prisons overflow, state parks are chronically underfunded and the conundrum of illegal immigration from Mexico, which fills a critical cheap labor shortage (especially in agriculture), continues to vex the state.

CALIFORNIA FACTS

» **Nickname** Golden State

» **Population** 37 million

» **Area** 155,959 sq miles

» **Capital city** Sacramento (population 466,488)

» **Other cities** Los Angeles (population 3,792,620), San Diego (population 1,307,402), San Francisco (population 805,235)

» **Sales tax** 8.25%

» **Birthplace of** author John Steinbeck (1902–68), photographer Ansel Adams (1902–84), US president Richard Nixon (1913–94), pop-culture icon Marilyn Monroe (1926–62)

» **Home of** the highest and lowest points in the contiguous US (Mt Whitney and Death Valley), world's oldest, tallest and biggest living trees (ancient bristlecone pines, coast redwoods and giant sequoias)

» **Politics** majority Democrat (multiethnic), minority Republican (mostly white), one in five Californians votes independent

» **Famous for** Disneyland, earthquakes, Hollywood, hippies, tree huggers, Silicon Valley, surfing

» **Kitschiest souvenir** 'Mystery Spot' bumper sticker

» **Driving distances** Los Angeles to San Francisco 380 miles, San Francisco to Yosemite Valley 190 miles

Local Culture

Currently the world's eighth-largest economy, California is a state of extremes, where

CALIFORNIA IN...

One Week

California in a nutshell. Start in **Los Angeles**, detouring to **Disneyland**. Head up the breathtaking Central Coast, stopping in **Santa Barbara** and **Big Sur**, before soaking up a dose of big-city culture in **San Francisco**. Head inland to **Yosemite National Park**, then zip back to LA.

Two Weeks

Follow the one-week itinerary above, but at a saner pace. Add jaunts to NorCal's **Wine Country**; **Lake Tahoe**, perched high in the Sierra Nevada; the beaches of **Orange County** and laid-back **San Diego**; or **Death Valley** and **Joshua Tree National Park**, near the hip-again desert resort of **Palm Springs** outside LA.

One Month

Do everything described above, and more! From San Francisco, head up the north coast, starting in Marin County at **Point Reyes National Seashore**. Stroll Victorian-era **Mendocino** and **Eureka**, find yourself on the **Lost Coast** and ramble through fern-filled **Redwood National & State Parks**. Inland, snap a postcard-perfect photo of **Mt Shasta**, detour to **Lassen Volcanic National Park** and get dirty in California's historic **Gold Country**. Trace the backbone of the **Eastern Sierra** before winding down into the **Deserts**.

grinding poverty shares urban corridors with fabulous wealth. Waves of immigrants keep arriving, and neighborhoods are often mini-versions of their homelands. Tolerance for others is the social norm, but so is intolerance, which you'll encounter if you smoke or dare to drive on the freeway during rush hour.

Untraditional and unconventional attitudes continue to define California, a trendsetter by nature. Image is an obsession, appearances are stridently youthful and outdoorsy, and self-help all the rage. Whether it's a luxury SUV or Nissan Leaf, a car may define who you are and also how important you consider yourself to be, especially in SoCal.

Think of California as the USA's most futuristic social laboratory. If technology identifies a new useful gadget, Silicon Valley will build it at light speed. If postmodern celebrities, bizarrely famous merely for the fact of being famous, make a fashion statement or get thrown in jail, the nation pays attention. Perhaps no other state's pop culture has as big an effect on how the rest of us work, play, eat, love, consume and, yes, recycle.

LOS ANGELES

While 'All-American' isn't the first thought that comes to mind when thinking of Los Angeles, LA County – America's largest – represents this vast nation in extremes. Its people are among America's richest and poorest, most established and newest arrivals, most refined and roughest, most beautiful and most plain, most erudite and most airheaded. Even the landscape is a microcosm of the USA, from fabled beaches to snowcapped mountains, skyscrapers, suburban sprawl and even wilderness.

The one thing that binds Angelenos is that they are seekers – or descendants of seekers – drawn by a dream, from fame on the silver screen to money to send back to the family. Success can be spectacular and failure equally so. If that's not America, we don't know what is.

If you think you've already got LA figured out – celebrity culture, smog, traffic, Botox babes and wannabes – think again. Although it's the world's entertainment capital, the city's truths aren't delivered on movie screens or reality shows; rather, in small portions of everyday experiences. Chances are, the more you explore, the more you'll enjoy.

Now is an exciting time to visit LA. Hollywood and Downtown are undergoing an urban renaissance, and art, music, fashion and food are all in high gear.

History

The hunter-gatherer existence of the Gabrieleño and Chumash peoples ended with the arrival of Spanish missionaries and pioneers in the late 18th century. Spain's first civilian settlement here (1781), El Pueblo de la Reina de Los Angeles, remained an isolated

Greater Los Angeles

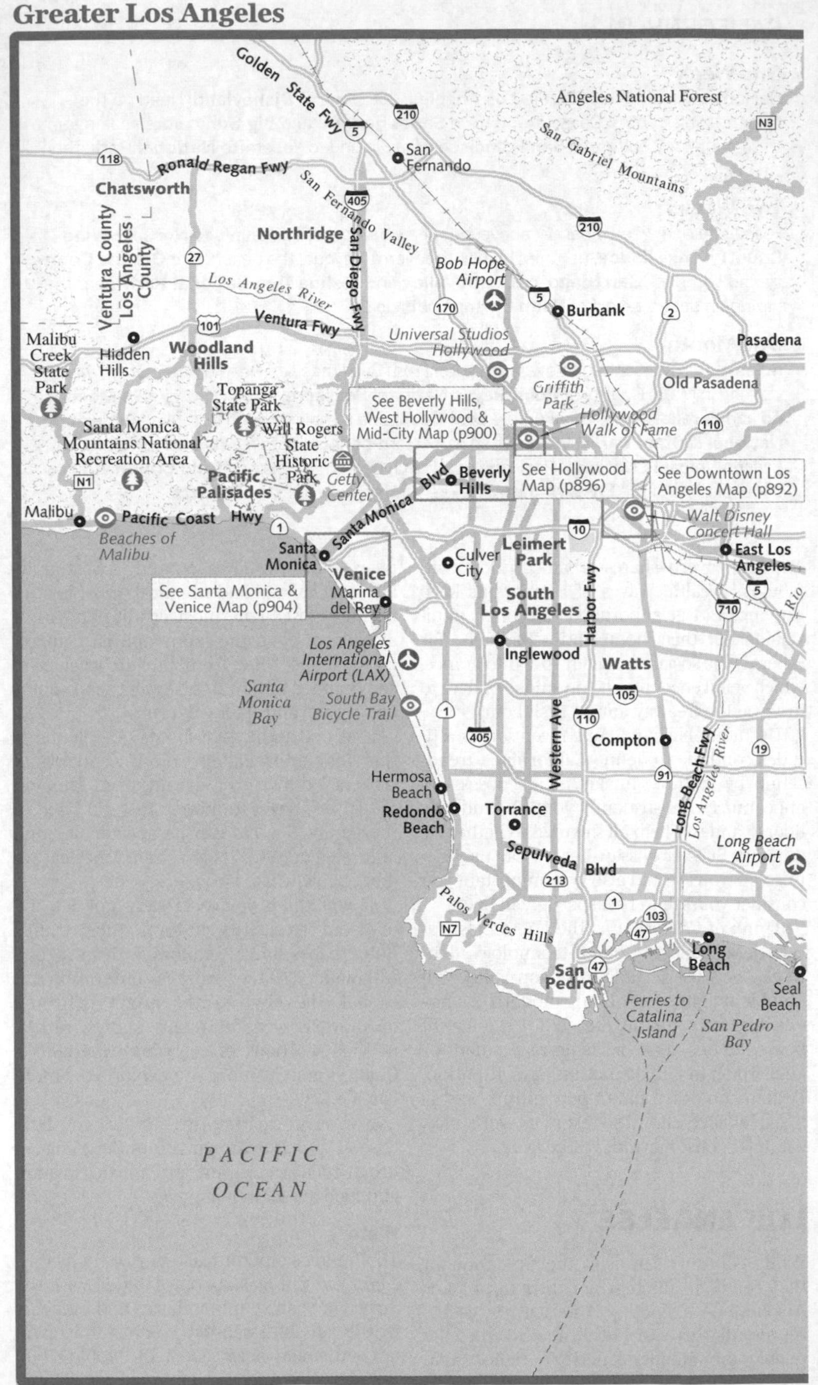

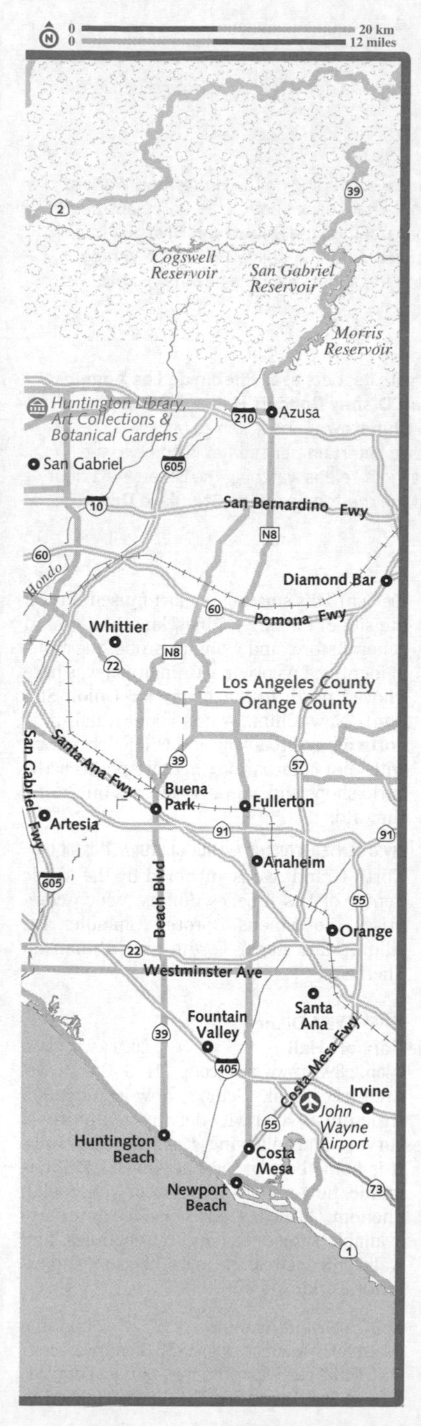

farming outpost for decades. LA was incorporated as a California city in 1850, and by 1830 its population had swollen thanks to the collapse of the Northern California gold rush, the arrival of the transcontinental railroad, the citrus industry, the discovery of oil, the launch of the port of LA, the birth of the movie industry and the opening of the California Aqueduct. The city's population has boomed from some 1.5 million in 1950 to almost four million today.

LA's growth has caused problems, including suburban sprawl and air pollution – though thanks to aggressive enforcement, smog levels have fallen annually since records have been kept. Traffic, a struggling public-education system, a fluctuating real-estate market and the occasional earthquake or forest fire remain nagging concerns, but with a strong and diverse economy and a decreasing crime rate, all things considered, LA's a survivor.

Sights

LA County is vast (88 cities in over 4000 square miles), but the areas of visitor interest are fairly well defined. About 12 miles inland, Downtown combines history, highbrow culture and global-village pizzazz. Hip-again Hollywood is to the northwest, and urban-designer chic and lesbi-gays rule West Hollywood. South of here, Museum Row is Mid-City's main draw, while further west are ritzy Beverly Hills, Westwood and the hilltop Getty Center. Santa Monica is the most tourist-friendly beach town; others include swish but low-key Malibu, boho Venice and hopping Long Beach. Stately Pasadena lies northeast of Downtown.

Getting around is easiest by car, although if you're not in a hurry public transport is usually adequate to most of these neighborhoods.

DOWNTOWN

For decades, Downtown was LA's historic core, and main business and government district – and empty nights and weekends. No more. Crowds fill Downtown's performance and entertainment venues, and young professionals and artists have moved by the thousands into new lofts, bringing bars, restaurants and galleries. Don't expect Manhattan just yet, but for adventurous urbanites, now is an exciting time to be Downtown.

Downtown is easily explored on foot or by subway or DASH minibus. Parking is cheapest (about $6 all day) around Little Tokyo and Chinatown.

LOS ANGELES IN...

Distances are ginormous in LA, so allow for traffic and don't try to pack too much into a day.

One Day

Fuel up for the day at the **Waffle** and then go star-searching on the **Hollywood Walk of Fame** along revitalized Hollywood Blvd. Up your chances of spotting actual celebs by hitting the fashion-forward boutiques on paparazzi-infested **Robertson Blvd** and having lunch at the **Ivy**. Then drive to lofty **Getty Center**, before heading west to the **Venice Boardwalk** to see the seaside sideshow. Watch the sunset over the ocean in **Santa Monica**.

Two Days

Explore rapidly evolving Downtown LA. Start with its roots at **El Pueblo de Los Angeles**, and catapult to the future at the dramatic **Walt Disney Concert Hall** and **Cathedral of our Lady of the Angels**. Dim sum brunch in **Chinatown** is best walked off with a stroll among the nearby art galleries. The new LA Live entertainment center is home to the **Grammy Museum**, and if you're lucky you can join celebs watching the Lakers next door at **Staples Center**. Top it off with cocktails at the rooftop bar of the **Standard Downtown LA**.

EL PUEBLO DE LOS ANGELES & AROUND

Compact, colorful and car-free, this historic district is an immersion in LA's Spanish-Mexican roots. Its spine is **Olvera St**, a festive tack-o-rama where you can chomp on tacos and stock up on handmade candy, folkloric trinkets and bric-a-brac.

FREE Avila Adobe HISTORIC BUILDING

(Map p892; ☎213-628-1274; Olvera St; ⏰9am-4pm) This 1818 ranch home claims to be the city's oldest existing building. It's decorated with period furniture, and a video gives history and highlights of the neighborhood.

La Plaza de Cultura y Artes MUSEUM

(Map p892; www.lapca.org; 501 Main St; adult/child $9/5; ⏰noon-7pm Wed-Sun; 🅿) This new museum (opened 2010) chronicles the Mexican-American experience in Los Angeles, in exhibits about city history from the Zoot Suit Riots to the Chicana movement. Calle Principal re-creates Main St in the 1920s.

FREE Union Station LANDMARK

(Map p892; 800 N Alameda St; 🅿) This majestic 1939 edifice is the last of America's grand rail stations; its glamorous art-deco interior can be seen in *Blade Runner, Bugsy, Rain Man* and many other movies.

Chinese American Museum MUSEUM

(Map p892; ☎213-485-8567; www.camla.org; 425 N Los Angeles St; adult/child $3/2; ⏰10am-3pm Tue-Sun) This small but smart museum is on the site of an early Chinese apothecary and general store, and exhibits probe questions of identity. LA's original Chinatown was here (moved north to make way for Union Station). 'New' Chinatown is about a half-mile north along Broadway and Hill St, crammed with dim sum parlors, herbal apothecaries, curio shops and edgy art galleries on Chung King Rd.

CIVIC CENTER & GRAND AVENUE CULTURAL CORRIDOR

North Grand Ave is anchored by the Music Center of Los Angeles County, which comprises the famous Dorothy Chandler Pavilion, Mark Taper Forum and Ahmanson Theater.

FREE Walt Disney Concert Hall CULTURAL BUILDING

(Map p892; www.laphil.com; 111 S Grand Ave) Architect Frank Gehry's now-iconic 2003 structure is a gravity-defying sculpture of curving and billowing stainless-steel walls. It is home base of the Los Angeles Philharmonic, now under the baton of Venezuelan phenom Gustavo Dudamel. Free tours are available subject to concert schedules, and walkways encircle the maze-like roof and exterior. Parking is $9.

MOCA Grand Avenue MUSEUM

(Map p892; www.moca.org; 250 S Grand Ave; adult/child $10/free, 5-8pm Thu free; ⏰11am-5pm Mon & Fri, to 8pm Thu, to 6pm Sat & Sun) Housed in a building by Arata Isozaki, which many consider his masterpiece, the Museum of Contemporary Art offers headline-grabbing special exhibits; its permanent collection presents heavy hitters from the 1940s to the present. Parking is $9, at Walt Disney Concert Hall. There are two other branches: the Geffen Contemporary at MOCA (Map p892) in Little Tokyo and at the Pacific Design Center in West Hollywood.

FREE Cathedral of Our Lady of the Angels CHURCH
(Map p892; www.olacathedral.org; 555 W Temple St; ⌚6:30am-6pm Mon-Fri, from 9am Sat, 7am-6pm Sun) Architect José Rafael Moneo mixed Gothic proportions with bold contemporary design for the main church of LA's Catholic Archdiocese. Built in 2002 it teems with art, and soft light through alabaster panes lends serenity. Tours (1pm Monday to Friday) and recitals (12:45pm Wednesday) are both free and popular. Unless you're coming for Mass, weekday parking is expensive – $4 per 15 minutes ($18 maximum) until 4pm, $5 on Saturday.

FREE City Hall LANDMARK
(Map p892; www.lacity.org; 200 N Spring St; ⌚8am-5pm Mon-Fri) Until 1966 no LA building stood taller than City Hall. The 1928 building, with its ziggurat-shaped top, has cameoed in the *Superman* and *Dragnet* TV series and the 1953 sci-fi thriller *War of the Worlds*. There are some cool views of Downtown and the mountains from the observation deck. Tours are available by reservation, seven days in advance.

LITTLE TOKYO

Little Tokyo swirls with shopping malls, Buddhist temples, public art, traditional gardens, authentic sushi bars and *izakaya* (pubs), some of LA's hippest new restaurants and a branch of MOCA, Geffen Contemporary, at 152 N Central Ave.

Japanese American National Museum MUSEUM
(Map p892; www.janm.org; 369 E 1st St; adult/child $9/5; ⌚11am-5pm Tue, Wed & Fri-Sun, to 8pm Thu) Get an in-depth look at the Japanese immigrant experience, including the painful chapter of the WWII internment camps.

SOUTH PARK

The southwestern corner of Downtown, South Park isn't a park but an emerging neighborhood, including Staples Center arena, LA Convention Center, and the dining and entertainment hub **LA Live** (Map p892), which includes a dozen restaurants, live music venues, a 54-story hotel tower and the Nokia Theatre, which is home to the MTV Music Awards and *American Idol* finals.

Parking is in private lots ($8 to $20). South Park is near the Blue Line light-rail.

Grammy Museum MUSEUM
(Map p892; www.grammymuseum.org; 800 W Olympic Blvd; adult/child $12.95/10.95; ⌚11:30am-7:30pm Mon-Fri, from 10am Sat & Sun) Opened in 2008, with mind-expanding interactive displays of the history of American music and plenty of listening opportunities.

EXPOSITION PARK & AROUND

Just south of Downtown LA, this neighborhood has a full day's worth of kid-friendly museums, historic sports facilities and green spaces. Landmarks include the **Rose Garden** (admission free; ⌚9am-dusk mid-Mar–Dec) and the 1923 **Los Angeles Memorial Coliseum**, site of the 1932 and 1984 Summer Olympic Games.

Natural History Museum MUSEUM
(www.nhm.org; 900 Exposition Blvd; adult/child $12/5; ⌚9:30am-5pm) Dinos to diamonds, bears to beetles, hissing roaches to an ultra-rare megamouth shark – the old-school museum will take you around the world and back millions of years in time. Kids love digging for fossils in the Discovery Center and making friends with creepy crawlies in the Insect Zoo.

FREE California Science Center MUSEUM
(www.californiasciencecenter.org; 700 State Dr; ⌚10am-5pm) A simulated earthquake, hatching baby chicks and a giant techno-doll named Tess bring out the kid in all of us at this great hands-on science museum. As we went to press, the museum was preparing to become the permanent home of the Space Shuttle *Endeavour*. The **IMAX** (☎213-744-7400; adult/child $8.25/5) theater caps off an action-filled day.

FREE California African American Museum MUSEUM
(www.caamuseum.org; 600 State Dr; ⌚10am-5pm Tue-Sat, from 11am Sun) A more grown-up attraction, this museum is a handsome showcase of African American art, culture and history.

Downtown Los Angeles

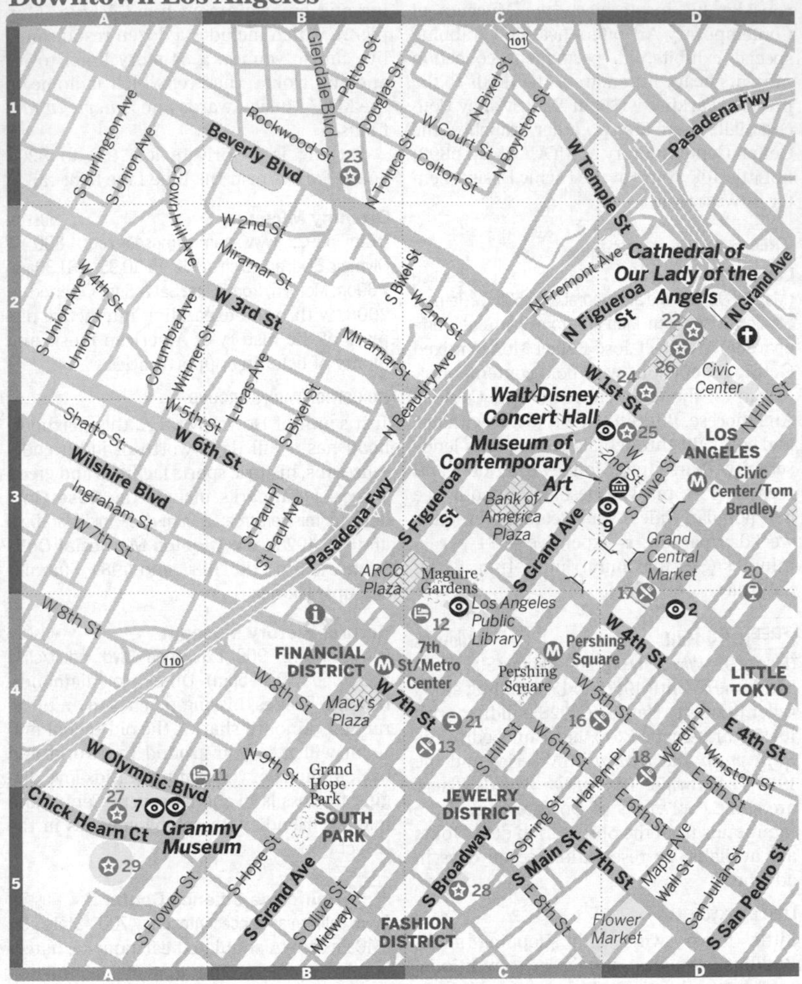

Watts Towers MONUMENT

(www.wattstowers.org; 1727 E 107th St; tours adult/child $7/free; ⌚art center 10am-4pm Wed-Sat, from noon Sun, tours every 30min 11am-3pm Thu & Fri, from 10:30am Sat, from 12:30pm Sun Oct-Jun, from 10:30am Thu-Sat, from 12:30pm Sun Jul-Sep; P) The area south of Exposition Park, known as South Los Angeles, is no stranger to poverty and crime. But one good reason to venture here is the world-famous Watts Towers, a huge and fantastical free-form sculpture cobbled together from found objects – from green 7-Up bottles to seashells and pottery shards – by artist Simon Rodía. Admission is by tour only.

HOLLYWOOD

Just as aging movie stars get the occasional facelift, so has central Hollywood. While it still hasn't recaptured its Golden Age glamour of the 1920s and '40s, much of its late-20th-century seediness is gone.

The Metro Red Line stops beneath Hollywood & Highland, a multistory mall with nicely framed views of the **Hollywood Sign** 2.5 miles away, erected in 1923 as an advertisement for a land development called Hol-

lywoodland. Validated parking here costs $2 for four hours.

Grauman's Chinese Theatre CINEMA
(Map p896; 6925 Hollywood Blvd) Even the most jaded visitor may thrill in the Chinese's famous forecourt, where generations of screen legends have left their imprints in cement: feet, hands, dreadlocks (Whoopi Goldberg), and even magic wands (the young stars of the *Harry Potter* films). Actors dressed as Superman, Marilyn Monroe and the like pose for photos (for tips), and you may be offered free tickets to TV shows.

The theater is on the **Hollywood Walk of Fame**, which honors over 2000 celebrities with stars embedded in the sidewalk. Other historic theaters include the flashy **El Capitan Theater** (Map p896; 6838 Hollywood Blvd) and the 1922 **Egyptian Theater** (Map p896; ☎323-466-3456; www.americancinematheque.com; 6712 Hollywood Blvd), home to American Cinematheque, which presents arty retros and Q&As with directors, writers and actors.

Kodak Theatre THEATER
(Map p896; www.kodaktheatre.com; adult/child $15/10; ⏰10:30am-4pm) Real-life celebs sashay along the Kodak's red carpet for the Academy Awards – columns with names of Oscar-winning films line the entryway. Pricey 30-minute tours take you inside the auditorium, VIP room and past an actual Oscar statuette. Cirque du Soleil presents **Iris** (www.cirquedusoleil.com; tickets $43-253) here, a new film-themed show.

Hollywood Museum MUSEUM
(Map p896; www.thehollywoodmuseum.com; 1660 N Highland Ave; adult/child $15/5; ⏰10am-5pm Wed-Sun) The slightly musty museum is a 35,000-sq-ft shrine to the stars, crammed with kitsch, costumes, knickknacks and props from Charlie Chaplin to *Glee*.

GRIFFITH PARK, SILVER LAKE & LOS FELIZ

FREE **Griffith Park** PARK
(Map p888; www.laparks.org/dos/parks/griffithpk; ⏰6am-10pm, trails close at dusk; P) America's largest urban park is five times the size of New York's Central Park. It embraces an outdoor theater, zoo, observatory, museum, antique trains, golf, tennis, playgrounds, bridle paths, 53 miles of hiking trails, Batman's caves and the Hollywood Sign. The **Ranger Station** (4730 Crystal Springs Dr) has maps.

Griffith Observatory OBSERVATORY, PLANETARIUM
(www.griffithobservatory.org; 2800 Observatory Rd; observatory free, planetarium shows adult/child $7/3; ⏰noon-10pm Tue-Fri, from 10am Sat & Sun, closed occasional Tue; P) Above Los Feliz loom the iconic triple domes of this 1935 observatory, which boasts a super-techie planetarium and films in the Leonard Nimoy Event Horizon Theater. During clear nighttime skies, you can often peer through the telescopes at heavenly bodies.

Los Angeles Zoo ZOO
(www.lazoo.org; 5333 Zoo Dr; adult/child $14/9; ⏰10am-5pm; P) Make friends with 1100

Downtown Los Angeles

Top Sights

Cathedral of Our Lady of the Angels ... D2
El Pueblo de Los Angeles ... E2
Grammy Museum ... A5
Museum of Contemporary Art ... D3
Walt Disney Concert Hall ... D3

Sights

1 Avila Adobe ... E2
2 Bradbury Building ... D4
3 Chinese American Museum ... E3
4 City Hall ... E3
5 Geffen Contemporary at MOCA ... E4
6 Japanese American National Museum ... E4
7 LA Live ... A5
8 La Plaza de Cultura y Artes ... E2
9 MOCA Grand Avenue ... D3
10 Union Station ... F3

Sleeping

11 Figueroa Hotel ... A4
12 Standard Downtown LA ... C4

Eating

13 Bottega Louie ... C4
14 Daikokuya ... E4
15 Empress Pavilion ... E1
16 Gorbals ... C4
17 Grand Central Market ... D4
18 Nickel Diner ... D4
19 Philippe the Original ... E2

Drinking

20 Edison ... D4
Rooftop Lounge@Standard Downtown LA ... (see 12)
21 Seven Grand ... C4

Entertainment

22 Ahmanson Theatre ... D2
23 Bob Baker Marionette Theater ... B1
24 Los Angeles Opera ... D2
25 Los Angeles Philharmonic ... D3
26 Mark Taper Forum ... D2
27 Nokia Theatre ... A5
28 Orpheum Theater ... C5
29 Staples Center ... A5

Shopping

30 Tokyo ... E4

finned, feathered and furry creatures, including in the Campo Gorilla Reserve and the Sea Cliffs, which replicate the California coast complete with harbor seals.

Museum of the American West MUSEUM
(www.autrynationalcenter.org; 4700 Western Heritage Way; adult/child $10/4, free 2nd Tue each month; ⏲10am-4pm Tue-Fri, to 5pm Sat & Sun; P) Exhibits on the good, the bad and the ugly of America's westward expansion rope in even the most reluctant of cowpokes. Star exhibits include an original stagecoach, a Colt firearms collection and a nymph-festooned saloon.

WEST HOLLYWOOD

Rainbow flags fly proudly over Santa Monica Blvd. Celebs keep gossip rags happy by misbehaving at clubs on the fabled Sunset Strip. Welcome to the city of West Hollywood (WeHo), 1.9 sq miles of pure personality.

Boutiques on Robertson Blvd and Melrose Ave purvey the sassy and chic for Hollywood royalty, Santa Monica Blvd is gay central, and Sunset Blvd bursts with clubs, chichi hotels and views across LA. WeHo's also a hotbed of cutting-edge interior design, particularly along the **Avenues of Art and Design** around Beverly Blvd and Melrose Ave.

Pacific Design Center MUSEUM
(PDC; Map p900; www.pacificdesigncenter.com; 8687 Melrose Ave; 9am-5pm Mon-Fri) Some 130 galleries fill the monolithic blue and green 'whales' of the Cesar Pelli–designed Pacific Design Center (a red whale was also under construction as we went to press), including a branch of **MOCA** (www.moca.org; admission free). Visitors are welcome to window-shop, though most sales are to the trade. Parking is $6 per hour.

Schindler House HOUSE
(Map p900; www.makcenter.org; 835 N Kings Rd; adult/child $7/6, 4-6pm Fri free; ⏲11am-6pm Wed-Sun) A point of pilgrimage, pioneering modernist architect Rudolph Schindler (1887–1953) made this building his home. It houses changing exhibits and lectures.

MID-CITY

Some of LA's best museums line Museum Row, a short stretch of Wilshire Blvd just east of Fairfax Ave.

Los Angeles County Museum of Art MUSEUM

(LACMA; Map p900; www.lacma.org; 5905 Wilshire Blvd; adult/child under 17yr $15/free; ⏲noon-8pm Mon, Tue & Thu, to 9pm Fri, 11am-8pm Sat & Sun) One of the country's top art museums and the largest in the western USA. The collection in the Renzo Piano–designed **Broad Contemporary Art Museum** (B-CAM) includes seminal pieces by Jeff Koons, Roy Lichtenstein and Andy Warhol, and two gigantic works in rusted steel by Richard Serra.

Other LACMA pavilions brim with paintings, sculpture and decorative arts: Rembrandt, Cézanne and Magritte; ancient pottery from China, Turkey and Iran; photographs by Ansel Adams and Henri Cartier-Bresson; and a jewel box of a Japanese pavilion. There are often headline-grabbing touring exhibits. Parking is $10.

Petersen Automotive Museum MUSEUM

(Map p900; www.petersen.org; 6060 Wilshire Blvd; adult/child $10/3; ⏲10am-6pm Tue-Sun) A four-story ode to the auto, the museum exhibits shiny vintage cars galore, plus a fun LA streetscape showing how the city's growth has been shaped by the automobile. Parking is $8.

La Brea Tar Pits ARCHAEOLOGICAL SITE

(Map p900) Between 10,000 and 40,000 years ago, tarlike bubbling crude oil trapped saber-toothed cats, mammoths and other extinct ice-age critters, which are still being excavated at the La Brea Tar Pits. Check out their fossilized remains at the **Page Museum** (Map p900; www.tarpits.org; 5801 Wilshire Blvd; adult/child $11/5, 1st Tue each month free; ⏲9:30am-5pm). New fossils are being discovered all the time, and an active staff of archaeologists works behind glass. Parking is $7.

BEVERLY HILLS

The mere mention of Beverly Hills conjures images of Maseratis, manicured mansions and megarich moguls. Stylish and sophisticated, this is a haven for the well-heeled and famous. Stargazers could take a guided bus tour to scout for stars' homes.

No trip to LA would be complete without a saunter along pricey, pretentious **Rodeo Drive**, the famous three-block ribbon of style. Here sample-size fembots browse for fashions from international houses – from Armani to Zegna – in killer-design stores. If the prices make you gasp, Beverly Dr, one block east has more budget-friendly boutiques.

Municipal lots and garages offer two hours of free parking in central Beverly Hills.

Paley Center for Media BROADCASTING MUSEUM

(Map p900; www.paleycenter.org; 465 N Beverly Dr; suggested donation adult/child $10/5; ⏲noon-5pm Wed-Sun) TV and radio addicts can indulge their passion at this mind-boggling archive of TV and radio broadcasts from 1918 through the internet age. Pick your faves, grab a seat at a private console and enjoy. There's an active program of lectures and screenings.

WESTWOOD & AROUND

University of California, Los Angeles UNIVERSITY

Westwood is dominated by the vast campus of the prestigious University of California, Los Angeles (UCLA). The excellent, university-run **Hammer Museum** (www.hammer.ucla.edu; 10899 Wilshire Blvd; adult/child $10/free, Thu free; ⏲11am-7pm Tue, Wed, Fri & Sat, to 9pm Thu, to 5pm Sun) has cutting-edge contemporary art exhibits. Hammer parking is $3.

HIGHLIGHTS OF HISTORIC DOWNTOWN

Pershing Square, the center of Downtown's historic district, was LA's first public park (1866) and has been modernized many times since. Now encircled by high-rises, there's public art and summer concerts.

Nearby, some turn-of-the-last century architecture remains as it once was. Latino-flavored Broadway has the 1893 **Bradbury Building** (Map p892; 304 S Broadway; ⏲9am-6pm Mon-Fri, to 5pm Sat & Sun), whose dazzling galleried atrium featured prominently in *Blade Runner*.

In the early 20th century, Broadway was a glamorous shopping and theater strip, where megastars such as Charlie Chaplin leapt from limos to attend premieres at lavish movie palaces. Some – such as the **Orpheum Theater** (Map p892; 842 Broadway) – have been restored and once again host screenings and parties. The best way to get inside is on tours run by the **Los Angeles Conservancy** (☎213-623-2489; www.laconservancy.org; tours $10).

Hollywood

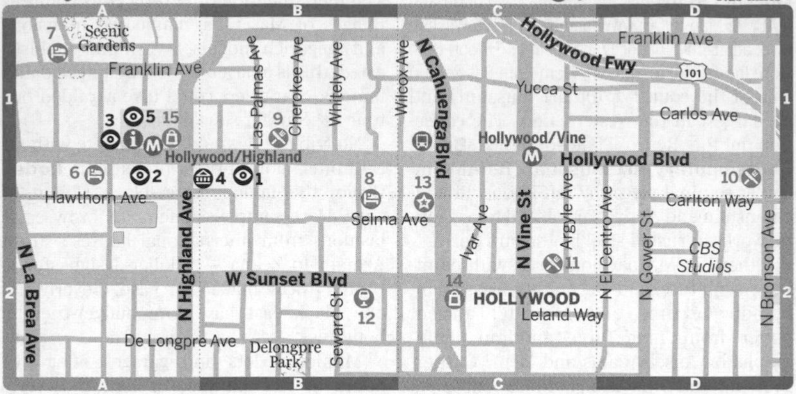

Hollywood

Sights

1 Egyptian Theatre B1
2 El Capitan Theatre A1
3 Grauman's Chinese Theatre A1
4 Hollywood Museum B1
5 Kodak Theatre A1

Sleeping

6 Hollywood Roosevelt Hotel A1
7 Magic Castle Hotel A1
8 USA Hostels Hollywood B2

Eating

9 Musso & Frank Grill B1
10 Palms Thai D1
11 Waffle C2

Drinking

12 Cat & Fiddle B2

Entertainment

13 Hotel Cafe C2

Shopping

14 Amoeba Music C2
15 Hollywood & Highland A1

FREE **Annenberg Space for Photography** MUSEUM
(www.annenbergspaceforphotography.org; 2000 Ave of the Stars, No 10; ⏲11am-6pm Wed-Sun) This fine, camera-shaped museum is just east of Westwood, in the skyscraper village known as Century City. Parking is $3.50 from Wednesday to Friday, $1 on Saturday and Sunday or after 4:30pm daily.

FREE **Getty Center** MUSEUM
(Map p888; www.getty.edu; 1200 Getty Center Dr; ⏲10am-5:30pm Sun & Tue-Thu, to 9pm Fri & Sat) Triple delights: a stellar art collection, Richard Meier's fabulous architecture and Robert Irwin's ever-changing gardens. On clear days, add breathtaking views of the city and ocean to the list. Visit in the late afternoon after the crowds have thinned. Parking is $15.

Museum of Tolerance MUSEUM
(www.museumoftolerance.com; 9786 W Pico Blvd; adult/child $15/11; ⏲10am-5pm Mon-Thu, to 3:30pm Fri, 11am-5pm Sun; P) This museum uses interactive technology to make visitors confront racism and bigotry. There's a particular focus on the Holocaust, including Nazi-era artifacts and letters by Anne Frank. A history wall celebrates diversity, exposes intolerance and champions rights in America. Reservations recommended.

FREE **Westwood Village Memorial Park** CEMETERY
(1218 Glendon Ave; ⏲8am-5pm) Tucked among Westwood's high-rises, this postage-stamp-sized park is packed with such famous 6ft-under residents as Marilyn Monroe, Burt Lancaster and Rodney Dangerfield.

MALIBU

Hugging 27 spectacular miles of Pacific Coast Hwy, Malibu has long been synonymous with surfing, stars and a hedonistic lifestyle, but it actually looks far less posh than the glossy mags make it sound. Still, it's been celebrity central since the 1930s. Leo, Brangelina, Streisand and other A-listers have homes here, and can often be spotted shopping at the villagelike **Malibu Country Mart** (3835 Cross Creek Rd; P) and the more utilitarian **Malibu Colony Plaza** (23841 W Malibu Rd; P).

Malibu's twin natural treasures are the Santa Monica Mountains National Recreation Area and its beaches, including the aptly named **Surfrider**.

FREE **Getty Villa** MUSEUM

(www.getty.edu; 17985 Pacific Coast Hwy; ⏲10am-5pm Wed-Mon; P) Malibu's cultural star, a replica Roman villa that's a fantastic showcase of Greek, Roman and Etruscan antiquities. Admission is by timed ticket (no walk-ins). Parking is $15.

SANTA MONICA

Santa Monica is the belle by the beach, mixing urban cool with a laid-back vibe. Tourists, teens and street performers make car-free, chain-store-lined **Third Street Promenade** the most action-packed zone. There's free two-hour parking in public garages on 2nd and 4th Sts ($3 after 6pm).

For more local flavor, shop celeb-favored **Montana Avenue** or down-homey **Main Street**, backbone of the neighborhood once nicknamed 'Dogtown' as the birthplace of skateboard culture.

Santa Monica Pier AMUSEMENT PARK

(Map p904) Kids love the venerable pier, where attractions include a quaint carousel, a solar-powered Ferris wheel and tiny aquarium with touch tanks.

Bergamot Station Arts Center MUSEUM

(2525 Michigan Ave; ⏲10am-6pm Tue-Sat; P) Art fans gravitate inland toward this avant-garde center, a former trolley stop that now houses 35 galleries and the progressive **Santa Monica Museum of Art** (www.smmoa.org; 2525 Michigan Ave; suggested donation $5; ⏲11am-6pm Tue-Sat).

VENICE

The **Venice Boardwalk** (Ocean Front Walk) is a freak show, a human zoo, a wacky carnival and an essential LA experience. This cauldron of counterculture is the place to get your hair braided or a *qi gong* back massage, or pick up cheap sunglasses or a woven bracelet. Encounters with bodybuilders, hoop dreamers, a Speedo-clad snake charmer or a roller-skating Sikh minstrel are pretty much guaranteed, especially on hot summer afternoons. Alas, the vibe gets a bit creepy after dark.

To escape the hubbub, meander inland to the **Venice Canals**, a vestige of Venice's early days when gondoliers poled visitors along quiet man-made waterways. Today ducks preen and locals lollygag in rowboats in this serene, flower-festooned neighborhood.

The hippest Westside strip is funky, sophisticated **Abbot Kinney Boulevard**, a palm-lined mile of restaurants, yoga studios, art galleries and eclectic shops selling mid-century furniture and handmade fashions.

There's street parking around Abbot Kinney, and parking lots ($6 to $15) on the beach.

LONG BEACH

The port of Los Angeles and Long Beach dominate LA County's southern flank, the world's third-busiest container port after Singapore and Hong Kong. But Long Beach's industrial edge has worn smooth in its humming downtown and restyled

TOURING THE STUDIOS

Half the fun of visiting Hollywood is hoping you'll see stars. Up the odds by being part of the studio audience of a sitcom or game show, which usually tape between August and March. For free tickets, contact **Audiences Unlimited** (☎818-260-0041; www.tvtickets.com).

For an authentic behind-the-scenes look, take a small-group tour by open-sided shuttle at **Paramount Pictures** (☎323-956-1777; www.paramount.com; 5555 Melrose Ave, Hollywood; tours $40, minimum age 12yr; ⏲10am-2pm Mon-Fri) or **Warner Bros Studios** (☎818-972-8687; www.wbstudiotour.com; 3400 Riverside Dr, Burbank, San Fernando Valley; tours $45, minimum age 8yr; ⏲8:30am-4pm Mon-Fri; P), or a walking tour of **Sony Pictures Studios** (☎310-244-8687; 10202 W Washington Blvd, Culver City; tours $33, minimum age 12yr; ⏲tours 9:30am, 10:30am, 12:30pm, 1:30pm & 2:30pm Mon-Fri; P). All of these tours show you around sound stages and backlots (outdoor sets), and into such departments as wardrobe and make-up. Reservations are required; bring photo ID.

waterfront. Pine Ave is chockablock with restaurants and clubs popular with everyone from coiffed conventioneers to the testosterone-fuelled frat pack.

The Blue Line (55 minutes) connects Long Beach with Downtown LA, and **Passport** (www.lbtransit.org) minibuses shuttle you around the major sights for free ($1.25 elsewhere in town).

Queen Mary OCEAN LINER
(www.queenmary.com; 1126 Queens Hwy; adult/child from $25/13; ⌚10am-6pm) Long Beach's 'flagship' is the grand (and supposedly haunted!) British ocean liner, which is permanently moored here. Larger and fancier than the *Titanic*, it transported royals, dignitaries, immigrants and troops during its 1001 Atlantic crossings between 1936 and 1964. Parking is $12.

Aquarium of the Pacific AQUARIUM
(www.aquariumofpacific.org; 100 Aquarium Way; adult/child $25/13; ⌚9am-6pm) Children will probably have a better time here, providing a high-tech romp through an underwater world in which sharks dart, jellyfish dance and sea lions frolic. Imagine the thrill of petting a shark! Parking is $8 to $15. *Queen Mary*/Aquarium combination tickets cost adult/child aged three to 11 years $36/20.

Museum of Latin American Art MUSEUM
(www.molaa.org; 628 Alamitos Ave; adult/child $9/free, Sun free; ⌚11am-5pm Wed-Sun; P) One of California's best, as it is the only museum in the western USA specializing in contemporary art from south of the border. The permanent collection highlights spirituality and landscapes, and special exhibits are first-rate.

PASADENA

Resting below the lofty San Gabriel Mountains, this city of 147,000 drips wealth and gentility, and feels a world apart from urban LA. It's famous for art museums, fine arts-and-crafts architecture and the Rose Parade on New Year's Day.

The main fun zone is **Old Town Pasadena** (Map p888), along Colorado Blvd and between Pasadena Ave and Arroyo Pkwy. Metro Gold Line trains connect Pasadena and Downtown LA.

Norton Simon Museum MUSEUM
(www.nortonsimon.org; 411 W Colorado Blvd; adult/child $10/free; ⌚noon-6pm Wed-Thu & Sat-Mon, to 9pm Fri; P) Stroll west and you'll see Rodin's *The Thinker*, a mere overture to the full symphony of European art at this museum. Don't skip the basement, with fabulous Indian and Southeast Asian sculpture.

Gamble House ARCHITECTURE
(www.gamblehouse.org; 4 Westmoreland Pl; adult/child $10/free; ⌚admission by tour only noon-3pm Thu-Sun; P) A masterpiece of California arts-and-crafts architecture, the 1908 Gamble House by Charles and Henry Greene was Doc Brown's home in the movie *Back to the Future*. Admission is by one-hour guided tour.

WORTH A TRIP

UNIVERSAL STUDIOS HOLLYWOOD

Universal Studios (Map p888; www.universalstudioshollywood.com; 100 Universal City Plaza; admission over/under 48in $77/69) first opened to the public in 1915, when studio head Carl Laemmle invited visitors at a quaint 25¢ each (including a boxed lunch) to watch silent films being made. Nearly a century later, Universal remains one of the world's largest movie studios.

Your chances of seeing an actual movie shoot are approximately nil at Universal's current theme park incarnation, yet generations of visitors have had a ball here. Start with the 45-minute narrated studio tour aboard a giant, multicar tram that takes you past working soundstages and outdoor sets like *Desperate Housewives*. Also prepare to survive a shark attack à la *Jaws* and an 8.3-magnitude earthquake. It's hokey but fun.

Among the dozens of other attractions, the **Simpsons Ride** is a motion-simulated romp 'designed' by Krusty the Clown, and you can splash down among the dinos of **Jurassic Park**, while **Special Effects Stages** illuminate the craft of movie-making. **Water World** may have bombed as a movie, but the live action show based on it is a runaway hit, with stunts including giant fireballs and a crash-landing seaplane.

Parking is $12, or arrive via Metro Red Line.

Huntington Library MUSEUM, GARDENS
(Map p888; www.huntington.org; 1151 Oxford Rd; adult/child Tue-Fri $15/6, Sat, Sun & holidays $20/6, 1st Thu each month free; ⏲10:30am-4:30pm Tue-Sun Jun-Aug, Sat & Sun Sep-May, noon-4:30pm Tue-Fri Sep-May; P) LA's biggest understatement does have a library of rare books, including a Gutenberg Bible, but it's the collection of great British and French art and exquisite gardens that make it special. The Rose Garden boasts more than 1200 varieties (and a lovely tearoom; reserve ahead, adult/child $28/15), the Desert Garden has a Seussian quality, and the Chinese garden has a small lake crossed by a stone bridge.

Activities

Bicycling & In-line Skating

Get a scenic exercise kick skating or riding along the paved **South Bay Bicycle Trail** (Map p888), which parallels the beach for most of the 22 miles between Pacific Palisades and Torrance. Rental outfits are plentiful in beach towns. Warning: crowded on weekends.

Hiking

Turn on your celeb radar while strutting it with the hot bods along **Runyon Canyon Park** above Hollywood. **Griffith Park** (Map p888) is also laced with trails. For longer rambles, head to the Santa Monica Mountains, where **Will Rogers State Historic Park**, **Topanga State Park** and **Malibu Creek State Park** (Map p888) are all excellent gateways to beautiful terrain. Parking costs $10 to $12.

Swimming & Surfing

Top beaches for swimming are Malibu's **Zuma**, **Santa Monica State Beach** (Map p904) and **Hermosa Beach** (Map p888). **Surfrider Beach** in Malibu is a legendary surfing spot.

'Endless Summer' is, sorry to report, a myth, so much of the year you'll want to wear a wet suit in the Pacific. Water temperatures become tolerable by June and peak at about 70°F (21°C) in August and September. Water quality varies; check the 'Beach Report Card' at www.healthebay.org.

Los Angeles for Children

Keeping the rug rats happy is child's play in LA. The sprawling Los Angeles Zoo in family-friendly Griffith Park is a sure bet. Dino-fans dig the Page Museum at La Brea Tar Pits and the Natural History Museum, while budding scientists love the California Science Center next door. For live sea creatures, head to the Aquarium of the Pacific; teens might get a kick out of the ghost tours of the *Queen Mary*.

Among LA's amusement parks, Santa Monica Pier is meant for kids of all ages. Activities for younger children are more limited at Universal Studios Hollywood. See also Disneyland and Knott's Berry Farm.

TOP CHOICE **Noah's Ark at Skirball Cultural Center** PLAYGROUND
(☎tickets 877-722-4849; www.skirball.org; 2701 N Sepulveda Blvd; adult/under 12yr $10/5, Thu free; ⏲noon-5pm Tue-Fri, from 10am Sat & Sun; P) This indoor playground of imaginative creatures made from car mats, couch springs, metal strainers and other recycled items is great for those rare days when the weather doesn't cooperate.

Kidspace MUSEUM
(www.kidspacemuseum.org; 480 N Arroyo Blvd, Pasadena; admission $8, ⏲9:30am-5pm Mon-Fri, from 10am Sat & Sun; P) Hands-on exhibits, outdoor learning areas and gardens lure the single-digit set. It's best after 1pm, when the field-trip crowd has left.

Bob Baker Marionette Theater THEATER
(www.bobbakermarionettes.com; 1345 W 1st St; admission $15, reservations required; ⏲10:30am Tue-Fri, 2:30pm Sat & Sun; P) Adorable singing and dancing marionettes have enthralled generations of wee Angelenos.

Tours

Esotouric HISTORY, LITERATURE
(☎323-223-2767; www.esotouric.com; bus tours $58) Hip, offbeat, insightful and entertaining walking and bus tours themed around famous crime sites (Black Dahlia), literary lions (Chandler to Bukowski) and historical neighborhoods.

Los Angeles Conservancy ARCHITECTURE
(☎213-623-2489; www.laconservancy.org; tours $10) Thematic walking tours, mostly of Downtown LA, with an architectural focus. Check the website for self-guided tours.

Melting Pot Tours CULINARY, WALKING
(☎800-979-3370; www.meltingpottours.com; tours from $58; ⏲Wed-Sun) Snack your way through the Original Farmers Market and the aromatic alleyways of Old Town Pasadena.

Beverly Hills, West Hollywood & Mid-City

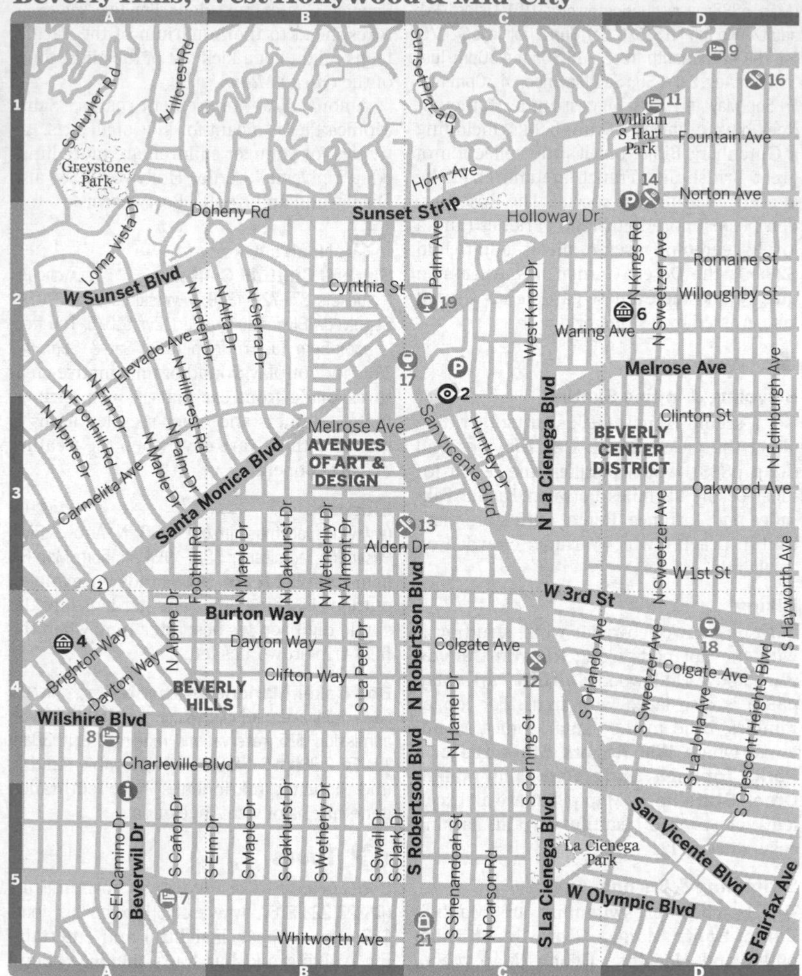

Six Taste CULINARY, WALKING
(☎888-313-0936; www.sixtaste.com; tours $55-65) Walking tours of restaurants in LA neighborhoods including Downtown, Little Tokyo, Chinatown, Thai Town and Santa Monica.

Out & About GAY
(www.outandabout-tours.com; tours $60; ⏲Sat & Sun) Enthusiastic guides show landmarks of LA's gay and lesbian history; there's a lot more than you think!

Red Line Tours WALKING, BUS
(☎323-402-1074; www.redlinetours.com; tours from $25) 'Edutaining' walking tours of Hollywood and Downtown using headsets that cut out traffic noise.

Starline Tours BUS
(☎323-463-333; www.starlinetours.com; tours from $39) Narrated bus tours of the city, stars' homes and theme parks.

Festivals & Events

In addition to the following annual events, monthly street fairs include the gallery and shop open houses and food truck meet-ups of **Downtown LA Art Walk** (www.downtownartwalk.com; ⏲2nd Thu each month) and **First**

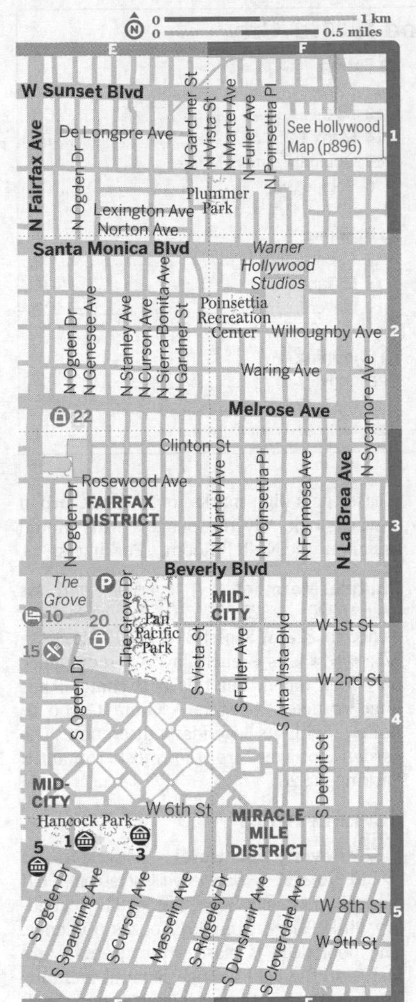

Fridays (1st Fri each month) on Abbot Kinney Blvd in Venice.

Tournament of Roses PARADE
(626-449-4100; www.tournamentofroses.com) New Year's Day cavalcade of flower-festooned floats along Pasadena's Colorado Blvd, followed by the Rose Bowl football game.

Toyota Grand Prix of Long Beach AUTO RACE
(888-827-7333; www.longbeachgp.com) Week-long auto-racing spectacle in mid-April drawing world-class drivers.

Fiesta Broadway STREET FAIR
(310-914-0015; www.fiesta broadway.la) Mexican-themed fair along historic Broadway in Downtown, with performances by Latino stars. Last Sunday in April.

Sunset Junction STREET FAIR
(323-661-7771; www.sunsetjunction.org) Silver Lake weekend street party with grub, libations and edgy bands in late August.

West Hollywood Halloween Carnival STREET FAIR
(323-848-6400; www.visitwesthollywood.com) Eccentric, and often NC17-rated, costumes fill Santa Monica Blvd, on October 31.

Sleeping

For seaside life, base yourself in Santa Monica, Venice or Long Beach. Cool-hunters and party people will be happiest in Hollywood or WeHo; culture-vultures, in Downtown. Expect a lodging tax of 12% to 14%; always inquire about discounts.

DOWNTOWN

TOP CHOICE **Standard Downtown LA** HOTEL $$
(Map p892; 213-892-8080; www.standardhotel.com; 550 S Flower St; r from $165;) This 207-room design-savvy hotel in a former office building goes for a young, hip and shag-happy crowd – the rooftop bar fairly pulses – so don't come here with kids or to get a solid night's sleep. Mod, minimalist rooms have platform beds and peek-through showers. Parking is $33.

Figueroa Hotel HISTORIC HOTEL $$
(Map p892; 213-627-8971; www.figueroahotel.com; 939 S Figueroa St; r $148-184, ste $225-265;) A rambling 1920s oasis across from LA Live, the Fig welcomes guests with a richly tiled Spanish-style lobby that segues to a sparkling pool and buzzy outdoor bar. Rooms are furnished in a world-beat mash-up of styles (Morocco, Mexico, Zen…), comfy but varying in size and configuration. Parking is $12.

HOLLYWOOD

Hollywood Roosevelt Hotel HOTEL $$$
(Map p896; 323-466-7000; www.hollywoodroosevelt.com; 7000 Hollywood Blvd; r from $269;) This venerable hotel has hosted elite players since the first Academy Awards were held here in 1929. It pairs a palatial Spanish lobby with sleek Asian contemporary rooms, a busy pool scene and rockin' restos. Parking is $33.

Beverly Hills, West Hollywood & Mid-City

Sights

La Brea Tar Pits .... (see 3)
1 Los Angeles County Museum of Art E5
2 Pacific Design Center C2
3 Page Museum E5
4 Paley Center for Media A4
5 Petersen Automotive Museum E5
6 Schindler House D2

Sleeping

7 Avalon Hotel A5
8 Beverly Wilshire A4
9 Chateau Marmont D1
10 Farmer's Daughter Hotel E3
11 Standard Hollywood D1

Eating

12 Bazaar C4
13 Ivy C3
14 Marix Tex Mex D1
15 Original Farmers Market E4
16 Veggie Grill D1

Drinking

17 Abbey C2
18 El Carmen D4
19 Eleven C2

Shopping

20 Grove E4
21 It's a Wrap C5
22 Melrose Trading Post E2

Magic Castle Hotel APARTMENT $$$
(Map p896; ☎323-851-0800; www.magiccastlehotel.com; 7025 Franklin Ave; r $154-304;) Walls are thin, but this renovated former apartment building around a courtyard boasts contemporary furniture, attractive art, comfy bathrobes and fancy bath amenities. Most rooms have a separate living room. For breakfast: freshly baked goods and gourmet coffee on your balcony or poolside. Ask about access to the namesake private club for magicians. Parking is $10.

USA Hostels Hollywood HOSTEL $
(Map p896; ☎323-462-3777; www.usahostels.com; 1624 Schrader Blvd; incl breakfast & tax dm $30-40, r $70-85;) Not for introverts, this energetic hostel puts you within steps of Hollywood's party circuit. Make new friends during staff-organized BBQs, comedy nights and tours, or during free pancake breakfast in the guest kitchen.

WEST HOLLYWOOD & MID-CITY

Standard Hollywood HOTEL $$$
(Map p900; ☎323-650-9090; www.standardhotel.com; 8300 W Sunset Blvd; r $165-250, ste from $350;) This white-on-white property on the Sunset Strip is a scene, with Astroturf-fringed pool with a view across LA and sizable shagadelic rooms with silver beanbag chairs, orange-tiled bathrooms and Warhol poppy-print curtains. Parking is $29.

Farmer's Daughter Hotel MOTEL $$$
(Map p900; ☎323-937-3930; www.farmersdaughterhotel.com; 115 S Fairfax Ave; r $219-269;) Opposite the Original Farmers Market, Grove and CBS Studios, this perennial pleaser gets high marks for its sleek 'urban cowboy' look. Adventurous lovebirds should ask about the No Tell Room... Parking is $18.

Chateau Marmont HISTORIC HOTEL $$$
(Map p900; ☎323-656-1010; www.chateaumarmont.com; 8221 W Sunset Blvd; r $415, ste $500-875;) Its French-flavored indulgence may look dated, but this faux-chateau has long attracted A-listers – Greta Garbo to Bono – with its legendary discretion. The garden cottages are the most romantic. Parking is $28.

BEVERLY HILLS

TOP CHOICE **Beverly Hills Hotel** LUXURY HOTEL $$$
(☎310-276-2251; www.beverlyhillshotel.com; 9641 Sunset Blvd; r from $530;) The legendary Pink Palace from 1912 oozes opulence. The pool deck is classic, the grounds are lush, and the Polo Lounge remains a clubby lunch spot for the well-heeled and well-dressed. Rooms are comparably old-world, with gold accents and marble tile. Parking is $33.

Avalon Hotel HOTEL $$$
(Map p900; ☎310-277-5221; www.avalonbeverlyhills.com; 9400 W Olympic Blvd; r $228-370;) Midcentury modern gets a 21st-century spin at this fashion-crowd fave, Marilyn Monroe's old pad in its days as an apartment building. The beautiful, moneyed and metrosexual now vamp it up in the chic restaurant-bar overlooking a sexy hourglass-shaped pool. Rooms facing the other direction are quieter. Parking is $30.

Beverly Wilshire HOTEL $$$
(Map p900; ☎310-275-5200; www.fourseasons.com/beverlywilshire; 9500 Wilshire Blvd; r $495-545, ste $695-1795;) It has corked Rodeo Dr since 1928, yet amenities are very much up-to-the-minute, both in the original Italian Renaissance wing and in the newer addition. And yes, this is the very hotel from which Julia Roberts first stumbled then strutted in *Pretty Woman*. Parking costs $33.

SANTA MONICA & VENICE

Viceroy HOTEL $$$
(Map p904; ☎310-260-7500; www.viceroysantamonica.com; 1819 Ocean Ave, Santa Monica; r from $370;) Ignore the high-rise eyesore exterior and plunge headlong into *Top Design*'s Kelly Wearstler's campy 'Hollywood Regency' decor and color palette from dolphin gray to mamba green. Look for poolside cabanas, Italian designer linens, and chic bar and restaurant. Parking is $33.

Hotel Erwin HOTEL $$
(☎310-452-1111; www.jdvhotels.com; 1679 Pacific Ave, Venice; r from $169;) A worthy emblem of Venice. Rooms aren't the biggest and in most there's a low traffic hum, but you're steps from the beach and your room features graffiti- or anime-inspired art and an honor bar containing sunglasses and '70s-era soft drinks. The rooftop bar offers spellbinding coastal vistas. Parking is $28.

Embassy Hotel Apartments BOUTIQUE HOTEL $$$
(Map p904; ☎310-394-1279; www.embassyhotelapts.com; 1001 3rd St, Santa Monica; r $169-390;) This hushed 1927 Spanish-Colonial hideaway delivers charm by the bucket. A rickety elevator takes you to units oozing old-world flair and equipped with internet. Kitchens make many rooms well suited to do-it-yourselfers. No air con.

HI Los Angeles-Santa Monica HOSTEL $
(Map p904; ☎310-393-9913; www.lahostels.org; 1436 2nd St, Santa Monica; r $26-30;) Near the beach and Promenade, the location is the envy of much fancier places. Its 200 beds in single-sex dorms and bed-in-a-box doubles with shared bathrooms are clean and safe, and there are plenty of groovy public spaces to lounge and surf; party people are better off in Hollywood.

> **FUN FACT**
>
> At 10.2 million residents, if LA County were a state, it would be the eighth largest in population.

LONG BEACH

Queen Mary Hotel SHIP $$$
(☎562-435-3511; www.queenmary.com; 1126 Queens Hwy, Long Beach; r $110-395;) Take a trip without leaving the dock aboard this grand ocean liner. Staterooms brim with original art-deco details – avoid the cheapest ones that are on the inside. Rates include admission to guided tours. Parking is $12 to $15.

Hotel Varden BOUTIQUE HOTEL $$
(☎562-432-8950; www.thevardenhotel.com; 335 Pacific Ave; r from $109;) The designers clearly had a field day with their modernist renovation of the 35 diminutive rooms in this 1929 hotel: tiny desks, tiny sinks, lots of right angles, cushy beds, white, white and more white. Rates include simple continental breakfast and wine hour. It's a block from Pine Ave's restaurants and night spots. Parking is $10.

Eating

LA's culinary scene is one of the world's most vibrant and eclectic, from celebrity chefs whipping up farmers-market-fab to authentic international cooking.

DOWNTOWN

Downtown's restaurant scene has exploded. Great neighborhoods for browsing include 7th St east of Grand Ave, Little Tokyo (not just for Japanese cuisine anymore), LA Live (Map p892) and the food stalls of the **Grand Central Market** (Map p892; 317 S Broadway; 9am-6pm).

Bottega Louie ITALIAN $$
(Map p892; ☎213-802-1470; www.bottegalouie.com; 700 S Grand Ave; mains $11-18; 10:30am-11pm Mon Fri, Sat & Sun from 9am) The wide marble bar has become a magnet for the artsy loft set and office workers alike. The open-kitchen crew, in chef's whites, grills housemade sausage and wood-fires thin-crust pizzas in the white-on-white, big-as-a-gym dining room. Always busy, always buzzy.

Gorbals JEWISH $$
(Map p892; ☎213-488-3408; www.thegorbals.com; 501 S Spring St; small plates $8-17; 6pm-midnight Mon-Wed, to 2am Thu-Sat) *Top Chef* winner Ilan

Hall tweaks traditional Jewish comfort food: bacon-wrapped matzo balls, potato latkes with smoked applesauce, *gribenes* (fried chicken fat) served BLT style. It's hidden in the back of the Alexandria Hotel lobby.

Nickel Diner DINER **$$**
(Map p892; ☎213-623-8301; 524 S Main St; mains $8-14; ⏲8am-3:30pm Tue-Sun, 6-11pm Tue-Sat) In Downtown's boho historic district, this red vinyl joint feels like a throwback to the 1920s. Ingredients are 21st century, though: artichokes stuffed with quinoa salad, burgers piled with poblano chilies. Must-try dessert: maple-glazed bacon doughnut.

Santa Monica & Venice

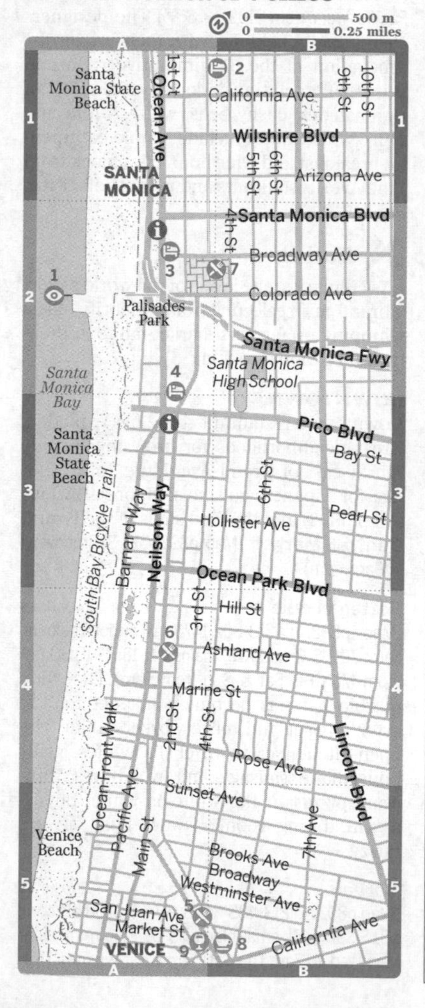

Philippe the Original DINER **$**
(Map p892; ☎213-628-3781; www.philippes.com; 1001 N Alameda St; sandwiches $6-7.50; ⏲6am-10pm; P) LAPD hunks, stressed-out attorneys and Midwestern vacationers all flock to this legendary 'home of the French dip sandwich,' dating back to 1908 at the edge of Chinatown. Order your choice of meat on a crusty roll dipped in *jus,* and hunker down at the tables on the sawdust-covered floor. Coffee is just 10¢ (no misprint). It accepts cash only.

HOLLYWOOD

Osteria Mozza & Pizzeria Mozza ITALIAN **$$$**
(☎323-297-0100; www.mozza-la.com; 6602 Melrose Ave, Mid-City; mains Osteria $17-29, Pizzeria $10-18; ⏲lunch & dinner) Reserve weeks ahead at LA's hottest Italian eatery, run by celebrity chefs Mario Batali and Nancy Silverton. Two restaurants share the same building: a wide-ranging menu at the Osteria, and precision-made pizzas baked before your eyes at the **Pizzeria** (☎323-297-0101, 641 N Highland Ave).

Musso & Frank Grill BAR & GRILL **$$$**
(Map p896; ☎323-467-7788; 6667 Hollywood Blvd; mains $12-35; ⏲11am-11pm Tue-Sat) Hollywood history hangs thickly in the air at the boulevard's oldest eatery. Waiters balance platters of steaks, chops, grilled liver and other dishes harking back to the days when cholesterol wasn't part of our vocabulary. Service is smooth, so are the martinis.

Waffle MODERN AMERICAN **$$**
(Map p896; ☎323-465-6901; 6255 W Sunset Blvd; mains $9-12; ⏲6:30am-2:30am Sun-Thu,

Santa Monica & Venice

Sights
1 Santa Monica Pier A2

Sleeping
2 Embassy Hotel Apartments B1
3 HI Los Angeles-Santa Monica A2
4 Viceroy A2

Eating
5 3 Square Café & Bakery A5
6 Library Alehouse A4
7 Santa Monica Place B2

Drinking
8 Intelligentsia B5
9 Roosterfish A5

EATING LA: ESSENTIAL ETHNIC NEIGHBORHOODS

Taking nothing away from LA's top-end eateries, some of the city's greatest food treasures are its ethnic restaurants. With some 140 nationalities in LA, we can just scratch the surface, but here are some of the most prominent neighborhoods for authentic cuisine and fun things to do nearby.

Little Tokyo

Daikokuya JAPANESE
(Map p892; ☎213-626-1680; 327 East 1st St; ⊙11am-2:30pm & 5pm-midnight Mon-Sat) In Downtown LA, the essential dish is a steaming bowl of ramen from Daikokuya. While you're there, shop for J-pop culture at **Tokyo** (Map p888; 114 Japanese Village Plaza).

Chinatown

Empress Pavilion CHINESE
(Map p892; ☎213-617-9898; 2nd fl, 988 N Hill St; dim sum per plate $2-6, most mains $10-25; ⊙10am-2:30pm & 5:30-9pm, to 10pm Sat & Sun) In Downtown LA, the essential dish is dim sum. While there, view contemporary art in galleries along Chung King Rd.

Boyle Heights

La Serenata de Garibaldi MEXICAN
(☎323-265-2887; 1842 E 1st St; mains $10-25; ⊙11:30am-10:30pm Mon-Fri, from 9am Sat & Sun) In east LA, the essential dish in this Mexican neighborhood is gourmet tortilla soup. While there, listen to mariachis at Mariachi Plaza.

Koreatown

Chosun Galbee KOREAN
(☎323-734-3330; 3300 Olympic Blvd; mains $12-24; ⊙11am-11pm) West of Downtown LA, the essential dish is barbecue cooked at your table with lots of *banchan* (side dishes). While there, browse the giant Koreatown Galleria mall (Olympic Blvd and Western Ave) for housewares and more food.

Thai Town

Palms Thai THAI
(Map p896; ☎323-462-5073; 5900 Hollywood Blvd; mains $6-19; ⊙11am-midnight Sun-Thu, to 2am Fri & Sat) In East Hollywood, the essential dish is curry with accompaniment by an Elvis impersonator. While there, pick up a flower garland at Thailand Plaza shopping center (5321 Hollywood Blvd).

to 4:30am Fri & Sat) After a night out clubbing, do you really feel like filling yourself with garbage? Us, too. But the Waffle's 21st-century diner food – cornmeal-jalapeño waffles with grilled chicken, carrot cake waffles, mac 'n' cheese, samiches, heaping salads – is organic and locally sourced, so it's (almost) good for you.

WEST HOLLYWOOD, MID-CITY & BEVERLY HILLS

TOP CHOICE **Bazaar** MODERN SPANISH **$$**
(Map p900; ☎310-246-5555; 465 S La Cienega Blvd; dishes $8-18; ⊙6-11pm, brunch 11am-3pm Sat & Sun) In the SLS Hotel, the Bazaar dazzles with over-the-top design by Philippe Starck and 'molecular gastronomic' tapas by José Andrés. Caprese salad pairs cherry tomatoes with mozzarella balls that explode in your mouth, or try cotton-candy foie gras or a Philly cheesesteak on 'air bread.' A word of caution: those small plates add up.

Ivy CALIFORNIAN **$$$**
(Map p900; ☎310-274-8303; 113 N Robertson Blvd; mains $20-38; ⊙11:30am-11pm Mon-Fri, from 11am Sat, from 10am Sun) In the heart of Robertson's fashion frenzy, the Ivy's picket-fenced porch and rustic cottage are *the* power lunch spot. Chances of catching A-lister babes nibbling on a carrot stick or studio execs discussing sequels over the lobster omelet are excellent.

Marix Tex Mex MEXICAN $$

(Map p900; ☎323-656-8800; 1108 N Flores St; mains $9-19; ⏰11:30am-11pm) Many an evening in Boystown has begun flirting on Marix's patios over kick-ass margaritas, followed by fish tacos, fajitas, chipotle chicken sandwiches and all-you-can-eat on Taco Tuesdays.

Veggie Grill VEGETARIAN $

(Map p900; ☎323-822-7575; www.veggiegrill.com; 8000 Sunset Blvd; mains $7-9.50; ⏰11am-11pm; ✎) If Santa Fe crispy chickin' or a carne asada sandwich don't sound vegetarian, know that this cheery local chain uses seasoned vegetable proteins (mostly tempeh). Try sides of 'sweetheart' sweet potato fries or steamin' kale with miso dressing.

Original Farmers Market MARKET $

(Map p900; cnr 3rd St & Fairfax Ave) The market hosts a dozen worthy, budget-priced eateries, most alfresco. Try the classic diner Dupar's, Cajun-style cooking at the Gumbo Pot, ¡Loteria! Mexican grill or Singapore's Banana Leaf.

SANTA MONICA & VENICE

3 Square Café & Bakery CALIFORNIAN $$

(Map p904; ☎310-399-6504; 1121 Abbot Kinney Blvd; mains $8-20; ⏰cafe 8am-10pm Mon-Thu, to 11pm Fri, 9am-11pm Sat, 9am-10pm Sun, bakery 7am-7pm) Tiny, modernist cafe at which you can devour Hans Röckenwagner's German-inspired pretzel burgers, gourmet sandwiches and apple pancakes. Bakery shelves are piled high with rustic breads and fluffy croissants.

Library Alehouse PUB $$

(Map p904; ☎310-399-7892; www.libraryalehouse.com; 2911 Main St; mains $12-20; ⏰11:30am-midnight) Locals gather as much for the food as the 29 beers on tap, at this wood-paneled gastropub with a cozy outdoor back patio. Angus burgers, fish tacos and hearty salads sate the 30-something regulars.

Santa Monica Place SHOPPING CENTER $$

(Map p904; www.santamonicaplace.com; 3rd fl, cnr 3rd St & Broadway; 👪) We wouldn't normally eat at a mall, but the indoor-outdoor dining deck sets standards: Latin-Asian fusion at Zengo (think Peking duck tacos), sushi at Ozumo, wood-oven-baked pizzas at Antica. Most restaurants have seating with views across adjacent rooftops – some to the ocean. Stalls in the Market do *salumi* to soufflés.

LONG BEACH

Number Nine VIETNAMESE $

(☎562-434-2009; www.numberninenoodles.com; 2118 E 4th St; mains $7-9; ⏰noon-midnight) Maximalist portions of Vietnamese noodles and five-spice chicken with egg roll, in minimalist surrounds on Retro Row. Meats and poultry are sustainably raised.

George's Greek Café GREEK $$

(☎562-437-1184; www.georgesgreekcafe.com; 135 Pine Ave; mains $8-19; ⏰11am-10pm Sun-Thu, to 11pm Fri & Sat) George himself may greet you at the entrance on the generous patio, heart of the Pine Ave restaurant row, both geographically and spiritually. Locals cry *'Opa!'* for the *saganaki* (flaming cheese) and lamb chops.

Drinking

TOP CHOICE Edison BAR

(Map p892; www.edisondowntown.com; 108 W 2nd St, off Harlem Alley, Downtown; ⏰Wed-Sat) *Metropolis* meets *Blade Runner* at this industrial-chic basement boîte, where you'll be sipping *mojitos* surrounded by turbines and other machinery back from its days as a boiler room. Don't worry: it's all tarted up nicely with cocoa leather couches, three cavernous bars and a dress code.

Seven Grand BAR

(Map p892; ☎213-614-0737; 515 W 7th St, Downtown) It's as if hipsters invaded Mummy and Daddy's hunt club, amid the tartan-patterned carpeting and deer heads on the walls. Whiskey is the drink of choice: choose from over 100 from Scotland, Ireland and even Japan.

Cat & Fiddle PUB

(Map p896; www.thecatandfiddle.com; 6530 W Sunset Blvd; ⏰11:30am-2am; Ⓟ) Morrissey to Frodo, you never know who might be popping by for Boddingtons or Sunday-night jazz. Still, this Brit pub with leafy beer garden is more about friends and conversation than faux-hawks and deal-making.

Dresden RETRO BAR

(1760 N Vermont Ave, Los Feliz) Dresden's answer to Bogey & Bacall is the campy songster duo Marty & Elayne. They're an institution: you saw them crooning 'Stayin' Alive' in *Swingers*.

El Carmen BAR

(Map p900; 8138 W 3rd St; ⏰5pm-2am Mon-Fri, from 7pm Sat & Sun; Ⓟ) Mounted bull heads and *lucha libre* (Mexican wrestling) masks create an over-the-top 'Tijuana North' look and pull in an entertainment-industry-heavy crowd at LA's ultimate tequila and mezcal tavern (over a hundred to choose from).

Intelligentsia CAFE
(Map p904; www.intelligentsiacoffee.com; 1331 Abbot Kinney Blvd, Venice; ⏲6am-8pm Mon-Wed, to 11pm Thu & Fri, 7am-11pm Sat, 7am-8pm Sun; 📶) In this hip, minimalist monument to the coffee gods, skilled baristas never short you on foam or caffeine, and scones and muffins are addictive. Also at 3920 W Sunset Blvd in Silver Lake (open 6am to 8pm Sunday to Wednesday, to 11pm Thursday to Saturday).

☆ Entertainment

LA Weekly (www.laweekly.com) and the *Los Angeles Times* (www.latimes.com/theguide) have extensive entertainment listings. Snag tickets online, at the box office or through **Ticketmaster** (☎213-480-3232; www.ticketmaster.com). For half-price tickets to selected stage shows, visit the visitor centers in Hollywood and Downtown LA; try **Goldstar** (www.goldstar.com) for stage, concerts and events, or **LAStage Alliance** (www.theatrela.org) or **Plays 411** (www.plays411.com) for the theater.

Live Music & Nightclubs

Legendary music venues on the Sunset Strip include Whisky A-Go-Go and House of Blues.

TOP CHOICE **Spaceland** LIVE MUSIC
(www.clubspaceland.com; 1717 Silver Lake Blvd, Silver Lake) Beck played some early gigs at what is still LA's best place for indie and alternasounds. When the ad says 'special guest,' you never know what level of star might show up for quick and dirty impromptu sessions.

Hotel Cafe LIVE MUSIC
(Map p896; www.hotelcafe.com; 1623-1/2 N Cahuenga Blvd; tickets $10-15) The 'it' place for handmade music sometimes features big-timers such as Suzanne Vega, but it's really more of a stepping stone for message-minded newbie balladeers. Get there early and enter from the alley.

McCabe's Guitar Shop LIVE MUSIC
(☎310-828-4403; www.mccabes.com; 3101 Pico Blvd, Santa Monica) This mecca of musicianship sells guitars and other instruments, and the likes of Jackson Browne, Liz Phair and Michelle Shocked have performed live in the postage-stamp-sized back room.

Classical Music & Opera

Los Angeles Philharmonic ORCHESTRA
(Map p892; ☎323-850-2000; www.laphil.org; 111 S Grand Ave, Downtown) The world-class LA Phil performs classics and cutting-edge works at the Walt Disney Concert Hall, under the baton of Venezuelan phenom Gustavo Dudamel.

TOP CHOICE **Hollywood Bowl** AMPHITHEATER
(☎323-850-2000; www.hollywoodbowl.com; 2301 N Highland Ave, Hollywood; ⏲late Jun-Sep) This historic natural amphitheater is the LA Phil's summer home and also a stellar place to catch big-name rock, jazz, blues and pop acts. Come early for a preshow picnic (alcohol is allowed).

Los Angeles Opera OPERA
(Map p892; ☎213-972-8001; www.laopera.com; Dorothy Chandler Pavilion; 135 N Grand Ave, Downtown) Helmed by Plácido Domingo, this renowned opera ensemble plays it pretty safe with crowd-pleasers.

Theater

Centre Theatre Group THEATER
(☎213-628-2772; www.centretheatregroup.org) New and classic plays and musicals, including some Broadway touring companies, are presented in – count 'em – three venues: Ahmanson Theatre (Map p892) and Mark Taper Forum (Map p892) in Downtown LA, and Kirk Douglas Theatre in Culver City. Phone for $20 'Hot Tix' to shows (when available).

Actors' Gang THEATER
(www.theactorsgang.com; 9070 Venice Blvd, Culver City) Cofounded by Tim Robbins, this socially mindful troupe has won many awards for its bold and offbeat interpretations of classics and new works pulled from ensemble workshops.

Will Geer Theatricum Botanicum AMPHITHEATER
(www.theatricum.com; 1419 N Topanga Canyon Blvd, Malibu) Enchanting summer repertory in the woods.

Sports

Dodger Stadium BASEBALL
(www.dodgers.com; 1000 Elysian Park Dr, Downtown) LA's Major League Baseball team plays from April to October in this legendary stadium.

LA: SO GAY

LA is one of America's gayest cities. The *Advocate* magazine, PFLAG (Parents and Friends of Lesbians and Gays), and America's first gay church and synagogue all started here. Gays and lesbians fill every segment of society: entertainment, politics, business and actors/waiters/models.

'Boystown,' Santa Monica Blvd in West Hollywood (WeHo), is gay ground zero. Dozens of high-energy bars, cafes, restaurants, gyms and clubs here are especially busy from Thursday to Sunday; most cater to gay men. Elsewhere, the gay scenes are considerably more laid-back. Silver Lake, LA's original gay enclave, has evolved from largely leather and Levi's to encompass cute multiethnic hipsters. Long Beach also has a significant gay community.

LA's **Gay Pride** (www.lapride.org) celebration in mid-June attracts hundreds of thousands for nonstop partying and a parade down Santa Monica Blvd. Here are some party places to get you started the rest of the year. Freebie listings magazines and www.losangeles.gaycities.com have comprehensive listings.

Weho

Abbey BAR

(Map p900; www.abbeyfoodandbar.com; 692 N Robertson Blvd; mains $9-24; ⌚9am-2am) LA's essential gay bar and restaurant. Take your pick of preening and partying spaces at the Abbey, spanning a leafy patio to slick lounge, and enjoy flavored martinis and *mojitos* and upscale pub grub.

Eleven BAR

(Map p900; www.eleven.la; 8811 Santa Monica Blvd; mains $13-29; ⌚6-10pm Tue-Sun, 11am-3pm Sat & Sun) This glam spot occupies a historic building, serves New American cuisine and offers different theme nights from Musical Mondays to high-energy dance parties; check the website for club nights.

Silver Lake

Akbar BAR

(www.akbarsilverlake.com; 4356 W Sunset Blvd) Best jukebox in town, a Casbah atmosphere, and a crowd that's been known to change from hour to hour – gay, straight or just hip, but not too-hip-for-you. Some nights, the back room's a dancefloor; other nights, you'll find comedy, craft-making or 'Bears in Space.'

MJ's CLUB

(www.mjsbar.com; 2810 Hyperion Ave) Popular contempo hangout for dance nights, 'porn star of the week' and cruising. Young but diverse crowd.

Beach Cities

Roosterfish BAR

(Map p904; www.roosterfishbar.com; 1302 Abbot Kinney Blvd, Venice) The Westside's last remaining gay bar, the 'Fish has been serving the men of Venice for over three decades, but still feels current and chill, with a pool table and back patio. Friday nights are busiest.

Silver Fox BAR

(www.silverfoxlongbeach.com; 411 Redondo Ave, Long Beach) Despite its name, all ages frequent this mainstay of gay Long Beach, especially on karaoke nights. It is a short drive from shopping on Retro Row.

Staples Center SPECTATOR SPORT

(Map p892; www.staplescenter.com; 1111 S Figueroa St, Downtown) All the high-tech trappings fill this flying-saucer-shaped home to the Lakers, Clippers and Sparks basketball teams, and the Kings ice hockey team. Headliners – Britney Spears to Katy Perry – also perform here.

Shopping

Beverly Hills's **Rodeo Drive** (btwn Wilshire & Santa Monica Blvds) may be the world's most famous shopping street, but LA drips with other options for retail therapy. Fashionistas, and their paparazzi piranhas, flock to **Robertson Boulevard** (btwn Beverly Blvd & 3rd St) and **Montana Avenue** (btwn Lincoln Blvd & 20th St) in Santa Monica. **Melrose Avenue** (btwn San Vicente Blvd & La Brea Ave) in Hollywood and West Hollywood is still a fave of Gen-Y hipsters.

Hollywood is ground zero for groovy tunes at **Amoeba Music** (Map p896; 323-245-6400; 6400 W Sunset Blvd). East of here, Silver Lake has cool kitsch, collectibles and emerging LA designers, especially around **Sunset Junction** (Sunset Blvd, btwn Santa Monica & Griffith Park Blvds). Other chain-free strips are Main St in Santa Monica, Abbot Kinney Blvd in Venice and Larchmont Blvd in Hollywood.

In Long Beach, **Retro Row** (E 4th St, btwn Junipero & Cherry Aves) brims with shops selling vintage clothing and mid-century furniture at prices from 'how much?' to '*how* much?'.

Shoppers with couture taste but bargain budgets: head to Downtown's market districts. The 90-block **Fashion District** (Map p892; www.fashiondistrict.org) is a head-spinning selection of samples, knockoffs and original designs at cut-rate prices. The atmosphere is more street market than Rodeo Dr, and haggling is ubiquitous. Gold and diamonds are the main currency in the **Jewelry District** (Map p892) along Hill St, and the **Flower Market** (Map p892; Wall St, btwn 7th & 8th Sts; admission Mon-Fri/Sat $2/1; 8am-noon Mon, Wed & Fri, from 6am Tue, Thu & Sat) is the largest in the country, dating from 1913.

Bookstores include **Book Soup** (310-659-3110; www.booksoup.com; 8818 W Sunset Blvd, West Hollywood), with frequent celeb sightings, and **Distant Lands** (www.distantlands.com; 626-449-3220; 56 S Raymond Ave, Pasadena), a treasure chest of travel books, guides and gadgets.

Bargains await at two of LA's leading flea markets.

Rose Bowl Flea Market FLEA MARKET
(www.rgcshows.com; 1001 Rose Bowl Dr, Pasadena; admission $8-20; 5am-4:30pm 2nd Sun of the month) The 'mother' of all flea markets, with more than 2500 vendors; monthly.

Melrose Trading Post FLEA MARKET
(Map p900; www.melrosetradingpost.com; Fairfax High School, 7850 Melrose Ave, West Hollywood; admission $2; 9am-5pm Sun) Good weekly flea market which brings out hipsters in search of retro treasure.

Information

Emergency & Medical Services

Cedars-Sinai Medical Center (310-423-3277; 8700 Beverly Blvd, West Hollywood; 24hr emergency)

Rite-Aid pharmacies (800-748-3243) Call for the nearest branch; some are open 24 hours.

Internet Access

Coffee shops, including the local chain **Coffee Bean & Tea Leaf** (www.cbtl.com), offer wi-fi with a purchase. Libraries offer free access.

Los Angeles Public Library (213-228-7000; www.lapl.org; 630 W 5th St, Downtown;)

Santa Monica Public Library (310-458-8600; www.smpl.org; 601 Santa Monica Blvd;)

Media

KCRW 89.9 FM (www.kcrw.org) A Santa Monica–based National Public Radio (NPR) station that plays cutting-edge music and airs well-chosen public affairs programming.

KPCC 89.3 FM (www.kpcc.org) Pasadena-based NPR station with NPR and BBC programming and intelligent local talk shows.

LA Weekly (www.laweekly.com) Free alternative news and listings magazine.

Los Angeles Magazine (www.losangelesmagazine.com) Glossy lifestyle monthly with a useful restaurant guide.

Los Angeles Times (www.latimes.com) The West's leading daily newspaper and winner of dozens of Pulitzer Prizes. Embattled but still useful.

Money

Travelex (310-659-6093; US Bank, 8901 Santa Monica Blvd, West Hollywood; 9am-5pm Mon-Thu, to 6pm Fri, to 1pm Sat)

Post

Call 800-275-8777 or visit www.usps.com for the nearest branch.

IT'S A WRAP

Dress just like a movie star – in their actual clothes! Packed-to-the-rafters **It's a Wrap** (Map p900; 310-246-9727; www.itsawrap.com; 1164 S Robertson Blvd, Mid-City; 11am-8pm Mon-Fri, to 6pm Sat & Sun) sells wardrobe castoffs – tank tops to tuxedos – worn by actors and extras working on TV or movie shoots. Tags are coded, so you'll be able to brag with the knowledge of which person's clothing you are wearing.

Telephone

LA County is covered by 10 area codes. Dial 1+area code before all numbers.

Tourist Information

Beverly Hills (☎310-248-1015; www.lovebeverlyhills.org; 239 S Beverly Dr; ⊙8:30am-5pm Mon-Fri)

Downtown LA (☎213-689-8822; http://discoverlosangeles.com; 685 S Figueroa St; ⊙8:30am-5pm Mon-Fri)

Hollywood (☎323-467-6412; http://discoverlosangeles.com; Hollywood & Highland complex, 6801 Hollywood Blvd; ⊙10am-10pm Mon-Sat, to 7pm Sun)

Long Beach (☎562-628-8850; www.visitlongbeach.com; 3rd fl, One World Trade Center; ⊙11am-7pm Sun-Thu, 11:30am-7:30pm Fri & Sat Jun-Sep, 10am-4pm Fri-Sun Oct-May)

Santa Monica (☎310-393-7593; www.santamonica.com) Visitor center (1920 Main St; ⊙9am-6pm); Information kiosk (☎1400 Ocean Ave; ⊙9am-5pm Jun-Aug, 10am-4pm Sep-May)

Websites

Daily Candy LA (www.dailycandy.com) Little bites of LA style.

Discover Los Angeles (http://discoverlosangeles.com) Official tourist office site.

Gridskipper LA (www.gridskipper.com/travel/los-angeles) Urban travel guide to the offbeat.

LA Observed (www.laobserved.com) News blog that rounds up – and often scoops – other media.

LA.com (www.la.com) Clued-in guide to shopping, dining, nightlife and events.

Getting There & Away

Air

LA's main gateway is **Los Angeles International Airport** (LAX; ☎310-646-5252; www.lawa.org/lax), one of the world's five busiest. The nine terminals are linked by the free shuttle bus A, on the lower (arrival) level. Hotel and car-rental shuttles stop here as well.

Long Beach Airport (LGB) and Burbank's **Bob Hope Airport** (BUR) handle mostly domestic flights.

Bus

The main **Greyhound bus terminal** (☎213-629-8401; 1716 E 7th St) is in an unsavory part of Downtown, so avoid arriving after dark. Some buses go directly to the **Hollywood terminal** (☎323-466-6381; 1715 N Cahuenga Blvd).

Car

The usual international car-rental agencies have branches throughout Los Angeles (see p1174 for central reservation numbers and websites).

Train

Amtrak trains roll into Downtown's historic **Union Station** (☎800-872-7245; www.amtrak.com; 800 N Alameda St). The *Pacific Surfliner* travels daily to San Diego ($36, 2¾ hours), Santa Barbara ($29, 2½ hours) and San Luis Obispo ($40, 4¾ hours).

Getting Around

To & From the Airport

At LAX, door-to-door shared-ride vans operated by **Prime Time** (☎800-473-3743; www.primetimeshuttle.com) and **Super Shuttle** (☎310-782-6600; www.supershuttle.com) leave from the lower level of all terminals. Typical fares to Santa Monica, Hollywood or Downtown are $20, $25 and $16, respectively. **Disneyland Express** (☎714-978-8855; www.grayline.com) travels at least hourly between LAX and Disneyland-area hotels for one way/round-trip $22/32.

Curbside dispatchers will summon a taxi for you. There's a flat fare of $46.50 to Downtown LA. Otherwise, metered fares ($2.85 at flag fall plus $2.70 per mile) average $30 to Santa Monica, $42 to Hollywood and up to $90 to Disneyland. There is a $4 surcharge for taxis departing LAX.

LAX Flyaway Buses (☎866-435-9529; www.lawa.org) depart LAX terminals every 30 minutes, from about 5am to midnight, nonstop to both Westwood ($5, 30 minutes) and Union Station ($7, 45 minutes) in Downtown LA.

Other public transportation is slower and less convenient but cheaper. From the lower level outside any terminal, catch a free shuttle bus to parking lot C, next to the LAX Transit Center, the hub for buses serving all of LA. You can also take shuttle bus G to Aviation Station and the Metro Green Line light-rail, from where you can connect to the Blue Line and Downtown LA or Long Beach (40 minutes).

Car & Motorcycle

Unless time is no factor or money is extremely tight, you'll probably find yourself behind the wheel. Driving in LA doesn't need to be a hassle (a GPS device helps), but be prepared for some of the worst traffic in the country during rush hour (roughly 7:30am to 9am and 4pm to 6:30pm).

Parking at motels and cheaper hotels is usually free, while fancier ones charge from $8 to $36. Valet parking at nicer restaurants, hotels and nightspots is commonplace, with rates ranging from $2.50 to $10.

For local parking recommendations, see each of the neighborhoods in the Sights section.

Public Transportation

Tickets cost $1.50 per boarding (get a transfer when boarding if needed). There are no free

ACTUALLY, SOME PEOPLE DO WALK IN LA

'No one walks in LA,' the '80s band Missing Persons famously sang. That was then. Fed up with traffic, smog and high gas prices, the city that defined car culture is developing a foot culture. Angelenos are moving into more densely populated neighborhoods and walking, cycling and taking public transit.

The Metro Red Line subway connects Union Station in Downtown LA to the San Fernando Valley via Koreatown, Hollywood and Universal Studios. Base yourself near one of the arty stations, and you may not need a car at all. Unlimited-ride tickets at $6 a day are a downright bargain; plus, given LA's legendary traffic, it's often faster to travel below ground than above.

While eventual plans call for a 'Subway to the Sea,' for now you'll be busing it to Mid-City, Beverly Hills, Westwood and Santa Monica. The easiest transfer is to the Rapid 720 bus (at Wilshire/Vermont station on the Red Line or Wilshire/Western on the Purple Line), which makes limited stops along Wilshire Blvd. For more information visit www.metro.net.

transfers between trains and buses, but the 'TAP card' unlimited ride passes cost $6/20/75 per day/week/month. Purchase train tickets and TAP cards at vending machines throughout stations, or check out metro.net to search for other vendors.

Local **DASH minibuses** (☎your area code + 808-2273; www.ladottransit.com; fare 35¢) serve Downtown and Hollywood. Santa Monica–based **Big Blue Bus** (☎310-451-5444; www.bigbluebus.com, fare $1) serves much of the western LA area and LAX. Its Line 10 Freeway Express connects Santa Monica with Downtown LA ($2, one hour).

Trip-planning help is available via LA's **Metro** (☎800-266-6883; www.metro.net), which operates about 200 bus lines and six subway and light-rail lines:

Blue Line Downtown (7th St/Metro Center) to Long Beach.

Expo Line Downtown (7th St/Metro Center) to Culver City, via Exposition Park (scheduled opening winter 2011–12).

Gold Line Union Station to Pasadena and east LA.

Green Line Norwalk to Redondo Beach.

Purple Line Downtown to Koreatown.

Red Line Union Station to North Hollywood, via Downtown, Hollywood and Universal Studios.

Taxi

Except for taxis lined up outside airports, train stations, bus stations and major hotels, it's best to phone for a cab. Fares are metered, $2.85 at flag fall plus $2.70 per mile. Taxis serving the airport accept credit cards, though sometimes grudgingly.

Checker (☎800-300-5007)

Independent (☎800-521-8294)

Yellow Cab (☎800-200-1085)

SOUTHERN CALIFORNIA COAST

Disneyland & Anaheim

The mother of all West Coast theme parks, also known as the 'Happiest Place on Earth,' Disneyland is a parallel world that's squeaky-clean, enchanting and wacky all at once. Because it's smaller and somewhat more modest than Florida's Disneyworld, many visitors don't realize that Disneyland was, in fact, Walt Disney's original theme park. He famously dreamt of a 'magical park' where children and their parents could have fun together. For all his visions of waterfalls, castles and gigantic teacups, Disney was a practical businessman, too, choosing to construct his fantastical park within easy reach of the Los Angeles metropolitan area.

The park opened to great fanfare in 1955 and Anaheim grew up around it; today the Disneyland Resort comprises both the original park and the newer California Adventure Park. Though the city of Anaheim doesn't have a strong identity that's independent from Disney – especially after serious revitalization efforts in the 1990s – a few attractions and a large conference center bring in a crowd of visitors who've never posed in front of Sleeping Beauty Castle.

Sights & Activities

You can see either **park** (☎714-781-4565, 714-781-4400; www.disneyland.com; 1313 Harbor Blvd, Anaheim; 1-day pass adult/child 3-9yr $80/74, both parks $105/99) in a day, but going on all the rides requires at least two days (three if

Disneyland Resort

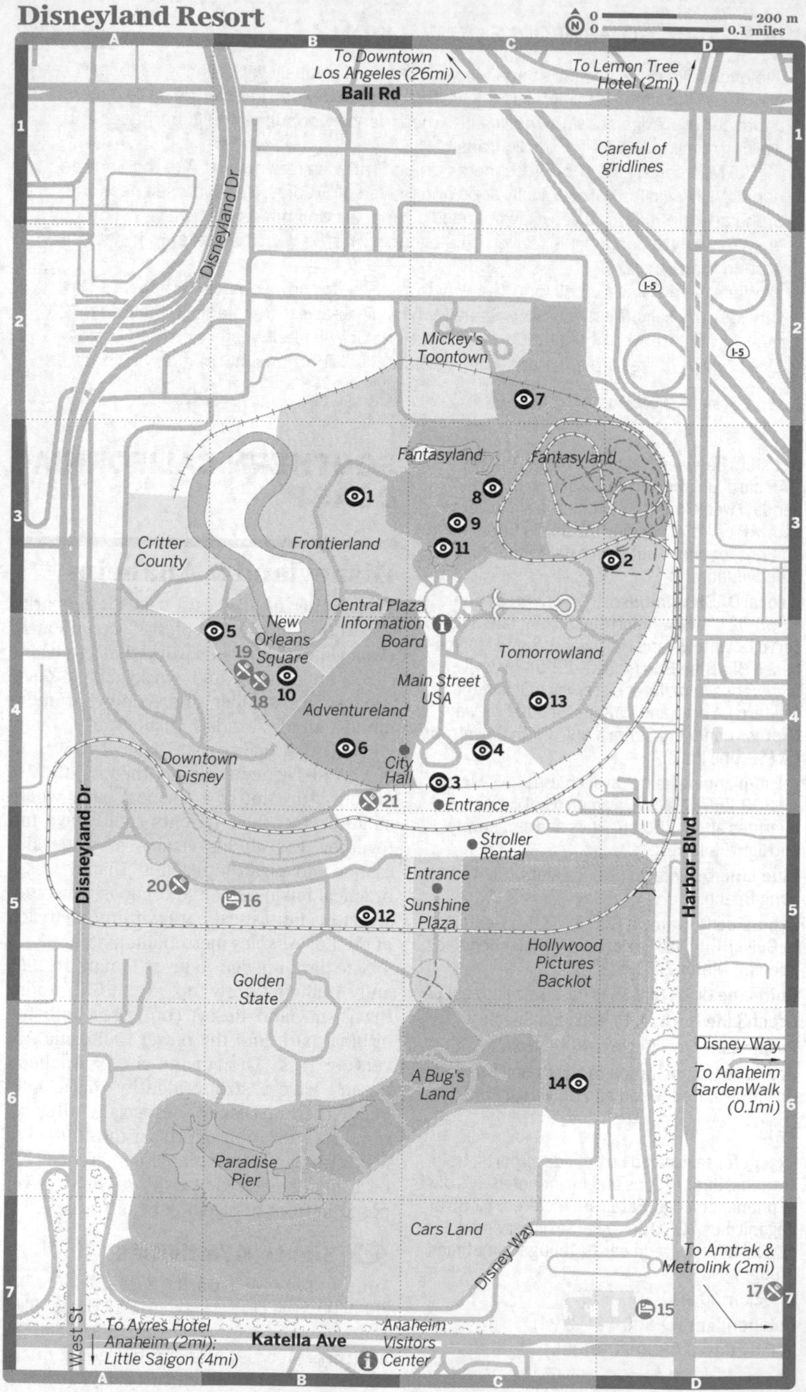

0 200 m
0 0.1 miles
To Downtown Los Angeles (26mi)
To Lemon Tree Hotel (2mi)
Ball Rd
Careful of gridlines
Disneyland Dr
I-5
Mickey's Toontown
Fantasyland
Fantasyland
Frontierland
Critter County
Central Plaza Information Board
New Orleans Square
Tomorrowland
Main Street USA
Adventureland
Downtown Disney
City Hall
Entrance
Stroller Rental
Entrance
Sunshine Plaza
Hollywood Pictures Backlot
Golden State
Harbor Blvd
Disney Way
To Anaheim GardenWalk (0.1mi)
A Bug's Land
Paradise Pier
Cars Land
Disney Way
To Amtrak & Metrolink (2mi)
West St
To Ayres Hotel Anaheim (2mi); Little Saigon (4mi)
Katella Ave
Anaheim Visitors Center

Disneyland Resort

Sights

1	Big Thunder Mountain Railroad	B3
2	Disneyland Monorail	D3
3	Disneyland Railroad Station	C4
4	Disneyland Story: presenting Great Moments with Mr Lincoln	C4
5	Haunted Mansion	B4
6	Indiana Jones Adventure	B4
7	It's a small world	C2
8	Mad Tea Party	C3
9	Peter Pan's Flight	C3
10	Pirates of the Caribbean	B4
11	Sleeping Beauty Castle	C3
12	Soarin' Over California	B5
13	Space Mountain	C4
14	Twilight Zone Tower of Terror	C6

Sleeping

15	Candy Cane Inn	D7
16	Disney's Grand Californian Hotel & Spa	B5

Eating

17	Anaheim GardenWalk	D7
18	Blue Bayou	B4
19	Café Orleans	B4
20	Catal Restaurant & Uva Bar	A5
	Napa Rose	(see 16)
21	Picnic Area	B4

visiting both parks), as waits for top attractions can be an hour or more. To minimize wait times, especially in summer, arrive midweek before the gates open and use the Fastpass system, which assigns boarding times for selected attractions. A variety of multiday passes are available. Check the website for discounts and seasonal park hours. Parking is $15.

Disneyland Park AMUSEMENT PARK

Spotless, wholesome Disneyland is still laid out according to Walt's original plans: **Main Street USA**, a pretty thoroughfare lined with old-fashioned ice-cream parlors and shops, is the gateway into the park. Though kids will make a beeline for the rides, adults will enjoy the antique photos and history exhibit just inside the main park entrance at the **Disneyland Story**: presenting Great Moments with Mr Lincoln.

At the far end of the street is Sleeping Beauty Castle, an obligatory photo op and a central landmark worth noting – its towering blue turrets are visible from many areas of the park. The sections of Disneyland radiate from here like spokes on a wheel. **Fantasyland** is your best bet for meeting princesses and other characters in costume; it's also home to a few notable rides like the famous spinning teacups of Mad Tea Party, Peter Pan's Flight and 'it's a small world.' For something a bit more fast-paced, head to the exhilarating Space Mountain roller coaster in **Tomorrowland** or the popular Indiana Jones Adventure ride in **Adventureland**. Nearby **New Orleans Square** offers several worthwhile attractions, too – the Haunted Mansion (not too scary for older kids) and the otherworldly Pirates of the Caribbean cruise, where cannons shoot across the water, wenches are up for auction and the mechanical Jack Sparrow character is creepily lifelike. Find Big Thunder Mountain Railroad, another popular roller coaster, in the Old West–themed **Frontierland**. If you've got little ones in tow, you'll likely spend time in kid-focused **Critter Country** and **Mickey's Toontown**, too.

Disney's California Adventure AMUSEMENT PARK

Disneyland resort's larger but less crowded park, California Adventure celebrates the natural and cultural glories of the Golden State but lacks the density of attractions and depth of imagination. The best rides are Soarin' Over California, a virtual hang-glide, and the famous Twilight Zone Tower of Terror that drops you 183ft down an elevator chute.

Downtown Disney PLAZA

Disney's open-air pedestrian mall, sandwiched between the two parks, offers plenty of opportunities to drop even more cash in its stores, restaurants and entertainment venues.

Sleeping

Chain hotels are a dime a dozen in the surrounding city of Anaheim.

Disney's Grand Californian Hotel & Spa LUXURY HOTEL $$$

(☎714-635-2300; http://disneyland.disney.go.com/grand-californian-hotel; 1600 S Disneyland Dr; d $384-445; P❄📶🏊👪) Along the promenade of Downtown Disney, you'll see the entrance to this splurgeworthy arts-and-crafts-style hotel offering family-friendly scavenger hunts, swimming pools bordered by private cabanas and a private entrance to California Adventure. Nonguests can soak up some of the hotel's glamour by stopping for lunch or a glass of wine at Napa Rose, the on-site wine bar and eatery; **Disney Dining** (714-781-3463) handles reservations.

Lemon Tree Hotel HOTEL **$$**
(866-311-5595; http://lemon-tree-hotel.com; 1600 E Lincoln Ave; r $89-119, ste $159;) Disneygoers and road-trippers appreciate the great value and communal BBQ facilities at this Aussie-owned inn. The simple but appealing accommodations include studios with kitchenettes and a two-room, three-bed suite with a kitchen that's ideal for families.

Ayres Hotel Anaheim HOTEL **$$**
(714-634-2106; www.ayreshotels.com/anaheim; 2550 E Katella Ave; r $129-149;) For something a bit more upscale but still affordable, try this French country-style hotel where amenities include complimentary evening receptions, large flat-screen TVs and pillow-top beds.

Candy Cane Inn MOTEL **$$**
(714-774-5284; www.candycaneinn.net; 1747 S Harbor Blvd; r $123-144;) At this flowery and family-friendly motel, rates include a fitness center and poolside continental breakfast.

> WORTH A TRIP
>
> **KNOTT'S BERRY FARM**
>
> What, Disney's not enough for you? Find even more thrill rides and cotton candy at the smaller, less commercial **Knott's Berry Farm** (714-220-5200; www.knotts.com; 8039 Beach Blvd, Buena Park; adult/child 3-11yr $57/25; from 10am). The Old West–themed amusement park teems with packs of speed-crazed adolescents testing their mettle on a line-up of rides. Gut-wrenchers include the wooden GhostRider and the '50s-themed Xcelerator, while the single-digit-aged find tamer action at Camp Snoopy. If your stomach's up for it, wrap up a visit with Mrs Knott's classic fried-chicken dinner (mains $12 to $18). Save time and money by printing tickets online. Parking costs $14 (free for restaurant patrons). Closing times vary from 5pm to 1pm; check website.

Eating

There are dozens of dining options inside the theme parks; it's part of the fun to hit the walk-up food stands for treats like huge dill pickles, turkey legs and sugar-dusted churros. If you need to sit down, some of the more memorable eateries include the cafeteria-style **Café Orleans** in New Orleans Square, serving jambalaya and mint juleps (virgin – the park is dry), and the surprisingly romantic **Blue Bayou** restaurant inside the Pirates of the Caribbean complex – whatever the time of day, you'll feel like you're dining outside under the stars as the ride's boats float peacefully by. For reservations or information on these and other Disneyland Resort eating options, including Character Dining, call **Disney Dining** (714-781-3463). Budget-conscious visitors and families with kids will also appreciate the picnic area just outside the park's main entrance; there's a nearby set of lockers where you can leave your picnic fixings when you arrive in the morning.

Downtown Disney offers generic but family-friendly chain restaurants; the same is true of the **Anaheim GardenWalk**, an outdoor mall on Katella Ave near the parks.

Catal Restaurant & Uva Bar MEDITERRANEAN **$$$**
(714-774-4442; www.patinagroup.com/catal; 1580 S Disneyland Dr; mains breakfast $9-14, dinner $23-38; 8am-10pm;) Looking for something more sophisticated without having to move the car from the Disneyland parking lot? Your best bet is the Mediterranean-inspired cuisine and cocktail menu at Catal; reserve ahead for balcony seating.

Little Saigon VIETNAMESE **$$**
If you need to steer totally clear of Mickey Mouse for a few hours, consider driving a few miles southwest to the ethnic community of Little Saigon (near the junction of I-405 and Hwy 22.) In the commercial district around the intersection of Bolsa and Brookhurst Aves, you'll find authentic, no-frills Vietnamese food – many menus aren't in English, so just point at the photo of your chosen dish.

Information

Stroller Rental
Rent a stroller for $15 per day ($25 for two strollers) outside the main entrance of Disneyland

Park. Rental strollers may be taken into both theme parks.

Tourist Information

Anaheim/Orange County Visitor & Convention Bureau (☎714-765-8888; www.anaheimoc.org; 800 W Katella Ave) Provides maps, tickets and planning tools for the region.

Central Plaza Information Board (☎714-781-4565; Main St USA, Disneyland Park) One of several information centers in the theme parks.

Websites

Mouse Wait (www.mousewait.com) This free iPhone app offers up-to-the-minute updates on ride wait times and what's happening in the parks.

Touring Plans (www.gaslamp.org) The 'unofficial guide to Disneyland' since 1985, this online resource offers no-nonsense advice, a crowd calendar and a 'lines app' for most mobile devices.

Getting There & Around

The Disneyland Resort is just off I-5 (Santa Ana Fwy), about 30 miles southeast of Downtown LA. As you approach the Disney area, giant easy-to-read overhead signs indicate which ramps you need to take for the theme parks, hotels or Anaheim's streets.

If you're arriving by train, you'll stop at the depot next to Angel Stadium, a quick shuttle or taxi ride east of Disneyland. **Amtrak** (☎714-385-1448; www.amtrak.com; 2150 E Katella Ave) and **Metrolink** (☎800-371-5465; www.metrolinktrains.com) commuter trains connect Anaheim to LA's Union Station ($14, 50 minutes) and San Diego ($27, two hours).

Once you're in the parks, a free tram connects the Disneyland Resort's main parking garage and Downtown Disney, a short walk from the theme parks' main entrance. Trams operate from one hour before Disneyland opens until one hour after the park closes.

Orange County Beaches

If you've seen *The OC* or *Real Housewives*, you *think* you know what to expect from this giant quilt of suburbia connecting LA and San Diego: affluence, aspiration and anxiety. (And if you were a fan of *Arrested Development*, you'll associate the region with frozen bananas, Segways and struggling actors – perhaps a more realistic picture?) But indeed, there is much living large in Orange County: shopping is a pastime, and resorts and restaurants serve its affluent residents. But it's also home to a burgeoning arts community and 42 miles of glorious beaches.

WHAT THE...?

Hey, did that painting just move? Welcome to the **Pageant of the Masters** (☎949-497-6582; www.pageanttickets.com; admission $15-100; ⏰8:30pm Jul & Aug), in which elaborately costumed humans step into painstaking re-creations of famous paintings on an outdoor stage. The pageant began in 1933 as a sideshow to Laguna Beach's **Festival of the Arts** (www.lagunafestivalofarts.org) and has been a prime attraction ever since. Our favorite part: watching the paintings deconstruct.

Hummer-driving hunks and Botoxed beauties mix it up with surfers and artists to give Orange County's beach towns their distinct vibe. Just across the LA–OC county-line, **Seal Beach** is refreshingly noncommercial with its pleasantly walkable downtown, while gentrified **Huntington Beach** (aka Surf City, USA) epitomizes the California surfing lifestyle. Fish tacos and happy-hour specials abound along Main St.

Next up is the ritziest of the OC's beach communities: **Newport Beach**, portrayed in *The OC* and nirvana for luxe shoppers. Families should steer toward Balboa Peninsula for its beaches, vintage wooden pier and quaint amusement center. Near the Ferris wheel on the harbor side, the **Balboa Island Ferry** (www.balboaislandferry.com; 410 S Bayfront; car & driver/adult/child $2/1/50¢; ⏰6:30am-midnight) shuttles passengers across the bay to ritzy Balboa Island for ice-cream cones, strolls past historic beach cottages, and the boutiques along Marine Ave.

Laguna Beach is the OC's most cultured and charming seaside town, where secluded beaches, glassy waves and eucalyptus-covered hillsides create a Riviera-like feel. Art galleries dot Pacific Coast Hwy here, and Laguna's summer arts festivals are institutions. To soak up the region's natural beauty right in the center of town, grab your morning café au lait and croissants at **C'est La Vie** (www.cestlavierestaurant.com; 373 S Coast Hwy) and enjoy them on a nearby park bench facing the ocean – there's an incredibly scenic playground right here if you're traveling with kids.

TOP CHOICE **Mission San Juan Capistrano** (☎949-234-1300; www.missionsjc.com; cnr Ortega Hwy & Camino Capistrano; incl audio tour adult/child $9/5; ⏲8:30am-5pm), about 10 miles south and inland from Laguna, is one of California's most beautiful missions – and the only mission in the OC – featuring lush gardens and the charming Serra Chapel.

San Diego

San Diegans shamelessly yet endearingly promote their hometown as 'America's Finest City.' Smug? Maybe, but it's easy to see why. The weather is practically perfect, with coastal high temperatures hovering around 72°F (22°C) all year. Beaches or forests are rarely more than 10 minutes' drive away. Its population (about 1.3 million) makes it America's eighth-largest city (or about 1.5 times the size of San Francisco), yet we're hard-pressed to think of a more laid-back big city anywhere.

The city languished as a relative backwater until WWII, when the Japanese attack on Pearl Harbor prompted the US Navy to relocate the US Pacific Fleet from Hawaii to San Diego's natural harbor. Growth in the military, tourism, education and research (especially medicine and oceanography), alongside high-tech companies cropping up in the inland valleys, helped to develop the city. It all makes San Diego seem more all-American than its California *compadres*, despite the borderland location.

Sights

San Diego's compact downtown revolves around the historic Gaslamp Quarter, a beehive of restaurants, bars and boutiques with the convention center just to its south. Southwest of here, Coronado is reached via a stunning bridge, while Little Italy and museum-rich Balboa Park (home of the San Diego Zoo) are to the north. The park segues into Hillcrest, the city's lesbi-gay hub. West of here are tourist-oriented Old Town, and the water playground around Mission Bay.

Heading north along the coast, Ocean Beach, Mission Beach and Pacific Beach epitomize the laid-back SoCal lifestyle, while La Jolla sits pretty and privileged. The I-5 Fwy cuts through the region north–south, while the I-8 is the main east–west artery. The CA163 Fwy heads north from downtown through Balboa Park.

DOWNTOWN

In 1867 creative real-estate wrangling by developer Alonzo Horton created the so-called 'New Town' that is today's downtown San Diego. Downtown's main street, 5th Ave, was once a notorious strip of saloons, gambling joints and bordellos known as Stingaree. These days, Stingaree has been beautifully restored as the thumping heart of downtown San Diego and rechristened the **Gaslamp Quarter** (Map p920), a playground of restaurants, bars, clubs, shops and galleries. The commercial focal point of downtown is **Westfield Horton Plaza** (Map p920; Broadway & 4th St; Ⓟ), a colorful, maze-like shopping mall.

In northern downtown, **Little Italy** (Map p920; www.littleitalysd.com) has evolved into one of the city's hippest places to live, eat and shop. India St is the main drag.

William Heath Davis House HISTORIC BUILDING
(Map p920; ☎619-233-4692; www.gaslampquarter.org; 410 Island Ave; adult/child $5/4; ⏲10am-6pm Tue-Sat, 9am-3pm Sun) For a full historical picture, peruse the exhibits inside this museum; the saltbox house was the onetime home of William Heath Davis, the man credited with starting the development of modern San Diego. Self-guided tours are available and the foundation also offers guided walking tours of the quarter (adult/child $10/8; tours 11am Saturday).

Petco Park STADIUM
(Map p920; ☎619-795-5011; www.padres.com; 100 Park Blvd; tours adult/child $11/7; ⏲tours 10:30am, 12:30pm & 2:30pm Tue-Sun May-Aug, 10:30am & 12:30pm Apr & Sep, subject to game schedule) Just a quick stroll southeast of the Gaslamp Quarter is one of downtown's newer landmarks, home of the San Diego Padres baseball team. Take an 80-minute behind-the-scenes tour; highlights often include the bullpen and press box.

Museum of Contemporary Art MUSEUM
(Map p920; ☎858-454-3541; www.mcasd.org; 1001 & 1100 Kettner Blvd; adult/child $10/free; ⏲11am-5pm Thu-Tue, to 7pm 3rd Thu each month, 5-7pm free) Emphasizes minimalist and pop art, as well as conceptual works and cross-border art. The 1100 Kettner Bldg is at the historic Santa Fe Depot. Another branch is in La Jolla; one ticket admits you to all venues.

USS Midway Museum MUSEUM
(Map p920; ☎619-544-9600; www.midway.org; Navy Pier; adult/child $18/10; ⏲10am-5pm) Step

Greater San Diego

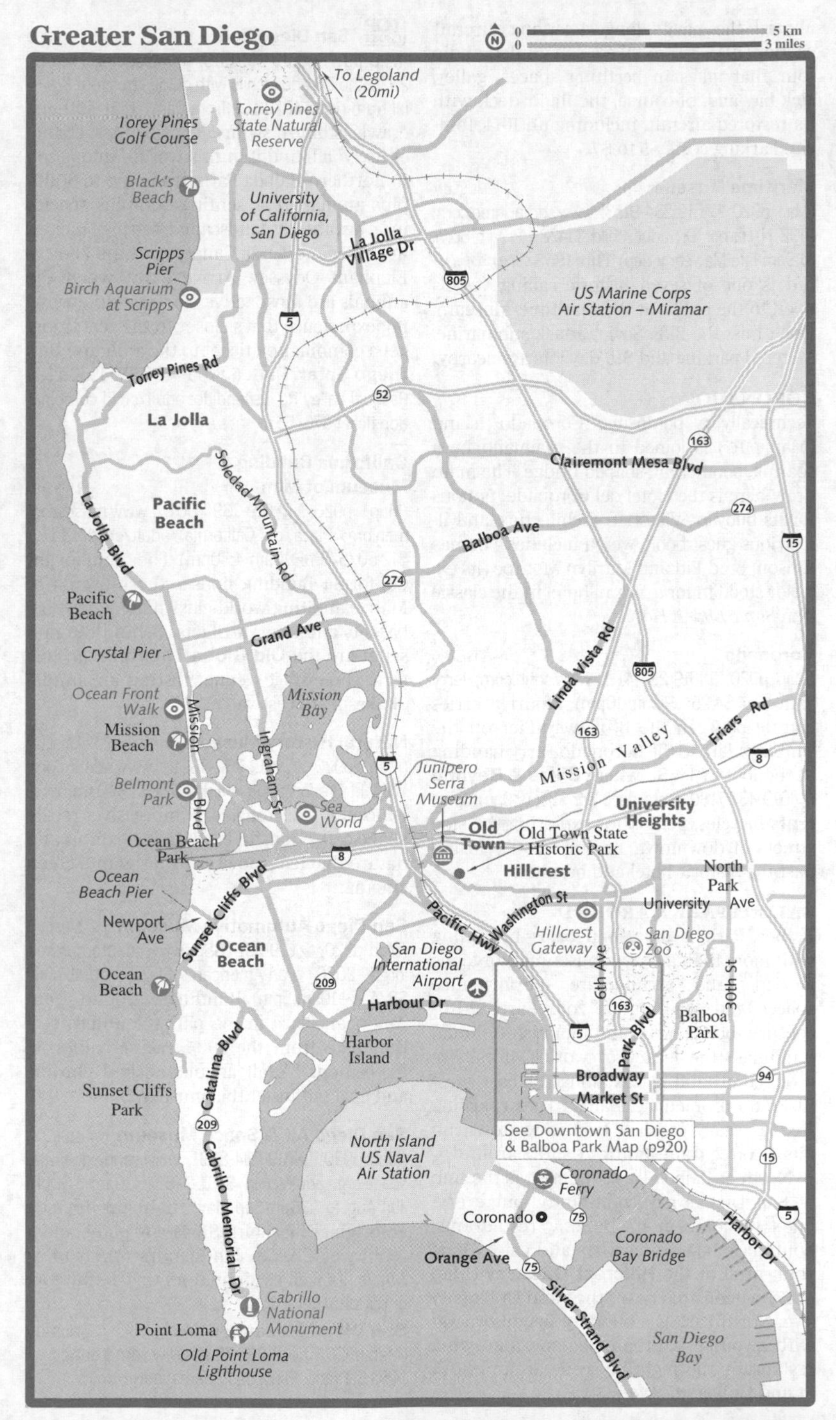

aboard the navy's longest-serving aircraft carrier (1945–91) to take a self-guided audio tour that takes in berthing spaces, galley, sick bay and, of course, the flight deck with its restored aircraft, including an F-14 Tomcat. Parking costs $5 to $7.

Maritime Museum MUSEUM
(Map p920; ☎619-234-9153; www.sdmaritime.com; 1492 N Harbor Dr; adult/child $14/8; ⏲9am-8pm, to 9am late May-early Sep) The 1863 *Star of India* is one of seven historic sailing vessels open to the public at the Maritime Museum. Don't miss the B-39 Soviet attack submarine. Metered parking and $10 day lots are nearby.

CORONADO

Technically a peninsula, Coronado Island (Map p917) is joined to the mainland by a soaring, boomerang-shaped bridge. The main draw here is the Hotel del Coronado, famous for its buoyant Victorian architecture and illustrious guest book, which includes Thomas Edison, Brad Pitt and Marilyn Monroe (its exterior stood in for a Miami hotel in the classic film *Some Like it Hot*).

Coronado ISLAND
(Map p920; ☎619-234-4111; www.sdhe.com; ferry each way $4.25; ⏲9am-10pm) Hourly ferries shuttle between the Broadway Pier on the Embarcadero to the Coronado Ferry Landing at the foot of 1st St, where **Bikes & Beyond** (☎619-435-7180; rental per 1-2hr $25; ⏲9am-8pm) rents bicycles, perfect for exploring the side streets of downtown La Jolla and cruising past the historic hotel and beaches.

BALBOA PARK & AROUND

Balboa Park is an urban oasis brimming with more than a dozen museums, gorgeous gardens and architecture, performance spaces and the famous zoo. Early 20th-century beaux arts and Spanish-Colonial buildings (the legacy of world's fairs) are grouped around plazas along the east–west El Prado promenade. Balboa Park (parking free) is easily reached from downtown on bus 7. A free tram shuttles visitors around.

North of Balboa Park, Hillcrest is the hub of San Diego's gay community, but everyone's welcome in its buzzing restaurants, boutiques, bookstores, bars and cafes. Start your stroll at the **Hillcrest Gateway** (Map p917), a neon arch near 5th St and University Ave. North Park is a budding neighborhood with a youngish, urban vibe and a growing restaurant and nightlife scene around 30th St and University Ave.

TOP CHOICE **San Diego Zoo** ZOO
(Map p917; ☎619-231-1515; www.sandiegozoo.org; 2920 Zoo Dr; adult/child with guided bus tour & aerial tram ride $40/30; ⏲from 9am) If it slithers, crawls, stomps, swims, leaps or flies, chances are you'll find it in this world-famous zoo in northern Balboa Park. It's home to 3000-plus animals representing 800-plus species in a beautifully landscaped setting, including the giant Panda Canyon and the 7.5-acre Elephant Odyssey. Arrive early, when the animals are most active. For a wildlife viewing experience that's closer to the real thing, get a combination ticket to the affiliated **San Diego Safari Park** (☎760-747-8702; 15500 San Pasqual Valley Rd, Escondido; adult/child combination ticket $76/56).

California Building & Museum of Man MUSEUM
(Map p920; ☎619-239-2001; www.museumofman.org; Plaza de California; adult/child/13-17yr $12.50/5/8; ⏲10am-4:30pm) The flamboyant California Building houses the Museum of Man, exhibiting world-class pottery, jewelry, baskets and other artifacts. Behind the museum are the **Old Globe Theaters**, an historic three-stage venue hosting an annual Shakespeare Festival.

Natural History Museum MUSEUM
(Map p920; ☎619-232-3821; www.sdnhm.org; 1788 El Prado; adult/child $17/11; ⏲10am-5pm) Dinosaur skeletons, an impressive rattlesnake collection, an earthquake exhibit and nature-themed movies in a giant-screen cinema.

San Diego Automotive Museum MUSEUM
(Map p920; ☎619-231-2886; www.sdautomuseum.org; 2080 Pan-American Plaza; adult/child $8/4; ⏲10am-5pm) Buildings around Pan-American Plaza in the park's southern section date from the 1935 Pacific-California Exposition. It's all about polished chrome and cool tailfins at this museum.

San Diego Air & Space Museum MUSEUM
(Map p920; ☎619-234-8291; www.sandiegoairandspace.org; adult/child $16.50/6; ⏲10am-5:30pm Jun-Aug, to 4:30pm Sep-May) Highlights include an original Blackbird SR-71 spy plane and a replica of Charles Lindbergh's *Spirit of St Louis,* as well as simulators that require an extra charge.

San Diego Museum of Art MUSEUM
(Map p920; ☎619-232-7931; www.sdmart.org; 1450 El Prado, Plaza de Panama; adult/child

$12/4.50; ⌚10am-5pm Tue-Sat, from noon Sun, to 9pm Thu Jun-Sep) Gets accolades for its European old masters and good collections of American and Asian art.

Mingei International Museum MUSEUM
(Map p920; ☎619-239-0003; www.mingei.org; 1439 El Prado, Plaza de Panama; adult/child $7/4; ⌚10am-4pm Tue-Sun) Exhibits folk art from around the globe; don't miss the lovely museum store here.

FREE **Timken Museum of Art** MUSEUM
(Map p920; ☎619-239-5548; www.timkenmuseum.org; 1500 El Prado; ⌚10am-4:30pm Tue-Sat, from 1:30pm Sun) Small but exquisite, the museum showcases European and American heavyweights, from Rembrandt to Cézanne and John Singleton Copley.

Museum of Photographic Arts MUSEUM
(Map p920; ☎619-238-7559; www.mopa.org; 1649 El Prado; adult/child $8/free; ⌚10am-5pm Tue-Sun) Exhibits fine-art photography and hosts an ongoing film series.

San Diego Model Railroad Museum MUSEUM
(Map p920; ☎619-696-0199; www.sdmrm.org; 1649 El Prado; adult/child $7/6; ⌚11am-4pm Tue-Fri, to 5pm Sat & Sun) One of the largest of its kind, with brilliantly 'landscaped' train sets.

Reuben H Fleet Science Center MUSEUM
(Map p920; ☎619-238-1233; www.rhfleet.org; 1875 El Prado; adult/child $10/8.75, incl Imax theater $14:50/11.75; ⌚from 10am) Family-oriented hands-on museum-cum-Imax theater in Plaza de Balboa.

OLD TOWN & MISSION VALLEY

In 1769 a band of missionaries led by the Franciscan friar Junípero Serra founded the first of the 21 California missions on San Diego's Presidio Hill; a small village (pueblo) grew around it. The spot turned out to be less than ideal for a mission, however, and in 1774 the mission was moved about 7 miles upriver, closer to a steady water supply and fertile land.

Mission Basilica San Diego de Alcalá CHURCH
(☎619-281-8449; www.missionsandiego.com; 10818 San Diego Mission Rd; adult/child $3/1; ⌚9am-4:45pm) Secluded in a corner of what's now called Mission Valley, the 'Mother of the Missions' was relocated here in 1774. Come at sunset for glowing views over the valley and the ocean beyond.

Junípero Serra Museum MUSEUM
(Map p917; ☎619-232-6203; www.sandiegohistory.org; 2727 Presidio Dr; adult/child $6/2; ⌚10am-5pm Sat & Sun) On the site of the original mission in Old Town stands this handsome museum, which highlights life during the city's rough-and-tumble early period.

Old Town State Historic Park HISTORIC SITE
(Map p917; ☎619-220-5422; www.parks.ca.gov; San Diego Ave, at Twiggs St; ⌚visitor center 10am-5pm; P) Preserves five original adobe buildings and several re-created structures from the first pueblo, including a schoolhouse and a newspaper office. Most now contain museums, shops or restaurants. The visitor center operates free tours daily at 11am and 2pm.

POINT LOMA

This peninsula wraps around the entrance to crescent-shaped San Diego Bay.

Cabrillo National Monument MONUMENT
(Map p917; ☎619-557-5450; www.nps.gov/cabr; per car/person $5/3; ⌚9am-5pm; P) Enjoy stunning bay panoramas from the monument, which honors the leader of the first Spanish exploration of the West Coast. The nearby 1854 **Old Point Loma Lighthouse** helped guide ships until 1891 and is now a museum.

MISSION BAY & BEACHES

After WWII, coastal engineering turned the mouth of the swampy San Diego River into a 7-sq-mile playground of parks, beaches and bays. Amoeba-shaped Mission Bay sits just inland. Surfing is popular in Ocean Beach and Mission Beach, and all the beaches are naturals for swimming, kite-flying and cycling along miles of paved bike paths.

San Diego's three major beaches are ribbons of hedonism where armies of tanned, taut bodies frolic in the sand and surf. South of Mission Bay, hippie-flavored **Ocean Beach** (OB; Map p917) has a fishing pier, beach volleyball, sunset BBQs and good surf. Newport Ave is chockablock with bohemian bars, eateries and shops selling beachwear, surf gear and antiques.

West of Mission Bay, **Mission Beach** (MB) and its northern neighbor, **Pacific Beach** (PB), are connected by the car-free **Ocean Front Walk**, which swarms with skaters, joggers and cyclists year-round. The small **Belmont Park** amusement park in MB beckons with a historic wooden roller coaster and large indoor pool.

Downtown San Diego & Balboa Park

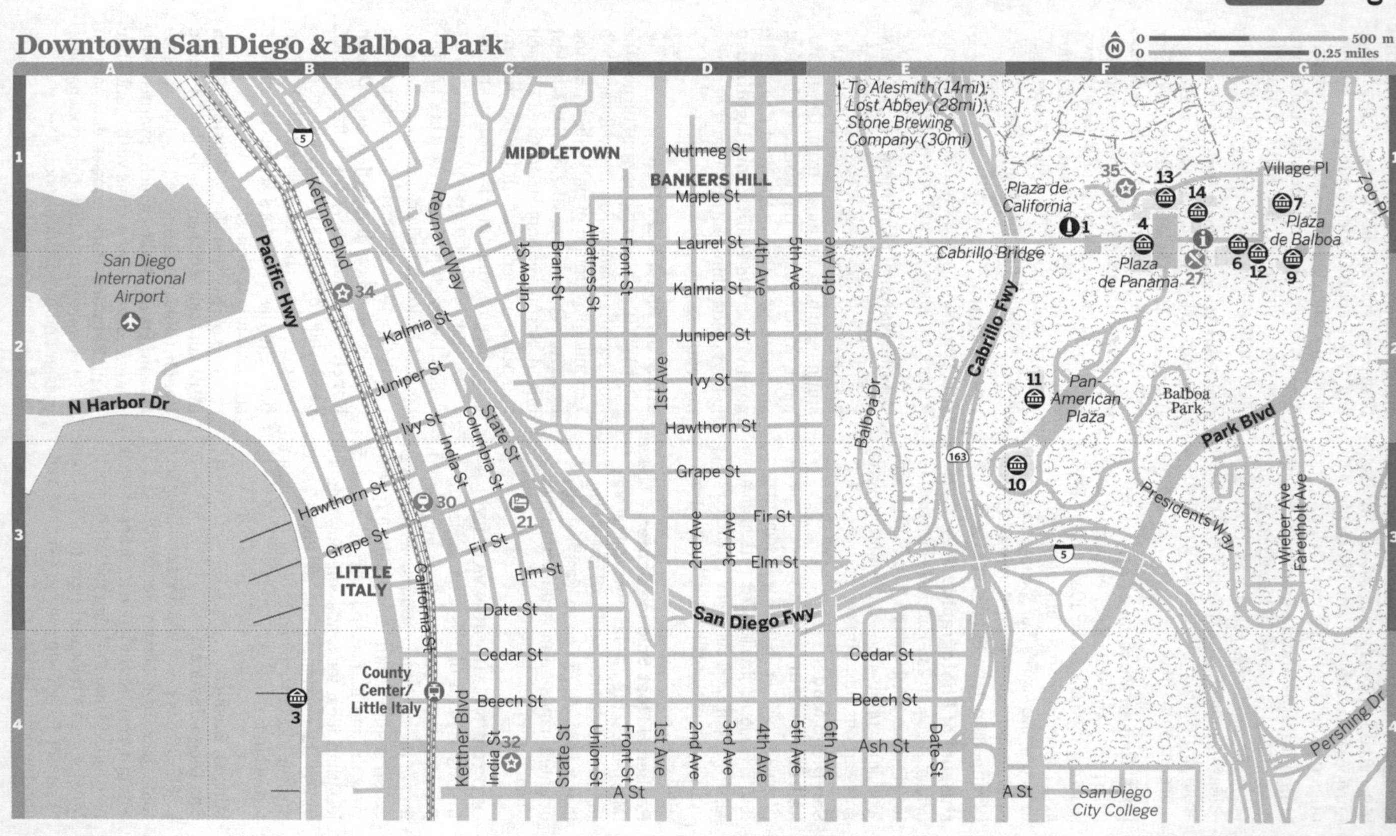

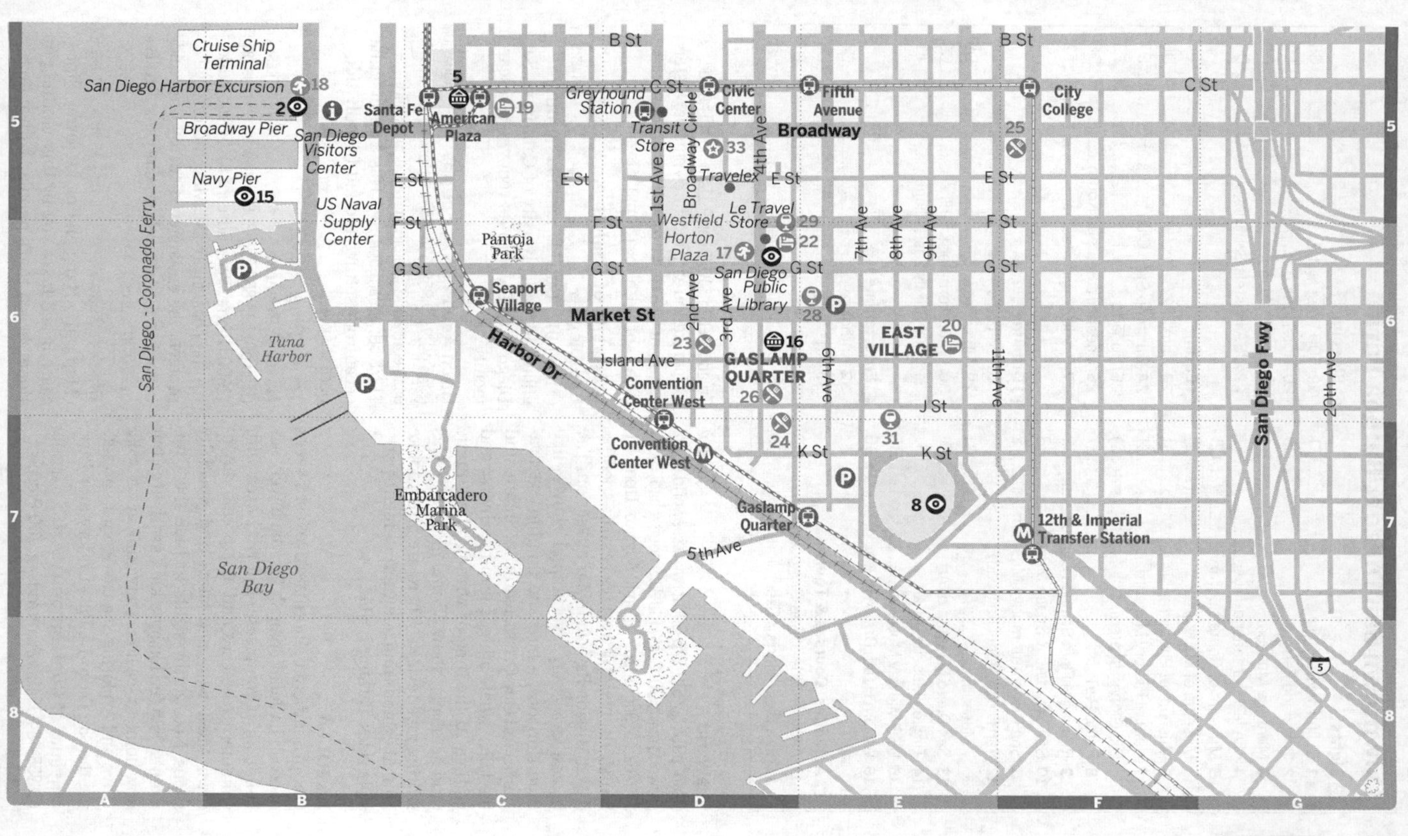
Cruise Ship Terminal
San Diego Harbor Excursion
18
2
Broadway Pier
Navy Pier
15
San Diego Visitors Center
US Naval Supply Center
Santa Fe Depot
5
American Plaza
19
Greyhound Station
Transit Store
Broadway Circle
Civic Center
33
Travelex
Le Travel Store
Westfield Horton Plaza
17
22
29
San Diego Public Library
28
Fifth Avenue
Broadway
City College
25
Pantoja Park
Seaport Village
Market St
Harbor Dr
Island Ave
Convention Center West
Convention Center West
23
16
GASLAMP QUARTER
26
24
EAST VILLAGE
20
31
8
Gaslamp Quarter
12th & Imperial Transfer Station
Embarcadero Marina Park
Tuna Harbor
San Diego Bay
San Diego - Coronado Ferry
San Diego Fwy
5
B St
C St
E St
F St
G St
J St
K St
1st Ave
2nd Ave
3rd Ave
4th Ave
5th Ave
6th Ave
7th Ave
8th Ave
9th Ave
11th Ave
20th Ave
A
B
C
D
E
F
G
5
6
7
8

Downtown San Diego & Balboa Park

Sights

1 California Building ... F1
2 Coronado Ferry ... B5
3 Maritime Museum ... B4
4 Mingei International Museum ... F1
5 Museum of Contemporary Art ... C5
Museum of Man ... (see 1)
6 Museum of Photographic Arts ... G1
7 Natural History Museum ... G1
Old Globe Theaters ... (see 35)
8 Petco Park ... E7
9 Reuben H Fleet Science Center ... G2
10 San Diego Air & Space Museum ... F3
11 San Diego Automotive Museum ... F2
12 San Diego Model Railroad Museum ... G1
13 San Diego Museum of Art ... F1
14 Timken Museum of Art ... F1
15 USS Midway Museum ... B5
16 William Heath Davis House ... D6

Activities, Courses & Tours

17 Another Side of San Diego ... D6
18 San Diego Harbor Excursion ... B5

Sleeping

19 500 West Hotel ... C5
20 Hotel Indigo ... E6
21 Little Italy Inn ... C3
22 USA Hostels San Diego ... D6

Eating

23 Café 222 ... D6
24 Gaslamp Strip Club ... D7
25 Hodad's ... F5
26 Oceanaire Seafood Room ... D6
27 Prado ... F2

Drinking

28 Prohibition ... E6
29 Tipsy Crow ... D5
30 Waterfront Bar & Grill ... C3
31 Wine Steals East Village ... E7

Entertainment

32 Anthology ... C4
33 Arts Tix ... D5
34 Casbah ... B2
35 Old Globe Theaters ... F1

SeaWorld AQUARIUM
(Map p917; ☎619-226-3901; www.seaworld.com/seaworld/ca; 500 SeaWorld Dr; adult/child 3-9yr $70/62; ⏲9am-10pm Jul–mid-Aug, to 11pm Fri-Sun, shorter hr rest of year) It's easy to spend a day at Mission Bay's four-star attraction. The biggest draws are live animal shows, like Blue Horizons, a bird and dolphin extravaganza, and One Ocean, featuring Shamu and his killer whale amigos leaping, diving and gliding. At the time of writing, the aquatic (and acrobatic) show *Cirque de la Mer* was scoring rave reviews. There are also zoolike animal exhibits and a few amusement-park-style rides. Parking is $14.

LA JOLLA

One of Southern California's loveliest sweeps of coast, La Jolla (Spanish for 'the jewel;' say la-*hoy*-ah, if you please) is a ritzy area with shimmering beaches and an upscale downtown filled with boutiques and specialty shops. Noteworthy sights include the **Children's Pool** (no longer a kids' swim area but now home to sea lions), kayaking at **La Jolla Cove** and exploring sea caves, and snorkeling the San Diego-La Jolla Underwater Park.

Museum of Contemporary Art MUSEUM
(☎858-454-3541; www.mcasd.org; 700 Prospect St; adult/child $10/free; ⏲11am-5pm Thu-Tue, to 7pm 3rd Thu each month, 5-7pm free) Sister venue of the downtown branch (same ticket for both locations).

University of California, San Diego UNIVERSITY
(Map p917) Outside La Jolla's central village is the University of California, San Diego (UCSD), with its renowned research facilities.

Birch Aquarium at Scripps AQUARIUM
(Map p917; ☎858-534-3474; http://aquarium.ucsd.edu; 2300 Exhibition Way; adult/child $12/8.50; ⏲9am-5pm; P) Has a spectacular oceanfront setting and kid-friendly tide pool displays.

Torrey Pines State Natural Reserve WILDLIFE RESERVE
(Map p917; ☎858-755-2063; www.torreypine.org; 12600 N Torrey Pines Rd; car $10; ⏲8am-dusk) Up the coast near Del Mar, the reserve protects the endangered Torrey pine and is perfect for leisurely ocean-view strolls on 2000 acres.

Black's Beach BEACH
(Map p917) Hang-gliding at Torrey Pines State Beach takes you by this 'clothing optional' beach that's popular with naturists.

Activities

Surfing and windsurfing (for surf reports, call ☎619-221-8824) are both excellent, although in some areas territorial locals are a major irritation.

Pacific Beach Surf School SURFING
(☎858-373-1138; www.pacificbeachsurfschool.com; 4150 Mission Blvd, Suite 161, Pacific Beach; private/semiprivate lessons per person $80/65) Learn to hang 10 at surf school or just rent a board and wetsuit (half-day $25) at San Diego's oldest surf shop.

San Diego-La Jolla Underwater Park SNORKELING, DIVING
Snorkeling and scuba diving here, you'll encounter glowing orange garibaldi flitting around giant kelp forests.

OEX Dive & Kayak DIVING, KAYAKING
(☎858-454-6195; www.oexcalifornia.com; 2243/2132 Avenida de la Playa, La Jolla) For gear or instruction, including spearfishing seminars and stand-up paddleboard lessons, head to this one-stop resource in La Jolla.

Tours

Another Side of San Diego WALKING, BOAT
(Map p920; ☎619-239-2111; www.anothersideofsandiegotours.com; 300 G St) This highly rated tour company does Segway tours of Balboa Park, horseback riding on the beach and Gaslamp Quarter food tours.

Hike, Bike, Kayak San Diego CYCLING, KAYAKING
(☎858-551-9510; www.hikebikekayak.com; 2246 Avenida de la Playa, La Jolla) Just what it says.

Old Town Trolley Tours TROLLEY
(☎619-298-8687; www.trolleytours.com; adult/child $34/17) Hop-on, hop-off loop tour to the main attractions; board at Old Town.

San Diego Harbor Excursion BOAT
(Map p920; ☎619-234-4111; www.sdhe.com; 1050 N Harbor Dr; adult/child from $22/11) A variety of bay and harbor cruises.

Sleeping

Rates quoted here are 'rack' rates; they skyrocket downtown during big conventions and the summer peak, then plummet at other times.

DOWNTOWN

USA Hostels San Diego HOSTEL $
(Map p920; ☎619-232-3100; www.usahostels.com; 726 5th Ave; dm/d incl breakfast from $28/72; ❄@📶) In a former Victorian-era hotel, this convivial Gaslamp hostel has cheerful rooms, a full kitchen and an inviting movie lounge. Rates include a pancake breakfast and laundry facilities; the nightly family-style dinner costs $5.

Little Italy Inn B&B $$
(Map p920; ☎619-230-1600; www.littleitalyhotel.com; 505 W Grape St; r with shared/private bath $89/109, apt from $149; 📶) If you can't get enough of Little Italy's charm, this pretty B&B is an ideal place to hang your hat. The 23-room Victorian-style inn boasts comfortable beds, cozy bathrobes in each room, a casual European-style breakfast and wine socials on weekend evenings.

500 West Hotel HOSTEL $
(Map p920; ☎619-231-4092; www.500westhotelsd.com; 500 W Broadway; s/d with shared bath from $50/62; @📶) Rooms are shoebox-sized and baths are down the hallway in this renovated 1920s YMCA, but hipsters on a budget love the bright decor, flat-screen TVs, communal kitchen and fitness studio.

Hotel Indigo BOUTIQUE HOTEL $$
(Map p920; ☎619-727-4000; www.hotelsandiegodowntown.com; 509 9th Ave; r from $146; P❄@📶🏊) The first Leadership in Energy and Environmental Design (LEED) certified hotel in San Diego, Hotel Indigo is smartly designed and ecofriendly. The design is contemporary but colorful; guest rooms feature huge floor-to-ceiling windows, spa-style baths and large flat-screen TVs. Parking is $35.

BEACHES

Inn at Sunset Cliffs HOTEL $$
(☎619-222-7901; www.innatsunsetcliffs.com; 1370 Sunset Cliffs Blvd, Point Loma; r from $175; P❄@📶🏊) Hear the surf crashing onto the rocky shore at this breezy charmer wrapped around a flower-bedecked courtyard. Recently renovated rooms are light-filled but on the small side; recent efforts to decrease the hotel's water and plastic consumption have made the place greener.

TOP CHOICE **Hotel del Coronado** LUXURY HOTEL $$$
(☎619-435-6611; www.hoteldel.com; 1500 Orange Ave, Coronado; r from $325; P❄@📶🏊) San Diego's iconic hotel, the Del provides more than a century of history, tennis courts, spa, shops, splashy restaurants, manicured grounds and a white-sand beach. Book the original building. Parking is $25.

Ocean Beach Hotel HOTEL $$
(☎619-223-7191; www.obhotel.com; 5080 Newport Ave, Ocean Beach; d from $129; ❄@🛜) This recently remodeled hotel is just across the street from the beach. Spotless guest rooms are on the smaller side; the French provincial look is a bit dated but all feature refrigerators and complimentary wi-fi.

La Valencia LUXURY HOTEL $$$
(☎858-454-0771; www.lavalencia.com; 1132 Prospect St, La Jolla; r from $285; P❄@🛜) This 1926 landmark, the Mediterranean-style 'Pink Lady,' was designed by William Templeton Johnson. Its 116 rooms are rather compact, but it wins for Old Hollywood romance; recent ecofriendly efforts add to the charm. Parking is $32.

Eating

With more than 6000 restaurants, San Diego's dynamic dining scene caters to all tastes. Generally speaking, you'll find fine steakhouses and seafood institutions downtown, casual seafood along the beaches, ethnic food in and around Hillcrest, and tacos and margaritas, well, everywhere.

DOWNTOWN & EMBARCADERO

Café 222 BREAKFAST $
(Map p920; ☎619-236-9902; www.cafe222.com; 222 Island Ave; mains $7-11; ⏲7am-1:45pm) Downtown's favorite breakfast place for pumpkin waffles, orange-pecan or granola pancakes, and farm-fresh eggs Benedict. The French toast stuffed with peanut butter and bananas was featured on the Food Network.

C Level SEAFOOD $$$
(☎619-298-6802; www.islandprime.com; 880 Harbor Island Dr; mains $14-30; ⏲from 11am) The bay views are stunning from this airy, elegant eatery on Harbor Island, west of downtown; well-prepared seafood dishes include the popular seared Hawaiian 'ahi tuna, lobster truffle mac 'n' cheese and Japanese-style sesame salmon. The Social Hour (3:30pm to 5:30pm Monday to Friday) offers $5 'bites and libations.'

Gaslamp Strip Club STEAKHOUSE $$
(Map p920; ☎619-231-3140; www.gaslampsteak.com; 340 5th Ave; mains $14-24; ⏲5-10pm Sun-Thu, to midnight Fri & Sat) Pull a bottle from the wine vault and then char your favorite cut of steak, chicken or fish on the open grills in this retro-Vegas dining room.

Oceanaire Seafood Room SEAFOOD $$$
(Map p920; ☎619-858-2277; www.theoceanaire.com; 400 J St; mains $24-40; ⏲5-10pm Sun-Thu, to 11pm Fri & Sat) The look is art-deco ocean liner and the service is just as refined, with an oyster bar (get them for a buck during happy hour, 5pm to 6pm Monday to Friday) and inventive creations including Maryland blue crab cakes and horseradish-crusted Alaskan halibut.

BALBOA PARK & OLD TOWN

TOP CHOICE **Prado** MEDITERRANEAN $$$
(Map p920; ☎619-557-9441; www.pradobalboa.com; 1549 El Prado, Balboa Park; mains lunch $10-15, dinner $21-34; ⏲11:30am-3pm Mon-Fri, from 5pm Tue-Sun, 11am-3pm Sat & Sun; 👪) This classic lunch spot in the museum district of Balboa Park serves up fresh Mediterranean cuisine like steamed mussels, shrimp paella and grilled portobello sandwiches. Breezy outdoor seating and the Mexican-tiled interior are equally inviting; happy hour food and drink specials (4pm to 6pm Tuesday to Friday) are a steal.

Old Town Mexican Café MEXICAN $$
(☎619-297-4330; www.oldtownmexcafe.com; 2489 San Diego Ave, Old Town; mains $4-15; ⏲7am-2am; 👪) Watch the staff turn out fresh tortillas in the window while waiting for a table. Besides breakfast (great *chilaquiles* – soft tortilla chips covered with mole), there's *pozole* (spicy pork stew), avocado tacos and margaritas at the festive central bar.

HILLCREST & NORTH PARK

Bread & Cie BAKERY $
(www.breadandciecatering.com; 350 University Ave, Hillcrest; mains $6-10; ⏲7am-7pm Mon-Fri, to 6pm Sat, 9am-6pm Sun) The fantastic sandwiches and decadent pastries (try the almond croissant or the ridiculously oversized *pain au chocolat*) make this busy bakery a Hillcrest institution.

Alchemy INTERNATIONAL $$$
(☎619-255-0616; www.alchemysandiego.com; 1503 30th St, North Park; mains $13-25; ⏲4pm-midnight Sun-Thu, to 1am Fri & Sat, 10am-2pm Sat & Sun) It's a spin-the-globe menu of local ingredients from small plates (including charcuterie or Parmesan frites with garlic aioli), and Jidori chicken with bok choy and shiitake dumplings, in an art-filled blond-wood room.

Linkery PUB $$$
(☎619-255-8778; www.thelinkery.com; 3794 30th St, North Park; mains $10-25; ⏲5-11pm Mon-Thu,

noon-midnight Fri, 11am-midnight Sat, 11am-10pm Sun) A daily changing menu of housemade sausages and hand-cured meats from sustainably raised animals is the thing here – on a roll, on a board with cheese or in *choucroute* (French stew).

Saigon on Fifth VIETNAMESE $$
(☎619-220-8828; 3900 5th Ave, Hillcrest; mains $11-16; ⊙11am-late; P) This Vietnamese place tries hard and succeeds, with dishes such as fresh spring rolls, fish of Hue (with garlic, ginger and lemongrass) and rockin' 'spicy noodles.' Elegant but not overbearing.

BEACHES

TOP CHOICE **Cafe 1134** CAFE $
(1134 Orange Ave, Coronado; mains $8-10; ⊙9am-7pm) This cool coffee shop on Coronado's main drag offers more than your morning fix: think delicious Greek-style egg scramblers, grilled panini, spinach salads, high-end teas, and a wine and beer list. Prices are slashed as part of the 'Money Wise Menu' on Sunday, Monday and Tuesday evenings.

George's at the Cove MODERN AMERICAN $$$
(☎858-454-4244; www.georgesatthecove.com; 1250 Prospect St, La Jolla; mains $11-48; ⊙11am-11pm) Chef Trey Foshee's Euro-Cal cuisine is as dramatic as this eatery's oceanfront location. George's has graced just about every list of top restaurants in California. Three venues allow you to enjoy it at different price points: **George's Bar** (mains lunch $9-16), **Ocean Terrace** (mains lunch $11-18) and **George's California Modern** (mains dinner $28-48). Walk-ins welcome at the bar, but reservations are recommended for the latter two.

Hodad's BURGERS $
(www.hodadies.com; 5010 Newport Ave, Ocean Beach; burgers $4-9; ⊙5am-10pm) OB's legendary burger joint serves great shakes, massive baskets of onion rings and succulent hamburgers wrapped in paper. The walls are covered in license plates and your bearded, tattooed server might sidle into your booth to take your order. A second location recently opened **downtown** (Map p920; 945 Broadway Ave).

World Famous SEAFOOD $$$
(☎858-272-3100; www.worldfamous.signonsandiego.com; 711 Pacific Beach Dr, Pacific Beach; mains breakfast & lunch $9-16, dinner $15-25; ⊙7am-11pm) Watch the surf while enjoying 'California coastal cuisine,' an ever-changing menu of inventive dishes from the sea (think banana rum mahi and bacon-and-spinach-wrapped scallops), plus steaks, salads, lunchtime sandwiches and burgers.

Drinking

TOP CHOICE **Wine Steals** WINE BAR
(☎619-295-1188; www.winestealssd.com; 1243 University Ave, Hillcrest) Laid-back wine tastings (go for a flight or choose a bottle off the rack in the back), live music, gourmet pizzas and cheese platters bring in a nightly crowd to this low-lit wine bar. Look for two newer branches in San Diego, **Wine Steals East Village** (Map p920; 793/5 J St, Downtown) and

SAN DIEGO MICROBREWERIES

San Diegans take their craft beers seriously – even at a dive bar, you might overhear local guys talking about hops and cask conditioning. Various microbreweries around the city specialize in India Pale Ale (IPA) and Belgian-style brews. The following venues are beer enthusiast favorites.

Stone Brewing Company BREWERY
(off Map p920; ☎760-471-4999; www.stonebrew.com; 1999 Citracado Pkwy, Escondido; ⊙11am-9pm). Take a free tour before a guided tasting of Oaked Arrogant Bastard Ale and Stone Barley Wine.

Lost Abbey BREWERY
(off Map p920; ☎800-918-6816; www.lostabbey.com; 155 Mata Way, Suite 104, San Marcos; ⊙1-6pm Wed-Thu, 3-9pm Fri, noon-6pm Sat & Sun) More than 20 brews ($1 per taste) are on tap in the tasting room – try Lost and Found Abbey Ale.

AleSmith BREWERY
(off Map p920; ☎858-549-9888; www.alesmith.com; 9368 Cabot Dr; ⊙2-7pm Thu-Fri, noon-6pm Sat, noon-4pm Sun) Wee Heavy and the potent Old Numbskull ($1 per taste) are the stand-out brews.

Lounge-Point Loma (2970 Truxtun Rd, Point Loma).

Tipsy Crow BAR, LOUNGE
(Map p920; www.thetipsycrow.com; 770 5th Ave, Downtown) There are three distinct levels at this historic Gaslamp building that's been turned into an atmospheric watering hole: the main floor with its long mahogany bar, the lounge-like 'Nest' (thought to be the site of a former brothel), and the brick-walled 'Underground' with a dancefloor and live music acts.

Nunu's Cocktail Lounge COCKTAIL BAR
(www.nunuscocktails.com; 3537 5th Ave, Hillcrest) Dark and divey, this hipster haven started pouring when JFK was president and still looks the part with its curvy booths, big bar and lovably kitsch decor.

Bourbon Street GAY
(www.bourbonstreetsd.com; 4612 Park Blvd, North Park) This gay spot's warren of bars, courtyards and dancefloor makes for easy mingling (it's hetero-friendly too.) Look for billiards, guest DJs and wickedly cheap martini happy hours.

Waterfront Bar & Grill BAR
(Map p920; www.waterfrontbarandgrill.com; 2044 Kettner Blvd, Little Italy) Beer and burgers are the orders of choice at this cheerful neighborhood bar, opened in 1933 shortly after Prohibition was outlawed.

☆ Entertainment

Check the *San Diego Reader* (www.sandiegoreader.com) or the Thursday edition of the *San Diego Union-Tribune* (www.signonsandiego.com) for the latest happenings around town. **Arts Tix** (p920; ☎858-381-5595; www.sdartstix.com; 3rd Ave & Broadway, Downtown; ⏲9:30am-5pm Tue-Thu, to 6pm Fri & Sat), in a kiosk on Broadway outside Horton Plaza, has half-price tickets for same-day evening or next-day matinee performances and discounted tickets to all types of other events.

Anthology LIVE MUSIC
(Map p920; ☎619-595-0300; www.anthologysd.com; 1337 India St, Downtown; cover free-$60) Near Little Italy, Anthology presents live jazz, blues and indie music in a swank supper-club setting, from both up-and-comers and big-name performers.

Casbah LIVE MUSIC
(Map p920; ☎619-232-4355; www.casbahmusic.com; 2501 Kettner Blvd, Little Italy; cover free-$20) Liz Phair, Alanis Morissette and the Smashing Pumpkins all rocked the funky Casbah on their way up the charts; catch local acts and headliners like Bon Iver.

Prohibition JAZZ
(Map p917; www.prohibitionsd.com; 548 5th Ave, Downtown; cover free) This sophisticated 1930's-style jazz bar takes music and cocktails (made with gin or rye whiskey) seriously. The house rules aren't a joke either; you have to reserve online, no cell phones are allowed at the bar, and a dress code is enforced.

ⓘ Information

Internet Access

For wi-fi hotspot locations, check www.jiwire.com.

San Diego Public Library www.sandiego.gov/public-library; 820 E St, Downtown; 📶) Call or check the website for branch locations.

Media

Gay & Lesbian Times (www.gaylesbiantimes.com) Free weekly.

KPBS 89.5 FM (www.kpbs.org) National public radio.

San Diego Magazine (www.sandiegomagazine.com) Glossy monthly.

San Diego Reader (www.sdreader.com) Free tabloid-sized listings magazine.

San Diego Union-Tribune (www.signonsandiego.com) The city's major daily.

Medical Services

Rite-Aid pharmacies (☎800-748-3243) Call for the nearest branch.

Scripps Mercy Hospital (☎619-294-8111; 4077 5th Ave, Hillcrest) Has a 24-hour emergency room.

Money

Travelex (⏲10:30am-7pm Mon-Fri, 10am-6pm Sat, 11am-4pm Sun) Airport (☎619-295-2501; ⏲8am-5pm); Downtown (☎619-235-0901; Horton Plaza); La Jolla (☎858-457-2412; University Towne Centre mall, 4417 La Jolla Village Dr) Foreign currency exchange services.

Post

Call ☎800-275-8777 or log on to www.usps.com for the nearest branch.

Tourist Information

Balboa Park Visitors Center (☎619-239-0512; www.balboapark.org; 1549 El Prado; ⏲9:30am-4:30pm) In the House of Hospitality, the visitor center sells park maps and the **Passport to Balboa Park** (adult/child $45/24, with zoo admission $77/42), which allows one-time entry to 14 of the park's museums within seven days. Ask about the museums that occasionally have free admission on Tuesday.

San Diego Visitor Information Centers (☎619-236-1212; www.sandiego.org) Downtown (cnr W Broadway & Harbor Dr; ⏰9am-5pm Jun-Sep, to 4pm Oct-May); La Jolla (7966 Herschel Ave; ⏰11am-5pm) The downtown location is designed for international visitors.

Websites

Accessible San Diego (www.asd.travel) Excellent resource for barrier-free travel around San Diego.

Gaslamp.org (www.gaslamp.org) Everything you need to know about the bustling Gaslamp Quarter, including parking secrets.

San Diego Convention & Visitors Bureau (www.sandiego.org) Search hotels, sights, dining, rental cars and more, and make reservations.

San Diego.com (www.sandiego.com) Comprehensive ad-based portal to all things San Diegan, from fun stuff to serious business.

Getting There & Away

San Diego International Airport (Lindbergh Field; ☎619-400-2404; www.san.org) sits about 3 miles west of Downtown; plane-spotters will thrill watching jets come in for a landing over Balboa Park.

Greyhound (☎619-515-1100; 120 W Broadway, Downtown) has hourly direct buses to Los Angeles (one way/round-trip $19/31, two to three hours).

Amtrak (☎800-872-7245; www.amtrak.com) runs the *Pacific Surfliner* several times daily to Los Angeles ($36, three hours) and Santa Barbara ($41, 5½ hours) from the **Santa Fe Depot** (1055 Kettner Blvd, Downtown).

All major car-rental companies have desks at the airport, or call the national toll-free numbers (p1174). **Eagle Rider** (☎619-546-5066; www.eaglerider.com; 4236 Taylor St, Old Town; ⏰9am-5pm) rents motorcycles and scooters.

Getting Around

Bus 992 ('the Flyer,' $2.25) operates at 10- to 15-minute intervals between the airport and downtown, with stops along Broadway. Airport shuttles such as **Super Shuttle** (☎800-974-8885; www.supershuttle.com) charge $8 to $10 to downtown. A taxi fare to downtown from the airport is $10 to $15.

Local buses and the San Diego Trolley, which travels south to the Mexican border, are operated by **Metropolitan Transit System** (MTS; www.sdmts.com). The **Transit Store** (☎619-234-1060; Broadway & 1st Ave; ⏰9am-5pm Mon-Fri) has route maps, tickets and Day Tripper passes for $5/9/12/15 for one/two/three/four days. Single-day passes are available for purchase onboard buses. Taxi fares start at $2.20 for the first 1/10 mile and $2.30 for each additional mile.

Around San Diego

SAN DIEGO ZOO SAFARI PARK

Take a walk on the 'wild' side at this 1800-acre open-range **zoo** (☎760-747-8702; www.sandiegozoo.org; 15500 San Pasqual Valley Rd, Escondido; general admission incl tram adult/child $40/30, with San Diego Zoo $76/56; ⏰from 9am). Giraffes graze, lions lounge and rhinos romp more or less freely on the valley floor. For that instant safari feel, board the Journey to Africa tram ride, which tours you around the second-largest continent in under half an hour.

The park is in Escondido, about 35 miles north of downtown San Diego. Take I-15 Fwy to the Via Rancho Pkwy exit and then follow the signs. Parking is $10.

LEGOLAND

This fun fantasy **park** (☎760-918-5346; www.california.legoland.com; 1 Legoland Dr, Carlsbad; adult/child $69/59; ⏰from 10am) of rides, shows and attractions is mostly suited to the elementary-school set. Tots can dig for dinosaur bones, pilot helicopters and earn their driver's license. From downtown San Diego (about 32 miles), take the I-5 Fwy north to the Cannon Rd E exit. Parking is $12.

PALM SPRINGS & THE DESERTS

From swanky Palm Springs to intriguing Death Valley, the California desert region – swallowing 25% of California – is a land of contradictions: vast yet intimate, searing yet healing. Over time, you may find that what first seemed harrowingly barren will transform in your mind's eye to perfect beauty: weathered volcanic peaks, sensuous sand dunes, purple-tinged mountains, cactus gardens, tiny wildflowers pushing up from hard-baked soil in spring, lizards scurrying beneath colossal boulders, and in the night sky uncountable stars. California's deserts are serenely spiritual, surprisingly chic and ultimately irresistible, whether you're a boho artist, movie star, rock climber or 4WD adventurer.

Palm Springs

The Rat Pack is back, baby – or, at least, its hangout is. In the 1950s and '60s, Palm Springs (population 44,500), some 100 miles east of LA, was the swinging getaway of Sinatra, Elvis and other big stars. Once the Rat Pack packed it in, however, Palm Springs surrendered to retirees in golf clothing. In the 1990s, a new generation rediscovered the city's retro-chic charms: kidney-shaped pools, starchitect bungalows, vintage boutique hotels, and piano bars serving perfect martinis. Today retirees mix comfortably with hipsters and a significant gay and lesbian contingent.

Sights & Activities

Palm Springs is the principal city of the Coachella Valley, a string of desert towns ranging from ho-hum Cathedral City to glamtastic Palm Desert, all linked by Hwy 111. In Palm Springs' compact downtown, Hwy 111 runs one way south as Palm Canyon Dr, paralleled by northbound Indian Canyon Dr.

TOP CHOICE **Palm Springs Aerial Tramway** CABLE CAR
(760-325-1449; www.pstramway.com; 1 Tram Way; adult/child $23.25/16.25; 10am-8pm Mon-Fri, from 8am Sat & Sun, last tram down 9:45pm) Enjoy dizzying views as you're whisked 2.5 miles from sunbaked desert to a pine-scented alpine wonderland atop Mt San Jacinto. It gets chilly up here, so bring a jacket. Hiking trails through the wilderness of **Mt San Jacinto State Park** include a 5.5-mile nontechnical summit trek. In winter, rent snowshoes and cross-country skis at the mountain station's **Adventure Center** (10am-4pm Thu-Mon, last rental 2:30pm).

Indian Canyons CANYON
(760-323-6018; www.indian-canyons.com; off S Palm Canyon Dr; adult/child $9/5, 90min guided hike $3/2; 8am-5pm Oct-Jun, Fri-Sun only Jul-Sep) Shaded by fan palms and flanked by soaring cliffs, these ancestral lands of the Cahuilla tribe are a hiker's delight, especially during the spring wildflower bloom.

Tahquitz Canyon CANYON
(760-416-7044; www.tahquitzcanyon.com; 500 W Mesquite Ave; adult/child $12.50/6; 7:30am-5pm Oct-Jun, Fri-Sun only Jul-Sep, last entry 3:30pm) Featured in Frank Capra's 1937 movie *Lost Horizon,* this canyon is famous for its seasonal waterfall and ancient rock art. Explore on your own or join a ranger-guided hike.

Palm Springs Art Museum MUSEUM
(760-322-4800; www.psmuseum.org; 101 Museum Dr; adult/child $12.50/free, 4-8pm Thu free; 10am-5pm Tue-Wed & Fri-Sun, noon-8pm Thu) This art beacon is a good place for keeping tabs on the evolution of American painting, sculpture, photography and glass art over the past century or so.

Living Desert Zoo & Gardens ZOO
(760-346-5694; www.livingdesert.org; 47900 Portola Ave, off Hwy 111, Palm Desert; adult/child $14.25/7.75; 9am-5pm Oct-May, 8am-1:30pm Jun-Sep) At this engaging park you can pet exotic animals, hitch a camel ride or take a spin on the endangered species carousel. It's educational fun and worth the 30-minute drive down-valley.

Knott's Soak City AMUSEMENT PARK
(760-327-0499; www.knotts.com/public/park/soakcity; 1500 S Gene Autry Trail, Palm Springs; adult/child $32/22; mid-Mar–Sep) A great place to keep cool on hot days, Knott's boasts a massive wave pool, towering water slides and tube rides. Parking is $10.

Sleeping

Rates are lower during midweek. High-season winter rates are quoted below; summer savings can be significant. Chain motels are on Hwy 111 south of downtown.

TOP CHOICE **El Morocco Inn & Spa** BOUTIQUE HOTEL $$$
(760-288-2527; www.elmoroccoinn.com; 66814 4th St, Desert Hot Springs; r incl breakfast $169-249;) Heed the call of the Kasbah at this exotic adult-only hideaway whose 10 rooms wrap around a pool deck and perks include a spa, DVD library and homemade lemonade. No kids. In Desert Hot Springs, about a 20-minute drive north of Palm Springs.

Ace Hotel & Swim Club HOTEL $$
(760-325-9900; www.acehotel.com/palmsprings; 701 E Palm Canyon Dr; r $119-190, ste $200-440; P@) Palm Springs goes Hollywood – with all the sass but *sans* attitude – at this hipster hangout. Rooms (many with patio) sport a glorified tent-cabin look and are crammed with lifestyle essentials (big flat-screen TVs, MP3 plugs). Good on-site restaurant and bar to boot.

Orbit In HOTEL **$$$**
(☎760-323-3585; www.orbitin.com; 562 W Arenas Rd; r incl breakfast $149-259;) Swing back to the '50s at this quintessential mid-century property set around a quiet saline pool. Rooms sport designer furniture (Eames, Noguchi et al), while freebies include cocktail hour, bike rentals, and daytime sodas and snacks.

Palm Springs Travelodge MOTEL **$$**
(☎760-327-1211; www.palmcanyonhotel.com; 333 E Palm Canyon Dr; r incl breakfast $60-140;) Travelodge 2.0 with a sleek lobby, mod black furniture and a cool pool with barbecue, fire pits and canopied lounge beds.

Caliente Tropics MOTEL **$$**
(☎760-327-1391; www.calientetropics.com; 411 E Palm Canyon Dr; d $66-111;) This impeccably kept tiki-style motor lodge, where Elvis once frolicked poolside, is a premier budget pick with spacious rooms and comfy beds.

Eating

Note that many restaurants are closed in July and August.

TOP CHOICE **Trio** MODERN AMERICAN **$$$**
(☎760-864-8746; www.triopalmsprings.com; 707 N Palm Canyon Dr; mains $13-28; ⏲4-10pm) The winning formula in this '60s modernist space: updated American comfort food (awesome Yankee pot roast!), eye-catching artwork and picture windows. The $19 'early bird' three-course dinner (served 4pm to 6pm) is a steal.

Cheeky's MODERN AMERICAN **$$**
(☎760-327-7595; www.cheekysps.com; 622 N Palm Canyon Dr; mains $6-13; ⏲8am-2pm Wed-Mon) Waits can be long and service only so-so, but the farm-to-table menu dazzles with witty inventiveness. Actual dishes change weekly, but custardy scrambled eggs, arugula pesto frittata and bacon bar 'flights' keep making appearances.

Wang's in the Desert ASIAN **$$**
(☎760-325-9264; www.wangsinthedesert.com; 424 S Indian Canyon Dr; mains $12-20; ⏲5-9:30pm Sun-Thu, to 10:30 Fri & Sat) This mood-lit gay-fave with indoor koi pond delivers creatively crafted Chinese classics and has a busy daily happy hour.

Sherman's DELI **$$**
(☎760-325-1199; www.shermansdeli.com; 401 E Tahquitz Canyon Way; sandwiches $9-12; ⏲7am-9pm;) With a breezy sidewalk patio, this 1950s kosher-style deli pulls in an all-ages crowd with its 40 sandwich varieties (great hot pastrami!), finger-lickin' rotisserie chicken and to-die-for pies.

Copley's on Palm Canyon AMERICAN **$$$**
(☎760-327-9555; www.copleyspalmsprings.com; 621 N Palm Canyon Dr; mains $27-38; ⏲6pm-late Jan-Apr, closed Mon May, Jun & Sep-Dec) Swoon-worthy American fare on the former Cary Grant estate.

Tyler's Burgers BURGERS **$**
(149 S Indian Canyon Dr; burgers $4.50-9; ⏲11am-4pm Mon-Sat) The best burgers in town. Enough said. Expect a line.

Native Foods VEGAN **$**
(☎760-416-0070; www.nativefoods.com; Smoke Tree Village, 1775 E Palm Canyon Dr; mains $8-11; ⏲11:30am-9:30pm Mon-Sat;) Organic and meatless without sacrificing a lick to the taste gods.

Drinking & Entertainment

Arenas Rd, east of Indian Canyon Dr, is lesbi-gay nightlife central.

Birba BAR
(622 N Palm Canyon Dr; ⏲6-11pm Wed-Fri, from 9:30am Sat & Sun) It's cocktails and pizza at this fabulous indoor-outdoor space where floor-to-ceiling sliding glass doors separate the long marble bar from a hedge-fringed patio with sunken fire pits.

Shanghai Red's BAR
(235 S Indian Canyon Dr; ⏲5pm-late) Behind a casual fish restaurant, this joint has a busy courtyard, an intergenerational crowd and live blues on Friday and Saturday nights.

Melvyn's BAR
(200 W Ramon Rd) Join the Bentley pack for stiff martinis and quiet jazz at this former Sinatra haunt at the Ingleside Inn. Shine your shoes.

Shopping

For art galleries and indie boutiques, head 'Uptown' to North Palm Canyon Dr. If you're riding the retro wave, ferret for treasure in thrift shops and consignment boutiques scattered along Hwy 111. For the local version of Rodeo Dr, drive 14 miles down-valley to El Paseo in Palm Desert. For bargain-hunters, there's the huge Desert Hills Premium Outlets, 20 minutes west on the I-10.

WHAT THE...?

West of Palm Springs, you may do a double-take when you see the **World's Biggest Dinosaurs** (☎951-922-0076; www.cabazondinosaurs.com; 50770 Seminole Dr, off I-10 exit Main St, Cabazon; adult/child $7/6; ⏲10am-6pm). Claude K Bell, a sculptor for Knott's Berry Farm, spent over a decade crafting these concrete behemoths, now owned by Christian creationists who contend that God created the original dinosaurs in one day, along with the other animals. In the gift shop, alongside the sort of dino-swag you might find at science museums, you can read about the alleged hoaxes and fallacies of evolution and Darwinism.

Information

Desert Regional Medical Center (☎800-491-4990; 1150 N Indian Canyon Dr; ⏲24hr) Emergency room.

Palm Springs Official Visitors Center (☎760-778-8418; www.visitpalmsprings.com; 2901 N Palm Canyon Dr; ⏲9am-5pm) Inside a 1965 Albert Frey–designed gas station at the tramway turnoff north of downtown.

Post office (333 E Amado Rd; ⏲8am-5pm Mon-Fri, 9am-3pm Sat)

Public library (300 S Sunrise Way; ⏲9am-8pm Tue-Wed, to 6pm Thu-Sat; @ wi-fi)

Getting There & Around

Ten minutes' drive from downtown, **Palm Springs International Airport** (PSP; www.palmspringsairport.com; 3400 E Tahquitz Canyon Way) is served by domestic and Canadian airlines; major car-rental agencies are on-site.

Thrice-weekly Amtrak trains to/from LA ($37, 2¾ hours) stop at the unstaffed, kinda-creepy North Palm Springs Station, 5 miles north of downtown, as do several daily Greyhound buses to/from LA ($32.50, three hours). **SunLine** (www.sunline.org; single ride/day pass $1/3) runs slow-moving local buses throughout the valley.

Joshua Tree National Park

Like figments from a Dr Seuss book, the whimsical Joshua trees (actually tree-sized yuccas) welcome visitors to this 794,000 acre (321,000 hectare) park at the convergence of the Sonora and Mojave Deserts. The park is hemmed in by the I-10 in the south and by Hwy 62 (Twentynine Palms Hwy) in the north, and you'll find most of the attractions, including all of the Joshua trees, in its northern half.

Joshua Tree is popular with rock climbers and day hikers, especially in spring when the trees send up a huge single cream-colored flower. The mystical quality of this stark, boulder-strewn landscape has inspired many artists, most famously the band U2.

There are no park facilities aside from restrooms, but you can gas and stock up in the trio of desert communities linked by Twentynine Palm Hwy (Hwy 62) along its northern boundary. Of these, Yucca Valley has the most facilities and arty Joshua Tree the best eating. Twentynine Palms, home to the country's largest US marine base, is more down-to-earth.

Sights & Activities

The epic **Wonderland of Rocks**, a mecca for climbers, dominates the park's north side. Sunset-worthy **Keys View** overlooks the San Andreas Fault and as far as Mexico. For Western pioneer history, visit **Keys Ranch** (☎reservations 760-367-5555; 90min walking tour adult/child $5/2.50; ⏲10am & 1pm year-round, plus 7pm Tue, Thu-Sat Oct-May). Hikers can search out native desert fan-palm oases like **49 Palms Oasis** (3-mile round-trip) or **Lost Palms Oasis** (7.2-mile round-trip). Kid-friendly nature trails include **Barker Dam** (1.1-mile loop), which passes Native American petroglyphs; **Skull Rock** (1.7-mile loop); and **Cholla Cactus Garden** (0.25-mile loop). For a scenic 4WD route, tackle the bumpy 18-mile **Geology Tour Road**, also open to mountain bikers.

Sleeping

The national park itself has only camping, but there's plenty of lodging along Hwy 62, as well as the deliciously kooky Pioneertown Motel.

Desert Lily B&B $$
(☎760-366-4676; www.thedesertlily.com, Joshua Tree Highlands; s/d incl breakfast $140/155; ⏲closed Jul & Aug; @ wi-fi) The charming Carrie presides over this three-room adobe retreat and will happily dole out insider tips about the area. Breakfasts are scrumptious.

Spin & Margie's Desert Hide-a-Way CABIN $$
(☎760-366-9124; www.deserthideaway.com; 64491 Twentynine Palms Hwy; ste $125-175; air-con wi-fi)

This hacienda-style inn harbors five boldly colored suites with striking design using corrugated tin, old license plates and cartoon art.

29 Palms Inn HOTEL $$$
(☎760-367-3505; www.29spalmsinn.com; 73950 Inn Ave, Twentynine Palms; r & cottages incl breakfast $95-258;) History oozes from every nook and cranny in these historic adobe-and-wood cabins dotted around a palm oasis.

High Desert Motel MOTEL $
(☎760-366-1978; www.highdesertmotel.com; 61310 Twentynine Palms Hwy, Joshua Tree; r $50-70;) Near the park entrance, rooms here are plain-Jane plus minifridges and microwaves.

Camping CAMPGROUNDS $
(campsites $10-15) Of the park's eight campgrounds, only Cottonwood and Black Rock have potable water, flush toilets and dump stations. Indian Cove and Black Rock accept **reservations** (☎877-444-6777; www.recreation.gov); the others are first-come, first-served. None have showers. Backcountry camping (no campfires) is allowed 1 mile from any trailhead or road and 100ft from water sources; free self-registration is required at the park's 13 staging areas. **Joshua Tree Outfitters** (☎760-366-1848; 61707 Twentynine Palms Hwy, Joshua Tree) rents quality camping gear.

WHAT THE...?

Just north of Yucca Valley, **Pioneertown** (www.pioneertown.com; admission free) was built as a Hollywood Western movie set in 1946, and it hasn't changed much since. On Mane St, witness mock gunfights at 2:30pm on Saturdays and Sundays from April to October. Enjoy BBQ, cheap beer and live music at honky-tonk **Pappy & Harriet's Pioneertown Palace** (☎760-365-5956; www.pappyandharriets.com; 53688 Pioneertown Rd; burgers $5-12, mains $16-30; 11am-2am Thu-Sun, 5pm-midnight Mon). Then bed down at **Pioneertown Motel** (☎760-365-7001; www.pioneertown-motel.com; 5040 Curtis Rd; r $50-100;), where yesteryear silver-screen stars once slept and rooms are now crammed with Western-themed memorabilia.

Eating & Drinking

Ricochet Gourmet INTERNATIONAL $$
(www.ricochetjoshuatree.com; 61705 Twentynine Palm Hwy, Joshua Tree; mains $8-15; 7am-5p Mon-Sat, from 8am Sun;) At this much adored cafe-cum-deli, the menu bounces from breakfast frittatas to curry chicken salad and fragrant soups, all of them homemade using organic and seasonal ingredients.

Restaurant at 29 Palms Inn AMERICAN $$
(☎760-367-3505, www.29spalmsinn.com; 73950 Inn Ave, Twentynine Palms; mains lunch $7.50-10, dinner $9-21;) The well-respected restaurant has its own organic garden and does burgers and salads at lunchtime and grilled meats and yummy pastas for dinner.

Joshua Tree Saloon AMERICAN $$
(http://thejoshuatreesaloon.com; 61835 Twentynine Palms Hwy, Joshua Tree; mains $9-17; 8am-late;) For rib-sticking burgers and steaks, report to this raucous watering hole that also offers nightly entertainment (over 21s only).

Sam's PIZZA, INDIAN $
(☎760-366-9511; 61380 Twentynine Palms Hwy, Joshua Tree; mains $8-11; 11am-9pm Mon-Sat, 3-8pm Sun;) Sure, there's pizza but clued-in locals flock here for the flavor-packed Indian curries, many of them meatless. Takeout available.

Information

Joshua Tree Outfitters (☎760-366-1848; 61707 Twentynine Palms Hwy, Joshua Tree) has internet access for $2 per 15 minutes.

Park entry permits ($15 per vehicle) are valid for seven days and come with a map and newspaper guide. Get information at the **visitor centers** (☎760-367-5500; www.nps.gov/jotr) Cottonwood (north of I-10, Cottonwood Springs; 9am-3pm); Joshua Tree (Park Blvd, off Hwy 62; 8am-5pm); Oasis (Utah Trail & National Park Dr, Twentynine Palms; 8am-5pm).

Anza-Borrego Desert State Park

Shaped by an ancient sea and tectonic forces, Anza-Borrego is the largest state park in the USA outside Alaska. Cradling the park's only commercial hub – tiny Borrego Springs (pop 2535) – are 600,000 acres of mountains, canyons and badlands; a fabulous variety of plants and wildlife; and intriguing relics

WHAT THE...?

East of Anza-Borrego and south of Joshua Tree awaits a most unexpected sight: the **Salton Sea** (www.saltonsea.ca.gov), California's largest lake in the middle of its biggest desert, created in 1905 when the Colorado River breached its banks. Originally a tourist destination, it's reputation has been tainted since the 1980s by the annual fish die-offs caused by chemical runoff from surrounding farmland. It's an environmental nightmare with no easy solutions.

An even stranger sight near the lake's eastern shore is **Salvation Mountain** (www.salvationmountain.us), a 100ft-high hill blanketed in colorful paint and found objects, and inscribed with religious messages. The vision of Leonard Knight, it's become one of the great works of American folk art and has even been recognized as a national treasure in the US Senate. It's in Niland, about 3 miles off Hwy 111, via Main St.

of native tribes, Spanish explorers and gold-rush pioneers. Wildflower season (usually March to May; for updates call ☎760-767-4684) is peak season and right before the Hades-like heat makes exploring dangerous.

Sights

Park highlights include: **Fonts Point** desert lookout; **Clark Dry Lake** for birding; the **Elephant Tree Discovery Trail**; Split Mountain's wind caves; and **Blair Valley**, with its Native American pictographs and *morteros* (seed-grinding stones). Further south, **Agua Caliente County Park** has hot springs.

Sleeping & Eating

Aside from developed **Borrego Palm Canyon** (☎reservations 800-444-7275; www.reserveamerica.com; tent/RV sites $25/35), there are a handful of primitive campgrounds with vault toilets but no water. Free backcountry camping is permitted anywhere that's off-road and at least 100ft from water but open ground fires and vegetation gathering are *verboten*.

For country-style B&Bs and famous apple pie, the gold-mining town of **Julian** (www.julianca.com) is a 45-minute drive southwest of Borrego Springs.

TOP CHOICE **Borrego Valley Inn** BOUTIQUE HOTEL **$$$**
(☎760-767-0311; www.borregovalleyinn.com; 405 Palm Canyon Dr, Borrego Springs; r incl breakfast $185-275;) This intimate spa-resort inn has 15 adobe-style rooms brimming with Southwestern decor, plus two pools (one clothing-optional) and a hot tub.

Palms at Indian Head BOUTIQUE HOTEL **$$$**
(☎760-767-7788; www.thepalmsatindianhead.com; 2200 Hoberg Rd, Borrego Springs; r $169-249;) This former haunt of Cary Grant, Marilyn Monroe and other old-time celebs has been reborn as a chic mid-century-modern retreat. Connect with the era over martinis and chicken cordon bleu at the on-site bar and grill while enjoying enchanting desert views.

Carlee's Place AMERICAN **$$**
(660 Palm Canyon Dr, Borrego Springs; mains lunch $7-14, dinner $12-23; 11am-9pm) Join the locals for casual American fare, karaoke nights and pool.

Information

Borrego Springs has stores, ATMs, gas stations, a post office, supermarket and a public library with free internet access and wi-fi. The park's comprehensive **visitor center** (☎760-767-4205; www.parks.ca.gov; 200 Palm Canyon Dr; 9am-5pm Nov-Apr, Sat & Sun only May-Oct) is 2 miles west. For additional information, see www.california-desert.org. Driving through the park is free, but if you camp, hike or picnic, a day fee of $8 per car applies. You'll need a 4WD to tackle the 500 miles of back-country dirt roads. For hikes or mountain biking along dirt roads, pack extra water and don't go at midday.

Mojave National Preserve

If you're on a quest for the 'middle of nowhere,' you'll find it in the wilderness of the **Mojave National Preserve** (☎760-252-6100; www.nps.gov/moja; admission free), a 1.6-million-acre jumble of sand dunes, Joshua trees, volcanic cinder cones and habitats for desert tortoises, jackrabbits and coyotes. No gas is available here.

Southeast of Baker and the I-15 Fwy, Kelbaker Rd crosses a ghostly landscape of cinder cones before arriving at **Kelso Depot**, a handsome 1920s railroad station in Spanish mission revival style, which now houses the park's **visitor center** (☎760-252-6108; ⏰9am-5pm) with excellent natural and cultural history exhibits and an old-fashioned **lunch counter** (dishes $3.50-8.50). It's another 11 miles southwest to the 'singing' **Kelso Dunes** which, at 600ft high, are the country's third-tallest sand dunes. When conditions are right, they emanate low humming sounds that are caused by shifting sands – running downhill sometimes jump-starts the effect.

From Kelso Depot, Kelso–Cima Rd takes off northeast. After 19 miles, Cima Rd heads back toward I-15 around **Cima Dome**, a 1500ft-high hunk of granite with crusty lava outcroppings. Its slopes are smothered in the world's largest **Joshua tree forest**. For close-ups, summit Teutonia Peak (3 miles round-trip); the trailhead is 6 miles northwest of Cima.

East off the Kelso–Cima Rd, Mojave Rd is the backdoor route to two first-come, first-served **campgrounds** (sites $12) with potable water at Mid Hills (no RVs) and Hole-in-the-Wall. They bookend a rugged 10-mile scenic drive along **Wild Horse Canyon Rd**. Ask at Hole-in-the-Wall's **visitor center** (☎760-252-6104; ⏰9am-4pm Wed-Sun Oct-Apr, Fri-Sun only May-Sep) about the slot-canyon **Rings Loop Trail**. Roads in this area are mostly unpaved but well maintained.

Southwest of Hole-in-the-Wall, the splendid **Mitchell Caverns** (☎760-928-2586) unlock a world of quirky limestone formations but tours were suspended until further notice at press time.

Sleeping & Eating

Free backcountry and roadside **camping** is permitted throughout the preserve in areas already used for this purpose. Check the website for locations or ask at the visitor center. Baker is the nearest town with bare-bones motels.

For more ambience, detour to the **Hotel Nipton** (☎760-856-2335; www.nipton.com; 107355 Nipton Rd, Nipton; d incl breakfast $79; ⏰reception 8am-6pm; Wi-Fi) in a century-old adobe villa in a remote railway outpost northeast of the preserve. Check-in is at the well-stocked trading post adjacent to the **cafe-bar** (dishes $7-10; ⏰11am-6pm, dinner by arrangement). There's also a **campground** (per site $25) and **tent cabins** ($65).

Death Valley National Park

The name itself evokes all that is harsh and hellish – a punishing, barren and lifeless place of Old Testament severity. Yet closer inspection reveals that in Death Valley nature is putting on a spectacular show with water-sculpted canyons, singing sand dunes, palm-shaded oases, eroded mountains and plenty of endemic wildlife. It's a land of superlatives, holding the US records for hottest temperature (134°F, or 57°C), lowest point (Badwater, 282ft below sea level) and largest national park outside Alaska (over 5000 sq miles). Peak tourist season is when spring wildflowers bloom. Furnace Creek is the park's commercial hub.

Sights & Activities

Drive up to **Zabriskie Point** at sunrise or sunset for spectacular valley views across golden badlands eroded into waves, pleats and gullies. Some 20 miles further south, at **Dante's View**, you can simultaneously see the highest (Mt Whitney, 14,505ft) and lowest (Badwater) points in the contiguous USA. En route, consider detouring along the bone-rattling scenic one-way loop through **Twenty Mule Team Canyon**.

Badwater itself, a timeless landscape of crinkly salt flats, is a 17-mile drive south of Furnace Creek. Along the way, narrow **Golden Canyon** and **Natural Bridge** are both easily explored on short hikes. On the **Devils Golf Course**, crystallized salt has piled up into saw-tooth mini mountains. A 9-mile detour along **Artists Drive** is best in the late afternoon when eroded hillsides erupt in fireworks of color.

North of Furnace Creek, near Stovepipe Wells, you can scramble along the smooth marble walls of **Mosaic Canyon** or roll down the Saharan-esque **Mesquite Flat sand dunes** – magical during a full moon.

Another 36 miles north is whimsical **Scotty's Castle** (☎760-786-2392; adult/child $11/6; ⏰tours 9am-5pm Nov-Apr, to 4pm May-Oct), where costumed guides bring to life the strange tale of con-man Death Valley Scotty.

In summer, stick to paved roads (dirt roads can quickly overheat vehicles), limit your exertions and visit higher-elevation areas. For example, the scenic drive up **Emigrant Canyon Road**, starting west of Stovepipe Wells, ends 21 miles later at the historic beehive-shaped **Charcoal Kilns**, near the trailhead for the 8.4-mile round-trip hike up

Wildrose Peak (9064ft). At the park's western edge, utterly remote **Panamint Springs** offers volcanic vistas, Joshua tree forests and the scenic Darwin Falls.

Activities back at Furnace Creek Ranch include horseback riding and golf.

Sleeping & Eating

In-park lodging is pricey and often booked solid in springtime when even first-come first-served campgrounds fill by midmorning, especially on weekends. The closest town with cheaper lodging is Beatty in Nevada (44 miles from Furnace Creek), although choices are more plentiful in Las Vegas (120 miles southeast) and Ridgecrest (122 miles west).

Stovepipe Wells Village MOTEL **$$**
(760-786-2387; www.escapetodeathvalley.com; Hwy 190; RV sites $31, r $80-155;) Newly spruced-up rooms feature quality linens beneath cheerful Native American bedspreads as well as coffeemakers. The small pool is cool and the cowboy-style restaurant (mains $5 to $25) delivers three square meals a day.

Furnace Creek Ranch RESORT **$$**
(760-786-2345; www.furnacecreekresort.com; cabins $130-162, r $162-213;) Tailor-made for families, this rambling resort has been subjected to a vigorous facelift resulting in rooms dressed in desert-color decor, updated bathrooms and porches with comfortable patio furniture. The grounds encompass a playground, spring-fed swimming pool, tennis courts and the Forty-Niner Café (mains $12 to $25), which cooks up decent American standards. The next-door Wrangler serves juicy steak dinners (mains $22 to $39) and run-of-the-mill breakfast and lunch buffets ($11.25/14.95).

Furnace Creek Inn HOTEL **$$$**
(760-786-2345; www.furnacecreekresort.com; r $330-460; early Oct-early May;) At this elegant, mission-style hotel you can count the colors of the desert while unwinding by the spring-fed pool with sweeping valley views. The restaurant (dress code) serves upscale American fare (lunch mains $13 to $17, dinner $24 to $38) and an opulent Sunday brunch.

Camping CAMPGROUNDS **$**
(campsites free-$18) Of the park's nine campgrounds, only Furnace Creek accepts **reservations** (877-444-6777; www.recreation.gov) from mid-April to mid-October. In summer, Furnace Creek is first-come, first-served, and the only other campgrounds open are Mesquite Spring, near Scotty's Castle, and those along Emigrant Canyon Rd west of Stovepipe Wells. Some are accessible to high-clearance vehicles only. Other valley-floor campgrounds – like roadside Stovepipe Wells, Sunset and shadier Texas Springs – cater primarily to RVs; they're open October to April.

Backcountry camping (no campfires) is allowed 2 miles off paved roads and away from developed and day-use areas, and 100yd from any water source; pick up free permits at the visitor center.

Furnace Creek Ranch and Stovepipe Wells Village offer public showers ($5, including swimming-pool access).

Information

Entry permits ($20 per vehicle) are valid for seven days and sold at self-service pay stations throughout the park. For a free map and newspaper, show your receipt at the **visitor center** (760-786-3200; www.nps.gov/deva; 8am-5pm) in Furnace Creek, which has a general store, gas station, post office, ATM, internet access, lodging and restaurants. Stovepipe Wells, a 30-minute drive northwest, has a general store, gas station, ATM, motel and cafe. Panamint Springs, on the park's western edge, has gas and snacks. Cell-phone reception is poor to nonexistent in the park.

CENTRAL COAST

No trip to California would be worth its salt without a jaunt along the surreally scenic Central Coast. Hwy 1, one of the USA's most iconic roads, skirts past posh Santa Barbara, retro Pismo Beach, collegiate San Luis Obispo, fantastical Hearst Castle, soul-stirring Big Sur, down-to-earth Monterey Bay and hippie Santa Cruz. Slow down – this idyllic coast deserves to be savored, not gulped. (That same advice goes for locally grown wines.)

Santa Barbara

Life is certainly sweet in Santa Barbara, a coastal Shangri-La where the air is redolent with citrus and jasmine, flowery bougainvillea drapes whitewashed buildings with Spanish-esque red-tiled roofs, and it's all cradled by pearly beaches. Just ignore those pesky oil derricks out to sea. State St, the

WHAT THE...?

Four miles west of Beatty, NV, look for the turnoff to the ghost town of **Rhyolite** (www.rhyolitesite.com; Hwy 374; admission free; ⏲sunrise-sunset), which epitomizes the hurly-burly, boom-and-bust story of so many Western gold-rush mining towns. Don't overlook the 1906 'bottle house' or the skeletal remains of a three-story bank. Next door is the bizarre **Goldwell Open Air Museum** (www.goldwellmuseum.org; admission free; ⏲24hr), a trippy art installation started by Belgian artist Albert Szukalski in 1984.

main drag, abounds with bars, cafes, theaters and boutique shops.

Sights

Mission Santa Barbara CHURCH
(www.sbmission.org; 2201 Laguna St; adult/child $5/1; ⏲9am-4:30pm) Established in 1786, California's hilltop 'Queen of the Missions' was the only one to escape secularization under Mexican rule. Look for Chumash artwork inside the vaulted church and a moody cemetery out back.

Santa Barbara Museum of Art MUSEUM
(www.sbma.net; 1130 State St; adult/child $9/6; ⏲11am-5pm Tue-Sun) These downtown galleries hold an impressive, well-edited collection of contemporary California artists, modern masters like Matisse and Chagall, 20th-century photography and Asian art, with provocative special exhibits. Sundays are pay-what-you-wish.

FREE **County Courthouse** HISTORIC BUILDING
(www.santabarbaracourthouse.org; 1100 Anacapa St; ⏲8am-5pm Mon-Fri, 10am-4:30pm Sat & Sun) Built in Spanish-Moorish-revival style, it's an absurdly beautiful place to stand trial. Marvel at hand-painted ceilings and intricate murals, then climb the *Vertigo*-esque clock tower for panoramic views. Free tours.

Santa Barbara Historical Museum MUSEUM
(www.santabarbaramuseum.com; 136 E De La Guerra St; donations welcome; ⏲10am-5pm Tue-Sat, from noon Sun) By a romantic cloistered adobe courtyard, peruse a fascinating mishmash of local memorabilia, including Chumash woven baskets, and learn about odd historical footnotes like the city's involvement in toppling the last Chinese monarchy.

Santa Barbara Botanic Garden GARDEN
(www.sbbg.org; 1212 Mission Canyon Rd; adult/child 2-12yr/youth 13-17yr $8/4/6; ⏲9am-6pm, to 5pm Nov-Feb) Uphill from the mission, this garden is devoted to California's native flora. Rolling trails meander through cacti and wildflowers past the historic mission dam and aqueduct. Nearby is a natural-history museum for kiddos.

Santa Barbara Maritime Museum MUSEUM
(www.sbmm.org; 113 Harbor Way; adult/child $7/4, 3rd Thu of month free; ⏲10am-5pm Thu-Tue, to 6pm Jun-Aug) At the harbor, this museum celebrates the town's briny history with historical artifacts, hands-on and virtual-reality exhibits, and a small documentary-movie theater.

Activities

On the waterfront and good for a stroll, 1872 **Stearns Wharf** is the West's oldest continuously operating wooden pier, strung with restaurants and touristy shops. Outside town along Hwy 101, look for palm-fringed **state beaches** (www.parks.ca.gov; per car $10; ⏲8am-sunset) at Carpinteria, about 12 miles east, and El Capitan and Refugio, over 20 miles west.

Wheel Fun CYCLING
(www.wheelfunrentals.com; 22 State St & 23 E Cabrillo Blvd; ⏲8am-8pm) Rents bicycles (from $8 per hour) for the paved recreational trail that skirts miles of beautiful city beaches.

Paddle Sports KAYAKING, SURFING
(☎805-899-4925; www.kayaksb.com; 117b Harbor Way; kayak/SUP rentals from $25/40, 2hr SUP lesson from $80) Friendly kayaking and stand-up paddle boarding (SUP) outfitter.

Santa Barbara Adventure Co KAYAKING, SURFING
(☎805-884-9283; www.sbadventureco.com; tours/lessons from $50/99) Guided kayaking tours and traditional board-surfing and SUP lessons.

Santa Barbara Sailing Center KAYAKING, SAILING
(☎805-962-2826; www.sbsail.com; 133 Harbor Way; kayak rental per hr $10-15, cruises/tours from $25/60) Rents kayaks, teaches sailing and offers sunset cocktail cruises and guided paddling tours.

Condor Express WHALE-WATCHING (805-882-0088; www.condorcruises.com; 301 W Cabrillo Blvd; adult/child from $48/25) Narrated year-round whale-watching tours.

Sleeping

Prepare for sticker shock: even basic rooms command over $200 in summer. Search out motel bargains along upper State St, north of downtown. For state-beach campgrounds off Hwy 101, make **reservations** (800-444-7275; www.reserveamerica.com; campsites $35-50).

Inn of the Spanish Garden BOUTIQUE HOTEL $$$ (805-564-4700; http://spanishgardeninn.com; 915 Garden St; d incl breakfast $259-519;) Elegant Spanish-revival-style downtown hotel has two dozen romantic luxury rooms and suites facing a gracious fountain courtyard. Concierge services are top-notch.

TOP CHOICE **El Capitan Canyon** CABINS, CAMPGROUND $$ (805-685-3887; www.elcapitancanyon.com; 11560 Calle Real, off Hwy 101; safari tents $155, cabins $225-350;) Go 'glamping' in this car-free zone near El Capitan State Beach, a 30-minute drive up Hwy 101. Safari tents are rustic, while creekside cedar cabins come with heavenly mattresses, kitchenettes and outdoor fire pits.

Presidio Motel MOTEL $$$ (805-963-1355; http://thepresidiomotel.com; 1620 State St; r incl breakfast $119-220;) Like the H&M of motels, this affordable gem has panache and personality thanks to arty flair, dreamy bedding and free loaner bikes. Noise can be an issue. Its sister motel, the nearby Agave Inn, is cheaper.

Brisas del Mar HOTEL $$$ (805-966-2219; www.sbhotels.com; 223 Castillo St; r incl breakfast $145-290;) Big kudos for the freebies (DVDs, wine and cheese, milk and cookies) and Mediterranean-style front section, although the motel wing is unlovely. Its sister properties away from the beach are typically lower-priced.

Eating

Olio Pizzeria ITALIAN $$$ (805-899-2699; www.oliopizzeria.com; 11 W Victoria St; dishes $3-24; 11:30am-2pm Mon-Sat, 5-10pm Sun-Thu, to 11pm Fri & Sat) Cozy, high-ceilinged pizzeria and enoteca with a happening wine bar proffers a tempting selection of crispy pizzas, imported cheeses and meats, traditional antipasti and *dolci* (desserts).

TOP CHOICE **Santa Barbara Shellfish Company** SEAFOOD $$ (www.sbfishhouse.com; 230 Stearns Wharf; dishes $5-19; 11am-9pm) 'From sea to skillet to plate' best describes this end-of-the-wharf crab shack that's more of a counter joint. Great lobster bisque, ocean views and the same location for 25 years.

Silvergreens CAFE $ (www.silvergreens.com; 791 Chapala St; dishes $4-10; 7:30am-10pm Mon-Fri, from 11am Sun;) Who says fast food can't be fresh and tasty? With the tag line 'Eat smart, live well,' this sun-drenched cafe makes nutritionally sound salads, soups, sandwiches, burgers, breakfast burritos and more.

D'Angelo Pastry & Bread CAFE $ (25 W Gutierrez St; dishes $2-8; 7am-2pm) Retrolicious bakery with shiny-silver sidewalk bistro tables is a perfect quick breakfast or brunch spot, whether for a buttery croissant or Iron Chef Cat Cora's favorite 'Eggs Rose.'

Lilly's Taquería MEXICAN $ (310 Chapala St; items from $1.50; 11am-9pm Mon & Wed-Thu, to 10pm Fri & Sat, to 9:30pm Sun) There's almost always a line, so be snappy with your order – locals fight over *adobada* (marinated pork) tacos.

Drinking & Entertainment

Nightlife revolves around lower State St. Pick up the free alt-weekly *Santa Barbara Independent* (www.independent.com) for an events calendar. You can ramble between a dozen wine-tasting rooms (and a microbrewery, too) along the city's **Urban Wine Trail** (www.urbanwinetrailsb.com).

Soho LIVE MUSIC (805-962-7776; www.sohosb.com; 1221 State St; cover $12-25) Unpretentious brick room located upstairs behind a McDonald's has live bands nightly, from indie rock, funk and folk to jazz and blues.

Brewhouse BREWERY (www.brewhousesb.com; 229 W Montecito St; 11am-11pm Sun-Thu, to midnight Fri & Sat;) Rowdy dive down by the railroad tracks crafts its own unique small-batch beers and has rockin' live music Wednesday to Saturday nights.

IF YOU HAVE A FEW MORE DAYS

Remote, rugged **Channel Islands National Park** (www.nps.gov/chis) earns the nickname 'California's Galápagos' for its unique wildlife. The islands offering superb snorkeling, scuba diving and sea kayaking too. Spring when wildflowers bloom is a gorgeous time to visit; summer and fall can be bone-dry, and winter stormy.

Anacapa, an hour's boat ride from the mainland, is the best island for day-tripping, with easy hikes and unforgettable views. Santa Cruz, the biggest island, is for overnight excursions, offering camping, hiking and kayaking. Other islands require longer channel crossings and multiday trips: San Miguel is often shrouded in fog; tiny Santa Barbara supports seabird and seal colonies, as does Santa Rosa, which also protects Chumash archaeological sites.

Boats leave from Ventura Harbor, off Hwy 101, where the park's **visitor center** (805-658-5730; 1901 Spinnaker Dr; 8:30am-5pm) has info and maps. The main tour-boat operator is **Island Packers** (805-642-1393; www.islandpackers.com; 1691 Spinnaker Dr; adult/child from $33/24); book ahead. Primitive island **campgrounds** (reservations 877-444-6777; www.recreation.gov; tent sites $15) require reservations; bring food and water.

French Press CAFE
(1101 State St; 6am-7pm Mon-Fri, from 7am Sat, 8am-5pm Sun;) With shiny silver espresso machines from Italy and beans roasted in Santa Cruz, these baristas know how to pull their shots.

Information

Santa Barbara Car Free (www.santabarbaracarfree.org) Helpful website for ecotravel tips and valuable discounts.

Visitor center (805-965-3021; www.santabarbaraca.com; 1 Garden St; 9am-5pm Mon-Sat, from 10am Sun) Near the waterfront, offers maps and self-guided tour brochures.

Getting There & Around

Amtrak (209 State St) Trains run south to LA ($25, three hours) and north to San Luis Obispo ($29, 2¾ hours).

Greyhound (34 W Carrillo St) A few daily buses to LA ($18, three hours), San Luis Obispo ($26, 2¼ hours) or San Francisco ($53, nine hours).

Metropolitan Transit District (805-963-3366; www.sbmtd.gov) Runs city-wide buses (fares $1.75) and electric shuttles (25¢) from State St downtown to Stearns Wharf and along beachfront Cabrillo Blvd.

Santa Barbara to San Luis Obispo

You can speed up to San Luis Obispo in just two hours along Hwy 101, or take all day detouring to wineries, a historical mission and hidden beaches.

A scenic backcountry drive north of Santa Barbara follows Hwy 154, where you can go for the grape in the **Santa Ynez & Santa Maria Valleys** (www.sbcountywines.com). Keep an eye out for *Sideways* (2004) film locations. For ecoconscious vineyard tours, check **Sustainable Vine** (805-698-3911; www.sustainablevine.com; all-day tour $125). Or start DIY explorations at **Los Olivos Cafe & Wine Merchant** (805-688-7265; www.losolivoscafe.com; 2879 Grand Ave, Los Olivos; mains $11-25; 11:30am-8:30pm), a Cal-Mediterranean bistro with a tasting bar, then follow the **Foxen Canyon Wine Trail** (www.foxencanyonwinetrail.com) north to cult winemakers' vineyards.

Further south, the Danish-immigrant village of **Solvang** (www.solvangusa.com) is a kitsch lovers' dream with decorative windmills and fairytale-esque bakeries. For a picnic lunch or BBQ takeout, swing by **El Rancho Marketplace** (www.elranchomarket.com; 2886 Mission Dr/Hwy 246, Solvang; 6am-10pm). Nearer Hwy 101, **Hitching Post II** (805-688-0676; www.hitchingpost2.com; 406 E Hwy 246, Buellton; mains $22-48; 5-9:30pm Mon-Fri, 4-9:30pm Sat & Sun) is an old-guard steakhouse that makes its own Pinot Noir (which is damn good, by the way); reservations are essential.

Follow Hwy 246 about 15 miles west of Hwy 101 to **La Purísima Mission State Historic Park** (www.lapurisimamission.org; 2295 Purisima Rd, Lompoc; per car $6; 9am-5pm). Exquisitely restored, it's one of California's most evocative Spanish-Colonial missions, with flowering gardens, livestock pens and adobe buildings. South of Lompoc off Hwy 1, Jalama Rd travels 14 twisting miles to utterly isolated **Jalama Beach County Park**

(☎805-736-3504; www.sbparks.org; per car $10). Its crazy-popular **campground** (tent/RV sites $25/40, cabins $80-200) only accepts reservations for its newly built cabins – otherwise, look for the 'campground full' sign a half-mile south of Hwy 1.

Heading north on Hwy 1, rough-and-tumble **Guadalupe** is the gateway to North America's largest coastal dunes. Here the **Lost City of DeMille** (www.lostcitydemille.com), the movie set of the 1923 version of *The Ten Commandments,* lies buried beneath the sands. Scenes from *Pirates of the Caribbean: At World's End* (2007) were shot here. The best dunes access is west of town via Hwy 166. Downtown, dig into juicy steaks at genuine Old West–flavored **Far Western Tavern** (☎805-343-2211; www.farwesterntavern.com; 899 Guadalupe St; dinner mains $22-35; ⊙11am-8:30pm Tue-Thu, to 9pm Fri & Sat, 9am-8pm Sun).

Where Hwy 1 rejoins Hwy 101, **Pismo Beach** has a long, lazy stretch of sand and a **butterfly grove** (www.monarchbutterfly.org), where migratory monarchs perch in eucalyptus trees from late October to February. The grove stands south of **Pismo State Beach campground** (☎reservations 800-444-7275; www.reserveamerica.com; Hwy 1; campsites $35;), which offers beach access and hot showers. Pismo Beach has dozens of motels by the beach and off Hwy 101, but rooms fill quickly, especially on weekends. **Pismo Lighthouse Suites** (☎805-773-2411; www.pismolighthousesuites.com; 2411 Price St; ste incl breakfast $149-329;) has everything vacationing families need, from kitchenette suites to a life-sized outdoor chessboard.

By Pismo's seaside pier, lines go out the door at scruffy, hole-in-the-wall **Splash Cafe** (www.splashcafe.com; 197 Pomeroy Ave; dishes $4-10; ⊙8am-9pm;), famed for its clam chowder served in homebaked sourdough-bread bowls. Nearby, **Old West Cinnamon Rolls** (www.oldwestcinnamon.com; 861 Dolliver St; snacks $3-5; ⊙6:30am-5:30pm) bakery is sugary goodness. Uphill at the **Cracked Crab** (www.crackedcrab.com; 751 Price St; mains $9-50; ⊙11am-9pm Sun-Thu, to 10pm Fri & Sat), make sure you don a plastic bib before that fresh bucket o' seafood gets dumped on your table.

The nearby town of Avila Beach has a waterfront promenade. Grab a chipotle tri-tip sandwich from **Avila Grocery & Deli** (354 Front St; mains $5-11; ⊙7am-7pm). Nearer Hwy 101, pick berries and feed the goats at **Avila Valley Barn** (http://avilavalleybarn.com; 560 Avila Beach Dr; ⊙9am-6pm, reduced winter hr) farm stand, then do some private stargazing from a redwood hot tub at **Sycamore Mineral Springs** (☎805-595-7302; www.sycamoresprings.com; 1215 Avila Beach Dr; 1hr per person $12.50-17.50; ⊙8am-midnight, last reservation 10:45pm).

San Luis Obispo

Halfway between LA and San Francisco, San Luis Obispo is a low-key place. But CalPoly university students inject a healthy dose of hubbub into the streets, pubs and cafes, especially during the weekly **farmers market** (⊙6-9pm Thu), which turns downtown's Higuera St into a street festival with live music and sidewalk BBQs.

Like many other California towns, SLO grew up around a Spanish Catholic **mission** (☎805-543-6850; www.missionsanluisobispo.org; 751 Palm St; donation $2; ⊙9am-4pm), founded in 1772 by Padre Junípero Serra. These days, SLO is just a grape's throw from thriving **Edna Valley wineries** (www.slowine.com), known for Chardonnays and Pinots.

Sleeping

San Luis Obispo's motel row is north of downtown along Monterey St, with cheaper chains along Hwy 101.

Peach Tree Inn MOTEL **$$**
(☎805-543-3170; www.peachtreeinn.com; 2001 Monterey St; r incl breakfast $79-200;) Folksy, nothing-fancy motel rooms are relaxing, especially those set creekside or with rocking chairs overlooking a rose garden. Hearty breakfasts include homemade breads.

WHAT THE...?

The fabulously campy **Madonna Inn** (☎805-543-3000; www.madonnainn.com; 100 Madonna Rd; r $179-299;) is a garish confection visible from Hwy 101. Japanese tourists, vacationing Midwesterners and irony-loving hipsters adore the 110 themed rooms – including Yosemite Rock, Caveman and hot-pink Floral Fantasy (check out photos online). The urinal in the men's room is a bizarre waterfall. But the best reason to stop here? Old-fashioned cookies from the storybook bakery.

HI Hostel Obispo HOSTEL $
(805-544-4678; www.hostelobispo.com; 1617 Santa Rosa St; dm $24-27, r from $45; check-in 8-10am & 4:30-10pm;) Cozy solar-powered ecohostel inhabits a converted Victorian one block from the train station. Amenities include a kitchen and bike rentals (from $10 per day). No credit cards; BYOT (bring your own towel).

Eating & Drinking

Downtown overflows with cafes, restaurants, wine-tasting rooms, brewpubs and the USA's first solar-powered cinema, **Palm Theatre** (805-541-5161; www.thepalmtheatre.com; 817 Palm St), showing indie art-house flicks.

Luna Red FUSION $$$
(805-540-5243; www.lunaredslo.com; 1009 Monterey St; small plates $4-15, dinner mains $18-26; 11am-9pm Mon-Thu, to 10pm Fri, 4-10pm Sat, 5-9pm Sun) A locally inspired chef spins Californian, Mediterranean and Asian tapas, with a keen eye toward freshness and spice, bounty from the land and sea, and crazily creative cocktails, all with a surprisingly sophisticated ambience.

Big Sky Café CALIFORNIAN $$$
(www.bigskycafe.com; 1121 Broad St; mains $6-22; 7am-9pm Mon-Wed, to 10pm Thu-Fri, 8am-10pm Sat, 8am-9pm Sun;) With the tagline 'analog food for a digital world,' this airy, ecoconscious cafe gets top marks for market-fresh breakfasts (served until 1pm daily), although big-plate dinners trend toward bland.

Firestone Grill BARBECUE $$
(www.firestonegrill.com; 1001 Higuera St; mains $5-12; 11am-10pm Sun-Wed, to 11pm Thu-Sun;) Sink your teeth into an authentic Santa Maria–style tri-tip steak sandwich on a toasted garlic roll, or a rack of succulent pork ribs.

Information

Car-free SLO (http://slocarfree.org) Helpful website for ecotravel tips and valuable discounts.

Visitor center (805-781-2777; www.visitslo.com; 1039 Chorro St; 10am-5pm Sun-Wed, to 7pm Thu-Sat) Downtown, off Higuera St.

Getting There & Around

Amtrak (1011 Railroad Ave) Daily Seattle–LA *Coast Starlight* and twice-daily *Pacific Surfliner* trains stop 0.6 miles east of downtown en route to/from Santa Barbara ($29, 2¾ hours) and LA ($34, 5½ hours).

Greyhound (1023 Railroad Ave) Runs a few daily buses to Santa Barbara ($26, 2¼ hours), LA ($38, 5¼ hours) or San Francisco ($48, 6½ hours).

SLO Regional Transit Authority (805-541-2228; www.slorta.org; fares $1.50-3, day pass $5) County-wide buses with limited weekend services converge on downtown's **transit center** (cnr Palm & Osos Sts).

Morro Bay to Hearst Castle

A dozen miles northwest of SLO via Hwy 1, **Morro Bay** is home to a commercial fishing fleet and Morro Rock, a volcanic peak jutting up from the ocean floor – your first hint of the coast's upcoming drama. (Too bad about those power-plant smokestacks obscuring the views, though.) Buy boat-tour tickets and rent kayaks along the Embarcadero, where **Giovanni's Fish Market & Galley** (www.giovannisfishmarket.com; 1001 Front St; mains $7-13; 9am-6pm;), a classic California seafood shack, cooks killer garlic fries and fish-and-chips. Midrange motels cluster uphill off Harbor and Main Sts. Downtown's **Shine Café** (www.sunshinehealthfoods-shinecafe.com; 415 Morro Bay Blvd; mains $5-14; 11am-5pm Mon-Fri, from 9am Sat, 10am-4pm Sun;) offers takeout karma-cleansers like tempeh tacos and tofu scrambles.

Nearby are fantastic state parks for coastal hiking and **camping** (reservations 800-444-7275; www.reserveamerica.com). South of the Embarcadero, **Morro Bay State Park** (www.parks.ca.gov; tent/RV sites $35/50) has a natural-history museum and heron rookery. Further south in Los Osos, west of Hwy 1, wilder **Montaña de Oro State Park** (www.parks.ca.gov; campsites $20-25) features coastal bluffs, tide pools, sand dunes, peak-hiking and mountain-biking trails, and primitive camping. Its Spanish name ('mountain of gold') comes from native California poppies that blanket the hillsides in spring.

Heading north along Hwy 1, surfers love the Cal-Mexican **Taco Temple** (2680 Main St, Morro Bay; mains $7-13; 11am-8:30pm Sun, to 9pm Mon & Wed-Sat), a cash-only joint, and **Ruddell's Smokehouse** (www.smokerkjim.com; 101 D St, Cayucos; items $5-12; 11am-6pm), serving smoked-fish tacos by the beach in small-town Cayucos. Vintage motels line Cayucos' Ocean Ave, including cutesy, family-run **Seaside Motel** (805-995-3809; www.seasidemotel.com; 42 S Ocean Ave, Cayucos; d $80-160;), offering kitchenettes. In a historic sea captain's home, **Cass House Inn** (805-995-3669; www.casshouseinn.com; 222 N Ocean Ave, Cayucos; d incl breakfast $165-325;) has plush rooms, some with soaking tubs and antique fireplaces to ward off chilly coastal fog. Downstairs is a creative, seasonally inspired French-Californian **restaurant** (prix-fixe dinner $65; 5-9pm Thu-Mon).

Less than 4 miles north of Hwy 46, which leads east into the vineyards of **Paso Robles wine country** (www.pasowine.com), quaint **Cambria** has lodgings along unearthly pretty Moonstone Beach. The charming, pet-friendly **Blue Dolphin Inn** (805-805-927-3300; www.cambriainns.com; 6470 Moonstone Beach Dr; d incl breakfast $159-329;) harbors crisp, modern rooms with romantic fireplaces. Inland, **HI Cambria Bridge Street Inn** (805-927-7653; www.bridgestreetinncambria.com; 4314 Bridge St; dm $22-25, r $45-80, all with shared bath; check-in 5-9pm;) sleeps like a hostel but feels like a grandmotherly B&B. The artisan cheese and wine shop **Indigo Moon** (www.indigomooncafe.com; 1980 Main St; lunch mains $6-13; 10am-4pm Mon-Sat, to 3pm Sun, 5-9pm Wed-Sun) has breezy bistro tables, market-fresh salads and gourmet sandwiches for lunch. With a sunny patio and takeout counter, **Linn's Easy as Pie Cafe** (www.linnsfruitbin.com; 4251 Bridge St; mains $6-9; 10am-7pm;) is famous for its olallieberry pie and preserves.

Another 10 miles north of Cambria, hilltop **Hearst Castle** (805-927-2020; www.hearstcastle.org; tours adult/child from $25/12; tours from 9am) is California's most famous monument to wealth and ambition. William Randolph Hearst, the newspaper magnate, entertained Hollywood stars and royalty at this fantasy estate dripping with European antiques, accented by shimmering pools and surrounded by flowering gardens. Try to make tour reservations in advance, especially for Christmas holiday evening living-history programs. On the opposite side of Hwy 1, historic **Sebastian's Store** (442 San Simeon Rd; mains $7-12; 11am-5pm Tue-Sun) sells cold drinks, Hearst Ranch beef burgers, giant deli sandwiches and salads for beach picnics. Five miles back south off Hwy 1, **San Simeon State Park** (reservations 800-444-7275; www.reserveamerica.com; campsites $20-35) has creekside campsites.

Heading north, Point Piedras Blancas is home to an enormous **elephant-seal colony** that breeds, molts, sleeps, frolics and, occasionally, goes aggro on the beach. Keep your distance from these wild animals who move faster on the sand than you can. The main viewpoint, 4.5 miles north of Hearst Castle, has interpretive panels. Seals haul out here year-round, but the exciting birthing and mating season runs January through March, peaking on Valentine's Day. Nearby, the 1875 **Piedras Blancas Lightstation** (805-927-7361; www.piedrasblancas.org; tours adult/child $10/5) is an outstandingly scenic spot.

Big Sur

Much ink has been spilled extolling the raw beauty and energy of this 100-mile stretch of craggy coastline shoehorned south of the Monterey Peninsula. More a state of mind than a place you can pinpoint on a map, Big Sur has no traffic lights, banks or strip malls. When the sun goes down, the moon and stars provide the only illumination – if summer fog hasn't extinguished them. Lodging, food and gas are all scarce and pricey. Demand for rooms is high year-round, so book ahead. The free, info-packed newspaper *Big Sur Guide* (www.bigsurcalifornia.org) is available everywhere along the way. The $10 parking fee at Big Sur's state parks is valid for same-day entry to all.

It's about 25 miles from Hearst Castle to blink-and-you-miss-it Gorda, home of **Treebones Resort** (877-424-4787; www.treebonesresort.com; 71895 Hwy 1; d with shared bath incl breakfast $169-199;), which offers back-to-nature cliff-top yurts, some with ocean-view decks. Don't expect much privacy though. Basic **USFS campgrounds** (877-444-6777; www.campone.com, www.recreation.gov; campsites $22) are just off Hwy 1 at Plaskett Creek and Kirk Creek.

Ten miles north of Lucia is the new-agey **Esalen Institute** (831-667-3047; www.esalen.org; 55000 Hwy 1), famous for its esoteric workshops and ocean-view hot-springs baths. With a reservation you can frolic nekkid in the latter from 1am to 3am ($20, credit cards only). It's surreal.

Three miles north, **Julia Pfeiffer Burns State Park** harbors California's only coastal waterfall, 80ft-high McWay Falls, which is reached via a quarter-mile stroll. Two more miles north, a steep dirt trail descends from a hairpin turn on Hwy 1 to **Partington Cove**, a raw and breathtaking spot where crashing surf salts your skin – truly scenic, but swimming isn't safe.

Around 7 miles further north, nestled among redwoods and wisteria, the quaint restaurant at **Deetjen's Inn** (☎831-667-2377; www.deetjens.com; 48865 Hwy 1; mains breakfast $10-12, dinner $24-36; ⊙8-11:30am & 6-9pm) serves country-style comfort food. Just north, the beatnik **Henry Miller Memorial Library** (☎831-667-2574; www.henrymiller.org; Hwy 1; ⊙11am-6pm Wed-Mon; @📶) is the art and soul of Big Sur bohemia, with a jam-packed bookstore, live-music concerts and DJs, open-mic nights and outdoor film screenings. Opposite, food takes a backseat to dramatic ocean views at cliff-top **Nepenthe** (☎831-667-2345; 48510 Hwy 1; mains $14-39; ⊙11:30am-10pm), meaning 'island of no sorrow.' Its Ambrosia burger is mighty famous.

Heading north, USFS rangers at **Big Sur Station** (☎831-667-2315; ⊙8am-4pm Wed-Sun Nov-Mar, daily Apr-Oct) can clue you in about hiking trail conditions and camping options. They also issue overnight parking ($5) and campfire permits (free) for backpacking trips into the Ventana Wilderness, including the popular 10-mile trek to Sykes Hot Springs. Across the road, turn onto obscurely marked Sycamore Canyon Rd, which drops two narrow, twisting miles to crescent-shaped **Pfeiffer Beach** (per car $5; ⊙9am-8pm), with a towering offshore sea arch and strong currents too dangerous for swimming. But dig down into the sand – it's purple!

Next up, **Pfeiffer Big Sur State Park** is crisscrossed by sun-dappled trails through redwood forests, including a 1.4-mile round-trip to seasonal Pfeiffer Falls. Make campground **reservations** (☎800-444-7275; www.reserveamerica.com; campsites $35-50) or stay at the rambling, old-fashioned **Big Sur Lodge** (☎831-667-3100; www.bigsurlodge.com; 47225 Hwy 1; d $199-319; 🏊), which has rustic attached cottages (some with kitchens and wood-burning fireplaces), a well-stocked general store and a simple **restaurant** (mains $9-27; ⊙7:30am-9pm; 👪).

Most of Big Sur's commercial activity is concentrated along the next 2 miles, including a post office, shops, gas stations, private campgrounds, motels and restaurants. At **Glen Oaks Motel** (☎831-667-2105; www.glenoaksbigsur.com; Hwy 1; d $175-350; 📶), a chic, redesigned 1950s redwood-and-adobe motor lodge, snug rooms and woodsy cabins all have gas fireplaces. Pick up a giant burrito or deli sandwich at the Big Sur River Inn's **general store** (http://bigsurdeli.com; 47520 Hwy 1; dishes $1.50-7; ⊙7am-8pm). Nearby, **Maiden Publick House** (☎831-667-2355) has an encyclopedic beer menu and live-music jams.

Heading north, many visitors overlook **Andrew Molera State Park**, a trail-laced pastiche of grassy meadows, waterfalls, ocean bluffs, rugged beaches and wildlife watching. Learn all about endangered California condors at the park's **Discovery Center** (☎831-620-0702; www.ventanaws.org; admission free; ⊙9am-4pm Fri-Sun late May–mid-Sep) and the on-site bird-banding lab. From the parking lot, a half-mile trail leads to a first-come, first-served **campground** (tent sites $25).

Six miles before the famous Bixby Bridge, take a tour of 1889 **Point Sur Lightstation** (☎831-625-4419; www.pointsur.org; tour adult/child from $10/5). Meet your guide at the locked gate a quarter-mile north of Point Sur Naval Facility; arrive early because space is limited (no reservations).

Carmel

Once a bohemian artists' seaside resort, quaint Carmel-by-the-Sea now has the well-manicured feel of a country club. Simply plop down in any cafe and watch the parade of behatted ladies toting fancy-label shopping bags to lunch and dapper gents driving top-down convertibles along Ocean Ave, the village's slow-mo main drag.

Sights & Activities

Not always sunny, Carmel Beach is a gorgeous white-sand crescent, where pampered pups excitedly run off-leash.

Point Lobos State Reserve PARK
(www.pointlobos.org; per car $10; ⊙8am-30min after sunset) They bark, they bray, they bathe and they're fun to watch – sea lions are the stars here, 4 miles south of Carmel, where a dramatically rocky coastline offers excellent tide-pooling. The full perimeter hike is 6 miles, but shorter walks take in Bird Island, Piney Woods and the Whalers Cabin. Arrive early on weekends; parking is limited.

San Carlos Borroméo de Carmelo Mission CHURCH
(www.carmelmission.org; 3080 Rio Rd; adult/child $6.50/2; ⊙9:30am-5pm Mon-Sat, from 10:30am Sun) A mile south of downtown, this gorgeous mission is an oasis of calm and solemnity,

ensconced in flowering gardens. Its stone basilica is filled with original art, while a separate chapel holds the memorial tomb of California missions founder Junípero Serra.

Tor House HISTORIC BUILDING
(☎831-624-1813; www.torhouse.org; 26304 Ocean View Ave; tour adult/child $10/5; ⏰10am-3pm Fri & Sat) Even if you've never heard of 20th-century poet Robinson Jeffers, a pilgrimage to this house, which was built with his own hands, offers fascinating insights into bohemian Old Carmel (reservations required). A porthole in the Celtic-inspired Hawk Tower reputedly came from the wrecked ship that carried Napoleon from Elba.

Eating & Drinking

La Bicyclette FRENCH, ITALIAN $$$
(www.labicyclетterestaurant.com; Dolores St, at 7th Ave; lunch mains $7-16, 3-course prix-fixe dinner $28; ⏰11:30am-4pm & 5-10pm) Rustic European comfort food using seasonal local ingredients packs canoodling couples into this bistro, with an open kitchen delivering wood-fired pizzas. Excellent local wines by the glass.

Mundaka TAPAS $$
(www.mundakacarmel.com; San Carlos St, btwn Ocean & 7th Aves; small plates $4-19; ⏰5:30-10pm Sun-Wed, to 11pm Thu-Sat) This courtyard hideaway is a svelte escape from Carmel's stuffy 'newly wed and nearly dead' crowd. Take Spanish tapas plates for a spin and sip housemade sangria while DJs or flamenco guitars play.

Carmel Belle CALIFORNIAN $$
(www.carmelbelle.com; Doud Craft Studios, cnr Ocean Ave & San Carlos St; brunch mains $5-12; ⏰8am-5pm) Fresh, often organic ingredients flow from Carmel Valley farms onto tables at this charcuterie, cheese and wine shop hidden in a mini mall.

Bruno's Market & Deli GROCERY STORE $
(www.brunosmarket.com; cnr 6th & Junípero Aves; sandwiches $5-8; ⏰7am-8pm) Makes a saucy tri-trip beef sandwich and stocks all the accoutrements for a beach picnic.

Monterey

Working-class Monterey is all about the sea. Today it lures visitors with a top-notch aquarium that's a veritable temple to Monterey Bay's underwater universe. A National Marine Sanctuary since 1992, the bay begs for exploration by kayak, boat, scuba or snorkel. Meanwhile, downtown's historic quarter preserves California's Spanish and Mexican roots. Don't waste too much time on the tourist ghettos of Fisherman's Wharf and Cannery Row, the latter immortalized by novelist John Steinbeck back when it was the hectic, smelly epicenter of the sardine-canning industry, Monterey's lifeblood till the 1950s.

Sights

Monterey Bay Aquarium AQUARIUM
(☎831-648-4800, tickets 866-963-9645; www.montereybayaquarium.org; 886 Cannery Row; adult/child $30/20; ⏰10am-5pm Sep-May, 9:30am-6pm Mon-Fri, to 8pm Sat & Sun Jun-Aug) We dare you not to be mesmerized and enriched by this ecoconscious aquarium. Give yourself at least half a day to see sharks and sardines play hide-and-seek in kelp forests, observe the antics of frisky otters, meditate upon ethereal jellyfish and get touchy-feely with sea cucumbers, bat rays and other tide-pool creatures. Feeding times are best, especially for watching penguins. To avoid the worst crowds, get tickets in advance and arrive when the doors open.

Monterey State Historic Park PARK
(☎831-998-9458; www.parks.ca.gov; tours $3-10) Downtown, Old Monterey has a cluster of lovingly restored 19th-century brick-and-adobe buildings, including novelist Robert Louis Stevenson's one-time boarding house and the Cooper-Molera Adobe, a sea captain's house. Admission to the gardens is free, but the buildings' opening hours and tour times vary. Pick up walking-tour maps and check schedules at the **Pacific House Museum** (☎831-649-7118; 20 Custom House Plaza; ⏰10am-4:30pm), which has in-depth period exhibits on California's multinational history.

Monterey History & Maritime Museum MUSEUM
(☎831-372-2608; http://montereyhistory.org; 5 Custom House Plaza; admission $5; ⏰11am-5pm Wed-Sat, 1-4pm Sun) Near the waterfront, this voluminous modern exhibition hall illuminates Monterey's salty past, including the roller-coaster-like rise and fall of the local sardine industry that brought Cannery Row to life. Gems include a ship-in-a-bottle collection and the historic Fresnel lens from Point Sur Lightstation.

Point Pinos Lighthouse LIGHTHOUSE
(www.ci.pg.ca.us/lighthouse; adult/child $2/1; ⏲1-4pm Thu-Mon) The West Coast's oldest continuously operating lighthouse has been warning ships off this peninsula's hazardous point since 1855. Inside are exhibits on its history and its failures: local shipwrecks.

FREE **Monarch Grove Sanctuary** PARK
(www.ci.pg.ca.us/monarchs; Ridge Rd, Pacific Grove; ⏲dawn-dusk) Between October and February, migratory monarch butterflies cluster in a thicket of eucalyptus trees off Lighthouse Ave.

Activities

Diving and snorkeling reign supreme, although the water is rather frigid, even in summer. Year-round, Fisherman's Wharf is the launch pad for whale-watching trips. Another favorite four-seasons activity is walking or cycling the paved 18-mile **Monterey Peninsula Recreation Trail**, which edges the coast past Cannery Row, ending at Lovers Point in Pacific Grove. The overhyped **17-Mile Drive** (www.pebblebeach.com; per car/bicycle $9.50/free) toll road connects Monterey and Pacific Grove with Carmel-by-the-Sea.

Monterey Bay Kayaks KAYAKING
(☎800-649-5357; www.montereybaykayaks.com; 693 Del Monte Ave; rental kayak per day $30-50, tours adult/child from $50/40) Kayak and SUP rentals, lessons and guided tours of Monterey Bay and Elkhorn Slough, including full-moon paddles.

Sanctuary Cruises WHALE-WATCHING
(☎831-917-1042; www.sanctuarycruises.com; adult/child under 3yr/child 3-12yr $48/10/38) Departing from Moss Landing, 20 miles north of Monterey, this biodiesel boat runs recommended whale-watching and dolphin-spotting tours (reservations essential).

Monterey Bay Dive Charters SCUBA DIVING
(☎831-383-9276; www.mbdcscuba.com; scuba rental $79, shore/boat dive from $49/199) Rent a full scuba kit including wetsuit, book a small-group dive or take the plunge with a three-hour beginners' dive experience ($159, no PADI certification required).

Adventures by the Sea KAYAKING, CYCLING
(☎831-372-1807; www.adventuresbythesea.com; 299 Cannery Row & 210 Alvarado St; rental kayak per day $30, bicycle per hr/day $7/25) Also offers sunset kayaking tours at Lovers Point and SUP rentals and lessons.

Bay Bikes CYCLING
(☎831-655-2453; www.baybikes.com; 585 Cannery Row; per hr/day from $8/32) Cruiser, tandem, hybrid and mountain-bike rentals near the aquarium.

Sleeping

Skip the frills and save a bunch of dough at chain and indie motels along Munras Ave south of downtown or on N Fremont St, east of Hwy 1.

InterContinental–Clement HOTEL $$$
(☎831-375-4500; www.intercontinental.com; 750 Cannery Row; r $200-455; ❄@🛜≋👪) Like an upscale version of a millionaire's seaside clapboard house, this sparkling resort presides over Cannery Row. For utmost luxury, book an ocean-view suite with a balcony and private fireplace, then breakfast in bayfront C Restaurant. Parking $18.

TOP CHOICE **Asilomar Conference Grounds** LODGE $$
(☎831-372-8016; www.visitasilomar.com; 800 Asilomar Ave, Pacific Grove; r incl breakfast $115-175; 🛜≋👪) Coastal state-park lodge has buildings designed by architect Julia Morgan, of Hearst Castle fame. Historic rooms are small and thin-walled, but charming nonetheless. The lodge's fireside rec room has ping-pong and pool tables. Bicycle rentals available.

Monterey Hotel HOTEL $$$
(☎831-375-3184; www.montereyhotel.com; 406 Alvarado St; r $70-310; 🛜) Right downtown, this quaint 1904 edifice harbors small, somewhat noisy but freshly renovated rooms sporting reproduction Victorian furniture. No elevator. Parking $17.

HI Monterey Hostel HOSTEL $
(☎831-649-0375; www.montereyhostel.org; 778 Hawthorne St; dm $25-28, r $59-75; ⏲check-in 4-10pm; @) Four blocks from Cannery Row, this simple, clean hostel is just the ticket for backpackers on a budget (reservations strongly recommended). No private bathrooms. Take MST bus 1 from downtown's Transit Plaza.

Veterans Memorial Park CAMPGROUND $
(☎831-646-3865; www.monterey.org; campsites $27) Forested hilltop public campground has 40 well-kept, grassy nonreservable sites with hot showers, drinking water and fire pits (three-day maximum stay).

Eating & Drinking

Many more eateries, bars, live-music venues and cinemas line Cannery Row and downtown's Alvarado St.

TOP CHOICE Passionfish SEAFOOD $$$
(☎831-655-3311; www.passionfish.net; 701 Lighthouse Ave, Pacific Grove; mains $17-26; ⏰5-10pm) Eureka! Finally, a perfect, chef-owned seafood restaurant where the sustainable fish is dock-fresh, every preparation fully flavored and the wine list more than affordable. Reservations recommended.

First Awakenings DINER $$
(www.firstawakenings.net; American Tin Cannery, 125 Oceanview Blvd, Pacific Grove; mains $5-12; ⏰7am-2pm Mon-Fri, to 2:30pm Sat & Sun; 👪) Sweet and savory creative breakfasts and lunches, plus bottomless pitchers of coffee, make this hideaway cafe in an outlet mall near the aquarium worth seeking out.

Montrio Bistro CALIFORNIAN $$$
(☎831-648-8880; www.montrio.com; 414 Calle Principal; mains $14-29; ⏰5-10pm Sun-Thu, to 11pm Fri & Sat; 👪) Inside a 1910 firehouse, this classy restaurant's tables are covered in butcher paper with crayons for kids. Seasonal New American cooking and Monterey County wines satisfy.

East Village Coffee Lounge CAFE $
(www.eastvillagecoffeelounge.com; 498 Washington St; snacks & drinks $3-6; ⏰6am-late Mon-Fri, from 7am Sat & Sun) Sleek coffeehouse with a liquor license and live-music, DJ and open-mic nights.

Crêpes of Brittany SNACKS $
(www.vivalecrepemonterey.com; 6 Old Fisherman's Wharf; snacks $4-9; ⏰8:30am-7pm Sun-Thu, to 8pm Sun) Authentic savory and sweet crepes swirled by a French expat; expect long lines and shorter hours in winter.

Information

Visitor center (☎831-657-6400; www.seemonterey.com; 401 Camino El Estero; ⏰9am-6pm Mon-Sat, to 5pm Sun, closing 1hr earlier Nov-Mar) Ask for a free *Monterey County Film & Literary Map*.

Getting Around

Monterey-Salinas Transit (☎888-678-2871; www.mst.org; fares $1-3, day pass $8) Local buses converge on downtown's Transit Plaza (cnr Pearl and Alvarado Sts), including routes to Pacific Grove, Carmel, Big Sur and Salinas. In summer, a free trolley loops around downtown Monterey and Cannery Row daily from 10am until 7pm or later.

Santa Cruz

SoCal beach culture meets NorCal counterculture in Santa Cruz. The UCSC student population makes this old-school radical town youthful, hip and lefty-political. Some worry that Santa Cruz's weirdness quotient is dropping, but you'll disagree when you witness the freak show (and we say that with love) along Pacific Ave, downtown's main drag. For the beach and boardwalk, head south.

Sights & Activities

In Santa Cruz most of the action takes place at the beach.

Beach Boardwalk AMUSEMENT PARK
(☎831-423-5590; www.beachboardwalk.com; 400 Beach St; rides $3-5, all-day pass $30; ⏰daily May-Sep, off-season hr vary) A short walk from the municipal wharf, this slice of Americana boasts the West Coast's oldest beachfront amusement park, with the 1924 Giant Dipper roller coaster and 1911 Looff carousel. Free Friday-night summer concerts.

Surfing Museum MUSEUM
(www.santacruzsurfingmuseum.org; 701 W Cliff Dr; donations welcome; ⏰noon-4pm Thu-Mon Sep-Jun, 10am-5pm Wed-Mon Jul & Aug) About a mile south along the coast, the old lighthouse is packed with memorabilia, including vintage redwood boards. It overlooks experts-only **Steamers Lane** and beginners' **Cowell's**, both popular surf breaks.

Natural Bridges State Beach BEACH
(www.parks.ca.gov; per car $10; ⏰8am-sunset) Further west, this beach bookends a scenic coastal drive or cycle, about 3 miles from the wharf. There are tide pools for exploring and leafy trees in which monarch butterflies roost from October through February.

Seymour Marine Discovery Center MUSEUM
(www2.ucsc.edu/seymourcenter; end of Delaware Ave; adult/child $6/4; ⏰10am-5pm Tue-Sat, from noon Sun, plus 10am-5pm Mon Jul & Aug) University-run Long Marine Lab has cool interactive science exhibits for kids, including touch tanks, with the world's largest blue-whale skeleton outside.

Santa Cruz State Parks HIKING
(www.santacruzstateparks.org; per car $10; ⌚sunrise-sunset) Streamside trails through old-growth redwood forests await at Henry Cowell Redwoods and Big Basin Redwoods, off Hwy 9 north in the Santa Cruz Mountains, and the Forest of Nisene Marks, off Hwy 1 south near Aptos. Mountain bikers ride Wilder Ranch, off Hwy 1 west.

Roaring Camp Railroads TRAIN RIDES
(☎831-335-4484; www.roaringcamp.com; adult/child from $24/17) For family fun, hop aboard a narrow-gauge steam train up into the redwoods or a standard-gauge train leaving from the beach boardwalk. Check the website or call ahead for seasonal opening hours.

Venture Quest KAYAKING
(☎831-427-2267; www.kayaksantacruz.com; Municipal Wharf; kayak rentals/tours/lessons from $30/55/85; ⌚10am-7pm Mon-Fri, from 9am Jun-Sep, off-season hr vary) Experience the craggy coastline with sea-cave and whale-watching kayak tours, including to Elkhorn Slough and moonlight paddles.

Santa Cruz Surf School SURFING
(☎831-426-7072; www.santacruzsurfschool.com; 322 Pacific Ave; 2hr lesson $80-90) Near the wharf, these folks can get you out there, all equipment included.

O'Neill Surf Shop SURFING
(☎831-475-4151; www.oneill.com; 1115 41st Ave; wetsuit/surfboard rental $10/20; ⌚9am-8pm Mon-Fri, from 8am Sat & Sun) Head east to Capitola to this internationally renowned surfboard maker. Downtown branch is at 110 Cooper St.

Sleeping

For motels, try Ocean St near downtown and Mission St by the UCSC campus. Make **reservations** (☎800-444-7275; www.reserveamerica.com; campsites $35-65) for state-park campgrounds at nearby beaches and in the Santa Cruz Mountains.

Dream Inn HOTEL $$$
(☎831-426-4330; www.dreaminnsantacruz.com; 175 W Cliff Dr; r $200-380; ❄@📶🏊) Overlooking the wharf from its hillside perch, this retro-chic boutique-on-the-cheap hotel is as stylish as Santa Cruz gets. Rooms have all mod cons, while the beach is just steps away. Hit happy hour at ocean-view Aquarius restaurant.

Adobe on Green B&B B&B $$
(☎831-469-9866; www.adobeongreen.com; 103 Green St; r incl breakfast $149-199; 📶) Peace and quiet are the mantras here. The hosts are practically invisible, but their thoughtful touches are everywhere: from boutique-style amenities inside spacious, stylish and solar-powered rooms to breakfast spreads from the organic gardens.

Pacific Blue Inn B&B $$$
(☎831-600-8880; http://pacificblueinn.com; 636 Pacific Ave; r incl breakfast $170-240; 📶) Downtown courtyard B&B is truly ecoconscious, with water-saving fixtures and renewable and recycled building materials. Clean-lined rooms have pillow-top beds, fireplaces and flat-screen TVs with DVD players. Free loaner bikes.

Pelican Point Inn INN $$
(☎831-475-3381; www.pelicanpointinn-santacruz.com; 21345 E Cliff Dr; ste $99-199; @👪) Ideal for families, these roomy apartment-style lodgings near kid-friendly Twin Lakes Beach are equipped with everything you'll need for a lazy beach vacation, including kitchenettes and high-speed internet. Weekly rates available.

HI Santa Cruz Hostel HOSTEL $
(☎831-423-8304; www.hi-santacruz.org; 321 Main St; dm $25-28, r $55-105; ⌚check-in 5-10pm; @) Budget overnighters dig this cute hostel at the Carmelita Cottages in a flowery garden setting, two blocks from the beach. One bummer: the 11pm curfew. Make reservations. Shared bath.

Eating

Downtown, especially Pacific Ave, is chockablock with just-OK cafes. Mission St near the UCSC campus and neighboring Capitola offer cheap takeout and ethnic eats.

Soif BISTRO $$$
(☎831-423-2020; www.soifwine.com; 105 Walnut Ave; small plates $5-17, mains $19-28; ⌚5-10pm Sun-Thu, to 11pm Fri & Sat) Downtown wine shop where bon vivants flock for a heady selection of 50 international wines by the glass paired with a sophisticated, seasonally driven Euro-Cal menu.

Engfer Pizza Works PIZZERIA $$$
(www.engferpizzaworks.com; 537 Seabright Ave; pizzas $8-23; ⌚4-9:30pm Tue-Sun; 👪) Detour to find this old factory, where wood-fired pizzas

are made from scratch with love – the no-name specialty is almost like a giant salad on roasted bread. Play ping-pong and down draft microbrews while you wait.

Tacos Moreno MEXICAN $
(www.tacosmoreno.com; 1053 Water St; dishes $2-6; ⏲11am-8pm) Who cares how long the line is, especially at lunchtime? Seekers will find taqueria heaven here – from pork, chicken and beef soft tacos and quesadillas to stuffed burritos.

Penny Ice Creamery DESSERT $
(www.thepennyicecreamery.com; 913 Cedar St; items $2-4; ⏲noon-9pm Sun-Wed, to 11pm Thu-Sat) With a cult following, this artisan ice-cream shop makes zany flavors from scratch using wild local ingredients like avocado, roasted barley or cherry balsamic.

Drinking & Entertainment

Pacific Ave downtown is jam-packed with bars, live-music lounges and coffeehouses. Check the free *Santa Cruz Weekly* (www.santacruzweekly.com) tabloid for more venues and events.

Caffe Pergolesi CAFE
(www.theperg.com; 418 Cedar St; ⏲7am-11pm; 📶) On a leafy sidewalk verandah, discuss art and conspiracy theories over strong coffee, organic juices or beer.

Santa Cruz Mountain Brewing BREWERY
(www.santacruzmountainbrewing.com; 402 Ingalls St; ⏲noon-10pm) Bold, organic brews west of downtown off Mission St, squeezed between local winery tasting rooms.

Surf City Billiards & Café BAR
(www.surfcitybilliards.com; 931 Pacific Ave; ⏲4-11pm Mon-Thu, to 1am Fri & Sat, 10am-11pm Sun) For shooting stick, dartboards, big-screen TVs and darn good pub grub.

Moe's Alley MUSIC
(☎831-479-1854; www.moesalley.com; 1535 Commercial Way) Tiny venue for jazz, blues, folk, rock, reggae and world beats.

Kuumbwa Jazz Center MUSIC
(☎831-427-2227; www.kuumbwajazz.org; 320 Cedar St) Books big-name jazz sounds.

Information

KPIG (107.5 FM) Plays the classic Santa Cruz soundtrack – think Bob Marley, Janis Joplin and Willie Nelson.

Visitor center (☎831-425-1234; www.santacruzca.org; 303 Water St; ⏲9am-5pm Mon-Fri, 10am-4pm Sat & Sun; @) Free public internet terminal.

Getting There & Away

Greyhound (920 Pacific Ave) A few daily buses to San Francisco ($16, three hours), Santa Barbara ($50, six hours) and Los Angeles ($57, nine hours).

Santa Cruz Metro (☎831-425-8600; www.scmtd.com; single ride/day pass $1.50/4.50) Local and regional buses converge on downtown's Metro Center (920 Pacific Ave).

Santa Cruz to San Francisco

Far more scenic than any freeway, this curvaceous, 70-mile stretch of coastal Hwy 1 is bordered by wild beaches, organic farm stands and sea-salted villages, all scattered like loose diamonds in the rough.

About 20 miles northwest of Santa Cruz, **Año Nuevo State Park** (☎tour reservations 800-444-4445; www.parks.ca.gov; per car $10, tour per person $7; ⏲8:30am-3:30pm Apr-Aug, to 3pm Sep-Nov, tours mid-Dec–Mar) is home base for the world's largest colony of northern elephant seals. Call ahead to reserve space on a 2½-hour, 3-mile guided walking tour, given during the cacophonous winter birthing and mating season. On a quiet windswept coastal perch further north, green-certified **HI Pigeon Point Lighthouse Hostel** (☎650-879-0633; www.norcalhostels.org/pigeon; dm $24-29, r $72-156; ⏲check-in 3:30-10:30pm; @📶👪) inhabits historic lightkeepers' quarters. It's popular (especially for its cliff-top hot tub), so book ahead.

Five miles north, **Pescadero State Beach & Marsh Natural Preserve** (www.parks.ca.gov; per car $8; ⏲8am-sunset) attracts beachcombers and birders. Inland Pescadero village is home to famed **Duarte's Tavern** (☎650-879-0464; www.duartestavern.com; 202 Stage Rd; mains $8-35; ⏲7am-9pm), where creamy artichoke soup and homemade pies are crowd-pleasers. For a beach picnic, visit the bakery-deli at **Arcangeli Grocery Co** (287 Stage Rd; ⏲10am-6pm) and family-owned **Harley Farms Cheese Shop** (250 North St; ⏲11am-5pm), which offers weekend goat-dairy farm tours.

Less than 20 miles north, busy Half Moon Bay is defined by pretty **Half Moon Bay State Beach** (www.parks.ca.gov; per car $10, campsites $35-50), offering scenic campsites. To get out on the water, talk to **Half Moon**

Bay Kayak (☎650-773-6101; www.hmbkayak.com; 2 Johnson Dr, Pillar Point Harbor; kayak rentals from $20, tours $65-150). For oceanfront luxury, the pet-friendly **Inn at Mavericks** (☎650-728-1572; www.innatmavericks.com; 364 Princeton Ave; r $199-239;) offers spacious, romantic roosts. It overlooks Pillar Point Harbor, which has a decent brewpub with a sunset-view patio. Back south in Half Moon Bay's quaint downtown, cafes, restaurants and eclectic shops line Main St, just inland from Hwy 1. Nearby, **Flying Fish Grill** (www.flyingfishgrill.net; 211 San Mateo Rd; dishes $5-15; ⊙11am-8pm) is the tastiest seafood shack around.

Six miles north of downtown, follow the signs to **Moss Beach Distillery** (www.mossbeachdistillery.com; 140 Beach Way; appetizers $4-30; ⊙noon-8:30pm Mon-Thu, to 9pm Fri & Sat, 11am-8:30pm Sun), a historic bootleggers' joint with a dog-friendly deck for sunset drinks. Just north, **Fitzgerald Marine Reserve** (http://fitzgeraldreserve.org; California St, off Hwy 1) protects tide pools teeming with colorful sea life. Another mile north, **HI Point Montara Lighthouse Hostel** (☎650-728-7177; www.norcalhostels.org; Hwy 1 & 16th St; dm $26-31, r $70-105; ⊙check-in 3:30-10:30pm; @) is an airy, ecofriendly hostel with a small private beach (reservations essential). From there, it's just 20 more miles to San Francisco via Devil's Slide.

SAN FRANCISCO & THE BAY AREA

San Francisco

If you've ever wondered where the envelope goes when it's pushed, here's your answer. Psychedelic drugs, newfangled technology, gay liberation, green ventures, free speech and culinary experimentation all became mainstream long ago in San Francisco. After 160 years of booms and busts, losing your shirt has become a favorite local pastime at the clothing-optional Bay to Breakers race, Pride Parade and hot Sundays on Baker Beach. This is no place to be shy: out here among eccentrics of every stripe, no one's going to notice a few tan lines. So long, inhibitions; hello, San Francisco.

History

Oysters and acorn bread were prime dinner options in the Mexico-run Ohlone settlement of San Francisco c 1848 – but a year and some gold nuggets later, Champagne and chow mein were served by the bucket. Gold found in the nearby Sierra Nevada foothills had turned a waterfront village of 800 into a port city of 100,000 prospectors, con artists, prostitutes and honest folk trying to make an honest living – good luck telling which was which. That friendly bartender might drug your drink, and you'd wake up a mile from shore, shanghaied into service on some ship bound for Argentina.

By 1850 California was nabbed from Mexico and fast-tracked for US statehood, and San Francisco attempted to introduce public order to 200 saloons and untold numbers of brothels and gambling dens. Panic struck when Australia glutted the market with gold in 1854, and ire turned irrationally on SF's Chinese community, who from 1877 to 1945 were restricted to living and working in Chinatown by anti-Chinese laws. The main way out of debt was dangerous work building railroads for the city's robber barons, who dynamited, mined and clear-cut their way across the Golden West, and built grand Nob Hill mansions above Chinatown.

The city's lofty ambitions and 20-plus theaters came crashing down in 1906, when earthquake and fire left 3000 dead, 100,000 homeless and much of the city reduced to rubble – including almost every mansion on Nob Hill. Theater troupes and opera divas performed for free amid smoldering ruins downtown, establishing SF's tradition of free public performances in parks.

Ambitious public works projects continued through the 1930s, when Diego Rivera, Frida Kahlo and federally funded muralists began the tradition of leftist politics in paint visible in some 400 Mission murals.

WWII brought seismic shifts to San Francisco's community as women and African Americans working in San Francisco shipyards created a new economic boom, and President Franklin Delano Roosevelt's Executive Order 9066 mandated the internment of the city's historic Japanese American community. A 40-year court battle ensued, ending in an unprecedented apology from the US government. San Francisco became a testing ground for civil rights and free speech, with Beat poet Lawrence Ferlinghetti and City Lights Bookstore winning a landmark 1957 ruling against book banning over the publication of Allen Ginsberg's splendid, incendiary *Howl and Other Poems*.

San Francisco & the Bay Area

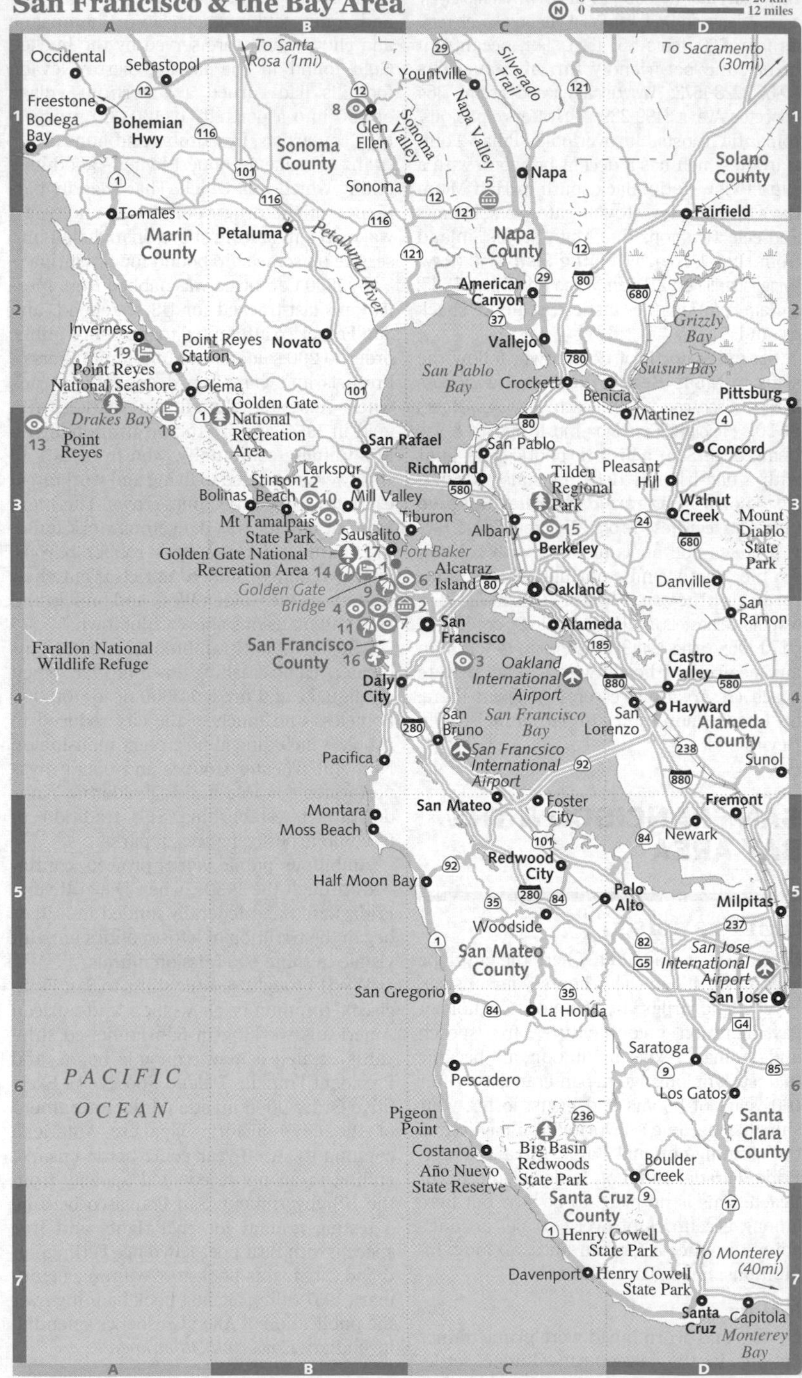

San Francisco & the Bay Area

Sights

1 Baker Beach B3
2 California Palace of the Legion of Honor B4
3 Candlestick Park C4
4 Cliff House B4
5 di Rosa Art + Nature Preserve C1
6 Fort Point C3
7 Golden Gate Park B4
8 Jack London Historic State Park B1
9 Lands End B4
10 Muir Woods National Monument B3
11 Ocean Beach B4
12 Pantoll Station B3
13 Point Reyes Lighthouse A3
14 Rodeo Beach B3
15 University of California, Berkeley C3

Activities, Courses & Tours

16 Aqua Surf Shop B4
Sutro Baths .... (see 4)

Sleeping

17 HI Marin Headlands Hostel B3
18 HI Point Reyes Hostel A3
19 Motel Inverness A2

The Central Intelligence Agency (CIA) hoped an experimental drug called LSD might turn San Francisco test subject Ken Kesey into the ultimate fighting machine, but instead the author of *One Flew Over the Cuckoo's Nest* slipped some into Kool-Aid and kicked off the psychedelic '60s. The Summer of Love meant free food, love and music in the Haight until the '70s, when enterprising gay hippies founded an out-and-proud community in the Castro. San Francisco witnessed devastating losses from AIDS in the 1980s, but the city rallied to become a model for disease treatment and prevention.

Geeks and cyberpunks converged on SF in the mid-1990s, spawning the web and dot-com boom – until the bubble popped in 2000. But risk-taking SF continues to float new ideas, and as recession hits elsewhere, social media, mobile apps and biotech are booming in San Francisco. Congratulations: you're just in time for San Francisco's next wild ride.

Sights

Let San Francisco's 43 hills and more than 80 arts venues stretch your legs and imagination, and take in some (literally) breathtaking views. The 7 x 7-mile city is laid out on a staid grid, but its main street is a diagonal contrarian streak called Market St. Downtown sights are within walking distance of Market St, but keep your city smarts and wits about you, especially around South of Market (SoMa) and the Tenderloin (5th to 9th Sts). SF's most historic landmarks are in the Mission, while exciting new destinations are inside Golden Gate Park.

SOMA

Cartoon Art Museum MUSEUM
(Map p952; ☎415-227-8666; www.cartoonart.org; 655 Mission St; adult/child $7/5; ⏰11am-5pm Tue-Sun) Comics earn serious consideration with shows of original *Watchmen* covers, too-hot-to-print political cartoons and lectures with local Pixar studio heads. Even fanboys will learn something from lectures about 1930s efforts to unionize overworked women animators, and shows on SF underground comics legends like R Crumb, Spain Rodriguez and Trina Robbins.

Contemporary Jewish Museum MUSEUM
(Map p952; ☎415-655-7800; www.jmsf.org; 736 Mission St, at 3rd St; adult/child $10/free; ⏰11am-5:30pm Fri-Tue, 1-8:30pm Thu) In 2008 architect Daniel Liebskind reshaped San Francisco's 1881 power plant with a blue steel extension to form the Hebrew word *l'chaim* ('to life'). Inside this architectural statement are lively shows, ranging from a retrospective of modern art instigator and Bay Area native Gertrude Stein to Linda Ellia's *Our Struggle: Artists Respond to Mein Kampf,* for which 600 artists from 17 countries were invited to alter one page of Hitler's book.

Museum of African Diaspora MUSEUM
(Map p952; ☎415-358-7200; www.moadsf.org; 685 Mission; adult/child $10/5; ⏰11am-6pm Wed-Sat, noon-5pm Sun) An international cast of characters tell the epic story of diaspora, from Ethiopian painter Qes Adamu Tesfaw's three-faced icons to quilts by India's Siddi community, descended from 16th-century African slaves. Themed interactive displays vary in interest and depth, but don't miss

SAN FRANCISCO IN...

One Day

Since the gold rush, great San Francisco adventures have started in **Chinatown**, where you can still find hidden fortunes – in cookies, that is. Beat it to **City Lights Bookstore** to revel in Beat poetry, then pass the **Transamerica Pyramid** en route to dumplings at **City View**. Hit **SFMOMA** and the downtown **gallery scene**, then head over to the **Asian Art Museum**, where art transports you across centuries and oceans within an hour. Toast hearts lost and inspiration found in SF with wine on tap and sensational small plates at **Frances**. End the night with silver-screen revivals at the **Castro Theatre**, or swaying to glam-rock anthems at **Café du Nord**.

Two Days

Start your day amid mural-covered garage doors lining **Balmy Alley**, then window-shop to **826 Valencia** for pirate supplies and ichthyoid antics in the Fish Theater. Break for burritos, then hoof it to the Haight for flashbacks at vintage boutiques and the Summer of Love site: **Golden Gate Park**. Glimpse Golden Gate Bridge views atop the **MH de Young Museum**, take a walk on the wild side inside the **California Academy of Sciences** rainforest dome, then dig into organic Cal-Moroccan feasts at **Aziza**.

the moving video of slave narratives recounted by Maya Angelou.

UNION SQUARE

The paved square is nothing special, but offers front-row seating for downtown drama: bejeweled theater-goers dodging clanging cable cars, trendy teens camped out overnight for limited-edition sneakers, and business travelers heading into the Tenderloin for entertainment too scandalous to include on expense reports. The action begins with shoppers clustered around the Powell St cable-car turnaround, gets dramatic along the Geary St Theater District and switches on the red lights south of Geary.

CIVIC CENTER

Asian Art Museum MUSEUM

(Map p952; ☎415-581-3500; www.asianart.org; 200 Larkin St; adult/child $12/7; ⏰10am-5pm Tue, Wed, Fri-Sun, to 9pm Thu) Imaginations race from ancient Persian miniatures to cutting-edge Japanese fashion through three floors spanning 6000 years of Asian arts. Besides the largest collection outside Asia – 17,000 works – the Asian offers excellent programs for all ages, from shadow-puppet shows and yoga for kids to monthly over-21 Matcha mixers with cross-cultural cocktails and DJ mashups.

City Hall HISTORIC BUILDING

(Map p952; ☎docent tours 415-554-6139; www.sfgsa.org; 400 Van Ness Ave; ⏰8am-8pm Mon-Fri, tours 10am, noon & 2pm Mon-Fri) Rising from the ashes of the 1906 earthquake, this beaux-arts building houses San Francisco's signature mixture of idealism, corruption and opposition politics under a splendid Tennessee pink marble and Colorado limestone rotunda. Historic firsts here include America's first sit-in on the grand staircase in 1960, the 1977 election and 1978 assassination of openly gay Supervisor Harvey Milk, and 4037 same-sex marriages in 2004. Intriguing art shows are in the basement and weekly Board of Supervisors meetings are open to the public (2pm Tuesday).

FINANCIAL DISTRICT

Back in its Barbary Coast heyday, loose change would buy you time with loose women in this neighborhood – now you'd be lucky to see a loose tie during happy hour. But the area still has redeeming quirks: a redwood grove has taken root in the remains of old whaling ships below the rocket-shaped **Transamerica Pyramid** (Map p952; www.thepyramidcenter.com; 600 Montgomery St), and eccentric art collectors descend from hilltop mansions for First Thursday gallery openings at **14 Geary**, **49 Geary** and **77 Geary** (Map p952; www.sfada.com; San Francisco Art Dealers Association; ⏰10:30am-5:30pm Tue-Fri, 11am-5pm Sat).

Ferry Building LANDMARK

(Map p952; ☎415-983-8000, www.ferrybuildingmarketplace.com; ⏰10am-6pm Mon-Fri, from 9am Sat, 11am-5pm Sun) Hedonism is alive and well at this transit hub turned gourmet emporium, where foodies happily miss their ferries slurping local oysters and bubbly. Star chefs are frequently spotted at the **farmers market** (⏲10am-2pm Tue & Thu, from 8am Sat) that wraps around the building year-round.

CHINATOWN

Since 1848 this community has survived riots, earthquakes, bootlegging gangsters and politicians' attempts to relocate it down the coast.

Chinese Historical Society of America Museum MUSEUM

(CHSA; Map p952; ☎415-391-1188; www.chsa.org; 965 Clay St; adult/child $5/2, 1st Tue of month free; ⏲noon-5pm Tue-Fri, 11am-4pm Sat) Picture what it was like to be Chinese in America during the gold rush, transcontinental railroad construction or the Beat heyday at the nation's largest Chinese American historical institute. Rotating exhibits are across the courtyard in CHSA's graceful red-brick, green-tile-roofed landmark building, built as Chinatown's YWCA in 1932 by Julia Morgan, chief architect of Hearst Castle.

Chinese Culture Center GALLERY

(Map p952; ☎415-986-1822; www.c-c-c.org; 3rd fl, Hilton Hotel, 750 Kearny St; donation requested; ⏲10am-4pm Tue-Sat) You can see all the way to China on the 3rd floor of the Hilton inside this cultural center, which hosts exhibits of traditional Chinese arts; Xian Rui (Fresh & Sharp) cutting-edge art installations, such as Stella Zhang's discomfiting toothpick-studded pillows; and Art at Night, showcasing Chinese-inspired art, jazz and food. Check the center's online schedule for concerts, hands-on arts workshops, Mandarin classes, genealogy services and Chinatown arts festivals.

NORTH BEACH

Beat Museum MUSEUM

(Map p952; ☎800-537-6822; www.thebeatmuseum.org; 540 Broadway; admission $5; ⏲10am-7pm Tue-Sun) Beat writers Jack Kerouac, Allen Ginsberg and Lawrence Ferlinghetti made North Beach the proving ground for free spirits and free speech in the 1950s, as shown in this rambling, shambling museum of literary curios and vintage video. Entry to the bookstore and frequent readings are free.

RUSSIAN HILL & NOB HILL

Gardeners, fitness freaks and suckers for sunsets brave the climbs west of North Beach up Russian and Nob Hills. Drivers test themselves on the crooked 1000 block of Lombard St, but many obliviously roll past one of the best sunset vista points over the Golden Gate Bridge at **George Sterling Park** (Map p952) and a Diego Rivera mural at **Art Institute** (Map p952; ☎415-771-7020; www.sfai.edu; 800 Chestnut St; ⏲9am-7:30pm).

Grace Cathedral CHURCH

(Map p952; ☎415-749-6300; www.gracecathedral.com; 1100 California St; suggested donation adult/child $3/2; ⏲7am-6pm Mon-Fri, from 8am Sat, 8am-7pm Sun, services with choir 8:30am & 11am Sun) Take a shortcut to heaven: hop the cable car uphill to SF's progressive Episcopal church, where the AIDS Interfaith Memorial Chapel features a bronze Keith Haring altarpiece; stained-glass 'Human Endeavor' windows illuminate Albert Einstein in a swirl of nuclear particles; and pavement labyrinths offer guided meditation for restless souls.

DON'T MISS

SAN FRANCISCO MUSEUM OF MODERN ART

Bold moves have set the **San Francisco Museum of Modern Art** (SFMOMA; Map p952; ☎415-357-4000; www.sfmoma.org; 151 3rd St; adult/child $18/free, 1st Tue of month free; ⏲11am-6pm Fri-Tue, to 9pm Thu) apart since 1935, with curatorial gambles on then-controversial contemporary painters like Diego Rivera and Frida Kahlo, and history-making works by local photographers Dorothea Lange, Eadweard Muybridge, Ansel Adams and Edward Weston. The museum moved into architect Mario Botta's light-filled brick box just in time for the tech boom in 1995, making room for new media mavericks such as San Franciscan Matthew Barney, who debuted his dazzling Vaseline-smeared videos at SFMOMA. Today installations fill the atrium, sculpture sprouts from the rooftop garden and a $480 million expansion is under way to accommodate 1100 major modern works donated by the Fisher family (local founders of the Gap) alongside emerging niches: conceptual architecture, wall-drawing installations and relational art. Go Thursday nights after 6pm for half-price admission and the most artful flirting in town.

Downtown San Francisco

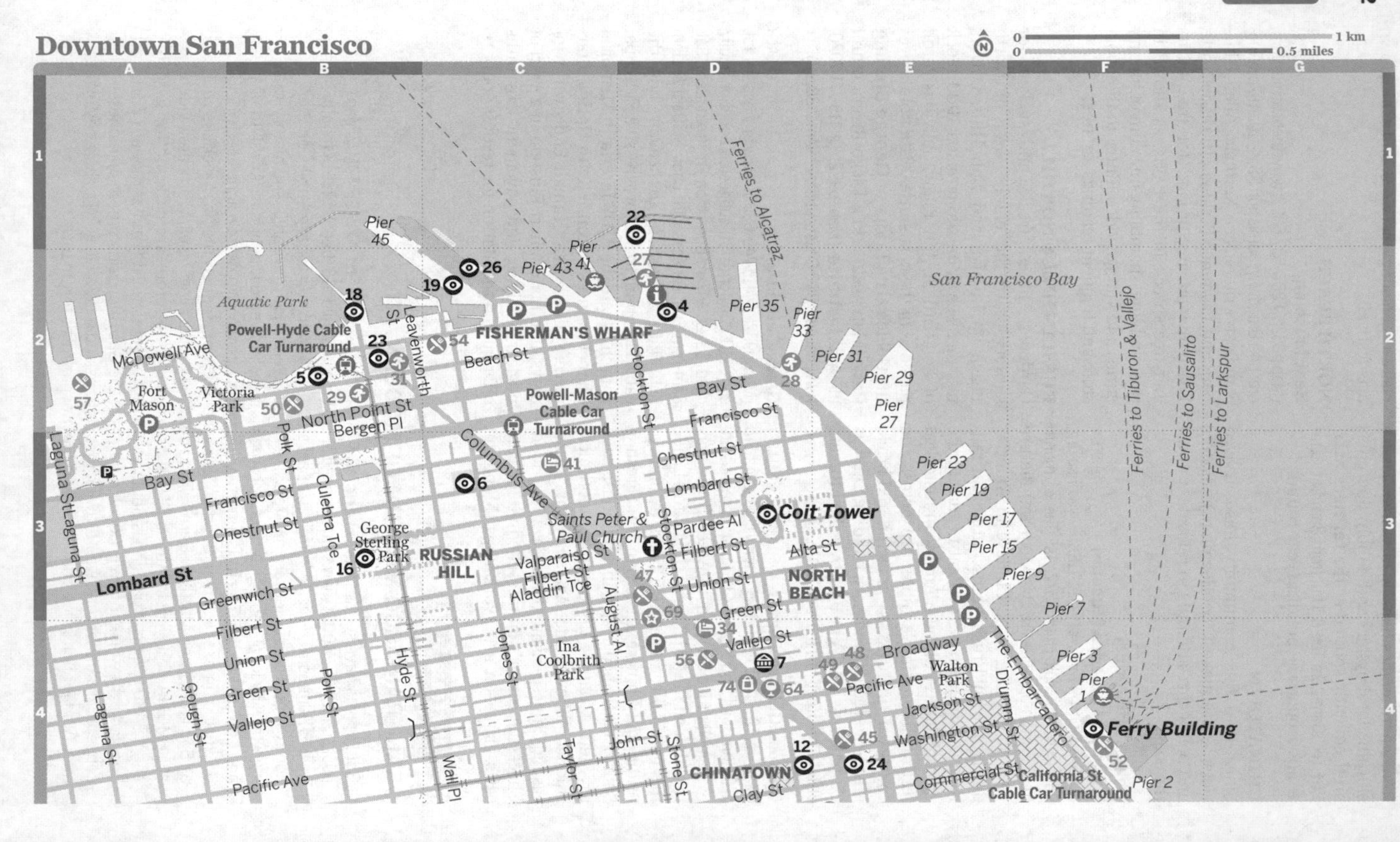

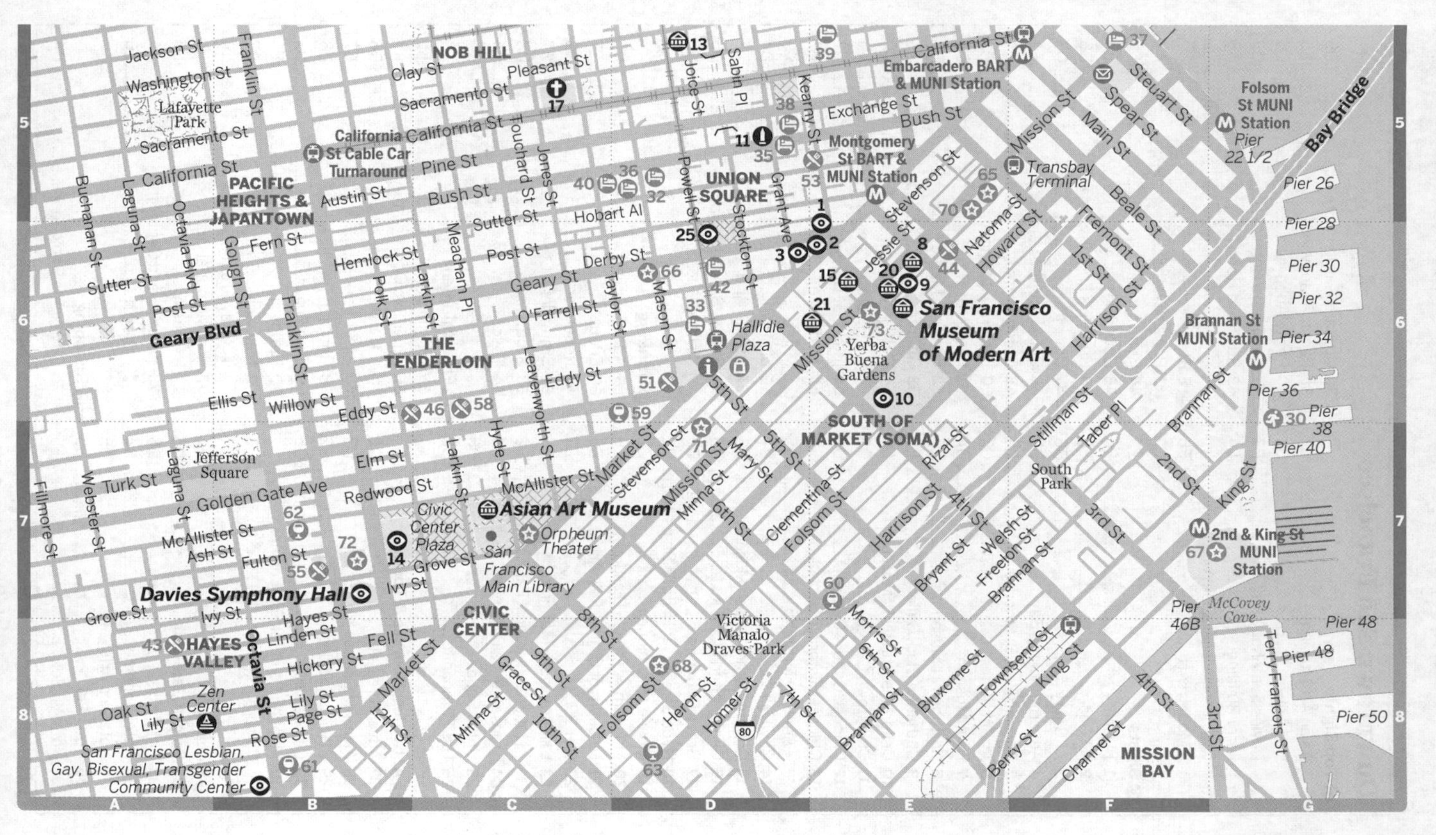
Jackson St
Washington St
Lafayette Park
Sacramento St
California St
Franklin St
NOB HILL
Clay St
Pleasant St
Sacramento St
California St Cable Car Turnaround
California St
Pine St
Bush St
Touchard St
Jones St
Joice St
Sabin Pl
Kearny St
Exchange St
Bush St
California St
Embarcadero BART & MUNI Station
Steuart St
Spear St
Main St
Mission St
Folsom St MUNI Station
Pier 22 1/2
Bay Bridge
Buchanan St
Laguna St
Octavia Blvd
PACIFIC HEIGHTS & JAPANTOWN
Austin St
Sutter St
Hobart Al
UNION SQUARE
Powell St
Stockton St
Grant Ave
Montgomery St BART & MUNI Station
Stevenson St
Transbay Terminal
Beale St
Pier 26
Pier 28
Pier 30
Pier 32
Pier 34
Pier 36
Pier 38
Pier 40
Fern St
Gough St
Hemlock St
Post St
Derby St
Geary St
Jessie St
Natoma St
Howard St
Fremont St
1st St
Harrison St
Sutter St
Post St
Geary Blvd
Franklin St
Polk St
Larkin St
Meacham Pl
O'Farrell St
Taylor St
Mason St
Hallidie Plaza
Mission St
Yerba Buena Gardens
San Francisco Museum of Modern Art
Brannan St MUNI Station
THE TENDERLOIN
Leavenworth St
Eddy St
5th St
SOUTH OF MARKET (SOMA)
Brannan St
Ellis St
Willow St
Eddy St
Stillman St
Taber Pl
Jefferson Square
Elm St
Larkin St
Hyde St
Market St
Stevenson St
Mission St
Mary St
Minna St
Rizal St
South Park
2nd St
King St
Fillmore St
Webster St
Turk St
Laguna St
Golden Gate Ave
Redwood St
McAllister St
Asian Art Museum
Clementina St
Folsom St
6th St
Harrison St
4th St
3rd St
McAllister St
Ash St
Fulton St
Civic Center Plaza
Grove St
Orpheum Theater
San Francisco Main Library
Welsh St
Freelon St
Bryant St
Brannan St
2nd & King St MUNI Station
Davies Symphony Hall
Ivy St
CIVIC CENTER
Pier 46B
McCovey Cove
Grove St
Ivy St
Hayes St
Linden St
8th St
Victoria Manalo Draves Park
Morris St
Pier 48
HAYES VALLEY
Octavia St
Hickory St
Fell St
Market St
9th St
Grace St
6th St
Townsend St
King St
Terry Francois St
Pier 48
Zen Center
Oak St
Lily St
Lily St
Page St
Rose St
12th St
Minna St
10th St
Folsom St
Heron St
Homer St
7th St
Brannan St
Bluxome St
4th St
3rd St
Pier 50
San Francisco Lesbian, Gay, Bisexual, Transgender Community Center
Berry St
Channel St
MISSION BAY

Downtown San Francisco

Top Sights
Asian Art Museum ... C7
Coit Tower ... D3
Davies Symphony Hall ... B7
Ferry Building ... F4
San Francisco Museum of Modern Art ... E6

Sights
1 14 Geary ... E6
2 49 Geary ... E6
3 77 Geary ... D6
4 Aquarium of the Bay ... D2
5 Aquatic Park Bathhouse ... B2
6 Art Institute ... C3
7 Beat Museum ... D4
8 Cartoon Art Museum ... E6
9 Catharine Clark Gallery ... E6
10 Children's Creativity Museum ... E6
11 Chinatown Gate ... D5
12 Chinese Culture Center ... D4
13 Chinese Historical Society of America Museum ... D5
14 City Hall ... B7
15 Contemporary Jewish Museum ... E6
16 George Sterling Park ... B3
17 Grace Cathedral ... C5
18 Hyde Street Pier Historic Ships ... B2
19 Musée Mécanique ... C2
20 Museum of African Diaspora ... E6
21 Museum of Craft & Folk Arts ... E6
22 Pier 39 ... D1
23 San Francisco Maritime National Historical Park ... B2
24 Transamerica Pyramid ... E4
25 Union Square ... D6
26 Uss Pampanito ... C2

Activities, Courses & Tours
27 Adventure Cat ... D2
28 Alcatraz Cruises ... D2
29 Blazing Saddles ... B2
30 City Kayak ... G6
31 Meeting Point for Fire Engine Tours ... B2

Sleeping
32 Golden Gate Hotel ... D5
33 Hotel Abri ... D6
34 Hotel Bohème ... D4
35 Hotel des Arts ... D5
36 Hotel Rex ... D5
37 Hotel Vitale ... F5
38 Orchard Garden Hotel ... D5
39 Pacific Tradewinds ... E5
40 Petite Auberge ... C5
41 San Remo Hotel ... C3
42 Stratford Hotel ... D6

Eating
43 Bar Jules ... A8
44 Benu ... E6
45 Bocadillos ... E4
46 Brenda's French Soul Food ... B6
47 Cinecittà ... D3
48 Coi ... E4
49 Cotogna ... E4
50 Crown & Crumpet ... B2
51 Farmerbrown ... D6
52 Farmers Market ... F4
53 Gitane ... E5
Gott's Roadside ... (see 52)
Hog Island Oyster Company ... (see 52)
54 In-N-Out Burger ... C2
55 Jardinière ... B7
Mijita ... (see 52)
56 Molinari ... D4
57 Off the Grid ... A2
58 Saigon Sandwich Shop ... C6
Slanted Door ... (see 52)

Drinking
59 Aunt Charlie's ... D6
60 Endup ... E7
61 Rebel Bar ... B8
62 Smuggler's Cove ... B7
63 Stud ... D8
64 Tosca Cafe ... D4

Entertainment
65 111 Minna ... E5
66 American Conservatory Theater ... D6
67 AT&T Park ... G7
68 Cat Club ... D8
69 Club Fugazi ... D3
70 Harlot ... E5
71 Mezzanine ... D7
TIX Bay Area ... (see 25)
72 War Memorial Opera House ... B7
73 Yerba Buena Center for the Arts ... E6

Shopping
74 City Lights Bookstore ... D4

FISHERMAN'S WHARF

FREE **Aquatic Park Bathhouse** HISTORIC BUILDING
(Map p952; ☎415-447-5000; www.nps.gov/safr; 499 Jefferson St, at Hyde St; ⏲10am-4pm) A monumental hint to sailors in need of a scrub, this recently restored, ship-shape 1939 streamline moderne landmark is decked out with Works Progress Administration (WPA) art treasures: playful seal and frog sculptures by Beniamino Bufano, Hilaire Hiler's surreal underwater dreamscape murals and recently uncovered wood reliefs by Richard Ayer. Acclaimed African American artist Sargent Johnson created the stunning carved green slate marquee doorway and the verandah's mesmerizing aquatic mosaics, which he deliberately left unfinished on the east side to protest plans to include a private restaurant in this public facility. Johnson won: the east wing is now a maritime museum office.

Musée Mécanique AMUSEMENT ARCADE
(Map p952; ☎415-346-2000; www.museemecaniquesf.com; Pier 45; ⏲10am-7pm Mon-Fri, to 8pm Sat & Sun) Where else can you guillotine a man for a quarter? Creepy 19th-century arcade games like the macabre French Execution compete for your spare change with the diabolical Ms Pac-Man.

Pier 39 LANDMARK
(Map p952; www.pier39.com) With the notable exception of sea lions gleefully belching after fish dinners at Pier 39, most of Fisherman's Wharf is packed with landlubbers attempting to digest sourdough-bread bowls of gloppy clam chowder (don't bother: can't be done).

USS Pampanito MUSEUM
(Map p952; ☎415-775-1943; www.maritime.org; Pier 45; adult/child $10/4; ⏲9am-5pm) Explore a restored WWII submarine that survived six tours of duty, while listening to submariners' tales of stealth mode and sudden attacks in a riveting audio tour ($2) that makes surfacing afterwards a relief (caution claustrophobes).

Hyde Street Pier Historic Ships HISTORIC SITE
(Map p952; ☎415-447-5000; www.nps.gov/safr; 499 Jefferson St, at Hyde St; adult/child $5/free; ⏲9am-5pm) Tour 19th-century ships moored here as part of the Maritime National Historical Park, including triple-masted 1886 **Balclutha** and 1890 steamboat **Eureka**; summer sailing trips are available aboard elegant 1891 schooner **Alma** (adult/child $40/20; ⏲Jun-Nov).

THE MARINA & PRESIDIO

TOP CHOICE **Exploratorium** MUSEUM
(☎415-561-0360; www.exploratorium.edu; 3601 Lyon St; adult/child $15/10, incl Tactile Dome $10; ⏲10am-5pm Tue-Sun) Budding Nobel Prize winners swarm this hands-on discovery museum, learning the scientific secrets to skateboarding and groping through the Tactile Dome (ages seven+). Mad-scientist cocktails, live performances and scientific experiments draw the over-21 crowd to **After Dark** (⏲6-10pm Thu). With exhibits that won designers a McArthur Genius Grant, the Exploratorium is outgrowing its picturesque Palace of Fine Arts location and moving to the piers in 2013. Meanwhile, ducklings march past the Exploratorium through Bernard Maybeck's faux-Roman 1915 **rotunda**, where friezes depict Art under attack by Materialists, with Idealists leaping to her rescue.

Crissy Field WATERFRONT, BEACH
(☎415-561-7690; www.crissyfield.org) The Presidio's army airstrip has been stripped of asphalt and reinvented as a haven for coastal birds, kite-fliers and windsurfers enjoying sweeping views of Golden Gate Bridge.

Baker Beach BEACH
(Map p948; ⏲sunrise-sunset) Unswimmable waters (except when the tide's coming in) but unbeatable views of the Golden Gate make this former Army beachhead SF's tanning location of choice, especially the

WORTH A TRIP

COIT TOWER

Adding an exclamation mark to San Francisco's landscape, **Coit Tower** (Map p952; ☎415-362-0808; elevator rides $5; ⏲10am-6pm) offers views worth shouting about – especially after you climb the giddy, steep Filbert St steps to get here. Check out 360-degree views of downtown from the viewing platform, and wrap-around 1930s lobby murals glorifying SF workers – once denounced as communist but now a beloved landmark. To see more murals hidden inside Coit Tower's stairwell, take free docent-led tours at 11am Saturdays.

clothing-optional north end – at least until the afternoon fog rolls in.

Fort Mason HISTORIC SITE
(☎415-345-7500; www.fortmason.org) Army sergeants would be scandalized by the frolicking at this former military outpost, including comedy improv workshops, kiddie art classes, and **Off the Grid** (http://offthegridsf.com), where gourmet trucks circle like pioneer wagons.

Fort Point HISTORIC SITE
(Map p948; ☎415-561-4395; www.nps.gov/fopo) Despite its impressive guns, this Civil War fort saw no action – at least until Alfred Hitchcock shot scenes from *Vertigo* here, with stunning views of the Golden Gate Bridge from below.

THE MISSION

Mission Dolores CHURCH
(Map p958; ☎415-621-8203; www.missiondolores.org; cnr Dolores & 16th Sts; adult/child $5/3; ⏲9am-4pm) The city's oldest building and its namesake, the whitewashed adobe Misión San Francisco de Asis was founded in 1776 and rebuilt in 1782 with conscripted Ohlone and Miwok labor – note the ceiling patterned after Native American baskets. In the cemetery beside the adobe mission, a replica Ohlone hut is a memorial to the 5000 Ohlone and Miwok who died in 1814 and 1826 mission measles epidemics. The mission is overshadowed by the adjoining ornate 1913 basilica, where stained-glass windows commemorate the 21 original California missions, from Santa Cruz to San Diego.

Balmy Alley STREET
(Map p958; off 24th St, near Folsom St) Mission activist artists set out in the 1970s to transform the political landscape, one mural-covered garage door at a time. Today, a one-block walk down Balmy Alley leads past three decades of murals, from an early memorial for El Salvador activist Archbishop Óscar Romero to an homage to the golden age of Mexican cinema. Nonprofit Precita Eyes restores these murals, commissions new ones and offers mural tours (see p961).

826 Valencia CULTURAL BUILDING
(Map p958; ☎415-642-5905; www.826valencia.org; 826 Valencia St; ⏲noon-6pm) 'No buccaneers! No geriatrics!' warns the sign above the vat of sand where kids rummage for buried pirates' booty. The eccentric Pirate Supply Store sells eye patches, scoops from an actual tub o' lard, and McSweeney's literary magazines to support a teen writing nonprofit and the Fish Theater, where a puffer fish is immersed in Method acting.

Creativity Explored GALLERY
(Map p958; ☎415-863-2108; www.creativityexplored.org; 3245 16th St; donations welcome; ⏲10am-3pm Mon-Fri, to 7pm Thu, 1-6pm Sat) Fresh perspectives on themes ranging from superheroes to architecture by critically acclaimed, developmentally disabled artists – don't miss joyous openings with the artists, their families and fans.

Dolores Park PARK
(Map p958) Sunshine and politics come with the Mission territory: protests are held almost every weekend, alongside soccer, tennis and hillside tanning.

THE CASTRO

Rainbow flags fly high over **Harvey Milk Plaza** (Map p958) in San Francisco's historic out-and-proud neighborhood, home of the nation's first openly gay official.

GLBT History Museum MUSEUM
(Map p958; ☎415-621-1107; www.glbthistory.org/museum; 4127 18th St; admission $5, 1st Wed of month free; ⏲11am-7pm Tue-Sat, noon-5pm Sun-Mon) America's first gay-history museum captures proud moments and historic challenges: Harvey Milk's campaign literature, interviews with trailblazing bisexual author Gore Vidal, matchbooks from long-gone bathhouses and pages of the 1950s penal code banning homosexuality.

THE HAIGHT

Better known as the hazy hot spot of the Summer of Love, the Haight has hung onto its tie-dyes, ideals and certain habits – hence the Bound Together Anarchist Book Collective, the Haight Ashbury Free Clinic and high density of medical marijuana dispensaries (sorry, dude: prescription required). Fanciful 'Painted Lady' Victorian houses surround **Alamo Square Park** (Hayes & Scott Sts) and the corner of Haight and Ashbury Sts, where Jimi Hendrix, Janis Joplin and the Grateful Dead crashed during the Haight's hippie heyday.

JAPANTOWN & PACIFIC HEIGHTS

Atop every Japantown sushi counter perches a *maneki neko,* the porcelain cat with one paw raised in permanent welcome: this is your cue to unwind with shiatsu massages at Kabuki Hot Springs, eco-entertainment and non-GMO popcorn at Sundance Kabuki Cinema, world-class jazz at Yoshi's or mind-blowing rock at the Fillmore.

GOLDEN GATE PARK & AROUND

San Francisco was way ahead of its time in 1865, when the city voted to turn 1017 acres of sand dunes into the world's largest city stretch of green, Golden Gate Park (Map p948). This ambitious green scheme scared off Frederick Law Olmstead, the celebrated architect of New York's Central Park, and thwarted real estate speculators' plans to turn Golden Gate Park into a theme-park resort. Instead of hotels and casinos, park architect William Hammond Hall insisted on botanical gardens and a Japanese Tea Garden.

GAY/LES/BI/TRANS SAN FRANCISCO

Doesn't matter where you're from, who you love or who's your daddy: if you're here, and queer, welcome home. The intersection of 18th and Castro Sts is the heart of the gay cruising scene, but dancing queens and slutty boys head South of Market (SoMa) for thump-thump clubs. The Mission is the preferred 'hood of alt-chicks, trans FTMs (female-to-males) and flirty femmes. *Bay Area Reporter* (aka BAR; www.ebar.com) covers community news and listings; *San Francisco Bay Times* (www.sfbaytimes.com) also has good resources for transsexuals; and free mag *Gloss Magazine* (www.glossmagazine.net) covers nightlife.

To find out where the party is, check **Honey Soundsystem** (www.honeysoundsystem.com) for roving queer dance parties; **Betty's List** (www.bettyslist.com) for parties, fund-raisers and power-lesbian mixers; and **Juanita More** (www.juanitamore.com) for fierce circuit parties thrown by a drag superstar. **Sisters of Perpetual Indulgence** (www.thesisters.org), 'the leading-edge order of queer nuns,' organizes parties, guerrilla street theater and the subversive 'Hunky Jesus Contest' in Dolores Park at Easter.

Other top GLBT venues:

Stud BAR
(Map p952; ☎415-252-7883; www.studsf.com; 399 9th St; admission $5-8; ⏰5pm-3am) Rocking the gay scene since 1966, and branching out beyond leather daddies with rocker-grrrl Mondays, Tuesday drag variety shows, raunchy comedy/karaoke Wednesdays, Friday art-drag dance parties, and performance-art cabaret whenever hostess/DJ Anna Conda gets it together.

Rebel Bar BAR
(Map p952; ☎415-431-4202; 1760 Market St; ⏰5pm-3am Mon-Thu, to 4am Fri, 11am-4am Sat & Sun) Funhouse southern biker disco, complete with antique mirrored walls, Hell's Angel cocktails (Bulleit bourbon, Chartreuse, OJ) and exposed pipes. The crowd is mostly 30-something, gay and tribally tattooed; on a good night, poles get thoroughly worked.

Aunt Charlie's BAR
(Map p952; ☎415-441-2922; www.auntcharlieslounge.com; 133 Turk St; ⏰9am-2am) Total dive, with the city's best classic drag show Fridays and Saturdays at 10pm. Thursday nights, art-school boys freak for bathhouse disco at Tubesteak ($5).

Endup BAR
(Map p952; ☎415-646-0999; www.theendup.com; 401 6th St; admission $5-20; ⏰10pm-4am Mon-Thu, 11pm-11am Fri, 10pm Sat-4am Mon) Home of Sunday 'tea dances' (gay dance parties) since 1973, though technically the party starts Saturday – bring a change of clothes and Endup watching Monday's sunrise over the freeway on-ramp.

Lexington Club LESBIAN
(Map p958; ☎415-863-2052; 3464 19th St; ⏰3pm-2am) The baddest lesbian bar in the West, with pool, pinball and grrrrls galore.

Cafe Flore CAFE
(Map p958; ☎415-621-8579; http://cafeflore.com; 2298 Market St; mains $8-11; ⏰7am-2am; 📶) Coffee, wi-fi and hot beefy dishes – and the burgers aren't bad either.

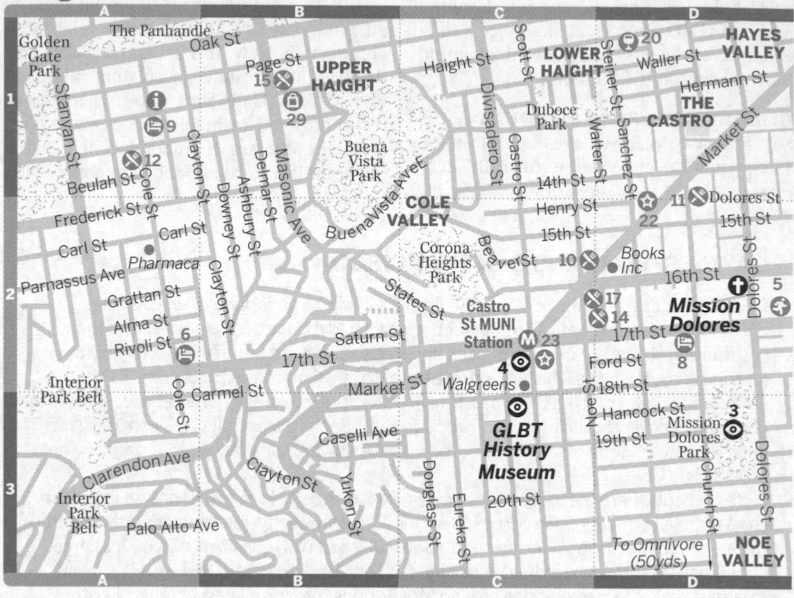

Haight & the Mission

Top Sights

- 826 Valencia E3
- Balmy Alley E2
- GLBT History Museum C3
- Mission Dolores D2

Sights

- 1 Alamo Square Park E1
- 2 Creativity Explored E2
- 3 Dolores Park D3
- 4 Harvey Milk Plaza C2

Activities, Courses & Tours

- 5 18 Reasons D2

Sleeping

- 6 Belvedere House A2
- 7 Inn San Francisco F3
- 8 Parker Guest House D2
- 9 Red Victorian A1

Eating

- 10 Cafe Flore C2
- 11 Chilango D1
- 12 Cole Valley Cafe A1
- 13 Commonwealth E2
- 14 Frances D2
- 15 Magnolia Brewpub B1
- 16 Pizzeria Delfina E2
- Rosamunde Sausage Grill .... (see 20)
- 17 Starbelly C2

Drinking

- 18 Bar Agricole F1
- 19 Lexington Club E3
- 20 Toronado D1
- 21 Zeitgeist E1

Entertainment

- 22 Café du Nord D2
- 23 Castro Theatre C2
- 24 DNA Lounge F1
- 25 Marsh E3
- 26 Roxie Cinema E2
- 27 Slim's F1

Shopping

- 28 Adobe Books E2
- 29 Bound Together Anarchist Book Collective B1

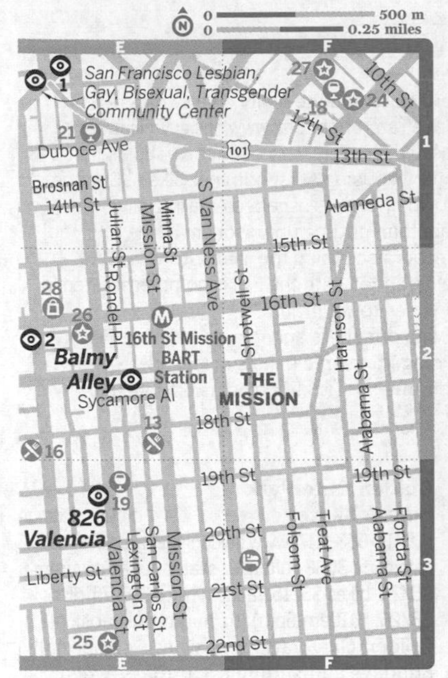

Toward Ocean Beach, the park's scenery turns quixotic, with bison stampeding in their paddock toward windswept windmills. At the north end of Ocean Beach, the recently restored **Cliff House** (Map p948; www.cliffhouse.com) restaurant overlooks the splendid ruin of **Sutro Baths**, where Victorian ladies and dandies once converged by the thousands for bracing baths in rented itchy wool bathing suits. Follow the partly paved hiking trail above Sutro Baths around **Lands End** (Map p948) for end-of-the-world views of Marin and the Golden Gate Bridge.

California Academy of Sciences WILDLIFE RESERVE
(☎415-379-8000; www.calacademy.org; 55 Concourse Dr; adult/child $29.95/24.95, $3 discount with Muni ticket, 6-10pm Thu $10 (age 21+ only); ⊙9:30am-5pm Mon-Sat, from 11am Sun) Architect Renzo Piano's 2008 landmark LEED-certified green building houses 38,000 weird and wonderful animals in a four-story rainforest and split-level aquarium under a 'living roof' of California wildflowers. After the penguins nod off to sleep, the wild rumpus starts at kids'-only Academy Sleepovers and over-21 NightLife Thursdays, when rainforest-themed cocktails encourage strange mating rituals among shy internet daters.

MH de Young Fine Arts Museum MUSEUM
(☎415-750-3600; www.famsf.org/deyoung; 50 Hagiwara Tea Garden Dr; adult/child $10/free, $2 discount with Muni ticket, 1st Tue of month free; ⊙9:30am-5:15pm Tue-Sun, to 8:45pm Fri) Follow sculptor Andy Goldsworthy's artificial fault line in the sidewalk into Herzog & de Meuron's sleek, copper-clad building that's oxidizing green to blend into the park. Don't be fooled by the de Young's camouflaged exterior: shows here boldly broaden artistic horizons from Oceanic ceremonial masks and Balenciaga gowns to sculptor Al Farrow's cathedrals built from bullets.

California Palace of the Legion of Honor MUSEUM
(Map p948; ☎415-750-3600; http://legionofhonor.famsf.org; 100 34th Ave; adult/child $10/6, $2 discount with Muni ticket, 1st Tue of month free; ⊙9:30am-5:15pm Tue-Sun) Never doubt the unwavering resolve of a nude model: sculptor's model and heiress 'Big Alma' de Bretteville Spreckels donated her fortune to build this monumental tribute to Californians killed in France in WWI. Featured artworks range from Monet water lilies to John Cage soundscapes, Iraqi ivories to R Crumb comics – part of the Legion's Achenbach collection of 90,000 graphic artworks.

Ocean Beach BEACH
(Map p948; ☎415-561-4323; www.parksconservancy.org; ⊙sunrise-sunset) The park ends in this blustery beach, too chilly for bikini-clad clambakes but ideal for wet-suited pro surfers braving rip tides (casual swimmers beware). Bonfires are permitted in designated fire pits only; no alcohol allowed.

Conservatory of Flowers GARDEN
(☎415-666-7001; www.conservatoryofflowers.org; Conservatory Dr West; adult/child $7/2; ⊙10am-4pm Tue-Sun) This recently restored 1878 Victorian greenhouse is home to outer-space orchids, contemplative floating lilies and creepy carnivorous plants that reek of insect belches.

Japanese Tea Garden GARDEN
(http://japaneseteagardensf.com; Hagiwara Tea Garden Dr; adult/child $7/5; ⊙9am-6pm) Since 1894, this picturesque 5-acre garden and bonsai grove has blushed with cherry blossoms in spring, turned flaming red with maple leaves in fall, and lost all track of time in the meditative Zen Garden.

WORTH A TRIP

ALCATRAZ

For 150 years, the name has given the innocent chills and the guilty cold sweats. **Alcatraz** (Alcatraz Cruises 415-981-7625; www.alcatrazcruises.com, www.nps.gov/alcatraz; adult/child day $26/16, night $33/19.50; call center 8am-7pm) has been the nation's first military prison, a maximum-security penitentiary housing A-list criminals like Al Capone, and hotly disputed Native American territory. No prisoners escaped Alcatraz alive, but since importing guards and supplies cost more than putting up prisoners at the Ritz, the prison was closed in 1963. Native American leaders occupied the island from 1969 to '71 to protest US occupation of Native lands; their standoff with the FBI is commemorated in a dockside museum and 'This is Indian Land' water-tower graffiti.

Day visits include captivating audio tours, with prisoners and guards recalling life on 'the Rock,' while night tours are led by a park ranger; reserve tickets at least two weeks ahead. Ferries depart Pier 33 every half-hour from 9am to 3:55pm, plus 6:10pm and 6:45pm.

Stow Lake LAKE
(http://sfrecpark.org/StowLake.aspx; per hr paddleboats/canoes/rowboats/tandem bikes/bikes $24/20/19/15/8; rentals 10am-4pm) Huntington Falls tumble down 400ft Strawberry Hill into the lake, near a romantic Chinese pavilion and a 1946 boathouse offering boat and bike rentals.

SAN FRANCISCO BAY

Golden Gate Bridge BRIDGE
(www.goldengatebridge.org) Imagine a squat concrete bridge striped black and caution yellow spanning the San Francisco Bay – that's what the US Navy initially had in mind. Luckily, engineer Joseph B Strauss and architects Gertrude and Irving Murrow insisted on a soaring art-deco design and International Orange paint of the 1937 Golden Gate Bridge. Cars pay a $6 toll to cross from Marin to San Francisco; pedestrians and cyclists stroll the east sidewalk for free.

Activities

Kabuki Hot Springs SPA
(415-922-6000; www.kabukisprings.com; 1750 Geary Blvd; admission $22-25; 10am-9:45pm) Soak muscles worked by SF's 43 hills in Japanese baths. Men and women alternate days, and bathing suits are required on coed Tuesdays.

Oceanic Society Expeditions BOATING
(415-474-3385; www.oceanic-society.org; per person $100-120; office 8:30am-5pm Mon-Fri, trips Sat & Sun) Whale sightings aren't a fluke on naturalist-led, ocean-going weekend boat trips during mid-October through December migrations.

Golden Gate Park Bike & Skate CYCLING, SKATING
(415-668-1117; www.goldengateparkbikeandskate.com; 3038 Fulton St; skates per hr/day from $5/20, bikes $3/15, tandem bikes $15/75, discs $6/25; 10am-6pm) To make the most of Golden Gate Park, rent wheels – especially Sundays and summer Saturdays, when JFK Dr is closed to vehicular traffic – or disc golf equipment.

Blazing Saddles CYCLING
(415-202-8888; www.blazingsaddles.com; 2715 Hyde St; bikes per hr/day from $8/$32; 8am-7:30pm) From this bike rental shop's Fisherman's Wharf outposts, cyclists can cross the Golden Gate Bridge and take the Sausalito ferry back to SF (weather permitting).

18 Reasons COOKING
(Map p952; 415-252-9816; www.18reasons.org; 593 Guerrero St; 6:30am-5pm Mon-Sat, 7am-4:30pm Sun) Go gourmet at this local food community nonprofit offering knife-skills and edible perfume workshops, wine and cheese tastings, and more.

City Kayak KAYAKING
(Map p952; 415-357-1010; http://citykayak.com; South Beach Harbor; kayak rentals per hr $35-65, 3hr lesson & rental package $59, tours $65-75) Experienced paddlers hit the choppy waters beneath the Golden Gate Bridge or take a moonlit group tour, while newbies venture calm waters near the Bay Bridge.

Adventure Cat SAILING
(Map p952; 415-777-1630; www.adventurecat.com; Pier 39; adult/child $35/15, sunset cruise $50) Three daily catamaran cruises depart

March to October; weekends only November to February.

FREE **Potrero del Sol/La Raza Skatepark** SKATING
(www.sfgov.org; 25th & Utah Sts) Skate the bowl or watch in awe as pro street skaters hit air and padded kindergartners scoot along.

Aqua Surf Shop SURFING
(Map p948; 415-876-2782; www.aquasurfshop.com; 1742 Haight St; 11am-7pm; rental per day board/wetsuit $25/15) Even kooks (newbies) become mavericks with Aqua's wetsuit rentals, tide updates and lesson referrals.

Tours

Chinatown Alleyway Tours WALKING
(415-984-1478 www.chinatownalleywaytours.org; adult/child $18/5/; 11am Sat & Sun) Neighborhood teens lead two-hour tours for up-close-and-personal peeks into Chinatown's past (weather permitting). Book five days ahead or pay double for Saturday walk-ins; cash only.

Precita Eyes Mission Mural Tours WALKING
(415-285-2287; www.precitaeyes.org; adult $12-15, child $5; 11am, noon & 1:30pm Sat & Sun) Muralists lead two-hour tours on foot or bike covering 60 to 70 murals in a six- to 10-block radius of mural-bedecked Balmy Alley; proceeds fund mural upkeep.

FREE **Public Library City Guides** WALKING
(www.sfcityguides.org) Volunteer local historians lead tours by neighborhood and theme: Art Deco Marina, Gold Rush Downtown, Pacific Heights Victorians, North Beach by Night, and more. See website for upcoming tours.

Festivals & Events

Chinese New Year Parade CULTURAL
(www.chineseparade.com) Chase the 200ft dragon, and see lion dancers and toddler kung-fu classes parade through Chinatown in February.

SF International Film Festival FILM
(www.sffs.org) Stars align and directors launch premieres each April at the nation's oldest film festival.

Bay to Breakers RACE
(www.baytobreakers.com; race registration $44-48) Run costumed or naked from Embarcadero to Ocean Beach the third Sunday in May, while joggers dressed as salmon run upstream.

Carnaval CULTURAL
(www.carnavalsf.com) Brazilian, or just faking it with a wax and a tan? Shake your tail feathers in the Mission the last weekend of May.

SF Pride Celebration CULTURAL
A day isn't enough to do SF proud: June begins with **International LGBT Film Festival** (www.frameline.org), and goes out in style

SAN FRANCISCO FOR CHILDREN

Although it has the least kids per capita of any US city – according to recent SFSPCA data, there are about 19,000 more dogs than kids under age 18 in town – San Francisco is packed with attractions for kids, including Golden Gate Park, Exploratorium, California Academy of Sciences, Cartoon Art Museum and Museé Mechanique. For babysitting, **American Child Care** (415-285-2300; www.americanchildcare.com; 580 California St, Suite 1600) charges $20 per hour plus gratuity; four-hour minimum.

Children's Creativity Museum MUSEUM
(415-820-3320; www.zeum.org; 221 4th St; admission $10; 11am-5pm Tue-Sun) Technology that's too cool for school: robots, live-action video games, DIY music videos and 3D animation workshops with Silicon Valley innovators.

Aquarium of the Bay AQUARIUM
(Map p952; www.aquariumofthebay.com; Pier 39; adult/child $17/8; 9am-8pm summer, 10am-6pm winter) Glide through glass tubes underwater on conveyer belts as sharks circle overhead.

Fire Engine Tours TOUR
(Map p952; 415-333-7077; www.fireenginetours.com; Beach St at the Cannery; adult/child $50/30; tours depart 1pm) Hot stuff: a 75-minute, open-air vintage fire-engine ride over Golden Gate Bridge.

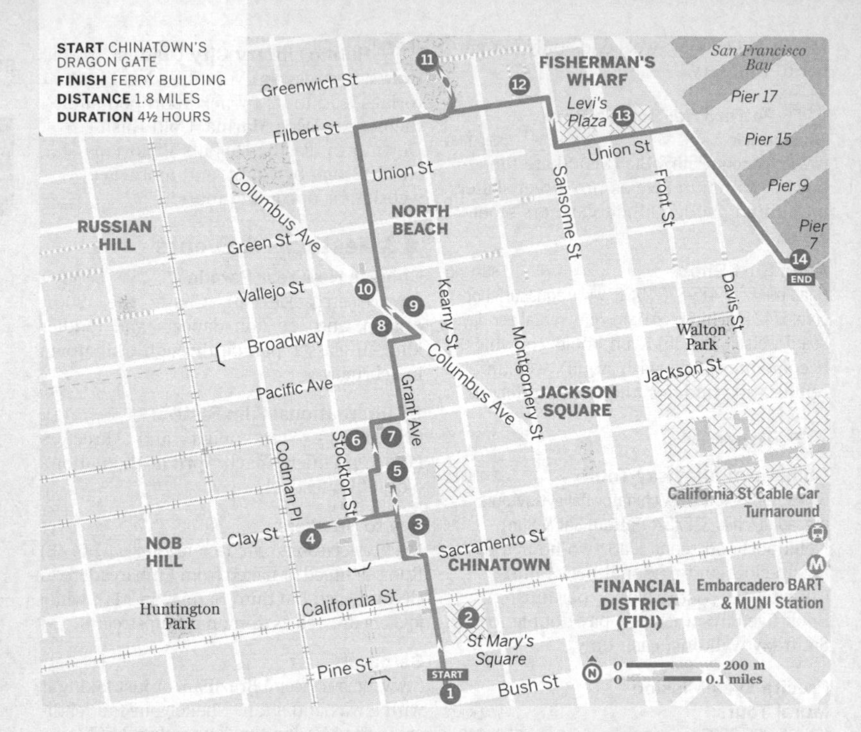

Walking Tour
Chinatown

Limber up and look sharp: on this walk, you'll discover revolutionary plots, find hidden fortunes, see controversial art and go gourmet with Gandhi.

Starting at 1 **Chinatown's Dragon Gate**, head past Grant St's gilded dragon lamps to 2 **Old St Mary's Square**, site of a brothel leveled in the 1906 fire where renegade skateboarders turn a different kind of tricks under the watchful eye of Beniamino Bufano's 1929 statue of Chinese revolutionary Sun Yat-Sen. Walk uphill to spot flag-festooned temple balconies along 3 **Waverly Place**, then head up to the 4 **Chinese Historical Society of America Museum**, in the majestic Chinatown YWCA built by Julia Morgan.

Backtrack past Stockton to 5 **Spofford Alley**, where mahjong tiles click, Chinese orchestras warm up and beauticians gossip indiscreetly over blow-dryers. Once you might have heard Prohibition bootlegger turf wars, or Sun Yat-Sen at No 36 plotting the 1911 overthrow of China's last dynasty. Once packed with brothels, 6 **Ross Alley** was more recently pimped as the picturesque setting for such forgettable sequels as *Karate Kid II* and *Indian Jones and the Temple of Doom.* At No 56, get your fortune while it's hot, folded into warm cookies at 7 **Golden Gate Fortune Cookie Factory**.

Back on Grant, take a shortcut through 8 **Jack Kerouac Alley**, where poetry marks where the binge-prone author sometimes wound up *On the Road*. The light at the end of the alley is 9 **City Lights Bookstore**, champion of Beat poetry and free speech. Savor poetry with espresso at 10 **Caffe Trieste** at 601 Vallejo St, under the Sicilian mural where Francis Ford Coppola legendarily wrote *The Godfather* script.

Climb to 11 **Coit Tower** for viewing-platform panoramas and 1930s lobby murals critics have called communist, courageous, or both. Take 12 **Filbert Steps** downhill past wild parrots and hidden cottages to 13 **Levi's Plaza**, named for San Francisco's denim inventor. Head right on Embarcadero to the 14 **Ferry Building** for lunch Bayside, with a gaunt bronze Gandhi peeking over your shoulder.

the last weekend with Pink Saturday's **Dyke March** (www.dykemarch.org) and the frisky, million-strong **Pride Parade** (www.sfpride.org).

Folsom Street Fair STREET FAIR
(www.folsomstreetfair.com) Work that leather look and enjoy public spankings for local charities the last weekend of September.

Hardly Strictly Bluegrass MUSIC
(www.strictlybluegrass.com) SF celebrates Western roots with three days of free Golden Gate Park concerts and headliners ranging from Elvis Costello to Gillian Welch in early October.

LitQuake CULTURAL
(www.litquake.org) Authors tell stories at the biggest lit fest in the West and spill trade secrets over drinks at the legendary Lit Crawl; second week in October.

SF Jazz Festival MUSIC
(www.sfjazz.org) Old-school greats and breakthrough talents blow horns and minds in late October.

Sleeping

San Francisco is the birthplace of the boutique hotel, offering stylish rooms for a price: $100 to $200 rooms midrange, plus 15.5% hotel tax (hostels exempt) and $35 to $50 for overnight parking. For vacancies and deals, check SF Visitor Information Center's **reservation line** (☎415-391-2000; www.onlyinsanfrancisco.com), **Bed & Breakfast SF** (☎415-899-0060; www.bbsf.com) and **Lonely Planet** (http://hotels.lonelyplanet.com).

UNION SQUARE & CIVIC CENTER

Hotel Rex BOUTIQUE HOTEL **$$$**
(Map p952; ☎415-433-4434; www.jdvhotels.com; 562 Sutter St; r $169-279; P❄@📶) Noir-novelist chic, with 1920s literary lounge and compact rooms with hand-painted lampshades, local art and sumptuous beds piled with down pillows.

Orchard Garden Hotel BOUTIQUE HOTEL **$$$**
(Map p952; ☎415-399-9807; www.theorchardgardenhotel.com; 466 Bush St; r $179-249; ❄@📶) SF's first all-green-practices hotel has soothingly quiet rooms with luxe touches, like Egyptian-cotton sheets, plus an organic rooftop garden.

Hotel des Arts HOTEL **$$**
(Map p952; ☎415-956-3232; www.sfhoteldesarts.com; 447 Bush St; r with bath $139-199, without bath $99-149; 📶) A budget hotel for art freaks, with specialty rooms painted by underground artists – it's like sleeping inside an art installation. Standard rooms are less exciting, but clean and good value; bring earplugs.

Petite Auberge B&B **$$$**
(Map p952; ☎415-928-6000; www.jdvhotels.com; 863 Bush St; r $169-219; @📶) An urban French-provincial country inn with cheerful rooms, some with gas fireplaces; don't miss chatty fireside wine hour.

Hotel Abri BOUTIQUE HOTEL **$$$**
(Map p952; ☎415-392-8800; www.hotel-abri.com; 127 Ellis St; r $149-229; ❄@📶) Snazzy boutique hotel with bold black-and-tan motifs and ultramod cons: iPod docking stations, pillow-top beds, flat-screen TVs and rainfall showerheads.

Golden Gate Hotel HOTEL **$$**
(Map p952; ☎415-392-3702; www.goldengatehotel.com; 775 Bush St; r without/with bath $105/165; @📶) A homey Edwardian hotel with kindly owners, homemade cookies and a cuddly cat, safely uphill from the Tenderloin. Most rooms have private baths, some with claw-foot tubs.

Stratford Hotel HOTEL **$$**
(Map p952; ☎415-397-7080; hotelstratford.com; 242 Powell St; r incl breakfast $89-149; @📶) Simple, smallish, clean rooms with rainfall showers; request rooms facing away from clanging Powell St cable cars.

FINANCIAL DISTRICT & NORTH BEACH

TOP CHOICE **Hotel Bohème** BOUTIQUE HOTEL **$$**
(Map p952; ☎415-433-9111; www.hotelboheme.com; 444 Columbus Ave; r $174-194; @📶) A love letter to North Beach's Beat era, with vintage photos, retro orange, black and sage-green color schemes, and Chinese parasols for lampshades; no elevator.

TOP CHOICE **Hotel Vitale** LUXURY HOTEL **$$$**
(Map p952; ☎415-278-3700; www.hotelvitale.com; 8 Mission St; d $239-379; ❄@📶) The shagadelic-chic Vitale is SF's sexiest splurge, with roof hot tubs at the on-site spa, silky 450-threadcount linens on sumptuous beds, and some sweeping bay views.

San Remo Hotel HOTEL **$**
(Map p952; ☎415-776-8688; www.sanremohotel.com; 2237 Mason St; d $65-99; @📶) The 1906

San Remo is long on old-fashioned charm, with mismatched turn-of-the-century furnishings and shared bathrooms. Bargain rooms face the corridor.

Pacific Tradewinds HOSTEL $
(Map p952; ☎415-433-7970; www.sanfranciscohostel.org; 680 Sacramento St; dm $29.50; @☎) SF's smartest-looking hostel has a blue-and-white nautical theme, full kitchen and spotless glass-brick showers. Three flights up; no elevator.

FISHERMAN'S WHARF & THE MARINA

Hotel Del Sol MOTEL $$
(☎415-921-5520; www.thehoteldelsol.com; 3100 Webster St; d $149-199; P❄@☎) A colorful, revamped 1950s motor lodge, with heated outdoor pool, board games and family suites with trundle beds.

Marina Motel MOTEL $
(☎415-928-1000; www.marinainn.com; 3110 Octavia Blvd; r $79-109; ☎) Bougainvillea-bedecked 1930s motor court, offering some rooms with kitchens ($10 extra) and free parking. Request one of the quiet rooms at the back.

HI San Francisco Fisherman's Wharf HOSTEL $
(☎415-771-7277; www.sfhostels.com; Fort Mason, Bldg 240; dm $25-30, r $65-100; P@☎) Barracks converted to dorms, with unparalleled waterfront park setting, communal showers, limited free parking, no curfew and no daytime heat (dress warmly year-round).

THE MISSION

Inn San Francisco B&B $$$
(Map p958; ☎415-641-0188; www.innsf.com; 943 S Van Ness Ave; r incl breakfast $175-285, with shared bath $120-145, cottage $335; P@☎) Impeccably maintained and packed with antiques, this 1872 Italianate-Victorian mansion contains a redwood hot tub in the English garden, genteel guestrooms with freshly cut flowers and featherbeds, and limited parking.

THE CASTRO

Parker Guest House B&B $$$
(Map p958; ☎415-621-3222; www.parkerguesthouse.com; 520 Church St; r incl breakfast $149-229; P@☎) SF's best gay B&B has cushy rooms in adjoining Edwardian mansions, a steam room and garden.

Belvedere House B&B $$
(Map p958; ☎415-731-6654; www.belvederehouse.com; 598 Belvedere St; r incl breakfast $125-190; @☎) Castro's romantic getaway on a leafy side street, with vintage chandeliers and eclectic art in six cozy rooms.

THE HAIGHT

Red Victorian B&B $$
(Map p958; ☎415-864-1978; www.redvic.net; 1665 Haight St; r incl breakfast $149-229, with shared bath $89-129; ☎) Peace, love and nature worship live on in themed rooms at the tripped-out Red Vic. Four of 18 rooms have baths, but all include organic breakfasts; wi-fi and meditation pillows available in the lobby.

Eating

Hope you're hungry – there are 10 times more restaurants per capita in San Francisco than in any other US city. Graze your way across SF, with stops at the Ferry Building farmers market, Omnivore (p970) for signed cookbooks, knife-skills workshops at nonprofit 18 Reasons (p960) and gourmet food trucks at Off the Grid (p966). Most of SF's top restaurants are quite small, so reserve now.

SOMA, UNION SQUARE & CIVIC CENTER

TOP CHOICE **Benu** CALIFORNIAN FUSION $$$
(Map p952; ☎415-685-4860; www.benusf.com; 22 Hawthorne St; mains $25-40; ⊙5:30-10pm Tue-Sat) SF has refined fusion cuisine over 150 years, but no one rocks it quite like chef Corey Lee, who remixes local fine-dining staples and Pacific Rim flavors with a SoMa DJ's finesse. Velvety Sonoma foie gras with tangy, woodsy yuzu-sake glaze makes taste buds bust wild moves, while Dungeness crab and black truffle custard bring such outsize flavor to faux-shark's fin soup, you'll swear there's Jaws in there. The tasting menu is steep ($160) and beverage pairings add $110, but you won't want to miss star-sommelier Yoon Ha's flights of fancy – including a rare 1968 Madeira with your soup.

Jardinière CALIFORNIAN $$$
(Map p952; ☎415-861-5555; www.jardiniere.com; 300 Grove St; mains $19-37; ⊙5-10:30pm Tue-Sat, to 10pm Sun-Mon) Iron Chef and Top Chef Master Traci Des Jardins is better known locally as a mastermind of sustain-

able, salacious California cuisine, lavishing braised oxtail ravioli with summer truffles, and stuffing crispy pork belly with salami and Mission figs. Go on Mondays, when $45 scores three decadent courses with wine pairings.

Saigon Sandwich Shop SANDWICHES $
(Map p952; ☎415-474-5698; 560 Larkin St; ⏲6:30am-5:30pm) Join the line for Vietnamese *banh mi,* baguettes piled with roast meat, pâté, meatballs and/or tofu with pickled carrots, jalapeño, onion and cilantro. Order two now, and spare yourself a return trip.

Brenda's French Soul Food CREOLE $$
(Map p952; ☎415-345-8100; www.frenchsoulfood.com; 652 Polk St; mains $8-12; ⏲8am-3pm Sun-Tue, to 10pm Wed-Sat) Chef-owner Brenda Buenviaje combines Creole cooking with French technique in hangover-curing Hangtown fry (omelet with cured pork and corn-breaded oysters), shrimp-stuffed po'boys, and fried chicken with collard greens and hot-pepper jelly – all worth inevitable waits on a sketchy stretch of sidewalk.

Bar Jules CALIFORNIAN $$$
(Map p952; ☎415-621-5482; www.barjules.com; 609 Hayes St; mains $10-26; ⏲6-10pm Tue, 11:30am-3pm & 6-10pm Wed-Sat, 11am-3pm Sun) Small and succulent is the credo at this corridor-sized neighborhood bistro, where the short daily menu packs a wallop of local flavor – think duck breast with cherries, almonds and arugula. Waits are a given, but so is unfussy, tasty food.

Farmerbrown MODERN AMERICAN $$$
(Map p952; ☎415-409-3276; www.farmerbrownsf.com; 25 Mason St; mains $12-23; ⏲6-10:30pm Tue-Sun, weekend brunch 11am-2pm) A rebel from the wrong side of the block, dishing up seasonal watermelon margaritas with a cayenne-salt rim, ribs that stick to yours and coleslaw with kick. Chef-owner Jay Foster works with local organic and African American farmers to provide food with actual soul, in a shotgun-shack setting with live funk bands.

FINANCIAL DISTRICT, CHINATOWN & NORTH BEACH

TOP CHOICE **Coi** CALIFORNIAN $$$
Map p952; ☎415-393-9000; http://coirestaurant.com; 373 Broadway; set menu per person $145; ⏲6-10pm Tue-Fri, from 5:30pm Fri & Sat;) Chef Daniel Patterson's wild tasting menu featuring foraged morels, wildflowers and Pacific seafood is like licking the California coastline. Black and green noodles are made from clams and Pacific seaweed, and purple ice-plant petals are strewn atop Sonoma duck's tongue, wild-caught abalone and just-picked arugula. Only-in-California flavors and intriguing wine pairings ($95; pours generous enough for two to share) will keep you California dreaming for a while afterwards.

Cotogna ITALIAN $$$
(Map p952; ☎415-775-8508; www.cotognasf.com; 470 Pacific Av; mains $14-24; ⏲noon-3pm & 7-10pm Mon-Sat;) No wonder chef-owner Michael Tusk won the 2011 James Beard Award: his rustic Italian pastas and toothsome pizzas magically balance a few pristine, local flavors. Book ahead; the $24 prix-fixe is among San Francisco's best dining deals.

City View CHINESE $
(Map p952; ☎415-398-2838; 662 Commercial St; small plates $3-5; ⏲11am-2:30pm Mon-Fri, from 10am Sat & Sun) Dim sum aficionados used to cramped quarters and surly service are wowed by impeccable shrimp and leek dumplings, tender black-bean asparagus and crisp Peking duck, all served with a flourish in a spacious, sunny room.

Bocadillos MEDITERRANEAN $$
(Map p952; ☎415-982-2622; www.bocasf.com; 710 Montgomery St; dishes $9-15; ⏲7am-10pm Mon-Fri, 5-10:30pm Sat) Lunchtime fine dining that won't break the bank or pop buttons, with just-right Basque bites of lamb burger, snapper ceviche with Asian pears, Catalan sausages and wines by the glass.

Molinari ITALIAN SANDWICHES $
(Map p952; ☎415-421-2337; 373 Columbus Ave; sandwiches $5-8; ⏲9am-5:30pm Mon-Fri, from 7:30am Sat) Grab an Italian roll and get it stuffed with translucent sheets of Parma prosciutto, milky buffalo mozzarella, marinated artichokes and legendary house-cured salami.

Cinecittà PIZZERIA $$
(Map p952; ☎415-291-8830; 663 Union St; pizzas $9-14; ⏲noon-10pm Sun-Thu, to 11pm Fri & Sat) That aroma you followed into this 18-seat eatery is thin-crust Roman pizza, probably the savory Trastevere (fresh mozzarella, arugula and prosciutto). Drink locally – Anchor

FIVE TASTY REASONS TO MISS THAT FERRY

When it comes to California dining, you'll be missing the boat unless you stop and taste the local treats at the Ferry Building (Map p952).

» Today's catch at **Hog Island Oyster Company** (☎415-391-7117; www.hogislandoysters.com; half-dozen oysters $15-17; ⏲11:30am-8pm Mon-Fri, 11am-6pm Sat & Sun, happy hour 5-7pm Mon & Thu), including $1 oysters at happy hour.

» Gourmet picnic supplies from the **farmers market** (☎415-291-3276; www.cuesa.org; ⏲10am-2pm Tue & Thu, from 8am Sat) – especially Andante cheeses, 4505 artisan meats, Donna's tamales and Namu's Korean tacos.

» Chef Traci des Jardins' *nuevo* Mexican street eats at **Mijita** (☎399-0814; www.mijitasf.com; menu items under $10; ⏲10am-7pm Mon-Wed, to 8pm Thu-Sat, to 4pm Sun;).

» Free-range beef burgers and sweet-potato fries at **Gott's Roadside** (☎415-318-3423; www.gotts.com; burgers $7-10; ⏲10:30am-10pm).

» Cal-Vietnamese Dungeness crab over cellophane noodles at Charles Phan's family-operated **Slanted Door** (☎415-861-8032; http://slanteddoor.com; mains $13-36; ⏲11am-10pm).

Steam on tap or Claudia Springs Zin – and save room for housemade tiramisu.

Gitane MEDITERRANEAN **$$$**
(Map p952; ☎415-788-6686; www.gitanerestaurant.com; 6 Claude Lane; mains $15-25; ⏲5:30pm-midnight Tue-Sat, bar to 1am;) Slip out of the Financial District and into something more comfortable at this boudoir-styled bistro, featuring Basque- and Moroccan-inspired stuffed squash blossoms, silky pan-seared scallops, herb-spiked lamb tartare and craft cocktails.

FISHERMAN'S WHARF

Crown & Crumpet DESSERTS, SANDWICHES **$$**
(Map p952; ☎415-771-4252; www.crownandcrumpet.com; 207 Ghirardelli Sq; dishes $8-12; ⏲10am-9pm Mon-Fri, from 9am Sat, 9am-6pm Sun;) Designer style and rosy cheer usher teatime into the 21st century: dads and daughters clink teacups with crooked pinkies, Lolita goth teens nibble cucumber sandwiches, and girlfriends rehash dates over scones and Champagne. Reservations recommended weekends.

In-N-Out Burger BURGERS **$**
(Map p952; ☎800-786-1000; www.in-n-out.com; 333 Jefferson St; meals under $10; ⏲10:30am-1am Sun-Thu, to 1:30am Fri & Sat;) Serving burgers for 60 years the way California likes them: with prime chuck ground on-site, fries and shakes made with pronounceable ingredients, served by employees paid a living wage. Ask for yours 'wild style,' cooked in mustard with grilled onions.

THE MARINA

Off the Grid FOOD TRUCKS **$**
(Map p952; http://offthegridsf.com; Fort Mason parking lot; dishes under $10; ⏲5-10pm Fri) Some 30 food trucks circle their wagons at SF's largest mobile-gourmet hootenanny (other nights/locations attract less than a dozen trucks; see website). Arrive before 6:30pm or expect 20-minute waits for Chairman Bao's clamshell buns stuffed with duck and mango, Roli Roti's free-range herbed roast chicken, and dessert from the Crème Brûlée Man. Cash only; take dinner to nearby docks for Golden Gate Bridge sunsets.

Greens VEGETARIAN **$$**
(☎415-771-6222; www.greensrestaurant.com; Fort Mason Center, Bldg A; mains $7-20; ⏲noon-2:30pm Tue-Sat, 5:30-9pm Mon-Sat, 9am-4pm Sun;) Career carnivores won't realize there's no meat in roasted eggplant panini or hearty black bean chili with crème fraîche and pickled jalapeños. Book ahead or enjoy takeout at redwood-stump cafe tables or wharfside benches.

Warming Hut CAFE
(⏲9am-5pm) When the fog rolls into Crissy Field, head here for Fair Trade coffee, organic pastries and hot dogs within walls insulated with recycled denim; all purchases support Crissy Field conservation.

THE MISSION

TOP CHOICE **La Taquería** MEXICAN **$**
(☎415-285-7117; 2889 Mission St; burritos $6-8; ⏲11am-9pm Mon-Sat, to 8pm Sun) No debatable

tofu, saffron rice, spinach tortilla or mango salsa here: just classic tomatillo or mesquite salsa, marinated, grilled meats and flavorful beans inside a flour tortilla – optional housemade spicy pickles and sour cream highly recommended.

Commonwealth CALIFORNIAN **$$**
(Map p958; ☎415-355-1500; www.commonwealthsf.com; 2224 Mission St; small plates $5-16; ⏰5:30-10pm Tue-Thu & Sun, to 11pm Fri & Sat;) California's most imaginative farm-to-table dining isn't in some quaint barn, but the converted cinderblock Mission dive where chef Jason Fox serves crispy hen with toybox carrots cooked in hay (yes, hay), and sea urchin floating on a bed of farm egg and organic asparagus that looks like a tide pool and tastes like a dream. Savor the $65 prix-fixe knowing $10 is donated to charity.

Pizzeria Delfina PIZZERIA **$$$**
(Map p958; ☎415-437-6800; www.delfinasf.com; 3611 18th St; pizzas $11-17; ⏰11:30am-10pm Tue-Thu, to 11pm Fri, noon-11pm Sat & Sun, 5:30-10pm Mon;) One bite explains why SF is so obsessed with pizza lately: Delfina's thin crust supports the weight of fennel sausage and fresh mozzarella without drooping or cracking, while white pizzas let chefs freestyle with Cali-foodie ingredients like maitake mushrooms, broccoli rabe and artisan cheese. No reservations; sign up on the chalkboard and wait with wine at Delfina bar next door.

THE CASTRO

TOP CHOICE **Frances** CALIFORNIAN **$$**
(Map p958; ☎415-621-3870; www.frances-sf.com; 3870 17th St; mains $14-27; ⏰5-10.30pm Tue-Sun) Chef/owner Melissa Perello earned a Michelin star for fine dining, then ditched downtown to start this market-inspired neighborhood bistro. Daily menus showcase bright, seasonal flavors and luxurious textures: cloud-like sheep's-milk ricotta gnocchi with crunchy breadcrumbs and broccolini, grilled calamari with preserved Meyer lemon, and artisan wine served by the ounce, directly from Wine Country.

Chilango MEXICAN **$$**
(Map p952; ☎415-552-5700; chilangorestaurantsf.com; 235 Church St; dishes $8-12; ⏰11am-10pm) Upgrade from to-go taquerias to organic, *chilango* (Mexico City native) dishes worthy of a sit-down dinner, including grass-fed filet mignon tacos, sustainable pork *carnitas* and sensational free-range chicken *mole*.

Starbelly CALIFORNIAN **$$**
(Map p958; ☎415-252-7500; www.starbellysf.com; 3583 16th St; dishes $6-19; ⏰11:30am-11pm, to midnight Fri & Sat) Reclaimed wood decor to match the food: market-fresh salads, scrumptious pâté, roasted mussels with housemade sausage and juicy grass-fed burgers. Reserve ahead to lounge amid flowering herbs on the heated patio, or join the communal table.

THE HAIGHT

Rosamunde Sausage Grill SAUSAGES **$**
(Map p958; ☎415-437-6851; 545 Haight St; sausages $4-6; ⏰11:30am-10pm) Impress a dinner date for $10: load up classic brats or fig-duck links with complimentary roasted peppers, grilled onions, wholegrain mustard and mango chutney, washed down with microbrews at Toronado next door.

Cole Valley Cafe SANDWICHES **$**
(Map p958; ☎415-668-5282; www.colevalleycafe.com; 701 Cole St; sandwiches $5-6; ⏰6:30am-8:30pm Mon-Fri, to 8pm Sat & Sun;) Powerful coffee, free wi-fi and hot gourmet sandwiches that are a bargain at any price, let alone $6 for lip-smacking thyme-marinated chicken with lemony avocado spread.

Magnolia Brewpub CALIFORNIAN **$$**
(Map p958; ☎415-864-7468; www.magnoliapub.com; 1398 Haight St; mains $11-20; ⏰noon-midnight Mon-Thu, to 1am Fri, 10am-1am Sat, 10am-midnight Sun) Organic pub grub and homebrew samplers keep conversation flowing at communal tables, while grass-fed Prather Ranch burgers satisfy stoner appetites in side booths – it's like the Summer of Love is back, only with better food.

JAPANTOWN & PACIFIC HEIGHTS

Tataki SUSHI **$$**
(☎415-931-1182; www.tatakisushibar.com; 2815 California St; dishes $12-20; ⏰11:30am-2pm & 5:30-10:30pm Mon-Fri, 5-11:30pm Sat, 5-9:30pm Sun) Rescue dinner dates and the oceans with sensational, sustainable sushi: silky Arctic char drizzled with yuzu-citrus and capers replaces dubious farmed salmon, and the Golden State Roll is a local hero with spicy line-caught scallop, Pacific tuna, organic apple slivers and edible gold.

Aziza NORTH AFRICAN $$$
(☎415-752-2222; www.azizasf.com; 5800 Geary Blvd; mains $16-29; ⊙5:30-10:30pm Wed-Mon; ✎) Mourad Lahlou's inspiration is Moroccan and his produce organic Californian, but his flavors are out of this world: Sonoma duck confit melts into caramelized onion in flaky pastry *basteeya,* while sour cherries rouse slow-cooked local lamb shank from its barley bed.

Namu KOREAN $$
(☎415-386-8332; www.namusf.com; 439 Balboa St; small plates $8-16; ⊙6-10:30pm Sun-Tue, to midnight Wed-Sat, 10:30am-3pm Sat & Sun) Organic ingredients, Silicon Valley inventiveness and Pacific Rim roots are showcased in Namu's Korean-inspired soul food, including house-made kimchee, umami-rich shiitake mushroom dumplings and NorCal's definitive *bibimbap:* organic vegetables, grass-fed local steak and a Sonoma farm egg served sizzling on rice in a stone pot.

Drinking

TOP CHOICE Smuggler's Cove THEME BAR
(Map p952; http://smugglerscovesf.com; 650 Gough St; ⊙5pm-2am) Yo-ho-ho and a bottle of rum…or make that 200 at this Barbary Coast shipwreck of a tiki bar. With tasting flights and 70 cocktail recipes gleaned from around the world, you won't be dry-docked.

Zeitgeist BAR
(Map p958; www.zeitgeistsf.com; 199 Valencia St; ⊙9am-2am) When temperatures rise, bikers and hipsters converge on Zeitgeist's huge outdoor beer garden for 40 brews on tap and late-night tamales.

Bar Agricole BAR
(Map p958; ☎415-355-9400; www.baragricole.com; 355 11th St; ⊙6-10pm Sun-Wed, 6pm-late Thu-Sat) Drink your way to a history degree with well-researched cocktails: Bellamy Scotch Sour with egg whites passes the test, but Tequila Fix with lime, pineapple gum and hellfire bitters earns honors.

Toronado PUB
(Map p958; www.toronado.com; 547 Haight St) Glory hallelujah, beer-lovers: 50-plus microbrews, with hundreds more in bottles. Stumble next door to Rosamunde for sausages.

Tosca Cafe COCKTAIL BAR
(Map p952; http://toscacafesf.com; 242 Columbus Ave; ⊙5pm-2am Tue-Sun) With red vinyl booths and a jukebox of opera and Sinatra, Tosca is classic North Beach.

Entertainment

TIX Bay Area (Map p952; ☎415-433-7827; www.tixbayarea.org; ⊙Tue-Sun) sells last-minute theater tickets half-price. More options:

7x7 (www.7x7.com)

SF Bay Guardian (www.sfbg.com)

SF Weekly (www.sfweekly.com)

Squid List (http://squidlist.com/events)

Live Music

Fillmore LIVE MUSIC
(www.thefillmore.com; 1805 Geary Blvd; tickets from $20) Hendrix, Zeppelin, Janis – they all played the Fillmore, where the 1250 capacity means you're close to the stage. Don't miss the psychedelic poster-art gallery upstairs. Nightly shows.

Yoshi's JAZZ
(www.yoshis.com; 1300 Fillmore St; tickets $12-50; ⊙most shows 8pm) San Francisco's definitive jazz club draws the world's top talent, and adjoins a pretty good sushi restaurant.

Slim's LIVE MUSIC
(Map p958; ☎415-255-0333; www.slims-sf.com; 333 11th St; tickets $11-28; ⊙5pm-2am) Guaranteed good times by Gogol Bordello, Tenacious D and AC/DShe (the hard-rocking female tribute band) fill the bill at this mid-sized club, where Prince and Elvis Costello have turned up to play impromptu sets unannounced.

Mezzanine LIVE MUSIC
(Map p952; ☎415-625-8880; www.mezzaninesf.com; 444 Jessie St; admission $10-40) The best sound system in SF bounces off the brick walls at breakthrough hip-hop shows by Quest Love, Method Man, Nas and Snoop Dogg, plus throwback alt-classics like the Dandy Warhols and Psychedelic Furs.

Café du Nord LIVE MUSIC
(Map p958; www.cafedunord.com; 2170 Market St) The historic speakeasy in the basement of the Swedish-American Hall with glam-rock, afrobeats, retro-rockabilly and indie-record-release parties almost nightly.

Nightclubs

Cat Club CLUB
(Map p952; www.catclubsf.com; 1190 Folsom St; admission after 10pm $5; ⊙9pm-3am Tue-Sun) Thursday's '1984' is a euphoric bi/straight/

gay party scene from a lost John Hughes movie; other nights vary from Saturday power pop to Bondage-a-Go-Go.

DNA Lounge CLUB

(Map p958; www.dnalounge.com; 375 11th St; admission $3-25; ⏲9:30pm-3am Fri & Sat, other nights vary) SF's mega-club hosts live bands and big-name DJs. Second and fourth Saturdays bring Bootie, the kick-ass original mashup party; Mondays mean Goth Death Guild, with free tea servicc.

El Rio CLUB

(☎415-282-3325; www.elriosf.com; 3158 Mission St; admission $3-8; ⏲5pm-2am Mon-Thu, from 4pm Fri, from noon Sun) 'Salsa Sundays' are legendary: arrive at 3pm for lessons. Other nights: oyster happy hours, eclectic music, pan-sexual crowd flirting on the patio.

Harlot CLUB

(Map p952; www.harlotsf.com; 46 Minna St; admission $10-20, 5-9pm Wed-Fri free; ⏲5pm-2am Wed-Fri, from 9pm Sat) Aptly named after 10pm, when the bordello-themed lounge cuts loose to house Thursdays, indie-rock Wednesdays and women-only Fem Bar parties.

111 Minna CLUB

(Map p952; www.111minnagallery.com; 111 Minna St) Street-wise art gallery by day, after-work lounge and club after 9pm, when '90s and '80s dance parties take the back room by storm.

Classical Music & Opera

Rivaling City Hall's grandeur is SF's 1932 **War Memorial Opera House** (Map p952; 301 Van Ness Ave), home to **San Francisco Opera** (www.sfopera.com), whose season runs from June to December, and **San Francisco Ballet** (www.sfballet.org), performing January to May. For more, check **SF Classical Voice** (www.sfcv.org).

TOP CHOICE **Davies Symphony Hall** CLASSICAL MUSIC

(Map p952; ☎415-864-6000; www.sfsymphony.org; 201 Van Ness Ave) Home of nine-time Grammy-winning SF Symphony, conducted with verve by Michael Tilson Thomas. The season runs September to July.

Yerba Buena Center for the Arts CONCERT VENUE

(Map p952; ☎415-978-2787; www.ybca.org; 701 Mission St) Hosts concerts and modern dance innovators Liss Fain Dance, Alonzo King's Lines Ballet and Smuin Ballet.

Theater

SF is home to the cutting-edge professional **American Conservatory Theater** (ACT; ☎415-749-2228; www.act-sf.org; 415 Geary St). **SHN** (☎415-512-7770; www.shnsf.com) hosts touring Broadway shows. See also **Theatre Bay Area** (www.theatrebayarea.org).

Club Fugazi COMEDY, CABARET

(Map p952; ☎415-421-4222; www.beachblanketbabylon.com; 678 Green St; seats $25-78) Home of ribald, satirical *Beach Blanket Babylon,* featuring giant hats and belly laughs.

Magic Theater THEATER

(☎415-441-8822; www.magictheatre.org; Fort Mason, Bldg D) Risk-taking original productions from major playwrights, including Sam Shepard, Edna O'Brien and Terrence McNally, starring actors like Ed Harris and Sean Penn.

Marsh THEATER

(Map p958; ☎415-826-5750; www.themarsh.org; 1062 Valencia St; tickets $15-35) Choose your seat wisely: you'll spend the evening on the edge of it, with one-acts, monologues and works-in-progress that involve the audience.

Cinema

TOP CHOICE **Castro Theatre** CINEMA

(Map p958; www.thecastrotheatre.com; 429 Castro St; adult/child $10/7.50) The city's grandest movie place screens vintage, foreign, documentary and new films.

Sundance Kabuki Cinema CINEMA

(www.sundancecinemas.com/kabuki.html; 1881 Post St; admission $10-14) The silver screen gone green, from recycled-fiber reserved seating to local Hangar vodka cocktails at 21+ shows.

Roxie Cinema CINEMA

(Map p958; www.roxie.com; 3117 16th St; adult/child $10/6.50) Documentaries, indie premieres, rare imports.

Sports

San Francisco Giants BASEBALL

(Map p952; http://sanfrancisco.giants.mlb.com; AT&T Park; tickets $5-135) Watch and learn how the World Series is won – bushy beards, women's underwear and all.

San Francisco 49ers FOOTBALL

(☎415-656-4900; www.sf49ers.com) For NFL football, beer and garlic fries, head to Candlestick Park (Map p948).

Shopping

All those rustic-chic dens, well-stocked spice racks and fabulous outfits don't just pull themselves together – San Franciscans scoured their city for it all. Here's where to find what:

Hayes Valley Local and independent designers, home design, sweets, shoes.

Valencia St Bookstores, local design collectives, art galleries, vintage whatever.

Haight St Head shops, music, vintage, skate, snow and surf gear.

Upper Fillmore & Union Sts Date outfits, girly accessories, wine and design.

Powell & Market Sts Department stores, megabrands, discount retail, Apple store.

Grant St From Chinatown souvenirs to eccentric North Beach boutiques.

Ferry Building Local food, wine and kitchenware.

Bookstores

City Lights Bookstore BOOKS
(Map p952; www.citylights.com; 261 Columbus Ave; 10am-midnight) Landmark bookseller, publisher and free-speech champion; browse Muckraking and Stolen Continents sections downstairs and find Nirvana upstairs in Poetry.

Adobe Books BOOKS
(http://adobebooksbackroomgallery.blogspot.com; 3166 16th St; 11am-midnight) Books you never knew you needed used and cheap, hidden among sofas, cats and art installations.

Omnivore BOOKS
(415-282-4712; www.omnivorebooks.com; 3885a Cesar Chavez St; 11am-6pm Mon-Sat, noon-5pm Sun) Salivate over books signed by chef-legend Alice Waters and rare Civil War cookbooks; check events calendar for standing-room-only events with star chefs.

Bound Together Anarchist Book Collective BOOKS
(Map p958; www.boundtogetherbooks.com; 1369 Haight St; 11:30am-7:30pm) All-volunteer bookstore featuring conspiracy-theory comics, alternative histories, organic farming manuals and other radical notions.

Green Apple BOOKS
(415-387-2272; www.greenapplebooks.com; 506 Clement St; 10am-10:30pm Sun-Thu, to 11:30pm Fri & Sat) Three stories of new releases, remaindered titles and used nonfiction; mags, music and used novels two doors down.

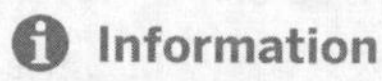

Information

Emergency & Medical Services

American College of Traditional Chinese Medicine (415-282-9603; www.actcm.edu; 450 Connecticut St; 8:30am-9pm Mon-Thu, 9am-5:30pm Fri & Sat) Acupuncture and herbal remedies.

Haight Ashbury Free Clinic (415-746-1950; www.hafci.org; 558 Clayton St) Free doctor visits by appointment; substance abuse and mental health services.

Pharmaca (415-661-1216; www.pharmaca.com; 925 Cole St; 8am-8pm Mon-Fri, from 9am Sat & Sun) Pharmacy and naturopathic remedies.

Police, fire & ambulance (911)

San Francisco General Hospital (emergency room 415-206-8111, main 415-206-8000; www.sfdph.org; 1001 Potrero Ave) Open 24 hours.

Trauma Recovery & Rape Treatment Center (415-437-3000; http://traumarecoverycenter.org) A 24-hour hotline.

Walgreens (415-861-3136; www.walgreens.com; 498 Castro ST; 24hr) Pharmacy with locations citywide (see website).

Internet Access

SF has free wi-fi hot spots citywide – locate one nearby with www.openwifispots.com. Connect for free in Union Sq, and most cafes and hotel lobbies.

Apple Store (www.apple.com/retail/sanfrancisco; 1 Stockton St; 9am-9pm Mon-Sat, 10am-8pm Sun;) Free wi-fi and internet terminal usage.

San Francisco Main Library (http://sfpl.org; 100 Larkin St; 10am-6pm Mon & Sat, 9am-8pm Tue-Thu, noon-5pm Fri & Sun;) Free 15-minute internet terminal usage; spotty wi-fi access.

Media

KALW 91.7 FM (www.kalw.org) National Public Radio (NPR) affiliate.

KPFA 94.1 FM (www.kpfa.org) Alternative news and music.

KPOO 89.5 FM (www.kpoo.com) Community radio with jazz, R & B, blues and reggae.

KQED 88.5 FM (www.kqed.org) NPR and Public Broadcasting (PBS) affiliate offering podcasts and streaming video.

San Francisco Bay Guardian (www.sfbg.com) San Francisco's free, alternative weekly covers topics such as politics, theater, music, art and movie listings.

San Francisco Chronicle (www.sfgate.com) Main daily newspaper with news, entertainment and event listings.

Money

Bank of America (www.bankamerica.com; 1 Market Plaza; ⌚9am-6pm Mon-Fri)

Post

Rincon Center post office (www.usps.com; 180 Steuart St; ⌚8am-6pm Mon-Fri, 9am-2pm Sat) Postal services plus historic murals.

Tourist Information

San Francisco's Visitor Information Center (☎415-391-2000; www.onlyinsanfrancisco.com; lower level, Hallidie Plaza; ⌚9am-5pm Mon-Fri, to 3pm Sat & Sun)

Websites

Craigslist (http://sfbay.craigslist.org) SF-based source for jobs, dates, free junk, Buddhist babysitters, the works.

Twitter (www.twitter.com) SF-based social media alerts on SF pop-up shops, food trucks, free shows and weekend recommendations from Lonely Planet authors.

Yelp (www.yelp.com) Locals trade verbal fisticuffs on this San Francisco–based review site that covers shopping, bars, services and restaurants.

ℹ Getting There & Away

Air

San Francisco International Airport (SFO; www.flysfo.com) is 14 miles south of downtown off Hwy 101 and accessible by Bay Area Rapid Transit (BART).

Bus

Until the new terminal is complete in 2017, San Francisco's intercity hub remains the **Temporary Transbay Terminal** (Howard & Main Sts), where you can catch buses on **AC Transit** (www.actransit.org) to the East Bay, **Golden Gate Transit** (http://goldengatetransit.org) north to Marin and Sonoma Counties, and **SamTrans** (www.samtrans.com) south to Palo Alto and the Pacific coast. **Greyhound** (☎800-231-2222; www.greyhound.com) buses leave daily for Los Angeles ($56.50, eight to 12 hours), Truckee near Lake Tahoe ($33, 5½ hours) and other destinations.

Train

Amtrak (☎800-872-7245; www.amtrakcalifornia.com) offers low-emissions, leisurely travel to and from San Francisco. *Coast Starlight*'s spectacular 35-hour run from Los Angeles to Seattle stops in Oakland, and the *California Zephyr* takes its sweet time (51 hours) traveling from Chicago through the Rockies to Oakland. Both have sleeping cars and dining/lounge cars with panoramic windows. Amtrak runs free shuttle buses to San Francisco's Ferry Building and CalTrain station.

CalTrain (www.caltrain.com; cnr 4th & King Sts) connects San Francisco with Silicon Valley hubs and San Jose.

ℹ Getting Around

For Bay Area transit options, departures and arrivals, check ☎511 or www.511.org.

To/From San Francisco International Airport

BART (www.bart.gov; one way $8.10) Offers a fast, direct ride to downtown San Francisco.

SamTrans (www.samtrans.com; one way $5) Express bus KX gets you to the Temporary Transbay Terminal in about 30 minutes.

SuperShuttle (☎800-258-3826; www.supershuttle.com; one way $17) Door-to-door vans depart from baggage-claim areas, taking 45 minutes to most SF locations.

Taxi To downtown San Francisco costs $35 to $50.

To/From Oakland International Airport

BART is the cheapest way to get to San Francisco from the Oakland airport. AirBART shuttle ($3) operates every 10 to 20 minutes to the Coliseum station to catch BART to downtown SF ($3.80, 25 minutes). Taxis from Oakland airport average $25 to Oakland and around $50 to $60 to San Francisco. **SuperShuttle** (☎800-258-3826; www.supershuttle.com) offers shared van rides to downtown SF for $25 to $30. **Airport Express** (☎800-327-2024; www.airportexpressinc.com) runs a scheduled shuttle every two hours (from 6am to midnight) between Oakland airport and Sonoma ($32) and Marin ($24) counties.

Boat

Blue & Gold Ferries (www.blueandgoldfleet.com) operates the Alameda–Oakland ferry from Pier 41 and the Ferry Building. **Golden Gate Ferry** (www.goldengate.org) runs from the Ferry Building to Sausalito and Larkspur in Marin County.

Car

Avoid driving in San Francisco: street parking is harder to find than true love, and meter readers are ruthless. Downtown parking lots are at Embarcadero Center, 5th and Mission Sts, Union Sq, and Sutter and Stockton Sts. National car-rental agencies have airport and downtown offices.

Public Transportation

MUNI (Municipal Transit Agency; www.sfmuni.com) operates bus, streetcar and cable-car lines. Two cable-car lines leave from Powell and Market Sts; a third leaves from California and Markets Sts. A detailed *MUNI Street & Transit Map* is available free online and at the Powell MUNI kiosk ($3). Standard fare for buses or streetcars is $2; cable-car fare is $6. A **MUNI Passport** (1/3/7 days $14/21/27) allows unlimited travel on all MUNI transport, including cable cars; it's sold at San Francisco's Visitor Information Center and at the TIX Bay Area kiosk at Union Sq. A seven-day **City Pass** (adult/child $69/39) covers Muni and admission to five attractions.

BART links San Francisco with the East Bay and runs beneath Market St, down Mission St and south to SFO and Millbrae, where it connects with CalTrain.

Taxi

Fares run about $2.25 per mile; meters start at $3.50.

DeSoto Cab (☎415-970-1300)

Green Cab (☎415-626-4733; www.626green.com) Fuel-efficient hybrids; worker-owned collective.

Luxor (☎415-282-4141)

Yellow Cab (☎415-333-3333)

Marin County

Majestic redwoods cling to coastal hills just across the Golden Gate Bridge in woodsy, wealthy, laid-back **Marin** (www.visitmarin.org). **Sausalito**, the southernmost town, is a cute, touristy bayside destination for bike trips over the bridge (take the ferry back). At the harbor, the **San Francisco Bay-Delta Model** (☎415-332-3871; www.spn.usace.army.mil/bmvc; 2100 Bridgeway Blvd; admission free; ⏱9am-4pm Tue-Fri, plus 10am-5pm Sat & Sun in summer) is a way-cool 1.5-acre hydraulic recreation of the entire bay and delta.

MARIN HEADLANDS

The windswept, rugged headlands are laced with hiking trails, providing stunning views of SF and the Golden Gate. To reach the **visitor center** (☎415-331-1540; www.nps.gov/goga/marin-headlands.htm; ⏱9:30am-4:30pm), take the Alexander Ave exit from the Golden Gate Bridge, turn left under the freeway, and then turn right on Conzelman Rd and follow signs. Attractions include the **Point Bonita Lighthouse** (⏱12:30-3:30pm Sat-Mon), climbable Cold War–era bunkers and **Rodeo Beach** (Map p948). At Fort Baker, **Bay Area Discovery Museum** (☎415-339-3900; www.baykidsmuseum.org; 557 McReynolds Rd, Sausalito; adult/child $10/8; ⏱9am-4pm Tue-Fri, 10am-5pm Sat & Sun) is a cool destination for kids.

Near the visitor center, the **HI Marin Headlands Hostel** (Map p948; ☎415-331-2777; www.norcalhostels.org/marin; dm $22-26, r $72-92; @) occupies two historic 1907 buildings on a forested hill. Private rooms in the former officer's house are sweet.

MT TAMALPAIS STATE PARK

Majestic 2571ft 'Mt Tam' is fantastic for mountain biking and hiking. **Mt Tamalpais State Park** (☎415-388-2070; www.mttam.net; parking $8) encompasses 6300 acres of parklands, plus over 200 miles of trails; don't miss the East Peak lookout. Panoramic Hwy climbs from Hwy 1 through the park to **Stinson Beach**, a mellow seaside town with a great 3-mile-long sandy beach. Park headquarters are at **Pantoll Station** (Map p948; 801 Panoramic Hwy; tent sites $25; wi-fi), the nexus of many trails and location of a wooded first-come, first-served campground. Or hike in food, linen and towels to the rustic, electricity-free **West Point Inn** (☎415-646-0702; www.westpointinn.com; 1000 Panoramic Hwy, Mill Valley; r per adult/child $50/25); reservations required.

Near park headquarters, **Mountain Home Inn** (☎415-381-9000; www.mtnhomeinn.com; 810 Panoramic Hwy; r incl breakfast $195-345, dinner $38, brunch $10-21; ⏱restaurant 11:30am-3pm & 5:30-8pm Wed-Sun, to 9pm Fri & Sat; wi-fi) sits atop a wooded ridge. Its romantic, woodsy rooms have gorgeous views; the restaurant serves good brunches and prix-fixe dinners.

MUIR WOODS NATIONAL MONUMENT

Wander among an ancient stand of the world's tallest trees in 550-acre **Muir Woods National Monument** (Map p948; ☎415-388-2595; www.nps.gov/muwo; adult/child under 16yr $5/free), 12 miles north of the Golden Gate. The easy 1-mile Main Trail Loop leads past thousand-year-old redwoods at Cathedral Grove and returns via Bohemian Grove. Come midweek to avoid crowds; otherwise arrive early morning or late afternoon. Take Hwy 101 to the Hwy 1 exit, and follow the signs.

The **Muir Woods shuttle** (☎415-455-2000; www.goldengatetransit.org; adult/child $3/1) bus 66 operates weekends and holidays, May to September, and runs about every 30 minutes from Marin City and Mill Valley, with limited connections with the Sausalito ferry terminal.

POINT REYES NATIONAL SEASHORE

The windswept peninsula of Point Reyes National Seashore juts 10 miles out to sea on an entirely different tectonic plate, and covers 110 sq miles of beaches, lagoons and forested hills.

TOP CHOICE **Point Reyes Lighthouse** (Map p948; ⏰10am-4:30pm Thu-Mon), crowns the peninsula's westernmost point and is ideal for whale-watching. To see Tule elk, hike the bluff-top Tomalcs Point Trail on the peninsula's north tip, reached via Pierce Point Rd. The **Bear Valley Visitors Center** (☎415-464-5100; www.nps.gov/pore) is just past Olema and has trail maps and cool displays. Point Reyes has four hike-in **campgrounds** (☎reservations 415-663-8054; tent sites $15), two near the beach.

The **West Marin Chamber of Commerce** (☎415-663-9232; www.pointreyes.org) has information on cozy inns and cottages. The bayside **Tomales Bay Resort** (☎415-669-1389; www.tomalesbayresort.com; 12938 Sir Francis Drake Blvd, Inverness; r $120-225; 📶🏊) has pleasant motel rooms, with bargain rates from Sunday through Thursday and in winter.

Nature lovers bunk at the only in-park lodging, **HI Point Reyes Hostel** (Map p948; ☎415-663-8811; www.norcalhostels.org/reyes; dm/r $24/68; @), off Limantour Rd, 8 miles from the visitor center. Kayaking scenic Tomales Bay gets you up close to seals, birds and the occasional elk, and **Blue Waters Kayaking** (☎415-669-2600; www.bwkayak.com; guided trips $68-98, 4hr rentals $60-130) has locations in Inverness and Marshall.

TOP CHOICE **Drake's Bay Oyster Company** (☎415-669-1149; 1 dozen oysters to go/on the half shell $15/24; ⏰8:30am-4:30pm), off Sir Francis Drake Blvd in the park, is the place for oyster-lovers. Nearby, cute little Point Reyes Station has excellent restaurants.

Berkeley

Not much has changed since the 1960s heyday of anti-Vietnam War protests – except the bumper stickers: 'No Blood for Oil' has supplanted 'Make Love Not War.' Birkenstocks and pony tails remain perennially in fashion. You can't walk around nude on campus anymore, but 'Berserkeley' remains the Bay Area's radical hub, crawling with university students, scoffing skateboarders and aging hippies. Stroll its wooded university grounds and surrounding streets to soak up the vibe.

Sights & Activities

University of California, Berkeley UNIVERSITY

(Map p948) 'Cal' is one of the country's top universities and home to 35,000 diverse, politically conscious students. The **Visitor Services Center** (☎510-642-5215; http://visitors.berkeley.edu; 101 Sproul Hall; tours 10am Mon-Sat, 1pm Sun) has info and leads free campus tours (reservations required). Cal's landmark is the 1914 Sather Tower (also called the Campanile), with elevator rides ($2) to the top. The Bancroft Library displays the small gold nugget that started the California gold rush in 1848.

Leading to the campus's south gate, **Telegraph Avenue** is as youthful and gritty as San Francisco's Haight St, packed with cafes, cheap eats, record stores and bookstores.

UC Berkeley Art Museum MUSEUM

(☎510-642-0808; www.bampfa.berkeley.edu; 2626 Bancroft Way; adult/child $10/7; ⏰11am-5pm Wed-Sun) A campus highlight with 11 galleries showcasing a wide range of works, from ancient Chinese to cutting-edge contemporary. Across the street, its world-renowned **Pacific Film Archive** (☎510-642-1124; 2575 Bancroft Way; adult/child $9.50/6.50) screens little-known independent and avant-garde films. Both are scheduled to move to a new Oxford St location by 2014.

Tilden Regional Park PARK

(www.ebparks.org/parks/tilden) In the Berkeley hills, this 2079-acre park has hiking, picnicking, swimming at Lake Anza, and fun stuff for kids, including a merry-go-round and steam train.

Sleeping

Basic and midrange motels are clustered west of campus along University Ave.

Hotel Durant BOUTIQUE HOTEL **$$**

(☎510-845-8981; www.hoteldurant.com; 2600 Durant Ave; r from $134; @📶) A block from campus, this 1928 hotel cheekily highlights that connection. The lobby's adorned with embarrassing yearbook photos and a ceiling mobile of exam books, and smallish rooms have dictionary-covered shower curtains and bongs repurposed into bedside lamps.

IF YOU HAVE A FEW MORE DAYS

Right across the bay, gritty-urban Oakland's got attitude, the A's baseball team and deep African American roots that shine through in world-celebrated arts and food. It has a lovely historic downtown, saltwater lake for joggers and kids, and some happening clubs and restaurants.

Oakland Museum of California MUSEUM
(510-238-2200; www.museumca.org; cnr 10th & Oak Sts; adult/child $12/6; 11am-5pm Wed-Sun, to 9pm Fri) A must-see. Relevant, fascinating rotating exhibits plus permanent galleries dedicated to California's history and ecology.

Heinhold's First & Last Chance Saloon BAR
(48 Webster St) In Jack London Sq, this lopsided quake survivor and National Literary Landmark is open daily for inspirational drinking. Yes, your beer *is* sliding off the counter.

Yoshi's CLUB
(510-238-9200; www.yoshis.com; 510 Embarcadero West; admission $12-40) One of the country's major jazz clubs; also a sushi restaurant.

YMCA HOSTEL $
(510-848-6800; www.baymca.org/dt/downtown-hotel.aspx; 2001 Allston Way; s/d with shared bath $49/81;) The recently remodeled 100-year-old downtown Y building is still the best budget option in town. Rates for the austere private rooms include use of the pool, fitness center and kitchen facilities.

Downtown Berkeley Inn MOTEL $$
(510-843-4043; www.downtownberkeleyinn.com; 2001 Bancroft Way; r $89-109;) A 27-room budget boutique-style motel with good-sized rooms and correspondingly ample flat-screen TVs.

Eating & Drinking

TOP CHOICE **Chez Panisse** AMERICAN $$$
(restaurant 510-548-5525, cafe 510-548-5049; 1517 Shattuck Ave; restaurant $60-95, cafe mains $18-29; restaurant dinner Mon-Sat) Genuflect at the temple of Alice Waters: the birthplace of California cuisine remains at the pinnacle of Bay Area dining. Book one month ahead for its legendary prix-fixe meals (no substitutions); or book upstairs at the less-expensive, à la carte cafe.

Café Intermezzo CAFETERIA $
(2442 Telegraph Ave; sandwiches & salads $6.50;) Mammoth salads draw a constant crowd, and we're not talking about delicate little rabbit food plates. Bring a friend, or you might drown while trying to polish one off yourself.

Cheese Board Pizza PIZZERIA $
(1512 Shattuck Ave; pizza slice $2.50; 11:30am-3pm & 4:30-8pm Tue-Sat;) Sit down for a slice of the fabulously crispy one-option-per-day veggie pizza at this worker-owned collective where there's often live music.

Caffe Strada CAFE $
(2300 College Ave; 6am-midnight;) University students get wired on caffeine on the giant outdoor patio and study, ardently talk philosophy or make eyes at each other.

Triple Rock Brewery & Ale House BREWERY $
(1920 Shattuck Ave) One of the country's first brewpubs, the house beers and pub grub are quite good, and the antique wooden bar and rooftop sun deck are delightful.

Entertainment

Berkeley Repertory Theatre THEATER
(510-647-2949; www.berkeleyrep.org; 2025 Addison St) A highly respected company that has produced bold versions of classical and modern plays since 1968.

Freight & Salvage Coffeehouse LIVE MUSIC
(510-644-2020; www.thefreight.org; 2020 Addison St) This legendary club has over 40 years of history and features great traditional folk and world music. All ages; half-price tickets for under 21s.

Getting There & Around

AC Transit (510-817-1717, 511; www.actransit.org) runs local buses in Berkeley, as well as between Berkeley and Oakland ($2.10), and Berkeley and San Francisco ($4.20). **BART** (www.bart.gov) trains run from SF to downtown Berkeley ($3.50), which is four blocks from the main campus gate.

NORTHERN CALIFORNIA

The Golden State goes wild in Northern California, with giant redwoods emerging from coastal mists, wallows in volcanic mud amid Wine Country vineyards, and the majestic Sierra Nevada mountains framing Yosemite and Lake Tahoe. Northern California's backwoods are surprisingly forward-thinking, with organic diners, ecoresorts, and the nation's earliest national and state parks. Pack your trash and be mindful of private property – local goatherds and medical-marijuana growers can get touchy about trespassers. Come for the scenery, but stay for superb wine and cheese, the obligatory hot tub, and conversations that begin with 'Hey dude!' and end hours later.

Wine Country

A patchwork of vineyards stretches from sunny inland Napa to chilly coastal Sonoma – America's premier wine-growing region. Napa has art-filled tasting rooms by big-name architects, with prices to match; in down-to-earth Sonoma, you'll drink in sheds and probably meet the vintner's dog. NB: There are three Sonomas: the town, the valley and the county.

NAPA VALLEY

Some 230 wineries crowd 30-mile-long Napa Valley along three main routes. Main Hwy 29 is lined with blockbuster wineries; it jams weekends. Parallel-running Silverado Trail moves faster; it's lined with boutique wineries, bizarre architecture and cult-hit cabs. Hwy 121 (aka Carneros Hwy) runs west toward Sonoma, with landmark wineries specializing in sparkling wines and Pinot Noir.

Traveling south to north, **Downtown Napa** – the valley's workaday hub – lacks rusticity, but has trendy restaurants, tasting rooms and mansions reinvented as B&Bs. Picky picnickers head to Oxbow Public Market; bargain hunters hit **Napa Valley Welcome Center** (☎707-260-0107; www.legendarynapavalley.com; 600 Main St; ⏲9am-5pm) for spa deals, wine-tasting passes and winery maps.

Formerly a stagecoach stop, tiny **Yountville** – home of famous French Laundry – has more Michelin-starred eateries per capita than anywhere else in America.

Charming **St Helena** – the Beverly Hills of Napa – is where traffic jams, but there's great strolling and shopping, if you find parking.

Folksy **Calistoga** – Napa's least-gentrified town – is home to hot-spring spas and mud-bath emporiums that use volcanic ash from adjacent Mt St Helena. To find spas, contact **Calistoga Visitors Center** (☎707-942-6333; www.calistogavisitors.com; 1133 Washington St; ⏲9am-5pm).

Sights & Activities

Most Napa wineries require reservations. Book one appointment, then build your day around it. Plan to see no more than three in one day. The following are in south-to-north order.

di Rosa Art + Nature Preserve GALLERY
(Map p948; ☎707-226-5991; www.dirosapreserve.org; 5200 Carneros Hwy 121; ⏲gallery 9:30am-3pm Wed-Fri, by appointment Sat) When you notice scrap-metal sheep grazing Carneros vineyards, you've spotted di Rosa Art + Nature Preserve, one of the best-anywhere collections of Northern California art. Reservations are highly recommended for tours.

Vintners' Collective TASTING ROOM
(☎707-255-7150; www.vintnerscollective.com; 1245 Main St, Napa; tasting $25; ⏲11am-6pm) Inside a former 19th-century brothel, VC represents 20 high-end boutique wineries too small to have their own tasting rooms.

DON'T MISS

DON'T MISS...

» Dig into farm-to-table cooking at **Zazu** (p979) and **Ad Hoc** (p977)

» Cycle Sonoma's sun-dappled Dry Creek Valley, braking for Zin in a cave at **Bella Vineyards** (p979) and Pinot in a tool shed at **Porter Creek Vineyards** (p979)

» Wander beneath 1000-year-old redwoods at **Armstrong Redwoods State Reserve** (p979)

» Find inspiration among vineyards, peacocks and surreal sculptures at Napa's **di Rosa Art + Nature Preserve**

» Race otters down the lazy **Russian River** in a canoe (p978)

» Wallow in **volcanic-mud baths** at Calistoga's Indian Springs (p976)

Twenty Rows WINERY
(☎707-287-1063; www.vinoce.com; 880 Vallejo St, Napa; tasting $10; ⏰11am-5pm Tue-Sat) Downtown Napa's only working winery crafts light-on-the-palate Cabernet Sauvignon for a mere $20 a bottle.

Hess Collection WINERY, GALLERY
(☎707-255-1144; www.hesscollection.com; 4411 Redwood Rd, Napa; tasting $10; ⏰10am-4pm) Northwest of downtown, Hess pairs monster cabs with blue-chip art by mega-modernists like Francis Bacon and Robert Motherwell. Reservations suggested.

Darioush WINERY
(☎707-257-2345; www.darioush.com; 4240 Silverado Trail, Napa; tasting $18-35; ⏰10:30am-5pm) Stone bulls glower from atop pillars lining the driveway of Darioush, a jaw-dropping Persian-temple winery that crafts monumental Merlots.

Frog's Leap WINERY
(☎707-963-4704; www.frogsleap.com; 8815 Conn Creek Rd, Rutherford; tours with tasting $20; ⏰by appointment) Meandering paths wind through magical gardens surrounding an 1884 barn at this LEED-certified winery, known for Sauvignon Blanc and Cabernet. Reservations required.

Culinary Institute of America at Greystone COOKING SCHOOL
(☎707-967-2320; 2555 Main St, St Helena; mains $25-29, cooking demonstration $20; ⏰restaurant 11:30am-9pm, cooking demonstrations 1:30pm Sat & Sun) An 1889 stone chateau houses a gadget-filled culinary shop, fine restaurant, and weekend cooking demonstrations and wine-tasting classes.

Cade WINERY
(☎707-965-2746; www.cadewinery.com; 360 Howell Mountain Rd, Angwin; tasting $20; ⏰by appointment) Ascend Mt Veeder for drop-dead vistas at Napa's oh-so-swank, first-ever LEED gold-certified winery, which crafts Bordeaux-style Cabernet Sauvignon. Hawks ride thermals at eye level. Reservations required.

Pride Mountain WINERY
(☎707-963-4949; www.pridewines.com; 4026 Spring Mountain Rd, St Helena; tasting $10; ⏰10:30am-3:45pm by appointment) Cult-favorite Pride straddles the Sonoma–Napa border and makes stellar Cabernet, Merlot and Viognier at an unfussy hilltop estate with spectacular picnicking. Reservations required.

Casa Nuestra WINERY
(☎866-844-9463; www.casanuestra.com; 3451 Silverado Trail, St Helena; tasting $10; ⏰10am-4:30 by appointment) A peace flag and portrait of Elvis greet you at this tiny mom-and-pop winery, known for its unusual varietals. Goats frolic beside the picnic area.

Castello di Amorosa WINERY
(☎707-967-6272; www.castellodiamorosa.com; 4045 Hwy 29, Calistoga; tasting $10-15, tour adult/child $32/22; ⏰by appointment) You'll need reservations to tour this near-perfect re-creation of a 12th-century Italian castle, complete with moat and torture chamber. The respectable Italian varietals include a good Merlot blend, great with pizza.

Lava Vine TASTING ROOM
(☎707-942-9500; www.lavavine.com; 965 Silverado Trail, Calistoga; tasting $10; ⏰10am-5pm, appointment suggested) The party kids at Lava Vine take a lighthearted approach to seriously good wine, offering food pairings with tastings. Kids and dogs play outside. Bring a picnic. Reservations recommended.

Indian Springs SPA
(☎707-942-4913; www.indianspringscalistoga.com; 1712 Lincoln Ave, Calistoga; ⏰9am-8pm) Book ahead for a volcanic-mud bath at Calistoga's original 19th-century hot-springs resort; treatments ($85) include access to the hot-springs-fed pool.

Sleeping

Napa's best values are midweek and off-season in Calistoga and at downtown Napa motels and B&Bs – see www.lonelyplanet.com and www.legendarynapavalley.com for more options.

Eurospa Inn MOTEL $$
(☎707-942-6829; www.eurospa.com; 1202 Pine St, Calistoga; r $139-189; ❄📶🏊) Immaculate single-story motel.

El Bonita Motel MOTEL $$
(☎707-963-3216; www.elbonita.com; 195 Main St, St Helena; r $119-179; ❄@📶🏊) Book well ahead for this mid-valley motel; up-to-date rooms, hot tub and sauna.

Chablis Inn MOTEL $$
(☎707-257-1944; www.chablisinn.com; 3360 Solano Ave, Napa; r weekday $89-109, weekend $159-179; ❄@📶🏊) Good-value motel, on Napa's suburban strip.

Calistoga Inn INN $$
(☎707-942-4101; www.calistogainn.com; 1250 Lincoln Ave, Calistoga; r midweek/weekend $69/119) Bargain inn upstairs from a brewery-restaurant (bring earplugs). No TVs, shared bathrooms.

Mountain Home Ranch B&B, RESORT $$
(☎707-942-6616; www.mountainhomeranch.com; 3400 Mountain Home Ranch Rd, Calistoga; r $109-119, cabins $69-144;) Secluded, rustic 1913 guest ranch on 340 acres, with hiking, canoeing and farm animals.

Bothe-Napa Valley State Park CAMPGROUND $
(☎707-942-4575, reservations 800-444-7275; www.parks.ca.gov; campsites $35;) Hillside campsites with hiking beneath moss-covered oaks.

Eating

Wine Country restaurants cut their hours in winter and spring. Plan to eat dinner by 8pm in the off-season.

Oxbow Public Market MARKET $
(☎707-226-6529; www.oxbowpublicmarket.com; 610 & 644 1st St, Napa; ⏲9am-7pm Mon-Sat, 10am-5pm Sun) Oxbow showcases sustainably produced artisanal foods by multiple vendors. Feast on Hog Island oysters (six for $15), Pica Pica's Venezuelan cornbread sandwiches ($8) and Three Twins certified organic ice-cream ($4 cones).

Gott's Roadside/Taylor's Automatic Refresher BURGERS $$
(☎707-963-3486; www.gottsroadside.com; 933 Main St, St Helena; dishes $8-15; ⏲10:30am-9pm;) A 1950s drive-in diner with 21st-century sensibilities: burgers are all-natural Niman Ranch beef or lean 'ahi tuna, with optional sides of chili-dusted sweet-potato fries.

JoLé CALIFORNIAN $$
(☎707-942-5938; www.jolerestaurant.com; 1457 Lincoln Ave, Calistoga; mains $15-20; ⏲5-9pm) Small plates, modest prices and outsize flavor – chef-owned JoLé evolves seasonally and scores high marks for consistency and farm-to-table flavors.

TOP CHOICE **Ad Hoc** AMERICAN $$$
(☎707-944-2487; www.adhocrestaurant.com; 6476 Washington St, Yountville; ⏲5-9pm Wed-Mon, 10:30am-2pm Sun brunch) Don't ask for a menu at Thomas Keller's most innovative restaurant since French Laundry: chef Dave Cruz dreams up his four-course, $48 market menu daily. No substitutions (except for dietary restrictions), but none needed – every dish is comforting, fresh and spot-on.

Ubuntu VEGETARIAN $$$
(☎707-251-5656; www.ubuntunapa.com; 1140 Main St, Napa; dishes $14-18; ⏲11:30am-2:30pm Sat & Sun, 5:30-8:30pm daily;) The Michelin-starred seasonal, vegetarian menu features wonders from the kitchen garden, satisfying hearty eaters with four-to-five inspired small plates, and eco-savvy drinkers with 100-plus sustainably produced wines.

French Laundry CALIFORNIAN $$$
(☎707-944-2380; www.frenchlaundry.com; 6640 Washington St, Yountville; fixed-price menu $270; ⏲11:30am-2:30pm Sat & Sun, 5:30-9pm daily) A high-wattage culinary experience on par with the world's best, French Laundry is ideal for marking lifetime achievements. Book exactly two months ahead: call at 10am (or try OpenTable.com at midnight). If you can't score a table, console yourself at Keller's nearby note-perfect French brasserie Bouchon; or with chocolate cake at Bouchon Bakery.

SONOMA VALLEY

More casual, less commercial than Napa, Sonoma Valley has 70 wineries around Hwy 12 – and unlike Napa, most welcome picnicking.

Sights & Activities

Sonoma Plaza SQUARE
(Napa, Spain & 1st Sts, Sonoma) Downtown Sonoma was once the capital of a rogue nation. Today's plaza – the state's largest town square – looks stately with chic boutiques, historical buildings and stone **visitor center** (☎707-996-1090; www.sonomavalley.com; 453 1st St E; ⏲9am-5pm), but it gets lively during summer evenings and **farmers markets** (⏲9am-noon Fri, 5:30-8pm Tue Apr-Oct).

Gundlach-Bundschu WINERY
(☎707-938-5277; www.gunbun.com; 2000 Denmark St, Sonoma; tasting $10; ⏲11am-4:30pm) West of downtown, Gundlach-Bundschu dates to 1858 and looks like a storybook castle. Winemakers craft legendary Tempranillo and signature Riesling and Gewürztraminer. GunBun also operates nearby **Bartholomew Park Winery** (☎707-939-3026; www.bartpark.com; 1000 Vineyard Lane; tasting $5-10; ⏲11am-4:30pm), a 400-acre preserve with vineyards cultivated in 1857, now

certified organic, yielding citrusy Sauvignon Blanc and smoky Merlot.

Jack London Historic State Park HISTORIC SITE
(Map p948; ☎707-938-5216; www.jacklondonpark.com; 2400 London Ranch Rd, Glen Ellen; per car $8; ⏱10am-5pm Thu-Mon) Up Hwy 12, obey the call of the wild at Jack London State Historic Park, where adventure-novelist Jack London moved in 1910 to build his dream house – which burned on the eve of completion in 1913. His widow built the house that now stands as a museum to London. Miles of **hiking trails** (some open to mountain bikes) weave through 1400 hilltop acres; an easy 2-mile loop meanders to a lake, great for picnicking.

Kaz Winery WINERY
(☎707-833-2536; www.kazwinery.com; 233 Adobe Canyon Rd, Kenwood; tasting $5-10; ⏱11am-5pm Fri-Mon) Veer off Hwy 12 near Kenwood for offbeat, organically grown, cult-favorite wines, poured inside a barn.

FREE **Cornerstone** GARDENS
(☎707-933-9474, 707-933-3010; www.corenerstonegardens.com; 23570 Hwy 121; ⏱10am-5pm) There's nothing traditional about this tapestry of gardens, south of downtown Sonoma, showcasing 25 renowned avant-garde landscape designers.

Sleeping

At the northern end of Sonoma Valley, Santa Rosa has chain hotels near Railroad Sq.

TOP CHOICE **Beltane Ranch** RANCH $$$
(☎707-996-6501; www.beltaneranch.com; 11775 Hwy 12; r incl breakfast $150-240;) Surrounded by pasturelands, Beltane's cheerful 1890s ranch house occupies 100 acres and has double porches lined with swinging chairs and white wicker. Five rooms. No phones or TVs.

Sonoma Hotel HISTORIC HOTEL $$
(☎707-996-2996; www.sonomahotel.com; 110 W Spain St, Sonoma; r incl breakfast midweek/weekend Nov-Mar $140/170, Apr-Oct $170/200) Charming 1880 landmark hotel on happening Sonoma Plaza, with larger/smaller rooms for $30 more/less; two-night minimum weekends. No elevator or parking lot.

Hillside Inn MOTEL $
(☎707-546-9353; www.hillside-inn.com; 2901 4th St, Sonoma; s/d Nov-Mar $70/82, Apr-Oct $74/86;) One of Santa Rosa's best-kept (if dated) motels lies close to wineries; add $4 for kitchens.

Sugarloaf Ridge State Park CAMPGROUND $
(☎707-833-5712, reservations 800-444-7275; www.parks.ca.gov; Adobe Canyon Rd; tent sites $30) Northeast of Kenwood wineries, find 50 sites (no hookups) in two hilltop meadows. Superb hiking.

Eating

Fremont Diner AMERICAN $
(☎707-938-7370; 2698 Fremont Dr/Hwy 121, Sonoma; mains $8-11; ⏱8am-3pm Mon-Fri, 7am-4pm Sat & Sun;) Feast on Southern-inspired, farm-to-table cooking at this order-at-the-counter diner. Arrive early to avoid queues.

Fig Cafe & Winebar CALIFORNIAN $$
(☎707-938-2130; www.thefigcafe.com; 13690 Arnold Dr, Glen Ellen; mains $15-20; ⏱10am-2:30pm Sat & Sun, 5:30-9pm daily) Sonoma's take on comfort food: organic salads, Sonoma duck cassoulet and free corkage on Sonoma wines, in a convivial room with vaulted wooden ceilings.

Cafe La Haye MODERN AMERICAN $$$
(☎707-935-5994; www.cafelahaye.com; 140 E Napa St, Sonoma; mains $19-26; ⏱from 5:30pm Tue-Sat) This tiny bistro, with open kitchen, creates earthy New American dishes from ingredients sourced within 60 miles. Reservations essential.

Red Grape PIZZERIA $$
(☎707-996-4103; www.theredgrape.com; 529 1st St W, Sonoma; pizzas $10-16; ⏱11:30am-10pm;) Thin-crust pizza with local cheeses, plus small-production Sonoma wines.

Sonoma Market DELI $
(☎707-996-3411; 500 W Napa St, Sonoma; ⏱6am-9pm) Superior grocery-store deli with hot-pressed panini and picnic fixings.

RUSSIAN RIVER VALLEY

The West preserves its wild ways in woodsy Russian River, two hours north of San Francisco (via Hwys 101 and 116) in western Sonoma County (aka West County), where redwoods tower over small wineries.

Sebastopol has good shopping, with antique shops lying south of downtown. Find clever crafts at **Renga Arts** (☎707-874-9407; rengaarts.com; 2371 Gravenstein Hwy S, Sebastopol; ⏱Thu-Mon) and vintage-thrift at **Aubergine** (☎707-827-3460; auberginea fterdark.com; 755 Petaluma Ave, Sebastopol). Lunch in the beer garden at **Hopmonk Tavern** (707-829-9300; www.hopmonk.com; 230 Petaluma Ave, Sebastopol; mains $10-20; 11:30am-9:30pm), or gather picnic supplies at **Pacific Market** (www.fiestamkt.com; 550 Gravenstein Hwy N).

Guerneville is the main river town, with hippie craft galleries and gay-friendly honky-tonks; its **visitor center** (707-869-9000; www.russianriver.com; 16209 1st St, Guerneville; 10am-5pm) provides winery maps and lodging info. Explore old-growth redwoods at 805-acre **Armstrong Redwoods State Reserve** (707-869-2015; www.parks.ca.gov; 17000 Armstrong Woods Rd; entry per car $8, camping $25; 8am-sunset), which includes the 308ft, 1400-year-old Colonel Armstrong Tree. Paddle downriver, past herons and otters, with **Burke's Canoe Trips** (707-887-1222; www.burkescanoetrips.com; 8600 River Rd, Forestville; canoes $60). Or head south to sip bubbly – the label the White House pours – at the outdoor hilltop tasting bar at **Iron Horse Vineyards** (707-887-1507; www.ironhorsevineyards.com; 9786 Ross Station Rd, Sebastopol; tasting $10-15; 10am-4:30pm). Find other excellent wineries along rural Westside Rd, which follows the river to Healdsburg.

Guerneville's best eats are at California-smart **Boon Eat + Drink** (707-869-0780; www.eatatboon.com; 16248 Main St, Guerneville; lunch mains $9-11, dinner $12-22; 11am-3pm & 5-9pm). Dinner and a movie await at **Rio Theater** (707-865-0913; www.riotheater.com; 20396 Bohemian Hwy, Monte Rio; adult/child $8/6; Wed-Sun), a converted 1940s Quonset hut, featuring Oscar contenders and gourmet hot dogs ($7). For bona fide farm-to-table cooking, detour southeast to roadhouse-restaurant **Zazu** (707-523-4814; 3535 Guerneville Rd, Santa Rosa; brunch mains $11-15, dinner $18-26; 5:30-8:30pm Wed-Mon, 9am-2pm Sun), which farms its own pigs and chickens for earthy-delicious Italian-inspired comfort cooking.

South of Guerneville, the 10-mile-long, aptly named **Bohemian Highway** (www.bohemianconnection.com) runs to tiny **Occidental**, great for strolling. For a spectacular scenic drive to the ocean, take Coleman Valley Rd. Meet locals at Occidental's weekly organic **farmers market** (707-793-2159; www.occidentalfarmersmarket.com, 4pm-dusk Fri Jun-Oct). **Howard Station Cafe** (707-874-2838; www.howardstationcafe.com; 3811 Bohemian Hwy, Occidental; mains $8-11; 7am-2:30pm) serves hearty breakfasts and lunches.

HEALDSBURG TO BOONVILLE

More than 90 wineries dot the Russian River, Dry Creek and Alexander Valleys within a 30-mile radius of **Healdsburg**, where upscale eateries, wine-tasting rooms and stylish inns surround the Spanish-style plaza. For tasting passes and maps, hit the **Healdsburg Visitors Center** (707-433-6935; www.healdsburg.org; 217 Healdsburg Ave, Healdsburg; 9am-5pm Mon-Fri, to 3pm Sat, 10am-2pm Sun).

Picture-perfect farmstead wineries await discovery in Dry Creek Valley, across Hwy 101 from downtown Healdsburg. Rent a bike downtown and pedal for Zin tasting in the caves at **Bella Vineyards** (707-473-9171; www.bellawinery.com; 9711 West Dry Creek Rd; tasting $5-10; 11am-4:30pm), or drive southwest to certified-biodynamic **Porter Creek Vineyards** (707-433-6321; www.portercreekvineyards.com; 8735 Westside Rd; tasting free; 10:30am-4:30pm) for Pinot Noir served on a bar made from a bowling-alley lane.

North of Healdsburg, take Hwy 128 to **Anderson Valley** for organic eats and award-winning beer amid vineyards and orchards. In **Boonville**, brake for disc-golf and beer-tasting at solar-powered **Anderson Valley Brewing Company** (707-895-2337; www.avbc.com; 17700 Hwy 253, Boonville; tasting $5; 11am-6pm, tours 1:30pm & 3pm).

Sleeping & Eating

Best Western Dry Creek MOTEL **$$$**
(707-433-0300; www.drycreekinn.com; 198 Dry Creek Rd, Healdsburg; r weekday $59-129, weekend $199-259;) Spiffy motel.

L&M Motel MOTEL **$$**
(707-433-6528; www.landmmotel.com; 70 Healdsburg Ave, Healdsburg; r $100-140;) Old-fashioned motel.

Bovolo ITALIAN **$$**
(707-431-2962; www.bovolorestaurant.com; 106 Matheson St, Healdsburg; lunch mains $8-14; 9am-4pm Mon, Wed & Thu, to 8pm Tue, Fri & Sat, to 6pm Sun) Bovolo puts a Slow Food spin on fast food, with salads, panini and pizza made with house-cured salumi.

Cyrus CALIFORNIAN **$$$**
(707-433-3311; www.cyrusrestaurant.com; 29 North St, Healdsburg; fixed-price menus $102-130; 11:30am-2pm Sat, 6-10pm Thu-Mon) Critics rave about ultra-chic Cyrus, but the local secret is the bar, where mad-scientist cocktails accompany truffle-laced dishes.

Boonville General Store CAFE $$
(☎707-895-9477; 14077 Hwy 128, Boonville; ⊙8am-3pm; 👪) House-baked pastries and pizza, plus locally grown organic salads.

ℹ Getting There & Around

Wine Country begins 75 minutes north of San Francisco, via Hwy 101 or I-80. For transit information, dial ☎511.

Public Transportation

Slow, but possible. Take **Vallejo Ferry** (www.baylinkferry.com; adult/child $13/6.50) from San Francisco's Ferry Building; weekday boats leave hourly, 6:30am to 7pm, and every two hours weekends, 11am to 7:30pm. In Vallejo, connect with **Napa Valley Vine** (www.napavalleyvine.net; adult/child $2.90/2.15) buses to Napa and Calistoga. Alternatively, take BART to El Cerrito, then transfer to **Vallejo Transit** (www.vallejotransit.com; $5) to Vallejo and connect with Napa buses.

For Sonoma, **Greyhound buses** (www.greyhound.com) connect San Francisco and Santa Rosa ($22). **Golden Gate Transit** (goldengatetransit.org) links San Francisco to Petaluma ($8.80) and Santa Rosa ($9.70), where you connect with **Sonoma County Transit** (www.sctransit.com).

Napa Valley Vine provides public transit within Napa Valley; Golden Gate Transit and Sonoma County Transit provide transit around Sonoma.

Bicycle

Rentals cost about $25 to $45 per day; inquire about wine pick-up.

Calistoga Bike Shop (☎707-942-9687; www.calistogabikeshop.com; 1318 Lincoln Ave, Calistoga) Bike rental.

Getaway Adventures (☎707-568-3040; www.getawayadventures.com) Offers easy 'Sip-n-Cycle' tours around Calistoga ($149, six hours).

Napa River Vélo (☎707-258-8729; www.naparivervelo.com; 680 Main St, Napa) Bike rental; rear of building.

Napa Valley Adventure Tours (☎707-259-1833; www.napavalleyadventuretours.com; Oxbow Public Market, 610 1st St, Napa) Rents bikes and leads wine-tasting bicycle trips with lunch and introductions to winemakers.

Sonoma Valley Cyclery (☎707-935-3377; www.sonomacyclery.com; 20091 Broadway, Sonoma) Bike rental.

Spoke Folk Cyclery (☎707-433-7171; www.spokefolk.com; 201 Center St, Healdsburg) Bike rental.

Train

Napa Valley Wine Train (☎707-253-2111; www.winetrain.com; per person from $89-189) Cushy, touristy three-hour trips with an optional winery stop.

North Coast

Valleys of redwoods amble into the moody crash of the Pacific along the North Coast, home to hippies, hoppy microbrews and flora that famously includes the tallest trees and most potent marijuana in the world.

Road-tripping in this part of California is best if you just keep driving: the winding coastal drive gets more rewarding with every gorgeous, white-knuckled mile of road. Along the jagged edge of the continent, the metropolitan charms of San Francisco, only a few hours behind in the rear view mirror, feel eons away from the frothing, frigid crash of Pacific tide and the two-stoplight towns.

BODEGA BAY TO FORT BRAGG

Compared to the famous Big Sur coast, the serpentine stretch of Hwy 1 up the North Coast is more challenging, more remote and more *real:* it passes farms, fishing towns and hidden beaches. Drivers use roadside pull-outs to scan the hazy Pacific horizon for migrating whales and explore a coastline dotted with rock formations that are relentlessly pounded by the surf. The drive between Bodega Bay and Fort Bragg takes four hours of daylight driving without stops. At night in the fog, it takes steely nerves and much, much longer.

Bodega Bay is the first pearl in a string of sleepy fishing towns and the setting of Hitchcock's terrifying 1963 avian psycho-horror flick *The Birds*. The skies are free from bloodthirsty gulls today (though you best keep an eye on the picnic); it's Bay Area weekenders who descend en masse for extraordinary **Sonoma Coast State Beaches** between here and Jenner, 10 miles north. This system of beaches has arched rocks, wildflower-covered bluffs and tons of coves for lovers to spread a blanket and watch the fog roll in. **Bodega Charters** (www.bodegacharters.com; 1410 Bay Flat Rd, Bodega Bay) and several other one-boat outfits run whale-watching trips ($35 per person, 3½ to four hours). Migrating whales are most active between January and May. **Bodega Bay Surf Shack** (www.bodegabaysurf.com; 1400 N Hwy 1, Bodega Bay; surfboards per day $15, kayaks per 4hr single/double $45/65) rents surfboards, wetsuits and kayaks. Landlubbers can enjoy the views of the coastline and rolling inland hills on horseback with **Chanslor Riding**

Stables (www.chanslorranch.com; 2660 N Hwy 1, Bodega Bay; 1hr rides from $70).

There isn't much to **Jenner**, just a cluster of shops and restaurants dotting the coastal hills where the wide, lazy Russian River meets the Pacific. The main attraction is the resident harbor seal colony. Look for them from Hwy 1 turnouts north of town. Volunteers protect the seals and educate tourists at **Goat Rock State Beach** (Mile 19.15) during pupping season, between March and August.

The salt-weathered structures of **Fort Ross State Historic Park** (☎707-847-3286; www.fortrossstatepark.org; 19005 Hwy 1; per car $8), 12 winding miles north of Jenner, were an 1812 trading post and Russian Orthodox church. It's a quiet place, but the history is riveting; this was once the southernmost reach of Tsarist Russia's North American trading expeditions. The small, wood-scented museum offers historical exhibits and respite from windswept cliffs. Budget cuts have impacted seasonal hours, but the park is almost always open on weekends.

Salt Point State Park (☎800-444-7275; www.reserveamerica.com; Mile 39; per car/campsites $8/35) has hiking trails, tide pools and two campgrounds where pink blooms spot the misty green woods in springtime. Cows graze the surrounding rock-strewn fields on the bluffs, which are home to organic dairy cooperatives.

Eight miles north of Elk, **Van Damme State Park** (☎800-444-7275; www.reserveamerica.com; per car/campsites $8/35) has the popular **Fern Canyon Trail**, which passes through a pygmy forest and a fern- and elderberry-lined canyon. The car-accessible camping is pleasant, but an easy 2-mile hike-in offers a secluded option and the hill-top sites are situated around a grassy clearing and good for families.

The most popular village on this stretch is **Mendocino**, a salt-washed historical gem perched on a gorgeous headland. For 40- and 50-somethings from the Bay Area, the New England saltbox B&Bs and quaint shops make the town seem like a baby step from heaven. A headland walk passes berry bramble and wildflowers, where cypress trees stand guard over dizzying cliffs (ideal for a picnic). Nature's power is evident everywhere: from driftwood littered fields and cave tunnels to the raging surf. The **visitor center** (www.gomendo.com; 735 Main St, Mendocino; ⌚11am-4pm) is in the Ford House and is the place to start.

Medocino's scrappy sister city, **Fort Bragg** is trying to lure some of the well-heeled weekenders a bit further north, but it still has a way to go. You'll find cheap gas, large motels and a mess of fast food, but it's not without its charm. The elegant and well-balanced brews at **North Coast Brewing Co** (www.northcoastbrewing.com; 455 N Main St, Fort Bragg; pint $4, 10-beer sampler $12) are reason enough to pull over. Fort Bragg also boasts the 1885 **Skunk Train** (☎800-866-1690; www.skunktrain.com; adult/child 3-11yr $49/24), whose diesel and steam engines make half-day trips through the woods to Ukiah.

Sleeping & Eating

Every other building in Mendocino seems to be a B&B; there are dozens to choose from and many are stuffed with frilly decor and return guests.

TOP CHOICE **Mar Vista Cottages** CABIN $$
(☎707-884-3522; www.marvistamendocino.com; 35101 S Hwy 1, Anchor Bay; cottages from $155; wi-fi) The elegantly renovated 1930s fishing cabins of Mar Vista are a simple, stylish seaside escape with vanguard commitment to sustainability. The harmonious environment, situated in the sunny 'Banana Belt' of the North Coast, is the result of pitch-perfect details: linens are line-dried over lavender, guests browse the organic vegetable garden to harvest their own dinner, and chickens cluck around the grounds laying the next morning's breakfast. Often requires a two-night stay.

Andiorn CABIN $$
(☎800-955-6478; www.theandiorn.com; 6051 N Hwy 1, Mendocino; r $99-149; wi-fi) Styled with hip vintage decor, this cluster of 1950s roadside cottages is a refreshingly playful option amid the stuffy cabbage-rose and lace aesthetic of Mendocino. Each cabin houses two rooms with complementing themes: 'Read' has old books, comfy vintage chairs and hip retro eyeglasses, while the adjoining 'Write' features a huge chalk board and ribbon typewriter. A favorite for travelers? 'Here' and 'There,' themed with old maps, 1960s airline paraphernalia and collectables from North Coast's yesteryear.

Gualala Point Regional Park CAMPGROUND $
(www.sonoma-county.org/parks; 42401 S Highway 1, Gualala; campsites $28) Shaded by a stand of redwoods and fragrant California bay laurel trees, a short trail connects this creekside

campground to the windswept beach. The quality of sites, including several secluded hike-in spots, makes it the best drive-in camping on this part of the coast.

Brewery Gulch Inn B&B $$$
(800-578-4454; www.brewerygulchinn.com; 9401 N Hwy 1, Mendocino; r $210-450;) Just south of Mendocino; this place wins with modern fireplace rooms, hosts who pour heavily at the wine hour and sweets for midnight snacking. Breakfast is served in a small dining room overlooking the distant water.

TOP CHOICE **Piaci Pub & Pizzeria** PIZZERIA $$
(www.piacipizza.com; 120 W Redwood Ave, Fort Bragg; pizza $8-12; 11am-4pm Mon-Fri, 4-9pm Sun-Thu, to 10pm Fri & Sat) Fort Bragg's must-visit pizzeria is the place to chat up locals while enjoying microbrews and a menu of fantastic wood-fired, brick-oven, 'adult' pizza. The 'Gustoso' – an immaculate selection with chevre, pesto and seasonal pears – speaks to the carefully orchestrated thin-crust pies. It's tiny, loud and fun, but expect to wait at peak times.

Spud Point Crab Company SEAFOOD $
(www.spudpointcrab.com; 1860 Bay Flat Rd, Bodega Bay; dishes $4-10; 9am-5pm Thu-Tue;) In the classic tradition of dockside crab shacks, Spud Point serves salty-sweet crab cocktails and *real* clam chowder, served at picnic tables overlooking the marina.

Café Beaujolais CALIFORNIA FUSION $$$
(707-937-5614; www.cafebeaujolais.com; 961 Ukiah St, Mendocino; lunch $9-16, mains $24-36; 11:30am-2:30pm Wed-Sun, from 5:30pm daily) Mendocino's iconic, beloved country Cal/French restaurant occupies an 1896 house restyled into a monochromatic urban-chic dining room, perfect for holding hands by candlelight. The refined and inspired cooking draws diners from San Francisco, who make this the centerpiece of their trip. The locally sourced menu changes with the seasons, but the Petaluma duck breast served with crispy skin is a gourmand's delight.

Bones Roadhouse BARBECUE $$
(www.bonesroadhouse.com; 39350 S Hwy 1, Gualala; mains $10-20; 11:30am-9pm Sun-Thu, to 10pm Fri & Sat) Savory smoked meats make this Gualala's best lunch. On weekends, a codgerly blues outfit may be growling out 'Mustang Sally.'

Patterson's Pub PUB $$
(www.pattersonspub.com; 10485 Lansing St, Mendocino; mains $10-15) If it's late, you'll thank heavens for this pub, which stays open after all the fancier options close to serve big salads and first-class pub fare.

Getting There & Away

Although Hwy 1 is popular with cyclists, a car is nearly a necessity along Hwy 1. Those determined to travel via bus can connect through the **Mendocino Transit Authority** (MTA; 800-696-4682; www.4mta.org), which operates a daily ride from Fort Bragg south to Santa Rosa via Willits and Ukiah ($21, three hours); at Santa Rosa, catch San Francisco-bound bus 80 ($8.80), operated by **Golden Gate Transit** (415-923-2000; www.goldengate.org). Neither Greyhound nor Amtrak serves towns along Hwy 1.

UKIAH TO SCOTIA

If the coastal route along Hwy 1 is ideal for ambling, much of the traffic that heads between Ukia and Scotia on Hwy 101 is rushing toward remote regions beyond the so-called 'Redwood Curtain.' Still, there are a number of worthy diversions, including excellent vineyards around Ukiah, redwood forests north of Leggett and the abandoned wilds of the Lost Coast.

Although **Ukiah** is mostly a place to gas up or get a bite, it boasts the nearby Vichy Springs Resort.

North of tiny **Leggett** on Hwy 101, take a dip at the **Standish-Hickey State Recreation Area** (707-925-6482, 69350 Hwy 101; per car $8). It has river swimming and fishing, as well as 9 miles of hiking trails in virgin and second-growth redwoods (look for the 225ft-tall Miles Standish tree). Fourteen miles further north is **Richardson Grove State Park** (per car/campsites $8/35), for 1400 acres of more virgin redwoods and camping.

The **Lost Coast** tops a serious hiker's itinerary, offering the most rugged coastal camping in California. It became 'lost' when the state's highway bypassed the rugged mountains of the King Range, which rise 4000ft within several miles of the ocean, leaving the region largely undeveloped. The scenery is stunning. From Garberville it's 23 miles along a rough road to Shelter Cove, the main supply point for Lost Coast's adventurers, little more than a seaside subdivision with a deli, restaurant and motels. Heed those 'no trespassing' signs before wandering off trail, lest you encounter farmers who are extremely protective of the region's illicit cash crop.

Along Hwy 101, 80-sq-mile **Humboldt Redwoods State Park** (www.humboldtredwoods.org; campsites $20-35) protects some of the world's oldest redwoods and has three-quarters of the world's tallest 100 trees. Tree huggers take note: these groves rival (and many say surpass) those in Redwood National Park, which is a long drive further north. Even if you don't have time to hike, drive the park's awe-inspiring **Avenue of the Giants**, a 32-mile, two-lane road parallel to Hwy 101. Book ahead for magnificent campsites near the informative **visitor center** (☎707-946-2409; ⏰9am-5pm).

Sleeping & Eating

The camping options are plentiful and extremely high quality, and every one-horse town guarantees at least a deli, a taqueria and a dog-earned motel. The Avenue of the Giants has *excellent* camping – the best of which is in Humboldt Redwoods State Park – and scads of musty midcentury motels, to be approached with caution.

Vichy Springs Resort RESORT, SPA **$$$**
(☎707-462-9515; www.vichysprings.com; 2605 Vichy Springs Rd, Ukiah; lodge s/d $135/195, creekside r $195/245, cottages from $280; ❄📶🏊) This 700-acre resort has the only warm-water, naturally carbonated mineral baths in North America (two hours/all-day use $30/50). Unlike other nearby hot springs, it requires swimwear – you'll be thankful.

Benbow Inn HISTORIC HOTEL **$$**
(☎800-355-3301; www.benbowinn.com; 445 Lake Benbow Dr, Garberville, r $130-200; 📶) Though the English countryside decor has a comically highbrow quality, this Tudor-style manor is a memorable getaway. There's complimentary decanted sherry in each room. The white-tablecloth restaurant and wood-paneled bar are inviting on foggy evenings.

Ukiah Brewing Company BREWERY **$$$**
(www.ukiahbrewingco.com; 102 S State St, Ukiah; dinner mains $15-25; ⏰11:30am-9pm Sun-Thu, to 9:30pm Fri & Sat, 📶) The brews might outshine the food, but the dancefloor gets a bit rowdy to live music on the weekend. The menu has a strong organic and sustainable bent, with plenty of vegan and raw options.

Getting There & Around

Greyhound (☎800-231-2222; www.greyhound.com) operates from San Francisco to Ukiah ($40). The **Redwood Transit System** (www.hta.org, 📶) operates buses Monday through Saturday between Scotia and Trinidad ($2.50, 2½ hours).

EUREKA TO CRESCENT CITY

Passing the strip malls that sprawl from the edges, **Eureka** is unlikely to have you shouting the town's name from the hills; however, it does have an Old Town with fine Victorians, inviting shops and restaurants. You can blow right by on Hwy 101 without getting much of a hint of the town's charm though – for the best window-shopping, head to 2nd St between D and G Sts.

The **Eureka visitor center** (www.eurekachamber.com; 2112 Broadway, Eureka; ⏰8:30am-5pm Mon-Fri, 10am-4pm Sat) has maps and information. In Old Town, **Going Places** (328 2nd St, Eureka; ⏰10:30am-5:30pm Mon-Sat, 11am-5pm Sun) is a fabulous travel bookstore with tons of guidebooks and gear.

The best thing going in Eureka is **Blue Ox Millworks** (www.blueoxmill.com; adult/child 6-12yr $7.50/3.50; ⏰9am-4pm Mon-Sat), one of a small handful of mills in the nation that hand-tools Victorian detailing using traditional carpentry and 19th-century equipment. Fascinating self-guided tours let you watch the craftsmen work.

Cruising the harbor aboard the blue-and-white 1910 **Madaket** (☎707-445-1910; www.humboldtbaymaritimemuseum.com; adult/child 5-12yr $15/7.50; ⏰May-Oct) is also fun. It departs from the foot of F St and the $10 sunset cocktail cruise serves from the smallest licensed bar in the state.

Nine miles north of Eureka, **Arcata** is a patchouli-dipped bastion of radical politics set around a quaint square, where trucks run on biodiesel and recycling gets picked up by tandem bicycle. On the northeast side of town lies the pretty campus of **Humboldt State University** (www.humboldt.edu). At the junction of Hwys 299 and 101 is a **California Welcome Center** (www.arcatachamber.com; ⏰9am-5pm; 📶), with area info.

Trinidad, a working fishing town 16 miles north of Arcata, sits on a bluff overlooking a glittering harbor. There are lovely sand beaches and short hikes on Trinidad Head. Nearby Luffenholtz Beach is popular (but unpatrolled) for surfing; north of town, Patrick's Point Rd is dotted with lodging and forested campgrounds. **Patrick's Point State Park** (www.reserveamerica.com; day use/campsites $8/35) has stunning rocky headlands, tide pools and camping.

Highway 101 passes the **Redwood National & State Parks Visitor Center** (www.nps.gov/redw; 9am-5pm). Together, Redwood National Park and three state parks – Prairie Creek, Del Norte and Jedediah Smith – are a designated World Heritage Site containing almost half the remaining old-growth redwood forests in California. The national park is free; the state parks have an $8 day-use fee in some areas and the only developed campsites ($35). Peering out of the tent at the surreal size of the trunks makes this excellent camping. The visitor center has info about the parks and free permits for backcountry camping. At first glance it's a bit confusing to understand this patchwork of state and federally managed land, as the combined park area stretches all the way north to the Oregon border and is interspersed with several towns.

From south to north, you'll first encounter **Redwood National Park**, which is under Federal jurisdiction and includes the Lady Bird Johnson Grove and Tall Trees Grove, home to several of the world's tallest trees. Dispersed backcountry camping along Redwood Creek is free with a permit and idyllic.

Several miles north of tiny Klamath, **Del Norte Coast Redwoods State Park** contains redwood groves and 8 miles of unspoiled coastline. The Damnation Creek Trail is only 4 miles long, but the (1100ft) elevation change and cliff-side redwood makes it the park's best hike. The unmarked trailhead starts from a parking area off Hwy 101 at mile mark 16.

Jedediah Smith Redwoods State Park is the northernmost park in the system, 5 miles northeast of Crescent City. It's less crowded than the other parks but also beautiful. The redwood stands are so dense that there are few trails, but the outstanding 11-mile Howland Hill Scenic Drive is the best way to see the forest if you can't hike.

Sprawling over a crescent-shaped bay, **Crescent City** is a drab little town, but the only sizable coastal settlement north of Arcata. More than half the town was destroyed by a tidal wave in 1964 and rebuilt with ugly utilitarian architecture. When the tide's out, you can check out the 1865 **Battery Point Lighthouse** (admission $3; 10am-4pm Wed-Sun Apr-Oct) at the south end of A St.

Sleeping & Eating

A mixed bag of midcentury motels are scattered throughout every town along Hwy 101. In Eureka, the cheapest options are south of downtown. The best food and widest variety is in Arcata.

Requa Inn B&B **$$**
(707-482-1425; www.requainn.com; 451 Requa Rd, Klamath; r $85-155;) Built in 1914, this simple historic inn caters to hikers, with a big breakfast and country-style rooms overlooking the river.

Hotel Arcata HISTORIC HOTEL **$$**
(707-826-0217; www.hotelarcata.com; 708 9th St, Arcata; r $96-156;) On the Arcata town square, the stately 1915 hotel is a bit stuffy but right in the center of town.

Carter House Inns B&B **$$$**
(707-444-8062; www.carterhouse.com; 301 L St, Eureka; r incl breakfast $185-213;) The cushy option near Old Town Eureka is this complex of several lovingly tended Victorians. French fusion at Restaurant 301 is the most haute dining around.

TOP CHOICE **Six Rivers Brewery** BREWERY **$$**
(www.sixriversbrewery.com; 1300 Central Ave, McKinleyville; mains $11-18; 11:30am-midnight Tue-Sun, from 4pm Mon) One of the first female-owned breweries in California, the 'brew with a view' kills it in every category: great beer, community vibe, occasional live music and delicious hot wings. The spicy chili pepper ale is amazing.

Getting There & Around

Greyhound (www.greyhound.com) serves Arcata; from San Francisco budget $53 and seven hours. **Redwood Transit** (www.hta.org) buses serve Arcata and Eureka on the Trinidad–Scotia routes ($2.50, 2½ hours), which don't run on Sunday. Though hitchhiking is still fairly rare and safety concerns should be taken seriously, a culture of hippies of all ages and transient marijuana harvesters makes this the easiest region in California to thumb a ride.

Sacramento

Sacramento was the first nonmission European settlement in California, and the state's capital is an anomalous place: the first city to shoot up from gold discovery is flat and fairly bland with shady trees, withering summer heat and jammed highways.

In 1839 eccentric Swiss immigrant John Sutter built a fort, and after gold was discovered nearby in 1848, the town's population exploded. In 1854, after several years of legislative waffling, it became California's capital. Old Sacramento remains the visitor's magnet – a riverside area with raised wooden sidewalks that can feel like a ye olde tourist trap. Better food and culture lie hidden among the grid of streets in midtown, where a fledgling arts scene is quietly defying the city's reputation as a cow town. During **Second Saturday** (www.2nd-sat.com) events, the galleries and shops in midtown draw loads of boozy stumblers.

Sights

TOP CHOICE California Museum MUSEUM
(www.californiamuseum.org; 1020 O St; adult/child 6-13yr $8.50/7; ⏲10am-5pm Mon-Sat, from noon Sun) The attractive, modern California Museum is home to the California Hall Of Fame – perhaps the only place to simultaneously encounter Cesar Chavez, Mark Zuckerburg and Amelia Earhart. The newly opened exhibit *California Indians: Making A Difference* is the state's best view of the traditions and culture of California's first residents, past and present.

State Capitol HISTORIC BUILDING
The 19th-century state capitol at 10th St is the brilliant white jewel rising from the manicured Capitol Mall. The **Capitol Museum** (www.statecapitolmuseum.com; admission free; ⏲9am-5pm) gives tours through period-furnished chambers. The Assembly and Senate rooms are open to the public.

California State Railroad Museum MUSEUM
(www.californiastaterailroadmuseum.org; 125 I St; adult/child 6-17yr $9/4; ⏲10am-5pm) A must-stop for train-lovers, allows visitors to board dozens of meticulously restored beasts of steam and diesel; ride a steam train (adult/child $10/5) at summer weekends. The museum is in Old Sacramento, at the river.

Old Town Sacramento HISTORIC DISTRICT
(www.oldsacramento.com) It's more than a little stagey, where candy-scented streets rumble with baby boomers on Harleys, but this walkable district holds California's largest concentration of historic buildings and a few fine museums.

Sutter's Fort HISTORIC FORT
(cnr 27th & L Sts; adult/child 5 $5/3; ⏲10am-5pm) Restored to its 1850s appearance, the fort has historical actors in summer and some Saturdays throughout the year.

Sleeping & Eating

Sacramento's hotels cater to those doing business at the capitol, so there are serious weekend bargains, especially with last-minute bookings on Priceline. Midtown has a glut of midrange chain hotels. For restaurants, make for J St between 16th and 25th Sts.

TOP CHOICE Citizen Hotel BOUTIQUE HOTEL $$$
(☎916-492-4460; 926 J St; r $159, ste from $215; 📶) With an elegant, ultrahip upgrade by the Joie de Vivre group, the long-vacant Citizen has suddenly become one of the coolest stays in this part of the state. Rooms are lovely with luxurious linen, bold patterned fabrics and stations for your iPod. The little touches make a big impression too: vintage political cartoons adorning the walls, loaner bikes and a nightly wine reception. There's an upscale farm-to-table restaurant on the ground floor (a daily menu of seasonal mains starts around $25).

HI Sacramento Hostel HOSTEL $
(www.norcalhostels.org/sac; 925 H St; dm/r $28/55.75; P@📶) This is a *hostel*? Sweet! The public areas in this restored Victorian mansion are nearly B&B quality, the spacious dorms are clean and the staff knows the local nightlife.

TOP CHOICE Andy Nguyen's THAI $$
(www.andynguyenvegetarianrestaurant.com; 2007 Broadway; meals $8-16; ⏲11:30am-9pm Sun-Mon, to 9:30pm Tue-Thu, to 10pm Fri & Sat; 🥬) The best vegetarian fare in all of California might be at this tranquil Buddhist Thai diner. Try the steaming curries and artful fake meat dishes (the 'chicken' leg has a little wooden bone).

Mulvaney's B & L CALIFORNIA $$$
(☎916-441-6022; www.mulvaneysbl.com; 1215 19th St; mains $20-40; ⏲11:30am-2:30pm & 5-10pm Tue-Fri, 5-10pm Sat) The class place in town; an expert French-touched menu changes every day.

Rubicon BREWERY $
(www.rubiconbrewing.com; 2004 Capitol Ave; sandwiches $7-11; ⏲11am-11:30pm Mon-Thu, to 12:30am Fri & Sat, to 10pm Sun) For award-winning IPAs and decent pub grub.

Getting There & Around

Sacramento is 91 miles east of San Francisco via I-80, and 386 miles north of LA via I-5. **Sacramento International Airport** (www.sacairports.org) is a great small airport to access Lake Tahoe, 15 miles north of downtown off I-5.

Sacramento's **Amtrak** (www.capitolcorridor.org; cnr 5th & I Sts) is the best way to travel to the Bay Area, with frequent trains on the Capitol Corridor line. The depot is near downtown. Trains leave daily for Oakland ($26, two hours) and Los Angeles ($57, 14 hours). **Greyhound** (www.greyhound.com; 7th & L Sts) connects to San Francisco ($22, two hours) or Los Angeles ($66, nine hours) and all points beyond. **Sacramento Regional Transit** (www.sacrt.com) runs a bus and light-rail system (fare $2.25).

Gold Country

Hard to believe, but this is where it all began – the quiet hill towns and drowsy oak-lined byways of Gold Country belie the wild, chaotic, often violent establishment of California. Shortly after a glint of gold caught James Marshall's eye in Sutters Creek in 1848, the rush for gold brought a 300,000-stong stampede of 'forty-niners' to the Sierra foothills. By the time the dust settled, several of the first urban areas in the West were booming, immigration routes were traced from Asia and the Americas, and the 31st state was founded. The frenzy for gold paid little heed to the starched moral decorum of the Victorian society but only traces of environmental havoc and lawless boom towns remain. Traveling here might be a thrill ride for history buffs – the fading historical markers tell tales of bloodlust and banditry – but more tactile pleasures await the traveler willing to plunge into a swimming hole or rattle down single-track mountain-bike trails.

Situated along Hwy 49, Gold Country warrants a two-day detour, where tiny towns survive on selling antiques, ice-cream and gold-rush ephemera. For something adventurous, try a white-water trip down the American River; its three forks are inviting for beginners and experts alike.

In the summer when temperatures soar, there's reprieve in the icy currents of the American, Tuolumne, Kings and Stanislaus Rivers. **All-Outdoors California Whitewater Rafting** (www.aorafting.com) is the favorite; the family-run outfitter does single- and two-day wilderness adventures. **Wolf Creek Wilderness** (www.wolfcreekwilderness.com; 595 E Main St, Grass Valley; kayaks per day from $40) has kayak rentals and lessons ($40 to $150).

The **Gold Country Visitors Association** (www.calgold.org) has detailed local tourist information.

NORTHERN MINES

Highway 50 divides the Northern and Southern Mines; the former stretch south from Nevada City to Placerville. Winding Hwy 49, which connects it all, has plenty of pull-outs and vistas of the surrounding hills. If it's sweltering and you see a line of cars parked roadside, it's likely a swimming hole. Don't ask questions; just park, strip and jump. One of the best is where North and South forks of the American River join up, 3 miles south of Auburn on Hwy 49.

Nevada City was known as the 'Queen City of the Northern Mines,' and her streets gleam with lovingly restored buildings, an arty folk scene, organic cafes and boutiques. The **chamber of commerce** (www.nevadacitychamber.com; 132 Main St, Nevada City; ⌚9am-5pm Mon-Fri, 11am-4pm Sat, 11am-3pm Sun) has self-guided walking tours and excellent information. The **Tahoe National Forest Headquarters** (☎530-265-4531; ⌚8am-4:30pm Mon-Fri, plus Sat in summer), on Hwy 49 at the north end of Coyote St, has hiking and backcountry info, including details about mountain-biking trails.

About 5 miles southwest, **Grass Valley** is Nevada City's functional sister, where artists, hippies and ranchers get their oil changed. Two miles east of town, the landscaped **Empire Mine State Historic Park** (www.empiremine.org; adult/child 6-16yr $7/3; ⌚10am-5pm) marks the site of one of the richest mines in California; from 1850 to 1956 it produced 5.8 million ounces of gold – about $5 billion in today's market.

Coloma is where the gold rush started, and the **Marshall Gold Discovery State Historic Park** (☎530-622-3470; per car $8; ⌚8am-dusk) makes an eerily quiet tribute to the riotous discovery, with a replica of Sutter's Mill, restored buildings and short hikes. There's a statue of Sutter himself, who, in one of the many ironic twists of the gold rush, died a ward of the state.

Sleeping & Eating

Cafes, ice-cream parlors and upscale eateries are in nearly every sizable town along Hwy 49. Nevada City has a spread of eating and sleeping options (including *tons* of B&Bs), and is the cutest place to stay.

TOP CHOICE **Broad Street Inn** B&B **$$**
(☎530-265-2239; www.broadstreetinn.com; 517 E Broad St, Nevada City; r $110-120; ❄📶) It seems as if there are a million bed and breakfasts in town, but this six-room inn is a favorite

because it keeps it simple. (No weird old dolls, no yellowing lace doilies.) The rooms are modern, brightly furnished and elegant, the breakfast is delicious and it's an amazing value.

Outside Inn MOTEL **$$**
(☎530-265-2233; www.outsideinn.com; 575 E Broad St, Nevada City; r $75-150; ❄📶🏊👪) The most fun of the motels just south of town, this has clean, themed rooms, grills for guests to use and is run by exceedingly friendly outdoor enthusiasts.

Holbrooke Hotel HISTORIC HOTEL **$$**
(☎800-933-7077; www.holbrooke.com; 212 W Main St, Grass Valley; r from $105; ❄📶) The register of this 1852 hotel boasts Ulysses Grant and Mark Twain. Elegant Victorian rooms have claw-foot tubs. A recommended restaurant is on-site.

TOP CHOICE **Ikedas** BURGERS **$**
(www.ikedas.com; 13500 Lincoln Way; ⏲8am-7pm, to 8pm Sat & Sun) If you're cruising this part of the state without time to explore, the best pit stop is off I-80 at exit 121. This place feeds Tahoe-bound travelers thick, grass-fed burgers, homemade pies and snacks. The seasonal fresh peach shake is deliriously good.

SOUTHERN MINES

The towns of the Southern Mines – from Placerville to Sonora – receive less traffic and the dusty streets still have a whiff of Wild West, today evident in the motley assortment of Harley cruisers, weed farmers, outsider winemakers and gold prospectors (still!) who populate them. Some, like **Plymouth** (Ole Pokerville) and **Mokelumne Hill** (Moke Hill), are virtual ghost towns, slowly crumbling into photogenic oblivion. Others, like **Jackson**, **Murphys** and **Sutter Creek**, are frilly slices of Americana. Get off the beaten path for family-run vineyards (especially around Plymouth in Amador County, a region that invented Zinfandel) and underground caverns, where geological wonders reward those willing to navigate the touristy gift shops above.

Columbia (www.columbiacalifornia.com) is Gold Country's best historic site, with four square blocks of authentic 1850s buildings and concessionaires in period costumes right in the middle of town. It's crazy with kids panning for gold. The park itself doesn't close, but most businesses are open from 10am to 5pm.

Sleeping & Eating

This area's best-value camping is in the national forests, which is free. Lacy B&Bs are in nearly every town and usually priced over $100 per night. Busy Sonora is a bit drab, but it's just over an hour from Yosemite National Park and has serviceable midrange hotels.

Gunn House Hotel HISTORIC HOTEL **$$**
(☎209-532-3421; www.gunnhousehotel.com; 286 S Washington St, Sonora; r $79-115; P❄🏊👪) For a lovable alternative to Gold Country's cookie-cut chains, this historic hotel hits the sweet spot. Rooms feature period decor and guests take to rocking chairs on the wide porches in the evening. Stuffed bears, a nice pool and a big breakfast also make it a hit with families.

City Hotel & Fallon Hotel HISTORIC HOTELS **$$**
(☎800-532-1479; www.cityhotel.com; r incl breakfast from $90-145; 📶) These co-run hotels have 24 stunning, rooms and common spaces, decked out with museum-quality pieces. The City Hotel has an acclaimed **restaurant** (meals $14-30) frequented by a Twain impersonator. The Fallon hosts a repertory theater.

Volcano Union Inn HISTORIC HOTEL **$$**
(☎209-296-4458; www.volcanounion.com; 16104 Main St, Volcano; r incl breakfast $109-129; ❄@📶) The preferred of two historic hotels in Volcano, there are four lovingly updated rooms with crooked floors and two have street-facing balconies. The Union Pub has a menu designed by the guys from Taste and will host the occasional old-time fiddler.

TOP CHOICE **Taste** CALIFORNIAN, FRENCH **$$$**
(☎209-245-3463; www.restauranttaste.com; 9402 Main St, Plymouth; mains $31-50; ⏲5-10pm Thu-Mon, 11:30am-2pm Sat) The antidote to Gold Country's dependence on burgers and chops, Taste plates artful, fresh, seasonal dishes which come well paired with bold Zinfandels from the surrounding hills of Amador County.

Lighthouse Deli & Ice Cream Shop DELI **$**
(www.thelighthousedeli.com; 28 S Washington, Sonora; sandwiches $7-9; ⏲10am-4pm Mon-Fri, 11am-3pm Sat) The flavors of N'awlins make this unassuming deli an unexpected delight. The muffeletta – a toasted piece of Cajun paradise that's stacked with ham, salami, cheese and olive tapenade – is the best sandwich within 100 miles.

Getting There & Around

About 26 miles northeast of Sacramento, Hwy 49 intersects I-80 in the town of Auburn. Local bus systems include **Gold Country Stage** (☎530-477-0103), which links Nevada City, Grass Valley and Auburn (fare $1.50 to $3), and **Placer County Transit** (☎530-885-2877). No public transit serves the Southern Mines on Hwy 49.

Northern Mountains

Remote, empty and eerily beautiful, the Northern Mountains are some of California's least-visited turf; it's an endless show of geological wonders, alpine lakes, rivers and desert. The major peaks – Lassen, Shasta, Lava Beds National Monument and the Trinity Alps – have virtually zero geological features in common, but all offer isolated backcountry camping under sparkling skies. The towns dotting the regions aren't attractions, but are good enough to supply a launch into the wild.

REDDING TO YREKA

Much of the drive north of Redding is dominated by **Mt Shasta**, a 14,179ft snow-capped goliath that rises out of the Central Valley as dramatically as the anticipation felt by outdoor enthusiasts who seek adventure along its slopes. An extremely helpful pit stop just off I-5 is the **Shasta-Cascade Wonderland Association** (www.shastacascade.com; ⏲9am-10pm Mon-Fri, to 4pm Sat & Sun). It's 10 miles south of Redding in the Shasta Factory Outlets Mall.

Don't believe the tourist brochures; **Redding**, the largest town in the region, is a snooze. The best reason to stop is the **Sundial Bridge**, a glass-deck pedestrian marvel designed by world-class architect Santiago Calatrava. It leads over the Sacramento River and to the **Turtle Bay Exploration Park** (www.turtlebay.org; 840 Auditorium Dr, Redding; adult/child 4-12yr $14/10; ⏲9am-5pm in summer, 9am-4pm Wed-Sat, from 10am Sun in winter), a kid-friendly science center.

Eight miles west of Redding on Hwy 299 (the Trinity Scenic Byway) is the **Whiskeytown National Recreation Area**, home of Whiskeytown Lake, a vast reservoir with hiking, camping and several sandy beaches. The **visitor center** (☎530-246-1225; ⏲9am-6pm summer, 10am-4:30pm winter) has maps, permits and information. **Weaverville**, another 35 miles west, is the launching point for mountains, and a lovely detour from Redding. The **Weaverville Ranger Station** (☎530-623-2121; 210 N Main St, Weaverville; ⏲8am-5pm Mon-Fri, to 4:30pm Sat) issues backcountry permits to surrounding **Trinity Alps**, some of the most pristine wilderness in California.

North of Redding, I-5 crosses deep-blue **Shasta Lake**, California's biggest reservoir, which is surrounded by hiking trails and RV parks. High in the limestone megaliths at the north end of the lake are the prehistoric caves of **Lake Shasta Caverns** (www.lakeshastacaverns.com; adult/child 3-11yr $22/13; ⏲tours 9am-4pm). Tours come with a pontoon ride.

Dunsmuir is a teeny historic railroad town, a bit down on its luck due to the crummy economy, but distinguished with a healthy scene for culture and cuisine. If for no other reason, stop to fill your bottle from the public fountains; Dunsmuir claims it's got the best H_20 on earth.

Gorgeous **Mt Shasta town** lures climbers, burnouts and back-to-nature types, all of whom revere the majestic mountain that looms overhead with varying degrees of mystical and physical engagement. **Mt Shasta visitor center** (☎530-926-4865; www.mtshastachamber.com; 300 Pine St, Mt Shasta; ⏲9am-5:30pm Mon-Thu, to 6pm Fri & Sat, to 4pm Sun) is a useful info hub.

Everitt Memorial Hwy climbs the mountain to 7900ft; to access it, simply head east from town on Lake St and keep going. Ten-thousand-foot-plus climbs require a $20 Summit Pass from the **Mt Shasta Ranger Station** (☎530-926-4511; 204 W Alma St, Mt Shasta; ⏲8am-4:30pm Mon-Sat). Campers note: even in summer, temperatures on the mountain drop below freezing.

Sleeping & Eating

The best option in this part of the state is to camp. Midcentury motels are abundant in all but the remote northeast. Redding has the most chain lodging, but clustered near major thoroughfares, it can be noisy.

Railroad Park Resort BOUTIQUE HOTEL **$$**
(☎800-974-7245; www.rrpark.com; d from $115; ❄📶🏊) The most memorable indoor stay is in a wood-paneled caboose, off I-5 just south of Dunsmuir.

Sengthongs THAI **$$**
(www.sengthongs.com; 5855 Dunsmuir Ave; mains $15-22; ⏲5-9pm Thu-Mon) An excellent Thai restaurant; also hosts live music in an adjoining room.

DON'T MISS

SIERRA NEVADA PARKS

Bodie State Historic Park (p997) A real gold-rush ghost town

Mono Lake (p997) Unearthly, mysterious-looking mineral formations

Ancient Bristlecone Pine Forest (p997) The world's oldest living trees

Manzanar National Historic Site (p997) Uncensored history of WWII-era internment camps

Mammoth Mountain (p996) Lofty winter sports and mountain biking

Getting There & Around

Amtrak (www.amtrak.com) services Redding and Dunsmuir; **Greyhound** (800-231-2222; www.greyhound.com) buses serve Redding and Yreka. By car, San Francisco to Redding is 215 miles (four hours). For updated road conditions call **Siskiyou County** (530-842-4438).

NORTHEAST CORNER

Site of one of the last major Indian wars and a half-million years of volcanic destruction, **Lava Beds National Monument** is a quiet monument to centuries of turmoil. This park's got it all: lava flows, craters, cinder and spatter cones, and more than 500 lava tubes. It was the site of the Modoc War, and Native Americans maintain a strong presence here today – their ancestors' petroglyphs adorn some cave walls. Info, maps and flashlights (for cave exploring) are available at the **visitor center** (530-667-8113; www.nps.gov/labe; 1 Indian Well; 8am-6pm May-Oct, to 5pm Nov-Sep). Nearby is the park's only **campground** (campsites $10). The simple sites (no showers) are suitable for tents and small RVs.

Just north, the **Klamath Basin National Wildlife Refuges** consists of six separate refuges. This is a prime stopover on the Pacific Flyway and an important wintering site for bald eagles. The **visitor center** (http://klamathbasinrefuges.fws.gov; 4009 Hill Rd; 8am-4:30pm Mon-Fri, 10am-4pm Sat & Sun) is along the road to Lava Beds Monument on Hwy 161. Self-guided 10-mile auto tours (free) of the Lower Klamath and Tule Lake reserves provide excellent viewing. For commercial services, go to Klamath Falls, OR, just over the border.

Modoc National Forest blankets over 3000 sq miles of California's northeast. Camping is free and no reservations are accepted, though permits are required for campfires. **Medicine Lake**, 14 miles south of Lava Beds Monument on Hwy 49, is a pristine, gleaming blue crater lake surrounded by pine forest, hulking volcanic formations and cool, secluded campgrounds (also free). Twenty-four miles east of Alturas, on the California–Nevada border, is the high desert of **Surprise Valley**, which is the gateway to the wild **Warner Mountains** – possibly the least visited range in the state.

The impressive **Lassen Volcanic National Park** (per car $10, campsites $10-18) has hydrothermal sulfur pools and cauldrons with names like 'Devil's Kitchen.' At 10,462ft, Lassen Peak is the world's largest plug-dome volcano. The park has two entrances with visitor centers: the smaller on Hwy 44 at Manzanita Lake, and a newly remodeled one off Hwy 89, where **park headquarters** (530-595-4444; www.nps.gov/lavo; 8am-4:30pm Jul-Sep, Mon-Fri Oct-Jun) is located. Hwy 89 through the park is open to cars from June to October (and to cross-country skiers in winter).

SIERRA NEVADA

The mighty Sierra Nevada – baptized the 'Range of Light' by naturalist John Muir – is California's backbone. This 400-mile phalanx of craggy peaks, chiseled and gouged by glaciers and erosion, both welcomes and challenges outdoors enthusiasts. Cradling three national parks (Yosemite, Sequoia and Kings Canyon), the Sierra is a magical wonderland of both wilderness and superlatives, embracing the contiguous USA's highest peak (Mt Whitney), North America's tallest waterfall and the world's biggest trees.

Yosemite National Park

There's a reason why everybody's heard of it: the granite-peak heights are dizzying, the mist from thunderous waterfalls drenching, the Technicolor wildflower meadows amazing, and the majestic, hulking silhouettes of El Capitan and Half Dome almost shocking

Yosemite Valley

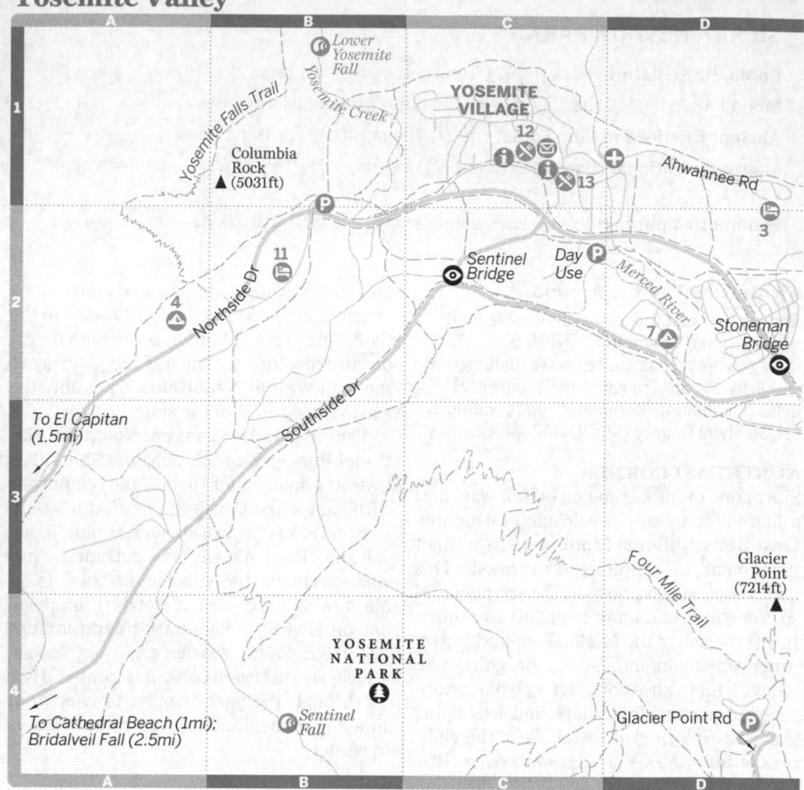

against a crisp blue sky. It's a landscape of dreams, relentlessly surrounding us oh-so-small people on all sides. Then, alas, the hiss and belch of another tour bus, disgorging dozens, rudely breaks the spell. While staggering crowds can't be ignored, these rules will shake most of 'em:

» Avoid summer in the valley. Spring's best, especially when waterfalls gush in May. Autumn is blissfully peaceful, and snowy winter days can be magical too.

» Park your car and leave it – simply by hiking a short distance up almost any trail, you'll lose the car-dependent majority of visitors.

» To hell with jet lag. Get up early, or go for moonlit hikes and do unforgettable stargazing.

Sights

Yosemite's entrance fee ($20 per car, $10 on bicycle, motorcycle or foot) is valid for seven days and includes a free map and helpful newspaper guide. The primary entrances are loctaed at: Arch Rock (Hwy 140), South Entrance (Hwy 41), Big Oak Flat (Hwy 120 west) and Tioga Pass (Hwy 120 east). Open seasonally, Hwy 120 traverses the park as Tioga Rd, connecting Yosemite Valley with Hwy 395 in the Eastern Sierra Nevada.

Overrun, traffic-choked Yosemite Village is home to the park's main visitor center, museum, general store and many other services. Curry Village is another Yosemite Valley hub, offering showers, wi-fi and outdoor equipment rental and sales, including for camping. Along scenic Tioga Rd, high-altitude Tuolumne (pronounced *twol*-uh-mee) Meadows draws hikers, backpackers and climbers to the park's northern region. Wawona, near the southern entrance, has a pioneer history village, golf course and giant sequoias.

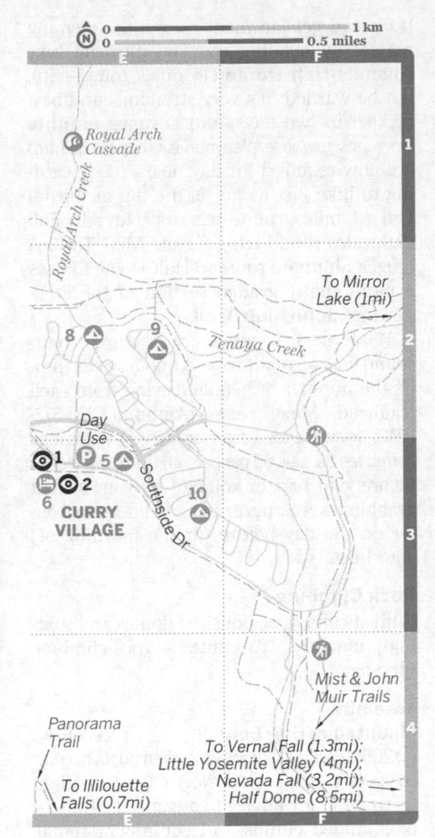

Yosemite Valley

Activities, Courses & Tours

1 Curry Village Ice Rink E3
2 Yosemite Mountaineering School E3

Sleeping

3 Ahwahnee Hotel D2
4 Camp 4 Campground A2
5 Campground Reservation Office E3
6 Curry Village E3
7 Housekeeping Camp D2
8 Lower Pines Campground E2
9 North Pines Campground E2
10 Upper Pines Campground E3
11 Yosemite Lodge at the Falls B2

Eating

Ahwahnee Dining Room .... (see 3)
Degnan's Deli .... (see 12)
12 Degnan's Loft C1
Mountain Room .... (see 11)
13 Village Store C1

YOSEMITE VALLEY

From the ground up, this dramatic valley cut by the meandering Merced River is song-inspiring: rippling green meadowgrass; stately pines; cool, impassive pools reflecting looming granite monoliths and cascading, glacier-cold white-water ribbons.

You can't ignore monumental **El Capitan** (7569ft), an El Dorado for rock climbers, while toothed **Half Dome** (8842ft) is Yosemite's spiritual centerpiece. The classic photo-op is up Hwy 41 at **Tunnel View**. Sweat it out and you'll get better views – sans crowds – from the **Inspiration Point Trail** (2.6 miles round-trip), starting near the tunnel. Early or late in the day, head up the 2-mile round-trip trail to **Mirror Lake** to catch the ever-shifting reflection of Half Dome in the still waters, full only in spring and early summer.

Spring snowmelt turns the valley's famous waterfalls into thunderous cataracts; most are reduced to a mere trickle by late summer. **Yosemite Falls** is North America's tallest, dropping 2425ft in three tiers. A wheelchair-accessible trail leads to the bottom of this cascade or, for solitude and different perspectives, you can trek the grueling switchback trail to the top (7.2 miles round-trip). No less impressive are nearby **Bridalveil Fall** and other waterfalls scattered throughout the valley. A strenuous staircase climb beside **Vernal Fall** leads you, gasping, right to the top edge of the falls for a vertical view – look for rainbows in the clouds of mist.

GLACIER POINT & WAWONA

Rising 3200ft above the valley floor, dramatic **Glacier Point** (7214ft) practically puts you at eye level with Half Dome. It's about an hour's drive from Yosemite Valley up Glacier Point Rd (usually open late May to mid-November) off Hwy 41, or a strenuous hike along the **Four Mile Trail** (actually, 4.8 miles one way) or the less-crowded, waterfall-strewn **Panorama Trail** (8.5 miles one way). To avoid backtracking, reserve a seat on the hikers' shuttle bus.

At Wawona, a 45-minute drive south of Yosemite Valley, drop by the **Pioneer Yosemite History Center**, with its covered bridge, pioneer cabins and historic Wells Fargo office. Further south, wander giddily in the

IMPASSABLE TIOGA PASS

Hwy 120 is the only road connecting Yosemite National Park with the Eastern Sierra, climbing through Tioga Pass (9945ft). Most California maps mark this road 'closed in winter,' which, while literally true, is also misleading. Tioga Rd is usually closed from the first heavy snowfall in October or November until May or June. If you are planning a trip through Tioga Pass in spring, you'll likely be out of luck. The earliest date that the road through the pass is plowed is April 15, yet it has only opened in April once since 1980. In 1998 it didn't open until July 1! Call ☎209-372-0200 or check www.nps.gov/yose/planyourvisit/conditions.htm for current road and weather conditions.

Mariposa Grove, home of the 1800-year-old Grizzly Giant and other giant sequoias.

TUOLUMNE MEADOWS

A 90-minute drive from Yosemite Valley, Tuolumne Meadows (8600ft) is the Sierra Nevada's largest subalpine meadow. It's a vivid contrast to the valley, with wildflower fields, azure lakes, ragged granite peaks and domes, and cooler temperatures. Hikers and climbers will find a paradise of options; swimming and picnicking by lakes are also popular. Access is via scenic Tioga Rd (Hwy 120), which follows a 19th-century wagon road and older Native American trading route. West of the meadows and **Tenaya Lake**, stop at **Olmsted Point** for epic vistas of Half Dome.

HETCH HETCHY

It's the site of perhaps the most controversial dam in US history. Despite not existing in its natural state, Hetch Hetchy Valley remains pretty and mostly crowd-free. It's a 40-minute drive northwest of Yosemite Valley. **Wapama Falls**, approached via a 5-mile round-trip hike across the dam and through a tunnel, lets you get thrillingly close to an avalanche of water crashing down into the sparkling reservoir. In spring, you'll get drenched.

Activities

Hiking & Backpacking

With over 800 miles of varied hiking trails, you're spoiled for choice. Easy valley floor trails can get jammed; escape the teeming masses by heading up. The ultimate hike summits **Half Dome** (14 miles round-trip), but be warned: it's very strenuous and best tackled in two days, and advance **permits** (www.nps.gov/yose/planyourvisit/hdpermits.htm) are now required for day hikes. It's rewarding to hike just as far as the top of **Vernal Fall** (3 miles round-trip) or **Nevada Fall** (5.8 miles round-trip) via the **Mist Trail**. A longer, alternate route to Half Dome follows a more gently graded section of the long-distance **John Muir Trail**.

Wilderness permits are required year-round for overnight trips. A quota system limits the number of people leaving from each trailhead. Make **reservations** (☎209-372-0740; www.nps.gov/yose/planyourvisit/wpres.htm; permit fee $5, plus $5 per person) up to 24 weeks before your trip, or you can try your luck at grabbing a free permit at a wilderness center on the day before (or the morning of) your hike.

Rock Climbing

With sheer spires, polished domes and soaring monoliths, Yosemite is rock-climbing nirvana.

Yosemite Mountaineering School ROCK CLIMBING
(☎209-372-8344; www.yosemitemountaineering.com; Curry Village; ⌚Apr-Nov) Offers topflight instruction for novice to advanced climbers, plus guided climbs and equipment rental. During peak summer season, it also operates at Tuolumne Meadows.

Winter Sports

Badger Pass SKIING
(☎209-372-8430; www.badgerpass.com; lift ticket adult/child $42/23; ⌚9am-4pm mid-Dec–late Mar) Gentle slopes are perfect for beginning skiers and snowboarders. Cross-country skiers can schuss along 25 miles of groomed tracks and 90 miles of marked trails, which are also great for snowshoers. Equipment rental and lessons are available.

Curry Village Ice Rink SKATING
(adult/child $8/6, skate rental $3) At Curry Village in Yosemite Valley.

Sleeping & Eating

Concessionaire **Delaware North Companies** (DNC; ☎801-559-4884; www.yosemitepark.com) has a monopoly on park lodging and eating establishments, including mostly forgettable food courts, cafeteria buffets and snack bars. All park accommodations, campgrounds and eateries are shown on the free map and newspaper guide given out to visitors as they enter the park. Lodging reservations (available up to 366 days in advance) are essential from May to September. In summer, DNC sets up simple canvas-tent cabins at riverside **Housekeeping Camp** (cabins $93) in Yosemite Valley, busy **Tuolumne Meadows Lodge** (cabins $107) and serene **White Wolf Lodge** (cabins $99-120) off Tioga Rd. Tuolumne Meadows is about a 90-minute drive northeast of the valley, while White Wolf is an hour away.

Curry Village CABINS **$$**
(Yosemite Valley; tent cabins $112-120, cabins without/with bath $127/168, cottage r $191;) With a nostalgic summer-camp atmosphere, Curry Village has hundreds of helter-skelter units scattered beneath towering evergreens. Tent cabins resemble Civil War army barracks with scratchy wool blankets; wooden cabins are smaller but cozy.

Yosemite Lodge at the Falls MOTEL **$$$**
(Yosemite Valley; r $191-218;) Spacious motel-style rooms have patios or balconies overlooking Yosemite Falls, meadows or the parking lot. Fork into grass-fed steaks, river trout and organic veggies at the lodge's Mountain Room (dinner mains $17 to $35), open nightly (no reservations). The food court has a decent range of cafeteria fare and the casual lounge has a convivial open-pit fireplace.

Wawona Hotel HISTORIC HOTEL **$$$**
(Wawona; r without/with bath incl breakfast $147/217;) Filled with character, this Victorian-era throwback has wide porches, manicured lawns and a golf course. Half the thin-walled rooms share baths. The romantic dining room with vintage details serves three meals a day (dinner mains $19 to $30). Wawona is about a 45-minute drive south of the valley.

Ahwahnee Hotel HISTORIC HOTEL **$$$**
(Yosemite Valley; r from $449;) Sleep where Charlie Chaplin, Eleanor Roosevelt and JFK bedded down at this national historic landmark, built in 1927. Sit a spell by the roaring fireplace beneath soaring sugar-pine timbers. Skip the formal dining room, serving overpriced Californian fare (dinner mains $26 to $46), for the lobby bar with its small plates and inspired cocktails.

Degnan's Deli & Loft DELI, PIZZERIA **$**
(Yosemite Village; mains $6-10; deli 7am-5pm year-round, restaurant 5-9pm Mon-Fri, to 9pm Sat & Sun Apr-Oct) Grab a custom-made deli sandwich and bag of chips downstairs before hitting the trail. After dark, head upstairs for cold brewskies and crispy pizzas.

Camping

All campgrounds have bearproof lockers and campfire rings; most have potable water.

In summer, most campgrounds are noisy and booked to bulging, especially **North Pines** (tent & RV sites $20; Apr-Sep), **Lower Pines** (tent & RV sites $20; Mar-Oct) and **Upper Pines** (tent & RV sites $20; year-round) in Yosemite Valley; and **Tuolumne Meadows** (tent & RV sites $20; Jul-late Sep) off Tioga Rd, a 90-minute drive northeast of the valley.

Camp 4 (shared tent sites per person $5; year-round), a rock climber's hangout in the valley, and **Bridalveil Creek** (tent & RV sites $14; Jul-early Sep), a 45-minute drive south of the valley off Glacier Point Rd, are first-come, first-served and often full by noon, especially on weekends. Also 45 minutes south is pretty riverside **Wawona** (tent & RV sites $20; year-round).

Looking for a quieter, more rugged experience? Try smaller primitive spots like **Tamarack Flat** (tent sites $10; Jul-Sep), **Yosemite Creek** (tent sites $10; Jul–mid-Sep) and **Porcupine Flat** (tent & RV sites $10; Jul-Sep) off Tioga Rd.

OUTSIDE YOSEMITE NATIONAL PARK

Gateway towns that sometimes have lodgings include Fish Camp, Oakhurst, El Portal, Midpines, Mariposa, Groveland and Lee Vining.

Yosemite Bug Rustic Mountain Resort CABINS, HOSTEL **$**
(209-966-6666; www.yosemitebug.com; 6979 Hwy 140, Midpines; dm $25, tent cabins $45-75, r $75-155, cabins with shared bath $65-100;)

YOSEMITE CAMPING RESERVATIONS

In summer, many campgrounds require **reservations** (518-885-3639; www.recreation.gov), which are available starting five months in advance. Campsites routinely sell out online within *minutes*. See www.nps.gov/yose/planyourvisit/camping.htm for sale dates.

Tucked into a forest about 25 miles west of Yosemite Valley, this mountain hostelry hosts globetrotters who dig the clean rooms, yoga studio and gorgeous spa, shared kitchen access and laundry. The cafe's fresh, organic and vegetarian-friendly meals (dinner mains $8.50 to $18) get raves.

TOP CHOICE **Evergreen Lodge** RESORT **$$$**
(209-379-2606; www.evergreenlodge.com; 33160 Evergreen Rd, Groveland; tents $75-110, cabins $175-350;) Near the entrance to Hetch Hetchy, this classic 90-year-old resort lets roughing-it guests cheat with comfy, prefurnished tents and deluxe mountain cabins. Outdoor recreational activities abound, with equipment rentals available. There's a general store, tavern with a pool table and a restaurant (dinner mains $18 to $28) serving three hearty meals every day.

Narrow Gauge Inn INN **$$$**
(559-683-7720; www.narrowgaugeinn.com; 48571 Hwy 41, Fish Camp; r incl breakfast $145-220; restaurant 5:30-9pm Wed-Sun Apr-Oct;) Swiss chalet-esque, this small inn has 26 comfy rooms, each with balcony or patio, and the Yosemite Mountain Sugar Pine steam railway next door. The 'buffalo bar' is authentic, and elk, venison and rib-eye appear on the Euro-Cal menu. It's 4 miles south of the park.

Information

Yosemite Village, Curry Village and Wawona stores all have ATMs. Drivers should fill up the tank before entering the park, or buy high-priced gas at Wawona or Crane Flat year-round or at Tuolumne Meadows in summer. Cell phone service is spotty throughout the park; Verizon and AT&T have some coverage. Pay internet kiosks are available adjacent to Degnan's Deli, and at Yosemite Lodge, which also has fee-based wi-fi.

Curry Village Lounge (Curry Village, behind registration office) Free wi-fi.

Mariposa County Public Library Wawona (Chilnualna Falls Rd; 1-6pm Mon-Fri, 10am-3pm Sat); Yosemite Valley (Girls Club Bldg, 58 Cedar Ct, Yosemite Valley; 8:30am-11:30am Mon, 2-5pm Tue, 8:30am-12:30pm Wed, 4-7pm Thu) Free internet terminals available.

Valley Wilderness Center (209-372-0745; Yosemite Village; 7:30am-5pm, shorter winter hr) Backcountry permits and bear-canister rentals; also available seasonally at Wawona, Tuolumne Meadows and Big Oak Flat.

Yosemite Medical Clinic (209-372-4637; Ahwahnee Dr, Yosemite Valley; 9am-7pm, emergencies 24hr) Also runs a dental clinic.

Yosemite Valley Visitor Center (209-372-0299; www.nps.gov/yose; Yosemite Village; 9am-7:30pm, shorter winter hr) Smaller visitor centers at Wawona, Tuolumne Meadows and Big Oak Flat are open seasonally.

Getting There & Around

The nearest Greyhound and Amtrak stations are in Merced. **YARTS** (209-388-9589; www.yarts.com) buses travel from Merced to the park along Hwy 140, stopping at towns along the way. In summer, YARTS buses run from the valley to Mammoth Lakes along Hwy 120. One-way tickets including the park-entry fee cost $13 from Merced, $15 from Mammoth Lakes.

Free shuttle buses loop around Yosemite Valley and, in summer, the Tuolumne Meadows and Wawona areas. DNC runs hikers' buses from the valley to Tuolumne Meadows (one way/round-trip $14.50/23) or Glacier Point (one way/round-trip $25/41). Bike rentals (per hour/day $10/28) are available at Yosemite Lodge and Curry Village, both in the valley. In winter, valley roads are plowed and the highways to the parks are kept open (except Tioga Rd/Hwy 120) – although snow chains may be required – and a free twice-daily shuttle bus connects Yosemite Valley with Badger Pass.

Sequoia & Kings Canyon National Parks

In these neighboring parks, the famous rust-red giant sequoia trees are bigger – up to 30 stories high! – and more numerous than anywhere else in the Sierra Nevada. Tough and fire-charred, they'd easily swallow two freeway lanes each. Giant, too, are the mountains – including Mt Whitney (14,505ft), the tallest peak in the lower 48 states. Finally, there is the giant Kings Canyon, carved out of granite by ancient glaciers and a powerful river. These are what lure the vast majority of 1.6 million annual visitors here; however, for quiet, solitude and close-up sightings of wildlife, including black bears, hit the trail to quickly lose yourself in the epic wilderness.

Sights

Sequoia was designated a national park in 1890; Kings Canyon, in 1940. Though distinct, the two parks operate as one unit with a single admission fee (valid for seven days) of $20 per car, $10 on motorcycle, bicycle or foot. For updates and general info, call 559-565-3341 or check the park website (www.nps.gov/seki).

From the south, Hwy 198 enters Sequoia National Park beyond the town of Three Rivers at Ash Mountain, from where it ascends the zigzagging Generals Hwy. From the west, Hwy 180 leads to the Big Stump entrance near Grant Grove before plunging into Kings Canyon.

SEQUOIA NATIONAL PARK

We dare you to try hugging the trees in **Giant Forest**, a 3-sq-mile grove protecting the park's most gargantuan specimens; the world's biggest is the **General Sherman Tree**. With sore arms and sticky sap fingers, lose the crowds by venturing onto any of the many forested trails (bring a map).

Giant Forest Museum MUSEUM
(☎559-565-4480; Generals Hwy; ⊙9am-5pm mid-May–late May & mid-Aug–mid-Oct, to 6pm late May–late Jun, to 7pm late Jun–mid-Aug, sometimes to 4pm mid-Oct–mid-May) Four miles south of Lodgepole Village, a number of hiking trails start here, including a wheelchair-accessible route. For 360-degree views of the Great Western Divide, climb the steep quarter-mile staircase up **Moro Rock**.

Crystal Cave CAVE
(☎559-565-3759; www.sequoiahistory.org; Crystal Cave Rd; tours adult/child from $13/7; ⊙mid-May–late Oct) Discovered in 1918, the cave has marble formations estimated to be 10,000 years old. Tickets for the 45-minute basic tour are available at the Lodgepole and Foothills visitor centers, *not* at the cave. Bring a jacket.

Mineral King HISTORIC SITE
Worth a detour is Mineral King, a late-19th-century mining and logging camp ringed by craggy peaks and alpine lakes. The 25-mile one-way scenic drive – navigating almost 700 hair-raising hairpin turns – is usually open from late May to late October.

KINGS CANYON NATIONAL PARK & SCENIC BYWAY

North of Grant Grove Village, **General Grant Grove** brims with majestic giants. Beyond here, Hwy 180 begins its 35-mile descent into **Kings Canyon**, serpentining past chiseled rock walls laced with spring waterfalls. The road meets the Kings River, its roar ricocheting off granite cliffs soaring over 4000ft high, making this one of North America's deepest canyons.

Boyden Cavern CAVE
(☎559-965-8243; www.boydencavern.com; Hwy 180; 45min tour adult/child $13/8; ⊙May–mid-Nov) While smaller and less impressive than Crystal Cave in Sequoia National Park, the beautiful and whimsical formations here require no advance tickets.

Cedar Grove Village LANDMARK
The last outpost of civilization before the rugged grandeur of the Sierra Nevada backcountry. A popular day hike climbs 4 miles one way to roaring **Mist Falls** from Roads End; continue uphill alongside the river 2.5 more miles to **Paradise Valley**. A favorite of birders, an easy 1.5-mile nature trail loops around **Zumwalt Meadow**, just west of Roads End. Watch for rattlesnakes, black bear and mule deer.

Activities

Hiking is why people come here – with over 850 miles of marked trails to prove it. Cedar Grove and Mineral King offer the best backcountry access. Trails usually begin to open by mid-May, though there's hiking year-round in the Foothills area. Overnight backcountry trips require wilderness permits ($15), subject to a quota system in summer; for details, see www.nps.gov/seki/planyourvisit/wilderness.htm.

You can take a naturalist-led field trip with the **Sequoia Natural History Association** (☎559-565-3759; www.sequoiahistory.org). Horseback riding is offered at **Grant Grove Village** (☎559-335-9292) and the **Cedar Grove Pack Station** (☎559-565-3464). In summer,

SUPERSIZED FORESTS

In California you can stand under the world's oldest trees (ancient bristlecone pines) and its tallest (coast redwoods), but the record for biggest in terms of volume belongs to the giant sequoias *(Sequoiadendron giganteum)*. They grow only on the western slope of the Sierra Nevada range and are most abundant in Sequoia, Kings Canyon and Yosemite national parks. John Muir called them 'Nature's forest masterpiece,' and anyone who's ever craned their neck to take in their soaring vastness has probably done so with the same awe. These trees can grow 300ft tall and nearly 60ft in diameter, with bark up to 2ft thick. The Giant Forest Museum in Sequoia National Park has exhibits about the trees' unusual ecology.

cool off by swimming at Hume Lake, on national forest land off Hwy 180, and at riverside swimming holes in both parks. In winter, you can cross-country ski or snowshoe among the snow-draped giant sequoias. Equipment rental is available at Grant Grove Village and Wuksachi Lodge; for the best cross-country skiing and other winter sports, visit old-fashioned Montecito Sequoia Lodge, off the Generals Hwy between the two parks.

Sleeping & Eating

Outside Sequoia's southern entrance, several independent and chain motels line Hwy 198 through unexciting Three Rivers town.

Camping **reservations** (☎518-885-3639; www.recreation.gov) are accepted only at Lodgepole and Dorst in Sequoia National Park. The parks' dozen other campgrounds are first-come, first-served. Most have flush toilets; sites cost $10 to $20. Lodgepole, Azalea, Potwisha and South Fork are open year-round. Overflow camping is available in the surrounding Sequoia National Forest.

The markets in Grant Grove, Lodgepole and Cedar Grove have limited, pricey groceries; the latter two have snack bars serving burgers and basic meals for under $10, while Grant Grove has a simple restaurant and a cozy pizzeria. The Wuksachi Lodge's upscale **restaurant** (☎559-565-4070; dinner mains $18-38; ⊙7-10am, 11am-2:30pm & 5-9:45pm) is hit-or-miss.

John Muir Lodge & Grant Grove Cabins LODGE, CABINS **$$**
(☎559-335-5500; www.sequoia-kingscanyon.com; Hwy 180, Grant Grove Village; d $69-190;) The woodsy lodge has good-sized, if generic, rooms and a cozy lobby with a stone fireplace and board games. Oddly assorted cabin types range from thin-walled canvas tents to nicely furnished historical cottages with private bathrooms.

Cedar Grove Lodge MOTEL **$$**
(☎559-335-5500; www.sequoia-kingscanyon.com; Hwy 180, Cedar Grove Village; r $119-135; ⊙mid-May–mid-Oct;) The 21 motel-style rooms with common porches overlooking Kings River are simple and well worn, but they're still your best option down the canyon.

Montecito Sequoia Lodge RESORT **$$**
(☎559-565-3388; www.mslodge.com; 63410 Generals Hwy, btwn Sequoia & Kings Canyon national parks; d incl meals $119-169;) Basic, recently renovated rooms include all meals. Family-fun camps keep things raucous all summer long; in winter there's cross-country skiing lessons and 50 miles of groomed trails.

Wuksachi Lodge HOTEL **$$$**
(☎559-565-4070; www.visitsequoia.com; off Generals Hwy, 4 miles north of Lodgepole Village; r $215-335;) Don't be misled by the grand lobby – because oversized motel-style rooms are nothing to brag about.

Bearpaw High Sierra Camp CABINS **$$**
(www.visitsequoia.com; tent cabin & meals per person $175; ⊙mid-Jun–mid-Sep) An 11-mile back-country hike and unforgettable wilderness adventure.

Information

Lodgepole Village (☎559-565-4436; ⊙mid-Apr–mid-Oct), in Sequoia, and **Grant Grove Village** (☎559-565-4307; ⊙year-round), in Kings Canyon, are the main hubs. Both have visitor centers, post offices, markets, ATMs and public showers (summer only).

Foothills Visitor Center (☎559-565-3135) at Ash Mountain is open year-round. **Cedar Grove Visitor Center** (☎559-565-3793) and the **Mineral King Ranger Station** (☎559-565-3768) are open during summer. Check the free park newspaper for opening hours of visitor centers and other services.

Expensive gas is available at Hume Lake (year-round) and Stony Creek (summer only) outside park boundaries on national forest land.

Getting There & Around

In summer, free shuttle buses cover the Giant Forest and Lodgepole Village areas of Sequoia National Park, while the **Sequoia Shuttle** (☎877-287-4453; www.sequoiashuttle.com) connects the park with Three Rivers and Visalia (round-trip fare $15), with onward connections to Amtrak; reservations are required. Currently, there is no public transportation into Kings Canyon National Park.

Eastern Sierra

Vast, empty and majestic, here jagged peaks plummet down into the Great Basin desert, a dramatic juxtaposition that creates a potent scenery cocktail. Hwy 395 runs the entire length of the Sierra Nevada range, with turn-offs leading to pine forests, wildflower-strewn meadows, placid lakes, simmering hot springs and glacier-gouged canyons. Hikers, back-packers, mountain bikers, fishers and skiers love to escape here. The main visitor hubs are Mammoth Lakes and Bishop.

At **Bodie State Historic Park** (☎760-647-6445; www.parks.ca.gov; Hwy 270; adult/child $7/5; ⏰9am-6pm Jun-Aug, to 3pm Sep-May), a gold-rush ghost town is preserved in a state of 'arrested decay.' Weathered buildings sit frozen in time on a dusty, windswept plain. To get there, head east for 13 miles (the last three unpaved) on Hwy 270, about 7 miles south of Bridgeport. The access road is often snowed in during winter.

Further south, **Mono Lake** (www.monolake.org) is famous for its unearthly tufa towers, which rise from the alkaline water like drip sand castles. The best photo ops are from the south shore's **South Tufa Reserve** (adult/child $3/free). Off Hwy 395, **Mono Basin Scenic Area Visitor Center** (☎760-647-3044; ⏰8am-5pm mid-Apr–Nov) has excellent exhibits and schedules of guided walks and talks. From the nearby town of Lee Vining, Hwy 120 heads west into Yosemite National Park via the Tioga Pass.

Continuing south on Hwy 395, detour along the scenic 16-mile **June Lake Loop** or push on to **Mammoth Lakes**, a popular four-seasons resort guarded by 11,053ft **Mammoth Mountain** (☎760-934-2571, 24hr snow report 888-766-9778; www.mammothmountain.com; Minaret Rd; lift ticket adult/child $92/46), a top-notch skiing area. The slopes morph into a mountain-bike park in summer, when there's also camping, fishing and day hiking in the Mammoth Lakes Basin and Reds Meadow areas. Nearby are the near-vertical, 60ft-high basalt columns of **Devils Postpile National Monument** (☎760-934-2289; www.nps.gov/depo; shuttle fee adult/child $7/4), formed by volcanic activity. Hot-springs fans can soak in primitive pools off Benton Crossing Rd, 9 miles south of town, or view the geysering water at the **Hot Creek Geological Site** ⏰sunrise-sunset), 3 miles south. The **Mammoth Lakes Welcome Center & Ranger Station** (☎888-466-2666, 760-924-5500; www.visitmammoth.com; Hwy 203; ⏰8am-5pm) has maps and information about all of these places.

Further south, Hwy 395 descends into the Owens Valley, soon arriving in frontier-flavored **Bishop**, whose minor attractions include art galleries and an interesting railroad museum. Bishop provides access to the best fishing and rock climbing in the entire Eastern Sierra, and it's the main gateway for packhorse trips.

To check out some of the earth's oldest living things, budget a half-day for the thrilling trip up to the **Ancient Bristlecone Pine Forest** (☎760-873-2500; per car $5). These gnarled, otherworldly looking trees are found above 10,000ft on the slopes of the parched White Mountains, where you'd think nothing could grow. The oldest tree – called Methuselah – is estimated to be over 4700 years old. The road (usually open May to October) is paved to the visitor center at Schulman Grove, where there are hikes of varying lengths. From Hwy 395 in Big Pine, take Hwy 168 east for 12 miles and then head uphill another 10 miles from the marked turnoff.

Hwy 395 barrels on south to Independence and **Manzanar National Historic Site** (☎760-878-2194; www.nps.gov/manz; admission free; ⏰visitor center 9am-4:30pm, to 5:30pm Apr-Oct), which memorializes the war relocation camp where some 10,000 Japanese Americans were unjustly interned during WWII following the attack on Pearl Harbor. Interpretive exhibits and a short film vividly chronicle life at the camp.

South of here, in Lone Pine, you finally catch a glimpse of 14,505ft **Mt Whitney** (www.fs.usda.gov/inyo), the highest mountain in the lower 48 states. The heart-stopping, 11-mile scenic drive up **Whitney Portal Road** (closed in winter) is spectacular. Climbing the peak is hugely popular, but requires a permit issued on a lottery basis. West of Lone Pine, the bizarrely shaped boulders of the **Alabama Hills** have enchanted filmmakers of such Hollywood Western classics as *How the West Was Won* (1962). Peruse vintage memorabilia and movie posters at the **Museum of Lone Pine Film History** (☎760-876-9909; www.lonepinefilmhistorymuseum.org; 701 S Main St; admission $5; ⏰10am-6pm

SCENIC DRIVES IN THE SIERRA NEVADA

Tioga Road (Hwy 120; p992) Yosemite's rooftop of the world

Generals Highway (Hwy 198; p994) Historic byway past giant sequoias

Kings Canyon Scenic Byway (Hwy 180; p995) Dive into North America's deepest canyon

Eastern Sierra Scenic Byway (US 395; p996) Where snowy mountains overshadow the desert

Mon-Wed, to 7pm Thu-Sat, to 4pm Sun). At the Hwy 395/136 junction, the **Eastern Sierra InterAgency Visitor Center** (☎760-876-6222; www.fs.fed.us/r5/inyo; ⊙8am-5pm, extended summer hr) issues wilderness permits and dispenses information about regional parks, forests and deserts.

Sleeping

The Eastern Sierra is freckled with campgrounds. Backcountry camping requires a wilderness permit, reservable in advance or available at ranger stations. Bishop, Lone Pine and Bridgeport have the most motels. Mammoth Lakes has countless inns, B&Bs and condo and vacation rentals.

Tamarack Lodge & Resort RESORT **$$**
(☎760-934-2442; www.tamaracklodge.com; off Lake Mary Rd, Mammoth Lakes; r $99-169, cabins $169-599; @📶) In business since 1924, this woodsy lakeside resort offers lodge rooms and cabins with kitchens, ranging from very simple to simply deluxe, and some even have wood-burning stoves.

Redwood Motel MOTEL **$**
(☎760-932-7060; www.redwoodmotel.net; 425 Main St, Bridgeport; d from $59-89; ⊙Apr-Nov; ❄📶) Wacky farm animal sculptures give a cheerful welcome to this spotless motel. Your host will shower you with travel tips.

Whitney Portal Hostel HOSTEL **$**
(☎760-876-0030; www.whitneyportalstore.com; 238 S Main St, Lone Pine; dm/q $20/60; ❄@📶) The carpeted bunk-bed rooms are a popular launching pad for Whitney hikes, and public showers are available. Reserve two months ahead for July and August.

Chalfant House B&B **$$**
(☎760-872-1790; www.chalfanthouse.com; 213 Academy, Bishop; d incl breakfast $80-110; ❄📶) Lace curtains and Victorian accents swirl through the six rooms of this restored historic home.

Eating & Drinking

Good Life Café CALIFORNIAN **$**
(126 Old Mammoth Rd, Mammoth Lakes; mains $8-10; ⊙6:30am-3pm) Stomach-stuffing Mexican breakfasts, healthy veggie wraps, brawny burgers and big salad bowls make this place perennially popular.

TOP CHOICE **Whoa Nellie Deli** MODERN AMERICAN **$$**
(Hwys 120 & 395, Lee Vining; mains $8-19; ⊙7am-9pm mid-Apr–Oct) Great food in a gas station? Really, you gotta try this amazing kitchen, where chef Matt 'Tioga' Toomey serves up delicious fish tacos, wild buffalo meatloaf and other tasty morsels.

Raymond's Deli DELI **$**
(206 N Main St, Bishop; sandwiches $7-9; ⊙10am-6pm; ✎) A sassy den of kitsch, pinball and Pac-Man, it serves heaping sandwiches with names like 'When Pigs Fly,' 'Flaming Farm' and 'Soy U Like Tofu.' Kick back with a Lobotomy Bock.

Mammoth Brewing Company Tasting Room BREWERY
(☎760-934-7141; www.mammothbrewingco.com; 94 Berner St, Mammoth Lakes; ⊙10am-6pm) Free samples anyone? Try some of the dozen brews on tap, then buy some IPA 395 or Double Nut Brown to go.

Lake Tahoe

Shimmering in myriad blues and greens, Lake Tahoe is the nation's second-deepest lake. Driving around its spellbinding 72-mile scenic shoreline gives you quite a workout behind the wheel. The north shore is quiet and upscale; the west shore, rugged and old-timey; the east shore, undeveloped; and the south shore, busy and tacky with aging motels and flashy casinos. The horned peaks surrounding the lake, which straddles the California–Nevada state line, are four-seasons playgrounds.

Tahoe gets packed in summer, on winter weekends and holidays, when reservations are essential. **Lake Tahoe Visitors Authority** (☎800-288-2463; www.tahoesouth.com) and **North Lake Tahoe Visitors' Bureaus** (☎888-434-1262; www.gotahoenorth.com) can help with accommodations and tourist information. There's camping in **state parks** (☎800-444-7275; www.reserveamerica.com) and on **USFS lands** (☎877-444-6777; www.recreation.gov).

SOUTH LAKE TAHOE & WEST SHORE

With retro motels and eateries lining busy Hwy 50, South Lake Tahoe gets crowded. Gambling at Stateline's casino hotels, just across the Nevada border, attracts thousands, as does the world-class ski resort of **Heavenly** (☎775-586-7000; www.skiheavenly.com; 3860 Saddle Rd). In summer, a trip up Heavenly's gondola (adult/child $32/20) guarantees fabulous views of the lake and **Desolation Wilderness** (www.fs.fed.us/r5/ltbmu).

This starkly beautiful landscape of raw granite peaks, glacier-carved valleys and alpine lakes is a favorite with hikers. Get maps, information and overnight **wilderness permits** (per adult $5-10; www.recreation.gov) from the **USFS Taylor Creek Visitor Center** (530-543-2674; Hwy 89; daily May-Oct, winter hr vary). It's 3 miles north of the 'Y' intersection of Hwys 50/89, at **Tallac Historic Site** (tour $5; 10am-4:30pm mid-Jun–Sep, Fri & Sat only late May–mid-Jun), which preserves early-20th-century vacation estates. **Lake Tahoe Cruises** (800-238-2463; www.zephyrcove.com; adult/child from $39/15) ply the 'Big Blue' year-round. Back on shore, vegetarian-friendly **Sprouts** (3123 Harrison Ave; mains $6-10; 8am-9pm;) is a delish natural-foods cafe.

Hwy 89 threads northwest along the thickly forested west shore to **Emerald Bay State Park** (www.parks.ca.gov; per car/campsites $8/35; late May-Sep), where granite cliffs and pine trees frame a fjordlike inlet, truly sparkling green. A steep 1-mile trail leads down to **Vikingsholm Castle** (tours adult/child $5/3; 10:30am-4:30pm). From this 1920s Scandinavian-style mansion, the 4.5-mile **Rubicon Trail** ribbons north along the lakeshore past an old lighthouse and petite coves to **DL Bliss State Park** (www.parks.ca.gov; entry per car $8, campsites $35-45; late May-Sep), offering sandy beaches. Further north, **Tahoma Meadows B&B Cottages** (530-525-1553; www.tahomameadows.com; 6821 W Lake Blvd, Tahoma; d incl breakfast $109-269) rents darling country cabins (pet fee $20).

NORTH & EAST SHORES

The north shore's commercial hub, **Tahoe City** is great for grabbing supplies and renting outdoor gear. It's not far from **Squaw Valley USA** (530-583-6985; www.squaw.com; off Hwy 89), a megasized ski resort that hosted the 1960 Winter Olympics. Après-ski crowds gather for beer 'n' burgers at woodsy **Bridgetender Tavern** (www.tahoebridgetender.com; 65 W Lake Blvd; mains $8-12; 11am-11pm Sun-Thu, to midnight Fri & Sat) back in town, or fuel up on French toast and eggs Benedict at downhome **Fire Sign Cafe** (1785 W Lake Blvd; dishes $6-12; 7am-3pm).

In summer, swim or kayak at Tahoe Vista or Kings Beach. Spend a night at **Franciscan Lakeside Lodge** (530-546-6300; www.franciscanlodge.com; 6944 N Lake Blvd, Tahoe Vista; d $80-265;), where simple cabins, cottages and suites have kitchenettes. East of Kings Beach, which has cheap, filling lakeshore eateries, Hwy 28 barrels into Nevada. Try your luck at the gambling tables or catch a live-music show at the **Crystal Bay Club Casino** (775-831-0512; www.crystalbaycasino.com; 14 Hwy 28). But for more happening bars and bistros, drive further to **Incline Village**.

With pristine beaches, lakes and miles of multiuse trails, **Lake Tahoe-Nevada State Park** (http://parks.nv.gov/lt.htm; per car $7-12) is the east shore's biggest draw. Summer crowds splash in the turquoise waters of **Sand Harbor**. The 15-mile **Flume Trail** (775-749-5349; www.theflumetrail.com; trailhead bike rental $45-65, shuttle $5-10), a mountain biker's holy grail, starts further south at **Spooner Lake**.

TRUCKEE & AROUND

North of Lake Tahoe off I-80, Truckee is not in fact a truck stop but a thriving mountain town, with organic-coffee shops, trendy boutiques and dining in downtown's historical district. Ski bunnies have several area resorts to pick from, including glam **Northstar-at-Tahoe** (800-466-6784; www.northstarattahoe.com; off Hwy 267); kid-friendly **Sugar Bowl** (530-426-9000; www.sugarbowl.com; off Hwy 40), cofounded by Walt Disney; and **Royal Gorge** (530-426-3871; www.royalgorge.com; off I-80), paradise for cross-country skiers.

West of Hwy 89, Donner Summit is where the infamous Donner Party became trapped during the fierce winter of 1846–47. Led astray by their guidebook, less than half survived – by cannibalizing their dead friends. The grisly tale is chronicled at the museum inside **Donner Memorial State Park** (www.parks.ca.gov; Donner Pass Rd; per car/campsites $8/35; museum 9am-4pm year-round, campground mid-May–mid-Sep), where **Donner Lake** is popular with swimmers and windsurfers.

Ecoconscious **Cedar House Sport Hotel** (530-582-5655; www.cedarhousesporthotel.com; 10918 Brockway Rd; r incl breakfast $170-270;) is green building-certified, and has an outdoor hot tub and stylishly modern boutique rooms (pet fee $50). For live jazz and wine, **Moody's Bistro & Lounge** (530-587-8688; www.moodysbistro.com; 10007 Bridge St; dinner mains $18-40; 11:30am-9:30pm Sun-Thu, to 10pm Fri & Sat) sources locally ranched meats and seasonal produce. Down pints of 'Donner Party Porter' at **Fifty Fifty Brewing Co** (www.fiftyfiftybrewing.com; 11197 Brockway Rd) across the tracks.

Getting There & Around

South Tahoe Express (☎866-898-2463; www.southtahoeexpress.com) runs frequent shuttles from Nevada's **Reno-Tahoe International Airport** to Stateline (one way adult/child $27/15). **North Lake Tahoe Express** (☎866-216-5222; www.northlaketahoeexpress.com) connects Reno's airport with Truckee, Squaw Valley and north-shore towns (one way/round-trip $40/75).

Truckee's **Amtrak depot** (10065 Donner Pass Rd) has daily trains to Sacramento ($37, 4½ hours) and Reno ($15, 1½ hours), and twice-daily Greyhound buses to Reno ($18, one hour), Sacramento ($42, 2½ hours) and San Francisco ($40, six hours). Amtrak Thruway buses connect Sacramento with South Lake Tahoe ($34, three hours).

Tahoe Area Regional Transit (TART; ☎800-736-6365; www.laketahoetransit.com; single ride/24hr pass $1.75/3.50) runs local buses to Truckee and around the north and west shores. South Lake Tahoe is served by **BlueGO** (☎530-541-7149; www.bluego.org; single ride/day pass $2/6), which operates a summer-only trolley up the west shore to Tahoma, connecting with TART.

If you're driving, tire chains are often required in winter on I-80, US 50, Hwy 89 and Mt Rose Hwy, any or all of which may close during and after snowstorms.

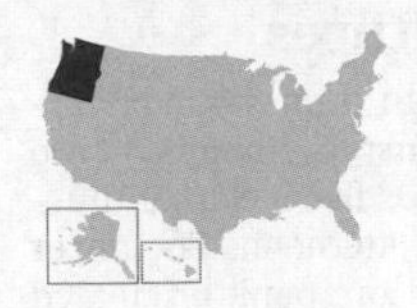

Pacific Northwest

Includes »

Washington 1007
Seattle 1007
Olympic Peninsula 1022
San Juan Islands 1027
North Cascades 1029
South Cascades 1031
Oregon 1034
Portland 1034
Willamette Valley 1046
Columbia River Gorge 1049
Oregon Cascades 1049
Oregon Coast 1056

Best Places to Eat

» Seeds Bistro & Bar (p1026)

» Allium (p1028)

» Paley's Place (p1041)

» New Sammy's Cowboy Bistro (p1054)

Best Places to Stay

» Sun Mountain Lodge (p1030)

» Ace Hotel – Portland (p1039)

» McMenamins Old St Francis School (p1051)

» Enzian Inn (p1029)

Why Go?

As much a state of mind as a geographical region, the US's northwest corner is a land of subcultures and new trends, where evergreen trees frame snow-dusted volcanoes, and inspired ideas scribbled on the back of napkins become tomorrow's business start-ups. You can't peel off the history in layers here, but you *can* gaze wistfully into the future in fast-moving, innovative cities such as Seattle and Portland, sprinkled with food carts, streetcars, microbrews, green belts, coffee connoisseurs and weird urban sculpture.

Ever since the days of the Oregon Trail, the Northwest has had a hypnotic lure for risk-takers and dreamers, and the metaphoric carrot still dangles. There's the air, so clean they ought to bottle it; the trees, older than many of Rome's Renaissance palaces; and the end-of-the-continent coastline, holding back the force of the world's largest ocean. Cowboys take note; it doesn't get much more 'wild' or 'west' than this.

When to Go

Seattle

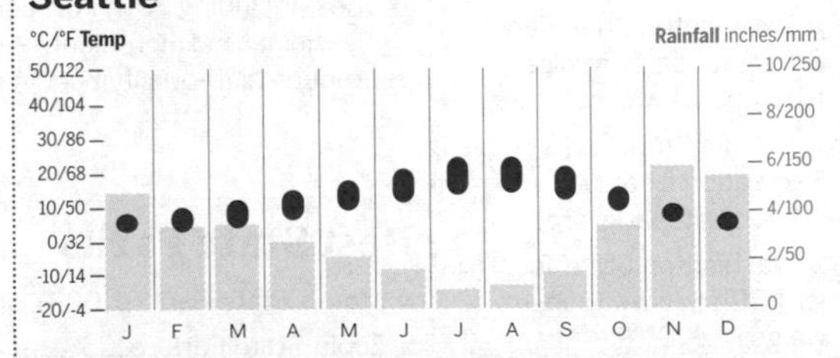

Jan-Mar Most reliable snow cover for skiing in the Cascades and beyond.

May Festival season: Portland Rose, Northwest Folklife, the Seattle International Film Festival.

Jul-Sep The best hiking window in-between the spring snowmelt and the first fall flurries.

DON'T MISS

Between them, the states of Washington and Oregon harbor four of the US's most spectacular national parks: Mt Rainier (established 1899), Crater Lake (1902), Olympic (1938) and North Cascades (1968).

Fast Facts

» Population: Seattle (608,660), Portland (583,770)

» Distances from Seattle: Portland (174 miles), Spokane (280 miles)

» Time zone: Pacific Standard

» States covered in this chapter: Washington, Oregon

Did You Know?

Over the winter of 1998–99, the Mt Baker ski resort in northwest Washington received 1140in of snow in a single season, the largest annual snowfall ever recorded.

Resources

» Washington State Parks & Recreation Commission (www.parks.wa.gov)

» Oregon State Parks & Recreation Dept (www.oregonstateparks.org)

» Washington State Tourism Office (www.tourism.wa.gov)

» Oregon Tourism Commission (www.traveloregon.com)

Grunge & Other Subcultures

Synthesizing Generation X angst with a questionable approach to personal hygiene, grunge first dive-bombed onto Seattle's music scene in the early 1990s like a clap of thunder on an otherwise dry and sunny afternoon. The anger had been fermenting for years. Hardcore punk originated in Portland in the late 1970s, led by resident contrarians the Wipers, whose antifashion followers congregated in legendary dive bars such as Satyricon. Another musical blossoming occurred in Olympia, where DIY-merchants Beat Happening invented 'lo-fi' and coyly mocked the corporate establishment. Scooping up the fallout of a disparate youth culture, Seattle quickly became grunge's pulpit, spawning bands like Pearl Jam, Soundgarden and Alice in Chains. The genre went global in 1991 when Nirvana's *Nevermind* album knocked Michael Jackson off the number-one spot, but the movement was never meant to be successful and the kudos quickly killed it. Since the mid '90s the Pacific Northwest has kept its subcultures largely to itself, though the music's no less potent or relevant.

MICROBREWERIES

'Beer connoisseurship' is a nationwide phenomenon these days, but the campaign to put a dash of flavor back into insipid commercially brewed beer was first ignited in that longstanding bastion of good taste, the Pacific Northwest, in the 1980s.

One of America's first microbreweries was the mercurial, if short-lived, Cartwright Brewing Company, set up in Portland in 1980. The nation's first official brewpub was the now defunct Grant's, which opened in the Washington city of Yakima in 1982. The trend went viral in 1984 with the inauguration of Bridgeport Brewing Company in Portland, followed a year later by Beervana's old-school brewing brothers Mike and Brian McMenamin, whose quirky beer empire still acts as a kind of personification of the craft-brewing business in the region.

Today the Pacific Northwest has over 200 microbreweries (including 30 in Portland alone), all of which take classic natural ingredients – malt, hops and yeast – to produce high-quality beer in small but tasty batches.

Best State Parks

» Moran State Park (p1028), on Orcas Island

» Ecola State Park (p1058), at Cannon Beach

» Deception Pass State Park (p1025), on Whidbey Island

» Fort Worden State Park (p1023), in Port Townsend

» Lime Kiln Point State Park (p1028), on San Juan Island

» Cape Blanco State Park (p1060), near Port Orford

» Smith Rock State Park (p1051), near Bend

History

Native American societies, including the Chinook and the Salish, had long-established coastal communities by the time Europeans arrived in the Pacific Northwest in the 18th century. Inland, on the arid plateaus between the Cascades and the Rocky Mountains, the Spokane, Nez Percé and other tribes thrived on seasonal migration between river valleys and temperate uplands.

Three hundred years after Columbus landed in the New World, Spanish and British explorers began probing the northern Pacific coast, seeking the fabled Northwest Passage. In 1792 Capt George Vancouver was the first explorer to sail the waters of Puget Sound, claiming British sovereignty over the entire region. At the same time, an American, Captain Robert Gray, found the mouth of the Columbia River. In 1805 the explorers Lewis and Clark crossed the Rockies and made their way down the Columbia to the Pacific Ocean, extending the US claim on the territory.

In 1824 the British Hudson's Bay Company established Fort Vancouver in Washington as headquarters for the Columbia region. This opened the door to waves of settlers but had a devastating impact on the indigenous cultures, assailed as they were by the double threat of European diseases and alcohol.

In 1843 settlers at Champoeg, on the Willamette River south of Portland, voted to organize a provisional government independent of the Hudson's Bay Company, thereby casting their lot with the USA, which formally acquired the territory from the British by treaty in 1846. Over the next decade, some 53,000 settlers came to the Northwest via the 2000-mile Oregon Trail.

Arrival of the railroads set the region's future. Agriculture and lumber became the pillars of the economy until 1914, when WWI and the opening of the Panama Canal brought increased trade to Pacific ports. Shipyards opened along Puget Sound, and the Boeing aircraft company set up shop near Seattle.

Big dam projects in the 1930s and '40s provided cheap hydroelectricity and irrigation. WWII offered another boost for aircraft manufacturing and shipbuilding, and agriculture continued to thrive. In the postwar period, Washington's population, especially around Puget Sound, grew to twice that of Oregon. But hydroelectricity production and the massive irrigation projects along the Columbia have nearly destroyed the river's ecosystem, and logging has also left its scars, especially in Oregon. The environment remains a contentious issue in the Northwest; flash points are the logging of old-growth forests and the destruction of salmon runs in streams and rivers.

In the 1980s and '90s, the economic emphasis shifted again with the rise of the high-tech industry, embodied by Microsoft in Seattle and Intel in Portland. The region has also reinvigorated its eco credentials,

THE PACIFIC NORTHWEST IN...

Four Days

Hit the ground running in **Seattle** with the main sights, Pike Place Market and the Seattle Center, on days one and two. On day three, take the train down to **Portland** where you can rent a bike and spin around the bars, cafes, food carts and nightlife.

One Week

Add in some extra sights along the I-5 corridor, such as Washington state capital **Olympia**, the pastoral fields of **Whidbey Island** or the magnificent University of Oregon campus in left-field **Eugene**. You may also have time for day sorties to spectacular **Cannon Beach** on the Oregon Coast, or the historic seaport of **Port Townsend** on the Olympic Peninsula.

Two Weeks

It's time to visit some national parks. **Mount Rainier** is doable in a day trip from Seattle, while **Crater Lake** can be combined with a trip to **Ashland** and its Shakespeare Festival. Don't miss the ethereal **San Juan Islands** up near the watery border with Canada, or **Bend**, Oregon, the region's biggest outdoor draw. If time allows, head across the Cascades to the dramatically different east. **Walla Walla** is wine-quaffing heaven, while **Steens Mountain** is a lightly trodden wilderness that feels as remote as parts of Alaska.

Pacific Northwest Highlights

1. Use human-powered bikes and kayaks to get around the quieter corners of the **San Juan Islands** (p1027)
2. Admire trees older than Europe's Renaissance castles in Washington's **Olympic National Park** (p1022)
3. View one of the greatest pages of American history in the Columbia River's **Lewis & Clark National & State Historical Parks** (p1057)
4. Watch the greatest outdoor show in the Pacific Northwest in Seattle's theatrical **Pike Place Market** (p1007)
5. Ride a bike around clean, green, serene **Portland** (p1034), energized by beer, coffee and food-cart pizza
6. Descend on **Bend** (p1051) in Oregon to review the most multifarious list of outdoor activities in the state

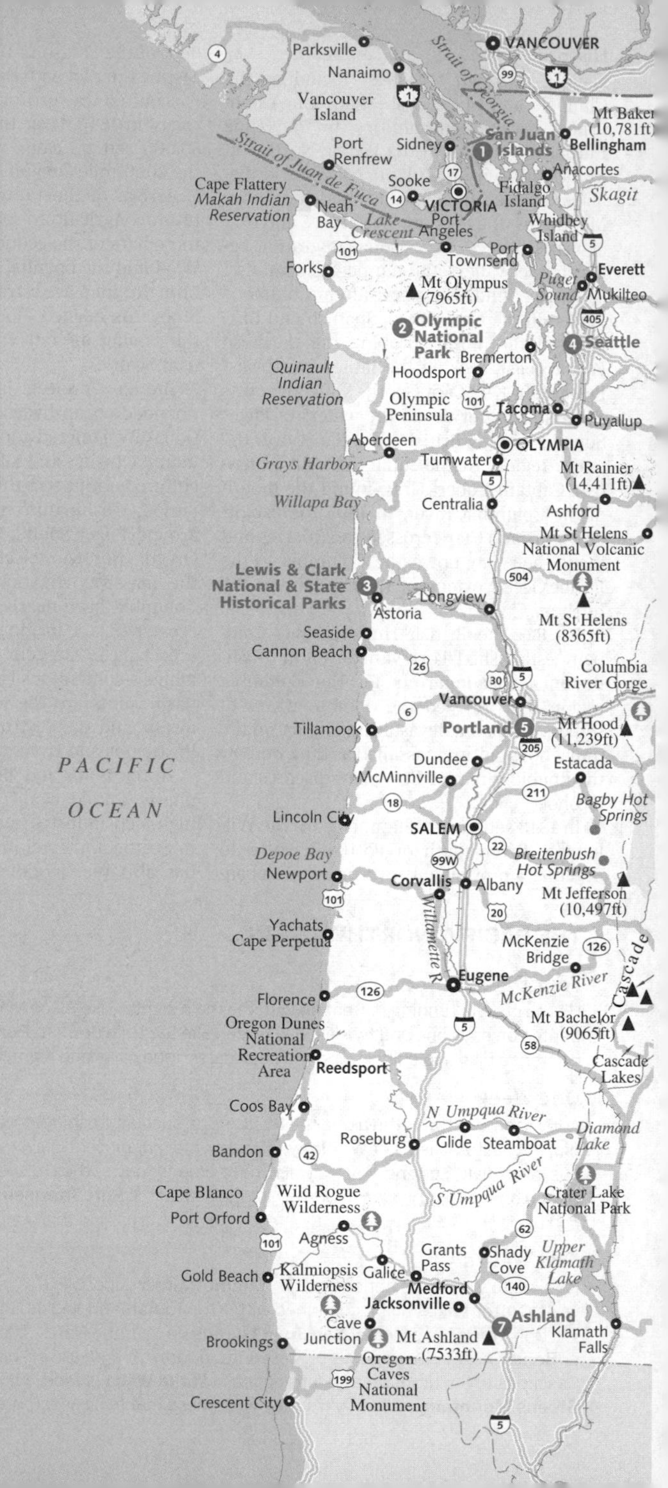

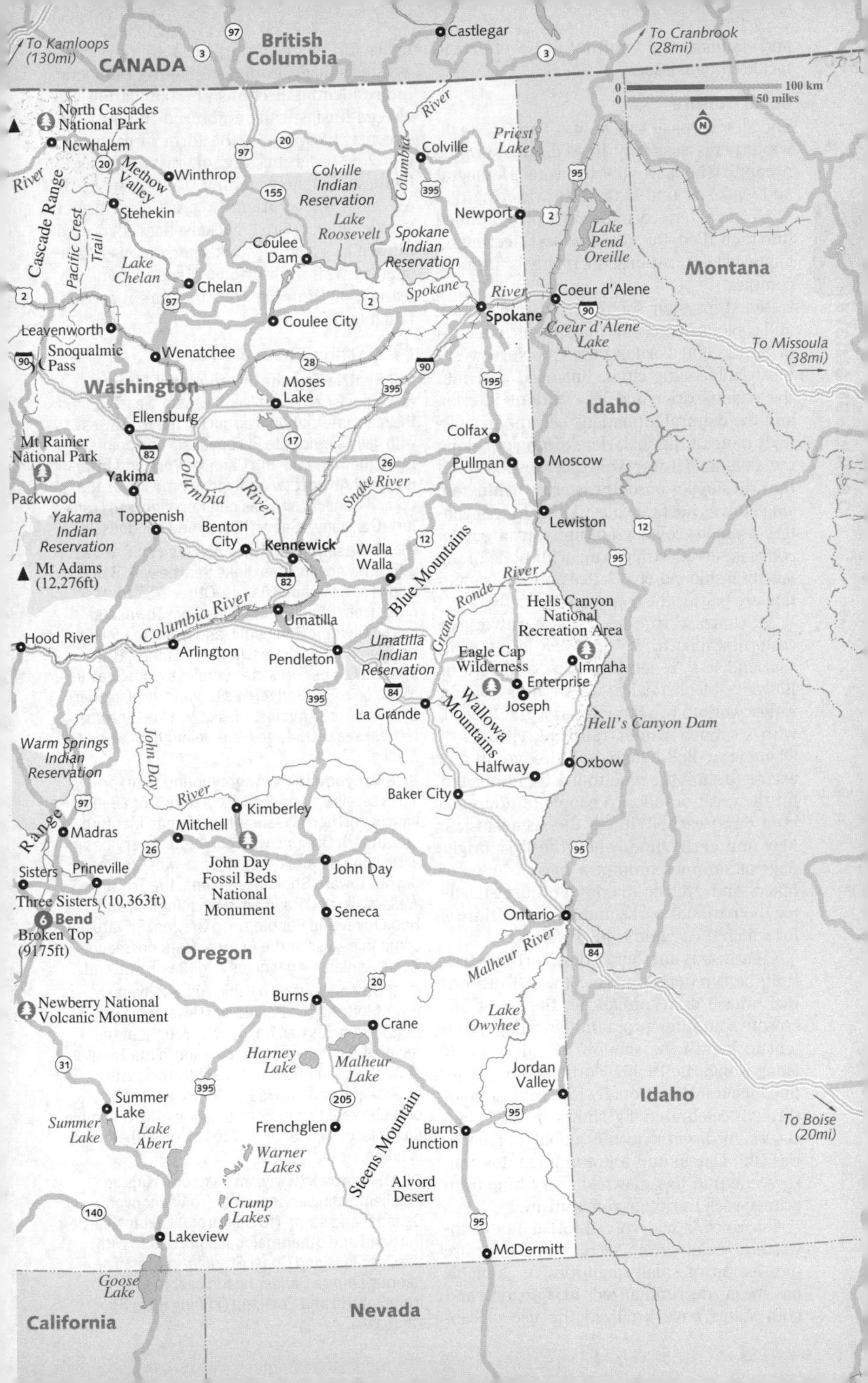

To Kamloops (130mi)
CANADA
British Columbia
Castlegar
To Cranbrook (28mi)
100 km
50 miles
North Cascades National Park
Newhalem
Methow Valley
Winthrop
Stehekin
Cascade Range
Pacific Crest Trail
River
Lake Chelan
Chelan
Colville Indian Reservation
Columbia River
Colville
Priest Lake
Newport
Lake Roosevelt
Spokane Indian Reservation
Coulee Dam
Lake Pend Oreille
Montana
Spokane River
Spokane
Coeur d'Alene
Coeur d'Alene Lake
Coulee City
Leavenworth
Snoqualmie Pass
Wenatchee
Washington
Moses Lake
To Missoula (38mi)
Idaho
Ellensburg
Mt Rainier National Park
Yakima
Columbia River
Colfax
Pullman
Moscow
Snake River
Packwood
Yakama Indian Reservation
Toppenish
Benton City
Kennewick
Lewiston
Walla Walla
Blue Mountains
Mt Adams (12,276ft)
Grand Ronde River
Columbia River
Umatilla
Hells Canyon National Recreation Area
Hood River
Arlington
Pendleton
Umatilla Indian Reservation
Eagle Cap Wilderness
Imnaha
Enterprise
Joseph
La Grande
Wallowa Mountains
Hell's Canyon Dam
Warm Springs Indian Reservation
John Day River
Oxbow
Halfway
Baker City
Kimberley
Range
Madras
Mitchell
Sisters
Prineville
John Day
John Day Fossil Beds National Monument
Three Sisters (10,363ft)
Seneca
Bend
Broken Top (9175ft)
Ontario
Oregon
Malheur River
Burns
Newberry National Volcanic Monument
Crane
Lake Owyhee
Harney Lake
Malheur Lake
Jordan Valley
Idaho
Summer Lake
Summer Lake
Lake Abert
Frenchglen
Steens Mountain
Burns Junction
To Boise (20mi)
Warner Lakes
Alvord Desert
Crump Lakes
Lakeview
McDermitt
Goose Lake
California
Nevada

and stands at the forefront of US efforts to tackle climate issues.

Local Culture

The stereotypical image of a Pacific Northwesterner is a casually dressed, latte-supping urbanite who drives a Prius, votes Democrat and walks around with an unwavering diet of Nirvana-derived indie rock programmed into their iPod. But, as with most fleeting regional generalizations, the reality is far more complex.

Noted for their sophisticated cafe culture and copious microbrew pubs, the urban hubs of Seattle and Portland are the Northwest's most emblematic cities. But head east into the region's drier and less verdant interior, and the cultural affiliations become increasingly more traditional. Here, strung out along the Columbia River Valley or nestled amid the arid steppes of southeastern Washington, small towns host raucous rodeos, tourist centers promote cowboy culture, and a cup of coffee is served 'straight up' with none of the fancily fashioned chai lattes and icy frappés that are par for the course in Seattle.

In contrast to the USA's hardworking eastern seaboard, life out West is more casual and less frenetic than in New York or Boston. Idealistically, Westerners would rather work to live than live to work. Indeed, with so much winter rain, the citizens of Olympia or Bellingham will dredge up any excuse to shun the nine-to-five treadmill and hit the great outdoors a couple of hours (or even days) early. Witness the scene in late May and early June, when the first bright days of summer prompt a mass exodus of hikers and cyclists making enthusiastically for the national parks and wilderness areas for which the region is justly famous.

Creativity is another strong Northwestern trait, be it redefining the course of modern rock music or reconfiguring the latest Microsoft computer program. No longer content to live in the shadow of California or Hong Kong, the Pacific Northwest has redefined itself internationally in recent decades through celebrated TV shows (*Frasier* and *Grey's Anatomy*), iconic global personalities (Bill Gates) and a groundbreaking music scene that has spawned everything from grunge rock to riot grrrl feminism.

Tolerance is widespread in Pacific Northwestern society, from recreational drug use (possession of small quantities of cannabis has been decriminalized in Oregon, and both states have legalized the use of cannabis for medical purposes) to physician-assisted suicide. Commonly voting Democrat in presidential elections, the population has also enthusiastically embraced the push for 'greener' lifestyles in the form of car clubs, recycling programs, organic restaurants and biodiesel whale-watching tours. An early exponent of ecofriendly practices, former Seattle mayor Greg Nickels has advocated himself as a leading spokesperson on climate change, while salubrious Portland regularly features high in lists of America's most sustainable cities.

ℹ Getting There & Around

AIR Seattle-Tacoma International Airport (www.portseattle.org/seatac), aka 'Sea-Tac,' is the main international airport in the Northwest, with daily services to Europe, Asia and points throughout the US and Canada. **Portland International Airport** (www.flypdx.com) serves the US and Canada, and has nonstop flights to Frankfurt (Germany), Seoul (Korea) and London (UK).

BOAT Washington State Ferries (WSF; www.wsdot.wa.gov/ferries) links Seattle with Bainbridge and Vashon Islands. Other WSF routes cross from Whidbey Island to Port Townsend on the Olympic Peninsula, and from Anacortes through the San Juan Islands to Sidney, BC. Victoria Clipper operates services from Seattle to Victoria, BC, and ferries to Victoria also operate from Port Angeles. Alaska Marine Highway ferries (see p1064) go from Bellingham, WA, to Alaska.

BUS Greyhound (www.greyhound.com) provides service along the I-5 corridor from Bellingham in northern Washington down to Medford in southern Oregon, with connecting services across the US and Canada. East–west routes fan out toward Spokane, Yakima, the Tri-Cities, Walla Walla and Pullman in Washington, and Hood River and Pendleton in Oregon. Private bus companies also serve Astoria, Cannon Beach, Bend, Ashland, Anacortes and Port Townsend.

CAR Driving your own vehicle is a convenient way of touring the Pacific Northwest. Major rental agencies can be found throughout the region. I-5 is the major north–south road artery. In Washington I-90 heads east from Seattle to Spokane and into Idaho. In Oregon I-84 branches east from Portland along the Columbia River Gorge via Pendleton to link up with Boise in Idaho.

TRAIN Amtrak (www.amtrak.com) runs an excellent train service north (to Vancouver, Canada) and south (to California) linking Seattle, Portland and other major urban centers with the *Cascades* and *Coast Starlight* routes. The famous *Empire Builder* heads east to Chicago from Seattle and Portland (joining up in Spokane, WA).

WASHINGTON

Divided in two by the spinal Cascade Mountains, Washington isn't so much a land of contrasts as a land of polar opposites. Centered on Seattle, the western coastal zone is wet, urban, liberal and famous for its fecund evergreen forests; splayed to the east between the less celebrated cities of Spokane and Yakima, the inland plains are arid, rural, conservative and covered by mile after mile of scrublike steppe.

Of the two halves it's the west that harbors most of the quintessential Washington sights, while the more remote east is less heralded, understated and full of surprises.

WASHINGTON FACTS

» **Nickname** Evergreen State

» **Population** 6,724,540

» **Area** 71,342 sq miles

» **Capital city** Olympia (population 46,480)

» **Other cities** Seattle (population 608,660), Spokane (population 208,915), Yakima (population 91,065), Bellingham (population 80,000), Walla Walla (population 31,730)

» **Sales tax** 6.5%

» **Birthplace of** singer and actor Bing Crosby (1903–77), guitarist Jimi Hendrix (1942–70), computer geek Bill Gates (b 1955), political commentator Glen Beck (b 1964), musical icon Kurt Cobain (1967–94)

» **Home of** Mt St Helens, Microsoft, Starbucks, Nordstrom, Evergreen State College

» **Politics** Democrat governor, Democrat senators, Democrat in presidential elections since 1988

» **Famous for** grunge rock, coffee, *Grey's Anatomy*, *Twilight*, volcanoes, apples, wine, precipitation

» **State vegetable** Walla Walla sweet onion

» **Driving distances** Seattle to Portland 174 miles, Spokane to Port Angeles 365 miles

Seattle

Combine the brains of Portland, Oregon, with the beauty of Vancouver, BC, and you'll get something approximating Seattle. It's hard to believe that the Pacific Northwest's largest metropolis was considered a 'secondary' US city until the 1980s, when a combination of bold innovation and unabashed individualism turned it into one of the dot-com era's biggest trendsetters, spearheaded by an unlikely alliance of coffee-supping computer geeks and navel-gazing musicians. Reinvention is the buzzword these days in a city where grunge belongs to the history books and Starbucks is just one in a cavalcade of precocious indie coffee providers eking out their market position.

Surprisingly elegant in places and coolly edgy in others, Seattle is notable for its strong neighborhoods, top-rated university, monstrous traffic jams and proactive city mayors who harbor green credentials. Although it has fermented its own pop culture in recent times, it has yet to create an urban mythology befitting Paris or New York, but it does have 'the Mountain.' Better known as Rainier to its friends, Seattle's unifying symbol is a 14,411ft mass of rock and ice, which acts as a perennial reminder to the city's huddled masses that raw wilderness and potential volcanic catastrophe are never far away.

Sights

DOWNTOWN

TOP CHOICE **Pike Place Market** MARKET

(www.pikeplacemarket.org) Take a bunch of small-time businesses and sprinkle them liberally around a spatially challenged waterside strip amid crowds of bohemians, restaurateurs, tree-huggers, bolshie students, artists, vinyl lovers and artisans. The result: Pike Place Market, a cavalcade of noise, smells, personalities, banter and urban theater that's almost London-like in its cosmopolitanism. In operation since 1907, Pike Place Market is famous for many things, not least its eye-poppingly fresh fruit and vegetables, its anarchistic shops and its loquacious fish-throwing fishmongers. Improbably, it also spawned the world's first Starbucks, which is still there (if you can get past the tourists) knocking out the old 'joe' from under its original brown logo. But, more importantly, Pike Place is Seattle in a bottle, a wonderfully 'local' experience that highlights the city for what it really is: all-embracing, eclectic and proudly singular.

Seattle

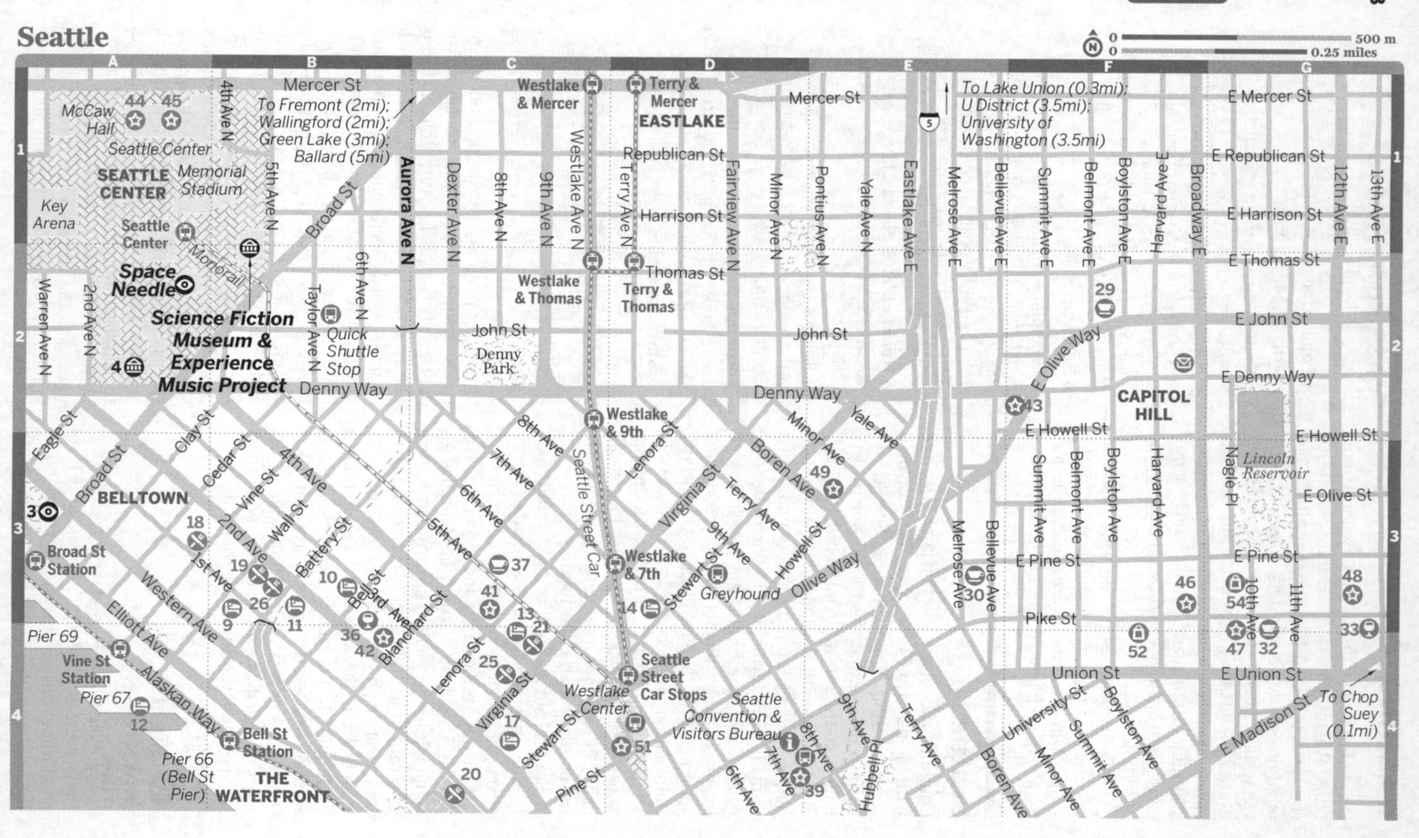

500 m
0.25 miles
McCaw Hall
Seattle Center
SEATTLE CENTER
Memorial Stadium
Key Arena
Seattle Center
Monorail
Space Needle
Science Fiction Museum & Experience Music Project
To Fremont (2mi); Wallingford (2mi); Green Lake (3mi); Ballard (5mi)
Quick Shuttle Stop
Westlake & Mercer
Terry & Mercer
EASTLAKE
Westlake & Thomas
Terry & Thomas
Denny Park
To Lake Union (0.3mi); U District (3.5mi); University of Washington (3.5mi)
CAPITOL HILL
Lincoln Reservoir
Westlake & 9th
Seattle Street Car
Westlake & 7th
Greyhound
Seattle Street Car Stops
Westlake Center
Seattle Convention & Visitors Bureau
BELLTOWN
Broad St Station
Vine St Station
Bell St Station
Pier 69
Pier 67
Pier 66 (Bell St Pier)
THE WATERFRONT
To Chop Suey (0.1mi)
Mercer St
E Mercer St
Republican St
E Republican St
Harrison St
E Harrison St
Thomas St
E Thomas St
John St
E John St
Denny Way
E Denny Way
E Olive Way
E Howell St
E Olive St
E Pine St
Pike St
Union St
E Union St
E Madison St
University St
Warren Ave N
2nd Ave N
4th Ave N
5th Ave N
Taylor Ave N
6th Ave N
Aurora Ave N
Dexter Ave N
8th Ave N
9th Ave N
Westlake Ave N
Terry Ave N
Fairview Ave N
Minor Ave N
Pontius Ave N
Yale Ave N
Eastlake Ave E
Melrose Ave E
Bellevue Ave E
Summit Ave E
Belmont Ave E
Boylston Ave E
Harvard Ave E
Broadway E
12th Ave E
13th Ave E
Nagle Pl
10th Ave
11th Ave
Melrose Ave
Bellevue Ave
Summit Ave
Belmont Ave
Boylston Ave
Harvard Ave
Broad St
Eagle St
Clay St
Cedar St
Vine St
Wall St
Battery St
Bell St
Blanchard St
Lenora St
Virginia St
Stewart St
Pine St
Howell St
Olive Way
Western Ave
Elliott Ave
Alaskan Way
1st Ave
2nd Ave
3rd Ave
4th Ave
5th Ave
6th Ave
7th Ave
8th Ave
9th Ave
Terry Ave
Boren Ave
Minor Ave
Yale Ave
Hubbell Pl

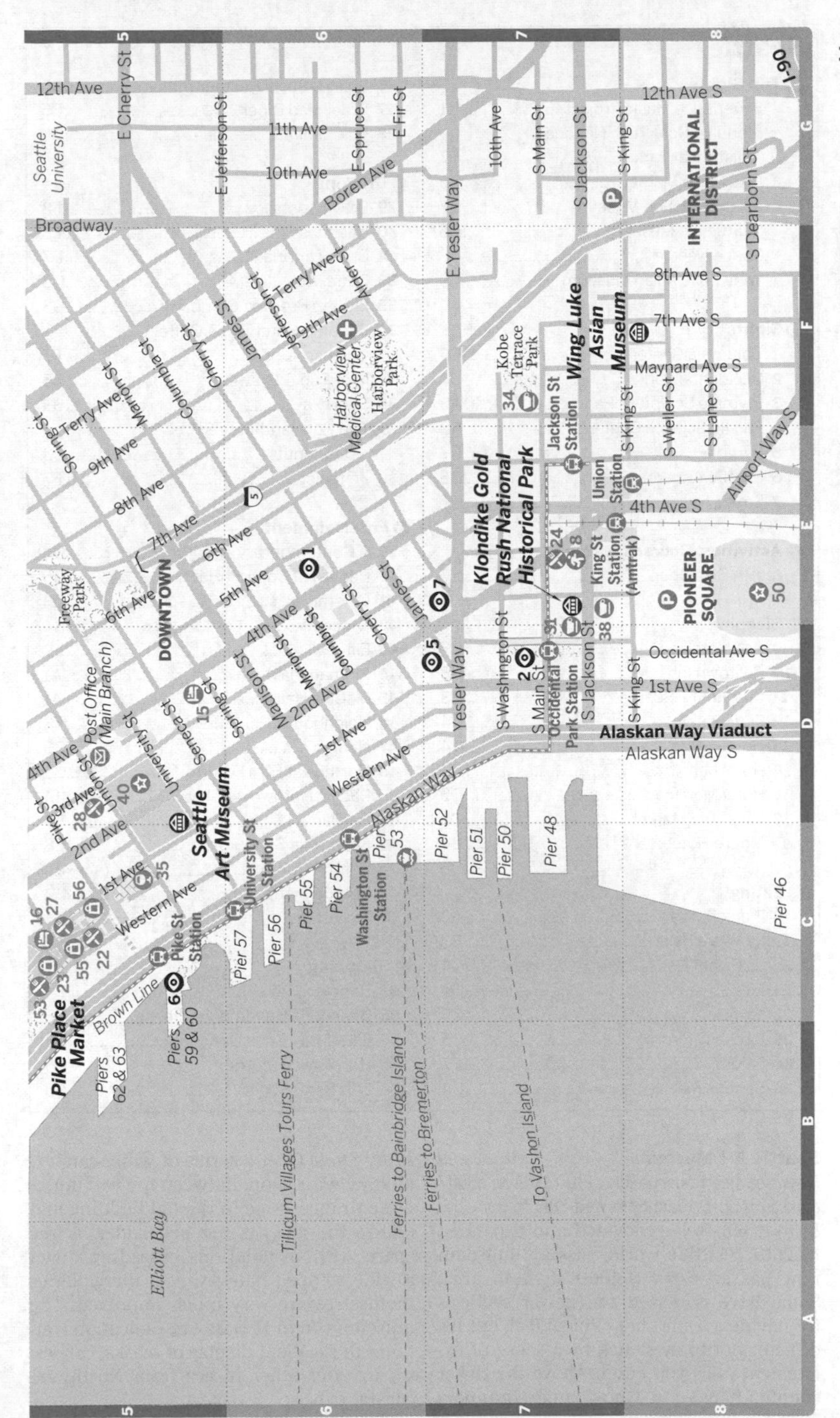
Pike Place Market
Seattle Art Museum
DOWNTOWN
Klondike Gold Rush National Historical Park
Wing Luke Asian Museum
PIONEER SQUARE
INTERNATIONAL DISTRICT
Seattle University
Freeway Park
Harborview Medical Center
Harborview Park
Kobe Terrace Park
Post Office (Main Branch)
Elliott Bay
Piers 62 & 63
Piers 59 & 60
Pier 57
Pier 56
Pier 55
Pier 54
Pier 53
Pier 52
Pier 51
Pier 50
Pier 48
Pier 46
Brown Line
Pike St Station
University St Station
Washington St Station
Occidental Park Station
Jackson St Station
Union Station
King St Station (Amtrak)
Alaskan Way Viaduct
Alaskan Way
Alaskan Way S
Western Ave
1st Ave
2nd Ave
3rd Ave
4th Ave
5th Ave
6th Ave
7th Ave
8th Ave
9th Ave
Terry Ave
Boren Ave
Broadway
10th Ave
11th Ave
12th Ave
12th Ave S
E Cherry St
E Jefferson St
E Spruce St
E Fir St
E Yesler Way
Yesler Way
Pike St
Union St
University St
Seneca St
Spring St
Madison St
Marion St
Columbia St
Cherry St
James St
Jefferson St
Alder St
S Washington St
S Main St
S Jackson St
S King St
S Weller St
S Lane St
S Dearborn St
Occidental Ave S
1st Ave S
4th Ave S
Maynard Ave S
7th Ave S
8th Ave S
Airport Way S
I-90
Tillicum Villages Tours Ferry
Ferries to Bainbridge Island
Ferries to Bremerton
To Vashon Island

Seattle

Top Sights

Experience Music Project B1
Klondike Gold Rush National Historical Park E7
Pike Place Market C5
Science Fiction Museum B2
Seattle Art Museum D5
Space Needle A2
Wing Luke Asian Museum F8

Sights

1 Columbia Center E6
2 Occidental Park D7
3 Olympic Sculpture Park A3
4 Pacific Science Center A2
5 Pergola D7
6 Seattle Aquarium C5
7 Smith Tower E7

Activities, Courses & Tours

8 JRA Bike Shop E7

Sleeping

9 Ace Hotel B3
10 Belltown Inn B3
11 City Hostel Seattle B3
12 Edgewater A4
13 Hotel Andra C4
14 Hotel Max D3
15 Hotel Monaco D5
16 Inn at the Market C5
17 Moore Hotel C4

Eating

18 Black Bottle A3
19 La Vita é Bella B3
20 Le Pichet C4
21 Lola C4
22 Lowells C5
23 Piroshky Piroshky C5
24 Salumi E7
25 Serious Pie C4
26 Shiro's Sushi Restaurant B3
27 Steelhead Diner C5
28 Wild Ginger D5

Drinking

29 B&O Espresso F2
30 Bauhaus E3
31 Caffè Umbria D7
32 Caffé Vita G3
33 Elysian Brewing Company G3
34 Panama Hotel Tea & Coffee House F7
35 Pike Pub & Brewery C5
36 Shorty's B3
37 Top Pot Hand-Forged Doughnuts C3
38 Zeitgeist E7

Entertainment

39 A Contemporary Theater D4
40 Benaroya Concert Hall D5
41 Cinerama C3
42 Crocodile B4
43 Elite F2
44 Intiman Playhouse A1
45 McCaw Hall A1
46 Neighbours F3
47 Neumo's G3
48 Northwest Film Forum G3
Pacific Nothwest Ballet .... (see 45)
49 Re-Bar E3
50 Seahawks Stadium E8
Seattle Opera .... (see 45)
Seattle Symphony .... (see 45)
51 TicketMaster D4

Shopping

52 Babeland F4
53 Beecher's Handmade Cheese C5
54 Elliott Bay Book Company G3
55 Holy Cow Records C5
56 Left Bank Books C5

Seattle Art Museum MUSEUM
(www.seattleartmuseum.org; 1300 1st Ave; adult/child $15/12; ⏲10am-5pm Wed-Sun, to 9pm Thu & Fri) Extensively renovated and expanded in 2007, Seattle's world-class art museum now has an extra 118,000 sq ft in area. Some have criticized the newer sections for having a somewhat clinical feel, but it's difficult not to be struck by a sense of excitement once you enter. Above the ticket counter hangs Cai Guo-Qiang's *Inopportune: Stage One,* a series of white cars exploding with neon. Between the two museum entrances (one in the old building and one in the new) is the 'art ladder,' a free space with installations cascading down a wide stepped hallway. And the galleries themselves are very much improved. The museum's John H Hauberg Collection contains an excellent display of masks, canoes, totems and other pieces from Northwest coastal tribes.

Belltown NEIGHBORHOOD

Where industry once fumed, glassy condos now rise in the thin walkable strip of Belltown. The neighborhood gained a reputation for trend-setting nightlife in the 1990s and two of its bar-clubs, the Crocodile and Shorty's, can still claim legendary status. Then there are the restaurants – over 100 of them – and not all are prohibitively expensive.

FREE **Olympic Sculpture Park** PARK

(2901 Western Ave; ⏰sunrise-sunset) After sharing lattes with the upscale condo crowd in Belltown, you can stroll over to the experimental new sculpture park (an outpost of the Seattle Art Museum) overlooking Elliott Bay.

PIONEER SQUARE

Pioneer Sq is Seattle's oldest quarter, which isn't saying much if you're visiting from Rome or London. Most of the buildings here date from just after the 1889 fire (a devastating inferno that destroyed 25 city blocks, including the entire central business district), and are referred to architecturally as Richardson Romanesque, a redbrick revivalist style in vogue at the time. In the early years, the neighborhood's boom-bust fortunes turned its arterial road, Yesler Way, into the original 'skid row' – an allusion to the skidding logs that were pulled downhill to Henry Yesler's pier-side mill. When the timber industry fell on hard times, the road became a haven for the homeless and its name subsequently became a byword for poverty-stricken urban enclaves countrywide.

Thanks to a concerted public effort, the neighborhood avoided being laid to waste by the demolition squads in the 1960s and is now protected in the Pioneer Sq–Skid Rd Historic District.

The quarter today mixes the historic with the seedy, while harboring art galleries, cafes and nightlife. Its most iconic building is the 42-story **Smith Tower** (cnr 2nd Ave S & Yesler Way; observation deck adult/child $7.50/5; ⏰10am-dusk), completed in 1914 and, until 1931, the tallest building west of the Mississippi. Other highlights include the 1909 **Pergola**, a decorative iron shelter reminiscent of a Parisian Metro station, and **Occidental Park**, containing totem poles carved by Chinook artist Duane Pasco.

FREE **Klondike Gold Rush National Historical Park** MUSEUM

(www.nps.gov/klse; 117 S Main St; ⏰9am-5pm) A shockingly good museum with exhibits, photos and news clippings from the years of the 1897 Klondike gold rush, when a Seattle-on-steroids acted as a fueling depot for prospectors bound for the Yukon in Canada. It would cost $10 anywhere else; in Seattle it's free!

INTERNATIONAL DISTRICT

For 'international' read Asian. East of Pioneer Sq, the shops and businesses are primarily Chinese, Vietnamese and Filipino.

Wing Luke Asian Museum MUSEUM

(www.wingluke.org; 719 S King St; adult/child $12.95/8.95; ⏰10am-5pm Tue-Sun) Relocated and refurbished in 2008, the Wing Luke examines Asian and Pacific American culture, focusing on prickly issues such as Chinese settlement in the 1880s and Japanese internment camps in WWII. There are also art exhibits and a preserved immigrant apartment. Guided tours are available and recommended.

SEATTLE CENTER

The remnants of the futuristic 1962 World's Fair hosted by Seattle and subtitled Century 21 Exposition are now into their sixth decade at the Seattle Center. And what remnants! The fair was a major success, attracting 10 million visitors, running a profit (rare for the time) and inspiring a skin-crawlingly kitschy Elvis movie, *It Happened at the World's Fair* (1963).

Space Needle LANDMARK

(www.spaceneedle.com; adult/child $18/11; ⏰9:30am-11pm Sun-Thu, to 11:30pm Fri & Sat) Standing apart from the rest of Seattle's skyscrapers, the needle is the city's undisputed modern symbol. Built for the World's

HIGHER THAN THE SPACE NEEDLE

Everyone makes a rush for the iconic Space Needle, but it's neither the tallest nor the cheapest of Seattle's glittering viewpoints. That honor goes to the sleek, tinted-windowed **Columbia Center** (701 5th Ave), built in 1985, which at 932ft high is the loftiest building in the Pacific Northwest. From the plush **observation deck** (adult/child $5/3; ⏰8:30am-4:30pm Mon-Fri) on the 73rd floor you can look down on ferries, cars, islands, roofs and – ha, ha – the Space Needle!

Fair in 1962, it was the highest structure in Seattle at the time, topping 605ft, though it has since been easily usurped. Visitors make for the 520ft-high observation station with a revolving restaurant.

Monorail TRAIN
(www.seattlemonorail.com; adult/child $4/1.50; ⌚9am-11pm) Floating like a low-flying spaceship through Belltown, this 1.5-mile experiment in mass transit was so ahead of its time that some American cities have still to cotton on to it. The slick raised train runs every 10 minutes daily from downtown's Westlake Center to a station next to the Experience Music Project.

TOP CHOICE **Experience Music Project** MUSEUM
(EMP; www.empmuseum.org; 325 5th Ave N; adult/child $15/12; ⌚10am-5pm Sep-May, to 7pm Jun-Aug) This modern architectural marvel or monstrosity (depending on your view), the brainchild of Microsoft cofounder Paul Allen, is a dream fantasy to anybody who has picked up an electric guitar and plucked the opening notes to 'Stairway to Heaven.' The ultramodern Frank Gehry building houses 80,000 music artifacts, many of which pay homage to Seattle's local music icons. There are handwritten lyrics by Nirvana's Kurt Cobain, a Fender Stratocaster demolished by Jimi Hendrix, Ray Charles' first album and the stage suits worn by power pop duo Heart.

Science Fiction Museum MUSEUM
(www.sfhomeworld.org; 325 5th Ave N; adult/child $15/12; ⌚10am-5pm Sep-May to 8pm Jun-Aug) Attached to the EMP, this is a nerd paradise of costumes, props and models from sci-fi movies and TV shows. Admission is included with your EMP ticket.

CAPITOL HILL

Millionaires mingle with goth musicians in irreverent Capitol Hill, a well-heeled but liberal neighborhood rightly renowned for its fringe theater, alternative music scene, indie coffee bars, and vital gay and lesbian culture. You can take your dog for a herbal bath here, go shopping for ethnic crafts on Broadway, or blend in (or not) with the young punks and the old hippies on the eclectic Pike-Pine Corridor. The junction of Broadway and E John St is the nexus from which to navigate the quarter's various restaurants, brewpubs, boutiques and dingy, but not dirty, dive bars.

Seattle Asian Art Museum MUSEUM
(www.seattleartmuseum.org; 1400 E Prospect St; adult/child $7/5, 1st Thu & Sat of month free; ⌚10am-5pm Wed-Sun, to 9pm Thu; P) In stately Volunteer Park, the museum houses the extensive art collection of Dr Richard Fuller, who donated this severe art-moderne-style gallery to the city in 1932.

Volunteer Park PARK
Seattle's most manicured park merits a wander in its own right. Check out the glass-sided Victorian **conservatory** (admission free), filled with palms, cacti and tropical plants, and don't depart before you've taken in the opulent mansions that embellish the streets immediately to the south.

FREMONT

The humorously coined 'Artist's Republic of Fremont' about 2 miles north of Seattle Center is known for its lefty inclinations, nude solstice cyclists, farmers market and wacky public sculpture.

Fremont Sunday Market MARKET
(www.fremontmarket.com; Stone Way & N 34th St; ⌚10am-5pm Sun) People come from all over town for the market. It features fresh fruit and vegetables, arts and crafts, and all kinds of people getting rid of junk.

Public Sculpture MONUMENTS
Public art has never been as provocative as it is in Fremont. Look out for **Waiting for the Interurban** (cnr N 34th St & Fremont Ave N), a cast-aluminum statue of people awaiting a train that never comes: the Interurban linking Seattle and Everett stopped running in the 1930s (it started up again in 2001 but the line no longer passes this way). Check out the human face on the dog; it's Armen Stepanian, once Fremont's honorary mayor, who made the mistake of objecting to the sculpture. Equally eye-catching is the **Fremont Troll** (cnr N 36th St & Troll Ave), a scary-looking 18ft troll crushing a Volkswagen Beetle in its left hand. The **Fremont Rocket** (cnr Evanston Ave & N 35th St) is a rocket that was found lying around in Belltown in 1993 and that now sticks out of a building – mmm, interesting. Fremont's most controversial art is the **Lenin statue** (cnr Evanston Ave & N 36th) salvaged from Slovakia after it was toppled during the 1989 revolution. Even if you hate the politics, you have to admire the art – and audacity!

THE U DISTRICT

University of Washington UNIVERSITY

(www.washington.edu) Seattle's university (founded 1861) is almost as old as the city itself and is highly ranked worldwide. The beautiful 700-acre campus sits at the edge of Lake Union about 3 miles northeast of downtown and affords views of Mt Rainier. The main streets are University Way, known as 'the Ave,' and NE 45th St, both lined with coffee shops, restaurants and bars. The core of the campus is **Central Plaza**, known as Red Sq because of its brick base. Get information and a campus map at the **visitor center** (4014 University Way; ⏲8am-5pm Mon-Fri).

Burke Museum MUSEUM

(adult/child $9.50/7.50; ⏲10am-5pm) The best museum of natural history in the Northwest is situated near the junction of NE 45th St and 16th Ave. The main collections are of fossils, plus artifacts from 19 different Native American cultures.

Henry Art Gallery MUSEUM

(adult/child $10/6, Thu free; ⏲11am-4pm Wed, Sat & Sun, to 8pm Thu & Fri) At the corner of NE 41st St and 15th Ave is a sophisticated space centered on a remarkable permanent exhibit by light-manipulating sculptor James Turrell, featuring various temporary and touring collections.

BALLARD

Despite its recent veneer of hipness, Ballard still has the feel of an old Scandinavian fishing village – especially around the locks, the marina and the Nordic Heritage Museum. Six miles northwest of downtown, the old town has become a nightlife hot spot, but even in the daytime its historic buildings and cobblestoned streets make it a pleasure to wander through.

Hiram M Chittenden Locks LOCKS

(3015 NW 54th St; ⏲24hr) Here, the waters of Lake Washington and Lake Union flow through the 8-mile-long Lake Washington Ship Canal and into Puget Sound. Construction of the canal began in 1911; today 100,000 boats a year pass through the locks, about a half-mile west of Ballard, off NW Market St. Take bus 17 from downtown at 4th Ave and Union St. On the southern side of the locks you can watch from underwater glass tanks or from above as salmon navigate a **fish ladder** on their way to spawning grounds in the Cascade headwaters of the Sammamish River, which feeds Lake Washington.

Activities

Hiking

There are great hiking trails through old-growth forest at Seward Park, which dominates the Bailey Peninsula that juts into Lake Washington, and longer but flatter hikes in 534-acre Discovery Park northwest of Seattle.

Sierra Club WALKING

(www.sierraclub.org) Leads day-hiking and car-camping trips on weekends; most day trips are free.

Cycling

A cycling favorite, the 16.5-mile **Burke-Gilman Trail** winds from Ballard to Log Boom Park in Kenmore on Seattle's Eastside. There, it connects with the 11-mile **Sammamish River Trail**, which winds past the Chateau Ste Michelle winery in Woodinville before terminating at Redmond's Marymoor Park.

More cyclists pedal the popular loop around **Green Lake**, situated just north of Fremont and 5 miles north of the downtown core. From Belltown, the 2.5-mile **Elliott Bay Trail** runs along the Waterfront to Smith Cove.

Get a copy of the *Seattle Bicycling Guide Map,* published by the City of Seattle's **Transportation Bicycle & Pedestrian Program** (www.cityofseattle.net/transportation/bikemaps.htm) online or at bike shops.

The following are recommended for bicycle rentals and repairs:

Recycled Cycles CYCLING

(www.recycledcycles.com; 1007 NE Boat St; rentals per 6/24hr $20/40; ⏲10am-8pm Mon-Fri, to 6pm Sat & Sun; 👪) A friendly U District shop, this place also rents out chariots and trail-a-bike attachments for kids.

JRA Bike Shop CYCLING

(www.jrabikeshop.com; 311 3rd Ave S; ⏲9am-5pm Mon-Fri) The handiest rental outlet for downtown is JRA, bivouacked close to Pioneer Sq and King Street train station.

Counterbalance Bicycles CYCLING

(www.counterbalancebicycles.com; 2943 NE Blakeley St; ⏲7:30am-7pm Mon-Fri, 10am-6pm Sat & Sun) Counterbalance is handily situated on the Burke-Gilman cycling trail as it cuts its way through the U District.

SEATTLE FOR CHILDREN

Make a beeline for the Seattle Center, preferably on the monorail, where food carts, street entertainers, fountains and green space will make the day fly by. One essential stop is the **Pacific Science Center** (www.pacsci.org; 200 2nd Ave N; adult/child $14/9, plus Imax show $4; ⏲10am-5pm Mon-Fri, to 6pm Sat & Sun), which entertains and educates with virtual-reality exhibits, laser shows, holograms, an Imax theater and a planetarium – parents won't be bored either.

Downtown on Pier 59, **Seattle Aquarium** (www.seattleaquarium.org; 1483 Alaskan Way, at Pier 59; adult/child $19/12; ⏲9:30am-5pm) is a fun way to learn about the natural world of the Pacific Northwest. The centerpiece of the aquarium is a glass-domed room where sharks, octopuses and other deepwater denizens lurk in the shadowy depths.

Water Sports

Seattle is not just on a network of hiking and cycling trails. With Venice-like proportions of downtown water, it is also strafed with kayak-friendly marine trails. The **Lakes to Locks Water Trail** links Lake Sammamish with Lake Washington, Lake Union and – via the Hiram M Chittenden Locks – Puget Sound. For launching sites and maps, check the website of the **Washington Water Trails Association** (www.wwta.org).

Northwest Outdoor Center Inc KAYAKING
(www.nwoc.com; 2100 Westlake Ave N; kayaks per hr $13-20) On Lake Union, rents kayaks and offers tours and instruction in sea and whitewater kayaking.

 Tours

Argosy Cruises Seattle Harbor Tour CRUISE
(www.argosycruises.com; adult/child $22.50/8.50) Argosy's popular Seattle Harbor Tour is a one-hour narrated tour of Elliott Bay, the Waterfront and the Port of Seattle. It departs from Pier 55.

Coffee Crawl COFFEE
(www.seattlebyfoot.com; tours $22; ⏲10am Thu-Mon) Touring Seattle's coffee bars is a local experience akin to exploring Rome's ruins. This two-hour caffeine-fueled romp starts at Pike Place Market under the famous coffee sign and continues along Post Alley, with explanations on the city's coffee history and culture.

Seattle Food Tours FOOD
(www.seattlefoodtours.com; tours $39) A culinary hike in and around Pike Place Market, this 2½-hour excursion takes in a bakery, chowder house, Vietnamese restaurant and Mexican kitchen. You'll also get some historical and artistic background.

 Festivals & Events

Northwest Folklife Festival MUSIC
(www.nwfolklife.org) International music, dance, crafts, food and family activities held at Seattle Center on the Memorial Day weekend in May.

Seafair WATER
(www.seafair.com) Huge crowds attend this festival held on the water in late July/August, with hydroplane races, a torchlight parade, an air show, music and a carnival.

Bumbershoot MUSIC, LITERATURE
(www.bumbershoot.com) A major arts and cultural event at Seattle Center on the Labor Day weekend in September, with live music, author readings and lots of unclassifiable fun.

Seattle International Film Festival FILM
(SIFF; www.siff.net; tickets $13-30) Held in mid-May, the city's biggest film festival uses a half-dozen cinemas but also has its own dedicated cinema, in McCaw Hall's **Nesholm Family Lecture Hall** (321 Mercer St, Seattle Center).

Seattle Lesbian & Gay Film Festival FILM
(www.threedollarbillcinema.org; tickets $6-8) This popular festival in October shows new gay-themed films from directors worldwide at the **Three Dollar Bill Cinema** (1122 E Pine St).

Sleeping

From mid-November through to the end of March, most downtown hotels offer Seattle Super Saver Packages – generally 50% off rack rates, with a coupon book for savings on dining, shopping and attractions. Make reservations online at www.seattlesuper saver.com.

TOP CHOICE **Belltown Inn** HOTEL **$$**
(☎206-529-3700; www.belltown-inn.com; 2301 3rd Ave; s/d $109/119; P❄@🛜) Can it be true? The Belltown is such a bargain and in such a prime location that it's hard not believe it hasn't accidently floated over from a smaller, infinitely cheaper city. But no, clean functional rooms, handy kitchenettes, roof terrace, free bikes and – vitally important – borrow-and-return umbrellas are all yours for the price of a posh dinner.

Hotel Andra BOUTIQUE HOTEL **$$**
(☎206-448-8600; www.hotelandra.com; 2000 4th Ave; r $189-229; P❄🛜) It's in Belltown (so it's trendy), and it's Scandinavian-influenced (so it has lashings of minimalist style), plus the Andra's fine location is complemented by leopard-skin fabrics, color accents, well-stocked bookcases, fluffy bathrobes, Egyptian-cotton bed linen and a complimentary shoe-shine. The Lola restaurant next door does room service. Say no more.

Ace Hotel HOTEL **$$**
(☎206-448-4721; www.acehotel.com; 2423 1st Ave; r with shared/private bath $99/190; P🛜) Emulating (almost) its hip Portland cousin, the Ace sports minimal, futuristic decor (everything's white or stainless steel, even the TV), antique French army blankets, condoms instead of pillow mints and a copy of *Kama Sutra* in place of the Bible. Parking costs $15.

City Hostel Seattle HOSTEL **$**
(☎206-706-3255; www.hostelseattle.com; 2327 2nd Ave; 6-/4-bed dm $28/32, d $73; @🛜) Sleep in an art gallery for peanuts – in Belltown, no less. That's the reality in this new 'art hostel', which will make your parent's hostelling days seem positively spartan by comparison. Aside from arty dorms, expect a common room, hot tub, in-house movie theater (with free DVDs) and all-you-can-eat breakfast.

Mediterranean Inn HOTEL **$$**
(☎206-428-4700; www.mediterranean-inn.com; 425 Queen Anne Ave N; r from $119; P❄@) There's something about the surprisingly un-Mediterranean Med Inn that just clicks. Maybe it's the handy cusp-of-downtown location, or the genuinely friendly staff, or the kitchenettes in every room, or the small downstairs gym, or the surgical cleanliness in every room. Don't try to define it – just go there and soak it up.

Hotel Max BOUTIQUE HOTEL **$$**
(☎206-441-4200; www.hotelmaxseattle.com; 620 Stewart St; s/d from $188/219; P@) Original artworks hang in the small but cool guest rooms, and it's tough to get any hipper than the Max's super-saturated color scheme – not to mention package deals such as the Grunge Special or the Gaycation. Rooms feature menus for your choice of pillows and spirituality services.

Edgewater HOTEL **$$$**
(☎206-728-7000; www.edgewaterhotel.com; Pier 67, 2411 Alaska Way; r 289-349; P❄@🛜) Fame and notoriety once stalked the Edgewater. Perched over the water on a pier, it was once the hotel of choice for every rock band that mattered, including the Beatles, the Rolling Stones and, most infamously, Led Zeppelin, who took the 'you can fish from the hotel window' advertising jingle a little too seriously and filled their suite with sharks. These days, the fishing – and Led Zeppelin – is prohibited, but the rooms are still deluxe with a capital 'D.

Hotel Monaco BOUTIQUE HOTEL **$$$**
(☎206-621-1770; www.monaco-seattle.com; 1101 4th Ave; r $260-400; P@🛜) Whimsical, with dashes of European elegance, the downtown Monaco is worthy of all four of its illustrious stars. Bed down amid the stripy wallpaper and heavy drapes.

College Inn HOTEL **$**
(☎206-633-4441; www.collegeinnseattle.com; 4000 University Way NE; s/d incl breakfast from $65/75; @🛜) This pretty, half-timbered building in the U District, left over from the 1909 Alaska-Yukon-Pacific Exposition, has 25 European-style guest rooms with sinks and shared baths. Pub in the basement!

Inn at the Market BOUTIQUE HOTEL **$$$**
(☎206-443-3600; www.innatthemarket.com; 86 Pine St; r with/without water view $370/255; P❄🛜) The only lodging in venerable Pike Place Market, this elegant 70-room boutique hotel has large rooms, many of which enjoy views onto market activity and Puget Sound. Parking costs $20.

Moore Hotel HOTEL **$**
(☎206-448-4851, www.moorehotel.com; 1926 2nd Ave; s/d with shared bath $59/71, with private bath $74/86; 🛜) Old-world and a little moth-eaten, the Moore nonetheless has a friendly front desk and a prime location. If that doesn't swing you, the price should.

Eating

The best budget meals are to be found in Pike Place Market. Take your pick and make your own from fresh produce, baked goods, deli items and take-out ethnic foods.

TOP CHOICE **Lola** GREEK $$$
(☎206-441-1430; www.tomdouglas.com; 2000 4th Ave; mains $22-32) Seattle's ubiquitous cooking maestro, Tom Douglas, goes Greek in this new Belltown adventure and delivers once again with gusto. Stick in trendy clientele, some juicy kebabs, heavy portions of veg, shared meze dishes and pita with dips, and you'll be singing Socratic verse all the way home.

La Vita é Bella ITALIAN $$
(www.lavitaebella.us; 2411 2nd Ave; pasta $10-14) As any Italian food snob will tell you, it's very hard to find authentic home-spun Italian cuisine this side of Sicily. Thus extra kudos must go to La Vita é Bella for trying and largely succeeding in a difficult field. Judge the pizza margherita as a good yardstick, though the *vongole* (clams), desserts and coffee are also spot on. As in all good Italian restaurants, the owners mingle seamlessly with the clientele with handshakes and good humor.

Serious Pie PIZZERIA $$
(www.tomdouglas.com; 316 Virginia St; pizzas $16-18) Gourmet pizza sounds like an oxymoron until you stumble upon this place in Belltown which adds ingredients no one else would dare use to embellish its crispy Italianate crusts. Bank on truffles, Brussels sprouts, clams, eggs and a variety of herbs and cheeses.

Lowells DINER $
(www.eatatlowells.com; 1519 Pike Pl; mains $6-9) 'Fish-and-chips' is a simple meal often done badly – but not here. Slam down your order for Alaskan cod at the front entry and take it up to the top floor for delicious views over Puget Sound. It also serves corned-beef hash and an excellent clam chowder.

Piroshky Piroshky BAKERY $
(www.piroshkybakery.com; 1908 Pike Pl; snacks $2-7; ⏲8am-6:30pm Oct-Apr, from 7:30am May-Sep) Proof that not all insanely popular Pike Pl holes-in-the-wall go global (à la Starbucks), Piroshky is still knocking out its delectable mix of sweet and savory Russian pies and pastries in a space barely big enough to swing a small kitten. Join the melee and order one 'to go.'

Salumi SANDWICHES $
(www.salumicuredmeats.com; 309 3rd Ave S; sandwiches $7-10, plates $11-15; ⏲11am-4pm Tue-Fri) The queue outside Mario Batali's dad's place has long been part of the sidewalk furniture. It's even formed its own community of chatterers, note comparers, Twitter addicts and gourmet sandwich experts. When you get in, the sandwiches come with any of a dozen types of cured meat and fresh cheese. Great for a picnic!

Paseo CUBAN $
(www.paseoseattle.com; 4225 Fremont Ave N; sandwiches $6-9; ⏲11am-9pm Tue-Fri, to 8pm Sat) Proof that most Seattleites aren't posh (or pretentious) is the local legend known as Paseo, a Cuban hole-in-the-wall that's in a nondescript part of Fremont and which people alter their commute drive to visit. The fuss centers on the sandwiches; in particular the Midnight Cuban Press with pork, ham, cheese and banana peppers, and the Cuban Roast (slow roasted pork in marinade). Grab plenty of napkins.

Peso's Kitchen & Lounge MEXICAN $$
(www.pesoskitchen.com; 605 Queen Anne Ave N; breakfast $7-10, dinner $10-15; ⏲9am-2am) A place that wears many sombreros, Pesos serves fine Mexican food in the evenings amid a cool trendy 'scene' that is anything but Mexican. But the trump card comes the next morning, after the beautiful people have gone home, with an acclaimed egg-biased breakfast.

Shiro's Sushi Restaurant JAPANESE $$$
(www.shiros.com; 2401 2nd Ave; mains $26.75; ⏲5:30-9:45pm) There's barely room for all the awards and kudos that cram the window in this sleek Japanese joint. Grab a pew behind the glass food case and watch the experts concoct delicate and delicious Seattle sushi.

5 Spot BREAKFAST $
(1502 Queen Anne Ave N; brunch $8-10, dinner $13-17; ⏲8:30am-midnight) Top of the hill, top of the morning and top of the pops; the queues outside 5 Spot at 10am on a Sunday testify to a formidable brunch. The crowds mean a great atmosphere and the hearty menu, which has perfected French toast, *huevos rancheros* and plenty more American standards, will shift even the most stubborn of hangovers.

Black Bottle MODERN AMERICAN $
(www.blackbottleseattle.com; 2600 1st Ave; plates $8-12; ⏲4:30pm-2am) This trendy minimalist bar-restaurant showcases the new Belltown of smart condo dwellers and avid wine quaf-

fers. The food is mainly appetizers, but with menu items such as grilled lamb and sumac hummus, and braised artichoke heart and greens, even the nostalgic grunge groupies of yore will find it hard to resist.

Steelhead Diner SEAFOOD **$$**
(206-625-0129; www.steelheaddiner.com; 95 Pine St; sandwiches $9-13, mains $15-33; 11am-10pm Tue-Sat, 10am-3pm Sun) Homey favorites such as fish-and-chips, grilled salmon or braised short ribs and grits become fine cuisine when they're made with the best of what Pike Place Market has to offer.

Wild Ginger ASIAN **$$**
(www.wildginger.net; 1401 3rd Ave; mains $15-28) All around the Pacific Rim – via China, Indonesia, Malaysia, Vietnam and Seattle, of course – is the wide-ranging theme at this highly popular downtown fusion restaurant. Try the fragrant duck first.

Le Pichet FRENCH **$$**
(www.lepichetseattle.com; 1933 1st Ave; lunch/mains $9/18; 8am-midnight) Say *bienvenue* to Le Pichet just up from Pike Place Market, a *très français* bistro with pâtés, cheeses, wine, *chocolat* and a refined Parisian feel.

Drinking

You'll find cocktail bars, dance clubs and live music on Capitol Hill. The main drag in Ballard has brick taverns old and new, filled with the hard-drinking older set in daylight hours and indie rockers at night. Belltown has gone from grungy to shabby chic, but has the advantage of many drinking holes neatly lined up in rows.

Coffeehouses

Starbucks is the tip of the iceberg. Seattle has spawned plenty of smaller indie chains, many with their own roasting rooms. Look out for Uptown Espresso, Caffe Ladro and Espresso Vivace.

TOP CHOICE **Bauhaus** CAFE
(www.bauhauscoffee.net; 301 E Pine St; 6am-1am Mon-Fri, from 7am Sat, from 8am Sun) Drink coffee, browse books, nibble pastries, stay awake…until 1am! Bauhaus positively encourages lingering with its mezzanine bookshelves, Space Needle view and lazy people-watching opps. One senses that the next great American novel could be getting drafted here.

Top Pot Hand-Forged Doughnuts CAFE
(www.toppotdoughnuts.com; 2124 5th Ave; 6am-7pm) Top Pot is to doughnuts what champagne is to wine – a different class. And its cafes – this one in an old car showroom with floor-to-ceiling library shelves and art-deco signage – are equally legendary.

B&O Espresso CAFE
(www.b-oespresso.com; 204 Belmont Ave E; 7am-late Mon-Thu, from 8am Fri-Sun) Full of understated swank, this piece of the Capitol Hill furniture (open since 1976) is the place to go for Turkish coffee – if you can get past the pastry case up front.

Caffé Vita CAFE
(www.caffevita.com; 1005 E Pike St; 6am-11pm) The laptop fiend, the date, the radical student, the homeless hobo, the philosopher, the business guy on his way to work: watch the whole neighborhood pass through this Capitol Hill institution (one of four in Seattle) with its own on-site roasting room visible through a glass partition.

Panama Hotel Tea & Coffee House CAFE
(607 S Main St; 8am-7pm Mon-Sat, from 9am Sun) The Panama, a historic 1910 building containing the only remaining Japanese bathhouse in the US, doubles as a memorial to the neighborhood's Japanese residents forced into internment camps during WWII.

Zeitgeist CAFE
(www.zeitgeistcoffee.com; 171 S Jackson St; 6am-7pm Mon-Fri, from 8am Sat & Sun;) Plug into the spirit of the times with the rest of the laptop crew at this lofty, brick-walled cafe near the train station.

Caffè Umbria CAFE
(www.caffeumbria.com; 320 Occidental Ave S; 6am-6pm Mon-Fri, from 7am Sat, 8am-5pm Sun) Premier roasters of blended coffee, the Bizzarri family, from Perugia in Italy, founded this European-flavored outlet in Pioneer Sq in 1986.

Bars

Shorty's BAR
(www.shortydog.com; 2222 2nd Ave) A cross between a pinball arcade and the Korova Milk Bar in the film *A Clockwork Orange*, Shorty's is a Belltown legend where you can procure cheap beer, hot dogs, alcohol slushies and a back room of pinball heaven.

Pike Pub & Brewery BREWERY
(www.pikebrewing.com; 1415 1st Ave) Leading the way in the microbrewery revolution, this

brewpub opened in 1989 underneath Pike Place Market. Today it still serves great burgers and brews in a neo-industrial multilevel space that's a beer nerd's heaven.

Blue Moon BAR
(712 NE 45th St) A legendary counterculture dive that's near the university and first opened in 1934 to celebrate the repeal of the prohibition laws, the Blue Moon has served its mellow beer to the likes of Dylan Thomas, Allen Ginsberg and Tom Robbins. It's lost its luster a bit in recent times, but be prepared for impromptu poetry recitations, jaw-harp performances and inspired rants.

Brouwer's BEER HALL
(400 N 35th St; 11am-2am) This dark cathedral of beer in Fremont has rough-hewn rock walls and a black metal grate in the ceiling. Behind an epic bar are tantalizing glimpses into a massive beer fridge. A replica *Mannequin Pis* statue at the door and the Belgian crest everywhere clue you in to the specialty.

Copper Gate BAR
(6301 24th Ave NW) Formerly one of Seattle's worst dives, the Copper Gate in Ballard is now an upscale bar-restaurant focused on meatballs and naked ladies. A Viking longship forms the bar, with a peepshow pastiche for a sail and a cargo of helmets and gramophones.

Hale's Ales Brewery BREWERY
(www.halesbrewery.com; 4301 Leary Way NW) Hale's makes fantastic beer, notably its ambrosial Cream Ale. Its flagship brewpub in Fremont feels like a business-hotel lobby, but it's worth a stop. There is a self-guided tour near the entrance.

Elysian Brewing Company BREWERY
(www.elysianbrewing.com; 1221 E Pike St) On Capitol Hill, the Elysian's huge windows are great for people-watching – or being watched, if your pool game's good enough.

☆ Entertainment

Consult the *Stranger, Seattle Weekly* or the daily papers for listings. Tickets for big events are available at **TicketMaster** (206-628-0888), which operates a **discount ticket booth** (206-233-1111) at Westlake Center.

Live Music

Crocodile LIVE MUSIC
(www.thecrocodile.com; 2200 2nd Ave) Reopened in March 2009 after a year in the doldrums, the sole survivor of Belltown's once influential grunge scene (formerly known as the Crocodile Café) will have to work hard to reclaim an audience who grew up listening to Nirvana, Pearl Jam and REM at this hallowed music venue.

Neumo's LIVE MUSIC
(www.neumos.com; 925 E Pike St) A punk, hip-hop and alternative-music venue that counts Radiohead and Bill Clinton (not together) among its former guests, Neumo's (formerly known as Moe's) fills the big shoes of its original namesake. You can mark the passage of time at 'Sad Bastards Mondays', which offer 'tunes to cry into your beer to.'

Chop Suey LIVE MUSIC
(www.chopsuey.com; 1325 E Madison St) Chop Suey is a dark, high-ceilinged space with a ramshackle faux-Chinese motif and eclectic bookings.

Cinema

Northwest Film Forum CINEMA
(www.nwfilmforum.org; 1515 12th Ave) Impeccable programming, from restored classics to cutting-edge independent and international films. In Capitol Hill, of course!

Cinerama CINEMA
(www.cinerama.com; 2100 4th Ave) One of the very few Cineramas left in the world, it has a fun, sci-fi feel.

Harvard Exit CINEMA
(www.landmarktheatres.com; cnr E Roy St & Harvard Ave) Built in 1925, this is Seattle's first independent theater.

Performing Arts

Seattle Opera CLASSICAL MUSIC
(www.seattleopera.org) At McCaw Hall, features a program of four or five full-scale operas every season, including a Wagner's *Ring* cycle that draws sellout crowds in summer.

Intiman Playhouse THEATER
(www.intiman.org; 201 Mercer St) The Intiman Theatre Company, Seattle's oldest, takes the stage at this playhouse.

Pacific Northwest Ballet BALLET
(www.pnb.org) The foremost dance company in the Northwest puts on more than 100 shows a season from September through June at Seattle Center's McCaw Hall.

Seattle Symphony CLASSICAL MUSIC
(www.seattlesymphony.org) A major regional ensemble. It plays at the Benaroya Concert

Hall, which you'll find downtown at 2nd Ave and University St.

A Contemporary Theatre THEATER
(ACT; www.acttheatre.org; 700 Union St) One of the three big companies in the city, fills its $30-million home at Kreielsheimer Place with performances by Seattle's best thespians and occasional big-name actors.

Gay & Lesbian Venues

Elite BAR
(1520 Olive Way; 📶) An extremely friendly Capitol Hill establishment with darts, pool, not-too-loud music and decent cocktails.

Re-Bar CLUB
(1114 Howell St) Storied dance club, where many of Seattle's defining cultural events happened (such as Nirvana album releases), welcomes gay, straight, bi or undecided revelers to its lively dance floor.

Neighbours CLUB
(1509 Broadway Ave E) Check out the always-packed dance factory for the gay club scene and its attendant glittery straight girls.

Sport

Seattle Mariners BASEBALL
(www.mariners.org; tickets $7-60) The beloved baseball team plays in Safeco Field just south of downtown.

Seattle Seahawks FOOTBALL
(www.seahawks.com; tickets $42-95) The Northwest's only National Football League (NFL) franchise plays in the 72,000-seat Seahawks Stadium.

Shopping

The main big-name shopping area is downtown between 3rd and 6th Aves and University and Stewart Sts. Pike Place Market is a maze of arts-and-crafts stalls, galleries and small shops. Pioneer Sq and Capitol Hill have locally owned gift and thrift shops. The following are some only-in-Seattle shops to seek out.

Elliott Bay Book Company BOOKS
(www.elliottbaybook.com; 1521 10th Ave; ⏰10am-10pm, to 11pm Sat, 11am-9pm Sun) Perish the day when ebooks render bookstores obsolete. What will happen to the Saturday-afternoon joy of Elliott Bay books, where 150,000 titles inspire author readings, discussions, reviews and hours of serendipitous browsing?

Beecher's Handmade Cheese FOOD
(www.beechershandmadecheese.com; 1600 Pike Pl; ⏰9am-6pm) Artisan beer, artisan coffee... next up, Seattle brings you artisan cheese and it's made as you watch in this always-crowded Pike Pl nook, where you can buy all kinds of cheese-related paraphernalia. Don't leave without tasting the wonderful home-made mac 'n' cheese.

Babeland ADULT
(www.babeland.com; 707 E Pike St; ⏰11am-10pm Mon-Sat, noon-7pm Sun) Remember those pink furry handcuffs and that glass dildo you needed? Well, look no further.

Holy Cow Records MUSIC
(1501 Pike Pl, Suite 325; ⏰10am-10pm Mon-Sat, to 7pm Sun) Proceed to Pike Place Market and let your fingers flick through the aging vinyl at this shrine to music geekdom; you might just stumble upon that rare Psychedelic Furs 12-inch that has been eluding you since 1984.

Left Bank Books BOOKS
(www.leftbankbooks.com; 92 Pike St; ⏰10am-7pm Mon-Sat, 11am-6pm Sun) This 35-year-old collective displays 'zines in *español,* revolutionary pamphlets, a 'fuck authority' notice board and plenty of Chomsky. You're in Seattle, just in case you forgot.

Information

Emergency & Medical Services

45th St Community Clinic (☎206-633-3350; 1629 N 45th St, Wallingford) Medical and dental services.

Harborview Medical Center (☎206-731-3000; 325 9th Ave) Full medical care, with emergency room.

Seattle Police (☎206-625-5011)

Seattle Rape Relief (☎206-632-7273)

Washington State Patrol (☎425-649-4370)

Internet Access

Seattle is a computer geek's heaven and practically every bar and coffee shop has free wi-fi, as do most hotels.

Cyber-Dogs (909 Pike St; 1st 20min free, then per hr $6; ⏰10am-midnight) A veggie hot-dog stand (dogs $2 to $5), espresso bar, internet cafe and youngster hangout and pick-up joint.

Online Coffee Company (www.onlinecoffeeco.com; 1st 30min free, then per hr $1; ⏰7:30am-midnight) Olive Way (1720 E Olive Way); Pine St (1404 E Pine St) The Olive Way location is in a cozy former residence, while the Pine St shop is more utilitarian-chic. The first hour is free for students.

Internet Resources

Seattle's Convention and Visitors Bureau (www.visitseattle.org)

Seattlest (www.seattlest.com) A blog about various goings-on in and around Seattle.

Media

KEXP 90.3 FM Legendary independent music and community station.

Seattle Times (www.seattletimes.com) The state's largest daily paper.

Seattle Weekly (www.seattleweekly.com) Free weekly with news and entertainment listings.

The Stranger (www.thestranger.com) Irreverent weekly edited by Dan Savage of 'Savage Love' fame.

Money

American Express (Amex; 600 Stewart St; ⌚8:30am-5:30pm Mon-Fri)

Travelex-Thomas Cook Currency Services Airport (⌚6am-8pm); Westlake Center (400 Pine St, Level 3; ⌚9:30am-6pm Mon-Sat, 11am-5pm Sun) The booth at the main airport terminal is behind the Delta Airlines counter.

Post

Post office (301 Union St; ⌚8:30am-5:30pm Mon-Fri)

Tourist Information

Seattle Convention & Visitors Bureau (www.visitseattle.org; cnr 7th Ave & Pike St; ⌚9am-5pm Mon-Fri) Inside the Washington State Convention and Trade Center; it opens weekends June to August.

Getting There & Away

Air

Seattle-Tacoma International Airport (SEA; www.portseattle.org/seatac), aka 'Sea-Tac,' 13 miles south of Seattle on I-5, has daily services to Europe, Asia, Mexico and points throughout the USA and Canada, with frequent flights to and from Portland, OR, and Vancouver, BC.

Boat

Victoria Clipper (www.victoriaclipper.com) operates several high-speed passenger ferries to Victoria, BC, and to the San Juan Islands. It also organizes package tours that can be booked in advance through the website. Victoria Clipper runs from Seattle to Victoria up to six times daily (round-trip adult/child $147/73).

The **Washington State Ferries** (www.wsdot.wa.gov/ferries) website has maps, prices, schedules, trip planners and weather updates, plus estimated waiting times for popular routes. Fares depend on the route, vehicle size and trip duration, and are collected either for round-trip or one-way travel depending on the departure terminal.

Bus

The **Bellair Airporter Shuttle** (www.airporter.com) has daily buses between Seattle, Sea-Tac Airport, Ellensburg, Yakima, Anacortes and Bellingham. Reserve in advance.

Greyhound (www.greyhound.com; 811 Stewart St; ⌚6am-midnight) connects Seattle with cities all over the country, including Chicago, IL ($206 one way, two days, three daily), Spokane, WA ($74, five to seven hours, three daily), San Francisco, CA ($89, 20 hours, four daily), and Vancouver, BC ($28, three to four hours, six daily).

More comfortable and offering free on-board wi-fi is the super-efficient **Quick Shuttle** (www.quickcoach.com) that runs five times daily along I-5 between Sea-Tac Airport and Central Vancouver (BC), also stopping in downtown Seattle (at the Best Western Executive Inn, 200 Taylor Ave N), Bellingham airport and Vancouver airport.

Train

Amtrak (www.amtrak.com) serves Seattle's **King Street Station** (303 S Jackson St; ⌚6am-10:30pm, ticket counter 6:15am-8pm). Three main routes run through town: the *Amtrak Cascades* (connecting Vancouver, Seattle, Portland and Eugene), the very scenic *Coast Starlight* (connecting Seattle, Oakland and Los Angeles) and the *Empire Builder* (a cross-continental roller coaster to Chicago).

Chicago, IL From $205, 46 hours, daily

Oakland, CA $154, 23 hours, daily

Portland, OR $31, three to four hours, five daily

Vancouver, BC $38, three to four hours, five daily

Getting Around

To/From the Airport

There are a number of options for making the 13-mile trek from the airport to downtown Seattle. The most efficient is via the new light-rail service run by Sound Transit.

Gray Line's **Airport Express** (www.grayline seattle.com) fetches passengers in the parking lot outside door 00 at the south end of the baggage-claim level. It will drop you at a choice of eight different downtown hotels (one way $11 to $15).

Taxis and limousines (about $35 and $40, respectively) are available at the parking garage on the 3rd floor. Rental-car counters are located in the baggage-claim area.

Car & Motorcycle

Trapped in a narrow corridor between mountains and sea, Seattle is a horrendous traffic bottleneck and its nightmarish jams are famous. I-5 has a high-occupancy vehicle lane for vehicles carrying two or more people. Otherwise, try to work around the elongated rush 'hours.'

Public Transportation

Buses are operated by **Metro Transit** (www.transit.metrokc.gov), part of the King County Department of Transportation. Fares cost $2 to $2.75. Bus travel within the central core demarcated by Bell St, 6th Ave, I-5 and S King St is free.

The recently installed **Seattle Street Car** (www.seattlestreetcar.org) runs from the Westlake Center to Lake Union along a 2.6-mile route. There are 11 stops allowing interconnections with numerous bus routes.

Seattle's brand new light-rail train, **Sound Transit** (www.soundtransit.org), runs between Sea-Tac Airport and downtown (Westlake Center) every 15 minutes between 5am and midnight. The ride takes 36 minutes and costs $2.50. There are additional stops in Pioneer Sq and the International District.

Taxi

All Seattle taxi cabs operate at the same rate, set by King County; at the time of research the rate was $2.50 at meter drop, then $2.50 per mile.

Orange Cab Co (206-444-0409; www.orangecab.net)

Yellow Cab (206-622-6500; www.yellowtaxi.net)

Around Seattle

OLYMPIA

Small in size but big in clout, state capital Olympia is a musical, political and outdoor powerhouse that punches well above its 46,480 population. Look no further than the street-side buskers on 4th Ave belting out acoustic grunge, the smartly attired bureaucrats marching across the lawns of the resplendent state legislature, or the Goretex-clad outdoor fiends overnighting before rugged sorties into the Olympic Mountains. Truth is, despite its classical-Greek-sounding name, creative, out-of-the-box Olympia is anything but ordinary. Progressive Evergreen college has long lent the place an artsy turn (creator of *The Simpsons,* Matt Groening studied here), while the dive bars and secondhand guitar shops of downtown provided an original pulpit for riot grrrl music and grunge.

Sights & Activities

FREE **Washington State Capitol** LANDMARK
(8am-4:30pm) Looking like a huge Grecian temple, the Capitol complex, set in a 30-acre park overlooking Capitol Lake, dominates the town. The campus' crowning glory is the magnificent **Legislative Building** (1927), a dazzling display of craning columns and polished marble, topped by a 287ft dome that is only slightly smaller than its namesake in Washington, DC. Free guided tours are available.

State Capital Museum MUSEUM
(211 W 21st Ave; admission $2; 10am-4pm Tue-Fri, from noon Sat) Preserves the general history of Washington State, from the Nisqually tribe to the present day.

Olympia Farmers Market MARKET
(10am-3pm Thu-Sun Apr-Oct, Sat & Sun Nov-Dec) At the north end of Capitol Way, this is one of the state's best markets, with fresh local produce, crafts and live music.

Sleeping & Eating

Phoenix Inn Suites HOTEL $
(360-570-0555; 415 Capitol Way N; s/d $99/109;) The town's most upmarket accommodations is slick, efficient and well tuned to dealing with demanding state government officials.

Batdorf & Bronson CAFE $
(Capitol Way S; 6am-7pm Mon-Fri, 7am-6pm Sat & Sun) Olympia's most famous java comes from a local roaster offering ethical coffee. Aside from this downtown cafe, you can buy or try the latest blends at its popular **Tasting Room** (200 Market St NE; 9am-4pm Wed-Sun).

TOP CHOICE **Oyster House** SEAFOOD $$
(320 W 4th Ave; seafood dinners $15-20; 11am-11pm, to midnight Fri & Sat) Olympia's most celebrated restaurant also specializes in its most celebrated cuisine, the delicate Olympia oyster, best served pan-fried and topped with a little cheese and spinach.

Spar Bar Café CAFE $
(www.mcmenamins.com; 114 4th Ave E; breakfast $4-5, lunch $5-8; 7am-9pm) A cozy old-school cafe-cum-bar-cum-cigar store run by McMenimans with good brews, classic comfort food and supersonic service.

Drinking

The city's never-static music scene still makes waves on 4th Ave at the retrofitted **4th Avenue Tavern** (210 4th Ave E) or the graffiti-decorated **Le Voyeur** (404 4th Ave E), an anarchistic, vegan-friendly dive bar with a busker invariably guarding the door.

Information

The **State Capitol Visitor Center** (cnr 14th Ave & Capitol Way) offers information on the capitol campus, the Olympia area and Washington State.

Olympic Peninsula

Surrounded on three sides by sea and exhibiting many of the insular characteristics of a full-blown island, the remote Olympic Peninsula is about as 'wild' and 'west' as America gets. What it lacks in cowboys it makes up for in rare, endangered wildlife and dense primeval forest. The peninsula's roadless interior is largely given over to the notoriously wet Olympic National Park, while the margins are the preserve of loggers, Native American reservations and a smattering of small but interesting settlements, most notably Port Townsend. Equally untamed is the western coastline, America's isolated end point, where the tempestuous ocean and misty old-growth Pacific rainforest meet in aqueous harmony.

OLYMPIC NATIONAL PARK

Declared a national monument in 1909 and a national park in 1938, the 1406-sq-mile **Olympic National Park** (www.nps.gov/olym) shelters one of the world's only temperate rainforests and a 57-mile strip of Pacific coastal wilderness that was added in 1953 – it exists as one of North America's last great wilderness areas. Opportunities for independent exploration abound, with visitors enjoying such diverse activities as hiking, fishing, kayaking and skiing.

EASTERN ENTRANCES

The graveled Dosewallips River Rd follows the river from US 101 (turn off approximately 1km north of Dosewallips State Park) for 15 miles to **Dosewallips Ranger Station**, where the trails begin; call ☎360-565-3130 for road conditions. Even hiking smaller portions of the two long-distance paths – with increasingly impressive views of heavily glaciated **Mt Anderson** – is reason enough to visit the valley. Another eastern entry for hikers is the **Staircase Ranger Station** (☎360-877-5569; ⊙May-Sep), just inside the national park boundary, 15 miles from Hoodsport on US 101. Two state parks along the eastern edge of the national park are popular with campers: **Dosewallips State Park** (☎888-226-7688; tent/RV sites $21/28) and **Lake Cushman State Park** (☎888-226-7688; tent/RV sites $22/28). Both have running water, flush toilets and some RV hookups. Reservations are accepted.

NORTHERN ENTRANCES

The park's easiest – and hence most popular – entry point is at **Hurricane Ridge**, 18 miles south of Port Angeles. At the road's end, an interpretive center overlooks a stupendous view of Mt Olympus (7965ft) and dozens of other peaks. The 5200ft altitude can mean inclement weather and the winds here (as the name suggests) can be ferocious. Aside from various summer trekking opportunities, the area maintains one of only two US national-park-based ski runs, operated by the small, family-friendly **Hurricane Ridge Ski & Snowboard Area** (www.hurricaneridge.com).

Popular for boating and fishing is **Lake Crescent**, the site of the park's oldest and most reasonably priced **lodge** (☎360-928-3211; www.olympicnationalparks.com; 416 Lake Crescent Rd; lodge r with shared bath $76, cottages $142-224; ⊙May-Oct; P❄📶). Delicious sustainable food is served in the lodge's ecofriendly restaurant. From **Storm King Information Station** (☎360-928-3380; ⊙May-Sep) on the lake's south shore, a 1-mile hike climbs through old-growth forest to Marymere Falls.

Along the Sol Duc River, the **Sol Duc Hot Springs Resort** (☎360-327-3583; www.northolympic.com/solduc; 12076 Sol Duc Hot Springs Rd, Port Angeles; RV sites $33, r $131-189; ⊙late Mar-Oct; ❄≋) has lodging, dining, massage and, of course, hot-spring pools (adult/child $10/7.50), as well as great day hikes.

WESTERN ENTRANCES

Isolated by distance and one of the country's rainiest microclimates, the Pacific side of the Olympics remains its wildest. Only US 101 offers access to its noted temperate rainforests and untamed coastline. The **Hoh River Rainforest**, at the end of the 19-mile Hoh River Rd, is a Tolkienesque maze of dripping ferns and moss-draped trees. You can get better acquainted with the area's complex yet delicate natural ecosystems at the **Hoh visitor center and campground** (☎360-374-6925; campsites $12; ⊙9am-6pm Jul & Aug, to 4:30pm Sep-Jun), which has information on guided walks and longer backcountry hikes. There are no hookups or showers; first come first served.

A little to the south lies **Lake Quinault**, a beautiful glacial lake surrounded by forested peaks. It's popular for fishing, boating and swimming, and is punctuated by some of the nation's oldest trees. **Lake Quinault Lodge** (☎360-288-2900; www.visitlakequinault.com; 345 S Shore Rd; lodge r $134-167, cabins $125-243;), a luxury classic of 1920s 'parkitecture,' has a heated pool and sauna, a crackling fireplace and a memorable dining room noted for its sweet-potato breakfast pancakes. For a cheaper sleep nearby, try the ultrafriendly **Quinault River Inn** (☎360-288-2237; www.quinaultriverinn.com; 8 River Dr; r $75-115; P) in Amanda Park, a favorite with anglers.

A number of short hikes begin just outside the Lake Quinault Lodge, or you can try the longer **Enchanted Valley Trail**, a medium-grade 13-miler that begins from the Graves Creek Ranger station at the end of South Shore Rd and climbs up to a large meadow resplendent with wildflowers and copses of alder trees.

Information

The park entry fee is $5/15 per person/vehicle, valid for one week, payable at park entrances. Many park visitor centers double as United States Forestry Service (USFS) ranger stations, where you can pick up permits for wilderness camping ($5 per group, valid up to 14 days, plus $2 per person per night).

Forks Visitor Information Center (1411 S Forks Ave, Forks; 10am-4pm) Suggested itineraries and seasonal information.

Olympic National Park Visitor Center (3002 Mt Angeles Rd, Port Angeles; 9am-5pm) The best overall center is situated at the Hurricane Ridge gateway, a mile off Hwy 101 in Port Angeles.

Wilderness Information Center (3002 Mt Angeles Rd, Port Angeles; 7:30am-6pm Sun-Thu, to 8pm Fri & Sat May-Sep, 8am-4:30pm daily Oct-Apr) Directly behind the visitor center, you'll find maps, permits and trail information.

PORT TOWNSEND

Historical relics are rare in the Pacific Northwest, which makes time-warped Port Townsend all the more fascinating. Small, nostalgic and culturally vibrant, this showcase of 1890s Victorian architecture is the 'New York of the West that never was,' a one-time boomtown that went bust at the turn of the 20th century, only to be rescued 70 years later by a group of far-sighted locals. Port Townsend today is a buoyant blend of inventive eateries, elegant fin de siècle hotels and quirky annual festivals.

Sights

Jefferson County Historical Society Museum MUSEUM
(210 Madison St; adult/12yr & under $4/1; 11am-4pm Mar-Dec) The local historic society runs this well-maintained exhibition area that includes mock-ups of an old courtroom and jail cell, along with the full lowdown on the rise, fall and second coming of this captivating port town.

Fort Worden State Park PARK
(www.parks.wa.gov/fortworden; 200 Battery Way; 6:30am-dusk Apr-Oct, from 8am Nov-Mar) This attractive park located within Port Townsend's city limits is the remains of a large fortification system constructed in the 1890s. The extensive grounds and array of historic buildings have been refurbished in recent years into a lodging, nature and historical park. The **Commanding Officer's Quarters** (admission $4; 10am-5pm Jun-Aug, 1-4pm Sat & Sun Mar-May & Sep-Oct), a 12-bedroom mansion, is open for tours, and part of one of the barracks is now the **Puget Sound Coast Artillery Museum** (admission $2; 11am-4pm Tue-Sun), which tells the story of early Pacific coastal fortifications.

Hikes lead along the headland to **Point Wilson Lighthouse Station** and some wonderful windswept beaches.

Sleeping

Palace Hotel HISTORIC HOTEL $
(☎360-385-0773; www.palacehotelpt.com; 1004 Water St; r $59-109;) Built in 1889, this beautiful Victorian building is a former brothel that was once run by the locally notorious Madame Marie, who managed her dodgy business from the 2nd-floor corner suite. Reincarnated as an attractive period hotel with antique furnishings and old-fashioned claw-foot baths, the Palace's former seediness is now a thing of the past.

Manresa Castle HISTORIC HOTEL $$
(☎360-385-5750; www.manresacastle.com; cnr 7th & Sheridan Sts; d & ste $109-169) This 40-room mansion-castle, built by the town's first mayor, sits high on a bluff above the port and is supposedly haunted. The vintage rooms may be a little spartan for some visitors, but in a setting this grandiose it's the all-pervading sense of history that counts.

Eating

TOP CHOICE **Waterfront Pizza** PIZZERIA $
(951 Water St; large pizzas $11-19) Arguably the best pizza in the state, this buy-by-the-slice

outlet inspires huge local loyalty and will satisfy even the most querulous of Chicago-honed palates with its crisp sourdough crusts and creative toppings.

Salal Café BREAKFAST **$**
(634 Water St; breakfast $7-8, lunch $8-9; ⌚7am-2pm) The Salal specializes in eggs. Scrambled, poached, frittatas, stuffed into a burrito or served up as an omelet – you can ponder all varieties here during a laid-back breakfast or a zippy lunch.

Information

To get the lowdown on the city's roller-coaster boom-bust history, call in at the **visitor center** (www.ptchamber.org; 2437 E Sims Way; ⌚9am-5pm Mon-Fri, to 4pm Sat & Sun).

Getting There & Away

Port Townsend can be reached from Seattle by a ferry-bus connection via Bainbridge Island and Poulsbo (bus 90 followed by bus 7). **Washington State Ferries** (www.wsdot.wa.gov/ferries) goes to and from Keystone on Whidbey Island (car and driver $11.70/foot passenger $2.75, 35 minutes).

PORT ANGELES

Despite the name, there's nothing Spanish or particularly angelic about Port Angeles, propped up by the lumber industry and backed by the steep-sided Olympic Mountains. Rather than visiting to see the town per se, people come here to catch a ferry for Victoria, BC, or plot an outdoor excursion into the nearby Olympic National Park. The **visitor center** (121 E Railroad Ave; ⌚8am-8pm May-Oct, 10am-4pm Nov-Apr) is adjacent to the ferry terminal. For information on the national park, the **Olympic National Park Visitor Center** (3002 Mt Angeles Rd, Port Angeles; ⌚9am-5pm) is just outside town.

The **Olympic Discovery Trail** (www.olympicdiscoverytrail.com) is a 30-mile off-road hiking and cycling trail between Port Angeles and Sequim, starting at the end of **Ediz Hook**, the sand spit that loops around the bay. Bikes can be rented at **Sound Bikes & Kayaks** (www.soundbikekayaks.com; 120 Front St; bike rental per hr/day $9/30).

Port Angeles' most comfortable accommodations, hands down, is the **Olympic Lodge** (☎360-452-2993; www.olympiclodge.com; 140 Del Guzzi Drive; r from $119; ❄@📶🏊), with a swimming pool, on-site bistro, so-clean-they-seem-new rooms and complementary cookies and milk.

Bella Italia (118 E 1st St; mains $12-20; ⌚from 4pm) has been around a lot longer than Bella, the heroine of the *Twilight* saga, but its mention in the book as the place where Bella and Edward Cullen go for their first date has turned an already popular restaurant into an icon. Try the clam linguine, chicken marsala or smoked duck breast washed down with an outstanding wine from a list featuring 500 selections.

THE TWILIGHT ZONE

Forks, a small lumber town on Hwy 101, was little more than a speck on the Washington state map when publishing phenomenon Stephenie Meyer set the first of her now famous *Twilight* vampire novels here in 2003. Ironically, Meyer – America's answer to JK Rowling – had never been to Forks when she resurrected the ghoulish legacy of Bela Lugosi et al with the first of what has become a series of insanely popular 'tweenage' books. Not that this has stopped the town from cashing in on its new-found literary fame. Forks has apparently seen a 600% rise in tourism since the *Twilight* film franchise began in 2008, the bulk of the visitors comprising of gawky, wide-eyed under 15-year-old girls who are more than a little surprised to find out what Forks really is – chillingly ordinary (and wet).

A fresh bit of color was needed and it was provided in November 2008 with the opening of **Dazzled by Twilight** (www.dazzledbytwilight.com; 11 N Forks Ave; ⌚10am-6pm), which runs two *Twilight* merchandise shops in Forks (and another in Port Angeles) as well as the Forks **Twilight Lounge** (81 N Forks Ave). The lounge hosts a downstairs restaurant along with an upstairs music venue that showcases regular live bands and a blood-curdling Saturday-night 'tween' karaoke (5pm to 8pm). The company also runs four daily **Twilight Tours** (adult/child $39/25; ⌚8am, 11:30am, 3pm & 6pm) visiting most of the places mentioned in Meyer's books. Highlights include Forks High School, the Treaty Line at the nearby Rivers Resort and a sortie out to the tiny coastal community of La Push.

The ferry that runs from Port Angeles to Victoria, BC, is called the **Coho Vehicle Ferry** (www.cohoferry.com; passenger/car $15.50/55). The crossing takes 1½ hours. **Olympic Bus Lines** (www.olympicbuslines.com) runs twice daily to Seattle ($39) from the public transit center at the corner of Oak and Front Sts. **Clallam Transit** (www.clallamtransit.com) buses go to Forks and Sequim, where they link up with other transit buses, enabling you to circumnavigate the whole Olympic Peninsula.

NORTHWEST PENINSULA

Several Native American reservations cling to the extreme northwest corner of the continent and welcome interested visitors. Hit hard by the decline in the salmon-fishing industry, the small settlement of Neah Bay on Hwy 112 is characterized by its weather-beaten boats and craning totem poles. It's home to the Makah Indian Reservation, whose **Makah Museum** (www.makah.com; 1880 Bayview Ave; admission $5; ⏲10am-5pm) displays artifacts from one of North America's most significant archaeological finds. Exposed by tidal erosion in 1970, the 500-year-old Makah village of Ozette quickly proved to be a treasure trove of Native American history, unearthing a huge range of materials including whaling weapons, canoes, spears and combs. Seven miles beyond the museum, a short boardwalk trail leads to **Cape Flattery**, a 300ft promontory that marks the most northwesterly point in the lower 48 states.

Convenient to the Hoh River Rainforest and the Olympic coastline is **Forks**, a one-horse lumber town that's now more famous for its *Twilight* paraphernalia. Get cozy in the amiable **Forks Motel** (☎360-374-6243; www.forksmotel.com; 432 S Forks Ave; s/d $65/70; ❄📶🏊) with kitchen suites, a small pool and a very friendly welcome.

Northwest Washington

Wedged between Seattle, the Cascades and Canada, northwest Washington draws influences from three sides. Its urban hub is collegiate Bellingham, while its outdoor highlight is the pastoral San Juan Islands, an extensive archipelago that glimmers like a sepia-toned snapshot from another era. Equally verdant, and simpler to reach, Whidbey Island contains beautiful Deception Pass State Park and the quaint oyster-fishing village of Coupeville. Situated on Fidalgo Island and attached to the mainland via a bridge, the settlement of Anacortes is the main hub for ferries to the San Juan Islands and Victoria, BC. If your boat's delayed you can pass time in expansive Washington Park or sample the local halibut and chips in a couple of classic downtown restaurants.

WHIDBEY ISLAND

Whidbey Island is an idyllic emerald escape beloved of stressed-out Seattleites. While not as detached or nonconformist as the San Juans (there's a bridge connecting it to adjacent Fidalgo Island at its northernmost point), life is certainly slower, quieter and more pastoral here. Having six state parks is a bonus, along with a plethora of B&Bs, two historic fishing villages (Langley and Coupeville), famously good clams and a thriving artist's community.

Deception Pass State Park (☎360-675-2417; 41229 N State Hwy 20) straddles the eponymous steep-sided water chasm that flows between Whidbey and Fidalgo Islands, and incorporates lakes, islands, campsites and 27 miles of hiking trails.

Ebey's Landing National Historical Reserve (www.nps.gov/ebla; admission free; ⏲8am-5pm mid-Oct–Mar, 6:30am-10pm Apr–mid-Oct) comprises 17,400 acres encompassing working farms, sheltered beaches, two state parks and the town of **Coupeville**. This small settlement is one of Washington's oldest towns and has an attractive seafront, antique stores and a number of old inns, including the **Coupville Inn** (☎800-247-6162; www.thecoupevilleinn.com; 200 Coveland St; r with/without balcony $140/105; P❄@📶), which bills itself as a French-style motel (if that's not an oxymoron) with fancy furnishings and a substantial breakfast. For the famous fresh local clams, head to **Christopher's** (www.christophersonwhidbey.com; 103 NW Coveland St; mains $17-26), which offers exciting and creative modern cooking in huge portions.

Washington State Ferries (www.wsdot.wa.gov/ferries) link Clinton to Mukilteo (car and driver $9/foot passenger free, 20 minutes, every 30 minutes) and Keystone to Port Townsend (car and driver $11.70 /foot passenger $2.75, 30 minutes, every 45 minutes). Free **Island Transit buses** (www.islandtransit.org) run the length of Whidbey every hour daily, except Sunday, from the Clinton ferry dock.

BELLINGHAM

Imagine a slightly less eccentric slice of Portland, Oregon, broken off and towed 250 miles to the north. Welcome to laid-back Bellingham, a green, liberal and famously livable settlement that has taken the libertine, nothing-is-too-weird ethos of Oregon's 'City of Roses' and given it a peculiarly Washingtonian twist. Mild in both manners and weather, the 'city of subdued excitement,' as a local mayor once dubbed it, is an unlikely alliance of espresso-supping students, venerable retirees, all-weather triathletes and placard-waving Peaceniks. Publications such as *Outside Magazine* have consistently lauded it for its abundant outdoor opportunities, while adventure organizations such as the American Alpine Institute call it home base.

Activities

Bellingham offers outdoor activities by the truckload. **Whatcom Falls Park** is a natural wild region that bisects Bellingham's eastern suburbs. The change in elevation is marked by four sets of waterfalls, including **Whirlpool Falls**, a popular summer swimming hole. The substantial intra-urban trails extend south as far as Larabee State Park, with a popular 2.5-mile section tracking Bellingham's postindustrial waterfront. **Fairhaven Bike & Mountain Sports** (1103 11th St) rents bikes from $20 a day and has all the info (and maps) on local routes.

Victoria/San Juan Cruises (www.whales.com; 355 Harris Ave) has whale-watching trips to Victoria, BC, via the San Juan Islands. Boats leave from the Bellingham Cruise Terminal in Fairhaven.

Sleeping

TOP CHOICE **Hotel Bellwether** BOUTIQUE HOTEL **$$$**
(360-392-3100; www.hotelbellwether.com; 1 Bellwether Way; r $156-272, lighthouse from $473;) Bellingham's finest and most charismatic hotel is positioned on a redeveloped part of the waterfront, and offers European-style furnishings in 66 luxury rooms and an adjoining lighthouse condominium.

Guesthouse Inn MOTEL **$**
(360-671-9600; www.bellinghamvaluinn.com; 805 Lakeway Dr; s/d $81/91;) The secret of a good 'chain' hotel is that it doesn't seem like a chain at all. To put this theory into practice, check out the clean, personable Guesthouse Inn, just off I-5 and an easy 15-minute walk from downtown.

Eating

TOP CHOICE **Pepper Sisters** MODERN AMERICAN **$$**
(www.peppersisters.com; 1055 N State St; mains $9-13; from 5pm Tue-Sun;) People travel from

WORTH A TRIP

LA CONNER

Celebrated for its tulips, wild turkeys, erudite writer's colony and (among other culinary treats) enormous doorstep-sized cinnamon buns, La Conner's myriad attractions verge on the esoteric. Abstract writer Tom Robbins lives here, if that's any measuring stick, along with about 840 other creative souls.

Aside from three decent museums, the zenith of La Conner's cultural calendar is its annual Tulip Festival, when the surrounding fields are embellished with a colorful carpet of daffodils (March), tulips (April) and irises (May). But they're not the only valuable crops. The flat, fertile Lower Skagit River delta worked by hardworking second-, third- and fourth-generation Dutch farmers also produces copious amounts of vegetables, including 100% of the nation's parsnips and Brussels sprouts.

Many of the products find their way into La Conner's stash of creative restaurants. Situated inside the old Tillinghurst Seed building, **Seeds Bistro & Bar** (www.seedsbistro.com; 623 Morris St; mains $18-25) is the cream of the crop, offering a rare combo of classy food and brunch-cafe-style friendliness. The fresh flavors of the surrounding farmland are mixed with equally fresh fish plucked from the nearby ocean to concoct unparalleled ling cod, off-the-ratings-scale crab cakes, and a raspberry and white chocolate bread pudding you'll still be talking about months later.

The size of the cinnamon buns at **Calico Cupboard** (www.calicocupboardcafe.com; 720 S 1st St; 7:30am-4pm Mon-Fri, to 5pm Sat & Sun) beggar belief, and their quality (there are four specialist flavors) is equally good. Factor in a 10-mile run through the tulip fields before you tackle one and you should manage to stave off instant diabetes.

far and wide to visit this cult restaurant with its bright turquoise booths. The hard-to-categorize food is Southwestern with a Northwest twist. Try the cilantro-and-pesto quesadillas, or blue corn rellenos.

Swan Cafe CAFE $
(www.communityfood.coop; 220 N Forest St; dishes $5-7; 8am-9pm;) A Community Food Co-op with an on-site cafe-deli that offers an insight into Bellingham's organic, fair-trade, community-based mentality.

Colophon Café CAFE $
(1208 11th St; mains $7-10; 9am-10pm) The toast of the Fairhaven district is known for its African peanut soup and chocolate brandy cream pies.

Information

The best downtown tourist information can be procured at the **Visitor Info Station** (www.downtownbellingham.com; 1304 Cornwall St; 9am-6pm).

Getting There & Away

San Juan Islands Shuttle Express (www.orcawhales.com) offers daily summer service to the Orcas and San Juan Islands ($20). Alaska Marine Highway ferries (see p1064) go to Juneau (60 hours) and other southeast Alaskan ports (from $363 without car). The **Bellair Airporter Shuttle** (www.airporter.com) runs to Sea-Tac Airport ($34), with connections en route to Anacortes and Whidbey Island.

San Juan Islands

Take the ferry west out of Anacortes and you'll feel like you've dropped off the edge of the continent. A thousand metaphoric miles from the urban inquietude of Puget Sound, the nebulous San Juan archipelago conjures up Proustian flashbacks from another era and often feels about as American as – er – Canada (which surrounds it on two sides). Street crime here barely registers, fast-food franchises are a nasty mainland apparition, and cars – those most essential of US travel accessories – are best left at home.

There are 172 landfalls in this expansive archipelago but unless you're rich enough to charter your own yacht or seaplane, you'll be restricted to seeing the big four – San Juan, Orcas, Shaw and Lopez Islands – all served daily by Washington State Ferries. Communally, the islands are famous for their tranquility, whale-watching opportunities, sea kayaking and seditious nonconformity.

The best way to explore the San Juans is by sea kayak or bicycle. Kayaks are available for rent on Lopez, Orcas and San Juan Islands. Expect a guided half-day trip to cost $45 to $65. Note that most beach access is barred by private property, except at state or county parks. Cycling-wise, Lopez is flat and pastoral and San Juan is worthy of an easy day loop, while Orcas offers the challenge of undulating terrain and a steep 5-mile ride to the top of Mt Constitution.

Information

For good general information about the San Juans, contact the **San Juan Islands Visitor Information Center** (360-468-3663; www.guidetosanjuans.com; 10am-2pm Mon-Fri).

Getting There & Around

Airlines serving the San Juan Islands include **San Juan Airlines** (www.sanjuanairlines.com) and **Kenmore Air** (www.kenmoreair.com).

Washington State Ferries (www.wsdot.wa.gov/ferries) leave Anacortes for the San Juans; some continue to Sidney, BC, near Victoria. Ferries run to Lopez Island (45 minutes), Orcas Landing (60 minutes) and Friday Harbor on San Juan Island (75 minutes). Fares vary by season; the cost of the entire round-trip is collected on westbound journeys only (except those returning from Sidney, BC). To visit all the islands, it's cheapest to go to Friday Harbor first and work your way back through the other islands.

Shuttle buses ply Orcas and San Juan Island in the summer months.

LOPEZ ISLAND

If you're going to Lopez – or 'Slow-pez,' as locals prefer to call it – take a bike. With its undulating terrain and salutation-offering locals (who are famous for their three-fingered 'Lopezian wave'), this is the ideal cycling isle. A leisurely pastoral spin can be tackled in a day with good overnight digs available next to the marina in the **Lopez Islander Resort** (360-468-2233; www.lopezislander.com; 2864 Fisherman Bay Rd; d from $120;), which has a restaurant, gym and pool and offers free parking in Anacortes (another incentive to dump the car). If you arrive bikeless, call up **Lopez Bicycle Works** (www.lopezbicycleworks.com; 2847 Fisherman Bay Rd; 10am-6pm May-Sep), which can deliver a bicycle to the ferry terminal for you.

SAN JUAN ISLAND

San Juan Island is the archipelago's unofficial capital, a harmonious mix of low forested hills and small rural farms that resonate with a dramatic and unusual 19th-century history. The only settlement is Friday Harbor, where the **chamber of commerce** (www.sanjuanisland.org; 135 Spring St; ⏲10am-5pm Mon-Fri, to 4pm Sat & Sun) is bivouacked inside a small mall off the main street.

Sights & Activities

FREE San Juan Island National Historical Park HISTORIC SITE
(www.nps.gov/sajh; ⏲8:30am-4pm) San Juan Island hides one of the 19th-century's oddest political confrontations, the so-called 'Pig War' between the USA and Britain. This curious 19th-century cold war stand-off is showcased in two separate historical parks on either end of the island that once housed opposing American and English military encampments. On the southern flank of the island, the **American Camp** hosts a small **visitors center** (admission free; ⏲8:30am-4:30pm Thu-Sun, daily Jun-Sep) with the remnants of an old fort, desolate beaches and a series of interpretive trails. At the opposite end of the island, **English Camp**, 9 miles northwest of Friday Harbor, contains the remains of the British military facilities dating from the 1860s.

Lime Kiln Point State Park PARK
(⏲8am-5pm mid-Oct–Mar, 6:30am-10pm Apr–mid-Oct) Clinging to the island's rocky west coast, this beautiful park overlooks the deep Haro Strait and is, reputedly, one of the best places in the world to view whales from the shoreline.

San Juan Vineyards WINERY
(www.sanjuanvineyards.com; 3136 Roche Harbor Rd; ⏲11am-5pm) Washington's unlikeliest winery has a tasting room next to an old schoolhouse built in 1896. Open-minded tasters should try the Siegerrebe and Madeleine Angevine varieties.

Sleeping & Eating

There are hotels, B&Bs and resorts scattered around the island, but Friday Harbor has the best concentration.

TOP CHOICE Earthbox Motel & Spa BOUTIQUE MOTEL $$
(☎360-378-4000; www.earthboxmotel.com; 410 Spring St; r from $197; P 📶 🏊) Reaching out to retro-lovers, Earthbox styles itself as a 'boutique motel,' a hybrid of simplicity and sophistication that has taken a former motor inn and embellished it with features more commonly associated with a deluxe hotel. The only downside is the prices, which aren't very motel-like.

Market Chef DELI $
(225a St; ⏲10am-6pm) Several hundred locals can't be wrong, can they? The 'Chef's' specialty is deli sandwiches and very original ones at that. Join the queue and watch staff prepare the goods with fresh, local ingredients.

ORCAS ISLAND

Precipitous, unspoiled and ruggedly beautiful, Orcas Island is the San Juans' emerald icon, excellent for hiking and, more recently, gourmet food. The ferry terminal is at Orcas Landing, 8 miles south of the main village, Eastsound. On the island's eastern lobe is **Moran State Park** (⏲6:30am-dusk Apr-Sep, from 8am Oct-Mar), dominated by Mt Constitution (2409ft), with 40 miles of trails and an amazing 360-degree mountaintop view.

Kayaking in the calm island waters is a real joy here. **Shearwater** (www.shearwaterkayaks.com; 138 North Beach Rd, Eastsound) has the equipment and know-how. Three-hour guided trips start at $69.

Sleeping

TOP CHOICE Rosario Resort & Spa RESORT $$$
(☎360-376-2222; www.rosario-resort.com; 1400 Rosario Rd, Eastsound; r $188-400; P ❄ 📶 🏊) A magnificent seafront mansion built by former shipbuilding magnate Robert Moran in 1904 and now converted into an exquisite, upscale resort and spa.

Outlook Inn HOTEL $$
(☎360-376-2200; www.outlookinn.com; 171 Main St, Eastsound; r with shared/private bath $89/119; P ❄ 📶) Eastsound village's oldest building (1888) is an island institution that has kept up with the times by expanding into a small bayside complex. Also onsite is the rather fancy New Leaf Café.

Eating

Allium INTERNATIONAL $$$
(☎360-376-4904; www.alliumonorcas.com; 310E Main St, Eastsound; dinner mains $30; ⏲10am-2pm Sat & Sun, 5-8pm Thu-Mon) Orcas got a destination restaurant in 2010 with the opening of the illustrious Allium, where the secret is simplicity (local ingredients, limited opening hours and only five mains on the menu). The result: food worth visiting the island for.

Cafe Olga CAFE $
(11 Point Lawrence Rd, Olga; mains $9-11; ⏲9am-6pm Mon-Fri, to 8pm Sat & Sun, closed Wed Mar-Apr) Tucked inside a barn alongside a crafts gallery, 6 miles southeast of Eastsound, Olga specializes in homemade pies and provides a sweet treat for cyclists and hikers who've just conquered lofty Mt Constitution.

North Cascades

Geologically different from their southern counterparts, the North Cascade Mountains are peppered with sharp, jagged peaks, copious glaciers and a preponderance of complex metamorphic rock. Thanks to their virtual impregnability, the North Cascades were an unsolved mystery to humans until relatively recently. The first road was built across the region in 1972 and, even today, it remains one of the Northwest's most isolated outposts.

MT BAKER

Rising like a ghostly sentinel above the sparkling waters of upper Puget Sound, Mt Baker has been mesmerizing visitors to the Northwest for centuries. A dormant volcano that last belched smoke in the 1850s, this haunting 10,781ft peak shelters 12 glaciers and in 1999 registered a record-breaking 95ft of snow in one season.

Well-paved Hwy 542, known as the Mt Baker Scenic Byway, climbs 5100ft to **Artist Point**, 56 miles from Bellingham. Near here you'll find the **Heather Meadows Visitor Center** (Mile 56, Mt Baker Hwy; ⏲8am-4:30pm May-Sep) and a plethora of varied hikes including the 7.5-mile Chain Lakes Loop that leads you around a half-dozen icy lakes surrounded by huckleberry meadows.

Receiving more annual snow than any ski area in North America, the undone **Mt Baker Ski Area** (www.mtbakerskiarea.com) has 38 runs, eight lifts and a vertical rise of 1500ft. Due to its rustic facilities, ungroomed terrain and limited après-ski options, the resort has gained something of a cult status among snowboarders, who have been coming here for the Legendary Baker Banked Slalom every January since 1985.

On the 100 or so days a year when Baker breaks through the clouds, the views from the deck at the **Inn at Mount Baker** (☎360-599-1359; www.theinnatmtbaker.com; 8174 Mt Baker Hwy; r $155-165; P❄@) can divert your attention away from breakfast. Situated 7 miles east of Maple Falls, this six-room B&B is welcoming, private and mindful of its pristine setting.

LEAVENWORTH

Blink hard and rub your eyes. This isn't some strange Germanic hallucination. This is Leavenworth, a former lumber town that underwent a Bavarian makeover back in the 1960s after the rerouting of the cross-continental railway threatened to put it permanently out of business. Swapping wood for tourists, Leavenworth today has successfully reinvented itself as a traditional Romantische Strasse village, right down to the beer and sausages and the lederhosen-loving locals (25% of whom are German). The classic *Sound of Music* mountain setting helps, as does the fact that Leavenworth serves as the main activity center for sorties into the nearby Alpine Lakes Wilderness.

The **Leavenworth Ranger Station** (600 Sherbourne St; ⏲7:30am-4:30pm daily mid-Jun–mid-Oct, from 7:45am Mon-Fri mid-Oct–mid-Jun) can advise on the local outdoor activities. Highlights include the best climbing in the state at **Castle Rock** in Tumwater Canyon, about 3 miles northwest of town off US 2.

The Devil's Gulch is a popular off-road bike trail (25 miles, four to six hours). Local outfitters **Der Sportsmann** (www.dersportsmann.com; 837 Front St) rents bikes from $25 a day.

Sleeping

TOP CHOICE **Enzian Inn** HOTEL $$
(☎509-548-5269; www.enzianinn.com; 590 Hwy 2; d $125-155; ❄📶🏊) Taking the German theme up a notch, the Enzian goes way beyond the call of duty with an 18-hole putting green, a racquetball court, a sunny breakfast room and a lederhosen-clad owner who entertains guests with an early-morning blast on the alphorn.

Bavarian Lodge HOTEL $$
(☎509-548-7878; www.bavarianlodge.com; 810 Hwy 2; d/ste $149/249; P❄📶🏊) This lodge takes the Bavarian theme to luxury levels in a plush, clutter-free establishment with modern – but definably German – rooms complete with gas fires, king beds and funky furnishings. Outside there's a heated pool and hot tub.

Eating

Café Christa GERMAN $$
(www.cafechrista.com; upstairs 801 Front St; mains $14-18) Christa's features quaint

European decor, discreet yet polite service, and a menu that rustles up German classics such as bratwurst, Wiener schnitzel and Jäger schnitzel.

München Haus GERMAN $
(www.munchenhaus.com; 709 Front St; snacks from $6; ⌚11am-11pm May-Oct, closed Mon-Fri Nov-Apr) An alfresco beer garden that serves the best charbroiled Bavarian sausages this side of Bavaria.

LAKE CHELAN

Long, slender Lake Chelan is central Washington's water playground. **Lake Chelan State Park** (☎509-687-3710; S Lakeshore Rd; tent/RV sites $21/28) has 144 campsites; a number of lakeshore campgrounds are accessible only by boat. The town of **Chelan**, at the lake's southeastern tip, is the primary base for accommodations and services, and has a **USFS ranger station** (428 Woodin Ave). **Link Transit** (www.linktransit.com) buses connect Chelan with Wenatchee and Leavenworth ($1).

Beautiful **Stehekin**, on the northern tip of Lake Chelan, is accessible only by **boat** (www.ladyofthelake.com; round-trip from Chelan $39), **seaplane** (www.chelanairways.com; round-trip from Chelan $159) or a long hike across Cascade Pass, 28 miles from the lake. Most facilities are open mid-June to mid-September.

METHOW VALLEY

The Methow's combination of powdery winter snow and abundant summer sunshine has transformed the valley into one of Washington's primary recreation areas. You can bike, hike and fish in the summer, and cross-country ski on the second-biggest snow trail network in the US in the winter.

The 200km of trails are maintained by the nonprofit organization **Methow Valley Sport Trails Association** (MVSTA; www.mvsta.com), which, in the winter, provides the most comprehensive network of hut-to-hut (and hotel-to-hotel) skiing in North America. An extra blessing is that few people seem to know about it. For classic accommodations and easy access to the skiing, hiking and cycling trails, decamp at the exquisite **Sun Mountain Lodge** (☎509-996-2211; www.sunmountainlodge.com; Box 1000, Winthrop, WA 98862; r $170-350, cabins $275-460; ❄📶🏊), 10 miles west of the town of Winthrop.

NORTH CASCADES NATIONAL PARK

The wildest of all Pacific Northwest wildernesses, the lightly trodden **North Cascades National Park** (www.nps.gov/noca) has no settlements, no overnight accommodations and only one unpaved road. The names of the dramatic mountains pretty much set the tone: Desolation Peak, Jagged Ridge, Mt Despair and Mt Terror. Not surprisingly, the region offers some of the best backcountry adventures outside of Alaska.

The **North Cascades Visitor Center** (502 Newhalem St; ⌚9am-4:30pm mid-Apr–Oct, closed Mon-Fri Nov-Mar), in the small settlement of Newhalem on Hwy 20, is the best orientation point for visitors and is staffed by expert rangers who can enlighten you on the park's highlights.

Built in the 1930s for loggers working in the valley that was soon to be flooded by Ross Dam, the floating cabins at the **Ross Lake Resort** (☎206-386-4437; www.rosslakeresort.com; cabins d $145-169, cabins q $210; ⌚mid-Jun–Oct) on the eponymous lake's west side are the state's most unique accommodations. There's no road in – guests can either hike the 2-mile trail from Hwy 20 or take the resort's tugboat-taxi-and-truck shuttle from the parking area near Diablo Dam.

Northeastern Washington

SPOKANE

Washington's second-biggest population center is one of the state's latent surprises and a welcome break after the treeless monotony of the eastern scablands. Situated at the nexus of the Pacific Northwest's so-called 'Inland Empire,' this understated yet confident city sits clustered on the banks of the Spokane River, close to where British fur traders founded a short-lived trading post in 1810. Though rarely touted in national tourist blurbs, Spokane hosts the world's largest mass participation running event (May's annual Bloomsday), a stunning Gilded Age hotel (the Davenport) and a spectacular waterfall throwing up angry white spray in the middle of its downtown core.

Sights & Activities

Riverfront Park PARK
(www.spokaneriverfrontpark.com) On the former site of Spokane's 1974 World's Fair, the park provides a welcome slice of urban greenery in the middle of downtown. It has been redeveloped in recent years with a 17-point **sculpture walk**, along with plenty of bridges and trails to satisfy the city's plethora of amateur runners. The park's centerpiece is **Spokane Falls**, a gush-

ing combination of scenic waterfalls and foaming rapids. There are various viewing points over the river, including a short **gondola ride** (adult/child $7.25/4; ⏲11am-6pm Sun-Thu, to 10pm Fri & Sat Apr-Sep) that takes you directly above the falls. Walkers and joggers crowd the interurban **Spokane River Centennial Trail** (www.spokanecentennialtrail.org), which extends for 37 miles to the Idaho border and beyond.

Northwest Museum of Arts & Culture MUSEUM
(www.northwestmuseum.org; 2316 W 1st Ave; adult/child $7/5; ⏲10am-5pm Wed-Sat) Encased in a striking state-of-the-art building in the posh Browne's Addition neighborhood, the museum has – arguably – one of the finest collections of indigenous artifacts in the Northwest.

Sleeping

Davenport Hotel HISTORIC HOTEL $$
(☎509-455-8888; www.thedavenporthotel.com; 10 S Post St; standard/deluxe r $139/159;) A historic Spokane landmark (opened in 1914) that is considered one of best hotels in the US. If you can't afford a room, linger in the exquisite lobby.

Montvale Hotel BOUTIQUE HOTEL $$
(☎509-747-1919; www.montvalehotel.com; 1005 W 1st Ave; queen/king r $119/189;) The Montvale is situated in a former brothel, but don't be fooled by the small, rather plain lobby. Upstairs a refined inner quadrangle has a distinct European feel.

Hotel Ruby BOUTIQUE MOTEL $
(☎509-747-1041; www.hotelrubyspokane.com; 901 W 1st Ave; d from $69; P) This new boutique motel has replaced an old Rodeway Inn. Furnished with modern gadgets and funky color accents, it has an unbeatable downtown location opposite the Davenport.

Frank's Diner BREAKFAST $
(www.franksdiners.com; 516 W 2nd Ave; breakfast $5-9) A little west of downtown, but worth the walk, this restored vintage railway car knocks out a classic breakfast including extraordinarily good eggs and no-frills biscuits and gravy. Arrive early to beat the queues.

Rock City Grill INTERNATIONAL $$
(www.rockcitygrill. Com; 505 W Riverside Ave; mains $12-19) An atmospherically lit, youthful bar-restaurant with an expansive menu of old staples prepared in imaginative ways.

Drinking & Entertainment

With a vibrant student population based at Gonzaga University, Spokane has a happening nighttime scene.

Northern Lights Brewing Company BREWERY
(www.northernlightsbrewing.com; 1003 E Trent Ave) You can sample the locally handcrafted ales at Spokane's best microbrewery, near the university campus.

Dempsey's Brass Rail CLUB
(www.dempseysbrassrail.net; 909 W 1st; ⏲9pm-2am) An alternative gay-friendly nighttime establishment.

Bing Crosby Theater THEATER
(www.mettheater.com; 901 W Sprague Ave) The former Met, now named after local hero Bing, presents concerts, plays, film festivals and the Spokane Opera in a fairly intimate setting.

Information

Spokane Area Visitor Information Center (www.visitspokane.com; 201 W Main Ave at Browne St; ⏲8:30am-5pm Mon-Fri, 9am-6pm Sat & Sun) keeps a raft of information.

Getting There & Away

Buses and trains depart from the **Spokane Intermodal Transportation Station** (221 W 1st Ave). **Amtrak** (www.amtrak.com) has a daily service on the esteemed *Empire Builder* to Seattle ($48, 7½ hours), Portland ($48, 9½ hours) and Chicago ($205, 45 hours).

South Cascades

The South Cascades are taller but less clustered than their northern counterparts, extending from Snoqualmie Pass east of Seattle down to the mighty Columbia River on the border with Oregon. The highpoint in more ways than one is 14,411ft Mt Rainier. Equally compelling for different reasons is Mt St Helens (8365ft), still recovering from a devastating 1980 volcanic eruption. Lesser known Mt Adams (12,276ft) is renowned for the huckleberries and wildflowers that fill its grassy alpine meadows during the short but intense summer season.

MT RAINIER NATIONAL PARK

The USA's fourth-highest peak (outside Alaska), Majestic Mt Rainier is also one of its most beguiling. Encased in a 368-sq-mile national park (the world's fifth national park when it was inaugurated in 1899), the mountain's snowcapped summit and forest-covered foothills harbor numerous hiking trails, huge swaths of flower-carpeted meadows and an alluring conical peak that presents a formidable challenge for aspiring climbers.

The park has four entrances. Nisqually, on Hwy 706 via Ashford, near the park's southwest corner, is the busiest and most convenient gate, being close to the park's main nexus points and open year-round. The other entrances are Ohanapecosh, via Hwy 123; White River, off Hwy 410; and Carbon River, the most remote entryway, at the northwest corner. Call ☎800-695-7623 for road conditions. For information on the park, check out the National Park Service (NPS) website at www.nps.gov/mora, which includes downloadable maps and descriptions of 50 park trails.

Park entry is $15 per car or $5 per pedestrian. For overnight trips, get a wilderness camping permit (free) from ranger stations or visitor centers. The six campgrounds in the park have running water and toilets, but no RV hookups. **Reservations** (☎800-365-2267; www.mount.rainier.national-park.com/camping.htm; reserved campsites $12-15) are strongly advised during summer months and can be made up to two months in advance by phone or online.

The park's two main nexus points are Longmire and Paradise. Longmire, 7 miles inside the Nisqually entrance, has a **Museum & Information Center** (admission free; ⏲9am-6pm Jun-Sep, to 5pm Oct-May), a number of important trailheads and the rustic **National Park Inn** (☎360-569-2275; www.guestservices.com/rainier; r with shared/private bath $104/139, units $191; P❄) complete with an excellent restaurant. More hikes and interpretive walks can be found 12 miles further east at loftier Paradise, which is served by the informative **Henry M Jackson Visitor Center** (⏲10am-7pm daily Jun-Oct, to 5pm Sat & Sun Oct-Dec), completely rebuilt and reopened in 2008, and the vintage **Paradise Inn** (☎360-569-2275; www.mtrainierguestservices.com; r with shared/private bath $105/154; ⏲May-Oct; P❄📶), a historic 'parkitecture' inn constructed in 1916 and long part of the national park's fabric. Climbs to the top of Rainier leave from the inn; excellent four-day guided ascents are led by **Rainier Mountaineering Inc** (www.rmiguides.com; 30027 SR706 E, Ashford) for $944.

The **Wonderland Trail** is a 93-mile path that completely circumnavigates Mt Rainier via a well-maintained unbroken route. The hike is normally tackled over 10 to 12 days, with walkers staying at one of 18 registered campsites along the way. Before embarking you'll need to organize a free backcountry permit from the **Wilderness Information Center** (www.nps.gov/mora; 55210 238th Ave E, Ashford, WA 98304-9751); forms are available online.

The remote Carbon River entrance gives access to the park's inland rainforest. The **ranger station** (☎360-829-9639), just inside the entrance, is open daily in summer.

Gray Line (www.graylineseattle.com) runs guided bus tours from Seattle between May and September (one/two days $85/179).

MT ST HELENS NATIONAL VOLCANIC MONUMENT

Thanks to a 1980 eruption that set off an explosion bigger than the combined power of 1500 atomic bombs, Washington's 87th-tallest mountain needs little introduction. What it lacks in height, Mt St Helens makes up for in fiery infamy – 57 people perished on the mountain on that fateful day in May 1980 when an earthquake measuring 5.1 on the Richter scale sparked the biggest landslide in human history and buried 230 sq miles of forest under millions of tons of volcanic rock and ash.

For the carless, Mt St Helens can be seen on a day trip by bus from Portland with **Eco Tours of Oregon** (www.ecotours-of-oregon.com) for $69.50. If traveling independently, your first port of call should be the **Silver Lake Visitor Center** (3029 Spirit Lake Hwy; admission $3; ⏲9am-5pm), 5 miles east of Castle Rock on Hwy 504, which showcases films, exhibits and free information on the mountain.

For a closer view of the destructive power of nature, venture to the **Johnston Ridge Observatory** (⏲10am-6pm May-Oct), situated at the end of Hwy 504 and looking directly into the mouth of the crater. The observatory's exhibits take a more scientific look at the geologic events surrounding the 1980 blast.

A welcome B&B in an accommodations-lite area, the **Blue Heron Inn** (☎360-274-9595; www.blueheroninn.com; Hwy 504; d/ste $175/215; 📶) offers seven rooms including a Jacuzzi suite in a large house opposite the Silver Lake Visitor Center.

Central & Southeastern Washington

While they're rarely the first places visitors to Washington head for, the central and southeastern parts of the state harbor one secret weapon: wine. A Johnny-come-lately to the viticultural world, the fertile land that borders the Nile-like Yakima and Columbia River valleys is awash with enterprising new wineries producing quality grapes that now vie with California for national recognition. Yakima and its smaller and more attractive cousin Ellensburg have traditionally held the edge, but look out too for emerging Walla Walla, where talented restaurateurs and a proactive local council have begun to craft a wine destination par excellence.

YAKIMA & ELLENSBURG

Situated in its eponymous river valley, the city of Yakima is a rather bleak trading center that doesn't really live up to its 'Palm Springs of Washington' tourist label. The main reason to stop here is to visit one of the numerous wineries that lie between Yakima and Benton City; pick up a map at the **Yakima Valley Visitors & Convention Bureau** (www.visityakima.com; 10 N 8th St; ⌚9am-5pm Mon-Sat, 10am-4pm Sun).

A better layover is Ellensburg, a diminutive settlement 36 miles to the northwest that juxtaposes the state's largest rodeo (each Labor Day) with a town center that has more coffee bars per head than anywhere else in the world (allegedly). Grab your latte at local roaster **D&M Coffee** (www.dmcoffee.com; 301 N Pine St), browse the history section in the **Kittitas County Historical Museum** (www.kchm.org; donations accepted; ⌚10am-4pm Mon-Sat Jun-Sep, from noon Tue-Sat Oct-May) opposite, and stay over in **Inn at Goose Creek** (☎509-962-8030; www.innatgoosecreek.com; 1720 Canyon Rd; r from $99; 📶), one of the most imaginative motels in the Pacific Northwest with 10 completely different offbeat rooms, including the Victorian Honeymoon Suite, the Ellensburg Rodeo Room (cowboy memorabilia) and the I Love Christmas Room (with a red-and-green Santa carpet).

WALLA WALLA

Over the last decade, Walla Walla has converted itself from an obscure agricultural backwater, famous for its sweet onions and large state penitentiary, into the hottest wine-growing region outside of California's Napa Valley. While venerable Marcus Whitman College is the town's most obvious cultural attribute, you'll also find zany coffee bars here, along with cool wine-tasting rooms, fine Queen Anne architecture and one of the state's freshest and most vibrant farmers markets.

Sights & Activities

You don't need to be sloshed on wine to appreciate Walla Walla's historical and cultural heritage. Its Main Street has won countless historical awards, and to bring the settlement to life, the local **chamber of commerce** (www.wallawalla.org; 29 E Sumach St; ⌚8:30am-5pm Mon-Fri, 9am-4pm Sat & Sun May-Sep) has concocted some interesting walking tours, complete with leaflets and maps. For information on the region's wine culture, check out **Walla Walla Wine News** (www.wallawallawinenews.com), an excellent online resource.

Fort Walla Walla Museum MUSEUM
(755 Myra Rd; adult/child $7/6; ⌚10am-5pm Apr-Oct) A pioneer village of 17 historic buildings, with the museum housed in the old cavalry stables. There are collections of farm implements, ranching tools and what could be the world's largest plastic replica of a mule team.

Walla Walla Wineworks WINE TASTING
(www.waterbrook.com; 31 E Main St; ⌚10am-6pm Mon-Thu & Sun, to 8pm Fri & Sat) A good starting point for aspiring wine-quaffers in the town center, this new tasting room is affiliated with the local Waterbrook winery. It offers good Cabernet Sauvignons accompanied by cheese, cured meats and live music at weekends.

Sleeping & Eating

Marcus Whitman Hotel HOTEL $$
(☎509-525-2200; www.marcuswhitmanhotel.com; 6 W Rose St; r/ste $139/279; ❄📶) Walla Walla's best known landmark is impossible to miss with its distinctive rooftop turret visible from all around. In keeping with the settlement's well-preserved image, the red-bricked 1928 beauty has been elegantly renovated with ample rooms kitted out in rusts and browns, and embellished with Italian-crafted furniture.

TOP CHOICE **Saffron Mediterranean Kitchen** MEDITERRANEAN $$$
(☎509-525-2112; www.saffronmediterraneankitchen.com; 125 W Alder St; mains $15-27; ⌚2-10pm, to 9pm in winter) This place isn't about cooking,

it's about alchemy; Saffron takes seasonal, local ingredients and turns them into – well – pure gold. The Med-inspired menu lists dishes like pheasant, ricotta gnocchi, amazing flatbreads and weird yogurt-cucumber combo soups that could stand up against anything in Seattle.

Olive Marketplace & Café CAFE $

(21 E Main St; breakfast & sandwiches $7-12; ⏲7am-9pm) Run by local gourmet restaurateurs T Maccerones and set in the historic 1885 Barrett Building, this breezy cafe-market is famous for its breakfast (until 11am) and is a good place to line your stomach for the impending wine-tasting.

OREGON

Spatially larger than Washington but with only half the population, Oregon is the Pacific Northwest's warm, mild-mannered elder cousin (it joined the union 30 years earlier than Washington). Physically, the state shares many characteristics with its northern neighbor, including a rain-lashed coast, a spectacular spinal mountain range and a drier, more conservative interior plateau. But, with better urban planning laws and less sprawl, Oregon retains a more laid-back and tranquil feel.

OREGON FACTS

- » **Nickname** Beaver State
- » **Population** 3,831,074
- » **Area** 95,997 sq miles
- » **Capital city** Salem (population 154,637)
- » **Other cities** Portland (population 583,776), Eugene (population 156,185), Bend (population 76,639)
- » **Sales tax** Oregon has no sales tax
- » **Birthplace of** former US president Herbert Hoover (1874–1964), writer and Merry Prankster Ken Kesey (1935–2001), actress and dancer Ginger Rogers (1911–95), *The Simpsons* creator Matt Groening (b 1954), filmmaker Gus Van Sant (b 1952)
- » **Home of** Oregon Shakespeare Festival, tree-sitting, Nike, McMenamins
- » **Politics** Democratic governor, Democrat majorities in Congress, Democrat in Presidential elections since 1984
- » **Famous for** the Oregon Trail, forests, rain, beer, not being able to pump your own gas
- » **State beverage** milk (dairy's big here)
- » **Driving distances** Portland to Eugene 110 miles, Pendleton to Astoria 295 miles

Portland

If you want to see what the future looks like, come to Portland, Oregon, a city that is 10 years ahead of its time and as definitive of its age as the Rome of Caesar or the Paris of Haussmann. What Portland lacks in Coliseums and baroque opera houses, it makes up for in innovation and ideas that start from the ground up. No thought is too outlandish here, and no behavioral pattern too weird. Urban growth boundaries (which have prevented ugly suburban sprawl) were established in 1973, a light-rail network was instituted in 1986, and the first community bike projects hit the streets in 1994. Prone to becoming daring rather than depressed during economic downturns, Portland's pugnacious DIY attitude has charitably endowed the metro area (and, in some cases, the nation) with food carts, microbreweries, hardcore punk rock, bike culture, indie 'zines and a traffic-calmed downtown that feels more small town than big city. While the results might often look distinctly European, the 'can-do' ethos behind it is 100% American.

Sights

DOWNTOWN

Tom McCall Waterfront Park PARK

In case you hadn't noticed, Portland is famous for its parks. Sinuous, 2-mile-long Tom McCall Waterfront Park flanks the west bank of the Willamette River and is both an unofficial training ground for lunchtime runners and a commuter path for the city's avid army of cyclists.

The east side of the river is embellished by the **Eastbank Esplanade**, a path that tracks below the roaring overpasses that carry traffic north and south. You can loop back over half a dozen bridges.

Steel Bridge BRIDGE

'City of bridges' is one of numerous Portland monikers, and in this case it's justified; there are 11 of these river-spanning edifices across the Willamette. If you've only got time to traverse one, then walk, cycle, drive or catch the train across the multimodal, vertical-lift Steel Bridge built in 1912, the city's second-oldest.

Pioneer Courthouse Square LANDMARK
Portland's downtown hub is Pioneer Courthouse Sq, a redbricked people-friendly square with minimal traffic interference and where you'll find chess players, sunbathers, lunching office workers, buskers and the odd political activist. Formerly a car park, and before that a posh hotel, the square today hosts concerts, festivals and rallies. Across 6th Ave is the muscular **Pioneer Courthouse** (1875), the oldest federal building in the Pacific Northwest.

Portland Building LANDMARK
(cnr SW 5th Ave & SW Main St) In a downtown devoid of big skyscrapers, the city's signature structure is the emblematic, if architecturally dull, Portland Building, designed in 1980 by Michael Graves. A triumph of postmodernism to some, but a mine of user unfriendliness to others, the 15-story utilitarian block is embellished by the Neptune-like **Portlandia** statue, added above the front door in 1985, representing the Goddess of Commerce.

Oregon Historical Society MUSEUM
(www.ohs.org; 1200 SW Park Ave; adult/child $11/9; ⌚10am-5pm Tue-Sat, from noon Sun) Along the tree-shaded South Park Blocks sits the state's primary history museum, which dedicates most of its space to the story of Oregon and the pioneers who made it. There are interesting sections on Native American tribes and the travails of the Oregon Trail. Temporary exhibits furnish the downstairs space.

Portland Art Museum MUSEUM
(www.portlandartmuseum.org; 1219 SW Park Ave; adult/child under 17yr $10/free; ⌚10am-5pm Tue, Wed & Sat, to 8pm Thu & Fri, noon-5pm Sun) Just across the park, the art museum's excellent exhibits include Native American carvings, Asian and American art, and English silver. The museum also houses the Whitsell Auditorium, a first-rate theater that frequently screens rare or international films.

Aerial Tram CABLE CAR
(www.gobytram.com; 3303 SW Bond Ave; ⌚5:30am-9:30pm Mon-Fri, 9am-5pm Sat) Portland's aerial tram runs from the south Waterfront (there's a streetcar stop) to Marquam Hill. The tram runs along a 3300ft line up a vertical ascent of 500ft. The ride takes three minutes and costs $4 round-trip. The tram opened in 2007, smashing its budget predictions and causing much public controversy.

OLD TOWN & CHINATOWN

The core of rambunctious 1890s Portland, the once-notorious Old Town still exhibits a slightly seedy, if innocuous, underbelly. Among the poster-covered brick buildings and doorways full of down-and-outs lie several of the city's better music clubs and – slightly to the north – the city's main 'gayborhood.'

Shanghai Tunnels HISTORIC SITE
(www.shanghaitunnels.info; adult/child $13/8) Running beneath Old Town's streets is this series of underground corridors through which, in the 1850s, unscrupulous people would kidnap or 'shanghai' drunken men and sell them to sea captains looking for indentured workers. Tours run Fridays and Saturdays at 6:30pm and 8pm. Book online.

Chinatown NEIGHBORHOOD
Don't expect flashbacks of Shanghai in Portland's lackluster Chinese quarter, which begins (and largely ends) at the deceptively impressive pagoda-style **Chinatown Gates** (cnr W Burnside St & NW 4th Ave). Aside from some token chow mein takeouts, the main attraction here is the terribly overpriced **Classical Chinese Garden** (www.portlandchinesegarden.org; cnr NW 3rd Ave & NW Everett St; adult/child $8/7; ⌚10am-5pm), a deliciously tranquil block of reflecting ponds and manicured greenery, but for $8! Thankfully, tours are included with admission.

Saturday Market MARKET
(www.portlandsaturdaymarket.com; ⌚10am-5pm Sat, 11am-4:30pm Sun Mar-Dec) The best time to hit the river walk is on a weekend to catch the famous market, which showcases handicrafts, street entertainers and food carts.

Skidmore Fountain FOUNTAIN
Victorian-era architecture and the attractive Skidmore Fountain give the area beneath the Burnside Bridge some nostalgic flair.

NORTHWEST PORTLAND

Pearl District NEIGHBORHOOD
(www.explorethepearl.com) Slightly to the northwest of downtown, the Pearl District is an old industrial quarter that has transformed its once grotty warehouses into expensive lofts, upscale boutiques and creative restaurants.

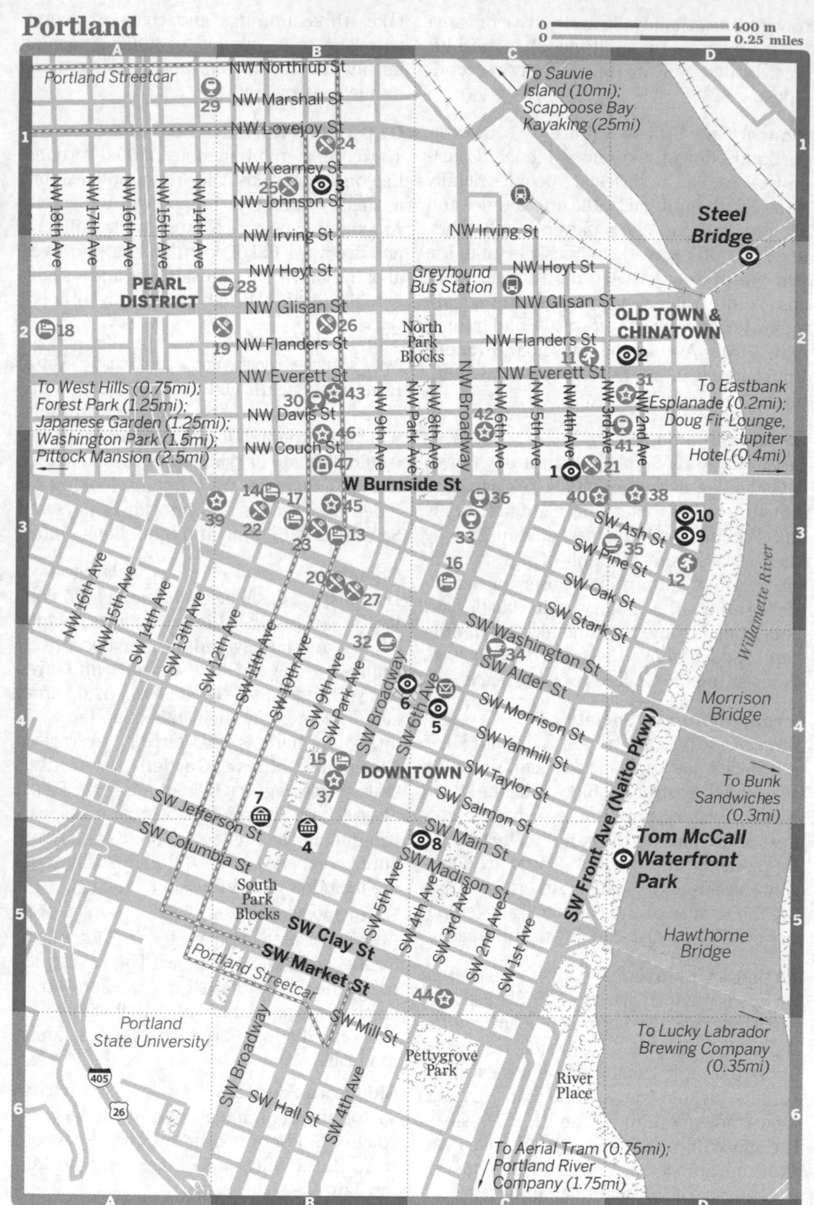

On the first Thursday of every month, the zone's abundant **art galleries** extend their evening hours and the area turns into a fancy street party of sorts. The **Jamison Square Fountain** (cnr NW Johnson St & NW 10th Ave) is one of its prettier urban spaces.

Nob Hill NEIGHBORHOOD

Nob Hill – or 'Snob Hill' to its detractors – has its hub on NW 23rd Ave, a trendy neighborhood thoroughfare that brims with clothing boutiques, home decor shops and cafes. The restaurants – including some of Portland's

Portland

Top Sights
Steel Bridge D2
Tom McCall Waterfront Park D5

Sights
1 Chinatown Gates C3
2 Classical Chinese Garden D2
3 Jamison Square Fountain B1
4 Oregeon Historical Society B5
5 Pioneer Courthouse C4
6 Pioneer Courthouse Sq B4
7 Portland Art Museum B4
8 Portland Building C5
9 Saturday Market D3
10 Skidmore Fountain D3

Activities, Courses & Tours
11 Portland Bicycle Tours C2
12 Waterfront Bicycles D3

Sleeping
13 Ace Hotel B3
14 Crystal Hotel B3
15 Heathman Hotel B4
16 Hotel Lucia C3
17 Mark Spencer Hotel B3
18 Northwest Portland Hostel A2

Eating
19 Andina B2
20 El Cubo de Cuba B3
21 Gaufre Gourmet C3
22 Jake's Famous Crawfish B3
23 Kenny & Zuke's B3
24 Lovejoy Bakers B1
25 Piazza Italia B1
26 Silk B2
27 Ziba's Pitas B3

Drinking
28 Barista B2
29 Bridgeport Brewpub A1
30 Deschutes Brewery B2
31 Hobo's D2
32 Public Domain Coffee B4
33 Saucebox C3
34 Spella Caffè C4
35 Stumptown Coffee D3
Stumptown Coffee .... (see 13)
36 Tugboat Brewery C3

Entertainment
37 Arlene Schnitzer Concert Hall B4
38 Berbati's Pan D3
39 Crystal Ballroom B3
40 Dante's C3
41 Darcelle XV D2
42 Embers C2
43 Jimmy Mak's B2
44 Keller Auditorium C5
45 Living Room Theater B3
46 Portland Center Stage B3

Shopping
47 Powell's City of Books B3

finest, lie mostly along NW 21st Ave. This is a perfect neighborhood for strolling, window-shopping and looking at houses you'll never be able to afford.

WEST HILLS

Behind downtown Portland is the West Hills area, known for its exclusive homes, huge parks and – if you're lucky – peek-a-boo views of up to five Cascade volcanoes.

Forest Park PARK

Not many cities have 5100 acres of temperature rainforest within their limits, but then not many cities are like Portland. Abutting the more manicured Washington Park to the west (to which it is linked by various trails) is the far wilder Forest Park, whose dense foliage harbors plants, animals and an avid hiking fraternity. The **Portland Audubon Society** (www.audubonpoerland.com; 5151 NW Cornell Rd; ⌚store 10am-6pm Mon-Sat, to 5pm Sun) maintains a bookstore, wildlife rehabilitation center and 4 miles of trails within its Forest Park sanctuary.

The main sight in the park is the **Pittock Mansion** (www.pittockmansion.com; 3229 NW Pittock Dr; adult/child $7/4; ⌚11am-4pm; P), a grand mansion built in 1914 by Henry Pittock, who revitalized the Portland-based *Oregonian* newspaper. It's worth visiting the (free) grounds just to check out the spectacular views – bring a picnic.

Washington Park PARK

West of Forest Park, the more tamed Washington Park contains a good half-day's worth of attractions within its 400 acres of greenery. **Hoyt Arboretum** (www.hoytarboretum.org; 4000 Fairview Blvd; admission free; ⌚trails 6am-10pm, visitor center 9am-4pm Mon-Fri, to 3pm

Sat) showcases more than 1000 species of native and exotic trees and has 12 miles of walking trails. It's prettiest in the fall. The **International Rose Test Gardens** (www.rosegardenstore.org; admission free; ⏲sunrise-sunset) is the centerpiece of Portland's famous rose blooms; there are 400 types on show here, plus great city views. Further uphill is the **Japanese Garden** (www.japanesegarden.com; 611 SW Kingston Ave; adult/child $9.50/6.75; ⏲noon-7pm Mon, from 10am Tue-Sun; P), another oasis of tranquility.

NORTHEAST & SOUTHEAST

Across the Willamette River from downtown is the **Lloyd Center** shopping mall (1960), the usual fluorescent amalgamation of fast-food franchises and chain stores, of interest only because it was – apparently – the first of its kind in the US. A few blocks to the southwest is the equally ugly glass-towered **Oregon Convention Center** and the **Rose Garden Arena**, home of local basketball heroes, the Trailblazers.

Further up the Willamette, **N Mississippi Avenue** used to be full of run-down buildings but has undergone a yuppification in recent times. Northeast is artsy **NE Alberta Street**, a ribbon of art galleries, boutiques and cafes. **SE Hawthorne Boulevard** (near SE 39th Ave) is affluent hippy territory; think tie-dye T-shirts, homeopaths and cafes where every menu item can be veganized. One leafy mile to the south, the connecting thoroughfare of **SE Division Street** has in recent years become a kind of SE Delicious Street with an ample quota of excellent new restaurants, bars and pubs.

Activities

Hiking and mountain biking are to Portland what driving is to LA – part of the cultural make-up.

Hiking

The best hiking is found in **Forest Park**, which harbors an unbelievable 70 miles of trails and often feels more like Mt Hood's foothills than Portland's city limits. The park's all-encompassing **Wildwood Trail** starts at the Hoyt Arboretum and winds through 30 miles of forest, with many spur trails that allow for loop hikes. Other trailheads into Forest Park are located at the western ends of NW Thurman and NW Upshur Sts.

Cycling

Coming to Portland and not cycling isn't really playing the game – and you'll get few better opportunities to pedal freely in an urban area in North America.

Two unbroken trails head out from downtown. To the east the **Springwater Corridor** starts near the Oregon Museum of Science & Industry (as an extension of the Eastbank Esplanade) and goes all the way to the suburb of Gresham – 21 miles away. In the northwest the **Leif Erikson Drive** is an old logging road leading 11 miles into Forest Park and offering occasional peeks over the city.

PORTLAND FOR CHILDREN

Fear not, overworked parent. Kids love Portland for multiple reasons, and you might not even need the car seat. **Waterfront Bicycles** (www.waterfrontbikes.com) rents out tandem bikes ($75 per day), trek trailer kid extensions ($30) or chariots ($30) from its SW Ash St store. Throw your kid on the back and discover Portland on two wheels. On the riverside, the **Oregon Museum of Science & Industry** (OMSI; www.omsi.edu; 1945 SE Water Ave; adult/child $12/9; ⏲9:30am-5:30pm Tue-Sun, to 7pm Jun-Aug) has playful science exhibits for the whole age range. There's also an Omnimax theater, planetarium shows and a submarine tour (all separate charge).

Three further kid-orientated sights are located in expansive Washington Park, with its ample tearing-around possibilities. The **Children's Museum** (www.portlandcm.org; 4015 SW Canyon Rd; admission $9; ⏲9am-5pm Mon-Sat, from 11am Sun) is more a play centre than a museum, with numerous opportunities to crawl, climb, paint and create. Nearby, the **World Forestry Center** (www.worldforestry.org; 4033 SW Canyon Rd; adult/child $8/5; ⏲10am-5pm) offers similar experiences but with a woodsy twist.

The default sight for pacifying parents is **Oregon Zoo** (www.oregonzoo.org; 4001 SW Canyon Rd; adult/child $9.75/6.75; ⏲8am-6pm Apr-Sep), connected in summer to Washington Park's rose garden by the Zoo Train. Don't miss 'zoolights' during the holiday season, when the complex is filled with lit-up trees and animal figures.

For scenic farm country, head to **Sauvie Island**, 10 miles northwest of downtown Portland. This island is prime cycling land – it's flat, has relatively little traffic and much of it is wildlife refuge.

For bike rental, try **Waterfront Bicycles** (www.waterfrontbikes.com; 10 SW Ash St), where the ballpark price for day rental is $35. The tourist office gives out an excellent free cycling map.

Kayaking

Situated close to the confluence of the Columbia and Willamette Rivers, Portland has miles of navigable waterways. Kayaking is a popular water-based pursuit. Rentals start at approximately $10 per hour ($50 per day), and you can also sign up for instruction and guided tours.

Portland River Company KAYAKING
(503-459-4050; www portlandrivercompany.com.; 6320 SW Macadam Ave) Kayaking rentals and tours including a three-hour circumnavigation of Ross Island on the Willamette River for $45.

Scappoose Bay Kayaking KAYAKING
(503-397-2161, www.scappoosebaykayaking.com; 57420 Old Portland Rd) Rentals, instruction and wildlife-biased tours around Sauvie Island.

Tours

Portland Bicycle Tours BICYCLE
(503-360-6815; www.intrepidexperience.com; 345 NW Everett St) Bike the 'City of Roses' on a parks, bridges or market tour energized with plenty of Stumptown coffee. Two-hour tours with own/rented bike cost $30/40.

Eco Tours of Oregon NATURE
(503-245-1428; www.ecotours-of-oregon.com) Naturalist tours of northwest Oregon and Washington, including the Columbia River Gorge, Mt St Helens and the wine country.

PDX Running Tours RUNNING
(503-334-7334; www.pdxruntours.com; tours $30-45) Discover both weird and wild Portland with your own personal trainer-cum-guide on these cross-city running tours for all abilities.

Festivals & Events

Portland International Film Festival FILM
(www.nwfilm.org) Oregon's biggest film event highlights nearly 100 films from over 30 countries. Held mid- to late February.

Portland Rose Festival ROSES
(www.rosefestival.org) Rose-covered floats, dragon-boat races, fireworks, roaming packs of sailors and the crowning of a Rose Queen all make this Portland's biggest celebration. Held late May to early June.

Queer Pride Celebration GAY & LESBIAN
(www.pridenw.org) Keep Portland queer in mid-June: enjoy a kick-off party, take a cruise or join the parade.

Oregon Brewers Festival BEER
(www.oregonbrewfest.com) Quaff microbrews during the summer (late July) in Tom McCall Waterfront Park and during the winter (early December) at Pioneer Courthouse Sq.

Sleeping

Reserve ahead in summer.

TOP CHOICE **Ace Hotel** BOUTIQUE HOTEL $$
(503-228-2277; www.acehotel.com; 1022 SW Stark St; d with shared/private bath from $107/147;) A microcosm of the Portland scene, Ace is what the word 'hipster' was invented for. The reception area is a good indication of what's to come: big sofas, retro-industrial decor, the Ramones on the sound system and the comforting aroma of Stumptown coffee wafting in through the connecting door. If you make it upstairs you'll find chic minimalist rooms (some with shared bath) kitted out with wonderfully comfortable beds.

Crystal Hotel HOTEL $$
(503-972-2670, www.mcmenamins.com; 303 SW 12th Ave; queen/king r $105/165;) Room furnishings that blend Grateful Dead–inspired psychedelia with the interior of a Victorian boudoir can only mean one thing. Welcome to the latest McMenamins hotel, an action-packed accommodations option, bar, cafe and restaurant that shares a name and ownership with the famous Ballroom across the road.

Jupiter Hotel BOUTIQUE MOTEL $$
(503-230-9200; www.jupiterhotel.com; 800 E BurnsideSt; d $114-149; P) Take a dull concept – in this case a motel – give it a sleek makeover and behold! The Jupiter has hijacked America's most ubiquitous cheap-sleep idea and personalized it with retro furnishings, chalkboard doors (on which you can write instructions to the room maid) and vivid color accents. No two rooms are

alike (ironic given the motel shell) and the adjacent Doug Fir Lounge is one of the city's coolest live-music venues. Hit the bar with the band roadies and check in after midnight for a discount.

Northwest Portland Hostel HOSTEL **$**
(503-241-2783; www.nwportlandhostel.com; 425 NW 18th Ave; dm $20-26, d $42-68; P ❄ @ wifi) Perfectly located between the Pearl District and NW 21st and 24th Aves, this highly rated hostel is spread across a couple of quintessential Northwest District houses and features plenty of common areas (including a small deck), good rooms and bike rentals. Non-HI members pay $3 extra.

McMenamins Edgefield HOTEL **$$**
(503-669-8610; www.mcmenamins.com; 2126 SW Halsey St, Troutdale; dm $30, d with shared bath $60-80, with private bath $110-145; ❄ @ wifi) This former county poor farm, restored by the McMenamin brothers, is now a one-of-a-kind, 38-acre hotel complex with a dizzying variety of services. Taste wine and homemade beer, play golf, watch movies, shop at the gift store, listen to live music, walk the extensive gardens and eat at one of its restaurants. It's about a 20-minute drive east from downtown.

Kennedy School HOTEL **$$**
(503-249-3983, www.mcmenamins.com; 5736 NE 33rd Ave; d $109-130; P @ wifi) At this Portland institution, a former elementary school, you can relive those halcyon days when you used to fall asleep in biology classes. A few miles from the city center, the school is now home to a hotel (yes, the bedrooms are converted classrooms), a restaurant, several bars, a microbrewery and a movie theater. There's a soaking pool, and the whole school is decorated with mosaics, fantasy paintings and historical photographs.

Mark Spencer Hotel HOTEL **$$**
(503-224-3293, www.markspencer.com; 409 SW 11th Ave; d incl breakfast from $129; ❄ @ wifi) If the Ace is just too trendy, head next door to this more refined and down-to-earth (some would say 'boring') choice where spacious, unmemorable rooms, all with kitchens, are economically priced for such a well-placed, comfortable city-center option. There's complimentary tea with cookies during the afternoon.

Hotel Lucia BOUTIQUE HOTEL **$$$**
(503-225-1717; www.hotellucia.com; 400 SW Broadway; d $199-299; ❄ @ wifi) A boutique hotel with sleek black-and-white furnishings topped with arty displays of polished (but still edible) apples. Rooms are design-show funky and geek-friendly gadgets include wi-fi, flat-screen TVs and iPod docking stations. The downtown location is handy for everywhere.

DON'T MISS

PORTLAND'S FOOD CARTS

Perhaps one of the best (and cheapest) ways to uncover Portland's cultural pastiche is to explore its diverse **food carts** (www.foodcartsportland.com). Largely a product of the last decade, these semipermanent kitchens-on-wheels inhabit parking lots around town and are usually clustered together in rough groups or 'pods,' often with their own communal tables, ATMs and portaloos. As many of the owners are recent immigrants (who can't afford a hefty restaurant start-up), the carts are akin to an international potluck with colorful kitchen hatches offering soul food from everywhere from Bosnia and Czechoslovakia to Vietnam and Mexico. While prices are low ($5 to $6 for a filling and tasty lunch), standards of hygiene – thanks to tight city regulations – are kept high and the banter between customer and proprietor is a kind of geography lesson meets recipe exchange.

Food-cart locations vary, though the most significant cluster is on the corners of SW Alder St and SW 9th Ave. Some of the newer carts have no fixed abode and announce their daily whereabouts on Facebook and Twitter. Highlights in a highly competitive field:

Ziba's Pitas (SW 9th Ave & SW Alder St) Stuffed flat-breads from Bosnia.

Potato Champion (SE 12th Ave & Hawthorne) Twice-fried *pommes frites* with dips.

El Cubo de Cuba (SW 10th Ave & SW Alder St) *Ropa vieja* (shredded stewed beef) and classic Cuban sandwiches.

Gaufre Gourmet (NW 4th Ave & W Burnside St) Liège-style Belgian waffles with innovative toppings.

Inn at Northrup Station HOTEL $$
(☎503-224-0543; www.northrupstation.com; 2025 NW Northrup St; d incl breakfast from $156; P❄@📶) Almost over the top with its bright color scheme and funky decor, this super-trendy hotel boasts huge artsy suites, many with a patio or balcony. There's a cool rooftop patio with plants.

Heathman Hotel LUXURY HOTEL $$$
(☎503-241-4100; www.heathmanhotel.com; 1001 SW Broadway; d from $200; ❄@📶) Portland's token old-school 'posh' hotel has a doorman dressed as a London beefeater (without the accent) and one of the best restaurants in the city. It also hosts high tea in the afternoons, jazz in the evenings and a library stocked with signed books by authors who have stayed here. Rooms are elegant, stylish and luxurious. Parking costs $30.

Eating

Portland's rapidly evolving food scene tore up the rule book years ago and has branched out into countless genres, subgenres, and subgenres of subgenres. Vegetarianism is well represented, as is brunch, Asian fusion and the rather loose concept known as 'Pacific Northwest.' Then there are the international food carts, cramming the entire cuisine of planet Earth into a single city block.

Paley's Place FRENCH, FUSION $$$
(☎503-243-2403; www.paleysplace.net; 1204 NW 21st Ave; mains $20-32; ⏰5:30-10pm Mon-Thu, to 11pm Fri & Sat, 5-10pm Sun) It takes a special kind of talent to win a Food Network *Iron Chef*, but, truth be told, Vitaly Paley, a recent recipient of the honor, had been serving up top-drawer duck confit, Kobe burger and veal sweetbreads long before reality TV came knocking. Paley's Gallic-leaning Portland restaurant occupies a refined perch above a spa in salubrious Nob Hill. Eating there is a memorable experience.

Andina SOUTH AMERICAN $$$
(☎503-228-9535; www.andinarestaurant.com; 1314 NW Glisan St; mains $25-30) Always the trend-setter, Portland's restaurant-of-the-moment is not French, Italian or Thai but…novo-Peruvian. The hook? Take locally grown ingredients and inject them with flavors reminiscent of the High Andes. The result? Food that's daring, delicious and – above all – different.

Piazza Italia ITALIAN $$
(☎503-478-0619; www.piazzaportland.com; 1129 NW Johnson; pasta $12-18; ⏰11:30am-3pm & from 5pm) Remember that great *ragù* (meat sauce) you last had in Bologna or those memorable *vongole* (clams) you once polished off in Sicily. Well, here they are again courtesy of Piazza Italia, a highly authentic restaurant that succeeds where so many fail: replicating the true essence of Italian food in North America.

Kenny & Zuke's DELI $$
(www.kennyandzukes.com; 1038 SW Stark St; sandwiches $9-13; ⏰7am-8pm Sun-Thu, to 9pm Fri & Sat) Portland takes on New York in this traditional Jewish-style deli next to the Ace Hotel, where the *pièce de résistance* is – surprise, surprise – the hand-sliced pastrami (cured for five days, smoked for 10 and steamed for three). Try the classic pastrami on rye, and leave room for a blintz, latke or formidable dessert.

Silk VIETNAMESE $$
(1012 NW Glisan St; mains $9-14; ⏰11am-3pm & 5-10pm Mon-Sat) An interesting modern take on Vietnamese cuisine, for Silk read Slick. The clean-lined minimalist decor offers sit-down or cocktail-bar options but the atmosphere is laid-back (lots of single diners) and the prices are very reasonable. Highlights include the banana-blossom salad, the prawn and chicken spring rolls and the pho (noodle soups).

Pambiche CUBAN $$
(☎503-233-0511; www.pambiche.com; 2811 NE Glisan St; mains $11-17; ⏰11am-10pm Sun-Thu, to midnight Fri & Sat) Most good Cuban food emigrated with two million others after the revolution in 1959, meaning the best place to find it these days is in Miami, New Jersey or – slightly more serendipitously – this multicolored restaurant in the northeast district of Portland. Open all day, *la hora del amigo* (Cuban happy hour, 2pm to 6pm Monday to Friday, 10pm to midnight Friday and Saturday) is the best time to chow: lashings of *ropa vieja* (shredded beef), snapper in coconut sauce and that rich Cuban coffee. Warning – the place is insanely popular, but tiny. Arrive early!

Jake's Famous Crawfish SEAFOOD $$$
(☎503-226-1419; 401 SW 12th Ave; mains $17-32; ⏰11am-11pm Mon-Thu, to midnight Fri, noon-midnight Sat, 3-11pm Sun) Portland's best seafood lies within this elegant old-time venue, which serves up divine oysters, revelatory crab cakes and a horseradish salmon made in heaven. Come at 3pm and praise the lord for (cheap) happy hour.

Lovejoy Bakers BAKERY, SANDWICHES $
(www.lovejoybakers.com; 939 NW 10th Ave; lunch $7-10; ⌚) Another typically stylish Pearl District abode; this bakery has on-site ovens, creative breads and an inviting streamline dmoderne cafe where you can embellish the home-baked stuff with exotic sandwich fillings.

Bunk Sandwiches SANDWICHES $
(www.bunksandwiches.com; 621 SE Morrison St; light meals $5-7; ⌚8am-3pm) This unfussy hole-in-the-wall brunch-lunch spot necessitates multiple napkins. Choose from a blackboard of po'boys, tuna melts and meatball parmigianas and find out why.

Drinking

Coffeehouses

The Seattle coffee boom is ancient history. Portland grabbed the 'best coffee-making city' baton a decade ago and has been running with it ever since. You ain't seen nothing yet!

TOP CHOICE **Stumptown Coffee** CAFE
(www.stumptowncoffee.com; 📶) Ace Hotel (1022 SW Stark St); Belmont (3356 SE Belmont St); Division (3377 SE Division St); Downtown (128 SW 3rd Ave) The godfather of the micro-roasting revolution still takes some beating. The Ace Hotel location is the coolest nook, where trendy baristas compare asymmetrical haircuts over an Iggy Pop soundtrack. You'll be back multiple times.

Barista CAFE
(www.baristapdx.com) Pearl District (539 NW 13th Ave); Alberta (1725 NE Alberta St) Pro baristas serve made-to-perfection coffee with charm at these two newish locations that showcase different roasts every week and get their fresh pastries from a nearby Pearl district bakery.

Coava Coffee CAFE
(www.coava.myshopify.com; 1300 SE Grand Ave; ⌚7am-5pm Mon-Fri, from 8am Sat & Sun) Despite having no menu and a decor that takes the concept of 'neo-industrial' to ridiculous extremes (think school woodwork classes), Coava delivers where it matters – java that tastes so good you wonder if they've been out hand-picking it bean by bean. Unmissable!

Public Domain Coffee CAFE
(www.publicdomaincoffee.com; 603 SW Broadway, cnr Alder St; 6am-7pm Mon-Fri from 7am Sat & Sun) A swanky new downtown outlet owned by long-time indie roasters Coffee Bean International. Admire the plush wood and shiny high-end espresso machines, and call in for the public cuppings (2pm weekends) and home-brewing classes (first Saturday of the month).

Spella Caffè CAFE
(www.spellacaffe.com; 520 SW 5th; ⌚7:30am-4pm Mon-Fri) A former food-cart coffee specialist now bivouacked in a tiny standing-room-only shop, Andrea Spella roasts his Brazilian beans with the precision of an experienced oenologist and dispatches espresso from a unique hand-operated, piston-style machine.

Bars & Brewpubs

It's enough to make a native Brit jealous. Portland has about 30 brewpubs within its borders – more than any other city on earth. A good way to taste as much as possible without going into liver failure is to order four to eight beer samplers.

TOP CHOICE **Bridgeport Brewpub** BREWERY
(www.bridgeportbrew.com; 1313 NW Marshall St) This huge, relaxing unpretentious bar (which also sells great food) hides a small piece of history. This is where the micro-brewing industry in the US was kick-started in 1984. And yes, it's still here working the magic.

Lucky Labrador Brewing Company BREWERY
(www.luckylab.com) Hawthorne (915 SE Hawthorne Blvd); Pearl District (1945 NW Quimby St) The name's no joke. Dogs are welcome at this mild-mannered and mild-beer-ed pub; there's even a dog-friendly back patio at the Hawthorne branch where movies are shown in summer.

Deschutes Brewery BREWERY
(www.deschutesbrewery.com; 210 NW 11th Ave) Proof that not all good ideas start in Portland is Deschutes, an import from Bend that serves great pub grub and beer from its swanky perch in the Pearl District. The beer is brewed on-site.

Saucebox BAR
(www.saucebox.com; 214 SW Broadway) Trendy downtowners slink into this ubersleek downtown restaurant with pretty bar staff serving upscale Asian-fusion cuisine; but entertainment-seeking out-of-towners are welcome to pop by for a creative cocktail. DJs fire up at 10pm.

Tugboat Brewery BREWERY
(711 SW Ankeny; ⌚5-10pm Mon, 4pm-midnight Tue-Thu, 4pm-1am Fri & Sat) Dive-bar-ish and, well, different, the Tugboat is on the periphery of the shabby Old Town and has an English front parlor feel to its small interior lined with bookshelves and jovial locals.

Horse Brass Pub BAR
(www.horsebrass.com; 4534 SE Belmont St) Portland's most authentic English pub, cherished for its dark-wood atmosphere, excellent fish and chips, and 50 beers on tap. Play some darts, watch soccer on TV or just take it all in.

Crush BAR
(www.crushbar.com; 1400 SE Morrison St) Slip into this sexy lounge with all the pretty people and order one of the exotic cocktails. The menu's gourmet (try brunch) and there's a 'vice' room just for smokers. Great for a girls' night out, straight or lesbian.

LaurelThirst Pub BAR
(2958 NE Glisan St) Crowds sometimes spill onto the sidewalk at this dark, funky neighborhood joint. Regular live music is free in the early evening, but incurs a cover charge after 9pm. Good beer and wine selection (but no liquor), along with fine breakfasts.

Amnesia Brewing BREWERY
(832 N Beech St) Hip N Mississippi Ave's main brewery, with a casual feel and picnic tables out front. Excellent beer – try the Desolation IPA or Wonka Porter. Outdoor grill offers burgers and sausages.

Hopworks Urban Brewery BREWERY
(www.hopworksbeer.com; 2944 SE Powell Blvd) One of the newer kids on the brewpub block has furnished Portland with its first 100% ecobrewery – all organic ales, local ingredients, composting and even a 'bicycle bar.'

Hair of the Dog Brewing BREWERY
(www.hairofthedog.com; 61 SE Yamhill; ⌚2-8pm Wed-Sun) Beer connoisseurship took a leaf out of the wine snob's guidebook when this beer geek's heaven opened in 2010, billing itself as a 'tasting room' as opposed to a pub. Complex 'bottled-conditioned' beer is brewed on the premises with all the precision of a scientific experiment.

☆ Entertainment

That cozy brewpub was just the ice-breaker. Portland has been manifesting a dynamic music scene, ever since hardcore punk merchants the Wipers stood up and yelled 'Is This Real?' in 1979. Then there are the cinemas, wonderfully congenial places where wait staff will bring your food orders into the auditorium *during the movie!*

Check the *Mercury* or *Willamette Week* for entertainment schedules and cover charges.

Live Music

Doug Fir Lounge LIVE MUSIC
(www.dougfirlounge.com; 830 E Burnside St) Since the closing of the legendary Satyricon nightclub in the late 2000s, Portland's musical baton has been passed onto the Doug Fir, a bar-lounge with a personality that's more middle-aged rock star than angry young punk. But, true to form, the Fir still delivers where it matters, luring edgy, hard-to-get talent into a venue that pits tattooed youths against suburban yuppies. Its ascent has enlivened the new trendy neighborhood of South Burnside, recently christened with the acronym SoBu.

Dante's LIVE MUSIC
(www.danteslive.com; 1 SW 3rd Ave) This steamy red bar near Chinatown books vaudeville shows along with national acts such as the Dandy Warhols and Concrete Blonde. Drop in on a Monday night for the ever-popular 'Karaoke from Hell.'

Berbati's Pan LIVE MUSIC
(www.berbati.com; 10 SW 3rd Ave) An established rock club that nabs some of the more interesting acts in town, including big band, swing, acid rock and R & B. Outdoor seating and pool tables are a plus.

Crystal Ballroom LIVE MUSIC
(www.mcmenamins.com; 1332 W Burnside St) Opened in 1914, the Crystal saw it all – jazz, beat poets and psychedelic – until a 1968 closure led to it becoming the city's favorite squat. The McMenamin brothers rescued it from oblivion in 1997 and it's back to its '50s high-water mark, complete with a 'floating' dance floor that bounces at the slightest provocation.

Jimmy Mak's LIVE MUSIC
(www.jimmymaks.com; 221 NW 10th Ave ⌚music from 8pm) Stumptown's premier jazz venue serves excellent Mediterranean food in its posh dining room. There's a casual smoking bar-lounge in the basement.

Cinema

Living Room Theater CINEMA
(www.livingroomtheaters.com; 341 SW 10th Ave) Almost too good to be true! These six movie

theaters with cutting-edge digital technology screen art-house, foreign and retro films while the staff bring you drinks and tapas to enjoy in front of the big screen. There's an adjacent bar with wine, wi-fi, coffee and comfy sofas.

Kennedy School CINEMA
(www.mcmenamins.com; 5736 NE 33rd Ave) The McMenamin brothers' premier Portland venue. You can watch movies in the old school gym.

Bagdad Theater CINEMA
(www.mcmenamins.com; 3702 SE Hawthorne Blvd) Another historic McMenamins venue over on the eastside; has bargain flicks.

Cinema 21 CINEMA
(www.cinema21.com; 616 NW 21st Ave) Portland's premier art-house and foreign-film theater.

Performing Arts

Portland Center Stage THEATER
(☎503-445-3700; www.pcs.org; 128 NW 11th Ave) The city's main theater company now performs in the Portland Armory – a newly renovated Pearl District landmark with state-of-the-art features.

Arlene Schnitzer Concert Hall CLASSICAL MUSIC
(☎503-228-1353; www.pcpa.com/events/asch.php; 1037 SW Broadway) The Oregon Symphony performs in this beautiful, if not acoustically brilliant, downtown venue.

Artists Repertory Theatre THEATER
(☎503-241-1278; www.artistsrep.org; 1516 SW Alder St) You can catch some of Portland's best plays, including regional premieres, in this intimate space.

Keller Auditorium THEATER
(☎503-248-4335; www.pcpa.com/events/keller.php; 222 SW Clay St) The Portland Opera, Oregon Ballet Theatre and Oregon Children's Theatre all stage performances here.

Gay & Lesbian Venues

For current listings, see *Just Out*, Portland's free gay biweekly. Or grab a *Gay and Lesbian Community Yellow Pages* (www.pdxgayyellowpages.com) for other services.

Darcelle XV CABARET
(www.darcellexv.com; 208 NW 3rd Ave) Portland's premier drag show, featuring queens in big wigs, fake jewelry and overstuffed bras. Male strippers perform at midnight on weekends.

Embers CLUB
(110 NW Broadway) Regulars come to meet up for the music (from '80s tunes to techno and pop), amateur drag shows, a fun dance floor and friendly camaraderie. Mixed crowd.

Hobo's BAR
(www.hobospdx.com; 120 NW 3rd Ave) Past the old historic storefront is a classy restaurant-piano bar popular with older gay men. It's a quiet, relaxed place for a romantic dinner or drink.

Sports

Portland's only major-league sports team is the **Trail Blazers** (www.nba.com/blazers), which plays basketball at Rose Garden Arena.

PGE Park hosts the Portland's minor-league baseball team, the **Portland Beavers** (www.portlandbeavers.com), along with the A-League soccer team, the **Portland Timbers** (www.portlandtimbers.com). The Timbers, now in their fourth incarnation, were first formed in 1975 and logged some early successes in the erstwhile NASL. They are well known for their vociferous supporters, the *Timbers Army,* and long succession of British coaches.

Shopping

Portland's downtown shopping district extends in a two-block radius from Pioneer Courthouse Sq and displays all of the usual suspects. Pioneer Pl, an upscale mall, is be-

DON'T MISS

POWELL'S CITY OF BOOKS

Remember those satisfying weekend afternoons in the 1980s and '90s, when you could bivouac yourself inside the local bookstore with a takeout coffee and let your eye carry you spontaneously from shelf to shelf? Well, it's not all ancient history – at least, not yet. Like a Proustian flashback from a pre-ebook era, **Powell's City of Books** (www.powells.com; 1005 W Burnside St; ⏲9am-11pm) reacquaints incurable bookworms with dog-eared dust jackets, geeky assistants and unexpected literary epiphanies. Founded in 1971, it claims to be the largest independent bookstore in the world and its labyrinthine interior takes up a whole city block.

tween SW Morrison and SW Yamhill Sts, east of the square. The Pearl District is dotted with high-end galleries, boutiques and home-decor shops. On weekends, you can visit the quintessential Portland Saturday Market by the Skidmore Fountain.

Eastside has lots of trendy shopping streets that also host a few restaurants and cafes. SE Hawthorne Blvd is the biggest, N Mississippi Ave is the most recent and NE Alberta St is the most artsy and funky. Down south, Sellwood is known for its antique shops.

Information

Emergency & Medical Services

Legacy Good Samaritan Hospital & Medical Center (☎503-413-7711; 1015 NW 22nd Ave)

Portland Police (☎503-823-0000)

Walgreens (☎503-238-6053; 940 SE 39th Ave) Has a 24-hour pharmacy in the city's east.

Internet Access

Backspace (www.backspace.bz; 115 NW 5th Ave; ⏲7am-11pm Mon-Wed, to midnight Thu & Fri, 10am-midnight Sat, to 11pm Sun) Youth-oriented hangout with arcade games, coffee and long hours.

Urban Grind Coffeehouse (www.urbangrindcoffee.com) NE Oregon St (2214 NE Oregon St); NW 14th Ave (911 NW 14th Ave; ⏲6am-10:30pm) Slick cafe with computers and free wi-fi.

Internet Resources

City of Portland (www.portlandonline.com) Stumptown's official website.

Gay Oregon (www.gaypdx.com) A resource for Portland's gay and lesbian communities.

PDX Guide (www.pdxguide.com) Fun and spot-on food and drink reviews by a guy who knows, plus other happenings around town.

Portland Independent Media Center (www.portland.indymedia.org) Community news and lefty activism.

Media

Just Out (www.justout.com) Free biweekly serving Portland's gay community.

KBOO 90.7 FM Progressive local station run by volunteers; alternative news and views.

Portland Mercury (www.portlandmercury.com) The local sibling of Seattle's *Stranger*, this free weekly is published on Thursdays.

Willamette Week (www.wweek.com) Free alt-weekly covering local news and culture, published on Wednesdays.

Money

Travelex (⏲5:30am-4:30pm) Downtown (900 SW 6th Ave); Portland International Airport (main ticket lobby) Foreign-currency exchange.

Post

Post office Main branch (715 NW Hoyt St); University Station (1505 SW 6th Ave)

Tourist Information

Portland Oregon Visitors Association (www.travelportland.com; 701 SW 6th Ave; ⏲8:30am-5:30pm Mon-Fri, 10am-4pm Sat, 10am-2pm Sun) Super-friendly volunteers man this office in Pioneer Courthouse Sq. There's a small theater with a 12-minute film about the city, and Tri-Met bus and light-rail offices inside.

Getting There & Away

Air

Portland International Airport (PDX; www.flypdx.com) has daily flights all over the US, as well as to four international destinations. It's situated just east of I-5 on the banks of the Columbia River (20 minutes' drive from downtown). Amenities include money changers, restaurants, bookstores (including three Powell's branches) and business services like free wi-fi.

Bus

Greyhound (www.greyhound.com; 550 NW 6th Ave) connects Portland with cities along I-5 and I-84. Destinations include Chicago, IL (50 hours, $197), Boise, WA (9½ hours, $69), Denver, CO (28 hours, $135), San Francisco, CA (17½ hours, $87), Seattle, WA (four hours, $28) and Vancouver, BC (8½ hours, $55).

Train

Amtrak (www.amtrak.com; cnr NW 6th Ave & NW Irving St) serves Chicago, IL ($267, two days, two daily), Oakland, CA ($122, 18 hours, one daily), Seattle, WA ($31, 3½ hours, four daily) and Vancouver, BC ($58, four hours, two daily).

Getting Around

To/From the Airport

Tri-Met's MAX light-rail train runs between PDX airport and downtown ($2.35, 45 minutes). Taxis from the airport cost about $30.

Bicycle

Portland is regularly touted as the most bike-friendly city in the US and there are miles of dedicated paths. Rentals start at $35. Some hotels (eg Ace Hotel) offer bikes free of charge.

Bus, Light Rail & Streetcar

Another Portland tour de force is its comprehensive public transportation network. The city runs standard local buses, a MAX light-rail system – run by Tri-Met, and with an **information center** (www.trimet.org; ⏲8:30am-5:30pm Mon-Fri) at Pioneer Courthouse Sq – and a streetcar (tram) introduced in 2001, which runs from Portland State University, south of downtown, through the Pearl District to NW 23rd Ave. Within the downtown core, public transportation is free; outside downtown, fares run $2 to $2.35. Services run until 1:30am.

Car

Major car-rental agencies have outlets at Portland International Airport and around town. Oregon law prohibits you from pumping your own gas. Most of downtown is metered parking; a free option is to park along an inner-southeast street and walk across a bridge to the city center.

Taxi

Cabs are available 24 hours by phone. Downtown, you can often just flag them down. Try **Broadway Cab** (503-227-1234) or **Radio Cab** (503-227-1212).

Around Portland

Beer, coffee and wine: Portland excels at all three. For the latter you'll have to venture a little out of town to the wineries that embellish the Willamette Valley, in particular those around the towns of Dundee and McMinnville along Hwy 99W. **Willamette Valley Wineries Association** (www.willamettewines.com) is a good information portal for this alluring region.

For a decent overview of the area's many wineries, visit **Ponzi Vineyards** (14665 SW Winery Lane, Beaverton; 10am-5pm), 30 minutes southwest of downtown Portland, where you can taste current releases and visit the historic cellars and vineyards.

Meandering through plush green hills on winding country roads from one wine-tasting room to another is a delightful way to spend an afternoon (just make sure you designate a driver). Alternatively, Portland-based **Pedal Bike Tours** (http://pedalbiketours.com) runs five-hour spins ($89) from the town of Dundee on Hwy 99W. Wine in Oregon is all about its premier grape variety – Pinot Noir. One of the earliest planters was **Erath Winery** (www.erath.com; 9409 NE Worden Hill Rd, Dundee; 11am-5pm), harvesting grapes since 1969 – there's no better place to start your tasting. For some oenological back-up, contact **Grape Escape** (www.grapeescapetours.com), which specializes in wine-country tours.

For something different (or to sober up), head to McMinnville's **Evergreen Aviation Museum** (www.sprucegoose.org; 500 NE Capt Michael King Smith Way; adult/child $20/18; 9am-5pm) and check out Howard Hughes' **Spruce Goose**, the world's largest wood-framed airplane. There's also a replica of the Wright brothers' Flyer, along with an Imax theater (movie admission separate).

There are several fine restaurants in the area, but for something spectacular consider **Joel Palmer House** (503-864-2995; www.joelpalmerhouse.com; 600 Ferry St, Dayton; mains $29-38; 5-9pm Tue-Sat); its dishes are peppered with wild mushrooms collected by hand from the surrounding woods by the chefs! And if you need an interesting place to stay, consider **McMenamins Hotel Oregon** (503-472-8427; www.mcmenamins.com; 310 NE Evans St, McMinnville; d $60-130;), an older building renovated into a charming hotel. It has a pub (of course) with a wonderful rooftop bar.

Willamette Valley

The Willamette Valley, a fertile 60-mile-wide agricultural basin, was the Holy Grail for Oregon Trail pioneers who headed west more than 150 years ago. Today it's the state's breadbasket, producing more than 100 kinds of crops – including renowned Pinot Noir grapes. Salem, Oregon's capital, is about an hour's drive from Portland at the northern end of the Willamette Valley, and most of the other attractions in the area make easy day trips as well. Toward the south is Eugene, a dynamic college town worth a few days of exploration.

SALEM

Less interesting than Washington's state capital, Olympia, Oregon's legislative center is day-trip fodder, renowned for its cherry trees, art-deco capitol building and Willamette University. You can get orientated at the helpful **Visitors Information Center** (www.travelsalem.com; 181 NE High St; 8:30am-5pm Mon-Fri, 10am-4pm Sat).

Following an Oregon trend, Salem's best museum is housed in the local university. Willamette University's **Hallie Ford Museum of Art** (900 State St; adult/senior $3/2; 10am-5pm Tue-Sat, from 1pm Sun) showcases the state's best collection of Pacific Northwest art, including an impressive Native American gallery.

The **Oregon State Capitol** (900 Court St NE), built in 1938, looks like a background prop from a lavish Cecil B DeMille movie. Free tours run hourly between 9am and 4pm in summer. Rambling 19th-century

WORTH A TRIP

HOT SPRINGS

Oregon trumps its northern neighbor Washington in its abundance of hot springs and there are a couple of good ones within easy striking distance of the state capital, Salem. Two hours' drive east of the city is **Bagby Hot Springs** (www.bagbyhotsprings.org), a revitalizing free hot tub in a rustic forest bathhouse 1.5 miles down a hiking trail. From Estacada, head 26 miles south on Hwy 224 (which becomes Forest Rd 46); turn right onto Forest Rd 63 and go 3 miles to USFS Rd 70. Turn right and drive 6 miles to the parking area ($5 Northwest Forest Pass required).

If the communal bathing doesn't cut it, enjoy more salubrious climes at **Breitenbush Hot Springs** (www.breitenbush.com), a fancier spa with massages, yoga and the like. Day-use prices are $14 to $26. Breitenbush is east of Salem on Hwy 46, just past the settlement of Detroit.

Bush House (600 Mission St SE; adult/child $4/2; ⌚noon-5pm Tue-Sun) is an Italianate mansion now preserved as a museum with historic accents, including original wallpapers and marble fireplaces.

On the main Oregon north–south artery, Salem is served daily by **Greyhound** (450 Church St NE) buses and **Amtrak** (500 13th St SE) trains.

EUGENE

Zany has long passed for 'normal' in countercultural Eugene, a bolshie offshoot of metro Portland that invented tree-sitting as a means of protest, stoked bike friendliness decades before it was trendy, and has long manifested a uniquely West Coast spirit of sedition.

While the downtown's no oil painting, Eugene wins kudos for its academic institution, the magnificently landscaped University of Oregon, which also doubles up as an arboretum. Elsewhere Eugene is an underneath-the-surface kind of place where some gentle prodding reveals running trails, workers coops and the odd aging Merry Prankster. The Prankster's original psychedelic bus, *Further,* remains at the farm of former Eugene resident Ken Kesey in Pleasant Hill, 10 miles away.

Sights & Activities

As the city that gave the world Nike, Eugene (or 'Tracktown' as it likes to call itself) safeguards some of the best running facilities in the nation. Many trails hug the Willamette River and some are floodlit after dark.

Alton Barker Park PARK

Eugene's largest park is renowned for its running trails, most notably the wood-chip **Pre's Trail** named for Eugene's Olympian running icon Steve Prefontaine, who was killed in a car crash in 1975. The **Adidas Oregon Trail** (cnr 24th Ave & Amazon Pkwy) is a 1-mile loop popular with interval runners (it's floodlit at night). The park is divided roughly in half, demarcating wild and manicured areas. Abutting the Willamette River, it connects to the city's wider trail network via three footbridges. **Skinner Butte** (682ft) is a landmark hill on the opposite side of the river replete with lawns, hiking trails and a prime city view.

University of Oregon UNIVERSITY, MUSEUM

(1680 E 15th Ave; adult/child $3/2; ⌚11am-5pm Wed-Sun) What America lacks in cobbled Italianate piazzas it makes up for in beautifully laid-out university campuses, and few are as authentic and salubrious as this one. Showcased on the 295-acre campus you'll find a splendid art museum, a top research library, illustrious Romanesque revival architecture and an arboretum with over 500 species of tree. Previous alumni include Ken Kesey (writer) and Steve Prefontane (athlete). A campus highlight is the **Jordan Schnitzer Museum of Art** (1430 Johnson Lane; adult/child $5/3; ⌚11am-8pm Wed, to 5pm Tue & Thu-Sun), offering a rotating permanent collection of world-class art from Korean scrolls to Rembrandt paintings.

Sleeping

Eugene's accommodations consist of mainly unexciting chain hotels and motels, with the odd B&B thrown in to break the monotony.

C'est La Vie Inn B&B **$$**

(☎541-302-3014; www.cestlavieinn.com; 1006 Taylor St; d $125-140; ❄@📶) Break the monotony of the utilitarian downtown in this classic turreted Queen Anne B&B that

WHAT THE...?

It stands to reason that the city that invented tree-sitting as a means of environmental protest would be equally expert in the art of tree-*climbing*. Re-creating one of our strongest childhood impulses, the **Pacific Tree Climbing Institute** (☎866-653-8733; www.pacifictreeclimbing.com; 605 Howard Ave) offers day and overnight trips to a nearby forest where you can shin up an old-growth Sitka spruce or Douglas fir with all the exuberance of a 10-year-old. If the primate in you still isn't satisfied, the institute offers the opportunity to spend the night amid the leafy branches in a specially rigged hammock. Climbs start at $200.

dates from the late 19th century but offers comforts more in keeping with the internet age. C'est La Vie is run by a French woman (no surprise there) and La France is evident in everything from the coffee mugs to the furniture.

Campus Inn MOTEL $
(☎541-343-3376; www.campus-inn.com; 390 E Broadway; d from $66; ❄@📶) An independent and comfortable family-run motel perched between the university and downtown with friendly helpful staff, a Jacuzzi and a small gym. Prices depend on the season but are negotiable.

Courtesy Inn MOTEL $
(☎541-345-3391; www.courtesyinneugene.com; 345 W 6th Ave; d from $60; P📶) Friendly nook near the train station that is above average in the motel stakes and offers free wi-fi, HBO and a snack breakfast. The town and parks are within walking distance.

Eating & Drinking

TOP CHOICE **Sweet Life Patisserie** CAFE, BAKERY $
(www.sweetlifedesserts.com; 755 Monroe St; pastries $2-5; ⏲7am-11pm Mon-Fri, from 8am Sat & Sun) You might want to warm up on Tracktown's ample trails before you hit this sugarfest situated on a quiet street on the cusp of downtown. Everything is homemade with the emphasis on sweet – pies, cheesecakes, pastries, cup cakes, the works. The coffee's good as well.

McMenamins PUB $
(⏲11am-11pm Sun-Thu, to midnight Fri & Sat) E 19th St (1485 E 19th St); High St (1243 High St); North Bank (22 Club Rd) Gloriously located on the banks of the mighty Willamette, the North Bank pub-restaurant has riverside patio tables. The other two locations lack water views but offer similar fare ('classic pub food with a Northwest kick' – pasta, salads, burgers and steaks).

Morning Glory Café VEGETARIAN $
(450 Willamette St; ⏲7:30am-3:30pm; ✎) Eugene in a nutshell (or should that be a nut roast?). This sustainable place is good for breakfast, lunch and brunch, and rarely will vegans have a better choice – everything on the menu is either vegan or can be made vegan. Try the biscuits, tofu sandwiches or cookies, and as the in-shop sign says 'make tea not war.'

Beppe & Gianni's Trattoria ITALIAN $$
(☎541-683-6661; www.beppeandgiannis.net; 1646 E 19th Ave; mains $16-20; ⏲5-9pm Sun-Thu, to 10pm Fri & Sat) An insanely popular local Italian place where you can choose from antipasti, *primi* and *secondi* plates, or enjoy all three. The homemade pastas are the best.

Voodoo Doughnuts CAFE, DESSERTS $
(www.voodoodoughnut.com; 20 E Broadway; ⏲24hr) This weird and wonderful Portland import recently introduced Eugene to 24-hour doughnuts with flavors such as 'bacon and maple,' and 'iced fruit-loop' served in a psychedelic downtown cafe.

Information

For more information, visit the **Visitors Association** (www.visitlanecounty.com; 754 Olive St; ⏲8am-5pm Mon-Fri, 10am-4pm Sat & Sun).

Getting There & Around

Eugene's plush **Amtrak station** (www.amtrak.com; cnr E 4th Ave & Willamette St) runs daily trains to Vancouver, BC, and LA, and everywhere in between on its *Cascade* and *Coast Starlight* lines. **Greyhound** (www.greyhound.com; 987 Pearl St) runs north to Salem and Portland, and south to Grants Pass and Medford. **Porter Stage Lines** runs a daily bus from outside the train station to Coos Bay in the west, and Bend and Ontario in the east. Book tickets through Amtrak.

Local bus service is provided by **Lane Transit District** (www.ltd.org). For bike rentals, try **Paul's Bicycle Way of Life** (152 W 5th St; ⏲9am-7pm Mon-Fri, 10am-5pm Sat & Sun) near the train station.

Columbia River Gorge

The fourth-largest river in the US by volume, the mighty Columbia runs 1243 miles from Alberta, Canada, into the Pacific Ocean just west of Astoria. For the final 309 miles of its course, the heavily dammed waterway delineates the border between Washington and Oregon and cuts though the Cascade Mountains via the spectacular Columbia River Gorge. Showcasing numerous ecosystems, waterfalls and magnificent vistas, the land bordering the river is protected as a National Scenic Area and is a popular sporting nexus for windsurfers, cyclists, anglers and hikers.

HOOD RIVER & AROUND

The surrounding apple orchards and wineries are just the wrapping paper. The small town of Hood River, 63 miles east of Portland on I-84, is famous for its legendary windsurfing (on the Columbia River), arguably the best in the world, and – to a lesser extent – its mountain biking south of town off Hwy 35 and Forest Rd 44. A sporting triumvirate is completed by year-round skiing facilities on nearby Mt Hood. For more on the outdoor bounty, call in at the **chamber of commerce** (www.hoodriver.org; 720 E Port Marina Dr; ⌚9am-5pm Mon-Fri, from 10am Sat & Sun).

Sights & Activities

In operation since 1906, the 22-mile **Mount Hood Railroad** (110 Railroad Ave; www.mthoodrr.com; adult/child $27/17) was built to carry lumber to the Columbia River. Today it serves mainly as a tourist train. Spectacular two-hour trips run Wednesdays to Sundays from April through December, starting from the historic rail depot in Hood River on the corner of 1st St and Cascade Ave.

For Hood River's real deal, check in with **Hood River Waterplay** (www.hoodriverwaterplay.com; Port of Hood River Marina), where you can procure windsurfing rentals ($60 per day) and partake in lessons ($199 for a two-day beginners course).

Sleeping & Eating

Columbia River Gorge Hostel HOSTEL **$**
(☎509-493-3363; www.bingenschool.com; cnr Cedar & Humbolt Sts; dm/r from $19/49; ❄@📶) Across the Columbia in Bingen on the Washington side, this hostel has simple and affordable lodging in an old schoolhouse.

Hood River Hotel HISTORIC HOTEL **$$**
(☎541-386-1900; www.hoodriverhotel.com; 102 Oak St; d $99-164; ❄📶) A vintage 1913 hotel in the heart of downtown that still scores highly with its old-fashioned four-poster beds and general air of conviviality.

Full Sail Brewery PUB **$$**
(www.fullsailbrewing.com; 506 Columbia St; mains $9-23; ⌚11:30am-8pm) This cozy tasting-room bar has a small pub menu and good river views. Free 30-minute microbrewery tours end up here.

Getting There & Away

Hood River is connected to Portland by daily **Greyhound** (www.greyhound.com) buses. Alternatively, take the **Amtrak** (www.amtrak.com) *Empire Builder* and disembark at Bingen on the Washington side.

Oregon Cascades

An extension of their Washington cousins, the Oregon Cascades offer plenty of dramatic stand-alone volcanoes that dominate the skyline for miles around. Mt Hood, overlooking the Columbia River Gorge, is the state's highest peak and has year-round skiing plus a relatively straightforward summit ascent. Tracking south you pass Mt Jefferson and the Three Sisters before reaching Crater Lake, the ghost of erstwhile Mt Mazama that collapsed in on itself after blowing its top approximately 7000 years ago.

MT HOOD

If the Cascade Mountains were people, Mt Hood – Oregon's highest peak at 11,239ft – would be the congenial, easy-to-get-to-know one. There are plenty of reasons to admire its ethereal snowcapped beauty. You can ski Hood year-round (unique to the US), ascend it inside a day without Reinhold Messner-like climbing skills, circumnavigate it on a well-trodden 40-mile path known as the Timberline trail, and reach it within a one-hour drive from Portland. But like all people, Hood has its bad days when it walks off and sulks and the sky turns black with ugly, potentially lethal storms. The Native Americans knew the score. They called the mountain Wy'east, after a legendary native chief, and witnessed the dormant stratovolcano's latent anger on more than one occasion, most recently during an eruption in the 1790s.

Hood was named by the 1792 Vancouver expedition after Samuel Hood, a British admiral who somewhat ironically fought patriotically *against* the Americans in the American War of Independence.

Activities

SKIING

Hood is rightly revered for its skiing. There are six ski areas on the mountain, including **Timberline** (www.timberlinelodge.com; lift tickets adult/child $48/30), which lures Canadians and Californians (as well as Oregonians) with the only year-round skiing in the US. Closer to Portland, **Mt Hood SkiBowl** (www.skibowl.com; lift tickets adult/child $44/24) is no slacker either. It's the nation's largest night-ski area and popular with city slickers who ride up for an evening of powder play from the metro zone. The largest ski area on the mountain is **Mt Hood Meadows** (www.skihood.com; lift tickets adult/child $69/39) and the best conditions usually prevail here.

HIKING

The Mt Hood National Forest protects an astounding 1200 miles of trails. A Northwest Forest Pass ($5) is required at most trailheads.

One popular trail loops 7 miles from near the village of Zigzag to beautiful **Ramona Falls**, which tumbles down mossy columnar basalt. Another heads 1.5 miles up from US 26 to **Mirror Lake**, continues a half-mile around the lake, then tracks 2 miles beyond to a ridge.

The 41-mile **Timberline Trail** circumnavigates Mt Hood through scenic wilderness. Noteworthy portions include the hike to McNeil Point and the short climb to Bald Mountain. From Timberline Lodge, Zigzag Canyon Overlook is a 4.5-mile round-trip.

Climbing Mt Hood should be taken seriously, as deaths do occur, though dogs have made it to the summit and the climb can be done in a long day. Contact **Timberline Mountain Guides** (541-312-9242; www.timberlinemtguides.com) for guided climbs.

Sleeping & Eating

Reserve **campsites** (877-444-6777; www.reserveusa.com; campsites $12-18) in summer. On US 26 are streamside campgrounds Tollgate and Camp Creek. Large and popular Trillium Lake has great views of Mt Hood.

TOP CHOICE **Timberline Lodge** LODGE $$
(800-547-1406; www.timberlinelodge.com; d $115-290;) Stanley Kubrick fans will have no trouble recognizing this historic 1937 lodge as the fictional Overlook Hotel from the film *The Shining* (exterior shots only). 'All work and no play makes Jack a dull boy,' typed Jack Nicholson repeatedly in the movie. If only he'd known about the year-round skiing, the hikes, the cozy fires and the hearty restaurant.

Huckleberry Inn INN $
(503-272-3325; www.huckleberry-inn.com; 88611 E Government Camp Loop, Government Camp; d $85-180;) A family-run rustic inn and restaurant with dorm and private rooms, along with a 24-hour restaurant serving up formidable milk shakes and – as the name suggests – huckleberry pie! It's handily located in Government Camp village.

Ice Axe Grill PUB $$
(www.iceaxegrill.com; 87304 E Government Camp Loop, Government Camp; mains $12-18; 11:30am-9pm Tue-Thu, from 7am Fri & Sat, 7am-8pm Sun) Anyone up for fine-dining after a day of skiing and/or wilderness hiking? Thought not. All the more reason to drop into Government Camp's only brewery-restaurant to fill that hole with shepherd's pie, bacon burgers and thick pizzas.

Rendezvous Grill & Tap Room MODERN AMERICAN $$$
(503-622-6837; 67149 E US 26, Welches; mains $20-30; 11:30am-9pm) Outstanding dishes such as porterhouse steak and Dungeness crab linguine are served here. Also great desserts and wine list.

Information

If you're approaching from Hood River, visit the **Hood River Ranger Station** (6780 Hwy 35, Parkdale; 8am-4:30pm Mon-Sat). The **ZigZag Ranger Station** (70220 E Hwy 26, Zigzag; 7:45am-4:30pm Mon-Sat) is more handy for Portland arrivals. There's another helpful office in Government Camp. The weather changes quickly here; carry chains in winter. For road conditions, dial 800-977-6368.

Getting There & Away

The prettiest approach to Hood by car is from Hood River (44 miles) on Hwy 35. Alternatively, you can take Hwy 26 directly from Portland (56 miles). The **Breeze Shuttle** (www.cobreeze.com) between Bend and Portland stops briefly at Government Camp, 6 miles from the Timberline Lodge. There are regular **shuttles** (www.skihood.com) from Portland to the ski areas during the winter.

SISTERS

Named for the trio of eponymous 10,000ft-plus peaks that dominate the skyline, Sisters is the unofficial 'sister' of Bend, 22 miles to the southeast, a town with which it shares a penchant for the gritty outdoors. The main difference between the two is size. Sisters is a one-horse town of Hollywood 'Western' folklore, where cowboy-themed shop-fronts hide modern boutiques and art galleries. There's nothing faux about the surroundings though – raw mountains, roller-coaster single-track bike trails, and wilderness of the highest order.

For local orientation, see the **chamber of commerce** (www.sisterschamber.com; 291 Main St; ⏲9am-5pm). The most accessible bike trail is the recently extended **Peterson Ridge Trail** system, 28 miles of moderate single-track with loop-back possibilities that starts half a mile south of town.

At the southern end of Sisters, the city park has **camping** (sites $10), but no showers. For ultra-comfort, bag a room in the **Five Pine Lodge** (☎866-974-5900; www.fivepinelodge.com; 1021 Desperado Trail; d $149-219, cottages $199-219; ❄📶🏊), ridiculously luxurious for a so-called cowboy town, though none of the guests are complaining. On the quieter and cheaper side is **Sisters Motor Lodge** (☎541-549-2551; www.sistersmotorlodge.com; 511 W Cascade St; d from $89; ❄📶), offering 11 individually crafted rooms with a nonmotel-like atmosphere.

It's hard to drive past **Bronco Billy's Ranch Grill & Saloon** (www.broncobillysranchgrill.com; 190 E Cascade Ave; mains $10-25; ⏲11:30am-9pm), the town's most obvious Wild West facade, a historic hotel reincarnated as a restaurant with a carnivorous menu anchored by hamburgers and steaks.

ℹ Getting There & Away

A daily **Porter Stage Line** bus runs through town on its way between Eugene and Bend. There's no official stop, but you should be able to be dropped off. Bookings are through **Amtrak** (www.amtrak.com).

BEND

Sandwiched in between the east's high desert plateau and the west's snow-choked Cascade Mountains, Bend is where the two radically different halves of Oregon meet. And what a collision! Herein lies the best mountain biking in the state, the best skiing in the state, the best rock climbing in the state...and all of this before you've even got round to examining the town itself, whose lush riverside parks do a good impersonation of a Monet canvas.

Sights

TOP CHOICE High Desert Museum MUSEUM
(www.highdesertmuseum.org; 59800 S US 97; adult/child $15/12; ⏲9am-5pm) This extraordinary museum, 6 miles south of Bend, is undoubtedly one of the best in the state. It charts the settlement of the West, along with the region's natural history. The sea-otter exhibit and trout pool are highlights.

Activities

Couch potatoes will be deathly bored in Bend, where most things are orientated around outdoor pursuits.

CYCLING

Within riding distance of the town center lies one of the most comprehensive networks of mountain-biking trails in the nation – 300 miles worth and counting. **Cog Wild** (www.cogwild.com; 255 SW Century Dr) offers bike rental (from $30 per day), along with organized tours and shuttles out to the best trailheads.

CLIMBING

Not 25 miles northeast of Bend lies **Smith Rock State Park** (www.oregonstateparks.org; day use $5), where 800ft ballast cliffs guarding the Crooked River have become the G-spot of sport climbing in the US. The park's 1800-plus routes are, without question, among the best in the nation. Guides for both experienced and inexperienced climbers can be procured with **Smith Rock Climbing Guides Inc** (www.smithrockclimbingguides.com; excursions $90-225).

SKIING

As improbable as it may seem on a hot spring day, Bend hosts Oregon's best skiing, 22 miles southwest of the town at the glorious **Mount Bachelor Ski Resort** (www.mtbachelor.com; lift tickets adult/child 6-12yr $50/29), famous for its 'dry' powdery snow, long season (until late May) and ample terrain (it's the largest ski area in the Pacific Northwest). The mountain has long advocated cross-country skiing in tandem with downhill and maintains 35 miles of groomed trails.

Sleeping & Eating

TOP CHOICE McMenamins Old St Francis School HOTEL $$
(☎541-382-5174; www.mcmenamins.com; 700 NW Bond St; d $145-175, cottages $190-330; ❄@📶) It's the usual McMenamins quandary. How do you tear yourself away from the establishment's fine eating-sleeping-cinema triumvirate and see the town? Old St Francis

School is what it says it is: an old Catholic school remodeled into a classy 19-room hotel complete with saltwater Turkish bath, restaurant-pub, pool tables and a movie theater. It's a destination in itself.

Oxford Hotel BOUTIQUE HOTEL **$$$**
(☎877-440-8436; www.oxfordhotelbend.com; 10 NW Minnesota Ave; d $199-259; P❄☺≋) Central Oregon was crying out for a decent boutique hotel to break the monotony of the usual suspects on its all-too-familiar motel strip. So, along came the Oxford to embellish Bend's already salubrious downtown and blow away most of the opposition with huge luxurious rooms, a gym, a fancy on-site restaurant and free bikes.

Victorian Café BREAKFAST **$**
(1404 NW Galveston Ave; mains $7-12; ⊙7am-2pm) A Bend classic and a must-see for anyone with a hearty morning appetite, the Victorian is a formidable American brunch stop housed in an inviting red chalet in the city's leafy western suburbs. Brave the weekend queues to get in – you won't regret it.

Bourbon Street CAJUN **$$**
(www.bourbonstreetbend.com; 5 NW Minnesota Ave; mains $16-34) Fresh farmed local goods with a Cajun twist are on offer in this remodeled fire station in recently trussed-up Minnesota Ave.

Deschutes Brewery & Public House BREWERY **$$**
(1044 NW Bond St; ⊙11am-11pm Mon-Thu, to midnight Fri & Sat, to 10pm Sun) Bend's first microbrewery, gregariously serving up plenty of food and handcrafted beers.

Information

Information is available at the **visitor and convention bureau** (www.visitbend.com; 917 NW Harriman St; ⊙9am-5pm Mon-Fri, 10am-4pm Sat).

Getting There & Away

The **Breeze Shuttle** (www.cobreeze.com) runs once a day between Bend (Sugarloaf Mountain Motel, US 97 62980) and Portland. **Porter Stage Lines** also runs a daily bus east to Ontario and west to Eugene. Book tickets online through **Amtrak** (www.amtrak.com).

NEWBERRY NATIONAL VOLCANIC MONUMENT

Weird landscapes get ever weirder as you head south out of Bend. Case in point is the Newberry National Volcanic Monument (day use $5), which showcases 500,000 years of dramatic seismic activity. Start your visit at the **Lava Lands Visitor Center** (☎541-593-2421; ⊙9am-5pm Jul-Sep, limited hours May, Jun, Sep & Oct, closed Nov-Apr), 13 miles south of Bend. Nearby attractions include **Lava Butte**, a perfect cone rising 500ft, and **Lava River Cave**, Oregon's longest lava tube. Four miles west of the visitor center is **Benham Falls**, a good picnic spot on the Deschutes River.

Newberry Crater was once one of the most active volcanoes in North America, but after a large eruption a caldera was born. Close by are **Paulina Lake** and **East Lake**, deep lakes rich with trout, while looming above is 7985ft **Paulina Peak**.

CRATER LAKE NATIONAL PARK

Get ready for a sharp intake of breath. It may be a cliché but it certainly isn't an exaggeration: the still, deep blue waters of Crater Lake reflect the surrounding cliffs like a giant mirror. The secret lies in the water's purity. No rivers or streams feed the lake, meaning its H_2O content is made up entirely of rain and melted snow. It is also exceptionally deep – indeed at 1949ft (maximum) it's the deepest lake in the US. The classic tour is the 33-mile self-guided rim drive (open approximately June to mid-October), but there are also exceptional hiking and cross-country skiing opportunities. As Oregon's sole national park, there's a $10 vehicle fee to enter the Crater Lake area. It receives some of the highest snowfalls in North America and the rim drive and north entrance are sometimes closed up until early July. Check ahead. For more park information, head to **Steel Visitor Center** (☎541-594-3100; ⊙9am-5pm May-Sep, 10am-4pm Nov-Apr).

You can stay overnight from early June to early October at the **Cabins at Mazama Village** (☎541-830-8700; www.craterlakelodges.com; d $124; P) or the majestic old **Crater Lake Lodge** (☎541-594-2255; www.craterlakelodges.com; d $149-275; P❄), opened in 1915 as a classic example of rustic 'parkitecture.' The updated facilities still retain their rustic elegance. Nearby campgrounds include the large **Mazama Campground** (www.craterlakelodges.com; tent/RV sites $21/27), managed by Crater Lake Lodge.

Southern Oregon

With a warm and sunny climate that belongs in nearby California, southern Oregon is the state's banana belt. Rugged landscapes, scenic rivers and a couple of attractive towns top the highlights list.

ASHLAND

Oregon was unknown territory to the Elizabethan explorers of William Shakespeare's day, so it might seem a little strange to find that the pretty settlement of Ashland in southern Oregon has established itself as the English playwright's second home. The irony probably wouldn't have been lost on Shakespeare himself. 'All the world's a stage,' the great Bard once opined, and fittingly people come from all over the world to see Ashland's famous Shakespeare Festival, which has been held here under various guises since the 1930s.

The 'festival' moniker is misleading; the shows here are a semipermanent fixture occupying nine months of the annual town calendar and attracting up to 400,000 theatergoers per season. Even without them, Ashland is an attractive town, propped up by various wineries, upscale B&Bs and fine restaurants. For information, visit the **chamber of commerce** (www.ashlandchamber.com; 110 E Main St; ⊙9am-5pm Mon-Fri).

Sights & Activities

The Shakespearian attractions contrast sharply with Ashland's other main draw: the outdoors.

Lithia Park PARK

Adjacent to the three splendid theaters (one of which is outdoors) lies what is arguably the loveliest city park in Oregon, whose 93 acres wind along Ashland Creek above the center of town. Unusually, the park is in the National Register of Historic Places and is embellished with fountains, flowers, gazebos and an ice-skating rink (winter only).

Schneider Museum of Art MUSEUM

(www.sou.edu/sma; 1250 Siskiyou Blvd; suggested donation $5; ⊙10am-4pm Mon-Sat) Like all good Oregonian art museums, this one's on the local university campus and displays a kind of global potluck of paintings, sculptures and artifacts.

Jackson Wellsprings SPA

(☎541-482-3776; www.jacksonwellsprings.com; 2253 Hwy 99) For a good soak, try this casual New Age–style place, which maintains an 85°F (29°C) mineral-fed swimming pool ($8) and 103°F (39°C) private Jacuzzi tubs ($25 to $35 for 75 minutes). It's 2 miles north of town.

Mt Ashland Ski Resort SKI AREA

(www.mtashland.com; lift pass adult/child $39/29) Powdery snow is surprisingly abundant here, 18 miles southwest on Mt Ashland (7533ft), which has some excellent advanced terrain.

Siskiyou Cyclery CYCLING

(www.siskiyoucyclery.com; 1729 Siskiyou Blvd; per day $35; ⊙10am-5:30pm Tue-Sat) Pedal-pushers can rent a bike here and explore the countryside on the semicompleted Bear Creek Greenway, a 21-mile bike path between Ashland and the town of Central Point.

Sleeping

Reserve in summer when the thespians descend in their droves.

TOP CHOICE **Columbia Hotel** HOTEL $

(☎541-482-3726, www.columbiahotel.com; 262 1/2 E Main St; d $89-149; ❄@📶) Get in a Shakespearean mood at this quaint European-style hotel with period rooms (some with shared baths), a comfy sitting area, complimentary morning coffee and an ideal theater-side location.

Ashland Springs Hotel HISTORIC HOTEL $$$

(☎541-488-1700; www.ashlandspringshotel.com; 212 E Main St; d $179-269; ❄@📶🏊) An Ashland institution and National Historic Landmark that was painstakingly restored in 2000, the Springs glistens with plenty of Shakespearean splendor, although it actually dates from 1925. Elegant rooms are bedizened with pastel colors and common areas include a grand ballroom, a conservatory, an English garden and Larks Restaurant.

Ashland Hostel HOSTEL $

(☎541-482-9217; www.theashlandhostel.com; 150 N Main St; dm $28, d $59-89; ❄📶) It might sound like an oxymoron, but Ashland's rather 'posh' hostel should quickly banish memories of those youth hostelling free-for-alls of yore with clean dorms and the options to go private in compact doubles with their own bath.

Cowslip's Belle B&B B&B $$

(☎541-488-2901, www.cowslip.com; 159 N Main St; d/ste $170/245; ❄📶) A top-rated B&B with four luxurious rooms in a 1913 bungalow along with a couple of suites in a separate town house. Highlights include a beautiful garden, love seats, rockers, private decks and Jacuzzi tubs.

Manor Motel MOTEL $

(☎541-482-2246; www.manormotel.net; 476 N Main St; d $69-125; ❄📶) Handily located independent hotel on the threshold of the central area with 11 rooms, friendly service and plenty of greenery.

Eating

TOP CHOICE New Sammy's Cowboy Bistro MODERN AMERICAN **$$$**
(☎541-535-2779; 2210 S Pacific Hwy, Talent; mains $23-36; ⊙5-8:30pm Thu-Sun) Sammy's might sound like a French cowboy restaurant, but there are no such oxymorons at this funky spot, considered by some to be Oregon's best restaurant. It's small, understated and located 3 miles north of Ashland in the village of Talent. Reserve weeks in advance to taste its highly creative cuisine.

Sesame Asian Kitchen ASIAN **$$**
(www.sesameasiankitchen.com; 21 Winburn Way; mains $11-16; ⊙11:30am-9pm) This is a chic but relatively cheap Asian-fusion restaurant where quick service and hearty but healthy portions make for an ideal pre-Shakespeare dinner. Try the tangerine chicken or the Mongolian beef short ribs as you discuss the merits of *Hamlet* over *The Merchant of Venice*.

Chateaulin FRENCH **$$$**
(☎503-482-2264; www.chateaulin.com; 50 E Main St; mains $24-36; ⊙5-9pm Wed-Sun) More European fantasies are stirred at this fine-dining French bistro right next to the theaters. The decor and menu are *très* Parisian (dishes include duck, vol-au-vent and *filet mignon*) but the wine list stays patriotically local with some hard-to-find Oregonian vintages. There's a wine shop next door.

JACKSONVILLE

This small but endearing ex-gold-prospecting town is the oldest settlement in southern Oregon and a National Historic Landmark. The main drag is lined with well-preserved buildings dating from the 1880s, now converted into boutiques and galleries. Music-lovers can't miss the September **Britt Festival** (www.brittfest.org), a world-class musical experience with top-name performers. Seek more enlightenment at the **chamber of commerce** (www.jacksonvilleoregon.org; 185 N Oregon St; ⊙10am-5pm Mon-Fri, 11am-4pm Sat & Sun).

Jacksonville is full of fancy B&Bs; for budget motels head 6 miles east to Medford. The **Jacksonville Inn** (☎541-899-1900; www.jacksonvilleinn.com; 175 E California St; d $159-199; ❄☜) is the most pleasant abode, shoehorned downtown in an 1863 building with regal antique-stuffed rooms. There's a restaurant on-site.

WILD ROGUE WILDERNESS

Yes, it's *wild* and it's *rogue*. Situated between the town of Grants Pass on I-5 and Gold Beach on the Oregon coast, the aptly named Wild Rogue Wilderness is anchored by the turbulent Rogue River, which cuts through 40 miles of untamed, roadless canyon. People regularly underestimate the powerful force of nature here and the area is known for challenging white-water rafting (classes III and IV) and long-distance hikes.

Basking in its own warm microclimate, the medium-sized town of **Grants Pass** is the gateway to adventures along the Rogue. The **chamber of commerce** (www.visitgrantspass.org; 1995 NW Vine St; ⊙8am-5pm Mon-Fri) is right off I-5, exit 58. For raft permits and backpacking advice, contact the Bureau of Land Management's **Smullin Visitors Center** (☎541-479-3735; www.blm.gov/or/resources/recreation/rogue/index.php; 14335 Galice Rd; ⊙7am-3pm) in Galice.

Rafting the Rogue is legendary, but not for the faint of heart; a typical trip takes three days and costs upward of $650. A good outfitter is **Rogue Wilderness Adventures** (☎800-336-1647; www.wildrogue.com). Kayaking the river is equally exhilarating; for instruction and guidance (and you'll need it!), contact **Sundance River Center** (☎541-386-1725; www.sundanceriver.com).

Another highlight of the region is the 40-mile **Rogue River Trail**, once a supply route from Gold Beach. The full trek takes four to five days; day hikers might aim for Whiskey Creek Cabin, a 6-mile round-trip from the Grave Creek trailhead. The trail is dotted with rustic lodges ($110 to $140 per person with meals; reservations required) – try **Black Bar** (☎541-479-6507; www.blackbarlodge.net; d $120). There are also primitive campgrounds along the way.

NORTH UMPQUA RIVER

This 'Wild and Scenic' river boasts world-class fly-fishing, fine hiking and serene camping. The 79-mile **North Umpqua Trail** begins near Idleyld Park and passes through Steamboat en route to the Pacific Crest Trail. A popular sideline is pretty **Umpqua Hot Springs**, east of Steamboat near Toketee Lake. Not far away, stunning, two-tiered **Toketee Falls** (113ft) flows over columnar basalt, while **Watson Falls** (272ft) is one of the highest waterfalls in Oregon. For information, stop by Glide's **Colliding Rivers Information Center** (18782 N Umpqua Hwy, Glide; ⏲9am-5pm May-Oct). Adjacent is the **North Umpqua Ranger District** (☎541-496-3532; ⏲8am-4:30pm Mon-Fri).

Between Idleyld Park and Diamond Lake are dozens of riverside campgrounds; these include lovely **Susan Creek** and primitive **Boulder Flat** (no water). A few area accommodations fill up quickly in summer; try the log-cabin-like rooms at **Dogwood Motel** (☎541-496-3403; www.dogwoodmotel.com; 28866 N Umpqua Hwy; d $70-75; ❄).

OREGON CAVES NATIONAL MONUMENT

This very popular cave (there's only one) lies 19 miles east of Cave Junction on Hwy 46. Three miles of passages are explored via 90-minute **walking tours** (☎541-592-2100; www.nps.gov/orca; adult/child $8.50/6; ⏲9am-6pm Jun-Sep, hours vary Oct-May) that include 520 rocky steps and dripping chambers running along the River Styx. Dress warmly, wear shoes with good traction and be prepared to get dripped on.

Cave Junction, 28 miles south of Grants Pass on US 199 (Redwood Hwy), provides the region's services. Here you'll find the decent **Junction Inn** (☎541-592-3106; 406 Redwood Hwy; d from $70; ❄), along with a few restaurants. For fancy lodgings right at the cave there's the impressive **Oregon Caves Chateau** (☎541-592-3400, www.oregoncaves chateau.com; d from $90-165; ⏲May-Oct); grab a milk shake at the old-fashioned soda fountain here. Campers should head to **Cave Creek Campground** (☎541-592-2166; campsites $10), 14 miles up Hwy 46, about 4 miles from the cave.

Eastern Oregon

Mirroring Washington, Oregon east of the Cascades bears little resemblance to its wetter western cohort either physically or culturally. Few people live here – the biggest town, Pendleton, numbers only 20,000 – and the region hoards high plateaus, painted hills, alkali lakebeds and the country's deepest river gorge.

JOHN DAY FOSSIL BEDS NATIONAL MONUMENT

Within the soft rocks and crumbly soils of John Day country lies one of the world's greatest fossil collections, laid down between six and 50 million years ago. Roaming the forests at the time were saber-toothed nimravids, pint-sized horses, bear-dogs and other early mammals.

The national monument includes 22 sq miles at three different units: Sheep Rock Unit, Painted Hills Unit and Clarno Unit. Each has hiking trails and interpretive displays. To visit all of the units in one day requires quite a bit of driving, as more than 100 miles separate the fossil beds. See www.nps.gov/joda for more details.

Visit the excellent **Thomas Condon Paleontology Center** (32651 Hwy 19, Kimberly; ⏲9am-5pm), 2 miles north of US 26 at the Sheep Rock Unit. Displays include a three-toed horse and petrified dung-beetle balls, along with many other fossils and geologic history exhibits. If you feel like walking, take the short hike up the **Blue Basin Trail**, which will make you feel like you've just landed on the sunny side of the moon.

The **Painted Hills Unit**, near the town of Mitchell, consists of low-slung, colorfully banded hills formed about 30 million years ago. Ten million years older is the **Clarno Unit**, which exposes mud flows that washed over an Eocene-era forest and eroded into distinctive, sheer white cliffs topped with spires and turrets of stone.

Rafting is popular on the John Day River, the longest free-flowing river in the state. **Oregon River Experiences** (☎800-827-1358; www.oregonriver.com) offers trips of up to five days. There's also good fishing for smallmouth bass and rainbow trout. Enquire at the **Oregon Department of Fish & Wildlife** (☎541-575-1167; www.dfw.state.or.us).

Every little town in the area has at least one hotel; these include the clean, economical **Oregon Hotel** (☎541-462-3027; 104 E Main St; dm $15, d $39-89) in Mitchell and the friendly **Sonshine B&B** (☎541-575-1827; www.sonshinebedandbreakfast.com; 210 NW Canton St; d $85-95; ❄), in John Day itself, which has four rooms, formidable breakfasts and a warm welcome. There are several public campgrounds in the area including Lone Pine and Big Bend (sites $5) on Hwy 402.

WALLOWA MOUNTAINS

The Wallowa Mountains, with their glacier-hewn peaks and crystalline lakes, are among the most beautiful natural areas in Oregon. The only drawback is the large number of visitors who flock here in summer, especially to the pretty Wallowa Lake area. Escape them all on one of several long hikes into the nearby **Eagle Cap Wilderness** area, such as the 6-mile one-way jaunt to **Aneroid Lake** or the 9-mile trek on the **West Fork Trail**. From the upper Lostine Valley, or from the Sheep Creek Summit of USFS Rd 39, there is easier day-hike access to the Eagle Cap's high country.

Just north of the mountains, in the Wallowa Valley, **Enterprise** is a homely backcountry town with several motels such as the **Ponderosa** (541-426-3186; www.ponderosamotel.hotels.officelive.com; 102 E Greenwood St; d $70-80;). If you like beer, don't miss the town's microbrewery, **Terminal Gravity** (www.terminalgravitybrewing.com; 803 School St; mains $7-11). Just 6 miles south is Enterprise's fancy cousin, the upscale town of **Joseph**. Expensive bronze galleries and artsy boutiques line the main strip, and accommodations comprise mostly B&Bs.

HELLS CANYON

North America's deepest river gorge (yes – even deeper than the Grand Canyon) provides Oregon with its northeastern border (with Idaho) and visitors with one of the state's wildest and jaw-dropping vistas. The mighty Snake River (a 1000-mile-long tributary of the even mightier Columbia) has taken 13 million years to carve its path through the high plateaus of eastern Oregon to its present depth of 8000ft. The canyon itself is a true wilderness bereft of roads but open to the curious and the brave.

For perspective, drive 30 miles from Joseph to Imnaha, where a 24-mile slow gravel road leads up to the excellent lookout at **Hat Point** (USFS Rd 4240). From here you can see the Wallowa Mountains, Idaho's Seven Devils, the Imnaha River and the wilds of the canyon itself. This road is open from late May until snowfall; give yourself two hours each way for the drive.

For white-water action and spectacular scenery, head down to **Hells Canyon Dam**, 25 miles north of the small community of Oxbow. Just past the dam, the road ends at the **Hells Canyon Visitor Center** (541-785-3395; 8am-4pm May-Sep), which has good advice on the area's campgrounds and hiking trails. Beyond here, the Snake River drops 1300ft in elevation through wild rapids accessible only by jet boats and rafts. **Hells Canyon Adventures** (541-785-3352; www.hellscanyonadventures.com; 4200 Hells Canyon Dam Rd) is the main operator running raft trips and jet-boat tours from May through September (reservations required).

The area has many campgrounds. Just outside Imnaha is the huntsman-style **Imnaha River Inn** (541-577-6002; www.imnahariverinn.com; s/d $70/130), a B&B replete with Hemingway-esque animal trophies, while Oxbow has the good-value **Hells Canyon B&B** (541-785-3373; www.hellscanyonb-b.com; 49922 Homestead Rd; d $70;). For more services, head to the towns of Enterprise, Joseph and Halfway.

STEENS MOUNTAIN & ALVORD DESERT

Wonderfully remote, Steens Mountain, the highest peak (9670ft) in southeastern Oregon, is like an alpine island towed off the Cascades and plonked in the middle of the stark Alvord Desert, near the Nevada border. On the west slope of the range, ice-age glaciers bulldozed massive U-shaped valleys into the flanks of the mountain. To the east, delicate alpine meadows and lakes flank the Steens, dropping off dizzyingly into the Alvord Desert, 5000ft below.

Beginning in Frenchglen, the 66-mile gravel **Steens Mountain Loop Road** offers access to Steens Mountain Recreation Area; it's open from late June to October (depending on the weather) and requires a high-clearance vehicle in parts. Call the **Bureau of Land Management** (BLM; 541-573-4400; www.blm.gov; 7:45am-4:30pm Mon-Fri) for information. If you happen to be in the area outside these months or have a low-clearance vehicle, consider seeing the Steens via the flat eastern gravel road through the scenic Alvord Desert. Take a full gas tank and prepare for weather changes year-round.

There are campgrounds on the Steens Mountain Loop, such as the BLM's pretty Page Springs and fine South Steens Campgrounds (campsites $6 to $8, water available). Free 'dispersed' camping is allowed in the Steens and Alvord Desert (bring water). The historic **Frenchglen Hotel** (541-493-2825; fghotel@yahoo.com; 39184 Hwy 205, Frenchglen; d $70-110; mid-Mar–Oct;) in the eponymous hamlet has small, cute rooms with shared bath, plus five modern rooms with private bath. Dinners are available (reserve ahead).

Oregon Coast

While Washington's coast is speckled with islands and inland seas, Oregon's 362 miles get full exposure to the crashing waves of the Pacific. This magnificent littoral is paralleled by view-hugging US 101, a scenic

LEWIS & CLARK: JOURNEY'S END

In November 1805 William Clark and his fellow explorer Meriwether Lewis of the Corps of Discovery staggered, with three dozen others, into a sheltered cove on the Columbia River, 2 miles west of the present-day Astoria-Megler Bridge, after completing what was indisputably the greatest overland trek in American history. After setting up a temporary camp, the party trekked west to what is now **Cape Disappointment State Park** (Hwy 100; ⌚dawn-dusk) to gaze upon the Pacific and search for a winter bivouac. Located on a high bluff inside the park not far from the Washington town of Ilwaco, the sequentially laid-out **Lewis & Clark Interpretive Center** (Hwy 100; adult/child $5/2.50; ⌚10am-5pm) faithfully recounts the Corps of Discovery's cross-continental journey using a level of detail the journal-writing explorers would have been proud of. A succinct 20-minute film backs up the permanent exhibits.

After the first truly democratic ballot in US history (in which a woman and a black slave both voted), the party elected to make their winter bivouac across the Columbia River in present-day Oregon. A replica of the original **Fort Clatsop** (adult/child $3/free; ⌚9am-6pm Jun-Aug, to 5pm Sep-May), where the Corps spent a miserable winter in 1805–06, lies 5 miles south of Astoria. Also on-site are trails, a visitor's center and historical reenactments (summer only).

There are 10 additional sites in the so-called **Lewis & Clark National & State Historical Parks** (www.nps.gov/lewi), all of them clustered around the mouth of the Columbia River and each relating important facts about the Corps of Discovery and its historic mission to map the American West.

highway that winds its way through towns, resorts, state parks (over 70 of them) and wilderness areas.

ASTORIA

There are three alluring reasons to visit Astoria, Oregon: first, it's the oldest Caucasian-founded settlement west of the Rockies; second, it's awash with poignant Lewis & Clark memorabilia; and third, the historic seaport is speckled with attractive Victorian heritage houses akin to a mini San Francisco.

Sitting at the wide mouth of the Columbia River, Astoria was founded by America's first multimillionaire, John Jacob Astor, in 1811. The town is dominated by the impossible-to-miss 4.1-mile-long **Astoria-Megler Bridge** (1966), which takes US 101 into Washington state and is the world's longest continuous truss bridge.

Sights & Activities

Aside from the not-to-be-missed Lewis and Clark sites, Astoria has a handful of other lures.

Columbia River Maritime Museum MUSEUM
(www.crmm.org; 1792 Marine Dr; adult/child $10/8; ⌚9:30am-5pm) The 150-year-old seafaring and river heritage is well interpreted at this fine museum, with mock-up lifeboats and details of the hundreds of shipwrecks that litter the river mouth.

Heritage Museum MUSEUM
(www.cumtux.org; 1618 Exchange St; adult/child $4/3; ⌚10am-5pm) The decidedly less flashy Heritage Museum contains historical exhibits, which include Ku Klux Klan (KKK) paraphernalia.

Flavel House HISTORIC BUILDING
(www.cumtux.org; 441 8th St; adult/child $5/4; ⌚10am-5pm) Extravagant Flavel House is a Queen Anne Victorian built by Captain George Flavel, one of Astoria's leading citizens during the 1880s.

Astoria Column LOOKOUT
(recommended donation $1) For a fantastic view, head uphill to this 125ft tower painted with scenes from the westward sweep of US exploration and settlement.

Fort Stevens State Park PARK
(tent/RV sites $18/22, yurts $30) Located about 10 miles west of Astoria off US 101, this park commemorates the historic military reservation that once guarded the mouth of the Columbia River. There's beach access, camping and bike trails. Reservations are accepted.

Sleeping & Eating

Astoria has two revitalized historic hotels and a stash of interesting independent bars and coffeehouses.

TOP CHOICE **Hotel Elliott** HISTORIC HOTEL **$$**
(☎503-325-2222; www.hotelelliott.com; 357 12th St; d $149-169; ❄📶) Encased in the oldest part of the oldest town in the Pacific Northwest, the elegant Elliott is a period piece that has clawed its way up to boutique standard without losing its historical significance.

Commodore Hotel BOUTIQUE HOTEL **$$**
(☎503-325-4747; www.commodoreastoria.com; 258 14th St; d with shared/private bath from $69/129; @📶) Even trendier and equally historic is this early-20th-century wonder that reopened in 2009 after 45 years as a pigeon coop. The birds and moths have been replaced by a stylish set of European-style rooms and suites. Don't miss the Portland-esque 14th Street Coffee House next door, with its fine java and neo-industrial decor.

TPaul's Urban Café INTERNATIONAL **$$**
(1119 Commercial St; mains $9-16; ⏰9am-9pm Mon-Thu, to 10pm Fri & Sat, 11am-4pm Sun) Cooks up formidable lunchtime quesadillas served with nachos and a homemade salsa dip.

Baked Alaska SEAFOOD **$$$**
(1 12th St; mains $18-24; ⏰11am-10pm) Astoria's finest fine-dining is perched on stilts over the water with great views and equally memorable seafood.

Information

Find information at the **visitor center** (www.oldoregon.com; 111 W Marine Dr; ⏰9am-5pm).

Getting There & Away

A daily bus run by **Northwest Point** (www.northwest-point.com) connects Astoria with Portland's Amtrak station ($18, 2½ hours) via Cannon Beach.

CANNON BEACH

The low-key antidote to gaudy Seaside, 9 miles to the north, Cannon Beach is a sensitively laid-out small resort where upmarket serenity is juxtaposed with thunderous Pacific breakers and fickle weather. Immense basalt promontories and a sweeping sandy beach have given the town its tourist-brochure wrapping paper, but Cannon Beach is uniquely beautiful and far from spoiled. The town itself is replete with small art galleries and esoteric shops.

Sights & Activities

Photogenic **Haystack Rock**, a 295ft sea stack, is the most spectacular landmark on the Oregon coast and accessible from the beach. Birds cling to its ballast cliffs and tide pools ring its base.

The coast to the north, protected inside **Ecola State Park**, is the Oregon you may have already visited in your dreams: sea stacks, crashing surf, hidden beaches and gorgeous pristine forest. The park is 1.5 miles from town and is crisscrossed by paths, including part of the Oregon Coast Trail, which leads over Tillamook Head to the town of Seaside.

The Cannon Beach area is good for surfing – though not the beach itself. The best spots are Indian Beach in Ecola State Park, 3 miles to the north, and Oswald West State Park, 10 miles south. **Cleanline Surf Shop** (www.cleanlinesurf.com; 171 Sunset Blvd) is a friendly local shop that rents out boards and mandatory wetsuits for $35 a day.

Sleeping & Eating

Cannon Beach Hotel HISTORIC HOTEL **$$**
(☎503-436-1392; www.cannonbeachhotel.com; 1116 S Hemlock St; d $132-242; @📶) A classy joint with small but meticulously turned-out rooms in a historic wooden arts-and-crafts building dating from 1914. A downstairs lounge and cafe-bistro add to the charm.

Blue Gull Inn Motel MOTEL **$**
(☎800-507-2714; www.haystacklodgings.com; 487 S Hemlock St; d/cottages from $69/125; @📶) Proving that Cannon Beach can still deliver to the budget-conscious is this modest but pleasant arc of motel-style rooms clustered around an outdoor fountain.

Newman's FRENCH, ITALIAN **$$$**
(☎503-436-1151; www.newmansat988.com; 988 S Hemlock St; mains $19-28; ⏰dinner Tue-Sun) Fuse the world's two greatest cuisines (Italian and French) to create a regionally lauded fine-dining experience in this historic beach house turned restaurant.

Sleepy Monk Coffee CAFE **$**
(www.sleepymonkcoffee.com; 1235 S Hemlock St; ⏰8am-4pm Fri-Sun) Slide under the skin of this free-and-easy beach town with a pastry and a cup of homemade joe (beans roasted on-site).

Information

For a full Cannon Beach rundown, look in at the **chamber of commerce** (www.cannonbeach.org; 207 N Spruce St; ⏰10am-5pm Mon-Sat, 11am-4pm Sun).

Getting There & Away

NorthWest Point (www.northwest-point.com) runs two comfortable daily buses (with on-board wi-fi) to and from Portland Amtrak station ($17), continuing on to Astoria. The bus stop is at the Beach Store at 1108 S Hemlock St.

NEWPORT

Oregon's second-largest commercial port, Newport is a lively tourist city with several fine beaches and a world-class aquarium. Good restaurants – along with some tacky attractions, gift shops and barking sea lions – abound in the historic Bayfront area, while bohemian Nye Beach offers art galleries and a friendly village atmosphere. The **Newport Seafood & Wine Festival** in late February draws the West's top chefs and literally dozens of wineries from California up to Washington. Get information at the **visitor center** (www.newportchamber.org; 555 SW Coast Hwy; ⏲8am-5pm Mon-Fri, 10am-3pm Sat).

The top-notch **Oregon Coast Aquarium** (www.aquarium.org; 2820 SE Ferry Slip Rd; adult/child $15.95/9.95; ⏲9am-6pm) is well known on the scenic coast, featuring a sea otter pool, surreal jellyfish tanks and Plexiglas tunnels through a shark tank. An alternative is the **Oregon Coast History Center** (www.oregoncoast.history.museum; 545 SW 9th St; suggested donation $2; ⏲10am-5pm Tue-Sun), housed in the turreted Burrows House and adjacent Log Cabin. There's more history at the breezy **Yaquina Head Outstanding Area** (750 Lighthouse Dr; admission $7; ⏲sunrise-sunset), site of the coast's tallest lighthouse and an interesting interpretive center.

Campers can head to **South Beach State Park** (☎541-867-4715; www.oregonstateparks.org; RV sites/yurts $27/40), which is 2 miles south on US 101, and has 227 reservable campsites and 27 yurts. Book-lovers shouldn't miss the **Sylvia Beach Hotel** (☎541-265-5428; www.sylviabeachhotel.com; 267 NW Cliff St; d incl breakfast $100-193), with simple but comfy rooms, each named after a famous author (Steinbeck, JK Rowling, Dr Seuss); reservations are mandatory. For a fancy meal, try **Saffron Salmon** (☎541-265-8921; www.saffronsalmon.com; 859 SW Bay Blvd; mains $22-30; ⏲11:30am-2:30pm & 5-8:30pm Thu-Tue). Once you get past the stellar wall-to-wall view, dig into grilled wild salmon fillet or rack of lamb with sumac. Reserve for dinner.

YACHATS & AROUND

Tiny Yachats (population 675) is what travel magazines describe as 'up-and-coming'; (read: unspoiled and hoping to stay that way). There are some interesting festivals here, including an October Mushroom Festival and a November Celtic Music Festival, but the real beauty is in the setting, in particular lofty **Cape Perpetua**, 3 miles to the south and first sighted by Captain Cook in 1778. Volcanic intrusions have formed a beautifully rugged shoreline, with dramatic features such as the Devil's Churn, where powerful waves crash through a 30ft inlet. Hikes start from the **visitors center** (www.fs.fed.us/r6/siuslaw; ⏲10am-5pm May-Sep, to 4pm Wed-Sun Sep-May), including the 1.2-mile Captain Cook Trail down to Cook's Chasm and tide pools, and the precipitous 1.3-mile St Perpetus Trail through meadows to an astounding viewpoint.

Fifteen miles to the south on US 101 is the almost tourist trap but fun **Sea Lion Caves** (www.sealioncaves.com; adult/child $12/8; ⏲8am-6pm Jul & Aug, 9am-5:30pm Sep-Jun), a noisy grotto filled with groaning sea lions accessed via an elevator.

Camp at **Beachside State Park** (☎541-563-3220; www.oregonstateparks.org.com; tent/RV sites $21/26, yurts $40), 5 miles north on US 101 (reservations accepted). A mile further on is the quirky lesbian-owned **See Vue Motel** (☎541-547-3227; www.seevue.com; 95590 Hwy 101 S; d $95-120; @📶), whose 11 individually crafted rooms are perched high above the Pacific breakers. In town you can bed down at the posher **Overleaf Lodge** (☎541-547-4880; www.overleaflodge.com; 280 Overleaf Lodge Lane; d $190-290; @📶), a highly popular resort-spa where all rooms have ocean views and some also have balconies, Jacuzzis and fireplaces.

OREGON DUNES NATIONAL RECREATION AREA

Stretching for 50 miles between Florence and Coos Bay, the Oregon Dunes form the largest expanse of coastal dunes in the USA. The dunes tower up to 500ft and undulate inland as far as 3 miles to meet coastal forests, harboring curious ecosystems that sustain an abundance of wildlife. Hiking trails, bridle paths, and boating and swimming areas are available, but avoid the stretch south of Reedsport as noisy dune buggies dominate this area. Inform yourself at the Oregon Dunes National Recreation Area's **headquarters** (☎541-271-3495; www.fs.fed/us/r6/sius law; 855 Highway Ave; ⏲8am-4:30pm Mon-Fri, to 4pm Sat & Sun) in Reedsport.

State parks include popular **Jessie M Honeyman** (☎541-997-3641; US 101; tent/RV sites $17/22, yurts $29), 3 miles south of Florence, and pleasant **Umpqua Lighthouse**

(☎541-271-4118; US 101; tent/RV sites/yurts/cabins $16/20/27/35), 6 miles south of Reedsport. USFS campgrounds include **Eel Creek** (☎877-444-6777; US 101; campsites $17), 10 miles south of Reedsport.

PORT ORFORD

Occupying a rare natural harbor and guarding plenty of spectacular views, the hamlet of Port Orford (population 2000) sits on a headland wedged between two magnificent state parks. **Cape Blanco State Park**, 4 miles to the north, is the second most-westerly point in the continental USA, and the trail-crisscrossed promontory is often lashed by fierce 100mph winds. As well as hiking, visitors can tour the **Cape Blanco Lighthouse** (adult/child $2/free; ⏲10am-3:30pm Tue-Sun Apr-Oct), built in 1870, and the oldest and highest operational lighthouse in Oregon.

Six miles south of Port Orford, in **Humbug Mountain State Park**, mountains and sea meet in aqueous disharmony with plenty of angry surf. You can climb the 1750ft peak on a 3-mile trail through old-growth cedar groves.

For an affordable B&B call in at **Home by the Sea** (☎877-332-2855; www.homebythesea.com; 444 Jackson St; d $105-115; @📶), where crashing waves will (hopefully) lull you to sleep and first-class hospitality will wake you up. Food in this fishing village means a visit to the slick, view-embellished confines of newly opened **Redfish** (☎541-336-2200; 517 Jefferson St; mains $15-20; ⏲7am-10pm Wed-Sun) for organic Northwest haute cuisine.

GOLD BEACH

Situated at the mouth of the fabulous Rogue River, Gold Beach attracts anglers and adventurers looking to zip upstream via jet boat into the Wild Rogue Wilderness area. Hikers can appreciate the area's spectacular coastline; visit **Cape Sebastian State Park**, a rocky headland 7 miles south, for a panorama stretching from California to Cape Blanco. Get details at the **visitors center** (www.goldbeach.org; 94080 Shirley Lane; ⏲9am-5pm).

For rustic, modern or beach cabins (along with RV sites), head to **Ireland's Rustic Lodges** (☎541-247-7718; www.irelandsrusticlodges.com; 29346 Ellensburg Ave; d $79-149; 📶). There's a glorious garden area in front and beach views in back. Tasty cheeses, meats, soup and sandwiches can be had at **Patti's Rollin 'n Dough Bistro** (☎541-247-4438; 94257 N Bank Rogue Rd; mains $9-15; ⏲9am-3pm Tue-Sun summer, Wed-Sun winter), one of the coast's best cheap eats (reserve ahead).

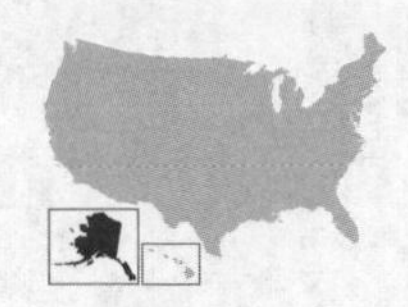

Alaska

Includes »

Southeast Alaska 1064
Ketchikan 1065
Wrangell 1066
Petersburg 1066
Sitka 1067
Juneau 1068
Haines 1071
Skagway 1072
Anchorage 1074

Best Places to Stay

» Copper Whale Inn (p1075)

» Black Bear Inn (p1065)

» Juneau International Hostel (p1069)

» Beach Roadhouse (p1071)

» Alaskan Sojourn Hostel (p1073)

Best Places to Eat

» Snow City Café (p1076)

» Ludvig's Bistro (p1068)

» Tracy's King Crab Shack (p1070)

» Coastal Cold Storage (p1067)

» Sack's Café (p1076)

Why Go?

Big, beautiful and wildly bountiful. Far away, rurally isolated and very expensive. Alaska is a traveler's dilemma.

There are few places in the world with such grandeur and breathtaking beauty. Mt McKinley, the highest peak in North America, is a stunning sight when you catch its alpenglow in Wonder Lake. Forty bald eagles perched on a single tree is something seen in Haines, not Iowa.

Alaska is also a remote and costly destination for anybody tripping through the rest of the country, a place where accommodations are expensive and transportation options meager. But, from the Northwest, a slice of Alaska can be an affordable side trip, whether it's a few days cruising the Southeast on the state ferry or a 2½-hour flight to Anchorage for the weekend. Once there you'll marvel at the grandeur of the land and begin plotting your ultimate adventure, a summer in Alaska.

When to Go

Anchorage

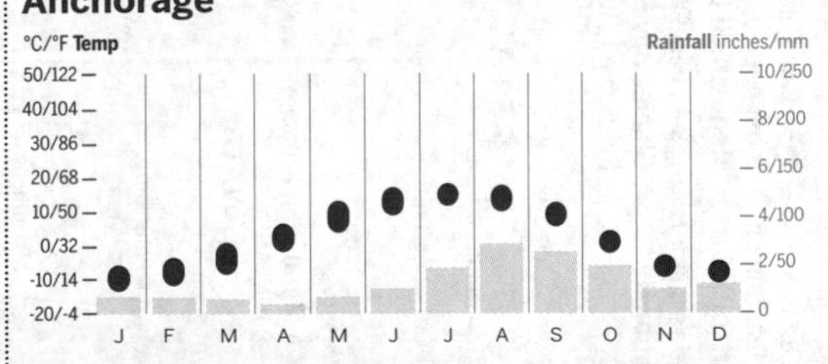

Jun Enjoy summer solstice festivals and 20-hour days. Stay up and play outdoors.

Jul Salmon runs, with millions of spawning fish choking streams, hit their peaks.

Late Sep The mystical northern lights begin to appear in the night skies.

Alaska Highlights

1. Zip-lining down to a stream full of bears feasting on salmon in **Ketchikan** (p1065)
2. Uncovering Russia's history in Alaska at **Sitka National Historical Park** (p1067)
3. Hiking alongside Alaska's most popular river of ice, **Mendenhall Glacier** (p1069)
4. Kayaking with seals at **Glacier Bay National Park & Preserve** (p1070)
5. Following the Klondike stampedes of 1898, hiking the **Chilkoot Trail** (p1073)
6. Exploring Alaska's history and culture at the **Anchorage Museum** (p1074)
7. Watching **Childs Glacier** (p1076) calf giant icebergs into the Copper River near Cordova
8. Exploring Kennecott and McCarthy in **Wrangell-St Elias National Park** (p1076)
9. Looking for bears and Mt McKinley in **Denali National Park & Preserve** (p1076)
10. Enjoying a mountain hike then a soothing soak at **Chena Hot Springs** (p1076)

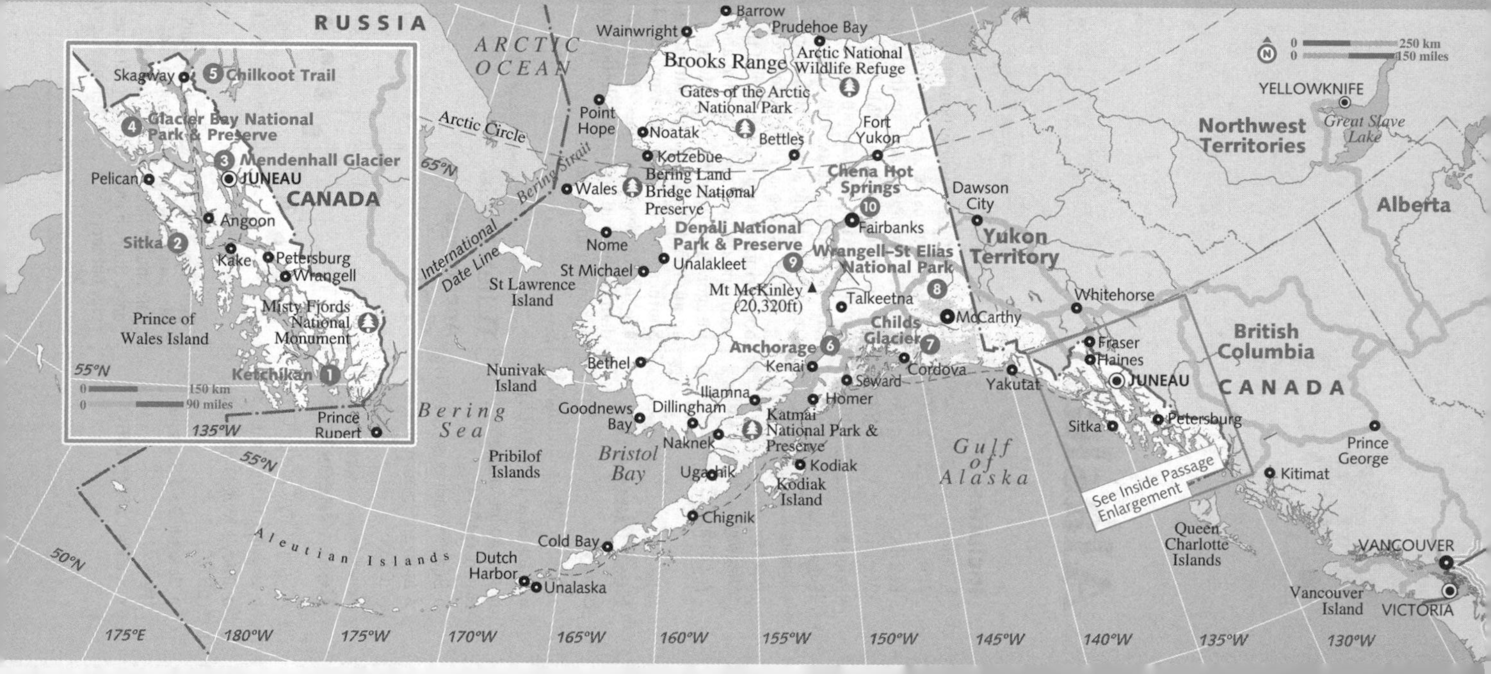

History

Indigenous Alaskans – Athabascans, Aleuts and Inuit, and the coastal tribes Tlingits and Haidas – migrated over the Bering Strait land bridge 20,000 years ago. In the 18th century waves of Europeans arrived: first British and French explorers, then Russian whalers and fur traders, naming land formations, taking otter pelts and leaving the cultures of the Alaska Native peoples in disarray.

With the Russians' finances badly over-extended by the Napoleonic Wars, US Secretary of State William H Seward was able to purchase the territory from them for $7.2 million – less than 2¢ an acre – in 1867. There was uproar over 'Seward's Folly,' but the land's riches soon revealed themselves: whales initially, then salmon, gold and finally oil.

After Japan bombed and occupied the Aleutian Islands in WWII, the military built the famous Alcan (Alaska-Canada) Hwy, which connected the territory with the rest of the USA. The 1520-mile Alcan contributed greatly to postwar Alaska becoming a state in 1959. The Good Friday earthquake in 1964 left Alaska in a shambles, but recovery was boosted when oil was discovered under Prudhoe Bay, resulting in the construction of a 789-mile pipeline to Valdez.

In 2006 Sarah Palin, a former mayor of Wasilla, stunned the political world by beating the incumbent governor to become Alaska's first female governor as well as its youngest at age 42. Two years later presidential candidate John McCain named her as his running mate on the Republican ticket. Even though they lost and Palin resigned as governor later that year, she is now considered one of the top presidential contenders for 2012.

Land & Climate

Simply put, Alaska is huge. Or, as residents love to point out: if Alaska was divided in half, each half would rank as the top two largest states in the country, dropping Texas to third. At latitudes spanning the Arctic Circle, the main body of Alaska is about 800 sq miles, with the arc of the Aleutian Islands chain stretching some 1600 miles south and west, and a 'panhandle' strip running 600 miles southeast down the North American coast.

The coastal regions, such as Southeast and Prince William Sound, have lush coniferous forests, while the Interior is dominated by boreal forest of white spruce, cottonwood and birch. Further north is a taiga zone – a moist, subarctic forest characterized by muskeg, willow thickets and stunted spruce – then the treeless Arctic tundra, with grass, mosses and a variety of tiny flowers thriving briefly in summer.

Alaska's size is the reason for its extremely variable climate. The Interior can top 90°F (32°C) during the summer, while the Southeast and Southcentral maritime regions will average 55°F (13°C) to 70°F (21°C). In the Southeast it rains almost daily from late September through October, while in June you'll experience the longest days of the year. In Anchorage that means 19 hours of sunshine while in Barrow the sun never sets at all.

The peak tourist season runs from early July to mid-August, when the best-known parks are packed and it's essential to make reservations for ferries and accommodations. In May and September you'll still find mild weather, but fewer crowds and lower prices.

Parks & Activities

Alaska has room to play outdoors and plenty of parks to do it in. Travelers come here for

ALASKA FACTS

- **Nickname** Final Frontier
- **Population** 676,9873
- **Area** 586,400 sq miles
- **Capital City** Juneau (population 31,275)
- **Other cites** Anchorage (population 291,826), Fairbanks (population 35,252), Ketchikan (population 13,477), Kodiak (population 13,049)
- **Sales tax** There is no state sales tax
- **Birthplace of** singer and poet Jewel (b 1974), cartoonist Virgil F Partch (1916-84)
- **Home of** Iditarod Sled Dog Race, tallest mountain in North America, Sarah Palin
- **Politics** Red state
- **Famous for** giant veggies, including a 127-pound cabbage grown in 2010, and giant king crab
- **Best souvenir** moose nugget ear rings
- **Driving distances** Anchorage to Fairbanks 586 miles, Anchorage to Denali National Park 425 miles

the mountains, the trails, the wildlife, the camping – the adventure. Hiking trails are boundless and are the best way to escape the summer crowds in places like Juneau and the Kenai Peninsula. Mountain biking is allowed on many trails, and bikes can be rented throughout the state. You can also rent kayaks throughout the Southeast, where paddlers enjoy sea kayaking in protective fjords, often within view of glaciers. Other popular outdoor activities are rafting, bear- and whale-watching, fishing, zip-lining and just pulling over on the road and admiring the scenery.

The best places to play and see wildlife are Alaska's many parks and preserves. Within the state the National Park Service administers 54 million acres as national parks, preserves and monuments. The most popular national parks are **Klondike Gold Rush National Historical Park** (☎907-983-2921; www.nps.gov/klgo) in Skagway, **Denali National Park & Preserve** (☎907-683-2294; www.nps.gov/dena) in the Interior and **Kenai Fjords National Park** (☎907-224-2125; www.nps.gov/kefj) near Seward. **Tongass National Forest** (☎907-586-8800; www.fs.fed.us/r10/tongass) covers most of Southeast while **Chugach State Park** (☎907-345-5014; dnr.alaska.gov/parks/units/chugach), on the edge of Anchorage, is the country's third-largest state park at 773 sq miles.

Information

The **Alaska Travel Industry Association** (www.travelalaska.com) is the official tourism marketing arm for the state and publishes a vacation planner with listings of B&Bs, motels, tours and more. An excellent source for tour companies and outfitters committed to responsible tourism is **Alaska Wilderness Recreation and Tourism Association** (☎907-258-3171; www.visitwildalaska.com).

The best place for information on national parks, state parks and all public land agencies along with their cabin rental programs is one of the four Alaska Public Lands Information Centers (APLICs) scattered around the state. Anchorage has the largest **APLIC** (☎907-644-3661; www.alaskacenters.gov) and the Southeast Alaska Discovery Center in Ketchikan is another.

Getting There & Around

AIR The vast majority of visitors to Alaska fly into **Ted Stevens Anchorage International Airport** (ANC; www.dot.state.ak.us/anc; wi-fi). **Alaska Airlines** (☎800-252-7522; www.alaskaair.com) Has direct flights to Anchorage from Seattle, Chicago, Los Angeles and Denver. It also flies between many towns within Alaska, including daily northbound and southbound flights year-round through Southeast Alaska, with stops at all main towns including Ketchikan and Juneau.

Continental (☎800-525-0280; www.continental.com) Flies nonstop from Houston, Chicago, Denver and San Francisco.

Delta (☎800-221-1212; www.delta.com) Direct flights from Minneapolis, Phoenix and Salt Lake City.

BOAT The **Alaska Marine Highway** (☎800-642-0066; www.ferryalaska.com) ferries connect Bellingham, WA, with 14 towns in Southeast Alaska. The complete trip (Bellingham–Haines, $353, 3½ days) stops at ports along the way and should be scheduled in advance. Trips within the Inside Passage include Ketchikan–Petersburg ($60, 11 hours), Sitka–Juneau ($45, five hours) and Juneau–Haines ($37, two hours). The ferries are equipped to handle cars (Bellingham–Haines $462), but space must be reserved months ahead. The ferries also service five towns in Southcentral Alaska, and twice a month make a special run across the Gulf of Alaska from Juneau to Whittier ($221).

BUS From Anchorage bus service is available to many areas of the state.

Alaska Direct Bus Line (☎800-770-6652; www.alaskadirectbusline.com) Goes to Tok ($115, eight hours)

Alaska Yukon Trails (☎800-770-7275; www.alaskashuttle.com) Links to Denali National Park ($75, six hours) and Fairbanks ($99, nine hours).

Seward Bus Lines (☎888-420-7788; www.sewardbuslines.net) Connects to Seward ($50, three hours).

TRAIN The **Alaska Railroad** (☎907-265-2494; www.akrr.com) offers service between Seward and Anchorage and from Anchorage to Denali, before ending in Fairbanks. Book seats in advance on this popular train.

SOUTHEAST ALASKA

The Southeast is as close as Alaska comes to continental USA, but most of it is inaccessible by road. It's possible to fly to the panhandle for a quick visit, but a better option, if you can spare a week, is to cruise the Inside Passage, a waterway made up of thousands of islands, glacier-filled fjords and a mountainous coastline. You can jump on a state ferry and stop at a handful of ports for hiking, kayaking and whale-watching.

Ketchikan

Ketchikan, the first stop of the Alaska Marine Highway and most cruise ships, is one long, thin town: several miles long, never more than 10 blocks wide and crammed with Alaskan character, adventure and the scenery you came looking for.

Sights & Activities

Dolly's House MUSEUM
(24 Creek St; adult/child $5/free; 8am-5pm) The star of Ketchikan's former red-light district, Creek St, this place is the parlor of Ketchikan's most famous madam, Dolly Arthur.

FREE **Totem Bight State Historical Park** HISTORIC SITE
(N Tongass Hwy; 6am-10pm) Ten miles north of downtown Ketchikan is this seaside park that contains 14 restored totem poles, a colorful community house and viewing deck overlooking Tongass Narrows. Next door to the state park is the equally intriguing **Potlatch Park** (www.potlatchpark.com; 9809 Totem Bight Rd; admission free; 7:30am-4pm), home to another dozen totems and five beautiful tribal houses.

Alaska Canopy Adventures EXTREME SPORTS
(907-225-5503; www.alaskacanopy.com; 116 Wood Rd; $190 per person) Fly through the trees! Uses eight zip lines, three suspension bridges and 4WD vehicles so you can zip 4600ft down a mountain. Afterwards you can watch bears feast on a salmon run.

Deer Mountain Trail HIKING
This 3-mile walking trail begins near the city center and provides access to the alpine world above the timberline and wonderful views of the town.

Totem Heritage Center MUSEUM
(601 Deermont St; adult/child $5/free; 8am-5pm) Features a collection of 19th-century totems in a spiritual setting.

Sleeping

TOP CHOICE **Black Bear Inn** B&B $$$
(907-225-4343; www.stayinalaska.com; 5528 N Tongass Hwy; r $160-230; @) This incredible B&B, 2.5 miles north of downtown, offers both rooms and small apartments. Among the many amenities is a covered outdoor hot tub where you can soak while watching eagles soaring overhead.

DON'T MISS

MISTY FJORDS NATIONAL MONUMENT

In the wilderness neighborhood that surrounds Ketchikan, this 3750-sq-mile monument is packed with wildlife-watching opportunities and spectacular views of 3000ft sheer granite walls that rise from the ocean. **Allen Marine Tours** (907-225-8100, 877-686-8100; www.allenmarinetours.com; adult/child $159/109) runs a four-hour trip around the monument but a more enjoyable adventure is to spend a few days paddling the fjords. **Southeast Sea Kayaks** (907-225-1258; www.kayakketchikan.com; 1621 Tongass Ave; 1-/2-person kayak per day $45/59) can supply rentals and water-taxi service into the heart of this watery wilderness, letting you bypass the long open-water paddle from Ketchikan.

New York Hotel BOUTIQUE HOTEL $$
(907-225-0246, 866-225-0246; www.thenewyorkhotel.com; 207 Stedman St; r $149-189, ste $209; @) A historic boutique hotel in the heart of town but far enough away to escape the cruise-ship madness. Its rooms and unique suites are filled with antiques and overlook the waterfront or Creek St.

Ketchikan Hostel HOSTEL $
(907-225-3319; www.ketchikanhostel.com; 400 Main St; dm $20) A friendly, clean hostel, with separate male and female dorms and located in a Methodist church downtown. It's open only from June through August.

Gilmore Hotel HISTORIC HOTEL $$
(907-225-9423; www.gilmorehotel.com; 326 Front St; d $115-155; @) Built in 1927, the Gilmore has 38 'historically proportioned' (ie small) rooms that include cable TV, coffeemakers and hair dryers.

Eating & Drinking

TOP CHOICE **Bar Harbor Restaurant** MODERN AMERICAN $$$
(907-225-2813; 2813 Tongass Ave; mains $18-34; 5-8pm Tue-Thu & Sun, 5-9pm Fri & Sat) A cozy place with a covered outdoor deck, between downtown and the ferry terminal. Yea, they serve seafood here – who doesn't in Southeast? – but the signature dish is Ketchikan's best prime rib.

Sushi Harbor SUSHI $
(☎907-225-1233; 629 Mission St; lunch specials $9-11, rolls $7-14; ⊙10am-10pm Mon-Sat, to 9pm Sun). This Japanese restaurant bustles with locals and cruise-ship workers alike. There are almost 40 types of roll on the menu but just a bowl of the udon noodles will fuel you all afternoon.

Burger Queen BURGERS $
(518 Tongass Ave; burgers $6-9; ⊙11am-3pm Mon, 11am-7pm Tue-Sat) Ketchikan's favorite shake-and-burger joint will deliver your hamburger to the Arctic Bar across the street where you can be sipping a beer.

First City Saloon LOUNGE
(830 Water St; wi-fi) A sprawling club that rocks with live music during the summer, often impromptu performances when cruise-ship bands are looking to let loose.

Information

Ketchikan Visitor Information & Tour Center (☎907-225-6166; www.visit-ketchikan.com; 131 Front St; ⊙7am-6pm) Helpful staff will book tours and accommodations.

Seaport Cyber (No 5 Salmon Landing; internet per hr $6; ⊙8:30am-5pm) Internet, wi-fi, phone cards and phones for international calls.

Southeast Alaska Discovery Center (☎907-228-6220; www.fs.fed.us/r10/tongass/districts/discoverycenter; 50 Main St; adult/child $5/free; ⊙8am-5pm) Houses an impressive exhibit hall; provides details of outdoor activities.

Getting There & Around

Alaska Airlines and Alaska Marine Highway ferries service Ketchikan. For wheels, try **Alaska Car Rental** (☎907-225-5123; 2828 Tongass Ave; compacts $57).

Wrangell

Strategically located near the mouth of the Stikine River, Wrangell is the only town to have existed under three flags and been ruled by four nations – Tlingit, Russia, Britain and the USA. Today it is one of the few ports in which the state ferries dock downtown, so at the very least jump off the boat for a quick look around town.

Sights & Activities

For its size, Wrangell has an impressive collection of totems. Pick up the free *Wrangell Guide* at the visitor center and spend an afternoon locating them all. Make sure you stop at **Chief Shakes Island**, near the boat harbor downtown.

Wrangell Museum MUSEUM
(296 Outer Dr; adult/child/family $5/3/12; ⊙10am-5pm Mon-Sat) In this museum at the Nolan Center you can learn about gold-rush Wrangell or why Wyatt Earp filled in as the town's deputy marshal for 10 days.

Sleeping & Eating

Stikine Inn MOTEL $$
(☎907-874-3388, 888-874-3388; www.stikineinn.com; 107 Stikine Ave; s $115-143, d $134-151; wi-fi) Recently renovated, Wrangell's largest motel is on the waterfront near the ferry dock and includes 34 rooms and a restaurant with tables overlooking the boat traffic on the water.

Alaskan Sourdough Lodge LODGE $$
(☎907-874-3613; www.akgetaway.com; 1104 Peninsula St; s/d $114/124; @wi-fi) This family-owned lodge offers 16 rooms, a sauna, steam bath and a front deck full of wicker furniture and a view of the harbor.

Diamond C Café CAFE $$
(223 Front St; breakfast $6-12, lunch $8-17; ⊙6am-3pm) Eat what the locals eat (eggs, biscuits and deep-fried fish-and-chips) while listening to the conservative pulse of this community.

Wrangell Hostel HOSTEL $
(☎907-874-3534; 220 Church St; dm $20) In the Presbyterian church

Information

Wrangell Visitor Center (☎907-874-3901; www.wrangell.com; 296 Outer Dr; ⊙10am-5pm Mon-Sat; @) At the Nolan Center.

Petersburg

At the north end of the spectacular Wrangell Narrows lies the picturesque community of Petersburg, a town known for its Norwegian roots and home to one of Alaska's largest fishing fleet.

Sights & Activities

The center of Old Petersburg is **Sing Lee Alley**, which winds past weathered homes and boathouses perched on pilings above the water.

Tongass Kayak Adventures KAYAKING
(☎907-772-4600; www.tongasskayak.com; 1-/2-person kayak $55/65) Offers rentals and drop-

off transportation, as well as several guided paddles, including a day-long paddle at **LeConte Glacier** ($265), North America's southernmost tidewater glacier and often the site of spectacular falling ice and breaching whales.

Clausen Memorial Museum MUSEUM
(203 Fram St; adult/child $3/free; 10am-5pm Mon-Sat) Features local artifacts and fishing relics, and a small but excellent museum store.

Sleeping

Scandia House HOTEL $$
(907-772-4281; www.scandiahousehotel.com; 110 Nordic Dr; s/d $110/130;) The most impressive place in town, this hotel has 33 modern rooms (some with kitchenettes), a courtesy shuttle service and a main-street location.

Nordic House B&B $$
(907-772-3620; www.nordichouse.net; 806 S Nordic Dr; r without bath $82-149;) Within an easy walk of the ferry terminal, this place offers five large rooms and a common area overlooking the boat harbor.

Tides Inn MOTEL $$
(907-772-4288; www.tidesinnalaska.com; 307 1st St; s $100-110, d $115-130; @) Largest motel in town, with 45 rooms, some with kitchenettes.

Eating & Drinking

TOP CHOICE **Coastal Cold Storage** SEAFOOD $
(306 N Nordic Dr; breakfast $4-8, lunch $8-12; 7am-3pm Mon-Sat;) The local specialty is halibut beer bits and this place serves the best ones in this seafood town.

Beachcomber Inn AMERICAN $$
(907-772-3888; 384 Mitkof Hwy; mains $19-30; 5-9pm Tue-Sat) This wonderful restaurant is built on pilings over the sea so every table has a fabulous maritime-and-mountain view.

Harbor Bar BAR
(310 Nordic Dr;) The classic place for deckhands and cannery workers, with pool tables, free popcorn and an excellent beer selection. In that great Alaskan tradition, patrons have started pinning dollar bills to the walls.

Information

Petersburg Chamber of Commerce (907-772-4636; www.petersburg.org; cnr Fram & 1st Sts; 9am-5pm Mon-Sat, noon-4pm Sun) Has B&B and USFS (United States Forest Service) information.

Sitka

Russians established Southeast Alaska's first nonindigenous settlement here in 1799, and the town flourished on fur. Today Sitka sees itself as both the cultural center of the Southeast and, because it's the only one facing the Pacific Ocean, the region's most beautiful city.

Sights & Activities

Sitka has superb hiking, and the **Gaven Hill Trail** into the mountains is accessible from the downtown area. There are also many kayaking trips around Baranof and Chichagof Islands.

Thanks to Sitka's ocean location, marine-wildlife boat tours have mushroomed in the town.

Sitka National Historical Park HISTORIC SITE
(Lincoln St; adult/child $4/free; 8am-5pm) Alaska's smallest national park has an intriguing trail that winds past 15 totem poles, while inside its visitor center are Russian and indigenous artifacts and traditional carving demonstrations.

Alaska Raptor Center WILDLIFE RESERVE
(www.alaskaraptor.org; 101 Sawmill Creek Rd; adult/child $12/6; 8am-4pm;) For an eye-to-eye encounter with a bald eagle, head to this center where injured birds relearn to fly.

St Michael's Cathedral CHURCH
(240 Lincoln St; admission $5; 9am-4pm Mon-Fri when cruise ships are in) A replica of the original 1840s Russian Orthodox cathedral destroyed by fire in 1966 and still the centerpiece of Sitka. The original icons and religious objects were salvaged and are on display.

FREE **Baranof's Castle** MONUMENT
Castle Hill is the site of Baranof's Castle, where Alaska was officially transferred from Russia to the USA.

Russian Bishop's House HISTORIC BUILDING
(Lincoln St; adult/child $4/free; 9am-5pm) Built in 1842, this is Sitka's oldest intact Russian building.

Sheldon Jackson Museum MUSEUM
(104 College Dr; adult/child $4/free; 9am-5pm) Houses an excellent indigenous culture collection.

Sitka Sound Ocean Adventures KAYAKING
(907-752-0660; www.kayaksitka.com; 1-/2-person kayak $65/80) Rents kayaks and runs guided trips; its office is a blue bus at the Centennial Building.

Allen Marine Tours CRUISE
(907-747-8100, 888-747-8101; www.allenmarinetours.com; adult/child $99/69; 1:30-4:30pm Sat) Offers three-hour tours, in a fully enclosed catamaran with wraparound windows, that often include spotting otters and whales.

Sleeping

Shee Atika Totem Square Inn HOTEL $$$
(907-747-3693, 866-300-1353; www.totemsquareinn.com; 201 Katlian St; r $179-249; @) Extensively renovated, this is Sitka's finest hotel, with 68 large, comfortable rooms perched above a harbor that bustles with boats bringing in the day's catch.

Ann's Gavan Hill B&B B&B $
(907-747-8023; www.annsgavanhill.com; 415 Arrowhead St; s/d $75/95; @) An easy walk from downtown, this lovely Alaskan home has three guest rooms and a wraparound deck with two hot tubs. Ahhh!

Sitka International Hostel HOSTEL $
(907-747-8661; sitkahostel.org; 109 Jeff Davis St; dm $24; @) Sitka's new – and only – hostel is downtown less than a block from Crescent Harbor and features five single-sex dorm rooms and one family room.

Sitka Hotel HOTEL $$
(907-747-3288, 888-757-3288; www.sitkahotel.net; 118 Lincoln St; s/d $99/105; @) This venerable hotel is right downtown and its back rooms are large, comfortable and feature views of Sitka Sound.

Eating & Drinking

TOP CHOICE **Ludvig's Bistro** MEDITERRANEAN $$$
(907-966-3663; www.ludvigsbistro.com; 256 Katlian St; tapas $12-16, mains $24-34; 4-10pm) Sitka's boldest restaurant is also the Southeast's best. The menu is described as 'rustic Mediterranean fare' and almost everything is local, even the sea salt.

Kenny's Wok & Teriyaki CHINESE $
(210 Katlian St; lunch $7-10, dinner $9-12; 11am-9pm Mon-Fri, noon to 9pm Sat & Sun) This Chinese restaurant also in the Katlian district seems to be always full, partly because it has only nine tables but mostly because the locals love the portions and the prices.

Victoria's BREAKFAST $$
(118 Lincoln St; breakfast $8-14, lunch $9-14, dinner $15-29; 4:30am-9pm) Sitka's early morning breakfast joint, it's open no matter when your charter captain decides to shove off to chase kings and cohos.

Highliner Coffee CAFE $
(www.highlinercoffee.com; 327 Seward St, Seward Sq Mall; light fare under $5; 5:30am-6pm Mon-Fri, 5:30am-5pm Sat, 7am-4pm Sun; @) At the Highliner they like their coffee black and their salmon wild. Come here to catch the buzz from a latte and the local issues.

Fly-in Fish Inn Bar BAR
(485 Katlian St) A delightful little six-stool bar on the back side of a inn. On the covered deck outside you can watch deckhands unload the day's catch.

Information

Sitka Convention & Visitors Bureau (907-747-5940; www.sitka.org; 330 Harbor Dr; 8am-5pm Mon-Fri) Across the street from St Michael's Cathedral, and also staffs a desk in the Centennial Building.

USFS office (907-747-6671; 204 Siginaka Way; 8am-4:30pm Mon-Fri) Can provide hiking and kayaking information for the area.

Getting There & Away

Sitka Airport (SIT; 907-966-2960), on Japonski Island, is served by **Alaska Airlines** (800-252-7522; www.alaskaair.com).

Northstar Rental (907-966-2552; Sitka Airport) has midsize cars from $69 per day.

Alaska Marine Highway (907-747-8737; www.ferryalaska.com) ferries stop almost daily at the terminal, which is 7 miles north of town. **Ferry Transit Bus** (907-747-8443; one way/round-trip $8/12) will take you into town.

Juneau

The first town to be founded after Alaska's purchase from the Russians, Juneau became the territorial capital in 1906 and today is the most scenic capital in the country. Its historic downtown clings between snow-capped mountains and a bustling waterfront. The rest of the city spreads north into the Mendenhall Valley. Juneau is also Alaska's cruise-ship capital and the gateway to many attractions, including Tracy Arm and Glacier Bay National Park.

Sights & Activities

Mendenhall Glacier GLACIER

Juneau's famous 'drive-in' glacier is one of the most picturesque attractions in Southeast Alaska. This frozen river and its informative **USFS Visitor Center** (Glacier Spur Rd; adult/child $3/free; ⊙8am-7:30pm) is 12 miles from the city. **Mendenhall Glacier Transport** (☎907-789-5460; round-trip $16) runs buses from downtown.

Last Chance Mining Museum HISTORIC SITE

(☎907-586-5338; 1001 Basin Rd; adult/child $4/free; ⊙9:30am-12:30pm & 3:30-6:30pm) The compressor building of Alaska Juneau Gold Mining Company is now a museum and the only building open to the public from Juneau's Gold Rush era.

Hiking HIKING

Hiking is the most popular activity in the area, and some trails access USFS cabins. **Juneau Parks & Recreation** (☎907-586-0428; www.juneau.org/parksrec) organizes free hikes. **West Glacier Trail**, which sidles along Mendenhall Glacier, has the most stunning scenery. The **Mt Roberts Trail** is the most popular hike to the alpine country above Juneau.

Taku Glacier Lodge TOUR

(☎907-586-6275; www.wingsairways.com; adult/child $280/225) The most popular tours in Juneau are flightseeing, glacier viewing and salmon bakes and a trip to this historic camp combines all three. You reach it via a floatplane that includes flying across a half-dozen glaciers. At the log lodge you enjoy an incredible meal of wild salmon to the view of Taku Glacier.

Alaska State Museum MUSEUM

(www.museums.state.ak.us; 395 Whittier St; adult/child $5/free; ⊙8:30am-5:30pm; 👪) Has artifacts from Alaska's six major indigenous groups, plus a full-size eagles' nest atop a two-story tree.

Mt Roberts Tram CABLE CAR

(☎www.goldbelttours.com; 490 S Franklin St; adult/child $27/13.50; ⊙noon-9pm Mon, 8am-9pm Tue-Fri, 9am-9pm Sat & Sun; 👪) Takes passengers from the cruise-ship dock to the timberline, where there is a nature center and a restaurant.

Juneau-Douglas City Museum MUSEUM

(www.juneau.org/parkrec/museum; 114 W 4th St; adult/child $4/free; ⊙9am-5pm Mon-Fri, 10am-5pm Sat & Sun) Highlights the area's gold-mining history and offers a **Historic Downtown Walking Tour** (adult/child incl museum $15/10; ⊙1:30pm Tue-Thu).

> DON'T MISS
>
> ### GLACIERS OF TRACY ARM
>
> This steep-sided fjord, 50 miles southeast of Juneau, has a pair of tidewater glaciers and a gallery of icebergs floating down its length. Tracy Arm makes an interesting day trip, far less expensive and perhaps even more satisfying than a visit to Glacier Bay. You're almost guaranteed to see seals inside the arm, and you might spot whales on the way there. **Adventure Bound Alaska** (☎907-463-2509; www.adventureboundalaska.com; adult/child $150/95; 👪) is the longtime tour operator to Tracy Arm and uses a pair of boats that leave daily from the Juneau waterfront. Reserve a seat in advance if you can (the full-day tour is popular with cruise ships) and pack a lunch along with your binoculars.

Alaska Boat & Kayak Center KAYAKING

(☎907-364-2333; www.juneaukayak.com; 11521 Glacier Hwy; 1-/2-person kayak $50/70; ⊙9am-6pm) Rents boats and offers a self-guided Mendenhall Lake paddle ($99).

Orca Enterprises CRUISE

(☎907-789-6801, 888-733-6722; www.alaskawhalewatching.com; adult/child $119/59) Uses a 42ft jet boat for three-hour whale-watching tours.

Sleeping

Juneau International Hostel HOSTEL $

(☎907-586-9559; www.juneauhostel.net; 614 Harris St; dm adult/child $10/5; @🛜) Alaska's best hostel is a five-minute walk from the state capitol.

Silverbow Inn BOUTIQUE HOTEL $$$

(☎907-586-4146; www.silverbowinn.com; 120 2nd St; r $189-219; @🛜) A wonderful boutique inn on top of a downtown bagel shop. Along with 11 rooms, there's an outdoor hot tub with a view of the mountains.

Driftwood Lodge MOTEL $$

(☎907-586-2280; www.driftwoodalaska.com; 435 Willoughby Ave; r $95-135; 🛜) The rooms are no-frills but clean, and many have kitchenettes. There's a courtesy airport and ferry van, a coin laundry and bike rental.

Juneau Hotel HOTEL **$$$**
(☎907-586-5666; www.juneauhotels.net; 1200 W 9th St; ste $189; @) An all-suites hotel located within easy walking distance of the downtown attractions.

Eating & Drinking

S Franklin St is Juneau's historic and at times colorful drinking sector.

TOP CHOICE **Tracy's King Crab Shack** SEAFOOD **$$**
(www.kingcrabshack.com; 356 S. Franklin St; crab $10-27; 10:30am-7pm) Squeezed between the Library Parking Garage and the Cruise Ship Docks, this little hut serves up crab, from outstanding bisque to mini-cakes. A bucket of king crab pieces ($60) is 2lb of the sweetest seafood you'll ever have.

Island Pub PIZZERIA **$$**
(www.theislandpub.com; 1102 2nd St; large pizza $13-20; 11:30am-10pm) Across the channel in Douglas is the capital city's best pizzeria, serving firebrick-oven focaccias and gourmet pizza to a mountainous view.

Twisted Fish SEAFOOD **$$**
(550 S Franklin St; dinner mains $16-40; 11am-10pm) Beef be gone! Located between Taku Smokeries and a wharf where commercial fishermen unload their catch, this restaurant is all about local seafood. Even half the pizzas on the menu have something from the sea on them.

Thane Ore House SEAFOOD **$$**
(☎907-586-3442; 4400 Thane Rd; salmon bake adult/child $24/12; 11am-9pm) Juneau's best salmon bake, 4 miles south of town, is an all-you-can-eat affair of grilled salmon and halibut that takes place in a rambling log lodge full of Alaskan artifacts. There's courtesy-van transportation from major downtown hotels.

Red Dog Saloon BAR
(☎907-463-3658; 278 S Franklin St) The (in) famous Red Dog Saloon has a sawdust floor and relic-covered walls.

Alaskan Hotel BAR
(☎907-586-1000; 167 S Franklin St) Hidden here is a unique bar with historic ambience and occasional live music.

Information

Juneau Convention & Visitors Bureau (☎907-586-2201, 888-581-2201; www.traveljuneau.com; 101 Egan Dr; 9am-5pm) In Centennial Hall.

Juneau Library (☎907-586-5249; 292 Marine Way; 11am-8pm Mon-Thu, noon-5pm Fri-Sun; @) Gorgeous views and free internet.

WORTH A TRIP

GLACIER BAY NATIONAL PARK & PRESERVE

Eleven tidewater glaciers that spill out of the mountains and fill the sea with icebergs of all shapes, sizes and shades of blue have made Glacier Bay National Park and Preserve an icy wilderness renowned worldwide. This can be an expensive side trip from Juneau but, for most people who include it on their itinerary, well worth the extra funds.

Gustavus (www.gustavusak.com) is a weekly stop ($33, 4½ hours) for the **Alaska Marine Highway** (☎800-642-0066; www.ferryalaska.com). **Alaska Airlines** (☎800-252-7522; www.alaskaair.com) has daily flights between Gustavus and Juneau.

Food, lodging and transportation to Bartlett Cove in the park is available in Gustavus. **Annie Mae Lodge** (☎907-697-2346; www.anniemae.com; Grandpa's Farm Rd; s $120-150, d $170-200) has 11 rooms, most with private entrances and bathrooms; **Beartrack Mercantile** (☎907-697-2358; Dock Rd) has limited groceries.

The **park headquarters** (☎907-697-2230; www.nps.gov/glba; 1 Park Rd; 8am-4:30pm Mon-Fri) in Bartlett Cove maintains a free campground and a **visitor center** (☎907-697-2627; 7am-9pm) at the dock, which provides backcountry permits and maps. Or you can stay at **Glacier Bay Lodge** (☎888-229-8687; www.visitglacierbay.com; 199 Bartlett Cove Rd; r $199-224) the only hotel and restaurant at Bartlett Cove.

To see the glaciers, board the *Fairweather Express* operated by **Glacier Bay Lodge & Tours** (☎907-264-4600, 888-229-8687; www.visitglacierbay.com; adult/child $190/95) for an eight-hour cruise up the West Arm of Glacier Bay.

The only developed hiking trails are in Bartlett Cove, but there is excellent kayaking; rent equipment from **Glacier Bay Sea Kayaks** (☎907-697-2257; www.glacierbayseakayaks.com; 1-/2-person kayak per day $45/50).

Juneau Ranger Station (☎907-586-8800; 8510 Mendenhall Loop Rd; ⏰8am-5pm Mon-Fri) Head to the Mendenhall Valley for information on cabins, trails and kayaking.

Getting There & Around

AIR The main airline serving Juneau is **Alaska Airlines** (☎800-252-7522; www.alaskaair.com). Smaller companies such as **Wings of Alaska** (☎907-789-0790; www.wingsofalaska.com) provide services to isolated communities.

BOAT The terminal for the **Alaska Marine Highway** (☎800-642-0066; www.ferryalaska.com) is 14 miles from downtown; M/V *LeConte* runs to Angoon ($37, five hours) and Tenakee Springs ($35, eight hours), while the high-speed M/V *Fairweather* connects to Petersburg ($66, four hours) and Sitka ($45, 4½ hours).

BUS Juneau's public bus system, **Capital Transit** (☎907-789-6901; www.juneau.org/capitaltransit; adult/child $1.50/1), can take you from the airport to the city center, but not the ferry terminal.

CAR Numerous car-rental places offer pick up, drop off and unlimited mileage. Compacts at **Rent-A-Wreck** (☎907-789-4111, 888-843-4111; 2450c Industrial Blvd) are $59.

Haines

Haines is Southeast Alaska's most scenic departure point and a crucial link to the Alcan Hwy for thousands of RVers (recreational vehicle drivers) every summer on their way to Interior Alaska. The Northwest Trading Company arrived here in 1878, followed by gold prospectors and the US Army, which built its first permanent post in Alaska, Fort Seward, in 1903. The perceived threat of a Japanese invasion in WWII resulted in the construction of the Haines and Alcan Hwys, connecting Haines to the rest of the USA. If mammoth cruise ships depress you, Haines is a much better destination choice than Skagway.

Sights & Activities

Hiking HIKING

Haines offers two major hiking-trail systems – Mt Riley and Mt Ripinsky – as well as afternoon walking tours of **Fort Seward** (the visitor center has details).

Sheldon Museum MUSEUM

(www.sheldonmuseum.org; 11 Main St; adult/child $5/free; ⏰10am-5pm Mon-Fri, 1-4pm Sat & Sun) Features indigenous artifacts upstairs, and gold-rush relics downstairs.

American Bald Eagle Foundation MUSEUM

(www.baldeagles.org; 113 Haines Hwy; adult/child $10/5; ⏰10am-5pm Mon-Fri, 1-5pm Sat & Sun; 👪) Displays almost 180 species of animals, including almost two dozen eagles, in their natural habitat.

Hammer Museum MUSEUM

(www.hammermuseum.org; 108 Main St; adult/child $3/free; ⏰10am-5pm Mon-Fri) For something quirky, a 1500-hammer monument to owner Dave Pahl's obsession with the tool.

Chilkat Guides RAFTING

(☎907-766-2491; www.raftalaska.com; adult/child $94/65) Runs a four-hour Chilkat River raft float.

Sleeping

TOP CHOICE **Beach Roadhouse** B&B $$

(☎907-766-3060, 866-741-3060; www.beachroadhouse.com; Mile 1 Beach Rd; r/cabins $105/145; 📶) This large cedar home is perched above Lynn Canal in a tranquil, woodsy setting, offering four rooms with kitchenettes and two lovely cabins.

Alaska Guardhouse Lodging B&B $$

(☎907-766-2566, 866-290-7445; www.alaskaguardhouse.com; 15 Seward Dr; s/d $105/135; 📶) A building that was used to jail misbehaving soldiers now houses visitors in four large and comfortable bedrooms.

Captain's Choice Motel MOTEL $

(☎907-766-3111; www.capchoice.com; 108 2nd Ave N; s/d $123/133; @📶) Haines' largest motel has the best view of the Chilkat Mountains and Lynn Canal and a huge sundeck to enjoy it.

Fort Seward Lodge MOTEL $

(☎766-2009, 877-617-3418; www.ftsewardlodge.com; 39 Mud Bay Rd; r $110, without bath $75; 📶) The former Post Exchange of Fort Seward offers Haines' best value in accommodations, with updated rooms and a friendly bar.

Bear Creek Cabins & Hostel HOSTEL $

(☎907-766-2259; www.bearcreekcabinsalaska.com; Small Tract Rd; dm/cabins $20/68) To escape the metropolis of Haines, head a mile out of town to this pleasant hostel on the edge of the woods.

Eating & Drinking

Mosey's Cantina MEXICAN $$

(www.moseyscantina.com; 31 Tower Rd; lunch $8-14, dinner $16-24; ⏰11:30am-2:30pm & 5:30-8:30pm Wed-Mon) This may be Haines but Mosey's offers some of the best Mexican fare outside of Anchorage, in a cute and cozy setting.

Fireweed Restaurant BISTRO $$
(37 Blacksmith St; sandwiches $8-13, large pizza $25; mains $13-17; 11:30am-3pm Wed-Sat, 4:30-9pm Tue-Sat;) This bright and laid-back bistro looks like it belongs in California with words like 'organic' and 'veggie' on its menu as opposed to 'deep fried' and 'captain's special.'

Klondike PIZZA $$
(Dalton City; medium pizza $14-18; 5-8pm) Haines' newest restaurant serves excellent wood-fired pizza, salads and beer that's brewed only two doors down.

Haines Brewing Company BREWERY
(Dalton City; 1-6pm Mon-Sat) It's well worth the walk to the town's delightful one-room brewery.

Information

Haines Convention & Visitors Bureau (907-766-2234; www.haines.ak.us; 122 2nd Ave; 8am-5pm Mon-Fri, 9am-4pm Sat & Sun)

Getting There & Away

Several air-charter companies service Haines, the cheapest being **Wings of Alaska** (907-789-0790; www.wingsofalaska.com).

VALLEY OF THE EAGLES

The 75-sq-mile **Alaska Chilkat Bald Eagle Preserve**, along the Chilkat River, protects the world's largest-known gathering of bald eagles. The greatest numbers, up to 4000 birds, are spotted in December and January, but Haines comes alive during its **Alaska Bald Eagle Festival** (www.baldeagles.org/festival) in the second week of November, a five-day event that attracts hundreds of birders from around the country to witness the event.

But you can see eagles here any time during summer, albeit not as many. Head north on the Haines Hwy and pull over at the posted lookouts on the Haines between Miles 18 and 22, the best spots to search for eagles. Don't have wheels? During the summer **Alaska Nature Tours** (907-766-2876; www.alaskanaturetours.net; adult/child $75/60;) offers a Valley of the Eagles Nature Tour, a 3½-hour tour up the Chilkat River with a naturalist.

Haines-Skagway Fast Ferry (907-766-2100, 888-766-2103; www.hainesskagwayfastferry.com; one way adult/child $35/18) will get you to and from Skagway.

Eagle Nest Car Rentals (907-766-2891; 1183 Haines Hwy), in the Eagle Nest Motel, has cars available for $57 per day with 100 miles included.

Skagway

The northern terminus of the Alaska Marine Highway, Skagway was a gold-rush town infamous for its lawlessness. In 1887 the population was two; 10 years later it was Alaska's largest city, with 20,000 residents. Today Skagway survives entirely on tourism and gets packed when a handful of cruise ships pull in and thousands of passengers converge on the town as if the Klondike gold rush was still on.

Sights & Activities

FREE **Klondike Gold Rush National Historical Park** HISTORIC SITE
(983-9223; www.nps.gov/klgo; visitor center Broadway St at 2nd Ave; 8am-6pm) A seven-block corridor along Broadway St that features 15 restored buildings, false fronts and wooden sidewalks from Skagway's golden era as a boom town. Thanks to the cruise ships, it's the most popular national park in Alaska. To best appreciate this amazing moment in Skagway's history, join a free, ranger-led walking tour, at the visitor center on the hour from 9am to 4pm.

Skagway Museum MUSEUM
(cnr 7th Ave & Spring St; adult/child $2/1; 9am-5pm Mon-Fri, 10am-5pm Sat, 10am-4pm Sun) One of the best museums in the Southeast, and its gold-rush relics are some of the most interesting exhibits in a town filled with museums.

White Pass & Yukon Route Railroad TOUR
(907-983-2217; www.wpyr.com; 231 2nd Ave; adult/child $112/56) Offers the best tour: the three-hour Summit Excursion climbs the high White Pass in a historic narrow-gauge train.

FREE **Mascot Saloon** MUSEUM
(290 Broadway St; 8am-6pm) A museum devoted to Skagway's heyday as the 'roughest place in the world.'

CHILKOOT TRAIL

The Chilkoot is the ultimate Alaska trek, combining great scenery, a historical site and an incredible sense of adventure. It was the route used by the Klondike gold miners in the 1898 gold rush, and walking it is not so much a wilderness adventure as a history lesson. The 33-mile trek takes four days and includes the Chilkoot Pass – a steep climb up to 3525ft that has hikers scrambling on all fours. The highlight for many is riding the historic White Pass & Yukon Route Railroad (p1074) back to Skagway.

Interested? Stop at the **Trail Center** (☎907-983-9234; www.nps.gov/klgo; Broadway St at 2nd Ave; ⊙8am-5pm) to obtain backpacking permits and set up the hike.

Sleeping

Alaskan Sojourn Hostel HOSTEL $
(☎907-983-2040; www.alaskansojourn.net; 488 8th Ave; dm/r $25/75; 📶) Skagway's newest hostel is open and airy, has dorms, private rooms, free coffee in the morning and a barbecue in a courtyard for the evening.

Sgt Preston's Lodge MOTEL $$
(☎907-983-2521, 866-983-2521; http://sgtprestons.eskagway.com; 370 6th Ave; s $85-115, d $90-125; @📶) This motel is the best bargain in Skagway and just far enough from Broadway St to escape most of the cruise-ship crush.

Skagway Inn INN $$
(☎907-983-2289, 888-752-4929; www.skagwayinn.com; Broadway St at 7th Ave; r incl breakfast $119-199; @📶) In a restored 1897 Victorian house that was originally one of the town's brothels – what building still standing in Skagway wasn't? – the inn is downtown and features 10 rooms, four with shared baths. All are small but filled with antique dressers, iron beds and chests. A delicious breakfast is included.

Mile Zero B&B B&B $$
(☎907-983-3045; www.mile-zero.com; 901 Main St; r $135-145; @) This B&B is like a motel with the comforts of home as the six large rooms have their own bath and a private entrance on the wraparound porch.

Eating & Drinking

In 2012, Skagway's restaurants and bars became a smoke-free zone.

TOP CHOICE **Stowaway Café** CAJUN $$
(☎907-983-3463; 205 Congress Way; sandwiches $9-12, mains $20-24; ⊙10am-9pm) Near the Harbor Master's office, this funky and fantastic cafe serves excellent fish and Cajun-style steak dinners. Make sure you try the wasabi salmon.

Starfire THAI $$
(4th Ave at Spring St; lunch $12-15, dinner $14-19; ⊙11am-10pm; 🖉) Order pad Thai or curry dishes in five colors (purple is *Fire with Flavor!*) here and then enjoy it with a beer on the outdoor patio.

Skagway Fish Company SEAFOOD $$$
(☎907-983-3474; Congress Way; lunch $10-17, dinner $16-36; ⊙11am-10pm) Despite a menu loaded with seafood, what locals rave about at this restaurant, located next to Stowaway Café, are its ribs – great barbecue even if you weren't in Alaska.

Glacial Smoothies & Espresso CAFE $
(336 3rd Ave; breakfast $4-7, sandwiches $7-9; ⊙6am-6pm; 🖉) Skagway's favorite for breakfast bagels, healthy sandwiches and smoothies named Gold Rush (peaches, pineapple, banana) and Cabin Fever (peanut butter, chocolate, banana). This is where you come to idle away a rainy afternoon with a white-chocolate mocha.

Red Onion Saloon BAR
(205 Broadway St) This former brothel is now Skagway's liveliest bar. Naturally.

Information

Klondike Gold Rush National Historical Park Visitors Center (☎907-983-9223; www.nps.gov/klgo; 154 Broadway St; ⊙8am-6pm) For everything outdoors; local trails, public campgrounds and National Park Service (NPS) programs.

Skagway Convention & Visitors Bureau (☎907-983-2854; www.skagway.com; cnr Broadway St & 2nd Ave; ⊙8am-6pm Mon-Fri, 8am-5pm Sat & Sun) In the can't-miss Arctic Brotherhood Hall (think driftwood).

Getting There & Away

Regularly scheduled flights from Skagway to Juneau, Haines and Glacier Bay are available from **Wings of Alaska** (☎907-983-2442; www.wingsofalaska.com).

Alaska Marine Highway (800-642-0066; www.ferryalaska.com) has ferries departing every day in summer, and **Haines-Skagway Fast Ferry** (907-766-2100, 888-766-2103; www.hainesskagwayfastferry.com; one way adult/child $35/18) runs daily to Haines.

Sourdough Car Rentals (907-983-2523; www.sourdoughrentals.com; 350 6th Ave) has compacts for $69 a day with unlimited miles.

Yukon-Alaska Tourist Tours (866-626-7383, in Whitehorse 867-668-5944; www.yukonalaskatouristtours.com) offers a minibus service to Whitehouse (one way $60) Monday to Saturday.

White Pass & Yukon Route Railroad (907-983-2217; www.wpyr.com; 231 2nd Ave) goes to Fraser, British Columbia, where there's a bus connection to Whitehorse (adult/child $119/60).

ANCHORAGE

Anchorage offers the comforts of a large US city but is only a 30-minute drive from the Alaskan wilderness. Founded in 1914 as a work camp for the Alaska Railroad, the city was devastated by the 1964 Good Friday earthquake but quickly rebounded as the industry headquarters for the Prudhoe Bay oil boom. Today almost half the state's residents live in or around the city, as Anchorage (population 283,938) serves as the economic and political heart of Alaska. Sorry, Juneau.

Sights & Activities

TOP CHOICE **Anchorage Museum** MUSEUM
(www.anchoragemuseum.org; 625 C Street; adult/child $12/7; 9am-6pm;) A $75-million renovation has made this Alaska's best cultural experience. Spend an afternoon viewing paintings by Alaskan masters, including Sydney Laurence, on the 1st floor and learning about Alaska's history on the 2nd.

Alaska Native Heritage Center CULTURAL BUILDING
(www.alaskanative.net; 8800 Heritage Center Dr; adult/child $25/17; 9am-5pm) This cultural center is spread over 26 acres and includes studios with artists carving baleen or sewing skin-boats, a small lake and five replica villages. Other than traveling to the Bush, this is the best place to see how humans survived – even thrived – before central heating.

FREE **Alaska Heritage Museum** MUSEUM
(301 W Northern Lights Blvd; noon-4pm Mon-Fri) This museum-in-a-bank is home to the largest private collection of original paintings and Alaska Native artifacts in the state. The collection is so large there are displays in the elevator lobbies throughout the bank.

Alaska Aviation Heritage Museum MUSEUM
(www.alaskaairmuseum.org; 4721 Aircraft Dr; adult/child $10/6; 9am-5pm) Ideally located on Lake Hood, the world's busiest floatplane lake, this museum is a tribute to Alaska's colorful bush pilots and includes 25 of their faithful planes.

Alaska Zoo ZOO
(www.alaskazoo.org; 4731 O'Malley Rd; adult/child $12/6; 9am-6pm Sat-Mon, Wed & Thu, 9am-9pm Tue & Fri;) The unique wildlife of the Arctic is on display at the only zoo in North America that specializes in northern animals, ranging from all three species of Alaskan bear to wolverines, moose, caribou and Dall sheep.

Flattop Mountain HIKING
A three- to five-hour, 3.4-mile round-trip of Alaska's most-climbed peak starts from a trailhead on the outskirts of Anchorage. Maps are available at the Alaska Public Lands Information Center and the **Flattop Mountain Shuttle** (907-279-5293; www.hike-anchorage-alaska.com; round-trip adult/child $22/15) will run you to the trailhead.

Tony Knowles Coastal Trail HIKING
On the other side of the creek from the Flattop Mountain trail, beginning at the west end of 2nd Ave, this 11-mile trail is the most scenic of the city's 122 miles of paved path.

Downtown Bicycle Rental CYCLING
(www.alaska-bike-rentals.com; 333 W 4th Ave; 3/24hr rental $16/32; 8am-8pm) Anchorage has been called a 'Bike Utopia.' Rent a bike and find out why.

CULTURE PASS JOINT TICKET

Anchorage's top two attractions, the Alaska Native Heritage Center and Anchorage Museum, can both be enjoyed at a 22% discount with a special joint-admission ticket. The Culture Pass Joint Ticket is $29 per person and includes admission to both museums as well as shuttle transportation between them. You can purchase the joint pass from the ticket offices at either location.

Tours

Rust's Flying Service SCENIC FLIGHT
(907-243-1595; www.flyrusts.com; 4525 Enstrom Circle) Has 30-minute tours ($100), a three-hour flight to view Mt McKinley in Denali National Park ($375) and a 1½-hour tour of Knik Glacier ($225).

Anchorage City Trolley Tours BUS TOUR
(907-775-5603, 888-917-8687; www.alaskatrolley.com; 612 W 4th Ave; adult/child $15/7.50; tours 9am-5pm) One-hour rides in a bright red trolley depart on the hour, passing Lake Hood, Earthquake Park and Cook Inlet, among other sights.

Sleeping

TOP CHOICE **Copper Whale Inn** INN $$$
(907-258-7999; www.copperwhale.com; W 5th Ave & L St; r $185-220; @) An ideal downtown location, recently remodeled rooms and a bright and elegant interior make this gay-friendly inn one of the best top-end places in Anchorage. Many rooms and the breakfast lounge give way to views of Cook Inlet. Are those beluga whales out there?

Wildflower Inn B&B $$
(907-274-1239; www.alaska-wildflower-inn.com; 1239 I St; r incl breakfast $129-139; @) In a historic home just three blocks south of Delaney Park, this B&B offers three large rooms, pleasant sitting areas and a full breakfast in the morning, including caramelized French toast.

Anchorage Downtown Hotel BOUTIQUE HOTEL $$$
(907-258-7669, 886-787-2423; www.anchoragedowntownhotel.com; 826 K St; r $189-212;) Recently remodeled, this midtown hotel (despite its name) is a very pleasant place to stay, with 16 colorful and comfortable rooms that feature private baths, coffeemakers and small refrigerators. In the morning you're handed a newspaper, in the evening a glass of wine.

Qupqugiaq Inn INN $
(907-563-5633; www.qupq.com; 640 W 36th Ave; dm $25, s/d $96/106, without bath $80/90; @) This colorful establishment has a continental breakfast that includes French-pressed coffee and roll-your-own oats. The large dorms sleep eight, and the private rooms are bright and clean.

Alaska Backpackers Inn HOSTEL $
(907-277-2770; www.alaskabackpackers.com; 327 Eagle St; dm/s/d $25/60/70; @) A bit east of central downtown, this roomy and comfortable hostel is still within walking distance of restaurants and bars. Plus it has a foosball table!

Long House Alaskan Hotel HOTEL $$
(907-243-2133, 888-243-2133; www.longhousehotel.com; 4335 Wisconsin St; s/d $143/153;) A block off Spenard Rd, this log hotel has 54 huge rooms and lots of amenities including 24-hour shuttle to the airport.

Spenard Hostel HOSTEL $
(907-248-5036; www.alaskahostel.org; 2845 W 42nd Pl; dm $25; @) This friendly, independent hostel is near the airport and has 24-hour check-in – great for red-eye arrivals in Alaska. There's free coffee in the morning and bike rentals ($3 per hour) are available.

Anchorage Guest House HOSTEL $
(907-274-0408; www.akhouse.com; 2001 Hillcrest Dr; dm/r $35/89; @) This beautiful place feels more like a B&B than a hostel, and the prices reflect that. Rent a bike ($5 per hour) for the nearby Tony Knowles Coastal Trail.

Puffin Inn MOTEL $$
(907-243-4044; www.puffininn.net; 4400 Spenard Rd; r $119-159;) Arriving on the red-eye? This motel offers free 24-hour airport shuttle as well as four tiers of fine rooms, from 26 sardine-can economy rooms to full suites.

Millennium Alaskan Hotel HOTEL $$$
(907-243-2300; www.millenniumhotels.com; 4800 Spenard Rd; r $249-340; @) A large, 248-room resort with a woodsy lodge feel overlooking Lake Spenard, 4 miles from downtown. Kids love the mounted animals and fish.

City Garden B&B B&B $$
(907-276-8686; www.citygarden.biz; 1352 W 10th Ave; r $100-150;) This open, sunny, gay-and-lesbian-friendly place has three rooms, one with a private bath.

Eating

In Anchorage you'll enjoy great menus, from Polynesian and Mexican to good old burgers, and clean air. All restaurants and bars are smoke-free.

THE BEST OF THE REST OF ALASKA

Came for a quick peek and are so smitten by the grandeur of Alaska you want to linger? Go ahead; skip Nebraska and stay another week or two. Here's more of Alaska that's worth changing your travel plans for:

» A breathtaking wilderness, **Denali National Park & Preserve** (www.nps.gov/dena) includes North America's highest peak and an amazing array of wildlife.

» At the tip of the Kenai Peninsula, **Homer** (www.homeralaska.org) is a scenic town with good eating, a great art scene and giant halibut offshore.

» There's great hiking in Chena River State Recreation Area and Mother Nature's own Jacuzzi to soak in afterwards at **Chena Hot Springs** (www.chenahotsprings.com).

» To watch giant brown bears snag salmon in mid-air or to hike in the Valley of 10,000 Smokes, come to **Katmai National Park** (www.nps.gov/katm).

» Another scenic Kenai Peninsula town, **Seward** (www.sewardak.org) is the place to go for marine wildlife in Kenia Fjords National Park or Alaska SeaLife Center.

» Stretching between Seward and Fairbanks, the **Alaska Railroad** (www.akrr.com) is one of the most amazing train rides in the world.

» Walk the same streets that Wyatt Earp did in the colorful gold-rush town of **Nome** (www.nomealaska.org) or pan for some color on Golden Sands Beach.

» At the end of the McCarthy Road in the heart of Wrangell–St Elias National Park, the country's largest, are the twins towns of **Kennecott & McCarthy** (www.nps.gov/wrst), full of history, artifacts and glaciers.

» Childs Glacier alone makes it worth jumping on the Alaska Marine Highway for the fishing port of **Cordova** (www.cordovachamber.com) in Prince William Sound.

» The most amazing ferry trip in the USA is the **Trusty Tushy Run to UnAlaska** (www.ferryalaska.com), a four-day cruise from Homer to the Aleutian Islands.

TOP CHOICE Snow City Café CAFE **$$**
(www.snowcitycafe.com; 1034 W 4th Ave; breakfast $7-15, lunch $9-13; ⏰7am-3pm Mon-Fri, 7am-4pm Sat & Sun; 📶) This hip and busy cafe serves healthy grub to a mix of clientele that ranges from the tattooed to the up-and-coming. Surrounding all of them are walls adorned with local art.

Sack's Café FUSION **$$$**
(☎907-274-4022; www.sackscafe.com; 328 G St; lunch mains $12-16, dinner mains $24-34; ⏰11am-2:30pm & 5-9pm Sun-Thu, 11am-2:30pm & 5-10pm Fri & Sat) A bright, colorful restaurant serving Asian-Mediterranean fusion fare that is consistently creative (reservations recommended).

Moose's Tooth Pub & Pizzeria PIZZERIA **$$**
(www.moosestooth.net; 3300 Old Seward Hwy; large pizza $16-25; ⏰10:30am-11pm Mon-Thu, to midnight Fri & Sat, 11am-11pm Sun; 🖉) An Anchorage institution serving a dozen custom-brewed beers including monthly specials, and 40 gourmet pizzas including 10 veggie options.

Bear Tooth Grill TEX-MEX **$$**
(http://beartooththeatre.net; 1230 W 27th St; burgers $10-14, mains $12-20; ⏰11am-11:30pm Mon-Fri, 10am-11:30pm Sat & Sun) A popular hangout with an adjacent movie theater, the Bear Tooth Grill serves excellent burgers and seafood as well as Tex-Mex dishes.

Humpy's Great Alaskan Alehouse PUB **$$**
(www.humpys.com; 610 W 6th Ave; mains $15-21; ⏰11am-midnight Mon-Fri, 9am-midnight Sat & Sun; 📶) Anchorage's most beloved beer place, with almost 60 beers on tap. There's also ale-battered halibut, gourmet pizzas, outdoor tables and live music most nights.

Jen's Restaurant EUROPEAN **$$$**
(☎907-561-5367; www.jensrestaurant.com; 701 W 36th Ave; lunch mains $13-26; dinner mains $18-40; ⏰11am-2pm Mon-Fri, 6-10pm Tue-Sat) Innovative, Scandinavian-accented cuisine that emphasizes fresh ingredients and elaborate presentation. There's also a wine bar with music and a menu of tapas.

Glacier Brewhouse BREWERY **$$$**
(www.glacierbrewhouse.com; 737 W 5th Ave; lunch $11-18, dinner $19-30; ⏰11am-9:30pm Mon, 11am-

10pm Tue-Thu, 11am-11pm Fri & Sat, noon-9:30pm Sun) Grab a table overlooking the three giant copper brewing tanks and enjoy Alaskan seafood and rotisserie-grilled ribs and chops with a pint of oatmeal stout.

Arctic Roadrunner BURGERS **$**
(5300 Old Seward Hwy; burgers $5-7; ⏲10:30am-9pm Mon-Sat) Since 1964 this place has been turning out beefy burgers that can be enjoyed outdoors while watching salmon spawn up Campbell Creek.

Ray's Place VIETNAMESE **$**
(www.raysplaceak.com; 32412 Spenard Rd; mains $8-15; ⏲10am-3pm & 5-9pm Mon-Fri; ✎) Leave Chilkoot Charlie's dance floor early and cross the street to this Vietnamese restaurant that does great cold-noodle salads and stir fries and stocks Vietnamese beer.

Charlie's Bakery CHINESE **$$**
(2729 C St; mains $10-15; ⏲11am-8:30pm Mon-Sat) The most authentic Chinese food you'll find in Anchorage, sold next to French baguettes.

New Sagaya's City Market SUPERMARKET **$**
(www.newsagaya.com; W 13th Ave; ⏲6am-10pm Mon-Sat, 8am-9pm Sun) Eclectic and upscale, this grocery store has a great deli specializing in Asian fare and seating indoors and outdoors.

Drinking

Bernie's Bungalow Lounge LOUNGE
(626 D St) Pretty people, pretty drinks: this is the place to see and be seen. The outdoor patio, with a water-spewing serpentine, is the city's best and on summer weekends it rocks late into the night with live music.

Crush WINE BAR
(343 W 6th Ave) This swanky club and restaurant is a great place for a glass of wine or the entire bottle.

Snow Goose & Sleeping Lady Brewing Co BREWERY
(717 W 3rd Ave) If the sun is setting over Cook Inlet and the Alaska Range, head to the rooftop deck of this brewpub. Only the beer is better than the view.

Entertainment

Check the *Anchorage Press* for the latest entertainment listings.

TOP CHOICE **Chilkoot Charlie's** LIVE MUSIC
(www.koots.com; 2435 Spenard Rd) 'Koots,' as locals call this beloved landmark, is big and brash, with 10 bars, four dance floors and sawdust everywhere. There's live music every night and $2 pints until 10pm.

Tap Root LIVE MUSIC
(www.taprootalaska.com; 3300 Spenard Rd) With the addition of Tap Root, Spenard cemented its reputation as the heart of Anchorage nightlife. The lively bar has 20 microbrews on tap, an impressive list of single-malt Scotch whiskeys and live bands every night of the week.

Cyrano's Theatre Company THEATER
(☎907-274-2599; www.cyranos.org; 413 D St) This may be the best live theater in town, staging everything from Hamlet to a Mel Brooks' jazz musical with a strong commitment to local theater artists and Alaskan playwrights.

Mad Myrna's DANCE
(☎907-276-9762; 530 E 5th Ave) A fun, cruisy bar with line-dancing on Wednesday, drag shows on Friday and dance music most other nights after 9pm.

Shopping

Oomingmak Musk Ox Producers Co-op CLOTHING
(www.qiviut.com; 604 H St) Handles a variety of very soft, very warm and very expensive garments made of arctic musk-ox wool, hand-knitted in isolated Inupiaq villages.

REI OUTDOOR EQUIPMENT
(1200 W Northern Lights Blvd; ⏲10am-8pm Mon-Fri, 10am-7pm Sat, 11am-6pm Sun) The expanded REI has the city's finest selection of backpacking, kayaking and camping gear.

MORE AFFORDABLE CAR RENTALS

Avoid renting a car at the airport if at all possible as you will be hit with a 34% rental tax. Rental agencies within Anchorage will tack on only 18% tax and generally have cheaper rates. And while they can't pick you up at the airport, if you drop the car off during business hours some rental places will provide you with a ride to the airport.

Finally, if you can rent a vehicle in May or September as opposed to June or August, you will usually save more than 30%.

ANC Auxiliary Craft Shop ARTS & CRAFTS
(☎907-729-1122; 4315 Diplomacy Dr; ⊙10am-2pm Mon-Fri, 11am-2pm 1st & 3rd Sat of month) On the 1st floor of the Alaska Native Medical Center; has some of the finest Alaska Native arts and crafts available to the public.

ℹ Information

Internet Access

ZJ Loussac Public Library (☎907-343-2975; 3600 Denali St; ⊙10am-9pm Mon-Thu, to 6pm Fri & Sat, 1-5pm Sun) Free internet access.

Media

Tourist freebies are available everywhere, including the *Official Anchorage Visitors Guide*.

Anchorage Daily News (www.adn.com) This daily has the largest circulation in the state.

Anchorage Press (www.anchoragepress.com) A fabulous free weekly with events listings and social commentary.

Medical Services

Alaska Regional Hospital (☎907-276-1131; 2801 DeBarr Rd; ⊙24hr) For emergency care.

First Care Medical Center (☎907-248-1122; 3710 Woodland Dr, Suite 1100; ⊙7am-midnight) Walk-in clinic in midtown.

Providence Alaska Medical Center (☎907-562-2211; 3200 Providence Dr)

Money

Key Bank (☎907-257-5500; 601 W 5th Ave) Downtown.

Wells Fargo (☎800-869-3557; 301 W Northern Lights Blvd) The main bank is in midtown.

Post

Post office (344 W 3rd Ave) Downtown in the Village at Ship Creek Center.

Tourist information

Alaska Public Lands Information Center (☎907-644-3661, 866-869-6887; www.alaskacenters.gov; 605 W 4th Ave, Suite 105; ⊙9am-5pm) Has park, trail and cabin information as well as excellent displays.

Log Cabin Visitor Center (☎907-257-2363; www.anchorage.net; 524 W 4th Ave; ⊙8am-7pm) Has pamphlets, maps, bus schedules and city guides in several languages.

ℹ Getting There & Around

To/From the Airport

Alaska Shuttle (☎907-338-8888, 907-694-8888; www.alaskashuttle.net) offers door-to-door transportation between the airport and downtown and South Anchorage (one to three people $30) and Eagle River ($45). The city's bus service (People Mover) picks up from the South Terminal (bus 7) on a route that heads back downtown.

Air

Ted Stevens Anchorage International Airport (ANC; ☎907-266-2525; www.dot.state.ak.us/anc/index.shtml) has frequent inter- and intrastate flights. Terminals are off International Airport Rd.

Alaska Airlines (☎800-252-7522; www.alaskaair.com) Flies to 19 Alaskan towns, including Fairbanks, Juneau, Nome and Barrow.

Era Aviation (☎800-866-8394; www.flyera.com) Flies to Cordova, Valdez, Kodiak and Homer.

Pen Air (☎800-448-4226; www.penair.com) Serves southwest Alaska.

Bus

Alaska Direct Bus Line (☎800-770-6652; www.alaskadirectbusline.com) Regular services to Glennallen ($75, three hours), and Tok ($115, eight hours).

Alaska/Yukon Trails (☎800-770-7275; www.alaskashuttle.com) Goes to Denali ($75, six hours) and Fairbanks ($99, nine hours).

Seward Bus Lines (☎907-563-0800, 888-420-7788; www.sewardbuslines.net) Goes to Seward ($50, three hours).

Homer Stage Lines (☎907-235-2252; http://stagelineinhomer.com) To Homer ($90, 4½ hours) and points in between.

People Mover (☎907-343-6543; www.peoplemover.org; adult/child $1.75/1) The local bus service; its main terminal is located at the **Downtown Transit Center** (cnr W 6th Ave & G St).

Car

Midnight Sun Car & Van Rental (☎907-243-8806, 888-877-3585; 4211 Spenard Rd) rents compacts ($61/370 per day/week), as does **Denali Car Rental** (☎907-276-1230; 1209 Gambell St), for $65/390.

Train

Alaska Railroad (☎907-265-2494; www.akrr.com) chugs its way south to Whittier (adult/child $65/33, 2½ hours) and Seward ($75/38, four hours), and north to Denali ($146/73, eight hours) and then Fairbanks ($210/105, 12 hours).

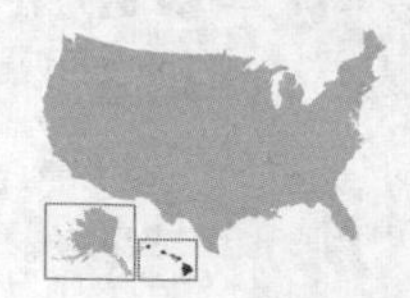

Hawaii

Includes »

O'ahu 1082
Honolulu & Waikiki 1082
Hawai'i The Big Island 1087
Mauna Kea 1089
Hilo 1090
Hawai'i Volcanoes National Park 1091
Maui 1091
Kaua'i 1095

Best Places to Eat

» Roy's–Waikiki Beach (p1084)

» Ted's Bakery (p1087)

» Sansei (p1092)

» Mama's Fish House (p1094)

» Kona Brewing Company (p1088)

Best Places to Stay

» Royal Hawaiian (p1083)

» Mauna Lani Bay Hotel & Bungalows (p1089)

» Ka'awa Loa Plantation (p1089)

» Hotel Hana-Maui (p1095)

» Hanalei Colony Resort (p1097)

Why Go?

Truth: this string of emerald islands in the cobalt-blue Pacific, more than 2000 miles from any continent, takes work to get to. And aren't the islands totally crushed by sun-baked tourists and cooing honeymooners? Cue the galloping *Hawaii Five-0* theme music, Elvis crooning and lei-draped beauties dancing hula beneath wind-rustled palms.

Hawaii, as tourist bureaus and Hollywood constantly remind us, is 'paradise.' Push past the hype and you may find they're not far off. Hawaii is diving coral-reef cities in the morning and listening to slack-key guitar at sunset. It's slurping chin-dripping *liliko'i* (passion fruit) with hibiscus flowers in your hair. It's Pacific Rim cuisine, fiery volcanoes and breaching whales. The islands are an expression of nature at its most divine, blessed with a multicultural society rooted in Polynesia, Asia, America and even Europe.

Locals know Hawaii isn't always paradise, but on any given day it can sure feel like it.

When to Go

Honolulu

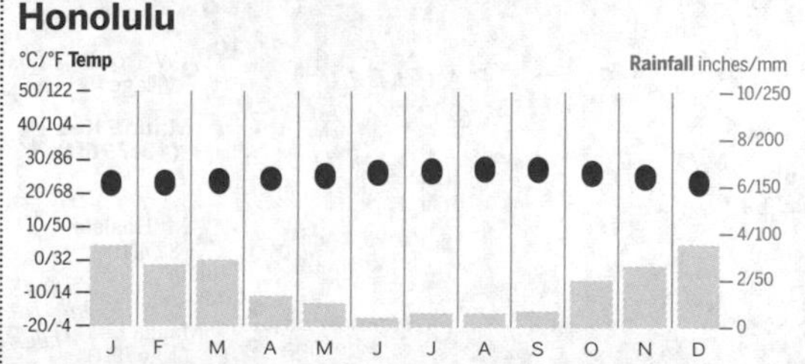

Dec–Apr Slightly cooler, wetter winter weather; peak season for tourism, surfing and whale-watching.

May–Sep Mostly sunny, cloudless days and huge crowds of families taking summer vacations.

Oct–Nov Weather is extremely hot and humid, but fewer visitors mean cheaper accommodations.

Hawaii Highlights

1. Exploring multicultural **Honolulu** (p1082), from eye-popping museums to ethnic eats
2. Snorkeling with tropical fish in O'ahu's **Hanauma Bay** (p1086)
3. Seeing the smoldering crust of a living volcano at **Hawai'i Volcanoes National Park** (p1091)
4. Stargazing atop Hawaii's highest mountain, sacred **Mauna Kea** (p1089)
5. Catching dawn over Maui's 'house of the rising sun' in **Haleakalā National Park** (p1095)
6. Driving Maui's twisting seaside **Hana Highway** (p1095) past jungle valleys and waterfalls
7. Kayaking or trekking Kaua'i's sculpted **Na Pali Coast** (p1097)

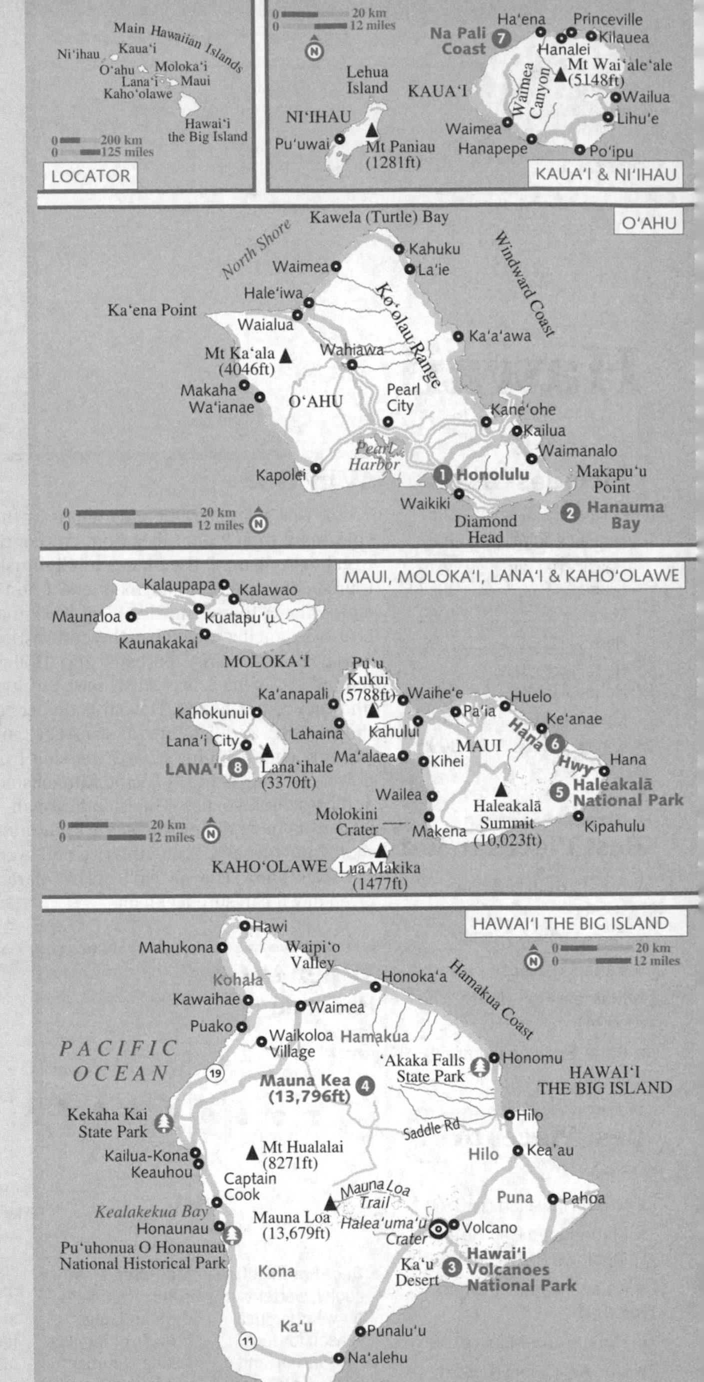

History

Little is known about Hawaii's first settlers, who arrived around AD 500. Tahitians had landed by AD 1000 and, for the next 200 years, navigated thousands of miles back and forth across the ocean in double-hulled canoes. Ruled by chiefs, ancient Hawaiian society was matriarchal and its religion followed strict laws known as *kapu*.

Beginning in the 1790s, King Kamehameha, chief of the Big Island, conquered and united the Hawaiian Islands. He is credited with bringing peace and stability to a society that was often in flux due to wars and the power struggles of the ruling class. After Kamehameha's death in 1819, his son Liholiho inherited the throne, while Kamehameha's favorite wife, Queen Ka'ahumanu, became regent. In a stunning repudiation of traditional Hawaiian religion, Liholiho and Ka'ahumanu deliberately violated *kapu* and destroyed many temples.

Christian missionaries arrived soon after and, in the midst of Hawaii's social and spiritual chaos, began to 'save souls.' New England whalers also arrived, seeking different quarry, and by the 1840s Lahaina and Honolulu were the busiest whaling towns in the Pacific. Meanwhile, foreigners made a grab for Hawaii's fertile land, turning vast tracts into sugarcane plantations; needing field workers, they encouraged a flood of immigrants from Asia and Europe. This gave rise to Hawaii's multiethnic culture, but also displaced Native Hawaiians, most of whom became landless.

In 1893 a group of American businessmen overthrew the Hawaiian monarchy. The US government was initially reluctant to support the coup, but soon rationalized colonialism by citing the islands' strategic importance, annexing Hawaii in 1898. Hawaii played an infamous role in history when a surprise attack on Pearl Harbor in 1941 catapulted the US into WWII. Hawaii became the 50th state in 1959.

Local Culture

Compared to 'the mainland' – a blanket term for the rest of the USA – Hawaii may as well be another country. In fact, some Native Hawaiians would like to restore its status as an independent nation. Both geologically and culturally speaking, Hawaii developed in isolation and, like its flora and fauna, its ways are unique.

No ethnicity can claim a majority, but this racial diversity is also distinct from typical US multiculturalism. Hawaii has large Asian populations and tiny African American and Latino communities. Less than 10% of residents identify themselves as Native Hawaiian.

As befits a tropical island paradise, Hawaii is decidedly casual. Except in cosmopolitan Honolulu, aloha shirts and sandals ('rubbah slippahs') are acceptable attire for any occasion, socializing revolves around food and family, and fun means sports and

HAWAII IN...

Four Days

Anyone on a trans-Pacific stopover will land at **Honolulu**, so spend the few days you have on **O'ahu**. In between surfing and sunning on **Waikiki Beach**, check out Honolulu's museums and wander the city's **Chinatown**, summit **Diamond Head** and snorkel **Hanauma Bay**. In winter, admire monster waves on the **North Shore**.

One Week

With a week, fit in another island – say, **Maui**. Explore the old whaling town of **Lahaina**, head to **Haleakalā National Park** to see the sunrise above the volcano summit, take a whale-watching cruise, snorkel or dive **Molokini Crater**, drive the serpentine **Road to Hana** and take a dip in waterfall pools at **Oheo Gulch**.

Two Weeks

With two weeks, as well as the above, visit another island. On the **Big Island**, glimpse ancient Hawaii at **Pu'uhonua O Honaunau National Historical Park**, kayak and snorkel in **Kealakekua Bay**, lounge on **North Kona & South Kohala** beaches, visit coffee farms in **South Kona**, and say aloha to Pele at **Hawai'i Volcanoes National Park**.

If you choose **Kaua'i**, kayak the **Wailua River**, hike **Waimea Canyon** and **Koke'e State Park**, hang ten at **Hanalei Bay**, snorkel **Ke'e Beach** and trek or paddle the **Na Pali Coast**.

HAWAII FACTS

» **Nickname** Aloha State

» **Population** 1.3 million

» **Area** 6423 sq miles

» **Capital city** Honolulu (population 375,750)

» **Sales tax** 4% (4.5% on O'ahu) plus 9.25% room tax

» **Birthplace of** Olympian Duke Kahanamoku (1890–1968), entertainer Don Ho (1930–2007), President Barack Obama (b 1961), actor Nicole Kidman (b 1967)

» **Home of** ukuleles and the USA's only royal palace

» **Politics** majority vote Democrat, minority Native Hawaiian separatists

» **Famous for** surfing, hula, mai tais, the world's most active volcano

» **State fish** *humuhumunukunukuapua'a* ('fish with a nose like a pig')

outdoor pursuits. Caring for the land and the community are intertwined.

Then there is aloha – or *alooooooHA,* as they say at luau (Hawaiian feasts). It is of course a greeting, but, more than that, it describes a gentle, everyday practice of openness, hospitality and loving welcome – one that's extended to everyone, local and visitor.

LANGUAGE

Hawaii has two official state languages, English and Hawaiian, and one unofficial language, pidgin. The Hawaiian language has experienced a renaissance but, outside of a formal setting (eg classroom, performance), you are unlikely to hear it spoken. All residents speak English, but when locals 'talk story' with each other they may reach for the relaxed, fun-loving cadences of pidgin. Pidgin developed on sugar plantations as a common tongue for diverse foreign workers.

O'AHU

O'ahu is the *ali'i* (chief) of Hawaii's main islands – so much so that others are referred to as 'Neighbor Islands.' O'ahu is the center of Hawaii's government, commerce and culture, while Waikiki's beaches gave birth to the whole tiki-craze Hawaii fantasia. If you want to take the measure of Hawaii's diversity, O'ahu offers the full buffet in one tidy package: in the blink of an eye you can go from crowded metropolis to turquoise bays teeming with sea life – and surfers.

Getting There & Around

Honolulu International Airport (HNL; http://hawaii.gov/hnl) is a major Pacific air hub. From the US mainland, fares start around $400 from California. **Roberts Hawaii** (808-441-7800; www.robertshawaii.com) runs 24-hour airport shuttles to/from Waikiki (one way/round-trip $9/15).

Hawaiian Airlines (800-367-5320; www.hawaiianair.com) and **go!** (888-435-9462; www.iflygo.com) are the main carriers flying between islands. Service is frequent and flight times are short, but fares vary wildly from $65 to $180.

O'ahu's extensive public transit system, **TheBus** (808-848-5555; www.thebus.org), covers most of O'ahu, but not most hiking trailheads or scenic lookouts; fares are $2.50 (four-day pass $25).

Honolulu & Waikiki

Among its many museums and cultural offerings, Honolulu has the USA's only royal palace. It's also a foodie heaven with everything from cheap noodle joints to gourmet Pacific Rim fusion cuisine. Saunter over to Waikiki Beach to lounge on the sand, play in the water, and hear Hawaiian music and watch hula dancers sway after sunset.

Sights

Immediately north of downtown Honolulu, **Chinatown** is an intriguing quarter that lends itself to exploring. Bring an appetite – you'll be grazing in pan-Asian markets and cafes as you wander among herbalists, temples and contemporary art galleries.

'Iolani Palace HISTORIC BUILDING
(808-538-1471, tour reservations 808-522-0832/0823; www.iolanipalace.org; 364 S King St; adult/child 5-12yr from $13/6; 9am-4pm Mon-Sat) At the heart of downtown Honolulu, this historical site where the monarchy was overthrown offers a unique glimpse into the Kingdom of Hawai'i's late-19th-century history. Phone for tour schedules.

Bishop Museum MUSEUM
(808-847-3511; www.bishopmuseum.org; 1525 Bernice St; adult/child 4-12yr $18/15; 9am-5pm

Wed-Mon;) Considered the world's finest Polynesian anthropological museum, here impressive cultural displays include the regal Hawaiian Hall. The Science Adventure Center puts kids inside an erupting volcano; call ahead to check planetarium show times.

Honolulu Academy of Arts MUSEUM
(tour reservations 866-385-3849; www.honoluluacademy.org; 900 S Beretania St; adult/child under 12yr $10/free; 10am-4:30pm Tue-Sat, 1-5pm Sun) Displays must-see collections of Asian, European and Pacific art. Phone to make reservations for tours ($25) of Doris Duke's former mansion Shangri La, a trove of Islamic art.

Also worth seeing:

FREE **Hawai'i State Art Museum** MUSEUM
(www.hawaii.gov/sfca; 2nd fl, 250 S Hotel St; 10am-4pm Tue-Sat, 5-9pm 1st Fri of month) Showcases traditional and modern works by multicultural island artists.

Lyon Arboretum GARDENS
(www.hawaii.edu/lyonarboretum; 3860 Manoa Rd; admission by donation; 8am-4pm Mon-Fri, 9am-3pm Sat) Nature trails and a Hawaiian ethnobotanical garden.

Waikiki Aquarium AQUARIUM
(www.waquarium.org; 2777 Kalakaua Ave; adult/child 5-12yr/youth 13-17yr $9/2/4; 9am-5pm, last entry 4:30pm;) Fantastic educational exhibits and hands-on touch tanks.

Activities

Beaches BEACHES
It's all about loooong **Waikiki Beach**. Catamarans and outrigger canoes offering rides pull right up onto the sand, while concession stands rent surfboards, kayaks and windsurfing gear and offer lessons. For a swim without the tourist crowds, head to mile-long **Ala Moana Beach Park** (1201 Ala Moana Blvd), just west of Waikiki.

Hiking Trails HIKING
Several hiking trails offer sweeping city views in the verdant Upper Manoa and Makiki Valleys above downtown and the University of Hawai'i. Few trails are just barely accessible by bus, including the 0.8-mile-long route to **Manoa Falls**. Consult **Na Ala Hele** (www.hawaiitrails.org) for more information and directions.

Festivals & Events

For many more celebrations on all islands, browse www.gohawaii.com.

Waikiki Spam Jam FOOD, MUSIC
(www.spamjamhawaii.com) In late April, this street festival goes nuts for tinned meat.

Pan-Pacific Festival CULTURAL
(www.pan-pacific-festival.com) Three days of Japanese, Hawaiian and South Pacific entertainment in mid-June.

Aloha Festivals CULTURAL
(www.alohafestivals.com) September's statewide cultural festival brings a royal court and block party to Waikiki.

Hawaii International Film Festival FILM
(www.hiff.org) Celluloid celebration of Pacific Rim and homegrown films in late October.

Sleeping

Waikiki is the center of the action, and Kalakaua Ave, the main beachfront strip, is lined with swanky high-rise hotels; for better value, head inland. Overnight parking averages $20 or more. Party-hardy independent backpacker hostels line back-alley Lemon Rd.

Royal Hawaiian RESORT $$$
(808-923-7311, 866-716-8110; www.royal-hawaiian.com; 2259 Kalakaua Ave; r $345-615; P@) With its Moorish-style turrets and archways, the aristocratic, oh-so-pink Royal Hawaiian was Waikiki's first true luxury hotel. It's now spiffier than ever, thanks to multimillion-dollar renovations. For old-school ambience, ask for the historic building; for ocean views, the modern tower.

Hotel Renew BOUTIQUE HOTEL $$
(808-687-7700, 888-485-7639; www.hotelrenew.com; 129 Pa'oakalani Ave; r incl breakfast $150-225; P@) Just a half-block from the beach, this ecoconscious, gay-friendly boutique hotel satisfies sophisticated urbanites nursing romantic island dreams with stylish, design-savvy rooms, attentive staff and lots of little niceties.

Hostelling International–Waikiki HOSTEL $
(808-926-8313; www.hostelsaloha.com; 2417 Prince Edward St; dm/r from $25/58; reception 7am-3am; @) In an bright-aqua converted apartment building, this tidy hostel is set back from the beach. There are sex-segregated dorms plus kitchen, laundry and lockers; no curfew, alcohol or smoking. Reservations essential.

Recommended Hawaii-based chain hotels and condos:

TOP CHOICE Aqua BOUTIQUE HOTELS $$
(☎866-971-2782; www.aquaresorts.com; r from $99; P ❄ @ ≈) Best hotels: Coconut Waikiki, Bamboo, Palms and Lots.

Aston HOTELS, APARTMENTS $$
(☎866-956-4262; www.astonhotels.com; r/1br condo from $105/130; P ❄ @ ≈) Has all the best family-friendly picks: Waikiki Beach Tower, Waikiki Beach and Waikiki Banyan.

Outrigger & Ohana HOTELS, RESORTS $$
(☎866-956-4262; www.outrigger.com; r/1br condo from $105/189; P ❄ @ ≈) Best locations: Reef on the Beach and Regency on Beachwalk.

Eating

Honolulu is a multiethnic chowhound capital, from Chinatown's kitchens to local joints scattered around Ala Moana Center mall to top chef's kitchens in Waikiki.

TOP CHOICE Roy's–Waikiki Beach FUSION $$$
(☎808-923-7697; www.roysrestaurant.com; 226 Lewers St; mains $28-45; ⊙11am-10pm) Groundbreaking Hawaii chef Roy Yamaguchi doesn't actually cook here, but his signature *misoyaki* butterfish, blackened 'ahi (tuna), macnut-encrusted mahimahi and deconstructed sushi rolls are always on the menu. Reservations essential.

WHAT THE...?

'Local grinds' is a catch-all pidgin term for the satisfying comfort foods of Hawaii's polyglot cultures. It means Native Hawaiian favorites such as *kalua* pork (traditionally roasted in an underground oven), *laulau* (savory meat wrapped and steamed in *ti* leaves) and poi (mashed fermented taro). It includes endless varieties of *poke* (cubed, marinated raw fish). It's a morning loco moco (rice, two fried eggs, hamburger patty and gravy) followed by an afternoon plate lunch (fried or grilled meat, 'two-scoop' rice and potato-macaroni salad) and for dessert, Chinese crack seed (preserved fruit) or a classic rainbow shave ice.

In Honolulu, the daily **Hawaii Food Tours** (☎808-926-3663; www.hawaiifoodtours.com; van tour $99) sample Chinatown's holes-in-the-wall, island-style mixed-plate lunches, famous bakeries, crack-seed candy shops and more (reservations required).

Sushi Izakaya Gaku JAPANESE $$
(☎808-589-1329; 1329 S King St; shared plates $6-28; ⊙5-11pm Mon-Sat) Wildly popular *izakaya* (Japanese gastropub) plates traditional, supremely fresh sushi and hard-to-find specialties such as *chazuke* (tea-soaked rice porridge) and *natto* (fermented soybeans). Reservations recommended.

Side Street Inn BAR & GRILL $$
(☎808-591-0253; www.sidestreetinn.com; 1225 Hopaka St; shared plates $7-28; ⊙2pm-2am) Outside it looks like hell, but Honolulu's top chefs hang out after work at this late-night sports bar with Naugahyde (fake leather) booths. Divinely tender *kalbi* (korean-style barbecue) short ribs and pork chops are signature dishes. Bring a group; make reservations. Also in Waikiki.

Haili's Hawaiian Food HAWAIIAN $$
(http://mybackyardluau.ning.com; 760 Palani Ave; meals $10-15; ⊙10am-3pm Mon, 10am-7pm Tue-Thu, 10am-8pm Fri & Sat, 11am-3pm Sun) Locals shoehorn themselves in for heaping plates of *kalua* pig, *lomilomi* salmon and *laulau* (meat wrapped in *ti* leaves and steamed) served with scoops of poi or rice.

Little Village Noodle House CHINESE $$
(☎808-545-3008; www.littlevillagehawaii.com; 1113 Smith St; mains $10-22; ⊙10:30am-10:30pm Sun-Thu, to midnight Fri & Sat; P) An air-con cafe in Chinatown? For noodles in black-bean sauce, this is Honolulu's gold standard. Regional Chinese classics are made garlicky, fiery or with just the right dose of salt.

Ramen Nakamura JAPANESE $$
(2141 Kalakaua Ave; mains $9-14; ⊙11am-11:30pm) You'll have to strategically elbow aside Japanese tourists toting Gucci bags to dig into hearty bowls of oxtail or *tonkotsu kim-chi* ramen soup topped with crunchy fried garlic.

Me BBQ LOCAL $
(151 Uluniu Ave; meals $4-11; ⊙7am-8:45pm Mon-Sat) No-nonsense takeout counter delivers island-style mixed plates fast and plentiful. Chow down at plastic picnic tables outside or hit the beach.

Ruffage Natural Foods VEGETARIAN $
(2443 Kuhio Ave; items $4-8; ⊙9am-6pm; ✓) Pint-sized health-food store whips up taro

burgers, veggie burritos, vegan chili and fruit smoothies to revitalize your bod.

For sweet endings (or beginnings!):

Leonard's BAKERY $
(www.leonardswaikiki.com; 933 Kapahulu Ave; snacks 75¢-$2; ⏲5:30am-9pm Sun-Thu, 5:30am-10pm Fri & Sat) O'ahu's best hot *malasadas* (filled Portuguese doughnuts).

Royal Kitchen BAKERY $
(http://royalkitchenhawaii.com; Chinatown Cultural Plaza, 100 N Beretania St; snacks $1-2; ⏲5:30am-4:30pm Mon-Fri, 6:30am-4:30pm Sat, 6:30am-2:30pm Sun) Sweet and savory *manapua* (baked buns) in Chinatown.

Drinking & Entertainment

Waikiki has plenty of Hawaiian-style hula and live music on offer. Honolulu's hippest nightlife scene revolves around N Hotel St and Nu'uanu Ave in Chinatown, once a notorious red-light district. Free tabloid *Honolulu Weekly* (www.honoluluweekly.com) covers bars, clubs, entertainment and more.

TOP CHOICE **Kuhio Beach Torch Lighting & Hula Show** TRADITIONAL DANCE
(Kuhio Beach Park; admission free; ⏲usually 6:30-7:30pm Tue, Thu, Sat & Sun;) Bask in the warm aloha with performances by local hula troupes and talented musicians at this city-sponsored show near Waikiki's Duke Kahanamoku statue.

House Without a Key LOUNGE
(www.halekulani.com; Halekulani, 2199 Kalia Rd; ⏲7am-9pm) At this genteel open-air oceanfront bar beside a century-old kiawe tree, catch live Hawaiian music and hula dancing by former Miss Hawaii pageant winners (live music usually 5:30 to 8:30pm).

Duke's Waikiki BAR
(www.dukeswaikiki.com; Outrigger Waikiki, 2335 Kalakaua Ave; ⏲4pm-midnight) Duke's hosts a raucous, surf-themed party most nights, with baby-boomer crowds spilling onto the sand during weekend concerts (live music usually 4pm to 6pm Friday to Sunday).

Hula's Bar & Lei Stand GAY BAR
(www.hulas.com; Castle Waikiki Grand, 134 Kapahulu Ave, 2nd fl; ⏲10am-2am; @) Waikiki's top gay venue is a breezy balcony bar with views of Diamond Head and Queen's Surf Beach, a prime destination for a sun-worshipping LGBTQ crowd.

Shopping

Native Books/Nā Mea Hawai'i BOOKS, GIFTS
(☎808-596-8885; www.nativebookshawaii.com; Ward Warehouse, 1050 Ala Moana Blvd; ⏲10am-8:30pm Mon-Thu, 10am-9pm Fri & Sat, 10am-6pm Sun) Specializes in Hawaiiana books, CDs and handmade artisan crafts; also hosts free cultural workshops in hula dancing, Hawaiian languagc, feather lei-making and *lauhala* weaving, ukulele playing etc.

TOP CHOICE **Bailey's Antiques & Aloha Shirts** CLOTHING
(www.alohashirts.com; 517 Kapahulu Ave; ⏲10am-6pm) Waikiki's most famous collection of vintage and used aloha shirts promises 15,000 choices, so you're guaranteed to find something memorable, including contemporary island labels.

Also worth browsing:

Island Slipper SHOES
(www.islandslipper.com; Ward Warehouse, 1050 Ala Moana Blvd; ⏲10am-9pm Mon-Sat, to 6pm Sun) Hawaii's comfiest 'rubbah slippah' (flip-flops).

Kamaka Hawaii SOUVENIRS
(www.kamakahawaii.com; 550 South St; ⏲8am-4pm Mon-Fri) Handcrafted ukuleles made on O'ahu since 1916.

Information

Waikiki and the University of Hawai'i area have many cybercafes; surfing averages $6 to $12 an hour.

Hawaii Visitors and Convention Bureau (☎800-464-2924; www.gohawaii.com; 2270 Kalakaua Ave, suite 801) Waikiki tourist office.

Honolulu Star-Advertiser (www.staradvertiser.com) Hawaii's largest daily newspaper.

Public Library (www.librarieshawaii.org; 478 S King St; ⏲10am-5pm Mon & Wed, 9am-5pm Tue, Fri & Sat, 9am-8pm Thu; @) Temporary visitor card ($10) allows free internet access at any branch statewide.

Queen's Medical Center (☎808-538-9011; www.queensmedicalcenter.net; 1301 Punchbowl St; ⏲24hr) Full-service hospital in downtown Honolulu.

Pearl Harbor

On December 7, 1941, a Japanese attack on Pearl Harbor took 2500 lives, sank 21 ships and fatefully catapulted the US into WWII. Today almost 1.4 million people a year remember 'a date which will live in infamy'

PEARL HARBOR 411

Strict security measures are in place at Pearl Harbor's memorials, museums and visitor centers. You may not bring in any items that allow concealment (eg purses, camera bags, fanny packs, backpacks, diaper bags). Personal-sized cameras and camcorders are allowed. Don't lock valuables in your car – use the storage facility (per item $3) outside the entrance instead.

by visiting the **USS Arizona Memorial**. The memorial sits directly over the sunken USS *Arizona;* visitors look down at the shallow wreck, still a tomb for 1177 sailors. On shore, the **NPS visitor center & museum** (808-422-3300; www.nps.gov/valr; 1 Arizona Memorial Pl; admission & tour free; 7am-5pm, boat departures 8am-3pm) runs 75-minute tours including a documentary film and boat ride to the memorial. Tour tickets are first-come, first-served and may all be given away by noon. Show up early to avoid long lines.

If you have to wait, visit the adjacent **USS Bowfin Submarine Museum & Park** (www.bowfin.org; 11 Arizona Memorial Dr; museum & self-guided tour adult/child 4-12yr $10/4; 7am-5pm, last entry 4:30pm) to poke around WWII relics and clamber down inside the submarine nicknamed the 'Pearl Harbor Avenger'. From Bowfin Park, shuttle buses head over to the **USS Missouri** (877-644-4896; www.ussmissouri.org; admission incl standard tours adult/child 4-12yr $20/10, incl guided tour $45/22; 8am-5pm) battleship memorial and hangar-sized **Pacific Aviation Museum** (www.pacificaviationmuseum.org; adult/child 4-12yr $20/10, incl guided tour $30/20; 9am-5pm) on Ford Island. Interestingly, the 'Mighty Mo' hosted the Japanese surrender ending WWII.

From Waikiki and Honolulu, buses 42 and 20 go to Pearl Harbor ($2.50, one hour).

Diamond Head & Southeast O'ahu

O'ahu's glamorous southeast coast abounds in dramatic scenery and offers plenty of activities. For windy panoramas, make the 0.8-mile climb up **Diamond Head** (www.hawaiistateparks.org; off Diamond Head Rd; pedestrian/car $1/5; 6am-6pm, last trail entry 4:30pm), the 760ft extinct volcano crater visible from Waikiki Beach.

The best place on O'ahu to go eyeball to eyeball with tropical fish is at **Hanauma Bay Nature Preserve** (www.honolulu.gov/parks/facility/hanaumabay/; Hwy 72, Hawai'i Kai; adult/child under 13yr $7.50/free; 6am-7pm Wed-Mon Apr-Oct, to 6pm rest of yr;), a gorgeous turquoise bathtub set in a rugged volcanic ring. For the best snorkeling conditions, arrive early in the morning. You can rent snorkel gear on-site. Parking costs $1; when the lot fills, often by mid-morning, visitors arriving by car will be turned away.

Long and lovely **Sandy Beach Park**, along Hwy 72 northeast of Hanauma, offers very challenging, even life-risking bodysurfing with punishing shorebreaks, making it a favorite of pros – and exhilarating to watch!

From Waikiki, bus 22 ($2.50, hourly, no service Tuesday) stops near Diamond Head and at Hanauma Bay and Sandy Beach.

Kailua & Windward Coast

The deeply scalloped Ko'olau Range forms a scenic backdrop for the entire Windward Coast. From Honolulu, drive the Pali Hwy (Hwy 61) over the mountains, stopping for the very windy **Nu'uanu Pali Lookout** (1200ft).

Beneath the windswept *pali* (cliffs) sits beautiful **Kailua Beach**, O'ahu's top windsurfing spot, while offshore islands are popular with kayakers. Water-sports gear rental, lessons and tours are available from several outfitters, including **Kailua Sailboards & Kayaks** (808-262-2555, 888-457-5737; www.kailuasailboards.com; 130 Kailua Rd; kayak rental $40-65) near the beach. **Kailua** has plenty of sleeping and eating options, and makes a good adventure base camp. For B&Bs, cottages and condos, ask **Affordable Paradise** (808-261-1693; www.affordable-paradise.com).

Other jewel-like Windward Coast beaches include reef-protected **Waimanalo Bay**, cinematic **Kualoa Regional Park**, and **Malaekahana State Recreation Area**, a dramatic stretch near La'ie for swimming, windsurfing or snorkeling, especially over at Moku'auia (Goat Island) a near-shore bird sanctuary. To see where Hurley built his *Lost* golf course, Godzilla left his footprints and *Jurassic Park* dinosaurs rampaged, tour **Kualoa Ranch** (808-237-7321; www.kualoa.com; 49-560 Kamehameha Hwy; tours adult/child 3-12yr from $23/15;).

Run by the Mormon church, La'ie's **Polynesian Cultural Center** (☎808-293-3333; www.polynesia.com; 55-370 Kamehameha Hwy; adult/child 5-11yr $50/36; ⏰noon-5pm Mon-Sat) is a theme park (and all that implies) with villages, performances and luau buffets. Only Pearl Harbor draws more visitors.

Further north in **Kahuku**, roadside stands and trucks sell plates of grilled and fried shrimp for around $15 – expect long lines around lunchtime.

Hale'iwa & North Shore

O'ahu's North Shore is legendary for the massive 30ft winter swells that thunder against its beaches. In the 1950s surfers first learned to ride these deadly waves, and today the North Shore hosts the world's most awesome surf competitions, especially the **Triple Crown of Surfing** (www.vanstriplecrownofsuring.com) in November and December.

The gateway to the North Shore, **Hale'iwa** is the region's only real town – along its main road you'll find a funky surf museum, shops selling surf gear and bikinis, and rusty pickup trucks with surfboards tied to the roof. When the surf's up, folks really do drop everything to hit the waves. They don't have to go far: **Hale'iwa Ali'i Beach Park**, right in town, gets towering swells.

The North Shore's most popular beach, **Waimea Bay Beach Park**, flaunts a dual personality. In summer the water can be as calm as a lake and ideal for swimming and snorkeling; in winter it rips with the island's highest waves. **Sunset Beach Park**, another classic winter surf spot, is famous for its tricky breaks. At 'Ehukai Beach Park, **Banzai Pipeline** breaks over a shallow reef, creating a death-defying ride for pro surfers only. Snorkelers, divers and tide-poolers gather at **Pupukea Beach Park**, a marine-life conservation district. For calmer swimming, head to resort-backed **Kawela (Turtle) Bay**.

Team Real Estate (☎808-637-3507; www.teamrealestate.com; 1-/2-/3-bedroom apt from $100/150/200) rents accommodations, from studio apartments to beachfront luxury homes, along the North Shore; book well in advance. **Food trucks** trundle along the Kamehameha Hwy and park on the south side of Hale'iwa town. Opposite Sunset Beach, **Ted's Bakery** (www.tedsbakery.com; 59-024 Kamehameha Hwy; dishes $1-8; ⏰7am-6pm Mon-Tue, to 8pm Wed-Sun; 👪) is legendary for island-style plate lunches and chocolate-*haupia* (coconut pudding) pie.

In Hale'iwa, an après-surf crowd knocks back margaritas and chomps on beer-battered mahimahi tacos at **Luibueno's** (www.luibueno.com; 66-165 Kamehameha Hwy; mains $7-25; ⏰11am-midnight), a Mexican faux-adobe joint. Day-trippers queue for syrupy rainbow shave ice at **Matsumoto's** (www.matsumotosshaveice.com; 66-087 Kamehameha Hwy; ⏰9am-6pm; 👪) tin-roofed 1950s general store.

HAWAI'I THE BIG ISLAND

Almost twice the size of the other Hawaiian Islands combined, the Big Island contains a whole continent-worth of adventures. Even more thrillingly, it's still growing. Hawai'i's most active volcanoes, Kilauea, has been erupting almost nonstop for three decades. Along with red-hot lava, the Big Island offers stargazing from subarctic mountaintops, ancient Hawaiian places of refuge, rugged hikes into forgotten valleys, and a full range of hypnotizing beaches, from bone-white strands to green or black cratered with lava-rock tide pools.

Getting There & Around

Mainland and interisland flights arrive at **Kona** (http://hawaii.gov/koa) or **Hilo** (http://hawaii.gov/ito) **International Airports**, which both have taxis and car-rental booths. **Hele-On** (☎808-961-8744; www.heleonbus.org) public buses circle the island (fares 50¢ to $1), but with limited Monday-to-Saturday commuter-oriented routes.

Kailua-Kona

It's the sort of sun-drenched tourist town where you sit in open-air cafes and count sunburnt vacationers for amusement. But with gold-medal beaches heading north and south and stacks of ocean-centric activities at hand, this condo-rich area makes an affordable base for wider explorations.

Sights & Activities

Near Kailua Pier, **Kamakahonu Beach** was once Kamehameha the Great's royal residence and includes the restored **Ahu'ena Heiau** (http://ahuena.net; ⏰no public entry), the temple where King Kamehameha died in 1819. Meander south on Ali'i Dr to visit lava-rock **Moku'aikaua Church** (www.mokuaikaua.org; 75-5713 Ali'i Dr; admission free; ⏰8am-5pm), built in 1837 by Hawaii's first Christian missionaries. Across the street, but closed for post-tsunami repairs at the time of writing, **Hulihe'e Palace** (☎808-329-1877; www.daughtersofhawaii.org; 75-5718 Ali'i Dr; adult/child $6/1) was a vacation spot for Hawaiian royalty. Its museum is packed with memorabilia and historical artifacts. Call ahead for hours.

Several miles south of town on Ali'i Dr, sun yourself at sparkling **White Sands Beach**, but don't swim in winter when the sand disappears. In Keauhou, **Kahalu'u Beach Park** offers fab snorkeling with sea turtles and stand-up paddle boarding (SUP). Myriad outfitters in Kailua-Kona offer water-sports gear rental and guided tours, including amazing nighttime snorkeling and diving with **manta rays** (www.mantapacific.org).

Sleeping

King Kamehameha's Kona Beach Hotel HOTEL **$$$**
(☎808-329-2911, reservations 800-367-2111; www.konabeachhotel.com; 75-5660 Palani Rd; r $185-250; P❄📶🏊) Anchoring Ali'i Dr, the mammoth 'King Kam' sports sleekly renovated rooms, killer views and a classic poolside bar for mai tais. Avoid noisy rooms facing the street.

TOP CHOICE **Kona Tiki Hotel** HOTEL **$**
(☎808-329-1425; www.konatikihotel.com; 75-5968 Ali'i Dr; r incl breakfast $79-100; P📶🏊) It's all about the price, the location and the surf crashing right outside your window. Motel-style rooms are straightforward (no TVs or phones); some have kitchenettes. No credit cards.

Koa Wood Hale Inn/Patey's Place HOSTEL **$**
(☎808-329-9663; www.alternative-hawaii.com/affordable/kona.htm; 75-184 Ala Ona Ona St; dm/s/d from $25/55/65, 2-bedroom apt $130; P@📶) A short walk from Ali'i Dr, this well-managed hostel is Kona's best budget deal, with plain, clean dorms and private rooms. No-alcohol policy equals low-key vibe.

For condos, check with **ATR Properties** (☎808-329-6020, 888-311-6020; www.konacondo.com) or **Kona Hawaii Vacation Rentals** (☎808-329-3333; www.konahawaii.com).

Eating & Drinking

Kona Brewing Company BREWPUB **$$**
(☎808-334-2739; www.konabrewingco.com; 75-5629 Kuakini Hwy; mains & pizza $11-26; ⊙11am-9pm Sun-Thu, to 10pm Fri & Sat; 👪) The Big Island's original microbrewery makes top-notch ales with a Hawaiian touch, along with thin-crust pizzas and juicy burgers. The torch-lit patio packs 'em in nightly. Call for reservations and brewery tour schedules.

Island Lava Java CAFE **$$**
(www.islandlavajava.com; 75-5799 Ali'i Dr; snacks around $5, mains $9-24; ⊙6:30am-9:30pm; @📶) A favorite gathering spot for sunny breakfasts, this almost oceanfront cafe offers an irresistible combo of 100% Kona coffee, sea breezes and local seafood, organic farm salads and homemade sandwiches and desserts.

Big Island Grill LOCAL **$$**
(75-5702 Kuakini Hwy; mains $10-20; ⊙7:30am-9pm Mon-Sat) Hawaiian-style home cooking draws everyone and their auntie to this beloved institution (aka Biggie's). Look no further than island plate lunches and loco mocos, all with 'two scoop' rice.

TOP CHOICE **Kanaka Kava** CAFE **$$**
(www.kanakakava.com; Coconut Grove Marketplace, 75-5803 Ali'i Dr; mains $14-16; ⊙10am-10pm Sun-Wed, to 11pm Thu-Sat) Join locals for some mildly intoxicating kava (juice of the *'awa* plant) at this tiny, tropical cafe. The Hawaiian fare is fresh and tasty.

South Kona Coast

Linger along the verdant South Kona coast, visiting its fragrant coffee farms, ancient Hawaiian sites and characterful small towns. For a window on local life, sit down at **Teshima Restaurant** (☎808-322-9140; 79-7251 Mamalahoa Hwy, Honalo; mains $13-23; ⊙6:30am-1:45pm & 5-9pm), where families and coffee pickers have been ordering up Japanese comfort food since the 1940s (cash only).

Off Hwy 11, a side road leads to sparkling, mile-wide **Kealakekua Bay**. On its north side is Ka'awaloa Cove (where Captain Cook was killed in 1779), now the Big Island's premier **snorkeling** destination. You can hike to it, but it's more fun to kayak – talk to Hawaiian-owned **Aloha Kayak Company** (☎808-322-2868, 877-322-1444; www.alohakayak.com; 79-7248 Mamalahoa Hwy, Honalo; kayak rental $25-85, tours $90-130). For snorkel and dive cruises, try **Sea Paradise** (☎808-322-2500; www.seaparadise.com; snorkel cruise adult/child 4-12yr $99/59) in Keauhou.

WORTH A TRIP

KONA COFFEE FARMS

Gourmet 100% Kona coffee is grown on South Kona's small family-run farms. With harvesting still done by hand, the region has a lost-in-time feel, seemingly unchanged from when 19th-century immigrants established themselves here. In Captain Cook, the excellent **Kona Coffee Living History Farm** (808-323-2006; www.konahistorical.org; Hwy 11, Mile 110; self-guided tour adult/child 5-12yr $20/5; 10am-2pm Mon-Thu, last entry 1:15pm) evocatively re-creates Japanese immigrants' rural lifestyle. In November, don't miss the 10-day **Kona Coffee Cultural Festival** (www.konacoffeefest.com).

In **Captain Cook**, the 1917 **Manago Hotel** (808-323-2642; www.managohotel.com; 82-6155 Mamalahoa Hwy; r with/without bath from $56/33, mains $4-14) is a classic experience: stay in the simple, no-frills roadhouse rooms and order the restaurant's signature pork chops. **Ka'awa Loa Plantation** (808-323-2686; www.kaawaloaplantation.com; 82-5990 Napo'opo'o Rd; r incl breakfast $125-149, ste $159-199;), a stylish garden estate with four-poster beds and a sunset-view lanai (veranda), is perfect for romantics.

South of Kealakekua Bay, awesome **Pu'uhonua O Honaunau National Historical Park** (www.nps.gov/puho; per car $5; 7am-7pm) is an ancient place of refuge *(pu'uhonua)*, a sanctuary where *kapu*-breakers could have their lives spared – with evocative royal grounds and a reconstructed temple. Immediately north of the park is a terrific snorkeling spot called **Two-Step**. Afterwards, refresh yourself with an organic smoothie from **South Kona Fruit Stand** (www.southkonafruitstand.com; 84-4770 Mamalahoa Hwy, Honaunau; 9am-6pm Mon-Sat).

North Kona & Kohala Coasts

The lava-blackened coast running north of Kailua-Kona is strung with secluded palm-lined beaches, ancient Hawaiian sites and posh resorts. Stand-out strands, all off Hwy 19, include dreamy sugar-colored **Kekaha Kai State Park** (4WD required), black-sand **Kiholo Bay**, windsurfers' **Anaeho'omalu Beach Park**, kid-friendly **Beach 69** and the **Puako** tide pools, resort-backed **Mauna Kea Beach** on crescent-shaped Kauna'ola Bay, and swoon-worthy **Mau'umae Beach** (respect territorial locals).

The Waikaloa resort area is home to ancient Hawaiian **petroglyphs** and two shopping malls offering free entertainment daily. Blurring the line between resort and theme park is **Hilton Waikoloa Village** (808-886-1234; www.hiltonwaikoloavillage.com; 69-425 Waikoloa Beach Dr; r from $199; P), with pools, lagoons and activities to please all ages, although almost everything costs extra, even parking ($15).

The Mauna Lani resort area also has ancient Hawaiian sites – fishponds, lava tubes and over 3000 petroglyphs – near the eco-conscious **Mauna Lani Bay Hotel & Bungalows** (808-885-6622; www.maunalani.com; 68-1400 Mauna Lani Dr; r $445-965, ste from $995;), a full-service oceanfront resort with towering palms and genuine Hawaiian spirit.

To boogie under the stars, head north to Kawaihae's **Blue Dragon Musiquarium** (808-882-7771; www.bluedragonhawaii.com; 61-3616 Kawaihae Rd; mains $18-36; 5:30-10pm Thu-Sun, bar to 11pm), offering eclectic surf-and-turf and an engaging roster of island musicians.

Mauna Kea

When measured from its base beneath the sea, this sacred mountain (13,796ft) is the planet's tallest, and its summit is clustered with world-class astronomical observatories.

Partway up the mountain, the **Onizuka Center for International Astronomy** (808-961-2180; www.ifa.hawaii.edu/info/vis; admission free; 9am-10pm) visitor information station (VIS) offers educational displays and awesome stargazing programs almost nightly. Continuing to the summit for sunset is unforgettable, but it requires either 4WD, a challenging 6-mile, high-altitude hike (10 hours round-trip), or a guided tour with **Mauna Kea Summit Adventures** (808-322-2366, 888-322-2366; www.maunakea.com; tours $200).

To reach the Onizuka Center, you must first drive the 50-mile Saddle Rd (Hwy 200) connecting the Kona and Hilo coasts; although scenic, it's accident prone and some car-rental companies prohibit driving on it. From the marked turn-off near mile marker 28, it's another 6 miles uphill along Mauna Kea's summit road to the VIS.

WORTH A TRIP

HAMAKUA COAST

The Hamakua Coast offers some of the Big Island's most spectacular scenery. It's a *Lost*-worthy show of deep ravines, lush jungle valleys and cascading waterfalls.

Most scenic of all is **Waipi'o Valley**, the largest of seven magnificent amphitheater valleys on the windward coast. Hwy 240 dead-ends at a dramatic overlook: the road down is so steep that only 4WDs can make it. It's worth the mile-long hike down – *and* the grueling return uphill – to meditate on the thunderous black-sand beach, backgrounded by ribbony waterfalls feeding ancient taro patches.

Heading south, **'Akaka Falls State Park** (Hwy 220, Honomu; pedestrian/car $5/1) has two stunning waterfalls easily accessed along a half-mile rainforest loop trail.

Hilo

The Big Island's capital has been dubbed the 'rainiest city in the USA,' and that soggy reputation tends to keep tourists away. It's their loss, however, because Hilo, with its working-class waterfront and century-old buildings downtown, brims with weather-beaten charm. Ethnically diverse, this town is an evocative slice of real Hawaii.

Sights & Activities

TOP CHOICE **'Imiloa Astronomy Center of Hawai'i** MUSEUM
(www.imiloahawaii.org; 600 'Imiloa Pl; adult/child 4-12yr $17.50/9.50; ⏲9am-4pm Tue-Sun) One of Hawaii's most fascinating museums explores Native Hawaiian culture, ecology and the environment, with astronomical discoveries filtered through the lens of Mauna Kea. It's an eye-popping, thought-provoking journey.

Pacific Tsunami Museum MUSEUM
(www.tsunami.org; 130 Kamehameha Ave; adult/child 6-17yr $8/4; ⏲9am-4pm Mon-Sat) Hilo has survived several major tsunamis and this dramatic museum brings these chilling events to life, with multimedia exhibits including documentary film footage.

Lyman Museum & Mission House MUSEUM
(www.lymanmuseum.org; 276 Haili St; adult/child $10/3; ⏲9:30am-4:30pm Mon-Sat; 👪) For a kid-friendly overview of Hawaii's natural and cultural history. Catch a guided tour of the 1830s mission house next door (usually 11am and 2pm daily).

Farmers Market MARKET
(www.hilofarmersmarket.com; cnr Mamo St & Kamehameha Ave; ⏲6am-4pm Wed & Sat) Time your visit for a Hilo market day, an event that's equal parts gossip and shopping, both for fresh produce and local crafts.

Sleeping

Dolphin Bay Hotel HOTEL $$
(☎808-935-1466, 877-935-1466; www.dolphinbayhotel.com; 333 Iliahi St; studio/1-/2br condo from $119/159/169; 📶👪) This family-run small hotel is a perennial favorite with volcano-bound travelers who like to settle in. Apartment-style units aren't snazzy, but they're comfortably clean and have kitchens.

TOP CHOICE **Shipman House** B&B $$$
(☎808-934-8002; www.hilo-hawaii.com; 131 Ka'iulani St; r incl breakfast $219-249; 📶) Hilo's most gracious and historic B&B occupies a Victorian mansion packed with museum-quality Hawaiiana. Queen Lili'uokalani once entertained on the grand piano.

Hilo Bay Hostel HOSTEL $
(☎808-933-2771; www.hawaiihostel.net; 101 Waianuenue Ave; dm $27, r with/without bath $77/67; @📶) Perfectly situated in a historic building downtown, this airy, spic-and-span hostel welcomes a diverse all-ages crowd.

Eating

Hilo Bay Café CAFE $$$
(☎808-935-4939; www.hilobaycafe.com; Waiakea Center, 315 Maka'ala St; mains $15-26; ⏲11am-9pm Mon-Sat, 5-9pm Sun) Unpretentious yet sophisticated dishes featuring organic ingredients whipped up at this incongruously urban-chic cafe – in a strip mall! – will keep your honey's heart warm even when the rain is pounding.

TOP CHOICE **Miyo's** JAPANESE $$
(☎808-935-2273; Waiakea Villas, 400 Hualani St; mains $8-15; ⏲11am-2pm & 5:30-8:30pm Mon-Sat) Like a rustic teahouse, with shoji doors opening toward Waiakea Pond, here you'll find tasty Japanese home-style cooking. Locally caught seafood specials are especially delish.

Also recommended:

Suisan Fish Market SEAFOOD $
(93 Lihiwai St; items $5-13; ⌚8am-5pm Mon-Fri, to 4pm Sat) Fresh harborfront *poke* and rice bowls to take away.

Ken's House of Pancakes DINER $$
(1730 Kamehameha Ave; mains $6-12; ⌚24hr) Mac-nut pancakes and Spam omelets.

Hawai'i Volcanoes National Park

Even among Hawaii's many natural wonders, this **park** (☎808-985-6000; www.nps.gov/havo; 7-day entry pass per car $10) stands out: its two active volcanoes testify to the ongoing birth of the islands. Majestic Mauna Loa (13,677ft) looms like a sleeping giant, while young Kilauea – the world's most active volcano – has been erupting almost continually since 1983. With luck, you'll witness the primal event of molten lava tumbling into the sea. But the park contains much more too, including overwhelming lava deserts, steaming craters, lava tubes and ancient rainforests.

Near the entrance, the **Kilauea Visitor Center & Museum** (☎808-985-6017; ⌚7:45am-5pm) makes a great introduction; rangers provide updates on hiking trail conditions, volcanic activity and guided walks. The nearby **Volcano Art Center** (☎808-967-7565, 866-967-7565; www.volcanoartcenter.org; ⌚9am-5pm) gallery coordinates special events, Hawaiian cultural classes and performances.

Note that shifting eruptions can cause unexpected road and trail closures. When open, the 11-mile **Crater Rim Drive** circles Kilauea Caldera, offering almost nonstop views of the goddess Pele's scorched, smoldering home. Visit the **Jaggar Museum** (admission free; ⌚8:30am-8pm), with working seismographs, lava displays and a stupendous vista of **Halema'uma'u Crater** (where eruption activity resumed in 2008). Don't miss **Thurston Lava Tube**, an enormous cave left by flowing lava, or the 4-mile **Kilauea Iki Trail**, which crosses a crater moonscape. The park's equally scenic 20-mile **Chain of Craters Road** leads down to the coast, ending abruptly where modern lava flows have buried it.

The national park maintains two free, drive-up **campgrounds** (no reservations). The nearby village of Volcano has arty, heart-warming B&Bs, rainforest cottages and vacation homes. **Volcano Gallery** (☎800-967-8617; www.volcanogallery.com) is a locally managed rental agency.

The small, friendly **Holo Holo In** (☎808-967-7950; www.volcanohostel.com; 19-4036 Kalani Honua Rd; dm $25, r $65-80; @) hostel is an acceptable budget choice.

With a variety of country-cozy B&B rooms, the rambling **Kilauea Lodge** (☎808-967-7366; www.kilauealodge.com; 19-3948 Old Volcano Rd; r incl breakfast $170-205;) is appealing. Plus, it runs the area's only fine-dining restaurant, serving hearty chophouse staples (*hassenpfeffer*, anyone?) and, for breakfast, island-style comfort fare.

TOP CHOICE **Volcano Country Cottages** (☎808-967-7690; www.volcanocottages.com; 19-3990 Old Volcano Rd; cottages incl breakfast $105-135) offers your own private rainforest retreat. These lovingly restored plantation cottages have everything a hideaway needs, from airy lanai to Hawaiian CDs and books. DIY breakfast fixings provided.

Inspired by Pele, perhaps, the superior Thai cuisine at **Thai Thai Restaurant** (☎808-967-7969; 19-4084 Old Volcano Rd; mains $15-26; ⌚noon-9pm Thu-Tue) is satisfyingly hot and fairly authentic, if overpriced. Leftovers make the perfect trail lunch. It has a popular bar, too.

WHERE'S THE LAVA?

For lava updates, check with the **USGS** (http://hvo.wr.usgs.gov) and the **Hawaiian Lava Daily website** (http://hawaiianlavadaily.blogspot.com). Park rangers and visitor center staff can advise you on how, or if it's possible, to hike to the active flow outside the park. As this book went to press, **Hawai'i County Civil Defense** (☎808-961-8093; www.lavainfo.us) maintained a lava-viewing site outside the park at Kalapana, in the Puna district; a tell-tale steam plume marks the spot where lava enters the water. Stay for sunset when darkness brings out the fiery glow.

MAUI

According to some, you can't have it all. Perhaps those folks haven't been to Maui, which consistently lands atop travel-magazine reader polls as one of the world's most romantic islands. And why not? With its sandy beaches, deluxe resorts, gourmet cuisine, fantastic luau and world-class windsurfing, whale-watching, snorkeling, diving and hiking, it leaves most people a little more in love than when they arrived.

Getting There & Around

Most visitors arrive on US mainland or inter-island flights at **Kahului International Airport** (OGG; http://hawaii.gov/ogg). From the airport, bio-diesel **Speedi Shuttle** (☎877-242-5777; www.speedishuttle.com) charges $35 to Kihei, $50 to Lahaina.

The island's public **Maui Bus** (☎808-871-4838; www.mauicounty.gov/bus) system operates several daily routes (fares $1) that stop at some main towns, but exclude many tourist destinations (eg Haleakala National Park). To rent your own wheels, consider an ecofriendly car or Jeep from **Bio-Beetle** (☎808-873-6121; www.bio-beetle.com).

Lahaina & West Maui

For the megahotel and resort experience, bunk down in West Maui, with its prime sunset beaches. For historical atmosphere, entertainment and dining out, make time for Lahaina, a 19th-century whaling town rich in well-preserved period architecture.

Sights & Activities

The focal point of Lahaina is its bustling small-boat harbor, backed by the historic **Pioneer Inn** and Banyan Tree Sq, the latter home to the largest **banyan tree** in the US. The main tourist drag is oceanside Front St, lined with shops, galleries and restaurants. Within walking distance of the waterfront are several small but diverting museums, missionary homes, prisons built for rowdy sailors and a Chinese immigrants' colorful meeting hall. The visitor center inside the old courthouse has free walking-tour maps.

Beaches BEACHES
For those world-famous beaches, head north and keep going: between Ka'anapali and Kapalua, one impossible perfect strand follows another. Three top-ranked gems are **Kahekili Beach Park**, **Kapalua Beach** and **DT Fleming Beach Park**. All water sports are possible, and tour outfitters abound.

FREE **Whalers Village Museum** MUSEUM
(www.whalersvillage.com; 2435 Ka'anapali Pkwy; ⌚10am-6pm) In Ka'anapali, stop here to inspect scrimshaw carvings and whistle sea shanties.

Sleeping

Plantation Inn BOUTIQUE HOTEL $$$
(☎808-667-92255; www.theplantationinn.com; 174 Lahainaluna Rd; r/ste incl breakfast from $159/239; ❄📶🏊) Forget cookie-cutter resorts – if you want an authentic taste of Old Hawaii, book a romantic if small room at this genteel oasis, furnished with antiques and Hawaiian quilts on four-poster beds.

TOP CHOICE **Napili Surf** APARTMENTS $$
(☎808-669-8002, 888-627-4547; www.napilisurf.com; 50 Napili Pl; studio/1-br condo from $125/250; 🏊📶) On a curving bay perfectly poised between Ka'anapali and Kapalua, this low-slung oceanfront complex feels like staying with *ohana* (family and friends), especially during Wednesday night mai-tai parties. No credit cards.

Ka'anapali Beach Hotel HOTEL $$
(☎808-661-0011; www.kbhmaui.com; 2525 Ka'anapali Pkwy; r incl breakfast from $159; ❄📶🏊👪) While not the fanciest, newest or biggest, this low-key Ka'anapali resort hotel has an enviable beach location and, most of all, genuine Hawaiian aloha. Free family-friendly lessons in ukulele, hula and lei-making.

Eating

Mala Ocean Tavern SEAFOOD, HAWAIIAN $$$
(☎808-667-9394; www.malaoceantavern.com; 1307 Front St; dinner mains $23-39; ⌚11am-9:30pm Mon-Fri, 9am-9:30pm Sat, 9am-9pm Sun) For Lahaina's best waterfront fine dining, stop searching. Mala features nouveau Hawaii cuisine using organic, farm-fresh ingredients and a bounty of just-caught seafood.

TOP CHOICE **Sansei** SUSHI, SEAFOOD $$$
(☎808-669-6286; www.sanseihawaii.com; 600 Office Rd; mains $16-45; ⌚5:30-10pm Sat-Wed, 5:30pm-1am Thu & Fri) In Kapalua, trendy Sansei is always packed, serving out-of-this-world sushi and intriguing Japanese-Hawaiian fusion fare. Food orders placed by 6pm are discounted 25%. No reservations? Line up *before* 5pm.

Aloha Mixed Plate LOCAL $
(www.alohamixedplate.com; 1285 Front St; meals $7-13; ⌚10:30am-10pm; 👪) This rubbah-slippah Lahaina beach shack keeps it local with heaping plates of Hawaii-style home cooking, or catch sunset with a tropical drink and a few *pupu* (snacks).

Drinking & Entertainment

Around sunset, catch a free torch-lighting and cliff-diving ceremony at Pu'u Keka'a (Black Rock), at the north end of Ka'anapali Beach.

TOP CHOICE Old Lahaina Lu'au LUAU
(☎808-667-1998; www.oldlahainaluau.com; 1251 Front St; adult/child 2-12yr $95/65; ⊙5:45-8:45pm; 👪) For a night to remember, this beachside luau is unsurpassed for its authenticity and all-around aloha – the hula is first-rate and the feast darn good. Book far ahead.

Feast at Lele LUAU
(☎808-667-5353, 866-244-5353; www.feastatlele.com; 505 Front St; ⊙6-9pm) No half-hearted buffet, this gourmet luau (adult/child two to 12 years $110/80) is a delicious culinary tour of Pacific cultures, accompanied by excellent music-and-dance performances.

Pioneer Inn BAR
(658 Wharf St; ⊙11am-10pm) With its whaling-era atmosphere and harborside veranda, this century-old landmark is unquestionably Lahaina's most popular place for an ocean-view drink. Even Captain Ahab would agree.

Hula Grill & Barefoot Bar BAR
(Whalers Village, 2435 Ka'anapali Pkwy; ⊙11am-11pm) It's your Maui postcard: coconut-frond umbrellas, sunset mai tais, sand beneath your sandals and the lullaby sounds of Hawaiian slack-key guitar. Skip the food, though.

Information

Lahaina Visitor Center (☎808-667-9193; www.visitlahaina.com; 648 Wharf St; ⊙9am-5pm) Inside the old courthouse.

Ma'alaea

Ma'alaea Bay runs along the low isthmus separating the West Maui Mountains from Haleakalā volcano. Prevailing trade winds funnel between the mountain masses, creating strong midday gusts and some of the best **windsurfing** conditions on Maui.

Maui Ocean Center (www.mauioceancenter.com; 192 Ma'alaea Rd; adult/child 3-12yr $26/19; ⊙9am-5pm, to 6pm Jul & Aug; 👪), the USA's largest tropical aquarium, is a feast for the eyes (but not your stomach!). Dedicated to Hawaii's marine life, exhibits are as close as you can get to being underwater without scuba gear.

Kihei & South Maui

Sun-kissed beaches run for miles and miles south of **Kihei**, which is decidedly less ritzy than West Maui. Vacationers flock to this more affordable coast for excellent swimming, snorkeling, windsurfing, kayaking and abundant condos. **South Pacific Kayaks** (☎808-875-4848; www.southpacifickayaks.com; 1-/2-person kayak rental $40/60, tours $59-139) leads adventurous coastline paddles and teaches surfing and stand-up paddle boarding.

Maui's most upscale seaside community, **Wailea** boasts million-dollar homes and extravagant resorts with prices to match – all because this stretch of coastline cradles tawny beaches of dreamy perfection. South of Wailea, **Makena** has several knockout undeveloped beaches – particularly **Big Beach** and secluded **Little Beach** – as well as the **'Ahihi-Kina'u Natural Area Reserve**,

DON'T MISS

WHALE-WATCHING

Every winter from late November through mid-May, around 10,000 humpback whales crowd the shallow waters along Maui's western shores to breed, calve and nurse. These truly awesome creatures can be easily spotted from the shore, particularly when they perform their acrobatic breaches. You can eavesdrop on their singing online at www.whalesong.net.

To get a closer look, take a whale-watching cruise with the nonprofit **Pacific Whale Foundation** (☎808-249-8811; www.pacificwhale.org; 2hr cruise adult/child 7-12yr $49/17; 👪), which sails out of Lahaina and Ma'alaea harbors. Another place to get acquainted with these majestic mammals is at Kihei's shoreline **Hawaiian Islands Humpback Whale National Marine Sanctuary Headquarters** (☎808-879-2818; http://hawaiihumpbackwhale.noaa.gov; 726 S Kihei Rd; ⊙10am-3pm Mon-Fri), which has educational displays and telescopes for spotting whales offshore.

which encompasses trails, historic ruins and hidden coves for snorkeling.

To reach **Molokini**, an underwater volcanic crater that's Maui's best snorkeling and diving spot, take a ride with Kihei-based **Maui Dreams Dive Co** (☎808-874-5332; www.mauidreamsdiveco.com; 2-tank dive $129) or **Blue Water Rafting** (☎808-879-7238; www.bluewaterrafting.com; snorkel tour adult/child from $50/39).

Sleeping

Begin sorting through Kihei's condo possibilities with **Bello Realty** (☎808-879-3328; www.bellomaui.com).

Punahoa APARTMENTS $$$
(☎808-879-2720; www.punahoabeach.com; 2142 Ili'ili Rd; studio/1-/2-bedroom apt from $145/205/255;) This tasteful boutique condo, hidden on a side street, fronts a quiet beach frequented by sea turtles. Who needs a pool? All apartments have ocean lanai; penthouses get air-con.

Kihei Kai Nani APARTMENTS $$
(☎808-879-9088; www.kiheikainani.com; 2495 S Kihei Rd; 1-bedroom apt $110-170;) Opposite Kihei's beach, this retro low-rise complex has roomy one-bedroom condos (some with air-con and wi-fi); decor ranges from dated to chic. Ask about weekly discounts.

Two Mermaids on Maui B&B $$
(☎808-874-8687; www.twomermaids.com; 2840 Umalu Pl; r/ste incl breakfast $115/140; @) For a more personal touch, try the two kitchenette units at this friendly, cheerful B&B. The ocean-themed suite has a private hot tub and bamboo-shaded lanai.

Eating

South Maui's best restaurants are actually branches of other island restaurants, including **Da Kitchen Express** (a branch of Da Kitchen, p1094) and **Sansei** (p1092) in Kihei, and **Mala** (p1092) in Wailea.

808 Bistro BISTRO $$
(☎808-879-8008; www.808bistro.com; 2511 S Kihei Rd; mains breakfast $7-15, dinner $15-20; ⏰7am-noon & 5-9pm) Creative comfort food – think braised short ribs, fresh mahimahi, mango-chutney pork chops, banana-bread French toast and 'whale pie' – dished up on an airy lanai. Hit next-door 808 Deli for lunchtime salads and sandwiches.

Joy's Place CAFE $$
(www.joysplacemaui.com; 1993 S Kihei Rd; dishes $7-11; ⏰8am-3pm Mon-Sat;) Little kitchen for organic, free-range and locally harvested fare, including healthy raw salads, custom-order wraps, tropical smoothies and daily specials that attract a loyal following.

Eskimo Candy SEAFOOD $$
(www.eskimocandy.com; 2665 Wai Wai Place; mains $7-17; ⏰10:30am-7pm Mon-Fri;) If you've never tried *poke,* this local fish market is a required stop. 'Ahi wraps, fish tacos, fish-and-chips and tempura fried shrimp round out the casual menu.

Kahului & Wailuku

Maui's two largest communities flow together into one urban sprawl. Kahului hosts Maui's windsurfing shops, whose staff give lessons at perpetually breezy **Kanaha Beach** near the airport. On the outskirts of Wailuku, **'Iao Valley State Monument** (www.hawaiistateparks.org; 'Iao Valley Rd; car $5; ⏰7am-7pm) centers on picturesque 'Iao Needle rock pinnacle, rising 1200ft above the valley floor.

Step back into the 1920s in the **Old Wailuku Inn** (☎808-244-5897; www.mauiinn.com; 2199 Kaho'okele St, Wailuku; r $165-195;), an elegant period home built by a wealthy banker and authentically restored by gracious innkeepers. Spacious rooms are comfy, with traditional Hawaiian quilts.

At **Da Kitchen** (www.da-kitchen.com; 425 Koloa St, Kahului; mains $8-16; ⏰11am-9pm Mon-Sat;) Unbeatable island-style *'ono grinds* ('good eats') fill plates big enough to feed two, and the *kalua* pork is, as they say, 'so tender it falls off da bone.' Expect a crowd, but service is fast.

Pa'ia

A former sugar plantation town, Pai'a is Maui's windsurfing and surfing capital. To gawk at all the action, head to **Ho'okipa Beach**. Nearby, **Mama's Fish House** (☎808-579-8488; www.mamasfishhouse.com; 799 Poho Pl; mains $38-50; ⏰11am-3pm & 4:15-9pm) is Maui's most celebrated seafood restaurant, pairing beachside romance with impeccably prepared fish (reservations essential).

Downtown Pa'ia has a burgeoning row of restaurants and boutique shops. **Pa'ia Fish Market** (www.paiafishmarket.com; 100 Hana Hwy;

SCENIC DRIVE: ROAD TO HANA

One of Hawaii's most spectacular scenic drives, the **Hana Highway** (Hwy 360) winds its way past jungle valleys and back out above a rugged coastline. The road is a real cliff-hugger with 54 one-lane bridges, roadside waterfalls and head-spinning views. Gas up and buy snacks and drinks in Pa'ia before starting out.

Swimming holes, heart-stopping vistas and awesome hikes call out almost nonstop. Detour to explore the ancient coastal trails and black-sand beach at **Wai'anapanapa State Park**, offering basic tent camping ($18) and cabins ($90); for overnight reservations (required), contact the **Division of State Parks** (☎808-984-8109; www.hawaiistateparks.org).

mains $9-16; ⊙11am-9:30pm) is the go-to place for fish-and-chips. **Flatbread Company** (http://flatbreadcompany.com; 89 Hana Hwy; pizzas $11-20; ⊙11:30am-10pm) crafts addictive wood oven–fired pizzas topped with local, often organic ingredients.

Hana

The mainland influences so evident everywhere else on Maui are missing in Hana, where many residents are Native Hawaiian, and they treasure the town's sleepy pace and rural isolation. Families splash at **Hana Bay Beach Park**, which has a snack bar, and at gorgeous gray-sand **Hamoa Beach** (Haneo'o Rd), just beyond town.

The road south from Hana is incredibly beautiful, passing organic farms and fruit stands. 'Ohe'o Stream cuts its way through **'Ohe'o Gulch** in a gorgeous series of wide pools and waterfalls, each tumbling into the one below. Part of the coastal section of Haleakala National Park, there you'll also find hiking trails through bamboo groves and free primitive **camping** (no reservations) – bring water and insect repellent!

Can't pull yourself away? Hana has one famed resort that breathes tranquility: **Hotel Hana-Maui** (☎808-248-8211; www.hotelhanamaui.com; 5031 Hana Hwy; r from $325), where airy rooms and sea cottages don't even have alarm clocks. Unwind with a Hawaiian *lomolomi* (Hawaiian) massage at the hotel's spa.

Haleakalā National Park

No trip to Maui is complete without visiting this sublime **national park** (www.nps.gov/hale; 3-day entry pass per car $10), containing East Maui's mighty volcano. From the towering volcano's rim near the summit, there are dramatic views of a lunarlike surfacc and multicolored cinder cones. For an unforgettable (and chilly) experience, arrive in time for sunrise – an event Mark Twain called the 'sublimest spectacle' he'd ever seen. Check weather conditions and sunrise times (☎866-944-5025) before driving up.

The adventure needn't stop at roadside viewpoints: with a good pair of hiking boots and warm, waterproof clothing layers, you can hike down into the crater on the Halemau'u or Sliding Sands Trails. Find free drive-up dispersed tent camping (no reservations) at Hosmer Grove, near the park entrance. A more amazing overnight option are the **wilderness cabins** (https://fhnp.org/wcr; per night $60-75) on the crater floor; demand is high, so you should book online up to 90 days in advance.

KAUA'I

On Hawaii's oldest major island, nature's fingers have had time to dig deep – carving the Na Pali Coast's unbelievable fluted cliffs and the tremendous depths of Waimea Canyon. Lush, rural Kaua'i is beloved by outdoor enthusiasts of all stripes, but especially hikers and kayakers. It has been the darling of honeymooners ever since Elvis tied the knot here in *Blue Hawaii*. Forget coddling spa resorts or bustling nightlife. Come to 'the Garden Isle' for its heavenly temple – the one you'll find outside, that is. The price for salvation? Just a pair of boots and a little sweat.

ℹ Getting There & Around

Frequent interisland flights and limited US mainland services land at **Lihu'e Airport** (LIH; http://hawaii.gov/lih), where taxis and major car-rental companies are available. The limited **Kaua'i Bus** (☎808-241-6410; www.kauai.gov; one way $2) reaches most towns, but not all tourist destinations, with reduced weekend services.

Lihu'e

This former plantation town is Kaua'i's capital and commercial center. Pick up information at **Kaua'i Visitors Bureau** (☎808-245-3971; www.kauaidiscovery.com; 4334 Rice St; ⏰8am-4:30pm Mon-Fri). The insightful **Kaua'i Museum** (www.kauaimuseum.org; 4428 Rice St; adult/child 6-12yr $10/2, 1st Sat of month free; ⏰10am-5pm Mon-Sat) traces the island's independent history.

Garden Island Inn (☎808-245-7227; www.gardenislandinn.com; 3445 Wilcox Rd; r/ste from $99/125;) offers modestly cheerful rooms just minutes from Kalapaki Beach. Fish lovers may find themselves at **Fish Express** (3343 Kuhio Hwy; mains $6-9; ⏰10am-6pm Mon-Sat, to 4pm Sun, grill 10am-3pm Mon-Fri) every day for its gourmet island-style takeout. A Kaua'i institution, hot-box hole-in-the-wall **Hamura Saimin** (2956 Kress St; mains $4-8; ⏰10am-10pm Mon-Thu, to 11:30pm Fri & Sat, to 9pm Sun) specializes in homemade *saimin* (local-style noodle soup) and *liliko'i* chiffon pie.

Wailua & Eastside

You wouldn't know it from the shopping strip-lined Kuhio Hwy, but the Wailua area contains great outdoor opportunities. Families should head to **Lydgate Beach Park** (www.kamalani.org;), with the best kids' playground in Hawaii and safe swimming at a protected beach. The mountains above Wailua hold some recommended **hikes**, such as the Kuilau Ridge Trail, the Moalepe Trail and the Nounou Mountain Trails.

However, most come to kayak the **Wailua River**. The easy, bucolic 5-mile kayak – including swimming holes and waterfall hikes – is so popular that it's restricted almost completely to guided tours (daily except Sunday). Book a day ahead with **Kayak Kaua'i** (☎808-826-9844; www.kayakkauai.com; 2-person kayak rental per person $27, tours adult/child under 12yr $85/60) or smaller, family-owned **Kayak Wailua** (☎808-822-3388; www.kayakwailua.com; tour $45).

Hostellers will be forever spoiled by **Rosewood Kaua'i** (☎808-822-5478; www.rosewoodkauai.com; 872 Kamalu Rd, Kapa'a; r without bath $50-60;), where meticulously tidy private bunkrooms come with kitchenettes (there's a $25 cleaning fee). The owner also rents beach cottages and condos nearby. A surf-casual walk-up counter, **Mermaids Cafe** (4-1384 Kuhio Hwy, Kapa'a; mains $9-11; ⏰11am-8:45pm) concocts sizeable seafood wraps, market-fresh salads and homemade dishes jazzed up with lemongrass and organic greens.

Hanalei & North Shore

Unspoiled and unhurried, Kaua'i's mountainous north shore features otherworldly scenery and enough outdoor adventures for a lifetime.

Stop at **Kilauea Point National Wildlife Refuge** (www.fws.gov/kilaueapoint; adult/child under 16yr $5/free; ⏰10am-4pm) to enjoy its historic lighthouse and thriving seabird sanctuary. Gentle **'Anini Beach Park** () has calm waters perfect for kids, lazy kayaking, easy snorkeling and Kaua'i's best begin-

WORTH A TRIP

MOLOKA'I & LANA'I

Sparsely populated by mostly Native Hawaiians and largely undeveloped for tourism, rural Moloka'i is ideal for those seeking the 'other' Hawaii: unpackaged, traditional, still wild and exuding genuine aloha. Its untamed landscape recalls Hawaii's awe-inspiring natural beauty as it might have looked a century or more ago. To reach Moloka'i's Ho'olehua airport, **Island Air** (☎800-652-6541; www.islandair.com), **go! Mokulele** (☎866-260-7070; www.mokuleleairlines.com) and **Pacific Wings** (☎888-575-4546; www.pacificwings.com) have daily flights from Honolulu and Kahului, Maui. **Molokai Ferry** (☎866-307-6524; www.molokaiferry.com; adult/child $60/30) runs daily round-trips from Lahaina, Maui.

Once home to Hawaii's largest pineapple plantation, Lana'i – to the south - has been refashioned into a plaything for the wealthy. Home to a pair of Hawaii's most elite resorts and two world-class golf courses, Lana'i makes a quick day or overnight getaway from Maui. **Expeditions** (☎808-661-3756; www.go-lanai.com; adult/child one way $30/20) runs five daily round-trip ferries to Lana'i from Lahaina, Maui. Island Air and go! Mokulele have daily flights from Honolulu.

ner windsurfing. Camping is allowed nightly (except Tuesday); get advance permits from Kaua'i's **Department of Parks & Recreation** (☎808-241-4463; www.kauai.gov; tent sites per person $3).

Known for glamorous resort living (think: golf, tennis, horseback riding and spas), Princeville provides glorious sunset perches, such as at the tiny but magnificent **Pali Ke Kua (Hideaways) Beach** (accessible through the St Regis resort). Condo-like 'ocean villas' at the **Westin Princeville** (☎808-827-8700; www.westinprinceville.com; 3838 Wyllie Rd, Princeville; studio/1 br from $275/365;) boast full kitchens and whirlpool tubs.

In **Hanalei**, the hippie-surfer vibe is palpable and, indeed, in magnificent **Hanalei Bay** the surfing is spectacular; it really swells in winter. Also popular are quiet, easy kayak trips up the **Hanalei River** – talk to **Kayak Kaua'i** (☎808-826-9844; www.kayakkauai.com; 5-5070-A Kuhio Hwy; 1-/2-person kayak rental $29/54), which also rents bicycles and camping and surfing gear. With Hawaiiana and surf-inspired stylings by the beach, **Hanalei Surfboard House** (☎808-826-9825; www.hanaleisurfboardhouse.com; 5459 Weke Rd; r $225, cleaning fee $75;) has two kitchenette studios with all mod cons.

Hanalei makes a good meal stop. Doubters become converts at **Hanalei Taro & Juice Co** (5-5070b Kuhio Hwy; snacks $3-7; 11am-4pm Mon-Fri), where the taro-based smoothies are exquisite; the other Hawaiian fare is great too. Organic snacks, a salad bar and smoothie station complement natural-foods **Harvest Market** (5-5156 Kuhio Hwy; 8am-8pm). For trendy atmosphere, killer **Bar Acuda** (☎808-826-7081; 5-5161 Kuhio Hwy; shared dishes $6-16; 6-9:30pm) tapas and wine bar features local produce like North Shore honeycomb and Kailani Farms greens.

Marking the western end of Hwy 56, at the little village of **Ha'ena**, are **Makua (Tunnels) Beach** and **Ke'e Beach**, both of which have excellent snorkeling in summer. Nearby, lush **Limahuli Garden** (www.ntbg.org; 5-8291 Kuhio Hwy; adult/child under 12yr $15/free; 9:30am-4pm Tue-Sat) conserves Hawaii's native botanical wealth. Camping is allowed Thursday, Friday and Saturday nights (advance permit required) at **Ha'ena Beach Park** (☎808-241-4463; www.kauai.gov; tent sites per person $3). The **Hanalei Colony Resort** (☎808-826-6235; www.hcr.com; 5-7130 Kuhio Hwy, Ha'ena; 2br condo from $205;) has a tad dated 1970s-era decor, but the peaceful condos (no TVs or phones) are in a secluded waterfront location.

WORTH A TRIP

NA PALI COAST

Hikers visiting Kaua'i shouldn't miss the challenging but oh-so-rewarding 11-mile **Kalalau Trail**, which runs along the dizzying Na Pali cliffs and winds through a series of lush valleys inside **Na Pali Coast State Park**. To hike beyond Hanakapi'ai Valley and for backcountry camping ($20 nightly per person), you need a **permit** (☎808-274-3444; www.hawaiistateparks.org); reserve up to a year in advance.

Hard-core paddlers can admire the same scenery from the sea along the strenuous 17-mile Na Pali Coast kayak. It takes all day (and feels longer) and is only possible between May and September. **Na Pali Kayak** (☎808-826-6900; www.napalikayak.com; full-day tour $200) is one experienced local outfitter.

Po'ipu & South Shore

Sunny, family-friendly **Po'ipu** fronts a fabulous run of sandy beaches. It's good for swimming and snorkeling year-round and for surfing in summer. Tour the stunning **National Tropical Botanical Garden** (☎808-742-2623; www.ntbg.org; 4425 Lawa'i Rd; adult/child 6-12yr $20/10, guided tour $45; 8:30am-5pm) or admire windswept cliffs, tide pools and pristine beaches along the 4-mile round-trip **Maha'ulepu Heritage Trail** (www.hikemahaulepu.org).

Po'ipu is awash with resorts, condos and vacation rentals for all budgets; browse listings by **Parrish Collection Kaua'i** (☎808-742-2000; www.parrishkauai.com), **Po'ipu Connection Realty** (☎800-742-2260; www.poipuconnection.com) or **Po'ipu Beach Vacation Rentals** (☎808-742-2850; www.pbvacationrentals.com). The magnificent valley views from **Marjorie's Kaua'i Inn** (☎808-332-8838; www.marjorieskauaiinn.com; Hailima Rd, Lawa'i; r incl breakfast $130-195;) could be a trip highlight, and tropical rooms have kitchenettes.

At dinnertime, head to chef-owned **Josselin's Tapas Bar & Grill** (☎808-742-7117; www.josselins.com; 2829 Ala Kalanikaumaka St; shared dishes $9-18; 5-10pm), which crafts

Asian fusion cuisine and thirst-slaking *liliko'i* and lychee sangria. Worth a detour, tiny **Koloa Fish Market** (5482 Koloa Rd, Koloa; mains $5-10; ⌚10am-6pm Mon-Fri, to 5pm Sat) lines up locals for outstanding *poke*, Japanese-inspired bento boxes and island plate lunches.

Waimea & Westside

The top destinations here are **Waimea Canyon** – the 'Grand Canyon of the Pacific' with cascading waterfalls – and adjacent **Koke'e State Park**. Both feature breathtaking views and a vast network of hiking trails; some, like Koke'e's Awa'awapuhi and Nu'alolo Trails, stroll along the knife-edge of precipitously eroded cliffs. Waimea Canyon Dr (Hwy 550) starts in the town of Waimea and is peppered with scenic lookouts. Pick up trail information at the park's **Koke'e Museum** (☎808-335-9975; www.kokee.org; 3600 Koke'e Rd; donation $1; ⌚10am-4pm).

Pitch your rainproof tent at the park's campground; for advance permits (required), contact the **Division of State Parks** (☎808-274-3444; www.hawaiistateparks.org; tent sites $18-30). A former plantation town, **Waimea** makes a civilized base for Westside explorations. **Inn Waimea** (☎808-338-0031; www.innwaimea.com; 4469 Halepule Rd; ste from $110, cottages $150; @📶) is a lovely old missionary home with four guest rooms and two-bedroom cottages. **Ishihara Market** (9894 Kaumuali'i Hwy; ⌚6am-8:30pm Mon-Fri, 7am-8:30pm Sat & Sun) is an ad-hoc lesson in local cuisine from spicy 'ahi *poke* and lobster salad to barbecue bento boxed lunches.

Also worth exploring is **Hanapepe**, a quaint, historic town with false-fronted Old West buildings housing art galleries, shops and tasty eateries, including **Hanapepe Cafe & Bakery** (3830 Hanapepe Rd; mains $7-10; ⌚7am-3pm Mon-Thu), serving veg-friendly soups, salads, sandwiches and home-baked desserts. Just outside town, **Salt Pond Beach Park** is perfect for swimming with kids. Nearby **Port Allen** offers snorkeling and whale-watching cruises and Zodiac tours of the Na Pali Coast.

Understand the USA

THE USA TODAY **1100**

Hot topics of the day: from endless wars and economic hard times to greener cities, changing diets and sustainability.

HISTORY **1103**

Shaped by Native Americans, colonists, revolutionaries, Reconstructionists, New Dealers and Civil Rights fighters.

THE WAY OF LIFE **1115**

Keys to understanding the American cultural landscape: through lifestyles, immigration, religion and sports.

NATIVE AMERICANS **1120**

Overview of some of the great Native American tribes, plus the lowdown on crafts and iconic texts.

AMERICAN CUISINE **1122**

Top tips on feasting a la Americana, from Maryland crabs to Texas BBQ, Southern biscuits 'n' gravy to California fusion.

WINE, BEER & BEYOND **1128**

Venerable vineyards, magnificent microbreweries and top tipples, plus the ever-enduring coffee craze.

ARTS & ARCHITECTURE **1132**

Providing a window into the American identity, through literature, painting, theater and architecture.

THE MUSIC SCENE **1142**

The Great American sound in all its beauty and dissonance from blues and jazz to country, folk, rock and hip-hop.

THE LAND & ENVIRONMENT **1146**

Geology, natural disasters, environmentalism and today's green movement have all helped shape the national conscience.

WILD THINGS **1150**

A peek at some great American creatures, including bears, buffalo and wolves – plus the complex landscapes they live among.

The USA Today

Memories from the Past

The 21st century has certainly been a tumultuous one for the USA. As Americans looked toward the future, many found it difficult to leave the past behind. This was not surprising since wars in Afghanistan and in Iraq, launched a decade prior, continued to simmer on the backburner of the ever-changing news cycle. Add to that the 10-year anniversary of September 11, which again brought back memories of that day when thousands perished in terrorist attacks. Earlier in 2011, in a subterfuge operation vetted by president Obama, Navy Seals raided Osama Bin Laden's Pakistan hideout, bringing an end to America's greatest public enemy.

» **Population** 312 million

» **Gross Domestic Product** $14.66 trillion

» **Gross Domestic Product per capita** $47,200

» **Unemployment** 9.7%

» **Population below poverty line** 12.8%

» **Annual inflation** 1.4%

Economic Woes

Following his sober announcement describing the raid, Obama saw his approval ratings jump by 11%. The president for his part certainly needed a boost. The economy remained in bad shape, and the ambitious $800 billion stimulus package passed by congress in 2009 hadn't born much fruit in the eyes of many Americans.

These were, after all, unprecedented times economically, with the US in the largest financial crisis since the Great Depression. What started as a collapse of the US housing bubble in 2007, spread to the banking sector, with the meltdown of major financial institutions. The shockwave spread and by 2008 many industrialized nations across the globe were experiencing a full-blown recession.

Tea Party

With lost jobs, overvalued mortgages and little relief in sight, millions of Americans found themselves adrift. This was not a recession they could spend their way out of, as Obama's predecessor had suggested. People

Travel Lit

» **On the Road** (1957) Jack Kerouac on post-WWII America.

» **Travels with Charley** (1962) John Steinbeck's trek across America with his poodle.

» **On the Rez** (2000) Ian Frazier's portrait of life on Native American reservations.

Classic Reads

» **Walden** (1854) Thoreau's transcendentalist masterpiece of self-reliance and living simply among nature.

» **Huckleberry Finn** (1884) Mark Twain's moving tale of journey and self-discovery.

» **The Color Purple** (1982) Powerful portrait of life for African Americans in the 1800s by Alice Walker.

belief systems

(% of population)

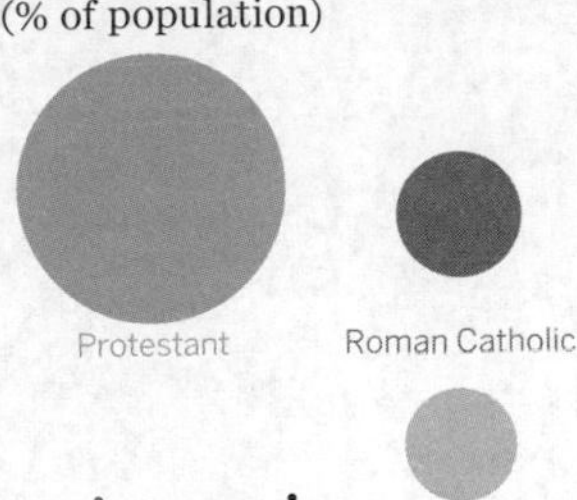

if the USA were 100 people

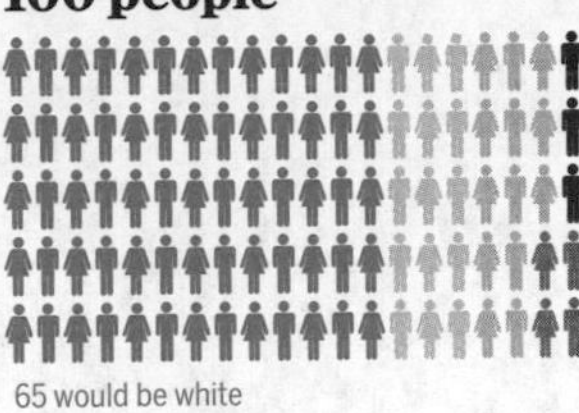

65 would be white
15 would be Hispanic
13 would be African American
4 would be Asian American
3 would be other

were upset and gathered in big numbers to voice their anger. This in turn gave birth to the Tea Party (www.teapartypatriots.org), a wing of political conservatives who believed that Obama was leaning too far to the left, and that government handouts would destroy the economy and thus America. High federal spending, government bailouts (the banking and auto industries) and especially Obama's healthcare reform ('Obamacare') particularly captured their ire.

Healthcare for All

For democrats, however, Obama's healthcare bill, which became law in 2010, was a victory in bringing healthcare coverage to more Americans, lowering the cost of healthcare and closing loopholes that allowed insurance companies to deny coverage to individuals. Critics from both sides reined down blows – from the right: 'this is socialism!' From the left: 'where's the public option?' (ie a government-backed plan, which would not force consumers to remain at the mercy of insurance companies).

Big-City Appeal

On other fronts, great changes were unfolding across the county, affecting many spheres of American life. The city, once regarded as a place of crime and urban decay, was now seen as a place where multiculturalism, the arts, and great restaurants flourished. Indeed cities had become greener, more livable and more appealing (shorter commutes, mostly car-free living). Americans – not just singles but families too – were moving back into the city. Some suburban areas, meanwhile, were beginning to adopt elements of urban living – many Americans wanted more than just a house in a sidewalk-free gated community. They wanted farmers markets, entertainment options or cultural attractions, and a better sense of community.

» **Gallon (3.76 liters) of gasoline** $3.88

» **Car/bicycle hire per day** $35/20

» **Broadway show** $100-300

» **Major League Baseball game** $30

» **Dinner for two at top restaurant** $200

» **Highest point (in lower 48)** 14,495ft (Mt Whitney, CA)

» **Lowest recorded temperature** -80°F (Prospect Creek, AK)

» **Highest recorded temperature** 134°F (Death Valley, CA)

Classic Films

» **Singin' in the Rain** (1952) Among the best in the era of musicals, with an exuberant Gene Kelly and a timeless score.

» **Godfather** (1972–90) Famed trilogy that looks at American society through immigrants and organized crime.

» **Unforgiven** (1992) Clint Eastwood's searing western drama.

Road Movies

» **Easy Rider** (1969) Bikers on a tragic journey of discovery.

» **Blues Brothers** (1980) Belushi and Akroyd find redemption in music.

» **Thelma & Louise** (1991) Two gals on the run beneath big western skies.

Changing Eating Habits

In terms of diet, Americans were doing some soul-searching. No one could deny that many Americans were obese (shows like *The Biggest Loser* and Jamie Oliver's quest to change diets in America's 'fattest city' – were constant reminders that things were deeply wrong). Fast food, soft drinks and too much TV have all been vilified in recent years; whether this brings substantive change – or just higher ratings for weight-loss shows – remains to be seen.

Sustainable Agriculture

Diet, of course, isn't just about dieting, and awareness of problems in American agriculture is growing in leaps and bounds. The documentary film *Food, Inc;* and books by Michael Pollan *(The Omnivore's Dilemma)*, Eric Schlosser *(Fast Food Nation)* and others have illuminated the disheartening way food is produced in America, and its enormous unseen costs on society – from both a health- and environmental perspective. As a result, more Americans are eating organic food, and supporting local, sustainably raised products.

Greener Lifestyles

Speaking of sustainability, the word 'green' seems to be on everyone's mind. Owing in part to high fuel prices, Americans are less eager to own a gas-guzzling SUV. Recycling, energy-efficiency, and renewable energy are the buzz words of the moment. And big projects are underway – with large solar and wind-power plants in the works, greener cities (eco-friendly architecture and infrastructure, more parks) and even electric cars soon to bring changes to the American landscape.

Faux Pas

» Don't assume you can smoke – even if you're outside. Most Americans have little tolerance for smokers and have even banned smoking from many parks, boardwalks and beaches.

» Do be on time. Many folks in the US consider it rude to be kept waiting.

» Don't be overly physical if you greet someone. Some Americans will hug; urbanites may exchange cheek kisses, but most – especially men – shake hands.

Myths Debunked

» Urban residents are sophisticated and rural folk hillbillies... You'll find foodies in Appalachia and hicks in Manhattan.

» Americans are monolingual. Spanish is common across the United States.

History

The startling New World for Europeans was ancient homeland for thousands of indigenous tribes. Sadly, introduced diseases would decimate their numbers, followed by centuries of warfare to push them off the land.

The earliest colonies struggled to survive. By the 17th century, however, British colonials in present-day Virginia and Massachusetts put down permanent roots. From there, the American colony flourished, helped along by slaves and a plantation economy.

By 1776, the colonists waged war for independence. Washington, Adams, Jefferson, Franklin and others laid the foundations for an ingenious new type of government by the people.

In the 19th century the survival of the fledgling nation was at stake when the slave-owning south seceded from the union. Seeing no other way to keep the nation intact, Abraham Lincoln led the nation into a bloody, four-year-long Civil War.

The republic survived, and more importantly slavery was abolished. The north helped rebuild the south, but bitterness lived on. Freed blacks soon found themselves disenfranchised, and 'separate but equal' became a justification for overt discrimination. America became deeply segregated.

World war soon overshadowed racial strife, followed by the 'roaring twenties'. The good times didn't last, and the Great Depression erupted in 1929, destroying banks, farms and businesses and leaving millions unemployed. Roosevelt's New Deal helped pull the nation back together, while an even more devastating world war reeled in America.

The 1950s were boom days once again, with suburban homes and fancy highways all the rage. Unfortunately, the threat of nuclear annihilation seemed ever-present as the Cold War kicked into high gear (with proxy wars against communism waged in Korea and Vietnam).

Assassinations (John F Kennedy, Martin Luther King, Robert F Kennedy), riots, a devastating and unpopular war, political corruption (Watergate) and

The People: Indians of the American Southwest (1993), by Stephen Trimble, is a diverse account of indigenous history and contemporary culture as related by Native Americans themselves.

TIMELINE

20,000-40,000 BC

The first peoples to the Americas arrive from Central Asia by migrating over a wide land bridge between Siberia and Alaska (when sea levels were lower than today).

8000 BC

Widespread extinction of ice-age mammals including the woolly mammoth, due to cooperative hunting by humans and a warming climate. Indigenous peoples begin hunting smaller game and gathering native plants.

7000 BC-AD 100

'Archaic period' marked by nomadic hunter-gatherer lifestyle. By the end of this period, corn, beans and squash (the agricultural 'three sisters') and permanent settlements are well established.

sexual liberation ensure there's never a dull moment in the tumultuous 1960s and '70s. It's also a time of momentous change as African Americans achieve hard-won victories in the realm of civil rights.

The 1980s see decaying cities and a stratified society as whites take flight to the suburbs. Communism ends with a bang as the Berlin Wall collapses and the USSR dissolves. It's good times again in the 1990s, with peace and prosperity, budget surpluses and a growing high-tech sector. The 21st century starts off badly, with a devastating attack on New York and Washington, DC, followed by two costly wars lasting well into the next decade.

Authoritative and sobering, *Bury My Heart at Wounded Knee* (1970), by Dee Brown, tells the story of the late-19th-century Indian Wars from the perspective of Native Americans.

Turtle Island

According to oral traditions and sacred myths, indigenous peoples have always lived on the North American continent, which some called Turtle Island. When Europeans arrived, approximately two to 18 million Native American people occupied the turtle's back north of present-day Mexico and spoke more than 300 languages.

Among North America's most significant prehistoric cultures were the Mound Builders, who inhabited the Ohio and Mississippi River valleys from around 3000 BC to AD 1300. In Illinois, Cahokia (p535) was once a metropolis of 20,000 people, the largest in pre-Columbian North America.

In the Southwest, Ancestral Puebloans occupied the Colorado Plateau from around AD 100 to AD 1300, until warfare, drought and scarcity of resources likely drove them out. You can still see their cliff dwellings at Colorado's Mesa Verde National Park (p740) and desert adobe pueblos at New Mexico's Chaco Culture National Historic Park (p874).

It was the Great Plains cultures that came to epitomize 'Indians' in the popular American imagination, in part because these tribal peoples put up the longest fight against the USA's westward expansion. Oklahoma is rich in sites that interpret Native American life before Europeans arrived, including at Anadarko (p648) and along the Trail of Tears (p650).

In 1502, Italian explorer Amerigo Vespucci used the term Mundus Novus (New World) to describe his discoveries. His reward? In 1507, new maps labeled the western hemisphere 'America.'

Enter the Europeans

In 1492, Italian explorer Christopher Columbus, backed by Spain, voyaged west – looking for the East Indies. He found the Bahamas. With visions of gold, Spanish explorers quickly followed: Cortés conquered much of today's Mexico; Pizarro conquered Peru; Ponce de León wandered through Florida looking for the fountain of youth. Not to be left out, the French explored Canada and the Midwest, while the Dutch and English cruised North America's eastern seaboard.

European explorers left in their wake diseases to which indigenous peoples had no immunity. More than any other factor – war, slavery or

1492

Italian explorer Christopher Columbus 'discovers' America, making three voyages throughout the Caribbean. He names the indigenous people 'Indians,' mistakenly thinking he had reached the Indies.

1607

The English found the first English colony, the Jamestown settlement on marshland in present-day Virginia. The first few years are hard, with many dying from sickness and starvation.

DENNIS JOHNSON/LONELY PLANET IMAGES ©

» Memorial, Jamestown

1620

The *Mayflower* lands at Plymouth with 102 English Pilgrims, who have come to the New World to escape religious persecution. The Wampanoag tribe saves them from starvation.

THE AFRICAN AMERICAN EXPERIENCE: THE STRUGGLE FOR EQUALITY

It's impossible to properly grasp American history without taking into account the great struggles and hard-won victories of African Americans who come from all spheres of life.

Slavery

From the early 17th century until the 19th century, an estimated 600,000 slaves were brought from Africa to America. Those who survived the horrific transport on crowded ships (which sometimes had 50% mortality rates) were sold in slave markets (African males cost $27 in 1638). The majority of slaves ended up in southern plantations where conditions were usually brutal – whipping and branding were commonplace.

All (White) Men are Created Equal

Many of the founding fathers – George Washington, Thomas Jefferson and Benjamin Franklin – owned slaves, though privately expressed condemnation for the abominable practice. The abolition movement however wouldn't appear until the 1830s, long after the appearance of the rousing but ultimately hollow words 'all men are created equal' on the Declaration of Independence.

Free at Last

While some revisionist historians describe the Civil War as being about states' rights, most scholars agree that the war was really about slavery. Following the Union victory at Antietam, Lincoln drafted the Emancipation Proclamation, which freed all blacks in occupied territories. African Americans joined the Union effort, with more than 180,000 serving by war's end.

Jim Crow Laws

During Reconstruction (1865–77) federal laws provided civil rights protection for newly freed blacks. Southern bitterness, however, coupled with centuries of prejudice, fueled a backlash. By the 1890s, the Jim Crow laws (named after a derogatory character in a minstrel show) appeared. African Americans were effectively disenfranchised, and America became a deeply segregated society.

Civil Rights Movement

Beginning in the 1950s, a movement was underway in African American communities to fight for equality. Rosa Parks, who refused to give up her seat to a white passenger, inspired the Montgomery bus boycott. There were sit-ins at lunch counters where blacks were excluded; massive demonstrations led by Martin Luther King Jr in Washington, DC; and harrowing journeys by 'freedom riders' that aimed to end bus segregation. The work of millions paid off: In 1964, President Johnson signed the Civil Rights Act, which banned discrimination and racial segregation.

1675

For decades, the Pilgrims and local tribes live fairly cooperatively, but deadly conflict erupts in 1675. King Philip's War lasts 14 months and kills over 5000 people (mostly Native Americans).

1756-63

In the Seven Years' War (or the 'French and Indian War'), France loses to England and withdraws from Canada. Britain now controls most territory east of the Mississippi River.

1773

To protest a British tax on tea, Bostonians dress as Mohawks, board East India Company ships and toss their tea overboard during what would be named the Boston Tea Party.

1775

Paul Revere rides from Boston to warn colonial 'Minutemen' that the British are coming. The next day, 'the shot heard round the world' is fired at Lexington, starting the Revolutionary War.

famine – disease epidemics devastated Native populations by anywhere from 50% to 90%. By the 17th century, indigenous North Americans numbered only about a million, and many of the continent's once-thriving societies were in turmoil and transition.

In 1607, English noblemen established North America's first permanent European settlement in Jamestown (p301). Earlier settlements had ended badly, and Jamestown almost did too: the English chose a swamp, planted their crops late and died from disease and starvation. Some despairing colonists ran off to live with the local tribes, who provided the settlement with enough aid to survive.

For Jamestown and America, 1619 proved a pivotal year: the colony established the House of Burgesses, a representative assembly of citizens to decide local laws, and it received its first boatload of 20 African slaves.

The next year was equally momentous, as a group of radically religious Puritans pulled ashore at what would become Plymouth, Massachusetts (p185). The Pilgrims were escaping religious persecution under the 'corrupt' Church of England, and in the New World they saw a divine opportunity to create a new society that would be a religious and moral beacon. The Pilgrims signed a 'Mayflower Compact,' one of the seminal texts of American democracy, to govern themselves by consensus.

Colonial Sights

» Williamsburg, Virginia

» Jamestown, Virginia

» Plymouth, Massachusetts

» North End, Boston

» Philadelphia

» Annapolis, Maryland

» Charleston, South Carolina

Capitalism & Colonialism

For the next two centuries, European powers competed for position and territory in the New World, extending European politics into the Americas. As Britain's Royal Navy came to rule Atlantic seas, England increasingly profited from its colonies and eagerly consumed the fruits of their labors – sweet tobacco from Virginia, sugar and coffee from the Caribbean.

Over the 17th and 18th centuries, slavery in America was slowly legalized into a formal institution to support this plantation economy. By 1800, one out of every five persons was a slave.

Meanwhile, Britain mostly left the American colonists to govern themselves. Town meetings and representative assemblies, in which local citizens (that is, white men with property) debated community problems and voted on laws and taxes, became common.

However, by the end of the Seven Years' War in 1763, Britain was feeling the strains of running an empire: it had been fighting France for a century and had colonies scattered all over the world. It was time to clean up bureaucracies and share financial burdens.

The colonies, however, resented English taxes and policies. Public outrage soon culminated in the 1776 Declaration of Independence. With this document, the American colonists took many of the Enlightenment ideas then circulating worldwide – of individualism, equality and free-

If history is a partisan affair, Howard Zinn makes his allegiance clear in *A People's History of the United States* (1980 & 2005), which tells the often-overlooked stories about laborers, minorities, immigrants, women and radicals.

1776
On July 4, the colonies sign the Declaration of Independence. Famous figures who helped create this document include John Hancock, Samuel Adams, John Adams, Benjamin Franklin and Thomas Jefferson.

1787
The Constitutional Convention in Philadelphia draws up the US Constitution. Power is balanced between the presidency, Congress and judiciary.

1791
Bill of Rights adopted as constitutional amendments outlining citizens' rights, including free speech, assembly, religion and the press; the right to bear arms; and prohibition of 'cruel and unusual punishments.'

1803
France's Napoleon sells the Louisiana Territory to the US for just $15 million, thereby extending the boundaries of the new nation from the Mississippi River to the Rocky Mountains.

dom; of John Locke's 'natural rights' of life, liberty and property – and fashioned a new type of government to put them into practice.

Frustrations came to a head with the Boston Tea Party in 1773, after which Britain clamped down hard, shutting Boston's harbor and increasing its military presence. In 1774 representatives from 12 colonies convened the First Continental Congress in Philadelphia's Independence Hall to air complaints and prepare for the inevitable war ahead.

The New World (2005), directed by Terrence Malick, is a brutal but passionate film that retells the tragic story of the Jamestown colony and the pivotal peacemaking role of Pocahontas, a Powhatan chief's daughter.

Revolution & The Republic

In April 1775, British troops skirmished with armed colonists in Massachusetts, and the Revolutionary War began. George Washington, a wealthy Virginia farmer, was chosen to lead the American army. Trouble was, Washington lacked gunpowder and money (the colonists resisted taxes even for their own military), and his troops were a motley collection of poorly armed farmers, hunters and merchants, who regularly quit and returned to their farms due to lack of pay. On the other side, the British 'Redcoats,' represented the world's most powerful military. The inexperienced General Washington had to improvise constantly, sometimes wisely retreating, sometimes engaging in 'ungentlemanly' sneak attacks. During the winter of 1777–78, the American army nearly starved at Valley Forge.

Meanwhile, the Second Continental Congress tried to articulate what exactly they were fighting for. In January 1776, Thomas Paine published the wildly popular *Common Sense,* which passionately argued for independence from England. Soon, independence seemed not just logical, but noble and necessary, and on July 4, 1776, the Declaration of Independence was finalized and signed. Largely written by Thomas Jefferson, it elevated the 13 colonies' particular gripes against the monarchy into a universal declaration of individual rights and republican government.

However, to succeed on the battlefield, General Washington needed help, not just patriotic sentiment. In 1778, Benjamin Franklin persuaded France (always eager to trouble England) to ally with the revolutionaries, and they provided the troops, material and sea power that helped win the war. The British surrendered at Yorktown, Virginia, in 1781, and two years later the Treaty of Paris formally recognized the 'United States of America.'

At first, the nation's loose confederation of fractious, squabbling states were hardly 'united.' So the founders gathered again in Philadelphia, and in 1787 drafted a new-and-improved Constitution: the US government was given a stronger federal center, with checks and balances between its three major branches; and to guard against the abuse of centralized power, a citizen's Bill of Rights was approved in 1791.

With the Constitution, the scope of the American Revolution solidified to a radical change in government; and the preservation of the economic

The HBO miniseries *John Adams* (2008) is a riveting story, told from all sides, of the years when the American Revolution hung in the balance and fate could have swung either way.

1803-6

President Thomas Jefferson sends Meriwether Lewis and William Clark west. Guided by the Shoshone tribeswoman Sacajawea, they trailblaze from St Louis, Missouri, to the Pacific Ocean and back.

1812

The War of 1812 begins with battles against the British and Native Americans in the Great Lakes region. Even after the 1815 Treaty of Ghent, fighting continues along Gulf Coast.

1823

President Monroe articulates the Monroe Doctrine, seeking to end European military interventions in America. Roosevelt later extends it to justify US interventions in Latin America.

1841

Wagon trains follow the Oregon Trail, which extends the route Lewis and Clark followed. By 1847, over 6500 emigrants a year are heading West, to Oregon, California and Mormon-dominated Utah.

and social status quos. Rich landholders kept their property, which included their slaves; Native Americans were excluded from the nation; and women were excluded from politics. These blatant discrepancies and injustices, which were widely noted, were the results of both pragmatic compromise (eg to get slave-dependent Southern states to agree) and also widespread beliefs in the essential rightness of things as they were.

Westward, Ho!

As the 19th century dawned on the young nation, optimism was the mood of the day. With the invention of the cotton gin in 1793 – followed by threshers, reapers, mowers and later combines – agriculture was industrialized, and US commerce surged. The 1803 Louisiana Purchase doubled US territory, and expansion west of the Appalachian Mountains began in earnest.

Relations between the US and Britain – despite lively trade – remained tense, and in 1812, the US declared war on England again. The two-year conflict ended without much gain by either side, although the British abandoned their forts, and the US vowed to avoid Europe's 'entangling alliances.'

In the 1830s and 1840s, with growing nationalist fervor and dreams of continental expansion, many Americans came to believe it was 'Manifest Destiny' that all the land should be theirs. The 1830 Indian Removal Act aimed to clear one obstacle, while the building of the railroads cleared another hurdle, linking Midwestern farmers with East Coast markets.

In 1836 a group of Texans fomented a revolution against Mexico. (Remember the Alamo? See p667.) Ten years later, the US annexed the Texas Republic, and when Mexico resisted, the US waged war for it – and while they were at it, took California too. In 1848, Mexico was soundly defeated and ceded this territory to the US. This completed the USA's continental expansion.

By a remarkable coincidence, only days after the 1848 treaty with Mexico was signed, gold was discovered in California. By 1849, surging rivers of wagon trains were creaking west filled with miners, pioneers, entrepreneurs, immigrants, outlaws and prostitutes, all seeking their fortunes. This made for exciting, legendary times, but throughout loomed a troubling question: as new states joined the USA, would they be slave states or free states? The nation's future depended on the answer.

LEWIS & CLARK

You can follow the Lewis and Clark expedition on its extraordinary journey west to the Pacific and back again online at www.pbs.org/lewisandclark, which features historical maps, photo albums and journal excerpts.

The Civil War

The US Constitution hadn't ended slavery, but it had given Congress the power to approve (or not) slavery in new states. Public debates raged constantly over the expansion of slavery, particularly since this shaped the balance of power between the industrial North and the agrarian South.

1849

After the 1848 discovery of gold near Sacramento, an epic cross-country gold rush sees 60,000 'forty-niners' flock to California's Mother Lode. San Francisco's population explodes from 850 to 25,000.

JOHN ELK III/LONELY PLANET IMAGES ©

» San Francisco

1861-65

American Civil War erupts between North and South (delineated by the Mason-Dixon line). The war's end on April 9, 1865, is marred by President Lincoln's assassination five days later.

1870

Freed black men are given the vote, but the South's segregationist 'Jim Crow' laws (which remain until the 1960s) effectively disenfranchise blacks from every meaningful sphere of daily life.

TECUMSEH'S CURSE

According to legend, a curse spanning more than 100 years hung over every president elected in a year ending in zero (every 20 years). It all began with future president William Henry Harrison, who in 1811 led the Battle of Tippecanoe against revered Shawnee chief Tecumseh. The battle devastated the Shawnee, putting an end to Tecumseh's hope of a pan-Indian alliance. After the bitter defeat, Tecumseh (or in some accounts his medicine man and half-brother Tenskwatawa) placed a curse, uttering something along the lines of 'Harrison will die, and after him every great chief chosen 20 years thereafter will also die. And when each dies, let everyone remember the death of my people'.

In 1840 William Henry Harrison was elected president. He served just 32 days in office – the shortest term in presidential history. Three weeks after his inauguration, he caught a cold, which turned into pneumonia, and he died.

The next to die in office was Abraham Lincoln, who was elected in 1860, reelected in 1864, and assassinated just five days after the end of the Civil War.

In 1880, James Garfield was shot; he died several months later from infection.

In 1900, William McKinley was elected to his second term in office. A year later he was shot and killed (the ultimate cause of death was gangrene) by an anarchist.

In 1920, Warren G Harding became president. His death came in 1923 from a stroke suffered on a visit to San Francisco.

Franklin Roosevelt, elected to his third of four terms in 1940, also died in office – in April 1945 from a stroke, just a month before the surrender of Nazi Germany in WWII.

In 1960, young, charismatic John F Kennedy was elected president and was violently gunned down in 1963.

The curse was broken in 1980, when Reagan was elected. He narrowly avoided dying in office, however, following the 1981 assassination attempt by John Hinckley (whose bullet lodged an inch from Reagan's heart).

Since the founding, Southern politicians had dominated government and defended slavery as 'natural and normal,' which an 1856 *New York Times* editorial called 'insanity.' The Southern proslavery lobby enraged northern abolitionists. But even many Northern politicians feared that ending slavery would be ruinous. Limit slavery, they reasoned, and in the competition with industry and free labor, slavery would wither without inciting a violent slave revolt – a constantly feared possibility. Indeed, in 1859, radical abolitionist John Brown tried unsuccessfully to spark just that at Harpers Ferry.

The economics of slavery were undeniable. In 1860, there were more than four million slaves in the US, most held by Southern planters – who grew 75% of the world's cotton, accounting for more than half of US exports. Thus, the Southern economy supported the nation's economy, and

1880-1920

Millions of immigrants flood in from Europe and Asia, fueling the age of cities. New York, Chicago and Philadelphia swell in size, becoming global centers of industry and commerce.

1882

Racist sentiment, particularly in California (where over 50,000 Chinese immigrants have arrived since 1848) leads to the Chinese Exclusion Act, the only US immigration law to exclude a specific race.

1896

In *Plessy v. Ferguson*, the US Supreme Court rules that 'separate but equal' public facilities for blacks and whites are legal, arguing that the Constitution addresses only political, not social, equality.

1898

Victory in the Spanish-American War gives US control of the Philippines, Puerto Rico and Guam, and indirect control of Cuba. But Philippine's bloody war for independence deters future US colonialism.

it required slaves. The 1860 presidential election became a referendum on this issue, and the election was won by a young politician who favored limiting slavery: Abraham Lincoln.

In the South, even the threat of federal limits was too onerous to abide, and as President Lincoln took office, 11 states eventually seceded from the union and formed the Confederate States of America. Lincoln faced the nation's greatest moment of crisis. He had two choices: let the southern states secede and dissolve the union or wage war to keep the union intact. He chose the latter, and war soon erupted.

It began in April 1861, when the Confederacy attacked Fort Sumter in Charleston, South Carolina, and raged on for the next four years – in the most gruesome combat the world had ever known until that time. By the end, more than 600,000 soldiers, nearly an entire generation of young men, were dead; Southern plantations and cities (most notably Atlanta) lay sacked and burned. The North's industrial might provided an advantage, but its victory was not preordained; it unfolded battle by bloody battle.

As fighting progressed, Lincoln recognized that if the war didn't end slavery outright, victory would be pointless. In 1863, his Emancipation Proclamation expanded the war's aims and freed all slaves. In April 1865, Confederate General Robert E Lee surrendered to Union General Ulysses S Grant in Appomattox, Virginia. The Union had been preserved, but at a staggering cost.

WASHINGTON

According to legend, George Washington was so honest that after chopping down his father's cherry tree when he was just a child, he admitted, 'I cannot tell a lie. I did it with my little hatchet.'

Great Depression, The New Deal & World War II

In October 1929, investors, worried over a gloomy global economy, started selling stocks, and seeing the selling, everyone panicked until they'd sold everything. The stock market crashed, and the US economy collapsed like a house of cards.

Thus began the Great Depression. Frightened banks called in their dodgy loans, people couldn't pay, and the banks folded. Millions lost their homes, farms, businesses and savings, and as much as 50% of the American workforce became unemployed.

In 1932, Democrat Franklin D Roosevelt was elected president on the promise of a 'New Deal' to rescue the US from its crisis, which he did with resounding success. When war once again broke out in Europe in 1939, the isolationist mood in America was as strong as ever. However, the extremely popular President Roosevelt, elected to an unprecedented third term in 1940, understood that the US couldn't sit by and allow victory for fascist, totalitarian regimes. Roosevelt sent aid to Britain and persuaded a skittish Congress to go along with it.

1906

Upton Sinclair publishes *The Jungle*, an exposé of Chicago's unsavory meatpacking industry. Many workers suffer through poverty and dangerous, even deadly, conditions in choking factories and sweatshops.

1908

The first Model T (aka 'Tin Lizzie') car is built in Detroit, MI; assembly-line innovator Henry Ford is soon selling one million automobiles annually.

1914

Panama Canal opens, linking Atlantic and Pacific Oceans. US won the right to build and run the canal by inciting a Panamanian revolt over independence from Colombia.

1917

President Woodrow Wilson enters US into WWI. The US mobilizes 4.7 million troops, and suffers around 110,000 of the war's 9 million military deaths.

Then, on December 7, 1941, Japan launched a surprise attack on Hawaii's Pearl Harbor, killing more than 2000 Americans and sinking several battleships. As US isolationism transformed overnight into outrage, Roosevelt suddenly had the support he needed. Germany also declared war on the US, and America joined the Allied fight against Hitler and the Axis powers. From that moment, the US put almost its entire will and industrial prowess into the war effort.

Initially, neither the Pacific nor European theaters went well for the US. In the Pacific, fighting didn't turn around until the US unexpectedly routed the Japanese navy at Midway Island in June 1942. Afterward, the US drove Japan back with a series of brutal battles recapturing Pacific islands.

In Europe, the US dealt the fatal blow to Germany with its massive D-Day invasion of France on June 6, 1944: unable to sustain a two-front war (the Soviet Union was savagely fighting on the eastern front), Germany surrendered in May 1945.

Nevertheless, Japan continued fighting. Newly elected President Harry Truman – ostensibly worried that a US invasion of Japan would lead to unprecedented carnage – chose to drop experimental atomic bombs on Hiroshima and Nagasaki in August 1945. Created by the government's top-secret Manhattan Project, the bombs devastated both cities, killing over 200,000 people. Japan surrendered days later. The nuclear age was born.

James McPherson is a preeminent Civil War historian, and his Pulitzer Prize–winning *Battle Cry of Freedom* (1988) somehow gets the whole heartbreaking saga between two covers.

The Red Scare, Civil Rights & the Wars in Asia

The US enjoyed unprecedented prosperity in the decades after WWII but little peace.

Formerly wartime allies, the communist Soviet Union and the capitalist USA soon engaged in a running competition to dominate the globe. The superpowers engaged in proxy wars – notably the Korean War (1950–53) and Vietnam War (1959–75) – with only the mutual threat of nuclear annihilation preventing direct war. Founded in 1945, the UN couldn't overcome this worldwide ideological split and was largely ineffectual in preventing Cold War conflicts.

Meanwhile, with its continent unscarred and its industry bulked up by WWII, the American homeland entered an era of growing affluence. In the 1950s, a mass migration left the inner cities for the suburbs, where affordable single-family homes sprang up. Americans drove cheap cars using cheap gas over brand-new interstate highways. They relaxed with the comforts of modern technology, swooned over TV, and got busy, giving birth to a 'baby boom.'

Great Presidential Reads

» *Washington*, Ron Chernow

» *Thomas Jefferson*, RB Bernstein

» *Lincoln*, David Herbert Donald

» *Mornings on Horseback*, David McCullough

» *The Bridge*, David Remnick

1920s

Spurred by African American migration to northern cities, the Harlem Renaissance inspires an intellectual flowering of literature, art and music. Important figures include WEB Du Bois and Langston Hughes.

1941-45

WWII: America deploys 16 million troops and suffers 400,000 deaths. Overall, civilian deaths outpace military deaths two to one, and total 50 to 70 million people from over 50 countries.

1948-51

The US-led Marshall Plan funnels $12 billion in material and financial aid to help Europe recover from WWII. The plan also aims to contain Soviet influence and reignite America's economy.

1963

On November 22, President John F Kennedy is publically assassinated by Lee Harvey Oswald while riding in a motorcade through Dealey Plaza in Dallas, Texas.

FIGHTING FOR CHANGE: FIVE WHO SHAPED HISTORY

American history is littered with larger-than-life figures who brought dramatic change through bold deeds, sometimes at great personal cost. While presidents tend to garner all the attention, there are countless lesser-known visionaries who have made enormous contributions to civic life.

Rachel Carson (1907–64) An eloquent writer with a keen scientific mind, Carson helped spawn the environmental movement. Her pioneering work *Silent Spring* illustrated the ecological catastrophe unleashed by pesticides and unregulated industry. The ensuing grassroots movement spurred the creation of the Environmental Protection Agency.

Cesar Chavez (1927–93) A second-generation Mexican-American who grew up in farm labor camps (where entire families labored for $1 a day), Chavez was a charismatic and inspiring figure – Gandhi and Martin Luther King Jr were among his role models. He gave hope, dignity and a brighter future to thousands of poor migrants by creating the United Farm Workers.

Harvey Milk (1930–78) California's first openly gay public servant was a tireless advocate in the fight against discrimination, encouraging gays and lesbians to 'come out, stand up and let the world know. Only that way will we start to achieve our rights'. Milk, along with San Francisco mayor George Moscone, was assassinated in 1978.

Betty Friedan (1921–2006) Founder of the National Organization of Women (NOW), Friedan was instrumental in leading the feminist movement of the 1960s. Friedan's groundbreaking book *The Feminine Mystique* inspired millions of women to envision a life beyond mere 'homemaker'.

Ralph Nader (1934–) The frequent presidential contender (in 2008, Nader received 738,000 votes) is one of America's staunchest consumer watchdogs. The Harvard-trained lawyer has played a major role in insuring Americans have safer cars, cheaper medicines and cleaner air and water.

Middle-class whites did, anyway. African Americans remained segregated, poor and generally unwelcome at the party. Echoing 19th-century abolitionist Frederick Douglass, the Southern Christian Leadership Coalition (SCLC), led by African American preacher Martin Luther King Jr (p383), aimed to end segregation and 'save America's soul': to realize color-blind justice, racial equality and fairness of economic opportunity for all.

Beginning in the 1950s, King preached and organized nonviolent resistance in the form of bus boycotts, marches and sit-ins, mainly in the South. White authorities often met these protests with water hoses and batons, and demonstrations sometimes dissolved into riots, but with the 1964 Civil Rights Act, African Americans spurred a wave of legislation

1965-75

US involvement in the Vietnam War tears the nation apart as 58,000 Americans die, along with four million Vietnamese and 1.5 million Laotians and Cambodians.

1969

American astronauts land on the moon, fulfilling President Kennedy's unlikely 1961 promise to accomplish this feat within a decade and culminating the 'space race' between the US and USSR.

RICHARD CUMMINS/LONELY PLANET IMAGES ©

» US astronaut suit

1973

In *Roe v. Wade*, the Supreme Court legalizes abortion. Today, this decision remains controversial and divisive, pitting 'right to choose' advocates against the 'right to life' anti-abortion lobby.

that swept away racist laws and laid the groundwork for a more just and equal society.

Meanwhile, the 1960s saw further social upheavals: rock 'n' roll spawned a youth rebellion, and drugs sent Technicolor visions spinning in their heads. President John F Kennedy was assassinated in Dallas in 1963, followed by the assassinations in 1968 of his brother, Senator Robert Kennedy, and of Martin Luther King. Americans' faith in their leaders and government were further shocked by the bombings and brutalities of the Vietnam War, as seen on TV, which led to widespread student protests.

Yet President Richard Nixon, elected in 1968 partly for promising an 'honorable end to the war,' instead escalated US involvement and secretly bombed Laos and Cambodia. Then, in 1972, the Watergate scandal broke: a burglary at Democratic Party offices was, through dogged journalism, tied to 'Tricky Dick,' who, in 1974, became the first US president to resign from office.

The tumultuous 1960s and '70s also witnessed the sexual revolution, women's liberation, struggles for gay rights, energy crises over the supply of crude oil from the Middle East, and, with the 1962 publication of Rachel Carson's *Silent Spring,* the realization that the USA's industries had created a polluted, diseased environmental mess (p1147).

This Republic of Suffering (2008), by historian Drew Gilpin Faust, is a poignant look at the Civil War through the eyes of loved ones left behind by fallen soldiers on both sides of the Mason-Dixon line.

Pax Americana & The War On Terror

In 1980, Republican California governor and former actor Ronald Reagan campaigned for president by promising to make Americans feel good about America again. The affable Reagan won easily, and his election marked a pronounced shift to the right in US politics.

Reagan wanted to defeat communism, restore the economy, deregulate business and cut taxes. To tackle the first two, he launched the biggest peacetime military build-up in history, and dared the Soviets to keep up. They went broke trying, and the USSR collapsed.

Military spending and tax cuts created enormous federal deficits, which hampered the presidency of Reagan's successor, George HW Bush. Despite winning the Gulf War – liberating Kuwait in 1991 after an Iraqi invasion – Bush was soundly defeated in the 1992 presidential election by Southern Democrat Bill Clinton. Clinton had the good fortune to catch the 1990s high-tech internet boom, which seemed to augur a 'new economy' based on white-collar telecommunications. The US economy erased its deficits and ran a surplus, and Clinton presided over one of America's longest economic booms.

In 2000 and 2004, George W Bush, the eldest son of George HW Bush, won the presidential elections so narrowly that the divided results seemed to epitomize an increasingly divided nation. 'Dubya' had the

In *The Souls of Black Folk* (1903), WEB Du Bois, who helped found the National Association for the Advancement of Colored People (NAACP), eloquently describes the racial dilemmas of politics and culture facing early-20th-century America.

1980s

New Deal–era financial institutions, deregulated under President Reagan, gamble with their customers' savings and loans, and fail, leaving the government with the bill: $125 billion.

1989

The 1960s-era Berlin Wall is torn down, marking the end of the Cold War between the US and the USSR (now Russia). The USA becomes the world's last remaining superpower.

1990s

The World Wide Web debuts in 1991. Silicon Valley, CA, leads a high-tech internet revolution, remaking communications and media, and overvalued tech stocks drive the massive boom (and subsequent bust).

2001

On September 11, Al-Qaeda terrorists hijack four commercial airplanes, flying two into NYC's twin towers, and one into the Pentagon (the fourth crashes in Pennsylvania); nearly 3000 people are killed.

Suspicious of political factoids? Fact.check.org is a nonpartisan, self-described 'consumer advocate' that monitors the accuracy of statements made by US politicians during debates, speeches, interviews and in campaign ads. It's a great resource for parsing truth from bombast and is particularly handy during election cycles.

misfortune of being president when the high-tech bubble burst in 2000, but he nevertheless enacted tax cuts that returned federal deficits even greater than before. He also championed the right-wing conservative 'backlash' that had been building since Reagan.

On September 11, 2001, Islamic terrorists flew hijacked planes into New York's World Trade Center and the Pentagon in Washington, DC. This catastrophic attack united Americans behind their president as he vowed revenge and declared a 'war on terror.' Bush soon attacked Afghanistan in an unsuccessful hunt for Al-Qaeda terrorist cells, then he attacked Iraq in 2003 and toppled its anti-US dictator, Saddam Hussein. Meanwhile, Iraq descended into civil war.

Following scandals and failures – torture photos from Abu Ghraib, the federal response in the aftermath of Hurricane Katrina and the inability to bring the Iraq War to a close – Bush's approval ratings reached historic lows in the second half of his presidency. Hungry for change, Americans responded by electing political newcomer, Barack Obama, who became America's first African American president in 2008.

2003

After citing evidence that Iraq possesses weapons of mass destruction, President George W Bush launches a preemptive war that will cost over 4000 American lives and some $3 trillion.

2005

On August 29, Hurricane Katrina hits the Mississippi and Louisiana coasts, rupturing poorly maintained levees and flooding New Orleans. Over 1800 people die, and cost estimates exceed $110 billion.

2008-9

Barack Obama becomes the first African American president. The stock market crashes due to mismanagement by major American financial institutions. The crisis spreads worldwide .

2010

America's worst natural disaster occurs when a deep-water oil rig off the Louisiana coast explodes, killing 11 workers and releasing an estimated 5 million barrels of oil into the Gulf.

The Way of Life

For all their differences – Americans don't look alike, eat the same foods or worship alike – they do share a common thread: the belief that America is a land of possibility, and if you apply yourself, you can achieve your dreams. As simplistic as it sounds, it's the core of the national psyche.

When the founding fathers laid out their take on democracy, government by and for the people, liberty and the pursuit of happiness, they laid the mold for the American character. People expect a large slate of individual rights, and for those rights to prevail if the government tries to curb them. It's also a group effort, where everyone has to trust 'the basic good sense and stability of the great American consensus,' as John F Kennedy once put it.

One thing's for sure: freedom gets its due each Fourth of July, during the nation's whopping Independence Day celebration. Almost every city holds a fireworks-laden parade or festival to rock the nation's birthday. In Chicago, for instance, more than a million people fill downtown to watch red, white and blue pyrotechnics explode over a score of patriotic music. The scene plays out across the country, complemented by barbecues, picnics and ever-flowing beer.

Multiculturalism

From the get-go, America was called a 'melting pot,' which presumed that newcomers came and blended into the existing American fabric. The country hasn't let go of that sentiment completely. On one hand, diversity is celebrated (Cinco de Mayo, Martin Luther King Day and Chinese New Year all get their due), but on the other hand, many Americans are comfortable with the status quo.

Immigration is at the crux of the matter. Immigrants currently make up about 12% of the population. About 470,000 newcomers enter the US legally each year, with the majority from Mexico, followed by Asia and Europe. Another 11 million or so are in the country illegally. This is the issue that makes Americans edgy, especially as it gets politicized.

'Immigration reform' has been a Washington buzzword for more than a decade. Some people believe the nation's current system deals with illegal immigrants too leniently – that walls should be built on the border, immigrants who are here unlawfully should be deported and employers who hire them should be fined. Other Americans think those rules are too harsh – that immigrants who have been here for years working, contributing to society and abiding by the law deserve amnesty. Perhaps they could pay a fine and fill out the paperwork to become citizens while continuing to live here with their families. Despite several attempts, Congress has not been able to pass a comprehensive package addressing illegal immigration, though it has put through various measures to beef up enforcement.

Age has a lot to do with Americans' multicultural tolerance. When asked in a recent survey if immigration strengthens the nation, only

ROCK STARS

NPR radio host Terry Gross interviews Americans from all walks of life, from rock stars to environmental activists to nuclear scientists. Listen online at www.npr.org/freshair.

KNOW YOUR GENERATIONS

American culture is often stratified by age groups. Here's a quick rundown to help you tell Generation X from Y, and then some.

» **Baby Boomers** – those born from 1946 to 1964. After American soldiers came home from WWII, they got busy with the ladies, and the birthrate exploded (hence the term 'baby boom'). Youthful experimentation, self-expression and social activism was often followed by midlife affluence.

» **Generation X** – those born between 1961 and 1981. Characterized by their rejection of Baby Boomer values, skepticism and alienation are X's pop-culture hallmarks.

» **Generation Y** – those born from roughly the early 1980s to early 1990s (aka Millennials). Known for being brash and self-confident, they were the first to grow up with the internet.

» **Generation Next** – overlaps with Gen Y, but basically applies to those born in the 1990s. Weaned on iPods, text messaging, instant messaging and social-networking websites, they are a work in progress. Stay tuned (and check their Facebook page for updates).

about one-third of older Americans said yes, whereas more than half of 18- to 26-year-olds said yes, according to the Pew Research Center. In a similar survey, those aged 60 and older were asked if it's acceptable for whites and African Americans to date each other: 35% said no, but that dropped to 6% when asked of Americans aged 30 and younger.

The US holds the world's second-largest Spanish-speaking population, behind Mexico and just ahead of Spain. Hispanics are also the fastest-growing minority group in the nation.

Many people point to the election of President Barack Obama as proof of America's multicultural achievements. It's not just his personal story (white mother, black father, Muslim name, has lived among the diverse cultures of Hawaii, Indonesia and the Midwest, among others). Or that he's the first African American to hold the nation's highest office (in a country where as recently as the 1960s blacks couldn't even vote in certain regions). It's that Americans of all races and creeds voted overwhelmingly to elect the self-described 'mutt' and embrace his message of diversity and change.

Religion

When the Pilgrims (early settlers to the United States who fled their European homeland to escape religious persecution) came ashore, they were adamant that their new country would be one of religious tolerance. They valued the freedom to practice religion so highly they refused to make their Protestant faith official state policy. What's more, they forbade the government from doing anything that might sanction one religion or belief over another. Separation of church and state became the law of the land.

Americans are increasingly defining their spiritual beliefs outside of organized religion. The proportion of those who say they have 'no religion' is now around 16%. Some in this catch-all category disavow religion altogether (around 4%), but the majority sustain spiritual beliefs that simply fall outside the box.

Today, Protestants are on the verge of becoming a minority in the country they founded. According to the Pew Research Center, Protestant numbers have declined steadily to just over 50%. Meanwhile, other faiths have held their own or seen their numbers rise.

The country is also in a period of exceptional religious fluidity. Forty-four percent of American adults have left the denomination of their childhood for another denomination, another faith or no faith at all, according to Pew. A unique era of 'religion shopping' has been ushered in. As for the geographic breakdown: the USA's most Catholic region is shifting from the Northeast to the Southwest; the South is the most evangelical; and the West is the most unaffiliated.

All that said, America's biggest schism isn't between religions or even between faith and skepticism. It's between fundamentalist and progressive interpretations within each faith. Most Americans don't care much if you're Catholic, Episcopalian, Buddhist or atheist. What they do care about are your views on abortion, contraception, gay rights, stem-cell research, teaching of evolution, school prayer and government displays of religious icons. The country's Religious Right (the oft-used term for evangelical Christians) has pushed these issues onto center stage, and the group has been effective at using politics to codify its conservative beliefs into law. This effort has prompted a slew of court cases, testing the nation's principles on separation of church and state. The split remains one of America's biggest culture wars, and it almost always plays a role in politics, especially elections.

Key Sports Sites

» www.mlb.com – baseball

» www.nfl.com – football

» www.nba.com – basketball

» www.nascar.com – auto-racing

Lifestyle

The USA has one of the world's highest standards of living. The median household income is around $51,000, though it varies by region (with higher earnings in the Northeast and West followed by the Midwest and the South. Wages also vary by ethnicity, with African Americans and Hispanics earning less than whites and Asians ($34,000 and $38,000 respectively, versus $52,000 and $66,000, according to census data).

Nearly 87% of Americans are high-school graduates, while some 30% go on to graduate from college with a four-year bachelor's degree.

More often than not there are two married parents in an American household, and both of them work. Single parents head 9% of households. Twenty-eight percent of Americans work more than 40 hours per week. Divorce is common – more than 40% of first marriages go kaput – but both divorce and marriage rates have declined over the last three decades. Despite the high divorce rate, Americans spend more than $160 billion annually on weddings. The average number of children in an American family is two.

Four million Americans tune in every week to Midwestern raconteur Garrison Keillor's old-timey radio show, *A Prairie Home Companion;* listen to the live music, sketches and storytelling online at http://prairiehome.publicradio.org.

While many Americans hit the gym or walk, bike or jog regularly, over 50% don't exercise at all during their free time, according to the Centers for Disease Control (CDC). Health researchers speculate this lack of exercise and Americans' fondness for sugary and fatty foods have led to rising obesity and diabetes rates. More than two-thirds of Americans are overweight, with one-third considered obese, the CDC says.

About 26% of Americans volunteer their time to help others or help a cause. This is truer in the Midwest, followed by the West, South and Northeast, according to the Corporation for National and Community Service. Eco-consciousness has entered the mainstream: over 75% of Americans recycle at home, and most big chain grocery stores – including Wal-Mart – now sell organic foods.

Americans tend to travel close to home. Just over one-third of Americans have passports so most people take vacations within the 50 states.

STATES & TRAITS

Regional US stereotypes now have solid data behind them, thanks to a 2008 study titled *The Geography of Personality*. Researchers processed more than a half-million personality assessments collected from individual US citizens, then looked at where certain traits stacked up on the map. Turns out 'Minnesota nice' is for real – the most 'agreeable' states cluster in the Midwest, Great Plains and South. These places rank highest for friendliness and cooperation. The most neurotic states? They line up in the Northeast. But New York didn't place number one, as you might expect; that honor goes to West Virginia. Many of the most 'open' states lie out West. California, Nevada, Oregon and Washington all rate high for being receptive to new ideas, although they lag behind Washington, DC, and New York. The most dutiful and self-disciplined states sit in the Great Plains and Southwest, led by New Mexico. Go figure.

According to the US Department of Commerce's Office of Travel and Tourism Industries, Mexico and Canada are the top countries for international getaways, followed by the UK, Italy, France, Germany and Japan. America's reputation as the 'no-vacation nation,' with many workers having only five to 10 paid annual vacation days, contributes to this stay-at-home scenario.

Sports

What really draws Americans together, sometimes slathered in blue body paint or with foam-rubber cheese wedges on their heads, is sports. It provides a social glue, so whether a person is conservative or liberal, married or single, Mormon or pagan, chances are come Monday at the office they'll be chatting about the weekend performance of their favorite team.

The Super Bowl costs America $800 million dollars in lost workplace productivity as employees gossip about the game, make bets and shop for new TVs online.

SUPER BOWL

The fun and games go on all year long. In spring and summer there's baseball nearly every day. In fall and winter, a weekend or Monday night doesn't feel right without a football game on, and through the long days and nights of winter there's plenty of basketball to keep the adrenaline going. Those are the big three sports. Car racing has revved up interest in recent years. Major League Soccer (MLS) is attracting an ever-increasing following. And ice hockey, once favored only in northern climes, is popular nationwide, with three Stanley Cup winners since 2000 hailing from either California or the South.

Baseball

Despite high salaries and its biggest stars being dogged by steroid rumors, baseball remains America's pastime. It may not command the same TV viewership (and subsequent advertising dollars) as football, but baseball has 162 games over a season versus 16 for football.

Besides, baseball isn't about seeing it on TV, it's all about the live version: being at the ballpark on a sunny day, sitting in the bleachers with a beer and hot dog, and indulging in the seventh-inning stretch, when the entire park erupts in a communal singalong of 'Take Me Out to the Ballgame.' The play-offs, held every October, still deliver excitement and unexpected champions. The New York Yankees, Boston Red Sox and Chicago Cubs continue to be America's favorite teams, even when they're abysmal (the Cubs haven't won a World Series in more than 100 years).

Tickets are relatively inexpensive – seats average about $14 at most stadiums – and are easy to get for most games. Minor-league baseball games cost half as much, and can be even more fun, with lots of audience participation, stray chickens and dogs running across the field and wild throws from the pitcher's mound. For info, click to www.minorleaguebaseball.com.

Football

Football is big, physical and rolling in dough. With the shortest season and least number of games of any of the major sports, every match takes on the emotion of an epic battle, where the results matter and an unfortunate injury can deal a lethal blow to a team's play-off chances.

Football's also the toughest because it's played in fall and winter in all manner of rain, sleet and snow. Some of history's most memorable matches have occurred at below-freezing temperatures. Green Bay Packers fans are in a class by themselves when it comes to severe weather. Their stadium in Wisconsin, known as Lambeau Field, was the site of the infamous Ice Bowl, a 1967 championship game against the Dallas Cowboys where the temperature plummeted to –13°F – mind you, that was with a wind-chill factor of –48°F.

The rabidly popular Super Bowl is pro football's championship match, held in late January or early February. The bowl games (such as Rose Bowl and Orange Bowl) are college football's title matches, held on and around New Year's Day.

Even college and high-school football games enjoy an intense amount of pomp and circumstance, with cheerleaders, marching bands, mascots, songs and mandatory pre- and post-game rituals, especially the tailgate – a full-blown beer-and-barbecue feast that takes place over portable grills in parking lots where games are played.

Basketball

The teams bringing in the most fans these days include the Chicago Bulls (thanks to the lingering Michael Jordan effect), Detroit Pistons (a rowdy crowd in which riots have broken out), Cleveland Cavaliers, the San Antonio Spurs and last but not least, the Los Angeles Lakers, which won five championships between 2000 and 2010. Small-market teams like Sacramento and Portland have true-blue fans, and such cities can be great places to take in a game.

College level basketball also draws millions of fans, especially every spring when March Madness rolls around. This series of college play-off games culminates in the Final Four, when the four remaining teams compete for a spot in the championship game. The Cinderella stories and unexpected outcomes rival the pro league for excitement. The games are widely televised – and bet on. This is when Las Vegas bookies earn their keep.

Native Americans

Although a fraction of its pre-Columbian size, there are more than three million Native Americans from 500 tribes, speaking some 175 languages and residing in every region of the United States. Not surprisingly, North America's indigenous people are an extremely diverse bunch with unique customs and beliefs, molded in part by the landscapes they inhabit – from the Inuit living in the frozen tundra of Alaska, to the many tribes of the arid, mountainous Southwest.

Culturally speaking, America's tribes today grapple with questions about how to prosper in contemporary America while protecting their traditions from erosion and their lands from further exploitation, and how to lift their people from poverty while maintaining their sense of identity and the sacred.

Always observe reservation etiquette. Most tribes ban alcohol. Ask before taking pictures or drawing; if granted permission, a tip is polite and often expected. Treat ceremonies like church services; watch respectfully (no photos), and wear modest clothing. Ask before discussing religion and respect each person's boundaries. Silent listening shows respect.

The Tribes

The Cherokee, Navajo, Chippewa and Sioux are the largest tribal groupings in the lower 48 (ie barring Alaska and Hawaii). Other well-known tribes include the Choctaw (descendants of a great mound-building society originally based in the Mississippi valley), the Apache (a nomadic hunter-gatherer tribe that fiercely resisted forced relocation) and the Hopi (a Pueblo people with Southwest roots dating back 2000 years).

Cherokee

The Cherokee (www.cherokee.org) originally lived in an area of more than 80 million acres, covering a huge swath of the south (including Tennessee, Virginia, the Carolinas and Kentucky). However, in 1830 they

NATIVE AMERICAN ART & CRAFTS

It would take an encyclopedia to cover the myriad artistic traditions of America's tribal peoples, from pre-Columbian rock art to the contemporary multimedia scene.

What ties such diverse traditions together is that Native American art and crafts are not just functional for everyday life, but can also serve ceremonial purposes and have social and religious significance. The patterns and symbols are woven with meanings that provide a window into the heart of Native American peoples. This is as true of Zuni fetish carvings as it is of patterned Navajo rugs, Southwestern pueblo pottery, Sioux beadwork, Inuit sculptures and Cherokee and Hawaiian woodcarvings, to name just a few examples.

In addition to preserving their culture, contemporary Native American artists have used sculpture, painting, textiles, film, literature and performance art to reflect and critique modernity since the mid-20th century, especially after the civil rights activism of the 1960s and cultural renaissance of the '70s. *Native North American Art,* by Berlo and Phillips, offers an introduction to North America's varied indigenous art .

Many tribes run craft outlets and galleries, usually in the main towns of reservations. The **Indian Arts & Crafts Board** (IACB; www.iacb.doi.gov) lists Native American–owned galleries and shops state-by-state online (click on 'Source Directory of Businesses'.)

were forcibly relocated east of the Mississippi and today reside largely in Oklahoma (home to more than 200,000 Cherokee). Tahlequah has been the Cherokee capital since 1839.

Cherokee society was originally matrilineal, with bloodlines traced through the mother. Like some other native tribes, the Cherokee recognize seven cardinal directions: north, south, east and west along with up, down and center (or within).

Navajo

The Navajo Reservation (www.discovernavajo.com) is by far the largest and most populous in the US. Also called the Navajo Nation and Navajoland, it covers 17.5 million acres (over 27,000 sq miles) in Arizona and parts of New Mexico and Utah.

The Navajo were feared nomads and warriors who both traded with and raided the Pueblos and who fought settlers and the US military. They also borrowed generously from other traditions: they acquired sheep and horses from the Spanish, learned pottery and weaving from the Pueblos, and picked up silversmithing from Mexico. Today, the Navajo are renowned for their woven rugs, pottery and inlaid silver jewelry, as well as for their intricate sandpainting, which is used in healing ceremonies.

Chippewa

Although Chippewa or Ojibway is the commonly used term for this tribe, members prefer to be called Anishinabe. They are based in Minnesota, Wisconsin and Michigan. According to legend, the Chippewa once lived on the Atlantic coast and gradually migrated west over 500 years. They traditionally survived by fishing, hunting and farming corn and squash. They also harvested (by canoe) wild rice, which remains an essential Chippewa tradition.

Sioux

Like the Iroquois, the Sioux is not one tribe but a consortium of three major tribes (and various subbranches) speaking different dialects but sharing a common subculture. Prior to European arrival they lived in the northeast of present-day North America but slowly migrated to the Great Plains by 1800. The Sioux were fierce defenders of their lands, and fought many battles to preserve them, although the slaughter of the buffalo (on whom they had survived) did more to remove them from their lands than anything else. Today, they live in Minnesota, Nebraska, North Dakota and South Dakota – the latter contains the 2-million-acre Pine Ridge Reservation, the nation's second-largest.

700-1400

North America's largest ancient city, Cahokia, supports a population of 10,000 to 20,000 at its peak. By 1400 it is mysteriously abandoned.

750-1300

Ancestral Pueblo peoples living near Chaco Canyon flourish. This advanced desert civilization develops adobe dwellings in enormous complexes.

1831

Following the 1830 *Indian Removal Act*, Cherokee and other tribes are forced to abandon homelands to areas west of the Mississippi. Thousands die on the 1000-mile Trail of Tears.

1876

Lakota chief Sitting Bull defeats Custer at the Battle of Little Big Horn, one of the last military victories by Native Americans in the effort to protect their lands.

1968

The American Indian Movement is founded. Through protests, marches and demonstrations, AIM brings attention to marginalized peoples.

1968

Navajo Community College becomes the first college on any reservation founded and run by Native Americans. Later, other tribal community colleges are founded, growing to 30 today.

1975

President Nixon passes the *Indian Self-Determination Act*, empowering Native Americans to control how federal moneys are spent on native matters.

American Cuisine

Long before the iconic golden arches of McDonald's reigned over the vast, agriculturally rich lands of the USA, Wampanoag tribespeople brought food to help the Pilgrims stave off starvation over the winter of 1620, thus kicking off the very first Thanksgiving.

Since then Americans have mixed myriad food cultures to create their own, based on the rich bounty of the continent. Americans took pride in that bounty, drawing on the seafood of the North Atlantic, Gulf of Mexico and Pacific Ocean; the fertility of Midwest farmlands; and vast western ranchlands that made beef, pork and chicken everyday staples.

Classic American Diners

» **Miss Worcester Diner**, Worcester, MA

» **Mickey's Diner**, St. Paul, MN

» **Bob's Café**, Sioux Falls, SD

» **Ann's Chicken Fry House**, Oklahoma City, OK

» **Peppermill**, Las Vegas

» **Lone Spur Cafe**, Prescott, AZ

» **Gus Balon's**, Tucson, AZ

Massive waves of immigrants enriched American gastronomy by adapting foreign ideas to home kitchens, from Italian pizza and German hamburgers to Eastern European borscht, Mexican huevos rancheros and Japanese sushi. Later, a vast market and transportation system made fresh, canned, boxed and frozen foods available to everyone – so much so, it can be argued, that many Americans grew fat (and even obese) on the abundance of fast food and junk food. It is not by accident that phrases such as 'grab a bite,' and 'pick up some takeout' are quintessential American colloquialisms, along with 'road food' and 'the munchies.' Such ideas had the effect of American cooking not being taken seriously by the rest of the world.

Not until the 1960s did food and wine become serious topics for newspapers, magazines and TV, led by a Californian named Julia Child who taught Americans how to cook French food through black-and-white programs broadcast from Boston's public TV station. By the 1970s, everyday folks (and not just hippies) had started turning their attention to issues of organic, natural foods and sustainable agriculture. In the 1980s and '90s, the 'foodie revolution' – choosing 'arugula over iceberg' lettuce, as *Time* magazine put it in 2007 – encouraged entrepreneurs to open restaurants featuring regional American cuisine, from the South to the Pacific Northwest, that would rank with Europe's best.

Staples & Specialties

Americans have such easy access to regional foods that once-unique specialties are now often readily available everywhere: a Bostonian might just as easily have a taco or barbecue ribs for lunch as a Houstonian would eat Maine lobster for dinner.

Breakfast

Long billed by American nutritionists as 'the most important meal of the day,' morning meals in America are big business – no matter how many folks insist on skipping them. From a giant stack of buttermilk pancakes at a vintage diner to a quick Egg McMuffin at the McDonald's drive-thru window, to lavish Sunday brunches, Americans love their eggs and bacon, their waffles and hashbrowns, and their big glasses of orange juice. Most of all, they love that seemingly inalienable American right: a steaming cup of morning coffee with unlimited refills. (Try asking for a free refill in other nations, and you'll get anything from an eye-roll to a smirk to downright confusion.)

Lunch

Usually after a midmorning coffee break, an American worker's lunch hour affords only a sandwich, quick burger or hearty salad. The formal 'business lunch' is more common in big cities like New York, where food is not necessarily as important as the conversation.

While you'll spot diners drinking a beer or a glass of wine with their lunch, long gone are the days when the 'three martini lunch' was socially acceptable. It was a phenomenon common enough in the mid-20th century to become a kind of catchphrase for indulgent business lunches, usually written off as a corporate, tax-deductible expense. The classic noontime beverage, in fact, is a far cry from a martini: iced tea (and yes, almost always with unlimited refills).

Top Food TV Shows

- Anthony Bourdain: No Reservations (Travel Channel)
- Top Chef (Bravo)
- Iron Chef America (Food Network)
- Diners, Drive-ins and Dives (Food Network)
- Bizarre Foods with Andrew Zimmern (Travel Channel)

Dinner

Usually early in the evening, Americans settle in to a more substantial weeknight dinner, which, given the workload of so many two-career families, might be takeout (eg pizza or Chinese food) or prepackaged meals cooked in a microwave. Desserts tend toward ice cream, pies and cakes. Some families still cook a traditional Sunday night dinner, when relatives and friends gather for a big feast, or grill outside and go picnicking on weekends.

Quick Eats

Eating hot dogs or pretzels from city street carts or tacos and barbecue from roadside trucks carries a small risk that you might pick up some nasty bacteria, but generally fast food tends to be safe and vendors are usually supervised by the local health department. At festivals and county fairs, you can take your pick from cotton candy, corn dogs, candy apples, funnel cakes, chocolate-covered frozen bananas and plenty of tasty regional specialties. Farmers markets often have more wholesome, affordable prepared foods.

NYC: Foodie Heaven

They say that you could eat at a different restaurant every night of your life in New York City, and not exhaust the possibilities. Considering that according to the Zagat Guide, there are more than 23,000 restaurants in the five boroughs, it's true (that is, unless you live until 100). Owing to its huge immigrant population and an influx of 49 million tourists annually, New York captures the title of America's greatest restaurant city, hands down. Its diverse neighborhoods serve up authentic Italian food and thin-crust pizza, all manner of Asian food, French *haute cuisine* and

THE AMERICAN DIET CRAZE

America's almost as well know for its fad diets as it is for its fast food. Some of the most bizarre diets? In the 1920s and 1930s, there was the Cigarette Diet, the Bananas and Skim Milk Diet and the Grapefruit Diet – also called the Hollywood Diet. The 1960s brought the Steak and Martini Diet; the 1980s ushered in the Cabbage Soup Diet. In the 1990s, fat free and high carb was all the rage – until, that is, the Atkins Diet came in with its low-carb mantra. Stars embraced the 'Master Cleanse,' aka the Lemonade Diet, and then just as quickly abandoned it.

classic Jewish deli food, from bagels to piled-high pastrami on rye. More exotic cuisines are found here as well, from Ethiopian to Slavic.

Arthur Schwartz's New York City Food (2008), by famous foodie Arthur Schwartz, reveals where to find every NYC specialty, from bagels and pizza to Gray's Papaya juice and cheesecake, and includes more than 100 recipes. Finally, don't let NYC's image as expensive get to you: according to the Zagat Guides the average cost of a meal – including drink, tax, and tip – is $42. There may be no free lunch in New York, but compared to other world cities, eating here can be a bargain.

New England: Clam Bakes & Lobster Boils

New England's claim to have the nation's best seafood is hard to beat, because the North Atlantic offers up clams, mussels, oysters and huge lobsters, along with shad, bluefish and cod. New Englanders love a good chowder (seafood stew) and a good clambake, an almost ritual meal where the shellfish are buried in a pit fire with corn, chicken, potatoes and sausages. Fried clam fritters and lobster rolls (lobster meat with mayonnaise served in a bread bun) are served throughout the region. There are excellent cheeses made in Vermont, cranberries (a Thanksgiving staple) harvested in Massachusetts and maple syrup from New England's forests. Maine's coast is lined with lobster shacks; baked beans and brown bread are Boston specialties; and Rhode Islanders pour coffee syrup into milk and embrace traditional cornmeal johnnycakes.

Mid-Atlantic: Cheesesteaks, Crabcakes & Scrapple

From New York down through Maryland and Virginia, the middle Atlantic states share a long coastline and a cornucopia of apple, pear and berry farms. New Jersey and New York's Long Island are famous for their spuds (potatoes). Chesapeake Bay's blue crabs are the finest anywhere and Virginia salt-cured 'country-style' hams are served with biscuits. In Philadelphia, you can gorge on 'Philly' cheesesteaks, made with thin, sautéed beef and onions and melted cheese on a bun. In Pennsylvania Dutch country, stop by a farm restaurant for chicken pot pie, noodles and meatloaf-like scrapple. The wines of New York's Finger Lakes, Hudson Valley and Long Island are well worth sampling.

The South: BBQ, Biscuits & Gumbo

No region is prouder of its food culture than the South, which has a long history of mingling Anglo, French, African, Spanish and Native American foods in dishes such as slow-cooked barbecue, which has as many meaty and saucy variations as there are towns in the South. Southern fried chicken is crisp outside and moist inside. In Florida, dishes made with alligator, shrimp and conch incorporate hot chili peppers and tropical spices. Breakfasts are as big as can be, and treasured dessert recipes tend to produce big layer cakes or pies made with pecans, bananas and citrus. Light, fluffy hot biscuits are served well buttered, and grits (ground corn cooked to a porridge-like consistency) are a passion among Southerners, as are cool mint julep cocktails.

Louisiana's legendary cuisine is influenced by colonial French and Spanish cultures, Afro-Caribbean cooking and Choctaw Indians' traditions. Cajun food is found in the bayou country and marries native spices such as sassafras and chili peppers with provincial French cooking. Creole food is more urban, and centered in New Orleans, where dishes such as shrimp remoulade, crabmeat ravigote, crawfish étouffée and beignets are ubiquitous.

FOOD TRUCKS

The hottest dining craze on wheels is food trucks. From crab-cake tacos to red velvet cupcakes, there's no telling what creative, healthy, gourmet, decadent, or downright bizarre twist on 'fast food' you'll discover. To find the best trucks, visit Portland, Austin, Minneapolis, Los Angeles, New York, Las Vegas, and Miami.

Midwest: Burgers, Bacon, & Beer

Throughout the Midwest they eat big and with plenty of gusto. Portions are huge – this is farm country, where people need sustenance to get their day's work done. So you might start off the day with eggs, bacon and toast; have a double cheeseburger and potato salad for lunch; and fork into steak and baked potatoes for dinner – all washed down with a cold brew, often one of the growing numbers of microbrews. Barbecue is very popular here, especially in Kansas City, St Louis and Chicago. Chicago is also an ethnically diverse culinary center, with some of the country's top restaurants. One of the best places to sample Midwestern foods is at a county fair, which offers everything from bratwurst to fried dough to grilled corn on the cob. Elsewhere at diners and family restaurants, you'll taste the varied influences of Eastern European, Scandinavian, Latino and Asian immigrants, especially in the cities.

Louisiana is renowned among epicures for its French-influenced Cajun and Creole cuisine. Famous dishes include gumbo, a roux-based stew of chicken and shellfish, or sausage and often okra; jambalaya, a rice-based dish with tomatoes, sausage and shrimp; and blackened catfish.

The Southwest: Chile, Steak & Smoking Hot Salsa

Two ethnic groups define southwestern food culture: the Spanish and Mexicans, who controlled territories from Texas to California until well into the 19th century. While there is little actual Spanish food today, the Spanish brought cattle to Mexico, which the Mexicans adapted to their own corn-and-chile-based gastronomy to make tacos, tortillas, enchiladas, burritos, chimichangas and other dishes made of corn or flour pancakes filled with everything from chopped meat and poultry to beans. Don't leave New Mexico without trying a bowl of spicy green chile stew. Steaks and barbecue are always favorites on Southwestern menus, and beer is the drink of choice for dinner and a night out. Don't miss the fist-sized burritos in San Francisco's Mission District and fish tacos in San Diego.

VEG HEAVEN

Some of the most highly regarded American restaurants cater exclusively to vegetarians and vegans. Vegetarian and vegan restaurants abound in major US cities, though not always in small towns and rural areas away from the coasts. Eateries that are exclusively vegetarian or vegan are noted throughout this book using the 🖉 symbol. To find more vegetarian and vegan restaurants, browse the online directory at www.happycow.net. Here are a few of our go-to faves for when the veggie cravings hit.

- **Green Elephant**, Portland, ME (p235)
- **Veggie Planet**, Cambridge, MA (p180)
- **Counter**, NYC (p100)
- **Blossom**, NYC (p101)
- **Moosewood Restaurant**, Ithaca, NY (p121)
- **Mama's Vegetarian**, Philadelphia (p146)
- **Café Zenith**, Pittsburgh (p159)
- **Grit**, Athens, Georgia (p390)
- **Green** (p670)
- **Bouldin Creek Coffeehouse** (p660)
- **Poco**, Bisbee, AZ (p837)
- **Fresh Mint**, Scottsdale, AZ (p815)
- **Andy Nguyen's**, Sacramento, CA (p985)
- **Ubuntu**, Napa Valley (p977)

California: Farm-to-Table Restaurants & Taquerías

Owing to its vastness and variety of microclimates, California is truly America's cornucopia for fruits and vegetables, and a gateway to myriad Asian markets. The state's natural resources are overwhelming, with wild salmon, Dungeness crab and oysters from the ocean; robust produce year-round; and artisanal products such as cheese, bread, olive oil, wine and chocolate. Starting in the 1970s and '80s, star chefs such as Alice Waters and Wolfgang Puck pioneered 'California cuisine' by incorporating the best local ingredients into simple, yet delectable, preparations. The influx of Asian immigrants, especially after the Vietnam War, enriched the state's urban food cultures with Chinatowns, Koreatowns and Japantowns, along with huge enclaves of Mexican Americans who maintain their own culinary traditions across the state. Global fusion restaurants are another hallmark of California's cuisine scene.

Regional Weird Foods

» Scrapple (rural Pennsylvania)

» Lutefisk (Minnesota)

» Deep-fried cheese curds (Wisconsin)

» Beef on Weck (Western New York)

» Frito Pie (Texas)

» Spiedie (Binghamton, NY)

» Akutaq (Alaska)

» Spam sushi (Hawaii)

Pacific Northwest: Salmon & Starbucks

The cuisine of the Pacific Northwest region draws on the traditions of the local tribes of Native Americans, whose diets traditionally centered on game, seafood – especially salmon – and foraged mushrooms, fruits and berries. Seattle spawned the modern international coffeehouse craze with Starbucks; and the beers and wines from both Washington and Oregon have come up to international standards, especially Pinot Noirs and Rieslings.

Hawaii: Island Style

In the middle of the Pacific Ocean, Hawaii is rooted in a Polynesian food culture that takes full advantage of locally caught fish such as mahimahi, 'opakapaka, 'ono and 'ahi. Traditional luau celebrations include cooking kalua pig in an underground pit layered with hot stones and ti leaves. Hawaii's contemporary cuisine incorporates fresh, island-grown produce and borrows liberally from the islands' many Asian and European immigrant groups. This also happens to be the only state to grow coffee commercially; 100% Kona beans from the Big Island have the most gourmet cachet.

Celebrations

The late historian Arthur Schlesinger Jr noted that after just a single generation, the children of American immigrants lost nearly all ties to their ethnicities – except with regard to food culture.

Thanksgiving may be the only holiday (held the last Thursday in November) where most Americans would agree on the menu – roast turkey, stuffing, mashed potatoes, cranberry sauce and, perhaps, pumpkin pie – but even then appetizers, side dishes and desserts might be Latino, African or Hawaiian.

SLOW, LOCAL, ORGANIC

The Slow Food movement, along with renewed enthusiasm for eating local, organically grown fare is a leading trend in American restaurants. The movement, which was arguably started in 1971 by chef Alice Waters at Berkeley's Chez Panisse (p974), continues with First Lady Michelle Obama – the First Lady of food if there ever was one – and her daughters, who have planted an organic garden on the White House lawn. Recently, farmers markets have been popping up all across the country and they're a great place to meet locals and take a big bite out of America's cornucopia of foods, from heritage fruit and vegetables to fresh, savory and sweet regional delicacies.

That said, these days the weak US dollar makes the occasional foray into a posh restaurant far less expensive than in cities such as London, Paris and Tokyo. If you go for it, always call to make a reservation (or ask your hotel concierge to do so), ask if there is a dress code, and be prepared to accept a very early or quite late table at popular star-chefs restaurants.

For typical restaurant opening hours, see p1156, and for average meal costs, see p1157.

Habits & Customs

Americans tend to eat early at restaurants and at home, so don't be surprised to find a restaurant half full at noon or 5:30pm. In smaller towns, it may be hard to find anywhere to eat after 8:30pm or 9pm. Dinner parties for adults usually begin around 6:30pm or 7pm with cocktails followed by a buffet or sit-down meal. If invited to dinner, it's polite to be prompt: ideally, you should plan to arrive within 15 minutes of the designated time.

Americans are notoriously informal in their dining manners, although they will usually wait until everyone is served before eating. Many foods are eaten with the fingers, and an entire piece of bread may be buttered and eaten all at once. To the surprise of some foreign visitors, the sight of beer bottles on the dinner table is not uncommon.

Do's & Don'ts

» Do tip: 15% of the total bill is standard; tip 20% (or more) for excellent service.

» It's customary to place your napkin on your lap, even more the meal is served

» In general, try to avoid putting your elbows on the table.

» Wait until everyone is served to begin eating.

» In formal situations, diners customarily wait to eat until the host(ess) has lifted her fork.

» Many Americans say a prayer before meals; it's fine to sit quietly if you prefer not to participate.

Cooking Courses

Even more Americans are realizing that they want to be able to cook better (or just plain cook). Cooking shows have become popular on TV, and cooking classes taught by culinary professionals are now offered at some high-end cookware shops such as **Williams-Sonoma** (www.williams-sonoma.com) and **Sur la Table** (www.surlatable.com).

Cooking schools that offer courses for enthusiastic amateur chefs on vacation include the following, though this list is by no means exhaustive:

California Sushi Academy (www.sushi-academy.com) Apprentice in the art of finessing raw fish in Los Angeles.

Central Market Cooking School (www.centralmarket.com) Heat things up in the kitchen in major Texas cities.

Chopping Block Cooking School (www.thechoppingblock.net) Master knife skills; meet the 'Wine Goddess' in Chicago.

Cookin' Cajun Cooking School (www.cookincajun.com) Feast on Cajun and Creole delicacies in New Orleans.

Cook's World (www.cooksworld.net) Try rustic bread baking or street-food recipes from around the world in Seattle.

Heat and Spice Cooking School (http://heatandspice.com) Vegetarian, grilling, New Orleans-style, Floribbean and world cuisine classes in Chicago.

International Culinary Center (www.internationalculinarycenter.com) Hosts the French Culinary Institute and Italian Culinary Academy in New York City.

Kitchen Window (www.centralmarket.com) Hosts market tours and restaurant crawls, plus classes on baking, outdoor grilling, and world cuisine in Minneapolis.

Natural Gourmet Cookery School (www.naturalgourmetschool.com) Focuses on vegetarian and healthy 'flexitarian' cooking in NYC.

New School of Cooking (www.newschoolofcooking.com) Learn ethnic cooking from around the world in Los Angeles County.

Santa Fe School of Cooking (www.santafeschoolofcooking.com) Unlock the chili-spiced secrets of Southwestern cuisine in New Mexico.

Tante Marie's Cooking School (www.tantemarie.com) Shares farmers market recipes and passes on world culinary traditions in San Francisco.

Wine, Beer & Beyond

Go ahead, crack open that beer: work-hard, play-hard Americans are far from teetotalers. About 67% of American adults drink alcohol, with the majority preferring beer to wine.

Beer

It's hard to deny that beer is about as American as Chevrolet, football, and apple pie: just tune in to the Super Bowl commercials (America's most popular yearly televised event, featuring its most expensive advertisements) and you'll see how beer has become intertwined with American cultural values. Just look at the slogans, celebrating individuality ('This Bud's for You'), sociability ('It's Miller Time!'), ruggedness ('Head for the Mountains') and authenticity ('Real Men Drink Bud Light').

While alcohol sales in the USA have soared to record highs in recent years, only about 20% of Americans drink wine on a regular basis; beer is far more popular. It's more than a thirst-quencher; it is a social beverage that's almost essential for a good picnic, a day at the beach or a 'tailgate party' held outside a sports stadium before the game.

Tips on Tipping

In the USA, where restaurants and bars often pay the legal minimum wage (or less), servers rely on tips for their livelihood. A good rule: tip at least a dollar per drink, or roughly 15% to 20% of the total bill.

After establishing the American beer industry in Milwaukee, 19th-century German immigrants developed ways to make beer in vast quantities and to deliver it all over America. Today about 80% of domestic beer still comes from the Midwest.

Despite their ubiquity, popular brands of American beer have long been the subject of ridicule abroad due to their low alcohol content and 'light' taste. The antithesis to strong European beers, American lager is by far and away the most popular variety of beer, with a relatively low alcohol content of between 3% and 5%. Regardless of what the critics say, sales indicate that American beer is more popular than ever – and now, with the meteoric rise of microbreweries and craft beer, even beer snobs admit that American beer has reinvented itself.

Craft & Local Beer

Today, beer aficionados (otherwise known as beer geeks) sip and savor beer as they would wine, and some urban restaurants even have beer 'programs,' 'sommeliers' and cellars. Many brewpubs and restaurants host beer dinners, a chance to experience just how beers pair with different foods.

Microbrewery and craft beer production is rising meteorically, accounting for 11% of the domestic market in 2010. With more than 1500 craft breweries across the USA, Vermont boasts the most microbreweries per capita. In recent years, it's become possible to 'drink local' all over the country as microbreweries pop up in urban centers, small towns, and unexpected places.

Wine

In the seminal 1972 film *The Godfather*, Marlon Brando's Vito Corleone muses, 'I like to drink wine more than I used to.' The country soon followed suit, and nearly four decades later, Americans are still drinking more wine than ever. According to the *Los Angeles Times*, 2010 marked the first year that the US actually consumed more wine than France.

To the raised eyebrows of European winemakers, who used to regard even California wines as second class, many American wines are now even (gulp!) winning prestigious international awards. In fact, the nation is the world's 4th-largest producer of wine, behind Italy, France and Spain.

Wine isn't cheap in the US, as it's considered a luxury rather than a staple – go ahead and blame the Puritans for that. But it's possible to procure a perfectly drinkable bottle of American wine at a liquor or wine shop for around US$8 or $10.

DUI (driving under the influence) is taken very seriously in the USA (see p1176). Designating a sober driver who doesn't drink has become a widespread practice among groups of friends consuming alcohol at restaurants, bars, nightclubs and parties.

Wine Regions

Today almost 90% of US wine comes from California, while Oregon, Washington and New York wines have achieved international status.

Without a doubt, the country's hotbed of wine tourism is in Northern California, just outside of the Bay Area in Napa and Sonoma Valleys. As other regions, from Oregon's Willamette Valley to Texas' Hill Country to New York's Finger Lakes have evolved as wine regions, they have spawned an entire industry of bed-and-breakfast tourism that seem to go hand and hand with the quest to find the perfect Pinot Noir.

So, what are the best American wines? Amazingly, though it's only been a few decades since many American restaurants served either 'red,' 'white,' or sometimes 'pink' wine, there are many excellent 'New World' wines that have flourished in the rich American soil. The most popular white varietals made in the US are Chardonnay and Sauvignon Blanc; best-selling reds include Cabernet Sauvignon, Merlot, Pinot Noir and Zinfandel.

The Hard Stuff

You might know him by his first name, Jack. (Hint: Daniels is his last name). Good ole Jack Daniels remains the most well-known brand of American whiskey around the world, and is also the oldest continually operating US distillery, going strong since 1870.

While whiskey and bourbon are the most popular American exports, rye, gin and vodka are also crafted in the USA. Bourbon, made from corn, is the only native spirit and traditionally it is made in Kentucky.

Cocktails were invented in America before the Civil War. Born in New Orleans, an appropriately festive city to launch America's contribution to booze history, the first cocktail was the Sazerac – a mix of rye whiskey or brandy, simple syrup, bitters and a dash of absinthe (before it was banned in 1912, that is). American cocktails created at bars in the late

WHEN COCKTAILS IMITATE TELEVISION

Among many American women who came of age during the 1990s and 2000s, *Sex and the City* was not only one of cable television's most beloved shows but one of *the* definitive pop-culture commentaries on love, sex, and relationships around the new millennium. In bars, the TV show inspired sudden allegiance to Cosmopolitans, the show's trademark reddish drink that Carrie, Samantha, Charlotte and Miranda could be seen languidly sipping from a martini glass in almost every episode. Soon, it seemed as though millions of women (and a few sheepish guys, too) were ordering 'Cosmos,' a heady concoction of vodka, triple sec, cranberry juice, and lime.

LEGENDARY AMERICAN DISH ABOUT DRINKING

While these Americans are all lauded for their talents in the arts or entertainment, they were undeniably (and often infamously) associated with the boozing life. Here are a few choice words they have on the subject.

» Ernest Hemingway: 'Always do sober what you said you'd do drunk. That will teach you to keep your mouth shut.'

» Frank Sinatra: 'Alcohol may be man's worst enemy, but the Bible says "love your enemy."'

» Dorothy Parker: 'I'd rather have a bottle in front of me than a frontal lobotomy.'

» WC Fields: 'A woman drove me to drink, and I never had the courtesy to thank her.'

» William Faulkner: 'The tools I need for my work are paper, tobacco, food, and a little whiskey.'

» Homer Simpson: 'Beer – the cause of and solution to all of life's problems.'

19th and early 20th centuries include such long-standing classics as the martini, the Manhattan, and the old-fashioned.

The Vintage Cocktail Craze

Across US cities, it's become decidedly cool to party like it's 1929 by drinking retro cocktails from the days – less than a century ago – that alcohol was illegal to consume across the entire United States. Good old Prohibition, of course, instead of spawning a nation of teetotalers, only solidified a culture in which the forbidden became appealing, it felt good to be bad, fast girls carried flasks of gin in their purses, and so-called respectable citizens congregated in secret 'speakeasies' to drink homemade moonshine and dance to hot jazz.

Fast forward to the 21st century. While Prohibition isn't in danger of being reinstated, you'll find plenty of bars where the spirit of the Roaring 20s –and the illicit 1930s – lives on. Inspired by vintage recipes featuring spirits and elixirs – remember, back in the day you couldn't just grab a bottle of scotch at the grocery store! – these cocktails, complete with ingredients like small-batch liqueurs, whipped egg whites, hand-chipped ice and fresh fruits, are lovingly concocted by nattily dressed bartenders who regard their profession as something between an art and a science.

Blame it on Hollywood: Merlot is just not that cool anymore. Paul Giametti's Academy Award–winning performance in the film *Sideways* singlehandedly destroyed its sophisticated reputation through the following line: 'If anyone orders Merlot, I'm leaving. I am *not* drinking any f*&%ing Merlot!' In the film, he favors Pinot Noir.

Nonalcoholic drinks

Tap water in the USA is safe to drink, though its taste varies depending on the region and city. Most nonalcoholic drinks are quite sugary and served over ice, from Southern-style iced 'sweet tea' and lemonade to quintessential American soft drinks such as Coca-Cola, Pepsi and Dr Pepper, along with retro and nouveau soft-drinks, often made with cane sugar instead of corn syrup.

Interestingly, carbonated nonalcoholic beverages have different nicknames depending on where you order them. In many parts of the South, a 'coke' means any kind of soda, so you may have to specify which kind you mean, for example, if you say 'I'll have a Coke,' the waiter might ask, 'Which kind?' In the Midwest, soda is called 'pop.' On the East Coast and elsewhere, it's called 'soda.' Go figure…

The Coffee Craze

While Americans kick back with beer, and unwind with wine, the country runs on caffeine. The coffee craze has only intensified in the last 25 years, ever since coffeehouse culture exploded in urban centers and spread throughout the country.

Blame it on Starbucks – the coffee that America loves (or loves to hate, or hates to love) above all others. The world's biggest coffee chain was born amidst the Northwest's progressive coffee culture in 1971, when Starbucks opened its first location across from Pike Place Market in Seattle. The idea, to offer a variety of roasted beans from around the world in a comfortable cafe, helped start filling the American coffee mug with more refined, complicated (and expensive) drinks compared to the ubiquitous Folgers and diner cups of joe. By the early 1990s, specialty coffeehouses began springing up across the country, everywhere from cities to university towns.

While many coffee chains only have room for a few chairs and a take-out counter, independent coffee shops support a coffeehouse culture that encourages lingering; think free wi-fi, comfortable indoor and outdoor seating, and little pressure to buy more food and drink, even after camping out at a table for hours. At the most high-level cafes, experienced baristas will happily banter about the origins of any roast and will share their ideas about bean grinds and more.

The most infamous rumor about Coca-Cola, developed in 1886 at an Atlanta pharmacy, is true: once marketed as a medicine, it did indeed contain trace amounts of cocaine. Having once contained about 9 milligrams per glass, cocaine was eliminated from the product in 1903.

Arts & Architecture

Geography and race together create the varied regionalism that is key to understanding America's arts. And despite a popular affinity for technology, nature and wilderness still inspire the nation's soul and, consequently, much of its art.

There is no question that digital technology is currently unmaking and remaking every medium and influencing every aesthetic in the US. America is in the middle of a global revolution, in which economics, production, distribution, tools, community, performance, expression and audience experience are all changing.

Yet to understand the art of tomorrow, you've got to first look at the history of the arts in America – including literature, architecture, painting, photography, theater and dance – today.

Film

Hollywood and American film are virtually inseparable. No less an American icon than the White House itself, Hollywood is increasingly the product of an internationalized cinema and film culture. This evolution is partly pure business: Hollywood studios are the showpieces of multinational corporations, and funding flows to talent that brings the biggest grosses, regardless of nationality.

But this shift is also creative. It's Hollywood's recognition that if the studios don't incorporate the immense filmmaking talent emerging worldwide, they will be made irrelevant by it. Co-option is an old Hollywood strategy, used most recently to subvert the challenge posed by the independent film movement of the 1990s that kicked off with daring homegrown films like *Sex, Lies, and Videotape* and *Reservoir Dogs*, and innovative European imports. That said, for the most part, mainstream American audiences remain steadfastly indifferent to foreign films.

If digital technology isn't killing celluloid, it is at least its archenemy: movies can now be made and shown without using film. With celluloid increasingly out of the picture, production and distribution, once so prohibitively expensive and complex they were easily controlled by a few privileged gatekeepers (ie studios) have never been more accessible. Some praise film's new democratic nature, while others bemoan a culture in which anyone, regardless of talent or skill, can ostensibly make a film for the price of a laptop and an inexpensive digital camera.

JHUMPA LAHIRI

Jhumpa Lahiri won the Pulitzer Prize for her first breathtaking collection of stories, *The Interpreter of Maladies*, about the experience of Indian immigrants in the contemporary United States.

Television

In the 20th century, it could be argued that TV was the defining medium of the modern age. An average American still watches 35 hours of TV a week, an all-time high. Americans *love* TV, but they are watching differently: recording or downloading online, viewing according to their schedules (not the networks') and skipping the commercials. As the internet messes with the economics of this corporate-owned, ad-driven entertainment, TV executives shudder.

TV was developed in the USA and Europe in the 1920s and '30s, and the first commercial TV set was introduced at the 1939 New York World's Fair. After WWII, owning a set became a status symbol for America's blossoming middle class, and radio and movies wilted under TV's cathode-tube glow. Cable arrived in the 1980s and satellite services rapidly grew in the 1990s, expanding TV's handful of channels into dozens, and then hundreds.

For many decades, critics sneered that TV was lowbrow, and movie stars wouldn't be caught dead on it. But well-written, thought-provoking shows have existed almost since the beginning. In the 1950s, the original *I Love Lucy* show was groundbreaking: shot on film before a live audience and edited before airing, it pioneered syndication. It established the sitcom ('situation comedy') formula, and showcased a dynamic female comedian, Lucille Ball, in an interethnic marriage.

In its brief history, TV has proved to be one of the most passionately contested cultural battlegrounds in American society, blamed for a whole host of societal ills, from skyrocketing obesity to plummeting attention spans and school test scores. On the other hand, as cable TV has emerged as the frontier for daring and innovative programming, some of the TV shows of the past decade have proved as riveting and memorable as anything Americans viewers (and the scores of people around the world who watch American TV) have ever seen. Praised for their intellectual and cultural weight in addition to their sheer entertainment values, these recent small screen heavyweights prove that 'good TV' doesn't have to be an oxymoron.

Of course, 'good' American TV has been around for a long time, whether through artistic merit or cultural and political importance. The 1970s comedy *All in the Family* aired an unflinching examination of prejudice, as embodied by bigoted patriarch Archie Bunker, played by Carroll O'Connor. Similarly, the sketch-comedy show *Saturday Night Live*, which debuted in 1975, pushed social hot buttons with its subversive, politically charged humor.

In the 1980s, videotapes brought movies into American homes, blurring the distinction between big and small screens, and the stigma Hollywood attached to TV slowly faded. Another turning point in this decade was *The Cosby Show*, starring comedian Bill Cosby. While not the first successful African American show, it became the nation's highest-rated program and spurred more multicultural TV shows.

In the 1990s, TV audiences embraced the unformulaic, no-holds-barred weird cult show *Twin Peaks*, leading to a slew of provocative idiosyncrasies like *The X-Files*.

Now, YouTube, Blip.tv and its ilk are changing the rules again. The networks have responded by creating more edgy, long-narrative serial dramas, like *Lost* and *24*, as well as cheap-to-produce, 'unscripted' reality TV: what *Survivor* started in 2000, the contestants and 'actors' of *American Idol*, *Dancing with the Stars*, *Project Runway* and *The Jersey Shore* keep alive today, for better or for worse.

Literature

Not so long ago, the nation's imagination stirred when critics heralded the next Great American Novel. For more than a century the novel was still the vital engine of US culture and art. Yet in today's glutted multimedia environment, American writers have to fight for wallets – and ever-decreasing attention spans – so much so some wonder if the Great

Upton Sinclair's *The Jungle* (1906) shocked the public with its harrowing exposé of Chicago's meatpacking industry, and instantly became a modern classic. Nearly a century later, Eric Schlosser's *Fast Food Nation* (2001) similarly alerted America to the dark underside of the fast food industry.

On the subject of Mark Twain's influence on American letters, Ernest Hemingway once declared, 'All modern American literature comes from one book by Mark Twain called *Huckleberry Finn*. There was nothing before. And there has been nothing as good since.'

American Novel is a phenomenon of another age whose extinction is imminent.

Yet reading survives. According to the most recent US census, even during the recession and with the publishing business under siege from digital media, Americans spent more than $16.5 billion a year on books in 2010. That's more than they spend on music and movie tickets combined. Yet writers, publishers and readers alike fear that physical bookstores – and indeed, the act of reading a lovingly battered printed book – are suffering due to web-retailers, an explosion of free online 'content,' and digital reading devices for ebooks.

At least one thing is sacred: Americans are in no danger of losing their love of a well-told tale, even though the distinction between literature and genre fiction is often playfully blurred. Each year reveals a pluralistic wealth of new and talented voices, all feverishly digesting what life in these United States is really all about.

Books Once Banned in America

» *The Catcher in the Rye,* JD Salinger

» *1984,* George Orwell

» *Adventures of Huckleberry Finn,* Mark Twain

» *Are You There, God? It's Me, Margeret,* Judy Blume

» *The Color Purple,* Alice Walker

» *Lord of the Flies,* William Golding

American Identity through Literature

America first articulated a vision of itself through its literature. Until the American Revolution, the continent's citizens identified largely with England, but after independence, an immediate call went out to develop an American national voice. Not until the 1820s, however, did writers take up the two aspects of American life that had no counterpart in Europe: the untamed wilderness and the frontier experience.

James Fenimore Cooper is credited with creating the first truly American literature with *The Pioneers* (1823). In Cooper's 'everyman' humor and individualism, Americans first recognized themselves.

In his essay *Nature* (1836), Ralph Waldo Emerson articulated similar ideas, but in more philosophical and spiritual terms. Emerson claimed that nature reflected God's instructions for humankind as plainly as the Bible did, and that individuals could understand these through rational thought and self-reliance. Emerson's writings became the core of the transcendentalist movement, which Henry David Thoreau championed in *Walden; or, Life in the Woods* (1854).

Literary highlights of this era include Herman Melville's ambitious *Moby Dick* (1851) and Nathaniel Hawthorne's examination of the dark side of conservative New England in *The Scarlet Letter* (1850). Canonical poet Emily Dickinson wrote haunting, tightly structured poems, which were first published in 1890, four years after her death.

Famous American Literary Recluses

These writers have rarely given interviews – or, in some cases – were seen publicly at all. Is that why they remain so fascinating to us?

» Emily Dickinson, 19th-century poet

» JD Salinger, 20th-century novelist

» Don DeLillo, 20th- and 21st-century novelist

» Harper Lee, 20th-century novelist

The Civil War & Beyond

The celebration of common humanity and nature reached its apotheosis in Walt Whitman, whose poetry collection *Leaves of Grass* (1855) signaled the arrival of an American literary visionary. In Whitman's informal, intimate, rebellious free verse were songs of individualism, democracy, earthy spirituality, taboo-breaking sexuality and joyous optimism that encapsulated the heart of a throbbing new nation.

But not everything was coming up roses. Abolitionist Harriet Beecher Stowe's controversial novel *Uncle Tom's Cabin* (1852) depicted African American life under slavery with Christian romanticism but also enough realism to inflame passions on both sides of the 'great debate' over slavery, which would shortly plunge the nation into civil war.

After the Civil War (1861–65), two enduring literary trends emerged: realism and regionalism. Regionalism was especially spurred by the rapid late-19th-century settlement of the West; novelist Jack London serialized his adventures for popular magazines such as the *Saturday Evening Post*.

However, it was Samuel Clemens (aka Mark Twain) who came to define American letters. In *Adventures of Huckleberry Finn* (1884), Twain made explicit the quintessential American narrative of an individual journey of self-discovery. The image of Huck and Jim – a poor white teenager and a runaway black slave – standing outside society's norms and floating together toward an uncertain future down the Mississippi River challenges American society still. Twain wrote in the vernacular, loved 'tall tales' and reveled in satirical humor and absurdity, while his folksy, 'anti-intellectual' stance endeared him to everyday readers.

Sylvia Plath became America's most famous – and infamous – literary suicide when she stuck her head in an oven in her London apartment in 1963, at age 30. Her last poetry collection, the acclaimed *Ariel*, was written just before her death and sealed her fate as one of the nation's greatest contemporary poets.

Disillusionment & Diversity

With the dramas of world wars and a newly industrialized society for artistic fodder, American literature came into its own in the 20th century.

Dubbed the 'Lost Generation,' many US writers, most famously Ernest Hemingway, became expats in Europe. His novels exemplified the era, and his spare, stylized realism has often been imitated, yet never bettered. Other notable American figures at Parisian literary salons included modernist writers Gertrude Stein and Ezra Pound, and iconoclast Henry Miller, whose semiautobiographical novels were published in Paris, only to be banned for obscenity and pornography in the USA until the 1960s.

F Scott Fitzgerald eviscerated East Coast society life with his fiction, while John Steinbeck became the great voice of rural working poor in the West, especially during the Great Depression. William Faulkner examined the South's social rifts in dense prose riddled with bullets of black humor.

Between the world wars, the Harlem Renaissance also flourished, as African American intellectuals and artists took pride in their culture and undermined racist stereotypes. Among the most well known writers were poet Langston Hughes and novelist Zora Neale Hurston.

After WWII, American writers delineated ever-sharper regional and ethnic divides, pursued stylistic experimentation and often caustically repudiated conservative middle-class American values. Writers of the 1950s Beat Generation, such as Jack Kerouac, Allen Ginsburg and Lawrence Ferlinghetti, threw themselves like Molotov cocktails onto the profusion of smug suburban lawns. Meanwhile, novelists JD Salinger, Russian immigrant Vladimir Nabokov, Ken Kesey and poet Sylvia Plath darkly chronicled descents into madness by characters who struggled against stifling social norms.

The South, always ripe with paradox, inspired masterful short-story writers and novelists Flannery O'Connor and Eudora Welty and novelist Dorothy Allison. The mythical romance and modern tragedies of the West have found their champions in Chicano writer Rudolfo Anaya, Larry McMurtry and Cormac McCarthy, whose characters poignantly tackle the rugged realities of Western life.

As the 20th century ended, American literature became ever more personalized, starting with the 'me' decade of the 1980s. Narcissistic, often nihilistic narratives by writers such as Jay McInerney and Brett Easton Ellis, catapulted the 'Brat Pack' into pop culture.

Since the 1990s, an increasingly diverse, multiethnic panoply of voices reflects the kaleidoscopic society Americans live in. Ethnic identity (especially that of immigrant cultures), regionalism and narratives of self-discovery remain at the forefront of American literature, no matter how experimental. The quarterly journal *McSweeney's,* founded by Dave Eggers (*A Heartbreaking Work of Staggering Genius,* 2000), publishes titans of contemporary literature such as prolific Joyce Carol Oates and Michael Chabon, both Pulitzer Prize winners. Watch out for the next novel by emerging novelists like Nicole Krauss, Junot Diaz, Gary Shytengart, and Jonathan Safran-Foer. For a sweeping, almost panoramic look at American society, read Jonathan Franzen's *The Corrections* or *Freedom,* the 2010 novel that wowed critics at home and abroad, prompting London's *Guardian* to deem it 'the novel of the century.'

African American Experience

African American writers rose in the 20th century, led by Richard Wright (*Black Boy,* 1945) and Ralph Ellison (*Invisible Man,* 1952). James Baldwin became a groundbreaking openly gay writer (*Giovanni's Room,* 1956) while African American women writers were led by Toni Morrison (*The Bluest Eye,* 1970), Maya Angelou (*I Know Why the Caged Bird Sings,* 1971) and Alice Walker (*The Color Purple,* 1982).

Painting & Sculpture

An ocean away from Europe's aristocratic patrons, religious commissions and historic art academies, colonial America was not exactly fertile ground for the visual arts. Since then, thankfully, times have changed: once a swampy Dutch trading post, New York is the red-hot center of the art world, and its make-or-break influence shapes tastes across the nation and around the globe.

Top American Photographers

- Ansel Adams
- Walker Evans
- Man Ray
- Alfred Stieglitz
- Richard Avedon
- Robert Frank
- Dorothea Lange
- Cindy Sherman
- Edward Weston
- Diane Arbus
- Lee Friedlander

Shaping a National Identity

Artists played a pivotal role in the USA's 19th-century expansion, disseminating images of far-flung territories and reinforcing the call to Manifest Destiny. Thomas Cole and his colleagues in the Hudson River School translated European romanticism to the luminous wild landscapes of upstate New York, while Frederic Remington offered idealized, often stereotypical portraits of the Western frontier.

After the Civil War and the advent of industrialization, realism increasingly became prominent. Eastman Johnson painted nostalgic scenes of rural life, as did Winslow Homer, who later became renowned for watercolor seascapes.

An American Avant-Garde

Polite society's objections to Eakins' painting had nothing on the near-riots inspired by New York's Armory Show of 1913. This exhibition introduced the nation to European modernism and changed the face of American art. It showcased impressionism, fauvism and cubism, including the notorious 1912 *Nude Descending a Staircase, No. 2* by Marcel Duchamp, a French artist who later became an American citizen.

New York's 1913 Armory Show was merely the first in a series of exhibitions evangelizing the radical aesthetic shifts of European modernism, and it was inevitable that American artists would begin to grapple with what they had seen. Alexander Calder, Joseph Cornell and Isamu Noguchi produced sculptures inspired by surrealism and constructivism; the precisionist paintings of Charles Demuth, Georgia O'Keeffe and Charles Sheeler combined realism with a touch of cubist geometry.

In the 1930s, the Works Progress Administration's (WPA) Federal Art Project, part of FDR's New Deal, commissioned murals, paintings and sculptures for public buildings nationwide. WPA artists borrowed from Soviet social realism and Mexican muralists to forge a socially engaged figurative style with regional flavor.

In February 2011, the United States' second-largest bookstore chain, Borders, declared bankruptcy, prompting cries of the 'death' of the publishing industry. Meanwhile, sales of Amazon's e-reader, Kindle, are booming.

Abstract Expressionism

In the wake of WWII, American art underwent a sea change at the hands of New York school painters such as Franz Kline, Jackson Pollock and Mark Rothko. Moved by surrealism's celebration of spontaneity and the unconscious, these artists explored abstraction and its psychological potency through imposing scale and the gestural handling of paint. The movement's 'action painter' camp went extreme; Pollock, for example, made his drip paintings by pouring and splattering pigments over large canvases.

Having stood the test of time, abstract expressionism is widely considered to be the first truly original school of American art.

Art + Commodity = Pop

Once established in America, abstract expressionism reigned supreme. However, stylistic revolts had begun much earlier, in the 1950s. Most notably, Jasper Johns came to prominence with thickly painted renditions of ubiquitous symbols, including targets and the American flag, while Robert Rauschenberg assembled artworks from comics, ads and even – à la Duchamp – found objects (a mattress, a tire, a stuffed goat). Both artists helped break down traditional boundaries between painting and sculpture, opening the field for pop art in the 1960s.

America's postwar economic boom also influenced pop. Not only did artists embrace representation, they drew inspiration from consumer images such as billboards, product packaging and media icons. Employing mundane mass-production techniques to silkscreen paintings of movie stars and Coke bottles, Andy Warhol helped topple the myth of the solitary artist laboring heroically in the studio. Roy Lichtenstein combined newsprint's humble Benday dots with the representational conventions of comics. Suddenly, so-called 'serious' art could be political, bizarre, ironic and fun – and all at once.

Horror & mystery

Edgar Allan Poe was the first American writer to achieve international acclaim. His gruesome stories (such as 'The Tell-Tale Heart,' 1843) helped popularize the short-story form, and he is credited with inventing the mystery story, the horror story and science fiction, all extremely popular and enduring genres in America.

Minimalism & Beyond

What became known as minimalism shared pop's interest in mass production, but all similarities ended there. Like the abstract expressionists, artists such as Donald Judd, Agnes Martin and Robert Ryman eschewed representational subject matter; their cool, reductive works of the 1960s and '70s were often arranged in gridded compositions and fabricated from industrial materials.

The '80s & Beyond

By the 1980s, civil rights, feminism and AIDS activism had made inroads in visual culture; artists not only voiced political dissent through their work but embraced a range of once-marginalized media, from textiles and graffiti to video, sound and performance. The decade also ushered in the so-called Culture Wars, which commenced with tumult over photographs by Robert Mapplethorpe and Andres Serrano. In 1998, the Supreme Court ruled that the National Endowment for the Arts could withhold funding from artists violating 'general standards of decency and respect for the beliefs and values of the American public.'

To get the pulse of contemporary art in the US, check out works by artists like Jenny Holzer, Kara Walker, Chuck Close, Martin Puryear and Frank Stella.

From 1996 to 2011, Oprah Winfrey ran what was the world's most influential book club from her syndicated *Oprah Winfrey Show*, launching the career of new writers, bringing classics back to life, sparking literary controversies, and encouraging a nation – and, indeed, the whole world – to read.

Theater

American theater is a three-act play of sentimental entertainment, classic revivals and urgent social commentary. From the beginning, Broadway musicals (www.livebroadway.com) have aspired to be 'don't-miss-this-show!' tourist attractions. From mid-2010 to mid-2011, Broadway shows sold over a billion dollars worth of tickets – a new record even as costly shows like *Spiderman: Turn Off the Dark* close and reopen amidst bad reviews and artistic feuds, they've apparently succeeded.

Independent theater arrived in the 1920s and '30s, with the Little Theatre Movement, which emulated progressive European theater and developed into today's 'off-Broadway' scene. Always struggling and scraping, and mostly surviving, the country's 1500 nonprofit regional theaters are breeding grounds for new plays and foster new playwrights. Some also develop Broadway-bound productions, while others sponsor festivals dedicated to the Bard himself, William Shakespeare.

Eugene O'Neill – the first major US playwright, and still widely considered the best – put American drama on the map. After WWII, American playwrights joined the nationwide artistic renaissance. Two of the most famous were Arthur Miller, who famously married Marilyn Monroe and wrote about everything from middle-class male disillusionment to the dark psychology of the mob mentality of the Salem witch trials, and the prolific Southerner Tennessee Williams.

FROM CABARET TO CATS

Is the musical the true American art form? Its devoted (some might say insane) fans – the ones who have lined up to see *Wicked* or *Chicago* for the sixteenth time – would say (or, more likely, sing) a resounding 'yes!!!' in the key of C sharp. Here are a few musicals that are exemplary of this big, brash, all-American form.

» *Showboat*, Jerome Kern and Oscar Hammerstein II

» *Oklahoma*, Richard Rodgers and Hammerstein

» *West Side Story*, Leonard Bernstein and Stephen Sondheim

» *Carousel*, Rodgers and Hammerstein

» *Guys & Dolls*, Cole Porter

» *Rent*, Jonathan Larson

» *Into the Woods*, Stephen Sondheim

» *My Fair Lady*, Alan Jay Lerner and Frederick Lowe

» *A Chorus Line*, Marvin Hamlisch and Edward Kleban

» *Cabaret*, John Kander and Fred Ebb

» *The Producers*, Mel Brooks

As in Europe, absurdism and the avant-garde marked American theater in the 1960s. Few were more scathing than Edward Albee, who started provoking bourgeois sensibilities. Neil Simon arrived at around the same time; his ever-popular comedies kept Broadway humming for 40 years.

Other prominent, active American dramatists emerging in the 19790s include David Mamet, Sam Shephard and innovative 'concept musical' composer Stephen Sondheim. August Wilson created a monumental 10-play 'Pittsburgh Cycle' dissecting 20th-century African American life.

Today, American theater is evolving in its effort to remain a relevant communal experience in an age of ever-isolating media. One-person shows, such as *Bridge & Tunnel* (2004), by Sarah Jones, and *Let Me Down Easy* (2008), by Anna Deavere Smith, are increasingly popular. Meanwhile, contemporary playwrights like Suzan-Lori Parks, Tony Kushner and Sarah Ruhl keep experimenting.

Pop art icon Andy Warhol turned the art world on its head in the early 1960s with his celebrity portraits of figures such as Marilyn Monroe and Jackie Onassis that at once commented on celebrity and commercial culture while making the American public look at these legendary figures in a startling new light.

Architecture

In the 21st century, computer technology and innovations in materials and manufacturing allow for curving, asymmetrical buildings once considered impossible, if not inconceivable. Architects are being challenged to 'go green,' and the creativity unleashed is riveting, transforming skylines and changing the way Americans think about their built environments. The public's architectural taste remains conservative, but never mind: avant-garde 'starchitects' are revising urban landscapes with radical visions that the nation will catch up with – one day.

The Colonial Period

Perhaps the only lasting indigenous influence on American architecture has been the adobe dwellings of the Southwest. In the 17th and 18th centuries, Spanish colonists incorporated elements of what they called the Native American *pueblo* (village). It reappeared in late-19th and early-20th-century architecture in both the Southwest's Pueblo Revival style and Southern California's Mission Revival style.

Elsewhere until the 20th century, immigrant Americans mainly adopted English and continental European styles and followed their trends. For most early colonists in the eastern US, architecture served necessity rather than taste, while the would-be gentry aped grander English homes, a period well preserved in Williamsburg, Virginia.

After the Revolutionary War, the nation's leaders wanted a style befitting the new republic and adopted neoclassicism. Virginia's capitol, designed by Thomas Jefferson, was modeled on an ancient Roman temple, and Jefferson's own private estate, Monticello, sports a Romanesque rotunda.

Professional architect Charles Bulfinch helped develop the more monumental federal style, which paralleled the English Georgian style. The grandest example is the US Capitol in Washington, DC, which became a model for state legislatures nationwide. As they moved into the 19th century, Americans, mirroring English fashions, gravitated toward the Greek and Gothic Revival styles, still seen today in many churches and college campuses.

Building the Nation

Meanwhile, small-scale architecture was revolutionized by 'balloon-frame' construction: a light frame of standard-milled timber joined with cheap nails. Easy and economical, balloon-frame stores and houses made possible swift settlement of the expanding west and, later, the surreal proliferation of the suburbs. Home-ownership was suddenly within

AMERICA DANCES

America fully embraced dance in the 20th century. New York City has always been the epicenter for dance innovation and the home of many premier dance companies, but every major city supports resident and touring troupes, both ballet and modern.

Modern ballet is said to have begun with Russian-born choreographer George Balanchine's *Apollo* (1928) and *Prodigal Son* (1929). With these, Balanchine invented the 'plotless ballet' – in which he choreographed the inner structure of music, not a pantomimed story – and thereby created a new, modern vocabulary of ballet movement. In 1934, Balanchine founded the School of American Ballet; in 1948 he founded the New York City Ballet, turning it into one of the world's foremost ballet companies. Jerome Robbins took over that company in 1983, after achieving fame choreographing huge Broadway musicals, such as *West Side Story* (1957). Broadway remains an important venue for dance today. National companies elsewhere, like San Francisco's Lines Ballet, keep evolving contemporary ballet.

The pioneer of modern dance, Isadora Duncan, didn't find success until she began performing in Europe at the turn of the 20th century. Basing her ideas on ancient Greek myths and concepts of beauty, she challenged the strictures of classical ballet and sought to make dance an intense form of self-expression.

Martha Graham founded the Martha Graham School for Contemporary Dance in 1926 after moving to New York, and many of today's major American choreographers developed under her tutelage. In her long career she choreographed more than 140 works and developed a new dance technique, now taught worldwide, aimed at expressing inner emotion and dramatic narrative. Her most famous work was *Appalachian Spring* (1944).

Merce Cunningham, Paul Taylor and Twyla Tharp succeeded Graham as leading exponents of modern dance; they all have companies that are active today. In the 1960s and '70s, Cunningham explored abstract expressionism in movement, collaborating famously with musician John Cage. Taylor experimented with everyday movements and expressions, while Tharp is known for incorporating pop music, jazz and ballet.

Another student of Martha Graham, Alvin Ailey, was part of the post-WWII flowering of African American culture. He made his name with *Revelations* (1960), two years after he founded the still-lauded Alvin Ailey American Dance Theater in New York City.

Other celebrated postmodern choreographers include Mark Morris and Bill T Jones. Beyond New York, San Francisco, Los Angeles, Chicago, Minneapolis and Philadelphia are noteworthy for modern dance.

reach of average middle-class families, making real the enduring American Dream.

After the Civil War, influential American architects studied at Paris' École des Beaux-Arts, and American buildings began to show increasing refinement and confidence. Major examples of the beaux-arts style include Richard Morris Hunt's Biltmore Estate (p336) in North Carolina and New York's Public Library (p79).

Art in Out-of-the-Way Places

- Marfa, TX
- Santa Fe, NM
- Traverse City, MI
- Park City, UT
- Bellingham, WA
- Beacon, NY
- Provincetown, MA

In San Francisco and other cities across America, Victorian architecture appeared as the 19th century progressed. Among well-to-do classes, larger and fancier private houses added ever more adornments: balconies, turret, towers, ornately painted trim and intricate 'gingerbread' wooden millwork.

In a reaction against Victorian opulence, the Arts and Crafts movement arose after 1900 and remained popular until the 1930s. Its modest bungalows, such as the Gamble House in Pasadena, California, featured locally handcrafted wood- and glasswork, ceramic tiles and other artisan details.

Reaching for the Sky

By the 1850s, internal iron-framed buildings had appeared in Manhattan, and this freed up urban architectural designs, especially after the advent of Otis hydraulic elevators in the 1880s. The Chicago School of architecture transitioned beyond beaux-arts style to produce the skyscraper – considered the first truly 'modern' architecture, and America's most prominent architectural contribution to the world at that time.

In the 1930s, the influence of art deco – which became instantly popular in the US after the Paris Exposition of 1925 – meant that urban high-rises soared, becoming fitting symbols of America's technical achievements, grand aspirations, commerce and an affinity for modernism.

THE GREAT AMERICAN NOVEL: A CRASH COURSE

- *The Age of Innocence*, Edith Wharton
- *My Antonia*, Willa Cather
- *The Sun Also Rises*, Ernest Hemingway
- *Tropic of Cancer*, Henry Miller
- *The Great Gatsby*, F Scott Fitzgerald
- *The Sound and the Fury*, William Faulkner
- *The Grapes of Wrath*, John Steinbeck
- *Native Son*, Richard Wright
- *Their Eyes Were Watching God*, Zora Neale Hurston
- *To Kill a Mockingbird*, Harper Lee
- *One Flew Over the Cuckoo's Nest*, Ken Kesey
- *Fahrenheit 451*, Ray Bradbury
- *Lolita*, Vladimir Nabokov
- *Slaughterhouse Five*, Kurt Vonnegut
- *The Moviegoer*, Walker Percy
- *Beloved*, Toni Morrison
- *Underworld*, Don DeLillo
- *Rabbit Run*, John Updike
- *Housekeeping*, Marilynne Robinson
- *Independence Day*, Richard Ford
- *Infinite Jest*, David Foster Wallace
- *American Pastoral*, Phillip Roth

Modernism & Beyond

When the Bauhaus school fled the rise of Nazism in Germany, architects such as Walter Gropius and Ludwig Mies van der Rohe brought their pioneering modern designs to American shores. Van der Rohe landed in Chicago, where Louis Sullivan, considered to be the inventor of the modern skyscraper, was already working on a simplified style of architecture in which 'form ever follows function.' This evolved into the International style, which favored glass 'curtain walls' over a steel frame. IM Pei, who designed Cleveland's Rock and Roll Hall of Fame, is considered the last living high-modernist architect in America.

In the mid-20th century, modernism transitioned into America's suburbs, especially in Southern California. Midcentury modern architecture was influenced not only by the organic nature of Frank Lloyd Wright homes but also the spare, geometric, clean-lined designs of Scandinavia. Post-and-beam construction allowed for walls of sheer glass that gave the illusion of merging indoor and outdoor living spaces. Today, a striking collection of midcentury modern homes and public buildings by Albert Frey, Richard Neutra and other luminaries can be found in Palm Springs, CA.

Rejecting modernism's 'ugly boxes' later in the 20th century, postmodernism reintroduced decoration, color, historical references and whimsy. In this, architects like Michael Graves and Philip Johnson took the lead. Another expression of postmodernism is the brash, mimetic architecture of the Las Vegas Strip, which Pritzker Prize–winning architect Robert Venturi held up as the triumphant antithesis of modernism (he sardonically described the latter as 'less is a bore').

Today, aided and abetted by digital tools, architectural design favors the bold and the unique. Leading this plunge into futurama has been Frank Gehry; his Walt Disney Concert Hall in Los Angeles is but one example. Other notable contemporary architects include Richard Meier (Los Angeles' Getty Center), Thom Mayne (San Francisco's Federal Building) and Daniel Libeskind (San Francisco's Contemporary Jewish Museum and the Denver Art Museum's Hamilton Building).

Even as the recession crippled the American economy in 2008 and stalled new construction, several phenomenal new examples of visionary architecture have burst upon the scene in American cities. Notable examples include Jeanne Gang's Acqua building in Chicago, Peter Bohlin's already-iconic glass cube at New York City's Fifth Avenue Apple Store, and Renzo Piano's stunning (and sustainable) California Academy of Sciences in San Francisco, which includes a 2.5-acre living roof made of 1.7 million native plants.

Remarkable examples of art deco skyscrapers include New York City's Chrysler Building and Empire State Building. Art deco simultaneously appeared nationwide in the design of movie houses, train stations, and office buildings across the country, and in neighborhoods like Miami's South Beach.

SKYSCRAPERS

The Music Scene

American popular music is the nation's heartbeat and its unbreakable soul. It's John Lee Hooker's deep growls and John Coltrane's passionate cascades. It's Hank Williams' yodel and Elvis' pout. It's Beyoncé and Bob Dylan, Duke Ellington and Patti Smith. It's the sound of Janis Joplin's heart breaking, Kurt Cobain's tortured cry, and Johnny Cash's hypnotic refrain to 'walk the line.' It's a feeling as much as a form – always a foot-stomping, defiant good time, whether folks are boot scooting to bluegrass, sweating to zydeco, jumping to hip-hop or stage-diving to punk rock.

No other American art has been as influential. Blues, jazz, country, rock and roll, hip-hop: download them to your iPod and you've got the soundtrack for the story of American music as it evolved in the 20th century and continues to explode into the next. The rest of the world has long returned the love, and American music today is a joyful, freewheeling multicultural feast, in which genres and styles are mixed, matched, blended and blurred. Every time it seems like pop music can't be reinvented again (just watch Gwen Stefani, Britney Spears or Lady Gaga all riff off Madonna's pioneering style and reinterpret it in a daring new way) it bends genre, defies expectations and breaks the rules all over again.

One-Hit Wonders

- » 'Tell Him,' The Exciters (1962)
- » 'Just One Look,' Doris Troy (1963)
- » 'Cruel to Be Kind,' Nick Lowe (1979)
- » 'Video Killed the Radio Star,' The Buggles (1979)
- » 'Funkytown,' Lipps, Inc. (1980)
- » 'Turning Japanese,' The Vapors (1980)
- » 'Mickey,' Toni Basil (1982)
- » 'Tainted Love,' Soft Cell (1982)
- » 'Come on Eileen,' Dexys Midnight Runners (1983)
- » 'Rock Me Amadeus,' Falco (1985)
- » 'Baby Got Back,' Sir Mix-a-Lot (1992)
- » 'Whoomp... There it Is,' Tag Team (1993)
- » 'Crazy,' Gnarls Barkley (2006)

Blues

The South is the mother of American music, most of which has roots in the frisson and interplay of black-white racial relations. The blues developed after the Civil War out of the work songs, or 'shouts,' of black slaves and out of black spiritual songs and their 'call-and-response' pattern, both of which were adaptations of African music.

Improvisational and intensely personal, the blues remain at heart an immediate expression of individual pain, suffering, hope, desire and pride. Nearly all subsequent American music has tapped this deep well.

At the turn of the 20th century, traveling blues musicians, and particularly female blues singers, gained fame and employment across the South. Early pioneers included Robert Johnson, WC Handy, Ma Rainey, Huddie Ledbetter (aka Lead Belly) and Bessie Smith, who some consider the best blues singer who ever lived. At the same time, African American Christian choral music evolved into gospel, whose greatest singer, Mahalia Jackson, came to prominence in the 1920s.

After WWII, blues from Memphis and the Mississippi Delta dispersed northward, particularly to Chicago, in the hands of a new generation of musicians like Muddy Waters, Buddy Guy, BB King, John Lee Hooker and Etta James.

Jazz

Down in New Orleans, Congo Sq, where slaves gathered to sing and dance from the late 18th century onward, is considered the birthplace of jazz. There ex-slaves adapted the reed, horn and string instruments used by the city's often French-speaking, multiracial Creoles – who themselves preferred formal European music – to play their own African-influenced music. This fertile cross-pollination produced a steady stream of innovative sounds.

The first variation was ragtime, so-called because of its 'ragged,' syncopated African rhythms. Beginning in the 1890s, ragtime was popularized by musicians like Scott Joplin, and was made widely accessible through sheet music and player-piano rolls.

Dixieland jazz, centered on New Orleans' infamous Storyville red-light district, soon followed. In 1917 Storyville shut down and New Orleans' jazz musicians dispersed. In 1919, bandleader King Oliver moved to Chicago, and his star trumpet player, Louis Armstrong, soon followed. Armstrong's distinctive vocals and talented improvisations led to the solo becoming an integral part of jazz throughout much of the 20th century.

The Jazz Age & Beyond

The 1920s and '30s are known as the Jazz Age, but music was just part of the greater flowering of African American culture during New York's Harlem Renaissance. Swing – an urbane, big band jazz style – swept the country, led by innovative bandleaders Duke Ellington and Count Basie. Jazz singers Ella Fitzgerald and Billie Holiday combined jazz with its Southern sibling, the blues.

After WWII, bebop (aka bop) arose, reacting against the smooth melodies and confining rhythms of big-band swing. A new crop of musicians came of age, including Charlie Parker, Dizzy Gillespie and Thelonious Monk. Critics at first derided such 1950s and '60s permutations as cool jazz, hard-bop, free or avant-garde jazz, and fusion (which combined jazz and Latin or rock music) – but there was no stopping the postmodernist tide deconstructing jazz. Pioneers of this era include Miles Davis, Dave Brubeck, Chet Baker, Charles Mingus, John Coltrane, Melba Liston and Ornette Coleman.

PRINCE

One of rock music's most phenomenal success stories, Prince, was born Prince Rogers Nelson in 1950s Minneapolis. He originally tried out for the high school basketball team, but being too short at 5ft 2in, he was cut. His back-up hobby? He took up the guitar.

Country

Early Scottish, Irish and English immigrants brought their own instruments and folk music to America, and what emerged over time in the secluded Appalachian Mountains was fiddle-and-banjo hillbilly, or 'country,' music. In the Southwest, steel guitars and larger bands distinguished 'western' music. In the 1920s, these styles merged into 'country-and-western' music and became centered on Nashville, Tennessee, especially once the *Grand Ole Opry* began its radio broadcasts in 1925. Country musicians that are now 'classics' include Hank Williams, Johnny Cash, Willie Nelson, Patsy Cline and Loretta Lynn.

Country music influenced rock and roll in the 1950s, while rock-flavored country was dubbed 'rockabilly.' In the 1980s, country and western achieved new levels of popularity with stars like Garth Brooks. Today, country music stations dominate other genres. Musicians with record-breaking success include Shania Twain, Dwight Yoakam, Tim McGraw and Taylor Swift. Occupying the eclectic 'alt country' category are Lucinda Williams and Lyle Lovett.

Folk

The tradition of American folk music was crystallized in Woody Guthrie, who traveled the country during the Depression singing politically conscious songs. In the 1940s, Pete Seeger emerged as a tireless preserver of America's folk heritage. Folk music experienced a revival during 1960s protest movements, but then-folkie Bob Dylan ended it almost single-handedly when he plugged in an electric guitar to shouts of 'traitor!'

Rock & Roll

Most say rock and roll was born in 1954 the day Elvis Presley walked into Sam Phillips' Sun Studio and recorded 'That's All Right.' Initially, radio stations weren't sure why a white country boy was singing black music, or whether they should play it. Two years later Presley scored his first big breakthrough with 'Heartbreak Hotel.'

Musically, rock and roll was a hybrid of guitar-driven blues, black rhythm and blues (R & B), and white country-and-western music. R & B evolved in the 1940s out of swing and the blues and was then known as 'race music.' With rock and roll, white performers and some African American musicians transformed 'race music' into something that white youths could embrace freely – and oh, did they.

Rock and roll instantly abetted a social revolution even more significant than its musical one: openly sexual as it celebrated youth and dancing freely across color lines, rock scared the nation. Authorities worked diligently to control 'juvenile delinquents' and to sanitize and suppress rock and roll, which might have withered if not for the early 1960s 'British invasion,' in which the Beatles and the Rolling Stones, emulating Chuck Berry, Little Richard and others, shocked rock and roll back to life.

The 1960s witnessed a full-blown youth rebellion, epitomized by the drug-inspired psychedelic sounds of the Grateful Dead and Jefferson Airplane, and the electric wails of Janis Joplin and Jimi Hendrix. Ever since, rock has been about music *and* lifestyle, alternately torn between hedonism and seriousness, commercialism and authenticity.

Punk arrived in the late 1970s, led by the Ramones and the Dead Kennedys, as did the working-class rock of Bruce Springsteen and Tom Petty.

ONLY THE GOOD DIE YOUNG?

American singer Billie Joel famously sang 'Only the good die young,' yet in the music industry, it's not exactly true. Some of the most notoriously hard-living musicians of the past century did, in fact, die tragically young, commonly from drugs, alcohol, violence, accidents, or suicide.

The deaths of Jimi Hendrix, Janis Joplin, Jim Morrison and Bryan Jones – all at 27 – prompted some observers to speculate if there was a kind of morbid synchronicity about rock stars dying at 27. Later, when Kurt Cobain committed suicide, his name was added to the fateful list. And now Amy WInehouse has joined them. In any case, these untimely deaths have ensured that these American artists live as large in their deaths as they did in their short lives. To this day, the legacy of rapper Tupac Shakur (murdered at age 25) lives on as much through his music as it does through the seemingly unsolvable question 'Who shot Tupac?'

Here are just a few of the many legendary American pop, rock, soul and blues artists who died young, and the medically determined cause of their deaths.

» Robert Johnson, age 27 (poisoned, 1938)

» Jim Croce, age 30 (airplane crash, 1973)

» Buddy Holly, age 22 (airplane crash, 1956)

» Sam Cooke, age 33 (homicide, 1964)

» Otis Redding, age 26 (airplane crash, 1967)

» Janis Joplin, age 27 (drug overdose, 1970)

» Jimi Hendrix, age 27 (drug overdose, 1970)

» GG Allin, age 36 (drug overdose, 1993)

» Kurt Cobain, age 27 (suicide by shotgun, 1994)

» Notorious BIG, age 24 (murder, 1997)

» Jeff Buckley, age 30 (drowning, 1997)

As the counterculture became the culture in the 1980s, critics prematurely pronounced 'rock is dead.' Rock was saved (including by the Talking Heads, REM, Nirvana, Sonic Youth, Pavement and Pearl Jam) as it always has been: by splintering and evolving, whether it's called new wave, heavy metal, grunge, indie rock, world beat, skate punk, hardcore, goth, emo or electronica.

Even though hip-hop has become today's outlaw sound, rock remains relevant, and it's not going anywhere. Cue up the Killers, the Yeah Yeah Yeahs, Kings of Leon, Arcade Fire or the Strokes to hear why.

Hip-Hop

From the ocean of sounds coming out of the early 1970s – funk, soul, Latin, reggae and rock and roll – young DJs from the Bronx in New York City began to spin a groundbreaking mixture of records together in an effort to drive dance floors wild.

And so hip-hop was born. Groups like Grandmaster Flash and the Furious Five were soon taking the party from the streets to the trendy clubs of Manhattan and mingling with punk and new wave bands like the Clash and Blondie. Break-out artists Futura 2000, Keith Haring and Jean-Michel Basquiat moved from the subways and the streets to the galleries, and soon to the worlds of fashion and advertising.

As groups like Run-DMC, Public Enemy and the Beastie Boys sold millions, the sounds and styles of the growing hip-hop culture rapidly diversified. The daring 'gangsta rap' sound of Niggaz With Attitude came out of Los Angeles, and the group got both accolades and bad press for its daring sounds and social commentary – which critics called battle cries for violence – on racism, drugs, sex and urban poverty.

Come the turn of the millennium, what started as some raggedy gang kids playing their parents' funk records at illegal block parties had evolved into a multibillion-dollar business. Russell Simmons and P Diddy stood atop media empires, and stars Queen Latifah and Will Smith were Hollywood royalty. A white rapper from Detroit, Eminem, sold millions of records and hip-hop overtook country as America's second-most-popular music behind pop rock.

Today, many view hip-hop as a vapid wasteland of commercial excess – glorifying consumerism, misogyny, homophobia, drug use and a host of other social ills. But just as the hedonistic days of arena rock and roll gave birth to the rebel child of punk, the evolving offspring of hip-hop and DJ culture are constantly breaking the rules to create something new and even more energizing.

TECHNOLOGY

The country that spawned the world's most successful recording industry also popularized the technology accused of killing it. From the emergence of file sharing to Apple's 2011 unveiling of the new iCloud, a new music streaming service, it's no surprise that the American music industry is under stress – though from its ability to evolve, you'd hardly know it.

The Land & Environment

The USA is big, no question. Covering more than 3.5 million sq miles, it's the world's third-largest country, trailing only Russia and Canada, its friendly neighbor to the north. The continental USA is made up of 48 contiguous states ('the lower 48'), while Alaska, its largest state, is northwest of Canada, and the volcanic islands of Hawaii, the 50th state, are 2600 miles southwest of the mainland in the Pacific Ocean.

Geologists believe that roughly 460 million years ago the Appalachian Mountains were the highest mountains on earth – higher even than the Himalayas are today.

It's more than just size, though. America feels big because of its incredibly diverse topography, which began to take shape around 50 to 60 million years ago.

In the contiguous USA, the east is a land of temperate, deciduous forests and contains the ancient Appalachian Mountains, a low range that parallels the Atlantic Ocean. Between the mountains and the coast lies the country's most populated, urbanized region, particularly in the corridor between Washington, DC, and Boston, MA.

To the north are the Great Lakes, which the USA shares with Canada. These five lakes, part of the Canadian Shield, are the greatest expanse of fresh water on the planet, constituting nearly 20% of the world's supply.

Going south along the East Coast, things get wetter and warmer till you reach the swamps of southern Florida and make the turn into the Gulf of Mexico, which provides the USA with a southern coastline.

West of the Appalachians are the vast interior plains, which lie flat all the way to the Rocky Mountains. The eastern plains are the nation's breadbasket, roughly divided into the northern 'corn belt' and the southern 'cotton belt.' The plains, an ancient sea bottom, are drained by the mighty Mississippi River, which together with the Missouri River forms the world's fourth-longest river system, surpassed only by the Nile, Amazon and Yangtze Rivers. Going west, farmland slowly gives way to cowboys and ranches in the semiarid, big-sky Great Plains.

By turns self-effacing and earnest, Bill McKibben talks with Vermont farmers and friends about how to turn an ecological mind-set into a practical everyday reality in *Wandering Home* (2005).

The young, jagged Rocky Mountains are a complex set of tall ranges that run all the way from Mexico to Canada, providing excellent skiing. West of these mountains are the Southwestern deserts, an arid region of extremes that has been cut to dramatic effect by the Colorado River system. This land of eroded canyons leads to the unforgiving Great Basin as you go across Nevada. Also an ancient sea bottom, the Great Basin is where the military practices and where the USA plans to bury its nuclear waste.

Then you reach America's third major mountain system: the southern, granite Sierra Nevada and the northern, volcanic Cascades, which both parallel the Pacific Coast. California's Central Valley is one of the most fertile places on earth, while the coastline from San Diego to Seattle is celebrated in folk songs and Native American legends – a stretch of sandy beaches and old-growth forests, including coast redwoods.

But wait, there's more. Northwest of Canada, Alaska reaches the Arctic Ocean and contains tundra, glaciers, an interior rainforest and the lion's share of federally protected wilderness. Hawaii, in the Pacific Ocean, is a string of tropical island idylls.

The Environmental Movement

The USA is well known for its political and social revolutions, but it also birthed environmentalism. The USA was the first nation to make significant efforts to preserve its wilderness, and US environmentalists often spearhead preservation efforts worldwide.

America's Protestant settlers believed that civilization's Christian mandate was to bend nature to its will. Not only was wilderness deadly and difficult, but it was a potent symbol of humanity's godless impulses, and the Pilgrims set about subduing both with gusto.

Then, in the mid-19th-century, taking their cue from European Romantics, the USA's transcendentalists claimed that nature was not fallen, but holy. In *Walden; or, Life in the Woods* (1854), iconoclast Henry David Thoreau described living for two years in the woods, blissfully free of civilization's comforts. He persuasively argued that human society was harmfully distant from nature's essential truths. This view marked a profound shift toward believing that nature, the soul and God were one.

Reading Climate Change

» *Field Notes From a Catastrophe*, Elizabeth Kolbert

» *The Weather Makers*, Tim Flannery

» *Eaarth*, Bill McKibben

» *The Great Disruption*, Paul Gilding

John Muir & National Parks

The continent's natural wonders – vividly captured by America's 19th-century landscape painters – had a way of selling themselves, and rampant

AMERICA'S WORST NATURAL DISASTERS

Earthquakes, wildfires, tornadoes, hurricanes and blizzards – the US certainly has its share of natural disasters. A few of the more infamous events that have shaped the national conscience:

» **Galveston Hurricane** In 1900, Galveston – then known as 'the jewel of Texas' – was practically obliterated by a category-4 hurricane. Fifteen-foot waves destroyed buildings and at one point the entire island was submerged. More than 8000 perished, making it America's deadliest natural disaster.

» **1906 San Francisco Earthquake** A powerful earthquake (estimated to be around the 8 Richter-scale range) leveled the city followed by even more devastating fires. The quake was felt as far away as Oregon and Central Nevada. An estimated 3000-plus died, while more than 200,000 people (of a population of 410,000) were homeless.

» **Dust Bowl** During a prolonged drought of the 1930s, the overworked topsoil of the Great Plains dried up, turned to dust and billowed eastward in massive windstorm-fueled 'black blizzards' – reaching all the way to NYC and Washington, DC. Millions of acres of crops were decimated and more than 500,000 people were left homeless. The great exodus westward by stricken farmers and migrants was immortalized in John Steinbeck's *The Grapes of Wrath*.

» **Hurricane Katrina** August 29, 2005, is not a day easily forgotten in New Orleans. A massive category-5 hurricane swept across the Gulf of Mexico and slammed into Louisiana. As levees failed, floods inundated more than 80% of the city. The death toll reached 1836, with more than $100 billion in estimated damages – making it America's costliest natural disaster. Heartbreaking images of the destroyed city and anger over the government's response still linger.

» **Tornado Alley** In 2011, the US experienced its largest tornado outbreak in recorded history. More than 300 tornadoes raged across 21 states over three harrowing days. Amazingly, this occurred just weeks after the second-largest tornado outbreak in US history. The storms left more than 300 dead and $10 billion in damages.

nationalism led to a desire to promote them. In the late 1800s, US presidents began setting aside land for state and national parks.

Scottish naturalist John Muir soon emerged to champion wilderness for its own sake. Muir considered nature superior to civilization, and he spent much of his life wandering the Sierra Nevada mountain range and passionately advocating on its behalf. Muir was the driving force behind the USA's emerging conservation movement, which had its first big victory in 1890 when Yosemite National Park was established. Muir founded the Sierra Club in 1892 and slowly gained national attention.

The Sierra Club (www.sierraclub.org) was the USA's first conservation group and it remains the nation's most active, with educational programs, organized trips and tons of information.

The Science of Ecology

By the end of the 19th century, the nation was realizing the limits of its once boundless resources. In 1891 the *Forest Reserve Act* was passed to maintain and manage forests to ensure they'd keep fueling America's growth. This epitomized the conservation movement's central conflict: whether to preserve nature for human use or for its own sake.

In the early 20th century, the science of ecology emerged. Ecology proved yet another humbling moment for humankind – already knocked from the center of the universe, and swinging arm in arm with monkeys, thanks to Charles Darwin – with its assertion that people were in fact dependent on nature, not in charge of it.

With ecology, America's 19th-century conservation movement became the modern environmental movement. Aldo Leopold was the first writer

IT'S NOT EASY BEING GREEN

The USA has long been one of the world's greatest consumers of energy, accounting for a quarter of the world's greenhouse gases. Sustainability, however, seems to be on everyone's lips these days, and interest in renewable energy is at an all-time high.

Though enormous obstacles lie ahead, the US has made marked advances in lowering its carbon footprint:

» **Winds of Change** Although wind energy generates just more than 2% of the nation's electricity, the US is the world's second-largest producer of wind energy (after China), and has enormous potential for growth. The US Department of Energy envisions 20% of the nation's power supplied by this clean energy by 2030.

» **Solar Power** Interest in solar power is high – with solar power growing at a rate of 40% per year. The US currently generates roughly half of the world's solar energy. Ambitions are grand for solar plants (including the $2.2 billion, 392MW Ivanpah plant, the world's largest), though private citizens and small businesses are also contributing – adding solar panels to help meet energy needs.

» **Biofuels** The USA is now the world's largest producer of ethanol (fuels made from corn and other common crops). As of 2011, it accounted for roughly 10% of the nation's total domestic fuel consumption – a big jump from 2001 when it was only 1%.

» **Electric Cars** American automobile manufacturers, once wedded to gas-guzzling SUVs and trucks, have responded to consumer demand for more fuel-efficient cars. Ford and GM have both ramped up production of electric vehicles. Ford will produce 100,000 electrified cars by 2013. GM's full-size Chevrolet Volt would see production jump from 16,000 to 60,000 between 2011 and 2012.

» **Ecofriendly Architecture** Green buildings have arrived and are garnering much attention at home and abroad. Energy-efficient windows, more ecofriendly building materials and water conservation features (like greywater systems that utilize rainwater) are just a few features of LEED-certified buildings emerging nationwide.

» **Greenways** Back in the 1980s, the notion of riding a bicycle down Broadway in New York City seemed pure suicide. Today, Gotham – along with Chicago, Washington, DC, and other cities – has added hundreds of miles of bike lanes, and urbanites are finding greener (and sometimes faster) ways of getting around town.

to popularize an ecological world view with his idea of a 'land ethic,' which proposed that humans must act with respectful stewardship toward all of nature, rather than celebrating the parts they like and abusing the rest. The 1962 publication of *Silent Spring,* by Rachel Carson, provided the shocking proof: this exposé of how chemicals such as DDT were killing animals and poisoning the land horrified the nation and inspired a wide-ranging grass-roots movement.

Aldo Leopold's *A Sand County Almanac* (1949) became a touchstone for American naturalists, and it remains a humble, unpretentious and powerfully moving testimony to the power of leaving wilderness undisturbed.

Environmental Laws & Climate Change

Over the following decades, the USA passed a series of landmark environmental and wildlife laws that resulted in significant improvements in the nation's water and air quality, and the partial recovery of many near-extinct plants and animals. The movement's focus steadily broadened – to preserving entire ecosystems, not just establishing parks – as it confronted devastation wrought by pollution, overkill of species, habitat destruction through human impact, and the introduction of nonnative species.

Today, environmentalism is a worldwide movement, one that understands that each nation's local problems also contribute to a global threat: climate change. In the USA, the dangers of global warming are inspiring an environmental awareness as widespread as at any time in US history. Whether or not average Americans believe God speaks through nature, they're increasingly disturbed by the messages they are hearing.

Wild Things

The USA is home to creatures both great and small, from the ferocious grizzly to the industrious beaver, with colossal bison, snowy owls, soaring eagles, howling coyotes and doe-eyed manatees all part of the great American menagerie. The nation's varied geography – coastlines along two oceans, mountains, deserts, rain forests and massive bay and river systems – harbor ecosystems where an extraordinary array of plant and animal life can flourish.

Unusual Wildlife Reads

» *Rats*, by Robert Sullivan

» *Pigeons*, by Andrew Blechman

» *Cod*, by Mark Kurlansky

» *Ants*, by Bert Hölldobler & EO Wilson

» *Secret Life of Lobsters*, by Trevor Corson

Land Mammals

Nineteenth-century Americans did not willingly suffer competing predators, and federal eradication programs nearly wiped out every single wolf and big cat and many of the bears in continental US. Almost all share the same story of abundance, precipitous loss and, today, partial recovery.

The grizzly bear, a subspecies of brown bear, is one of North America's largest land mammals. Male grizzlies can stand 7ft tall, weigh up to 850lb and consider 500 sq miles home. At one time, perhaps 50,000 grizzlies roamed the West, but by 1975 fewer than 300 remained. Conservation efforts, particularly in the Greater Yellowstone Region, have increased the population in the lower 48 states to around 1300. By contrast, Alaska remains chock-full of grizzlies, with upwards of 30,000. Despite a decline in numbers, black bears survive nearly everywhere. Smaller than griz-

WILDLIFE WATCHING: USA'S ENDANGERED SPECIES

Currently, more than 1300 plants and animals are listed in the USA as either endangered or threatened. Although all endangered species are vital to the ecosystem, if it's brag-worthy animals that you're keen to see (and photograph), here are places to spot them before (gulp) it's too late:

» **Bighorn sheep** Anza-Borrego Desert State Park, CA (p931) and Zion National Park, UT (p855)

» **California condor** Big Sur, CA (p940) and Grand Canyon National Park, AZ (p823)

» **Desert tortoise** Mojave National Preserve, CA (p932)

» **Florida panther** Everglades National Park, FL (p463)

» **Gray wolf** Yellowstone National Park, WY (p744)

» **Hawaiian goose** Haleakalā National Park (p1095)

» **Hawaiian monk seal** Waikiki Aquarium, HI (p1083)

» **Manatee** Everglades National Park, FL (p463)

» **Mexican long-nosed bat** Big Bend National Park, TX (p694)

» **Whooping cranes** Aransas National Wildlife Refuge, TX (p680) and Bosque del Apache National Wildlife Refuge, NM (p875)

RETURN OF THE WOLF

The wolf is a potent symbol of America's wilderness. This smart, social predator is the largest species of canine – averaging more than 100lb and reaching nearly 3ft at the shoulder. An estimated 400,000 once roamed the continent from coast to coast, from Alaska to Mexico.

Wolves were not regarded warmly by European settlers. The first wildlife legislation in the British colonies was a wolf bounty. As 19th-century Americans tamed the West, they slaughtered the once-uncountable herds of bison, elk, deer and moose, replacing them with domestic cattle and sheep, which wolves found equally tasty.

To stop wolves from devouring the livestock, the wolf's extermination soon became official government policy. Up until 1965, for $20 to $50 an animal, wolves were shot, poisoned, trapped and dragged from dens until in the lower 48 states only a few hundred gray wolves remained in northern Minnesota and Michigan.

In 1944, naturalist Aldo Leopold called for the return of the wolf. His argument was ecology, not nostalgia. His studies showed that wild ecosystems need their top predators to maintain a healthy biodiversity; in complex interdependence, all animals and plants suffered with the wolf gone.

Despite dire predictions from ranchers and hunters, gray wolves were reintroduced to the Greater Yellowstone Region in 1995–96 and red wolves to Arizona in 1998.

Protected and encouraged, wolf populations have made a remarkable recovery, with more than 5500 now counted in the wild.

zlies, these opportunistic, adaptable and curious animals can survive on very small home ranges.

Another extremely adaptable creature is the coyote, which looks similar to a wolf but is about half the size, ranging from 15lb to 45lb. An icon of the Southwest, coyotes are found all over, even in cities. The USA has one primary big-cat species, which goes by several names: mountain lion, cougar, puma and panther. In the east, a remnant population of panthers is defended within Everglades National Park. In the west, mountain lions are common enough for human encounters to be on the increase. These powerful cats are about 150lb of pure muscle, with short tawny fur, long tails and a secretive nature.

The story of the great American buffalo is a tragic one. These massive herbivores numbered as many as 65 million in 1800 – in herds so thick they 'darkened the whole plains,' as explorers Lewis and Clark wrote. They were killed for food, hides, sport and to impoverish Native Americans, who depended on them for survival. By the 20th century, only a few hundred bison remained. Overcoming near extinction, new herds arose from these last survivors, so that one of America's noblest animals can again be admired in its gruff majesty – among other places, in Yellowstone, Grand Teton and Badlands National Parks.

Wilderness Films

» *Winged Migration*, by Jacques Perrin

» *Grizzly Man*, by Werner Herzog

» *Into the Wild*, by Sean Penn

» *White Fang*, by Randal Kleiser

Marine Mammals & Fish

Perhaps no native fish gets more attention than salmon, whose spawning runs up Pacific Coast rivers provide famous spectacles. However, both Pacific and Atlantic salmon are considered endangered; hatcheries release millions of young every year, but there is debate about whether this practice hurts or helps wild populations.

As for marine life, gray, humpback and blue whales migrate annually along the Pacific Coast, making whale-watching very popular. Alaska and Hawaii are important breeding grounds for whales and marine mammals, and Washington's San Juan Islands are visited by orcas. The Pacific Coast is also home to ponderous elephant seals, playful sea lions and endangered sea otters.

In California, Channel Islands National Park and Monterey Bay preserve unique, highly diverse marine worlds. For coral reefs and tropical fish, Hawaii and the Florida Keys are the prime destinations. The coast of Florida is also home to the unusual, gentle manatee, which moves between freshwater rivers and the ocean. Around 10ft long and weighing on average 1000lb, these agile, expressive creatures number around 3800 today, and may once have been mistaken for mermaids.

The Gulf of Mexico is another vital marine habitat, perhaps most famously for endangered sea turtles, which nest on coastal beaches.

High in the White Mountains (a small range just east of California's Sierra Nevada) stand the oldest single living plant species on earth. Known as bristlecone pines, these bare and dramatically twisted trees date back more than 4000 years and have long mystified scientists for their extraordinary longevity.

Birds

Birding is the most popular wildlife-watching activity in the US, and little wonder – all the hemisphere's migratory songbirds and shorebirds rest here at some point, and the USA consequently claims some 800 native avian species.

The bald eagle was adopted as the nation's symbol in 1782. It's the only eagle unique to North America, and perhaps half a million once ruled the continent's skies. By 1963, habitat destruction and, in particular, poisoning from DDT had caused the population to plummet to 487 breeding pairs in the lower 48. However, by 2006, bald eagles had recovered so well, increasing to almost 9800 breeding pairs across the continent (plus 50,000 in Alaska), that they've been removed from the endangered species list.

Another impressive bird is the endangered California condor, a prehistoric, carrion-eating bird that weighs about 20lb and has a wingspan over 9ft. Condors were virtually extinct by the 1980s (reduced to just 22 birds), but they have been successfully bred and reintroduced in California and northern Arizona, where they can sometimes be spotted soaring above the Grand Canyon.

Plants

The eastern United States was originally one endless, complex deciduous forest that mixed with evergreens depending on altitude and latitude. Great Smoky Mountains National Park contains all five eastern forest types – spruce fir, hemlock, pine-oak, and northern and cove hardwood – which support more than 100 native species of trees. Spring wildflower and colorful autumn foliage displays are a New England specialty.

The fastest bird in North America is believed to be the peregrine falcon, which has been clocked diving for prey at speeds of up to 175mph.

In Florida, the Everglades is the last subtropical wilderness in the US. This vital, endangered habitat is a fresh- and saltwater world of marshes, sloughs and coastal prairies that support mangroves, cypresses, sea grasses, tropical plants, pines and hardwoods.

The grasslands of the interior plains are perhaps America's most abused ecosystem. The 19th-century 'sodbusters' converted them largely to agriculture, particularly the eastern tallgrass prairies, of which less than 4% remains. The semi-arid shortgrass prairies have survived somewhat better, but farmers have still cultivated them for monoculture row crops by tapping the underground aquifer. Theodore Roosevelt National Park in North Dakota is a good destination to see America's remaining grasslands.

The Southwest deserts are horizon-stretching expanses of sage, scrub and cacti that abut western mountain ranges, where abundant wildflowers in spring and yellow quaking aspens in fall inspire pilgrimages.

West of the Cascades in wet, milder Washington and Oregon are the last primeval forests in America. These diverse, ancient evergreen stands, of which only 10% remain, contain hemlocks, cedars, spruces and towering Douglas firs.

California is famous for its two species of sequoias (redwoods). The coast redwood is the world's tallest tree, with the tallest specimens in Redwood National Park. Its relative, the giant sequoia, is the world's biggest tree by volume; Sequoia National Park has the biggest.

Survival Guide

DIRECTORY A–Z . . . 1154
Accommodations 1154
Business Hours 1156
Customs Regulations . . . 1156
Electricity 1156
Embassies & Consulates 1157
Food 1157
Gay & Lesbian Travelers 1157
Health 1157
Insurance 1158
Internet Access 1158
Legal Matters 1159
Maps 1159
Money 1160
Photography & Video . . . 1160
Post 1161
Public Holidays 1161
Safe Travel 1161
Telephone 1162
Time 1162
Tourist Information 1163
Travelers with Disabilities 1163
Visas 1164
Volunteering 1166
Women Travelers 1166
Work 1167

TRANSPORTATION . . 1168
GETTING THERE & AWAY 1168
Entering the USA 1168
Air 1168
Land 1169
Sea 1170
Tours 1170
GETTING AROUND 1170
Air 1170
Bicycle 1171
Boat 1171
Bus 1171
Car & Motorcycle 1172
Hitchhiking 1176
Local Transportation 1176
Tours 1177
Train 1177

Directory A-Z

Accommodations

The listings in the accommodations sections of this guidebook are in order of preference. For all but the cheapest places and the slowest seasons, reservations are advised. In high-season tourist hot spots, hotels can book up months ahead. In general, many hotels offer specials on their websites, but low-end chains sometimes give a slightly better rate over the phone. Chain hotels also increasingly offer frequent-flyer mileage deals and other rewards programs; ask when booking. Online travel booking, bidding and comparison websites (see p1169) are another good way to find discounted hotel rates – but are usually limited to chain hotels; also check out **Hotels.com** (www.hotels.com) and **Hotwire** (www.hotwire.com).

B&Bs

In the USA, many B&Bs are high-end romantic retreats in restored historic homes that are run by personable, independent innkeepers who serve gourmet breakfasts. These B&Bs often take pains to evoke a theme – Victorian, rustic, Cape Cod and so on – and amenities range from merely comfortable to indulgent. Rates normally top $100, and the best run are $200 to $300. Some B&Bs have minimum-stay requirements, and some exclude young children.

Still, European-style B&Bs exist: these may be rooms in someone's home, with plainer furnishings, simpler breakfasts, shared baths and cheaper rates. These often welcome families.

B&Bs can close out of season and reservations are essential, especially for top-end places. To avoid surprises, always ask about bathrooms (whether shared or private). B&B agencies are sprinkled throughout this guide. Also check listings online:

Bed & Breakfast Inns Online (www.bbonline.com)

BedandBreakfast.com (www.bedandbreakfast.com)

BnB Finder (www.bnbfinder.com)

Pamela Lanier's Bed & Breakfast Inns (www.lanierbb.com)

Select Registry (www.selectregistry.com)

Hostels

Hostels are mainly found in urban areas, in the northeast, the Pacific Northwest, California and the Southwest.

Hostelling International USA (HI-USA; ☎301-495-1240; www.hiusa.org; annual membership adult/child/senior $28/free/$18) runs more than 50 hostels in the US. Most have gender-segregated dorms, a few private rooms, shared baths and a communal kitchen. Overnight fees for dorm beds range from $21 to $45. HI-USA members are entitled to small discounts. Reservations are accepted (you can book online) and advised during high season, when there may be a three-night maximum stay.

The USA has many independent hostels not affiliated with HI-USA. For online listings, check the following:

Hostels.com (www.hostels.com)

Hostelworld.com (www.hostelworld.com).

Hostelz.com (www.hostelz.com)

Camping

Most federally managed public lands and many state parks offer camping. First-come, first-served 'primitive' campsites offer no facilities; overnight fees range from free to less than $10. 'Basic' sites usually provide toilets (flush or pit), drinking water, fire pits and picnic tables; they cost $5 to $15 a night,

> **BOOK YOUR STAY ONLINE**
>
> For more accommodations reviews by Lonely Planet authors, check out hotels.lonelyplanet.com/USA. You'll find independent reviews, as well as recommendations on the best places to stay. Best of all, you can book online.

and some or all may be reserved in advance. 'Developed' campsites, usually in national or state parks, have nicer facilities and more amenities: showers, barbecue grills, RV sites with hookups etc. These are $13 to $40 a night, and many can be reserved in advance.

Camping on most federal lands – including national parks, national forests, Bureau of Land Management land – can be reserved through **Recreation.gov** (☎518-885-3639, 877-444-6777; www.recreation.gov). Camping is limited to 14 days and can be reserved up to six months in advance. For some state park campgrounds, you can make bookings through **ReserveAmerica** (www.reserveamerica.com). Both websites let you search for campground locations and amenities, check availability and reserve a site, view maps and get driving directions.

Private campgrounds tend to cater to RVs and families (tent sites may be few and lack atmosphere). Facilities may include playgrounds, convenience stores, wi-fi access, swimming pools and other activities. Some rent camping cabins, ranging from canvas-sided wooden platforms to log-frame structures with real beds, heating and private baths. **Kampgrounds of America** (KOA; http://koa.com) is a national network of

PRACTICALITIES

Electricity

» AC 110V is standard; buy adapters to run most non-US electronics.

Newspapers & Magazines

» National newspapers: *New York Times, Wall Street Journal, USA Today*

» Mainstream news magazines: *Time, Newsweek, US News & World Report*

Radio & TV

» Radio news: National Public Radio (NPR), lower end of FM dial

» Broadcast TV: ABC, CBS, NBC, FOX, PBS (public broadcasting)

» Major cable channels: CNN (news), ESPN (sports), HBO (movies), Weather Channel

Video Systems

» NTSC standard (incompatible with PAL or SECAM)

» DVDs coded for Region 1 (US and Canada only)

Weights & Measures

» Weight: ounces (oz), pounds (lb), tons

» Liquid: oz, pints, quarts, gallons (gal)

» Distance: feet (ft), yards (yd), miles (mi)

Smoking

» As of 2011, about half the states, the District of Columbia and many municipalities across the US were entirely smoke-free in restaurants, bars and workplaces. You may still encounter smoky lobbies in chain hotels and budget-minded inns, but most other accommodations are smoke-free. For more on smoking, see www.cdc.gov.

Currency

» The currency is the US dollar ($).

Discount Cards

» The following passes can net you savings on museums, accommodations and some transport (including Amtrak): **International Student Identity Card** (ISIC; www.isiccard.com), for international nonstudents under 26; **Student Advantage Card** (www.studentadvantage.com), for US and foreign travelers; the **American Association of Retired Persons** (AARP; www.aarp.org) for US travelers age 50 and older. Membership in the **American Automobile Association** (AAA; www.aaa.com) and reciprocal clubs in the UK, Australia and elsewhere can also earn discounts.

private campgrounds with a full range of facilities. You can order KOA's free annual directory (shipping fees apply) or browse its comprehensive campground listings and make bookings online.

Hotels

Hotels in all categories typically include in-room phones, cable TV, alarm clocks, private baths and a simple continental breakfast. Many midrange properties provide minibars, microwaves, hairdryers, internet access, air-conditioning and/or heating, swimming pools and writing desks, while top-end hotels add concierge services, fitness and business centers, spas, restaurants, bars and higher-end furnishings.

Even if hotels advertise that children 'sleep free,' cots or rollaway beds may cost extra. Always ask about the hotel's policy for telephone calls; all charge an exorbitant amount for long-distance and international calls, but some also charge for dialing local and toll-free numbers.

Motels

Motels – distinguishable from hotels by having rooms that open onto a parking lot – tend to cluster around interstate exits and on main routes into town. Some remain smaller, less-expensive 'mom-and-pop' operations; breakfast is rarely included; and amenities might be a phone and TV (maybe with cable). Motels often have a few rooms with simple kitchenettes.

Although many motels are of the bland, cookie-cutter variety, these can be good for discount lodging or when other options fall through.

Don't judge a motel solely on looks. Facades may be faded and tired, but the proprietor may keep rooms spotlessly clean. Of course, the reverse could also be true. Try to see your room before you commit.

> **PRICE GUIDE**
>
> Accommodations rates in this guide are based on double occupancy for high season (generally May to September), and don't include taxes, which can add 10% to 15%. When booking, ask for the rate including taxes.
>
> » $ less than $100
>
> » $$ $100 to $200
>
> » $$$ more than $200

Business Hours

Reviews won't list operating hours unless they deviate from the following normal opening times:

» Bars: 5pm-midnight Sun-Thu, to 2am Fri & Sat

» Banks: 8:30am-4:30pm Mon-Thu, to 5:30pm Fri (and possibly 9am-noon Sat)

» Nightclubs: 10pm-2am Thu-Sat

» Post offices: 9am-5pm Mon-Fri

» Shopping Malls: 9am-9pm

» Stores: 10am-6pm Mon-Sat, noon-5pm Sun

» Supermarkets: 8am-8pm, some open 24hr

Customs Regulations

For a complete list of US customs regulations, visit the official portal for **US Customs and Border Protection** (www.cbp.gov).

Duty-free allowance per person is as follows:

» 1L of liquor (provided you are at least 21 years old)

» 100 cigars and 200 cigarettes (if you are at least 18)

» $100 worth of gifts and purchases ($800 if a returning US citizen)

» If you arrive with $10,000 in US or foreign currency, it must be declared.

There are heavy penalties for attempting to import illegal drugs. Forbidden items include drug paraphernalia, lottery tickets, items with fake brand names, and most goods made in Cuba, Iran, North Korea, Myanmar (Burma), Angola and Sudan. Fruit, vegetables, or other food or plant material must be declared or left in the arrival area bins.

Electricity

Embassies & Consulates

In addition to the following foreign embassies in Washington, DC (see www.embassy.org for a complete list), most countries have an embassy for the UN in New York City. Some countries have consulates in other large cities; look under 'Consulates' in the yellow pages, or call local directory assistance.

Australia (☎202-797-3000; www.usa.embassy.gov.au; 1601 Massachusetts Ave NW)

Canada (☎202-682-1740; www.canadainternational.gc.ca; 501 Pennsylvania Ave NW)

France (☎202-644-6000; www.info-france-usa.org; 4101 Reservoir Rd NW)

Germany (☎202-298-4000; www.germany.info; 2300 M St NW)

Ireland (☎202-462-3939; www.embassyofireland.org; 2234 Massachusetts Ave NW)

Mexico (☎202-728-1600; http://embamex.sre.gob.mx/eua; 1911 Pennsylvania Ave NW)

Netherlands (☎877-388-2443; http://dc.the-netherlands.org; 4200 Linnean Ave NW)

New Zealand (☎202-328-4800; www.nzembassy.com/usa; 37 Observatory Circle NW)

UK (☎202-588-6500; http://ukinusa.fco.gov.uk; 3100 Massachusetts Ave NW)

Food

Rates for main meals in Eating sections are:

» $ less than $10
» $$ $10 to $20
» $$$ more than $20

Gay & Lesbian Travelers

It's never been a better time to be gay in the USA. GLBT travelers will find lots of places where they can be themselves without thinking twice. Naturally, beaches and big cities typically are the gayest destinations.

Hot Spots

Manhattan is too crowded and cosmopolitan to worry about who's holding hands, while Fire Island is the sandy gay mecca on Long Island. Other East Coast cities that flaunt it are Boston, Philadelphia, Washington, DC, Massachusetts' Provincetown and Delaware's Rehoboth Beach. Even Maine brags a gay beach destination: Ogunquit.

In the South, there's always steamy 'Hotlanta' and Texas gets darn-right gay-friendly in Austin and parts of Houston. In Florida, Miami and the 'Conch Republic' of Key West support thriving gay communities, though Fort Lauderdale attracts bronzed boys and girls too. Of course, everyone gets their freak on in New Orleans.

In the Midwest, seek out Chicago and Minneapolis. You will have heard of San Francisco, the happiest gay city in America, and what can gays and lesbians do in Los Angeles and Las Vegas? Hmmm, just about anything. In fact, when LA or Vegas gets to be too much, flee to the desert resorts of Palm Springs.

Lastly, for an island idyll, Hawaii is generally gay-friendly, especially in Waikiki.

Attitudes

Most major US cities have a visible and open GLBT community that is easy to connect with. In this guide, many cities include a boxed text or section that describes the city's best GLBT offerings.

The level of acceptance varies nationwide. In some places, there is absolutely no tolerance whatsoever, and in others acceptance is predicated on GLBT people not 'flaunting' their sexual preference or identity. Sadly, bigotry still exists. In rural areas and extremely conservative enclaves, it's unwise to be openly out, as violence and verbal abuse can sometimes occur. When in doubt, assume locals follow a 'don't ask, don't tell' policy. Same-sex marriage, a hotly debated topic, is now legal in a handful of states.

Resources

Gay Travel (www.gaytravel.com) Online guides to dozens of US destinations.

Damron (www.damron.com) Publishes the classic gay travel guides, but they're advertiser-driven and sometimes outdated.

OutTraveler (www.outtraveler.com) Has useful online city guides and travel articles to various US and foreign destinations.

Purple Roofs (www.purpleroofs.com) Lists gay-owned and gay-friendly B&Bs and hotels nationwide.

Advocate (www.advocate.com) Gay-oriented news website reports on business, politics, arts, entertainment and travel.

Gay & Lesbian National Help Center (☎888-843-4564; www.glnh.org; ⏲1-9pm PST Mon-Fri, 9am-2pm PST Sat) A national hotline for counseling, information and referrals.

Gay Yellow Network (www.gayyellow.com) Yellow-page listings for more than 30 US cities. Also available as smartphone app (GLYP).

National Gay & Lesbian Task Force (www.thetaskforce.org) National activist group's website covers news, politics and current issues.

The Queerest Places: A Guide to Gay and Lesbian Historic Sites, by Paula Martinac, is full of juicy details and history, and covers the country.

Health

The USA offers possibly the finest health care in the world. The problem is that, unless you have good insurance, it can be prohibitively expensive. It's essential to purchase travel health insurance if your regular policy doesn't cover you when you're abroad.

Bring any medications you may need in their original containers, clearly labeled. A signed, dated letter from your physician that describes all medical conditions and medications, including generic names, is also a good idea.

If your health insurance does not cover you for medical expenses abroad, consider supplemental insurance. Check the Travel Services section of the **Lonely Planet** (www.lonelyplanet.com) website for more information. Find out in advance if your insurance plan will make payments directly to providers or reimburse you later for overseas health expenditures. For more information on insurance, see p1158.

Medical Checklist

Recommended items for a medical kit:

» acetaminophen (Tylenol) or aspirin

» adhesive or paper tape

» antibacterial ointment (eg Bactroban) for cuts and abrasions

» antihistamines (for hay fever and allergic reactions)

» anti-inflammatory drugs (eg ibuprofen)

» bandages, gauze, gauze rolls

» DEET-containing insect repellent for the skin

» permethrin-containing insect spray for clothing, tents and bed nets

» pocket knife

» scissors, safety pins, tweezers

» steroid cream or cortisone (for poison ivy and other allergic rashes)

» sunblock

» thermometer

Resources

The World Health Organization publishes a superb book, called *International Travel and Health,* which is revised annually and is available free online at www.who.int/ith/en. **MD Travel Health** (www.mdtravelhealth.com) provides travel health recommendations for every country, updated regularly.

It's usually a good idea to consult your government's travel health website before departure:

Australia (www.smarttraveller.gov.au)

Canada (www.hc-sc.gc.ca/index-eng.php)

UK (www.dh.gov.uk/travellers)

USA (wwwn.cdc.gov/travel)

Availability & Cost Of Health Care

In general, if you have a medical emergency, the best bet is for you to find the nearest hospital and go to its emergency room. If the problem isn't urgent, you can call a nearby hospital and ask for a referral to a local physician, which is usually cheaper than a trip to the emergency room. Stand-alone, for-profit urgent-care centers can be convenient, but may perform large numbers of expensive tests, even for minor illnesses.

Pharmacies are abundantly supplied, but you may find that some medications that are available over-the-counter in your home country require a prescription in the USA and, as always, if you don't have insurance to cover the cost of prescriptions, they can be shockingly expensive.

Insurance

No matter how long or short your trip, make sure you have adequate travel insurance, purchased before departure. At a minimum, you need coverage for medical emergencies and treatment, including hospital stays and an emergency flight home if necessary. Medical treatment in the USA is of the highest caliber, but the expense could kill you.

You should also consider getting coverage for luggage theft or loss and trip cancellation. If you already have a home-owner's or renter's policy, see what it will cover and consider getting supplemental insurance to cover the rest. If you have prepaid a large portion of your trip, cancellation insurance is a worthwhile expense. A comprehensive travel insurance policy that covers all these things can cost up to 10% of the total cost of your trip.

If you will be driving, it's essential that you have liability insurance. Car rental agencies offer insurance that covers damage to the rental vehicle and separate liability insurance, which covers damage to people and other vehicles. See p1173 for details.

Worldwide travel insurance is available at www.lonelyplanet.com/bookings/insurance.do. You can buy, extend and claim online anytime – even if you're already on the road.

Internet Access

Travelers will have few problems staying connected in the tech-savvy USA.

This guide uses an internet icon (@) when a place has a net-connected computer for public use and the wi-fi icon (wi-fi) when it offers wireless internet access, whether free or fee-based. These days, most hotels and some motels have either a public computer terminal or wi-fi (sometimes free, sometimes for a surcharge of $10 or more per day); ask when reserving. For more on wi-fi hotspots, see the boxed text, p1159.

Big cities have a few internet cafes, but in smaller towns, you may have to head to the public library or a copy center to get online if you're

WI-FI

Wi-fi hotspots don't entirely cover the USA yet, but wireless internet access is common. Most cities and college towns have neighborhood hotspots, and even the smallest towns usually have at least one coffee shop, internet cafe or hotel with wi-fi. You can even connect in the woods: private campgrounds (like KOA) increasingly offer it, and so do some state parks (for example, in California, Michigan, Kentucky and Texas).

The following websites provide lists of free and fee-based wi-fi hotspots nationwide:

» www.hotspot-locations.com

» www.jiwire.com

» www.wi-fi.org (run by the nonprofit Wi-Fi Alliance).

» www.wififreespot.com

» www.wi-fihotspotlist.com

not packing a laptop or other web-accessible device. Most libraries have public terminals (though they have time limits) and often wi-fi. Occasionally out-of-state residents are charged a small fee.

If you're not from the US, remember that you will need an AC adapter for your laptop, plus a plug adapter for US sockets; both are available at larger electronics shops, such as **Best Buy** (☎888-237-8289; www.bestbuy.com).

Legal Matters

In everyday matters, if you are stopped by the police, bear in mind that there is no system of paying traffic or other fines on the spot. Attempting to pay a fine to an officer is frowned upon at best and may result in a charge of bribery. For traffic offenses, the police officer or highway patroller will explain the options to you. There is usually a 30-day period to pay a fine. Most matters can be handled by mail.

If you are arrested, you have a legal right to an attorney, and you are allowed to remain silent. There is no legal reason to speak to a police officer if you don't wish, but never walk away from an officer until given permission to do so. Anyone who is arrested is legally allowed to make one phone call. If you can't afford a lawyer, a public defender will be appointed to you free of charge. Foreign visitors who don't have a lawyer, friend or family member to help should call their embassy; the police will provide the number upon request.

As a matter of principle, the US legal system presumes a person innocent until proven guilty. Each state has its own civil and criminal laws, and what is legal in one state may be illegal in others.

Drinking

Bars and stores often ask for photo ID to prove you are of legal drinking age (ie 21 or over). Being 'carded' is standard practice; don't take it personally. The sale of liquor is subject to local government regulations; some counties prohibit liquor sales on Sunday, after midnight or before breakfast. In 'dry' counties, liquor sales are banned altogether.

Driving

In all states, driving under the influence of alcohol or drugs is a serious offense, subject to stiff fines and even imprisonment. For more information on driving in the USA and road rules, see p1176.

Drugs

Recreational drugs are prohibited by federal and state laws. Some states, such as California and Alaska, treat possession of small amounts of marijuana as a misdemeanor, though it is still punishable with fines and/or imprisonment.

Possession of any illicit drug, including cocaine, ecstasy, LSD, heroin, hashish or more than an ounce of pot, is a felony potentially punishable by a lengthy jail sentence. For foreigners, conviction of any drug offense is grounds for deportation.

Maps

For a good road atlas or driving maps, try **Rand McNally** (www.randmcnally.com) and its Thomas Brothers city guides; both are stocked at many bookstores and some gas stations. If you are a member of an automobile association (p1173), you can get free high-quality maps from regional offices; AAA has reciprocal agreements with some international auto clubs. For online driving directions and free downloadable maps, visit **Google Maps** (http://maps.google.com).

If you're heading into the wilderness backcountry, don't venture out on the trail without a good topographic map, often sold at park visitor centers, outdoor outfitters and supply stores. The most detailed topo maps are published by the **US Geological Survey** (USGS; ☎877-275-8747; http://store.usgs.gov), which offers online downloads and orders; the website has a comprehensive list of retailers. You can pay to create custom, downloadable topo maps at **Trails.com** (www.trails.com) or buy personalized topo-map creation software from **National Geographic** (www.nationalgeographic.com), whose online store has all the mapping products you'd ever want.

For on- and off-road driving and outdoor adventures on foot and bicycle, GPS gear and mapping software are available from **Garmin** (www.garmin.com) and **Magellan** (www.magellangps.com). Of course, GPS units can sometimes fail and may not work in all areas of the country, such as in thick forests or deep canyons.

Money

See p19 for exchange rates and costs.

Most locals do not carry large amounts of cash for everyday use, relying instead on credit cards, ATMs and debit cards. Smaller businesses may refuse to accept bills larger than $20. Prices quoted in this book are in US dollars and exclude taxes, unless otherwise noted.

ATMs

ATMs are available 24/7 at most banks, and in shopping centers, airports, grocery stores and convenience shops. Most ATMs charge a service fee of $2.50 or more per transaction and your home bank may impose additional charges. Withdrawing cash from an ATM using a credit card usually incurs a hefty fee; check with your credit-card company first.

For foreign visitors, ask your bank or credit card company for exact information about using its cards in stateside ATMs. If you will be relying on ATMs (not a bad strategy), bring more than one card and carry them separately. The exchange rate on ATM transactions is usually as good as you'll get anywhere. Before leaving home, notify your bank and credit-card providers of your upcoming travel plans. Otherwise, you may trigger fraud alerts with atypical spending patterns, which may result in your accounts being temporarily frozen.

Credit Cards

Major credit cards are almost universally accepted. In fact, it's almost impossible to rent a car or make phone reservations without one (though some airlines require your credit card billing address to be in the USA – a hassle if you're booking domestic flights once there). It's highly recommended that you carry at least one credit card, if only for emergencies. Visa and MasterCard are the most widely accepted.

If your credit cards are lost or stolen, contact the issuing company immediately:

American Express (☎800-528-4800; www.americanexpress.com)

Diners Club (☎800-234-6377; www.dinersclub.com)

Discover (☎800-347-2683; www.discovercard.com)

MasterCard (☎800-627-8372; www.mastercard.com)

Visa (☎800-847-2911; www.visa.com)

Currency Exchange

Banks are usually the best places to exchange foreign currencies. Most large city banks offer currency exchange, but banks in rural areas may not. Currency-exchange counters at the airport and in tourist centers typically have the worst rates; ask about fees and surcharges first. **Travelex** (☎877-414-6359; www.travelex.com) is a major currency-exchange company, but **American Express** (☎800-528-4800; www.americanexpress.com) travel offices may offer better rates.

Taxes

Sales tax varies by state and county; see each state's 'Facts' boxed text in the regional chapters for specifics. Hotel taxes vary by city, and these are listed under cities' Sleeping sections.

Tipping

Tipping is *not* optional; only withhold tips in cases of outrageously bad service.

Airport & hotel porters $2 per bag, minimum per cart $5

Bartenders 10-15% per round, minimum per drink $1

Hotel maids $2-4 per night, left under the card provided

Restaurant servers 15-20%, unless a gratuity is already charged on the bill

Taxi drivers 10-15%, rounded up to the next dollar

Valet parking attendants At least $2 when handed back the keys

Traveler's Checks

Since the advent of ATMs, traveler's checks are becoming obsolete, except as a trustworthy backup. If you carry them, buy them in US dollars; local businesses may not cash them in a foreign currency. Keep a separate record of their numbers in case they are lost or stolen. American Express and Visa traveler's checks are the most widely accepted.

Photography & Video

Print film can be found in drugstores and at specialty camera shops. Digital camera memory cards are widely available at chain retailers such as Best Buy and Target.

Some Native American tribal lands prohibit photography and video completely; when it's allowed, you may be required to purchase a permit. Always ask permission if you want to photograph someone close up; anyone who then agrees to be photographed may expect a small tip.

For more advice on picture-taking, consult Lonely Planet's *Travel Photography* book.

Post

For 24-hour postal information, including post office locations and hours, contact the **US Postal Service** (USPS; ☎800-275-8777; www.usps.com), which is reliable and inexpensive.

For sending urgent or important letters and packages either domestically or internationally, **Federal Express** (FedEx; ☎800-463-3339; www.fedex.com) and **United Parcel Service** (UPS; ☎800-742-5877; www.ups.com) offer more-expensive door-to-door delivery services.

Postal Rates

When this book went to print, the postal rates for 1st-class mail within the USA were 44¢ for letters weighing up to 1oz (20¢ for each additional ounce) and 29¢ for postcards. First-class mail goes up to 13oz, and then priority-mail rates apply.

International airmail rates (except to Canada and Mexico) are 98¢ for a 1oz letter or a postcard; to Canada and Mexico it's 80¢.

Sending & Receiving Mail

If you have the correct postage, you can drop mail weighing less than 13oz into any blue mailbox. To send a package weighing 13oz or more, you must go to a post office.

Poste-restante mail can usually be sent to you c/o General Delivery at any post office that has its own zip code. Domestic mail is usually held for 10 days and international mail for 30 days before it's returned to the sender; you might ask the sender to write 'Hold for Arrival' on the envelope. You'll need photo ID to collect mail. In some big cities, general-delivery mail is not held at the main post office but at a postal facility away from downtown.

Public Holidays

On the following national public holidays, banks, schools and government offices (including post offices) are closed, and transportation, museums and other services operate on a Sunday schedule. Holidays falling on a weekend are usually observed the following Monday.

New Year's Day January 1

Martin Luther King Jr Day Third Monday in January

Presidents' Day Third Monday in February

Memorial Day Last Monday in May

Independence Day July 4

Labor Day First Monday in September

Columbus Day Second Monday in October

Veterans' Day November 11

Thanksgiving Fourth Thursday in November

Christmas Day December 25

During spring break, high school and college students get a week off from school so they can overrun beach towns and resorts. This occurs throughout March and April. For students of all ages, summer vacation runs from June to August.

Safe Travel

Despite its seemingly Babylonian list of dangers – guns, violent crime, riots, earthquakes, tornadoes – the USA is actually a pretty safe country to visit. The greatest danger for travelers is posed by car accidents (buckle up – it's the law).

Crime

For the traveler, petty theft is the biggest concern, not violent crime. When possible, withdraw money from ATMs during the day, or at night in well-lit, busy areas. When driving, don't pick up hitchhikers, and lock valuables in the trunk of your car before arriving at your destination. In hotels, you can secure valuables in room or hotel safes.

Scams

Pack your street smarts. In big cities, don't forget that three-card-monte card games are always rigged, and that expensive electronics, watches and designer items sold on the cheap from sidewalk tables are either fakes or stolen. Those truly fascinated by all the myriad ways small-time American hucksters make a living today (usually with credit card, real estate and investment frauds) can browse the 'Consumer Guides' on the government's website, www.usa.gov.

Natural Disasters

Most areas with predictable natural disturbances – tornadoes in the Midwest, tsunamis in Hawaii, hurricanes in the South, earthquakes in California – have an emergency siren system to alert communities to imminent danger. These sirens are tested periodically at noon, but if you hear one and suspect trouble, turn on a local TV or radio station, which will be broadcasting safety warnings and advice.

The **US Department of Health & Human Services**

GOVERNMENT TRAVEL ADVICE

- **Australia** (www.smartraveller.gov.au)
- **Canada** (www.voyage.gc.ca)
- **New Zealand** (www.safetravel.govt.nz)
- **UK** (www.fco.gov.uk)

(www.phe.gov) has preparedness advice, news and information on all the ways your vacation could go horribly, horribly wrong. But relax: it probably won't.

Telephone

The US phone system comprises regional service providers, competing long-distance carriers and several mobile-phone and pay-phone companies. Overall, the system is very efficient, but it can be expensive. Avoid making long-distance calls on a hotel phone or on a pay phone. It's usually cheaper to use a regular landline or cell phone. Most hotels allow guests to make free local calls.

Telephone books can be handy resources: some list community services, public transportation and things to see and do as well as phone and business listings. Online phone directories include www.411.com and www.yellowpages.com.

Cell Phones

In the USA cell phones use GSM 1900 or CDMA 800, operating on different frequencies from other systems around the world. The only foreign phones that will work in the USA are GSM tri- or quad-band models. If you have one of these phones, check with your service provider about using it in the USA. Ask if roaming charges apply, as these will turn even local US calls into pricey international calls.

It might be cheaper to buy a compatible prepaid SIM card for the USA, like those sold by AT&T or Cingular, which you can insert into your international mobile phone to get a local phone number and voicemail. **Planet Omni** (www.planetomni.com) and **Telestial** (www.telestial.com) offer these services, as well as cell phone rentals.

If you don't have a compatible phone, you can buy inexpensive, no-contract (pre-paid) phones with a local number and a set number of minutes, which can be topped up at will. Virgin Mobile, T-Mobile, AT&T and other providers offer phones starting at US$15, with a package of minutes starting around $40 for 400 minutes. Electronics stores such as Radio Shack and Best Buy sell these phones.

Huge swathes of rural America, including many national parks and recreation areas, don't pick up a signal. Check your provider's coverage map.

Dialing Codes

All phone numbers within the USA consist of a three-digit area code followed by a seven-digit local number. Typically, if you are calling a number within the same area code, you only have to dial the seven-digit number; however, some places now require you to dial the entire 10-digit number even for a local call. If dialing the seven-digit number doesn't work, try all 10.

If you are calling long distance, dial ☎1 plus the area code plus the phone number. If you're not sure whether the number is local or long distance (new area codes are added all the time, confusing even residents), try one way, and if it's wrong, usually a recorded voice will correct you.

Toll-free numbers begin with ☎800, ☎888, ☎877 and ☎866 and when dialing, are preceded by ☎1. Most can only be used within the USA, some only within the state, and some only from outside the state. You won't know until you try dialing. The 900-series of area codes and a few other prefixes are for calls charged at a premium per-minute rate – phone sex, horoscopes, jokes etc.

- ☎1 is the international country code for the USA if calling from abroad (the same as Canada, but international rates apply between the two countries).
- ☎011 to make an international call from the USA (followed by country code, area code and phone number)
- ☎00 for assistance making international calls
- ☎411 directory assistance nationwide
- ☎800-555-1212 directory assistance for toll-free numbers

Pay Phones

Pay phones are an endangered species in an ever-expanding mobile-phone world. Local calls at pay phones that work (listen for a dial tone before inserting coins) cost 35¢ to 50¢ for the first few minutes; talking longer costs more. Only put in the exact amount because pay phones don't give change. Some pay phones (eg in national parks) only accept credit cards or prepaid phone cards. Local calls from pay phones get expensive quickly, while long-distance calls can be prohibitive, especially if you use the operator (☎0) to facilitate long-distance or collect (reverse-charge) calls. It's usually cheaper to use a prepaid phone card or the access line of a major carrier like **AT&T** (☎800-321-0288).

Phone Cards

A prepaid phone card is a good solution for travelers on a budget. Phone cards are easy to find in larger towns and cities, where they are sold at newsstands, convenience stores, supermarkets and major retailers. Be sure to read the fine print, as many cards contain hidden charges such as 'activation fees' or per-call 'connection fees' in addition to the rates. AT&T sells a reliable phone card that is widely available in the USA.

Time

The USA uses Daylight Saving Time (DST). On the second Sunday in March, clocks are set one hour ahead ('spring forward'). Then, on the first Sunday of November, clocks are turned back one hour ('fall back'). Just to keep you on your toes, Arizona (except the Navajo Nation), Hawaii and much of Indiana don't follow DST.

The US date system is written as month/day/year. Thus, 8 June 2012 becomes 6/8/12.

Tourist Information

There is no national office promoting US tourism. However, visit the federal government's official web portal (www.usa.gov), go to the 'Travel and Recreation' page, and you'll find links to every US state and territory tourism office and website, plus more links to indoor and outdoor recreation, from museums and historical landmarks to scenic byways, national parks and, uh, migratory bird hunting.

In this book, state tourism offices are listed in the Information section at the start of each regional chapter, while city and county visitor information centers are listed throughout the regional chapters.

Any tourist office worth contacting has a website, where you can download free travel e-guides. They also field phone calls; some local offices maintain daily lists of hotel room availability, but few offer reservation services. All tourist offices have self-service racks of brochures and discount coupons; some also sell maps and books.

State-run 'welcome centers,' usually placed along interstate highways, tend to have materials that cover wider territories, and offices are usually open longer hours, including weekends and holidays.

Many cities have an official convention and visitors bureau (CVB); these sometimes double as tourist bureaus, but since their main focus is drawing the business trade, CVBs can be less useful for independent travelers.

Keep in mind that, in smaller towns, when the local chamber of commerce runs the tourist bureau, their lists of hotels, restaurants and services usually mention only chamber members; the town's cheapest options may be missing.

Similarly, in prime tourist destinations, some private 'tourist bureaus' are really agents who book hotel rooms and tours on commission. They may offer excellent service and deals, but you'll get what they're selling and nothing else.

Travelers with Disabilities

If you have a physical disability, the USA can be an accommodating place. The Americans with Disabilities Act (ADA) requires that all public buildings, private buildings built after 1993 (including hotels, restaurants, theaters and museums) and public transit be wheelchair accessible. However, call ahead to confirm what is available. Some local tourist offices publish detailed accessibility guides.

Telephone companies offer relay operators, available via teletypewriter (TTY) numbers, for the hearing impaired. Most banks provide ATM instructions in Braille and via earphone jacks for hearing-impaired customers. All major airlines, Greyhound buses and Amtrak trains will assist travelers with disabilities; just describe your needs when making reservations at least 48 hours in advance. Service animals (guide dogs) are allowed to accompany passengers, but bring documentation.

Some car rental agencies, such as Budget and Hertz, offer hand-controlled vehicles and vans with wheelchair lifts at no extra charge, but you must reserve them well in advance. **Wheelchair Getaways** (☎800-642-2042; www.wheelchairgetaways.com) rents accessible vans throughout the USA. In many cities and towns, public buses are accessible to wheelchair riders and will 'kneel' if you are unable to use the steps; just let the driver know that you need the lift or ramp. Cities with underground transport have elevators for passengers needing assistance; DC has the best network (every station has an elevator); NYC's elevators are few and far between.

Many national and some state parks and recreation areas have wheelchair-accessible paved, graded dirt or boardwalk trails. US citizens and permanent residents with permanent disabilities are entitled to a free 'America the Beautiful' Access Pass. Go online (www.nps.gov/findapark/passes.htm) for details.

Some helpful resources for travelers with disabilities:

Access-Able Travel Source (☎303-232-2979; www.access-able.com) General travel website with useful tips and links.

Disabled Sports USA (☎301-217-0960; www.dsusa.org) Offers sports and recreation programs for those with disabilities and publishes *Challenge* magazine.

Flying Wheels Travel (☎507-451-5005, 877-451-5006; www.flyingwheelstravel.com) A full-service travel agency.

Mobility International USA (☎541-343-1284; www.miusa.org) Advises disabled travelers on mobility issues and runs educational international-exchange programs.

Moss Rehabilitation Hospital (☎215-663-6000; www.mossresourcenet.org/travel.htm) Extensive links and tips for accessible travel.

Society for Accessible Travel & Hospitality (☎212-447-7284; www.sath.org) Advocacy group provides general information for travelers with disabilities.

Visas

Warning: all of the following information is highly subject to change. US entry requirements keep evolving as national security regulations change. All travelers should double-check current visa and passport regulations *before* coming to the USA.

The **US State Department** (www.travel.state.gov/visa) maintains the most comprehensive visa information, providing downloadable forms, lists of US consulates abroad and even visa wait times calculated by country.

Visa Applications

Apart from most Canadian citizens and those entering under the Visa Waiver Program (see p1164), all foreign visitors will need to obtain a visa from a US consulate or embassy abroad. Most applicants must schedule a personal interview, to which you must bring all your documentation and proof of fee payment. Wait times for interviews vary, but afterward, barring problems, visa issuance takes from a few days to a few weeks.

Your passport must be valid for at least six months after the end of your intended stay in the USA. You'll need a recent photo (2in by 2in), and you must pay a non-refundable $140 processing fee, plus in a few cases an additional visa issuance reciprocity fee. You'll also need to fill out the online DS-160 nonimmigrant visa electronic application.

Visa applicants are required to show documents of financial stability (or evidence that a US resident will provide financial support), a round-trip or onward ticket and 'binding obligations' that will ensure their return home, such as family ties, a home or a job. Because of these requirements, those planning to travel through other countries before arriving in the USA are generally better off applying for a US visa while they are still in their home country, rather than while on the road.

The most common visa is a nonimmigrant visitor's visa, type B-1 for business purposes, B-2 for tourism or visiting friends and relatives. A visitor's visa is good for multiple entries over one or five years, and specifically prohibits the visitor from taking paid employment in the USA. The validity period depends on what country you are from. The actual length of time you'll be allowed to stay in the USA is determined by US immigration at the port of entry.

If you're coming to the USA to work or study, you will need a different type of visa, and the company or institution to which you are going should make the arrangements. Other categories of nonimmigrant visas include an F-1 visa for students attending a course at a recognized institution; an H-1, H-2 or H-3 visa for temporary employment; and a J-1 visa for exchange visitors in approved programs. See p1167 for more information about working in the USA.

Visa Waiver Program

Currently under the Visa Waiver Program (VWP), citizens of the following countries may enter the USA without a visa for stays of 90 days or fewer: Andorra, Australia, Austria, Belgium, Brunei, Czech Republic, Denmark, Estonia, Finland, France, Germany, Greece, Hungary, Iceland, Ireland, Italy, Japan, Latvia, Liechtenstein, Lithuania, Luxembourg, Malta, Monaco, the Netherlands, New Zealand, Norway, Portugal, San Marino, Singapore, Slovakia, Slovenia, South Korea, Spain, Sweden, Switzerland and the UK.

If you are a citizen of a VWP country, you do not need a visa *only if* you have a passport that meets current US standards (see p1168) *and* you have gotten approval from the Electronic System for Travel Authorization (ESTA) in advance. Register online with the Department of Homeland Security at https://esta.cbp.dhs.gov at least 72 hours before arrival; once travel authorization is approved, your registration is valid for two years. The fee, payable online, is $14.

Visitors from VWP countries must still produce at the port of entry all the same evidence as for a nonimmigrant visa application. They must demonstrate that their trip is for 90 days or less, and that they have a round-trip or onward ticket, adequate funds to cover the trip and binding obligations abroad.

In addition, the same 'grounds for exclusion and deportation' apply, except that you will have no opportunity to appeal or apply for an exemption. If you are denied under the Visa Waiver Program at a US point of entry, you will have to use your onward or return ticket on the next available flight.

Grounds for Exclusion & Deportation

If on your visa application form you admit to being a subversive, smuggler, prostitute, drug addict, terrorist or an ex-Nazi, you may be excluded. You can also be refused a visa or entry to the USA if you have a 'communicable disease of public health significance' or a criminal record, or if you've ever made a false statement in connection with a US visa application. However, if these last three apply, you are still able to request an exemption;

many people are granted them and then given visas.

The US immigration department has a very broad definition of a criminal record. If you've ever been arrested or charged with an offense, that's a criminal record, even if you were acquitted or discharged without conviction. Don't attempt to enter through the VWP if you have a criminal record of any kind; assume US authorities will find out about it.

Communicable diseases include tuberculosis, the Ebola virus, SARS and most particularly HIV. US immigration doesn't test people for disease, but officials at the point of entry may question anyone about his or her health. They can exclude anyone whom they believe has a communicable disease, perhaps because they are carrying medical documents, prescriptions or AIDS/HIV medicine. Being gay is not grounds for exclusion; being an IV drug user is. Visitors may be deported if US immigration finds out they have HIV but did not declare it. Being HIV-positive is not grounds for deportation, but failing to provide accurate information on the visa application is.

Often USCIS (United States Citizenship & Immigration Services) will grant an exemption (a 'waiver of ineligibility') to a person who would normally be subject to exclusion, but this requires referral to a regional immigration office and can take some time (allow at least two months). If you're tempted to conceal something, remember that US immigration is strictest of all about false statements. It will often view favorably an applicant who admits to an old criminal charge or a communicable disease, but it is extremely harsh on anyone who has ever attempted to mislead it, even on minor points. After you're admitted to the USA, any evidence of a false statement to US immigration is grounds for deportation.

Prospective visitors to whom grounds of exclusion may apply should consider their options *before* applying for a visa.

Entering the USA

If you have a non-US passport, you must complete an arrival/departure record (form I-94) before you reach the immigration desk. It's usually handed out on the plane along with the customs declaration. For the question, 'Address While In the United States,' give the address where you will spend the first night (a hotel address is fine).

No matter what your visa says, US immigration officers have an absolute authority to refuse admission to the USA or to impose conditions on admission. They will ask about your plans and whether you have sufficient funds; it's a good idea to list an itinerary, produce an onward or round-trip ticket and have at least one major credit card. Showing that you have over $400 per week of your stay should be enough. Don't make too much of having friends, relatives or business contacts in the USA; the immigration official may decide that this will make you more likely to overstay. It also helps to be neatly dressed and polite.

The Department of Homeland Security's registration program, called **US-VISIT** (www.dhs.gov/us-visit), includes every port of entry and nearly every foreign visitor to the USA. For most visitors (excluding, for now, most Canadian and some Mexican citizens), registration consists of having a digital photo and electronic (inkless) fingerprints taken; the process takes less than a minute.

The National Security Entry/Exit Registration System (NSEERS) applies to certain citizens of countries that have been deemed particular risks; however, US officials can require this registration of any traveler. Currently, the countries included are Iran, Iraq, Libya, Sudan and Syria, but be sure to visit www.ice.gov for updates. Registration in these cases also includes a short interview in a separate room and computer verification of all personal information on travel documents.

Visa Extensions

To stay in the USA longer than the date stamped on your passport, go to a local **USCIS** (☎800-375-5283; www.uscis.gov) office to apply for an extension well *before* the stamped date. If the date has passed, your best chance will be to bring a US citizen with you to vouch for your character, and to produce lots of other verification that you are not trying to work illegally and have enough money to support yourself. However, if you've overstayed, the most likely scenario is that you will be deported. Travelers who enter the USA under the VWP are ineligible for visa extensions.

Short-Term Departures & Re-entry

It's temptingly easy to make trips across the border to Canada or Mexico, but upon return to the USA, non-Americans will be subject to the full immigration procedure. Always take your passport when you cross the border. If your immigration card still has plenty of time on it, you will probably be able to re-enter using the same one, but if it has nearly expired, you will have to apply for a new card, and border control may want to see your onward air ticket, sufficient funds and so on.

Traditionally, a quick trip across the border has been a way to extend your stay in the USA without applying for an extension at a USCIS office. Don't assume this still works. First, make sure you hand in your old immigration card to the immigration authorities when you leave the USA, and when you return make sure you have all the necessary application documentation from when you first entered the country. US immigration will be very suspicious of anyone who leaves for a few days and returns immediately hoping for a new six-month stay; expect to be questioned closely.

Citizens of most Western countries will not need a visa to visit Canada, so it's really not a problem at all to cross to the Canadian side of Niagara Falls, detour up to Québec or pass through on the way to Alaska. Travelers entering the USA by bus from Canada may be closely scrutinized. A round-trip ticket that takes you back to Canada will most likely make US immigration feel less suspicious. Mexico has a visa-free zone along most of its border with the USA, including the Baja Peninsula and most of the border towns, such as Tijuana and Ciudad Juárez. You'll need a Mexican visa or tourist card if you want to go beyond the border zone. See Border Crossings, p1169.

Volunteering

Volunteer opportunities abound in the USA, and they can be a great way to break up a long trip. They can also provide truly memorable experiences: you'll get to interact with people, society and the land in ways you never would by just passing through.

Casual, drop-in volunteer opportunities are plentiful in big cities, where you can socialize with locals while helping out nonprofit organizations. Check weekly alternative newspapers for calendar listings, or browse the free classified ads online at **Craigslist** (www.craigslist.org). The public website **Serve.gov** (www.serve.gov) and private websites **Idealist.org** (www.idealist.org) and **VolunteerMatch** (www.volunteermatch.org) offer free searchable databases of short- and long-term volunteer opportunities nationwide.

More-formal volunteer programs, especially those designed for international travelers, typically charge a hefty fee of $250 to $1000, depending on the length of the program and what amenities are included (eg housing, meals). None cover travel to the USA.

Recommended volunteer organizations:

Green Project (☎504-945-0240; www.thegreenproject.org) Working to rebuild New Orleans post-Katrina in sustainable, green ways.

Habitat for Humanity (☎800-422-4828; www.habitat.org) Focuses on building affordable housing for those in need.

Sierra Club (☎415-977-5500; www.sierraclub.org) 'Volunteer vacations' restore wilderness areas and maintain trails, including in national parks and nature preserves.

Volunteers for Peace (☎802-540-3060; www.vfp.org) Grassroots, multiweek volunteer projects emphasize manual labor and international exchange.

Wilderness Volunteers (☎928-556-0038; www.wildernessvolunteers.org) Week-long trips helping maintain national parklands and outdoor recreation areas.

World Wide Opportunities on Organic Farms-USA (☎949-715-9500; www.wwoofusa.org) Represents more than 1000 organic farms in all 50 states that host volunteer workers in exchange for meals and accommodation, with opportunities for both short- and long-term stays.

Women Travelers

Women traveling alone or in groups should not expect to encounter any particular problems in the USA. The community website www.journeywoman.com facilitates women exchanging travel tips, and has links to other helpful resources. The booklet *Her Own Way*, published by the Canadian government, is filled with general travel advice, useful for any woman; click to www.voyage.gc.ca/publications/menu-eng.asp to download the PDF or read it online.

These two national advocacy groups might also be helpful:

National Organization for Women (NOW; ☎202-628-8669; www.now.org)

Planned Parenthood (☎800-230-7526; www.plannedparenthood.org) Offers referrals to women's health clinics throughout the country.

In terms of safety issues, single women just need to practice common-sense street smarts.

When first meeting someone, don't advertise where you are staying, or even that you are traveling alone. Americans can be eager to help and even take in solo travelers. However, don't take all offers of help at face value. If someone who seems trustworthy invites you to his or her home, let someone (eg hostel or hotel manager) know where you're going. This advice also applies if you go for a hike by yourself. If something happens and you don't return as expected, you want to know that someone will notice and know where to begin looking for you.

Some women carry a whistle, mace or cayenne-pepper spray in case of assault. If you purchase a spray, contact a police station to find out about local regulations. Laws regarding sprays vary from state to state; federal law prohibits them being carried on planes.

If you are assaulted, consider calling a rape-crisis hotline before calling the police, unless you are in immediate danger, in which case you should call ☎911. But be aware that not all police have as much sensitivity training or experience assisting sexual assault survivors, whereas rape-crisis-center staff will tirelessly advocate on your behalf and act as a link to other community services, including hospitals and the police. Telephone books have listings of local rape-crisis centers, or contact the 24-hour **National Sexual Assault Hotline** (☎800-656-4673; www.rainn.org). Alternatively, go straight to a hospital emergency room.

Work

If you are a foreigner in the USA with a standard nonimmigrant visitor's visa, you are expressly forbidden to partake in paid work in the USA and will be deported if you're caught working illegally. Employers are required to establish the bona fides of their employees or face fines, making it much tougher for a foreigner to get work than it once was.

To work legally, foreigners need to apply for a work visa before leaving home. A J-1 visa, for exchange visitors, is issued to young people (age limits vary) for study, student vacation employment, work in summer camps, and short-term traineeships with a specific employer. Organizations that can help arrange international student exchanges, work placements and J-1 visas:

American Institute for Foreign Study (☎866-906-2437; www.aifs.com)

Au Pair in America (☎800-928-7247; www.aupairinamerica.com)

BUNAC (in the UK ☎020-7251-3472; www.bunac.org)

Camp America (in the UK ☎020-7581-7373; www.campamerica.co.uk)

Council on International Educational Exchange (☎207-553-4000; www.ciee.org)

InterExchange (☎212-924-0446; www.interexchange.org)

International Exchange Programs (IEP) Australia (☎1300-300-912; www.iep.org.au); New Zealand (☎0800-443-769; www.iep.co.nz)

For nonstudent jobs, temporary or permanent, you need to be sponsored by a US employer who will have to arrange an H-category visa. These are not easy to obtain, since the employer has to prove that no US citizen or permanent resident is available to do the job.

Seasonal work is possible in national parks and at tourist attractions and ski resorts. Contact park concessionaire businesses, local chambers of commerce and ski-resort management. Lonely Planet's *Gap Year Book* has more ideas on how best to combine work and travel.

Transportation

GETTING THERE & AWAY

Flights and tours can be booked online at www.lonely planet.com/travel_services.

Entering the USA

If you are flying to the US, the first airport that you land in is where you must go through immigration and customs, even if you are continuing on the flight to another destination. Upon arrival, all international visitors must register with the US-VISIT program, which entails having your fingerprints scanned and a digital photo taken. For more information on visa requirements for visiting the USA, including the Electronic System for Travel Authorization (ESTA) now required before arrival for citizens of the Visa Waiver Program (VWP) countries, see p1164.

Once you go through immigration, you collect your baggage and pass through customs (p1156). If you have nothing to declare, you'll probably clear customs without a baggage search, but don't assume this. If you are continuing on the same plane or connecting to another one, it is your responsibility to get your bags to the right place. There are usually airline representatives just outside the customs area who can help you.

If you are a single parent, grandparent or guardian traveling with anyone under 18, carry proof of legal custody or a notarized letter from the nonaccompanying parent(s) authorizing the trip. This isn't required, but the USA is concerned with thwarting child abduction, and not having authorizing papers could cause delays or even result in being denied admittance to the country.

Passports

Every visitor entering the USA from abroad needs a passport. Your passport must be valid for at least six months longer than your intended stay in the USA. Also, if your passport does not meet current US standards, you'll be turned back at the border. If your passport was issued before October 26, 2005, it must be 'machine readable' (with two lines of letters, numbers and <<< at the bottom); if it was issued between October 26, 2005, and October 25, 2006, it must be machine readable and include a digital photo; and if it was issued on or after October 26, 2006, it must be an e-Passport with a digital photo and an integrated RFID chip containing biometric data.

Air

Airports

The USA has more than 375 domestic airports, but only a baker's dozen are the main international gateways. Many other airports are called

CLIMATE CHANGE & TRAVEL

Every form of transport that relies on carbon-based fuel generates CO_2, the main cause of human-induced climate change. Modern travel is dependent on aeroplanes, which might use less fuel per kilometer per person than most cars but travel much greater distances. The altitude at which aircraft emit gases (including CO_2) and particles also contributes to their climate change impact. Many websites offer 'carbon calculators' that allow people to estimate the carbon emissions generated by their journey and, for those who wish to do so, to offset the impact of the greenhouse gases emitted with contributions to portfolios of climate-friendly initiatives throughout the world. Lonely Planet offsets the carbon footprint of all staff and author travel.

'international' but may have only a few flights from other countries – typically Mexico or Canada. Even travel to an international gateway sometimes requires a connection in another gateway city (eg London–Los Angeles flights may involve transferring in Houston).

International gateway airports in the USA:

Atlanta Hartsfield-Jackson International (ATL; www.atlanta-airport.com)

Boston Logan International (BOS; www.massport.com/logan)

Chicago O'Hare International (ORD; www.flychicago.com)

Dallas-Fort Worth (DFW; www.dfwairport.com)

Honolulu (HNL; www.honoluluairport.com)

Houston George Bush Intercontinental (IAH; www.fly2houston.com)

Los Angeles (LAX; www.lawa.org/lax)

Miami (MIA; www.miami-airport.com)

New York John F Kennedy (JFK; www.panynj.gov)

Newark Liberty International (EWR; www.panynj.gov)

San Francisco (SFO; www.flysfo.com)

Seattle Seattle-Tacoma International (SEA; www.portseattle.org/seatac)

Washington, DC Dulles International (IAD; www.metwashairports.com/dulles)

Tickets

Flying midweek and in the off-season (usually, fall to spring, excluding holidays) is always less expensive, but fare wars can start anytime. To ensure you've found the cheapest possible ticket for the flight you want, check every angle: compare several online travel booking sites with the airline's own website. Engage a living, breathing travel agent if your itinerary is complex.

Keep in mind your entire itinerary. Some deals for travel within the USA can only be purchased overseas in conjunction with an international air ticket, or you may get discounts for booking air and car rental together. Or, you may find domestic flights within the USA are less expensive when added on to your international airfare.

For a good overview of online ticket agencies, visit **Airinfo** (http://airinfo.aero), which also lists travel agencies worldwide. The big three US travel-booking websites are **Travelocity** (www.travelocity.com), **Orbitz** (www.orbitz.com) and **Expedia** (www.expedia.com). Similar to these and worth trying are **Cheap Tickets** (www.cheaptickets.com) and **Lowest Fare** (www.lowestfare.com). Typically, these sites don't include budget airlines such as Southwest.

Meta sites like **Kayak** (www.kayak.com) and **Mobissimo** (www.mobissimo.com). are good for price comparisons, as they gather from many sources (but don't provide direct booking).

Bidding for travel can be very successful, but read the fine print carefully before bidding. Try **Hotwire** (www.hotwire.com), **Skyauction** (www.skyauction.com) and **Priceline** (www.priceline.com).

Land

Border Crossings

The USA has more than 20 official border crossings with Canada in the north and almost 40 with Mexico in the south. It is relatively easy crossing from the USA into either country; it's crossing *into* the USA that can pose problems if you haven't brought all your documents (see p1164). US Customs & Border Protection tracks current wait times (see http://apps.cbp.gov/bwt) at every border crossing. Some borders are open 24 hours, but most are not.

Busy entry points with Canada include those at Detroit (MI)/Windsor, Buffalo (NY)/Niagara Falls and Blaine (WA)/British Columbia.

The main USA–Mexico posts are San Diego (CA)/Tijuana, Nogales West (AZ)/Nogales East, El Paso (TX)/Ciudad Juárez and Brownsville (TX)/Matamoros. As always, have your papers in order, be polite and don't make jokes or casual conversation with US border officials.

At research time, cartel violence and crime were serious dangers along the US–Mexico border. Before heading out, check the latest warnings of the **US State Department** (http://travel.state.gov).

Canada

BUS

Greyhound has direct connections between main cities in Canada and the northern USA, but you may have to transfer to a different bus at the border. Book through **Greyhound USA** (☎800-231-2222, international customer service 214-849-8100; www.greyhound.com) or **Greyhound Canada** (☎in Canada 800-661-8747; www.greyhound.ca). Greyhound's Discovery Pass (p1172) allows unlimited travel in both the USA and Canada.

CAR & MOTORCYCLE

If you're driving into the USA from Canada, bring the vehicle's registration papers, proof of liability insurance and your home driver's license. Canadian auto insurance is typically valid in the USA, and vice-versa. Canadian driver's licenses are also valid, but an International Driving Permit (IDP) is a good supplement (p1173).

If your papers are in order, taking your own car across the US–Canadian border is usually fast and easy, but occasionally the authorities of either country decide to search a car *thoroughly*.

On weekends and holidays, especially in summer, traffic at the main border crossings can be heavy and waits long.

TRAIN

Amtrak (☎800-872-7245; www.amtrak.com) and **VIA Rail Canada** (☎888-842-7245; www.viarail.ca) operate daily services between Montreal and New York, Toronto and New York via Niagara Falls, Toronto and Chicago via Detroit, and Vancouver and Seattle. Customs inspections occur at the border.

Mexico

BUS

Greyhound US (☎800-231-2222, international customer service 214-849-8100; www.greyhound.com) and **Greyhound México** (☎in Mexico 800-710-8819; www.greyhound.com.mx) operate direct bus routes between main towns in Mexico and the USA.

For connections to smaller destinations south of the border, there are numerous domestic Mexican bus companies; **Ticketbus** (☎in Mexico 5133-5133, 800-009-9090; www.ticketbus.com.mx) is an alliance of several.

CAR & MOTORCYCLE

If you're driving into the USA from Mexico, bring the vehicle's registration papers, proof of liability insurance and your driver's license from your home country. Mexican driver's licenses are valid, but an IDP (p1173) is a good supplement.

Very few car-rental companies will let you take a car from the US into Mexico. US auto insurance is not valid in Mexico, so even a short trip into Mexico's border region requires you to buy Mexican car insurance, available for around $25 per day at most border crossings, as well as from **AAA** (☎800-874-7532; www.aaa.com).

For a longer driving trip into Mexico beyond the border zone or Baja California, you'll need a Mexican *permiso de importación temporal de vehículos* (temporary vehicle import permit). See Lonely Planet's *Mexico* guide for details, or call Mexico's tourist information number in the USA on ☎800-446-3942.

Sea

If you're interested in taking a cruise ship to America – as well as to other interesting ports of call – a good specialized travel agency is **Cruise Web** (☎800-377-9383; www.cruiseweb.com).

You can also travel to and from the USA on a freighter, though it will be much slower and less cushy than a cruise. Nevertheless, freighters aren't spartan (some advertise cruise-ship-level amenities), and they are much cheaper (sometimes by half). Trips range from a week to two months; stops at interim ports are usually quick.

For more information:

Cruise & Freighter Travel Association (☎800-872-8584; www.travltips.com)

Freighter World Cruises (☎800-531-7774; www.freighterworld.com).

Tours

Group travel can be an enjoyable way to get to and tour the USA. For tours once you're in the country, see p1177.

Reputable tour companies:

American Holidays (☎01-673-3840; www.americanholidays.com) Ireland-based company specializes in tours to North America.

Contiki (☎866-266-8454; http://contiki.com) Party-hardy sightseeing tour-bus vacations for 18- to 35-year-olds.

North America Travel Service (☎020-7569-6710; www.northamericatravelservice.co.uk) UK-based tour operator arranges luxury US trips.

Trek America (☎in North America 800-873-5872, in the UK 0844-576-1400; www.trekamerica.com) For active outdoor adventures; group sizes are kept small.

GETTING AROUND

Air

When time is tight, book a flight. The domestic air system is extensive and reliable, with dozens of competing airlines, hundreds of airports and thousands of flights daily. Flying is usually more expensive than traveling by bus, train or car, but it's the way to go when you're in a hurry.

Main 'hub' airports in the USA include all international gateways (p1168) plus many other large cities. Most cities and towns have a local or county airport, but you usually have to travel via a hub airport to reach them.

The website www.parkingaccess.com offers information, reservations and discounts on parking at most major airports.

Airlines in the USA

Overall, air travel in the USA is very safe (much safer than driving out on the nation's highways); for comprehensive details by carrier, check out **Airsafe.com** (www.airsafe.com).

The main domestic carriers:

AirTran Airways (☎800-247-8726; www.airtran.com) Atlanta-based airline; primarily serves the South, Midwest and eastern US.

Alaska Airlines/Horizon Air (☎800-252-7522, 800-547-9308; www.alaskaair.com) Serves Alaska and western US, with flights to the East Coast and Hawaii.

American Airlines (☎800-433-7300; www.aa.com) Nationwide service.

Continental Airlines (☎800-523-3273; www.continental.com) Nationwide service.

Delta Air Lines (☎800-221-1212; www.delta.com) Nationwide service.

Frontier Airlines (☎800-432-1359; www.frontierairlines.com) Denver-based airline with nationwide service, including to Alaska.

Hawaiian Airlines (☎800-367-5320; www.hawaiianair.com) Serves the Hawaiian Islands and West Coast, plus Las Vegas and Phoenix.

JetBlue Airways(☎800-538-2583; www.jetblue.com) Nonstop connections between eastern and western US cities, plus Florida, New Orleans and Texas.

Southwest Airlines (☎800-435-9792; www.southwest.com) Service across the continental USA.

Spirit Airlines (☎800-772-7117; www.spiritair.com) Florida-based airline; serves many US gateway cities.

United Airlines (☎800-864-8331; www.united.com) Nationwide service.

US Airways (☎800-428-4322; www.usairways.com) Nationwide service.

Virgin America (☎877-359-8474; www.virginamerica.com) Flights between East and West Coast cities and Las Vegas.

Air Passes

International travelers who plan on doing a lot of flying might consider buying a North American air pass. Passes are normally available only to non-North American citizens, and they must be purchased in conjunction with an international ticket. Conditions and cost structures can be complicated, but all passes include a certain number of domestic flights (from two to 10) that typically must be used within a 60-day period. Often you must plan your itinerary in advance, but sometimes dates (and even destinations) can be left open. Talk with a travel agent to determine if an air pass will save you money. Two of the biggest airline networks offering air passes are **Star Alliance** (www.staralliance.com) and **One World** (www.oneworld.com).

Bicycle

Regional bicycle touring is popular. It means coasting winding backroads (because bicycles are often not permitted on freeways), and calculating progress in miles per day, not miles per hour. Cyclists must follow the same rules of the road as automobiles, but don't expect drivers to respect your right of way. **Better World Club** (p1173) offers a bicycle roadside assistance program.

For highlights of the USA's cycling and mountain-biking trails, see p43. For epic cross-country journeys, get the support of a tour operator; it's about two months of dedicated pedaling coast to coast.

For advice, and lists of local bike clubs and repair shops, browse the **League of American Bicyclists website** (www.bikeleague.org). If you're bringing your own bike to the USA, visit the **International Bicycle Fund website** (www.ibike.org), which lists bike regulations by airline and has lots of advice. In the past, most international and domestic airlines have carried bikes as checked baggage without charge when they're in a box; recently, many have changed their regulations and imposed or increased fees (from $50 to upwards of $250 each way). Amtrak trains and Greyhound buses will transport bikes within the USA, sometimes charging extra.

It's not hard to buy a bike once you're here and resell it before you leave. Every city and town has bike shops; if you prefer a cheaper, used bicycle, try garage sales, bulletin boards at hostels and colleges, or the free classified ads at **Craigslist** (www.craigslist.org). These are also the best places to sell your bike, though stores selling used bikes may also buy from you.

Long-term bike rentals are also easy to find; recommended rental places are listed throughout this guide. Rates run from $100 per week and up, and a credit card authorization for several hundred dollars is usually necessary as a security deposit.

Boat

There is no river or canal public transportation system in the USA, but there are many smaller, often state-run, coastal ferry services, which provide efficient, scenic links to the many islands off both coasts. Most larger ferries will transport private cars, motorcycles and bicycles. For details, see the regional chapters.

The most spectacular coastal ferry runs are on the southeastern coast of Alaska and along the Inside Passage (p1066). The Great Lakes have several islands that can be visited only by boat, such as Mackinac Island, MI (p570); the Apostle Islands, off Wisconsin (p582); and remote Isle Royale National Park (p571), MN. Off the coast of Washington, ferries reach the scenic San Juan Islands (p1027).

Bus

To save money, travel by bus, particularly between major towns and cities. Gotta-go middle-class Americans prefer to fly or drive, but buses let you see the countryside and meet folks along the way. As a rule, buses are reliable, cleanish and comfortable, with air-conditioning, barely reclining seats, lavatories and no smoking.

Greyhound (800-231-2222; www.greyhound.com) is the major long-distance bus company, with routes throughout the USA and Canada. To improve efficiency and profitability, Greyhound has recently stopped service to many small towns; routes generally trace major highways and stop at larger population centers. To reach country towns on rural roads, you may need to transfer to local or county bus systems; Greyhound can usually provide their contact information.

Competing with Greyhound are the 75-plus franchises of **Trailways** (703-691-3052; www.trailways.com). Trailways may not be as useful as Greyhound for long trips, but fares can be competitive. Upstart long-distance bus lines that may offer cheaper fares include **Megabus** (877-462-6342; www.megabus.com), primarily operating routes in the Northeast and Midwest.

Most baggage has to be checked in; label it loudly and clearly to avoid it getting lost. Larger items, including skis, surfboards and bicycles, can be transported, but there may be an extra charge. Call to check.

The frequency of bus services varies widely, depending on the route. Despite the elimination of many tiny destinations, nonexpress Greyhound buses still stop every 50 to 100 miles to pick up passengers, and long-distance buses will stop for meal breaks and driver changes.

Many bus stations are clean and safe, but some are in dodgy areas; if you arrive in the evening, it's worth spending the money on a taxi. Some towns have just a flag stop. If you are boarding at one of these, pay the driver with exact change.

Bus Passes

Greyhound's **Discovery Pass** (www.discoverypass.com), which is available to both domestic and international travelers, allows unlimited, unrestricted travel for periods of seven ($246), 15 ($356), 30 ($456) or 60 ($556) consecutive days in both the USA and Canada. Besides the length of the pass, the only real decision to make is which country you want to start your travels in. This pass is also accepted by a few dozen regional bus companies; check with Greyhound for a list.

You can buy passes at select Greyhound terminals up to two hours before departure, or purchase them online at least 14 days in advance, then pick them up using the same credit card, with photo ID, at least an hour before boarding.

Costs

For lower fares on Greyhound, purchase tickets at least seven days in advance (purchasing 14 days in advance will save even more). Round trips are also cheaper than two one-way fares. Special promotional fares are regularly offered on Greyhound's website, especially for online bookings. If you're traveling with family or friends, Greyhound's companion fares let up to three additional travelers get 50% off with a minimum three-day advance purchase.

As for other Greyhound discounts: tickets for children aged two to 11 get 25% off; seniors over 62 get 5% off; and students get 20% off if they have purchased the $20 **Student Advantage Discount Card** (www.studentadvantage.com).

Reservations

Tickets for some Trailways and other buses can only be purchased immediately prior to departure. Greyhound bus tickets can be bought over the phone or online. You can print tickets at home or pick them up at the terminal using 'Will Call' service.

Seating is normally first-come, first-served. Greyhound recommends arriving an hour before departure to get a seat.

BUS DETAILS

Here are some sample standard one-way adult fares and trip times on Greyhound:

SERVICE	PRICE ($)	DURATION (HR)
Boston–Philadelphia	55	7
Chicago–New Orleans	133	23
Los Angeles–San Francisco	55	8
New York–Chicago	108	18
New York–San Francisco	252	72
Washington, DC–Miami	160	28

Car & Motorcycle

For maximum flexibility and convenience, and to explore rural America and its wide-open spaces, a car is essential. Although petrol prices are high, you can often score fairly inexpensive rentals (NYC excluded), with rates as low as $20 per day.

For recommended driving routes, turn to the special Road Trips & Scenic Drives chapter (p35).

Automobile Associations

The **American Automobile Association** (AAA; ☎800-874-7532; www.aaa.com) has reciprocal membership agreements with several international auto clubs (check with AAA and bring your membership card from home). For its members, AAA offers travel insurance, tour books, diagnostic centers for used-car buyers and a wide-ranging network of regional offices. AAA advocates politically for the auto industry.

A more ecofriendly alternative, the **Better World Club** (☎866-238-1137; www.betterworldclub.com) donates 1% of revenue to assist environmental cleanup, offers ecologically sensitive choices for every service it provides and advocates politically for environmental causes.

In either organization, the primary member benefit is 24-hour emergency roadside assistance anywhere in the USA. Both also offer trip planning, free travel maps, travel agency services, car insurance and a range of travel discounts (eg on hotels, car rentals, attractions).

Bring Your Own Vehicle

For details on driving your own car over the border from Canada, see p1169, and from Mexico, see p1170. Unless you're moving to the USA, don't even think about freighting your car.

Drive-Away Cars

'Drive-away cars' refers to the business of driving cars across the country for people who are moving or otherwise can't transport their cars themselves. For flexible travelers, they can be a dream come true: you can cover the long distances between A and B for the price of gas. Timing and availability are key.

To be a driver you must be at least 23 years old with a valid driver's license (non-US citizens should have an International Driving Permit); you'll also need to provide a $350 deposit – sometimes requested in cash – which is refunded upon safe delivery of the car, a printout of your 'clean' driving record from home, a major credit card and/or three forms of identification (or a passport).

The drive-away company provides insurance; you pay for gas. The stipulation is that you must deliver the car to its destination within a specified time and mileage, which usually requires that you drive no more than eight hours and about 400 miles a day along the shortest route (ie no sightseeing). Availability depends on demand.

One major company is **Auto Driveaway** (☎800-346-2277; www.autodriveaway.com), which has more than 40 offices nationwide.

Driver's License

Foreign visitors can legally drive a car in the USA for up to 12 months using their home driver's license. However, an IDP will have more credibility with US traffic police, especially if your home license doesn't have a photo or isn't in English. Your automobile association at home can issue an IDP, valid for one year, for a small fee. Always carry your home license together with the IDP.

To drive a motorcycle in the USA, you will need either a valid US state motorcycle license or an IDP specially endorsed for motorcycles.

Insurance

Don't put the key into the ignition if you don't have insurance, which is legally required. You risk financial ruin and legal consequences if there's an accident. If you already have auto insurance, or if you buy travel insurance that covers car rentals, make sure your policy has adequate liability coverage for where you will be driving; it probably does, but beware that states specify different minimum levels of coverage.

Rental-car companies will provide liability insurance, but most charge extra. Rental companies almost never include collision-damage insurance for the vehicle. Instead, they offer an optional Collision Damage Waiver (CDW) or Loss Damage Waiver (LDW), usually with an initial deductible cost of between $100 and $500. For an extra premium, you can usually get this deductible covered as well. Paying extra for some or all of this insurance increases the cost of a rental car by as much as $30 a day.

Many credit cards offer free collision damage coverage for rental cars, if you rent for 15 days or less and charge the total rental to your card. This is a good way to avoid paying extra fees to the rental company, but note that if there's an accident, sometimes you must pay the rental car company first and then seek reimbursement from the credit-card company. There may be exceptions that are not covered, too, such as 'exotic' rentals (eg 4WD Jeeps, convertibles). Check your credit-card policy.

Purchase

Buying a car is usually much more hassle than it's worth, particularly for foreign visitors and trips less than four months. Foreigners will have the easiest time arranging this if they have stateside friends or relatives who can provide a fixed address for registration, licensing and insurance.

To find a new or used auto, check newspapers and websites and visit dealers. To evaluate used-car prices, check the **Kelley Blue Book** (www.kbb.com). It's smart to pay an independent auto mechanic to inspect any used car before you buy it. Once purchased, the car's transfer of ownership papers must be registered with the state's Department of Motor Vehicles (DMV) within 10 days; you'll need the bill of sale, the title (or 'pink slip') and proof of insurance. Some states also require a 'smog certificate.' This is the seller's responsibility, so don't buy a car without a current certificate. A dealer will submit all necessary paperwork to the DMV for you.

For foreigners, independent liability insurance is difficult to virtually impossible to arrange without a US driver's license. A car dealer or AAA may be able to suggest an insurer who will do this. Even with a local license, insurance can be expensive and difficult to obtain if you don't have evidence of a good driving record. Bring copies of your home auto-insurance policy if it helps establish that you are a good risk. All drivers under 25 will have problems getting insurance.

Finally, selling a car can become desperate business. Selling to dealers gets you the worst price but involves a minimum of paperwork. Otherwise, fellow travelers and college students are the best bets – but be sure the DMV is properly notified about the sale, or you may be on the hook for someone else's traffic tickets later on.

Based in Seattle, WA, **Auto Tour USA** (☎206-999-4686; www.autotourusa.com) specializes in helping foreign visitors purchase, license and insure cars. For US citizens, **Adventures on Wheels** (☎800-943-3579; www.adventuresonwheels.com) offers a six-month buy-back program: you buy one of their cars, they register and insure it, and when your trip's done, they buy it back for a pre-established price.

Rental

CAR

Car rental is a competitive business in the USA. Most rental companies require that you have a major credit card, be at least 25 years old and have a valid driver's license. Some major national companies may rent to drivers between the ages of 21 and 24 for an additional charge of around $25 per day. Those under 21 are usually not permitted to rent at all.

Good independent agencies are listed in this guide. Online, **Car Rental Express** (www.carrentalexpress.com) rates and compares independent agencies in US cities; it's particularly useful for searching out cheaper long-term rentals.

Major national car-rental companies:

Alamo (☎877-222-9075; www.alamo.com)

Avis (☎800-230-4898; www.avis.com)

Budget (☎800-527-0700; www.budget.com)

Dollar (☎800-800-3665; www.dollar.com)

Enterprise (☎800-261-7331; www.enterprise.com)

Hertz (☎800-654-3131; www.hertz.com)

National (☎877-222-9058; www.nationalcar.com)

Rent-a-Wreck (☎877-877-0700; www.rentawreck.com)

Thrifty (☎800-847-4389; www.thrifty.com)

Car-rental prices vary wildly. As when buying plane tickets, shop around, checking every angle and several websites. Airport locations may have cheaper rates but higher fees; city-center offices may do pick-ups and drop-offs. Adjusting the days of your rental even slightly can completely change the rate; weekend and weekly rates are usually cheaper. The average daily rate for a small car ranges from around $30 to $75, or $200 to $500 per week. If you belong to an auto club or frequent-flier program, you may get a discount (or earn rewards points or miles). Check out arranging a cheaper fly-drive package, too. No matter what, advance reservations are recommended.

Some other things to keep in mind: most national agencies make 'unlimited mileage' standard on all cars, but independents might charge extra for this. Tax on car rentals varies by state and agency location; always ask for the total cost *including* all taxes and fees. Most agencies charge more if you pick the car up in one place and drop it off in another; usually only national agencies even offer this option. Be careful about adding extra days or turning in a car early; extra days may be charged at a premium rate, or an early return may jeopardize any weekly or monthly discounts you originally arranged.

Some major national companies, including Avis, Budget and Hertz, offer 'green' fleets of hybrid rental cars (eg Toyota Priuses, Honda Civics), although you'll usually have to pay a lot extra to rent a more fuel-efficient car. Some independent local agencies, especially on the West Coast, also offer hybrid-vehicle rentals. Try Southern California's **Simply Hybrid** (www.simplyhybrid.com) and Hawaii's **Bio-Beetle** (p1092).

For car-sharing rentals in cities and towns in more than 30 states, **Zipcar** (☎866-494-7227; www.zipcar.com) charges hourly/daily rental fees with free gas, insurance and limited mileage included; prepayment is required. Check the website for locations and to apply (some foreign drivers are OK). No one-way rentals are allowed.

MOTORCYCLE & RECREATIONAL VEHICLE (RV)

If you dream of cruising across America on a Harley, **EagleRider** (☎888-900-9901; www.eaglerider.com) has offices in major cities nationwide and rents other kinds of adventure vehicles, too. Beware that motorcycle rental and insurance are expensive.

Driving Distances & Times

0 — 200 km
0 — 120 miles

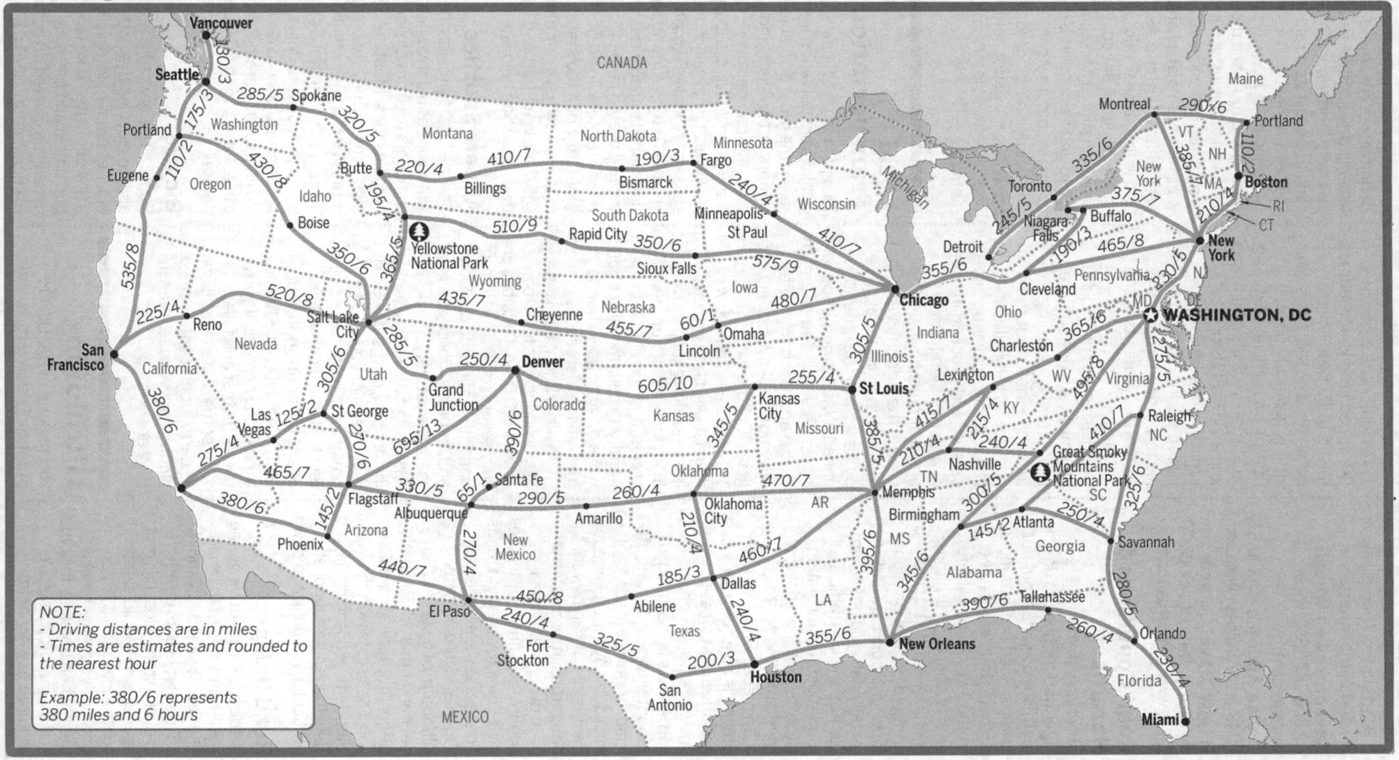
CANADA
MEXICO
Vancouver
130/3
Seattle
285/5
Spokane
320/5
175/3
Portland
110/2
Eugene
535/8
430/8
Washington
Oregon
Idaho
Montana
Boise
Butte
220/4
Billings
410/7
195/4
Yellowstone National Park
510/9
365/5
350/6
North Dakota
Bismarck
190/3
Fargo
Minnesota
240/4
Minneapolis-St Paul
South Dakota
Rapid City
350/6
Sioux Falls
575/9
410/7
Wisconsin
Michigan
Wyoming
435/7
Cheyenne
Nebraska
455/7
Lincoln
60/1
Omaha
480/7
Iowa
Chicago
San Francisco
225/4
Reno
520/8
Salt Lake City
Nevada
California
Utah
285/5
250/4
Denver
Grand Junction
Colorado
605/10
Kansas City
255/4
St Louis
305/5
Illinois
Indiana
Ohio
Kansas
Missouri
380/6
Las Vegas
125/2
St George
305/6
275/4
465/7
270/6
695/13
390/6
Flagstaff
330/5
65/1
Santa Fe
Albuquerque
290/5
Amarillo
260/4
Oklahoma
Oklahoma City
345/5
470/7
380/6
145/2
Phoenix
Arizona
New Mexico
270/4
440/7
El Paso
450/8
Abilene
185/3
Dallas
210/4
460/7
240/4
Texas
240/4
Fort Stockton
325/5
San Antonio
200/3
Houston
355/6
New Orleans
LA
395/6
AR
Memphis
385/5
415/7
210/4
Nashville
TN
215/4
KY
Lexington
240/4
Birmingham
MS
345/6
Alabama
145/2
Atlanta
300/5
Georgia
250/4
Great Smoky Mountains National Park
390/6
Tallahassee
260/4
Orlando
Florida
230/4
Miami
280/5
Savannah
325/6
SC
Raleigh
NC
410/7
495/8
Virginia
WV
Charleston
365/6
275/5
WASHINGTON, DC
MD
DE
NJ
230/5
Detroit
355/6
Cleveland
Pennsylvania
465/8
190/3
Niagara Falls
Buffalo
245/5
Toronto
335/6
375/7
New York
New York
Montreal
385/7
VT
NH
MA
RI
CT
210/4
Boston
110/2
Portland
290/6
Maine
NOTE:
- Driving distances are in miles
- Times are estimates and rounded to the nearest hour
Example: 380/6 represents 380 miles and 6 hours

Companies specializing in RV and camper rentals:

Adventures on Wheels (☎866-787-3682; www.wheels9.com)

Cruise America (☎800-671-8042; www.cruiseamerica.com)

Happy Travel Camper Rental & Sales (☎800-370-1262; www.camperusa.com)

Road Conditions & Hazards

America's highways are legendary ribbons of unblemished asphalt, but not always. Road hazards include potholes, city commuter traffic, wandering wildlife and, of course, cell-phone-wielding, kid-distracted and enraged drivers. Caution, foresight, courtesy and luck usually gets you past them. For nationwide traffic and road-closure information, click to www.fhwa.dot.gov/trafficinfo/index.htm.

In places where winter driving is an issue, many cars are fitted with steel-studded snow tires; snow chains can sometimes be required in mountain areas. Driving off-road, or on dirt roads, is often forbidden by rental-car companies, and it can be very dangerous in wet weather.

In deserts and range country, livestock sometimes graze next to unfenced roads. These areas are signed as 'Open Range' or with the silhouette of a steer. Where deer and other wild animals frequently appear roadside, you'll see signs with the silhouette of a leaping deer. Take these signs seriously, particularly at dusk and dawn.

Road Rules

In the USA, cars drive on the right-hand side of the road. The use of seat belts and child safety seats is required in every state. Most car rental agencies rent child safety seats for around $12 per day, but you must reserve them when booking. In some states, motorcyclists are required to wear helmets.

On interstate highways, the speed limit is sometimes raised to 75mph. Unless otherwise posted, the speed limit is generally 55mph or 65mph on highways, 25mph to 35mph in cities and towns and as low as 15mph in school zones (strictly enforced during school hours). It's forbidden to pass a school bus when its lights are flashing.

Unless signs prohibit it, you may turn right at a red light after first coming to a full stop – note that turning on right on red is illegal in NYC. At four-way stop signs, cars should proceed in order of arrival; when two cars arrive simultaneously, the one on the right has the right of way. When in doubt, just politely wave the other driver ahead. When emergency vehicles (ie police, fire or ambulance) approach from either direction, pull over safely and get out of the way.

Most states have laws against (and hefty fines for) littering along the highway. In an increasing number of states, it is illegal to talk on a handheld cell (mobile) phone while driving; use a hands-free device instead.

The maximum legal blood-alcohol concentration for drivers is 0.08%. Penalties are very severe for 'DUI' – driving under the influence of alcohol and/or drugs. Police can give roadside sobriety checks to assess if you've been drinking or using drugs. If you fail, they'll require you to take a breath test, urine test or blood test to determine the level of alcohol or drugs in your body. Refusing to be tested is treated the same as if you'd taken the test and failed.

In some states it is illegal to carry 'open containers' of alcohol in a vehicle, even if they are empty.

Hitchhiking

Hitchhiking in the USA is potentially dangerous and definitely not recommended. Indeed, drivers have heard so many lurid reports they tend to be just as afraid of those with their thumbs out. Hitchhiking on freeways is prohibited. You'll see more people hitchhiking in rural areas and in Alaska and Hawaii, but these places aren't safer than anywhere else, and with sparse traffic, you may well get stranded. In and around national parks, hitching to and from trailheads is common, but a safer bet is to check ride-share boards at hostels, park visitor centers and wilderness information stations.

Local Transportation

Except in large US cities, public transportation is rarely the most convenient option for travelers, and coverage can be sparse to outlying towns and suburbs. However, it is usually cheap, safe and reliable. For details, see the Getting Around sections for the main cities and towns covered in the On the Road chapters. In addition, more than half the states in the nation have adopted ☎511 as an all-purpose local-transportation help line.

Airport Shuttles

Shuttle buses provide inexpensive and convenient transport to/from airports in most cities. Most are 12-seat vans; some have regular routes and stops (which include the main hotels) and some pick up and deliver passengers 'door to door' in their service area. Costs range from $15 to $30 per person.

Bicycle

Some cities are more amen able to bicycles than others, but most have at least a few dedicated bike lanes and paths, and bikes can usually be carried on public transportation. See p1171 for more on bicycling in the USA, including rentals.

Bus

Most cities and larger towns have dependable local bus systems, though they are often designed for commuters and provide limited service in the evening and on weekends. Costs range from free to between $1 and $3 per ride.

Subway & Train

The largest systems are in New York, Chicago, Boston, Philadelphia, Washington, DC, Chicago, Los Angeles and the San Francisco Bay Area. Other cities may have small, one- or two-line rail systems that mainly serve downtown.

Taxi

Taxis are metered, with flagfall charges of around $2.50 to start, plus $1.50 to $2 per mile. They charge extra for waiting and handling baggage, and drivers expect a 10% to 15% tip. Taxis cruise the busiest areas in large cities; otherwise, it's easiest to phone and order one.

Tours

Hundreds of companies offer all kinds of organized tours of the USA; most focus on either cities or regions. See Tours in the city sections throughout this book for more recommendations.

Backroads (☎510-527-1555, 800-462-2848; www.backroads.com) Designs a range of active, multisport and outdoor-oriented trips for all abilities and budgets.

Gray Line (☎800-966-8125; www.grayline.com) For those short on time, Gray Line offers a comprehensive range of standard sightseeing tours across the country.

Green Tortoise (☎415-956-7500, 800-867-8647; www.greentortoise.com) Offering budget adventures for independent travelers, Green Tortoise is famous for its sleeping-bunk buses. Most trips leave from San Francisco, traipsing through the West and nationwide.

Road Scholar (800-454-5768; www.roadscholar.org) For those aged 55 and older, this venerable nonprofit offers 'learning adventures' in all 50 states.

Train

Amtrak (☎800-872-7245; www.amtrak.com) has an extensive rail system throughout the USA, with Amtrak's Thruway buses providing connections to and from the rail network to some smaller centers and national parks. Compared with other modes of travel, trains are rarely the quickest, cheapest, timeliest or most convenient option, but they turn the journey into a relaxing, social and scenic all-American experience.

Amtrak has several long-distance lines traversing the nation east to west, and even more running north to south. These connect all of America's biggest cities and many of its smaller ones. Long-distance services (on named trains) mostly operate daily on these routes, but some run only three to five days per week. See Amtrak's website for detailed route maps, as well as the Getting There & Around sections in this guide's regional chapters.

Commuter trains provide faster, more frequent services on shorter routes, especially the northeast corridor from Boston, MA, to Washington, DC. Amtrak's high-speed Acela Express trains are the most expensive, and rail passes (p1178) are not valid on these trains. Other commuter rail lines include those serving the Lake Michigan shoreline near Chicago, IL, major cities on the West Coast and the Miami, FL, area.

Classes & Costs

Amtrak fares vary according to the type of train and seating; on long-distance lines, you can travel in coach seats (reserved or unreserved), business class, or 1st class, which includes all sleeping compartments. Sleeping cars include simple bunks (called 'roomettes'), bedrooms with en-suite facilities and suites sleeping four with two bathrooms. Sleeping-car rates include meals in the dining car, which offers everyone sit-down meal service (pricey if not included). Food service on commuter lines, when it exists, consists of sandwich and snack bars. Bringing your own food and drink is recommended on all trains.

Various one-way, round-trip and touring fares are available from Amtrak, with

TRAIN DETAILS

Sample standard, one-way, adult coach-class fares and trip times on Amtrak's long-distance routes:

SERVICE	PRICE ($)	DURATION (HR)
Chicago–New Orleans	112	20
Los Angeles–San Antonio	136	29
New York–Chicago	88	19
New York–Los Angeles	248	68
Seattle–Oakland	154	23
Washington, DC–Miami	125	27

ALL ABOARD!

Who doesn't enjoy the steamy puff and whistle of a mighty locomotive as glorious scenery streams by? Dozens of historic narrow-gauge railroads still operate today as attractions, rather than as transportation. Most trains only run in the warmer months, and they can be extremely popular – so book ahead.

Here are some of the best:

Cass Scenic Railroad Nestled in the Appalachian Mountains in West Virginia (p317).

Cumbres & Toltec Scenic Railroad Living, moving museum from Chama, NM, into Colorado's Rocky Mountains (p874).

Durango & Silverton Narrow Gauge Railroad Ends at historic mining town Silverton in Colorado's Rocky Mountains (p734).

Great Smoky Mountain Railroad Rides from Bryson City, NC, through the Great Smoky Mountains (p339).

Mount Hood Railroad Winds through the scenic Columbia River Gorge outside Portland, OR (p1049).

1880 Train Classic steam train running through rugged Black Hills country (p631).

Skunk Train Runs between Fort Bragg, CA, on the coast and Willits farther inland, passing through redwoods (p981).

White Pass & Yukon Route Railroad Klondike Gold Rush–era railroad has departures from Skagway, AK (p1074), and Fraser (British Columbia) and Carcross and Whitehorse (Yukon) in Canada.

Also worth riding are the vintage steam and diesel locomotives of Arizona's **Grand Canyon Railway** (p819), New York State's **Delaware & Ulster Line** (p119) and Colorado's **Pikes Peak Cog Railway** (p716).

discounts of 15% for seniors aged 62 and over and for students with a 'Student Advantage' card ($20) or an International Student Identity Card (ISIC), and 50% discounts for children aged two to 15 when accompanied by a paying adult. AAA members get 10% off. Web-only 'Weekly Specials' offer deep discounts on certain undersold routes.

Generally, the earlier you book, the lower the price. To get many of the standard discounts, you need to reserve at least three days in advance. If you want to take an Acela Express or Metroliner train, avoid peak commute times and aim for weekends.

Amtrak Vacations (☎800-268-7252; www.amtrakvacations.com) offers vacation packages that include rental cars, hotels, tours and attractions. Air-Rail packages let you travel by train in one direction, then return by plane the other way.

Reservations

Reservations can be made any time from 11 months in advance up to the day of departure. Space on most trains is limited, and certain routes can be crowded, especially during summer and holiday periods, so it's a good idea to book as far in advance as you can; this also gives you the best chance of fare discounts.

Train Passes

Amtrak's USA Rail Pass offers coach-class travel for 15 ($389), 30 ($579) or 45 ($749) days, with travel limited to eight, 12 or 18 one-way 'segments,' respectively. A segment is *not* the same as a one-way trip. If reaching your destination requires riding more than one train (for example, getting from New York to Miami with a transfer in Washington, DC) that one-way trip will actually use two segments of your pass.

Present your pass at an Amtrak office to pick up your ticket(s) for each trip. Reservations should be made by phone (call ☎800-872-7245, or ☎215-856-7953 from outside the USA) as far in advance as possible. Each segment of the journey must be booked. At some rural stations, trains will only stop if there's a reservation. Tickets are not for specific seats, but a conductor on board may allocate you a seat. Business-class, 1st-class and sleeper accommodations cost extra and must be reserved separately.

All travel must be completed within 180 days of purchasing your pass. Passes are not valid on the Acela Express, Auto Train, Thruway motorcoach connections or the Canadian portion of Amtrak routes operated jointly with Via Rail Canada.

behind the scenes

SEND US YOUR FEEDBACK

We love to hear from travelers – your comments keep us on our toes and help make our books better. Our well-traveled team reads every word on what you loved or loathed about this book. Although we cannot reply individually to postal submissions, we always guarantee that your feedback goes straight to the appropriate authors, in time for the next edition. Each person who sends us information is thanked in the next edition – and the most useful submissions are rewarded with a free book.

Visit **lonelyplanet.com/contact** to submit your updates and suggestions or to ask for help. Our award-winning website also features inspirational travel stories, news and discussions.

Note: We may edit, reproduce and incorporate your comments in Lonely Planet products such as guidebooks, websites and digital products, so let us know if you don't want your comments reproduced or your name acknowledged. For a copy of our privacy policy visit lonelyplanet.com/privacy.

OUR READERS

Many thanks to the travelers who used the last edition and wrote to us with helpful hints, useful advice and interesting anecdotes:
David Angus, Olivia Ann, Emma Åsenius, Jyri-Peter Backman, Martin Ballard, Walter Bertschinger, Feather Biedess, Raymond Bishop, Chris Campbell, Kevin Carleton-Reeves, Lin Chen, Brendan Cotter, Benjamin Davenport, Megan De Bruyn, Christopher Enders, Tore Flo, Adrienne Frasher, Roberto Gasparini, Kolby Granville, Susan Gurr, Harald, Aaron Heflich Shapiro, Barbara Lauener, Carol Lea Benjamin, Wolfgang Meisen, Christian Montag, Chiara Motta, Giovanna O'Grady, Wendy Parnell, Leo Paton, Stephen Pickhardt, Sunny Reynolds, Paula Robertson, David Schon, Erik Schwartz, Lisa Sebena, Thomas Seymour, Brian Sherman, August Welsh.

AUTHOR THANKS

Regis St Louis

Thanks go to Suki and my talented co-authors who did such a stellar job bringing America to life. Thanks to Eve and friends for top tips in Washington and to the Krishna friends at New Vrindaban for a magical visit. Big hugs to Cassandra, Magdalena and Genevieve for joining on the big southern road trip. Lastly, thank you the Kaufman gang for letting us join in the Wrightsville Beach holiday.

Amy C Balfour

Thanks to Suki, Regis and the Southwest team for top-notch editing and writing. Many thanks to Deb Corcoran, Tucson's greatest docent, and Judy Hellmich-Bryan, who provided the latest news for Grand Canyon National Park. A special shout out to Lucy and Michael Gordon for their hospitality and Phoenix insights, and a toast to Mark Baker and the in-the-know barflies as Bisbee Brewing Company and Café Roka. And Ninette Crunkleton and Melissa Peeler, thanks for the Arizona leads!

Michael Benanav

Thank you Whitney George in Ruidoso, for a great story about one Mike the Midget and a mysterious village beneath Bonita Lake. I owe the biggest thanks to Kelly and Luke, who always let me go and always welcome me back.

Andrew Bender

Thank you Suki Gear, Sam Benson, Regis St Louis and Justin Flynn, for the opportunity and their good cheer and advice.

Sara Benson

Thanks to Suki Gear, Regis St Louis, my talented *USA* co-authors and everyone at Lonely Planet for making this book happen. I'm grateful to all those I met on the road who shared their local expertise and tips, from park rangers to brewpub barflies, and also to my friends and family who live in the Golden State, especially the Picketts for their Lake Tahoe hospitality. PS to MSC Jr: Whew! Glad that avalanche didn't kill us.

Alison Bing

Many thanks and crushing California bear hugs to editor Suki Gear, *San Francisco* city guide co-author John Vlahides, co-authors Regis St Louis and Sam Benson, editors Anna Metcalfe and Sasha Baskett, but above all Marco Flavio Marinucci, who made waiting for a Muni bus the adventure of a lifetime.

Jeff Campbell

First, Regis and Suki, you made this easy. For their Florida tips, thanks to Anne Higgins, Ali DeLargy, Kathleen Ogle, Michelle Kratochvil (and Judi!), Ed in St Pete, and Bruce in Tampa. To Darby's own, James, Karen and son William: thanks for your companionship to Cayo Costa and great advice. As always, endless thanks to my children, Jackson and Miranda, and my wife, Deanna, for all their love and support, and for not minding my tan.

Nate Cavalieri

Thanks to my partner Florence Chien for joining my research travels through Northern California. (Sorry about the speeding tickets.) Thanks also to the lovely people at Lonely Planet and particularly for the enthusiasm of commissioning editor and mentor Suki Gear.

Sarah Chandler

Suki Gear, thanks for trusting me to get into enough (but not too much) trouble in Sin City. My trusty co-pilot, the intrepid Jennifer Christensen, deserves serious props for remaining calm during flat tires, blizzards, and a losing streak in the smokey blackjack room of the Hotel Nevada. Finally, to Jack and everyone at the Hard Rock, thanks for showing me how the locals rock Vegas nightlife (fearlessly, of course).

Jim DuFresne

Thanks to my long time Alaskan friends of Todd, Ed, Sue, Jeff, Dragon and Buckwheat for putting me up and putting up with me. I'll always be indebted to Annette, Dave, Aurora, Brian and the rest of the gang at the Clarkston Post Office for keeping the home front stable while I was gone. Finally here's to Postcard Margaret, Rachelle, Marlena and, most of all, my son Michael for high adventures on the Chilkoot and memorable evenings in Juneau.

Lisa Dunford

I always meet so many kindred spirits on the Utah road. Thanks go to Nan Johnson, Peggy Egan, Trista Rayner, Nicole Muraro, David Belz, Jessica Kunzer, Lisa Varga and Ty Markham, among others. I very much enjoyed talking to you all. Thanks, too, to the many park rangers I met, for the ever-helpful job they do.

Ned Friary & Glenda Bendure

We'd like to thank everyone who shared their tips with us and chimed in on their favorite spots, especially Gretchen Grozier, Bob Prescott, Steve Howance, Julie Lipkin, Ken Merrill, Bill O'Neill and Bryan Lantz. And of course thanks to the many travelers we met along the way.

Bridget Gleeson

I'm grateful to my sister Molly, my brother-in-law Germán Parra, and my dear friend Starla Silver for their hospitality in southern California – and to all their friends for their dining recommendations (and willingness to go to Disneyland). Thanks to my mother, as always, for joining me on the road.

Michael Grosberg

To Rebecca Tessler who is always in my heart. Special thanks to Carly Neidorf for her presence and support, on the road and off, and her navigational abilities. Radie Kaighin-Shields and Annie Humphrey for help on Pittsburgh; to Caitlin Larussa and Olwyn Conway for West Philly tips and my parents for their Philly suggestions; and to all my NYC friends who joined me for research meals and drinks.

Beth Kohn

All the usual suspects get thanks again, especially the fabulous multitasking Suki Gear and the dynamo known as Sam Benson. California cohorts and experts this time around included Agent 'Pedal-to-the-metal' Moller, Felix 'Hella Loves Oakland' Thomson, Jenny 'Stink' G, Dillon 'The Scientist' Dutton and Julia 'Wawona' Brashares, plus all the helpful and patient rangers at Yosemite National Park. Kudos to Regis St Louis, Alison Lyall and Anna Metcalfe for all their crucial work.

Mariella Krause

I'd like to wish a permanent and ongoing thank you to my husband Tim Bauer, who I met the first day I moved to Texas three million years ago. He's an integral part of every project I take on, whether it's lending me words when I run out, taking part in late-night proofreading sessions, or just making sure I don't forget to eat. Plus, he's just generally awesome and writes funny plays about zombies.

Emily Matchar

Thanks to Suki Gear and the rest of the Lonely Planet team. Thanks to Kerry Crawford for sharing her copious Memphis knowledge, to Julie Montgomery for her spot-on Charleston recommendations, to Meg, Maggie, Daniel and every other friend and/or fellow Twitterer for their excellent steers. Special thanks to Leslie Jamison for helping me brave surreal Memphis discos at midnight, and to Jamin Asay, my partner in travel and in life, for his tireless map-reading and, well, everything else.

Bradley Mayhew

Thanks to all the Yellowstone Park rangers who took to answer my many questions and to my wife Kelli who gave me her opinon on the best mussels from Billings to Bozeman.

Carolyn McCarthy

Sincere thanks goes out to all those who helped me, especially the park rangers who are so committed to preserving our great wilderness. Richard Carrier proved adept at attacking the snowy passes of southern Colorado. Thanks also to Louise, Conan, Anne and the Cameron Johns family for their thoughtful hospitality. Virtual beers go out to ace authors Bradley Mayhew, Brendan Sainsbury and Regis St Louis for their collaboration.

Kevin Raub

Special thanks to my wife, Adriana Schmidt Raub, whose second opinion in Georgia and New Orleans proved invaluable. Along the way, Jason and Jennifer Hatfield, Dave and Aynsley Corbett, Jeff Fenn, Adam Skolnick, Tracy and Jeff Knapp, Fran Raub, Americas Coffee Shop in Lafayette, Leah Simon, JR & Pam Rivera, Shack Up Inn, Liz Carroll, Marika Cackett, Heidi Flynn Barnett, Vickie Ashford, Rachel Rosenberg, Kelly Norris, Wendy James, Erica Backus, Jason and Bianca Raub, Tom McDermott and Grace Wilson.

Brendan Sainsbury

Thanks to all the untold bus drivers, tourist info volunteers, restaurateurs, national park rangers, weather forecasters, oenologists and innocent bystanders who helped me during my research. Special thanks to Andy McKee, for his hiking company in the Glacier National Park; and Scott Davies, for his intriguing insights into Pike Place Market in Seattle. Thanks also to my wife Liz and five-year-old son Kieran for their company on the road.

Andrea Schulte-Peevers

Big thanks to Suki Gear for letting me have another shot at California. A heartfelt thank you also to my husband David for being such good company while tooling around the desert. Big kudos to all the good folks who shared their local insights, steered me in the right direction and made helpful introductions, including Hillary Angel, Mark Graves, Cheryl Chipman and Christopher Vonloudermilk.

Ryan Ver Berkmoes

Serious thanks to my parents who believed in the value of road trips. In Iowa I was again reunited with my senior prom date Kathy Berge while in South Dakota I saw winter formal date Sue Hegland (both following the unworn path *out* of Santa Cruz, CA for the Plains). At Lonely Planet, wide open thanks to Suki and Regis for their hard work. And more special thanks go to unnamed Plains cooks everywhere: burnt ends, garlic salad, etc etc etc.

John A Vlahides

I owe heartfelt thanks to my commissioning editor, Suki Gear, and co-authors, Sam Benson and Regis St Louis, for their stellar assistance and always-sunny dispositions. And to you, the readers, thank you for letting me be your guide to California Wine Country. Have fun. I know you will.

Karla Zimmerman

Many thanks to Denis Agar, Lisa Beran, Marie Bradshaw, Sarah Chandler, Sasha Chang, Lisa DiChiera, Jim DuFresne, Ruggero Fatica, Jill Hurwitz, Joe Kelley, Julie Lange, Katie Law, Kari Lydersen, the McCabe clan, Amanda Powell, Kristin Reither, Betsy Riley, Tamara B Robinson, Jim and Susan Stephan and the Chicago and Cleveland CVBs. Thanks most to Eric Markowitz, the world's best partner-for-life, who indulges all my hare-brained, pie-filled road trips.

ACKNOWLEDGMENTS

Climate map data adapted from Peel MC, Finlayson BL & McMahon TA (2007) 'Updated World Map of the Köppen-Geiger Climate Classification', *Hydrology and Earth System Sciences*, 11, 1633–44.

Cover photograph: Monument Valley, Utah; Rob Blakers/LPI. Many of the images in this guide are available for licensing from Lonely Planet Images: www.lonelyplanetimages.com.

THIS BOOK

For this 7th edition of Lonely Planet's *USA*, Regis St Louis coordinated a stellar author team (see Our Writers, p1208). Sara Benson coordinated the 6th edition and Jeff Campbell the 5th edition. This guidebook was commissioned in Lonely Planet's Oakland office, and produced by the following:

Commissioning Editor Suki Gear

Coordinating Editor Justin Flynn

Coordinating Cartographer Mark Griffiths

Coordinating Layout Designer Carlos Solarte

Managing Editor Anna Metcalfe

Managing Cartographer Alison Lyall

Managing Layout Designer Chris Girdler

Assisting Editors Janet Austin, Elin Berglund, Janice Bird, Cathryn Game, Carly Hall, Victoria Harrison, Kim Hutchins, Anne Mulvaney, Katie O'Connell, Helen Yeates

Assisting Cartographers Andras Bogdanovits, Valeska Canas, Xavier Di Toro, Brendan Streager

Cover Research Naomi Parker

Internal Image Research Sabrina Dalbesio

Thanks to Ryan Evans, Martin Heng, Asha Ioculari, Yvonne Kirk, Bella Li, Virginia Moreno, Trent Paton, Wibowo Rusli, Sophie Splatt, Gerard Walker

NOTES

index

ABBREVIATIONS

AK Alaska
AL Alabama
AR Arkansas
AZ Arizona
CA California
CO Colorado
CT Connecticut
DC District of Columbia
DE Delaware
FL Florida
GA Georgia
HI Hawaii
IA Iowa
ID Idaho
IL Illinois
IN Indiana
KS Kansas
KY Kentucky
LA Louisiana
MA Massachusetts
MD Maryland
ME Maine
MI Michigan
MN Minnesota
MO Missouri
MS Mississippi
MT Montana
NC North Carolina
ND North Dakota
NE Nebraska
NH New Hampshire
NJ New Jersey
NM New Mexico
NV Nevada
NY New York
OH Ohio
OK Oklahoma
OR Oregon
PA Pennsylvania
RI Rhode Island
SC South Carolina
SD South Dakota
TN Tennessee
TX Texas
UT Utah
VA Virginia
VT Vermont
WA Washington
WI Wisconsin
WV West Virginia
WY Wyoming

000 Map pages
000 Photo pages

A

Abilene 642
Abingdon 313-14
Abiquiu 870-1
Abita Springs 426
Absaroka Beartooth Wilderness 756-7
Acadia National Park 239-40, 776, **776-7**
accommodations 1154-6, *see also individual locations*
Acoma Pueblo 863
activities 42-8, *see also individual locations*
Adel 618
African Americans 1105
  festivals 384
  museums 142, 169, 252, 271-4, 415, 427, 558, 711, 891
  slavery 324, 1105
  writers 1136
agriculture 1102
air travel
  air tickets 1169
  to/from the USA 1168-9
  within the USA 1170-1
airlines 1170-1
airports 1168-9
Alabama 397-401, **322**
Alamo, the 667
Alamogordo 878
Alaska 55, 1061-78, **1062**
  accommodations 1061
  climate 1061
  food 1061
  highlights 1062
  travel seasons 1061
Alaska Marine Highway 1070
Alaska Railroad 1076
Albany 121
Albuquerque 858-63
Alcatraz 960
Alexandria 294
Alexandria Bay 123
Alpine 698-9
Alton 535
Alvord Desert 1056
Amana Colonies 619-20
Amelia Island 481
American Museum of Natural History 82
Ames 620
Amicalola Falls 389
Amish Country 542, 548-9
Amish people 151
amusement parks
  Breckenridge 728
  Busch Gardens 301
  Cedar Point 547
  Disneyland 911-15, **912**
  Knott's Berry Farm 914
  New Orleans 417
  Nickelodeon Universe 592
  Orlando 491
  Pittsburgh 157
  Santa Cruz 944
  Universal Studios 489-90, 898
  Valleyfair 587
  Walt Disney World 493, **10**
  Washington, DC 261
Anacostia 259-60
Anaheim 911-15
Anchorage 1074-8
animals
  bats 661
  bears 748, 1150, **774**
  birds 1152
  bison 748, **13**
  buffaloes 1151
  coyotes 1151
  endangered species 1150
  manatees 482, 487, 1152
  salmon 1151
  whales 1151
  wolves 1151
Ann Arbor 562-4
Annapolis 281-2
Antelope Island State Park 844
Anza-Borrego Desert State Park 931-2
Apache people 1120
Apalachicola 496
Apostle Islands 581-2
Appalachian Trail 215, 243, 310
aquariums
  Baltimore 271
  Boston 171
  Chicago 512
  Coney Island 88
  Dallas 683
  Daytona Beach 477
  Duluth 593
  Georgia 379
  Honolulu 1083
  Los Angeles 898
  Miami (FL) 453

aquariums *continued*
Monterey Bay 942
Mystic 209
New Orleans 416
Newport (RI) 1059
North Carolina 326
San Diego 922
South Carolina 342
Tampa 482
Tennessee 368
Virginia Beach 304-5
Woods Hole 188
Aquinnah Cliffs 197
Aransas National Wildlife Refuge 680-1
Arcata 983
Arch Rock 568
Arches National Park 780, 850, **781**
architecture 512, 1138-41
Brooklyn Bridge 63
Chrysler Building 81
Empire State Building 80
Golden Gate Bridge 960, **9**, **1108**
Grand Central Station 80
Willis Tower 511
area codes 1162
Arizona 808-37, **788-9**
Arizona-Sonora Desert Museum 832
Arkansas 433-9, **322-3**
Arkansas River Valley 437
Arlington 292-4
art galleries, *see* museums & galleries
Art Institute of Chicago 511
arts 455, 1132-41, *see also* architecture
Asbury Park 130
Asheville 336-8
Ashfall Fossil Beds 638
Ashland 1053-4
Ashley River Plantations 346-7
Aspen 731-3
Assateague Island 285
Astoria 90, 1057-8
Atchafalaya Basin 431
Athens 389-91, 550
Atlanta 379-89, **380-1**
Atlantic City 132-3
ATMs 1160
Auburn 542
auctions 81
Augusta 242
Austin 14, 656, **658**

000 Map pages
000 Photo pages

B

Badlands National Park 626-7, 778, **628-9**
Badwater 933
Baker 807
bald eagles 1072, 1152
ballet 1139
ballooning 860
Baltimore 271-81, **272-3**
Bandelier National Monument 870
Bandera 666
Bangor 242
Banner Elk 334
Bar Harbor 240-1
barbecue 16, 652, **16**
Barnegat Peninsula 131
Bartlesville 650
baseball 122, 275, 372, 1118
basketball 198, 1119
Bath 236
Baton Rouge 427-8
bats 661
Baxter State Park 243
beaches
Amelia Island 481
Big Sur 941
Brighton Beach 88
Canaveral National Seashore 475
Cape Cod National Seashore 14, 190
Cape Hatteras National Seashore 326
Chicago 514
Falmouth 187
Fort Lauderdale 459
Fort Myers Beach 487
Hanauma Bay 1086, **17**
Hyannis 188
Islamorada 468
Kailua 1086
Kailua-Kona 1088
Lahaina 1092
Lake Winnipesaukee 225
Long Island 114
Marathon (FL) 469
Miami Beach 447
Montauk 115
Nantucket 194
Ocean County 131
Orange County 915-16
Padre Island National Seashore 681
Point Reyes National Seashore 973
Rhode Island 206-7
Rockaway Beach 92
San Diego 919
Sandwich 186-7
Waikiki 1083
Wellfleet 190
Wilmington 329
Beals 241
Bear Mountain State Park 116
bears 748, 1150, **774**
Beartooth Highway 757
Beaufort 328, 347
beer 514, 1128
breweries 426, 480, 573, 608, 671
festivals 28, 712, 1039
Bellevue 619
Bellingham 1026-7
Bemidji 597
Bend 1051-2
Bennington 214-15
Bentsen-Rio Grande Valley State Park 682
Berkeley 973-4
Berkeley Springs 317
Berkshires, the 199-201
Berlin (MD) 284
Berlin (OH) 548
Bethany Beach 290
Bethel 242-3
Bethlehem 151
Beverly Hills 895, **900-1**
bicycling, *see* cycling, mountain-biking
Big Bend National Park 694-5
Big Bend Ranch State Park 696-7
Big Island 1087-91
Big Sur 940-1
Bighorn Mountains 753
Bill Baggs Cape Florida State Recreation Park 452
Billings 757
birds 1152
birdwatching
Acadia National Park 240
Alaska Chilkat Bald Eagle Preserve 1072
Aransas National Wildlife Refuge 680-1
Assateague Island 285
Big Bend National Park 694
Block Island 206
Blue Ridge Parkway 40
Cape May 133
Chatham 189
Chicago 532
Custer State Park 632
Dauphin Island 401
Great Wass Island 241
New York City 82, 92
Okefenokee National Wildlife Refuge 396
Pine Barrens 132
World Birding Center 682

Birmingham 397-9
Bisbee 837
Biscayne National Park 464
Bishop 997
Bismarck 622-3
bison 748, **13**
Black Hills 627-34, **628-9**
Black Hills National Forest 628-9
Block Island 206
Bloomington 540
Blowing Rock 334
Blue Hill 239
Blue Ridge Parkway 14, 39-40, 312, 335, **15**
Bluegrass Country 374-5
blues music 1142
Bluff 851
boat travel
  to/from the USA 1170
  within the USA 1171
Bob Marshall Wilderness Complex 760-1
Bodega Bay 980
Bodie State Historic Park 997
Boise 763-5
books 1100, 1111, 1134-5, 1140, *see also* literature
Boone 334
Boonville 979
Boothbay Harbor 236-7
border crossings
  Canada 128, 1169-70
  Mexico 699, 1170
Boston 14, 167-84, **170-1**, **176-7**, **15**
  accommodations 175-8
  drinking 181
  entertainment 181-2
  festivals 173-5
  food 178-81
  internet access 182-3
  medical services 183
  shopping 182
  sights 168-73
  sports 182
  tourist offices 183
  tours 173
  travel to/from 183
  travel within 183-4
  walking tour 174, **174**
Boulder (CO) 718-22
Boulder (UT) 852-3
bourbon, *see* whiskey
Bozeman 754-6
Bradley Beach 131
Brandywine Valley 150, 290-1
Branson 611-12
Brattleboro 212-14
Breaux Bridge 431
Breckenridge 727-9
Bretton Woods 228
Brevard 338
breweries
  Abita 426
  Anheuser-Busch 480, 608
  Lakefront 573
  Spoetzl 671
  Sprecher 573
Brewster 189
Bridgehampton 115
Brighton Beach 88
Brooklyn Bridge 63
Brownsville 682
Brunswick 395-6
Bryce Canyon National Park 780, 854, **771**
Bryson City 338-9
budgeting 18, 1101
Buffalo 124-6
Buffalo Bill Ranch State Historical Park 638
Buffalo Gap National Grassland 627
Buffalo National River 439
buffaloes 1151
Burlington (IA) 619
Burlington (VT) 219-22
Burning Man 29, 805
bus travel
  to/from the USA 1169, 1170
  within the USA 1171-2
Bush, George W 1113-14
business hours 1156

C

Cadillac Mountain 239
Cahokia Mounds State Historic Site 535
Cajun Country 429-32
Calais 242
California 55, 882-1000, **884-5**
  accommodations 882
  climate 882
  food 882, 1126
  highlights 884-5
  internet resources 883
  itineraries 887
  travel seasons 882
Calistoga 975
Calumet 596
Cambridge 171-3
Camden 237-9
Cameron 829
camping 1154-6
Canaveral National Seashore 475
Cane River Country 432
Cannon Beach 1058-9
canoeing & kayaking 46
  Apostle Islands 581-2
  Bar Harbor 240
  Bethel 242
  Boundary Waters 596
  Charlotte 333
  Chicago 520
  Francis Marion National Forest 350
  Glacier Bay National Park 1070
  Juneau 1069
  Kealakekua Bay 1088
  Key Largo 467
  Key West 472
  Manchester (VT) 216
  Marathon (FL) 469
  Misty Fjords National Monument 1065
  Monterey 943
  Na Pali 1097
  Petersburg 1066-7
  Portland (ME) 234
  Portland (OR) 1039
  San Diego 923
  San Francisco 960
  Santa Barbara 935
  Santa Cruz 945
  Sitka 1068
  Valentine 638
  Wailua 1096
Canterbury Shaker Village 224
Canton 546
Canyonlands National Park 850-1
Cape Cod 185-94, **186**
Cape Cod National Seashore 14, 190
Cape Cod Rail Trail 190
Cape Flattery 1025
Cape Hatteras National Seashore 326
Cape Henlopen State Park 288
Cape May 133-4
Cape Perpetua 1059
Cape Vincent 123
Capital Region 53, 249-319, **246**
  accommodations 244
  climate 244
  food 244
  highlights 246
  internet resources 245
Capitol Hill 256
Capitol Reef National Park 852
Capone, Al 513
Captain Cook 1089
Captiva Islands 488
Capulin Volcano National Monument 875
car travel 1169-70, 1172-6, *see also* road trips
Caratunk 243
Carhenge 638
Carlsbad 880-1

Carlsbad Caverns National Park 881
Carmel 941-2
Carson City 806
Carson, Rachel 1112
casinos 791-4, 804
Cathedral Gorge State Park 808
cathedrals, *see* churches & cathedrals
Catoosa 646
Catskills 118
Cedar Breaks National Monument 854
Cedar City 854
Cedar Point Amusement Park 547
cell phones 19, 1162
Central Park 82, **84-5**
Chaco Culture National Historic Park 874
Chama 874-5
Chamberlain 625
Channel Islands National Park 937
Chapel Hill 331-3
Chapin Mesa 740
Charleston 340-6
Charleston County Sea Islands 347
Charlevoix 567
Charlotte 333-4
Charlottesville 306-8
Charm 548
Chatham 189-90
Chattanooga 368-9
Chavez, Cesar 1112
Chelan 1030
Cherokee people 334, 1120
Cherokee town 338
cherry blossoms 26
Cheyenne 742-3
Chicago 10, 505-31, **506**, **508-9**, **10**
  accommodations 521-3
  activities 517-18
  Andersonville 515, **516**
  drinking 526-7
  entertainment 527-9
  festivals 520-1
  food 523-6
  Gold Coast 513-14
  internet access 530
  itineraries 507
  Lincoln Park 514
  Loop, the 507-12
  medical services 530
  Near North 513
  shopping 529-30
  sights 507-17
  South Loop 512-13
  South Side 516-22
  sports 529
  tourist offices 530
  tours 518-20
  travel to/from 530-1
  travel within 531
  walking tour 519, **519**
  Wrigleyville 515, **516**
children, travel with 49-51, *see also* amusement parks, aquariums, water parks, zoos
  Albuquerque 860
  Atlanta 385
  Boston 179
  Chicago 520
  Hershey's Chocolate World 154
  Houston 673
  Las Vegas (NV) 796
  Legoland 927
  Los Angeles 899
  Miami (FL) 453
  Minneapolis 587
  New York City 92
  Phoenix 813
  Portland (OR) 1038
  Salt Lake City 841
  San Francisco 961
  Santa Fe 866
  Seattle 1014
  SeaWorld 490-1, 922
  St Paul 591
Chilkoot Trail 1073
Chincoteague 306
Chinese New Year 26
Chinook people 1003
Chippewa people 1121
Chiricahua National Monument 836-7
Choctaw people 1120
Chrysler Building 81
churches & cathedrals
  Cathedral of Our Lady of the Angels 891
  Cathedral of St John the Baptist 391
  Cathedral of St John the Divine 83
  Ebenezer Baptist Church 383
  First Gospel Tabernacle Church 355
  Gateway Walk Churches 340
  Grace Cathedral 951
  Mission Dolores 956
  Old First Church 214
  Old North Church 169
  San Francisco de Asís Church 872
  St Augustine's Church 415
  Washington National Cathedral 259
Cimarron 875
Cincinnati 551-5
City Island 90
Civil War 340, 653, 1103, 1108-10
  books 1134-5
  museums 296, 341, 415, 537
  sites 342, 406, 533, 956
Claremore 650
Clark, William 1057
Clarksdale 404-5
Clayton 123
Cleveland 542-6
climate 18, *see also individual locations*
climate change 1149, 1168
Clinton 647
Clinton, Bill 1113
Clyde 547
C&O Canal National Historic Park 286
cocktails 1129-30
Coconino National Forest 820
Cody 744
Coeur d'Alene 768
coffee 1089, 1130-1
Coloma 986
Colonial Williamsburg 299-300
Colorado 709-41, **706-7**
Columbia (MO) 611
Columbia (TN) 350
Columbia River Gorge 1049
Columbus (IN) 539
Columbus (OH) 549-50
Columbus, Christopher 1104
Concord 184, 224-5
condors 1152
Coney Island 88
Congaree National Park 350
Connecticut 207-12, **164-5**
consulates 1157
Conway Scenic Railroad 226
cooking courses 417
Cooperstown 122
Cordova 1076
Cornucopia 581
Corolla 325
Corpus Christi 681
Cosmosphere & Space Center 641
costs 18, 1101
country music 1143
Country Music Hall of Fame & Museum 359-61
Coupeville 1025
Covington 426
coyotes 1151
Crater Lake National Park 1052, **772**
Crawford 688
Crawford Notch State Park 228
Crazy Horse Memorial 632
credit cards 1160
Crescent City 984

000 Map pages
000 Photo pages

Crested Butte 733
crime 1161
Crisfield 283
Crooked Road 314-15
cruise ships 1170
Crystal Coast 328-9
culture 1100-2
Cumberland 286-7
Cumberland Island 396
Custer, General George 758
Custer State Park 632-3
customs 1102, 1127
customs regulations 1156
cycling 43-4, 1171, *see also* mountain-biking
- Aspen 731
- Bend 1051
- Cape Cod 187
- Cape Cod Rail Trail 190
- Chicago 517-18
- Cumberland 287
- Delaware 288
- Miami (FL) 453
- Missoula 759
- Moab 849
- Monterey 943
- Nantucket 194
- New York City 91-2
- Portland (OR) 1038-9
- Provincetown 191
- San Francisco 960
- Santa Barbara 935
- Seattle 1013

D

Dahlonega 389
Dalí Museum 485
Dallas 682-9, **684**, **690**
dance 1139
dangers, *see* safety
Daniel Boone National Forest 377
Dauphin Island 401
Dayton 550-1
Daytona Beach 476-8
Daytona International Speedway 476
Dead Horse Point State Park 851
Deadwood 630-1
Dearborn 562
Death Valley National Park 782, 933-4, **783**
Declaration of Independence 1106-7
Deep Creek Lake 287
Delaware 287-91, **246-7**
Delaware Water Gap 129
Denali National Park & Preserve 1076
Denton 688
Denver 709-16, **710**
Des Moines 617-18
Detroit 555-62, **556**
Devil's Tower National Monument 753
Dewey 288-9
dialing codes 1162
Diamond Head 1086
diet crazes 1123
Dinosaur National Monument 847
disabilities, travelers with 1163
discount cards 1155
Disneyland 911-15, **912**, *see also* Walt Disney World
distilleries
- Buffalo Trace 376
- Four Roses 376
- Heaven Hill 376
- Jack Daniel's 364
- Jim Beam 376
- Maker's Mark 376
- Moss Beach 947
- Ole Smoky Moonshine 370
- Tom Moore 376
- Wild Turkey 376
- Woodford Reserve 376

diving & snorkeling 47-8
- Kailua-Kona 1088
- Key Largo 467
- Key West 472
- La Jolla 923
- Looe Key 470
- Molokini 1094
- Monterey 943
- Outer Banks 327
- San Diego 923

Dodge City 644
Douglas 565
Dover 291
drinks, *see also* beer, breweries, distilleries
- cocktails 1129-30
- coffee 1089, 1130-1
- tipping 1128
- whiskey 364, 376, 1129
- wine 9, 1129

driver's licenses 1173
driving, *see* car travel
Dry Tortugas National Park 471
Dubuque 620
Duck 325
Duke University 332
Duluth 593-5
Durham 331-3
Dylan, Bob 594

E

earthquakes 1147
East Haddam 210
East Hampton 115
Eastern Panhandle 315-17
Echo Lake State Park 226
economy 1100
ecotravel 441, 466
Edgartown 196-7
Edisto Island 347
El Camino Del Rio 696
El Morro National Monument 863
El Paso 699-702
El Reno 647
El Santuario de Chimayo 870
electricity 1155, 1156
Elk City 647
Elkins 317
Elko 807
Ellensburg 1033
Elsah 535
Ellis Island 65
embassies 1157
Empire State Building 80
Enchanted Rock State Natural Area 665
environment 1146-9
Escalante 853-4
Essex 210
Estes Park 724-5
Eugene 1047-8
Eunice 432
Eureka 983
Eureka Springs 438-9
Evanston 532
events, *see* festivals & events
Everglades City 465-6
Everglades National Park 463-4, 776, **776**
exchange rates 19

F

Fairmount 539
Fairmount Park 143
Fairy Falls 748
Falmouth 187-8
Fargo 621-2
farmers markets 50
- Ann Arbor 563
- Bird-in-Hand 152
- Boston 180
- Burlington (VT) 221
- Charleston 343
- Hilo 1090
- Ithaca 120
- Los Angeles 906
- Madison (WI) 576
- Minneapolis 583
- Nashville (TN) 361
- New York City 75
- Occidental 979
- Olympia 1021
- Richmond 298

farmers markets *continued*
- Roanoke 313
- Salt Lake City 841
- San Francisco 951, 966
- San Luis Obispo 938
- Santa Fe 868
- Soulard 607
- Trenton 129
- Wichita 640

Farmington 874
fauna, *see* animals
Fayetteville 318
Fenway Park 25, 182
Fenwick Island 290
festivals & events 26-9, *see also individual locations*
- African American 384
- art 455
- bald eagles 1072
- balloons 717
- beer 28, 712, 1039
- Burning Man 29, 805
- coffee 1089
- film 26, 29, 93, 738, 845, 961, 1014
- flowers 26
- food 92, 613
- gay & lesbian 26, 27, 93, 192, 384, 418, 455, 961-3, 1014, 1039
- Gullah people 348
- horses 276
- ice climbing 737
- literature 418
- lobster 237-8
- motor racing 537
- music 26-7, 28, 29, 199, 355, 372, 384, 404, 418, 559, 657, 731, 738
- Native American 27, 866
- sandcastles 131
- snow 728
- theater 200

film 1132
film festivals 26, 29, 93, 738, 845, 961, 1014
Finger Lakes Region 118-21
fishing 756, 759, 768
Flagstaff 818-19
Flaming Gorge National Recreation Area 847
Flathead Lake 760
flora 1152
Florida 53, 440-99, **442**
- accommodations 440
- climate 440
- food 440
- highlights 442
- internet resources 441
- travel seasons 440

Florida City 464-5
Florida Keys 466-74
Florida Panhandle 495-9
Floyd 314
folk music 1143
food 163, 321, 1102, 1122-7, **2**, **8**, *see also* farmers markets
- barbecue 16, 652, **16**
- blue crab 284
- cooking courses 417
- deep-dish pizza 523
- festivals 92, 613
- hot dogs 834
- price ranges 1157

food carts 20, 1124
- Austin 660
- Chicago 525
- Hale'iwa 1087
- Portland (OR) 1040

football 1118-19
Forest Park 605
Forks 1024, 1025
Fort Bragg 981
Fort Davis 697
Fort Lauderdale 459-61
Fort McHenry National Monument & Historic Shrine 275-6
Fort Myers 487
Fort Myers Beach 487
Fort Raleigh National Historic Site 326
Fort Worth 689-93, **690**
Four Corners Navajo Tribal Park 830
Foyil 646
Francis Marion National Forest 350
Franconia Falls 225
Franconia Notch State Park 228
Frankfort 375
Franklin 365
Frederick 286
Fredericksburg (TX) 665-6
Fredericksburg (VA) 295-6
Freeport 236
Friedan, Betty 1112
Front Range 716-25
Front Royal 310

G

Galax 314-15
Galena 532-3
galleries, *see* museums & galleries
Gallup 863
Galveston 679-80
Gary 541
Gathering of Nations 27
Gatlinburg 370
gay travelers 1157
- Atlanta 384
- Austin 662
- Baltimore 279-80
- Boston 181
- Chicago 521
- Dallas 687
- festivals 26, 27, 93, 192, 384, 418, 455, 961-3, 1014, 1039
- Fort Lauderdale 460
- Los Angeles 908
- Minneapolis 588
- Portland (OR) 1044
- San Francisco 957
- Seattle 1019
- Washington, DC 267

geography 1146-7
geology 1146-7
George Washington National Forest 310
Georgia 378-97, **322-3**
Gettysburg 153-4
Glacier Bay National Park 1070
Glacier National Park 704, 761-3, 778, **769**, **778-9**
Glacier Point 991
Gold Beach 1060
Gold Country 986-8
gold rush 947, 986, 1108
Golden Gate Bridge 960, **9**, **1108**
Governor's Island National Monument 65-7
Graceland 354-5
Grafton 535
Grand Canyon National Park 7, 780, 823-8, **824**, **7**, **770-1**, **773**, **780-1**
Grand Canyon Skywalk 828
Grand Canyon West 828
Grand Central Station 80
Grand Forks 624
Grand Island 637-8
Grand Marais 595
Grand Rapids 564-5
Grand Staircase-Escalante National Monument 853
Grand Teton National Park 704, 750-1, **746**, **13**, **774**
Grants Pass 1054
Grass Valley 986
Grassy Key 469
Grauman's Chinese Theatre 893
Grayton Beach State Park 497
Great Barrington 199
Great Basin National Park 807
Great Depression 1110
Great Lakes 53, 500, **502-3**
- accommodations 500
- climate 500
- food 500

000 Map pages
000 Photo pages

highlights 502-3
internet resources 501
itineraries 504
travel seasons 500
Great Plains 17, 54, 598-650, **600-1**
accommodations 598
climate 598
food 598
highlights 600-1
internet resources 599
itineraries 602
travel seasons 598
Great River Road 40-1
Great Salt Lake 844
Great Sand Dunes National Park 704, 734
Great Smoky Mountains National Park 338, 369-70, 776, **777**
Great Wass Island 241
Green Bay 580-1
Green Country 650
Green River 848
Greenbrier 319
Greenbrier Valley 318-19
Greenport 116
Gruene 664-5
Guadalupe 938
Guadalupe Mountains National Park 702
Guerneville 979
Gulf Coast 409
Gullah people 348

H

Haines 1071-2
Haleakalā National Park 1095
Halloween 29
Hampton Roads 302-4
Hana 1095
Hanalei 1096-7
Hanapepe 1098
Hannibal 610-11
Hanover 229-30
Harbor Country 565
Harmony 593
Harpers Ferry 316-17
Hartford 210-11
Harvard University 171-2
Hatteras Island 325
Havasu Canyon 828
Hawaii 17, 55, 1079-98, **1080**, **17**
accommodations 1079
climate 1079
food 1079, 1126
highlights 1080
itineraries 1081
travel seasons 1079
Hawai'i Volcanoes National Park 1091, **784**
Hayden Valley 748
Hays 643
Healdsburg 979
health 1101, 1157-8
Heber Valley 846-7
Helena 757-8
Hells Canyon 1056
Hells Canyon National Recreation Area 704
Hemingway, Ernest 568, 766
Hershey 153
Hibbing 596
High Line, the 20, 59, 73
Highlands 130
hiking 43, 44
Acadia National Park 239-40
Anchorage 1074
Appalachian Trail 215, 243, 310
Big Bend National Park 694
Bethel 242
Blue Ridge Parkway 312
Chilkoot Trail 1073
C&O Canal National Historic Park 286
Eureka Springs 438
Flagstaff 818
Franconia Notch State Park 228
Glacier National Park 761-2
Grand Canyon National Park 7, 825, 827, **7**
Grand Teton National Park 704, 750, **13**
Great Smoky Mountains National Park 338, 370
Haines 1071
Juneau 1069
Ketchikan 1065
Kings Canyon National Park 995
Lake Tahoe 999
Marquette 570-1
Mauna Kea 1089
Mesa Verde National Park 740
Missoula 759
Mt Hood 1050
Mt Rainier National Park 1032
Mt Washington 229
Na Pali 1097
Newport (RI) 204
Olympic National Park 1022
Pike's Peak 717
Portland (OR) 1038
Rocky Mountain National Park 722
Santa Cruz 945
Sequoia National Park 995
Shenandoah National Park 309
Stowe 218
Superior Hiking Trail 596
Telluride 739
Vail 729-30
Yellowstone National Park 745-8
Yosemite National Park 991, 992
Zion National Park 855
Hill City 631-2
Hillsboro 643
Hilo 1090-1
hip-hop 1145
Historic Triangle 299-302
history 1103-14, *see also* Civil War
European invasion 1104-6
gold rush 947, 986, 1108
Great Depression 1110
Korean War 1111
slavery 324, 1105
Vietnam War 1111
WWI 612
WWII 1063, 1081, 1111
hitchhiking 1176
Hoboken 128
Hocking County 550
Hohokam people 787
holidays 1161
Holland 566
Hollywood 892-3, **896**
Homer 1076
Homestead 464-5
Honolulu 1082-5
Hood River 1049
Hoover Dam 802-3
Hope 437
Hopi Nation 830
Hopi people 1120
horseback riding 48
Grand Canyon National Park 825, 827
Lexington 374, 375
Moab 849
Mt Washington Valley 226
Outer Banks 327
hot dogs 834
Hot Springs (AR) 436-7
Hot Springs (NE) 634
Hot Springs (SC) 338
Houston 672-9, **674-5**, **678**
Hovenweep National Monument 852
Hudson 117
Hudson, Henry 62
Hudson Valley 116-18
Hueco Tanks State Historical Park 702
Huntington Beach 915
Hurricane Katrina 411, 1147
hurricanes 411, 1147
Hyannis 188-9
Hyde Park 117

I

ice hockey 1118
ice skating
  Chicago 518
  Cleveland 543
  Dallas-Fort Worth 688
  Minneapolis 585
  New York City 79
  St Louis 605
ice wine 546
Idaho 763-8, **706-7**
Illinois 505-35, **502-3**
immigration 1115, 1168
Independence (MO) 616
Independence Day 28
Independence National Historic Park 135-9
Indian Canyons 928
Indiana 535-42, **502-3**
Indiana Dunes 541
Indianapolis 536-9
Ingalls Wilder, Laura 625
Inlet Beach 131
insurance 1158, 1173
Intercourse 152
internet access 1158-9, *see also individual locations*
internet resources 19, 59, 163, *see also individual locations*
  air tickets 1169
  cycling 44
  hiking 43
  road trips 37, 40, 41
Iowa 616-20, **600-1**
Iowa City 618-19
Iron Range District 596-7
Islamorada 467-9
Isle of Palms 346
Isle Royale National Park 571
Ithaca 119-20
itineraries 30-4, **30**, **31**, **33**, **34**

J

Jack Daniel's Distillery 364
Jack London Historic State Park 978
Jackson (CA) 987
Jackson (MS) 407-8
Jackson (WY) 751-4
Jacksonville (FL) 480
Jacksonville (OR) 1054
James River Plantations 302
Jamestown 301
jazz music 1142-3
Jekyll Island 396

000 Map pages
000 Photo pages

Jenner 981
Jerome 821-2
Jersey City 128
Jersey Shore 130-1
Jewel Cave National Monument 633
Jewish heritage
  museums 68, 83-6, 139, 254-5, 275, 485, 949
  synagogues 69-70, 205
Jim Thorpe 154
John Day Fossil Beds National Monument 1055
John Pennekamp Coral Reef State Park 467
Jonesport 241
Joshua Tree National Park 782, 930-1, **772**
Juneau 1068-71

K

Kahuku 1087
Kahului 1094
Kailua 1086-7
Kailua-Kona 1087-8
Kamas 845
Kanab 854-5
Kancamagus Pass 225
Kansas 639-44
Kansas City 612-15, **600-1**
Kartchner Caverns State Park 836
Katrina, Hurricane 411, 1147
Kaua'i 1095-8
kayaking, *see* canoeing & kayaking
Kayenta-Monument Valley 821
Kealakekua Bay 1088
Kearney 638
Kelleys Island 547-8
Kennebec River 243
Kennebunkport 232-3
Kennecott 1076
Kennedy Space Center 474-5
Kentucky 370-8, **322-3**
Ketchikan 1065-6
Ketchum 765-7
Key Biscayne 452
Key Largo 466-7
Key West 470-4
Keystone 632
Kiawah Island 347
Kidron 548
Kihei 1093
Kill Devil Hills 325
Killington 217
King Jr, Martin Luther 383, 1112
  historic site 383
  memorials 257
  place of death 353
Kingman 831
Kings Canyon National Park 994-6
Kitty Hawk 325
Knott's Berry Farm 914
Kodachrome Basin State Park 854
Korean War 1111

L

La Conner 1026
Lafayette 429-31
Laguna Beach 915
Lahaina 1092-3
Lahiri, Jhumpa 1132
Lajitas 696
Lake City 736
Lake George 122
Lake Havasu City 832
Lake Mead 802-3
Lake Placid 122-3
Lake Powell 828-9
Lake Tahoe 998-1000
Lake Travis 664
Lake Waramaug 212
Lake Winnipesaukee 225-6
Lamar Valley 748
Lambertville 151
Lana'i 1096
Lancaster 151-2
Lander 743-4
Lanesboro 593
Langlade 581
language 18
Lansing 564
Laramie 743
Las Vegas (NM) 869-70
Las Vegas (NV) 11, 790-802, **792**, **11**
Lava Beds National Monument 989
Lead 631
Leavenworth 1029-30
legal matters 1159
Leggett 982
Legoland 927
Lemmon 633
Lenox 199-200
lesbian travelers 1157
  Atlanta 384
  Austin 662
  Baltimore 279-80
  Boston 181
  Chicago 521
  Dallas 687
  festivals 26, 27, 93, 192, 384, 418, 455, 961-3, 1014, 1039
  Fort Lauderdale 460
  Los Angeles 908
  Minneapolis 588
  Portland (OR) 1044
  San Francisco 957

Seattle 1019
Washington, DC 267
Lewes 288
Lewis, Meriwether 1057
Lexington 184, 311-12, 374-5
lifestyle 1117-18
Lihu'e 1096
Lincoln (NE) 636-7
Lincoln (NH) 227-8
Lincoln (NM) 879-80
Lincoln, Abraham 1103
house of 533
memorials 255
museums 533
tomb 533-4
Lincoln Park 514
Litchfield 211-12
Litchfield Hills 211-12
literature 418, 1133-5, *see also* books
Little Rock 434-5
Little Washington 293
Lockport 126
Lollapalooza 29
Long Beach 897-8
Long Beach Island 131
Long Branch 130
Long Island 114-16
Long Island City 90-1
Looe Key 470
Lopez Island 1027
Los Alamos 870
Los Angeles 16, 887-911, **888-9**, **16**
accommodations 901-3
activities 899
Beverly Hills 895, **900-1**
Downtown 889-92, **892-3**
drinking 906-7
entertainment 907-8
festivals 900-1
food 903
Hollywood 892-3, **896**
internet access 909
itineraries 890
Long Beach 897-8
Malibu 896-7
medical services 909
Pasadena 898-9
Santa Monica 897, **904**, **25**
shopping 908-9
sights 889-99
tourist offices 910
tours 899-900
travel to/from 910
travel within 910-11
Venice 897, **904**
Louisiana 409-33, **322-3**
Louisiana State Museum 414
Louisville 371-4
Lower Connecticut River Valley 210
Lower Keys 470
Lubec 241-2
Lucas 642-3
Luckenbach 666, **32**
Ludington 566

M

Ma'alaea 1093
Machias 241
Mackinac Island 568-9
Mackinaw City 567-8
Madeline Island 582
Madison (IN) 540
Madison (WI) 576-8
Madison County 618
magazines 1155
Maine 230-43, **164-5**, **231**
Makena 1093
Malibu 896-7
Mall of America 592
Mammoth 745
Mammoth Cave National Park 377-8, 776
Mamou 432
Manassas 295
manatees 482, 487, 1152
Manchester (NH) 224
Manchester (VT) 215-16
Manitou Islands 567
Manoa Falls 1083
Manteo 325
maps 1159-60
Marathon (FL) 469
Marathon (TX) 699
Marin County 972
Marquette 570-1
Marsh-Billings-Rockefeller National Historical Park 216
Martha's Vineyard 195-7, **186**
Martin Luther King Jr National Historic Site 383
Maryland 270-87, **246-7**
Massachusetts 167-201, **164-5**
Maui 1091-5
Mauna Kea 1089
McCarthy 1076
measures 1155
medical services 1158, *see also individual locations*
Medicine Bow Mountains 753
Medora 623-4
Memphis 351-8, **352**
Mendenhall Glacier 1069
Mendocino 981
Menemsha 197
Merritt Island National Wildlife Refuge 475
Mesa 811
Mesa Verde National Park 704, 740-1, 778
Mesilla 876
Methow Valley 1030
Metropolitan Museum of Art 83
Meyer, Stephanie 1024
Miami (FL) 12, 445-59, 446, **12**
accommodations 455-7
activities 453
Coconut Grove 451-3, **452**
Coral Gables 451-3, **452**
Downtown 447-9, **450**
drinking 457
entertainment 457
festivals 453-7
food 455-7
internet access 458
Little Haiti 451
Little Havana 449, **452**
medical services 459
Miami Beach 447, **448**
shopping 458
sights 445-52
tourist offices 459
tours 453
travel to/from 459
travel within 459
walking tour 454, **454**
Miami (OK) 646
Michigan 555-72, **502-3**
Middle Bass Island 547
Middleburg 293
Middlebury 217-18
Milan 546
Milford 154
Milk, Harvey 1112
Millennium Park 507-11
Millersburg 548
Milwaukee 572-6
Minneapolis 582-90, **584-5**
Minnesota 582-97, **502-3**
Minot 624
Minuteman Missile National Historic Site 626
Minuteman Missile State Historic Site 623
Mississippi 402-9, **322-3**
Mississippi Delta 403
Missoula 758-60
Missouri 602-16, **600-1**
Misty Fjords National Monument 1065
Mitchell 625, **17**
Moab 848-50
Mobile 401
mobile phones 19, 1162
Mogollon people 787

Mojave National Preserve 932-3
Mokelumne Hill 987
Moloka'i 1096
Molokini 1094
Monadnock State Park 224
money 1160
Monhegan Island 237
Monongahela National Forest 317
Montana 754-63, **706-7**
Montauk 115
Monterey 942-4
Montgomery 400-1
Monticello 306-7
Montpelier 218
Monument Rocks 643
Monument Valley 852
Mormon church 856
Morro Bay 939
motorcycle travel 1169-70, 1170, 1172-6
Motown Records 560
Mound City 550
Mount Vernon 294-5
mountain-biking 45, *see also* cycling
movies 1101
Mt Anderson 1022
Mt Baker 1029
Mt Equinox 215
Mt Hood 1049-50
Mt Mansfield 218
Mt Pleasant 346
Mt Rainier National Park 782, 1031-2, **782**
Mt Rogers National Recreation Area 313
Mt Rushmore 632
Mt Shasta 988
Mt Snow 214
Mt St Helens National Volcanic Monument 1032
Mt Tamalpais State Park 972
Mt Trashmore 305
Mt Washington 229
Mt Washington Valley 226
Mt Whitney 997
Muir Woods National Monument 972
multiculturalism 1115-16
Mummers Parade 26
Murphys 987
museums & galleries
- American Museum of Natural History 82
- Anchorage Museum 1074
- Arizona-Sonora Desert Museum 832
- Art Institute of Chicago 511
- Cloisters 87
- Cosmosphere & Space Center 641
- Country Music Hall of Fame & Museum 359-61
- Dalí Museum 485
- Dallas Museum of Art 683
- Louisiana State Museum 414
- Metropolitan Museum of Art 83
- Museum of Fine Arts, Houston 673
- Museum of Modern Art (MoMa) 75-9
- National Civil Rights Museum 353
- National Gallery of Art 254
- North Carolina Museum of Art 330-1
- Oklahoma City National Memorial Museum 645
- Philadelphia Museum of Art 141
- Ringling Museum Complex 486
- San Francisco Museum of Modern Art 951
- Seattle Art Museum 1010
- Sixth Floor Museum 683
- Smithsonian Institution Museums 252-4, **22**
- Solomon R Guggenheim Museum 83

music 321, 1142-5
- festivals 26-7, 28, 29, 199, 355, 372, 384, 404, 418, 559, 657, 731, 738
- museums 354, 359-61, 404, 543, 648

Muskegon 566
Muskogee 650
Mystic 209-10

000 Map pages
000 Photo pages

N

Nader, Ralph 1112
Nags Head 325
Nantucket 194-5, **186**
Napa 20, 21, 975
Napa Valley 20, 975-7, **32**
Naples 488-9
Nashville (IN) 539
Nashville (TN) 359-67, **360-1**
Natchez 408-9
Natchez Trace Parkway 368
National Civil Rights Museum 353
National Gallery of Art 254
National Mall 12, 249-56, **12**
national parks 59, 769-84, 786, 1148-9
- Acadia 239-40, 776, **776-7**
- Arches 780, 850, **781**
- Badlands 626-7, 778, **628-9**
- Big Bend 694-5
- Biscayne 464
- Bryce Canyon 780, 854, **771**
- Canyonlands 850-1
- Capitol Reef 852
- Carlsbad Caverns 881
- Channel Islands 937
- Congaree 350
- Crater Lake 1052, **772**
- Death Valley 782, 933-4, **783**
- Denali 1076
- Dry Tortugas 471
- Everglades 463-4, 776, **776**
- Glacier 704, 761-3, 778, **769**, **778-9**
- Glacier Bay 1070
- Grand Canyon 7, 780, 823-8, **824**, **7**, **770-1**, **773**, **780-1**
- Grand Teton 704, 750-1, **746**, **13**, **774**
- Great Basin 807
- Great Sand Dunes 704, 734
- Great Smoky Mountains 338, 369-70, 776, **777**
- Guadalupe Mountains 702
- Haleakalā 1095
- Hawai'i Volcanoes 1091, **784**
- Isle Royale 571
- Joshua Tree 782, 930-1, **772**
- Kings Canyon 994-6
- Mammoth Cave 377-8, 776
- Mesa Verde 704, 740-1, 778
- Mt Rainier 782, 1031-2, **782**
- North Cascades 1030
- Olympic 782, 1022-3, **770**
- Redwood 782, 984
- Rocky Mountain 704, 722-4, 778, **778**
- Saguaro 780, 832, **780**
- Sequoia 994-6
- Shenandoah 309, 776
- Theodore Roosevelt 623-4
- Voyageurs 597
- Wind Cave 633
- Yellowstone 8, 704, 744-50, 778, **746**, **8**, **775**, **779**
- Yosemite 13, 782, 990-3, **13**, **773**, **782-3**
- Zion 780, 855, **775**

Native American Scenic Byway 633
Native Americans 627, 829, 830, 1120-1, *see also individual peoples*
- cultural centers 650
- festivals 27, 860, 866
- museums 254, 645, 865
- sites 15, **15**

Natural Bridge 312
Natural Bridges National Monument 851-2
natural disasters 1147
Navajo Nation 829-30

Navajo people 1121
Nebraska 634-9, **600-1**
Nevada 790-808, **788-9**
Nevada City 986
New Bedford 185
New Castle 291
New England 9, 52, 162-243, **164-5**, **9**
  accommodations 162
  climate 162
  food 162, 1124
  highlights 164-5
  internet resources 163
  travel seasons 162
New Hampshire 222-30, **164-5**, **213**
New Harmony 541
New Haven 207-9
New Hope 151
New Jersey 52, 127-34, **60-1**
  accommodations 58
  climate 58
  food 58
  highlights 60-1
  internet resources 59, 127-8
  travel seasons 58
New Mexico 857-81, **788-9**
New Orleans 8, 410-26, **412-13**, **28**
  accommodations 418-21
  drinking 423-4
  entertainment 424
  festivals 418
  food 421-3
  French Quarter 411-15
  internet access 425-6
  medical services 425
  shopping 424
  sights 411-17
  tourist offices 425
  tours 418
  travel to/from 425
  travel within 425-6
  Tremé 415
  walking tour 419, **419**
New Paltz 117
New River Gorge National River 318
New York City 6, 62-113, **64**, **6**, **28**
  accommodations 93-7
  activities 91-2
  Bronx, the 89-90
  Brooklyn 88-9
  Central Park 82, **84-5**
  Chelsea 73-5, **76-7**
  Chinatown 69, **66-7**
  drinking 103-6
  East Village 70-3, **70-1**
  entertainment 106-9
  festivals 92-3
  Flatiron District 75
  food 97-103
  Gramercy Park 75
  Harlem 87
  internet access 110-11
  Little Italy 69
  Lower East Side 69-70
  Lower Manhattan 63-7, **66-7**
  Meatpacking District 73
  medical services 111
  Midtown 75-81, **76**
  Morningside Heights 83
  Queens 90-1
  shopping 109-10
  sights 63-91
  SoHo 69
  sports 109
  Staten Island 91
  Times Square 79, **76-7**
  tourist offices 111
  tours 92
  travel to/from 111-12
  travel within 112-13
  Tribeca 69
  Union Square 75
  Upper East Side 82-3, 83-7
  walking tour 74, **74**
  Wall St 67-8
  Washington Heights 87
  West Village 73, **70-1**
New York state 52, 113-27, **60-1**
  accommodations 58
  climate 58
  food 58
  highlights 60-1
  internet resources 59
  travel seasons 58
Newark 129
Newberry National Volcanic Monument 1052
Newport (OR) 1059
Newport (RI) 203-6, **204**
Newport Beach 915
newspapers 1155
Niagara Falls 126-7
Nicodemus 643
Nixon, Richard 1113
Nome 1076
Norfolk 302-4
North Carolina 324-39, **322-3**
North Carolina Museum of Art 330-1
North Cascade Mountains 1029-30
North Cascades National Park 1030
North Dakota 620-4, **600-1**
North Fork 116
North Wildwood 133
North Woodstock 227-8
Northampton 198-9
Nuevo Progreso 682

O

O'ahu 1082-7
Oak Alley Plantation 427, **11**
Oak Bluffs 195-6
Oak Creek Canyon 821
Oak Park 531-2
Obama, Barack 249, 517, 1100-1, 1116
Oberlin 546
Occidental 979
Ocean City 133, 285-6
Ocean Grove 130-1
Ocean Springs 409
Ochopee 465
Ocracoke Island 325, 326-7
Ogunquit 232
Ohio 542-55, **502-3**
Ohio River 540-1
OK Corral 837
Okefenokee National Wildlife Refuge 396-7
Oklahoma 644-50, **600-1**
Oklahoma City 644-7
Old Faithful 745
Olympia 1021-2
Olympic National Park 782, 1022-3, **770**
Olympic Peninsula 1022-5
Omaha 634-6
Opelousas 431
opening hours 1156
Ophir Pass 736
Orange County 915-16
Oregon 1034-60, **1004-5**
Oregon Caves National Monument 1055
Oregon Dunes National Recreation Area 1059-60
Organ Pipe Cactus National Monument 835-6
Orlando 489-93, **490**
Ouachita National Forest 437
Ouray 737-8
Outer Banks 325-8
Oxford (MS) 402-3
Oxford (WA) 283-4
Ozark Mountains 437-9
Ozarks, the 611-12

P

Pacific Coast Highway 38-9, **11**
Pacific Northwest 55, 1001-60, **1004-5**
  accommodations 1001
  climate 1001
  food 1001, 1126
  highlights 1004-5
  internet resources 1002
  itineraries 1003
  travel seasons 1001

Padre Island 681
Padre Island National Seashore 681
Pai'a 1094-5
painting 1136-7
Palm Beach 461-2
Palm Springs 928-30
Palo Duro Canyon State Par 702
Panama City Beach 496-7
Park City 844-6
Pasadena 898-9
passports 1165, 1168
Pawleys Island 350
Pearl Harbor 1081, 1085-6, 1111
Pelee Island 548
Pemaquid Peninsula 237
Pennsylvania 52, 134-61, **60-1**
  accommodations 58
  climate 58
  food 58
  highlights 60-1
  internet resources 59
  travel seasons 58
Pennsylvania Dutch Country 151-3
Pensacola 497-9
Pentagon 293
Petersburg 535, 1066-7
Petoskey 567
Petrified Forest National Park 831
Pfeiffer Big Sur State Park 941
Philadelphia 134-50, **136-7**
  accommodations 144
  Center City 139
  Chinatown 142
  drinking 148
  entertainment 148-9
  Fairmount Park 143
  festivals 144
  food 145-7
  Manayunk 143
  medical services 149
  Old City 139, **140**
  Penn's Landing 142
  Rittenhouse Square 139
  sights 135-43
  Society Hill 139
  South Philadelphia 142
  South Street 141-2
  sports 149
  tourist offices 149
  tours 143
  travel to/from 149-50
  travel within 150
  University City 142

000 Map pages
000 Photo pages

Phoenicia 119
Phoenix 809-18, **810-11**, **814**
phone cards 1162
photography 1160
Pictured Rocks National Lakeshore 570
Piedmont, the 306-9
Pierre 625-6
Pikes Peak 716
Pine Barrens 132
Pine Ridge Indian Reservation 627
Pioneertown 931
Pittsburgh 154-61
Pittsfield 200-1
Plaisance 432-3
planning 18-19, 36, *see also individual locations*
  calendar of events 26-9
  children 49-51
  itineraries 30-4, **30**, **31**, **33**, **34**
  repeat visitors 20
  travel seasons 18
  USA's regions 52-5
plantations
  Aitken-Rhett House 341
  Ashley River 346-7
  Boone Hall 346
  James River 302
  Laura 427
  Melrose 432
  Monticello 306-7
  Nashville (TN) 362-3
  Oak Alley 427, **11**
  Plimoth 185
  Shirley 302
  St Francisville 428
  Vacherie 427
plants 1152
Plath, Sylvia 1135
Plymouth (CA) 987
Plymouth (MA) 185
Poconos 154
Po'ipu 1097-8
Point Lobos State Reserve 941
Point Pleasant 131
Point Reyes National Seashore 973
Polson 760
polygamy 856
Ponderosa Pine Scenic Byway 767
population 1100, 1101
Porcupine Mountains Wilderness State Park 571-2
Port Allen 1098
Port Angeles 1024-5
Port Aransas 680
Port Orford 1060
Port Townsend 1023-4
Portland (ME) 233-6

Portland (OR) 1034-46, **1036**
Portsmouth 223
postal services 1161
Poughkeepsie 118
Prairie du Chien 579
Prescott 822-3
Presley, Elvis 1144
  birthplace 402
  Graceland 354-5
Prince 1143
Princeton 129
Providence 201-3
Provincetown 191-4
Provo Canyon 847
public holidays 1161
Pu'uhonua O Honaunau National Historical Park 1089

Q

Quad Cities 533
Quandary Peak 716
Quechee 216-17

R

Rachel 808
Racine 578-9
radio 1155
rafting 46
  Big Bend National Park 695
  Bluff 851
  Charlotte 333
  Fayetteville 318
  Gold Country 986
  Hells Canyon 1056
  John Day River 1055
  Kennebec River 243
  Langlade 581
  Reno 804
  Santa Fe 866
  Stanley 767-8
  Taos 872
  Valentine 638
  Yellowstone National Park 748
Raleigh 330-1
Ramona Falls 1050
Rapid City 629-30
Reagan, Ronald 1113
Red Bank 130
Red Cliff 581
Red Rock Canyon 802
Red Wing 592
Redding 988
Redwood National Park 782, 984
Rehoboth 288-9
religion 1101, 1116-17
Reno 803-6
Revere, Paul 169
Rhinebeck 117

Rhode Island 201-7, **164-5**
Rhyolite 935
Richmond 296-9
Ringling Museum Complex 486
road distance chart 1175
road rules 1176
road trips 59, **37**
  Blue Ridge Parkway 39-40, **15**
  Great River Road 40-1
  Pacific Coast Highway 38-9, **11**
  planning 36
  Route 66 7, 35-7, **7**
Roanoke 313
Roanoke Island 325
rock climbing 47, 724
Rock Island 533
rock & roll music 1144-5
Rocky Mountain National Park 704, 722-4, 778, **778**
Rocky Mountains 13, 703-68, **706-7**, **726**
  accommodations 703
  climate 703
  food 703
  highlights 706-7
  internet resources 704
  itineraries 705
  travel seasons 703
rodeos
  Albuquerque 860
  Cheyenne 742
  Cody 744
  Fort Worth 691
  Houston 673
  San Antonio 669
  Tucson 833
Roswell 880
Route 66 7, 35-7, **7**
  Arizona 831
  Illinois 534
  Kansas 640
  Missouri 610
  Oklahoma 646-7
  Texas 694
Rugby 624
Ruidoso 878-9
Russian River Valley 978-9

S

Sabbaday Falls 225
Sabbathday Lake 242
Sackets Harbor 123
Sacramento 984-6
safety 1161-2
Sag Harbor 115
Saguaro National Park 780, 832, **780**
sailing 238
Sainte Genevieve 615
Salem (MS) 184-5
Salem (OR) 1046-7
Salish people 1003
salmon 1151
Salmon River Scenic Byway 767
Salt Lake City 838-43
Salton Sea 932
San Antonio 14, 666-72, **668-9**, **15**
San Diego 916-27, **917**, **920-1**
San Francisco 9, 947-72, **948**, **952-3**, **9**
  accommodations 963-4
  activities 960-1
  Castro, the 956-7
  Chinatown 951
  drinking 968
  entertainment 968-9
  festivals 961-3
  Financial District 950-1
  Fisherman's Wharf 955
  food 964-8
  Haight, the 956, **958-9**
  internet access 970
  itineraries 950
  medical services 970
  Mission, the 956, **958-9**
  shopping 970
  sights 949-60
  SoMa 949-50
  tourist offices 971
  tours 961
  travel to/from 971
  travel within 971-2
  walking tour 962, **962**
San Juan Islands 1027-9
San Juan Mountain Passes 736
San Luis Obispo 938-9
Sandhills 637
Sandpoint 768
Sandusky 547
Sandwich 186-7
Sandy Hook Gateway National Recreation Area 130
Sanibel 488
Santa Barbara 934-7
Santa Cruz 944-6
Santa Fe 863-9, **864-5**
Santa Monica 897, **904**, **25**
Saranac Lake 123
Sarasota 486-7
Saratoga Spa State Park 121
Saratoga Springs 121-2
Saugatuck 565-6
Sault Ste Marie 569-70
Savannah 391-5, **392**
Sawtooth Scenic Byway 767
scenic drives, *see* road trips
Schoodic Peninsula 241
Scotts Bluff National Monument 638
Scottsdale 810-11
scuba diving, *see* diving & snorkeling
sculpture 1136-7
Seal Beach 915
Seaside 497
Seaside Heights 131
Seattle 15, 1007-21, **1008-9**, **15**
  accommodation 1014-15
  activities 1013-14
  Ballard 1013
  Capitol Hill 1012
  Downtown 1007-11
  drinking 1017-18
  entertainment 1018-19
  festivals 1014
  food 1015-17
  Fremont 1012
  internet access 1019
  medical services 1019
  Pioneer Square 1011
  Seattle Center 1011-12
  shopping 1019
  sights 1007-13
  tourist offices 1020
  tours 1014
  travel to/from 1020
  travel within 1020-1
  U District 1013
SeaWorld 490-1, 922
Sebastopol 978
Sedona 820-1
Selma 401
Seminole people 461
September 11 62, 65, 1114
Sequoia National Park 994-6
Seven Mile Bridge 469
Seven Years' War 1106
Shasta Lake 988
Shelter Island 116
Shem Creek 346
Shenandoah National Park 309, 776
Shenandoah Valley 309-12
Sheridan 753
Shiloh National Military Park 358-9
Shreveport 433
Sierra Nevada 989-1000
Silver City 877
Silverton 736-7
Sioux Falls 625
Sioux people 1121
Sisters 1050-1
Sitka 1067-8
Skagway 1072-4
skiing & snowboarding 46-7
  Albuquerque 860
  Ashland 1053
  Aspen 729, 731

skiing & snowboarding *continued*
Bend 1051
Bethel 242
Big Sky 756
Bozeman 755
Breckenridge 727, 729
Bretton Woods 228
Crested Butte 733
Duluth 594
Durango 735
Flagstaff 818
Jackson Hole 729, 752
Killington 217
Lake Tahoe 998
Mt Baker 1029
Mt Hood 1050
Mt Mansfield 218
Mt Snow 214
Park City 844
Porcupine Mountains Wilderness State Park 571
Rocky Mountain National Park 722
Ruidoso 879
Salt Lake City 843-4
Santa Fe 866
Steamboat Mountain 727
Sun Valley 765
Taos 872
Telluride 729
Vail 729
Whitefish 761
Winter Park 725
Yosemite National Park 992
slavery 324, 1105
Sleeping Bear Dunes National Lakeshore 566
Slide Rock State Park 820
Smith Island 283
Smithsonian Institution Museums 252-4, **22**
smoking 1155
snorkeling 47-8, *see also* diving & snorkeling
Snow Canyon State Park 856
Snow Hill 284-5
snowboarding, *see* skiing & snowboarding
soccer 1118
Solvang 937
Sonoma Valley 977-8
Sony Pictures Studios 897
South Bass Island 547
South Bend 541-2
South Carolina 339-50, **322-3**

000 Map pages
000 Photo pages

South Dakota 624-34, **600-1**
South Padre Island 681-2
South, the 11, 53, 320-439, **322-3**
accommodations 320
climate 320
food 320, 321, 1124
highlights 322-3
internet resources 321
itineraries 324
travel seasons 320
Southampton 115
Southern Shores 325
Southwest 54, 785-881, **788-9**
accommodations 785
climate 785
food 785, 1125
highlights 788-9
internet resources 786
itineraries 787
travel seasons 785
Space Center Houston 672
Space Coast 474-6
Spearfish 630
Sperryville 293
Spokane 1030-1
sports 1118, *see also individual sports*
Spring Green 579
Spring Lake 131
Springdale 855-6
Springfield (IL) 533-5
Springfield (MA) 198
St Augustine 478-9
St Charles 609-10
St Francisville 428-9
St George 856-7
St Helena 975
St Helena Island 347
St Ignace 568
St Joseph 616
St Louis 603-9, **604**
St Martinville 431
St Marys 396
St Michaels 283
St Patricks Day 26
St Paul 590-2
St Petersburg 484-6
St Simons Island 396
Stanley 767-8
Staten Island 91
Statue of Liberty 63-5, **2**
Staunton 310-11
Steamboat Springs 725-7
Steens Mountain 1056
Stehekin 1030
Stillwater 592
Stinson Beach 972
Stockbridge 199
Stone City 618
Stowe 218-20
Straits of Mackinac 567
Study Butte 695-6
Sturgis 630
Sullivan's Island 346
Sun Valley 765-7
Super Bowl 1118
Superior Hiking Trail 596
surfing 44-6
Bodega Bay 980
Hawaii 1087, 1097
Los Angeles 899
museums 944
San Diego 923
San Francisco 959, 961
Santa Barbara 935
Santa Cruz 945
Space Coast 475
Sutter Creek 987
swamp tours 426

T

Tahlequah 650
Tahoe City 999
Tahquamenon Falls 570
Tahquitz Canyon 928
Tallahassee 495-6
Tampa 481-4
Taos 871-4
taxes 1160
Tecumseh's Curse 1109
telephone services 19, 1162
television 1132-3
Telluride 738-40
Tempe 811
Tennessee 350-70, **322-3**
Terlingua 695-6
Texas 54, 651-702, **654-5**
accommodations 651
climate 651
food 651
highlights 654-5
internet resources 652
itineraries 656
travel seasons 651
Texola 647
Thanksgiving 29
theater 200, 1137-8
Theodore Roosevelt Inaugural National Historic Site 125
Theodore Roosevelt National Park 623-4
Thousand Islands Region 123
Tilghman Island 283
time 19, 1162

tipping 1128, 1160
Toketee Falls 1054
Tombstone 837
Topeka 642
tornadoes 635, 1147
Torrey 852
tours 426, 1170, 1177, *see also individual locations*, walking tours
train travel
  to/from the USA 1170
  within the USA 1177-8
travel seasons 18
traveler's checks 1160
Traverse City 566-7
trekking, *see* hiking
Trenton 129
Trinidad 983
Truth or Consequences 875-6
Tubac 836
Tucson 832-5
Tulsa 646, 648-9
Tuolumne Meadows 992
Tupelo 402
TV 1132-3, 1155
Twain, Mark 610
Two Harbors 595
Tyler 688

U

Ukiah 982
Universal Studios 489-90, 898
University of California, Berkeley 973
University of California, Los Angeles 895
University of Chicago 517
University of Minnesota 584
University of Nebraska 636
University of North Carolina 332
University of Notre Dame 541-2
Up-Island 197
US Space & Rocket Center 399
Utah 837-57, **788-9**

V

vacations 1161
Vail 729-31
Valentine 638-9
Valley Forge 150
vegan travelers 1125
vegetarian travelers 1125
Venice 897, **904**
Vermont 212-22, **164-5**, **213**
Vernal 847
video systems 1155, 1160
Vietnam War 1111
Vineyard Haven 196
Virginia 291-315
Virginia Beach 304-6
Virginia City 806-7, **246-7**
Viroqua 579
visas 19, 1164-6
volunteering 1166
Voyageurs National Park 597

W

Wabasha 593
Waikiki 1083
Wailea 1093
Wailua 1096
Wailuku 1094
Waimea 1098
Waimea Canyon 1098
Waipi'o Valley 1090
Waitsfield 218
walking, *see* hiking
walking tours
  Boston 174, **174**
  Chicago 519, **519**
  Miami (FL) 454, **454**
  New Orleans 419, **419**
  New York City 74, **74**
  San Francisco 962, **962**
Wall 626
Walla Walla 1033-4
Wallowa Mountains 1055-6
Walnut Canyon National Monument 818
Walt Disney World 493-4, **10**, *see also* Disneyland
Wapama Falls 992
Warhol, Andy 1138
Warner Bros Studios 897
Warren 218
Washington 1007-34, **1004-5**
Washington, DC 53, 248-70, **250-1**
  accommodations 261-3
  activities 260
  Capitol Hill 256
  Downtown 257-8
  drinking 266-8
  Dupont Circle 259
  entertainment 266-8
  Foggy Bottom 258
  food 263-6
  Georgetown 259
  internet access 269
  medical services 269
  National Mall 12, 249-56, **12**
  sights 249-60
  sports 269
  Tidal Basin 257
  tours 261
  travel to/from 269-70
  travel within 270
Washington, George 1107, 1110
  Masonic National Memorial 294
  monuments of 615
water 1130
water parks
  Charlotte 333
  Ocean City 133
  Orlando 489, 490-1
  Phoenix 813
  Tampa 483
  Williamsburg (WA) 301
waterfalls
  Amicalola 389
  Fairy 748
  Franconia 225
  Linville 335
  Manoa 1083
  Niagara 126
  Ramona 1050
  Sabbaday 225
  Tahquamenon 570
  Toketee 1054
  Wapama 992
  Watson 1054
Waterville Valley 226
Watson Falls 1054
weather 18, *see also individual regions*
Weaverville 988
websites, *see* internet resources
weights 1155
Weirs Beach 225
Wellesley Island State Park 124
Wellfleet 190-1
Weslaco 682
West Virginia 315-19, **246-7**
Wetherill Mesa 740
whales 1151
whale-watching
  Bar Harbor 240
  Bellingham 1026
  Cape Cod 191
  Maui 1093
  Monterey 943
  Santa Barbara 936
Whatcom Falls Park 1026
Whidbey Island 1025
whiskey 364, 376, 1129
White House 258
White Mountain National Forest 225
White Mountains 226-9
White River State Park 536
White Sands National Monument 878
Whitefish 761
white-water rafting, *see* rafting
Wichita 639-41
Wild Rogue Wilderness 1054
wildflowers 664

wildlife, *see* animals
Wildwood 133
Wildwood Crest 133
Willamette Valley 1046-8
Williams 819-20
Williamsburg (NY) 89
Williamsburg (WA) 299-301
Wilmington (NC) 329-30
Wilmington (VT) 214
Wilmington (WA) 290
Wind Cave National Park 633
windsurfing 1093
wine 9, 1129
wine regions 1129
  Healdsburg 979
  Lake Waramaug 212
  Long Island 116
  Napa Valley 975-7, **32**
  Ohio 546
  Russian River 978-9
  San Juan Island 1028
  San Luis Obispo 937
  Sonoma Valley 977-8
  Virginia 307
  Walla Walla 1033-4
  Willamette Valley 1046-8
  Williamsburg 300
Winfrey, Oprah 1137
Winnemucca 807
Winslow 830-1
Winter Park 725
Wisconsin 572-82, **502-3**
witchcraft 184
Wolfeboro 225-6
wolves 1151
women travelers 1166-7
Woods Hole 188
Woodstock (NY) 118
Woodstock (VT) 216-17
Worcester 197-8
work 1167
Wrangell 1066
Wrigley Field 515, 529
WWI 612
WWII 1063, 1081, 1111
Wynwood 451
Wyoming 741-54, **706-7**

Y

Yachats 1059
Yakima 1033
Yale University 208
Yankee Stadium 90, 109
Yellow Springs 550-1
Yellowstone National Park 8, 704, 744-50, 778, **746**, **8**, **775**, **779**
Yorktown 301-2
Yosemite National Park 13, 782, 990-3, **13**, **773**, **782-3**
Yosemite Valley 991, **990-1**
Yountville 975

Z

Zion National Park 780, 855, **775**
zoos
  Anchorage 1074
  Baltimore 276
  Brownsville 682
  Chicago 514
  Los Angeles 893-4
  Memphis 354
  Miami (FL) 453
  Minnesota 587
  New York City 82, 90
  Philadelphia 143
  Salt Lake City 841
  San Diego 918
  Tampa 482
  Washington, DC 259

000 Map pages
000 Photo pages

how to use this book

These symbols will help you find the listings you want:

- Sights
- Beaches
- Activities
- Courses
- Tours
- Festivals & Events
- Sleeping
- Eating
- Drinking
- Entertainment
- Shopping
- Information/ Transport

These symbols give you the vital information for each listing:

- Telephone Numbers
- Opening Hours
- Parking
- Nonsmoking
- Air-Conditioning
- Internet Access
- Wi-Fi Access
- Swimming Pool
- Vegetarian Selection
- English-Language Menu
- Family-Friendly
- Pet-Friendly
- Bus
- Ferry
- Metro
- Subway
- Tram
- Train

Reviews are organised by author preference.

Look out for these icons:

TOP CHOICE Our author's recommendation

FREE No payment required

A green or sustainable option

Our authors have nominated these places as demonstrating a strong commitment to sustainability – for example by supporting local communities and producers, operating in an environmentally friendly way, or supporting conservation projects.

Map Legend

Sights

- Beach
- Buddhist
- Castle
- Christian
- Hindu
- Islamic
- Jewish
- Monument
- Museum/Gallery
- Ruin
- Winery/Vineyard
- Zoo
- Other Sight

Activities, Courses & Tours

- Diving/Snorkelling
- Canoeing/Kayaking
- Skiing
- Surfing
- Swimming/Pool
- Walking
- Windsurfing
- Other Activity/ Course/Tour

Sleeping

- Sleeping
- Camping

Eating

- Eating

Drinking

- Drinking
- Cafe

Entertainment

- Entertainment

Shopping

- Shopping

Information

- Post Office
- Tourist Information

Transport

- Airport
- Border Crossing
- Bus
- Cable Car/ Funicular
- Cycling
- Ferry
- Monorail
- Parking
- Subway
- Taxi
- Train/Railway
- Tram
- Tube Station
- U-Bahn
- Underground Train Station/ Muni & BART
- Other Transport

Routes

- Tollway
- Freeway
- Primary
- Secondary
- Tertiary
- Lane
- Unsealed Road
- Plaza/Mall
- Steps
- Tunnel
- Pedestrian Overpass
- Walking Tour
- Walking Tour Detour
- Path

Boundaries

- International
- State/Province
- Disputed
- Regional/Suburb
- Marine Park
- Cliff
- Wall

Population

- Capital (National)
- Capital (State/Province)
- City/Large Town
- Town/Village

Geographic

- Hut/Shelter
- Lighthouse
- Lookout
- Mountain/Volcano
- Oasis
- Park
- Pass
- Picnic Area
- Waterfall

Hydrography

- River/Creek
- Intermittent River
- Swamp/Mangrove
- Reef
- Canal
- Water
- Dry/Salt/ Intermittent Lake
- Glacier

Areas

- Beach/Desert
- Cemetery (Christian)
- Cemetery (Other)
- Park/Forest
- Sportsground
- Sight (Building)
- Top Sight (Building)

Karla Zimmerman

Great Lakes As a life-long Midwesterner, Karla is well-versed in the region's beaches, ballparks, breweries and pie shops. When she's not home in Chicago watching the Cubs, er, writing for newspapers, books and magazines, she's out exploring. For this gig, she curled in Minnesota, caught a wave in Michigan, heard the curds squeak in Wisconsin and drank an embarrassing number of milkshakes in Ohio. Karla has written for several Lonely Planet guidebooks covering the USA, Canada, Caribbean and Europe.

Read more about Karla at:
lonelyplanet.com/members/karlazimmerman

Bradley Mayhew

Rocky Mountains An expat Brit, Bradley currently calls southeastern Montana home. Half a lifetime of travels through Central Asia, Tibet and Mongolia has made him feel quite at home in Big Sky country. He is the coordinating author of a dozen Lonely Planet guides, including *Tibet, Bhutan, Nepal, Central Asia* and *Yellowstone & Grand Teton National Parks* and he hikes nearby Yellowstone Park and the Beartooth Mountains every chance he gets. See what he's up to at www.bradleymayhew.blogspot.com.

Carolyn McCarthy

Rocky Mountains Carolyn became enamored of the Rockies as an undergraduate at Colorado College. She studied, skied and hiked her way through the region, even working as a boot fitter. In the last seven years she has contributed to over a dozen Lonely Planet titles and has written for *National Geographic, Outside, Lonely Planet Magazine* and other publications. You can follow her Americas blog at www.carolynswildblueyonder.blogspot.com.

Kevin Raub

The South Though Indiana born, Kevin grew up in Atlanta and started his career as a music journalist in New York, working for *Men's Journal* and *Rolling Stone* magazines. The rock 'n' roll lifestyle took its toll, so he needed an extended vacation and took up travel writing while ditching the States for Brazil. This homecoming, covering Georgia, Alabama, Mississippi, Arkansas and Louisiana, only reaffirmed a bumper sticker he has contemplated for years: *Hoosier by Birth, Southern by the Grace of God*! This is Kevin's 13th Lonely Planet guide. You can find him at www.kevinraub.net.

Brendan Sainsbury

Rocky Mountains, Pacific Northwest UK-born Brendan lives in White Rock, Canada within baseball-pitching distance (almost) of the USA and the Pacific Northwest. He has been researching the area for Lonely Planet since 2007 and his forays across the border have included fine-dining in the San Juan Islands, hitchhiking in western Montana and running 100 miles unassisted across the Cascade Mountains in a so-called endurance race. Brendan is also a co-author of Lonely Planet's *Washington, Oregon & the Pacific Northwest* guidebook.

Read more about Brendan at:
lonelyplanet.com/members/brendansainsbury

Andrea Schulte-Peevers

California Andrea fell in love with California – its pizzazz, people and sunshine – almost the instant she landed in the Golden State. She grew up in Germany, lived in London and traveled the world before getting a degree from UCLA and embarking on a career in travel writing. Andrea has written or contributed to some 60 Lonely Planet books, including several editions of this one as well as *California, Los Angeles* and *Southern California*.

Ryan Ver Berkmoes

Great Plains Ryan first drove across the Great Plains with his family in the 1960s. Among his treasured memories are a pair of Wild West six-shooters he got at Wall Drugs in South Dakota and which he still has (in a box someplace *not* under his pillow). Through the years he never passes up a chance to wander the backroads of America's heartland finding beauty and intrigue where you least expect it. Find more at www.ryanverberkmoes.com.

Read more about Ryan at:
lonelyplanet.com/members/ryanverberkmoes

John A Vlahides

California John cohosts the TV series *Lonely Planet: Roads Less Travelled,* screening on National Geographic Channels International. John studied cooking in Paris with the same chefs who trained Julia Child, and is a former luxury-hotel concierge and member of *Les Clefs d'Or,* the international union of the world's elite concierges. He lives in San Francisco, where he sings tenor with the San Francisco Symphony, and spends free time skiing the Sierra Nevada. For more, see johnvlahides.com and twitter.com.johnvlahides.

Read more about John at:
lonelyplanet.com/members/johnvlahides

Ned Friary & Glenda Bendure

New England Ned and Glenda hail from Cape Cod, their home since the 1980s. Ocean swims, long bike rides and road trips around New England are favorite pastimes. The highlight of their latest trip was a climb to the summit of Acadia Mountain in Acadia National Park, where the jaw-dropping views reminded them just how wildly diverse New England is. They've written extensively on the region and are co-authors of Lonely Planet's *New England* and *Discover USA's Best National Parks* guides.

Bridget Gleeson

California A journalist who divides her time between California and Argentina, Bridget has written about food, wine, hotels and adventure travel for Budget Travel, Afar, Delta Sky, Jetsetter, Continental, Tablet Hotels and Mr & Mrs Smith. Follow her travels at www.bridgetgleeson.com.

Read more about Bridget at:
lonelyplanet.com/members/bridgetgleeson

Michael Grosberg

New York, New Jersey & Pennsylvania Growing up Michael spent family holidays crisscrossing NY, NJ and PA and with his large New York City family and grew to know their neighborhoods as if they were his own. After several long overseas trips and many careers, some abroad, Michael returned to New York City for graduate school and taught literature in colleges. He's lived in three of the five boroughs and takes every opportunity to hit the road and explore these diverse states.

Beth Kohn

California A lucky long-time resident of San Francisco, Beth loves to be playing outside or splashing in big puddles of water. For this guide, she hiked and biked Bay Area byways, lugged a bear canister along the John Muir Trail and selflessly soaked in hot springs – for research purposes, of course. An author of Lonely Planet's *Yosemite, Sequoia & Kings Canyon National Parks* and *California* guides, you can see more of her work at www.bethkohn.com.

Mariella Krause

Texas Although she currently lives in California, Mariella will always consider Texas home. She lived in Austin for 15 years and still sprinkles her language with Texanisms whenever possible, much to the amusement of those who don't consider 'ya'll' a proper pronoun. Fresh off last year's *Texas* guide, Mariella is as proud as a kitten in a pickup to once again share her favorite places in the Lone Star state.

Emily Matchar

The South A native Tarheel, Emily lives and works in Chapel Hill, North Carolina (when she's not bopping around the globe, that is). Though she doesn't have a Southern accent, she does know how to smoke a hog, hotwire a pickup truck and bake a mean coconut cake. She writes about culture, food and travel for a variety of national magazines and newspapers, and has contributed to a dozen Lonely Planet guides.

Read more about Emily at:
lonelyplanet.com/members/emilymatchar

OUR STORY

A beat-up old car, a few dollars in the pocket and a sense of adventure. In 1972 that's all Tony and Maureen Wheeler needed for the trip of a lifetime – across Europe and Asia overland to Australia. It took several months, and at the end – broke but inspired – they sat at their kitchen table writing and stapling together their first travel guide, *Across Asia on the Cheap*. Within a week they'd sold 1500 copies. Lonely Planet was born.

Today, Lonely Planet has offices in Melbourne, London and Oakland, with more than 600 staff and writers. We share Tony's belief that 'a great guidebook should do three things: inform, educate and amuse'.

OUR WRITERS

Regis St Louis

Coordinating Author, Washington, DC & the Capital Region A Hoosier by birth, Regis grew up in a sleepy riverside town where he dreamed of big-city intrigue. In 2001, he settled in New York, which had all that and more. He has also lived in San Francisco and Los Angeles and has crossed the country by train, bus and car, while visiting remote corners of America. Favorite memories from his most recent trip include chasing the bluegrass scene across southern Virginia, chanting with Krishna devotees in West Virginia and crab feasting all over Maryland. Regis has contributed to more than 30 Lonely Planet titles, including Washington, DC and NYC.

Read more about Regis at:
lonelyplanet.com/members/regisstlouis

Amy C Balfour

Southwest Amy has hiked, biked, skied and gambled her way across the Southwest, finding herself returning again and again to Flagstaff, Monument Valley and, always, the Grand Canyon. On this trip she fell hard for Bisbee and Chiricahua National Monument. When she's not daydreaming about red rocks and green chile hamburgers, she's writing about food, travel and the outdoors. Amy has authored or co-authored 11 guidebooks for Lonely Planet, including *Los Angeles Encounter*, *California*, *Hawaii* and *Arizona*.

Read more about Amy at:
lonelyplanet.com/members/amycbalfour

Michael Benanav

Southwest Michael came to New Mexico in 1992 and quickly fell under its spell; soon after, he moved to a rural village in the Sangre de Cristo foothills, where he still lives. A veteran international traveler, he can't imagine a better place to come home to after a trip. Aside from his work for Lonely Planet, he's authored two nonfiction books and writes and photographs for magazines and newspapers. His website is www.michaelbenanav.com.

Andrew Bender

California Andrew is a true Angeleno, not because he was born in Los Angeles but because he's made it his own. Two decades ago, this native New Englander packed up the car and drove cross-country to work in film production, and eventually realized that the joy was in the journey (and writing about it). His work has since appeared in the *Los Angeles Times*, *Forbes*, over two dozen Lonely Planet titles, and on his blog, www.wheres-andy-now.com. Current obsessions: discovering LA's next great ethnic enclave, and winter sunsets over the bike path in Santa Monica.

OVER PAGE MORE WRITERS

Published by Lonely Planet Publications Pty Ltd
ABN 36 005 607 983
7th edition – Mar 2012
ISBN 978 1 74179 900 2

10 9 8 7 6 5 4 3 2 1
Printed in Singapore

Sara Benson

USA's National Parks, California, Hawaii After graduating from college in Chicago, Sara jumped on a plane to California with just one suitcase and $100 in her pocket. She has bounced around the Golden State ever since, in between stints living in Asia and Hawaii and working as a national park ranger. The author of 50 travel and nonfiction books, Sara dodged avalanches in Lake Tahoe and rockslides along Big Sur's splendid coast while writing this guide. Follow her adventures online at www.indietraveler.blogspot.com and www.twitter.com/indie_traveler.

Read more about Sara at:
lonelyplanet.com/members/Sara_Benson

Alison Bing

California After 18 years in San Francisco, Alison has done everything you're supposed to do in the city and some things you're not, including falling in love on the Haight St bus and eating a Mission burrito in one sitting. Alison holds degrees in art history and international relations – respectable diplomatic credentials she regularly undermines with opinionated culture commentary for newspapers, magazines, TV, radio and books, including Lonely Planet's *USA Trips*, *California*, *San Francisco* and *San Francisco Encounter* guides.

Jeff Campbell

Florida Jeff is the great-grandson of Florida pioneers who cleared the pines, mined the phosphate, and paved the roads in central Florida. As a child, he remembers searching for alligators in the local lake, and riding Space Mountain the year it opened. As an adult, he's been a travel writer for Lonely Planet since 2000. He was the coordinating author of *Florida*, as well as three editions of *USA*, among other US titles.

Nate Cavalieri

California A native of central Michigan, Nate lives in Northern California and has crisscrossed the region's back roads by bicycle, bus and rental car on a tireless search for the biggest trees, the best camping and the hoppiest pints of craft beer. In addition to authoring guides on *California* and *Latin America* for Lonely Planet, he writes about jazz and pop music and is the jazz editor at Rhapsody Music Service. Photos from his travels in Northern California and other writing can be found at www.natecavalieri.com.

Read more about Nate at:
lonelyplanet.com/members/natecavalieri

Sarah Chandler

Southwest Long enamored of Sin City's gritty enchantments, Sarah jumped at the chance to sharpen her blackjack skills while delving into the atomic and alien mysteries of rural Nevada. In Vegas, Sarah learned the secret art of bypassing velvet ropes, bounced from buffets to pool parties, and explored the seedy vintage glamour of downtown. Sarah is currently based between the US and Amsterdam, where she works as a writer, actress, and lecturer at Amsterdam University College. When in doubt, she always doubles down.

Read more about Sarah at:
lonelyplanet.com/members/sarahchandler

Jim DuFresne

Alaska Jim has lived, worked and wandered across Alaska and even cashed a Permanent Fund Dividend check. As the sports and outdoors editor of the *Juneau Empire*, he was the first Alaskan sportswriter to win a national award from Associated Press. As a guide for Alaska Discovery he has witness Hubbard Glacier shed icebergs the size of pickup trucks off its 8-mile-wide face. Jim now lives in Michigan writing for www.MichiganTrailMaps.com and regularly returns to the Far North to update Lonely Planet's *Alaska*.

Lisa Dunford

Southwest As one of the possibly thousands of great, great grand-daughters of Brigham Young, ancestry first drew Lisa to Utah. But it's the incredible red rocks that keep her coming back. Driving the remote backroads outside Bluff, she was reminded of how here the earth seems at its most elemental. Before becoming a freelance author 10 years ago, Lisa was a newspaper editor and writer in South Texas. Lisa co-authored Lonely Planet's *Zion & Bryce Canyon National Parks*.